MW01502923

Employment Discrimination Law

Fourth Edition
Volume II

BNA Books Authored by the
ABA Section of Labor and Employment Law

Age Discrimination in Employment Law, 2006 Supplement

Covenants Not to Compete: A State-by-State Survey

The Developing Labor Law

Discipline and Discharge in Arbitration

Elkouri & Elkouri: How Arbitration Works

Employee Benefits Law

Employee Duty of Loyalty: A State-by-State Survey

Employment Discrimination Law

Employment Termination: Rights and Remedies, 2003 Supplement

Equal Employment Law Update

The Fair Labor Standards Act

The Family and Medical Leave Act

How ADR Works

How to Take a Case Before the NLRB

International Labor and Employment Laws

Labor Arbitration: A Practical Guide for Advocates

Labor Arbitration: Cases and Materials for Advocates

Labor Arbitrator Development: A Handbook

Labor Union Law and Regulation

Occupational Safety and Health Law

The Railway Labor Act

Tortious Interference in the Employment Context: A State-by-State Survey

Trade Secrets: A State-by-State Survey

Wage and Hour Laws: A State-by-State Survey

For details on these and other related titles, please visit BNA Books Web site at **bnabooks.com** or call **1-800-960-1220** to request a catalog. All books are available on a 30-day free examination period.

Employment Discrimination Law

Fourth Edition
Volume II

Barbara T. Lindemann
Seyfarth Shaw LLP
Los Angeles, CA

Paul Grossman
Paul, Hastings, Janofsky & Walker LLP
Los Angeles, CA

Editor-in-Chief
C. Geoffrey Weirich
Paul, Hastings, Janofsky & Walker LLP
Atlanta, GA

Executive Editors

Linda M. Dardarian
Goldstein, Demchak, Baller, Borgen & Dardarian
Oakland, CA

Paul W. Mollica
Meites, Mulder, Mollica & Glink
Chicago, IL

Marilyn S. Teitelbaum
Schuchat, Cook & Werner
St. Louis, MO

Associate Editor
William C. Barker
Paul, Hastings, Janofsky & Walker LLP
Atlanta, GA

Assistant Editors

Melissa B. Garrett
Paul, Hastings, Janofsky & Walker LLP
Atlanta, GA

Eric R. Magnus
Paul, Hastings, Janofsky & Walker LLP
Atlanta, GA

Equal Employment Opportunity Committee
Section of Labor and Employment Law
American Bar Association

BNA Books, *A Division of BNA*, Washington, DC

The materials contained herein represent the opinions of the authors and editors and should not be construed to be those of either the American Bar Association or the Section of Labor and Employment Law. Nothing contained herein is to be considered as the rendering of legal advice for specific cases, and readers are responsible for obtaining such advice from their own legal counsel. These materials and any forms and agreements herein are intended for educational and informational purposes only.

Library of Congress Cataloging-in-Publication Data

Lindemann, Barbara, 1935-
 Employment discrimination law / Barbara T. Lindemann, Paul Grossman ;
editor-in-chief, C. Geoffrey Weirich ... [et al.]. -- 4th ed.
    p. cm.
 Includes bibliographical references and index.
 ISBN 978-1-57018-430-7 (two-volume set) -- ISBN 978-1-57018-533-5
(volume I) -- ISBN 978-1-57018-692-9 (volume II)
 1. Discrimination in employment--Law and legislation--United States.
I. Grossman, Paul, 1939- II. Weirich, C. Geoffrey. III. Title.
 KF3464.L56 2007
 344.7301'133--dc22

                                                         2007025818

Published by BNA Books, *A Division of BNA*, Washington, DC 20037
bnabooks.com

International Standard Book Numbers
978-1-57018-430-7 (two-volume set)
978-1-57018-533-5 (Vol. I)
978-1-57018-692-9 (Vol. II)
Printed in the United States of America

SUMMARY TABLE OF CONTENTS
VOLUMES I & II

Volume I

DETAILED TABLE OF CONTENTS
VOLUME II

[See Volume I for Chapters 1–24]

PART V: PROCEDURAL ISSUES

Part VII: Remedies and Resolution

Part V

Procedural Issues

CHAPTER 25

EEOC ADMINISTRATIVE PROCESS

I. STRUCTURE AND STATUTES ENFORCED

A. Structure of the EEOC

Section 705 of Title VII[1] created the Equal Employment Opportunity Commission. Its five Commissioners and General Counsel are appointed by the President and confirmed by the Senate.[2] Today the agency employs about 2,500 persons at its Washington, D.C., headquarters and its district offices throughout the country.[3]

The EEOC's staff is organized into 10 divisions, called "offices." They are: Office of Communications and Legislative Affairs, Office of Federal Operations, Office of Legal Counsel, Office of Inspector General, Office of Field Programs, Office of Equal Opportunity, Office of Human Resources, Office of Research, Information and Planning, Office of Information Technology, and Office of Chief Financial Officer and Administrative Services. The field offices report to the Director of Field Management Programs, who in turn reports to the Director of Field Programs.[4]

Many districts have satellite "area" or "local" offices, bringing the total number of field offices to about 51.[5] Each district has a legal unit responsible for litigating charges in the district courts and advising and assisting field officers in handling charges from intake through resolution. Each legal unit is headed by a regional attorney, who reports to the Office of General Counsel.[6]

B. Statutes Enforced

1. Title VII

The EEOC is responsible for the administrative intake, investigation, and conciliation of charges of discrimination under Title VII.[7] Since the 1972 Title VII amendments, the EEOC also has had authority to initiate litigation under § 706(f)(1) and (2)[8] and to

---

[1]42 U.S.C. § 2000e-4 (2000).

[2]*Id.* § 2000e-4(a) & (b)(1).

[3]EEOC Order 110, Organization, Mission, and Functions (as amended through July 1, 1994), *reprinted in* 1 EEOC COMPL. MAN. (BNA) §§ 110:0101 & 110:0201.

[4]EEOC Performance and Accountability Report FY 2004: EEOC at a Glance.

[5]*Id.*

[6]*Id.*

[7]*See* Sections III.C, III.I, and III.J *infra.*

[8]*See* EEOC v. Waffle House, Inc., 534 U.S. 279, 285–88 (2002) (describing EEOC's authority to obtain remedies in enforcement actions). *See generally* Chapter 29 (EEOC Litigation).

intervene in private litigation under § 706(f)(1).[9] In addition, the EEOC has numerous educational responsibilities under Title VII.[10]

2. ADEA and EPA

Enforcement of the Equal Pay Act (EPA)[11] and the Age Discrimination in Employment Act (ADEA)[12] rests with the EEOC.[13] In addition to its administrative charge-handling authority, the EEOC may sue to enforce the EPA[14] and the ADEA.[15] As under Title VII, the EEOC also has numerous educational responsibilities under the ADEA.[16]

3. ADA

Title I of the Americans with Disabilities Act (ADA)[17] prohibits discrimination in employment on the basis of disability and vests the EEOC with responsibility for enforcing the ADA's provisions, using remedies and procedures contained in Title VII.[18] As under Title VII, the EEOC is responsible for providing technical assistance about the ADA,[19] as well as investigating charges and litigating cases.

---

[9]*Id.*

[10]*See, e.g.,* 42 U.S.C. § 2000e-4(g)(3) (2000) (provide respondents with technical assistance to comply with Title VII); *id.* § 2000e-4(g)(4) (assist respondents whose employees or members refuse or threaten to refuse to comply with Title VII); *id.* § 2000e-4(g)(5) (study and report on matters appropriate to effectuate the purposes of Title VII); *id.* § 2000e-4(h) (educational and promotional activities).

[11]29 U.S.C. § 206(d) (2000).

[12]29 U.S.C. § 621 et seq.

[13]Reorg. Plan No. 1 of 1978, *reprinted in* 1978 U.S.C.C.A.N. 9799 (issued pursuant to the Reorganization Act of 1977, Pub. L. No. 95-17, 1977 U.S.C.C.A.N. (91 Stat.) 29 (codified at 5 U.S.C. §§ 901–912)). The Reorganization Plan later was codified at 5 U.S.C. § 906.

[14]*See* 29 U.S.C. §§ 216(c), 217 (2000).

[15]*See id.* §§ 625, 626(a) & (b).

[16]*See, e.g., id.* § 622(a) (authorizing research and dissemination of information on employment of older workers); *id.* § 625 (authorizing technical assistance).

[17]Pub. L. No. 101-336, 1990 U.S.C.C.A.N. (104 Stat.) 327 (codified at 42 U.S.C. § 12101 et seq.). *See generally* Chapter 13 (Disability).

[18]*See* 42 U.S.C. § 12117(a) (2000); EEOC v. Waffle House, Inc., 534 U.S. 279, 285 (2002).

[19]*See id.* § 12206(c)(2).

II. GENERAL ADMINISTRATIVE POWERS

A. Rulemaking Powers

Congress specifically has authorized the EEOC to issue "procedural" regulations to carry out Title VII,[20] regulations to carry out and to establish reasonable exemptions to the ADEA,[21] and regulations to carry out the ADA.[22] The EEOC takes the position that it has implicit authority to issue regulations to carry out the EPA.[23]

The EEOC issued procedural regulations and interpretations under Title VII throughout the 1970s and early 1980s.[24] In 1999, the EEOC revised its sex discrimination guidelines and national origin guidelines following the Supreme Court decisions in *Faragher v. City of Boca Raton*[25] and *Burlington Industries v. Ellerth*,[26] to reflect the Court's opinion regarding employer liability for harassment by supervisors. As for the EPA, the EEOC issued procedural regulations in 1984[27] and substantive interpretations in

---

[20]42 U.S.C. § 2000e-12(a) (2000); *see* General Elec. Co. v. Gilbert, 429 U.S. 125, 141 & n.20, 13 FEP 1657 (1976) (although not specifically authorized, the EEOC can and does issue interpretive regulations that should be treated as guidelines only, and not accorded the force of law); *see also* Edelman v. Lynchburg Coll., 535 U.S. 106, 114 n.7, 88 FEP 321 (2002) (EEOC procedural regulation under Title VII does not have to comply with the notice and comment requirements of the Administrative Procedure Act (APA), 5 U.S.C. § 553); Associated Dry Goods Corp. v. EEOC, 720 F.2d 804, 812, 33 FEP 181 (4th Cir. 1983) (notice and comment requirements of the APA apply only to substantive rulemaking).

[21]29 U.S.C. § 628 (2000). Although substantive rulemaking under the Administrative Procedure Act is authorized under the ADEA, the EEOC has utilized that power only rarely.

[22]The EEOC has clear congressional authority under the ADA to issue regulations with the force of law. *See* 42 U.S.C. §12116 (2000) (authorizing the EEOC to issue guidelines implementing Title I of the ADA).

[23]*See* 29 U.S.C. § 211 (2000) (administrative enforcement of the FLSA, incorporated by reference by the EPA); *cf. Associated Dry Goods*, 720 F.2d at 810 ("while an administrative agency might be without statutory authority to issue substantive rules, still it [has] inherent power to issue what are characterized as interpretive rules").

[24]Title VII procedural regulations appear at 29 C.F.R. pt. 1601; substantive guidelines appear at 29 C.F.R. pts. 1604 (sex), 1605 (religion), 1606 (national origin), 1607 (employee selection procedures), and 1608 (affirmative action).

[25]524 U.S. 775, 77 FEP 14 (1998). *See generally* Chapter 10 (Sex).

[26]524 U.S. 742, 77 FEP 1 (1998). *See generally* Chapter 10 (Sex).

[27]29 C.F.R. pt. 1621 (2005).

1986.[28] The Commission's ADEA substantive interpretations first appeared in 1981,[29] followed by procedural regulations in 1983.[30] In 1998, the EEOC promulgated regulations regarding waivers of rights and claims under the ADEA.[31] In 1999, the EEOC issued a follow-up Notice of Proposed Rulemaking[32] and published a final rule on December 11, 2000, which is based on the EEOC's interpretation of *Oubre v. Entergy Operations, Inc.*[33] The EEOC's final rules implementing the ADA were published on July 26, 1991.[34] They draw upon the regulations implementing § 504 of the Rehabilitation Act of 1973, as amended,[35] and the cases interpreting those regulations. The ADA procedural regulations were published on March 7, 1991, in the form of revisions to the Commission's Title VII procedural regulations.[36] On June 8, 2000, the EEOC amended the Interpretive Guidance on Title I of the Americans with Disabilities Act[37] in accordance with the Supreme Court decision in *Sutton v. United Airlines.*[38]

The courts, to varying degrees, generally defer to the EEOC's regulations and guidelines (especially procedural ones),[39] except

---

[28]*Id.* pt. 1620.

[29]*Id.* pt. 1625.

[30]*Id.* pt. 1626.

[31]29 C.F.R. § 1625.22 (1999) (waivers of rights and claims under ADEA).

[32]*Id.* § 1625.23 (2001) (tender back of consideration).

[33]522 U.S. 422, 75 FEP 1255 (1998) (holding that the individual is not required to return consideration received in exchange for waiver of rights before challenging that waiver and pursuing an ADEA claim).

[34]56 Fed. Reg. 35,726 (1991) (codified at 29 C.F.R. pt. 1630).

[35]*See* 34 C.F.R. pt. 104. *See generally* Chapter 13 (Disability).

[36]56 Fed. Reg. 9623 (1991) (amending 29 C.F.R. pt. 1601).

[37]*See* 65 Fed. Reg. 36,327–01 (rescinding sentences in 29 C.F.R. § 1630.2(h) and (j) that address mitigating measures used by persons with impairments in light of the Supreme Court's decisions in *Sutton v. United Airlines, Inc.*, 527 U.S. 471, 9 AD 673 (1999), and *Murphy v. United Parcel Serv., Inc.*, 527 U.S. 516, 9 AD 691 (1999), that such measures may be considered in determining whether the individual is substantially limited).

[38]527 U.S. 471, 9 AD 673 (1999).

[39]*See, e.g.*, Edelman v. Lynchburg Coll., 535 U.S. 106, 114, 88 FEP 321 (2002) (upholding the validity of 29 C.F.R. § 1601.12(b), which permits a charge of discrimination to be verified after the expiration of the applicable limitations period, holding that it does not conflict with the requirements of Title VII of the Civil Rights Act, 42 U.S.C. § 2000e-5(e)(1)); Walters v. Metropolitan Educ. Enter., Inc., 519 U.S. 202, 207, 72 FEP 1211 (1997) (noting that in its administration of Title VII, the EEOC has expressed certain preference for interpreting/defining "employer" in its Policy Guidance, but it lacks rulemaking authority over the issue); *see also* EEOC

where they are viewed to be contrary to law.[40] The standard of deference accorded to the EEOC varies depending on whether the

---

v. Seafarers Union (SIU), 394 F.3d 197, 202, 95 FEP 35 (4th Cir. 2005) (deferring to EEOC's substantive ADEA regulation, promulgated after public notice and comment, which extends ADEA to apprenticeship programs); Tice v. Centre Area Trans. Auth., 247 F.3d 506, 515 (3d Cir. 2001) (court defers to the EEOC interpretation of § 12112(d) of the ADA regarding medical examinations and inquiries); Lovejoy Wilson v. Noco Motor Fuel, Inc., 263 F.3d 208 (2d Cir. 2001) (deferring to the ADA interpretation of "direct threat" defense under ADA, 29 C.F.R. § 1630.2(r)); Navarro v. Pfizer Corp., 261 F.3d 90 (1st Cir. 2001) (rejecting the application of EEOC Guideline (29 C.F.R. § 1630.2(g)(1)) promulgated under ADA to analogous section of FMLA, under which Department of Labor had sole authority to issue regulations section); Rizzo v. Children's World Learning Ctrs., Inc., 173 F.3d 254, 258, 9 AD 436 (5th Cir. 1999) (noting that court's holding in prior proceeding relied on EEOC's interpretative guidance on ADA regulations); Ryan v. Grae & Rybicki, P.C., 135 F.3d 867, 870, 7 AD 1387 (2d Cir. 1998) (explaining that EEOC regulations under ADA, while "not binding," provide "guidance in interpreting the ADA"); Hendricks-Robinson v. Excel Corp., 154 F.3d 685, 693, 8 AD 875 (7th Cir. 1998) (EEOC's interpretation of ADA in its guidelines, while not controlling, is entitled to some deference); Arnold v. United Parcel Serv., Inc., 136 F.3d 854, 863, 7 AD 1489 (1st Cir. 1998) (same); EEOC v. Wal-Mart Stores, Inc., 156 F.3d 989, 993 n.1, 77 FEP 1611 (9th Cir. 1998) (EEOC guidelines constitute administrative interpretation of Title VII by enforcing agency, and consequently they are entitled to great deference); Gilday v. Mecosta County, 124 F.3d 760, 763 n.2, 7 AD 348 (6th Cir. 1997) ("because the appendix consists of interpretive, rather than legislative, rules, a reviewing court must conduct an independent evaluation of these guidelines, rather than simply following them if they are reasonable interpretations of the statute"); Trans. Union Corp. v. FTC, 81 F.3d 228, 230 (D.C. Cir 1996) (discussion of limited deference given to EEOC in its enforcement of Title VII due to its lack of rulemaking authority); EEOC v. Commercial Office Prods. Co., 486 U.S. 107, 115–16, 46 FEP 1265 (1988) (deference to the EEOC's deferral regulation is appropriate where it is supported by the language, legislative history, and purposes of the statute); *cf.* Firefighters Local 93 v. City of Cleveland, 478 U.S. 501, 518, 41 FEP 139 (1986) (the EEOC's affirmative action guidelines are not law but may be used for guidance); Meritor Sav. Bank v. Vinson, 477 U.S. 57, 65, 40 FEP 1822 (1986) (same); Gutierrez v. Municipal Court Se. Judicial Dist., 838 F.2d 1031, 1039–40 & n.7, 51 FEP 435 (9th Cir. 1988) (deferring to the EEOC's national origin guidelines concerning English-only rules), *vacated and remanded on other grounds*, 490 U.S. 1016, 51 FEP 457 (1989).

[40]*See* EEOC v. Arabian Am. Oil Co., 499 U.S. 244, 257, 55 FEP 449 (1991) (deference is not due to the EEOC's guidance stating that Title VII applies abroad, since the guidance contradicts the EEOC's prior position); Public Employees Ret. Sys. v. Betts, 492 U.S. 158, 175, 50 FEP 104 (1989) (invalidating former 29 C.F.R. § 1625.10 of the ADEA regulations, later to be codified by § 103 of the Older Workers Benefit Protection Act, 29 U.S.C. § 623(f)(2)(B)(i)); Fallon v. Illinois, 882 F.2d 1206, 1217–18, 50 FEP 954 (7th Cir. 1989) (the EEOC regulation stating that a violation of the Equal Pay Act is a violation of Title VII is not entitled to deference where it marks a change from past practice, there is no legislative history or explanation to support the change, and the guideline is at odds with case law that a Title VII violation requires intent).

EEOC has issued interpretive guidelines as opposed to legislative-type rules or regulations. As Justice O'Connor explained in her concurring opinion in *Edelman v. Lynchburg College*,[41] where the EEOC was not given rulemaking authority to interpret the substantive provisions of a statute, the Commission's substantive regulations are to be assessed pursuant to the standards established in *Skidmore v. Swift*,[42] which accord weight to the guidelines depending upon "the thoroughness evident in its consideration, the validity of its reasoning, its consistency with earlier and later pronouncements, and all those factors which give it power to persuade, if lacking power to control."[43] Although the Court determined in *Skidmore* that the Administrator's views are not controlling upon the courts, the Court recognized that they "do constitute a body of experience and informed judgment to which courts and litigants may properly resort for guidance."[44] By contrast, when the EEOC issues rules and regulations, which have gone through the notice and comment procedures, the court is more likely to defer to the agency, pursuant to the standard articulated in *Chevron U.S.A. Inc. v. Natural Resources Defense Council*.[45] In *Chevron*, a unanimous Supreme Court held that regulations are given "controlling weight" except in rare cases in which the regulation is deemed "arbitrary, capricious, or manifestly contrary to the statute."[46] Because the EEOC has been given the authority to issue suitable procedural regulations, those regulations are entitled to *Chevron* deference even when notice and comment procedures have not been followed.[47]

B. EEOC Posting Requirements

Section 711 of Title VII requires employers, employment agencies, and labor organizations to post EEOC notices summarizing the

---

[41]535 U.S. 106, 122–23, 88 FEP 321 (2002) (citing *Arabian Am. Oil*, 499 U.S. at 257).
[42]323 U.S. 134 (1944).
[43]*Id*. at 140.
[44]*Id*.
[45]467 U.S. 837 (1984).
[46]*Id*. at 843–44; *see Seafarers Union*, 394 F.3d at 202–07, 95 FEP 35 (applying two-step *Chevron* analysis to EEOC substantive regulation promulgated after public notice and comment).
[47]*Edelman*, 535 U.S. at 114, 123.

requirements of Title VII. A willful failure to display such notice is punishable by a fine of not more than $100 for each offense.[48] The ADEA also requires the posting of a notice prepared and approved by the EEOC.[49] Although the ADEA, unlike Title VII, does not contain penalties for failing to post, some (but not all) courts have held that the failure to post may extend the time period for filing a charge or court action under the ADEA.[50] Where an employer has prominently posted EEOC notices or otherwise disseminated information about employee rights, a court may infer knowledge, even if there is a claim that the plaintiff never saw or read the information.[51]

---

[48]42 U.S.C. § 2000e-10 (2000); *see* 29 C.F.R. § 1601.30 (2005). According to the EEOC, the poster requirement may be applicable to subsidiaries of covered companies even if they do not have the 15 employees necessary for independent Title VII coverage. EEOC Dec. 68-2-724E, CCH EEOC Dec. ¶ 6006 (1969). The EEOC further has held that failure to display the poster gives reasonable cause to believe that the employer willfully violated § 711(a). EEOC Dec. CL7-6-694, CCH EEOC Dec. ¶ 6009 (1969).

[49]29 U.S.C. § 627 (2000); *see* 29 C.F.R. § 1627.10 (2005).

[50]*E.g.*, EEOC v. Kentucky State Police Dep't, 80 F.3d 1086, 1094–95, 71 FEP 1495 (6th Cir. 1996) (failure to post ADEA notices, coupled with lack of actual or constructive knowledge by employees regarding their rights under ADEA, requires tolling of limitations period); Marley v. Addus Healthcare, Inc., 122 F. Supp. 2d 954, 957–58 (N.D. Ill. 2000) (employee not able to invoke equitable tolling doctrine where employer admittedly failed to post notice of employees' ADEA rights, as court found she had actual notice of her ADEA rights); Nicolai v. Trustmark Ins. Co., 1998 WL 292384, at *2–3 (N.D. Ill. May 20, 1998) (recognizing failure to post notice of ADEA and ADA rights would toll limitations period unless plaintiff knew or should have known of rights); Fairbanks v. Home Sav., 72 FEP 1162 (S.D.N.Y 1996) (same; ADEA claim); Quicker v. American V. Mueller, 712 F. Supp. 824, 828, 49 FEP 1319 (D. Colo. 1989) (the charge-filing period is tolled where the employer failed to post the notice and the charging party filed the charge 2 days after being notified of his rights). *Contra* Kazanzas v. Walt Disney World Co., 704 F.2d 1527, 1530–31, 31 FEP 1590 (11th Cir. 1983) (the ADEA limitations period is not tolled by failure to post the notice); Schroeder v. Copley Newspaper, 879 F.2d 266, 271–72, 50 FEP 447 (7th Cir. 1989) (no tolling due to the employer's failure to post, where another employee told the charging party that he thought the employer was discriminating; the charging party was "generally aware of his right to obtain redress"); Downey v. Firestone Tire & Rubber Co., 35 FEP 30, 31 (D.D.C. 1984) (the ADEA limitations period is not tolled by the failure to post the notice, where the complainant was represented by counsel during the limitations period), *aff'd*, 762 F.2d 137, 37 FEP 1072 (D.C. Cir. 1985). *See generally* Chapter 26 (Timeliness).

[51]*E.g.*, German v. Peña, 88 F. Supp. 2d 216, 221 (S.D.N.Y. 2000) (federal employee denied opportunity to rely on equitable tolling argument where employer posted required notice); *Nicolai*, 1998 WL 292384, at *1 (when notice is prominently posted, presumption is that employee could have learned about federally protected rights); *Fairbanks*, 72 FEP at 1164–65 (so long as defendant made information regarding

Constructive knowledge can likewise be inferred where an employee was represented by counsel.[52]

The ADA requires the posting of a notice "in an accessible format" that describes that Act "in the manner prescribed by section 711" of Title VII.[53] The EEOC's basic poster incorporates information not only on Title VII, the ADEA, and the ADA, but also on the EPA, Executive Order 11246, the Rehabilitation Act of 1973, the Vietnam Era Veterans' Readjustment Assistance Act, Title VI of the Civil Rights Act of 1964, and Title IX of the Education Amendments of 1972.[54]

C. Records and Reports

Section 709(c) of Title VII, incorporated by reference by the ADA,[55] provides in part:

> Every employer, employment agency, and labor organization subject to this title shall (1) make and keep such records relevant to the determinations of whether unlawful employment practices have been or are being committed, (2) preserve such records for such periods, and (3) make such reports therefrom as the Commission shall prescribe by regulation or order . . . .[56]

Section 7(a) of the ADEA provides that the "EEOC shall have the power to . . . require the keeping of records necessary or appropriate for the administration of this act in accordance with the

---

employee rights under ADEA readily available, that plaintiff did not actually read the information does not entitle her to tolling of limitations period).

[52]*E.g.*, Scruggs v. University Health Servs., 134 F. Supp. 2d 1375, 1384 (S.D. Ga. 2001) (attorney representation for part of time that limitations period was running weighs against equitable tolling), *rev'd in part and vacated in part*, 281 F.3d 1285 (11th Cir. 2001); Zellars v. Philadelphia Sch. Dist., 1997 WL 230803 (E.D. Pa. May 1, 1997) (no equitable tolling of 300-day limitations period for filing Title VII claim, because plaintiff was represented by counsel), *aff'd*, 127 F.3d 1098 (3d Cir. 1997).

[53]42 U.S.C. § 12115 (2000). The EEOC's revised poster regulation, 29 C.F.R. § 1601.30 (2005), indicates that the Title VII penalty provision is incorporated into the ADA.

[54]*See* Consolidated EEO Poster, *reprinted in* 8 FEP MAN. (BNA) 441:153.

[55]42 U.S.C. § 12117(a) (2000).

[56]*Id.* § 2000e-8(c). Section 709(c) further requires especially detailed reports from apprenticeship or training programs, and allows applications to the EEOC for exemptions from the recordkeeping and reporting requirements if they "would result in undue hardship." *Id.* Court review is available of any denial by the EEOC of such exemption request; the EEOC also is authorized to apply for court orders requiring compliance. *Id.*

powers provided in [§ 11] of the Fair Labor Standards Act."[57] Section 11(c) of the FLSA authorizes the EEOC to require employers covered by either the ADEA or the Equal Pay Act to make and preserve records and to make such reports as the EEOC "shall prescribe by regulation or order."[58]

1. Reports Required Under Title VII

Employers with 100 or more employees are required to file by September 30 of each year Standard Form 100, also known as the employer information report or EEO-1.[59] The EEO-1 report shows the relationship of minority and female workers to the employer's total workforce in specified job categories.[60] For classification purposes, the employer may use visual surveys or post employment records as to the identity of persons if this is permitted by state law.[61]

Other forms are required of unions,[62] political jurisdictions,[63] and educational institutions and school districts.[64] Willfully false

---

[57]29 U.S.C. § 626(a) (2000). Section 9 of the ADEA, 29 U.S.C. § 628, authorizes the EEOC to establish "reasonable exemptions to and from any or all provisions of this Chapter."

[58]29 U.S.C. § 211(c) (2000).

[59]29 C.F.R. § 1602.7 (2005). The Commission mails these forms to every employer it knows to be subject to the reporting requirement, and mails additional forms to its district offices. Forms are available from the Commission. *Id.*

[60]The job categories are (1) officials and managers, (2) professionals, (3) technicians, (4) sales workers, (5) office and clerical, (6) craft workers (skilled), (7) operatives (semi-skilled), (8) laborers (unskilled), and (9) service workers. *See* EEO-1 Report, *reprinted in* 8 FEP MAN. (BNA) 441:273–74 & 3 EEOC COMPL. MAN. (BNA) N:5071 (Apr. 1, 1995).

[61]29 C.F.R. § 1602.13 (2005). The regulation recommends that these records be segregated from the individual's personnel file. *Id.*; *see also* EEOC Joint Reporting Comm., Standard Form 100 Instruction Booklet 4–5, *reprinted in* 8 FEP MAN. (BNA) 441:275, 275–81. The instruction booklet also provides that no one person can be counted in more than one race-ethnic category and that "Hispanic" is deemed to include all persons of Mexican, Puerto Rican, Cuban, Central or South American, or other Spanish culture or origin, regardless of race.

[62]29 C.F.R. § 1602.22 (2005) (local unions must file biennial EEO-3 reports if they have 100 or more members). Although § 1601.15, which requires annual EEO-2 reports from joint labor-management committees that control apprenticeship programs, still is in existence, in fact the EEOC has not distributed those reporting forms since 1980.

[63]*Id.* § 1602.32 (political jurisdictions with more than 100 employees, and some with 15 or more, must file EEO-4 reports by September 30 of each year).

[64]*Id.* § 1602.41 (elementary and secondary schools must file EEO-5 reports by November 30 biennially); *id.* § 1601.50 (institutions of higher education must file EEO-6 reports by November 30 biennially).

statements on EEO reports violate 18 U.S.C. § 1001, which prohibits the giving of false statements to officials, and are punishable by fine or imprisonment.[65]

Section 709(c) of Title VII specifically authorizes court orders to enforce compliance with the reporting and disclosure requirements,[66] and some courts have issued such orders.[67] If the
reporting criteria are not readily adaptable to the respondent, special reporting procedures may be requested.[68] Special or supplemental reports also may be required.[69]

Once collected, the statistical information is reduced to computer printouts and is available to all EEOC offices, the Office of
Federal Contract Compliance Programs (OFCCP) within the Department of Labor, the Civil Rights Divisions of the Departments
of Justice and Education, and the state and local fair employment
practice agencies with which the EEOC contracts. The data then
are analyzed for use in the EEOC's research reports[70] and statistical

---

[65]See id. § 1602.8 (employers); id. § 1602.16 (joint labor-management committees); id. § 1602.23 (local unions); id. § 1601.33 (political jurisdictions); id. § 1602.42
(elementary and secondary schools); id. § 1602.51 (institutions of higher education).

[66]42 U.S.C. § 2000e-8(c). The Commission amended its regulations implementing
these statutory provisions in July 1991, to add recordkeeping under the ADA and
other changes. 56 Fed. Reg. 35,753 (1991) (codified at 29 C.F.R. pts. 1602 & 1627;
amending then-existing 29 C.F.R. pt. 1602). Among the changes was the addition
of a new subpart that clarifies that the Commission has the authority to investigate
persons to determine whether they comply with the reporting and recordkeeping
requirements under Title VII and the ADA. See 29 C.F.R. § 1602.56. This may have
been prompted by a widely publicized case in which the EEOC discovered that two
employment referral services were destroying records; the EEOC successfully moved
for a temporary restraining order and preliminary injunction. See EEOC v. Recruit
U.S.A., Inc., 939 F.2d 746, 758, 56 FEP 721 (9th Cir. 1991).

[67]See, e.g., EEOC v. Rogers Bros., Inc., 470 F.2d 965, 965–66, 4 FEP 1123 (5th
Cir. 1972) (per curiam) (district court's denial of injunction vacated and remanded
with instructions to grant the injunction unless defendants "comply with the law";
"an injunction is . . . the only effective remedy for a deliberate refusal to obey the
law"); EEOC v. Merrill Lynch, Pierce, Fenner & Smith, 677 F. Supp. 918, 932, 58
FEP 1778 (N.D. Ill. 1987) (injunction issued requiring the employer to submit the
required reports to the EEOC).

[68]29 C.F.R. § 1602.10 (2005) (employer); id. § 1602.18 (apprenticeship); id.
§ 1602.25 (labor organization); id. § 1602.35 (political jurisdiction); id. § 1602.44
(elementary and secondary schools); id. § 1602.53 (higher education).

[69]Id. §§ 1602.11 & 1602.12 (employer); id. § 1602.19 (apprenticeship); id.
§ 1602.26 (labor organization); id. § 1602.37 (political jurisdiction); id. § 1602.45
(elementary and secondary school); id. § 1602.54 (higher education).

[70]E.g., EEOC, JOB PATTERNS FOR MINORITIES AND WOMEN IN PRIVATE INDUSTRY
(1989). Additionally, in the early 1990s a "Glass Ceiling Initiative" was launched

investigations. The data can be retrieved in summary form by industry[71] for all reporting employers in the same geographic area[72] or state, or for the nation as a whole. This allows the comparison of an individual respondent with other respondents in the same industry drawing generally upon the same available workforce.[73]

2. Records to Be Made or Kept

For purposes of Title VII and the ADA, "[t]he [EEOC] has not adopted any requirement, generally applicable to employers, that records be made or kept."[74] It has, however, adopted such requirements under the ADEA and the EPA.

Under the ADEA, covered employers are required to make and keep payroll-type records of their employees for three years.[75] Such records must contain each employee's name, address, date of birth, occupation, rate of pay, and compensation earned each week.[76]

Employers covered by the EPA are required to make and preserve records as required of employers under the FLSA.[77] Such records must contain each employee's name, address, date of birth (if under 19), sex, occupation, and specified detailed information on earnings, which information is more detailed for nonexempt than exempt employees.[78]

---

by the Department of Labor to identify and examine barriers to advancement in the workplace among women and minorities. Under this initiative, a commission of 21 members studied opportunities for and artificial barriers to the advancement of women and minorities to management and decision-making positions in business. *See* EEOC, *available at* www.eeoc.gov/35th/thelaw/cra.1991.html (last visited Aug. 6, 2003).

[71]Based on Standard Industrial Classifications (SIC).

[72]By Standard Metropolitan Statistical Area (SMSA).

[73]Where tabulations have previously been compiled by the EEOC and are available in documentary form, the information is available under the Freedom of Information Act, 5 U.S.C. § 552 et seq., so long as the tabulations involve at least three responding entities and do not reveal the identity of an individual or the dominant entity in a particular industry or area. 29 C.F.R. § 1610.18(a) (2005). This data is a valuable tool for employers to measure how they compare with others in their industry, and can be a valuable litigation tool for plaintiffs and defendants.

[74]29 C.F.R. § 1602.12 (2005).

[75]*Id.* § 1627.3(a).

[76]*Id.*

[77]*Id.* § 1620.32(a).

[78]*Id.* (incorporating by reference the Department of Labor FLSA regulations at *id.* § 516).

3. Preservation of Records Made or Kept

Although employers are not required to make or keep particular records under Title VII or the ADA, the EEOC requires retention of certain records if they are made in the first place. Such records must be maintained or kept for a minimum period of one year from the date of the making of the record or the personnel action involved.[79] If the records are relevant to a charge or action, they must be retained until "final disposition of the charge or action."[80] The types of records covered are specified in the regulations.[81]

Under the ADEA, in addition to the records required to be made and kept, employers must preserve for at least one year records relating to hiring, promotion, demotion, transfer, recall, and discharge.[82] Where a charge has been filed or the EEOC otherwise begins enforcement activities, the records must be preserved pending final disposition.[83]

Under the EPA, in addition to records required to be made or kept, employers must preserve for two years "records [the employer] makes . . . which explain the basis for payment of any wage differential" to employees of the opposite sex in the same establishment.[84]

Employers falling within the scope of the Uniform Guidelines on Employee Selection Procedures[85] are required to maintain records

---

[79]29 C.F.R. § 1602.14 (2005). Many states require longer record retention. *See, e.g.*, CAL. GOV'T CODE § 12946 (requiring 2-year retention).

[80]*Id.* Courts may or may not penalize a defendant who has failed to maintain records where the administrative process has been prolonged. *Compare* Smith v. Caterpillar, Inc., 338 F.3d 730 (7th Cir. 2003) (employer's loss of records and faded witnesses' memories pertinent to a suit filed by an employee 8.5 years after filing with the EEOC results in employer prejudice and the doctrine of laches precludes action) *with* Robinson v. American Int'l Adjustment Co., 53 FEP 898, 903 (D.N.J. 1990) (the employer was not prejudiced by a suit 6 years after discharge, even though the EEOC destroyed records, since the employer should have maintained them).

[81]*See* 29 C.F.R. § 1602.14 (2005) (employer recordkeeping); *id.* §§ 1602.20–.21 (apprenticeship program recordkeeping); *id.* §§ 1602.27–.28 (labor organization recordkeeping); *id.* §§ 1602.30–.31 (political jurisdictions recordkeeping); *id.* §§ 1602.39–.40 (recordkeeping by elementary and secondary school systems); *id.* §§ 1602.48–.49 (recordkeeping by institutions of higher education).

[82]*Id.* § 1627.3(b).

[83]*Id.* § 1627.3(b)(3); *see also id.* § 1627.4 (records to be retained by employment agencies for 1 year); *id.* § 1627.5 (records to be retained by labor organizations for 1 year, or until the disposition of an EEOC charge or enforcement action).

[84]*Id.* § 1620.32(c).

[85]29 C.F.R. pt. 1607. The Uniform Guidelines apply to all employers covered by Title VII and all federal contractors covered by Executive Order 11246.

or other information that disclose the impact of their selection procedures on employment opportunities, including records concerning the individual components of a selection process.[86]

4. Adverse Inference From Failure to Preserve

The Second Circuit has affirmed the availability of an adverse inference jury instruction where an employer allows destruction of records ordered to be preserved under § 709(c), irrespective of bad faith.[87]

III. THE EEOC ENFORCEMENT PROCESS[88]

On April 19, 1995, the EEOC significantly changed its charge-processing procedures in an attempt to streamline them.[89] The EEOC further ordered the development of both national and local enforcement plans.[90] This section focuses primarily on the EEOC enforcement process as it has existed and evolved since April 1995.[91]

---

[86]*Id.* §§ 1607.4, 1607.15; *cf.* Atonio v. Ward's Cove Packing Co., 54 FEP 1623, 1625 (W.D. Wash. 1991) (no adverse inference should be drawn against the employer, which had destroyed job applications, because the Uniform Guidelines' requirement to preserve records was not mandatory with respect to the jobs at issue, particularly since the jobs were seasonal), *aff'd*, 275 F.3d 797 (2001).

[87]*See* Zimmermann v. Associates First Capital Corp., 251 F.3d 376, 383–84, 85 FEP 1505 (2d Cir. 2001); Byrnie v. Town of Cromwell, 243 F.3d 93, 107–11 (2d Cir. 2001).

[88]The same procedures generally pertain to charges filed under each of the four statutes for which the EEOC has administrative-enforcement responsibility, except for differences mandated by the statutes themselves. *See, e.g.,* EEOC v. Home of Economy, 712 F.2d 356, 357, 32 FEP 599 (8th Cir. 1983) (the EEOC may file suit under the EPA, unlike under Title VII, without first attempting conciliation); 1 EEOC COMPL. MAN. (BNA) § 60.3(a), at 60:0001 (same).

[89]*Charge Processing Procedures Adopted by EEOC and Task Force Recommendations to Be Implemented by Chairman* (Apr. 19, 1995), *reprinted in* DAILY LAB. REP. (BNA) at E-5 (Apr. 20, 1995); *see* News and Background, *EEOC Adopts Charge-Priority System,* 149 LRR 13 (May 1, 1995).

[90]*Id.*

[91]A more extensive explication of the system that existed prior to April 1995 is contained in the earlier editions of this treatise. *See* BARBARA LINDEMANN SCHLEI & PAUL GROSSMAN, EMPLOYMENT DISCRIMINATION LAW 938–39 (2d ed. 1983); BARBARA LINDEMANN & PAUL GROSSMAN, EMPLOYMENT DISCRIMINATION LAW 1214–17 (3d ed. 1996) (P. Cane, ed.).

A. Evolution of the Current System

The EEOC's system for resolving charges since April 1995 evolved from the experiences with, and criticisms of, the Commission's prior approaches. The "rapid charge" processing system of the late 1970s and early 1980s[92] gave way to a "full remedy" approach in the mid-1980s.[93] In April 1995, the EEOC rescinded certain of its earlier policy statements[94] and began implementing a new "priority" charge-processing system, featuring a two-track enforcement approach. In some areas, the EEOC vested more discretion in its district offices; in other areas, such as those involving priority issues for litigation and class-type claims, central oversight continued to be exercised.[95]

During this period, the EEOC developed, and continues to rely on, a uniform case management and tracking system. Field managers and supervisors prioritize cases according to established guidelines.[96] Those personnel rely on reports (generated from the

---

[92]The agency implemented rapid charge processing to reduce a backlog of charges that had reached 70,000 by January 1978. The principal components of that system were (1) a backlog unit to reduce the charge inventory; (2) a rapid charge-processing system, which featured narrowed charges and resolved them principally through a face-to-face, fact-finding conference; and (3) an Early Litigation Identification (ELI) program under which some charges were winnowed out for expanded investigation and possible litigation.

[93]In December 1983 the EEOC adopted a system of case-by-case determinations. DAILY LAB. REP. (BNA) at A-5, D-1 (Dec. 12, 1983). The EEOC stated its expectation that there would be an adequate evidentiary basis for a merits determination before any charge would be resolved. EEOC, 19TH ANN. REP. 4–5 (1984). The September 1984 policy statement represented that all "cause" determinations failing conciliation would be considered by the Commission itself for litigation. DAILY LAB. REP. (BNA) at D-1 (Sept. 17, 1984). In February 1985, the Commission adopted its *Statement of Policy on Remedies and Relief in Individual Cases of Discrimination*, which established that the agency would seek in conciliation the full relief to which a charging party would be entitled if the case were successfully litigated. 1 EEOC COMPL. MAN. (BNA) § 60, exh. 60-A, at 60:0005.

[94]*See* DAILY LAB. REP. (BNA) at E-5 (Apr. 20, 1995) (rescinding the policy statements issued in December 1983, September 1984, and February 1985).

[95]The EEOC's April 1995 changes in charge-processing procedures ordered the development of a National Enforcement Plan:

That the Chairman develop, in consultation with the General Counsel, a National Enforcement Plan for approval by the Commission that will identify priority issues and set out a plan for administrative and litigation enforcement.

Id. at E-5.

[96]Charges that have priority include charges nearing the expiration of the statute of limitations, cases that call for a temporary restraining order (e.g., retaliation

Commission's Information Mission System (IMS))[97] that summarize the nature and status of all charges on file in each office.

B. Place for Filing Charge and Venue

A charge may be filed at any EEOC office or with any representative of the EEOC.[98] If the respondent has no facility within the district where the charge is filed, the district office forwards the charge for docketing and investigation to a district office with jurisdiction over the location (1) where the charging party worked, or (2) where the respondent facility responsible for the alleged discrimination is located.[99]

---

and ongoing sexual harassment) or otherwise require quick action (e.g., the witness is leaving town), and potential "cause" cases. Otherwise, charges generally are investigated in the order of their arrival ("docket order"). 1 EEOC COMPL. MAN. (BNA) § 2.8, at 2:0011–12.

[97]IMS is an automated management information system that was fully installed during FY 2003. It contains complete information on all charges filed with the EEOC. Data is entered into the national database from each of the field offices.

[98]29 C.F.R. § 1601.8 (2005) (Title VII, ADA); *id.* § 1626.5 (ADEA). Many state and local fair employment practices agencies have entered into contracts and "work-sharing agreements" with the EEOC providing that the filing with the state agency constitutes a filing with the EEOC and vice versa. *See id.* §§ 1601.13(a)(4)(ii), 1626.10(c). *See generally* Chapter 26 (Timeliness). A related topic, the "deferral" of charges to state agencies, is discussed in Section III.E *infra.*

[99]1 EEOC COMPL. MAN. (BNA) § 2.7(f), at 2:0011. The selection of the proper office is important where the EEOC office effectuates deferral to a state or local agency. By statute, deferral or referral must be to the state or local agency where the alleged unlawful employment practice occurred. *See* 42 U.S.C. § 2000e-5(d) (2000) (Title VII and ADA); 29 U.S.C. § 633(b) (2000) (ADEA). Failure to defer to the proper office may, under some circumstances, preclude the filing of a federal lawsuit. *See* Freeman v. CSX Transp. Co., 730 F. Supp. 1084, 1086–87, 51 FEP 761 (M.D. Ala. 1989) (case dismissed for failing to file a timely charge, where discrimination occurred in Alabama but plaintiff filed the charge with the Florida fair employment practices agency and the EEOC's Miami office; the extended 300-day federal charge-filing period was unavailable). *But see* Sofferin v. American Airlines, Inc., 923 F.2d 552, 555–60, 56 FEP 338 (7th Cir. 1991) (case of plaintiff who filed with the EEOC's Detroit office, where discrimination occurred in Illinois, will not be dismissed, where the EEOC transferred the charge to its Chicago office, which has a work-sharing agreement with Illinois providing for waiver of deferral); Husch v. Szabo Food Serv. Co., 851 F.2d 999, 1003–04, 47 FEP 566 (7th Cir. 1988) (equitable tolling permitted where plaintiff filed an age discrimination complaint with an agency in a state in which a reasonable person would believe discrimination occurred; action stayed pending referral to the proper state agency); McKee v. Painters, 51 FEP 1470, 471–72 (D.N.J. 1990) (ADEA action stayed pending referral to fair employment practices agency in District of Columbia, since that is where plaintiff

C. The Intake and Initial Investigation of a Charge

The charge-intake process is designed to screen out invalid charges at the earliest juncture and to elicit the evidence upon which a charging party rests his or her discrimination claim. Charging parties will be advised of the EEOC's jurisdictional requirements and will be informed that some charges may be dismissed at intake, with a notice of right to sue; however, a charging party will never be told that he or she cannot file a charge.[100]

Under priority charge-handling procedures, the field offices "categorize and prioritize charges" into one of three categories, based on the likely merit of a particular charge:

> The *first* category includes those high priority charges identified as falling within the national or local enforcement plans and those in which it appears more likely than not that discrimination has occurred; the *second* category includes those charges that initially appear to have some merit but will require additional evidence to determine whether it is more likely than not that a violation occurred; and the *third* category includes those charges appropriate for resolution just after intake or following a brief investigation.[101]

Subsequently, the EEOC elaborated on each of the three categories for classifying new charges.[102] The first category, in addition to including charges that fall within the national or local enforcement plan and charges where further investigation will probably result in a finding of discrimination, includes charges where "irreparable harm will result unless processing is expedited."[103] The second category is reserved for cases where additional information is needed to determine whether the cases should be assigned to either the first or third categories.[104] A charge may be placed in the third category and dismissed when the office has sufficient

---

was told to retire or be terminated and where the letter of resignation was sent; cause of action therefore arose in District of Columbia, although plaintiff lived in New Jersey); Porta v. Rollins Envtl. Servs., 654 F. Supp. 1275, 1281, 50 FEP 11 (D.N.J. 1987) (court will not dismiss Title VII action though plaintiff did not file with state and it was unclear whether the EEOC did; the EEOC's error will not redound to plaintiff's detriment), *aff'd mem.*, 845 F.2d 1014 (3d Cir. 1988).

[100]DAILY LAB. REP. (BNA) at E-5 (Apr. 20, 1995).

[101]*Id.* (emphasis added).

[102]Priority Charge Handling Procedures, *reprinted in* 1 FEP MAN. (BNA) 405:7311 (June 20, 1995).

[103]*Id.* at 7317.

[104]*Id.*

information from which to conclude that it is not likely that further investigation will result in a cause finding.[105] Examples of cases falling into the third category are where the Commission lacks jurisdiction, where the charges are unsupported by any evidence and the charging party was in a position to have such evidence, where the charging party is not credible, where the charging party has a history of filing repetitive charges and is not credible, where the charge is filed beyond the limitations period, and where the charging party has failed to cooperate with the EEOC.[106]

The EEOC adopted its National Enforcement Plan on February 8, 1996, in which the EEOC identified three major categories of priorities: (1) cases that by their nature have the potential of a significant impact beyond the parties to the particular dispute; (2) cases having the potential of promoting the development of law supporting the purposes of the statutes enforced by the EEOC; and (3) cases "involving the integrity or effectiveness of the Commission's enforcement process."[107]

This discussion to some extent has begged the threshold question of what *is* a "charge." A charge is a written statement made by the complainant that is "sufficiently precise to identify the parties, and to describe generally the practices complained of."[108] Correspondence that might constitute a charge is date-stamped and given to the Charge Receipt and Technical Information Unit (CR/TIU) to determine whether it contains all the elements necessary for a charge, to determine jurisdiction, and to seek follow-up information.[109] To constitute a charge, correspondence need not be received on an official EEOC charge form so long as it is in writing and contains the required information, e.g., the name of the respondent and the relevant facts of the alleged discrimination, including pertinent dates.[110]

The EEOC regulations provide that amendments to perfect, verify, or add to a charge relate back to the date the charge first

[105]*Id.* at 7313–14.

[106]*Id.*

[107]National Enforcement Plan (Feb. 8, 1996), *reprinted in* DAILY LAB. REP. (BNA) at D-20 (Feb. 9, 1996).

[108]29 C.F.R. §§ 1601.11 & 1601.12(a) (2005) (Title VII and ADA); 29 C.F.R. §§ 1626.6, 1626.8 (2005) (ADEA); *see also* Edelman v. Lynchburg Coll., 535 U.S. 106, 110 n.2, 88 FEP 321 (2002).

[109]1 EEOC COMPL. MAN. (BNA) § 1.6, at 1:0001–02; *id.* § 2.2, at 2:0001.

[110]*See* 29 C.F.R. §§ 1601.11 & 1601.12(a) (2005) (Title VII and ADA); *id.* §§ 1626.6, 1626.8 (ADEA); *see, e.g.*, Dupree v. Housing Auth., 55 FEP 163, 167

was received.[111] An unverified letter to the EEOC from a charging party may be an otherwise valid charge that can be perfected after the charge-filing period.[112] Additionally, several cases suggest that, at least in some circumstances, an unverified EEOC intake questionnaire, completed by the charging party, can be perfected after the charge-filing period.[113]

A filed charge "starts the [EEOC] down the road to investigation, conciliation and enforcement."[114] Once a charge is filed, "the EEOC has exclusive jurisdiction over the claim for 180 days. During

---

(D. Kan. 1991) (letters complaining of sex discrimination constituted valid charges, even though the EEOC ignored them and issued a notice of right to sue on the plaintiff's race charge only); Farr v. Continental White Cap, Inc., 762 F. Supp. 814, 816, 55 FEP 1330 (N.D. Ill.) (the plaintiff's letter alleging age discrimination constituted an ADEA charge), *vacated in part on other grounds on reconsideration*, 774 F. Supp. 522, 57 FEP 165 (N.D. Ill. 1991); Montgomery v. Atlanta Family Rests., Inc., 752 F. Supp. 1575, 1578–80, 55 FEP 653 (N.D. Ga. 1990) (a letter from the plaintiff's attorney constituted a charge, even though the EEOC rejected it). *But see* Bennett v. Russ Berrie & Co., 564 F. Supp. 1576, 1579, 32 FEP 225 (N.D. Ill. 1983) (a letter from the employee's attorney to the EEOC and the state FEP agency did not constitute a Title VII charge; the EEOC did not accept or treat the letter as a charge, process or investigate it, make attempts to conciliate the matter, or give the employer notice of the charge). *See generally* Chapter 29 (EEOC Litigation).

[111]29 C.F.R. § 1601.12(b) (2005); *see Edelman*, 535 U.S. at 110 n.2 (" 'a charge may be amended to cure technical defects or omissions, including failure to verify the charge, or to amplify allegations made therein' " and " 'such amendments . . . relate back to the date the charge was first received' ") (quoting 29 C.F.R. § 1601.12(b)); *see also* Peterson v. City of Wichita, 888 F.2d 1307, 1308, 51 FEP 525 (10th Cir. 1989) (verification of the original, unverified charge relates back to the date of original filing, pursuant to EEOC regulation). *But see* Austin v. Russell County Sch. Bd., 53 FEP 1749, 1750 (W.D. Va. 1990) (the relation-back doctrine does not apply where EEOC sought to perfect charge, but the plaintiff did not cooperate); Proffit v. Keycom Elec. Publ'g, 625 F. Supp. 400, 408, 40 FEP 1 (N.D. Ill. 1985) (plaintiff was not permitted to use relation-back doctrine to circumvent the filing deadlines where the "new" charge of discrimination occurred outside both the state and federal filing periods).

[112]Edelman v. Lynchburg Coll., 300 F.3d 400, 406 (4th Cir. 2002).

[113]Philbin v. General Elec. Capital Auto Lease, Inc., 929 F.2d 321, 323, 55 FEP 867 (7th Cir. 1991) (per curiam) ("[A]n intake questionnaire which is later verified may be sufficient to constitute a charge in some circumstances."); Clark v. Coates & Clark, Inc., 865 F.2d 1237, 1239–41, 49 FEP 99 (11th Cir. 1989) (finding timely a charge not perfected until after the limitations period had run, but that was based upon a valid, timely filed intake questionnaire); Casavantes v. California State Univ., 732 F.2d 1441, 1442, 34 FEP 1336 (9th Cir. 1984) ("[F]iling of an Intake Questionnaire satisfied the statutory obligation to initiate the administrative process within the required . . . period.").

[114]Edelman, 535 U.S. at 115. Although the practice varies somewhat among the EEOC's field offices, investigators typically also rotate into each field office's Charge Receipt and Technical Information Unit (CR/TIU), where they draft charges and exhaustively interview complainants. Each investigator typically is responsible for

that period, the employee must obtain a right-to-sue letter from the agency before prosecuting the claim.[115] In most instances, the investigation begins with an interview of the charging party, involving a several-part process. First, the investigative assistant or investigator explains the administrative process and suit procedure and reviews the matter for basic jurisdictional and timeliness information, including possible grounds for tolling.[116] Next, the investigator conducts an in-depth discussion with the complainant regarding the nature of his or her problem, seeking to identify the basis or bases for a charge, define the issues, and probe the type and quality of the evidence supporting the charging party's discrimination claim. If the complainant has not already done so, the investigator ultimately drafts the charge and reduces the charging party's statements to an affidavit. The session closes with postcharge counseling, in which the investigator discusses possible relief and the charging party's obligation to cooperate in the investigative process.[117]

In age cases, the complainant has the option of filing a confidential complaint rather than a charge, but such a complaint technically does not preserve private-suit rights.[118] An equal pay allegation that does not implicate Title VII also will be taken at the complainant's request. Here, though, a confidential complaint does not curtail private-suit rights because a charge is not a prerequisite for an EPA action to begin with.[119]

If a charge is not resolved during the initial investigation, further investigation follows. That process is discussed below in Section III.J.

D. Assignment of a Charge Number

The CR/TIU supervisor authorizes the assignment of a charge number to each charge.[120] The number has 12 digits. The first three

---

resolving the charges that he or she formulates at intake. EEOC, COMBINED ANN. REP. FISCAL YEARS 1986, 1987, 1988, at 3–7 (1988).

[115]EEOC v. Waffle House, Inc., 534 U.S. 279, 291 (2002); *see also* Section III.I *infra.*

[116]*See generally* Chapter 26 (Timeliness).

[117]1 EEOC COMPL. MAN. (BNA) §§ 2.1–2.6, at 2:0001–09.

[118]29 C.F.R. § 1626.4 (2005); 1 EEOC COMPL. MAN. (BNA) § 2.3(c), at 2:0002. In practice, however, such individuals generally file an anonymous third-party charge, and therefore retain their private-suit right.

[119]1 EEOC COMPL. MAN. (BNA) § 2.3(b), at 2:0002. *See generally* Chapter 18 (Compensation).

[120]1 EEOC COMPL. MAN. (BNA) § 2.7, at 2:0009.

digits identify the office that received the charge; the next four digits represent the fiscal year of receipt; and the last five digits indicate the sequence in which the charge was received in that year.[121]

E. Deferral and Contracts With State and Local Agencies

Section 706 of Title VII (incorporated by reference by the ADA) requires that before a charge may be filed with the EEOC, it first must be filed with the state or local fair employment practices agency, if any, where the alleged discrimination "occurred."[122] Somewhat similarly, § 14(b) and § 7(d) of the ADEA require resort to the state agency as a condition precedent to suit, though not as a condition precedent to filing with the EEOC.[123]

State and local agencies having the requisite jurisdiction and enforcement authority are designated by EEOC regulations as "FEP agencies" or "deferral agencies."[124] The EEOC defers Title VII and ADA charges initially received by the EEOC to FEP agencies for an initial 60-day period unless the agency earlier terminates its proceedings or waives its right exclusively to process a charge during the 60-day period.[125]

If a charge arises in a jurisdiction with an FEP agency but in a substantive area over which the FEP agency has waived its exclusive processing rights, EEOC regulations provide that the charge

---

[121]For example, "210-2003-00476" indicates that the charge was the 476th charge received in the Chicago district office during FY 2003.

[122]42 U.S.C. § 2000e-5 (2000); *see generally* Chapter 26 (Timeliness). At least one court has held that a state legislature's declaration that filing with the EEOC "shall be deemed" to constitute filing with the state does not mean that a plaintiff can bypass the state; failure also to file there precludes suit. Scheller v. Hydrotherm, Inc., 728 F. Supp. 377, 379–80, 51 FEP 979 (D. Md. 1989).

[123]29 U.S.C. § 633(b) (2000); Oscar Mayer & Co. v. Evans, 441 U.S. 750, 753, 19 FEP 1167 (1979) (§ 14(b) of the ADEA, 29 U.S.C. § 633(b), requires a complainant to file with an available state agency before instituting an ADEA action in federal court). *See generally* Chapter 12 (Age). *But see* Colgan v. Fisher Scientific Co., 935 F.2d 1407, 1414, 56 FEP 106 (3d Cir. 1991) (en banc) (an ADEA filing with the EEOC is viewed as filing with the state).

[124]29 C.F.R. §§ 1601.70 & 1601.71 (2005) (Title VII and ADA); *id.* §§ 1626.9 & .10 (ADEA). They formerly were known as "706 agencies," referring to § 706 of Title VII; the name was changed to prevent confusion with regard to charges filed under the ADA. *See* 56 Fed. Reg. 9623 (1991) (codified at 29 C.F.R. pt. 1601). Section 1601.74 lists FEP agencies, to which deferral procedures apply, and "Notice Agencies," to which deferral is not required but to which the EEOC sends notice of charges.

[125]29 C.F.R. § 1601.13(a)(3) (2005).

is filed upon initial receipt by the EEOC (and is timely so long as it is received within 300 days).[126]

Where the FEP agency has not waived its right to exclusive processing of a Title VII or an ADA charge, the EEOC district office sends the charge to the FEP agency by registered mail (unless the FEP agency and the EEOC have agreed to another method).[127] State/local proceedings are commenced on the date the charge is mailed or hand delivered by the EEOC.[128] The charging party then is advised of the deferral, and the Title VII or ADA charge is deemed automatically "filed" with the EEOC upon the expiration of 60 days.[129]

The EEOC is authorized by Title VII,[130] the ADA,[131] and the ADEA[132] to enter into agreements with state and local FEP agencies.

---

[126]*Id.* § 1601.13(a)(4)(ii)(A); *see* EEOC v. Commercial Office Prods., 486 U.S. 107, 115, 123, 46 FEP 1265 (1988) (waiver constitutes "termination" within the meaning of the statute, so the EEOC may deem a charge filed, even where the agency reserves the option to take further action after the EEOC completes its investigation; the extended 300-day period for filing an EEOC charge in a deferral state applies even if the charge is untimely under state/local law). In the wake of *Commercial Office Prods.*, most courts have held that waiver is self-executing, not dependent on the exchange of paperwork between the EEOC and the FEP agency. EEOC v. Techalloy Md., Inc., 894 F.2d 676, 678, 52 FEP 36 (4th Cir. 1990); Trevino-Barton v. Pittsburgh Nat'l Bank, 919 F.2d 874, 878–79, 56 FEP 291 (3d Cir. 1990); Green v. Los Angeles County Superintendent of Schools, 883 F.2d 1472, 1476 n.4, 50 FEP 1233 (9th Cir. 1989); Griffin v. Air Prods. & Chems., Inc., 883 F.2d 940, 943, 50 FEP 1444 (11th Cir. 1989). *But cf.* Sofferin v. American Airlines, Inc., 923 F.2d 552, 555–60, 56 FEP 338 (7th Cir. 1991) (remanding for district court to determine whether a work-sharing agreement made waiver self-executing, or whether waiver occurred only when the EEOC employee, who is the designated agent of the state, determines that waiver applies).

[127]29 C.F.R. § 1601.13(a)(4)(i)(B) (2005).

[128]*Id.* § 1601.14(a)(4)(i)(B).

[129]*Id.* § 1601.13(a)(4)(ii)(B). Prior to the lapse of 60 days, the EEOC reserves the right to make an immediate preliminary-relief investigation pursuant to § 706(f)(2) of Title VII. 29 C.F.R. § 1601.13(d) (2005).

[130]*See* 42 U.S.C. § 2000e-4(g)(1) (2000) (power to cooperate with local agencies); *id.* § 2000e-5(b) (the EEOC should "accord substantial weight" to findings of local agencies); *id.* § 2000e-8(b) (the EEOC may cooperate with state and local agencies, contribute to the cost of their research and projects, utilize their services, pay for said services, and join such agencies in work-sharing agreements).

[131]Section 107(a) of the ADA incorporates the powers of §§ 705 and 706 of Title VII. *See* 42 U.S.C. § 12117 (2000).

[132]*See* 29 U.S.C. § 625(b) (2000) (power to cooperate with state and local agencies); *id.* § 626(b) (incorporating § 11(b) of the FLSA (29 U.S.C. § 211), which permits the EEOC to utilize the services of state and local agencies, and reimburse them for those services).

Most district offices do so through contracts and "work-sharing agreements."[133] A work-sharing agreement is required as a condition of entering into a charge-resolution contract. Work-sharing agreements provide for the dual filing of charges and identify categories of charges for which the EEOC or the FEP agency has initial investigative responsibility.[134]

The EEOC awards annual contracts to designated FEP agencies to investigate and resolve Title VII, ADA, and ADEA charges. Under the funding principles approved by the Commission, the FEP agency must meet certain standards of capability, performance, and compatibility with the EEOC's charge investigation systems and methods to qualify for such a contract. The FEP agency contracts to investigate to conclusion a minimum number of charges at a fixed amount per charge.

Section 706(b) of Title VII (and, by incorporation, the ADA) requires that the EEOC accord "substantial weight" to the final findings and orders of FEP agencies when the EEOC makes its own determinations.[135] Many EEOC charges are resolved in this

---

[133]*See* 1 EEOC COMPL. MAN. (BNA) § 5, at 5:0001–08.

[134]*Id.* §§ 5.1 & 5.2, at 5:0001. Such agreements permit the staff of the agency receiving the charge to determine whether that agency is the one to investigate the charge initially, or whether under the terms of the agreement the charge initially is to be investigated by the other agency. Copies of all charges received by one agency are sent to the other with the appropriate transmittal forms (EEOC Form 212) and notices to respondents (EEOC Forms 131 and 131-A). The most common division of labor between agencies is to have the receiving office initially investigate. Agreements also can and do provide for specific categories of charges in which each agency might have a particular interest. In the wake of *Mohasco Corp. v. Silver*, 447 U.S. 807, 23 FEP 1 (1980), work-sharing agreements expressly provide that FEP agencies waive their exclusive processing rights over charges received between 240 and 300 days after an alleged violation. The EEOC will initially investigate these charges. In *Maynard v. Pneumatic Products Corp.*, 256 F.3d 1259, 1263–64, 11 AD 1790 (11th Cir. 2001), the Eleventh Circuit held that the failure of a plaintiff to enter a copy of the relevant work-sharing agreement into the record waived his timing argument.

[135]42 U.S.C. § 2000e-5(b) (2000); *see also* 29 C.F.R. § 1601.21(e) (2005). The EEOC has been challenged occasionally on this issue. *See, e.g.*, EEOC v. James Julian, Inc., 736 F. Supp. 59, 62, 53 FEP 458 (D. Del. 1990) (no procedural irregularity occurred where the EEOC found cause but the FEP agency found no cause; the EEOC had no reason to accord substantial weight where state and federal law differed); *cf.* EEOC v. Best Prods. Co., 53 FEP 883, 884 (N.D. Tex. 1990) (the EEOC officials' testimony sufficed on whether the EEOC accorded substantial weight to the FEP agency's decision; the EEOC should not have to litigate the question of whether the weight accorded was substantial enough).

manner, with the EEOC simply adopting the findings of the state or local agency.[136]

F. Service of the Charge on the Respondent

As amended in 1972, Title VII (and, by incorporation, the ADA) requires the EEOC to serve notice of a charge upon the respondent within 10 days.[137] Section 7(d) of the ADEA provides that the EEOC should "promptly notify" all named respondents that there is a charge.[138] Regardless of the violation charged, the EEOC typically serves respondents with notice (EEOC Form 131) and a copy of the actual charge.[139] The EEOC will not serve the respondent with notice of an otherwise sufficient charge until it has been verified.[140] If a charge is amended or perfected prior to service, the respondent is served only the amended charge.[141] On the back

---

[136]1 EEOC COMPL. MAN. § 5.8 (BNA) at 5:0007.

[137]42 U.S.C. § 2000e-5(b) & (e) (2000). Prior to 1972, the EEOC often delayed service until after it began its investigation—which was often several years after the charge was filed—to forestall any retaliatory action against the charging party or destruction of records by the respondent. Respondents, however, found that the practice frustrated early resolution of problems, built up back-pay liabilities that diminished the likelihood of settlements, and led to the unknowing destruction of relevant documents. *See* EEOC v. Shell Oil Co., 466 U.S. 54, 81 & n.38, 34 FEP 709 (1984).

[138]29 U.S.C. § 626(d) (2000).

[139]*See* 29 C.F.R. § 1601.14 (Title VII and ADA) (2005). ADEA charges are not themselves required to be sent. *Id.* § 1626.11. A copy of the charge will not be sent if the EEOC determines that to do so would impede its law enforcement functions. *Id.* § 1601.14. That may be the case (1) where the charge names more than one respondent; (2) where the charge is filed "on behalf of" an aggrieved person who could be identified from the charge; (3) where the charging party expresses concern about the charge being sent to respondent; (4) where the allegations are vague or incoherent, or otherwise of such a nature as not to facilitate resolution; or (5) where the charge has not yet been drafted on EEOC Form 5. 1 EEOC COMPL. MAN. (BNA) § 3.6, at 3:0003. In that event, the respondent receives a notice, stating the date, place, and circumstances of the alleged discrimination and, where appropriate, the identity of the person or organization filing the charge. 29 C.F.R. § 1601.14 (2005). Notice of the charge need contain only that information required to be included in the charge itself under § 1601.12(a)(3). *Shell Oil*, 466 U.S. at 78–79; EEOC v. K-Mart Corp., 796 F.2d 139, 144, 41 FEP 371 (6th Cir. 1986) (per curiam) (a charge that served as notice was sufficient under *Shell Oil*). *But see Shell Oil*, 466 U.S. at 91 (O'Connor, J., dissenting) (notice is sufficient only when it informs the respondent of the complainant's underlying reasons for filing the charge and is sufficient for a well-intentioned respondent to undertake immediate remedial measures if the charge is valid).

[140]Edelman v. Lynchburg Coll., 535 U.S. 106, 115, 88 FEP 321 (2002).

[141]1 EEOC COMPL. MAN. (BNA) § 3.6, at 3:0003.

of the notice, the EEOC reminds respondents to refrain from retaliation and to preserve records.

Most courts have held that the EEOC's failure to serve the charge or notice of the charge within the mandated 10 days does not affect subsequent private litigation by an individual claimant.[142] However, the EEOC's tardiness sometimes may bar its own suits.[143]

G. Administrative Closures

Some charges end with "administrative closure."[144] The most important of these are discussed below.

1. Withdrawal

The EEOC's regulation (29 C.F.R. § 1601.10) governing Title VII and ADA charges provides in part:

> A charge filed by or on behalf of a person claiming to be aggrieved may be withdrawn only by the person claiming to be aggrieved and only with the consent of the Commission.

---

[142]*E.g.*, Edelman v. Lynchburg Coll., 300 F.3d 400, 404–05 (4th Cir. 2002) ("Once a valid charge has been filed, a simple failure by the EEOC to fulfill its statutory duties regarding the charge does not preclude a Title VII claim.") (citing Walters v. Robert Bosch Corp., 683 F.2d 89, 92 (4th Cir. 1982)); Smith v. American President Lines, Ltd., 571 F.2d 102, 107 n.8, 16 FEP 712 (2d Cir. 1978); Brewster v. Shockley, 554 F. Supp. 365, 367, 30 FEP 1390 (W.D. Va. 1983); National Org. for Women v. Sperry Rand Corp., 457 F. Supp. 1338, 1342–43, 18 FEP 455 (D. Conn. 1978). Some courts say that even a respondent who never received formal notice at all may be named in a suit if it had actual or constructive notice of the charge. Bruce v. S & H Riggers & Erectors, Inc., 732 F. Supp. 1172, 1176–77, 52 FEP 1170 (N.D. Ga. 1990) (refusing to dismiss a company where notice was sent to the president of another company named in charge, who happens also to be president of the defendant). *See generally* Chapter 28 (Title VII Litigation Procedure).

[143]*Compare* EEOC v. Firestone Tire & Rubber Co., 626 F. Supp. 90, 93, 39 FEP 583 (M.D. Ga. 1985) (a 33-month delay in the service of the charge supports a laches defense) *with* EEOC v. Burlington N., Inc., 644 F.2d 717, 720–21, 25 FEP 499 (8th Cir. 1981) (the Commission's failure to serve the employer with notice of a charge within 10 days is not an absolute bar to enforcement; if the delay is not willful or in bad faith, a court must evaluate any evidence of prejudice to the employer) *and* EEOC v. Christie Lodge Assocs., Ltd., 51 FEP 916, 918 (N.D. Ill. 1989) (dismissal denied for lack of prejudice, where the employer had notice of the charge and officials not named in the charge had reason to believe that they would be sued). *See generally* Chapter 29 (EEOC Litigation).

[144]The following resolutions fall into the general category of "administrative closures": (1) dismissals for lack of jurisdiction or untimeliness; (2) withdrawals

District directors, and other specified officials, may approve a withdrawal, but only "where the withdrawal of a charge will not defeat the purposes of Title VII or the ADA."[145]

The director typically will grant a request to withdraw unless (1) the director suspects that the request is motivated by fear or intimidation; (2) there are other persons aggrieved by the challenged practice(s); or (3) the case is in conciliation and withdrawal would impede the Commission's policy on obtaining satisfactory relief.[146] If the charge requested to be withdrawn contains valid class allegations and any private settlement does not confer benefits on the class, the director may (1) deny withdrawal or (2) approve withdrawal of the individual charge while recommending the issuance of a Commissioner charge to pursue the class claims.[147] Under the EPA and the ADEA, the director can approve the withdrawal and, without any further charge, simply institute an investigation of the respondent.[148]

2. Failure to Locate/Failure to Cooperate

The EEOC may dismiss a charge where (1) the charging party no longer can be located despite reasonable efforts to do so; (2) there do not appear to be other persons aggrieved by the charged practice; and (3) the charging party has not responded within 30 days to a notice mailed to the party's last known address.[149] The agency also may dismiss a charge if the charging party fails or

---

without benefits (i.e., withdrawal not accompanying a settlement agreement between the parties); (3) dismissals for failure to locate the charging party; (4) dismissals in response to the charging party's refusal to cooperate; (5) dismissals when suit is brought by the charging party; (6) dismissals when the charging party refuses to accept full relief; and (7) dismissals following the issuance of notice of right to sue upon request. "Merit factor" closures include (1) withdrawal with benefits; (2) negotiated settlement prior to determination; and (3) cause determinations.

[145]29 C.F.R. § 1601.10 (2005). Section 1626.13 governs withdrawals of age charges.

[146]1 EEOC COMPL. MAN. (BNA) §§ 7.1(a), 7.3(a), 7.5(b), at 7:0001–03; *see also* Section III.K *infra* (identifying what relief is satisfactory).

[147]1 EEOC COMPL. MAN. (BNA) § 7.2(b), at 7:0001.

[148]*Id.; see* 29 C.F.R. §§ 1626.4 & .13 (2005) (ADEA); *id.* § 1620.30 (EPA).

[149]29 C.F.R. § 1601.18(c) (2005); 1 EEOC COMPL. MAN. (BNA) § 4.4(c), at 4:0004. The charge may be reopened at a later date if the charging party is located (§ 1601.21(b)(1)), with notice to respondent of the reopening (§ 1601.21(b)(2)).

refuses to cooperate in a manner that prevents completion of the investigation, unless there appear to be violations against other persons.[150]

3. Other Administrative Closures

The EEOC also will dismiss a charge where a state court decision has been rendered involving the same issues and parties in the pending charge,[151] where the charging party has died,[152] or where the charging party refuses a respondent's offer of full retroactive and prospective relief.[153]

H. EEOC's Mediation Program

In 1999, the EEOC considerably expanded its voluntary and free mediation program in hopes of resolving more cases before they enter the investigative stage.[154] The stated goal of the program is to eliminate unnecessary investigation and litigation, to save time and costs for employers and employees, and to allow EEOC investigators to concentrate on more pressing cases.[155] As of April 1999, the program was in place at every agency district office nationwide.[156]

---

[150]29 C.F.R. § 1601.18(b) (2005); 1 EEOC COMPL. MAN. (BNA) § 4.4(b), at 4:0004; *see also* Shikles v. Sprint United Mgmt. Co., 426 F.3d 1304, 1310, 96 FEP 1156 (10th Cir. 2005) (where claimant cancelled three interviews, repeatedly failed to return investigator's calls, and did not submit requested information, charging party did not cooperate with EEOC and therefore failed to exhaust administrative remedies). One court dismissed a plaintiff's subsequent suit, where he failed to cooperate with the EEOC. Davis v. Mid-South Milling Co., 54 FEP 1561, 1563 (W.D. Tenn. 1990). *But see* Jasch v. Potter, 302 F.3d 1092, 1095 (9th Cir. 2002) (reversing dismissal of plaintiff's subsequent suit, where his failure to cooperate with EEOC requests did not prevent agency from examining the merits of plaintiff's Title VII claim).

[151]1 EEOC COMPL. MAN. (BNA) § 4.3(f)(1), at 4:0003.

[152]The Commission will dismiss if, under state law, the cause of action does not survive or the charging party's testimony is necessary to make a determination, unless there are indications of class discrimination. *Id.* § 4.4(d), at 4:0004–05.

[153]The district director must make a specific written determination that the relief offered is what the party would have received in successful litigation. Note that rejection of full relief also can preclude later suit in the federal sector. Wrenn v. Secretary of V.A. Dep't, 918 F.2d 1073, 1078, 54 FEP 664 (2d Cir. 1990).

[154]*See* DAILY LAB. REP. (BNA) at C-1, E-20 (Feb. 12, 1999).

[155]*Id.*

[156]*See* EEOC Mediation Program Scores High Marks in Major Survey of Participants, *available at* http://www.eeoc.gov/press/9-26-00.html, at 2–3 (Sept. 26, 2000).

Under the program, at or about the time a charge is filed the Commission offers mediation services to charging parties whose cases have potential merit (based on the initial charge information) but are not priority cases.[157] If the employee accepts, the Commission encourages the employer to engage in a mediation session with a neutral mediator.[158] Mediators are drawn from three pools—independent mediators under contract to the EEOC (called "contract mediators"), volunteer mediators, and EEOC personnel who have been trained as mediators. Staff members performing EEOC mediations are forbidden from discussing any dispute they mediate with EEOC enforcement staff. Statements made during the mediation are confidential and cannot be used in any EEOC investigation or civil litigation if mediation fails.[159] Mediators who are EEOC staff members do not participate in the Commission's investigatory functions.[160]

Between September 1998 and September 2004, the EEOC resolved over 31,000 private sector charges[161] and obtained monetary benefits of $651 million for charging parties. The program has also enabled the EEOC to resolve charges in a more expeditious manner. Through September of fiscal year 2004, 65 percent of the cases that entered the mediation program were resolved in an average of 85 days.[162] Charges resolved through the administrative/investigative process remain pending for an average exceeding 180 days.[163]

I. Settlement—Pre-Determination Settlements, Negotiated Settlements, and Settlement of Commissioner Charges

Charging parties and respondents may settle a charge at any time during the administrative investigation of a charge.[164] Settlements

---

[157]DAILY LAB. REP. (BNA) at C-1 (Feb. 12, 1999).

[158]*Id.* at E-20.

[159]*Id.*

[160]*Id.* at C-1.

[161]EEOC and Intel Enter Mediation Partnership to Resolve Workplace Disputes, *available at* http://www.eeoc.gov/press/10-4-04.html, at 2 (Oct. 4, 2004).

[162]*See id.*

[163]EEOC Mediation Program Scores High Marks in Major Survey of Participants, *available at* http://www.eeoc.gov/press/9-26-00.html, at 2 (Sept. 26, 2000).

[164]The EEOC's April 1995 charge-processing procedures direct "[t]hat settlement efforts be encouraged at all stages of the administrative process." DAILY LAB. REP. (BNA) at E-5 (Apr. 20, 1995).

entered into prior to the EEOC issuing its determination are commonly called pre-determination settlements. The Commission's Title VII and ADA regulations authorize field office directors and directors within the Office of Field Programs to sign "any settlement agreement which is agreeable to both parties," so long as it is limited to the parties' current dispute.[165] The EEOC will sign as a party to an agreement that is acceptable to each party, unless it (1) contains an unlawful provision, (2) appears to ratify practices that the EEOC has not investigated, or (3) contains a waiver of the charging party's prospective rights.[166] The ADEA provides for conciliation attempts promptly after the charge is filed.[167]

Settlement, according to the charge-processing procedure, is generally "encouraged."[168] The EEOC does not attempt to facilitate settlement of cases that fall into the third category, i.e., the dismissal category, although the Commission will not stand in the way of parties who are interested in settling their dispute. Charges under investigation that fall into the first two categories but do not fall within the national or local enforcement plans may be settled at any time by the enforcement staff, without consultation with the legal staff.[169]

Typically, investigators will note after the intake interview whether a charging party is disposed to settle the charge.[170] The investigator may explore the prospect of settlement with a respondent after it has submitted a position statement or replied to the

---

[165]29 C.F.R. § 1601.20 (2005). The Commission's promise to cease processing a charge is made in consideration for the promises made by the other parties to the agreement. The regulation makes clear that "[s]uch an agreement shall not affect the processing of any other charge, including but not limited to, a Commissioner charge or a charge, the allegations of which are like and related to the individual allegations settled." Id.

[166]1 EEOC COMPL. MAN. (BNA) §§ 15.7 & 15.8, at 15:0002. Investigators may negotiate vigorously on behalf of a charging party whose claim appears meritorious. Additionally, agreements to which the EEOC is a party often contain provisions for affirmative relief (e.g., respondent's agreement to adopt a sexual harassment policy drafted by the Commission) to help ensure that the harm suffered by the charging party will not recur.

[167]29 U.S.C. § 626(d) (2000). The conciliation process is discussed in Section III.K infra.

[168]DAILY LAB. REP. (BNA) at E-5 (Apr. 20, 1995).

[169]EEOC Investigations: What an Employer Should Know, available at http://www.eeoc.gov/employers/investigations.html (last visited July 22, 2005).

[170]1 EEOC COMPL. MAN. (BNA) § 2.6(a), at 2:0008.

investigator's request for information.[171] At that juncture, the investigator is in a better position to assess the strengths and weaknesses in the charging party's claim. In general, the settlement level increases as the EEOC edges closer to finding a violation. For example, "the Commission may accept settlements providing 'substantial' relief when the evidence of record indicates a violation or 'appropriate' relief at an earlier stage in the investigation."[172]

"Negotiated settlements" are those in which the parties themselves reach an agreement, but to which the EEOC is not a party. In these circumstances, the EEOC does not sign the agreement.[173] Where necessary, the EEOC will facilitate settlement by agreeing to the charging party's request to withdraw the charge as part of a private settlement, when doing so will not defeat the purposes of the statute at issue.[174]

In settlements to which it is a party, and which it therefore has approved, the EEOC routinely includes a provision stating that "[t]he parties agree that this Agreement may be specifically enforced in court and may be used as evidence in a subsequent proceeding in which any of the parties allege a breach of this Agreement."[175] By contrast, the EEOC has no litigation authority with respect to a negotiated settlement agreement to which it is not a party.

Where the EEOC is a party to the settlement, and later determines that the respondent has not complied with the agreement and negotiation proves unsuccessful, the EEOC will review the case for possible court action.[176] Most courts recognize that the EEOC may bring an action in federal district court to enforce a settlement agreement to which it is a party, despite the absence of an investigation and a reasonable-cause determination.[177] When the

---

[171]*Id.* § 14.5, at 14:0002; *id.* § 14.8, at 14:0003.

[172]DAILY LAB. REP. (BNA) at E-5 (Apr. 20, 1995).

[173]1 EEOC COMPL. MAN. (BNA) § 15.8(b), at 15:0002.

[174]*Id.* § 7.5(a), at 7:0003.

[175]*Id.* § 15, exh. 15-A(2), ¶ 6, at 15:0007.

[176]*Id.* § 80.13(c), at 80:0007–08.

[177]*See, e.g.*, EEOC v. Henry Beck Co., 729 F.2d 301, 305–06, 34 FEP 373 (4th Cir. 1984) (jurisdiction to enforce a pre-determination settlement is implicit in § 706(f)(3) of Title VII and 28 U.S.C. §§ 1337 and 1343); EEOC v. Safeway Stores, Inc., 714 F.2d 567, 571–72, 32 FEP 1465 (5th Cir. 1983) (federal courts have jurisdiction over suits to enforce Title VII conciliation agreements); EEOC v. Cleveland

EEOC decides against litigation in such a case, it notifies the charging party of his or her right to file a breach of contract suit and/or to request a notice of right to sue for the charge that led to the agreement.[178] Most[179] but not all[180] federal courts accept jurisdiction

State Univ., 28 FEP 441, 443–44 (N.D. Ohio 1982) (the EEOC may bring suit to enforce a predetermination settlement agreement without a reasonable-cause determination or further conciliation efforts); EEOC v. Liberty Trucking Co., 695 F.2d 1038, 1044, 30 FEP 884 (7th Cir. 1982) (federal district courts have jurisdiction under Title VII over EEOC suits to enforce post determination conciliation agreements); Eatmon v. Bristol Steel & Iron Works, Inc., 769 F.2d 1503, 1508, 38 FEP 1364 (11th Cir. 1985) (recognizing a private right of action under Title VII to enforce a conciliation agreement where the individual plaintiff had released Title VII claims in return for the employer's compliance with the OFCCP conciliation agreement). *Contra* EEOC v. Pierce Packing Co., 669 F.2d 605, 608, 28 FEP 393 (9th Cir. 1982) (the EEOC acted without jurisdiction when it attempted to use a voluntary preconciliation settlement agreement to justify court enforcement when a breach occurred). Enforcement actions likely can be brought in state court, too, particularly in light of the Supreme Court's decision in *Yellow Freight Systems, Inc. v. Donnelly*, 494 U.S. 820, 821, 52 FEP 875 (1990), that state courts have jurisdiction to hear Title VII actions.

[178]1 EEOC COMP. MAN. (BNA) § 80.13(c), at 80:0007–08.

[179]*See, e.g.*, IMPACT v. Firestone, 893 F.2d 1189, 1196–97, 52 FEP 71 (11th Cir. 1990) (an employee need not exhaust administrative remedies for the court to enforce a conciliation agreement); Quarles v. Colorado Sec. Agency, Inc., 843 F.2d 557, 558–59 (D.C. Cir. 1988) (per curiam) (federal law controls enforcement of Title VII agreements; no separate charge/exhaustion is required); Morgan v. South Bend Community Sch. Corp., 797 F.2d 471, 474, 41 FEP 736 (7th Cir. 1986) (affirming enforcement of an oral settlement agreement); Brewer v. Muscle Shoals Bd. of Educ., 790 F.2d 1515, 1519, 40 FEP 1580 (11th Cir. 1986) (federal law controls enforcement of Title VII predetermination settlement agreements; it is not necessary to file an EEOC charge alleging breach); Perdue v. Roy Stone Transfer Corp., 690 F.2d 1091, 1093, 29 FEP 1673 (4th Cir. 1982) (a right-to-sue letter is not a prerequisite to an action for breach of a predetermination settlement); Gill v. Hercules, Inc., 54 FEP 427, 429 (D. Kan. 1990) (an employee can sue for breach of an oral settlement of a Title VII claim); Hamilton v. School Comm., 725 F. Supp. 641, 648–49, 51 FEP 1008 (D. Mass. 1989) (an employee can sue for breach of an agreement settling a prior Title VII suit without filing a new charge); *cf.* Eatmon v. Bristol Steel & Iron Works, Inc., 769 F.2d 1503, 1508, 38 FEP 1364 (11th Cir. 1985) (a third-party action to enforce an OFCCP conciliation agreement is "brought under Title VII" where the employees had released Title VII claims in return for compliance with the OFCCP conciliation agreement; Title VII charges need not be filed).

[180]*See, e.g.*, Parsons v. Yellow Freight Sys., Inc., 741 F.2d 871, 873, 35 FEP 1121 (6th Cir. 1984) (private enforcement of an EEOC settlement agreement must be premised upon the filing of a new charge and receipt of a right-to-sue letter); Weills v. Caterpillar Tractor Co., 553 F. Supp. 640, 642–43, 31 FEP 210 (N.D. Cal. 1982) (a Title VII suit must be brought within 90 days of receipt of a right-to-sue letter; federal question jurisdiction over a breach of settlement suit could not be based on any other Title VII provisions); *cf.* Morris v. City of Hobart, 39 F.3d 1105, 1111, 66 FEP 285 (10th Cir. 1994) (no federal jurisdiction of suit brought to enforce a private Title VII settlement—it is simply a contract action that must be enforced in state court).

over individual plaintiffs' suits to enforce settlement or conciliation agreements arising under Title VII or the ADEA even though administrative processes were not exhausted.

Settlements of Commissioner systemic charges,[181] on the other hand, typically are not made until the investigation nears completion. The EEOC in such cases usually seeks specific and substantial relief. Settlement attempts normally begin only when the EEOC has sufficient facts on each basis and issue raised in the charge to develop an informal settlement proposal. Settlement discussions may be delayed where the respondent's lack of cooperation prevents the EEOC from obtaining relevant information.[182] A proposed settlement of a systemic charge before agency decision must be approved by the district director, who may well consult the Commissioner who filed the charge. Individual charges against a respondent may be consolidated for processing with a systemic Commissioner charge; if so, settlement discussions usually[183] are handled by the systemic unit responsible for the systemic charge.[184]

J. Investigations and Determinations

1. The Assignment Process and the Respondent's Position Statement

Charges generally are assigned for investigation at the same time that notice is served on the respondent. The investigator who took the charge typically is assigned responsibility for resolving it, unless the charge is deferred to a state or local agency for investigation, "batched" with other charges in the office against the same respondent,[185] or is too complex for the investigator's grade

---

[181]*See* Section III.N *infra.*

[182]1 EEOC COMPL. MAN. (BNA) § 16.6(f), at 16:0005.

[183]*See* EEOC, *Priority Charge Handling Procedures*, at 19 (June 1995) [hereinafter cited as *Priority Procedures*].

[184]*Id.* § 16.8, at 16:0008; *id.* § 16.8(d), at 16:0009. For charges not consolidated, a negotiated settlement may be attempted by another EEOC unit. *Id.* § 16.8(f). However, conciliation agreements in a nonconsolidated individual charge involving a systemic respondent must be cleared by the headquarters or field systemic unit responsible for the systemic case. *Id.* § 16.8(g), at 16:0010.

[185]Charges are batched if they are similar with respect to bases and issues; they also may be batched simply because it is more efficient for one investigator to obtain information from a particular respondent.

level. Whether an investigation begins in earnest—and, if so, when—depends on the Commission's priorities and the size of the inventory in the particular EEOC office. If a charge appears to call for preliminary relief, it may be investigated on a priority basis in close coordination with the legal unit.[186]

The CR/TIU or the investigator's enforcement unit generally will ask the respondent to submit a position statement,[187] with supporting documentation,[188] within a specified time frame.

2. Requests for Information (RFIs) and On-Site Reviews

Where appropriate, a written request for information (RFI) may accompany notice to the respondent of the charge or be sent to the respondent shortly after the EEOC analyzes the respondent's position statement.[189] RFIs are used in most investigations, unless resolution of the allegations rests solely on testimonial evidence.[190]

The EEOC's policy is to tailor RFIs, both in terms of time frame and the respondent's organizational structure, and to seek specific information based on leads developed in the charging party's

---

[186]1 EEOC COMPL. MAN. (BNA) § 13, at 13:0001–05. The EEOC reaffirmed its commitment to seeking preliminary relief in appropriate cases in conjunction with implementation of the EEOC's April 1995 charge-processing procedures. Chairman Casellas made the following request:

> I am requesting the General Counsel to delegate to regional attorneys the authority to seek temporary relief pursuant to § 706(f)(2) of Title VII, without prior approval from the General Counsel or the Commission, in cases involving individual claims of disparate treatment not rising to a pattern of discrimination, when the District Director has concluded on the basis of a preliminary investigation that prompt judicial action is necessary to carry out the purposes of the Act.

DAILY LAB. REP. (BNA) at E-5–E-6 (Apr. 20, 1995).

[187]1 EEOC COMPL. MAN. (BNA) § 3.4(b)(2), at 3:0002–03; id. exh. 3-A, at 3:0005.

[188]Documentation could include records made at the time of the alleged violation and affidavits from involved officials attesting to the legitimate reasons for their action. Where the EEOC has interviewed witnesses that credibly testify to discriminatory practices, however, it will typically interview respondent officials in person, regardless of any earlier affidavits. Where the evidence of discrimination is weak or nonexistent, however, the respondent's documents, position statements, and/or affidavits may well comprise a sufficient evidentiary basis upon which the EEOC will dismiss a charge.

[189]1 EEOC COMPL. MAN. (BNA) § 3.4(b)(2), at 3:0002–03; id. § 14.2(b), at 14:0001; id. § 14.3, at 14:0002; id. § 22.3, at 22:0002–03; id. § 26.3, at 26:0002–03.

[190]Id. § 14.2(b), at 14:0001 (individual charges); id. § 22.2(b), at 22:0001–02 (extended and systemic investigations).

interview or in the systemic investigation preceding the issuance of a Commissioner charge. The questions also may seek information pertaining to other potential aggrieved persons if the charging party alleged class discrimination or if the charge (or information obtained during the investigation of a charge) suggests the possibility of a pattern or practice of discrimination affecting persons other than the charging party.[191]

The EEOC RFIs frequently ask respondents to compile data— e.g., to provide a list of all employees hired into Department X between June 1 and December 1, 2004, coded by race and sex. Although there is no statutory authority for the EEOC's use of written requests for information, the technique has been used with such frequency that it rarely is questioned by respondents. That is true because, as a practical matter, such compilations expedite the investigation, and a respondent may prefer to compile rather than to submit to an on-site examination by the investigator of the underlying files.[192] Moreover, the EEOC can resort to subpoenas to compel production of documents or the testimony of witnesses.[193] In the face of a refusal, the EEOC might (1) issue a subpoena, (2) draw an adverse inference against the respondent to support a cause determination, where appropriate,[194] or (3) simply issue a cause determination and authorize direct suit if the withheld information is not "absolutely necessary" to reaching a determination.[195] And, as noted above, the investigator may request an on-site visit, even in an individual disparate treatment case, for the purpose of face-to-face interviews, examination of documents, or inspection of facilities.[196]

3. Fact-Finding Conference

A fact-finding conference is an investigative tool that may be used in individual and limited-class disparate treatment cases.[197] A

---

[191]*Id.* § 3.4(b)(2), at 3:0002–03; *id.* § 14.2(b), at 14:0001; *id.* § 14.3, at 14:0002; *id.* § 22.3, at 22:0002–03; *id.* § 26.3, at 26:0002–03.

[192]As noted in Section IV *infra*, courts are divided on whether the EEOC may compel a respondent by subpoena to make such compilations.

[193]*See* Section IV *infra*.

[194]*See* Section III.J.4 *infra*.

[195]*Investigative Compliance Policy Statement* (July 14, 1986), *reprinted in* 1 EEOC COMPL. MAN. (BNA) § 22, exh. 22-C, at 22:0017.

[196]1 EEOC COMPL. MAN. (BNA) § 14.7(a)(5), at 14:0003; *id.* § 25.1, at 25:0001.

[197]*Id.* § 14.9(b), at 14:0003.

fact-finding conference generally will not be held in the following cases: (1) where the alleged discrimination arises from an acknowledged or documented policy; (2) in Commissioner charge cases; (3) where a charge is filed on behalf of an aggrieved individual who wishes his or her identity to remain confidential; (4) in ADEA and EPA complaint cases; and (5) where charges are being processed under expedited procedures prescribed by local or national settlement agreements or consent decrees (unless those procedures are compatible with the fact-finding procedures).[198]

The goals of the conference are: (1) to further define the issues, (2) to determine which elements are undisputed, (3) to clarify disputed issues and evidence, (4) to determine what other evidence may be necessary, and (5) to assist the parties to achieve a settlement, if that "is deemed to be appropriate."[199] The investigator, not the attorneys, elicits testimony from the parties and relevant witnesses; attorneys may serve an advisory role but cannot speak for the parties or cross-examine the opposing party.[200] The proceedings are on the record, but the EEOC's policy is generally not to permit tape recordings to be made by either the respondent or the charging party.[201]

4. Adverse Inference Rule

The EEOC will "draw an adverse inference against respondent as to the evidence sought, when a respondent knowingly destroys or knowingly fails to maintain records in anticipation of the filing of a charge, or because of the Commission's investigation, or otherwise with the intent to defeat the statutes enforced by the Commission."[202] In such cases, the district director may use the inference to establish facts relevant to a merits determination,[203]

---

[198]*Id.* § 14.9(c), at 14:0004.

[199]*Id.* § 14.9(b), at 14:0003.

[200]*Id.* §§ 14.10 & .11, at 14:0006–07.

[201]*Id.* § 14.11(b)(4), at 14:0006.

[202]*Id.* § 22.13(f), at 22:0012. The Second Circuit has drawn an adverse inference in the absence of willfulness. *See, e.g.,* Zimmerman v. Associates First Capital Corp., 251 F.3d 376, 383–84, 85 FEP 1505 (2d Cir. 2001); *see also* EEOC v. Protek of Albuquerque, Inc., 49 FEP 1110, 1113 (D.N.M. 1988) (the EEOC and an ex-employee are entitled to the presumption that the defendant employed 15 persons where records were incompletely maintained and destroyed through no fault of the employer).

[203]1 EEOC COMPL. MAN. (BNA) § 26.1(a), at 26:0001.

and the EEOC will urge the district court in any subsequent litigation to do the same.[204] The EEOC characterizes the rule as an analytical tool, not a sanction to compel production of documents.

5. Scope of the Investigation

Charge investigations are designed to afford the EEOC with a basis for determining whether there is reasonable cause to believe that the charge is true, and will probe evidence relevant to the complainant's prima facie case as well as the respondent's defenses to it.[205]

The scope of the charge does not necessarily define the scope of the EEOC's investigation. The Commission may, for instance, choose not to investigate every allegation in a charge. If the scope of the investigation has been so narrowed, any later determination by its terms may speak only to those allegations investigated and addressed.[206] Conversely, an individual charge may be expanded by the EEOC to include investigation of a potential pattern or practice, or an individual or pattern-or-practice charge investigation may be expanded to include "like and related" issues under Title VII[207] or the ADEA or EPA.[208] Title VII violations uncovered in an investigation of an age or equal pay charge may lead to a Commissioner charge.[209]

---

[204]*Investigative Compliance Policy Statement* (July 14, 1986), *reprinted in* 1 EEOC COMPL. MAN. (BNA) § 22, exh. 22-C, at 22:0017 & § 22.13(f), at 22:0012.

[205]The investigator usually drafts an investigative plan (IP) early in the process, which includes, among other things, a statement of the likely or enunciated respondent defenses and a description of the evidence required to test their validity. *Id.* § 14.2(a), at 14:0001; *id.* § 22.2(a), at 22:0001.

[206]29 C.F.R. § 1601.21(a) (2005); 1 EEOC COMPL. MAN. (BNA) § 2.6(b), at 2:0009.

[207]1 EEOC COMPL. MAN. (BNA) § 22.3(a), at 22:0002.

[208]*Id.* § 22.3(b), at 22:0002. Section 706(a) of Title VII (incorporated by reference by the ADA) allows the EEOC to investigate an employer only upon the filing of a valid charge. Under the equal pay and age statutes, however, the EEOC has independent investigative authority. 29 C.F.R. §§ 1620.30 (2005) (equal pay) & 1626.15 (2005) (age).

[209]1 EEOC COMPL. MAN. (BNA) § 25.7, at 25:0003–04. Where Title VII violations have been uncovered in an age or equal pay investigation, the only recourse is a Commissioner charge, since no Title VII investigation can proceed in the absence of a charge. *See* 42 U.S.C. § 2000e-5(a) (2000). *See generally* Chapter 29 (EEOC Litigation).

6. Determination Interview and the Investigative Memorandum

When sufficient evidence has been obtained to support a determination, the investigator may hold a determination interview (DI) with the party against whom the proposed determination runs (i.e., with respondent if the determination is cause, with charging party if it is to dismiss the charge).[210] In "cause" cases, the DI usually is held after the file is reviewed by the office director and the legal unit.[211] The investigator summarizes the evidence and invites the submission of additional evidence that could change the result. The DI can lead to further investigation, settlement, or the issuance of the proposed determination as it stands. When either party is represented by an attorney, the attorney is notified of the impending DI and may participate if the attorney and party so desire.[212]

When the case is ready to be finalized, the investigator (1) prepares an investigative memorandum (IM) supporting any recommended cause determination, (2) drafts a determination or dismissal, and (3) completes the running case log indicating all actions taken in the case.[213] He or she assembles the file containing the investigator's work product, jurisdictional items (charge, notice, and deferral/referral documents), charging party's evidence, respondent's evidence, and other evidence the investigator independently may have collected from other sources.[214] The case then is submitted up the chain of command (described below) for appropriate action.

7. EEOC Letters of Determination and EEOC Decisions

The Commission has delegated its authority to issue "letters of determination" to the directors of the Office of Field Programs

---

[210]1 EEOC COMPL. MAN. (BNA) § 22.15, at 22:0006; id. § 27, at 27:0001–02. Among its April 1995 charge-processing procedural changes, the EEOC eliminated its "no cause" determination. Where no cause is found, the charge should be dismissed "without particularized findings." DAILY LAB. REP. (BNA) at E-5 (Apr. 20, 1995). The pre-determination interview, however, was not eliminated: where an "investigation of a charge has not established reasonable cause to believe that discrimination has occurred . . . field offices are encouraged to share with charging parties the basis for EEOC's determination through such means as pre-determination interviews." Id.

[211]Id. § 27.1, at 27:0001; id. § 34.3, at 34:0001; id. § 40.3, at 40:0001.

[212]Id. § 27.2, at 27:0001; id. § 27.4, at 27:0002.

[213]Id. §§ 22.16 & 22.17, at 22:0012; id. § 29, at 29:0001–04.

[214]Id. § 28, at 28:0001–02.

and Field Management Programs and, upon further delegation, to the field directors.

In cases where there is no finding that a violation exists and governing Commission Decision Precedents (CDPs) are present, the dismissal is issued by the field directors upon recommendation by the enforcement unit.[215] The determination itself constitutes the charging party's notice of right to sue under Title VII and the ADA. The determination or decision is accompanied by an information sheet on filing suit in federal court.[216]

Cause determinations are typically closely coordinated with the legal unit in the district office.[217] Under the EEOC's "reasonable cause" standard, the question is whether "it is more likely than not" that there has been discrimination, a question to be assessed (in a disparate treatment case) by determining first whether a prima facie case exists, and then by analyzing any evidence of pretext.[218]

---

[215]When there is no finding that a violation exists, the EEOC provides the following uniform language: "Based upon the Commission's investigation, the Commission is unable to conclude that the information obtained establishes violations of the statutes. This does not certify that the respondent is in compliance with the statutes. No finding is made as to any other issue that might be construed as having been raised by this charge."

[216]1 EEOC COMPL. MAN. (BNA) § 4.5(a), at 4:0005 & exh. 4-J, at 4:0020. Between 1987 and 1991, a charging party could appeal a no-cause determination to the headquarters' Determinations Review Program. The Determinations Review Program was authorized to remand files for further investigation or information; forward recommendations to the Director of Program Operations to reverse the field, and issue "cause" determinations; or issue final no-cause determinations when field office determinations were sustained upon review or requests were withdrawn. The procedural regulations implementing this program are found at 52 Fed. Reg. 26,957 (1987) (previously codified at 29 C.F.R. § 1601.19(a)). The program was dismantled effective April 8, 1991, because so few determinations merited reversal or remand, and the EEOC's resources were needed elsewhere. See 56 Fed. Reg. 9623 (1991). And, as noted above, in April 1995 the Commission eliminated no-cause determinations entirely, in favor of dismissals "without particularized findings." See DAILY LAB. REP. (BNA) at E-5 (Apr. 20, 1995).

[217]1 EEOC COMPL. MAN. (BNA) § 12.3, at 12:0002–03. Courts have upheld the EEOC-issued regulation, 29 C.F.R. § 1621(d), which provides, inter alia, that the field office director has authority to issue most reasonable-cause determinations. See, e.g., EEOC v. Raymond Metals Prods. Co., 530 F.2d 590, 593–94, 12 FEP 38 (4th Cir. 1976); EEOC v. Laclede Gas Co., 530 F.2d 281, 285, 12 FEP 306 (8th Cir. 1976). The absence of a right of review by the full Commission is not constitutionally fatal since no "final rights" are adjudicated by these administrative determinations. Raymond Metals, 530 F.2d at 594. Any subsequent court action involves a trial de novo, although a cause determination often is given evidentiary weight. See generally Chapter 28 (Title VII Litigation Procedure).

[218]1 EEOC COMPL. MAN. (BNA) § 40.2, at 40:0001. This standard is the product of refinements enunciated in the EEOC's September 1984 "Statement of Enforcement

If the office director finds that the reasonable-cause standard has been met, he or she usually will forward the file to the legal unit for review. Depending upon the results of that review, the director can require further investigation or, after a DI with the respondent, change the determination to one of dismissal without particularized findings, or proceed to issue the cause determination.[219] Copies of the determination then are mailed to the parties and their attorneys, if any.[220] The final paragraphs of a cause determination inform the parties of the EEOC's intent to conciliate.[221]

8. Reconsideration

EEOC decisions and letters of determination are final when issued.[222] The regulations do not provide for charging parties or respondents to file motions for reconsideration, and there is no due process "right" to reconsideration or to a hearing on a motion for reconsideration.[223] Since the powers being utilized by the EEOC in producing their decisions and determinations are only investigative, as opposed to adjudicative, they do not constitute final orders for administrative law purposes. Thus, because such a preliminary determination is without legal effect in and of itself, due process rights do not attach.[224]

But both decisions and letters of determination in fact may be reconsidered upon motion of the Commission or a district director.[225]

Policy." *See* DAILY LAB. REP. (BNA) at D-1 (Sept. 17, 1984). Although the September 1984 policy statement was rescinded by the EEOC in April 1995, *see* DAILY LAB. REP. (BNA) at E-5 (Apr. 20, 1995), the EEOC offered no new "reasonable cause" standard. Until it does so, the EEOC likely will follow the standard enunciated above.

[219]The decision is the ultimate responsibility of the office director, not the regional attorney. 1 EEOC COMPL. MAN. (BNA) § 40.3(c), at 40:0001. However, inasmuch as the regional attorney must recommend to the Commission for or against litigation in the event conciliation fails, a director seldom issues a cause determination over the objection of the regional attorney.

[220]*Id.* § 40.6, at 40:0003.

[221]*Id.* § 40.4(e), at 40:0002. In an equal pay case, the final paragraphs of the letter of violation describe the specific relief that the respondent must provide and include the names of all aggrieved persons. *Id.* § 40.4(e)(3), at 40:0002.

[222]29 C.F.R. §§ 1601.19(b) & 1601.21(b), (d) (2005).

[223]Georator Corp. v. EEOC, 592 F.2d 765, 767–68, 19 FEP 70 (4th Cir. 1979); EEOC v. Sears, Roebuck & Co., 22 FEP 457, 462–63 (N.D. Ga. 1980).

[224]*Georator Corp.*, 592 F.2d at 768.

[225]29 C.F.R. §§ 1601.19(b) & 1601.21(b), (d) (2005). Reconsideration does not occur after a cause finding and conciliation failure where the respondent is a governmental agency. *Id.* § 1601.21(b).

However, reconsideration can only occur if one of the following circumstances exists: (1) there is evidence of misconduct by an agency official that may have affected the outcome; (2) there is substantial new and material evidence; or (3) there was an error in the interpretation of the law that may have affected the outcome. As a practical matter, reconsideration usually occurs when a party submits a written request presenting a persuasive case that a mistake was made. If the director agrees to reconsider, a notice of intent to reconsider is issued to all parties, vacating the prior dismissal or cause determination. If the Director issued to the charging party a dismissal notice, the notice of reconsideration renders the 90-day suit filing deadline inoperative. But the notice of reconsideration does not serve to revoke the notice of right to sue if (1) the reconsideration notice is issued after the 90-day suit-filing period has expired, (2) the charging party already has filed suit before the notice was deposited in the mail by the EEOC, or (3) the charging party had requested a notice of right to sue.[226] After reconsideration, the EEOC issues a new determination. When the EEOC revokes the prior right to sue, it issues a new right-to-sue notice.[227]

K. The Conciliation Process

In cases where the EEOC finds reasonable cause to believe that unlawful discrimination has occurred, it then attempts to remedy and eliminate the unlawful practice through conciliation.[228] The goal

---

[226]*Id.* § 1601.21(b); *see* Dougherty v. Barry, 869 F.2d 605, 610, 49 FEP 289 (D.C. Cir. 1989) (the second notice of right to sue is a nullity where the EEOC notice of reconsideration came after 90 days had expired from the first notice of right to sue); *see also* Martin v. Alamo Cmty. Coll. Dist., 353 F.3d 409, 413 (5th Cir. 2003) (when notice of reconsideration is issued (mailed) on same day that the charging party files suit, the reconsideration letter effectuates revocation of right to sue).

[227]29 C.F.R. § 1601.21(b) (2005).

[228]Section 706(b) of Title VII (incorporated by reference by the ADA) requires conciliation in the wake of a reasonable cause finding. 42 U.S.C. § 2000e-5(b). The statutory mandate is implemented in 29 C.F.R. § 1601.24. The same requirement is present in § 7(b) of the ADEA, 29 U.S.C. § 626(b), (d), which is implemented in 29 C.F.R. § 1626.15(b), (c). Under § 7(e)(2) of the ADEA, conciliation tolls the running of the statute of limitations for a period not to exceed 1 year. 29 C.F.R. § 1626.15(b). The EEOC takes the position that the tolling provision is applicable to both Commission and private litigation. *See* 29 C.F.R. § 1626.15(b) (2005). *See generally* Chapter 26 (Timeliness). Under the Equal Pay Act, the EEOC has the option of attempting settlement after a letter of violation and prior to an EEOC suit. *See* EEOC COMPL. MAN. (BNA) § 15.3(c), at 15:0001; § 60.3(c), at 60:0001–02.

of conciliation usually is to reach a tripartite agreement signed by the parties and the Commission. If the Commission is unable to obtain from the employer a conciliation agreement acceptable to the Commission, the EEOC may file suit against the employer.[229] The conciliation process will differ from case to case, but the Commission's conciliation efforts must be conducted in "good faith."[230] However, courts have held that the judiciary's role in reviewing the conciliation process is limited, and that the form and substance of EEOC conciliation proposals are generally within the discretion of the EEOC.[231] When the employer rejects the EEOC's counterproposals after good faith negotiations, then the EEOC is not required to continue the conciliation process.[232]

The EEOC encourages settlements throughout the administrative process. Although the Commission is obligated by statute to commence conciliation after finding reasonable cause to believe that unlawful discrimination has occurred, it may seek normal resolution of the dispute at any time during the charge process.

After investigation, the EEOC investigator often will initiate the conciliation process by sending a proposed conciliation agreement to the respondent; later, the investigator may hold conferences with the parties individually.[233]

---

[229]See § 706(f)(1).

[230]42 U.S.C. § 2000e-5(f)(1) (2000); see 3 EEOC COMPL. MAN. (BNA) N:3067–68. Compare EEOC v. Fenyves & Nerenberg, M.D.P.A., 1999 WL 134279 (N.D. Tex. Mar. 9, 1999) (no good faith effort by EEOC where it rejected employer's offer to mediate), EEOC v. First Midwest Bank, N.A., 14 F. Supp. 2d 1028, 1031–32, 77 FEP 1121 (N.D. Ill. 1998) (court stays judicial action where EEOC failed to respond sufficiently to employer's requests for in-person discussions, and EEOC quadrupled the amount of prior settlement demand without explanation) and EEOC v. Asplundh, 340 F.3d 1256 (11th Cir. 2003) (upholding dismissal of complaint and fee award, rejecting "all or nothing" approach and finding EEOC did not act in good faith when it ignored the employer's conciliation offer that arrived just beyond a deadline set by the EEOC) with EEOC v. Mitsubishi Motor Mfg., 990 F. Supp. 1059, 1091, 75 FEP 1379 (C.D. Ill. 1998) (good faith effort where EEOC began conciliation process and later provided what it considered acceptable terms, but employer rejected terms and said further negotiations would be futile) and EEOC v. Phillips Colleges, Inc., 984 F. Supp. 1464, 1470 (M.D. Fla. 1997) (further attempts by EEOC unnecessary after employer rejected offer and did not seriously entertain conciliation).

[231]See EEOC v. Dial Corp., 156 F. Supp. 2d 926, 940 (N.D. Ill. 2001) (and cases cited therein).

[232]See id. at 942.

[233]See 1 EEOC COMPL. MAN. (BNA) § 64, at 60:0001–03.

The investigator's job is to represent the interests of the EEOC, which often overlap substantially with those of the charging party. But that is not always true. For example, if the EEOC is unwilling to accept an agreement acceptable to the charging party and the respondent, the parties always can enter into a private settlement. On the other hand, the EEOC cannot enter into a conciliation agreement that is binding on a charging party unless the charging party also signs the agreement.[234] In these circumstances, the EEOC and the respondent still may enter into an agreement, but the agreement will expressly preserve the charging party's private right of action, and he or she will receive a right-to-sue letter.[235] Similarly, if the charging party and the EEOC enter into a conciliation agreement with one of two or more respondents, such agreement does not bar suit against the nonsignatory respondent(s).[236]

If a conciliation agreement is reached among all parties, the EEOC ceases its administrative processing of the charge, except for compliance follow-up to the extent specified in the conciliation agreement.[237] In Title VII and ADA cases, if conciliation fails, EEOC regulations require notice to be sent to the respondent that conciliation has failed.[238] The file then is forwarded to the district

---

[234]*See, e.g.*, Buckner v. ADCO Elec. Co., 332 F. Supp. 2d 950, 952 (S.D. Miss. 2004) ("conciliation does not refer to the agreement of respondent to [an EEOC] proposal, but a mutually satisfactory agreement of the charging party and the respondent"); Cox v. United States Gypsum Co., 284 F. Supp. 74, 84, 1 FEP 602 (N.D. Ind. 1968) (the employer agreed to an EEOC proposal that was not acceptable to the charging party), *aff'd as modified on other grounds*, 409 F.2d 289, 1 FEP 714 (7th Cir. 1969); Austin v. Reynolds Metals Co., 327 F. Supp. 1145, 1151–53, 2 FEP 451 (E.D. Va. 1970) (an agreement executed by the EEOC, respondent, and some charging parties is not binding on the nonsignatory charging parties).

[235]1 EEOC COMPL. MAN. (BNA) §§ 63.5 & 63.6, at 63:0001–02; Riddle v. Cerro Wire & Cable Group, Inc., 902 F.2d 918, 922, 53 FEP 47 (11th Cir. 1990) (a charging party can maintain suit where she disagreed with and refused to sign a conciliation agreement between the respondent and the EEOC).

[236]Manning v. General Motors Corp., 3 FEP 968, 970–72 (N.D. Ohio 1971), *aff'd sub nom.* Manning v. Auto Workers Local 913, 466 F.2d 812, 4 FEP 1282 (6th Cir. 1972).

[237]1 EEOC COMPL. MAN. (BNA) §§ 65.2(c)(1), (5), & (6), at 65:0001–02; *id.* § 65.6, at 65:0004.

[238]29 C.F.R. § 1601.25 (2005); *see* 1 EEOC COMPL. MAN. (BNA) § 66.2, at 66:0001. Although EEOC regulations do not require that a conciliation failure notice be sent in cases processed only under the ADEA, the EEOC must provide "a copy to the respondent's attorney." *Id.* § 66.2(b), at 66:0001.

office's regional attorney to consider for litigation by the EEOC.[239] If suit is not authorized by the Commission, the parties are sent a notice and the charging party is issued a right-to-sue letter for any claims under Title VII, ADA, and ADEA.[240] If the Commission is unable to reach conciliation with a governmental respondent in a Title VII or ADA case, the case is forwarded to the Attorney General who may bring a civil action against the respondent or issue a right-to-sue letter to the charging party.[241] Title VII, ADA, and ADEA plaintiffs have 90 days after receiving their right-to-sue notice to file a lawsuit. However, ADEA plaintiffs may file suit without obtaining a right-to-sue notice, but must first wait 60 days after the filing of the charge.[242] Because the EEOC has authority to sue governmental respondents under the ADEA and EPA, the EEOC itself can file a civil complaint only under these statutes in concurrent cases if it so chooses, and the Justice Department, which has control over the Title VII and ADA claims, may join.[243] Additionally, private parties and the EEOC may seek enforcement of conciliation agreements by suing in federal court. Private parties need not resort to further administrative action.[244]

---

[239]1 EEOC COMPL. MAN. (BNA) § 66.5, at 66:0002–03. If the regional attorney considers the case appropriate for litigation, he/she will make a recommendation for litigation to the Office of General Counsel (OGC). Regional attorneys have been delegated the authority to file most types of cases subject only to sending OGC a "notice of intent" briefly describing the case to be filed. Upon approval by OGC, the regional attorney is then authorized to file the litigation. In cases (1) under the ADA; (2) involving "novel" issues; or (3) likely to require the commitment of substantial EEOC resources, a more detailed recommendation called a presentation memorandum is submitted by the regional attorney to OGC. OGC then reviews the presentation memorandum and sends it along with its own recommendation to the Commissioners for a vote.

[240]42 U.S.C. § 2000e-5(b)(1) (2000); 29 C.F.R. § 1601.28(b) (2005); 1 EEOC COMPL. MAN. (BNA) § 66.6, at 66:0003–04.

[241]42 U.S.C. § 2000e-5(f)(1) (2000).

[242]29 U.S.C. § 626(d) (2000) ("No civil action may be commenced by an individual under this section until 60 days after a charge alleging unlawful discrimination has been filed with the Equal Employment Opportunity Commission."). One court has interpreted this section to require an ADEA charging party to cooperate with conciliation efforts during this 60-day period. See Kozlowski v. Extendicare Health Serv., Inc., 83 FEP 167 (E.D. Pa. 2000).

[243]Id.; 29 C.F.R. §§ 1601.28(d), 1601.29 (2005); 1 EEOC COMPL. MAN. (BNA) § 66.6(d), at 66:0004; id. § 84, at 84:0001–02. See generally Chapters 29 (EEOC Litigation) and 30 (Justice Department Litigation).

[244]Ruedlinger v. Jarrett, 106 F.3d 212, 215, 73 FEP 162 (7th Cir. 1997); Howell v. Department of the Army, 975 F. Supp. 1293, 1303 (M.D. Ala.), aff'd, 130 F.3d

L. Issuance of Notice of Right to Sue Under Title VII and the ADA

Whenever the EEOC ceases its administrative charge-handling process (in a case where the EEOC itself will not bring suit),[245] the claimant will be issued notice of the right to bring a private civil action. Statutory notice of right to sue thus may issue at any of five junctures in the administrative process: (1) upon a finding of no jurisdiction or upon any administrative closure;[246] (2) upon request of the charging party before the completion of the administrative process, either before or after the end of the 180-day period;[247] (3) after a dismissal "without particularized findings" (unable to conclude a violation of the statute exists);[248] (4) after a finding of reasonable cause and the entry of an agreement to which the charging party is not a signatory;[249] or (5) after a finding of reasonable cause, failure of conciliation, and a determination that the case will not be litigated by the government (EEOC or Department of Justice) itself.[250] A Title VII, ADA, or ADEA civil action must be filed within 90 days of receipt of the statutory notice of right to sue.[251]

An EEOC regulation continues to provide that the Commission may issue a right-to-sue letter to a charging party *prior to* the expiration of the 180-day period in which it is to perform its investigation and conciliation functions as long as an authorized person certifies in writing that it is probable that the EEOC will be unable to complete the administrative process within 180 days from

---

445 (11th Cir. 1997) (table) (federal courts have jurisdiction over breach of conciliation agreement claims without the parties "first having to bring timely administrative complaints and exhaust their remedies with the EEOC").

[245]*See generally* Chapter 29 (EEOC Litigation).

[246]29 C.F.R. §§ 1601.28(b)(3) & (d), 1601.19 (2005); 1 EEOC COMPL. MAN. (BNA) § 4, at 4:0001–06; *see* Section III.G *supra*.

[247]29 C.F.R. § 1601.28(a)(1), (2), & (d) (2005); *see also* 1 EEOC COMPL. MAN. (BNA) § 6.3, at 6:0001–02.

[248]29 C.F.R. § 1601.19(a) (2005); *see* Martin v. Alamo Cmty. Coll. Dist., 353 F.3d 409, 411 (5th Cir. 2003) ("if the EEOC determines there is no reasonable cause to believe that an unlawful employment practice has occurred, the EEOC issues a letter informing the aggrieved party that it has the right to sue in federal district court").

[249]29 C.F.R. § 1601.28(b)(2).

[250]*Id.* § 1601.28(b)(1) & (d)(1).

[251]42 U.S.C. 2000e-5(f)(1) (2000); 29 U.S.C. § 626(e) (2000). *See generally* Chapter 26 (Timeliness).

the filing of the charge.[252] All EEOC offices have the option of utilizing this regulation, but those without a backlog of charges usually do not. Some courts have upheld the validity of this regulation.[253] Others have held that the regulation is contrary to statutory authority and dismissed "premature" cases without prejudice to refiling once 180 days have elapsed after filing of the charge.[254] In *EEOC v. Waffle House, Inc.*,[255] the Supreme Court stated in dicta that once a charge is filed, "the EEOC has exclusive jurisdiction over the claim for 180 days. During that time the employee must obtain a right-to-sue letter from the agency before prosecuting the claim."[256] This statement by the Court casts doubt on the validity of those decisions dismissing cases filed within the 180-day period.

M. Role of Attorneys

1. During the Administrative Enforcement Process

The EEOC does not recognize counsel for a charging party or respondent until a written statement of representation is received.[257] Conversely, a party's assertion that an attorney no longer represents that party also must be submitted in writing.[258]

---

[252]29 C.F.R. § 1601.28(a)(2) (2005). The persons authorized to make the required certification are: "the District Director, the Area Director, the Local Director, the Program Director, Office of Program Operations or upon delegation, the Director of Systemic Programs, Office of Program Operations or the Directors, Field Management Programs, Office of Program Operations." *Id.*

[253]*E.g.*, Sims v. Trus Joist MacMillan, 22 F.3d 1059, 1061–62, 64 FEP 1766 (11th Cir. 1994); Brown v. Puget Sound Elec., 732 F.2d 726, 729, 34 FEP 1201 (9th Cir. 1984); Woelbling v. R.C. Wilson Co., 966 F. Supp. 858, 862–63, 74 FEP 223 (E.D. Mo. 1997); Figueira v. Black Entm't Television, Inc., 944 F. Supp. 299, 304, 76 FEP 1850 (S.D.N.Y. 1996); Rolark v. University of Chi. Hosp., 688 F. Supp. 401, 404, 47 FEP 431 (N.D. Ill. 1988).

[254]*E.g.*, Martini v. Federal Nat'l Mortgage Ass'n, 178 F.3d 1336, 80 FEP 1 (D.C. Cir. 1999); Robinson v. Red Rose Commc'ns, Inc., 77 FEP 379, 381–82 (E.D. Pa. 1998); Pearce v. Barry Sable Diamonds, 912 F. Supp. 149, 154–57, 69 FEP 1332 (E.D. Pa. 1996) (discussing probable invalidity of regulation before certifying question to Third Circuit); *see also* EEOC v. Hearst Corp., 103 F.3d 462, 466, 72 FEP 1541 (5th Cir. 1997) ("the statute is clear that in the first 180 days after the charge is filed, only the EEOC is permitted to sue").

[255]534 U.S. 279 (2002).

[256]*Id.* at 291.

[257]1 EEOC COMPL. MAN. (BNA) § 82.2, at 82:0001. The statement of representation must be submitted by the attorney on his or her stationery.

[258]*Id.*

Once a written statement of representation is received, the Commission's policy is to deal with the *respondent* entirely through its attorney unless requested in writing to do otherwise.[259] On the other hand, the Commission will contact directly even represented *charging parties*, but the charging party's attorney generally will be copied on all EEOC correspondence to the party, and the EEOC generally will inform the attorney in advance of any telephonic contact with the party.[260]

Any party has the right to counsel when being interviewed by an EEOC investigator. For respondents, this right obtains during interviews of its personnel, subject to two limitations. First, the EEOC takes the position that the respondent may not insist that counsel be present at interviews of nonmanagement employees. Second, as for interviews of management personnel, the EEOC takes the position that counsel may be present only if (1) the particular manager, after EEOC counseling, has not elected to provide a statement outside of counsel's presence, and (2) the manager's own employment circumstances are not under investigation.[261]

2. *In Court*

Charging parties have the right to go to court at any time under the EPA,[262] and 180 days after charge filing under Title VII and the ADA.[263] A charging party who has filed an ADEA charge may file a lawsuit after 60 days even without obtaining a notice of right to sue. The EEOC usually recommends that a charging party retain counsel if he or she wishes to terminate the administrative process and go to court immediately. Charging parties often find it easier to obtain competent legal counsel if the EEOC has developed an investigative record, especially where there is a cause finding. Where a Title VII or ADA claimant is in propria persona, he

---

[259]*Id.* § 82.5, at 82:0001.

[260]*Id.* § 82.4, at 82:0001.

[261]*Id.*

[262]29 U.S.C. § 216(b) (2000).

[263]42 U.S.C. § 2000e-(5)(f)(1) (2000) (Title VII, incorporated by reference by the ADA); 29 U.S.C. § 626(c) (2000) (ADEA). By regulation, the EEOC will issue a notice of right to sue in advance of the expiration of the 180 days where a charging party so requests and the field director certifies that the EEOC would not complete the investigation within 180 days. 29 C.F.R. § 1601.28(a)(2) (2005); *see also* EEOC v. Waffle House, Inc., 534 U.S. 279, 291 (2002) (dicta indicating that a charging party may obtain a right-to-sue letter and file suit during the 180-day period).

or she may petition the court to appoint an attorney.[264] Pro se clerks at federal district courts sometimes provide assistance to pro se litigants in drafting and filing complaints.

Courts may appoint attorneys to represent Title VII and ADA plaintiffs. Courts typically consider the following three factors in determining whether to appoint counsel: (1) the plaintiff's ability to pay for representation; (2) the merits of the claim; and (3) the plaintiff's efforts to secure counsel.[264a] Many courts also consider a fourth factor—the capacity of the plaintiff to present his or her case adequately without the aid of counsel.[265]

It is the EEOC's policy to assist charging parties in obtaining an attorney upon request.[266] Many field offices therefore maintain a panel of attorneys who have indicated their willingness to represent charging parties and to cooperate with the Commission. These

---

[264]Section 706(f)(1) of Title VII, incorporated by reference by § 107(a) of the ADA, provides that the court may appoint an attorney for the claimant; the statute does not, however, provide the court with any funds to pay the attorney, who must depend for compensation upon representing a "prevailing party" under § 706(k).

The attorney's fees provision of Title VII (incorporated by the ADA) can make representation attractive to a prospective lawyer if the plaintiff is likely to prevail. *See* 42 U.S.C. § 2000e-5(k) (2000). Under the ADEA or EPA, attorney's fees are available to prevailing plaintiffs under § 16(b) of the FLSA, 29 U.S.C. § 216(b) (2000). Attorney's fees also may be awarded to plaintiffs who prevail in actions against the United States pursuant to the Equal Access to Justice Act, if "the position of the United States was not substantially justified." 28 U.S.C. § 2412(b), (d)(1)(B) (2000). *See generally* Chapter 41 (Attorney's Fees).

[264a]*See* Johnson v. U.S. Treasury Dep't, 27 F.3d 415, 417, 65 FEP 159 (9th Cir. 1994) (considering three factors: "(1) the plaintiff's financial resources; (2) the efforts made by the plaintiff to secure counsel on his or her own; and (3) the merit of the plaintiff's claim"); Miles v. Department of the Army, 881 F.2d 777, 784 n.6, 50 FEP 1006 (9th Cir. 1989) (applying the three factors set forth by the Ninth Circuit in *Bradshaw v. Zoological Soc'y*, 662 F.2d 1301, 1318, 16 FEP 828 (9th Cir. 1978): (1) the plaintiff's financial resources, (2) the efforts made by the plaintiff to secure counsel, and (3) whether the plaintiff's claim has merit); Henry v. City of Detroit Manpower Dep't, 763 F.2d 757, 760, 37 FEP 1445 (6th Cir. 1985) (en banc) (same).

[265]*See* Walker v. United Parcel Serv., Inc., 240 F.3d 1268, 1270 (10th Cir. 2001) (four factors); Ficken v. Alvarez, 146 F.3d 978, 979–80, 77 FEP 293 (D.C. Cir. 1998) (four factors); Poindexter v. FBI, 737 F.2d 1173, 1185, 35 FEP 136 (D.C. Cir. 1984) (same); Jones v. WFYR Radio/RKO Gen., 626 F.2d 576, 577, 27 FEP 864 (7th Cir. 1980) (per curiam) (same); Melton v. Freeland, 1997 WL 382054 (M.D.N.C. Feb. 6, 1997) (same); Tyson v. Pitt County Gov't, 919 F. Supp. 205, 207 (E.D.N.C. 1996) (same); Young v. K-Mart Corp., 911 F. Supp. 210, 211 (E.D. Va. 1996) (same).

[266]*See* 29 C.F.R. §§ 1601.28(a)(4) & (b)(4) (2005); 1 EEOC COMPL. MAN. (BNA) § 81, at 81:0001–06.

attorneys review case files and provide legal advice and counseling upon request to charging parties contemplating litigation.[267] The regional attorney within each district is responsible for developing the panel;[268] membership requires the applicant attorney to complete an application detailing the attorney's civil rights experience and training.[269] Charging parties generally are referred to panel attorneys on a rotating basis.[270]

N. The Systemic Program

The EEOC's systemic program handles the development and resolution of Commissioner charges under Title VII.[271] A Commissioner charge must be in writing and under oath and must state the facts constituting the alleged discrimination.[272]

The systemic program traditionally has been "designed to raise the level of compliance within industries and occupations having a high incidence of non-compliance" with any of the statutes that the EEOC enforces.[273] Most Commissioner charges are generated by (1) a Commissioner's inquiry, or (2) the EEOC's field systemic units, from leads obtained in the course of investigating individual charges. Further, input from civil rights and advocacy groups is gathered via the EEOC's Local Enforcement Plans (LEP), which are used in conjunction with the National Enforcement Plan (NEP) to improve the collaboration between the charge-processing and litigation groups.[274] Some Commissioner charges also result from

---

[267]1 EEOC COMPL. MAN. (BNA) § 81.1, at 81:0001.

[268]*Id.* § 81.2, at 81:0001–02.

[269]*Id.* § 81.3, at 81:0002; *id.* exh. 81-A, at 81:0007.

[270]*Id.* § 81.5, at 81:0003–04.

[271]Section 706(b) of Title VII, incorporated by reference by § 107(a) of the ADA, empowers Commissioners to file charges so as to permit investigation of a targeted respondent. 42 U.S.C. § 2000e-5(b) (2000); *see also* 29 C.F.R. § 1601.7 (2005). Under the ADEA and the EPA, the Commission may conduct a "directed investigation" of a particular respondent even in the absence of a charge from the public or itself. 29 C.F.R. §§ 1620.30 & 1626.15 (2005).

[272]42 U.S.C. § 2000e-5(b) (2000); 29 C.F.R. § 1601.12(a)(3) (2005); *see* EEOC v. Shell Oil Co., 466 U.S. 54, 63 & n.11, 34 FEP 709 (1984) (§ 706(b) provides that "charges shall be in writing under oath" and should set forth the facts upon which the charge is based).

[273]1 EEOC COMPL. MAN. (BNA) § 8.2(c), at 82:0003.

[274]*See* 3 EEOC COMPL. MAN. (BNA) N:3065–66. In April 1998, former Acting Chairman Paul Igasaki directed the EEOC to take more responsibility for improving the collaboration between the Commission's charge-processing and litigation groups,

leads supplied by the media and the community within which a field office is situated, combined with a statistical analysis of the respondent's workforce.[275] But these are only the most common ways that a Commissioner charge arises; "any person or organization" may request that a Commissioner charge be issued.[276]

Traditionally, systemic charges were centrally investigated and monitored out of Washington, D.C.[277] The EEOC's current practice favors decentralization.[278] Among other things, district offices may select and recommend for investigation a manageable number of systemic targets.[279] If a Commissioner charge is signed, it is returned to the field systemic unit for investigation and resolution.[280] Field units may be assisted by the headquarters' Program Research and Surveys Division in the compilation and analysis of statistical data.[281] Headquarters is, and other district offices may be, notified when a systemic charge is issued, so that individual charges may be reviewed for consolidation. A Commissioner may withdraw his or her charge before a "cause" determination is made.[282]

Even now, however, the decision to litigate any systemic case that fails conciliation is made by the Commissioners upon recommendation of the General Counsel.[283] Once the EEOC authorizes a systemic case to be litigated, trial responsibility rests with the regional attorney for the district office in which the case arose, or with the Associate General Counsel of Systemic Litigation Services at headquarters.[284]

---

with input from those groups in the systemic program. To achieve that goal, Igasaki directed the EEOC's Office of General Counsel and Office of Field Programs, along with its district offices, to develop Local Enforcement Plans (LEP), which would be used in conjunction with the National Enforcement Plan (NEP).

[275]*Id.* § 8.2, at 8:0002–03.

[276]29 C.F.R. § 1601.6 (2005); 1 EEOC COMPL. MAN. (BNA) § 8.3(a), at 8:0004.

[277]*See, e.g.*, 1 EEOC COMPL. MAN. §§ 8, 9, 22, 33, 34, & 36. The EEOC's *Priority Charge Handling Procedures* (June 1995) [hereinafter cited as *Priority Procedures*] have eliminated this centralization; contrary provisions of the Compliance Manual now are superseded. *See Priority Procedures*, at 17.

[278]For example, the *Priority Procedures* state, at page 19:

Field offices should investigate Commission charges in the same manner as individually filed charges, without headquarters supervision. Field offices can settle, decide and conciliate these charges in the same manner as other cases.

[279]1 EEOC COMPL. MAN. (BNA) §§ 8.2 & 8.3, at 8:0001–05.

[280]*Id.* § 8.3(b)(2), at 8:0005.

[281]*Id.* § 26.3(a)(2), at 26:0002; *id.* § 26.5, at 26:0004.

[282]*Priority Procedures*, at 19.

[283]*Id.* § 36, at 36:0001.

[284]*Id.* § 36.1, at 36:0001.

O. Interagency Coordination

Under Executive Order 12,067,[285] the EEOC is responsible for coordinating the federal effort to enforce federal equal employment opportunity laws. Its roles include providing for information-sharing and for mutual consultation and review of issuances by the Commission and other agencies, where those issuances affect the obligations of employers, labor organizations, employment agencies, and other federal agencies.[286]

The EEOC coordinates with other agencies in carrying out overlapping mandates. For example, the Commission has entered into a memorandum of understanding with the Department of Labor's Office of Federal Contract Compliance Programs (OFCCP) to share information pertaining to the administration of their respective statutes and executive orders, to coordinate enforcement efforts, and to allocate investigative responsibility where both agencies have jurisdiction over a complaint of employment discrimination.[287] For example, the OFCCP normally will forward complaints of individual harm filed with the OFCCP to the EEOC for investigation; the EEOC then will notify the OFCCP when it finds cause, conciliation has failed, and the Commission has decided against litigation.[288]

Additionally, the OFCCP is permitted to serve as the EEOC's agent for the processing of the Title VII component of employment discrimination class claims filed with the OFCCP under Executive Order 11,246. The OFCCP will investigate Title VII class claims in a manner consistent with Title VII principles, will issue findings, and will attempt voluntary conciliation for damages where appropriate.[289] Coordination also exists between the EEOC, the

---

[285]43 Fed. Reg. 28,967 (1978).

[286]*See* 29 C.F.R. § 1690 et seq.

[287]46 Fed. Reg. 7435 (1981); *see* Memorandum of Understanding, 64 Fed. Reg. 17,664 (1999). *See generally* Chapter 38 (Federal Contractor Affirmative Action Compliance).

[288]*See generally* Chapter 38 (Federal Contractor Affirmative Action Compliance).

[289]Memorandum of Understanding, 64 Fed. Reg. 17,666 (1999). The OFCCP will issue Title VII right-to-sue notices in cases where it does not find reasonable cause to believe unlawful discrimination has occurred, but only the EEOC may issue those notices (or initiate litigation) where the OFCCP *does* make a reasonable-cause finding and is unsuccessful in conciliation. Furthermore, the OFCCP also has taken the position that it may seek punitive damages for "egregious" behavior. *See* DAILY LAB. REP. (BNA) at A-3 (Apr. 16, 1999).

OFCCP, and the Department of Labor's Wage and Hour Division, which have agreed to various duties related to enforcing laws prohibiting compensation discrimination, notably under the Equal Pay Act, Title VII, and Executive Order 11,246.[290]

The EEOC also has responsibility for investigating employment discrimination complaints against recipients of federal financial assistance subject to Title VI of the Civil Rights Act of 1964,[291] Title IX of the Education Amendment Acts of 1972,[292] and other similar statutes, where the complaints also allege Title VII, ADA,[293] or Equal Pay Act violations. The funding agency must transmit to the EEOC for resolution complaints over which the EEOC has exclusive jurisdiction and most individual complaints over which the agencies have concurrent jurisdiction.[294] In the latter case, if the EEOC dismisses a claim, the funding agency will give "due weight to EEOC's determination" in deciding whether it will do likewise.[295] On the other hand, if the EEOC finds cause, such a complaint may be resolved through conciliation[296] or enforcement by the funding agency.[297]

The EEOC has a memorandum of understanding with the Federal Communications Commission (FCC). The memorandum establishes procedures for the orderly exchange of information and for the resolution of employment discrimination complaints filed against broadcast licensees and cable operators.[298] Charges over

---

[290]Memorandum of Understanding, 64 Fed. Reg. 17,668 (1999). The EEOC has agreed to help train the Wage and Hour Division staff to better identify potential compensation discrimination cases. In addition, whenever the Wage and Hour Division learns of potential compensation discrimination, it may refer the case to the OFCCP. If the employer is not a federal contractor, the OFCCP may then refer the matter to the EEOC. The Commission, the OFCCP, and the Wage and Hour Division also have agreed to share information in order to improve the efficiency of their staffs.

[291]42 U.S.C. § 2000d et seq.

[292]20 U.S.C. § 1681 et seq.

[293]Because the EEOC has responsibility for the employment title of the ADA, its work-sharing arrangement includes claims of disability discrimination under § 504 of the Rehabilitation Act of 1973. See 59 Fed. Reg. 39,898 (1994).

[294]See 29 C.F.R. § 1691 et seq.; see also 28 C.F.R. pt. 42 (Justice Department regulations); 1 EEOC COMPL. MAN. (BNA) § 90, at 90:0001–04.

[295]29 C.F.R. § 1691.8 (2005).

[296]Id. § 1691.11.

[297]Id. § 1691.10.

[298]Administering FCC/EEOC Memo of Understanding (June 16, 1986), reprinted in 1 EEOC COMPL. MAN. (BNA) exh. 91-A, at 91:0005.

which the agencies have concurrent jurisdiction are investigated by the EEOC. When the EEOC finds reasonable cause, it notifies the FCC, which then decides what its own course of action should be if conciliation fails.[299]

The EEOC also has entered into a memorandum of understanding with the Office of Special Counsel (OSC) for Immigration Related Unfair Employment Practices of the Justice Department.[300] Under § 102 of the Immigration Reform and Control Act of 1986 (IRCA), the OSC has jurisdiction to investigate charges alleging national origin and citizenship employment discrimination covered by IRCA.[301] The memorandum provides for the exchange of information between the EEOC and the OSC and the receipt and referral of charges in cases where one or the other has exclusive jurisdiction. The memorandum was revised in 1998 to improve the coordination of discrimination charges based on national origin.[302] The revision allowed the EEOC and the OSC to serve as the other's agent for the sole purpose of receiving charges under Title VII and federal immigration laws.[303]

IV. EEOC INVESTIGATION AND SUBPOENA POWERS

A. Statutory Authority

1. Title VII and the ADA

Section 709(a) of Title VII (incorporated by reference by § 107(a) of the ADA) provides:

---

[299]1 EEOC COMPL. MAN. (BNA) § 91, at 91:0001–04.

[300]*Memorandum of Understanding, reprinted in* 1 EEOC COMPL. MAN. (BNA) exh. 94-A, at 94:0012.

[301]*See* 8 U.S.C. § 1324b (2000). *See generally* Chapter 7 (National Origin and Citizenship). IRCA provides that the OSC and the EEOC may not simultaneously entertain charges of discrimination based on the same facts—e.g., a charge filed with the EEOC for national origin discrimination under Title VII and a charge filed with the OSC for citizenship discrimination under IRCA, where the charges relate to the same events. 8 U.S.C. § 1324b(b)(2) (2000); *see* 28 C.F.R. § 44.300(d) (2005). The complainant, therefore, must choose with which agency to file.

[302]Memorandum of Understanding, 63 Fed. Reg. 5518 (1998), *reprinted in* 1 EEOC COMPL. MAN. (BNA) 94:0004.

[303]*Id.* at 5519; 1 EEOC COMPL. MAN. (BNA) at 94:0004. The memorandum describes generally how the agencies are to refer charges to each other when the

In connection with any investigation of a charge filed under [§ 706], the Commission or its designated representative shall at all reasonable times have access to, for the purposes of examination, and the right to copy any evidence of any person being investigated or proceeded against that relates to unlawful employment practices covered by this [title] and is relevant to the charge under investigation.[304]

Section 710, as amended in 1972,[305] provides:

For the purposes of all hearings and investigations conducted by the Commission or its duly authorized agents or agencies, Section 11 of the National Labor Relations Act (49 Stat. 455; 29 U.S.C. 161) shall apply.[306]

Section 11 of the NLRA[307] confers upon the federal agency the right to have access to and to copy all evidence, to require the attendance and testimony of witnesses, and to issue subpoenas in support thereof. It provides that within five days after the service of any such subpoena requiring the production of evidence, the party served may file a petition to revoke or modify the subpoena if the evidence subpoenaed does not relate to any matters under investigation or if the subpoena does not describe with sufficient particularity the evidence whose production is required.[308] If the

---

nonreceiving agency has exclusive jurisdiction. The memorandum also provides for liberal information sharing and coordinated investigative efforts for charges in which both the EEOC and OSC retain jurisdiction.

[304]42 U.S.C. § 2000e-8(a) (2000).

[305]Prior to amendment, § 710 authorized the EEOC to examine witnesses under oath and to require the production of documentary evidence by means of a written demand therefor, and required the respondent, if it did not intend to comply, to file a petition in the U.S. district court to set aside the demand. If a petition was not filed within 20 days, all defenses to such a demand were deemed waived if the EEOC sought court enforcement of its demand.

[306]42 U.S.C. § 2000e-9 (2000).

[307]29 U.S.C. § 161 (2000).

[308]Id. 29 C.F.R. § 1601.16(a) (2005) authorizes subpoenas to be issued by the district directors, other directors within the Office of Program Operations, "or any representatives designated by the Commission." Section 1601.16(b) provides that any person not intending to comply must, within 5 days from receipt, petition the issuing director, or the General Counsel where the subpoena is issued by the Commission, to revoke or modify. Within 8 days after receipt, if practicable, the director or General Counsel is to revoke or modify or make a determination on the petition and submit the proposed determination to the Commission for its review and final determination. See generally 1 EEOC COMPL. MAN. (BNA) § 24, at 24:0001–09; id. § 22, exh. 22-C, at 22:0017 (EEOC's July 1986 Investigative Compliance Policy Statement, which was issued out of a concern that "[t]he Commission's investigative processes should not be frustrated by a respondent's ability to provoke subpoena litigation in an attempt to delay reaching a determination on the merits of a charge

agency issuing the subpoena does not revoke or modify it, and the respondent refuses to comply, the agency may petition the district court to enforce its subpoena.[309]

A respondent wishing to resist a subpoena therefore must file a petition to revoke or modify the subpoena within five days after service. There is a split in the circuits over whether a respondent who fails to exhaust administrative remedies may challenge subsequent judicial enforcement of a subpoena.[310] The Fifth Circuit has held that the EEOC's investigative authority with respect to a charge, and hence, its subpoena power, ceases when the agency issues a right-to-sue letter and the charging party initiates litigation based on the charge.[311]

2. The ADEA and the EPA

Section 7(a) of the ADEA provides:

[The EEOC] shall have the power to make investigations . . . in accordance with the powers and procedures provided in section 9 . . . of the Fair Labor Standards Act of 1938, as amended.[312]

---

or to make settlement more attractive to charging parties because of the prospect of further delays in resolution." The statement authorizes district directors to reach cause determinations without the evidence a respondent withholds, if the file contains probative evidence of discrimination, or to draw an adverse inference against the respondent where the respondent knowingly destroys or fails to retain records in anticipation of the filing of a charge. The statement also calls for a shortened administrative subpoena appeal process, which is set forth at 29 C.F.R. § 1601.16(b)).

[309]See 29 U.S.C. § 161 (2000).

[310]Compare EEOC v. Cuzzens of Ga., Inc., 608 F.2d 1062, 1064, 21 FEP 803 (5th Cir. 1979) (per curiam) (finding waiver) with EEOC v. Lutheran Social Servs., 186 F.3d 959, 80 FEP 1009 (D.C. Cir. 1999) (finding that objections were not waived) and EEOC v. Food Town Stores, 27 FEP 111, 112 (M.D.N.C. 1981) (where "respondent has made diligent use of the administrative review process, . . . [it would be] unreasonable to require an employer to forego every argument it did not raise before an administrative tribunal"; court proceedings are de novo).

[311]EEOC v. Hearst Corp., 103 F.3d 462, 72 FEP 1541 (5th Cir. 1997); accord EEOC v. Federal Home Loan Mortgage Corp., 37 F. Supp. 2d 769, 79 FEP 451 (E.D. Va. 1999). The Fifth Circuit refused to enforce the subpoenas, concluding that the issuance of a right-to-sue notice and the initiation of litigation terminates the investigative portion of the EEOC's multi-stage administrative procedure. According to the court, keeping the various stages of the EEOC administrative proceedings separate is important because of the different roles that the EEOC plays as a charge progresses: administrator, investigator, mediator, and finally, enforcer. The court held that once a charge has entered the enforcement stage (here, through the initiation of the private lawsuit), the EEOC's investigative role ends. It may pursue any further interest in the matter only by intervening in the lawsuit and utilizing discovery mechanisms or, if appropriate, by filing a Commissioner charge.

[312]29 U.S.C. § 626(a) (2000).

Section 9 of the FLSA[313] also is the statutory authority for the EEOC's investigatory and subpoena powers under the Equal Pay Act,[314] which amended the FLSA. Section 9 makes applicable, for ADEA or EPA subpoenas, the provisions of 15 U.S.C. §§ 49 and 50, which govern Federal Trade Commission subpoenas. Section 49 confers upon the issuing agency the right of access to documentary evidence at all reasonable times for copying and examination and the right to compel the attendance and testimony of witnesses and the production of documents.

Although the access rights under 15 U.S.C. § 49 and under § 11 of the NLRA are comparable, their enforcement procedures differ.[315] If a respondent refuses to obey a subpoena in an age or equal pay case, the EEOC may apply for a writ of mandate to compel compliance. Under 15 U.S.C. § 50, failure to comply may result in a fine and imprisonment.[316] Moreover, refusal to comply may toll the running of the statute of limitations on the recovery of back pay under the Equal Pay Act.

B. The "Valid Charge" Requirement Under Title VII and the ADA

The Supreme Court in *EEOC v. Shell Oil Co.*[317] made it clear that the existence of a charge meeting the requirements of § 706(b)

---

[313]*Id.* § 209.

[314]*Id.* § 206(d).

[315]*Compare* 29 C.F.R. § 1620.31(b) (2005) (EPA regulations; "There is no right of appeal to the Commission from the issuance of such a subpoena.") *and id.* § 1626.16(c) (ADEA regulations; "A subpoena issued by the Commission or its designee pursuant to the Act is not subject to review or appeal.") *with id.* § 1601.16(b) (Title VII and ADA regulations; the respondent has 5 days to petition district director or General Counsel to modify or revoke a subpoena). Note also that a "member of the Commission" alone has the authority to issue an Equal Pay Act subpoena. *Id.* § 1620.31(a); 1 EEOC COMPL. MAN. (BNA) § 24.5(b), at 24:0004.

[316]15 U.S.C. § 50 (2000) permits the imposition of a fine of $1,000 to $5,000 or up to 1-year imprisonment.

[317]466 U.S. 54, 65 & n.15, 34 FEP 709 (1984). There is no comparable "valid charge" requirement in ADEA subpoena-enforcement actions. EEOC v. American & Effird Mills, Inc., 964 F.2d 300, 301, 58 FEP 1062 (4th Cir. 1992) (per curiam) (the EEOC has broad authority to investigate possible violations of the ADEA and bring suit independent of the existence of a valid charge by an employee; ordering a subpoena enforced against an employer that refused the agency's request on the ground that the employee's discrimination charge was untimely); EEOC v. Sears, Roebuck & Co., 55 FEP 482, 483 (D. Or. 1991) (the EEOC's power to investigate

of Title VII is a jurisdictional prerequisite to enforcement of a subpoena issued by the EEOC. The threshold question in determining whether a Title VII subpoena can be enforced, therefore, is the extent to which § 706(b) and 29 C.F.R. § 1601.12—which specify what information must be included in the underlying charge—have been satisfied.

The Supreme Court in *Shell Oil* explained what must be contained, in the context of subpoena enforcement based on a Commissioner pattern-or-practice charge:

> [The charge must] identify the groups of persons that [the Commissioner] has reason to believe have been discriminated against, the categories of employment positions from which they have been excluded, the methods by which the discrimination may have been effected, and the periods of time in which [the Commissioner] suspects the discrimination to have been practiced.[318]

Courts exercise deference and enforce most EEOC subpoenas, even where the underlying charge does not literally satisfy each of the four factors set out in *Shell Oil*.[319] For example, the Seventh Circuit upheld enforcement of an EEOC subpoena despite the fact that the underlying charge failed to state the categories of employment positions from which affected individuals allegedly were excluded.[320] The court explained that the *Shell Oil* test was not meant to be a rigid formula for scrutinizing an EEOC charge and that the omission was not deficient because it did not leave the charge without

---

under the ADEA does not require a timely charge); EEOC v. Allstate Ins. Co., 30 FEP 573, 575–76 (N.D. Ill. 1981) (enforcing an EEOC subpoena in an ADEA "directed investigation" over objections that no charge had been filed).

[318]466 U.S. at 73. The requirements of a valid charge are considered in more detail in Section III.C *supra*, and Chapters 21 (Employers) and 29 (EEOC Litigation).

[319]466 U.S. at 73 (four factors: (1) identification of persons the EEOC believes have been discriminated against; (2) categories of employment positions from which they have been excluded; (3) methods by which discrimination was effected; and (4) period during which EEOC suspects discrimination occurred).

[320]EEOC v. Quad/Graphics, Inc., 63 F.3d 642, 649, 68 FEP 1085 (7th Cir. 1995). The court explained that the four factors listed by the Supreme Court in *Shell Oil* should be applied pragmatically, and "the key inquiry must be whether the allegations in the charge, when assessed against these four factors, fulfill the legislative and regulatory command that the charging Commissioner identify as precisely as possible the appropriate area of inquiry to determine whether or not there is a violation of the Act." *Id.* at 647; *see also* EEOC v. Roadway Express, Inc., 86 FEP 833 (6th Cir. 2001) (enforcing subpoena seeking promotion data on job categories beyond the scope of the original charge).

"meaningful limitations." The Second Circuit held that the charge's identification of the groups and positions affected was sufficient to satisfy the *Shell Oil* test, where the respondent was given fair notice of the allegedly discriminatory nature of its conduct.[321]

Further, courts generally have enforced subpoenas over objections that an EEOC Commissioner charge is too indefinite to provide the basis for the investigation[322] or that the EEOC acted in bad faith.[323] Neither the charge nor the notice thereof need contain specific statistical data substantiating the allegations. Nor must a district court find that the charge is verifiable or factually or legally well founded.[324] Although a Title VII investigation cannot be based on an invalid charge, a court may enforce an EEOC subpoena to gather records that would help determine whether the EEOC had jurisdiction.[325] Moreover, where a charge at least fa-

[321]EEOC v. Superior Temporary Servs., Inc., 56 F.3d 441, 67 FEP 1700 (2d. Cir. 1995).

[322]*E.g., Shell Oil*, 466 U.S. at 73 (rejecting the respondent's "too indefinite" challenge); EEOC v. K-Mart Corp., 796 F.2d 139, 144–46, 41 FEP 371 (6th Cir. 1986) (per curiam) (same); New Orleans Pub. Serv., Inc. v. Brown, 507 F.2d 160, 164, 9 FEP 134 (5th Cir. 1975) (same); General Employment Enters., Inc. v. EEOC, 440 F.2d 783, 784, 3 FEP 310 (7th Cir. 1971) (per curiam) (same).

[323]*Quad/Graphics*, 63 F.3d at 649 (affirming district court's holding that EEOC did not issue subpoena in bad faith in retaliation for respondent's failure to cooperate fully with Department of Labor investigator during routine audit); *K-Mart*, 796 F.2d at 146 (the Commissioner's good faith is presumed because of the oath and affirmation requirement; denial of enforcement would require a substantial showing of abuse of process); EEOC v. Michael Constr. Co., 706 F.2d 244, 250–52, 31 FEP 1081 (8th Cir. 1983) (rejecting the employer's charge that the EEOC issued the subpoena solely to force settlement); EEOC v. Bay Shipbuilding Corp., 668 F.2d 304, 311, 27 FEP 1377 (7th Cir. 1981) (the employer failed to show that the investigation was undertaken for an ulterior motive); EEOC v. South Carolina Nat'l Bank, 562 F.2d 329, 332, 15 FEP 1141 (4th Cir. 1977) (subpoena enforced where there was no substantial showing of bad faith). *But see* EEOC v. First Ala. Bank, 440 F. Supp. 1381, 1385, 17 FEP 103 (N.D. Ala. 1977) (enforcement refused where the court determined that the subpoena was issued due to a personal vendetta held by the investigator), *aff'd*, 611 F.2d 132, 21 FEP 1633 (5th Cir. 1980).

[324]EEOC v. Shell Oil Co., 466 U.S. 54, 72 n.26, 34 FEP 709 (1984) ("Some of respondent's arguments are based on the assumption that a district court, when deciding whether to enforce a subpoena issued by the EEOC, may and should determine whether the charge of discrimination is 'well founded' or 'verifiable.' Nothing in the statute or its legislative history provides any support for this assumption.") (citation omitted); *see also* Brock v. Plumbers Local 375, 860 F.2d 346, 348, 129 LRRM 2826 (9th Cir. 1988) (agencies may issue subpoenas on suspicion of violation).

[325]*See, e.g.*, EEOC v. Sidley Austin Brown & Wood, 315 F.3d 696 (7th Cir. 2002) (limiting enforcement of subpoena to coverage issue); EEOC v. Superior Temporary

cially appears timely, courts generally will enforce the subpoena and leave the timeliness question for another day.[326] Some courts have enforced EEOC subpoenas over allegations that the claims are barred for other reasons, such as by reason of a prior consent decree[327] or because of res judicata or collateral estoppel.[328]

The permissible scope of discovery that may be undertaken by a respondent in opposing subpoena enforcement is not conclusively resolved, but appears limited.[329]

Servs., 56 F.3d 441, 447, 67 FEP 1700 (2d Cir. 1995) (enforcing subpoena and indicating that underlying charge was not substantially flawed because, without access to employer records, EEOC may not have had enough information to specify categories of jobs from which it contends individuals have been discriminatorily excluded); EEOC v. Kloster Cruise Ltd., 939 F.2d 920, 923, 56 FEP 1061 (11th Cir. 1991) (enforcing a Title VII subpoena against a Miami-based travel company that was incorporated in Bermuda and operated cruise ships under the flag of the Bahamas, on the ground that there was not clear evidence that the respondent was extraterritorial); Pacific Maritime Ass'n v. Quinn, 491 F.2d 1294, 1296, 7 FEP 482 (9th Cir. 1974) (affirming enforcement of the EEOC's subpoena to determine whether it has jurisdiction).

[326]EEOC v. Tire Kingdom, Inc., 80 F.3d 449, 70 FEP 744 (11th Cir. 1996); EEOC v. Norfolk Police Dep't, 45 F.3d 80, 85, 66 FEP 1425 (4th Cir. 1995) (EEOC has jurisdiction to investigate charge where untimeliness of individual charge is not "readily apparent"); EEOC v. Tempel Steel Co., 814 F.2d 482, 485, 43 FEP 557 (7th Cir. 1987) (alleged untimeliness of a charge is not a defense to subpoena enforcement); EEOC v. Roadway Express, Inc., 750 F.2d 40, 42, 36 FEP 867 (6th Cir. 1984) (per curiam) (the subpoena enforcement stage is not the appropriate time to decide the timeliness of a charge); EEOC v. United States Steel Corp., 534 F. Supp. 416, 417–18, 28 FEP 592 (S.D.W. Va. 1982) (same); see also EEOC v. Maryland Cup Corp., 785 F.2d 471, 476, 40 FEP 475 (4th Cir. 1986) (the district court's order declining to enforce the EEOC's subpoena was vacated and remanded; the information sought was relevant and material, and statutory due process requirements were satisfied).

[327]E.g., EEOC v. Children's Hosp. Med. Ctr., 719 F.2d 1426, 1429, 33 FEP 461 (9th Cir. 1983) (subpoena enforced even though the underlying claims might have been barred by a prior consent decree).

[328]E.g., New Orleans S.S. Ass'n v. EEOC, 680 F.2d 23, 25–26, 29 FEP 398 (5th Cir. 1982) (subpoena enforced over objection that the investigation was precluded by res judicata or collateral estoppel; the subsequent challenge by the EEOC sought different relief from the prior private suit); Channelmark Corp. v. Destination Prods. Int'l, Inc., 2000 U.S. Dist. LEXIS 9854, at *14 (N.D. Ill. July 12, 2000) (enforcing subpoena despite res judicata argument).

[329]Generally, the respondent may not engage in discovery on the merits of the underlying charge or depose a Commissioner concerning the facts surrounding its issuance. See In re United States v. Comley, 890 F.2d 539, 543 (1st Cir. 1989) ("Except in extraordinary circumstances, discovery is improper in a summary subpoena enforcement proceeding."); In re EEOC, 709 F.2d 392, 400, 32 FEP 361 (5th Cir. 1983) (as a general rule, a respondent is not entitled to engage in "counter-discovery" to

C. Permissible Scope of Inquiry

If an EEOC subpoena is properly issued in a Title VII case, a court normally will enforce it if the subpoenaed information is relevant and material.[330] In an age or equal pay investigation, the subpoena normally will be enforced if the data sought is within the scope of the statute and is being sought for a legitimate purpose.[331] Some cases suggest that the definition of "relevance" for subpoena purposes may be narrower than the "like and related" concept used to determine the scope of EEOC litigation that may arise from a charge.[332]

---

find grounds for resisting a subpoena; discovery on the merits may be conducted only after the respondent makes "a substantial demonstration of abuse based on meaningful evidence"); Food Town Stores v. EEOC, 708 F.2d 920, 925, 31 FEP 1327 (4th Cir. 1983) (EEOC was not required to issue a subpoena at the respondent's request to compel testimony of an EEOC Commissioner concerning the merits of the underlying charge; in enacting Title VII, Congress did not intend to allow extensive delay in the disposition of employment discrimination cases); EEOC v. K-Mart Corp., 694 F.2d 1055, 1065, 30 FEP 788 (6th Cir. 1982) (enforcement of the subpoena proffered by the respondent denied).

[330]E.g., EEOC v. United Air Lines, Inc., 287 F.3d 643, 649, 653, 88 FEP 1018 (7th Cir. 2002) (as long as the investigation is within the EEOC's authority, the subpoena is not too indefinite, and the information sought "might throw light upon" the inquiry raised in the complaint, the district court must enforce the subpoena); EEOC v. Southern Farm Bureau Casualty Ins. Co., 271 F.3d 209, 211, 87 FEP 332 (5th Cir. 2001) (district courts will enforce EEOC subpoenas when EEOC carries its burden of demonstrating that the information requested is relevant to the charge against the employer); EEOC v. South Carolina Nat'l Bank, 562 F.2d 329, 332, 15 FEP 1141 (4th Cir. 1977) (the standard to be applied in a demand for enforcement proceeding is relevance and materiality, not cause to believe the charge is true); *accord* EEOC v. Kloster Cruise Ltd., 939 F.2d 920, 922, 56 FEP 1061 (11th Cir. 1991) (citing cases); EEOC v. Chrysler Corp., 567 F.2d 754, 755, 16 FEP 500 (8th Cir. 1977) (citing cases).

[331]E.g., EEOC v. Bessemer Group Inc., 105 Fed. Appx. 411, 413 (3d Cir. 2004) (subpoena enforced in an ADEA case where the agency showed that "the investigation will be conducted pursuant to a legitimate purpose, that the inquiry is relevant, that the information demanded is not already within the agency's possession, and that the administrative steps required by the statute have been followed"); EEOC v. Peat, Marwick, Mitchell & Co., 589 F. Supp. 534, 539, 38 FEP 1843 (E.D. Mo. 1984) (subpoena enforced over the objection that the EEOC has no authority to issue a subpoena in an ADEA action), *aff'd*, 775 F.2d 928, 38 FEP 1846 (8th Cir. 1985); EEOC v. Allstate Ins. Co., 30 FEP 573, 575–76 (N.D. Ill. 1981) (subpoena enforced in an ADEA "directed investigation" case over objections that the EEOC had no authority to investigate on a companywide basis and in the absence of a charge).

[332]EEOC v. Occidental Life Ins. Co., 535 F.2d 533, 541, 12 FEP 1300 (9th Cir. 1976) (although the respondent arguably could have resisted the scope of EEOC inquiry at the investigation stage, the scope of a later EEOC suit is determined by the scope of the EEOC investigation and determination), *aff'd*, 432 U.S. 355, 14 FEP 1718 (1977).

Many courts have said that the EEOC's subpoena power is broad.[333] Courts enforce most EEOC subpoenas, including those that appear to be broad or that seek what an employer may view as marginally relevant information.[334] The EEOC's burden to show that the information it seeks is "relevant to the charge under investigation" is "not particularly onerous."[335] Still, the subpoena must relate to the charge. For example, most courts have refused to allow access to evidence pertaining to *bases* of discrimination clearly not raised in the charge (e.g., race information in a sex case).[336]

---

[333]Courts have continued to hold that a district court's role in reviewing EEOC subpoenas is deferential and limited to inquiry of: (1) whether the administrative investigation is within the agency's authority, (2) whether the agency's demand is too indefinite, and (3) whether the information sought is reasonably relevant. *See United Air Lines*, 287 F.3d at 649; EEOC v. Tire Kingdom, Inc., 80 F.3d 449, 450, 70 FEP 744 (11th Cir. 1996); EEOC v. Quad/Graphics, Inc., 63 F.3d 642, 645, 68 FEP 1085 (7th Cir. 1995); United States v. Florida Azalea Specialists, 19 F.3d 620, 623, 64 FEP 769 (11th Cir. 1994); *see also* New Orleans S.S. Ass'n v. EEOC, 680 F.2d 23, 26, 29 FEP 398 (5th Cir. 1982) (data that would show adverse impact in ranking is relevant where the challenged test was validated for pass/fail only); EEOC v. Elrod, 674 F.2d 601, 613, 28 FEP 607 (7th Cir. 1982) (documentary information and the testimony of a knowledgeable official concerning the basis for respondent's retirement policies were "reasonable requests for information" to determine whether there was a violation of the ADEA); EEOC v. University of Pittsburgh, 643 F.2d 983, 985–86, 25 FEP 508 (3d. Cir. 1981) (lists and information regarding all instructors and teaching positions in four professional schools is relevant to a charge of sex discrimination in compensation in the nursing school); Circle K Corp. v. EEOC, 501 F.2d 1052, 1054, 8 FEP 758 (10th Cir. 1974) (polygraph examination data must be produced even though the alleged discriminatee did not take the polygraph examination); Motorola, Inc. v. McLain, 484 F.2d 1339, 1345–46, 6 FEP 469 (7th Cir. 1973) (individual charges of promotion discrimination and harassment support a demand for information on all employees in all job classifications); Bowaters S. Paper Corp. v. EEOC, 428 F.2d 799, 800, 2 FEP 711 (6th Cir. 1970) (per curiam) ("It is to be said that there is no constitutional prohibition to Congress permitting investigations of corporate behavior based upon nothing more than official curiosity.") (quoting United States v. Morton Salt Co., 338 U.S. 632 (1950)).

[334]EEOC v. Milwaukee, 919 F. Supp. 1247, 1259 (E.D. Wis. 1996) (enforcing in large part subpoena that requested, among other things, applicant background investigation files for 1991–1995, all personnel files for employees who served probation from 1991 to present, internal affairs files created since 1989, all reports prepared on various topics, information regarding officers who underwent drug testing, and numerous other documents relating to individual claimants in connection with charge of pattern and practice of race discrimination).

[335]EEOC v. United Air Lines, Inc., 287 F.3d 643, 652–53, 88 FEP 1018 (7th Cir. 2002).

[336]*See, e.g.*, EEOC v. Southern Farm Bureau Casualty Ins. Co., 271 F.3d 209, 211–12, 87 FEP 332 (5th Cir. 2001) (EEOC failed to show the relevance of requested information about the gender of the company's employees to individual African-American male's race discrimination charge); General Ins. Co. v. EEOC, 491 F.2d 133, 136, 7 FEP 106 (9th Cir. 1974) (the EEOC is not entitled to "evidence going

In *EEOC v. Sidley Austin Brown & Wood*,[337] the Seventh Circuit ordered a subpoena for information to be enforced to assist in determining whether the subpoenaed party is within the agency's jurisdiction or is covered by the statute it administers with respect to the conduct in question. However, the court did limit the scope of the subpoena and held that coverage determinations need to be made before full compliance is mandated. But most courts have been more liberal in allowing the EEOC to seek information regarding *issues* not specified in the charge (e.g., promotion information in a discharge case).[338] Similarly, most courts have allowed classwide investigations,[339] or investigations—for comparative purposes—

---

to forms of discrimination not even charged or alleged"); EEOC v. Quick-Shop Mkts., 396 F. Supp. 133, 135–36, 10 FEP 1081 (E.D. Mo.) (access to evidence on race discrimination denied since only sex discrimination was alleged in the charge), *aff'd per curiam*, 526 F.2d 802 (8th Cir. 1975). *But see Milwaukee*, 919 F. Supp. 1259 (portion of subpoena requesting all information regarding sexual harassment complaints made during specified period deemed reasonably relevant in race discrimination investigation where it was alleged that sexual harassment complaints lodged against African-American officers were treated more seriously than those lodged against white officers) and EEOC v. U.S. Fidelity & Guar. Co., 414 F. Supp. 227, 244, 15 FEP 532 (D. Md.) (the EEOC should not be limited to investigating the retaliation and national origin charge and may require production of documents concerning sex and racial discrimination where allegations of the charge are broadly framed), *aff'd mem.*, 538 F.2d 324, 13 FEP 1005 (4th Cir.), *cert. denied*, 429 U.S. 1023 (1976).

[337]315 F.3d 696 (7th Cir. 2002).

[338]*See, e.g.*, EEOC v. Roadway Express, Inc., 261 F.3d 634, 638–39 (6th Cir. 2001) (permitting EEOC access to evidence of "patterns of racial discrimination" for job classifications and hiring situations other than those that the EEOC's charge specifically targeted); EEOC v. Cambridge Tile Mfg. Co., 590 F.2d 205, 206, 18 FEP 1378 (6th Cir. 1979) (per curiam) (information concerning sex discrimination in job classification is relevant to charges of sex and race discrimination in firing); Blue Bell Boots, Inc. v. EEOC, 418 F.2d 355, 358, 2 FEP 228 (6th Cir. 1969) (charges alleging discriminatory discharges support a subpoena seeking information on hiring job classifications and "records concerning every employee in every category of employment"). *But see* EEOC v. Southern Farm Bureau, 271 F.3d 209, 211 (5th Cir. 2001) (holding that the EEOC may only obtain evidence that "is relevant to the charge under investigation").

[339]*See, e.g.*, EEOC v. Quad/Graphics, Inc., 63 F.3d 642, 68 FEP 1085 (7th Cir. 1995) (subpoena enforced where charge alleged pattern and practice of discrimination in failing to recruit or hire protected individuals); EEOC v. Western Publ'g Co., 502 F.2d 599, 603, 8 FEP 629 (8th Cir. 1974) (where the complainant's charge alleged that the defendant "has been discriminating against my race," "the Commission is entitled to have access to . . . all evidence which is relevant and material to the . . . allegations that discrimination against [the complainant] and other Negroes prevailed in [the company] in regard to salaries, promotions, hiring, discharges and

regarding employees in positions different from the claimant.[340] Some courts have held that the EEOC's subpoena power also extends to third parties,[341] including the power to protect a witness from misuse of a subpoena.[342]

Although the subpoena power is broad, a court may modify a subpoena that it judges to be overbroad, burdensome, or directed at irrelevant material.[343] For example, the EEOC's former practice of utilizing a vague, catchall description in seeking evidence has been disapproved.[344] Courts also have imposed limitations on the

---

references"); Graniteville Co. v. EEOC, 438 F.2d 32, 39–42, 3 FEP 155 (4th Cir. 1971) (the EEOC is entitled to plantwide computer-generated information in its investigation of departmental discrimination).

[340]*See, e.g., Roadway Express*, 261 F.3d at 639; EEOC v. University of N.M., 504 F.2d 1296, 1299–1302, 8 FEP 1037 (10th Cir. 1974) (information concerning all faculty members in the college of engineering is relevant to an individual charge of retaliatory discharge); Georgia Power Co. v. EEOC, 412 F.2d 462, 468, 1 FEP 787 (5th Cir. 1969) ("Comparative evaluation of job qualifications is obviously essential to the EEOC's task."); EEOC v. Chrysler Corp., 14 FEP 656, 657–58 (E.D. Mo.) (enforcing an EEOC subpoena for information regarding the employer's treatment of clerical employees as relevant to a charge of discrimination against all African Americans and females, even though the charging party was a welder), *aff'd*, 567 F.2d 754, 16 FEP 500 (8th Cir. 1977).

[341]*See* EEOC v. Illinois Dep't Empl. Sec., 995 F.2d 106, 107 (7th Cir. 1993) (during investigation of an employer, court enforces EEOC subpoena for information from third-party state agency); *cf.* EEOC v. Bellemar Parts Indus., Inc., 868 F.2d 199, 200, 49 FEP 369 (6th Cir. 1989) (upholding an award of attorney's fees against the EEOC in a subpoena enforcement action where the respondent had not been named in the charge and had presented evidence to the EEOC that the charge against another respondent did not apply to it).

[342]EEOC v. Kim & Ted, Inc., 1995 U.S. Dist. LEXIS 14510, at *7 (N.D. Ill. Oct. 4, 1995) (EEOC may move to quash third-party subpoenas).

[343]*E.g.*, EEOC v. United Air Lines, Inc., 287 F.3d 643, 653–55, 88 FEP 1018 (7th Cir. 2002) (a subpoena seeking information about all benefits provided to all of defendant's French employees could not be enforced because the undue financial and administrative burden outweighed the tangential relevance of the information); EEOC v. Packard Elec. Div., 569 F.2d 315, 317–19, 17 FEP 9 (5th Cir. 1978) (a subpoena seeking plantwide information should not be enforced where the charges concerned narrow factual situations, and the EEOC had not shown that the relevant information unit was the entire facility); EEOC v. United States Fidelity & Guar. Co., 414 F. Supp. 227, 250, 15 FEP 532 (D. Md.) (the EEOC may not request that information be identified by race and sex where the charge alleges only sex discrimination and the charging party is Caucasian), *aff'd*, 538 F.2d 324, 13 FEP 1005 (4th Cir. 1976); EEOC v. Western Elec. Co., 382 F. Supp. 787, 793–95, 8 FEP 595, *modified on other grounds*, 8 FEP 815 *and* 1198 (D. Md. 1974) (the EEOC does not have power to compel answers to interrogatories).

[344]Manpower, Inc. v. EEOC, 346 F. Supp. 126, 128–29, 5 FEP 169 (E.D. Wis. 1972) (not enforcing the EEOC's broad catchall demand for "any like or related

time period for which records must be produced[345] and on the geographic scope of the inquiry, many times excluding data pertaining to unrelated facilities.[346]

Not all claims of undue burden are sustained, however. Some courts say that the trouble and expense of responding to administrative subpoenas is "part of the social burden of living under government."[347] Additionally, the presumption is that compliance should be enforced to further the EEOC's legitimate inquiry into

---

records"); H. Kessler & Co. v. EEOC, 53 F.R.D. 330, 333, 336, 3 FEP 956 (N.D. Ga. 1971) (refusing to enforce the "catchall" request of "any and all like or related records"), *aff'd*, 468 F.2d 25, 5 FEP 132 (5th Cir. 1972), *modified on other grounds*, 472 F.2d 1147, 5 FEP 405 (5th Cir. 1973).

[345]*E.g.*, Monsanto Co. v. EEOC, 2 FEP 50, 50 (N.D. Fla. 1969) (8-month period); Georgia Power Co. v. EEOC, 295 F. Supp. 950, 954, 1 FEP 351 (N.D. Ga. 1968) (5 years prior to the alleged violation), *aff'd*, 412 F.2d 462, 1 FEP 787 (5th Cir. 1969); *cf.* EEOC v. Recruit USA, Inc., 939 F.2d 746, 755, 56 FEP 721 (9th Cir. 1991) (3 to 4 years' worth of documents are not burdensome, and they are relevant where the biased acts could have occurred within that time period); EEOC v. Magnetics Div., 13 FEP 191, 192 (W.D. Pa. 1976) (discovery of information for the time period of 3½ years before the alleged discriminatory act is not unduly oppressive to the employer). In earlier days, however, courts allowed access to data pertaining to events occurring before the effective date of Title VII. *E.g.*, EEOC v. University of N.M., 504 F.2d 1296, 1304, 8 FEP 1037 (10th Cir. 1974) (the employer must produce data preceding 1972, when educational institutions first were covered by Title VII); United States v. Electrical Workers (IBEW) Local 309, 3 FEP 948, 951 (E.D. Ill. 1969) (the union was ordered to produce documents regarding its pre-Act conduct; the information was relevant regarding its post-Act activities and possible Title VII violations); *see also Georgia Power Co.*, 295 F. Supp. at 954 (absent some special showing of the need and relevancy of a longer period, demands for relevant data are limited to a 5-year period prior to the alleged violation), *aff'd*, 412 F.2d 462, 1 FEP 787 (5th Cir. 1969).

[346]*E.g.*, Joslin Dry Goods Co. v. EEOC, 483 F.2d 178, 184, 6 FEP 293 (10th Cir. 1973) (where "[i]t was not shown that there were any hiring or firing practices and procedures applicable to all of the stores," limiting EEOC discovery to a single location); *cf. Georgia Power Co.*, 295 F. Supp. at 954 (the parties agreed the EEOC's discovery should be limited to the city of Atlanta, where "all personnel records [for 18 locations] are maintained at one central office"). *But see* Parliament House Motor Hotel v. EEOC, 444 F.2d 1335, 1340–41, 3 FEP 663 (5th Cir. 1971) (affirming enforcement of a subpoena for records relating to another restaurant because of common management).

[347]Bradley Lumber Co. v. NLRB, 84 F.2d 97, 100 (5th Cir. 1936); *see, e.g.*, Federal Trade Comm'n v. Rockefeller, 591 F.2d 182, 190 (2d Cir. 1979) (a subpoena is not unduly burdensome unless compliance "pose[s] a threat to the normal operation of appellants' businesses"); EEOC v. Lockheed Martin Corp., 70 FEP 1457 (D. Md. 1996) (enforcing EEOC subpoena that required respondent to generate and provide EEOC with detailed description of its personnel computer files despite burden of such task where EEOC demonstrated that request ultimately would result in administrative convenience for respondent and that information would contribute to

matters of public interest.[348] Conclusory claims of undue burden generally are rejected, and several courts have held that in order to sustain such an objection, the employer must show that complying with EEOC's subpoena would have a significant impact on the normal operation of its business.[349] Some courts even have required respondents to compile subpoenaed information in the format requested by the EEOC.[350] A detailed description of the

---

efficiency and accuracy of EEOC's investigation), *aff'd*, 116 F.3d 110, 74 FEP 202 (4th Cir. 1997); EEOC v. Milwaukee, 919 F. Supp. 1247, 1259 (E.D. Wis. 1996) (rejecting respondent's contention that EEOC's subpoena was unreasonably burdensome); EEOC v. General Elec. Co., 447 F. Supp. 978, 981, 17 FEP 549 (E.D. Wis. 1978) (enforcement of the EEOC subpoena would not impose an undue burden where the subpoena itself permits the employer, as an alternative, to describe in detail the manner and method of storing documents requested and the persons having charge of them); EEOC v. U.S. Fidelity & Guar. Co., 414 F. Supp. 227, 244, 15 FEP 532 (D. Md.) ("[B]urdensomeness alone is not a sufficient basis for refusal to enforce a subpoena."), *aff'd*, 538 F.2d 324, 13 FEP 1005 (4th Cir. 1976); EEOC v. National Elec. Benefit Fund, 12 FEP 1006, 1007 (D.D.C. 1976) (the expenditure of $1,000 to $1,500 by the electric industry pension fund to comply with the EEOC's subpoena is not unduly burdensome or unreasonable).

[348]EEOC v. United Air Lines, Inc., 287 F.3d 643, 653, 88 FEP 1018 (7th Cir. 2002).

[349]*E.g., id.* at 653; EEOC v. Maryland Cup Corp., 785 F.2d 471, 478, 40 FEP 475 (4th Cir. 1986) (broadly interpreting the EEOC's subpoena power; the company is required to compile lists, conduct an internal investigation, and, if necessary, interview its employees to obtain data); EEOC v. Bay Shipbuilding Corp., 668 F.2d 304, 313, 27 FEP 1377 (7th Cir. 1981) (since the respondent was unable to show that "compliance would threaten the normal operation of [its] business," enforcement was not unduly burdensome); New Orleans Pub. Serv., Inc. v. Brown, 507 F.2d 160, 165, 9 FEP 134 (5th Cir. 1975) (district court's order quashing EEOC subpoena was reversed and remanded; the documents sought were relevant and based on a valid charge); Circle K Corp. v. EEOC, 501 F.2d 1052, 1055, 8 FEP 758 (10th Cir. 1974) (subpoena was enforced where the charge was on sufficient grounds and compliance would not be unduly burdensome); EEOC v. Grinnell Fire Prot. Sys. Co., 764 F. Supp. 623, 626, 56 FEP 139 (D. Kan. 1991) (enforcing an EEOC subpoena over the claim that it provides a "free round of discovery" for the charging party); EEOC v. Pan Am. World Airways, 31 FEP 1136, 1139 (S.D.N.Y. 1983) (although the district court found the subpoena to be "burdensome," enforcement was ordered because the court was unable to find that compliance would "unduly disrupt or seriously hinder normal operations"); *H. Kessler & Co.*, 53 F.R.D. at 336 (subpoena was enforced where the material sought was relevant and material to the charge; compliance is "part of the social burden of living under government"). *But see* Pacific Maritime Ass'n v. Quinn, 491 F.2d 1294, 1297, 7 FEP 482 (9th Cir. 1974) (on remand, the district court can "further restrict the breadth of the demand"); United States Steel Corp. v. United States, 6 FEP at 977, 983–84 (W.D. Pa.) (accepting "burdensome" defense as to only a portion of the EEOC's demand for documents), *aff'd mem.*, 487 F.2d 1396 (3d Cir. 1973).

[350]*See* EEOC v. Citicorp Diners Club, 985 F.2d 1036, 1037, 1039–40, 60 FEP 1242 (10th Cir. 1993) (an EEOC subpoena that requires the employer to search its

burden involved in complying with a subpoena will not defeat enforcement of the subpoena where the estimate appears to be an exaggeration or fails to account for an EEOC offer to limit the scope of the subpoena.[351] And, where a colorable claim of undue burden has been made, at least one court conditioned the production of documents upon the EEOC advancing the costs thereof.[352] Courts will, on occasion, limit the scope of grossly overbroad subpoenas that the court concludes seek wholly irrelevant information.[353] Indeed, the Sixth Circuit has refused the EEOC's request

---

personnel files, interview employees, and compile written summaries of the findings is not overly broad; the EEOC may compel an employer to compile information within its control in order to respond to a subpoena; rejecting the company's claim that the information sought did not exist and would require hundreds of hours to develop and compile). *Compare Maryland Cup Co.*, 785 F.2d at 478 (requiring compilation), *Bay Shipbuilding*, 668 F.2d at 313 (same), *New Orleans Pub. Serv.*, 507 F.2d at 164–65 (the trial court erred in limiting the EEOC subpoena power to information that need not be compiled), Motorola, Inc. v. McLain, 484 F.2d 1339, 1342, 1346, 6 FEP 469 (7th Cir. 1973) (upholding a subpoena requiring the respondent to produce a list of all employees broken down by race, sex, labor grade, job classification, department, and seniority date), Sunbeam Appliance Co. v. Kelly, 532 F. Supp. 96, 101, 28 FEP 180 (N.D. Ill. 1982) (requiring compilation), Oklahoma Publ'g Co. v. Powell, 22 FEP 1421, 1425 (W.D. Okla. 1976) (requiring the respondent to compile lists from computer data), *aff'd sub nom.* Oklahoma Publ'g Co. v. EEOC, 22 FEP 1429 (10th Cir. 1978), *and* Cameron Iron Works, Inc. v. EEOC, 320 F. Supp. 1191, 1194, 3 FEP 27 (S.D. Tex. 1970) (compilation of a promotion list is required despite the man-hours involved) *with United States Steel Corp.*, 6 FEP at 983–84; Monsanto Co. v. EEOC, 2 FEP 50, 52 (N.D. Fla. 1969) (same) *and Georgia Power Co.*, 295 F. Supp. at 953–54 (same). Because courts have relied by analogy on the federal discovery rules in evaluating EEOC investigative subpoenas, a respondent seeking to avoid compilation of data may want to point to the alternative provided in Rule 33(c) of the Federal Rules of Civil Procedure. That rule provides the option of making the raw evidence available to the requesting party where the burden of compilation would be the same for each party. The employer's duty to compile data in response to discovery requests made by a plaintiff in litigation is discussed generally in Chapter 33 (Discovery).

[351]EEOC v. Quad/Graphics, Inc., 63 F.3d 642, 648–49, 68 FEP 1085 (7th Cir. 1995) (respondent failed to meet its burden of establishing that compliance with subpoena would threaten its normal business operations and was therefore unduly burdensome where respondent's detailed affidavit setting forth precise burden it would undergo in complying with subpoena was exaggeration and failed to account for EEOC's offer to mitigate burden).

[352]*E.g., New Orleans Pub. Serv.*, 507 F.2d at 165 (using analogy to Rule 45(b), holding that a court may condition the denial of a motion to quash a subpoena "upon the advancement by the person on whose behalf the subpoena is issued of the reasonable cost of producing the book, papers, documents, or tangible things").

[353]EEOC v. Ford Motor Credit Co., 26 F.3d 44, 47–48, 65 FEP 65 (6th Cir. 1994) (limiting scope of subpoena and noting that despite broad subpoena power, EEOC

for all personnel records for employees who served at the charging party's location during the entirety of the charging party's employment on the ground that the "extremely tenuous" relevance of such information is outweighed by the burden to the employer of producing it.[354]

With few exceptions, claims of confidentiality and privacy have met with limited success.[355] Assertions of a "peer review" privilege in academia were rejected in *University of Pennsylvania v. EEOC*.[356] There, a unanimous Supreme Court rejected the university's claim of a peer review privilege in determining tenure of a professor. The Court held that a university does not enjoy a special privilege concerning materials pertinent to charges of discrimination in tenure decisions.[357] Employers have had somewhat better, but not uniform, success in invoking a self-critical analysis privilege.[358] Where disclosure is required, the respondent still may seek a protective order.[359]

Claims of laches generally have been rejected when offered as a complete defense to subpoena compliance.[360] Also unsuccessful have been requests to stay enforcement of an EEOC subpoena

---

is not entitled "to any material it deems relevant in its discretion"); EEOC v. Milwaukee, 919 F. Supp. 1247, 1259–60 (E.D. Wis. 1996) (refusing to enforce portions of subpoena that sought information regarding individual that was too indefinite and ambiguous, and portion that sought medical records of third parties).

[354]*Ford Motor Credit Co.*, 26 F.3d at 47; *see also* EEOC v. United Air Lines, Inc., 287 F.3d 643, 654, 88 FEP 1018 (7th Cir. 2002) (tangential relevance outweighed by undue financial and administrative burden of information sought).

[355]*See* EEOC v. Bay Shipbuilding Corp., 668 F.2d 304, 312, 27 FEP 1377 (7th Cir. 1981) (rejecting the employer's confidentiality assertion; criminal penalties of Title VII protect the employer from disclosure by EEOC employees); EEOC v. Massachusetts, 760 F. Supp. 685, 687, 55 FEP 488 (N.D. Ill. 1990) (enforcing an ADEA subpoena seeking personnel records where a state statute protecting privacy rights has been complied with). *But cf.* EEOC v. Food Town Stores, 27 FEP 111, 111–12 (M.D.N.C. 1981) (upholding refusal to provide access to the employer's computer tape on the ground that it contained valuable commercial information that the respondent did not want to disclose).

[356]493 U.S. 182, 189, 51 FEP 1118 (1990).

[357]*Id.* at 189–94. *See generally* Chapter 33 (Discovery).

[358]*See generally* Chapter 33 (Discovery).

[359]*See, e.g.*, EEOC v. Laborers Local 75, 30 FEP 1339, 1340 (N.D. Ill. 1982) (even though Title VII imposes criminal penalties on EEOC employees who publicize information gained during investigations, "[t]he court may . . . utilize a protective order to assure confidentiality").

[360]EEOC v. National City Bank, 865 F.2d 1267 (6th Cir. 1988) (recognizing that the application of the doctrine of laches has been denied in a number of cases, but

under the automatic stay provisions of the Bankruptcy Code; some courts have held that EEOC administrative proceedings are exempt from those provisions.[361]

One court has held that the EEOC's deviation from the subpoena provisions of its Compliance Manual will not forestall an enforcement order.[362]

V. ACCESS TO EEOC FILES AND ADMISSIBILITY OF THE EEOC DETERMINATION[363]

A. Access to EEOC Files

1. Statutory Framework

a. Title VII and the ADA. Parties and the public may have access to Title VII and ADA investigative files under the Freedom of

---

finding no reason for this when both elements of the doctrine have been established); EEOC v. South Carolina Nat'l Bank, 562 F.2d 329, 332, 15 FEP 1141 (4th Cir. 1977) (laches will not bar enforcement of a subpoena unless any resulting prejudice is established and the delay can be attributed to EEOC misconduct); EEOC v. Exchange Sec. Bank, 529 F.2d 1214, 1216–17, 12 FEP 1066 (5th Cir. 1976) (something more than time alone, such as proof of dilatory attitude by the EEOC, is required to sustain a finding that the EEOC's delay of more than 2 years was unreasonable); Associated Dry Goods Corp. v. EEOC, 454 F. Supp. 387, 393–94, 17 FEP 1219 (E.D. Va. 1978) (same), *aff'd sub nom.* EEOC v. Joseph Horne Co., 607 F.2d 1075, 20 FEP 1752 (4th Cir. 1979), *rev'd and remanded on other grounds sub nom.* EEOC v. Associated Dry Goods Corp., 449 U.S. 590, 24 FEP 1356 (1981); EEOC v. U.S. Fidelity & Guar. Co., 414 F. Supp. 227, 240–42, 15 FEP 532 (D. Md.) (enforcing the subpoena despite a 2-year delay; EEOC authority should not be circumscribed by rigid time limitations; there was no showing of prejudice, and the charge alleged a continuing violation), *aff'd,* 538 F.2d 324, 13 FEP 1005 (4th Cir. 1976). *But see* EEOC v. First Ala. Bank, 440 F. Supp. 1381, 1385–86, 17 FEP 103 (N.D. Ala. 1977) (EEOC is not entitled to enforcement of a subpoena where the respondent bank had undergone a major change in personnel, and enforcement clearly would result in the bank sustaining prejudice by the EEOC's unwarranted delay of almost 2 years), *aff'd,* 611 F.2d 132, 21 FEP 1633 (5th Cir. 1980).

[361]*E.g.,* EEOC v. Sambo's Rest., Inc., 34 FEP 1451, 1453 (S.D. Tex. 1982); AM Int'l, Inc. v. EEOC, 34 FEP 1535, 1536 (N.D. Ill. 1982).

[362]Sunbeam Appliance Co. v. Kelly, 532 F. Supp. 96, 99–100, 28 FEP 180 (N.D. Ill. 1982) (EEOC is under no duty to follow the procedures set forth in the Compliance Manual).

[363]This section deals with private suits; different rules apply where the EEOC is a litigant. *See generally* Chapter 29 (EEOC Litigation). On the question of party and public access to records in the possession of the OFCCP, see Chapter 38 (Federal Contractor Affirmative Action Compliance).

Information Act (FOIA),[364] except as limited by the confidentiality provisions of §§ 706(b) and 709(e) of Title VII and the FOIA's general exceptions to disclosure.[365] Sections 706(b) and 709(e) of Title VII (which are incorporated by reference in the ADA) together establish the confidentiality of information obtained by the EEOC (1) in a charge, (2) during the investigative process, (3) in settlement attempts, and (4) pursuant to EEOC recordkeeping and reporting requirements.[366] Both sections forbid EEOC personnel from "making public" the confidential information described and impose criminal sanctions on those who do.[367]

These provisions effectively allow the EEOC to offer a respondent an additional inducement to enter into a conciliation or

---

[364]5 U.S.C. § 552 et seq.

[365]*See* Section V.A.1.b *infra.*

[366]Section 706(b) provides that "[c]harges shall not be made public by the Commission," and nothing said or done in attempts to settle the charge shall be made public or be used as evidence in a subsequent proceeding without the written consent of the parties. 42 U.S.C. § 2000e-5(b). Section 709(e) provides that it shall be unlawful for an EEOC employee to "make public . . . any information obtained by the Commission pursuant to its authority under this section prior to the institution of any proceedings under this title involving such information." *Id.* § 2000e-8(e). Employees who violate either provision are subject to a fine of up to $1,000 or imprisonment of up to 1 year.

[367]*Id.* §§ 2000e-5(b) & 2000e-8(e). The parties are not considered members of the "public" for purposes of §§ 706(b) and 709(e). EEOC v. Associated Dry Goods Corp., 449 U.S. 590, 598, 24 FEP 1356 (1981). The two statutory sections are supplemented by EEOC procedural regulations. 29 C.F.R. § 1601.22 provides:

Neither a charge, nor information obtained during the investigation of a charge of employment discrimination under the ADA or Title VII, nor information obtained from records required to be kept or reports required to be filed . . . shall be made matters of public information . . . prior to the institution of any proceeding . . . . This provision does not apply to such earlier disclosures to charging parties, or their attorneys, respondents or their attorneys, or witnesses where disclosure is deemed necessary for securing appropriate relief. This provision also does not apply to such earlier disclosures to representatives of interested Federal, State, and local authorities as may be appropriate or necessary to the carrying out of the Commission's function . . . .

Section 1601.26(a) restates the prohibition against release of information pertaining to settlement attempts, and allows for release to federal, state, or local agencies, but adds that "the Commission may refuse to make disclosures to any such agency which does not maintain the confidentiality of such endeavors . . . or in any circumstances where the disclosures will not serve the purposes of the effective enforcement of Title VII or the ADA." Section 1601.26(b) provides that factual information obtained in conciliation, if otherwise obtainable under § 709 of Title VII, will be treated for disclosure purposes as if it were obtained in investigation. *Accord* Branch v. Phillips Petroleum, 638 F.2d 873, 881–82, 25 FEP 653 (5th Cir. 1981) (purely factual material is not covered by any privilege).

settlement agreement by providing that there will be no public identification of the respondent where a charge does not proceed to litigation.[368] Published EEOC decisions do not identify the respondent, and conciliation agreements are not released to the public, absent the consent of the parties.

Neither the EPA nor the ADEA contains comparable confidentiality provisions.[369] Disclosure of charge and charge-file materials under these statutes is governed by the Commission's regulations under the ADEA,[370] FOIA,[371] and the Privacy Act of 1974.[372]

   b. The Freedom of Information Act. The FOIA, which allows "the public" access to certain files of federal government agencies,

---

[368]Typically, charges and the facts underlying them become public when the charging party or the EEOC sues on the merits. But in *EEOC v. Recruit USA, Inc.,* 939 F.2d 746, 56 FEP 721 (9th Cir. 1991), the EEOC made charges public at an earlier stage by appending them to a suit seeking an injunction against the respondent's destruction of records. The court rejected the respondent's arguments that the EEOC's actions violated Title VII's confidentiality provisions and that its actions should be punished through the imposition of civil sanctions. *Id.* at 754.

[369]The Fifth Circuit, however, has held that § 706(b) prohibits the introduction of an EEOC file in an ADEA case between two private litigants. Olitsky v. Spencer Gifts, Inc., 842 F.2d 123, 126, 46 FEP 902 (5th Cir. 1988). *Contra* Binder v. Long Island Lighting Co., 933 F.2d 187, 193–94, 55 FEP 1525 (2d Cir. 1991) (defendant's statements to the EEOC during its investigation may be used in a subsequent ADEA action, because § 706(b) of Title VII does not apply to the ADEA).

[370]*See* 29 C.F.R. § 1626.4 (2005).

[371]*See id.* pt. 1610.

[372]5 U.S.C. § 552a (2000); *see* 29 C.F.R. pt. 1611 (2005); 1 EEOC COMPL. MAN. (BNA) §§ 83.1(a), (b), at 83:0001. The Privacy Act describes "systems of records" as any group of records that can be retrieved about a particular individual by the individual's name or by some identifying number or symbol. 5 U.S.C. § 552a(a)(5) (2000). Pursuant to § 552a(k)(2) (the Privacy Act), the EEOC has exempted from the Act's access, accounting, and notification requirements systems EEOC-1 (Age and Equal Pay Act discrimination case files) and EEOC-3 (Title VII and Americans with Disabilities Act discrimination case files). The EEOC has explained this exemption in its Privacy Act regulations. These files are exempted because they may contain information regarding unlawful employment practices other than those complained of by the individual who is the subject of the file, the disclosure of which would impede law enforcement activities; because the subject individuals of the files in these systems know of the file and its contents; because individuals with files in these systems have a means of access to their records under the FOIA and, for system EEOC-3, under § 83 of the EEOC Compliance Manual; and because individuals with files in these systems are given the opportunity during the EEOC's investigation to rebut information provided by the alleged discriminator. To allow "such individuals the additional right to amend or correct the records submitted by the allegedly discriminating employer would undermine the investigatory process and destroy the integrity of the administrative record." *Id.*

has seven exemptions, four of which are invoked by the EEOC in refusing disclosure. The four exemptions are for

> (3) [records] specifically exempted from disclosure by statute . . . ;
> (4) trade secrets and commercial or financial information obtained from a person and privileged or confidential;
> (5) inter-agency or intra-agency memorandums or letters which would not be available by law to a party other than an agency in litigation with the agency;
> . . .
> (7) records or information compiled for law enforcement purposes, but only to the extent that production of such law enforcement records or information (A) could reasonably be expected to interfere with enforcement proceedings, (B) would deprive a person of a right to a fair trial or an impartial adjudication, (C) could reasonably be expected to constitute an unwarranted invasion of personal privacy, (D) could reasonably be expected to disclose the identity of a confidential source . . . , (E) would disclose techniques and procedures for law enforcement investigations or prosecutions . . . , or (F) could reasonably be expected to endanger the life or physical safety of any individual;
> . . .
> Any reasonably segregable portion of a record shall be provided to any person requesting such record after deletion of the portions which are exempt under this subsection.[373]

The confidentiality provisions of §§ 706(b) and 709(e) of Title VII are specifically incorporated into the FOIA exemptions by § 552(b)(3).[374]

Whether charging parties and respondents are "members of the public" within the meaning of the FOIA, and thus subject to the § 552(b) exemptions to disclosure, was settled by the Supreme Court in *EEOC v. Associated Dry Goods Corp.*[375] The Court there ratified the EEOC's practice of disclosing the investigative file to a charging party contemplating litigation under Title VII, holding that the charging party is not a member of "the public" within the meaning of the statute.[376] The Court made clear, however, that the EEOC may disclose to the charging party appropriate information only from the charging party's *own* file. It may not disclose information from

[373]5 U.S.C. § 552(b) (2000).
[374]American Centennial Ins. Co. v. EEOC, 722 F. Supp. 180, 182–83, 50 FEP 1156 (D.N.J. 1989).
[375]449 U.S. 590, 24 FEP 1356 (1981).
[376]*Id.* at 598; *see* 1 EEOC Compl. Man. (BNA) § 83.2, at 83:0001.

other files against the same respondent because, as to those files, the charging party *is* a member of the public.[377] By similar reasoning, the EEOC holds that a respondent is barred from access to files generated from charges lodged against others by the same charging party.[378]

The fourth exemption—trade secrets and commercial or financial information—is especially important to employers resisting disclosure. In compliance with Executive Order 12,600,[379] the EEOC's FOIA regulations now provide a procedure whereby respondents that have submitted confidential commercial information in the course of an investigation may be notified of a FOIA request for the information and have an opportunity to object and seek judicial relief if necessary.[380]

The fifth exemption allows an agency to withhold certain interagency and intra-agency memoranda or letters. The Supreme Court in *Federal Trade Commission v. Grolier, Inc.*[381] made clear that the privileges incorporated by this exemption are those " 'which the Government enjoys under the relevant statutory and case law in the pretrial discovery context.' " The Court stated that the test under exemption five is whether "the documents would be 'routinely' or 'normally' disclosed upon a showing of relevance."[382] This

---

[377]449 U.S. at 603; *cf.* Broderick v. Shad, 117 F.R.D. 306, 312, 43 FEP 532 (D.D.C. 1987) (because §§ 706(b) and 709(c) of Title VII preclude disclosure by the EEOC of charges of discrimination, the plaintiff is not entitled to discovery from the employer of another employee's charge).

In the wake of the Supreme Court's ruling in *Associated Dry Goods*, the EEOC amended its policy to ensure that statistical and other information about an employer's general practices that are relevant to several charges are duplicated and placed in the file of each charging party before granting access to the file. *See* 1 EEOC COMPL. MAN. (BNA) § 83.7(c), at 83:0004.

[378]1 EEOC COMPL. MAN. (BNA) §§ 83.5 & 83.6(b)(4), at 83:0003; *see, e.g.,* Branch v. Phillips Petroleum Co., 638 F.2d 873, 880, 25 FEP 653 (5th Cir. 1981) (the respondent is a "member of the public" within the meaning of § 706(b) with respect to other charges filed by the charging party).

[379]52 Fed. Reg. 23,781 (1987).

[380]29 C.F.R. § 1610.19 (2005); *see also* Venetian Casino Resort v. EEOC, 409 F.3d 359, 364, 95 FEP 1373 (D.C. Cir. 2005) (employer contended EEOC disclosed trade secrets produced to it to charging parties without first notifying party submitting information; appeals court directed district court to determine whether EEOC's policy is inconsistent with Trade Secrets Act, Administrative Procedure Act, and FOIA).

[381]462 U.S. 19, 27 (1983).

[382]*Id.* at 20; *see also* United States v. Weber Aircraft Corp., 465 U.S. 792, 801–02 (1984) (a claim of privilege under exemption five, other than executive or attorney-client

exemption encompasses records such as those involving confidential intra-agency advisory opinions, the attorney-client privilege, and the attorney work-product privilege. Some cases suggest that, where the facts at issue already are available, there is no need to disclose them further.[383]

The seventh exemption, covering "records or information compiled for law enforcement purposes,"[384] allows an agency to withhold disclosure in a variety of circumstances and is the section most often cited by the EEOC in responding to FOIA requests.[385] Although there are six subparts to exemption seven, only two commonly are at issue. Indeed, the Fourth Circuit has held that the only issues relevant under exemption seven are whether disclosure of the files would (1) interfere with enforcement proceedings if released (subsection (A)) or (2) identify a confidential source (subsection (D)).[386]

As for subsection (A), except as noted below, the EEOC denies requests to disclose *open* investigative files on the ground that it would interfere with enforcement proceedings.[387] The Supreme Court in *NLRB v. Robbins Tire & Rubber Co.*[388] rejected respondent's argument that interference with law enforcement functions must be established on a document-by-document basis. Rather, the Court

---

privilege, must be viewed with caution; however, the legislative history of exemption five does not provide a comprehensive or exclusive list of privileges).

[383]*See, e.g.*, Public Citizen v. Department of State, 11 F.3d 198, 201 (D.D.C. 1993) (FOIA exemption for duplicates; plaintiff must establish that specific fact already has been placed in public domain); Montrose Chem. Corp. v. Train, 491 F.2d 63, 71 (D.C. Cir. 1974) (the facts sought were exempt from disclosure since they were already on the record); Morton-Norwich Prods., Inc. v. Mathews, 415 F. Supp. 78, 82 (D.D.C. 1976) (the facts sought had already been made public by the agency; they also may be withheld as exempt when they may be elsewhere ascertained from other documents available from the agency).

[384]5 U.S.C. § 552(b)(7) (2000).

[385]*See* 29 C.F.R. § 1610.17(a) (2005).

[386]Charlotte-Mecklenburg Hosp. Auth. v. Perry, 571 F.2d 195, 202, 16 FEP 680 (4th Cir. 1978); *see also* Southern Imperial Coatings Corp. v. EEOC, 27 FEP 701, 702–03 (E.D. La. 1981) (investigatory records are exempt as a matter of law under § 552(b)(7) during the pendency of administrative processing; the court will not inquire into whether or not disclosure will interfere with enforcement proceedings).

[387]*See* 5 U.S.C. § 552(b)(7)(A) (2000); 29 C.F.R. § 1610.17(g) (2005). The rationale for denying release of open files may be found in *Title Guarantee Co. v. NLRB*, 534 F.2d 484, 489, 91 LRRM 2993 (2d Cir. 1976), where the Second Circuit held that "such disclosure would interfere with enforcement proceedings."

[388]437 U.S. 214, 236, 98 LRRM 2617 (1978).

held, a determination regarding disclosure properly may be made generically—for example, by denying disclosure of all witness statements in the file.[389] However, where investigative files are closed, a document-by-document analysis must be made to see what other exemption, if any, might be applicable. For example, if the invasion of personal privacy exemption of § 552(b)(7)(C) would be used, only those records that would constitute an unwarranted invasion of personal privacy may be withheld.[390] Where portions of records are reasonably segregable, FOIA requires that the non-exempt portions be released.[391]

As for subsection (D), portions of records may be withheld if they disclose the identity of a confidential source. This exemption applies only if the witness has been promised confidentiality.[392] Thus, in open investigative files, witness statements may be withheld entirely under subsection (A); in closed files, by contrast, only the *names* of the confidential witness and any identifying information may be withheld under subsection (D).

2. The EEOC's Procedure on Disclosure of Files

The EEOC's June 1995 *Priority Charge Handling Procedures* state that, to help foster an understanding of the issues and to reduce

---

[389]*Id.* at 226; *accord Southern Imperial Coatings Corp.*, 27 FEP at 702–03 (pursuant to § 552(b)(7), the EEOC can refuse to disclose its investigatory files regarding pending investigations where disclosure could jeopardize future enforcement proceedings). *But see* J.P. Stevens & Co. v. Perry, 710 F.2d 136, 143, 32 FEP 40 (4th Cir. 1983) (rejecting the EEOC's contention that all investigatory records of an ongoing proceeding are exempt from disclosure under § 552(b)(7) of the FOIA, ruling that the exemption applies only to records that, if disclosed, would (1) "chill" witnesses and dry up sources of information, (2) hamper the free flow of ideas among Commission employees or between interested governmental agencies, (3) hinder the EEOC's ability to shape and control investigations, or (4) make more difficult the future investigation and enforcement of charges).

[390]The Supreme Court offered guidance on the § 552(b)(7)(C) exemption in *United States Department of Justice v. Reporters Committee*, 489 U.S. 749, 775–80 (1989), where it instructed that in deciding whether to disclose private documents, the agency must balance the affected individual's privacy interest against the public interest in shedding light on the conduct or actions of the government. If the charge is being litigated, the plaintiff's privacy interest declines, and the exemption probably could not shelter much in the file.

[391]5 U.S.C. § 552(b) (2000) ("Any reasonably segregable portion of a record shall be provided to any person requesting such record after deletion of the portions which are exempt under this subsection.").

[392]By regulation, the EEOC promises to keep confidential the identity of persons giving information regarding violations of the ADEA and the Equal Pay Act,

FOIA requests, the EEOC normally will give any party access to any other party's position statement and, in its discretion, "appropriate" documents.[393] Where FOIA requests to the EEOC are made, they are handled by the legal counsel and by the regional attorneys in each district office.[394]

Open ADEA and EPA case files ordinarily will be denied to the public under FOIA's seventh exemption.[395]

The EEOC will disclose an entire Title VII case file to the charging party (or aggrieved persons on whose behalf a charge was filed) at any time unless a right-to-sue notice has been issued and has expired; the EEOC will disclose a "closed" case file (after a right-to-sue notice has expired) only where the aggrieved person "arguably has a continuing right of judicial action."[396] Whether disclosure is to the charging party or to the respondent, the EEOC before disclosure requires that a nondisclosure agreement be executed.[397]

3. What the EEOC May and Must Remove From the File Prior to Disclosure to a Party

Under § 706(b), the EEOC must remove from a Title VII or ADA file prior to disclosure all information relating to conciliation.[398] The EEOC also must remove all references to other charges

---

unless disclosure is necessary in a court proceeding. 29 C.F.R. §§ 1620.30(c) (Equal Pay) & 1626.4 (ADEA).

[393]*Priority Procedures*, at 10.

[394]*See* 29 C.F.R. § 1610.8–.13 (2005).

[395]*Id.* § 1610.17(g). However, "[t]he general policy against disclosure from open files does not include disclosure to the parties or other persons incident to the investigation." 1 EEOC COMPL. MAN. (BNA) § 83.1(a), at 83:0001.

[396]1 EEOC COMPL. MAN. (BNA) § 83.5(a) & (b), at 83:0002–3; *id.* § 83.3(d), at 83:0002.

[397]*Id.* § 83.4(c), at 83:0002; *see id.* exh. 83-A, at 83:0007. The EEOC conditions disclosure to parties on their agreement in writing "not to make the information public except in the normal course of civil action or other proceeding instituted under Title VII." In *EEOC v. Associated Dry Goods Corp.*, on remand from the Supreme Court, the Fourth Circuit specifically approved these EEOC procedures, finding them not to be "unfair or discriminatory." 720 F.2d 804, 811, 33 FEP 181 (4th Cir. 1983).

[398]*See* 42 U.S.C. § 2000e-5(b) (2000); 1 EEOC COMPL. MAN. (BNA) § 83.6(b)(5), at 83:0003. Documents relating to predetermination settlement attempts are considered within the confidentiality provisions attaching to conciliation efforts. Frazier v. Indiana Dep't of Labor, 2003 U.S. Dist. LEXIS 9073, at *17 (S.D. Ind. Mar. 17, 2003) (redacting a DOL position paper that contained statements regarding settlement); Parker v. EEOC, 10 FEP 1239, 1240–41 (D.D.C. 1975), *aff'd*, 534 F.2d 977 (D.C. Cir. 1976). A court has held, however, that a charging party in a Title VII case

and respondents.[399] Additional documents and information may be deleted, too, pursuant to FOIA's exemptions. For example, both statements by and the identities of witnesses who were promised anonymity by the EEOC are deleted, pursuant to § 552b(c)(7).[400] Inter-agency and intra-agency memoranda containing recommendations or mental impressions as to strategy for settlement or litigation are deleted pursuant to § 552b(c)(5) and (7)(E).[401] According to one court, even a draft of a proposed charge can be part of the EEOC's deliberative process and exempt from disclosure pursuant to § 552b(c)(5).[402]

The EEOC takes the position that statistical data forms required pursuant to § 709(c) are disclosable whether or not physically contained in the charging party's case file.[403]

Information furnished to the EEOC by agencies with which the Commission has memoranda of understanding[404] generally is released in accordance with the statutory, regulatory, and policy provisions described above.[405] The unauthorized disclosure to a third party of a charge gives rise to a cause of action under the Privacy Act,[406] but there are no legal impediments to the exchange of EEO information between federal agencies.[407]

---

has a right to materials documenting the EEOC's conciliation efforts in his or her case. EEOC v. Fina Oil & Chem. Co., 145 F.R.D. 74, 75 (E.D. Tex. 1992) (ordering the EEOC to produce logs and letters reflecting EEOC efforts at conciliation); Greene v. Thalhimer's Dep't Store, 93 F.R.D. 657, 661, 28 FEP 918 (E.D. Va. 1982) (prohibiting the charging party from using the documents in any subsequent proceeding without the written consent of the persons concerned, and limiting disclosure to the charging party and her attorney).

[399]1 EEOC COMPL. MAN. (BNA) § 83.6(b)(4), at 83:0003.

[400]*Id.* § 83.6(b)(1), at 83:0003.

[401]*Id.* § 83.6(b)(3), at 83:0003.

[402]*See* Dresser Indus. Valve Operations v. EEOC, 28 FEP 1819, 1819 (W.D. La. 1982) (here, however, the EEOC's inadvertent disclosure of the draft's contents removed "the mantle of confidentiality" and constituted a waiver of the agency's right to rely on the exemption).

[403]1 EEOC COMPL. MAN. (BNA) §§ 83.7(a) & 83.7(c), at 83:0004.

[404]*See* Section III.O *supra.*

[405]Under the EEOC-OFCCP memorandum, for example, third-party requests for information are coordinated with the agency that compiled the information, except that the EEOC is authorized to release information to state and local fair employment deferral agencies that have bound themselves to §§ 706 and 709 of Title VII. Memorandum ¶ 5, 46 Fed. Reg. 7435, 7437 (1981).

[406]Swenson v. United States Postal Serv., 890 F.2d 1075, 1078, 51 FEP 899 (9th Cir. 1989).

[407]Emerson Elec. Co. v. Schlesinger, 609 F.2d 898, 905–06, 21 FEP 475 (8th Cir. 1979) (information exchange between agencies does not violate the Federal Reports

4. Federal Employees' Procedures

EEOC regulations provide that the identity of an aggrieved federal employee shall not be revealed, without his or her authorization, before the filing of a formal complaint.[408] The National Labor Relations Board held, however, that the purpose of this provision is to protect the employee from management, not to limit union participation at the precomplaint stage.[409]

The procedures for handling administrative complaints from federal employees are discussed extensively in Chapter 31 (Federal Employee Litigation).

B. Admissibility of EEOC Findings

The admissibility into evidence of the EEOC's final determination usually is left to the discretion of the trial court.[410] The Fifth

---

Act); Reynolds Metal Co. v. Rumsfeld, 564 F.2d 663, 668–69, 15 FEP 1185 (4th Cir. 1977) (information exchange does not violate any statute, including Title VII).

[408]29 C.F.R. § 1613.213(a) (2005).

[409]United States Postal Serv., 281 NLRB 1015, 1016, 123 LRRM 1209 and 123 LRRM 1213 (1986) (when the same situation leads both to grievances under the union contract and an informal complaint under Title VII, the union representative may not be denied the opportunity to participate in the conciliation process by the employer's invocation of the EEOC's regulation concerning confidentiality of the aggrieved party's identity).

[410]See, e.g., Astoria Fed. Sav. & Loan Ass'n v. Solimino, 501 U.S. 104, 110, 55 FEP 1503 (1991) (state administrative findings may be entered as evidence in a federal ADEA action); Chandler v. Roudebush, 425 U.S. 840, 863 n.39, 12 FEP 1368 (1976) (administrative findings may be admitted as evidence in a federal sector trial de novo); Coleman v. Home Depot, Inc., 306 F.3d 1333, 1344–45, 89 FEP 1876 (3d Cir. 2002) (adopting majority view that district courts have discretion to exclude EEOC letters of determination when the negative factors listed in Fed. R. Evid. 403 substantially outweigh the probative value of the EEOC determination); Paolitto v. John Brown E. & C., Inc., 151 F.3d 60, 65, 77 FEP 1351 (2d Cir. 1998) (adopting majority position that leaves "the question of whether to admit EEOC findings to the sound discretion of the district court"); Williams v. Nashville Network, 132 F.3d 1123, 1129 (6th Cir. 1997) ("it is within the sound discretion of the court whether to accept the EEOC's final investigation report into evidence"); Smith v. MIT, 877 F.2d 1106, 1113, 50 FEP 169 (1st Cir. 1989) (exclusion was not an abuse of discretion); Tulloss v. Near N. Montessori Sch., Inc., 776 F.2d 150, 154, 39 FEP 418 (7th Cir. 1985) (it was not reversible error to exclude the EEOC determination and file, where the evidence available to the EEOC was available to the trial court); Johnson v. Yellow Freight Sys., Inc., 734 F.2d 1304, 1309, 34 FEP 1503 (8th Cir. 1984) (exclusion of the EEOC's determination in a § 1981 jury trial was not an abuse of discretion); Whatley v. Skaggs Cos., 707 F.2d 1129, 1137, 31 FEP 1202 (10th Cir. 1983) (the admission of the EEOC investigative report was harmless error where the report was corroborated by trial testimony); Francis-Sobel v. University of Me., 597 F.2d 15, 18, 19 FEP 991 (1st Cir.

and Ninth Circuits have held, however, that the EEOC determination in a Title VII case is per se admissible.[411] The weight to be assigned the determination normally is left to the fact finder and a limiting instruction may be given.[412]

Courts generally have declined to admit the underlying documentation that appears in the EEOC investigative file unless the contents are independently admissible.[413]

1979) (exclusion of the cause determination was not error); Angelo v. Bacharach Instrument Co., 555 F.2d 1164, 1176, 14 FEP 1778 (3d Cir. 1977) (the district court in an Equal Pay Act case acted within its discretion in refusing to admit the EEOC determination letter; any minimal probative value was outweighed by the danger of unfair prejudice and misleading the jury). *But see* Estes v. Dick Smith Ford, Inc., 856 F.2d 1097, 1105–06, 47 FEP 1472 (8th Cir. 1988) (reversing, for abuse of discretion, the district court's ruling admitting a finding of no probable cause).

[411]*See* Plummer v. Western Int'l Hotels Co., 656 F.2d 502, 505, 26 FEP 1292 (9th Cir. 1981); Garcia v. Gloor, 618 F.2d 264, 272, 22 FEP 1403 (5th Cir. 1980) (EEOC reasonable cause determinations are per se admissible in Title VII cases). The Ninth Circuit came to a different conclusion, however, regarding "letters of violation" in ADEA cases, which it held are not per se admissible because of the risk of jury prejudice; rather, the district court must exercise its discretion:

> A finding of probable cause [under Title VII] does not suggest to the jury that the EEOC has already determined that there has been a violation. Rather, it suggests that preliminarily there is reason to believe that a violation has taken place . . . . A letter of violation, however, represents a determination by the EEOC that a violation of the [ADEA] has occurred and thus results in a much greater possibility of unfair prejudice.

Gilchrist v. Jim Slemons Imports, Inc., 803 F.2d 1488, 1500, 42 FEP 314 (9th Cir. 1986). Although the district court in *Gilchrist* believed that it had no discretion to refuse to admit the ADEA letter, the Ninth Circuit found the error harmless on the facts of that case. *Id.* at 1500; *see also* Lucas v. Wheeler Mach. Co., 53 FEP 1729, 1730–31 (D. Utah 1989) (admission of the fair employment agency's cause findings in ADEA litigation is error).

[412]EEOC v. Ford Motor Co., 1996 U.S. App. LEXIS 26263, at *39 (6th Cir. Sept. 30, 1996) (Wellford, J. concurring) (the weight to be given to EEOC determinations is within the discretion of the court); Gentile v. County of Suffolk, 926 F.2d 142, 160 (2d Cir. 1991) (weight to be given EEOC determinations to be decided by the trier of fact); Bradshaw v. Zoological Soc'y, 569 F.2d 1066, 1069, 16 FEP 828 (9th Cir. 1978) (the district court is to determine the degree of weight to be assigned to the determination); *see, e.g.,* Aguirre-Molina v. New York State Div. of Alcoholism & Alcohol Abuse, 675 F. Supp. 53, 57 n.4, 50 FEP 355 (N.D.N.Y. 1987) (giving no weight to the state fair employment agency's determination where the document lacked factual detail); Spray v. Kellos-Sims Crane Rental, Inc., 507 F. Supp. 745, 750, 25 FEP 422 (S.D. Ga. 1981) (the determination is given the same weight as any other testimony); Theobald v. Botein, Hays, Sklar & Herzberg, 493 F. Supp. 1, 2, 23 FEP 1300 (S.D.N.Y. 1979) (giving the determination some evidentiary value); Fearrington v. American Indem. Co., 22 FEP 1538, 1539 (S.D. Tex. 1978) (giving it less than controlling value).

[413]*See, e.g., Williams,* 132 F.3d at 1129 (excluding an EEOC letter from evidence); Haines v. Texas Workers Comp. Comm'n, 2005 U.S. App. LEXIS 5, at *3

It is unclear what effect courts will give to the EEOC's current practice of issuing dismissals "without particularized findings" instead of "no cause" findings. Employers may contend that they are the functional equivalent of "no cause" findings and should be admitted as such. Alternatively, employers facing "cause" findings may contend that they should be excluded.[414] The argument is that admitting "cause" findings while excluding employer-favorable resolutions gives plaintiffs collectively an unjust advantage: a leg up when the agency proceedings end favorably to the charging party, but no corresponding detriment when they do not. Plaintiffs, on the other hand, likely will argue that a "cause" determination is a finding on the merits, but a dismissal "without particularized findings" may be the product of a host of factors, including the inadequate investigatory resources of an overwhelmed agency, that may have no bearing on the merits.

(5th Cir. Jan. 3, 2005) (upholding exclusion of EEOC documents); Georator Corp. v. EEOC, 592 F.2d 765, 769, 19 FEP 70 (4th Cir. 1979) (exclusion of the record was not error); Watford v. Birmingham Stove & Range Co., 14 FEP 626, 629 (N.D. Ala. 1976) (excluding statements attributed to the plaintiff by the EEOC investigator in the EEOC investigative report); Kinsey v. Legg, Mason & Co., 10 FEP 1013, 1015 (D.D.C. 1974) (rejecting admission of the EEOC file, but admitting the investigative report), *rev'd and remanded on other grounds sub nom.* Kinsey v. First Reg'l Sec., Inc., 557 F.2d 830, 14 FEP 1143 (D.C. Cir. 1977); *cf.* Kimbrough v. Bowman Transp., Inc., 920 F.2d 1578, 1583, 54 FEP 1469 (11th Cir.) (any error in admitting an EEOC report arising from a charge filed by an employee other than the one bringing the § 1981 action was harmless, where the report was used to impeach the respondent's official and the court did not give it more than permissible weight), *vacated on other grounds*, 929 F.2d 599, 55 FEP 1024 (11th Cir. 1991). *But see* Peters v. Jefferson Chem. Co., 516 F.2d 447, 450–51, 11 FEP 296 (5th Cir. 1975) ("EEOC investigative files" should have been admitted); Frazier v. Independent Dep't of Labor, 2003 U.S. Dist. LEXIS 9073, at *16 (S.D. Ind. Mar. 17, 2003) (position statements admissible).

[414]EEOC v. Walner & Assoc., 91 F.3d 963, 968 n.3 (7th Cir. 1996) ("This determination of reasonable cause is only an administrative prerequisite to a court action and has no legally binding significance on subsequent litigation.").

TIMELINESS

I. OVERVIEW

A. History

Title VII was the product of an intense, protracted legislative struggle on issues of both substance and procedure. What emerged was an enforcement scheme far different from and more complicated than that originally envisioned.[1]

The procedural scheme detailed in § 706[2]—replete with diverse time limitations for filing with the Equal Employment Opportunity Commission (EEOC) and the court, involving two and sometimes three federal instrumentalities[3] and frequently a state or local agency—has been an exceedingly fertile source of procedural litigation.[4] During the seven years between Title VII's 1965 effective date and the 1972 amendments, courts were generally unreceptive to the numerous procedural defenses asserted to Title VII actions. The then-prevailing judicial attitude, perhaps most straightforwardly expressed in *Culpepper v. Reynolds Metals Co.*,[5] was that the congressional promise of federal protection against invidious discrimination, secured by resort to the courts, should not be rendered meaningless by procedural defaults, especially those resulting from the complexity of the statutory scheme. Accordingly, most procedural defenses, particularly where no actual prejudice was shown, were initially rejected.

---

[1]The 1964 legislative history is summarized in Francis J. Vaas, *Title VII: Legislative History*, 7 B.C. INDUS. & COM. L. REV. 431 (1966). In its own brief summary of that legislative history, one court of appeals praised the author for his "excellent delineation of Title VII's torrid conception, its turbulent gestation, and its frenzied birth." Miller v. International Paper Co., 408 F.2d 283, 286 & n.13, 1 FEP 647 (5th Cir. 1969).

[2]Pub. L. No. 88-352, tit. VII, § 706, 1964 U.S.C.C.A.N. (78 Stat. 241) 287, 309–11 (codified as amended at 29 U.S.C. § 2000e-5).

[3]The three are the Equal Employment Opportunity Commission (EEOC), the courts, and sometimes the U.S. Department of Justice. With respect to Executive Order 11246 and the Rehabilitation Act, there is a fourth: the U.S. Department of Labor and its Office of Federal Contract Compliance Programs (OFCCP). Exec. Order No. 11,246 (1965), *reprinted as amended in* FEDERAL CONT. COMPL. MAN. (BNA, Nov. 25, 1998); *see* the Rehabilitation Act of 1973, Pub. L. No. 93-111, § 503, 1973 U.S.C.C.A.N. (87 Stat. 355) 409, 453.

[4]*See, e.g.*, EEOC v. Wah Chang Albany Corp., 499 F.2d 187, 189, 8 FEP 203 (9th Cir. 1974) (describing "an intricate statute hedged about with definitional, substantive, and procedural limitations, restrictions, and requirements").

[5]421 F.2d 888, 891, 2 FEP 377, *supplemented*, 2 FEP 506 (5th Cir. 1970). There the court explained:

Title VII of the 1964 Civil Rights Act provides us with a clear mandate from Congress that no longer will the United States tolerate this form of discrimination. It is, therefore, the duty of the courts to make sure that the Act works, and the intent of Congress is not hampered by a combination of a strict construction of the statute and a battle with semantics.

Although the 1972 amendments increased the length of certain time periods, they left the basic structure of the Act relatively unchanged with respect to private actions. The legislative history of the 1972 amendments specifically stated that, except where a contrary intention was plainly manifested, pre-amendment case law should continue to control.[6]

Beginning in the mid 1970s, however, judicial attitudes shifted. Perhaps the courts were less inclined to forgive procedural defaults because plaintiffs' counsel were more prevalent and, presumably, more experienced in dealing with Title VII's intricacies. For whatever reason, courts were less willing to excuse noncompliance with procedural hurdles. The U.S. Supreme Court found procedural aspects of Title VII determinative of discrimination suits in a series of cases starting with *Electrical Workers (IUE) Local 790 v. Robbins & Myers, Inc.*[7] (in which the Court held that resort to a grievance-arbitration procedure does not toll the Title VII charge-filing period); continuing with *United Air Lines, Inc. v. Evans*[8] (in which the Court demonstrated a less receptive attitude toward claims alleging "continuing violations" than many courts previously had exhibited); followed by *Delaware State College v. Ricks*[9] (in which the Court emphasized that "time-limitations provisions themselves promote important interests"); and culminating with *Lorance v. AT&T Technologies, Inc.*[10] (in which the Court held that a discriminatory seniority system in some cases must be challenged when adopted rather than when applied).

---

[6]The section-by-section analysis of the 1972 amendments stated by way of preamble: "[I]n any areas where a specific contrary intention is not indicated, it was assumed that the present case law as developed by the courts would continue to govern the applicability and construction of Title VII." 118 CONG. REC. 7166 (1972) (section-by-section analysis by Sen. Williams). An identical version of the section-by-section analysis was submitted to each house of Congress by the respective chairs of the conferees for each house. 118 CONG. REC. 7563 (1972) (section-by-section analysis by Rep. Perkins).

[7]429 U.S. 229, 236, 13 FEP 1813 (1976).

[8]431 U.S. 553, 558, 14 FEP 1510 (1977).

[9]449 U.S. 250, 259, 24 FEP 827 (1980).

[10]490 U.S. 900, 909, 49 FEP 1656 (1989). *Lorance*, however, was legislatively overruled, at least in part, by the Civil Rights Act of 1991, Pub. L. No. 102-166, § 112, 1991 U.S.C.C.A.N. (105 Stat.) 1071, 1079 (codified as amended at 42 U.S.C. § 2000e-5(e)(2)).

One might think that now, more than 40 years after Title VII's enactment, procedural rules, especially those concerning timeliness, would be well settled. Yet that is not the case. Just a few years ago, the Supreme Court, in *National Railroad Passenger Corp. v. Morgan*,[11] provided important guidance in the application of the elusive continuing violation doctrine by clarifying how the concept applies in cases where discrete acts of discrimination occur versus situations involving hostile environment claims. Although some ambiguities have been resolved conclusively or at least have been clarified, many other doctrines remain unresolved and, at times, confusing. For example, the *Morgan* Court left open important questions, such as when the limitations period actually is triggered, whether application of the discovery rule is appropriate, and whether timeliness issues in pattern-or-practice cases should be resolved similarly. Moreover, Congress has not always acquiesced in the Supreme Court's resolution of disputed issues.[12] For all of these reasons, litigation under Title VII and the Age Discrimination in Employment Act (ADEA)[13] has remained a procedural battleground.

B. Scope

In *McDonnell Douglas Corp. v. Green*,[14] the Supreme Court noted the two "jurisdictional prerequisites" to a Title VII action: "filing timely charges of employment discrimination with the [EEOC] and . . . receiving and acting upon the Commission's statutory notice of the right to sue."[15]

This chapter deals with (1) filing a timely charge with the EEOC, and (2) filing a timely complaint in court after receiving statutory notice from the EEOC of the right to sue.

---

[11]536 U.S. 101, 88 FEP 1601 (2002).

[12]For example, as noted earlier, *Lorance* was one of the cases that spurred congressional passage of the Civil Rights Act of 1991, one portion of which legislatively overruled *Lorance* in part. *See id.*

[13]Pub. L. No. 90-202, 1967 U.S.C.C.A.N. (81 Stat.) 602, 658 (codified as amended at 29 U.S.C. §§ 621–634). Procedural issues unique to the ADEA, including timeliness, are discussed in Chapter 12 (Age).

[14]411 U.S. 792, 5 FEP 965 (1973).

[15]*Id.* at 798 (citation omitted). These prerequisites are not, however, truly "jurisdictional"; they are subject to equitable principles such as tolling or laches. *See* Section II.C.1 *infra*.

II. TIMELINESS OF FILING THE EEOC CHARGE

A. The 180/300-Day Limitations Periods

1. General Charge-Filing Requirements

Section 706(e)(1) of Title VII provides that a charging party must file an EEOC charge within either 180 or 300 days of the alleged unlawful employment practice, depending on whether the alleged practice occurred in a "deferral state" (one having its own state or local agency with authority to contest the challenged practice).[16] To be timely in nondeferral states, an EEOC charge must be filed within 180 days of the alleged unlawful occurrence.[17] In deferral states, that limitations period is extended to 300 days.[18]

---

[16]Section 706(e)(1) provides:

(1) A charge under this section shall be filed within one hundred and eighty days after the alleged unlawful employment practice occurred and notice of the charge (including the date, place and circumstances of the alleged unlawful employment practice) shall be served upon the person against whom such charge is made within ten days thereafter, except that in a case of an employment practice with respect to which the person aggrieved has initially instituted proceedings with a State or local agency with authority to grant or seek relief from such practice or to institute criminal proceedings with respect thereto upon receiving notice thereof, such charge shall be filed by or on behalf of the person aggrieved within three hundred days after the alleged unlawful employment practice occurred, or within thirty days after receiving notice that the State or local agency has terminated the proceedings under the State or local law, whichever is earlier, and a copy of such charge shall be filed by the Commission with the State or local agency.

42 U.S.C. § 2000e-5(e)(1) (2000).

[17]Id.

[18]Id.; see also White v. BFI Waste Servs., 375 F.3d 288, 94 FEP 73 (4th Cir. 2004) (under Title VII, 300-day period, rather than 180-day period, applies to filing of charge where state law also proscribes alleged employment discrimination and employee files with state or local employment discrimination agency either before filing with EEOC or concurrently therewith); Manatt v. Bank of Am., NA, 339 F.3d 792 (9th Cir. 2003) (employee's Title VII retaliation claim based on her transfer from trade finance department to private banking department was untimely where complaint was not filed with state Bureau of Labor and Industries within 300 days thereof); Hedrich v. Board of Regents of Univ. of Wis. Sys., 274 F.3d 1174 (7th Cir. 2001) (employee has 300 days from time she suffered adverse employment action allegedly based on gender to file her complaint with Wisconsin Personnel Commission or EEOC); Tinsley v. First Union Nat'l Bank, 155 F.3d 435, 439–41, 77 FEP 1753 (4th Cir. 1998) (resolving conflict between U.S. District Courts for Eastern and Western Districts of Virginia, Fourth Circuit determined that Virginia Council on

Section 706(c) requires a charging party, before filing with the EEOC, to first file with the appropriate state or local agency (the "706" or "deferral" agency) and then wait 60 days (or until the termination of state proceedings) before filing a charge with the EEOC.[19] However, under widely prevalent work sharing agreements between the EEOC and various state agencies, a complainant may file a charge with the EEOC instead of directly with the deferral agency.[20]

2. EEOC Deferral Procedure

In *Love v. Pullman Co.*,[21] the Supreme Court considered several issues under § 706 pertaining to the timeliness of and manner

---

Human Rights is "state deferral agency" within meaning of Title VII such that discrimination charges filed in Virginia are subject to 300-day limitations period instead of shorter 180-day period).

[19]Section 706(c) provides:

In the case of an alleged unlawful employment practice occurring in a State, or political subdivision of a State, which has a State or local law prohibiting the unlawful employment practice alleged and establishing or authorizing a State or local authority to grant or seek relief from such practice or to institute criminal proceedings with respect thereto upon receiving notice thereof, no charge may be filed under subsection (b) of this section by the person aggrieved before the expiration of sixty days after proceedings have been commenced under the State or local law, unless such proceedings have been earlier terminated, provided that such sixty-day period shall be extended to one hundred and twenty days during the first year after the effective date of such State or local law. If any requirement for the commencement of such proceedings is imposed by a State or local authority other than a requirement of the filing of a written and signed statement of the facts upon which the proceeding is based, the proceeding shall be deemed to have been commenced for the purposes of this subsection at the time such statement is sent by registered mail to the appropriate State or local authority.

42 U.S.C. § 2000e-5(c). The deferral requirement of § 706(c) is an expression of "[a] fundamental policy of the Equal Employment Opportunity Act . . . to avoid federal action whenever possible by making the state a partner in the enforcement of Title VII." EEOC v. Wah Chang Albany Corp., 499 F.2d 187, 190, 8 FEP 203 (9th Cir. 1974); *accord* Oscar Mayer & Co. v. Evans, 441 U.S. 750, 755, 19 FEP 1167 (1979) ("[Section 706(c)] is intended to give state agencies a limited opportunity to resolve problems of employment discrimination and thereby to make unnecessary, resort to federal relief by victims of the discrimination.").

[20]*See* Tewksbury v. Ottaway Newspapers, Inc., 192 F.3d 322, 325, 80 FEP 1594 (2d Cir. 1999) (deeming employee to have filed discrimination charge with state agency where employee filed only with EEOC); *see also* Millage v. City of Sioux City, 258 F. Supp. 2d 976, 984, 14 AD 504 (N.D. Iowa 2003) (same).

[21]404 U.S. 522, 4 FEP 150 (1972).

of pursuing an administrative charge of discrimination. *Love* arose when an employee was not satisfied with a resolution negotiated by the employer and the state agency. Love sent a letter to the EEOC alleging discrimination. To ensure compliance with Title VII procedure, the EEOC orally advised the state agency of the allegation. When that agency elected not to take further action, the EEOC proceeded with its own investigation and found merit to the discrimination allegation. *Love* held that:

(1) Prior resort to an appropriate state or local agency, if any, is necessary to the maintenance of a Title VII action.[22]

(2) The EEOC may act on a charging party's behalf to fulfill the deferral requirements.[23] Courts thus have rejected arguments that would require charging parties to file separately with the EEOC and a deferral agency.[24]

(3) Deferral need not be formal (and may even be oral).[25]

(4) A state's inaction with respect to (or waiver of) its right to attempt to resolve the charge cannot prevent resort to the EEOC and thus to the courts.[26]

(5) The EEOC may hold a charge in " 'suspended animation,' automatically filing it upon termination of state proceedings."[27]

---

[22]*See id.* at 523, 526 n.5. In *Oscar Mayer*, 441 U.S. at 756 & n.3, the Supreme Court repeated that deferral to state proceedings under Title VII is "require[d]" and "mandatory." As noted later, however, failure to comply with the deferral requirement can be cured in some circumstances. *See* EEOC v. Dinuba Med. Clinic, 222 F.3d 580 (9th Cir. 2000) (under Title VII provisions governing filing of complaint with state agency, state agency must be given 60-day window in which it has initial and exclusive right to process charge, free from premature federal intervention.); *see also* Section II.A.3 *infra.*

[23]*Love*, 404 U.S. at 525.

[24]*See, e.g.*, Shaffer v. National Can Corp., 565 F. Supp. 909, 911, 34 FEP 172 (E.D. Pa. 1983) (whether complaint sent to both entities arrived first at EEOC or state agency is immaterial to whether proceedings were "initially instituted" with state agency; however, EEOC cannot treat charge as "filed" until expiration of 60 days from filing with state, or upon earlier termination of state proceedings); Colgan v. Fisher Scientific Co., 935 F.2d. 1407 (3d Cir 1991) (under ADEA, claim need not be filed directly with deferral agency but may be dual-filed with EEOC).

[25]*Love*, 404 U.S. at 525.

[26]*Id.* at 524.

[27]*Id.* at 526; *see also* Puryear v. County of Roanoke, 214 F.3d 514 (4th Cir. 2000) (if charge of unlawful employment practices is first filed with EEOC, EEOC

The EEOC's current deferral policy is outlined at 29 C.F.R. § 1601.13.

3. When Prior Resort to a State or Local Agency Is Required

a. *State Law Must Authorize an Appropriate Agency to Prosecute the Claim of Discrimination.* Questions arise about the deferral requirement when the state law covers part but not all of the discrimination at issue or when the § 706 agency cannot give the same type of relief a court could grant under Title VII. For example, state law may require equal pay for equal work performed by men and women but may not prohibit sex discrimination in discharge or promotion. If a claim alleges sex discrimination with respect to pay rates, promotion, and discharge, is deferral necessary?

In one of the earliest deferral decisions, *EEOC v. Union Bank*,[28] the Ninth Circuit rejected the EEOC's position that the statute required deferral only to state agencies with general jurisdiction over discriminatory employment practices.[29] Prior resort is required if the state agency is authorized to enforce a state prohibition of *any* of the practices involved in the Title VII claim.[30] No deferral is required, however, if the state law does not prohibit the specific practice alleged,[31] or if the state law does not confer jurisdiction

---

may retain charge in "suspended animation" during state agency's period of exclusive jurisdiction, and, upon termination of state agency's proceedings, "suspended" charge is deemed filed with EEOC for purposes of Title VII's exhaustion requirement).

[28]408 F.2d 867, 1 FEP 429 (9th Cir. 1968).

[29]*Id.* at 869–70.

[30]*Id.; accord* Mitchell v. Mid-Continent Spring Co., 466 F.2d 24, 26–27, 4 FEP 1144 (6th Cir. 1972) (remanding claim of unequal wages to allow petitioner to seek redress through state wage discrimination law). The current EEOC regulations are consistent with this position. *See* 29 C.F.R. § 1601.70(a) (enumerating qualifications for designation as "FEP [706] agency").

[31]*See* Nueces County Hosp. Dist. v. EEOC, 518 F.2d 895, 897–98, 11 FEP 289 (5th Cir. 1975) (no deferral required because state law did not prohibit retaliation); Cunningham v. Litton Indus., 413 F.2d 887, 891, 1 FEP 861 (9th Cir. 1969) (no deferral required because, at time in question, California statutes did not prohibit sex discrimination except as to rate of pay); *see also* Volovsek v. Wisconsin Dep't of Agric., 344 F.3d 680, 92 FEP 1275 (7th Cir. 2003) (owing to absence of antiretaliation provision in Wisconsin law, differential charge-filing periods apply to plaintiff's claims—300 days for discrimination, 180 days for retaliation). The current EEOC regulations provide that a charge will not be deferred when the § 706 agency does not have subject-matter jurisdiction over the charge. 29 C.F.R. § 1601.13(a)(2) (2005).

over the employer.[32] But deferral is required, as the Ninth Circuit held in *Crosslin v. Mountain States Telephone & Telegraph Co.*,[33] when a state agency has jurisdiction, even though it lacks power to obtain relief comparable to that available through the courts under Title VII.[34]

Before broad-based state antidiscrimination laws were commonplace, questions arose as to what constituted a § 706 agency. In *General Insurance Co. of America v. EEOC*,[35] the Ninth Circuit held that the general authority of a state officer to prosecute violations of law did not render that officer a § 706 "agency."[36] But the Fifth Circuit reached a somewhat contrary conclusion in *White v. Dallas Independent School District*,[37] ruling that deferral is required under a Texas law that prohibits discrimination in government employment and designates district attorneys and county attorneys as appropriate state officials to entertain complaints.[38] This issue has become less significant with the proliferation of state fair employment practices (FEP) statutes providing for state administrative enforcement.

  b. No Need for Deferral With Respect to Every Incident. In *Oubichon v. North American Rockwell Corp.*,[39] the plaintiff filed two charges with the EEOC, the first alleging a retaliatory suspension

---

[32]*See* Keitz v. Lever Bros., 563 F. Supp. 230, 234, 31 FEP 1230 (N.D. Ind. 1983) (ADEA case; state law did not confer jurisdiction over employers covered by federal law; hence, state agency was not § 706 agency).

[33]422 F.2d 1028, 1030, 2 FEP 480 (9th Cir. 1970), *vacated on other grounds*, 400 U.S. 1004, 3 FEP 70 (1971); *see also* Watson v. Eastman Kodak Co., 235 F.3d 851 (3d Cir. 2000) (under Title VII and ADEA, plaintiffs residing in states having agency authorized to grant relief for federally prohibited employment discrimination must resort to that state remedy before they will be allowed access to federal judicial relief).

[34]*See* Maynard v. Pneumatic Prods. Corp., 256 F.3d 1259 (11th Cir. 2001) (in deferral state that prohibits challenged employment action and establishes authorities in which relief from such practice may be sought, no charge of ADA violation may be filed with EEOC by person aggrieved before expiration of 60 days after proceedings have started under state law; this gives deferral agency opportunity to investigate before federal agency gets involved).

[35]491 F.2d 133, 7 FEP 106 (9th Cir. 1974).

[36]*Id.* at 135.

[37]581 F.2d 556, 18 FEP 204 (5th Cir. 1978) (en banc).

[38]*Id.* at 561, 563 (case allowed to proceed, however, because of erroneous EEOC advice).

[39]482 F.2d 569, 6 FEP 171 (9th Cir. 1973).

for protesting alleged racial discrimination and the second alleging three subsequent incidents of discrimination: denial of training, unwarranted discipline, and denial of a transfer. Only the first charge was referred to the state agency, which summarily dismissed the charge because it had found similar charges brought by others to be without merit. The district court dismissed the plaintiff's claims on the three subsequent incidents of discrimination because no deferral had taken place with respect to those issues. The Ninth Circuit reversed, holding that deferral is not necessary for the additional allegations if the plaintiff can prove at trial that they were part of a continuing pattern of discrimination: "To force an employee to return to the state agency every time he claims a new instance of discrimination in order to have the EEOC and the courts consider the subsequent incidents along with the original ones would erect a needless procedural barrier."[40]

When the EEOC affords the local agency an opportunity for full investigation and the agency waives that opportunity, some courts have held that the EEOC need not defer again if its investigation reveals forms of discrimination different from those alleged in the charge.[41] By contrast, when the additional incidents, or additional EEOC charges, involve *parties* who have not been the subject of a prior charge referred to a local agency, deferral is likely required because of the absence of prior resort to the deferral agency with respect to the additional parties.[42]

---

[40]*Id.* at 571; *accord* Weise v. Syracuse Univ., 522 F.2d 397, 412, 10 FEP 1331 (2d Cir. 1975) (first charge, alleging denial of position and termination, was deferred to state agency and dismissed; second charge, alleging refusal to rehire, need not be deferred); *cf.* Ramirez v. National Distillers & Chem. Corp., 586 F.2d 1315, 1320, 18 FEP 966 (9th Cir. 1978) (when first EEOC charge was not deferred but second charge was, deferral requirement still was satisfied because second charge, which only substituted in-state address for employer, in effect was amendment of first).

[41]*See, e.g.*, EEOC v. Raymond Metal Prods. Co., 530 F.2d 590, 597, 12 FEP 38 (4th Cir. 1976) (no deferral of subsequent EEOC charge required when local agency had waived jurisdiction over initial charge). For a discussion of the extent to which the scope of an EEOC charge may limit a subsequent civil action, see Chapter 28 (Title VII Litigation Procedure).

[42]*See* Marcano v. H.J. Heinz Co., 9 FEP 26, 30 (W.D. Mich. 1974) (charges must be filed with state agency against defendant union before proceeding with claim against it); Workman v. Ravenna Arsenal, Inc., 6 FEP 149, 152 (N.D. Ohio 1973) (dismissing two parties who were not named in charges deferred to state agency). *But see* Cook v. Mountain States Tel. & Tel. Co., 397 F. Supp. 1217, 1223, 12 FEP

4. Deferral Mistakes by Charging Parties and Cure of Such Mistakes

Errors sometimes can be cured. Courts initially were divided on whether to dismiss private Title VII actions because of mistakes by the EEOC[43] or because of erroneous filings with the wrong state or local agency by an individual charging party.[44] In *Crosslin v. Mountain States Telephone & Telegraph Co.*,[45] the EEOC, which had by regulation purported to assume the obligation to defer to a local agency if the charge had not previously been filed there,[46]

---

99 (D. Ariz. 1975) (when "considerably more specific" second charge—characterized by court as "amendment" to first—was not deferred, "amended" charge related back to first; deferral of that first charge conferred jurisdiction over union, because of union's involvement in "common enterprise of discrimination" with company).

[43]*See* General Ins. Co. of Am. v. EEOC, 491 F.2d 133, 135 n.2, 7 FEP 106 (9th Cir. 1974) (stay of action to allow deferral to state agency would be appropriate only if failure to defer was result of good faith oversight or good faith error of law); Nichols v. Muskingum Coll., 318 F.3d 674 (6th Cir. 2003) (finding bizarre situation where, through misfeasance of state charging agency, it had failed to refer charge to itself for purposes of state filing; such failure should not be held against plaintiff).

[44]*Compare* Taylor v. Vocational Rehab. Ctr., 10 FEP 936, 941 (W.D. Pa. 1975) (EEOC pursuant to agreement erroneously deferred to city rather than state agency, which erroneously failed to refer matter on; "[b]ureaucratic *faux pas* will not stand as impediments to a judicial complaint") *and* Williams v. Warehouse Mkts., Inc., 637 F. Supp. 724, 726 (D. Nev. 1986) (failure to file ADEA charge with EEOC does not bar suit when charging party relied on state agency's representation that it would forward complaint to EEOC) *with* Cornett v. AVCO Fin. Servs., 792 F.2d 447, 450, 40 FEP 1763 (4th Cir. 1986) (failure by EEOC to file ADEA charge with agency in appropriate state barred plaintiff's age claim), EEOC v. Union Bank, 408 F.2d 867, 868–69, 1 FEP 429 (9th Cir. 1968) (individual's suit was dismissed for failure to defer properly; charging party was attorney), Abshire v. Chicago & E. Ill. R.R., 352 F. Supp. 601, 604, 5 FEP 296 (N.D. Ill. 1972) (failure to defer bars suit), Rucker v. Great Scott Supermkts., 11 FEP 473, 473–74 (E.D. Mich. 1974) (failure to defer to state agency not excused by fact that plaintiff believed state law did not apply once he turned 60), *aff'd*, 528 F.2d 393, 12 FEP 370 (6th Cir. 1976), *overruled on other grounds sub nom.* Wright v. Tennessee, 628 F.2d 949, 23 FEP 714 (6th Cir. 1980) *and* Lyda v. American Broad. Cos., 587 F. Supp. 670, 673, 34 FEP 1151 (S.D.N.Y. 1984) (no evidence of "multistate" discrimination that might justify filing with state agency other than one in plaintiff's state of residence and employment).

In explaining § 706 in 1964, Senator Humphrey stated:

> [Section 706] is carefully worded to protect an individual who, in good faith, unnecessarily seeks to comply with the requirement of initial resort to State or local authority. Such a person will not lose his right to seek Federal relief simply because the 90-day period for filing with the Federal Commission has elapsed while he seeks to pursue State remedies.

110 CONG. REC. 12,723 (1964).

[45]422 F.2d 1028, 2 FEP 480 (9th Cir. 1970), *vacated and remanded*, 400 U.S. 1004, 3 FEP 70 (1971).

[46]29 C.F.R. § 1601.13(a)(4)(i).

did not do so because of its later-discredited position that the particular agency did not have sufficient remedial powers.[47] The Ninth Circuit dismissed the individual's suit for lack of a proper deferral.[48] But the Supreme Court, in an ambiguous decision, vacated and remanded the case for consideration of a suggestion in the Solicitor General's brief that the trial court retain jurisdiction while suspending the proceedings to allow the state agency time to act.[49] This produced a line of cases holding that individual litigants who do not defer, but who timely file with the EEOC, will not have their cases dismissed, at least for a period of time, to allow the EEOC time to properly notify the state agency of the charge.[50]

Ultimately, in *Oscar Mayer & Co. v. Evans*,[51] the Supreme Court held that although resort to an appropriate state agency is mandatory for individual claimants under the ADEA (as it is under Title VII), the failure of the plaintiff to file a complaint with the state agency may be remedied subsequently, even if the state limitations period has run. The Court reasoned that § 14(b) of the ADEA requires only that the plaintiff "commence" state proceedings; it does not require that the state proceedings be *timely* commenced.[52] The Court accordingly remanded the case with instructions to hold it in abeyance until the plaintiff satisfied the deferral requirements.[53]

Subsequently, in *EEOC v. Commercial Office Products Co.*,[54] the Supreme Court applied to Title VII the reasoning of *Oscar*

---

[47]*Crosslin*, 422 F.2d at 1030.

[48]*Id.* at 1031–32.

[49]*Crosslin*, 400 U.S. at 1004.

[50]*See, e.g.*, Heiniger v. City of Phoenix, 625 F.2d 842, 844, 23 FEP 709 (9th Cir. 1980) (citing many prior Ninth Circuit decisions that allowed district court to retain jurisdiction pending proper deferral); Mitchell v. Mid-Continent Spring Co., 466 F.2d 24, 26, 4 FEP 1144 (6th Cir. 1972) (following *Crosslin*); Marcano v. H.J. Heinz Co., 9 FEP 26, 30 (W.D. Mich. 1974) (failure to name union along with company in state charge requires remand of union claim to state agency; court retained jurisdiction for sufficient time to allow state agency to complete its processing of union charge); *cf.* White v. Dallas Indep. Sch. Dist., 581 F.2d 556, 562, 18 FEP 204 (5th Cir. 1978) (en banc) (case allowed to proceed without deferral because of EEOC's erroneous advice to charging party). The Ninth Circuit has admonished the EEOC, however, holding that although this procedure "may be appropriate where the Commission's neglect was due to good faith oversight or error of law, it would hardly be appropriate otherwise." General Ins. Co. of Am. v. EEOC, 491 F.2d 133, 135 n.2, 7 FEP 106 (9th Cir. 1974). *See generally* Chapter 28 (Title VII Litigation Procedure).

[51]441 U.S. 750, 19 FEP 1167 (1979).

[52]*Id.* at 759.

[53]*Id.* at 764.

[54]486 U.S. 107, 46 FEP 1265 (1988).

Mayer, which had involved only the ADEA.[55] The Court held that failure to file a timely charge under state law does not bar a Title VII action. The Court reasoned that the "importation of state limitations periods into § 706(e) not only would confuse lay complainants, but also would embroil the EEOC in complicated issues of state law."[56]

5. Availability of the 300-Day Filing Period

In *Mohasco Corp. v. Silver*,[57] the Supreme Court made important holdings relating to the availability of the 300-day filing period in a deferral state. In *Mohasco*, the complainant, in a deferral state, filed a charge with the EEOC 291 days after the occurrence of the allegedly discriminatory act and had not previously filed a charge with the appropriate state agency.[58] The *Mohasco* Court first held that the 300-day filing period is available even though a complainant does not file a charge with the appropriate state or local agency within 180 days of the allegedly discriminatory act.[59] This holding, however, led to a second issue: if a complainant has not initially filed a charge with the appropriate state or local agency, but files a charge with the EEOC within the 300-day filing period, is it timely filed?[60] In *Mohasco*, where the charge was not "filed" within the 60 days, the 60 days elapsed, unless the state agency previously terminated its proceedings.[61] The *Mohasco* Court, in effect, held that a charge would be timely if a claimant filed a charge with the EEOC within 240 days after the allegedly discriminatory act, because the 60-day deferral period then would elapse before the 300th day.[62] If a claimant filed a charge after the 240-day mark, it could be timely if the state or local agency had

---

[55]*Id.* at 123.
[56]*Id.* at 124.
[57]447 U.S. 807, 23 FEP 1 (1980).
[58]*Id.* at 816–17.
[59]*Id.* at 814 n.16, 816, 817 & n.19 (resolving circuit split as to whether, in order to preserve Title VII right, complainant must, even in deferral state, initially file charge with either appropriate state agency or EEOC within 180 days of alleged discrimination, or file with either state agency or EEOC within 240 days of discriminatory act).
[60]*Id.*
[61]*Id.* at 817.
[62]*Id.* at 814 n.16.

terminated its proceedings by the 300th day from the allegedly discriminatory action.[63]

The effect of the *Mohasco* ruling prompted the EEOC to enter into "work sharing agreements"[64] with certain deferral agencies whereby the deferral agency waives its 60-day exclusive processing period whenever a charge is filed more than 240 days after the date of the alleged discrimination.[65] These work sharing agreements prompted a flurry of technical challenges to court jurisdiction. The Supreme Court put most of these to rest in *EEOC v. Commercial Office Products Co.*[66] In that case, the Supreme Court held that a state agency's waiver, pursuant to a work sharing agreement, of the exclusive 60-day processing period renders timely an EEOC charge filed after the 240th day.[67] The Court expressly held

---

[63]*Id.*

[64]*See* 29 C.F.R. § 1601.13(c) (giving EEOC power to enter into agreements with FEP agencies in order to establish effective and integrated procedures).

[65]*See* EEOC v. Commercial Office Prods. Co., 486 U.S. 107, 112, 46 FEP 1265 (1988) (noting that agreements provide that state or local agency will process certain charges, whereas EEOC will process others). In regard to the charges the EEOC processes, the state or local agency will waive the 60-day deferral period. The agreements also generally preserve the right of the state agency to take action subsequent to the waiver.

[66]*Id.*

[67]*Id.* at 125; *see, e.g.*, Johnson v. J.B. Hunt Transp., Inc., 280 F.3d 1125 (7th Cir. 2002) (holding that work sharing agreement wherein Wisconsin Equal Rights Division (ERD) waived exclusive jurisdiction for all Title VII charges initially processed by EEOC was "self-executing," and thus post-action filing of ERD employee who sent form to EEOC indicating that charge received more than 240 days after date of violation would be processed by ERD did not prevent state agency from constructively terminating charge at time of filing); Marlowe v. Bottarelli, 938 F.2d 807, 814, 56 FEP 1012 (7th Cir. 1991) (waiver of initial state jurisdiction in work sharing agreement is "self-executing," so that charge is "filed" with EEOC when filed with state agency, without further state action); Hong v. Children's Mem'l Hosp., 936 F.2d 967, 970, 56 FEP 612 (7th Cir. 1991) (work sharing agreement properly could designate EEOC employee as agent of state to determine whether state would waive exclusive initial processing); Sofferin v. American Airlines, Inc., 923 F.2d 552, 560, 56 FEP 338 (7th Cir. 1991) (reversing dismissal by district court and remanding for evidentiary hearing on whether particular work sharing agreement intended self-executing waiver of 706 agency jurisdiction); Trevino-Barton v. Pittsburgh Nat'l Bank, 919 F.2d 874, 880, 56 FEP 291 (3d Cir. 1990) (when work sharing agreement provided that charge initially would be processed by agency that first received charge, state proceedings "terminated" when EEOC identified charge as state waiver case in form sent to state—notwithstanding earlier letter claimant sent to state agency requesting state right-to-sue letter, which she erroneously believed necessary to take her charge to EEOC); EEOC v. Techalloy Md., Inc., 894 F.2d 676, 679, 52 FEP 36

that § 706(c) "permits state and local agencies to waive the sixty-day deferral period and, thus, authorize the EEOC to take immediate action."[68] It may be necessary, however, to ensure that evidence of the work sharing agreement is part of the court record to get the benefit of the FEP agency's waiver.[69]

Commercial Office Products also addressed whether the 300-day filing period is available to a claimant in a deferral state who failed to file a *timely* state charge.[70] The Supreme Court held that the 300-day period is available regardless of whether the state charge is timely.[71] Additionally, it is not necessary for the state agency to take further action on proceedings a claimant "initially instituted" in a state agency. In *Nichols v. Muskingum College*,[72] the Sixth Circuit was presented with a case where a plaintiff completed a charge with her state agency and indicated she wanted the charge filed with the EEOC. The state agency took no further action on the claim. Noting the well-settled law that a plaintiff will not be

---

(4th Cir. 1990) (waiver of jurisdiction is self-executing despite EEOC's failure to comply strictly with procedural requirements of work sharing agreement); Green v. Los Angeles County Superintendent of Sch., 883 F.2d 1472, 1480, 50 FEP 1233 (9th Cir. 1989) (waiver of initial state jurisdiction in work sharing agreement is "self-executing" so that charge is "filed" with EEOC when filed with state agency, without further state action); EEOC v. Hacienda Hotel, 881 F.2d 1504, 1510, 50 FEP 877 (9th Cir. 1989) (proceedings were "initially instituted" with state agency under work sharing agreement); Griffin v. Air Prods. & Chems., Inc., 883 F.2d 940, 943, 50 FEP 1444 (11th Cir. 1989) (even though both agencies began processing claim received 300 days after event, state waiver of exclusive jurisdiction for overlapping claims found in work sharing agreement resulted in "instantaneous 'constructive termination' " of state proceedings that made filing with EEOC timely); Urrutia v. Valero Energy Corp., 841 F.2d 123, 125, 46 FEP 601 (5th Cir. 1988) (in view of work sharing agreement ceding authority for initial processing of charges filed between 180 and 300 days after alleged violation, charge was "initially instituted" with state agency by EEOC's routine transmittal of complaint to state).

[68]*Commercial Office Prods.*, 486 U.S. at 121 (Court discussed similarities and dissimilarities in language of § 706(d) and § 706(c) and held that there is no reason why Congress would make deferral period waivable under § 706(d), but mandatory under § 706(c)).

[69]*See* Maynard v. Pneumatic Prods. Corp., 256 F.3d 1259 (11th Cir. 2001) (employee who filed his charge directly with EEOC 292 days after his termination did not meet his burden of showing that his EEOC filing constituted filing with state agency and that agency terminated its proceedings within 300-day period where work sharing agreement was not entered into record; agreement was necessary to determine if EEOC filing qualified as filing with state agency).

[70]*Commercial Office Prods.*, 486 U.S. at 123–24.

[71]*Id.* at 124–25.

[72]318 F.3d 674 (6th Cir. 2003).

harmed by the EEOC's failure to refer a charge to the state agency, the court held that the state agency's misfeasance "should not be held against the plaintiff."[73] "To initiate proceedings for the purpose of invoking the 300-day filing period under 42 U.S.C. § 2000e-5(e)(1) a charging party need only present a charge to the OCRC [Ohio Civil Rights Commission] and request that the charge be presented to the EEOC."[74]

In a case of first impression, the Second Circuit affirmed a decision holding that the Port Authority is a bi-state entity that lies outside the control of New York and New Jersey's antidiscrimination regimes.[75] Because neither state's antidiscrimination regime applies to the bi-state entity, the 300-day filing period is unavailable, and the default 180-day filing period applies.[76]

The Second, Third, Fourth, Fifth, Seventh, Eighth, Ninth, and Eleventh Circuits have held that a state or local agency's waiver of exclusive jurisdiction is self-executing, thus effecting the instantaneous termination of its proceedings, which permits the EEOC to commence its own proceedings when the charge is filed and makes the charge timely filed with the EEOC.[77]

Even in those jurisdictions with work sharing agreements, plaintiffs may still be required to prove to the district court that the provisions of the particular state's work sharing agreement ultimately provide them with the benefit of the 300-day limitations period.[78] The Ninth Circuit found a genuine issue of material

---

[73]*Id.* at 678.

[74]*Id.* at 679.

[75]Dezaio v. Port Auth., 205 F.3d 62, 82 FEP 377 (2d Cir. 2000) (citing Hess v. Port Auth. Trans-Hudson Corp., 513 U.S. 30, 42 (1994)) (stating that bi-state entities created by compact are not subject to unilateral control of either of states).

[76]*Dezaio*, 205 F.3d at 65.

[77]*See* Ford v. Bernard Fineson Dev. Ctr., 81 F.3d 304, 311, 70 FEP 825 (2d Cir. 1996) ("This holding is consistent with the rulings of the seven other circuits that have considered this issue, and with the reasoning of the district courts in our Circuit that have unanimously reached the same conclusion."); Griffin v. Dallas, 26 F.3d 610, 613–14, 65 FEP 784 (5th Cir. 1994); *cf.* EEOC v. Green, 76 F.3d 19, 23 nn.5–6, 70 FEP 88 (1st Cir. 1996) (citing case law from other circuits and advising EEOC and Massachusetts Commission Against Discrimination to clarify intent of ambiguous language in their work sharing agreement).

[78]*See* Russell v. Delco Remy Div. of Gen. Motors Corp., 51 F.3d 746, 750–51, 67 FEP 673 (7th Cir. 1995) (because "[w]orksharing agreements are to some degree particularized . . . [and] each embodies a particular state's intent regarding its relationship with the EEOC . . . some fact-finding is necessary to determine the intended effect of Indiana's worksharing agreement with the EEOC").

fact about whether Nevada's 1995 work sharing agreement waived the 60-day deferral provision for the plaintiff's Title VII sex harassment charge.[79]

6. Effect of State Action or Inaction on Title VII Rights

a. State Inaction. A charging party's rights cannot be affected merely because the state agency makes only perfunctory efforts,[80] elects to do nothing,[81] or waives its right to proceed.[82] Furthermore, the charging party has an obligation to cooperate with the state agency.[83]

---

[79]LaQuaglia v. Rio Hotel & Casino, Inc., 186 F.3d 1172, 1175–77, 80 FEP 848 (9th Cir. 1999).

[80]See, e.g., Nichols, 318 F.3d at 678 (state agency's failure to take further action on plaintiff's charge would not be held against him); see also Saulsbury v. Wismer & Becker, Inc., 644 F.2d 1251, 1255, 23 FEP 287 (9th Cir. 1980) (state agency failed to request complainant to file verified complaint, which was required under state law).

[81]See Pacific Mar. Ass'n v. Quinn, 465 F.2d 108, 110–11, 4 FEP 992 (9th Cir. 1972) ("If . . . state representatives choose to do nothing . . . the federal purpose [of deferral] has been fully met."); EEOC v. Fidelity & Guar. Co., 13 FEP 1005, 1006 (4th Cir. 1976) (deferral requirement is satisfied if state agency is given opportunity to act); see also EEOC v. Commercial Office Prods. Inc., 486 U.S. 107, 114–15, 46 FEP 1265 (1988) (state proceeding need not be finally ended in order for it to be considered "terminated" under Title VII; Court accepted EEOC contention that state agency terminates its proceedings when it declares that it will not proceed, if it does so at all, for specified interval of time); cf. Martinez v. Orr, 738 F.2d 1107, 1110 (10th Cir. 1984) (citing Carlile v. South Routt Sch. Dist., 652 F.2d 981, 986 (10th Cir. 1981)) (plaintiff's charge will not be time-barred when employer, state, or federal agencies "lull" plaintiff into inaction).

[82]See Love v. Pullman Co., 404 U.S. 522, 524, 4 FEP 150 (1972) (state agency entirely waived its right to proceed); see also Johnson v. J.B. Hunt Transp., Inc., 280 F.3d 1125, 1129–30 (7th Cir. 2002) (holding that, under work sharing agreement between EEOC and state agency, state agency can waive its right to exclusive jurisdiction under 42 U.S.C. § 2000e-5(c) for first 60 days after charge has been filed). The EEOC's procedural regulations specifically provide that a § 706 agency may waive the deferral period. 29 C.F.R. § 1601.13(a)(3)(iii) (2005).

[83]See Albano v. General Adjustment Bureau, Inc., 478 F. Supp. 1209, 1215, 21 FEP 323 (S.D.N.Y. 1979) (case dismissed because plaintiff refused request from deferral agency to file formal complaint and instead informed it (apparently through counsel) that she was filing with another agency), aff'd mem., 622 F.2d 572 (2d Cir. 1980); see also Scott v. University of Del., 385 F. Supp. 937, 943, 10 FEP 1064 (D. Del. 1974) (noncooperation within deferral period might affect court's jurisdiction). But cf. McKeever v. Atlantic Spring & Mfg. Co., 502 F. Supp. 684, 688, 24 FEP 1059 (E.D. Pa. 1980) (state acceded to plaintiff's request to waive its jurisdiction; case was not dismissed even though there was possibility state would have had jurisdiction).

   b. State Action. Questions frequently arise as to what preclusive effect should be given to state agency determinations. Generally, an unreviewed state or local agency determination does not
preclude the plaintiff from seeking relief under Title VII or from
obtaining supplemental relief. In *Astoria Federal Savings & Loan
Ass'n v. Solimino,*[84] an ADEA case, the Supreme Court reasoned
that federal consideration of age discrimination claims would be
rendered merely *"pro forma* if prior state administrative proceedings were given preclusive effect."[85]

   Different rules apply after state agency determinations are
reviewed in court. For example, in *Kremer v. Chemical Construction Corp.,*[86] the Supreme Court held that a final determination by
a state court on a state-law claim of discrimination adverse to the
plaintiff, could be preclusive in subsequent Title VII litigation if
the plaintiff had a full and fair opportunity to litigate the merits
under state law.[87] State administrative agency rulings that have been

---

[84]501 U.S. 104, 55 FEP 1503 (1991).

[85]*Id.* at 111.

[86]456 U.S. 461, 28 FEP 1412 (1982).

[87]*Id.* at 485; *see also* Garcia v. Village of Mount Prospect, 360 F.3d 630, 634
(7th Cir. 2004) (Illinois circuit courts could have exercised jurisdiction over Garcia's
independent federal civil rights claims either directly or after Garcia exhausted available administrative remedies; it was thus possible for Garcia to join those claims
with his administrative appeal of Board's decision; therefore he had full and fair
opportunity to litigate his civil rights claims and, consequently, res judicata applies);
Hirst v. California, 770 F.2d 776, 778, 38 FEP 1496 (9th Cir. 1985) (plaintiff was
precluded from relitigating under Title VII state court's finding that there was no
discrimination when elements of state and federal cases were same); Burney v. Polk
Cmty. Coll., 728 F.2d 1374, 1379, 34 FEP 727 (11th Cir. 1984) (preclusive effect
of judgment not undermined by fact that state court reviewed determination by community college board of trustees; state agency not authorized by statute to enforce
employment antidiscrimination laws); Unger v. Consolidated Foods Corp., 693 F.2d
703, 705–06, 30 FEP 441 (7th Cir. 1982) (final decision of state appeals court given
preclusive effect). Preclusion normally applies only when the issue of discrimination was or could have been fully and fairly litigated. Hence, there normally is no
preclusion where the issues are different. *See* Kirk v. Bremen Cmty. High Sch. Dist.
228, 811 F.2d 347, 353, 42 FEP 1473 (7th Cir. 1987) (significant differences in
underlying cause of action); Jalil v. Avdel Corp., 873 F.2d 701, 704, 49 FEP 1210
(3d Cir. 1989) (issues were different). Nor is there preclusion where there was insufficient opportunity to litigate. *See* Scroggins v. Kansas Dep't of Human Res., 802
F.2d 1289, 1293, 50 FEP 1294 (10th Cir. 1986) (no bar to Title VII suit because
there had been no full and fair opportunity to litigate discrimination issue in hearing first brought before state civil service board); Jones v. City of Alton, 757 F.2d
878, 886, 37 FEP 523 (7th Cir. 1985) (no preclusionary effect when plaintiff was
not allowed to present evidence on discrimination issue).

appealed to state courts may bar subsequent Title VII litigation even if they ultimately are dismissed for procedural reasons.[88] And, in *University of Tennessee v. Elliott*,[89] the Supreme Court held that even an unappealed state administrative ruling would bar a race discrimination claim under 42 U.S.C. §§ 1981 and 1983 if it would have had such preclusive effect under state law.[90]

7. *Effect of Complainant's Failure to Verify Charge*

Two procedural hurdles in the charge-filing process are (1) filing a timely charge and (2) verifying a charge with the EEOC. The Supreme Court recently took interest in the interplay of these two procedural stumbling blocks for complainants. In *Edelman v. Lynchburg College*,[91] the Supreme Court sustained an EEOC regulation[92] pursuant to which a timely unverified charge of discrimination filed with the Commission may be verified after the time for filing has expired.[93]

The Court gave two reasons for its decision. First, allowing a charge to be verified after the time for filing has expired protects the lay complainant who may not know that verification is required. Second, the relation-back doctrine is commonly used in courts and is no less appropriate in an agency regulation.[94] The Court concluded

---

[88]*See* Bray v. New York Life Ins., 851 F.2d 60, 64, 47 FEP 278 (2d Cir. 1988) (appeal dismissed because it was filed 1 day too late); *cf.* Brookins v. General Motors Corp., 843 F.2d 879, 882, 46 FEP 905 (6th Cir. 1987) (state court discrimination lawsuit dismissed for "lack of progress" bars Title VII claim).

[89]478 U.S. 788, 41 FEP 177 (1986).

[90]*Id.* at 799.

[91]535 U.S. 106, 88 FEP 321 (2002).

[92]The regulation called into question in *Edelman* states as follows:
Notwithstanding the provisions of paragraph (a) of this section, a charge is sufficient when the Commission receives from the person making the charge a written statement sufficiently precise to identify the parties, and to describe generally the action or practices complained of. A charge may be amended to cure technical defects or omissions, including failure to verify the charge, or to clarify and amplify allegations made therein. Such amendments and amendments alleging additional acts which constitute unlawful employment practices related to or growing out of the subject matter of the original charge will relate back to the date the charge was first received. A charge that has been so amended shall not be required to be redeferred.
29 C.F.R. § 1601.12(b) (2005).

[93]*Edelman*, 535 U.S. at 109.

[94]*Id.* at 113–16.

that its ruling was consistent with the broad remedial purpose of Title VII.

This decision effectively removes one of the grounds that had been available to employers to get an early exit from Title VII litigation. Charges not timely filed may still be time-barred but, according to the relation-back regulation, complainants can correct defects after the time for filing has expired. The Court remanded *Edelman*, however, for a determination about whether the letter submitted to the EEOC by the plaintiff's lawyer constituted a sufficient "charge."[95]

---

[95]*Id.* at 117–18; *see* Edelman v. Lynchburg Coll., 300 F.3d 400, 89 FEP 1053 (4th Cir. 2002) (on remand, court finds that employee's unverified letter to EEOC constituted valid sex discrimination charge, to which Form 5 charge relates back, despite fact that EEOC did not originally act on letter as charge; but Form 5 charge does not relate back with respect to claims of religious and national origin discrimination not included in original letter). Prior to *Edelman*, several circuits held that unsworn intake questionnaires cannot serve as an administrative charge under Title VII (or, by extension, the ADA). *See* Shempert v. Harwick Chem. Corp., 151 F.3d 793, 796–98, 78 FEP 615 (8th Cir. 1999); Schlueter v. Anheuser-Busch, Inc., 132 F.3d 455, 75 FEP 1358 (8th Cir. 1998); Park v. Howard Univ., 71 F.3d 904, 908–09, 71 FEP 1838 (D.C. Cir. 1995); Balazs v. Liebenthal, 32 F.3d 151, 156–57, 65 FEP 993 (4th Cir. 1994); Lawrence v. Cooper Cmtys., Inc., 132 F.3d 447, 451, 75 FEP 1661 (8th Cir. 1998) (preparation and filing of intake questionnaire may in some instances equitably toll limitations period for filing charge). Other circuits prior to *Edelman* held that a timely filed intake questionnaire can serve as an administrative charge if verified (at least during the pendency of an investigation). *See* Wilkerson v. Grinnell Corp., 270 F.3d 1314 (11th Cir. 2001) (holding intake questionnaire signed under penalty of perjury that includes basic information suggested by applicable regulation may constitute charge for purposes of Title VII statute of limitations when circumstances of case would convince reasonable person that charging party manifested her intent to activate administrative process by filing intake questionnaire with EEOC); Philbin v. General Elec. Capital Auto Lease, Inc., 929 F.2d 321, 322–25, 55 FEP 867 (7th Cir. 1991) (per curiam); Peterson v. City of Wichita, 888 F.2d 1307, 1308–09, 51 FEP 525 (10th Cir. 1989); Casavantes v. California State Univ., 732 F.2d 1441, 1442–44, 34 FEP 1336 (9th Cir. 1984); *cf.* LaQuaglia v. Rio Hotel & Casino, Inc., 186 F.3d 1172, 1175, 80 FEP 848 (9th Cir. 1999) (intake form filed with Nevada state agency that was signed under oath satisfied Title VII requirements, pursuant to state-federal work sharing agreement's dual-filing provision). Authorization for such verification is drawn from 29 C.F.R. § 1601.12(b), which permits a party to amend a charge to meet the verification requirement.

Unlike Title VII, the ADEA does not require that a charge be signed under oath. Courts differ about whether an unsigned intake questionnaire can serve as a charge under the ADEA. *See* Diez v. Minnesota Mining & Mfg. Co., 88 F.3d 672, 675–77, 71 FEP 383 (8th Cir. 1996) (intake form was not charge where it was not sufficiently definite to activate EEOC authority to investigate); Downes v. Volkswagen of Am., Inc., 41 F.3d 1132, 1138, 69 FEP 11 (7th Cir. 1994) ("to constitute a charge, notice to the EEOC must be of a kind that would convince a reasonable person that the

B. When Did the Discrimination Occur?

1. Individual Acts

In order to determine whether a charge has been timely filed, one first must determine (1) what adverse action is at issue, and (2) when it "occurred."[96] These determinations can be difficult. Multiple events, occurring at different times, may be part of an employment decision. For example, a hiring decision may involve each of the following events: interviews with several different persons; one or more recommendations, or tentative decisions, made over several different levels of decision making; and an ambiguous or nonexistent communication of the decision to the affected parties. If the company's decision allegedly was infected by unlawful discrimination, when did the discrimination "occur?"

A review of Supreme Court cases provides some guidance. In *Electrical Workers (IUE) Local 790 v. Robbins & Myers, Inc.*,[97] the Court held that a discharge "occurred" on the day the charging party stopped work, not on the day the processing of her grievance under the collective bargaining agreement concluded.[98] In *Delaware State College v. Ricks*,[99] the Court labeled a college's communication of its denial of tenure to the plaintiff as the discriminatory "occurrence," even though tenure denial did not cause actual termination for one additional academic year.[100] " '[T]he

---

plaintiff manifested an intent to activate the Act's machinery"; to determine intent courts may consider factors including, but not limited to, "whether the questionnaire is precise enough to identify the parties and generally describe the complained-of practices and whether the information in the questionnaire was subsequently used to complete the formal charge," as well as whether EEOC treated questionnaire as charge); Early v. Bankers Life & Cas. Co., 959 F.2d 75, 79–80, 63 FEP 363 (7th Cir. 1992) (charge filing may be equitably tolled); Clark v. Coats & Clark, Inc., 865 F.2d 1237, 1239–41, 49 FEP 99 (11th Cir. 1989) (verification could relate back to date of filing unsworn intake questionnaire).

[96]Section 706(e)(1) provides, in part, that "[a] charge under this section shall be filed within one hundred and eighty days after the alleged unlawful employment practice occurred." 42 U.S.C. § 2000e-5(e)(1) (2000).

[97]429 U.S. 229, 13 FEP 1813 (1976).

[98]*Id.* at 234–40.

[99]449 U.S. 250, 259, 24 FEP 827 (1980).

[100]*Id.* at 252 ("Like many colleges and universities, Delaware State has a policy of not immediately discharging a junior faculty member who does not receive tenure. Rather, such a person is offered a 'terminal' contract to teach one additional year. When that contract expires, the employment relationship ends.").

proper focus,' " the Court declared, " 'is upon the time of the *discriminatory acts*, not upon the time at which the *consequences* of the acts became most painful.' "[101] Accordingly, the Court rejected as the time of "occurrence" (1) the date the plaintiff's final contract expired; and (2) the date the college denied Ricks' grievance challenging the adverse tenure decision.[102] The Supreme Court further extended *Ricks* in *Chardon v. Fernandez*,[103] ruling untimely a § 1983 discharge action brought less than one year after the actual termination of employment; what mattered is that it was brought more than one year after the employee was notified of an impending discharge.[104]

Courts have continued to rely on *Ricks* and *Chardon* in holding that the accrual date of the cause of action for limitations purposes is the date on which the adverse employment action is *communicated* to the plaintiff,[105] although almost all courts now

---

[101]*Id.* at 258 (quoting Abramson v. University of Haw., 594 F.2d 202, 209, 19 FEP 439 (9th Cir. 1979)) (emphasis in *Ricks*). But cf. Gustovich v. AT&T Commc'ns, 972 F.2d 845, 847, 59 FEP 1060 (7th Cir. 1992) (employees whose jobs were eliminated after they received allegedly discriminatory poor performance evaluations could file discrimination charges within limitations period following layoff notice; time did not run from date of evaluations).

[102]*Ricks*, 449 U.S. at 258, 261 & n.15 ("limitations periods normally commence when the employer's decision is made," not thereafter; "Mere requests to reconsider . . . cannot extend the limitations period applicable to the civil rights laws.").

[103]454 U.S. 6, 27 FEP 57 (1981).

[104]*Id.* at 8; *accord* Cada v. Baxter Healthcare Corp., 920 F.2d 446, 453, 54 FEP 961 (7th Cir. 1990) (*Ricks* establishes that it is date of communication of adverse decision, not when action takes effect, that begins running of charge-filing period); English v. Whitfield, 858 F.2d 957, 961, 3 IER 1357 (4th Cir. 1988) (letter that removed employee from her position provided temporary assignment of 90 days from which to look for other positions in company and stated that if she did not find another position she involuntarily would be laid off; this letter provided unequivocal notice and began running of statute of limitations); Wislocki-Goin v. Mears, 831 F.2d 1374, 1380, 45 FEP 216 (7th Cir. 1987) (limitations period began to run when female employee learned that employer had hired allegedly less experienced male who had not applied for position she sought); Calhoun v. Federal Nat'l Mortgage Ass'n, 823 F.2d 451, 455–56, 44 FEP 761 (11th Cir. 1987) (employee was on notice when he had cleared out his office, stopped receiving further work assignments, sought letters of recommendation, and accepted work at another job); Janikowski v. Bendix Corp., 823 F.2d 945, 947, 47 FEP 544 (6th Cir. 1987) (that employer stated that employee could seek new position elsewhere in company did not toll statute of limitations).

[105]*See* Williams v. Giant Food, Inc., 370 F.3d 423, 427–28 (4th Cir. 2004) (failure-to-promote claim accrued on the date when the selection decision was communicated to the employee, not when the assignment commenced); Campbell v. BankBoston, N.A., 327 F.3d 1, 91 FEP 410 (1st Cir. 2003) (300-day period commenced

recognize (or at least consider) that the limitations period may be subject to equitable tolling. At least one court has permitted the

---

for purpose of age discrimination claim when company decision concerning his pension benefits was made and communicated to him, not when grievance procedure to correct decision was terminated); Bailey v. United Airlines, 279 F.3d 194, 88 FEP 22 (3d Cir. 2002) (statute of limitations began to run as soon as plaintiff was informed of adverse employment decision reached by employer and presented with offer to resign or be terminated); Watson v. Eastman Kodak Co., 235 F.3d 851, 855–58, 84 FEP 1164 (3d Cir. 2000) (charge filed fewer than 300 days after discharge from employment, but more than 300 days after removal from account executive position, was untimely because charge challenged decision to remove plaintiff from position rather than plaintiff's termination); Stewart v. Booker T. Washington Ins., 232 F.3d 844, 848–50, 84 FEP 665 (11th Cir. 2000) (180-day filing period runs from date plaintiff is told she will be terminated, not from date she is told her job may be in danger; however, claims of discriminatory transfer were untimely where plaintiff was told transfer was because of filing of EEOC charge, but transfer occurred more than 180 days earlier); Thomas v. Eastman Kodak Co., 183 F.3d 38, 47–53, 80 FEP 38 (1st Cir. 1999) (employee's notice of layoff, rather than receipt of negative performance evaluations, triggers charge-filing period); Martin v. Southwestern Va. Gas Co., 135 F.3d 307, 7 AD 1374 (4th Cir. 1998) (ADA plaintiff's cause of action accrued when defendant informed him that he would be discharged on later date certain); Norman-Bloodsaw v. Lawrence Berkeley Lab., 135 F.3d 1260, 1266, 75 FEP 1695 (9th Cir. 1998) ("a limitations period begins to run when the plaintiff knows, or has reason to know, of the injury which is the basis of the action"); Zotos v. Lindbergh Sch. Dist., 121 F.3d 356, 362, 74 FEP 1055 (8th Cir. 1997) (ADEA claim for discriminatory transfer accrued when plaintiff was notified of transfer); Peanick v. Morris, 96 F.3d 316, 321, 71 FEP 1711 (8th Cir. 1996) (30-day period of time for contacting EEO counselor started running when adverse employment action was communicated to plaintiff); Dring v. McDonnell Douglas Corp., 58 F.3d 1323, 1327–28, 70 FEP 481 (8th Cir. 1995) (accrual date of charge-filing period begins when adverse employment action is communicated to plaintiff); Hargett v. Valley Fed. Sav. Bank, 60 F.3d 754, 760–61, 68 FEP 852 (11th Cir. 1995) (ADEA claim is barred if claimant knew or reasonably should have known of challenged acts more than 180 days prior to filing his EEOC claim; plaintiff, who is aware that he is being replaced in position, which he believes he is able to perform, by person outside protected age group knows enough to support filing claim); Oshiver v. Levin, Fishbein, Sedran & Berman, 38 F.3d 1380, 1386, 66 FEP 429 (3d Cir. 1994) (discovery rule functions to delay initial running of limitations period, but only until plaintiff has discovered or, by exercising reasonable diligence, should have discovered (1) that he or she has been injured and (2) that this injury has been caused by another party's conduct; discovery rule is limited to discovery of actual fact of injury, not discovery of information showing that injury was legally wrong); Teumer v. General Motors Corp., 34 F.3d 542, 550 (7th Cir. 1994) (plaintiff is required to bring charge within "reasonable time" after he or she obtained, or could have obtained by due diligence, information regarding alleged wrongdoing); Hulsey v. K-Mart, Inc., 43 F.3d 555, 557–58, 66 FEP 1327 (10th Cir. 1994) (cause of action accrued as of date of discharge; rejecting plaintiffs' argument for equitable tolling based on their claims of constructive discharge by demotion and transfer as pretext for age discrimination, and holding that plaintiffs had duty to determine whether there was discriminatory motive for alleged constructive discharge).

jury to determine the event that triggers the commencement of the charge-filing period.[106]

Although these cases seem to establish a relatively simple "notice" rule as to when discrimination "occurs" (so as to start the running of the charge-filing period), courts continue to disagree on the subject of the notice. Most cases, relying on *Ricks* and *Chardon*, focus on notice of the adverse action.[107] Some, however, focus on notice of at least some facts suggesting discrimination.[108] The better reasoned cases distinguish between *accrual* of the cause of action and possible *tolling* of the limitations period; these cases find that the statute of limitations commences to run when the injury occurs, regardless of whether the claimant is on notice of possible discrimination.

---

[106]*See* Duty v. Norton-Alcoa Proppants, 293 F.3d 481, 13 AD 304 (8th Cir. 2002) (jury found that latest date plaintiff's action accrued was date of official termination letter, rather than earlier date when plaintiff received word by phone from individual who, although placed in management, lacked any firing authority over plaintiff).

[107]*See, e.g., Williams*, 370 F.3d at 429 (failure to promote claim accrued on the date when the selection decision was communicated to the employee, not when the assignment commenced); Hamilton v. 1st Source Bank, 928 F.2d 86, 89 & n.3, 54 FEP 1019 (4th Cir. 1990) (en banc) (charge of pay discrimination is untimely despite plaintiff's argument that he was not aware of pay disparity until discovery was conducted on his timely discharge claim); Mull v. Arco Durethene Plastics, Inc., 599 F. Supp. 158, 162, 36 FEP 1052 (N.D. Ill. 1984) (oral notice of discharge is sufficient even though employer's regular procedure is to give written notice), *aff'd*, 784 F.2d 284, 40 FEP 311 (7th Cir. 1986); *see* Monnig v. Kennecott Corp., 603 F. Supp. 1035, 1038, 37 FEP 193 (D. Conn. 1985) ("To constitute a notice of termination, a specific date on which employment will be discontinued must be stated."). *But cf.* De Los Angeles-Sanchez v. Puerto Rico Elec. Power Auth., 993 F.2d 1530 (1st Cir. 1993) (unpublished decision) (in constructive discharge case, actual effective date of resignation, not date employee tendered letter of resignation, controls; employee might change her mind).

[108]*See, e.g.,* Beamon v. Marshall & Ilsley Trust Co., 411 F.3d 854, 860–61 (7th Cir. 2005) (limitations period began to run when plaintiff was aware of facts that might give rise to a claim of discrimination); Jones v. Dillard's, Inc., 331 F.3d 1259, 1263–64 (11th Cir. 2003) (charge-filing deadline equitably tolled until plaintiff discovers evidence of the discriminatory intent behind an adverse employment action); Vaught v. R.R. Donnelley & Sons Co., 745 F.2d 407, 410–11, 35 FEP 1820 (7th Cir. 1984) (duty to file charge arises when claimant possesses knowledge of facts sufficient to establish prima facie case); *see also* Webb v. Indiana Nat'l Bank, 931 F.2d 434, 436, 437, 55 FEP 1238 (7th Cir. 1991) (statute begins to run when plaintiff knows or should know of discrimination; subsequent denials of promotion cannot revive statutory period once plaintiff knows or should know that she will never be considered for promotion); *cf.* Janowiak v. Corporate City of South Bend, 750 F.2d 557, 560, 36 FEP 737 (7th Cir. 1984) (claimant will be excused from learning of alleged unlawful conduct only by "circumstances beyond his control"), *vacated and remanded on other grounds*, 481 U.S. 1001, 43 FEP 640 (1987).

A somewhat different issue is presented in cases attacking an otherwise time-barred incident when the charge is prompted by additional disparate treatment within the limitations period.[109] These cases are best understood as involving a new violation (e.g., a discriminatory refusal to recall from layoff) or a possible claim of a "continuing violation" if the acts were part of a series of acts constituting one unlawful employment practice. These issues are discussed later in light of the Supreme Court's decision in *National Railroad Passenger Corp. v. Morgan*.[110]

The Second Circuit has held that in cases of constructive discharge the employee's claim accrues on the date the employee provides definite notice of his or her intention to resign, regardless of whether the last day of employment is in the future.[111] The court explained that this rule "is essentially the converse of the discriminatory discharge case where the date the employer gives notice to the employee is controlling for purposes of accrual."[112] The court linked the accrual date to the date the employee gives formal notice of resignation because only the employee can know when the assertedly discriminatory atmosphere created by the employer has become so intolerable that the employee allegedly is compelled to leave.[113]

---

[109]*See, e.g.*, Maki v. Allete, 383 F.3d 740 (8th Cir. 2004) (employer's failure to credit female employees with past service in pension plan constitutes a potential current violation of Title VII; limitations period commenced when allegedly discriminatory pension plan was actually applied to plaintiffs); Perez v. Laredo Junior Coll., 706 F.2d 731, 735 (5th Cir. 1983) (although professor's claims of salary discrimination under 42 U.S.C. §§ 1981 and 1983 were untimely based on when college denied him increase, plaintiff still could pursue the issue because he alleged that other similarly situated individuals received raises within limitations period); Ortiz v. Chicago Transit Auth., 639 F. Supp. 310, 312, 41 FEP 350 (N.D. Ill. 1986) (statute begins to run when similarly situated employee is allowed to return to work); Coleman v. Clark Oil & Ref. Co., 568 F. Supp. 1035, 1041, 36 FEP 758 (E.D. Wis. 1983) (charge alleging denial of promotion was timely because younger white employee was promoted during charge-filing period).

[110]536 U.S. 101, 88 FEP 1601 (2002); *see* Section II.B.3 *infra*.

[111]Flaherty v. Metromail Corp., 235 F.3d 133, 138, 84 FEP 1050 (2d Cir. 2000).

[112]*Id.* at 138–39.

[113]*Id.* (citing with approval Draper v. Coeur Rochester, Inc., 147 F.3d 1104, 1110, 77 FEP 188 (9th Cir. 1998) ("the date of discharge triggers the limitations period in a constructive discharge case, just as in all other cases of wrongful discharge")); *see also* Fielder v. UAL Corp., 218 F.3d 973, 988–89, 83 FEP 493 (9th Cir. 2000) ("the date of the resignation triggers the limitations period in a constructive discharge case"), *vacated*, 536 U.S. 919 (2002).

2. Application of Policies[114]

If the employer has a formal rule or policy of disparate treatment in either the allocation of jobs or the provision of benefits of employment and the system is maintained into the charge-filing period, the system or practice arguably may be attacked once there is a current injury occasioned by the operation of the system.[115] These cases, however, all generally predate the Supreme Court's decision in *National Railroad Passenger Corp. v. Morgan*,[116] in which the Court reserved the question of how its ruling would be applied in a pattern-or-practice case.[117]

In *Bazemore v. Friday*,[118] the Supreme Court considered an employer's salary structure that perpetuated pre-Act discrimination. The Fourth Circuit held that if the employer acted evenhandedly after the effective date of the 1972 amendments to Title VII prior salary disparities would not be actionable. The Supreme Court,

---

[114]*See generally* Chapter 17 (Seniority).

[115]*See, e.g.*, Rendon v. AT&T Techs., 883 F.2d 388, 395–96, 50 FEP 1587 (5th Cir. 1989) (work assignment and promotion system); Morelock v. NCR Corp., 586 F.2d 1096, 1103, 18 FEP 225 (6th Cir. 1978) (ADEA case; discriminatory seniority system); *see* Civil Rights Act of 1991, Pub. L. No. 102-166, § 112, 1991 U.S.C.C.A.N. (105 Stat.) 1071, 1079 (codified as amended at 42 U.S.C. § 2000e-5(e)(2)) (amending Title VII; with respect to discriminatory seniority systems, discrimination "occurs" when system is adopted, when individual becomes subject to system, *or* when person is injured by application of system); *cf.* Bartmess v. Drewrys U.S.A., Inc., 444 F.2d 1186, 1188, 3 FEP 795 (7th Cir. 1971) (upholding challenge to retirement system even before it was applied to plaintiff).

[116]536 U.S. 101, 88 FEP 1601 (2002).

[117]*Id.* at 115 n.9 ("[w]e have no occasion here to consider the timely filing question with respect to 'pattern or practice' claims brought by private litigants"). The Supreme Court may address this issue in *Ledbetter v. Goodyear Tire & Rubber Co.*, 421 F.3d 1169, 98 FEP 418 (11th Cir. 2005), *cert. granted*, 126 S. Ct. 2965 (2006), on which the Court heard arguments several months before this book went to press.

[118]478 U.S. 385, 41 FEP 92 (1986). Prior to the enactment of the Civil Rights Act of 1964, the North Carolina Agricultural Expansion Service formally designated one of its two branches a "Negro branch." This branch was composed entirely of African Americans and served only that community. The other branch employed only whites (but did sometimes serve African Americans). In response to the 1964 Act, the state merged the two branches into one organization, but the integration did not immediately eliminate " 'some disparities which had existed between the salaries of white personnel and black personnel.' " *Id.* at 387 n.1 (citation omitted). Title VII was expanded to include public employees in 1972. The Court acknowledged two distinct salary claims: those of employees hired before and after the merger. *Id.* at 397 n.8.

deeming this error "too obvious to warrant extended discussion,"[119] held that a salary system perpetuating pre-Act disparities constitutes present discrimination; "[e]ach week's pay check that delivers less to a black than to a similarly situated white is a wrong actionable under Title VII, regardless of the fact that this pattern was begun prior to the effective date of Title VII."[120]

The Court distinguished *United Airlines, Inc. v. Evans,*[121] a case in which the plaintiff's injury resulted from the operation of a nondiscriminatory seniority system combined with a historical violation that was not subject to a timely charge.[122] Compensation cases, by contrast, generally involve current and ongoing decisions to raise, freeze, or trim pay. Compensation seems to be an inherently mutable term or condition of employment and thus is arguably less susceptible to the *Evans* analysis.[123] Somewhat similarly, *Teamsters v. United States*[124] specifically recognized that if a union, because of past discrimination, had all white members, the otherwise neutral device of limiting new members to blood relatives of existing members would be current discrimination.[125] Where, in a pattern-or-practice case, a discriminatory policy is maintained into the current charge-filing period and applied, some courts have

---

[119]*Id.* at 395.

[120]*Id.* at 395–96. *But cf.* EEOC v. Penton Indus. Publ'g Co., 851 F.2d 835, 838–39, 47 FEP 458 (6th Cir. 1988) (Title VII and Equal Pay Act claims accrued during periods that male was paid more than females; it did not continue to accrue after his termination, when females continued to be paid less than male was paid).

[121]431 U.S. 553, 14 FEP 1510 (1977).

[122]*Bazemore,* 478 U.S. at 396 n.6 ("Because the employer was not engaged in discriminatory practices at the time the respondent in *Evans* brought suit, there simply was no violation of Title VII.").

[123]*See, e.g.,* Gandy v. Sullivan County, 24 F.3d 861, 865, 64 FEP 1607 (6th Cir. 1994) (woman who sued 9 years after she learned she was paid less than her male predecessor could bring cause of action for all violations occurring within 3-year limitations period immediately prior to suit; her rights were violated with every check she received); *cf.* Pallas v. Pacific Bell, 940 F.2d 1324, 1327, 56 FEP 1025 (9th Cir. 1991) (early retirement program treated former maternity leaves differently from other disabilities in determining eligibility; present discrimination). *But cf.* Ross v. Buckeye Cellulose Corp., 980 F.2d 648, 660, 60 FEP 822 (11th Cir. 1993) (although systemwide pay freeze locked in place effects of alleged prior discrimination, there was no continuing violation; every employee was thus locked in, regardless of race). As this book went to press, however, the continuing viability of *Bazemore* was before the U.S. Supreme Court in *Ledbetter v. Goodyear Tire & Rubber Co.,* 421 F.3d 1169, 98 FEP 418 (11th Cir. 2005), *cert. granted,* 126 S. Ct. 2965 (2006).

[124]431 U.S. 324, 365, 14 FEP 1514 (1977) (nonapplicants who are deterred may challenge discriminatory practices). *See generally* Chapter 15 (Hiring).

[125]431 U.S. at 349 n.32.

permitted plaintiffs to whom it was applied prior to the current period to pursue their claims on the "continuing" violation theory under *Bazemore*.[126]

It is less clear when less formal and less structured practices will be deemed a "system" of discrimination, arguably vulnerable to attack notwithstanding the absence of a specific, timely incident of discrimination against the plaintiff. Some courts have characterized even informal and unstructured employment practices as decision-making "systems." In *Reed v. Lockheed Aircraft Corp.*,[127] the plaintiff alleged that she had been maintained in the same position for 25 years while men were promoted over her and repeatedly paid more for essentially identical work. She also alleged that Lockheed closed its training programs to women and that employees did not apply for promotions or training programs. Instead, they were selected unilaterally by management for such opportunities. The district court dismissed her complaint because the most recent specific incident of alleged discrimination had occurred approximately four years before her charge. The Ninth Circuit reversed, stating that her complaint did not attack discrete acts, but rather was a "sweeping attack on Lockheed's systems of promotion, compensation and training."[128] The court concluded that she had challenged a "continuous policy of favoring males in selecting employees for promotions and training programs" and reasoned:

> [The district] court should focus on Lockheed's systems of promotion, admission to training programs and compensation, not just on isolated incidents. The findings below that Lockheed did not discriminate against Reed in 1963, 1969 and 1972, even if correct, are almost irrelevant in light of Reed's attack on Lockheed's policies. As in *Shehadeh v. Chesapeake & Potomac Tel. Co.*, 193 U.S. App. D.C. 326, 334, 340, 595 F.2d 711, 724–25[, 18 FEP 614] (D.C. Cir. 1978), "it is the ongoing program of discrimination, rather than any of its particular manifestations, that is the subject of attack."[129]

---

[126]*See, e.g.*, Abrams v. Baylor Coll. of Med., 805 F.2d 528 (5th Cir. 1986) (refusal to send Jewish doctors to Saudi Arabia could be basis for claim by time-barred plaintiffs where policy applied to one doctor plaintiff in limitations period). *But see* Section II.B.3 *infra* (discussing decision in National Railroad Passenger Corp. v. Morgan, 536 U.S. 101, 88 FEP 1601 (2002)).

[127]613 F.2d 757, 22 FEP 1049 (9th Cir. 1980).

[128]*Id.* at 759.

[129]*Id.* at 762; *accord* Williams v. Owens-Ill., Inc., 665 F.2d 918, 924, 27 FEP 1273 (9th Cir. 1982) (although terminations and refusals to hire cannot be continuing violations without more, court may consider discriminatory placements and denials

In these "discriminatory system" cases, plaintiffs challenge a presently maintained means of allocating employment opportunities or benefits, alleging that the system discriminates under Title VII. Even if the charging parties are unable to demonstrate that they were personally denied a specific opportunity or benefit during the charge-filing period, some courts have reasoned that the maintenance of a discriminatory employment practice adversely affects not just those who suffer the loss of tangible benefits, but all members of the same protected class,[130] as well as employees who are not protected class members but who have a right to a nondiscriminatory environment.[131] Similarly, when the challenged

---

of promotions occurring before charge-filing period if continuing violation is established); *see also* Sosa v. Hiraoka, 920 F.2d 1451, 1455, 54 FEP 892 (9th Cir. 1990) (earlier denial of conference leave and expenses could be part of "policy" of racial discrimination); Roberts v. North Am. Rockwell Corp., 650 F.2d 823, 826, 25 FEP 1615 (6th Cir. 1981) (challenge of hiring system that would not consider females); Patterson v. American Tobacco Co., 586 F.2d 300, 304, 18 FEP 378 (4th Cir. 1978) (promotional policies); Acha v. Beame, 570 F.2d 57, 65, 16 FEP 526 (2d Cir. 1978) (attacking "a continuous policy which limited opportunities for female participation in the police force"); Clark v. Olinkraft, Inc., 556 F.2d 1219, 1221–22, 15 FEP 374 (5th Cir. 1977) (discriminatory promotion and pay systems); Laffey v. Northwest Airlines, Inc., 567 F.2d 429, 472–73, 13 FEP 1068 (D.C. Cir. 1976) (disparate wages, expense allowances, and weight restrictions); Rich v. Martin Marietta Corp., 522 F.2d 333, 348, 11 FEP 211 (10th Cir. 1975) ("Plaintiffs here challenge the entire promotion system maintaining that it continually operated so as to hold them in lower echelons. Hence, the 90-day period prior to filing of the EEOC charge looms inconsequential in this kind of case.").

[130]*See* Bundy v. Jackson, 641 F.2d 934, 944–46, 24 FEP 1155 (D.C. Cir. 1981) (employer's toleration of pattern of sexual harassment constitutes maintaining discriminatory condition of employment); Bartmess v. Drewrys U.S.A., Inc., 444 F.2d 1186, 1188, 3 FEP 795 (7th Cir. 1971) ("The collective bargaining agreement in force at the time the plaintiff filed her charge provided that female employees must retire three years prior to their male counterparts. If such a contract is found to be discriminatory, its mere presence in a collective bargaining agreement would render female workers 'aggrieved persons' within the meaning of Title VII and would continue to do so for the entire time the individual was employed.").

[131]*See* Waters v. Heublein, Inc., 547 F.2d 466, 470, 13 FEP 1409 (9th Cir. 1976) (white employee may challenge practices aimed at African Americans and Hispanics); *cf.* Trafficante v. Metropolitan Life Ins. Co., 409 U.S. 205, 209–10 (1972) (both white and nonwhite residents have standing to sue, as both are injured by "loss of important benefits of interracial associations" caused by housing discrimination against nonwhites). *But see* Patee v. Pacific N.W. Bell Tel. Co., 803 F.2d 476, 478–79, 42 FEP 298 (9th Cir. 1986) (distinguishing *Waters*; male employees cannot bring Title VII action alleging that they received lower wages in job category that was predominantly women because employer discriminated against women; no discrimination against males based on sex was alleged and, unlike *Waters* and *Trafficante*, there was no allegation of adverse consequences from denial of interpersonal contacts).

"system" is part of a collective bargaining agreement to which the union is a party, courts generally have been receptive to claims of continuing violation.[132] Where the plaintiff fails to challenge the system itself that led to the otherwise time-barred discrete discriminatory act, the continuing violation theory will not be available.[133]

One interesting analytical variant of these problems arises when an employer uses the results of a discriminatory test over a period of time as the basis for employment decisions, e.g., promotion, hiring, or admission to an apprenticeship program. Must an aggrieved party file a charge within the statutory period running from the date of administration of the test, or is a charge timely if filed while the results are still being used as a basis for employment decisions? The courts are divided on this issue.[134]

The "discriminatory system" rationale normally does not permit challenges to ongoing employment practices by former employees who failed to file within the charge-filing period; the last possible limitations period commenced to run on the date of termination.[135] On the other hand, in a hiring case, persons who applied

---

[132]*E.g.*, Norman v. Missouri Pac. R.R., 414 F.2d 73, 84, 1 FEP 863 (8th Cir. 1969) (challenge to system of alleged unequal work assignments, promotional opportunities, and wage rates incorporated in collective bargaining agreements; allowing claim of continuing violation against union signatories); Glus v. G.C. Murphy Co., 329 F. Supp. 563, 565, 3 FEP 1094 (W.D. Pa. 1971) (allegation that union failed to attempt to rid its collective bargaining agreement of discriminatory provisions states continuing violation). *See generally* Chapter 22 (Unions).

[133]*See* Davidson v. America Online, Inc., 337 F.3d 1179 (10th Cir. 2003).

[134]*Compare* Guardians Ass'n v. Civil Serv. Comm'n, 633 F.2d 232, 249, 23 FEP 677 (2d Cir. 1980) (in suit brought by employees who claimed that, but for entry-level exams, they would have been hired earlier and accrued sufficient seniority to withstand layoffs, discriminatory act occurred each time plaintiff was denied chance to fill vacancy), *aff'd in part*, 463 U.S. 582, 32 FEP 250, *and cert. denied in part*, 463 U.S. 1228 (1983) *and* Gonzalez v. Firestone Tire & Rubber Co., 610 F.2d 241, 249, 21 FEP 1367 (5th Cir. 1980) (case remanded to district court to determine whether employer selected employees for job opportunities within charge-filing period based on earlier-administered discriminatory tests) *with* Dickerson v. United States Steel Corp., 23 FEP 1088, 1091 (E.D. Pa. 1980) (charge was untimely when not filed within 180 days of date charging party took apprenticeship admission test; no new violation occurred each time test results were used) *and* Bronze Shields v. New Jersey Dep't of Civil Serv., 667 F.2d 1074, 1083, 27 FEP 749 (3d Cir. 1981) (under *Ricks*, if discrimination occurred against applicants not placed on Civil Service hiring roster, it occurred when roster was promulgated not when it was used; courts must separate discriminatory employment practice from inevitable consequences of practice).

[135]*See* Terry v. Bridgeport Brass Co., 519 F.2d 806, 808, 11 FEP 628 (7th Cir. 1975) (discrimination no longer continuing once employment ends; rather, date of

before the charge-filing period might attack the continued maintenance of discriminatory selection practices on the ground that the
maintenance of the practices deterred them from reapplying.[136]

3. Continuing Violations

a. National Railroad Passenger Corp. v. Morgan. One area of
employment law that has evolved greatly in recent years is the
application of the continuing violation doctrine to the timeliness
of charge filing. The term "continuing violation" generally is used
to refer to a defendant's alleged maintenance over time of a discriminatory policy or system. Sometimes the term is used to refer
to a series of acts that, although perhaps different in kind, are alleged to constitute a related course of conduct. When a continuing
violation is found, a plaintiff is entitled to have the court consider
all relevant and sufficiently related actions allegedly taken pursuant to the employer's discriminatory policy or practice, including
those that would otherwise be time-barred.[137]

In *National Railroad Passenger Corp. v. Morgan*,[138] the Supreme Court provided much-needed clarification of this concept.
Prior to *Morgan*, the continuing violations doctrine was arguably
the most muddled area in all of employment discrimination law.
Although the long-term impact of the *Morgan* decision is not yet
known, it has had an immediate effect of reversing some trends in
the law and much pre-*Morgan* case law.[139] Further, although *Morgan*

---

discharge controls and former employee must file timely in relation to that date);
Olson v. Rembrandt Printing Co., 511 F.2d 1228, 1234, 10 FEP 27 (8th Cir. 1975)
(en banc) (same); Wetzel v. Liberty Mut. Ins. Co., 508 F.2d 239, 246, 9 FEP 211
(3d Cir. 1975) (employees "who left the employ of the company" could not secure
relief); EEOC v. United Ins. Co. of Am., 666 F. Supp. 915, 918, 46 FEP 250 (S.D.
Miss. 1986) (continuing violation theory may not be used by EEOC to add parties
who did not file timely charges after discharge); cf. Shehadeh v. Chesapeake &
Potomac Tel. Co., 595 F.2d 711, 726, 18 FEP 614 (D.C. Cir. 1978) (derogatory
references given to prospective employers were independent violations; charge was
timely as to alleged references, but untimely as to discharge); Tarvesian v. Carr Div.
of TRW, Inc., 407 F. Supp. 336, 339, 341, 16 FEP 348 (D. Mass. 1976) (same).
    [136]See Teamsters v. United States, 431 U.S. 324, 367–68, 14 FEP 1514 (1977)
(nonapplicants who are deterred may challenge discriminatory practices). See generally Chapter 15 (Hiring).
    [137]Van Zant v. KLM Royal Dutch Airlines, 80 F.3d 708, 713 (2d Cir. 1996).
    [138]536 U.S. 101, 88 FEP 1601 (2002).
    [139]See Sharpe v. Cureton, 319 F.3d 259 (6th Cir. 2003) (stating that "[p]revious
'continuing violation' law must be reexamined in light of the Supreme Court's recently

was a Title VII case, courts have readily adopted its holdings to other discrimination laws.[140]

In *Morgan*, the plaintiff brought claims for race discrimination, retaliation, and hostile work environment, which were based on events dating back to the beginning of his employment nearly four and one-half years before filing a charge of discrimination. Most of the events occurred prior to the 300-day filing period. The issue before the Court was "whether, and under what circumstances, a Title VII plaintiff may file suit on events that fall outside this statutory time period."[141]

Answering these questions, the Court first held that a continuing violation theory is not permitted for claims arising out of discrete acts of discrimination, such as termination, failure to promote, denial of transfer, or refusal to hire.[142] The Court concluded that "[t]here is simply no indication that the term 'practice' converts related discrete acts into a single unlawful practice for the purposes of timely filing."[143] Instead, the Court held that a discrete

---

imposed limits on the viability of the doctrine" and holding that *Morgan* overturns prior Sixth Circuit law addressing serial violations); Madison v. IBP, Inc., 330 F.3d 1051, 91 FEP 1673 (8th Cir. 2003) (holding that rule in *Ashley* limiting recovery for hostile environment claims to those acts occurring during charge-filing period may no longer be applied); Lyons v. England, 307 F.3d 1092, 89 FEP 1793 (9th Cir. 2002) (holding that *Morgan* overrules prior Ninth Circuit authority and invalidates circuit's previous application of continuing violations doctrine to discrete acts of discrimination and retaliation); Davidson v. America Online, Inc., 337 F.3d 1179, 1184 (10th Cir. 2003) (*Morgan* implicitly overturns prior Tenth Circuit law permitting plaintiffs to establish continuing violation for acts occurring prior to limitation period where they are sufficiently related to acts occurring within limitations period); Inglis v. Buena Vista Univ., 235 F. Supp. 2d 1009, 1021, 90 FEP 1506 (N.D. Iowa 2002) ("Indeed, prior to *Morgan*, the trend, though clearly not a universal one, was to interpret pay claims as continuing violations of Title VII, regardless of whether the plaintiff challenged a single act of wage discrimination or a discriminatory pay policy.").

[140]*See* Shenkan v. Potter, 2003 WL 21649506 (3d Cir. June 12, 2003) (ADA claim); Sharpe v. Cureton, 319 F.3d 259 (6th Cir. 2003) (§ 1983 claim); Sherman v. Chrysler Corp., 47 Fed. Appx. 716 (6th Cir. 2002) (ADEA claim); Madison v. IBP, Inc., 330 F.3d 1051, 91 FEP 1673 (8th Cir. 2003) (§ 1981 claim); Shields v. Fort James Corp., 305 F.3d 1280, 89 FEP 1646 (11th Cir. 2002) (§ 1981 claim); Lewis v. Norfolk S. Corp., 271 F. Supp. 2d 807 (E.D. Va. 2003) (ADEA claim); Kinley Norfolk S. Ry. Co., 230 F. Supp. 2d 770 (E.D. Ky. 2002) (§ 1981 claim).

[141]*Morgan*, 536 U.S. at 105.

[142]*Id.* at 114.

[143]*Id.* at 111. For the purpose of the Court's analysis, the critical sentence of the charge-filing provision, 42 U.S.C § 2000e-5(e), is: "a charge under this section *shall be filed* within one hundred and eighty days *after the alleged unlawful employment practice occurred.*" *Id.* at 109 (emphasis in original).

retaliatory or discriminatory act "occurred" on the day that it "happened." The Court unanimously rejected the Ninth Circuit's application of the continuing violations doctrine to "serial violations" and held that discrete acts are not actionable if time-barred, even when they are related to acts alleged in timely filed charges.[144] Instead, each discrete discriminatory act starts a new clock for filing charges alleging that act, and a claimant must file a charge of discrimination within the appropriate limitations period as to each such discrete act of discrimination that has occurred.[145] Nonetheless, time-barred charges can be used as background evidence, and the time period for filing a charge remains subject to equitable doctrines, such as tolling or estoppel, although such doctrines are to be applied "sparingly."[146]

By contrast, the *Morgan* Court found that hostile work environment claims are different from discrete acts because their very nature involves repeated conduct. The Court held 5–4 that the continuing violation doctrine applies to such claims where the unlawful employment practice cannot be said to occur on any particular day but can occur over a series of days.[147] The Court further stated:

> Given, therefore, that the incidents constituting a hostile work environment are part of one unlawful employment practice, the employer may be liable for all acts that are part of this single claim. In order for the charge to be timely, the employee need only file a charge within 180 or 300 days of any act that is part of the hostile work environment.[148]

The "act" need not be the last act: "As long as the employer has engaged in enough activity to make out an actionable hostile environment claim, an unlawful employment practice has 'occurred,' even if it is still occurring."[149]

Addressing concerns about hostile environment claims that extend over long periods of time, the *Morgan* Court reiterated that employers continue to have equitable defenses available to them, such as waiver, estoppel, and laches, which allow the Court to "honor

---

[144]*Id.* at 114.
[145]*Id.* at 113.
[146]*Id.*
[147]*Id.* at 115.
[148]*Id.* at 118.
[149]*Id.* at 117.

Title VII's remedial purpose 'without negating the particular purpose of the filing requirement, to give prompt notice to the employer.' "[150]

Yet, with all its clarity, *Morgan* left many important issues unresolved. It did not address claim accrual and application of the discovery rule, having no occasion to resolve that issue.[151] Thus, questions still remain, and the courts continue to grapple with the issue of whether a plaintiff may state a claim for a discriminatory act that falls outside the charge-filing period where the employee was unaware of the basis for the employer's decision.[152] The *Morgan* Court also specifically noted that it was not addressing the timely filing question with respect to "pattern-or-practice" claims brought by private litigants.[153]

b. Discrete Acts. *Morgan* defined a "discrete" act as an act that " 'occurred' on the day that it 'happened' " and constituted its own unlawful employment practice.[154] Since *Morgan*, the courts have been fairly rigorous in refusing to apply the continuing violation doctrine to easily identifiable discrete acts of discrimination that fall outside the 180- or 300-day charge-filing period. Claims involving denials of promotion, transfers, warning letters or poor performance evaluations, and failure to hire have been routinely denied where the event or events that formed the basis for the discrimination claim fell outside the charge-filing period.[155] The

---

[150]*Id.* at 121.

[151]*Id.* at 115 n.7.

[152]*Compare* Davidson v. America Online, Inc., 337 F.3d 1179 (10th Cir. 2003) (holding that notice or knowledge of employer's motivation is not prerequisite for cause of action to accrue) *and* Boyer v. Cordant Techs., Inc., 316 F.3d 1137, 90 FEP 1249 (10th Cir. 2003) (employee could not invoke continuing violations doctrine if employee knew or should have known that she was discriminated against at time of earlier incidents) *with* Tinner v. United Ins. Co. of Am., 308 F.3d 697, 89 FEP 1843 (7th Cir. 2002) (noting that in Seventh Circuit employee must sue upon discrete discriminatory acts if employee knew, or with exercise of reasonable diligence should have known, that each act, once completed, was discriminatory) *and* Campbell v. National R.R. Passenger Corp., 222 F. Supp. 2d 8 (D.D.C. 2002) (finding that to extent plaintiff was unaware of discriminatory nature of his termination, his claim could be equitably tolled).

[153]*Morgan*, 536 U.S. at 115 n.9.

[154]*Id.* at 110.

[155]*See* Williams v. Giant Foods, 370 F.3d 423, 427–28 (4th Cir. 2004) (various discrete actions, including denial of promotion, that occurred prior to limitations period do not constitute a continuing violation); Beamon v. Marshall & Ilsley Trust Co., 411 F.3d 854, 860, 95 FEP 1797 (7th Cir. 2005) (discrete discriminatory employment

Second Circuit has held that denials of requests for religious accommodations also fall within this "easily identifiable" group, because once the employer has rejected the proposed accommodation no periodic implementation of that decision occurs.[156]

Nonetheless, following *Morgan*, time-barred employment actions may be offered as "background" evidence to support timely claims by employees.[157] Conversely, however, timely discrete acts

---

actions such as terminations, failures to promote, denials of transfer, or refusals to hire are deemed to have been taken on the dates they occur, even if they form part of ongoing practice or are connected with other acts); Rivera v. Puerto Rico Aqueduct & Sewers Auth., 331 F.3d 183, 188–89, 92 FEP 1 (1st Cir. 2003) (continuing violation doctrine cannot operate to save alleged discriminatory transfer because transfer was discrete act that occurred more than 300 days prior to filing of charge); Miller v. New Hampshire Dep't of Corr., 296 F.3d 18, 21–22, 89 FEP 481 (1st Cir. 2002) (denying plaintiff's claim that continuing violation doctrine allowed him to include transfer and letter of warning within his claim because those events were connected to alleged retaliatory acts that occurred within limitations period; these were discrete acts upon which employee should have acted promptly); Shenkan v. Potter, 71 Fed. Appx. 893, 895 (3d Cir. 2003) (continuing violation doctrine not applicable where plaintiff, who suffered from bipolar disorder, was really complaining about two discrete failures to hire); Sharpe v. Cureton, 319 F.3d 259, 266–67 (6th Cir. 2003) (court held that plaintiffs' § 1983 claims regarding alleged discriminatory transfers were time-barred because they were discrete acts that fell outside limitations period); Tinner v. United Ins. Co. of Am., 308 F.3d 697, 709, 89 FEP 1843 (7th Cir. 2002) (employee could not "piggy-back" Title VII claims relating to series of discrete discriminatory acts to timely filed wrongful termination claims to form continuing violation); Tademe v. Saint Cloud State Univ., 328 F.3d 982, 988, 91 FEP 1446 (8th Cir. 2003) (claims of racial discrimination in tenure and promotion involved discrete acts and were not rendered timely under continuing violation theory); Lyons v. England, 307 F.3d 1092, 1105, 89 FEP 1793 (9th Cir. 2002) (finding that African-American military veterans' pre-limitation period claims, based on alleged discriminatory assignment of details, were time-barred); EEOC v. Joe's Stone Crabs, Inc., 296 F.3d 1265, 1271–72, 89 FEP 522 (11th Cir. 2002) (continuing violation doctrine did not apply because failures to hire women were discrete, one-time employment events that should have put plaintiffs on notice that cause of action had accrued); Lewis v. Norfolk S. Corp., 271 F. Supp. 2d 807, 813 (E.D. Va. 2003) (plaintiff's claims regarding discriminatory job transfer, denials of promotion, denial of merit-based pay increase, and negative performance evaluation were time-barred as discrete acts); Pegram v. Honeywell, Inc., 2003 WL 282448, at *5 (N.D. Tex. Feb. 5, 2003) (failure to train, failure to allow participation in MBA program, and transfer of accounts to white co-workers are discrete acts that do not trigger continuing violations doctrine), *aff'd*, 361 F.3d 272, 93 FEP 649 (5th Cir. 2004).

[156]Elmenayer v. ABF Freight Sys., Inc., 318 F.3d 130, 134, 90 FEP 1393 (2d Cir. 2003) (employer's rejection of employee's proposed religious accommodation is not continuing violation under Title VII but discrete act for which timeliness is measured from date when proposal is rejected).

[157]*See Lyons*, 307 F.3d at 1111–12 (veterans were permitted to offer evidence of their prelimitations period claims as "background" evidence of their timely failure-to-promote claims).

cannot be used to revive prelimitations discrete acts for purposes of recovering damages, because the former are separate and distinct unlawful employment practices.[158] Discrete acts that are untimely under federal law may also be relevant to claims under state antidiscrimination law pursuant to which courts are not bound by *Morgan*.[159]

   *c. Hostile Work Environment Claims in the Post-*Morgan *Era.* Prior to *Morgan*, the courts engaged a variety of analytical methodologies to determine whether they could consider acts that occurred before the charge-filing period for purposes of determining liability. There was not widespread agreement and much confusion existed, particularly with respect to harassment claims. Fortunately, *Morgan* has simplified the limitations inquiry in hostile work environment cases.[160]

   As *Morgan* explained, a hostile work environment claim is composed of a series of separate acts that collectively constitute one unlawful employment practice.[161] If the plaintiff can establish that at least one act contributing to the claim occurred during the charge-filing period, the entire time period of the hostile environment may be considered by the court for determining liability and for assessing damages other than back pay,[162] including claims for punitive damages.[163] The outcome is thus dependent on the plaintiff's

---

   [158]Mems v. City of St. Paul Dep't of Fire & Safety Servs., 327 F.3d 771, 91 FEP 1176 (8th Cir. 2003) (timely discrete acts of discrimination do not make other discriminatory acts that fall outside the period timely).

   [159]*See* Madison v. IBP, Inc., 330 F.3d 1051, 91 FEP 1673 (8th Cir. 2003) (holding that continuing series of discrete discriminatory acts may constitute continuing violation under Iowa Civil Rights Acts as long as one such act occurred within 180-day charge-filing period). *But cf. Mems*, 327 F.3d at 784 (holding that *Morgan* equally affects vitality of continuing violations doctrine as it applies to Minnesota Human Rights Act); Livey v. Flexible Packaging Ass'n, 92 FEP 809, 818 (D.C. 2003) (applying *Morgan*'s continuing violation analysis to plaintiff's hostile environment claims under District of Columbia Human Rights Act); Caggiano v. Fontoura, 804 A.2d 1193, 89 FEP 838 (N.J. Super. Ct. App. Div. 2002) (adopting *Morgan*'s analysis to plaintiff's hostile environment claims under New Jersey Law Against Discrimination).

   [160]*See* Watson v. Blue Circle, Inc., 324 F.3d 1252, 1258, 91 FEP 609 (11th Cir. 2003) (finding that Supreme Court has simplified limitations inquiry in hostile work environment cases).

   [161]National R.R. Passenger Corp. v. Morgan, 536 U.S. 101, 117 (2002).

   [162]Title VII contains a 2-year cap on back pay, measured from the date the charge of discrimination is filed. *See* 42 U.S.C. § 2000e(5)(g)(1) (2000). *See generally* Chapter 40 (Monetary Relief).

   [163]*Id.*; *see also* Crowley v. L.L. Bean, Inc., 303 F.3d 387, 395, 89 FEP 1656 (1st Cir. 2002) (court considered all evidence offered at trial regarding plaintiff's

ability to connect at least one event during the charge-filing period to the earlier events.[164]

The threshold required to connect the dots is not a substantial one. The Sixth Circuit allowed a sexual harassment claim to proceed under the continuing violations doctrine where the conduct that occurred during the charge-filing period included allegedly permitting a magazine to fall on the plaintiff's hand, refusing the plaintiff the option of working through lunch, and speaking to the plaintiff in a manner likely to cause her to lose esteem in the eyes of co-workers.[165] Generally, in the post-*Morgan* era, courts have expressed a readiness to apply the continuous violation doctrine even where only a small portion of the unlawful harassment occurred within the limitations time period or where the events that occurred during the filing period, although seemingly innocuous, taken one at a time, are related to more serious allegations of harassment lying outside the filing period.[166]

---

harassment claim from fall 1996 through July 1998 to determine whether it supported jury's verdict that company maintained hostile work environment).

[164]*See Madison*, 330 F.3d at 1061 n.6 (an individual act occurring outside the filing period is not time-barred if plaintiff shows evidence connecting the act to a series of acts that make up a hostile work environment); *Crowley*, 303 F.3d at 395 (if plaintiff can show that an act contributing to the claim occurred within the filing period, the entire time period of the hostile work environment may be considered by the court).

[165]McFarland v. Henderson, 307 F.3d 402, 408, 90 FEP 23 (6th Cir. 2002).

[166]*See* Porter v. California Dep't of Corr., 419 F.3d 885 (9th Cir. 2005) (supervisor's decision to deny employee transfer during 300 days prior to filing of charge may constitute tangible employment action that is part of harassment); West v. Ortho-McNeil Pharm. Corp., 405 F.3d 578, 95 FEP 961 (7th Cir. 2005) (timely acts of harassment could be combined with racial slurs uttered more than 300 days before filing of charge); Petrosino v. Bell Atl., 385 F.3d 210, 94 FEP 903 (2d Cir. 2004) (record established 9-year campaign of grabbing, disparaging remarks about plaintiff's body, graffiti, and sexist comments by supervisors; charge was timely because at least some events occurred within 300 days before charge was filed); Rowe v. Hussman Corp., 382 F.3d 775 (8th Cir. 2004) (plaintiff's claims are not time-barred in spite of a 7-month gap in harassing acts because the acts before and after the limitations period were similar in nature, frequency, and severity); Singletary v. District of Columbia, 351 F.3d 519, 92 FEP 1799 (D.C. Cir. 2003) (race harassment; chain of harassing events included employee being denied reviews and job description, assigned to poorly lit storage room, and denied promotions); Marrero v. Goya of P.R., 304 F.3d 7, 89 FEP 1361 (1st Cir. 2002) (single timely incident in which supervisor gave penetrating look with lust toward employee and made comments employee interpreted as sexually suggestive was sufficient to trigger continuing violations doctrine); *Crowley*, 303 F.3d at 396–400 (eight innocuous events that occurred during filing period were related to longstanding pattern of hostile and intimidating behavior that spanned over 1½ years); Jensen v. Henderson, 315 F.3d

One court has suggested that the employer's failure to act in response to allegations of harassment in and of itself may be sufficient to sustain a finding of a continuing violation where the inaction has continued up to the time of the charge filing.[167] Conversely, where an employer intervenes and causes the harassing conduct to cease, such conduct is disassociated from the remainder of the plaintiff's allegations and is no longer part of the plaintiff's hostile work environment claim and cannot be used to establish a continuing violation.[168] Similarly, where the complainant brings untimely supervisor harassment claims together with hostile environment claims that are not of the same kind or character, the latter cannot be used to save the former.[169] A lapse in time between the untimely and timely events that allegedly frame the hostile work environment may also result in a court's refusal to apply the continuing violations doctrine.[170]

854, 859, 90 FEP 898 (8th Cir. 2002) ("[o]nly the smallest portion of that 'practice' needs to occur within the limitations period to be timely") (citing Shields v. Fort James Corp., 305 F.3d 1280, 1282, 89 FEP 1280 (11th Cir. 2002) ("Put simply, if the smallest portion of that 'practice' occurred within the limitations time period, then the court should consider it as a whole")); Watson v. Blue Circle, Inc., 324 F.3d 1252, 91 FEP 609 (11th Cir. 2003) (where employer conceded that six incidents of harassment occurred within filing period, entire period of harassment may be considered for purposes of determining liability); Shields v. Fort James Corp., 305 F.3d 1280, 89 FEP 1646 (11th Cir. 2002) (claims by African-American plaintiffs that they were subject to hostile environment from 1981 through filing of their suit in 1999 remanded for consideration of whether, in their entirety, they present any issue as to any material fact); Khoury v. Meserve, 268 F. Supp. 2d 600, 92 FEP 384 (D. Md. 2003) (series of acts could be characterized as part of ongoing pattern of disrespect, abuse, and harassment that extended into federal employee's 45-day limitations period to file complaint with EEO counselor).

[167]Jensen v. Henderson, 315 F.3d 854, 90 FEP 898 (8th Cir. 2002) (finding that summary judgment was inappropriate based on timeliness where one of matters alleged to be discriminatory was employer's failure to act on allegations of discrimination during charge-filing period).

[168]See Watson v. Blue Circle, Inc., 324 F.3d 1252, 91 FEP 609 (11th Cir. 2003) (holding that intervening action by employer preventing further harassment by coworker rendered prior conduct no longer part of plaintiff's hostile environment claim).

[169]See Singleton v. Chicago Sch. Reform Bd. of Trs., 2002 WL 2017082 (N.D. Ill. Sept. 3, 2002) (holding that continuing violation doctrine could not be used to link claims that school board engaged in nonsexual harassment during charge-filing period with untimely charge that employee's supervisor sexually harassed her).

[170]See Serrano-Nova v. Banco Popular de P.R., Inc., 254 F. Supp. 2d 251 (D.P.R. 2003) (6-month gap between alleged employment discrimination and employee's resignation was too great a time period to find that employee had been constructively discharged in violation of Title VII, and thus employee could not use discharge as anchor for acts that fell outside charge-filing period).

d. Claims for Salary and Pay Discrimination. A consensus does not exist among the lower courts on whether the continuing violation doctrine can be used in cases involving allegations of salary or pay discrimination.[171] In *Bazemore v. Friday*,[172] the Supreme Court held that pay discrimination was a continually recurring series of violations. Thus, each paycheck delivered under a discriminatory pay system was a violation of Title VII.[173] Based on *Bazemore*, some courts held that each successive pay period was a continuing violation of an ongoing practice that began prior to the statute of limitations period.[174]

The *Morgan* Court did not discuss how its holding impacted *Bazemore*. As a result, *Morgan*'s distinction between discrete discriminatory acts and hostile environment claims has complicated the analysis for pay discrimination claims. Some courts, relying on the *Bazemore* decision and pre-*Morgan* precedent, take the position that the continuing violation doctrine applies because pay discrimination is a continually recurring series of violations.[175] Other courts have reached the opposite conclusion, treating each salary decision paycheck as a discrete allegedly discriminatory act that

---

[171]*See* Reese v. Ice Cream Specialties, Inc., 347 F.3d 1007, 92 FEP 1460 (7th Cir. 2003) (noting current state of affairs to be confusing).

[172]478 U.S. 385, 41 FEP 92 (1986).

[173]*Id.* at 395.

[174]*See, e.g.*, Goodwin v. General Motors Corp., 275 F.3d 1005, 87 FEP 1651 (10th Cir. 2002) (holding that plaintiff could bring claim even though discriminatory pay decision was made prior to 300-day filing period because each paycheck was actionable act), *cert. denied*, 537 U.S. 941, 89 FEP 1692 (2002); Miller v. Beneficial Mgmt. Corp., 977 F.2d 834 (3d Cir. 1992) (noting that most courts treat pay discrimination claims as continuing violations).

[175]*See* Hildebrandt v. Illinois Dep't of Natural Res., 347 F.3d 1014, 1028–29, 92 FEP 1441 (7th Cir. 2003) (employee may timely seek damages on paychecks issued within 300 days of charge filing); Reese v. Ice Cream Specialties, Inc., 347 F.3d 1007, 1011, 92 FEP 1460 (7th Cir. 2003) (discriminatory failure to raise hourly wage constitutes continuing violation; each paycheck is a new act of discrimination for limitations purposes); Tademe v. Saint Cloud State Univ., 328 F.3d 982, 988, 91 FEP 1446 (8th Cir. 2003) (even though initial salary determination was made years before filing of EEOC charge, court applied continuing violations doctrine because charge was filed within 300 days of receiving allegedly discriminatory paychecks); Rathbun v. Autozone, Inc., 253 F. Supp. 2d 226, 231, 91 FEP 852 (D.R.I. 2003) (holding that unequal pay claims were subject to application of continuing violations doctrine); EEOC v. Oilgear Co., 250 F. Supp. 2d 1193, 1196, 91 FEP 963 (D. Neb. 2003) (court held that allegedly unlawful promotion was discrete act that was time-barred but that discrimination claim was timely under continuing violations doctrine); Tomita v. University of Kan. Med. Ctr., 227 F. Supp. 2d 1171, 1180 (D. Kan. 2002) (discussing *Morgan* but nonetheless holding that pay discrimination claims constituted "continually recurring series of violations" that were each actionable under Title VII).

must be acted on within the charge-filing period.[176] One court has noted that the difference may lie in the fact that *Bazemore* was a pattern-or-practice case, and the *Morgan* Court was careful to point out that difference in its opinion.[177] The outcome may also turn on whether the discriminatory pay structure was still in place during the charge-filing period or was merely a lingering effect of past discrimination.[178] One court has taken a middle ground, holding that although the continuing violation doctrine does not apply, a plaintiff may still file a claim for the present effects of a single past discriminatory pay decision for all paychecks received during the 300-day period prior to filing the charge.[179]

---

[176]*See* Ledbetter v. Goodyear Tire & Rubber Co., 421 F.3d 1169, 1189, 98 FEP 418 (11th Cir. 2005) (where salary is reviewed annually, employee may reach back "no further than the last such decision immediately preceding the start of the limitations period"; such decisions are discrete acts), *cert. granted*, 127 S. Ct. 2965 (2006); Shea v. Rice, 409 F.3d 448, 451, 95 FEP 1555 (D.C. Cir. 2005) (each paycheck that employee received was a discrete discriminatory act; continuing violation doctrine was not applicable); White v. BFI Waste Servs., 375 F.3d 288, 293, 94 FEP 73 (4th Cir. 2004) (salary discrimination claims must be acted on within limitations period); City of Hialeah v. Rojas, 311 F.3d 1096, 90 FEP 467 (11th Cir. 2002) (continuing violations doctrine could not save plaintiffs' claim that they were denied equal longevity pay and retirement compensation as result of city's policy of classifying Hispanic employees as temporary workers longer than white workers); Verdecchia v. Prozan, Inc., 274 F. Supp. 2d 712, 724–25, 14 AD 1447 (W.D. Pa. 2003) (finding that failure to pay plaintiff while on leave is discrete discriminatory act and not ongoing violation); Maki v. Allete, Inc., 2003 WL 21980481, *3 (D. Minn. Aug. 18, 2003) (plaintiffs' claims regarding unequal pension benefits were time-barred where they were based on company policy of automatic termination of women who became pregnant or married that had long since been abolished); Clissuras v. Teachers' Ret. Sys. of N.Y., 2003 WL 1701992, at *4 (S.D.N.Y., Mar. 28, 2003) (continuing violations doctrine did not save plaintiffs' § 1983 claims where they received their first retirement checks in 1983 and 1986 but did not file their discriminatory pay claims until 2002); Inglis v. Buena Vista Univ., 235 F. Supp. 2d 1009, 1024, 90 FEP 1506 (W.D. Iowa 2002) (court refused to apply continuing violations doctrine to untimely pay discrimination claims based on *Bazemore* and *Morgan*).

[177]*Inglis*, 235 F. Supp. 2d at 1024 ("The *Morgan* Court was careful to point out that *Bazemore* was a pattern-or-practice case challenging a discriminatory pay structure in place prior to and following the implementation of Title VII" and noted that had plaintiffs brought suit to challenge defendant's compensation system within 300 days of its discontinuance, their claims would have been timely.).

[178]*Id.*; *see also* Peters v. City of Stamford, 2003 WL 1343265, at *4 (D. Conn. Mar. 17, 2003) (each paycheck plaintiff received within 300-day charge-filing period was actionable where discriminatory pay structure established prior to charge-filing period continued on into charge-filing period).

[179]Reese v. Ice Cream Specialties, Inc., 347 F.3d 1007, 1013, 92 FEP 1460 (7th Cir. 2003); *see also* Hildebrandt v. Illinois Dep't of Natural Res., 347 F.3d 1014, 1028–29, 92 FEP 1441 (7th Cir. 2003) (plaintiffs' claim covering all paychecks received during 300-day period that allegedly were tainted by earlier discrimination is timely).

4. The Present Effects of Past Discrimination

The "present effects of past discrimination" theory of continuing violation suffered a severe if not fatal blow in *United Airlines, Inc. v. Evans*.[180] The courts have viewed *Morgan* as reinforcing the principle established by *Evans*.[181] In *Evans*, the majority opinion, by focusing on "whether any present *violation* exists,"[182] appeared to foreclose claims based solely on the residual effects of discriminatory conduct not made the subject of a timely charge. Lower courts subsequently applied *Evans* to find no current violation in many contexts.[183] As discussed earlier, however, where past discriminatory acts are given new life by present policies, in some circumstances a valid continuing violation claim may be found.

---

[180]431 U.S. 553, 14 FEP 1510 (1977). For additional discussion of *Evans*, see Section II.B.2 *supra*.

[181]*See* City of Hialeah v. Rojas, 311 F.3d 1096, 1101–02, 90 FEP 467 (11th Cir. 2002) (holding that because time-barred discrete discriminatory conduct has no legal significance, neutral policies that give present effect to time-barred conduct do not create continuing violation); Inglis v. Buena Vista Univ., 235 F. Supp. 2d 1009, 1028, 90 FEP 1506 (N.D. Iowa 2002) (holding that *Morgan* Court's rejection of Ninth Circuit's "serial violation" interpretation precluded plaintiff from taking position that lingering effects of past discrimination can be challenged based on continuing violation).

[182]431 U.S. at 558.

[183]*See Rojas*, 311 F.3d 1096, 1101–02 (neutral policies that give present effect to time-barred conduct do not create continuing violation); Knox v. Davis, 260 F.3d 1009, 1013 (9th Cir. 2001) (continued affirmation by correctional facility of its prior decision to withdraw attorney's mail and visitation privileges with inmates at facility were merely continuing effect of original suspension and did not give rise to continuing violation); Fowler v. Birmingham News Co., 608 F.2d 1055, 1057, 21 FEP 833 (5th Cir. 1979) (discriminatory relative placement on seniority list at time of hire did not constitute claim of current discriminatory employment practices); Daughtry v. King's Dep't Stores, Inc., 608 F.2d 906, 909, 21 FEP 333 (1st Cir. 1979) (per curiam) (rejecting argument that, because plaintiff was laid off rather than fired, possibility of rehire existed, and therefore company's failure to rehire constituted continuing violation); Goldman v. Sears, Roebuck & Co., 607 F.2d 1014, 1018, 21 FEP 96 (1st Cir. 1979) (denial of requests to be retransferred back to original department after allegedly discriminatory initial transfer did not constitute continuing violation); Dobbs v. City of Atlanta, 606 F.2d 557, 559, 21 FEP 827 (5th Cir. 1979) (no present violation in allegation that African-American former employees receive lower pensions because of initial discriminatory placement during employment—provisions depend on function, not race); Trabucco v. Delta Airlines, 590 F.2d 315, 316, 19 FEP 177 (6th Cir. 1979) (lower pay after alleged discriminatory reclassification; no present violation); Masco v. United Air Lines, Inc., 574 F.2d 1127, 1130, 17 FEP 634 (3d Cir. 1978) (failure to reinstate after time-barred separation preceding maternity leave did not constitute present violation); Farris v. Board of Educ., 576 F.2d 765, 767, 17 FEP 859 (8th Cir. 1978) (present impact on salaries caused by loss of incremental raises during mandatory maternity leave did not constitute present violation); Martin v. Georgia-Pacific Corp., 568 F.2d 58, 62, 16 FEP 303 (8th Cir. 1977) (that two white employees had been given allegedly discriminatory seniority preference did not enable continuously

C. Tolling of the Charge-Filing Period

1. A Jurisdictional Prerequisite, or a Statute of Limitations That May Be Tolled for Equitable Reasons?

In 1982, in *Zipes v. Trans World Airlines, Inc.*,[184] the Supreme Court resolved an ongoing debate by holding that the failure to file a timely charge with the EEOC is not an absolute jurisdictional prerequisite to suit that would deprive the courts of subject matter jurisdiction, but rather a requirement that, like a statute of limitations, "is subject to waiver, estoppel, and equitable tolling."[185] The Court reaffirmed this holding in *Morgan*[186] but cautioned that "such doctrines . . . are to be applied sparingly."[187] As discussed earlier, the Court further ruled that the "continuing violations" theory could not be invoked to preserve discrete acts of discrimination that were time-barred.[188] Most courts conclude that a complete failure to file a charge with the EEOC remains jurisdictional, depriving the courts of subject matter jurisdiction, and is not subject to waiver, estoppel, or tolling.[189] The party who invokes equitable tolling bears the burden of demonstrating that it applies in his or her case.[190] Whatever the claimed basis for tolling or estoppel, the claim is substantially weakened or lost if the plaintiff was represented by counsel when the events underlying the asserted tolling or estoppel occurred.[191] The failure to raise the defense of an untimely charge in the district court waives the issue on appeal.[192]

---

employed plaintiff to bring suit 3 years later; refusing to distinguish *Evans* on basis of break in service); Cates v. Trans World Airlines, Inc., 561 F.2d 1064, 1070, 15 FEP 329 (2d Cir. 1977) (maintenance of date-of-hire seniority system determining layoffs did not constitute continuing violation of allegedly discriminatory refusal to hire).

[184]455 U.S. 385, 28 FEP 1 (1982).

[185]*Id.* at 393, 398.

[186]National R.R. Passenger Corp. v. Morgan, 536 U.S. 101 (2002).

[187]*Id.* at 121.

[188]*Id.* at 113.

[189]*See, e.g.*, Weigel v. Baptist Home of E. Tenn., 302 F.3d 367, 379 (6th Cir. 2002); Doan v. NSK Corp., 266 F. Supp. 629 (E.D. Mich. 2003) (citing Strauss v. Michigan Dep't of Corr., 250 F.3d 336, 342 (6th Cir. 2001)). *But see* Santa Maria v. Pacific Bell Tel., 202 F.3d 1170, 1176, 10 AD 245 (9th Cir. 2000).

[190]Ramirez v. City of San Antonio, 312 F.3d 178, 183 (5th Cir. 2002).

[191]*See, e.g.*, Leorna v. United States Dep't of State, 105 F.3d 548, 551 (9th Cir. 1997) (being represented by counsel gives plaintiff constructive notice of law's requirements); Jackson v. Richards Med. Co., 961 F.2d 575, 579 (6th Cir. 1992) (constructive knowledge attributed to individual represented by counsel).

[192]*E.g.*, Girard v. Rubin, 62 F.3d 1244, 68 FEP 1002 (9th Cir. 1995); Williams v. Meese, 926 F.2d 994, 996 n.1, 55 FEP 390 (10th Cir. 1991); Weaver v. Casa

2. *The Effect of Equitable Tolling or Estoppel*

Estoppel and tolling suspend the running of a statute of limitations for equitable reasons. For example, if the statute of limitations for filing a charge with the EEOC is 180 days and the statute is tolled from its inception, the charging party arguably would have 180 days after the expiration of the tolling period to file a charge. If the event starting the running of the tolling period occurred 120 days from the date of the discrimination, the charging party arguably would have the remaining 60 days from the end of the tolling period within which to file a charge. However, some cases reject a rule based on arithmetic computations, indicating instead that the court will take into consideration whether the plaintiff acted with due diligence before granting equitable modifications of the limitations periods.[193]

3. *Tolling Because of Resort to Another Forum*

The tolling doctrine was originally invoked in Title VII cases when an individual made two attempts to redress the same injury, first in one forum and then in another. The Supreme Court rejected this use of the tolling doctrine. In *Johnson v. Railway Express Agency, Inc.*,[194] the Court held that the filing of a Title VII charge with the EEOC does not toll the limitations period in a § 1981 action.[195] Subsequently, in *Electrical Workers (IUE) Local 790 v. Robbins & Myers, Inc.*,[196] the Court ruled that the utilization of grievance procedures does not toll the running of the limitations period,[197] stating that Congress defined the statutory period " 'with precision' "[198] and "did not leave to courts the decision as to which delays might or might not be 'slight.' "[199]

Gallardo, Inc., 922 F.2d 1515, 1521–22, 55 FEP 27 (11th Cir. 1991); Hernandez v. Hill Country Tel. Coop., Inc., 849 F.2d 139, 142, 47 FEP 318 (5th Cir. 1988).

[193]*See, e.g.*, Dodds v. Cigna Secs., Inc., 12 F.3d 346, 350 (2d Cir. 1993) (equitable tolling will stay running of statute only so long as plaintiff exercises reasonable care and diligence); Cada v. Baxter Healthcare Corp., 920 F.2d 446, 452–53, 54 FEP 961 (7th Cir. 1990) (equitable tolling does not necessarily bring about automatic extension of statute of limitations equal to length of tolling period; plaintiff must act within reasonable time after obtaining necessary information).

[194]421 U.S. 454, 10 FEP 817 (1975).

[195]*Id.* at 465–67.

[196]429 U.S. 229, 13 FEP 1813 (1976).

[197]*Id.* at 236–40.

[198]*Id.* at 240 (quoting Alexander v. Gardner-Denver Co., 415 U.S. 36, 47, 7 FEP 81 (1974)).

[199]429 U.S. at 240.

Courts have held that resort to various independent remedies does not toll the charge-filing period for Title VII, ADA, and ADEA claims.[200] This has included such remedies as those provided in or by state administrative proceedings,[201] the National Railroad Adjustment Board,[202] the U.S. Department of Transportation,[203] and the U.S. Department of Labor.[204] It should be noted, however, that a charge filed with the Office of Federal Contract Compliance Programs at the Department of Labor may be deemed filed with the EEOC.[205] Tolling does not apply during utilization of an informal "open door" policy,[206] a formal internal grievance procedure,[207] or a union grievance under a collective bargaining agreement.[208]

---

[200]*See, e.g.,* Santa Maria v. Pacific Bell, 202 F.3d 1170, 1176–79 (9th Cir. 2000) (equitable estoppel is unwarranted where ADA plaintiff had combined allegation of failure to accommodate with attempt to fraudulently conceal that wrong); American Airlines, Inc. v. Cardoza-Rodriguez, 133 F.3d 111, 124, 75 FEP 1217 (1st Cir. 1998) (refusing to apply equitable tolling where employees had actual knowledge of their ADEA rights); Currier v. Radio Free Europe/Radio Liberty, 159 F.3d 1363, 1367–68, 78 FEP 513 (D.C. Cir. 1998) (fact issue existed as to whether employer's affirmatively misleading statements that grievance will be resolved in employee's favor established equitable estoppel).

[201]*E.g.,* Dyer v. Jefferson Parish, 619 F. Supp. 284, 286–87, 38 FEP 698 (E.D. La. 1985) (no tolling during period plaintiff appealed termination to county personnel board); Daughtry v. King's Dep't Stores, Inc., 608 F.2d 906, 907–09, 21 FEP 333 (1st Cir. 1979) (per curiam) (late filing of racial claim with EEOC is not excused by 6-year delay by state agency).

[202]*E.g.,* Harris v. Norfolk & W. Ry. Co., 616 F.2d 377, 379–80, 22 FEP 472 (8th Cir. 1980) (filing with NRAB does not toll 180-day period for filing with EEOC).

[203]*E.g.,* Ryan v. New York State Thruway Auth., 889 F. Supp. 70, 78–79, 73 FEP 1525 (N.D.N.Y. 1995) (filing with federal agency other than Department of Labor's OFCCP does not constitute filing with EEOC and cannot toll limitations period).

[204]*E.g.,* Bledsoe v. Pilot Life Ins. Co., 473 F. Supp. 864, 866–67, 20 FEP 633 (M.D.N.C. 1978) (filing charge with Department of Labor (not OFCCP) does not toll EEOC charge-filing period), *aff'd per curiam,* 602 F.2d 652 (4th Cir. 1979).

[205]*See, e.g.,* Reynolds Metals Co. v. Rumsfeld, 564 F.2d 663, 667–70, 15 FEP 1185 (4th Cir. 1977) (upholding validity of EEOC-OFCCP agreement providing that charges filed with OFCCP are "deemed" filed with EEOC); Meckes v. Reynolds Metals Co., 604 F. Supp. 598, 600–04, 37 FEP 1269 (N.D. Ala.) (notwithstanding joint filing agreement between agencies, ADEA charge filed with OFCCP, which lacks jurisdiction over age discrimination matters, does not constitute proper filing with EEOC), *aff'd mem.,* 776 F.2d 1055 (11th Cir. 1985).

[206]*E.g.,* Vaught v. R.R. Donnelley & Sons Co., 745 F.2d 407, 412, 35 FEP 1820 (7th Cir. 1984) (resort to informal grievance procedure does not stop running of limitations period).

[207]*E.g.,* Delaware State Coll. v. Ricks, 449 U.S. 250, 260–61, 24 FEP 827 (1980) (discussed in Section II.B.1 *supra*) (college's internal tenure-review grievance procedure did not effect tolling).

[208]*E.g.,* Frank v. New York State Elec. & Gas, 871 F. Supp. 167, 172, 69 FEP 711 (W.D.N.Y. 1994); Yoonessi v. State Univ. of N.Y., 862 F. Supp. 1005, 1014

And, in a case labeled one of first impression, a district court has held that filing a claim under the Family and Medical Leave Act does not toll the time to file an EEOC charge for ADA violations based on the same facts.[209]

Courts do, however, permit tolling when the individual has mistakenly gone to the wrong forum.[210]

4. Other Grounds for Estoppel and Tolling

Although the courts have not always been clear on the distinction, most decisions have labeled as equitable estoppel situations where the employee has failed to file a timely charge because the employer's actions mislead the employee or concealed facts the employee needed to assert his or her rights, and have labeled as equitable tolling situations where the individual failed to act or lacked information necessary to act, but not as a result of employer misconduct. Although some differences occur, courts generally recognize the following situations as ones in which such relief from a lapsed limitations period is appropriate: employer misconduct or some other extraordinary circumstance causing a plaintiff, despite due diligence, not to file a timely charge; lack of mental capacity by the plaintiff; governmental conduct that in some way contributes to the plaintiff's failure to file a timely charge; and a mistaken filing by the plaintiff in the wrong forum.

a. Employer Misconduct. The First Circuit, taking a " 'narrow view' of equitable exceptions," allows tolling only where the employer actively misled the employee.[211] It is joined by the

---

(W.D.N.Y. 1994) ("In instituting an action under Title VII, the employee is not seeking review of the arbitrator's decision. Rather, he is asserting a statutory right independent of the arbitration process.").

[209]Peter v. Lincoln Technical Inst., 255 F. Supp. 2d 417, 428–29 (E.D. Pa. 2002) (filing Family and Medical Leave Act claim with Department of Labor does not toll charge-filing requirements for ADA claim where statutes had different remedies).

[210]*See* Section II.C.4.d *infra.*

[211]Thomas v. Eastman Kodak Co., 183 F.3d 38, 53, 80 FEP 537 (1st Cir. 1999) ("noting that the First Circuit's 'narrow view' of equitable tolling reaches only 'active deception' "); *see also* Mercado v. Ritz-Carlton San Juan Hotel, Spa & Casino, 410 F.3d 41, 46–47, 95 FEP 1464 (1st Cir. 2005) (employer's violation of an EEOC posting requirement may provide a basis for extending the filing period where the employee had no other actual or constructive knowledge of the complaint procedure); American Airlines, Inc. v. Cardoza-Rodriguez, 133 F.3d 111, 124, 75 FEP

Seventh[212] and District of Columbia[213] Circuits, both of which articulate a narrow view of equitable exceptions to the limitations period, requiring the employer to have actively misled the employee. The Second, Third, and Sixth Circuits also condition the availability of equitable estoppel on whether the defendant actively misled the plaintiff.[214]

1217 (1st Cir. 1998); Ramos v. Roman, 83 F. Supp. 2d 233, 243 (D.P.R. 2000); Lawton v. State Mut. Life Assurance Co. of Am., 924 F. Supp. 331, 339, 75 FEP 783 (D. Mass. 1996) ("To qualify for an exception, a complaining party must allege and prove, not only that she had no reason to be aware of the employer's improper motivation when the alleged violation occurred, but also that the employer actively misled her and that she relied on that misconduct to her detriment."), *aff'd*, 101 F.3d 218, 75 FEP 767 (1st Cir. 1996).

[212]*See* Williamson v. Indiana Univ., 345 F.3d 459, 463, 92 FEP 1057 (7th Cir. 2003) (history professor could not assert equitable estoppel absent showing that employer took affirmative steps to prevent her from filing claim); Shanoff v. Illinois Dep't of Human Servs., 258 F.3d 696, 702, 86 FEP 490 (7th Cir. 2001) (threats of retaliation, even physical harm, insufficient to extend equitable estoppel doctrine); Sharp v. United Airlines, Inc., 236 F.3d 368, 372, 84 FEP 1173 (7th Cir. 2001); Jackson v. Rockford Hous. Auth., 213 F.3d 389, 394, 83 FEP 149 (7th Cir. 2000); Speer v. Rand McNally & Co., 123 F.3d 658, 663, 74 FEP 1797 (7th Cir. 1997) (equitable estoppel applies when "the defendant takes active steps to prevent the plaintiff from suing in time, . . . such as by hiding evidence or promising not to plead the statute of limitations").

[213]*See* Washington v. Washington Metro. Area Transit Auth., 160 F.3d 750, 752–53, 78 FEP 639 (D.C. Cir. 1998) ("equitable principles favor tolling where, for example, a defendant engaged in 'affirmative misconduct,' or 'misled [a plaintiff] about the running of a limitations period' "); Currier v. Radio Free Europe/Radio Liberty, Inc., 159 F.3d 1363, 1367, 78 FEP 513 (D.C. Cir. 1998) (equitable estoppel in limitations context prevents defendant from asserting untimeliness where defendant has taken active steps to prevent plaintiff from litigating in time).

[214]*See* Amini v. Oberlin Coll., 259 F.3d 493, 498, 86 FEP 625 (6th Cir. 2001) (tolling not warranted where no allegations of misrepresentation or other wrongdoing); Oshiver v. Levin, Fishbein, Sedran & Berman, 38 F.3d 1380, 1387, 66 FEP 429 (3d Cir. 1994) (equitable tolling may be appropriate where defendant has actively misled plaintiff regarding plaintiff's cause of action, where plaintiff in some extraordinary way has been prevented from asserting his or her rights, or where plaintiff has timely asserted his or her rights mistakenly in wrong forum); Smith v. American President Lines, Ltd., 571 F.2d 102, 109, 16 FEP 712 (2d Cir. 1978) (expressing essentially same standard used by Third Circuit in *Schafer v. Board of Public Education*, 903 F.2d 243, 52 FEP 1492 (3d Cir. 1990); basing standards on statements made by Supreme Court in *Electrical Workers (IUE) Local 790 v. Robbins & Myers, Inc.*, 429 U.S. 229, 13 FEP 1813 (1976)). The Third Circuit has held that because the timeliness of exhaustion of administrative remedies is subject to waiver, estoppel, and tolling, a motion to dismiss a Title VII claim for failure to file a timely EEOC charge should be treated under Rule 12(b)(6) as a motion to dismiss for failure to state a claim rather than under Rule 12(b)(1) as a motion to dismiss for lack of jurisdiction. Robinson v. Dalton, 107 F.3d 1018, 1022, 73 FEP 387 (3d Cir. 1997).

The Fourth, Fifth, Eighth, and Ninth Circuits apply a somewhat broader test. In the Fifth Circuit, equitable estoppel is appropriate where the individual is actively misled by the defendants.[215] In addition, however, it has also held that equitable estoppel does not require intentional employer misconduct, but also can be warranted where the defendant's conduct, innocent or not, reasonably induced the plaintiff not to file within the limitation period.[216] In both equitable estoppel and equitable tolling, the Fifth Circuit requires some affirmative act by either the employer or the EEOC to mislead the party who fails to file a timely charge.[217] The Eighth Circuit also applies equitable estoppel to toll the limitations period where the employer has engaged in affirmative conduct that was deliberately designed to mislead or conduct the employer unmistakably should have understood was likely to mislead a plaintiff.[218] It applies equitable tolling where the plaintiff, despite due

---

[215]See Manning v. Chevron Chem. Co., 332 F.3d 874, 880 (5th Cir. 2003) (plaintiff's delay was not because of employer's affirmative acts but plaintiff's erroneous belief that his claims were already before court).

[216]See Tyler v. Union Oil Co., 304 F.3d 379, 385 (5th Cir. 2002) (employer should have "unmistakably understood" that its acts in giving plaintiff defective release would have delayed filing claim); Christopher v. Mobil Oil Corp., 950 F.2d 1209, 1215 (5th Cir. 1992) (plaintiff's lack of awareness of rights must be caused by employer misconduct, either deliberate or because of acts employer should "unmistakably" know would cause employee to delay).

[217]See Ramirez v. City of San Antonio, 312 F.3d 178, 184, 13 AD 1454 (5th Cir. 2002) (court will equitably toll a limitations period only when the employer's acts mislead the employee).

[218]See Garfield v. J.C. Nichols Real Estate, 57 F.3d 662, 666, 68 FEP 188 (8th Cir. 1995) (no tolling on equitable estoppel grounds unless failure to file is because of deliberate design by employer or to actions that employer should unmistakably have understood would cause employee to delay filing charge); Dunham v. O'Fallon, 945 F. Supp. 1256, 1261, 72 FEP 1878 (E.D. Mo. 1996) ("the equitable estoppel doctrine will not toll a statute of limitations unless an employee's failure to file in a timely manner is the result either of a deliberate design by the employer or of actions that the employer should have understood would cause the employee to delay filing the charge"), aff'd, 124 F.3d 207 (8th Cir. 1997). Despite the stringent language, however, the Eighth Circuit has applied this test somewhat loosely. See also Lawrence v. Cooper Cmtys., Inc., 132 F.3d 447, 451–52, 75 FEP 1661 (8th Cir. 1998) (employee presented sufficient evidence to equitably toll limitations period where, "based on the EEOC's instructions and its interpretation of the charge filing procedures, [she] reasonably believed that she had taken all of the required steps to activate the Title VII statutory machinery"; holding that "an affirmative misrepresentation is not a requisite to applying equitable tolling because 'ambiguous and misleading language' could also 'lead a reasonable person to believe' that the steps that were taken would activate the Title VII process").

diligence, is unable to obtain vital information bearing on the existence of the claim.[219] The Fourth Circuit appears to follow the Eighth Circuit test.[220] The Ninth Circuit also will apply equitable estoppel to permit the late filing of a charge where there is evidence that the employer had actual or constructive knowledge of the deceptive nature of its conduct.[221] Although earlier cases suggest that the Tenth Circuit followed only the "active deception" rule,[222] a recent case suggests that the Tenth Circuit may now also consider whether the employer unmistakably should have known that its actions would mislead the employee into delay.[223]

b. *Plaintiff's Lack of Due Diligence.* Courts have recognized that equitable tolling is applicable to excuse a claimant's failure to comply with the time limitations where he or she had neither actual nor constructive notice of the filing period.[224] A plaintiff must have acted with reasonable diligence when seeking to toll the charge-filing period to persuade a court to find that there was excusable delay. An individual who complains to her employer over a four-year period but never files a charge has not acted with reasonable

---

[219]Dorsey v. Pinnacle Automation Co., 278 F.3d 830, 836, 87 FEP 1675 (8th Cir. 2002) (reasonable person would have inquired about status of promotions).

[220]*See* Williams v. Giant Food, Inc., 370 F.3d 423, 430 n.4 (4th Cir. 2004) ("we conclude that tolling is not appropriate here, because Williams did not allege that Giant Food deceived or misled her about its promotion selections 'in order to conceal the existence of a cause of action.' ") (citation omitted); English v. Pabst Brewing Co., 828 F.2d 1047, 1049, 44 FEP 1385 (4th Cir. 1987) (no tolling on equitable estoppel grounds unless failure to file is because of employer's deliberate design or actions that employer unmistakably should have understood would cause delay in filing).

[221]Johnson v. Henderson, 314 F.3d 409, 414 (9th Cir. 2002) (dicta) (citing Santa Maria v. Pacific Bell, 202 F.3d 1170 (9th Cir. 2000)).

[222]*See* Bennett v. Coors Brewing Co., 189 F.3d 1221, 1236, 80 FEP 1197 (10th Cir. 1999) (plaintiffs presented genuine issue of material fact requiring remand to determine whether employer's alleged lie to employees about reasons their department was reorganized constituted active deception); Mascheroni v. Board of Regents, 28 F.3d 1554, 1562–63, 65 FEP 632 (10th Cir. 1994) (finding no equitable tolling because plaintiff did not allege active deception by employer, just business reasons and corporate culture that discouraged him from suing).

[223]Bennett v. Quark, Inc., 258 F.3d 1220 (10th Cir. 2001) (equitable estoppel appropriate only where employers actively misled plaintiff or should unmistakably have understood that acts would cause plaintiff to delay filing claim).

[224]*See* Johnson v. Henderson, 314 F.3d 409, 414, 90 FEP 829 (9th Cir. 2002) (doctrine of equitable tolling focuses on whether there was excusable delay by plaintiff); Leonora v. United States Dep't of State, 105 F.3d 548, 551, 6 AD 504 (9th Cir. 1997) (period tolled until plaintiff obtained counsel).

diligence.[225] In contrast, courts have been willing to toll the limitations period when the delay is short.[226] Courts have been reluctant to grant tolling where an employee heard rumors about being passed over for promotion but failed to take action to confirm those suspicions.[227] Where the plaintiff knew or reasonably should have known of the existence of a possible claim of discrimination within the time limit for filing a charge, the court will not toll the filing requirement.[228]

The Sixth Circuit has articulated a five-factor testing for deciding whether equitable tolling of the charge-filing requirements is appropriate: (1) lack of notice of the filing requirement; (2) lack of constructive knowledge of the filing requirement; (3) diligence in pursuing one's rights; (4) absence of prejudice to the employer; and (5) the employee's reasonableness in remaining ignorant of the particular legal requirement for filing his or her claim.[229]

The courts continue to face tolling issues when questions of employer misconduct and plaintiff's lack of diligence coincide in situations where the plaintiff lacks sufficient knowledge during the charge-filing period to file a claim and waits until additional facts make the deception apparent. An early example of this is *Reeb v. Economic Opportunity Atlanta, Inc.*[230] In *Reeb*, the employer told

---

[225]*See* Williams v. Widnall, 173 F.3d 431 (6th Cir. 1999) (informal complaints of discriminatory conduct insufficient to toll period after years of delay); Placides v. Rumsfeld, 79 Fed. Appx. 319, 320 (9th Cir. 2003) (affirming summary judgment where plaintiff did not contact EEOC until 19 months after leaving employment and more than 4 years after completing counseling to file complaint).

[226]*See* Merit v. Southeastern Pa. Transit Auth., 276 F. Supp. 2d 382 (E.D. Pa. 2003) (equitable tolling appropriate where lay person unfamiliar with complexities of administrative process and charge only 23 days late).

[227]*See* Dorsey v. Pinnacle Automation Co., 278 F.3d 830, 836 (8th Cir. 2002) (reasonable person would have been aware of promotions and acted).

[228]*See, e.g.*, Santa Maria v. Pacific Bell, 202 F.3d 1170, 1178–79 (9th Cir. 2000) (deadline for filing EEOC charge not equitably tolled because plaintiff knew or reasonably should have known of possible ADA claim within limitations period); Taxley v. Maricopa County, 237 F. Supp. 2d 1109, 1114–15, 91 FEP 417 (D. Ariz. 2002) (genuine issue of material fact whether plaintiff knew basis for employer action within filing period, thus defeating employer summary judgment).

[229]Amini v. Oberlin Coll., 259 F.3d 493 (6th Cir. 2001) (court evaluated each factor to reach decision that equitable tolling of EEOC charge-filing period was inappropriate); Truitt v. County of Wayne, 148 F.3d 644, 648 (6th Cir. 1998) (applying factors to consider when determining appropriateness of equitable tolling); Andrews v. Orr, 851 F.2d 146 (6th Cir. 1998) (applying pertinent factors to decision whether to apply equitable tolling).

[230]516 F.2d 924, 11 FEP 235 (5th Cir. 1975).

the plaintiff that she was terminated because the defendant had insufficient funds to continue her in its employ. She did not file a charge with the EEOC within the prescribed period. She learned that she had been replaced six months after termination and promptly thereafter filed a charge. The plaintiff alleged that the employer "actively sought to mislead [her] in informing her that adequate funds for her program no longer would be available."[231] The Fifth Circuit stated:

> In these circumstances we apply the familiar equitable modification to statutes of limitation: the statute does not begin to run until the facts which would support a cause of action are apparent or should be apparent to a person with a reasonably prudent regard for his rights. A corollary of this principle, often found in cases where wrongful concealment of facts is alleged, is that a party responsible for such wrongful concealment is estopped from asserting the statute of limitations as a defense. Mr. Justice Black gave a classic statement of this corollary in Glus v. Brooklyn Eastern District Terminal, [359 U.S. 231, 232 (1959)]: . . . "[N]o man may take advantage of his own wrong."[232]

In contrast, in *Thelen v. Marcia's Big Boy Corp.*,[233] the Seventh Circuit held that an employer's misrepresentation to the plaintiff regarding who would take over his duties should not result in equitable estoppel of his time to file an ADEA charge: "It is the view of this court that such a position would eviscerate the concept of a limitations period because '[i]t implies that a defendant is guilty of fraudulent concealment unless it tells the plaintiff, "We're firing you because of your age." ' "[234]

Some courts continue to follow the *Reeb* line of reasoning to permit tolling of the limitations period until the plaintiff had sufficient information to file a valid charge, expressing concern that the employer could evade the law by waiting to act.[235] Others have

---

[231]*Id.* at 930; *see also* Bennett v. Coors Brewing Co., 189 F.3d 1221, 1236, 80 FEP 1197 (10th Cir. 1999) (plaintiffs presented genuine issue of material fact about whether equitable tolling should apply where employer allegedly lied to employees about reasons their department was reorganized).

[232]*Reeb*, 516 F.2d at 930.

[233]64 F.3d 264 (7th Cir. 1995).

[234]*Id.* at 267–68 (citing Cada v. Baxter Healthcare Corp., 920 F.2d 446, 451, 54 FEP 961 (7th Cir. 1990)).

[235]*See, e.g.*, Jones v. Dillard's, Inc., 331 F.3d 1259, 1263, 92 FEP 28 (11th Cir. 2003) (charge-filing period tolled when plaintiff had only suspicion of discrimination that was insufficient to file valid charge; period tolled until she learned that someone

refused, especially where the plaintiff was not diligent when he or she finally had enough information to have more than a "suspicion" of discrimination but still did not act on a timely basis.[236]

Mental incapacity is theoretically available as a basis for equitable tolling of the charge-filing period, but courts take a narrow view of such claims.[237] The plaintiff faces two major obstacles. The first is whether the incapacity is substantial enough, even arguably, to warrant tolling.[238] The second is whether, under all the

---

had been hired in her place); Oshiver v. Levin, Fishbein, Sedran & Berman, 38 F.3d 1380, 1386, 66 FEP 429 (3d Cir. 1994) (statute of limitations will be tolled until facts that would support plaintiff's cause of action are apparent); Vaught v. R.R. Donnelley & Sons Co., 745 F.2d 407, 410–12 (7th Cir. 1984) (applying *Reeb* and referring to it as "seminal case" in area of equitable tolling); Wilkerson v. Siegfried Ins. Agency, Inc., 683 F.2d 344, 345–46 (10th Cir. 1982) (applying *Reeb*); Miranda v. B & B Cash Grocery Store, Inc., 975 F.2d 1518, 1531–32 (11th Cir. 1992) (same).

[236]*See, e.g.,* Amini v. Oberlin Coll., 259 F.3d 493, 500, 86 FEP 625 (6th Cir. 2001) (court followed *Thelen*, but ruled that charge-filing period not tolled until plaintiff learned who replaced him because he was not diligent in trying to find out, he had time to do so before limitation period expired, and there was no evidence of employer misrepresentation); Santa Maria v. Pacific Bell, 202 F.3d 1170, 1173, 10 AD 245 (9th Cir. 2000) (court rejected equitable tolling when plaintiff knew or should have known of existence of possible claim during limitations period); Juniel v. Park Forest-Chi. Heights Sch. Dist., 161 F. Supp. 2d 910, 914 (N.D. Ill. 2001) (*Thelen* invoked but not applied where no allegation that employer concealed facts); Taxley v. Maricopa County, 237 F. Supp. 2d 1109 (D. Ariz. 2002) (court reversed summary judgment for employer to permit plaintiff to prove whether she reasonably should have been expected to learn of facts to support charge within charge-filing period).

[237]*See* Boos v. Runyon, 201 F.3d 178, 185 (2d Cir. 2000) (holding that plaintiff's conclusory and vague claim of mental illness, without particularized description of how her condition adversely affected her pursuit of her rights, was "manifestly insufficient to justify any further inquiry into tolling"); Hood v. Sears, Roebuck & Co., 168 F.3d 231, 233, 79 FEP 605 (5th Cir. 1999) (plaintiff's mental illness did not justify tolling where she was able to retain counsel, thus indicating that her mental state did not prevent her from pursuing her legal rights during filing period); Steele v. Brown, 993 F. Supp. 918, 922 (M.D.N.C.) (plaintiff failed to demonstrate severe disability that precluded his ability to reason and function in society where he continued to work and take care of financial matters and attempted to secure legal representation, and where he was hospitalized after 90-day period had expired), *aff'd*, 155 F.3d 561 (4th Cir. 1998); Smoots v. CB Int'l, 1998 WL 418017, at *1 (N.D. Ill. July 6, 1998) (plaintiff's severe depression did not warrant tolling where she had separate counsel pursuing similar lawsuit against another former employer during filing period); Wilson v. West, 962 F. Supp. 939, 949 (S.D. Miss. 1997) (court unable to find any reported decisions within Fifth Circuit that adopted concept of tolling on basis of mental disability, but found that such disability justified tolling); Temparali v. Rubin, 1997 WL 361019, at *6 (E.D. Pa. June 19, 1997) (plaintiff's allegations that she was "extremely upset and distraught" and was "feeling completely insane" did not permit tolling where she continued to work after alleged sexual assault and harassment and consulted with counsel about other issues).

[238]*See* Cox v. Sears, Roebuck & Co., 1994 WL 143019, at *3 (M.D. Fla. Mar. 31, 1994) (stress and depression insufficient to effect tolling); Trynor v. Dalton, 64

facts, the plaintiff should have been able to proceed with litigation notwithstanding his or her condition.[239] The First Circuit rejected an absolute rule that tolling always would be applicable in the event of insanity.[240] Applying a fact-specific approach, the court found that tolling should not be applied because an attorney represented the plaintiff during the period in question.[241] The Seventh Circuit also rejected the contention that mental illness per se tolls statutes of limitations in all cases in which discrimination based on that mental illness is the basis of the suit.[242] The court saw no reason "to depart from the traditional rule that mental illness tolls a statute of limitations only if the illness in fact prevents the sufferer from managing his affairs and thus from understanding his rights and acting upon them."[243]

The Sixth Circuit has recognized that the mental illness of a claimant's attorney may be available as a basis for equitable tolling of the charge-filing period if the claimant pursued the claim

---

FEP 23, 25 (D. Me. 1994) (plaintiff with borderline-retarded IQ of 72 not excused from requirement of timely filing when her employer went to great lengths to assure that she knew of all filing requirements); Kerver v. Exxon Prod. Research Co., 40 FEP 1567, 1568–69 (S.D. Tex. 1986) (finding no basis for equitable tolling when employee who suffered from depression resulting from job loss handled his own affairs, did not consider himself mentally or emotionally ill, and did not claim he was legally incompetent), aff'd mem., 810 F.2d 196 (5th Cir. 1987); Steward v. Holiday Inns, Inc., 609 F. Supp. 1468, 1469, 40 FEP 191 (E.D. La. 1985) (alleged physical and mental incapacity of plaintiff who was fired while in hospital did not toll filing period for sex discrimination claim); Bassett v. Sterling Drug, Inc., 578 F. Supp. 1244, 1248, 35 FEP 382 (S.D. Ohio 1984) (ADEA limitations period, which had already begun to run, "may be tolled, in the discretion of the Court, for that period of time during which the claimant was adjudicated mentally incompetent or institutionalized under a diagnosis of mental incompetence"; tolling statute from date of hospitalization, not date of diagnosis, and dismissing action as time barred), appeal dismissed, 770 F.2d 165 (6th Cir. 1985).

[239]Compare Moody v. Bayliner Marine Corp., 664 F. Supp. 232, 235, 236, 44 FEP 468 (E.D.N.C. 1987) ("in rare circumstances, mental incapacity may equitably toll the statute of limitations period in Title VII cases"; period was not tolled here, however, because, despite her doctor's advice that it was too stressful, plaintiff was capable of filing claim and was represented by counsel) with Llewellyn v. Celanese Corp., 693 F. Supp. 369, 379, 47 FEP 993 (W.D.N.C. 1988) (plaintiff's mentally disabled condition and employer's failure to post statutory notice justified tolling of limitations period in Title VII case; severe emotional and physical symptoms combined with medication impaired plaintiff's ability to focus on sexual harassment).

[240]Lopez v. Citibank, N.A., 808 F.2d 905, 906–07, 42 FEP 1153 (1st Cir. 1987).

[241]Id. at 907.

[242]Miller v. Runyon, 77 F.3d 189, 191, 5 AD 415 (7th Cir. 1996).

[243]Id. at 191–92 ("Any other conclusion would perpetuate the stereotype of the insane as raving maniacs or gibbering idiots and impair their employment opportunities, thus stigmatizing [the plaintiff's] own class.").

diligently but was abandoned by his or her attorney because of the attorney's mental illness.[244]

c. *Government Misconduct or Negligence.* Conduct by the government that causes employees to fail to file a timely charge has been a consistent basis for equitable tolling. Courts have tolled the charge-filing requirements where the EEOC has misled the plaintiff[245] or where the EEOC has made mistakes, such as refusing to accept a charge for filing,[246] erroneously informing the plaintiff that he had completed all necessary paperwork when he had only filled out the intake questionnaire,[247] failing to schedule an intake meeting before the filing deadline,[248] erroneously telling the claimant that she had a year to file,[249] and perhaps other errors.[250] Similar actions by state agencies can serve as the basis for equitable tolling.[251] Where the EEOC's misleading information, however, is because of the plaintiff's failure to provide sufficient information to the EEOC, there is no basis for equitable tolling.[252] These issues are discussed more fully in Chapter 25 (EEOC Administrative Process).

---

[244]Cantrell v. Knoxville Cmty. Dev. Corp., 60 F.3d 1117, 1179–80 (6th Cir. 1995) (case remanded for factual determination where court would not take judicial notice of attorney's incapacitation and could not determine if claimant acted with due diligence after being abandoned).

[245]*See* Manning v. Chevron Chem. Co., 332 F.3d 874, 880 (5th Cir. 2003) (EEOC must give individual incorrect information that leads him to file untimely charge).

[246]*E.g.*, McKee v. McDonnell Douglas Technical Servs. Co., 700 F.2d 260, 264–65, 31 FEP 383 (5th Cir. 1983) (remanding to trial court for factual determination).

[247]Early v. Bankers Life & Cas. Co., 959 F.2d 75, 80 (7th Cir. 1992).

[248]Gray v. Phillips Petroleum Co., 858 F.2d 610, 616, 49 FEP 67 (10th Cir. 1988) (record established as matter of law that EEOC "misled or at least lulled plaintiffs into inaction").

[249]Alsaras v. Dominick's Finer Foods, Inc., 248 F.3d 1156, 2000 WL 1763350, at *2 (7th Cir. Nov. 22, 2000) (EEOC representative erroneously told plaintiff she had 1 year to file claim with EEOC); Browning v. AT&T Paradyne, 120 F.3d 222, 226, 74 FEP 1227 (11th Cir. 1997) (EEOC's letter incorrectly informing employee that incorrect statute of limitations applied to his ADEA claim operated to equitably toll limitations period).

[250]*See* Harris v. City of N.Y., 186 F.3d 242, 248 n.3 (2d Cir. 1999) (courts do not penalize litigants for EEOC mistakes and misinformation); Jackson v. Richards Med. Co., 961 F.2d 575, 587 n.11 (6th Cir. 1992) (no penalty for EEOC errors).

[251]*See* Newbold v. Wisconsin Pub. Defender, 310 F.3d 1013, 1016, 90 FEP 513 (7th Cir. 2003) (tolling might be applicable where state agency authoritatively addressed EEOC deadlines and gave erroneous information).

[252]*E.g.*, Ramirez v. City of San Antonio, 312 F.3d 178, 184–85 (5th Cir. 2002) (plaintiff told EEOC he was being transferred but not that he was being demoted).

d. Wrong Forum. Equitable tolling applies in the rare case where parties have been litigating an action in state court but discover they chose the wrong forum.[253] The doctrine is not applicable, however, where a plaintiff wrongly believes that his or her claim was already before a court.[254]

5. Piggybacking or Single-Filing Rule

In very limited circumstances, a plaintiff who fails to file a timely charge and who cannot justify tolling the limitations period on equitable grounds may still be able to pursue a claim. The majority of circuit courts have held that the "piggybacking" or "single-filing" rule, under which a grievant who does not file an EEOC charge may opt into a class action by "piggybacking" onto a timely charge filed by one of the named plaintiffs in the class action, applies both to Title VII and ADEA cases.[255] Moreover, the single-filing rule is not strictly limited to class actions; it can also permit a plaintiff to join an individual action filed by another person

---

[253]Manning v. Chevron Chem. Co., LLC, 332 F.3d 874, 880 (5th Cir. 2003) (equitable tolling may be justified if the parties pursue their claims in the wrong forum); Chappell v. Emco Mach. Works Co., 601 F.2d 1295, 1302 (5th Cir. 1979) (policy of repose inherent in timely filing requirement satisfied where parties litigated in wrong forum).

[254]*Manning*, 332 F.3d at 880 (court rejected equitable estoppel claim when erroneous belief about whether claim was pending in court led plaintiff to delay).

[255]*See* Hipp v. Liberty Nat'l Life Ins. Co., 252 F.3d 1208, 1217 (11th Cir. 2001) (piggybacking rule applies to ADEA opt-in cases when relied-upon charge is not invalid and claims of filing plaintiff and piggybacking plaintiff arise out of similar discriminatory treatment in same time frame); Howlett v. Holiday Inns, Inc., 49 F.3d 189, 194, 67 FEP 289 (6th Cir. 1995); Grayson v. K-Mart Corp., 79 F.3d 1086, 1101–02, 70 FEP 770 (11th Cir. 1996); Mooney v. Aramco Serv. Co., 54 F.3d 1207, 1223, 68 FEP 421 (5th Cir. 1995). A similar rule has been applied, with more limited effects, when an employee fails to file suit within the requisite 90-day period. *See* Winbush v. Iowa, 66 F.3d 1471, 1485–86, 69 FEP 1348 (8th Cir. 1995) (employee who filed his own charge but failed to file suit after receiving right-to-sue letter barred from recovering under Title VII for any injuries he suffered prior to expiration of his right-to-sue period; however, he could still piggyback on filings of other employees for his Title VII claims that might have accrued after expiration of his right-to-sue period); *cf.* Anderson v. Unisys Corp., 47 F.3d 302, 309, 67 FEP 317 (8th Cir. 1995) (plaintiff who filed separate administrative charge but failed to timely file suit barred by statute of limitations and cannot "piggyback" on another employee's timely charge or lawsuit); Communications Workers v. New Jersey Dep't of Pers., 282 F.3d 213 (3d Cir. 2002) (union local that did not file timely charge could not piggyback onto national union suit where national suit not class action). *See generally* Chapter 32 (Class Actions).

who is similarly situated, provided that the timely filed charge gave notice of the collective nature of the charge.[256] Construing the language of several circuit court decisions, one district court has held that the single-filing rule properly applies only to those individuals who could have filed a timely EEOC charge at the time the actual charge was filed.[257] The Fifth Circuit has held that the single-filing rule permits a plaintiff to join an existing individual action; the rule cannot be utilized to allow a noncharging plaintiff to file a separate suit based on the charge of a party who had not filed suit.[258]

Tolling issues often arise in class actions or ADEA collective action. These issues are discussed in Chapters 32 (Class Actions) and 12 (Age), respectively.

III. TIMELINESS OF FILING SUIT

A. Introduction

Filing a timely charge is not the plaintiff's only procedural obligation. Any subsequent lawsuit in court also must be timely.

A defendant's failure to contend that the lawsuit is untimely, premature, or barred by the statute of limitations as an affirmative defense in its answer (or before) may constitute a waiver of its right to rely on such defense.[259]

---

[256]*See Mooney*, 54 F.3d at 1223; *Howlett*, 49 F.3d at 195. The "piggybacking" rule may be applied only where (1) the relied-upon charge is not invalid, and (2) the individual claims of the filing and nonfiling plaintiff arise out of similar discriminatory treatment in the same time frame. *Grayson*, 79 F.3d at 1101–02 (citing Calloway v. Partners Nat'l Health Plans, 986 F.2d 446, 61 FEP 550 (11th Cir. 1993)).

[257]*See* Thiessen v. General Elec. Capital Corp., 996 F. Supp. 1071, 1077 (D. Kan. 1998) ("the vast majority of circuit courts that have addressed this question apply the single-filing rule only to those plaintiffs whose claims arise in the 'same time frame' as the filing plaintiff or who could have filed timely EEOC charges on the date which the filing plaintiff actually filed his or her EEOC charge"). The majority of the courts of appeals continue to recognize the validity of the single-filing rule. *See, e.g.,* Gitlitz v. Compagnie Nationale Air Fr., 129 F.3d 554 (11th Cir. 1997). The First Circuit recently recognized but failed to address the merits of the single-filing rule. Basch v. Ground Round, Inc., 139 F.3d 6, 8–10, 76 FEP 533 (1st Cir. 1998).

[258]Bettcher v. Brown Schs., Inc., 262 F.3d 492, 495, 86 FEP 929 (5th Cir. 2001).

[259]*See* O'Rourke v. City of Providence, 235 F.3d 713, 725 n.3, 85 FEP 1135 (1st Cir. 2001) (defendant waived right to complain about plaintiff's filing of her original court complaint before she filed her EEOC charge); Harris v. United States

B. Statutory and Regulatory Framework

Title VII specifies that the person aggrieved has 90 days to bring a civil action after receipt of the notice of right to sue from the EEOC.[260] The ADEA, as amended by the Civil Rights Act of 1991, contains a similar 90-day period.[261]

Dep't of Veterans Affairs, 126 F.3d 339, 344–45, 74 FEP 1835 (D.C. Cir. 1997) (under FED. R. CIV. P. 8(c), defendant could not raise untimeliness defense for first time in dispositive motion without ever having pled defense; reversing grant of summary judgment for defendant but holding that defendant could file motion for leave to amend its answer on remand); Bowden v. United States, 106 F.3d 433, 438–39, 73 FEP 395 (D.C. Cir. 1997) (defendant waived defense of untimely filing of administrative charge because it responded to merits of complaint without ever questioning its timeliness); Day v. Liberty Nat'l Life Ins. Co., 122 F.3d 1012, 1014–16, 74 FEP 1556 (11th Cir. 1997) (defendant waived former 2-year statute of limitations for nonwillful violations of ADEA by failing to plead it in its answer to pro se complaint alleging willful violation; defendant did not raise limitations defense until after jury in second trial returned verdict for plaintiff; also held that defendant would have waived defense by failing to include it in pretrial order); Venters v. City of Delphi, 123 F.3d 956, 962–65, 74 FEP 1095 (7th Cir. 1997) (defendants waived limitations defense on Title VII claim by failing to plead it in their answer and by first mentioning it in their reply memorandum in support of summary judgment); Funk v. F & K Supply, Inc., 43 F. Supp. 2d 205, 214, 79 FEP 1543 (N.D.N.Y. 1999) (failure to affirmatively plead defense of statute of limitations resulted in waiver); cf. Jackson v. Rockford Hous. Auth., 213 F.3d 389, 392–94, 83 FEP 149 (7th Cir. 2000) (where plaintiff's claim was filed 8 years after limitations period ended, court appropriately granted defendant leave to amend answer in order to add statute of limitations defense because plaintiff was well aware his claims were stale, had sufficient notice of the defense, and was not prejudiced by amendment); Figuero v. Buccaneer Hotel, Inc., 188 F.3d 172, 176, 80 FEP 938 (3d Cir. 1999) (rejecting plaintiff's argument that "shotgunned" nature of defendants' assertion of statute of limitations defense in their answer amounted to waiver); Zotos v. Lindbergh Sch. Dist., 121 F.3d 356, 361, 74 FEP 1055 (8th Cir. 1997) (rejecting plaintiff's argument that defendant waived its limitations defense to her ADEA claim, because its bare assertion of such defense was sufficient and defendant had no obligation in its pleading to specify particular period of limitations it was raising as defense); Morales v. Instituto Comercial de P.R. Junior Coll., 40 F. Supp. 2d 62, 65 (D.P.R. 1999) (court held that it is within court's discretion to raise statute of limitations issue on its own and dismiss plaintiff's claim on that basis where parties were permitted to brief issue, issue was readily ascertained from plaintiff's complaint, and there was no undue surprise to plaintiff), aff'd, 215 F.3d 1311 (1st Cir. 2000).

[260]Section 706(f)(1), 42 U.S.C. § 2000e-5(f)(1) (2000).

[261]Pub. L. No. 102-166, § 115(4), 1991 U.S.C.C.A.N. (105 Stat.) 1071, 1079 (codified as amended at 29 U.S.C. § 626(e)). Under the ADEA, the plaintiff need not receive a right-to-sue letter to sue; he or she need only wait 60 days following the filing of an EEOC charge. See Adams v. Burlington N. R.R., 838 F. Supp. 1461, 1467–69, 63 FEP 679 (D. Kan. 1993) (that ADEA has 90-day statute of limitations running from receipt of right-to-sue letter does not mean that age plaintiff cannot sue earlier). See generally Chapter 12 (Age).

According to the EEOC regulations, a notice of right to sue is issued (1) where the Commission has decided not to sue following a reasonable cause finding and a failure of conciliation; (2) where the Commission has entered into a conciliation agreement that the party claiming to be aggrieved has not joined; (3) where a charge is dismissed; or (4) where the Commission has made a finding of no reasonable cause.[262] If requested by the charging party, the notice of right to sue will be issued at an earlier time. With respect to governmental respondents, the procedure varies somewhat from the above.[263]

State statutes of limitations are inapplicable to the bringing of a Title VII action.[264] Relying on the established congressional intent as recognized in *Occidental Life Insurance Co. v. EEOC*[265] and decisions in the Sixth and Ninth Circuits, the Third Circuit ruled that Pennsylvania's two-year statute of limitations period did not bar plaintiff's Title VII claim where the claim was filed within the 90-day period, despite the fact that the EEOC right-to-sue letter was not requested by the plaintiff until nearly three and one-half years after the state and federal agency charges had been filed.[266]

In *EEOC v. W.H. Braum, Inc.*,[267] the Tenth Circuit pointed out that when Congress explicitly puts a limit on the time for enforcing a right that it created, there is an end to the matter and the congressional statute of limitations is definitive. The court overruled the district court, finding that it had mistakenly relied on the state statute of limitations for employment discrimination claims in an action under the ADA.[268] The court went on to explain that,

---

[262]29 C.F.R. §§ 1601.19(a), 1601.28(b) (2005). The EEOC's recent practice is not to issue "no cause" determinations but rather to terminate investigations "without particularized findings." *See generally* Chapter 25 (EEOC Administrative Process).

[263]29 C.F.R. § 1601.28(d) (2005). *See generally* Chapters 30 (Justice Department Litigation) and 31 (Federal Employee Litigation).

[264]*See, e.g.*, Kirk v. Rockwell Int'l Corp., 578 F.2d 814, 819, 17 FEP 1380 (9th Cir. 1978) ("Title VII does not borrow state statutes of limitations because the time limits for filing a charge and giving notice to the employer are a Congressionally established statute of limitations."); Draper v. United States Pipe & Foundry Co., 527 F.2d 515, 522, 11 FEP 1106 (6th Cir. 1975) ("Title VII establishes its own statute of limitations, and state law is irrelevant . . . .").

[265]432 U.S. 355 (1977).

[266]Burgh v. Borough Council, 251 F.3d 465, 469–75, 85 FEP 1452 (3d Cir. 2001).

[267]347 F.3d 1192 (10th Cir. 2003).

[268]*Id.* at 1197.

because Title I of the ADA expressly adopts the statutory scheme of Title VII, the court's analysis is whether there is a gap in the Title VII framework that should be filled with a state statute of limitations.[269] The court, in accordance with prior holdings, found that there is no gap in Title VII's scheme, that an employee has 90 days from receipt of a right-to-sue notice in which to file suit, and a state statute of limitations should not be imported.[270]

C. Time of Issuing Notice of Right to Sue

1. *The EEOC Is Not Required to Issue Notice Within a Specified Period After the Charge Is Filed*

Under § 706(d) of the Civil Rights Act of 1964 as originally enacted, the EEOC had 60 days to process a charge. If it did not obtain voluntary compliance, it was to "so notify the person aggrieved," who then had 30 days to file suit. Defendants, therefore, contended that, reading the statute literally, EEOC delays of greater than 90 days effectively extinguished the right to file suit. This contention was uniformly rejected, with the courts holding that the EEOC's 60-day time limit was not mandatory in the jurisdictional sense.[271]

Although the 1972 amendments expanded the time periods, the same issue was often presented. Read literally, § 706(f)(1), as amended in 1972, requires the EEOC to issue a right-to-sue letter 180 days after it assumes jurisdiction over a timely charge and gives the charging party 90 days thereafter within which to file suit.[272] As in the earlier cases, the courts consistently rejected the argument that the 180-day period marked the end of the EEOC's jurisdiction.[273]

---

[269]*Id.*

[270]*Id.* at 1198 (explaining that Congress provided benchmark for purposes of statute of limitations—date upon which EEOC charge is filed).

[271]*E.g.*, Cunningham v. Litton Indus., 413 F.2d 887, 890, 1 FEP 861 (9th Cir. 1969) ("period prescribed in the statute in which the EEOC is to act should be interpreted as directory and not mandatory in nature"); Miller v. International Paper Co., 408 F.2d 283, 286–87, 1 FEP 647 (5th Cir. 1969) (same; actions—or inactions—of EEOC cannot defeat private individual's rights).

[272]Pub. L. No. 92-261, § 4, 1972 U.S.C.C.A.N. (86 Stat. 103) 122, 125–26 (codified as amended at 42 U.S.C. § 2000e-5(f)(1)).

[273]*E.g.*, Tuft v. McDonnell Douglas Corp., 517 F.2d 1301, 1307, 10 FEP 929 (8th Cir. 1975) ("We believe that the language of the statute and its legislative history

2. Preliminary Relief Before Receiving Right-to-Sue Notice

Some plaintiffs have commenced actions without requesting a right-to-sue letter, or even without filing a charge. Their argument for jurisdiction is that they seek only to preserve the status quo ante (for instance, by requesting that an employee not be immediately fired or removed from work) pending the required period of resort to the EEOC, and thus that they are not acting in derogation of the Commission's jurisdiction, but in aid of it.[274] Several courts have concluded that jurisdiction exists to consider and, if appropriate, grant injunctive relief during the 180-day period.[275] Other courts, however, have reached the opposite conclusion,[276] primarily on the ground that Title VII specifically authorizes the Commission to seek preliminary relief on behalf of the employee, and the absence of a similar provision for private parties

---

support the conclusion that administrative enforcement of Title VII does not cease at the end of 180 days, and, thus, the 180-day provision does not serve as a time deadline for the Commission to issue any notice to the complaining party."); Turner v. Texas Instruments, Inc., 556 F.2d 1349, 1351–52, 15 FEP 481 (5th Cir. 1977) (rejecting employer's argument that EEOC is required to give notice after 180 days). In *Occidental Life Insurance Co. v. EEOC*, 432 U.S. 355, 366, 367, 14 FEP 1718 (1977), the Supreme Court, in holding that there was no statute of limitations that governed an EEOC suit, provided support for the contention that the EEOC need not issue a right-to-sue notice after 180 days.

[274]For a general discussion of preliminary relief, *see* Chapter 39 (Injunctive and Affirmative Relief).

[275]*E.g.*, Holt v. Continental Group, 708 F.2d 87, 90, 31 FEP 1468 (2d Cir. 1983) (jurisdiction exists to preserve or restore status quo ante); Duke v. Langdon, 695 F.2d 1136, 1137, 1138, 30 FEP 1059 (9th Cir. 1983) (Kilkenny, J., concurring) (jurisdiction to consider issue exists even though federal employee had filed EEOC charge only a day or so before seeking injunction), *supplemented on other grounds*, 701 F.2d 768 (9th Cir. 1983); Sheehan v. Purolator Courier Corp., 676 F.2d 877, 886, 887, 28 FEP 202 (2d Cir. 1982) (1972 amendments to Title VII did not restrict court's inherent equity powers); Berg v. Richmond Unified Sch. Dist., 528 F.2d 1208, 1211–12, 11 FEP 1285 (9th Cir. 1975) (jurisdiction exists to grant injunction where there is high probability of success and threat of irreparable injury), *vacated and remanded on other grounds per curiam*, 434 U.S. 158 (1977); Karmel v. City of N.Y., 200 F. Supp. 2d 361 (S.D.N.Y. 2002) (city's interrogation of female city police detective presented threat of irreparable harm to her right of access to courts and to her ability to vindicate rights under Title VII, for purposes of showing irreparable harm on motion for preliminary injunction to prevent such interrogation).

[276]*See, e.g.*, Doerr v. B.F. Goodrich Co., 484 F. Supp. 320, 323, 22 FEP 345 (N.D. Ohio 1979) (court does not have jurisdiction prior to exhaustion of Title VII remedies); Hunter v. Ward, 476 F. Supp. 913, 917, 20 FEP 1643 (E.D. Ark. 1979) (same).

indicates congressional intent to foreclose such actions.[277] Still others have denied preliminary injunctive relief on grounds of absence of irreparable harm or failure to state a claim, without deciding the jurisdictional issue.[278] Some appellate courts have avoided reviewing the issue of whether preliminary relief ever is available by holding that, after a right-to-sue letter is or could have been issued, the issue is moot.[279]

The failure to exhaust the EEOC's administrative procedures also may bear on the proof required for preliminary relief.[280] For example, at least two courts of appeals have presumed irreparable injury in Title VII cases where administrative remedies have been exhausted, but not where the remedies have not been exhausted.[281]

---

[277]*E.g.*, Fields v. Village of Skokie, 502 F. Supp. 456, 459, 24 FEP 834 (N.D. Ill. 1980) (court should not allow plaintiff to "circumvent administrative procedure"; EEOC has right to seek temporary relief).

[278]*E.g.*, Bailey v. Delta Air Lines, Inc., 722 F.2d 942, 944, 33 FEP 713 (1st Cir. 1983) (although not deciding jurisdictional issue, indicating that preliminary relief might be available if degree of irreparable injury justified disruption of EEOC's administrative process); Jerome v. Viviano Food Co., 489 F.2d 965, 966, 7 FEP 145 (6th Cir. 1974) (suggesting doubt as to jurisdiction, but affirming dismissal on ground that no irreparable injury was alleged); Fagan v. National Cash Register Co., 481 F.2d 1115, 1126, 5 FEP 1335 (D.C. Cir. 1973) (affirming dismissal, without discussing district court's jurisdiction, on ground that no cause of action was stated); Howard v. Evans, 193 F. Supp. 2d 221 (D.D.C. 2002) (federal employee not likely to succeed on merits of Title VII claim against employer, as required for preliminary injunction preventing employer from assigning her to office space she considered detrimental to her health; employee did not exhaust administrative remedies before bringing Title VII claim).

[279]*See, e.g.*, Gutierrez v. Municipal Court, 838 F.2d 1031, 1053–54, 51 FEP 435 (9th Cir. 1988) (any jurisdictional problem created by initial lack of right-to-sue letter cured by subsequent issuance), *vacated as moot*, 490 U.S. 1016, 51 FEP 457 (1989); Berg v. LaCrosse Cooler Co., 548 F.2d 211, 213, 14 FEP 618 (7th Cir. 1977) (moot, as notice of right to sue now may be requested); Troy v. Shell Oil Co., 519 F.2d 403, 404–05, 10 FEP 1447 (6th Cir. 1975) (same).

[280]The Supreme Court was faced with a roughly analogous issue in *Sampson v. Murray*, 415 U.S. 61, 91–92 (1974), in which it held that a district court should not have issued an injunction to preserve the status quo pending resort to the Civil Service Commission. The Court stated that the analytically distinct questions of whether the court had jurisdiction to issue an injunction and whether the relief issued was proper could not be "bifurcated into two watertight compartments." *Id.* at 68. The Court then held that, although the district court may have had jurisdiction to issue relief pendente lite, it could not appropriately do so without the clearest showing of irreparable harm. *Id.* at 84, 88, 91–92.

[281]*See* United States v. Jefferson County, 720 F.2d 1511, 1520, 33 FEP 829 (11th Cir. 1983) (no presumption of irreparable harm applies where administrative remedies are not pursued); Middleton-Keirn v. Stone, 655 F.2d 609, 612, 26 FEP 1154

3. Premature Issuance of Right-to-Sue Notices and Premature Filing of Suit

The EEOC regulations provide for the premature issuance of notices of right to sue before the expiration of the 180-day period.[282] The regulations apply only to nongovernmental respondents and only when it is improbable that the Commission's processing of the charge will be completed within 180 days of filing.[283]

Even though the regulations seem to permit the premature issuance of right-to-sue notices, there is disagreement in the circuits about whether a plaintiff may proceed to file a civil action under Title VII on a right-to-sue letter issued by the EEOC fewer than 180 days from the date of the charge.[284] Some courts have

---

(5th Cir. 1981) (presumption applies where administrative remedies were exhausted and notice of right to sue had been issued); *cf.* Moteles v. University of Pa., 730 F.2d 913, 917, 34 FEP 424 (3d Cir. 1984) (plaintiff's bypass of administrative remedies is factor to be considered in determining whether equitable relief should be granted). *See generally* Chapter 39 (Injunctive and Affirmative Relief).

[282]29 C.F.R. § 1601.28(a)(2) (2005) provides as follows:

When a person claiming to be aggrieved requests, in writing, that a notice of right to sue be issued, and the charge to which the request relates is filed against a respondent other than a government, governmental agency or political subdivision, the Commission may issue such notice as described in § 1601.28(e) with copies to all parties, at any time prior to the expiration of 180 days from the date of filing the charge with the Commission; provided, that the District Director, the Area Director, the Local Director, the Program Director, Office of Program Operations or upon delegation, the Director of Systemic Programs, Office of Program Operations or the Directors, Field Management Programs, Office of Program Operations has determined that it is probable that the Commission will be unable to complete its administrative processing of the charge within 180 days from the filing of the charge and has attached a written certificate to that effect.

[283]*Id.*

[284]*See* Walker v. United Parcel Serv., 240 F.3d 1268, 1270, 85 FEP 1841 (10th Cir. 2001) (siding with Eleventh and Ninth Circuits [and Second Circuit's preregulation analysis] and explaining that EEOC has authority to accede to or deny request to issue early right-to-sue notice and that private parties do not have ability to affect that power; therefore suit filed before expiration of 180 days should not be dismissed); Martini v. Federal Nat'l Mortgage Ass'n, 178 F.3d 1336, 1347, 80 FEP 1 (D.C. Cir. 1999) (holding that plaintiff was required to wait 180 days after filing charge to bring suit and that EEOC regulation to contrary was invalid); Portis v. Ohio, 141 F.3d 632, 634 (6th Cir. 1998) (employee's failure to receive right-to-sue letter prior to filing suit did not provide basis for dismissal where right-to-sue letter was obtained 1 week after complaint was filed and there was no prejudice to defendant); Roe v. Cheyenne Mountain Conference Resort, Inc., 124 F.3d 1221, 1228, 7 AD 779 (10th Cir. 1997) (EEOC's immediate issuance of right-to-sue letter upon plaintiff's request, even after suit had already been filed, was at most affirmative defense that defendant waived by failing to take cross-appeal from

allowed[285] and others have rejected[286] such suits prior to the expiration of the 180-day period.

In an unusual case, a former employee filed suit on his second administrative charge (which was untimely) before he had received a right-to-sue notice on his timely first charge, and the

---

district court's award in favor of employee); Hall v. FlightSafety Int'l, Inc., 106 F. Supp. 2d 1171, 1182 (D. Kan. 2000) (issuance of right-to-sue notice by EEOC in fewer than 180 days does not preclude immediate filing of federal lawsuit); Shepherd v. United States Olympic Comm., 94 F. Supp. 2d 1136, 1145 (D. Colo. 2000) (holding that suit filed prior to expiration of 180 days allotted to EEOC is violation of 180-day waiting period); West v. Merillat Indus., Inc., 92 F. Supp. 2d 558, 561 (W.D. Va. 2000) (upholding EEOC practice of issuing right-to-sue letters before expiration of 180 days because agency regulation is based on permissible construction of Title VII); Kane v. Iowa Dep't of Human Servs., 955 F. Supp. 1117, 1136–39, 75 FEP 1093 (N.D. Iowa 1997) (employee's receipt of right-to-sue letter from Department of Justice that was required because suit was against governmental entity sufficient to cure defect of prematurely filed Title VII lawsuit; holding that in order to bar premature claim, there must be some prejudice to employer's ability to defend against claims, "such as a change in [employer's] legal theories, the need for additional discovery or trial preparation, or tardiness in asserting a stale claim"); Gadbois v. Rock-Tenn Co., Mill Div., Inc., 984 F. Supp. 811, 817 (D. Vt. 1997) (employee's subsequent receipt of right-to-sue letter during pendency of state court lawsuit cured any defect caused by premature filing of complaint); see also Sims v. Trus Joist MacMillan, 22 F.3d 1059, 1061, 64 FEP 1766 (11th Cir. 1994) (requirement that right-to-sue letter issued by EEOC be issued after expiration of 180 days is not jurisdictional prerequisite; regulation does not prohibit EEOC from issuing letter early); Menchaca v. American Med. Response of Ill., Inc., 6 F. Supp. 2d 971 (N.D. Ill. 1998) (allowing EEOC, pursuant to its regulations, to issue right-to-sue notices before expiration of 180-day period where EEOC determines it would be unable to complete its process within 180 days from filing of charge).

[285]E.g., Walker v. United Parcel Serv., 240 F.3d 1268, 1274 (10th Cir. 2001) (finding that early right-to-sue letters do not preclude suit); Brown v. Puget Sound Elec. Apprenticeship & Training Trust, 732 F.2d 726, 729, 34 FEP 1201 (9th Cir. 1984) (pre-180-day suit letter is valid); McGrath v. Nassau Health Care Corp., 217 F. Supp. 2d 319, 325–28 (E.D.N.Y. 2002) (explaining that Second Circuit has not addressed issue of early right-to-sue letters but finding arguments that permit suits on early right-to-sue letters more compelling).

[286]E.g., Martini v. Federal Nat'l Mortgage Ass'n, 178 F.3d 1336, 1347 (D.C. Cir. 1999) (holding that suits in district court based on early right-to-sue letters are premature); New York ex rel. Abrams v. Holiday Inns, Inc., 656 F. Supp. 675, 680, 35 FEP 1308 (W.D.N.Y. 1984) (pre-180-day suit letter not valid); Spencer v. Banco Real, S.A., 87 F.R.D. 739, 747, 23 FEP 1558 (S.D.N.Y. 1980) (EEOC regulations authorizing early issuance of notice are inconsistent with congressional intent); Grimes v. Pitney Bowes, Inc., 480 F. Supp. 1381, 1385, 21 FEP 811 (N.D. Ga. 1979) (same); Hiduchenko v. Minneapolis Med. & Diagnostic Ctr., Ltd., 467 F. Supp. 103, 107, 19 FEP 460 (D. Minn. 1979) (early issuance is inconsistent with language of Title VII itself and its legislative history); see also Occidental Life Ins. Co. v. EEOC, 432 U.S. 355, 361, 14 FEP 1718 (1977) (charging party's private right of action does not arise until 180 days after EEOC charge has been filed; dictum).

district court dismissed his suit.[287] The employee then filed suit on the timely first charge after receiving the right-to-sue notice, and the district court dismissed on res judicata grounds. The Second Circuit reversed, holding that the dismissal of the initial suit on the second charge was not a judgment on the merits and that res judicata therefore did not bar the employee from bringing a second Title VII action based on his timely first charge.[288]

The Eleventh Circuit held that employees who filed charges of discrimination with the EEOC after filing their lawsuit did not fail to meet the conditions precedent for filing suit under Title VII, given that the employees filed an amendment to their complaint after the EEOC issued notices of right to sue and prior to the expiration of the 90-day period.[289]

In a case of first impression, the Fifth Circuit addressed whether an EEOC right-to-sue letter is interchangeable with a state-issued right-to-sue letter for the purposes of filing a claim under the Texas Human Rights Act where the plaintiff had not checked the dual filing box on the EEOC form and cited only an ADEA violation, not a violation of any state law.[290] The court held that the plaintiff's claim was premature because the plaintiff had not received a right-to-sue letter from the state agency, hence had not exhausted all state administrative remedies.[291]

Some of the disapproving courts have suspended rather than dismissed the proceedings while the case is resubmitted to the EEOC for the remainder of the 180-day period.[292]

---

[287]Criales v. American Airlines, Inc., 105 F.3d 93, 95–96, 72 FEP 1690 (2d Cir. 1997).

[288]*Id.* at 96. In contrast, the Sixth Circuit found that an employee's Title VII action *was* barred by res judicata where the employee could and should have litigated her race discrimination claim in her prior § 1981 action, even though she did not receive her right-to-sue letter from the EEOC until after judgment was entered against her in the first action. Rivers v. Barberton Bd. of Educ., 143 F.3d 1029, 1031–33, 76 FEP 1545 (6th Cir. 1998). In that case, the employee could have obtained the right-to-sue letter and perfected her prior Title VII claim from the outset or during the 2-year pendency of the prior action. *Id.* at 1033; *see also* Heyliger v. State Univ. & Cmty. Coll. Sys., 126 F.3d 849, 855–56, 90 FEP 516 (6th Cir. 1997) (same).

[289]Cross v. Alabama Dep't of Mental Health & Mental Retardation, 49 F.3d 1490, 1504, 67 FEP 844 (11th Cir. 1995).

[290]Jones v. Grinnell Corp., 235 F.3d 972, 84 FEP 1301 (5th Cir. 2001).

[291]*Id.* at 974; *see also* Vielma v. Eureka Co., 218 F.3d 458, 464, 83 FEP 729 (5th Cir. 2000) (holding that right-to-sue letters are not interchangeable in terms of triggering 60-day filing requirement under Texas Human Rights Act).

[292]*E.g., Holiday Inns*, 656 F. Supp. at 680 (action held in abeyance); *Spencer*, 87 F.R.D. at 747 (action suspended).

A different but related problem occurs when plaintiffs bring suit prior to the expiration of the 180-day period without obtaining any right-to-sue notice. Many courts have not dismissed such suits, but have found the defect cured by a subsequently issued right-to-sue notice.[293] Other courts have dismissed the action without prejudice pending the receipt of the notice.[294] Some courts allow an action to be brought if a plaintiff is entitled to receive a right-to-sue notice and the EEOC fails to respond to the plaintiff's request to provide it.[295]

D. Timely Court Filing

1. Form of Right-to-Sue Notice and Multiple Notices

The form of the right-to-sue notice currently used by the EEOC specifically informs charging parties of their right to file a court action within 90 days from the receipt of the notice and informs them that, if they do not, their right to sue will be lost.[296] Once a

---

[293]*E.g.*, Gooding v. Warner-Lambert Co., 744 F.2d 354, 357–58, 35 FEP 1707 (3d Cir. 1984) (requirement not jurisdictional and can be fulfilled by subsequent notice); Wrighten v. Metropolitan Hosps., Inc., 726 F.2d 1346, 1351, 33 FEP 1714 (9th Cir. 1984) (defect was cured by notice issued approximately 2 years after filing of suit, where defendants had made no motion to dismiss; no showing of prejudice, and state not precluded from performing its administrative function by filing); Williams v. Washington Metro. Area Transit Auth., 721 F.2d 1412, 1418 n.12, 33 FEP 581 (D.C. Cir. 1983) (per curiam) (receipt during pendency of action cures defect); Pinkard v. Pullman-Standard, 678 F.2d 1211, 1218–19, 29 FEP 216 (5th Cir. 1982) (no motion to dismiss filed prior to receipt of notice); Henderson v. Eastern Freight Ways, Inc., 460 F.2d 258, 260, 4 FEP 726 (4th Cir. 1972) (per curiam) (it is "general policy of law to find a way in which to prevent loss of valuable rights, not because something was done too late but rather because it was done too soon"); Soble v. University of Md., 572 F. Supp. 1509, 1517, 33 FEP 611 (D. Md. 1983) (action not dismissed, as notice now has been received).

[294]*E.g.*, Hill v. Potter, 352 F.3d 1142, 1145 (7th Cir. 2003) (suggesting that if plaintiffs could sue before receiving their right-to-sue notice then "the time of the courts and of lawyers would be wasted with cases that ended up being resolved or abandoned at the administrative level"); *see also* Cox v. United States Gypsum Co., 409 F.2d 289, 291–92, 1 FEP 714 (7th Cir. 1969) (case dismissed without prejudice to commence timely action); Campbell v. Burger King Corp., 10 FEP 1214, 1215 (S.D. Fla. 1975) (specifically stating that plaintiff could apply for right-to-sue letter and, if he obtained one, file new suit with same judge).

[295]Perdue v. Roy Stone Transfer Corp., 690 F.2d 1091, 1095, 29 FEP 1673 (4th Cir. 1982) (regulations did not permit EEOC to issue right-to-sue letter following negotiated settlement, even though defendant allegedly breached its entire agreement with agency and the plaintiff); Kahn v. Pepsi Cola Bottling Group, 526 F. Supp. 1268, 1270, 27 FEP 770 (E.D.N.Y. 1981) (EEOC had misplaced Title VII charge and refused to issue letter).

[296]*See* 29 C.F.R. § 1601.28(e) (2005).

facially valid notice of right to sue is issued and the 90-day period expires, a second notice of right to sue cannot be issued.[297]

Where the EEOC reconsiders its earlier determination and then issues a second notice of right to sue following the reconsideration, courts have upheld the validity of the second notice if the EEOC revokes the original notice during the 90-day period following the charging party's receipt of the original notice.[298] The Eleventh Circuit held that a former employee's receipt of a second right-to-sue notice was ineffective to start the 90-day limitations period running again where there was no evidence that the EEOC reconsidered the merits of the employee's first charge prior to issuing the second notice. Accordingly, the employee's suit filed pursuant to the second right-to-sue notice was dismissed as untimely.[299]

In attempting to reduce confusion surrounding multiple notices, these judicially created rules are now reflected in the EEOC's regulations.[300]

---

[297]*E.g.*, Brown v. Mead Corp., 646 F.2d 1163, 1167–68, 25 FEP 684 (6th Cir. 1981) (facially valid notice of right to sue was issued, and plaintiff did not sue before 90-day period expired; although original notice was issued by District Director without authority, second notice issued 4 years later was invalid); Cleveland v. Douglas Aircraft Co., 509 F.2d 1027, 1030, 10 FEP 192 (9th Cir. 1975) (second right-to-sue notice is legal nullity); Ford v. General Motors Corp., 452 F. Supp. 355, 356–57, 21 FEP 1365 (E.D. Mo. 1978) (action dismissed although filed within 90 days of second right-to-sue notice; even if EEOC wrongfully had issued first notice, EEOC lacked power to issue second one). *But cf.* Hiduchenko v. Minneapolis Med. & Diagnostic Ctr., Ltd., 475 F. Supp. 1175, 1179–80, 20 FEP 1395 (D. Minn. 1979) (first case was dismissed because notice of right to sue was issued prematurely, but second notice issued by EEOC was valid; characterizing *Cleveland* result as "unduly harsh").

[298]*E.g.*, Lute v. Singer Co., 678 F.2d 844, 846, 847, 28 FEP 1700 (9th Cir. 1982) (limiting time to revoke protects parties' interests in speedy resolutions without unduly restricting EEOC's abilities to correct its own errors), *modified on other grounds and reh'g en banc denied*, 696 F.2d 1266, 34 FEP 1372 (1983); Trujillo v. General Elec. Co., 621 F.2d 1084, 1086–87, 22 FEP 1575 (10th Cir. 1980) (second notice upheld where first notice was revoked within initial 90-day period); Gonzalez v. Firestone Tire & Rubber Co., 610 F.2d 241, 245–46, 21 FEP 1367 (5th Cir. 1980) (EEOC may issue second notice, provided that parties are given notice of reconsideration within 90-day period).

[299]Gitlitz v. Compagnie Nationale Air Fr., 129 F.3d 554, 557 (11th Cir. 1997) (second notice not effective if there is no reconsideration); *see also* Santini v. Cleveland Clinic Fla., 232 F.3d 823, 825, 84 FEP 321 (11th Cir. 2000) (holding that second notice issued by EEOC did not equitably toll statutory filing period because plaintiff had actual notice from first, albeit, undated notice of right to sue).

[300]29 C.F.R. §§ 1601.19(b), 1601.21(b)(1) & (d)(1) (2005) (first notice of right to sue may be revoked if (1) notice of intent to reconsider is issued within 90 days

Courts have held, however, that a second notice of right to sue was not valid when reconsideration was granted *after* the initial 90-day period.[301] The Fifth Circuit has addressed the question of which prevails when the notice of reconsideration and the filing of the lawsuit occur simultaneously. The court held that the notice of reconsideration trumps. Therefore, when the notice of reconsideration is issued on the same day the complaint is filed, the notice of right to sue on which suit is filed is no longer effective; the plaintiff must wait for the second notice of right to sue to file a valid court claim.[302]

Where cause has been found, the EEOC now issues a notice of right to sue following (1) the failure of conciliation, and (2) a subsequent decision by the EEOC not to bring suit, unless notice is earlier requested by the charging party.[303]

2. What Triggers Commencement of the 90-Day Period

Under § 706(f)(1), the 90-day period begins to run from "the giving" of the notice of right to sue. It is the *receipt* of the notice,

---

of receipt of first notice, (2) charging party has not already filed suit, and (3) charging party did not request issuance of initial notice). These regulations have been upheld on subsequent attack. *See* Jackson v. Richards Med. Co., 961 F.2d 575, 585, 58 FEP 869 (6th Cir. 1992) (regulations found procedural and reasonably related to § 713(a)).

[301]*E.g.*, Dougherty v. Barry, 869 F.2d 605, 612–13, 49 FEP 289 (D.C. Cir. 1989) (second notice of right to sue issued by Justice Department not valid, and facts do not justify equitable estoppel); Pradia v. Gulf Oil Co., 20 FEP 876, 877 (S.D. Tex. 1979) (EEOC redetermination of reasonable cause and issuance of second notice cannot revive cause of action not filed within 90 days of receipt of first notice).

[302]Martin v. Alamo Cmty. Coll. Dist., 353 F.3d 409, 413, 15 AD 160 (5th Cir. 2003) (court found that simultaneous filing merely means on same day and is regardless of hours and minutes). In its analysis of the timing of the two simultaneous events, the court also determined that a notice of reconsideration is "issued" by the EEOC on the date that it is deposited in the mail by the EEOC. *Id.* at 413.

[303]*See* 29 C.F.R. § 1601.28(b)(1) (2005). This is a change of practice. The EEOC earlier used a controversial "two-letter" procedure. After conciliation failed, the EEOC would send the charging party a letter advising that conciliation had failed and asking if the charging party wished the notice of right to sue to issue. Only if the charging party responded in the affirmative would the EEOC issue the right-to-sue letter. The defendants argued that this put total control of the statute of limitations in the hands of the charging party, who could wait an indefinite period of time before requesting the notice of right to sue. The defendants contended that the limitations period should run from the receipt of the first letter. The courts of appeals were divided on the validity of the EEOC's practice. The split became moot when the EEOC abandoned its earlier practice. It now issues the notice of right to sue at the termination of its proceedings, unless earlier requested.

however, rather than the Commission's *sending* of the notice, that triggers the running of the suit-filing period.[304]

But receipt by whom? Difficult questions arise where an individual other than the charging party receives the notice, or where the notice for some reason goes undelivered. In *Irwin v. Department of Veterans Affairs*,[305] the Supreme Court held that a notice of right to sue was received, for purposes of § 717(c), when it arrived at the office of the charging party's attorney.[306] The court action was filed 44 days after it was received at the attorney's office, but only 29 days after the charging party claimed to have received it. In applying the then-required[307] 30-day filing limit for federal government employees, the Supreme Court found that the filing was untimely. The Court reasoned that if Congress had intended to depart from the accepted practice of providing actual notice through counsel, it would have made this clear in the statute.[308]

Similar issues arise when the notice of right to sue is received by a third person at the charging party's address. Most[309] but not

---

[304]McDonnell Douglas Corp. v. Green, 411 U.S. 792, 798, 5 FEP 965 (1973). Because the period runs from *actual* receipt, courts generally have rejected efforts to deem constructive receipt by (for example) adding 3 days to the 90-day time period. *E.g.*, Taylor v. Books-A-Million, Inc., 296 F.3d 376, 89 FEP 577 (5th Cir. 2002), *cert. denied*, 537 U.S. 1200 (2003); Peete v. American Standard Graphic, 885 F.2d 331, 331–32, 50 FEP 1377 (6th Cir. 1989); Mosel v. Hills Dep't Store, Inc., 789 F.2d 251, 253, 40 FEP 1049 (3d Cir. 1986); Norris v. Florida Dep't of Health & Rehabilitative Servs., 730 F.2d 682, 683, 35 FEP 1505 (11th Cir. 1984). *But see* Hunter v. Stephenson Roofing, Inc., 790 F.2d 472, 475, 40 FEP 1193 (6th Cir. 1986) (90 days begins to run 5 days after notice is mailed where plaintiff fails to inform EEOC of new address and notice is received by former roommate).

[305]498 U.S. 89, 54 FEP 577 (1990).

[306]*Id*. at 92–93. The charging party's attorney had actually been out of the country when the letter arrived. The Supreme Court, however, rejected the idea that there was a "material difference" between receipt by an attorney and his or her office. *Id.* at 93. Instead, it observed that notice to an attorney's office acknowledged by a representative of that office qualifies as notice to the client. *Id.*

[307]The Civil Rights Act of 1991 subsequently changed the time period for federal employees to file suit from 30 to 90 days. Pub. L. No. 102-166, § 114, 1991 U.S.C.C.A.N. (105 Stat.) 1071, 1079 (codified as amended at 29 U.S.C. § 2000e-16).

[308]*Irwin*, 498 U.S. at 93.

[309]*See, e.g.*, Morehardt v. Spirit Airlines, Inc., 174 F. Supp. 2d 1272, 1277 (M.D. Fla. 2001) (receipt of letter by spouse or counsel is binding on plaintiff); Hunter-Reed v. City of Houston, 244 F. Supp. 2d 733, 740 (S.D. Tex 2003) (90-day filing period begins to run on date right-to-sue letter was issued to office of formally designated counsel or to claimant); Scholar v. Pacific Bell, 963 F.2d 264, 267, 58 FEP 1248 (9th Cir. 1992) (return receipt signed by charging party's daughter); Harvey v. City of New Bern Police Dep't, 813 F.2d 652, 654, 43 FEP 401 (4th Cir. 1987)

all[310] courts have held that receipt by a third person triggers the beginning of the limitations period. The circuits that have spoken on the issue—the Fourth, Fifth, Ninth, Tenth, and Eleventh—have taken the approach that the 90-day period begins to run when there has been receipt by a member of plaintiff's household at the plaintiff's address unless the plaintiff establishes equitable considerations that would justify tolling.[311] The circuits are split, however, over the effect that a complainant's receipt of a postal notice of attempted delivery of the right-to-sue letter has on the commencement of the 90-day period.[312] The circuits also are split on

---

(charging party's wife signed for letter); Espinoza v. Missouri Pac. R.R., 754 F.2d 1247, 1250, 37 FEP 415 (5th Cir. 1985) (charging party was out of town); Bell v. Eagle Motor Lines, 693 F.2d 1086, 1087, 30 FEP 951 (11th Cir. 1982) (same); Law v. Hercules, Inc., 713 F.2d 691, 692–93, 32 FEP 1291 (11th Cir. 1983) (letter was picked up at post office by charging party's 17-year-old son at request of charging party's wife).

[310]*See, e.g.*, Stallworth v. Wells Fargo Armored Servs. Corp., 936 F.2d 522, 524–25, 56 FEP 618 (11th Cir. 1991) (notice was received by plaintiff's nephew; plaintiff never saw it; and EEOC failed to follow plaintiff's counsel's instructions (and its own compliance manual) to send copy of notice to counsel).

[311]*See* Million v. Frank, 47 F.3d 385, 387–88, 67 FEP 254 (10th Cir. 1995) ("If the rule were otherwise, a plaintiff would be permitted to 'enjoy a manipulable, open-ended time extension which could render the statutory limitation meaningless.' ") (citation omitted); Rasmussen v. Sigma Corp. of Am., 27 F. Supp. 2d 388, 392, 78 FEP 1820 (E.D.N.Y. 1998) (suit filed more than 90 days after employee's teenage daughter accepted delivery of right-to-sue letter was untimely); Simpkins v. Washington Metro. Area Transit Auth., 2 F. Supp. 2d 52, 57 (D.D.C. 1998); Roberson v. Bowie State Univ., 899 F. Supp. 235, 238, 72 FEP 899 (D. Md. 1995) (plaintiff's daughter signed for letter that plaintiff first saw 17 days later; 90-day period began to run upon receipt by daughter).

[312]*Compare* Graham-Humphreys v. Memphis Brooks Museum of Art, Inc., 209 F.3d 552, 558–60 (6th Cir. 2000) (90-day period begins to run 5 days after plaintiff received constructive notice that certified mail notification was delivered to plaintiff's last-known address), *Hunter-Reed*, 244 F. Supp. 2d at 741 (90-day filing period begins to run on date right-to-sue letter sent by certified mail is presumptively available for pick-up at post office upon passage of 7 days after issuance) *and* Lee v. Henderson, 75 F. Supp. 2d 591, 593 (E.D. Tex. 1999) (90-day period triggered upon delivery of first notice of certified mail, not when letter actually picked up) *with* Houston v. Sidley & Austin, 185 F.3d 837, 839, 80 FEP 417 (7th Cir. 1999) ("when the EEOC sends a right-to-sue letter by certified mail, the 90-day limitations period begins to run on the day the plaintiff actually received the letter, so long as she picks it up within the time that the Post Office's notice gives her before it will be returned to the sender"), Jackson v. Continental Cargo-Denver, 183 F.3d 1186, 1188–90, 80 FEP 564 (10th Cir. 1999) (90 days runs only from actual receipt of letter, not simply notice of attempted delivery), Zillyette v. Capital One Fin. Corp., 179 F.3d 1337, 1341–42, 9 AD 925 (11th Cir. 1999) (90 days commences 3 days after complainant receives notice of attempted delivery; analogizing to FED. R. CIV. P. 6(e)) *and* Watts-Means v. Prince

which party bears the burden of proof to establish whether the complaint was filed within the 90-day period.[313]

Courts have also generally found that the suit-filing period runs from the date the right-to-sue letter is received at the address most recently listed with the EEOC—even though the letter was not actually received by the plaintiff because of the plaintiff's failure to provide the EEOC with a current address.[314]

Courts have also suggested that the initial presumptions surrounding the triggering of the 90-day period (i.e., that a mailed document is received three days after its mailing, and notice provided by a government agency has been mailed on the date shown on

---

George's Family Crisis Ctr., 7 F.3d 40, 42 (4th Cir. 1993) (90-day period presumptively runs from date when plaintiff received notice of attempted delivery, but allowing equitable tolling when plaintiff was unaware of letter's contents).

[313]*Compare* Ebbert v. DaimlerChrysler Corp., 319 F.3d 103, 108 (3d Cir. 2003) (because limitations is affirmative defense, defendant bears burden of proof) *with* Green v. Union Foundry Co., 281 F.3d 1229 (11th Cir. 2002) (record showed that case was filed 97 days after mailing of right-to-sue notice by EEOC, while charging party was incarcerated, and wife received letter but could not place date of receipt; plaintiff did not meet burden of establishing compliance with deadline).

[314]*E.g.*, Hill v. John Chezik Imps., 869 F.2d 1122, 1124, 49 FEP 493 (8th Cir. 1989) (period normally runs from date letter is received at most recent address provided to EEOC; barring action, even though EEOC failed to send copy of notice to charging party's attorney); Ball v. Abbott Adver., Inc., 864 F.2d 419, 421 (6th Cir. 1988) (same; providing new address to state human rights agency insufficient); St. Louis v. Alverno Coll., 744 F.2d 1314, 1316–17, 35 FEP 1715 (7th Cir. 1984) (period runs from date letter is received at most recent address given to EEOC; failure to receive letter was charging party's fault); Nelmida v. Shelly Eurocars, Inc., 112 F.3d 380, 384, 73 FEP 1313 (9th Cir. 1997) (refusing to apply equitable tolling where EEOC delivered right-to-sue letter to address that plaintiff had given even though she did not reside there and often failed to receive mail at that address and where she had left state for several weeks without informing EEOC of her absence); Ortez v. Washington County, 88 F.3d 804, 807, 71 FEP 584 (9th Cir. 1996) (suit-filing period begins to run when notice of right to sue is received at plaintiff's mailing address); Choate v. National R.R. Passenger Corp., 132 F. Supp. 2d 569 (E.D. Mich. 2001) (when plaintiff has changed addresses and does not notify EEOC of said change, 90-day period begins to run 5 days after date that EEOC mails notice to plaintiff's address of record as demonstrated by postmark on envelope); Bobbitt v. Freeman Cos., 132 F. Supp. 2d 1110, 85 FEP 412 (N.D. Ill. 2000) (failure to check one's mail for 4 weeks because of extensive business travel did not extend 90-day period for filing Title VII suit); Harding v. Fort Wayne Foundry/Pontiac Div., Inc., 919 F. Supp. 1223, 1231–32, 70 FEP 1074 (N.D. Ind. 1996) (dismissing plaintiff's claim even though he had provided change of address to local agency rather than EEOC, because agency had no duty under work sharing agreement to transmit information to EEOC, and plaintiff's claim that local agency and EEOC had apparent authority agency relationship lacked merit).

the notice) are not dispositive.[315] If a claimant can present sworn testimony or other admissible evidence from which it reasonably could be inferred either that the notice was mailed later than its typewritten date or that it took longer than three days by mail, then the presumption of the date of receipt may be rebutted.[316]

The Eleventh Circuit engaged in an extensive analysis and determined that although the 90-day limitations period was tolled while the plaintiffs were putative members of a class action, that period resumed running as to the excluded putative class members on the date of the district court's order denying class certification, given that "the named plaintiffs no longer have a duty to advance the interests of the excluded putative class members."[317]

The Fifth Circuit examined the relationship between the state agency and the EEOC and the receipt of a right-to-sue letter. In *Vielma v. Eureka*,[318] the court found that the receipt of a right-to-sue letter from the EEOC did *not* trigger the 60-day period for filing suit under the Texas Commission on Human Rights Act. The court also held that, because the right-to-sue letter is the "exclusive mechanism" for commencing the federal 90-day period, the receipt of a state letter does not trigger the federal period.[319]

In addressing a novel question, the Third Circuit found that expiration of the 90-day period for filing suit provided in Title VII does not prevent joining a successor corporation as an additional defendant after the expiration of the 90-day period.[320]

---

[315]*See* Sherlock v. Montefiore Med. Ctr., 84 F.3d 522, 525–26, 70 FEP 1377 (2d Cir. 1996).

[316]*Id.*; *see also* Peltier v. Apple Health Care, Inc., 130 F. Supp. 2d 285, 291 (D. Conn. 2000) (plaintiff's sworn affidavit stating that she never received right-to-sue letter, saw it for first time in litigation, and had no reason to suspect that letter had, or would be, sent in light of EEOC's letter informing her that right-to-sue letter was not prerequisite to filing suit under ADEA sufficient to rebut presumption of receipt); Gardner v. Honest Weight Food Co-op, Inc., 96 F. Supp. 2d 154, 158–59 (N.D.N.Y. 2000) (plaintiff's sworn affidavit that she was "confident" she received her right-to-sue notification days after presumed date of receipt sufficient to create genuine issue of fact as to when limitations period ran).

[317]Armstrong v. Martin Marietta Corp., 138 F.3d 1374, 1380–81, 76 FEP 1007 (11th Cir. 1998).

[318]218 F.3d 458 (5th Cir. 2000).

[319]*Vielma*, 218 F.3d at 466–67.

[320]Brzozowski v. Correctional Physician Servs., Inc., 360 F.3d 173 (3d Cir. 2004) (finding that relation-back rule under rules of civil procedure was not applicable in determining whether joinder of successor employer as additional defendant was timely).

Although courts have held that certain events are sufficient to start the running of the 90-day suit-filing period, other cases have focused on events that are *insufficient* to start the running of the 90-day filing period. Courts have deemed insufficient the receipt of a defective right-to-sue notice that fails to apprise a plaintiff of the correct limitations period,[321] the U.S. Postal Service's placing a notice in a lay plaintiff's post office box that a certified letter addressed to her had been received,[322] and receipt of the right-to-sue letter by a claimant's former attorney.[323]

At least one court has held that in computing the day that the 90-day time period commences under Federal Rule of Civil Procedure 6(a), the day after receipt of the right-to-sue letter is day one, and therefore the plaintiff's complaint filed on the 91st day after receipt of the right-to-sue letter was timely.[324]

In *Ebbert v. DaimlerChrysler Corp.*,[325] the Third Circuit considered the novel issue of whether a notice of dismissal must be in writing. Declining to give *Chevron*[326] deference to the EEOC's regulations requiring written notice, the court held that oral notice from the EEOC of the dismissal of a charge can commence the limitations period for filing an ADA action, but the notice must be equivalent to written notice.[327]

---

[321]Wilson v. Peña, 79 F.3d 154, 163–64, 72 FEP 67 (D.C. Cir. 1996) (court held that "[w]hen an agency or department has taken final action but has failed to issue a proper notice, an employee can bring an action in the district court within a reasonable time" where EEOC notice erroneously apprised plaintiff that he had only 30 days to file suit instead of 90).

[322]Holmes v. World Wildlife Fund, Inc., 908 F. Supp. 19, 21, 69 FEP 1181 (D.D.C. 1995) (in refusing to dismiss complaint filed 94 days after delivery of such notice to plaintiff's post office box, court relied on fact that plaintiff actually received right-to-sue letter 87 days before filing, and letter stated that suit could be filed "within 90 days of . . . receipt of this letter"); *cf.* Biester v. Midwest Health Servs., Inc., 77 F.3d 1264, 1266, 70 FEP 397 (10th Cir. 1996) (impliedly holding that plaintiff's suit-filing period started running when he picked up his right-to-sue letter at post office, after receiving two or three notices that he had certified letter).

[323]Coates v. Shalala, 914 F. Supp. 110, 112, 72 FEP 644 (D. Md. 1996) (focusing on attorney's lack of authority to accept service for or act as representative of plaintiff), *aff'd*, 133 F.3d 914 (4th Cir. 1997).

[324]Bowens v. Big K-Mart Corp., 117 F. Supp. 2d 288 (E.D.N.Y. 2000).

[325]319 F.3d 103 (3d Cir. 2003).

[326]Chevron U.S.A., Inc. v. Natural Res. Def. Council, 467 U.S. 837 (1984).

[327]319 F.3d at 115–16; *see also* Hunter-Reed v. City of Houston, 244 F. Supp. 2d 733, 742 (S.D. Tex. 2003) (oral notice of dismissal is sufficient to begin 90-day limitation period); Kerr v. McDonald's Corp., 2005 U.S. App. LEXIS 21613, at *16–17

Courts seem to examine all the facts and circumstances, including any equitable considerations, when determining the timing of the commencement of the 90-day suit-filing period.

3. What Constitutes a "Filing"

Section 706(f)(1) provides that within 90 days after the giving of the notice of right to sue, "a civil action may be brought against the respondent named in the charge."[328] Rule 3 of the Federal Rules of Civil Procedure provides that "[a] civil action is commenced by the filing of a complaint with the court."[329]

Sometimes, however, unsophisticated persons attempt to initiate proceedings in a less formal way. In *Baldwin County Welcome Center v. Brown*,[330] the Supreme Court provided some guidance about what constitutes an adequate "filing." The plaintiff in *Baldwin* mailed the notice of right to sue to the court and requested the appointment of counsel, within the 90-day period. In response, a magistrate entered an order requiring the plaintiff to make formal application for appointed counsel using the court's motion form and supporting questionnaire. The magistrate also reminded the plaintiff of the necessity of complying with the 90-day period. The plaintiff subsequently did not file a complaint, the motion, or the questionnaire within the 90-day period. The Supreme Court concluded that the plaintiff had not timely commenced an action[331] and that this was not an appropriate case in which to apply equitable tolling.[332]

The Eleventh Circuit has held that the filing of the original EEOC charge with the court is sufficient to constitute a complaint.[333]

(11th Cir. Oct. 6, 2005) (telephone notice that EEOC terminated investigation triggered inquiry notice for charging parties; failure to discover until 6 weeks later that EEOC mailed right-to-sue letters did not excuse belated filing of civil action).

[328]42 U.S.C. § 2000e-5(f)(1) (2000).

[329]*See* Fed. R. Civ. P. 3.

[330]466 U.S. 147, 34 FEP 929 (1984) (per curiam).

[331]*Id.* at 149–50.

[332]*Id.* at 151–52.

[333]Judkins v. Beech Aircraft Corp., 745 F.2d 1330, 1331–32, 36 FEP 367 (11th Cir. 1984) (charge more than adequately complies with "short and plain statement" requirement of Federal Rule of Civil Procedure 8(a)(2)); *cf.* Mahroom v. Defense Language Inst., 732 F.2d 1439, 1440, 34 FEP 1334 (9th Cir. 1984) (filing found where request for counsel included copy of EEOC's determination describing nature of claim).

The effect of a pending application for court-appointed counsel without an accompanying complaint is less clear. The Court in *Baldwin* distinguished the plaintiff's situation from one where a more or less formal motion for appointment of counsel is pending: there, equity might justify tolling the statutory period until a ruling on the motion.[334] But courts are divided on the sufficiency of an application for appointment of counsel where a complaint is not included with the application.[335]

Courts continue to provide greater leeway to pro se plaintiffs in terms of what constitutes a "filing." The Fifth Circuit held that a pro se complaint was timely filed even though it was devoid of the essential elements of a complaint, because it was submitted to the clerk for filing within the 90-day period and the court gave the plaintiff free leave to amend the defective allegations in that pleading.[336] Other courts have held that a plaintiff who *submits* a complaint within the period, with an application for appointment of counsel or to proceed in forma pauperis, would be considered timely, even though the clerk does not actually *file* the complaint until later.[337]

---

[334]*Baldwin*, 466 U.S. at 151–52 (citing Harris v. Walgreen's Distrib. Ctr., 456 F.2d 588, 591, 592, 4 FEP 342 (6th Cir. 1972) (all papers necessary to support motion for counsel were filed within then-applicable 30-day period)); *see, e.g.*, Jarrett v. US Sprint Commc'ns Co., 22 F.3d 256, 262 (10th Cir. 1994) (in such cases, "[t]he facts must be examined and any granting of equity must be made on a case-by-case basis"; limitations period was tolled while plaintiff's in forma pauperis petition was pending, but it was not tolled during pendency of plaintiff's subsequent motion for appointment of counsel, where plaintiff showed her ability to file complaint by presenting one to clerk with her in forma pauperis petition, but plaintiff did not pay filing fee until 5 months after her petition was denied).

[335]*Compare* Brown v. J.I. Case Co., 756 F.2d 48, 51, 36 FEP 1399 (7th Cir. 1985) (filing of request for appointment of counsel with notice of right to sue tolls limitations period, unless plaintiff has failed to exercise diligence or otherwise has engaged in inequitable conduct) *with* Firle v. Mississippi State Dep't of Educ., 762 F.2d 487, 488–89, 37 FEP 1817 (5th Cir. 1985) (filing request for appointment of counsel, notice of right-to-sue, and copy of termination notice not sufficient).

[336]McClellon v. Lone Star Gas Co., 66 F.3d 98, 101–02, 69 FEP 36 (5th Cir. 1995).

[337]*See* Hernandez v. Aldridge, 902 F.2d 386, 388, 52 FEP 1769 (5th Cir. 1990) (complaint deemed filed within statutory period, as it was in custody of clerk); Toliver v. County of Sullivan, 841 F.2d 41, 42, 46 FEP 1175 (2d Cir. 1988) (where complaint with application to proceed in forma pauperis was received by clerk within 90 days, action was deemed timely even though clerk did not file complaint until after application was granted); Gilardi v. Schroeder, 833 F.2d 1226, 1233, 45 FEP 346 (7th Cir. 1987) (district clerk acted improperly in returning plaintiff's papers,

Service of process need not be made within the 90-day period. The 90-day limitations period may, however, have a bearing on the plaintiff's ability later to add or change defendants. In this regard, courts have considered whether the amendment satisfies the requirements of Federal Rule of Civil Procedure 15(c).[338]

Similarly, an amended Title VII complaint filed after the 90-day limitations period will be allowed if it "relates back" to an earlier complaint filed within the requisite time period under the standard set forth in Rule 15(c) of the Federal Rules of Civil Procedure.[339] The same rule applies if the amended complaint filed outside the 90-day period seeks to add a new defendant. Rule 15(c) allows the addition of a new defendant when the new defendant knew or should have known of a mistake concerning the identity of the proper party and where the new defendant cannot establish the requisite prejudice.[340] Courts continue to apply the rules of relation back restrictively, however, particularly where a plaintiff seeks to add parties or new claims.[341] In general, the question of

---

including complaint and in forma pauperis petition, on basis of technical filing inadequacies); *see also* Loya v. Desert Sands Unified Sch. Dist., 721 F.2d 279, 280–81, 33 FEP 739 (9th Cir. 1983) (deeming complaint filed even though clerk had refused to accept it because plaintiff had used wrong size paper; local rules not jurisdictional requirements).

[338]*See, e.g.,* Archuleta v. Duffy's, Inc., 471 F.2d 33, 35, 5 FEP 347 (10th Cir. 1973) (naming incorrect corporation based on misinformation supplied by secretary of state not misnomer but was substitution of parties not complying with Rule 15(c)). This issue also has arisen where a federal employee sues the wrong government entity or person. *Compare* Warren v. Department of the Army, 867 F.2d 1156, 1160–61, 49 FEP 141 (8th Cir. 1989) (period was tolled by misleading EEOC notice; requirements of Rule 15(c) were satisfied during tolled period) *with* Johnson v. United States Postal Serv., 861 F.2d 1475, 1479–81, 48 FEP 686 (10th Cir. 1988) (facts do not justify tolling, and requirements of Rule 15(c) were not met) *and* Bates v. Tennessee Valley Auth., 851 F.2d 1366, 1368–69, 47 FEP 905 (11th Cir. 1988) (denying addition of proper defendants because elements of Rule 15(c) were not satisfied).

[339]Kaup v. First Bank Sys., Inc., 926 F. Supp. 155, 158 (D. Colo. 1996).

[340]*See* Graham v. Gendex Med. X-Ray, Inc., 176 F.R.D. 288, 290 (N.D. Ill. 1997) (plaintiff made an inadvertent mistake concerning the identity of proper party, and new defendant received notice that it was potential party to suit and would not be prejudiced because it had opportunity to settle case when it was filed with EEOC); Rowe v. Florida Sch. for Deaf & Blind, 176 F.R.D. 646, 649 (M.D. Fla. 1997) (defendant was on notice of action and aware of misidentification well before period for service ended, defendant failed to establish any prejudice, and there was no undue delay in seeking leave to amend).

[341]*See* Anderson v. Unisys Corp., 47 F.3d 302, 307–09, 67 FEP 317 (8th Cir. 1995) (claims of additional plaintiffs under amended complaint held not to relate

relation back of an untimely complaint is still largely determined by the specific facts of each case.[342]

4. Tolling

Before the Supreme Court's decision in *Zipes v. Trans World Airlines, Inc.*,[343] most courts had concluded that the 90-day period was jurisdictional.[344] After *Zipes* held that the *charge-filing* period was not jurisdictional,[345] courts increasingly reached the same conclusion about the 90-day *suit-filing* period.[346]

Although the Supreme Court has not explicitly so held, it has given pointed clues. In *Crown, Cork & Seal Co. v. Parker*,[347] the Court rejected an argument that the "jurisdictional" nature of the

---

back to filing of original complaint because they filed their own ADEA charges with EEOC, received their own right-to-sue letters, and deliberately decided not to file suit within limitations period); Sanders v. Venture Stores, Inc., 56 F.3d 771, 774–75, 75 FEP 637 (7th Cir. 1995) (district court did not abuse discretion in denying plaintiffs' motion for leave to amend time-barred Title VII complaint where summary judgment motion was pending, discovery cutoff had passed, plaintiffs offered no reason for their delay in asserting proposed new claims, and allowing such amendment would result in additional discovery costs for employer, undue delay, and prejudice to parties and court); Cornwell v. Robinson, 23 F.3d 694, 705, 64 FEP 1254 (2d Cir. 1995) (amended complaint that adds new individual defendants outside limitations period does not relate back to original timely complaint unless individuals knew or should have known that such action would be brought against them for mistake in identity of proper party).

[342]*See, e.g.*, Davis v. Virginia Commonwealth Univ., 180 F.3d 626, 627–28, 9 AD 1151 (4th Cir. 1999) (Title VII plaintiff not required to comply with 90-day limitations period for filing second amended complaint that simply updated events alleged in first amended complaint); Wilson v. Fairchild Republic Co., 143 F.3d 733, 738–39, 76 FEP 1521 (2d Cir. 1998) (employee's first failure-to-promote claim under § 1981, which was never raised in EEOC charges or in employee's pleadings, did not relate back to his original complaint and was time-barred; employee's second failure-to-promote claim was not newly made but was timely raised in original Title VII complaint).

[343]455 U.S. 385, 28 FEP 1 (1982).

[344]*E.g.*, Hinton v. CPC Int'l, Inc., 520 F.2d 1312, 1315, 10 FEP 1423 (8th Cir. 1975) ("filing a complaint within 90 days is jurisdictional"); Cleveland v. Douglas Aircraft Co., 509 F.2d 1027, 1030, 10 FEP 192 (9th Cir. 1975) ("requirement is jurisdictional").

[345]*Zipes*, 455 U.S. at 1135.

[346]*E.g.*, Rice v. New Eng. Coll., 676 F.2d 9, 10, 28 FEP 1191 (1st Cir. 1982) ("tenor" of *Zipes* requires same conclusion for suit-filing period); Gordon v. National Youth Worth Alliance, 675 F.2d 356, 360, 28 FEP 980 (D.C. Cir. 1982) ("logic" of *Zipes* extends to suit-filing period).

[347]462 U.S. 345, 31 FEP 1697 (1983).

90-day suit-filing requirement prevented tolling of the limitations period during the pendency of a motion to certify a class in an action in which the plaintiff would have been a member of the class.[348] The plaintiff filed an individual action within 90 days following the denial of class certification. This was sufficient, the Court held, because the plaintiff had not received his right-to-sue letter until after the putative class action had been filed.[349]

In *Baldwin County Welcome Center v. Brown*,[350] the Court assumed, without explicitly stating, that equitable tolling would be applicable to the suit-filing period under appropriate factual circumstances. In *Irwin v. Department of Veterans Affairs*,[351] the Supreme Court indicated that the suit-filing period for Title VII actions against the federal government may be subject, in an appropriate case, to equitable tolling (noting, in dictum, that "the statutory time limits applicable to lawsuits against private employers under Title VII are subject to equitable tolling").[352] Thus, it now appears relatively certain that the 90-day suit-filing period is not jurisdictional and may be tolled.[353]

---

[348]*Id.* at 349 n.3.

[349]*Id.* at 353–54.

[350]466 U.S. 147, 151, 34 FEP 929 (1984) (per curiam) (discussed in Section III.D.3 *supra*) ("Nor do we find anything in the record to call for the application of the doctrine of equitable tolling"; distinguishing cases where plaintiff had received inadequate notice, where motion for appointment of counsel was pending, where court had led plaintiff to believe that further action was unnecessary, or where affirmative misconduct by defendant lulled plaintiff into inaction.).

[351]498 U.S. 89, 95–96, 54 FEP 577 (1990).

[352]*Id.* at 95 (citing Zipes v. Trans World Airlines, Inc., 455 U.S. 385, 394, 28 FEP 1 (1982), and Crown, Cork & Seal Co. v. Parker, 462 U.S. 345, 349 n.3, 31 FEP 1697 (1983)).

[353]*See* Hill v. John Chezik Imps., 869 F.2d 1122, 1124, 49 FEP 493 (8th Cir. 1989) (limitations period not jurisdictional and subject to equitable tolling); Valenzuela v. Kraft, Inc., 801 F.2d 1170, 1174, 41 FEP 1849 (9th Cir. 1986) (recognizing that Supreme Court overruled prior cases holding that period was jurisdictional), *supplemented*, 815 F.2d 570, 47 FEP 644 (9th Cir. 1987); Espinoza v. Missouri Pac. R.R., 754 F.2d 1247, 1248, 1249 & n.1, 37 FEP 415 (5th Cir. 1985) (90-day period is "akin to a statute of limitations" and is subject to equitable tolling); Jones v. Madison Serv. Corp., 744 F.2d 1309, 1314, 35 FEP 1711 (7th Cir. 1984) (90-day period may be equitably tolled when circumstances warrant); Johnson v. Al Tech Specialties Steel Corp., 731 F.2d 143, 146, 34 FEP 861 (2d Cir. 1984) ("time limit may be equitably tolled"); *cf.* Fouche v. Jekyll Island-State Park Auth., 713 F.2d 1518, 1526, 33 FEP 303 (11th Cir. 1983) (requirement that Attorney General issue right-to-sue letter in action against state entity is not jurisdictional and is subject to equitable modification).

It does not necessarily follow, however, that the same bases sufficient to toll the charge-filing period are sufficient to toll the suit-filing period. In *Irwin*, for example, the Court declined to apply equitable tolling to a "garden variety claim of excusable neglect."[354] Several cases have held that the pendency of an action later dismissed without prejudice does not toll the 90-day period with respect to a similar or identical subsequently filed action.[355] Reasons commonly proffered for tolling the charge-filing period are the claimant's lack of suspicion of discrimination and lack of access to facts. Presumably, these are insufficient to toll the suit-filing period, because by definition at this stage the plaintiff at least suspects discrimination (as there was an earlier, verified charge alleging discrimination) and additional fact-gathering can occur later (through discovery). The Supreme Court in *Irwin* indicated in dictum that equitable tolling arises "in situations where the claimant has actively pursued his judicial remedies by filing a defective pleading during the statutory period, or where the complainant has been induced or tricked by his adversary's misconduct into allowing the filing deadline to pass."[356]

In general, courts continue to apply *Irwin* in narrowly construing the doctrine of equitable tolling with respect to the suit-filing period.[357] As such, equitable tolling may not be allowed where

---

[354]*Irwin*, 498 U.S. at 96 (the plaintiff claimed that his attorney was out of the country when the notice arrived on March 23, and the plaintiff did not personally get the letter until April 7); *see also* Hallgren v. United States Dep't of Energy, 331 F.3d 588 (8th Cir. 2003) (suit-filing period for ADEA claim would not be tolled where employee's attorney mailed complaint on day before it was to be filed in city 450 miles away and it was not filed on time).

[355]*E.g.*, Brown v. Hartshorne Pub. Sch. Dist. #1, 926 F.2d 959, 961, 55 FEP 349 (10th Cir. 1991) (limitations period not tolled during pendency of action voluntarily dismissed because of plaintiff's attorney's back injury); Price v. Digital Equip. Corp., 846 F.2d 1026, 1027, 47 FEP 136 (5th Cir. 1988) (per curiam) (dismissal of first action for failure to prosecute does not toll period for subsequent action); Wilson v. Grumman Ohio Corp., 815 F.2d 26, 28, 43 FEP 733 (6th Cir. 1987) (per curiam) (no tolling after dismissal for failure to perfect service within 120 days).

[356]*Irwin*, 498 U.S. at 96 (footnote omitted); *see also* Threadgill v. Moore U.S.A., Inc., 269 F.3d 848, 850 (7th Cir. 2001) (tolling is reserved for situations where claimant has made good faith error, for example, brought suit in wrong court or was prevented in some extraordinary way from filing his complaint in time).

[357]*See, e.g.*, Williams v. Thomson Corp., 383 F.3d 789, 791, 94 FEP 543 (8th Cir. 2004) (equitable tolling of limitations period for filing suit not warranted where right-to-sue notice reached employee through forwarding address, where employee failed to update her address with EEOC when she moved, despite her pending appeal);

the complainant received oral notice of the issuance of a right-to-sue letter.[358] In certain circumstances, however, usually where the plaintiff is the victim of affirmative misinformation from the EEOC or his or her attorney, courts may be receptive to tolling arguments.[359]

Ebbert v. DaimlerChrysler Corp., 319 F.3d 103, 117–18 (3d Cir. 2003) (court declined to toll 90-day period where employee did not ask for right-to-sue letter after phone conversation with EEOC informing her of dismissal of her claim and where she did not make any inquiry into status of her EEOC charge until nearly 1 year later); Doster v. West, 165 F.3d 27, 30–31 (6th Cir. 1998) (no basis for equitable tolling where plaintiff failed to contact EEOC counselor until 1½ years after expiration of relevant 30-day period, even though plaintiff's lawyer was absent from his office when EEOC notice was received); Anderson v. Board of Regents, 140 F.3d 704, 706, 76 FEP 929 (7th Cir. 1998) (court refused to apply equitable tolling because "the Personnel Commission's promise to forward a copy of the complaint to the EEOC is not equivalent to an assurance that filing with the state is tantamount to simultaneously filing with the EEOC" and plaintiff failed to make inquiries into terms of work sharing agreement); Witt v. Roadway Express, 136 F.3d 1424, 1430, 76 FEP 1705 (10th Cir. 1998) (allegedly confusing letter from Kansas Human Rights Commission saying that case was closed but that plaintiff could have action reviewed by EEOC did not amount to active deception sufficient to warrant equitable tolling); Robinson v. Dalton, 107 F.3d 1018, 1022, 73 FEP 387 (3d Cir. 1997) (one phone call from EEOC counselor indicating that plaintiff did not need to file additional complaint for retaliatory discharge did not actively mislead plaintiff sufficiently to provide basis for equitable tolling); Nelmida v. Shelly Eurocars, Inc., 112 F.3d 380, 384–85, 73 FEP 1313 (9th Cir. 1997) (fact that Postal Service was unable to deliver right-to-sue notice did not entitle employee to equitable tolling where employee was not diligent in ensuring that she receive such notice in that she provided address at which she did not reside and left state for several weeks without informing EEOC, and employee provided no explanation for 10-week delay in filing after receipt of notice); Carney v. City of Shawnee, 24 F. Supp. 2d 1185, 1188–89 (D. Kan. 1998) (although plaintiffs' attorney requested copies of right-to-sue letters and never received them, plaintiffs had actual notice of 90-day period and EEOC directly issued them their right-to-sue notices, thus precluding equitable tolling); Pauling v. Secretary of Dep't of Interior, 960 F. Supp. 793 (S.D.N.Y. 1997) (no basis for equitable tolling).

[358]See Ebbert v. DaimlerChryler Corp., 319 F.3d 103, 106, 13 AD 1806 (3d Cir. 2003) (oral notice from EEOC of dismissal of charge can suffice to start 90-day period if it is equivalent to written notice); see also Hunter-Reed v. City of Houston, 244 F. Supp. 2d 733, 742 (S.D. Tex. 2003) (claimant not entitled to equitable tolling of 90-day filing period where EEOC orally notified claimant of its issuance of right-to-sue letter).

[359]See Walsh v. National Computer Sys., Inc., 332 F.3d 1150, 1157, 92 FEP 140 (8th Cir. 2003) (90-day period properly tolled in Title VII action because of conduct of employer's attorney, which lulled employee into delaying refiling of her complaint in federal court while parties were engaged in settlement negotiations); Seitzinger v. Reading Hosp. & Med. Ctr., 165 F.3d 236, 239–41, 79 FEP 48 (3d Cir. 1999) (although "usual rule is that attorney errors will be attributed to their clients," plaintiff's attorney's affirmative misrepresentations, in response to plaintiff's persistent questioning whether he had filed complaint on time, created issues of

Similarly, failure of the plaintiff's employer to post required legal notices of certain rights may warrant equitable tolling.[360]

The Third and Tenth Circuits have held that a federal employee's timely filed request for reconsideration of an adverse EEOC or agency decision tolls the 90-day limitations period, but that an untimely petition will have no tolling effect.[361]

The Sixth, Seventh, and Tenth Circuits have held that the filing of an in forma pauperis (IFP) petition serves as a proper basis for equitably tolling the suit-filing period and that the 90-day limitations period begins to run again once the IFP petition is denied; however, the failure to pay the required filing fee within 90 days after the denial of IFP status will generally render such tolling inappropriate and the complaint untimely.[362]

---

material fact sufficient to withstand summary judgment as to whether limitations should be equitably tolled); Armstrong v. Martin Marietta Corp., 138 F.3d 1374, 1393, 76 FEP 1007 (11th Cir. 1998) (court equitably tolled limitations period for those plaintiffs who were affirmatively misinformed by EEOC regarding statute of limitations); Browning v. AT&T Paradyne, 120 F.3d 222, 225–27, 74 FEP 1227 (11th Cir. 1997) (court equitably tolled limitations period where right-to-sue notice did not inform plaintiff of any filing deadline and EEOC investigator told plaintiff that her case was governed by old 2-year/3-year limitations period); Ryczek v. Guest Servs., Inc., 877 F. Supp. 754, 758, 67 FEP 461 (D.D.C. 1995) (limitations period may be tolled where plaintiff can demonstrate that she failed to receive right-to-sue letter because of "fortuitous circumstances" or "events beyond [her] control" or "no fault" of her own, as where EEOC mistakenly sent notice to plaintiff at wrong address and failed to send copy to plaintiff's attorney, despite request by attorney).

[360]Kephart v. Institute of Gas Tech., 581 F.2d 1287, 1289 (7th Cir. 1978) (where employer failed to post notice of ADEA rights, filing period is equitably tolled until plaintiff retains attorney or acquires knowledge of his rights). *But see* Marley v. Addus Healthcare, Inc., 122 F. Supp. 2d 954, 957–59 (N.D. Ill. 2000) (equitable tolling refused even where employer failed to post notice of employees' ADEA rights conspicuously, in violation of 29 USC § 627, based on plaintiff's knowledge of ADEA rights from other sources, such as employee's own drafting of employer's handbook that covered ADEA).

[361]Holley v. Department of Veterans Affairs, 165 F.3d 244, 246, 79 FEP 228 (3d Cir. 1999) (when request for reconsideration is timely filed, EEOC's decision on appeal becomes "final" only when that request is granted or denied); Belhomme v. Widnall, 127 F.3d 1214, 1216–17, 79 FEP 739 (10th Cir. 1997) ("a timely petition for reconsideration will toll the filing deadline . . . but an untimely petition will have no tolling effect").

[362]Truitt v. County of Wayne, 148 F.3d 644, 648, 77 FEP 657 (6th Cir. 1998) (no abuse of discretion in refusing to toll limitations period where plaintiff waited 4 months to pay filing fee after denial of IFP status; noting, however, that "there may be circumstances in which equitable tolling is appropriate after denial of a plaintiff's application for IFP status"); Williams-Guice v. Board of Educ., 45 F.3d 161, 162 (7th Cir. 1995) (limitations period suspended pending resolution of IFP

Courts continue to reject most efforts to argue that a plaintiff's mental incapacity tolls the 90-day filing period. However, in *Stoll v. Runyon*,[363] the Ninth Circuit reversed the district court's dismissal of a Title VII action as time-barred, holding that the plaintiff had demonstrated the type of "extraordinary circumstances" necessary to warrant tolling the limitations period for filing suit on the basis of mental incapacity.[364] In that case, the plaintiff had suffered severe psychological damage as a result of being sexually harassed, raped, and abused by supervisors and co-workers at the Sacramento Post Office. She attempted suicide several times and was unable to read, open mail, or otherwise function in society. Although the plaintiff was represented by counsel at the time, the court found that the plaintiff's mental incapacity impaired her relationship with her attorney and rendered her unable to communicate with him or to protect her legal rights. The court concluded: "To state the matter bluntly, if ever equity demanded tolling a statute of limitations, it does so here."[365]

Absent such egregious facts, however, courts remain largely unwilling to toll the 90-day limitations period on the basis of alleged mental incapacity or disability of the plaintiff.[366]

---

petition resumed running on date application denied; plaintiff's failure to pay docket fee before expiration of resumed limitations period made complaint untimely); Jarrett v. US Sprint Commc'ns, Inc., 22 F.3d 256, 259–60, 67 FEP 1026 (10th Cir. 1994) (statute of limitations was tolled while petition to proceed IFP pending); Madison v. BP Oil Co., 928 F. Supp. 1132, 1135–36 (S.D. Ala. 1996) (complaint was submitted within 90 days, with motion to proceed in forma pauperis; complaint not considered formally filed until filing fee paid, following denial of motion, but deemed constructively filed as of date of initial submission); Woods v. Bentsen, 889 F. Supp. 179, 184–85, 72 FEP 1554 (E.D. Pa. 1995) (same). There is some disagreement, however, as to whether the plaintiff seeking IFP status must pay the filing fee at the time of filing suit. *Compare Truitt*, 148 F.3d at 648 *with Williams-Guice*, 45 F.3d at 164.

[363]165 F.3d 1238, 78 FEP 1312 (9th Cir. 1999).

[364]*Id.* at 1242–43.

[365]*Id.* at 1242.

[366]*See* Bravo Perazza v. Commission of P.R., 218 F. Supp. 2d 176 (D.P.R. 2002) (equitable tolling only available if plaintiff can show that his mental disability is so severe that plaintiff is unable to engage in rational thought and deliberate decision making sufficient to pursue his claim alone or through counsel); Smith-Haynie v. District of Columbia, 155 F.3d 575, 579–80, 77 FEP 1499 (D.C. Cir. 1998) (employee's statements that she was confused by and did not understand her right-to-sue letter and that she was further traumatized and unable to psychologically deal with it, without any evidence that she was unable to manage her affairs or function

5. Laches and Related Issues

Laches may bar a Title VII action if the plaintiff unreasonably and inexcusably delays in bringing the lawsuit, and the defendant is prejudiced as a result of the delay.[367] In *Smith v. Caterpillar, Inc.*,[368] the Seventh Circuit stated the general principle that "the decision to apply the doctrine of laches lies on a sliding scale: the longer the plaintiff delays in filing her claim, the less prejudice the defendant must show in order to defend on laches."[369]

A number of courts of appeals have dismissed actions brought by the EEOC where delay and prejudice have been established.[370]

---

in society, insufficient to establish that she was non compos mentis during limitation period so as to warrant tolling); Biester v. Midwest Health Servs., Inc., 77 F.3d 1264, 1268, 70 FEP 397 (10th Cir. 1996) (suit-filing period not tolled by fact that plaintiff was suffering from major depression and attendant symptoms, given that necessary exceptional circumstances were not present); Steele v. Brown, 993 F. Supp. 918, 922 (M.D.N.C.) (plaintiff's alleged disability during limitations period not severe enough to toll limitations period where plaintiff attempted to secure legal representation, worked 40 hours per week, and otherwise supported himself during that period and where plaintiff's hospitalization for mental illness occurred *after* 90-day period had expired), *aff'd*, 155 F.3d 561 (4th Cir. 1998); Zillyette v. Capital One Fin. Corp., 1 F. Supp. 2d 1435 (M.D. Fla. 1998) (plaintiff's depression and suicidal ideation held insufficient to toll 90-day limitations period), *aff'd*, 179 F.3d 1337 (11th Cir. 1999); Thornton v. South Cent. Bell Tel. Co., 906 F. Supp. 1110, 1118 (S.D. Miss. 1995) (plaintiff's mental breakdown held not to toll 90-day limitations period).

[367]*See* Brown-Mitchell v. Kansas City Power & Light Co., 267 F.3d 825 (8th Cir. 2001) (holding that laches applied to preclude employee's suit based on her unreasonable and inexcusable delay in filing); EEOC v. Great Atl. & Pac. Tea Co., 735 F.2d 69, 80, 34 FEP 1412 (3d Cir. 1984) (assuming arguendo possible availability of laches to EEOC actions, but finding—as matter of law—that elements were not established; raising question of whether laches can be invoked against arm of sovereign).

[368]338 F.3d 730, 92 FEP 595 (7th Cir. 2003).

[369]*Id.* at 734.

[370]*E.g.*, EEOC v. Dresser Indus., Inc., 668 F.2d 1199, 1202–04, 29 FEP 249 (11th Cir. 1982) (action filed more than 5 years after employee filed initial charge; prejudice shown by death or unavailability of key witnesses, complete turnover of employer's personnel staff, and loss of records); EEOC v. Alioto Fish Co., 623 F.2d 86, 88–89, 23 FEP 251 (9th Cir. 1980) (same); EEOC v. Liberty Loan Corp., 584 F.2d 853, 857–58, 18 FEP 303 (8th Cir. 1978) (action filed more than 4 years after employee filed initial charge; prejudice shown in that drastic reorganization of company following financial losses meant that all employee's supervisors and almost all related corporate managers had left company, and it was difficult to locate records). *But see Great Atlantic & Pacific Tea Co.*, 735 F.2d at 81–84 (inexcusable delay not established even though more than 7 years had elapsed since commissioner charge); *cf.* EEOC v. American Nat'l Bank, 574 F.2d 1173, 1174–76, 17 FEP 213 (4th Cir. 1978) (vacating and remanding for further fact development; trial court dismissed

Courts generally agree that laches also may be applied against a private plaintiff. What, however, if the private plaintiff was simply awaiting EEOC action, which was long delayed? Because of a concern that a private plaintiff should not automatically be penalized for delays caused by the EEOC, some courts have required a showing of lack of diligence on the plaintiff's part. What "diligence" is required is unclear. Although several courts of appeals have dismissed actions where the plaintiff has not made sufficient inquiry of the agency during the period of the delay,[371] others have refused to dismiss actions where the plaintiff waited for the completion of the administrative process.[372]

In *Ashley v. Boyle's Famous Corned Beef Co.*,[373] the Eighth Circuit determined that separation of powers principles dictate that federal courts not apply laches to bar a federal statutory claim that is timely filed under an express federal statute of limitations.[374]

EEOC action alleging pattern or practice of discrimination filed 6 years after initial charge; district court's finding of prejudice "rested primarily on the lost evidence" concerning initial charge; loss may justify denying relief to initial charging party but not dismissal of Commission's own suit).

[371]*E.g.*, Brown-Mitchell v. Kansas City Power & Light Co., 267 F.3d 825, 827–28 (8th Cir. 2001) (finding that attempting to contact administrative agency five times within 6-year period not sufficient diligence on part of plaintiff); Garrett v. General Motors Corp., 844 F.2d 559, 562, 46 FEP 985 (8th Cir. 1988) (plaintiff's contact with EEOC between 1972 and 1980 "minimal," and plaintiff did not "actively pursue" claim until 1984; defendant was prejudiced by 12-year delay); Cleveland Newspaper Guild Local 1 v. Plain Dealer Publ'g Co., 839 F.2d 1147, 1154, 45 FEP 1869 (6th Cir. 1988) (en banc) (upholding dismissal of action brought 10 years after filing of charge; plaintiff union could not reasonably account for its "inaction," especially in view of its knowledge of EEO matters); Jeffries v. Chicago Transit Auth., 770 F.2d 676, 679–82, 38 FEP 1282 (7th Cir. 1985) (after certain EEOC officials told him to wait to hear from agency, plaintiff did not contact EEOC for at least 9 years; defendant was prejudiced by hardship of locating former employees and by loss of records).

[372]*E.g.*, Howard v. Roadway Express, Inc., 726 F.2d 1529, 1533, 34 FEP 341 (11th Cir. 1984) (action brought 5 years after filing of charge; waiting for completion of EEOC processes not inexcusable delay); Bernard v. Gulf Oil Co., 596 F.2d 1249, 1257, 19 FEP 1682 (5th Cir. 1979) (plaintiffs' failure to file their action until completion of EEOC process not inexcusable delay, even though 9 years had elapsed since filing of charge), *adopted in relevant part en banc*, 619 F.2d 459, 463, 23 FEP 20 (5th Cir. 1980), *aff'd*, 452 U.S. 89 (1981).

[373]66 F.3d 164, 68 FEP 1261 (8th Cir. 1995).

[374]*Id.* at 169–70 (rejecting defendant's argument that plaintiff should be barred from pursuing pay discrimination claims because she waited until her layoff, more than 7 years after initial hiring, to challenge pay disparity; noting that equal pay claim was still timely because each paycheck was potentially actionable wrong).

The court went on to note, however, that although only statutes of limitations are relevant in determining whether a plaintiff's claims are time-barred, "laches, like other equitable principles, may be relevant in determining the extent to which [a plaintiff] is entitled to equitable remedies."[375] The Second Circuit has agreed, holding that laches cannot bar a federal statutory claim seeking legal relief where the statute contains an express limitations period within which the action is timely.[376] The starting point in any such inquiry, therefore, must include a consideration of whether the alleged discriminatory conduct is a discrete event, such as hiring or termination, or a nondiscrete violation, such as harassment.[377]

Cases concerning laches and the time for filing suit largely turn on the specific facts involved.[378] Courts remain wary, however, of applying laches to bar Title VII and related claims, especially where the EEOC has filed suit on behalf of the aggrieved

---

[375]*Id.*

[376]*See* Ivani Contracting Corp. v. New York, 103 F.3d 257, 259–60 (2d Cir. 1997) (laches not available to bar legal claims for damages under § 1983 where claims were timely filed under applicable 3-year limitations period).

[377]*See* National R.R. Passenger Corp. v. Morgan, 536 U.S. 101 (2002).

[378]In *National Association of Government Employees v. City Public Service Board*, 40 F.3d 698, 67 FEP 1013 (5th Cir. 1994), for example, the Fifth Circuit affirmed the district court's grant of summary judgment to the defendant on the Title VII claims on laches grounds, where there had been a delay of 9 years in bringing suit on plaintiff's EEOC charges. *Id.* at 708–11. The court found that the plaintiffs' delay was inexcusable, given their continuous representation by counsel since 3 years after they filed their EEOC charges, the active involvement of the plaintiff union, the plaintiffs' failure to demand right-to-sue letters, and the plaintiffs' failure to make inquiry with the Department of Justice or the EEOC, and that such delay unduly prejudiced the defendant, including by the substantial loss of witness testimony over time. *Id.*; *see also* Waddell v. Small Tube Prods., Inc., 799 F.2d 69, 77, 41 FEP 988 (3d Cir. 1986) (remanding case in which plaintiff wrote to EEOC twice and then took no action for 4½ years; "plaintiffs have some obligation to monitor the progress of their charge and do not have the absolute right to await termination of EEOC proceedings where it would appear to a reasonable person that no administrative resolution will be forthcoming"); Brown v. Continental Can Co., 765 F.2d 810, 815, 38 FEP 695 (9th Cir. 1985) (remanding to trial court for additional necessary factual inquiry regarding action brought 6 years after plaintiff filed first charge; noting that "complainants are not required to terminate the administrative process by requesting a notice of right-to-sue"); Holsey v. Armour & Co., 743 F.2d 199, 211, 35 FEP 1064 (4th Cir. 1984) (laches not applicable, as plaintiff's decision to await completion of administrative processes was not inexcusable delay; action was filed 4½ years after charge); Rozen v. District of Columbia, 702 F.2d 1202, 1204, 31 FEP 618 (D.C. Cir. 1983) (per curiam) (pro se plaintiff did not unreasonably delay by failing to seek right-to-sue letter after EEOC

employee or employees, and sometimes even in rather extreme circumstances involving lengthy periods of delay.[379]

6. *Effect of Tolling Statute*

In *Raygor v. Regents of the University of Minnesota*,[380] the Supreme Court determined that the tolling provisions of the federal supplemental jurisdiction statute[381] did not extend Minnesota's period of limitations for filing a Minnesota Human Rights Act (MHRA) suit where the defendant was a state entity with Eleventh Amendment immunity. In *Raygor*, the plaintiffs sued the University of Minnesota in federal court alleging violations of the ADEA and the MHRA. The plaintiffs requested that the court assert supplemental jurisdiction over the state law claim pursuant to 28 U.S.C. § 1367. After the court ruled that the claims could not be brought because of the Eleventh Amendment, the plaintiffs filed their pendent state claims in state court, but the claims were time-barred. The plaintiffs argued in state court that § 1367(d) tolled the state statute of limitations. Ultimately, the state supreme court ruled that the federal statute could not constitutionally toll the state

---

informed him one would be coming; fact that he waited 21 months for suit letter not grounds for laches); Boone v. Mechanical Specialties Co., 609 F.2d 956, 959–60, 21 FEP 789 (9th Cir. 1979) (action dismissed where EEOC charge had been pending for almost 7 years during which time EEOC frequently had asked plaintiff if he wished to receive notice of right to sue).

[379]*See* Springer v. Partners in Care, 17 F. Supp. 2d 133, 136–38 (E.D.N.Y. 1998) (lawsuit filed more than *10 years* after pro se plaintiff filed charge with EEOC and state agency held not barred by laches where plaintiff made occasional phone calls during that period regarding status of charge, received nothing from EEOC after state agency issued no-cause determination, and employer failed to make specific showing of prejudice or to provide affidavits that necessary witnesses were unavailable); EEOC v. Mitsubishi Motor Mfg. of Am., Inc., 990 F. Supp. 1059, 1088–89, 75 FEP 1379 (C.D. Ill. 1998) (refusing to bar Title VII pattern-or-practice suit on basis of laches where EEOC took 4½ years to file suit from date of filing of charge but employer failed to establish inexcusable delay or prejudice; holding that "[a]pplication of the laches defense in a case such as this would certainly undermine and impair the EEOC's statutory duty to investigate and extirpate any pattern or practice of discrimination"); EEOC v. Phillips Colls., 984 F. Supp. 1464 (M.D. Fla. 1997) (refusing to bar suit on basis of laches; although there was inexcusable delay by EEOC in taking 14 months to investigate charge, 8 more months to issue its own determination letter, and 4 years to file suit, defendant's ability to defend such suit was not substantially prejudiced by such delay).

[380]534 U.S. 533 (2002).

[381]28 U.S.C. § 1367 (2000).

statute as against nonconsenting state defendants. The U.S. Supreme Court agreed, indicating that a contrary result would "raise serious constitutional doubt."[382]

---

[382]534 U.S. at 536.

JURISPRUDENTIAL BARS TO ACTION

I. PRECLUSION

A. Preclusion Issues Resulting From Prior Resort to Another Forum

1. Introduction

The doctrine of res judicata, commonly referred to as claim preclusion, bars claims that either were previously raised or could have been raised in an earlier proceeding between the same parties (or their privies) that resulted in a final judgment on the same claim.[1] The related doctrine of collateral estoppel, also known as issue preclusion, prevents the relitigation of particular issues that have been actually litigated and necessarily decided.[2] When applying these doctrines, courts analyze competing interests. Although res judicata and collateral estoppel serve the laudable purpose of protecting parties[3] and courts[4] from unnecessary and duplicative litigation, courts must also consider the intent of employment discrimination laws to provide an avenue for plaintiffs to litigate their claims.[5] These doctrines also seek to advance comity between state and federal courts when a state court has already adjudicated a claim or issue.[6]

Res judicata and collateral estoppel are affirmative defenses, and a defendant's failure to raise these issues before the federal district court may render the defenses waived.[7]

---

[1]*See* EEOC v. Pemco Aeroplex, Inc., 383 F.3d 1280, 1285, 94 FEP 848 (11th Cir. 2004) ("res judicata can be applied only if all of four factors are shown: (1) the prior decision must have been rendered by a court of competent jurisdiction; (2) there must have been a final judgment on the merits; (3) both cases must involve the same parties or their privies; and (4) both cases must involve the same causes of action") (citations and quotations omitted), *cert. denied*, 126 S. Ct. 42 (2005).

[2]*Id.* ("collateral estoppel can apply only when the parties are the same (or in privity) and if the party against whom the issue was decided had a full and fair opportunity to litigate the issue in the earlier proceeding") (citations and quotations omitted).

[3]*See* Parklane Hosiery Co. v. Shore, 439 U.S. 322, 326 (1979) (preclusion protects litigants from burden of relitigating issues already decided).

[4]*Id.* (preclusion promotes judicial economy).

[5]*See* University of Tenn. v. Elliott, 478 U.S. 788, 799 n.7 (1986) (Title VII contemplated that some normal preclusion rules would have to yield to societal goal of eliminating discrimination); Alexander v. Gardner-Denver Co., 415 U.S. 36, 44–45, 7 FEP 81 (1974) (discussing purposes underlying Title VII's remedial scheme).

[6]Kremer v. Chemical Constr. Corp., 456 U.S. 461, 467, 28 FEP 1412 (1982) (citing Allen v. McCurry, 449 U.S. 90, 96 (1980)).

[7]Rizzo v. Sheahan, 266 F.3d 705, 714, 87 FEP 1583 (7th Cir. 2001) (defendant waived affirmative defense of res judicata where it failed to raise issue with district

Many of the principles examined in this section apply to both res judicata and collateral estoppel. Rules unique to collateral estoppel are examined in Section I.C *infra*.

2. Preclusive Effect of Prior State Court Judgments and Reviewed State Administrative Decisions

In *Kremer v. Chemical Construction Corp.*,[8] the seminal employment case on preclusion, the Supreme Court held that a state court decision that upheld a decision of a state administrative agency must be given full faith and credit by the federal court in a subsequent Title VII suit.[9] Thus, if a state court would bar a subsequent Title VII suit or claim on res judicata or collateral estoppel grounds, so too must a federal court.[10] In *Kremer*, the plaintiff filed a charge with the Equal Employment Opportunity Commission (EEOC) alleging religion and national origin discrimination. The EEOC deferred the plaintiff's charge to a state agency, which subsequently found no probable cause. The plaintiff then sought review of that determination in state court, lost, obtained a Title VII right-to-sue letter, and instituted a federal Title VII action. The Supreme Court held that the state court decision was preclusive.[11] The Court reviewed the administrative agency's procedures for determining whether there was discrimination, as well as the state court's procedures for review of the agency determination. Because both satisfied the Due Process Clause, the state court decision barred the subsequent Title VII action.[12]

In *Sondel v. Northwest Airlines*,[13] a class certified in a federal court adverse impact case under Title VII was found to be bound,

---

court, resulting in court considering otherwise-barred Title VII claim that was previously before administrative agency and later reviewed by state court); *see also* Huffman v. Pursue, Ltd., 420 U.S. 592, 607–08 n.19 (1975).

[8]456 U.S. 461, 28 FEP 1412 (1982).

[9]456 U.S. at 485.

[10]*Id.* at 475; *accord* Jarrett v. Gramling, 841 F.2d 354, 356 (10th Cir. 1988) (§ 1983 action barred by judgment in earlier state action; "Full Faith and Credit Act . . . requires a federal court to give the same preclusive effect to a state court judgment that the judgment would be given in the courts of the state in which the judgment was rendered"). *But see* Staats v. County of Sawyer, 220 F.3d 511, 516–17, 10 AD 1433 (7th Cir. 2000) (claim preclusion did not bar plaintiff from bringing his federal claims in federal court where state law would have allowed claims to be split).

[11]*Kremer*, 456 U.S. at 485.

[12]*Id.* at 484.

[13]56 F.3d 934 (8th Cir. 1995).

on res judicata principles, by the outcome of a corollary state court suit initiated by the named class representatives. Subsequent to certification of the class in the federal court case, the named representatives brought a discrimination action in state court under state law in their individual capacities based on the alleged discriminatory policy. Summary judgment was granted to the employer in the state court action. The defendant then moved for summary judgment in the federal action on the grounds of res judicata. Affirming summary judgment in favor of the defendant, the Eighth Circuit held that the named class representatives had a fiduciary relationship with the unnamed class members that extended beyond "the four corners of the federal lawsuit"[14] and created privity among all class members for res judicata purposes, binding all class members to the actions of the named representatives. Notice adequate to satisfy due process must be provided before absent class members may be barred from pursuing their monetary relief claims in subsequent lawsuits.[14a]

3. Preclusive Effect of State Court Judgments on Claims Not Raised

The *Kremer* Court did not decide whether preclusion rules bar claims that could have been, but were not raised in the prior proceeding.[15] In *Migra v. Warren City School District Board of Education*,[16] the Supreme Court resolved that issue. The Court held

---

[14]*Id.* at 939 ("Accordingly, by virtue of their fiduciary duties to refrain from taking any action prejudicial to the Class, the certified representatives were representing the interests of the Class at the state trial.").

[14a]*See* Johnson v. General Motors Corp., 598 F.2d 432, 433–34, 438, 20 FEP 239 (5th Cir. 1979) (prior race discrimination employment class action certified pursuant to Fed. R. Civ. P. 23(b)(2) that obtained classwide injunctive relief but did not seek or obtain classwide monetary relief and did not provide absent class members with notice or opportunity to opt out to pursue monetary relief claims would not preclude subsequent class action for monetary relief; "due process . . . require[s] notice before the individual monetary claims of absent class members may be barred"); *see also* Crowder v. Lash, 687 F.2d 996, 1008 (7th Cir. 1982) (same; § 1983 action); Penson v. Terminal Transp. Co., 634 F. 2d 989, 995, 26 FEP 828 (5th Cir. 1981) (same; Title VII action).

[15]Somewhat similarly, in *Allen v. McCurry*, 449 U.S. 90, 97 n.10, 105 (1980), the Supreme Court had held that collateral estoppel precluded the relitigation, in a § 1983 action, of issues that were decided in an earlier state court action. The Court declined to rule on whether res judicata also barred claims asserted in the § 1983 action that the plaintiff could have raised, but did not raise, in the prior state proceeding against the same adverse party.

[16]465 U.S. 75, 33 FEP 1345 (1984).

that res judicata barred §§ 1983 and 1985 claims in a federal law-suit that the plaintiff could have raised—but failed to—in a prior state court action for breach of the employment contract.[17] The *Migra* Court explained that the preclusive effect of the prior state court decision is determined by the law of the state that rendered the decision in the original action.[18] Indeed, in *Marrese v. American Academy of Orthopaedic Surgeons*,[19] the Supreme Court held that federal courts must apply state preclusion law even when ruling on federal statutory claims over which the original state court lacked jurisdiction.[20]

---

[17]465 U.S. at 84–85; *see also* Balcerzak v. Milwaukee Police Dep't, 163 F.3d 993, 997, 78 FEP 512 (7th Cir. 1998) (plaintiff's § 1983 claims precluded where he chose not to raise race discrimination of defendant as defense to his discharge in state proceedings); Bolling v. City of Denver, 790 F.2d 67, 68, 40 FEP 1274 (10th Cir. 1986) (per curiam) (§§ 1981 and 1983 claims barred by state court's affirmance of civil service board decision, even though discrimination claim was not raised); Brown v. St. Louis Police Dep't, 691 F.2d 393, 396, 30 FEP 18 (8th Cir. 1982) (prior state court proceeding appealing discharge of African-American police officer barred §§ 1981, 1983, and 1985 claims, even though race discrimination issue had not been raised in state proceeding).

[18]*Migra*, 465 U.S. at 81. *Compare* Welch v. Johnson, 907 F.2d 714, 721–23, 54 FEP 529 (7th Cir. 1990) (claims under Title VII and § 1983 for discriminatory discharge and retaliation barred by state court's affirmance of state agency determination that discharge was warranted; under Illinois res judicata law, federal claims should have been raised in state proceedings; but Title VII claim for discriminatory failure to promote constituted separate cause of action that was not barred by Illinois law), Puckett v. Cook, 864 F.2d 619, 621 (8th Cir. 1989) (under Arkansas law of claim preclusion, plaintiff's state-law constructive discharge claim barred by prior judicially affirmed denial of unemployment benefits), Bray v. New York Life Ins., 851 F.2d 60, 64, 47 FEP 278 (2d Cir. 1988) (affirmance by state court of dismissal of petition on statute of limitations grounds precluded Title VII and § 1981 action; New York law treats dismissal on statute of limitations grounds as dismissal on merits for res judicata purposes), Yancy v. McDevitt, 802 F.2d 1025, 1028–32, 46 FEP 260 (8th Cir. 1986) (plaintiff in §§ 1981 and 1983 action barred from litigating issue of discriminatory discharge under Iowa law of issue preclusion) *and* Peavey v. Polytechnic Inst. of N.Y., 768 F. Supp. 35, 37, 55 FEP 1690 (E.D.N.Y 1990) (New York law gives preclusive effect to dismissal for want of prosecution) *with* Al-Khazraji v. St. Francis Coll., 784 F.2d 505, 509, 40 FEP 397 (3d Cir. 1986) (Pennsylvania law affords no preclusive effect to state court dismissal for want of prosecution), *aff'd*, 481 U.S. 604, 43 FEP 1305 (1987) *and* Ross v. Communications Satellite Corp., 759 F.2d 355, 362, 37 FEP 797 (4th Cir. 1985) (judicially affirmed findings of Maryland unemployment insurance agency not accorded preclusive effect in Title VII case because Maryland law would deny issue preclusion where issue arose in second proceeding under substantially different statute).

[19]470 U.S. 373 (1985).

[20]*Id.* at 379–86. In *Marrese*, an antitrust case, the Supreme Court did not decide the question of Illinois preclusion law. It noted in dictum, however, that under most states' laws, claim preclusion will not apply if the new claim at issue could not have been brought in the earlier state proceeding. *Id.* at 382.

Following *Kremer* and *Migra*, many federal courts have given preclusive effect to a state court judgment[21] or a state court's review of a state administrative determination[22] in a subsequent action[23]

---

[21]*E.g.*, Boateng v. InterAmerican Univ., Inc., 210 F.3d 56, 62–63, 90 FEP 425 (1st Cir. 2000) (plaintiff's second suit barred by res judicata as second suit and original state court action both concern same set of facts, and state court found no discrimination on part of defendant; plaintiff "had a full bite of the apple—and the choice of the bite was his. He is not entitled to another nibble"); Hogue v. Royse City, 939 F.2d 1249, 1254, 56 FEP 1264 (5th Cir. 1991) (police chief lost wrongful discharge claim in state court and then sued in federal court under ADEA; plaintiff cannot "bring a parade of suits each raising a new theory on the motive for his firing"); Atkins v. Hancock County Sheriff's Merit Bd., 910 F.2d 403, 405 (7th Cir. 1990) (under Indiana's "identity of evidence" approach to res judicata, plaintiff's federal civil rights suit alleging violations of his First and Fourteenth Amendment rights was barred by prior action in state court); Singal v. General Motors Corp., 56 FEP 479, 479–80, 1990 U.S. Dist. LEXIS 19225 (E.D. Mich. May 10, 1990) (claims of race and age discrimination were barred by previous state court suit arising out of same transaction or occurrence and seeking recovery for same injury; claims were asserted or could have been asserted in earlier state court complaint), *aff'd mem.*, 924 F.2d 1059, 56 FEP 479 (6th Cir. 1991).

[22]*E.g.*, Butler v. City of N. Little Rock, 980 F.2d 501, 506, 60 FEP 612 (8th Cir. 1992) (discharged African-American police officer precluded from litigating Title VII and § 1983 claims in federal court action where state court affirmed ruling of civil service commission upholding discharge; officer had "full and fair opportunity" to litigate his disparate treatment claims at state level even though officer failed to avail himself of certain specific procedures); Welch v. Johnson, 907 F.2d 714, 719–23, 54 FEP 529 (7th Cir. 1990) (claims under Title VII and § 1983 for discriminatory discharge and retaliation barred by state court affirmance of state agency determination that discharge was warranted; under Illinois law of res judicata, federal claims should have been raised in state proceedings); Swapshire v. Baer, 865 F.2d 948, 950–52, 48 FEP 1439 (8th Cir. 1989) (state court judgment affirming administrative decision to discharge African-American police officer precluded subsequent suit under §§ 1981 and 1983 because issue of race was raised before administrative commission); *cf.* Bradley v. Pittsburgh Bd. of Educ., 913 F.2d 1064, 1070–74, 53 FEP 1481 (3d Cir. 1990) (§ 1983 claim not precluded by state court's affirmance of plaintiff's dismissal where plaintiff reserved § 1983 claims for determination by federal court; plaintiff was, however, collaterally estopped to extent that issues actually were determined by state court).

[23]*E.g.*, Balcerzak v. Milwaukee Police Dep't, 163 F.3d 993, 997, 78 FEP 512 (7th Cir. 1998) (police officers' suit against chief of police under § 1983 barred by claim preclusion because of former state action against board of commissioners concerning same fact situation); Carpenter v. Reed *ex rel.* Dep't of Pub. Safety, 757 F.2d 218, 219, 50 FEP 1331 (10th Cir. 1985) (§ 1981 action barred by state court affirmance of prior personnel board decision); Gorin v. Osborne, 756 F.2d 834, 836 (11th Cir. 1985) (§ 1983 action barred by state court affirmance of state administrative ruling); Davis v. United States Steel Supply, 688 F.2d 166, 170, 29 FEP 1202 (3d Cir. 1982) (§ 1981 claim barred by res judicata because of prior state court reversal of agency decision on same alleged discriminatory acts); Lee v. City of Peoria, 685 F.2d 196, 200, 29 FEP 892 (7th Cir. 1982) (§§ 1981, 1983, and 1985 action barred on res judicata grounds by prior review of administrative judgment that arose from same set of operative facts). *But see* Hill v. Coca-Cola Bottling Co., 786 F.2d

involving either the same claim or a claim that could have been raised in the prior action. Federal courts have thus given prior state court judgments preclusive effect in federal actions brought under §§ 1981, 1983, and 1985;[24] Title VII;[25] the Age Discrimination in

---

550, 553, 40 FEP 639 (2d Cir. 1986) (just cause determination in state unemployment compensation proceedings does not necessarily negate discrimination claims under Title VII and § 1981, particularly absent fair opportunity to litigate discrimination claim).

[24]*See, e.g.*, Bolling v. City of Denver, 790 F.2d 67, 68, 40 FEP 1274 (10th Cir. 1986) (per curiam) (§§ 1981 and 1983 claims barred by state court's affirmance of civil service board decision, even though discrimination claim was not raised, because plaintiff "could have joined her claims for that relief in [the] . . . state court proceeding"); Brown v. St. Louis Police Dep't, 691 F.2d 393, 396, 30 FEP 18 (8th Cir. 1982) (prior state court proceeding appealing discharge barred §§ 1981, 1983, and 1985 claims even though race discrimination issue had not been raised in state proceeding); *cf.* Capers v. Long Island R.R., 34 FEP 892, 893–94 (S.D.N.Y. 1984) (§ 1983 claim barred by state court judgment reversing state fair employment practices (FEP) agency's ruling for former employee, even though constitutional claim was not raised in state proceeding). *But see* Tolefree v. City of Kan. City, 980 F.2d 1171, 1175, 60 FEP 666 (8th Cir. 1992) (fire fighter who appealed his discharge to personnel appeals board, which decision was reviewed by state court, not barred on res judicata grounds from bringing federal discrimination claim; he was not obliged to raise discrimination issue before personnel board).

[25]*See, e.g.*, Heyliger v. State Univ. & Cmty. Coll. Sys., 126 F.3d 849, 856, 90 FEP 516 (6th Cir. 1997) (Title VII action precluded where plaintiff could have sought right-to-sue letter and amended complaint in state court lawsuit to include Title VII claim); Zanders v. National R.R. Passenger Corp., 898 F.2d 1127, 1133–34, 52 FEP 769 (6th Cir. 1990) (state court determination that employee's posttermination agreement not to disclose confidential information did not violate public policy and was properly accorded preclusive effect in subsequent Title VII retaliation action); Rider v. Pennsylvania, 850 F.2d 982, 989–92, 47 FEP 198 (3d Cir. 1988) (state court decision vacating arbitrator's award had issue-preclusive effect on subsequent Title VII action); Levitt v. University of Tex., 847 F.2d 221, 226–27, 47 FEP 90 (5th Cir. 1988) (discharged professor's Title VII claim barred where district court reviewed tribunal's finding that professor received full and fair opportunity to litigate his claim); Brown v. J.I. Case Co., 813 F.2d 848, 852–54, 43 FEP 355 (7th Cir. 1987) (state court decision overturning state administrative agency's finding of racial discrimination is res judicata with respect to subsequent Title VII action); Burney v. Polk Cmty. Coll., 728 F.2d 1374, 1379, 34 FEP 727 (11th Cir. 1984) (Title VII claim barred by state court's affirmance of decision of community college board of trustees); Butland v. New Hampshire Dep't of Corr., 229 F. Supp. 2d 75, 90 FEP 337 (D.N.H. 2002) (plaintiff precluded from relitigating her sexual harassment claim under Title VII in federal court because of prior state court action under state civil rights act). *But cf.* Cooper v. City of N. Olmstead, 795 F.2d 1265, 1268–70, 41 FEP 425 (6th Cir. 1986) (no estoppel of Title VII or § 1981 claim created by state court affirmance of adverse ruling in unemployment compensation proceeding because race/sex discrimination was not directly present or ruled on); Ross v. Communications Satellite Corp., 759 F.2d 355, 362, 37 FEP 797 (4th Cir. 1985) (judicially affirmed findings of Maryland unemployment insurance agency not entitled to preclusive effect in Title VII case because Maryland law would deny issue preclusion where issue arose in second proceeding under substantially different statute); Carpenter v. Reed, 757 F.2d 218, 220, 50 FEP 1331 (10th Cir. 1985)

Employment Act (ADEA);[26] and the Americans with Disabilities Act (ADA).[27] The Eighth and Eleventh Circuits have rejected plaintiffs' contentions that state court review was not meaningful because the standard of "review of an administrative decision need not be *de novo* in order for the state court's judgment to be entitled

---

(Title VII and § 1981 claims accorded preclusive effect only if plaintiff was required by state law to raise discrimination claims and only if state administrative agency had authority to hear them); Harding v. Ramsay, Scarlett & Co., 599 F. Supp. 180, 184, 36 FEP 717 (D. Md. 1984) (state court affirmance of unemployment compensation decision did not bar race discrimination claim because that claim was not litigated).

[26]Bechtold v. City of Rosemount, 104 F.3d 1062, 1068–69, 72 FEP 1704 (8th Cir. 1997) (state court ruling that city had substantial legitimate reasons for discharge bars subsequent ADEA claim); Clark v. Haas Group, Inc., 953 F.2d 1235, 1238–39, 57 FEP 1276 (10th Cir. 1992) (ADEA suit barred by res judicata where prior action for overtime under Fair Labor Standards Act (FLSA) was dismissed with prejudice; although two actions involved different legal theories, they both involved same parties, and claims would best have been tried in single action; employee cannot pursue employer sequentially under different statutes with different theories); Hogue v. Royse City, 939 F.2d 1249, 1254, 56 FEP 1264 (5th Cir. 1991) (state wrongful discharge suit barred subsequent ADEA suit where issue in both cases was whether there was justification for discharge; plaintiff "alleged a single wrong—one wrongful discharge—and the policies underlying the doctrine of *res judicata* surely would be offended if [plaintiff] were allowed to bring a parade of [such] suits each raising a new theory on the motive for his firing"); DiAngelo v. Illinois Dep't of Pub. Aid, 891 F.2d 1260, 1263, 51 FEP 1108 (7th Cir. 1989) (ADEA action barred by adverse decision on wrongful discharge claim by Human Rights Commission that was affirmed by state appellate court); Stillians v. Iowa, 843 F.2d 276, 282–83, 46 FEP 645 (8th Cir. 1988) (ADEA claim precluded by state administrative determination that employee had been discharged for just cause; no reason to believe that Congress intended "to deviate from traditional rules of preclusion" with respect to ADEA); Nichols v. City of St. Louis, 837 F.2d 833, 835, 45 FEP 1433 (8th Cir. 1988) (ADEA claim collaterally estopped by state court ruling affirming state administrative decision; state findings of fact precluded showing plaintiff was qualified for her job). *But see* Whitfield v. City of Knoxville, 756 F.2d 455, 460, 37 FEP 288 (6th Cir. 1985) (ADEA claim not barred because plaintiff could not raise claim in prior state proceeding).

[27]Shields v. BellSouth Adver. & Publ'g Co., 254 F.3d 986, 986–87, 11 AD 1716 (11th Cir. 2001) (plaintiff's ADA claim barred by collateral estoppel where previous state court proceedings denying him unemployment benefits found no evidence that plaintiff was discharged because he was HIV-positive); Jones v. United Parcel Serv., 214 F.3d 402, 406–07, 10 AD 1064 (3d Cir. 2000) (res judicata barred plaintiff's relitigation of issue within ADA claim where court found in previous workers' compensation action that plaintiff had fully recovered from his work-related injury and was able to return to his position as package car driver); Hapgood v. City of Warren, 127 F.3d 490, 7 AD 616 (6th Cir. 1997) (where fire fighter could have raised his ADA claim in state court action involving retaliation for filing workers' compensation claim, res judicata doctrine bars subsequent ADA action).

to preclusive effect."[28] Similar principles have been applied to federal court review of federal administrative decisions.[29]

Some courts have held, however, that a prior decision is not preclusive where the prior state court decision did not reach the merits of the underlying claim;[30] the state proceeding could not provide

---

[28]Swapshire v. Baer, 865 F.2d 948, 951, 48 FEP 1439 (8th Cir. 1989); *accord* Gorin v. Osborne, 756 F.2d 834, 837 (11th Cir. 1985) (state court affirmance held preclusive even though court's review was limited to whether there was "any evidence" in the record to support the administrative agency's factual findings).

[29]*E.g.*, Collier v. United States, 720 F. Supp. 75, 78 (W.D. La. 1989) (issue preclusion barred federal employee from pursuing in federal court Title VII and Rehabilitation Act claims where issues had been determined adversely to plaintiff in federal court of appeals' review of administrative agency decisions), *aff'd mem. sub nom.* Collier v. U.S. Dep't of Justice, 896 F.2d 550 (5th Cir. 1990); *see also* United States v. Utah Constr. & Mining Co., 384 U.S. 394, 422 (1966) (where federal administrative agency is acting in judicial capacity and resolves disputed issues of fact properly before it, which parties have had adequate opportunity to litigate, courts may give issue-preclusive effect to agency's findings). *But cf.* Quinones Candelario v. Postmaster Gen., 906 F.2d 798, 800–01, 53 FEP 355 (1st Cir. 1990) (reversing summary judgment for federal employee; postmaster not barred from first raising issue of employee's failure to mitigate damages in compliance action in district court).

[30]*See, e.g.*, Johnson v. Burnley, 887 F.2d 471, 474, 54 FEP 944 (4th Cir. 1989) ("Dismissal of a case for lack of subject matter jurisdiction carries with it no claim preclusive effects. By contrast, disposal of a case on the merits (including a grant of summary judgment) or for failure to comply with the statute of limitations . . . does operate as *res judicata* barring subsequent litigation of the same claim in federal court.") (citations omitted); Patzer v. University of Wis. Bd. of Regents, 763 F.2d 851, 854–55, 37 FEP 1847 (7th Cir. 1985) (state court dismissal for lack of personal jurisdiction did not constitute judgment on merits); Mack v. Kent County Vocational & Technical Sch. Dist., 757 F. Supp. 364, 377 (D. Del.) (state court affirmance of school board's decision to discharge plaintiff did not collaterally estop subsequent Title VII action where state court did not affirm board's findings on basis that plaintiff was incompetent), *aff'd*, 944 F.2d 897, 62 FEP 160 (3d Cir. 1991); EEOC v. Sears, Roebuck & Co., 55 FEP 482, 483, 1991 U.S. Dist. LEXIS 3321 (D. Or. Mar. 12, 1991) (EEOC investigation of ADEA claim not barred by dismissal for want of prosecution of claimant's previous wrongful termination claim under state law because there was no final determination on merits of plaintiff's age discrimination claim); Van Abrahams v. Pioneer Elec., 52 FEP 1010, 1011 (C.D. Cal. 1989) (state court decision dismissing plaintiff's state-law claims on statute of limitations grounds has no res judicata effect on § 1981 claim); Clinton v. Georgia Ports Auth., 37 FEP 593, 594 (S.D. Ga. 1985) (res judicata held not applicable where state court dismissal pertained to procedural untimeliness issues); Griffin v. George B. Buck Consulting Actuaries, Inc., 551 F. Supp. 1385, 1386 n.2, 31 FEP 405 (S.D.N.Y. 1982) (state court's refusal to set aside state agency's dismissal of claim for failure to file timely notice of appeal did not constitute judicial review on merits). *But see* DuBose v. Minnesota, 893 F.2d 169, 171, 51 FEP 1252 (8th Cir. 1990) (dismissal with prejudice for failure to prosecute constitutes merits adjudication with

relief for the federal claims;[31] the plaintiff lacked a full and fair opportunity to litigate, especially where the claims are different;[32]

---

res judicata effect); Bray v. New York Life Ins., 851 F.2d 60, 64, 47 FEP 278 (2d Cir. 1988) (once party has entered state court system, employee is bound by preclusion rules governing that system, including dismissal on timeliness grounds); Santos v. Todd Pac. Shipyards Corp., 585 F. Supp. 482, 484–85, 35 FEP 681 (C.D. Cal. 1984) (state court judgment on statute of limitations issue is final judgment entitled to res judicata effect).

[31]*See, e.g.*, Jones v. American State Bank, 857 F.2d 494, 498–99, 47 FEP 1686 (8th Cir. 1988) (plaintiffs permitted to seek attorney's fees in Title VII actions where state proceedings they were required to invoke did not provide for such relief). *But cf.* Swanson v. Best Buy Co., 731 F. Supp. 914, 916–18 (S.D. Iowa 1990) (small claims court decision had preclusive effect in subsequent FLSA retaliation action where plaintiff chose to limit his prayer for relief so he could utilize small claims process).

[32]*E.g.*, Thomas v. Contoocook Valley Sch. Dist., 150 F.3d 31, 40, 8 AD 599 (1st Cir. 1998) (no res judicata effect because state court only affirmed State Board of Education's decision to uphold nonrenewal of plaintiff's contract; factual issue in ADA claim is distinct); Dici v. Pennsylvania, 91 F.3d 542, 549, 71 FEP 801 (3d Cir. 1996) (legal issues in workers' compensation proceeding not identical to those in Title VII litigation); Tolefree v. City of Kan. City, 980 F.2d 1171, 1175, 60 FEP 666 (8th Cir. 1992) (fire fighter who appealed discharge to personnel appeals board, decision of which was later reviewed by state court, not barred from bringing discrimination claims in federal court because discrimination claims are "of an entirely different nature from the earlier appeal"); Crowley v. Prince George's County, 890 F.2d 683, 688, 51 FEP 799 (4th Cir. 1989) (under Maryland law, findings of state personnel board approving pay-level downgrade that were affirmed by state court did not preclude Title VII suit because of "substantial differences" between Title VII and governing provisions of county code); Carlisle v. Phenix City Bd. of Educ., 849 F.2d 1376, 1379–82, 47 FEP 616 (11th Cir. 1988) (neither res judicata nor collateral estoppel barred § 1983 and Title VII claims; state law gives no preclusive effect to state administrative proceeding where issue of racial bias was not considered and arguably could not even have been raised before tenure committee on appeal); McNasby v. Crown Cork & Seal Co., 888 F.2d 270, 276–77, 50 FEP 1826 (3d Cir. 1989) (no preclusion where neither administrative commission nor reviewing court had authority to decide Title VII claim); Barnes v. McDowell, 848 F.2d 725, 731–32 (6th Cir. 1988) (§ 1983 action not barred under Kentucky law by state court's review of administrative determination affirming discharge, where issue of unconstitutional bias was not in issue in state judicial proceedings); Scroggins v. Kansas, 802 F.2d 1289, 1291–92, 50 FEP 1294 (10th Cir. 1986) (state civil service decision upholding employee's discharge, even though judicially affirmed, did not preclude Title VII or § 1983 action where employee was not afforded full and fair opportunity to litigate discrimination claim); Jones v. City of Alton, 757 F.2d 878, 885–87, 37 FEP 523 (7th Cir. 1985) (state court's affirmance of civil service commission discharge decision did not bar Title VII or § 1983 claims because plaintiff lacked full and fair opportunity to litigate issue); Henry v. City of Tallahassee, 216 F. Supp. 2d 1299, 1313–14, 89 FEP 548 (N.D. Fla. 2002) (plaintiff's second action not barred where plaintiff was not yet discharged at time of first cause of action and plaintiff did not raise issue of discharge even though in first action plaintiff stated that certain actions taken by defendant were "contrived to effect his termination" and could "result in his termination").

or the parties to the litigation were not identical.[33] Generally, it is immaterial, for preclusion purposes, whether the plaintiff or defendant initiates the judicial review of the state administrative decision.[34] Courts disagree, however, over whether subsequent litigation will be barred where a plaintiff declines to pursue state court review of a state administrative determination, where such review is available.[35]

---

[33]*E.g.*, Gray v. Lacke, 885 F.2d 399, 406–07, 50 FEP 1575 (7th Cir. 1989) (§ 1983 suit against county employees acting in their official capacity not res judicata in subsequent § 1983 action against same employees in their individual capacities, nor did it collaterally estop claims against employees under First and Fourteenth Amendments); Gjellum v. City of Birmingham, 829 F.2d 1056, 1061 (11th Cir. 1987) (where plaintiff was not party to and was not permitted to intervene in defendant's state court appeal of personnel board decision, plaintiff not barred by state court judgment); Grann v. City of Madison, 738 F.2d 786, 789, 35 FEP 296 (7th Cir. 1984) (no privity of parties); Foulks v. Ohio Dep't of Rehab. & Corr., 713 F.2d 1229, 1231, 32 FEP 829 (6th Cir. 1983) (neither res judicata nor collateral estoppel bars § 1981 suit against supervisors who could not have been sued in prior state proceedings because, under state FEP statute, they were not "employers" subject to suit); Mohammed v. May Dep't Stores, 273 F. Supp. 2d 531, 537, 92 FEP 540 (D. Del. 2003) (plaintiff in privity with EEOC in earlier EEOC action where her claim provided sole basis for EEOC lawsuit; plaintiff barred from bringing suit in later private action where EEOC prosecuted plaintiff's claim with due diligence and reasonable prudence even though plaintiff did not pursue her opportunity with EEOC to vigorously assert her claims); *cf.* EEOC v. United States Steel Corp., 921 F.2d 489, 496–97, 54 FEP 1044 (3d Cir. 1990) ("Private litigation in which the EEOC is not a party cannot preclude the EEOC from maintaining its own action because private litigants are not vested with the authority to represent the EEOC"; however, "individuals who fully litigated their own claims under the ADEA are precluded by *res judicata* from obtaining individual relief in a subsequent EEOC action based on the same claims.").

[34]*See, e.g.*, Trujillo v. County of Santa Clara, 775 F.2d 1359, 1368–69, 44 FEP 954 (9th Cir. 1985) (res judicata and collateral estoppel applicable to Title VII, § 1981, and § 1983 claims even though it was employer who appealed state administrative decision to state court); Hickman v. Electronic Keyboarding, Inc., 741 F.2d 230, 233, 35 FEP 1281 (8th Cir. 1984) (although state agency, not employee, was party in prior proceeding, employee was in privity and thus bound by prior proceeding, even though review was requested by employer); Gonsalves v. Alpine Country Club, 727 F.2d 27, 29, 33 FEP 1817 (1st Cir. 1984) (Title VII action barred regardless of who sought state court review of earlier proceeding); Davis v. United States Steel Corp., 688 F.2d 166, 170–74, 29 FEP 1202 (3d Cir. 1982) (state court judgment on state discrimination claims bars § 1981 action regardless of which party sought state court judgment; mutuality of estoppel principle applies).

[35]*Compare* McInnes v. California, 943 F.2d 1088, 1095–96, 56 FEP 1257 (9th Cir. 1991) (plaintiff need not seek reversal of administrative decision through state judicial appeals prior to filing action in federal court) *and* Carlisle v. Phenix City Bd. of Educ., 849 F.2d 1376, 1378–79, 47 FEP 616 (11th Cir. 1988) (same) *with* Eilrich v. Remas, 839 F.2d 630, 632–33 (9th Cir. 1988) (if adequate opportunity for review is available, losing party cannot avoid preclusive effect of state administrative decision simply by foregoing appeal; federal claims do not necessarily mandate federal forum; administrative decisions should be given same preclusive effect that they would receive under state law).

It is possible to bypass the effect of res judicata through agreement between the parties. In *Simmons v. New Public School District Number Eight*,[36] the parties settled the first action after a decision by the North Dakota State Supreme Court that reversed the lower court's determination regarding her discharge. The settlement specifically gave the plaintiff the right to pursue the claims enumerated in her EEOC charge.[37] The Eighth Circuit noted that, although the claims alleged in the plaintiff's EEOC charge normally would be precluded by the settlement of the first action, the fact that the parties explicitly reserved her right to bring these claims allowed for their survival.[38]

4. Preclusive Effect of Prior Unreviewed State Administrative Decisions

Unreviewed state administrative decisions have limited preclusive effect. In *Kremer v. Chemical Construction Corp.*,[39] the Supreme Court noted in dictum that "unreviewed administrative determinations by state agencies . . . should not preclude [federal court] review even if such a decision were to be afforded preclusive effect in a State's own courts."[40]

Subsequently, in *University of Tennessee v. Elliott*,[41] the Supreme Court explicitly held that unreviewed administrative decisions do not bar subsequent Title VII actions that raise the same issues.[42] The Court held, however, that actions under §§ 1981, 1983,

---

[36]251 F.3d 1210, 1214, 85 FEP 1685 (8th Cir. 2001).
[37]*Id.* at 1214.
[38]*Id.*
[39]456 U.S. 461, 28 FEP 1412 (1982).
[40]*Id.* at 470 n.7. *But see* Waid v. Merrill Area Pub. Schs., 91 F.3d 857, 866, 71 FEP 577 (7th Cir. 1996) (court opted to use same common law test Wisconsin state court would apply in determining whether to give preclusive effect to unreviewed state agency proceeding); Eilrich v. Remas, 839 F.2d 630, 632–33 (9th Cir. 1988) (same); *see also* Moodie v. Federal Reserve Bank, 58 F.3d 879, 68 FEP 327 (2d Cir. 1995) (barring federal court from hearing claim previously brought before state FEP agency where state law expressly denies relitigation before state court of same jurisdiction).
[41]478 U.S. 788, 41 FEP 177 (1986).
[42]*Id.* at 795–96; *accord, e.g.*, Kosereis v. Rhode Island, 331 F.3d 207, 212, 92 FEP 241 (1st Cir. 2003) (relying on *Elliott* in holding that because state administrative decision regarding plaintiff's layoff was not reviewed by court, it did not have preclusive effect on plaintiff's Title VII claims); Roth v. Koppers Indus., Inc., 993 F.2d 1058, 1062, 61 FEP 1387 (3d Cir. 1993) (unemployment compensation board's finding that discharged employee had been subjected to discrimination and harassment had no collateral estoppel effect; it was simply state administrative board decision unreviewed by any court).

or 1985 are treated differently; in such actions, administrative decisions must be given the same preclusive effect to which they would be entitled in state court, provided that (1) the state agency acted in a judicial capacity to resolve disputed issues of fact properly before it, and (2) the parties were afforded an adequate opportunity to litigate their claims.[43] The reason for the different treatment of claims under the nineteenth-century Civil Rights Acts is found in the legislative histories of those Acts and Title VII, respectively. The *Elliott* Court explained that "Congress, in enacting the Reconstruction civil rights statutes, did not intend to create an exception to general rules of preclusion."[44] However, the legislative history of Title VII is clear in indicating that Congress decided the policy of according finality to state administrative proceedings was outweighed by other values,[45] such as the elimination of racial discrimination. Accordingly, the majority of courts continue to hold that an unreviewed state administrative decision cannot be given preclusive effect[46] in Title VII cases, but the decision may be introduced into evidence at trial.[47]

Following *Elliot*, courts have held that decisions of state agencies that involve claims later raised under §§ 1981, 1983, or 1985 preclude such subsequent litigation, provided that the agency acted in a judicial capacity to resolve disputed fact issues before it and

---

[43]*Elliott*, 478 U.S. at 796–99; *accord* Long v. Laramie County Cmty. Coll. Dist., 840 F.2d 743, 749, 751, 46 FEP 264 (10th Cir. 1988) (unreviewed findings of fact in state administrative proceedings that were favorable to plaintiff have no collateral estoppel effect in Title VII case but are given preclusive effect in §§ 1983 and 1985 actions); Buckhalter v. Pepsi-Cola Gen. Bottlers, 820 F.2d 892, 895, 43 FEP 1615 (7th Cir. 1987) (unreviewed decisions of human rights commission not entitled to preclusive effect in Title VII action, but are res judicata with respect to § 1983 claims); *cf.* Yancy v. McDevitt, 802 F.2d 1025, 1028–31, 46 FEP 260 (8th Cir. 1986) (school board termination proceeding later upheld by arbitrator had preclusive effect in subsequent §§ 1981 and 1983 action).

[44]478 U.S. at 796–97.

[45]*Id.* at 799 n.7.

[46]*See, e.g.*, Raniola v. Bratton, 243 F.3d 610, 624, 85 FEP 882 (2d Cir. 2001) (plaintiff's Title VII action not precluded by earlier administrative finding as to her discharge although she failed to appeal issue in state courts); Pernice v. City of Chi., 237 F.3d 783, 787 n.5, 11 AD 608 (7th Cir. 2001) (employee not bound by city personnel board's ruling that employee was discharged for drug possession); Crapp v. City of Miami Beach Police Dep't, 242 F.3d 1017, 1021–22, 85 FEP 353 (11th Cir. 2001) (unreviewed decision of city's personnel board that plaintiff engaged in conduct unbecoming officer has no preclusion effect in his subsequent Title VII action).

[47]*See, e.g.*, McInnes v. California, 943 F.2d 1088, 1093, 1096, 56 FEP 1257 (9th Cir. 1991) (unreviewed decision of state personnel board not given issue-preclusive effect in subsequent Title VII action but may be entered into evidence at trial).

the parties were afforded an adequate opportunity to litigate their claims.[48] Federal courts, however, are reluctant to preclude §§ 1981, 1983, or 1985 suits where the administrative body did not have authority to fully address the issues raised by such suits or where there were no factual findings pertinent to the federal claims.[49]

In *Astoria Federal Savings & Loan Ass'n v. Solimino*,[50] an ADEA case, the Supreme Court held that unreviewed state administrative determinations have no preclusive effect but may be introduced into evidence at trial.[51]

Although most federal courts refuse to give preclusive effect to unreviewed state administrative decisions,[52] some courts have held that adjudicative proceedings by state agencies bar later actions under the Family and Medical Leave Act (FMLA) and the ADA.[53] The Ninth Circuit and at least one district court, however,

---

[48]*See* Misischia v. Pirie, 60 F.3d 626, 628 (9th Cir. 1995) (judicially unreviewed decision of state board of examiners denying dental license barred § 1983 suit in federal court); Odunmbaku v. New York Blood Ctr., 72 FEP 202 (S.D.N.Y. Sept. 10, 1996) (§ 1981 claim barred based on collateral estoppel effect because of no probable cause finding of state FEP agency applying state-law principles because plaintiff was provided with full and fair hearing before agency), *decision adhered to on reconsideration*, 72 FEP 1564 (S.D.N.Y. 1996); Lindas v. Cady, 515 N.W.2d 458, 71 FEP 791 (Wis. 1994) (Wisconsin Personnel Commission's dismissal of discrimination-based complaint precluded relitigation of issue of sex discrimination in plaintiff's § 1983 state-commenced action because she was afforded adequate opportunity to litigate sex discrimination complaint before that state agency).

[49]*E.g.*, Frazier v. King, 873 F.2d 820, 824–25 (5th Cir. 1989) (subsequent § 1983 action not barred where agency had no authority to award full relief); Kelley v. TYK Refractories Co., 860 F.2d 1188, 1198, 48 FEP 262 (3d Cir. 1988) (§ 1981 suit not precluded by decision of state unemployment commission review board where federal claims were not addressed by board); *cf.* Nelson v. Jefferson County, 863 F.2d 18, 19 (6th Cir. 1988) (administrative determination given preclusive effect in § 1983 suit because review board had authority to and did hear plaintiff's claims of unconstitutional treatment surrounding discharge). *But see* DeCintio v. Westchester County Med. Ctr., 821 F.2d 111, 116–17, 44 FEP 33 (2d Cir. 1987) (unreviewed state administrative decision barred §§ 1981 and 1983 claims even though claims had not been raised at administrative hearing).

[50]501 U.S. 104, 55 FEP 1503 (1991).

[51]*Id.* at 113–14.

[52]*See, e.g.*, Bishop v. City of Birmingham Police Dep't, 361 F.3d 607, 610, 93 FEP 533 (11th Cir. 2004) (factual findings of state personnel board, if unreviewed by court, not entitled to preclusive effect in Title VII cases) (citing cases from several circuits).

[53]Settle v. S.W. Rodgers Co., 998 F. Supp. 657, 664, 4 WH2d 822 (E.D. Va. 1998) ("In appropriate circumstances, the factual findings of an administrative body . . . should be given preclusive effect in actions alleging discrimination in violation

have held that collateral estoppel may act to bar subsequent claims where the plaintiff did not pursue a review of state administrative determinations where such a review was available.[54]

5. Preclusive Effect of Prior Federal Proceedings

Generally, courts rely on res judicata to preclude claims that were or could have been raised in a previous federal proceeding.[55]

---

of Federal rights."), aff'd, 182 F.3d 909 (4th Cir. 1999); Roberts v. County of Fairfax, 937 F. Supp. 541, 547, 8 AD 919 (E.D. Va. 1996) (Civil Service Commission's finding that just cause existed for plaintiff's demotion precludes his ADA claim).

[54]Tarin v. County of L.A., 123 F.3d 1259, 1265, 79 FEP 1284 (9th Cir. 1997) ("If a state administrative agency is acting in a judicial capacity, an unreviewed agency decision has the same preclusive effect as that accorded in the state's own courts."); Misischia v. Pirie, 60 F.3d 626, 628 (9th Cir. 1995) (dentist who repeatedly failed state dental qualifying examination precluded from bringing federal § 1983 action against state board of dental examiners because he did not exhaust his state appeals of board's decision upholding his failure); Miller v. County of Santa Cruz, 39 F.3d 1030, 1034–35 (9th Cir. 1994) (county sheriff employee who had been discharged precluded from bringing federal § 1983 action because he failed to seek state court review of civil service board's confirmation of his discharge); Adamczyk v. Chief, Baltimore County Police Dep't, 952 F. Supp. 259, 262 n.7, 8 AD 515 (D. Md. 1997) (finding that where plaintiff did not appeal decision of administrative board, its findings of fact were given preclusive effect), aff'd, 134 F.3d 362 (4th Cir. 1998).

[55]E.g., Havercombe v. Department of Educ., 250 F.3d 1, 7–8, 85 FEP 1724 (1st Cir. 2001) (plaintiff's second action under § 1981, Title VII, and ADEA barred by res judicata because of earlier federal action where plaintiff failed to allege fresh claims in second action; "it was plaintiff's burden to make allegations from which the existence of a new cause of action could be gleaned"); Rivers v. Barberton Bd. of Educ., 143 F.3d 1029, 1033, 76 FEP 1545 (6th Cir. 1998) (claim preclusion applies to Title VII action when claim could and should have been litigated in prior action and where plaintiff had opportunity and burden of perfecting her Title VII claim in pendency of prior action); Jackson v. Widnall, 99 F.3d 710, 715, 72 FEP 608 (5th Cir. 1996) (action could not be revived where it had been dismissed for failure to timely file suit); Woods v. Dunlop Tire Corp., 972 F.2d 36, 41, 59 FEP 887 (2d Cir. 1992) (res judicata barred Title VII suit where plaintiff earlier had challenged discharge under § 301 of Taft-Hartley Act; plaintiff could have followed simple alternatives to preserve Title VII claim while administrative proceedings were in progress and could have sought stay of action while EEOC completed its procedures); Prochotsky v. Baker & McKenzie, 966 F.2d 333, 334–35, 59 FEP 418 (7th Cir. 1992) (res judicata barred Title VII action where plaintiff brought prior ERISA action in which plaintiff claimed that her discharge was motivated by desire to deprive her of medical insurance; Title VII claim should have been pursued as alternative in ERISA action because both actions arose from discharge); Clark v. Haas Group, Inc., 953 F.2d 1235, 1238–39, 57 FEP 1276 (10th Cir. 1992) (ADEA suit barred by res judicata; earlier FLSA overtime suit had been dismissed with prejudice); Fleming v. Travenol Labs., Inc., 707 F.2d 829, 833–34, 31 FEP 1219 (5th Cir. 1983) (Title VII suit for alleged sex discrimination barred by previous unsuccessful

A federal jury's findings in cases involving claims of intentional discrimination under Title VII, the ADA, and the Rehabilitation Act[56] generally have a preclusive effect on nonjury findings on common factual issues.[57] Where jury claims are erroneously dismissed, an

---

action under § 1983 and Fourteenth Amendment for alleged racial discrimination); Poe v. John Deere Co., 695 F.2d 1103, 1105–07, 30 FEP 827 (8th Cir. 1982) (res judicata barred tort claims in second federal diversity lawsuit even though plaintiff was denied leave to add tort claims to earlier § 1981 complaint); Yaba v. Roosevelt, 961 F. Supp. 611, 621, 8 AD 815 (S.D.N.Y. 1997) (where senior partner had been dismissed from Title VII claim, res judicata barred subsequent claim against him under § 1981). *But see* Curtis v. Citibank, N.A., 226 F.3d 133, 140, 83 FEP 1697 (2d Cir. 2000) (claim preclusion did not bar litigation of events arising after employee's first amended complaint where some of Title VII claims in second suit could not have been brought in earlier action); Wu v. Thomas, 863 F.2d 1543, 1548, 52 FEP 3 (11th Cir. 1989) (Title VII claim for retaliation not barred where retaliation was not subject of prior Title VII action, although some testimony at trial touched on retaliatory actions taken by defendant).

    [56]42 U.S.C. § 1981a(c) (2000).

    [57]*See* Marseilles Hydro Power, LLC v. Marseilles Land & Water Co., 299 F.3d 643, 650 (7th Cir. 2002) (common issues "must be tried to a jury in order to prevent a judge's determination from foreclosing a party's right to have the issues in a common lawsuit tried by a jury"); Pals v. Schepel Buick & GMC Truck, Inc., 220 F.3d 495, 501, 10 AD 1345 (7th Cir. 2000) ("an issue may be tried to [a] jury 'with the consent of both parties' even if the issue is 'not triable of right by a jury' "; therefore, jury findings have preclusive effect); Heno v. Sprint/United Mgmt. Co., 208 F.3d 847, 82 FEP 837 (10th Cir. 2000) (elements of Title VII and § 1981 claims have been construed as identical, and jury verdict on issue of liability under § 1981 is normally conclusive on issue of liability in parallel action under Title VII when based on same facts); Thomas v. Denny's, Inc., 111 F.3d 1506, 1513, 73 FEP 1333 (10th Cir. 1997) ("[j]ury's findings on factual issues common to claims under § 1981 and Title VII are binding on the district court"); Hashimoto v. Dalton, 118 F.3d 671 (9th Cir. 1997) (error in submitting Title VII claim to jury is used when trial court enters independent findings); Lebow v. American Trans. Air, Inc., 86 F.3d 661, 672–73, 152 LRRM 2463 (7th Cir. 1996) ("the jury's factual findings are binding on the judge" when awarding equitable relief); Dranchak v. Akzo Nobel, Inc., 88 F.3d 457, 459, 71 FEP 284 (7th Cir. 1996) (where jury verdict is vacated because of issues regarding its reliability, judge is not bound by jury's findings); Melendez v. Illinois Bell Tel. Co., 79 F.3d 661, 70 FEP 589 (7th Cir. 1996) (court not bound by jury verdict regarding plaintiff's § 1981 disparate treatment claim in resolving nonjury Title VII adverse impact case because issues presented in respective causes of action were not identical); Dombeck v. Milwaukee Valve Co., 40 F.3d 230, 66 FEP 497 (7th Cir. 1994) (in effort to cure error made by district court in submitting Title VII claim to jury, Seventh Circuit remanded to district court to enter independent findings of fact and conclusion of law); Ways v. City of Lincoln, 871 F.2d 750, 755–56, 49 FEP 865 (8th Cir. 1989) (although district court could make independent findings of fact on Title VII claim, it was without power to render verdict inconsistent with that of jury in related § 1983 claim); Garza v. City of Omaha, 814 F.2d 553, 577, 43 FEP 572, 1 IER 1687 (8th Cir. 1987) (§ 1983 and Title VII case tried

adverse ruling on nonjury claims will not estop the subsequent reinstatement of the jury claims.[58]

Federal court consent decrees also are afforded preclusive effect. Pursuant to § 108 of the Civil Rights Act of 1991,[59] an employment practice that implements and is within the scope of a consent judgment or order that resolves a claim of employment discrimination under the U.S. Constitution or a federal civil rights law generally may not be challenged.[60] Prior to the entry of judgment or order, however, a person whose interests or legal rights might be adversely affected by that judgment or order must have had actual notice of the proposed judgment or order and an opportunity to present objections to such judgment or order by a specific

---

simultaneously; jury found discrimination under § 1983, which precluded contrary finding by judge under Title VII); Kitchen v. Chippewa Valley Sch., 825 F.2d 1004, 1014, 44 FEP 663 (6th Cir. 1987) (jury finding on state claim bound judge on nonjury federal claim because standards of liability for both claims were identical); Green v. Kinney Shoe Corp., 728 F. Supp. 768, 772, 54 FEP 566 (D.D.C. 1989) (jury's factual conclusions on § 1981 claim were binding on judge's factual decisions on Title VII claim).

[58]See Lytle v. Household Mfg., 494 U.S. 545, 552–53, 52 FEP 423 (1990) (Seventh Amendment right to jury trial precluded giving collateral estoppel effect to district court's determination of issues common to claims under Title VII and § 1981 where district court had erroneously dismissed § 1981 claims); see Tomasello v. Rubin, 167 F.3d 612, 79 FEP 523 (D.C. Cir. 1999) (where Seventh Amendment concerns are not implicated and there are overlapping issues, remand to district court was unnecessary despite improper dismissal of one claim); Perkins v. Mari Trend, Inc., 1996 U.S. Dist. LEXIS 4613, 70 FEP 930 (E.D. La. Apr. 10, 1996) (in enacting 42 U.S.C. § 1981a, Congress showed its intent to allow parties access to jury trial on issue of liability when compensatory and punitive damages were sought; therefore, plaintiffs were entitled to have all issues relating to claim of compensatory and punitive damages resolved by jury, including issues common to both legal and equitable claims).

[59]42 U.S.C. §2000e-2(n)(1) (2000).

[60]See EEOC v. United Ass'n of Journeymen, 235 F.3d 244 (6th Cir. 2000) (§ 108 not to be applied retroactively, and no error in subjecting parties to consent decree to ensure complete relief); Boston Police Superior Officers Fed'n v. City of Boston, 147 F.3d 13, 91 FEP 803 (1st Cir. 1998) (§ 108 bar applies "only if the challenged employment practice implements and is within the scope of a litigated or consent judgment or order resolving a federal claim of employment discrimination"); Donnelly v. Glickman, 159 F.3d 405, 78 FEP 724 (9th Cir. 1998) (§ 108 generally bars independent challenges to remedial orders in employment discrimination actions but expressly states that statute shall not "alter the standards for intervention under Rule 24 of the Federal Rules of Civil Procedure"); Edwards v. City of Houston, 78 F.3d 983 (5th Cir. 1996) (analyzing effect of § 108 on nonparty's ability to intervene); Maitland v. University of Minn., 43 F.3d 357, 66 FEP 796 (8th Cir. 1994) (§ 108 "does not govern" in cases that arose before statute became effective).

future date certain.[61] Similarly, notice adequate to satisfy due process must be provided before absent class members may be barred from pursuing their monetary relief claims in subsequent lawsuits.[62]

Alternatively, a person cannot challenge a consent decree if that person's interests were adequately represented by another person who had previously challenged the judgment or order on the same legal grounds and with a similar factual situation, unless there has been an intervening change in law or fact.[63]

A finding that the defendant engaged in a pattern or practice of unlawful discrimination as to an identified class of persons may estop the defendant from denying such discrimination in subsequent litigation brought by individuals included in the class.[64] However, the fact that class certification was denied does not preclude the United States from bringing suit based on pattern-or-practice discrimination.[65]

The ADEA specifically requires that in order to become a part of a collective action an eligible employee must affirmatively "opt in."[66]

---

[61]42 U.S.C. §§ 2000e-2(n)(1)(B)(i)(I)–(II) (2000); *see also* Riddle v. Cerro Wire & Cable Group, Inc., 902 F.2d 918, 921, 53 FEP 47 (11th Cir. 1990) (plaintiff's Title VII action not barred by consent decree between EEOC and defendant employer in suit brought by EEOC based on plaintiff's charge; EEOC informed plaintiff that if she did not agree with consent decree she could refuse to sign required release and retain right to sue for individual damages).

[62]*See* Johnson v. General Motors Corp., 598 F.2d 432, 433–34, 438, 20 FEP 239 (5th Cir. 1979) (prior race discrimination employment class action certified pursuant to Fed. R. Civ. P. 23(b)(2) that obtained classwide injunctive relief but did not seek or obtain classwide monetary relief and did not provide absent class members with notice or opportunity to opt out to pursue monetary relief claims would not preclude subsequent class action for monetary relief; "due process . . . require[s] notice before the individual monetary claims of absent class members may be barred"); *see also* Crowder v. Lash, 687 F.2d 996, 1008 (7th Cir. 1982) (same; § 1983 action); Penson v. Terminal Transp. Co., 634 F. 2d 989, 995, 26 FEP 828 (5th Cir. 1981) (same; Title VII action).

[63]42 U.S.C. § 2000e-2(n)(1)(B)(ii) (2000).

[64]McKnight v. Circuit City Stores, Inc., 168 F.R.D. 550, 72 FEP 28 (E.D. Va. 1996) (defendant would be precluded from relitigating pattern-and-practice issue in subsequent cases, in event of adverse outcome on that issue, notwithstanding that class action was decertified), *aff'd*, 158 F.3d 742 (4th Cir. 1998), *cert. granted and judgment vacated on other grounds*, 527 U.S. 1031 (1999).

[65]*See, e.g.*, United States v. Denver, 927 F. Supp. 1396, 1398, 5 AD 1322 (D. Colo. 1996) (Attorney General could sue city of Denver under § 707 of ADA, alleging "pattern or practice" of discrimination, where city forced police officers with work-related injuries to take disability retirement when they could no longer perform functions of their original positions).

[66]29 U.S.C. § 216(b) (2000) ("[n]o employee shall be a party plaintiff to any . . . action [under it] unless he gives his consent in writing"); Sondel v. Northwest Airlines,

In *Tice v. American Airlines, Inc.*,[67] the Seventh Circuit held that a group of former pilots were not precluded from litigating their ADEA claims where they had not opted to join a similar collective action that had previously been brought by other employees.

6. Preclusion Where the First Action Is Dismissed on Procedural Grounds

In *Nilsen v. City of Moss Point*,[68] the Fifth Circuit, sitting en banc, held that res judicata precluded the plaintiff's action under § 1983 because the plaintiff's earlier lawsuits, which sought essentially the same relief under Title VII, had been dismissed as untimely. Where the first action was dismissed for reasons of timelines or jurisdictional concerns, courts generally follow *Nilsen*.[69]

In *Davila v. Delta Air Lines, Inc.*,[70] the Eleventh Circuit held that res judicata barred the plaintiff's ADA claim even though the federal court in the previous action "couched its holding in jurisdictional terms."[71] In *Davila*, the district court was reviewing the

---

56 F.3d 934, 973–74 (8th Cir. 1995); *see also* Frank v. United Airlines, Inc., 216 F.3d 845, 83 FEP 1 (9th Cir. 2000) (judgment in prior class action did not preclude subsequent Title VII class action where class representatives in prior action did not adequately represent interests of future flight attendants when they chose not to appeal adverse ruling).

[67] 162 F.3d 966, 78 FEP 1019 (7th Cir. 1998).

[68] 701 F.2d 556, 561, 31 FEP 612 (5th Cir. 1983) (en banc).

[69] *E.g.*, Serlin v. Arthur Andersen & Co., 3 F.3d 221, 223–24, 62 FEP 1207 (7th Cir. 1993) (dismissing second ADEA action that was brought during pendency of motion to dismiss first ADEA action (because complaint had not been served within 120 days of filing action), on ground that actions were duplicative and that no special factors outweighed interest in efficient judicial administration); Shaver v. F.W. Woolworth Co., 840 F.2d 1361, 1365, 3 IER 46 (7th Cir. 1988) (wrongful discharge claim precluded by earlier ADEA claim that had been dismissed as untimely); Miller v. United States Postal Serv., 825 F.2d 62, 63–64, 44 FEP 1049 (5th Cir. 1987) (adverse judgment in Title VII action is res judicata on subsequent claim of disability discrimination under § 501, which could have been raised in original proceeding, where Title VII action was dismissed as untimely); *cf.* Talley v. City of De Soto, 37 FEP 375, 376, 1986 U.S. Dist. LEXIS 29006 (N.D. Tex. Feb. 22, 1985) (action under § 1983 barred by prior Title VII action based on same facts that was dismissed on jurisdictional grounds).

[70] 326 F.3d 1183, 14 AD 304 (11th Cir. 2003).

[71] *Id.* at 1188. The Ninth Circuit has also looked beyond the terminology used by a district court in determining whether a previous action was a judgment on the merits or was a decision rendered on a jurisdictional basis. *See* Stewart v. U.S. Bancorp, 297 F.3d 953, 957 (9th Cir. 2002) (res judicata barred action where previous ERISA action was dismissed for lack of jurisdiction because district court had to analyze complaint to determine if federal preemption defense applied, and such analysis constituted decision on merits). *But see* Criales v. American Airlines, Inc.,

determination of Delta's System Board of Adjustment, which had previously found that the plaintiff's discharge was justified. The appellate court noted that although the district court stated that it lacked jurisdiction over the case's subject matter in dismissing the case, "it was only after reaching the very merits of [the plaintiff's] challenge to the System Board's determination that the court found subject matter jurisdiction to be lacking."[72] Further, the district court never concluded that it did not have the power to decide the case before it.

In *Criales v. American Airlines, Inc.*,[73] the plaintiff had filed two charges with the EEOC—one timely and another untimely— and had filed the first action based on the right-to-sue notice received on the untimely charge. The Second Circuit held that the plaintiff's second Title VII action was not precluded by the dismissal of his previous Title VII action, which was based on the absence of a notice of right to sue from the EEOC. The Second Circuit determined that the earlier dismissal was not on the merits, as the plaintiff had merely failed to comply with a precondition necessary to the court's ability to determine the merits of his claim.[74] Because the plaintiff could still comply with the necessary precondition by filing an action after he received a right-to-sue notice on the timely charge, the dismissal of the first complaint should not operate to bar the second action.[75]

Similarly, in *Truvillion v. King's Daughters Hospital*,[76] the Fifth Circuit held that dismissal of the EEOC's Title VII action (for failure to conduct a good faith investigation and failure to give the employer a sufficient opportunity to conciliate) was not a judgment on the merits and therefore did not bar a subsequent action by either the EEOC or the charging party.[77]

---

105 F.3d 93, 97–98, 72 FEP 1690 (2d Cir. 1997) (plaintiff's second Title VII action not precluded by dismissal of prior Title VII action, which was based on absence of right-to-sue notice from EEOC; earlier dismissal not on merits but because of procedural omission later corrected by plaintiff upon EEOC's issuance of notice to sue).

[72]*Davila*, 326 F.3d at 1188.
[73]105 F.3d at 93, 72 FEP 1690 (2d Cir. 1997).
[74]*Id.* at 97.
[75]*Id.*
[76]614 F.2d 520, 22 FEP 554 (5th Cir. 1980).
[77]*Id.* at 524–25.

The Second Circuit considered the relationship between an EEOC Title VII action and a separate private action in *Williamson v. Bethlehem Steel Corp.*[78] The court held that a decree obtained in a prior government suit would not prevent persons on whose behalf the government had sought relief from seeking additional relief that had not been requested by the government. The court reasoned that the private plaintiffs were not bound by the Attorney General's actions because they then were neither parties to the case nor in privity with the Attorney General.[79] The doctrine of stare decisis also did not apply because the government case did not seek the relief sought by the private plaintiffs. There was, accordingly, no ruling in the earlier case on the availability of such relief.[80]

7. Preclusion Based on Prior Federal Agency Determination

Federal courts may be required to give preclusive effect to federal agency determinations where the agency has acted in a judicial capacity[81] to resolve disputed issues of fact and the parties have had an adequate opportunity to litigate, or where the defendant has established a dispositive affirmative defense in the agency proceeding.[82]

However, in *Stafford v. Muscogee County Board of Education*,[83] the Eleventh Circuit determined that the unsuccessful pursuit

---

[78]468 F.2d 1201, 5 FEP 204 (2d Cir. 1972).

[79]*Id.* at 1203.

[80]*Id.* at 1203–04.

[81]*See* Durko v. OI-NEG TV Prods., 870 F. Supp. 1278, 1281 (M.D. Pa. 1994) (defining elements required for acting in judicial capacity).

[82]*See* Ali v. Jeng, 86 F.3d 1148 (4th Cir. 1996) (per curiam) (court dismissed plaintiffs' §§ 1983 and 1985 actions because same claims were brought in their prior employment discrimination case, which was dismissed as untimely); Lee v. Kroger Co., 901 F. Supp. 1218, 70 FEP 425 (N.D. Tex. 1995) (dismissing second Title VII action because of res judicata effect of dismissal of prior Title VII action for failure to timely commence that action); *cf.* Bradley v. Americold Servs. Inc., 75 FEP 8 (D. Kan. 1997) (NLRB decision that employer discharged African-American employee for assaulting co-worker did not estop him from asserting racial bias claim under Title VII). *But see* Burrell v. United States Postal Serv., 164 F. Supp. 2d 805, 812 (E.D. La. 2001) (no res judicata over subsequent Title VII suit where claims previously brought before federal Merit Systems Protection Board but dismissed for lack of jurisdiction).

[83]688 F.2d 1383, 29 FEP 1773 (11th Cir. 1982).

of an administrative proceeding under Title VI does not preclude a race bias complaint in federal court under either Title VII or § 1981 where the administrative proceeding is narrower in scope and not a competent forum for the Title VII and § 1981 claims.[84]

Federal courts do not give preclusive effect to EEOC determinations.[85] Determinations by the EEOC may, however, be considered as evidence by district courts.[86]

8. Preclusion Based on Federal Agency and Individual Litigation

The EEOC's authority to proceed with an action or obtain relief may be somewhat circumscribed by principles of res judicata.[87] For example, in *EEOC v. Harris Chernin, Inc.*,[88] the Seventh Circuit held that the EEOC cannot sue for individual remedies for a protected-age employee who already had sued under the ADEA.[89]

---

[84]*Id.* at 1391–92.

[85]*See, e.g.*, Castner v. Colorado Springs Cablevision, 979 F.2d 1417, 1422, 60 FEP 566 (10th Cir. 1992) ("When examining the merits, the district court may not give preclusive effect to an EEOC finding that the evidence does not support a finding of discrimination.").

[86]*Id.* (EEOC's administrative finding is factor to be considered); *see also* Johnson v. City of Port Arthur, 892 F. Supp. 835, 840, 6 AD 547 (E.D. Tex. 1995) (determination reached by EEOC should not be ignored, but court should inquire as to validity of determination). *See generally* Chapter 28 (Title VII Litigation Procedure).

[87]*See* EEOC v. North Gibson Sch. Corp., 266 F.3d 607, 615–16, 86 FEP 1275 (7th Cir. 2001) (denying EEOC authority to proceed with ADEA action where charges filed were untimely); EEOC v. United States Steel Corp., 921 F.2d 489, 496–97, 54 FEP 1044 (3d Cir. 1990) (EEOC's claim for individual monetary relief was barred by res judicata); *cf.* EEOC v. Pasta House Co., 70 FEP 61 (E.D. Mo. 1996) (although individual plaintiff whose suit was dismissed with prejudice may not join with EEOC as party to subsequent suit, she may still be called as witness in EEOC's case). *But see* EEOC v. Goodyear Aerospace Corp., 819 F.2d 1539, 1542–43 (9th Cir. 1987) (res judicata does not bar EEOC from proceeding to obtain injunction against employer despite individual private action against same defendant); New Orleans S.S. Ass'n v. EEOC, 680 F.2d 23, 25 (5th Cir. 1982) ("The EEOC may challenge a transaction which was the subject of prior judicial scrutiny in a private suit, if the subsequent challenge seeks different relief."); EEOC v. Kimberly-Clark Corp., 511 F.2d 1352, 1362–62 (6th Cir. 1975) (EEOC not privy to private settlement); EEOC v. Huttig Sash & Door Co., 511 F.2d 453, 455–56, 10 FEP 529 (5th Cir. 1975) (termination of private party's Title VII suit does not estop EEOC from bringing suit on identical charges).

[88]10 F.3d 1286, 1291, 63 FEP 616 (7th Cir. 1993).

[89]*Accord* EEOC v. Continental Oil Co., 548 F.2d 884, 889, 14 FEP 365 (10th Cir. 1977) (in Title VII case, Tenth Circuit determined that EEOC cannot sue on basis of charge on which private party previously had brought action); EEOC v. Pic Pac Supermarkets, Inc., 689 F. Supp. 607, 608, 47 FEP 1556 (S.D. W.Va. 1988) (EEOC

However, the doctrine of res judicata did not prevent the EEOC from bringing suit to enjoin the employer from future ADEA violations, using the evidence of the individual's claim, because the EEOC represents a broader public interest than the individual grievant.[90] As the Eleventh Circuit explained in *EEOC v. Pemco Aeroplex, Inc.*,[91] unless the EEOC is a party to the prior litigation, it will rarely be barred from proceeding in its subsequent action because privity will most likely be lacking: "Quite simply, it is so unusual to find privity between a governmental agency and private plaintiffs because governmental agencies have statutory duties, responsibilities and interests that are far broader than the discrete interests of a private party."[92] "The EEOC's comprehensive mandate and authority to petition for broad injunctive and pecuniary relief stands in stark contrast to the interests of individual plaintiffs in employment actions."[93] Thus, the *Pemco* court held that "the overwhelming weight of precedent in this Circuit and elsewhere weighs heavily against finding privity between the EEOC and the private plaintiffs."[94]

The Eleventh Circuit has held that an employee was not bound by a consent decree issued in the EEOC's action against the employer—even a decree that covered the plaintiff's individual claim—where there was a substantial showing that the plaintiff's interests were not congruent with those of the EEOC.[95]

---

could not institute suit against employer and was limited to seeking intervention in previously instituted Title VII suit arising out of same events).

[90]*Harris Chernin, Inc.*, 10 F.3d at 1291; *see also* EEOC v. Jacksonville Shipyards, Inc., 696 F. Supp. 1438, 1441–42, 48 FEP 66 (M.D. Fla. 1988) (dismissal of individual plaintiff's suit does not collaterally estop discrimination suit by EEOC to vindicate public interest).

[91]383 F.3d 1280, 94 FEP 848 (11th Cir. 2004) (EEOC's systemic action charging employer with companywide racial harassment not barred by earlier judgment in employer's favor in separate action by 22 employees alleging racial harassment because there was no privity between EEOC and private plaintiffs in prior action).

[92]*Id.* at 1291; *see also* Secretary of Labor v. Fitzsimmons, 805 F.2d 682, 692 (7th Cir. 1986) (en banc) ("the Government is not barred by the doctrine of res judicata from maintaining independent actions asking courts to enforce federal statutes implicating both public and private interests merely because independent private litigation has also been commenced or concluded").

[93]383 F.3d at 1294.

[94]*Id.*

[95]Riddle v. Cerro Wire & Cable Group, Inc., 902 F.2d 918, 921–22, 53 FEP 47 (11th Cir. 1990) (where plaintiff expressed her dissatisfaction with EEOC's handling of her interests prior to entry of consent decree between EEOC and employer, no privity existed between plaintiff and EEOC, and plaintiff's subsequent suit was not

Some courts have precluded subsequent private lawsuits based on the same charge as the earlier EEOC lawsuit, or where the lawsuits involve the same practices. In *Jones v. Bell Helicopter Co.*,[96] the Fifth Circuit held that the dismissal of the EEOC's Title VII action under Rule 41(b) for failure to comply with the Administrative Procedure Act was a dismissal on the merits, and thus res judicata barred the charging party's subsequent Title VII action based on the same claim.[97] In *Vines v. University of Louisiana at Monroe*,[98] the Fifth Circuit held that a federal court injunction was warranted to prevent state court relitigation of whether the university's policy prohibiting reemployment of retirees constituted age discrimination; the state claim by affected individuals was collaterally estopped by the dismissal of an EEOC suit seeking relief for the individuals.[99]

9. Preclusive Effect of Prior Arbitration Decisions [100]

In the landmark decision in *Alexander v. Gardner-Denver Co.*,[101] the Supreme Court first considered the preclusive effect of a prior arbitration. In *Gardner-Denver*, the discharged employee brought a Title VII claim. The Court determined that a prior arbitration should not have preclusive effect and specifically concluded:

> [T]he federal policy against discriminatory employment practices can best be accommodated by permitting an employee to pursue fully both his remedy under the grievance-arbitration clause of a

---

precluded); *cf.* Cooper v. Federal Reserve Bank, 467 U.S. 867, 880, 35 FEP 1 (1984) (finding of no class discrimination does not preclude subsequent individual claims).

[96]614 F.2d 1389, 1390, 22 FEP 773 (5th Cir. 1980).

[97]*See* McClain v. Wagner Elec. Corp., 550 F.2d 1115, 1119, 14 FEP 817 (8th Cir. 1977) (private plaintiff cannot maintain independent action on his charge after EEOC has sued, even if he was not informed of EEOC action; even after judgment, his remedy was to intervene); *see also* Doninger v. Pacific N.W. Bell, Inc., 564 F.2d 1304, 1310, 16 FEP 316 (9th Cir. 1977) (class certification refused where potential class members accepted individual relief under consent decree); Franklin v. General Elec. Co., 15 FEP 1084, 1085 (W.D. Va. 1977) (court refused to certify class action because issues at trial would have been identical to those raised in EEOC's action concerning same matter).

[98]398 F.3d 700 (5th Cir. 2005), *cert. denied*, 126 S. Ct. 1019 (2006).

[99]*Id.* at 712.

[100]This section will not address the propriety of mandatory arbitration provisions or prospective waivers of statutory claims; instead, it will simply assume that a case has previously proceeded to arbitration and will analyze the effect thereof. This section will primarily focus on arbitration agreements negotiated through collective bargaining as opposed to individually negotiated arbitration agreements.

[101]415 U.S. 36, 7 FEP 81 (1974).

collective bargaining agreement and his cause of action under Title VII. The federal court should consider the employee's claim *de novo*. The arbitral decision may be admitted as evidence and accorded such weight as the court deems appropriate.[102]

---

[102]*Id.* at 59–60; *see also* EEOC v. Waffle House, Inc., 534 U.S. 279, 12 AD 1001 (2002) (open question whether arbitration judgment would affect validity of EEOC claim or character of relief EEOC may seek); Ciambriello v. County of Nassau, 292 F.3d 307, 170 LRRM 2173 (2d Cir. 2002) (where party never received notice of or opportunity to participate in arbitration or state court confirmation proceeding, no preclusive effect on judgment confirming award); Collins v. New York City Transit Auth., 305 F.3d 113, 119, 89 FEP 1473 (2d Cir. 2002) (where arbitration decision, based upon substantial evidence and rendered by a neutral board, upholds termination following evidentiary hearing at which discrimination claims are litigated, Title VII plaintiff can survive a summary judgment motion only with "strong evidence that the decision was wrong as a matter of fact—e.g., new evidence not before the tribunal—or that the impartiality of the proceeding was somehow compromised"); Fayer v. Town of Middlebury, 258 F.3d 117, 123–24 (2d Cir. 2001) (First Amendment claim not precluded by prior arbitration reviewed in Connecticut state court); EEOC v. Indiana Bell Tel. Co., 256 F.3d 516, 522, 86 FEP 1 (7th Cir. 2001) (en banc) (reaffirming that "a union cannot surrender employee's rights under Title VII" through CBA); Kennedy v. Superior Printing Co., 215 F.3d 650 (6th Cir. 2000) (where employee brings wrongful discharge claim to arbitration under CBA that also includes antidiscrimination provision, employee's allegation that employer violated federal antidiscrimination law does not necessarily waive employee's right to federal judicial forum for federal statutory rights); Bell v. Conopco, Inc., 186 F.3d 1099, 80 FEP 971 (8th Cir. 1999) (prior arbitration decision did not bar plaintiff's Title VII and Missouri Human Rights Act discrimination claims); Bromley v. Michigan Educ. Ass'n-NEA, 82 F.3d 686, 152 LRRM 2070 (6th Cir. 1996) (statutory right to have Article III court adjudicate suits brought pursuant to § 1983 for vindication of rights secured by First Amendment cannot be foreclosed by non-statutory arbitration conducted by privately appointed decision maker); Kulavic v. Chicago & Ill. Midland Ry., 1 F.3d 507 (7th Cir. 1993) (fact-finding procedures inadequate to convince court that facts determined in arbitration should be given preclusive effect in Federal Employers' Liability Act case); Ryan v. City of Shawnee, 13 F.3d 345, 63 FEP 1281 (10th Cir. 1993) (state judicial proceeding to review arbitration not entitled to preclusive effect); United States v. Teamsters, 954 F.2d 801, 139 LRRM 2646 (2d Cir. 1992) (federal court need not defer to arbitrator's decision when plaintiff's labor-related claim stems from source of legal rights that are separate from, although possibly co-extensive with, CBA); National Labor Relations Bd. v. Yellow Freight Sys., Inc., 930 F.2d 316, 55 FEP 998 (3d Cir. 1991) (refusing to give preclusive effect to state court judgment affirming arbitration award); Bolden v. Southeastern Pa. Transp. Auth., 953 F.2d 807 (3d Cir. 1991) (grievance settlement did not preclude § 1983 claim under res judicata or collateral estoppel); Blumenthal v. Merrill Lynch, Pierce, Fenner & Smith, Inc., 910 F.2d 1049 (2d Cir. 1990) (no res judicata or collateral estoppel effect when arbitrators considered different issues or when arbitrator may be unable to grant full relief); Owens v. Texaco, Inc., 857 F.2d 262, 48 FEP 147 (5th Cir. 1988) (employee may pursue fully both his right to arbitration under CBA and his cause of action under Title VII, and findings of arbitrator with regard to discrimination issues are not binding on court; however, arbitral decision is final and binding to extent it resolves questions of contractual rights); Cooper v. Asplundh Tree Expert Co., 836 F.2d 1544, 45 FEP 1386 (10th Cir. 1988) (arbitrator's award should not foreclose ADEA claim); McAlester v. United Air Lines,

The Supreme Court further stated:

> We adopt no standards as to the weight to be accorded an arbitral decision, since this must be determined in the court's discretion with regard to the facts and circumstances of each case. Relevant factors include the existence of provisions in the collective-bargaining agreement that conform substantially with Title VII, the degree of procedural fairness in the arbitral forum, adequacy of the record with respect to the issue of discrimination, and the special competence of particular arbitrators. Where an arbitral determination gives full consideration to an employee's Title VII rights, a court may properly accord it great weight. This is especially true where the issue is solely one of fact, specifically addressed by the parties and decided by the arbitrator on the basis of an adequate record. But courts should ever be mindful that Congress, in enacting Title VII, thought it necessary to provide a judicial forum for the ultimate resolution of discriminatory employment claims. It is the duty of courts to assure the full availability of this forum.[103]

In *Barrentine v. Arkansas-Best Freight System*,[104] the Supreme Court reviewed the preclusive effect of a prior arbitration in the

---

Inc., 851 F.2d 1249, 47 FEP 512 (10th Cir. 1988) (*Gardner-Denver* indicates admission of arbitrator's decision is discretionary, not mandatory); Kirk v. Board of Educ. of Bremen Cmty. High Sch. Dist. No. 228, 811 F.2d 347, 42 FEP 1473 (7th Cir. 1987) (no preclusion under state law because judicial review of prior arbitration decision did not involve same "cause of action," and there was no decision on merits of case); Wilmington v. J.I. Case Co., 793 F.2d 909, 40 FEP 1833 (8th Cir. 1986) (arbitral awards do not foreclose plaintiff's exercise of § 1981 rights); Bottini v. Sadore Mgmt. Corp., 764 F.2d 116 (2d Cir. 1985) (arbitration proceeding does not supplant comprehensive statutory scheme of Title VII that Congress enacted to prohibit various types of discriminatory employment practices, and claim preclusion principles will not bar employment discrimination suit in federal court, even when same dispute was subject of arbitration); Rodgers v. Fisher Body Div., 739 F.2d 1102, 35 FEP 349 (6th Cir. 1984) (prior arbitration does not have preclusive effect under § 1981); Becton v. Detroit Terminal of Consol. Freightways, 687 F.2d 140, 142, 29 FEP 1078 (6th Cir. 1982) ("[T]he court may consider the arbitration decision as persuasive evidence that the grounds found by the arbitrator to be just cause for discharge under the [CBA] are sufficient to amount to just cause. The court should defer to the arbitrator's construction of the contract. Moreover, an arbitration decision in favor of the employer is sufficient to carry the employer burden of articulating 'some legitimate nondiscriminatory reason for the employee's rejection.' However, to allow that decision to answer conclusively questions raised in the final step of the McDonnell Douglas analysis unnecessarily limits the plaintiff's opportunity to vindicate his statutory and constitutional rights. We hold . . . that a federal court may in the course of trying a Title VII or section 1981 action, reconsider evidence rejected by the arbitrator in previous proceedings"); Kelly v. Classic Rest. Corp., 92 FEP 1222 (S.D.N.Y. 2003) (refusing to dismiss ADEA claims on collateral estoppel or res judicata grounds).

[103]*Gardner-Denver*, 415 U.S. at 60.
[104]450 U.S. 728, 24 WH 1284 (1981).

context of a wage and hour claim. "Because Congress intended to give individual employees the right to bring their minimum-wage claims under the FLSA [Fair Labor Standards Act] in court, and because these congressionally granted FLSA rights are best protected in a judicial rather than in an arbitral forum, we hold that petitioners' claim is not barred by the prior submission of their grievances to the contractual dispute-resolution procedures."[105]

Three years after *Barrentine*, the Supreme Court revisited this issue in *McDonald v. City of West Branch*,[106] a § 1983 case. The issue was whether a federal court could accord preclusive effect to an unappealed arbitration award. The Sixth Circuit had determined that such awards had a preclusive effect. The Supreme Court disagreed and reversed. The Court reiterated that the full faith and credit statute[107] does not apply to an arbitration award because it is not a judicial proceeding.[108] The Court then considered the propriety of a judicially created preclusive effect. Based on *Gardner-Denver* and *Barrentine*, the Court concluded that res judicata and collateral estoppel were inapplicable to the § 1983 claim.[109]

In the backdrop of *Gardner-Denver* and its progeny, the lower courts generally have held that a judicially unreviewed arbitration decision has no preclusive effect on subsequent litigation. The Fifth Circuit, however, has determined that an arbitral decision is final and binding to the extent it resolves questions of contractual rights.[110]

---

[105]*Id.* at 745.

[106]466 U.S. 284, 115 LRRM 3646 (1984).

[107]28 U.S.C. § 1738 (2000) provides: "judicial proceedings [of any court of any state] shall have the same full faith and credit in every court within the United States . . . as they have . . . in the courts of such State." Accordingly, the federal courts must "give the same preclusive effect to [the] state court judgments that those judgments would be given in the courts of the State from which the judgments emerged."

[108]466 U.S. at 288.

[109]*Id.* at 292; *see also* Dean Witter Reynolds Inc. v. Byrd, 470 U.S. 213 (1985) ("it is far from certain that arbitration proceedings will have any preclusive effect on the litigation of nonarbitrable federal claims"); NLRB v. Yellow Freight Sys., Inc., 930 F.2d 316, 320, 55 FEP 998 (3d Cir. 1991) (NLRB not required to give issue-preclusive effect to factual determinations of arbitrator; NLRB is not court); Caldeira v. County of Kauai, 866 F.2d 1175, 1178 (9th Cir. 1989) (state court confirmation of arbitration decision entitled to full faith and credit and therefore was issue preclusive); Rider v. Pennsylvania, 850 F.2d 982, 990–95, 47 FEP 198 (3d Cir. 1988) (state court decision vacating arbitrator's ruling giving collateral estoppel effect, resulting in dismissal of Title VII action).

[110]*See* Owens v. Texaco, Inc., 857 F.2d 262, 48 FEP 147 (5th Cir. 1988) (district court bound by arbitrator's interpretation of bargaining agreements and status

The Eighth Circuit held that when statutory claims were specifically submitted to arbitration, "there is nothing in *Alexander* that would indicate that the arbitrator's decision should not be given its normal preclusive effect."[111]

B. Judicial Estoppel and Preclusive Effect of Prior Sworn Statements

A plaintiff may be barred by the doctrine of judicial estoppel[112] from pursuing litigation if he or she has taken a contrary position in another forum, the inconsistent positions were made under oath, and the inconsistencies "are shown to have been calculated to make a mockery of the judicial system."[113]

---

of parties); *see also* Manion v. Nagin, 394 F.3d 1062 (8th Cir. 2005) (arbitration award counts as final judgment for collateral estoppel purposes), *cert. denied*, 545 U.S. 1128 (2005).

[111]Merrill Lynch, Pierce, Fenner & Smith, Inc. v. Nixon, 210 F.3d 814, 817, 82 FEP 1030 (8th Cir. 2000), *overruled in part by* EEOC v. Waffle House, Inc., 534 U.S. 279 (2002); *see also* Clarke v. UFI, Inc., 98 F. Supp. 2d 320, 82 FEP 1681 (E.D.N.Y. 2000) (where motion to confirm arbitration award was unnecessary to judicial action giving effect to such award, arbitration award had issue-preclusive effect, even in absence of judicial confirmation of award, particularly when parties had benefit of plenary proceedings to develop their claims) (citing Benjamin v. Traffic Exec. Ass'n E.R.R., 869 F.2d 107 (2d Cir. 1989)); Handley v. Phillips, 715 F. Supp. 657, 52 FEP 195 (M.D. Pa. 1989) (decision of arbitrator pursuant to CBA did not have claim-preclusive effect on subsequent causes of action under Title VII and § 1983 where plaintiff did not have full and fair opportunity to raise claims during state court proceeding; however, plaintiff was precluded by collateral estoppel from relitigating issues actually decided during arbitration). *But see* Fayer v. Town of Middlebury, 258 F.3d 117 (2d Cir. 2001) (judicial review of prior arbitration did not have preclusive effect because of Connecticut's state law governing preclusion, limited scope of judicial review, and state policy against arbitral preclusion); Coppinger v. Metro-North Commuter R.R., 861 F.2d 33, 129 LRRM 2817 (2d Cir. 1988) (arbitrator's decision not res judicata as to § 1983 claim because constitutional issues were not raised during arbitration and arbitrator did not have authority to grant complete relief); Aleem v. General Felt Indus., Inc., 661 F.2d 135, 137, 27 FEP 569 (9th Cir. 1981) (Although Aleem's Title VII claim arose from same set of facts as his arbitration claim, claims involved different injuries and different causes of action; "The maintenance of the Title VII action after judicial review of the arbitration decision therefore [did] not involve splitting a cause of action so as to render the second action barred by res judicata. . . . Collateral estoppel [was] equally inapplicable, for Congress in enacting Title VII made it clear that prior administrative adjudications were not to prevent de novo review of Title VII claims in federal court.").

[112]" 'Judicial estoppel is an equitable concept invoked at a court's discretion' and [is] 'designed to prevent the perversion of the judicial process.' " Parker v. Wendy's Int'l, Inc., 365 F.3d 1268, 1271 (11th Cir. 2004) (quoting Burnes v. Pemco Aeroplex, Inc., 291 F.3d 1282, 1285 (11th Cir. 2002)).

[113]*Parker*, 365 F.3d at 1271.

In *Cleveland v. Policy Management Systems Corp.*,[114] the employee filed for Social Security Disability Insurance (SSDI) benefits and subsequently brought suit under the ADA. The district court granted summary judgment in the employer's favor. The Fifth Circuit affirmed, holding that the receipt of SSDI benefits created a rebuttable presumption that the recipient was judicially estopped from asserting that she was a "qualified individual with a disability."[115] The Supreme Court held that although the SSDI and ADA allegations were ostensibly divergent, they could be consistent with each other; accordingly, the receipt of SSDI benefits should not automatically estop the employee from pursuing an ADA claim.

The factors considered by the Supreme Court in *Cleveland* recognize that the definition of "disability" differed under the statutory schemes of the ADA and SSDI; that the Social Security Administration occasionally awards or continues previously awarded disability benefits to persons who are working; that the nature of an employee's disability may change, so that a previously accurate disability statement on an SSDI application may not reflect that person's capacities at the time of the relevant employment decision; and that if an employee had merely applied for, but not received, SSDI benefits, that inconsistency is allowed under the legal system.[116]

---

[114]526 U.S. 795, 9 AD 491 (1999).

[115]Cleveland v. Policy Mgmt. Sys. Corp., 120 F.3d 513, 518, 7 AD 1031 (5th Cir. 1997), *cert. granted in part*, 525 U.S. 808 (1998), *judgment vacated*, 526 U.S. 795 (1999).

[116]*Cleveland*, 526 U.S. at 805; *see also* Giles v. General Elec. Co., 245 F.3d 474, 11 AD 844 (5th Cir. 2001) (inconsistent statements in employee's SSDI application did not prevent him from asserting claim under ADA where he failed to obtain Social Security benefits); Parker v. Columbia Pictures Indus., 204 F.3d 326, 10 AD 396 (2d Cir. 2000) (employee's statements in SSDI and long-term disability applications did not subject him to estoppel on issue of ability to work in ADA action where statements did not result in irreconcilable conflict with ADA claim); Motley v. New Jersey State Police, 196 F.3d 160, 166, 9 AD 1505 (3d Cir. 1999) (ADA claim not automatically barred by prior representations of disability; however, "the attainment of disability benefits is certainly some evidence" that should be considered in determining whether plaintiff is qualified individual with disability); Totty v. International Bus. Machs., 198 F.3d 247 (6th Cir. 1999) (per curiam) (grant of summary judgment for employer in ADA case not proper when premised on basis of plaintiff's receipt of SSDI benefits); Norris v. Sysco Corp., 191 F.3d 1043, 1048, 9 AD 1262 (9th Cir. 1999) (applying principles of *Cleveland* but noting that court felt "some discomfort about facts which regularly show up in this area of the law and enable a claimant to first obtain one recovery and then another").

Notwithstanding other possible explanations, the Court in *Cleveland* stated that an ADA plaintiff is not free to ignore her previous contention that she was too disabled to work.[117] To survive a motion for summary judgment, the employee must explain why the previous contention is consistent with her present contention that she can perform the essential functions of the job, such as by using a reasonable accommodation.[118] The explanation, according to the Court, must be sufficient to warrant a reasonable juror's conclusion that, assuming the truth of, or the employee's good-faith belief in, the earlier statement, the employee could nonetheless "perform the essential functions" of her job, with or without reasonable accommodation.[119]

The doctrine of judicial estoppel has been applied to bar a plaintiff's employment discrimination action when the plaintiff is a debtor in bankruptcy court, fails to list the claim as an asset, and the failure was intentional or a bad faith effort to deceive the court.[120] Not surprisingly, courts that apply this standard in employment discrimination cases have reached different results.[121]

---

[117]*Cleveland*, 526 U.S. at 806–07; *see also* Feldman v. American Mem'l Life Ins. Co., 196 F.3d 783, 9 AD 1717 (7th Cir. 1999) (plaintiff's ADA claim not estopped simply because she applied for or received SSDI benefits; however, she cannot avoid summary judgment merely by asserting she is qualified individual if she made prior inconsistent statements in applying for SSDI).

[118]*Cleveland*, 526 U.S. at 806–07; *see also* EEOC v. Stowe-Pharr Mills, Inc., 216 F.3d 373, 10 AD 1153 (4th Cir. 2000) (employee's statement in SSDI application does not preclude EEOC from establishing genuine issue of material fact where statement in SSDI application did not take into account possibility of reasonable accommodation).

[119]*Cleveland*, 526 U.S. at 806–07; *see also* Lee v. City of Salem, Ind., 259 F.3d 667, 676, 12 AD 10 (7th Cir. 2001) (plaintiff who stated under oath in SSDI application that he could not return to work because "[i]t was too strenuous for me and my back pain is just too great to keep aggravating [sic] it every day" failed burden under *Cleveland* to explain inconsistency).

[120]Burnes v. Pemco Aeroplex, Inc., 291 F.3d 1282, 88 FEP 1281 (11th Cir. 2002). In *Burnes*, the Eleventh Circuit held that the plaintiff's employment discrimination claim was barred by the doctrine of judicial estoppel because the record contained "sufficient evidence from which to infer intentional discrimination." 291 F.3d at 1287. The Eleventh Circuit has since questioned the application of judicial estoppel in *Burnes*, suggesting that the appropriate defense in that case was not judicial estoppel but whether the debtor lacked standing. *See* Parker v. Wendy's Int'l, Inc., 365 F.3d 1268, 1272 (11th Cir. 2004).

[121]*Compare Burnes*, 291 F.3d at 1288 (applying judicial estoppel to bar employment discrimination action when it was not disclosed to bankruptcy court), De Leon v. Comcar Indus., Inc., 321 F.3d 1289, 1292, 91 FEP 105 (11th Cir. 2003) (same),

C. Issue Preclusion

Collateral estoppel, or issue preclusion, bars litigation of certain issues that arise in a second lawsuit. Unlike its sister doctrine, res judicata, issue preclusion normally applies only when an issue was actually raised, litigated, and resolved. Many of the same principles and rules of law discussed in Sections I.A and I.B *supra* apply to both doctrines. This section addresses certain issues specific to issue preclusion.

In *Kremer v. Chemical Construction Corp.*,[122] the Supreme Court held: "Under collateral estoppel, once a court decides an issue of fact or law necessary to its judgment, that decision precludes relitigation of the same issue on a different cause of action between the same parties."[123] On the other hand, "[u]nder res judicata, a final judgment on the merits of an action precludes the parties or their privies from relitigating issues that were or could have been raised in that action."[124]

In order for issue preclusion to bar the relitigation of an issue, the party sought to be precluded in the second suit must have been a party, or in privity with a party, to the original lawsuit; the issue sought to be precluded must be the same as the issue involved in the prior action; that issue must have been actually litigated in the prior action; and must have been determined by a valid and final judgment; and the determination in the prior action must have been essential to the prior judgment.[125]

Traylor v. Gene Evans Ford, LLC, 185 F. Supp. 2d 1338, 1340 (N.D. Ga. 2002) (same) *and* Lott v. Sally Beauty Co., 88 FEP 669 (M.D. Fla. 2002) (same) *with* EEOC v. Apria Healthcare Group, Inc., 222 F.R.D. 608, 612, 15 AD 1522 (E.D. Mo. 2004) (refusing to apply judicial estoppel to EEOC action where former employee on whose behalf EEOC sued did not practice knowing misrepresentation or fraud on courts when she failed to list EEOC proceeding on her bankruptcy schedule) *and* Taylor v. Comcast Cablevision of Ark., Inc., 252 F. Supp. 2d 793, 799, 14 AD 277 (E.D. Ark. 2003) ("mere failure to list the EEOC charge in the bankruptcy proceeding will not support a finding of intent").

[122]456 U.S. 461, 28 FEP 1412 (1982). *Kremer* is more thoroughly discussed in Section I.A.2 *supra*.

[123]*Id.* at 467 (citing Montana v. United States, 440 U.S. 147, 153 (1979); Parklane Hosiery Co. v. Shore, 439 U.S. 322, 326 n.5 (1979)).

[124]456 U.S. at 467 (citing Allen v. McCurry, 449 U.S. 90, 94 (1980); Cromwell v. County of Sac, 94 U.S. 351, 352 (1877)).

[125]*See* Anderson v. Genuine Parts Co., 128 F.3d 1267, 1273, 75 FEP 593 (8th Cir. 1997) (citing Tyus v. Schoemehl, 93 F.3d 449, 453 (8th Cir. 1996)); *see also*

Issue preclusion does not bar an issue from being relitigated where the issue was not settled in the earlier proceeding[126] where there were factual distinctions between the claims,[127] where the defendant did not have a full and fair opportunity to litigate the claim,[128] and where there was not a final judgment on the merits.[129]

Similar to claim preclusion, issue preclusion does not generally bar issues from being relitigated that were raised in an earlier, unreviewed administrative proceeding.[130] Collateral estoppel may be used to prevent government agencies from relitigating issues previously established in other actions brought by the government.[131]

Maniccia v. Brown, 171 F.3d 1364, 1368, 80 FEP 901 (11th Cir. 1999) (Eleventh Circuit upheld finding of district court that plaintiff was collaterally estopped from arguing in federal court that she did not lie, disseminate confidential information, or misuse her patrol car where earlier finding of civil service board on these issues existed); Brewer v. Dupree, 2003 U.S. Dist. LEXIS 25327 (M.D. Ala. Feb. 12, 2003) (no res judicata because parties not in privity; collateral estoppel applied to claims in subsequent suit actually litigated in prior Title VII suit, but not as to allegations identified but not litigated).

[126]See Heyliger v. State Univ. & Cmty. Coll. Sys., 126 F.3d 849, 853–54, 90 FEP 516 (6th Cir. 1997) (state court's determination regarding plagiarism of plaintiff not settled issue sufficient to constitute legitimate, nondiscriminatory reason for plaintiff's termination and defeat his Title VII claim; however, case was dismissed on res judicata grounds).

[127]See Anderson, 128 F.3d at 1273 (court refused to apply issue preclusion to affect judgment for plaintiff on ADA claim where court did not feel defendant should be bound to ADEA judgment in previous case on behalf of another plaintiff; "discrimination claims are in and of themselves very factual, and, consequently . . . applying the doctrine of issue preclusion to situations such as that in Anderson is inappropriate"); Dici v. Pennsylvania, 91 F.3d 542, 548–49, 71 FEP 801 (3d Cir. 1996) (issue preclusion not applicable where legal issues in workers' compensation hearing were not identical to issues in plaintiff's later Title VII claim). But see Meredith v. Beech Aircraft Corp., 18 F.3d 890, 894, 64 FEP 473 (10th Cir. 1994) (court applied issue preclusion to prevent defendant from asserting that its actions in promoting male were motivated by nondiscriminatory reasons because jury, in prior suit by another female co-employee, found that defendant had discriminated by promoting male in question).

[128]See Lindsey v. Prive Corp., 161 F.3d 886, 891, 78 FEP 1857 (5th Cir. 1998) (no preclusive effect on age discrimination claim where defendant's bankruptcy trustee settled claim with plaintiffs against estate, and defendant was denied opportunity to defend merit of judgment).

[129]See Grey v. Wilburn, 14 AD 528 (E.D. Mo. 2003) (plaintiff's ADA claims not barred by either issue preclusion or claim preclusion because no final judgment on merits where state administrative proceeding was unreviewed as plaintiff entered into consent agreement in which he waived his right to hearing before state commission).

[130]See Russo v. Lightning Fulfillment, Inc., 196 F. Supp. 2d 203, 209–10, 89 FEP 548 (D. Conn. 2002) (collateral estoppel does not operate to bar unreviewed administrative regardless of whether plaintiff fully participated in administrative proceedings).

[131]See Exxon Corp. v. U.S. Dep't of Labor, 12 AD 1665 (N.D. Tex. 2002) (Department of Labor estopped from litigating issue of whether individual was qualified

The offensive use of collateral estoppel has been allowed by some[132] but not all[133] courts, largely depending on whether the same issues had been resolved.[134] In *Harrison v. Eddy Potash, Inc.*,[135] the Tenth Circuit held that although issue preclusion did not preclude the plaintiff's Title VII claim, it did bar the defendant from relitigating the issue of whether the plaintiff consented to the advances of the harasser. In the first action, the jury found for the plaintiff on her battery claim, concluding that the harasser had intentionally touched her without her consent; because the jury had already decided this issue against the defendant, it could not be relitigated.[136]

II. EXHAUSTION OF REMEDIES[137]

Private sector employees generally are not required to complete state administrative remedies before pursuing a Title VII, ADA, or ADEA claim.[138] Where the alleged discrimination occurs in a

---

individual with disability where exact issue was litigated previously in action brought by EEOC; court found that DOL and EEOC were in privity).

[132]*See* Hawkins v. Hennepin Technical Ctr., 900 F.2d 153, 156, 52 FEP 885 (8th Cir. 1990) (directing district court on remand to consider whether findings of fact against defendant in related sexual harassment suit should be given offensive collateral estoppel effect under *Parklane Hosiery Co. v. Shore*, 439 U.S. 322 (1979)); *see also* Davis v. West Cmty. Hosp., 786 F.2d 677, 682, 40 FEP 800 (5th Cir. 1986) (Title VII suit; although offensive use of collateral estoppel not applied, court recognized possibility for offensive use; "district court has broad discretion to determine whether offensive collateral estoppel is appropriate").

[133]*E.g.*, Comeaux v. Uniroyal Chem. Corp., 849 F.2d 191, 194, 47 FEP 455 (5th Cir. 1988) (finding in state unemployment compensation hearing that plaintiff did not violate safety rule could not be used offensively in Title VII or § 1981 suit to establish issue via doctrine of preclusion where issue in hearing—whether there was good cause for plaintiff's discharge—differed from issue of racial discrimination); *Davis*, 786 F.2d at 682–83 (no offensive use of determination in prior § 1981 claim because issue litigated not necessarily related to discharge at issue in later Title VII claim).

[134]*See generally* Parklane Hosiery Co. v. Shore, 439 U.S. 322, 331 (1979) (declining to create bright-line rule on circumstances in which courts should allow litigants offensive use of collateral estoppel; Court instead "grant[ed] trial courts broad discretion to determine when it should be applied").

[135]248 F.3d 1014, 1022–23, 85 FEP 990 (10th Cir. 2001).

[136]*Id.* at 1021–23.

[137]This section does not discuss EEOC exhaustion requirements, exhaustion of state administrative statutes, or mandatory arbitration provisions in a CBA. *See generally* Chapters 25 (EEOC Administrative Process) and 28 (Title VII Litigation Procedure).

[138]Patsy v. Board of Regents, 457 U.S. 496, 29 FEP 12 (1982); Zugay v. Progressive Care, 180 F.3d 901, 80 FEP 462 (7th Cir. 1999) (Title VII does not require

"deferral" state, special exhaustion requirements do apply.[139] Moreover, at least one court has held that when a plaintiff files a discrimination complaint with a state commission, the employee is obliged to exhaust state administrative remedies.[140]

Federal employee litigation involves a different remedial scheme.[141]

III. JUSTICIABILITY DOCTRINES AS BARS TO ACTION

A. Introduction

Article III of the U.S. Constitution limits the federal courts to deciding "cases" or "controversies."[142] From this requirement, the

---

plaintiff to complete state administrative process before starting federal proceedings); Smith v. McClammy, 740 F.2d 925, 35 FEP 1316 (11th Cir. 1984) (individual not required to exhaust state administrative remedies before instituting action under § 1983); Holt v. Continental Group, Inc., 708 F.2d 87, 31 FEP 1468 (2d Cir. 1983) (plaintiff's § 1981 claim not subject to exhaustion requirement); Lilly v. Harris-Teeter Supermkt., 720 F.2d 326, 33 FEP 195 (4th Cir. 1983) (same); United States v. Texas Educ. Agency, 459 F.2d 600, 9 FEP 1203 (5th Cir. 1972) (invocation of state administrative remedies does not bar simultaneous resort to equitable relief in federal courts for redress of constitutional wrongs); Claps v. Moliterno Stone Sales, Inc., 819 F. Supp. 141, 147, 63 FEP 1131 (D. Conn. 1993) ("[A CBA] cannot—at least as a general matter—require an employee to arbitrate individual statutory claims"); True v. New York State Dep't of Corr. Servs., 613 F. Supp. 27, 33, 36 FEP 1048 (W.D.N.Y. 1984) (state administrative remedies need not be exhausted and Title VII procedures need not be instituted before commencing § 1983 action in federal court); Cummings v. Walsh Constr. Co., 561 F. Supp. 872, 878, 31 FEP 930 (S.D. Ga. 1983) (no duty to exhaust employer's own internal grievance procedure); Maryland Nat'l Capital Park & Planning Comm'n v. Crawford, 475 A.2d 494, 501, 34 FEP 1731 (Md. Ct. Spec. App. 1984) (state administrative remedies need not be exhausted before suit under § 1983 in state court), aff'd, 511 A.2d 1079 (Md. 1986).

[139]See 29 U.S.C. § 633(b) (2000); 42 U.S.C. § 2000e-5(c) (2000); 42 U.S.C. § 2000e-5(e)(1) (2000); 42 U.S.C. § 12117(a) (2000) (ADA incorporates Title VII administrative procedures); Dao v. Auchan Hypermarket, 96 F.3d 787, 5 AD 1633 (5th Cir. 1996) (§ 2000e-5(e)(1) provides that before commencing civil action under Title VII in federal court, plaintiff must file timely charge with EEOC or with state or local agency with authority to grant or seek relief from alleged unlawful employment); Vielma v. Eureka Co., 218 F.3d 458, 83 FEP 729 (5th Cir. 2000) (general discussion of federal-state dual systems); Davis v. North Carolina Dep't of Corr., 48 F.3d 134, 67 FEP 258 (4th Cir. 1995); Marshall v. West Essex Gen. Hosp., 575 F.2d 1079, 17 FEP 702 (3d Cir. 1978); Garces v. Sagner Int'l, Inc., 534 F.2d 987, 12 FEP 1122 (1st Cir. 1976); Cordero v. Wal-Mart PR, Inc., 235 F. Supp. 2d 95 (D.P.R. 2002). See generally Chapter 25 (EEOC Administrative Process).

[140]Holt, 708 F.2d at 89–90.

[141]See generally Chapter 31 (Federal Employee Litigation).

[142]U.S. CONST., art. III, § 2; see Allen v. Wright, 468 U.S. 737, 750 (1984).

U.S. Supreme Court has articulated several justiciability doctrines, including standing,[143] ripeness,[144] and mootness,[145] among others.[146] These doctrines, at their bare minimum, govern who can sue (standing) and when that litigation may occur (ripeness and mootness).

1. The Justiciability Doctrine of Standing

Standing is arguably the most important justiciability doctrine,[147] and it is "an essential and unchanging part" of Article III.[148] Every plaintiff must have constitutional standing under Article III of the U.S. Constitution to bring suit in federal court.[149] The Supreme Court has held that "the question of standing is whether the litigant is entitled to have the court decide the merits of the dispute or of particular issues."[150] To have standing, plaintiffs must allege that they (1) have suffered, or imminently will suffer, an injury;[151]

---

[143]*See, e.g.*, Bennett v. Spear, 520 U.S. 154, 162–66 (1997); *Wright*, 468 U.S. at 752; Warth v. Seldin, 422 U.S. 490, 498 (1975); *see also* Section III.A.1 *infra*.

[144]*See* Abbott Labs. v. Gardner, 387 U.S. 136, 148 (1967); *see also* Section III.A.2 *infra*.

[145]*See* Board of Sch. Comm'rs v. Jacobs, 420 U.S. 128, 130 (1975); *see also* Section III.A.2 *infra*.

[146]Other justiciability doctrines include the political question doctrine and the prohibition against advisory opinions. *See* Baker v. Carr, 369 U.S. 186, 217 (1962) (discussing criteria to consider in resolving political questions); Preiser v. Newkirk, 422 U.S. 395, 401 (1975) (courts cannot give advisory opinions and "decide questions that cannot affect the rights of litigants in the case" before it).

[147]*See* Cotter v. City of Boston, 323 F.3d 160, 166 (1st Cir. 2003) (standing is "most important" Article III doctrine).

[148]Lujan v. Defenders of Wildlife, 504 U.S. 555, 560 (1992).

[149]*See Bennett*, 520 U.S. at 162. There are two aspects of standing—constitutional standing and prudential standing. *Id.* In most cases, plaintiffs have to satisfy both constitutional (Article III) standing and prudential standing (additional judicially imposed limits on the exercise of federal jurisdiction), unless Congress has granted an express right of action under the statute to persons who would otherwise be barred by prudential standing rules. *Id.* Prudential standing requires that the plaintiff be within the "zone of interests" protected by the statute. *Id.* Another prudential standing limitation includes the prohibition against generalized grievances. Warth v. Seldin, 422 U.S. 490, 499 (1975); *Defenders of Wildlife*, 504 U.S. 555. Courts are split, and the Supreme Court has not ruled, on whether and to what extent plaintiffs in Title VII cases must meet the qualifications of prudential standing, or whether Congress intended standing in Title VII cases to be as broad as Article III standing. *See* Leibovitz v. New York City Transit Auth., 252 F.3d 179, 186, 85 FEP 1543 (2d Cir. 2001) (discussing split in precedent).

[150]*Warth*, 422 U.S. at 498; *see also* Raines v. Byrd, 521 U.S. 811, 818 (1997) ("the standing inquiry focuses on whether the plaintiff is the proper party to bring this suit").

[151]An injury must be personal, particularized, concrete, and otherwise judicially cognizable. *Raines*, 521 U.S. at 819; *see also Leibovitz*, 252 F.3d at 185 (plaintiff,

(2) that the injury is fairly traceable to the defendant's conduct; and (3) that a favorable federal court decision is likely to redress the injury.[152]

The federal courts have interpreted Title VII's standing requirement liberally.[153] A plaintiff need not establish a prima facie case to have standing under statutes such as Title VII or the ADA.[154] Standing has been challenged in cases involving affirmative action policies where the plaintiff cannot show an injury or that the injury was caused by the defendant's affirmative action policy.[155]

Third parties generally do not have standing to sue on behalf of other persons.[156] In jurisdictions that apply prudential standing requirements to employment discrimination cases, plaintiffs must allege their own injuries and not the injuries of other parties.[157] Exceptions to this limitation include where the third party is unlikely

---

by alleging emotional harm from hostile work environment, established injury for purposes of standing).

[152]*Bennett*, 520 U.S. at 162.

[153]*See Leibovitz*, 252 F.3d at 185; Fair Employment Council of Greater Wash., Inc. v. BMC Mktg. Corp., 28 F.3d 1268, 1278, 65 FEP 512 (D.C. Cir. 1994) (Congress intended to grant standing under Title VII to any person that satisfied Article III standing); Gray v. Greyhound Lines, E., 545 F.2d 169 (D.C. Cir. 1976) (same).

[154]*See, e.g.*, Roe v. Cheyenne Mountain Conf. Resort, Inc., 124 F.3d 1221, 1229, 13 IER 257 (10th Cir. 1997) (plaintiffs need not be disabled under ADA to have standing); *cf.* Phillips v. Cohen, 400 F.3d 388 (10th Cir. 2005) (federal employees who failed to submit affidavits asserting that they were injured by an agency's allegedly discriminatory promotion scheme did not have standing to assert adverse impact claims).

[155]*See* Byers v. City of Albuquerque, 150 F.3d 1271, 1274–75, 78 FEP 100 (10th Cir. 1998) (white police officers did not have standing because they failed to show causal relationship between defendant's decisions not to promote them and defendant's affirmative action policies).

[156]*See* Warth v. Seldin, 422 U.S. 490, 499 (1975) ("even when the plaintiff has alleged injury sufficient to meet the 'case or controversy' requirement, the Court has held that the plaintiff generally must assert his own legal rights and interests, and cannot rest his claim to relief on the legal rights and interests of third parties"). Third-party standing requirements are prudential rather than constitutional in nature. Moore v. Consolidated Edison Co. of N.Y., Inc., 409 F.3d 506, 511 n.5, 95 FEP 1441 (2d Cir. 2005).

[157]*See, e.g.*, Bermudez v. TRC Holdings, Inc., 138 F.3d 1176, 1180–81, 76 FEP 467 (7th Cir. 1998) (suggesting that white female does not have standing to sue for harassment directed at black employees); Childress v. City of Richmond, 134 F.3d 1205, 75 FEP 1167 (4th Cir. 1998) (white male police officers do not have standing under Title VII or § 1983 to sue for hostile work environment based on disparaging remarks directed toward black and female police officers); Patee v. Pacific Nw. Bell Tel., 803 F.2d 476, 478 (9th Cir. 1986) ("The male workers cannot assert the right of their female co-workers to be free from discrimination based on their sex."). Courts are split as to whether and to what extent prudential limitations on standing apply to Title VII actions. *See Moore*, 409 F.3d at 511 n.5.

to be able to sue,[158] where there is a close relationship between the third party and the plaintiff,[159] and under the overbreadth doctrine in First Amendment cases.[160]

2. The Justiciability Doctrines of Ripeness and Mootness

The ripeness and mootness justiciability doctrines determine the temporal juncture when judicial review is appropriate. The ripeness doctrine applies when matters are premature for review because the injury is too speculative and may never occur.[161] In deciding whether an employee may seek review of an adverse employment action before it occurs,[162] federal courts look at (1) the hardship to the parties of withholding court consideration, and (2) the fitness of the issues for judicial decision.[163] The "basic rationale" of the ripeness doctrine is "to prevent the courts, through

---

[158]Also known as associational standing or organizational standing, this exception is often utilized by organizations suing on behalf of their members. *See, e.g.,* NAACP v. City of Parma, 263 F.3d 513, 524, 86 FEP 936 (6th Cir. 2001) (NAACP has standing to sue on behalf of its member).

[159]*See, e.g.,* Pierce v. Society of Sisters, 268 U.S. 510 (1925) (parochial school had standing to sue on behalf of students' parents); Craig v. Boren, 429 U.S. 190 (1976) (vendors may assert rights of customers); Singleton v. Wulff, 428 U.S. 106 (1976) (doctors have standing to sue for patients). *But see* Holt v. JTM Indus., Inc., 89 F.3d 1224, 1227, 71 FEP 809 (5th Cir. 1996) (husband who is co-worker and passive observer of wife's protected activities does not have standing to sue for retaliation under ADEA).

[160]*See* Village of Scaumburg v. Citizens for a Better Env't, 444 U.S. 620, 634 (1980). Some courts have held that plaintiffs have standing under Title VII where plaintiffs have claimed that discrimination against third parties caused the plaintiffs to lose the benefits of interracial association. *See, e.g.,* Clayton v. White Hall Sch. Dist., 875 F.2d 676, 679–80 (8th Cir. 1989) (plaintiff has standing alleging hostile work environment as result of "lost benefits of associating with persons of other racial groups"); Stewart v. Hannon, 675 F.2d 846, 850 (7th Cir. 1982) (same); EEOC v. Mississippi Coll., 626 F.2d 477, 483 (5th Cir. 1980) (holding that white female "may charge a [Title VII] violation of her own personal right to work in an environment unaffected by racial discrimination," provided she meets Article III's requirements); Waters v. Heublein, Inc., 547 F.2d 466, 469 (9th Cir. 1976) (granting white female standing to sue to enjoin racial discrimination against co-workers). Other courts have allowed third-party standing if the plaintiff alleges a pecuniary injury. *See, e.g.,* Anjelino v. New York Times Co., 200 F.3d 73, 92, 81 FEP 641 (3d Cir. 1999) (white male employees have standing to sue based on discrimination directed at female co-workers because they alleged pecuniary harm); Rosen v. Public Serv. & Gas Co., 477 F.2d 90 (3d Cir. 1972) (where male retiree alleged Title VII claim that former employer's pension plan was discriminatory, he alleged pecuniary harm).

[161]*See, e.g.,* Abbott Labs. v. Gardner, 387 U.S. 136, 148 (1967).

[162]*See City of Parma,* 263 F.3d at 533 (NAACP's Title VII claims are ripe).

[163]*Abbott Labs.,* 387 U.S. at 149.

avoidance of premature adjudication, from entangling themselves in abstract disagreements."[164]

The mootness doctrine generally applies when a change in the facts of the case ends the controversy.[165] A case is not moot, however, where

• a collateral consequence or injury survives after the plaintiff's primary claim has been resolved;[166]

• the wrong is one capable of repetition yet evading review;[167]

• the defendant voluntarily ceases the alleged unlawful action but is free to resume it;[168] or

• in a certified class action, the named plaintiff's individual claims are rendered moot.[169]

IV. PREEMPTION AS A BAR TO ACTION

Under the doctrine of preemption, federal law may alter or even completely supercede applicable state laws. "Preemption

---

[164]*Id.* at 148.

[165]*See, e.g.*, Board of Sch. Comm'rs v. Jacobs, 420 U.S. 128, 130 (1975) (case or controversy no longer existed when all named plaintiffs had graduated from school system); *see also City of Parma*, 263 F.3d at 513 (NAACP's claim not moot); EEOC v. Goodyear Aerospace Corp., 813 F.2d 1539, 1543, 43 FEP 875 (9th Cir. 1987) (EEOC's claim on behalf of individual is moot under Title VII when individual has settled claim because public interest in back pay award is minimal).

[166]In *Firefighters Local 1784 v. Stotts*, 467 U.S. 561, 34 FEP 1702 (1984), a plaintiff seeking both reinstatement and back pay for alleged discrimination was permitted to continue to pursue the case even once reinstatement was granted or no longer sought. *Id.* at 568; *see also* Super Tire Eng'g Co. v. McCorkle, 416 U.S. 115 (1974) (employers' suit challenging state law allowing striking employees to receive welfare benefits not moot when strike ended because decision in case could affect future labor-management negotiations).

[167]*See, e.g.*, Roe v. Wade, 410 U.S. 113, 125 (1973). This exception has primarily been applied to prior restraints on free speech and challenges to elections. *See* Nebraska Press Ass'n v. Stuart, 427 U.S. 539, 546 (1976) (applying exception in prior restraint case); Moore v. Ogilvie, 394 U.S. 814, 816 (1969) (applying exception to election challenge case). *But see* DeFunis v. Odegaard, 416 U.S. 312, 316–17 (1974) (refusing to apply exception to white male student's challenge to affirmative action program because trial court issued injunction admitting him while case was pending).

[168]*See, e.g.*, United States v. W.T. Grant Co., 345 U.S. 629, 632 (1953) (case not moot where "defendant is free to return to his old ways").

[169]*See, e.g.*, Sosna v. Iowa, 419 U.S. 393, 399 (1975) (plaintiff's action to have state's 1-year divorce residency requirement declared unconstitutional would have been moot because 1-year period elapsed while case was pending, but was not moot because controversy still existed for certified class).

derives from the Supremacy Clause of the United States Constitution, which provides that the laws of the United States 'shall be the supreme Law of the Land . . . any Thing in the Constitution or Laws of any State to the Contrary notwithstanding.' "[170] Although federal law generally will trump state law,[171] there are different forms of preemption, depending on what federal law is at issue and what state law the party asserting it seeks to preempt.[172]

In *California Federal Savings & Loan Ass'n v. Guerra*,[173] the Supreme Court addressed preemption in relation to Title VII and the Pregnancy Discrimination Act (PDA).[174] As the Court explained in *Guerra*, there are generally three ways in which a federal law preempts a state law—express preemption, field preemption, and conflict preemption.[175] Express preemption exists where Congress, acting within constitutional limits, so expressly states.[176] Field preemption exists and is inferred where Congress intends to leave no room for supplementary state regulation by enacting a comprehensive scheme of federal regulation.[177] Conflict preemption exists in areas where Congress has not completely displaced state regulation, yet federal law nonetheless conflicts with state law.[178]

In *Guerra,* the issue was whether the California pregnancy discrimination statute conflicted with Title VII as amended by the PDA. The Supreme Court noted that the "narrow scope of preemption available under [§ 708 and § 1104 of the Civil Rights Act of 1964] reflects the importance Congress attached to state antidiscrimination laws in achieving Title VII's goals of equal employment opportunity."[179] Title VII is the floor, not the ceiling.[180] Thus, a state law may supplement Title VII's requirements, but it cannot conflict with them.[181] The Court held that the state statute in *Guerra*

---

[170]St. Thomas-St. John Hotel & Tourism Ass'n, Inc. v. Government of U.S.V.I., 218 F.3d 232, 237, 16 IER Cases 779 (3d Cir. 2000) (citing U.S. CONST. art. VI, cl. 2).
[171]*Id.*
[172]*See* California Sav. & Loan Ass'n v. Guerra, 479 U.S. 272, 280–82 (1987).
[173]479 U.S. 272 (1987).
[174]*Id.* at 280–82.
[175]*Id.; see also St. Thomas-St. John,* 218 F.3d at 238.
[176]*See Guerra,* 479 U.S. at 280–81.
[177]*Id.* at 281.
[178]*Id.*
[179]*Id.* at 282–83.
[180]*Id.* at 285.
[181]*Id.* at 283–84; *see also* Shaw v. Delta Air Lines, Inc., 463 U.S. 85, 100–04 (1983).

was not preempted by Title VII: "We conclude that 'permit' in § 708 must be interpreted to preempt only those state laws that expressly *sanction* a practice unlawful under Title VII; the term does not preempt state laws that are silent on the practice."[182] The ADEA and the ADA are treated similarly.[183]

The Employee Retirement Income Security Act of 1974 (ERISA; specifically §§ 502 and 514);[184] the Labor Management Relations Act of 1947 (LMRA; specifically § 301);[185] and, to a lesser extent, the National Labor Relations Act (NLRA; specifically § 9)[186] similarly have been held to preempt state law.[187] Generally, federal statutes like ERISA, the LMRA, and the NLRA cannot "preempt" another federal statute, but a plaintiff can only pursue a claim under these statutes concurrently with an employment discrimination claim when the latter is merely collateral and it provides an independent federal remedy.[188]

---

[182]479 U.S. at 291.

[183]*See, e.g.*, Devlin v. Transportation Comm'cns Union, 173 F.3d 94, 100 (2d Cir. 1999) (ADEA, like Title VII, provides joint state and federal enforcement); *see also* Gregory v. Ashcroft, 501 U.S. 452 (1991) (ADA).

[184]29 U.S.C. §§ 1132, 1144 (2000); *see* Metropolitan Life Ins. Co. v. Taylor, 481 U.S. 58 (1987) (ERISA preempted former employee common law claims against former employer and its insurer alleging breach of contract, retaliatory discharge, and wrongful termination of disability benefits); Ingersoll-Rand Co. v. McClendon, 498 U.S. 133 (1990) (ERISA preempted employee's state-law wrongful discharge claim based on allegation that his discharge was based on his employer's desire to avoid making contributions to his pension fund). For ERISA preemption, it is important to distinguish between § 502 preemption, which can provide federal removal jurisdiction, and § 514 preemption, which is only an affirmative defense.

[185]29 U.S.C. § 185 (2000); *see* Avco Corp. v. Machinists, 390 U.S. 557 (1968) (§ 301 of LMRA preempts state-law claims); *cf.* Caterpillar, Inc. v. Williams, 482 U.S. 386, 125 LRRM 2521 (1987) (suit for breach of individual employment contract, even if defendant's action also constituted breach of entirely separate CBA, not preempted by § 301 of LMRA).

[186]29 U.S.C. § 159(a) (2000); *see* Machinists v. Wisconsin Employment Relations Comm'n, 427 U.S. 132, 146 (1976) (quoting Teamsters v. Morton, 377 U.S. 252, 260 (1964)) (NLRA preempts state law that "upset[s] the balance of power between labor and management expressed in our national labor policy"); San Diego Bldg. Trades Council v. Garmon, 359 U.S. 236 (1959) (state law that infringes on NLRB's primary jurisdiction over unfair labor practice charges is preempted).

[187]For further discussion of preemption under ERISA, the LMRA, or the NLRA, see STEVEN J. SACHER, ET AL., EMPLOYEE BENEFITS LAW ch. 11 (BNA 2d ed. 2000), and AMERICAN BAR ASSOCIATION, SECTION OF LABOR & EMPLOYMENT LAW, The Developing Labor Law ch. 28 (J.E. Higgins, Jr. ed., 5th ed. BNA Books 2006).

[188]*See, e.g.*, Britt v. Grocers Supply Co., 978 F.2d 1441, 1447 (5th Cir. 1992) (NLRA does not preempt ADEA claim).

CHAPTER 28

TITLE VII LITIGATION PROCEDURE

I. OVERVIEW

This chapter focuses on discrimination claims that require the exhaustion of administrative remedies with the Equal Employment Opportunity Commission (EEOC), including Title VII and the Americans with Disabilities Act.[1]

II. EFFECT OF DEFICIENCIES IN THE EEOC ADMINISTRATIVE PROCESS ON CHARGING PARTY'S RIGHT TO SUE

A. Introduction

Consistent with the recognition that Title VII is a remedial statute, the courts construe it liberally to avoid imposing technical

---

[1]*See* 42 U.S.C. § 2000e-5(e)(1) (2000) (Title VII). Title I of the Americans with Disabilities Act of 1990 (ADA) incorporates the same powers, remedies, and procedures established for Title VII. *See* 42 U.S.C. § 12117(a) (2000). Many states have parallel fair employment practices statutes that may be subject to different procedural requirements.

obstacles to relief. The basic structure of Title VII involves the early identification of offending practices through the timely filing of an administrative charge under oath, naming the violators charged and the violations alleged in at least general language, together with prompt notice to the employer, investigation of the charge, and rendering of a determination of whether there is "reasonable cause" to believe the charging party's allegations. Commencement of private litigation then may follow notice from the agency to the charging party. This notice commences another limitations period (90 days), within which the charging party may initiate a civil action against the parties named in the charge for the violations alleged in that charge. Courts have held that the EEOC's failure to comply with certain of Title VII's procedural requirements does not bar a Title VII suit by the charging party,[2] although such non-compliance might result in dismissal of a suit brought by the EEOC.[3]

---

[2]*See, e.g.*, EEOC v. W.H. Braum, Inc., 347 F.3d 1192, 1200–01, 14 AD 1768 (10th Cir. 2003) (where aggrieved employee files suit after expiration of 180-day period during which EEOC has exclusive jurisdiction, federal court jurisdiction exists even if right-to-sue letter not actually received); McGrath v. Nassau Health Care Corp., 217 F. Supp. 2d 319, 325 (E.D.N.Y. 2002) (issuance of premature right-to-sue letter by EEOC did not warrant dismissal of Title VII claim due to failure to comply with administrative requirements; dismissing such cases was unsound as policy matter and would be inequitable); Gray v. Phillips Petroleum Co., 858 F.2d 610, 615–16, 49 FEP 67 (10th Cir. 1988) (charge-filing period tolled where EEOC area office director misled charging parties regarding when to file charges and there was no prejudice to employer); Steffen v. Meridian Life Ins. Co., 859 F.2d 534, 542–44, 48 FEP 173 (7th Cir. 1988) (EEOC's failure to act on ADEA intake questionnaire does not bar ADEA action); Albright v. City of Phila., 399 F. Supp. 2d 575, 583, 96 FEP 1466 (E.D. Pa. 2005) (when EEOC fails to ever issue right-to-sue letter, statute of limitations on those claims does not run); Quarles v. General Inv. & Dev. Co., 260 F. Supp. 2d 1, 17, 91 FEP 623 (D.D.C. 2003) (plaintiff's late receipt of right-to-sue notice from EEOC during pendency of Title VII action cures defect caused by failure to receive notice before filing Title VII claim in federal court); Canty v. Wackenhut Corr. Corp., 255 F. Supp. 2d 113, 117, 91 FEP 1143 (E.D.N.Y. 2003) (employee not required to obtain right-to-sue letter from EEOC where employee filed grievance); McInnis v. North Carolina Dep't of Envtl. & Natural Res., 223 F. Supp. 2d 758, 761 (M.D.N.C. 2002) (it is the entitlement to a right-to-sue notice from EEOC, rather than its actual issuance or receipt, which is prerequisite to jurisdiction of federal courts).

[3]*See* EEOC v. Asplundh Tree Expert Co., 340 F.3d 1256, 1259, 92 FEP 661 (11th Cir. 2003) (affirming dismissal because EEOC failed to make bona fide effort to conciliate); EEOC v. LJax, Inc., 442 F. Supp. 2d 267, 268 (D. Md. 2006) (dismissing EEOC's complaint where EEOC failed to attempt conciliation for 30 days prior to suing company for unlawful employment practices); EEOC v. American Express Publ'g Corp., 681 F. Supp. 216, 220–22, 47 FEP 1596 (S.D.N.Y. 1988) (dismissal of EEOC ADEA suit on behalf of plaintiffs not named in charge or referred to in investigation or conciliation). *But cf.* EEOC v. UMB Bank, N.A., 432 F. Supp. 2d 948, 953, 17 AD 1367 (W.D. Mo. 2006) (where EEOC's conciliation

Courts have imposed limitations where the charging party fails to participate in the administrative and investigative process in good faith,[4] including dismissal of the later civil action.[5] This is particularly true where an employer is prejudiced by delays in the process and claims that the equitable doctrine of laches requires dismissal.[6]

---

efforts are insufficient, dismissal is too harsh a remedy absent grossly unreasonable conduct or substantial prejudice to the employer; instead, appropriate remedy is temporary stay); EEOC v. First Midwest Bank, N.A., 14 F. Supp. 2d 1028, 1031, 77 FEP 1121 (N.D. Ill. 1998) (if district court finds improper conciliation efforts by EEOC, appropriate remedy is not dismissal but stay of proceedings so that conciliation may take place); EEOC v. Jacksonville Shipyards, 696 F. Supp. 1438, 1444–45, 48 FEP 66 (M.D. Fla. 1988) (rejected EEOC settlement offer constituted sufficient conciliation, even though specific charges were not discussed expressly). *See generally* Chapter 29 (EEOC Litigation).

[4]*See* Shikles v. Sprint/United Mgt. Co., 426 F.3d 1304, 1317, 96 FEP 1156 (10th Cir. 2005) (employee's failure to make good faith effort to cooperate with EEOC in its investigation constitutes failure to exhaust administrative remedies); Crawford v. Babbitt, 186 F.3d 1322, 1326–27, 80 FEP 1119 (11th Cir. 1999) (by failing to respond to EEOC's requests for additional information, employee did not participate in good faith in administrative proceedings and therefore did not exhaust her administrative remedies).

[5]*See, e.g., Shikles*, 426 F.3d at 1317 (failure to cooperate may deprive district court of jurisdiction to adjudicate claim); *Crawford*, 186 F.3d at 1326–27 (plaintiff's claim for compensatory damages properly dismissed because she failed to participate in good faith in administrative proceedings); Briley v. Carlin, 172 F.3d 567, 574, 79 FEP 1630 (8th Cir. 1999) (district court properly granted summary judgment to defendant because plaintiff failed to participate in good faith in administrative process); Artis v. Greenspan, 158 F.3d 1301, 1306–08, 78 FEP 74 (D.C. Cir. 1998) (affirming dismissal of discrimination complaint for failure to participate adequately in administrative process); Barnes v. Levitt, 118 F.3d 404, 408 (5th Cir. 1997) (reversing verdict for plaintiff because of plaintiff's failure to cooperate with EEOC investigation). *But see* Doe v. Oberweis Dairy, 456 F.3d 704, 709, 98 FEP 958 (7th Cir. 2006) (rejecting *Shikles* approach).

[6]*Compare* Smith v. Caterpillar, Inc., 338 F.3d 730, 733–34, 92 FEP 595 (7th Cir. 2003) (plaintiff filed charge in 1991, bypassed evidentiary hearing in 1998 before state agency, took additional year to obtain right-to-sue letter from EEOC; district court did not abuse discretion in applying laches where employer documented that witnesses—including key decision maker—had retired or were otherwise unavailable, that memories had faded and witnesses could not recall critical facts, loss of documents, and accumulation of 9 years' worth of back pay prejudgment interest placed employer at unfair disadvantage), National Ass'n of Gov't Employees v. City Pub. Serv. Bd., 40 F.3d 698, 708–11, 67 FEP 1013 (5th Cir. 1994) (defendant successfully asserted laches defense based on 9-year delay between failure of conciliation and filing of lawsuit) *and* Henderson v. Anne Arundel County Bd. of Educ., 54 F. Supp. 2d 481, 482 (D. Md. 1998) (defendant successfully asserted laches defense based on 20-year delay between date of alleged discrimination and filing of lawsuit) *with* Anderson v. Anheuser-Busch, Inc., 65 F. Supp. 218, 225–26, 81 FEP 598 (S.D.N.Y. 1999) (defendant unsuccessfully asserted laches defense based

Neither the charging party[7] nor respondent[8] has a right of action against the EEOC under Title VII or the U.S. Constitution for its administrative failures.

The consequences of errors by the EEOC in relation to the filing or processing of the charge are treated elsewhere.[9]

B. EEOC Failure to Serve Charge on Respondent

Title VII provides that the EEOC must notify respondents of charges against them within 10 days of receipt.[10] For various reasons, this notification is not always effected within that period.

---

on 2-year delay between conclusion of administrative investigation and filing of lawsuit), *aff'd*, 229 F.3d 1135 (2d Cir. 2000). *See generally* Chapter 26 (Timeliness); William T. Goglia, Annotation, *Laches as Defense to Action Under Title VII of Civil Rights Act of 1964 Brought by Private Individual*, 52 A.L.R. FED. 218 (2001). Several courts have dismissed on laches grounds, even where the delay may have been due to the EEOC administrative process. *See, e.g.*, EEOC v. Autozone, Inc., 258 F. Supp. 2d 822, 826–27, 91 FEP 921 (W.D. Tenn. 2003) (EEOC may be barred by laches from filing suit if it has delayed inexcusably and defendant has been materially prejudiced by delay). However, other courts have limited such dismissal to cases where the plaintiff is at least partly responsible. *See, e.g.*, National R.R. Passenger Corp. v. Morgan, 536 U.S. 101, 121–22 (2002) (if employee unreasonably delays in filing Title VII claim and as result harms employer, then employer may raise laches defense); Brown-Mitchell v. Kansas City Power & Light Co., 267 F.3d 825, 827–28 (8th Cir. 2001) (laches is proper defense to claims of discrimination and retaliatory discharge under Title VII when based upon plaintiff's post-charge delay in filing lawsuit).

[7]*See, e.g.*, Skibinski v. Zevnik, 2003 U.S. App. LEXIS 3991, at *2 (2d Cir. Mar. 4, 2003) ("employees have no express or implied cause of action under Title VII to sue the EEOC for improper investigation or processing of employment discrimination claims"); Jordan v. Summers, 205 F.3d 337, 342, 82 FEP 311 (7th Cir. 2000) ("[i]t is well established that a private-sector employee has no cause of action against the EEOC for its failure to process a charge of discrimination"); Smith v. Casellas, 119 F.3d 33, 34, 74 FEP 854 (D.C. Cir. 1997) ("no cause of action against the EEOC exists for challenges to its processing of a claim"); Terry v. Director, Complaint Adjudication Div., United States EEOC, Office of Fed. Operations, 21 F. Supp. 2d 566, 569 (E.D. Va. 1998) ("[c]ourts have uniformly held that no cause of action exists with respect to the EEOC's handling of discrimination claims"), *aff'd*, 1999 U.S. App. LEXIS 2964 (4th Cir. Feb. 25, 1999); Forbes v. Reno, 893 F. Supp. 476, 482, 73 FEP 51 (W.D. Pa. 1995) (Title VII does not grant plaintiff express or implied right to bring suit against EEOC for inadequate or improper investigation of charge of discrimination), *aff'd without opinion*, 91 F.3d 123, 73 FEP 192 (3d Cir. 1996).

[8]*See, e.g.*, Sears v. EEOC, 42 FEP 1890, 1892 (D.D.C. 1987) (Title VII and Rehabilitation Act provide no cause of action against EEOC to challenge its investigation or processing of a charge).

[9]*See generally* Chapters 25 (EEOC Administrative Process) and 26 (Timeliness).

[10]42 U.S.C. § 2000e-5(b) (2000).

Dismissal of a later civil action brought by the EEOC may be appropriate where there is substantial prejudice to the respondent from an unreasonable delay or failure of notice.[11]

C. EEOC Failure to Investigate and/or Conciliate

The structure of Title VII gives primacy to the administrative investigation of charges without the publicity that attends formal litigation, giving the parties the opportunity for notice of the claim, participation in an investigation, and, perhaps more important, if the EEOC issues a cause determination, the opportunity to conciliate in an effort to avoid litigation. Disruption or lack of cooperation by the charging party in the administrative investigation, which has the effect of preventing an adequate investigation by the EEOC, has been the basis for a denial of the right to proceed with private litigation.[12]

The effect of the EEOC's failure to conciliate differs with the circumstances. The EEOC's obligation to conciliate is neither a jurisdictional prerequisite nor a condition precedent to private suits under Title VII.[13] Therefore, the courts have held that the failure of the EEOC to attempt conciliation with a party does not affect

---

[11]*E.g.*, EEOC v. AirGuide Corp., 29 FEP 236, 240–41 (S.D. Fla. 1978) (substantial prejudice where EEOC failed to notify employer until almost 1 year after the filing of the charge; records had been destroyed and back-pay claim grew). *But see* EEOC v. Wayside World Corp., 646 F. Supp. 86, 88, 42 FEP 253 (W.D. Va. 1986) (6-month delay in notification of charge filing did not cause substantial prejudice, where witnesses were still available).

[12]*See* Shikles v. Sprint/United Mgmt. Co., 426 F.3d 1304, 1310, 96 FEP 1156 (10th Cir. 2005) (employee's non-cooperation that prevents effective EEOC investigation constitutes failure to exhaust, barring ADEA action; employee failed to make himself available for interview and failed to provide documents requested by agency, and plaintiff's attorney did not respond to EEOC attempts to reach him); Hill v. Potter, 352 F.3d 1142, 1146, 93 FEP 188 (7th Cir. 2003) (employee's refusal to cooperate with EEOC after filing charge constituted failure to exhaust administrative remedies); Jasch v. Potter, 302 F.3d 1092, 1094, 89 FEP 1377 (9th Cir. 2002) (employee's failure to cooperate with EEOC prevents exhaustion of administrative remedies when it prevents agency from making determination on merits of charge); Barnes v. Levitt, 118 F.3d 404, 409 (5th Cir. 1997) (Title VII plaintiffs who resort to administrative process but do not cooperate therein can fail to exhaust administrative remedies; EEOC did not abuse discretion by dismissing charge for failure to cooperate). *But see* Doe v. Oberweis Dairy, 456 F.3d 704, 710, 98 FEP 958 (7th Cir. 2006) (no duty of cooperation imposed on charging party under Title VII); Adair v. Broadlawns Med. Ctr., 102 F. Supp. 2d 1092, 1096 (S.D. Iowa 1999) (dismissal of Title VII suit due to plaintiff's failure to cooperate with agency's investigation not appropriate when plaintiff's default does not prevent agency from timely deciding merits of complaint).

[13]*See* Sedlacek v. Hach, 752 F.2d 333, 336, 36 FEP 1253 (8th Cir. 1985); *see also* Hodge v. New York Coll. of Podiatric Med., 157 F.3d 164, 168, 78 FEP 80 (2d

the complaining party's substantive rights under Title VII,[14] although non-compliance with required informal conciliation efforts might result in dismissal of a suit brought by the EEOC.[15]

By contrast, where the administrative failure to include a party in the charge, such as a parent corporation, deprives it of the opportunity for notice and the opportunity to conciliate on its own behalf, a later civil action against that entity may be dismissed.[16] This may also be true where the charging party has failed to specify the claim against the employer in the charge documents.[17]

D. Charge Not Under Oath

Title VII requires that a charge be made under oath or affirmation.[18] The EEOC by regulation, however, has allowed charges

---

Cir. 1998) (district court's jurisdiction over ADEA claim does not depend on EEOC's having taken action in response to a filed charge).

[14]*Sedlacek*, 752 F.3d at 335; *Hodge*, 157 F.3d at 168 (plaintiff can sue in court even if EEOC has not completed investigation or attempts at conciliation); Donaldson v. Cafritz Co., 30 FEP 436, 438 (D.D.C. 1981) (failure of EEOC to attempt conciliation is no basis for dismissal and does not mandate a stay, because the conciliation requirement is not jurisdictional). *But see* EEOC v. Asplundh Tree Expert Co., 340 F.3d 1256, 92 FEP 661 (11th Cir. 2003) (awarding attorney's fees to defendant because EEOC failed to make bona fide effort to conciliate).

[15]*See, e.g.*, 42 U.S.C. §§ 2000e-5(b), (f) (2000) (upon finding cause, the EEOC must attempt conciliation before filing suit). *See generally* Chapter 29 (EEOC Litigation).

[16]*See, e.g.*, Adorno-Rosado v. Wackenhut P.R., Inc., 98 F. Supp. 2d 181, 186 (D.P.R. 2000) (plaintiff's failure to name defendant in charge prevented it from participating in conciliation, which supported dismissal of the claim); Secrist v. Burns Int'l Sec. Servs., 926 F. Supp. 823, 825–26, 71 FEP 162 (E.D. Wis. 1996) (dismissing claims against defendant not named by pro se litigant in her EEOC charge); Vakharia v. Little Co. of Mary Hosp. & Health Care Ctrs., 917 F. Supp. 1282, 1294 (N.D. Ill. 1996) (claim dismissed with respect to defendants not named in charge due to failure of adequate notice of the charge and opportunity to participate in conciliation). *But see* Virgo v. Riviera Beach Assocs., 30 F.3d 1350, 1358–59, 65 FEP 1317 (11th Cir. 1994) (defendant had opportunity to participate in conciliation); Harris v. Stallman Trucking Co., 951 F. Supp. 134, 136–37 (N.D. Ill. 1996) (absence of prejudice to defendant precludes dismissal).

[17]*See* Fairchild v. Forma Scientific, 147 F.3d 567, 575–76, 77 FEP 251 (7th Cir. 1998) (plaintiff's failure to include disability discrimination allegation in timely filed charge prevented defendant from having opportunity to participate in conciliation relating to that allegation; summary judgment granted); Meek v. Swift Transp., 83 FEP 1503, 1511 (D. Kan. 2000) (plaintiff's failure to include constructive discharge allegation in charge prevented opportunity to participate in conciliation related to that allegation; summary judgment for defendant); Hoffman v. Rhode Island Enters., 50 F. Supp. 2d 393, 399, 80 FEP 449 (M.D. Pa. 1999) (failure to include class action allegation in charge prevented defendant from participating in conciliation related to that allegation; class certification denied).

[18]42 U.S.C. § 2000e-5(b) (2000).

to be liberally amended, so that a complainant may file a later formal charge under oath that relates back by amendment to the initial document, usually an intake questionnaire.[19]

The Supreme Court approved this practice in *Edelman v. Lynchburg College*, where it held that a Title VII complainant may cure the failure of charge verification, even after the filing deadline, by submitting a properly verified document, and that this cure will relate back to the time when an unverified charge was initially submitted.[20]

By contrast, ADEA charges are not required to be made under oath or affirmation.[21]

E. EEOC Failure to Issue Notice of Right to Sue When Charging Party Is Entitled to It

Title VII provides that, upon completion of the investigative and/or conciliation process, the charging party's right to commence a civil action depends on receipt of a notice from the EEOC of the charging party's right to initiate suit.[22] Courts have not treated this requirement as a jurisdictional prerequisite to suit under Title VII, but rather as a condition precedent to suit[23] that may be cured[24] or

---

[19]*See* 29 C.F.R. § 1601.12(b) (2005). *But see* Bost v. Federal Express Corp., 372 F.3d 1233, 93 FEP 1705 (11th Cir.) (intake interview should not be treated as charge where it was not served on employer, claimant was not misinformed by EEOC, intake interview form itself stated in a disclaimer that it was not a charge, and plaintiff did eventually file a charge), *cert. denied*, 543 U.S. 1020 (2004).

[20]535 U.S. 106, 118–19, 88 FEP 321 (2002). *But cf.* Balazs v. Liebenthal, 32 F.3d 151, 157, 65 FEP 993 (4th Cir. 1994) (once EEOC has issued right-to-sue letter, suit has been instituted, and EEOC has closed its file, "there is no longer a charge pending before the EEOC which is capable of being amended"); Danley v. Book-of-the-Month Club, 921 F. Supp. 1352, 1354, 70 FEP 1281 (M.D. Pa. 1996) (once right-to-sue letter has been issued by EEOC and its file has been closed, defective unverified charge cannot be cured by amendment), *aff'd mem.*, 107 F.3d 861, 80 FEP 896 (3d Cir. 1997).

[21]29 U.S.C. § 626(d) (2000).

[22]42 U.S.C. § 2000e-5(f) (2000).

[23]*See* Worth v. Tyer, 276 F.3d 249, 258–59, 87 FEP 994 (7th Cir. 2001) (notice is not jurisdictional prerequisite, and receipt of notice prior to dismissal cures any defect); Parry v. Mohawk Motors of Mich., 236 F.3d 299, 309–10, 11 AD 538 (6th Cir. 2000) (receipt of right-to-sue letter is merely condition precedent to ADA suit and failure to satisfy can be cured after suit is filed); Rivers v. Barberton Bd. of Educ., 143 F.3d 1029, 1032, 76 FEP 1545 (6th Cir. 1998) (same); Portis v. Ohio, 141 F.3d 632, 634–35, 84 FEP 1258 (6th Cir. 1998) ("no prejudice in this case," where right-to-sue letter arrived 1 week after the filing of complaint).

[24]*See* Shanks v. Calvin Walker & Doctor's Assocs., 116 F. Supp. 2d 311, 313 (D. Conn. 2000) (receipt of right-to-sue letter after commencement of lawsuit); Alarcon v. Bill

even waived.[25] Some courts have held that it is the entitlement to a right-to-sue letter, rather than the actual receipt of the letter, that is necessary to support federal court jurisdiction.[26] However, if the EEOC initiates suit without issuing a right-to-sue notice, the charging party has a right to intervene.[27]

Consistent with this approach, courts may equitably toll the 90-day filing period in some circumstances, such as where the right-to-sue letter has been issued but not received by the charging party even though the charging party used due care in notifying the EEOC of address changes; such tolling, however, will be available only where the equities are in the plaintiff's favor.[28]

III. SUIT AGAINST PARTIES NOT NAMED IN EEOC CHARGE

A. Introduction

Section 706(f)(1) provides that a "civil action may be brought against a respondent named in the charge."[29] This language often

---

Rodgers Buick, Inc., 110 F. Supp. 2d 656, 657 (E.D. Tenn. 2000) (same); Kane v. Iowa Dep't of Human Servs., 955 F. Supp. 1117, 1135–40, 75 FEP 1093 (N.D. Iowa 1997) (receipt of notice after commencement of civil action sufficient); Gilday v. Mecosta County, 920 F. Supp. 792, 794 n.1, 5 AD 758 (W.D. Mich. 1996) (absence of notice "a curable defect"), rev'd on other grounds, 124 F.3d 760, 7 AD 348 (6th Cir. 1997).

[25]See Francis v. City of N.Y., 235 F.3d 763, 768–69 (2d Cir. 2000) ("We hold that presentation of a Title VII claim to the EEOC 'is not a jurisdictional [prerequisite], but only a precondition to bringing a Title VII action that can be waived by the parties or the court,' and that defendants waived that precondition in this case.") (citation omitted); Pietras v. Board of Fire Comm'rs, 180 F.3d 468, 473–74, 80 FEP 307 (2d Cir. 1999) (affirming decision to excuse absence of right-to-sue letter because plaintiff had attempted to obtain one, but state agency and EEOC had wrongfully failed to provide one based on erroneous belief that plaintiff was not an "employee").

[26]See Worth v. Tyer, 276 F.3d 249, 259, 87 FEP 994 (7th Cir. 2001); McInnis v. North Carolina Dep't of Envtl. & Natural Res., 223 F. Supp. 2d 758, 761–62 (M.D.N.C. 2002); Henderson v. Anne Arundel County Bd. of Educ., 54 F. Supp. 2d 481, 482 (D. Md. 1998). But see Garcia v. Los Banos Unified Sch. Dist., 418 F. Supp. 2d 1194, 1212 (E.D. Cal. 2006) (receipt of right-to-sue letter is jurisdictional prerequisite to maintaining Title VII action).

[27]42 U.S.C. § 2000e-5(f)(1) (2000); see also Nevilles v. EEOC, 511 F.2d 303, 305 (8th Cir. 1975) ("aggrieved employee had an absolute right to intervene in a civil action brought by the EEOC").

[28]See generally Chapter 26 (Timeliness). Where the charging party has not been diligent in providing an updated address most courts will utilize the "constructive receipt" doctrine and decline to equitably toll the filing period. See, e.g., Kerr v. McDonald's Corp., 427 F.3d 947, 96 FEP 1086 (11th Cir. 2005); Taylor v. Books A Million, Inc., 296 F.3d 376, 89 FEP 577 (5th Cir. 2002), cert. denied, 537 U.S. 1200 (2003).

[29]42 U.S.C. § 2000e-5(f)(1) (2000).

serves as the basis for motions to dismiss claims against parties or entities who are not named in an EEOC charge that forms the basis for a later civil action. Nevertheless, there are numerous circumstances in which the courts have applied this limitation flexibly to advance the remedial purposes of Title VII.[30]

The parent corporation of a subsidiary is not a proper party to a civil action when it was not named in the charge.[31] Similarly, in states where individuals may be liable under the antidiscrimination laws, individual defendants and managers generally may not be sued where they were not named in the charge.[32]

The courts focus on equitable issues such as the reasonable scope of the investigation by the EEOC,[33] actual notice of the investigation

---

[30]*See* Triplett v. Midwest Wrecking Co., 155 F. Supp. 2d 932, 937 (N.D. Ill. 2001) ("a party not named in the EEOC charge may be sued where the unnamed party received adequate notice of the charge"); Frazier v. Smith, 12 F. Supp. 2d 1362, 1369 (S.D. Ga. 1998) (refusing to dismiss county sheriff not named specifically in EEOC charge where plaintiff did name county sheriff's department and described acts taken by sheriff in EEOC charge); Kramer v. Windsor Park Nursing Home, 943 F. Supp. 844, 851, 75 FEP 899 (S.D. Ohio 1996) (even if there was no identity of interest between named and unnamed defendants, unnamed defendant received adequate notice because such defendant was named specifically in actions described in body of EEOC charge); Alfano v. Costello, 940 F. Supp. 459, 465–66, 80 FEP 1507 (N.D.N.Y. 1996) (same), *rev'd in part on other grounds*, 294 F.3d 365, 89 FEP 193 (2d Cir. 2002); Compton v. Chinn Enters., 936 F. Supp. 480, 487 (N.D. Ill. 1996) (corporate owner received adequate notice of retaliation charge where named as respondent in plaintiff's sexual harassment charge); Scales v. Sonic Indus., 887 F. Supp. 1435, 1437 (E.D. Okla. 1995) (informal reference to franchiser's trade name linked charge sufficiently to otherwise unnamed franchiser); Afande v. National Lutheran Home for the Aged, 868 F. Supp. 795, 800 (D. Md. 1994) (purposes of naming requirement met where supervisor had notice of charge and participated in conciliation process), *aff'd*, 69 F.3d 532 (4th Cir. 1995). *But see* Bishop v. Okidata, Inc., 864 F. Supp. 416, 425, 3 AD 1283 (D.N.J. 1994) (naming requirement not necessarily met where plaintiff names individuals in affidavit accompanying EEOC charge).

[31]*See* Cellini v. Harcourt Brace & Co., 51 F. Supp. 2d 1028, 1034, 83 FEP 483 (S.D. Cal. 1999) (subsidiary not agent of parent corporation for purposes of holding parent liable on agency theory for employment discrimination allegedly perpetrated against subsidiary's former employee); Krahel v. Owens-Brockway Glass Container, Inc., 971 F. Supp. 440, 456, 74 FEP 465 (D. Or. 1997) (parent corporation not liable for Title VII violations of wholly owned subsidiary).

[32]*See generally* Chapter 21 (Employers).

[33]*See* Nogueras v. University of P.R., 890 F. Supp. 60, 63, 69 FEP 1007 (D.P.R. 1995) (allegations in charge sufficient to give notice to EEOC and unnamed parties that plaintiff considered unnamed parties to be culpable); Brogdon v. Alabama Dep't of Econ. & Cmty. Affairs, 864 F. Supp. 1161, 1165, 66 FEP 325 (M.D. Ala. 1994) (conduct of head of state agency was within reasonable scope of investigation where

to the unnamed respondent,[34] and the identity of interest between the named and unnamed parties in the charge.[35] Dismissal is most likely when the unnamed party had no notice of conciliation efforts and was prejudiced by the failure to be named in the charge.[36] The Supreme

---

agency itself was named in charge); Ajaz v. Continental Airlines, 156 F.R.D. 145, 147 (S.D. Tex. 1994) (unreasonable to conclude that EEOC investigation arising out of charge would focus on unnamed immediate supervisor where only individual named in charge was shift manager who notified plaintiff of discharge). *Compare* Walls v. Mississippi State Dep't of Pub. Welfare, 730 F.2d 306, 317–18, 34 FEP 1114 (5th Cir. 1984) (applicant's claims could include a challenge to state examinations even though the charge failed to name the state's Merit System Council, which administers the tests; the charge could be read to encompass a claim against the entire state system), Wright v. Manatee County, 717 F. Supp. 1493, 1497, 50 FEP 1194 (M.D. Fla. 1989) (county commissioners not named in charge may be sued because policy makers reasonably were within scope of EEOC investigation) *and* Schuth v. Louisiana State Univ., 50 FEP 853, 856–57 (E.D. La. 1989) (university officials not named in charge may be sued if their involvement was within the reasonable scope of the EEOC investigation) *with* Hamm v. Board of Regents, 708 F.2d 647, 649–50, 32 FEP 441 (11th Cir. 1983) (complaint dismissed against two state agencies not named in charge because it was unclear whether scope of EEOC investigation would have reasonably included them).

[34]*See* Roberts v. Michaels, 219 F.3d 775, 778, 83 FEP 653 (8th Cir. 2000) (unnamed employer could be added where corporation received actual notice of suit when its president and general manager were personally served with initial complaint and participated in EEOC investigation); Campbell, 69 F. Supp. 2d at 388 (expansion of claim to unnamed international union improper where international had no notice of charges against it).

[35]*See* Georgiu v. Sterling Mounting & Finishing, 1 Fed. Appx. 47, 49–50 (2d Cir. 2001) (employment discrimination action may proceed against party who was not named in EEOC charge where there is clear identity of interest); Knowlton v. Teltrust Phones, Inc., 189 F.3d 1177, 1185, 80 FEP 1062 (10th Cir. 1999) (Title VII action may proceed against defendant not named in EEOC charge when there is clear identity of interest between unnamed defendant and party named in charge); Alexander v. Laborers Local 496, 177 F.3d 394, 411, 79 FEP 1057 (6th Cir. 1999) (party must be named in EEOC charge unless there is clear identity of interest).

[36]*See* Olsen v. Marshall & Ilsley Corp., 267 F.3d 597, 604, 86 FEP 1404 (7th Cir. 2001) (affirming dismissal of employer's parent company not named in charge because it did not have adequate notice or opportunity to conciliate); Causey v. Balog, 162 F.3d 795 (4th Cir. 1998) (purposes of requirement that civil action can be brought only against respondent named in charge include putting charged party on notice and allowing EEOC to attempt conciliation); Wells v. Hospital Group of Ill., Inc., 2003 U.S. Dist. LEXIS 12822, at *9–12 (N.D. Ill. July 23, 2003) (same); Kern v. General Elec., 2003 U.S. Dist. LEXIS 10331, at *16–18 (N.D. Tex. June 17, 2003) (rejecting dismissal of unnamed subsidiary because it had opportunity to conciliate and there was clear identity of interest between named parent company and unnamed subsidiary). *Compare* Chandler v. Fast Lane, Inc., 868 F. Supp. 1138, 1141, 66 FEP 675 (E.D. Ark. 1994) (unnamed owner and operator of named corporate defendant had requisite notice and opportunity) *and* Johnson v. County of Cook, 864 F. Supp. 84, 86–87 (N.D. Ill. 1994) (unnamed sheriff's office had constructive notice because

Court's decision in *Northwest Airlines, Inc. v. Transport Workers*,[37] narrowly read, holds that the employer cannot rely on an implied statutory or common law right of contribution under either Title VII or the Equal Pay Act to bring in a co-defendant,[38] but the case may also stand for the proposition that no relief may be obtained against a party who has not been made the subject of an EEOC charge, a notice of right to sue and a timely filed civil action.[39]

One approach to address this issue is to stay the action to permit correction of the procedural defect, but this can be unsatisfactory where the relatively short statutory limitations period of Title VII has already expired.[40] Courts are more likely to hold the charging party responsible for naming prospective defendants in the administrative charge where they have been represented by counsel in the charge-filing process.[41]

---

it initiated discharge proceedings and was represented by same attorney as named department of corrections) *with* Banks v. Chicago Bd. of Educ., 895 F. Supp. 206, 210, 68 FEP 1333 (N.D. Ill. 1995) (plaintiff failed to allege that unnamed principals of elementary schools had notice of charge) *and* Smith v. Sheet Metal Workers Local 28, 877 F. Supp. 165, 172–73, 148 LRRM 2856 (S.D.N.Y. 1995) (unnamed union representatives not provided with constructive notice even though plaintiff named union in charge), *aff'd*, 100 F.3d 943, 152 LRRM 2384 (2d Cir. 1996).

[37]451 U.S. 77, 25 FEP 737 (1981).

[38]*Id.* at 94–95, 97–98.

[39]*See id.* at 89–90 & n.23; *see also* Section III.D *infra*.

[40]*See* King v. One Unknown Fed. Corr. Officer, 201 F.3d 910, 914 (7th Cir. 2000) (Rule 15(c)(3) does not allow plaintiff to add new defendant by amendment after limitations period has run when plaintiff had failed to identify proper party); Vakharia v. Swedish Covenant Hosp., 824 F. Supp. 769, 773, 61 FEP 1065 (N.D. Ill. 1993) (time-barred Title VII claims in amended complaint adding new defendants do not relate back to time of original filing); Fuchilla v. Prockop, 682 F. Supp. 247, 256, 52 FEP 259 (D.N.J. 1987) (29 C.F.R. § 1601.12, which allows for relation back of amended EEOC charges curing technical defects or omissions, does not provide for naming a new party to relate back to filing of original charge).

[41]*Compare* Strine v. Marion Cent. Sch. Dist., 2003 U.S. Dist. LEXIS 15709, at *8–9 (W.D.N.Y. Aug. 18, 2003) (allowing pro se plaintiff to supplement record with evidence supporting suit against unnamed school district), Garner v. Knoll Bros. Quick Marts, Inc., 962 F. Supp. 1115, 1119–20 (N.D. Ind. 1997) (refusing to dismiss unnamed owner and corporation that operated store that employed plaintiff where plaintiff was unrepresented during EEOC proceedings and did name store that employed him), Dortz v. New York, 904 F. Supp. 127, 143, 72 FEP 205 (S.D.N.Y. 1995) (because plaintiff was proceeding pro se and was told by EEOC investigator not to change her charge, plaintiff permitted to pursue claims against unnamed employer of alleged harasser despite knowledge of employment relationship at time charges were filed) *and* Gilmore v. List & Clark Constr. Co., 862 F. Supp. 294, 297 (D. Kan. 1994) (because EEOC charges are written by laypersons not versed in technicalities of

B. Circumstances in Which Joinder of an Unnamed Party Has Been Permitted

1. Joinder Where Injustice Would Otherwise Result to Plaintiff and Defendant Named in EEOC Charge

To determine whether a party that is neither named nor referenced in an administrative charge may nevertheless be joined, courts examine:

> 1) whether the role of the unnamed party could through reasonable efforts by the complainant be ascertained at the time of the filing of the EEOC complaint; 2) whether, under the circumstances, the interests of a named [party] are so similar as the unnamed party's that for the purpose of obtaining voluntary conciliation and compliance it would be unnecessary to include the unnamed party in the EEOC proceedings; 3) whether its absence from the EEOC proceedings resulted in actual prejudice to the interests of the unnamed party; 4) whether the unnamed party has in some way represented to the complainant that its relationship with the complainant is to be through the named party.[42]

---

pleading or Title VII's jurisdictional requirements, charges must be construed liberally) *with* Crosten v. Kamauf, 932 F. Supp. 676, 682, 70 FEP 1144 (D. Md. 1996) (court aided in its conclusion that no exception to naming requirement was justified when plaintiff was represented by counsel during entire administrative process), Bonner v. Guccione, 68 FEP 47, 50 (S.D.N.Y. 1995) (finding significant fact that plaintiff was represented by counsel at time EEOC complaint was filed) *and* Sanders v. Bethlehem Steel Corp., 68 FEP 695, 699 (D. Md. 1995) (plaintiff's argument that she was unrepresented by counsel when charges drafted by EEOC investigator were filed failed to persuade court to allow plaintiff to bring claims against unnamed defendant), *aff'd*, 91 F.3d 133 (4th Cir. 1996).

[42]Glus v. G.C. Murphy Co., 562 F.2d 880, 888, 15 FEP 998 (3d Cir. 1977); *see also Alexander*, 177 F.3d at 411–12 (applying *Glus* factors to find sufficient identity of interest between local and international union to allow liability of international union to begin to accrue as of date of first EEOC filing); Cook v. Arrowsmith Shelburne, Inc., 69 F.3d 1235, 1241–42, 69 FEP 392 (2d Cir. 1995) (applying *Glus* factors to find substantial identity of interest and thus lack of prejudice to unnamed party by allowing joinder as defendant); Winbush v. Iowa, by Glenwood State Hosp., 66 F.3d 1471, 1478 n.9 (8th Cir. 1995) (applying *Glus* factors to find that purpose of Title VII's notice and conciliation requirements had been met); Virgo v. Riviera Beach Assocs., 30 F.3d 1350, 1358–59 (11th Cir. 1994) (same); Brown v. Vitelcom, Inc., 47 F. Supp. 2d 595, 604 (D.V.I. 1999) (applying *Glus* factors and stating that the "jurisdictional prerequisite is construed liberally in favor of complainants"); Stafford v. Radford Cmty. Hosp., Inc., 908 F. Supp. 1369, 1373 (W.D. Va. 1995) (applying *Glus* factors to find that plaintiff failed to meet burden of showing that unnamed and named parties had substantial identity of interest), *aff'd*, 120 F.3d 262 (4th Cir. 1997).

Many courts have been reluctant to dismiss a plaintiff's lawsuit for failure to name a third party in the charge.[43] Some will permit joinder;[44] others find that the third party is dispensable after all under Rule 19.[45]

2. Joinder of Parties Necessary for Purposes of Modifying Seniority Provisions of Collective Bargaining Agreements

Particularly in the earlier days of Title VII, the EEOC brought a number of cases in which it sought to join unnamed parties (usually labor unions) as defendants under Rule 19. The Commission contended that it was not charging such a party with a violation of Title VII, or seeking monetary relief against it, but only seeking joinder because that entity is a party to a collective bargaining agreement that must be modified to provide full relief. The Sixth Circuit approved the joinder of a union for such a purpose in *EEOC v. MacMillan Bloedel Containers, Inc.*,[46] relying on a number of grounds: the charging party may not understand the relevance of the collective bargaining agreement and the union's role until after the statute of limitations has run; joinder will allow the charging party an opportunity for full and complete relief; the union was subject to an EEOC investigation relating to the alleged unlawful employment practices of the employer regardless of whether it was named in the charge; the union will have a full opportunity to participate in the litigation and the formulation of any proposed relief against the employer; the union will have the opportunity to protect adequately the interests of its members; the suit will be

---

[43]*See, e.g.*, Secrist v. Burns Int'l Sec. Servs., 926 F. Supp. 823, 825 (E.D. Wis. 1996) (before rejecting joinder of unnamed party, court considered whether plaintiff would be deprived of Title VII remedy); Johnson v. County of Cook, 864 F. Supp. 84, 87 (N.D. Ill. 1994) (court considered fact that if claims were not permitted against unnamed defendant, plaintiff would be left with no Title VII remedy because named defendant was not suable entity).

[44]*See* EEOC v. Rockwell Int'l Corp., 23 F. Supp. 2d 892, 894, 8 AD 1153 (N.D. Ill. 1998) (joinder of union and its local as defendants was proper even though union was not named in EEOC charge where union was needed to effect complete relief); EEOC v. Electrical Workers (IBEW) Local 103, 476 F. Supp. 341, 349–50, 20 FEP 1461 (D. Mass. 1979).

[45]*E.g.*, Eldredge v. Carpenters 46 N. Cal. Counties Joint Apprenticeship & Training Comm., 662 F.2d 534, 536–38, 27 FEP 479 (9th Cir. 1981) (employers not indispensable parties to lawsuit against apprenticeship committee). The issue of indispensable parties is discussed in Section III.C *infra*.

[46]503 F.2d 1086, 8 FEP 897 (6th Cir. 1974).

tried at one time and in one forum; Title VII's grant of broad equitable powers to the courts to eradicate the effects of discrimination is consistent with joining the union; and nothing in Title VII specifically restricts the courts' joinder authority otherwise available under the Federal Rules of Civil Procedure.[47] Other courts have followed a similar approach.[48]

The distinction between "real" defendants and "interest" defendants has been criticized.[49] First, numerous cases have held that each of the parties to a discriminatory collective bargaining agreement commits a violation of Title VII.[50] Second, the concept of the "interest" defendant potentially allows the individual charging party or the EEOC to designate which of the alleged joint violators of Title VII will be exposed to back-pay liability and which will not.[51]

Nevertheless, a party not guilty of discrimination may not be subjected to injunctive relief that requires it to share the financial costs of implementing a remedial decree.[52] Upon an appropriate

---

[47]*Id.* at 1095–96. The Supreme Court cited *EEOC v. MacMillan Bloedel* in support of the proposition that a union that has not violated the statute may be retained in a lawsuit for the purposes of providing full injunctive relief. *See* Teamsters v. United States, 431 U.S. 324, 356 n.43, 14 FEP 1514 (1977). *Teamsters*, however, was a Justice Department-initiated civil action, not one based on a charge of discrimination filed with the EEOC. *Id.* at 348 n.30.

[48]*Rockwell Int'l Corp.*, 23 F. Supp. 2d at 894 (joining union as defendant where retroactive seniority was element of remedial relief; union needed to effect complete relief because union represented members' seniority rights under CBA and award of retroactive seniority absent joinder could leave corporation open to suit by union for violation of bargaining agreement).

[49]*See, e.g.*, Chrapliwy v. Uniroyal, Inc., 509 F. Supp. 442, 446, 25 FEP 445 (N.D. Ind. 1981), *aff'd in relevant part*, 670 F.2d 760, 28 FEP 19 (7th Cir. 1982) (where a collective bargaining agreement violates Title VII, the cost of rectifying the discrimination should be shared by the employer and union); *cf.* Johnson v. Thomson Brush Moore, Inc., 7 FEP 921, 925 (N.D. Ohio 1974) (union whose contract is affected is an indispensable party for injunctive purposes and, if unnamed in the charge, it cannot be joined; thus, no injunctive relief is available against the company, but money claims against the company may proceed).

[50]Wright v. Universal Maritime Serv. Corp., 525 U.S. 70, 76 (1998) (statutory cause of action cannot be waived by union's agreement); EEOC v. Indiana Bell Tel. Co., 256 F.3d 516, 522, 86 FEP 1 (7th Cir. 2001) (terms of labor agreements do not exculpate conduct that would violate Title VII if undertaken unilaterally by employers). *See generally* Chapter 22 (Unions).

[51]*Cf.* Northwest Airlines, Inc. v. Transport Workers, 451 U.S. 77, 86–91, 25 FEP 737 (1981) (refusing to recognize a right of contribution, and thus arguably allowing the named joint violator to bear the full financial burden of the violation).

[52]General Bldg. Contractors Ass'n v. Pennsylvania, 458 U.S. 375, 399, 29 FEP 139 (1982) (no injunctive relief available "against a party found not to have violated any substantive right").

evidentiary showing, however, a party may be retained in a lawsuit and subjected to "minor and ancillary" provisions of an injunctive order necessary to grant complete relief.[53]

3. Joinder Where There Is an Agency Relationship or Substantial Identity Between the Named Party and the Unnamed Defendant

A Title VII action ordinarily may be brought only against a party previously named in an EEOC charge.[54] However, under the "identity of interests" doctrine, "an employment discrimination action may proceed against an unnamed party where there is a clear identity of interest between the unnamed defendant and the party named in the administrative charge."[55]

One line of "identity of interests" cases focuses on when the named and unnamed parties are so interrelated that they should be considered a "single employer."[56] This theory may apply when the named and unnamed entities are: a parent or sister corporation and its subsidiary,[57] a local union and its international,[58] an "integrated

---

[53]Id.; see also Zipes v. Trans World Airlines, 455 U.S. 385, 400 & n.14, 28 FEP 1 (1982) (Court reaffirmed its holding in Teamsters that a union not guilty of discrimination should remain in the lawsuit so that full relief can be awarded).

[54]42 U.S.C. § 2000e-5(f)(1) (2000).

[55]Georgiu v. Sterling Mounting & Finishing, 1 Fed. Appx. 47, 50 (2d Cir. 2001); Knowlton v. Teltrust Phones, Inc., 189 F.3d 1177, 1185, 80 FEP 1062 (10th Cir. 1999) (Title VII action may proceed against defendant not named in EEOC charge when there is a clear identity of interest between unnamed defendant and party named in administrative charge); Alexander v. Laborers Local 496, 177 F.3d 394, 411, 79 FEP 1057 (6th Cir. 1999) (party must be named in EEOC charge before that party may be sued under Title VII unless there is a clear identity of interest between the unnamed party and a party named in the charge).

[56]See Knowlton, 189 F.3d at 1185 (subsidiary, parent, and sister corporations constituted single employer); Virgo v. Riviera Beach Assocs., 30 F.3d 1350, 1359, 65 FEP 1317 (11th Cir. 1994) (general partners "functionally identical" to partnership and should not be protected by naming requirement); Darby v. Pasadena Police Dep't, 939 F.2d 311, 314–15, 56 FEP 1253 (5th Cir. 1991) (plaintiff may amend complaint to name city as defendant; the city's police department is not a legally separate entity).

[57]See Knowlton, 189 F.3d at 1185 (employee's failure to name employer's parent and sister corporations in EEOC charge did not preclude employee from including them in Title VII suit). But see Knafel v. Pepsi-Cola Bottlers of Akron, Inc., 899 F.2d 1473, 1480 (6th Cir. 1990) (EEOC charge that named a subsidiary was not sufficient to give the court jurisdiction over the corporate parent; the parent-subsidiary relationship is not an alter ego relationship for the purposes of allowing an unnamed party to be sued under Title VII).

[58]See Alexander, 177 F.3d at 412 (local and international unions interrelated; "we conclude that the district court did not abuse its discretion by determining that

enterprise" under common control,[59] holding themselves out as being closely related,[60] or entities with an agency relationship.[61] Factors to examine in determining whether two companies constitute a single employer include "common management, centralized control of labor relations, common financial control, and interrelation of operations."[62]

The second line of cases is based on the theory of "identity of interest" derived from the four-part test articulated in *Glus*,[63]

---

the parent union's liability began to accrue at the same time as the local union's liability on February 1, 1982").

[59]*See* Colindres v. QuitFlex Mfg., 235 F.R.D. 347, 364–65 (S.D. Tex. 2006) (summary judgment precluded where parent and subsidiary were an "integrated enterprise" that could be held liable as a joint employer); Rowland v. Franklin Career Servs., LLC, 272 F. Supp. 2d 1188, 1202 (D. Kan. 2003) (summary judgment precluded where genuine issue of material fact existed as to degree of centralized control of labor relations between parent and subsidiary LLCs); Smith v. K&F Indus., Inc., 190 F. Supp. 2d 643, 647 (S.D.N.Y. 2002) (genuine issue of material fact existed as to whether two corporations were integrated enterprises, precluding summary judgment); Platt v. Kini L.C., 10 F. Supp. 2d 1229, 1233 (D. Kan. 1998) (rejecting summary judgment and finding material question of fact as to "entanglement of management control" between management company and corporation that does business as cellular phone company).

[60]*See* Boateng v. Apple Health Care, Inc., 156 F. Supp. 2d 247, 253 (D. Conn. 2001) (clear identity of interest existed between health care center and its managing entity where employee may have been led to believe she was to deal exclusively with health care center); Dunn v. Tutera Group, 181 F.R.D. 653, 658 (D. Kan. 1998) (where there was little reason for the plaintiff to believe the corporate owner of her nursing home employer was her true employer, employee's failure to name corporate owner excused); Kopec v. Elmhurst, 966 F. Supp. 640, 646–47, 80 FEP 1829 (N.D. Ill. 1997) (plaintiff understandably believed city's unnamed board of fire and police commissioners was part of named city defendant where board held itself out as part of city under guise of city's letterhead), *summary judgment granted*, 8 F. Supp. 2d 1082 (N.D. Ill. 1998), *aff'd*, 193 F.3d 894 (7th Cir. 1999).

[61]*See* Sosa v. Hiraoka, 920 F.2d 1451, 1459 (9th Cir. 1990) (if the respondent named in an EEOC charge is a principal or agent of an unnamed party, suit may proceed against the unnamed party); Efird v. Riley, 342 F. Supp. 2d 413, 423 (M.D.N.C. 2004) (exception to general rule that defendant must be administratively charged arises where named and unnamed parties have agency relationship); Zakeri v. Oliver, 19 F. Supp. 2d 553, 556–57 (E.D. Va. 1998) (court would consider employee's Title VII action against city director and assistant director of public works, city manager, city human resources employee, and city engineer as action against defendants in their capacity as agents of city and its public works department, even though individuals were not named as defendants in EEOC charge).

[62]Scelta v. Delicatessen Support Servs., Inc., 57 F. Supp. 2d 1327, 1354 (M.D. Fla. 1999); *see also* Schiele v. Charles Vogel Mfg. Co., 787 F. Supp. 1541, 1547 (D. Minn. 1992) (factors include "interrelation of operations, common management, centralized control of labor relations, and common ownership or financial control").

[63]Glus v. G.C. Murphy Co., 562 F.2d 880, 15 FEP 998 (3d Cir. 1977).

designed to ensure that the statutory naming requirement's twin purposes of notice to the respondent and an opportunity to participate in conciliation are both met.[64] Courts that apply this theory generally focus on the second and third *Glus* factors: whether the interests of the named and unnamed party are so similar that the unnamed party's presence in EEOC proceedings was not necessary to obtain voluntary conciliation and compliance, and whether the unnamed party's absence from the proceedings resulted in actual prejudice to that party.[65]

---

[64]*Lawsuit allowed against unnamed defendant based on identity of interest*: Alexander v. Laborers Local 496, 177 F.3d 394, 411, 79 FEP 1057 (6th Cir. 1999) (international and local unions shared identity of interest such that unnamed party may be sued under Title VII where unnamed party possessed sufficient notice of claim to participate in voluntary conciliation proceedings); Cook v. Arrowsmith Shelburne, Inc., 69 F.3d 1235, 1241–42 (2d Cir. 1995) (identity of interest between unnamed parent company and subsidiary); Winbush v. Iowa, by Glenwood State Hosp., 66 F.3d 1471, 1478 n.9 (8th Cir. 1995) (identity of interest between unnamed individual school officials and school); Virgo v. Riviera Beach Assocs., 30 F.3d 1350, 1358–59, 65 FEP 1317 (11th Cir. 1994) (identity of interest between unnamed sole owner and named employer); Kern v. General Elec., 2003 U.S. Dist. LEXIS 10331, at *16–18 (N.D. Tex. June 17, 2003) (identity of interest between unnamed subsidiary and named parent company and affiliate); Aguirre v. McCaw RCC Commc'ns, 923 F. Supp. 1431, 1433–34 (D. Kan. 1996) (identity of interest between unnamed employer and named unincorporated association); Rivera v. Puerto Rican Home Attendants Servs., Inc., 922 F. Supp. 943, 946–48, 73 FEP 1215 (S.D.N.Y. 1996) (identity of interest between unnamed city and named agency that provided services on behalf of city).

Lawsuit not allowed against unnamed defendant based on lack of identity of interest: Olsen v. Marshall & Ilsley Corp., 267 F.3d 597, 604, 86 FEP 1404 (7th Cir. 2001) (employer's parent company not named in EEOC charge dismissed from Title VII action even though parent had notice of charges and participated in administrative proceedings; parent did not have notice of any charges against it and did not have opportunity to conciliate on its own behalf); Vital v. Interfaith Med. Ctr., 168 F.3d 615, 620, 80 FEP 281 (2d Cir. 1999) (employer and union did not have identity of interest such that employee could maintain Title VII claim against union after naming only employer in his administrative discrimination charge; interests of union and employer were dissimilar and union did not have notice of any charge against it); Causey v. Balog, 162 F.3d 795, 800–01, 78 FEP 1241 (4th Cir. 1998) (plaintiff's EEOC charge failed to put individual defendants on notice they were potentially subject to personal liability for the alleged violations; therefore, individual defendants may not be held personally liable for alleged violations of Title VII or the ADEA).

[65]*See, e.g., Cook*, 69 F.3d at 1241–42 (applying identity of interest exception to naming requirement where factors two and three from *Glus* test weighed strongly in favor of plaintiff, though court found it arguable that plaintiff could easily have included unnamed defendant in charge).

4. *Joinder Where Named Party Since Has Been Acquired, Merged With, or Succeeded by a Different Entity*

Successor entities, whether corporations or unions, ordinarily may be substituted for predecessor defendants where there is continuity of interest and notice.[66] The policy underlying the successor liability doctrine is "to protect an employee when the ownership of his employer suddenly changes."[67]

In order for successor liability to apply, "there must be some type of sale, merger, or consolidation" because "[t]here must be . . . privity between the predecessor and successor employers."[68] There is no statute of limitations applicable to joinder of a successor employer after a suit is timely brought against the predecessor

---

[66]*See* Brzozowski v. Correctional Physician Servs., Inc., 360 F.3d 173, 178, 93 FEP 436 (3d Cir. 2004) (holding that employee who brought employment discrimination suit against employer should have been allowed to amend complaint to add successor employer); EEOC v. SWP, Inc., 153 F. Supp. 2d 911, 918, 86 FEP 717 (N.D. Ind. 2001) (when successor company knows about predecessor's liability for employment discrimination judgment, presumption is in favor of successor liability); Brennan v. National Tel. Dir. Corp., 850 F. Supp. 331, 339, 67 FEP 218 (E.D. Pa. 1994) (claim against corporation under doctrine of successor liability would not be dismissed, though corporation was not named in employee's EEOC charge, where employee moved to amend her complaint to include corporation once she was notified of change in corporate status); EEOC v. Sheet Metal Workers Local 638, 700 F. Supp. 739, 740, 49 FEP 1224 (S.D.N.Y. 1988) (successorship, determined by labor law principles, bound union to nondiscrimination order against predecessor). *But see* Cibulka v. Trans World Airlines, Inc., 92 Fed. Appx. 366, 368 (8th Cir. 2004) (upholding denial of employee's motion to amend complaint against bankrupt employer to add employer's successor in interest where public policy supported transfer of employer's assets free and clear of discrimination claims; testimony established that if employer could not sell its assets, employer would likely liquidate and over 20,000 employees could lose their jobs); Catagnus v. Aramark Corp., 235 F. Supp. 2d 413, 417 (E.D. Pa. 2002) (court did not have jurisdiction over successor supervisor in his personal capacity where only employer and two other supervisors had been named in EEOC charge).

[67]*See* Rego v. ARC Water Treatment Co., 181 F.3d 396, 401, 80 FEP 311 (3d Cir. 1999) (finding no successor liability because of the lack of continuity in the operations and workforce of the predecessor and successor); McKee v. American Transfer & Storage, 946 F. Supp. 485, 488 (N.D. Tex. 1996) (same).

[68]Korlin v. Chartwell Health Care, Inc., 128 F. Supp. 2d 609, 614, 85 FEP 142 (E.D. Mo. 2001) (where successor corporation assumed operations pursuant to negotiations with owner of real property on which former employer located, there was no privity and therefore no successor liability; *see also Rego*, 181 F.3d at 401 (successor liability applies where the assets of the defendant employer are transferred to another entity).

employer.[69] In *Brzozowski v. Correctional Physician Services, Inc.*,[70] the Third Circuit listed three factors required in order to impose successor liability in the employment discrimination field:

'(1) continuity in operations and work force of the successor and predecessor employers; (2) notice to the successor-employer of its predecessor's legal obligation; and (3) ability of the predecessor to provide adequate relief directly.'[71]

Although some courts base their holdings on successor liability exclusively on the notice factor,[72] most consider whether there has been "sufficient continuity in the business operations of the predecessor and the successor."[73] The continuity inquiry includes such things as:

(a) whether the new employer uses the same plant; (b) whether it uses the same or substantially the same work force; (c) whether it uses the same or substantially the same supervisory personnel; (d) whether the same jobs exist under substantially the same working conditions; (e) whether the successor uses the same machinery, equipment, and methods of production; and (f) whether he produces the same product.[74]

---

[69]*See Brzozowski*, 360 F.3d at 180 (Title VII does not contain statute of limitations applicable to joinder of successor employer after suit is timely brought against predecessor employer; rather, doctrine of laches is applicable in determining whether joinder timely).

[70]360 F.3d 173, 93 FEP 436 (3d Cir. 2004).

[71]*Id.* at 178 (citing *Rego*, 181 F.3d at 401). Other circuits have articulated a similar test. *See, e.g.*, Rojas v. TK Commc'ns, Inc., 87 F.3d 745 (5th Cir. 1996) (discussing successor liability in Title VII context); EEOC v. G-K-G, Inc., 39 F.3d 740 (7th Cir. 1994) (same); Desporte-Bryan v. Bank of Am., 147 F. Supp. 2d 1356, 1362, 86 FEP 432 (S.D. Fla. 2001) (same). The Tenth Circuit has adopted a nine-factor test to determine whether a purchaser company is a "mere continuation of the predecessor company such that successor liability may be imposed." Gamez v. Country Cottage Care & Rehab., 377 F. Supp. 2d 1103, 1116 (D.N.M. 2005) (citing Trujillo v. Longhorn Mfg. Co., 694 F.2d 221, 224–25 (10th Cir. 1982)).

[72]*See* Moriarty v. Consolidated Funeral Servs., Inc., 65 F. Supp. 2d 853, 865 (N.D. Ill. 1999) (successor companies not liable where successors had no notice before their acquisition of predecessors that they would be liable); Coleman v. Keebler Co., 997 F. Supp. 1094, 1100 (N.D. Ind. 1998) (buyer of business did not have adequate notice of employee's discrimination charge against its predecessor and, thus, buyer could not be held directly liable).

[73]*Desporte-Bryan*, 147 F. Supp. 2d at 1362; Rego v. ARC Water Treatment Co., 181 F.3d 396, 401–02, 80 FEP 311 (3d Cir. 1999) (lack of continuity in the operations and workforce of the predecessor employer and the successor employer weights against imposing successor liability in employment discrimination actions).

[74]*Desporte-Bryan*, 147 F. Supp. 2d at 1362; *see also* Berg Chilling Sys., Inc. v. Hull Corp., 435 F.3d 455, 470 (3d Cir. 2006) (no successor liability where no continuity

C. Necessary and Indispensable Parties

Rule 19 of the Federal Rules of Civil Procedure draws a distinction between "persons needed for just adjudication" and those that are "indispensable."[75] Necessary parties are those that must participate if there is to be a just disposition of the issues in the case.[76] A finding of indispensability, on the other hand, "must meet a higher standard than necessity."[77] If the absent party is found only to be "necessary" and not "indispensable," then the absent party will be joined if joinder is feasible and the court will continue adjudication of the case.[78] If, on the other hand, the absent party is found to be "indispensable," then the case must be dismissed for failure to join an essential party.[79]

Since 1991, courts' decisions on whether absent parties are necessary to a pending case seeking a consent decree have been colored by § 108 of the Civil Rights Act of 1991 (CRA).[80] Section

of stock ownership and no continuation of the selling entity's business by the successor); Ed Peters Jewelry Co. v. C&J Jewelry Co., 124 F.3d 252, 272 (1st Cir. 1997) (among considerations pertinent to business continuity aspect of successor liability under "mere continuation" theory are whether corporations had identical products, whether their operations were conducted at same physical premises, and whether acquiring corporation retained employees of divesting corporation).

[75]*Compare* FED. R. CIV. P. 19(a) *with* FED. R. CIV. P. 19(b).

[76]*See* Merrill Lynch, Pierce, Fenner & Smith, Inc. v. ENC Corp., 446 F.3d 1019, 1024 (9th Cir. 2006) (Republic of the Philippines a necessary party to have a just disposition of the assets). In determining whether an absent party is "necessary," the court first considers whether, in the absence of the non-party, complete relief can be accorded among the existing parties. *See* Dawavendewa v. Salt River Project Agric. Improvement & Power Dist., 276 F.3d 1150, 1155, 87 FEP 1106 (9th Cir. 2002) (considering whether the Navajo nation was a necessary party in order for Dawavendewa to be accorded complete relief). "Completeness is determined on the basis of those persons who are already parties, and not as between a party and the absent person whose joinder is sought." Angst v. Royal Maccabees Life Ins. Co., 77 F.3d 701, 705 (3d Cir. 1996).

[77]*Id.*

[78]*See* Rishell v. Jane Phillips Episcopal Mem'l Med. Ctr., 94 F.3d 1407, 1411 (10th Cir. 1996) (court must first determine whether party is necessary and can therefore be joined if joinder is feasible); Pit River Home & Agric. Co-op Ass'n v. United States, 30 F.3d 1088, 1099 (9th Cir. 1994) (after determining that the party is necessary, the court should determine whether that party can be joined).

[79]*See* FED. R. CIV. P. 19(b); *Rishell*, 94 F.3d at 1411 (if party is indispensable, suit must be dismissed due to failure to join); *Pit River*, 30 F.3d at 1099 (finding that a party is indispensable renders dismissal of the case necessary); Janney Montgomery Scott, Inc. v. Shepard Niles, Inc., 11 F.3d 399, 409 (3d Cir. 1993) (if an absent party is indispensable, the action cannot go forward).

[80]Pub. L. 102-166 (1991), codified at 42 U.S.C. § 2000e-2(n) (2000).

108 limits the rights of non-parties to attack consent decrees by barring any challenges from parties who knew or should have known of the decree or who were adequately represented by the original parties.[81] This legislation overturned the Supreme Court's 1989 decision in *Martin v. Wilks*,[82] which permitted a group of white firefighters who had not been party to prior litigation establishing a consent decree governing the hiring and promotion of black firefighters in the Birmingham, Alabama fire department to bring suit to challenge the decree.[83] Congress recognized that "[o]nce an employment dispute has reached the courts, the parties, all non-litigants with a stake in the outcome, and the public have a strong interest in bringing the litigation to an expeditious end. [Accordingly], all related interests and claims should be adjudicated in one proceeding."[84] Whereas *Martin* "placed the burden on the parties to join all persons who might be affected by a decree under Federal Rule of Civil Procedure 19's mandatory joinder provisions,"[85] Section 108 of the CRA places the burden on necessary third parties to intervene in the initial lawsuit if their rights are likely to be affected by a decree.

D. Joinder of One Defendant by Another

In many cases defendants (usually employers) have sought to join absent unnamed parties (usually unions) so that the absent party will be held jointly liable for any monetary relief. Before the Supreme Court's decision in *Northwest Airlines, Inc. v. Transport Workers*,[86] most cases allowed such joinder; the theory generally was that the absent party was necessary and should be joined if feasible, and that Title VII does not deprive the court or the named defendants of their rights under the Federal Rules of Civil Procedure to compel joinder of all potentially liable persons.[87]

---

[81]*See* 42 U.S.C. § 2000e-2(n)(1)(B) (2000).

[82]490 U.S. 755, 49 FEP 1641 (1989).

[83]*Id.* at 767.

[84]H.R. Rep. 40(I), 102d Cong., 1st Sess. 53 (1991), *reprinted in* 1991 U.S.C.C.A.N. 549, 591.

[85]Edwards v. City of Houston, 78 F.3d 983, 997 (5th Cir. 1996).

[86]451 U.S. 77, 86–90, 25 FEP 737 (1981).

[87]*See, e.g.*, Torockio v. Chamberlain Mfg. Co., 51 F.R.D. 517, 519, 3 FEP 10 (W.D. Pa. 1970) (joinder of international union on motion of the defendant employer;

Northwest Airlines undermined those cases, at least in part. *Northwest Airlines* rejected an employer's claim for post-judgment contribution against a union and cast doubt on whether the union could be joined as a full party defendant at all, at least in the absence of an EEOC charge against the union.[88] Thus, for example, a union does not have a right to contribution or indemnity against an employer to whom it referred workers.[89] Although joinder for purposes of obtaining contribution is improper under *Northwest Airlines*, some decisions hold that joinder among defendants to secure other "complete and final relief" may be possible.[90] And even joinder for purposes of a monetary cross-claim arguably may be permitted if the right procedural foundation is laid. Justice White, at oral argument in the *Northwest Airlines* case, suggested that the proper procedure would be for an employer to file an EEOC charge against the union and obtain a right-to-sue letter.[91]

Similar issues also arise in other contexts. In several cases, local governments sued under Title VII were held not entitled to contribution from the United States.[92]

---

nothing in Title VII deprives the court of power to order joinder under Rule 19(a)). Other cases permitted cross-claims or counterclaims. *E.g.*, Gilbert v. General Elec. Co., 59 F.R.D. 267, 270–72, 5 FEP 989 (E.D. Va. 1973).

[88]*Northwest Airlines*, 451 U.S. at 81 n.5. Joinder for the limited purpose of modification of a collective bargaining agreement is a different question; the union was joined as a nonaligned party in *Northwest Airlines*. *See generally* Chapter 22 (Unions).

[89]*E.g.*, Anderson v. Electrical Workers (IBEW) Local 3, 582 F. Supp. 627, 633, 34 FEP 517 (S.D.N.Y. 1984) (rejecting union's claim that it was entitled to contribution or indemnity), *aff'd*, 751 F.2d 546, 36 FEP 1249 (2d Cir. 1984).

[90]*See, e.g.*, Forsberg v. Pacific N.W. Bell Tel. Co., 623 F. Supp. 117, 120, 54 FEP 1852 (D. Or. 1985) (where relief could alter collective bargaining agreement, joinder of union is proper), *aff'd*, 840 F.2d 1409, 54 FEP 1873 (9th Cir. 1988); McCooe v. Town of Manchester, 101 F.R.D. 339, 341, 35 FEP 463 (D. Conn. 1984) (union has an interest in litigation, where collective bargaining agreement forms some basis of plaintiff's action).

[91]*See* Summary of Oral Argument, 49 U.S.L.W. 3461, 3461 (U.S. Jan. 6, 1981). *But see* Smart v. Electrical Workers Local 702, 315 F.3d 721, 727, 90 FEP 461 (7th Cir. 2002) (court skeptical that employer can sue union under statute that prohibits employment discrimination). For a more expansive discussion of this and other procedural issues involving unions, see Chapter 22 (Unions).

[92]*See* Walls v. Mississippi Dep't of Pub. Welfare, 730 F.2d 306, 323, 34 FEP 1114 (5th Cir. 1984) (right of contribution barred by sovereign immunity); Liberles v. County of Cook, 709 F.2d 1122, 1134–35, 31 FEP 1537 (7th Cir. 1983) (contribution denied pursuant to *Northwest Airlines*; court refused to decide claim for indemnification under other federal statutes).

IV. SCOPE OF EEOC CHARGE AS LIMITING THE SCOPE OF A TITLE VII LAWSUIT

A. Basic Rationale

In enacting Title VII, Congress created an agency under whose jurisdiction there would be an opportunity for the parties to resolve employment issues without public litigation. The intent was that, by avoiding publicity, employees might be spared embarrassment, and employers might be more willing to adjust their employment practices if they were not subjected to the glare of public accusation and recrimination. Congress imposed short limitations periods for bringing claims and made it a condition precedent to the public litigation of those claims that an employee must first seek administrative relief through the EEOC within 90 days (now 180 or 300 days depending on the existence of a state deferral agency). The purposes underlying the administrative charge requirement include giving the charged party notice of the claim,[93] narrowing the issues for speedier and more effective adjudication and decision,[94] and giving the EEOC and the employer an opportunity to resolve the dispute.[95] If the EEOC finds reasonable cause to believe that a violation has occurred it must attempt to eliminate the practice through conciliation, conference, and persuasion before commencing a lawsuit.[96]

---

[93]See Wallace v. DTG Operations, Inc., 442 F.3d 1112, 1123, 97 FEP 1292 (8th Cir. 2006) (information contained in an EEOC charge must be sufficient to give the employer notice of the subject matter of the charge); McGoffney v. Vigo County Div. of Fam. & Children, Fam. & Soc. Servs. Admin., 389 F.3d 750, 752, 94 FEP 1485 (7th Cir. 2004) (limiting a Title VII plaintiff to claims included in her EEOC charge serves the purpose of giving the employer some warning of the conduct about which the employee is aggrieved); Foster v. Ruhrpumpen, Inc., 365 F.3d 1191, 1194, 93 FEP 1511 (10th Cir. 2004) (finding exhaustion requirement satisfied where despite using the word "termination" in charge, employer was no doubt on notice that workers were accusing company of discrimination stemming from a failure to hire); Manning v. Chevron Chem. Co., 332 F.3d 874, 878 (5th Cir. 2003) (one of the central purposes of the charge is to put employers on notice of the existence and nature of the charges against them), *cert. denied*, 540 U.S. 1107 (2004).

[94]B.K.B. v. Maui Police Dep't, 276 F.3d 1091, 1099, 87 FEP 1306 (9th Cir. 2002).

[95]See Geldon v. South Milwaukee Sch. Dist., 414 F.3d 817, 819, 96 FEP 109 (7th Cir. 2005) (rule is meant both to give the EEOC and employer an opportunity to settle the dispute and to give the employer fair notice of the conduct about which the employee is complaining).

[96]See 42 U.S.C. § 2000e-5(b) (2000); *see also* Conner v. Illinois Dep't of Natural Res., 413 F.3d 675, 680, 95 FEP 1833 (7th Cir.) (EEOC charge process gives the

In litigation brought by private parties, rather than litigation brought by the EEOC itself,[97] courts generally have applied this statutorily prescribed structure flexibly, as a condition precedent to litigation.[98] Although this issue arises in a variety of circumstances, the two most frequent contexts are complaints that: (1) assert *issues* that are beyond those identified in the EEOC charge or (2) allege an additional *basis* of discrimination beyond those alleged in the charge.

B. Application of Rationale

1. Issues and Bases of Discrimination Not Asserted in the Charge

The first step is establishing what issues and bases of discrimination were in fact alleged in the EEOC charge. The charge contains both a factual statement and a series of boxes that the claimant must check to identify the appropriate basis of discrimination

---

agency a chance to investigate allegedly discriminatory conduct and to seek voluntary compliance or conciliation without lawsuit), *cert. denied*, 126 S. Ct. 804 (2005); Dezaio v. Port Auth. of N.Y. & N.J., 205 F.3d 62, 65, 82 FEP 377 (2d Cir. 2000) (the reason for the ADEA's requirement that a charge be filed with the EEOC is to exhaust administrative remedies with an eye toward conciliation and resolution of the alleged practice that brought about the discrimination claim without the need to resort to litigation).

[97]Different principles apply where the litigation is brought by the EEOC rather than by a private litigant. *See, e.g.*, EEOC v. Caterpillar, Inc., 409 F.3d 831, 833, 95 FEP 1371 (7th Cir. 2005) (EEOC decision to expand claim in litigation beyond scope of original charge not judicially reviewable). *See generally* Chapter 29 (EEOC Litigation).

[98]*See* Josephs v. Pacific Bell, 443 F.3d 1050, 1061 (9th Cir. 2006) (liberally construing employment discrimination charges filed before the EEOC for the purpose of determining whether the employee has met the administrative exhaustion requirement prior to filing a discrimination lawsuit); Deravin v. Kerik, 335 F.3d 195, 201, 92 FEP 472 (2d Cir. 2003) (allowing for "reasonably related" claims to those filed in the EEOC charge is "an allowance of loose pleading" based on the recognition that charges frequently are filled out by employees without counsel); Simmons v. New Pub. Sch. Dist. No. Eight, 251 F.3d 1210, 1216, 85 FEP 1685 (8th Cir. 2001) (administrative complaint must be construed liberally); Nelson v. General Elec. Co., 2 Fed. Appx. 425, 428 (6th Cir. 2001) (court should construe administrative complaint liberally); Cable v. Ivy Tech State Coll., 200 F.3d 467, 477 (7th Cir. 1999) ("The EEOC charge-filing requirement is not intended to erect 'elaborate pleading requirements' or 'let the form of the purported charge prevail over its substance.' "). *But see* Martin v. Central States Emblems, Inc., 150 Fed. Appx. 852, 856 (10th Cir. 2005) (court imposes exhaustion requirement by finding that a complaint for termination based on race resulting in prison disciplinary proceedings could not be brought based on an EEOC charge alleging that the prison discipline was the discrimination itself rather than the termination), *cert. denied*, 126 S. Ct. 1392 (2006).

(e.g., race, age, disability, sex, etc.). The statement provides the claimant an opportunity to discuss the issues comprising the alleged discrimination, while the boxes indicate the alleged bases of discrimination. Some courts have noted that "[t]he crucial element of a charge of discrimination" in considering whether a particular allegation was made in a charge "is the factual statement contained therein" rather than which boxes the claimant checked.[99] The general consensus is that courts may not consider bases of discrimination that are not asserted in the charge.[100]

---

[99]*B.K.B.*, 276 F.3d at 1100; *see also* Tisdale v. Federal Express Corp., 415 F.3d 516, 528, 96 FEP 65 (6th Cir. 2005) (employee allowed to go forward with retaliation claim even though employee failed to check the box on the EEOC form marked "retaliation"); Schlueter v. Anheuser-Busch, Inc., 132 F.3d 455, 459, 75 FEP 1358 (8th Cir. 1998) (court's inquiry into whether employee intended EEOC questionnaire to function as charge under ADEA focuses on the contents of the questionnaire itself); Annett v. University of Kansas, 371 F.3d 1233, 1238, 93 FEP 1789 (10th Cir. 2004) (employee could not bring retaliation claim based on distinction between receiving adjunct lecturer position rather than adjunct professor position when such distinction was not mentioned as probative of discrimination in EEOC charge); *Deravin*, 335 F.3d at 201 (the focus should be on the factual allegations made in the charge itself in deciding whether the complaint is reasonably related to the charge). *But see* Moraga v. Ashcroft, 110 Fed. Appx. 55, 60–61 (10th Cir. 2004) (employee could not bring sex discrimination claim where she did not allege sex discrimination in her EEOC charge or check the box marked "sex"); Teffera v. North Tex. Tollway Auth., 121 Fed. Appx. 18, 21 (5th Cir. 2004) (former employee failed to exhaust retaliation claim where she did not make any reference to retaliation or check the retaliation box on her EEOC charge, instead referencing only her claim for national origin discrimination).

[100]*See* Hillemann v. University of Cent. Fla., 167 Fed. Appx. 747, 749–50 (11th Cir. 2006) (applicant's Title VII gender and race discrimination claims arising from university's failure to hire him were procedurally barred where charge only asserted age discrimination); Chacko v. Patuxent Inst., 429 F.3d 505, 511, 96 FEP 1633 (4th Cir. 2005) (employee failed to exhaust administrative remedies where his claim alleged national origin epithets and no mention of such discrimination existed in EEOC charge); Atkins v. Southwestern Bell Tel. Co., 137 Fed. Appx. 115, 118 (10th Cir. 2005) (by failing to raise retaliation with EEOC, employee failed to adequately exhaust her administrative remedies with respect to that claim); Anderson v. City of Dallas, 116 Fed. Appx. 19, 25 (5th Cir. 2004) (employee failed to exhaust administrative remedies with respect to sex and age claims where charge alleged racial discrimination and retaliation); Ajayi v. Aramark Bus. Servs., Inc., 336 F.3d 520, 527, 92 FEP 106 (7th Cir. 2003) (when EEOC charge alleges particular theory of discrimination, allegations of a different type of discrimination are not reasonably related unless the new allegations can be reasonably inferred from the facts alleged in the charge); Young v. DaimlerChyrsler Corp., 52 Fed. Appx. 637, 640 (6th Cir. 2002) (applicant's race discrimination claim could not go forward when EEOC charge alleged only age discrimination in his failure to be hired); Spindler v. Southeastern Penn. Transp. Auth., 47 Fed. Appx. 92, 94 (3d Cir. 2002) (employee's racial discrimination claims were

In deciding whether a Title VII claim could reasonably be expected to grow out of an EEOC charge, the court "may consider 'such factors as the alleged basis of the discrimination, dates of discriminatory acts specified within the charge, perpetrators of discrimination named in the charge, and any locations at which discrimination is alleged to have occurred.' "[101]

Courts have concluded that an EEOC charge and claims asserted in court are "reasonably related" where:

    a.   an employee alleges a discriminatory termination in his or her charge and brings a claim based on a refusal to reinstate,[102]

---

not administratively exhausted where charges were disability claims); Wiseman v. County of Washoe, 44 Fed. Appx. 776, 778 (9th Cir. 2002) (employee failed to exhaust administrative remedies where his charge concerned only disability discrimination, not sexual or religious harassment). This may include the circumstance when the new basis of discrimination is retaliation for asserting the underlying charge. *Compare* Duncan v. Manager, Dep't of Safety, City & County of Denver, 397 F.3d 1300, 1314, 95 FEP 311 (10th Cir. 2005) (police officer failed to exhaust remedies as to her claim that transfer to police academy was in retaliation for filing EEOC charge in that she did not file additional EEOC charge alleging retaliation), Peters v. Renaissance Hotel Operating Co., 307 F.3d 535, 550, 91 FEP 293 (7th Cir. 2002) (retaliation claim could not proceed where charge identified no protected activity or resulting adverse action so as to suggest retaliation claim), Kowalow v. Correctional Servs. Corp., 35 Fed. Appx. 344, 347–48 (9th Cir. 2002) (failure of employee to describe retaliatory conduct in EEOC charge barred her from asserting the claim in court), *and* O'Hara v. Memorial Sloan-Kettering Cancer Ctr., 27 Fed. Appx. 69, 70 (2d Cir. 2001) (district court did not err in dismissing retaliation claim where plaintiff neither alleged retaliation in her charge nor pled the facts upon which she based the claim) *with* Wedow v. City of Kansas City, 442 F.3d 661, 674, 97 FEP 1217 (8th Cir. 2006) (retaliation claims based on prior lawsuit not barred where charges predated alleged retaliatory conduct), Webster v. Rumsfeld, 156 Fed. Appx. 571, 580–81 (4th Cir. 2005) (separate administrative charge not prerequisite to Title VII suit complaining about retaliation for filing the first charge), Smith v. Kentucky State Univ., 97 Fed. Appx. 22, 26 (6th Cir. 2004) (professor's claim of retaliation reasonably related to underlying discrimination charge), Vasquez v. County of L.A., 349 F.3d 634, 645–46, 92 FEP 1630 (9th Cir. 2003) (retaliation claim administratively exhausted even though EEOC charge alleged only harassment), Terry v. Ashcroft, 336 F.3d 128, 151, 92 FEP 447 (2d Cir. 2003) (claims not raised in an EEOC charge are sufficiently related to complaints alleging retaliation by the employer for filing EEOC charge) *and* Gawley v. Indiana Univ., 276 F.3d 301, 313–14, 87 FEP 1116 (7th Cir. 2001) (employee seeking to exhaust remedies prior to bringing retaliation claim is not required to file a separate EEOC charge when the retaliation occurs in response to the filing of the original charge).

[101]*Vasquez*, 349 F.3d at 644, 92 FEP 1630 (quoting B.K.B. v. Maui Polic Dep't, 276 F.3d 1091, 1100 (9th Cir. 2002)).

[102]*See Josephs*, 443 F.3d at 1062 (any EEOC investigation of his discharge claim would have encompassed his grievance proceeding with the employer, in which he asserted the discriminatory refusal to reinstate claim).

b. an employee alleges hostile work environment in his or her charge and brings a claim based on an inadequate response to that charge,[103]

c. an employee brings charges resulting in retaliation in response to the filing of the charges,[104]

d. an employee adds additional incidents of discrimination carried out in the same manner as those alleged in the EEOC charge,[105] and

---

[103]*See* Cottrill v. MFA, Inc., 443 F.3d 629, 635, 97 FEP 1487 (8th Cir. 2006) (female employees, whose charge alleged that their manager created a hostile work environment by peeping into women's restrooms for years, exhausted administrative remedies and were not precluded from suing on claims that management had inadequately responded to reports of such activity), *cert. denied*, 127 S. Ct. 394 (2006).

[104]*See* Wedow v. City of Kansas City, 442 F.3d 661, 674, 97 FEP 1217 (8th Cir. 2006) (retaliation claims based on prior lawsuit not barred where charges predated alleged retaliatory conduct); *Webster*, 156 Fed. Appx. 571, 580–81 (separate administrative charge not prerequisite to Title VII suit complaining about retaliation for filing the first charge); Smith v. Kentucky State Univ., 97 Fed. Appx. 22, 26 (6th Cir. 2004) (professor's claim of retaliation reasonably related to underlying discrimination charge); *Vasquez*, 349 F.3d at 645–46 (retaliation claim administratively exhausted even though EEOC charge alleged only harassment); *Terry*, 336 F.3d at 151, 92 FEP 447 (claims not raised in an EEOC charge are sufficiently related to complaints alleging retaliation by the employer for filing EEOC charge); *Gawley*, 276 F.3d at 313–14, 87 FEP 1116 (employee seeking to exhaust remedies prior to bringing retaliation claim is not required to file a separate EEOC charge when the retaliation occurs in response to the filing of the original charge). *But see* Duncan v. Manager, Dep't of Safety, City & County of Denver, 397 F.3d 1300, 1314, 95 FEP 311 (10th Cir. 2005) (police officer failed to exhaust remedies as to her claim that transfer to police academy was in retaliation for filing EEOC charge in that she did not file additional EEOC charge alleging retaliation); Peters v. Renaissance Hotel Operating Co., 307 F.3d 535, 550, 91 FEP 293 (7th Cir. 2002) (retaliation claim could not proceed where charge identified no protected activity or resulting adverse action so as to suggest retaliation claim); Kowalow v. Correctional Servs. Corp., 35 Fed. Appx. 344, 347–48 (9th Cir. 2002) (failure of employee to describe retaliatory conduct in EEOC charge barred her from asserting the claim in court); O'Hara v. Memorial Sloan-Kettering Cancer Ctr., 27 Fed. Appx. 69, 70 (2d Cir. 2001) (district court did not err in dismissing retaliation claim where she neither alleged retaliation in her charge nor pled the facts upon which she based the claim).

[105]*See* Jute v. Hamilton Sundstrand Corp., 420 F.3d 166, 177 (2d Cir. 2005) (circumstances surrounding employer's failure to list employee for potential hire by related company would be considered in claim of retaliation even though employee did not specifically raise it in EEOC charge since conduct was related to employee's other assertions of retaliatory conduct); *Terry*, 336 F.3d at 151 (claims not raised in EEOC charge sufficiently related to complaints alleging further incidents of discrimination carried out in precisely same manner as those alleged in EEOC charge).

e. an employee brings a constructive discharge claim premised on the same facts as a claim asserted in the EEOC charge.[106]

Courts have concluded that a charge and subsequent claim are not reasonably related where:

a. a claimant alleges only disparate treatment in his or her charge and attempts to bring an adverse impact claim in the subsequent lawsuit,[107]

b. a claimant alleges sexual harassment in his or her charge and attempts to bring "retaliation charges for complaining about antecedent harassment,"[108]

c. a claimant alleges hostile work environment in his or her charge and attempts to bring a disparate treatment claim such as discriminatory failure to promote, demotion, or retaliation in the subsequent lawsuit (and vice versa),[109]

---

[106]See Harris v. Parker Coll. of Chiropractic, 286 F.3d 790, 795, 88 FEP 663 (5th Cir. 2002) (plaintiffs could assert constructive discharge claims even though they did not raise them in EEOC charge because claims were premised on the same facts as the claims for discrimination in employment).

[107]See, e.g., Pacheco v. Mineta, 448 F.3d 783, 788 (5th Cir. 2006) (employee failed to administratively exhaust Title VII disparate impact claim by filing charge alleging he has been passed over for promotion because of his race; charge failed to identify any neutral employment policy that could form the basis of disparate impact claim, and named only incidents of disparate treatment), cert. denied, 127 S. Ct. 299 (2006). But see Farrell v. Butler Univ., 421 F.3d 609, 616 (7th Cir. 2005) (adverse impact claim preserved by EEOC charge complaining about faculty cash award policy despite charge being devoid of adverse impact reference); Watkins v. City of Chi., 992 F. Supp. 971, 973 (N.D. Ill. 1998) (charge that plaintiff "had been disqualified based on results of a background investigation which indicated that [she] had been arrested and charged with a felony" set forth claim that "may have a disparate impact on African-Americans").

[108]Duncan v. Delta Consol. Indus., Inc., 371 F.3d 1020, 1025–26, 93 FEP 1843 (8th Cir. 2004); see also Sitar v. Indiana Dep't of Transp., 344 F.3d 720, 726, 92 FEP 1148 (7th Cir. 2003) (normally, retaliation, sex discrimination, and sexual harassment charges are not "like or reasonably related" to one another to permit charge of one type of wrong to support subsequent Title VII suit for another); Holtz v. Rockefeller & Co., 258 F.3d 62, 84, 86 FEP 305 (2d Cir. 2001) (employee failed to exhaust remedies prior to bringing claim that she was denied bonus and overtime pay in retaliation for complaints about alleged sexual harassment).

[109]See Cottrill, 443 F.3d at 634–35 (female employees, whose charge alleged that their manager created a hostile work environment by peeping into women's restrooms for years, failed to exhaust administrative remedies and thus were precluded from suing on claims of disparate treatment); Chacko v. Patuxent Inst., 429 F.3d 505, 511,

d. a claimant alleges discriminatory discharge in his or her charge and attempts to bring either a failure-to-accommodate, failure-to-promote, or retaliation claim in the subsequent lawsuit (or vice versa),[110]

e. a claimant's EEOC charge contains allegations of discrimination by a different actor than the allegations contained in the Title VII suit,[111]

---

96 FEP 1633 (4th Cir. 2005) (employee failed to exhaust administrative remedies where lawsuit was based on hostile work environment and charge alleged discriminatory failure to promote, demotion, and retaliation); Green v. Elixir Indus., Inc., 152 Fed. Appx. 838, 841 (11th Cir. 2005) (EEOC charge asserting racially discriminatory termination could not support claim of discrimination based on hostile work environment), *cert. denied*, 126 S. Ct. 2024 (2006); Dandy v. United Parcel Serv., Inc., 388 F.3d 263, 270, 94 FEP 1156 (7th Cir. 2004) (employee's claims of unequal pay or hostile work environment not mentioned in EEOC charge that alleged employee was denied promotions and retaliated against because of race); Mitchell v. City & County of Denver, 112 Fed. Appx. 662, 666–67 (10th Cir. 2004) (employees' charge that asserted claim for retaliation from failure to promote could not reasonably have been expected to lead to a hostile work environment claim); Alfano v. Costello, 294 F.3d 365, 381, 89 FEP 193 (2d Cir. 2002) (claim alleging discriminatory disciplinary action based on sex not reasonably related to hostile work environment claim raised in charge). *But see* Harris v. Parker Coll. of Chiropractic, 286 F.3d 790, 795, 88 FEP 663 (5th Cir. 2002) (charge stating claim for harassment could support later complaint for constructive discharge).

[110]*See* Kolupa v. Roselle Park Dist., 438 F.3d 713, 715–16, 97 FEP 643 (7th Cir. 2006) (employee's claims that employer failed to accommodate his religious beliefs, failed to promote him, and retaliated against him when he tried to protect his rights were not reasonably related to allegations in charge that claimed religious discrimination in discharge); Bryant v. Bell Atl. Md., Inc., 288 F.3d 124, 132, 88 FEP 1089 (4th Cir. 2002) (employee failed to exhaust administrative remedies with respect to claim regarding termination where charge based on alleged suspension and verbal warning). *But see* Wedow v. City of Kansas City, 442 F.3d 661, 674, 97 FEP 1217 (8th Cir. 2006) (although plaintiffs did not specifically charge that employer conduct was retaliatory, claims were like or reasonably related to EEOC charges of discrimination); Tisdale v. Federal Express Corp., 415 F.3d 516, 528, 96 FEP 65 (6th Cir. 2005) (although plaintiff failed to mention "retaliation" in charge, claim was foreseeable in light of allegations related to discrimination claim); Dixon v. Ashcroft, 392 F.3d 212, 218–19, 94 FEP 1743 (6th Cir. 2004) (statement in EEOC charge that plaintiff suffered discrimination "because the Applicant Program was removed from his direct supervision because of continued harassment" put agency on notice that he alleged retaliation as well).

[111]*See Chacko*, 429 F.3d at 511 (employee failed to exhaust administrative remedies where charge alleged specific instances of discrimination by supervisors and claimed later that co-workers continually made derogatory remarks); Vasquez v. County of L.A., 349 F.3d 634, 645, 92 FEP 1630 (9th Cir. 2003) (Title VII claim not administratively exhausted where EEOC charge was based on alleged conduct of a supervisor whereas retaliation claim rested on allegations of wrongdoing by facility director).

    f. a claimant alleges a discriminatory layoff in his or her charge and attempts to bring a claim for failure to rehire or promote,[112] and

    g. a claimant alleges a specific incident in his or her charge and attempts to assert a claim for a continuing violation.[113]

2. Incidents Occurring Subsequent to the Filing of the EEOC Charge

A frequently recurring issue is whether plaintiffs may litigate, without filing a new charge, incidents that take place after the initial charge on which the civil action is based. It is difficult to harmonize the decisions on this issue. They tend to turn on fact-specific analyses.

Most courts will exercise jurisdiction over allegations of retaliation that occur after the filing of the original charge.[114] Where

---

[112]*See* Shelton v. Boeing Co., 399 F.3d 909, 913, 95 FEP 606 (8th Cir. 2005) (employee's charge regarding his layoff insufficient to meet exhaustion requirement regarding employer's subsequent failure to rehire him; layoff and failure to rehire are discrete employment actions); Parisi v. Boeing Co., 400 F.3d 583, 586, 95 FEP 596 (8th Cir. 2005) (same); Nelson v. General Elec. Co., 2 Fed. Appx. 425, 428–29 (6th Cir. 2001) (plaintiff failed to exhaust administrative remedies with regard to three failure-to-promote claims where charge dealt only with subsequent layoff).

[113]*See* Martinez v. Potter, 347 F.3d 1208, 1210, 92 FEP 1483 (10th Cir. 2003) (charge alleging retaliation in 1999 cannot be used to litigate later continuing alleged acts of retaliation); Freeman v. Oakland Unified Sch. Dist., 291 F.3d 632, 638, 88 FEP 1646 (9th Cir. 2002) (although teacher's EEOC charge mentioned racial discrimination, it in no way suggested the teacher was asserting a continuing violation because sole focus of charge was one election among school faculty).

[114]*See* Jones v. Denver Post Corp., 203 F.3d 748, 755, 82 FEP 61 (10th Cir. 2000) (allegations of retaliatory conduct subsequent to filing of EEOC charge were reasonably related to underlying discrimination claims stated in charge); Siko v. Kassab, Archbold & O'Brien, L.L.P., 77 FEP 1032, 1033 (E.D. Pa. 1998) (retaliation claims were reasonably related to pregnancy discrimination claim in plaintiff's original charge because reasonable investigation of pregnancy discrimination allegations would have examined job performance and discharge); Saladin v. Turner, 936 F. Supp. 1571, 1580, 6 AD 945 (N.D. Okla. 1996) (although retaliatory acts subsequent to EEOC charge will be reasonably related to underlying discrimination in charge, court will refuse to consider retaliatory acts that predate filing of original charge); Edwards v. Nederland Indep. Sch. Dist., 930 F. Supp. 272, 276 (E.D. Tex. 1996) (court has jurisdiction over retaliation claims alleged in plaintiff's complaint but not included in EEOC charge where retaliation occurred after filing of charge); *cf.* Scott v. University of Miss., 148 F.3d 493, 514, 77 FEP 1085 (5th Cir. 1998) (refusing to exercise jurisdiction over failure-to-hire claim that plaintiff failed to include in original charge, reasoning that court's jurisdiction over claims that "grow out of" EEOC charge

the alleged retaliation occurs prior to or contemporaneous with the filing of the initial charge, however, a majority of courts have required that plaintiffs specifically include that retaliation claim in the charge at the risk of losing it as a basis for civil action.[115]

---

was limited to retaliation claims); Daulo v. Commonwealth Edison, 892 F. Supp. 1088, 1093, 72 FEP 1566 (N.D. Ill. 1995) (in Seventh Circuit, "[f]or retaliation for the filing of the base EEOC charge itself, no subsequent EEOC charge is required," but refusing to consider retaliation claims that were not even "hinted at" in original charge). *Compare* Duncan v. Manager, Dep't of Safety, City & County of Denver, 397 F.3d 1300, 1314, 95 FEP 311 (10th Cir. 2005) (police officer failed to exhaust remedies as to her claim that transfer to police academy was in retaliation for filing EEOC charge in that she did not file additional EEOC charge alleging retaliation), Peters v. Renaissance Hotel Operating Co., 307 F.3d 535, 550, 91 FEP 293 (7th Cir. 2002) (retaliation claim could not proceed where charge identified no protected activity or resulting adverse action so as to suggest retaliation claim), Kowalow v. Correctional Servs. Corp., 35 Fed. Appx. 344, 347–48 (9th Cir. 2002) (failure of employee to describe retaliatory conduct in EEOC charge barred her from asserting the claim in court) *and* O'Hara v. Memorial Sloan-Kettering Cancer Ctr., 27 Fed. Appx. 69, 70 (2d Cir. 2001) (district court did not err in dismissing retaliation claim where she neither alleged retaliation in her charge nor pled the facts upon which she based the claim) *with* Wedow v. City of Kansas City, Mo., 442 F.3d 661, 674, 97 FEP 1217 (8th Cir. 2006) (retaliation claims based on prior lawsuit not barred where charges predated alleged retaliatory conduct), Webster v. Rumsfeld, 156 Fed. Appx. 571, 580–81 (4th Cir. 2005) (separate administrative charge not prerequisite to Title VII suit complaining about retaliation for filing the first charge), Smith v. Kentucky State Univ., 97 Fed. Appx. 22, 26 (6th Cir. 2004) (professor's claim of retaliation reasonably related to underlying discrimination charge), *Vasquez*, 349 F.3d at 645–46 (retaliation claim administratively exhausted even though EEOC charge alleged only harassment), Terry v. Ashcroft, 336 F.3d 128, 151, 92 FEP 447 (2d Cir. 2003) (claims not raised in an EEOC charge are sufficiently related to complaints alleging retaliation by the employer for filing EEOC charge) *and* Gawley v. Indiana Univ., 276 F.3d 301, 313–14, 87 FEP 1116 (7th Cir. 2001) (employee seeking to exhaust remedies prior to bringing retaliation claim is not required to file a separate EEOC charge when the retaliation occurs in response to the filing of the original charge).

[115]*See* Holtz v. Rockefeller & Co., 258 F.3d 62, 83, 86 FEP 305 (2d Cir. 2001) (plaintiff's claims of religion and national origin discrimination and retaliation dismissed because plaintiff failed to raise them in her EEOC charge, despite fact that events underlying those claims occurred prior to the filing of the charge); Sloop v. Memorial Mission Hosp., Inc., 198 F.3d 147, 149, 81 FEP 1068 (4th Cir. 1999) (plaintiff failed to exhaust administrative prerequisites for retaliation claim where alleged retaliatory conduct predated filing of charge but where charge failed to raise Title VII retaliation claim, or refer to Title VII at all); Wallin v. Minnesota Dep't of Corr., 153 F.3d 681, 688–89, 8 AD 1012 (8th Cir. 1998) (allegations of retaliatory conduct that occurred before charge was filed, but that were not included in charge, will be procedurally barred unless such allegations "grew out of" initial charge filed with EEOC); Abeita v. TransAmerica Mailings, Inc., 159 F.3d 246, 254, 78 FEP 364 (6th Cir. 1998) (although courts generally will exercise jurisdiction over retaliation claims not included in EEOC charge, "this exception does not apply to retaliation claims based on conduct that occurred before the EEOC charge was filed"); Scott v. Florida Dep't of Revenue, 81 FEP 924, 930 (M.D. Fla. 1999) (alleged retaliatory

Courts sometimes will allow litigation if the subsequent events are "reasonably related" to the events at issue in the charge, and the EEOC actually did investigate (or at least had a reasonable opportunity to investigate) the subsequent events.[116] Other courts take the contrary view, however, particularly where the subsequent, uncharged events were not actually investigated by the EEOC, where the uncharged acts were different in kind from those alleged in the charge, or where, under the circumstances, the charging party might have been expected to file a new charge.[117]

---

failure to promote predated EEOC charge and, therefore, did not "grow out of" initial charge of discrimination); Fry v. Holmes Freight Lines, Inc., 72 F. Supp. 2d 1074, 1079–80, 81 FEP 1356 (W.D. Mo. 1999) (allegations of retaliatory conduct that occurred before EEOC charge was filed were not reasonably related to sexual harassment claim in initial charge because such allegations did not "grow out of" EEOC charge and investigation); Cordero v. Heyman, 1998 WL 730558, at *5 (S.D.N.Y. Oct. 19, 1998) (although retaliation claim for filing of EEOC charge is reasonably related to the initial charge of discrimination, allegations of retaliation prior to filing administrative charge cannot be considered by court).

[116]*See* Hansen v. City of Seattle, 79 FEP 671, 674 (W.D. Wash. 1999) (alleged racial discrimination after plaintiff filed EEOC charge reasonably related to race discrimination claims in charge because allegations of both claims stemmed from same incident); Johnson v. City of Camden Police Dep't, 78 FEP 1649, 1654 (D.N.J. 1998) (alleged acts of racial discrimination that occurred after plaintiff filed original charge would have been included in reasonable investigation by EEOC of charge, involved the same type of discrimination alleged in charge, and would be considered "part of the same overall episode" of alleged racial discrimination) (internal quotations omitted), *aff'd*, 208 F.3d 206 (3d Cir. 2000); Bonds v. Heyman, 950 F. Supp. 1202, 1208, 72 FEP 1589 (D.D.C. 1997) (where initial complaint filed with administrative agency alleges discrimination and retaliation for previous grievances lodged against employer, "it is unnecessary for an employee to refile a new complaint upon every new instance" of discrimination or retaliation, as long as employer is given notice of the claims against it and has the opportunity to conciliate with the employee); Webb v. District of Columbia, 864 F. Supp. 175, 184, 73 FEP 451 (D.D.C. 1994) (similar acts of discrimination and retaliation occurring after filing of charge are properly before court despite plaintiff's failure to amend or file new charge; to hold otherwise would "erect a needless procedural barrier" for plaintiffs); Sims v. Unified Gov't of Wyandotte County/Kansas City, Kan., 120 F. Supp. 2d 938, 951–52 (D. Kan. 2000) (although allegations of retaliatory conduct occurring after filing of EEOC charge are reasonably related to claims in initial charge, same rule does not apply to claims of discriminatory conduct after termination of EEOC investigation).

[117]*E.g.*, Leong v. Potter, 347 F.3d 1117, 1121–22, 92 FEP 1384 (9th Cir. 2003) (dismissing disability claim because plaintiff's charge alleged discrimination on basis of race, color, religion, sex, national origin, and/or age); Sitar v. Indiana Dep't of Transp., 344 F.3d 720, 726–27, 92 FEP 1148 (7th Cir. 2003) (dismissing plaintiff's claims for sex discrimination and harassment because charge only alleged termination in retaliation for making internal report of discrimination); Stuart v. General Motors Corp., 217 F.3d 621, 631, 84 FEP 871 (8th Cir. 2000) (plaintiff could not pursue claim for discipline because charge only alleged that termination from employment

3. Suit Alleging Class-Wide Discrimination Where the Charge Relates to Individual Treatment

Courts have allowed plaintiffs to assert class action claims based on allegations in their individual EEOC charges, as long as those charges have put the defendant employer on notice of the class-wide nature of their allegations.[118] Decisions vary on whether class members who did not file individual charges with the EEOC may "piggyback" their claims on the charges of others. Generally, the courts will allow putative class members to participate in the litigation under the "single-filing rule" as long as their allegations do not expand the scope of the litigation beyond that properly presented by the named plaintiff in the charge filed with the EEOC.[119]

---

was retaliatory); Bland v. Kansas City., Kan. Comm. Coll., 271 F. Supp. 2d 1280, 1283–85 (D. Kan. 2003) (dismissing plaintiff's Title VII and ADA claims because charge alleged age discrimination).

[118]See Communications Workers v. New Jersey Dep't of Pers., 282 F.3d 213, 217, 88 FEP 315 (3d Cir. 2002) (allowing class suit where at least one plaintiff filed EEOC charge and charge provided notice of collective or class-wide nature of charge to employer); Bettcher v. Brown Sch., Inc., 262 F.3d 492, 494, 86 FEP 929 (5th Cir. 2001) (same); Gitlitz v. Compagnie Nationale Air France, 129 F.3d 554, 558, 84 FEP 404 (11th Cir. 1997) (same); Paige v. California, 102 F.3d 1035, 1041–42 (9th Cir. 1996) (permitting class action for failure to promote on basis of race where classwide allegations "[could] *reasonably be expected* to grow out of" individual plaintiff's EEOC charge); Fellows v. Universal Rests., Inc., 701 F.2d 447, 451–52, 31 FEP 483 (5th Cir. 1983) (allegations of disparate treatment and unequal pay on basis of sex alleged by class members are classwide allegations that could reasonably be expected to grow out of EEOC investigation of individual plaintiff's gender discrimination charge); Mooney v. Aramco Serv. Co., 54 F.3d 1207, 1223, 68 FEP 421 (5th Cir. 1995) (individual plaintiff precluded from filing class action where his EEOC charge failed to put employer on notice of class-based nature of disparate treatment claim and scope of class).

[119]*Compare* Holowecki v. Federal Express Corp., 440 F.3d 558, 564, 97 FEP 1037 (2d Cir. 2006) (according to the "piggybacking" or single filing rule, where one plaintiff has filed a timely EEOC complaint, other non-filing plaintiffs may join in the action if their individual claims arise out of similar discriminatory treatment in the same time frame), White v. BFI Waste Servs., LLC, 375 F.3d 288, 293, 94 FEP 73 (4th Cir. 2004) (single-filing rule allows plaintiffs who have not exhausted EEOC administrative requirements to join in lawsuits with other plaintiffs who have, provided that plaintiffs' claims are substantially similar and EEOC charge gave notice of charge's collective nature), Bost v. Federal Express Corp., 372 F.3d 1233, 1239, 93 FEP 1705 (11th Cir. 2004) (in lawsuit under ADEA, plaintiff who has not filed his own charge with the EEOC may piggyback on another plaintiff's charge provided that the relied-upon charge is valid and the individual claims of the filing and non-filing plaintiff arise out of similar discriminatory treatment in the same time frame) *and* Foster v. Ruhrpumpen, Inc., 365 F.3d 1191, 1198–99, 93 FEP 1511 (10th Cir. 2004) (single filing doctrine applicable to claims brought by four workers alleging age discrimination; non-filing workers' claims arose out of same circumstances and

In those cases where the EEOC seeks to litigate or intervene in a class action, courts generally permit the EEOC to become a party to the litigation so long as its judicial complaint is "like or reasonably related" to the allegations raised in the individual class members' initial charges and will not expand the scope of existing litigation.[120]

4. Pleading Requirements of the Complaint

In *Swierkiewicz v. Sorema*,[121] the Supreme Court resolved a split in the circuits regarding the proper pleading standard for employment discrimination cases. Although most courts had held that plaintiffs did not need to plead allegations sufficient to state a prima facie case of discrimination in their complaint,[122] some

---

occurred within same general time frame as charge, and charge stated it was on behalf of all others similarly situated) *with* Price v. Choctaw Glove & Safety Co., 459 F.3d 595, 599, 98 FEP 1101 (5th Cir. 2006) (employees who failed to exhaust administrative remedies with EEOC before bringing Title VII sex discrimination claim against employer could not use single filing rule to piggyback on EEOC charge filed by plaintiff in class action with which their case was later consolidated) *and* Williams v. Henderson, 129 Fed. Appx. 806, 812–13 (4th Cir. 2005) (assuming first three African-American employees who had failed to exhaust administrative remedies with EEOC were similarly situated with second three African-American employees who had exhausted their administrative remedies, first group could not piggyback their unexhausted claims on the exhausted claims of second group; no one made any effort to pursue class complaint before EEOC, and piggybacking through single-filing rule would conflict with EEOC's established procedure for class complaints, which enabled federal employees to preserve claims of others while putting government on notice that it would have to defend itself against wider array of claims), *cert. denied*, 126 S. Ct. 387 (2005).

[120]*See* EEOC v. Golden Lender Fin. Group, 82 FEP 1253, 1254 (S.D.N.Y. 2000) (dismissing race and national origin pattern-or-practice claims brought by EEOC on grounds that such claims not reasonably related to charges filed by former employees that involved only individual allegations of racial discrimination by employer; however, gender pattern-or-practice claim was reasonably related to allegations in EEOC charges, which were not limited to individual instances of discrimination but involved conduct that would fall reasonably within scope of EEOC investigation); EEOC v. Air Line Pilots Ass'n, 885 F. Supp. 289, 293, 67 FEP 1363 (D.D.C. 1995) (in order to effectuate EEOC's broad remedial purpose, "the EEOC has independent authority to file a civil suit based on a new claim arising from an investigation of a valid charge provided that the additional discrimination is included in the reasonable cause determination followed by compliance with proper conciliation procedures"). *But see* Reid v. Lockheed Martin Aeronautics Co., 85 FEP 602 (N.D. Ga. 2001) (denying EEOC motion to intervene due to unreasonable delay and prejudice to original parties).

[121]534 U.S. 506 (2002).

[122]*See, e.g.*, Sparrow v. United Air Lines, Inc., 216 F.3d 1111, 1114, 83 FEP 556 (D.C. Cir. 2000) (discrimination plaintiff need not set forth elements of prima facie case at pleading stage); Bennett v. Schmidt, 153 F.3d 516, 518, 77 FEP 1210

courts—such as the lower court in *Swierkiewicz*—held that a complaint in an employment discrimination suit must contain factual allegations sufficient to support each element of a prima facie case.[123]

The Supreme Court held in *Swierkiewicz* that employment discrimination complaints were governed by the same notice pleading rules as other complaints, and plaintiffs did not have to plead facts sufficient to set forth the prima facie case of discrimination. The Court noted that it had long rejected the argument that a Title VII complaint requires greater "particularity," because this would "too narrowly constrict the role of the pleadings."[124] Under a notice pleading system, the Court stated it is not appropriate to require a plaintiff to plead facts establishing a prima facie case because the *McDonnell Douglas* framework does not apply in every employment discrimination case.[125] The Court also noted that the precise requirements of the prima facie case can vary.[126] Further, imposing a heightened standard of pleading in employment discrimination cases conflicts with Federal Rule of Civil Procedure 8(a)(2), which provides that a complaint need only include "a short and plain statement of the claim showing that the pleader is entitled to relief."[127]

V. VENUE

Venue in Title VII cases is governed by the specific venue provisions of the statute,[128] not by the general venue provisions of

---

(7th Cir. 1998) (complaints "need not plead law or match facts to every element of a legal theory").

[123]*See, e.g.*, Tarshis v. Riese Org., 211 F.3d 30, 35, 82 FEP 1261 (2d Cir. 2000) (complaint must allege set of facts supporting each claim that would entitle plaintiff to relief); Jackson v. Columbus, 194 F.3d 737, 751–52, 18 IER 305 (6th Cir. 1999) (to survive motion to dismiss, complaint must assert factual allegations that support each element of a prima facie case).

[124]*Swierkiewicz*, 534 U.S. at 511 (quoting McDonald v. Santa Fe Trail Transp. Co., 427 U.S. 273, 283 n.11 (1976)).

[125]*Swierkiewicz*, 534 U.S. at 511 (citing McDonnell Douglas Corp. v. Green, 411 U.S. 792, 5 FEP 965 (1973)).

[126]*Swierkiewicz*, 534 U.S. at 512.

[127]*Id.* at 512–14 (citing FED. R. CIV. P. 8(a)(2)).

[128]42 U.S.C. § 2000e-5(f)(3) (2000). Section 706(f)(3) of Title VII specifically provides:

Each United States district court and each United States court of a place subject to the jurisdiction of the United States shall have jurisdiction of actions brought under this title. Such an action may be brought in any judicial district

28 U.S.C. § 1391.[129] Venue is proper primarily in three places. The first is the state where the alleged unlawful employment practice took place.[130] In determining where the alleged unlawful employment

---

in the State in which the unlawful employment practice is alleged to have been committed, in the judicial district in which the employment records relevant to such practice are maintained and administered, or in the judicial district in which the aggrieved person would have worked but for the alleged unlawful employment practice, but if the respondent is not found within any such district, such an action may be brought within the judicial district in which the respondent has his principal office. For purposes of sections 1404 and 1406 of title 28 of the United States Code, the judicial district in which the respondent has his principal office shall in all cases be considered a district in which the action might have been brought.

[129]*Id.*; *see, e.g.*, Gwin v. Reynolds & Reynolds Co., 86 FEP 559, 561 (N.D. Ill. 2001) (granting defendant's motion to transfer venue to Ohio, where defendant's principal office was located and all employment records were maintained, where factual dispute existed as to whether, but for defendant's alleged unlawful employment practices, plaintiff would have continued to work in Illinois); Cox v. NFL, 75 FEP 553, 556 (N.D. Ill. 1997) (denying defendant's motion to transfer venue to New York where decision to impose fine on plaintiff, a professional football player, was made in New York but acts of imposing fine and paying fine by mailing plaintiff's game check to NFL were performed by team management in Illinois); Geiger v. E.I. DuPont de Nemours & Co., 1997 WL 83291, at *6 (S.D.N.Y. Feb. 14, 1997) (under Title VII, venue is proper in any judicial district in the state in which alleged discrimination occurred; court denied plaintiffs' motion to transfer to different district in New York based on convenience of parties and witnesses); Launer v. Buena Vista Winery, Inc., 916 F. Supp. 204, 212 (E.D.N.Y. 1996) (denying defendant's motion to dismiss Title VII claims for improper venue where substantial part of events giving rise to discrimination claim occurred in New York); Wexler v. Runyon, 1996 WL 209978, at *1 (S.D.N.Y. Apr. 30, 1996) (granting defendant's motion to transfer venue to New Jersey where plaintiff was hired by, worked for, and was fired by New Jersey post office, and where all pertinent records and witnesses were located in New Jersey); Blazy v. Woolsey, 64 FEP 724, 725 (D.D.C. 1994) (granting defendant's motion to transfer venue to Eastern District of Virginia notwithstanding factual dispute as to whether any employment records were maintained in District of Columbia, where relevant conduct occurred in Virginia and it appeared that, but for alleged unlawful employment practices, plaintiff would have continued to work in Virginia); Johnson v. Payless Drug Stores, 950 F.2d 586, 587–88, 66 FEP 355 (9th Cir. 1991) (per curiam); Trujillo v. Total Bus. Sys., Inc., 704 F. Supp. 1031, 1032–33, 49 FEP 285 (D. Colo. 1989).

[130]*See, e.g.*, Ramos de Almeida v. Powell, 90 FEP 1235, 1237–38 (S.D.N.Y. 2002) (venue in New York improper where almost all aspects of case are directly related to events, documents, and persons located in District of Columbia, where allegedly unlawful employment practice took place); Amirmokri v. Abraham, 217 F. Supp. 2d 88, 90, 89 FEP 1788 (D.D.C. 2002) (alleged unlawful employment practices that were subject of employee's race and national origin discrimination action occurred in Maryland rather than in District of Columbia, and thus venue of Title VII action was proper only in Maryland); Adams v. Cal-Ark Int'l, Inc., 159 F. Supp. 2d 402, 409 (E.D. Tex. 2001) (venue in Title VII action was appropriate in any judicial district in Texas because unlawful employment practices occurred in Texas); Cameli v. WNEP-16 The News Station, 134 F. Supp. 2d 403, 405 (E.D. Pa. 2001) (Middle

practice took place, courts look to the "events having operative significance in the case."[131] Generally, the decision to hire, fire, or deny employment is considered to be such an event. That a position was advertised in a particular state or that correspondence concerning an application was mailed to or from that state is not enough, without more, to obtain proper venue in that state.[132] Second, venue is proper in the judicial district where the employment records relevant to the suit are maintained or administered.[133] Third, a plaintiff may bring suit in the judicial district where the plaintiff would have worked but for the alleged discrimination.[134]

District of Pennsylvania appropriate venue for ADA case because unlawful employment practice allegedly was committed there); EEOC v. Mustang Mobile Homes, Inc., 88 F. Supp. 2d 722, 724 (W.D. Tex. 1999) ("because this cause arises out of actions allegedly taken by Defendant in Lubbock, and because the Western District of Texas is a judicial district in the State . . . in which the unlawful employment practice is alleged to have been committed, . . . the Court finds venue for this cause is proper in the Western District of Texas").

[131]Cole v. Appalachian Power Co., 1995 U.S. Dist. LEXIS 22239, at *18 n.5 (S.D. W. Va. Mar. 30, 1995); see also EEOC v. ICON Benefit Adm'rs Inc., 91 FEP 116, 121 (W.D. Tex. 2003) (where the convenience of the parties and witnesses, the place of the alleged wrong, and the location of the employment records all weighed in favor of the Northern District of Texas, the defendant's motion to transfer was granted); Ramos de Almeida, 90 FEP at 1237–38 (S.D.N.Y. 2002) (case transferred to District of Columbia where the alleged discrimination took place and the employment records and the employer itself were located); Murray v. Plantation Mgmt. Co., LLC, 90 FEP 926, 928 (E.D. La. 2002) (where the alleged wrong, the employment records, and the witnesses were located in the Middle District of Louisiana, transfer was appropriate); Donnell v. National Guard Bureau, 568 F. Supp. 93, 94–95, 32 FEP 589 (D.D.C. 1983).

[132]See Sconion v. Thomas, 603 F. Supp. 66, 68–69, 36 FEP 618 (D.D.C. 1984) (venue improper in district where the defendant had sent plaintiff's employment records "for her perusal"); Templeton v. Veterans Admin., 540 F. Supp. 695, 697, 31 FEP 909 (S.D.N.Y. 1982) (venue proper in California where a discriminatory act occurred and where plaintiff might have been employed, or in Missouri where relevant records were maintained); Matthews v. Trans World Airlines, Inc., 478 F. Supp. 1244, 1246, 21 FEP 481 (S.D.N.Y. 1979) (venue proper in New York even though discriminatory act occurred in Kansas and relevant documents were stored in Kansas or Missouri, when plaintiff would have been assigned to New York).

[133]42 U.S.C. § 2000e-5(f) (2000); see James v. Booz-Allen & Hamilton, Inc., 227 F. Supp. 2d 16, 24–25, 89 FEP 1401 (D.D.C. 2002) (court transferred case to the Eastern District of Virginia because the alleged discriminatory decision took place outside of the District of Columbia, the plaintiff's employment records and the employer's principal place of business were located in the Eastern District of Virginia, and defendant did not challenge the transfer); Dais v. Mobil Oil Corp., 20 FEP 874, 875–76 (S.D.N.Y. 1979) (proper venue is in the district where employee's primary records are kept).

[134]42 U.S.C. § 2000e-5(f) (2000); see Quarles v. General Inv. & Dev. Co., 260 F. Supp. 2d 1, 91 FEP 623, 632 (D.D.C. 2003) (defendant's motion to dismiss for

If venue cannot be had in one of the above three districts, the court may look to the district in which the employer's "principal office" is located.[135] This aspect of the Title VII venue provision was enacted to cover the "rare case" when the employer cannot be found in one of the other three districts.[136]

The venue provisions of Title VII are exclusive.[137] Thus, in a case where the alleged unlawful employment practice occurred in New York, the employment records were located in New York, and the aggrieved plaintiff would have worked in New York but for the alleged unlawful practice, venue was proper only within one of the four judicial districts of New York, even though the defendant corporation was licensed to do business in Georgia.[138]

Plaintiff has the burden of establishing proper venue. Therefore, a mere allegation that the unlawful employment decision was made in a particular state will be insufficient to establish venue when there is contradictory evidence.[139]

___

lack of venue as to plaintiff A in class action claim denied based on plaintiff A's well-pled allegation in the complaint that, but for the alleged unlawful employment practice, she would have accepted the position she applied for in the District of Columbia); Johnson v. Payless Drug Stores, 950 F.2d 586, 587–88, 66 FEP 355 (9th Cir. 1991) (proper venue is where employee was working and where employment records were maintained); *Matthews*, 478 F. Supp. at 1246 (venue lay in district in which employee would have worked but for termination); Cowgill v. Management Placement, 12 FEP 1778, 1779 (D.D.C. 1976) (proper venue is in district where plaintiff would have worked absent alleged unlawful discrimination).

[135]42 U.S.C. § 2000e-5(f) (2000); Worthy v. Aspin, 64 FEP 65, 67–68 (W.D. Pa. 1994) (granting motion to transfer venue to Eastern District of Virginia where alleged discrimination occurred in Japan and Okinawa, plaintiff's employment records were maintained in Okinawa, plaintiff would have continued to work in Japan had he not been discharged, and defendant Les Aspin's principal office, the Pentagon, was located in Eastern District of Virginia).

[136]*See* Arrocha v. Panama Canal Comm'n, 609 F. Supp. 231, 234, 37 FEP 1789 (E.D.N.Y. 1985) (the court may look to the district in which the employer's principal office is located only if venue cannot be had in one of the other three possible districts specified in the statute).

[137]*See* Pierce v. Shorty Small's of Branson, Inc., 137 F.3d 1190, 1191, 77 FEP 1471 (10th Cir. 1998); Amirmokri v. Abraham, 217 F. Supp. 2d 88, 89–90, 89 FEP 1788 (D.D.C. 2002); Phillips v. Rubin, 76 F. Supp. 2d 1079, 1080, 81 FEP 906 (D. Nev. 1999).

[138]Kravec v. Chicago Pneumatic Tool Co., 579 F. Supp. 619, 622, 36 FEP 266 (N.D. Ga. 1983). *But cf.* Hoffman v. United Telecomms., Inc., 575 F. Supp. 1463, 1484, 35 FEP 1215 (D. Kan. 1983) (venue may be proper where a parent corporation is located if the parent controls the subsidiary's personnel policies and practices).

[139]*See* Zughni v. Peña, 851 F. Supp. 300, 302–03 (N.D. Ill. 1994) (granting defendants' motion to transfer venue where plaintiff made only unsupported assertion that decision to discharge her was made in Illinois but defendants provided documentation

VI. SUMMARY JUDGMENT

A. Introduction

The parties to employment discrimination cases, and especially defendants, commonly file summary judgment motions before trial. A large percentage of the cases cited throughout this book, in fact, arise in the posture of employer contentions that it should prevail as a matter of law, either on summary judgment, directed verdict, or judgment notwithstanding the verdict.

B. General Principles

Summary judgment is appropriate when no genuine issue of material fact exists and the moving party is entitled to judgment as a matter of law.[140] Prior to 1986, courts frequently denied summary judgment in employment discrimination cases, stating that subjective issues such as the defendant's motive or intent usually rendered summary judgment inappropriate.[141]

In 1986, however, the Supreme Court made clear in three opinions, known as the *Celotex* trilogy,[142] that summary judgment

---

supporting their contention that disputed decision was made in Ohio), *aff'd*, 56 F.3d 82 (Fed. Cir. 1995).

[140]FED. R. CIV. P. 56(c) (summary judgment shall be rendered "if the pleadings, depositions, answers to interrogatories, and admissions on file, together with the affidavits, if any, show that there is no genuine issue as to any material fact and that the moving party is entitled to a judgment as a matter of law").

[141]*See, e.g.*, Thornbrough v. Columbus & Greenville R.R., 760 F.2d 633, 640, 37 FEP 1414 (5th Cir. 1985) ("In general, summary judgment is an inappropriate tool for resolving claims of employment discrimination, which involve nebulous questions of motivation and intent."); Keys v. Lutheran Family & Children's Servs., 668 F.2d 356, 358, 29 FEP 253 (8th Cir. 1981) ("where motive, intent and credibility are key factors, summary judgment is generally inappropriate"); Kephart v. Institute of Gas Tech., 630 F.2d 1217, 1218, 23 FEP 1412 (7th Cir. 1980) (per curiam) (summary judgment is improper in a discrimination case if it involves any weighing of conflicting indications of motive and intent); Hayden v. First Nat'l Bank, 595 F.2d 994, 997, 19 FEP 1342 (5th Cir. 1979) (summary judgment is especially questionable in employment discrimination cases).

[142]Anderson v. Liberty Lobby, Inc., 477 U.S. 242, 248 (1986) (only evidence of a factual dispute that might affect the suit's outcome and could lead a reasonable jury to return a verdict for the nonmoving party will properly preclude summary judgment); Celotex Corp. v. Catrett, 477 U.S. 317, 324, 327 (1986) (the nonmoving party must go beyond the pleadings and must produce evidence showing a genuine issue of material fact; summary judgment is not a disfavored procedural shortcut but an integral part of the Federal Rules); Matsushita Elec. Indus. Co. v. Zenith Radio Corp., 475 U.S. 574, 586–87 (1986) (the nonmoving party cannot simply show that

is not a "disfavored procedural shortcut."[143] Accordingly, since 1986 courts have granted summary judgment more readily in employment discrimination cases.[144]

C. The Impact of *Reeves*

In *Reeves v. Sanderson Plumbing Products, Inc.*,[145] the Supreme Court addressed the type and amount of evidence necessary

---

some metaphysical doubt exists but must present specific facts showing a genuine issue of material fact).

[143]*Celotex*, 477 U.S. at 327.

[144]*See, e.g.*, Wilson v. B/E Aerospace, Inc., 376 F.3d 1079, 1086, 93 FEP 1825 (11th Cir. 2004) (rejecting contention that summary judgment should seldom be used in employment discrimination cases because they involve examination of motivation and intent); Abdu-Brisson v. Delta Air Lines, Inc., 239 F.3d 456, 466, 85 FEP 161 (2d Cir. 2001) ("It is now beyond cavil that summary judgment may be appropriate even in the fact-intensive context of discrimination cases [because] the 'salutary purposes of summary judgment—avoiding protracted, expensive and harassing trials—applies no less to discrimination cases than to . . . other areas of litigation.' ") (quoting Meiri v. Dacon, 759 F.2d 989, 998 (2d Cir. 1985)); Wallace II v. SMC Pneumatics, Inc., 103 F.3d 1394, 1396, 72 FEP 1635 (7th Cir. 1997) (many of the more than 90% of employment discrimination cases resolved before trial are on summary judgment in favor of the employer); Earley v. Champion Int'l Corp., 907 F.2d 1077, 1081, 53 FEP 968 (11th Cir. 1990) ("Summary judgments for defendants are not rare in employment discrimination cases."); Summers v. State Farm Mut. Auto. Ins. Co., 864 F.2d 700, 709, 48 FEP 1107 (10th Cir. 1988) (although "courts are, or perhaps were, slow to grant summary judgments in discrimination cases . . . recent cases indicate" that it is "not an impossibility and that obvious cases should be weeded out before trial"). *But see* Phelan v. Cook County, 463 F.3d 773, 779–80, 98 FEP 1601 (7th Cir. 2006) (for an employee to defeat summary judgment in a Title VII discrimination claim, all that is required is evidence from which a rational trier of fact could reasonably infer that the defendant had fired the employee because the latter was a member of a protected class); Simpson v. Des Moines Water Works, 425 F.3d 538, 542, 17 AD 225 (8th Cir. 2005) (summary judgment is disfavored in employment discrimination cases, as such cases are inherently fact-based); Dominguez-Curry v. Nevada Transp. Dep't, 424 F.3d 1027, 1037, 96 FEP 744 (9th Cir. 2005) (at summary judgment, the degree of proof necessary to establish a prima facie Title VII employment discrimination case is minimal and does not even need to rise to the level of a preponderance of the evidence); Forsyth v. Federation Employment & Guidance Serv., 409 F.3d 565, 569–70, 95 FEP 1545 (2d Cir. 2005) (more caution should be exercised in affirming the grant of summary judgment in a discrimination case because smoking gun evidence of discriminatory intent is rare and most often must be inferred); Back v. Hastings on Hudson Union Free Sch. Dist., 365 F.3d 107, 124, 93 FEP 1430 (2d Cir. 2004) (unless defendants' proffered nondiscriminatory reason for adverse employment action is dispositive and forecloses any issue of material fact, summary judgment is inappropriate on employment discrimination claim). A more expansive treatment of the standards generally applicable to summary judgment motions in employment cases is beyond the intended scope of this book.

[145]530 U.S. 133, 82 FEP 1748 (2000).

to sustain a jury verdict in an individual disparate treatment case under the ADEA. The Supreme Court also commented further in *Reeves* on principles applicable generally to motions for judgment as a matter of law.[146] Addressing what appeared to be differing approaches among the circuits about the evidence a court is to consider in ruling on a motion for judgment as a matter of law, the Court held that the trial court must review all of the evidence in the record.[147]

> In doing so, however, the court must draw all reasonable inferences in favor of the nonmoving party, and it may not make credibility determinations or weigh the evidence .... Thus, although the court should review the record as a whole, it must disregard all evidence favorable to the moving party that the jury is not required to believe .... That is, the court should give credence to the evidence favoring the nonmovant as well as that "evidence supporting the moving party that is uncontradicted and unimpeached, at least to the extent that the evidence comes from disinterested witnesses."[148]

Reeves also clarified that although an individual plaintiff's establishment of a prima facie case of disparate treatment, combined

---

[146]The Court reiterated that the "standard for granting summary judgment 'mirrors' the standard for judgment as a matter of law, such that 'the inquiry under each is the same.'" 530 U.S. at 150 (quoting Anderson v. Liberty Lobby, Inc., 477 U.S. 242, 250–51 (1986)).

[147]530 U.S. at 150; *see, e.g.*, McCowan v. All Star Maint., Inc., 273 F.3d 917, 921, 926, 87 FEP 596 (10th Cir. 2001) (reversing summary judgment for defendant in termination case because district court failed to indulge all reasonable inferences in favor of the nonmoving party and "ignored some of the facts presented, permitting it to resolve what otherwise would be material facts more appropriately reserved for a rational jury").

[148]530 U.S. at 150 (citations omitted) (quoting 9A CHARLES ALAN WRIGHT & ARTHUR R. MILLER, FEDERAL PRACTICE & PROCEDURE § 2529, at 300 (2d ed. 1995)). The Seventh Circuit addressed this language from *Reeves* in *Traylor v. Brown*, 295 F.3d 783, 89 FEP 1438 (7th Cir. 2002). In *Traylor*, the plaintiff argued that summary judgment was inappropriate because "a trier of fact *could* disbelieve [the employer's] proffered reasons because they were not offered by 'disinterested witnesses.'" 295 F.3d at 790. The Seventh Circuit disagreed, explaining that such an interpretation of *Reeves* would require a court to ignore uncontroverted testimony of company employees and thereby prevent any employer from prevailing on summary judgment. *Id.* at 791. On the other hand, the jury does not have to accept biased testimony and a reviewing court must view the record in that light. *See* Wilson v. Brinker Int'l, Inc., 382 F.3d 765, 770, 94 FEP 585 (8th Cir. 2004) (manager's testimony, which jury could disbelieve, did not warrant entry of judgment as a matter of law); Tart v. Illinois Power Co., 366 F.3d 461, 478 (7th Cir. 2004) (interested witnesses' testimony did not have to be credited).

with evidence sufficient to find that the employer's asserted justifications are false, may permit a finding of unlawful discrimination, such a showing will not always be adequate to sustain a jury verdict.[149] Rather, the appropriateness of judgment as a matter of law in any particular case will depend on a number of factors, including strength of the prima facie case, probative value of the proof that the employer's explanation is false, and any other evidence that supports the employer's case and that may be considered properly on a motion for judgment as a matter of law.[150] The Court refrained from determining all circumstances and factors that might be weighed in this analysis. The Court, however, observed by way of example that the employer would be entitled to judgment as a matter of law if the record revealed conclusively some other nondiscriminatory reason for the decision, or if the plaintiff created only a weak issue of fact as to whether the employer's reasons were untrue and there was abundant and uncontroverted independent evidence that discrimination had not occurred.[151]

Reeves establishes that a court must consider the entire record in evaluating a discrimination claim at the summary judgment phase. It did not, however, relax "the requirement that plaintiffs make a showing that the defendant's proffered reasons were pretextual."[152] The "ultimate question" in any individual disparate treatment employment discrimination case remains "whether the employer intentionally discriminated" against the plaintiff.[153]

---

[149]*Reeves*, 530 U.S. at 147.

[150]*Id.* at 148–49.

[151]*Id.* at 148; *see, e.g.*, Chuang v. University of Cal. Davis Bd. of Trs., 225 F.3d 1115, 1127, 86 FEP 1551 (9th Cir. 2000) (evidence establishing plaintiff's prima facie case of race and national origin discrimination was "sufficiently strong to raise a genuine issue of material fact regarding the truth of [the employer's] proffered non-discriminatory reasons" for its decision to deny plaintiff a full-time teaching position and forcible relocation of plaintiff's laboratory); Collins v. New York City Transit Auth., 305 F.3d 113, 118 (2d Cir. 2002) (plaintiff has higher burden to prove that employer's decision was motivated by racial animus where neutral arbitrator decided, after full and fair hearing, that company's action was justified).

[152]*See* Abdu-Brisson v. Delta Air Lines, Inc., 239 F.3d 456, 470, 85 FEP 161 (2d Cir. 2001).

[153]*Reeves*, 530 U.S. at 146–47. The circuits have applied this requirement in a variety of ways. *See* Thanongsinh v. Board of Educ., 462 F.3d 762, 780, 98 FEP 1730 (7th Cir. 2006) (to show that defendant's explanation for adverse employment action is pretextual, plaintiff must show more than that the decision was mistaken, ill considered, or foolish; as long as the employer honestly believes those reasons,

pretext has not been shown, as pretext means a dishonest explanation—a lie rather than an oddity or an error); Mickelson v. New York Life Ins. Co., 460 F.3d 1304, 1315, 98 FEP 1485 (10th Cir. 2006) (Title VII plaintiff can show pretext by revealing such weaknesses, implausibilities, inconsistencies, incoherencies, or contradictions in the employer's proffered legitimate reasons for its action that a reasonable fact finder could rationally find them unworthy of credence); Azimi v. Jordan's Meats, Inc., 456 F.3d 228, 246, 98 FEP 1258 (1st Cir. 2006) (in assessing pretext, court's focus must be on whether employer believed its stated reason to be credible; although employer's good faith belief is not automatically conclusive, it is not enough for plaintiff merely to impugn veracity of employer's justification, and he must elucidate specific facts that would enable jury to find reason given is not only a sham, but a sham intended to cover up employer's real and unlawful motive of discrimination); Twymon v. Wells Fargo & Co., 462 F.3d 925, 935 (8th Cir. 2006) (to prove pretext for discrimination, plaintiff must both discredit employer's asserted reason for termination and show that the circumstances permit drawing the reasonable inference that real reason for terminating plaintiff was discriminatory); Wright v. Murray Guard, Inc., 455 F.3d 702, 707, 98 FEP 833 (6th Cir. 2006) (in discrimination case, pretext may be shown either directly by persuading the trier of fact that discriminatory reason more likely motivated employer or indirectly by showing that employer's proffered explanation is unworthy of credence); Brooks v. County Comm'n of Jefferson County, 446 F.3d 1160, 1163, 97 FEP 1587 (11th Cir. 2006) (to avoid summary judgment, plaintiff must introduce significantly probative evidence showing that asserted reason for employer's action is merely pretext for discrimination; a reason is not pretext for discrimination unless it is shown both that the reason was false and that discrimination was the real reason); Atkinson v. Lafayette Coll., 460 F.3d 447, 454, 98 FEP 1515 (3d Cir. 2006) (in order for employee bringing discrimination claim to prove that employer's proffered legitimate reasons for adverse employment action are pretextual, employee can: (1) present evidence that casts sufficient doubt upon each legitimate reason proffered so that fact finder could reasonably conclude that each reason was fabrication, or (2) provide evidence that allows fact finder to infer that discrimination was more likely than not motivating or determinative cause of challenged action); Dominguez-Curry v. Nevada Transp. Dep't, 424 F.3d 1027, 1037, 96 FEP 744 (9th Cir. 2005) (employee may show pretext, as required to rebut employer's proffered nondiscriminatory reason for adverse employment action, either by (1) showing that unlawful discrimination more likely motivated the employer, or (2) showing that the employer's proffered explanation is unworthy of credence because it is inconsistent or otherwise not believable); Diamond v. Colonial Life & Accident Ins. Co., 416 F.3d 310, 318, 96 FEP 287 (4th Cir. 2005) (plaintiff may avert summary judgment through two avenues of proof: plaintiff may present direct or circumstantial evidence that raises a genuine issue of material fact as to whether impermissible factor motivated employer's adverse employment decision, or, alternatively, plaintiff may, after establishing prima facie case of discrimination, demonstrate that employer's proffered reason for taking adverse employment action is actually a pretext for discrimination), *cert. denied*, 126 S. Ct. 1033 (2006); Back v. Hastings on Hudson Union Free Sch. Dist., 365 F.3d 107, 123, 93 FEP 1430 (2d Cir. 2004) (to defeat summary judgment, plaintiff asserting employment discrimination claim not required to show employer's proffered reasons were false or played no role in challenged employment decision, but only that proffered reasons were not the only reasons and that alleged prohibited factor was at least one of the motivating factors); Kanida v. Gulf Coast Med. Personnel LP, 363 F.3d 568, 576, 9 WH 865 (5th Cir. 2004) (to prevail in discrimination case, plaintiff must show actual discriminatory intent; successfully rebutting defendant's asserted

D. Common Procedural Issues

1. Inadmissible Evidence and Motions to Strike

In moving for or opposing summary judgment, the parties must submit evidence to establish their respective positions on the motion. This evidence can be in the form of depositions, answers to interrogatories, admissions, and affidavits.[154] In particular, in response to a properly supported motion for summary judgment, the non-moving party "may not rest upon mere allegations or denials . . . but must set forth specific facts showing there is a genuine issue for trial."[155] In considering whether summary judgment is appropriate, the court must review the totality of this record evidence.[156]

There is no requirement that a party submit an affidavit to support or oppose a motion for summary judgment.[157] To the extent that an affidavit is submitted, however, Rule 56(e) contains specific evidentiary requirements. First, affidavits must be based on personal knowledge of the facts stated.[158] An affidavit that does

---

justifications for adverse action may not itself be sufficient); Sparrow v. United Air Lines, Inc., 216 F.3d 1111, 1117, 83 FEP 556 (D.C. Cir. 2000) (even where employer carries its burden of articulating nondiscriminatory reason, plaintiff must then have an opportunity to prove by a preponderance of the evidence that the legitimate reasons offered by defendant were not its true reasons, but were a pretext for discrimination).

[154]FED. R. CIV. P. 56(c).

[155]Anderson v. Liberty Lobby, Inc., 477 U.S. 242, 256 (1986). To make this showing, the non-moving party can use any of the evidentiary materials listed in Rule 56(c); although the rules of evidence generally apply to such submissions, the non-moving party is not required to "produce evidence in a form that would be admissible at trial," and the non-moving party therefore can submit an affidavit instead of deposing his or her own witness. See Celotex Corp. v. Catrett, 477 U.S. 317, 324 (1986); see also Stinnett v. Iron Works Gym/Executive Health Spa, Inc., 301 F.3d 610, 613, 89 FEP 1282 (7th Cir. 2002) (although evidence submitted for summary judgment "need not be admissible in form . . . it must be admissible in content").

[156]FED. R. CIV. P. 56(c).

[157]Celotex, 477 U.S. at 323 (Rule 56(a) and (b) provide that the claimant and defending party may move for summary judgment "with or without supporting affidavits").

[158]FED. R. CIV. P. 56(e); see, e.g., Bryant v. Farmers Ins. Exch., 432 F.3d 1114, 1117, 97 FEP 202 (10th Cir. 2005) (district court abused discretion by striking portions of non-moving employee's affidavit under Rule 56(e), FRE 602, and FRE 701; employee as former supervisor had personal knowledge that audit results were not intended to be used to dismiss employees and that poor audit results should not be attributed to another employee's actions); Haynes v. Williams, 392 F.3d 478, 482,

not establish personal knowledge is insufficient and should not be considered by the court.[159] Second, affidavits must "set forth facts as would be admissible in evidence."[160] Third, the affidavit must show that the affiant is competent to testify as to the facts stated.[161]

---

16 AD (D.C. Cir. 2004) (plaintiff in ADA case could supply own affidavit on limitation of major life activity of sleeping); Gillen v. Fallon Ambulance Serv., Inc., 283 F.3d 11, 25–26, 12 AD 1633 (1st Cir. 2002) (district court erred in disregarding plaintiff's own affidavit on lifting restrictions, submitted in opposition to summary judgment, which clarified that at the time she was scheduled to take her qualifying test she could have lifted 70 or more pounds); Volovsek v. Wisconsin Dep't of Agric., Trade & Consumer Prot., 344 F.3d 680, 690 (7th Cir. 2003) (plaintiff's affidavit was based on personal knowledge because it recounted alleged discriminatory comments that she overheard); Bryant v. Bell Atl. Md. Inc., 288 F.3d 124, 134–35 n.9 (4th Cir. 2002) (although affidavits of defendant's officers do not state that they are based on personal knowledge, "the affidavits contain sufficient information, including a description of the affiants' job titles and duties, to establish that the statements were based on personal knowledge"; on the other hand, affidavits submitted by plaintiff were not based on personal knowledge, but rather mere subjective belief, including statements such as "I believe [supervisor] is a racist").

[159]See, e.g., Lopez-Carrasquillo v. Rubianes, 230 F.3d 409, 414 (1st Cir. 2000) (affidavit stating that it was "correct in all parts to the best of my knowledge" and merely repeating the conclusory allegations in the complaint was not sufficient to oppose summary judgment); Fowler v. Tillman, 97 F. Supp. 2d 602, 607 (D.N.J. 2000) (court refused to consider portions of affidavits that stated that plaintiff "believe[d]" and "felt" that the defendant took action in violation of the Fair Housing Act because affidavits did not meet requirements of Rule 56(e)); Keating v. Bucks County Water & Sewer Auth., 2000 WL 1888770, at *4 (E.D. Pa. Dec. 29, 2000) (court could not consider paragraph 17 of plaintiff's affidavit because it stated that a fact "was generally known around the Authority" but did not state that the fact was known by the affiant-plaintiff).

[160]FED. R. CIV. P. 56(e); see, e.g., Patterson v. County of Oneida, 375 F.3d 206, 227, 94 FEP 129 (2d Cir. 2004) (anonymous affidavit from separate litigation and conclusory affidavit from co-worker that African-American guards were selectively disciplined held inadmissible); Pamintuan v. Nanticoke Mem'l Hosp., 192 F.3d 378, 387 (3d Cir. 1999) (court properly refused to consider inadmissible evidence submitted in plaintiff's affidavit to establish pretext on discrimination claim); Galindo v. Precision Am. Corp., 754 F.2d 1212, 1216 (5th Cir. 1985) (declarations that set forth ultimate or conclusory facts are insufficient under Rule 56(e)); Franzon v. Massena Mem'l Hosp., 89 F. Supp. 2d 270, 276–77 (N.D.N.Y. 2000) (court could not consider portions of affidavit that contain double hearsay—that is, portions detailing affiant's out-of-court conversation with a witness who recounted an out-of-court conversation between two other witnesses—even though the alleged first-level hearsay statements, if true, would be persuasive evidence on plaintiff's claims).

[161]FED. R. CIV. P. 56(e); see, e.g., Foster v. AlliedSignal Inc., 293 F.3d 1187, 1192 n.1 (10th Cir. 2002) (court did not consider telephone logs attached to affidavit submitted by plaintiff's attorney because attorney did not have any personal knowledge of the log's source or authenticity and, therefore, was incompetent to testify about the documents); Murphy v. Ford Motor Co., 170 F.R.D. 82, 85 (D. Mass.

Fourth, documents referred to in the affidavit should be attached.[162] Any documents submitted in support of the motion or opposition to summary judgment must be properly authenticated—pursuant to Federal Rules of Evidence 901–903—to be considered by the court.[163]

In addition to affidavits, the court may consider other evidentiary materials. At the summary judgment stage answers to interrogatories submitted by a party are generally held to the same evidentiary standards as affidavits, such that the answers must be based on personal knowledge and set forth admissible evidence.[164] Deposition testimony may be submitted in support of or in opposition to the motion itself, and must contain admissible evidence to be considered by the court.[165] Under Rule 56(c), admissions on

---

1997) (striking portions of plaintiff's affidavit testifying as to accident reconstruction and automotive engineering because plaintiff had not established his qualifications as an expert on those matters).

[162]FED. R. CIV. P. 56(e).

[163]*See, e.g.,* Carmona v. Toledo, 215 F.3d 124, 131 (1st Cir. 2000) (defendants' failure to authenticate documents attached to their summary judgment motion precluded consideration of the documents); IBP, Inc. v. Mercantile Bank of Topeka, 6 F. Supp. 2d 1258, 1263 (D. Kan. 1998) (although business records may be admissible at trial as a hearsay exception, on summary judgment, they must be authenticated by a person through whom the records could be admitted at trial).

[164]*See, e.g.,* BMG Music v. Martinez, 74 F.3d 87, 90 (5th Cir. 1996) (on appeal from summary judgment, court could not consider answers to interrogatories and affidavit by debtor's sister to whom debtor had transferred property because it was not clear that sister had personal knowledge of any agreement between her brother and father); Gross v. Burggraf Constr. Co., 53 F.3d 1531, 1541, 68 FEP 88 (10th Cir. 1995) (female employee's interrogatory response was not based on personal knowledge and, thus, could not be considered by court when reviewing order granting employer's and supervisor's motions for summary judgment in employment discrimination action).

[165]FED. R. CIV. P. 56(c), (e); *see, e.g.,* Kirk v. City of Tulsa, 72 Fed. Appx. 747, 750 (10th Cir. 2003) (deposition excerpt in which city contractor stated that he had heard secondhand that city supervisor made disparaging comments about former employee's handling of project was hearsay that could not be considered by district court in deciding summary judgment motion); Boyce v. Moore, 314 F.3d 884, 889 (7th Cir. 2002) (prisoner's deposition testimony was hearsay and thus was not admissible in opposition to supervisor's motion for summary judgment on prisoner's claim that supervisor was deliberately indifferent to threat of harm to prisoner in violation of Eighth Amendment); Orr v. Bank of Am., 285 F.3d 764, 774, 779 (9th Cir. 2002) (extract from deposition of defendant's employee was not properly authenticated and was hearsay, and thus was inadmissible on summary judgment); Gleklen v. Democratic Cong. Campaign Comm., Inc., 199 F.3d 1365, 1369 (D.C. Cir. 2000) (plaintiff's deposition testimony that someone told her about a conversation

file may include formal admissions made in response to a request under Federal Rule of Civil Procedure 36 or informal admissions by a party in documents, interrogatory answers, and testimony or statements on the record.[166]

If the materials submitted do not meet the evidentiary requirements, a party may move to strike the materials from the record and prevent their consideration by the court for purposes of deciding the summary judgment motion.[167] Thus, for example, a party may move to strike documents not properly authenticated, or to strike affidavits, answers to interrogatories, or deposition testimony (in whole or in part) that contain hearsay statements not subject to a valid exception or that contain information not based on personal knowledge.[168]

2. Affidavit in Conflict With Deposition

Pursuant to Federal Rule of Civil Procedure 56(c), the court may consider affidavits submitted by the moving or non-moving party in deciding whether summary judgment is appropriate. If the

---

between two witnesses is "sheer hearsay"; therefore, plaintiff could not testify regarding this conversation at trial).

[166]11 JAMES WM. MOORE ET AL., MOORE'S FEDERAL PRACTICE ¶ 56.14[2][d] (3d ed. 2003).

[167]Id. ¶ 56.14[4][a] (explaining that the party may file a formal motion to strike or, in the alternative, notify the court of the specific objection to the evidentiary materials and the grounds for striking the materials).

[168]See, e.g., Rogers v. City of Chi., 320 F.3d 748, 752, 91 FEP 273 (7th Cir. 2003) (affirming district court's refusal to consider plaintiff's affidavit because it contained inadmissible hearsay, relied on unauthenticated documents, and contradicted her deposition testimony); Green v. Pittsburgh Plate & Glass Co., 224 F. Supp. 2d 1348, 1358–59 (N.D. Ala. 2002) (granting motion to strike portions of plaintiff's deposition testimony that contained inadmissible hearsay, conclusory statements, and statements not based on personal knowledge; stricken testimony included statements that "everybody knew" that a certain employee had an alcohol problem and "[y]ou just hear things around the plant"); Murphy v. Ford Motor Co., 170 F.R.D. 82, 84–85 (D. Mass. 1997) (striking paragraphs of plaintiff's affidavit based on his belief and conclusory allegations, rather than personal knowledge); Duff v. Lobdell-Emery Mfg. Co., 926 F. Supp. 799, 802–03 (N.D. Ind. 1996) (granting plaintiff's motion to strike defendant's answers to interrogatories, submitted by defendant in support of summary judgment, because answers were signed by a person with no personal knowledge of the facts stated therein); Mustfov v. Superintendent of Chi. Police Dep't, 733 F. Supp. 283, 287 (N.D. Ill. 1990) (striking unauthenticated documents submitted by plaintiffs in response to summary judgment; plaintiffs' contention that the documents could be authenticated at trial "miss[es] the mark" because, to be considered at summary judgment, documents must be authenticated).

record evidence, including any affidavits,[169] establishes a genuine issue of material fact, then summary judgment must be denied.[170]

A party cannot attempt to create a material issue of fact by submitting an affidavit that flatly contradicts or is materially inconsistent with that party's deposition testimony. "When a party has given clear answers to unambiguous questions which negate the existence of any genuine issue of material fact, that party cannot thereafter create such an issue with an affidavit that merely contradicts, without explanation, previously given clear testimony."[171]

Faced with conflicting submissions, a court can disregard the affidavit unless the party can provide a legitimate explanation for

---

[169]A party may submit a declaration under penalty of perjury pursuant to 28 U.S.C. § 1746 instead of an affidavit.

[170]See FED. R. CIV. P. 56(c).

[171]See Cleveland v. Policy Mgmt. Sys. Corp., 526 U.S. 795, 806 (1999) (recognizing, without endorsing, "sham affidavit" holdings of every circuit; "a party cannot create a genuine issue of fact sufficient to survive summary judgment simply by contradicting his or her own previous sworn statement (by, say, filing a later affidavit that flatly contradicts that party's earlier sworn deposition) without explaining the contradiction or attempting to resolve the disparity"); see also Moore v. LaFayette Life Ins. Co., 458 F.3d 416, 434 (6th Cir. 2006) (exclusion of summary judgment affidavit warranted when affidavit could not be reconciled with claimant's earlier deposition testimony); In re CitX Corp., Inc., 448 F.3d 672, 679 (3d Cir. 2006) (affiant's deposition testimony that uncovered untruths in affiant's prior affidavit warranted district court's discounting of affidavit pursuant to sham affidavit doctrine); Orta-Castro v. Merck, Sharp & Dohme Quimica P.R., Inc., 447 F.3d 105, 110, 17 AD 1573 (1st Cir. 2006) (in action brought by female former employee against employer alleging disability discrimination, district court did not abuse discretion in disregarding affidavit because statements therein conflicted with answers employee had given in her deposition, and employee failed to provide satisfactory explanation for subsequent change in testimony); City of St. Joseph v. Southwestern Bell Tel., 439 F.3d 468, 475–76 (8th Cir. 2006) (city engineer's affidavit amounted to sham affidavit designed to create genuine issue of material fact where the engineer never claimed in his affidavit that he was confused or that he needed to clarify statements he made in his deposition); Beckel v. Wal-Mart Assocs., Inc., 301 F.3d 621, 623, 89 FEP 1208 (7th Cir. 2002) ("affidavits offered to contradict the affiant's deposition are so lacking in credibility as to be entitled to zero weight in summary judgment proceedings unless the affiant gives a plausible explanation for the discrepancy"). But cf. Briggs v. Potter, 463 F.3d 507, 512–13, 98 FEP 1722 (6th Cir. 2006) (no evidence that plaintiff's affidavit was a sham because trial court's finding that affidavit and deposition were inconsistent was premised on credibility determination that was contrary to court's obligation to view evidence in light most favorable to employee); Fast v. Southern Union Co., 149 F.3d 885, 892 n.7, 77 FEP 643 (8th Cir. 1998) (no evidence that plaintiff's affidavit was a sham because, in deposition testimony, plaintiff provided evidence that defendant's decision to discharge plaintiff as part of a reduction in force was motivated by age).

the inconsistencies. If the plaintiff establishes a satisfactory explanation, the affidavit may be considered.[172] Courts also disregard affidavits of non-party witnesses that contradict their prior testimony or sworn statements.[173] One court has applied the "sham affidavit" principle to a plaintiff's material modification of his deposition testimony by submitting an errata sheet.[174]

---

[172]*See* Burns v. Board of County Comm'rs, 330 F.3d 1275, 1282, 91 FEP 1726 (10th Cir. 2003) (factors a court should consider in deciding whether an affidavit is a sham include whether the party was cross-examined during deposition, whether the party had access to relevant evidence at the time of the deposition, whether there is newly discovered evidence, and whether the affidavit explains a point of confusion in the deposition); *Beckel*, 301 F.3d at 623–25 (plaintiff did not provide plausible explanation for inconsistency between affidavit and deposition testimony because, although plaintiff argued that defense counsel did not address the issue of an alleged threat by management to terminate plaintiff, plaintiff's lawyer could have asked plaintiff questions about the alleged threat at the deposition); Bailey v. United Airlines, 279 F.3d 194, 201, 88 FEP 22 (3d Cir. 2002) (plaintiff's deposition testimony that he received phone call May 4, 1993, from employer to come to San Francisco May 6 "to be terminated" was ambiguous, and could be supplemented with clarifying affidavit that stated that phone call did not specify termination, plus affidavits of other witnesses at meeting May 6, 1993, who were surprised to learn about the termination on that date); Williams v. Raytheon Co., 220 F.3d 16, 20, 88 FEP 1748 (1st Cir. 2000) (no explanation offered for deposition-affidavit conflict as to when plaintiff became aware of his discharge from employment; at deposition, plaintiff testified he was discharged on July 11, 1995, but, in affidavit, claimed he did not know of discharge until August); *Raskin*, 125 F.3d at 63 (plaintiff could not create an issue of fact on his age discrimination claim of failure to promote by filing an affidavit "at odds" with his deposition testimony; at deposition, plaintiff testified that he could not recall what was discussed during a meeting with company president but, then, in an affidavit, claimed that the president expressed concern that plaintiff would not remain with the company long enough to learn the new position); *Halperin*, 128 F.3d at 197–98 (plaintiff could not create a genuine issue of fact on ADA claim by submitting affidavit stating that, at the time defendant discharged him, he was able to return to work, when he testified on deposition that he was unable to work for at least another 5 months); Gonzalez Garcia v. Puerto Rico Elec. Power Auth., 214 F. Supp. 2d 194, 203–04 (D.P.R. 2002) (court will not consider plaintiff's affidavit that she received harassing phone calls from supervisors because it "directly contravenes her earlier deposition testimony that she received frequent, apparently social phone calls" from management while she was at home recovering from an injury); *see also* Pryor v. Seyfarth, Shaw, Fairweather & Geraldson, 212 F.3d 976, 978 (7th Cir. 2000) (court refused to consider plaintiff's affidavit because it attempted to "bolster" her prior deposition testimony regarding the alleged incidents of sexual harassment).

[173]*E.g.*, Darnell v. Target Stores, 16 F.3d 174, 177–79, 64 FEP 53 (7th Cir. 1994) (plaintiff could not create issues of fact by relying on affidavits of co-workers that contradicted their own previous deposition testimony, and assertion that plaintiff's job was difficult and required him to perform unpleasant task under an insufferable boss).

[174]*Burns*, 330 F.3d at 1281–82. In *Burns*, the plaintiff alleged that he was discriminatorily discharged. On the deposition errata sheet, plaintiff modified his

An affidavit that supplements or explains that party's deposition testimony may properly be considered by the court.[175]

3. *Federal Rule of Civil Procedure 56(f)*

Federal Rule of Civil Procedure 56(f) provides that:

> Should it appear from the affidavits of a party opposing the [summary judgment] motion that the party cannot for reasons stated present by affidavit facts essential to justify the party's opposition, the court may refuse the application for judgment or may order a continuance to permit affidavits to be obtained or depositions to be taken or discovery to be had or may make such other order as is just.[176]

Courts generally require that a party seeking additional discovery under Rule 56(f) show that it was diligent in seeking discovery prior to the filing of the summary judgment motion.[177] This involves consideration of several factors, including examination of

---

straightforward responses to two questions to significantly change the import of the response, and particularly to suggest, contrary to the deposition testimony, that the employee's misconduct was only one of the reasons for his discharge. *Id.* at 1281. The Tenth Circuit concluded that the district court correctly disregarded plaintiff's modified testimony as an "attempt to rewrite portions of his deposition." *Id.* at 1281–82; *cf.* Norelus v. Denny's Inc., 2000 WL 33541630 (S.D. Fla. Mar. 21, 2000) (plaintiff submitted 63-page errata sheet making 868 changes to her deposition testimony; changes in testimony did not prevent summary judgment and resulted in fee award against plaintiff's counsel), *rev'd and remanded sub nom.* Amlong & Amlong, P.A. v. Denny's, Inc., 457 F.3d 1180, 98 FEP 1617 (11th Cir. 2006).

[175]*See* Scamihorn v. General Truck Drivers, 282 F.3d 1078, 1085–86 n.7, 82 FEP 40 (9th Cir. 2002) (in FMLA case, plaintiff alleged that he was not returned to same position after leave to care for his father who was suffering from depression; in light of the corroborating statements from his doctors, father's affidavit regarding his alleged depression and seeking of counseling did not contradict earlier deposition testimony that downplayed his emotional problems and treatment); Selenke v. Medical Imaging of Colo., 248 F.3d 1249, 1258 (10th Cir. 2001) (plaintiff's subsequent affidavit, detailing her alleged breathing difficulties, clarified her ambiguous deposition testimony regarding the "major life activities" affected by her sinusitis, her alleged disability); Rollins v. TechSouth, Inc., 833 F.2d 1525, 1531 (11th Cir. 1987) (affidavit was not in conflict with deposition so as to warrant its exclusion; at deposition, plaintiff was questioned about age-related comments at meetings plaintiff attended, but she was not asked whether the supervisor made any age-related comments in personal conversations).

[176]Fed. R. Civ. P. 56(f).

[177]*See, e.g.*, Ayala-Gerena v. Bristol Myers-Squibb Co., 95 F.3d 86, 92 (1st Cir. 1996) (appellants failed to exercise due diligence before motion for summary judgment was filed as the discovery period was extended twice, for a total of 18 months, and appellants did not file any discovery requests until after the first extension and

the earlier efforts to obtain and reasonableness of access to the discovery, the nature and amount of discovery already taken, and whether the party could reasonably have anticipated a need for the requested additional discovery.[178]

The motion must be supported by an affidavit that demonstrates how additional discovery will assist the party in opposing a pending summary judgment motion.[179] The affidavit cannot simply state that that additional discovery is needed or speculate as to what information might be uncovered. Rather, the affidavit must contain specific information, such as: "(1) the nature of the uncompleted discovery, such as what facts are reasonably expected to create a

---

only 2 weeks before the discovery deadline); Williams v. R.H. Donnelley, Inc., 199 F. Supp. 2d 172, 179–80 (S.D.N.Y. 2002) (denying request for additional discovery submitted after late filing of plaintiff's opposition to summary judgment where witness was identified during discovery period, but plaintiff failed to depose him), aff'd, 368 F.3d 123 (2d Cir. 2004).

[178]See, e.g., Majewski v. Automatic Data Processing, Inc., 274 F.3d 1106, 1114, 87 FEP 1074 (6th Cir. 2001) ("Where the full period for pretrial discovery has run its course, a party should generally be precluded from reopening discovery months after it has closed in a last-ditch attempt to salvage a deficient claim or defense."); Dyson v. Winfield, 113 F. Supp. 2d 35, 42 (D.D.C. 2000) (denying request to continue discovery because the pretrial discovery period was 2 years long, and plaintiff failed to alert court to discovery issues until 5 months after defendant moved for summary judgment), aff'd, 21 Fed. Appx. 2 (D.C. Cir. 2001); City of Rome v. Glanton, 958 F. Supp. 1026, 1039 (E.D. Pa.), aff'd mem., 133 F.3d 909 (3d Cir. 1997) (denying Rule 56(f) motion because defendants had sufficient time to conduct discovery, a large amount of information regarding both plaintiff and defendants' claims already had been produced, and court had mediated discovery disputes).

[179]See, e.g., White v. BFI Waste Servs., LLC, 375 F.3d 288, 295, 94 FEP 73 (4th Cir. 2004) (Rule 56(f) motion properly denied upon magistrate's finding that plaintiff did not exercise sufficient diligence to obtain requested discovery by waiting until just before the discovery cutoff to demand certain documents); Stella v. Mineta, 284 F.3d 135, 147, 88 FEP 854 (D.C. Cir. 2002) (remanding for additional consideration of summary judgment and Rule 56(f) motions because district court applied wrong legal standard on plaintiff's failure-to-promote claim and, applying the correct legal standard, the requested discovery might be necessary; plaintiff's affidavit specified that she was seeking discovery as to which employees received promotions and that she had not obtained the discovery because defendant failed to respond to discovery requests); Bradley v. United States, 299 F.3d 197 (3d Cir. 2002) (affirming denial of Rule 56(f) motion because plaintiff failed to identify with specificity what information she was seeking and how it would preclude summary judgment); Roark v. City of Hazen, 189 F.3d 758, 762 (8th Cir. 1999) (plaintiff's motion failed to state what discovery was needed and, instead, "did little more than detail the other cases that were occupying his counsel's time"); Stanback v. Best Diversified Prod., Inc., 180 F.3d 903, 911, 75 FEP 45 (8th Cir. 1999) (denying request for additional discovery because plaintiff never submitted a Rule 56(f) affidavit and her contention as to what the proposed discovery would show was unsupported speculation).

genuine issue of material fact; (2) the manner by which those facts are reasonably expected to create a genuine issue of material fact; (3) the efforts the affiant has made to obtain those facts; and (4) the reasons these efforts were unsuccessful."[180]

A Rule 56(f) motion may be submitted within a reasonable time after the motion for summary judgment is filed, or can be submitted with the party's opposition to that motion.[181] In response to such a motion, the court may deny the request for additional discovery, order a continuance to take discovery, or "make such other order as is just,"[182] such as denying the motion for summary judgment without prejudice or continuing a hearing, if the non-moving party "has not had an opportunity to make full discovery."[183]

---

[180]MOORE'S FEDERAL PRACTICE ¶ 56.10[8][c] (3d ed. 1997); *see, e.g.*, Oneida Indian Nation v. City of Sherrill, 337 F.3d 139, 167–68 (2d Cir. 2003) (affirming denial of Rule 56(f) motion because city had sufficient opportunity to conduct discovery on issues for summary judgment and had failed to specify what facts or documents it was requesting and, instead, simply submitted a list of issues on which it wanted more information); Horvath v. Keystone Health Plan E., Inc., 333 F.3d 450, 458 (3d Cir. 2003) (no abuse of discretion in district court's denial of plaintiff's Rule 56(f) motion because the requested discovery had previously been denied by the court on two motions to compel); Allen v. CSX Transp., Inc., 325 F.3d 768, 775–76 (6th Cir. 2003) (district court did not abuse its discretion in denying plaintiffs' Rule 56(f) motion because discovery sought had no bearing on the legal question at issue); Fairclough v. Board of County Comm'rs, 244 F. Supp. 2d 581, 586, 91 FEP 268 (D. Md. 2003) (granting plaintiff additional time for discovery; plaintiff's affidavit identified the specific items for discovery, and these would have bearing on his claims of discriminatory discharge on the basis of religion).

[181]MOORE'S FEDERAL PRACTICE ¶ 56.10[8][a] (3d ed. 1997) (citations omitted); *see, e.g.*, Kalis v. Colgate-Palmolive Co., 231 F.3d 1049, 1058 n.5 (7th Cir. 2000) (although there is not a specific time requirement, plaintiff's Rule 56(f) motion was not timely because it was filed 3 months after submission of the summary judgment motion and 1 month past the deadline for plaintiff's response); Rodriguez-Cuervos v. Wal-Mart Stores, Inc., 181 F.3d 15, 22–23 (1st Cir. 1999) (affirming denial of 56(f) motion where plaintiff made the request for further discovery after the court granted summary judgment to defendant; "a party may not attempt to meet a summary judgment challenge head-on but fall back on Rule 56(f) if its first effort is unsuccessful") (internal quotation omitted); *Ayala-Gerena*, 95 F.3d at 92 (plaintiff's Rule 56(f) motion was not timely because it was first made at the pretrial conference and after plaintiffs filed their opposition and supplemental opposition to summary judgment, which made no reference to the need for additional discovery); Nguyen v. CNA Corp., 44 F.3d 234, 242 (4th Cir. 1995) ("non-moving party on a motion for summary judgment may not sit idly by as the deadline to respond approaches; instead, the non-moving party must respond to the motion once the moving party has satisfied its initial burden").

[182]FED. R. CIV. P. 56(f).

[183]Celotex Corp. v. Catrett, 477 U.S. 317, 326 (1986). As the Supreme Court has explained, the remedies provided in Rule 56(f) are adequate for dealing with "potential problems [from] premature motions" for summary judgment. *Id.*

VII. JURY TRIAL

A. Issues Tried to Jury and Bench

Since the enactment of the 1991 Civil Rights Act amendments, jury trials are available to the parties in most employment discrimination cases alleging disparate treatment.[184] A jury, however, is not required if the plaintiff either abandons or loses by way of summary judgment or judgment as a matter of law his or her claims for compensatory damages and punitive damages.[185] Claims for back wages and other equitable relief remain issues for the judge on which there is no right to a jury trial.[186]

Similarly, issues of post-judgment relief, such as reinstatement to employment or "front pay," remain issues for the court and not the jury.[187] Generally, the cases hold that an employee who has

---

[184]See 42 U.S.C. § 1981a(c) (2000).

[185]See 42 U.S.C. § 1981a(c)(1) (2000) ("If a complaining party seeks compensatory or punitive damages under this section . . . any party may demand a trial by jury."); 42 U.S.C. § 1981a(b)(2) (2000) ("Compensatory damages awarded under this section shall not include backpay . . . or any other type of relief authorized under [42 U.S.C. § 2000e-5(g).]"); see also Lutz v. Glendale Union High Sch., 403 F.3d 1061, 1063, 16 AD 1031 (9th Cir. 2005) (plaintiff waived jury for liability issues by not making timely demand).

[186]See 42 U.S.C. § 2000e-5(g) (2000) ("If court finds that the respondent has intentionally engaged in . . . an unlawful employment practice . . . , the court may enjoin such unlawful employment practice, and order such affirmative action as may be appropriate, which may include, . . . reinstatement or hiring of employees, with or without back pay . . . , or any other equitable relief as the court deems appropriate."); see also Lutz, 403 F.3d at 1069–70 (no Seventh Amendment right to jury determination of back pay); Kramer v. Banc of Am. Sec., LLC, 355 F.3d 961, 964, 15 AD 141 (7th Cir. 2004) (42 U.S.C. § 1981a(a)(2) does not allow compensatory and punitive damages or a jury trial for retaliation claims under the ADA, because the above remedy section fails to specifically incorporate the ADA retaliation section), cert. denied, 542 U.S. 932 (2004); McCue v. Kansas Dep't of Human Res., 165 F.3d 784, 791–92, 78 FEP 1183 (10th Cir. 1999) ("Damages awarded under section 2000e-5(g) are equitable relief to be determined by the court."); Allison v. Citgo Petroleum Corp., 151 F.3d 402, 423 n.19, 81 FEP 501 (5th Cir. 1998) (right to a jury trial provided in 42 U.S.C. § 1981a(c) "does not include the power to determine the availability of back pay or front pay" as "[t]hese are equitable remedies to which no right to jury trial attaches"). But see Rhoads v. Federal Deposit Ins. Corp., 286 F. Supp. 2d 532, 537, 14 AD 1701 (D. Md. 2003) (although court granted judgment as matter of law at close of all evidence, plaintiff was still entitled to a jury trial because defendant never specifically objected to having jury determine back pay and even proposed a jury instruction on back pay), aff'd, 94 Fed. Appx. 187 (4th Cir.), cert. denied, 543 U.S. 927 (2004).

[187]See 42 U.S.C. § 2000e-5(g) (2000); EEOC v. W&O, Inc., 213 F.3d 600, 618–19, 83 FEP 117 (11th Cir. 2000) (because front pay and reinstatement are forms of

prevailed on a discharge claim will be entitled to reinstatement, rather than front pay, unless circumstances make that impracticable, such as hostility in the workplace.[188]

In awarding equitable relief, the court may hold a separate evidentiary hearing following the jury verdict[189] or may be assisted by an advisory jury in determining the amount of back pay or front pay to award.[190] With the consent of the parties, the issues of back pay and front pay may be tried to the jury; such a verdict will have "the same effect as if a trial by jury had been a matter of right."[191]

---

equitable relief, the award of such relief is for the judge, not the jury, to decide); *McCue*, 165 F.3d at 791 (vacating jury award of front pay because appropriate amount of award should be determined by judge); Martini v. Federal Nat'l Mortgage Ass'n, 178 F.3d 1336, 1348–49, 80 FEP 1 (D.C. Cir. 1999) (front pay is an equitable remedy); *see also* Pollard v. E.I. Du Pont de Nemours, 532 U.S. 843, 848, 85 FEP 1217 (2001) (front pay not an element of compensatory damages under the 1991 Civil Rights Act amendments).

[188]*See, e.g.*, Che v. Massachusetts Bay Transp. Auth., 342 F.3d 31, 42, 43 & n.1., 44, 92 FEP 895 (1st Cir. 2003) (factors considered by the district court include: "(1) the strength of the evidence . . . ; (2) whether the discharged employee has found comparable work; (3) the absence of a property right in the position . . . ; and (4) the ineligibility of the employee for the position, due to failure to meet established qualifications" (quoting Quint v. A.E. Staley Mfg. Co., 172 F.3d 1, 19 (1st Cir. 1999)); Julian v. City of Houston, 314 F.3d 721, 728, 90 FEP 887 (5th Cir. 2002) ("Although reinstatement is the preferred equitable remedy for a discriminatory discharge, . . . front pay—money awarded for future lost compensation—is appropriate when reinstatement is not feasible"); *W&O, Inc.*, 213 F.3d at 619 (in deciding whether to award front pay, rather than reinstatement, courts look at various factors, including "whether discord and antagonism between the parties would render reinstatement ineffective as a make-whole remedy") (internal quotation omitted); Williams v. Pharmacia, Inc., 137 F.3d 944, 951, 76 FEP 310 (7th Cir. 1998) (front pay is only awarded if reinstatement is "inappropriate, such as when there is no position available or the employer-employee relationship is pervaded by hostility").

[189]*See, e.g.*, Gotthardt v. National R.R. Passenger Corp., 191 F.3d 1148, 1156, 80 FEP 1528 (9th Cir. 1999) (affirming district court's determination, after an evidentiary hearing, that reinstatement was impossible because plaintiff was suffering from post-traumatic stress disorder and unable to perform any job and that front pay was appropriate). *But see* Davoll v. Webb, 194 F.3d 1116, 1142–43 (10th Cir. 1999) (district court did not abuse its discretion in refusing to hold an evidentiary hearing on issues of back pay and front pay because defendant agreed to have equitable relief decided on basis of parties' written submissions, and defendant could have presented relevant evidence at trial).

[190]*See* FED. R. CIV. P. 39(c).

[191]FED. R. CIV. P. 39(c); *see Julian*, 314 F.3d at 728 (district court should determine whether front pay is appropriate and the amount, although the court may be assisted by an advisory jury to establish the amount of award); Pals v. Schepel Buick & GMC Truck, Inc., 220 F.3d 495, 501, 10 AD 1345 (7th Cir. 2000) (affirming jury's award of back pay because defendant demanded a jury trial of all issues in its answer to plaintiff's complaint).

B. Jury Instructions and Verdict Forms

Under the Federal Rules of Civil Procedure, objections to jury instructions must be made before the jury begins to deliberate.[192] Courts prefer that errors in jury instructions be corrected immediately upon detection of the errors by resubmitting correct instructions to the jury, although the use of post-verdict instructions is not automatically reversible.[193]

In addition to being timely, the objection must specifically state the material objected to and the basis for the objection.[194] Some courts require that the objecting party also propose an alternate instruction.[195] A properly preserved objection to an instruction will be governed by the "harmless error" standard of Federal Rule of Civil Procedure 61. An error in a jury instruction is harmless if the appellant suffered no prejudice.[196] If, however, the objection is

---

[192]See FED. R. CIV. P. 51; see also Estes v. Georgetown Univ., 231 F. Supp. 2d 279, 283, 90 FEP 698 (D.D.C. 2002) (defendant's objection to instruction was untimely because it was made after jury retired to deliberate). But cf. Rose v. New York City Bd. of Educ., 257 F.3d 156, 160, 86 FEP 380 (2d Cir. 2001) (plaintiff's failure to object after judge read instruction to jury did not constitute waiver of the objection because plaintiff had already twice objected to the proposed jury instruction and further objection would have been futile).

[193]See Bonner v. Guccione, 178 F.3d 581, 588 (2d Cir. 1999) (upholding postverdict supplemental instructions and submission of additional jury verdict form where incorrect instruction as to applicable statute of limitations likely led jury to award no damages, and language of supplemental instruction was not coercive; but instructing that trial court should have corrected error immediately upon detection and not waited until after jury returned a verdict).

[194]See FED. R. CIV. P. 51; see also Zhang v. American Gem Seafoods, Inc., 339 F.3d 1020, 1030, 92 FEP 641 (9th Cir. 2003) (appellants waived objection to instruction because they failed to specify grounds of objection, i.e., that "substantial factor" and "motivating factor" standards should be identical), cert. denied, 541 U.S. 902 (2004); Foley v. Commonwealth Elec. Co., 312 F.3d 517, 521–22, 90 FEP 895 (1st Cir. 2002) (objection by plaintiff's counsel did not satisfy standard of Fed. R. Civ. P. 51 because counsel did not state any grounds for the objection, but simply made a general reference to the instruction at issue); Romano v. U-Haul Int'l, 233 F.3d 655, 663, 84 FEP 795 (1st Cir. 2000) (general awareness by court and parties that alternative instruction could have been given does not excuse appellant's failure to specifically object to given instruction).

[195]See, e.g., Kehoe v. Anheuser-Busch, Inc., 96 F.3d 1095, 1104 (8th Cir. 1996). But see Pavon v. Swift Transp. Co., 192 F.3d 902, 907–08, 80 FEP 1557 (9th Cir. 1999) (simply providing an alternative instruction is not sufficient; party must tell court it has made error).

[196]E.g., Pivirotto v. Innovative Sys., Inc., 191 F.3d 344, 357–58, 80 FEP 1269 (3d Cir. 1999) (trial court erroneously instructed jury that plaintiff in Title VII gender

not properly preserved, a reviewing court will reverse only if the instructions constitute plain error.[197] This demanding standard requires a showing of substantial injustice.[198] When a party invites the error by requesting the substance of the instructions given, the objection is waived and no plain error will be found.[199]

Although the trial court's decision on whether to give a specific jury instruction is reviewed for an abuse of discretion,[200] the

---

case must prove that she was replaced by male, but error was harmless because "in light of the total record . . . no jury would have found [for the defendant] solely on the basis of the [erroneous instruction]"). *But see* Norville v. Staten Island Univ. Hosp., 196 F.3d 89, 100–101, 81 FEP 324 (2d Cir. 1999) (trial court's failure to instruct jury that offer of inferior position when comparable position is available does not qualify as reasonable accommodation under ADA gave misimpression that employer may offer any accommodation, including reassignment to inferior position, and that plaintiff is required to accept any such accommodation defendant offers, and was prejudicial error because jury found for plaintiff on all elements of her claim except reasonable accommodation issue).

[197]*See, e.g.*, Gray v. Genlyte Group, Inc., 289 F.3d 128, 133–34, 88 FEP 1055 (1st Cir.), *cert. denied*, 537 U.S. 1001 (2002) (court would review jury instructions for plain error only because plaintiff failed to make specific objections before jury retired to deliberate); Medlock v. Ortho Biotech, Inc., 164 F.3d 545, 553, 78 FEP 1592 (10th Cir. 1999) (although defendant objected generally to propriety of giving mixed-motive instruction, it did not object to specific language in verdict form that, on appeal, it claims is misleading; therefore, review is limited to whether it was "plain error"); Rizzo v. Children's World Learning Ctrs., Inc., 173 F.3d 254, 262 (5th Cir. 1995) (because error was first raised on appeal, reversal is proper only if error was so significant as to " 'seriously affect the fairness, integrity or public reputation of judicial proceedings' ") (quoting United States v. Olano, 507 U.S. 725 (1993)).

[198]*See* Farley v. Nationwide Mut. Ins. Co., 197 F.3d 1322, 1329–30, 10 AD 87 (11th Cir. 1999) (reversal for plain error in jury instructions or verdict form will occur "only in exceptional cases where the error is so fundamental as to result in a miscarriage of justice" and the appellant must prove that "the challenged instruction was an incorrect statement of the law and [that] it was probably responsible for an incorrect verdict, leading to substantial injustice") (internal quotation omitted). *Compare* Hernandez v. Crawford Bldg. Material Co., 321 F.3d 528, 532–33, 91 FEP 97 (5th Cir. 2003) (holding that district court committed plain error because jury instruction that the defendant's counterclaim for theft "could support a finding of retaliatory employment action" was an "obvious misstatement of the law that led to substantial injustice to the defendant") *with* Kozlowski v. Hampton Sch. Bd., 77 Fed. Appx. 133, 145–46 (4th Cir. 2003) (although instruction that ADEA makes it unlawful to refuse to renew an employment contract "solely because of" age was erroneous, instruction did not rise to the level of plain error because court gave a correct and extended instruction that age had to be a "determining factor").

[199]*See, e.g.*, *Farley*, 197 F.3d at 1331; Johnson v. Paradise Valley Unified Sch. Dist., 251 F.3d 1222, 1226 n.3, 11 AD 1389 (9th Cir. 2001) (defendant-employer's stipulation to specific instruction at trial precludes it from challenging instruction on appeal).

[200]*See, e.g.*, Moore v. Robertson Fire Prot. Dist., 249 F.3d 786, 789, 89 FEP 350 (8th Cir. 2001) (trial court did not abuse discretion by refusing to instruct jury

instructions are reviewed de novo to determine whether, on the whole, they accurately stated the law and properly guided the jury on the issues.[201] Courts have held generally that jury instructions are not deficient simply because they do not contain certain key words or phrases, as long as they accurately state the law.[202]

Whether the jury ought to be charged on the *McDonnell Douglas* prima facie case receives different answers among the circuits. Some courts reject such an instruction on the ground of jury confusion.[203] Other circuits allow or even demand such a charge. In

---

specifically as to "pretext" where charge as a whole provided proper legal standard, evidence of pretext was scant, and, in any event, plaintiff was allowed to argue pretext to jury and, therefore, suffered no prejudice); Beachy v. Boise Cascade Corp., 191 F.3d 1010, 1013, 9 AD 1258 (9th Cir. 1999) (trial court's refusal in ADA case to instruct jury on perceived disability not an abuse of discretion where undisputed evidence established that plaintiff did have impairment); Banks v. Travelers Cos., 180 F.3d 358, 366, 80 FEP 30 (2d Cir. 1999) (trial court did not abuse discretion by refusing to give a "same actor" instruction where, although requested instruction properly stated law, trial court allowed defendant's counsel to make argument to jury and jury did not need an instruction to "draw this commonsensical inference").

[201]See Foster v. Time Warner Entm't Co., L.P., 250 F.3d 1189, 1197–98 (8th Cir. 2001) (review of jury instructions is limited to whether they "viewed on the whole, fairly and adequately represent the evidence and applicable law in light of the issues presented to the jury in a particular case"); Pavon v. Swift Transp. Co., 192 F.3d 902, 907, 80 FEP 1557, 1560 (9th Cir. 1999) (district court's formulation of jury instructions is reviewed for abuse of discretion, but when claim is that instruction misstated law, review is de novo); Medlock v. Ortho Biotech, Inc., 164 F.3d 545, 552, 78 FEP 1592, 1597 (10th Cir. 1999) ("Instructions as a whole need not be flawless, but we must be satisfied that, on hearing the instructions, the jury understood the issues to be resolved and its duty to resolve them.").

[202]See, e.g., Gibson v. City of Louisville, 336 F.3d 511, 514 (6th Cir. 2003) (affirming jury instruction using phrase "because of," rather than "motivating factor" as requested by plaintiff; although instruction could have been more precise, it was accurate as jury was clearly charged with answering whether plaintiff was the victim of unlawful discrimination); Hartley v. Dillards, Inc., 310 F.3d 1054, 1059, 91 FEP 1217 (8th Cir. 2002) (no harmful error where instruction stated that age must be "a" determining factor, rather than "the" factor, because, taken as a whole, the jury instructions were a correct statement of the law); White v. New Hampshire Dep't of Corr., 221 F.3d 254, 263–64, 83 FEP 851 (1st Cir. 2000) (trial court did not err by refusing to explicitly instruct jury that plaintiff had to prove that defendant's given reason for discharge was pretext and that real reason was retaliatory intent where instruction stated that plaintiff had to prove that "the employer took the adverse employment action because she had filed a sexual harassment claim"); *Farley*, 197 F.3d at 1333 (upholding trial court's instructions that plaintiff's disability had to be "a motivating factor in the discharge" and that plaintiff's age had to be "one of the reasons" for plaintiff's discharge and a factor that "made a difference in the outcome").

[203]See, e.g., Sanghvi v. City of Claremont, 328 F.3d 532, 538–41 (9th Cir. 2003) (barring an instruction on the prima facie case in housing discrimination case), *cert.*

Perez v. Texas Department of Criminal Justice,[204] the court found plain error in a Title VII charge that described the fourth element of the prima facie case as follows:

> [t]o establish discrimination by using indirect evidence in this case, the plaintiff must prove by a preponderance of the evidence that one or more similarly situated non-Hispanic employees who engaged in criminal activity were treated more favorably. In comparing the nature of the offense at issue and the nature of the discipline imposed, the quantity and quality of the other employees' misconduct must be of comparable seriousness to the misconduct of the plaintiff.[205]

The circuits also disagree on whether the jury should be instructed that it may infer discrimination if it disbelieves the employer's proffered explanation (the "pretext" instruction).

The Second, Third, and Tenth Circuits support a pretext instruction, in some instances finding it mandatory. These courts regard the pretext formula as important or even essential to proving discrimination, and conclude that juries are unlikely to intuit this standard on their own.[206] The Seventh Circuit, however, discourages the

---

denied, 540 U.S. 1075 (2004); Achor v. Riverside Golf Club, 117 F.3d 339, 341 (7th Cir. 1997) ("elements that make up a 'prima facie case' are for the judge, not the jury").

[204] 395 F.3d 206, 94 FEP 1729 (5th Cir. 2004), *cert. denied,* 126 S. Ct. 545 (2005).

[205] *Id.* at 211–12; *see also* Rodriguez-Torres v. Caribbean Forms Mfr., Inc., 399 F.3d 52, 58–59, 95 FEP 353 (1st Cir. 2005) (endorsing jury charge on prima facie case; district court erred only in its description of the fourth element, but error was harmless); Watson v. Southeastern Pa. Transp. Auth., 207 F.3d 207, 221–22 (3d Cir. 2000) (holding that it is proper "to instruct the jury that it may consider whether the factual predicates necessary to establish the prima facie case have been shown," though it is otherwise error to instruct the jury on the *McDonnell Douglas* burden-shifting scheme); Kehoe v. Anheuser-Busch, Inc., 96 F.3d 1095, 1105, 71 FEP 1749 (8th Cir. 1996) ("the district courts in this circuit are constrained to instruct juries on the elements of the prima facie case").

[206] *See, e.g.,* Miller v. Eby Realty Group LLC, 396 F.3d 1105, 1115, 95 FEP 65 (10th Cir. 2005) (pretext instruction "is required where, as here, a rational finder of fact could reasonably find the [employer's] explanation false and could 'infer from the falsity of the explanation that the employer is dissembling to cover up a discriminatory purpose' ") (quoting Townsend v. Lumbermens Mut. Cas. Co., 294 F.3d 1232, 1241 (10th Cir. 2002)); Smith v. Borough of Wilkinsburg, 147 F.3d 272, 279–81, 77 FEP 119 (3d Cir. 1998) ("the jurors must be instructed that they are entitled to infer, but need not, that the plaintiff's ultimate burden of demonstrating intentional discrimination by a preponderance of the evidence can be met if they find that the facts needed to make up the prima facie case have been established and they disbelieve the employer's explanation for its decision"; finding refusal to give pretext instruction reversible error); Cabrera v. Jakabovitz, 24 F.3d 372, 382 (2d Cir. 1994)

use of pretext instructions, finding that permissive inferences seldom require instructions and the concept of pretext is liable to confuse the jury.[207] Other circuits less decisively discourage their use.[208]

The Sixth and Eleventh Circuits appear neither to require nor discourage such instructions.[209] And although the Fifth Circuit in *Ratliff v. City of Gainesville, Texas*[210] supported a pretext instruction, a subsequent panel reviewing an FLSA verdict followed *Ratliff* only grudgingly, and urged the full court to review the case and overrule it en banc.[211]

One court has held that failure to give a "business judgment" instruction is reversible error if the employer can show that the error caused it prejudice.[212] Prejudice may be shown where the instruction goes to the heart of the defense, such as when the employer argues that a termination was based on budgetary constraints[213] or that the use of a physical test to screen job applicants

---

(in Title VIII housing discrimination case, "the jury needs to be told . . . [that it] is entitled to infer, but need not infer, that this burden has been met if they find that the [facts needed to make a prima facie case] have been established and they disbelieve the defendant's explanation," though finding failure to give instruction harmless in context of entire charge).

[207]Gehring v. Case Corp., 43 F.3d 340, 343 (7th Cir. 1994) (instruction on permissible inference where employer's explanation not believed is "unnecessary"; "the judge may and usually should leave the subject to the argument of counsel").

[208]*See, e.g.,* Moore v. Robertson Fire Prot. Dist., 249 F.3d 786, 790 & n.9, 89 FEP 350 (8th Cir. 2001) ("[w]e do not express any view as to whether it ever would be reversible error for a trial court to fail to give a pretext instruction, though we tend to doubt it"); Fite v. Digital Equip. Corp., 232 F.3d 3, 7, 84 FEP 524 (1st Cir. 2000) (expressing doubt "that such an explanation is compulsory, even if properly requested"). Although these decisions do not go so far as to find pretext instructions reversible error, they clearly set a different tone for the district courts charging juries in these circuits.

[209]Williams v. Eau Claire Pub. Schs., 397 F.3d 441, 446, 95 FEP 382 (6th Cir.) (jury instructions not required to "be cast in the language of pretext or the framework of shifting burdens of McDonnell Douglas"), *cert. denied,* 126 S. Ct. 68 (2005); Conroy v. Abraham Chevrolet-Tampa, 375 F.3d 1228, 1233, 94 FEP 107 (11th Cir.) (circuit does not require pretext instruction), *cert. denied,* 543 U.S. 1035 (2004).

[210]256 F.3d 355, 359–60, 86 FEP 472 (5th Cir. 2001).

[211]*See* Kanida v. Gulf Coast Med. Pers. LP, 363 F.3d 568, 573–77 (5th Cir. 2004).

[212]*See* Scamardo v. Scott County, 189 F.3d 707, 711, 80 FEP 1140 (8th Cir. 1999).

[213]*Id.* (granting new trial where defendant's position was that plaintiff was terminated due to budgetary constraints and trial court rejected proposed instruction, stating "you may not return a verdict for plaintiff just because you might disagree with defendant's decision or believe it to be harsh or unreasonable"). *But see* Munoz v. Oceanside Resorts, Inc., 223 F.3d 1340, 1347 (11th Cir. 2000) (upholding trial

is "job-related and consistent with business necessity" under the ADEA.[214]

Since the Supreme Court's decisions in *Faragher v. City of Boca Raton*[215] and *Burlington Industries, Inc. v. Ellerth*,[216] courts have addressed the propriety and content of an instruction on the employer's affirmative defense to alleged sexual harassment.[217] In addition, since the Supreme Court's decision in *Kolstad v. American Dental Ass'n*,[218] courts of appeal have addressed the propriety and content of punitive damages instructions.[219]

Courts generally hold that if the evidence is sufficient to allow a jury to find that both forbidden and permissible motives played a role in the employment decision, then the jury should be given a mixed-motive instruction, shifting the burden to the defendant

---

court's refusal to supplement pretext instruction that required jury to find both that employer's reasons were false and that discrimination was real reason with statement that "a plaintiff may not establish that an employer's proffered reason is pretextual merely by questioning the wisdom of the employer's reason"; original instruction's falsity requirement was more onerous to plaintiff than requested supplemental language).

[214]*See* Belk v. Southwestern Bell Tel. Co., 194 F.3d 946, 953 (8th Cir. 1999) (trial court's failure to instruct on "business necessity" was prejudicial error where defendant presented relevant and persuasive evidence that physical performance test was job-related and consistent with business necessity).

[215]524 U.S. 742 (1998).

[216]524 U.S. 775 (1998).

[217]*See, e.g.*, Harrison v. Eddy Potash, Inc., 248 F.3d 1014, 1024, 85 FEP 990 (10th Cir. 2001) (affirming trial court's rejection of defendant-employer's proposed instruction as contrary to law of *Faragher/Ellerth*, and finding no abuse of discretion by trial court's refusal to instruct jury that generalized fear of retaliation does not excuse failure to report sexual harassment where, although this requested instruction properly stated law, court's general instruction on *Faragher/Ellerth* defense properly conveyed issue and law to jury); Savino v. C.P. Hall Co., 199 F.3d 925, 934, 82 FEP 1245 (7th Cir. 1999) (upholding trial court's decision to issue affirmative defense instruction and its content).

[218]527 U.S. 526 (1999).

[219]*See, e.g.*, Godinet v. Management & Training Corp., 91 FEP 1024, 1031 (10th Cir. 2003) (district court's instruction on punitive damages properly reflected the law following *Kolstad*; instruction's use of the phrase "prevent and remedy" accurately "stressed the employer's need to enforce anti-discrimination policies"); Foster v. Time Warner Entm't Co., L.P., 250 F.3d 1189, 1198 (8th Cir. 2001) (upholding trial court's instruction to jury that defendant must have acted with malice or reckless indifference to federally protected right and that jury " 'should not award damages if the acts of [defendant's] managers were contrary to its good faith efforts to comply with federal law' ") (quoting *Kolstad*, 527 U.S. at 545).

to prove that it would have made the same decision absent the unlawful motive.[220] In *Desert Palace v. Costa*,[221] the Supreme Court clarified that a plaintiff is not required to present direct evidence of discrimination to obtain a mixed-motive jury instruction.[222] Rather, "a plaintiff need only present sufficient evidence for a reasonable jury to conclude, by a preponderance of the evidence, that 'race, color, religion, sex, or national origin was a motivating factor for any employment practice.' "[223] In *Desert Palace*, the plaintiff presented evidence at trial that she was singled out by a supervisor, she was disciplined more harshly than male employees, male employees were treated more favorably for overtime, and supervisors " 'stacked' her disciplinary record and 'frequently used or tolerated' sex-based slurs against her."[224] The Supreme Court affirmed the Ninth Circuit's opinion that although there was no direct evidence of gender discrimination the plaintiff had submitted sufficient evidence to warrant a mixed-motive instruction.[225]

---

[220]*See, e.g.*, Rose v. New York City Bd. of Educ., 257 F.3d 156, 161–63, 86 FEP 380 (2d Cir. 2001) (plaintiff's evidence of decision maker's comments that he would replace plaintiff with someone younger and cheaper was sufficient to allow jury to find both permissible and impermissible motives); Matima v. Celli, 228 F.3d 68, 80, 83 FEP 1660 (2d Cir. 2000) (mixed-motive instruction appropriate because evidence included conduct or statements of decision makers that could be viewed as "directly reflecting" alleged retaliatory attitude); Medlock v. Ortho Biotech, Inc., 164 F.3d 545, 552–53, 78 FEP 1592 (10th Cir. 1999) (affirming trial court's mixed-motive instruction in retaliation case where termination letter explicitly referenced plaintiff's deposition testimony in his pending race discrimination case and came only 1 month after deposition and, therefore, directly reflected defendant's retaliatory animus).

[221]539 U.S. 90 (2003).

[222]*Id.* at 101.

[223]*Id.* (quoting 42 U.S.C. § 2000e-2(m)).

[224]*Id.* at 95–96.

[225]*Id.* at 98, 101; *see also* Rowland v. American Gen. Fin. Inc., 340 F.3d 187, 193, 92 FEP 734 (4th Cir. 2003) (district court abused its discretion in refusing to give a mixed-motive instruction on plaintiff's failure-to-promote claim because evidence showed that supervisor knew of plaintiff's qualifications and interest in position, had power to promote plaintiff, and told plaintiff that he did not need any more females in the position).

After *Desert Palace*, questions remain as to the line separating single and mixed-motive cases. This distinction is significant because of the differing burdens of proof on plaintiff: in a single motive case, the plaintiff has to prove that the employment practice was "because of" discrimination, whereas in a mixed-motive case a plaintiff only needs to prove that discrimination was a "motivating factor" in the employment practice. *Compare* 42 U.S.C. § 2000e-2(a)(1) (2000) *and* McDonnell Douglas Corp. v. Green, 411 U.S. 792 (1973) *with* 42 U.S.C. § 2000e-2(m) (2000) *and* Price Waterhouse v. Hopkins, 490 U.S. 228 (1989). The implications of the *Desert Palace* decision on the burden of proof in disparate treatment cases are discussed in

When a plaintiff asserts multiple claims, in order to avoid an ambiguous verdict the trial court should provide a verdict form that differentiates each claim and requires the jury to specify on which claims it finds for the plaintiff and on which claims it does not.[226] Similarly, when one claim is based on multiple grounds, the jury should be instructed to address each asserted ground in its verdict.[227] If a special verdict results in inconsistencies, the trial court should ask the jury to resolve the conflict.[228] The trial court should make every effort to reconcile the jury's answers to special interrogatories before ordering a new trial.[229]

In an effort to assist district court judges, several courts of appeal have now adopted pattern or model jury instructions and verdict forms for employment discrimination claims,[230] although

---

Chapter 2 (Disparate Treatment). *See also* Liu v. Amway Corp., 347 F.3d 1125, 1141, 92 FEP 1486 (9th Cir. 2003) (declining to apply *McDonnell Douglas* analysis because plaintiff presented a mixed-motive case); Dare v. Wal-Mart Stores Inc., 267 F. Supp. 2d 987, 990–92 (D. Minn. 2003) (analyzing the consequences of the *Desert Palace* decision).

[226]*See* Galdieri-Ambrosini v. National Realty & Dev. Corp., 136 F.3d 276, 286, 76 FEP 290 (2d Cir. 1998) (trial court erred by submitting only single liability question of whether defendant engaged in gender discrimination where plaintiff had asserted claims for gender discrimination and retaliation; error was harmless in light of appellate court's further rulings).

[227]*See, e.g.*, Rutherford v. Harris County, 197 F.3d 173, 185, 81 FEP 1775 (5th Cir. 1999) (trial court's failure to require jury to consider each individual factual basis for plaintiff's disparate treatment claim requires reversal where plaintiff asserted several different bases for claim and appellate court cannot determine whether verdict rested on basis supported by sufficient evidence).

[228]*See* Heno v. Sprint/United Mgmt. Co., 208 F.3d 847, 853, 82 FEP 837 (10th Cir. 2000) (ordering new trial for defendant where jury found against corporate defendant on Title VII claim, but found no liability under § 1981 on part of individual defendant who was corporate decision maker, and instructing that "[o]rdinarily, a trial judge should point out apparent inconsistencies in the special verdict to the jury and ask the jury to resolve the conflict").

[229]*See, e.g.*, Tolbert v. Queen's Coll., 242 F.3d 58, 74–75 (2d Cir. 2001) (reversing trial court's entry of judgment as matter of law for defendant-employer and concluding that, based on evidence, jury's finding of liability and awards of $0 in compensatory damages and $50,000 in punitive damages were consistent); Norris v. Sysco Corp., 191 F.3d 1043, 1048, 9 AD 1262 (9th Cir. 1999) (upholding trial court's conclusion in ADA case that jury could properly conclude that defendant-employer neither refused to reinstate plaintiff nor offered her reasonable accommodation). *But see* Wilbur v. Correctional Servs. Corp., 393 F.3d 1192, 1199, 95 FEP 100 (11th Cir. 2004) (upholding trial court's conclusion that jury's answers to special interrogatories required judgment in favor of employer even though jury awarded damages, rather than returning the jury for further deliberations or ordering new trial).

[230]*See, e.g.*, United States Court of Appeals Fifth Judicial Circuit Pattern Jury Instructions 1999 (Civil Cases); Manual of Model Civil Jury Instructions for the Dist.

these instructions are not typically binding on the district courts.[231] As explained by the Committee of District Court Judges in the Eleventh Circuit, the purpose of developing pattern or model instructions is generally "to provide in words of common usage and understanding a body of brief, uniform jury instructions, fully stating the law without needless repetition [and] to facilitate rapid assembly of a complete jury charge on each case, suitable for submission to the jury in written form."[232] These instructions, however, are not "one size fits all" because "each case turns on unique facts." The model instructions therefore "should be . . . adapted to conform to the facts in each case."[233]

Courts of the Eighth Circuit (Apr. 2001); Federal Civil Jury Instructions of the Seventh Circuit, chs. 3–5 (2005); Ninth Circuit Manual of Model Civil Jury Instructions (rev. 2002–2003); Eleventh Judicial Circuit Pattern Jury Instructions 1999 (Civil Cases).

[231]*See, e.g.*, United States v. Norton, 846 F.2d 521, 525 (8th Cir. 1988).

[232]Eleventh Judicial Circuit Pattern Jury Instructions 1999 (Civil Cases), Preface; *see also* Manual of Model Civil Jury Instructions for the Dist. Courts of the Eighth Circuit (Apr. 2001), Introduction (the "model instructions were prepared to help judges communicate more effectively with juries" and "to provide judges and lawyers with models of clear, brief and simple instructions calculated to maximize juror comprehension").

[233]Manual of Model Civil Jury Instructions for the Dist. Courts of the Eighth Circuit (Apr. 2001), Introduction.

EEOC LITIGATION

I. HISTORICAL PERSPECTIVE

The Equal Employment Opportunity Commission (EEOC) is the federal government's principal litigation arm in enforcing Title VII. Prior to the 1972 amendments to Title VII, however, the EEOC had no such enforcement power. Initially, § 707 of Title VII authorized the U.S. Attorney General to bring pattern-or-practice suits against defendants in the public sector, and § 706 of Title VII authorized individual parties, after receipt of an EEOC right-to-sue letter, to bring suits against defendants in the private sector.

In 1972, Congress amended Title VII to give the EEOC the broad litigation powers formerly held by the Attorney General.[1] In 1979, pursuant to President Carter's Reorganization Plan,[2] the EEOC also received the U.S. Secretary of Labor's judicial and administrative enforcement authority with respect to the Age Discrimination in Employment Act (ADEA)[3] and the Equal Pay Act (EPA).[4]

Suits by the EEOC frequently are characterized as being brought in the public interest and not simply to vindicate private

---

[1]*See* 118 CONG. REC. 7564–65 (1972) (analysis of H.R. 1746, 92d Cong. § 4 (1972)); *see also* H.R. REP. NO. 29-238 (1971), *reprinted in* 1972 U.S.C.C.A.N. 2137, 2137–86 (hereinafter H.R. REP. NO. 92-238). *See generally* Chapter 30 (Justice Department Litigation).

[2]Reorganization Plan No. 1 of 1978, 3 C.F.R. § 321 (1978), *reprinted in* 5 U.S.C. app. at 205 (2000).

[3]29 U.S.C. §§ 621–634 (2000). *See generally* Chapter 12 (Age).

[4]29 U.S.C. § 206(d) (2000). *See generally* Chapter 18 (Compensation). The EEOC's authority to enforce the ADEA and EPA pursuant to the 1978 Presidential Reorganization Plan was questioned as a result of the Supreme Court's decision in *Immigration & Naturalization Service v. Chadha*, 462 U.S. 919 (1983). In *Chadha*, the Supreme Court held unconstitutional the one-house legislative veto provision of the Immigration and Naturalization Act. Following *Chadha*, a number of respondents around the country challenged the EEOC's right to litigate cases under the ADEA or the EPA, whereas the EEOC maintained that its authority was unaffected by that decision. Cases were split on the issue. Congress then mooted the issue by enacting Pub. L. No. 98-532, 1984 U.S.C.C.A.N. (98 Stat.) 2705. That statute retroactively ratified and affirmed as law all reorganization plans implemented prior to the date of its enactment. Courts thereafter uniformly held that the statute eliminated any questions regarding the EEOC's enforcement authority. *E.g.*, EEOC v. First Citizens Bank of Ill., 758 F.2d 397, 400, 45 FEP 1337 (9th Cir. 1985) (Pub. L. No. 98-532 made clear that EEOC not only has authority to bring future EPA actions, but also has retroactive authority with respect to any previous actions it instituted); EEOC v. Westinghouse Elec. Corp., 765 F.2d 389, 391–93, 45 FEP 1342 (3d Cir. 1985) (neither manifest injustice nor due process violation by retroactive application of Pub. L. No. 98-532 results in either manifest injustice or violations of due process); *see also* EEOC v. CBS, Inc., 748 F.2d 124, 125, 36 FEP 575 (2d Cir. 1984) (per curiam) (Pub. L. No. 98-532 ratified 1978 reorganization plan).

rights.[5] As the U.S. Supreme Court stated in *General Telephone Co. v. EEOC*,[6] "[w]hen the EEOC acts, albeit at the behest of and for the benefit of specific individuals, it acts also to vindicate the public interest in preventing employment discrimination."[7]

II. ADMINISTRATIVE PREREQUISITES TO SUIT

A. Administrative Prerequisites to Suit Under § 706 and the ADEA[8]

Section 706 sets forth a series of procedural steps the EEOC must take before suing under Title VII.[9] In an early case, *EEOC v. Container Corp.*,[10] the district court addressed whether these steps

---

[5]*E.g.*, EEOC v. Waffle House, Inc., 534 U.S. 279, 296,12 AD 1001 (2002) ("whenever the EEOC chooses from among the many charges filed each year to bring an enforcement action in a particular case, the agency may be seeking to vindicate a public interest, not simply provide make-whole relief for the employee, even when it pursues entirely victim-specific relief"); EEOC v. General Elec. Co., 532 F.2d 359, 372–73, 12 FEP 21 (4th Cir. 1976) (public enforcement necessary because Congress recognized discrimination in employment as societal wrong); *see* EEOC v. Kimberly-Clark Corp., 511 F.2d 1352, 1359, 10 FEP 38 (6th Cir. 1975) (public interests transcend private interests). Courts generally remain cognizant that rights important to the charging party are at issue as well. *See* EEOC v. Burlington N., Inc., 644 F.2d 717, 720, 25 FEP 499 (8th Cir. 1981) ("Although an EEOC suit is brought, in part, to vindicate the public interest in preventing employment discrimination, it is evident from the relief requested here that the Commission sues on behalf of the charging party. Thus, that the EEOC is the nominal plaintiff in this action does not obviate the prejudice to [the charging party's] interests which would result if the action were barred by the Commission's procedural default." (citations and footnotes omitted)). *Compare* EEOC v. Occidental Life Ins. Co., 535 F.2d 533, 537, 12 FEP 1300 (9th Cir. 1976) (both injunctive relief and back pay vindicated public interest), *aff'd*, 432 U.S. 355, 14 FEP 1718 (1977) *with* EEOC v. Griffin Wheel Co., 511 F.2d 456, 459, 10 FEP 531 (insofar as government sues to recover back pay, it acts to vindicate private rights; insofar as it seeks injunctive relief, it vindicates public rights), *reh'g denied and opinion clarified on other grounds*, 521 F.2d 223, 11 FEP 988 (5th Cir. 1975) (per curiam).

[6]446 U.S. 318, 22 FEP 1196 (1980).

[7]*Id.* at 326.

[8]There are no jurisdictional prerequisites to suit by the EEOC to enforce the EPA.

[9]*See* 42 U.S.C. § 2000e-5 (2000). The § 706 requirements include the following: (1) a timely charge (§ 706(e)); (2) service of notice of such charge on the respondent within 10 days (§ 706(b), (e)); (3) deferral to the state agency, if any (§ 706(c), (d)); (4) a Commission investigation (§ 706(b)); (5) a determination of reasonable cause (§ 706(b)); and (6) an unsuccessful attempt at conciliation with the respondent (§ 706(b), (f)(1)).

[10]352 F. Supp. 262, 5 FEP 108 (M.D. Fla. 1972). The defendants in *Container Corp.* contended that some of them had not been served with the charge, that the

were jurisdictional. The EEOC argued that the steps were not juris-dictional and, indeed, "that the administrative decision to sue is not reviewable" at all.[11] The court disagreed:

> The Court views each one of the deliberate steps in this statutory scheme—charge, notice, investigation, reasonable cause, concilia-tion—as intended by Congress to be a condition precedent to the next succeeding step and ultimately legal action. Certainly, the EEOC does not contend that it could skip one or more of these steps at will. The language of the Act is mandatory as to each step and the Commission must complete each step before moving to the next.[12]

The ADEA requirements differ. An EEOC suit is not necessarily related to or limited by a charge that may have been filed with the EEOC[13] or administrative processing of a charge.[14] However, an

---

Commission had made no investigation whatsoever, and that with respect to at least some defendants, the Commission had not attempted conciliation.

[11]*Id.* at 266; *cf.* Zipes v. Trans World Airlines, Inc., 455 U.S. 385, 393, 28 FEP 1 (1982) ("[F]iling a timely charge with the EEOC is not a jurisdictional prerequi-site to suit in federal court, but a requirement that, like a statute of limitations, is subject to waiver, estoppel, and equitable tolling."). *See generally* Section VI *infra* and Chapter 26 (Timeliness).

[12]*Container Corp.*, 352 F. Supp. at 265; *accord* EEOC v. Asplundh Tree Ex-pert Co., 340 F.3d 1256, 92 FEP 661 (11th Cir. 2003) (case dismissed because of agency's failure to engage in good faith conciliation when it conducted 3-year in-vestigation in individual case, gave company 12 business days to accept nationwide conciliation agreement, and declined request by employer to set forth basis for its determination); EEOC v. Klingler Elec. Corp., 636 F.2d 104, 106, 25 FEP 555 (5th Cir. 1981) (per curiam) (although EEOC not required to plead compliance specifi-cally, EEOC must in fact satisfy all conditions precedent to suit). In *EEOC v. Shell Oil Co.*, 466 U.S. 54 (1984), however, the Supreme Court noted that "lower courts have taken a more forgiving view of the relation between the steps in the Title VII enforcement sequence," and accordingly have not dismissed cases even though the EEOC failed to provide notice to the employer within 10 days, where there has been no showing of bad faith or prejudice. 466 U.S. at 66 n.16.

[13]EEOC v. Sidley Austin Brown & Wood, LLP, 406 F. Supp. 2d 991, 993–94 (N.D. Ill. 2005) (EEOC can seek damages on behalf of older law firm partners even though partners had not filed individual claims with the EEOC), *aff'd*, 437 F.3d 695 (7th Cir. 2006); Gilmer v. Interstate/Johnson Lane Corp., 500 U.S. 20, 28, 55 FEP 1116 (1991) (ADEA action; "the EEOC's role in combating discrimination is not dependent on the filing of a charge"); EEOC v. Sears, Roebuck & Co., 55 FEP 482, 483 (D. Or. 1991) (EEOC's power to investigate age discrimination not dependent on timely filing of valid claim); *see* EEOC v. Ritenour Sch. Dist., 692 F. Supp. 1068, 1069, 47 FEP 421 (E.D. Mo. 1988) (timely charge not prerequisite to EEOC in-vestigation or subsequent lawsuit under ADEA). *See generally* Chapter 25 (EEOC Administrative Process).

[14]However, the ADEA prescribes steps for charge processing in *private* suits. They include (1) a timely charge (29 U.S.C. § 626(d)); (2) prompt service of notice of such charge on the named respondents (29 U.S.C. § 626(d)); (3) deferral to the

attempt to conciliate remains a statutory prerequisite to an ADEA suit by the EEOC.[15] Whether that prerequisite is jurisdictional, however, is not totally clear.[16] Where no conciliation has occurred, most courts have stayed the litigation for that purpose,[17] but some courts have dismissed the case entirely.[18]

1. A Timely Charge[19]

An EEOC Title VII suit, like a private suit, must be based on a timely and valid charge.[20] In 2002, the Supreme Court upheld the validity of the EEOC's regulation permitting an otherwise timely

---

state agency, if any (29 U.S.C. § 633(b)); (4) investigation to determine whether there is an alleged unlawful practice (29 U.S.C. § 626(a)); and (5) efforts to eliminate an alleged unlawful practice by "conciliation, conference, and persuasion" (29 U.S.C. § 626(d) [sic]). *See generally* Chapter 12 (Age).

[15]29 U.S.C. § 626(b) provides: "Before instituting any action under this section, the [EEOC] shall attempt to eliminate the discriminatory practice or practices alleged, and to effect voluntary compliance with the requirements of this [Act] through informal methods of conciliation, conference, and persuasion."

[16]In the conference committee report that accompanied the 1978 amendments, the committee stated that conciliation was not a jurisdictional prerequisite to suit. S. REP. NO. 95-493, at 13 (1977), *reprinted in* 1978 U.S.C.C.A.N. 504, 516.

[17]*E.g.*, EEOC v. Fox Point-Bayside Sch. Dist., 24 FEP 668, 669 (E.D. Wis. 1980) (action stayed as to some claims to permit conciliation); Marshall v. Sun Oil Co., 605 F.2d 1331, 1339 n.8, 21 FEP 257 (5th Cir. 1979) (when EEOC has not discharged its statutory duty to attempt conciliation, action will be stayed pending attempt); Brennan v. Ace Hardware Corp., 495 F.2d 368, 376, 7 FEP 657 (8th Cir. 1974) (conciliation not jurisdictional prerequisite; court should stay proceedings).

[18]*E.g.*, Dunlop v. Resource Scis. Corp., 410 F. Supp. 836, 843, 15 FEP 38 (N.D. Okla. 1976) (conciliation is jurisdictional prerequisite; failure to conciliate required dismissal).

[19]For a general discussion of what constitutes a timely charge, see Chapter 26 (Timeliness).

[20]*See* EEOC v. United Ins. Co., 666 F. Supp. 915, 918, 46 FEP 250 (S.D. Miss. 1986) (former employees failed to file charges; waiving requirement of filing for them would have revived claims that otherwise would have been barred if brought as individual actions); EEOC v. Procter & Gamble Co., 15 FEP 1132, 1133 (S.D. Ohio 1977) (enforcement of EEOC's subpoena against respondent denied and complaint dismissed; underlying charge not timely); *cf.* EEOC v. Nicholson File Co., 408 F. Supp. 229, 234–35, 12 FEP 1405 (D. Conn. 1976) (timely charge requirement met; time period for filing charge tolled between time (then) Office of Federal Contract Compliance (OFCC) received charge and time that EEOC received charge). The defense of untimeliness is subject to "waiver, estoppel, and equitable tolling," however. Zipes v. Trans World Airlines, Inc., 455 U.S. 385, 393, 28 FEP 1 (1982); *see, e.g.*, EEOC v. Mico Oil Co., 48 FEP 1206, 1207 (D. Kan. 1988) (defendants waived defense by admitting in their answer that "all conditions precedent to the institution of this lawsuit have been fulfilled"). *See generally* Chapter 26 (Timeliness).

charge to be verified by a sworn amendment submitted after the expiration of the 180/300-day limitation period.[21] The Court remanded the case, however, on the issue of whether the document originally submitted constituted a "charge."[22] On remand, the Fourth Circuit held that the document, a letter that the plaintiff-employee sent to the EEOC in which he related his allegations of discrimination, constituted a valid charge.[23]

The EEOC may bring suit on behalf of several aggrieved persons even if only one of them files a timely charge, as long as the charge contains "sufficient information to notify defendant of its potential liability . . . and to permit the EEOC to engage in conciliation of all . . . claims."[24] Where there is such a timely charge, the EEOC may sue on behalf of other injured parties identified through its investigation of that charge, even when the EEOC eventually decides not to pursue the charging party's claims.[25] However, the EEOC may not use a timely charge to "piggyback" untimely claims that are not part of a "continuous and ongoing course of discriminatory conduct"; there must be "a timely charge upon which EEOC has made a determination of reasonable cause."[26] Moreover, the EEOC is precluded from pursuing claims after it consents to the withdrawal of the filed charge.[27]

Demonstration of the timeliness of the underlying charge is not a prerequisite to judicial enforcement of an EEOC subpoena or to the EEOC's jurisdiction to investigate allegations of discrimination; enforcement may be precluded, however, where it is apparent from the face of the charge, "otherwise apparent," or conceded that the charge is untimely.[28]

---

[21]Edelman v. Lynchburg Coll., 535 U.S. 106 (2002).

[22]*Id.* at 118–19.

[23]Edelman v. Lynchburg Coll., 300 F.3d 400, 404–05 (4th Cir. 2002) (deficiencies pointed out by college—i.e., lack of EEOC charge number and fact EEOC did not forward copy to college or to Virginia Council on Human Rights—not shortcomings of charge, but failures of EEOC to carry out its responsibilities under Title VII). *See generally* Chapter 25 (EEOC Administrative Process).

[24]EEOC v. Sara Lee Corp., 923 F. Supp. 994, 999, 70 FEP 57, 59 (W.D. Mich. 1995) (four employees covered by one charge concerning single reduction in force).

[25]*See* EEOC v. Air Line Pilots Ass'n, 885 F. Supp. 289, 292–93, 67 FEP 1363 (D.D.C. 1995).

[26]*See* EEOC v. Harvey L. Walner & Assocs., 91 F.3d 963, 967, 71 FEP 683 (7th Cir. 1996).

[27]*See id.*

[28]EEOC v. Norfolk Police Dep't, 45 F.3d 80, 83, 66 FEP 1425, 1427 (4th Cir. 1995).

The 300-day time period is available when there is a state deferral agency with conciliation authority, even if that agency has no authority to impose remedies for discrimination.[29] The deferral agency has an exclusive 60-day period to process the charge. Upon either the expiration of the 60-day period or the termination of the deferral agency's proceedings, the charge is deemed to have been filed with the EEOC.[30] The deferral agency need not actually conduct an investigation of the charge as a prerequisite to waiving its right if the agency and the EEOC have instituted a work-sharing agreement.[31] When the deferral agency and the EEOC have a memorandum of understanding that requires actual referral, however, the charge will not be deemed to have been automatically filed with the EEOC.[32]

Under the ADEA, an individual charge is not a prerequisite for a suit by the EEOC following a directed investigation.[33]

When required under § 706(c), the charge must first be deferred to the appropriate state or local agency.[34] The Supreme Court, in *EEOC v. Commercial Office Products Co.*,[35] upheld a procedure in which a state fair employment practices (FEP) agency waives its exclusive 60-day period for initial processing of a discrimination

---

[29]*See* Tinsley v. First Union Nat'l Bank, 155 F.3d 435, 439–40, 77 FEP 1753 (4th Cir. 1998).

[30]EEOC v. Dinuba Med. Clinic, 222 F.3d 580, 585, 83 FEP 1655 (9th Cir. 2000).

[31]*See* Puryear v. County of Roanoke, 214 F.3d 514, 519, 84 FEP 155 (4th Cir. 2000).

[32]*See* Walker v. Novo Nordisk Pharm. Indus., Inc., 225 F.3d 656 (table), 2000 WL 1012960 (4th Cir. July 24, 2000).

[33]*See* EEOC v. Johnson & Higgins, Inc., 91 F.3d 1529, 71 FEP 818 (2d Cir. 1996) (EEOC may challenge mandatory retirement policy for board of directors although no director objects; dissent argues directors should be treated as employers rather than employees).

[34]*See id.* Several cases, such as *Crosslin v. Mountain States Telephone & Telegraph Co.*, 422 F.2d 1028, 1029, 2 FEP 480 (9th Cir. 1970), *vacated on other grounds*, 400 U.S. 1004 (1971), and its progeny, including *EEOC v. Wah Chang Albany Corp.*, 499 F.2d 187, 189 n.3, 8 FEP 203 (9th Cir. 1974) (per curiam), and *Motorola, Inc. v. EEOC*, 460 F.2d 1245, 1246, 4 FEP 755 (9th Cir. 1972), suggest that the EEOC's action generally will not be dismissed when it mistakenly failed to defer to a state agency. Rather, the court will stay the action under § 706(f)(1) to permit the EEOC to defer the charge to the state agency.

[35]486 U.S. 107, 46 FEP 1265 (1988); *see* EEOC v. Western States Mach. Co., 17 FEP 1356, 1357 (S.D. Ohio 1978) (upholding legality of EEOC agreement with state agency where state agency waived jurisdiction over all charges initially received by EEOC, deeming charges immediately filed with EEOC).

charge filed first with the EEOC, thereby "terminating" the agency's proceedings under § 706(c), so that the EEOC may deem the charge immediately filed.[36]

The state limitations period for filing discrimination claims does not determine the applicable federal limitations period.[37]

If the underlying Title VII charge is by an EEOC commissioner, it must be under oath.[38] The Supreme Court explicated the standards for a commissioner charge based on a Title VII violation in *EEOC v. Shell Oil Co.*[39] Applying the governing regulation,[40] the Supreme Court held that, at least in a pattern-or-practice case, a commissioner charge should identify

> the groups of persons that he has reason to believe have been discriminated against, the categories of employment positions from which they have been excluded, the methods by which discrimination may have been effected and the periods of time in which he suspects the discrimination to have been practiced.[41]

---

[36]*Commercial Office Prods.*, 486 U.S. at 121–22; *see* EEOC v. Techalloy Md., Inc., 894 F.2d 676, 679, 52 FEP 36 (4th Cir. 1990) (waiver by state FEP agency of the initial processing of a charge is self-executing; state agency's proceedings were commenced and terminated no later than date state agency received charge); Green v. Los Angeles County Superintendent of Schs., 883 F.2d 1472, 1479–80, 50 FEP 1233 (9th Cir. 1989) (waiver is self-executing); Griffin v. Air Prods. & Chems., Inc., 883 F.2d 940, 943, 50 FEP 1444 (11th Cir. 1989) (agreement between EEOC and state agency created instantaneous "constructive termination"); *cf.* EEOC v. Hacienda Hotel, 881 F.2d 1504, 1510, 50 FEP 877 (9th Cir. 1989) (EEOC's referral of copies of claimant's charges to state agency sufficient to "institute" proceedings with state agency).

[37]*Commercial Office Prods.*, 486 U.S. at 123; *accord* EEOC v. Hansa Prods., Inc., 844 F.2d 191, 192, 46 FEP 951 (4th Cir. 1988) (claimant's untimely filing under state law does not prohibit application of federal 300-day filing period when claimant simultaneously mailed charge to both EEOC and Maryland Human Relations Commission; claimant merely needs to file with state agency in sufficient time to effect filing with EEOC within 300 days).

[38]*See* Section VI *infra*.

[39]466 U.S. 54, 34 FEP 709 (1984).

[40]29 C.F.R. § 1601.12(a) provides: "Each charge should contain . . . [a] clear and concise statement of the facts, including pertinent dates, constituting the alleged unlawful employment practices . . . ."

[41]*Shell Oil*, 466 U.S. at 73. The Court determined that the charge in *Shell Oil* met these standards when it (1) identified African Americans and women as the victims of discrimination; (2) specified six occupational categories to which African Americans, and seven to which women, allegedly had been denied equal access; (3) alleged that the employer had discriminated in "recruitment, hiring, selection, job assignment, training, testing, promotion, and terms and conditions of employment"; and (4) charged the employer with discriminatory practices since at least the effective

2. Notice of the Charge

Under § 706(b), the EEOC is required to serve notice of a Title VII charge on the named respondent within 10 days after its filing. The question naturally arises: What happens if the agency makes a mistake? The legislative history suggests an answer: "It is not intended [by Congress], however, that failure to give notice of the charge to the respondent within ten days would prejudice the rights of the aggrieved party."[42] In *EEOC v. Airguide Corp.*,[43] after the trial court dismissed an EEOC suit because the respondent did not receive notice of the charge, the Fifth Circuit reversed and remanded for a determination of the extent of prejudice, if any.[44]

A related issue is what must be disclosed in the notice. The Supreme Court held in *Shell Oil* that § 706(b) requires the Commission, within 10 days of the filing of a charge, simply to reveal

---

date of the Civil Rights Act. *Id.* Justice O'Connor, whose opinion concurring in part and dissenting in part was joined by three other Justices, agreed that the charge in *Shell Oil* was sufficient, but only because the regulation did not require the charge to contain a more detailed description of the circumstances of discrimination. *Id.* at 83–85 (citing 29 C.F.R. § 1601.12(b) ("Notwithstanding the provisions of paragraph (a) of this section, a charge is sufficient when the Commission receives from the person making the charge a written statement sufficiently precise to identify the parties, and to describe generally the action or practices complained of.")). The majority suggested, without resolving the issue, that § 1601.12(b) might apply only to charges filed by laypersons, and not to commissioner charges. *Id.* at 74 n.28; *see also* EEOC v. Astronautics Corp. of Am., 660 F. Supp. 838, 841–42, 43 FEP 1569 (E.D. Wis. 1987) (charges of discrimination that set forth class of persons allegedly discriminated against and nature of such discrimination sufficient).

[42]Section-by-section analysis of H.R. 1746, 92d Cong., § 4 (1972), 118 CONG. REC. 7564 (1972); *see also* H.R. REP. NO. 92-238. *See generally* Chapter 25 (EEOC Administrative Process).

[43]539 F.2d 1038, 13 FEP 904 (5th Cir. 1976).

[44]*Id.* at 1042 n.7 ("Even if substantial prejudice is found to have occurred, this would not necessarily defeat the whole case but only those portions of the case affected by that prejudice."); *see also* EEOC v. Burlington N., Inc., 644 F.2d 717, 720–21, 25 FEP 499 (8th Cir. 1981) (where notice was sent late and received 25 days late, late notice not fatal unless it was willful or in bad faith or unless substantial prejudice was shown; however, court refused to hold (as urged by EEOC) that there can be no prejudice as matter of law if notice is given within charge-filing period); *cf.* Occidental Life Ins. Co. v. EEOC, 432 U.S. 355, 372 n.32, 14 FEP 1718 (1977) ("Prompt notice of a reasonable cause determination also serves to cure any deficiencies in the 10-day notice that may result from EEOC amendment of the claimed violation after investigation."). *But see* EEOC v. Brown Transp. Corp., 15 FEP 1062, 1068 (N.D. Ga. 1976) (scope of EEOC's case limited to notice of violations given to defendant within 10-day period).

to the employer the information that must be included in the charge itself.[45] Later cases have not required that the notice provide substantial information about the factual basis for the charge.[46]

One district court has found that the EEOC may pursue investigations of charges through the enforcement of subpoenas despite the fact that the charging party is prepared to settle his or her claim.[47]

3. Investigation

Although the statute does not specify what type of investigation of a Title VII charge the EEOC shall make, the EEOC's regulations and its compliance manual set out the investigation procedures to be followed by the EEOC's field personnel.[48] Although disputes have arisen where employers perceived that the EEOC's investigation was substandard, the courts continue to allow broad EEOC investigations and enforcement of subpoenas where voluntary compliance with the investigation is not obtained.[49] Employers

---

[45]466 U.S. at 81. Four dissenting Justices disagreed, concluding that § 706(b) "expressly requires more in the notice of charge than in the charge itself. A charge need only allege an unlawful employment practice and 'contain such information and be in such form as the Commission requires.' " *Id.* at 86 (O'Connor, J., dissenting). By contrast, the dissenters asserted, a "notice of charge . . . must 'includ[e] the date, place and circumstances of the alleged unlawful employment practice.' " *Id.* The dissent concluded that service on the employer of the "brief, formal, and wholly uninformative 'charge,' . . . did not comport with the language and purposes of [§ 706(b)'s] notice requirement." *Id.* at 89.

[46]*E.g.*, EEOC v. Bethlehem Steel Corp., 765 F.2d 427, 430 & n.2, 38 FEP 345 (4th Cir. 1985) (notice of charge, which was worded similarly to one in *Shell Oil*, sufficiently notified employer of circumstances of alleged discrimination); *cf.* EEOC v. Reichhold Chems., Inc., 700 F. Supp. 524, 528 & n.2, 47 FEP 186 (N.D. Fla. 1988) (EEOC has no additional duty to "apprise an employer of the course or focus of its investigation"; EEOC could amend its complaint to add claim of retaliation for bringing underlying charge of discrimination).

[47]EEOC v. Morgan Stanley & Co., 132 F. Supp. 2d 146, 152–53, 86 FEP 100 (S.D.N.Y. 2000) ("if the EEOC were foreclosed from pursuing investigations whenever the charging party whose charge occasioned the inquiry wished to settle with his or her employer, employers would be able to forestall investigations . . . by buying off any victim who had the temerity to complain").

[48]*See* Chapter 25 (EEOC Administrative Process).

[49]*See* University of Pa. v. EEOC, 493 U.S. 182, 191 (1990) (when court is asked to enforce Commission subpoena, its responsibility is to satisfy itself that charge is valid, that material requested is relevant to charge, and to assess any contentions by employer that demand for information is too indefinite or has been made for illegitimate purpose) (quoting EEOC v. Shell Oil Co., 466 U.S. 54, 72 n.26 (1984)); EEOC

cannot intervene to block issuance of third-party subpoenas,[50] nor can employers block the enforcement of subpoenas when the employer has failed to exhaust its administrative remedies or claims that the requested information is "confidential."[51]

Courts generally have found the EEOC's allegation that it conducted an investigation to be sufficient to satisfy the statutory prerequisite to suit.[52] However, where the EEOC is attempting to expand the litigation beyond bases or issues described in the charge, courts have considered whether the expanded bases or issues were in fact investigated and whether such investigation provided fair notice to the respondent of what ultimately was at issue.[53] Thus,

---

v. Lockheed Martin Corp., 116 F.3d 110, 74 FEP 202 (4th Cir. 1997) (materials sought relevant and no argument made of burdensomeness); EEOC v. United Airlines, Inc., 287 F.3d 643, 653, 88 FEP 1018 (7th Cir. 2002) (EEOC's burden not particularly onerous; requirement of relevance, like charge requirement itself, is designed to cabin EEOC's authority and prevent "fishing expeditions") (citing EEOC v. K-Mart Corp., 694 F.2d 1055 (6th Cir. 1982)); EEOC v. Sidley Austin Brown & Wood, 315 F.3d 696 (7th Cir. 2002) (although court did not rule that 32 demoted law partners were employees within meaning of ADEA, it did find there was enough doubt about whether demoted partners were covered by ADEA to entitle EEOC to full compliance with that part of its subpoena); EEOC v. Dillard Dep't Stores, 1998 WL 25548 (N.D. Tex. Jan. 9, 1998) (generous construction of relevance); EEOC v. Optical Cable Corp., 76 FEP 1552 (W.D. Va. 1998) (broad construction of subpoena authority).

[50]See EEOC v. Illinois Dep't of Employment Sec., 6 F. Supp. 2d 784, 77 FEP 107 (N.D. Ill. 1998).

[51]See EEOC v. City of Milwaukee, 54 F. Supp. 2d 885, 891, 86 FEP 62 (E.D. Wis. 1999); EEOC v. Guess?, Inc., 176 F. Supp. 2d 416 (E.D. Pa. 2001) (citing EEOC v. Lutheran Soc. Servs., 186 F.3d 959 (D.C. Cir. 1999)) (employer's failure to first petition Commission for modification or revocation of its subpoena does not bar it from objecting to subpoena before court on basis of attorney-client privilege and work product doctrine; on merits, court determined that employer failed to meet its burden of demonstrating applicability of either attorney-client or work product doctrines to its robbery investigative file).

[52]E.g., EEOC v. Keco Indus., Inc., 748 F.2d 1097, 1100, 36 FEP 511 (6th Cir. 1984) (lower court erred by inquiring into sufficiency of EEOC investigation of charge); Newsome v. EEOC, 301 F.3d 227, 231 (5th Cir. 2002) (court, in denying employee's lawsuit seeking writ of mandamus compelling Commission to further investigate her charge, stated that "the nature and extent of an EEOC investigation into a discrimination claim is a matter within the discretion of that agency") (citing Keco Indus., Inc., 748 F.2d at 1100); EEOC v. Nestle Co., 29 FEP 491, 492 (E.D. Cal. 1982) (EEOC adequately investigated alleged "white collar" sex discrimination claim); EEOC v. American Mach. & Foundry, Inc., 13 FEP 1634, 1640 (M.D. Pa. 1976) ("The EEOC is not required . . . to conduct a full-scale, almost adversarial investigation that would run down every lead and confront every fact relevant to the charge.").

[53]Compare EEOC v. St. Anne's Hosp., Inc., 664 F.2d 128, 131, 27 FEP 170 (7th Cir. 1981) (prerequisites to suit satisfied when employer was informed, prior to reasonable cause determination, that retaliatory discharge was issue) and EEOC

where the preceding prerequisites were met, the EEOC has been allowed to expand the geographic scope of its litigation from the site identified in the cause determination.[54]

Courts express differing views over whether the EEOC's authority to investigate alleged discriminatory practices against a protected group extends widely enough to permit investigation of practices with respect to other protected groups.[55]

Respondents generally have been unsuccessful in restricting the EEOC's ability to investigate charges by claiming inadequate notice of the charge,[56] excessive delays,[57] and undue burden.[58] Courts

---

v. Bumble Bee Seafoods Co., 19 FEP 854, 856 (D. Or. 1979) (investigation of allegations of sex discrimination against women in sex-segregated jobs amounted to sufficient investigation of discrimination against men as well) *with* EEOC v. Allegheny Airlines, 436 F. Supp. 1300, 1307, 15 FEP 891 (W.D. Pa. 1977) (EEOC may not litigate issue of discrimination in job classifications that were not investigated, even though that issue was included in cause determination), EEOC v. Brown Transp. Corp., 15 FEP 1062, 1068–70 (N.D. Ga. 1976) (defendant's motion for partial summary judgment granted where charge alleged only race discrimination and investigation of sex discrimination was not complete) *and* EEOC v. Bailey Co., 563 F.2d 439, 449, 15 FEP 972 (6th Cir. 1977) ("if conciliation is to work properly, charges of discrimination must be fully investigated"). For a discussion of the relationship of scope of the charge and investigation to scope of the complaint in private litigation, see Chapter 28 (Title VII Litigation Procedure).

[54]*See* Lucky Stores, Inc. v. EEOC, 714 F.2d 911, 913, 32 FEP 1281 (9th Cir. 1983) (EEOC may challenge employer's practices not only at warehouse named in reasonable cause determination but also at two other warehouses where same alleged discrimination occurred, because employer had adequate notice during investigation of issue being litigated).

[55]*Compare* EEOC v. Roadway Express, Inc., 261 F.3d 634, 639–41, 86 FEP 833 (6th Cir. 2001) (Commissioner charge that alleged failure to hire women as operators and laborers and failure to promote blacks to sales and upper-management positions allowed EEOC to obtain data regarding promotion of women to sales and upper-management positions and hiring of blacks as operators and laborers) *with* EEOC v. Southern Farm Bureau Cas. Ins. Co., 271 F.3d 209, 211, 87 FEP 332 (5th Cir. 2001) (charge specifying race discrimination did not give Commission authority to investigate sex discrimination as well).

[56]*See* EEOC v. Shell Oil Co., 466 U.S. 54, 75 (1984) (Congress did not envision notice requirement as substantive constraint on EEOC's investigative authority); Mississippi Chem. Corp. v. EEOC, 786 F.2d 1013, 1017–18, 40 FEP 609 (11th Cir. 1986).

[57]*See* EEOC v. Great Atl. & Pac. Tea Co., 735 F.2d 69, 82–83 34 FEP 1412 (3d Cir. 1984) (31 months between end of employer's resistance to investigation and EEOC's determination of reasonable cause not excessive). *But see* EEOC v. National City Bank, 694 F. Supp. 1287, 1294, 47 FEP 401 (N.D. Ohio 1987) (4-year delay in investigating charge prejudiced employer; EEOC subpoena therefore not enforced).

[58]*See* EEOC v. Maryland Cup Corp., 785 F.2d 471, 477–78, 40 FEP 475 (4th Cir. 1986) (EEOC subpoena of relevant and material information enforceable, and employer not entitled to reimbursement for reproduction costs unless employer demonstrates

also have supported the EEOC's administrative use of discovery tools such as subpoenas[59] and (according to one court) interrogatories,[60] have granted a preliminary injunction to prevent an employer from impeding the EEOC's investigation,[61] have ruled that the automatic stay provisions of the Bankruptcy Code do not prevent an EEOC investigation,[62] and have held that prior investigation and

---

that producing documents would seriously disrupt its normal business operations; employer's conclusory allegations that it needs constant access to all documents and that it fears EEOC will lose documents insufficient).

[59]See, e.g., University of Pa. v. EEOC, 493 U.S. 182, 201, 51 FEP 1118 (1990) (upholding EEOC's subpoena of peer review materials in investigation of tenure denial case; EEOC had broad right of access under § 2000e-8(a); nothing more than relevance required to compel disclosure); EEOC v. Kloster Cruise, Ltd., 939 F.2d 920, 922, 56 FEP 1061 (11th Cir. 1991) (enforcing EEOC subpoena; documents sought were relevant to EEOC's jurisdictional inquiry, and no clear absence of jurisdiction; court's role in proceeding to enforce administrative subpoena limited to determining whether discovery sought was material and relevant to lawful purpose of agency); EEOC v. American Express Centurion Bank, 758 F. Supp. 217, 221, 225, 56 FEP 1817 (D. Del. 1991) (EEOC subpoena upheld despite release allegedly barring age discrimination claim; in general, party may not defeat agency's authority to investigate by raising defense to potential lawsuit; when charge was valid and material sought was relevant, burden was on employer to show EEOC's abuse of its investigative authority); EEOC v. State Farm Mut. Auto. Ins. Co., 34 FEP 1073, 1074 (N.D. Cal. 1982) (EEOC may issue subpoena before deciding whether it has jurisdiction over employer), aff'd in part and vacated in part mem., 707 F.2d 519 (9th Cir. 1983); EEOC v. Quadrant Club, Inc., 35 FEP 195, 196–97 (N.D. Tex. 1984) (EEOC entitled to enforcement of subpoena seeking information about employer's recruitment and hiring practices; information sought is relevant to charge of age discrimination); EEOC v. W.A. Krueger Co., 1984 WL 1108, at *2–3 (E.D. Wis. Oct. 10, 1984) (enforcing subpoena; EEOC charge, which failed to specify dates or alleged discriminatory acts, was proper). But see EEOC v. National City Bank, 694 F. Supp. 1287, 1293, 47 FEP 401 (N.D. Ohio 1987) (refusing to enforce EEOC's subpoena when Commission's 4-year delay in investigating charge prejudiced employer). See generally EEOC v. Peat, Marwick, Mitchell & Co., 775 F.2d 928, 930, 38 FEP 1846 (8th Cir. 1985) (EEOC has authority to issue subpoena duces tecum in age discrimination action).

[60]See State Farm, 34 FEP at 1074–75 (employers can be required to compile lists and answer interrogatories under EEOC subpoena).

[61]See EEOC v. United States Steel Corp., 583 F. Supp. 1357, 1363, 34 FEP 973 (W.D. Pa. 1984) (EEOC granted preliminary injunction when employer's actions hindered EEOC's investigation and administrative processes); cf. EEOC v. Recruit U.S.A., Inc., 939 F.2d 746, 755, 56 FEP 721 (9th Cir. 1991) (EEOC obtained injunction regarding preservation of certain business records "essential to its investigation"; that injunction did not have time limit not determinative, because injunction covered evidence that might be relevant, and defendant had been incorporated for less than 5 years).

[62]See AM Int'l, Inc. v. EEOC, 34 FEP 1535, 1536 (Bankr. N.D. Ill. 1982) (EEOC may investigate employer that has filed petition under Chapter 11); cf. EEOC v.

even settlement of a charge by a state FEP agency do not preclude an EEOC investigation.[63]

The EEOC takes the position that respondents face a risk even in asserting some of the preceding arguments. An EEOC policy statement asserts that an employer's unjustified refusal to provide relevant information in an EEOC investigation will allow the EEOC to adopt inferences adverse to the employer on open factual issues, which may form the basis for a reasonable cause determination and a Commission decision to litigate.[64]

Investigation is not a condition precedent to suit under the ADEA[65] except to the extent it is subsumed by the conciliation requirement.[66]

Whatever may be the deficiencies in the EEOC's investigation and fact finding, dissatisfied charging parties and respondents generally must direct their objections to the Commission itself, or at most to the court hearing the resulting litigation. Separate suits against the EEOC have not been allowed.[67]

McLean Trucking Co., 834 F.2d 398, 402, 45 FEP 679 (4th Cir. 1987) (automatic stay provisions of Bankruptcy Code do not apply to actions filed by EEOC).

[63]See EEOC v. Peterson, Howell & Heather, Inc., 702 F. Supp. 1213, 1217–18, 48 FEP 1185 (D. Md. 1989) (EEOC may investigate charge filed by its commissioners, even though state FEP agency had already investigated and settled charge of discrimination against same defendant).

[64]1 EQUAL EMPL. COMPL. MAN. (BNA) § 26.1(a), (c), at 26:0001.

[65]E.g., EEOC v. Westinghouse Elec. Corp., 632 F. Supp. 343, 362, 40 FEP 643 (E.D. Pa. 1986) (EEOC does not have to conduct exhaustive investigation of all charges before it can file ADEA action), rev'd on other grounds, 925 F.2d 619 (3d Cir. 1991).

[66]See Marshall v. Sun Oil Co., 605 F.2d 1331, 1335, 21 FEP 257 (5th Cir. 1979) (to meet conciliation requirement, EEOC "must . . . also present a reasonable showing of discrimination. . . . To acquire evidence, the [EEOC] must necessarily undertake some independent investigation or verification of evidence supplied by others; however, investigation is not a separate requirement of the Act.").

[67]See Baba v. EEOC, 111 F.3d 2 (2d Cir. 1997) (citing Ward v. EEOC, 719 F.2d 311, 313 (9th Cir. 1983)) (plain text of Title VII contains no express cause of action against EEOC, and it is evident—under traditional analysis used to determine whether federal statute provides implied private right of action—that Title VII does not impliedly authorize suits against EEOC; implying cause of action against EEOC contradicts Title VII's policy of individual enforcement of equal employment opportunity laws and could dissipate limited resources of EEOC in fruitless litigation with charging parties); Forbes v. Reno, 893 F. Supp. 476, 482, 73 FEP 51 (W.D. Pa. 1995), aff'd, 91 F.3d 123, 73 FEP 192 (3d Cir. 1996); Becker v. Sherwin Williams, 717 F. Supp. 288, 294 (D.N.J. 1989), aff'd mem., 9 F.3d 1539 (3d Cir. 1993) (no cause of action against EEOC for its failure to properly prosecute or investigate complaint under ADEA); Circuit City Stores v. EEOC, 75 F. Supp. 2d 491, 505 (E.D.

Generally, "the EEOC may not continue to investigate a charge once formal litigation by the charging party has commenced."[68] As a result, courts may deny enforcement of an EEOC subpoena after issuance of a right-to-sue letter.[69] However, courts have enforced subpoenas requesting information concerning events that occurred after a commissioner's charge was issued.[70]

Memoranda of EEOC investigators may be sheltered from disclosure under the Freedom of Information Act (FOIA) to the extent they are protected by the "deliberative process privilege."[71] Confidential portions of charge files maintained by the EEOC likewise have been shielded from FOIA discovery by employers or others.[72]

Va. 1999), *aff'd mem.*, 232 F.3d 887 (4th Cir. 2000); Terry v. Director, Complaint Adjudication Div., 21 F. Supp. 2d 566 (E.D. Va. 1998), *aff'd mem.*, 173 F.3d 425 (4th Cir. 1999); Reed v. EEOC, 100 F.3d 957, 1996 U.S. App. LEXIS 29032, at *3–4 (6th Cir. Oct. 30, 1996); McCottrell v. EEOC, 726 F.2d 350, 351–52, 33 FEP 1880 (7th Cir. 1984) (employee has no right to challenge EEOC's determination of no reasonable cause; only remedy is pursuing normal private suit in district court against respondent, where employee will have chance to prove that EEOC was wrong); Garcia v. International Rehab. Assocs., 29 F.3d 631 (9th Cir. 1994); Smith v. Casellas, 119 F.3d 33, 74 FEP 854 (D.C. Cir. 1997); Borg-Warner Protective Servs. Corp. v. EEOC, 81 F. Supp. 2d 20, 26, 81 FEP 1052 (D.D.C. 2000), *aff'd*, 245 F.3d 831, 85 FEP 673 (D.C. Cir. 2001); Dillon v. EEOC, 1996 WL 3900 (E.D. La. Jan. 3, 1996); Saccardo v. United States Postal Serv., 51 FEP 424, 425–26 (D. Mass. 1989) (there exists no right to sue EEOC based on dissatisfaction with its findings); Sears v. EEOC, 42 FEP 1890, 1892 (D.D.C. 1987) (Title VII does not provide plaintiffs with cause of action to challenge EEOC's investigation and handling of their charges); Adams v. EEOC, 932 F. Supp. 660, 663, 70 FEP 1357 (E.D. Pa. 1996); Materson v. Stokes, 166 F.R.D. 368, 371, 70 FEP 1630 (E.D. Va. 1996); Askew v. Human Rights Div., 1998 WL 299943 (S.D.N.Y. June 9, 1998); Hartnett v. Texas Commerce Bank, 1997 WL 538744 (N.D. Tex. Aug. 25, 1997); Muniz v. New York, 1997 WL 576033 (S.D.N.Y. Sept. 15, 1997).

[68]EEOC v. Hearst Corp., 103 F.3d 462, 468–69, 72 FEP 1541, 1541 (5th Cir. 1997) (also suggesting that courts have been too lenient in failing to require EEOC to adhere to strict timetables in processing of charges, with consequence that cases often end up in "administrative limbo" for years).

[69]*Id.*

[70]*See, e.g.*, EEOC v. Roadway Express, Inc., 261 F.3d 634, 641–42, 86 FEP 833 (6th Cir. 2001).

[71]*See* Greyson v. McKenna & Cuneo, 879 F. Supp. 1065, 1069, 67 FEP 792, 794 (D. Colo. 1995) ("facts intertwined with the agency's policy and decisionmaking processes are protected" unless "adopted or incorporated by reference into the agency's final decision"); *see also* Section IX *infra*.

[72]*See* Frito-Lay v. EEOC, 964 F. Supp. 236 (W.D. Ky. 1997) (substantial discussion of policy and statutory construction issues); *see also* Venetian Casino Resort, LLC v. EEOC, 409 F.3d 359, 95 FEP 1373 (D.C. Cir. 2005) (challenge to EEOC Compliance Manual § 83, regarding disclosure of information in open case files

4. Reasonable Cause Determination

The EEOC may not bring a Title VII suit unless it[73] first issues a reasonable cause determination[74] that covers the issues to be raised in the suit.[75] In determining whether reasonable cause exists, the EEOC is required to "accord substantial weight to final findings and orders made by State or local authorities in proceedings commenced under State or local law."[76] Once the determination is

---

without notice to employer, ripe where EEOC presently possessed asserted trade secrets or proprietary information).

[73]Courts have approved the Commission's delegation to its district directors of the authority to make cause or dismissal determinations. *See* EEOC v. Raymond Metal Prods. Co., 530 F.2d 590, 592, 12 FEP 38 (4th Cir. 1976) (EEOC suit may be based on cause determination issued by district director without Commission review); EEOC v. MFC Servs., 10 FEP 942, 943 (S.D. Miss. 1975) (same).

[74]*See, e.g.,* EEOC v. Pierce Packing Co., 669 F.2d 605, 608, 28 FEP 393 (9th Cir. 1982) (after allegations that pre-decision settlement agreement between EEOC and employer had been violated, EEOC investigated and sued under Title VII; suit dismissed on ground that EEOC must find cause and attempt conciliation); EEOC v. Westvaco Corp., 372 F. Supp. 985, 994, 7 FEP 579 (D. Md. 1974) (summary judgment for defendants; EEOC sought but failed to obtain "pre-decision settlement," but no reasonable cause determination had been issued and no conciliation had been attempted).

[75]*E.g.,* Wright v. Olin Corp., 697 F.2d 1172, 1176–77, 30 FEP 889 (4th Cir. 1982) (EEOC may not rely on vague and conclusory stipulation that it complied with "administrative and procedural requirements of Title VII material to this action and with all conditions precedent to bringing this action"; each claim must be subject of cause determination); EEOC v. Brown Transp. Corp., 15 FEP 1062, 1064 (N.D. Ga. 1976) (EEOC's finding of no reasonable cause precludes Commission suit on that issue). *Compare* EEOC v. General Elec. Co., 532 F.2d 359, 366, 12 FEP 21 (4th Cir. 1976) (EEOC can sue on matters not in charge if they were developed in course of reasonable investigation of that charge, "provided such discrimination was included in the reasonable cause determination of the EEOC and was followed by compliance with the conciliation procedures fixed in the Act") *with* EEOC v. Sherwood Med. Indus., Inc., 452 F. Supp. 678, 681–84, 17 FEP 441 (M.D. Fla. 1978) (charge alleged race discrimination, but EEOC sued on race and sex bases; sex discrimination allegations were dismissed because there was no reasonable cause determination and no conciliation efforts thereon) *and* EEOC v. Upjohn Corp., 445 F. Supp. 635, 639, 16 FEP 180 (N.D. Ga. 1977) ("the judicial inquiry is limited to those allegations . . . upon which the EEOC made a reasonable cause determination"). *But cf.* EEOC v. Kimberly-Clark Corp., 511 F.2d 1352, 1362 n.13, 10 FEP 38 (6th Cir. 1975) (issuance of cause determination may not be prerequisite to EEOC suit; dictum); EEOC v. Pierce & Stevens Chem. Corp., 434 F. Supp. 1162, 1166–67, 15 FEP 1451 (W.D.N.Y. 1977) (expansion of suit approved where attorneys on staff of EEOC General Counsel followed "pre-suit" procedure specified in EEOC General Counsel Manual and informed defendant of additional allegations; information was exchanged, and there was opportunity to resolve those issues).

[76]42 U.S.C. § 2000e-5(b) (2000); *see* EEOC v. Best Prods. Co., 53 FEP 883, 884 (N.D. Tex. 1990) (deposition testimony by EEOC's local coordinator and affidavit

made, however, the courts' task normally is simply to try the lawsuit, not review the basis for or correctness of the EEOC's cause determination.[77] However, in considering whether a suit should be allowed to proceed on a basis or an issue arguably different from that presented in the charge, a few courts have looked at the adequacy of the EEOC's fact finding.[78] Even where *a court* would lack jurisdiction to second guess (much less vacate) a cause determination, the EEOC *itself* may reconsider its cause determinations.[79]

Under the ADEA, a determination that a probable violation exists has been held to be a necessary element of conciliation and therefore a condition precedent to an EEOC suit.[80]

Sometimes settlements are reached before the EEOC makes a reasonable cause determination. In these circumstances, courts may have jurisdiction to enforce the settlement agreements even in the

---

of its compliance manager showed that substantial weight was accorded to state agency; no basis to question EEOC's cause determination); EEOC v. James Julian, Inc., 736 F. Supp. 59, 62, 53 FEP 458 (D. Del. 1990) (EEOC not bound by findings of state agency; less deference to state agency required when state law does not prohibit retaliation); *cf.* EEOC v. Carolina Freight Carriers Corp., 686 F. Supp. 309, 311, 47 FEP 419 (S.D. Fla. 1988) (when local agency found no cause and EEOC found reasonable cause, EEOC not bound to accord any weight to state agency's conclusions of law for purpose of applying federal law).

[77]*E.g.*, EEOC v. Food & Commercial Workers Local 1105, 48 FEP 1895, 1895 (D. Or. 1988) (allegations of misconduct by EEOC in arriving at its reasonable cause determination insufficient as matter of law to state affirmative defense to Title VII action); EEOC v. Sears, Roebuck & Co., 24 FEP 937, 940 (N.D. Ga. 1980) (not duty of court to review sufficiency of evidence underlying EEOC determination of reasonable cause); EEOC v. Western Elec. Co., 382 F. Supp. 787, 794, 8 FEP 595 (D. Md. 1971) (same); *see* EEOC v. E.I. du Pont de Nemours & Co., 373 F. Supp. 1321, 1338, 7 FEP 759 (D. Del. 1974) ("It is one thing for courts to insist upon procedural compliance with the Act and quite another for them to test the factual basis for Commission action."), *aff'd*, 516 F.2d 1297, 10 FEP 916 (3d Cir. 1975); EEOC v. Purex Corp., 9 FEP 171, 172 (E.D. Mo. 1974) (failure of EEOC cause determination to mention adverse ruling by state agency not basis for summary judgment against EEOC where state held no hearing). *Contra* EEOC v. King's Daughters Hosp., 12 FEP 484, 489–90 (S.D. Miss. 1976) ("complete failure" of EEOC to make good faith investigation; complaint dismissed).

[78]*E.g.*, EEOC v. New York Times Broad. Serv., Inc., 364 F. Supp. 651, 654, 6 FEP 563 (W.D. Tenn. 1973) (court dismissed race allegation in EEOC's complaint; statistics did not support EEOC's cause determination on that issue, and allegation was too far removed from underlying sex discrimination charge).

[79]*See* 29 C.F.R. § 1601.21(b); *cf.* EEOC v. Jacksonville Shipyards, Inc., 696 F. Supp. 1438, 1441, 48 FEP 66 (M.D. Fla. 1988) (previous finding of no reasonable cause for particular charge does not estop EEOC from subsequently including charge in larger pattern-or-practice lawsuit).

[80]Marshall v. Sun Oil Co., 605 F.2d 1331, 1337, 21 FEP 257 (5th Cir. 1979) (burden is met by making out prima facie case).

absence of a cause determination.[81] The plaintiff, however, is limited to enforcing the agreement and may not litigate the underlying charge.

The admissibility of EEOC cause determinations was extensively examined by the Sixth Circuit in *EEOC v. Ford Motor Co.*[82] The court found that "district courts should be free to adopt a general rule that refuses to admit these cause determinations in any sort of trial, whether to the court or to a jury" because the courts' fact-finding process should not be influenced by "what the EEOC thought the facts were when it brought the case before the district court."[83] The court concluded that an EEOC cause determination "carries an evidentiary value of practically zero."[84] A concurring judge would have prohibited the EEOC from using cause determinations in its own litigation, but would have permitted their use in private litigation.[85]

The Fifth Circuit has explained that although it considers EEOC determinations of reasonable cause to be presumptively admissible, district courts still retain discretion regarding the admissibility of such letters.[86] Moreover, the court found that an EEOC "letter of violation" is more likely to be excluded than a "letter of reasonable cause" because the former threatens greater prejudice by stating a "categorical legal conclusion," whereas the latter is "more tentative."[87]

Admissibility of no-cause determinations may be an issue of historical interest only since the EEOC's 1996 Enforcement Plan dispensed with the practice of issuing no-cause determinations.[88]

---

[81]EEOC v. Henry Beck Co., 729 F.2d 301, 305–06, 34 FEP 373 (4th Cir. 1984) (employee, employer, and EEOC entered into predetermination settlement agreement after employee filed charge with EEOC, but before EEOC issued reasonable cause determination; employer then breached agreement; because Title VII encourages voluntary compliance, action by EEOC to enforce agreement is "brought directly under" Title VII, and district court therefore had jurisdiction); *cf.* Eatmon v. Bristol Steel & Iron Works, Inc., 769 F.2d 1503, 1513, 38 FEP 1364 (11th Cir. 1985) (employees who never filed charges with EEOC executed releases, accepting benefits under conciliation agreement between employer and Office of Federal Contract Compliance Programs; district court had jurisdiction to hear employees' action to enforce settlement).

[82]98 F.3d 1341 (table), 1996 WL 557800, at *5 (6th Cir. Sept. 30, 1996).

[83]*Id.* at *9–10.

[84]*Id.* at *13.

[85]*Id.* (Wellford, J., concurring).

[86]EEOC v. Manville Sales Corp., 27 F.3d 1089, 1095, 65 FEP 804, 809 (5th Cir. 1994).

[87]*Id.*

[88]EEOC, *National Enforcement Plan*, DAILY LAB. REP. (BNA), at E-1 (Feb. 9, 1996).

EEOC reasonable cause determinations are immune from review by the courts. Employers may not seek judicial review of EEOC reasonable cause determinations because the determinations are not final Commission actions ripe for adjudication.[89]

5. Conciliation

Title VII requires that, if the Commission finds cause, it "shall endeavor to eliminate any such alleged unlawful employment practice by informal methods of conference, conciliation and persuasion"[90] and may file suit only if it "has been unable to secure . . . a conciliation agreement acceptable to the [EEOC]."[91] Similarly, the ADEA requires that "[b]efore instituting any action" the EEOC "shall attempt to eliminate" the discrimination "and to effect voluntary compliance . . . through informal methods of conciliation, conference, and persuasion."[92]

Courts have required that conciliation afford a fair opportunity to defendants to address issues to be raised in litigation,[93] and

---

[89]See AT&T Co. v. EEOC, 270 F.3d 973, 976, 87 FEP 385 (D.C. Cir. 2001) (noting that "to allow AT&T to institute litigation with the Commission over the lawfulness of its [pension calculation] policy would be to preempt the Commission's discretion to allocate its resources as between this issue and this employer, as opposed to other issues and other employers, as well as its ability to choose the venue for its litigation, as the statute contemplates"); Borg-Warner Protective Servs. Corp. v. EEOC, 245 F.3d 831, 834–35, 85 FEP 673 (D.C. Cir. 2001) (pre-suit determination of probable cause by Commission not judicially reviewable under Administrative Procedure Act (APA)); Bell Atl. Cash Balance Plan v. EEOC, 182 F.3d 906, 81 FEP 96 (4th Cir. 1999); Georator Corp. v. EEOC, 592 F.2d 765, 767 (4th Cir. 1979) (no review under APA or Title VII).

[90]42 U.S.C. § 2000e-5(b).

[91]Id. § 2000e-5(f)(1).

[92]29 U.S.C. § 626(b).

[93]See EEOC v. Sears, Roebuck & Co., 650 F.2d 14, 18–19, 25 FEP 1338 (2d Cir. 1981) (nationwide conciliation did not provide fair opportunity to discuss practices at two specific stores at issue); EEOC v. Sears, Roebuck & Co., 490 F. Supp. 1245, 1257–58, 22 FEP 1479 (M.D. Ala. 1980) (EEOC's "all or nothing" nationwide conciliation effort too broad to constitute attempt to conciliate issues at single Sears facility named in suit); EEOC v. Fox Point-Bayside Sch. Dist., 24 FEP 668, 669 (E.D. Wis. 1980) (when EEOC has not discharged its statutory duty to conciliate as to some claims, those claims will be stayed to permit conciliation); EEOC v. Griffin Wheel Co., 12 FEP 523, 525 (N.D. Ala. 1975) (EEOC cannot file suit unless claims are revealed during investigation, employer has opportunity to comment, and claim is subject to conciliation); EEOC v. E.I. du Pont de Nemours & Co., 373 F. Supp. 1321, 1336, 7 FEP 759 (D. Del. 1974) (not intention of Congress that "the Commission could attempt conciliation on one set of issues and, having failed, litigate a

that conciliation be attempted with every respondent.[94] The courts are divided on whether, in a class-type or other collective action, the EEOC must attempt to conciliate on behalf of each potential claimant.[95] Although the EEOC generally may not pursue legal *claims* that were not the subject of conciliation, it is not required to seek in conciliation all the *relief* that it may later pursue in court.[96]

---

different set"), *aff'd*, 516 F.2d 1297 (3d Cir. 1975); EEOC v. Westvaco Corp., 372 F. Supp. 985, 992, 994, 7 FEP 579 (D. Md. 1974) (EEOC held to higher standard than private litigant; case dismissed because there was neither reasonable cause finding nor opportunity for conciliation). *But cf.* EEOC v. Sears, Roebuck & Co., 50 FEP 1123, 1124–25 (N.D. Cal. 1989) (where employer denied all wrongdoing, EEOC permitted to include claim of age discrimination in its complaint even though age claim was not included in proposed conciliation agreement concerning race discrimination); EEOC v. Sara Lee Corp., 923 F. Supp. 994, 999–1000, 70 FEP 57, 60 (W.D. Mich. 1995) (declining to dismiss or stay action where EEOC submitted no proof that it discussed merits of individual claims for which relief was sought with defendant); *accord* EEOC v. Dolphin Cruise Line, Inc., 945 F. Supp. 1550, 1557, 6 AD 187, 191–92 (S.D. Fla. 1996); EEOC v. Johnson & Higgins, Inc., 887 F. Supp. 682, 689, 68 FEP 1481, 1489 (S.D.N.Y. 1995), *aff'd*, 91 F.3d 1529, 71 FEP 818 (2d Cir. 1996); EEOC v. Acorn Niles Corp., 1995 WL 519976 (N.D. Ill. Aug. 30, 1995). *But see* EEOC v. Warshawsky & Co., 1994 WL 384041 (N.D. Ill. July 21, 1994) (EEOC may not receive relief for pre-1984 pregnant employees because it did not conciliate with employer with respect to that group).

[94]*See* EEOC v. United States Pipe & Foundry Co., 375 F. Supp. 237, 243–45, 248, 7 FEP 977 (N.D. Ala. 1974) (when no effort had been made to conciliate with labor union, court lacked jurisdiction over union; moreover, because union was indispensable party, employer should be granted summary judgment; court rejected EEOC's request to remand case to it for 60 days, because conciliation must be completed before EEOC files suit); EEOC v. Raymond Metal Prods. Co., 385 F. Supp. 907, 912, 8 FEP 1199 (D. Md. 1974) (granting union defendant summary judgment; EEOC had not attempted to conciliate with union after conciliation with employer failed), *rev'd in part on other grounds*, 530 F.2d 590, 12 FEP 38 (4th Cir. 1976).

[95]*Compare* EEOC v. Rhone-Poulenc, Inc., 876 F.2d 16, 17, 50 FEP 86 (3d Cir. 1989) (per curiam) (ADEA class-type action may include individuals for whom no specific conciliation efforts were undertaken; EEOC not required to provide documentation of individual attempts to conciliate on behalf of each potential claimant) *with* EEOC v. American Express Publ'g Corp., 681 F. Supp. 216, 221–22, 47 FEP 1596 (S.D.N.Y. 1988) (dismissing EEOC claims on behalf of unnamed individuals for whom EEOC did not make "strong, affirmative attempts" at conciliation).

[96]*See* EEOC v. Massey-Ferguson, Inc., 622 F.2d 271, 277, 22 FEP 1330 (7th Cir. 1980) (conciliation need not include "every possible form of relief which might be sought in order to remedy these practices"; EEOC may request back pay in court even though that was not sought in conciliation); EEOC v. Akron Nat'l Bank & Trust Co., 497 F. Supp. 733, 737, 22 FEP 1665 (N.D. Ohio 1980) (if EEOC is to fulfill Congress' desire for conciliation, it "must be willing to accept conciliation agreements that afford less relief than it thinks would be afforded by a court following a trial"; proposed conciliation agreement therefore is inadmissible).

Considerable litigation has focused on the sufficiency of the EEOC's conciliation efforts.[97] The EEOC's obligation to conciliate is discharged when the respondent refuses to conciliate.[98] Although most courts will not assess the substance of the conciliation,[99] courts do require the EEOC to make a good faith effort at conciliation.[100]

---

[97]*See* EEOC v. Johnson & Higgins, Inc., 91 F.3d 1529 (2d Cir. 1996) (quoting EEOC v. New Cherokee Corp., 829 F. Supp. 73, 80 (S.D.N.Y. 1993)) (EEOC fulfills its duty to conciliate before initiating litigation if it (1) outlines to employer reasonable cause for its belief that employer is in violation of the Act; (2) offers opportunity for voluntary compliance; and (3) responds in reasonable and flexible manner to reasonable attitude of employer; in this case EEOC satisfied its duty to conciliate where it sent employer letter of determination and where employer refused to accommodate EEOC's repeated requests for information about salaries of retired directors in order to negotiate question of damages); EEOC v. Equicredit Corp. of Am., 2002 U.S. Dist. LEXIS 19985 (E.D. Pa. Oct. 8, 2002) (for EEOC to satisfy requirements of attempted conciliation, this circuit requires EEOC to (1) inform employer of how to come into compliance with Act; (2) inform employer that terminated employees may recover back pay; (3) notify employers that EEOC may initiate legal proceedings; and (4) assure employer that it may respond to violations, in light of possible remedy) (citing EEOC v. Rhone-Poulenc, Inc., 677 F. Supp. 264, 266 (D.N.J. 1988)), *aff'd*, 2002 U.S. App. LEXIS 22808 (3d Cir. 2002).

[98]*E.g.*, EEOC v. Radiator Specialty Co., 610 F.2d 178, 183, 21 FEP 351 (4th Cir. 1979) (good faith attempt at conciliation enough); Marshall v. Sun Oil Co., 605 F.2d 1331, 1337, 21 FEP 257 (5th Cir. 1979) (ADEA action; when EEOC makes out case of discrimination and employer refuses to discuss evidence, EEOC need not conduct further investigation or conciliation efforts); EEOC v. Jacksonville Shipyards, Inc., 696 F. Supp. 1438, 1444–45, 48 FEP 66 (M.D. Fla. 1988) (EEOC efforts sufficient when employer categorically denied allegation contained in charge and rejected EEOC's settlement offer); EEOC v. Rymer Foods, Inc., 50 FEP 787, 788 (N.D. Ill. 1989) (EEOC made good faith effort to conciliate when it gave employer draft of its proposed settlement offer and employer rejected proposal and refused to concede past discrimination); EEOC v. Procter & Gamble Mfg. Co., 20 FEP 170, 172 (D. Md. 1979) (defendant refused to discuss violations found in determination that it felt lacked factual basis); EEOC v. North Cent. Airlines, 475 F. Supp. 667, 670, 20 FEP 957 (D. Minn. 1979) (defendant's ambiguous response to EEOC's conciliation proposal justified termination of conciliation); Marshall v. Hartford Fire Ins. Co., 78 F.R.D. 97, 107, 18 FEP 15 (D. Conn. 1978) (EEOC has no further duty to conciliate when employer, after being properly informed, refuses to conciliate).

[99]*See* EEOC v. Pierce & Stevens Chem. Corp., 434 F. Supp. 1162, 1166, 15 FEP 1451 (W.D.N.Y. 1977) (conciliation prerequisite satisfied even though EEOC raised new issues after conciliation; efforts to resolve these issues during pre-suit procedures cured any deficiency); EEOC v. Rexall Drug Co., 10 FEP 450, 453 (E.D. Mo. 1974) (court will not dismiss where "Commission engaged in at least some minimal dialogue (telephone call) with the defendant union"); *cf.* EEOC v. Bumble Bee Seafoods Co., 19 FEP 854, 856 (D. Or. 1979) (agreement of parties that pre-decision settlement efforts would satisfy conciliation requirement valid). *But see* EEOC v. Sherwood Med. Indus., Inc., 452 F. Supp. 678, 684, 17 FEP 441 (M.D. Fla. 1978) (rejecting as "frivolous" contention that court cannot inquire into merits of conciliation, and ordering stricken sex discrimination claim that EEOC did not attempt to conciliate).

[100]*See* EEOC v. Keco Indus., Inc., 748 F.2d 1097, 1101–02, 36 FEP 511 (6th Cir. 1984) (EEOC under no duty to attempt further conciliation with employer after

Thus, in *Patterson v. American Tobacco Co.*,[101] the Fourth Circuit remanded with directions to dismiss the union defendant because of the EEOC's failure to appropriately attempt conciliation.[102] The dispositive deficiency there was that the EEOC representative concededly lacked the authority to settle. In assessing whether particular conciliation efforts were sufficient to permit the EEOC to proceed with a lawsuit, courts generally have avoided setting bright-line rules.[103] One court has held that the EEOC's obligation to conciliate in good faith requires, at a minimum, that the employer "be told how to achieve compliance."[104] Flexibility on both sides

---

employer rejects good faith conciliation effort; form and substance of conciliation are within discretion of EEOC; court should determine only whether attempt was made); EEOC v. Best Prods. Co., 53 FEP 883, 884–85 (N.D. Tex. 1990) (multiple telephone calls, letters between parties, and unsuccessful conciliation conference constitute good faith effort to conciliate); EEOC v. Rymer Foods, Inc., 50 FEP 787, 788 (N.D. Ill. 1989) (when EEOC conducted conciliation negotiations and provided defendant with draft of proposed settlement, EEOC acted in good faith in light of defendant's flat rejection of proposal); EEOC v. Cabot Corp., 48 FEP 1136, 1137 (E.D. Pa. 1988) (EEOC reasonably determined that further efforts to conciliate on behalf of unnamed employees would be futile); EEOC v. KDM Sch. Bus Co., 612 F. Supp. 369, 374, 38 FEP 602 (S.D.N.Y. 1985) (EEOC's letter to employer school district adequate conciliation, under standard of "reasonableness and responsiveness . . . under all the circumstances"; EEOC's action challenged state mandatory retirement regulation that school district had no discretion to disregard, and school district's only response to EEOC's letter was that EEOC should reverse its position); EEOC v. Riss Int'l Corp., 525 F. Supp. 1094, 1099, 35 FEP 416 (W.D. Mo. 1981) (conciliation efforts on employee's charge adequate when EEOC did not consider conciliation efforts unsuccessful until employer stated that it would provide no further information and when employer made clear that it would not be likely to conciliate on any terms); EEOC v. St. Louis-S.F. Ry., 35 FEP 86, 88–89 (N.D. Okla. 1980) (EEOC attempted conciliation, even though its efforts fell far short of exhaustive efforts; made stringent demands on employer; and did not change its position as to its offers), *rev'd on other grounds*, 743 F.2d 739, 35 FEP 1163 (10th Cir. 1984).

[101]535 F.2d 257, 12 FEP 314 (4th Cir. 1976).

[102]*Id.* at 271–72.

[103]*See* EEOC v. Mack Trucks, Inc., 10 FEP 1028, 1029 (D. Md. 1974) (whether EEOC attempted conciliation in good faith is question of fact not to be resolved on motion for summary judgment); *Rymer Foods*, 50 FEP at 787 ("Conciliation is a flexible, responsive process that by necessity differs from case to case."). EEOC regulations formerly required the agency to issue a "last chance" notice before finally terminating conciliation (former 29 C.F.R. § 1601.23). Some courts then held that failure to send such notice constituted a fatal defect barring subsequent litigation. *See, e.g.*, EEOC v. United States Pipe & Foundry Co., 375 F. Supp. 237, 248, 249, 7 FEP 977 (N.D. Ala. 1974) (summary judgment granted where EEOC did not send § 1601.25 "last chance" notice). However, the EEOC has amended its procedural regulations; they no longer require a "last chance" notice. 29 C.F.R. § 1601.25.

[104]EEOC v. Westinghouse Elec. Corp., 632 F. Supp. 343, 360, 40 FEP 643 (E.D. Pa. 1986) ("Specifically, the employer should be informed (1) of the ways compliance may be achieved, (2) that affected employees may receive 'make whole' remedies,

often is mentioned as essential.[105] In *EEOC v. Pet, Inc.*,[106] the court held that the EEOC's refusal to conciliate the class issues because the respondent refused to conciliate the claims of the individual charging party is

> not the sort of good-faith attempt at conciliation on the part of EEOC that Title VII contemplates. To withdraw from discussions while the other party is offering to negotiate the broad issues, merely because an impasse has occurred as to the charging party, smacks more of coercion than of conciliation. Such an all-or-nothing approach on the part of a commission, one of whose most essential functions is to attempt conciliation, will not do.[107]

Courts have reached different results as to whether to stay or dismiss a Title VII action after finding that appropriate conciliation did not occur. Most[108] but not all[109] courts prefer a stay pending further conciliation rather than dismissal.

---

(3) that the Commission may institute legal action, and (4) that the employer may respond to the Commission's allegations."), *rev'd in part on other grounds*, 869 F.2d 696 (3d Cir.), *vacated on other grounds*, 493 U.S. 801 (1989).

[105]*E.g.*, EEOC v. City of Chi., 51 FEP 499, 501 (N.D. Ill. 1987) (EEOC should (1) outline to employer its basis for belief that violation of ADEA had occurred; (2) give employer opportunity to comply voluntarily with law; and (3) react in flexible and responsive way to reasonable attitudes of employer).

[106]612 F.2d 1001, 22 FEP 370 (5th Cir. 1980) (per curiam).

[107]*Id.* at 1002.

[108]*E.g.*, *id.* (dismissal is "a sanction far too harsh where, as here, conciliation has at least been attempted in good faith, though prematurely aborted"); EEOC v. Zia Co., 582 F.2d 527, 533–35, 17 FEP 1201 (10th Cir. 1978) (although court "should not examine the details of the offers and counteroffers between the parties, nor impose its notions of what the agreement should provide," EEOC "acted improperly" when it terminated conciliation without allowing sufficient time for reasonable negotiations with another federal agency, which had indemnification obligation; however, court refused to dismiss action, instead ordering stay of proceedings pending further conciliation efforts); *cf.* EEOC v. Prudential Fed. Sav. & Loan Ass'n, 763 F.2d 1166, 1169, 37 FEP 1691 (10th Cir. 1985) ("when the EEOC initially makes a sufficient albeit limited effort to conciliate, the minimal jurisdictional requirement of the [ADEA] is satisfied.... Once this initial effort is made, 'if the district court finds that further conciliation efforts are required the proper course is to stay proceedings until such informal conciliation can be concluded.' " (citation omitted)); EEOC v. Hugin Sweda, Inc., 750 F. Supp. 165, 168, 54 FEP 1140 (D.N.J. 1990) (EEOC's efforts met minimal conciliation requirements, but action still was stayed to allow EEOC to do even more); EEOC v. Die Fliedermaus, L.L.C., 77 F. Supp. 2d 460, 467, 82 FEP 1809 (S.D.N.Y. 1999); EEOC v. Pacific Mar. Ass'n, 188 F.R.D. 379, 381 (D. Or. 1999); EEOC v. HBH, Inc., 1999 WL 508403, at *3 (E.D. La. July 19, 1999); EEOC v. First Midwest Bank, N.A., 14 F. Supp. 2d 1028, 77 FEP 1121 (N.D. Ill. 1998); *City of Chi.*, 66 FEP at 226.

[109]*See* EEOC v. Sears, Roebuck & Co., 650 F.2d 14, 19, 25 FEP 1338 (2d Cir. 1981) (affirming dismissal; court below had dismissed when it found existence of suit would "put a pall" over meaningful conciliation; court affirms, even though "we

In EPA cases, the Fifth and Eighth Circuits have allowed the EEOC to sue without prior conciliation efforts.[110] Failure of conciliation neither signals that the EEOC's administrative process has ended nor starts the clock for filing suit: "the EEOC has power to take administrative actions . . . until the matter is formally closed or referred to litigation."[111] After the employer rejects the EEOC's offer, the EEOC is under no obligation to continue negotiations.[112] The substance of the EEOC's conciliation offers are within its discretion and not reviewable by the courts.[113] However, EEOC refusal to allow reasonable inquiry of the conciliation offer's terms may warrant a stay to permit further conciliation.[114] One district court allowed an employer to raise lack of conciliation as an affirmative defense because the EEOC had rejected the employer's offer to mediate.[115] Another district court disallowed a failure-to-conciliate defense because the employer previously refused to respond to the EEOC's offer to mediate.[116] The EEOC's obligation to conciliate following a cause determination is distinct from EEOC mediation, which is voluntary.

The EEOC cannot amend its complaint to include additional parties without conciliation on behalf of the added parties.[117]

---

think it would have been preferable for the district court to stay proceedings to promote renewed conciliation rather than dismiss the action. The extensiveness of the Commission's conciliation efforts militate against dismissal. However, the statute contemplates that the decision of whether to stay proceedings or dismiss the action is committed to the trial court's discretion." (citation omitted)).

[110]*See* EEOC v. Hernando Bank, Inc., 724 F.2d 1188, 1193–94, 34 FEP 15 (5th Cir. 1984) (no requirement that EEOC attempt conciliation as precondition to filing EPA suit); EEOC v. Home of Econ., Inc., 712 F.2d 356, 357–58, 32 FEP 599 (8th Cir. 1983) (same).

[111]EEOC v. CNA Ins. Cos., 96 F.3d 1039, 1042–43, 5 AD 1769, 1771 (7th Cir. 1996).

[112]*See* EEOC v. Bernina of Am., 2000 U.S. Dist. LEXIS 8336, at *6 (N.D. Ill. June 13, 2000) (the EEOC is under no duty to attempt further conciliation after an employer rejects its offer).

[113]*Id*. at *7.

[114]*See* EEOC v. Golden Lender Fin. Group, 82 FEP 1253, 1257 (S.D.N.Y. 2000) (where employer met other terms requested by EEOC but requested information regarding extent of damages of alleged victims other than charging parties, EEOC's failure to respond is unreasonable and warrants stay).

[115]*See* EEOC v. Fenyves & Nerenberg, 1999 WL 134279, at *8 (M.D. Pa. Mar. 9, 1999) (denying EEOC's motion for summary judgment with respect to employer's affirmative defense that EEOC did not properly fulfill responsibilities precedent to bringing a Title VII action).

[116]*See* EEOC v. Charoen Pokphand USA, Inc., 133 F. Supp. 2d 1237, 1244 (M.D. Ala. 2001).

[117]*See* EEOC v. HBH, Inc., 1999 WL 319213, at *2 (E.D. La. July 19, 1999).

B. Administrative Prerequisites to Pattern-or-Practice Suits Under § 707

Under the 1972 amendments to Title VII, the EEOC acquired the Attorney General's former authority to bring § 707 pattern-or-practice suits against nongovernmental defendants.[118] Although there had been no procedural prerequisites for the Attorney General to bring a pattern-or-practice suit, the 1972 amendments added § 707(e), which provides:

> [T]he Commission shall have authority to investigate and act on a charge of a pattern or practice of discrimination, whether filed by or on behalf of a person claiming to be aggrieved or by a member of the Commission. *All such actions shall be conducted in accordance with the procedures set forth in [§ 706] of this title.*[119]

Section 707(e) thus provides that there must be an individual or commissioner charge and compliance with all of the § 706 prerequisites to suit before a pattern-or-practice suit can be filed. In *EEOC v. United Air Lines, Inc.*,[120] the court explained:

> The Commission's new authority under 707(e), unlike the Attorney General's authority under 707(a), is required to be exercised in accordance with the procedures set forth in section 706(b), which includes efforts to conciliate with the respondent prior to the institution of suit.[121]

However, in *United States v. Allegheny-Ludlum Industries, Inc.*,[122] the Fifth Circuit held that the incorporation of § 706 jurisdictional procedures into § 707(e) did not incorporate the intervention provisions of § 706.[123] Thus, individual aggrieved parties do not have an absolute right to intervene in a pattern-or-practice suit brought by the government under § 707.[124]

One court, finding "no statutory language, no regulation, no case, and no commentator which definitely holds that there is any

---

[118]*See generally* Chapter 30 (Justice Department Litigation).
[119]42 U.S.C. § 2000e-6(e) (emphasis added).
[120]12 FEP 1592 (N.D. Ill. 1975), *aff'd as modified on other grounds*, 560 F.2d 224, 15 FEP 310 (7th Cir. 1977).
[121]*Id.* at 1594.
[122]517 F.2d 826, 11 FEP 167 (5th Cir. 1975).
[123]*Id.* at 843–44.
[124]*See* Section VII.B *infra*. The *Allegheny-Ludlum* court went on in dictum to state:
Under § 707, the EEOC (formerly the Attorney General) may institute a "pattern or practice" suit anytime it has "reasonable cause" to believe such a suit necessary. Section 707 does not make it mandatory that anyone file a charge against the employer or follow administrative timetables before suit may be

limitations period applicable to a § 707 pattern or practice case initiated by the filing of a Commissioner's charge," held that there is no statute of limitations applicable to a commissioner's charge initiating a § 707 case.[125] The court reasoned that, given the nature of the commissioner's charge process, it would be arbitrary to apply the 300-day period backward from the date of the charge and that such a statute of limitations would be "inconsistent with the very nature of a pattern-or-practice violation."[126] Another court found that it had no jurisdiction to hear a pattern-or-practice suit brought by the EEOC because the individual claims were not reasonably related to a pattern or practice of race or national origin discrimination.[127]

III. EEOC INTERNAL PROCESSES

A. Statutory Authority

The 1972 amendments, which gave the EEOC the authority to litigate, also established within the EEOC a quasi-independent, presidentially appointed General Counsel. Section 705(b)(1) provides that the

> General Counsel shall have responsibility for the conduct of litigation as provided in [§§ 706 and 707] of this title. The General Counsel shall have such other duties as the Commission may prescribe or as may be provided by law and shall concur with the Chairman of the Commission on the appointment and supervision of regional attorneys.[128]

Section 705(b)(2) provides that "[a]ttorneys appointed under this section may, at the direction of the Commission, appear for

---

brought. It was unquestionably the design of Congress in the enactment of § 707 to provide the government with a swift and effective weapon to vindicate the broad public interest in eliminating unlawful practices, at a level which may or may not address the grievances of particular individuals.
517 F.2d at 843 (citations omitted); *see also* EEOC v. Stroh Brewery Co., 83 F.R.D. 17, 30, 19 FEP 1099 (E.D. Mich. 1979) (to require "§ 706 type of reasonable cause . . . for each and every allegation that cumulatively establishes the pattern or practice" in § 707 pattern-or-practice suits would unnecessarily restrict use of § 707).
[125]EEOC v. Mitsubishi Motor Mfg., 990 F. Supp. 1059, 1083, 75 FEP 1379 (C.D. Ill. 1998).
[126]*Id.* at 1085.
[127]EEOC v. Golden Lender Fin. Group, 82 FEP 1253, 1256 (S.D.N.Y. 2000).
[128]42 U.S.C. § 2000e-4(b)(1). Section 705(a) specifies that the EEOC Chairman "shall be responsible on behalf of the Commission for the administrative operations of the Commission." *Id.* § 2000e-4(a).

and represent the Commission in any case in court, provided that the Attorney General shall conduct all litigation to which the Commission is a party in the Supreme Court."[129]

B. Organization of the Office of General Counsel

The Office of General Counsel (OGC) of the EEOC contains three divisions that enforce Title VII, the ADA, the ADEA, and the EPA.[130] The first division, Litigation Management Services, is responsible for conducting trial court litigation and recommending cases to the Commission for litigation. Litigation Management Services, headed by an associate general counsel, has lawyers in the Washington, D.C., headquarters office and in more than 20 field office legal units.[131] The second division, Appellate Services, conducts litigation in the U.S. courts of appeals and the U.S. Supreme Court (in conjunction with the Solicitor General of the United States). Appellate Services also acts on behalf of the Commission in appearances amicus curiae in state and federal courts.[132] The third division, Systemic Litigation Services, conducts certain cases alleging a pattern or practice of unlawful employment discrimination.[133]

In addition to those three litigating divisions, the Office of Legal Counsel in the Washington, D.C., headquarters office is responsible for assisting in the development of policy statements for

---

[129]*Id.* § 2000e-4(b)(2).

[130]*Structure of the Office of General Counsel*, REGIONAL ATTORNEYS' DESKBOOK (BNA) GC:1003–04 (Sept. 30, 1990). As noted earlier in this chapter, President Carter's Reorganization Plan No. 1 of 1978 transferred to the General Counsel the responsibilities and functions of the Department of Labor in enforcing and litigating actions under the ADEA and the EPA. 3 C.F.R. § 321 (1978), *reprinted in* 5 U.S.C. app. at 205 (2000).

[131]*Structure of the Office of General Counsel*, at GC:1004. The field legal units presently are located in Atlanta, Baltimore, Birmingham, Charlotte, Chicago, Cleveland, Dallas, Denver, Detroit, Houston, Indianapolis, Los Angeles, Memphis, Miami, Milwaukee, New Orleans, New York, Philadelphia, Phoenix, San Antonio, San Francisco, Seattle, and St. Louis. Each is headed by a regional attorney, who reports to (1) the Associate General Counsel for Litigation Management Services in connection with conducting litigation and (2) the district director in the field office in connection with providing legal support for investigations and conciliations.

[132]*Id.*

[133]*Id.* OGC also maintains a Research and Analytical Services Staff composed of economists, psychologists, statisticians, and social science analysts to provide assistance, in complex cases, to the litigation divisions of OGC.

the Commission and conducting defensive litigation on behalf of the Commission when the EEOC is sued by present or former employees.

The *Regional Attorneys' Deskbook* (published by BNA) contains internal guidance on EEOC litigation. But the mere failure to abide by regulations (much less internal guidance) does not preclude a suit by the EEOC. Instead, substantial compliance with regulations is sufficient and not reviewable absent an affirmative showing of substantial prejudice to the affected party.[134]

IV. EEOC SUITS IN THE NATURE OF CLASS ACTIONS

A. Compliance With Federal Rule of Civil Procedure 23 Not Required

In *General Telephone Co. v. EEOC*,[135] the Supreme Court held that EEOC Title VII suits that seek relief for others in addition to the original charging party are not subject to the requirements that govern Rule 23 class actions.[136] The defendant there contended that the EEOC lacked authority to seek class-type relief without complying with Rule 23. The Court held, however, that

> the EEOC need look no farther than § 706(f) for its authority to bring suit in its own name for the purpose . . . of securing relief for a group of aggrieved individuals. Its authority to bring such actions is in no way dependent upon Rule 23, and the Rule has no application to a § 706 suit.[137]

Courts have generally held that the *General Telephone* rule applies to a private action in which the EEOC intervenes.[138]

---

[134]*See* EEOC v. Appleton Elec. Co., 487 F. Supp. 1207 (N.D. Ill. 1980).

[135]446 U.S. 318, 22 FEP 1196 (1980).

[136]*Id.* at 324.

[137]*Id.*; *accord In re* Bemis Co., 279 F.3d 419 (7th Cir. 2002) (EEOC exempt from Rule 23 even when it seeks compensatory and punitive damages and does not allege pattern or practice of discrimination); EEOC v. United Parcel Serv., 860 F.2d 372, 375, 48 FEP 245 (10th Cir. 1988) (EEOC may act to further overriding public interest in equal employment opportunity); EEOC v. Astronautics Corp., 660 F. Supp. 838, 842, 43 FEP 1569 (E.D. Wis. 1987) (Rule 23 requirements do not apply to EEOC subpoena enforcement action).

[138]*See, e.g.*, Fields v. Beech Aircraft Corp., 95 F.R.D. 1, 6, 38 FEP 1239 (1981) (presence of EEOC as intervenor made issue of class certification academic because

Courts recognize the EEOC's authority to bring suits that could not be brought as class actions by private individuals.[139]

The EEOC likewise is exempt from the procedural requirements governing a private collective action when it is pursuing an action under the ADEA[140] or the EPA.[141] EEOC actions seeking relief for persons under the ADEA and EPA are brought pursuant to §§ 16(c) and 17 of the Fair Labor Standards Act (FLSA)[142] and are exempt from the FLSA "opt-in" provisions that apply to private suits.[143] By incorporating the enforcement procedures of the FLSA, the ADEA authorizes the EEOC to intervene on behalf of multiple plaintiffs "whether or not they are 'similarly situated,' common questions of law or fact 'predominate,' or claims arise out of the same action or 'occurrence.' "[144]

EEOC could seek classwide relief without comporting with Rule 23), *modified on reh'g on other grounds*, 39 FEP 582 (D. Kan. 1982); Harris v. Amoco Prods. Co., 768 F.2d 669, 680–83, 38 FEP 1226 (5th Cir. 1985) (EEOC is advocate of public interest and can litigate its suit in intervention even though private plaintiffs' case not certified pursuant to Rule 23; private plaintiffs settled with defendants and ceased litigation; and EEOC had not previously met § 706(f)(1) jurisdictional prerequisites— investigation, decision, and conciliation—for independent government suit); United Telecomms., Inc. v. Saffels, 741 F.2d 312, 313–14, 35 FEP 1232 (10th Cir. 1984) (employer not entitled to writ of mandamus requiring district court to make EEOC, an intervenor, satisfy Rule 23 before seeking classwide relief; Rule 23 does not apply to EEOC, even in intervention).

[139]*See* EEOC v. United Parcel Serv., 94 F.3d 314, 318, 71 FEP 1301 (7th Cir. 1996) (no need for EEOC to obtain class certification); EEOC v. Air Line Pilots, 885 F. Supp. 289, 291–92, 67 FEP 1363, 1364 (D.D.C. 1995) (Title VII religion case); *see also* EEOC v. Dinuba Med. Clinic, 222 F.3d 580, 588 (9th Cir. 2000) (EEOC empowered to file representative action that is not class action).

[140]*See, e.g.*, EEOC v. Chrysler Corp., 546 F. Supp. 54, 75, 29 FEP 1385 (E.D. Mich. 1982) (EEOC suit enforcing ADEA under § 16(c) not subject to either Rule 23 or "opt-in" provisions of § 16(c); individual claimants do not have to consent to being joined as party plaintiffs in order to be represented by EEOC), *aff'd*, 733 F.2d 1183, 34 FEP 1401 (6th Cir. 1984). *See generally* Chapter 12 (Age).

[141]*See* Dunlop v. Pan Am. World Airways, Inc., 672 F.2d 1044, 1049 n.6, 28 FEP 290 (2d Cir. 1982) (settlement between Secretary of Labor and defendant did not have to comply with Rule 23(e)'s requirements regarding settlement); Donovan v. University of Tex., 643 F.2d 1201, 1204–06, 25 FEP 1050 (5th Cir. 1981) (suit by Secretary of Labor prior to transfer of authority to EEOC). *See generally* Chapter 18 (Compensation).

[142]29 U.S.C. §§ 216(c), 217 (2000).

[143]*See generally* Chapter 12 (Age).

[144]*See* Flavel v. Svedala Indus., Inc., 875 F. Supp. 550, 553–54, 75 FEP 915, 917 (E.D. Wis. 1994).

B. Damages Caps

The EEOC may seek damages up to the Title VII statutory cap for each aggrieved individual.[145]

C. EEOC Settlement of Actions on Behalf of Multiple Claimants

The Ninth Circuit has held that the EEOC's discretion in conducting ADEA enforcement actions is limited only by due process requirements. Therefore, the EEOC need only provide "constitutionally adequate" notice to potential ADEA claimants before depriving them of the right to join a lawsuit.[146]

D. Defendants' Communication With Persons for Whom the EEOC Seeks Relief

A number of courts have held that communications between EEOC attorneys and claimants for whom the EEOC seeks relief are privileged.[147] As a result, a number of courts prohibit or limit a defendant's attempts to contact persons who have advised the EEOC that they wish the EEOC to seek relief for them in a suit,[148] or persons whom the EEOC in an ADEA suit had designated as persons for whom it seeks relief.[149]

Similarly, courts disfavor a defendant's attempts to obtain a settlement or secure a waiver through direct communications with

---

[145]EEOC v. Dinuba Med. Clinic, 222 F.3d 580, 589 (9th Cir. 2000); EEOC v. W&O, Inc., 213 F.3d 600, 613 (11th Cir. 2000).

[146]EEOC v. Pan Am. World Airways, Inc., 897 F.2d 1499, 1507–08, 52 FEP 990 (9th Cir. 1990) (court rejected claimants' request to share benefits of consent decree in ADEA action, settled on behalf of 106 pilots; earlier notice "constitutionally adequate").

[147]See EEOC v. International Profit Assocs., Inc., 206 F.R.D. 215 (N.D. Ill. 2002); EEOC v. Chemsico, 203 F.R.D. 432, 87 FEP 278 (E.D. Mo. 2001); Bauman v. Jacobs Suchard, Inc., 136 F.R.D. 460 (N.D. Ill. 1990); EEOC v. Pasta House Co., 1996 WL 120648, 70 FEP 61 (E.D. Mo. Jan. 29, 1996); EEOC v. Chemtech Int'l Corp., 4 AD 1465, 1466 (S.D. Tex. 1995).

[148]See EEOC v. Dana Corp., 202 F. Supp. 2d 827 (N.D. Ind. 2002); EEOC v. Morgan Stanley Co., 206 F. Supp. 2d 559 (S.D.N.Y. 2002).

[149]See EEOC v. NEBCO Evans Distrib., Inc., 1997 WL 416423, at *4 (D. Neb. June 9, 1997).

claimants.[150] However, if a person has never filed a charge of discrimination and has not otherwise sought the EEOC's representation, an employer may communicate a settlement offer directly to that person.[151]

In a private class action in which the EEOC had been permitted to intervene, in a post-certification order that later was vacated, one court (1) directed an employer to disseminate a notice to all class members to "cure" misimpressions employees may have had from prior internal communications by the employer; (2) ordered that the employer include in any subsequent communications concerning the lawsuit a statement to the effect that such communications were merely the employer's opinion and providing class counsel's phone number; and (3) limited ex parte communications by the employer with class members to those who were managerial employees.[152]

V. STATUTES OF LIMITATIONS AND LACHES

A. Statutes of Limitations

1. Title VII and the ADA

Although the language of § 706(f)(1) contains language arguably suggesting that the EEOC should act (or not act) within 180 days,[153] the Supreme Court held in *Occidental Life Insurance Co. v. EEOC*[154] that neither the expiration of this 180-day period nor a state statute of limitations bars the EEOC from bringing suit.[155] The Court allowed, however, that prejudice resulting from undue

---

[150]*See* EEOC v. Johnson & Higgins, Inc., 78 FEP 1127, 1131–32 (S.D.N.Y. 1998) (identifying date the privileged relationship with EEOC commenced is critical to assessing proper measure of damages).

[151]*See* EEOC v. McDonnell Douglas Corp., 948 F. Supp. 54, 55–56 (E.D. Mo. 1996).

[152]*See* Shores v. Publix Super Mkts., Inc., 1996 WL 859985 (M.D. Fla. Nov. 25, 1996) (EEOC, as intervenor, sought same communications restrictions as private class counsel), *vacated*, 1997 WL 714787 (M.D. Fla. Jan. 27, 1997).

[153]Section 706(f)(1) provides that certain events shall occur "[i]f . . . within one hundred and eighty days from the filing of [a] charge . . . the Commission has not filed a civil action under this section."

[154]432 U.S. 355, 14 FEP 1718 (1977).

[155]*Id.* at 366–68.

delay on the EEOC's part may be addressed in other ways.[156] The most significant of these—the laches doctrine—is discussed in Section V.B *infra*. Courts continue to follow *Occidental Life* in permitting the EEOC to reach back more than 300 days prior to the charge in its litigation.[157]

Statute of limitations issues may also arise when the EEOC attempts to join additional defendants during litigation. Rule 15(c)(3) of the Federal Rules of Civil Procedure governs whether claims against a newly added party will "relate back" to the date of the original complaint. If the new claims do not relate back under Rule 15(c)(3), they may be barred.[158] In the Sixth Circuit, Rule 15(c)(3) is understood only to allow for "correction of misnomers"; thus, any amendment "which adds a new party creates a new cause of action and there is no relation back."[159]

2. The ADEA and the EPA

Although there is no statute of limitations applicable to any *injunctive relief* the EEOC may pursue on behalf of discriminatees under the EPA or the ADEA,[160] the *back pay* that the EEOC may recover on behalf of any discriminatee is limited pursuant to statute.[161]

---

[156]*Id.* at 373.

[157]*See, e.g.*, EEOC v. Warshawsky & Co., 1994 WL 384041 (N.D. Ill. July 21, 1994) (allowing EEOC to bring suit on behalf of employees injured more than 300 days before first-filed charge but cutting off certain claims as barred by laches).

[158]*See* EEOC v. Regency Windsor Mgmt. Co., 862 F. Supp. 189, 190, 65 FEP 1777 (W.D. Mich. 1994) (citing cases); *cf.* Edelman v. Lynchburg Coll., 535 U.S. 106, 108–14 (2002).

[159]*See* Regency Windsor Mgmt. Co., 862 F. Supp. at 190.

[160]*See* 29 U.S.C. § 217 (2000).

[161]For discriminatees under the EPA, the back-pay period is 2 years (measured from the time the cause of action accrues until the date the complaint is filed), unless the violation was "willful" (in which case the back-pay period is 3 years). Section 6(a) of the Portal-to-Portal Act of 1947, 29 U.S.C. § 255(a). Formerly the same rule applied under the ADEA, but § 115 of the Civil Rights Act of 1991, Pub. L. No. 102-166, 105 Stat. 1071 (1991), made this provision inapplicable to the ADEA. The ADEA now requires the EEOC to notify the alleged discriminatee if the EEOC dismisses a charge or otherwise terminates its proceedings, and a civil action may be brought against the respondent within 90 days after such notice is received. *Id.* (codified at 29 U.S.C. § 626(e)); *see* EEOC v. AT&T, 36 F. Supp. 2d 994, 77 FEP 913 (S.D. Ohio 1998); Wilkerson v. Martin-Marietta Corp., 875 F. Supp. 1456, 1459, 67 FEP 279, 281 (D. Colo. 1995); EEOC v. Sara Lee Corp., 923 F. Supp. 994, 999, 70 FEP 57, 59 (W.D. Mich. 1995). *See generally* Chapters 18 (Compensation) and 12 (Age).

B. Laches

The applicability of the doctrine of laches as a defense to the EEOC's right to investigate a charge[162] or to an action by a private litigant[163] is primarily discussed elsewhere. There is no fixed period of time that is unreasonable for EEOC delay prior to filing suit. One court, citing numerous cases, found the facts insufficient to judge whether a four-year-and-four-month delay was unreasonable, breaking the time into an investigative activity period, a concilia-tion period, and a suit authorization period.[164] Another court held that the doctrine of laches did not bar a suit with a four-month delay between the breakdown in conciliation and the EEOC's fil-ing of the complaint.[165] The biggest stumbling block an employer faces in asserting the defense of laches is proving that it suffered material prejudice because of the EEOC's delay. The accrual of additional back-pay liability, without more, does not amount to material prejudice.[166] Nor will an employer be found to be materi-ally prejudiced by the absence of former employee witnesses, ab-sent a showing by the employer that it attempted to locate them.[167]

Charging parties who wait to sue until the administrative pro-cess has run its course often contend that the delay is not their fault and that they had a right to await completion of the govern-ment processes, no matter how long that took.[168] However, when

---

[162]See generally Chapter 25 (EEOC Administrative Process).

[163]See generally Chapters 26 (Timeliness) and 40 (Monetary Relief).

[164]EEOC v. Admiral Maint. Serv., L.P., 1998 WL 102748 (N.D. Ill. Feb. 26, 1998).

[165]EEOC v. Premier Operator Servs., Inc., 75 F. Supp. 2d 550, 561 (N.D. Tex. 1999).

[166]EEOC v. Acorn Niles Corp., 1995 WL 519976, at *4 (N.D. Ill. Aug. 29, 1995) (4-year delay by EEOC, including 21-month period where EEOC "did nothing at all," was unreasonable in case against small employer; however, mere showing that back-pay liability might extend for longer period, absent witness unavailability or other factors, "will not suffice to demonstrate prejudice").

[167]Admiral Maint., 1998 WL 102748, at *10.

[168]See, e.g., Sangster v. United Air Lines, Inc., 438 F. Supp. 1221, 1228, 16 FEP 617 (N.D. Cal. 1977) (plaintiff not guilty of laches because of EEOC's 8-year de-lay in charge processing; "reliance on the EEOC to conciliate her dispute with United cannot be characterized as lack of diligence on her part"), aff'd, 633 F.2d 864, 24 FEP 845 (9th Cir. 1980); Tunis v. Corning Glass Works, 698 F. Supp. 452, 55 FEP 1655 (S.D.N.Y. 1988) (plaintiff not guilty of laches where there was 10-year delay between time plaintiff filed charge and when EEOC adopted findings of Division

suit is brought by the EEOC, sometimes after lengthy delays in the administrative process, the defense of laches may have greater success. The Supreme Court noted in *Occidental Life* that when a defendant is prejudiced by inordinate EEOC delay, the court has the "discretionary power 'to locate a just result' in light of the circumstances peculiar to the case."[169] The delay, however, must be attributable to the EEOC itself, and not some other agency.[170]

Despite the dictum in *Occidental Life*, the Third Circuit has questioned whether laches can ever be applied against the EEOC,[171] because the EEOC is a governmental agency and the defense of laches traditionally applies against the government only with statutory authority.[172] That court noted that the language in *Occidental Life* "may well speak" only to the discretion respecting back-pay liability and not to prospective equitable relief.[173]

---

of Human Rights and issued right-to-sue letter; evidence showed that over 10-year period plaintiff had inquired of EEOC or State Division of Human Rights regarding progress of her case).

[169]432 U.S. 355, 373, 14 FEP 1718 (1997).

[170]*See* EEOC v. Navy Fed. Credit Union, 424 F.3d 397, 96 FEP 641 (4th Cir. 2005) (no finding of laches where delay was attributable to local agency with which EEOC had work-sharing agreement), *cert. denied*, 126 S. Ct. 1629 (2006).

[171]*See* EEOC v. Great Atl. & Pac. Tea Co., 735 F.2d 69, 80, 34 FEP 1412 (3d Cir. 1984) (issue not decided; 9½ years between filing charge and filing complaint not inordinate delay, considering complexity of case, difficulty of discovery, and absence of prejudice to employer).

[172]*Id.* That court did not address whether the Administrative Procedure Act (APA), 5 U.S.C. § 706, may provide the necessary statutory authority, but others since then have. *See* EEOC v. May & Co., 572 F. Supp. 536, 543 (N.D. Ga. 1983) (APA § 706 defense possible only when defendant shows prejudice to its defense as result of unreasonable delay). Some courts find in § 706 a separate, laches-like defense to tardy agency action. *E.g.*, EEOC v. Westinghouse Elec. Corp., 592 F.2d 484, 486, 19 FEP 42 (8th Cir. 1979) (both laches and APA § 706 defenses applicable); EEOC v. American Petrofina Co., 22 FEP 1321, 1325 (E.D. Tex. 1977) (same). Other courts that question the availability of laches have recognized that, in an appropriate case, APA § 706 may provide a defense. *E.g.*, EEOC v. Bell Helicopter Co., 426 F. Supp. 785, 790–91, 792–93, 14 FEP 658 (N.D. Tex. 1976) (laches not applicable to EEOC; but § 706 of APA bars action, because employer prejudice is shown); EEOC v. Moore Group, Inc., 416 F. Supp. 1002, 1004–05, 12 FEP 1758 (N.D. Ga. 1976) (same; suit brought 1½ years after conciliation failed, and agency had displayed dilatory attitude, both of which prejudiced employer); *cf.* EEOC v. Federated Mut. Ins. Co., 16 FEP 820, 821 (N.D. Ga. 1976) (laches not applicable against EEOC; APA § 706 does not bar agency action here, because there was no showing of employer prejudice).

[173]*Great Atl. & Pac. Tea Co.*, 735 F.2d at 80.

Most courts, however, either recognize explicitly or assume that laches is a potential defense to EEOC actions. Two questions then are presented: (1) what type of prejudice—and how much—must be shown; and (2) what consequences follow if laches is established. As for the first issue, some courts have found the absence of prejudice by citing the notice given by the EEOC at the time of the charge[174] or the employment recordkeeping requirements established by EEOC regulations.[175] Under both theories, these courts say, the employer should have preserved evidence for its defense and thereby avoided only prejudice.

Defendants have asserted several responses. First, because the ultimate litigation may be considerably broader than the charge, maintaining records pertaining to the initial notice may be inadequate to avoid prejudice. Second, records are not a substitute for firsthand testimony by live witnesses who have unaided recollections of the events in question. Third, prejudice results from delay

---

[174]*E.g., May & Co.*, 572 F. Supp. at 543 (any prejudice obviated by requirement that EEOC attempt to secure conciliation with respondents named in charge); EEOC v. Integrated Food Sys., 1988 U.S. Dist. LEXIS 10429, at *2–4 (S.D.N.Y. Sept. 16, 1988) (employer not unfairly prejudiced by 3½-year delay; EEOC notified company of charge when witnesses were still employed at company and advised company of its Title VII obligation to preserve personnel records relevant to action); EEOC v. Jacksonville Shipyards, Inc., 690 F. Supp. 995, 999–1000, 47 FEP 267 (M.D. Fla. 1988) (mere fact of delay of over 5 years between filing of charge and bringing of lawsuit not inexcusable; defendant did not suffer prejudice from delay, as EEOC had promptly informed defendant of pending charges); EEOC v. Autozone, Inc., 258 F. Supp. 2d 822 (W.D. Tenn. 2003) (5-year, 4-month delay between filing of charge and filing of lawsuit not unreasonable; reasonableness of EEOC's delay does not depend on total amount of time between filings, but on EEOC's reason for delay; court separated delay time into three distinct periods and found that in third period, which constituted time after which conciliation failed and 22 months later when EEOC filed lawsuit, EEOC took no further action; EEOC offered no specific reason for its inactivity; court found EEOC's inactivity amounted to unreasonable delay in case; although Autozone met first requirement for proving laches, court went on to find Autozone not materially prejudiced by delay, and therefore unable to prove laches).

[175]29 C.F.R. § 1602.14 (2005); *see Great Atl. & Pac. Tea Co.*, 735 F.2d at 84 ("any records unavailable by virtue of A & P's failure to comply with the record-preservation requirements of 29 C.F.R. § 1602.14 would not, of course, qualify as establishing prejudice"); *cf.* EEOC v. Bethlehem Steel Corp., 765 F.2d 427, 430–31, 38 FEP 345 (4th Cir. 1985) (respondent failed to show prejudice in subpoena-enforcement proceeding; subpoena sought only production of documents and because company by definition could produce only documents it still possessed, there was no possible prejudice).

because of the escalation of damages, even if all evidence pertinent to liability somehow could be preserved.[176]

The second major laches issue is determining the consequences that flow from a finding of laches. Courts have variously barred an action in its entirety,[177] barred specific causes

---

[176]Several courts have recognized that the undue prejudice requirement is not restricted to situations in which the delay impaired the defendant's ability to disprove liability. Instead, they have held that a defendant may be unduly prejudiced when the plaintiff's delay in filing suit exposes it to unfairly inflated damages. *E.g.*, EEOC v. Peterson, Howell & Heather, Inc., 702 F. Supp. 1213, 1222, 48 FEP 1185 (D. Md. 1989) ("Where a defendant faces unfairly accentuated potential monetary damages directly attributable only to a plaintiff's unreasonable delays, that defendant suffers an even more palpable prejudice than the difficulty of defending itself at trial."); EEOC v. Vucitech, 842 F.2d 936, 943, 46 FEP 550 (7th Cir. 1988) (dictum; laches may apply even if delay did not impair defendant's ability to defend itself on merits).

[177]For example, in *EEOC v. Alioto Fish Co.*, 623 F.2d 86, 23 FEP 251 (9th Cir. 1980), the court ruled that the entire action was barred by laches. The charge in that case was filed in 1971, the EEOC's reasonable cause decision was issued in 1973, conciliation efforts began 10 months after the cause determination and failed in 1974, and suit was brought in 1976, 20 months after the failure of conciliation. The court found that the 62-month lapse between charge filing and suit filing constituted unreasonable delay, rejecting the EEOC's argument that the delay was excused by its workload. The court found that the delay prejudiced the defendant because of the death of witnesses, the age of the defendant's principal official, the death or unavailability of the EEOC's investigator and conciliator, the disappearance of documentary evidence by the defendant, the dimming of memories among witnesses generally, and the dramatic increase in the defendant's back-pay exposure. 623 F.2d at 88–89; *see also* EEOC v. Liberty Loan Corp., 584 F.2d 853, 857–58, 18 FEP 303 (8th Cir. 1978) (affirming district court's dismissal of case brought more than 4 years after charge filing; prejudice resulted from complete turnover of supervisors); EEOC v. C & D Sportswear Corp., 398 F. Supp. 300, 302–03, 10 FEP 1131 (M.D. Ga. 1975) (6-year delay in filing suit prejudicial to defendant; records were destroyed in reliance on EEOC's regulations at that time); EEOC v. Bray Lumber Co., 478 F. Supp. 993, 997–98, 21 FEP 510 (M.D. Ga. 1979) (53-month delay between charge filing and suit filing, including 1½ years between failure of conciliation and suit; delay prejudiced defendant not familiar with EEOC procedures, as it failed to preserve evidence for its defense); EEOC v. Atlanta Big Boy Mgmt., Inc., 17 FEP 344, 346 (N.D. Ga. 1978) (EEOC action barred by laches because employer had not been effectively notified of charge for 3 years, thus losing its opportunity to present defense); EEOC v. Louisiana Power & Light Co., 51 FEP 849 (E.D. La. 1989) (defense of laches found appropriate where 12½ years elapsed between when charge was filed and when EEOC filed lawsuit; delay unreasonable because of periods of total inactivity and lengthy periods of "inter-office paper shuffling" that occurred; court also found employer was unduly prejudiced by delay in that half of people who were responsible for decisions concerning alleged discriminatory practices were unavailable because of either death, their having left company under adverse circumstances, or retirement; court also determined that given extended delay, many potential witnesses would have "faded memories" about event that happened years

of action,[178] or limited back-pay liability.[179] Even courts that decline to apply laches sometimes take any prejudice that resulted from the EEOC's delay into account in fashioning relief.[180]

Courts are more likely to apply laches against the EEOC when the EEOC has unreasonably delayed in suing and thereby unduly prejudiced defendants.[181] However, courts normally require a showing

---

earlier; court determined that company's claimed loss of 10% of personnel records of employee group on which EEOC was to focus was prejudicial to employer); *American Petrofina Co.*, 22 FEP at 1325–26 (case dismissed when witness and evidence problems were compounded by 5-year delay, including 3½ years after reasonable cause finding and by death or termination of some of respondent's supervisors who would have been involved in suit, sale of company, and loss of control of records).

[178]*See Westinghouse Elec. Corp.*, 592 F.2d at 486–87 (affirming dismissal of claims arising before 1971 because of destruction of records, turnover of supervisory personnel, and erosion of memories; remanding claims arising between 1971 and 1976 for further proceedings; reversing dismissal of claims arising after 1976 because of lack of prejudice and notice to defendant of processing of charge and suit).

[179]*See* EEOC v. American Mach. & Foundry, Inc., 13 FEP 1634, 1636 (M.D. Pa. 1976) (court dismissed complaint as to monetary (back pay) relief because there was sufficient proof of delay and prejudice; however, district court refused to dismiss claim for injunctive relief).

[180]*See* EEOC v. American Nat'l Bank, 574 F.2d 1173, 1176, 17 FEP 213 (4th Cir. 1978) ("Whether the Commission's delays caused prejudice that will justify a limitation of the relief ... can best be considered after the facts have been fully developed, if the Commission ultimately prevails."); EEOC v. Chesapeake & Ohio Ry. Co., 577 F.2d 229, 234, 17 FEP 815 (4th Cir. 1978) (same); EEOC v. Joint Apprenticeship Comm., 8 FEP 176, 177–78 (N.D. Cal. 1974) (6-year delay between filing of charge and suit not unreasonable, as it was caused by administrative overload; dismissal not warranted, but court stated that it would consider delay in fashioning relief); *cf.* EEOC v. Beaver Welding Supply Co., 21 FEP 152, 153 (W.D. Tenn. 1979) (question of prejudice left open for reconsideration at trial).

[181]*Compare* EEOC v. Vucitech, 842 F.2d 936, 942–43, 46 FEP 550 (7th Cir. 1988) (18-month delay not unreasonable when EEOC used time to attempt to settle matter), EEOC v. Rollins Acceptance Corp., 48 FEP 360, 362 (N.D. Ga. 1988) (equitable defense available but inapplicable under facts at bar) *and* EEOC v. Jacksonville Shipyards, Inc., 690 F. Supp. 995, 1000–01, 47 FEP 267 (M.D. Fla. 1988) (delay of over 5 years between filing of charge and bringing of lawsuit excusable when defendant did not suffer prejudice from delay and EEOC had promptly informed him of pending charges) *with* EEOC v. Peterson, Howell & Heather, Inc., 702 F. Supp. 1213, 1224, 48 FEP 1185 (D. Md. 1989) (EEOC's inexcusable 36-month delay, combined with significant hardship to defendant, compelled district court to apply laches), *Louisiana Power & Light Co.*, 51 FEP at 851–53 (laches applied where a 12½-year delay between charge and suit was unreasonable and defendant suffered undue prejudice as result of delay; witnesses had died or disappeared and records were lost), EEOC v. Star Tool & Die Works, Inc., 699 F. Supp. 120, 122–23, 47 FEP 39 (E.D. Mich. 1987) (EEOC's action barred by laches because of EEOC's inexcusable delay and undue prejudice to defendant; suit brought 7½ years after charges were filed; records were lost and crucial witnesses either died or were missing) *and*

of prejudice and will not presume prejudice from delay alone, even if the delay is unreasonable.[182]

VI. Scope of the Litigation

Both the EEOC and private plaintiffs sometimes seek to expand litigation beyond what was specified in the initial administrative charge. Most frequently at issue are the number and identity of the defendants (e.g., suit against affiliated companies not named in the charge), bases (e.g., a sex case based on a race charge), issues

---

EEOC v. National City Bank, 694 F. Supp. 1287, 1294, 47 FEP 401 (N.D. Ohio 1987) (subpoena enforcement case; defendant successfully asserted laches based on unreasonable delay; prejudice caused by duplicative discovery, greater back-pay liability, and harm to defendant's ability to defend), *remanded per curiam*, 865 F.2d 1267, 49 FEP 656 (6th Cir. 1988) (defendant would be required to comply with subpoena in part, limited to certain readily available documents; refusing to decide whether laches would bar EEOC action on merits, as no action had yet been filed).

[182]*See* EEOC v. Massey-Ferguson, Inc., 622 F.2d 271, 275–76, 22 FEP 1330 (7th Cir. 1980) (57-month delay between filing of charge and filing of complaint unreasonable, but no showing that delay prejudiced defendant when witnesses were still available and destruction of records by company during charge processing was as likely to have caused prejudice as EEOC's delay); EEOC v. Radiator Specialty Co., 610 F.2d 178, 182–83, 21 FEP 351 (4th Cir. 1979) (mere delay in processing charge insufficient to prove prejudice); EEOC v. North Hills Passavant Hosp., 544 F.2d 664, 672–73, 13 FEP 1129 (3d Cir. 1976) (EEOC action filed 3 years after private lawsuit was begun not barred by laches; no showing of inexcusable delay, lack of diligence, or sufficient employer prejudice); EEOC v. Christie Lodge Assocs., Ltd., 51 FEP 916, 919 (N.D. Ill. 1989) (laches not applied when defendant did not show that EEOC's delay "substantially," "materially," or "seriously" prejudiced its ability to defend action); EEOC v. Mistletoe Express Serv., 45 FEP 777, 777–78 (S.D. Tex. 1987) (motion to dismiss based on laches denied when no undue prejudice found); EEOC v. CW Transp., Inc., 658 F. Supp. 1278, 1296, 43 FEP 782 (W.D. Wis. 1987) (laches claim not necessarily established because of unreasonable delay of 12 years from time of consent decree until inspection; evidentiary hearing on question of material prejudice to respondent required); *Beaver Welding Supply Co.*, 21 FEP at 153 (2-year delay between conciliation failure and filing of suit may not establish prejudice); EEOC v. North Cent. Airlines, 475 F. Supp. 667, 670–71, 20 FEP 957 (D. Minn. 1979) (6-year delay between charge filing and suit filing held not unreasonable where delay caused both by EEOC backlog and actions of defendant); EEOC v. Pinkerton's, Inc., 14 FEP 1431, 1434 (W.D. Pa. 1977) (24-month delay between charge and suit not sufficient to bar action because delay was short, any destruction of records after notice was contrary to agency regulations, and no other prejudice was shown); EEOC v. American Express Co., 14 FEP 615, 617 (S.D.N.Y. 1977) (delay of 5 years between charge and suit held insufficient to bar action absent showing of employer prejudice), *appeal dismissed*, 558 F.2d 102, 15 FEP 74 (2d Cir. 1977).

(e.g., a discharge case based on a promotion charge), and geographic scope (e.g., a broad-based case based on a facility-specific charge). The proper resolution of such issues in private suits is discussed elsewhere.[183] This section discusses only those aspects of the problem that may be unique to EEOC suits.

The scope of EEOC litigation under Title VII and the ADEA is limited by the scope of the reasonable cause finding and conciliation.[184] There is no comparable scope limitation on EEOC suits under the EPA, except the substantive limitations imposed by the statute itself.[185]

A. Additional Defendants

Although § 706(f)(1) by its terms specifies that the EEOC under Title VII may only sue a "respondent . . . named in the charge," the EEOC has had some limited success in adding additional defendants. Most commonly, this has occurred when there is an agency[186] or a successor[187] relationship, although some cases

---

[183]See generally Chapter 28 (Title VII Litigation Procedure).

[184]See Section II supra.

[185]The EPA by its terms is limited to a single basis and issue and applies only to employers, not unions. See generally Chapter 18 (Compensation).

[186]See, e.g., EEOC v. Raymond Metal Prods. Co., 385 F. Supp. 907, 911, 8 FEP 199 (D. Md. 1974) (EEOC may name international union as full party defendant, although only local union was named in charge, because of agency relationship between local and international), rev'd in part on other grounds, 530 F.2d 590, 12 FEP 38 (4th Cir. 1976); EEOC v. Tesko Welding & Mfg. Co., 47 FEP 939, 940 (N.D. Ill. 1988) (officers/shareholders of closely held family-operated corporation may be sued, even though they were not named in charge, when each individual had notice of charge and corporation's refusal to settle made it unlikely that individuals would have settled even if named); EEOC v. Charleston Elec. Joint Apprenticeship Training Comm., 587 F. Supp. 528, 530–31, 35 FEP 473 (S.D. W. Va. 1984) (denying summary judgment to union and contractor not named in charge; factual questions existed as to whether union or contractor could be considered agent of apprenticeship committee, whether they had received notice of alleged violation, and whether they had opportunity to participate in conciliation process).

[187]See, e.g., EEOC v. MacMillan Bloedel Containers, Inc., 503 F.2d 1086, 1094, 8 FEP 897 (6th Cir. 1974) (new defendant was successor); Braswell v. Great Expectations of Wash., D.C., 1997 U.S. Dist. LEXIS 13600 (E.D.N.C. Aug. 5, 1997) (when liability is based on successor liability and not on personal involvement in Title VII violations, there is no need for plaintiff to name all defendants in EEOC charge). The court in MacMillan Bloedel set out nine factors to be considered in determining whether a successor corporation should be held liable for the Title VII violations of the predecessor: (1) whether the successor corporation had notice of the charge; (2) the ability of the predecessor to provide relief; (3) whether there has been a substantial continuity of business operations; (4) whether the new employer uses the same

require the new defendant to have had prior notice of the charge,[188] an opportunity to conciliate,[189] or both. Some courts, however, have permitted the addition of defendants neither named in charges nor investigated for violation of employment discrimination laws on the ground that they were merely "relief defendants" necessary for according full relief against the properly named defendants.[190] Another district court allowed the EEOC to maintain a suit against an unnamed respondent because the party was adequately notified of the charge and provided an opportunity to participate in conciliation negotiations.[191]

When only the employer is initially named in a Title VII charge but a resolution of the unlawful employment practice requires a change in a collective bargaining agreement, the EEOC ordinarily attempts to join the uncharged union as a defendant under Rule 19 of the Federal Rules of Civil Procedure, for the limited purpose of affording full relief, but without alleging that the union itself has violated Title VII. Many courts have allowed such joinder.[192]

---

plant; (5) whether the new employer uses the same or substantially the same workforce; (6) whether the new employer uses the same or substantially the same supervisory personnel; (7) whether the same jobs exist under substantially the same working conditions; (8) whether the new employer uses the same machinery, equipment, and methods of production; and (9) whether the new employer produces the same product. No one factor is determinative, and all must be considered in fashioning an equitable resolution. 503 F.2d at 1094.

[188]*E.g.*, EEOC v. Blue Ox Rest., 1986 U.S. Dist. LEXIS 29263, at *1–2 (N.D. Ill. Feb. 14, 1986) (on motion to reconsider, district court found that failure to use defendant's registered corporate name rather than restaurant's name did not void judgment, as restaurant was equivalent of corporation and individual owner-defendants were on notice that corporation was being sued).

[189]*See, e.g.*, EEOC v. Christie Lodge Assocs., Ltd., 51 FEP 916, 919 (N.D. Ill. 1989).

[190]*See* EEOC v. Rockwell Int'l Corp., 23 F. Supp. 2d 892, 893, 8 AD 1153 (N.D. Ill. 1998) (union that cannot be "liability defendant" under ADA may be named under Fed. R. Civ. P. 19(a) to effect complete relief consisting of retroactive seniority); EEOC v. JRG Fox Valley, Inc., 976 F. Supp. 1161, 1163, 74 FEP 1793 (N.D. Ill. 1997) (recipients of monetary distributions from defunct defendant corporation allowed as "relief defendants") (citing Wilson v. City of Chi., 120 F.3d 681 (7th Cir. 1997) (§ 1983 case)).

[191]EEOC v. Earl Scheib of Kan., Inc., 2000 WL 382008, at *2 (D. Kan. Mar. 15, 2000).

[192]*E.g., MacMillan Bloedel Containers*, 503 F.2d at 1095 (joinder "will allow the Union to protect adequately the interests of its members [and] will provide the discriminatee with full and complete relief"); EEOC v. Hearst Corp., 27 FEP 1108, 1111 (W.D. Wash. 1979) ("The principal function of their presence in the case will be to give them a chance to be heard on whether the provisions of the collective bargaining agreements are discriminatory." (citing with approval the reasoning in

When the EEOC has not discharged its obligation to conciliate with respect to a properly added new defendant, the action may be stayed pending conciliation.[193]

B. Expansion of Basis and Issues

There is a split in authority over whether the EEOC may expand litigation to include a basis or issue not addressed in a charge of discrimination. *Sanchez v. Standard Brands, Inc.*[194] and its progeny generally allow a private litigant to sue on Title VII issues that are "like and related" to, or grow out of, those specified in the underlying charge.[195] In the context of EEOC litigation, the Sixth Circuit[196] adopted the like-and-related test of *Sanchez* and held that the EEOC may litigate only claims "reasonably expected to grow out of the charge of discrimination."[197] When the investigation uncovers discrimination unrelated to the original charge, then the EEOC is required to file a commissioner charge to pursue such unrelated discrimination so as to give the respondent notice and an opportunity to participate in the investigation and conciliation process before a cause determination is made.[198]

MacMillan Bloedel Containers)); EEOC v. Rexall Drug Co., 10 FEP 450, 454 (E.D. Mo. 1974) ("joinder of a union not named in the original charge may be allowed where necessary to avoid a duplicity of lawsuits or where interpretation of a collective bargaining agreement is involved"). *See generally* Chapters 22 (Unions) and 28 (Title VII Litigation Procedure).

[193]*See, e.g.*, Patterson v. American Tobacco Co., 535 F.2d 257, 271–72, 12 FEP 314 (4th Cir. 1976) (district court had provided EEOC with opportunity to conciliate with union defendant after suit was filed).

[194]431 F.2d 455, 2 FEP 788 (5th Cir. 1970).

[195]*Id.* at 466.

[196]EEOC v. Bailey Co., 563 F.2d 439, 448, 450–54, 15 FEP 972 (6th Cir. 1977) (charge by white female originally alleged sex discrimination but later was amended to allege discrimination against African-American females; charge could form basis of EEOC suit alleging sex and race discrimination, but not religious discrimination; latter issue not "within the scope of an EEOC investigation reasonably related to" charge; irrelevant that information on religious discrimination "emerged during a legitimate investigation of sex discrimination"; indeed, "[a]bsent the amendment to . . . [the] charge, . . . [the] allegations of race discrimination . . . were even more unrelated to . . . [the] sex discrimination" charge than were allegations of religious discrimination).

[197]*Id.* at 446. *But cf.* EEOC v. Keco Indus., Inc., 748 F.2d 1097, 1101, 36 FEP 511 (6th Cir. 1984) (EEOC allowed to broaden scope of litigation to include class of discriminatees; class-based claim could reasonably be expected to grow out of individual complaint of discrimination).

[198]*Bailey Co.*, 563 F.2d at 449. The court elaborated:
It is our belief that if conciliation is to work properly, charges of discrimination must be fully investigated after the employer receives notice in a charge

The Seventh Circuit takes the position that a decision by the EEOC to expand litigation to encompass a claim beyond the scope of the original charge is not judicially reviewable.[199]

The Fourth[200] and Ninth[201] Circuits have permitted expansion when the new basis or issue was uncovered in the EEOC's investigation and was included in the cause determination and conciliation attempts. These courts have found that the Title VII charge serves only as a " 'jurisdictional springboard to investigate whether the employer is engaged in any discriminatory practices' " and that the EEOC may include in its determination " 'all facts developed in the course of a reasonable investigation of that charge.' "[202] Both circuits rejected the contention that the EEOC should file a commissioner charge when it uncovers such additional discrimination; the reasonable cause determination and subsequent conciliation

---

alleging unlawful discriminatory employment practices. The requirement that a member of the EEOC file a charge when facts suggesting unlawful discrimination are discovered that are unrelated to the individual party's charge does serve the purposes of treating the employer fairly and forcing the employer and the EEOC to focus attention during investigation on the facts of such possible discrimination and thereby does serve the goal of obtaining voluntary compliance with Title VII.

We are thus unable to accept the EEOC's argument that . . . it would be a matter of placing form over substance, resulting in the waste of administrative resources and the delay in the enforcement of rights, by requiring . . . [filing] a charge with respect to allegations of discrimination uncovered in an EEOC investigation which were of a kind not raised by the individual party . . . .

Id.

[199]*See* EEOC v. Caterpillar, Inc., 409 F.3d 831, 95 FEP 1371 (7th Cir. 2005).

[200]*See* EEOC v. Chesapeake & Ohio Ry., 577 F.2d 229, 231–32, 17 FEP 815 (4th Cir. 1978) (EEOC may expand charge alleging denial of transfer opportunities to include hiring and promotion claims; new issues were found in course of reasonable EEOC investigation and were included in cause determination and conciliation effort); EEOC v. General Elec. Co., 532 F.2d 359, 368, 373–74, 12 FEP 21 (4th Cir. 1976) (when African-American male alleged race discrimination in hiring tests, expansion was allowed to sex discrimination because tests at issue represented " 'a root source of discrimination' that [was] both racial and sexual").

[201]*See* EEOC v. Hearst Corp., 553 F.2d 579, 580, 13 FEP 1360 (9th Cir. 1977) (per curiam) (expansion allowed from sex (male) to race (African American), sex (female), and other minority groups; rule that private suit allegations must be like or reasonably related to those in underlying charge not applicable to EEOC); *see* EEOC v. Occidental Life Ins. Co., 535 F.2d 533, 540–42, 12 FEP 1300 (9th Cir. 1976) (when married female alleged discrimination in denial of maternity leave and other benefits, expansion permitted to discrimination against unmarried females in pregnancy benefits and against males in retirement program), *aff'd*, 432 U.S. 355, 14 FEP 1718 (1977).

[202]*E.g., General Elec.*, 532 F.2d at 364 (quoting EEOC v. E.I. du Pont de Nemours & Co., 373 F. Supp. 1321, 1335 (D. Del. 1974)).

provide the requisite notice.[203] The Fourth Circuit noted, however, that the EEOC's actions in raising a new basis or issue should not prejudice the defendant; thus, the two-year limitation on the accrual of back pay under § 706(g) must be measured from the actual date on which the respondent was given notice of the additional claim.[204]

The Supreme Court, in dictum in *General Telephone Co. v. EEOC*,[205] with respect to whether the Rule 23 class action requirements apply to the EEOC, appeared to share the view of the Fourth and Ninth Circuits:

> [T]he Courts of Appeals have held that EEOC enforcement actions are not limited to the claims presented by the charging parties. Any violations that the EEOC ascertains in the course of a reasonable investigation of the charging party's complaint are actionable. Th[is] approach is far more consistent with the EEOC's role in the enforcement of Title VII than is imposing the strictures of Rule 23, which would limit the EEOC action to claims typified by those of the charging party.[206]

Thus, although many of the older cases embrace the Sixth Circuit's view,[207] most of the cases since *General Telephone*—including

---

[203]*See id.* at 365 ("If the EEOC uncovers during that investigation facts which support a charge of another discrimination than that in the filed charge, it is neither obliged to cast a blind eye over such discrimination nor to sever those facts and the discrimination so shown from the investigation in process and file a Commissioner charge thereon, thereby beginning again a repetitive investigation of the same facts already developed in the ongoing investigation." (footnotes omitted)); *Hearst Corp.*, 553 F.2d at 580–81, 13 FEP 1360 (9th Cir. 1976) (although EEOC "could have, itself, brought a separate administrative charge upon race discrimination based upon information reasonably acquired in connection with an original sex discrimination charge . . . [w]e agree with *EEOC v. Occidental* that to require EEOC to pursue that route, rather than to allow it to include the new charge in its 'reasonable cause' determination, its conciliation proceedings and in its eventual suit, would be to champion form over substance").

[204]*General Elec.*, 532 F.2d at 371–72 (allowing back pay to commence earlier could "substantially prejudice" employer).

[205]446 U.S. 318, 22 FEP 1196 (1980).

[206]*Id.* at 331.

[207]*E.g.*, EEOC v. Federated Mut. Ins. Co., 16 FEP 820, 822 (N.D. Ga. 1976) (where underlying charge, investigation, and determination related only to hiring, complaint could not seek to litigate terms and conditions of employment); EEOC v. Winn-Dixie, Inc., 13 FEP 250, 252 (E.D. La. 1976) (sex discrimination allegation stricken because sex issue cannot be "like or related" to race discrimination); EEOC v. New York Times Broad. Serv., Inc., 364 F. Supp. 651, 654, 6 FEP 563 (W.D. Tenn. 1973) (where charge was by white woman alleging sex discrimination and EEOC also found race discrimination based on statistics, court struck race allegation, partly on ground it was not reasonably related and partly on ground that statistics did not establish prima facie case of race discrimination).

one within the Sixth Circuit itself [208]—have been more liberal.[209] Still, the more prudent practice may be for the EEOC to seek to amend the original charge.[210]

Under either test, however, the new allegations must in fact have been investigated, made the subject of the cause finding, and conciliated.[211]

A recurring factual scenario occurs where the EEOC lawsuit alleges other victims besides the charging party. In these circumstances—provided that the allegations regarding these alleged victims

---

[208]EEOC v. Akron Nat'l Bank & Trust Co., 497 F. Supp. 733, 738, 22 FEP 1665 (N.D. Ohio 1980) (EEOC may sue for assignment discrimination when that issue was like and related to promotion issue alleged in charge).

[209]E.g., EEOC v. St. Anne's Hosp., Inc., 664 F.2d 128, 130, 27 FEP 170 (7th Cir. 1981) (EEOC may sue where retaliatory discharge was "reasonably related" to original charge of sex and religious discrimination, and cause determination was issued on retaliation claim); EEOC v. National Cleaning Contractors, Inc., 56 FEP 1081, 1082–83 (S.D.N.Y. 1991) (charging party permitted to intervene in EEOC suit to assert quid pro quo sexual harassment, which was "reasonably related" to underlying charge of hostile environment sexual harassment); EEOC v. Tempel Steel Co., 723 F. Supp. 1250, 1253, 50 FEP 985 (N.D. Ill. 1989) (EEOC may sue employer for alleged discriminatory recruitment and hiring practices even though employee's charge merely alleged that employer unlawfully failed to rehire him; charge identified racial discrimination as basis of complaint, and rehiring and recruitment decisions are closely related practices); EEOC v. World's Finest Chocolate, Inc., 701 F. Supp. 637, 640, 48 FEP 845 (N.D. Ill. 1988) (EEOC may sue employer for both race and sex discrimination even though charge alleged only race discrimination; factual narrative of charge implied that discrimination against women also was occurring); EEOC v. Chicago Miniature Lamp Works, 640 F. Supp. 1291, 1297 & n.10, 41 FEP 911 (N.D. Ill. 1986) (expansion-of-issues doctrine could allow litigation of recruitment and hiring claims under "reasonable investigation" test; as for beginning of back-pay liability, defendant may have been put on notice of scope of investigation by EEOC's letter and questionnaire), rev'd on other grounds, 947 F.2d 292, 57 FEP 408 (7th Cir. 1991).

[210]See, e.g., EEOC v. Reichhold Chems., Inc., 700 F. Supp. 524, 527, 47 FEP 186 (N.D. Fla. 1988) (EEOC may amend charge to include retaliation claim when factual basis for it was uncovered in reasonable investigation of underlying charge), rev'd on other grounds, 988 F.2d 1564, 61 FEP 1001 (11th Cir. 1993).

[211]See EEOC v. Sherwood Med. Indus., Inc., 452 F. Supp. 678, 683–84, 17 FEP 441 (M.D. Fla. 1978) (striking sex discrimination cause of action because it was not included in cause determination or conciliation of original charge based on race); EEOC v. Allegheny Airlines, 436 F. Supp. 1300, 1306–07, 15 FEP 891 (W.D. Pa. 1977) (EEOC may not include in its complaint issues of discrimination against African Americans and women in management, professional, and technical jobs; superficial investigation prevented meaningful conciliation); EEOC v. National Cash Register Co., 405 F. Supp. 562, 566–67, 14 FEP 1118 (N.D. Ga. 1975) (striking issues that were not subject of statutorily required investigation, determination, and conciliation); see also EEOC v. Fifth Third Bank, 2004 U.S. Dist. LEXIS 3410 (N.D. Ill. Mar. 5, 2004) (reasonable nexus between constructive discharge allegations in lawsuit and sex discrimination and retaliation allegations in employee's EEOC charge;

were in fact investigated and conciliated[212]—courts generally have allowed the EEOC's class-type suit to proceed, even if the original charging party's individual claim was found to lack merit.[213]

For claims under statutes other than Title VII, the rules are liberal. The EEOC may raise any age discrimination issue that was raised in conciliation.[214] Further, because of the lack of any jurisdictional prerequisites to suit under the EPA, it would appear that the EEOC may raise an equal pay issue without regard to the scope of the administrative process.

C. Geographic Scope

Most courts apply the same rules in evaluating disputes about the geographic scope of EEOC litigation as they apply to disputes over the substantive scope of the bases and issues that may be pursued by the EEOC. In general, the geographic scope of the complaint is limited to the geographic scope of the administrative processing of the charge.[215] However, where the practices then at

---

EEOC provided employer notice of broader claims during conciliation); EEOC v. T.S.S.O., Inc., 85 FEP 619 (N.D. Fla. 2000) (permitting EEOC to seek additional complainants and witnesses by newspaper advertising where defendant failed to keep appropriate records); EEOC v. Pathmark, Inc., 1998 U.S. Dist. LEXIS 1329 (E.D. Pa. Feb. 10, 1998) (where charge alleged only race discrimination and retaliation, claims of sex discrimination were permitted because they were within scope of EEOC investigation; litigation of claims of religious discrimination, ethnic intimidation, and overtime discrimination not permitted), aff'd, 181 F.3d 85 (3d Cir. 1999); EEOC v. St. Michael Hosp., 6 F. Supp. 2d 809, 77 FEP 86 (E.D. Wis. 1998) (litigation of retaliation and racially hostile environment claims permitted, even though not in charge, where EEOC had investigated such claims); EEOC v. Dillard Dep't Stores, 1994 WL 738971, at *3 (E.D. Mo. Nov. 2, 1994) (failure-to-accommodate claims of possible religious discrimination in hiring).

[212]*Compare* EEOC v. Keco Indus., Inc., 748 F.2d 1097, 1100–01, 36 FEP 511 (6th Cir. 1984) (reversing summary judgment; EEOC could broaden scope of litigation from individual plaintiff to include class of discriminatees because EEOC had issued reasonable cause determination and had attempted conciliation of class-based claim and because class-based claim could be reasonably expected to grow out of individual complaint of discrimination) *with* EEOC v. Mallinckrodt, Inc., 22 FEP 311, 314 (E.D. Mo. 1980) (EEOC may not expand individual allegation of denial of promotion to include a class; investigation and determination limited to charging party's claim only).

[213]*E.g.*, EEOC v. Brookhaven Bank & Trust Co., 614 F.2d 1022, 1025, 22 FEP 703 (5th Cir. 1980) (dismissal reversed even though EEOC found no merit to individual's charge; affected class found by investigation).

[214]*See* Section II.A *supra*.

[215]*E.g.*, EEOC v. E.I. du Pont de Nemours & Co., 373 F. Supp. 1321, 1337–38, 7 FEP 759 (D. Del. 1974) (EEOC suit may include only facilities covered by its cause determination), aff'd, 516 F.2d 1297, 10 FEP 916 (3d Cir. 1975).

issue are common to other areas and set by a central decision maker, some courts have allowed the litigation to cover those other areas.[216] The EEOC takes the position that it may expand the investigation of one branch of an establishment upon a determination that violations appear to exist in "other respondent facilities."[217]

VII. THE RELATIONSHIP BETWEEN EEOC AND PRIVATE LITIGATION

A. Rights of Charging Parties When the EEOC Has Filed Suit

1. The ADEA and the EPA

The filing of an action by the EEOC under the ADEA or the EPA cuts off the right of private suit by the charging party, as well as the right to seek permissive intervention.[218]

---

[216]*See, e.g.*, EEOC v. American Nat'l Bank, 652 F.2d 1176, 1186, 26 FEP 472 (4th Cir. 1981) (even though investigation and conciliation focused on hiring practices at one branch, suit could be expanded to include other branches where "all [were] subject to unified supervision and control" and hiring practices were similar; conciliation, had it been successful, would have resulted in changes at all branches); EEOC v. Thurston Motor Lines, Inc., 124 F.R.D. 110, 112–13, 50 FEP 1759 (M.D.N.C. 1989) (expansion of EEOC litigation to other facilities of employer permissible when investigation that reasonably grew out of charge dealt with company policies generally); EEOC v. Westinghouse Elec. Corp., 632 F. Supp. 343, 363–64, 40 FEP 643 (E.D. Pa. 1986) (geographical expansion in second amended ADEA complaint properly related back, as severance pay plan at issue was in effect nationwide; Title VII principles apply), *rev'd on other grounds*, 925 F.2d 619 (3d Cir. 1991); EEOC v. Akron Nat'l Bank & Trust Co., 497 F. Supp. 733, 737, 22 FEP 1665 (N.D. Ohio 1980) (EEOC may attack practices at defendant's headquarters as well as branch offices when cause determination cited evidence of discrimination companywide); EEOC v. General Tel. Co., 27 FEP 1518, 1522–23 (W.D. Wash. 1979) (same; evidence of discrimination at several facilities); EEOC v. Georgia-Pac. Corp., 450 F. Supp. 1227, 1240, 24 FEP 386 (N.D. Miss. 1977) (EEOC may include in its suit all company facilities statewide, even though not all facilities had been included in administrative charge processing; "there exists a single industry with operations at separate locations, but all subject to one source of supervision and control").

[217]1 EEOC COMPL. MAN. (BNA) § 22.3(c), at 22:0003.

[218]Section 16(b) of the FLSA, 29 U.S.C. § 216(b), provides that a complaint by the EEOC for injunctive relief under § 17, *id.* § 217, terminates the right of an employee to bring an action or "to become a party plaintiff to any such action." An action by the EEOC under § 16(c), the section authorizing the EEOC to seek back pay, similarly terminates the right of an employee to bring an action for back wages, or "to become a party plaintiff to any such action." *See* EEOC v. Pan Am. World Airways, Inc., 897 F.2d 1499, 1509, 52 FEP 990 (9th Cir. 1990) (when EEOC commences suit, individual's right to bring suit under ADEA terminates); Usery v. Board of Pub. Educ., 418 F. Supp. 1037, 1038–39, 14 FEP 376 (W.D. Pa. 1976) (government

The rule that an EEOC ADEA suit bars subsequent private actions[219] does not prevent private parties from opting into a private collective action when their prior motion seeking to opt in has not been acted on at the time the EEOC files suit.[220] On the other hand, plaintiffs who attempt to opt in after the EEOC files its complaint are barred.[221]

2. Title VII and the ADA

If the EEOC files a Title VII suit first, the charging party may intervene as a matter of right.[222] Because the EEOC does not issue a right-to-sue letter if it has decided to file suit,[223] as a practical matter the charging party's rights under Title VII typically are limited to intervention.[224]

EPA suit terminates right of any employee to become plaintiff, including by intervention); *cf.* EEOC v. American Tel. & Tel. Co., 506 F.2d 735, 739, 9 FEP 53 (3d Cir. 1974) (petitioning intervenors did not contest district court's holding that there was no right of permissive intervention in actions brought under § 17 of FLSA). *But see* EEOC GENERAL COUNSEL MAN. (BNA) ch. 2, § X-E-1, at 1110:0062 (July 1980) (permissive intervention should be available to discriminatees in EEOC ADEA or EPA actions).

[219]*See* EEOC v. Transit Mgmt., 78 FEP 934, 936 (E.D. La. 1998) (employee has no right to intervene in EEOC action to enforce ADEA; her rights terminated when EEOC commenced action).

[220]Wilkerson v. Martin Marietta Corp., 875 F. Supp. 1456, 1463–64, 67 FEP 279, 285 (D. Colo. 1995) (opt-in notices considered "functionally equivalent to bringing an action under the ADEA").

[221]*Id.*

[222]Section 706(f)(1), 42 U.S.C. § 2000e-5(f)(1) (2000); *see, e.g.*, EEOC v. National Cleaning Contractors, Inc., 56 FEP 1081, 1082 (S.D.N.Y. 1991) (charging party had unconditional right to intervene in EEOC's hostile environment suit based on her charge; however, upon intervention her right to raise allegations outside scope of her EEOC complaint was no greater than what she would have had in her own Title VII action); EEOC v. General Motors Corp., 46 FEP 597, 598 (D. Kan. 1987) (individual who was the only subject of EEOC complaint could intervene; private party whose interest may be affected by EEOC lawsuit has unqualified right to intervene if intervention was sought in timely fashion); *cf.* EEOC v. Rappaport, Hertz, Cherson, & Rosenthal, 273 F. Supp. 2d 260, 264 (E.D.N.Y. 2003) (charging party bound by arbitration agreement may intervene in EEOC suit, but her claim will be stayed pending arbitration while EEOC suit may proceed).

[223]*See* § 706(f)(1) ("[I]f . . . the Commission has not filed a civil action under this section . . . the Commission . . . shall so notify the person aggrieved and within ninety days after the giving of such notice a civil action may be brought against the respondent named in the charge . . . .").

[224]*Id.*, *cf.* Truvillion v. King's Daughters Hosp., 614 F.2d 520, 525, 22 FEP 554 (5th Cir. 1980) (no bar to private suit where dismissal of EEOC suit not on merits).

Although individuals may intervene as a matter of right following the filing of a Title VII suit by the EEOC,[225] intervention may be denied as untimely where late intervention would prejudice the existing parties by, for example, disturbing settlement negotiations,[226] adding tenuous state law claims or unrelated parties,[227] or interfering with efforts to terminate a consent decree that "has long outlived its original purpose."[228] Permissive intervention in a Title VII matter may be allowed to enable a complainant to obtain sealed records from a federal action settled by the EEOC and the employer.[229]

3. Attorney's Fees

When a suit involves both the EEOC and private plaintiffs, questions sometimes arise concerning what attorney's fees are proper for the private plaintiffs' attorneys. Although courts will not deny attorney's fees simply because the EEOC commenced or was involved in the litigation,[230] courts have reduced fee requests by such plaintiffs where plaintiffs' counsel duplicated work done by the EEOC.[231]

B. The Impact on EEOC Litigation of Arbitration Agreements or Settlements Entered Into by Private Parties

Settlement by a charging party does not affect the EEOC's right to enforce subpoenas against the employer in order to determine

---

[225]EEOC v. Federal Express Corp., 1995 WL 569446, at *4 (W.D. Wash. Aug. 8, 1995) (permitting intervention despite delay because defendant had not been prejudiced).

[226]See EEOC v. United Air Lines, 1995 U.S. Dist. LEXIS 2581, at *9 (N.D. Ill. Mar. 2, 1995) (denying motions to intervene because they were untimely filed and would cause substantial prejudice to original parties, who had already concluded settlement negotiations).

[227]See EEOC v. Domino's Pizza, Inc., 870 F. Supp. 655, 657, 66 FEP 888, 889 (D. Md. 1994) (putative party seeking to add time-barred tort claims denied intervention); see also EEOC v. Dillard Dep't Stores, Inc., 1994 WL 396307 (E.D. La. July 27, 1994) (dismissal of claims under state fair employment law).

[228]See United Air Lines, 1995 U.S. Dist. LEXIS 2581, at *9.

[229]See EEOC v. National Children's Ctr., Inc., 146 F.3d 1042, 1047–49 (D.C. Cir. 1998) (district court had abused its discretion in not permitting intervention for limited purpose of obtaining documents).

[230]See EEOC v. State, County & Mun. Employees, 1996 WL 663971, at *4 (N.D.N.Y. Nov. 12, 1996).

[231]See EEOC v. Clear Lake Dodge, 60 F.3d 1146, 1154–55, 68 FEP 663, 669 (5th Cir. 1995) (on remand, court should deduct for "redundant and unnecessary"

whether other persons were injured by alleged employment discrimination.[232]

The Supreme Court has held that even if a charging party has signed and is bound by an agreement to arbitrate an employment dispute, that does not prevent the EEOC from seeking victim-specific relief for him or her, such as back pay, reinstatement, and damages.[233] Moreover, the inability of the charging party to maintain his or her suit will not affect the EEOC's ability to seek prospective injunctive relief because the EEOC's role is to protect the public from employment discrimination.[234]

On the other hand, if a charging party has already accepted a monetary settlement, the Supreme Court in *Waffle House* held that "any recovery by the EEOC would be limited accordingly" because courts should "preclude double recovery by an individual."[235]

C. The Impact on EEOC Litigation of the Resolution of a Private Lawsuit

The Supreme Court in *Waffle House* stated that if an individual already has litigated his or her own claim, he or she could be precluded by res judicata from obtaining individual relief in a later EEOC action based on the same claim.[236]

If a complainant on whose behalf the EEOC sues has settled his or her claim for monetary relief, the EEOC may still seek injunctive relief.[237]

---

work of private counsel); EEOC v. AIC Sec. Investigations, Ltd., 1994 WL 395119, at *6 (N.D. Ill. July 28, 1994) (where three EEOC trial attorneys handled "the bulk of the trial and the preparation" for trial, attorney's fee reduction of 50% was appropriate), *aff'd*, 55 F.3d 1276 (7th Cir. 1995). *See generally* Chapter 41 (Attorney's Fees).

[232]*See* EEOC v. Morgan Stanley & Co., 132 F. Supp. 2d 146, 152 (S.D.N.Y. 2000); *see also* EEOC v. Severn Trent Servs., Inc., 358 F.3d 438, 444–45, 93 FEP 251 (7th Cir. 2004) (declining to invalidate nondisparagement agreement between employer and potential witness in EEOC investigation as Commission had access to compulsory process to obtain evidence directly from witness; district court injunction vacated).

[233]EEOC v. Waffle House, Inc., 534 U.S. 279, 296–98 (2002).

[234]*See* General Tel. Co. v. EEOC, 446 U.S. 318, 325–26 (1980).

[235]*Waffle House*, 534 U.S. at 296.

[236]*Id.*

[237]EEOC v. Goodyear Aerospace Corp., 813 F.2d 1539, 1543, 43 FEP 875 (9th Cir. 1987) (private plaintiff's settlement did not moot EEOC's right of action seeking injunctive relief).

D. The Impact on EEOC Litigation of a Pending Private Suit

The right of the EEOC to file its own suit when there is a private suit pending based on the same charge is supported by the Supreme Court's dictum in *Waffle House* that "the EEOC has exclusive authority over the choice of forum and the prayer for relief once a charge has been filed."[238] Courts that have squarely faced whether the EEOC may file suit when there is a pending private Title VII suit based on the same charge are divided.[239] Some courts have held that the EEOC is limited to permissive intervention once a private Title VII suit has been filed,[240] even if the EEOC seeks to litigate broader issues.[241] But other courts have held that a private Title VII suit does not limit the right of the EEOC to file its own suit[242] and have permitted such a suit when the private suit had

---

[238]*Waffle House*, 534 U.S. at 296.

[239]Since a § 1981 action is completely independent of Title VII, Johnson v. Railway Express Agency, Inc., 421 U.S. 454, 460–61, 10 FEP 817 (1975), the filing of a private § 1981 action is not a bar to an EEOC suit under Title VII. *See, e.g.*, Patterson v. American Tobacco Co., 8 FEP 778, 781 (E.D. Va. 1974) (private § 1981 action filed before EEOC Title VII action; "dismissal of either action would not be warranted"), *rev'd in part on other grounds*, 535 F.2d 257, 12 FEP 314 (4th Cir. 1976).

[240]*See* EEOC v. Continental Oil Co., 548 F.2d 884, 888–90, 14 FEP 365 (10th Cir. 1977) (EEOC limited to intervention when private suit was filed earlier on same charge); EEOC v. Harris Chernin, Inc., 767 F. Supp. 919, 925, 63 FEP 803 (N.D. Ill. 1991) (same), *rev'd in part on other grounds*, 10 F.3d 1286, 63 FEP 616 (7th Cir. 1993); EEOC v. Pic Pac Supermkts., Inc., 689 F. Supp. 607, 609, 47 FEP 1556 (S.D. W. Va. 1988) (same); EEOC v. U.S. Pipe & Foundry Co., 8 FEP 335, 335–36 (E.D. Tenn. 1974) (when subject matter is identical, EEOC suit should be dismissed); EEOC v. Union Oil Co., 369 F. Supp. 579, 586, 6 FEP 1298 (N.D. Ala. 1974) (EEOC limited to intervention upon filing of private suit "involving the same charge"); *see also* EEOC v. Pacific Press Publ'g Ass'n, 535 F.2d 1182, 1186, 12 FEP 1312 (9th Cir. 1976) ("initiation of a private action . . . terminated EEOC's opportunity to bring suit" on that charge).

[241]*See* Johnson v. Nekoosa-Edwards Paper Co., 558 F.2d 841, 848, 14 FEP 1658 (8th Cir. 1977) (EEOC as intervenor may litigate issues in addition to those alleged in private complaint, provided that it attempted to conciliate additional issues; district court ordered to stay proceedings for 60 days to permit that conciliation effort); EEOC v. Missouri Pac. R.R., 493 F.2d 71, 75, 7 FEP 177 (8th Cir. 1974) (when private suit is filed, EEOC is limited to intervention; district court should "permit intervention and enlargement of the scope of the action by the Commission if necessary to the rendering of full and complete justice").

[242]*See* EEOC v. Pemco Aeroplex, Inc., 383 F.3d 1280, 1292–94, 94 FEP 848 (11th Cir. 2004) (EEOC not precluded by judgment in private pattern-or-practice case from proceeding with its own action where district court denied EEOC's motions

been settled[243] or dismissed for reasons other than a judgment on the merits.[244] Other courts have held that a private suit cuts off the right of the EEOC to file a separate *duplicative* suit, but not a *broader* suit, even though they may be based on the same charge.[245]

Does an ADEA or EPA private suit limit the EEOC in any later suit? The Fifth Circuit, noting that the ADEA (unlike Title VII) does not specifically mention EEOC intervention in pending private suits, held that the EEOC is not restricted to intervention in a private ADEA lawsuit but may bring its own duplicative suit.[246] The Seventh Circuit held that the EEOC has "an unequivocal statutory right to sue to enforce the age-discrimination law" and thus

---

to consolidate actions and EEOC did not direct or act in privity with private plaintiffs), *cert. denied*, 126 S. Ct. 42 (2005); EEOC v. North Hills Passavant Hosp., 544 F.2d 664, 672, 13 FEP 1129 (3d Cir. 1976) ("The plain words [of § 706(f)(1)] say that the EEOC may bring a civil action against a non-governmental respondent. They do not say that the EEOC loses that power when a private party brings a suit based on the same facts or charges . . . . Any burden arising [from prior] lawsuit . . . can be resolved in proceedings under Fed. R. Civ. P. 42(a).").

[243]*See, e.g.*, EEOC v. McLean Trucking Co., 525 F.2d 1007, 1010–11, 11 FEP 833 (6th Cir. 1975) (EEOC can sue on charge despite prior court-approved settlement by charging party); EEOC v. C.M.I., Inc., 45 FEP 521, 521–22 (D. Kan. 1987) (when charging party settled lawsuit with employer before EEOC could intervene, EEOC permitted to sue on behalf of other African-American employees allegedly subjected to same discriminatory practices); EEOC v. American Express Co., 14 FEP 615, 616 (S.D.N.Y.) (EEOC could file suit based on charge that had been basis of previously settled suit), *appeal dismissed*, 558 F.2d 102, 15 FEP 74 (2d Cir. 1977).

[244]*See, e.g., North Hills*, 544 F.2d at 673 (previously filed private action had been dismissed on procedural grounds); EEOC v. Huttig Sash & Door Co., 511 F.2d 453, 455, 10 FEP 529 (5th Cir. 1975) (private suit had been voluntarily dismissed before EEOC suit was filed); EEOC v. Bagas Rests., 55 FEP 172, 173 (D. Kan. 1990) (EEOC allowed to proceed with suit filed 5 days after Title VII action had been filed by individual; individual's suit dismissed without prejudice on procedural grounds); EEOC v. Eagle Iron Works, 367 F. Supp. 817, 822, 6 FEP 1077 (S.D. Iowa 1973) (EEOC can sue on same charge despite dismissal, as untimely filed, of prior suit).

[245]*See* EEOC v. Kimberly-Clark Corp., 511 F.2d 1352, 1363, 10 FEP 38 (6th Cir. 1975) ("If it appears that the EEOC investigation . . . could reasonably have been expected to disclose" broader discrimination, the EEOC was entitled to bring its own suit.); *cf.* EEOC v. Government Employees (AFGE) Local 1617, 657 F. Supp. 742, 750–51, 42 FEP 1500 (W.D. Tex. 1987) (district court dismissed EEOC suit when complaint was not broader than allegations of charging party and charging party's damages had been fully satisfied).

[246]EEOC v. Wackenhut Corp., 939 F.2d 241, 243–44, 56 FEP 1070 (5th Cir. 1991). One court, however, held that res judicata barred a subsequent, duplicative EEOC action under the ADEA, because the charging party's action was dismissed on the merits. EEOC v. Harris Chernin, Inc., 767 F. Supp. 919, 923–25, 63 FEP 803 (N.D. Ill. 1991), *rev'd in part on other grounds*, 10 F.3d 1286, 63 FEP 616 (7th Cir. 1993).

upheld a separate EEOC suit when a private suit based on the same charge had already been filed.[247]

E. The Impact of an EEOC Suit on a Pending Private ADEA Suit

The effect of a later-filed EEOC suit on the pending private ADEA suit is unresolved. The Fourth Circuit suggested that the pending private suit is "suspended" by an EEOC action.[248] But several other courts have held to the contrary.[249]

F. Permissive Intervention by the EEOC in a Pending Action

If the charging party files suit first and the EEOC wishes to intervene, it is limited to permissive intervention. Section 706(f)(1) of Title VII provides: "Upon timely application, the court may, in its discretion, permit the Commission . . . to intervene in such civil action upon certification that the case is of general public importance."

In ADEA and EPA cases, there is no express statutory authorization for EEOC intervention, but the same general principles apply pursuant to Rule 24(b) of the Federal Rules of Civil Procedure. Rule 24(b) provides:

> Upon timely application anyone may be permitted to intervene in an action: (1) when a statute of the United States confers a conditional right to intervene . . . . In exercising its discretion the court shall consider whether the intervention will unduly delay or prejudice the adjudication of the rights of the original parties.

---

[247]EEOC v. G-K-G, Inc., 39 F.3d 740, 744, 66 FEP 344, 347 (7th Cir. 1994). Because the two suits had been consolidated, however, the Seventh Circuit held that the district court may preclude the EEOC from redeposing previously deposed witnesses, examining or cross-examining trial witnesses, making lengthy opening and closing arguments, or otherwise duplicating the efforts of the employee's counsel. *Id.* at 745.

[248]Vance v. Whirlpool Corp., 707 F.2d 483, 489–90, 31 FEP 1115, *supplemental opinion on other grounds*, 716 F.2d 1010, 32 FEP 1391 (4th Cir. 1983).

[249]*See* EEOC v. Eastern Airlines, Inc., 736 F.2d 635, 640–41, 35 FEP 503 (11th Cir. 1984) (prior private suit remained viable after EEOC suit ended with consent decree); Castle v. Sangamo Weston, Inc., 744 F.2d 1464, 1465, 36 FEP 113 (11th Cir. 1984) (per curiam) (pending private suit neither terminated nor preempted by EEOC's subsequent action), *rev'g* 31 FEP 324 (M.D. Fla. 1983); Howard v. Daiichiya-Love's Bakery, Inc., 714 F. Supp. 1108, 1111, 50 FEP 1713 (D. Haw. 1989) (EEOC's action, filed 26 days after private action, does not automatically terminate private action); *see also* Burns v. Equitable Life Assurance Soc'y, 696 F.2d 21, 22–23, 30 FEP 873 (2d Cir. 1982) (affirming district court's holding that various private suits had not been preempted where private suit by more than 100 employees was followed 2 years later by EEOC action).

Permissive intervention by the EEOC in private ADEA or EPA cases has been allowed.[250]

1. Conditions Precedent to Permissive Intervention

The EEOC's certification that the issue is one of "general public importance" is a prerequisite to intervention in a private Title VII suit.[251] The decision to issue the certification is not reviewable.[252] Thus, the EEOC is not required to demonstrate a need for intervention.[253]

Although the EEOC must have completed its administrative processing of a charge before filing its own suit, completion of such processes usually is not a prerequisite to intervention,[254] but compliance with the prerequisites to direct suit often is required with respect to added issues.[255]

---

[250]*See, e.g.*, Brennan v. McDonnell Douglas Corp., 519 F.2d 718, 720, 14 FEP 1585 (8th Cir. 1975) (intervention in age case permitted by court), *rev'd in part on other grounds sub nom.* Houghton v. McDonnell Douglas Corp., 553 F.2d 561, 14 FEP 1594 (8th Cir. 1977).

[251]*See* Love v. Pullman Co., 12 FEP 330, 330–31 (D. Colo. 1973) (intervention not allowed when certificate was not filed).

[252]*E.g.*, Bennett v. McDonald's Sys., Inc., 13 FEP 326, 327–28 (N.D. Ohio 1976) (certification committed to agency discretion and not reviewable); Jones v. Holy Cross Hosp. Silver Spring, Inc., 64 F.R.D. 586, 591, 8 FEP 1024 (D. Md. 1974) ("There is no merit in defendant's argument that the court should review the determination of the EEOC that the case is one of general public importance."). The legislative history of the 1972 amendments to § 706(f)(1) suggests that the EEOC's determination to issue a complaint is "not reviewable in any court." H.R. REP. NO. 92-238 (1971), *reprinted in* 1972 U.S.C.C.A.N. 2137, 2162.

[253]*See* Meyer v. Macmillan Publ'g Co., 85 F.R.D. 149, 150–51, 25 FEP 1003 (S.D.N.Y. 1980) (EEOC's "decision that this case warrants the allocation of its limited resources is entitled to appropriate judicial deference").

[254]*See* Mills v. Bartenders Int'l Union, Local 41, 21 FEP 42, 44 (N.D. Cal. 1975) (EEOC not required to complete preliminary procedural processes prior to intervention; "Congress intended the E.E.O.C. to have the power to intervene to protect the public interest in private . . . lawsuits that might well be filed long before the E.E.O.C. had engaged in sufficient investigation to justify initiation of its own lawsuit. . . . [C]onsiderations that apply when a private suit has already been filed are entirely different than when no action has been filed."); NOW, Inc. v. Minnesota Mining & Mfg. Co., 11 FEP 720, 720 (D. Minn. 1975) (once charging party filed suit, EEOC's "functions as conciliator or persuader are at an end"); Stuart v. Hewlett-Packard Co., 66 F.R.D. 73, 75–77, 10 FEP 70 (E.D. Mich. 1975) (no need to establish independent jurisdictional basis when EEOC seeks to intervene and pursue injunctive or declaratory remedies where claims are identical, even though EEOC seeks to represent larger class).

[255]*Compare* Johnson v. Nekoosa-Edwards Paper Co., 558 F.2d 841, 847–48, 14 FEP 1658 (8th Cir. 1977) (action stayed 60 days to permit conciliation of additional claims) *and* Mead v. United States Fidelity & Guar. Co., 442 F. Supp. 109, 113–14,

2. Factors Considered

A court's discretion to grant[256] or deny[257] permissive intervention is broad[258] and, in practice, rarely disturbed.[259]

The timeliness of the EEOC's motion to intervene often has been an important factor, particularly for those courts denying intervention.[260] As the Second Circuit stated:

> In view of the 21 months that went by before EEOC filed its motion although it was aware of the cases almost from the start, the state of discovery when the motion was made, the possibility of

---

18 FEP 136 (D. Minn. 1977) (allowing intervention on issues broader than private plaintiff's claim, but staying that aspect of action for 60 days to permit conciliation) *with* Sobel v. Yeshiva Univ., 438 F. Supp. 625, 627–28, 21 FEP 47 (S.D.N.Y. 1977) (no requirement for EEOC to complete prerequisites for direct suit where EEOC and private litigant's claims were co-extensive after private litigant amended complaint) *and* Willis v. Allied Maint. Corp., 75 F.R.D. 622, 624, 13 FEP 766 (S.D.N.Y. 1976) (per curiam) (no requirement to complete prerequisites to direct suit where intervention does not expand scope of litigation).

[256]As one court explained:

> First, the court finds this motion to be timely. . . . Here, the court can find no harm that would compel nonintervention. . . .
>
> In sum, intervention by EEOC will cause no more than the ordinary and minimal delay and prejudice which is necessarily incidental to the addition of any party to a lawsuit. Further, the court is swayed by the fact that the public interest will be served by the intervention of an agency with special expertise in the area of Title VII law. Such intervention should materially expedite a resolution of the rights of all parties to this action.

Williams v. Continental Air Lines, Inc., 11 FEP 639, 640 (S.D. Tex. 1975); *see* Stuart v. Hewlett-Packard Co., 66 F.R.D. 73, 77–78, 10 FEP 70 (E.D. Mich. 1975) (EEOC's pursuit of class-type relief in public interest preferable to problems presented by private Rule 23 class actions).

[257]*See* Blowers v. Lawyers Co-op. Publ'g Co., 11 FEP 1119, 1119–20 (W.D.N.Y.), *aff'd per curiam*, 527 F.2d 333, 11 FEP 1316 (2d Cir. 1975) ("Intervention would not protect any interest not already protected. The Commission expressly recognizes . . . that it considers plaintiff's counsel competent to litigate this action. There is a danger that intervention may reopen or duplicate discovery that has already occurred. There is a danger that intervention may result in different views between plaintiff's counsel and the Commission, particularly as to possible appeals, which will delay the action.").

[258]*See* United States Fidelity & Guar. Co. v. Lord, 585 F.2d 860, 866, 18 FEP 171 (8th Cir. 1978) (district court has broad discretion on permissive intervention questions); *Blowers*, 527 F.2d at 334 (per curiam) (same); Van Hoomissen v. Xerox Corp., 497 F.2d 180, 181, 8 FEP 56 (9th Cir. 1974) (same).

[259]*See* Railroad Trainmen v. Baltimore & Ohio R.R., 331 U.S. 519, 524 (1947) ("in the absence of an abuse of discretion . . . intervention is a permissive matter within the discretion of the court"); Cisneros v. Corpus Christi Indep. Sch. Dist., 560 F.2d 190, 191 (5th Cir. 1977) (per curiam) (when request was for permissive intervention, Fifth Circuit would not "disturb the denial" unless there was abuse of discretion).

[260]Both Fed. R. Civ. P. 24(b) and § 706(f)(1) of Title VII require a timely application for permissive intervention.

delay, and the continued permission EEOC has to participate as amicus, the district judge could properly deny the motion. District courts should not be niggardly in allowing a government agency to intervene in cases involving a statute it is required to enforce; indeed, a hospitable attitude is appropriate. But on this record we cannot say there was an abuse of discretion.[261]

Timeliness thus is evaluated based on what has transpired in the litigation and on the effect intervention would have on a speedy resolution of the matter. The time the action already has been pending is relevant, but some courts hold it not to be dispositive.[262]

Especially important to courts in permitting[263] or denying[264] intervention is the court's balance of the possibility of undue delay,

---

[261]*Blowers*, 527 F.2d at 334.

[262]*Compare* Sinyard v. Foote & Davies, 8 FEP 477, 478 (N.D. Ga. 1974) (action already pending 20 months; intervention denied, even though parties would not be substantively prejudiced, because it would precipitate extensive discovery disputes and delay action), *aff'd mem.*, 502 F.2d 784 (5th Cir. 1974) *and* Patterson v. Youngstown Sheet & Tube Co., 62 F.R.D. 351, 352, 7 FEP 360 (N.D. Ind. 1974) (intervention denied when case had been at issue for "more than two years" and "ripe for final determination") *with* Meyer v. Macmillan Publ'g Co., 85 F.R.D. 149, 150, 25 FEP 1003 (S.D.N.Y. 1980) (although suit was pending for a year and a half, defendant had not shown that intervention would delay resolution of dispute), Muka v. Nicolet Paper Co., 24 FEP 671, 672 (E.D. Wis. 1979) (intervention motion, filed 18 months into case, not untimely; motion filed shortly after amended complaint, case still was at pleading stage, and EEOC agreed to coordinate discovery to avoid repetition), Le Beau v. Libbey-Owens-Ford Co., 16 FEP 1503, 1504 (N.D. Ill. 1975) (EEOC intervention granted even though EEOC waited 3 years to seek to intervene) *and* Hughes v. Timex Corp., 9 FEP 62, 64 (E.D. Ark. 1974) (intervention granted even though 3 years elapsed after original complaint was filed; more discovery still was needed, case still was not ready for trial, and any prejudice to defendant from intervention was outweighed by benefit to public).

[263]*See Meyer*, 85 F.R.D. at 150 (intervention granted, but EEOC would "not be permitted to extend the time required for trial"); Williams v. Continental Air Lines, Inc., 11 FEP 639, 640 (S.D. Tex. 1975) (no delay, because "defendant itself is still seeking to join additional parties"); NOW, Inc. v. Minnesota Mining & Mfg. Co., 11 FEP 720, 720 (D. Minn. 1975) (discovery only in preliminary stages; intervention would not cause undue delay); Marshall v. Electric Hose & Rubber Co., 65 F.R.D. 599, 607–08, 10 FEP 1070 (D. Del. 1974) (intervention allowed; although case had been pending "for some time," no responsive pleadings had been filed or discovery commenced); *cf. Hughes*, 9 FEP at 64 (citing judicial economy and public interest in support of intervention).

[264]*See* Spirt v. Teachers Ins. & Annuity Ass'n, 93 F.R.D. 627, 638 & n.2, 28 FEP 489 (S.D.N.Y.) (EEOC's application to intervene denied in part; EEOC had known of issues raised by changing party for 7 years without seeking to intervene), *rev'd in part on other grounds*, 691 F.2d 1054, 29 FEP 1599 (2d Cir. 1982), *vacated and remanded on other grounds*, 463 U.S. 1223 (1983); Molthan v. Temple Univ.-Commonwealth Sys. of Higher Educ., 93 F.R.D. 585, 587–88, 28 FEP 430 (E.D.

confusion,[265] or prejudice against the improvement of the administration of justice. One factor some courts find important on the latter issue is the competence of the plaintiff's private counsel.[266]

On occasion, intervention by the EEOC is conditioned on the EEOC's representation that its presence will not delay or prejudice the adjudication of the rights of the original parties, but rather will materially aid in the expeditious determination of the issues.[267] The EEOC is subject to later dismissal from the action for noncompliance or lack of cooperation.[268]

Pa. 1982) (denying EEOC's motion to intervene 6½ years after complaint was filed, because "its presence [would] further delay or prejudice the adjudication of the rights of the parties"), aff'd, 778 F.2d 955, 39 FEP 816 (3d Cir. 1985); *Blowers*, 527 F.2d at 334 (per curiam) (upholding denial of intervention in this case even though it urged courts generally to have "hospitable attitude"); Stallworth v. Monsanto Co., 13 FEP 832, 833–34 (N.D. Fla. 1975) (amicus curiae role adequate); *Sinyard*, 8 FEP at 478 (denial based on likelihood of "another year of discovery disputes"); Love v. Pullman Co., 12 FEP 330, 331 (D. Colo. 1973) (unlikely that EEOC as intervenor would "contribute to the progress of this lawsuit in any greater degree" than as amicus curiae).

[265]One court cited the "likely probability of trial confusion" as a reason for denying intervention; where this is true, denying leave to intervene "is not an abuse of discretion even though there is a well defined issue common to all the claims." Lipsett v. United States, 359 F.2d 956, 959–60 (2d Cir. 1966). Similarly, as noted by Judge (later, Justice) Blackmun in *Stadin v. Union Electric Co.*, 309 F.2d 912 (8th Cir. 1962):

> It seems unquestionably clear to us from the pleadings of the intervener that his desired incorporation . . . will bring into these lawsuits added complexity; the inevitable problems attendant upon additional witnesses, interrogatories and depositions; expanded pretrial activity; greater length of trial; and elements of confusion. These in themselves suggest delay and the clouding of the issues involved in the original causes of action. More than one trial court has observed that "[a]dditional parties always take additional time" and that "they are the source of additional questions, objections, briefs, arguments, motions and the like which tend to make the proceeding a Donnybrook Fair."

309 F.2d at 920 (citations omitted).

[266]*See, e.g., Blowers*, 11 FEP at 1119 (competence of private plaintiff's counsel and potential for conflict between EEOC and private counsel were factors militating against intervention), aff'd, 527 F.2d 333, 11 FEP 1316 (2d Cir. 1975) (per curiam); Rosario v. New York Times Co., 16 FEP 76, 76 (S.D.N.Y. 1975) (competence of plaintiffs' private counsel was one reason for denying intervention); Patterson v. Youngstown Sheet & Tube Co., 62 F.R.D. 351, 352, 7 FEP 360 (N.D. Ind. 1974) (same).

[267]*See Muka*, 24 FEP at 672 (EEOC represented that it would not subject defendants to repetition of discovery and would coordinate discovery with private plaintiff).

[268]Van Bronkhorst v. Safeco Corp., 529 F.2d 943, 947–48, 12 FEP 178 (9th Cir. 1976) (EEOC dismissed from case because its participation as intervenor delayed finalization of consent decree).

Many courts that have denied intervention have noted that the EEOC's contribution to the action can equally well be effected as amicus curiae.[269]

What happens to an EEOC intervening claim after the private plaintiff settles for monetary relief? The Supreme Court, in *EEOC v. Waffle House, Inc.*,[270] noted that courts "should preclude double recovery by an individual."[271] But *Waffle House* also stated that the EEOC is not the "proxy" for an employee.[272] Thus, the EEOC should be able to continue to seek relief other than that already achieved by a private plaintiff.[273]

VIII. PRELIMINARY RELIEF[274]

A. Statutory Authority

Section 706(f)(2) provides for preliminary relief in Title VII actions "pending final disposition" of an EEOC charge.[275] It provides:

---

[269]*See, e.g., Sinyard*, 8 FEP at 478 (EEOC's interests could be "fully protected" as amicus curiae), *aff'd mem.*, 502 F.2d 784 (5th Cir. 1974); *cf.* Brewer v. Republic Steel Corp., 64 F.R.D. 591, 593, 8 FEP 519 (N.D. Ohio 1974) (in denying motion to intervene by state FEP agency, district court suggested that amicus brief would be welcome), *aff'd*, 513 F.2d 1222, 10 FEP 606 (6th Cir. 1975); *Love*, 12 FEP at 331 (denying intervention; EEOC's contribution as party would be no greater than as amicus curiae). This may be particularly true when the EEOC's proposed complaint is substantially the same as the plaintiff's. *See* Crosby Steam Gage & Valve Co. v. Manning, Maxwell & Moore, Inc., 51 F. Supp. 972, 973 (D. Mass. 1943) ("Where he presents no new questions, a third party can contribute usually most effectively and always most expeditiously by a brief amicus curiae and not by intervention.").

[270]534 U.S. 279 (2002).

[271]*Id.* at 296 (charging party's arbitration agreement does not preclude suit by EEOC).

[272]*Id.*

[273]*Cf.* EEOC v. United Parcel Serv., 860 F.2d 372, 374, 48 FEP 245 (10th Cir. 1988) (when employee on whose behalf action was brought had settled, EEOC still could challenge allegedly discriminatory policy; it could affect unidentifiable others); EEOC v. Goodyear Aerospace Corp., 813 F.2d 1539, 1543, 43 FEP 875 (9th Cir. 1987) (private plaintiff's settlement did not moot EEOC's right of action seeking injunctive relief); Harris v. Amoco Prod. Co., 768 F.2d 669, 681–82, 38 FEP 1226 (5th Cir. 1985) (EEOC should not have been dismissed as matter of law after private plaintiffs settled, but may maintain suit thereafter, subject to court's sound discretion). *But cf.* Horn v. Eltra Corp., 686 F.2d 439, 441, 29 FEP 1266 (6th Cir. 1982) (EEOC's intervention revoked; its appeal held moot after charging party's Title VII action was settled; EEOC had not issued "reasonable cause" determination or engaged in conciliation).

[274]*See generally* Chapter 39 (Injunctive and Affirmative Relief).

[275]*See* EEOC v. Pacific Press Publ'g Ass'n, 535 F.2d 1182, 1186–87, 12 FEP 1312 (9th Cir. 1976) (because purpose is to prevent interference with administrative

Whenever a charge is filed with the Commission and the Commission concludes on the basis of a preliminary investigation that prompt judicial action is necessary to carry out the purposes of this Act, the Commission, or the Attorney General in a case involving a government, governmental agency, or political subdivision, may bring an action for appropriate temporary or preliminary relief pending final disposition of such charge. Any temporary restraining order or other order granting preliminary or temporary relief shall be issued in accordance with Rule 65 of the Federal Rules of Civil Procedure. It shall be the duty of a court having jurisdiction over proceedings under this section to assign cases for hearing at the earliest practicable date and to cause such cases to be in every way expedited.[276]

Section 107 of the ADA incorporates the above provision.[277]

Section 706(f)(2) itself requires (1) a "preliminary investigation" and (2) determination that "prompt judicial action is necessary." The district director has been delegated the authority to certify that "prompt judicial action is necessary."[278] Chapter 13 of the EEOC Compliance Manual addresses litigation for temporary or preliminary relief.[279]

The charging party may intervene in the § 706(f)(2) action after it has been filed by the EEOC.[280]

There is no special statutory provision for preliminary relief in either the ADEA or the EPA. As a result, preliminary proceedings are governed by Rule 65 of the Federal Rules of Civil Procedure.[281] The EEOC Compliance Manual indicates that the lack of an ADEA

---

process, there is no right to § 706(f)(2) relief once administrative process ends when charging parties file their own Title VII suit).

[276]42 U.S.C. § 2000e-5(f)(2).

[277]42 U.S.C. § 12117.

[278]29 C.F.R. § 1601.23(a). Such determination has been held unreviewable. EEOC v. American Koyo Corp., 16 FEP 1375, 1375 (N.D. Ohio 1975) (court denied discovery as to EEOC's reasons for bringing § 706(f)(2) action).

[279]Section 13.1 thereof provides in part:

EEOC views § 706(f)(2) broadly to authorize suits to preserve the status quo and to prevent actions which would deprive or tend to deprive any person of Title VII/ADA rights or which would interfere with EEOC's efforts to carry out the purposes of the Act. Thus, it might be appropriate to seek interim relief to prevent a person from destroying relevant records or from discharging or otherwise retaliating against any person who opposed a practice made unlawful by Title VII/ADA; made a charge; or testified, assisted or participated in any manner in an EEOC investigation, proceeding or hearing.

[280]Section 706(f)(1) provides for intervention as of right by the charging party in "a civil action brought by the Commission." 42 U.S.C. § 2000e-5(f)(1).

[281]For a discussion of the Rule 65 standards, see Chapter 39 (Injunctive and Affirmative Relief).

provision analogous to § 706(f)(2) means that conciliation efforts are a condition precedent to an action for interim relief, although the scope of the conciliation efforts may be limited to the scope of the interim relief sought.[282]

B. Standards for Relief

The legislative history of Title VII provides little guidance as to what standards should govern issuance of such relief.[283]

The traditional Rule 65 requirements are the inadequacy of the remedy at law, existence of irreparable injury, likelihood of prevailing on the merits, whether preliminary relief would effectively end the lawsuit, the balance of hardships, and the public interest.[284]

Courts have reached different conclusions on whether these traditional requirements apply under Title VII.[285]

---

[282]1 EEOC COMPL. MAN. (BNA) § 13.9.

[283]The legislative history describing the final conference bill does not specify the standard for preliminary relief. The Senate and House bills that went into the conference differed on the point. The Senate's bill specified no standard at all ("may bring an action for appropriate temporary or preliminary relief pending final disposition of such charge"). S. 2515, 92d Cong., 118 CONG. REC. 4945 (1972). The House bill specified something akin to the traditional standard ("*Provided*, that no . . . relief shall be issued absent a showing that substantial and irreparable injury to the aggrieved party will be unavoidable."). H.R. 1746, 92d Cong., 117 CONG. REC. 31,980 (1971); *see also* H.R. REP. NO. 92-238 (1971), *reprinted in* 1972 U.S.C.C.A.N. 2137–86. The Act's final language, in § 706(f)(2), described only how relief should issue once the decision is made that it is appropriate: "in accordance with Rule 65 of the Federal Rules of Civil Procedure."

[284]*See, e.g.*, EEOC v. Severn Trent Servs., Inc., 358 F.3d 438, 442 (7th Cir. 2004) (Rule 65 standards apply; declining to grant injunction to invalidate "nondisparagement" clause in agreement with potential witness where EEOC had not yet sought to obtain witness' testimony by compulsory process); Direx Israel, Ltd. v. Breakthrough Med. Corp., 952 F.2d 802, 812 (4th Cir. 1991) (enumerating Rule 65 requirements); QSI-Fostoria DC, LLC v. GE Capital Bus. Asset Funding Corp., 2005 U.S. Dist. LEXIS 521, at *13 (N.D. Ohio Jan. 14, 2005) (same).

[285]*See* EEOC v. Pacific Press Publ'g Ass'n, 535 F.2d 1182, 1187, 12 FEP 1312 (9th Cir. 1976) (Rule 65 requirements relaxed); EEOC v. Atlantic Richfield Co., 30 FEP 551, 552–53 (C.D. Cal. 1979) (same); EEOC v. Union Bank, 12 FEP 527, 530 (D. Ariz. 1976) (same); EEOC v. Astra USA, Inc., 94 F.3d 738, 742–43, 71 FEP 1267 (1st Cir. 1996) (traditional standards, including irreparable harm and adequacy of legal relief, apply in Title VII action); EEOC v. Anchor Hocking Corp., 666 F.2d 1037, 1043, 27 FEP 809 (6th Cir. 1981) (required showing either irreparable injury to charging party or that in fact EEOC's ability to prosecute pending charge has been impeded); EEOC v. Phoenix Newspapers, Inc., 23 FEP 1726, 1728–29 (D. Ariz. 1980) (same; no mention of *Pacific Press*); EEOC v. Bay Shipbuilding Corp., 480 F. Supp. 925, 927–28, 21 FEP 747 (E.D. Wis. 1979) (criticizing *Pacific Press* and requiring

C. Typical Situations in Which Preliminary Relief Is Sought

1. Retaliation Cases

Most § 706(f)(2) cases involve allegations of retaliation in violation of the participation clause of § 704(a).[286] Courts have reached different conclusions on whether the chilling effects of a retaliatory discharge will be presumed[287] or whether the EEOC must prove them in each case.[288] One court has said that the preliminary investigation must show a prima facie case of retaliation.[289]

Actions that "might constitute retaliation" for filing complaints with the EEOC were found sufficient to justify a preliminary injunction prohibiting the employer from entering into "any [alternative dispute resolution (ADR)] policy which would cause an employee to pay the costs of ADR proceedings" or "preclude or interfere with" an employee's right to file a complaint with the EEOC or subsequently sue under Title VII.[290]

Retaliatory conduct also has been enjoined in ADEA cases.[291]

---

showing of irreparable harm either to EEOC or charging party); *see also* EEOC v. Recruit U.S.A., Inc., 939 F.2d 746, 752, 56 FEP 721 (9th Cir. 1991) (traditional Rule 65 standards applied); EEOC v. New York, 51 FEP 969, 970–71 (S.D.N.Y. 1989) (same), *rev'd on other grounds*, 907 F.2d 316 (2d Cir. 1990); EEOC v. Hammond Ready Mix, Inc., 1989 WL 113992, at *3 (E.D. La. Sept. 22, 1989) (same); EEOC v. Chateau Normandy, 658 F. Supp. 598, 602–04, 43 FEP 1652 (S.D. Ind. 1987) (EEOC's petition for preliminary injunction denied because EEOC could not demonstrate irreparable injury; court evaluated petition under traditional standards of Rule 65); EEOC v. United States Steel Corp., 583 F. Supp. 1357, 1361, 34 FEP 973 (W.D. Pa. 1984) (applying irreparable injury standard to claim for preliminary relief pending completion of administrative proceedings), *rev'd on other grounds*, 921 F.2d 489, 54 FEP 1044 (3d Cir. 1990); EEOC v. Target Stores, Inc., 36 FEP 543, 544 (D. Minn. 1984) (EEOC satisfied standard for relief under *Anchor Hocking*).

[286]*See Pacific Press*, 535 F.2d at 1187 ("Preliminary injunctive relief under [§ 706(f)(2)] is an important tool in protecting Title VII rights, especially in cases involving retaliation for the exercise of those rights."). *See generally* Chapter 14 (Retaliation).

[287]*See Atlantic Richfield*, 30 FEP at 552 (describing serious effects of retaliatory discharge on employee, as well as on EEOC's processes); EEOC v. Union Bank, 12 FEP 527, 529 (D. Ariz. 1976) (injunction necessary or employees would be "reluctant to participate" in both administrative and judicial proceedings).

[288]*E.g.*, EEOC v. Phoenix Newspapers, Inc., 23 FEP 1726, 1728–29 (D. Ariz. 1980) (EEOC required to show that discharge interfered with investigation or chilled fellow employees' exercise of rights under Title VII); *Anchor Hocking*, 666 F.2d at 1043–44 (same); *Bay Shipbuilding*, 480 F. Supp. at 928 (same).

[289]*Union Bank*, 12 FEP at 530.

[290]EEOC v. River Oaks Imaging & Diagnostic, 1995 WL 264003, at *1, 67 FEP 1243, 1243–44 (S.D. Tex. Apr. 19, 1995).

[291]*See* EEOC v. Cosmair, Inc., 821 F.2d 1085, 1090 (5th Cir. 1987).

2. Interference With EEOC Investigations

Courts have enjoined employers' requirements that employees promise not to aid the EEOC's investigation of charges.[292] Courts also have enjoined agreements prohibiting employees from filing charges of discrimination.[293]

3. Destruction of Records

The threat of immediate and irreparable injury to an EEOC investigation has been found sufficient to justify a temporary restraining order to prevent the destruction of employee records.[294]

4. Mandatory Retirement

Courts have granted preliminary relief under the ADEA in regard to mandatory retirement.[295] One court has denied such relief.[296]

IX. DISCOVERY AGAINST THE EEOC[297]

A. Facts in the Possession of the EEOC

The EEOC generally must produce factual material from its administrative file on the charge of discrimination.[298] In an EEOC

---

[292]See EEOC v. Astra USA, Inc., 94 F.3d 738, 743–45, 71 FEP 1267 (1st Cir. 1996) ("Clearly, if victims of or witnesses to sexual harassment are unable to approach the EEOC or even to answer its questions, the investigatory powers that Congress conferred would be sharply curtailed and the efficacy of investigations would be severely hampered."); see also EEOC v. Morgan Stanley & Co. Inc., 89 FEP 1791, 1792 (S.D.N.Y. 2002) (granting preliminary injunction voiding policy that interfered with EEOC's ability to communicate with witnesses).

[293]See EEOC v. United States Steel Corp., 583 F. Supp. 1357, 1361, 1363, 34 FEP 973 (W.D. Pa. 1984) (granting preliminary injunction because use of release "hindered and impeded the EEOC's investigative and administrative processes").

[294]See EEOC v. Cornwell Pers. Assocs., 1995 WL 661154, at *1 (E.D. Wis. Aug. 15, 1995) (granting temporary restraining order because otherwise EEOC "will suffer immediate and irreversible injury to its ability to investigate and determine the charges of discrimination" if any documents are altered, destroyed, or removed).

[295]See EEOC v. Chrysler Corp., 738 F.2d 167, 168, 41 FEP 1011 (6th Cir. 1984) (upholding injunction that reinstated forced retirees to layoff status); EEOC v. City of Bowling Green, 607 F. Supp. 524, 525, 37 FEP 963 (W.D. Ky. 1985) (pending involuntary retirement qualified as irreparable injury).

[296]See EEOC v. New Jersey, 620 F. Supp. 977, 980, 39 FEP 516 (D.N.J. 1985).

[297]See generally Chapter 33 (Discovery).

[298]See EEOC v. St. Francis Cmty. Hosp., 70 F.R.D. 592, 595, 12 FEP 423 (D.S.C. 1976) (EEOC required to produce in camera all correspondence with charging party

lawsuit,[299] the EEOC must disclose the identities of the individual claimants in response to the respondent's discovery requests.[300]

B. Privileged Material

The scope of discovery in the federal courts is defined by Rule 26 of the Federal Rules of Civil Procedure, which permits discovery of matters "not privileged." Courts have recognized distinct governmental privileges protecting the deliberative processes of government, the identity of government informants, and certain information given to the government on a pledge of confidentiality.[301] The EEOC may also invoke privileges applicable to private litigants.

1. Informer's Privilege

The "informer's privilege" protects information given by a witness during the EEOC administrative investigation on the condition of confidentiality.[302] But the "informer's privilege" does not insulate the EEOC from identifying persons known to have knowledge of relevant facts.[303] In one ADEA case, the court accepted the EEOC's claim of informer's privilege as it pertained to identities of witnesses but rejected the claim of privilege as to information

---

and certain third persons; any interest in confidentiality outweighed by defendant's right to prepare its best defense); *see also* EEOC v. Los Alamos Constructors, Inc., 382 F. Supp. 1373, 1383, 1386, 8 FEP 963 (D.N.M. 1974) (EEOC may not rely on executive privilege or informer's privilege to refuse to submit to defendant, in answers to interrogatories, names of persons known by EEOC to have knowledge of facts); Hoffman v. United Telecomms., Inc., 117 F.R.D. 436, 438 (D. Kan. 1987) (EEOC as intervenor required to identify in interrogatory responses policies that EEOC contended were discriminatory).

[299]*See Hoffman*, 117 F.R.D. at 444.

[300]*Id.*

[301]*See* Association for Women in Sci. v. Califano, 566 F.2d 339, 343 (D.C. Cir. 1977) (listing governmental privileges).

[302]*See* EEOC v. G-K-G, Inc., 131 F.R.D. 553, 555, 53 FEP 817 (N.D. Ill. 1990) (sustaining informer's privilege regarding disclosure of two confidential witnesses; no demonstration by employer that its need for disclosure outweighed public interest in maintaining privilege). For a discussion of the informer's privilege under the FLSA, see Brennan v. Engineered Prods., Inc., 506 F.2d 299, 302, 9 FEP 987 (8th Cir. 1974) (enforcement highly dependent on cooperation of employees; justifying privilege); Dunlop v. J.D.C.N., Inc., 67 F.R.D. 505, 507, 11 FEP 614 (E.D. Mich. 1975) (privilege under FLSA not disputed and will cover statements even when identity of informer is known); Brennan v. Glen Falls Nat'l Bank & Trust Co., 9 FEP 1000, 1001 (N.D.N.Y. 1974) (privilege is "essential to effective enforcement" of FLSA).

[303]*See Los Alamos Constructors*, 382 F. Supp. at 1383, 1386.

regarding witnesses already identified, based on the employer's need for adequate trial preparation.[304]

2. Deliberative Process Privilege

In *EEOC v. Wagner Electric Corp.*,[305] the EEOC had previously produced its investigator's final report but had omitted four paragraphs covering his opinion; the court sustained this omission.[306] One district court disallowed Rule 30(b)(6) depositions of EEOC investigators because EEOC reasonable cause determinations are protected by the "deliberative process privilege."[307]

3. EEOC Thought Processes and Internal Procedures

Courts generally reject attempts to gain discovery of EEOC thought processes and internal procedures unless there is a substantial showing of an abuse of process.[308] In an action to enforce an EEOC subpoena issued as part of an investigation of a commissioner charge, the Sixth Circuit vacated a district court's discovery order requiring the EEOC to produce for depositions a former commissioner and certain current employees.[309]

---

[304]EEOC v. Consolidated Edison Co., 37 FEP 1660, 1661–62 (S.D.N.Y. 1981).

[305]9 FEP 170 (E.D. Mo. 1973).

[306]*Id.* (holding privileged EEOC investigator's opinion); *see also* EEOC v. Stauffer Chem. Co., 1990 WL 19967, at *2 (N.D. Ill. 1990) (EEOC may assert deliberative process privilege as to "predecisional" and "deliberative" documents, but privilege does not extend to factual or objective material; EEOC must show that privilege applies, and court must balance need for disclosure with need for secrecy; court ordered in camera inspection to determine need for secrecy).

[307]EEOC v. Venator Group, 83 FEP 609, 610 (S.D.N.Y. 2000).

[308]*See* Food Town Stores, Inc. v. EEOC, 708 F.2d 920, 925, 31 FEP 1327 (4th Cir. 1983) (defining abuse of process by EEOC to include investigations intended "for harassment or for other ulterior or improper purpose"); EEOC v. St. Regis Paper Co.-Kraft Div., 717 F.2d 1302, 1304, 32 FEP 1849 (9th Cir. 1983) (discovery allowed only when "exceptional circumstances" indicate abuse of process by EEOC); *In re* EEOC, 709 F.2d 392, 401–02, 32 FEP 361 (5th Cir. 1983) (statement of charging party's spouse to effect that she had friends who could get commissioner to make sure that company "paid," followed by issuance of broad-based commissioner charge, insufficient to raise substantial question of abuse of process). Defendants likely will contend, however, that it generally is impossible to prove an abuse of process without the disputed discovery.

[309]*See* EEOC v. K-Mart Corp., 694 F.2d 1055, 1064–65, 30 FEP 788 (6th Cir. 1982) (district court had directed former EEOC commissioner and other EEOC employees to submit to depositions in subpoena enforcement proceeding based on

Discovery concerning the EEOC's investigative and cause-finding processes has been denied.[310]

4. Conciliation

Courts are split on whether the EEOC must disclose information about conciliation efforts.[311]

5. Work Product Privilege

Even though Commission attorneys represent the agency rather than the claimant, the EEOC may invoke the work product privilege to protect communications between EEOC attorneys and claimants.[312] The privilege, however, does not cover the entire EEOC investigative file.[313] A defendant will not be allowed to depose an

---

commissioner charge; Sixth Circuit vacated district court's order and remanded; no proper basis for discovery directed toward circumstances surrounding issuance of charge; validity of charge must be determined from its face); *see also* EEOC v. Roadway Express, Inc., 580 F. Supp. 1063, 1066, 35 FEP 842 (W.D. Tenn.) (district court refused to allow deposition of EEOC district director in subpoena enforcement proceeding; allegations of bad faith must be buttressed by specific facts and must put in issue good faith of *agency*, and not just *agent* handling matter), *aff'd*, 750 F.2d 40, 36 FEP 867 (6th Cir. 1984).

[310]*See* EEOC v. Windsor Court Hotel, Inc., 1999 WL 407610, at *1 (E.D. La. June 17, 1999); Mace v. EEOC, 37 F. Supp. 2d 1144, 1149 (E.D. Mo.), *aff'd*, 197 F.3d 329 (8th Cir. 1999); EEOC v. St. Michael Hosp., 75 FEP 124, 125 (E.D. Wis. 1997) (no discovery permitted concerning reasons for agency's finding of reasonable cause); *see also Venator Group*, 83 FEP at 610 (disallowing Rule 30(b)(6) depositions of EEOC investigators because EEOC reasonable cause determinations are protected by "deliberative process privilege"); EEOC v. Exxon Corp., 1998 WL 50464, at *1 (N.D. Tex. Jan. 20, 1998) (prohibiting deposition of EEOC chair absent showing of "extraordinary circumstance" concerning official actions of chair).

[311]*Compare* EEOC v. E.I. du Pont de Nemours & Co., 9 FEP 65, 66 (W.D. Ky. 1974) (parties cannot depose EEOC official about conciliation negotiations because disclosure would injure conciliation efforts) *with* EEOC v. Missouri Federated Coop. Servs., 8 FEP 731, 734 (S.D. Miss. 1974) (confidentiality provisions pertaining to conciliation efforts are for benefit of parties and not for benefit of EEOC).

[312]*See* EEOC v. Pasta House Co., 70 FEP 61, 63 (E.D. Mo. 1996) (in class sex hiring discrimination case, completed questionnaires and notes of claimant interviews conducted by EEOC's attorney or paralegal assistant protected as work product, but EEOC required to produce names and addresses of those who completed questionnaires) (citing Upjohn Co. v. United States, 449 U.S. 383, 399 (1981) (disclosing attorney's notes of witness' oral statements would tend to reveal attorney's mental processes)).

[313]*See* EEOC v. Consolidated Edison Co., 37 FEP 1660, 1664 (S.D.N.Y. 1981) (requiring in camera inspection of documents to protect against disclosure of EEOC investigator's mental impressions).

EEOC attorney unless the defendant can show that there is no other way to obtain relevant, nonprivileged information that is crucial to the defendant's preparation of the case, and the information cannot be obtained by any other reasonable means.[314] A damages questionnaire prepared in anticipation of litigation may be protected by work product privilege.[315]

6. Attorney-Client Privilege

EEOC communications with charging parties and claimants have been afforded protection by the courts based on the attorney-client privilege, because where Congress has authorized enforcement of statutes through government suits on individual claims, its purposes can be fully accomplished only if the government attorneys have the same right as private counsel to communicate confidentially with the aggrieved individuals.[316] Courts have also found that the Commission's communications are protected by the common interest rule, which protects communications between an individual (or entity) or the individual's attorney and an attorney representing a person or entity that shares a common interest with

---

[314]*See* EEOC v. HBE Corp., 157 F.R.D. 465, 466 (E.D. Mo. 1994).

[315]*See* EEOC v. General Motors, 75 FEP 1734, 1736 (E.D. Mo. 1997) (questionnaire not completed in every case but prepared in anticipation of litigation; no showing of need).

[316]*See* EEOC v. International Profit Assocs., Inc., 206 F.R.D. 215, 220 (N.D. Ill. 2002) (holding that notes from interviews by EEOC with former and current employees, after litigation was filed, were privileged and that privilege was not waived by EEOC disclosing investigative file); EEOC v. Chemsico, 203 F.R.D. 432, 433 87 FEP 278 (E.D. Mo. 2001) (holding that information requested by defendant in discovery was protected by attorney-client privilege to extent interrogatory requested any oral or written statement made by charging party to EEOC's attorney, identity of persons who made written or oral statements to EEOC's attorney or to her agents, and notes prepared by EEOC's attorney or her agents of oral statements made to attorney or her agents by persons other than charging party); Bauman v. Jacobs Suchard, Inc., 136 F.R.D. 460, 463 (N.D. Ill. 1990) (denying defendant's motion to compel production of EEOC questionnaires completed by former employees of defendant who were not plaintiffs in lawsuit but for whom EEOC was seeking relief in separate lawsuit); EEOC v. Georgia Pac. Corp., 11 FEP 722, 725 (D. Or. 1975) (determining that written communications between EEOC staff and charging party were privileged where she sought legal advice from EEOC after private attorney terminated representation); *see also* EEOC v. HBE Corp., 64 FEP 1518, 1520 (E.D. Mo. 1994) (communication between plaintiff and EEOC protected by privilege where both have sued employer); EEOC v. Chemtech Int'l Corp., 4 AD 1465, 1466 (S.D. Tex. 1995) (EEOC represented claimant's interests).

the individual with respect to the legal matter to which the communications relate.[317]

C. The Defendant's Contacts With Claimants

The Commission takes the position that American Bar Association Model Rule of Professional Conduct 4.2 and related state ethical rules barring ex parte communications by opposing lawyers with represented parties applies to contacts by defense counsel with claimants in EEOC suits. The purpose of Rule 4.2 is to prevent lawyers from taking advantage of uncounseled laypersons, as well as to permit attorneys to develop their cases without interference by the adverse party.[318] Courts generally prohibit or limit a defendant's attempts to contact EEOC claimants directly.[319] Similarly, courts generally disfavor a defendant's attempts to obtain a

---

[317]*See HBE Corp.*, 64 FEP 1518 (finding that EEOC and charging party had common interest in litigation because both brought suit for alleged discrimination by defendant); *Chemtech Int'l*, 4 AD 1465, 1466 (finding that "because the EEOC and the private citizen have many identical interests, the attorney-client privilege is essentially a joint prosecution privilege that extends to communications between a party and the attorney for a co-litigant" (citations omitted)); *Bauman*, 136 F.R.D. at 462 (in refusing to compel production of EEOC questionnaire responses, court stated that "[T]he EEOC and the other plaintiffs . . . are aligned together. The privilege applies to communications between a party and the attorney for a co-litigant.").

[318]Pursuant to Rule 4.2, courts in certified private class actions prohibit defendants and their attorneys from contacting class members during litigation. *See, e.g.*, Kleiner v. First Nat'l Bank of Atlanta, 751 F.2d 1193, 1206–07 (11th Cir. 1985); RESTATEMENT (THIRD) OF THE LAW GOVERNING LAWYERS § 99, cmt. 1 & reporter's note to cmt. 1 (2000); MANUAL FOR COMPLEX LITIGATION (FOURTH) § 21.33, at 300–02 (2004). There is also some authority for limiting the nature of such communications prior to certification, *see* Dondore v. NGK Metals Corp., 152 F. Supp. 2d 662, 665–66 (E.D. Pa. 2001); Abdallah v. Coca-Cola Co., 186 F.R.D. 672, 678 (N.D. Ga. 1999), although broad bans on precertification communications require a clear record and specific findings, and may be unconstitutional, *see* Gulf Oil Co. v. Bernard, 452 U.S. 89, 101–02 (1981). EEOC class cases, although not governed by Rule 23, are directly authorized by § 706 of Title VII and §§ 16(c) and 17 of the FLSA (no opt-in requirement), and therefore arguably should be treated as equivalent to certified private class actions for purposes of the applicability of Rule 4.2.

[319]*See* EEOC v. Dana Corp., 202 F. Supp. 2d 827, 830 (N.D. Ind. 2002) (court found that until those individuals characterized as "potential class members" established attorney-client relationship, defendant would be permitted to engage in such ex parte communications; however, court noted that defendant's counsel ran risk of "running afoul of Rule 4.2" if it conducted any ex parte communication with represented party and cautioned defendant to "be extremely careful before . . . conducting such interviews"); EEOC v. Morgan Stanley Co., 206 F. Supp. 2d 559, 562–63

settlement or secure a waiver through direct communications with claimants once the EEOC has filed suit.[320]

X. SETTLEMENT

Settlement of litigation with the EEOC differs from settlement with a private plaintiff in three ways: (1) the EEOC may be more interested than private plaintiffs in injunctive relief or structural change, because the EEOC's mandate is to litigate in the public interest;[321] (2) the monetary component of settlement with the EEOC does not involve issues relating to payment of plaintiffs' attorney's fees; and (3) EEOC settlements, subject to fairly elaborate policy guidelines, in many cases are less negotiable than private settlements.[322] For example, confidentiality, normally a key nonfinancial term for a defendant, is difficult and sometimes impossible to negotiate in EEOC cases.[323]

(S.D.N.Y. 2002) (court, which had earlier ruled that defendant could not contact ex parte women who had affirmatively joined in EEOC's lawsuit, held that because case turned on statistical evidence and not individual testimony of female employees, defendant could contact potential class members who had not yet agreed to join suit, but said that because of possibility of coercive communication safeguards were warranted); EEOC v. Mitsubishi Motor Mfg. of Am., Inc., 960 F. Supp. 164, 168 (C.D. Ill. 1997) (after EEOC objected to ex parte interviews of female employees, defendant agreed to discontinue such contacts with individuals identified by EEOC as potential claimants and to conduct all future interviews as noticed depositions under federal rules); EEOC v. Nebco Evans Distrib., Inc., 1997 U.S. Dist. LEXIS 23111 (D. Neb. June 5, 1997) (prohibiting defendant from informally interviewing claimant applicants without prior consent of counsel for EEOC).

[320]See EEOC v. Johnson & Higgins, Inc., 78 FEP 1127, 1131–32 (S.D.N.Y. 1998) (holding waivers obtained by defendant invalid because court had previously found employer liable and therefore "EEOC was, at the very least, a necessary party to any discussions of settlement or other negotiations between J & H and the retirees"); cf. Nagy v. Jostens, Inc., 91 F.R.D. 431, 432 (D. Minn. 1981) (court issued injunction prohibiting defendant from requesting any releases or waivers of employment discrimination claims or confidentiality agreements with respect to defendant's employment policies from any class members).

[321]See, e.g., General Tel. Co. v. EEOC, 446 U.S. 318, 326, 22 FEP 1196 (1980).

[322]The EEOC General Counsel in 1987 issued Guidelines on Goals and Timetables in Consent Decrees, which are excerpted in the REGIONAL ATTORNEYS' DESKBOOK (BNA) GC:4503–06 (1993); see Charles Shanor, Affirmative Action in EEOC Litigation, 21 GA. L. REV. 1059, 1090–94 (1987). A variety of additional settlement issues are set forth in the General Counsel's Standards and Procedures for Consent Decrees and Settlement Agreements, REGIONAL ATTORNEYS' DESKBOOK (BNA) at GC:4507–20.

[323]See REGIONAL ATTORNEYS' DESKBOOK (BNA) at GC:4512.

Whether EEOC intervention will reduce or enhance private plaintiffs' chances of obtaining a satisfactory settlement will depend on the particular case and parties.[324] In the high-profile *Texaco* race discrimination class action, the EEOC initially indicated that it was not satisfied with a settlement that provided $176.1 million to class members because, in the EEOC's view, the equitable relief was insufficient.[325] The Commission later joined in the settlement, which was modified slightly to meet the EEOC's objections.[326] In *EEOC v. McDonnell Douglas Corp.*,[327] however, a consent decree to which the EEOC had agreed was approved as fair, adequate, and reasonable despite objections from some individual class members, in part because the court found that the EEOC's support of the consent decree had "great weight in light of the Commission's expertise in employment discrimination litigation."[328]

The EEOC has had some success in opposing the sealing of records in two different contexts. First, it has successfully opposed the sealing of a consent decree even though the plaintiff-intervenors in a Title VII action did not object to the employer's request to seal the record.[329] Second, the EEOC was able to discover information contained in a confidential settlement agreement between the employer and an intervening plaintiff, subject to a protective order barring the EEOC from "disclosing this information or using it for any purpose, except to decide whether the public interest requires further prosecution of this case."[330]

Where the EEOC filed a lawsuit seeking injunctive relief compelling the employer to correct employment actions that violate

---

[324]*See* EEOC v. G-K-G, Inc., 39 F.3d 740, 744, 66 FEP 344, 347 (7th Cir. 1994).

[325]DAILY LAB. REP. (BNA) at AA-1 (Nov. 21, 1996); Roberts v. Texaco, Inc., 979 F. Supp. 185 (S.D.N.Y. 1997).

[326]DAILY LAB. REP. (BNA) at AA-1 (Jan. 6, 1997).

[327]894 F. Supp. 1329, 68 FEP 1115 (E.D. Mo. 1995).

[328]*Id.* at 1335; *see also* EEOC v. New York, 1997 WL 159435, at *3 (N.D.N.Y. Feb. 11, 1997) (consent decree in ADEA case approved even though it excluded group of retirees because of statute of limitations issues; district court's finding that group was barred from relief left EEOC with issue of whether to settle remaining claims or appeal statute of limitations issue); EEOC v. Johnson & Higgins, Inc., 1999 WL 544721, at *3 (S.D.N.Y. July 26, 1999) (consent decree regarding disbursement of settlement proceeds approved despite objections of two employees who received no compensation; court gave "considerable deference" to "years of litigation and discussion" undergone by EEOC).

[329]*See* EEOC v. National Children's Ctr., Inc., 98 F.3d 1406, 1409–11, 72 FEP 314 (D.C. Cir. 1996).

[330]EEOC v. Rush Prudential Health Plans, 1998 WL 156718, at *1 (N.D. Ill. Mar. 31, 1998).

Title VII, the court found that the EEOC did have authority to bring the lawsuit, even though the employee and her employer had entered into a private settlement.[331]

XI. DECREE ENFORCEMENT

Normally, the district court will retain jurisdiction over the operation of a consent decree. Where the EEOC is a plaintiff, the EEOC may seek contempt orders to remedy noncompliance.[332]

Administration and termination of court orders and consent decrees have continued to present the courts with vastly divergent factual and legal situations.[333]

Some courts have held that the EEOC may sue to enforce a voluntary conciliation agreement.[334] One court, however, held that

---

[331]*See* EEOC v. Bay Ridge Toyota, Inc., 327 F. Supp. 2d 167, 173–74 (E.D.N.Y. 2004).

[332]*E.g.*, EEOC v. Longshoremen (ILA) Locals 829 & 858, 10 FEP 551, 553 (D. Md. 1975) (even if district court does not retain jurisdiction over decree, court has inherent power to protect and effectuate its decree; EEOC can come before it without satisfying normal prerequisites required for original suits; EEOC could secure relief against persons who are not parties to original decree if they acted in concert with named defendants to frustrate its purpose), *appeal dismissed*, 541 F.2d 1062, 13 FEP 971 (4th Cir. 1976).

[333]*See* EEOC v. Sheet Metal Workers Local 638, 889 F. Supp. 642, 658 (S.D.N.Y. 1995), *modified*, 921 F. Supp. 1126 (S.D.N.Y.), *aff'd in part and rev'd in part on other grounds*, 81 F.3d 1162 (2d Cir. 1996) (court rejected union's defense of impossibility in connection with 29.23% nonwhite membership goal, despite demographic changes in 20 years after court's order was entered). The Ninth Circuit en banc held that a consent decree that establishes a procedure for dealing with post–consent decree claims of discrimination cannot strip the EEOC of jurisdiction at least to issue a subpoena and investigate charges filed by employees governed by the decree. *See* EEOC v. Children's Hosp. Med. Ctr., 719 F.2d 1426, 1428, 33 FEP 461 (9th Cir. 1983) (en banc) (any preclusive effect of consent decree could be properly asserted after EEOC brought action). A court may compel compliance with instructions from a special master who has broad powers to enforce recordkeeping obligations contained in an earlier court order; *see also* EEOC v. Sheet Metal Workers Local 638, 1995 WL 334688, at *5 (S.D.N.Y. June 6, 1995), *rev'd in part on other grounds*, 81 F.3d 1162 (2d Cir. 1996).

[334]*See* EEOC v. Liberty Trucking Co., 695 F.2d 1038, 1040, 30 FEP 884 (7th Cir. 1982) ("Although Title VII does not explicitly provide the EEOC with the authority to seek enforcement of conciliation agreements in the federal courts, . . . Congress intended to provide the EEOC with a federal forum to enforce conciliation agreements."); EEOC v. Safeway Stores, Inc., 714 F.2d 567, 571–73, 32 FEP 1465 (5th Cir. 1983) (it "would be antithetical to Congress' strong commitment to

the EEOC could not sue for enforcement of a settlement agreement unless the settlement agreement was incorporated in the court order approving it.[335] Moreover, courts differ on whether the EEOC can sue to enforce a predetermination settlement agreement absent a reasonable cause determination.[336]

When a consent decree expires, the court's authority to enforce the order ends.[337] In some cases, it may be unclear when or whether a consent decree has expired, especially if it contains a continuing jurisdiction clause and no clear termination clause.[338] When the parties to a consent decree demonstrate "substantial attainment of the goals obtained therein," the consent decree may be terminated.[339]

XII. EEOC LIABILITY FOR ATTORNEY'S FEES AND COSTS

Section 706(k) of Title VII provides:

> In any action or proceeding under this title the court . . . may allow the prevailing party, other than the Commission or the United States, a reasonable attorney's fee as part of the costs, and the Commission and the United States shall be liable for costs the same as a private person.[340]

---

the conciliary process" if there was no federal forum in which EEOC could enforce such agreements).

[335]*See* EEOC v. University of Notre Dame du Lac, 629 F. Supp. 837, 839, 39 FEP 1265 (N.D. Ind. 1985) (EEOC could not bring action to compel compliance with class action settlement agreement because settlement was not incorporated into court order, and therefore was in nature of contract, not consent decree).

[336]*Compare* EEOC v. Pierce Packing Co., 669 F.2d 605, 608, 28 FEP 393 (9th Cir. 1982) (EEOC cannot sue to enforce settlement agreement entered into before reasonable cause determination and good faith attempts at conciliation) *with* EEOC v. Henry Beck Co., 729 F.2d 301, 305–06, 34 FEP 373 (4th Cir. 1984) (EEOC may seek to enforce predetermination settlement reached without reasonable cause determination, but it may not sue on underlying charge) *and Liberty Trucking Co.*, 695 F.2d at 1044 n.7 (dictum) (finding of reasonable cause not prerequisite to EEOC suit to enforce voluntary settlement agreement).

[337]*See* EEOC v. Iron Workers Local 40, 76 F.3d 76, 79–80 (2d Cir. 1996).

[338]*Id.*

[339]*See* EEOC v. United Air Lines, 1995 U.S. Dist. LEXIS 2604, at *1 (N.D. Ill. Mar. 2, 1995) (dissolving consent decree as recommended by parties who had demonstrated that 18-year-old consent decree had been complied with in good faith and "no longer serve[d] any useful function").

[340]42 U.S.C. § 2000e-5(k).

The Supreme Court's ruling in *Christiansburg Garment Co. v. EEOC*[341] sets forth the standards governing awards of attorney's fees against the EEOC as a party litigant.[342] A court may award attorney's fees to a prevailing defendant if it finds that the plaintiff's action was "frivolous, unreasonable, or without foundation."[343] The defendants' claims for attorney's fees against the EEOC accordingly are very fact-sensitive.[344]

The Equal Access to Justice Act (EAJA) provides for EEOC liability for attorney's fees in ADEA cases. The EEOC is liable

---

[341]434 U.S. 412, 16 FEP 502 (1978).

[342]*Id.* at 421. *See generally* Chapter 41 (Attorney's Fees).

[343]*Christiansburg Garment*, 434 U.S. at 421.

[344]*Fees Denied*: EEOC v. L.B. Foster Co., 123 F.3d 746, 78 FEP 485 (3d Cir. 1997) (fees denied where EEOC established prima facie case but lost); EEOC v. Hampton Mem'l Gardens, Inc., 52 F.3d 320 (table), 1995 WL 231843 (4th Cir. Apr. 20, 1995) (fee denial not abuse of discretion where EEOC lost case but did not act unreasonably or without foundation); EEOC v. Shoney's, Inc., 28 F.3d 1213, 1994 WL 325995, at *4 (6th Cir. July 5, 1994) (had EEOC brought only national origin suit, court would have awarded fees because EEOC investigation was "grossly inadequate"; however, fees were denied because EEOC showed prima facie case of race discrimination); EEOC v. Columbia Lakeland Med. Ctr., 1999 WL 35292, at *1–2 (E.D. La. Jan. 26, 1999) (attorney's fees denied where EEOC established prima facie case); EEOC v. Borg-Warner Protective Servs. Corp., 1996 WL 384622 (E.D. La. July 9, 1996) (fees denied where EEOC case not frivolous); EEOC v. Northwest Structural Components, Inc., 897 F. Supp. 249, 252, 67 FEP 1761, 1763 (M.D.N.C. 1995) (though court was not convinced discrimination occurred, claim was not frivolous); EEOC v. Tandem Computers, Inc., 158 F.R.D. 224, 229 (D. Mass. 1994) (EEOC had initially found "no cause" and was ultimately unsuccessful, but had "a legally sufficient evidentiary basis upon which to put its ADEA claim to the jury" and therefore defendant's fee request was denied); EEOC v. Sears, Roebuck & Co., 114 F.R.D. 615, 631–33, 42 FEP 1358 (N.D. Ill. 1987) (employer could not recover attorney's fees from EEOC when action was not frivolous; extensive discovery and statistical analysis, and case was proven defective only after EEOC's presentation of its case-in-chief).

Fees Awarded: EEOC v. E.J. Sacco, Inc., 102 F. Supp. 2d 413, 420 (E.D. Mich. 2000) (when EEOC failed to use "sound judgment" before filing suit and moved forward despite being notified of "patent defects," court ordered defendant to "be made whole" by assessing attorney's fees against EEOC); EEOC v. Hendrix Coll., 53 F.3d 209, 211, 76 FEP 465 (8th Cir. 1995) (EEOC's failure to investigate alleged recordkeeping violations before filing suit showed lawsuit initiated in bad faith); EEOC v. Kim & Ted, Inc., 69 FEP 1499, 1504 (N.D. Ill. 1995) (EEOC ordered to pay fees for defendant's motion for sanctions concerning failure to seek employee tax records); EEOC v. Bellemar Parts Indus., Inc., 868 F.2d 199, 200, 49 FEP 369 (6th Cir. 1989) (attorney's fees properly awarded against EEOC; EEOC knew that employer had not been named in charge); EEOC v. American Fed'n of Teachers Local 571, 761 F. Supp. 536, 542 (N.D. Ill. 1991) (EEOC required to pay attorney's fees when it failed to recognize legal bar to suit against school district, a governmental entity).

for attorney's fees in ADEA cases unless its position was "substantially justified."[345]

Fees also have been assessed against the EEOC under Rule 26(b)(4) of the Federal Rules of Civil Procedure for expert witnesses,[346] under the FOIA for failure to comply with a request,[347] and as a general equitable remedy for improper disclosure of confidential and incorrect information regarding settlement.[348]

---

[345]*See* EEOC v. O & G Spring & Wire Forms Specialty Co., 38 F.3d 872, 880–81, 65 FEP 1823, 1830 (7th Cir. 1994); EEOC v. Complete Dewatering, Inc., 16 F. Supp. 2d 1362, 1369 (S.D. Fla. 1998) (plaintiff potentially eligible for fees because EEOC action not substantially justified in ADEA case), *aff'd mem.*, 190 F.3d 540 (11th Cir. 1999); Johnson v. EEOC, 1996 WL 432394, at *4 (N.D. Ill. July 30, 1996) (no fees awarded concerning EEOC's rescission of rulemaking under ADEA where plaintiffs failed to prove their suit prompted EEOC action); *see also* EEOC v. Consolidated Serv. Sys., 30 F.3d 58, 59, 66 FEP 185, 185 (7th Cir. 1994) (holding EAJA inapplicable to EEOC litigation under Title VII); *Northwest Structural Components*, 897 F. Supp. at 251 (same).

[346]*See* EEOC v. Johnson & Higgins, Inc., 79 FEP 210, 214–15 (S.D.N.Y. 1999).

[347]*See* GRMI, Inc. v. EEOC, 149 F.3d 449, 452, 77 FEP 225 (6th Cir. 1998) (employer may be eligible for fees where EEOC belatedly turned over documents requested under FUTA).

[348]*See* EEOC v. Union Camp Corp., 1998 U.S. Dist. LEXIS 16922, at *2–3 (S.D. Ga. June 30, 1998) (EEOC's improper release of confidential information regarding a settlement agreement made the grant of attorney's fees and costs an equitable remedy).

JUSTICE DEPARTMENT LITIGATION

I. Overview

The Attorney General of the United States and the Department of Justice (Justice Department or DOJ) that he or she heads, rather than the Equal Employment Opportunity Commission (EEOC), have the authority and responsibility to enforce Title VII with respect to an alleged pattern or practice of discrimination by a government, governmental agency, or political subdivision.[1] The

---

[1] Section 707(a) of Title VII, 42 U.S.C. § 2000e-6(a) (2000), provides that "whenever the Attorney General has reasonable cause to believe that any person or group of persons is engaged in a pattern or practice of resistance to the full enjoyment of any of the rights secured by this subchapter, and that the pattern or practice is of such a nature and is intended to deny the full exercise of the rights herein described, the

DOJ also enforces Title I of the Americans with Disabilities Act (ADA)[2] against such governmental bodies. The Justice Department may bring such pattern-or-practice actions on behalf of public employees,[3] and also may intervene in private actions brought by public employees.[4] Additionally, where the EEOC determines that prompt judicial action is necessary to carry out the purposes of Title VII, the Attorney General may bring an action against a governmental body for "appropriate temporary or preliminary relief pending final disposition of such charge."[5]

Before the 1972 amendments to Title VII, the Attorney General had both the power now conferred on the EEOC to sue private employers for alleged violations of Title VII and also the opportunity to intervene in employment discrimination actions brought by employees against private employers.[6] The 1972 amendments extended Title VII's coverage to governments, governmental agencies, and political subdivisions.[7] Pursuant to these amendments,

---

Attorney General may bring a civil action." The usage of the terms "Department of Justice," "United States," and "Attorney General" can be confusing. The party in such litigation is the United States. The representative of the United States authorized by statute to conduct such litigation is the Attorney General, and the governmental entity that exercises these responsibilities is the Department of Justice, which is headed by the Attorney General. To some extent, these terms are interchangeable in this context.

[2]The Justice Department's authority under Title I of the ADA is coextensive with its authority under Title VII because Title I follows the procedures of Title VII. 42 U.S.C. § 12117 (2000); see Board of Trs. of Univ. of Ala. v. Garrett, 531 U.S. 365, 374 n.9 (2001) (affirming Justice Department's authority to pursue relief on behalf of individuals under ADA). The Justice Department also has enforcement authority under Titles II and III of the ADA.

[3]"In the case of a respondent which is a government, governmental agency, or political subdivision, if the Commission has been unable to secure from the respondent a conciliation agreement acceptable to the Commission, the Commission shall take no further action and shall refer the case to the Attorney General who may bring a civil action against such respondent in the appropriate United States district court." 42 U.S.C. § 2000e-5(f)(1) (2000).

[4]"Upon timely application, the court may, in its discretion, permit the Commission or the Attorney General in a case involving a government, governmental agency, or political subdivision, to intervene in such civil action upon certification that the case is of general public importance." 42 U.S.C. § 2000e-5(f)(1) (2000). For example, according to the Department of Justice website, the Attorney General regularly intervenes in matters where public employers have raised Eleventh Amendment challenges in antidiscrimination suits. See http://www.usdoj.gov/crt/crt-home.html (fact sheet: civil rights accomplishments released July 23, 2003).

[5]42 U.S.C. § 2000e-5(f)(2) (2000).

[6]Pub. L. No. 92-261 (1972).

[7]Id.

the DOJ became responsible for enforcement actions against governments, governmental agencies, and political subdivisions, whereas the EEOC became responsible for enforcement actions against private employers.[8] Additionally, the 1972 amendments provided that the Attorney General's power to bring pattern-or-practice litigation against an employer would be transferred to the EEOC effective March 24, 1974.[9]

Even after March 24, 1974, the Justice Department investigated and initiated pattern-or-practice litigation against public sector employers because the Attorney General interpreted the provision in the 1972 amendments as transferring to the EEOC only the power to investigate and pursue pattern-or-practice litigation against private employers.[10] Some courts, however, interpreted the 1972 amendments as requiring the Justice Department to obtain a referral from the EEOC prior to filing a pattern-or-practice action against a public sector employer.[11] The dispute was settled by executive order in 1978. The 1972 amendments permitted the President to return to the Justice Department the authority to investigate and initiate prosecution of actions alleging a pattern or practice of discrimination.[12] In his reorganization plan submitted in February 1978, the President explained to Congress that the plan, in part, was designed to clarify the Attorney General's authority to initiate pattern-or-practice suits under Title VII in the public sector.[13] Congress approved the plan as to the DOJ's responsibilities in June 1978.[14]

The Civil Rights Division of the Justice Department is responsible for the Department's enforcement obligations under Title VII and the ADA.

---

[8]42 U.S.C. § 2000e-5(f)(1) (2000).

[9]*Id.* § 2000e-6(c).

[10]*See* United States v. Fresno Unified Sch. Dist., 592 F.2d 1088, 1091 n.1, 1092 n.2 (9th Cir. 1979) (explaining Attorney General's position that 1972 amendments did not affect Justice Department's power to initiate pattern-or-practice litigation against public sector employer without referral from EEOC).

[11]*See* United States v. Board of Educ., Garfield Heights, 581 F.2d 791, 791–92 (6th Cir. 1978) (no independent authority in Justice Department to initiate pattern-or-practice litigation); United States v. South Carolina, 445 F. Supp. 1094, 1110–11 (D.S.C. 1977) (same), *aff'd*, 436 U.S. 1026 (1978).

[12]42 U.S.C. § 2000e-6(c) (2000); *see also* 5 U.S.C. § 906 (2000) (authorizing president to transfer governmental functions from one agency to another).

[13]43 Fed. Reg. 19,807 (Feb. 23, 1978) (Message of the President); *see also Fresno Unified Sch. Dist.*, 592 F.2d at 1092 n.2.

[14]Exec. Order No. 12068, 43 Fed. Reg. 28,971 (July 5, 1978).

II. JURISDICTION AND PROCEDURE FOR JUSTICE DEPARTMENT LITIGATION

A. Enforcement Upon Referral by the EEOC: Individual Charges

Pursuant to the 1972 amendments and the 1978 reorganization, the EEOC performs the same functions with respect to charges filed against state and local government employers as it does with respect to private sector employers, but only up to, and not including, the point of litigation. At that point, under § 706(f)(1) of Title VII, the Justice Department may pursue legal action against a government, governmental agency, or political subdivision on behalf of an individual only after receiving a referral of the charge from the EEOC.[15] In practical terms, the Justice Department will litigate for individual relief only where the EEOC finds that a governmental body violated Title VII or the ADA and the EEOC is unable to obtain voluntary compliance through conciliation. According to the Regional Attorneys' Deskbook, the Office of General Counsel for the EEOC provides the Attorney General a positive recommendation to litigate, along with all investigative and conciliation materials generated by the EEOC.[16]

There was initially some dispute over whether EEOC notices of right to sue to individuals pursuing actions against public employers were effective.[17] Ultimately, the EEOC and the Justice

---

[15]42 U.S.C. § 2000e-5(f)(1) (2000) ("if the Commission has been unable to secure from the respondent a conciliation agreement acceptable to the Commission, the Commission shall take no further action and shall refer the case to the Attorney General who may bring a civil action against such respondent"); *see* 29 C.F.R. § 1601.29 (2005) ("If the Commission is unable to obtain voluntary compliance in a charge involving a government, governmental agency or political subdivision, it shall inform the Attorney General of the appropriate facts in the case with recommendations for the institution of a civil action by him or her against such respondent or for intervention by him or her in a civil action previously instituted by the person claiming to be aggrieved."); *see also* United States v. City & County of Denver, 927 F. Supp. 1396, 1399 n.3 (D. Colo. 1996) (Attorney General may sue to obtain relief for individuals allegedly having suffered discrimination).

[16]EEOC Compliance Manual, VOL. III, Regional Attorneys' Deskbook, § IV, at GC 4808.

[17]*See* Hiller v. Oklahoma, 327 F.3d 1247, 1250, 1252 (10th Cir. 2003) (although public employee must have notice of right to sue from Attorney General, equitable considerations may permit use of EEOC notice of right to sue, depending on

Department developed a work-sharing arrangement with respect to such right-to-sue notices.[18] The EEOC is required to investigate charges filed against governmental entities.[19] Where the EEOC does not find reasonable cause to believe discrimination has occurred with respect to a governmental respondent, the EEOC will dismiss the charge and issue the notice of right to sue in accordance with 29 C.F.R. § 1601.28(e).[20] Where the EEOC has found reasonable cause as to at least part of the charge, however, it must refer the charge to the Attorney General, who then will either pursue legal action or issue a notice of right to sue.[21] Additionally, the Attorney General is authorized to issue the notice of right to sue if the charging party requests it during the investigation.[22]

B. Enforcement Under Independent Authority: Pattern-or-Practice Violations

Pursuant to § 707 of Title VII, the Attorney General may bring a civil action in district court against an employer that the Attorney General has "reasonable cause" to believe is engaged in a "pattern or practice of resistance to the full enjoyment of any rights secured by this chapter."[23] According to the 1972 amendments to Title VII, the Attorney General no longer had this authority as of March 1974. However, Reorganization Plan No. 1 of 1978 provided that EEOC functions relating to litigation against state or local government or political subdivisions under § 707 of Title VII (2000e-6) "and all necessary functions related thereto, including

---

circumstances); Dougherty v. Barry, 869 F.2d 605, 612 (D.C. Cir. 1989) (EEOC notice of right to sue proper if finding of no cause); Fouche v. Jekyll Island-State Park Auth., 713 F.2d 1518, 1526 (11th Cir. 1983) (equitable considerations warrant waiving requirement of right to sue issued by Attorney General); Thames v. Oklahoma Historical Soc'y, 646 F. Supp. 13, 16 (W.D. Okla. 1985) (state employee must have right to sue issued by Attorney General to sue under Title VII), aff'd per curiam, 809 F.2d 669 (10th Cir. 1987).

[18]*Hiller*, 327 F.3d at 1250 (explaining work-sharing agreement); *Dougherty*, 869 F.2d at 612 (same).

[19]*See Hiller*, 327 F.3d at 1249 (explaining the impact of 42 U.S.C. § 2000e-5(b) (2000)).

[20]29 C.F.R. § 1601.28(d) (2005); *Dougherty*, 869 F.2d at 611–12.

[21]29 C.F.R. § 1601.28(d) (2005).

[22]*Id.*

[23]42 U.S.C. § 2000e-6(a) (2000).

investigation, findings, notice and an opportunity to resolve the matter without contested litigation, are hereby transferred to the Attorney General" or to his or her designee within the Department of Justice.[24] In practice, cases filed pursuant to this section of Title VII usually are resolved by consent decree prior to trial.[25]

Although some courts initially ruled that the Attorney General could not bring cases pursuant to § 707 without EEOC referral, it seems well settled now that the Attorney General has independent authority regarding pattern-or-practice litigation against governmental entities. The Ninth Circuit explicitly stated that "courts have been mistaken in holding that the Attorney General lost independent authority to initiate public sector pattern or practice suits."[26] Similarly, the Fourth and Fifth Circuits have acknowledged the Attorney General's independent authority in public sector pattern-or-practice actions.[27] Arguably, the Justice Department is required to engage in pre-suit procedures similar to those followed by the EEOC,[28] but some courts have not held the Justice Department to that standard.[29]

Additionally, some debate exists about whether the Justice Department must have evidence of an ongoing violation to maintain pattern-or-practice litigation. Under § 707(a) of Title VII, the Justice Department has authority to maintain an action against a governmental body that "is engaged in a pattern of resistance to

---

[24]Reorganization Plan No. 1 of 1978, § 5, 43 Fed. Reg. 19,807, 92 Stat. 3781 (Feb. 23, 1978).

[25]See http://www.usdoj.gov/crt/crt-home.html (Civil Rights Division Activities and Programs, employment litigation section).

[26]United States v. Fresno Unified Sch. Dist., 592 F.2d 1088, 1093 (9th Cir. 1979).

[27]United States v. City of Miami, 664 F.2d 435, 436–37 (5th Cir. 1981); United States v. Virginia, 620 F.2d 1018, 1022 (4th Cir. 1980); United States v. North Carolina, 587 F.2d 625, 626 (4th Cir. 1978) (per curiam) (Reorganization Plan and Executive Order cured any jurisdictional deficiency).

[28]Fresno Unified Sch. Dist., 592 F.2d at 1095–96 (logically applicable procedural prerequisites of § 706 are required in § 707 litigation by Attorney General); United States v. Allegheny-Ludlum, Inc., 517 F.2d 826, 869 (5th Cir. 1975) (6-month negotiation leading to consent decrees satisfied any duty to conciliate).

[29]United States v. Northern Mariana Islands, 63 FEP 534, 537 (D.N. Mar. I. 1993) (determination of reasonable cause by Attorney General only prerequisite to pattern-or-practice suit); United States v. City of Yonkers, 592 F. Supp. 570, 582–85 (S.D.N.Y.1984) (no prerequisites to suit other than "reasonable cause" certification in complaint); United States v. New Jersey, 473 F. Supp. 1199, 1204–05 (D.N.J. 1979) (same); United States v. Masonry Contractors Ass'n of Memphis, Inc., 497 F.2d 871, 875–76 (6th Cir. 1974) (no prerequisite other than "reasonable cause").

full enjoyment of rights secured by this Title."[30] The use of the phrase "is engaged" suggests that an ongoing violation is necessary for subject matter jurisdiction to exist. On the other hand, even if no violation presently exists, where the respondent has failed to provide remedial relief, the Justice Department arguably has authority to litigate so that the aggrieved individuals may obtain the "full enjoyment of rights secured by this Title."[31]

The Fourth Circuit addressed the need for proof of an ongoing violation in *United States v. State of North Carolina*,[32] where the U.S. Attorney General alleged that the defendant was engaged in a pattern or practice of discrimination against female applicants and female correctional officers employed in the state's prisons for men.[33] The district court held that proof of a continuing violation was necessary even to support a consent decree. The parties agreed on a 51-page settlement proposal, but the district court refused to enter the consent decree based in part on the court's conclusion that a material change in circumstances had occurred since the filing of the lawsuit.[34] The court was persuaded that there was no violation because North Carolina had engaged in aggressive remedial measures with respect to the hiring, assignment, and promotion of women as employees.[35]

The court of appeals reversed, holding that the district court abused its discretion by failing to enter the consent decree.[36] As the Fourth Circuit explained, North Carolina's strides toward eliminating gender discrimination would merely permit the district court to consider evidence in support of modifying the consent decree after its entry.[37] The Fourth Circuit reasoned, in part, that evidence of increased hiring of females was unrelated to remedying discrimination suffered by past victims and that no evidence indicated that the central goal of the decree had been accomplished by improvements to the hiring process.[38] Accordingly, the court of appeals

---

[30]42 U.S.C. § 2000e-6(a) (2000).
[31]*Id.*
[32]914 F. Supp. 1257 (E.D.N.C. 1996), *rev'd*, 180 F.3d 574, 579 (4th Cir. 1999).
[33]914 F. Supp. at 1259.
[34]180 F.3d at 579.
[35]*Id.*
[36]*Id.* at 577.
[37]*Id.* at 582.
[38]*Id.*

remanded and instructed the district court to enter the decree.[39] The Fourth Circuit's analysis suggests that the Attorney General is authorized to pursue relief based on past discrimination without having to prove an ongoing violation.

III. JUSTICE DEPARTMENT ENFORCEMENT OF TITLE VII AND THE ADA

A. Title VII

The reported cases involving the Justice Department's enforcement of Title VII focus on the propriety of entering consent decrees. These cases demonstrate that race-conscious remedies, either in the form of voluntary affirmative action or as a part of a consent decree, are closely scrutinized.

In *United States v. Illinois State University Board of Trustees,*[40] the Justice Department brought suit on behalf of white males alleging a pattern or practice of discrimination against white men. The university hired no white men in nine years, although white males made up nearly half the relevant labor pool.[41] White applicants were told that a specific learner program for service workers was designed for women and minorities.[42] The court found that the university violated Title VII by implementing an affirmative action program designed to circumvent a lawful veterans preference program.[43] The court entered an injunction to ensure that individuals denied the opportunity to compete for the contested position would be able to do so in the future.[44]

A related issue is the right of affected individuals to intervene in Title VII litigation brought by the Justice Department. In *Brennan v. New York City Board of Education,*[45] the DOJ asserted that the New York City Board of Education was engaging in a pattern

---

[39]*Id.* at 583.

[40]944 F. Supp. 714 (C.D. Ill. 1996).

[41]*Id.* at 718–19.

[42]*Id.* at 718.

[43]*Id.* at 723.

[44]*Id.*

[45]260 F.3d 123, 133 (2d Cir. 2001), *rev'g*, United States v. New York City Bd. of Educ., 85 F. Supp. 2d 130, 138 (E.D.N.Y. 2000).

or practice of race discrimination with respect to hiring custodians and custodian engineers.[46] The district court found that the statistical analysis proved a prima facie case of disparate impact in testing and recruitment,[47] and a proposed settlement included race-conscious remedies affecting seniority rights. The district court denied intervention under Rule 24(a)(2) of the Federal Rules of Civil Procedure to three current white employees because the white employees' interest was not a "vested property right" and in any event was remote and speculative.[48]

The Second Circuit reversed, concluding that the district court abused its discretion by denying the white employees' motion to intervene. Rejecting the defendant's argument that it could adequately protect white employees' interests, the court held that the white employees had shown a cognizable interest sufficient to warrant intervention under Rule 24(a)(2).[49] The court remanded with instructions that the white employees be permitted to intervene and obtain discovery for a full development of the record regarding the fairness and constitutionality of the agreement.[50]

B. The ADA

In *United States v. Mississippi Department of Public Safety*,[51] the district court held that a governmental defendant could successfully assert an Eleventh Amendment immunity defense to an action by the Attorney General under the ADA seeking money damages on behalf of an individual.[52] The district court acknowledged that § 706(f) of Title VII[53] specifically permits the Attorney General to pursue a remedy for an individual instance of discrimination, but the district court interpreted literally the Supreme Court's holding in *University of Alabama Board of Trustees v. Garrett*[54] that an individual is not permitted to seek money damages against

---

[46]85 F. Supp. 2d at 136.
[47]*Id.* at 143, 145.
[48]*Id.* at 155–56.
[49]260 F.3d at 130–32.
[50]*Id.* at 133.
[51]159 F. Supp. 2d 374 (S.D. Miss. 2001), *rev'd*, 321 F.3d 495 (5th Cir. 2003).
[52]*Id.* at 377.
[53]42 U.S.C. § 2000e-5(f) (2000).
[54]531 U.S. 356 (2001).

a state.[55] The district court reasoned that the Attorney General "stepped into the shoes of a private individual" by suing for only individual relief under § 706(f) and therefore had no more power to obtain a money damages remedy than would the individual.[56] The Fifth Circuit reversed,[57] pointing out that the Supreme Court's statement in *Garrett* that the ADA "can be enforced by the United States in actions for money damages"[58] is not limited to pattern-or-practice cases. The Fifth Circuit also cited other statements by the Supreme Court that states retain no sovereign immunity as against the federal government, which has a real interest in ensuring a state's compliance with federal law.[59] The Fifth Circuit further rejected Mississippi's argument that the United States was a mere proxy for the individual in a § 706 lawsuit because the individual had "no right to compel the United States to bring suit or to dictate its complaint or prayer for relief in any way."[60]

IV. JUSTICE DEPARTMENT ENFORCEMENT OF OTHER STATUTES

A. The Immigration Reform and Control Act

The Immigration Reform and Control Act of 1986 (IRCA) prohibits discrimination on the basis of national origin or

---

[55]159 F. Supp. 2d at 377.

[56]*Id.* The district court also dismissed the Justice Department's claim for equitable relief based on its interpretation of *Ex parte Young*, 209 U.S. 123 (1908). 159 F. Supp. 2d at 378.

[57]United States v. Mississippi Dep't of Pub. Safety, 321 F.3d 495 (5th Cir. 2003).

[58]531 U.S. at 374 n.9.

[59]321 F.3d at 498 (citing Board of Trs. v. Garrett, 531 U.S. 365, 374 n.9 (2001); Alden v. Maine, 527 U.S. 706, 755–56 (1999); Seminole Tribe of Fla. v. Florida, 517 U.S. 44, 71 n.14 (1996); West Virginia v. United States, 479 U.S. 305, 312 n.4 (1987)).

[60]321 F.3d at 499. Similarly, a defendant should not be able to assert a statute of limitations defense against the United States, even in an ADA action seeking money damages on behalf of an individual. *Cf.* United States v. McHenry County, 1994 WL 447419, at *3 (N.D. Ill. Aug. 17, 1994) (Title VII limitations periods do not run against United States as sovereign); United States v. City of Yonkers, 592 F. Supp. 570, 40 FEP 941 (S.D.N.Y. 1984).

citizenship status.[61] The IRCA's coverage is broader than Title VII, as employers with more than three employees are subject to the Act.[62]

IRCA regulations require that a charge be filed within 180 days of the alleged act of discrimination.[63] A division of the Justice Department designated as the Office of Special Counsel for Immigration Related Unfair Labor Practices ("OSC") investigates the charges, which are filed either by the aggrieved individual or by an Immigration and Naturalization Service official.[64] Charges must allege a "knowing and intentional discriminatory activity" or a "pattern or practice of discriminatory activity."[65] The statute permits enforcement only where the violation involves intentional discrimination; adverse impact theories of liability are not recognized.[66]

The Special Counsel for the Justice Department may "propound interrogatories, requests for production of documents, and requests for admissions" during the investigation of the charge.[67] Similar to the EEOC, the OSC either advises the complaining party that the Justice Department will proceed to enforce the statute or issues a notice of right to sue to the individual upon completion of the investigation.[68] However, the IRCA requires enforcement actions to be heard by an administrative law judge (ALJ).[69]

Upon finding a violation, the ALJ may award back pay and reinstatement as well as impose fines ranging from $250 per harmed individual to $10,000 for repeat violators.[70] Within 60 days of an ALJ's decision being dated and made public, a party has a right to appeal the decision to the court of appeals for the circuit where

---

[61]8 U.S.C. § 1324b (2000). *See generally* Chapter 7 (National Origin and Citizenship).

[62]*Id.* § 1324b(a)(2); 28 C.F.R. § 44.200(b) (2005).

[63]8 U.S.C. § 1324b(d)(3) (2000).

[64]*Id.* § 1324b(c).

[65]*Id.* § 1324b(d)(2).

[66]28 C.F.R. § 44.200(a) (2005).

[67]*Id.* § 44.302.

[68]8 U.S.C. § 1324b(d)(1) & (2) (2000).

[69]28 C.F.R. § 44.303 (2005).

[70]8 U.S.C. § 1324b(g)(B) (2000).

the alleged violation occurred or where the employer resides or transacts business.[71]

B. The Omnibus Crime Control and Safe Streets Act

The Omnibus Crime Control and Safe Streets Act of 1968 authorizes federal financial and technical assistance to law enforcement agencies at the state and local levels.[72] The Act further prohibits discrimination on the basis of race, color, religion, sex, or national origin in any program or activity that receives such federal assistance.[73] The Attorney General is authorized to enforce this provision through pattern-or-practice actions against recipients believed to have engaged in discrimination.[74] One court has held that the Attorney General is not required to exhaust administrative remedies prior to initiating a lawsuit.[75] Nonetheless, the Act requires the Attorney General to engage in pre-suit measures such as providing notice, engaging in an investigation, providing the respondent an opportunity to submit evidence in its defense, holding a hearing, and attempting to obtain voluntary compliance.[76]

V. ENFORCEMENT OF GOVERNMENT CONTRACT ANTIDISCRIMINATION PROVISIONS

Government contractors have certain obligations as employers under Executive Order 11246.[77] Section 209(a)(2) of the Executive Order authorizes the Attorney General, upon referral from the Secretary of Labor,[78] to sue a federal contractor for breach of

---

[71]*Id.* § 1324b(i)(1); *see also* Mesa Airlines v. United States, 951 F.2d 1186, 1187–88 (10th Cir. 1991).

[72]42 U.S.C. § 3711 et seq. (2000).

[73]*Id.* § 3789d(c)(1).

[74]*Id.* § 3789d(c)(3).

[75]United States v. City of Yonkers, 592 F. Supp. 570, 585 (S.D.N.Y. 1984).

[76]42 U.S.C. § 3789d(c)(2) (2000).

[77]*See* 41 C.F.R. § 60-1.1 et seq. (regulations pertaining to government contractors' obligations as employers). *See generally* Chapter 38 (Federal Contractor Affirmative Action Compliance).

[78]Pursuant to 41 C.F.R. § 60-1.2 (2005), all responsibilities of the Secretary of Labor with respect to enforcing these requirements are delegated to the Deputy Assistant Secretary, Office of Federal Contract Compliance Programs.

a nondiscrimination-in-employment clause and to sue any individual who seeks to prevent a government contractor from performing its obligation not to discriminate.[79] The required equal opportunity language that would be the subject of such litigation can be found in the regulations.[80]

Once the matter has been referred to the DOJ by the Office of Federal Contract Compliance Programs ("OFCCP"), there are no procedural prerequisites the Justice Department must satisfy to enforce a claim under Executive Order 11246.[81] Specifically, the Justice Department is not required to engage in conciliation efforts.[82] The Justice Department is authorized, however, to provide to the respondent notice of the DOJ's findings, of the Attorney General's intent to sue, and of actions deemed necessary for compliance.[83]

In addition to enforcement actions following a referral from the OFCCP, the Justice Department may initiate an independent investigation of a contractor reasonably believed to be out of compliance.[84] The Department must obtain approval from the OFCCP to engage in the independent investigation.[85] If the investigation results in a finding of a violation, the Justice Department must attempt to secure voluntary compliance, and, if those efforts are unsuccessful, must obtain OFCCP approval prior to the Attorney General initiating a lawsuit.[86]

The Attorney General also represents federal agencies sued by government contractors for alleged overzealous enforcement of federal laws that prohibit discrimination.[87]

---

[79]41 C.F.R. § 60-1.26(c) (2005); *see, e.g.*, United States v. Duquesne Light Co., 423 F. Supp. 507, 509–10 (W.D. Pa. 1976) (seeking back-pay relief for individuals based on alleged violation of Executive Order requirements by government contractor); United States v. Mississippi Power & Light Co., 10 FEP 1084, 1091 (S.D. Miss. 1975) (seeking enforcement of nondiscrimination section of Executive Order 11246 for individuals based on alleged violation by public utility). *See generally* Chapter 38 (Federal Contractor Affirmative Action Compliance).

[80]41 C.F.R. § 60-1.4 (2005).

[81]*Id.* § 60-1.26(c)(1).

[82]*Id.*

[83]*Id.* § 60-1.25(c)(4).

[84]*Id.* § 60-1.26(d).

[85]*Id.*

[86]*Id.*

[87]*See* http://www.usdoj.gov (Civil Rights Division Activities and Programs, Employment Litigation Section).

CHAPTER 31

FEDERAL EMPLOYEE LITIGATION

I. Introduction and Historical Overview

A. Statutory Background

Sovereign immunity bars suit for monetary relief against an agency of the United States, unless Congress has expressly waived immunity.[1] With regard to federal employment, Congress has done just that. Federal executive agencies are subject to most of the same substantive discrimination principles concerning equal pay,[2]

---

[1]Lane v. Peña, 518 U.S. 187, 5 AD 973 (1996) (finding no waiver of sovereign immunity from monetary damage awards in Rehabilitation Act case brought by plaintiff dismissed from Merchant Marine Academy due to diabetes); Lehman v. Nakshian, 453 U.S. 156, 160, 26 FEP 65 (1981) (the United States, as sovereign, is immune from suit except where it has consented to be sued).

[2]*See generally* Chapter 18 (Compensation).

age,[3] disability,[4] and the bases covered by Title VII[5] as are private employers and state and local governments. Following passage

---

[3]*See generally* Chapter 12 (Age). Principal differences in the statutory provisions applicable to federal, as compared to private sector, employees include:

(1) Federal employees suing under the ADEA have no right to jury trial. *See Lehman*, 453 U.S. at 160.

(2) The ADEA does not provide for attorney's fees in federal employee actions and courts therefore generally have denied fees in such cases. *See, e.g.*, Lewis v. Federal Prison Indus., Inc., 953 F.2d 1277, 1281, 58 FEP 127 (11th Cir. 1992). Plaintiffs may argue, however, that they are entitled to attorney's fees under the Equal Access to Justice Act (EAJA), 28 U.S.C. § 2412, which allows fees against the United States "[u]nless expressly prohibited by statute." *See* Boehms v. Crowell, 139 F.3d 452, 461–63, 76 FEP 1368 (5th Cir. 1998) (ADEA subsection providing that plaintiff in civil action could receive such legal and equitable relief as would effectuate purposes of ADEA may not be used to award attorney's fees against federal government; however, Equal Access to Justice Act enables trial court to award attorney's fees against federal government in ADEA cases); Nowd v. Rubin, 76 F.3d 25, 28, 69 FEP 1587 (1st Cir. 1996) (ADEA does not provide for it, but EAJA empowers courts in their discretion to award prevailing federal employee attorney fees against the United States in ADEA actions); Craig v. O'Leary, 870 F. Supp. 1007, 1010, 69 FEP 452 (D. Colo. 1994) (Equal Access to Justice Act is itself an express waiver of governmental immunity for fees and also reflects congressional determination to permit award of attorney fees).

(3) Section 15(f) of the ADEA, 29 U.S.C. § 633a(f) (2000), provides that federal "personnel actions" are not "subject to, or affected by, any provisions of [the ADEA] other than the provisions of § 12(b) [the age coverage requirement] and the provisions of this section [15]." *See Lehman*, 453 U.S. at 166–68 (§ 15 "prescribed a distinct statutory scheme applicable only to the federal sector," which was "self-contained and unaffected by other sections" of the ADEA). This would appear to eliminate the FLSA procedural restrictions, which are incorporated by reference in the ADEA for lawsuits in the private sector. For this reason, some courts have permitted Rule 23 class actions in federal employee ADEA litigation. *See, e.g.*, Moysey v. Andrus, 481 F. Supp. 850, 854, 21 FEP 836 (D.D.C. 1979) (since the amended ADEA does not incorporate the FLSA provisions for lawsuits by federal employees and legal as well as equitable relief is available, a class action, although not available to private sector employees under the ADEA, is available to federal employees).

(4) Section 15(b) gives the Office of Personnel Management (OPM) authority to establish general BFOQ age requirements for federal employees. 29 U.S.C. § 633a(b) (2000).

[4]Although federal executive agencies are exempt from the Americans with Disabilities Act (ADA), they are covered by § 501 of the Rehabilitation Act of 1973, 29 U.S.C. § 791 (2000), which incorporate the "remedies, procedures and rights" set forth in Title VII (42 U.S.C. § 2000e-16(c)) for federal employees. 29 U.S.C. § 794a(a)(1) (2000); *see* Taylor v. Small, 350 F.3d 1286, 1291 (D.C. Cir. 2003) (§ 501 of the Rehabilitation Act covers federal employees, while § 504 applies to programs receiving federal funds); Rivera v. Heyman, 982 F. Supp. 932, 936–39 (S.D.N.Y. 1997) (reviewing split in circuits over applicability of § 504 to federal employees), *aff'd*, 157 F.3d 101 (2d Cir. 1998). Federal *legislative* bodies are covered by § 501 of the Rehabilitation Act, as well as by § 509 of the ADA. *See* 42 U.S.C. § 12209 (2000).

Besides requiring *nondiscrimination*, § 501 of the Rehabilitation Act requires federal agencies to undertake *affirmative action* in the recruitment and placement of disabled individuals. *See* 29 U.S.C. § 791(b) (2000). *See generally* Chapter 13 (Disability).

[5]*See* 42 U.S.C. § 2000e-16 (2000); *see also* Section I.B *infra*.

of the Civil Rights Act of 1991[6] and the Congressional Account-ability Act of 1995,[7] federal legislative branch employees attained comparable rights.[8]

Even where Congress has applied a civil rights law to federal agency employers, however, it sometimes has restricted the remedies available. For example, liquidated damages are not available under the ADEA in suits against federal agencies.[9] As with other public agency defendants, courts may not award punitive damages against federal agency defendants.[10]

Courts often apply general Title VII principles of proof[11] and procedure[12] in suits brought by federal employees. But there remain some significant differences relating to coverage, the exhaustion of administrative remedies, the exclusive nature of remedies, the

---

[6]*See* Section I.E *infra.*

[7]*See* Section I.F *infra.*

[8]Only employees of the judicial branch who hold positions in the competitive service are covered by the substantive protections against discrimination. 42 U.S.C. § 2000e-16(a) (2000); 29 C.F.R. § 1614.103(b)(4) (2005). *See generally* Section II.C *infra.*

[9]*See* Smith v. Office of Pers. Mgmt., 778 F.2d 258, 263–64, 39 FEP 1851 (5th Cir. 1985) (if Congress had intended to allow liquidated damages, it would have expressly provided for them); Mitchell v. Chao, 358 F. Supp. 2d 106, 114 (N.D.N.Y. 2005) (liquidated damages not included within section of ADEA applicable to federal employees); Edwards v. Shalala, 846 F. Supp. 997, 1001 n.8, 68 FEP 1410 (N.D. Ga. 1994), *aff'd*, 64 F.3d 601 (11th Cir. 1995).

[10]Robinson v. Runyon, 149 F.3d 507, 517 (6th Cir. 1998). It is doubtful that the waiver of a federal agency's sovereign immunity through a "sue and be sued" clause could be stretched far enough to allow a punitive damages claim against the agency. *See* Pereira v. United States Postal Serv., 964 F.2d 873, 876–77 (9th Cir. 1992) (such language should not be construed to create broad waivers of sovereign immunity; affirming dismissal of a constitutional tort claim against the Postal Service). *See* generally Chapter 40 (Monetary Relief).

[11]*See, e.g.*, Pesterfield v. Tennessee Valley Auth., 941 F.2d 437, 440–43, 56 FEP 1005 (6th Cir. 1991) (applying Title VII principles to a case alleging disparate treatment because of disability); Griffin v. Carlin, 755 F.2d 1516, 1520–27, 37 FEP 741 (11th Cir. 1985) (applying Title VII principles of statistical proof in a case alleging disparate treatment in discipline and adverse impact resulting from the use of scored tests); Page v. Bolger, 645 F.2d 227, 232–34, 25 FEP 593 (4th Cir. 1981) (en banc) (applying Title VII principles to uphold the dismissal of a federal employee's disparate treatment complaint).

[12]*See, e.g.*, Ong v. Cleland, 642 F.2d 316, 318–20, 25 FEP 994 (9th Cir. 1981) (applying Title VII principles to determine whether the scope of the federal employee's court complaint was reasonably related to the scope of the administrative charge and investigation); Eastland v. Tennessee Valley Auth., 704 F.2d 613, 618–28, 31 FEP 1578 (11th Cir. 1983) (same).

available relief, and other issues that trace their origins from (1) the historical context that led to the extension of Title VII to the federal government, (2) remnants of sovereign immunity, and (3) the federal personnel system[13] itself.

---

[13]Familiarity with the federal personnel system is essential to attorneys and fact finders involved in federal EEO cases. The civil service system has three basic components: (1) the classified or competitive service, (2) the excepted service, and (3) the Senior Executive Service. The primary reference source is the *Federal Personnel Manual* (FPM). Since the passage of the Civil Service Reform Act of 1978 (CSRA), Pub. L. No. 95-454, 1978 U.S.C.C.A.N. (92 Stat.) 1111 (codified in various sections of 5 U.S.C.), federal agencies have substantial discretion in running their own personnel systems. Therefore, the agency's own personnel manual and regulations should be studied with care, particularly for agencies with many excepted service positions.

Following is a brief, nonexhaustive outline of the federal nonpolitical appointee system:

Most employees are in either wage grade (WG, nonsupervisory blue-collar) or general schedule (GS, white-collar) positions. The blue-collar line has wage leader (WL) and wage supervisor (WS) positions. High-level positions (above GS-15) in the white-collar line are in the Senior Executive Service (SES-1 through SES-5). Excepted positions may have different classifications.

In theory, all federal workers at a particular grade, and, therefore, pay level— such as GS-9—are performing work of comparable complexity and requiring a comparable level of expertise, regardless of the particular job that is held. The Office of Personnel Management (OPM) established the basic qualifications required for competitive service jobs. *See* OPM HANDBOOK X-118 (1981) (GS positions); *id.* at X-118C (WG positions). In addition, the OPM set the standards by which these positions are classified as to job title, job series, and grade level. *See* OPM, CLASSIFICATION STANDARDS FOR POSITIONS IN GENERAL SCHEDULE (1981). The employing agency does the actual classification.

Initial appointment to competitive positions in the federal service is done largely through civil service registers (the few exceptions are discussed in Chapter 213 (Excepted Service Appointments) of the FPM). The OPM certifies applicants as eligible based on their education, performance on tests, veterans preference (if any), past employment experience, and other factors. The OPM phased out use of the Professional and Administrative Career Examination's (PACE) Test No. 500, as a result of the consent decree in *Luevano v. Campbell*, 93 F.R.D. 68, 80, 27 FEP 721 (D.D.C. 1981). Since 1984, agencies have used a variety of methods to screen applicants. The hiring agency makes the actual appointments from OPM registers, considering outside applicants along with employees who seek competitive promotions.

Chapter 335 (Promotion and Internal Placement) of the FPM governs competitive selections, including competitive promotions. As for promotions, the position first is reviewed to determine whether it is properly classified, then the vacancy is formally announced, and promotion applications are accepted. Some agencies maintain an updated register of the qualifications of current employees, who automatically are considered for vacancies without having to apply. *See, e.g.*, Salone v. United States, 645 F.2d 875, 877, 25 FEP 680 (10th Cir. 1981). All applications are screened

B. 1964–1972: No Coverage of Federal Employees Under Title VII

The original 1964 version of Title VII specifically excluded the federal government from its definition of "employer."[14] Nevertheless, § 701 contained a proviso that the government's policy was that all employment actions regarding federal employees were

---

to determine whether the applicant meets the minimum qualifications for the position and grade level as established by the OPM. Panels of staffing specialists in the agency personnel office then rate and rank those found qualified either as "highly" or "best" qualified, or simply as "qualified." Lists of the most highly qualified then are sent to the selecting official who generally is free to select any one of them. *See* Evaluation of Employees for Promotion and Internal Placement, subch. S4 (1980), in FPM, Supp. 335-1. FPM Chapter 335 requires agencies to validate all selection procedures and standards, including the rating and ranking factors, according to the Uniform Guidelines on Employee Selection Procedures (29 C.F.R. pt. 1607 (2005)). FPM Supp. 335-1, subch. S3-4(a); 5 C.F.R. § 300.103(c).

Employees may be transferred laterally on a noncompetitive basis into open positions. They also may be promoted noncompetitively, usually through a career ladder series. This involves competitive entry into a job series at a low level, and then noncompetitive promotion as the incumbent's duties increase. After reaching that level, further promotions usually are obtained through competition. Noncompetitive promotion also may occur by reclassification or the accretion of duties. FPM ch. 335, subch. 1–5.

Each grade (i.e., GS-1, GS-2, etc.) has 10 basic rates of pay beginning with a minimum (step 1) and gradually increasing up to the maximum (step 10). Pay rate increases, which are usually given annually, are given incrementally within a certain grade, from step 1 to step 10. Salary levels are set up so that an employee at the tenth step in a given GS grade level actually will have a higher salary than an employee at the first step in the next higher grade level.

Although appearing to be objective, the system provides wide latitude for discretion and subjectivity. For instance, the position description, which usually is written by the immediate supervisor, determines the grade level, job series, job title, job qualifications, duties, and opportunities for training. *See* FPM ch. 312 (Position Management), subch. 3; *id.* ch. 511 (Position Classification), subch. 4. To limit the discretion of agencies in terminating federal employees for poor performance OPM regulations require that the critical elements of each job be identified, and that employees be rated on those alone. *See* FPM, chs. 430 (Performance Appraisal), subch. 2 & 432 (Performance-Based Reduction in Grade and Removal Actions).

[14]*See* Pub. L. No. 88-352, § 701(b), 1964 U.S.C.C.A.N. (78 Stat.) 287, 302 (codified as amended at 42 U.S.C. § 2000e(b) (2000)). The exclusion of the federal government from Title VII's definition of "employer" remains in force; the Equal Employment Opportunity Act of 1972, however, later enacted a special section to cover the federal government. *See* 42 U.S.C. § 2000e-16 (2000); *see also* Section I.C *infra.*

to be free of discrimination.[15] It also authorized the President to issue appropriate executive orders. One such order, Executive Order No. 11246, authorized the U.S. Civil Service Commission (CSC) to issue regulations dealing with charges of discrimination.[16] The CSC issued comprehensive regulations that provided formal procedures by which federal employees in the executive agencies could file charges of discrimination.[17] The regulations imposed obligations on agencies to correct discriminatory practices and to develop affirmative action programs.[18] Executive Order No. 11478,[19] in part superseding Executive Order No. 11246, was issued in 1969; the CSC at that time revised its regulations regarding investigations of discrimination complaints brought by federal employees.[20]

Even though some forms of discrimination against federal employees then were prohibited by the Constitution,[21] statute,[22] executive order,[23] and regulation,[24] the protections embodied in the

---

[15]After original codification as 5 U.S.C. § 7151, that proviso now appears at 5 U.S.C. § 7201(b) (2000).

[16]30 Fed. Reg. 12,319 (1965). *See generally* Chapter 38 (Federal Contractor Affirmative Action Compliance).

[17]*See, e.g.*, 31 Fed. Reg. 3069 (1966) (codified at 5 C.F.R. pt. 713). An earlier version of 5 C.F.R. pt. 713 simply stated a general policy that there should be no discrimination in federal employment, without establishing any formal enforcement mechanism. *See* 28 Fed. Reg. 10,081 (1963).

[18]5 C.F.R. § 713.203 (2005).

[19]34 Fed. Reg. 12,985 (1969) (Equal Employment Opportunity in the Federal Government).

[20]*See id.* at 13,656 (investigation of discrimination complaints); *id.* at 14,023 (Rules and Regulations: Administrative Personnel).

[21]*See* Brown v. GSA, 425 U.S. 820, 835, 12 FEP 1361 (1976) (federal government employees could invoke the Constitution to sue for employment discrimination prior to 1972, when Title VII coverage was extended to certain federal government employees; Congress intended, however, that after 1972, Title VII would be the exclusive remedy for covered federal government employees); *cf.* Davis v. Passman, 442 U.S. 228, 235, 19 FEP 1390 (1979) (employees of Congress, who were not covered by § 717, could sue directly under the Constitution). *See generally* Chapter 35 (The Civil Rights Acts of 1866 and 1871). The exclusivity of Title VII's remedy for discrimination in the federal government is discussed in more detail in Section III.E *infra*.

[22]5 U.S.C. § 7151 (later redesignated 5 U.S.C. § 7201(b) (2000)).

[23]Exec. Order No. 11478, *reprinted in* 34 Fed. Reg. 12,985 (1969).

[24]5 C.F.R. pt. 713 (2005).

concept of sovereign immunity left the existence of a meaningful judicial remedy in serious doubt.[25]

C. The Equal Employment Opportunity Act of 1972: Title VII Was Amended to Cover Certain Federal Employees

In 1972 Congress added § 717 to Title VII, which expanded Title VII's coverage to employees of federal executive agencies and other specified categories of federal employees.[26] The hearings and reports on the 1972 amendments revealed four concerns.[27]

---

[25]*Compare* Chambers v. United States, 451 F.2d 1045, 1054, 3 FEP 1033 (Ct. Cl. 1971) (federal employees can obtain judicial relief) *with* Gnotta v. United States, 415 F.2d 1271, 1276, 2 FEP 111 (8th Cir. 1969) (Blackmun, J.) (sovereign immunity barred employment discrimination suits against the federal government).

[26]*See* 42 U.S.C. § 2000e-16 (2000). This section now defines its scope and coverage as follows:

> All personnel actions affecting employees or applicants for employment (except with regard to aliens employed outside the limits of the United States) in military departments as defined in section 102 of Title 5, in executive agencies as defined in section 105 of Title 5 (including employees and applicants for employment who are paid from nonappropriated funds), in the United States Postal Service and the Postal Rate Commission, in those units of the Government of the District of Columbia having positions in the competitive service, and in those units of the judicial branch of the Federal Government having positions in the competitive service, in the Smithsonian Institution, and in the Government Printing Office, the Government Accountability Office, and the Library of Congress shall be made free from any discrimination based on race, color, religion, sex, or national origin.

42 U.S.C. § 2000e-16(a) (2000). The Smithsonian, Government Printing Office, and Government Accountability Office were added in various amendments subsequent to 1972. *Cf.* Lawrence v. Staats, 640 F.2d 427, 429, 24 FEP 1711 (D.C. Cir. 1981) (only employees of the General Accounting Office who are in the competitive service are covered by § 717); Bethel v. Jefferson, 589 F.2d 631, 640, 18 FEP 789 (D.C. Cir. 1978) (District of Columbia police officers are covered under § 717); Dorsey v. Federal Reserve Bank, 451 F. Supp. 683, 684, 17 FEP 1076 (E.D. Mo. 1978) (Federal Reserve Bank employees are covered under § 717, not § 706).

This scope of coverage has been adopted for disability discrimination complaints under the Rehabilitation Act, *see* 29 U.S.C. § 794(a) (2000), and, with only minor differences, for age discrimination complaints under the ADEA, *see* 29 U.S.C. § 633a(a) (2000). The definition of covered employees under the Equal Pay Act, 29 U.S.C. § 203(e)(2)(A) & (B) (2000), is the same except that it excludes applicants, covers the District of Columbia (although in a different section, 29 U.S.C. § 203(c) (2000)), and differently defines civilian personnel in military departments.

[27]The Senate's Subcommittee on Labor, Committee on Labor and Public Welfare, made an invaluable compilation of the House and Senate reports, floor debates, and versions of the bill, which is published as *Legislative History of the Equal Employment Opportunity Act of 1972* (hereinafter cited as *Legis. Hist.*).

First, virtually all federal agencies showed distributions of employees by race and sex suggestive of possible discrimination.[28] Second, among the prime causes of this pattern were CSC tests and qualification standards.[29] Third, the administrative procedures for the resolution of EEO charges were ineffective because they were in the hands of the employing agencies and because they focused entirely on deliberate discrimination by individuals rather than systemic or institutional causes of discrimination.[30] Fourth, there existed, in light of sovereign immunity, no clear judicial remedy for discrimination by federal agencies.[31]

Congress addressed these concerns in a variety of ways in adding § 717 to Title VII. The section requires affirmative action plans, which must include provisions for training so that all employees may "perform at their highest potential."[32] The House version of the amendments proposed to transfer to the EEOC jurisdiction over federal employees. But the Senate version, which prevailed (temporarily, as it later developed), left jurisdiction with the CSC, and gave it broad powers to require agencies to comply with its regulations and directives implementing § 717. The CSC was empowered to award back pay as well as all other relief necessary to make claimants whole.[33] Finally, § 717(c) established a clear right to a judicial remedy,[34] substantially eroding the federal government's shield of sovereign immunity.

Although 42 U.S.C. § 2000e-16(a) constitutes a waiver of the government's immunity from suit, this waiver applies only to suits

---

[28]White males were concentrated heavily in the higher grade levels; women and minorities were in the lower grades with few opportunities for movement into professional and administrative positions. *Legis. Hist.* at 83.

[29]*Id.* at 423–24 ("Civil Service selection and promotion techniques and requirements are replete with artificial requirements that place a premium on 'paper' credentials [that can result in perpetuating patterns of discrimination].").

[30]*Id.* at 83–84; *see* Brown v. GSA, 425 U.S. 820, 825–26, 12 FEP 1361 (1976); Morton v. Mancari, 417 U.S. 535, 546, 8 FEP 105 (1974). The Senate report mandated that all selection and qualification criteria be brought into compliance with the standards of *Griggs v. Duke Power Co.*, 401 U.S. 424, 3 FEP 175 (1971). *Legis. Hist.* at 424–25. *See generally* Chapter 3 (Adverse Impact).

[31]*Legis. Hist.* at 425; *see Brown*, 425 U.S. at 826–27.

[32]42 U.S.C. § 2000e-16(b) (2000).

[33]*Legis. Hist.* at 1851; *see* 42 U.S.C. § 2000e-16(b) (2000).

[34]*See* 42 U.S.C. § 2000e-16(c) (2000); *see also* Brown v. GSA, 425 U.S. 820, 827–32, 12 FEP 1361 (1976). Congress in 1972 did not, however, include within this expanded scope of Title VII federal employees in the *judicial* or *legislative* branches, or certain other employees that were not within the competitive service.

by civilian employees of the military departments, and not members of the armed forces.[35]

D. The Civil Service Reform Act of 1978 (CSRA): Administrative Enforcement of § 717 Was Restructured

Dissatisfaction with the CSC, including its administrative enforcement of § 717, continued after 1972. Reorganization Plan No. 1 of 1978[36] transferred, from the CSC to the EEOC, jurisdiction over § 717 and a number of other statutes. The effective date of the transfer was delayed until January 1, 1979, to coincide with the effective date of the CSRA.[37]

The CSRA statutorily abolished the CSC and divided its functions (other than § 717 enforcement) between two new agencies. The Office of Personnel Management (OPM) was charged with carrying out the CSC's management functions,[38] while the Merit Systems Protection Board (MSPB) was given its adjudicatory responsibilities.[39] In this way, appeals were to be decided by a more independent agency. The CSRA gave the EEOC sole jurisdiction over "pure" EEO cases (those raising only discrimination issues, or where there existed no appeal rights to the MSPB) and gave the MSPB sole authority over "pure" civil service cases (those involving appeal rights to the MSPB, where no claims of discrimination had been raised). The MSPB was given concurrent jurisdiction with the EEOC over "mixed" cases—those involving personnel actions appealable to the MSPB in which discrimination issues had been raised. The EEOC was given jurisdiction to review

---

[35]*See* Brown v. United States, 227 F.3d 295, 298–99 (5th Cir. 2000) (plaintiff, a dual-status employee, could not bring claim over his discharge from Air Force Reserve, which resulted in termination of his civilian employment with military, because claim arose from military service and thus was not cognizable under Title VII).

[36]*See generally* Chapters 25 (EEOC Administrative Process) and 30 (Justice Department Litigation).

[37]Pub. L. No. 95-454, § 907, 1978 U.S.C.C.A.N. (92 Stat.) 1111, 1227 (codified in various sections of 5 U.S.C.).

[38]Pub. L. No. 95-454, § 201(a), 1978 U.S.C.C.A.N. (92 Stat.) 1118, 1119 (codified at 5 U.S.C. §§ 1101–1105 (2000)).

[39]*Id.* §§ 202(a), 205 (codified as amended at 5 U.S.C. §§ 1201–1206, 7701–7703 (2000)).

only the EEO aspects of MSPB decisions in "mixed" cases.[40] The CSRA made clear that federal employees had the right to judicial trial de novo over all EEO claims, regardless of the administrative body adjudicating them.[41]

When the EEOC took over jurisdiction on January 1, 1979, it repromulgated the majority of then-existing CSC regulations, along with specified CSC guidance letters.[42] Over the years, the EEOC promulgated a variety of amendments to its regulations and, on October 1, 1992, substantially revised and republished them.[43] The new regulations and subsequent interpretations of them are discussed in detail in Sections II and III below.

E. The Civil Rights Act of 1991: New Remedies, a Limitations Period, and Expanded Coverage of § 717

The Civil Rights Act of 1991 (the 1991 Act) had a profound effect on employment discrimination litigation in general. Several provisions specifically affected federal employee litigation. First, § 114 of the 1991 Act amended § 717(d) of Title VII to provide that "the same interest to compensate for delay in payment shall be available [against federal agencies] as in cases involving nonpublic parties."[44] *Library of Congress v. Shaw*[45] had held that interest on judgments against the federal government was not available in the absence of express statutory authority. The 1991 Act provided that authority.

---

[40]5 U.S.C. §§ 7701–7702 (2000); *see* S. REP. NO. 969, 95th Cong., 2d Sess. 56–60, *reprinted in* 1978 U.S.C.C.A.N. 2723, 778–82; H.R. CONF. REP. NO. 1717, 95th Cong., 2d Sess. 136–42, *reprinted in* 1978 U.S.C.C.A.N. 2860, 2869–72. Administrative enforcement of federal employee EEO complaints is discussed in greater detail in Section II *infra*.

[41]5 U.S.C. §§ 7702(e)(3), 7703(c) (2000). The Supreme Court previously had identified this right with respect to Title VII claims in *Chandler v. Roudebush*, 425 U.S. 840, 848, 12 FEP 1368 (1976). *See* Section III.C *infra*.

[42]43 Fed. Reg. 60,900 (1978). The EEOC adopted the following FPM letters: 713-19, 713-21, 713-30, 713-32, 713-36, 713-38, 713-40, 713-42, 713-44, and 551-9, along with CSC bulletins 713-43 and 713-50. *See generally* FPM Ch. 713 (Equal Employment Opportunity).

[43]*See* 29 C.F.R. pt. 1613 (2005). Following the intent of the CSRA, the EEOC's regulations require a separation of agency functions in the administration of the complaint process. *See* EEOC, Management Directive 110, at 1-1 (Oct. 22, 1992).

[44]Pub. L. No. 102-166, § 114(2), 1991 U.S.C.C.A.N. (105 Stat.) 1071, 1079 (codified at 42 U.S.C. § 2000e-16(d) (2000)).

[45]478 U.S. 310, 319, 41 FEP 85 (1986).

Second, § 114(1) of the 1991 Act amended § 717(c) to provide the same 90-day period for filing suit after a final agency or EEOC decision that is allowed to nonfederal employees.[46] However, Congress did not amend 5 U.S.C. § 7703(a)(2), which governs filings in district court following final MSPB decisions on "mixed" cases under 5 U.S.C. § 7702. Thus, such suits still must be filed within 30 days after receipt of the MSPB decision.

Third, federal employees, like their private sector counterparts, now can obtain awards of compensatory damages and try claims of intentional discrimination to juries pursuant to 42 U.S.C. § 1981a. In *West v. Gibson*,[47] the Supreme Court resolved a conflict between the Fifth, Seventh, and Eleventh Circuits as to the EEOC's authority to award compensatory damages in the administrative process.[48] The Court confirmed that the 1991 Act gave federal employees the right to seek compensatory damages from their government employers in the administrative process, holding that EEOC administrative judges have the authority to award compensatory damages.[49]

---

[46]Pub. L. No. 102-166, § 114(1), 1991 U.S.C.C.A.N. (105 Stat.) 1071, 1079 (codified at 42 U.S.C. § 2000e-16(c) (2000)). The 90-day period for private sector plaintiffs is found at 42 U.S.C. § 2000e-5(f)(1) (2000). *See generally* Chapters 26 (Timeliness) and 29 (EEOC Litigation).

[47]527 U.S. 212, 79 FEP 1537 (1999).

[48]*Compare* Gibson v. Brown, 137 F.3d 992, 995–97, 76 FEP 450 (7th Cir. 1998) (employee not required to exhaust EEOC administrative remedies before suing in federal court on claim for compensatory damages), *vacated by* 527 U.S. 212 (1999) *and* Crawford v. Babbitt, 148 F.3d 1318, 77 FEP 700 (11th Cir. 1998) (EEOC cannot award compensatory damages), *vacated by* 527 U.S. 1018 (1999) *with* Fitzgerald v. Secretary, Veterans Affairs, 121 F.3d 203, 207, 75 FEP 46 (5th Cir. 1997) (congressional mandate to EEOC to redress discrimination under Title VII by issuing "such rules, regulations, orders and instructions as it deems necessary and appropriate to carry out its responsibilities" includes issuance of awards of compensatory damages; collecting EEOC decisions).

[49]The Court held (in a 5–4 decision) that the EEOC's legal authority to enforce § 717 of Title VII, 42 U.S.C. § 2000e-16, includes requiring federal agencies to pay compensatory damages when they discriminate in employment in violation of Title VII. The Court found the grant of such authority to the EEOC consistent with the language, purposes, and history of both the 1972 extension of Title VII to cover federal employees and provide appropriate remedies, and the 1991 Amendment providing for compensatory damages under Title VII. The Court noted that the 1991 Act waives sovereign immunity as to awards of compensatory damages: "the statutory language, taken together with statutory purposes, history, and the absence of any convincing reason for denying the EEOC the relevant power," satisfies the standard for narrowly construing such waiver. *Id.* at 220; *see also* Jackson v. Runyon, EEOC Appeal No. 01923399, p. 3 (Nov. 12, 1992) ("the Civil Rights Act of 1991 . . . makes compensatory

Federal employees cannot sue for punitive damages.[50] Courts have confirmed that although the 1991 Act gave federal employees the right to seek compensatory damages from their government employers, they remain ineligible for awards of punitive damages.[51] The Sixth and Seventh Circuits have also held that, despite Congress' unequivocal waiver of sovereign immunity of the United States Postal Service, the Postal Service is a "government agency" exempt from punitive damages for purposes of the Civil Rights Act of 1991.[52]

Fourth, §§ 301 to 325 of the 1991 Act comprised the "Government Employee Rights Act of 1991."[53] This Act for the first time established statutory rights against employment discrimination for employees of the U.S. Senate[54] and certain other federal government entities not previously covered by Title VII, including presidential appointees.[55] This Act was superseded in major part by the Congressional Accountability Act of 1995, which became law on January 23, 1996.[56]

F. The Congressional Accountability Act of 1995: New Protection for Employees of Congress

The first statute enacted in the 104th Congress extended to congressional employees many protections comparable to those enjoyed by other employees. The Congressional Accountability Act

---

damages available to federal employee complaints"). The determination of the amount of compensatory damages following a finding of liability rests with the EEOC administrative judge. See 29 C.F.R. § 1614.109 (2005).

[50]Pub. L. No. 102-166, § 307, 1991 U.S.C.C.A.N. (105 Stat.) 1088, 1092 (codified at 42 U.S.C. § 1981a(a)(1), (b)(1) (2000)).

[51]Mukaida v. Hawaii, 159 F. Supp. 2d 1211, 1240 (D. Haw. 2001) (punitive damages against federal government not allowed under Title VII either pre- or post-Civil Rights Act of 1991), aff'd, 85 Fed. Appx. 631 (9th Cir. 2004); Erickson v. West, 876 F. Supp. 239, 244 (D. Haw. 1995) (same).

[52]Robinson v. Runyon, 149 F.3d 507, 517 (6th Cir. 1998) (Congress has not waived sovereign immunity on behalf of the agency); Baker v. Runyon, 114 F.3d 668, 670, 74 FEP 160 (7th Cir. 1997) (same); see also Ausfeldt v. Runyon, 950 F. Supp. 478, 487–88, 74 FEP 1725 (N.D.N.Y. 1997); Miller v. Runyon, 932 F. Supp. 276, 277, 71 FEP 1024 (M.D. Ala. 1996).

[53]Pub. L. No. 102-166, §§ 301–325, 1991 U.S.C.C.A.N. (105 Stat.) 1088, 1088–99 (codified at 2 U.S.C. §§ 1201–1224 (2000)).

[54]See 2 U.S.C. § 1202 (2000).

[55]See id. § 1219.

[56]Pub. L. No. 104-1, § 201(d), 1995 U.S.C.C.A.N. (109 Stat.) 3, 7.

of 1995 (the 1995 Act) provides, among other things, that the antidiscrimination provisions of Title VII, the ADA, the ADEA, and the Rehabilitation Act will apply to employees of Congress.[57] The substantive language of the 1995 Act tracks § 717 and provides that "all personnel actions affecting covered employees shall be made free from any discrimination based on" the categories covered by the incorporated antidiscrimination statutes.[58] A specific provision bars retaliation or other discrimination against a covered employee who has exercised his or her rights under the Act or otherwise has opposed unlawful discrimination.[59]

The 1995 Act made the remedial provisions of the various acts, including the provision for compensatory damages enacted as part of the Civil Rights Act of 1991, applicable to covered employees.[60] Attorney's fees (including expert fees) and interest are available to congressional employees on the same basis as under Title VII.[61] The 1995 Act is the exclusive remedy for the rights and protections it affords, and only persons who have exhausted certain required administrative prerequisites may obtain a remedy under it.[62]

The 1995 Act[63] provides, however, that it does not constitute a waiver of the immunity from suit of members of Congress under the Speech and Debate Clause of the Constitution.[64] The scope of this constitutional immunity is unclear.[65]

---

[57]Pub. L. No. 104-1, 1995 U.S.C.C.A.N. (109 Sta.), 2 U.S.C. §§ 1301–1438 (2000). The following additional statutes also are made applicable to legislative branch employees: the Family and Medical Leave Act of 1993 (FMLA); the Occupational Safety and Health Act of 1970 (OSHA); 5 U.S.C. ch. 71 (relating to federal service labor-management relations); the Employee Polygraph Protection Act of 1988; the Worker Adjustment and Retraining Notification Act (WARN Act); the Fair Labor Standards Act of 1938 (FLSA); and 38 U.S.C. ch. 43 (relating to veterans' employment and reemployment).

[58]Pub. L. No. 104-1, § 201, 1995 U.S.C.C.A.N. (109 Stat.) 3, 7. Section 225 provides that the definitions and exemptions in the various laws made applicable by the 1995 Act shall apply under the 1995 Act, except where they are inconsistent with the definitions and exemptions set out in the Act itself.

[59]*Id.* § 207.

[60]*See id.* § 225(c) (but prohibiting civil penalties or punitive damages).

[61]*Id.* § 225.

[62]*Id.*

[63]*Id.* § 413.

[64]U.S. CONST. art. I, § 6, cl. 1.

[65]*See* Davis v. Passman, 442 U.S. 228, 233, 19 FEP 1390 (1979) (allowing an employee of Congress to maintain an action against a congressman under the Constitution for discrimination based on sex, but declining to rule whether the Speech and Debate Clause barred relief). *See generally The Application of Federal Laws to Congress*, 50 REC. ASS'N BAR CITY N.Y. 270, 282–88 (1995).

The 1995 Act has its own administrative procedure that is enforced by Congress. It specifically provides that the executive branch (e.g., the EEOC) is not authorized to enforce its provisions.[66] Administrative enforcement is discussed below.[67]

The 1995 Act does not cover employees of the judicial branch. It required, however, that the Judicial Conference of the United States prepare a report for the Chief Justice to submit to Congress discussing application to the judicial branch of the statutes that the 1995 Act applied to legislative employees. The report was to include any recommendations of the Judicial Conference for legislation to provide to judicial employees the rights, protections, and procedures under the listed laws, "including administrative and judicial relief."[68]

G. The Workforce Investment Act of 1998: New Protection for Employees of the Smithsonian Institution

On August 7, 1998, the President signed into law the Workforce Investment Act of 1998, bringing Smithsonian employees within the protection of certain employment discrimination laws.[69] This statute amends Title VII and § 501 of the Rehabilitation Act to cover the Smithsonian Institution and applied to all cases pending on the date of enactment.[70]

II. ADMINISTRATIVE ENFORCEMENT

A. Employees Covered by § 717

1. General Overview of Procedures and Timeliness

Section 717 provides "a careful blend of administrative and judicial enforcement powers."[71] Federal employees must follow

---

[66]Pub. L. No. 104-1, § 225(f), 1995 U.S.C.C.A.N. (109 Stat.) 3, 22.

[67]*See* Section II.B *infra.*

[68]Pub. L. No. 104-1, § 505, 1995 U.S.C.C.A.N. (109 Stat.) 3, 22.

[69]Pub. L. No. 105-220, 112 Stat. 936 (1998), *amending* 42 USC § 2000e-16 (2000).

[70]*See* Misra v. Smithsonian Astrophysical Observatory, 248 F.3d 37, 39 (1st Cir. 2001) (Workforce Investment Act waived sovereign immunity for Smithsonian under Title VII); Rivera v. Heyman, 157 F.3d 101, 102 (2d Cir. 1998) (applying Workforce Investment Act to reverse lower court dismissal of claims under Rehabilitation Act on grounds that Smithsonian is not subject to Act because it is not in the executive branch).

[71]Brown v. GSA, 425 U.S. 820, 833, 12 FEP 1361 (1976).

carefully the applicable administrative procedures and time provisions prescribed, which the Supreme Court described as "preconditions" that Congress attached to the right to sue.[72]

The ADEA, by contrast, does not require exhaustion of administrative procedures as a condition precedent to filing suit. It permits—if the complainant elects not to pursue administrative remedies—direct access to court after giving a 30-day notice of intent to file suit.[73] The 30-day notice to the EEOC is intended to provide the government an opportunity to "take any appropriate action to assure the elimination of any unlawful practice."[74] The Equal Pay Act requires neither resort to administrative procedures nor notice.[75] EEOC regulations, however, permit (but do not require) federal employees to raise with the EEOC individual or class claims of discrimination under the ADEA and the EPA.[76]

A suit under the Equal Pay Act, for which exhaustion of administrative remedies is not required, must be filed within two years of the violation or, if the violation is willful, within three years.[77] If an employee decides not to invoke the administrative process in an age discrimination case, circuits differ on the applicable statute of limitations.[78]

---

[72]*Id.* at 832; *accord* Morales v. Runyon, 844 F. Supp. 1435, 1437 (D. Kan. 1994) (federal employee's belief that the administrative process was futile, no matter how well founded, did not excuse cooperating with the EEO investigation for 180 days); *see* Section III.A *infra*.

The § 717 procedures for Title VII suits apply likewise to federal employee suits brought under the Rehabilitation Act. Section 505(a)(1) of the Rehabilitation Act, 29 U.S.C. § 794(a)(1) (2000), applies the "rights, remedies, and procedures" of § 717 to handicap complaints under § 501 of the Rehabilitation Act, 29 U.S.C. § 791 (2000).

[73]29 U.S.C. § 633a(b), (c), & (d) (2000); 29 C.F.R. § 1614.201 (2005). Notice must be filed within 180 days of the alleged unlawful act and at least 30 days before suit is filed. *Cf.* Jorge v. Rumsfeld, 404 F.3d 556, 564 (1st Cir. 2005) (employee's notice of intent to sue under the ADEA did not satisfy the Title VII requirement to exhaust administrative remedies). The statute was construed in *Stevens v. Department of Treasury*, 500 U.S. 1, 6–7, 55 FEP 845 (1991) but, because the government changed its position on the issue, the Court refused to rule on whether administrative remedies, once invoked, must be exhausted before suit can be filed. The Court did, however, hold that the 30-day notice period is *not* a statute of limitations within which suit must be filed. *See* Bankston v. White, 345 F.3d 768, 777 (9th Cir. 2003) (employee's withdrawal of MSPB appeal 61 days after filing did not bar district court jurisdiction over ADEA claim).

[74]29 U.S.C. § 633a(d) (2000).

[75]*See generally* Chapter 18 (Compensation).

[76]29 C.F.R. § 1614.202 (2005).

[77]29 C.F.R. § 1614.408 (2005).

[78]*Compare* Rossiter v. Potter, 357 F.3d 26, 35, 93 FEP 129 (1st Cir. 2004) (adopting the 2-year limitations period in the Fair Labor Standards Act as the most analogous

The EEOC's regulations governing federal sector complaint processing were amended significantly, effective November 9, 1999.[79] The new regulations applied to all new cases filed after that date, as well as to all pending cases. As detailed further below, among the more significant features of the amended regulations are those dealing with alternative dispute resolution (ADR), coverage, dismissals, complaint consolidation, elimination of certified offers of full relief, finality of the administrative judge's decision, class certification and settlement agreements, and attorney's fees.[80]

Short time periods delimit when a complainant must act. The EEOC regulations require that a complaint be initiated by contacting the employing agency's EEO counselor within 45 days of the alleged violation.[81] If the complaint cannot be resolved informally, a formal written complaint must be filed within 15 days of the notice of the failure of the EEO counselor to resolve the matter.[82] A court action must be filed within 90 days of receipt of notice of final action on the formal written complaint.[83]

The agency investigation is to be completed within 180 days of the date the complaint or last amendment was filed, or within

---

statute) *with* Edwards v. Shalala, 64 F.3d 601, 605–06 (11th Cir. 1995) (once the 30 days have elapsed following employee's filing of notice intent to sue, a new 30-day statute begins running, yielding an ultimate 60-day statute of limitations), Long v. Frank, 22 F.3d 54 (2d Cir. 1994) (Title VII is most analogous statute from which to "borrow" limitations period to apply to federal employee ADEA actions), Lavery v. Marsh, 918 F.2d 1022, 1024–25 (1st Cir. 1990) (ADEA statute of limitations is same as that for Title VII) *and* Rebar v. Marsh, 959 F.2d 216, 218 n.5 (11th Cir. 1992) (collecting cases).

[79]29 C.F.R. §§ 1614.102(b)(2) and 1614.105(b)(2) (1999) had a delayed effective date of January 1, 2000, for agencies that did not have ADR programs at the time of the amendment. November 9, 1999, was the effective date of these provisions for agencies already possessing an ADR program. These provisions require that every agency establish or make available an ADR program for both the pre-complaint and formal complaint process. At the counseling stage, the aggrieved party may choose between participation in the ADR program, as available, and traditional counseling.

[80]*See* 29 C.F.R. pt. 1614 (2005). The relationship of federal EEO complaint processes to the related processes of negotiated grievance procedures, mixed-case complaints, and appeals is not changed by the amendments to the regulations (§§ 1614.301 and 1614.302–.310). Nor are there changes in §§ 1614.502–504 respecting compliance with final Commission decisions.

[81]The continuing violation doctrine has been applied to extend the 45-day period. *See* Burkett v. Glickman, 327 F.3d 658, 660 (8th Cir. 2003) (applying continuing violation doctrine to sexual harassment allegations). *See generally* Chapter 26 (Timeliness).

[82]29 C.F.R. §§ 1614.105(a)(1), .106(b) (2005); *see* Smith v. Potter, 445 F.3d 1000, 97 FEP 1854 (7th Cir. 2006) (phone call to EEO counselor not sufficient).

[83]42 U.S.C. § 2000e-16(c) (2000); *see* Section III.B *infra*.

360 days of the date the original complaint was filed, whichever is earlier.[84] A complainant's request for a hearing is made to the EEOC district or area office in the geographic area where the complaint arose, with a copy forwarded to the agency.[85]

Because of the interplay between § 717 and the CSRA,[86] it sometimes is no easy task to identify the agency with adjudicatory authority in a particular case. The answer depends generally on the nature of the personnel action at issue, the complainant's job tenure and status, whether the complaint alleges solely discrimination (where jurisdiction is with the EEOC),[87] solely a procedural violation (where jurisdiction is with the MSPB),[88] or both (a so-called "mixed" case, where jurisdiction is with both the EEOC and the MSPB),[89] whether the complainant is covered by a collective bargaining agreement,[90] and whether the charge is individual or class based.[91] Because of the potential for confusion and inadvertent error, a mixed-case claim will not be deemed untimely—even if filed with the correct agency only belatedly—as long as the claim was timely filed with *some* federal agency.[92]

---

[84]*Id.* § 1614.108.

[85]Hearing requests are no longer directed to the agency. Rather, within 15 days of receiving a copy of the request for hearing, the agency must send a copy of the complaint file to the EEOC district or area office with jurisdiction over the geographic area where the complaint arose. *Id.*

[86]*See* Section I.D *supra.*

[87]*See* Section II.A.2.a *infra.*

[88]Such cases by definition do not raise employment discrimination issues and therefore are beyond the scope of this book.

[89]*See* Section II.A.2.b *infra.*

[90]*See* Section II.A.4 *infra.*

[91]*See* Sections II.A.2 & II.A.3 *infra. See generally* H.R. REP. NO. 1717, 95th Cong., 2d Sess. (1978) 140–42 (conference report on the CSRA), *reprinted in* 1978 U.S.C.C.A.N. 2860, 2872–75. The various administrative procedures available to federal employees and applicants for employment are discussed in Charles Stephen Ralston, *Peculiarities of the EEO Process for Federal Employees*, in KENT SPRIGGS, REPRESENTING PLAINTIFFS IN TITLE VII ACTIONS ch. 9 (1994). Agency and installation manuals and directives, as well as the FPM and 5 C.F.R., should be studied to determine whether any basis for relief beyond the discrimination issue exists. Of particular importance in promotion cases will be the Merit Promotion Plan, Merit Staffing Plan, or similar document (such as an applicable labor agreement), which sets out the procedures that must be followed in promotion actions.

[92]5 U.S.C. § 7702(f) (2000) (a case "required" to be filed under § 7701, and "timely file[d] . . . with an agency other than" the correct one, will be treated as having been timely filed "as of the date it is filed with the proper agency").

2. Individual Complaints

As explained above,[93] the CSRA divided responsibility for processing federal employee EEO complaints between the EEOC and the MSPB: the EEOC has exclusive jurisdiction over appeals of "pure" EEO complaints—where discrimination is the only allegation—and the MSPB and EEOC have concurrent jurisdiction over "mixed" cases—which involve both discrimination and other, procedural-type allegations.

a. Individual Discrimination Complaints Not Appealable to the MSPB ("Pure EEO Cases"). Seven categories of federal employees (and applicants) and agencies are covered by the administrative process for discrimination cases that are not appealable to the MSPB.[94] These are employees in: (1) nonuniformed military departments; (2) executive agencies; (3) U.S. Postal Service, Postal Rate Commission, and Tennessee Valley Authority positions; (4) all units of the judicial branch having positions in the competitive service, except for complaints under the Rehabilitation Act; (5) the National Oceanic and Atmospheric Administration Commissioned Corps; (6) the Government Printing Office; and (7) the Smithsonian Institution.[95]

The individual complaint process at the agency level has five stages: (1) precomplaint processing and counseling, (2) filing of a formal written agency complaint, (3) investigation, (4) an administrative law judge hearing and decision, and (5) a final written agency decision.

(i.) Precomplaint and counseling stage. To begin the mandatory counseling step, the complainant must contact an EEO counselor

---

[93]*See* Section I.D *supra.*

[94]29 C.F.R. §§ 1614.105–.110, 1614.401–.409 (2005). This process covers complaints under § 717 of Title VII, § 501 of the Rehabilitation Act, § 15(c) of the ADEA, and the Equal Pay Act, including formal complaints of retaliation under those statutes. *See* 29 C.F.R. § 1614.103 (2005). Administrative complaints under the ADEA and the EPA are optional. *See* Section II.A.1 *supra.*

[95]29 C.F.R. § 1614.103(a), (b) (2005). Excluded employees are: uniformed member of the military, employees of the Government Accounting Office and the Library of Congress, aliens located outside the United States, and—for Equal Pay Act complaints—employees working in foreign countries and certain U.S. territories. 29 C.F.R. § 1614.103(d) (2005).

at the employing agency within 45 days of the allegedly discriminatory event or of the effective date of a challenged personnel action.[96]

EEO counselors provide information to the aggrieved individual concerning how the federal sector EEO process works, including time frames and appeal procedures, and attempt to informally resolve the matter. At the initial counseling session, counselors must advise individuals in writing of their rights and responsibilities in the EEO process, including the right to request a hearing before an EEOC administrative judge or an immediate final decision from the agency following its investigation of the complaint. The counselors must also inform the individuals of their right to proceed directly to court to pursue a lawsuit under the Age Discrimination in Employment Act, of their duty to mitigate damages, and that only claims raised in precomplaint counseling may be alleged in a subsequent complaint filed with the agency.[97]

Counseling must be completed within 30 days of the date the aggrieved person contacted the agency's EEO office to request counseling. If the matter is not resolved in that time period, the counselor must inform the individual in writing of the right to file a discrimination complaint. This notice (Notice of Final Interview) must inform the individual that a complaint must be filed within 15 days of receipt of the notice, identify the agency official with whom the complaint must be filed, and reference the individual's duty to inform the agency if he or she is represented.[98] The 30-day counseling period may be extended for an additional 60 days (1) where the individual agrees to such extension in writing or (2) where the aggrieved person chooses to participate in an alternative dispute resolution procedure. If the claim is not resolved prior to 90 days, the Notice of Final Interview described above must be issued to the individual.[99]

---

[96]29 C.F.R. § 1614.105(a)(1) (2005); see Brown v. Snow, 440 F.3d 1259, 1265 (11th Cir. 2006) (discussing 45-day requirement); Douglas v. Norton, 2006 WL 137403, at *9 (10th Cir. Jan. 19, 2006) (claim time-barred due to failure to contact EEO counselor within 45 days, even though employee had earlier contacted counselor but then abandoned the process to instead file a grievance); cf. Delaware State Coll. v. Ricks, 449 U.S. 250, 259, 24 FEP 827 (1980) (limitations periods begin to run upon notice of an allegedly discriminatory event, such as a future discharge, which may be given before its effective date). See generally Chapter 26 (Timeliness).
[97]29 C.F.R. § 1614.105(b)(1) (2005).
[98]29 C.F.R. § 1614.105(d) (2005).
[99]29 C.F.R. § 1614.105(e), (f) (2005).

Beginning January 1, 2000, all agencies were required to establish or make available an alternative dispute resolution (ADR) program. The programs must be available for both the precomplaint and the formal complaint process.[100] At the initial counseling session, counselors must advise individuals that, where an agency agrees to offer ADR in a particular case, the individual may choose between participating in the ADR program and EEO counseling.[101]

(ii.) Agency complaints. A complaint must be filed with the agency that allegedly discriminated against the complainant within 15 days of receipt of the Notice of Final Interview. The complaint must be a signed statement from the complainant or the complainant's attorney, containing the complainant's (or representative's) telephone number and address, and must be sufficiently precise to identify the complainant and the agency, and describe generally the action or practice that forms the basis of the complaint.[102]

A complainant may amend a complaint at any time prior to the conclusion of the investigation to include issues or claims like or related to those raised in the complaint. After requesting a hearing, a complainant may file a motion with the administrative judge to amend a complaint to include issues or claims like or related to those raised in the complaint.[103]

When a complaint is filed, the EEO counselor must submit a written report to the agency's EEO office concerning the issues discussed and the actions taken during counseling.[104]

The requirements of a formal agency complaint are not stringent.[105] However, the agency complaint can be rejected for a number

---

[100] 29 C.F.R. § 1614.102(b)(2) (2005).

[101] 29 C.F.R. § 1614.105(b)(2) (2005).

[102] 29 C.F.R. § 1614.106 (2005).

[103] 29 C.F.R. § 1614.106(d) (2005).

[104] 29 C.F.R. § 1614.105(c) (2005). The EEOC published EEOC Management Directive 110 (Oct. 22, 1992), which sets forth interpretations and guidance on the administrative process under 29 C.F.R. pt. 1614. MD 110, in accordance with the provision of 42 U.S.C. § 2000e-16(b), states that it is binding on agencies. MD 110, intro. ¶ 7, at 3. The EEOC regulations in various places incorporate management directives and require agencies to comply with them. *See, e.g.*, 29 C.F.R. § 1614.102(a)(2) (2005) (agency complaint process); *id.* § 1614.104(a)(1) (procedures adopted by agency); *id.* § 1614.105(c) (agency counseling activities); *id.* § 1614.108(b) (agency investigations). MD 110 is available from the EEOC, *see* 29 C.F.R. § 1614.102(d) (2005), and should be consulted, as well as the regulations themselves, for guidance in all cases.

[105] 29 C.F.R. § 1614.106 (2005). A standard form complaint usually is supplied by or is available from the agency. It can be submitted by the complainant's attorney

of procedural reasons, such as duplicating an earlier complaint, not counseling on the matter or counseling in an untimely manner, or failing to cooperate by not providing information reasonably requested by the agency.[106]

The 1999 amendments to the EEOC regulation eliminated a provision permitting dismissal for failure to accept a certified offer of full relief on an individual, nonclass complaint. However, an agency may now make an "offer of resolution" before a hearing is held. Attorney's fees are limited where a complainant does not accept an offer and the relief awarded in the final decision is not greater than the relief offered by the agency.[107]

(iii.) Investigation. Once the complaint is accepted, an agency investigator will interview and obtain sworn statements from the complainant and witnesses, and the investigator may look into broader issues at the agency that are not alleged in the complaint. The agency must develop an impartial and appropriate factual record upon which to make findings on the claims raised by the complaint. An appropriate factual record is defined in the regulations as one that allows a reasonable fact finder to draw conclusions as to whether discrimination occurred.[108]

The investigation must be completed within 180 days from the filing of the complaint. A copy of the investigative file must be provided to the complainant, along with a notification that, within 30 days of receipt of the file, the complainant has the right to request a hearing and a decision from an EEOC administrative judge, who will submit recommendations to the agency, or may request an immediate final decision from the agency.[109]

(iv.) Administrative hearings and decisions. Requests for hearing must be sent by the complainant to the EEOC office indicated in the agency's acknowledgment letter, with a copy to the agency's

---

on the complainant's behalf. The attorney's right to fees, if the client is successful, depends on the promptness of the attorney's appearance in the EEO process once the complaint is filed. The attorney can use a standard agency appearance form or make a signed, written submission to the agency. The regulations provide that prefiling activity normally cannot be compensated. *Id.* § 1614.501(e)(iv).

[106]*Id.* § 1614.107(a), (b), & (g).

[107]*Id.* § 1614.109(c). This provision is similar to an offer of judgment under FED. R. CIV. P. 68.

[108]29 C.F.R. § 1614.108(b) (2005).

[109]29 C.F.R. § 1614.108(f) (2005).

EEO office. Within 15 days of receipt of the request for a hearing, the agency must provide a copy of the complaint file to EEOC. The EEOC will then appoint an administrative judge to conduct a hearing.[110] Prior to the hearing, the parties may conduct discovery to obtain relevant information either by stipulation or by obtaining authorization from the administrative judge.[111]

Only employees approved as witnesses by the administrative judge may attend the hearing. Hearings are considered part of the investigative process, and are closed to the public. The administrative judge conducts the hearing and receives relevant information or documents as evidence. The hearing is recorded and the agency is responsible for paying for the transcripts of the hearing. Rules of evidence are not strictly applied to the proceedings. If the judge determines that some or all facts are not in genuine dispute, he or she may limit the scope of the hearing or issue a decision without a hearing.[112]

A procedure analogous to summary judgment is available to litigants who can show there is no genuine dispute as to some or all material facts.[113] A party may file a statement with the administrative judge at least 15 days prior to any hearing in an effort to establish there is no genuine issue as to any material facts.[114]

The administrative judge has discretion to permit amendment of the complaint to include "like and related" claims.[115] Substantially similar complaints filed by two or more complainants may be consolidated by the agency or the Commission for joint processing.[116]

The administrative judge may award fees and costs, as may the agency or Commission. There is a strong presumption that the calculated "lodestar" amount constitutes a reasonable fee. Generally, fees are payable for work performed after a formal complaint

---

[110]29 C.F.R. § 1614.108(g) (2005).

[111]29 C.F.R. § 1614.109(d) (2005). For a more detailed description of discovery procedures, see EEOC Management Directive 110, Chapter 6.

[112]29 C.F.R. § 1614.109(e), (f) (2005).

[113]29 C.F.R. § 1614.109(g) (2005). While similar to summary judgment in federal court proceedings under Fed. R. Civ. P. 56, the EEOC procedure includes an additional requirement that there be "no genuine issue as to credibility."

[114]29 C.F.R. § 1614.109(g) (2005).

[115]29 C.F.R. § 1614.106(d) (2005).

[116]29 C.F.R. § 1614.606 (2005).

is filed, plus a reasonable precomplaint fee in connection with obtaining representation. Otherwise, attorney's fees are not typically payable for work performed prior to the filing of a complaint. However, the regulations permit fees for work performed during the precomplaint process where the Commission affirms on appeal an administrative judge's decision that an agency declined to implement.[117]

The administrative judge must conduct the hearing and issue a decision on the complaint within 180 days of receipt of the complaint file from the agency, unless good cause exists for an extension. The judge is to send copies of the hearing record, the transcript and the decision to the parties.[118]

(v.) Final written agency decision. If an agency does not issue a final order within 40 days of receipt of the administrative judge's decision, then the decision becomes the final action by the agency in the matter.[119]

The final order must notify the complainant whether or not the agency will fully implement the decision of the administrative judge, and it must provide notice of the complainant's right to appeal to the EEOC or to file a civil action. If the final order does not fully implement the decision of the judge, the agency must simultaneously file an appeal with the EEOC and attach a copy of the appeal to the final order.[120]

When an administrative judge has not issued a decision (i.e., when an agency dismisses an entire complaint under § 1614.107, receives a request for an immediate final decision, or does not receive a reply to the notice providing the complainant the right to either request a hearing or an immediate final decision), the agency must take final action by issuing a final decision. The agency's final decision will consist of findings by the agency on the merits of each issue in the complaint. Where the agency has not processed certain allegations in the complaint for procedural reasons set out in 29 C.F.R. § 1614.107, it must provide the rationale for its decision not to do so. The agency's decision must be

---

[117]*See id.* § 1614.501(e)(1)(iv). This fees and costs provision applies to Title VII and Rehabilitation Act claims.
[118]29 C.F.R. § 1614.109(i) (2005).
[119]29 C.F.R. § 1614.109(i) (2005).
[120]29 C.F.R. § 1614.110(a) (2005).

issued within 60 days of receiving notification that the complainant has requested an immediate final decision. The agency's decision must contain notice of the complainant's right to appeal to the EEOC, or to file a civil action in federal court.[121]

If the complainant decides to appeal the agency decision to the EEOC Office of Federal Operations rather than filing suit, then he or she must file the appeal within 30 days of receiving the decision.[122] However, an appeal to the EEOC is not required prior to filing a civil suit seeking de novo review of the administrative decision.[123] The agency also may appeal an administrative judge's decision.[124]

Once a final EEOC decision issues and is received, the 90-day filing period starts to run.[125] Depending on the circumstances of the administrative process, the applicable timelines require that the complainant file suit (1) within 90 days of receiving the final action where no administrative appeal has been filed; (2) after 180 days from the date of filing an agency complaint if an administrative appeal has not been filed and final action has not been taken; (3) within 90 days of receipt of the EEOC's final decision on appeal; or (4) after 180 days from the filing of an appeal with the EEOC if there has been no final decision by the EEOC.[126]

b. Individual Discrimination Complaints Appealable to the MSPB ("Mixed Cases"). A case qualifies as a "mixed" case under the CSRA if it includes claims of a violation of civil service laws appealable to the MSPB and of discrimination appealable to the EEOC.[127] If the substance of the claim qualifies it as a mixed case, the EEOC requires that it be so treated, even if the employee characterizes the complaint as one of discrimination only.[128] A claim

---

[121]29 C.F.R. § 1614.110(b) (2005).

[122]29 C.F.R. §§ 1614.401(a), .402(a) (2005).

[123]Farrell v. Principi, 366 F.3d 1066, 1067–68, 15 AD 901 (9th Cir. 2004) (rejecting government's contention that the suit was actually an action for enforcement of the agency's decision for which an individual must notify the EEO Director within 30 days of the noncompliance).

[124]29 C.F.R. § 1614.401(b) (2005).

[125]42 U.S.C. § 2000e-16(c) (2000); 29 C.F.R. § 1614.407 (2005).

[126]29 C.F.R. § 1614.407 (2005).

[127]5 U.S.C. §§ 7701–7702 (2000); 29 C.F.R. § 1614.302 (2005).

[128]29 C.F.R. § 1614.302(b) (2005). *See generally* EEOC Management Directive 110 (Oct. 22, 1992), at 2-11 to 2-16, 3-16 to 3-17.

of discrimination contained within a petition to enforce a settlement agreement does not create a mixed case.[129]

(i.) Overview of mixed cases. As discussed more fully below, the employee must elect to proceed with a complaint as a "mixed-case complaint" under the Part 1614 regulations discussed above or as a "mixed-case appeal" before the MSPB, but not both.[130]

Mixed-case complaints are processed like other complaints of discrimination, with the following notable exceptions: (1) the agency has only 120 days from the date of the filing of the mixed-case complaint to issue a final decision, and the complainant may appeal the matter to the MSPB or file a civil action any time thereafter; (2) the complainant must appeal the agency's decision to the MSPB, not the EEOC, within 30 days of receipt of the agency's decision; (3) at the completion of the investigation the complainant does not have the right to request a hearing before an EEOC administrative judge, and the agency must issue a decision within 45 days.[131]

Individuals who have filed either a mixed-case complaint or a mixed-case appeal, and who have received a final decision from the MSPB, may petition the EEOC to review the MSPB final decision.[132]

In contrast to non-mixed matters, individuals who wish to file a civil action in mixed-case matters must file within 30 days (not 90) of receipt of: (1) the agency's final decision; (2) the MSPB's final decision; or (3) the EEOC's decision on a petition to review. Alternatively, a civil action may be filed after 120 days from the date of filing the mixed-case complaint with the agency or the mixed-case appeal with the MSPB if there has been no final decision on the complaint or appeal, or 180 days after filing a petition to review with EEOC if there has been no decision by EEOC on the petition.[133]

(ii.) Covered employees and personnel actions. A "mixed" case may be filed with the MSPB by nonprobationary individuals in the competitive service, career appointees in the Senior Executive Service, "preference eligibles" in the excepted service with one or

---

[129]Oja v. Department of the Army, 405 F.3d 1349, 1355 (Fed. Cir. 2005).
[130]29 C.F.R. § 1614.302 (2005); 5 C.F.R. §1201.151 (2005).
[131]29 C.F.R. § 1614.302(d) (2005).
[132]29 C.F.R. § 1614.303 (2005).
[133]29 C.F.R. § 1614.310 (2005).

more years of current continuous service, and nonpreference eligibles in the excepted service with two or more years of current continuous service, but excluding those at certain agencies.[134] In 2000, Congress restored to the MSPB jurisdiction over "mixed case" FAA employee complaints.[135] Several courts have found the MSPB lacks jurisdiction over appeals involving screener positions with the Transportation Security Administration (TSA), a component of the Department of Homeland Security, pursuant to the Aviation and Transportation Security Act.[136]

A covered employee may choose to pursue the claim (1) through the agency's EEO complaint procedure and appeal to the MSPB or EEOC,[137] (2) by a direct appeal to the MSPB—bypassing the employing agency—with appeal to the EEOC, or (3) in some cases, through the applicable collective bargaining agreement.[138]

---

[134]*See* 5 U.S.C. §§ 7511(a)(1) & (b), 2302(a)(2)(B) & (C) (2000); EEOC, Management Directive 110 (Oct. 22, 1992), at 3.2 to 3.3. Mixed-case claims were restricted, prior to 1990, to nonprobationary employees in the competitive service and "preference eligibles" with 1 year's current continuous service in the excepted service, subject to a number of exceptions. The statute was amended in 1991 to provide MSPB administrative remedies for more employees in view of the Supreme Court's holding in *United States v. Fausto*, 484 U.S. 439, 447–48 (1988), that the CSRA was exclusive and preclusive for employees not having MSPB administrative rights thereunder. *See* Pub. L. No. 101-376, § 2, 1990 U.S.C.C.A.N. (104 Stat.) 461, 461; H.R. REP. NO. 101-328, 101st Cong., 2d Sess. (1989), *reprinted in* 1990 U.S.C.C.A.N. 695.

[135]Pursuant to the 1996 Act, Pub. L. No. 104-50 § 347(a), (b), 109 Stat. 436, 460 (1995), effective April 1, 1996, FAA employees were removed from the general jurisdiction of the federal personnel system established in Title 5 of the U.S. Code, and MSPB no longer had jurisdiction of mixed-case FAA employee complaints. Section 307(a) of the Wendell H. Ford Aviation Investment and Reform Act, Pub. L. No. 106-181, 114 Stat. 61, amended the 1996 Act by revising 49 U.S.C. § 40122(g), essentially restoring FAA employees' rights to appeal to the MSPB and to seek judicial review of MSPB decisions. The MSPB asserted retroactive jurisdiction over FAA adverse action claims effective April 1, 1996.

[136]Conyers v. MSPB, 388 F.3d 1380, 1383 (Fed. Cir. 2004) (§ 111(d) of Aviation and Transportation Security Act allows Under Secretary of Transportation to hire, discipline, terminate, and control the terms of employment for screeners "notwithstanding any other provision of law"), *cert. denied*, 543 U.S. 1171 (2005); *see also* Springs v. Stone, 362 F. Supp. 2d 686, 698 (E.D. Va. 2005) (TSA Under Secretary exempt from constraints of "any other provision of law," including veterans' preference standards included in Federal Aviation Administration (FAA) personnel management system and incorporated into ATSA, when it designed and implemented RIF procedures).

[137]5 C.F.R. §§ 1201.151–.156 (2005).

[138]29 C.F.R. § 1614.301 (2005); *see* Section II.A.4 *infra*.

Only federal employees and applicants, not employees of government contractors, have appeal rights to the MSPB. An employee of an independent government contractor whose employment was subject to his ability to obtain a security clearance was held not an applicant for employment who was entitled to appeal his dismissal to the MSPB.[139]

There are appeal rights to the MSPB only with respect to certain types of personnel actions.[140] A major category of personnel actions over which the MSPB has jurisdiction is labeled "adverse actions," which include a removal (i.e., termination), a suspension for more than 14 days, a reduction in grade or pay, or a furlough of 30 days or less.[141] Reductions in pay and grade for unacceptable performance also are covered.[142] The MSPB also has jurisdiction over reductions in force and other actions where the OPM has granted appeal jurisdiction,[143] as well as other statutory appeals of determinations relating to disability retirement, health insurance and annuities,[144] certain actions involving those in the Senior Executive Service,[145] and specified probationary period terminations.[146]

If the action complained about were to be, for instance, a two-day suspension or the denial of a promotion, neither of which is an "adverse action" from which an appeal to the MSPB lies,[147] the employee's exclusive remedy would be under § 717 and the EEOC regulations.[148] Similarly, a probationary employee or one in the

---

[139]Thompson v. MSPB, 421 F.3d 1336, 1339 (Fed. Cir. 2005).

[140]See 5 U.S.C. § 7512 (2000); 5 C.F.R. § 1201.3 (2005); EEOC, Management Directive 110 (Oct. 22, 1992), at 3-13 to 3-14.

[141]5 U.S.C. § 7512 (2000); 5 C.F.R. § 1201.3(a)(2) (2005) .

[142]5 U.S.C. § 4303 (2000); 5 C.F.R. § 1201.3(a)(1) & (5) (2005).

[143]5 C.F.R. § 1201.3(a)(7), (9)–(19) (2005).

[144]Id. § 1201.3(a)(6).

[145]Id. § 1201.3(a)(3), (4), & (20).

[146]Id. § 1201.3(a)(8).

[147]See, e.g., 5 U.S.C. §§ 7501–7503 (2000) (suspensions of 14 days or less are not appealable to the MSPB); Nigg v. MSPB, 321 F.3d 1381, 1385 (Fed. Cir. 2003) (reduction in postal inspector's premium pay, as opposed to base pay, did not involve an adverse action); Williams v. Department of Army, 651 F.2d 243, 244 (4th Cir. 1981) (per curiam) (denial of a promotion is not an adverse action appealable to the MSPB).

[148]The employee also may be able to grieve a short suspension or promotion denial under a collective bargaining agreement allowing EEO claims. Such an employee must elect between the EEO complaint procedure or the grievance procedure, under 29 C.F.R. § 1614.301 (2005).

excepted service without sufficient time in service would not be a covered employee, and the MSPB's appeal procedures would not be available;[149] the sole administrative remedy in such cases would be through the EEOC.

(iii.) Administrative procedures in mixed cases. A covered complainant in a "mixed" case may elect to file a direct appeal with the MSPB within 30 days of the complained-of agency action[150] or may file a timely formal discrimination charge with the agency.[151] If initial filing with the agency is elected, the complainant may file an appeal with the MSPB within 20 days of receipt of the agency's final decision[152] or after the complaint has been filed with the agency and 120 days have elapsed without decision.[153]

An employee who complains about discrimination by the OPM rather than the employing agency, e.g., regarding an OPM-devised test with an alleged adverse impact, also may appeal such a claim directly to the MSPB.[154] If the complained-of test or standard is

---

[149]5 C.F.R. § 300.104(a) (2005). Discrimination on the basis of disability is not expressly covered by § 300.102 or § 300.103. Hence no internal complaint procedure prior to the MSPB appeal is provided for disability discrimination claims. *But see* 5 U.S.C. §§ 2301, 2302 (2000). However, if the complaint relates to a candidate's examination rating on an OPM test, an appeal is filed with the OPM itself. *See* 5 C.F.R. § 300.104(b) (2005); FPM ch. 337 (Examining System). The MSPB has appellate jurisdiction over "appeals from agency actions when the appeals are authorized by law, rule or regulation." 5 C.F.R. § 1201.3(a) (2005).

[150]5 C.F.R. § 1201.56 (2005); *see* Garcia v. Department of Homeland Sec., 437 F.3d 1322 (Fed. Cir. 2006) (en banc) (employee has burden at hearing of establishing MSPB jurisdiction by showing one of the adverse actions enumerated in 5 U.S.C. § 7512; overruling decisions that permitted jurisdiction based merely on finding of a nonfrivolous allegation). *Garcia* remanded a constructive discharge claim to the MSPB, and in doing so affirmed the jurisdictional standard in *Cruz v. Department of the Navy*, 934 F.2d 1240, 1248 (Fed. Cir. 1991), where an employee's failure to establish a constructive or involuntary discharge divested the MSPB of jurisdiction. Where the MSPB rules it does not have jurisdiction, the employee may pursue the discrimination claim before the EEOC.

[151]5 U.S.C. § 7702(a)(2) (2000); 5 C.F.R. § 1201.154(a) (2005); 29 C.F.R. § 1614.302(b) (2005). The EEOC regulation, 29 C.F.R. § 1614.302(b) (2005), provides that an aggrieved person may "initially file a mixed complaint with an agency pursuant to this part or an appeal on the same matter with the MSPB pursuant to 5 C.F.R. § 1201.151, but not both."

[152]29 C.F.R. § 1614.303(d)(1)(ii) (2005).

[153]5 C.F.R. § 1201.154(b) (2005); 29 C.F.R. § 1614.302(d)(1) (2005). No formal hearing is held by the agency in a mixed case under the EEOC regulations (29 C.F.R. § 1614.302(d)(2) (2005)); the MSPB hearing on appeal is the only hearing.

[154]5 C.F.R. § 300.104(a) (2005).

administered or required by the agency, the employee or applicant would have the additional option of proceeding through the agency's EEO complaint procedure, or through the agency grievance procedure (if a violation of a collective bargaining agreement is alleged).[155]

MSPB appeals are heard by an administrative judge and include the opportunity to conduct discovery prior to the formal hearing.[156] In a mixed case, the agency bears the burden of proof on the appealable issue and the aggrieved employee or applicant bears the burden of proof on the discrimination claim.[157] After the administrative judge's initial decision, the dissatisfied party may file a petition for review by the full board.[158] If no petition is filed, the administrative judge's decision becomes final. If the employee prevails, he or she may apply for attorney's fees within 10 days after the decision becomes final. Title VII standards govern awards of attorney's fees to employees who have prevailed on the discrimination claim in a mixed case.[159]

---

[155]*Id.* pt. 771; *see* Harrison v. Lewis, 559 F. Supp. 943, 950–52, 40 FEP 181 (D.D.C. 1983) (a complaint that OPM qualification standards used by an agency had an adverse impact on African-American applicants for promotions could be brought under the agency's EEO procedures); Brown v. Schlesinger, 434 F. Supp. 1004, 1006, 18 FEP 863 (E.D. Va. 1977) (pre-CSRA case; a part 300 complaint "is an alternative, not a mandatory procedure, for an employee who alleges that a particular [OPM] test or standard is discriminatory"; where the complained-of test or standard is required or administered by an agency, the complainant may proceed under the agency's EEO complaint procedure); *cf.* Chisholm v. United States Postal Serv., 516 F. Supp. 810, 867–69, 25 FEP 1778 (W.D.N.C. 1980) (discrimination in administration and use of written tests was reasonably related to the discrimination claims addressed in the administrative complaint), *aff'd in part and vacated in part on other grounds*, 665 F.2d 482, 27 FEP 425 (4th Cir. 1981).

[156]5 C.F.R. §§ 1201.71–.75 (2005). The MSPB has subpoena power, which it will exercise for hearings. 5 C.F.R. §§ 1201.81–.85 (2005).

[157]*Id.* § 1201.56; *see* Hodgson v. Department of Air Force, 704 F. Supp. 1035, 1037, 50 FEP 630 (D. Colo. 1989) (an employee who sought to establish a prohibited personnel practice and age discrimination had the burden of proof on the latter issue).

[158]5 C.F.R. § 1201.113 (2005).

[159]5 U.S.C. § 7701(g)(2) (2000); 5 C.F.R. § 1201.37(a) (2005). If the MSPB decision is in the employee's favor on the merits of the appealable action rather than on the discrimination claim, attorney's fees are awarded only if "warranted in the interest of justice." 5 U.S.C. § 7701(g)(1) (2000); *see* Price v. Social Sec. Admin., 398 F.3d 1322, 1326 (Fed. Cir. 2005) (affirming denial of fees under § 7701(g) to employee who was awarded back pay with interest for suspension without due process hearing); James v. Santella, 328 F.3d 1374, 1376–77 (Fed. Cir. 2003) (analyzing provision in 5 U.S.C. § 1204(m)(1) that is identical to § 7701(g) standard of "warranted in the interest of justice"); Allen v. United States Postal Serv., 2 MSPB 582, 586 (1980) ("interest of justice" standard in § 7701(g) is not co-extensive with "prevailing party" standard).

If a party files a petition for review with the MSPB, the board's decision becomes final when it either denies or rules on the petition, disposing of the case.[160] The employee then has the additional option of petitioning the EEOC for review of the claim within 30 days. The EEOC has 30 days to decide whether to review the decision and, if it does so, another 60 days to render its decision.[161] If the EEOC rejects or modifies the board's decision, the case is remanded back to the MSPB, which has 30 days in which to concur or disagree with the EEOC. The MSPB may make factual findings regarding discrimination, but must defer to the EEOC's interpretation of the discrimination laws.[162] If the board disagrees with the EEOC, it may refer the matter to a special panel composed of one board member, one Commission member, and a person appointed by the President to the position of chairman for a six-year term.[163]

(iv.) Judicial review in mixed cases. The complexities of the statute's provisions for judicial review parallel its administrative complexities. Basically, the mixed-case complainant can go to court any time there is a final decision (a "judicially reviewable action") issued by an agency in the process. "Notwithstanding any other provision of law . . . any such case [subject to § 7702] . . . must be filed within 30 days after the date the individual . . . received notice of the judicially reviewable action."[164]

---

[160]5 C.F.R. § 1201.113(b), (c), & (e) (2005).

[161]5 U.S.C. § 7702(b) (2000); 5 C.F.R. § 1201.161 (2005); 29 C.F.R. § 1614.303 (2005). The EEOC's procedure on such petitions is outlined in 29 C.F.R. §§ 1614.304 & .305 (2005).

[162]5 U.S.C. § 7702(c) (2000); *see, e.g.*, Lynch v. Bennett, 665 F. Supp. 62, 66, 44 FEP 651 (D.D.C. 1987) (the EEOC, after deciding that the MSPB had applied an incorrect standard, properly referred the case back to the MSPB; however, the MSPB exceeded the scope of its regulatory authority by reopening prior to a final decision).

[163]5 U.S.C. § 7702(d) (2005). Most cases have ended administratively with an MSPB administrative judge's decision. Virtually none have gone to the special panel, which was the final compromise between the House version of the CSRA, which would have given the EEOC the final decision, and the Senate version, which would have sent disputes between the EEOC and the MSPB to the District of Columbia Circuit for resolution. *See* Pub. L. No. 95-454, § 205, 1978 U.S.C.C.A.N. (92 Stat.) 1111, 1143; H.R. CONF. REP. NO. 1717, 95th Cong., 2d Sess. 142–43, *reprinted in* 1978 U.S.C.C.A.N. 2860, 2876.

[164]5 U.S.C. § 7703(b)(2) (2000). This 30-day time limit was not extended by the Civil Rights Act of 1991. *See* EEOC, Management Directive 110 (Oct. 22, 1992),

Thus, the complainant may file suit when no subsequent appeal steps are taken and (1) the employing agency issues its final decision, (2) the MSPB initial decision becomes final, (3) the MSPB denies a petition for review or issues its final decision, (4) the EEOC decides not to consider an MSPB decision or concurs in it, (5) the MSPB concurs and adopts "in whole" an EEOC decision, or (6) the special panel resolves a dispute between the MSPB and the EEOC. The complainant may also file suit where no agency decision has been issued, after any of the following time periods lapse: (1) 120 days after filing with the employing agency, if there has been no decision or appeal to the MSPB, (2) 120 days after filing with the MSPB if it has not yet made a decision, or (3) 180 days after filing with the EEOC, if there has been no final decision in the process leading to the special panel.[165]

A complainant must file a mixed case in federal district court, under the appropriate discrimination statute, if he or she wishes to preserve the discrimination claim.[166] If the discrimination claim is waived, or is frivolous,[167] so that only the issue appealable to the MSPB remains (i.e., the procedural, or pure civil-service issue), then the only appellate review available is in the U.S. Court of Appeals for the Federal Circuit. Agencies—except, in limited

---

at 10-5. Cases not involving discrimination, which must be filed in the Court of Appeals for the Federal Circuit, must be filed within *60 days* of receiving the final order or decision of the MSPB. 5 U.S.C. § 7703(b)(1) (2000).

[165]5 U.S.C. § 7702 (2000); 5 C.F.R. § 1201.175(b) (2005); *see* 29 C.F.R. § 1614.310 (2005) (summarizing time limits); *see also* Ballard v. Tennessee Valley Auth., 768 F.2d 756, 764–65, 38 FEP 904 (6th Cir. 1985).

[166]5 U.S.C. § 7703(b)(2) (2000); Chappell v. Chao, 388 F.3d 1373, 1379 (11th Cir. 2004) (appeal of adverse decision from MSPB to Court of Appeals for Federal Circuit waived right to assert in separate district court action discrimination claims arising out of same facts); Williams v. Department of Army, 715 F.2d 1485, 1491, 36 FEP 1518 (Fed. Cir. 1983) (court of appeals lacked jurisdiction over MSPB appeal in which discrimination was alleged basis of adverse action); Wiggins v. United States Postal Serv., 653 F.2d 219, 220, 35 FEP 1286 (5th Cir. 1981) (jurisdiction for discrimination claim rests with district court, rejecting bifurcation of claims between district and circuit court due in part to "tremendous waste of judicial resources"); Coffey v. United States, 939 F. Supp. 185, 192 (E.D.N.Y. 1996) (dismissing appeal of MSPB decision because complaint failed to allege sufficient facts to show whether case involved allegation of employment discrimination).

[167]*See* Hill v. Department of Air Force, 796 F.2d 1469, 1470, 41 FEP 528 (Fed. Cir. 1986) ("[I]f . . . the employee presented no more than a frivolous allegation of discrimination then there never was a 'mixed case,' and review . . . lies exclusively with the Federal Circuit.").

circumstances and at the discretion of the Federal Circuit, the OPM—have no right to court review of MSPB decisions under § 7702.[168]

The circuits are split on whether the Federal Circuit has exclusive jurisdiction over the MSPB's dismissal of discrimination appeals on procedural grounds.[169] In *Sloan v. West*, the Ninth Circuit discussed the distinction between a mixed-case complaint and an appeal, noting that the MSPB must decide that it has jurisdiction over a case before it becomes a mixed-case appeal.[170] The *Sloan* decision discusses the choices required of a federal employee who wishes to preserve a nondiscrimination claim coupled with a discrimination claim.

Sloan affirmed that, in a mixed case proceeding, although the district court reviews the MSPB's determination of the federal employee's nondiscrimination claim under a deferential standard, the discrimination claim is reviewed de novo.[171] *Sloan* also affirmed that the MSPB may not exercise jurisdiction over a claim of discrimination that is divorced from a personnel action otherwise within its jurisdiction.[172]

3. Class Complaints

Class complaints of discrimination begin with an administrative process similar to that which is followed for individual

---

[168]*See* 5 U.S.C. § 7703(a)(1) & (d) (2000); 28 U.S.C. § 1295(a)(9) (2000).

[169]*Compare* Powell v. Department of Def., 158 F.3d 597 (D.C. Cir. 1998) (appeal of MSPB decision that it lacked jurisdiction of mixed case complaint was properly venued in Federal Circuit, not in district court) *and* Ballentine v. MSPB, 738 F.2d 1244, 1247 (Fed. Cir. 1984) (same) *with* Harms v. IRS, 321 F.3d 1001, 1008 (10th Cir. 2003) (when MSPB has jurisdiction over an appeal but dismisses it on procedural—rather than jurisdictional—grounds, federal district court has jurisdiction to review that decision de novo) *and* Downey v. Runyon, 160 F.3d 139, 144–45 (2d Cir. 1999) (same).

[170]Sloan v. West, 140 F.3d 1255, 1262, 85 FEP 975 (9th Cir. 1998). The court ruled that a mixed-case appeal is not a subset of a mixed-case complaint, i.e., a case presenting an appealable nondiscrimination claim coupled with a discrimination claim. Rather, the MSPB must decide it has jurisdiction over a mixed case before it can become a mixed-case appeal.

[171]*Id.* at 1260; Downey v. Runyon, 160 F.3d 139, 8 AD 1469 (2d Cir. 1998) (Civil Service Reform Act entitled federal employee plaintiff to seek de novo review of discrimination claim in federal district court after MSPB dismissed his "mixed appeal" as untimely without reaching merits of his discrimination claim).

[172]*Sloan*, 140 F.3d at 1260.

discrimination claims; the employee or applicant who wishes to file a class complaint must first seek counseling.[173]

Once the counseling stage is completed, however, the class complaint is not investigated by the respondent agency. Instead, the class complaint is forwarded to the nearest EEOC field or district office, where an EEOC administrative judge decides whether to accept or dismiss the class complaint. The administrative judge should examine the class to determine whether it meets the class certification requirements of numerosity, commonality, typicality, and adequacy of representation. The judge may dismiss the class complaint, or any portion thereof, because it fails to meet any of these class certification requirements, or for any of the reasons for dismissal discussed above for individual complaints.[174]

A class complaint may begin as an individual complaint of discrimination. If it becomes apparent that there are more individuals affected by the issues raised in the individual complaint, the complainant may move for class certification at any reasonable point in the process.[175] A pro se plaintiff cannot litigate a class action on behalf of other federal employees.[176]

After the administrative judge transmits his or her decision to accept or dismiss a class complaint to the complainant and the agency, the agency must then take final action by issuing a final order within 40 days of receipt. The final order must notify the complainant whether or not the agency will implement the decision of the administrative judge. If the agency's final order does not implement the judge's decision, the agency must simultaneously appeal the judge's decision to the EEOC's Office of

---

[173]29 C.F.R. § 1614.204(b) (2005).

[174]29 C.F.R. § 1614.204(d) (2005); *see* Monreal v. Potter, 367 F.3d 1224, 1236–37 (10th Cir. 2004) (affirming dismissal of proposed class action on behalf of postal employees under Fed. R. Civ. P. 23(b)(2) and (b)(3) analysis).

[175]29 C.F.R. § 1614.204(b) (2005). Likewise, an individual claim of discrimination can be exhausted by its inclusion in a class administrative complaint; EEOC regulations do not mandate exclusive presentation of individual claims in individual complaints. *Monreal*, 367 F.3d at 1232. *But see* Ransom v. United States Postal Serv., 2006 WL 308265, at *3 (10th Cir. Feb. 10, 2006) (pro se employee's individual complaint, with brief references to maltreatment of other employees, did not exhaust administrative remedies for a class complaint).

[176]*See Ransom*, 2006 WL 308265, at *5.

Federal Operations. The agency must append a copy of its appeal to the agency's final order.[177]

A dismissal of a class complaint must inform the class agent either that the complaint is being filed on that date as an individual complaint and processed accordingly, or that the complaint is also dismissed as an individual complaint for one of the reasons for dismissal. In addition, a dismissal must inform the class agent of the right to appeal to the EEOC's Office of Federal Operations or to file a civil action in federal court.

When a class complaint is accepted, the agency must use reasonable means to notify the class members of the acceptance of the class complaint, a description of the issues accepted as part of the complaint, an explanation of the binding nature of the final decision or resolution on the class members, and the name, address, and telephone number of the class representative.[178]

Because the agency does not investigate the class complaint, the EEOC administrative judge develops a record through discovery and a hearing. The administrative judge then issues a recommended decision to the agency.[179] Within 60 days of receipt of the judge's recommended decision on the merits of the class complaint, the agency must issue a final decision that either accepts, rejects, or modifies the recommended decision. If the agency fails to issue a decision within that time frame, the administrative judge's recommended decision becomes the agency's final decision in the class complaint.[180]

When the final decision finds discrimination and a class member believes that he or she is entitled to relief, the class member may file a written claim with the agency within 30 days of receipt of notification by the agency of its final decision. The EEOC administrative judge retains jurisdiction over the complaint in order to resolve disputed claims by class members. The claim for relief must contain a specific showing that the claimant is a class member entitled to relief. The EEOC's regulations provide that, when a finding of discrimination against a class has been made, there is

---

[177]29 C.F.R. § 1614.204(d)(7) (2005).
[178]29 C.F.R. § 1614.204(e) (2005).
[179]29 C.F.R. § 1614.204(f) (2005).
[180]29 C.F.R. § 1614.204(j) (2005).

a presumption of discrimination as to each member of the class. The agency must show by clear and convincing evidence that any individual class member is not entitled to relief. The agency must issue a final decision on each individual claim for relief within 90 days of filing. The individual class member may appeal the agency's decision to the EEOC's Office of Federal Operations or file a civil action in federal court.[181]

The agency and the class representative may resolve a class complaint at any time. Notice of any such resolution must be provided to all class members, and it must be reviewed and approved by an EEOC administrative judge. If the administrative judge finds that the proposed resolution is not fair to the class as a whole, the judge can issue a decision vacating the agreement, and replace the class representative with some other eligible class member to further process the class complaint. The class representative may appeal such a decision by the administrative judge to EEOC. If the administrative judge finds that the resolution is fair to the class as a whole, then it becomes binding on all class members.[182]

Class actions in mixed cases appealed directly to the MSPB are not as tightly governed by regulations. The administrative judge has 30 days after filing within which to determine whether to hear the appeal as a class action. Except as the administrative judge may direct, there are no other special rules for processing class charges; the regulations simply state that decisions are to be guided—but not controlled—by the Federal Rules of Civil Procedure.[183] The presiding official may certify a ruling, such as one concerning a class charge, for an interlocutory appeal to the full board.[184] There is also a provision for permissive intervention by class members.[185] Only parties, including intervenors, may seek review by the full board.[186]

---

[181]29 C.F.R.§ 1614.204(l) (2005).

[182]29 C.F.R. § 1614.204(g) (2005).

[183]See 5 C.F.R. § 1201.27(c) (2005). The regulations require putative class members to keep up with the class proceedings at their peril. *Id.* § 1201.27(b).

[184]*Id.* §§ 1201.91–.93.

[185]*Id.* § 1201.34(c).

[186]*Id.* § 1201.114. 5 U.S.C. § 7703(a)(1) (2000) provides that "[a]ny employee or applicant for employment *adversely affected* or aggrieved *by a final order or decision* of the [MSPB] may obtain judicial review of the order or decision." (emphasis added.) This suggests that an affected class member may seek judicial review. That conclusion is strengthened by the statement in 5 U.S.C. § 7703(b)(2) (2000) that a mixed case may be filed under § 717(c) "[n]otwithstanding any other provision of law."

4. Employees Covered by Collective Bargaining Agreements

Employees who are covered by a collective bargaining agreement that is subject to 5 U.S.C. § 7121(d)[187] may elect to raise a claim of unlawful discrimination under the agreement, if it covers such claims, or under the EEOC's procedures in 29 C.F.R. part 1614.[188] Employees must elect which remedy to pursue; they may not pursue both.[189]

The Federal Labor-Management Relations Act (FLMRA) requirement that most federal employees pursuing discrimination claims must elect whether to pursue a remedy under an applicable collective bargaining agreement or through the EEOC's procedures represents an important distinction between the rights of federal employees and private sector employees.[190] In the private sector, attempts to bar an employee's pursuit of a grievance under a collective bargaining agreement (or other employee right) concurrently with a claim before the EEOC would likely run afoul of antiretaliation provisions because such attempts could be construed as interference with the employee's nonwaivable right to engage in protected activity.[191]

---

[187]Different rules apply to agencies exempt from § 7121(d). The major exempt agencies are the Postal Service and the TVA. Applicable procedures for those agencies are in 29 C.F.R. § 1614.301(c) (2005) and EEOC Management Directive 110 (Oct. 22, 1992), at 2-9, 3-8.

[188]29 C.F.R. § 1614.301 (2005). A suspected violation of an employee's rights may be raised under the grievance procedure by the union representing the employee. 5 U.S.C. § 7103(a)(9)(B) (2000).

[189]5 U.S.C. § 7121(d) (2000); 29 C.F.R. § 1614.301(a) (2005). The regulations require the employing agency's EEO counselor to inform employees of their statutory election right. 29 C.F.R. §§ 1614.105, .301(a) (2005). Nevertheless, the filing of a grievance under the collective bargaining agreement regarding the facts at issue irrevocably elects that remedy, even if the employee has not been informed of the requirement to make an election or has not raised a discrimination claim in the grievance. Id. § 1614.301(a). The statute speaks of the "aggrieved employee" having to make the binding election. 5 U.S.C. § 7121(d) (2000). On the other hand, the regulation uses the word "person," which, under the statute, includes the union. See 5 U.S.C. § 7103(a)(1) (2000). Therefore, it is not clear whether a union's election of the grievance procedure to pursue a claim of one of its members would prevent the employee from filing an EEO complaint.

[190]The FLMRA's election of remedies provision requires federal employees with exclusive representation to elect to pursue their employment discrimination claims under *either* statutory process *or* the union grievance process, unless the grievance procedure specifically excludes discrimination claims. Employees cannot pursue both avenues, and the election is irrevocable. 5 U.S.C. § 7121 (2000); 29 C.F.R. § 1614.107(d) (2005). *See generally* Chapter 27 (Jurisprudential Bars to Action).

[191]*See, e.g.,* Fasold v. Justice, 409 F.3d 178, 189, 95 FEP 1445 (3d Cir. 2005) (denial of grievance due to employee's filing of post-termination age discrimination

Whether a federal employee elects to pursue the grievance procedure pursuant to a collective bargaining agreement or a charge via the EEOC, he or she must pursue the chosen remedy to exhaustion as a prerequisite to filing suit.[192] Postal employees are exempt from this requirement, however.[193]

An arbitrator's decision on the employee's grievance may be appealed to the Federal Labor Relations Authority (FLRA), with the FLRA's final decision appealable to either the EEOC or the MSPB.[194] The bargaining agreement grievance procedure serves as an alternative to the agency investigation and EEO administrative hearing in discrimination matters appealable to the EEOC. The grievance procedure is also an alternative to the agency complaint stage in mixed discrimination matters appealable to the MSPB.[195]

The same regulations that govern judicial review of an agency-processed discrimination complaint under § 717(c) of Title VII govern claims of discrimination litigated administratively pursuant to negotiated grievance systems.[196] The employee grievant may

---

claim established prima facie case of retaliation); EEOC v. Board of Governors, 957 F.2d 424, 431, 58 FEP 292 (7th Cir. 1992) (finding unlawful retaliation where collective bargaining agreement allowed termination of employee's administrative grievance proceeding upon filing of charge with EEOC).

[192]Rosell v. Wood, 357 F. Supp. 2d 123, 129 (D.D.C. 2004) (employee failed to exhaust administrative remedy by affirmatively choosing not to amend retaliation charge to add disability and age claims); Macy v. Dalton, 853 F. Supp. 350, 353, 64 FEP 1718 (E.D. Cal. 1994) (plaintiffs who were in process of pursuing grievance procedure under collective bargaining agreement with respect to RIF, without expressly alleging discrimination, were barred from bringing claim in court as to same employment action).

[193]*See, e.g.*, Maddox v. Runyon, 139 F.3d 1017, 1020–21, 76 FEP 1549 (5th Cir. 1998) (FLMRA election-of-remedies provision did not apply to postal employee so as to preclude simultaneous pursuit of union-assisted arbitration and EEO procedures, and thus did not render final agency decision invalid for purposes of timeliness of employee's Title VII action filed subsequent to arbitration decision); Stahl v. MSPB, 83 F.3d 409, 411 (Fed. Cir. 1996) (5 U.S.C. § 7121(d) does not apply to Postal Service employees).

[194]5 U.S.C. §§ 7121(d), 7122 (2000). The jurisdiction of each would depend upon the jurisdiction over the employee and the personnel action at issue. One court has held that if the employee elects to pursue the claim under a collective bargaining agreement, he or she *must* appeal an unfavorable arbitrator's decision to the EEOC in order to exhaust administrative remedies before filing in federal court. Johnson v. Peterson, 996 F.2d 397, 399–400, 62 FEP 232 (D.C. Cir. 1993).

[195]For the procedure for appealing the decision of an arbitrator or the FLRA to the EEOC, see 29 C.F.R. § 1614.403 (2005).

[196]*See* Sections II.A.2.a *supra* & III *infra*.

file in the appropriate district court within 90 calendar days after receiving notice of the final decision of the agency, or of the Office of Federal Operations if the matter is appealed to the EEOC. Federal employees may proceed to court after 180 calendar days from the filing of a grievance with their agency or an appeal to the EEOC, if there has been no decision by either since the time of filing.[197]

5. Retaliation

Retaliation claims may be processed under the regular EEO complaint procedures discussed above, and a complaint of retaliation may be consolidated with the original EEO complaint, if any.[198] Injunctive court relief can provide expedited protection from retaliation.[199]

Some courts require that a federal employee plaintiff seeking injunctive relief meet a heightened standard by showing that "extraordinary harm" would result if interim relief were denied.[200] In *Bonds v. Heyman*,[201] the court agreed that such a showing was required but found the federal employee, a 58-year-old woman who had worked for the Smithsonian Institution for nearly 40 years (and who had brought a previous discrimination claim that was settled), met this standard with respect to a pending reduction in force.[202]

---

[197] 29 C.F.R. § 1614.408 (2005).

[198] *Id.* § 1614.606.

[199] *See, e.g.,* Wagner v. Taylor, 836 F.2d 566, 570, 45 FEP 1184 (D.C. Cir. 1987) (interim injunctive relief from retaliatory acts is available for federal employees); Mitchell v. Secretary of Commerce, 715 F. Supp. 409, 410, 68 FEP 482 (D.D.C. 1989) (a permanent injunction properly was granted against future acts of retaliation), *aff'd sub nom.* Brown v. Secretary of Army, 918 F.2d 214, 68 FEP 485 (D.C. Cir. 1990). *But see* Knopp v. Magaw, 9 F.3d 1478, 1479, 63 FEP 353 (10th Cir. 1993) (injunctive relief from retaliatory acts was not necessary where the agency's decision and order to the employee occurred *before* the filing of his EEOC complaint).

[200] White v. Carlucci, 862 F.2d 1209, 1212 (5th Cir. 1989) (loss of employment fails to constitute irreparable harm); Wagner v. Taylor, 836 F.2d 566, 575 n.66, 45 FEP 1184 (D.C. Cir. 1987) (questioning whether heightened standard applies in Title VII cases); Garcia v. Lawn, 805 F.2d 1400, 1406, 42 FEP 873 (9th Cir. 1986) (same); Stromfeld v. Smith, 557 F. Supp. 995, 998, 31 FEP 204 (S.D.N.Y. 1983) (requiring showing of "extraordinary harm," and finding that involuntary transfer of employee from Atlantic City to Miami was not enough).

[201] 950 F. Supp. 1202, 1215, 72 FEP 1589 (D.D.C. 1997).

[202] 950 F. Supp. at 1215. The court premised this finding in part on the assumption that the plaintiff would be unlikely to find comparable, if any, employment in

A complainant also may file a retaliation charge with the Office of Special Counsel of the MSPB.[203] The Special Counsel has authority to investigate, make recommendations, and file original actions with the MSPB.[204] Although such charges generally would be referred to the employing agency for processing,[205] the Special Counsel on occasion has retained jurisdiction and filed actions with the MSPB in EEO retaliation cases.[206]

6. Affirmative Action

Section 717(b) imposes on federal agencies an obligation to develop affirmative action plans, which must include programs to provide training to enable employees to advance according to their potential.[207] The CSRA states that its prohibitions against discrimination "shall not be construed to extinguish or lessen any effort to achieve equal employment opportunity through affirmative action,"[208] and mandates special minority recruitment programs to correct any underrepresentation of minorities in any job category.[209] The CSRA also requires that persons in the Senior Executive Service be rated on whether they meet affirmative action goals as well as achieve EEO requirements.[210]

---

the event of her layoff, notwithstanding the fact that she was eligible for retirement with full benefits and at 80% of her top 3 years' salary.

[203]5 C.F.R. § 1800.1 (2005).

[204]Id. §§ 1201.121–.123, 1810.1.

[205]Id. § 1810.1.

[206]The log of special counsel filings with the MSPB is published in the GOVERN-MENT EMPLOYEE RELATIONS REPORT (BNA) (1987). The full extent of the Special Counsel's authority is beyond the scope of this book.

[207]42 U.S.C. § 2000e-16(b) (2000). Affirmative action obligations also are imposed by § 501 of the Rehabilitation Act, 29 U.S.C. § 791 (2000), with respect to handicapped employees and applicants with disabilities. An agency, as part of its affirmative action obligation under the Rehabilitation Act, must offer to reassign disabled employees who no longer can perform the duties of their positions even with reasonable accommodation, unless the agency demonstrates that reassignment would be an undue hardship. 29 C.F.R. § 1614.203(g) (2005). Affirmative action obligations of government contractors are considered in Chapter 38 (Federal Contractor Affirmative Action Compliance).

[208]5 U.S.C. § 2302(d) (2000).

[209]Id. § 7201.

[210]Id. § 4313. Performance evaluations of all other employees subject to this statute must be based on "objective criteria . . . related to the job in question." 5 U.S.C. § 4302(b)(1) (2000). This provision was intended to embody Title VII standards and to avoid the possibly discriminatory adverse effect of using subjective criteria for

One court has rejected claims that an agency's failure to carry out the § 717 and CSRA affirmative obligations creates enforceable rights in affected employees,[211] or is evidence of a Title VII violation.[212]

Federal agencies also must be cognizant of *reverse* discrimination claims regarding affirmative action plans, especially after the Supreme Court's holding in *Adarand Constructors, Inc. v. Peña*.[213] In *Adarand,* the Court held that "race-based preference" programs created by the federal government will be subjected to "the strictest judicial scrutiny," and programs that fall short of this test violate the Constitution.[214] In arriving at this holding, the Court specifically overruled the more lenient, "intermediate" scrutiny test for federal government affirmative action programs established in *Metro Broadcasting, Inc. v. FCC*.[215]

B. Employees of Congress

Section 717 covers only those legislative branch employees "having positions in the competitive service" (i.e., certain federal civil service jobs).[216] Not until passage of the Congressional

---

determining access to promotional and other employment opportunities. *See* Wells v. Harris, 1 MSPB 199, 223 (1979).

[211]*See, e.g.,* Liao v. Tennessee Valley Auth., 867 F.2d 1366, 1369 (11th Cir. 1989) (rejecting the plaintiff's claim that an employer is required to adhere to its voluntarily established affirmative action plan); Maddox v. Claytor, 764 F.2d 1539, 1557, 38 FEP 713 (11th Cir. 1985) (the defendant's failure to implement an affirmative action plan did not give rise to a Title VII claim; the burden is on the plaintiff to show discriminatory impact or treatment).

[212]Antol v. Perry, 82 F.3d 1291, 1301, 70 FEP 993 (3d Cir. 1996) (evidence that employer failed to live up to its voluntary affirmative action plan is relevant to question of discriminatory intent); Milburn v. West, 854 F. Supp. 1, 13 (D.D.C. 1994) (liability cannot be based on noncompliance with affirmative action plan, but noncompliance was considered with other factors as evidence of discriminatory intent), *aff'd,* 1995 WL 117983 (D.C. Cir. Feb. 7, 1995); Gonzales v. Police Dep't, San Jose, 901 F.2d 758, 761, 52 FEP 1132 (9th Cir. 1990) (same); Yatvin v. Madison Metro. Sch. Dist., 840 F.2d 412, 415–16, 45 FEP 1862 (7th Cir. 1988) (same). *But see Liao*, 867 F.2d at 1369 ("failure to give a preference under [a voluntary] plan cannot be used to support an allegation of discrimination").

[213]515 U.S. 200, 67 FEP 1828 (1995). *See generally* Chapters 37 ("Reverse" Discrimination and Affirmative Action) and 38 (Federal Contractor Affirmative Action Compliance).

[214]515 U.S. at 224.

[215]*Id.* at 225–27, *overruling* 497 U.S. 547, 53 FEP 161 (1990).

[216]42 U.S.C. § 2000e-16(a) (2000).

Accountability Act of 1995 (the 1995 Act)[217] were employees of Congress covered by any comprehensive antidiscrimination statute.

The Office of Compliance, created by the 1995 Act as an independent office in the legislative branch, administratively enforces the 1995 Act.[218] The chair of the office is appointed from among its five-member board of directors, which is appointed jointly by the leaders of the House and the Senate. The chair, with the board's approval, appoints an executive director and a general counsel. The executive director adopts procedural rules; the board adopts substantive regulations.[219] Proposed regulations must be published in the *Congressional Record* for a 30-day comment period. The House and Senate must approve any regulations after adoption by the board of directors.[220]

A complainant under the 1995 Act first must request counseling by the Office of Compliance not later than 180 days after the date of the alleged violation.[221] After a 30-day counseling period, which can be shortened by agreement, the complainant has 15 days to file a request for mandatory mediation. The mediation period lasts for 30 days, beginning on the date the request for mediation is received, and may be extended.[222]

If counseling and mediation do not resolve the claim, the complainant may elect between filing a complaint with the Office of Compliance or filing a civil action in district court. The election must be made not later than 90 days after the complainant

---

[217]*See* Section I.F *supra*. Under the 1995 Act, a "covered employee" is defined as "any employee of—(A) the House of Representatives; (B) the Senate; (C) the Capitol Guide Service; (D) the Capitol Police; (E) the Congressional Budget Office; (F) the Office of the Architect of the Capitol; (G) the Office of the Attending Physician; (H) the Office of Compliance; or (I) the Office of Technology Assessment." 2 U.S.C. § 1301(3).

[218]Pub. L. No. 104-1, § 301, 1995 U.S.C.C.A.N. (109 Stat.) 3, 24 (codified at 2 U.S.C. § 1381). Section 506 provides for the transition between the Government Employees Rights Act of 1991 and the 1995 Act. *See* Sections I.D & I.E *supra*. In brief, any complaints begun pursuant to the 1991 Act before the effective date of the 1995 Act continued to be subject to the pre-1995 procedures.

[219]Pub. L. No. 104-1, §§ 303–304, 1995 U.S.C.C.A.N. (109 Stat.) 3, 28–29 (codified at 2 U.S.C. §§ 1383, 1384 (2000)).

[220]*Id*. § 304(c).

[221]*Id*. § 402(a) (codified at 2 U.S.C. § 1402 (2000)); Britton v. Office of Compliance, 412 F.3d 1324, 1328 (Fed. Cir. 2005) (FMLA claim time-barred because counseling not sought within 180 days of leave being denied).

[222]*Id*. § 403 (codified at 2 U.S.C. § 1403 (2000)).

receives notice of the end of the mediation period, but no sooner than 30 days after receipt of such notification.[223]

If the complainant elects to go to district court, the action proceeds as a civil action (and, therefore, as a trial de novo),[224] with the right to a jury trial if compensatory damages are sought.[225] Just as in private sector Title VII and ADA cases under 42 U.S.C. § 1981a, the court may not inform the jury of the maximum amount of compensatory damages available.[226] The named defendant is the employing office that allegedly committed the violation or the office in which the violation allegedly occurred.[227] This differs from actions under § 717 involving executive agencies, which requires that the agency head be the named defendant.[228]

If the complainant elects to file a complaint with the Office of Compliance, the right to a trial de novo and jury trial are lost. Post-proceeding judicial review lies only in the U.S. Court of Appeals for the Federal Circuit. Similar to review in MSPB cases, the Federal Circuit can set aside a final administrative decision only if (1) it is arbitrary, capricious, an abuse of discretion, or otherwise not consistent with law; (2) it is not made consistent with required procedures; or (3) it is not supported by substantial evidence.[229]

If the administrative complaint option is taken, the respondent is the employing office. The executive director of the Office of Compliance appoints an independent hearing officer to hear the complaint, which the hearing officer may dismiss if it fails to state a claim upon which relief may be granted.[230]

Prehearing discovery is permitted, but the hearing (conducted in closed session) must commence not later than 60 days after the

---

[223]*Id.* § 404 (codified at 2 U.S.C. § 1404 (2000)). Venue lies either in the district of employment or in the District of Columbia. *Id.*

[224]*See* Sections III.A & III.C *infra.*

[225]Pub. L. No. 104-1, § 408, 1995 U.S.C.C.A.N. (109 Stat.) 3, 33 (codified at 2 U.S.C. § 1408(c) (2000)).

[226]*Id.*

[227]*Id.* (codified at 2 U.S.C. § 1408(b) (2000)).

[228]*See* Section III.A *infra.*

[229]Britton v. Office of Compliance, 412 F.3d 1324, 1327 (Fed. Cir. 2005) (citing 2 U.S.C. § 1407(d)). *Compare* Pub. L. No. 104-1, § 407, 1995 U.S.C.C.A.N. (109 Stat.) 3, 35 (codified at 2 U.S.C. § 1407 (2000)) *with* 5 U.S.C. § 7703(c) (2000).

[230]Pub. L. No. 104-1, § 405, 1995 U.S.C.C.A.N. (109 Stat.) 3, 33 (codified at 2 U.S.C. § 1405 (2000)).

complaint is filed. (The hearing officer may allow a 30-day extension for good cause.) Subpoena power exists. The general counsel (with board permission) may apply to the federal district court for an enforcement order if a person refuses to comply with a subpoena.[231]

The hearing officer has 90 days after the conclusion of the hearing to issue an opinion containing findings of fact and conclusions of law. The hearing officer is to be guided by judicial decisions and board decisions.[232]

Any aggrieved party has 30 days after the hearing officer issues an opinion to file a petition for review by the board.[233] The parties may make written submissions and, in the board's discretion, present oral argument. The board has the same limited scope of review as that of the Federal Circuit, as described above.[234]

The final step in the process is for an aggrieved party to file a petition for review with the Federal Circuit. Unlike the procedure under § 717 or in mixed cases, both the employing agency and the complainant have the right to seek review.[235]

C. Employees of the Judicial Branch

Employees of the judicial branch not in "competitive service" positions are not covered by the various antidiscrimination statutes.[236] However, the federal courts have set up internal EEO complaint processes, and these administrative processes should be

---

[231]*Id.* § 405(d)–(f).

[232]*Id.* § 405(g)–(h).

[233]The 30-day time limit for petitions to the Board of Directors of Office of Compliance seeking review of a hearing officer's decision is measured from the date of the decision being entered in the records of the office, not the date of the petitioner's receipt thereof. Britton v. Office of Compliance, 412 F.3d 1324, 1327 (Fed. Cir. 2005).

[234]Pub. L. No. 104-1, § 406 (codified at 2 U.S.C. § 1406 (2000)).

[235]*Id.* § 407 (codified at 2 U.S.C. § 1407 (2000)); *cf.* 42 U.S.C. § 2000e-16(c) (2000) (only a federal employee or an applicant for employment may bring a civil action, which must be asserted within 90 days of final agency action); 5 U.S.C. § 7703(a)(1) & (d) (2000) (federal employees or applicants for employment *and* director of OPM may obtain judicial review of an order or decision of the MSPB).

[236]*See* Dotson v. Griesa, 398 F.3d 156, 95 FEP 248 (2d Cir. 2005) (no cause of action for federal probation officer under § 1981, Civil Service Reform Act, or *Bivens*). Section 717 covers only those members in the judicial branch "having positions in the competitive service" (i.e., certain federal civil service jobs). *See* 42 U.S.C. § 2000e-16(a) (2000).

exhausted before an action is brought in federal court for discrimination made illegal by the Constitution.[237]

III. LITIGATION PROCEDURE

A. Administrative Exhaustion

A federal employee litigant may have a trial de novo in federal district court.[238] "Attached to that right, however, are certain preconditions."[239] A federal employee suing under Title VII or the Rehabilitation Act is required to timely comply with the statutory and administrative requirements reviewed in Section II, above.[240] Courts discuss the federal litigant's requirements in terms of exhaustion of administrative remedies and timeliness[241] and not infrequently conflate the two.

In *Brown v. GSA*, the Supreme Court held that § 717 requires exhaustion of the administrative process as a condition precedent to suit.[242] The provisions for the ADEA[243] differ from those of Title VII and the Rehabilitation Act, as do the provisions for EPA

---

[237]*See* Davis v. Passman, 442 U.S. 228, 234, 19 FEP 1390 (1979) (an employee of Congress, not covered by Title VII, could bring a *Bivens* action directly under the Constitution for alleged employment discrimination based on sex).

[238]Chandler v. Roudebush, 425 U.S. 840, 12 FEP 1368 (1976); *see also* Section III.C *infra*.

[239]Brown v. GSA, 425 U.S. 820, 835, 12 FEP 1361 (1976).

[240]*E.g., Brown*, 425 U.S. at 834–35 (upholding dismissal of Title VII claim because suit had not been filed within the applicable period specified by § 717(c)).

[241]*E.g.*, Boos v. Runyon, 201 F.3d 178, 10 AD 198 (2d Cir. 2000) (where former employee filed suit under Rehabilitation Act after filing EEOC appeal but prior to lapse of 180 days or receipt of final decision, court separately discussed exhaustion and timeliness requirements, as counseling contact was made after 45-day regulatory deadline). EEOC regulations provide that filing a civil action under Title VII, the ADEA, Rehabilitation Act, or EPA terminates EEOC processing of an appeal pending on that matter. 29 C.F.R. § 1614.409 (2005). For further discussion of timeliness, see Section III.B *infra*. *See generally* Chapter 26 (Timeliness).

[242]425 U.S. 820, 834–35, 12 FEP 1361 (1976); *accord* Misra v. Smithsonian Astrophysical Observatory, 248 F.3d 37, 39 (1st Cir. 2001) (citing *Brown*; Title VII provides the exclusive judicial remedy for claims of discrimination in federal employment).

[243]An ADEA claimant may file suit after giving 30 days' notice to EEOC within 180 days of the alleged discrimination, rather than proceeding through the administrative process. However, after initiating the administrative process, the employee must comply with its requirements. 29 C.F.R. §§ 1614.201, .407 (2005).

claimants,[244] but the ADEA claimant who invokes the administrative process must then exhaust administrative remedies.[245]

Federal employees filing under Title VII, the ADEA, or the Rehabilitation Act must exhaust their administrative remedies before filing suit; failure to do so constitutes grounds for dismissal or summary judgment in favor of the employer.[246] Although failure

---

[244]The EPA-based claimant is bound by the statutory time frames of the FLSA, regardless of whether he or she pursued any administrative complaint process. *See* Rossiter v. Potter, 357 F.3d 26, 28 (1st Cir. 2004).

[245]*E.g.*, Belgrave v. Peña, 254 F.3d 384, 386–87 (2d Cir. 2001) (ADEA and Title VII claims barred as untimely; employee failed to file formal administrative complaint within 15 days of notice of right to file formal complaint); Velazquez-Rivera v. Danzig, 234 F.3d 790, 795 (1st Cir. 2000) (federal employee failed to exhaust administrative remedies prior to filing ADEA claim because he made no contact with EEO counselor within 45 days; where "pre-complaint" letter filed with Navy EEO counselor alleged discrimination only on basis of disability but subsequent complaint form checked age and disability, plaintiff's failure to bring age claim to attention of counselor foreclosed the administrative investigation and ameliorative action contemplated by the exhaustion requirement); *accord* Jenkins v. Potter, 271 F. Supp. 2d 557 (S.D.N.Y. 2003) (appeal to EEOC untimely, notwithstanding administrative judge's clarification of relief ordered, issued 1 week after agency notice of final action; filing of suit within 90 days could not cure untimeliness of appeal, and terminal illness of wife of plaintiff's union representative did not warrant equitable tolling of time to file notice of appeal) (citing Conway v. Runyon, 1995 WL 88976, at *2 (N.D. Ill. Feb. 24, 1995)) (EEOC notice of right to file within 90 days is required by federal regulation but " 'does not serve to abrogate initial filing deadlines.' ").

[246]*Brown*, 425 U.S. at 834–35; *Belgrave*, 254 F.3d at 386–87; *Velazquez-Rivera*, 234 F.3d at 794–95 (summary judgment for agency, finding failure to exhaust administrative remedies prior to filing ADEA claim because federal employee did not raise age claim with EEO counselor within 45 days; continuing violation would only excuse untimely filing, not failure to exhaust an administrative requirement); Boos v. Runyon, 201 F.3d 178, 178, 10 AD 198 (2d Cir. 2000) (affirming dismissal on summary judgment where Rehabilitation Act plaintiff failed to timely seek EEO counseling); Randel v. U.S. Dep't of Navy, 157 F.3d 392, 395 (5th Cir. 1998) (found reprisal claim timely, but upheld denial of subject matter jurisdiction as to claim of race discrimination; employee failed to exhaust administrative remedies where he initiated second EEO proceeding alleging reprisal for filing a previous claim of race discrimination but had not raised claim of race discrimination in his second proceeding); Knopp v. Magaw, 9 F.3d 1478, 1479 (10th Cir. 1993) (requirement to exhaust EEOC administrative remedies before filing suit acts as a jurisdictional bar; district court lacked jurisdiction over federal employee's request for preliminary injunction where employee filed in district court before either issuance of a final decision or expiration of 180 days from date of his formal administrative complaint); Blank v. Donovan, 780 F.2d 808 (9th Cir. 1986) (employment contract negotiated as a result of an EEO complaint could not be enforced until all Title VII administrative remedies have been exhausted); Ethnic Employees v. Boorstin, 751 F.2d 1405, 1413 (D.C. Cir. 1985) (failure to file administrative complaint barred employee's Title VII claims); Hoffman v. Boeing, 596 F.2d 683, 686 (5th Cir. 1979) (per curiam) (affirming dismissal because federal employee did not exhaust his administrative remedies); Bush v. Engleman, 266 F. Supp. 2d 97, 101 (D.D.C. 2003) (plaintiff

to exhaust administrative remedies against the agency is a juris-dictional bar and may be fatal to a federal employee's § 717 discrimination claim,[247] the exhaustion rule is not an end in itself. "[I]t is a practical and pragmatic doctrine that must be tailored to fit the peculiarities of the administrative system Congress has created."[248] Thus, the exhaustion-of-remedies requirement is not absolute or insurmountable, and is considered in light of the purposes of the exhaustion rule.[249]

Equitable tolling applies to suits against the United States just as it does to suits against private defendants.[250] Generally, failure to comply with procedural requirements is not a jurisdictional bar to suit but is subject to equitable tolling, estoppel, and waiver.[251]

---

waived agency dismissal of claims; although she was not required to file a brief in support of her notice of appeal to the EEOC, even if her notice proffered that such a brief would be submitted, plaintiff's subsequent inaction amounted to abandonment of her appeal absent evidence, or complainant's allegation, that she appealed dismissal of those claims) (citing Watson v. Henderson, 222 F.3d 320, 322 (7th Cir. 2000)); Marshall v. James, 276 F. Supp. 2d 41, 50–51 (D.D.C. 2003) (although federal employee contacted counselor within 45-day limit, she did not file EEO complaint within 15-day deadline and failed to show basis for equitable tolling); Ramirez v. Runyon, 971 F. Supp. 363, 368–69 (C.D. Ill. 1997) (summary judgment granted against plaintiff who failed to exhaust administrative remedies with respect to breach of contract claim based on settlement agreement resolving prior EEO claim); Matos v. Hove, 940 F. Supp. 67 (S.D.N.Y. 1996) (employee failed to exhaust administrative remedies by refusing to provide requested information on specific acts of alleged discrimination to enable agency to investigate complaint).

[247]E.g., Knopp v. Magaw, 9 F.3d 1478, 1479 (10th Cir. 1993) (court lacked subject matter jurisdiction to issue preliminary injunction where 180 days had not elapsed prior to filing of civil action).

[248]President v. Vance, 627 F.2d 353, 363 (D.C. Cir. 1980) (reversing lower court decision limiting plaintiff's right to seek promotion as relief where agency admitted race discrimination but agreed that employee may not litigate promotion unless, at the administrative level, he sought promotion to a specific position or grade).

[249]Brown v. Marsh, 777 F.2d 8, 14 (D.C. Cir. 1985) ("Exhaustion under Title VII . . . should never be allowed to become so formidable a demand that it obscures the clear congressional purpose of rooting out . . . every vestige of employment discrimination within the federal government.") (internal quotation marks omitted).

[250]Irwin v. Department of Veterans Affairs, 498 U.S. 89, 96 (1990) (equitable tolling was not warranted where plaintiff's attorney was absent from his office when the EEOC notice was received).

[251]See Gibson v. West, 201 F.3d 990, 993 (7th Cir. 2000) (failure to exhaust administrative remedies is not a jurisdictional flaw but a precondition subject to doctrines of equitable tolling and estoppel), *vacated on other grounds*, West v. Gibson, 527 U.S. 212 (2000); Bowden v. United States, 106 F.3d 433, 437 (D.C. Cir. 1997) ("Like the suit-filing time limits [in § 717], the administrative time limits created by the EEOC erect no jurisdictional bars to bringing suit. . . . Like statutes of limitations, these time limits are subject to equitable tolling, estoppel, and waiver.").

Untimely exhaustion of administrative remedies is an affirmative defense to be demonstrated by the employer. An agency-defendant has the burden to prove by a preponderance of the evidence a plaintiff's failure to exhaust administrative remedies.[252] Under appropriate circumstances, the court may permit limited jurisdictional discovery on the narrow issue of whether plaintiff satisfied the obligation to engage in counseling at the administrative level and thus exhausted administrative remedies.[253] At least one circuit has held that if an agency wrongly dismisses a complaint for a purported failure to comply with a provision of the regulations the case will not be remanded for further administrative proceedings; rather, the complainant is entitled to proceed to trial de novo in federal court.[254] A valid election to pursue the grievance process under a collective bargaining agreement, as discussed above in Section II, will preclude an EEO complaint where the employee fails to exhaust the administrative remedies.[255]

---

[252]*See* Boos v. Runyon, 201 F.3d 178 (2d Cir. 2000) (counseling contact within 45 days is nonjurisdictional exhaustion requirement subject to equitable tolling, but plaintiff's vague and conclusory claim without particularized description of how her condition adversely affected her capacity to function generally or in pursuit of her rights was "manifestly insufficient" to meet her burden); *Bowden,* 106 F.3d at 437 ("Because untimely exhaustion of administrative remedies is an affirmative defense, the defendant bears the burden of pleading and proving it."); Herron v. Veneman, 305 F. Supp. 2d 64 (D.D.C. 2004) (agency-defendant has burden to prove failure to exhaust by preponderance of the evidence); Marshall v. James, 276 F. Supp. 2d 41, 50–52 (D.D.C. 2003) (failure to comply with procedural requirements, including timely exhaustion of remedies, is not a jurisdictional bar to suit but is affirmative defense that employer must plead and prove).

[253]*See* Artis v. Greenspan, 223 F. Supp. 2d 149, 155–56 (D.D.C. 2002) (where Board contended that plaintiff secretaries failed to provide its EEO counselors with specific and detailed information regarding the claims of racial discrimination and court determined that Board secretaries proffered evidence that EEO counseling was used to prevent a civil action in a federal district court, it was appropriate to permit the secretaries to conduct limited jurisdictional discovery on narrow issue of whether obligation to engage in counseling had been satisfied and that secretaries thus exhausted their administrative remedies); Pueschel v. Veneman, 185 F. Supp. 2d 566, 574 (D. Md. 2002) (discovery required on equitable tolling issue raised for first time in response to motion to dismiss Title VII action for failure to exhaust administrative remedies).

[254]*See* Wade v. Secretary of Army, 796 F.2d 1369, 1378 (11th Cir. 1986).

[255]*See, e.g.,* Douglas v. Norton, 2006 WL 137403, at *9 (10th Cir. Jan. 19, 2006) (employee contacted EEO counselor, abandoned the process to file a grievance, but the matter was not grievable; claim held to be time-barred due to failure to contact EEO counselor within 45 days and exhaust that process); Fitzgerald v. Secretary,

In *Brown*, the Supreme Court described the federal administrative exhaustion requirements and time limitations as "rigorous."[256] The agency accused of discrimination controls the counseling and investigation of the complaint and is in possession of much of the evidence. In 2002, Congress passed a bill directing a review of the EEOC's federal discrimination complaint administrative process requirements.[257] Under the current regulations, courts may find the exhaustion requirement has been satisfied where the complainant meets the various time periods set forth in the regulations and cooperates fully during the 180-day period provided for agency action by § 717.[258] Courts maintain that the doctrine of equitable

---

U.S. Dep't of Veterans Affairs, 121 F.3d 203, 206 (5th Cir. 1997); Vinieratos v. Secretary, U.S. Dep't of Air Force, 939 F.2d 762, 768, 772 (9th Cir. 1991) (where federal employee obstructs the smooth functioning of a properly elected administrative process and abandons that process to pursue a remedy elsewhere, he fails to exhaust his chosen remedy and thereby forecloses judicial review); Nichols v. Billington, 402 F. Supp. 2d 48, 77 (D.D.C. 2005) (employee failed to exhaust administrative remedy by pursuing negotiated grievance procedures but then failing to either appeal arbitrator's decision or file timely complaint with EEOC), *aff'd*, 2006 U.S. App. LEXIS 5853 (D.C. Cir. Mar. 7, 2006); Taylor v. Dam, 244 F. Supp. 2d 747 (S.D. Tex. 2003) (dismissing action for lack of subject matter jurisdiction, court held that federal employee irrevocably elected to pursue her claims through the negotiated grievance procedure rather than statutory EEO procedure; abandonment of grievance process and attempt to file an EEO complaint resulted in failure to exhaust the elected remedy, thus her Title VII claim was barred).

[256]Brown v. GSA, 425 U.S. 820, 833, 12 FEP 1361 (1976).

[257]The Notification and Federal Employee Anti-discrimination and Retaliation ("No Fear") Act of 2002 directs the General Accounting Office (GAO) to study "the effects of eliminating the requirement that Federal employees . . . exhaust administrative remedies before filing complaints with the Equal Employment Opportunity Commission." 116 Stat. 566, 571 (May 15, 2002) (citing 29 C.F.R. § 1614.206(a)(1)).

[258]*Compare* Martinez v. Department of Army, 317 F.3d 511 (5th Cir. 2003) (appellate court reversed dismissal and reinstated complaint where Army employee abandoned administrative process and filed action against Army; Army failed to take final action on employee's initial administrative complaint within 180 days and employee's abandonment of process after 180 days lapsed did not constitute a lack of cooperation with administrative proceedings or failure to exhaust), Tolbert v. United States, 916 F.2d 245, 249 (5th Cir. 1990) ("A Title VII plaintiff who appeals to the EEOC must await a decision by that office, or 180 days, whichever comes first, before filing in federal court."), Charles v. Garrett, 12 F.3d 870, 875 (9th Cir. 1993) (complainants who had cooperated for the required 180 days had fully exhausted their administrative remedies), Munoz v. Aldridge, 894 F.2d 1489, 1493–94 (5th Cir. 1990) (same) *and* Clark v. Chasen, 619 F.2d 1330, 1337 (9th Cir. 1980) (where the complainant had fully cooperated for "a period far in excess of the requisite 180 days," the district court erred in dismissing the plaintiff's complaint for failure to exhaust administrative remedies) *with* Jorge v. Rumsfeld, 404 F.3d 556, 564, 95 FEP 964

tolling applies "only in extraordinary and carefully circumscribed circumstances."[259] Courts have held equitable tolling not warranted where: plaintiff's attorney was absent from the office when the EEOC notice was received;[260] plaintiff's sleep apnea may have contributed to his inability to meet filing deadlines;[261] or plaintiff's union representative's wife suffered from terminal illness.[262] Moreover, an employee's prior experience with the EEO process may

---

(1st Cir. 2005) (in absence of affirmative misconduct, equitable estoppel not applicable to extend filing deadline based on Assistant U.S. Attorney suggesting plaintiff dismiss action due to difficulty finding witnesses), Burzynski v. Cohen, 264 F.3d 611, 620 (6th Cir. 2001) (application of equitable tolling doctrine not justified where statement in letters from EEO officers suggesting that employee might have 6 years within which to file ADEA suit were ambiguous), Khader v. Aspin, 1 F.3d 968, 971 (10th Cir. 1993) (plaintiff failed to provide additional information, abandoned the process, and filed in court; the case properly was dismissed), Vinieratos v. United States, 939 F.2d 762, 775 (9th Cir. 1991) (plaintiff tried to follow multiple administrative remedies but abandoned all of them before the 180 days had expired; this failure to exhaust barred suit), Johnson v. Bergland, 614 F.2d 415, 417–18 (5th Cir. 1980) (per curiam) (suit dismissed for failure to exhaust; plaintiff failed to comply with the valid administrative requirement that he make his generalized complaints more specific), Koch v. Donaldson, 260 F. Supp. 2d 86 (D.D.C. 2003) (15-day period for filing formal complaint equitably tolled where plaintiff demonstrated diligence by numerous attempts to fax complaint on due date and mailing and faxing it the next day; claim nevertheless dismissed for failure to exhaust administrative remedies because plaintiff's sleep apnea did not excuse failure to file timely notice of appeal to EEOC), aff'd, 2004 U.S. App. LEXIS 7015 (D.C. Cir. Apr. 7, 2004) and Taylor, 244 F. Supp. 2d at 759–60 (initial election to pursue Title VII claim through negotiated grievance procedure and subsequent abandonment of grievance process by attempting to file EEO claim resulted in failure to exhaust administrative remedies).

[259]Mondy v. Secretary of Army, 845 F.2d 1051, 1057 (D.C. Cir. 1988) (time limit set forth in 42 U.S.C. § 2000e-16 is nonjurisdictional and subject to equitable tolling); Cristwell v. Veneman, 224 F. Supp. 2d 54, 60 (D.D.C. 2002) (equitable tolling allows a plaintiff to avoid the bar of the limitations period if he is unable to obtain vital information bearing on the existence of his claims); Moore v. Potter, 217 F. Supp. 2d 364, 374 (E.D.N.Y. 2002) (pro se plaintiff did not actively pursue his judicial remedies during prescribed time limits; where there was no evidence that government tricked him into missing deadlines, no court led plaintiff to believe that he had done all that is required, and plaintiff was no stranger to the administrative process, plaintiff's failure to exhaust administrative remedies was due to his own lack of due diligence and equitable tolling not applied).

[260]Irwin v. Department of Veterans Affairs, 498 U.S. 89, 96 (1990).

[261]Koch, 260 F. Supp. 2d at 90–91.

[262]Jenkins v. Potter, 271 F. Supp. 2d 557, 560–61 (S.D.N.Y. 2003) (filing of suit within 90 days could not cure untimeliness of appeal; terminal illness of wife of plaintiff's union representative also did not warrant equitable tolling of time to file notice of appeal).

preclude a claim of equitable tolling due to imputed constructive notice.[263]

Courts have followed Title VII precedent to limit the scope of a judicial complaint to those issues that could have reasonably been expected to grow out of the administrative complaint or that were raised or addressed in the administrative process.[264] "A court can exercise jurisdiction over only those claims contained in a plaintiff's administrative complaint, or claims like and reasonably related to allegations in the administrative complaint, that were exhausted."[265]

---

[263]*Id.* at 563–64; *Moore*, 217 F. Supp. 2d at 374.

[264]*See, e.g.*, Marshall v. James, 276 F. Supp. 2d 41, 49 (D.D.C. 2003) (Title VII suit following an EEO complaint is limited to claims that are like or reasonably related to the allegations of the charge and growing out of such allegations); Watson v. Henderson, 222 F.3d 320, 321–22 (7th Cir. 2000) (employee who prevailed in EEOC administrative action was entitled to district court review of claim that Postal Service failed to implement EEOC decision to promote him with back pay and interest as remedy for race discrimination, but forfeited claim for compensatory damages where he claimed failure to implement was retaliation yet failed to present reprisal claim to EEO counselor); Randel v. U.S. Dep't of Navy, 157 F.3d 392, 395 (5th Cir. 1998) (finding reprisal claim timely, but upholding denial of subject matter jurisdiction as to employee's claim of race discrimination; employee failed to exhaust administrative remedies, even though the employee had initiated second EEO proceeding alleging reprisal (for filing a previous claim of race discrimination) where he failed to raise race discrimination claims in his second proceeding; plaintiff's race discrimination claim is "separate and distinct from his reprisal claim[;] . . . he must exhaust his administrative remedies on that claim before seeking review in federal court). *But see* Brown v. Snow, 2005 WL 975772 (D.D.C. Apr. 24, 2005) (agency not entitled to dismissal or summary judgment based on plaintiff's failure to raise claims in his EEO complaint; employee's claims of retaliation, hostile work environment, and failure to accommodate were "*legal claims*" or "*theories*" not to be confused with the "*factual allegations*" relied upon to support these claims, which had been raised in EEO complaints, and court would address viability of each theory) (emphasis in original); Roepsch v. Bentsen, 846 F. Supp. 1363, 1367–68 (E.D. Wis. 1994) (discussing the applicability of the "like or reasonably related" and "reasonably grow out of" standards in federal sector cases; holding that such claims are cognizable in court even though not specifically stated in the administrative process).

[265]Herron v. Veneman, 305 F. Supp. 2d 64, 71 (D.D.C. 2004) (internal citation and quotation marks omitted); *see also* Eastland v. Tennessee Valley Auth., 714 F.2d 1066, 1067–68 (11th Cir. 1983) (per curiam) (in class action construing the "like or related" rule, claims that were not raised by the class representatives in the administrative complaint disallowed); Ray v. Freeman, 626 F.2d 439, 443 (5th Cir. 1980) (plaintiff could not include in the court action subsequent acts not included in, considered in, or reasonably related to the administrative charge); President v. Vance, 627 F.2d 353, 362–63 (D.C. Cir. 1980) (where administrative claim alleged that African

The named defendant in suits brought under § 717(c) must be the agency or department head, not any other agency official or the agency or department itself.[266] A court *may* permit relation back to cure a failure to name and serve the head of the agency or department. For example, some courts have permitted a late amendment naming the correct defendant under the doctrine of equitable tolling, finding that the wording of the EEOC Notice of Right to File Civil Action, which states "[y]ou must name the appropriate official agency or department head as the defendant," is ambiguous and misleading.[267] Some courts have also permitted amendments under Federal Rule of Civil Procedure 15(c) to relate back to the original complaint, where amendment is made to cure a failure to name as a party and serve the head of the government agency;[268] other courts— where the notice element of the relation-back doctrine was absent— have not.[269] The Fourth Circuit has permitted a federal employee's

---

Americans were denied promotional opportunities above a specific GS level, but did not request promotion as a remedy, exhaustion was satisfied; exhaustion relates to discrimination issues, not remedies); Kulkarni v. Alexander, 662 F.2d 758, 762 (D.C. Cir. 1978) (where the plaintiff alleged that RIF notices were in retaliation for having filed a discrimination claim, there is no requirement to file a separate charge each time a RIF notice is received).

[266]Section 717(c) provides that in civil actions "the head of the department, agency, or unit, as appropriate, shall be the defendant." 42 U.S.C. § 2000e-16(c) (2000); *see* Mulhall v. Ashcroft, 287 F.3d 543 (6th Cir. 2002) (proper defendant in Title VII action by police officer dismissed from joint task force of FBI was U.S. Attorney General, not FBI; held district court order granting summary judgment to FBI was final order even though order failed to specify dismissal of Attorney General, neither party prejudiced by treating order as final, and Attorney General, not FBI, was proper defendant); Bates v. Tennessee Valley Auth., 851 F.2d 1366, 1368 (11th Cir. 1988) (dismissing as named defendants the federal agency and the director of the division in which the plaintiff was employed).

[267]*E.g.,* Brezovski v. United States Postal Serv., 905 F.2d 334, 336–37 (10th Cir. 1990) (it is unclear whether "head" modifies only "department" or also "agency"); Warren v. Department of Army, 867 F.2d 1156, 1160 (8th Cir. 1989) (same). *But see* Gardner v. Gartman, 880 F.2d 797, 799 (4th Cir. 1989) (no relation back permitted; finding statutory language clear and unambiguous; no discussion of equitable tolling).

[268]*E.g.,* Jarrell v. United States Postal Serv., 753 F.2d 1088, 1091 (D.C. Cir. 1985) (on remand the plaintiff was allowed a reasonable time to amend his complaint to name the head of the government agency (Postmaster General)); Allen v. Bolger, 597 F. Supp. 482, 484 (D. Kan. 1984) (where the action was properly commenced within the 30-day statutory period, the court allowed the plaintiff's amendment to relate back).

[269]*See, e.g., Bates,* 851 F.2d at 1369 (the relation-back doctrine does not apply where the proper defendants were neither served with nor put on notice of the complaint within the 30-day limitations period); Koucky v. Department of Navy, 820 F.2d 300, 302 (9th Cir. 1987) (same); Romain v. Shear, 799 F.2d 1416, 1418–19 (9th Cir. 1986) (per curiam) (same); Hale v. United States Postal Serv., 663 F. Supp. 7, 9, 41 (N.D. Ill. 1986) (same), *aff'd mem.,* 826 F.2d 1067 (7th Cir. 1987).

claim under the ADA against a union and union local where the labor union constitutes a labor organization as defined in Title VII and, by proxy, the ADA.[270]

B. Timeliness

In pure, non-mixed, EEO cases, federal sector complainants may file suit within 90 days after notice of a final order by the employing agency following an administrative judge's decision,[271] after notice of a final agency decision,[272] or after giving the agency 180 days to act.[273] An employee who brings an action where the agency fails to take final action within the required 180 days may have exhausted his or her administrative remedies.[274] If an administrative appeal is taken to the EEOC, the complainant may file suit within 90 days after notice of the EEOC's final decision or, absent a final decision, 180 days after the appeal was first filed with the EEOC.[275]

In mixed EEO cases initiated with the employer agency,[276] there are nine points at which a complainant may file suit. An employee who has not appealed his or her mixed case to the MSPB may file a discrimination action in federal district court within 30 days of a final decision by the employing agency or after 120 days have

---

[270]Jones v. Postal Workers, 192 F.3d 417 (4th Cir. 1999) (Postal Service employee could pursue claim under the ADA against union and union local because labor union that represents federal employees constitutes a labor organization as defined in Title VII and by ADA; EEOC engaged in permissible statutory construction in so concluding; Rehabilitation Act did not bar Postal Service employee from maintaining disability discrimination suit against union and union local under ADA).

[271]29 C.F.R. § 1614.110(a) (2005).

[272]*Id.* § 1614.407(a).

[273]*Id.* § 1614.407(b).

[274]Martinez v. White, 317 F.3d 511 (5th Cir. 2003) (plaintiff entitled to proceed in district court where Army failed to take final action on employee's administrative complaint of race and gender discrimination within 180 days and employee abandoned administrative process by withdrawing request for EEO hearing after 180 days had elapsed).

[275]29 C.F.R. §1614.407(c), (d) (2005). *Compare* Brown v. Snow, 440 F.3d 1259, 1262–63 (11th Cir. 2006) (early filing prior to expiration of 180 days did not deprive court of jurisdiction where plaintiff had cooperated in good faith with EEOC) *with* Charles v. Garrett, 12 F.3d 870, 874 (9th Cir. 1993) (federal employee must sue in federal court under Title VII not more than 180 days after first filing an administrative appeal to the EEOC, even if a subsequent appeal is filed) *and* Tolbert v. United States, 916 F.2d 245, 249 (5th Cir. 1990) (a premature filing in federal court before the expiration of 180 days after filing appeal to EEOC is not cured by intervening issuance of final decision by EEOC).

[276]*See* Section II.A.2.b *supra.*

passed without a decision. An employee who has appealed his mixed case to the MSPB may file a discrimination action in federal district court within 30 days of the MSPB's final decision if he has not petitioned the EEOC to review the decision, or after 120 days have passed without a final decision.[277] However, once an employee has chosen to appeal the mixed case to the EEOC or the MSPB, she must exhaust her claims in that forum before filing suit in federal district court.[278] Mixed cases must be appealed to the district courts.[279] An appeal to a federal district court from an MSPB decision in a mixed case must identify a "judicially reviewable action" in order for a federal district court to exercise de novo review of the discrimination claim.[280]

Failure to file a Title VII action within 90 days of receipt of a final agency decision warrants dismissal of claims in federal district

---

[277]The legislative history of the CSRA, H.R. CONF. REP. NO. 95-1717, 95th Cong., 2d Sess. 141–42, *reprinted in* 1978 U.S.C.C.A.N. 2860, 2875, states those times to be as follows:

(1)   120 days after filing a complaint with the employing agency even if the agency has not issued a final decision by that time.
(2)   30 days after the employing agency's initial decision.
(3)   120 days after filing a petition with the MSPB if the MSPB has not yet made a decision.
(4)   30 days after an MSPB decision. If the employee petitions EEOC to review the matter and EEOC denies the petition, the 30-day period in this case runs from the denial of such a petition by EEOC.
(5)   30 days after the EEOC decision, if EEOC agrees with the MSPB.
(6)   30 days after MSPB reconsideration if MSPB agrees with the EEOC.
(7)   30 days after the Special Panel makes a decision.
(8)   180 days after filing a petition with the EEOC for reconsideration of an MSPB decision, if a final agency decision by EEOC, MSPB, or the Panel has not been reached by that time.

The first two steps do not apply if the claim is initiated by direct appeal to the MSPB.
[278]*E.g.*, Hill v. Potter, 2002 WL 226755, at *8 (N.D. Ill. Feb. 14, 2002) (court dismissed seven EEO claims, finding no "judicially reviewable action" by the MSPB and plaintiff failed to exhaust administrative remedies: "[P]ermitting Hill to maintain these claims in the present action would render the requirements for a 'judicially reviewable action' and exhaustion of remedies meaningless. Hill made a token attempt to exhaust his remedies by appealing to the MSPB. That token effort should not be rewarded." Once employees chose to appeal a mixed case to a particular agency (such as the EEOC or the MSPB), they must exhaust their claims in that forum before filing suit in federal district court.); McAdams v. Reno, 64 F.3d 1137, 1142 (8th Cir. 1995) (same).
[279]Coffey v. United States, 939 F. Supp. 185, 192 (E.D.N.Y. 1996). *But see* Davidson v. United States Postal Serv., 24 F.3d 223, 224 (Fed. Cir. 1994) (mixed case presented to MSPB may be appealed to Federal Circuit if petitioner files an explicit waiver of the discrimination claim).
[280]5 U.S.C. § 7702(a)(3) (2000).

court.[281] The EEOC's position is that a federal employee who chooses to pursue administrative remedies must file an ADEA action within the same time period as an action under Title VII.[282] After the Civil Rights Act of 1991,[283] the Title VII time period is 90 days from the conclusion of the administrative process.[284] Although finding the filing period nonjurisdictional and subject to equitable tolling, most courts accept the EEOC's position that the would-be federal ADEA litigant who pursues administrative remedies must file suit within the 90-day Title VII period.[285] Neither notice nor

---

[281]*See, e.g.*, Irwin v. Department of Veterans Affairs, 498 U.S. 89, 96 (1990) (federal employee's action, filed after the statutory limitations period—then 30 days after receipt of the EEOC's right-to-sue letter—properly was dismissed; receipt by the plaintiff's lawyer's office of the right-to-sue letter began the running of the statutory period; the attorney's excusable neglect was not grounds for equitable tolling); Maddox v. Runyon, 139 F.3d 1017 (5th Cir. 1998) (Title VII action filed more than 90 days after final agency decision was untimely; pursuit of internal grievance procedures did not meet exhaustion requirement and thus agency failure to defer EEO complaint until completion of grievance/arbitration process did not excuse untimeliness of Title VII action); Grey v. Potter, 2003 WL 1923733 (M.D.N.C. Apr. 21, 2003) (claims alleging failure to accommodate disability and race and disability disparate treatment dismissed where employee failed to make timely EEO counseling contact within requisite 45-day period; additional claims held untimely where employee failed to file civil action within 90 days of notice of final action); Johnston v. O'Neill, 272 F. Supp. 2d 696 (N.D. Ohio 2003) (federal employee failed to exhaust administrative remedies as to Title VII claim of hostile work environment where agency dismissed that claim for failure to state a claim and untimeliness, and informed employee of right to appeal to EEOC within 30 days or to file action in federal court within 90 days, and employee failed to do so). *But cf.* Williams v. Hidalgo, 663 F.2d 183, 188 (D.C. Cir. 1980) (a settlement agreement preserving the right to apply to court for attorney's fees was a final agency action, but the 30-day suit-filing period did not begin to run in the absence of proper notice of final agency action, as required by the regulations).
[282]29 C.F.R. § 1614.408(c) (2005); 57 Fed. Reg. 12,640 (1992). The ADEA plaintiff has the option of (1) filing suit after giving the EEOC at least 30 days' written notice of the intent to file suit, which notice must issue within 180 days of the alleged discriminatory act (29 U.S.C. § 633a(d) (2000); 29 C.F.R. § 1614.201 (2005)) or (2) first pursuing administrative remedies for EEO (29 U.S.C. § 633a(d) (2000); 29 C.F.R. § 1614.201 (2005)) or mixed-case complaints, and then filing suit within the Title VII time period. 29 U.S.C. § 633a(d) (2000); 29 C.F.R. § 1614.201 (2005); *cf.* Edmondson v. Simon, 24 FEP 1031, 1033 (N.D. Ill. 1978) (that an age complaint was pending before the CSC for more than 2 years did not bar suit on the same issue; the exhaustion requirement was satisfied after 180 days).
[283]5 C.F.R. § 1201.151 (2005); 29 C.F.R. § 1614.302 (2005).
[284]*See* Lavery v. Marsh, 918 F.2d 1022, 1024–25 (1st Cir. 1990) ("The appropriate statute of limitations in ADEA cases where the employee first pursues agency relief is 'the same as that for claims pursuant to Title VII of the Civil Rights Act—thirty days [now 90 days, pursuant to an amendment to Title VII] following receipt of the final administrative order.' ").
[285]*See, e.g.*, Montoya v. Chao, 296 F.3d 952 (10th Cir. 2002) (as a matter of first impression in the Tenth Circuit, the period of limitation prescribed by the CSRA

resort to administrative processes is required for suits brought under the Equal Pay Act.[286]

The time period for filing suit begins to run from the date the complainant's attorney receives, on behalf of the complainant, an EEOC notice of final action (or, if earlier, the date the complainant himself or herself is deemed to have received notice).[287] At least one court has explicitly stated that reliance on the EEOC's regulation providing that "time frames for receipt of materials shall be computed from the time of receipt by the attorney"[288] is "misplaced."[289]

---

for bringing an action in federal court was not jurisdictional and was subject to equitable tolling; ADEA complaint dismissed; equitable tolling of the limitations period was not warranted on ground that former federal employee was misdirected and given bureaucratic runaround absent assertion that he was actively or intentionally misled); Burzynski v. Cohen, 264 F.3d 611 (6th Cir. 2001) (Title VII's 90-day limitations period for filing civil action is appropriate period to apply to ADEA claim brought by federal employee pursuing administrative remedies before going to court; correspondence from EEO officers stating that employee might have 6 years within which to file age discrimination suit was not basis for equitable tolling of such period; ambiguity reflected in letters did not amount to affirmative misconduct that would justify equitable tolling); Edwards v. Shalala, 64 F.3d 601, 606 (11th Cir. 1995) (Title VII limitations period for private sector actions is the appropriate analogous limitations period to apply to federal employee ADEA claims); Jones v. Runyon, 32 F.3d 1454, 1456 (10th Cir. 1994) (Title VII limitations period applicable to federal employee Title VII claims applies to federal employee ADEA claim).

[286]29 C.F.R. § 1614.408 (2005).

[287]29 C.F.R. § 1614.605(d) (2005) ("When the complainant designates an attorney as representative, service of all official correspondence shall be made on the attorney and the complainant, but time frames for receipt of materials shall be computed from the time of receipt by the attorney."); see Irwin v. Department of Veterans Affairs, 498 U.S. 89, 92 (1990) (affirming Fifth Circuit's holding that notice of a final action is considered received by a claimant when the notice reaches either a claimant or the claimant's attorney, whichever comes first, and that attorney's absence from office at time of receipt did not justify tolling: "[P]rinciples of equitable tolling . . . do not extend to what is at best a garden variety claim of excusable neglect."); see also id. at 97 (White, J., concurring) ("I agree with the Court that the 30-day period under 42 U.S.C. § 2000e-16(c) begins to run when the notice from the EEOC is delivered either to the claimant or the claimant's attorney."); McKay v. England, 55 Fed. R. Serv. 3d 169 (D.D.C. 2003) (summary judgment granted because plaintiff failed to file in district court within 90 days of date that he received the Navy's final order, notwithstanding that complaint was filed timely based on later receipt of final order by plaintiff's attorney).

[288]29 C.F.R. § 1614.605(d) (2005).

[289]McKay, 55 Fed. R. Serv. 3d 169 (court noted that the same regulation requires the complainant "at all times be responsible for proceeding with the complaint whether or not he or she has designated a representative") (citing 29 C.F.R. § 1614.605(e)).

The court reasoned that the regulation applies to administrative proceedings before the EEOC and does not purport to apply to the limitations period for filing suit in federal court.[290] The cases are in conflict as to whether notice may be imputed to the plaintiff when the EEOC sends notice to the plaintiff's former attorney where the plaintiff has not notified the EEOC that he or she is no longer represented by the attorney.[291]

Courts will dismiss actions based on the plaintiff's failure to initiate the administrative charge procedure within the time period required by the regulations[292] or at all,[293] or for failure to comply

---

[290]*Id.*

[291]*Compare* Mosley v. Peña, 100 F.3d 1515, 1518 (10th Cir. 1996) (notice of final action to former attorney properly imputed to plaintiff because plaintiff had not notified EEOC that she was no longer represented by counsel) *with* Coates v. Shalala, 914 F. Supp. 110, 112 (D. Md. 1996) (EEOC notice of decision to attorney not imputed to plaintiff where attorney-client relationship had been terminated prior to attorney's receipt of notice), *aff'd*, 133 F.3d 914 (4th Cir. 1997).

[292]*See, e.g.*, Downey v. Runyon, 160 F.3d 139, 143–46 (2d Cir. 1998) (Civil Service Reform Act entitled federal employee to seek de novo review of discrimination claim in federal district court after MSPB dismissed his mixed appeal on grounds of untimeliness without reaching merits of his discrimination claim; employee would not ultimately be entitled to review on merits in district court if court determined employee failed to exhaust his administrative remedies under discrimination statutes); Bickham v. Miller, 584 F.2d 736, 738 (5th Cir. 1978) (per curiam) (dismissal was upheld where complaint procedures were not initiated within 30 days of learning of the denial of the promotion application); Grey v. Potter, 2003 WL 1923733 (M.D.N.C. Apr. 23, 2003) ("A court is not required to consider a complaint whose allegations are not raised with an EEO counselor within 45 days of the alleged discriminatory action even if the agency investigates the claim."); Cones v. Shalala, 945 F. Supp. 342, 348 (D.D.C. 1996) (failure to file administrative complaint within 45 days bars subsequent lawsuit), *rev'd*, 199 F.3d 512 (D.C. Cir. 2000); Kennedy v. Runyon, 933 F. Supp. 480, 485 (W.D. Pa. 1996) (same); Aikens v. Bolger, 23 FEP 1138, 1141 (D.D.C. 1979) (issues not the subject of a timely administrative complaint were excluded from the court complaint), *rev'd and remanded on other grounds sub nom.* Aikens v. United States Postal Serv. Bd. of Governors, 642 F.2d 514 (D.C. Cir. 1980), *vacated and remanded*, 453 U.S. 902 (1981); *see also* Cox v. Rumsfeld, 2003 WL 21691044 (W.D. Wis. Jun. 19, 2003) (discussing 29 C.F.R. § 1614.105(a)(1) and citing cases with differing interpretations of the requirement that federal employee initiate contact with an EEO counselor within 45 days after the date of alleged discriminatory act; actual contact required for "discrete acts") (citing National R.R. Passenger Corp. v. Morgan, 536 U.S. 101 (2002) (unless discriminatory acts are part of a "continuing violation" as in a hostile work environment claim, timely meeting administrative requirements for one act will not be sufficient to satisfy exhaustion requirement for other acts)); Cherosky v. Henderson, 330 F.3d 1243, 14 AD 673 (9th Cir. 2003) (applying *Morgan* to claim under Rehabilitation Act).

[293]*See* Section III.A *supra*.

with the time periods for filing formal complaints or appeals.[294] The EEOC's regulations provide, however, that the administrative time periods are not jurisdictional and "are subject to waiver, estoppel, and equitable tolling."[295] The same is true of the limitations periods for filing suit.[296] Thus, some cases suggest that a court will excuse lateness when the complainant was unaware, through no fault of his or her own, of the time limitations for initiating an administrative complaint[297] or where the failure to comply was attributable to

---

[294]*E.g.*, Marshall v. James, 276 F. Supp. 2d 41 (D.D.C. 2003) (discrimination claim barred; although federal employee contacted counselor within 45-day limit, she did not file EEO complaint within 15-day deadline and failed to show basis for equitable tolling); Parker v. Boorstin, 23 FEP 365, 366 (D.D.C. 1980) (dismissing complaint for failure to exhaust; after counseling, the plaintiff was given a written notice and orally was advised that he had 10 days within which to file a formal charge, but he did not do so for a month and a half and gave no reason justifying the delay); Quintana v. Bergland, 23 FEP 1489, 1490–91 (D.N.M. 1980) (dismissing the case for failure to exhaust where the notice of adverse agency decision provided the plaintiff with notice that the employee had 15 days to appeal or 30 days to file suit, and the appeal was filed 5 or 6 days late).

[295]29 C.F.R. § 1614.604(c) (2005); *see* Boddy v. Dean, 821 F.2d 346, 350 (6th Cir. 1987) (the then 30-day period for timely filing a charge with the EEOC is not a jurisdictional prerequisite for a federal employee's discrimination filing in a district court).

[296]Irwin v. Department of Veterans Affairs, 498 U.S. 89, 95–96 (1990) (equitable tolling has been allowed where claimant actively pursued his judicial remedies by filing a defective pleading during the statutory period, or has been induced or tricked by adversary's misconduct into allowing the filing deadline to pass; declining to apply equitable tolling to late filing); Johnston v. O'Neill, 272 F. Supp. 2d 696 (N.D. Ohio 2003) (in determining whether equitable tolling is available, a court considers (1) lack of actual notice of filing requirement, (2) lack of constructive knowledge of filing requirement, (3) diligence in pursuing one's rights, (4) absence of prejudice to the defendant, and (5) a plaintiff's reasonableness in remaining ignorant of the notice requirement; deadline not tolled where employee had actual notice of filing requirements; fact that plaintiff was pro se during administrative process did not justify equitable tolling).

[297]*Compare* Bayer v. Department of Treasury, 956 F.2d 330, 334 (D.C. Cir. 1992) (the employee's affidavit stating that he had no knowledge of the applicable time limits raised an issue of fact to be determined on credibility grounds) *and* Wells v. Perry, 22 FEP 665, 668 (D.D.C. 1977) (the 15-day time period for filing a formal complaint did not start to run automatically upon the expiration of the regulatory time period where an EEO counselor failed to provide the complainant with the requisite notice necessary to trigger the deadline) *with* White v. Bentsen, 31 F.3d 474, 475 (7th Cir. 1994) (inaccuracies in the hearing transcript are not grounds for tolling the limitations period for appealing an agency decision to the EEOC where the employee was aware of the time limits) *and* Taylor v. Espy, 816 F. Supp. 1553, 1559–60 (N.D. Ga. 1993) (no equitable tolling allowed where plaintiff's attorney failed to file suit in a timely manner after he received EEOC's decision; "each party . . . is considered to have notice of all facts . . . charged upon the attorney").

the agency.[298] Courts may find an agency to have waived the exhaustion requirement where failure to exhaust was not raised at the administrative stage of the matter.[299] However, an agency investigation of an allegation without more does not rise to the level of affirmative misconduct so as to waive timeliness.[300]

Courts may equitably toll the 45-day period for initiating a counseling contact where an employee is sufficiently mentally disabled to justify tolling.[301] Commenting that the 45-day limitation

---

[298]See, e.g., Burzynski v. Cohen, 264 F.3d 611, 620 (6th Cir. 2001) (application of equitable tolling doctrine not justified where court determined that ambiguity in letters from EEO officers stating that employee might have 6 years within which to file ADEA suit did not constitute affirmative misconduct and was not a basis for equitable tolling; nor was attorney's withdrawal from case where withdrawal took place several months after filing deadline passed); Weick v. O'Keefe, 26 F.3d 467, 470–71 (4th Cir. 1994) (equitable tolling appropriate when complainant was falsely told that problems giving rise to the EEOC complaint had been resolved); Richerson v. Jones, 572 F.2d 89, 95–96 (3d Cir. 1978) (where, at the urging of an EEO counselor and without notice about the effect of withdrawal, plaintiff withdrew his formal charge to permit informal handling, and then later sought to reinstate it, the subsequent suit was timely even though it was filed less than 180 days after the charge-reinstatement letter).

[299]Ester v. Principi, 250 F.3d 1068, 1072–73 (7th Cir. 2001) (court found waiver of exhaustion defense where agency failed to assert defense and issued final agency decision on the merits).

[300]See Grey v. Potter, 2003 WL 1923733, at *9 (M.D.N.C. Apr. 21, 2003) (mere investigation of employee's harassment allegation does not rise to level of affirmative misconduct so as to waive agency's timeliness objection first raised in district court); Kammaapel v. Hudson, 1993 WL 498234, at *10 (4th Cir. Dec. 3, 1993) (same); Rowe v. Sullivan, 967 F.2d 186, 191 (5th Cir. 1992) (EEO counselor's decision to investigate does not create an automatic claim for equitable estoppel of the 45-day deadline); Boyd v. United States Postal Serv., 752 F.2d 410, 414 (9th Cir. 1985) ("mere receipt and investigation of a complaint does not waive objection to failure to comply with original filing deadline when the investigation does not result in administrative finding of discrimination"); see also Blount v. Shalala, 1999 WL 978892, at *1 (4th Cir. Oct. 28, 1999) (agency does not waive timeliness defense by accepting and investigating an employment discrimination claim filed after the 15-day deadline).

[301]Boos v. Runyon, 201 F.3d 178, 181, 10 AD 198 (2d Cir. 2000) (45-day period for counseling contact is nonjurisdictional exhaustion requirement subject to equitable tolling; nevertheless, court affirmed grant of summary judgment because plaintiff bears burden of demonstrating that circumstances justify equitable tolling and whether a person is sufficiently mentally disabled to justify tolling of a limitation period is highly case-specific; plaintiff's vague and conclusory claim of "paranoia, panic attacks, and depression," without a particularized description of how her condition adversely affected her capacity to function generally or in relationship to pursuit of her rights was manifestly insufficient to justify further inquiry into equitable tolling) (citing Miller v. Runyon, 77 F.3d 189, 191 (7th Cir. 1996)); Nunnally v. MacCausland, 996 F.2d 1, 5 (1st Cir. 1993) (mental illness provides an available

period for initiating counseling contact is "unusually short," the Second Circuit found that an employee should not have been charged with knowledge of the time limit on the basis of his awareness that he was obligated to contact an EEO counselor.[302] Although the employee is required to initiate a counseling contact at the employing agency, courts have occasionally misidentified the counselor or investigator as an EEOC employee.[303]

Failure to timely comply with the administrative process may limit the scope of the complaint. Courts have excluded from judicial complaints incidents occurring before more than the regulatory period (formerly 30 days, now 45 days) for initiating administrative procedures with the employing agency.[304] Where the plaintiff

---

ground for equitable tolling); Downey v. Runyon, 160 F.3d 139, 145–45 (2d Cir. 1998) (timeliness is not jurisdictional prerequisite but is subject to equitable tolling); Briones v. Runyon, 101 F.3d 287, 290 (2d Cir. 1996).

[302]See Pauling v. Secretary, Dep't of the Interior, 160 F.3d 133, 136 (2d Cir. 1998) (finding federal employee's affidavit sufficient to raise triable issue of material fact as to whether informational posters placed him on constructive notice of 45-day limitation period for commencing administrative proceedings; employee should not have been charged with knowledge of time limit on basis of his awareness of EEO process generally and awareness of obligation to contact EEO counselor did not preclude extension of 45-day period under 29 C.F.R. § 1614.105(a)(2)); see also Pueschel v. Veneman, 185 F. Supp. 2d 566 (D. Md. 2002) (where daughter brought Title VII claim on behalf of deceased federal employee, motion to dismiss denied without prejudice to permit discovery on equitable tolling issue as to whether agency official affirmatively lulled federal employee, either personally or through her daughter, into not making informal contact with EEO counselor within 45 days of alleged discrimination).

[303]See Gibson, 201 F.3d at 990, 992 (7th Cir. 2000) (court noted its previous holding that request to an EEOC investigator for "monetary cash award" did not put EEOC on notice he was seeking compensatory damages). The EEO investigators in the federal sector are not employed by EEOC but rather by the agency that is the subject of the investigation. Generally, the EEOC does not enter the process until complainant appeals an agency final order or requests a hearing before an EEOC administrative judge. 29 C.F.R. §§ 1614.102–.109 (2005); see also Velazquez-Rivera v. Danzig, 234 F.3d 790, 794 (1st Cir. 2000) (reference to EEOC counselor at initial counseling stage with agency EEO counselor).

[304]E.g., Burzynski v. Cohen, 264 F.3d 611, 617–18 (6th Cir. 2001) (denying claim of continuing violation, finding no present discriminatory activity or longstanding demonstrable policy of discrimination that would give rise to claim of continuing violation, inasmuch as employees failed to allege circumstances of nonselections, failed to provide evidence of discriminatory animus linking various nonselections, and provided no evidence of policy of discrimination); Boos, 201 F.3d at 184 (Rehabilitation Act claim dismissed for failure to seek counseling within 45 days of alleged incidents of discrimination); Aikens v. United States Postal Serv., 642 F.2d 514, 516–17 (D.C. Cir. 1980) (issues that arose more than 30 days prior to initiating charge properly are excluded), vacated and remanded on other grounds, 453 U.S. 902 (1981).

demonstrates a continuing violation under prevailing legal precedent,[305] a plaintiff may revive otherwise time-barred incidents.[306] Complainant's failure to exhaust or to pursue compensatory damages in an administrative proceeding may result in forfeiture.[307]

Although Rehabilitation Act actions are subject to equitable tolling, courts have required an appropriate explanation for a delay in filing.[308] The Eleventh Circuit declined to hold that the Supreme

---

[305]*See generally* Chapters 26 (Timeliness) and 28 (Title VII Litigation Procedures). Cases applying the continuing violation theory prior to the Supreme Court's decision in *National Railroad Passenger Corp. v. Morgan*, 536 U.S. 101 (2002), should be interpreted in light of *Morgan*. *See, e.g.*, Costanzo v. Potter, 2003 WL 1701998 (S.D.N.Y. Mar. 31, 2003) (claims concerning discrete acts—as opposed to those allegedly part of an ongoing hostile work environment—occurring before the 45-day cutoff period and as to which employee failed to contact EEO counselor within 45 days, cannot be converted into a single unlawful practice for purposes of timely filing and thus were time-barred; claims are thus " 'not actionable if time barred, even when they are related to acts alleged in timely filed charges' ").

[306]*Compare* Anderson v. Reno, 190 F.3d 930 (9th Cir. 1999) (sexual harassment over 7-year period constituted continuing violation) *and* Ciafrei v. Bentsen, 877 F. Supp. 788, 794 (D.R.I. 1995) (allowing plaintiff to invoke continuing violation theory as to allegations that she was harassed and discriminated against due to her gender, coupled with her appearance and size) *with* Burzynski, 264 F.3d at 617–18 (denying class claim of continuing violation, finding no present discriminatory activity or longstanding demonstrable policy of discrimination that would give rise to claim of continuing violation, inasmuch as employees failed to allege circumstances of nonselections, failed to provide evidence of discriminatory animus linking various nonselections, and provided no evidence of policy of discrimination), Janneh v. Runyon, 932 F. Supp. 412, 418 (N.D.N.Y. 1996) (employee's allegations that he was consistently denied reemployment were insufficient to constitute continuing violation so as to toll 45-day limitations period), *aff'd*, 108 F.3d 329 (2d Cir. 1997) *and* Cones v. Shalala, 945 F. Supp. 342, 347 (D.D.C. 1996) (rejecting plaintiff's continuing violation argument; seven separate instances of denial of promotion or reassignment to different positions shared no common nexus), *rev'd and remanded*, 199 F.3d 512, 81 FEP 1650 (D.C. Cir. 2000).

[307]Watson v. Henderson, 222 F.3d 320, 321–22 (7th Cir. 2000) (employee forfeited claim for compensatory damages by failing to present such claim to EEOC; employee engaged in an administrative adjudication must specifically identify relief sought).

[308]*See, e.g.*, Harms v. IRS, 321 F.3d 1001 (10th Cir. 2003) (equitable tolling not permitted on basis of mental incapacity where employee failed to present evidence explaining 3-year delay in filing complaint after regaining mental competency; Treasury Complaint Center had improperly instructed complainant to take his suspension claims to MSPB); Boos v. Runyon, 201 F.3d 178, 184–85, 10 AD 198 (2d Cir. 2000) ("Mental illness tolls a statute of limitations only if the illness *in fact* prevents the sufferer from managing his affairs and thus from understanding his legal rights and acting upon them.") (emphasis in original); Nunnally v. MacCausland, 996 F.2d 1, 5 (1st Cir. 1993) (plaintiff entitled to equitable tolling only if she could demonstrate that she was unable to engage in rational thought and deliberate decision making sufficient to pursue claim alone or through counsel).

Court's decision in *Lorance v. AT&T Technologies, Inc.*[309]—that running of the limitations period for Title VII purposes is triggered at the time of adoption of an allegedly discriminatory classification system—also controls for claims brought under the Rehabilitation Act.[310]

A federal employee's timely request for reconsideration of an EEOC decision on appeal tolls the 90-day deadline for filing suit in federal court.[311] By contrast, the filing of a civil action terminates the processing of the plaintiff's appeal with the EEOC.[312]

In cases involving the MSPB, the CSRA protects complainants who timely file with the wrong agency.[313] The Ninth Circuit

---

[309]490 U.S. 900, 911 (1989). This holding was later abrogated by the Civil Rights Act of 1991, which provides that "with respect to a seniority system that has been adopted for an intentionally discriminatory purpose in violation of this title [42 U.S.C. 2000e et seq.]," the unlawful employment practice occurs when the seniority system is adopted, when an individual becomes subject to the system, or when an individual is injured by its application. 42 U.S.C. § 2000e-5(e)(2) (2000); *see* EEOC v. Plumbers & Pipefitters Local 350, 998 F.2d 641, 644–45 (9th Cir. 1992); Banas v. American Airlines, 969 F.2d 477, 481–82 (7th Cir. 1992).

[310]*See* Mullins v. Crowell, 228 F.3d 1305, 1311–12 (11th Cir. 2000) (limitations period for employees to file Rehabilitation Act claims against employer that placed them in separate disability-based classifications while they were receiving Federal Employees Compensation Act payments began to run when classification system was used to terminate them in reduction in force, not when they were placed in their classifications; classification system was facially discriminatory and employees did not feel effects of classification until RIF occurred).

[311]*See, e.g.*, Holley v. Department of Veterans Affairs, 165 F.3d 244 (3d Cir. 1999) (EEOC regulation at 29 C.F.R. § 1614.405(b)(1), providing that EEOC decision on appeal is final unless either party files timely request for reconsideration pursuant to § 1614.407, means that timely filed request for reconsideration tolls 90-day deadline for filing court action; employee filed her complaint more than 180 days after date on which she filed her appeal with EEOC and before she received EEOC's "final ruling" on her motion to reconsider decision on appeal); Belhomme v. Widnall, 127 F.3d 1214, 1216–17 (10th Cir. 1997) (timely petition for reconsideration will toll filing deadline for suit in district court, but untimely petition will have no tolling effect).

[312]*See Holley*, 165 F.3d at 246 (EEOC has no authority to consider complaint appeal once civil action is filed); *cf.* Randel v. U.S. Dep't of Navy, 157 F.3d 392, 396–97 (5th Cir. 1998) (federal employee's abandonment of disability claim before EEOC by including it in his then-pending district court action did not terminate his entire proceeding before EEOC and deprive EEOC of jurisdiction of his second claim (reprisal), so as to prevent exhaustion of remedies, where no evidence presented that employee failed to cooperate with agency or attempted to frustrate administrative process).

[313]5 U.S.C. § 7702(f) (2005); *see, e.g.*, Miller v. Department of Army, 987 F.2d 1552, 1555 (Fed. Cir. 1993) (reversing dismissal of the complaint where the complainant filed with the wrong agency; regardless of the reason for the error, "the Board was obligated to treat [the complaint] as timely filed").

has held that, in a mixed case complaint, the limitations period for filing a discrimination claim with the agency's equal opportunity office or with the EEOC is tolled by an appeal of the MSPB's jurisdictional decision. An MSPB determination that it lacks jurisdiction to hear a claim is appealable only to the Court of Appeals for the Federal Circuit.[314] The tolling period lasts until the employee receives a final jurisdictional determination from the Court of Appeals for the Federal Circuit.[315] Absent waiver of EEO claims, review of an MSPB determination on a federal employee's mixed appeal, involving claims of unlawful discrimination related to or stemming from employment, lies solely in district court (rather than the Court of Appeals for the Federal Circuit). Thus, the employee is deemed to have exhausted his or her administrative remedies and may obtain federal court de novo review, despite an MSPB determination that discrimination claims lacked merit.[316]

C. Trial de Novo

Federal employees' right to trial de novo emerged as a critical issue following passage of § 717. However, the Supreme Court in *Chandler v. Roudebush*[317] affirmed that federal plaintiffs[318] enjoy an absolute right to trial de novo under § 717:

> The legislative history . . . reinforces the plain meaning of the statute and confirms that Congress intended to accord federal employees the same right to a trial *de novo* as is enjoyed by private-sector

---

[314]*See* Mulhall v. Ashcroft, 287 F.3d 543 (6th Cir. 2002) (Federal Circuit has exclusive jurisdiction of constructive discharge claim dismissed by MSPB).

[315]*See* Sloan v. West, 140 F.3d 1255, 1262–63 (9th Cir. 1998).

[316]*See* Coffman v. Glickman, 328 F.3d 619 (10th Cir. 2003) (federal employee who has fully exhausted his administrative remedies in MSPB appeal process is not required to prevail on discrimination claims and matter may remain a "mixed case" subject to de novo review in district court).

[317]425 U.S. 840 (1976).

[318]The government does not enjoy a comparable right, but rather is bound by a final agency decision in favor of the federal employee. Pecker v. Heckler, 801 F.2d 709, 711 n.3 (4th Cir. 1986), *overruled on other grounds*, Laber v. Harvey, 438 F.3d 44, 427–28 (4th Cir. 2006); Moore v. Devine, 780 F.2d 1559, 1563–64 (11th Cir. 1986). *But cf.* Diamond v. Atwood, 43 F.3d 1538, 1541 (D.C. Cir. 1995) (an agency is not bound by the agency investigator's findings in a proposed disposition of an EEO complaint where the agency never adopted such findings). Section 717 and the ADEA allow only the aggrieved employee, not the government, to file in district court.

employees and employees of state governments and political subdivisions under [Title VII].[319]

Trial de novo likewise has been held available in age[320] and disability[321] cases.

In mixed cases, trial de novo is afforded only on the discrimination claims; other personnel matters are reviewed on the MSPB
record.[322]

Title VII entitles federal employees to bring agency discrimination cases in federal court to enforce final agency actions.[323] Thus,
as an alternative to trial de novo, a federal employee may seek from
the appropriate district court an order enforcing a favorable EEOC
ruling without risking de novo review.[324] In *Hashimoto v. Dalton*,[325]

---

[319]425 U.S. at 848. Employees of the General Accounting Office (GAO) who
bring discrimination claims before the GAO's Personnel Appeals Board for administrative review, however, are statutorily denied the right to trial de novo in district
court. *See* General Accounting Office Personnel Act of 1980, Pub. L. No. 96-191,
1980 U.S.C.C.A.N. (94 Stat.) 27, 34 (extending § 717's coverage to employees of
the GAO). Jurisdiction over the board's final decisions in discrimination cases is
vested in the Court of Appeals for the Federal Circuit and, as such, is conducted
only by review on the record. 31 U.S.C. § 755(a) (2000); *see, e.g.*, Ramey v. Bowsher,
9 F.3d 133, 134 (D.C. Cir. 1993) (GAO employee was denied a trial de novo in district
court on the Personnel Appeals Board decision and the case was transferred to the
Court of Appeals for the Federal Circuit).

[320]*See* Bak v. United States Postal Serv., 52 F.3d 241, 243 (9th Cir. 1995).

[321]*See* Shirey v. Devine, 670 F.2d 1188, 1197 (D.C. Cir. 1982). Disability cases
brought under the Rehabilitation Act since 1978 have been required by statute to be
conducted in accordance with "[t]he remedies, procedures, and rights set forth in
section 717 of [Title VII]." 29 U.S.C. § 794a(a)(1) (2000).

[322]*See* Romain v. Shear, 799 F.2d 1416, 1421 (9th Cir. 1986) (in a mixed case,
the petitioner has a right to a trial de novo on the discrimination claim; the nondiscrimination claim is reviewed only on the administrative record); Kline v. Tennessee Valley Auth., 805 F. Supp. 545, 547 (E.D. Tenn. 1992) (the district court's review of the MSPB's decision on nondiscrimination-related claims "must be on the
record . . . [and] it does not involve de novo adjudication of the issue"); *see also*
Rana v. United States, 812 F.2d 887, 890 (4th Cir. 1987) (age and national origin
discrimination claims only; the district court is entitled to review both the newly
introduced evidence and the MSPB's formal record).

[323]*See* Herron v. Veneman, 305 F. Supp. 2d 64, 74–75 (D.D.C. 2004).

[324]*See* Haskins v. Department of Army, 808 F.2d 1192, 1199 (6th Cir. 1987) (employee not required to litigate favorable liability finding at administrative level, but
such administrative finding did not entitle employee to back pay and promotion where
findings included no determination as to whether employee would be denied promotion in absence of discrimination); Moore v. Devine, 780 F.2d 1559, 1563 (11th
Cir. 1986) (courts "have uniformly granted requests for enforcement of favorable
final agency and EEOC decisions without requiring de novo review of the merits of
the discrimination claims").

[325]870 F. Supp. 1544, 1557 (D. Haw. 1994) (plaintiff allowed to accept EEOC
finding that defendant had acted with retaliatory animus while relitigating issue of

the district court permitted the plaintiff to accept the favorable portion of the EEOC's finding while relitigating de novo the unfavorable portion. However, the employee is not entitled to limited or fragmented trial de novo in order to challenge an administrative damages award without having to relitigate favorable findings on liability.[326] Moreover, a reviewing court is not automatically compelled to follow previous administrative findings.[327] Thus, the federal litigant who seeks partial review of an EEOC decision on the merits of the discrimination claim may be faced with a trial de novo of all the issues in the particular case, not just those challenged as erroneous.[328] Similarly, if the plaintiff seeks additional relief, the employee faces a trial de novo on the entire complaint.[329]

D. Class Actions

The Federal Rules of Civil Procedure and court precedent applicable to private-sector Title VII class actions also govern federal sector Title VII class actions.[330] Rule 23 class actions may be available to federal employees alleging age discrimination as well.[331]

---

whether she would have been offered job in absence of retaliatory, negative employment reference), *aff'd*, 118 F.3d 671 (9th Cir. 1997).

[326]*See* Morris v. Rumsfeld, 420 F.3d 287, 294 (3d Cir. 2005) (in suit challenging administrative disposition, court is not bound by prior administrative results), *cert. denied*, 126 S. Ct. 1769 (2006); *see also Herron*, 305 F. Supp. 2d at 76 (collecting cases).

[327]*Herron*, 305 F. Supp. 2d at 79 (prior finding of discrimination by the EEOC or an agency's acknowledgment of discrimination is clearly relevant to a district court's findings in a trial de novo but court is not compelled to follow previous administrative findings in action to challenge, not enforce, a final agency determination).

[328]*See* Barney v. Caldera, 2001 WL 1168163 (S.D. Ind. Aug. 6, 2001) (federal district court proceedings are de novo, so discovery sanction imposed during the administrative proceedings (finding Army admissions where it failed to timely respond to requests for admissions) does not carry over to proceedings in court); Cocciardi v. Russo, 721 F. Supp. 735, 737 (E.D. Pa. 1989) (even though the federal employee sought only partial review of the EEOC's findings, a "fragmented" trial de novo is not allowed and full trial de novo in such cases is mandated).

[329]*See* Laber v. Harvey, 438 F.3d 404, 427–28 (4th Cir. 2006) (Title VII does not authorize a federal sector employee to bring civil action alleging only that the administrative remedy granted was insufficient; agency's finding of discrimination at issue in civil suit); Ellis v. England, 432 F.3d 1321, 1325, 17 AD 703 (11th Cir. 2005) (rejecting argument employee was entitled to de novo review of damages only); Timmons v. White, 314 F.3d 1229, 1234 (10th Cir. 2003) (employee could not limit the district court's review in de novo civil action to the issue of remedy, and the employer was not bound by a prior adverse finding by EEOC).

[330]*See* Eastland v. Tennessee Valley Auth., 553 F.2d 364, 372 (5th Cir. 1977). *See generally* Chapter 32 (Class Actions).

[331]Moysey v. Andrus, 481 F. Supp. 850, 853–54 (D.D.C. 1979) (§ 15(c) of the ADEA, unlike the remedy provision applicable to nonfederal employees and applicants,

The failure of plaintiffs to exhaust administrative class remedies, however, is fatal to maintaining a class action in court.[332] Plaintiffs must clearly exhaust their administrative remedies on behalf of a class prior to maintaining a class action in court.[333]

E. Exclusivity of Remedy

In *Brown v. GSA*, the Supreme Court held that § 717 provides the exclusive remedy for discrimination by the employing agency.[334] The Court found that in enacting § 717, Congress intended to repeal any remedies for such discrimination by agencies that may have existed before the passage of the 1972 amendments to Title VII.[335] Federal employees therefore cannot invoke the Civil Rights Act of 1866 (42 U.S.C. § 1981)[336] or the Constitution[337] to sue the

---

does not reference the Fair Labor Standards Act, so the FLSA "opt-in" class action limitations do not apply to federal employee ADEA actions). *See generally* Chapter 12 (Age). The regulations governing federal employee EEO litigation specifically provide for administrative class complaints raising claims of discrimination based on race, color, religion, sex, national origin, age, or disability. 29 C.F.R. § 1614.204(a)(1) (2005).

[332]*See* 29 C.F.R. §§ 1613.601–.643 (2005); *see also* Gulley v. Orr, 905 F.2d 1383, 1385 (10th Cir. 1990) (class certification barred by plaintiff's failure to assert the class claims in her formal administrative complaint and pursued only an individual complaint); Wade v. Secretary of Army, 796 F.2d 1369, 1373 (11th Cir. 1986) ("A federal employee plaintiff seeking to litigate class claims of Title VII discrimination in federal court is required to have exhausted administrative remedies relating to class complaints."); Patton v. Brown, 95 F.R.D. 205, 207 (E.D. Pa. 1982) (the named plaintiff who files a Title VII class action complaint must exhaust all administrative remedies by filing a class complaint of discrimination at the agency level). However, where the burden of pleading and proving failure to exhaust is on the agency, its failure to do so constitutes a waiver of the defense. Brown v. Marsh, 777 F.2d 8, 15 (D.C. Cir. 1985).

[333]Ransom v. United States Postal Serv., 2006 WL 308265, at *4 (10th Cir. Feb. 10, 2006) (pro se employee's individual complaint with brief references to maltreatment of other employees did not exhaust administrative remedies for a class) (citing Belhomme v. Widnall, 127 F.3d 1214, 1217 (10th Cir. 1997)); Murphy v. West, 945 F. Supp. 874, 877 (D. Md. 1996) (Title VII class claims dismissed due to failure to exhaust class or individual administrative remedies, rejecting plaintiff's argument that perceived futility of raising claims at administrative level should excuse exhaustion requirement).

[334]425 U.S. 820, 835 (1976); *cf.* Bush v. Lucas, 462 U.S. 367, 390 (1983) (the administrative process enacted by Congress provides the sole remedy for the claim of a federal employee that his First Amendment rights had been violated).

[335]*Brown*, 425 U.S. at 832–34.

[336]*Id.* at 834 (affirming dismissal of plaintiff's § 1981 claim).

[337]In *Bivens v. Six Unknown Named Agents of the Federal Bureau of Narcotics*, 403 U.S. 388 (1971), the Supreme Court held that the victim of a violation of the

federal government for employment discrimination otherwise covered by Title VII.[338] Related claims, such as common law assault,[339] intentional infliction of emotional distress,[340] or, according to a minority of courts, the deprivation of procedural due process,[341] still may be allowed in proper circumstances.

Constitution under color of authority could obtain redress in an action for damages. But under *Brown*, such redress is allowed only where there exists no comprehensive remedial statute, like Title VII, providing relief for the acts complained of. *See* Grenci v. United States, 36 FEP 1044, 1046 (W.D. Pa. 1984) (Title VII displaces both § 1983 and Fifth Amendment claims to the extent such claims are founded on allegations of discrimination). By its terms, federal employees cannot invoke 42 U.S.C. § 1983, which applies only to *state* government action. Hogan v. Runyon, 15 Fed. Appx. 458 (9th Cir. 2001) (holding that Title VII provides the exclusive judicial remedy for claims of discrimination in federal employment). *See generally* Chapter 35 (The Civil Rights Acts of 1866 and 1871).

[338]*See* Ethnic Employees v. Boorstin, 751 F.2d 1405, 1415–16 (D.C. Cir. 1985) (Title VII is the exclusive remedy; an organization of employees cannot recast Title VII claims as constitutional claims; but constitutional claims that are not covered by Title VII are not barred and are remanded); Postal Workers v. Postmaster Gen., 35 FEP 1484, 1488 n.19 (N.D. Cal. 1984) (Title VII does not displace a federal employee's First Amendment freedom-of-religion claims), *rev'd and remanded on other grounds*, 781 F.2d 772, 39 FEP 1847 (9th Cir. 1986); Weiss v. Marsh, 543 F. Supp. 1115, 1117 (M.D. Ala. 1981) (an Equal Pay Act claim was not displaced by § 717).

[339]*See, e.g.*, Lage v. Thomas, 585 F. Supp. 403, 406 (N.D. Tex. 1984) (refusing to dismiss a pendent common law assault claim); Quillen v. United States Postal Serv., 564 F. Supp. 314, 321 (E.D. Mich. 1983) (an assault and battery claim was not dismissed because it does not constitute a cause of action for employment discrimination).

[340]*See* Boyd v. O'Neill, 273 F. Supp. 2d 92, 98 (D.D.C. 2003) (to the extent that a federal employee's claim of intentional infliction of emotional distress is based on an alleged assault and not the alleged harassment, it is not precluded by Title VII). *Compare* Pfau v. Reed, 167 F.3d 228, 229 (5th Cir. 1999) (the operative facts of the non-Title VII claim must be sufficiently distinct from the Title VII facts to avoid preemption) *and* Mathis v. Henderson, 243 F.3d 446 (8th Cir. 2001) *with* Wallace v. Henderson, 138 F. Supp. 2d 980, 986 (S.D. Ohio 2000) (closely scrutinizing factual allegations, court found intentional infliction of emotional distress claim was not preemptive where plaintiff suffered "highly personal injury" beyond retaliation and discrimination).

[341]*Compare* Ray v. Nimmo, 704 F.2d 1480, 1485–87 (11th Cir. 1983) (per curiam) (a claim that the defendant violated the plaintiff's due process rights by not following its own regulations or affirmative action plan was distinct from a claim of discrimination, but it was nevertheless subject to dismissal if the plaintiff was a federal employee who must submit such claims through administrative channels), Nolan v. Cleland, 686 F.2d 806, 815 (9th Cir. 1982) (dismissing the plaintiff's due process claim, alleging that she was forced to resign because of her employer's deceit, coercion, and duress, which allegedly constituted a taking of her property; pursuant to *Brown*, Title VII provides the exclusive judicial remedy for claims of discrimination in federal employment) *and* Valentine v. Drug Enforcement Admin., 544 F. Supp.

The Fifth and Eighth Circuits are divided on whether the exclusive-remedy principle enunciated in *Brown* means that unions, which are not covered under § 717(a), may not be sued under § 1981.[342]

The Second Circuit has applied the holding in *Brown v. GSA*[343] to a claim of disability and reprisal discrimination, dismissing the plaintiff's state human rights law claims on the ground that § 717 of the Civil Rights Act of 1964 provides the exclusive judicial remedy for federal employee claims of employment discrimination, and concluding that § 501 of the Rehabilitation Act[344] provides the sole remedy for a federal employee's disability discrimination claims.[345] Nongovernment employees who nevertheless work

---

830, 834–35 (N.D. Ill. 1982) (a claim that a lack of notice of the employer's affirmative action plan deprived the plaintiff of due process under the Fifth Amendment was duplicative of his Title VII claim, which provided the exclusive remedy) *with* McKenna v. Weinberger, 729 F.2d 783, 791 (D.C. Cir. 1984) (the district court erred by dismissing a separate claim under the Administrative Procedure Act (APA) for failure to follow the agency's own rules), Houseton v. Nimmo, 670 F.2d 1375, 1377 (9th Cir. 1982) (an APA action lies to enforce a CSC/EEOC decision granting relief against the agency), Perry v. Boorstin, 29 FEP 1227, 1228 (D.D.C. 1982) (allowing a Fifth Amendment due process claim concerning the decision of the agency to delegate responsibility to investigate internal discrimination complaints to private entities) *and* Kulkarni v. Hoffman, 22 FEP 1463, 1465 (D.D.C. 1976) (the exclusive remedy of § 717 does not preclude an action under the APA, 5 U.S.C. §§ 701–706, for the purpose of determining whether the agency complied with the APA's requirement to issue a final decision within 30 days of the CSC examiner's recommended decision).

[342]*Compare* Newbold v. United States Postal Serv., 614 F.2d 46, 46 (5th Cir. 1980) (per curiam) (it follows from *Brown* that labor organizations representing federal employees may not be sued under § 1981, even though the unions themselves are not covered by § 717) *with* Jennings v. Postal Workers, 672 F.2d 712, 716 (8th Cir. 1982) (exclusivity of remedy under Title VII does not preclude an action under § 1981 against a union representing federal employees).

[343]425 U.S. 820, 12 FEP 1361 (1976).

[344]29 U.S.C. § 701 (2000).

[345]*See* Rivera v. Heyman, 157 F.3d 101, 104 (2d Cir. 1998) (concurring in dismissal of disability claims under Rehabilitation Act § 504; joining Seventh, Ninth, and Tenth Circuits in holding that § 501 is federal employee's sole remedy for claim of disability discrimination under Rehabilitation Act, and rejecting the conclusion of the Fifth, Sixth, and Eighth Circuits that §§ 501 and 504 overlap and thus permit federal employees to sue under both provisions). *Compare* Taylor v. Small, 350 F.3d 1286, 1291 (D.C. Cir. 2003) (federal employers may sue under § 501 of Act, but not § 504, which applies only to programs receiving federal funds) *with* Morgan v. United States Postal Serv., 798 F.2d 1162, 1164–65 (8th Cir. 1986) (federal employee may sue under either § 501 or § 504 but must exhaust administrative remedies through EEOC under both sections).

for a federal program or activity are entitled to bring discrimination claims under § 504.[346] Furthermore, the Rehabilitation Act does not bar a Postal Service employee from maintaining a disability discrimination suit against the employee's union and union local under the ADA.[347]

Eight years after *Brown*, the Supreme Court held in *Davis v. Passman*[348] that employees of Congress, who were not covered by § 717, could sue for employment discrimination directly under the Constitution. The majority rejected the argument that such a claim was inconsistent with *Brown*, explaining that *Brown* applied only when employees covered by § 717 seek to redress "the violation of rights granted by that statute."[349] The Congressional Accountability Act of 1995 now provides a comprehensive remedy for discrimination against employees of Congress. Arguably, *Davis* no longer controls.[350] By contrast, judicial branch employees not in the competitive service are not yet covered by any antidiscrimination statute;[351] such employees presumably still can sue directly under the Constitution based on the *Davis v. Passman* theory.

---

[346]29 U.S.C. § 794(a) (2000); *see* Redd v. Summers, 232 F.3d 933 (D.C. Cir. 2000) (although plaintiff was not employee under § 501 of Rehabilitation Act for purposes of section prohibiting discrimination on the basis of disability, she was entitled to show that her tour guide contract with Bureau of Engraving and Printing constituted a federal program or activity under § 504, in which case she would be entitled to bring a claim of discrimination under § 504; reversing summary judgment for employer).

[347]*See* Jones v. Postal Workers, 192 F.3d 417 (4th Cir. 1999) (Postal Service employee could pursue claim under the ADA against union and union local where labor union that represents federal employees constitutes a labor organization, as defined in Title VII and, by proxy, ADA).

[348]442 U.S. 228 (1979).

[349]*Id.* at 248–49.

[350]*See* Lee v. Hughes, 145 F.3d 1272, 1275 (11th Cir. 1998) (*Davis v. Passman* did not consider the preemptive effect of CSRA, which had just been passed).

[351]*See* Dotson v. Griesa, 398 F.3d 156 (2d Cir. 2005) (*Bivens* action precluded by CSRA, where review of probation officer's termination was defined by internal administrative grievance procedure of his employer, even though CSRA failed to afford administrative or judicial review; probation officer was not entitled to damages to redress allegedly unconstitutional termination from federal employment), *cert. denied*, 126 S. Ct. 2859 (2006); *see also* Blankenship v. McDonald, 176 F.3d 1192, 1194–95 (9th Cir. 1999) (federal circuit court reporter alleged that her termination was in retaliation for her EEO testimony, in violation of Fifth Amendment due process; while acknowledging that CSRA afforded the reporter "no effective remedies," nevertheless congressional decision in promulgating CSRA was not inadvertent regarding federal employee's procedural due process rights).

F. Scope of Relief

The *Brown* Court also held that § 706 of Title VII governs "the scope of relief" for federal employees suing under § 717. One of the prime purposes of § 717 was to remove doubts as to the availability of "back pay or other compensatory relief" for federal employees.[352] Section 114 of the Civil Rights Act of 1991 overturned *Library of Congress v. Shaw*[353] and amended § 717 to provide for attorney's fee awards and interest on back pay against the federal government.[354] The 1991 Act provides that federal employees can seek compensatory, but not punitive, damages under 42 U.S.C. § 1981a for proven discrimination.[355]

In *West v. Gibson*,[356] the Supreme Court confirmed that the 1991 Civil Rights Act gave federal employees the right to seek compensatory damages from their government employers in the administrative process, holding that EEOC administrative judges have the authority to award compensatory damages.[357] The Court vacated a Seventh Circuit decision holding that a federal employee was not required to exhaust EEOC administrative remedies before suing on a claim for compensatory damages.[358]

Courts have confirmed that, although the 1991 Civil Rights Act gave federal employees the right to seek compensatory damages from their government employers, they remain ineligible for awards of punitive damages.[359] The Sixth and Seventh Circuits have also held that, despite Congress' unequivocal waiver of sovereign immunity of the United States Postal Service, the Postal Service

---

[352]Brown v. GSA, 425 U.S. 820, 826, 832, 12 FEP 1361 (1976).

[353]478 U.S. 310, 320 (1986).

[354]Pub. L. No. 102-166, § 114, 1991 U.S.C.C.A.N. (105 Stat.) 1071, 1079 (codified at 42 U.S.C. § 2000e-16(d) (2000)).

[355]*Id.* § 102 (codified at 42 U.S.C. § 1981a (2000)).

[356]527 U.S. 212 (1999).

[357]*Id.* at 220 (EEOC's legal authority to enforce § 717 of Title VII (42 U.S.C. § 2000e-16 (2000)) includes requiring federal agencies to pay compensatory damages when they discriminate in employment in violation of Title VII).

[358]Gibson v. Brown, 137 F.3d 992, 995–97 (7th Cir. 1998) (employee not required to exhaust EEOC administrative remedies before suing in federal court on claim for compensatory damages), *vacated by* 527 U.S. 212 (1999).

[359]*See, e.g.*, Robinson v. Runyon, 149 F.3d 507 (6th Cir. 1998) (Congress has not waived sovereign immunity on behalf of the agency); Baker v. Runyon, 114 F.3d 668, 670, 74 FEP 160 (7th Cir. 1997) (punitive damages against federal government not allowed under Title VII either prior to or after Civil Rights Act of 1991).

is a "government agency" exempt from punitive damages for purposes of the Civil Rights Act of 1991.[360]

Courts have held that in order to afford full relief to a plaintiff injured by unlawful discrimination, it may be necessary to "bump" an incumbent employee.[361]

G. Attorney's Fees

Attorney's fees are available under Title VII to federal employees who meet the standards of a "prevailing party"[362] on the same basis as they are available to private employees.[363] In *New York Gaslight Club, Inc v. Carey*[364] the Supreme Court cited with approval earlier appellate decisions[365] holding that federal employees and applicants may recover attorney's fees for time spent in the

---

[360]*See* Robinson v. Runyon, 149 F.3d 507 (6th Cir. 1998) (to permit suit for punitive damages against federal agency Congress must have waived sovereign immunity on behalf of the agency *and* the substantive law must permit punitive damages) (citing Baker v. Runyon, 114 F.3d 668, 670 (7th Cir. 1997)); *see also* Ausfeldt v. Runyon, 950 F. Supp. 478, 487–88 (N.D.N.Y. 1997); Miller v. Runyon, 932 F. Supp. 276, 277 (M.D. Ala. 1996).

[361]*See, e.g.*, Doll v. Brown, 75 F.3d 1200, 1205 (7th Cir. 1996) ("No one has a right to occupy a position that he obtained as a result of unlawful discrimination, even if he himself was not complicit in the discrimination."); Hayes v. Shalala, 933 F. Supp. 21, 25 (D.D.C. 1996) (ordering reinstatement of federal employee even though incumbent had to be "bumped" as a result; hostility engendered by litigation could not be used as a justification for denial of promotion).

[362]*See, e.g.*, Petite v. Reno, 822 F. Supp. 815, 816 (D.D.C. 1993) (former federal employee who received through settlement significant portion of relief he sought in bringing a Title VII action qualified as a "prevailing party" entitled to attorney's fees, even though there was no adjudication of his discrimination claim and no admission of liability by the employer); *cf.* Villescas v. Abraham, 311 F.3d 1253 (10th Cir. 2002) (court of appeals could not sustain attorney's fees under either the ADEA or the Equal Access to Justice Act (EAJA), 28 U.S.C. § 2412, once it reversed plaintiff's award of only compensatory damages).

[363]Section 717(d) incorporates by reference the attorney's fees provision in § 706(k). *See* Kulkarni v. Alexander, 662 F.2d 758, 765 (D.C. Cir. 1978) (U.S. Army employee who prevailed on a substantial portion of his discrimination claims is entitled to attorney's fees under § 717); Smith v. Kleindienst, 8 FEP 753, 754 (D.D.C. 1974) (attorney's fees awarded to prevailing federal employee following grant of summary judgment in her favor), *aff'd mem. sub nom.* Smith v. Levi, 527 F.2d 853 (D.C. Cir. 1975). Section 717(d) likewise applies to actions under § 501 of the Rehabilitation Act, 29 U.S.C. § 791. *See* 29 U.S.C. § 794a(a)(1) (2000). *See generally* Chapter 41 (Attorney's Fees).

[364]447 U.S. 54, 66 (1980).

[365]*See* Parker v. Califano, 561 F.2d 320 (D.C. Cir. 1977); Johnson v. United States, 554 F.2d 632 (4th Cir. 1977).

administrative process, as well as in court proceedings.[366] However, at least one court has held that prevailing plaintiffs who settle claims during the course of the Title VII administrative process may not bring separate federal court actions to recover attorney's fees.[367] Instead, these plaintiffs must pursue a modified award for attorney's fees via the EEOC process.

The ADEA does not authorize awarding attorney's fees against the U.S. government.[368] Some courts, however, have permitted an award of attorney's fees under the Equal Access to Justice Act,[369] which allows an award of fees against the United States "[u]nless expressly prohibited by statute," reasoning that the EAJA provides the basis for a discretionary award of fees to a prevailing plaintiff.[370]

In *Copeland v. Martinez*,[371] the District of Columbia Circuit held that prevailing federal agencies may recover attorney's fees against plaintiffs under the standards of *Christiansburg Garment*

---

[366]*See* 29 C.F.R. § 1614.501(e) (2005) (setting forth the procedures and standards for obtaining attorney's fees in the administrative process); 5 C.F.R. § 1201.37 (2005) (procedures in mixed cases). The regulations allow fees only for the period beginning after the filing of the formal complaint, thus excluding the counseling phase.

[367]*See* Chris v. Tenet, 221 F.3d 648, 655 (4th Cir. 2000) ("The jurisdictional grant of 42 U.S.C.§ 2000e-5(f)(3) does not extend to an independent action solely for attorney's fees and costs incurred during the course of the Title VII administrative process.").

[368]*See, e.g.*, Villescas v. Abraham, 311 F.3d 1253, 1256–62 (10th Cir. 2002) (ADEA did not waive government's sovereign immunity from damages for emotional distress arising from retaliation and employee was not entitled to attorney's fees and expenses as "prevailing party"); Lewis v. Federal Prison Indus., Inc., 953 F.2d 1277, 1281 (11th Cir. 1992) (rejecting plaintiff's claim for attorney's fees because no express waiver in ADEA, without addressing possible entitlement under Equal Access to Justice Act).

[369]28 U.S.C. § 2412 (1999) (2000).

[370]Boehms v. Crowell, 139 F.3d 452, 461–63 (5th Cir. 1998) (ADEA subsection providing that plaintiff in civil action could receive such legal and equitable relief as would effectuate purposes of ADEA may not be used to award attorney's fees against federal government; however, Equal Access to Justice Act enables trial court to award attorney's fees against federal government in ADEA cases); Nowd v. Rubin, 76 F.3d 25, 27–28 (1st Cir. 1996) (Equal Access to Justice Act permits attorney's fee award to prevailing federal employee); Craig v. O'Leary, 870 F. Supp. 1007, 1010 (D. Colo. 1994) (rejecting *Lewis*; allowing federal employee to seek attorney's fees in ADEA action based in part upon Equal Access to Justice Act).

[371]603 F.2d 981, 991–92 (D.C. Cir. 1979); *accord* Blue v. Department of Army, 914 F.2d 525, 538 (4th Cir. 1990) (adopting the rule articulated in *Copeland*; no congressional intent in § 706(k) to preclude all awards of sanctions to the government).

Co. v. EEOC,[372] despite the seemingly contrary language of § 706(k).[373]

H. Federal Officials as Defendants

In *Westfall v. Erwin*,[374] the Supreme Court held that federal employees are not absolutely immune from state law tort liability for conduct within the scope of their employment, unless policy dictates that absolute immunity is warranted to protect the decision-making process. To guard against the possibility of such awards, Congress enacted the Federal Employees Liability Reform and Tort Compensation Act of 1988, commonly known as the Westfall Act.[375] To invoke the statute's protection against individual tort liability, the Attorney General must certify "that the defendant employee was acting within the scope of his office or employment[376] at the time of the incident out of which the claim arose."[377] After proper

---

[372]434 U.S. 412 (1978); *see also* Stewart v. Department of Health & Hosps., 117 Fed. Appx. 918 (5th Cir. 2004) (Under Title VII of the Civil Rights Act of 1964, a prevailing party may be awarded attorney's fees at the discretion of the court (citing 42 U.S.C. § 2000e-5(k) (2000)). Prevailing defendants may recover such fees only where the court finds that the plaintiff's action was frivolous, unreasonable, or without foundation, even though not brought in subjective bad faith.). *See generally* Chapter 41 (Attorney's Fees).

[373]Section 706(k) provides: "In any action or proceeding under this subchapter the court . . . may allow the prevailing party, other than . . . the United States, a reasonable attorney's fee . . . ." 42 U.S.C. § 2000e-5(k) (2000).

[374]484 U.S. 292, 300 (1988).

[375]Pub. L. No. 100-694, 1988 U.S.C.C.A.N. (102 Stat.) 4564 (codified at 28 U.S.C. § 2679 (2000)).

[376]*See* Gutierrez de Martinez v. Lamagno, 515 U.S. 417 (1995). In *Gutierrez de Martinez*, the Supreme Court held that the propriety of the Attorney General's scope of employment certification under § 2679 (d) of the Westfall Act is subject to judicial review, and thus not conclusively binding on the district court for purposes of substitution of parties. For purposes of removal, however, certification is binding. This distinction may lead to jurisdictional dilemmas for circuit courts where certification is rejected in a removed case.

[377]28 U.S.C. § 2679(d)(1) (2000). When the action is brought in state court, the Attorney General's certification constitutes grounds for removal to federal court at any time before trial. *Id.* § 2679(d)(2); *see* Counts v. Guevara, 328 F.3d 212, 214 (5th Cir. 2003) (under Westfall Act, United States may remove action to federal court and substitute itself as defendant following certification that the government employee was acting within the scope of his employment at the time of the allegedly tortious act). Courts faced with the issue hold that they may review the propriety of the Attorney General's § 2679(d) certification. *See* Schrob v. Catterson, 967 F.2d 929, 934 & n.9 (3d Cir. 1992) (certification is prima facie evidence that the challenged

certification,[378] the proceeding is deemed to be against the United States, which is substituted as the sole party defendant and can assert all available defenses under the Federal Tort Claims Act.[379] In effect, the former defendant employee receives absolute immunity if the tort was committed within the scope of employment.[380]

---

conduct occurred within the scope of employment; plaintiff challenging the certification has the burden of coming forward with specific facts rebutting it); Larsen v. Frederiksen, 277 F.3d 1040, 1041 (8th Cir. 2002) (same); S.J. & W. Ranch v. Lehtinen, 913 F.2d 1538, 1540–44 (11th Cir. 1990) ("Although we are persuaded by the statutory language that the plaintiff has the burden of proving that the employee's conduct was not encompassed by the scope of his employment, we agree with the majority of federal courts that the district court determines scope de novo."), *amended on other grounds*, 924 F.2d 1555 (11th Cir. 1991); Nasuti v. Scannell, 906 F.2d 802, 808 (1st Cir. 1990) (although deferring to the scope of certification for removal purposes, the federal district court will exercise its customary adjudicative jurisdiction over scope of employment disputes); Arbour v. Jenkins, 903 F.2d 416, 421 (6th Cir. 1990) (same); Borawski v. Henderson, 265 F. Supp. 2d 475 (D.N.J. 2003) (a court may rely on pleadings, evidentiary documents, affidavits, and the scope of the certification made by the Attorney General in ruling on a motion to substitute the United States as defendant). Some courts have held that the right of review is necessary in order to avoid constitutional problems. *See, e.g.*, McHugh v. University of Vt., 966 F.2d 67, 74 (2d Cir. 1992) ("judicial review of a certification of scope of employment must be inferred to avoid serious constitutional problems"). *Contra* Johnson v. Carter, 983 F.2d 1316, 1320 (4th Cir. 1993) (Attorney General's certification is conclusive; "Legislative history is irrelevant to the interpretation of an unambiguous statute . . . . Congress enacted [the statute], not its accompanying legislative reports.") (citations omitted).

[378]An example of an improper certification is provided by *Wood v. United States*, 995 F.2d 1122 (1st Cir. 1993). There, the sexual harassment plaintiff filed federal claims and state law tort claims alleging assault and battery against her alleged harasser. Her claims under federal law eventually were dismissed, and the U.S. Attorney filed a Westfall Act certificate asserting that the Army major who was the alleged harasser had been acting within the scope of his employment, on the ground that the complained-of incidents never had occurred. The federal district court held that harassment would be outside the scope of employment and that the Attorney General cannot make it within the scope of employment simply by denying that the injury-causing incident ever occurred. *Id.* at 1128–29.

[379]*See* United States v. Smith, 499 U.S. 160, 173 n.16 (1991) ("The exclusive remedy provision . . . is intended to substitute the United States as the solely permissible defendant in all common law tort actions against Federal employees who acted in the scope of employment.") (internal quotations omitted) (quoting H.R. REP. NO. 100-700, at 6, *reprinted in* 1988 U.S.C.C.A.N. 5950). A parallel provision governing the Tennessee Valley Authority appears at 16 U.S.C. § 831c(2) (2000).

[380]*See* Buckles v. Indian Health Serv./Belcourt Serv. Unit, 268 F. Supp. 2d 1101 (D.N.D. 2003) (claims in tort were deemed actions by the United States, upon certification by Attorney General that employees were acting in the scope of federal employment at all times relevant to the claim); *see also* Rivera v. Heyman, 157 F.3d 101, 105 (2d Cir. 1998) (Westfall Act certification provision applies only to tort claims

If no certificate is granted, or if the certificate is found improper by a court, the district court possesses the discretion either to retain jurisdiction over the case and adjudicate the controversy or, in removal cases, to remand the tort claims to state court.[381]

The Supreme Court has held that the propriety of the Attorney General's "scope of employment" certification under § 2679(d) of the Westfall Act is not conclusively binding on the district court for purposes of substitution of parties, but rather is subject to judicial review.[382] The Court did, however, hold that the certification is conclusive for purposes of removal. This difference leads to a jurisdictional difficulty when a certification is rejected on review in a removed case. The circuits continue to diverge on whether a district must retain jurisdiction in such a case. The Fourth and Fifth Circuits have ruled that district courts are required to retain jurisdiction of state law claims against federal officers and may not remand the action to state court.[383] Other courts hold that remand to state court is discretionary or even mandatory.[384] Failure of the United States to enter as a substitute defendant does not constitute an admission that supervisors were acting outside the scope of

---

and not to discrimination claims under the Human Rights Laws of New York; United States' failure to substitute itself as defendant did not permit suit against federal employee's supervisors individually under state antidiscrimination laws).

[381]*See, e.g.*, Haddon v. United States, 68 F.3d 1420, 1426–27 (D.C. Cir. 1995) (requiring remand to state court following rejection of Attorney General's certification based, in part, on concerns over district court's jurisdiction to decide state law claims); Nadler v. Mann, 951 F.2d 301, 306 n.9 (11th Cir. 1992) (remand is discretionary); Green v. Hill, 968 F.2d 1098, 1098–99 (11th Cir. 1992) (if the district court finds that the supervisor acted outside the scope of his employment, the district court has the discretion to retain jurisdiction over the assault claim or remand the case to state court); Owens v. United States, 822 F.2d 408, 410–12 (3d Cir. 1987) (the doctrine of official immunity did not shield a staff physician against state common law claims of verbal and physical sexual harassment because these were outside the physician's duties; the claims against the supervisors for failing to act on the plaintiffs' complaints were remanded); Toboas v. Mlynczak, 149 F.3d 576, 578 (7th Cir. 1998) (denial of United States' motion for substitution is effectively a denial of immunity for the defendant; hence, the doctrine of collateral order applies.)

[382]Gutierrez de Martinez v. Lamagno, 515 U.S. 417 (1995).

[383]Garcia v. United States, 88 F.3d 318, 324 (5th Cir. 1996); Borneman v. United States, 213 F.3d 819 (4th Cir. 2000).

[384]*See, e.g.*, Haddon v. United States, 68 F.3d 1420, 1426–27 (D.C. Cir. 1995) (requiring remand to state court following rejection of Attorney General's certification based, in part, on concerns over district court's jurisdiction to decide state law claims); Nadler v. Mann, 951 F.2d 301, 306 n.9 (11th Cir. 1992) (remand is discretionary).

employment so as to permit suit against individual defendants where a state or city antidiscrimination statute is invoked.[385]

The Seventh Circuit has joined the Second, Fourth, Ninth, Eleventh, and District of Columbia Circuits in explicitly holding that a denial of the United States' motion for substitution under the Westfall Act (based on certification that defendants were acting within the scope of their employment) is immediately appealable under the collateral order doctrine.[386]

Although it is generally recognized that, under the Westfall Act, evidentiary hearings are permissible to resolve factual disputes on the preliminary scope-of-employment issue,[387] a dispute exists among the circuits regarding the appropriate range of issues that may be decided in such a hearing.[388]

---

[385]See Rivera v. Heyman, 157 F.3d 101, 105 (2d Cir. 1998) (Westfall Act certification provision applies only to tort claims and not to discrimination claims under Human Rights Laws of State and City of New York; United States' failure to substitute itself as defendant did not permit suit against federal employee's supervisors individually under state antidiscrimination laws).

[386]See Toboas v. Mlynczak, 149 F.3d 576, 578 (7th Cir. 1998) (denial of United States' motion for substitution is effectively denial of immunity for defendant employee; therefore, collateral order doctrine applies in this context as it does to other claims of qualified or absolute immunity). The Seventh Circuit noted in *Toboas* that the collateral order was appealable because denial in this instance was based on finding that, as matter of law, defendants acted outside the scope of their employment. Immediate appeal of a denial of immunity would not be available under the collateral order doctrine where the court's summary judgment denial rests on a determination that there are disputed facts. 149 F.3d at 580; *see also* Flohr v. Mackovjak, 84 F.3d 386, 390 (11th Cir. 1996) (same).

[387]See, e.g., *Toboas*, 149 F.3d at 580 (citing Jamison v. Wiley, 14 F.3d 222, 236 (4th Cir. 1994) (collecting cases)).

[388]See *Toboas*, 149 F.3d at 580.

CHAPTER 32

CLASS ACTIONS

I. The Application of Rule 23 to Title VII Class Actions

A. Basic Requirements

Title VII class actions brought by private plaintiffs are governed by Rule 23 of the Federal Rules of Civil Procedure.[1] "An individual litigant seeking to maintain a class action under Title VII must meet 'the prerequisites of numerosity, commonality, typicality, and adequacy of representation' specified in Rule 23(a)."[2] In addition, a plaintiff must also satisfy the requirements of one of the three types of class actions defined by Rule 23(b).[3] Typically, Title VII class actions involve certification under either Rule 23(b)(2)

---

[1]General Tel. Co. of the Sw. v. Falcon, 457 U.S. 147, 161, 28 FEP 1745 (1982) ("[W]e reiterate today that a Title VII class action, like any other class action, may only be certified if the trial court is satisfied, after a rigorous analysis, that the prerequisites of Rule 23(a) have been satisfied.").

[2]*Id.* at 156 (citation omitted). Rule 23(a) provides:
    (a) Prerequisites to a Class Action. One or more members of a class may sue or be sued as representative parties on behalf of all only if (1) the class is so numerous that joinder of all members is impracticable, (2) there are questions of law or fact common to the class, (3) the claims or defenses of the representative parties are typical of the claims or defenses of the class, and (4) the representative parties will fairly and adequately protect the interests of the class.

[3]Rule 23(b) provides:
    (b) Class Actions Maintainable. An action may be maintained as a class action if the prerequisites of subdivision (a) are satisfied, and in addition:

or (b)(3), rather than Rule 23(b)(1). Class actions brought under Rule 23(b)(3) must, in addition, comply with the notice requirement of Rule 23(c)(2), which allows individual class members to "opt out" of the class or be represented by separate counsel.[4]

Title VII pattern-or-practice actions brought by the Equal Employment Opportunity Commission (EEOC) or the U.S. Department of Justice on behalf of groups of aggrieved persons are not governed by Rule 23.[5] Similarly, class suits under the Age Discrimination in Employment Act (ADEA) and Equal Pay Act (EPA) are not governed by Rule 23.[6]

Prior to 1991, Title VII class actions were typically certified under Rule 23(b)(2).[7] The focus of these actions was injunctive

---

(1) the prosecution of separate actions by or against individual members of the class would create a risk of
   (A) inconsistent or varying adjudications with respect to individual members of the class which would establish incompatible standards of conduct for the party opposing the class, or
   (B) adjudications with respect to individual members of the class which would as a practical matter be dispositive of the interests of the other members not parties to the adjudications or substantially impair or impede their ability to protect their interests; or
(2) the party opposing the class has acted or refused to act on grounds generally applicable to the class, thereby making appropriate final injunctive relief or corresponding declaratory relief with respect to the class as a whole; or
(3) the court finds that the questions of law or fact common to the members of the class predominate over any questions affecting only individual members, and that a class action is superior to other available methods for the fair and efficient adjudication of the controversy. The matters pertinent to the findings include: (A) the interest of members of the class in individually controlling the prosecution or defense of separate actions; (B) the extent and nature of any litigation concerning the controversy already commenced by or against members of the class; (C) the desirability or undesirability of concentrating the litigation of the claims in the particular forum; (D) the difficulties likely to be encountered in the management of a class action.
   [4]FED. R. CIV. P. 23(c)(2). There also may be constitutional notice and "opt-out" requirements in other kinds of class actions. *See* Phillips Petroleum Co. v. Shutts, 472 U.S. 797, 811–12 (1985) (notice and opportunity to opt out are required to subject out-of-state class members to personal jurisdiction of forum state where class action is brought under state law).
   [5]General Tel. Co. of the Nw., Inc. v. EEOC, 446 U.S. 318, 324, 329, 22 FEP 1196 (1980).
   [6]29 U.S.C. §§ 621–634 (2000). *See generally* Chapter 12 (Age).
   [7]Amchem Prods., Inc. v. Windsor, 521 U.S. 591, 614 (1997) ("Civil rights cases against parties charged with unlawful, class-based discrimination are prime examples

relief—plaintiffs would seek a court order to change employment practices alleged to be discriminatory.[8] Although plaintiffs might also seek equitable relief in the form of back pay and reinstatement, Rule 23(b)(2) certification was still considered appropriate if the monetary relief was not the exclusive or predominant remedy.[9]

The Civil Rights Act of 1991 amended Title VII by adding new damage remedies and jury trial rights for disparate treatment claims.[10] The courts continue to grapple with how these changes affect certification of employment discrimination class actions under Rule 23.[11]

B. 2003 Revisions to Rule 23

Rule 23 was substantially amended in 2003.[12] The changes to Rule 23 apply to both pending and future cases.[13] The purpose of the amendments was to increase the role of the district court in supervising the conduct of class actions.[14] The amendments did not alter the requirements for certification under Rules 23(a) and (b).[15] Instead, the revised rule implements new standards or procedures

---

[of Rule 23(b) (2) cases].”); Wetzel v. Liberty Mut. Ins. Co., 508 F.2d 239, 250, 9 FEP 211 (3d Cir. 1975) (“the drafters of Rule 23 specifically contemplated that suits against discriminatory hiring and promotion policies would be appropriately maintained under (b)(2)”).

[8]Albemarle Paper Co. v. Moody, 422 U.S. 405, 415–18, 10 FEP 1181 (1975) (district courts have “not merely the power but the duty to render a decree which will so far as possible eliminate the discriminatory effects of the past as well as bar like discrimination in the future”).

[9]*Wetzel*, 508 F.2d at 250–52 (“since a Title VII suit is essentially equitable in nature, it cannot be characterized as one seeking exclusively or predominantly money damages”).

[10]42 U.S.C. § 1981a(b), (c) (2000).

[11]*See* Section IV *infra.*

[12]The changes became effective December 1, 2003. *See* Amendments to the Federal Rules of Civil Procedure, Communication From the Chief Justice, the Supreme Court of the United States, 215 F.R.D. 158, 161 (2003).

[13]*Id.*

[14]REPORT OF THE JUDICIAL CONFERENCE COMMITTEE ON RULES OF PRACTICE AND PROCEDURE TO THE CHIEF JUSTICE OF THE UNITED STATES AND MEMBERS OF THE JUDICIAL CONFERENCE OF THE UNITED STATES 8 (Sept. 2002), *available at* http://www.uscourts.gov/rules/jc09-2002/Report.pdf (“The overall goal of the advisory committee has been to develop rule amendments that provide the district courts with the tools, authority, and discretion to closely supervise class-action litigation.”).

[15]*Id.* (“The proposals focus on class-action procedures rather than on substantive certification standards.”).

for appointment of class counsel,[16] attorney's fees awards,[17] and settlement approval.[18] For purposes of employment discrimination class actions, one of the most significant changes is the amendment to Rule 23(c) to permit but not require class notice in cases certified under Rule 23(b)(2), at the discretion of the trial court.[19] The amendments to Rule 23 were not intended to change substantive class action law.[20]

II. MAJOR SUBSTANTIVE THEORIES FOR CLASS ACTION TREATMENT

A. Disparate Treatment Theory

Employment discrimination class actions may be based on a theory of disparate treatment.[21] A disparate treatment class action alleges that the employer has engaged in a pattern or practice of discriminatory treatment of the plaintiffs and members of the plaintiffs' protected class.[22] Plaintiffs frequently challenge an employer's subjective decision-making processes under a disparate treatment theory.[23] Disparate treatment class claims require proof of discriminatory motive.[24]

In *Teamsters v. United States*,[25] the U.S. Supreme Court articulated the order and burdens of proof in disparate treatment class actions, which are very different from those applicable to individual disparate treatment cases.[26] In disparate treatment class actions, the

---

[16]FED. R. CIV. P. 23(g); *see* Section III B.4 *infra*.

[17]FED. R. CIV. P. 23(h); *see* Section IX. E *infra*.

[18]FED. R. CIV. P. 23(e); *see* Section IX *infra*.

[19]FED. R. CIV. P. 23(c)(2)(A); *see* Section VII *infra*.

[20]The Rules Enabling Act provides that federal procedural rules "shall not abridge, enlarge or modify any substantive right." 28 U.S.C. § 2072(b).

[21]*See generally* Chapter 2 (Disparate Treatment).

[22]Teamsters v. United States, 431 U.S. 324, 334–35, 14 FEP 1514 (1977).

[23]*See* Section III.D.1 *infra*.

[24]*Teamsters*, 431 U.S. at 335 n.15 ("Proof of discriminatory motive is critical, although it can in some situations be inferred from the mere fact of differences in treatment.").

[25]431 U.S. 324.

[26]*See, e.g.*, McDonnell Douglas Corp. v. Green, 411 U.S. 792, 800–07, 5 FEP 965 (1973) (setting forth order and allocation of proof in individual disparate treatment cases).

plaintiff bears the burden of showing by a preponderance of the evidence that disparate treatment was the employer's "standard operating procedure."[27] Typically, the plaintiff will rely on a combination of statistical and anecdotal evidence, together with documents and testimony establishing the existence and nature of the disputed practice, to meet this prima facie burden.[28] The burden then shifts to the employer to rebut the showing. Employers often attack plaintiffs' statistical evidence, offer an alternative statistical analysis, or both.[29]

If the plaintiff proves liability, the case moves to the remedial phase, in which class members may seek individual relief. Class members are presumed to be victims of the discriminatory pattern or practice, and the employer bears the burden of rebutting the presumption at this phase.[30]

B. Adverse Impact Theory

Employment practices that are neutral on their face but have a disparate impact on a protected group are often challenged in a class action.[31] Unlike in disparate treatment cases, in adverse impact cases plaintiffs need not prove the existence of a discriminatory motive.[32]

---

[27]*Teamsters*, 431 U.S. at 336 & n.16; *see also McDonnell Douglas*, 411 U.S. at 804–05.

[28]*See, e.g., Teamsters*, 431 U.S. at 338–39 ("The Government bolstered its statistical evidence with the testimony of individuals who recounted over 40 specific instances of discrimination . . . [bringing] the cold numbers convincingly to life.").

[29]*See generally* Chapter 34 (Statistical and Other Expert Proof).

[30]*See Teamsters*, 431 U.S. at 361–62 ("[T]he question of individual relief does not arise until it has been proved that the employer has followed an employment policy of unlawful discrimination. The force of that proof does not dissipate at the remedial stage of the trial. The employer cannot, therefore, claim that there is no reason to believe that its individual employment decisions were discriminatorily based; it has already been shown to have maintained a policy of discriminatory decisionmaking.

"The proof of the pattern or practice supports an inference that any particular employment decision, during the period in which the discriminatory policy was in force, was made in pursuit of that policy. The Government need only show that an alleged individual discriminatee unsuccessfully applied for a job and therefore was a potential victim of the proved discrimination. As in *Franks*, the burden then rests on the employer to demonstrate that the individual applicant was denied an employment opportunity for lawful reasons.") (footnotes omitted).

[31]*See generally* Chapter 3 (Adverse Impact).

[32]Griggs v. Duke Power Co., 401 U.S. 424, 430–32, 3 FEP 175 (1971) ("The Act proscribes . . . practices that are fair in form, but discriminatory in operation.").

Under the Civil Rights Act of 1991, a plaintiff who brings an adverse impact claim must identify a specific practice or specific practices as the cause of the alleged adverse impact, unless the plaintiff establishes that the elements of the decision-making process are not capable of separation for analysis.[33] In the classic adverse impact case, the named plaintiffs have been excluded from an employment opportunity because of their failure to satisfy a facially neutral selection criterion; they seek to represent a class of persons likewise excluded, at a significantly disproportionate rate, from the same opportunity by the same criterion. Challenged practices might include, for example, a height or weight requirement,[34] a scored test,[35] or an education requirement.[36]

The Supreme Court ruled in *Watson v. Fort Worth Bank & Trust*[37] that "subjective or discretionary employment practices may be analyzed under the disparate impact approach in appropriate cases."[38]

Under the adverse impact approach, the burdens of production and persuasion initially rest with the plaintiff, who must establish a prima facie case of discrimination by demonstrating that the challenged employment practice or policy causes a substantial adverse impact on a protected group.[39] If adverse impact is established, the burdens of production and persuasion shift to the defendant to prove

---

[33]42 U.S.C. § 2000e-2(k)(1)(B) (2000). This legislation codified in part and modified in part the Supreme Court's holding in *Wards Cove Packing Co. v. Atonio*, 490 U.S. 642, 49 FEP 1519 (1989), that adverse impact plaintiffs must identify a specific practice of the employer that causes the adverse impact. 490 U.S. at 656–57.

[34]*See, e.g.*, Dothard v. Rawlinson, 433 U.S. 321, 324 n.2, 332, 15 FEP 10 (1977) (holding that Alabama statute establishing minimum height and weight requirements for all law enforcement officers, which resulted in discriminatory impact on female applicants, presented prima facie case of sex discrimination); Officers for Justice v. Civil Serv. Comm'n, 473 F. Supp. 801, 804 (N.D. Cal. 1979) (holding that preselection minimum height requirement that had adverse impact on Hispanics, Asians, and women presented prima facie case of employment discrimination), *aff'd*, 688 F.2d 615 (9th Cir. 1984).

[35]*Griggs*, 401 U.S. at 432 (holding, unanimously, that employment tests that are discriminatory in effect are violative of Title VII unless defendant employer meets "burden of showing that any given requirement . . . [has] a manifest relationship to the employment in question"); *see also* Albemarle Paper Co. v. Moody, 422 U.S. 405, 425–26, 436 (1975) (discussing concept of job relatedness with respect to employment tests).

[36]*Griggs*, 401 U.S. at 432–33.

[37]487 U.S. 977, 47 FEP 102 (1988).

[38]487 U.S. at 991; *see, e.g.*, McClain v. Lufkin Indus., Inc., 187 F.R.D. 267, 272 (E.D. Tex. 1999); *see also* Section III.D.1 *infra*.

[39]*See* 42 U.S.C. § 2000e-2(k)(1)(A)(i) (2000); *Albemarle Paper*, 422 U.S. at 425. Title VII, as amended by the 1991 Act, defines the phrase "demonstrates" as "meets the burdens of production and persuasion." 42 U.S.C. § 2000e(m) (2000).

that the practice or policy is "job related for the position in question and consistent with business necessity."[40] If the defendant employer meets the burden of proving that the challenged employment practice or policy is job-related, then the burden shifts back to the plaintiff to show that the employer refused to implement an effective alternative practice or hiring device that would have a lesser adverse impact.[41]

C. Hostile Environment Claims

In *Meritor Savings Bank v. Vinson*,[42] the Supreme Court recognized that a hostile work environment was a form of discrimination that violated Title VII. Although the *Meritor* case involved an individual case, class actions have been brought alleging a racially or sexually hostile work environment theory. The EEOC has also prosecuted pattern-or-practice enforcement actions under this theory; such EEOC actions, however, are not subject to Rule 23.[43] The Supreme Court has not yet addressed the issues presented by hostile work environment class claims.

The essence of a hostile work environment class action is that a protected group has been exposed to a workplace permeated with "discriminatory intimidation, ridicule and insult."[44] The class action challenges the practice of the employer in failing to provide adequate checks against discriminatory conduct and comment in the workplace. Hostile work environment class claims have been brought on their own or together with other disparate treatment

---

[40]42 U.S.C. § 2000e-2(k)(1)(A)(i) (2000); *see Griggs*, 401 U.S. at 431 ("The touchstone is business necessity.").

[41]42 U.S.C. § 2000e-2(k)(1)(A)(ii), (k)(1)(C) (2000); *see Albemarle Paper*, 422 U.S. at 425 ("Such a showing would be evidence that the employer was using its tests merely as a 'pretext' for discrimination."). The 1991 Act did not resolve the issue of whether the alternative must be "equally effective," stating instead that the necessary "demonstration" by the plaintiff "shall be in accordance with the law as it existed on June 4, 1989." 42 U.S.C. § 2000e-2(k)(1)(c) (2000).

[42]477 U.S. 57, 67, 40 FEP 1822 (1986). *See generally* Chapter 19 (Sexual and Other Forms of Harassment).

[43]EEOC v. Dial Corp., 259 F. Supp. 2d 710 (N.D. Ill. 2003) (establishing four-phase trial plan for sexual harassment pattern-or-practice case, including compensatory and punitive damages); EEOC v. Foster Wheeler Constructors, Inc., 1999 U.S. Dist. LEXIS 11226 (N.D. Ill. July 13, 1999) (rejecting defendant's argument that "subjective element of hostile work environment claims makes them inappropriate for class resolution"); EEOC v. Mitsubishi Motor Mfg. of Am., Inc., 990 F. Supp. 1059, 75 FEP 1379 (C.D. Ill. 1998) (establishing order and burdens of proof for sexually hostile work environment pattern-or-practice case).

[44]Harris v. Forklift Sys., Inc., 510 U.S. 17, 21, 63 FEP 225 (1993).

class allegations.[45] Some district courts have granted class certification in hostile work environment cases,[46] whereas others have not.[47]

---

[45]*See, e.g.*, Jenson v. Eveleth Taconite Co., 130 F.3d 1287 (8th Cir. 1997) (female employees brought class action alleging sex discrimination in promotions and sexual harassment in violation of Title VII and Minnesota Human Rights Act); Jones v. R.R. Donnelley & Sons, 305 F.3d 717 (7th Cir. 2002) (several subclasses of African-American former employees alleging discriminatory transfer, discriminatory termination, and racially hostile work environment), *rev'd and remanded on other grounds*, 541 U.S. 369 (2004); Allen v. International Truck & Engine Corp., 2003 U.S. Dist. LEXIS 4497, at *1–2, 91 FEP 709 (S.D. Ind. Mar. 21, 2003) (plaintiffs sought class certification of hostile work environment and race discrimination claims), *vacated and remanded for certification*, 358 F.3d. 469 (7th Cir. 2004).

[46]Latino Police Officers Ass'n v. City of N.Y., 209 F.R.D. 79, 81 (S.D.N.Y. 2002) (certifying class of Latino and African-American New York City police officers alleging race discrimination, racially hostile work environment, disparate disciplinary treatment, and retaliation); Adams v. R.R. Donnelley & Sons, 189 F.R.D. 383, 387 (N.D. Ill. 2001) (certifying racially hostile work environment subclasses of African-American workers in four different divisions); Wilfong v. Rent-A-Center, Inc., 87 FEP 1096 (S.D. Ill. 2001) (certifying sexually hostile work environment claims of workers in 2,200 stores nationwide); Beckmann v. CBS, Inc., 192 F.R.D. 608, 90 FEP 1379 (D. Minn. 2000) (certifying gender-related hostile environment claim covering women in five television stations in five states); BreMiller v. Cleveland Psychiatric Inst., 195 F.R.D. 1 (N.D. Ohio 2000) (denying employer's motion to decertify gender-related hostile environment claim covering facilities in four counties); Warnell v. Ford Motor Co., 189 F.R.D. 383, 388 (N.D. Ill. 1999) (substantially similar comments and behavior against women in same auto plant); Toney v. Rosewood Care Ctr., Inc., 1999 U.S. Dist. LEXIS 4744 (N.D. Ill. Mar. 31, 1999) (certifying racially hostile work environment subclass); Markham v. White, 171 F.R.D. 217, 223 (N.D. Ill. 1997) (certifying class of female police officers in sexual harassment suit against individual defendants); Neal v. Director, D.C. Dep't of Corr., 1995 U.S. Dist. LEXIS 11469 (D.D.C. Aug. 9, 1995) (classwide order of injunctive relief against defendant employer after final judgment found employer liable for hostile work environment); Adams v. Pinole Point Steel Co., 65 FEP 774 (N.D. Cal. 1994) (certifying race and gender discrimination subclass and hostile environment subclass); Jenson v. Eveleth Taconite Co., 139 F.R.D. 657, 667 (D. Minn. 1991) (certifying gender discrimination claim but denying preliminary injunction in hostile environment claim); *see also Allen*, 2003 U.S. Dist. LEXIS 4497, at *2–3 (in racially hostile work environment case, concluding that plaintiffs satisfied Rule 23(a) requirements but declining to allow plaintiffs to represent others similarly situated, foreclosing certification under Rule 23(b)(2) or (b)(3)).

[47]*See* Barabin v. Aramark Corp., 210 F.R.D. 152, 161–62, 90 FEP 349 (E.D. Pa. 2002) (in case alleging hostile work environment and disparate discipline against African-American employees, denying certification because individual issues predominated over common questions), *aff'd*, 2003 U.S. App. LEXIS 3532 (3d Cir. Jan. 24, 2003); Cooper v. Southern Co., 205 F.R.D. 596, 609–10 (N.D. Ga. 2001) (denying certification in case alleging racially hostile work environment, among other claims, because individualized issues predominated), *aff'd*, 390 F.3d 695 (11th Cir. 2004), *cert. denied*, 126 S. Ct. 478 (2005), *overruled in part on other grounds by* Ash v. Tyson Foods, Inc., 546 U.S. 454, 97 FEP 641 (2006); Miller v. Hygrade Food Prods.

To date, few courts of appeals have ruled on class treatment or other issues in hostile work environment putative class cases.[48]

The central question presented at class certification in hostile work environment cases is whether the plaintiffs have alleged a common policy or practice or simply a number of individual or isolated incidents.[49] Because plaintiffs in hostile work environment putative class actions typically seek compensatory and punitive damages, the issues that these remedies raise for Rule 23(b) class certification are also present.[50]

Corp., 198 F.R.D. 638, 641–45, 84 FEP 1755 (E.D. Pa. 2001) (denying certification in disparate treatment and racially hostile work environment case); Burrell v. Crown Cent. Petroleum, Inc., 197 F.R.D. 284, 290–91 (E.D. Tex. 2000) (denying class certification in hostile environment case because success of plaintiffs' claims would turn on individualized issues rather than on whether employer engaged in a pattern or practice of discrimination); Faulk v. Home Oil Co., 184 F.R.D. 645, 659, 82 FEP 451 (M.D. Ala. 1999) (determining that plaintiffs' hostile environment claim was "not subject to generalized proof" because "[a]pplicants who were not hired and never worked . . . could not have been subjected to a hostile working environment in the same manner as . . . employees," and diverse activities alleged to have occurred at different employment facilities "create[d] a formidable barrier to class certification"); Levels v. Akzo Nobel Salt, Inc., 178 F.R.D. 171, 177–78 (N.D. Ohio 1998) (refusing to certify hostile environment class action, finding that separate conditions that existed in different job locations prevented finding of commonality or typicality); Reyes v. Walt Disney World Co., 176 F.R.D. 654, 658, 76 FEP 338 (M.D. Fla. 1998) (denying certification, noting that any class would present "the very real danger of . . . splinter[ing] into an unmanageable plethora of individualized claims").

[48]See Allen v. International Truck & Engine Corp., 358 F.3d 469 (7th Cir. 2004) (vacating district court's denial of certification in racially hostile work environment case and directing district court to certify Rule 23(b)(2) class for injunctive purposes and to reconsider class treatment of damages); Barabin v. Aramark Corp., 2003 U.S. App. LEXIS 3532 (3d Cir. Jan. 24, 2003) (affirming denial of certification in racially hostile work environment case); Jenson v. Eveleth Taconite Co., 130 F.3d 1287, 75 FEP 852 (8th Cir. 1997) (in sexually hostile work environment class action, appellate court endorsed liability finding but remanded for reconsideration of compensatory and punitive damage claims).

[49]Compare Jenson v. Eveleth Taconite Co., 824 F. Supp. 847, 885 (D. Minn. 1993) ("[T]rier of fact must keep in mind that 'each successive episode has its predecessors, that the impact of the separate incidents may accumulate, and that the work environment created may exceed the sum of the individual episodes.' ") and In re Allstate Ins. Co., 400 F.3d 505, 508 (7th Cir. 2005) (in ERISA case, stating that "a single hearing may be all that's necessary to determine whether Allstate had a policy" of constructively discharging employees by a campaign of harassment, designed to prevent them from becoming eligible for severance pay) with Levels, 178 F.R.D. at 178, 180 ("In [plaintiffs' various work] positions, they are exposed to different co-employees, different supervisors, and different working conditions. . . . [T]he conduct each Plaintiff complains of varies with individual circumstances . . . .").

[50]See Section IV infra.

No appellate court has directly addressed the evidentiary standards and burdens of proof in a class hostile work environment trial.[51] District courts have taken different approaches to adapting the *Teamsters* burden shifting to the proof requirements for a hostile work environment claim.[52]

D. Reasonable Accommodation and Other Disability Class Claims

The Americans with Disabilities Act of 1990 (ADA) prohibits discrimination against qualified individuals with disabilities in public and private employment.[53] Class-based disability discrimination may be challenged using disparate treatment, disparate impact, or hostile work environment theories.[54]

In addition, Title I of the ADA requires employers to reasonably accommodate applicants and employees who have disabilities.[55] The duty of reasonable accommodation presents an additional class action theory. Under the ADA, however, whether a worker is disabled and whether an accommodation is reasonable

---

[51]In *Jenson*, 130 F.3d at 1299–1300, the Eighth Circuit panel endorsed burden shifting for Stage II constructive discharge claims as set forth in *Franks v. Bowman Transportation Co.*, 424 U.S. 747, 12 FEP 549 (1976), and in *Teamsters v. United States*, 431 U.S. 324, 14 FEP 1514 (1977).

[52]*See* EEOC v. Mitsubishi Motor Mfg., Inc., 990 F. Supp. 1059, 75 FEP 1379 (C.D. Ill. 1998) (upon showing of objectively hostile work environment, employer bears burden of demonstrating that it was not on notice and was not negligent with respect to particular claimant); EEOC v. Foster Wheeler Constructors, Inc., 1999 U.S. Dist. LEXIS 11226, at *2 (N.D. Ill. 1999) (declining to shift burden of production to employer on subjective element of pattern-or-practice harassment claim).

[53]42 U.S.C. § 12112(a), (b) (2000).

[54]Daggett v. Blind Enters. of Or., 1996 U.S. Dist. LEXIS 22465 (D. Or. Apr. 18, 1996) (certifying class challenging discriminatory pay to blind and partially blind employees but denying certification of reasonable accommodation class); Hendricks-Robinson v. Excel Corp., 164 F.R.D. 667 (C.D. Ill. 1996) (certifying class challenging medical layoff policy); Wilson v. Pennsylvania State Police Dep't, 1995 U.S. Dist. LEXIS 9981 (E.D. Pa. July 17, 1995) (certifying class challenging medical standards for police officers); Kimble v. Hayes, 1990 U.S. Dist. LEXIS 2418, 52 FEP 999 (E.D. Pa. 1990) (rejected applicants for police officer positions challenged vision standards under § 504 of Rehabilitation Act); Dyer-Neely v. City of Chi., 101 F.R.D. 83 (N.D. Ill. 1984) (certifying class challenging medical standards for police officers under Rehabilitation Act).

[55]42 U.S.C. §§ 12111(9), 12112(b)(5) (2000).

are typically fact-specific inquiries.[56] Courts have denied class certification in employment reasonable accommodation cases under the ADA because of the need for individualized assessments implicated by the plaintiffs' and putative class members' varying disabilities.[57] Reasonable accommodation class cases have been certified when challenging a specific, uniformly applied employment practice or policy.[58]

III. THE REQUIREMENTS OF RULE 23(A)

A. Commonality and Typicality

1. General Principles

Rule 23(a)(2) of the Federal Rules of Civil Procedure requires the plaintiff to establish that "there are questions of law or fact

---

[56]Sutton v. United Air Lines, Inc., 527 U.S. 471, 483 (1999) ("[W]hether a person has a disability under the ADA is an individualized inquiry."); Albertson's Inc. v. Kirkingburg, 527 U.S. 555 (1999) ("The [ADA] expresses [the statutory obligation to determine the existence of disabilities on a case-by-case basis] clearly by defining 'disability' 'with respect to an individual,' and in terms of the impact of an impairment on 'such individual.' ") (citations omitted).

[57]See, e.g., Sokol v. New United Motor Mfg., 9 AD 1767 (N.D. Cal. 1999) (denying class certification in ADA challenge to employer's procedures for assigning employees with medical restrictions to permanent positions because each claim would require individualized inquiry and claims, therefore, did not satisfy typicality requirement); Lintemuth v. Saturn Corp., 3 AD 1490, 1492–93 (M.D. Tenn. Aug. 29, 1994) (denying class certification in part because of "variance in the named plaintiffs' personal characteristics, coupled with the individualized, case-by-case analysis required by the ADA"); cf. Burkett v. United States Postal Serv., 175 F.R.D. 220, 224 (N.D. W.Va. 1997) (refusing to certify ADA class, reasoning that each class member would have to "introduce evidence concerning, inter alia, their medical history, the nature of their medical condition, and how their impairments were perceived by the Postal Service").

[58]See Bates v. United Parcel Serv., 204 F.R.D. 440, 443–44, 448 (N.D. Cal. 2001) (certifying nationwide class of hearing-impaired workers challenging blanket rule requiring drivers of all trucks to meet DOT hearing standards, even though DOT applies standard only to drivers of trucks exceeding 10,000 pounds; rejecting employer's argument that ADA requires individualized analyses that would prohibit class treatment), aff'd, 2006 WL 2864438, at *6 n.12 (9th Cir. Oct. 10, 2006); cf. Davoll v. Webb, 194 F.3d 1116, 1146–48, 9 AD 1533 (10th Cir. 1999) (affirming decision denying class certification for putative ADA private class action challenging prohibition of reassignment of police officers with disabilities but allowing U.S. government to pursue pattern-or-practice case using Teamsters framework).

common to the class." To satisfy the Rule 23(a) "commonality" requirement, plaintiffs need articulate only one issue of law or fact common to the class.[59] That issue, however, must be "a common issue the resolution of which will advance the litigation."[60] According to the Fifth Circuit, the common questions must "affect all or a substantial number of the class members," but the "threshold for 'commonality' is not high."[61] The Ninth Circuit has noted that, to satisfy commonality, "[t]he existence of shared legal issues with divergent factual predicates is sufficient, as is a common core of salient facts coupled with disparate legal remedies within the class."[62]

The "typicality" requirement of Rule 23(a)(3) seeks to ensure that "the claims or defenses of the representative parties are typical of the claims or defenses of the class."[63] Typicality, however, "does not mean that the claims of the class representative[s] must be identical or substantially identical to those of the absent class members."[64] The Seventh Circuit has noted that typicality "should be determined with reference to the company's actions, not with respect to particularized defenses it might have against certain class members."[65]

The Supreme Court recognized, in *General Telephone Co. v. Falcon*,[66] that the commonality and typicality inquiries are closely aligned:

> The commonality and typicality requirements of Rule 23(a) tend to merge. Both serve as guideposts for determining whether under the particular circumstances maintenance of a class action is economical and whether the named plaintiff's claim and the class claims

---

[59]Lightbourn v. County of El Paso, 118 F.3d 421, 426 (5th Cir. 1997) ("The commonality test is met when there is at least one issue, the resolution of which will affect all or a significant number of the putative class members."); *In re* American Med. Sys. Inc., 75 F.3d 1069, 1080–81 (6th Cir. 1996) (citing 1 HERBERT B. NEWBERG & ALBA CONTE, NEWBERG ON CLASS ACTIONS § 3.10 (3d ed. 1992)).

[60]Sprague v. General Motors Corp., 133 F.3d 388, 397 (6th Cir. 1998).

[61]Jenkins v. Raymark Indus., 782 F.2d 468, 472 (5th Cir. 1986).

[62]Staton v. Boeing Co., 327 F.3d 938, 953 (9th Cir. 2003) (quoting Hanlon v. Chrysler Corp., 150 F.3d 1011, 1019 (9th Cir. 1998)).

[63]FED. R. CIV. P. 23(a)(3).

[64]5 HERBERT B. NEWBERG & ALBA CONTE, NEWBERG ON CLASS ACTIONS § 24.25, at 24-105 (3d ed. 1992) [hereinafter NEWBERG ON CLASS ACTIONS (3d ed. 1992)].

[65]Wagner v. NutraSweet Co., 95 F.3d 527, 534, 72 FEP 284 (7th Cir. 1996).

[66]457 U.S. 147, 23 FEP 1745 (1982).

are so interrelated that the interests of the class members will be fairly and adequately protected in their absence.[67]

The commonality and typicality inquiries are also closely related to the adequacy of representation requirement.[68] Commonality and typicality, together with adequacy of representation,[69] are sometimes referred to as the "nexus" requirements because they share a basic theme: they all involve an analysis of the relationship or "nexus" between the named plaintiff(s) and the alleged class.[70] A demonstration of these three factors ensures that maintenance of a class action is economical and that the named plaintiff and the claimed class have substantially the same interests. This theme also is reflected in the Supreme Court's mandate in *East Texas Motor Freight Systems, Inc. v. Rodriguez* that the class representative must " 'possess the same interest and suffer the same injury' as the class members."[71]

Rule 23(a) inquiries in Title VII cases often compare the named plaintiffs and the alleged class in three areas: (1) the nature of the claims asserted, (2) the job classifications involved, and (3) the organizational units or geographic facilities involved.[72] Each of these issues is discussed in Section III.D *infra*.

---

[67]457 U.S. at 158 n.13.

[68]*Id.*; Amchem Prods., Inc. v. Windsor, 521 U.S. 591, 626 n.20 (1997); Stastny v. Southern Bell Tel. & Tel. Co., 628 F.2d 267, 274, 23 FEP 665 (4th Cir. 1980).

[69]See the discussion of Rule 23(a) adequacy of representation at Section III.B *infra* and Rule 23(g) appointment of class counsel at Section III.B.4 *infra*.

[70]*See, e.g.*, Dukes v. Wal-Mart, Inc., 474 F.3d 1214, 1232 n.10 (9th Cir. 2007) ("Commonality examines the relationship of facts and legal issues common to class members, while typicality focuses on the relationship of facts and issues between the class and its representatives.") (citing 1 NEWBERG ON CLASS ACTIONS § 3:13 at 317); Piazza v. Ebsco Indus., Inc., 273 F.3d 1341, 1346 (11th Cir. 2001) (typicality and commonality requirements focus on whether a sufficient nexus exists between the legal claims of the named class representatives and those of individual class members to warrant class certification); Washington v. Brown & Williamson Tobacco Corp., 959 F.2d 1566, 1569, 60 FEP 800 (11th Cir. 1992) ("commonality and typicality represent the 'nexus' necessary between class representatives and class members").

[71]431 U.S. 395, 403, 14 FEP 1505 (1977) (quoting Schlesinger v. Reservists Comm. to Stop the War, 418 U.S. 208, 216 (1974)); *accord* Harriston v. Chicago Tribune Co., 992 F.2d 697, 703, 63 FEP 319 (7th Cir. 1993); Aleknagik Natives Ltd. v. Andrus, 648 F.2d 496, 505 (9th Cir. 1980); Arnold v. Postmaster Gen., 667 F. Supp. 6 (D.D.C. 1987).

[72]*See, e.g.*, Harriss v. Pan Am. World Airways, Inc., 74 F.R.D. 24, 41, 15 FEP 1640 (N.D. Cal. 1977).

2. A Historical Perspective—Rejection of the Across-the-Board Approach and the General Policy of Discrimination Exception

Before the Supreme Court's decisions in *Rodriguez*[73] and *Falcon*,[74] many courts were more lenient in finding compliance with Rule 23(a) in Title VII cases than in other types of cases.[75] Without formally addressing the requirements of Rule 23(a), those courts permitted the named plaintiff to raise an "across-the-board" charge of employment discrimination against his or her employer and to represent all persons in the same protected class allegedly affected by discrimination, even those who had employment situations that were materially different from that of the named plaintiffs. For example, the broad across-the-board approach was held to allow a discharged employee who alleged race discrimination to represent all minority applicants, employees, and former employees of the defendant employer.[76] The primary rationale for this approach was that discrimination actions are "by their nature" class actions.[77]

The Supreme Court questioned the propriety of the broad across-the-board approach in *Rodriguez*,[78] where the Court considered for the first time the application of Rule 23 to Title VII actions. In a unanimous decision, the Court stated that, although Title VII cases can be class suits, they must nonetheless satisfy the requirements of Rule 23:

> We are not unaware that suits alleging racial or ethnic discrimination are often by their very nature class suits, involving classwide wrongs. Common questions of law or fact are typically present. But careful attention to the requirements of Fed. Rule Civ. Proc. 23 remains nonetheless indispensable. The mere fact that a complaint alleges racial or ethnic discrimination does not in itself ensure that the party who has brought the lawsuit will be an adequate

---

[73]431 U.S. 395.

[74]General Tel. Co. of the Sw. v. Falcon, 457 U.S. 147, 28 FEP 1745 (1982).

[75]*See, e.g.*, Johnson v. Georgia Highway Express, Inc., 417 F.2d 1122, 1127, 2 FEP 231 (5th Cir. 1969) (Godbold, J., concurring) ("The broad brush approach of some of the Title VII cases is in sharp contrast to the diligence with which in other areas we carefully protect those whose rights may be affected by litigation.").

[76]*See, e.g.*, Long v. Sapp, 502 F.2d 34, 43, 8 FEP 1079 (5th Cir. 1974).

[77]*See* Bowe v. Colgate-Palmolive Co., 416 F.2d 711, 719, 2 FEP 121 (7th Cir. 1969) ("A suit for violation of Title VII is necessarily a class action as the evil sought to be ended is discrimination on the basis of a class characteristic, *i.e.*, race, sex, religion or national origin.").

[78]431 U.S. 395, 14 FEP 1505 (1977).

representative of those who may have been the real victims of that discrimination.[79]

Five years later, in *Falcon*,[80] the Supreme Court reiterated the *Rodriguez* rule that Title VII classes are to be certified on the basis of Rule 23, not mere presumptions. The plaintiff must identify the questions of law and fact common to the class and show that the plaintiff's claims are typical of those of the class.[81] The Court emphasized that the error inherent in the broad across-the-board rule is the "failure to evaluate carefully the legitimacy of the named plaintiff's plea that he [is] a proper class representative" under Rule 23(a).[82] As noted earlier, rigorous compliance with Rule 23(a) would ensure that the "plaintiff's claim and the class claims are so interrelated that the interests of the class members will be fairly and adequately protected in their absence."[83]

Although the Supreme Court in *Falcon* restricted the use of across-the-board certification, the Court noted important exceptions. In its now-famous Footnote 15, the Court identified circumstances in which a plaintiff properly may represent others outside the plaintiff's job category:

> If petitioner used a biased testing procedure to evaluate both applicants for employment and incumbent employees, a class action on behalf of every applicant or employee who might have been prejudiced by the test clearly would satisfy the commonality and typicality requirements of Rule 23(a). Significant proof that an employer operated under a general policy of discrimination conceivably could justify a class of both applicants and employees if the discrimination manifested itself in hiring and promotion practices in the same general fashion, such as through entirely subjective decision-making processes.[84]

---

[79]*Id.* at 405–06.

[80]457 U.S. 147, 28 FEP 1745 (1982).

[81]*Id.* at 157.

[82]*Id.* at 161. In applying *Falcon* and Rule 23 to discrimination suits, courts have used various labels to describe their analyses. For example, one court concluded that the named plaintiff, as an incumbent employee, lacked the "representative capacity" to challenge testing and decision-making processes used to hire new employees. Griffin v. Dugger, 823 F.2d 1476, 1490–91, 44 FEP 938 (11th Cir. 1987). Another court held that a former employee did not have "standing" to represent those not hired because of alleged discriminatory practices. *See* Talley v. Leo J. Shapiro & Assocs., 713 F. Supp. 254, 257–58, 49 FEP 1260 (N.D. Ill. 1989).

[83]*Falcon*, 457 U.S. at 157 & n.13.

[84]*Id.* at 159 n.15.

The typical case now brought under this footnote involves allegations that all of the challenged decisions (only some of which affected the named plaintiffs) are made through a subjective process, in which a group of white and/or male supervisors exercised total or near-total discretion and did so in a discriminatory fashion. The issues presented by these cases are discussed in Section III.D.1 *infra*. Like all other employment class actions, cases falling under *Falcon*'s general policy of discrimination exception must still satisfy the rigorous analysis of Rule 23 requirements mandated by *Falcon*.[85]

B. Adequacy of Representation

Rule 23(a)(4) permits class certification only if "the representative parties will fairly and adequately protect the interests of the class." Adequacy of representation has been characterized as the most important Rule 23 prerequisite.[86] The requirement is especially important in Rule 23(b)(2) cases because notice to class members is not mandatory and class members seldom participate.[87]

Until the recent amendments to Rule 23, Rule 23(a)(4) required the court to assess the adequacy of both the proposed class representatives and proposed class counsel.[88] The 2003 revisions of Rule 23 added Rule 23(g), an entirely new provision that governs the appointment of class counsel.[89] The Advisory Committee notes to Rule 23(g) make clear that Rule 23(a)(4) now governs *only* the adequacy of the class representatives; scrutiny of counsel's adequacy is evaluated under Rule 23(g).[90] Appointment of class counsel is addressed in Section III.B.4 *infra*.

---

[85]*See, e.g.*, Caridad v. Metro-North Commuter R.R., 191 F.3d 283, 291–93, 80 FEP 627 (2d Cir. 1999).

[86]Harriss v. Pan Am. World Airways, Inc., 74 F.R.D. 24, 42, 15 FEP 1640 (N.D. Cal. 1977).

[87]*See* Gill v. Monroe County Dep't of Soc. Servs., 79 F.R.D. 316, 326–29, 19 FEP 540 (W.D.N.Y. 1978) (adequacy of representation criterion is most important because judgment will bind absent class members).

[88]*Cf.* Staton v. Boeing Co., 327 F.3d at 938, 957 (9th Cir. 2003) (to satisfy adequacy of representation requirement, two questions must be addressed: "(1) [d]o the representative plaintiffs and their counsel have any conflicts of interest with other class members, and (2) will the representative plaintiffs and their counsel prosecute the action vigorously on behalf of the class?").

[89]FED. R. CIV. P. 23(g).

[90]*Id.* The Notes of the Advisory Committee on the 2003 Amendments state that "Rule 23(a)(4) will continue to call for scrutiny of the proposed class representative, while this subdivision [Rule 23(g)] will guide the court in assessing proposed class counsel as part of the certification decision."

In determining whether the named plaintiffs are adequate class representatives, the courts focus on two inquiries: (1) whether the plaintiffs have the capacity and willingness to vigorously prosecute the action on behalf of the class, and (2) whether they have any conflicts of interest with the other class members.[91]

1. Capacity and Willingness of Named Plaintiff to Represent the Class

The named plaintiff must demonstrate sufficient interest in the action to warrant being entrusted with the duty of representing the rights and interests of absent members. He or she must also be available to assist with the litigation.[92] Potential named plaintiffs must have a working knowledge of the facts underlying the case.[93] Generally, class representatives are not required to prove that they can finance the litigation so long as class counsel is able and ethically permitted to do so.[94]

---

[91]*Staton*, 327 F.3d at 957.

[92]*See* Smith v. Merchants & Farmers Bank, 574 F.2d 982, 984, 17 FEP 566 (8th Cir. 1978) (named plaintiff was currently working more than 500 miles from defendant's bank); Jones v. Pacific Intermountain Express, 16 FEP 359, 360 (N.D. Cal. 1977) (plaintiff who was convicted murderer and presently incarcerated could not be class representative).

[93]Gunnells v. Healthplan Servs., Inc., 348 F.3d 417 (4th Cir. 2003) ("hornbook law" that class representatives in complex case do not need extensive knowledge), *cert. denied*, 542 U.S. 915 (2004); Buford v. H&R Block, Inc., 168 F.R.D. 340, 353 (S.D. Ga. 1996) ("This Court follows those courts which hold that an adequate representative must have some minimal degree of participation and knowledge of the action. If plaintiff has 'extremely limited or nonexistent' knowledge of the facts, then he is an inadequate class representative." (citations omitted)), *aff'd sub nom* Jones v. H&R Block Tax Servs., Inc., 117 F.3d 1433 (11th Cir. 1997); MANUAL FOR COMPLEX LITIGATION (FOURTH) § 21.26 (2004) ("courts have required that representatives be knowledgeable about issues in the case").

[94]Maudlin v. Wal-Mart Stores, Inc., 2002 WL 2022334, 89 FEP 1600 (N.D. Ga. Aug. 23, 2002) (where state bar ethical rule permits counsel to advance litigation expenses, plaintiff's uncertainty as to ability to fund litigation does not render her inadequate); Rodolico v. Unisys Corp., 199 F.R.D. 468, 477 (E.D.N.Y. 2001) ("[T]he representative plaintiffs together with several putative class members have agreed to fund the litigation. Thus, based on these representations, the Court finds that the named plaintiffs have demonstrated an ability and willingness to fund the litigation."); Krueger v. New York Tel. Co., 163 F.R.D. 433, 443 n.6 (S.D.N.Y. 1995) (in ADEA class action, sufficient if class representatives state they are "willing to pay their share"); Harris v. General Dev. Corp., 127 F.R.D. 655, 51 FEP 209 (N.D. Ill. 1989) ("If the lack of unlimited resources to fund all aspects of the class action were the basis for a finding of inadequacy of representation, class actions brought by natural persons would rarely be certified."); *see also* MANUAL FOR COMPLEX LITIGATION (FOURTH) § 21.141 (2004) (precertification discovery of plaintiffs' financial resources rarely appropriate in view of ethical rule permitting counsel to advance costs and expenses).

Extreme delay in bringing the class action and failure to move for class certification promptly once the suit is initiated[95] have caused some courts to find that the named plaintiff(s) failed to protect the interests of the class members.[96] Failure to file a timely EEOC charge will not render a named plaintiff an inadequate representative so long as another class member has filed a timely charge.[97] Other factors also may affect the named plaintiff's ability to serve as an adequate representative of the class.[98]

If the class representative's individual claim is found to be without merit *before* a class has been certified, the putative class

---

[95]Prior to being amended in 2003, Rule 23(c)(1)(A) required that a class certification motion be filed "as soon as practicable." The amended rule requires that the motion be filed at "an early practicable time." The Rule 23 Advisory Committee notes explain that this provision was amended to afford time "to gather information necessary to make the certification decision." FED. R. CIV. P. 23(c)(1) advisory committee's note. The advisory committee notes further suggest that courts "ensure that the class certification decision is not unjustifiably delayed." *Id.* Some courts establish specific time limits for filing the class certification motion through local court rules, which may change over time.

[96]East Tex. Motor Freight Sys., Inc. v. Rodriguez, 431 U.S. 395, 404–05, 14 FEP 1505 (1977) (class representatives' failure to move for class certification before trial was "strong indication[] that they would not 'fairly and adequately protect the interests of the class' "); Harriston v. Chicago Tribune, 992 F.2d 697, 63 FEP 319 (7th Cir. 1993) (class representative, who waited 2½ years to move for certification, found inadequate); Briggs v. Anderson, 796 F.2d 1009, 40 FEP 883 (8th Cir. 1986) (applicant class representatives inadequate for failing to move for certification); Percy v. Safeway Stores, Inc., 24 FEP 62, 62–63 (N.D. Tex. 1979) (failure to file motion or brief seeking class certification in accordance with court order and local rule demonstrated inadequacy of representation). *But see* Phillips v. Joint Legislative Comm. on Performance & Expenditure Review, 637 F.2d 1014, 1022–23, 25 FEP 120 (5th Cir. 1981) (delay in moving for certification not sufficient in itself to disqualify class representative).

[97]Robinson v. Sheriff of Cook County, 167 F.3d 1155, 1158, 79 FEP 203 (7th Cir. 1999) ("once a Title VII class action is up and running the class members are not required to inundate the EEOC with what amount to meaningless requests for right to sue letters"); Latino Officers Ass'n v. City of N.Y., 209 F.R.D. 79, 91–92 (S.D.N.Y. 2002) ("[While it is] correct that an individual plaintiff who failed to timely file an EEOC complaint may not later file suit under Title VII[,] [o]nce a class has been certified, however, there is no requirement that every class member have filed an EEOC charge . . . . [F]ailure to have filed their own EEOC charges does not impair the named plaintiffs' abilities to represent the class.").

[98]*See, e.g.,* Sondel v. Northwest Airlines, Inc., 63 FEP 415 (D. Minn. 1993) (where proposed named plaintiff did not decide to join class action until approached by class counsel, she was found to lack interest and involvement necessary to represent class); Barefield v. Chevron U.S.A., Inc., 44 FEP 1885, 1892 & n.2 (N.D. Cal. 1987) (rejecting argument that named plaintiffs would not provide adequate representation because they sought psychiatric treatment for stress associated with discrimination). *But see In re* American Med. Sys., 75 F.3d 1069, 1075, 1083 (6th Cir. 1996) (non-employment case; plaintiff's history of disabling psychological problems created concern about adequacy of representation).

action is typically dismissed without prejudice to the rights of absent putative class members to assert their rights individually or to bring another putative class action.[99] This spares the class from being bound by potentially wide-ranging negative rulings.[100] In determining whether to certify a class, however, "the question is not whether the . . . plaintiffs . . . will prevail on the merits, but rather whether the requirements of Rule 23 are met."[101] Once a class properly has been certified, and the class has prevailed on the issue of liability, the class claims survive even if the trier of fact determines that the representative plaintiff did not suffer any discrimination.[102] In such cases, the court may appoint a new class representative.[103]

---

[99]*Rodriguez*, 431 U.S. at 403–04 (trial court decision on merits made clear that named plaintiffs were not members of class they purported to represent); *Robinson*, 167 F.3d at 1158 (extremely weak individual claim raises doubt about adequacy of class representation); Trevino v. Holly Sugar Corp., 811 F.2d 896, 906, 43 FEP 280 (5th Cir. 1987) (plaintiff whose individual claim was dismissed no longer had nexus with membership of class; therefore, motion to certify properly denied); Wofford v. Safeway Stores, Inc., 78 F.R.D. 460, 477, 18 FEP 1645 (N.D. Cal. 1978) ("To permit a plaintiff to assert the claims of a class of which he is not a part [because he was not discriminated against] and to seek relief in which he has no concrete individual interest is to sanction a sham class action.").

[100]*Robinson*, 167 F.3d at 1158 (noting negative res judicata effect on class); Gilchrist v. Bolger, 733 F.2d 1551, 1556 n.4, 35 FEP 81 (11th Cir. 1984) (denial of certification affirmed in part because "any adverse consequences of denying class certification may well have been outweighed by the negative res judicata effects of certifying a class action with [a poor class representative]").

[101]Eisen v. Carlisle & Jacquelin, 417 U.S. 156, 178, 9 FEP 1302 (1974) (quoting Miller v. Mackey Int'l, Inc., 452 F.2d 424, 427 (5th Cir. 1971)).

[102]*See Rodriguez*, 431 U.S. at 406 n.12 (dicta; if class had been certified and class claims already tried, "and provided the initial certification was proper and decertification not appropriate, the claims of the class members would not need to be mooted or destroyed because subsequent events or the proof at trial had undermined the named plaintiffs' individual claims . . . . Where no class has been certified, however, and the class claims remain to be tried, the decision whether the named plaintiffs should represent a class is appropriately made on the full record, including the facts developed at the trial of the plaintiff's individual claims."); *Robinson*, 167 F.3d at 1157–58 (class certification properly denied; although the "fact that the named plaintiff in a class action turns out not to have a meritorious claim does not doom the class action," where the class representative has already been rejected by the court, any putative substitute class representative must independently satisfy the Rule 23 requirements, including having a timely claim); Scott v. City of Anniston, 682 F.2d 1353, 1356–57, 29 FEP 932 (11th Cir. 1982) (class should not be decertified after class prevails but individual named plaintiff does not); *cf.* Hill v. AT&T Techs., Inc., 731 F.2d 175, 181–82, 34 FEP 620 (4th Cir. 1984) (denying petition to intervene by would-be class representative who failed to file EEOC charge within 180 days and others who had filed charges had dissimilar claims).

[103]*Robinson*, 167 F.3d at 1157 (class member with "live" and comparable claim would be selected to replace class representative who lost individual claim at trial).

2. Potential Conflicts of Interest Between the Named Plaintiff and Absent Class Members

In *Amchem Products, Inc. v. Windsor*,[104] the Supreme Court emphasized that "[t]he adequacy inquiry under Rule 23(a)(4) serves to uncover conflicts of interest between named parties and the class they seek to represent."[105] To defeat certification, the conflict must be actual, not hypothetical or speculative.[106]

Disputes over potential conflicts of interest tend to focus on whether potential named plaintiffs can represent class members who have an employment status different from their own. There is no "per se rule concerning whether a named plaintiff can adequately represent employees at different levels of the employment hierarchy," such as supervisors or managers who represent hourly workers, or vice versa.[107] In *Staton v. Boeing*,[108] the Ninth Circuit held that "[t]he question of whether employees at different levels of the internal hierarchy have potentially conflicting interests is context-specific and depends upon the particular claims alleged in a case."[109] The court affirmed the district court's finding of adequacy of representation where objectors failed to identify a substantive issue for which there was a conflict of interest, the requested relief applied equally throughout the class, and a general discriminatory policy was alleged.[110] The court noted, however, that the adequacy concern, including supervisors and hourly workers in the same class, could be valid in some circumstances.[111] Some courts have concluded that named plaintiffs may not represent both supervisory

---

[104]521 U.S. 591 (1997).

[105]*Id.* at 626 (holding that class could not be certified because "named parties with diverse medical conditions sought to act on behalf of a single giant class" that encompassed currently injured plaintiffs as well as those who had been exposed to asbestos but as yet had no symptoms of injury, and that interests within class were not aligned in significant respects).

[106]Gunnells v. Healthplan Servs., 348 F.3d 417 (4th Cir. 2003); Cummings v. Connel, 316 F.3d 886, 896 (9th Cir.), *cert. denied*, 123 S. Ct. 2577 (2003); Social Serv. Union Local 535 v. County of Santa Clara, 609 F.2d 944, 948 (9th Cir. 1979); 5 JAMES WM. MOORE ET AL., MOORE'S FEDERAL PRACTICE ¶ 23.25[4][b][ii] (3d ed. 2002).

[107]Staton v. Boeing Co., 327 F.3d 938, 958 (9th Cir. 2003).

[108]*Id.*

[109]*Id.* at 958.

[110]*Id.* at 958–59.

[111]*Id.* (citing Wagner v. Taylor, 836 F.2d 578, 595 (D.C. Cir. 1987)).

and nonsupervisory employees;[112] others have concluded that they can.[113]

A named plaintiff's involvement, as an employee, in the very practices challenged by the class action may make his or her interests antagonistic to those of the class, thereby precluding certification.[114] If the plaintiff's authority was so limited that he or she

---

[112]*See* Bacon v. Honda of Am. Mfg., Inc., 370 F.3d 565, 571 (6th Cir. 2004) (plaintiffs failed to show how hourly and salaried employees would have same interests), *cert. denied*, 543 U.S. 1151 (2005); Wagner v. Taylor, 836 F.2d 578, 591, 595, 45 FEP 1199 (D.C. Cir. 1987) (plaintiff in high-level job not necessarily precluded from representing employees in lower-level jobs, but, on facts, interests of plaintiff and class were antagonistic); Donaldson v. Microsoft Corp., 205 F.R.D. 558, 568 (W.D. Wash. 2001) (named plaintiffs, who evaluated other class members, could not represent supervisors and nonsupervisors in case challenging rating system); Appleton v. Deloitte & Touche L.L.P., 168 F.R.D. 221, 233 (M.D. Tenn. 1996) (questions of adequacy of named plaintiffs representing supervisors and nonsupervisors weighs against certification); Wakefield v. Monsanto Co., 120 F.R.D. 112, 116–17, 46 FEP 1481 (E.D. Mo. 1988) (nonexempt employee cannot represent class that includes exempt employees because of inherent conflict of interest).

[113]*See* Dukes v. Wal-Mart, Inc., 474 F.3d 1214, 1233 (9th Cir. 2007) (no conflict of interest where named plaintiffs consist of persons who have worked in both supervisory and nonsupervisory roles and where requested injunctive and lost pay relief applies throughout class); Latino Officers Ass'n v. City of N.Y., 209 F.R.D. 79, 90–91 (S.D.N.Y. 2002) (hypothetical conflict will not prevent certification, but court will revisit adequacy if actual conflict arises); McReynolds v. Sodexho Marriott Servs., 208 F.R.D. 428, 447 (D.D.C. 2002) ("The mere fact that some putative class members were involved in the supervision and rating of other class members does not mean that the supervising class members perpetuated or contributed to any of Sodexho's alleged discriminatory policies."); Butler v. Home Depot, Inc., 1996 U.S. Dist. LEXIS 3370, at *11–12 (N.D. Cal. Nov. 6, 1996) (any conflict issues concerning inclusion of supervisors and nonsupervisors addressed by bifurcation); Shores v. Publix Super Mkts., Inc., 1996 WL 407850, at *8 (M.D. Fla. Mar. 12, 1996) (finding no inherent conflict where class includes both supervisory and nonsupervisory employees because "there is nothing to suggest that the elimination of sex discrimination for nonmanagerial employees would adversely affect managerial employees and vice versa"); Neal v. Moore, 1994 U.S. Dist. LEXIS 21339 (D.D.C. Dec. 23, 1994) ("an injunction against a few supervisory members of the class—who most likely did not exert significant influence over departmental policy-making—is fairly characterized as de minimis relative to the value of such an injunction in protecting those same supervisors from epidemic discrimination"); *see also* Hartman v. Duffey, 19 F.3d 1459, 1471 (D.C. Cir. 1994) (representation across job categories may be appropriate "where the primary practices used to discriminate in the different categories are themselves similar").

[114]*See, e.g.*, Wagner v. NutraSweet Co., 170 F.R.D. 448, 451–52 (N.D. Ill. 1997) (named plaintiff in challenge to salary practices as discriminatory against women was manager in personnel office but had no salary-setting authority with respect to class members). *But see Donaldson*, 205 F.R.D. at 568 (named plaintiffs inadequate because they implemented very system challenged).

could not be considered the employer's agent, however, the plaintiff may be deemed an adequate class representative.[115] Conflicts of interest can arise from evidence that the named plaintiff supports a practice challenged by the class.[116]

Courts have also addressed whether named plaintiffs can adequately represent both applicants and employees,[117] union and nonunion employees,[118] and current and former employees.[119] A class representative who has other litigation against the employer may also arguably be inadequate.[120]

Issues of adequacy of representation may arise when the named plaintiff chooses to pursue some but not all available claims or

---

[115]*Wagner*, 170 F.R.D. at 452.

[116]*See, e.g.*, Anderson v. Southern Pac. Transp. Co., 13 FEP 321, 322 (N.D. Cal. 1973) (class motion denied, inter alia, on grounds that one named plaintiff testified that he supported departmental seniority system that was challenged in class action); *cf.* Scott v. University of Del., 601 F.2d 76, 86, 19 FEP 1730 (3d Cir. 1979) (African-American former university professor with doctoral degree could not adequately represent applicant class challenging doctoral degree requirement because of conflict of interest).

[117]*See* General Tel. Co. of Nw. v. EEOC, 446 U.S. 318, 331, 22 FEP 1196 (1980) ("[C]onflicts might arise, for example, between employees and applicants who were denied employment and who will, if granted relief, compete with employees for fringe benefits or seniority. Under Rule 23, the same plaintiff could not represent these classes."); Hill v. Western Elec. Co., 596 F.2d 99, 101–02 (4th Cir. 1979) (after *Rodriguez*, court's certification of class where applicants challenging hiring discrimination were represented by individuals who had not been hired was erroneous); Powell v. Georgia Pac. Corp., 535 F. Supp. 713, 722, 30 FEP 21 (W.D. Ark. 1980) (present and former employees employed in defendant's plywood and paper mills were inadequate representatives of rejected applicants for clerical, sales, or upper-management positions). *But see Butler*, 1996 U.S. Dist. LEXIS 3370, at *11–12 (employee class representatives may represent applicants and employees where general policy of discrimination alleged).

[118]Latino Officers Ass'n v. City of N.Y., 209 F.R.D. 79, 90–91 (S.D.N.Y. 2002) (union members can adequately represent nonunion members where all share interest in elimination of race discrimination).

[119]Wetzel v. Liberty Mut. Ins. Co., 508 F.2d 239, 247 (3d Cir. 1975) (former employee can represent current employees); Slader v. Pearle Vision Inc., 84 FEP 834 (S.D.N.Y. 2000) (named plaintiffs who were former employees could not adequately represent class of current employees because former employees would primarily be interested in monetary recovery, whereas current employees may prefer injunctive relief); Drayton v. Western Auto Supply Co., 203 F.R.D. 520, 528 (M.D. Fla. 2000) (former employees will adequately represent current employees).

[120]*Latino Officers Ass'n*, 209 F.R.D. at 91 (other litigation did not make three named plaintiffs inadequate; one plaintiff subject to court order to discontinue participation found inadequate).

remedies on behalf of a class.[121] Conversely, a plaintiff who seeks a remedy at odds with the interests of other class members may give rise to a conflict of interest.[122] The defendant employer's inability to accommodate every class member in the remedial phase of litigation (so that class members might be competing with each other for the same jobs) will not necessarily lead to a finding of inadequate representation.[123] Differences in substantive or procedural strategy between the class representative and the absent members that do not rise to the level of conflicts in the claims of

---

[121]*Compare* Cooper v. Southern Co., 390 F.3d 695, 721, 94 FEP 1854 (11th Cir. 2004) (expressing concern that plaintiffs who would waive damages in favor of injunctive relief claims alone would not be adequate representatives), *cert. denied*, 546 U.S. 960 (2005), *overruled in part on other grounds by* Ash v. Tyson Foods, Inc., 546 U.S. 454, 97 FEP 641 (2006), Miller v. Baltimore Gas & Elec. Co., 202 F.R.D 195 (D. Md. 2001) (denying motion to amend complaint; concern that waiver of compensatory and punitive damages raised question about named plaintiffs' adequacy to represent class) *and* Zachery v. Texaco Exploration & Prod., Inc., 185 F.R.D. 230 (W.D. Tex. 1999) (named plaintiffs who waived compensatory and punitive damages to enhance chances of certification found inadequate) *with* In re Universal Serv. Fund Tel. Billing Practices Litig., 219 F.R.D. 661, 670 (D. Kan. 2004) ("mere fact that a named plaintiff elects not to pursue one particular claim does not necessarily create a conflict"), Coleman v. General Motors Acceptance Corp., 220 F.R.D. 64, 73 (M.D. Tenn. 2004) (rejecting argument that failure to include individual monetary claims made plaintiffs inadequate, distinguishing *Zachery*), Palmer v. Combined Ins. Co. of Am., 217 F.R.D. 430, 441 (N.D. Ill. 2003) ("If a class is willing to sacrifice compensatory relief in their class action to meet Rule 23 requirements, thus evincing a paramount desire to stop systemic discrimination and prevent future harm, they should be allowed to proceed.") *and* Beck v. Boeing Co., 203 F.R.D 459, 465 (W.D. Wash. 2001) (rejecting argument that named plaintiffs inadequate for failure to pursue certain remedies), *modified by slip op.* Dec. 27, 2001, *aff'd in part, vacated in part by unpublished decision*, 60 Fed. Appx. 38 (9th Cir. Feb. 25, 2003).

[122]*See, e.g.*, East Tex. Motor Freight Sys., Inc. v. Rodriguez, 431 U.S. 395, 405, 14 FEP 1505 (1977) (noting that fact that named plaintiffs sought remedy—merger of two bargaining units—which majority of alleged class had rejected by vote was "another factor" suggesting inadequacy of representation); *cf.* Robinson v. Metro-North Commuter R.R., 267 F.3d 147, 170–71, 86 FEP 1580 (2d Cir. 2001) (rejecting defendant's argument that named plaintiffs were not adequate representatives because they were personally entitled to only classwide injunctive relief and might therefore lack incentive to vigorously pursue monetary damage claims), *cert. denied*, 535 U.S. 951 (2002).

[123]*See* Dean v. International Truck & Engine Corp., 220 F.R.D. 319 (N.D. Ill. 2004) (finding that named plaintiff in disparate impact hiring case not inadequate because there are limited number of openings available); Hartman v. Duffey, 158 F.R.D. 525, 546–47 (D.D.C. 1994) (holding that limited promotional opportunities at remedial stage did not make named plaintiffs inadequate), *aff'd in part*, 88 F.3d 1232 (D.C. Cir. 1996) [Editor's Note: The defendant's name is misspelled as "Duffy"

the class are not sufficient to destroy the viability of the class or its representative.[124]

Named plaintiffs who negotiate class settlements that fail to protect the interests of the class may be found to be inadequate.[125]

Where named plaintiffs have potential conflicts of interest, rather than deny certification, some courts instead have bifurcated the liability and damages phase,[126] directed that additional named plaintiffs may be added later,[127] or approved subclasses.[128]

3. Organizations as Named Plaintiffs

Whether an organization, such as a labor union or civil rights association, can bring a class action as the named class representative depends on the same general factors that determine whether an individual can represent the class: the organization must be able

---

in the case caption at the district court level, reported at 158 F.R.D. 525.]; Meiresonne v. Marriott Corp., 124 F.R.D. 619, 625, 49 FEP 52 (N.D. Ill. 1989) ("that absurd proposition would of course doom almost every class action charging discrimination in promotion [or hiring]—a drastic rewrite of the law in this area"). *But see* Dickerson v. United States Steel Corp., 14 FEP 1450, 1451 (E.D. Pa. 1976) (excluding unsuccessful applicants because potential remedy of retroactive seniority could displace members of class of current employees).

[124]*See* Robinson v. Sears, Roebuck & Co., 111 F. Supp. 2d 1101, 1125 (E.D. Ark. 2000) (rejecting argument that named plaintiff's selection of statistician, whose analysis defendant challenged, demonstrated inadequacy); United States v. Trucking Employers, Inc., 75 F.R.D. 682, 687–88, 17 FEP 43 (D.D.C. 1977) (holding that objections to litigation strategy will not defeat claim of representative status).

[125]*See* Molski v. Gleich, 318 F.3d 937, 955–56 (9th Cir. 2003) (in ADA access class action, finding representation inadequate where named plaintiff did not suffer in same way as class; case settled in only 4 months, and settlement "waived practically all the class members' claims without compensation and allowed the defendants to escape with little penalty").

[126]*See* Drayton v. Western Auto Supply Co., 203 F.R.D. 520 (M.D. Fla. 2000) (noting that any conflicts among divergent interests may be resolved through bifurcation of liability and damages); Butler v. Home Depot, Inc., 1996 WL 421436, at *4 (potential conflict created by supervisors and nonsupervisors being members of same class is cured by bifurcating liability and remedial phases).

[127]*See* Robinson v. Metro-North Commuter R.R., 267 F.3d 147, 171, 86 FEP 1580 (2d Cir. 2001) (holding that if conflict arises at remedial stage, additional plaintiffs can be added).

[128]*See* Majeske v. City of Chi., 740 F. Supp. 1350, 1357, 53 FEP 574 (N.D. Ill. 1990) (noting that subclasses would have to be certified if African Americans, whites, and Hispanics were to be part of proposed class, as their interests would

to show both that it has standing to sue—typically through what is known as "associational standing"—and that it can meet the requirements of Rule 23(a).

In *Food & Commercial Workers Local 751 v. Brown Group, Inc.*,[129] the Supreme Court reaffirmed the requirements for associational standing and permitted a union to represent its members in a suit alleging violations of the Worker Adjustment & Retraining Notification (WARN) Act.[130] Associational standing is present when the organization's members would otherwise have standing to sue in their own right, the interests the organization seeks to protect are germane to the organization's purpose, and neither the claim asserted nor the relief requested requires the participation of individual members in the lawsuit.[131] Although many courts have held that organizations have standing to seek injunctive and declaratory relief for their members,[132] courts often hold that organizations often lack standing to assert claims for damages because

---

be antagonistic); FED. R. CIV. P. 23(c)(4); MANUAL FOR COMPLEX LITIGATION (FOURTH) § 21.142 (2004).

[129]517 U.S. 544 (1996) (citing Hunt v. Washington State Apple Adver. Comm'n, 432 U.S. 333 (1977)).

[130]Hunt v. Washington State Apple Adver. Comm'n, 432 U.S. 333, 343 (1977); *see also* Doe v. Stincer, 175 F.3d 879 (11th Cir. 1999) (applying requirements for associational standing set forth in *Hunt* and *Food & Commercial Workers Local 751*); Risinger v. Concannon, 117 F. Supp. 2d 61 (D. Me. 2000) (applying associational standing requirements set forth in *Food & Commercial Workers Local 751*).

[131]*Food & Commercial Workers Local 751*, 517 U.S. at 553 (citing *Hunt*); *accord* Auto Workers v. Brock, 477 U.S. 274, 288–90 (1986) (reaffirming *Hunt*; distinguishing associational suits from class actions); Retired Chi. Police Ass'n v. City of Chi., 7 F.3d 584, 600–07 (7th Cir. 1993); Associated Gen. Contractors of Cal., Inc. v. Coalition for Economic Equity, 950 F.2d 1401, 1405–09 (9th Cir. 1991); Humane Soc'y of U.S. v. Hodel, 840 F.2d 45, 52–60 (D.C. Cir. 1988); NAACP v. City of Evergreen, 693 F.2d 1367, 1369, 30 FEP 925 (11th Cir. 1982); Sierra Club v. Aluminum Co. of Am., 585 F. Supp. 842, 844–53 (N.D.N.Y. 1984).

[132]*See, e.g.*, California Rural Legal Assistance, Inc. v. Legal Servs. Corp., 917 F.2d 1171, 1175 (9th Cir. 1990) (affirming union as class representative); Clark Equip. Co. v. Allied Indus. Workers, 803 F.2d 878, 880 (6th Cir. 1986) (per curiam) (holding that union has standing to represent class, even if union alleges no specific injury as to it); Upper Valley Ass'n for Handicapped Citizens v. Mills, 168 F.R.D. 167, 171 (D. Vt. 1996); Auto Workers v. LTV Aerospace & Def. Co., 136 F.R.D. 113, 122–24, 55 FEP 1078 (N.D. Tex. 1991); Auto Workers v. Chicago, 45 FEP 463, 465–66 (E.D. Mich. 1987) (holding that union is appropriate class representative of both employees who were members of collective bargaining unit and those who were not).

individualized participation of members is considered necessary for an accurate allocation of damages and damages claims generally are not considered common to the entire membership.[133]

Some groups have been allowed to sue on behalf of themselves and their members for injunctive relief without invoking class action status and have thus avoided review under Rule 23.[134] More typically, however, an organization asserts such claims as a putative class action and therefore must also satisfy the requirements of Rule 23. Because Rule 23(a) requires a class action to be brought by "one or more *members* of the class," an organization may be denied class representative status because it is not an individual member of the class.[135] Unions have been deemed to satisfy Rule

---

[133]Warth v. Seldin, 422 U.S. 490, 515–17 (1975) (to obtain relief in damages, each member must be party to suit); Sanner v. Board of Trade, 62 F.3d 918, 923 (7th Cir. 1995) (because proof of damages ordinarily requires participation of association's members in lawsuit, "[w]e are unaware of any cases allowing associations to proceed on behalf of their members when claims for monetary as opposed to prospective relief are involved"); Firefighters Local 2665 v. City of Ferguson, 2001 U.S. Dist. LEXIS 23869 (E.D. Mo. Apr. 17, 2001) (union lacks standing to assert claim for damages on behalf of members); National Coalition Gov't of Union of Burma v. Unocal, Inc., 176 F.R.D. 329 (C.D. Cal. 1997) (union lacked standing to assert damage claim of members); Laborers v. Case Farms, Inc., 488 S.E.2d 632, 4 WH 2d (BNA) 159 (N.C. Ct. App. 1997) (union lacked associational standing to assert wage and hour claim and as class representative under Rule 23); Friends for Am. Free Enter. Ass'n v. Wal-Mart Stores, Inc., 284 F.3d 575 (5th Cir. 2002) (organization of manufacturing representatives lacked standing to assert claims of tortious interference); Gay-Straight Alliance Network v. Visalia Unified Sch. Dist., 262 F. Supp. 2d 1088 (E.D. Cal. 2001) (group has associational and direct standing to assert violation of members' constitutional rights).

[134]*See, e.g.*, Cleveland Branch, NAACP v. City of Parma, 263 F.3d 513 (6th Cir. 2001); Retail, Wholesale & Dep't Store Union Local 194 v. Standard Brands, Inc., 540 F.2d 864, 865, 13 FEP 499 (7th Cir. 1976) (finding that union could represent members without meeting Rule 23 requirements); New York Hotel & Motel Trades Council v. Hotel Ass'n of N.Y. City, Inc., 747 F. Supp. 1074, 1075, 54 FEP 120 (S.D.N.Y. 1990) (union may represent members in nonclass action); Vulcan Soc'y of Westchester County, Inc. v. Fire Dep't, 82 F.R.D. 379, 390–91, 25 FEP 910 (S.D.N.Y. 1979) (holding that Society of Black Firefighters had standing to sue but could not have representative status under Rule 23(a)). *But see* Miller v. Smith, 584 F. Supp. 149, 153, 36 FEP 96 (D.D.C. 1984) (questioning whether organization has standing to bring civil action under Title VII).

[135]Black Faculty Ass'n of Mesa Coll. v. San Diego Cmty. Coll. Dist., 664 F.2d 1153, 1156, 27 FEP 1037 (9th Cir. 1981) (holding that association lacks standing to challenge hiring and promotion practices; lack of evidence of association's purpose

23(a) requirements, however, and have been certified as class representatives.[136] Title VII specifically defines the term "person" to include labor unions.[137] Thus, under appropriate facts a union may be a "person aggrieved" or a "person claiming to be aggrieved" under the statute. Civil rights organizations have been certified as class representatives where the organization's primary function is to represent the interests of the class members.[138]

---

or goal precludes it from establishing injury to itself); Marin County Chapter of NOW v. County of Marin, 82 F.R.D. 605, 606 n.1, 19 FEP 1647 (N.D. Cal. 1979) ("NOW may not be the representative of a plaintiff class."); La Mar v. H & B Novelty & Loan Co., 489 F.2d 461, 465 (9th Cir. 1973) ("Obviously [the typicality] requirement is not met when the 'representative' plaintiff never had a claim of any type against any defendant."); Harriss v. Pan Am. World Airways, Inc., 74 F.R.D. 24, 39 n.10, 15 FEP 1640 (N.D. Cal. 1977) (holding that organization cannot be member of class and, therefore, normally cannot be class representative; possible exception is if raison d'être of organization is to represent class). *But see* Arkansas Educ. Ass'n v. Board of Educ., 446 F.2d 763, 766, 3 FEP 800 (8th Cir. 1971) (association and individual plaintiff can represent class of teachers).

[136]*See, e.g.*, International Woodworkers v. Chesapeake Bay Plywood Corp., 659 F.2d 1259, 1266–67, 26 FEP 1329 (4th Cir. 1981) (holding that union has associational standing and can represent class even though not technically class member); International Woodworkers v. Georgia-Pacific Corp., 568 F.2d 64, 66–67, 16 FEP 258 (8th Cir. 1977) (same).

[137]42 U.S.C. § 2000e(a) (2000). *See generally* Chapter 22 (Unions).

[138]*See, e.g.*, Upper Valley Ass'n for Handicapped Citizens v. Mills, 168 F.R.D. 167, 171 (D. Vt. 1996) (in action by disabled children based on educational rights, certifying class represented by two individuals and civil rights organization, citing "the ability of associations ... to act as class representatives ... provided that the underlying purpose of the organization is to represent the interests of the class"); Webb v. Missouri Pac. R.R., 95 F.R.D. 357, 360, 362 (E.D. Ark. 1982) (finding that coalition of organizations from several states that existed to assist minorities and females in achieving equal employment opportunities was proper class representative); League of United Latin Am. Citizens v. City of Salinas Fire Dep't, 88 F.R.D. 533, 542–44, 28 FEP 470 (N.D. Cal. 1980) (permitting organization devoted to achieving equal employment opportunities for Mexican Americans to act as class representative and noting that such groups may be less prone to conflicts with class and more suited to class representation than labor unions); IMAGE v. Bailar, 78 F.R.D. 549, 553, 24 FEP 1410 (N.D. Cal. 1978) (recognizing that organization could represent class, especially when it is raison d'être of organization); Women's Comm. for Equal Employment Opportunity v. National Broad. Co., 71 F.R.D. 666, 668, 671, 13 FEP 240 (S.D.N.Y. 1976) (certifying unincorporated association, along with individuals, as class representatives of female employees in sex discrimination case without comment on association's status as an organization); Percy v. Brennan, 384 F. Supp. 800, 809 (S.D.N.Y. 1974) (noting that representation of interests of minority members was primary reason

The EEOC is not required to meet Rule 23's requirements, regardless of whether it intervenes as a plaintiff or brings a direct action.[139]

4. Adequacy of Plaintiff's Counsel

The December 1, 2003, amendment to Rule 23 added subsection (g).[140] Rule 23(g) governs the standards and framework for the selection of class counsel. The new rule "responds to the reality that the selection and activity of class counsel are often critically important to the successful handling of a class action."[141] The adequacy of plaintiff's counsel is no longer evaluated under Rule 23(a)(4), which is now limited to determining the adequacy of the class representatives.[142]

---

for existence of two civil rights groups); *cf. Harriss*, 74 F.R.D. at 39 n.10 (noting that, although organization cannot be member of class and therefore normally cannot be class representative, possible exception exists if organization's raison d'être is to represent class).

[139]General Tel. Co. of the Nw. v. EEOC, 446 U.S. 318, 324, 329, 22 FEP 1196 (1980).

[140]FED. R. CIV. P. 23(g) (1) provides:

(1) Appointing Class Counsel.
   (A) Unless a statute provides otherwise, a court that certifies a class must appoint class counsel.
   (B) An attorney appointed to serve as class counsel must fairly and adequately represent the interests of the class.
   (C) In appointing class counsel, the court
      (i) must consider:
- the work counsel has done in identifying or investigating potential claims in the action,
- counsel's experience in handling class actions, other complex litigation, and claims of the type asserted in the action,
- counsel's knowledge of the applicable law, and
- the resources counsel will commit to representing the class.
      (ii) may consider any other matter pertinent to counsel's ability to fairly and adequately represent the interests of the class;
      (iii) may direct potential class counsel to provide information on any subject pertinent to the appointment and to propose terms for attorney fees and nontaxable costs; and
      (iv) may make further orders in connection with the appointment.

[141]FED. R. CIV. P. 23(g) advisory committee's note.

[142]*Id.* ("In the future, Rule 23(a)(4) will continue to call for scrutiny of the proposed class representative, while this subdivision will guide the court in assessing proposed class counsel as part of the class certification process.").

The new rule provides that, if a class is certified, class counsel must be appointed to represent the class and any subclass.[143] The obligation of class counsel is to "fairly and adequately represent the interests of the class."[144] The rule articulates four criteria that the district court *must* consider in evaluating the adequacy of proposed counsel[145] and *permits* the court to consider "any other [pertinent] matter."[146] The four mandatory considerations are counsel's prior experience in similar cases, counsel's knowledge of the applicable law, the extent of counsel's investigation in the action, and the resources that counsel will commit to the case.[147] The advisory committee noted that "[n]o single factor should necessarily be determinative in a given case."[148]

The court may ask potential class counsel to submit information on any subject "pertinent to the appointment," and to propose terms for attorney's fees and costs. This submission may be subject to a protective order to preserve confidential information from the defendant.[149]

Rule 23(g) also provides a procedure where there are competing applications for appointment as class counsel. The court must allow a reasonable period for attorneys to apply[150] and must "appoint the applicant best able to represent the interests of the class."[151]

The rule permits the court to appoint "interim class counsel" in the precertification period.[152] This provision recognizes that, prior to class certification, an attorney may need to take discovery, respond to motions, or engage in settlement negotiations on behalf of the class.[153]

---

[143]*Id.* at 23(g)(1) advisory committee's note (class counsel must also be appointed for "each subclass that the court certifies to represent divergent interests").

[144]*Id.* at 23(g)(1)(B); *id.* at 23(g)(1)(B) advisory committee's note ("[a]ppointment as class counsel means that the primary obligation of counsel is to the class rather than to the individual members of it").

[145]*Id.* at 23(g)(1)(C)(i).

[146]*Id.* at 23(g)(1)(C)(ii).

[147]*Id.* at 23(g)(1)(C)(i).

[148]*Id.* at 23(g)(1)(C) advisory committee's note.

[149]*Id.* at 23(g)(1)(C); *id.* at 23(g)(1)(C) advisory committee's note.

[150]*Id.* at 23(g)(2)(B).

[151]*Id.* at 23(g)(2)(C).

[152]*Id.* at 23(g)(2)(A); *id.* at 23(g)(2)(A) advisory committee's note.

[153]*Id.*

C. Numerosity

To satisfy the Rule 23(a)(1) numerosity requirement, the named plaintiff must show that "the class is so numerous that joinder of all members is impracticable."[154] The number of class members sufficient to satisfy the numerosity requirement of Rule 23(a) depends on the specific facts and circumstances of each case.[155] No specific number demonstrates numerosity. Courts have certified classes containing as few as 16 members and have refused to certify classes with more than 50 prospective members.[156]

"Counting" issues commonly arise. Some courts have counted future employees and "potential" applicants, i.e., persons who

---

[154]*Id.* at 23(a)(1).

[155]General Tel. Co. of Nw. v. EEOC, 446 U.S. 318, 330, 22 FEP 1196 (1980) ("The numerosity requirement requires examination of the specific facts of each case and imposes no absolute limitations."); Cox v. American Cast Iron Pipe Co., 784 F.2d 1546, 1553, 40 FEP 678 (11th Cir. 1986) ("while there is no fixed numerosity rule, 'generally less than twenty-one is inadequate, more than forty adequate, with numbers between varying according to other factors' " (quoting 3B JAMES WM. MOORE ET AL., MOORE'S FEDERAL PRACTICE ¶ 23.05[1], at n.7 (2d ed. 1978)).

[156]*General Tel. Co.*, 446 U.S. at 330 & n.14 (citing various decisions holding insufficient classes of fewer than 15 members); Government Employees (NAGE) v. City Pub. Serv. Bd., 40 F.3d 698, 715, 67 FEP 1013 (5th Cir. 1994) (finding potential class of 11 members, only 2 of whose claims concerned denial of promotion, insufficient); Roman v. ESB, Inc., 550 F.2d 1343, 1348–49, 14 FEP 235 (4th Cir. 1976) (holding that 55 is not enough to satisfy numerosity); Beckmann v. CBS, Inc., 192 F.R.D. 608, 613, 90 FEP 1379 (D. Minn. 2000) (holding that class of 71 employees satisfies numerosity); Massie v. Illinois Dep't of Transp., 1998 WL 312021, at *2, 78 FEP 111 (N.D. Ill. June 5, 1998) (finding 53 employees sufficient to certify class in race discrimination promotion case); Hendricks-Robinson v. Excel Corp., 164 F.R.D. 667, 671 (C.D. Ill. 1996) (in ADA case challenging employer's "medical layoff program," finding that 38 class members satisfied numerosity requirement); Rodger v. Electronic Data Sys. Corp., 160 F.R.D. 532, 535–37 (E.D.N.C. 1995) (holding that class of 57 was sufficient in wrongful discharge case and noting that circuit precedent certified classes with as few as 18 members); Hum v. Dericks, 162 F.R.D. 628, 634 (D. Haw. 1995) (denying certification of proposed class of 200 in medical malpractice case arising from use of specific medical procedure because proposed class members identifiable and joinder not impracticable; noting that courts have certified classes with as few as 13 members and denied certification of classes with more than 300 members); McCree v. Sam's Club, 159 F.R.D. 572, 576–77, 67 FEP 1271 (M.D. Ala. 1995) (in race discrimination case, finding that class of 15 members did not satisfy numerosity requirement).

allegedly did not apply for a job because they were "chilled" by discriminatory hiring policies.[157] Other courts disagree.[158]

Plaintiffs bear the burden of demonstrating numerosity.[159] Although they cannot rely on wholly conclusory allegations,[160] they

---

[157]*See, e.g.*, Phillips v. Joint Legislative Comm. on Performance & Expenditure Review, 637 F.2d 1014, 1022, 25 FEP 120, 126 (5th Cir. 1981) ("the alleged class includes future and deterred applicants, necessarily unidentifiable. In such a case the requirement of Rule 23(a)(1) is clearly met, for 'joinder of unknown individuals is certainly impracticable.' "); Jordan v. County of L.A., 669 F.2d 1311, 1319–20, 28 FEP 518 (9th Cir. 1982) (allowing class including unnamed and unknown future applicants; "joinder of unknown individuals is inherently impracticable"), *vacated on other grounds*, 459 U.S. 810, 29 FEP 1560 (1982); Bethesda Lutheran Homes & Servs., Inc. v. Leean, 165 F.R.D. 87, 88–89 (W.D. Wis. 1996) ("While potential future members of a class may be considered in the numerosity analysis, this is only true to the extent that the Court can reasonably approximate their number."); Johnson v. EEOC, 68 FEP 1712, 1721 (N.D. Ill. 1995) (numerosity requirement met in ADEA case when plaintiffs' evidence showed that individuals were deterred from applying to apprenticeship programs because of age restrictions); Slanina v. William Penn Parking Corp., 106 F.R.D. 419, 423–24, 34 FEP 1426 (W.D. Pa. 1984) (certifying class of 25 current employees where plaintiffs sought to include former and future employees; numerosity requirement not to be strictly applied where equitable relief is sought and class members fear reprisal if joined); Kilgo v. Bowman Transp., Inc., 87 F.R.D. 26, 29, 22 FEP 1007 (N.D. Ga. 1980) (finding that allegations of "an unknown number of deterred potential applicants and future applicants" show sufficient numerosity).

[158]Scott v. University of Del., 601 F.2d 76, 89, 19 FEP 1730 (3d Cir. 1979) (holding that allegation of discrimination against future faculty members is insufficient to satisfy numerosity requirement; "class of future faculty members is simply ephemeral on the facts of this case"); Frazier v. Consolidated Rail Corp., 851 F.2d 1447, 1456, 47 FEP 720 (D.D.C. 1988) ("the district court correctly refused to consider hypothetical future employees . . . . The plaintiffs attacked only the Training Program as it stood before being reformed, and not as it stands today."); *In re* Batesville Casket Co. EEO Litig., 35 FEP 1560, 1563 n.3 (D.D.C. 1984) (holding that future employees cannot be counted).

[159]*See, e.g.*, Adams v. Henderson, 197 F.R.D. 162, 169–70 (D. Md. 2000) ("the burden of satisfying the class certification requirements of Rule 23 is on the plaintiff"); Arenson v. Whitehall Convalescent & Nursing Home, Inc., 164 F.R.D. 659, 662 (N.D. Ill. 1996) (noting that plaintiff in class action bears burden of satisfying all four requirements of Rule 23(a), i.e., numerosity, commonality, typicality, and adequacy of representation).

[160]*See* Allen v. Chicago Transit Auth., 2000 WL 1207408, at *7 (N.D. Ill. July 31, 2000) (holding that uncertainty in calculating number of actual potential plaintiffs insufficient to prevent certification; "While plaintiffs may not rely on conclusory allegations or speculation that joinder is impracticable, the complaint need not specify the exact number of persons included in the class."); Cruz v. Coach Stores, Inc., 1998 U.S. Dist. LEXIS 18051, at *11–12 (S.D.N.Y. Nov. 17, 1998) (finding that plaintiff's conclusory allegations as to numerosity were unsupported by any evidence

need not identify each member of the class, demonstrate that each member of the proposed class actually was discriminated against, or show its exact size.[161] Some courts have found the numerosity requirement satisfied by the plaintiffs' general allegations that the employer, who has sole possession of information as to numerosity, refused to answer the plaintiffs' discovery.[162]

---

or even estimate of class size), *aff'd in part and vacated in part by, remanded by* 202 F.3d 560, 81 FEP 1762 (2d Cir. 2000); McCree v. Sam's Club, 159 F.R.D. 572, 576 (M.D. Ala. 1995) (noting that, despite extensive discovery, plaintiffs produced no evidence to support various conclusory allegations that class numbered several hundred members). *But see* Buttino v. Federal Bureau of Investigation, 1992 U.S. Dist. LEXIS 21919, at *5 (N.D. Cal. Sept. 24, 1992) ("Because plaintiff is seeking declaratory and injunctive relief, speculative assertions of class size are sufficient to meet the numerosity requirement.").

[161]*See, e.g., Allen*, 2000 WL 1207408, at *7 ("[plaintiffs] provide no method of determining how many of the 470 potential plaintiffs actually claim they were discriminated against on account of race. However, this uncertainty alone is insufficient to prevent certification of the class."); Robidoux v. Celani, 987 F.2d 931, 935 (2d Cir. 1993) ("[c]ourts have not required evidence of exact class size or identity of class members to satisfy the numerosity requirement"); Doe v. Bridgeport Police Dep't, 198 F.R.D. 325, 331 (D. Conn. 2001) (noting that identification of all class members or exact class size not required to satisfy numerosity); Kline v. Security Guards, Inc., 196 F.R.D. 261, 269 (E.D. Pa. 2000) (finding good faith estimate sufficient); Johnson v. Aronson Furniture Co., 1998 WL 641342, at *2 (N.D. Ill. Sept. 11, 1998) (ruling that estimate of 20–40 members per class met numerosity requirement, as exact number is not required); *Arenson*, 164 F.R.D. at 662–63 (noting that plaintiff is not required to specify exact number of class members so long as good faith estimate is provided, although estimate cannot be purely speculative); *cf.* BreMiller v. Cleveland Psychiatric Inst., 898 F. Supp. 573, 576–77 (N.D. Ohio 1995) (in sexual harassment class action, holding that defendants may not claim complete ignorance as to identities of class members or use plaintiffs' ignorance to defeat class certification when proposed class was composed of defendants' past and present employees and defendants could identify class members by reviewing own files); Rains v. City of Minneapolis, 1991 WL 238262, at *3 (D. Minn. July 31, 1991) (in sexual harassment class action, holding that plaintiffs' evidence of approximate number of female employees and testimony of six prospective class members with substantially similar claims satisfied numerosity requirement); Ruhe v. Philadelphia Inquirer, 14 FEP 1304, 1308–09 (E.D. Pa. 1975) (in gender discrimination class action, finding that plaintiffs' allegations of employment discrimination against defendant, a large employment agency with several offices across country, sufficient to suggest class so numerous as to satisfy numerosity requirement). *But see* Davoll v. Webb, 160 F.R.D. 142, 144–46 (D. Colo. 1995) (refusing to find that class met numerosity requirement in discrimination case based on work-related disabilities because class not sufficiently defined; not feasible for court to determine if particular individuals had "disabilities" qualifying them as class members), *aff'd*, 194 F.3d 1116 (10th Cir. 1999).

[162]Groves v. Insurance Co. of N. Am., 433 F. Supp. 877, 881–82, 17 FEP 776 (E.D. Pa. 1977) (rejecting defendant's claim that plaintiff's estimate of 200 class members was only speculative, noting defendant's refusal to answer interrogatories

In evaluating numerosity, courts also consider whether joinder of individuals would be impractical.[163] Relevant factors are the location and dispersion of class members,[164] the magnitude of the claims involved,[165] and whether harassment or retaliation by em-

---

addressed to that precise question); Society for Individual Rights, Inc. v. Hampton, 63 F.R.D. 399, 402, 11 FEP 1243 (N.D. Cal. 1973) (where defendant had refused to answer interrogatory as to number of persons discharged per year because of homosexual conduct, on ground that it would be "burdensome and oppressive," finding that admitted oppressiveness of counting indicated that number would be large and showed impracticality of individual joinder), *aff'd per curiam*, 528 F.2d 905 (9th Cir. 1975).

[163]Paxton v. Union Nat'l Bank of Little Rock, 688 F.2d 552, 559–60, 29 FEP 1233 (8th Cir. 1982) ("In addition to the size of the class, the court may also consider the nature of the action, the size of the individual claims, the inconvenience of trying individual suits, and any other factor relevant to the practicability of joining all the putative class members."); Rodriguez v. Carlson, 166 F.R.D. 465, 471–72 (E.D. Wash. 1996) (under numerosity evaluation, noting that court will examine not only mere number of plaintiffs but such factors as "geographical dispersion, degree of sophistication, and class members' reluctance to sue individually"). *But see* Ladegaard v. Hard Rock Concrete Cutters, Inc., 2000 WL 1774091, at *4 (N.D. Ill. Dec. 1, 2000) (suggesting that consideration of other factors such as judicial economy, financial resources of class members, and ability of claimants to bring individual lawsuits is necessary only where class size is smaller than 40).

[164]*See* Mullen v. Treasure Chest Casino, L.L.C., 186 F.3d 620, 624 (5th Cir. 1999) (finding that numerosity finding supported, in part, by inference that transient nature of gambling business would likely render some putative class members geographically dispersed and unavailable for joinder); Frazier v. Consolidated Rail Corp., 851 F.2d 1447, 1456 & n.10, 47 FEP 720 (D.C. Cir. 1988) (fewer than 40 members, most of whom resided nearby; no evidence of their reluctance to appear); Kilgo v. Bowman Transp., Inc., 789 F.2d 859, 878 (11th Cir. 1986) (holding that geographical dispersion supports numerosity finding); Kelley v. Norfolk & W. Ry. Co., 584 F.2d 34, 35–36 (4th Cir. 1978) (affirming denial of class certification; all 67 African-American employees lived and worked in area and could intervene); Sanft v. Winnebago Indus., Inc., 214 F.R.D. 514, 520 (N.D. Iowa 2003) (no geographical dispersion; cataloging cases on issue); Cervantes v. Sugar Creek Packing Co., Inc., 210 F.R.D. 611, 621 (S.D. Ohio 2002) (although current employees were local, former employees were geographically dispersed); Adams v. Henderson, 197 F.R.D. 162, 170 (D. Md. 2000) (where 67 class members lived and worked locally, holding that joinder not impractical and certification denied); Markham v. White, 171 F.R.D. 217, 221 (N.D. Ill. 1997) (finding numerosity is met when class members in five states); Martin v. City of Beaumont, 125 F.R.D. 435, 437–38, 50 FEP 246 (E.D. Tex. 1989) (denying class certification; 25 present and 27 former police officers in class, all of whom easily could be located); *Buttino*, 1992 U.S. Dist. LEXIS 21919, at *5 (finding proposed class members "geographically dispersed" where FBI employees work throughout United States).

[165]*See* Harriss v. Pan Am. World Airways, Inc., 74 F.R.D. 24, 45, 15 FEP 1640 (N.D. Cal. 1977) ("[p]racticability of joinder must be viewed in the light of all the circumstances, including the magnitude of the claim"); O'Neil v. Appel, 165 F.R.D. 479, 490 (W.D. Mich. 1996) (in securities fraud case, holding that magnitude of claims do not support numerosity finding).

ployers might prevent employees from joining.[166] Some courts have also weighed the financial resources of the potential class members and their ability to institute individual lawsuits.[167]

D. Frequently Contested Rule 23(a) Issues

1. Subjective Decision-Making Processes

As noted earlier, the Supreme Court in *Falcon*[168] recognized that plaintiffs could bring a disparate treatment class action to challenge a general policy of discrimination that "manifested itself . . . in the same general fashion, such as through entirely subjective decision-making processes."[169] In *Watson v. Fort Worth Bank & Trust*,[170] the Supreme Court ruled that "subjective or discretionary employment practices may [also] be analyzed under the adverse impact approach in appropriate cases."[171] The Court in *Watson* cautioned that "an employer's policy of leaving promotion decisions

---

[166]*See, e.g., Treasure Chest Casino, L.L.C.*, 186 F.3d at 624 (in mass tort action, finding that numerosity supported certification where casino workers might be reluctant to sue for fear of retaliation at their jobs); Arkansas Educ. Ass'n v. Board of Educ., 446 F.2d 763, 765, 3 FEP 800 (8th Cir. 1971) (certifying class of 20 public school teachers who might have "natural fear or reluctance to sue individually"); *Sanft*, 214 F.R.D. at 524 (finding insufficient evidence of potential retaliation); Ansoumana v. Gristede's Operating Corp., 201 F.R.D. 81, 85–86 (S.D.N.Y 2001) (finding that employees, many of whom were immigrants, feared reprisals); Adames v. Mitsubishi Bank, Ltd., 133 F.R.D. 82, 89, 58 FEP 1466 (E.D.N.Y. 1989) ("Since here a number of putative members are current employees, the concern for possible employer reprisal action exists and renders the alternative of individual joinder less than practicable."); *Buttino*, 1992 U.S. Dist. LEXIS 21919, at *5 ("assuming the existence of an anti-gay policy toward FBI employees, many individual claimants would have difficulty filing individual lawsuits out of fear of retaliation").

[167]*See* Robidoux v. Celani, 987 F.2d 931, 936 (2d Cir. 1993) (holding that, in determining numerosity, court may consider "financial resources of class members"); *Sanft*, 214 F.R.D. at 524 (finding inadequate information in record to determine whether financial resources supported numerosity finding); *Cervantes*, 210 F.R.D. at 621 (ruling that evidence that class had limited resources and plaintiffs could not afford bus fare to jurisdiction supported numerosity finding); *Buttino*, 1992 U.S. Dist. LEXIS 21919, at *5 ("The expense of litigation is an additional deterrent to individual class members instituting separate suits."); *cf.* Primavera Familienstiftung v. Askin, 178 F.R.D. 405, 411 (S.D.N.Y. 1998) (in securities fraud action, holding that financial resources of class members weighed against class certification).

[168]General Tel. Co. of Sw. v. Falcon, 457 U.S. 147, 28 FEP 1745 (1982).

[169]*Id.* at 159 n.15.

[170]487 U.S. 977, 47 FEP 102 (1988).

[171]*Id.* at 991.

to the unchecked discretion of lower level supervisors should it-self raise no inference of discriminatory conduct."[172] The Court recognized, however, that adverse impact analysis might be nec-essary to combat "the problem of subconscious stereotypes and prejudices": "If an employer's undisciplined system of subjective decision-making has precisely the same effects as a system per-vaded by impermissible intentional discrimination, it is difficult to see why Title VII's proscription against discriminatory actions should not apply."[173]

Broad class challenges to an employer's alleged policy of delegating subjective employment decisions to the discretion of lower-level supervisors are frequently brought under the theories of disparate treatment, disparate impact, or both. Although many courts have concluded that the particular practices alleged satisfy Rule 23(a) requirements,[174] other courts have concluded that the

---

[172]*Id.* at 990–91.

[173]*Id.*

[174]*See* Dukes v. Wal-Mart, Inc., 474 F.3d 1214, 1231 (9th Cir. 2007) (affirming certification of gender class challenging alleged discrimination in pay and promo-tion where class alleged excessive subjective decision making by individual store managers); Shipes v. Trinity Indus., 987 F.2d 311, 316, 66 FEP 375 (5th Cir. 1993) ("Allegations of similar discriminatory employments practices, such as the use of entirely subjective personnel processes that operate to discriminate, satisfy the com-monality and typicality requirements of Rule 23(a)."); Warren v. Xerox Corp., 2004 U.S. Dist. LEXIS 5080 (E.D.N.Y. Mar. 11, 2004) (adopting magistrate's recommen-dation to certify nationwide class of African-American salespersons challenging subjective assignment and compensation system); Mathers v. Northshore Mining Co., 217 F.R.D. 474, 485, 92 FEP 1360 (D. Minn. 2003) (certifying gender class chal-lenging discriminatory training, promotion, and overtime assignments); McReynolds v. Sodexho Marriott Servs., Inc., 208 F.R.D. 428, 441 (D.D.C. 2003) (certifying class of more than 2000 African-American employees in six divisions challenging dis-cretionary promotion practices); Wilfong v. Rent-A-Center, Inc., 2001 WL 1795093 (S.D. Ill. Dec. 27, 2001) (certifying class of female employees and applicants al-leging discrimination in hiring, promotion, demotion, termination, hostile work environment, and terms and conditions of employment); Beckmann v. CBS, Inc., 192 F.R.D. 608, 90 FEP 1379 (D. Minn. 2000) (certifying class claims of gender discrimination in assignments, promotion, training, overtime, and for hostile work environment; challenging, among other things, defendants' use of entirely subjec-tive personnel processes); Daniels v. Federal Reserve Bank, 194 F.R.D. 609, 615 (N.D. Ill. 2000) (granting class certification based on evidence of use of subjective decision-making process when choosing among qualified applicants for promotion); Robinson v. Sears, Roebuck & Co., 111 F. Supp. 2d 1101 (E.D. Ark. 2000) (certi-fying broad class of minority current and former employees alleging discrimination in job assignment, pay, and promotion); McClain v. Lufkin Indus., Inc., 187 F.R.D. 267, 275, 277–78 (E.D. Tex. 1999) (certifying class in race discrimination action

alleged practices do not.[175] These decisions turn on the individual
facts alleged in each case. The extent to which personnel practices

---

based on defendant's subjective employment practices); Faulk v. Home Oil Co., 184
F.R.D. 645, 657, 82 FEP 451 (M.D. Ala. 1999) (finding that Rule 23(a) requirements
met in action alleging discrimination through "one entirely subjective selection system
for all selection decisions"); Toney v. Rosewood Care Ctr., Inc., 1999 U.S. Dist. LEXIS
4744 (N.D. Ill. Mar. 31, 1999) (certifying broad class where plaintiffs "alleged a
specific policy and practice of discrimination with regard to implementation of the
disciplinary system"); Communities for Equity v. Michigan High Sch. Athletic Ass'n,
192 F.R.D. 568, 573 (W.D. Mich. 1999) (certifying class in sex discrimination action where there was "variety of alleged manifestations of discrimination," finding
that such discrimination was product of "underlying policy or practice of discrimination"); Battle v. White Cap, Inc., 1999 WL 199594, at *5 (N.D. Ill. Mar. 31, 1999)
(allowing broad class action where plaintiff demonstrated "centralized, subjective
discipline policy"); Orlowski v. Dominick's Finer Foods, Inc., 172 F.R.D. 370 (N.D.
Ill. 1997) (granting certification of broad class based on common questions of discriminatory policy and subjective decision-making system); Wagner v. NutraSweet
Co., 170 F.R.D. 448, 450 (N.D. Ill. 1997) (certifying class of women in various
positions at various facilities based on allegation that "company-wide salary guidelines . . . systematically undercompensated women"); Stewart v. Rubin, 948 F. Supp.
1077, 1093 (D.D.C. 1996) (approving certification of settlement class where plaintiffs' claims based on "excessive subjectivity in the employment-related decision-
making process"), aff'd, 124 F.3d 1309 (D.C. Cir. 1997) (table); Morgan v. United
Parcel Serv. of Am., Inc., 169 F.R.D. 349, 356, 77 FEP 165 (E.D. Mo. 1996) (certifying broad class action in race discrimination action, reasoning that defendant's
"personnel policies are uniform throughout the country" and that "[t]hese policies
include the subjective, decentralized system of decision-making which the plaintiffs
allege is discriminatory"); Stender v. Lucky Stores, Inc., 803 F. Supp. 259, 331, 62
FEP 11 (N.D. Cal. 1992) (finding employer liable for classwide gender discrimination based on subjective promotion and assignment practices).
    [175]See Cooper v. Southern Co., 390 F.3d 695 (11th Cir. 2004) (affirming denial
of certification where plaintiffs' evidence failed to establish general policy of race
discrimination and to demonstrate commonality and typicality), cert. denied, 126
S. Ct. 478 (2005), overruled in part by Ash v. Tyson Foods, Inc., 546 U.S. 454, 97
FEP 641 (2006); Vitug v. Multistate Tax Comm'n, 88 F.3d 506, 514, 71 FEP 1445
(7th Cir. 1996) ("It is not enough for a plaintiff to demonstrate that an employment
practice could theoretically be used to discriminate"; "Title VII does not forbid
subjective selection processes."); Grosz v. Boeing Co., 92 FEP 1690, 1695 (M.D.
Cal. 2003) (" 'Excessive subjectivity,' however, is a criticism, not an actual company-wide policy or practice."), aff'd, 136 Fed. Appx. 960 (9th Cir. 2005); Ellis v.
Elgin Riverboat Resort, 217 F.R.D. 415, 92 FEP 963 (N.D. Ill. 2003) (decertifying
racial hiring class because Rule 23(a) requirements not met); Rhodes v. Cracker Barrel
Old Country Store, Inc., 213 F.R.D. 619, 680 (N.D. Ga. 2003) (denying class certification where across-the-board channeling claim attacked multiple selection practices that included subjective and objective elements); Reid v. Lockheed Martin
Aeronautics Co., 205 F.R.D. 655, 677, 86 FEP 631 (N.D. Ga. 2001) (denying certification of "across-the-board" class because plaintiffs failed to demonstrate that
alleged subjective decision making was entirely subjective, resulted in statistically
significant disparities across job groups and pay grades, or was part of "general policy

are uniform and subject to centralized authority are often important factors in determining whether commonality has been satisfied in such cases.[176]

---

of intentional discrimination"); Donaldson v. Microsoft Corp., 205 F.R.D. 558, 568 (W.D. Wash. 2001) (denying certification of gender and race claims alleging discrimination in compensation and promotion); Latson v. GC Servs., 83 FEP 1778 (S.D. Tex. 2000) (denying class certification because plaintiffs failed to establish common discriminatory practice or methodology among several unique and independent business lines and divisions); Lott v. Westinghouse Savannah River Co., 200 F.R.D. 539 (D.S.C. 2000) (denying certification of "across the board" class where plaintiffs challenged broad range of employment decisions but failed to provide evidence proving centralized decision making); Hively v. Northlake Foods, Inc., 191 F.R.D. 661, 668, 82 FEP 324 (M.D. Fla. 2000) (denying certification of gender discrimination class action where case would revolve around individualized circumstances of each plaintiff and, therefore, did not satisfy typicality requirement); Riley v. Compucom Sys., Inc., 82 FEP 996 (N.D. Tex. 2000) (finding that typicality and commonality requirements not met where named plaintiffs' individual claims depended on discrete factual scenarios); Ramirez v. DeCoster, 194 F.R.D. 348, 353 (D. Me. 2000) (denying class certification of alleged race discrimination claims because plaintiffs did not establish that each member of proposed class was affected by discriminatory practice in same manner); Adams v. Henderson, 197 F.R.D. 162, 172 (D. Md. 2000) (refusing certification of statewide class of African-American supervisors in part because any liability or damages determinations would be based on individualized inquiries); LeGrand v. New York City Transit Auth., 83 FEP 1817 (E.D.N.Y. 1999) (holding that commonality and typicality absent when named plaintiff's circumstances varied from those of other named plaintiffs); Zachery v. Texaco Exploration & Prod., Inc., 185 F.R.D. 230, 239 (W.D. Tex. 1999) (rejecting broad class based on subjective decision making, reasoning that "[d]elving into the practice of each local business unit and conceivably even into the individual decisions is precisely the type of individualized inquiry that class actions were designed to avoid"); Bostick v. SHM, Inc., 78 FEP 1087, 1092 (N.D. Ga. 1998) (refusing to certify class, holding that defendant's consideration of subjective factors in personnel decisions "is not sufficient alone to establish a prima facie case of systemic gender based discrimination," and that individual issues would dominate in any such claims in any event); Appleton v. Deloitte & Touche L.L.P., 168 F.R.D. 221, 229–30 (M.D. Tenn. 1996) (determining that challenged employment practices involved varying elements of objective and subjective criteria, thus precluding finding of commonality and typicality); Brooks v. Circuit City Stores, Inc., 71 FEP 102 (D. Md. 1996) (holding that allegations of subjective decision making failed to meet commonality requirement of Rule 23(a) because "[t]he focus of the claim remains the individual employment decisions"); McKnight v. Circuit City Stores, Inc., 168 F.R.D. 550, 554 (E.D. Va. 1996) (decertifying class based on allegations of excess subjectivity, holding that "the focus of each plaintiff's proof, defendant's response to each plaintiff, and the jury's inquiry is whether each individual employment decision was motivated by intentional racial discrimination"), *aff'd*, 158 F.3d 742 (4th Cir. 1998), *vacated on other grounds*, 119 S. Ct. 2388 (1999).

[176]*See, e.g.*, Stastny v. Southern Bell Tel. & Tel. Co., 628 F.2d 267, 277 (4th Cir. 1980) (centralization of decision making and uniformity of practices among five factors to be considered in determining commonality); *Dukes*, 222 F.R.D. at 149–50 (consistent

Some courts have concluded that in subjectivity cases the *Falcon* Footnote 15 exception is limited to circumstances involving *entirely* subjective systems and that the use of any objective factors will defeat commonality.[177] Other courts have not, particularly where alleged objective factors are not consistently applied.[178]

---

corporate policy and culture of uniformity key to finding of commonality); Harriss v. Pan Am. World Airways, Inc., 74 F.R.D. 24, 41 (N.D. Cal. 1977) (same).

[177]*See* Bacon v. Honda of Am. Mfg., Inc., 370 F.3d 565, 571–72 (6th Cir. 2004) (where proposed class includes different types of employees, plaintiffs failed to show that class "subject to the same, exclusively-subjective, decision-making process"), *cert. denied*, 543 U.S. 1151 (2005); Griffin v. Dugger, 823 F.2d 1476, 1490–91 (11th Cir. 1987) ("By qualifying 'subjective decision-making processes' with 'entirely,' the Court implied that an employer's general policy of discrimination manifested, for example, by an objective hiring practice and by a subjective promotion practice would not be discrimination operating in 'the same general fashion'."); Vuyanich v. Republic Nat'l Bank of Dallas, 723 F.2d 1195, 1199–1200 (5th Cir. 1984) ("two objective inputs—education and experience—in its necessarily subjective hiring process . . . precludes reliance on [*Falcon*'s] 'general policy of discrimination' exception"); Rhodes v. Cracker Barrel Old Country Store, Inc., 213 F.R.D. 619, 680 (N.D. Ga. 2003) (denying class certification where channeling claim attacked multiple selection practices that included both subjective and objective elements); Webb v. Merck & Co., 206 F.R.D. 399, 406–07 (E.D. Pa. 2002) (finding no commonality where collective bargaining agreement included some objective factors for compensation and promotion); Garcia v. Veneman, 211 F.R.D. 15, 20 (D.D.C. 2002) ("[s]lavish adherence to the word 'entirely' would be unwise, but where, as here, a number of objective factors guide the decision-making process, the proposed class fits less neatly into the *Falcon* exception"); Lott v. Westinghouse Savannah River Co., 200 F.R.D. 539, 560 (D.S.C. 2000) (noting that presence of objective criteria is one factor in determining that commonality not met).

[178]*See* Staton v. Boeing Co., 327 F.3d 938, 954–55 (9th Cir. 2003) (where objectors contested commonality in settlement class on grounds that collective bargaining agreements provided objective criteria for promotions decisions affecting some class members, finding that *Falcon* did not bar finding of commonality: "Union employees under objective promotion systems may have been immune to discrimination in promotion, but they could still have been affected by other alleged axes of discrimination. We understand footnote fifteen of *Falcon* to present a demonstrative example rather than a limited exception to the overall skepticism toward broad discrimination class actions."); Vuyanich v. Republic Nat'l Bank of Dallas, 736 F.2d 160, 162 (5th Cir. 1984) (dissent from denial of rehearing; "[W]e have never required that a plaintiff prove the complete absence of objective criteria to establish the existence of a discriminatory policy."); Anderson v. Boeing Co., 222 F.R.D. 521, 537 (N.D. Okla. 2004) ("the court finds this list of 'objective factors' vague and is unconvinced that it defeats plaintiffs' claim regarding centralized policies which foster discriminatory subjective decision-making in order to establish commonality"); Warren v. Xerox Corp, 2004 U.S. Dist. LEXIS 5115, at *38 (E.D.N.Y. Jan. 26, 2004), *recommendation adopted*, 2004 U.S. Dist. LEXIS 5080 (E.D.N.Y. Mar. 11, 2004) ("the existence of some objective factors does not negate a claim that the process is 'entirely subjective' where those variables are alleged to have been inappropriately

2. Different Types of Claims Asserted

In *Falcon*, the Supreme Court emphasized that for a class action to be maintained, the plaintiff must demonstrate a sufficient nexus between the named plaintiff's individual claims and the claims of the class.[179] This nexus is particularly important where the plaintiff seeks to represent several groups that allegedly experienced different types of discriminatory practices.[180] As discussed earlier, the "general policy of discrimination" exception in *Falcon* may establish that nexus. A related issue is whether particular claims or employment practices have been properly raised in the named plaintiff's EEOC charge.[181]

Where a sufficient nexus exists, courts will allow different types of claims to be litigated within the same class. For example, courts have sometimes certified—and sometimes refused to certify—classes

---

applied"); Mathers v. Northshore Mining Co., 217 F.R.D. 474, 485, 92 FEP 1360 (D. Minn. 2003) ("it is not necessary that a defendant employ absolutely no objective criteria in its decision-making process [to satisfy commonality]"); McReynolds v. Sodexho Marriott Servs., Inc., 208 F.R.D. 428, 442 (D.D.C. 2002) ("although individual promotion decisions may in isolated cases be made based on some objective criteria, [employer's] overall promotion practices remain entirely subjective, because the decision of whether to use objective criteria—and if so, which criteria to use—is a matter left to the discretion of the individual manager"); Stender v. Lucky Stores, Inc., 57 FEP 1437, 1439 (N.D. Cal. 1990) (noting that, "in keeping with the rationale of *Falcon*, the ability of the named plaintiffs to represent those complaining of discrimination in their initial assignment should be analyzed under Rule 23" and thus allowing plaintiffs to include initial hiring claims based on "entirely subjective decisionmaking" in same class as post-hiring claims where alleged objective criteria were not applied consistently and objectively); Barefield v. Chevron U.S.A., Inc., 44 FEP 1885 (N.D. Cal. 1988) (noting that whether criteria are objective or subjective is merits issue).

[179]General Tel. Co. of the Sw. v. Falcon, 457 U.S. 147, 160, 28 FEP 1745 (1982); *accord* Wakefield v. Monsanto Co., 120 F.R.D. 112, 115–16, 46 FEP 1481 (E.D. Mo. 1988); *Barefield*, 44 FEP at 1890; State, County, & Mun. Employees v. County of Nassau, 664 F. Supp. 64, 68, 44 FEP 583 (E.D.N.Y. 1987).

[180]Griffin v. Dugger, 823 F.2d 1476, 1490–91 (11th Cir. 1987) (holding that employee challenging subjective promotion decisions could not represent those complaining of hiring practices, which relied on objective criteria); Walker v. Jim Dandy Co., 747 F.2d 1360, 1365, 36 FEP 928 (11th Cir. 1984) (finding that applicant with hiring claim could not represent class with claims concerning recruiting, job assignments, transfers, and promotions). *But see* Wynn v. Dixieland Food Stores, Inc., 125 F.R.D. 696, 699–701, 49 FEP 416 (M.D. Ala. 1989) (certifying class of African-American applicants and employees alleging discrimination in hiring, promotions, and terminations).

[181]See the discussion at Section V.A *infra*.

containing both incumbent employees and unsuccessful applicants, depending on the specific facts of the case.[182] Similarly, applicants have been allowed to represent current employees who originally were refused employment and then later hired.[183] Deterred applicants (those allegedly discouraged from applying by the disputed employment practice) may or may not be included in a class with applicants, depending on the facts.[184] Former employees have been allowed to

---

[182]*Compare* Adames v. Mitsubishi Bank, Ltd., 133 F.R.D. 82, 91, 58 FEP 1466 (E.D.N.Y. 1989) (holding that named plaintiffs need not have same employment status as class members; allowing named former employees to represent both former and current employees), Sandoval v. Saticoy Lemon Ass'n, 747 F. Supp. 1373, 1377, 56 FEP 1753 (C.D. Cal. 1990) (allowing companywide class of female employees who were rejected applicants, deferred applicants, or present employees), Simmons v. City of Kansas City, 129 F.R.D. 178, 180, 52 FEP 640 (D. Kan. 1989) (certifying class of former and current African-American police officers alleging racially discriminatory promotion policy), *Wynn*, 125 F.R.D. at 700–01 (holding that employee may represent both applicants and employees), *and* Wester v. Special Sch. Dist. No. 1, 35 FEP 199, 202–03 (D. Minn. 1984) (holding that employees seeking promotion to administrator could represent applicants for teaching positions) *with* Washington v. Brown & Williamson Tobacco Corp., 959 F.2d 1566, 1570, 60 FEP 800 (11th Cir. 1992) (denying class certification where plaintiffs sought to represent all present and past African-American employees and also all past unsuccessful African-American applicants), Holsey v. Armour & Co., 743 F.2d 199, 216, 35 FEP 1064 (4th Cir. 1984) ("Applying *Falcon*, we are unable to affirm single class treatment for both promotions and hiring claims because the district court made no finding that the supervisors who made the challenged promotions decisions were the same persons who made hiring decisions."), Freeman v. Motor Convoy, Inc., 700 F.2d 1339, 1345–47, 31 FEP 517 (11th Cir. 1983) (holding that rejected applicants cannot be included in class represented by incumbent employees), Talley v. Leo J. Shapiro & Assocs., 713 F. Supp. 254, 257–58, 49 FEP 1260 (N.D. Ill. 1989) (finding that because plaintiffs were hired, they lacked standing to assert claims on behalf of persons who were not hired), *and* Minority Police Officers Ass'n v. City of South Bend, 555 F. Supp. 921, 929, 32 FEP 398 (N.D. Ind. 1983) (holding that employees could not represent unsuccessful applicants), *aff'd and appeal dismissed in part*, 721 F.2d 197, 33 FEP 433 (7th Cir. 1983).

[183]*See, e.g.*, Hartman v. Wick, 678 F. Supp. 312, 324, 60 FEP 1527 (D.D.C. 1988) ("The law demands that any member of the plaintiff class who was ultimately employed by defendant obtain a remedy based on the amount of time in which she experienced discrimination and its effects. The fact that she subsequently achieved her goal cannot erase this basic right.").

[184]*See, e.g.*, Berger v. Iron Workers Local 201, 843 F.2d 1395, 1411, 46 FEP 780 (D.C. Cir. 1988) ("There is no reason why those who were unwilling to subject themselves to an allegedly unlawful regimen, but who would have taken the exam had this obstacle not been placed in their path, may not challenge that requirement."); Bouman v. Block, 940 F.2d 1211, 1218, 1232, 60 FEP 1000 (9th Cir. 1991) (allowing female sheriff's deputy who was denied promotion to represent female applicants, would-be applicants, and officers who were denied promotion or transfer). *But see* Harris v. General Dev. Corp., 127 F.R.D. 655, 659, 51 FEP 209 (W.D. Ill.

represent a class composed of both former and current employees alleging discriminatory denial of promotion opportunities.[185]

Courts vary on whether employees who have experienced one form of discrimination in the workplace can represent class members who have experienced different or additional forms of discrimination.[186] The Ninth Circuit has observed:

> [A]s we read *Falcon*, it does not generally ban all broad classes but rather precludes a class action that, on the basis of one form of discrimination against one or a handful of plaintiffs, seeks to adjudicate all forms of discrimination against all members of a group protected by Title VII, § 1981 or a similar statute.[187]

To head off a typicality challenge, plaintiffs often name a class representative who has suffered each of the alleged forms of discrimination.[188]

1989) (definition of class of both applicants and those discouraged from applying because of employer's alleged policy of discrimination in hiring and recruiting is "too imprecise and speculative to be certified").

[185]*See* Brown v. Eckerd Drugs, Inc., 663 F.2d 1268, 1275 n.5, 27 FEP 137 (4th Cir. 1981) (that proposed class representatives alleging discriminatory denial of promotions "are former employees does not affect their capacity to represent current employees"; collecting cases), *vacated on other grounds*, 457 U.S. 1128 (1982); *Adames*, 133 F.R.D. at 91. *But see* Sanchez v. City of Santa Ana, 936 F.2d 1027, 1035, 59 FEP 1854 (9th Cir. 1990) (affirming denial of class certification based on lack of typicality and commonality between plaintiffs who were no longer employed and all past, present, and future employees with Spanish surnames); Bowling v. Proctor-Silex, Inc., 50 FEP 871, 872 (W.D. Pa. 1989) (finding that, as matter of law, employee from closed plant was inadequate representative of class challenging employment conditions at other plants).

[186]*Compare* Vuyanich v. Republic Nat'l Bank of Dallas, 723 F.2d 1195, 1200 (5th Cir. 1984) ("Because [the named plaintiffs] can allege injuries only as a result of the Bank's hiring and termination practices, respectively, they lack standing to assert class claims arising from the bank's other employment practices—compensation, promotion, placement, and maternity practices.") *and* Rhodes v. Cracker Barrel Old Country Store, Inc., 213 F.R.D. 619, 679–82 (N.D. Ga. 2003) (holding that "channeling" claim is really host of separate employment practices and named plaintiffs' experiences not typical of range of practices) *with* Martens v. Smith Barney, Inc., 181 F.R.D. 243, 259, 77 FEP 532 (S.D.N.Y. 1998) ("Class certification is appropriate if the claims entail common issues and the injuries trace to the central employer's failings. This holds even where plaintiffs suffer varying forms of discrimination, where some plaintiffs hold managerial jobs while others do not, where plaintiffs assert diverse legal causes of action, or where some plaintiffs apply for positions while others do not.") (citations omitted).

[187]Staton v. Boeing Co., 327 F.3d 938, 955 (9th Cir. 2003).

[188]*See, e.g.*, Mathers v. Northshore Mining Co., 217 F.R.D. 474, 486, 92 FEP 1360 (D. Minn. 2003); Wright v. Stern, 2003 U.S. Dist. LEXIS 11589, 92 FEP 697 (S.D.N.Y. July 9, 2003).

3. Different Job Classifications

Another frequently contested Rule 23(a) issue is whether a putative class representative can represent persons in different jobs or job groups. Sometimes the court considers the issue of whether the named plaintiffs' claims are "typical" of those of the other class members[189] or whether the named plaintiff is an adequate representative, i.e., whether the interests of the named plaintiff are in conflict with those in other job groups.[190]

The case law on this point is not consistent. Some cases deny or narrow class certification where plaintiffs held jobs regarded as distinct from those held by alleged class members.[191] Other cases

---

[189]*See, e.g., Staton*, 327 F.3d at 957 (within trial court's discretion to find that class representatives' claims were typical of those of absent class members in multiple job categories).

[190]*See, e.g., Staton*, 327 F.3d at 958 ("The question of whether employees at different levels of the internal hierarchy have potentially conflicting interests is context-specific and depends upon the particular claims alleged in a case."); Wagner v. Taylor, 836 F.2d 578, 591, 595, 45 FEP 1199 (D.C. Cir. 1987) (plaintiff in high-level job not necessarily precluded from representing employees in lower-level jobs but, on facts, interests of plaintiff and class were antagonistic). See the discussion at Section III.B.2 *supra*.

[191]*See, e.g.,* Cooper v. Southern Co., 390 F.3d 695, 715 (11th Cir. 2004) (affirming denial of certification where employees worked in diverse job types in different facilities and geographic locations), *cert. denied*, 126 S. Ct. 478, *overruled in part by* Ash v. Tyson Foods, Inc., 126 S. Ct. 1195, 97 FEP 641 (2006); Bacon v. Honda of Am. Mfg., Inc., 370 F.3d 565, 571 (6th Cir. 2004) (commonality failed where class included hourly workers and supervisors and both production and administrative workers), *cert. denied*, 543 U.S. 1151 (2005); Walker v. Jim Dandy Co., 747 F.2d 1360, 1365, 36 FEP 928 (11th Cir. 1984) (applicants for supervisory positions not permitted to represent applicants for plant-level, nonsupervisory jobs); Troupe v. Randall's Food & Drugs, Inc., 1999 WL 552727 (N.D. Tex. July 28, 1999) (rejecting class consisting of current, past, and future employees, both supervisors and nonsupervisory positions, as well as past and future applicants); Cox v. Indian Head Indus., Inc., 187 F.R.D. 531 (W.D.N.C. 1999) (refusing to certify class of employees and applicants because "no named Plaintiff has alleged conduct involving her application for employment"); Jefferson v. Windy City Maint., Inc., 1998 U.S. Dist. LEXIS 12262 (N.D. Ill. Aug. 3, 1998) (modifying class definition "to exclude managers, and include only union janitorial employees" in order to preserve commonality); Gaines v. Boston Herald, Inc., 998 F. Supp. 91, 112, 76 FEP 1428 (D. Mass. 1998) (allowing named plaintiff in race discrimination action to represent individuals who applied for employment and were denied, but not those who were discouraged from applying altogether); Kresefsky v. Panasonic Commc'ns & Sys. Co., 169 F.R.D. 54, 63, 74 FEP 905 (D.N.J. 1996) (refusing to certify class in part because "various named plaintiffs worked in different groups . . . and in different job types with different responsibilities"); Morgan v. United Parcel Serv. of Am.,

have found that Rule 23(a) is satisfied where the plaintiffs can demonstrate that a common policy of discrimination similarly affected employees in various job categories.[192]

4. Multiple Organizational Units or Geographical Facilities

Employers often attempt to defeat or narrow class certification when the putative class covers multiple organizational units or geographical facilities. Where decision making or policy making

---

Inc., 169 F.R.D. 349, 356, 77 FEP 165 (E.D. Mo. 1996) (finding that named plaintiffs could not properly represent employees "below the level of center manager" or those "at higher levels").

[192]Dukes v. Wal-Mart, Inc., 474 F.3d 1214, 1232–33 (9th Cir. 2007) (affirming certification of class of salaried managers and hourly employees with regard to pay and promotion where only one named plaintiff was salaried manager and others were hourly workers); Holsey v. Armour & Co., 743 F.2d 199, 217, 35 FEP 1064 (4th Cir. 1984) (holding that persons seeking promotions to sales representative and to supervisor could be included in same class when at least one named plaintiff sought promotion to each classification); Carpenter v. Stephen F. Austin State Univ., 706 F.2d 608, 617, 31 FEP 1758 (5th Cir. 1983) (certifying class of salaried clerical and hourly custodial employees with regard to initial assignments, pay, and promotions); Giles v. Ireland, 742 F.2d 1366, 1372, 35 FEP 1718 (11th Cir. 1984) (excluding orderlies from mental health worker class where orderlies were not affected by salary and promotion claims raised by named plaintiffs); Paxton v. Union Nat'l Bank of Little Rock, 688 F.2d 552, 562, 29 FEP 1233 (8th Cir. 1982) ("Typicality is not defeated because . . . of the differing qualifications of the plaintiffs and class members . . . ."); Wright, 2003 U.S. Dist. LEXIS 11589 (holding that named plaintiffs in race discrimination case satisfied typicality and could represent supervisory, nonsupervisory, field office, and administrative employees challenging promotion, compensation, location segregation, and hostile work environment); Wilfong v. Rent-A-Center, 2001 U.S. Dist. LEXIS 22718, 87 FEP 1096 (S.D. Ill. Dec. 27, 2001) (certifying class of all female employees and applicants in all job positions alleging discrimination in hiring, promotion, demotion, termination, hostile work environment, and terms and conditions of employment); Bates v. United Parcel Serv., 204 F.R.D. 440, 445, 449 (N.D. Cal. 2001) (certifying class of all UPS employees and job applicants nationwide who have hearing impairments, use sign language as primary means of communication, and who were affected by defendant's failure to have process for addressing communication barriers); Faulk v. Home Oil Co., 184 F.R.D. 645, 658, 82 FEP 451 (M.D. Ala. 1999) (finding Rule 23(a) requirements met in class consisting of applicants who were not hired and employees who were not promoted because "defendant used an entirely subjective selection system"); Battle v. White Cap, Inc., 1998 U.S. Dist. LEXIS 14190 (N.D. Ill. Sept. 2, 1998) (allowing named plaintiff to represent several different job categories given defendant's alleged use of "centralized, subjective discipline policy"); Adames v. Mitsubishi Bank, Ltd., 133 F.R.D. 82, 91, 58 FEP 1466 (E.D.N.Y. 1989) ("[t]he named plaintiffs need not possess the same qualifications or have the same employment status as the purported class members").

is decentralized, certification of a multi-unit or multi-job class often is denied.[193] However, if an identifiable policy or practice in effect at all facilities is challenged in an adverse impact case, courts often find sufficient nexus between employees in different facilities.[194]

---

[193]*Bacon*, 370 F.3d at 571 (court viewed "with skepticism" class with workers in four different plants and more than 30 departments); Reid v. Lockheed Martin Aeronautics Co., 205 F.R.D. 655, 669, 86 FEP 631 (N.D. Ga. 2001) (declining to certify multi-facility class because "the facilities at issue in these cases were not subject to centralized and uniform employment practices such that plaintiffs have satisfied the commonality and typicality requirements"); Wright v. Circuit City Stores, Inc., 201 F.R.D. 526, 542 (N.D. Ala. 2000) (denying certification where "[p]laintiffs seek to represent individuals who worked in a multi-state geographical area, in different organizational divisions of the defendant, in separate facilities, at different times, reporting directly to and under the direct supervision of numerous autonomous decision-makers"); Zachery v. Texaco Exploration & Prod. Inc., 185 F.R.D. 230, 239 (W.D. Tex. 1999) (finding Rule 23(a) requirements not met in part because "the proposed class is spread across fifteen states in seventeen separate business units"); *Troupe*, 1999 WL 552727, at * 5 (refusing to certify class covering employees and applicants "from at least fifty separate stores spread over two large cities and their outlying suburbs"); Reyes v. Walt Disney World Co., 176 F.R.D. 654, 658, 76 FEP 338 (M.D. Fla. 1998) (finding Rule 23(a) requirements not met in part because "the representative plaintiffs were employed by three separate departments or divisions"); Bostron v. Apfel, 182 F.R.D. 188, 195, 77 FEP 1562 (D. Md. 1998) (reasoning that differences in demographics and labor force where defendant's various regional offices located precluded nationwide class); *Kresefsky*, 169 F.R.D. at 63 (refusing to certify class in part because "various named plaintiffs worked in . . . different geographical areas"); Rosenberg v. University of Cincinnati, 118 F.R.D. 591, 595 (S.D. Ohio 1988) ("[A]ny sex discrimination that occurred would have developed out of the autonomous decision-making within that department or college and would thus have had to have been unique and individual to that particular department or college."); *see also* Stastny v. Southern Bell Tel. & Tel. Co., 628 F.2d 267, 279–80, 23 FEP 665 (4th Cir. 1980) (statewide class covering multiple telephone company facilities inappropriate because of lack of proof of centralized control of employment policies); Duffy v. C. Itoh & Co., 53 FEP 815, 816 (S.D.N.Y. 1990) (nationwide class denied where there was insufficient evidence of centralized decision making).

[194]*See, e.g.*, Dukes v. Wal-Mart Stores, Inc., 222 F.R.D. 137, 152–53, 93 FEP 1629 (N.D. Cal. 2004) (finding commonality requirement is met despite localized decision making where "company maintains centralized corporate policies that provide some constraint on the degree of managerial discretion" and where company also "relies on its strongly imbued culture to guide managers in the exercise of their discretion"), *aff'd*, 474 F.3d 1214 (9th Cir. 2007); Coleman v. General Motors Acceptance Corp., 220 F.R.D. 64, 73 (M.D. Tenn. 2004) (in adverse impact challenge to retail loan markup policy, noting that "plaintiffs in this case have targeted a narrow, specific, facially neutral policy that they allege is created by a centralized decisionmaker with the power to set policy and utilized by all participating dealers who offer [defendant's] financing to customers, to observable discriminatory effect."); McReynolds v. Sodexho Marriott Servs., Inc., 208 F.R.D. 428, 441 (D.D.C. 2002)

Similarly, evidence of a challenged centralized policy or centralized decision making with respect to the employment practice in question can support certification of disparate treatment classes encompassing geographically separate facilities or different business units.[195]

(finding commonality requirement met in class action under disparate treatment and disparate impact theories on grounds that, although alleged discriminatory practice involved decentralized promotion processes at 5,000 different worksites across United States, promotion decisions were "linked to [defendant's] company-wide policy of not having any consistent promotion policy, guidelines, or requirements"); *Bates*, 204 F.R.D. at 445–46 (rejecting defendant's argument that decentralized decision-making process in sites across United States defeats commonality); Butler v. Home Depot, Inc., 1996 WL 421436, at *3 (N.D. Cal. Jan. 25, 1996) (finding that "statistical evidence of widespread discrimination" within defendant's West Coast Division satisfied commonality requirement in class action under disparate treatment and disparate impact theories); Shores v. Publix Super Mkts., Inc., 1996 WL 407850, at *7 (M.D. Fla. Mar. 12, 1996) (certifying class of female employees in 500 stores across three states where plaintiffs' challenge to company's allegedly subjective decision-making system raised common issues of law and fact under disparate impact and disparate treatment theories).

[195]*See, e.g., Dukes*, 474 F.3d at 1231–33 (affirming certification of nationwide class where company's allegedly discriminatory practices affect all plaintiffs in common manner); Warren v. Xerox Corp., 2004 U.S. Dist. LEXIS 5115 (E.D.N.Y. Jan. 26, 2004) (certification of nationwide class of African-American salespersons; rejecting argument that class members were assigned to numerous different sales organizations); Mathers v. Northshore Mining Co., 217 F.R.D. 474, 486, 92 FEP 1360 (D. Minn. 2003) (named plaintiffs satisfy typicality for claims across different operating units and departments); *McReynolds*, 208 F.R.D. at 445 ("[b]ecause plaintiffs have made a convincing showing of a common policy of discriminatory treatment that extends across divisions, units and geographic regions, including those where the proposed representatives worked, they have made a sufficient demonstration that the claims of the class representatives are largely typical of the class"); Duffy v. Massinari, 202 F.R.D. 437, 443 (E.D. Pa. 2001) (certifying ADEA class covering seven program centers nationwide); *Wilfong*, 2001 U.S. Dist. LEXIS 22718, at *6 (certifying class of all female employees and applicants in 2,200 stores nationwide); Latson v. GC Servs., 83 FEP 1778 (S.D. Tex. 2000) (refusing to certify, but noting that geographical dispersion of class members across nation is not reason to deny certification); *Bates*, 204 F.R.D. at 449 (certifying nationwide class of hearing-impaired employees); Beckmann v. CBS, Inc., 192 F.R.D. 608 (D. Minn. 2000) (certifying class of women working in five television stations in three states); Orlowski v. Dominick's Finer Foods, Inc., 172 F.R.D. 370 (N.D. Ill. 1997) (certifying class covering 80 stores in 4 different areas); *Butler*, 1996 WL 421436, at *3–4 (certifying both employees and applicants in national retail chain's West Coast division); *Shores*, 1996 WL 407850, at *7 (certifying class of female employees in retail stores companywide); *cf. Faulk*, 184 F.R.D. at 655 ("the locus of decision-making authority is an important consideration when determining whether class certification is appropriate for systemic discrimination claims involving multiple facilities").

IV. THE REQUIREMENTS OF RULE 23(b)

Title VII class actions generally have been maintained under Rule 23(b)(2), (b)(3), or both.[196] A Rule 23(b)(2) class action is appropriate when "the party opposing the class has acted or refused to act on grounds generally applicable to the class, thereby making appropriate final injunctive relief or corresponding declaratory relief with respect to the class as a whole."[197] Rule 23(b)(3) actions may be maintained where "the court finds that questions of law or fact common to members of the class predominate over any questions affecting only individual members, and that a class action is superior to other available methods for the fair and efficient adjudication of the controversy."[198] Title VII class actions have rarely been certified under Rule 23(b)(1), the subsection used for cases involving a "limited fund."[199]

A. Class Certification Prior to the 1991 Civil Rights Act

Before passage of the 1991 Civil Rights Act, most courts certified employment discrimination class actions under Rule 23(b)(2).

---

[196]*See, e.g.*, Wetzel v. Liberty Mut. Ins. Co., 508 F.2d 239, 248–57, 9 FEP 211 (3d Cir. 1975) (extensively discussing certification of "homogeneous" classes under subsection (b)(2)); Air Line Stewards & Stewardesses Ass'n Local 550 v. American Airlines, Inc., 490 F.2d 636, 643, 6 FEP 1197 (7th Cir. 1973) (subsection (b)(3) certification appropriate for class of discharged stewardesses); Barefield v. Chevron U.S.A, Inc., 48 FEP 907, 911 (N.D. Cal. 1988) (in § 1981 action, certifying liability and punitive damages under subsection 23(b)(2) and compensatory damages under Rule 23(b)(3)).

[197]FED. R. CIV. P. 23(b)(2). The traditional illustration of the Rule 23(b)(2) class action is in "the civil rights field where a party is charged with discriminating unlawfully against a class." FED. R. CIV. P. 23 advisory committee's note; *see* Amchem Prods. v. Windsor, 521 U.S. 591, 614 (1997) ("Civil rights cases against parties charged with unlawful, class-based discrimination are prime examples [of Rule 23(b)(2) cases].").

[198]FED. R. CIV. P. 23(b)(3).

[199]*See* Bacon v. Honda of Am. Mfg., Inc., 205 F.R.D. 466, 483 (S.D. Ohio 2001) (denying class certification under Rule 23(b)(1) in Title VII context); Levels v. Akzo Nobel Salt, Inc., 178 F.R.D. 171, 180 (N.D. Ohio 1998) (denying certification under Rule 23(b)(1) in Title VII context because there was (1) no risk of inconsistent adjudications where each plaintiff complained of individual circumstances; and (2) no risk that multiple adjudications would impair ability of other class members to pursue individual recourse). *But see* James v. Stockham Valves & Fittings Co., 559 F.2d 310, 313–14, 15 FEP 827 (5th Cir. 1977) (Rule 23(b)(1) certification appropriate where prosecution of separate actions would result in inconsistent standards of conduct for defendant).

Certification under Rule 23(b)(2) would ensure that all class members were included in the action, thereby promoting judicial economy and consistency of result.[200] In addition, Rule 23(b)(2) certification avoided the need to provide notice and opt-out rights or to prove that class treatment was superior to other available methods to resolve the controversy, both required under Rule 23(b)(3).[201] Although plaintiffs typically sought monetary relief in the form of back pay, courts concluded that this request did not preclude certification under Rule 23(b)(2) because such relief was considered to be an equitable remedy rather than a legal remedy of money damages.[202]

In some employment discrimination class cases, courts used one of three alternatives to Rule 23(b)(2) certification. A few courts, particularly in disparate treatment cases, determined that Rule 23(b)(3) treatment of the entire action was more appropriate.[203] Others certified classes under Rule 23(b)(2) as to injunctive relief, but deferred class certification as to claims for monetary relief.[204] Finally, some courts treated the back pay or damages remedial phase of the case under Rule 23(b)(3) and the injunctive relief part of the

---

[200]Robinson v. Union Carbide Corp., 544 F.2d 1258, 1260, 14 FEP 266, 267 (5th Cir. 1977) (reversing district court's certification under Rule 23(b)(3) and requiring that class members "opt in" if they sought to receive back pay; class should have been certified under Rule 23(b)(2), which compels inclusion and therefore promotes judicial economy, consistency of result, and binding adjudication more effectively than Rule 23(b)(3)).

[201]Wetzel v. Liberty Mut. Ins. Co., 508 F.2d 239, 252–53, 9 FEP 211 (3d Cir. 1975) (Rule 23(b)(3) procedural protections unnecessary for homogenous class).

[202]Allison v. Citgo Petroleum Corp., 151 F.3d 402, 415 (5th Cir. 1998), reh'g denied, 1998 U.S. App. LEXIS 24651, 81 FEP 501 (5th Cir. Oct. 2, 1998) (back pay has "long been recognized as an equitable remedy under Title VII . . . [that] conflicts in no way with the limitations of Rule 23(b)(2)"); Paxton v. Union Nat'l Bank, 688 F.2d 552, 563 (8th Cir. 1982) (Rule 23(b)(2) certification appropriate where back pay is incidental to injunctive relief claim).

[203]See, e.g., Air Line Stewards & Stewardesses Ass'n Local 550 v. American Airlines, Inc., 490 F.2d 636, 643, 6 FEP 1197 (7th Cir. 1973) ("As to the discharged stewardesses, the class actions would, even at the beginning, have had to be maintained under [Rule 23(b)(3)], with each such stewardess having the right to exclude herself, or appear through counsel.") (emphasis added); Roberts v. Marine Midland Bank, 22 FEP 326, 330 (S.D.N.Y. 1979) (although plaintiff selected Rule 23(b)(2), court found that "action is more appropriately certified in accordance with Rule 23(b)(3) in that the plaintiff has requested appropriate damages for himself and his class as well as injunctive and declaratory relief").

[204]See, e.g., Rich v. Martin Marietta Corp., 522 F.2d 333, 342 (10th Cir. 1975); Molthan v. Temple Univ., 83 F.R.D. 368, 376–77, 24 FEP 282 (E.D. Pa. 1979).

case under Rule 23(b)(2).[205] This was accomplished by bifurcating the case and using Rule 23(b)(2) for the Stage I "liability" proceeding and Rule 23(b)(3) for the Stage II "remedy" proceeding.[206]

With the 1991 amendments to Title VII, compensatory and punitive damages became available for the first time and, with them, the right to a jury trial. The central dispute regarding Rule 23(b) in the employment law arena now appears to be which type of certification, if any, is appropriate when plaintiffs seek compensatory and punitive damages.[207] The issue has centered on whether certification is proper under Rule 23(b)(2), Rule 23(b)(3), or some combination thereof. Each of these alternatives is discussed below.

B. Class Certification Under Rule 23(b)(2)

To date, the Second, Fifth, Sixth, Seventh, Ninth, and Eleventh Circuits have addressed whether Rule 23(b)(2) certification is appropriate in employment class cases that seek the damages remedies created by the 1991 amendments. The Fifth, Sixth, and Eleventh Circuits have questioned the availability of certification under Rule 23(b)(2) where compensatory and punitive damages are sought, given the likelihood, in the courts' view, that both forms of damages will require individualized inquiries into each class member's circumstances and predominate over the group remedies intended for Rule 23(b)(2) actions. The Second, Seventh, and Ninth Circuits by contrast have concluded that Rule 23(b)(2) certification may still be available in suits seeking compensatory and/or

---

[205]*See, e.g.*, Holmes v. Continental Can Co., 706 F.2d 1144, 1155, 31 FEP 1707 (11th Cir. 1983) ("The presence in a lawsuit of a significant number of atypical claims not common to the class activates a requirement that absent class members be given an opportunity to opt out . . . of a Title VII lawsuit or a settlement . . . . Because the monetary relief stage of this particular Title VII case is functionally more similar to a [Rule 23(b)(3)] class than to a [Rule 23(b)(2)] class, the opt out protection of [Rule 23(b)(3)] must be applied."); Officers for Justice v. Civil Serv. Comm'n, 688 F.2d 615, 622 (9th Cir. 1982); Barefield v. Chevron, U.S.A., Inc., 48 FEP 907, 911 (N.D. Cal. 1988).

[206]*Holmes*, 706 F.2d at 1158.

[207]Where plaintiffs do not seek compensatory and punitive damages, there is no controversy that certification is still appropriate under Rule 23(b)(2) or (b)(3), assuming that other Rule 23 requirements are satisfied. *See, e.g.*, Drayton v. Western Auto Supply Co., 203 F.R.D. 520, 529 (M.D. Fla. 2000). Similarly, adverse impact cases, by definition, are limited to equitable remedies and thus are still appropriate for Rule 23(b)(2) certification. *See* Section VIII.A *infra*.

punitive damages, although due process may require that class members be provided notice and an opportunity to opt out.

In *Allison v. Citgo Petroleum Corp.*,[208] the first appellate decision to consider the issue, the Fifth Circuit affirmed the district court's denial of class certification. The court prefaced its detailed conclusions by pointing to the determinative impact of the Civil Rights Act of 1991, noting that "[b]efore the passage of the Civil Rights Act of 1991, which for the first time provided plaintiffs with a right to compensatory and punitive damages as well as a jury trial (each demanded here), aspects of this case clearly would have qualified for class certification."[209] Following passage of the Act, however, the court concluded that "the plaintiffs' claims for money damages and the constitutional right of both parties to a jury trial, all with its substantive rights and procedural complications, ultimately render[ed] this case unsuitable for class certification under Rule 23."[210]

The Fifth Circuit considered whether the district court erred by holding that class certification was improper under Rule 23(b)(2) unless the requested relief relates predominantly to injunctive or declaratory relief rather than monetary damages.[211] The court found that the district court's use of a predominance requirement for Rule 23(b)(2) certification was fully consistent with applicable case law, and then considered the question of the proper definition of "incidental damages" for Rule 23(b)(2) actions.[212] The court concluded that Rule 23(b)(2) certification would be appropriate only where the damages flow directly from liability to the class as a whole, not from each class member's individual claim:

> [M]onetary relief predominates in [Rule 23(b)(2)] class actions unless it is incidental to requested injunctive or declaratory relief. By incidental, we mean damages that flow directly from liability to the class *as a whole* on the claims forming the basis of the injunctive or declaratory relief. Ideally, incidental damages should be only those to which class members automatically would be entitled once liability to the class (or subclass) as a whole is

---

[208]151 F.3d 402 (5th Cir. 1998), *reh'g denied*, 1998 U.S. App. LEXIS 24651, 81 FEP 501 (5th Cir. Oct. 2, 1998).

[209]*Id.* at 407.

[210]*Id.*

[211]*Id.* at 410–11.

[212]*Id.* at 411, 415–16.

established. . . . Moreover, such damages should at least be capable of computation by means of objective standards and not dependent in any significant way on the intangible, subjective differences of each class member's circumstances. Liability for incidental damages should not require additional hearings to resolve the disparate merits of each individual's case; it should neither introduce new and substantial legal or factual issues, nor entail complex individualized determinations. Thus, incidental damages will, by definition, be more in the nature of a group remedy, consistent with the forms of relief intended for [Rule 23(b)(2)] class actions.[213]

The panel then found that the district court had properly applied this standard to deny certification under Rule 23(b)(2).[214] Specifically, the court found that "[e]ntitlement to backpay and other equitable monetary remedies . . . required separate hearings in which each class member would have to show that the discrimination caused a loss," and "[s]imilarly, recovery of compensatory and punitive damages required particularly individualized proof of injury, including how each class member was personally affected by the discriminatory conduct."[215] The court thus affirmed the district court's finding that plaintiffs' claims for compensatory and punitive damages were not sufficiently incidental to the injunctive and declaratory relief to permit Rule 23(b)(2) certification.[216] It further noted that "[t]he very nature of these damages, compensating plaintiffs for emotional and other intangible injuries, necessarily implicates the subjective differences of each plaintiff's circumstances" and that, "by requiring individualized proof of discrimination and actual injury to each class member, compensatory damages introduce new

---

[213]*Id.* at 415 (citations omitted). The Fifth Circuit, however, also noted that this holding was not inconsistent with previous cases permitting back pay under Title VII in Rule 23(b)(2) class actions. Citing *Pettway v. American Cast Iron Pipe Co.*, 494 F.2d 211, 257, 7 FEP 1115 (5th Cir. 1974), the *Allison* court explained that "Rule 23(b)(2), by its own terms, does not preclude all claims for monetary relief. We construed [Rule 23(b)(2)] to permit monetary relief when it was an equitable remedy, and the defendant's conduct made equitable remedies appropriate. Back pay, of course, had long been recognized as an equitable remedy under Title VII . . . . In short, *Pettway* held that back pay could be sought in a [Rule 23(b)(2)] class action because, as an equitable remedy similar to other forms of affirmative injunctive relief permitted in [Rule 23(b)(2)] class actions, it was an integral component of Title VII's 'make whole' remedial scheme." *Id.*

[214]*Id.* at 416.

[215]*Id.*

[216]*Id.*

and substantial legal and factual issues."[217] The Fifth Circuit subsequently denied a motion for rehearing en banc in *Allison* and issued a somewhat cryptic order[218] that prompted one district court to question the precedential value of the original *Allison* opinion.[219]

In In re *Monumental Life Insurance Co.*,[220] the Fifth Circuit took a less rigid approach to the requirement articulated in *Allison* that monetary relief should "flow directly from liability to the class as a whole" and "not entail complex individualized determinations."[221] In this nonemployment case, the plaintiffs challenged life insurance sales practices that had allegedly discriminated against African Americans and sought equitable restitution in the form of a constructive trust.[222] The plaintiffs proposed calculating individual relief by constructing "restitution grids," which—although complex—would rely on objective factors.[223] The district court denied class certification under Rule 23(b), finding that the calculation of individual relief would be too complex under *Allison*.[224] The Fifth Circuit reversed and remanded to the district court for reconsideration of certification.[225] It rejected the notion that the monetary predominance test is subject to "a sweat-of-the-brow exception."[226]

---

[217]*Id.* at 417. The court also determined that the plaintiffs' claims for punitive damages were "not sufficiently incidental." Here, the court focused on the breadth and diversity of the plaintiffs' claims and observed that "[s]ome plaintiffs may have been subjected to more virile [*sic*] discrimination than others"; punitive damages must be reasonably related to the reprehensibility of the defendants' conduct and to the compensatory damages awarded to the plaintiffs; and punitive damages must therefore be determined after proof of liability to individual plaintiffs at the second stage of a pattern-or-practice case, not upon the mere finding of general liability to the class at the first stage. *Id.* at 417; *see also* Section IV.F *infra*.

[218]Allison v. Citgo Petroleum Corp., 81 FEP 501, 502 (5th Cir. 1998) ("[t]he trial court utilized consolidation under [Rule] 42 rather than class certification under [Rule] 23 to manage this case. We review that decision for abuse of discretion and we find no abuse in this case. We are not called upon to decide whether the district court would have abused its discretion if it had elected to bifurcate liability issues that are common to the class and to certify for class determination those discreet [*sic*] liability issues.").

[219]*See* Warnell v. Ford Motor Co., 189 F.R.D. 383, 389 (N.D. Ill. 1999).

[220]365 F.3d 408 (5th Cir.), *cert. denied*, 543 U.S. 870 (2004).

[221]*Id.* at 416 (quoting Allison v. Citgo Petroleum Corp., 151 F.3d 402, 416 (5th Cir. 1998)).

[222]*Id.* at 412.

[223]*Id.* at 419.

[224]*Id.* at 413.

[225]*Id.* at 411–12.

[226]*Id.* at 419.

Although it is arguable that the construction of thousands of restitution grids, though based on objective data, involves the sort of complex data manipulations forbidden by *Allison*, we read *Allison* to the contrary. The policy variables are identifiable on a classwide basis and, when sorted, are capable of determining damages for individual policyowners; none of these variables is unique to particular plaintiffs. The prevalence of variables common to the class makes damage computation "virtually a mechanical task."[227]

The Eleventh Circuit embraced the *Allison* analysis of Rule 23(b)(2) in a nonemployment class action, *Murray v. Auslander*.[228] It vacated a district court's class certification order under Rule 23(b)(2) and remanded the case for consideration of standing and whether the plaintiffs' damages claims could be certified under Rule 23(b)(3).[229] The court expressly adopted the *Allison* standard for determining whether damages are incidental to equitable relief[230] and concluded that because the plaintiffs sought damages "as a remedy for their alleged individual 'pain and suffering, mental anguish and humiliation,' " rather than "as a 'group remedy,' " these damages claims required "an inquiry into each class member's individual circumstances," and therefore predominated over the claims for equitable relief.[231] Accordingly, the court held that the district court's certification of such damages claims under Rule 23(b)(2) constituted an abuse of discretion.[232] In a subsequent employment discrimination class action, *Cooper v. Southern Co.*,[233] the Eleventh Circuit concluded that it was bound to apply the *Allison* test adopted in *Murray*.[234] It affirmed the denial of class certification under Rule 23(b)(2) because the plaintiffs sought compensatory and punitive damages, which would require an individualized assessment.[235]

---

[227]*Id.* (footnote and citations omitted).
[228]244 F.3d 807 (11th Cir. 2001) (alleging violations of Title XIX of Social Security Act, Fourteenth Amendment to U.S. Constitution, and ADA).
[229]*Id.* at 813–14.
[230]*Id.* at 812.
[231]*Id.*
[232]*Id.*
[233]390 F.3d 695 (11th Cir. 2004), *cert. denied*, 546 U.S. 960 (2005), *overruled in part on other grounds by* Ash v. Tyson Foods, Inc., 546 U.S. 454, 97 FEP 641 (2006).
[234]*Id.* at 721 n.12.
[235]*Id.* at 721.

In *Reeb v. Ohio Department of Rehabilitation & Correction*,[236] the Sixth Circuit also endorsed the *Allison* test. Reversing a district court's class certification order, the court concluded that "the claims for individual compensatory damages of members of a Title VII class necessarily predominate over requested declaratory or injunctive relief, and individual compensatory damages are not recoverable by a Rule 23(b)(2) class."[237] The court did, however, note that there are circumstances in which back pay may be appropriate in a Rule 23(b)(2) class due to its equitable nature and the relatively formulaic fashion in which it may be awarded.[238]

The Seventh Circuit has also addressed whether class actions in the employment discrimination context may be certified under Rule 23(b)(2). In *Jefferson v. Ingersoll International, Inc.*,[239] the Seventh Circuit vacated the district court's order, which certified a class of employees whose employment applications were allegedly rejected based on the applicants' race.[240] Citing *Allison*, the *Jefferson* court held that where a class seeks compensatory and punitive damages, certification under Rule 23(b)(2) is improper unless "monetary relief is incidental to the equitable remedy."[241] Because the district court failed to address this issue, the court remanded the case with instructions to determine whether the claimed monetary damages were incidental.[242]

Using a different analytic framework from that embraced by the *Allison* court, the Seventh Circuit expressed concern that certification under Rule 23(b)(2) did not provide class members with personal notice and an opportunity to opt out. The *Jefferson* court reasoned that the Supreme Court's decision in *Ortiz v. Fibreboard Corp.*[243] required notice and opt-out rights in actions involving

---

[236]435 F.3d 639 (6th Cir. 2006).

[237]*Id.* at 651.

[238]*Id.* at 650; *see also* Coleman v. General Motors Acceptance Corp., 296 F.3d 443, 445–46 (6th Cir. 2002) (in nonemployment case, court vacated certification of class under Rule 23(b)(2); "one critical factor" in determining whether certification under Rule 23(b)(2) is appropriate "is whether the compensatory relief requested requires individualized damages determination or is susceptible to calculation on a classwide basis").

[239]195 F.3d 894, 81 FEP 170 (7th Cir. 1999).

[240]*Id.* at 894–95.

[241]*Id.* at 898.

[242]*Id.* at 899.

[243]527 U.S. 815 (1999).

damages.[244] Accordingly, the *Jefferson* court suggested that the district court could still properly certify the action under Rule 23(b)(2) so long as the court ordered that class members be given the right to personal notice and the right to opt out.[245] Alternatively, the Seventh Circuit suggested that the district court could certify the action under Rule 23(b)(3) or employ "divided" or hybrid certification.[246]

In *Lemon v. Operating Engineers Local 139*,[247] the Seventh Circuit elaborated on its requirement that, for certification under Rule 23(b)(2), claims for declaratory and equitable relief must predominate over damages.[248] The court vacated the district court's order certifying a Rule 23(b)(2) class of racial minorities and women who had claimed that their labor union intentionally diverted work opportunities to white males.[249] The class sought injunctive and declaratory relief as well as compensatory and punitive damages.[250] Citing *Allison* and *Jefferson*, the court concluded that "incidental damages do not depend in any significant way on the intangible, subjective differences of each class member's circumstances and do not require additional hearings to resolve the disparate merits of each individual's case."[251] The court reasoned that certification was improper under Rule 23(b)(2) because to receive compensatory damages, "each individual plaintiff pursuing damages claims still would need to establish that [the union's] discrimination caused her personal injury," and to receive punitive damages the court would be obligated to engage in a "fact-specific inquiry" regarding each plaintiff's circumstances.[252] Accordingly, the court held that the requested monetary damages were not incidental to the requested injunctive and declaratory relief and vacated the district court's certification under Rule 23(b)(2). The *Lemon* court directed that

---

[244]195 F.3d at 897.
[245]*Id.* at 898.
[246]*Id.* at 897–98.
[247]216 F.3d 577, 83 FEP 63 (7th Cir. 2000).
[248]*Id.* at 580–82.
[249]*Id.* at 579–80.
[250]*Id.* at 579.
[251]*Id.* at 581.
[252]*Id.*

the district court instead consider the three alternatives for certification articulated in *Jefferson*.[253]

In *Robinson v. Metro-North Commuter Railroad*,[254] the Second Circuit rejected *Allison*'s "bright-line bar to [Rule 23(b)(2)] class treatment" for claims involving compensatory and punitive damages, which it labeled the "incidental damages approach."[255] Instead, the court adopted an ad hoc balancing test:

> The district court may allow [Rule 23(b)(2)] certification if it finds in its "informed, sound judicial discretion" that (1) "the positive weight or value [to the plaintiffs] of the injunctive or declaratory relief sought is predominant even though compensatory or punitive damages are also claimed," and (2) class treatment would be efficient and manageable, thereby achieving an appreciable measure of judicial economy.[256]

Rather than looking to whether damages are "incidental" or "nonincidental" to assess whether injunctive relief predominates, the court directed the district court, on remand, to determine whether the following hold true: "(1) even in the absence of a possible monetary recovery, reasonable plaintiffs would bring the suit to obtain the injunctive or declaratory relief sought; and (2) the injunctive or declaratory relief sought would be both reasonably necessary and appropriate were the plaintiffs to succeed on the merits."[257]

The Second Circuit vacated the denial of class certification and directed the district court to certify the adverse impact claim under Rule 23(b)(2) and to consider Rule 23(b)(2) certification for the disparate treatment claim based on the ad hoc standard.[258] In rejecting the *Allison* approach, the Second Circuit emphasized that district courts have historically been vested with discretion to determine certification on a case-by-case basis and a bright-line rule

---

[253]*Id.* at 581–82. The Seventh Circuit has endorsed a fourth alternative: the use of partial certification (liability and equitable relief only) in an employment discrimination class action. Allen v. International Truck & Engine Corp., 358 F.3d 469 (7th Cir. 2004).

[254]267 F.3d 147 (2d Cir. 2001), *cert. denied*, 535 U.S. 951 (2002).

[255]*Id.* at 164.

[256]*Id.* (quoting the dissent in Allison v. Citgo Petroleum Corp., 151 F.3d 402, 430 (5th Cir. 1998) (Dennis, J., dissenting)).

[257]*Id.*

[258]*Id.* at 172.

would nullify that discretion.[259] In addition, it reasoned that the ad hoc approach satisfies the underlying purposes of the incidental damages approach—achieving judicial efficiency and ensuring due process for absent class members.[260] Finally, the court noted that any due process concerns posed by the presence of nonincidental damages could be eliminated by affording notice and opportunity to opt out at the damages phase.[261] The court ordered that, in the event the district court concluded that Rule 23(b)(2) certification for the disparate treatment claim was inappropriate, it should certify the liability phase under Rule 23(b)(2).[262]

The Ninth Circuit has adopted the Second Circuit's analysis in *Robinson*. The court's initial decision in this regard was not in the employment context. In *Molski v. Gleich*,[263] the plaintiff, on behalf of a putative class of individuals with mobility impairments, alleged that the company's gasoline service stations failed to meet accessibility requirements under Title III of the ADA and California state law.[264] After agreeing to settle, the parties jointly moved the district court to certify the class under Rule 23(b)(2) for settlement purposes.[265] The proposed settlement included a consent decree awarding monetary damages of $5,000 to the plaintiff, $50,000 to the plaintiff's attorneys, and an aggregate $195,000 to eight California disability rights organizations, with the other class members releasing all nonphysical injury monetary claims against the defendant.[266] The consent decree also issued an injunction directing the defendant to (1) improve the accessibility of its service stations, (2) construct any new facilities in compliance with ADA guidelines, (3) implement written policies consistent with the ADA, and (4) allow class counsel to randomly inspect the defendant's facilities to confirm compliance.[267] Notwithstanding the objections of 30 class members, including an objection that class certification under Rule 23(b)(2) was inappropriate because the monetary

---

[259]*Id.* at 164–65.
[260]*Id.* at 165.
[261]*Id.* at 166.
[262]*Id.* at 172.
[263]318 F.3d 937 (9th Cir. 2003).
[264]*Id.* at 941.
[265]*Id.* at 942–43.
[266]*Id.* at 942.
[267]*Id.* at 943–44.

damages were more than incidental to the injunctive relief, the district court certified the class under Rule 23(b)(2) and approved the consent decree.[268]

On appeal, the Ninth Circuit affirmed class certification.[269] The court rejected the "bright-line rule" espoused by *Allison* and embraced the case-by-case analysis set forth in *Robinson*.[270] Rather than focusing on whether the monetary damages were incidental, the court looked to "the intent of the plaintiffs in bringing the suit."[271] Because the defendant acted in a manner generally applicable to the class and the consent decree did not release claims for physical injuries, the court determined that "the injunctive relief appeared to be the primary goal in the litigation" and held that, consequently, certification under Rule 23(b)(2) was appropriate because the injunctive relief predominated over monetary damages.[272] In *Dukes v. Wal-Mart, Inc.*,[273] the Ninth Circuit applied the *Molski/Robinson* approach and concluded that Rule 23(b)(2) certification was appropriate in a nationwide Title VII class action alleging gender discrimination and seeking injunctive relief, back pay, and punitive damages on behalf of more than 1.5 million women.[274]

As a result of the split in the circuit authority, district courts are divided on whether Rule 23(b)(2) certification is appropriate in cases involving compensatory and punitive damage claims. Some district courts have followed *Allison* and denied certification under Rule 23(b)(2),[275] especially where plaintiffs seek significant

---

[268]*Id.* at 943.

[269]*Id.* at 950.

[270]*Id.*

[271]*Id.*

[272]*Id.*

[273]474 F.2d 1214 (9th Cir. 2007).

[274]*Id.* at 1233–37.

[275]*See, e.g.*, Clayborne v. Omaha Pub. Power Dist., 211 F.R.D. 573, 599–600, 90 FEP 1340 (D. Neb. 2002) (denying certification under Rule 23(b)(2) because claims for compensatory damages and emotional distress would "depend on an individualized analysis of each class member's circumstances"); Reid v. Lockheed Martin Aeronautics Co., 205 F.R.D. 655, 679, 86 FEP 631 (N.D. Ga. 2001) (damages not "incidental to any injunctive relief also requested"); Cooper v. Southern Co., 205 F.R.D. 596, 627–28 (N.D. Ga. 2001) (compensatory and punitive damages "would require highly individualized fact findings" and "could not be termed merely incidental to an injunction or declaration"), *aff'd*, 390 F.3d 695 (11th Cir. 2004); Bacon v. Honda of Am. Mfg., Inc., 205 F.R.D. 466, 486 (S.D. Ohio 2001) (denying certification under Rule 23(b)(2) because claims for monetary relief were not incidental

compensatory and punitive damages awards.[276] Other district courts have instead followed the approach of the *Jefferson, Lemon,* and *Robinson* decisions and certified classes under Rule 23(b)(2), sometimes incorporating orders under Rule 23(d)(2) for personal notice and the opportunity to opt out.[277] Finally, some district courts

---

and claims for injunctive and declaratory relief did not otherwise predominate), *aff'd,* 370 F.3d 565 (6th Cir. 2004), *cert. denied,* 543 U.S. 1151 (2005); Adler v. Wallace Computer Servs., Inc., 202 F.R.D. 666, 671 (N.D. Ga. 2001) (denying class certification under Rule 23(b)(2) because plaintiffs' claims for compensatory and punitive damages are "dependent on the subjective differences of each class member's circumstances"); Miller v. Hygrade Food Prods. Corp., 198 F.R.D. 638, 641–42, 84 FEP 1755 (E.D. Pa. 2001) (denying certification under Rule 23(b)(2) because monetary relief predominated over class request for injunctive and declaratory relief); Ramirez v. DeCoster, 194 F.R.D. 348, 84 FEP 45 (D. Me. 2000) (denying certification under Rule 23(b)(2) where crux of class claims involved compensatory and punitive damages rather than equitable relief); Burrell v. Crown Cent. Petroleum, Inc., 197 F.R.D. 284, 289–90 (E.D. Tex. 2000) (denying certification under Rule 23(b)(2) because monetary damages sought were not incidental—each class member would be required to submit proof of actual injury to recover compensatory and punitive damages); Adams v. Henderson, 197 F.R.D. 162, 171 (D. Md. 2000) (denying certification under Rule 23(b)(2) because plaintiffs' claims for compensatory and punitive damages were not incidental to their claims for injunctive relief); Riley v. Compucom Sys., Inc., 2000 U.S. Dist. LEXIS 4096, 82 FEP 996, 1000 (N.D. Tex. 2000) (denying Rule 23(b)(2) certification because "[s]pecific individualized proof is needed" to recover monetary damages, which is "not incidental to the class-wide injunctive and declaratory relief"); Faulk v. Home Oil Co., 186 F.R.D. 660, 662 (M.D. Ala. 1999) (denying certification under Rule 23(b)(2) because compensatory damages require "specific individualized proof of actual injury"); Cwiak v. Flint Ink Corp., 186 F.R.D. 494, 498 (N.D. Ill. 1999) (denying certification under Rule 23(b)(2) where plaintiffs sought primarily payment of wrongfully withheld benefits); Adams v. Brookshire Grocery Co., 1999 U.S. Dist. LEXIS 21907 (E.D. Tex. Feb. 8, 1999) (denying certification under Rule 23(b)(2) because damages for future pecuniary loss, emotional pain, suffering, inconvenience, mental anguish, and loss of enjoyment of life do not "flow directly from liability to the class as a whole").

[276]LeGrand v. New York City Transit Auth., 83 FEP 1817 (E.D.N.Y. 1999) (denying certification under Rule 23(b)(2) where each class member sought $1 million in compensatory and punitive damages in addition to equitable relief); Saunders v. BellSouth Adver. & Publ'g Corp., 1998 U.S. Dist. LEXIS 20523 (S.D. Fla. Nov. 10, 1998) (denying certification where class collectively sought compensatory and punitive damages of $50 million).

[277]*See, e.g.,* Ellis v. Costco Wholesale Corp., 2007 WL 127800, at *12–14 (N.D. Cal. Jan. 11, 2007) (certifying gender class under Rule 23(b)(2) and ordering notice and opportunity to opt out; claims for compensatory and punitive damages do not predominate over injunctive and equitable relief claims); Dukes v. Wal-Mart Stores, Inc., 222 F.R.D. 137, 172, 93 FEP 1629 (N.D. Cal. 2004) (certifying class under Rule 23(b)(2) for punitive damages, back pay, and injunctive relief and providing all class members with notice and right to opt out), *aff'd,* 474 F.3d 1214 (9th Cir. 2007); Palmer v. Combined Ins. Co. of Am., 217 F.R.D. 430, 92 FEP 943 (N.D. Ill. 2003) (gender class action seeking injunctive relief and punitive damages certified

have adopted hybrid or partial certification, which is discussed further below.

C. Class Certification Under Rule 23(b)(3)

Rule 23(b)(3) is designed to cover cases that do not fall under either Rule 23(b)(1) or (b)(2) but nonetheless are suited to class treatment. Although *Amchem Products, Inc. v. Windsor*[278] was not decided in the Title VII context, it provides a detailed analysis of what is required to certify a class under Rule 23(b)(3). According to the Court, to qualify for certification under Rule 23(b)(3), a class must meet two requirements in addition to the Rule 23(a) prerequisites: common questions must "predominate over any questions affecting only individual members" and class resolution must be "superior to other available methods for the fair and efficient adjudication of the controversy."[279] Rule 23(b)(3) "predominance" requires more than the existence of issues common to the claimants. Rather, under *Amchem*, a plaintiff class must be cohesive in terms of the manner in which it suffered injury and the amount and nature of those injuries.[280]

The Fifth, Seventh, and Eleventh Circuits have addressed whether class certification is proper under Rule 23(b)(3) in employment discrimination actions. In *Allison*, the Fifth Circuit rejected

---

under Rule 23(b)(2) with notice and opt-out); Latino Officers Ass'n v. City of N.Y., 209 F.R.D. 79, 93 (S.D.N.Y. 2002) (following *Robinson*, class certified under Rule 23(b)(2) despite compensatory damages claim); Taylor v. District of Columbia Water & Sewer Auth., 205 F.R.D. 43 (D.D.C. 2002) (denying motion to dismiss class claims, concluding that certification was available under Rule 23(b)(2)–(b)(3), hybrid or partial approach, despite presence of compensatory damages); Wilfong v. Rent-A-Center, Inc., 2001 WL 1795093 (S.D. Ill. Dec. 27, 2001) (permitting class members to opt out of Rule 23(b)(2) hybrid certification); Bates v. United Parcel Serv., 204 F.R.D. 440, 448 (N.D. Cal. 2001) (certifying nationwide class of hearing-impaired employees under Rule 23(b)(2)); Robinson v. Sears, Roebuck & Co., 111 F. Supp. 2d 1101, 1127 (E.D. Ark. 2000) (certifying class under Rule 23(b)(2) for both monetary and equitable remedies and providing all class members with personal notice "as though the class was certified under Rule 23(b)(3)"); Jones v. CCH-LIS Legal Info. Servs., 78 FEP 254 (S.D.N.Y. 1998) (concluding that "Rule 23(b)(2) was intended for use in civil rights class actions, including employment discrimination cases"); Neal v. Moore, 1994 U.S. Dist. LEXIS 21336 (D.D.C. Aug. 25, 1994) (certifying and bifurcating sexual harassment and retaliation claims under Rule 23(b)(2)).

[278]521 U.S. 591 (1997).

[279]*Id.* at 615.

[280]*Id.* at 622.

the plaintiffs' argument that common questions of law predominated over questions affecting only individual members.[281] The court reasoned that the claims for compensatory and punitive damages would require a particularized inquiry into each class member's claims, rather than issues applicable to the class as a whole:

> The plaintiffs' claims for compensatory and punitive damages must therefore focus almost entirely on facts and issues specific to individuals rather than the class as a whole: what kind of discrimination was each plaintiff subjected to; how did it affect each plaintiff emotionally and physically, at work and at home; what medical treatment did each plaintiff receive and at what expense; and so on and so on. Under such circumstances, an action conducted nominally as a class action would "degenerate in practice into multiple lawsuits separately tried."[282]

The Eleventh Circuit adopted a similar analysis in *Cooper*, concluding that the case was inappropriate for Rule 23(b)(3) certification because "highly fact-specific" inquiries would be required for each plaintiff.[283] It has reached a similar result in nonemployment cases challenging discrimination in public accommodations[284] but affirmed certification of a nationwide conspiracy action under the Racketeer Influenced and Corrupt Organizations Act (RICO) by doctors against health maintenance organizations.[285]

---

[281]Allison v. Citgo Petroleum Corp., 151 F.3d 402, 420 (5th Cir. 1998).

[282]151 F.3d at 419 (citations omitted).

[283]Cooper v. Southern Co., 390 F.3d 695, 722–23, 94 FEP 1854 (11th Cir. 2004), *cert. denied*, 126 S. Ct. 478 (2005), *overruled in part by* Ash v. Tyson Foods, Inc., 546 U.S. 454, 97 FEP 641 (2006).

[284]Rutstein v. Avis Rent-A-Car Sys., Inc., 211 F.3d 1228 (11th Cir. 2000) (reversing certification of putative class under Rule 23(b)(3) because common questions of law did not predominate in action alleging discrimination against Jewish customers); Jackson v. Motel 6 Multipurpose, Inc., 130 F.3d 999 (11th Cir. 1997) (granting writ of mandamus and reversing certification of class of African-American customers who claimed that motel denied them rooms or provided them with inferior accommodations based on their race; certification under Rule 23(b)(3) improper because court would be required to address issues specifically related to individual members of class).

[285]Klay v. Humana, Inc., 382 F.3d 1241, 1257 (11th Cir. 2004) ("*Motel 6* and *Rutstein* were both cases in which individuals were seeking to litigate separate discrimination claims that arose from a variety of individual incidents together in the same class action simply because they alleged that the acts of discrimination occurred pursuant to corporate policies. . . . Thus, while corporate policies were only circumstantially relevant in the discrimination cases, and insufficient to overcome the tremendous individualized issues of fact that remained in those cases, they constitute the very heart of the plaintiffs' RICO claims here, and would necessarily have to be re-proven by every plaintiff if each doctor's claims were tried separately.").

In contrast, the Seventh Circuit has suggested that it may be proper to certify a class in the Title VII context under Rule 23(b)(3). In both *Lemon* and *Jefferson*, the Seventh Circuit stated that certification under Rule 23(b)(3) may be available where the class is unable to meet the predominance requirements of Rule 23(b)(2).[286] The Seventh Circuit, however, has yet to directly resolve the issue.[287]

The Sixth Circuit has also stated that plaintiffs "have the choice to proceed under Rule 23(b)(3) in an action for money damages or in an action under Rule 23(b)(2) for declaratory or injunctive relief alone or in conjunction with compensatory and punitive damages that inure to the group benefit."[288]

District courts have split on whether, by alleging that the defendant engaged in a pattern or practice of discrimination, a plaintiff class asserts "questions of law or fact common to the members of the class [which] predominate over any questions affecting only individual members."[289] A number of district courts have held that, even where a plaintiff class alleges that the defendant engaged in systemwide discriminatory conduct, the individual issues in question predominated over any common questions of law and fact, precluding certification under Rule 23(b)(3).[290] In contrast, other

---

[286]*See* Lemon v. Operating Eng'rs Local 139, 216 F.3d 577, 581, 83 FEP 63 (7th Cir. 2000); Jefferson v. Ingersoll Int'l, Inc., 195 F.3d 894, 899, 81 FEP 170 (7th Cir. 1999).

[287]*See* Allen v. International Truck & Engine Corp., 358 F.3d 469, 472 (7th Cir. 2004) (remanding Title VII race harassment case, stating that "because this litigation will proceed as a class action for equitable relief, it would be prudent for the district court to reconsider whether at least some of the issues bearing on damages . . . could be treated on a class basis (with opt-out rights under Rule 23(b)(3) or a hybrid Rule 23(b)(2) certification) even if some other issues . . . must be handled individually"); *Jefferson*, 195 F.3d at 899 (certification under Rule 23(b)(3) is possible if money damages "are more than incidental to the equitable relief in view"); *cf. In re* Allstate, 400 F.3d 505, 508 (7th Cir. 2005) (ERISA case; "[w]hen limited to incidental damages as the cases define the term, the award of damages by a judge does not run afoul of the Seventh Amendment's right to a jury trial in federal cases. For when calculation of damages is mechanical, there is no right to a jury trial because summary judgment would be granted. When, moreover, the basic relief sought in a case is equitable, the judge can award damages in the exercise of his equity powers, and thus without calling in a jury, under the 'clean up' doctrine of equity.").

[288]Reeb v. Ohio Dep't of Rehab. & Corr., 435 F.3d 639, 651, 97 FEP 353 (6th Cir. 2006).

[289]FED. R. CIV. P. 23(b)(3).

[290]Radmanovich v. Combined Ins. Co. of Am., 216 F.R.D. 424, 435–38, 92 FEP 371 (N.D. Ill. 2003) (denying certification under Rule 23(b)(3) because each plaintiff would "need to come forth with proof of how the pattern or practice impacted her" and, with respect to the harassment claims, each plaintiff would need to "establish

courts have held that "variances as to individual damages do not necessarily upset the predominance determination," and Rule 23(b)(3) certification therefore may be appropriate.[291]

---

a basis for employer liability"); Clayborne v. Omaha Pub. Power Dist., 211 F.R.D. 573, 600, 90 FEP 1340 (D. Neb. 2002) (denying certification under Rule 23(b)(3) because class claims "reflect[] highly individualized claims of discriminatory conduct"); Bacon v. Honda of Am. Mfg., Inc., 205 F.R.D. 466, 487–88 (S.D. Ohio 2001) (denying class certification under Rule 23(b)(3) because calculating "compensatory and punitive damages [would] require a highly individualized inquiry into the circumstances of each class member"), aff'd, 370 F.3d 565 (6th Cir. 2004), cert. denied, 543 U.S. 1151 (2005); Burrell v. Crown Cent. Petroleum, Inc., 197 F.R.D. 284, 292 (E.D. Tex. 2000) (denying certification under Rule 23(b)(3) because, although plaintiffs alleged that defendant engaged in systemwide discrimination by cultivating an environment that was openly hostile to African-American and female employees, "punitive damages cannot be assessed merely upon a finding that the defendant engaged in a pattern or practice of discrimination"); Adams v. Henderson, 197 F.R.D. 162, 172 (D. Md. 2000) (denying certification under Rule 23(b)(3) where plaintiffs claimed that U.S. Post Office systematically denied training and advancement opportunities to African-American employees; court held that "[c]ertification is not proper under [Rule 23(b)(3)] because of the individualized liability inquiries involved with determining whether each class member was denied advancement and promotional opportunities for discriminatory reasons"); Riley v. Compucom Sys., Inc., 82 FEP 996 (N.D. Tex. 2000) (denying certification under Rule 23(b)(3) where plaintiff class alleged that defendant company's headquarters applied subjective, racially discriminatory practices because "[p]laintiff's argument . . . fails to appreciate the overwhelming number of individual-specific issues in this case"); Ramirez v. DeCoster, 194 F.R.D. 348, 353, 84 FEP 45 (D. Me. 2000) (denying certification under Rule 23(b)(3) although plaintiffs alleged that defendant applied "discriminatory pattern or practice . . . common to the entire class," because "each worker's exposure to this subjective decision-making and hostile environment will vary in nature and degree, [and] any trial on class issues will quickly erode into a series of individual trials focused on issues specific to each worker"); Latson v. GC Servs., L.P., 83 FEP 1778 (S.D. Tex. 2000) (applying Allison); Faulk v. Home Oil Co., 186 F.R.D. 660, 664 (M.D. Ala. 1999) (denying plaintiffs' request to certify their class under Rule 23(b)(3) regarding a claim of pattern or practice because "recovery on the plaintiffs' claims for compensatory and punitive damages will come not merely from a finding of liability on the common issues, but from individualized proof of actual injury"); Adams v. Brookshire Grocery Co., 1999 U.S. Dist. LEXIS 21907 (E.D. Tex. Feb. 8, 1999) ("the procedural and substantive problems inherent in looking to one jury to resolve thousands of individual-specific issues destroys the efficiency-based purposes of the class-action device"); Saunders v. BellSouth Adver. & Publ'g Corp., 1998 U.S. Dist. LEXIS 20523 (S.D. Fla. Nov. 10, 1998) ("when plaintiffs allege a practice and policy of discrimination, as the [p]laintiffs have essentially alleged in this case, they do not create a class issue which predominates over the individual issues").

[291]See Taylor v. District of Columbia Water & Sewer Auth., 205 F.R.D. 43, 52 (D.D.C. 2002) (denying motion to dismiss class claims and concluding that certification was available under Rule 23(b)(2)–(b)(3) hybrid or partial approach, despite

D. Class Certification Under "Hybrid" of Rules 23(b)(2) and 23(b)(3)

In addition to certifying a class under either Rule 23(b)(2) or (b)(3), several courts of appeals have considered whether certification is proper under a hybrid of the two. Following the 1991 Amendments, the Second, Seventh, and District of Columbia Circuits have stated that, where a class seeks injunctive and declaratory relief in addition to compensatory and punitive damages, it may be appropriate to certify the class under Rule 23(b)(2) for equitable relief and under Rule 23(b)(3) for monetary damages.[292] The Seventh Circuit also reads the *Allison* per curiam opinion to endorse the use of a bifurcated approach.[293] Many district courts

---

presence of compensatory damages); Adams v. R.R. Donnelley & Sons, 2001 U.S. Dist. LEXIS 4247 (N.D. Ill. Apr. 6, 2001) (district court certified Rule 23(b)(3) class involving temporary employees denied permanent positions, employees subjected to hostile work environment, and employees discharged because of division shutdown); Daniels v. Federal Reserve Bank, 194 F.R.D. 609, 617 (N.D. Ill. 2000) (court changed certification from Rule 23(b)(2) to (b)(3) because of presence of damage claims); Warnell v. Ford Motor Co., 189 F.R.D. 383, 387 (N.D. Ill. 1999) (certifying class under Rule 23(b)(3) where female plaintiffs alleged that defendant's male employees severely and pervasively sexually harassed all female employees at defendant's Chicago area manufacturing facilities); *cf.* Carter v. West Publ'g Co., 79 FEP 1494 (M.D. Fla. 1999) (certifying class under Rule 23(b)(3) although court recognized "the potential problems with the individualized proof necessary to establish compensatory and thereafter perhaps punitive damages in the context of class certification"), *rev'd on other grounds*, 225 F.3d 1258 (11th Cir. 2000); Griffin v. Home Depot, Inc., 168 F.R.D. 187, 191 (E.D. La. 1996) (Rule 23(b)(3) certification permitted despite presence of damage claims, pending completion of discovery); Bremiller v. Cleveland Psychiatric Inst., 898 F. Supp. 573, 578 (N.D. Ohio 1995) (compensatory damages did not defeat commonality for Rule 23(b)(2) and (b)(3) certification).

[292]*See* Robinson v. Metro-North Commuter R.R., 267 F.3d 147, 167, 86 FEP 1580 (2d Cir. 2001), *cert denied*, 535 U.S. 951 (2002); Lemon v. Operating Eng'rs Local 139, 216 F.3d 577, 581, 83 FEP 63 (7th Cir. 2000); *Jefferson*, 195 F.3d at 899; Eubanks v. Billington, 110 F.3d 87, 96 (D.C. Cir. 1997). Prior to the 1991 amendments, the Eleventh Circuit remanded a proposed settlement with instructions to certify the settlement class under such a hybrid approach in order to provide those plaintiffs who wanted to pursue individual damages against the defendant the opportunity to opt out of the class. *See* Holmes v. Continental Can Co., 706 F.2d 1144 (11th Cir. 1983).

[293]*Jefferson*, 195 F.3d at 898. *But see In re* Allstate, 400 F.3d 505, 508 (7th Cir. 2005) (ERISA case; describing language from Seventh Circuit's *Lemon* decision as "dictum"; it would be "complicated and confusing" to order notice in Rule 23(b)(2) case).

have expressly adopted this approach,[294] but others have declined to do so.[295]

Bifurcation is further discussed in Section VIII.D. *infra*.

E. Partial Certification of Liability and Injunctive Relief Only

A number of courts have granted class certification under Rule 23(b)(2) for purposes of determining liability and injunctive and declaratory relief only, and deferring any certification of the remedies phase until after a finding of liability.[296]

---

[294]*See, e.g.*, Mathers v. Northshore Mining Co., 217 F.R.D. 474, 487, 92 FEP 1360 (D. Minn. 2003) (adopting hybrid certification for gender class action seeking equitable relief, compensatory and punitive damages); Wilfong v. Rent-A-Center, Inc., 2001 WL 1795093 (S.D. Ill. Dec. 27, 2001) (Rule 23(b)(2) certification for liability and injunctive relief and Rule 23(b)(3) certification for damages); *Taylor*, 205 F.R.D. at 52 (denying motion to dismiss class claims, concluding that certification was available under Rule 23(b)(2)–(b)(3), hybrid or partial approach despite presence of compensatory damages); Miller v. Baltimore Gas & Elec. Co., 202 F.R.D. 195, 199–200 (D. Md. 2001) (motion for partial summary judgment denied on class claims alleging compensatory and punitive damages; hybrid or partial certification possible alternative approaches); Beck v. Boeing Co., 203 F.R.D. 459 (W.D. Wash. 2001) (certifying liability and injunctive relief under Rule 23(b)(2) and punitive damage claims under Rule 23(b)(3)); Beckmann v. CBS, Inc., 192 F.R.D. 608, 615 (D. Minn. 2000) ("the hybrid class is the appropriate mechanism for the resolution of this case"); Adams v. Pinole Point Steel Co., 1994 U.S. Dist. LEXIS 6692, 65 FEP 774 (N.D. Cal. 1994); Barefield v. Chevron U.S.A., Inc., 48 FEP 907, 910 (N.D. Cal. 1988).

[295]*See, e.g.*, Adler v. Wallace Computer Servs., Inc., 202 F.R.D. 666, 673 (N.D. Ga. 2001) (bifurcation fails to resolve need for each individual plaintiff's proof of actual harm, and, under Seventh Amendment, litigants have right to determination of issues by single jury, which would cause confusion and be overly burdensome to court's resources); Cooper v. Southern Co., 205 F.R.D. 596, 625–31 (N.D. Ga. 2001) (denying certification; bifurcation would not resolve issue because common elements of proof still would not predominate), *aff'd*, 390 F.3d 695 (11th Cir. 2004), *cert. denied*, 126 S. Ct. 478 (2005), *overruled in part by* Ash v. Tyson Foods, Inc., 546 U.S. 454, 97 FEP 641 (2006).

[296]*See* Warren v. Xerox Corp., 2004 U.S. Dist. LEXIS 5115 (E.D.N.Y. Jan. 26, 2004), *recommendation adopted*, 2004 U.S. Dist. LEXIS 5080 (E.D.N.Y. Mar. 11, 2004) (Rule 23(b)(2) certification of liability and injunctive relief; court to revisit certification of damages if liability found); Wright v. Stern, 2003 U.S. Dist. LEXIS 11589 (S.D.N.Y. July 7, 2003) (race and national origin promotion and pay class certified under Rule 23(b)(2) for Stage I); McReynolds v. Sodexho Marriott Servs. Inc., 208 F.R.D. 428, 448–49 & n.35 (D.D.C. 2002) (Rule 23(b)(2) certification of liability and injunctive relief: "if liability established, the Court will then determine the most appropriate mechanism for determining remedies"); Morgan v. United Parcel Serv. of Am, Inc., 169 F.R.D. 349, 77 FEP 165 (E.D. Mo. 1996); Butler v. Home Depot, 1996 U.S. Dist. LEXIS 3370, 70 FEP 51 (N.D. Cal. Jan. 25, 1996); Shores v. Publix Super Mkts., Inc., 1996 WL 407850 (M.D. Fla. Mar. 12, 1996).

The Seventh Circuit recently endorsed this approach in *Allen v. International Truck & Engine Corp.*,[297] a racially hostile work environment class action on behalf of a class of 350 current and former black employees in the Indianapolis Navistar truck plant. The district court declined to certify the class under either Rule 23(b)(2) or (b)(3), concluding that common issues were "subordinate to" individual issues surrounding compensatory and punitive damages.[298] In addition, the district court declined to certify liability and equitable issues, believing that the Seventh Amendment precluded partial certification.[299]

The Seventh Circuit vacated the order and remanded with instructions to certify equitable matters and reconsider whether damages matters would also benefit from class treatment.[300] The appellate court disagreed with the trial court that management of 27 individual cases for the named plaintiffs would somehow be simpler than one class trial.[301] The *Allen* panel noted that injunctive relief was by necessity a class remedy: "The need for, if not inevitability of, class-wide treatment when injunctive relief is at stake is what Rule 23(b)(2) is about."[302] The court also rejected any constitutional concerns raised by the Seventh Amendment, concluding that the jury would resolve common factual disputes and those decisions would control the judge's determination of injunctive relief.[303]

In contrast to the Seventh Circuit, the Fifth and Eleventh Circuits have declined to certify solely the plaintiff's adverse impact claim, concluding that partial certification would run afoul of the Seventh Amendment.[304]

---

[297]358 F.3d 469 (7th Cir. 2004); *see also* Mejdrech v. Met-Coil Sys. Corp., 319 F.3d 910 (7th Cir. 2003) (in environmental mass tort case, Judge Posner endorsed use of partial certification of common legal question (causation) even where facts were highly individualized).

[298]*Allen*, 358 F.3d at 471.

[299]*Id.*

[300]*Id.* at 472.

[301]*Id.* at 471.

[302]*Id.*

[303]*Id.*

[304]*See* Allison v. Citgo Petroleum Corp., 151 F.3d 402, 424–25, 81 FEP 501 (5th Cir. 1998) ("[T]he business necessity defense to disparate impact claims and the legitimate nondiscriminatory reason defense to disparate treatment claims are not "so distinct and separable" from one another that they may be considered separately

F. Certification of Punitive Damage Claims

The law is very unsettled as to how punitive damages should be litigated in a Title VII class action. The crux of the dispute turns on whether punitive damages are analyzed as a victim-specific individual remedy or as a group remedy awardable to the class as a whole.

Prior to 1991, Title VII provided only equitable relief, such as a declaration or injunction, which could include back pay, to remedy intentional discrimination. The Civil Rights Act of 1991,[305] however, significantly expanded the remedies available under Title VII by permitting compensatory and punitive damages in cases of intentional discrimination.[306] The 1991 Act also allows a plaintiff to establish intentional discrimination when a protected characteristic is a "motivating factor" in an employment decision, even if the employer also has a legitimate reason for making the decision.[307] In such a case, the court can order a defendant to stop discriminating and award the complainants attorney's fees and costs, but cannot order reinstatement, hiring, promotion, or compensatory or punitive damages.[308]

In *Allison v. Citgo Petroleum Corp.*,[309] the Fifth Circuit analyzed punitive damages as an individual remedy. Specifically, the court concurred with the district court's conclusion that "recovery of compensatory and punitive damages required particularly individualized proof of injury, including how each class member was personally affected by the discriminatory conduct."[310] As such, the

---

by multiple factfinders without violating the Seventh Amendment. . . . [T]he existence of factual issues common between the plaintiffs' disparate impact and pattern or practice claims precludes trial of the disparate impact claim in a class action severed from the remaining nonequitable claims in the case. The claims for injunctive relief, declaratory relief, and any equitable or incidental monetary relief cannot be litigated in a class action bench trial (in the same case prior to certification of any aspects of the pattern or practice claim) without running afoul of the Seventh Amendment. . . ."); Cooper v. Southern Co., 390 F.3d 695, 722 (11th Cir. 2004) (for class certification to be appropriate, common questions must "predominate over any questions affecting only individual member") (citing FED. R. CIV. P. 23(b)(3)), *cert. denied*, 126 S. Ct. 478 (2005), *overruled in part by* Ash v. Tyson Foods, Inc., 546 U.S. 454, 97 FEP 641 (2006).

[305]42 U.S.C. § 1981a (2000).
[306]*Id.* § 1981a(a)(1).
[307]*Id.* § 2000e-2(m).
[308]*Id.* § 2000e-5(g)(2)(B).
[309]151 F.3d 402, 416 (5th Cir. 1998).
[310]*Id.*

panel concluded that punitive damages—like compensatory damages—were "non-incidental" damages and therefore were incompatible with class treatment under Rule 23(b)(2):

> [B]ecause punitive damages must be reasonably related to the reprehensibility of the defendant's conduct and to the compensatory damages awarded to the plaintiffs, recovery of punitive damages must necessarily turn on the recovery of compensatory damages. Thus, punitive damages must be determined after proof of liability to individual plaintiffs at the second stage of a pattern or practice case, not upon the mere finding of general liability to the class at the first stage. Moreover, being dependent on non-incidental compensatory damages, punitive damages are also non-incidental—requiring proof of how discrimination was inflicted on each plaintiff, introducing new and substantial legal and factual issues, and not being capable of computation by reference to objective standards.[311]

The court reasoned that because compensatory damages are "an individual, not class-wide, remedy," and punitive damages are "dependent on" compensatory damages, punitive damages must be an individual, nonincidental remedy and could only be decided *after* compensatory damages had been resolved.[312] In dicta, the *Allison* court determined that even if punitive damages might arguably be awarded on a classwide basis, the plaintiffs in *Allison* had not alleged a classwide injury.[313] Some courts have refused to certify Title VII class actions with claims for punitive damages, relying on the *Allison* analysis.[314]

---

[311]*Id.* at 417–18 (citations omitted).

[312]*Id.* at 418.

[313]*Id.* at 417 ("Assuming punitive damages may be awarded on a class-wide basis, without individualized proof of injury, where the entire class or subclass is subjected to the same discriminatory act or series of acts, no such discrimination is alleged in this case. The plaintiffs challenge broad policies and practices, but they do not contend that each plaintiff was affected by these policies and practices in the same way.").

[314]*See, e.g.*, Bacon v. Honda of Am. Mfg., Inc., 205 F.R.D. 466, 485–86 (S.D. Ohio 2001) ("If the criteria announced in *Allison* are employed, a class cannot be certified under Rule 23(b)(2) in this case because the compensatory and punitive damages sought by the plaintiffs would not flow automatically from a determination of liability on the part of the defendant to the class as a whole on the disparate impact and pattern or practice claims, and are thus not merely incidental."), *aff'd*, 370 F.3d 565 (6th Cir. 2004), *cert. denied*, 543 U.S. 1151 (2005); Burrell v. Crown Cent. Petroleum, Inc., 197 F.R.D. 284, 289 (E.D. Tex. 2000) (rejecting plaintiffs' argument that their claims for compensatory and punitive damages were incidental to their claims for injunctive and declaratory relief and finding that "[l]ike the plaintiffs in *Allison*, [p]laintiffs' request for compensatory and punitive damages would necessarily require this court to inquire into the individual circumstances of each plaintiff's claims").

In contrast to the Fifth Circuit's analysis in *Allison*, the Supreme Court has held in another context—in which the amended statutory language of Title VII regarding awards of punitive damages was not an issue—that punitive damages are analytically distinct from compensatory damages and focus instead not on individual harm but on punishment of the defendant:[315]

> Although compensatory damages and punitive damages are typically awarded at the same time by the same decisionmaker, they serve distinct purposes. The former are intended to redress the concrete loss that the plaintiff has suffered by reason of the defendant's wrongful conduct. The latter, which have been described as "quasi-criminal," operate as "private fines" intended to punish the defendant and deter future wrongdoing. A jury's assessment of the extent of a plaintiff's injury is essentially a factual determination, whereas its imposition of punitive damages is an expression of its moral condemnation.[316]

The Supreme Court has similarly affirmed that the "focus" of the inquiry regarding punitive damages is the defendant's state of mind.[317] In addition, numerous appellate courts have concluded that punitive damages under Title VII are not dependent on an award of compensatory damages and can instead be awarded based on nominal or actual damages.[318] Several courts have even

---

[315]*See* Cooper Indus., Inc. v. Leatherman Tool Group, Inc., 532 U.S. 424 (2001).

[316]*Id.* at 432 (citations omitted). One district court adopted a similar analysis in a race discrimination class action under § 1981, which does not require consideration of the statutory language of Title VII, as amended by the 1991 Civil Rights Act. *See* Barefield v. Chevron U.S.A., Inc., 48 FEP 907, 911 (N.D. Cal. 1988) ("Because the purpose of punitive damages is not to compensate the victim, but to punish and deter the defendant, any claim for such damages hinges, not on the facts unique to each class member, but on the defendant's conduct toward the class as a whole."). The *Cooper Industries* case also held that a jury's determination of the amount of punitive damages was not a finding of fact for Seventh Amendment purposes. 532 U.S. at 437.

[317]*See* Kolstad v. American Dental Ass'n, 527 U.S. 526, 535 (1999).

[318]*See* Corti v. Storage Tech. Corp., 304 F.3d 336, 342–43 (4th Cir. 2002) (holding that punitive damages award was supported by back-pay award; absence of compensatory damages award by jury did not undermine punitive damages award); EEOC v. W & O, Inc., 213 F.3d 600, 615, 85 FEP 117 (11th Cir. 2000) (ruling that compensatory damages need not be awarded to sustain punitive damages award and instead evaluating ratio between back pay and punitive damages); Provencher v. CVS Pharmacy, 145 F.3d 5, 17, 76 FEP 1569 (1st Cir. 1998) (holding that punitive damages award can be supported by back pay or nominal damages alone); Timm v. Progressive Steel Treating, Inc., 137 F.3d 1008, 76 FEP 321 (7th Cir. 1998) (holding that jury may award punitive damages in sex discrimination action even if no compensatory

approved an award of punitive damages without any award of damages.[319]

Some courts have concluded that punitive damages are a traditional group remedy, and, therefore, are not inconsistent with certification under Rule 23(b)(2), Rule 23(b)(3), or a bifurcated hybrid certification.[320]

V. JURISDICTIONAL AND PROCEDURAL REQUIREMENTS

A. Exhausting the EEOC Administrative Process

Under the "single-filing" rule, only the named plaintiff need exhaust the EEOC administrative process prior to filing a Title VII class action.[321] Class membership will, however, be restricted to

---

or nominal damages are awarded); Hennessy v. Penril Datacomm Networks, Inc., 69 F.3d 1344, 1352, 69 FEP 398 (7th Cir. 1995) (§ 1981 case that held that "nothing in the plain language of § 1981a conditions an award of punitive damages on an underlying award of compensatory damages"); *see also* Palmer v. Combined Ins. Co. of Am., 217 F.R.D. 430, 438, 92 FEP 943 (N.D. Ill. 2003) (rejecting argument that punitive damages in Title VII class action could only be awarded based on compensatory damages).

[319]Tisdale v. Federal Express Corp., 2005 WL 1653972, at *14 (6th Cir. July 14, 2005) ("there is no reason to condition punitive damages on the award of actual or nominal compensatory damages"); Cush-Crawford v. Adchem Corp., 271 F.3d 352, 359, 87 FEP 456 (2d Cir. 2001) ("we see no reason to make award of actual or nominal damages a prerequisite to the award of punitive damages"); *Timm*, 137 F.3d at 1010 ("[n]o reason comes to mind for reading a compensatory-punitive link into § 1981a or Title VII").

[320]*See, e.g.*, Dukes v. Wal-Mart Stores, Inc., 222 F.R.D. 137, 171–72, 93 FEP 1629 (N.D. Cal. 2004) (finding that claim of punitive damages is "consistent with the notion that the focus of a [Rule 23(b)(2)] action is the defendant's conduct toward persons sharing a common characteristic"), *aff'd*, 473 F.3d 1214 (9th Cir. 2007); *Palmer*, 217 F.R.D. at 438 (concluding that Title VII class action with punitive damage claims certifiable under Rule 23(b)(2) with notice and opt out or Rule 23(b)(3)); *Barefield*, 48 FEP at 911 (adopting hybrid certification of compensatory and punitive damage claims). *But cf.* Philip Morris USA v. Williams, 127 S. Ct. 1057, 1063 (2007) ("the Constitution's Due Process Clause forbids a state to use a punitive damages award to punish a defendant for injury that it inflicts upon nonparties or those whom they directly represent"; non-Title VII case not brought as putative class action, focusing on lack of opportunity to present individualized defenses).

[321]*See, e.g.*, Horton v. Jackson County Bd. of County Comm'rs, 343 F.3d 897, 92 FEP 929 (7th Cir. 2003) ("[r]equiring that every class member file a separate charge might drown agency and employer alike by touching off a multitude of fruitless negotiations"); Mistretta v. Sandia Corp., 639 F.2d 588, 594–95, 24 FEP 316 (10th Cir. 1980) (adopting single filing rule in ADEA action); Oatis v. Crown Zellerbach

those who *could* have filed a timely charge when the earliest filing named plaintiff did,[322] unless the discrimination is continuing.[323]
Some courts have held that the filing date of an EEOC charge by
a class member *other* than the named plaintiff also can be used to
establish the liability period in the class action.[324]

The claims of the class must be "like or related to" the claims
of its representatives.[325] Moreover, the scope of the class action
generally is limited by the scope of the EEOC charge. A class action
thus normally may be brought only when the representative's charge
puts the employer on notice of the class-based nature of the allegations.[326] But some courts have allowed class treatment where the

---

Corp., 398 F.2d 496, 498–99, 1 FEP 328 (5th Cir. 1968) ("it would be wasteful, if
not vain, for numerous employees, all with the same grievance, to have to process
many identical complaints with the EEOC").

[322]*See, e.g.*, Williams v. Owens-Ill., Inc., 665 F.2d 918, 923–24, 27 FEP 1273
(9th Cir. 1982); Ulloa v. City of Phila., 95 F.R.D. 109, 113–14, 34 FEP 906 (E.D.
Pa. 1982); Thornberry v. Delta Air Lines, 30 FEP 520, 529 (N.D. Cal. 1978) (limiting class to persons employed by defendant within 300 days prior to filing of first
EEOC charge by one of named plaintiffs).

[323]*See Williams*, 665 F.2d at 924 ("the relevant strain of continuing violation
doctrine is that a systematic policy of discrimination is actionable even if some or all
of the events evidencing its inception occurred prior to the limitations period"); Leach
v. Standard Register Co., 94 F.R.D. 621, 625, 34 FEP 1777 (W.D. Ark. 1982) (holding that, where continuing violations are alleged, only employees barred from class
are those who left employ of defendant more than 180 days prior to filing of charges);
Avagliano v. Sumitomo Shoji Am., Inc., 103 F.R.D. 562, 578, 38 FEP 561 (S.D.N.Y.
1984) (same; 300-day cutoff); Increase Minority Participation by Affirmative Change
Today of Nw. Fla., Inc. v. Firestone, 24 FEP 572, 577 (N.D. Fla. 1980) (noting that,
where continuing violation is alleged, class not limited to persons subjected to discrimination during 180-day period prior to charge filing), *rev'd on other grounds*,
893 F.2d 1189, 52 FEP 71 (11th Cir. 1990). *See generally* Chapter 26 (Timeliness).

[324]*See* Larkin v. Pullman-Standard Div., 854 F.2d 1549, 1563–65, 47 FEP 1732
(11th Cir. 1988), *vacated on other grounds sub nom.* Pullman-Standard, Inc. v. Swint,
493 U.S. 929 (1989); Harris v. Anaconda Aluminum Co., 479 F. Supp. 11, 18–19,
23 FEP 553 (N.D. Ga. 1979).

[325]Evans v. United States Pipe & Foundry Co., 696 F.2d 925, 929, 33 FEP 1620
(11th Cir. 1983) (holding that class can contain only those individuals whose claims
are "like or related" to those included in plaintiff's charge or in EEOC's "substantive inquiry"); *cf.* Vuyanich v. Republic Nat'l Bank, 723 F.2d 1195, 1200, 33 FEP
1521 (5th Cir. 1984) (finding that scope of Title VII class action is circumscribed
by scope of claims that named plaintiffs have standing to raise; no one has standing
to challenge practice that did not affect him or her personally).

[326]*See, e.g.*, Communications Workers Local 1033 v. New Jersey Dep't of Pers.,
283 F.3d 213, 217 (3d Cir. 2002) (EEOC charge filed by plaintiff who subsequently
files class action must allege class-based discrimination in EEOC charge); Basch v.
Ground Round, Inc., 139 F.3d 6, 9 (1st Cir. 1998) (EEOC charge must give "EEOC

class issues "could reasonably be expected to grow out of" the EEOC charge.[327] Similarly, subsequent allegations in a class action complaint may require no further exhaustion of administrative remedies where those allegations reasonably could be expected to grow from the original charge.[328]

B. Intervention

Some courts have held that intervenors, unlike the original named class representative, need not satisfy the jurisdictional requirements if their asserted claims "are so similar to those asserted by the original plaintiffs that no purpose would be served by requiring [them] to file independent . . . charges with [the] EEOC."[329]

---

and the employer adequate notice of allegations of class-wide discrimination" to allow subsequent lawsuit to survive).

[327]*See* Paige v. California, 102 F.3d 1035, 1041–42 (9th Cir. 1996) (finding that individual race discrimination charge could support class action); Fellows v. Universal Restaurants, Inc., 701 F.2d 447, 450–51, 31 FEP 483 (5th Cir. 1983) (noting that class should not be denied because EEOC charge and investigation did not cover class allegations: "[A] cause of action for Title VII employment discrimination may be based, not only upon the specific complaints made by the employee's initial EEOC charge, but also upon any kind of discrimination like or related to the charge's allegations, limited only by the scope of the EEOC investigation that could reasonably be expected to grow out of the initial charges of discrimination"); Miller v. Baltimore Gas & Elec. Co., 202 F.R.D. 195, 206–08 (D. Md. 2001) (finding that three separate charges alleging same series of discriminatory acts sufficient to satisfy exhaustion of class claims); Robinson v. Sears, Roebuck & Co., 111 F. Supp. 2d 1101, 1116 (E.D. Ark. 2000) (complaint alleging systemic discrimination in several conditions of employment supported by charge alleging only compensation discrimination). *But see* Mooney v. Aramco Servs. Co., 54 F.3d 1207, 1223, 68 FEP 421 (5th Cir. 1995) (holding individual charge inadequate to put employer on notice of class nature of claims); Schnellbaecher v. Baskin Clothing Co., 887 F.2d 124, 128, 50 FEP 1846 (7th Cir. 1989) (sending to EEOC revised charges incorporating class claims and claims against parent corporation 5 days before filing suit did not give adequate notice to defendants or provide opportunity for conciliation).

[328]*See* Nye v. Roberts, 97 F. Supp. 2d 677, 679, 82 FEP 1797 (D. Md. 2000) (court will consider retaliation claim even though not included in charge where alleged retaliation occurred while EEOC charge pending); Duffy v. Massinari, 202 F.R.D. 437, 440–41 (E.D. Pa. 2001) (plaintiff in ADEA opt-in class action satisfied exhaustion requirement for amended complaint where original charge contained allegations that could have led to discovery of such discrimination).

[329]*See* Winbush v. Iowa by Glenwood State Hosp., 66 F.3d 1471, 1478–79, 69 FEP 1348 (8th Cir. 1995) (intervenor need not independently satisfy jurisdictional prerequisite of filing EEOC charge if intervenor's claims have "similar and sufficient factual basis" to those of original plaintiffs); Foster v. Gueory, 655 F.2d 1319, 1323, 26 FEP 7 (D.C. Cir. 1981); *accord* Oatis v. Crown Zellerbach Corp., 398 F.2d

Courts disagree, however, on whether an intervenor with claims different from those of the original named plaintiff, who seeks to intervene to present claims that the named plaintiff cannot present because of *Falcon*, can satisfy Title VII by relying on the EEOC charges and other actions of the named plaintiff.[330] In all cases, the intervening class representative must have been in a position to pursue his or her own Title VII action, with respect to the newly presented claims, at the time the original plaintiff filed the charge.[331] Additionally, class members who never filed any EEOC charge may not intervene where the sole named class representative is dismissed for failing to meet the jurisdictional prerequisites to suit.[332] One

---

496, 499, 1 FEP 328 (5th Cir. 1968); Hartman v. Duffey, 158 F.R.D. 525, 531, 536 (D.D.C. 1994) (intervenors could rely on original EEOC charge because intervenors and original plaintiffs shared common complaint of discriminatory refusal to hire based on gender, albeit in different job categories), *aff'd*, 88 F.3d 1232 (D.C. Cir. 1996) [Editor's Note: The defendant's name is misspelled as "Duffy" in the case caption at the district court, reported at 158 F.R.D. 525.]; Martinez v. Oakland Scavenger Co., 680 F. Supp. 1377, 1389–90, 49 FEP 116 (N.D. Cal. 1987).

[330]*Compare* Vuyanich v. Republic Nat'l Bank, 723 F.2d 1195, 1201, 33 FEP 1521 (5th Cir. 1984) (named plaintiffs could represent only hiring and termination claims; intervenors, therefore, could not bring transfer, promotion, compensation, classification, and assignment claims in reliance on named plaintiffs' EEOC charges because named plaintiffs had no standing to assert such claims) *with* Lilly v. Harris-Teeter Supermkt., 720 F.2d 326, 334–35, 33 FEP 195 (4th Cir. 1983) (even though named plaintiffs could not present promotion claims, intervenors could rely on named plaintiffs' EEOC charges to bring their promotion claims; named plaintiffs' charges mentioned promotion, and there had been no indication that employer would conciliate any claims filed with EEOC, anyway) *and Hartman*, 158 F.R.D. at 531, 536 (intervenors could rely on original EEOC charge because intervenors and original plaintiffs shared common complaint of discriminatory refusal to hire based on gender, albeit in different job categories).

[331]*See* Salinas v. Roadway Express, Inc., 735 F.2d 1574, 1579, 35 FEP 533 (5th Cir. 1984) (intervention denied where intervenor's individual action had been dismissed on timeliness grounds; "to qualify as a named plaintiff, . . . [an individual] must have been in a position to pursue his own Title VII action"); *accord* Griffin v. Dugger, 823 F.2d 1476, 1492–93, 44 FEP 938 (11th Cir. 1987) ("single filing" rule encompasses only claims for which charge-filer has standing and for which class members seek relief).

[332]*See* Wakeen v. Hoffman House, Inc., 724 F.2d 1238, 1241–43, 33 FEP 1476 (7th Cir. 1983) (class members who do not meet procedural prerequisites for maintaining Title VII action may not intervene where named class representative's claim was dismissed because of res judicata); Schaulis v. CTB/McGraw-Hill, Inc., 496 F. Supp. 666, 676–78, 23 FEP 1185 (N.D. Cal. 1980) (persons who had not met jurisdictional requirements not permitted to intervene after summary judgment had been granted against only named plaintiff); *cf.* Hill v. AT&T Techs., Inc., 731 F.2d 175, 181–82, 34 FEP 620 (4th Cir. 1984) (denying petition to intervene where putative

court has concluded that if the original named plaintiff settles, intervening plaintiffs may continue the litigation even if some of them have not filed charges with the EEOC and those who have filed charges have not received right-to-sue letters.[333]

Although an individual seeking to intervene as class representative normally must make an application for intervention prior to a ruling on class certification,[334] intervention also may be permitted to challenge a consent decree.[335] In some cases, intervention has been permitted when a class has been decertified[336] or to cure defects in the class decertification.[337]

At the settlement stage, nonclass members can intervene to challenge a proposed consent decree.[338]

C. Tolling the Limitations Period

The filing of a class action tolls the applicable statute of limitations and permits all members of the putative class to file individual

---

intervenor failed to file EEOC charge within 180 days and others who had filed charges had dissimilar claims).

[333]*See Martinez*, 680 F. Supp. at 1389 ("In cases such as this—where the original class representatives settled their individual claims—intervenors have been allowed to continue the action and rely on the administrative compliance of the original plaintiffs.").

[334]*See* Walker v. Jim Dandy Co., 747 F.2d 1360, 1365–66, 36 FEP 928 (11th Cir. 1984).

[335]*See* Section X.C *infra.*

[336]*See* Winbush v. Iowa by Glenwood State Hosp., 66 F.3d 1471, 1478–79, 69 FEP 1348 (8th Cir. 1995) (putative class members permitted to intervene as plaintiffs following decertification of class).

[337]*Compare* Hartman v. Duffey, 158 F.R.D. 525, 531–32 (D.D.C. 1994) [Editor's Note: The defendant's name is misspelled as "Duffy" in the case caption at the district court level, reported at 158 F.R.D. 525.] (motion to intervene filed 25 days after appellate court remanded issue of class decertification for reconsideration was timely, although 16 years after initiation of litigation) *with* Griffin v. Singletary, 17 F.3d 356, 358, 64 FEP 516 (11th Cir. 1994) (denying class action status to individuals who attempted to join suit to represent potential employees subjected to challenged testing requirement; across-the-board class had been decertified pursuant to *Falcon*, and EEOC charge upon which new plaintiffs relied was filed by employee without standing to challenge testing requirement).

[338]*See* 42 U.S.C. § 2000e-2(n)(2) (2000) (listing allowable means to challenge consent decrees); Reynolds v. Roberts, 846 F. Supp. 948, 953–54, 954 n.8, 64 FEP 400 (M.D. Ala. 1994) (non–African-American employees can intervene to challenge race-conscious provisions of consent decree, but they also can challenge race-neutral provisions in their capacity as "objectors" under Civil Rights Act of 1991); *see also* Section X.C *infra.*

actions or to intervene,[339] if class certification is denied, "provided, of course, that those actions are instituted within the time that remains on the limitations period."[340] A member of a certified class who elects to opt out of the class similarly benefits from tolling of the statute of limitations, until the time of opting out.[341] A putative class member ordinarily cannot necessarily rely on class action tolling in order to file a subsequent class action.[342] Moreover, a plaintiff cannot rely on tolling under *American Pipe* if he or she files a separate suit before the class certification is denied.[343]

As a corollary to *American Pipe*, courts have held that, although the statute of limitations is tolled for members of the putative class while they are a part of a class action, the statute resumes running once class certification has been denied or a class has been certified that excludes the individuals in question.[344] These

---

[339]*See* Crown, Cork & Seal Co. v. Parker, 462 U.S. 345, 354, 31 FEP 1697 (1983) ("Once the statute of limitations has been tolled, it remains tolled for all members of the putative class until class certification is denied. At that point, class members may choose to file their own suits or to intervene as plaintiffs in the pending action."); American Pipe & Constr. Co. v. Utah, 414 U.S. 538, 554 (1974).

[340]Griffin v. Singletary, 17 F.3d 356, 359–61, 64 FEP 516 (11th Cir. 1994).

[341]*See* Tosti v. City of L.A., 754 F.2d 1485, 1488, 37 FEP 348 (9th Cir. 1985) ("when certification has been granted, the statute begins running anew from the date when the class member exercises the right to opt out because before this time, the class member is deemed to be actively prosecuting her rights").

[342]*See, e.g., Griffin*, 17 F.3d at 359–61; Korwek v. Hunt, 827 F.2d 874 (2d Cir. 1987). *But see* McKowan Lowe & Co. v. Jasmine Ltd., 295 F.3d 380 (3d Cir. 2002) (tolling applied to subsequent class action where denial of certification not related to suitability of claims for class treatment but to adequacy of class representative), *cert. denied sub nom.* Arthur Andersen, LLP v. Berger, 537 U.S. 1088 (2002).

[343]*Compare In re* WorldCom, Inc. Sec. Litig., 308 F. Supp. 2d 214, 230 (S.D.N.Y. 2004) (tolling not permitted) *and* Wyser-Pratte Mgmt. Co. v. Telxon Corp., 2005 WL 1515232, at *15 (6th Cir. June 28, 2005) (no tolling allowed) *with* Joseph v. Q.T. Wiles, 223 F.3d 1155, 1166–68 (10th Cir. 2000) (statutes of limitations and repose tolled for putative class member who filed separate lawsuit during pendency of alleged class action).

[344]*See* Nelson v. County of Allegheny, 60 F.3d 1010, 1013 (3d Cir. 1995) (holding that tolling period ended upon denial of class certification and therefore affirming lower court's dismissal of untimely claims and striking of untimely motions to intervene); Calderon v. Presidio Valley Farmers Ass'n, 863 F.2d 384, 390 (5th Cir. 1989) (per curiam) (holding that statute of limitations begins to run again upon entry of district court's order denying class certification, even if district court later reconsiders issue and certifies class); Andrews v. Orr, 851 F.2d 146, 149–50, 48 FEP 643 (6th Cir. 1988) (holding that instant suit "ceased to be a class action," and tolling ended, upon entry of order denying class certification); Fernandez v. Chardon, 681 F.2d 42, 48 (1st Cir. 1982) ("[T]olling would have ended, and the remaining portion

cases reason that once certification has been denied or the class has been narrowed to exclude such persons, it is no longer reasonable for plaintiffs to rely on the class action to protect their interests.[345] An additional question is raised by the amendment of Rule 23 to allow for discretionary interlocutory appeals of class certification decisions under Rule 23(f). Two district courts have concluded that tolling is extended until the Rule 23(f) appeal of the class certification order is resolved where a stay of proceedings was granted during the appeal.[346]

Under the ADEA, which is not governed by Rule 23 but instead permits a collective, opt-in action under 29 U.S.C. § 216(b), courts have likewise applied *American Pipe* and held that any tolling of the limitations period ceases upon interlocutory denial of judicial approval of the collective action.[347]

Of course, in order to toll the statute of limitations, the class must be adequately defined and clearly ascertainable, such that an individual's membership or nonmembership in the class may be readily determined. The extent of the identity necessary between claims of putative class members and the allegations of the tolling charge, however, has not conclusively been established.[348]

---

of the limitations period would have recommenced running . . . when the district court declined to certify the class."), *aff'd sub nom.* Chardon v. Soto, 462 U.S. 650 (1983).

[345]*See, e.g., Nelson,* 60 F.3d at 1013 ("to permit the tolling of the statute of limitations until final resolution on appeal of all claims would disable the essential purpose of the statute and encourage plaintiffs to sleep on their rights"). *See generally* Chapter 26 (Timeliness).

[346]*See* Monahan v. City of Wilmington, 2004 U.S. Dist. LEXIS 1322 (D. Del. Jan. 30, 2004); National Asbestos Workers Med. Fund v. Philip Morris, Inc., 2000 U.S. Dist. LEXIS 13910 (E.D.N.Y. Sept. 26, 2000).

[347]*See* Basch v. Ground Round, Inc., 139 F.3d 6, 76 FEP 533 (1st Cir. 1998) (without resolving whether *American Pipe* tolling applies under ADEA, court concludes that tolling rules do not permit what court describes as "stacking" of ADEA collective actions to toll limitations period); Armstrong v. Martin Marietta Corp., 138 F.3d 1374, 1394, 76 FEP 1007 (11th Cir. 1998) (en banc) (statute of limitations, which was tolled while plaintiffs had opted in and thus were putative members of ADEA collective action, resumed running when district court dismissed plaintiffs from class, even though district court's denial of certification in interlocutory order could still be reversed). *But see National Asbestos Workers,* 2000 U.S. Dist. LEXIS 13910 (limitations period tolled pending outcome of interlocutory appeal); *cf.* Realmonte v. Reeves, 169 F.3d 1280 (10th Cir. 1999) (statute of limitations tolled until plaintiff opted out of certified class).

[348]*See* Crown, Cork & Seal Co. v. Parker, 462 U.S. 345, 355, 31 FEP 1697 (1983) (Powell, J., concurring) ("[W]hen a plaintiff invokes [the tolling rule for intervening

The applicability of the continuing violations concept in the class action context will depend on the nature of the allegations in question. Although the Supreme Court held that a Title VII plaintiff alleging discrete discriminatory or retaliatory acts must file his or her charge within the applicable charge-filing period, the Court expressly stated that it was not called upon the consider the issue with respect to pattern-or-practice claims.[349] Courts continue to apply the continuing violation doctrine, in appropriate cases, where an ongoing systemic policy of discrimination is alleged.[350] Courts have refused to apply the continuing violation doctrine where the conduct within the liability period is merely the present effect of a past discriminatory act.[351]

---

in a class action, as set forth in *American Pipe*,] in support of a separate lawsuit, the district court should take care to ensure that the suit raises claims that 'concern the same evidence, memories, and witnesses as the subject matter of the original class suit,' so that 'the defendant will not be prejudiced.' Claims as to which the defendant was not fairly placed on notice by the class suit are not protected under *American Pipe* and are barred by the statute of limitations.") (citations omitted).

[349]*See* National R.R. Passenger Corp. v. Morgan, 536 U.S. 101, 115 n.9 (2002) (stating that applicability of continuing violations concept to pattern-or-practice claims was not before Court). The Court also held that a charge alleging a hostile work environment will not be time-barred if all acts constituting the claim are part of the same unlawful practice and at least one act falls within the charge-filing period.

[350]*See* Paige v. California, 291 F.3d 1141, 1149, 88 FEP 1666 (9th Cir. 2002), *cert. denied*, 537 U.S. 1189 (2003) (alleging systemic policy of discrimination in promotion decisions); Thiessen v. General Elec. Capital Corp., 267 F.3d 1095 (10th Cir. 2001) (applying continuing violation in ADEA opt-in class); Anderson v. Boeing Co., 222 F.R.D. 521, 547 (N.D. Okla. 2004) (rejecting defendant's opposition to use of continuing violation doctrine where plaintiffs' class claims are pattern-or-practice claims); Mathers v. Northshore Mining Co., 217 F.R.D. 474, 488 (D. Minn. 2003) (plaintiffs alleged specific facts suggesting that practice was ongoing during and before liability period, justifying application of continuing violation doctrine); Beckmann v. CBS, Inc., 192 F.R.D. 608, 620, 90 FEP 1379 (D. Minn. 2000) (hostile work environment claims not untimely because reasonable jury could find that practices were continuing violation); *cf.* Warren v. Xerox Corp., 2004 U.S. Dist. LEXIS 5115 (E.D.N.Y. Jan. 26, 2004) (magistrate recommended class certification; no determination of continuing violation until full discovery completed), *recommendation adopted*, 2004 U.S. Dist. LEXIS 5080 (E.D.N.Y. Mar. 11, 2004).

[351]*See* City of Hialeah v. City of Hialeah Employees' Ret. Sys., 311 F.3d 1096, 90 FEP 467 (11th 2002) (class certification reversed; denial of pension plan credit for temporary service not continuing violation); Carter v. West Publ'g Co., 225 F.3d 1258, 1265, 83 FEP 1523 (11th Cir. 2000) (women denied opportunity to purchase stock could not challenge failure to receive dividends that were present consequence of past discrimination, not continuing violation).

Courts have taken different approaches to determining timeliness issues for EEOC pattern-or-practice cases.[352]

D. The Employer in Bankruptcy

An issue of increasing importance is the maintenance of class claims against an employer in bankruptcy. The majority of bankruptcy courts hold that an individual may file a proof of claim on behalf of a class of persons who have not filed individual proofs of claims.[353] With the exception of the Tenth Circuit,[354] all other circuits that have considered the issue have held that class proofs of claim are permissible.[355]

VI. THE CLASS CERTIFICATION HEARING

A. Timing of the Hearing

Rule 23(c)(1)(A) was amended in 2003 to require that the court determine whether the case will be certified as a class action "at

---

[352]*Compare* EEOC v. Custom Cos., 93 FEP 1450, 1458 (N.D. Ill. 2004) (EEOC can seek relief, on basis of an individual charge, only for individuals who were employed after the commencement of the 300-day filing period before the charge was filed) *and* EEOC v. Optical Cable Corp., 169 F. Supp. 2d 539, 547 (W.D. Va. 2001) (180-day statute of limitations period applies to EEOC pattern-or-practice suit) *with* EEOC v. Dial Corp., 156 F. Supp. 2d 926, 944 (N.D. Ill. 2001) (300-day filing period not applicable to EEOC pattern-or-practice case) *and* EEOC v. Mitsubishi Motor Mfg. of Am., Inc., 990 F. Supp. 1059, 1084–87, 75 FEP 1379 (C.D. Ill. 1998) (denying motion to dismiss pattern-or-practice suit premised on statute of limitations; fact adduced will establish liability period, if any).

[353]*See, e.g., In re* Chateaugay Corp., 104 B.R. 626, 629–34, 50 FEP 1345 (S.D.N.Y. 1989) (and cases cited therein). *See generally* Joel R. Wolfson, *Class Actions in Bankruptcy: A Clash of Policies Reconciled*, 5 BANKR. DEV. J. 391 (1988) (advocating class proofs of claims in bankruptcy).

[354]*In re* Standard Metals Corp., 817 F.2d 625, 630 (10th Cir. 1987), *vacated in part on other grounds on reh'g sub nom.* Sheftelman v. Standard Metals Corp., 839 F.2d 1383 (10th Cir. 1987); *In re* Unioil, Inc., 962 F.2d 988, 991 (10th Cir. 1992). Courts have questioned the continuing validity of the Tenth Circuit's ruling in *Standard Metals. See, e.g., In re* Amdura Corp., 170 B.R. 445, 447–49 (D. Colo. 1994) (noting that case also distinguishable because class proof of claim was filed *after* district court had certified class); *In re* Charter Co., 876 F.2d 866, 869 n.4 (11th Cir. 1989).

[355]*In re* Birting Fisheries, Inc., 92 F.3d 939, 940 (9th Cir. 1996) (Bankruptcy Code should be construed to permit proof of claims filed on behalf of class); Reid

an early practicable time."[356] This language replaces the prior requirement that certification occur "as soon as practicable after commencement of an action." The old rule's mandate to resolve class certification quickly was often at odds with the need to ensure the rigorous analysis of certification requirements prescribed by the Supreme Court's *Falcon* decision.[357] As the Advisory Committee notes explain, "the 'as soon as practicable' exaction neither reflect[ed] prevailing practice nor capture[d] the many valid reasons that may justify deferring the initial certification decision."[358]

The revised rule anticipates that the trial court will actively supervise the timing of the class certification hearing to account for legitimate reasons for deferring the hearing, while at the same time avoiding unnecessary delay. The committee notes recognize that discovery is often necessary to make the certification decision: "Although an evaluation of the probable outcome on the merits is not properly part of the certification decision, discovery in aid of the certification decision often includes information required to identify the nature of the issues that actually will be presented at trial."[359]

The Advisory Committee noted two additional reasons for deferring the hearing—to give the party opposing the class an opportunity to "win dismissal or summary judgment as to the individual plaintiffs without certification" and to "explore designation of class counsel under Rule 23(g)."[360]

B. Discovery Before the Class Determination

Even before the 2003 amendment to Rule 23(c)(1)(A), several courts had declined to grant employer motions to strike class allegations if the plaintiffs had not been allowed to conduct discovery.[361] The difficult question is how much and what kind of discovery to allow.

---

v. White Motor Corp., 886 F.2d 1462 (6th Cir. 1989); *In re Charter Co.*, 876 F.2d at 873; *In re* American Reserve Corp., 840 F.2d 487, 488 (7th Cir. 1988).

[356]FED. R. CIV. P. 23(c)(1)(A) ("When a person sues or is sued as a representative of a class, the court must—at an early practicable time—determine by order whether to certify the action as a class action.").

[357]General Tel. Co. of Sw. v. Falcon, 457 U.S. 147, 161 (1982).

[358]FED. R. CIV. P. 23(c) (1) advisory committee's note.

[359]*Id.*

[360]*Id.; see also* Section III.B.4 *supra.*

[361]*See* Miller v. Baltimore Gas & Elec. Co., 202 F.R.D. 195 (D. Md. 2001) (denying motion to dismiss class claims because plaintiffs had not had opportunity

In the past, a distinction has often been drawn between "class" discovery (i.e., discovery directed to the Rule 23 requirements) and "merits" discovery (i.e., discovery to prove liability or damages). In practice, the distinction is easier to articulate than to apply.[362] The Advisory Committee has counseled a more practical approach to discovery in advance of class certification that focuses on the issues that will shape the trial:

> [D]iscovery in aid of the certification decision often includes information required to identify the nature of the issues that actually will be presented at trial. In this sense it is appropriate to conduct controlled discovery into the "merits," limited to those aspects relevant to making the certification decision on an informed basis. Active judicial supervision may be required to achieve the most effective balance that expedites an informed certification determination without forcing an artificial and ultimately wasteful division between "certification discovery" and "merits discovery." A critical need is to determine how the case will be tried.[363]

Although there are few reported cases that define the limits of discovery before the class determination,[364] some conclusions can be drawn. The defendant should be permitted to discover the

---

to conduct discovery); Abdallah v. Coca-Cola Co., 1999 WL 527835 (N.D. Ga. July 16, 1999) (shape and form of class action evolves through process of discovery, and it is premature to draw conclusion as to class certification before claim has taken form); Miller v. Hygrade Food Prods. Corp., 89 F. Supp. 2d 643, 654, 84 FEP 1744 (E.D. Pa. 2000) (denying motion to dismiss because not appropriate to determine the standing of named plaintiffs until class discovery has been completed); *see also* Gutierrez v. Johnson & Johnson, Inc., 2002 U.S. Dist. LEXIS 15418 (D.N.J. Aug. 12, 2002) ("The question of whether or not a class may be certified is not a basis to deny discovery.").

[362]*See* Gray v. First Winthrop Corp., 133 F.R.D. 39, 40–41 (N.D. Cal. 1990) (rejecting stay of "merits" discovery pending class certification as impracticable; "class" and "merits" issues are closely linked); Antonson v. Robertson, 1990 WL 58028, at *2 (D. Kan. Apr. 11, 1990) (recognizing difficulty of separating "class issues" from merits, but staying discovery on merits); Clark v. Virginia Paper Co., 17 FEP 581, 586 (D.S.C. 1978) ("[D]iscovery is limited solely to the issue of whether a class exists."); Karan v. Nabisco, Inc., 78 F.R.D. 388, 396, 17 FEP 507 (W.D. Pa. 1978) (class determination should be made before substantial discovery on merits has been conducted because broad discovery can require immense commitments of time, money, and resources that would be wasted if class action is not appropriate).

[363]FED. R. CIV. P. 23(c)(1) advisory committee's note.

[364]*Compare* National Org. for Women v. Sperry Rand Corp., 88 F.R.D. 272, 277–78 (D. Conn. 1980) (limiting plaintiffs' discovery to facilities at which named plaintiffs had worked or to which they had sought transfers, and to limited number of job titles) *with* Gutierrez v. Johnson & Johnson, Inc., 2002 U.S. Dist. LEXIS 15418 (D.N.J. Aug. 12, 2002) (refusing to limit plaintiffs' discovery to facilities in which named plaintiffs worked). *See generally* Chapter 33 (Discovery).

factual bases for the allegations of discrimination as well as other facts relevant to the named plaintiffs' satisfaction of the requirements of Rule 23. The plaintiffs should be permitted to discover facts relating to (1) the employment policies and practices that allegedly affected them and the members of their putative class; (2) the defendant's categories of jobs, job levels, departments, and other relevant categories; and (3) facts relating to the defendant's physical and organizational structure, including the allocation of decision-making authority over the challenged policies and practices. Plaintiffs are also entitled to personnel data relevant to the issues,[365] including electronic data versions of this information.[366] Although matters pertaining to discovery usually are committed to the discretion of the trial judge, unduly limited pre-class-determination discovery may constitute reversible error.[367]

C. Inquiry Into the Merits—Prohibited, Permitted, or Required?

Among the most difficult problems faced by courts in applying Rule 23 to Title VII actions is whether and to what extent the

---

[365]*See* Orlowski v. Dominick's Finer Foods, Inc., 1995 WL 516595, at *5 (N.D. Ill. Aug. 28, 1995) (granting detailed companywide discovery of computer database information and employment practices to determine scope of potential class); Zapata v. IBP, Inc., 1994 WL 649322, at *2–3 (D. Kan. Nov. 10, 1994) (granting plaintiff's request for companywide discovery of defendant's computerized work histories on grounds that such information was relevant to plaintiff's motion for class certification), *review denied*, 1995 WL 526527 (D. Kan. Sept. 1, 1995), *aff'd*, 1995 WL 646821 (D. Kan. Oct. 6, 1995).

[366]*See In re* Honeywell Int'l, Inc. Sec. Litig., 2003 U.S. Dist. LEXIS 20602, at *4–5 (S.D.N.Y. Nov. 18, 2003) (ordering defendant to produce papers in electronic form; prior production in hard copy insufficient); Storch v. IPCO Safety Prods. Co. of Pa., 1997 U.S. Dist. LEXIS 10118, at *5–6 (E.D. Pa. July 15, 1997) (defendant ordered to produce data on computer disk so plaintiff could avoid expense of recoding); Anti-Monopoly, Inc. v. Hasbro, Inc., 1995 U.S. Dist. LEXIS 16355, at *1 (S.D.N.Y. Nov. 3, 1995) ("The law is clear that data in computerized form is discoverable even if paper 'hard copies' of the information have been produced . . . ."; collecting cases); *Orlowski*, 1995 WL 516595, at *5 (finding that electronic information sought by plaintiffs was relevant as preclass certification discovery and that "production of such information and documents, in the form requested by [p]laintiffs, is not unduly burdensome"), *motion for reconsideration denied and clarification*, 1995 U.S. Dist. LEXIS 13197 (N.D. Ill. Sept. 11, 1995).

[367]*See* Duke v. University of Tex., 729 F.2d 994, 996–97, 34 FEP 982 (5th Cir. 1984) (limited discovery constituted reversible error).

parties should be allowed (or required) to present evidence on the "merits" prior to the initial class determination. The tension is created by two admonitions from the Supreme Court about class certification. In *Eisen v. Carlisle & Jacquelin*,[368] the Supreme Court expressly prohibited any inquiry into the merits at the class certification stage: "Nothing in either the language or history of Rule 23 . . . gives a court any authority to conduct a preliminary inquiry into the merits of a suit in order to determine whether it may be maintained as a class action."[369] Yet, in *Falcon*, the Supreme Court cautioned that "a Title VII class action, like any other class action, may only be certified if the trial court is satisfied, *after a rigorous analysis*, that the prerequisites of Rule 23(a) have been satisfied."[370] But, as one court has noted, in determining commonality, "the class action and merits inquiries essentially coincide."[371]

It remains unresolved whether and to what extent a court will inquire into the merits at the class certification stage. Most courts either permit or require such inquiry, at least insofar as it is necessary to determine whether the requirements of Rule 23 have been satisfied.[372] Disparate treatment cases, for example, require at least

---

[368]417 U.S. 156, 9 FEP 1302 (1974).

[369]*Id.* at 177; *cf.* Szabo v. Bridgeport Machs., Inc., 249 F.3d 672, 677 (7th Cir. 2001) ("The [*Eisen*] Court observed that the 1966 amendment to Rule 23 departed from the earlier handling of class claims by placing certification ahead of a decision on the merits. A class thus can lose as well as win, while in a permissive-intervention system the case is decided on the merits before the identities of the parties to be bound are known. The success of the 1966 amendments (which are still in force) depends on making a definitive class certification decision before deciding the case on the merits, and on judicial willingness to certify classes that have weak claims as well as strong ones. A court may not say something like 'let's resolve the merits first and worry about the class later' (Rule 23(c)(1) requires the certification decision to be made '[a]s soon as practicable after the commencement of an action brought as a class action') or 'I'm not going to certify a class unless I think that the plaintiffs will prevail.' "). *But see In re* Initial Public Offerings Sec. Litig., 471 F.3d 24, 41 (2d Cir. 2006) ("the obligation to make such [Rule 23] determinations is not lessened by overlap between a Rule 23 requirement and a merits issue, even a merits issue that is identical with a Rule 23 requirement"; noting that *Eisen* holding was in context of an assessment of merits issues for purposes of allocating the cost of notice, rather than for determining whether any Rule 23 requirement was satisfied).

[370]General Tel. Co. of Sw. v. Falcon, 457 U.S. 147, 161 (1982) (emphasis added).

[371]Stastny v. Southern Bell Tel. & Tel. Co., 628 F.2d 267, 274, 23 FEP 665 (4th Cir. 1980).

[372]*See, e.g.*, Wagner v. Taylor, 836 F.2d 578, 587, 45 FEP 1199 (D.C. Cir. 1987) ("[A] decision on class certification cannot be made in a vacuum" and "some inspection of the circumstances of the case is essential to determine whether the prerequisites

some inquiry into the merits at the class certification stage because class treatment depends on some showing of the existence of a common pattern of discrimination against a class.[373]

Courts generally require more than the factual allegations of the complaint to satisfy the Rule 23 requirements.[374] Although some courts steadfastly abstain from venturing into any resolution of disputed factual issues,[375] other courts not only consider the merits in assessing whether the Rule 23 requirements have been satisfied, but arguably travel well beyond the standard of "rigorous

---

of Federal Civil Rule 23 have been met."); Love v. Turlington, 733 F.2d 1562, 1564 (11th Cir. 1984) (trial court must be made privy to sufficient facts so that reasoned determination of whether plaintiff has met Rule 23 requirements can be made); Nelson v. United States Steel Corp., 709 F.2d 675, 679–80, 32 FEP 838 (11th Cir. 1983) (although advance adjudication of merits is not permitted, because evidence relating to commonality is intertwined with merits, some merits evidence must be offered); Wynn v. Dixieland Food Stores, Inc., 125 F.R.D. 696, 698, 49 FEP 416 (M.D. Ala. 1989) (question of class certification is procedural one distinct from merits; nevertheless, court must " 'evaluate carefully the legitimacy of the named plaintiff's plea that he is a proper class representative under Rule 23(a)' ") (quoting General Tel. Co. of the Sw. v. Falcon, 457 U.S. 147, 160 (1982)); Sperling v. Donovan, 104 F.R.D. 4, 6, 9, 35 FEP 983 (D.D.C. 1984) (mere allegation of classwide discrimination insufficient; plaintiffs must present competent evidence applicable to class).

[373]See, e.g., Sheehan v. Purolator, Inc., 839 F.2d 99, 102, 49 FEP 1000 (2d Cir. 1988) (affirming denial of class certification based on lack of classwide proof of aggrieved class); Wagner, 836 F.2d at 592–95 (statistics evidencing alleged discriminatory practice); Meiresonne v. Marriott Corp., 124 F.R.D. 619, 621–23, 49 FEP 52 (N.D. Ill. 1989) (statistics and documentary evidence supporting sex discrimination allegations). See generally Chapter 2 (Disparate Treatment).

[374]Szabo v. Bridgeport Machs., Inc., 249 F.3d 672, 677 (7th Cir. 2001) (holding that district court should not accept as incontestable allegations of complaint but must probe beyond pleadings); Coleman v. General Motors Acceptance Corp., 220 F.R.D. 64, 68 (M.D. Tenn. 2004) ("[A] class action may not be certified merely on the basis of its designation as such in the pleadings"). But cf. Falcon, 457 U.S. at 160 ("Sometimes the issues are plain enough from the pleadings to determine whether the interests of the absent parties are fairly encompassed within the named plaintiff's claim, and sometimes it may be necessary for the court to probe behind the pleadings before coming to rest on the certification question.").

[375]See, e.g., Hnot v. Willis Group Holdings, Ltd., 2007 WL 749675, at *5–6 (S.D.N.Y. Mar. 8, 2007) ("In this case, plaintiffs and defendant disagree on whose statistical findings and observations are more credible, but this disagreement is relevant only to the merits of plaintiffs' claim—whether plaintiffs actually suffered disparate treatment—and not to whether plaintiffs have asserted common *questions* of law or fact. By asking the Court to decide which expert report is more credible, defendants are requesting that the Court look beyond Rule 23 requirements and decide the issue on the merits, a practice In re [Initial Public Offerings] specifically cautions against.").

analysis" for Rule 23 purposes by making express or implicit findings on the merits.[376] The Second Circuit has cautioned that any
such findings at the class certification stage should be limited to
those aspects of the merits that overlap with a specific Rule 23
requirement,[377] and that the court should take care to ensure that
the class certification proceedings do "not become a pretext for a
partial trial of the merits."[378]

Although some older cases, pursuant to old Rule 23(c)(1), held
that a class certification order could be "conditional" subject to
reconsideration in light of discovery or trial,[379] "conditional" certification is no longer permitted under the 2003 revision of Rule 23.[380]

D. Types of Evidence in Support of and in Opposition to Class Certification

The plaintiff bears the burden of proving compliance with Rule
23.[381] Courts may hold evidentiary hearings at the Rule 23 stage,
but an evidentiary hearing is not required.[382] Courts have accepted

---

[376]*E.g.*, Cooper v. Southern Co., 390 F.3d 695, 719, 94 FEP 1854 (11th Cir. 2004)
(denial of certification affirmed where plaintiffs "did not establish pattern or practice discrimination common to the class"), *cert. denied*, 126 S. Ct. 478 (2005), *overruled in part by* Ash v. Tyson Foods, Inc., 546 U.S. 454, 97 FEP 641 (2006); *Sheehan*,
839 F.2d at 102 (affirming denial of class certification based on lack of classwide
proof of aggrieved class); *Wynn*, 125 F.R.D. at 700 (concluding that "overwhelming evidence presented at the hearing on class certification demonstrates that the
defendants have acted in a racially-discriminatory manner that applies to the entire
class"); Martin v. City of Beaumont, 125 F.R.D. 435, 438, 50 FEP 246 (E.D. Tex.
1989) (class certification denied after examining employer's proffered reasons that
some class members were terminated).

[377]*See In re* Initial Public Offerings Sec. Litig., 471 F.3d 24, 41 (2d Cir. 2006)
(although "the obligation to make such determinations is not lessened by overlap between
a Rule 23 requirement and a merits issue, . . . in making such determinations, a district
judge should not assess any aspect of the merits unrelated to a Rule 23 requirement").

[378]*Id.*

[379]*See, e.g.*, Martinez v. Oakland Scavenger Co., 680 F. Supp. 1377, 1396, 49
FEP 116 (N.D. Cal. 1987) (court conditionally certified class and redefined it more
narrowly after evaluating evidence at trial); *Meiresonne*, 124 F.R.D. at 624 (certifying class but stating that "if it turns out the class does not share common questions,
Rule 23(c)(1) permits a fresh look at the matter").

[380]*See* Section VI.E *infra.*

[381]Caridad v. Metro-North Commuter R.R., 191 F.3d 283, 290, *vacated and
remanded*, 267 F.3d 147, 86 FEP 1580 (2d Cir. 2001).

[382]*See* Grayson v. KMart Corp., 79 F.3d 1086, 1099 (11th Cir. 1996) ("A court
may hold an evidentiary hearing prior to certifying a class. The failure to hold an

statistical evidence, affidavits or declarations,[383] discovery responses,[384] and similar allegations by other employees[385] as evidence relevant to satisfaction of Rule 23.

Courts face a difficult challenge in determining how to evaluate competing statistical evidence at the class certification stage.[386] The Second Circuit at one point cautioned that class certification is not the appropriate venue for resolving so-called "statistical dueling,"[387] but later disavowed that determination. In *In re Initial Public Offerings Securities Litigation*,[388] the Second Circuit held that the district judge must "assess all of the relevant evidence admitted at the class certification stage," including statistical evidence,

---

evidentiary hearing, however, does not require reversal of the class certification unless the parties can show that the hearing, if held, would have affected their rights substantially." (citations omitted)); Bouman v. Block, 940 F.2d 1211, 1232, 60 FEP 1000 (9th Cir. 1991) (upholding certification and finding that "rigorous examination" of Rule 23(a) factors does not require evidentiary hearing); *see also* MANUAL FOR COMPLEX LITIGATION §21.21 (FOURTH) (2004) ("An evidentiary hearing may be necessary.").

[383]*See, e.g.*, Dukes v. Wal-Mart Stores, Inc., 222 F.R.D. 137, 145, 93 FEP 1629 (N.D. Cal. 2004), *aff'd*, 474 F.3d 1214 (9th Cir. 2007); State, County, & Mun. Employees v. City of N.Y., 599 F. Supp. 916, 918 n.1, 36 FEP 900 (S.D.N.Y. 1984); Sheehan v. Purolator, Inc., 103 F.R.D. 641, 649 (E.D.N.Y. 1984).

[384]*E.g.*, Evans v. United States Pipe & Foundry Co., 696 F.2d 925, 929–30, 33 FEP 1620 (11th Cir. 1983).

[385]*E.g.*, Ladele v. Consolidated Rail Corp., 95 F.R.D. 198, 203, 29 FEP 1547 (E.D. Pa. 1982).

[386]*See, e.g.*, Chaffin v. Rheem Mfg. Co., 904 F.2d 1269, 1275, 54 FEP 383 (8th Cir. 1990) (consideration of anecdotal and statistical evidence for purposes of determining satisfaction of Rule 23 requirements not impermissible inquiry into merits); Wagner v. Taylor, 836 F.2d 578, 594, 45 FEP 1199 (D.C. Cir. 1987) (evaluating statistics to determine whether they were specific enough to discern outline of class); Shelton v. Pargo, Inc., 582 F.2d 1298, 1312–13, 17 FEP 1413 (4th Cir. 1978) ("[a]n intelligent decision on class certification requires 'at least a preliminary exploration of the merits,' " which will aid court in making findings that are necessary before case can be certified as class action). In some early cases where the plaintiff initially introduced statistical proof in support of a motion to certify the class, the district courts allowed the defendant to present detailed statistics in rebuttal, under the rationale that the plaintiff had "opened the door" to statistical proof and should be estopped from raising an argument, based on *Eisen*, that the defendant's statistics should be ignored as too intertwined with the merits. *See, e.g.*, Abercrombie v. Bi-Lo, Inc., 21 FEP 1252, 1263 (D.S.C. 1979); Santos v. Thom. McAn Shoe Co., 19 FEP 1351, 1353 (W.D. Tex. 1979); Lim v. Citizens Sav. & Loan Ass'n, 430 F. Supp. 802, 809, 15 FEP 113 (N.D. Cal. 1976).

[387]*Caridad*, 191 F.3d at 293; *accord* Dukes v. Wal-Mart Stores, Inc., 222 F.R.D. 137, 155, 93 FEP 1629 (N.D. Cal. 2004), *aff'd*, 474 F.3d 1214 (9th Cir. 2007); Drayton v. Western Auto Supply Co., 203 F.R.D. 520, 527 n.1 (M.D. Fla. 2000); Robertson v. Sikorsky Aircraft Corp., 2000 U.S. Dist. LEXIS 21148 n.1 (D. Conn. Sept. 18, 2000).

[388]471 F.3d 24 (2d Cir. 2006).

but "should not assess any aspect of the merits unrelated to a Rule 23 requirement."[389] Some courts have concluded that conflicting statistical evidence does not defeat class certification and simply demonstrates the existence of common issues under Rule 23(a).[390] On the other hand, other courts have concluded that class certification should be denied at least in part because the plaintiff's statistical showing is inadequate to satisfy the Rule 23 requirements or because the plaintiff's statistical evidence is rebutted by the defendant's statistical showing.[391]

Courts have adopted varying approaches to challenges to expert testimony under the Supreme Court's decision in *Daubert v. Merrell Dow Pharmaceuticals, Inc.*[392] at the class certification stage. Some have concluded that *Daubert* does not apply at the class certification stage,[393] whereas others have applied a lower standard.[394]

---

[389]*Id.* at 41–42.

[390]*See, e.g.*, Hnot v. Willis Group Holdings, Ltd., 2007 WL 749675, at *5 (S.D.N.Y. Mar. 8, 2007) ("*In re [Initial Public Offerings]* does not stand for the proposition that the Court should, or is even authorized to, determine which of the parties' expert reports is more persuasive. . . . Instead, *In re IPO* reiterated that 'experts' disagreement *on the merits*—whether a discriminatory impact [can] be shown— [is] *not a valid basis* for denying class certification.'"; "in light of *In re IPO* an accurate statement of the law is that 'statistical dueling' is not relevant to the certification stage *unless such dueling presents 'a valid basis for denying class certification.*' " (quoting *In re IPO*, 471 F.3d at 35) (emphasis and alterations in original); Vuyanich v. Republic Nat'l Bank of Dallas, 82 F.R.D. 420, 432, 21 FEP 1380 (N.D. Tex. 1979) ("the sum of plaintiffs' and defendant's statistics points to the conclusion that in the liability phase of this proceeding, the court will have the duty of resolving certain contested issues of fact and law; that is, common questions do exist.").

[391]*See, e.g.*, Stastny v. Southern Bell Tel. & Tel. Co., 628 F.2d 267, 278–80, 23 FEP 665 (4th Cir. 1980); Rhodes v. Cracker Barrel Old Country Store, Inc., 213 F.R.D. 619, 653 (N.D. Ga. 2003); Cooper v. Southern Co., 205 F.R.D. 596, 610–15 (N.D. Ga. 2001), *aff'd*, 390 F.3d 695 (11th Cir. 2004), *cert. denied*, 546 U.S. 960 (2005), *overruled in part by* Ash v. Tyson Foods, Inc., 546 U.S. 454, 97 FEP 641 (2006).

[392]509 U.S. 579 (1993).

[393]*See In re* Visa Check/Mastermoney Antitrust Litig., 280 F.3d 124, 132 & n.4 (2d Cir. 2001) (*Daubert* challenge "involves an inquiry distinct from that for evaluating expert evidence in support of a motion for class certification"); Dean v. Boeing Co., 2003 U.S. Dist. LEXIS 8787 (D. Kan. Apr. 24, 2003) (*Daubert* not applicable at class certification stage; court considered whether expert evidence was so fatally flawed as to be inadmissible as matter of law); Vickers v. General Motors Corp., 204 F.R.D. 476, 479 (D. Kan. 2001) (*Daubert* analysis not required at class certification stage); Bacon v. Honda of Am. Mfg., Inc., 205 F.R.D. 466, 470 (S.D. Ohio 2001) (same), *aff'd*, 370 F.3d 565 (6th Cir. 2004), *cert. denied*, 543 U.S. 1151 (2005).

[394]*See* Dukes v. Wal-Mart Stores, Inc., 222 F.R.D. 189, 191, 93 FEP 1629 (N.D. Cal. 2004), *aff'd*, 474 F.3d 1214 (9th Cir. 2007); Anderson v. Boeing Co., 222 F.R.D. 521 (N.D. Okla. 2004) (*Daubert* standard applies at trial; "courts, therefore, are

E. The Class Certification Order

The 2003 revision of Rule 23 made three significant changes regarding class certification orders. First, the rule now contains explicit requirements about what a class certification order must address. Rule 23(c)(1)(B) provides that "[a]n order certifying a class action must define the class and the class claims, issues, or defenses, and must appoint class counsel under Rule 23(g)."[395]

Second, under revised Rule 23, a class certification order can no longer be "conditional."[396] As the Advisory Committee noted, a "court that is not satisfied that the requirements of Rule 23 have been met should refuse certification until they have been met."[397]

Finally, a class certification order may be altered or amended "before final judgment" under revised Rule 23(c)(1)(C).[398] The prior version of the rule set the cutoff point for alteration or amendment at "a decision on the merits." This change reflects that class action proceedings often continue well beyond a liability finding: "Following a determination of liability, for example, proceedings to define the remedy may demonstrate the need to amend the definition or subdivide the class."[399]

VII. CLASS COMMUNICATIONS AND NOTICE ISSUES

Rule 23(d) gives courts great flexibility to issue a broad range of orders to control the class action proceedings.[400] In *Gulf Oil*

---

unwilling to conduct a full *Daubert* analysis at the class certification stage."); Thomas & Thomas Rodmakers, Inc. v. Newport Adhesives & Composites, Inc., 209 F.R.D. 159, 162–63 (C.D. Cal. 2002) (lower *Daubert* standard applied at class certification stage; expert may rely on allegations in complaint).

[395]FED. R. CIV. P. 23(c)(1)(B).

[396]The language in Rule 23(c)(1)(C) that a certification order "may be conditional" was deleted in the 2003 revision. *Id.* at 23(c) advisory committee's note.

[397]*Id.* at 23(c)(1) advisory committee's notes.

[398]*Id.* at 23(c)(1)(C).

[399]*Id.* at 23(c)(1)(C) advisory committee's notes.

[400]Rule 23(d) provides:

In the conduct of actions to which this rule applies, the court may make appropriate orders: (1) determining the course of proceedings or prescribing measures to prevent undue repetition or complication in the presentation of evidence or argument; (2) requiring, for the protection of the members of the class or otherwise for the fair conduct of the action, that notice be given in such manner as

Co. v. Bernard,[401] the Supreme Court recognized that the district courts have both the "duty and broad authority to exercise control over a class action and to enter appropriate orders [under Rule 23(d)] governing the conduct of counsel and parties."[402]

A. Precertification Communications With Class Members

Although Rule 23(d) powers include the authority to enjoin communications in class actions in order to prevent abuse or undue interference,[403] the Supreme Court in *Gulf Oil* held that orders limiting communications in a class action should be narrowly drawn to limit speech as little as possible and should be issued only when a clear record and specific findings "reflect a weighing of the need for a limitation and the potential interference with the rights of the parties."[404] Therefore, under *Gulf Oil*, prior judicial approval is not required for precertification communication by parties or their counsel, except as necessary to prevent serious misconduct.[405]

---

the court may direct to some or all of the members of any step in the action or of the proposed extent of the judgment, or of the opportunity of members to signify whether they consider the representation fair and adequate, to intervene and present claims or defenses, or otherwise to come into the action; (3) imposing conditions on the representative parties or on intervenors; (4) requiring that the pleadings be amended to eliminate therefrom allegations as to representation of absent persons, and that the action proceed accordingly; (5) dealing with similar procedural matters. The orders may be combined with an order under Rule 16, and may be altered or amended as may be desirable from time to time.

[401]452 U.S. 89 (1981) (in employment discrimination suit, overturning district court's order imposing complete ban on all communications from named plaintiffs and class counsel to prospective class members concerning class action).

[402]*Id.* at 100. This duty and authority also applies in collective actions filed under § 216(b) of the Fair Labor Standards Act (FLSA). *See* Hoffmann-La Roche, Inc. v. Sperling, 493 U.S. 165, 171, 51 FEP 853 (1989) ("The same justifications [for Rule 23] apply in the context of an ADEA [collective form] action."); Belt v. EmCare Inc., 299 F. Supp. 2d 664, 667 (E.D. Tex. 2003) ("As in Rule 23 class actions, courts have the authority to govern the conduct of counsel and parties in § 216(b) collective actions.").

[403]*See In re* McKesson HBOC, Inc. Sec. Litig., 126 F. Supp. 2d 1239, 1242 (N.D. Cal. 2000) ("The court's Rule 23(d) powers include the authority to enjoin communications with class members to protect them from undue interference.") (citing Gulf Oil Co. v. Bernard, 452 U.S. 89 (1981)).

[404]*Gulf Oil*, 452 U.S. at 101.

[405]*See id.* at 94–95, 103; *see also* Parks v. Eastwood Ins. Servs., Inc., 235 F. Supp. 2d 1082, 1084 (C.D. Cal. 2002); MANUAL FOR COMPLEX LITIGATION (FOURTH) § 21.12 (2004) (Pre-certification Communications with the Proposed Class); Debra Lyn Bassett, *Pre-Certification Communication Ethics in Class Actions*, 36 GA. L.

The law is unsettled on the issue of whether local court rules that prohibit or limit precertification communication violate the *Gulf Oil* rule.[406] In the wake of the *Gulf Oil* holding, some district courts invalidated their local court rules that prohibited precertification communications,[407] whereas other courts have decided the matter on a case-by-case basis,[408] and yet other courts have addressed but not settled the issue.[409]

REV. 353 (2002) (providing analysis of major authorities addressing precertification attorney communications with putative class members).

[406]*See* HERBERT B. NEWBERG & ALBA CONTE, NEWBERG ON CLASS ACTIONS § 15:14 (4th ed. 2002) [hereinafter NEWBERG ON CLASS ACTIONS (4th ed. 2002)]("In the absence of a local court rule or a pretrial order prohibiting or restricting communications by the defendants with absent class members, the defendants may continue to communicate in the ordinary course of business with members of the class . . . .").

[407]*See, e.g.*, Abdallah v. Coca-Cola Co., 186 F.R.D. 672, 675, 79 FEP 1409 (N.D. Ga. 1999) (relying on *Gulf Oil* to invalidate local rule that banned all parties and their counsel in Rule 23(b)(3) action from any communication with putative class members prior to expiration of opt-out deadline). *But see* Hammond v. City of Junction City, 167 F. Supp. 2d 1271, 1276–77, 1281 (D. Kan. 2001) (holding that class counsel violated Kansas Rule of Professional Conduct 4.2 prohibiting litigation-related communications with "persons having a managerial responsibility on behalf of the [defendant] organization" despite affidavits that indicated subject employee initiated contact, denied having any management or policy making responsibility, requested counsel's representation, and was believed to be employee outside scope of local rule 4.2).

[408]*Compare* Domingo v. New Eng. Fish Co., 727 F.2d 1429, 1438–39, 34 FEP 584 (9th Cir. 1984) (giving *Gulf Oil* decision retroactive application, court held that local rule prohibiting communication violated Rule 23 and remanded "for a new hearing on the claims of class members who wish to refile their claims or to file new ones"), Marmol v. Adkins, 655 F.2d 594, 596 (5th Cir. 1981) (finding district court's broad "gag order" under local rules to be "almost precisely the same order that was before the Supreme Court in [*Gulf Oil*]" and concluding that imposition of the order was abuse of discretion for failure to meet *Gulf Oil* standards for limiting communication) *and* Impervious Paint Indus., Inc. v. Ashland Oil, 508 F. Supp. 720, 721–23 (W.D. Ky. 1981) (upholding district court's ruling invalidating standing order as overbroad "communications ban," but finding defendant who initiated communication with putative class members during opt-out period to be in violation of Code of Professional Responsibility and local rules because defense counsel had knowledge of their client's conduct and failed to advise against it) *with* Babbitt v. Albertson's, Inc., 1993 U.S. Dist. LEXIS 18801 (N.D. Cal. Jan. 28, 1993) (holding that defendant's ex parte communications with putative class members did not violate California Rule of Professional Conduct 2-100 nor present specific abuses under *Gulf Oil* sufficient to justify protective order, but, nevertheless, relying on *Gulf Oil*'s balancing analysis to order defendant "to instruct its agents to refrain from statements or conduct that serve to deter class members and putative class members from communicating with class counsel or their local union").

[409]*See, e.g.*, Kleiner v. First Nat'l Bank of Atlanta, 751 F.2d 1193, 1200 (11th Cir. 1985) (avoiding question of constitutional validity of local rule prohibiting opt-out solicitation requests and misleading communications, court found that defendants'

Plaintiffs and class counsel thus have authority to engage in precertification communication with potential class members.[410] Some courts have recognized the existence of a constructive attorney-client relationship between class counsel and putative class members;[411]

---

communications with putative class members violated protective and class notice orders); Jackson v. Motel 6 Multipurpose, Inc., 130 F.3d 999, 1002 (11th Cir. 1997) (where district court order granted relief to plaintiffs from local rule prohibiting communication with putative class members without prior court approval, court vacated order in its entirety on abuse of discretion grounds rather than *Gulf Oil* analysis and without addressing validity of local rule).

[410]*See* Gulf Oil Co. v. Bernard, 452 U.S. 89, 99 n.11, 101 (1981) (in overturning order banning communication between class counsel and putative class members, Court recognized that such communication is necessary to perform "the customary role of named plaintiffs, who seek to 'vindicat[e] the rights of individuals' " by informing potential class members of the existence of the lawsuit and obtaining information about the merits of the case from the persons they sought to represent (quoting Deposit Guaranty Nat'l Bank of Jackson v. Roper, 445 U.S. 326, 338 (1980))); *Abdallah*, 186 F.R.D. at 677 (holding that "[p]laintiffs and their counsel are entitled to speak freely about [the] lawsuit with any potential class member who contacts [class counsel]"); *see also* Newberg on Class Actions (4th ed. 2002) at § 15:12 ("[C]ommunications with absent class members are appropriate as long as they are not considered abusive within the guidelines created by *Gulf Oil Co. v. Bernard*.").

[411]*See* Newberg on Class Actions (4th ed. 2002) at § 15:14 & n.1 ("[S]ome courts have characterized . . . the constructive attorney-client relationship that exists between counsel for class representatives and members of the class."); *see, e.g., Babbitt*, 1993 U.S. Dist. LEXIS 18801, at *2 (recognizing that "it appears that some federal courts have found putative class members to be represented by class counsel"); Pollar v. Judson Steel Corp., 1984 WL 161273, 33 FEP 1870 (N.D. Cal. Feb. 3, 1984) (prior to certification of class, issuing temporary restraining order against defendant employer's publication of newspaper advertisements regarding affirmative action program for hiring women on grounds that, inter alia, advertisements were "attempt to solicit information from class members who are represented by counsel"); *Impervious Paint Industries*, 508 F. Supp. at 722–23 ("For purposes of the obligation to avoid compromising the rights of the class members, class counsel must treat them as clients; for purposes of the obligation to avoid unethical solicitation, class counsel must treat the class members as non-clients [but] the implication is unavoidable that defendants' counsel must treat plaintiff class members as represented by counsel, and must conduct themselves in accordance . . . ."); *Kleiner*, 751 F.2d at 1206–07 & n.28 ("[D]efense counsel had an ethical duty to refrain from discussing the litigation with members of the class as of the date of class certification, if not sooner . . . ."). Other courts recognize the existence of, at the very least, an "incipient fiduciary relationship" between class counsel and the class she seeks to represent. *See, e.g.,* Piambino v. Bailey, 757 F.2d 1112, 1144 (11th Cir. 1985) ("by asserting a representative role on behalf of the alleged class [as lead counsel did when they filed this suit, lead counsel] voluntarily accepted a fiduciary obligation towards the members of the putative class they [undertook] to represent"); Knuth v. Erie-Crawford Dairy Coop. Ass'n, 463 F.2d 470, 480 (3d Cir. 1972) (ordering new trial rather than reversal of jury verdict in plaintiffs' favor on grounds of fiduciary relationship between class counsel and all class members); *see also* Manual for Complex Litigation (Fourth) § 21.12 & n.753 (2004).

others have expressly rejected it.[412] Class counsel then is generally free to respond to inquiries by potential class members, seek information necessary to represent the class, and provide additional information to putative class members.[413]

The law is mixed on whether defendants may communicate with potential class members prior to class certification—some courts permit precertification communication with certain limitations,[414] whereas others disapprove of or prohibit such contact

---

[412]*See, e.g.,* Weight Watchers of Phila., Inc. v. Weight Watchers Int'l, Inc., 455 F.2d 770, 773 (2d Cir. 1972) (rejecting argument that "once a plaintiff brought suit on behalf of a class, the court may never permit communications between the defendant and other members"); Van Gemert v. Boeing Co., 590 F.2d 433, 440 n.15 (2d Cir. 1978) (noting certification makes class attorney's client), *aff'd,* 444 U.S. 472 (1980); Parks v. Eastwood Ins. Servs., Inc., 235 F. Supp. 2d 1082, 1084 (C.D. Cal. 2002) (citing *Weight Watchers* in holding that, "In a Rule 23 class action, precertification communication from the defense to prospective plaintiffs is generally permitted. The law is not settled on this issue, but the majority view seems to be against a ban on pre-certification communication between Defendant and potential class members.").

[413]MANUAL FOR COMPLEX LITIGATION (FOURTH) § 21.311 n.742 (2004) (discussing counsel's ability to operate Internet sites to disseminate information effectively); NEWBERG ON CLASS ACTIONS (4th ed. 2002) at §15-13 n.1 ("Plaintiffs who fail to communicate with class members to ascertain their interest in the litigation sometimes have been criticized for failing to supply information with respect to class determination."). *See, e.g.,* Williams v. Chartwell Fin. Servs. Ltd., 204 F.3d 748, 759 (7th Cir. 2000) (reversing trial court order prohibiting plaintiffs from communicating with putative class members where plaintiffs argued, inter alia, that protective order "deprived them of useful information to support [their] motion for class certification"); *Abdallah,* 186 F.R.D. at 677 (permitting plaintiffs to "(1) discuss the merits of the suit with potential class members who contact them; (2) determine whether that potential class member possesses any evidence relating to the Complaint allegations; (3) prepare affidavits or other testimony in support of class certification or the merits of the case; and (4) discuss with potential class members the possibility of representation by Plaintiffs' counsel and of providing legal services to them"); Hoffman-La Roche, Inc. v. Sperling, 493 U.S. 165, 167–70 (1989) (in § 216(b) collective action, ordering defendant employer to produce names and addresses of discharged employees and authorizing plaintiffs/respondents to mail court-approved notice and consent documents to all potential class members).

[414]*See, e.g., In re* School Asbestos Litig., 842 F.2d 671, 683 (3d Cir. 1988) (recognizing that, under *Gulf Oil* analysis, Rule 23(d) "authorizes the imposition of a restricting order to guard against the '*likelihood*' of serious abuses' [not a finding of actual harm]"; circuit court upheld portion of district court order imposing affirmative disclosure requirement on defendants' direct communications with class members); Bublitz v. E.I. du Pont de Nemours & Co., 196 F.R.D. 545, 547, 549 (S.D. Iowa 2000) (reasoning that "the at-will employer-employee relationship between [d]efendants and the putative class members produces a strong potential for coercion and thus justifies minimal protections"; court required that defendants' communication of settlement

altogether.[415] Recognizing the potential for abuse, several courts have noted that contacts by defendants with class members might undermine the purposes of Rule 23 in allowing defendants to "reduce their liability by encouraging potential class members not to join the litigation."[416] Generally then, opposing counsel may communicate with potential class members in the ordinary course of business so long as the communications do not involve litigation-related matters[417] and do not give false or misleading information[418] or attempt to influence or intimidate potential

---

offers directly to putative class members be in writing, with a copy provided to court and class counsel, and allowed 10 days for putative class member to respond); Hodges v. Board of Educ., 1997 WL 557299, at *2 (D. Kan. July 25, 1997) (prohibiting defendants and defense counsel from making any "contact or communication with [potential class members] which expressly refers to this litigation," but allowing defendants to continue communications "made in the ordinary course of providing educational services to [potential class members]"); see also MANUAL FOR COMPLEX LITIGATION (FOURTH) § 21.12 & n.749 (suggesting that copies of communications regarding pending litigation sent by defendants who have ongoing business relationships with putative class members should be provided to opposing counsel).

[415]See, e.g., Kleiner, 751 F.2d at 1197–99, 1206 (upholding order prohibiting litigation-related communication by defendant in suit where, after certification but prior to expiration of opt-out period and before court resolved issue of unsupervised contacts by defendant bank with potential class members, bank contacted over 3000 of its customers, urging them to opt out of litigation); Cobell v. Norton, 212 F.R.D. 14, 18, 20 (D.D.C. 2002) ("There is no apparent support in the available case law that permits an opposing party to engage in communications with class members that have the effect of extinguishing the rights of those class members.").

[416]Burrell v. Crown Cent. Petroleum, Inc., 176 F.R.D. 239, 243 (E.D. Tex. 1997) (race and gender discrimination action where defendant employer communicated with employees regarding lawsuit via e-mail, printed announcements, and information meetings); see also Kleiner, 751 F.2d at 1202–03; Bublitz, 196 F.R.D. at 547–48; Abdallah, 186 F.R.D. at 678.

[417]Cobell, 212 F.R.D. at 17 (citing HERBERT B. NEWBERG & ALBA CONTE, NEWBERG ON CLASS ACTIONS §15-18 (3d ed. 1992)). See also NEWBERG ON CLASS ACTIONS (4th ed. 2002) at §15-14 n.1.

[418]See Gulf Oil Co. v. Bernard, 452 U.S. 89, 100 n.12 (1981) ("Misleading communications to class members concerning the litigation pose a serious threat to the fairness of the litigation process, the adequacy of representation and the administration of justice generally."); Kleiner, 751 F.2d at 1202–03 (In Rule 23(b)(3) class action where defendants engaged in telephone and mail communications to putative class members in violation of protective order and without notice to court or class counsel, court reasoned that "it is critical that the class receive accurate and impartial information regarding the status, purposes and effects of the class action . . . unsupervised, unilateral communications with the plaintiff class sabotage the goal of informed consent by urging exclusion on the basis of a one-sided presentation of the facts, without opportunity for rebuttal. The damage from misstatements could well be irreparable.").

plaintiffs.[419] Thus, within these limitations, opposing counsel may engage in precertification communications in order to obtain information from potential class members regarding the matter in controversy[420] or negotiate settlements directly with putative class members.[421] Where the putative class member remains an employee of the defendant, however, some courts have found that the risk of coercion is sufficient to justify an order to limit or restrict such settlement communications by defendants.[422] Where

---

[419]*See In re* School Asbestos Litig., 842 F.2d 671, 683 (3d Cir. 1988) ("[C]ommunications that seek or threaten to influence the [putative class members'] choice of remedies are, in some instances, subject to the strictures of *Gulf Oil* and are therefore within a district court's discretion to regulate."); *see, e.g.*, Hampton Hardware, Inc. v. Cotter & Co., Inc., 156 F.R.D. 630, 632–33 (N.D. Tex. 1994) (holding, inter alia, that defendant wholesaler that had on three occasions contacted member hardware retailers warning retailers not to join class action would be prohibited from all litigation-related communication prior to class certification).

[420]*See, e.g.*, Weight Watchers of Phila., Inc. v. Weight Watchers Int'l, Inc., 455 F.2d 770, 773 (2d Cir. 1972) (permitting communications between defendants and putative class members concerning subject matter of action); Babbitt v. Albertson's, Inc., 1993 U.S. Dist. LEXIS 18801, at *7 (N.D. Cal. Jan. 28, 1993) (finding defense attorney's investigative communication with potential class members did not violate anti-contact rule).

[421]*See, e.g., Gulf Oil*, 452 U.S. at 95 n.5 (after class action had been commenced but before certification, defendant continued to deal directly with potential class members concerning offer of settlement that had been earlier negotiated with EEOC); Christensen v. Kiewit-Murdock Inv. Corp., 815 F.2d 206, 213 (2d Cir. 1987) ("*Weight Watchers* establishes that, at least prior to class certification, defendants do not violate Rule 23(e) by negotiating settlements with potential members of a class."). *But see In re* General Motors Corp. Engine Interchange Litig., 594 F.2d 1106, 1139–40 (7th Cir. 1979) ("[W]e think that the degree of judicial review should be concomitant with the potential for abuse that such communications create. The danger that the offer to settle individual claims would create is the possible misleading of class members about the strength and extent of their claims and the alternatives for obtaining satisfaction of those claims. Thus, an offer to settle should contain sufficient information to enable a class member to determine (1) whether to accept the offer to settle, (2) the effects of settling, and (3) the available avenues for pursuing his claim if he does not settle . . . . Whether the offer to settle should contain a statement by the plaintiff-objectors of their opinion of the adequacy of the settlement package in order to make the communication a full and complete disclosure is a matter left to the trial court's discretion.").

[422]*See* Bublitz v. E.I. du Pont de Nemours & Co., 196 F.R.D. 545, 547–48 (S.D. Iowa 2000) (relying on Eleventh Circuit's reasoning in *Kleiner* and district court's reasoning in *Abdallah* that "employer-employee relationship justifies certain minimal protections" in precertification communications with putative class members); *see also In re General Motors*, 594 F.2d at 1140 n.60 ("An offer to settle which offers only nominal consideration in return may amount to little more than a request that the class members opt-out of the class. Solicitations to opt-out tend to reduce the

a court finds that a defendant's communication has intimidated, unduly influenced, or caused confusion among potential class members, the court may order restrictive or corrective notice.[423]

B. Post-Certification Communications With Class Members and Decision Makers

After a class is certified, defense counsel may only communicate with class members about the lawsuit through class counsel: "[T]he rules governing communications apply as though each

---

effectiveness of [Rule 23(b)(3)] class actions for no legitimate reason." (citations omitted)); Abdallah v. Coca-Cola Co., 186 F.R.D. 672, 678–79, 79 FEP 1409 (N.D. Ga. 1999) (although "Coca-Cola has not given the Court any reason to suspect that it will attempt to mislead its employees and coerce them into nonparticipation in this case," court nevertheless prohibited employer's direct communication with putative class member employees about lawsuit, except to extent necessary to discuss with managerial employees their acts, omissions, or statements that could expose employer to liability in that action).

[423]*See* MANUAL FOR COMPLEX LITIGATION (FOURTH) § 21.12 (2004) ("If class members have received inaccurate precertification communications, the judge can take action to cure the miscommunication and prevent similar problems in the future."); NEWBERG ON CLASS ACTIONS (4th ed. 2002) at § 15:14 & n.6 ("When the communication can be shown to be abusive, the defendants may be ordered to retract their statements . . . ."); *see, e.g., In re School Asbestos Litig.*, 842 F.2d at 683 (imposing affirmative disclosure requirement on defendants' direct mailing to potential class members where communication at issue ("information booklet") was misleading, lacking in objectivity and neutrality, and would "surely result in confusion and adversely affect the administration of justice"); Belt v. Emcare, Inc., 299 F. Supp. 2d 664, 669 (E.D. Tex. 2003) (Ordering defendant to issue corrective notice where defendants' unapproved letter to absent class members was "misleading, coercive, and an attempt to undermine the purposes of a collective action. Defendants' conduct was more egregious in this collective action that it would be in a class action because potential class members must opt into the collective action rather than opt out as in a class action."); Bullock v. Automobile Club of S. Cal., 2002 WL 432003, at *2–3 (C.D. Cal. Jan. 28, 2002) (finding that defendant's communication to putative class members was improper, breached stipulated agreement, and may have discouraged all potential plaintiffs, court ordered defendant to issue corrective notice to all potential plaintiffs, not just those who received defendant's initial communication). *But see* Great Rivers Coop. of S.E. Iowa v. Farmland Indus., Inc., 59 F.3d 764, 765–66 (8th Cir. 1995) (reversing district court ruling ordering defendant to publish rebuttal by plaintiffs after defendants published opinion piece "denouncing" class action suit in employee newsletter on grounds that district court "made insufficient findings regarding misrepresentation and the likelihood of serious abuses"); *Hampton Hardware*, 156 F.R.D. at 632 (denying plaintiffs' request for corrective notice where "although a clear potential for abuse was established there was little evidence of actual harm [and corrective notice prior to class certification] would be premature and potentially confusing").

class member is a client of class counsel . . . defendant's attorneys [ ] may communicate through class counsel with class members on matters regarding the litigation."[424] This communications restriction extends to the defendants' nonlawyer personnel, such as its employees, agents, and representatives.[425] Even when it is the class members who initiate contact with the defendants to inquire about their legal rights, it "is probably more appropriate . . . for the defendant to refer the inquiring class member to class counsel or to the Rule 23(c)(2) notice, which outlines the rights of the class."[426]

When the potential class includes employees in managerial or supervisory positions, contact with those employees must generally "be limited to discussion of those acts, omissions and statements of those employees in their managerial capacity for which [the defendant] may be liable."[427] Where either party wishes to

---

[424]MANUAL FOR COMPLEX LITIGATION (FOURTH) § 21.33 & nn.915, 916 (2004); *see also* NEWBERG ON CLASS ACTIONS (4th ed. 2002) at § 15-18 n.1 ("After a court has certified a case as a class action and the time for exclusions has expired, the attorney for the named plaintiff represents all class members who are otherwise unrepresented by counsel."); Cobell v. Norton, 212 F.R.D. 14, 20, 22 (D.D.C. 2002) ("The two leading treatises on class action litigation warn against permitting defendants to communicate directly with class members.").

[425]*See* Kleiner v. First Nat'l Bank of Atlanta, 751 F.2d 1193, 1201 (11th Cir. 1985) (where defendant bank's marketing director and 175 loan officers contacted putative class members in furtherance of defense counsel's opt-out solicitation scheme, court held that "[t]he [district court] orders [regarding unsupervised communications], which were directed to counsel as agents of the Bank, were binding on the Bank in its capacity as principal"); Erhardt v. Prudential Group, Inc., 629 F.2d 843, 845, 847 (2d Cir. 1980) (recognizing that, where individual who was president and CEO of defendant company, but who was not named defendant in class action, personally mailed letters to class members urging them to opt out, district court, inter alia, ordered issuance of new class notice and enjoined defendants from further communications with class members; defendants did not appeal those portions of district court's order but CEO appealed finding of civil contempt, which Second Circuit vacated); Haffer v. Temple Univ. of Commonwealth Sys. of Higher Educ., 115 F.R.D. 506, 512 (E.D. Pa. 1987) (finding that defendants had improperly communicated with class members where communications were made not by defense counsel but by coaches of university athletic programs (who were not named defendants) as well as named defendant); Impervious Paint Indus., Inc. v. Ashland Oil, 508 F. Supp. 720, 723 (W.D. Ky. 1981) (holding that professional ethics were violated where communication with class members was initiated by corporate officers of defendant and not defense attorney).

[426]NEWBERG ON CLASS ACTIONS (4th ed. 2002) at §15:18.

[427]*See* Shores v. Publix Super Mkts., Inc., 1996 WL 859985, at *4 (M.D. Fla. Nov. 25, 1996), *vacated*, 1997 U.S. Dist. LEXIS 16778 (M.D. Fla. Jan. 27, 1997); *see also* Abdallah v. Coca-Cola Co., 186 F.R.D. 672, 677, 79 FEP 1409 (N.D. Ga. 1999) (Rejecting defendant's request that plaintiffs and class counsel be prohibited

contact upper-level or decision-making employees, courts may allow narrowly drawn orders for such communication. For example, in *Abdallah v. Coca-Cola Co.*,[428] the defendant requested permission to communicate with certain personnel, including managers and supervisors who had participated in the challenged employment decisions, on grounds that such communications were necessary to prepare a defense to the case.[429] Similarly, in preparing for class certification, class counsel requested permission to ask potential class members whether they were management or supervisory employees.[430] Relying on the guidelines articulated in *Jackson v. Motel 6 Multipurpose, Inc.*,[431] the court held that plaintiffs and their counsel were entitled to speak freely about the lawsuit with any potential class member, including any managerial employee who contacted them.[432] With respect to communications by the defendant employer, the court prohibited Coca-Cola from discussing the lawsuit directly with potential class members but allowed it to communicate with managerial employees to the extent necessary to investigate matters that may have exposed Coca-Cola to liability, even though those managers were potential class members.[433]

C. Notice Issues

For cases certified under Rule 23(b)(3), notice and an opportunity to opt out are mandatory.[434] Rule 23(c)(2)(B) provides that "[t]he court must direct to class members the best practicable notice under the circumstances, including individual notice to all members who can be identified through reasonable effort."[435] In

---

from communicating with "supervisory and managerial employees, any employees whose acts or admissions could be attributed to [defendant], employees involved in defending the action, and those likely to have privileged information [because] . . . upper level employees of [defendant] have a right to bring a discrimination claim against their employer. Therefore, to the extent that [those] employees wish to pursue employment claims against [defendant], they communicate freely [with the exception of privileged information] with Plaintiffs and their counsel.").

[428]186 F.R.D. 672, 79 FEP 1409 (N.D. Ga. 1999).
[429]*Id.* at 678.
[430]*Id.* at 677–78.
[431]130 F.3d 999 (11th Cir. 1997).
[432]*Abdallah*, 186 F.R.D. at 677.
[433]*Id.* at 679.
[434]FED. R. CIV. P. 23(c)(2) advisory committee's notes.
[435]*Id.* at 23(c)(2)(B).

Eisen v. Carlisle & Jacquelin,[436] the Supreme Court held that, in Rule 23(b)(3) cases, "best practicable notice" means individual notice by first-class mail, rather than published notice, where names and addresses are available.[437]

In 2003, Rule 23(c)(2)(B) was revised to mandate that the class notice specifically address six elements: (1) the nature of the action; (2) the definition of the class certified; (3) the class claims, issues, or defenses; (4) the right of the class member to enter an appearance through counsel; (5) the right of a class member to opt out and the time and method to do so; and (6) the binding effect of the class judgment on class members.[438] The revised rule also incorporated a requirement that the notice be written "concisely and clearly" in "plain, easily understood language."[439]

For cases certified under Rule 23(b)(2), notice and an opportunity to opt out have historically not been required.[440] Under the broad discretion conferred by Rule 23(d)(2),[441] however, district courts could exercise their discretion to order notice (or notice and an opportunity to opt out) in appropriate Rule 23(b)(2) cases.[442]

---

[436]417 U.S. 156 (1974).

[437]*Id.* at 176.

[438]FED. R. CIV. P. 23(c)(2)(B).

[439]*Id.*

[440]Eubanks v. Billington, 110 F.3d 87, 95, 77 FEP 211 (D.C. Cir. 1997). Notice has also not been required in cases certified under Rule 23(b)(1). *Id.*

[441]Rule 23(d)(2) provides in relevant part:
In the conduct of actions to which this rule applies, the court may make appropriate orders: . . . (2) requiring, for the protection of the members of the class or otherwise for the fair conduct of the action, that notice be given in such manner as the court may direct to some or all of the members of any step in the action or of the proposed extent of the judgment, or of the opportunity of members to signify whether they consider the representation fair and adequate, to intervene and present claims or defenses, or otherwise to come into the action; . . . .

[442]*See, e.g.*, Lemon v. Operating Eng'rs Local 139, 216 F.3d 577, 582, 83 FEP 63 (7th Cir. 2000) (district court could "exercise its plenary authority under Rules 23(d)(2) and 23(d)(5)" to order notice and opt-out rights in Rule 23(b)(2) action); *Eubanks*, 110 F.3d at 95 (recognizing authority of district court to permit notice and opt out in Rule 23(b)(2) action). *But see* Warren v. Xerox Corp., 2004 U.S. Dist. LEXIS 5115 (E.D.N.Y. Jan. 26, 2004), *recommendation adopted*, 2004 U.S. Dist. LEXIS 5080 (E.D.N.Y. Mar. 11, 2004) (Rule 23(b)(2) certification of liability and injunctive relief; court to revisit certification of damages if liability found); Wright v. Stern, 2003 U.S. Dist. LEXIS 11589 (S.D.N.Y. July 7, 2003) (race and national origin promotion and pay class certified under Rule 23(b)(2) for Stage I); McReynolds v. Sodexho Marriott Servs. Inc., 208 F.R.D. 428, 448–49 & n.35 (D.D.C. 2002) (Rule 23(b)(2) certification of liability and injunctive relief: "if liability established, the

The 2003 revisions to Rule 23 added language that expressly permits—but does not require—notice in Rule 23(b)(2) cases.[443] In determining whether to order notice in a Rule 23(b)(2) case, the district court should consider whether the cost of providing notice may deter the filing of class actions that do not seek damages.[444]

The standard for discretionary notice under Rule 23(b)(2) is "appropriate notice" rather than individual notice as required for Rule 23(b)(3) cases. The Advisory Committee's notes clarify that the trial court has significant "flexibility" in determining the method of notice and adds that "informal methods" may be effective.[445]

VIII. CLASS ACTION REMEDIES

A. Overview

In *Albemarle Paper Co. v. Moody*,[446] the Supreme Court ruled that one of the key purposes of Title VII is to "make persons whole for injuries suffered on account of unlawful employment discrimination."[447] In practice, "make whole" relief means that class members with valid claims should be compensated for all losses that they have suffered as a result of the defendant's wrongdoing.[448]

Court will then determine the most appropriate mechanism for determining remedies."); Morgan v. United Parcel Serv. of Am., Inc., 169 F.R.D. 349, 77 FEP 165 (E.D. Mo. 1996); Butler v. Home Depot, 1996 U.S. Dist. LEXIS 3370, 70 FEP 51 (N.D. Cal. Jan. 25, 1996); Shores v. Publix Super Mkts., Inc., 1996 WL 407850 (M.D. Fla. Mar. 12, 1996).

[443]Rule 23(c)(2) provides: "For any class certified under Rule 23(b) (1) or (2), the court may direct appropriate notice to the class."

[444]FED. R. CIV. P. 23(c)(2) advisory committee's notes. The advisory committee's notes explain that "the cost of providing notice . . . could easily cripple actions that do not seek damages. The court may decide not to direct notice after balancing the risk that notice costs may deter the pursuit of class relief against the benefits of notice." *Id.*

[445]*Id.* ("When the court does direct certification notice in a (b)(1) or (b)(2) class action, the discretion and flexibility established by subdivision (c)(2)(A) extend to the method of giving notice. Notice facilitates the opportunity to participate. Notice calculated to reach a significant number of class members often will protect the interests of all. Informal methods may prove effective. A simple posting in a place visited by many class members, directing attention to a source of more detailed information, may suffice. The court should consider the costs of notice in relation to the probable reach of inexpensive methods.").

[446]422 U.S. 405, 10 FEP 1181 (1975).

[447]*Id.* at 418.

[448]*Id.*

The trial court has "an obligation to fashion the most complete relief possible" and has very limited discretion to award class members any less than their full entitlement to relief.[449] Where the judge or jury in a Title VII class action has found that the employer is liable for discrimination against the class, the court may order injunctive relief.[450] In disparate treatment cases, class members may then be entitled to individual equitable remedies (back pay, front pay, reinstatement, or retroactive seniority) as well as compensatory and punitive damages.[451] In adverse impact cases, class members are limited to equitable remedies.[452] Title VII also provides for statutory attorney's fees under either theory.[453]

The Supreme Court has held that, at the remedies stage of a class action or pattern-or-practice case, class members have the benefit of a rebuttable presumption that they have been the victims of discrimination and are entitled to relief.[454]

B. Equitable and Injunctive Relief

The hallmark of the Title VII class action is the broad power of the district court to order injunctive relief to end discriminatory practices in the workplace.[455] These orders may involve enjoining the use of a biased employment test,[456] retraining managers,[457] or creating posting and bidding systems for promotions.[458]

---

[449]See Kraszewski v. State Farm General Ins. Co., 912 F.2d 1182, 1186 (9th Cir. 1990) (quoting Albemarle Paper Co. v. Moody, 422 U.S. 405, 10 FEP 1181 (1975)); see also Albemarle Paper Co. v. Moody, 422 U.S. 405, 421, 10 FEP 1181 (1975) ("given a finding of unlawful discrimination, backpay should be denied only for reasons which, if applied generally, would not frustrate the central statutory purposes of eradicating discrimination throughout the economy and making persons whole for injuries suffered through past discrimination").

[450]42 U.S.C. § 2000e-5(g)(1) (2005).

[451]Id. §1981a.

[452]Id. §1981a(a)(1)–(2).

[453]Id. § 2000e-5(k). See generally Chapter 41 (Attorney's Fees).

[454]See Teamsters v. United States, 431 U.S. 324, 360–61, 14 FEP 1514 (1977).

[455]See Albemarle Paper Co. v. Moody, 422 U.S. 405, 418, 10 FEP 1181 (1975) (district courts have "not merely the power but the duty to render a decree which will so far as possible eliminate the discriminatory effects of the past as well as bar like discrimination in the future."). See generally Chapter 39 (Injunctive and Affirmative Relief).

[456]See, e.g., Vulcan Pioneers, Inc. v. New Jersey Dep't of Civil Serv., 832 F.2d 811, 816–17, 53 FEP 703 (3d Cir. 1987).

[457]See, e.g., EEOC v. Gurnee Inn Corp., 48 FEP 871, 883–84 (N.D. Ill. 1988).

[458]See, e.g., James v. Stockham Valves & Fittings Co., 559 F.2d 310, 355, 15 FEP 827 (5th Cir. 1977).

The district court may also order affirmative relief, including gender- or race-conscious goals and timetables where there is a proven history of discrimination.[459]

Class members may also be entitled to individual injunctive relief. "Rightful place" relief is a remedy that awards class members a position or retroactive seniority that they were discriminatorily denied.[460] In practice, providing the class with rightful place relief can be a complicated process because there may be more class members than historical vacancies, and the interests of the incumbent job holders must be considered.[461] In some circumstances, where reinstatement is impractical, front pay has been paid in lieu of rightful place relief.[462]

C. Monetary Remedies

1. Back Pay and Front Pay

Following a liability finding, back pay will ordinarily be awarded to eligible class members.[463] Back pay is broadly defined to include lost wages, benefits (vacation, sick pay, overtime, bonuses, medical insurance),[464] and prejudgment interest.[465] The back-pay period in a class action runs from no more than two years before the filing of the first EEOC charge[466] until the date of judgment.[467] Under Title VII, back pay is an equitable remedy for the judge to award, as appropriate.[468]

---

[459]*See generally* Chapter 39 (Injunctive and Affirmative Relief).

[460]Franks v. Bowman Transp. Co., 424 U.S. 747, 779 n.41 (1976).

[461]*See generally* Chapter 39 (Injunctive and Affirmative Relief).

[462]*See, e.g.,* Williams v. Pharmacia, Inc., 137 F.3d 944, 952, 76 FEP 310 (7th Cir. 1998).

[463]*See* Albemarle Paper Co. v. Moody, 422 U.S. 405, 418, 10 FEP 1181 (1975) (Supreme Court established strong presumption in favor of back-pay award).

[464]*See generally* Chapter 40 (Monetary Relief).

[465]*See* Loeffler v. Frank, 486 U.S. 549, 46 FEP 1659 (1988) (prejudgment interest is element of back-pay remedy against private employer).

[466]42 U.S.C. § 2000e-5(g)(1) (2005); *see* Estate of Pitre v. Western Elec. Co., 975 F.2d 700, 704 (10th Cir. 1992) (remanding for district court to address failure to award back pay to class for entire 2-year period before EEOC charge).

[467]Kraszewski v. State Farm General Ins. Co., 912 F.2d 1182, 1186 (9th Cir. 1990); EEOC v. Monarch Mach. Tool Co., 737 F.2d 1444, 1453, 42 FEP 859 (6th Cir. 1980); Patterson v. American Tobacco Co., 535 F.2d 257, 269, 12 FEP 314 (4th Cir. 1976); EEOC v. Enterprise Ass'n Steamfitters Local 638, 542 F.2d 579, 590, 13 FEP 705 (2d Cir. 1976).

[468]42 U.S.C. § 2000e-5(g)(1) (2000); *see* Pals v. Schepel Buick & GMC Truck, Inc., 220 F.3d 495, 500 (7th Cir. 2000) ("Back pay and front pay are equitable remedies

Front pay is intended to compensate for continuing lost earnings after judgment but before a class member can be restored to his or her rightful place.[469] The Tenth Circuit affirmed a district court's order to pay front pay to class members until women comprised 50 percent of incumbents in two positions from which they had been discriminatorily excluded.[470] Because front pay is an equitable remedy, it too is determined by the district court, rather than the jury.[471]

There are two basic models for awarding relief in Stage II proceedings: individualized hearings and aggregate or formula proof of back-pay losses. Individualized hearings essentially attempt to recreate the historical hiring or promotion system, absent the discriminatory conditions.[472] Individual hearings can be complicated and can take from several weeks to years to complete.[473] They may be particularly appropriate where reinstatement is at issue, and the rights of other employees may be affected by the outcome.[474]

Courts have also recognized, however, that this exercise of recreating history can lead the court into a "quagmire of hypothetical judgments."[475] Accordingly, some courts in Title VII actions have allowed proof of aggregate monetary damages by means of expert statistical analysis.[476] The resulting sum of damages is

---

under § 706(g) (1)."); Simpson v. Lucky Stores, Inc., 1993 WL 414668, at *3 (N.D. Cal. Oct. 6, 1993) (injunctive relief and back pay are equitable remedies available under Title VII). Under the ADEA, back pay may be a jury question. See Sailor v. Hubbell, Inc., 4 F.3d 323, 325–26, 62 FEP 1444 (4th Cir. 1993) ("whether Hubbell is liable for discrimination against Sailor, as well as the appropriate amount of back pay and liquidated damages if Hubbell was found liable, were properly questions for a jury").

[469]See Patterson, 535 F.2d at 269.

[470]Estate of Pitre, 975 F.2d at 704.

[471]EEOC v. W&O, Inc., 213 F.3d 600, 618, 83 FEP 117 (11th Cir. 2000); see Pollard v. E.I. du Pont de Nemours & Co., 532 U.S. 843, 850, 85 FEP 1217 (2001) (front pay is equitable remedy, not subject to statutory caps).

[472]See Teamsters v. United States, 431 U.S. 324, 361, 14 FEP 1514 (1977).

[473]Id. at 372.

[474]Id. ("the District Court will . . . be faced with the delicate task of adjusting the remedial interests of discriminatees and the legitimate expectations of other employees innocent of any wrong doing").

[475]Pettway v. American Cast Iron Pipe Co., 494 F.2d 211, 260, 7 FEP 1115 (5th Cir. 1974).

[476]See, e.g., Shipes v. Trinity Indus., 987 F.2d 311, 316, 66 FEP 375 (5th Cir. 1993); Pitre v. Western Elec. Co., 843 F.2d 1262, 1274, 51 FEP 656 (10th Cir. 1988); Segar v. Smith, 28 FEP 935, 937 (D.D.C. 1982), aff'd in relevant part, 738 F.2d 1249, 35 FEP 31 (D.C. Cir. 1984); Domingo v. New Eng. Fish Co., 727 F.2d 1429, 1444–45, 34 FEP 584 (9th Cir. 1984); Pettway v. American Cast Iron Pipe Co., 681

then to be distributed among the class, either in a pro rata or weighted pro rata fashion.[477] This formula approach cannot resolve reinstatement claims, however.

2. Compensatory and Punitive Damages

With the 1991 amendments to Title VII, compensatory and punitive damages became available for victims of intentional discrimination, i.e., in disparate treatment claims.[478] The right to such damages already existed for § 1981 claims.[479] Where such damages are sought, both parties have the right to a jury trial on those issues.[480] The amount of compensatory and punitive damages that can be awarded under Title VII is subject to a statutory cap tied to the size of the employer (i.e., number of employees).[481] Several courts have held that, in an EEOC pattern-or-practice case, the statutory cap applies to *each* individual employee aggrieved by an unlawful employment practice.[482] The only federal court to address the issue to date in a Title VII class action reached the same result.[483]

The availability of compensatory and punitive damages has presented complicated issues for class certification, as discussed earlier.[484]

The Supreme Court established the standard for punitive damages in *Kolstad v. American Dental Ass'n.*[485] The majority of circuits to address the issue have held that an award of compensatory

---

F.2d 1259, 1266, 29 FEP 897 (11th Cir. 1982); Hameed v. Iron Workers, 637 F.2d 506, 520, 24 FEP 352 (8th Cir. 1980); Stewart v. General Motors Corp., 542 F.2d 445, 452–53, 13 FEP 1035 (7th Cir. 1976); United States v. United States Steel Corp., 520 F.2d 1043, 11 FEP 553 (5th Cir. 1975); *see also* NEWBERG ON CLASS ACTIONS (3d ed. 1992) at § 10:15, 10-13.

[477]*See Shipes*, 987 F.2d at 319.

[478]42 U.S.C. § 1981a (2000).

[479]*See* Patterson v. McLean Credit Union, 491 U.S. 164, 182 n.4, 49 FEP 1814 (1989).

[480]42 U.S.C. § 1981a(c) (2000).

[481]*Id.* § 1981a(c)(2).

[482]*See* EEOC v. Dinuba Med. Clinic, 222 F.3d 580, 588, 83 FEP 1655 (9th Cir. 2000); EEOC v. W&O, Inc., 213 F.3d 600, 613–14, 83 FEP 117 (11th Cir. 2000); EEOC v. Moser Foods, Inc., 1997 U.S. Dist. LEXIS 19798, 75 FEP 532 (D. Ariz. Nov. 5, 1997).

[483]Adams v. Pinole Point Steel Co., 1995 U.S. Dist. LEXIS 2036 (N.D. Cal. Feb. 10, 1995).

[484]*See* Section IV *supra*.

[485]527 U.S. 526, 79 FEP 1697 (1999). *See generally* Chapter 40 (Monetary Relief).

damages is not necessary for an award of punitive damages under Title VII.[486]

D. Procedures for Determining and Distributing Remedies

Courts have developed several procedural devices for determining and allocating relief in class actions.[487] Three principal devices—bifurcation of the trial, appointment of a special master, and use of proof-of-claim forms—are available to increase the efficiency and speed the resolution of classwide claims for relief.[488]

1. Bifurcation

The Federal Judicial Center's *Manual for Complex Litigation* states:

> Employment discrimination class actions have commonly been tried in separate stages under Rule 42(b). In some cases the class issues may themselves be severed, with the Phase I trials of different class issues conducted separately. The Phase I trial determines whether the defendants have discriminated against the class. Whether the merits of the individual claims of the class representatives should be tried in Phase I depends on whether proof of those claims is essential to establishing liability on the class claim. If class-wide discrimination is found, issues of relief are tried in Phase II. The 1991 [Civil Rights Act] entitles parties in disparate treatment cases to request a jury trial. If a jury is requested, the bifurcation of

---

[486]*See* Corti v. Storage Tech. Corp., 304 F.3d 336, 342–43, 89 FEP 1477 (4th Cir. 2002) (punitive damage award supported by back-pay award; absence of compensatory damage award by jury did not undermine punitive damage award); *W&O, Inc.*, 213 F.3d at 615 (compensatory damages need not be awarded to sustain punitive damage award; Eleventh Circuit instead evaluated ratio between back pay and punitive damages); Provencher v. CVS Pharmacy, 145 F.3d 5, 17, 76 FEP 1569 (1st Cir. 1998) (punitive damage award can be supported by back pay or nominal damages alone); Timm v. Progressive Steel Treating, Inc., 137 F.3d 1008, 76 FEP 321 (7th Cir. 1998) (jury may award punitive damages in sex discrimination action, even if no compensatory or nominal damages are awarded); Hennessy v. Penril Datacomm Networks, Inc., 69 F.3d 1344, 1352, 69 FEP 398 (7th Cir. 1995); Palmer v. Combined Ins. Co. of Am., 217 F.R.D. 430, 438, 92 FEP 943 (N.D. Ill. 2003) (rejecting argument that punitive damages in Title VII class action could only be awarded based on compensatory damages).

[487]Many of the procedures discussed below, derived from Title VII cases, also may be applicable to ADEA and EPA cases in which numerous persons have "opted in." *See* 29 U.S.C. § 216(b) (2000). *See generally* Chapter 12 (Age).

[488]Bifurcation and special masters may be used in individual actions as well. The determination of *which* class members are entitled to monetary relief, and how much, is discussed in Chapter 40 (Monetary Relief).

class actions will be substantially more complicated. Although the class-wide issue of discrimination is readily tried to a jury in Phase I, the trial of individual damage claims to a jury in Phase II will result in potentially lengthy trials. In some cases, Title VII permits recovery of front and back pay as well as compensatory damages, including future loss, and pain and suffering. Consider whether fairness to the parties requires that both liability and relief be tried to a single jury.

The individual damage claims of the class members should be resolved in Phase II. In some instances, a period of additional discovery may be necessary. In this second stage, the claimants—who, by proof of their membership in the class, are presumed to have been subjected to the discrimination practiced against the class— are permitted to present their individual claims of injury, subject to the right of the employer to raise defenses to those claims that were not resolved during Phase I proceedings.[489]

This procedure has been followed in most cases seeking class monetary relief.[490]

The court frequently will suspend discovery of individual relief issues until after the completion of Stage I. It may be desirable, however, to allow some overall discovery on relief issues so that the parties can determine the defendant's potential exposure and more readily assess settlement. The entry of a liability determination at the conclusion of Stage I may itself result in settlement.[491]

---

[489]MANUAL FOR COMPLEX LITIGATION (FOURTH) § 32.45 (2004) (Employment Discrimination—Case Management—Trial).

[490]See, e.g., Teamsters v. United States, 431 U.S. 324, 360–61, 14 FEP 1514 (1977) ("At the initial, 'liability' stage of a pattern-or-practice suit the Government is not required to offer evidence that each person for whom it will ultimately seek relief was a victim of the employer's discriminatory policy"; "When the Government seeks individual relief for victims of the discriminatory practice, a district court must usually conduct additional proceedings after the liability phase of the trial to determine the scope of individual relief."). Class actions typically employ the same bifurcated procedure that Teamsters advocated for its pattern-or-practice disparate treatment action. See, e.g., Segar v. Smith, 738 F.2d 1249, 1290, 35 FEP 31 (D.C. Cir. 1984); Domingo v. New Eng. Fish Co., 727 F.2d 1429, 1434, 34 FEP 584 (9th Cir.) (per curiam), modified on other grounds, 742 F.2d 520, 37 FEP 1303 (9th Cir. 1984); Sledge v. J.P. Stevens & Co., 585 F.2d 625, 637, 18 FEP 261 (4th Cir. 1978); United States v. United States Steel Corp., 520 F.2d 1043, 1053, 11 FEP 553 (5th Cir. 1974), modified on other grounds, 525 F.2d 1214, 15 FEP 581 (5th Cir. 1976); Pettway v. American Cast Iron Pipe Co., 494 F.2d 211, 257–58, 7 FEP 1115 (5th Cir. 1974). Notably, however, there have been very few trials of class actions seeking damages since the 1991 amendments to Title VII, and hence little recent precedent.

[491]For example, back-pay settlements were achieved after findings of liability in Albemarle Paper Co. v. Moody, 422 U.S. 405, 10 FEP 1181 (1975), Robinson v.

If a jury is requested, the bifurcation issues will be substantially more complicated.[492] The circuits are divided about whether the right to a jury trial provided by the 1991 amendments to Title VII creates Seventh Amendment problems for bifurcated proceedings. The Fifth Circuit, in *Allison v. Citgo Petroleum Corp.*,[493] considered this issue in the context of the plaintiffs' request that the court certify only their adverse impact claim, holding in abeyance the decision whether to certify their disparate treatment claim. The *Allison* court first noted that "the jury demand . . . extend[ed] to all issues that materially relate[d] to liability on the pattern or practice claims and the recovery of compensatory or punitive damages; on the other hand, the jury demand itself [did] not reach the disparate impact claim or any equitable relief."[494] Reviewing the plaintiffs' two types of claims, the court next determined that, because the same employment policies and practices were challenged under both claims, there were overlapping issues.[495] Reasoning that such factual overlap would occur with the plaintiffs' prima facie showing of disparity, as well as the defendant's rebuttal explanation of the disparity and its assertion of the business necessity defense, the Fifth Circuit concluded that "[t]he claims for injunctive relief, declaratory relief, and any equitable or incidental monetary relief [could not] be litigated in a class action bench trial . . . without running afoul of the Seventh Amendment."[496]

In *Robinson v. Metro-North Commuter Railroad*,[497] the Second Circuit explained that "sound case management" rather than wholesale abandonment of bifurcation could be used to avoid Seventh Amendment concerns. In the context of adverse impact claims coupled with and sharing common factual allegations with pattern-or-practice claims seeking compensatory damages, the court stated

---

Lorillard Corp., 444 F.2d 791, 3 FEP 653 (4th Cir. 1971), *United States v. Georgia Power Co.*, 474 F.2d 906, 5 FEP 587 (5th Cir. 1973), and *Payne v. Travenol Labs., Inc.*, 673 F.2d 798, 28 FEP 1212 (5th Cir. 1982). Settlement issues are discussed more extensively in Section IX *infra*.

[492]MANUAL FOR COMPLEX LITIGATION (FOURTH) § 32.45 (2004).
[493]151 F.3d 402, 81 FEP 501 (5th Cir. 1998), *reh'g denied*, 1998 U.S. App. LEXIS 24651 (5th Cir. Oct. 2, 1998).
[494]151 F.3d at 423.
[495]*Id.* at 424.
[496]*Id.* at 424–25.
[497]267 F.3d 147, 86 FEP 1580 (2d Cir. 2001), *cert. denied*, 535 U.S. 951 (2002).

that it could simply structure the trial so that the pattern-or-practice claims are tried first to a jury, thereby avoiding reconsideration of the jury's verdict, because the jury will have already determined all factual issues necessary to resolving the pattern-or-practice claims that are common to the adverse impact claims.[498] The court thus held that bifurcation was appropriate and that the trial court erred in failing to certify the adverse impact claims under Rule 23(b)(2).[499]

The Seventh Circuit, in *Jefferson v. Ingersoll International, Inc.*,[500] held in an interlocutory appeal of a class certification ruling that the district court could bifurcate the proceedings and certify a Rule 23(b)(2) class for equitable relief and a Rule 23(b)(3) class for damages. Subsequently, in *Lemon v. Operating Engineers Local 139*,[501] the Seventh Circuit instructed the district court to consider this type of "divided certification" in a case where a Title VII class sought both equitable relief and monetary damages.[502] The Seventh Circuit ruled that "a district court that proceeds with divided certification must adjudicate the damages claims first before a jury to preserve the Seventh Amendment right to a jury trial, even if adjudication of these claims decides the equitable claims as well."[503]

More recently, in *Allen v. International Truck & Engine Corp.*,[504] the Seventh Circuit reversed a district court's order refusing to certify the liability and injunctive phases of a hostile work environment class action. The court concluded that the district court erred in finding that the Seventh Amendment would preclude such partial certification: "[A] class proceeding for equitable relief vindicates the seventh amendment as fully as do individual trials, is no more complex than individual trials, yet produces benefits compared with the one-person-at-a-time paradigm."[505]

Some district courts have refused to bifurcate class claims based on the Fifth Circuit's reasoning in *Allison*.[506] Other district courts

---

[498]*Id.* at 170.
[499]*Id.*
[500]195 F.3d 894, 81 FEP 170 (7th Cir. 1999).
[501]216 F.3d 577, 83 FEP 63 (7th Cir. 2000).
[502]*Id.* at 581–82.
[503]*Id.* at 582.
[504]358 F.3d 469, 471–72 (7th Cir. 2004).
[505]*Id.* at 472.
[506]*See, e.g.*, Adler v. Wallace Computer Servs., Inc., 202 F.R.D. 666, 673 (N.D. Ga. 2001) (bifurcation fails to resolve need for each individual plaintiff's proof of

have followed the Second and Seventh Circuits and rejected arguments that bifurcation of employment discrimination class actions will violate the Seventh Amendment.[507]

---

actual harm and, under Seventh Amendment, litigants have right to determination of issues by single jury, which would cause confusion and be overly burdensome to court's resources); Reap v. Continental Cas. Co., 199 F.R.D. 536, 550 (D.N.J. 2001) (bifurcation of proposed sex and age discrimination class action into liability and damages phases would further complicate manageability problems because, under Seventh Amendment, jury that hears evidence in liability phase might also be required to hear evidence in damages phases); Miller v. Hygrade Food Prods. Corp., 198 F.R.D. 638, 644, 84 FEP 1755, 1760 (E.D. Pa. 2001) ("this Court would run afoul of the single jury requirement of the Seventh Amendment if it were to bifurcate issues to separate juries"); Burrell v. Crown Cent. Petroleum, Inc., 197 F.R.D. 284, 292 (E.D. Tex. 2000) (finding that plaintiffs' trial plan to bifurcate classwide liability and punitive damages phase from compensatory damages phase in race class action does not solve certification shortcomings because "it would be difficult to avoid violating the Seventh Amendment"); Ramirez v. DeCoster, 194 F.R.D. 348, 354 n.4, 84 FEP 45, 50 n.4 (D. Me. 2000) (questioning viability of bifurcation of § 1981 class action in light of Seventh Amendment's single jury requirement); Faulk v. Home Oil Co., 184 F.R.D. 645, 82 FEP 451 (M.D. Ala. 1999) (following *Allison*'s rejection of bifurcated approach to resolving class claims on Seventh Amendment grounds).

[507]*See, e.g.*, Taylor v. District of Columbia Water & Sewer Auth., 205 F.R.D. 43, 52 (D.D.C. 2002) (Seventh Amendment not obstacle to certification under either Rule 23(b)(2) or (3)); EEOC v. Dial Corp., 156 F. Supp. 2d 926, 958 (N.D. Ill. 2001); Beckmann v. CBS, Inc., 192 F.R.D. 608, 615, 90 FEP 1379 (D. Minn. 2000); Siddiqi v. Regents of Univ. of Cal., 2000 WL 33190435 (N.D. Cal. Sept. 6, 2000) (granting motion to bifurcate issues of equitable relief and individual damages in ADA and Rehabilitation Act class action, finding no substantial overlap of evidence between two phases and thus no impairment of defendants' Seventh Amendment rights); EEOC v. Foster Wheeler Constructors, Inc., 1999 WL 528200, at *3 (N.D. Ill. July 13, 1999) (bifurcating hostile environment class action, reasoning that "a well-constructed bifurcation scheme, used in tandem with clear instructions to the juries, can delineate the roles of the two juries in order to avoid reexamination of any factual issues"); EEOC v. Nebco Evans Distrib., Inc., 1997 U.S. Dist. LEXIS 23111 (D. Neb. June 5, 1997) (bifurcating trial in employment discrimination class action and ordering that damages stage will not immediately follow liability stage, notwithstanding defendant's argument that same jury should hear both phases); Orlowski v. Dominick's Finer Foods, Inc., 172 F.R.D. 370, 375 (N.D. Ill. 1997); Butler v. Home Depot, Inc., 70 FEP 51, 55–56 (N.D. Cal. 1996) (repetitive evidence should not be problem because issues regarding employer's liability for intentional discrimination against class of employees are distinct from issues involving individual class members' entitlement to damages); EEOC v. McDonnell Douglas Corp., 960 F. Supp. 203, 205, 72 FEP 769 (E.D. Mo. 1996) (rejecting notion in ADEA action that bifurcated trial would violate defendant's Seventh Amendment rights, reasoning that "the issues to be decided at the separate trials are wholly distinct"); Morgan v. United Parcel Serv. of Am., Inc., 169 F.R.D. 349, 356, 77 FEP 165 (E.D. Mo. 1996) (bifurcating trial and severing liability and injunctive relief from damages phase, certifying first phase under Rule 23(b)(2), and stating that "[i]f liability is established, then the Court will consider certifying the damages phase as a Rule

The Supreme Court has concluded, in a nonemployment case, that a jury's determination of punitive damages is not a finding of fact and does not implicate the Seventh Amendment.[508]

Regardless of whether a jury determines liability and the same or a different jury determines class members' *compensatory damages* claims,[509] a bench determination of class members' *back-pay* claims is desirable. Such determination would avoid the dangers of repetitive evidence and inconsistent adjudication because the court has heard the same evidence as the liability jury and will be hearing the same damages evidence as that of the compensatory damages jury. The court can apply any jury determinations of common facts, such as the existence of a violation as to a particular class member, and can also hear by itself whatever additional evidence is required solely for purposes of back pay. Separation of the § 706(g) award of equitable relief (including back pay) from the § 1981a award of damages also is desirable to enhance the administrability of § 1981a's caps on damages.[510]

2. Use of Special Masters

Because of their complexity, determinations of monetary relief in class actions often are made by special masters appointed

---

23(b)(3) class action"); *see also* Bates v. United Parcel Serv., 204 F.R.D. 440, 448–49 (N.D. Cal. 2001) (bifurcating ADA employment class action into liability and damages phases); Arnold v. United Artists Theatre Circuit, Inc., 158 F.R.D. 439, 459 (N.D. Cal. 1994) (bifurcating ADA Title III accessibility class action into liability and damages phases).

[508]Cooper Indus. v. Leatherman Tool Group, Inc., 532 U.S. 424, 437 (2001).

[509]In which proceedings punitive damages claims should be tried is a matter of debate. At least one court determined that punitive damages are an issue of classwide concern because their purpose is deterrence, not individual compensation. Therefore, the district court in *Barefield v. Chevron, U.S.A., Inc.*, 48 FEP 907, 911–12 (N.D. Cal. 1988), bifurcated the trial; the Stage I trial (certified as a Rule 23(b)(2) class action) was to determine classwide liability and what, if any, punitive damages to assess, and the Stage II trial, if necessary, was to be certified under Rule 23(b)(3) to determine individual monetary damages claims. The same procedure was adopted by the same court in *Butler*, 70 FEP at 56. More recently, the same district court concluded that "if punitive damages are at issue, plaintiffs also must prove liability for such damages [in the Stage I liability proceeding] by showing that the pattern or practice of discrimination was undertaken maliciously or recklessly in the face of a perceived risk that defendant's actions would not violate federal law." Dukes v. Wal-Mart Stores, Inc., 222 F.R.D. 137, 173, 93 FEP 1629 (N.D. Cal. 2004); *see also* Section IV.D *supra*.

[510]*See generally* Chapter 40 (Monetary Relief).

by the court.[511] The use of such masters expressly is authorized by § 706(f)(5) if the case has not been scheduled for trial within 120 days after the issue of § 706 relief has been joined[512]—that is to say, in virtually every case—and by Rule 53(b) of the Federal Rules of Civil Procedure.

In 2003, Rule 53 was substantially revised.[513] Appointment of a special master is limited to matters consented to by the parties, nonjury trial matters, and pretrial and post-trial matters.[514] The district court must give the parties notice and an opportunity to be heard before appointing a master.[515] The order of appointment must specifically address the duties of the special master, including any limits on authority, the circumstances—if any—in which ex parte communications may be made, time limits, the record, and the master's compensation.[516] The court will review the master's findings of fact and conclusions of law de novo.[517] Revised Rule 53 also sets standards for the payment and allocation of the special master's compensation.[518]

---

[511]*See* Berger v. Iron Workers Local 201, 170 F.3d 1111, 1117, 79 FEP 1018 (D.C. Cir. 1999) (per curiam) (referring race discrimination class action to special master to conduct proceedings to calculate back pay and to determine whether class members entitled to compensatory and punitive damages); Jenson v. Eveleth Taconite Co., 130 F.3d 1287, 1290, 75 FEP 852 (8th Cir. 1997) (referring sex discrimination class action to special master to determine compensatory and punitive damages awards); EEOC v. Sheet Metal Workers Local 638, 2001 WL 66327 (S.D.N.Y. Jan. 26, 2001) (referring discrimination class action to special master to determine eligibility for back pay); Kraszewski v. State Farm Gen. Ins. Co., 912 F.2d 1182, 1183 (9th Cir. 1990) (seven special masters used); Chisholm v. United States Postal Serv., 665 F.2d 482, 488, 498, 27 FEP 425 (4th Cir. 1981); Stewart v. General Motors Corp., 542 F.2d 445, 454, 13 FEP 1035 (7th Cir. 1976); Hairston v. McLean Trucking Co., 520 F.2d 226, 233, 11 FEP 91 (4th Cir. 1975); Meadows v. Ford Motor Co., 510 F.2d 939, 948, 9 FEP 180 (6th Cir. 1975); Trout v. Ball, 705 F. Supp. 705, 707, 49 FEP 150 (D.D.C. 1989); Kyriazi v. Western Elec. Co., 465 F. Supp. 1141, 1146–47, 26 FEP 398 (D.N.J. 1979), *aff'd*, 647 F.2d 388, 33 FEP 1147 (3d Cir. 1981).

[512]42 U.S.C. § 2000e-5(f)(5) (2000).

[513]FED. R. CIV. P. 53.

[514]*Id.* at 53(a)(1).

[515]*Id.* at 53(b)(1).

[516]*Id.* at 53(b)(2).

[517]*Id.* at 53(g)(3), (4). The parties may, however, stipulate that the findings of fact are final or to review the findings of fact for clear error instead. *Id.* at 53(g)(3)(A), (B).

[518]*Id.* at 53(h); *see also* Brock v. Ing, 827 F.2d 1426, 1428, 28 WH 566 (10th Cir. 1987) (Rule 53(a) permits but not does not require court to divide expenses of master between parties, and fairness may suggest one party should bear that expense; district court abused its discretion by requiring Secretary of Labor to pay half, instead

3. Claim Forms

Where a *Teamsters* hearing process is contemplated prior to the commencement of Stage II proceedings, the court will order that notice under Rule 23(d)(2) be sent to all class members. The notice typically will require those who believe that they have suffered a monetary loss through discrimination to file a proof-of-claim form within a specified time as a condition to being considered for monetary relief.[519] Similarly, proof-of-claim forms are often used to determine class participation, individual awards after settlement, and other similar individual issues.[520] The language of the notice should be clear and informative.[521] The court further may order that the defendant's records and assistance be made available

---

of requiring defendant, which had violated FLSA, as "wrong doer" to pay it all); Hairston v. McLean Trucking Co., 520 F.2d 226, 233, 11 FEP 91 (4th Cir. 1975) (discriminating employer is to bear costs of master).

[519]*See, e.g.,* Kyriazi v. Western Elec. Co., 647 F.2d 388, 395, 33 FEP 1147 (3d Cir. 1981) (upholding requirement that proof-of-claim forms be filed; "once liability against the defendant has been found, some appropriate notice must be given to the class members of their opportunity to obtain individual relief"); Sledge v. J.P. Stevens & Co., 585 F.2d 625, 652, 18 FEP 261 (4th Cir. 1978) ("In view of the large number of persons who qualify for membership in the class, an unknown portion of whom also qualify for individual relief, we find the filing proviso to be an appropriate first step toward the eventual assessment and resolution of the compensation claims."); Robinson v. Union Carbide Corp., 544 F.2d 1258, 1261, 14 FEP 266 (5th Cir. 1977) (in some class actions some affirmative action by class members is necessary as condition of recovery). The proof-of-claim requirement for sharing in class relief usually results in a substantial reduction in the number of class members sharing in the relief because "apathy, ignorance, burdensomeness, size of individual recovery involved, as well as myriad other factors will affect each claimant's decision whether or not to file such a response." NEWBERG ON CLASS ACTIONS (3d ed. 1992) at § 8:35, 8-114 to 8-115 (footnote omitted).

[520]*E.g.,* Eubanks v. Billington, 110 F.3d 87, 91 (D.C. Cir. 1997); Thornton v. Gayger's Montgomery Fair Co., 2000 WL 1785307, at *3 (M.D. Ala. Nov. 3, 2000); Wilkerson v. Martin Marietta Corp., 171 F.R.D. 273, 279 (D. Colo. 1997).

[521]*See* Mullane v. Central Hanover Bank & Trust Co., 339 U.S. 306, 315 (1950) ("The means employed must be such as one desirous of actually informing the absentee might reasonably adopt to accomplish it."; judicial settlement accounts case); *Kyriazi,* 647 F.2d at 395 ("Moreover, to satisfy due process, the notice, like any other affecting substantial rights, must be sufficiently informative and give sufficient opportunity for response, to satisfy due process."); *cf. Robinson,* 544 F.2d at 1261 ("While not necessarily erroneous, the language of the [notice] is not especially informative as to what relief was available to the class members. The district court should inform class members that back pay is included among possible types of relief."). *See generally* 2 NEWBERG ON CLASS ACTIONS (3d ed. 1992) at § 8:39, 8-122 ("Clarity and objectivity are of primary importance.").

for the purpose of making such claims.[522] Class members who do not respond in a timely fashion have been held barred from any back-pay relief,[523] although the court may exercise its discretion to waive the deadline for those who show good cause.[524] Because the requirement of proof-of-claim forms effectively is a type of "opt-in" requirement, completion of the forms should not be required before the determination of liability or preliminary approval of a settlement.[525]

IX. SETTLEMENT

A. Introduction

Courts strongly encourage settlement of Title VII disputes because voluntary compliance by the private parties contributes significantly to the ultimate achievement of Title VII's goals.[526] This

---

[522]Pettway v. American Cast Iron Pipe Co., 494 F.2d 211, 260, 7 FEP 1115 (5th Cir. 1974) ("The employer's records, as well as the employer's aid, would be made available to the plaintiffs for this purpose.").

[523]See, e.g., Bing v. Roadway Express, Inc., 485 F.2d 441, 449, 6 FEP 677 (5th Cir. 1973) (30-day deadline reasonable; "If an employee 'sleeps on his rights' the court is well within the bounds of its equitable discretion if it declines to extend relief.").

[524]See, e.g., Kyriazi, 647 F.2d at 396 (upholding constitutionality of claim-filing requirement where district court twice had given nonfiling class members opportunity to show good cause for their failure to file).

[525]Robinson, 544 F.2d at 1261 ("Although there may be some Title VII actions in which unnamed individual plaintiffs will have to come forward to establish their entitlement to portions of the recovery, such requirement should not be imposed upon them until *necessary* for adjudication. . . . [W]e cannot believe that [Rule 23(d)(2)] was intended to negate the clear thrust of the rule which is to minimize the requirement of active intervention by numerous members of an affected class.") (emphasis in original); see also 7B CHARLES A. WRIGHT ET AL., FEDERAL PRACTICE & PROCEDURE § 1787, at 216–17 (1986) ("[T]his additional requirement, which has the effect of obliging absent class members to opt-in, is directly contrary to the philosophy of Rule 23(c)(2). . . . On the other hand, once defendant's liability is established, the court may be justified in ordering a second notice sent pursuant to Rule 23(d)(2) requiring class members to file statements of their claims and barring those not presented at that time.") (footnote omitted).

[526]See, e.g., Carson v. American Brands, Inc., 450 U.S. 79, 88 n.14 (1981) ("In enacting Title VII, Congress expressed a strong preference for encouraging voluntary settlement of employment discrimination claims."). See generally Chapter 43 (Settlement).

is also true with respect to class actions. Under Rule 23(e), however, class actions may be settled only with the approval of the
district court and after notice of the proposed settlement to class
members.[527] Revisions to Rule 23(e) in 2003 introduced important
new procedures for the settlement of class actions. The Advisory
Committee's notes to revised Rule 23(e) underscore that "court
review and approval are essential to assure adequate representation of class members who have not participated in shaping the
settlement."[528]

B. Procedure for Approval of Class Settlements

Revised Rule 23(e)(1) clarifies that settlement approval and
class notice are only required for settlement or voluntary dismissal
of cases where there is a certified class or the proposed settlement
would otherwise bind class members.[529]

The Class Action Fairness Act of 2005 (CAFA), enacted February 18, 2005, amended the federal class action rules to require
defendants in all "interstate class actions" commenced on or after
the date of enactment that are filed in or removed to federal court
to provide notice of the proposed class settlement to "appropriate" federal and state governmental officials (such as the Attorney
General of the United States, and the state attorney general or the
"person in the State who has the primary regulatory or supervisory responsibility with respect to the defendant") within 10 days
of the date that the proposed settlement is filed with the court.[530]
The notice must include the complaint, notice of any scheduled
judicial hearing, the proposed notice to the class, the proposed
settlement agreement, any proposed side agreements, any final

---

[527]FED. R. CIV. P. 23(e).

[528]*Id.* at 23(e) advisory committee's note; *see* Officers for Justice v. Civil Serv.
Comm'n, 688 F.2d 615, 622, 29 FEP 1473 (9th Cir. 1982).

[529]FED. R. CIV. P. 23(e)(1)(A), (e)(1)(B). Ambiguity in the prior version of the
rule arguably required approval and notice for settlements that were limited to the
individual claims of the putative class representatives. *See id.* at advisory committee's
notes.

[530]Class Action Fairness Act of 2005 (CAFA), §§ 3(a), (b), & 9, 28 U.S.C.
§ 1715(a), (b). The CAFA also substantially expands federal diversity and removal
jurisdiction over interstate class actions that formerly were litigated in state court.
A full discussion of the impact of CAFA is beyond the scope of this chapter.

judgment or notice of dismissal, and any written judicial opinion relating to these materials. If feasible, the notice must also provide each appropriate state official with the names of class members who reside in the state and the members' estimated proportionate share of the claims.[531] In cases governed by CAFA, the court may not grant final settlement approval until at least 90 days after all appropriate federal and state officials have been served with the required notice.[532]

Rule 23(e), as revised, expressly requires that district courts direct notice in a reasonable manner to all class members of the settlement and hold a hearing on settlement fairness.[533] Typically, settlement approval is a two-step process. First, the court will make an initial determination that the settlement appears to be the result of good faith and arm's-length negotiations and to be fair, reasonable, and adequate.[534] This requires the court to preliminarily evaluate the fairness of the settlement. If the court determines that the settlement is within the range of possible approval, the court will then direct that notice be sent to class members informing them of the specific terms of the proposed settlement and that they may attend a hearing in person or submit written comments in favor of or in opposition to the proposed settlement.[535] Notice will also be sent to persons whose rights may be affected by the settlement.[536] Finally, the court will hold a fairness hearing to hear directly from proponents and opponents of the settlement.[537]

New Rule 23(e)(4) codifies that any class member may object to a proposed class settlement or binding voluntary dismissal.[538] Courts normally will make objections part of the record and afford

---

[531]*Id.*

[532]*Id.* § 3(d), 28 U.S.C. § 1715(d).

[533]FED. R. CIV. P. 23(e)(1)(B), (e)(1)(C).

[534]MANUAL FOR COMPLEX LITIGATION (FOURTH) § 21.632 (2004).

[535]*Id.*

[536]42 U.S.C. § 2000e-2(n)(1)(B) (2000). The Civil Rights Act of 1991 contains provisions that protect consent decrees from collateral attack. Therefore, settling parties and courts are going to even greater lengths to ensure that all interested parties are informed of the settlement. See the discussion at Section IX.G *infra.*

[537]MANUAL FOR COMPLEX LITIGATION (FOURTH) § 21.634 (2004).

[538]FED. R. CIV. P. 23(e)(4)(A) ("Any class member may object to a proposed settlement, voluntary dismissal, or compromise that requires court approval under Rule 23(e)(1)(C).").

objectors an opportunity to be heard at the fairness hearing.[539] Significantly, a class member may only withdraw an objection *with* court approval.[540] This new requirement gives the district court greater supervisory control to prevent the use of objections to obstruct or delay a settlement.[541]

Rule 23(e) now includes a provision that requires counsel to disclose to the court any side agreement made in connection with the proposed settlement agreement that may not expressly appear in the settlement agreement.[542]

C. Legal Standard of Review of Class Settlements

The district court may only approve a class settlement after a hearing and upon finding that the proposed settlement is "fair, reasonable, and adequate":[543]

> Fairness calls for a comparative analysis of the treatment of class members vis-à-vis each other and vis-à-vis similar individuals with similar claims who are not in the class. Reasonableness depends on an analysis of the class allegations and claims and the responsiveness of the settlement to those claims. Adequacy of settlement involves a comparison of the relief granted relative to what class members might have obtained without using the class action process.[544]

There is an initial presumption of fairness where the settlement has been arrived at by arm's-length bargaining, sufficient discovery has been conducted, the proponents of the settlement are experienced in similar litigation, and the number of objectors is relatively few.[545] The burden of persuasion that the proposed settlement

---

[539]*See, e.g.*, Mandujano v. Basic Vegetable Prod., Inc., 541 F.2d 832, 835–37, 13 FEP 694 (9th Cir. 1976) (trial court must hold hearing to consider "substantial" objections, allow objectors to be represented by counsel, and provide reasoned responses to objections on record); *accord* Pettway v. American Cast Iron Pipe Co., 576 F.2d 1157, 1218–19, 17 FEP 1712 (5th Cir. 1978).

[540]FED. R. CIV. P. 23(e)(4)(B) ("An objector may withdraw objections made under Rule 23(e)(4)(A) only with the court's approval.").

[541]*Id.* at 23(e)(4)(B) advisory committee's note.

[542]*Id.* at 23(e)(3).

[543]*Id.* at 23(e)(1)(C); MANUAL FOR COMPLEX LITIGATION (FOURTH) §§ 21.634–.635 (2004).

[544]MANUAL FOR COMPLEX LITIGATION (FOURTH) § 21.62 (2004). Judicial review of the proposed class settlement "must be exacting and thorough." *Id.* at §21.61.

[545]NEWBERG ON CLASS ACTIONS (4th ed. 2002) at § 11.41.

is fair, adequate, and reasonable is on the proponents of the settlement.[546] Among the factors relevant to the court's settlement review are (1) the strength of the plaintiffs' case; (2) the estimated length, complexity, and expense of the litigation; (3) the extent of discovery conducted; (4) the past history of negotiations and the circumstances surrounding the present settlement; (5) any suggestion of collusion; (6) the experience of counsel involved and whether they approve of the settlement; (7) the approval of the EEOC, if available; and (8) the attitude of members of the class, as expressed directly or by failure to object after notice of settlement has been sent.[547] This list is not exclusive and other factors may be appropriate in different circumstances.[548]

The relative importance to be attached to any particular factor depends on the circumstances of each case.[549] It is not necessary for the court to make a final determination of liability or damages, or to determine whether a better settlement might have been negotiated; rather, the court's proper role is only to determine whether the proposed settlement is fair, adequate, and reasonable.[550] Opposition by a significant number of class members will not necessarily prevent a court from approving a settlement as long as the settlement is otherwise fair, adequate, and reasonable.[551]

---

[546]MANUAL FOR COMPLEX LITIGATION (FOURTH) § 21.631 (2004).

[547]*See In re* Prudential Ins. Co. Am. Sales Practice Litig. Agent Actions, 148 F.3d 283, 316–24 (3d Cir. 1998) (cited with approval by advisory committee's notes to 2003 revision of Rule 23(e)); Torrisi v. Tucson Elec. Power Co., 8 F.3d 1370, 1374 (9th Cir. 1993); Franks v. Kroger Co., 670 F.2d 71, 72, 27 FEP 1433 (6th Cir. 1982); Cotton v. Hinton, 559 F.2d 1326, 1330–31 (5th Cir. 1977); *see also* MANUAL FOR COMPLEX LITIGATION (FOURTH) § 21.62 (2003) (additional factors noted).

[548]*Torrisi*, 8 F.3d at 1375.

[549]Officers for Justice v. Civil Serv. Comm'n, 688 F.2d 615, 625, 29 FEP 1473 (9th Cir. 1982); *see also* MANUAL FOR COMPLEX LITIGATION (FOURTH) § 21.62 (2004).

[550]Hanlon v. Chrysler Corp., 150 F.3d 1011, 1027 (9th Cir. 1998) (question is not whether "final product could be prettier, smarter or snazzier but whether it is fair, adequate and free from collusion").

[551]*See* Grant v. Bethlehem Steel Corp., 23 F.2d 20, 23–24, 44 FEP 250 (2d Cir. 1987) (of 126 class members, 45 objected to proposed settlement and nothing was heard from rest); Anderson v. Torrington Co., 755 F. Supp. 834, 844–45 (N.D. Ind. 1991) (extent of opposition generally is not entitled to great weight in determining fairness); *see also* Elliott v. Sperry Rand Corp., 680 F.2d 1225, 29 FEP 1281 (8th Cir. 1982) (790 class members out of 3000 objected); Parker v. Anderson, 667 F.2d 1204, 1207–08, 28 FEP 788 (5th Cir. 1982) (10 out of 11 named plaintiffs, as well as several unnamed class members, objected); *Cotton*, 559 F.2d at 1331 (50% of actively employed class objected); Bryan v. Pittsburgh Plate Glass Co., 494 F.2d 799, 803, 7 FEP 822 (3d Cir. 1974) (settlement approved despite opposition of more

If a settlement contains any provisions for affirmative action, courts must consider whether they are legal under the Fourteenth Amendment and Title VII.[552] To grant affirmative action relief, the court must determine that remedial action is justified based on the facts of the case and that the remedy proposed is narrowly tailored to the violation that exists. In the case of race-based affirmative action, there must be a compelling interest for the adoption of the remedy.[553] Courts have indicated that a remedy based on inclusion (e.g., attracting more qualified female or minority applicants through recruitment and other techniques) as opposed to one based on exclusion (i.e., selecting some candidates rather than others from a pool) is more likely to be acceptable.[554]

The 2003 revision to Rule 23(e) includes a provision permitting the district court or the parties by agreement to provide for a second opportunity for class members to elect exclusion from (i.e., opt out of) the class in Rule 23(b)(3) cases.[555] The Advisory Committee's notes outline some of the factors the district court should consider in exercising its discretion to order a second opt-out opportunity.[556] If the court determines that affording a second opt-out opportunity is appropriate, it should be incorporated into the settlement class notice.[557]

The district court is limited to approving or disapproving a proposed settlement; it cannot rewrite the agreement.[558] Both approval

---

than 20% of class); Boyd v. Bechtel Corp., 485 F. Supp. 610, 624, 20 FEP 944 (N.D. Cal. 1979) (settlement approved over objections of 16% of class); League of Martin v. City of Milwaukee, 588 F. Supp. 1004, 42 FEP 562 (E.D. Wis. 1984) (over 50% of class objected to all or part of agreement).

[552]*See* Shuford v. Alabama State Bd. of Educ., 897 F. Supp. 1535, 1550 (M.D. Ala. 1995) ("[u]nder the equal protection clause, the court must apply strict scrutiny to the race-conscious relief in the decree. . . . Sex-conscious relief, however, is subject to intermediate scrutiny"); *see also In re* Birmingham Reverse Discrimination Employment Litig., 20 F.3d 1525, 64 FEP 1032 (11th Cir. 1994).

[553]*See, e.g., Birmingham Reverse Discrimination*, 20 F.3d at 1544; Chicago Fire Fighters v. City of Chi., 1999 U.S. Dist. LEXIS 20310 (N.D. Ill. Dec. 30, 1999) (finding defendant city's affirmative action plan narrowly tailored to remediate lingering effects of past discrimination).

[554]*See Shuford*, 897 F. Supp. at 1551.

[555]Rule 23(e)(3) provides: "In an action previously certified as a class action under Rule 23(b)(3), the Rule 23(e)(1)(B) notice may state terms that afford individual class members a second opportunity to elect exclusion from the class."

[556]*See* FED. R. CIV. P. 23(e)(3) advisory committee's notes.

[557]*See id.* at 23(e)(3).

[558]MANUAL FOR COMPLEX LITIGATION (FOURTH) § 21.61 (2004).

and denial of approval of a class action settlement are appealable orders.[559] The standard of appellate review is whether there is a clear abuse of discretion by the district court.[560]

D. Review of Precertification Class Settlements

Where the district court is presented with a proposed class settlement *before* class certification has been resolved, the court must make two separate inquiries.[561] First, the court must determine whether the proposed settlement class meets the certification requirements of Rule 23(a) and 23(b). If it does, the court must then consider whether the settlement is fair, adequate, and reasonable under Rule 23(e).[562]

In *Amchem Products, Inc. v. Windsor*,[563] the Supreme Court addressed "the role settlement may play . . . in determining the propriety of class certification" in settlement-only classes.[564] The Court made clear that a district court may not certify for settlement purposes a class that it could not certify for litigation. Moreover, the Court explained that the class members' shared interest in receiving prompt compensation by settlement is not in itself sufficient to satisfy Rule 23(b)(3)'s requirement that common questions of law and fact predominate. A key exception, however, is that the existence of the settlement is relevant to class certification because it alleviates the need for the Rule 23(b)(3) inquiry about the manageability of a future trial.[565]

Since *Amchem*, numerous circuits have adopted a heightened standard of Rule 23(e) review for precertification settlements. In *Hanlon v. Chrysler Corp.*,[566] the Ninth Circuit explained:

---

[559]*See* Devlin v. Scardelletti, 536 U.S. 1, 14 (2002) (non-named plaintiff who timely objects at fairness hearing entitled to appeal approval of settlement without intervening); Carson v. American Brands, Inc., 450 U.S. 79, 82 n.6 (1981) (order refusing to approve consent decree appealable as interlocutory order).

[560]*See, e.g.*, Molski v. Gleich, 327 F.3d 938, 953 (9th Cir. 2003); Bailey v. Great Lakes Canning Co., 908 F.2d 38, 42, 59 FEP 1647 (6th Cir. 1990).

[561]Hanlon v. Chrysler Corp., 150 F.3d 1011, 1023–24 (9th Cir. 1998) ("*Amchem* cautioned against conflating the class certification requirements of [Rule 23(a) and (b)] into the 'fair, adequate and reasonable' preconditions [under Rule 23(e)]").

[562]Amchem Prods. v. Windsor, 521 U.S. 591, 617–23 (1997).

[563]521 U.S. 591 (1997).

[564]*Id.* at 619.

[565]*Id.* at 620.

[566]150 F.3d 1011 (9th Cir. 1998).

Several circuits have held that settlement approval that takes place prior to formal class certification requires a higher standard of fairness. The dangers of collusion between class counsel and the defendant, as well as the need for additional protections when the settlement is not negotiated by a court-designated class representative, weigh in favor of a more probing inquiry than may normally be required under Rule 23(e) . . . . Because settlement class actions present unique due process concerns for absent class members, we agree with our sister circuits and adopt this standard as our own.[567]

Applying this heightened scrutiny, the Ninth Circuit reversed approval of proposed precertification class settlements in two civil rights class actions.[568]

One significant issue in determining the fairness of precertification settlements is whether the class members are afforded a right to opt out. If the settlement releases significant monetary damages, the Supreme Court's decision in *Ortiz v. Fibreboard Corp.*[569] strongly suggests that a right to opt out must be afforded.[570]

E. Approval of Attorney's Fees

The 2003 revisions of Rule 23 significantly changed the procedure for approving attorney's fees to be awarded in connection with the settlement of a class action.[571] The revision added new section

---

[567]*Id.* at 1026; *accord In re* General Motors Pick-Up Truck Fuel Tank Prods. Liab. Litig., 55 F.3d 768, 805 (3d Cir. 1995); Mars Steel Corp. v. Continental Ill. Nat'l Bank & Trust, 834 F.2d 677, 681 (7th Cir. 1987); Weinberger v. Kendrick, 698 F.2d 61, 73 (2d Cir. 1982).

[568]Staton v. Boeing Co., 327 F.3d 938, 978 (9th Cir. 2003) (settlement approval reversed because attorney's fees were improperly calculated and certain class members were given disproportionate benefits); Molski v. Gleich, 318 F.3d 937, 953 (9th Cir. 2003) (certification and settlement rejected because substantial damages were released without proper notice or right to opt out nor adequate consideration).

[569]527 U.S. 815 (1999).

[570]In *Ortiz*, the Supreme Court vacated the lower court's approval of a limited fund settlement involving damages claims for asbestos exposure where class members were not provided the option of opting out of the class. The Court held that the elements of Rule 23(b)(1)(B) must be established before a class settlement of damages claims in a limited fund case may be certified without the right to opt out. Where a Title VII class settlement resolves claims for compensatory and punitive damages, it may be difficult after *Ortiz* to settle employment discrimination claims on a classwide basis unless class members are given the right to opt out. *See Molski*, 318 F.3d at 953. *But see* Thomas v. Albright, 139 F.3d 227 (D.C. Cir. 1998) (certification under Rule 23(b)(2) for settlement purposes only without opt-out right approved).

[571]FED. R. CIV. P. 23.

Rule 23(h), which requires that a motion for attorney's fees must be made pursuant to Rule 54(b)(2) of the Federal Rules of Civil Procedure, and fees can be awarded only after notice to the class.[572]

In the past, the parties to a class settlement would negotiate the amount of attorney's fees to be paid to class counsel and simply include it as one term in the settlement. The court was limited to considering the attorney's fees provision as part of the overall fairness of the settlement and was constrained to either approving or disapproving of the settlement in its entirety.[573] The current procedure ensures that the settlement is separately evaluated from the attorney's fees, and the court has flexibility to increase or decrease the amount proposed by the parties. As the Advisory Committee recognized, "[a]ctive judicial involvement in measuring fee awards is singularly important to the healthy operation of the class-action process."[574]

F. Incentive Awards and Distribution of Settlement Proceeds

The distribution of settlement proceeds among class members is subject to the same fairness scrutiny as the settlement agreement itself. Some courts have approved class settlements providing greater monetary amounts (often called incentive awards) to named plaintiffs than to other class members;[575] other courts have

---

[572]Rule 23(h) provides:

A claim for an award of attorney fees and nontaxable costs must be made by motion under rule 54(d)(2), subject to the provisions of this subdivision, at a time set by the court. Notice of the motion must be served on all parties and, for motions by class counsel, directed to class members in a reasonable manner.

[573]See Hanlon v. Chrysler, 150 F.3d 1011, 1026 (9th Cir. 1998) ("Neither the district court nor this court ha[s] the ability to 'delete, modify or substitute certain provisions.' The settlement must stand or fall in its entirety.") (citations omitted).

[574]FED. R. CIV. P. 23(h) advisory committee's notes. The notes for Rule 23(h) are extensive and very informative. See also Staton v. Boeing Co., 327 F.3d 938, 966, 974 (9th Cir. 2003) (in case that preceded revision to Rule 23, court reversed approval of class action settlement; in common fund approach to fees, the court must have discretion to set the fee, and value of injunctive relief should be included in common fund calculation only in the "unusual instance where the value to individual class members . . . can be accurately ascertained"). See generally Chapter 41 (Attorney's Fees).

[575]See, e.g., Ingram v. Coca-Cola, 200 F.R.D. 694 (N.D. Ga. 2001) (court approves payments of $300,000 for each class representative where funds over $100 million created, with average class member payout of approximately $38,000); Roberts v. Texaco, 979 F. Supp. 185, 204 (S.D.N.Y 1997) (court awards incentive payments

not.[576] There is no clear standard by which courts evaluate and approve named plaintiffs awards. In *Cook v. Niedert*,[577] the Seventh Circuit articulated some relevant considerations:

> Because a named plaintiff is an essential ingredient of any class action, an incentive award is appropriate if it is necessary to induce an individual to participate in the suit. . . . In deciding whether such an award is warranted, relevant factors include the actions the plaintiff has taken to protect the interests of the class, the degree to which the class has benefited from those actions, and the amount of time and effort the plaintiff expended in pursuing the litigation.[578]

Where awards of individualized relief to named plaintiffs are permitted, they are often justified on the basis that class representatives take on risks and perform services that are not required of the other

---

ranging from $2,500 to $85,000 where range of payments to class members was $60,000 to $80,000 and common fund totaled $115 million); Huguley v. General Motors Corp., 128 F.R.D. 81, 85, 52 FEP 1885 (E.D. Mich. 1989) (settlement provided specific monetary relief to named plaintiffs), *aff'd mem.*, 925 F.2d 1464 (6th Cir. 1991); United States v. City & County of San Francisco, 696 F. Supp. 1287, 1299–1300, 1311, 51 FEP 1500 (N.D. Cal. 1988) (consent decree provided certain named plaintiffs with promotions and implemented classwide affirmative action goals), *aff'd*, 890 F.2d 1438, 51 FEP 1542 (9th Cir. 1989); Green v. Battery Park City Auth., 44 FEP 623, 625, 627 (S.D.N.Y. 1987) (settlement provided class with injunctive and monetary relief and each named plaintiff with additional sum from separate fund).

[576]*See, e.g.*, Sheppard v. Consolidated Edison Co., 2000 U.S. Dist. LEXIS 20629, at *19–21 (E.D.N.Y. Dec. 21, 2000) (rejecting settlement where named plaintiffs would have received $400,000 each, compared to maximum of $3,502 for other class members); Holmes v. Continental Can Co., 706 F.2d 1144, 1148, 31 FEP 1707 (11th Cir. 1983) (named plaintiffs seeking preferential distribution of settlement proceeds bear heavy burden of proof; allocation of half of settlement proceeds to eight named plaintiffs—while remaining 118 members shared rest—held not justified); Plummer v. Chemical Bank, 97 F.R.D. 486, 488–89, 33 FEP 547 (S.D.N.Y. 1983) (proposed consent decree not approved; no apparent reason existed for providing named plaintiffs with immediate cash payments and guaranteed future benefits while making relief for class members contingent on future promotion or success under grievance procedure); *see also* Women's Comm. for Equal Opportunity v. National Broad. Co., 76 F.R.D. 173 (S.D.N.Y 1977) (expressing "doubts about a general policy of awarding class representatives a settlement on terms different from other class members" but approving awards).

[577]142 F.3d 1004 (7th Cir. 1998).

[578]*Id.* at 1015 (citation omitted); *see also* Van Vranken v. Atlantic Richfield, 901 F. Supp. 294, 300 (N.D. Cal. 1995) (criteria include (1) risk to class representative in commencing suit, both financial and otherwise; (2) notoriety and personal difficulties encountered by class representative; (3) amount of time and effort spent by class representative; (4) duration of litigation; and (5) personal benefit (or lack thereof) enjoyed by class representative as result of litigation).

class members who receive the benefit of those risks and services.[579] In addition, named plaintiffs often are required as part of the settlement of a class action to broadly release all claims against the defendant, of whatsoever nature, as opposed to the more limited release required of other class members of only the claims actually litigated in the suit.[580]

After settlement funds have been distributed to class members who can be identified and located, there are often unclaimed monies remaining in the class compensation fund. Courts have authorized cy pres distributions of these funds to nonprofit groups whose missions are consistent with the underlying purpose of the class action.[581] Other courts have questioned or rejected this approach in favor of a second distribution to class members.[582]

---

[579]See, e.g., Roberts v. Texaco, 979 F. Supp. 185 (S.D.N.Y. 1997) (risk of workplace retaliation relevant factor); Huguley, 128 F.R.D. at 85 ("Named plaintiffs . . . are entitled to more consideration than class members generally because of the onerous burden of litigation that they have borne."); Green v. Battery Park City Auth., 44 FEP 623, 627–28 (S.D.N.Y. 1987) (named plaintiffs received additional award from "Time and Effort Fund" to compensate them for special responsibilities they undertook and time and effort they expended as class representatives, although court found this "[t]he most troublesome aspect of the [settlement a]greement"); League of Martin v. City of Milwaukee, 588 F. Supp. 1004, 1024, 42 FEP 562 (E.D. Wis. 1984) (priority chance at promotion to named plaintiff was proper where that individual filed EEOC charges on which suit is based and was instrumental in prosecution of action); Lo Re v. Chase Manhattan Corp., 19 FEP 1366, 1370–71 (S.D.N.Y. 1979) (payment of $229,000 out of $1.5 million settlement fund to named plaintiffs approved where bulk of settlement funds would benefit class and where named plaintiffs risked their job security and their co-workers' goodwill in initiating suit; "The result of their efforts will confer wide-ranging benefits upon a substantial number of persons.").

[580]See, e.g., Lusardi v. Xerox Corp., 975 F.2d 964, 968 (3d Cir. 1992) (named plaintiffs signed general release, covenant not to sue, and stipulation of confidentiality).

[581]See Six Mexican Workers v. Arizona Citrus Growers, 904 F.2d 1301, 1307 (9th Cir. 1990) ("the district court's choice among distribution options should be guided by the objectives of the underlying statute and the interests of the silent class members"); In re Wells Fargo Sec. Litig., 991 F. Supp. 1193 (N.D. Cal. 1998) (approving distribution to law school securities program instead of bar association); Drennan v. Van Ru Credit Corp., 1997 U.S. Dist. LEXIS 7776 (N.D. Ill. May 30, 1997) (distribution to Mid-Minnesota Legal Assistance Foundation); In re Folding Carton Litig., 934 F.2d 323 (7th Cir. 1991) (over $2 million to National Association for Public Interest Law); Jones v. National Distillers, 56 F. Supp. 2d 355 (S.D.N.Y. 1999) (allowing distribution to Legal Aid Society Civil Division despite "thin" tie to purpose of litigation).

[582]See In re Wells Fargo Sec. Litig., 991 F. Supp. 1193 (N.D. Cal. 1998) (modifying fluid recovery plan to require additional pro rata distribution to class members with shares large enough to justify expense); Weber v. Goodman, 1999 U.S. Dist.

G. Collateral Attack on Consent Decrees

As a general rule, a judgment in a class action will bind all members of the class who do not opt out.[583] The exception to this rule is based on due process considerations. In determining whether a prior consent decree will bar an absent class member from subsequent suit, courts will review whether the class representative in the first action adequately represented the interests of the class members and whether the absent class member had actual or constructive knowledge of the prior suit and settlement.[584]

Following the Supreme Court's *Stotts*[585] decision, challenges were raised to consent decrees that included affirmative action plans on the ground that such plans benefitted persons who were not the actual victims of discrimination. Most courts rejected such challenges[586] and upheld settlement agreements that included affirmative

---

LEXIS 22832 (E.D.N.Y. Jan. 12, 1998) (fluid recovery premature until damage funds fully distributed); Fogie v. Thorn, 190 F.3d 889 (8th Cir. 1999) (same); *see also In re* Matzo Food Prods. Litig., 156 F.R.D. 600 (D.N.J. 1994) (refusing to approve class settlement with only cy pres distribution).

[583]*See* Kemp v. Birmingham News Co., 608 F.2d 1049, 1053, 21 FEP 830 (5th Cir. 1979) ("The main purpose of a class action is to dispose of the claims of numerous parties in one proceeding. If the defendants in class action lawsuits for employment discrimination could not rely on the binding effect of consent decrees they would have no incentive to settle such cases."); Harris v. General Dev. Corp., 126 F.R.D. 537, 538–39, 50 FEP 521 (N.D. Ill. 1989) (class action is res judicata as to all class members).

[584]*Compare* Penson v. Terminal Transp. Co., 634 F.2d 989, 992–93, 26 FEP 828 (5th Cir. 1981) (individual class member's suit not barred by prior judgment in class action where notice of consent decree did not advise him of his agreed-upon right to opt out of settlement) *and* Grigsby v. North Miss. Med. Ctr., Inc., 586 F.2d 457, 461–62, 18 FEP 1225 (5th Cir. 1978) (remanding to determine whether consent decree should be given res judicata effect as to class members in light of possible inadequate representation) *with Kemp*, 608 F.2d at 1054–55 (exception to general rule that judgment in class action binds members of class held not applicable because plaintiff was adequately represented, had actual knowledge, received back-pay award, and actually discussed pending decree with attorney) *and* Frank v. United Airlines, Inc., 216 F.3d 845, 851, 83 FEP 1 (9th Cir. 2000) (holding, inter alia, that judgment in prior class action does not preclude subsequent claims where second class action is based on alleged Title VII violations that arise after date of earlier judgment, even if such secondary claims arise out of continuing conduct that was basis for earlier suit, and second claim is based on employer policy enacted as part of post-judgment settlement in first suit).

[585]Firefighters Local 1784 v. Stotts, 467 U.S. 561, 34 FEP 1702 (1984). *See generally* Chapter 37 ("Reverse" Discrimination and Affirmative Action).

[586]*See, e.g.*, Williams v. City of New Orleans, 729 F.2d 1554, 1557, 34 FEP 1009 (5th Cir. 1984) (en banc) ("According to the government's argument, the last sentence

action plans.[587] The Civil Rights Act of 1991 amended Title VII to provide that no collateral attack may be brought by persons who had actual notice of the order or judgment and an opportunity to object prior to its entry, or who were adequately represented by another person who had challenged the judgment or order on the same legal ground and with a similar factual situation, unless there has been an intervening change in law or fact.[588] Nevertheless, challenges to consent decrees have been permitted on certain narrow grounds.[589] Settling parties and courts must be careful to comply with the provisions of Title VII that protect against collateral attacks.[590]

X. APPEALS

A. Rule 23(f) Appeals of Class Certification Orders

Federal Rule of Civil Procedure 23(f) allows discretionary interlocutory appeal of orders granting or denying class certification:

---

in § 706(g) of Title VII proscribes the use of any remedy which is not limited to actual victims of past discrimination . . . . We cannot accept this *per se* rule; the statute does not so require.").

[587]*E.g.*, Firefighters Local 93 v. City of Cleveland, 478 U.S. 501, 528, 41 FEP 139 (1986) (distinguishing *Stotts*; "Because § 706(g) [of Title VII] is not concerned with voluntary agreements by employers or unions to provide race-conscious relief, there is no inconsistency between it and a consent decree providing . . . the same relief after trial or, as in *Stotts*, in disputed proceedings to modify a decree entered upon consent."); Davis v. City & County of San Francisco, 890 F.2d 1438, 1445, 51 FEP 1542 (9th Cir. 1989) (approving consent decree containing affirmative action provisions). *See generally* Chapters 37 ("Reverse" Discrimination and Affirmative Action) and 39 (Injunctive and Affirmative Relief).

[588]42 U.S.C. § 2000e-2(n) (2000) (changing rules set forth in *Martin v. Wilks*, 490 U.S. 755, 49 FEP 1641 (1989)). A narrow exception exists for circumstances such as fraud or collusion. *Id. See generally* Chapter 37 ("Reverse" Discrimination and Affirmative Action).

[589]*See, e.g., In re* Birmingham Reverse Discrimination Employment Litig., 20 F.3d 1525 (11th Cir. 1994) (holding that § 1981 consent decree mandating that city select employees for promotion based on race could not withstand scrutiny under Title VII or Fourteenth Amendment); Ensley Branch, NAACP v. Seibels, 31 F.3d 1548 (11th Cir. 1994) (remanding case to district court for further modification of consent decree involving city employment practices to address changed circumstances).

[590]*See* Shuford v. Alabama State Bd. of Educ., 897 F. Supp. 1535, 1547 (M.D. Ala. 1995) (citing 42 U.S.C.A. § 2000e-2(n)(1)(B) (West 1994)); *see also* Allen v. Alabama State Bd. of Educ., 190 F.R.D. 602 (M.D. Ala. 2000) (notices of proposed settlement published in major newspapers throughout Alabama and sent to deans of

A court of appeals may in its discretion permit an appeal from an order granting or denying class action certification under this rule if application is made to it within ten days after entry of the order. An appeal does not stay proceedings in the district court unless the district judge or the court of appeals so orders.

Courts may consider "any" persuasive consideration in deciding whether to take the appeal:

> Permission to appeal may be granted or denied on the basis of any consideration that the court of appeals finds persuasive. Permission is most likely to be granted when the certification decision turns on a novel or unsettled question of law, or when, as a practical matter, the decision on certification is likely dispositive of the litigation.[591]

In *Prado-Steiman v. Bush*,[592] the Eleventh Circuit provided an extensive discussion of the standards for granting review in an interlocutory appeal from a class certification order under Rule 23(f):

> First, and most important, the court should examine whether the district court's ruling is likely dispositive of the litigation by creating a "death knell" for either plaintiff or defendant. . . . Second, a court should consider whether the petitioner has shown a *substantial* weakness in the class certification decision, such that the decision likely constitutes an abuse of discretion. . . . Third, a court

---

education of all Alabama colleges that operated teacher education programs and to presidents of all Alabama postsecondary institutions; both class and nonclass members permitted to submit written objections).

[591]FED. R. CIV. P. 23(f) advisory committee's note. Although the language of the advisory committee's note underscores the "unfettered discretion" of the courts to permit appeal, it also suggests that permission be granted only for compelling reasons. The courts have generally turned to the advisory committee's note for guidance in reviewing Rule 23(f) petitions. *See, e.g.*, Prado-Steiman v. Bush, 221 F.3d 1266, 1271 (11th Cir. 2000) (class action by developmentally disabled plaintiffs alleging denial of home- and community-based Medicaid services; "a good starting point is the Committee Note accompanying Rule 23(f), which articulates the drafters' view of how courts should resolve petitions for appeal under this new rule"); Waste Mgmt. Holdings, Inc. v. Mowbray, 208 F.3d 288, 293 (1st Cir. 2000) (class action alleging breach of contractual warranty in asset sale; "[u]sing the underlying purposes of [Rule 23(f)] as a beacon, we chart a middling course"); Blair v. Equifax Check Serv., Inc., 181 F.3d 832, 834 (7th Cir. 1999) (in class action under Fair Debt Collection Practices Act, allowing interlocutory appeal but refusing to vacate class certification; "[i]nstead of inventing standards, we keep in mind the reasons Rule 23(f) came into being").

[592]221 F.3d 1266, 1271 (11th Cir. 2000).

should consider whether the appeal will permit the resolution of an [important] unsettled legal issue [that is of specific and general importance]. . . . Fourth, a court should consider the nature and status of the litigation before the district court [i.e., the posture of the case and existence of an adequate record should influence the decision of whether to grant review]. . . . Finally, a court should consider the likelihood that future events [such as settlement or bankruptcy] may make immediate appellate review more or less appropriate.[593]

In providing guidance on how to weigh each factor for consideration, the Eleventh Circuit noted that "the foregoing list of factors is not intended to be exhaustive" and that "each relevant factor should be balanced against the others, taking into account any unique facts and circumstances."[594] Finally, the court cautioned that appellate courts must closely scrutinize appeals under Rule 23(f) because there are too many class actions filed each year to make routine review practicable.[595]

Most circuit courts have adopted the Eleventh Circuit's approach in *Prado-Steiman* with some variation, either elaborating on the principles set forth in *Prado-Steiman* or combining those factors with categories enumerated in other circuits.[596] The First and Seventh Circuits "allow appeal when a petition raises an unsettled and fundamental question of law, regardless [of] whether the district court likely erred,"[597] although "those same circuits

---

[593]*Id.* at 1274–77.

[594]*Id.* at 1276; *see also In re* Lorazepam & Clorazepate Antitrust Litig., 289 F.3d 98, 104 (D.C. Cir. 2002) ("[T]he second factor serves as a sliding scale; the more questionable the district court's decision, the less the remaining four factors need weigh in. The Eleventh Circuit recognized the possibility that when the district court's certification decision is clearly wrong, Rule 23(f) review 'may be warranted even if none of the other factors supports granting the Rule 23 petition.' " 221 F.3d at 1276 (citations omitted)).

[595]*Prado-Steiman*, 221 F.3d at 1273, 1276–77.

[596]*See In re Lorazepam*, 289 F.3d at 102–06 (antitrust litigation summarizing *Prado-Steiman* analysis and providing extensive discussion of development of Rule 23(f) review among various circuits).

[597]*Id.* at 104; *see Blair*, 181 F.3d at 834–35 (articulating three-pronged categorical approach to determining which cases are appropriate for 23(f) appeal: (1) when denial of class certification effectively ends case ("death knell"), (2) when grant of class status raises stakes of litigation so substantially that defendant likely will be pressured to settle, and (3) when appellate review will lead to clarification of fundamental issue of law; *Mowbray*, 208 F.3d at 293 (restricting *Blair*'s third category to "the resolution of an unsettled legal question that is important to the particular

caution that interlocutory appeal of an unsettled question of law is appropriate only when that question may evade effective appellate review at the end of the trial court proceedings."[598] The Second Circuit has concurred with the standards enumerated in *Blair v. Equifax Check Service, Inc.*,[599] *Waste Management Holdings, Inc. v. Mowbray*,[600] and *Prado-Steiman*, respectively, by adopting the "death knell" and "unsettled question of law" categories.[601] The Third and Fourth Circuits "permit appeal if the district court's decision is erroneous, regardless whether the other factors governing appeal under Rule 23(f) are present."[602] Of the remaining

---

litigation as well as important in itself and likely to escape effective review if left hanging until the end of the case," but leaving open question of what "unsettled" issue is); *see also* Allen v. International Truck & Engine Corp., 358 F.3d 469, 470 (7th Cir. 2004) (in Title VII hostile work environment claim, granting Rule 23(f) petition on grounds that "immediate review would promote the development of the law governing questions that have escaped resolution on appeal from final decisions . . . [and] that the district court committed an error best handled by a swift remand"); Jefferson v. Ingersoll Int'l, Inc., 195 F.3d 894, 81 FEP 170 (7th Cir. 1999) (in Title VII race discrimination class action, granting review of one portion of class certification order because "issue fits the third category of appropriate appeals discussed in *Blair* . . . situations in which the legal question is important, unresolved, and has managed to escape resolution by appeals from final judgments").

[598]*In re Lorazepam*, 289 F.3d at 104; *see also Mowbray*, 208 F.3d at 293; *Blair*, 181 F.3d at 835.

[599]181 F.3d 832.

[600]208 F.3d 288.

[601]*In re* Sumitomo Copper Litig. v. Credit Lyonnais Rouse, Ltd., 262 F.3d 134, 139 (2d Cir. 2001) ("[i]n line with our sister circuits, we hold that petitioners seeking leave to appeal pursuant to Rule 23(f) must demonstrate either (1) that the certification order will effectively terminate the litigation and there has been a substantial showing that the district court's decision is questionable, or (2) that the certification order implicates a legal question about which there is a compelling need for immediate resolution"). *Compare* National Asbestos Workers Med. v. Phillip Morris, 270 F.3d 984 (2d Cir. 2001) (denying, without discussion, interlocutory review of district court's orders denying class certification because "petitioners failed to satisfy the standard enunciated in *Sumitomo*") *with In re* Visa Check/MasterMoney Antitrust Litig., 280 F.3d 124, 132 & n.3 (2d Cir. 2001) (granting review of class certification order on grounds interlocutory appeal was appropriate to resolve uncertainty regarding certain legal questions).

[602]*In re Lorazepam*, 289 F.3d at 104. *Compare* Newton v. Merrill Lynch, Pierce, Fenner & Smith, Inc., 259 F.3d 154, 164 & n.5 (3d Cir. 2001) ("interlocutory review is not cabined by [the] circumstances [articulated in other circuits] . . . if the appellant demonstrates that the ruling on class certification is likely erroneous, 'taking into account the discretion the district judge possesses . . . and the correspondingly deferential standard of appellate review,' interlocutory review may be proper") *and* Lienhart v. Dryvit Sys., Inc., 255 F.3d 138, 145–46 (4th Cir. 2001) ("by adding the

circuits, the Fifth,[603] Sixth,[604] Eighth,[605] and Ninth[606] "have all entertained Rule 23(f) petitions without yet enumerating standards ... [whereas] [t]he Tenth Circuit has yet to publish any opinions in which a Rule 23(f) petition was considered."[607]

---

weakness of the district court's certification decision as an independent factor supporting review and noting that the impact of a question raised in a Rule 23(f) petition on related litigation can favor review, the *Prado-Steiman* court *broadened* the bases for a grant of review") *with Mowbray*, 208 F.3d at 293–94 *and Blair*, 181 F.3d at 834–35.

[603]*See* Bertulli v. Independent Ass'n of Cont'l Pilots, 242 F.3rd 290, 294 & n.11 (5th Cir. 2001) (in granting review of class certification order for abuse of discretion, holding that issue of standing may also be raised on appeal because it is "an inherent prerequisite to the class certification inquiry," but without articulating standards for Rule 23(f) review); Patterson v. Mobil Oil Corp., 241 F.3d 417, 418 (5th Cir. 2001) (certification of bifurcated class in RICO action reviewed on appeal for abuse of discretion); Bolin v. Sears, Roebuck & Co., 231 F.3d 970, 972 (5th Cir. 2000) (upholding constitutionality of "28 U.S.C. § 1292(e), the enabling authority for Rule 23(f), [as a proper] delegation of Congress' power to confer jurisdiction on the lower federal courts").

[604]*See, e.g.*, Reeb v. Ohio Dep't of Rehab. & Corr., 81 Fed. Appx. 550, 553–54 (6th Cir. 2003) (granting appeal of district court's class certification to address "novel and important legal question"); In re Delta Air Lines, 310 F.3d 953, 960 (6th Cir. 2002) (discussing standards for Rule 23(f) review articulated by other circuits), *cert. denied sub nom.* Northwest Airlines Corp. v. Chase, 539 U.S. 904 (2003).

[605]*See, e.g.*, Liles v. Del Campo, 350 F.3d 742, 746 & n.5 (8th Cir. 2003) (denying Rule 23(f) petition, reasoning that facts of case did not favor interlocutory appeal under any other circuit's formulations, but declining to "undertake ... the task of refining a[n Eighth] circuit standard for review of such petitions"); Glover v. Standard Fed. Bank, 283 F.3d 953, 958–59 (8th Cir. 2002) (holding that district court's modification of its class certification order broadening scope of class constituted "class certification" (of newly defined class members) for Rule 23(f) purposes rather than simply clarification (as order was labeled), and thus immediately appealable on grounds of abuse of discretion).

[606]*See, e.g.*, Dukes v. Wal-Mart, Inc., 474 F.3d 1214, 1223 (9th Cir. 2007) (affirming certification of nationwide gender class including managerial and nonmanagerial store employees); Zinser v. Accufix Research Inst., Inc., 253 F.3d 1180, 1186 (9th Cir. 2001) (review of district court's order denying class certification in mass tort action); Smith v. University of Wash. Law Sch., 233 F.3d 1188, 1992 (9th Cir. 2000) (granting review of district court's decertification of class of unsuccessful law school applicants challenging race-conscious admissions program).

[607]*See generally* 7B CHARLES ALAN WRIGHT & ARTHUR R. MILLER, FEDERAL PRACTICE & PROCEDURE § 1802 (2d ed. 2004); Aimee G. Mackay, Comment, *Appealability of Class Certification Orders Under Federal Rule of Civil Procedure 23(f): Toward a Principled Approach*, 96 Nw. U. L. REV. 755, 773–93 (2002) (providing extensive discussion of circuit court standards in reviewing Rule 23(f) petitions); Carey M. Erhard, Note, *A Discussion of the Interlocutory Review of Class Certification Orders Under Federal Rule of Civil Procedure 23(f)*, 51 DRAKE L. REV. 151, 172–73 (2002) (providing extensive examination of standards enumerated by circuit courts in granting Rule 23(f) petitions).

B. Post-Trial Appeals

An appeal of the grant or denial of class certification may also be made after a final judgment on the merits of the case.[608] For example, the Supreme Court has held that a putative class member may intervene for the purpose of appealing the denial of class certification even after the named plaintiffs' claims have been satisfied and judgment has been entered in their favor.[609] The Supreme Court also has held that the named plaintiffs themselves may appeal denial of class certification where a tender was made to them of the amounts claimed in their individual capacities and a judgment was entered on that basis over their objections[610] or after the plaintiffs' substantive claims were mooted due to an occurrence other than a judgment on the merits, as long as the plaintiff continues to have a "personal stake" in the class certification claim.[611] The Supreme Court has not yet decided the circumstances, if any, under which a "headless class" may seek review of a denial of class certification when the individual plaintiffs have gone on to lose their individual claims on the merits.[612]

---

[608]*See* Coopers & Lybrand v. Livesay, 437 U.S. 463, 469, 470–71 (1978) ("an order denying class certification is subject to effective review after final judgment at the behest of the named plaintiff or intervening class members") (citing United Airlines v. McDonald, 432 U.S. 385, 389–90, 14 FEP 1711 (1977)).

[609]United Airlines v. McDonald, 432 U.S. 385, 394–96 & n.15, 14 FEP 1711 (1977).

[610]Deposit Guar. Nat'l Bank v. Roper, 445 U.S. 326, 331–40 (1980) ("[T]o deny the right to appeal simply because the defendant has sought to 'buy off' the individual private claims of the named plaintiffs would be contrary to sound judicial administration . . . would frustrate the objectives of class actions . . . [and] invite waste of judicial resources.").

[611]United States Parole Comm'n v. Geraghty, 445 U.S. 388, 402 (1980).

[612]*See* Satterwhite v. City of Greenville, 445 U.S. 940, 22 FEP 439 (1980) (remanding to Fifth Circuit for consideration of denial of appeal in light of *Roper* and *Geraghty*); Simmons v. Brown, 611 F.2d 65, 67, 26 FEP 447 (4th Cir. 1979) ("headless class" remanded to district court with instructions to retain it on docket for reasonable period of time to permit proper plaintiff with similar grievances to come forward and prosecute action). The Supreme Court ruled that unnamed class members who object in a timely manner to approval of a class action settlement at the fairness hearing have the power to bring an appeal without first intervening. Devlin v. Scardelletti, 536 U.S. 1, 6 (2002) (noting mandatory nature of that class action because petitioner had no ability to opt out of settlement under Rule 23(b)(1)). However, at least one circuit has rejected extending the *Devlin* rationale to an appeal of class certification by a nonnamed plaintiff. Plaintiffs for African Centered Educ. v. School Dist. of Kan. City, 312 F.3d 341, 342–43 (8th Cir. 2002) (affirming district court's refusal to extend scope of *Devlin* in school desegregation case where plaintiffs brought appeal relying solely on *Devlin* and not under Rule 23(f)).

Where the named plaintiffs filed a notice of appeal, purportedly on behalf of themselves and all others similarly situated, but the class aspects of the action had been settled and class members had filed claims in accordance with the settlement, the Eleventh Circuit held that the appeal could encompass only the named plaintiffs, not any class members.[613]

On appeal from the denial of class certification and the trial on the merits of the individual claims, an appellate court will consider the full record, not just the record before the court at the certification hearing.[614] Thus, affirmance of a finding of no *individual* discrimination may prove fatal to the class certification claim because the individual will have no nexus with or membership in the proposed class.[615]

C. Post-Settlement Appeals

Approval of a class settlement may be appealed by an objector. In *Devlin v. Scardelletti*,[616] the Supreme Court held that an order approving a class settlement is immediately appealable where the settlement is approved over the objections of some class members and the order binds those class members to the settlement (such as in a Rule 23(b)(1) class with no opportunity to opt out).[617] An objector has standing to bring the appeal without formally intervening so long as he or she filed a timely objection to the proposed class settlement.[618] Several courts have also considered whether the *Devlin* rule is limited to mandatory class settlements where class members have no option to opt out.[619]

---

[613]Cotton v. U.S. Pipe & Foundry Co., 856 F.2d 158, 161, 47 FEP 1765 (11th Cir. 1988) ("Once members of the affected subclass filed their individual claims, however, those claims were no longer class claims. Rather, they were purely individual claims for back pay based on the individual facts of each person's employment. [Plaintiffs] cannot represent the interests of these employees in this appeal.").

[614]Everitt v. City of Marshall, 703 F.2d 207, 210, 31 FEP 985 (5th Cir. 1983).

[615]*Id.; accord* Walker v. Jim Dandy Co., 747 F.2d 1360, 1364, 36 FEP 928 (11th Cir. 1984) (affirming denial of class certification where individual claim was adjudicated as meritless).

[616]536 U.S. 1 (2002).

[617]*Id.* at 3, 9 ("[t]he District Court's approval of the settlement—which binds petitioner as a member of the class—amounted to a 'final decision of [petitioner's] right or claim' sufficient to trigger his right to appeal").

[618]*Id.* at 14.

[619]*See In re* General Am. Life Ins. Co. Sales Practices Litig., 302 F.3d 799, 800 (8th Cir. 2002) (on remand, questioning "whether *Devlin*'s holding applies to opt-out

Similarly, the district court's refusal to approve a proposed settlement is subject to immediate appeal. In *Carson v. American Brands, Inc.*,[620] the Supreme Court held that where denial of a proposed class settlement results in "serious, perhaps irreparable consequence," the order is immediately appealable. *Carson* involved a Title VII class action seeking both preliminary and permanent injunctive relief, where the district court denied the parties' joint motion to enter a proposed consent decree.[621] The Fourth Circuit dismissed the appeal, holding that the district court's order was neither a "final judgment" warranting appeal under 28 U.S.C.A. § 1291,[622] nor an interlocutory order "refusing an injunction" appealable under § 1292(a)(1).[623] Reversing the Fourth Circuit's ruling and resolving a conflict in the circuits, the Supreme Court held that the district court's denial of a proposed consent decree containing immediately effective injunctive provisions had the "practical effect of refusing an injunction" and thus was an appealable order under § 1292(a)(1).[624]

---

class actions certified under Rule 23(b)(3)" but reasoning that "[though] the limited reading of *Devlin* has considerable merit, we need not finally resolve the debate because . . . [the case at issue had] become moot"); Rutter & Wilbanks Corp. v. Shell Oil Co., 314 F.3d 1180, 1185 (10th Cir. 2002) (raising same question as *In re General American* but declining to narrow *Devlin*'s application, leaving "the scope of *Devlin* to another day"). *But cf. In re* Integra Realty Res., Inc. v. Fidelity Capital Appreciation Fund, 354 F.3d 1246, 1257 (10th Cir. 2004) (Holding that "a class member who does not opt out of a settlement but objects at the fairness hearing and against whom a final judgment is entered has the right to appeal the district court's approval of the settlement. This answers the question we left open in [*Rutter*] as to whether *Devlin* applies to opt-out settlements.") (citation omitted).

[620]450 U.S. 79 (1981).

[621]*Id.* at 81.

[622]*See* 28 U.S.C. § 1291 (2000), which provides, in pertinent part: "[t]he courts of appeals (other than the United States Court of Appeals for the Federal Circuit) shall have jurisdiction of appeals from all final decisions of the district courts of the United States . . . ."

[623]*Carson*, 450 U.S. at 82–83; *see also* 28 U.S.C. § 1292(a)(1) (2000), which provides, in pertinent part: "[e]xcept as provided in subsections (c) and (d) of this section, the courts of appeals shall have jurisdiction of appeals from: (1) Interlocutory orders of the district courts of the United States . . . ."

[624]*Carson*, 450 U.S. at 83–84 (but noting that "appeal as of right under § 1292(a)(1) will be available only in circumstances where an appeal will further the statutory purpose of 'permit[ting] litigants to effectually challenge interlocutory orders of serious, perhaps irreparable consequence' ").

DISCOVERY

I. INTRODUCTION

A general treatise on discovery issues is beyond the scope of this book. This chapter focuses on the particular application of discovery procedures to certain circumstances that often arise in employment discrimination litigation.

Generally, courts adhere to the principle that civil discovery rules are to be construed liberally in Title VII and Age Discrimination in Employment Act (ADEA) cases.[1] The Tenth Circuit has

---

[1]*See, e.g.*, Gomez v. Martin Marietta Corp., 50 F.3d 1511, 1520, 67 FEP 537, 543 (10th Cir. 1995) (discovery in Title VII cases "should not be narrowly circumscribed"); Owens v. Sprint United Mgmt. Co., 221 F.R.D. 649, 652, 94 FEP 765 (D. Kan. 2004) ("The scope of discovery is particularly broad in a Title VII case."); Jackson v. Montgomery Ward & Co., 173 F.R.D. 524, 526, 74 FEP 529, 530 (D. Nev. 1997) ("[I]n Title VII cases, courts should avoid placing unnecessary limitations on discovery."); Mackey v. IBP, Inc., 167 F.R.D. 186, 195–96 (D. Kan. 1996) (information about other facilities and corporatewide information about setting of policy that "may establish a

stated that "[i]t is well settled that in a Title VII suit, an employer's general practices are relevant even when a plaintiff is asserting an individual claim for disparate treatment."[2] Yet, even in discrimination cases, discovery is "not without limits."[3] Courts have required plaintiffs seeking "broad discovery" or discovery of confidential information to articulate the relevance of the information sought.[4] Courts have also shown a willingness to examine

---

pattern of discrimination is discoverable, even when the action is for individual relief only"); Ladson v. Ulltra E. Parking Corp., 164 F.R.D. 376, 378, 70 FEP 140, 141 (S.D.N.Y. 1996) (explaining that "[a]ll that must be shown is that the discovery requested possibly might be relevant, . . . or is reasonably calculated to lead to the discovery of admissible evidence"; court ordered defendant to produce personnel files of its current and former employees and supervisors); Peterson v. City Coll., 160 F.R.D. 22, 23–24, 70 FEP 259, 261–62 (S.D.N.Y. 1994) (when plaintiff's complaint alleges continuing pattern or practice of discrimination, plaintiff should be afforded broad scope of discovery regarding defendant's employment policies and procedures); Rodger v. Electronic Data Sys., 155 F.R.D. 537, 539, 2 WH 2d 1436, 1437 (E.D.N.C. 1994) ("Relevance is broadly construed . . . and 'encompass[es] any matter that bears on, or that reasonably could lead to any other matter that could bear on, any issue that is or that may be in the case.' [quotation omitted]. . . . This is especially the case with regard to discrimination claims, where the imposition of unnecessary discovery limitations is to be avoided.").

[2]*Gomez*, 50 F.3d at 1520, 67 FEP at 543; *see also Jackson*, 173 F.R.D. at 527–28 ("In a disparate treatment case, the scope of discovery must be broader than the specific individualized facts upon which the plaintiff's claim is based"; discovery of prior complaints of discrimination is permitted in individual disparate treatment case, because prior complaints may be relevant to proving that reasons given for adverse employment action are pretext for discrimination.).

[3]Wright v. AmSouth Bancorporation, 320 F.3d 1198, 1205, 91 FEP 41 (11th Cir. 2003) ("discovery in Title VII cases is 'not without limits. The information sought must be relevant and not overly burdensome to the responding party'.") (citations omitted); *see also* Kresefsky v. Panasonic Commc'ns & Sys. Co., 169 F.R.D. 54, 64, 74 FEP 905, 912 (D.N.J. 1996) ("[T]he scope of Title VII discovery is 'not without limits . . . . Discovery should be tailored to the issues involved in the particular case.' ") (citations omitted).

[4]*See* Schwab v. Wyndham Intl, Inc., 225 F.R.D. 538, 539 (N.D. Tex. 2005) (request for premise inspection made by claimant bringing Title VII claim overly broad because most departments had nothing to do with case and contained confidential and sensitive information); Smith v. Just for Feet, Inc., 80 FEP 1541, 1542–43 (E.D. La. 1999) (limiting discovery to plaintiffs' workplace and other facilities over which allegedly biased supervisor had authority, where action does not involve class or pattern-or-practice claims); Hicks v. Arthur, 159 F.R.D. 468, 470 (E.D. Pa. 1995) (denying plaintiffs' motion to compel interrogatory responses that would have required defendant to conduct survey of all its employees, past and present, over 8-year period when defendant at time of request employed over 1,000 people; plaintiffs "have not demonstrated the relevance of this expansive information"), *aff'd*, 72 F.3d 122 (3d Cir. 1995); Whittingham v. Amherst Coll., 164 F.R.D. 124, 127 (D. Mass. 1995) (rejecting plaintiff's request for personnel files of three other employees because

whether the discovery sought addresses the particular issues in the case.[5]

Parties to employment discrimination lawsuits should consider carefully not only what discovery to propound, but also what to oppose. Defendants' failure to cooperate in discovery, including unwarranted delay tactics, has resulted in sanctions.[6] Plaintiffs'

---

plaintiff offered only conclusory assertion that files were relevant, and this assertion did not outweigh three individuals' privacy interests).

[5]*See Owens*, 221 F.R.D. at 652 (limiting discovery to employing unit that was source of alleged discrimination); Ibrahim v. American Univ., 80 FEP 97, 98 (D.D.C. 1999) (allowing discovery of other candidates' employment files because "the very essence of Title VII is comparative evidence"); Gheesling v. Chater, 162 F.R.D. 649, 650, 68 FEP 965, 966 (D. Kan. 1995) ("In employment discrimination cases, discovery is usually limited to information about employees in the same department or office absent a showing of a more particularized need for, and the likely relevance of, broader information"; court would examine plaintiffs' proof to determine whether earlier discovery "could possibly indicate a hiring practice applicable to all employing units."). *Compare Rodger*, 155 F.R.D. at 539–42 (limiting discovery in age discrimination action; distinguishing *Hollander v. American Cyanamid Co.*, 895 F.2d 80, 51 FEP 1881 (2d Cir. 1990), *aff'd*, 172 F.3d 192 (2d Cir. 1999), on grounds that, in instant case, facility in which plaintiff worked exercised independent decision-making authority) *with* Kitchen v. Dial Page Co., 67 FEP 482, 484 (E.D. Tenn. 1995) (refusing to limit discovery to employing unit because decision to terminate plaintiff's employment was not made locally).

[6]*See, e.g.*, Phillips v. Cohen, 400 F.3d 388, 402, 95 FEP 520 (6th Cir. 2005) (finding that district court's grant of summary judgment for employer was abuse of discretion because it essentially imposed no sanctions on employer for discovery abuses when district court had found that such sanctions were warranted); Melendez v. Illinois Bell Tel. Co., 79 F.3d 661, 671–72, 70 FEP 589, 596–97 (7th Cir. 1996) (employer's statistical expert barred from testifying where employer failed to reveal, in response to plaintiff's request, expert's work in analyzing and reviewing standardized management test that allegedly had adverse impact on hiring Hispanics); Bonds v. District of Columbia, 93 F.3d 801, 812–13 (D.C. Cir. 1996) (reversing court's discovery sanction precluding defendant from offering any fact witness at trial, where defendant failed to respond in timely manner to interrogatory requesting names of all persons with knowledge of relevant events and instead restricting defendant's evidence to those witnesses made available for deposition and to those subjects testified to at deposition); Easley v. Anheuser-Busch, Inc., 758 F.2d 251, 258, 37 FEP 549 (8th Cir. 1985) (trial judge did not abuse his discretion by excluding testimony of expert witnesses who were not properly disclosed during discovery); Coles v. Perry, 217 F.R.D. 1, 6 (D.D.C. 2003) (sanctioning defense for failing to produce evidence by deadline by excluding such evidence unless defendant could establish that such failure was harmless); White v. Burt Enters., 200 F.R.D. 641, 643 (D. Colo. 2000) (requiring defendant to pay attorney's fees and costs incurred in connection with plaintiff's motion to compel as sanction for failure to comply with discovery orders); Trbovich v. Ritz-Carlton Hotel Co., 166 F.R.D. 30, 32, 70 FEP 991 (E.D. Mo. 1996) (requiring defendant to pay attorney's fees incurred by plaintiffs in attempting to obtain discovery from defendants as result of defendant's repeated failure to comply

failure to cooperate in discovery also has prompted sanctions,[7] including the sanction of dismissal where a plaintiff grossly abuses[8] or willfully or recurringly refuses to participate in the discovery process.[9] The Equal Employment Opportunity Commission (EEOC)

---

with discovery requests); Scarfo v. Cabletron Sys., 153 F.R.D. 9, 11–12, 64 FEP 222 (D.N.H. 1994) (awarding plaintiff attorney's fees and costs for defendant's resisting repeated requests to view personnel files, culling documents from files, and placing unreasonable deadlines on examination); Spurlock v. Nordyne, Inc., 59 FEP 1359, 1360 (E.D. Mo. 1992) (ordering defendant and its counsel to pay plaintiff's fees and costs for defense counsel's purposeful withholding of documents from plaintiff's personnel file that were responsive to earlier production request); Johnson v. Smith, 630 F. Supp. 1, 4–5, 40 FEP 1044 (N.D. Cal. 1986) (awarding attorney's fees to plaintiff as sanctions for excessive length of plaintiff's deposition and for interrogatories propounded to harass plaintiff); EEOC v. A.E. Staley Mfg. Co., 38 FEP 1803, 1804 (N.D. Ill. 1985) (attorney's fees and costs assessed for defendant's counsel's willful delay in complying with EEOC subpoena that court had previously ordered to be enforced); Shipes v. Trinity Indus., Inc., 40 FEP 1136, 1145–46 (E.D. Tex. 1981) (ordering defense counsel to pay plaintiff's attorney's fees and costs associated with repeated failure to comply with discovery orders); Fautek v. Montgomery Ward & Co., 96 F.R.D. 141, 144–47, 42 FEP 1395 (N.D. Ill. 1982) (sanctions issued against employer for giving plaintiff's counsel misinformation about its system of computerizing records and interpretive codes); EEOC v. Baby Prods. Co., 89 F.R.D. 129, 131–32, 24 FEP 1818 (E.D. Mich. 1981) (employer's history of noncooperation and extremely tardy responses to requests for admissions, without motion for relief, entitled plaintiffs to summary judgment).

[7]*E.g.*, Beavers v. American Cast Iron Pipe Co., 852 F.2d 527, 530–31, 47 FEP 925 (11th Cir. 1988) (sanctions less severe than dismissal appropriate where court did not find bad faith resistance to discovery orders), *rev'd in part on other grounds*, 975 F.2d 792 (11th Cir. 1992); Lomascolo v. Otto Oldsmobile-Cadillac Inc., 253 F. Supp. 2d 354, 360–61, 91 FEP 780 (N.D.N.Y. 2003) (plaintiff's failure to make initial disclosures of documents subsequently used at deposition of witness precludes their use in remainder of trial except for impeachment purposes); Pearson v. Metro-North R.R., 57 FEP 1589, 1594 (S.D.N.Y. 1990) (issue preclusion appropriate where plaintiff's failure to provide requested documents unduly hampered defendant's ability to prepare for trial); Gray v. Frito-Lay, Inc., 35 FEP 598, 605–06 (S.D. Miss. 1982) (plaintiff's failure to appear for deposition and failure to answer interrogatories both were in bad faith, warranting award of attorney's fees to employer).

[8]*E.g.*, Martin v. DaimlerChrysler Corp., 251 F.3d 691, 695, 86 FEP 123 (8th Cir. 2001) (plaintiff's false discovery responses provided "ample basis" for dismissal); Combs v. Rockwell Int'l Corp., 927 F.2d 486, 488 (9th Cir. 1991) (dismissal appropriate sanction where plaintiff authorized his counsel to change plaintiff's deposition answers on key questions).

[9]*E.g.*, Maynard v. Nygren, 372 F.3d 890, 893 (7th Cir. 2004) (affirming dismissal as sanction for willfully withholding doctor's letter from discovery), *cert. denied*, 543 U.S. 1049 (2005); Martin v. Daimler Chrysler, 251 F.3d 691, 695, 86 FEP 123 (8th Cir. 2001) (affirming district court's dismissal as sanction for plaintiff's misrepresentations made during deposition); Gratton v. Great Am. Commc'ns, 178 F.3d 1373, 1375, 80 FEP 162 (11th Cir. 1999) (per curiam) (affirming dismissal as sanction for

also has been sanctioned for withholding information.[10] Although discovery sanctions are reviewed on appeal only for an abuse of discretion, a terminating sanction—judgment for the plaintiff or dismissal—may be inappropriate where no bad faith is shown or less drastic measures would have sufficed.[11]

---

plaintiff's willful noncompliance with district court's discovery order); Baba v. Japan Travel Bureau Int'l, Inc., 111 F.3d 2, 3, 74 FEP 864 (2d Cir. 1997) (per curiam) (affirming dismissal as sanction for plaintiff's willful and repeated defiance of district court's discovery orders); Halas v. Consumer Serv., 16 F.3d 161, 164–65, 64 FEP 7 (7th Cir. 1994) (plaintiff's willful failure to appear at court-ordered deposition warranted dismissal of case); Sere v. Board of Trustees, 852 F.2d 285, 289–90, 47 FEP 563 (7th Cir. 1988) (race discrimination suit properly dismissed after plaintiff willfully ignored repeated warnings to participate in discovery); Tolliver v. Northrop Corp., 786 F.2d 316, 319, 40 FEP 470 (7th Cir. 1986) (court did not abuse discretion by dismissing and refusing to reinstate suit because of plaintiff's discovery abuses); Bluitt v. Arco Chem. Co., 777 F.2d 188, 191 (5th Cir. 1985) (plaintiff's willful disregard of discovery orders justified dismissal); Cross v. General Motors Corp., 721 F.2d 1152, 1155–56, 40 FEP 418 (8th Cir. 1983) (district court properly dismissed race discrimination suit without prejudice where plaintiff refused to comply with discovery);Young v. Office of U.S. Senate Sergeant at Arms, 217 F.R.D. 61, 67, 92 FEP 1047 (D.D.C. 2003) (dismissal is appropriate sanction for plaintiff's willful obstruction of discovery process and bad faith attempts to influence testimony of witnesses); Sanders v. Merry-Go-Round Enters., Inc., 61 FEP 431, 432 (D. Minn. 1993) (plaintiff's utter failure to respond to appropriate discovery requests resulted in dismissal of plaintiff's complaint); Morgan v. Massachusetts Gen. Hosp., 712 F. Supp. 242, 263–65, 53 FEP 1647 (D. Mass. 1989) (dismissing plaintiff's case for counsel's willful misconduct in failing to respond to court-ordered discovery), aff'd in relevant part, 901 F.2d 186, 53 FEP 1780 (1st Cir. 1990); Smith v. APAC-Carolina, Inc., 46 FEP 427, 428 (M.D.N.C. 1988) (dismissing pro se plaintiff's Title VII employment discrimination action for repeated failure to cooperate in discovery); Ford v. American Broad. Co., 101 F.R.D. 664, 667 (S.D.N.Y. 1983) (dismissal particularly appropriate where plaintiff-attorney refused to produce requested material because it would be damaging to his case), aff'd mem., 742 F.2d 1434 (2d Cir. 1984).

[10]See, e.g., EEOC v. New Enter. Stone & Lime Co., 74 F.R.D. 628, 633–35, 15 FEP 25 (W.D. Pa. 1977) (ordering EEOC to pay attorney's fees where EEOC's refusal to cooperate in extending defendant's deadline for answering interrogatories and requests for admission determined to be unfounded, meritless, frivolous, and vexatious). But see EEOC v. General Dynamics Corp., 999 F.2d 113, 115–17, 62 FEP 1120 (5th Cir. 1993) (trial court erred in excluding expert's vital testimony because EEOC's production of data in computer printouts instead of computer tapes was reasonable in light of general and vague order); EEOC v. First Nat'l Bank, 614 F.2d 1004, 1007, 22 FEP 706 (5th Cir. 1980) (trial court abused its discretion in dismissing EEOC's action where employer's discovery request related to counterclaim that was not properly maintainable); EEOC v. Carter Carburetor, 577 F.2d 43, 48, 17 FEP 706 (8th Cir. 1978) (mandamus issued ordering district court to withdraw its sanctions order against EEOC because both sides had used dilatory tactics).

[11]See Tisdale v. Federal Express Corp., 415 F.3d 516, 526, 96 FEP 65 (6th Cir. 2005) (affirming district court's denial of employer's motion to dismiss because

II. STRATEGY CONSIDERATIONS

A. Plaintiffs

Many courts have interpreted broadly the plaintiff's right to discovery in Title VII cases.[12] In so doing, courts sometimes have

---

employee took significant steps to try to comply with employer's extensive discovery requests); Computer Task Group, Inc. v. Brotby, 364 F.3d 1112, 1116–17 (9th Cir. 2004) (per curiam) (district court properly considered lesser sanctions for employee's noncompliance with discovery prior to ordering default in favor of former employer and dismissal of employee's counterclaims); *Gratton*, 178 F.3d at 1375 (dismissal as sanction not abuse of district court's discretion when lesser sanctions would not suffice); *General Dynamics*, 999 F.2d at 117 (district court abused its discretion by failing to consider possibility of lesser sanctions than total exclusion of EEOC's expert witness, which was tantamount to dismissal of EEOC's claim); Brooks v. Hilton Casinos, Inc., 959 F.2d 757, 767–68, 58 FEP 590 (9th Cir. 1992) (plaintiff's refusal to comply with discovery requests for information regarding his income taxes and employment was sanctionable, but order barring any recovery was excessive); John v. Louisiana, 828 F.2d 1129, 1133, 44 FEP 1769 (5th Cir. 1987) (dismissal reversed where there was "no clear record of delay or contumacious conduct, and lesser sanctions would have been more just"); Cox v. American Cast Iron Pipe Co., 784 F.2d 1546, 1555–57, 40 FEP 678 (11th Cir. 1986) (dismissal from suit of class members who failed to respond to interrogatories is abuse of discretion without finding of willfulness or bad faith); Batson v. Neal Spelce Assocs., Inc., 765 F.2d 511, 516, 38 FEP 867 (5th Cir. 1985) (valid reasons should be expressed to explain why sanction of dismissal is chosen over any other); Sova v. Wheaton Franciscan Servs., Inc. Health & Welfare Benefit Trust, 40 F. Supp. 2d 1031, 1043 (E.D. Wis. 1999) (dismissal of participant's ERISA claims not warranted because discovery violations could be addressed with less severe remedy).

[12]*See* Wards Cove Packing Co. v. Atonio, 490 U.S. 642, 657–58, 49 FEP 1519 (1989) ("liberal civil discovery rules give plaintiffs broad access to employers' records in an effort to document their claims"); Sempier v. Johnson & Higgins, 45 F.3d 724, 734–35, 66 FEP 1214, 1223 (3d Cir. 1995) (court of appeals vacated district court's discovery rulings after finding that they were improper "wholesale substitution of court-engineered discovery"; court of appeals stated that district court had no authority to "rewrite a party's questions and in effect serve its own set of interrogatories"); Gomez v. Martin Marietta Corp., 50 F.3d 1511, 1520, 67 FEP 537, 543 (10th Cir. 1995) (discovery in Title VII cases "should not be narrowly circumscribed"); Hollander v. American Cyanamid Co., 895 F.2d 80, 84, 51 FEP 1881 (2d Cir. 1990) (individual plaintiff entitled to companywide information regarding management employees, and such discovery should not be limited to facility in which plaintiff worked); Johnson v. Washington Times Corp., 208 F.R.D. 16, 18–19, 89 FEP 1 (D.D.C. 2002) (disagreeing with application in Title VII cases of hard and fast rules that purport to limit discovery); Cardenas v. Prudential Ins. Co. of Am., 91 FEP 82, 84 (D. Minn. 2003) ("in Title VII cases, in which plaintiffs are required to demonstrate pretext, courts have customarily allowed a wide discovery of personnel files"); Jackson v. Montgomery Ward & Co., 173 F.R.D. 524, 526, 74 FEP 529, 530 (D. Nev. 1997) ("[I]n Title VII cases, courts should avoid placing unnecessary limitations on discovery."); Mackey v. IBP, Inc., 167 F.R.D. 186, 195–96 (D. Kan. 1996) (information about other facilities, and corporatewide information about setting of policy, "which may establish a pattern of discrimination is discoverable, even when the action is for individual

rejected objections based on time and expense.[13] Courts allow the
EEOC broad discovery in subpoena enforcement actions,[14] but this
power is not without limits.[15]

---

relief only"); Ladson v. Ulltra E. Parking Corp., 164 F.R.D. 376, 378, 70 FEP 140,
141 (S.D.N.Y. 1996) (explaining that "[a]ll that must be shown is that the discovery
requested possibly might be relevant, . . . or is reasonably calculated to lead to the
discovery of admissible evidence"; court ordered defendant to produce personnel files
of its current and former employees and supervisors); Peterson v. City Coll., 160
F.R.D. 22, 23–24, 70 FEP 259, 261–62 (S.D.N.Y. 1994) (when plaintiff's complaint
alleges continuing pattern or practice of discrimination, plaintiff should be afforded
broad scope of discovery regarding defendant's employment policies and procedures);
Rodger v. Electronic Data Sys., 155 F.R.D. 537, 539, 2 WH 2d 1436, 1437 (E.D.N.C.
1994) ("Relevance is broadly construed . . . and 'encompass[es] any matter that bears
on, or that reasonably could lead to any other matter that could bear on, any issue
that is or that may be in the case.'. . . . This is especially the case with regard to
discrimination claims, where the imposition of unnecessary discovery limitations is
to be avoided.") (quotation omitted).

[13]See, e.g., Bryant v. Farmers Ins. Co., 2002 WL 1796045, at *4 (D. Kan. July
31, 2002) (former employee who was discharged for allegedly failing to meet audit
standards entitled to discovery pertaining to whether other claims departments in
defendant's four regional offices applied same standards; rejecting employer's contentions that request was unduly burdensome and time-consuming and should have
been limited to departments managed by employee's direct supervisor); Lyoch v.
Anheuser-Busch Inc., 164 F.R.D. 62, 66, 74 FEP 691 (E.D. Mo. 1995) (finding that
information's relevance and utility to plaintiff outweighed burden to defendant of
producing information); McLendon v. M. David Lowe Pers. Servs., 15 FEP 250,
253 (S.D. Tex. 1977) (ordering defendant to answer interrogatory seeking list by
race and/or national origin of all persons who applied unsuccessfully for certain
position during 4-year period even though it was estimated it would take between
1,250 and 2,500 hours to compile).

[14]See, e.g., EEOC v. Citicorp Diners Club, Inc., 985 F.2d 1036, 1038–39, 60
FEP 1242 (10th Cir. 1993) (EEOC may compel employer to compile information
within its control to respond to subpoenas, as EEOC's subpoena power is not limited
to production of documents already in existence; EEOC also may subpoena promotion policies relating to other bases of discrimination not alleged in complaint because EEOC seeks to vindicate public interest and not merely interests of charging
parties); EEOC v. University of Pa., 850 F.2d 969, 981, 47 FEP 189 (3d Cir. 1988)
(invalidity of Administrative Procedure Act agency rule does not invalidate EEOC's
statutory grant of investigative subpoena power), aff'd, 493 U.S. 182, 51 FEP 1118
(1990); EEOC v. Maryland Cup Corp., 785 F.2d 471, 479 (4th Cir. 1986) (ordering
defendant to provide information that exists only "in the minds of the supervisors
and workers" and requiring the defendant to interview supervisors and other employees regarding the race of former employees based on a questionnaire prepared
by the EEOC); EEOC v. City of Milwaukee, 54 F. Supp. 2d 885, 890, 86 FEP 62
(E.D. Wis. 1999) (in evaluating EEOC subpoena, court's only responsibility is to
satisfy itself that charge is valid and requested material is relevant to charge); EEOC
v. Deutz-Allis Corp., 49 FEP 97, 98 (W.D. Mo. 1989) (subpoena enforced where
burden of production and limits of investigation were reduced to proper range of
relevance). See generally Chapters 25 (EEOC Administrative Process) and 29 (EEOC
Litigation).

[15]See, e.g., EEOC v. Sidley Austin Brown & Wood, 315 F.3d 696, 700 (7th Cir.
2002) (subpoena issued by EEOC may be found unreasonable where "agency clearly

In litigated cases, the principal discovery methods used by the parties are (1) written interrogatories (under Rule 33 of the Federal Rules of Civil Procedure[16]); (2) document requests (under Rule 34); and (3) depositions of key decision makers (under Rules 30 and 31).[17] One frequently useful device is to notice a deposition pursuant to Rule 30(b)(6), which allows the deposition of a corporation with respect to any relevant subject matter.[18] The party noticing such a deposition is required to describe with reasonable particularity in the deposition notice the subject matter on which the deposition will be conducted. The burden then is on the defending party to produce one or more persons to testify on its behalf as to information known or reasonably available to the organization.[19] The advantage of this device is that it obviates the necessity of identifying the particular persons who have knowledge of

---

is ranging far beyond the boundaries of its statutory authority"; subpoena not enforced with respect to merits issues where coverage question still legitimately in dispute); EEOC v. Ford Motor Credit Co., 26 F.3d 44, 47, 65 FEP 65 (6th Cir. 1994) (EEOC not entitled to 12 years' worth of records from employer; although EEOC possesses broad subpoena powers, it is not entitled to any material *it* deems relevant—up to courts to determine what material is relevant); EEOC v. C&P Tel. Co., 813 F. Supp. 874, 876–77, 60 FEP 1217 (D.D.C. 1993) (EEOC entitled to discovery of employment tests only if it signs confidentiality agreement).

[16]In order to reduce the frequency and increase the efficiency of interrogatory practice, Rule 33 limits the number of interrogatories that a party may propound. Moreover, responses to interrogatories generally are less revealing than documents or deposition testimony, because they usually are drafted by attorneys and thus are less likely to elicit probative or damaging information.

[17]Requests for admission under Rule 36 are not commonly used in Title VII cases until the completion of discovery because the preparation of the requests presupposes that counsel knows the facts desired to be admitted. If there has been a prior EEOC investigation, requests for admission can be made for the purpose of introducing into evidence material or data contained in the investigative file.

[18]*See* Coleman v. General Elec. Co., 1995 WL 358089, at *5 (E.D. Pa. June 8, 1995) (permitting Rule 30(b)(6) deposition regarding defendant's hiring, promotion, and discharge decisions affecting employees in defendant's 250-employee human resources department); Crimm v. Missouri Pac. R.R., 750 F.2d 703, 708–09, 36 FEP 883 (8th Cir. 1984) (district court erred in excluding Rule 30(b)(6) deposition regarding defendant company's alleged unlawful discharge of employee on basis of age).

[19]The person the employer selects to testify on its behalf must be able to testify fully, completely, and unevasively as to the matters the plaintiff's deposition notice designates. *See* FED. R. CIV. P. 30(b)(6), Notes of Advisory Committee on Rule, 1970 Amendment. If the defending party, intentionally or otherwise, designates a witness who lacks knowledge of the matters specified in the notice, the deposing party may seek reimbursement of expenses, including reasonable attorney's fees, incurred in taking the deposition. FED. R. CIV. P. 26(g)(3), 37(a)(4).

any given subject area. Moreover, if the corporation is required under Rule 30(b)(6) to designate the witness to testify on its behalf, Rule 32(a)(2) deems that witness' testimony available for use "by an adverse party for any purpose." This eliminates evidentiary disputes over whether a particular employee is a "managing agent" within the meaning of the federal rules.[20]

A notice of deposition may include a request that the designated witness bring specified relevant documents to the deposition.[21] Because this essentially is a request to produce documents directed to a party, the 30-day period allowed by Rule 34 for production of documents is applicable.[22]

The leading case supporting the broad availability of statistical information through interrogatories is *Burns v. Thiokol Chemical Corp.*[23] In that class action, the district court refused to compel answers to the plaintiff's interrogatories seeking broad background and statistical data pertaining to African-American and white employees and job vacancies at the plant in question.[24] The employer prevailed at trial, but the Fifth Circuit reversed, citing the broad discovery provisions of the federal rules and, particularly, their applicability to Title VII litigation.[25] Statistical analyses also may be discoverable (1) to support "pattern or practice" allegations,[26]

---

[20]If the plaintiff notices the deposition of a particular company witness, rather than using Rule 30(b)(6), the testimony may not be admissible evidence at trial as a party's admission unless the witness was an "officer, director, or managing agent" at the time the deposition was taken. *See* FED. R. CIV. P. 32(a)(2).

[21]FED. R. CIV. P. 30(b)(5).

[22]Rule 30(b)(5) specifies that Rule 34's procedures apply to requests for production accompanying a notice of deposition. According to Rule 34(b), the responding party has 30 days after service of the request for production to respond to the request, and the court may allow a longer or shorter time.

[23]483 F.2d 300, 6 FEP 269 (5th Cir. 1973); *see also* Steger v. General Elec. Co., 318 F.3d 1066, 1071–72 (11th Cir. 2003) (plaintiff entitled to information used in determining employees' salaries for identified period); Orlowski v. Dominick's Finer Foods, Inc., 1995 WL 516595, at *5 (N.D. Ill. Aug. 28, 1995) (granting detailed companywide discovery of computer database information and employment practices to determine scope of potential class), *clarified*, 1995 WL 549096 (N.D. Ill. Sept. 11, 1995); Finch v. Hercules, Inc., 149 F.R.D. 60, 63, 62 FEP 295 (D. Del. 1993) (compelling defendant to answer interrogatories seeking statistical information on layoffs, terminations, and retirements).

[24]483 F.2d at 303–05.

[25]*Id.* at 307–08.

[26]*See* Lyoch v. Anheuser-Busch Cos., 164 F.R.D. 62, 65–68, 74 FEP 691, 695–97 (E.D. Mo. 1995) (permitting companywide discovery regarding hiring and promotion

and (2) to rebut as pretextual the defendant's purported nondiscriminatory reason for taking an adverse employment action.[27]

Where a defendant has failed to retain documents as required by law, a plaintiff may assert entitlement to an adverse inference—i.e., that the missing records would have supported his or her case.[28] However, courts will review the facts surrounding the defendant's failure to maintain the documents, and courts do not always find the adverse inference supported or impose sanctions on the defendant.[29] Plaintiffs may also be entitled to sanctions, including exclusion of evidence at trial, where the defendant has failed to disclose requested information.[30]

---

of employees similarly situated to plaintiffs who alleged pattern or practice of gender discrimination).

[27]*Id.* at 66 (granting companywide discovery of employment practices with regard to particular position at issue) (citing Hollander v. American Cyanamid Co., 895 F.2d 80, 84, 51 FEP 1881, 1884 (2d Cir. 1990), and Miles v. Boeing Co., 154 F.R.D. 117, 119–21 (E.D. Pa. 1994)); *cf.* Curry v. Morgan Stanley & Co., 193 F.R.D. 168, 175–76, 83 FEP 221, 226–27 (S.D.N.Y. 2000) (plaintiff, a first-year analyst whose employment was terminated for expense account abuse, not allowed to discover expense records of senior executives in order to show corporate culture of expense account abuse because plaintiff was not similarly situated to senior executives).

[28]*See* Byrnie v. Town of Cromwell Bd. of Educ., 243 F.3d 93, 108, 85 FEP 323 (2d Cir. 2001) (defendant's failure to retain records through pendency of lawsuit permits court to draw adverse inference that such documents would have supported plaintiff's claim); Hicks v. Gates Rubber Co., 833 F.2d 1406, 1418–19, 45 FEP 608 (10th Cir. 1987) (plaintiff entitled to presumption that destroyed clock charts and daily reports would have bolstered her case); Scott v. IBM Corp., 196 F.R.D. 233, 249 (D.N.J. 2000) (defendant's destruction of documents warrants inference that may provide evidence from which reasonable jury may disbelieve defendant's articulated reason for plaintiff's termination); Stender v. Lucky Stores, Inc., 803 F. Supp. 259, 318, 62 FEP 11 (N.D. Cal. 1992) (where employer has failed to retain records, plaintiff is entitled to adverse inference); *see also* Section IV *infra* regarding the employer's obligation to retain electronic records.

[29]Gomez v. Martin Marietta Corp., 50 F.3d 1511, 1519–20, 67 FEP 537, 542–43 (10th Cir. 1995) (magistrate judge could refuse to impose sanctions on employer where employer destroyed files that were summaries of original files but had already provided original files to plaintiff).

[30]*See* Melendez v. Illinois Bell Tel. Co., 79 F.3d 661, 671–72, 70 FEP 589, 596–97 (7th Cir. 1996) (employer's statistical expert barred from testifying where employer failed to reveal, in response to plaintiff's request, expert's work in analyzing and reviewing standardized management test that allegedly had adverse impact on hiring of Hispanics); Bonds v. District of Columbia, 93 F.3d 801, 812–13 (D.C. Cir. 1996) (reversing court's discovery sanction precluding defendant from offering any fact witness at trial, where defendant failed to respond in timely manner to interrogatory requesting names of all persons with knowledge of relevant events, and instead restricting defendant's evidence to those witnesses made available for deposition and to those subjects testified to at deposition).

B. Defendants

The defendant typically seeks to obtain a copy of the plaintiff's EEOC file, which often identifies potential witnesses.[31] This can be done informally via a request under the Freedom of Information Act (FOIA)[32] or formally by subpoena.[33]

The identity of testifying opposing experts and their opinions is discoverable. Rule 26 requires disclosure of certain information relating to expert testimony at least 90 days before the trial date, absent other direction from the court stipulation between the parties, unless the evidence is intended solely to contradict evidence identified by the other party.[34] Required disclosures include a complete statement of all opinions to be expressed and the basis and reasons therefor, the qualifications of the witness, a list of all publications authored by the witness in the preceding 10 years, and a listing of any other cases in which the witness has testified as an expert at trial or by deposition within the preceding four years.[35]

III. LIMITATIONS ON DISCOVERY

A. Discovery Sought by Plaintiffs

1. Privileged Materials

Several privilege issues unique to employment discrimination law have emerged. One such issue involves the discovery of matters arising from EEOC investigations. Under Title VII and the

---

[31]*See* EEOC v. Johnson & Higgins, 78 FEP 1127, 1131–32 (S.D.N.Y. 1998) (attorney-client privilege can cover communications between EEOC attorneys and employees on whose behalf EEOC prosecutes actions); EEOC v. Grinnell Fire Prot. Sys. Co., 764 F. Supp. 623, 626, 56 FEP 139, 141–42 (D. Kan. 1991) (information gathered during EEOC's nonadversarial investigation routinely provided to both parties). For the EEOC's Guidelines, consult 29 C.F.R. § 1610 (2005) (EEOC's FOIA regulations). *See generally* Chapter 25 (EEOC Administrative Process).

[32]5 U.S.C. § 552 (2000).

[33]Moreover, an EEOC policy directive allows the parties access to each side's position during the investigation. *See Charge Processing Procedures Adopted by EEOC and Task Force Recommendations to Be Implemented by Chairman* (Apr. 19, 1995), *reprinted in* DAILY LAB. REP. (BNA) at E-5 (Apr. 20, 1995).

[34]FED. R. CIV. P. 26(a)(2)(C).

[35]FED. R. CIV. P. 26(a)(2)(B).

Americans with Disabilities Act (ADA), it is unlawful for the EEOC to make *public* any information it has obtained until after the institution of any proceedings involving the information.[36] The ADEA does not contain a similar confidentiality provision.[37] However, the Supreme Court, in *EEOC v. Associated Dry Goods Corp.*,[38] held that the charging party was not intended to be included within the definition of "public."[39] Thus, charging parties have the right to obtain at least part of the EEOC's file.[40] Information from EEOC files regarding conciliation efforts and settlement discussions, however, normally is not discoverable.[41] Furthermore, the EEOC's

---

[36]42 U.S.C. § 2000e-8(e) (2000).

[37]*See* Codrington v. Anheuser-Busch, 81 FEP 263, 265 (M.D. Fla. Oct. 15, 1999) (ADEA does not contain confidentiality provision but plaintiff failed to demonstrate how disclosure would serve public interest under FOIA).

[38]449 U.S. 590, 24 FEP 1356 (1981).

[39]*Id.* at 598–603. This decision appears to abrogate *Sears, Roebuck & Co. v. EEOC*, 581 F.2d 941, 948, 17 FEP 897 (D.C. Cir. 1978), which held that the EEOC could not disclose to charging parties information it secured during an investigation. *See also* EEOC v. City of Milwaukee, 54 F. Supp. 2d 885, 893, 86 FEP 62 (E.D. Wis. 1999) ("No documents are released to charging parties who have settled a discrimination charge because the EEOC considers those persons to be members of the public to whom disclosure is forbidden."); EEOC v. Pasta House Co., 70 FEP 61, 63 (E.D. Mo. 1996) (limiting defendant's discovery of EEOC files to class members filing charges against defendant and denying access to any other files including class member charges against other employers, because defendant has no reason to know of class members' charges against other employers; therefore, defendant must be considered part of "public" as to those other charges); J.J.C. v. Fridell, 165 F.R.D. 513, 518 (D. Minn. 1995) (EEOC materials are discoverable by parties to agency proceeding because they could not logically be considered "public").

[40]*See* Comas v. United Tel. Co., 70 FEP 159, 160 (D. Kan. 1995) (allowing plaintiff to discover internal investigation file prepared by EEOC); *Codrington*, 81 FEP at 265 (EEOC need not disclose files concerning other charges of discrimination under Title VII and ADA filed by persons who are not parties, but must disclose files and documents relating to named employees, as well as information contained in files of other charging parties that are generally relevant to claims of parties).

[41]Olitsky v. Spencer Gifts, Inc., 964 F.2d 1471, 1477, 61 FEP 1507 (5th Cir. 1992) (letter written by employer's general counsel to EEOC denying discrimination and stating that plaintiff was fired because of inadequate sales discoverable because it set forth purely factual material and did not constitute conciliation material); Branch v. Phillips Petroleum Co., 638 F.2d 873, 880–81, 25 FEP 653 (5th Cir. 1981) (disclosure of conciliation efforts in error); Cason v. Builders FirstSource-Se. Group, Inc., 159 F. Supp. 2d 242, 249 (W.D.N.C. 2001) (mediation and settlement documents of EEOC charge filed by another black employee, who worked at same facility as plaintiff, not discoverable in plaintiff's race-based employment discrimination case); American Centennial Ins. Co. v. EEOC, 722 F. Supp. 180, 184, 50 FEP 1156 (D.N.J. 1989) (denying insurance company's FOIA request for conciliation agreement between its

deliberations are protected from disclosure by the deliberative process privilege.[42]

Some courts in discrimination cases have construed narrowly the scope of the attorney-client and work product privileges.[43]

Defendants often assert privacy concerns regarding employment information sought during discovery.[44] Blanket claims of privacy, even when based on statute or rule, often do not protect employee

---

insured and EEOC, holding that it is up to employer to decide with which members of public it wishes to share such information). *But see* Greene v. Thalhimer's Dep't Store, 93 F.R.D. 657, 660–61, 28 FEP 918 (E.D. Va. 1982) (court reluctantly permitted plaintiff to discover conciliation documents on condition that she not use materials as evidence without consent of persons concerned).

[42]Lang v. Kohl's Food Stores, Inc., 186 F.R.D. 525, 533 (W.D. Wis. 1998).

[43]*See, e.g.*, Colindres v. Quietflex Mfg., 228 F.R.D. 567, 572 (S.D. Tex. 2005) (unsolicited email that defendants' expert sent to defense counsel not protected from disclosure by work product doctrine); Freiermuth v. PPG Indus., Inc., 218 F.R.D. 694, 699 (N.D. Ala. 2003) (documents employer prepared in connection with reduction in force not protected as work product because there was no marking or notation demonstrating intent that these documents were confidential or privileged); Allen v. Chicago Transit Auth., 198 F.R.D. 495, 501 (N.D. Ill. 2001) (documents authored by EEO coordinator in course of employer's internal investigation of discrimination complaints by employees did not qualify for work product protection where employer's legal department was not consulted regarding the documents); Miller v. Federal Express Corp., 186 F.R.D. 376, 387 (W.D. Tenn. 1999) (documents prepared by employees in response to filing of internal grievance by black employee who had been disciplined not protected by work product doctrine because such documents were prepared uniformly every time internal grievance was filed); Hines v. Widnall, 183 F.R.D. 596, 600 (N.D. Fla. 1998) (computerized images of employment records did not constitute attorney work product even though computer imaging was done to facilitate review of documents by geographically dispersed attorneys; images did not contain attorneys' mental impressions or legal theories); Roberts v. Americable Int'l, Inc., 883 F. Supp. 499, 506, 79 FEP 1475 (E.D. Cal. 1995) (employee's tape recording of conversations with her supervisor and other employees not protected by attorney-client privilege because communications not made for purpose of seeking legal advice, but for purpose of acquiring evidence of harassing conversations). *But see* Jinks-Umstead v. England, 231 F.R.D. 13, 18 (D.D.C. 2005) (document prepared in anticipation of litigation protected by work product privilege even though it did not reflect counsel's mental impressions and conveyed trivial information); EEOC v. International Profit Assocs., Inc., 206 F.R.D. 215 (N.D. Ill. 2002) (interview notes of former and current employees prepared by EEOC protected as work product because employment discrimination suit had already been filed); Rauh v. Coyne, 744 F. Supp. 1181, 1185, 57 FEP 953 (D.D.C. 1990) (report prepared prior to date plaintiffs filed discriminatory discharge suit protected from discovery by work product doctrine because report prepared in anticipation of litigation by former employee in sexual discrimination suit).

[44]*See* Cardenas v. Prudential Ins. Co. of Am., 91 FEP 82, 84 (D. Minn. 2003) (discovery of personnel files implicating privacy concerns can be addressed through protective order); Tomanovich v. Autumn Glen, 89 FEP 1157, 1161 (S.D. Ind. 2002)

personnel files or similar information from discovery in discrimination cases.[45] Other courts have been considerably less willing to allow free-ranging discovery into these kinds of materials.[46]

(plaintiff permitted discovery of potential witnesses' phone numbers); Lyoch v. Anheuser-Busch Cos., 164 F.R.D. 62, 67, 74 FEP 691 (E.D. Mo. 1995) (defendant's legitimate confidentiality concerns regarding employees' salary information can best be accommodated by protective order).

[45]See, e.g., Webster v. Doe, 486 U.S. 592, 604, 46 FEP 1671 (1988) (court has discretion to balance plaintiff's need for access to documents against extraordinary security needs of Central Intelligence Agency); EEOC v. Illinois Dep't of Employment Sec., 995 F.2d 106, 107–09, 61 FEP 1385 (7th Cir. 1993) (state statute making unemployment compensation proceedings confidential does not bar EEOC from subpoenaing transcript of state unemployment proceeding; unemployment insurance privilege is even less compelling than other privileges, such as academic deliberation privilege); Garrett v. City & County of San Francisco, 818 F.2d 1515, 1519 n.6, 44 FEP 865 (9th Cir. 1987) (plaintiff entitled to discover personnel files of other fire fighters, despite defendant's claim that files are protected by state-created privileges); Weahkee v. Norton, 621 F.2d 1080, 1082, 22 FEP 1497 (10th Cir. 1980) (allowing plaintiff to discover personnel files of other employees promoted over him in order to permit him to compare qualifications and job performance); Ruran v. Beth El Temple of W. Hartford, Inc., 226 F.R.D. 165, 169 (D. Conn. 2005) (material in other employees' personnel files subject to exception to state statute protecting confidentiality of employee records, and hence discoverable); EEOC v. County of San Benito, 818 F. Supp. 289, 291, 61 FEP 946 (N.D. Cal. 1993) (state confidentiality laws prohibiting disclosure of peace officer's personnel records in any civil proceeding do not bar EEOC from obtaining those records in connection with sexual harassment claim; EEOC's mandate preempts state restrictions); Dinkins v. Ohio State Highway Patrol, 116 F.R.D. 270, 272 (N.D. Ohio 1987) (state law protecting as confidential law enforcement investigative reports does not extend to reports used in hiring decisions); Catherman v. Reynolds Metals Co., 28 FEP 668, 669 (N.D. Ga. 1980) (plaintiff may discover personnel files of other employees of defendant who have made similar complaints of discrimination).

[46]See, e.g., Ramirez v. Boehringer Ingelheim Pharm., Inc., 425 F.3d 67, 74, 96 FEP 1071 (1st Cir. 2005) (district court did not abuse its discretion with protective order denying plaintiff access to identifying information of witnesses who notified employer that plaintiff was not following company procedures; district court adequately balanced witnesses' privacy and safety interest with plaintiff's interest in discovery); Oleszko v. State Compensation Ins. Fund, 243 F.3d 1154, 85 FEP 483 (9th Cir. 2001) (plaintiff not entitled to discover communications between other employees and unlicensed counselors employed by state compensation insurance fund's employee assistance program because those communications were protected by psychotherapist-patient privilege); Sanchez v. City of Santa Ana, 936 F.2d 1027, 1034, 59 FEP 1854 (9th Cir. 1990) (protective order properly denied plaintiffs access to other peace officers' personnel files where files contained irrelevant information, and relevant information could have been obtained from other sources); Broderick v. Shad, 117 F.R.D. 306, 310–11, 43 FEP 532 (D.D.C. 1987) (government deliberative-process privilege precludes former Securities and Exchange Commission (SEC) employee from taking depositions of SEC's counsel regarding the inquiry they conducted in response to a complaint of misconduct); El Dorado Sav.

To ease discovery, parties often stipulate to blanket or umbrella protective orders, particularly in complex litigation.[47] Rule 26(c) requires an initial showing of good cause for the court to grant the stipulated protective order.[48]

Courts have yet to arrive at a definitive position regarding the existence of a privilege for information containing "self-critical analyses."[49] A number of courts have refused to recognize a self-critical analysis privilege at all,[50] at least with respect to the kinds of standard documents most often at issue, under the theory that the plaintiff's

---

& Loan Ass'n v. Superior Ct., 235 Cal. Rptr. 303, 305 (Cal. Ct. App. 1987) (even though employee whose records plaintiffs sought to discover in sex discrimination action was only similarly situated male, his personnel file is protected by his privacy right and is not discoverable absent showing that information cannot be obtained through less intrusive means—even then, court should review file in camera and order disclosure of only relevant material).

[47]*See* MANUAL FOR COMPLEX LITIGATION FOURTH § 11.423, at 64–65 (4th ed. 2004); 8 WRIGHT, MILLER, & MARCUS, FEDERAL PRACTICE & PROCEDURE: CIVIL § 2043 (2d ed. 1994); *see also* Rivera v. NIBCO, Inc., 364 F.3d 1057, 1064–66, 93 FEP 929 (9th Cir. 2004) (affirming magistrate judge's issuance of protective order precluding employer from using discovery to inquire into plaintiff's immigration status, and finding that allowing defendant to inquire into employees' immigration status would so chill bringing of civil rights actions as to unacceptably burden public interest), *cert. denied*, 544 U.S. 905 (2005); Parkway Gallery Furniture, Inc. v. Kittinger/Pennsylvania House Group, Inc., 121 F.R.D. 264, 267 (M.D.N.C. 1988) (blanket or umbrella protective orders agreed on by parties increasingly common to facilitate discovery, particularly in complex litigation).

[48]*See* Makar-Wellbon v. Sony Elecs., Inc., 187 F.R.D. 576, 577, 80 FEP 841 (E.D. Wis. 1999). *But see Parkway Gallery Furniture*, 121 F.R.D. at 268 (stipulated protective order requires no initial good cause showing).

[49]*See* Burden-Meeks v. Welch, 319 F.3d 897, 901, 19 IER 1111 (7th Cir. 2003) (fact that intergovernmental agency report was voluntarily disclosed to mayor of municipality makes it unnecessary to decide whether self-critical analysis privilege exists).

[50]*See, e.g.*, Holt v. KMI-Continental, Inc., 95 F.3d 123, 134, 73 FEP 1615, 1623 (2d Cir. 1996) (noting in Title VII case that there is no authority for existence of "self-evaluative" privilege under Connecticut law); Granberry v. Jet Blue Airways, 228 F.R.D. 647, 650 (N.D. Cal. 2005) (self-critical analysis privilege does not exist in Title VII cases, particularly within Ninth Circuit, which has not recognized privilege in any case); Roberts v. Hunt, 187 F.R.D. 71, 76, 80 FEP 607, 609 (W.D.N.Y. 1999) (self-evaluative privilege not available under federal law); Aramburu v. Boeing Co., 885 F. Supp. 1434, 1437–40, 74 FEP 1114 (D. Kan. 1995) (ordering production of defendant's affirmative action plan and documents related to development of and compliance with plan and declining to recognize self-critical analysis privilege "where Congress itself has not seen fit to create [a privilege] after almost 30 years of implementation of the Civil Rights Act of 1964"), *aff'd*, 112 F.3d 1398 (10th Cir. 1997); Hardy v. New York News, Inc., 114 F.R.D. 633, 641–42, 46 FEP 1199 (S.D.N.Y. 1987) (plaintiffs entitled to discover documents referring to defendant's analyses of

need for relevant evidence of discrimination contained in such reports outweighs the risk that disclosure will impede employers' self-evaluations.[51]

Some courts have acknowledged the self-critical analysis privilege in limited circumstances. These courts have found defendants' affirmative action plans to be at least partially privileged under the theory that voluntary efforts to eliminate underrepresentation will be impeded if the employer effectively is penalized for acknowledging that underrepresentation exists.[52] Other courts have

---

minority group employment and comparisons of minority group composition of its workforce with those of various labor pools, where plaintiffs' interest in gathering information necessary to prove their case outweighs interest in fostering candid self-analysis and voluntary compliance with equal employment laws; threat of disclosure would have insignificant deterrent effect on preparation of such documents); *cf.* Resnick v. American Dental Ass'n, 95 F.R.D. 372, 374–75, 31 FEP 1359 (N.D. Ill. 1982) (self-critical analysis privilege does not justify refusal to produce personnel practices study prepared by management consulting firm, or minutes and documents of defendant's ad hoc committee on employee relations; work product doctrine inapplicable even though work was initiated with advice of counsel); Cloud v. Superior Court, 58 Cal. Rptr. 2d 365, 369, 72 FEP 777, 780–81 (Cal. Ct. App. 1996) (self-critical analysis privilege not among privileges contained in California Evidence Code and court not free to create new privileges as matter of judicial policy; accordingly, in sex discrimination lawsuit plaintiff may discover defendant's affirmative action plan and related self-critical analyses).

[51]*See, e.g.,* Adams v. Pinole Point Steel Co., 65 FEP 782, 783–84 (N.D. Cal. 1994) (self-critical analysis privilege does not protect affirmative action plan that employers prepare in compliance with Office of Federal Contract Compliance Programs mandates; doubtful that employer truly has expectation of confidentiality in such reports; because such reports can contain crucial evidence in otherwise hard-to-prove discrimination cases, it serves public benefit to allow plaintiffs access to tools they need to prevail in discrimination actions); Etienne v. Mitre Corp., 146 F.R.D. 145, 148–49, 62 FEP 662 (E.D. Va. 1993) (self-critical analysis privilege does not protect documents relating to defendant's internal investigations or reviews regarding its compliance with ADEA where (1) documents are relevant, (2) no evidence that their disclosure would impair defendant's ability or incentive to conduct similar employment policy reviews in future, (3) public interest favors disclosure in employment cases, and (4) documents do not reveal confidential communications); Tharp v. Sivyer Steel Corp., 149 F.R.D. 177, 182–85, 62 FEP 570 (S.D. Iowa 1993) (refusing to apply self-critical analysis privilege to defendant's affirmative action materials; concluding that privilege should not be recognized in employment cases because discovery will not likely chill employers' self-evaluations, whereas privilege may impede employees' access to relevant information); Martin v. Potomac Elec. Power Co., 58 FEP 355, 358–61 (D.D.C. 1990) (rejecting self-critical analysis privilege as basis for avoiding production of employer's affirmative action plan and other EEO reports and records).

[52]*See, e.g.,* Reid v. Lockheed Martin Aeronautics Co., 199 F.R.D. 379, 387–88 (N.D. Ga. 2001) (precluding from discovery employer's internal diversity reports

examined closely the nature of the plan to see if it in fact contains a "self-critical analysis," which those courts consider a prerequisite to protection.[53] Some courts that have compelled production of affirmative action plans have done so with accompanying protective orders.[54] Attempts to limit discovery of other "confidential" business proprietary information have met with mixed results.[55]

---

on basis of self-critical analysis privilege); Sheppard v. Consolidated Edison Co. of N.Y., 893 F. Supp. 6, 7–8 (E.D.N.Y. 1995) (granting protective order in employment discrimination case for study of affirmative action because "disclosure would chill future voluntary self-critical analysis of companies who in good faith seek to improve their employment practices"); John v. Trane Co., 831 F. Supp. 855, 856, 63 FEP 223 (S.D. Fla. 1993) (ordering defendant to produce its affirmative action plan, except those portions that contain subjective evaluations made by company management); Jamison v. Storer Broad. Co., 511 F. Supp. 1286, 1297, 25 FEP 699 (E.D. Mich. 1981) (granting new trial; error to introduce into evidence candid internal evaluations employer made of its affirmative action posture), *aff'd in part, rev'd in part mem.*, 830 F.2d 194, 45 FEP 300 (6th Cir. 1987); Rosario v. New York Times Co., 84 F.R.D. 626, 631, 21 FEP 493 (S.D.N.Y. 1979) (qualified privilege of self-examination permits free discussion and examination of questioned documents with view to compliance with law); Stevenson v. General Elec. Co., 18 FEP 746, 747 (S.D. Ohio 1978) (affirmative action plan need not be released where it would interfere with public policy mandating frank self-criticism and evaluation); Sanday v. Carnegie-Mellon Univ., 12 FEP 101, 103 (W.D. Pa. 1975) (denying plaintiffs' motion to compel defendant to produce its affirmative action plans); *cf.* EEOC v. General Tel. Co., 885 F.2d 575, 578–79, 50 FEP 1316 (9th Cir. 1989) (when employer obtains order precluding discovery of self-critical analysis portion of its equal opportunity program, it cannot present evidence of that program); Coates v. Johnson & Johnson, 756 F.2d 524, 551–52, 37 FEP 467 (7th Cir. 1985) (self-critical portion of affirmative action plan is privileged, but privilege is qualified and can be waived if used by defendant to prove nondiscrimination).

[53]*See* Martin v. Potomac Elec. Power Co., 58 FEP 355, 360–61 (D.D.C. 1990) (employer cannot claim self-critical analysis privilege to shield documents analyzing or discussing its compliance with EEO laws); Mister v. Illinois Cent. Gulf R.R., 42 FEP 1710, 1714–15 (S.D. Ill. 1985) (affirmative action plans and EEO-1 forms covered by privilege of self-critical analysis, but only with respect to subjective self-evaluation statements therein); Penk v. Oregon State Bd. of Higher Educ., 99 F.R.D. 506, 37 FEP 918 (D. Or. 1982) (self-critical analyses are privileged; objective data is discoverable).

[54]*See, e.g.*, Riggs v. United Parcel Serv., 24 FEP 93, 94 (E.D. Mo. 1980) (rejecting defendant's contention as to confidentiality of its affirmative action plans, but entering protective order); EEOC v. ISC Fin. Corp., 16 FEP 174, 178–79 (W.D. Mo. 1977) (compelling production of affirmative action plans and programs, but confidentiality protected against persons not parties to action); Ligon v. Frito-Lay, Inc., 19 FEP 722, 723 (N.D. Tex. 1978) (plaintiff entitled to discovery of employer's affirmative action plan, but court will examine it in camera to eliminate privileged matters, and remaining material will be released under appropriate protective order).

[55]*Compare* Trevino v. Celanese Corp., 701 F.2d 397, 405–06, 33 FEP 1324 (5th Cir. 1983) (overturning broad order that denied discovery into management structure

Where disclosure is required, an appropriate protective order may be granted.[56]

In *University of Pennsylvania v. EEOC*,[57] an academic tenure dispute, the Supreme Court addressed the controversy surrounding the putative "academic privilege," which purported to protect from disclosure peer-review documentation. The Court held that a plaintiff's showing of relevance is sufficient to require disclosure of peer-review materials pertinent to charges of discrimination challenging tenure decisions.[58] The Court noted that Congress, in extending Title VII to educational institutions and in providing for broad EEOC subpoena powers, did not see fit to create a privilege for peer-review documents. The Court explained that it is "reluctant to recognize a privilege in an area where it appears that Congress

---

and policies of employer), Isaacson v. Keck, Mahin & Cate, 61 FEP 1140, 1143–44 (N.D. Ill. 1993) (in sexual harassment case, defendant not entitled to blanket protective order over pretrial discovery that could damage its reputation) *and* Schafer v. Parkview Mem'l Hosp., Inc., 593 F. Supp. 61, 65, 35 FEP 1489 (N.D. Ind. 1984) (ordering disclosure of peer-review committee meeting minutes after balancing competing factors and finding that plaintiff's need for discovery outweighed reasons underlying statutory privilege) *with* Rossini v. Ogilvy & Mather, Inc., 798 F.2d 590, 601, 42 FEP 1615 (2d Cir. 1986) (affirming order restricting plaintiff counsel's access to personnel files), Keyes v. Lenoir Rhyne Coll., 552 F.2d 579, 581, 15 FEP 925 (4th Cir. 1977) (defendant not compelled to produce confidential evaluations of faculty members where college had not sought to justify any male-female disparity on basis of evaluations), Price v. County of Erie, 40 FEP 115, 117 (W.D.N.Y. 1986) (files of county law department regarding its investigation of plaintiff and others held privileged in action against county) *and* Sanders v. Shell Oil Co., 678 F.2d 614, 619, 29 FEP 98 (5th Cir. 1982) (stolen documents ordered sealed pending ruling on relevance and need for confidentiality).

[56]*See, e.g.*, Haynes v. Shoney's, Inc., 59 FEP 163, 165, 167–68 (N.D. Fla. 1991) (ordering defendant to produce personal correspondence files of certain officers and executives and documents relating to minority-owned public relations firm that employer hired to combat adverse publicity generated by employees' action; also, issuing protective order that limited access to non-business-related correspondence with EEOC and conciliation of discrimination claims); Yee v. Multnomah County, 53 FEP 622, 624 (D. Or. 1990) (plaintiff entitled to review personnel files of other employees, but because of confidential nature of files protective order must be entered prior to inspection); Davis v. Burlington Indus., Inc., 34 FEP 917, 918 (N.D. Ga. 1983) (granting motion for protective order that prohibited plaintiff from disseminating confidential commercial data and placed data under seal); *cf.* Cook v. Yellow Freight Sys., 132 F.R.D. 548, 552, 53 FEP 1681 (E.D. Cal. 1990) (in sexual harassment case, court ordered procedure that allowed plaintiffs access to other female employees' addresses and telephone numbers, but that required those employees' consent before plaintiffs could contact them or review their files).

[57]493 U.S. 182, 51 FEP 1118 (1990).

[58]*Id.* at 188–94.

has considered the relevant competing concerns but has not provided the privilege itself."[59] The Court also weighed the costs to the academic institution in disclosing confidences against the substantial costs associated with illegal discrimination in institutions of higher learning and concluded that the balance favored disclosure of peer-review materials.[60]

In a sexual harassment action, the plaintiff typically will seek discovery pertaining to the alleged harasser. Evidence of the alleged harasser's prior habits, history, and behavior in the workplace may be discoverable with relation to (a) the employer's knowledge of the harassment, (b) the existence of a hostile work environment, and (c) the supervisor's motive, if not too remote in time.[61] Evidence of a harasser's sexual orientation or past sexual

---

[59]*Id.* at 189.

[60]*Id.* at 193.

[61]*See, e.g.*, Green v. Administrators of Tulane Educ. Fund, 284 F.3d 642, 660, 89 FEP 587 (5th Cir. 2002) (district court did not abuse its discretion when it admitted testimony during Title VII action that physician had previously been accused of sexual harassment by three employees he supervised to show that university was on notice that physician may have been sexually harassing women); Griffin v. City of Opa-Locka, 261 F.3d 1295, 1313, 86 FEP 1254 (11th Cir. 2001) (evidence of city manager's prior acts of sexual harassment at other jobs admissible because such evidence was directly relevant to plaintiff's claims that city had custom of condoning sexual harassment); Grant v. Murphy & Miller, Inc., 149 F. Supp. 2d 957, 967, 86 FEP 127 (N.D. Ill. 2001) (supervisor's prior offensive conduct would be admissible to show supervisor's unlawful intent); Waterson v. Plank Road Motel Corp., 43 F. Supp. 2d 284, 287, 79 FEP 1248 (N.D.N.Y. 1999) (testimony of another female employee regarding her own experiences of alleged sexual harassment while working for same employer relevant to support female employee's hostile work environment claim); Hunter v. Allis-Chalmers Corp., 797 F.2d 1417, 1424, 41 FEP 721 (7th Cir. 1986) (racial harassment case; evidence of prior disciplinary acts against alleged harasser relevant on issue of employer knowledge); Horn v. Duke Homes, 755 F.2d 599, 602, 37 FEP 228 (7th Cir. 1985) (trial court properly admitted evidence of harasser's prior voluntary workplace affair and prior harassment to show his propensity to use his supervisory power to "sexually exploit" women); Webb v. Hyman, 861 F. Supp. 1094, 1111–12 (D.D.C. 1994) (evidence of allegations of prior harassment by particular defendant toward other women admissible because it provides evidence as to intent); Jones v. Commander, Kan. Army Ammunitions Plant, 147 F.R.D. 248, 251–52 (D. Kan. 1993) (plaintiff allowed to obtain documents regarding alleged harasser's performance evaluations and other incidents of sexual harassment); Jones v. Lyng, 669 F. Supp. 1108, 1115, 42 FEP 587 (D.D.C. 1986) (allowing testimony from employees that alleged harasser had reputation as "womanizer" and had made unwanted sexual advances toward female employees); Priest v. Rotary, 634 F. Supp. 571, 575–76, 40 FEP 208 (N.D. Cal. 1986) (considering testimony of other women employees that defendant fondled them, made sexually suggestive comments about their breasts, and circulated obscene photograph); *see also*

history or behavior, apart from sexual harassment, is likely not discoverable.[62]

One recurring issue concerns the extent to which a plaintiff's counsel may investigate a case by contacting a defendant's employees. Defendants sometimes dispute opposing counsel's right to have ex parte contact with the defendant company's past or current employees.[63] Ex parte contact with current managerial employees, on topics that could be imputed to the company, is forbidden.[64] Courts

---

Stair v. Lehigh Valley Carpenters Local 600, 813 F. Supp. 1116, 1120, 66 FEP 1471 (E.D. Pa. 1993) (excluding evidence of past acts of discrimination and harassment that occurred more than 4 years prior to present claim because their remoteness caused probative value to be substantially outweighed by danger of unfair prejudice); Kresko v. Rulli, 432 N.W.2d 764, 768–69 (Minn. Ct. App. 1988) (excluding evidence of alleged harasser's relationship with other women; plaintiff intended to show pattern or habit of harassment, but incidents were not similar to plaintiff's—they were mostly consensual, and potential prejudice outweighed evidentiary value). See generally Chapter 19 (Sexual and Other Forms of Harassment).

[62]See Jones, 147 F.R.D. at 252 (barring discovery concerning alleged sexual harasser's sexual orientation and history of behavior, except for allegations of sexual harassment, because such information is irrelevant to victim's perspective and disclosure of such information would annoy and embarrass alleged harasser); Longmire v. Alabama State Univ., 151 F.R.D. 414, 418 (M.D. Ala. 1992) (plaintiff not entitled to discovery about alleged harasser's prior sexual conduct during previous employment).

[63]Ex parte contact with represented parties is prohibited under most attorney ethics rules. See, e.g., MODEL RULES OF PROFESSIONAL CONDUCT, Rule 4.2 ("In representing a client, a lawyer shall not communicate about the subject of the representation with a party the lawyer knows to be represented by another lawyer in the matter, unless the lawyer has the consent of the other lawyer or is authorized by law to do so.").

[64]See Weeks v. Independent School Dist. No. I-89 of Okla. County, 230 F.3d 1201, 1208, 84 FEP 823 (10th Cir. 2000) (prohibiting ex parte communications with employees of organization whose statements may constitute admission on part of organization); Wagner v. City of Holyoke, 183 F. Supp. 2d 289, 291–92 (D. Mass. 2001) (prohibiting ex parte contact on behalf of plaintiff's attorney with those persons within defendant organization whose acts and omissions could be imputed to organization), aff'd, 404 F.3d 504 (1st Cir.), cert. denied, 126 S. Ct. 552 (2005); Haynes v. Shoney's, Inc., 59 FEP 163, 168 (N.D. Fla. 1991) (plaintiffs allowed to communicate with unnamed class members but barred from any and all contact with current managerial employees of any named defendant); McKitty v. Board of Educ., Nyack Sch. Dist., 53 FEP 358, 359–61 (S.D.N.Y. 1987) (ethical rule barring attorney from communicating with party known to be represented by another attorney applies to employees who are entity's "alter ego" or individuals who can bind it to decision or settle controversies on its behalf); Massa v. Eaton Corp., 109 F.R.D. 312, 314–15, 39 FEP 1211 (W.D. Mich. 1985) (prohibiting ex parte communication with managerial employees and making evidence from such sources inadmissible); see also ABA Committee on Ethics & Professional Responsibility, Formal Op. 95-396 (1995) (when defendant is an organization, Rule 4.2 prohibits plaintiff's counsel from communicating ex parte with persons having current managerial responsibility for defendant, and with any other person whose act or omission in connection with lawsuit may be imputed to defendant, or whose statement may constitute admission by defendant).

are divided on contacts with former managerial employees.[65] Most courts allow contact with current lower-level employees.[66]

2. Burdensome or Irrelevant Discovery

Demands for voluminous amounts of information are evaluated on a case-by-case basis by balancing the relevance of the requests against the burden of producing the responsive information.[67] The

---

[65]*Compare* Cram v. Lamson & Sessions Co., 148 F.R.D. 259, 263, 62 FEP 685 (S.D. Iowa 1993) (as long as attorney-client confidences are not implicated, ex parte contact with any former employee is allowed, whether or not employee is managerial), Valassis v. Samelson, 143 F.R.D. 118, 123 (E.D. Mich. 1992) (same), Shearson Lehman Bros., Inc. v. Wasatch Bank, 139 F.R.D. 412, 417 (D. Utah 1991) (same), Hanntz v. Shiley, Inc., 766 F. Supp. 258, 269 (D.N.J. 1991) (same), Action Air Freight, Inc. v. Pilot Air Freight Corp., 769 F. Supp. 899, 903 (E.D. Pa. 1991) (same), *appeal dismissed*, 961 F.2d 207 (3d Cir. 1992), Dubois v. Gradco Sys., Inc., 136 F.R.D. 341, 346–47 (D. Conn. 1991) (same), Polycast Tech. Corp. v. Uniroyal, Inc., 129 F.R.D. 621, 629 (S.D.N.Y. 1990) (same), Siguel v. Trustees of Tufts Coll., 52 FEP 697, 700 (D. Mass. 1990) (same) *and* ABA Committee on Ethics & Professional Responsibility, Formal Op. 95-396 (1991) (Rule 4.2, prohibiting ex parte contact with separately represented parties does not apply to former employees) *with* Collier v. Ram Partners, Inc., 159 F. Supp. 2d 889, 893, 86 FEP 1008 (D. Md. 2001) (ex parte contact with former employees prohibited if they have been "extensively exposed" to confidential information protected by attorney-client privilege), Klier v. Sordoni Skanska Constr. Co., 766 A.2d 761 (N.J. Super. Ct. App. Div. 2001) (ex parte contacts with former managerial employees are forbidden if former manager possesses information that could be imputed to company with regard to litigation at issue), Rentclub v. Transamerica Rental Fin. Corp., 811 F. Supp. 651, 658 (M.D. Fla. 1992) (ex parte contacts with former managerial employees forbidden if former manager possesses information that could be imputed to company), *aff'd*, 43 F.3d 1439 (11th Cir. 1995), PPG Indus., Inc. v. BASF Corp., 134 F.R.D. 118, 121–22 (W.D. Pa. 1990) (same), Amarin Plastics, Inc. v. Maryland Cup Corp., 116 F.R.D. 36, 39–41 (D. Mass. 1987) (same) *and* Porter v. Arco Metals Co., 642 F. Supp. 1116, 1118 (D. Mont. 1986) (prohibiting ex parte communications with former managerial and control group employees).

[66]*E.g.*, Carter-Herman v. City of Phila., 897 F. Supp. 899, 903, 68 FEP 1690 (E.D. Pa. 1995) (plaintiffs in sexual harassment action could interview nonmanagerial employees of defendant police department); McCallum v. CSX Transp., Inc., 149 F.R.D. 104, 110 (M.D.N.C. 1993) ("It may be noted that nothing in this Court's interpretation of the ethical rule prevents a party from interviewing rank and file employees who merely witnessed an event, even though they relate facts prejudicial to their employer."); Chancellor v. Boeing Co., 678 F. Supp. 250, 253, 45 FEP 1808 (D. Kan. 1988) (allowing ex parte contact with company's current employees but not with current managers).

[67]*Compare* Sorosky v. Burroughs Corp., 826 F.2d 794, 805, 44 FEP 1180 (9th Cir. 1987) (lower court did not abuse its discretion in denying plaintiff's motion to compel where plaintiff failed to show that potential benefit of producing data regarding defendant's worldwide business operations outweighed burden), O'Neal v. Riceland Foods, 684 F.2d 577, 581, 29 FEP 956 (8th Cir. 1982) (employer not required to answer interrogatories pertaining to hiring because partial summary judgment

discoverability calculus should not be confused, however, with the test used to determine the information's eventual *admissibility*.[68]

---

previously had determined that hiring was not issue in case), Marshall v. District of Columbia Water & Sewage Auth., 214 F.R.D. 23, 25 (D.D.C. 2003) (employer in race discrimination suit should not be compelled to produce data on age and sex of all other employees in plaintiff's department because such information was irrelevant), Aikens v. Deluxe Fin. Servs., Inc., 217 F.R.D. 533, 538–40 (D. Kan. 2003) (plaintiff's request for all information or documents "regarding" or "relating to" lawsuit, 11 plaintiffs, and eight EEOC charges involved in suit were unduly burdensome and must be limited to information that would tend to show defendant's knowledge of litigation activities conducted by plaintiffs), Black v. Fluor Corp., 959 F. Supp. 1135, 1142 (E.D. Mo. 1996) (information regarding sale of former employer's company irrelevant to alleged age discrimination and thus not discoverable), Collins v. J.C. Nichols Co., 56 FEP 1713, 1714 (W.D. Mo. 1991) (interrogatory seeking information regarding all discrimination claims against defendant, not limited in time frame, is overly burdensome because it would require defendant to retrace its entire corporate history), Capellupo v. FMC Corp., 46 FEP 1193, 1198 (D. Minn. 1988) (upholding magistrate judge's decision to refuse plaintiff employee's request to discover documents spanning 10-year period) *and* Helt v. Metropolitan Dist. Comm'n, 113 F.R.D. 7, 12, 42 FEP 1561 (D. Conn. 1986) (in suit alleging sex discrimination in retirement benefits, not all documents interpreting or requesting interpretation of plan are relevant) *with* Sweat v. Miller Brewing Co., 708 F.2d 655, 658, 32 FEP 384 (11th Cir. 1983) (statistical information concerning employer's general policy and practice of minority employment may be relevant to establishing pretext and is therefore discoverable in individual discrimination case), Zubalake v. UBS Warburg LLC, 217 F.R.D. 309, 317, 91 FEP 1574 (S.D.N.Y. 2003) (former employee asserting gender discrimination and retaliation claims entitled to discovery of relevant emails that had been deleted and resided only on backup disks), Finch v. Hercules, Inc., 149 F.R.D. 60, 63, 62 FEP 295 (D. Del. 1993) (relevance of statistical evidence regarding layoffs, terminations, and retirees, as well as information regarding other adverse age bias rulings against employer, outweighs burden of production), Abel v. Merrill Lynch & Co., 1993 WL 33348, at *5 (S.D.N.Y. Feb. 4, 1993) ("Given the resources of [the employer] and the importance of enforcing the civil rights laws, plaintiff's need for information relevant to the impact of the company-wide workforce reduction on older employees outweighs the burden that production will impose upon the [company] in this situation."), Haynes v. Shoney's, Inc., 59 FEP 163, 167 (N.D. Fla. 1991) (past racial bias complaints against employer relevant and discoverable), Willis v. Golden Rule Ins. Co., 56 FEP 1451, 1454 (E.D. Tenn. 1991) (relevance to plaintiff's statistical case of data concerning all employer's directors and managers over 5-year period outweighs burden on employer to produce such data; relevance to plaintiff's pattern-or-practice claim of identities of all persons who filed age bias charges against employer outweighs burden), Morris v. Electrical Sys. Div., 54 FEP 292, 296 (N.D. Ind. 1990) (plaintiff entitled to discover records of other terminated employees despite defendant's claim that production is overly burdensome), Guruwaya v. Montgomery Ward, Inc., 119 F.R.D. 36, 39, 60 FEP 811 (N.D. Cal. 1988) (although collecting regionwide data regarding defendant's employment statistics would be burdensome, relevance of information required that it be produced), *and* Allen v. Colgate-Palmolive Co., 539 F. Supp. 57, 71, 27 FEP 1408 (S.D.N.Y. 1981) (compelling defendant to produce all evaluations prepared by supervisor that contain same discriminatory phrase as one in plaintiff's evaluation).

[68]*E.g.*, Siskonen v. Stanadyne, Inc., 124 F.R.D. 610, 612, 53 FEP 700 (W.D. Mich. 1989) (issue of whether information may be discovered not governed by whether

Certain issues recur, and time frame is a major one. Courts have used a reasonableness approach in considering the time period for which information must be made available. To the extent that one can discern a guideline, discovery often is allowed for a four- or five-year period, but the cases are not at all uniform.[69] In particular, cases differ in delimiting the period of discovery to a certain period of time preceding the liability period, the EEOC charge, the court complaint, or the date of the request.

As to the geographical scope of discovery, defendants often resist discovery targeted at departments, units, or businesses other than the one in which the plaintiff is or was employed. In these

---

its probative value outweighs its prejudicial effect); Aspgren v. Montgomery Ward & Co., 47 FEP 1425, 1427 (N.D. Ill. 1983) (discovery test is one of relevance, not weight or admissibility at trial).

[69]See, e.g., Tomanovich v. Autumn Glen, 89 FEP 1157, 1160 (S.D. Ind. 2002) (although plaintiff was only employed for 2 months, defendant improperly limited discovery period to 1 year: "A time period of five years is reasonable and appropriate in a case alleging disparate treatment where plaintiff may utilize statistical evidence to establish a prima facie case of discrimination."); Lyoch v. Anheuser-Busch Cos., 164 F.R.D. 62, 67, 74 FEP 691 (E.D. Mo. 1995) ("Information regarding Defendant's employment practices prior to plaintiff's employment may be relevant to establishing a pattern or practice of discrimination and showing that Defendant's proffered reason for disparate treatment is a pretext for discrimination."); Barnhart v. Safeway Stores, Inc., 60 FEP 751, 754–55 (E.D. Cal. 1992) (plaintiffs entitled to seek information regarding employer's policies and practices for 5 years prior to liability period); Collins v. J.C. Nichols Co., 56 FEP 1713, 1714 (W.D. Mo. 1991) (interrogatories containing no time frame will be limited to 4-year period preceding commencement of this action); Siskonen v. Stanadyne, Inc., 124 F.R.D. 610, 613, 53 FEP 700 (W.D. Mich. 1989) (request for employment information dating back to 1967 excessive where plaintiff was employed for less than 1 year). Other courts have limited discovery to shorter or longer time periods. Compare EEOC v. Kelly-Springfield Tire Co., 38 FEP 194, 197 (E.D.N.C. 1985) (period of 2 years prior to alleged acts is reasonable limitation on discovery), EEOC v. Delaware State Police, 618 F. Supp. 451, 453, 39 FEP 81 (D. Del. 1985) (enforcing EEOC subpoena for information that extended to 3 years prior to ADEA charge over objection by state police that EEOC ought to show "willfulness" before being allowed discovery predating 2-year limitation) and Williams v. United Parcel Serv., Inc., 34 FEP 1655, 1655 (N.D. Ohio 1982) (limiting interrogatory answers and production of documents to period beginning 1 year prior to earliest alleged act of discrimination) with Haynes v. Shoney's, Inc., 59 FEP 163, 166 (N.D. Fla. 1991) (plaintiffs entitled to discovery period dating back 11 years; but allowing discovery as far back as 1965 effective date of Title VII would be unmanageable), United States v. Board of Educ., 52 FEP 653, 655 (N.D. Ill. 1990) (ordering defendant to answer discovery regarding its practices that predated 1979 effective date of Title VII's pregnancy bias amendment), Capellupo v. FMC Corp., 46 FEP 1193, 1198 (D. Minn. 1988) (order permitting discovery for period exceeding 6 years, including 5 years before plaintiff filed suit, was reasonable) and Jacobs v. Sea-Land Serv., 23 FEP 1179, 1181 (N.D. Cal. 1980) (plaintiffs entitled to discovery going back to effective date of Act for ongoing discrimination only).

circumstances, some courts have allowed the discovery,[70] but others have not.[71]

---

[70]*E.g.*, Duke v. University of Tex., 729 F.2d 994, 996–97, 34 FEP 982 (5th Cir. 1984) (promotion and pay records of other departments of university are discoverable prior to class action certification hearing); Hollander v. American Cyanamid Co., 895 F.2d 80, 84, 51 FEP 1881 (2d Cir. 1990) (district court abused its discretion in refusing to compel defendant to respond to individual plaintiff's interrogatory requesting information pertaining to management employees throughout company); Diaz v. AT & T, 752 F.2d 1356, 1363–64, 36 FEP 1742 (9th Cir. 1983) (district court improperly denied plaintiff access to discovery regarding employer's hiring and promotion statistics for western region); Rich v. Martin Marietta Corp., 522 F.2d 333, 342–45, 11 FEP 211 (10th Cir. 1975) (district court improperly denied plaintiffs access to plantwide information that would have allowed plaintiffs to establish overall trends in defendant's hiring, promotion, demotion, and layoff practices); EEOC v. BASF Corp., 14 AD 535, 537 (E.D. Mo. 2003) ("where charging party has identified discrimination related to a company-wide policy, the relevant 'work unit' properly includes all employees subject to the policy"); Chambers v. Capital Cities/ABC, 154 F.R.D. 63, 66, 64 FEP 581 (S.D.N.Y. 1994) (plaintiffs entitled to discover personnel practices in corporate entities other than their direct employer); Willis v. Golden Rule Ins. Co., 56 FEP 1451, 1454 (E.D. Tenn. 1991) (plaintiff alleging pattern or practice of age discrimination allowed companywide geographic scope of discovery regarding hiring, promotion, and termination of managers in order to assess statistical case); Guruwaya v. Montgomery Ward, Inc., 119 F.R.D. 36, 39, 60 FEP 811 (N.D. Cal. 1988) (plaintiff entitled to discover regional statistics regarding management, even though decision to replace plaintiff was made on local level); Owens v. Bethlehem Mines Corp., 108 F.R.D. 207, 213–14, 39 FEP 782 (S.D. W. Va. 1985) (permitting companywide discovery to obtain pattern-or-practice evidence); Brown v. Marriott Corp., 33 FEP 550, 551 (N.D. Ga. 1983) (plaintiff entitled to discover promotion practices in hotels other than one at which he worked because transfers were common with promotions); Whalen v. McLean Trucking Co., 37 FEP 835, 837 (N.D. Ga. 1983) (plaintiff entitled to discover age discrimination claims without regard to any geographic restriction); Riggs v. United Parcel Serv., 24 FEP 93, 94 (E.D. Mo. 1980) (compelling defendants to answer interrogatories for entire Missouri district).

[71]*E.g.*, Scales v. J.C. Bradford & Co., 925 F.2d 901, 906–07, 55 FEP 612 (6th Cir. 1991) (denying plaintiff's request for companywide payroll records; discovery limited to department where plaintiff worked, because decisions were made locally); Earley v. Champion Int'l Corp., 907 F.2d 1077, 1084–85, 53 FEP 968 (11th Cir. 1990) (plaintiffs properly denied nationwide discovery in action claiming age discrimination in reduction in force because each plant given autonomy in deciding which employees should be terminated); Jhirad v. TD Sec. USA Inc., 91 FEP 1232, 1236 (S.D.N.Y. 2003) (where complaint did not allege facts that group of companies was employer, plaintiff was only entitled to statistics from his subsidiary company, not parent company and other subsidiaries); Hill v. Motel 6, 205 F.R.D. 490, 494, 87 FEP 652, 656 (S.D. Ohio 2001) (in disparate treatment case, plaintiff could not demonstrate good cause to permit discovery of all area managers' personnel files); Witten v. A.H. Smith & Co., 104 F.R.D. 398, 400–01, 36 FEP 268 (D. Md. 1984) (limiting discovery to three facilities under same umbrella as plaintiff's), *aff'd mem.*, 785 F.2d 306 (4th Cir. 1986); James v. Newspaper Agency Corp., 591 F.2d 579, 582, 18 FEP 1547 (10th Cir. 1979) (plaintiff limited to discovery of information for her own

Some courts have precluded discovery concerning non-similarly situated employees.[72] Other courts have limited discovery to the type of discrimination at issue in the particular case.[73]

Different discovery rules may apply in class actions, as a class suit by definition involves persons and circumstances beyond the particular named plaintiff or plaintiffs. As with other types of cases, courts in class actions have recognized the need to weigh competing considerations.[74] The Supreme Court has held that, at least in

---

department); Grigsby v. North Miss. Med. Ctr., 586 F.2d 457, 460, 18 FEP 1225 (5th Cir. 1978) (court did not abuse its discretion in limiting interrogatories to practices of medical center units at which employees and former employees were employed prior to class certification); Lute v. Consolidated Freightways, Inc., 59 FEP 394, 395 (N.D. Ind. 1992) (discovery limited to facility where plaintiff worked); Suggs v. Capital Cities/ABC, Inc., 122 F.R.D. 430, 431–32 (S.D.N.Y. 1988) (information concerning persons not employed in field producer positions irrelevant to evaluating plaintiff's claim that defendant promoted less-qualified people over her to field producer positions); Hendrix v. Safeway Stores, Inc., 39 FEP 118, 119 (W.D. Mo. 1985) (limiting discovery to division where plaintiff was employed; nationwide discovery denied); Prouty v. National R.R. Passenger Corp., 99 F.R.D. 545, 548 (D.D.C. 1983) (limiting individual plaintiff's discovery to department in which plaintiff worked).

[72]See, e.g., Banks v. CBOCS, W. Inc., 91 FEP 1019, 1021 (N.D. Ill. Apr. 16, 2003) (discovery limited to terminations of managers because nonmanagement employees were decidedly not similarly situated). But see Lyoch v. Anheuser-Busch Cos., 164 F.R.D. 62, 68, 74 FEP 691 (E.D. Mo. 1995) (information regarding jobs above plaintiff relevant to show career paths of employees beyond plaintiff's grade level); Capellupo v. FMC Corp., 46 FEP 1193, 1198–99 (D. Minn. 1988) (granting plaintiff's motion to compel production of documents pertaining to all employees, whether members of bargaining unit or not).

[73]See, e.g., Lyoch, 164 F.R.D. at 69 (in action alleging sex discrimination, statistics regarding race not relevant). But see Cardenas v. Prudential Ins. Co. of Am., 91 FEP 82, 84 (D. Minn. 2003) (plaintiffs demonstrated that claims, practices, and protected classes at issue are so wide-ranging that all requested information regarding other lawsuits, administrative charges, and informal complaints of discrimination was reasonably calculated to lead to discovery of admissible evidence).

[74]Compare Blum v. Gulf Oil Corp., 597 F.2d 936, 938, 20 FEP 108 (5th Cir. 1979) (employer not compelled to produce information for entire company, only department where plaintiff was employed) and National Org. for Women v. Sperry Rand Corp., 88 F.R.D. 272, 276–77, 24 FEP 781 (D. Conn. 1980) (although some discovery is necessary prior to determination of class certification, massive precertification document production request is unjustifiable) with Abram v. United Parcel Serv. of Am., Inc., 200 F.R.D. 424, 426 (E.D. Wis. 2001) (permitting discovery of statistical data relating to supervisor compensation for putative nationwide race discrimination class action prior to certification relevant to whether plaintiffs can make adequate showing of pattern of lower pay within proposed class of African-American supervisors), Barnhart v. Safeway Stores, Inc., 60 FEP 751, 756–57 (E.D. Cal. Dec. 14, 1992) (food department employees may conduct discovery to determine whether nonfood employees should be included in proposed class; full-time employees may

certain circumstances, plaintiffs seeking to maintain a collective action under the ADEA may discover the names and addresses of comparably situated employees or former employees.[75]

Although courts have held that before class certification plaintiffs are limited to discovery on the certification issue,[76] in practice much of this discovery will overlap with discovery on the merits.[77] Sufficient discovery will be allowed in order to enable the Court to determine the class certification issues and the proper scope of any class.[78]

---

conduct discovery to determine whether part-time employees should be included in proposed class) *and* Canty v. Philip Morris, U.S.A., 18 FEP 86, 88 (E.D. Pa. 1978) (plaintiff class entitled to disclosure of statistical information on nationwide basis, even though nationwide class has not yet been certified, because statistics would shed light on whether plaintiff's claims were typical of claims for national class or for smaller class; if national class is inappropriate, comparison with other division or regions might have probative value).

[75]Hoffman-La Roche, Inc. v. Sperling, 493 U.S. 165, 170, 51 FEP 853 (1989) (discovery of names and addresses of discharged employees relevant, and "there were no grounds to limit the discovery under the facts and circumstances of this case"); *see also* Willis v. Golden Rule Ins. Co., 56 FEP 1451, 1452–54 (E.D. Tenn. 1991) (demoted manager allowed to discover information about other managers in case of age discrimination).

[76]*E.g.*, Mueller v. CBS, Inc., 200 F.R.D. 242, 246 (W.D. Pa. 2001) (depositions of expert witnesses in ADEA class action relating to merits will be conducted in merits phase of discovery); Wilfong v. Rent-A-Center, Inc., 2001 WL 578262, at *2, 87 FEP 1094 (S.D. Ill. 2001) ("discovery on the merits has been stayed until ruling on plaintiff's motion for class certification"); Tracy v. Dean Witter Reynolds, Inc., 185 F.R.D. 303, 305 (D. Colo. 1998) (discovery on merits must not be completed prior to class certification).

[77]*See Mueller*, 200 F.R.D. at 245 ("class certification discovery may overlap substantially with merits discovery"); MANUAL FOR COMPLEX LITIGATION FOURTH § 21.14, at 256 (4th ed. 2004) ("Arbitrary insistence on the merits/class discovery distinction sometimes thwarts the informed judicial assessment that current class certification practice emphasizes. Allowing some merits discovery during the precertification period is generally more appropriate for cases that are large and likely to continue even if not certified. On the other hand, in cases that are unlikely to continue if not certified, discovery into the aspects of the merits unrelated to certification delays the certification decision and can create extraordinary and unnecessary expense and burden."). *See generally* Chapter 32 (Class Actions).

[78]*See* Pittman v. E.I. du Pont de Nemours & Co., 552 F.2d 149, 150, 29 FEP 876 (5th Cir. 1977) (certain amount of discovery is essential in order to determine existence and scope of class, but interrogatories as propounded here were overly broad and burdensome); Holley v. Pansophic Sys., 64 FEP 366, 367–68 (N.D. Ill. 1993) (affirming plaintiff's motion to compel discovery on broad allegations of systemic sex discrimination in order to demonstrate "class nature" of suit); *Barnhart*, 60 FEP at 754–56 (allowing broad discovery in order to enable parties to provide court with "all information that district court *might* find relevant in making class action determination")

B. Discovery Sought by Defendants

1. Privileged Materials

The EEOC has resisted discovery of portions of its files by claiming the "deliberative process" privilege.[79] Although the EEOC generally has been unsuccessful in wholly resisting defense discovery,[80] courts have granted protective orders with respect to certain information.[81]

(emphasis added); Zahorik v. Cornell Univ., 98 F.R.D. 27, 30, 31 FEP 1366 (N.D.N.Y. 1983) (plaintiffs, whose prior motion for class certification was denied without prejudice may engage in broad discovery relating to class claims), aff'd, 729 F.2d 85, 34 FEP 165 (2d Cir. 1984); Hawkins v. Fulton County, 95 F.R.D. 88, 94, 29 FEP 762 (N.D. Ga. 1982) ("class related discovery is permissible even though no class has been certified"); Nash v. City of Oakwood, 90 F.R.D. 633, 636, 28 FEP 279 (S.D. Ohio 1981) (discovery limited to determining maintainability of action as class). See generally Chapter 32 (Class Actions).

[79]See, e.g., Scott v. PPG Indus., Inc., 142 F.R.D. 291, 293–94, 58 FEP 1211 (N.D. W. Va. 1992) (deliberative process privilege bars employer from asking EEOC investigator deposition questions about or from reviewing EEOC documents concerning impressions and evaluations of its investigation of class sex discrimination charge).

[80]E.g., Williams v. E.I. du Pont de Nemours & Co., 119 F.R.D. 648, 651, 45 FEP 887 (W.D. Ky. 1987) (granting employer's request for discovery of documents used by EEOC to create its database, except for certain documents that were irrelevant to EEOC's method of analysis); EEOC v. Citizens Bank & Trust Co., 117 F.R.D. 366, 44 FEP 435 (D. Md. 1987) (EEOC's claim of "deliberative-process" privilege does not preclude employer from discovery of materials that private plaintiff would be compelled to make available); Winfield v. St. Joe Paper Co., 20 FEP 1094, 1095 (N.D. Fla. 1977) (employer may discover discussions occurring prior or subsequent to actual conciliation attempts); EEOC v. Anchor Continental, Inc., 74 F.R.D. 523, 526–29, 15 FEP 90 (D.S.C. 1977) (EEOC opposed discovery on grounds of attorney work product and executive privilege; court found exception to work product rule when its in camera inspection revealed that plaintiff had little evidence to support complaint; court ordered EEOC to produce all records requested, to answer all interrogatories, and to pay attorney's fees).

[81]E.g., Olitsky v. Spencer Gifts, Inc., 964 F.2d 1471, 1477, 61 FEP 1507 (5th Cir. 1992) (letter employer's general counsel wrote to EEOC responding to plaintiff's charge was discoverable because it set forth purely factual material and did not constitute conciliation material); EEOC v. Bice of Chi., 229 F.R.D. 581, 583 (N.D. Ill. 2005) (granting EEOC's motion for protective order barring discovery into charging party's immigration status); EEOC v. Howard Univ., 31 FEP 1263, 1264 (D.D.C. 1983) (allowing employer unrestricted deposition of witnesses on whose testimony EEOC intended to rely in support of its motion for preliminary injunction, but granting protective order to prohibit questioning about whether deponents had given statements to EEOC or whether they had cooperated with EEOC's investigation of other charges); EEOC v. Colgate-Palmolive Co., 4 FEP 1551, 1555 (S.D.N.Y. 1983) (defendant not entitled to discover whether EEOC's conciliation efforts were made in good faith where EEOC agents made clear that their proposals were subject to Commission approval).

Absent a showing of abuse of process by the EEOC, discovery sought by defendants resisting enforcement of an EEOC subpoena[82] or seeking to ascertain the underlying basis of a charge[83] is severely circumscribed. Except in limited circumstances,[84] discovery of the identity of governmental informers is not permitted.[85]

---

[82]*Compare* EEOC v. Ford Motor Credit Co., 26 F.3d 44, 65 FEP 65 (6th Cir. 1994) (affirming EEOC's subpoena order because scope of subpoena is not abuse of EEOC's authority), EEOC v. American Express Centurion Bank, 758 F. Supp. 217, 56 FEP 1817 (D. Del. 1991) (affirming EEOC's subpoena because it is not intended to serve purposes outside jurisdiction of agency), *In re* EEOC, 709 F.2d 392, 402–03, 32 FEP 361 (5th Cir. 1983) (EEOC commissioner required to submit to deposition with respect to reasons for issuance of charge only when charged party presents meaningful evidence that EEOC is attempting to abuse its investigative authority) *and* EEOC v. St. Regis Paper Co., 717 F.2d 1302, 1304, 32 FEP 1849 (9th Cir. 1983) (discovery against EEOC should be allowed only where exceptional circumstances show EEOC abused process) *with* EEOC v. Neches Butane Prods. Co., 31 FEP 1097, 1098 (E.D. Tex. 1981) (permitting deposition of EEOC official on "substantial showing" that Commission abused process).

[83]*See, e.g.*, EEOC v. K-Mart Corp., 694 F.2d 1055, 1067–68, 30 FEP 788 (6th Cir. 1982) (vacating order that required EEOC officials to submit to depositions on facts and circumstances surrounding their decision to issue charge; such discovery would divert EEOC from its primary purpose of determining whether Title VII was violated); Mayfield v. President Riverboat Casino, 84 FEP 318, 320 (E.D. Mo. 2000) (employer may not take deposition of EEOC investigator who attempted to resolve dispute between employee and employer using informal methods of conciliation); Evans v. F.W. Woolworth Co., 78 FEP 492, 493 (S.D. Fla. 1998) (denying defendant's right to depose EEOC investigator, based in part on finding that best evidence of factual information regarding EEOC's investigation is in nonprivileged documents in charge file); Valley Indus. Serv., Inc. v. EEOC, 570 F. Supp. 902, 906, 32 FEP 482 (N.D. Cal. 1983) (denying employer discovery as to validity of charge where it had not made requisite substantial showing of abuse of process and discovery would interfere with investigative process).

[84]*E.g.*, Hoffman v. United Telecomms., Inc., 117 F.R.D. 440, 445, 58 FEP 407 (D. Kan. 1987) (informer's privilege does not protect identities of potential claimants and facts on which claims are based from disclosure to employer, because information is vital to employer's preparation of its case; EEOC can mask identities of claimants who responded to questionnaires by mixing them with those from other sources); EEOC v. Consolidated Edison Co., 37 FEP 1660, 1664 (S.D.N.Y. 1981) (allowing limited discovery of documents by or concerning 163 persons known to defendant but declining as to other "informers" represented by EEOC).

[85]*See* Does I–XXIII v. Advanced Textile Corp., 214 F.3d 1058, 1072 (9th Cir. 2000) (permitting plaintiffs in Fair Labor Standards Act (FLSA) action brought by Secretary of Labor to use pseudonyms); Usery v. Ritter, 547 F.2d 528, 531, 15 FEP 1713 (10th Cir. 1977) (Secretary of Labor not compelled to supply identity of Secretary's informants in equal pay action); Martin v. New York City Transit Auth., 148 F.R.D. 56, 63 (E.D.N.Y. 1993) (identity of city transit authority employees who provided statements to Department of Labor in its investigation of city's alleged

Defendants have had some success in obtaining information claimed to be protected by the attorney-client privilege where circumstances indicate that the holder of the privilege has waived it.[86]

The psychotherapist-patient privilege, announced in *Jaffee v. Redmond*,[87] has been extended to information exchanged between employees and counselors in employee assistance programs.[88]

---

violation of travel time rules may remain confidential); Marting v. Albany Bus. Journal, 870 F. Supp. 927, 937 (N.D.N.Y. 1992) (withholding identity of Department of Labor employees bringing FLSA action even though employees revealed information only on being interviewed by government); EEOC v. G-K-G, Inc., 131 F.R.D. 553, 555–56, 53 FEP 817 (N.D. Ill. 1990) (employer being sued by EEOC not entitled to discover identities of two confidential informers); EEOC v. Citizens Bank & Trust Co., 117 F.R.D. 366, 367, 44 FEP 435 (D. Md. 1987) (informer's privilege warrants denial of employer's request for documents that would disclose identity of EEOC informers; employer not barred from discovering contents of statements and interviews with employees specifically named in complaint); Donovan v. Forbes, 614 F. Supp. 124, 126–27, 27 WH 669 (D. Vt. 1985) (employer not entitled to discover names of employee-informers or to obtain employee questionnaires, despite meritorious reasons for disclosure; other sources are available); Donovan v. First Fed. Sav. & Loan Ass'n, 26 WH 108, 110 (S.D. Iowa 1982) (finding insufficient employer's claim that it needed to know source of Labor Department investigation because it feared harassment from former employees); Donovan v. Fasgo, Inc., 25 WH 332, 333 (E.D. Pa. 1981) (institution of equal pay action did not waive government's privilege to withhold informer's identity).

[86]*E.g.*, Russell v. Curtin Matheson Scientific, Inc., 493 F. Supp. 456, 457–59, 23 FEP 739 (S.D. Tex. 1980) (defendants entitled to question plaintiffs regarding legal advice they received and problems they might have on procedural requirements and, if necessary, depose attorneys; plaintiffs waived any privilege by arguing that statutory period had been equitably tolled); Travers v. Travenol Labs., Inc., 94 F.R.D. 92, 93–94, 33 FEP 1457 (N.D. Ill. 1982) (defendant entitled to obtain from plaintiff's former counsel documents relating to discrimination charge plaintiff had filed against her prior employer; any privilege waived when documents were sent to EEOC), *aff'd mem.*, 723 F.2d 66 (7th Cir. 1983); Penk v. Oregon State Bd. of Higher Educ., 99 F.R.D. 511, 516–17 (D. Or. 1983) (in case certified as class action, work product doctrine may be abrogated by showing that information on class members' claims is necessary; information not protected by attorney-client privilege because class members are neither parties nor clients of plaintiffs' counsel). *But see* EEOC v. International Profit Assocs., 206 F.R.D. 215, 220 (N.D. Ill. 2002) (interview notes obtained from employees after case was filed protected by attorney-client privilege); Derderian v. Polaroid Corp., 121 F.R.D. 13, 15–16, 47 FEP 575 (D. Mass. 1988) (plaintiff's personal notes, which she kept in order to provide counsel with record of discriminatory events, are protected by attorney-client and work product privileges, even though plaintiff reviewed notes prior to testifying at deposition).

[87]518 U.S. 1, 9–12, 15–17 (1996).

[88]Oleszko v. State Compensation Ins. Fund, 243 F.3d 1154, 1159, 85 FEP 483 (9th Cir. 2001) (psychotherapist-patient privilege protects information held by unlicensed counselors).

2. Burdensome or Irrelevant Discovery

Courts apply a balancing process when considering the burdensomeness versus the relevance of discovery.[89] A defendant's discovery of private information regarding the plaintiff is illustrative. Rule 26(c) requires courts to balance the relevance of the evidence that a defendant seeks against the degree to which the discovery will invade the plaintiff's right to privacy.[90]

Sexual harassment cases involve special rules.[91] Previously limited to criminal cases, Rule 412 of the Federal Rules of Evidence was amended in 1994 to limit the admissibility of evidence in civil actions regarding the past sexual behavior of sexual harassment victims.[92] Rule 412(b)(2) prescribes a test that balances

---

[89]*See, e.g.*, Goff v. Kroger Co., 121 F.R.D. 61, 62, 47 FEP 465 (S.D. Ohio 1988) (denying defendant's motion to compel plaintiff's response to interrogatories; all information concerning issues in case was available through deposition testimony, and demanding answers to interrogatories would needlessly burden plaintiff); Lewis v. J.P. Stevens & Co., 11 FEP 364, 365–66 (D.S.C. 1975) (providing detailed information on plaintiff's preparation of proposed exhibits and name and address of all persons contacted in connection with action is burdensome, but plaintiffs must provide list of their witnesses and substance of testimony as well as names of those who have consented to being class members or indicated agreement).

[90]*See* Rivera v. NIBCO, Inc., 364 F.3d 1057, 1064 (9th Cir. 2004) (unfettered discovery into the immigration status of immigrant employees would impermissibly chill the enforcement of Title VII, be inconsistent with the policy of the Act, and is of no consequence as to whether the employer actually violated the Act), *cert. denied*, 544 U.S. 905 (2005); Hlinka v. Bethlehem Steel Corp., 863 F.2d 279, 282 (3d Cir. 1988) (affirming district court's order precluding defendants from access to circumstances of retirement and salaries of employees because such disclosure would be invasion of privacy), *superseded by statute on other grounds*, Bellas v. CBS, Inc., 221 F.3d 517 (3d Cir. 2000); Eggleston v. Chicago Journeymen Plumbers' Local 130, 657 F.2d 890, 903, 26 FEP 1192 (7th Cir. 1981) (despite liberal construction accorded term "relevance" in discovery, defendant should not ask plaintiff deposition questions that unnecessarily touch sensitive areas or go beyond reasonable limits); Cook v. Yellow Freight Sys., Inc., 132 F.R.D. 548, 552, 53 FEP 1681 (E.D. Cal. 1990) (when balance favors disclosure of private information, scope of disclosure will be narrowly circumscribed, permitted only to extent necessary for fair resolution of lawsuit); Priest v. Rotary, 98 F.R.D. 755, 761–62, 32 FEP 1064 (N.D. Cal. 1983) (balancing relevance of discovering intimate information about lives of sexual harassment plaintiff and her friends and acquaintances against potential that such requests would harass, intimidate, and discourage plaintiff from prosecuting her case).

[91]*See generally* Chapter 19 (Sexual and Other Forms of Harassment).

[92]The rule reads, in pertinent part, as follows:

(a) Evidence Generally Inadmissible. The following evidence is not admissible in any civil or criminal proceeding involving alleged sexual misconduct except as provided in subdivisions (b) and (c):

the probative value of the evidence against the danger of harm to the victim and the unfair prejudice to any party. The burden rests on the proponent to demonstrate admissibility. Moreover, commentary accompanying Rule 412 would raise the threshold for admission by requiring that the probative value of the evidence "*substantially* outweigh the specified dangers."[93]

Although amended Rule 412 is a rule of evidence, not of civil procedure, courts have deemed it of critical importance in considering the discoverability of a sexual harassment plaintiff's past sexual behavior. Courts that have examined the issue have been vigilant in balancing the respective interests to protect against unnecessary intrusion into a plaintiff's prior conduct.[94] Evidence that the plaintiff previously engaged in sexual activity within the workplace during

---

(1) Evidence offered to prove that any alleged victim engaged in other sexual behavior.
(2) Evidence offered to prove any alleged victim's sexual predisposition.
(b) Exceptions
. . .
(2) In a civil case, evidence offered to prove the sexual behavior or sexual predisposition of any alleged victim is admissible if it is otherwise admissible under these rules and its probative value substantially outweighs the danger of harm to any victim and of unfair prejudice to any party. Evidence of an alleged victim's reputation is admissible only if it has been placed in controversy by the alleged victim.
FED. R. EVID. 412.
[93]FED. R. EVID. 412, Notes of Advisory Committee on Rule.
[94]*See* B.K.B. v. Maui Police Dep't, 276 F.3d 1091, 1105 (9th Cir. 2002) ("courts have held . . . that the probative value of evidence of a victim's sexual sophistication or private sexual behavior with regard to the welcomeness of harassing behavior in the workplace does not substantially outweigh the prejudice to her."); Wolak v. Spucci, 217 F.3d 157, 160, 162 (2d Cir. 2000) (evidence of plaintiff's after-hours sexual behavior inadmissible under Rule 412 in sexual harassment case, but trial court's erroneous admission of such evidence was harmless because plaintiff offered no evidence to show that she was injured by hostile work environment); Rodriguez-Hernandez v. Miranda-Velez, 132 F.3d 848, 856 (1st Cir. 1998) (upholding district court's ruling that evidence concerning plaintiff's moral character or promiscuity and marital status of her boyfriend was inadmissible under Rule 412); Wade v. Washington Metro. Area Transit Auth., 2006 WL 890679, at *2 (D.D.C. Apr. 5, 2006) (granting defendant's Rule 412 motion to present evidence regarding plaintiff's alleged sexual behavior, subject to limitations); A.W. v. I.B. Corp., 224 F.R.D. 20, 94 FEP 179 (D. Me. 2004) (citing Rule 412, court refused to compel plaintiff to answer deposition questions regarding past sexual history); Chamblee v. Harris & Harris, Inc., 154 F. Supp. 2d 670 (S.D.N.Y. 2001) (evidence regarding plaintiff's work as call girl and her sex life outside work precluded pursuant to Rule 412); Barta v. City & County of Honolulu, 169 F.R.D. 132, 136 (D. Haw. 1996) ("The fact that the plaintiff may welcome sexual advances from certain individuals has absolutely no

a relevant time period generally is not barred by the considerations underlying Rule 412 because it arguably is relevant to the harassment claims.[95]

Prior case law is also instructive. A plaintiff's sexually provocative speech and dress in the workplace, for example, may be discoverable with respect to whether sexual advances were in fact unwelcome.[96] But where the defendant does not know of the plaintiff's workplace sexual history or does not believe that the conduct at issue is welcomed by the victim, evidence of the plaintiff's past conduct may not be discoverable.[97] Furthermore, a plaintiff's past sexual conduct *outside* the workplace is less relevant than sexual conduct *inside* the workplace; discovery of such outside-the-workplace conduct, whether to dispute liability[98]

---

bearing on the emotional trauma she may feel from sexual harassment that is unwelcome. Past sexual conduct does not callous one to subsequent, unwelcomed sexual advancements."); *see also* EEOC v. Danka Indus., Inc., 990 F. Supp. 1138, 1140, 75 FEP 685 (E.D. Mo. 1997) (plaintiff's sexual history of conduct outside of workplace not discoverable in sexual harassment action).

[95]Beard v. Flying J, Inc., 266 F.3d 792, 801 (8th Cir. 2001) (finding no error in introduction into evidence of plaintiff's sexual behavior in workplace because "an employee's workplace behavior is highly relevant to the question of whether the harassment was welcome"); *Wade*, 2006 WL 890679, at *1–2 (granting defendant's Rule 412 motion to present evidence regarding plaintiff's alleged sexual behavior, but excluding any evidence regarding which the alleged perpetrators were unaware, or regarding activity outside the workplace not involving the alleged perpetrators).

[96]*See* Meritor Sav. Bank v. Vinson, 477 U.S. 57, 69, 40 FEP 1822 (1986) ("While 'voluntariness' in the sense of consent is not a defense to such a claim, it does not follow that a complainant's sexually provocative speech or dress is irrelevant as a matter of law in determining whether he or she found particular sexual advances unwelcome. To the contrary, such evidence is obviously relevant."); *see also* Gan v. Kepro Circuit Sys., 28 FEP 639, 641 (E.D. Mo. 1982) (plaintiff "actively contributed to the distasteful working environment by her own profane and sexually suggestive conduct").

[97]*See* Steiner v. Showboat Operating Co., 25 F.3d 1459, 1464 n.5, 65 FEP 58 (9th Cir. 1994) (rejecting defendant's assertion that plaintiff somehow "welcomed" harassment because she herself talked like "drunken sailor"); Mitchell v. Hutchings, 116 F.R.D. 481, 484, 44 FEP 615 (D. Utah 1987) (evidence of plaintiff's sexual conduct that is remote in time or place to plaintiff's working environment irrelevant; evidence of plaintiff's sexual activity of which defendant was unaware or is unrelated to alleged incidents of sexual harassment not discoverable); Swentek v. USAir, Inc., 830 F.2d 552, 557, 44 FEP 1808 (4th Cir. 1987) ("Plaintiff's use of foul language or sexual innuendo in a consensual setting does not waive 'her legal protections against unwelcome harassment.' ") (citation omitted).

[98]*E.g.*, Priest v. Rotary, 98 F.R.D. 755, 761–62, 32 FEP 1064 (N.D. Cal. 1983) (evidence of prior sexual activity not admissible to prove propensity to engage in

or the degree of the plaintiff's damages,[99] generally will not be allowed.

There are several other issues that arise on a recurring basis in discovery sought by the defendant. These include discovery of the plaintiff's tax records,[100] discovery seeking to obtain

---

such conduct and is not discoverable because it would potentially discourage victims of sexual harassment from prosecuting Title VII lawsuits; denying defendant discovery of names of each sex partner plaintiff had during past 10 years); *see also* Burns v. McGregor Elec. Indus., 989 F.2d 959, 963, 61 FEP 592 (8th Cir. 1993) (plaintiff's having posed for nude magazine outside work hours not material to issue of whether she found employer's work-related conduct offensive; "[Plaintiff's] private life, regardless how reprehensible . . . did not provide lawful acquiescence to unwanted sexual advances at her work place by her employer. To hold otherwise would be contrary to Title VII's goal of ridding the work place of any kind of unwelcome sexual harassment."); Cronin v. United Serv. Stations, Inc., 809 F. Supp. 922, 932, 65 FEP 811 (M.D. Ala. 1992) (evidence that plaintiff had been abused at home by her boyfriend had no bearing as to whether she was sexually harassed at work). *But see* Weiss v. Amoco Oil Co., 142 F.R.D. 311, 314–17, 58 FEP 1352 (S.D. Iowa 1992) (plaintiff, who was terminated after person accused him of sexual harassment, *is* entitled to discover evidence of person's sexual conduct with co-workers because the accuser failed to prove it was irrelevant, and Iowa's statute restricting discovery of individual's sexual conduct applies only if that individual is plaintiff in sexual abuse or harassment case).

[99]*E.g.*, EEOC v. Danka Indus., Inc., 990 F. Supp. 1138, 1140, 75 FEP 685 (E.D. Mo. 1997) (information regarding plaintiff's past sexual history with persons not employed by company not discoverable in Title VII sexual harassment case); Mitchell v. Hutchings, 116 F.R.D. 481, 485, 44 FEP 615 (D. Utah 1987) (denying discovery of past welcomed sexual conduct or proclivities outside workplace because "[p]ast sexual conduct does not . . . create emotional calluses that lessen the impact of unwelcomed sexual harassment"); *cf.* Cal. Civ. Proc. Code § 2017(d) (barring discovery of plaintiff's prior sexual conduct with persons other than alleged perpetrator, absent "good cause" for such discovery); Vinson v. Superior Ct., 239 Cal. Rptr. 292, 299, 44 FEP 1174 (Cal. 1987) (federal and state constitutional rights to privacy preclude discovery of plaintiff's sexual history absent "specific facts showing good cause for that discovery"; history may be admissible, however, if plaintiff claims that harassment damaged her sexuality).

[100]*Compare* Reserve Solutions, Inc. v. Vernaglia, 238 F.R.D. 543, 543 (S.D.N.Y. 2006) (employee's personal income tax returns relevant to substantiate issues of material fact and thus were subject to discovery), Johnson v. Kraft Foods N. Am., Inc., 236 F.R.D. 535, 539 (D. Kan. 2006) (plaintiff in discrimination suit compelled to produce tax returns where plaintiff put income at issue by seeking economic losses), Maddow v. Proctor & Gamble Co., 107 F.3d 846, 853, 73 FEP 784 (11th Cir. 1997) (court did not abuse discretion in compelling discovery of plaintiff's tax records where arguably relevant to case) *and* Winbush v. Iowa by Glenwood State Hosp., 66 F.3d 1471, 1482, 69 FEP 1348 (8th Cir. 1995) (defendant entitled to tax records, but because defendant eventually got "all available information" it was within trial court's discretion to refuse to impose sanctions on basis of plaintiff's delays in providing such records) *with* Bujnicki v. American Paving & Excavating, Inc., 2004 WL 1071736,

information and documents regarding the plaintiff's immigration status,[101] and discovery to identify any criminal records regarding the plaintiff.[102]

Defendants may seek to discover "after-acquired evidence" in order to limit the plaintiff's entitlement to reinstatement, front pay, and back pay.[103] Plaintiffs often argue that such discovery should

---

at *14–15 (W.D.N.Y. Feb. 25, 2004) (denying discovery of plaintiff's income tax returns, despite relevance to plaintiff's emotional distress claim, because disclosure of plaintiff's W-2 and wage statements were sufficient to enable defendant to assess plaintiff's earnings), Denson v. Northeast Ill. Reg'l Commuter R.R., 2003 WL 1732984, at *4 (N.D. Ill. Mar. 31, 2003) (plaintiff need not produce income tax returns where she has instead produced copies of her W-2 forms), Gattegno v. Pricewaterhouse-Coopers, LLP, 205 F.R.D. 70, 72 (D. Conn. 2001) (plaintiff's income tax returns are entitled to a "qualified privilege" from discovery, which may be overcome when it is clear that returns are relevant to the issues raised in the action and there is compelling need for the returns because the relevant information contained therein is not otherwise readily obtainable; court denied discovery of tax returns, despite relevance on issues of mitigation and damages, where employer already had access to such information from other sources, including employee's W-2 and 1099 forms and earnings records subpoenaed from other employers) *and* Pedraza v. Holiday Housewares, Inc., 203 F.R.D. 40, 43 (D. Mass 2001) (adopting two-part test for discoverability of income tax returns: (1) they must be relevant to the action, and (2) the information contained therein must be otherwise unobtainable; the burden to show relevance lies with the party seeking disclosure, while the party resisting disclosure bears the burden of establishing alternative available sources for the information).

[101]*See, e.g.*, Rivera v. NIBCO, Inc., 364 F.3d 1057, 1064–65, 93 FEP 929 (9th Cir. 2004) (granting protective order to preclude questions regarding employees' immigration status), *cert. denied*, 544 U.S. 905 (2005); EEOC v. Restaurant Co., 448 F. Supp. 2d 1085, 1087 (D. Minn. 2006) (discovery regarding immigration status of plaintiffs in civil rights cases generally prohibited in early stages of litigation); Galaviz-Zamora v. Brady Farms, Inc., 230 F.R.D. 499, 501 (W.D. Mich. 2005) (immigration status of workers not subject to discovery in FLSA case; information irrelevant and burden would outweigh minimal legitimate value regarding credibility); EEOC v. Bice of Chicago, 229 F.R.D. 581, 583 (N.D. Ill. 2005) (EEOC entitled to protective order barring discovery of charging parties' immigration status; status not relevant to claims or defenses, questions were oppressive and constituted substantial burden on parties' and public interest, and such discovery would chill victims from coming forward to assert discrimination claims).

[102]*See, e.g.*, Schuurman v. Town of N. Reading, 139 F.R.D. 276, 278 (D. Mass. 1991) (defendant entitled to in camera inspection of criminal records requested in discovery where defendant provided adequate assurances that records would not be disseminated); Cumis Ins. Soc., Inc. v. South-Coast Bank, 610 F. Supp. 193, 197 (N.D. Ind. 1985) (Rule 26(b) qualified common-law privilege does not protect all law enforcement investigatory files from discovery, but only files relating to ongoing criminal investigations).

[103]*See* McKennon v. Nashville Banner Publ'g Co., 513 U.S. 352, 360–61, 66 FEP 1192 (1995) (after-acquired evidence of employee's wrongdoing, which would have led to termination if employer had known of it at time of discharge, cuts off

be restricted to matters that, had the defendant known of them at the time of the adverse employment action, would have been actual grounds for termination.[104] Although broad discovery generally is allowed into the plaintiff's background or job performance to find grounds to invoke the after-acquired evidence defense, such discovery has its limits. As discussed by the Ninth Circuit in *Rivera v. NIBCO, Inc.*,[105] the Supreme Court's decision in *McKennon v. Nashville Banner Publishing Co.*[106] regarding after-acquired evidence "authorizes district courts to invoke the Federal Rules of Civil Procedure when necessary to prevent [an] employer from using the discovery process to engage in wholesale searches for evidence that might serve to limit its damages for its wrongful conduct."[107]

In cases filed as class actions, the defendant's discovery as to the character or type of each named plaintiff's claim can be significant in challenging class certification.[108] For example, specific inquiries aimed at the adequacy of class representatives have been permitted.[109] Courts also have permitted the defendant in certain

---

employee's entitlement to back pay, front pay, and reinstatement). *See generally* Chapter 40 (Monetary Relief).

[104]513 U.S. at 358–60.

[105]364 F.3d 1057, 1070–72, 93 FEP 929 (9th Cir. 2004), *cert. denied*, 544 U.S. 905 (2005).

[106]513 U.S. at 361–62.

[107]*Rivera*, 364 F.3d at 1072.

[108]*See* MANUAL FOR COMPLEX LITIGATION FOURTH § 21.14, at 256 ("Discovery relevant to certification should generally be directed to the named parties."); *id.* § 21.141, at 258 (precertification discovery "may be necessary to determine if the plaintiff's claim is atypical"). *See generally* Chapter 32 (Class Actions).

[109]*E.g.*, Quintanilla v. Scientific-Atlanta, Inc., 28 FEP 1178, 1182–83 (N.D. Tex. 1982) (plaintiff's answers to interrogatories that he had "no knowledge" of other putative class members' claims held valid basis for denying certification), *appeal dismissed*, 33 Empl. Prac. Dec. (CCH) ¶ 34,050 (5th Cir. 1983); Dunn v. Midwest Buslines, Inc., 94 F.R.D. 170, 172–73, 28 FEP 1653 (E.D. Ark. 1982) (finding plaintiff to be inadequate representative in part because of lack of knowledge as to forms of discrimination allegedly suffered by other class members); Sessum v. Houston Cmty. Coll., 94 F.R.D. 316, 323, 32 FEP 1172 (S.D. Tex. 1982) (deposition demonstrated "highly individualized" nature of plaintiff's claims and her failure to satisfy commonality and adequacy of representation requirements of Rule 23); Rode v. Emery Air Freight Corp., 76 F.R.D. 229, 231, 15 FEP 1355 (W.D. Pa. 1977) (financial data concerning plaintiff relevant in determining adequacy of representation); Guse v. J.C. Penney Co., 409 F. Supp. 28, 30, 12 FEP 9 (E.D. Wis. 1976) (compelling plaintiff's representative to respond to inquiries relating to its ability to advance funds for action should it be maintainable as class action), *rev'd and remanded on other grounds*, 562 F.2d 6, 15 FEP 484 (7th Cir. 1977); *see also* Lim v. Citizens Sav. & Loan Ass'n,

circumstances to seek precertification discovery of the fee arrangement between class representatives and their attorney.[110]

Defendants have met with significant barriers in attempting to obtain individualized discovery regarding putative class members prior to class certification. In assessing a plaintiff's responses to class member interrogatories, courts have held that the named plaintiff is not required to answer interrogatories concerning the specific nature of the alleged discrimination against each of the class members. Although the information may be relevant to the defense of classwide liability claims, collecting such information would be overly burdensome.[111]

---

430 F. Supp. 802, 812, 15 FEP 113 (N.D. Cal. 1976) (were it not denying class certification on other grounds, court would require plaintiff to answer defendant's questions concerning financing of litigation).

[110]See MANUAL FOR COMPLEX LITIGATION FOURTH § 21.141, at 260 ("precertification inquiries into the named parties' finances or the financial arrangements between the class representatives and their counsel are rarely appropriate, except to obtain information necessary to determine whether the parties and their counsel have the resources to represent the class adequately"); see also Ferraro v. General Motors Corp., 105 F.R.D. 429, 433–34 (D.N.J. 1984) (allowing narrowly focused precertification discovery of "the agreement of counsel to advance fees and the willingness of the class representative to be liable for repayment" but denying discovery regarding the class representative's ability to repay his attorneys); cf. Trader v. Fiat Distribs., Inc., 30 FEP 1567, 1568–73 (D. Del. 1981) (permitting discovery regarding nature of fee arrangement between class plaintiffs and their attorneys as it is relevant to issue of adequacy of representation; declining to permit discovery of plaintiffs' financial resources without specific evidence to indicate that "class action may founder for lack of funds" where plaintiffs' counsel agreed to advance costs); Elster v. Alexander, 74 F.R.D. 503, 504 (N.D. Ga. 1976) ("Whether the personal financial circumstances of a class action named plaintiff and the fee arrangement he has with his attorney is relevant, discoverable information depends on the facts of each case."). Contra Stahler v. Jamesway Corp., 85 F.R.D. 85, 86 (E.D. Pa. 1979) (fee arrangement between class representatives and their lawyer not relevant to adequacy of representation and therefore not discoverable).

[111]See Cox v. American Cast Iron Pipe Co., 784 F.2d 1546, 1555–56, 40 FEP 678 (11th Cir. 1986) (interrogatories directed to individual class members to establish merits of individual claims improper because they were designed to reduce class size and were unnecessary in that focus of Stage I proceeding should be on broad pattern or practice at issue); Brennan v. Midwestern United Life Ins. Co., 450 F.2d 999, 1005 (7th Cir. 1971) (questions as to identity and claims of individual class members ordinarily should be deferred until after trial of class issues); Adkins v. Mid-America Growers, Inc., 141 F.R.D. 466, 468 (N.D. Ill. 1992) (discovery of individual class members appropriate only once class becomes well-defined); Brinkerhoff v. Rockwell Int'l Corp., 83 F.R.D. 478, 480, 20 FEP 1637 (N.D. Tex. 1979) (defendant not entitled to names and claims of putative class members before certification of class; such information is not relevant where defendant does not need it to oppose claims of numerosity and typicality); Kyriazi v. Western Elec.

3. Medical Records and Examinations

Where a plaintiff alleges pain and suffering, mental anguish and/or emotional distress and seeks recompense for that injury through an award of compensatory damages, some courts grant the defendant access to plaintiff's medical records without any showing that plaintiff has alleged a specific mental or emotional injury.[112] Other courts, however, have declined to grant such requests for medical records unless a plaintiff has alleged a particular mental or emotional injury, rather than mere "garden variety" emotional distress damages incidental to experiencing job-related discrimination.[113] Some defendants also request the opportunity to have their retained expert perform a mental or physical examination of the plaintiff in such circumstances, which raises additional issues.

Co., 74 F.R.D. 468, 473, 15 FEP 457 (D.N.J. 1977) (finding interrogatories asking named plaintiff to describe specific acts of discrimination against each class member overly burdensome); Bisgeier v. Fotomat Corp., 62 F.R.D. 118, 119 (N.D. Ill. 1973) (lengthy set of interrogatories sent to 5,000 class members after class certification thwarts concept of efficiency, which is fundamental to Rule 23). *But see* Southern Methodist Univ. Ass'n of Women Law Students v. Wynne & Jaffe, 599 F.2d 707, 713–14, 20 FEP 457 (5th Cir. 1979) (employer entitled to plaintiff association's membership list and identities of women it claimed were afraid to join association); Krueger v. New York Tel., 163 F.R.D. 446, 451 (S.D.N.Y. 1995) (serving interrogatories on all 162 class members in form of questionnaire on issues of individual liability appropriate in ADEA claim).

[112]*See, e.g.*, Owens v. Sprint/United Mgmt. Co., 221 F.R.D. 657, 660, 94 FEP 772 (D. Kan. 2004) (employer's request for production which sought medical records was relevant to claims in employee's Title VII suit in which she sought only "garden variety" damages for emotional distress); EEOC v. Grief Bros. Corp., 218 F.R.D. 59, 60, 64 (W.D.N.Y. 2003) (requested medical records were relevant to plaintiff's claim for emotional distress and therefore discoverable); Gattegno v. Pricewaterhouse-Coopers, LLP, 204 F.R.D. 228, 231 (D. Conn. 2001) (employee put emotional and mental state in controversy by seeking damages for mental anguish and physical and emotional distress, entitling employer to inspection of plaintiff's medical records).

[113]*See, e.g.*, Brown v. Kelly, 2007 WL 1138877, at *2 (S.D.N.Y. Apr. 16, 2007) ("for a garden variety claim of emotional distress resulting from the incident itself . . . , there is no need to examine plaintiff's full medical history"); EEOC v. Serramonte, 237 F.R.D. 220, 224 (N.D. Cal. 2006) (plaintiff's medical records are privileged by her right to privacy as she brings only a "garden variety" claim for emotional distress damages); Stevenson v. Stanley Bostitch, Inc., 201 F.R.D. 551, 553 (N.D. Ga. 2001) (plaintiff waives objection to production of medical records only where there is something other than garden variety emotional distress alleged); Burrell v. Crown Cent. Petroleum, Inc., 177 F.R.D. 376, 383 (E.D. Tex. 1997) (medical records are not required to support a claim for mental anguish in Title VII or § 1981 cases; claim for mental anguish or emotional harm does not necessarily put plaintiff's medical condition in controversy).

Under Rule 35(a), an order for a physical or mental examination may be made only on a "motion for good cause shown."[114] Even where "good cause" is shown, courts typically require that the condition to be examined be "in controversy" before ordering an examination.[115] For a mental condition to be "in controversy," most courts require the presence of one or more of the following factors:

(1) the plaintiff has asserted a specific cause of action for intentional or negligent infliction of emotional distress;

(2) the plaintiff has alleged a specific mental or psychiatric injury or disorder;

(3) the plaintiff has claimed unusually severe emotional distress;

(4) the plaintiff has offered expert testimony to support a claim of emotional distress damages; and/or

(5) the plaintiff has conceded that his or her mental condition is "in controversy."[116]

---

[114]FED. R. CIV. P. 35(a).

[115]*See* Smith v. Koplan, 215 F.R.D. 11, 12, 91 FEP 1652 (D.D.C. 2003) (plaintiff claiming that she suffered "physical, emotional and economic damages" as direct result of defendant's discriminatory behavior and that she continues to suffer depression and anxiety as result of defendant's conduct placed her ongoing mental illness in controversy).

[116]*See* Bowen v. Parking Auth. of City of Camden, 91 FEP 1200, 1206 (D.N.J. 2003) (examination denied despite plaintiff's allegations that he suffered "severe emotional distress, mental anguish, pain, suffering and humiliation" because of employer's actions and notwithstanding plaintiff's plan to introduce testimony of his treating physician); *Smith*, 215 F.R.D. at 12, 91 FEP at 1654 (granting examination where employee claimed that ongoing mental illness was caused by defendant's illegal discrimination); Nolan v. Teamsters Health & Welfare & Pension Funds, 199 F.R.D. 272, 276 (N.D. Ill. 2001) (denying Rule 35 psychological exam where sex harassment plaintiff's mental anguish was limited to general humiliation and embarrassment); Ricks v. Abbott Labs., 198 F.R.D. 647, 649–50, 85 FEP 364, 366–67 (D. Md. 2001) (mental condition not placed in controversy and plaintiff need not undergo mental exam where plaintiff did not assert specific cause of action for infliction of emotional distress, did not allege specific mental injury or severe distress, and did not seek to introduce expert psychiatric evidence); Bethel v. Dixie Homecrafters, Inc., 192 F.R.D. 320, 323, 82 FEP 345, 348 (N.D. Ga. 2000) (allowing mental examination of plaintiff in gender discrimination action where plaintiff alleged extreme and severe emotional distress caused by defendant); Bjerke v. Nash Finch Co., 2000 WL 33339658, at *1 (D.N.D. Feb. 1, 2000) (denying mental exam where plaintiff withdrew additional emotional distress claim but still sought compensatory damages for mental anguish and humiliation); Hertenstein v. Kimberly Home Health Care, Inc., 189 F.R.D. 620, 628, 80 FEP 355, 360 (D. Kan. 1999)

One of the factors some courts have considered in determining good cause is whether the defendant has used other discovery procedures before seeking a mental examination.[117]

IV. ELECTRONIC DISCOVERY

Although it is outside the parameters of this treatise to provide an in-depth overview of electronic discovery, it is of paramount importance that employment litigators familiarize themselves with

---

(allowing Rule 35 examination, but requiring expert to keep any inquiries and responses about plaintiff's sex life confidential per Fed. R. Evid. 412); Thiessen v. General Elec. Capital Corp., 178 F.R.D. 568, 570 (D. Kan. 1998) (allowing examination where plaintiff alleged specific injuries caused by defendant's age discrimination); Ford v. Contra Costa County, 179 F.R.D. 579, 580, 76 FEP 1849, 1850 (N.D. Cal. 1998) (denying defendant's motion to compel plaintiff to submit to Rule 35(a) psychiatric evaluation because even though plaintiff sought damages for emotional and mental distress, defendant did not demonstrate that plaintiff's mental condition was "in controversy" or that there was "good cause" for examination); Fox v. Gates Corp., 179 F.R.D. 303, 307 (D. Colo. 1998) (plaintiff's "garden variety" claim for emotional distress damages resulting from defendant's refusal to hire her did not place plaintiff's mental condition "in controversy" for purposes of Rule 35(a)); Burrell v. Crown Cent. Petroleum, Inc., 177 F.R.D. 376, 380 (E.D. Tex. 1997) ("asking for mental anguish damages does not place a plaintiff's physical or mental condition 'in controversy' and it will not justify a medical or psychological examination"; however, "just because the test for Rule 35 is not met does not mean that the medical records are unavailable"); EEOC v. Danka Indus., 990 F. Supp. 1138, 1143 (E.D. Mo. 1997) (plaintiff's claim of emotional distress as result of defendant's actions entitled defendant to conduct Rule 35 mental examination); O'Quinn v. New York Univ. Med. Ctr., 163 F.R.D. 226, 227–28, 68 FEP 1798, 1800 (S.D.N.Y. 1995) (denying defendant's request for psychiatric examination of plaintiff when plaintiff did not claim ongoing severe emotional injury but instead made boilerplate damages claim for emotional distress and humiliation), *motion granted in part, denied in part*, 933 F. Supp. 341 (S.D.N.Y. 1996); Turner v. Imperial Stores, 161 F.R.D. 89, 98 (S.D. Cal. 1995) (court "unwilling to set a precedent requiring a party to undergo an independent psychiatric examination merely because the party claims damages for emotional distress in her complaint"); Curtis v. Express, Inc., 868 F. Supp. 467, 469, 66 FEP 449, 450 (N.D.N.Y. 1994) (rejecting defendant's request for mental examination where plaintiff brought only her past emotional condition into issue and did not pursue separate tort claim for emotional distress).

[117]Anson v. Fickel, 110 F.R.D. 184, 186 (N.D. Ind. 1986) ("One of the factors which must be considered in determining good cause is whether the defendants have utilized other discovery procedures before seeking the mental examination."). *But see* Schlagenhauf v. Holder, 379 U.S. 104, 118 (1964) (good cause standard can be satisfied where plaintiff puts his or her medical or mental condition in issue in pleadings, e.g., in typical personal injury action).

this burgeoning area of the law. Employment attorneys must enter every case assuming that electronic discovery will be involved. Computer records, even those that have been "deleted," may be discoverable under Rule 34.[118] Although not the first court to address the issue,[119] the seminal decision in electronic discovery and its attendant obligations is *Zubulake v. UBS Warburg, LLC* (*Zubulake I*), a case alleging gender discrimination, retaliation, and failure to promote.[120] At issue was the plaintiff's request for all documents concerning communications by or between the defendant's employees concerning the plaintiff, including e-mails recoverable from the corporation's active directories, backup tapes, and archive systems. The defendant maintained that compliance with such a request constituted an undue burden. The court's decision in *Zubulake I* and its progeny (*Zubulake II–V*) have set the course in this field, including establishing a cost-shifting analysis applicable to electronic discovery disputes.

Electronic materials are often highly probative in employment cases and include (1) databases, such as personnel or payroll, containing fields of data that may be relevant to arguments for liability or exoneration; (2) drafts of documents or other preliminary materials, which in earlier years may have been shredded or destroyed and now may be electronically preserved; and (3) e-mail, where informality lends itself to frank and free-flowing dialogues that may reflect employee or employer intent. The scope of permitted discovery into such materials often will be critical to an employment discrimination case.

---

[118]Zubulake v. UBS Warburg LLC, 217 F.R.D. 309, 317 n.38 (S.D.N.Y. 2003) (*Zubulake I*).

[119]*See* Sattar v. Motorola, Inc., 138 F.3d 1164, 1171, 76 FEP 512, 517 (7th Cir. 1998) (approving district court's order that employer either download e-mail data from backup tapes to conventional computer disks or hard drive, loan plaintiff copy of software needed to read tapes, or provide plaintiff on-site access to employer's computer systems, rather than requiring employer to produce 210,000 pages of hard copy e-mail at employer's expense); *In re* Brand Name Prescription Drugs Antitrust Litig., 1995 WL 360526, at *1 (N.D. Ill. June 15, 1995) (ordering production of e-mail, including materials stored within computer system, and refusing to require class plaintiffs to pay for cost of retrieval of stored communications estimated at $50,000–$70,000). *cf.* Bass Pub. Ltd. Co. v. Promus Cos., 1994 WL 702052, at *1 (S.D.N.Y. Dec. 12, 1994) (ordering defendants to search system for e-mail to and from 10 individuals but denying more extensive search).

[120]217 F.R.D. at 309.

Because nearly every case likely implicates electronic discovery, every lawyer has electronic obligations. As with any other kind of document, a party is obligated to retain and preserve electronic documents once it is on notice that those documents are relevant to a claim.[121] The court in *Zubulake V* indicated that the employer's attorney must speak about the methods of data storage and retention with not just the client's information technology personnel, but with each "key player," and must investigate the potential existence of alternate repositories of data, such as a witness' personal data assistant, BlackBerry, home computer, or floppy disks.[122] Courts have imposed sanctions against parties who destroy electronic materials that are subject to discovery.[123]

In May 2004, the Committee on Rules of Practice and Procedure proposed revisions to the Federal Rules with regard to electronic discovery, which were approved by the Standing Committee in June 2005 and were passed by the Judicial Conference in September 2005.[124] Those new rules were approved by the Supreme Court and became effective on December 1, 2006.[125] The key areas of change include (1) requiring parties to give early attention to issues related to electronic discovery, including reviewing electronic documents for privilege; (2) guidelines on how parties should deal with electronic information that is not easily or readily accessible; (3) protecting against the likelihood of unintentional (not

---

[121]*See, e.g.*, Kronisch v. United States, 150 F.3d 112, 126 (2d Cir. 1998) (once party learns it has or may have information relevant to case, it is under duty to protect that information from spoliation).

[122]Zubulake v. UBS Warburg LLC, 229 F.R.D. 422, 432 (S.D.N.Y. 2004).

[123]*See, e.g.*, Metropolitan Opera Ass'n, Inc., v. HERE Int'l Local 100, 212 F.R.D. 178, 171 LRRM 2897 (S.D.N.Y. 2003) (court levied sanction against defendant for noncompliance during discovery, entering judgment in favor of plaintiff on all causes of action.)

[124]*See* Committee on Federal Rules of Civil Procedure, to the Committee on Rules of Practice and Procedure of the Judicial Conference of the United States, Submitting Proposals for Amendment of the Federal Rules of Civil Procedure (May 2004). The comments explain that:

The problems of electronic discovery reflect the extent of changes in technology. The stuff of discovery is information, and technology has fundamentally altered how information is created, stored, and exchanged. . . . The fact that changes in technology will continue to occur, at speeds and in ways that we cannot predict, requires that we proceed with caution. The discovery rules must recognize the fundamental changes that have already occurred, but remain flexible enough to accommodate changes that will develop in the future.

[125]*See* FED. R. CIV. P. 16(b), 26(b)(2)(B), 26(b)(5), 26(f), 33, 34(b), 37(f), 45(d).

just inadvertent) production of privileged materials; (4) the application of current discovery rules to electronic documents; and (5) a safe harbor from sanctions that are currently available under the Federal Rules for the loss of electronic information as a result of routine computer operations.[126]

---

[126]*See* Kenneth J. Withers, *Electronically Stored Information: The December 2006 Amendments to the Federal Rules of Civil Procedure*, 4 NW. J. TECH. & INTELL. PROP. 171, 192 (2006) (the driving force behind many of the Amendments to the Federal Rules was research that strongly indicated that many electronic discovery disputes could be prevented, managed, or resolved through early and direct communication between the parties); *see also* Phoenix Four, Inc. v. Strategic Res. Corp., 2006 WL 1409413, at *1 (S.D.N.Y. May 23, 2006) (as amended, Rule 26(b)(2)(B) will "reinforce the concept that a party must identify even those sources that are not reasonably accessible but exempts [that] party from having to provide discovery from such sources unless its adversary moves to compel discovery"); Cenveo Corp. v. Slater, 2007 U.S. Dist. LEXIS 8281, at *9 (E.D. Pa. Jan. 31, 2007) (in order to protect from unintentional production of privileged materials, court ordered third party computer forensics expert to first provide retrieved data to defendant who would have 45 days to review the information and produce anything deemed responsive, as well as a corresponding privilege log, to the plaintiff); DE Tech., Inc. v. Dell, Inc., 2007 U.S. Dist. LEXIS 2769, at *4–9 (W.D. Va. Jan. 12, 2007) (applying amended Fed. R. Civ. P. 34 to determine whether Dell produced electronic documents in a manner that fulfilled its obligation to produce documents as they were kept in the ordinary course of business).

CHAPTER 34

STATISTICAL AND OTHER EXPERT PROOF

I. USE OF EXPERTS IN LITIGATION

A. Introduction

Statistical analyses have long played a critical role in both disparate treatment and adverse impact cases. As the Supreme Court stated in *Teamsters v. United States*,[1] "[o]ur cases make it unmistakably clear that '[s]tatistical analyses have served and will continue to serve an important role' in cases in which the existence of discrimination is a disputed issue."[2] In addition, litigants in employment discrimination cases are increasingly relying on other types of experts as well, including labor economists, sociologists, social psychologists, survey researchers, medical psychologists, human resources experts, diversity consultants, industrial engineers, and damages analysts.[3] In *Brown v. Board of Education*,[4] the Supreme Court recognized the usefulness of social scientific evidence in discrimination cases.[5] In *Price Waterhouse v. Hopkins*,[6] the Supreme Court approvingly noted the district court's reliance on testimony by a social psychologist regarding gender stereotypes.[7]

---

[1]431 U.S. 324 (1977).

[2]*Id.* at 339.

[3]*See, e.g.*, Butler v. Home Depot, 984 F. Supp. 1257 (N.D. Cal. 1997) (denying *Daubert* motion to exclude testimony from social psychologist, sociologist, survey researcher, diversity consultant, and human resources expert). For a detailed discussion of *Daubert*, see Section I.B–I.D *infra*.

[4]347 U.S. 487 (1954).

[5]*Id.* at 495 n.11 (citing social science literature on effects of discrimination).

[6]490 U.S. 228 (1989).

[7]*Id.*; *see also* Lowery v. Circuit City Stores, Inc., 206 F.3d 431, 438 n.2 (4th Cir. 2000) (approvingly noting testimony by expert in field of human resources regarding whether employer's use of subjective criteria resulted in discrimination).

The Supreme Court's decisions in *Faragher v. City of Boca Raton*[8] and *Burlington Industries v. Ellerth*,[9] which created an affirmative defense to harassment claims for employers who put in place appropriate policies addressing harassment, gave rise to expert testimony from human resource experts regarding the adequacy of those policies. Courts are divided on whether such testimony assists the trier of fact.[10] Testimony from industrial psychologists regarding the validity of job selection criteria has been widely accepted.[11] In addition, expert testimony regarding disabilities, emotional distress, damages, and numerous other issues has been admitted in appropriate cases.

B. Federal Rule of Evidence 702

The standard for the admissibility of expert testimony in federal court is set forth in Rule 702 of the Federal Rules of Evidence (Testimony by Experts):

> If scientific, technical, or other specialized knowledge will assist the trier of fact to understand the evidence or to determine a fact in issue, a witness qualified as an expert by knowledge, skill, experience, training, or education, may testify thereto in the form of an opinion or otherwise, if (1) the testimony is based upon sufficient facts or data, (2) the testimony is the product of reliable principles and methods, and (3) the witness has applied the principles and methods reliably to the facts of the case.

---

[8]524 U.S. 775 (1998).

[9]524 U.S. 742 (1998).

[10]*Compare* Katt v. City of N.Y., 151 F. Supp. 2d 313, 326 (S.D.N.Y. 2001) (noting admission of testimony by professor of psychology and human resource management and expert in workplace sexual harassment) *and* Harper v. Southeast Ala. Med. Ctr., 998 F. Supp. 1289 (M.D. Ala. 1998) (noting testimony of social psychologist specializing in sexual harassment) *with* Wilson v. Muckala, 303 F.3d 1207 (10th Cir. 2002) (affirming district court exclusion of expert testimony), Murray v. Rent-A-Center, 2001 U.S. Dist. LEXIS 19339, at *16 (W.D. Mo. May 11, 2001) (testimony of "experts" in human resources not helpful regarding class certification motion) *and* Smith v. Borg-Warner, 2000 U.S. Dist. LEXIS 10200, at *9 (S.D. Ind. July 19, 2000) (granting *Daubert* motion to strike testimony by human resources expert). *See generally* Jayesh Shah, Comment, *Limiting Expert Testimony About Sexual Harassment Policies*, 1999 U. CHI. LEGAL F. 587 (1999)

[11]*See* Graffam v. Scott Paper Co., 60 F.3d 809, 71 FEP 736 (1st Cir. 1995) (finding employer established business necessity defense through industrial psychologist); *see also* Butler v. Home Depot, 984 F. Supp. 1257 (N.D. Cal. 1997) (admitting testimony of industrial psychologist regarding human resources policies and procedures).

The ultimate test is whether the use of expert testimony will assist the trier of fact.[12]

As initially drafted, Rule 702 was very broadly phrased. In 2000, Rule 702 was amended in response to *Daubert v. Merrell Dow Pharmaceuticals, Inc.*[13] and *Kumho Tire Co. v. Carmichael.*[14] In *Daubert*, the Supreme Court ruled that trial judges must assess the reliability of scientific evidence before admitting the evidence.[15] In *Kumho Tire*, the Court clarified that such a reliability assessment is appropriate in cases involving all expert testimony, not just scientific testimony.[16]

C. *Daubert* and Its Progeny

In *Daubert*, the Supreme Court held that a trial court has a "gatekeeping responsibility" to determine, as a preliminary matter, whether expert scientific testimony is both relevant and reliable.[17] Among the factors that a court may consider are (1) whether the expert's theory or technique can be and has been empirically tested, (2) whether the theory or technique has been subjected to peer review and publication, (3) whether the known or potential rate of error is acceptable, and (4) whether the theory or technique is generally accepted by the scientific community.[18] These factors are illustrative, rather than exhaustive, and need not be applied in every case.[19]

In *Kumho Tire*, the Court clarified that trial courts should also perform this gatekeeping function in cases involving nonscientific expert testimony. Once again, the Court confirmed that the weight accorded the factors, and whether a given factor is appropriately considered, will vary from case to case.[20]

Since *Daubert*, expert testimony offered in employment cases is sometimes challenged as not satisfying the *Daubert* criteria. As discussed in more detail in Sections VII and VIII *infra*, expert testimony

---

[12]*See* FED. R. EVID. 702, advisory committee's notes (quoting with approval Mason Ladd, *Expert Testimony*, 5 VAND. L. REV. 414, 418 (1952)).

[13]509 U.S. 579 (1993).

[14]526 U.S. 137 (1999).

[15]*Daubert*, 509 U.S. at 597.

[16]*Kumho Tire*, 526 U.S. at 147–48.

[17]*Daubert*, 509 U.S. at 589.

[18]*Id.* at 593–94.

[19]*See* Daubert v. Merrell Dow Pharms., Inc., 43 F.3d 1311, 1316–17 (9th Cir. 1995).

[20]*Kumho Tire*, 526 U.S. at 150–53.

from statisticians and from a variety of other experts often has been held to satisfy the *Daubert* test of reliability.[21]

D. Considerations in Selection and Use of Experts

1. Selection of the Expert

The first consideration when selecting an expert is whether expert testimony will assist the trier of fact regarding an issue in the case. Other important considerations include cost, whether the expert satisfies the *Daubert* criteria, whether the expert is credible, and whether the expert is an effective communicator. Academics are frequently credible witnesses and are likely to satisfy the *Daubert* criteria, and academics who teach are frequently good at communicating. Although there are often advantages to using experts who have experience testifying in court, there is a risk that such experts could be impeached with their prior testimony in other cases. Moreover, experts who appear to make a living by testifying at trial may lack the credibility of experts who testify less frequently.

2. Pretrial Use of the Expert

Prior to trial, experts may be used as consultants. Unlike communications with testifying experts, communications with nontestifying consultants are protected from production under the work product doctrine.[22] Once a witness is designated as a testifying expert,

---

[21]*See, e.g.*, Adams v. Ameritech Servs., Inc., 231 F.3d 414, 425–28, 84 FEP 178 (7th Cir. 2000) (expert's statistical analysis of employer's force reduction met *Daubert* standard of admissibility); Butler v. Home Depot, 984 F. Supp. 1257 (N.D. Cal. 1997) (plaintiffs' proffered expert testimony regarding diversity management, sexual stereotyping, social psychology, and interest surveying admissible under *Daubert*). Notably, *Daubert* challenges often arise in hybrid circumstances, such as motions for class certification, in which courts sometimes defer the ultimate ruling on reliability until the merits stage of the case. *See* Anderson v. Boeing Co., 222 F.R.D. 521, 526 (N.D. Okla. 2004) ("Courts do not conduct an inquiry into the merits at the class certification stage. . . . Courts, therefore, are unwilling to conduct a full *Daubert* analysis at the class certification stage.") (citing Vickers v. General Motors Corp., 204 F.R.D. 476, 479 (D. Kan. 2001) (*Daubert* analysis not required at class certification stage)).

[22]*See, e.g.*, Braun v. Lorillard Inc., 84 F.3d 230, 236 (7th Cir. 1996) (private communications between nontestifying consultant and counsel merited protection under work product doctrine as they reflected and implicated defendant's legal strategy regarding deposition taken as part of litigation); *In re* Cendant Corp. Sec. Litig., 343 F.3d 658 (3d Cir. 2003) (compelled disclosure of substance of conversations between defendant, his counsel, and nontestifying expert required disclosure of

however, all communications with that expert may be an appropriate subject of discovery, including communications before the designation.[23] There is a split of authority as to whether the immunity of work product produced to a testifying expert is waived.[24] A party therefore may want to use both a consultant and a testifying expert, notwithstanding the added cost.

---

communications protected by work product doctrine and were only discoverable on showing of rare and exceptional circumstances); *see also* Stanley D. Davis & Thomas D. Beisecker, *Discovering Trial Consultant Work Product: A New Way to Borrow an Adversary's Wits?*, 17 AM. J. TRIAL ADVOC. 581, 619 (1994) ("the attorney's discussions of case theory and the consultant's suggestions thereon should qualify for the higher protection accorded mental impressions").

[23]*See, e.g.*, QST Energy, Inc. v. Mervyn's, 2001 U.S. Dist. LEXIS 23266, at *3–5 (N.D. Cal. May 11, 2001) (in naming former consultant as witness, defendant waived work product and attorney-client privilege protection on all subjects on which expert was likely to offer testimony); Douglas v. University Hosp., 150 F.R.D. 165, 168 (E.D. Mo. 1993) (once nontestifying expert is designated as testifying expert, nontestifying expert subject to cross-examination). *But cf.* Messier v. Southbury Training Sch., 1998 WL 422858, at *2–4 (D. Conn. June 29, 1998) (where expert is retained as both consultant and testifying witness, work product doctrine may be invoked to protect work completed by expert in consultative capacity as long as there exists clear distinction between two roles and any ambiguity about which function was served by expert must be resolved in favor of discovery); B.C.F. Oil Ref. v. Consolidated Edison Co., 171 F.R.D. 57, 62 (S.D.N.Y. 1997) (directing disclosure of documents where it was "not clear" whether reviewed by expert solely in capacity of consultant or "whether they informed his expert opinion as well").

[24]*See, e.g.*, Lamonds v. General Motors Corp., 180 F.R.D. 302, 305 (W.D. Va. 1998) (work product discoverable when provided by attorney to expert for consideration in formulation of expert's opinion); Herman v. Marine Midland Bank, 207 F.R.D. 26, 29 (W.D.N.Y. 2002) (holding Rule 26(a)(2)(B) requires disclosure of core work product supplied by party to testifying expert); *In re* Pioneer Hi-Bred Int'l, Inc., 238 F.3d 1370, 1375 (Fed. Cir. 2001) (holding attorney-client privilege and work product protection waived by disclosure of confidential communications to expert witnesses, whether or not expert relies on information in preparing report); Johnson v. Gmeinder, 191 F.R.D. 638, 645–47 (D. Kan. 2000) (investigative report and other materials prepared by nontestifying expert in connection with investigation of automobile accident loses privileged status when disclosed to testifying expert). However, a number of courts considering the testifying expert issue have held that work product is protected, even when disclosed to a testifying expert. *See, e.g.*, Nexxus Prods. Co. v. CVS N.Y., Inc., 188 F.R.D. 7, 10 (D. Mass. 1999) (disclosures do not include core attorney work product considered by expert in forming his or her opinion); Estate of Chopper v. R.J. Reynolds Tobacco Co., 195 F.R.D. 648, 651 (N.D. Iowa 2000) (holding that opinion work product has near absolute immunity from discovery even when opinion work product is shared with expert witness); Krisa v. Equitable Life Assurance Soc'y, 196 F.R.D. 254, 260 (M.D. Pa. 2000) (attorney's mental impressions were shielded from discovery at expert's deposition); Haworth, Inc. v. Herman Miller, Inc., 162 F.R.D. 289, 292–94 (W.D. Mich. 1995) (holding work product is not discoverable in deposition of testifying expert).

Increasingly, experts are used in connection with class certification motions.[25] Because such expert testimony is presented to the court, not to a jury, courts have concluded there is less need for a trial court to perform the gatekeeping function described in *Daubert*. In *In re Visa Check/Master Money Antitrust Litigation*,[26] the Second Circuit held that *Daubert* scrutiny of an expert at the class certification stage should be less exacting and rigorous than at trial on the merits, but the trial court nevertheless must ensure that the expert opinion is not so flawed that it would be inadmissible as a matter of law. The less exacting test employed by the Second Circuit in the context of class certification is also employed during a bench trial, where there is also no gatekeeping issue.[27]

3. Expert Disclosures

Rule 26(a)(2) of the Federal Rules of Civil Procedure governs the disclosure of expert testimony. Subsection 26(a)(2)(B) governs the content of the report required to be produced prior to trial by any testifying expert. The report, which must be signed by

---

[25]*See, e.g.*, Beck v. Boeing, 60 Fed. Appx. 38, 39 (9th Cir. 2003) (affirming as not abuse of discretion class certification decision that based commonality finding in part on plaintiffs' statistical proof); Dukes v. Wal-Mart Stores, Inc., 222 F.R.D. 137, 93 FEP 1629 (N.D. Cal. 2004) (parties utilized statisticians, labor market economists, and sociologists to support and oppose class certification motion), *aff'd*, 474 F.3d 1214, 1230, 99 FEP 1285 (9th Cir. 2007) (district court did not abuse its discretion when it relied on plaintiff's statistical data and interpretation as a valid component of its commonality analysis).

[26]280 F.3d 124 (2d Cir. 2001), *cert. denied*, 536 U.S. 917 (2002).

[27]*See* Gibbs v. Gibbs, 210 F.3d 491, 500 (5th Cir. 2000) (standards in *Daubert* "are not as essential in a case such as this where a district judge sits as the trier of fact in place of a jury"); Seaboard Lumber Co. v. United States, 308 F.3d 1283, 1301–02 (Fed. Cir. 2002) (although misleading jury is not concern in bench trials, district courts must nevertheless satisfy relevance and reliability standards in *Daubert* when acting as trier of fact); United States v. Brown, 279 F. Supp. 2d 1238, 1243–45 (S.D. Ala. 2003) (finding it permissible in bench trials to relax *Daubert* standards when admitting expert testimony, but that court must nevertheless rely on expert testimony only if it is admissible and reliable); Ekotek Site PRP Comm. v. Self, 1 F. Supp. 2d 1282, 1296 n.5 (D. Utah 1998) (exercising its role as "gatekeeper" unnecessary when district court acts as trier of fact because of court and opposing counsel examining and ruling out flawed arguments in expert's testimony); SmithKline Beecham Corp. v. Apotex Corp., 247 F. Supp. 2d 1011, 1042–43 (N.D. Ill. 2003) (judges in bench trials need not follow *Daubert* standards strictly and should have discretion whether to admit questionable expert testimony because "*Daubert* requires a binary choice—admit or exclude").

the witness, "shall contain a complete statement of all opinions to be expressed and the basis and reasons therefor."[28] In addition, the report must contain

> the data or other information considered by the witness in forming the opinions; any exhibits to be used as a summary of or support for the opinions; the qualifications of the witness, including a list of all publications authored by the witness within the preceding ten years; the compensation to be paid for the study and testimony; and a listing of any other cases in which the witness has testified as an expert at trial or by deposition within the preceding four years.[29]

Rule 26(b)(4) permits deposing any person who has been identified as an expert whose opinions may be presented at trial.

4. Role of the Expert at Trial

As discussed herein, experts can provide useful, admissible trial testimony regarding a variety of issues in employment cases. Of course, before designating a person as a testifying expert, a party should ascertain whether the expert agrees generally with that party's positions on the important issues in the case. Because academics usually have publications, one can read those publications before contacting the expert, but one should ascertain the expert's views about the specific facts of the case presented before designating the expert. This task is complicated by the reality that a given expert might offer testimony that is helpful on some issues, but not others, and it will not always be possible to limit the testimony to a specific topic.

II. STATISTICAL PROOF

The allocation of proof in disparate treatment and adverse impact cases is discussed in Chapters 2 and 3. The following six sections of this chapter consider a certain type of proof—statistical proof—often used by plaintiffs and defendants to meet their respective burdens. Considered within are types of statistical comparisons, sources of statistics, the proper geographic scope and time frame of statistics, and the weight to be given different statistical conclusions.

---

[28]FED. R. CIV. P. 26(a)(2)(B).
[29]Id.

Statistics may be used in an attempt to establish or rebut a prima facie case of adverse impact discrimination[30] or classwide intentional discrimination,[31] or to assist in showing that the defendant's articulated reasons for an individual employment decision are pretextual.[32] It can be useful, but generally is not determinative on the question of discriminatory intent in individual cases.[33] In order to have probative value, statistics need not reach

---

[30]*E.g.*, Albemarle Paper Co. v. Moody, 422 U.S. 405, 425 (1975) (complaining party makes out prima facie case of adverse impact by showing significant racial disparities between selected applicants and applicant pool); Nash v. Consolidated City of Jacksonville, 905 F.2d 355, 358, 53 FEP 677 (11th Cir. 1990) (statistics showing disparate pass rate on promotion exam established prima facie case of adverse impact). *See generally* Chapter 3 (Adverse Impact).

[31]*See, e.g.*, Teamsters v. United States, 431 U.S. 324, 339, 14 FEP 1514 (1977) (pattern-or-practice disparate treatment case; "our cases make it unmistakably clear that '[s]tatistical analyses have served and will continue to serve an important role' in cases in which the existence of discrimination is a disputed issue"); McDonnell Douglas Corp. v. Green, 411 U.S. 792, 805, 5 FEP 965 (1973) ("[S]tatistics as to [defendant's] employment policy and practice may be helpful to a determination of whether [defendant's] refusal to rehire [plaintiff] . . . conformed to a general pattern of discrimination against blacks."); McAlester v. United Air Lines, Inc., 851 F.2d 1249, 1257–58, 47 FEP 512 (10th Cir. 1988) (statistics used to establish prima facie case of intentional race discrimination in disciplinary sanctions); Beck v. Boeing, 60 Fed. Appx. 38, 39 (9th Cir. 2003) (female employees seeking classwide injunctive or declaratory relief in case alleging systemic disparate treatment could establish prima facie case under Title VII through statistics alone); Diaz v. AT&T, 752 F.2d 1356, 1363, 36 FEP 1742 (9th Cir. 1985) ("Statistical data is relevant because it can . . . establish a general discriminatory pattern in an employer's hiring or promotion practices."); *cf.* Smith v. Horner, 839 F.2d 1530, 1537 & n.8, 46 FEP 513 (11th Cir. 1988) (plaintiff's use of statistical evidence to show inference of classwide intentional discrimination, while proper use of statistics, failed in this instance; statistics alone, however, cannot be used to establish prima facie case of discrimination in *individual* disparate treatment case). In many class cases, statistics provide "the only available avenue of proof." United States v. Iron Workers Local 86, 443 F.2d 544, 551, 3 FEP 496 (9th Cir. 1971) (government-brought pattern-or-practice action) (cited with approval in Teamsters v. United States, 431 U.S. 324, 340 n.20, 14 FEP 1514 (1977)). *See generally* Chapter 2 (Disparate Treatment).

[32]*See, e.g.*, Pottenger v. Potlatch Corp., 329 F.3d 740, 748, 91 FEP 1530 (9th Cir. 2003) (statistical evidence used to prove prima facie case may also be considered to show pretext); Hopson v. Daimler Chrysler Corp., 306 F.3d 427, 437, 89 FEP 1759 (6th Cir. 2002) (plaintiff's statistics, coupled with manager testimony, raised genuine issue of fact regarding pretext, precluding summary judgment); Cook v. Boorstin, 763 F.2d 1462, 1468 (D.C. Cir. 1985) (disparate treatment plaintiff can use statistics "to rebut explanatory defenses as pretextual").

[33]*See* Adams v. Ameritech Servs., 231 F.3d 414, 422–23, 84 FEP 178, 185 (7th Cir. 2000) (statistical evidence "obviously of central importance" to disparate impact case; it can also "be very useful" to prove discrimination in individual disparate treatment or pattern-or-practice case, but will generally not be sufficient by itself);

the level of scientific certainty, but must be of legal significance.[34] Among other things, that means that statistics should take into

---

EEOC v. Joe's Stone Crab, Inc., 220 F.3d 1263, 1274, 84 FEP 195 (11th Cir. 2000) (plaintiff in disparate impact sex discrimination suit must establish significant statistical disparity between proportion of women in available labor pool and proportion of women selected for position at issue); In re Employment Discrimination Litig., 198 F.3d 1305, 1311–12, 81 FEP 950 (11th Cir. 1999) (to prove disparate impact claim, plaintiff needs to offer evidence that shows what "impact is 'disparate' from"); Bullington v. United Air Lines, Inc., 186 F.3d 1301, 1319–20, 80 FEP 926 (10th Cir. 1999) (statistical evidence of employer's general hiring patterns considerably less probative in individual disparate treatment case); Scales v. Slater, 181 F.3d 703, 709 n.5, 82 FEP 485, 488 n.5 (5th Cir. 1999) (gross statistical disparities may be probative of discriminatory intent in individual disparate treatment case, but also may be "utterly insufficient" to show disparate impact); Lowery v. Circuit City Stores, Inc., 158 F.3d 742, 761, 77 FEP 1319 (4th Cir. 1998) (statistics alone cannot prove individual disparate treatment claim, although they are relevant), vacated on other grounds, 527 U.S. 1031, 80 FEP 64 (1999); EEOC v. Texas Instruments, Inc., 100 F.3d 1173, 1185, 72 FEP 980, 990–91 (5th Cir. 1996) (statistics will only rarely rebut employer's articulated nondiscriminatory reasons for discharge); Carman v. McDonnell Douglas Corp., 114 F.3d 790, 792, 73 FEP 1793 (8th Cir. 1997) (trial court did not abuse discretion in limiting employee's request for information because companywide statistics are usually not helpful in establishing pretext); Adreani v. First Colonial Bankshares Corp., 154 F.3d 389, 400, 77 FEP 1233 (7th Cir. 1998) (statistical evidence concerning discharged employees generally not relevant in analysis of reasons for firing of particular plaintiff). But see Kadas v. MCI Systemhouse Corp., 255 F.3d 359, 363, 85 FEP 1720 (7th Cir. 2001) (refusing to establish rule that statistical evidence alone can never establish prima facie case of intentional discrimination); Bell v. Environmental Prot. Agency, 232 F.3d 546, 552–53, 84 FEP 630 (7th Cir. 2000) (statistics can be utilized in establishing either individual's prima facie case of disparate treatment or in showing pretext); Smith v. Xerox Corp., 196 F.3d 358, 370, 81 FEP 343 (2d Cir. 1999) (in individual disparate treatment case, "statistical analyses that compare co-workers who competed directly against each other to receive a benefit . . . are appropriate"); Kidd v. Illinois State Police, 167 F.3d 1084, 1101, 1102 & n.16, 79 FEP 380 (7th Cir. 1999) (although its relevance was limited, district court erred in not considering statistical evidence in individual case proffered to establish pattern of discriminatory discharges); Carter v. Ball, 33 F.3d 450, 456, 65 FEP 1414 (4th Cir. 1994) ("In disparate treatment cases, we consider statistical evidence to be 'unquestionably relevant' " to plaintiff's prima facie case or showing of pretext.) (citation omitted); EEOC v. O & G Spring & Wire Forms Specialty Co., 38 F.3d 872, 876, 65 FEP 1823 (7th Cir. 1994) (rejecting argument that statistical evidence by itself could not be used to prove intentional discrimination). Statistical evidence of a balanced workforce alone, however, will not defeat an individual claim of discrimination. See Beaird v. Seagate Tech., Inc., 145 F.3d 1159, 1168, 76 FEP 1865 (10th Cir. 1998) ("statistical evidence cannot defeat the pretext claim of an individual plaintiff where the plaintiff's case rests on non-statistical evidence").

[34]See Bazemore v. Friday, 478 U.S. 385, 400, 41 FEP 92 (1986) (plaintiff's burden is only "to prove discrimination by a preponderance of the evidence," not with "scientific certainty"); see also Section VII infra.

account the appropriate labor pool[35] and account for significant nondiscriminatory factors, which typically is done using multiple regression analysis.[36]

Although a plaintiff's prima facie case of adverse impact can be established by statistics alone,[37] statistical evidence is not accepted uncritically.[38] The Supreme Court has cautioned that statistics " 'come in [an] infinite variety and . . . their usefulness depends on all of the surrounding facts and circumstances.' "[39] Cautioning against the use of data that may have been " 'segmented and particularized and fashioned to obtain a desired result,' "[40] courts focus on the probative value of the statistics presented. Only statistics regarding the plaintiff's protected group[41] and the employment practice at issue[42] are relevant. Courts have emphasized that statistics

---

[35]*See* Section IV *infra*.

[36]*See* Section III.E *infra*.

[37]*See generally* Chapter 3 (Adverse Impact).

[38]EEOC v. Federal Reserve Bank of Richmond, 698 F.2d 633, 646–47, 30 FEP 1137 (4th Cir. 1983), *rev'd on other grounds sub nom.* Cooper v. Federal Reserve Bank of Richmond, 467 U.S. 867, 35 FEP 1 (1984). The court of appeals stated:
    [S]tatistical evidence is circumstantial in character and its acceptability depends on the magnitude of the disparity it reflects, the relevance of its supporting data, and other circumstances in the case supportive of or in rebuttal of a hypothesis of discrimination. And, in reviewing statistical evidence and its supporting data, the Court must give consideration and evaluate fairly such conflicting opinions and hypotheses as may have been presented, tempering its conclusion with . . . "a pinch of common sense."
Id. (citation omitted).

[39]Watson v. Fort Worth Bank & Trust, 487 U.S. 977, 995 n.3, 47 FEP 102 (1988) (quoting Teamsters v. United States, 431 U.S. 324, 340, 14 FEP 1514 (1977)); *see also* Bilingual Bicultural Coalition on Mass Media, Inc. v. Federal Commc'ns Comm'n, 595 F.2d 621, 629 n.33, 17 FEP 409 (D.C. Cir. 1978) ("[c]onsidered in a vacuum, of course, naked statistical comparisons are meaningless").

[40]EEOC v. Western Elec. Co., 713 F.2d 1011, 1019, 32 FEP 708 (4th Cir. 1983) (quoting EEOC v. Datapoint Corp., 570 F.2d 1264, 1269, 17 FEP 281 (5th Cir. 1978)).

[41]*See* Baltazar v. Board of Educ., 52 FEP 1877, 1881 (D. Md. 1990) (statistical evidence concerning discharge of African Americans irrelevant to discharged Asian American's action); *cf.* Emanuel v. Marsh, 897 F.2d 1435, 1439, 52 FEP 616 (8th Cir. 1990) (rejecting relevance of disparities relating to irrelevant labor pool).

[42]*See* Powers v. Dole, 782 F.2d 689, 693, 39 FEP 1774 (7th Cir. 1986) (proof of discriminatory training programs has no weight in allegations of discriminatory grievance procedures); Box v. A & P Tea Co., 772 F.2d 1372, 1379–80, 38 FEP 1509 (7th Cir. 1985) (statistics regarding *promotions* "fail to create a genuine issue of fact whether the reason given for [the plaintiff's] *discharge* was a pretext") (emphasis added).

must be based on a sufficient sample size[43] and drawn "as narrowly as possible to avoid the effects of factors other than discriminatory practices."[44] However, some courts have rejected defendants' efforts to disaggregate employment data in order to create small samples where the statistics become less probative.[45]

III. TYPES OF STATISTICAL PROOF

A. Statistical Comparisons

The essence of statistical proof involves a comparison.[46] As the Ninth Circuit has stated, "[s]tatistical evidence is used to demonstrate how a particular employment practice causes a protected

---

[43]*E.g.*, Washington v. Electrical Joint Apprenticeship & Training Comm., 845 F.2d 710, 712, 46 FEP 1215 (7th Cir. 1988); Pitre v. Western Elec. Co., 843 F.2d 1262, 1267, 51 FEP 656 (10th Cir. 1988); *see* Section VII.C *infra*.

[44]*E.g.*, Powers v. Alabama Dep't of Educ., 854 F.2d 1285, 1297, 48 FEP 331 (11th Cir. 1988).

[45]*E.g.*, Ezell v. Mobile Hous. Bd., 709 F.2d 1376, 1382, 32 FEP 594 (11th Cir. 1983); Bouman v. Block, 940 F.2d 1211, 1226, 60 FEP 1000 (9th Cir. 1991).

[46]*See, e.g.*, Paige v. California, 291 F.3d 1141, 1147, 88 FEP 1666 (9th Cir. 2002) (only way to determine if any parts of promotion process have disparate impact against nonwhite officers is to use statistical analysis of comparable groups); Smith v. Leggett Wire Co., 220 F.3d 752, 761–62, 83 FEP 980, 985 (6th Cir. 2000) (court erred in admitting statistics related to percentage of minority supervisors because plaintiffs failed to offer statistics showing number of qualified minorities in labor market); Culley v. Trak Microwave Corp., 117 F. Supp. 2d 1317, 84 FEP 847, 849 (M.D. Fla. 2000) (fact that 64.29% of employees terminated over 6-year period were older than 40 years of age does not establish age discrimination when plaintiff failed to compare these figures to age of employer's workforce as whole); Carter v. Ball, 33 F.3d 450, 456–57, 65 FEP 1414 (4th Cir. 1994) (showing zero African-American employees in agency's management does not establish prima facie case; there must be comparison of percentage of African Americans in desired position with percentage of African Americans in qualified applicant pool); Hawkins v. Ceco Corp., 883 F.2d 977, 985, 50 FEP 1454 (11th Cir. 1989) (importance of evidence that plaintiff was only African-American salaried employee for 10-year period is difficult to assess without comparative evidence regarding number of salaried positions); Mack v. Great Atl. & Pac. Tea Co., 871 F.2d 179, 184, 50 FEP 971 (1st Cir. 1989) ("naked numbers, standing unadorned and unexplained, lacked sufficient convictive force"). *But see* Teamsters v. United States, 431 U.S. 324, 342 n.23, 14 FEP 1514 (1977) ("In any event, fine tuning of the statistics could not have obscured the glaring absence of minority line drivers . . . . [T]he company's inability to rebut the inference of discrimination came . . . from 'the inexorable zero.' ").

minority group to be underrepresented in a specific area of employment (for example, hiring or promotion)."[47] It also can be used for other comparisons, including relative rate of pay.[48] The composition of the pool of employees or applicants serves as the basis for courts to evaluate statistical proof.[49] For statistical evidence to be probative, the party offering the evidence must establish statistical evidence concerning groups of individuals who are in fact similarly situated.[50] For example, evidence that during a reduction in force (RIF)

---

[47]*Paige*, 291 F.3d at 1145.

[48]Cooper v. Southern Co., 260 F. Supp. 2d 1295, 1303 (N.D. Ga. 2003) (plaintiff's statistical comparison of persons with similar job functions and same pay grade does not adequately demonstrate compensation discrimination); Mathers v. Northshire Mining Co., 217 F.R.D. 474, 480–81, 92 FEP 1360 (D. Minn. 2003) (using records over time, plaintiff and defendant's experts found statistically significant indications of discrimination because of disparity in rate of pay between men and women).

[49]*See Paige*, 291 F.3d at 1147 (internal pool of all officers who applied for this particular promotion is proper comparative group in determining whether California's Highway Patrol promotional process favors white officers over nonwhite officers); EEOC v. Texas Instruments, Inc., 100 F.3d 1173, 1185, 72 FEP 980, 990–91 (5th Cir. 1996) (statistics will only rarely rebut employer's articulated nondiscriminatory reasons for discharge; rejecting analysis because plaintiffs were able to show statistically significant results only for subgroup of employees who were 46 through 51 years of age, but not for those 40 to 46, or those older than 51); Jones v. Pepsi-Cola Metro. Bottling Co., 871 F. Supp. 305, 310–11 (E.D. Mich. 1994) (finding that proper pool for comparison for purposes of analyzing challenged examination process should be based on pools of relevant groups who took exam).

[50]*See* Anderson v. Westinghouse Savannah River Co., 406 F.3d 248, 261–63, 95 FEP 1121 (4th Cir. 2005) (rejecting plaintiff's statistical analysis for failure to compare employees with similar job positions, title, performance, and rank); Pottenger v. Potlatch Corp., 329 F.3d 740, 748, 91 FEP 1530 (9th Cir. 2003) (affirming summary judgment against plaintiff whose statistical analysis failed to account for job performance, even though plaintiff's expert had obtained job performance data); Radue v. Kimberly-Clark Corp., 219 F.3d 612, 616, 83 FEP 741, 744 (7th Cir. 2000) (statistics regarding ages of employees terminated in RIF in separate division of company not probative of plaintiff's case); Martinez v. Wyoming, 218 F.3d 1133, 1139, 83 FEP 917, 920–21 (10th Cir. 2000) (statistics not probative in hiring case where they fail to account for differences in qualifications); Scott v. University of Miss., 148 F.3d 493, 510, 77 FEP 1085 (5th Cir. 1998) (plaintiff failed to compare persons hired to pool of qualified applicants); Schultz v. McDonnell Douglas Corp., 105 F.3d 1258, 1259, 75 FEP 385 (8th Cir. 1997) (statistics in age case not probative when plaintiffs ignored performance ratings of other employees); Furr v. Seagate Tech., Inc., 82 F.3d 980, 986–87, 70 FEP 1325 (10th Cir. 1996) (plaintiff's statistics did not account for differences in skill or specialty); Hutson v. McDonnell Douglas Corp., 63 F.3d 771, 777–78, 68 FEP 1209 (8th Cir. 1995) (statistics not probative where they did not control for similar characteristics).

an employer laid off a greater percentage of employees age 40 or over, compared to those younger than age 40, would not support a claim of intentional discrimination if older individuals tended to disproportionately occupy the positions that the employer eliminated.[51] Additionally, "[f]or statistical evidence to be probative, the statistical pool or sample used must logically be related to the employment decision at issue and the statistical method applied to the pool or sample must be meaningful and suitable under the facts and circumstances of the case."[52]

In order to grasp the meaning of the statistical evidence presented, some courts may require the party to substantiate the statistical evidence with expert testimony.[53] If courts do require such testimony, experts may disagree as to the basis for the statistical analysis. One common area of contention is whether an analysis should be done on a companywide or a position-by-position basis, with employees' experts often opting for the former and employers' experts using the latter.[54]

---

[51]Coleman v. Quaker Oats Co., 232 F.3d 1271, 1283, 84 FEP 602, 608–09 (9th Cir. 2000) (because older employees tended to occupy positions that had been eliminated and outsourced, statistics showing that older workers were more likely to be included in RIF insufficient to defeat summary judgment).

[52]*Jones*, 871 F. Supp. at 310; *see also Smith*, 220 F.3d at 761–62 (statistics regarding number of minority supervisors not relevant to plaintiff's discharge claim); Hallman v. Reynolds Metals Co., 82 FEP 1414 (N.D. Ala.) (plaintiff failed to present sufficient evidence because statistical analysis of RIF should distinguish employees who took voluntary retirement from those who were laid off involuntarily), *aff'd*, 235 F.3d 1346 (11th Cir. 2000); Lawton v. State Mut. Life Assurance Co., 101 F.3d 218, 220, 75 FEP 767, 768 (1st Cir. 1996) (fact that male employees were promoted more often and had higher salaries irrelevant to discharge analysis).

[53]*Compare* Carter v. Ball, 33 F.3d 450, 457, 65 FEP 1414 (4th Cir. 1994) ("if a plaintiff offers a statistical comparison without expert testimony as to methodology or relevance to plaintiff's claim, a judge may be justified in excluding the evidence") *and* Zuniga v. Koch Midstream Servs. Co., 82 FEP 380, 383 (W.D. Tex. 2000) (finding plaintiff's "statistical evidence even less compelling given the fact that it was not offered by an expert witness qualified in drawing the necessary inferences of discrimination from the data presented") *with* Luciano v. Olsten Corp., 110 F.3d 210, 217, 73 FEP 722, 728 (2d Cir. 1997) (trial court did not clearly err when it allowed plaintiff to introduce charts showing lower percentages of women in higher-level jobs without requiring expert testimony) *and* Stratton v. Department for the Aging, 922 F. Supp. 857, 863–64 (S.D.N.Y. 1996) (expert testimony about raw statistical data in form of charts not "absolute prerequisite"), *aff'd*, 132 F.3d 869 (2d Cir. 1997).

[54]*See, e.g.*, Caridad v. Metro-N. Commuter R.R., 191 F.3d 283, 292–93, 80 FEP 627, 633–34 (2d Cir. 1999) (although plaintiff's failure to disaggregate data involving different positions might prove fatal in trial of merits, it was sufficient to establish commonality for class certification purposes); *see also* Section III.D.4 *infra*.

The principal statistical comparisons used in employment discrimination cases are "selection rate" (including "potential selection rate") comparisons, "population/workforce" comparisons,[55] and multiple regression analyses.[56] Cohort and other statistical analyses also are used.[57]

In adverse impact cases, selection rate and potential selection rate comparisons are the most commonly used statistical analyses.[58] This is true because such comparisons lend themselves to isolating the alleged adverse effect of the *particular* employment practice at issue.[59] Pattern-or-practice disparate treatment cases, on the other hand—which usually involve nonstatistical evidence of intentional discrimination to buttress the statistical case[60]—may lend themselves to all types of statistical comparisons.

B. Selection Rate Comparisons

Selection rate statistics compare the percentage of the complainant's protected group that pass (or fail) a given test; meet (or do not meet) a given employment requirement; or are (or are not) actually hired, promoted, or otherwise selected with the corresponding success (or failure) rate for the majority group.[61]

---

[55]*See, e.g.*, Green v. Missouri Pac. R.R., 523 F.2d 1290, 1293–94, 10 FEP 1409, *amended*, 11 FEP 658 (8th Cir. 1975); *see also* Sections III.B–III.D *infra*.

[56]*See* Section III.E *infra*.

[57]*See* Section III.F *infra*.

[58]*See, e.g.*, Frank v. Xerox Corp., 347 F.3d 130, 92 FEP 1270 (5th Cir. 2003) (plaintiffs' reliance on statistical data gathered from 1994 to 1999 to show reduction in percentage of black employees created material issue of fact as to disparity).

[59]42 U.S.C. § 2000e-2(k)(1)(A)(i), 2(B)(i) (2000); *see* Section III.F *infra*. *See generally* Chapter 3 (Adverse Impact).

[60]*E.g.*, Teamsters v. United States, 431 U.S. 324, 339, 14 FEP 1514 (1977) (finding population/workforce comparison convincing, but noting that plaintiffs did not rely on statistics alone: "The individuals who testified about their personal experiences with the company brought the cold numbers convincingly to life."); *Frank*, 347 F.3d at 137 (existence of program targeted to balance representation of all racial and gender groups qualifies as sufficient evidence of pattern of discrimination). *See generally* Chapter 2 (Disparate Treatment).

[61]*See, e.g.*, Banks v. East Baton Rouge Parish Sch. Bd., 320 F.3d 570, 579 n.13, 91 FEP 280 (5th Cir. 2003) (defendant's statistical evidence demonstrated that of applicants that applied for new janitor position, 15.9% of total female applicants were selected, versus 11.9% of total male applicants); Shores v. Publix Super Mkts., Inc., 1996 WL 407850, at *4 (M.D. Fla. Mar. 12, 1996) (in certifying class action, court considered descriptive statistics suggesting job "segregation" between defendant's

Differences between selection rates of the protected class when compared with selection rates of the majority group can result from one, or a combination, of three things: (1) chance, (2) differences in the job-related qualifications of the protected group when compared with the majority group, or (3) the application of an illegal discriminatory selection criterion.[62] If a test of statistical significance rejects chance as the explanation for the differences in the selection rates between comparably qualified groups,[63] courts may infer that the disparate selection rates are attributable to discriminatory selection criteria.[64]

---

male and female employees). *See generally* Chapter 4 (Application of Adverse Impact to Employment Decisions). For example, in comparing the selection rates of the African-American applicants to those of the white applicants, the ultimate equation could be as follows:

(Number of successful African-American applicants) vs. (Total number of African-American applicants)	compared to	(Number of successful white applicants) vs. (Total number of white applicants)

For example:

(100 African Americans passed the test) vs. (500 African Americans took the test)	compared to	(500 whites passed the test) vs. (1,000 whites took the test)
20% African-American passing rate	compared to	50% white passing rate

In the hiring context, an example would be:

(80 African Americans hired) vs. (800 African Americans applied)	compared to	(400 whites hired) vs. (2,000 whites applied)
10% African-American hiring rate	compared to	20% white hiring rate

The significance of such disparities is discussed in Section VII *infra*.

[62]This latter explanation could include, inter alia, differences between the groups with respect to characteristics or qualifications that are not legitimate job-related considerations.

[63]*See* Section VII *infra*. A key point of contention in litigation, of course, concerns whether the analysis properly captures all legitimate job-related characteristics as to which the groups being compared may differ. *See generally* Chapter 3 (Adverse Impact).

[64]*See* Hameed v. Iron Workers Local 396, 637 F.2d 506, 512–13, 24 FEP 352 (8th Cir. 1980) ("If tests of statistical significance eliminate chance as a likely explanation for the differential pass rates, courts will presume that the disparate pass

To be admissible and probative, statistical analyses must account for relevant, nondiscriminatory factors in the employer's decision-making process. For example, in *EEOC v. American Airlines, Inc.*,[65] the Fifth Circuit found that the selection rate comparison offered by the EEOC was not credible as an indicator of discrimination in pilot hiring because it made only a superficial attempt to account for the qualifications of the job.[66] Specifically, the EEOC's analysis focused on just a few criteria assertedly relied on by the airline, such as experience, health, and failure to show up for an interview, but failed to account for other assertedly relevant criteria, such as passing a flight simulator test.[67]

Some courts have applied the "four-fifths rule"[68] proposed in the EEOC's Uniform Guidelines on Employee Selection Procedures to determine the significance of statistical evidence of discrimination.[69] Courts are cautious about applying this rule, however, because it may "produce inherently unreliable results" in some situations.[70] The Second Circuit rejected application of the rule to a

---

rates are attributable to racially discriminatory selection criteria."); *see also* Allen v. Seidman, 881 F.2d 375, 378, 50 FEP 607 (7th Cir. 1989) (evidence that 39% of African Americans passed promotion exam, whereas 84% of whites passed established adverse impact); Meacham v. Knolls Atomic Power Lab., 185 F. Supp. 2d 193, 211, 90 FEP 1791 (N.D.N.Y. 2002) (plaintiff's statistical evidence "determine[d] the probability that the statistical disparity between the predicted and actual results deviated from the norm by chance or for some other reasons, such as age discrimination"), *aff'd*, 381 F.3d 56 (2d Cir. 2004), *vacated and remanded sub nom.* KAPL, Inc. v. Meacham, 544 U.S. 957 (2005).

[65]48 F.3d 164, 67 FEP 754 (5th Cir. 1995).

[66]*Id.* at 172–73; *see also* Sheehan v. Daily Racing Form, Inc., 104 F.3d 940, 942, 72 FEP 1390, 1391 (7th Cir. 1997) (statistics showing correlation between age and job retention has no significance when statistician ignored job qualifications).

[67]*American Airlines*, 48 F.3d at 172.

[68]Under the four-fifths rule, "a selection practice is considered to have a disparate impact if it has a 'selection rate for any race, sex, or ethnic group which is less than four-fifths (4/5) (or eighty percent) of the rate of the group with the highest rate.' " Stout v. Potter, 276 F.3d 1118, 1124, 87 FEP 1255 (9th Cir. 2002) (quoting 29 C.F.R. § 1607.4(D) (2001)).

[69]Cotter v. City of Boston, 323 F.3d 160, 170–71, 92 FEP 65 (1st Cir. 2003) (state's interest of remedying past discrimination compelling for implementing affirmative action plan because statistical data revealed selection rate 20% below suggested "four-fifths rule").

[70]EEOC v. Joint Apprenticeship Comm., 186 F.3d 110, 118–19, 80 FEP 1518 (2d Cir. 1999) ("district court inappropriately sanctioned the application of the four-fifths rule to the fail ratio" because only small number of applicants failed to meet appropriate requirements).

"fail ratio" (i.e., the rate at which protected groups were not selected by an employer for a position) because of the small sample size in the case.[71] In *Stout v. Potter*,[72] however, the Ninth Circuit applied the "four-fifths rule" to a small sample and determined that plaintiffs failed to establish that the challenged employment practice had an adverse impact on female applicants because the selection rate for women was 81 percent of the selection rate for men.[73] In *Isabel v. City of Memphis*,[74] the Sixth Circuit cautioned that "notwithstanding a test's compliance with the four-fifths rule, other [statistical] analyses may still reveal an adverse impact."[75]

C. Potential Selection Rate Comparisons

Selection rate comparisons, which were discussed in the preceding section, can be effective when accurate and reliable applicant flow data is available. But courts have cautioned against relying on applicant flow for selection rate comparisons when the challenged application process or criterion itself might deter people from applying—thus potentially skewing the statistics in favor of the employer.[76] In those situations, courts sometimes approve comparisons of what are known as *potential* selection rates. Potential selection rate comparisons compare the percentage of the protected class in the potential applicant pool that meets a particular job requirement

---

[71]*Id.* at 118–19.

[72]276 F.3d 1118 (9th Cir. 2002).

[73]*Id.* at 1124.

[74]404 F.3d 404, 95 FEP 801 (6th Cir. 2005).

[75]*Id.* at 412.

[76]*See* Dothard v. Rawlinson, 433 U.S. 321, 330, 15 FEP 10 (1977) ("The application process might itself not adequately reflect the actual potential applicant pool, since otherwise qualified people might be discouraged from applying because of a self-recognized inability to meet the very standards challenged as being discriminatory."); EEOC v. Rath Packing Co., 787 F.2d 318, 337, 40 FEP 580 (8th Cir. 1986) (applicant flow data often best indicator of employer's discriminatory practices, but only when those same discriminatory practices do not deter people from applying); Kilgo v. Bowman Transp., Inc., 789 F.2d 859, 867–68, 40 FEP 1415 (11th Cir. 1986) (use of applicant flow data in sex discrimination case inappropriate where company posted experience requirement that probably deterred women from applying); Thompson v. Mississippi State Pers. Bd., 674 F. Supp. 198, 204, 45 FEP 530 (N.D. Miss. 1987) (actual applicant flow data are appropriate when evaluating discriminatory effect of college education requirement if there is no evidence of practices that discourage otherwise qualified women from applying). *See generally* Chapters 15 (Hiring) and 16 (Promotion, Advancement, and Reclassification).

(e.g., an educational credential) with the percentage of the majority group that meets the requirement.[77]

The Supreme Court has discussed potential selection rate statistics on at least three occasions. In *Griggs v. Duke Power Co.*,[78] for example—the Court's seminal adverse impact decision—the Court considered a challenge to an employer's high school diploma and intelligence test requirements. Although the parties did not dispute that the high school diploma requirement had an adverse impact on African Americans,[79] the Court in dictum cited the potential selection rate statistics that supported that conclusion—namely, that 34 percent of white males in North Carolina in 1960 had completed high school, but only 12 percent of African-American males had done so.[80]

---

[77]Using a high school diploma prerequisite as an example, the comparison would be as follows:

(Total number of African Americans in the relevant labor market with a high school diploma) vs. (Total number of African Americans in the relevant labor market)	compared to	(Total number of whites in the relevant labor market with a high school diploma) vs. (Total number of whites in the relevant labor market)

For example:

(100 African Americans in the relevant labor market have a high school diploma) vs. (150 African Americans in the relevant labor market)	compared to	(1,000 whites in the relevant labor market have a high school diploma) vs. (1,333 whites in the relevant labor market)
67% potential African American-applicants	compared to	75% potential white applicants

Alternatively, as noted in Section IV.B *infra*, plaintiffs can substitute "potential applicants"—using qualified workforce data—for applicants in the standard selection rate equation. Such a comparison differs from the "potential selection rate" equation in that it would compare the percentage of the protected group in the relevant labor pool with the percentage of the protected group that actually passed, rather than the percentage of the protected group in the relevant labor pool that "could" pass with the percentage of the majority or preferred group that could pass.

[78]401 U.S. 424, 3 FEP 175 (1971). *Griggs* is discussed extensively in Chapters 3 (Adverse Impact) and 4 (Application of Adverse Impact to Employment Decisions).

[79]*Griggs*, 401 U.S. at 430 n.6; *see* Griggs v. Duke Power Co., 420 F.2d 1225, 1239 & n.6, 2 FEP 310 (4th Cir. 1970), *rev'd*, 401 U.S. 424 (1971).

[80]*Griggs*, 401 U.S. at 430 n.6.

In *Dothard v. Rawlinson*,[81] the Court expressly sanctioned the use of potential selection rate statistics where the employer's use of a particular selection criterion likely chilled potential applicants of the protected class, thus rendering unreliable selection rate statistics based on applicant flow.[82] The *Dothard* Court considered the plaintiffs' adverse impact challenge to the state prison system's use of height and weight standards for hiring. The Court held that the following statistic made out a prima facie case of adverse impact: "When the height and weight restrictions are combined, Alabama's statutory standards would exclude 41.13% of the female population while excluding less than 1% of the male population."[83] That statistic, the Court held, was sufficient to shift to the defendant the burden of proving job-relatedness.[84]

In *New York City Transit Authority v. Beazer*,[85] the Court considered but rejected the plaintiffs' reliance on potential selection rate statistics. The plaintiffs challenged, on adverse impact grounds, the city's refusal to employ users of methadone, a narcotic often used by recovering heroin addicts. A typical potential selection rate comparison would compare the percentage of members of the protected group (in this case, African Americans and Hispanics) in the relevant population who pass or fail the requirement (i.e., who use methadone) with the percentage of whites who pass or fail the requirement. In *Beazer*, however, the plaintiffs instead offered statistics showing that 63 percent of all persons receiving methadone maintenance in New York public programs were African American or Hispanic. The Court rejected the statistics as "virtually irrelevant," primarily because they did not reflect those applying for, qualified for, or holding jobs with the defendant; thus, the 63 percent statistic was not reflective of those potentially subject to the challenged criterion.[86]

---

[81]433 U.S. 321, 15 FEP 10 (1977). *Dothard* is discussed further in Chapter 10 (Sex).

[82]433 U.S. at 330–31.

[83]*Id.* at 329–30.

[84]*Id.* at 330.

[85]440 U.S. 568, 19 FEP 149 (1979).

[86]*Id.* at 584–86. The Court also rejected the plaintiffs' statistics as being *underinclusive*, i.e., not reflecting the racial composition of persons treated with methadone in *private* facilities. *Id.* at 586. Moreover, even if the plaintiffs had established adverse impact, the Court noted that the defendant would prevail because it demonstrated the job-relatedness of its requirement. *Id.* at 587.

Beazer thus teaches that the population statistics used in potential selection rate comparisons must reflect those in the population "otherwise qualified" and available for the job in question.[87]

In hiring and promotion cases, an appropriate statistical analysis generally will begin with a measure of the percentage of members of the protected class in the potential qualified applicant pool.[88] In *Aiken v. City of Memphis*,[89] the city sought to justify its affirmative action program by demonstrating its own past discriminatory conduct and, toward that end, used potential selection rate comparisons. The city's statistical presentation showed that in 1971, 11 percent of patrol officers were African American, whereas only 5.9 percent of sergeants were African American, and in 1978, 25 percent of patrol officers were African American, whereas only 7.5 percent of sergeants were African American.[90] These statistics, the court held, were "probative enough to satisfy the City's burden of producing strong evidence that discrimination [had] occurred."[91]

In analyzing a claim of discrimination in connection with a RIF, the statistical analysis may consider either layoff rates or retention rates.[92]

---

[87]*See id.* at 585–86 (plaintiffs' statistic "tells us nothing about the class of otherwise-qualified applicants and employees who have participated in methadone maintenance programs for over a year—the only class improperly excluded by [the employer's] policy under the District Court's analysis"); *cf.* Bradley v. Pizzaco of Neb., Inc., 939 F.2d 610, 613, 68 FEP 242 (8th Cir. 1991) (pseudofolliculitis barbae, skin condition affecting primarily African Americans, likely to occur among potential job applicants in same ratio that it occurs in general population); Cox v. City of Chi., 868 F.2d 217, 222, 4 FEP 1674 (7th Cir. 1989) (relevant labor pool is number of persons who would be eligible to take test if at-issue rule were not in force). *See generally* Wards Cove Packing Co. v. Atonio, 490 U.S. 642, 651, 49 FEP 1519 (1989) ("[I]n cases where [qualified] labor market statistics will be difficult if not impossible to ascertain, we have recognized that . . . measures indicating the racial composition of 'otherwise-qualified applicants' for at-issue jobs [are probative].").

[88]Carter v. Ball, 33 F.3d 450, 456, 65 FEP at 1411 (4th Cir. 1994) ("The mere absence of minority employees in upper-level positions does not suffice to prove a prima facie case of [disparate treatment] without a comparison to the [qualified minorities in the] relevant labor pool."); *see also* Bullington v. United Air Lines, Inc., 186 F.3d 1301, 1313, 80 FEP 926 (10th Cir. 1999) (although applicant pool data were in some ways incomplete, failing to account for differences in male and female interviewees' aeronautical experience, they nonetheless raised genuine issue of material fact for trial on adverse impact).

[89]37 F.3d 1155, 65 FEP 1757 (6th Cir. 1994).

[90]*Id.* at 1163.

[91]*Id.*

[92]Council 31, State, Am. Fed'n of County & Mun. Employees v. Doherty, 169 F.3d 1068, 1074–75, 79 FEP 411 (7th Cir. 1999).

D. Population/Workforce Comparisons

Population/workforce comparisons compare the availability of the protected group in the general population or the relevant labor market with the percentage of the protected group in an employer's workforce (or portion thereof).[93]

The Supreme Court has considered population/workforce comparisons on several occasions. In *Teamsters v. United States*,[94] a pattern-or-practice disparate treatment case, the Court noted a gross disparity in the percentage of African Americans in the population with the percentage of African Americans employed as drivers by the defendant employer.[95] That disparity, along with other statistical

---

[93]In comparing African Americans in the employer's workforce with African Americans in the relevant labor market, the equation is as follows:

(Number of African Americans in the relevant labor pool)		(Number of African Americans employed by the employer)
vs.	compared to	vs.
(Number of all persons in the relevant labor pool)		(Number of all persons employed by the employer)

For example:

(80,000 African Americans in the relevant labor pool)		(25 African Americans employed by the employer)
vs.	compared to	vs.
(400,000 persons in the relevant labor pool)		(500 total employees)
20% African-American available labor market rate	compared to	5% African-American employment rate

A more narrowly defined population/workforce example (in the promotion context), *see* Sections IV–VI *infra*, would be as follows:

(200 African Americans in nonsupervisory positions with the requisite qualifications eligible for and interested in promotion)	compared to	(10 African Americans employed by the employer in supervisory positions)
vs.		vs.
(800 nonsupervisory employees qualified for and interested in promotion)		(100 supervisors in the employer's workforce)
25% African-American qualified and interested labor market rate	compared to	10% African-American employment rate

[94]431 U.S. 324, 14 FEP 1514 (1977).

[95]*Id.* at 337 & n.17. *Teamsters* is discussed extensively in Chapters 2 (Disparate Treatment), 15 (Hiring), and 40 (Monetary Relief).

and anecdotal indicia of discrimination, the Court held, was sufficient to meet the plaintiff's burden of proof of discrimination.[96]

In *Hazelwood School District v. United States*,[97] arguably the most significant Supreme Court decision on the subject of statistical proof, the Court established that substantial refinements on both sides[98] of the general population/workforce comparison would yield more probative evidence. On the left side of the equation, "population," the Court emphasized the necessity of determining the relevant geographic area,[99] as well as the qualified labor market,[100] when dealing with jobs involving skills that are not generally possessed or readily acquired.[101] On the right side of the equation, "employer's workforce," the Court for the first time focused its attention not on the *present* composition of the workforce (a static, snapshot analysis) but on the employment decisions that had been made during the relevant time period (time frame analysis).[102] At issue in *Hazelwood*—a pattern-or-practice race discrimination case—was the alleged disparate hiring of public school teachers. The Court rejected the plaintiff's proffered comparison of the percentage of African Americans employed by the school with the percentage of African Americans in the student population; the Court explained "that a proper comparison was between the racial composition of Hazelwood's teaching staff and the racial composition of the qualified public school teacher population in the relevant labor market."[103]

---

[96]431 U.S. at 338.

[97]433 U.S. 299, 15 FEP 1 (1977).

[98]The "left side" of the population/workforce comparison, as referred to in this chapter, is the percentage of members of the protected group in the relevant population (e.g., (500 African Americans)/(100,000 total relevant population) = 5%). The "right side" of the comparison is the percentage of members of the protected group in the employer's workforce (e.g., (6 African Americans)/(200 total relevant workforce) = 3%).

[99]*See* Section V *infra*.

[100]*See* Section IV.C.1 *infra*.

[101]*Hazelwood*, 433 U.S. at 309 n.13 ("When special qualifications are required to fill particular jobs, comparisons to the general population (rather than to the smaller group of individuals who possess the necessary qualifications) may have little probative value."). Although the Court permitted the use of general population data for entry-level jobs in *Teamsters*, it also cautioned that "evidence showing that the figures for the general population might not accurately reflect the pool of qualified job applicants would also be relevant." *Teamsters*, 431 U.S. at 339–40 n.20.

[102]*Hazelwood*, 433 U.S. at 309–12; *see* Section VI *infra*.

[103]*Hazelwood*, 433 U.S. at 308.

The Court again considered a population/workforce comparison in *Wards Cove Packing Co. v. Atonio.*[104] *Wards Cove* involved
an adverse impact challenge to an Alaskan salmon cannery's hiring and promotion practices. At issue were cannery and noncannery
jobs. The cannery jobs were almost entirely held by nonwhites;
the noncannery jobs—generally white-collar office jobs—were
almost entirely held by whites. This disparity proved discrimination, the plaintiffs argued. But *Wards Cove* echoed *Hazelwood* in
rejecting the plaintiffs' use of unrefined general population statistics and underscored the need for another, more refined comparison: "It is such a comparison—between the racial composition of
the qualified persons in the labor market and the persons holding
at-issue jobs—that generally forms the proper basis for the initial
inquiry in a disparate-impact case."[105]

In following the Supreme Court's rulings in these cases, lower
courts recognize that where a job requires special skills or experience,
the relevant labor pool for comparison is the segment of the local
labor force possessing those qualifications.[106] In these circumstances,
comparisons may not be based on general workforce classifications,
but must account for the qualifications needed for the position in
question.[107] Likewise, the data that provides the basis for the analysis
must not be overinclusive.[108] However, in cases where there are no

---

[104]490 U.S. 642, 650–51, 49 FEP 1519 (1989). *Wards Cove* was overruled in
part by the Civil Rights Act of 1991, but its requirement that qualified labor force
statistics be used on the left side of the population/workforce comparison survived.
See generally Chapter 3 (Adverse Impact).

[105]*Wards Cove*, 490 U.S. at 650–51. Other aspects of *Wards Cove* are discussed
in Sections III.F, III.G, and IV.C.4 *infra*.

[106]*See, e.g.*, Brown v. Coach Stores, Inc., 163 F.3d 706, 712, 78 FEP 917, 922
(2d Cir. 1998) (inappropriate to compare percentage of minorities in higher positions at company with percentage of minority employees in entire retail industry);
Moore v. Hughes Helicopters, Inc., 708 F.2d 475, 482–83 (9th Cir. 1983) ("If special skills are required for a job, the proxy pool must be that of the local labor force
possessing the requisite skills."); Sanchez v. Santa Ana, 928 F. Supp. 1494, 1503
(C.D. Cal. 1995) (limiting labor pool to those employed in company's lower-level
positions, where promotion was restricted to internal candidates).

[107]Alexander v. Fulton County, 207 F.3d 1303, 1327–28, 82 FEP 858, 874–76
(11th Cir. 2000) (comparison between racial composition of sheriff's department and
general demographics of surrounding eight-county metropolitan area not probative
when jobs are not entry level or of low skill level and general population is not readily
qualified for them).

[108]Thomas v. IBM, 48 F.3d 478, 486, 67 FEP 270 (10th Cir. 1995) (plaintiff's
study incorporated every possible group that may have been discriminated against,

special qualifications, comparisons between the workforce of the employer and the local population may be appropriate.[109]

E. Regression Analyses

Multiple regression analysis is a statistical technique designed to estimate the effect of several independent variables (e.g., education, experience, performance, age, race, sex) on a single dependent variable (e.g., salary).[110] The purpose of the methodology is to estimate the extent to which a particular independent variable (e.g., sex) influenced the dependent variable (e.g., pay rate); in other words, whether it was discrimination, or other factors, that caused the injury (e.g., a pay disparity).[111]

Multiple regression analyses are particularly necessary when comparing the wage rates paid to members of a protected group with those paid to whites or males, because a simple direct comparison of wages fails to take into account the legitimate differences caused by differing occupations, education levels, skills, and other relevant and nondiscriminatory factors.[112] Multiple regression

---

making it difficult for court to focus on specific age discrimination claim put forth).

[109]*See, e.g.*, Lalla v. City of New Orleans, 83 FEP 1269, 1273 (E.D. La. 1999) (proper to compare workforce to general population in hiring case involving position with no special qualifications).

[110]*See* David S. Evans, *Class Certification, the Merits and Expert Evidence*, 11 GEO. MASON L. REV. 1 (2002); David Sherwyn, Michael Heise, and Zev J. Eigen, *Don't Train Your Employees and Cancel Your "1-800" Harassment Hotline: An Empirical Examination and Correction of the Flaws in the Affirmative Defense to Sexual Harassment Charges*, 69 FORDHAM L. REV. 1265 (2001); Michael O. Finkelstein, *The Judicial Reception of Multiple Regression Studies in Race and Sex Discrimination Cases*, 80 COLUM. L. REV. 737, 742–45 (1980); Franklin M. Fisher, *Multiple Regression in Legal Proceedings*, 80 COLUM. L. REV. 702, 721–25 (1980).

[111]Fisher, 80 COLUM. L. REV. at 720. The explanatory power of a regression analysis is measured by its "R square," sometimes referred to as the "correlation coefficient." The R-square values quantify the proportion of the total variance in the dependent variable that is associated with variations in the independent variables. The R-square values range from 0 (which indicates no prediction) to 1 (which represents complete predictability).

[112]*See, e.g.*, Hemmings v. Tidyman's Inc., 285 F.3d 1174, 1183–84, 88 FEP 945 (9th Cir. 2002) (regression analysis used to establish gender disparities in wages); Churchill v. IBM, Inc., 759 F. Supp. 1089, 1097–99, 55 FEP 1004 (D.N.J. 1991) (regression analysis used to demonstrate salary discrimination); Pouncy v. Prudential Ins. Co., 499 F. Supp. 427, 449–50, 23 FEP 1349 (S.D. Tex. 1980) (same), *aff'd*, 668 F.2d 795, 28 FEP 121 (1982).

analyses also have been used in cases involving alleged discrimination in promotions, job assignments, and other issues.[113]

In *Bazemore v. Friday*[114]—a pattern-or-practice disparate treatment action—the Supreme Court approved the use of a multiple regression analysis in proving salary discrimination based on race.[115] The plaintiffs in *Bazemore* alleged that the government employer paid African Americans significantly less than it paid comparably situated white employees. In support, the plaintiffs offered several multiple regression analyses pinpointing statistically significant salary differences in particular years. The analyses attempted to isolate the effect of race on salary by accounting for legitimate effects of differences in education, tenure, and job title.[116] The district court found the plaintiffs' statistics nonprobative because they did not account for all variables that legitimately affect salary—in particular, salary differences from county to county.[117]

The Supreme Court reversed, distinguishing the *admissibility* of statistics from their *weight*. The Court held that regression analyses need not include all measurable variables thought to have an effect on salary in order to be admissible. But the omission of variables from a regression analysis affects the analysis' probative value, the Court recognized, and thus the weight to be attached to it.[118] In *Bazemore* itself, the regression analyses, especially when considered in light of other evidence presented by the plaintiffs, were held to be potentially sufficient to prove a pattern or practice of discrimination.[119]

---

[113]*E.g., Hemmings*, 285 F.3d at 1184 (plaintiff's expert used regression analysis to show gender disparity in promotions); EEOC v. General Tel. Co., 885 F.2d 575, 582–83, 50 FEP 1316 (9th Cir. 1989) (regression analysis used to show that certain employment practices resulted in women being denied access to higher-paying jobs within company); Segar v. Civiletti, 508 F. Supp. 690, 695–702, 25 FEP 1452 (D.D.C. 1981) (plaintiff successfully used multiple regression analysis to show discrimination in wages and initial job assignment), *vacated in part on other grounds*, 738 F.2d 1249, 35 FEP 31 (D.C. Cir. 1984).

[114]478 U.S. 385, 41 FEP 92 (1986).

[115]*Id.* at 400–01.

[116]*Id.* at 398.

[117]*See id.* at 399.

[118]*Id.* at 400. The Court noted that "[t]here may, of course, be some regressions so incomplete as to be inadmissible as irrelevant." *Id.* at 400 n.10.

[119]*Id.* at 403–04 (remanding case for court of appeals to apply proper standard of review to district court's rejection of plaintiffs' regression analyses).

When statistics are used to establish a prima facie case, some courts indicate a preference for regression analyses.[120] For example, in *Smith v. Xerox Corp.*,[121] the court noted that the plaintiffs should have conducted a regression analysis to eliminate other causes for the fact that older or male workers were more likely to be terminated; simply showing that "chance was most likely not responsible" for a disparity "could not, by itself, support a conclusion that discrimination must have been the cause."[122]

Courts will examine the variables included in the proponent's regression analyses, as well as those the opponent claims were improperly excluded.[123] The most probative analyses include all the major factors that influence the dependent variable[124] and exclude

---

[120]*See* Lavin-McEleney v. Marist Coll., 239 F.3d 476, 482, 84 FEP 1761 (2d Cir. 2001) ("It is undisputed that multiple regression analysis . . . is a scientifically valid statistical technique for identifying discrimination."); Adams v. Ameritech Servs., Inc., 231 F.3d 414, 425, 84 FEP 178 (7th Cir. 2000) (finding it "odd" that plaintiffs' expert did not run multiple regression analysis to isolate relevance of age as factor in defendants' termination and demotion decisions, but also stating that "we are not prepared to hold as a matter of law that nothing but regression analyses can produce evidence" that is reliable); *see also* Lowery v. Circuit City Stores, 158 F.3d 742, 764, 77 FEP 1319, 1334 (4th Cir. 1998) (plaintiffs' promotion analysis that failed to adequately control for factors other than race lacked probative value on issue of pretext), *vacated on other grounds*, 527 U.S. 1031, 80 FEP 64 (1999); Coward v. ADT Sys., Inc., 140 F.3d 271, 274, 76 FEP 899 (D.C. Cir. 1998) (multiple regression analysis that showed that employer paid African-American employees approximately 12% less than white employees was incomplete and not admissible in § 1981 action alleging intentional wage discrimination; analysis failed to account for job title or any other variable representing type of work performed), *aff'd in part and rev'd in part*, 194 F.3d 155 (D.C. Cir. 1999); Diehl v. Xerox Corp., 933 F. Supp. 1157, 1169, 71 FEP 723, 730 (W.D.N.Y. 1996) (plaintiff's statistical analysis fatally flawed because it failed to account for factors that contributed to RIF decisions).

[121]196 F.3d 358, 81 FEP 343 (2d Cir. 1999).

[122]196 F.3d at 371.

[123]*E.g.*, Smith v. Virginia Commonwealth Univ., 84 F.3d 672, 70 FEP 1248 (4th Cir. 1996) (en banc); Segar v. Smith, 738 F.2d 1249, 1275, 35 FEP 31 (D.C. Cir. 1984) (whether Title VII plaintiff has included necessary variables in statistical analyses requires careful examination).

[124]*Compare* Rudebusch v. Hughes, 313 F.3d 506, 516, 90 FEP 865 (9th Cir. 2002) (criticizing defendant's reliance on regression analysis of pay adjustments because analysis did not account for individual merit, an important factor for faculty compensation), EEOC v. Sears, Roebuck & Co., 839 F.2d 302, 324–27, 45 FEP 1257 (7th Cir. 1988) (district court could find that EEOC's regression analyses were not probative in view of their failure to include as independent variable applicants' interest in commission sales and in product to be sold), Sheehan v. Purolator, Inc., 839 F.2d 99, 102–03, 49 FEP 1000 (2d Cir. 1988) (district court did not err in rejecting plaintiff's statistical analysis because it did not account for differences in

those factors that would be "tainted" or affected by the employer's alleged discrimination.[125] Factors that a regression analysis must

---

education and work experience) *and* Sobel v. Yeshiva Univ., 839 F.2d 18, 34–35, 45 FEP 1785, *amended*, 47 FEP 912 (2d Cir. 1988) (employer challenged plaintiff's statistical analysis on basis that it did not consider all variables) *with* Hemmings v. Tidyman's Inc., 285 F.3d 1174, 1188, 88 FEP 945 (9th Cir. 2002) (disagreeing with employer's contention that plaintiff's statistical evidence was incomplete and inadmissible because analysis failed to include individual qualifications, preferences, and education), EEOC v. General Tel. Co., 885 F.2d 575, 582, 50 FEP 1316 (9th Cir. 1989) (crediting regression analyses for promotion even though they failed adequately to account for differences in job interests between men and women, where employer offered no explanation of how statistical disparities would have been eliminated if adjustments for job interest had been made), McAlester v. United Air Lines, Inc., 851 F.2d 1249, 1257–58, 47 FEP 512 (10th Cir. 1988) (although plaintiff's statistician did not consider each terminated employee's disciplinary history, defense did not establish that this missing factor would have mattered), Churchill v. IBM, Inc., 759 F. Supp. 1089, 1097–99, 55 FEP 1004 (D.N.J. 1991) (employer unsuccessfully argued that certain variables, such as time in job and prior salary history, should have been included in plaintiff's multiple regression analysis) *and* Segar v. Civiletti, 508 F. Supp. 690, 696 n.2, 25 FEP 1452 (D.D.C. 1981) (plaintiff cannot be expected to include all possible variables in regression analysis; only those variables that are "both objective in nature and quantifiable" need be included), *vacated in part on other grounds sub nom.* Segar v. Smith, 738 F.2d 1249, 35 FEP 31 (D.C. Cir. 1984).

[125] A variable should be excluded from a multiple regression analysis if (1) the variable, although perhaps related to productivity or worth, may reflect a qualification that had been denied to a protected group by the employer's discrimination; (2) the variable may reflect factors unrelated to productivity or worth and therefore might conceal discrimination; or (3) the data reflecting the variable may be unreliable. Michael O. Finkelstein, *The Judicial Reception of Multiple Regression Studies in Race and Sex Discrimination Cases*, 80 COLUM. L. REV. 737, 738–39 (1980); *see also Hemmings*, 285 F.3d at 1183 (plaintiff's expert "analyzed the progression of wages of women and men over time as a method of controlling for factors other than gender—such as experience—that might explain the initial wage differential"); *Segar*, 738 F.2d at 1276 (plaintiff's failure to include "specialized experience" as variable in regression analysis proper because "[s]uch subjective criteria may well serve as a veil of seeming legitimacy behind which illegal discrimination is operating"); James v. Stockham Valves & Fittings Co., 559 F.2d 310, 332, 15 FEP 827 (5th Cir. 1977) (rejecting "skill level" and "merit rating" variables because they were defined in such a way as to incorporate discrimination); Greenspan v. Automobile Club, 495 F. Supp. 1021, 1062, 1064, 22 FEP 184 (E.D. Mich. 1980) (plaintiff correctly excluded company-related variables—salary, job assignments, promotions, and disciplinary incidents, for example—on ground that these factors were tainted by company's own discriminatory practices). *But cf.* Ottaviani v. State Univ., 875 F.2d 365, 374–75, 51 FEP 330 (2d Cir. 1989) (rejecting plaintiff's argument that rank should not be used as independent variable; rank not tainted by sex discrimination); Coates v. Johnson & Johnson, 756 F.2d 524, 544, 37 FEP 467 (7th Cir. 1985) (plaintiff need not account for allegedly biased factor in establishing prima facie case; however, if defendant offers rebuttal statistics accounting for it, plaintiff must prove that factor is biased and therefore not valid).

include depend on the theory and facts of the particular case.[126] In a wage discrimination case, for example, a regression analysis that fails to account for the type of work performed may be disregarded.[127] However, most courts echo the Supreme Court in *Bazemore* that regression analyses need not include all measurable variables thought to have an effect on salary in order to be admissible; the failure to include such factors instead goes to the weight to be accorded the analysis.[128]

In cases involving employment decisions concerning supervisory, managerial, or professional positions, regression analyses may present an additional problem making them susceptible to challenge: many legitimate factors that influence wages or other employment decisions at those levels (e.g., skill, performance, quality of education, interest, and quality of experience) are subjective and difficult to quantify.[129]

The number of factors included in a multiple regression analysis (in addition to the alleged illegitimate factor, e.g., race or sex) has

---

[126]Factors used in multiple regression analyses—if themselves untainted by prior discrimination—include experience (years with the employer in question or in particular categories of jobs, years with other employers, quality of experience, and the relevance of such experience to the jobs in question), education (amount, areas of concentration, quality, and relevance to the job in question), employment level or rank, skills, performance ratings, absenteeism, prior salary, interest, and gaps or breaks in employment.

[127]Coward v. ADT Sys., Inc., 140 F.3d 271, 274, 76 FEP 899 (D.C. Cir. 1998). *But see* Maitland v. University of Minn., 155 F.3d 1013, 1016, 77 FEP 1661 (8th Cir. 1998) ("if a regression analysis omits variables, it is for the finder of fact to consider the variables that have been left out of an analysis, and the reasons given for the omissions, and then to determine the weight to accord the study's results—in this case, whether those results show a manifest or conspicuous imbalance in salaries"); Stender v. Lucky Stores, Inc., 803 F. Supp. 259, 299, 62 FEP 11 (N.D. Cal. 1992) (admitting into evidence expert human capital analysis even though regression analysis did not account for type of work performed).

[128]McMillan v. Massachusetts Soc'y for the Prevention of Cruelty to Animals, 140 F.3d 288, 303, 77 FEP 589, 597 (1st Cir. 1998). *But see* Bickerstaff v. Vassar Coll., 196 F.3d 435, 449–50, 81 FEP 624, 633 (2d Cir. 1999) (regression analysis inadmissible because it failed to account for merit score and seniority, two factors that employer claimed it used in determining merit raises).

[129]*See* Penk v. Oregon State Bd. of Higher Educ., 816 F.2d 458, 464, 48 FEP 1878 (9th Cir. 1987) (defendant entitled to challenge ability of mathematical regressions to approximate actual determinative factors in employment decision-making process); Presseisen v. Swarthmore Coll., 442 F. Supp. 593, 616, 15 FEP 1466 (E.D. Pa. 1977) (factors such as quality of teaching and scholarship very difficult to quantify), *aff'd mem.*, 582 F.2d 1275 (3d Cir. 1978).

ranged from just a few (e.g., years of experience and education)[130] to more than 100.[131]

F. Other Kinds of Statistical Comparisons

In analyzing statistics, there may be more than one acceptable methodology.[132] "Cohort analyses"[133] have been used in promotion and pay cases,[134] but these have been found by some courts to be less probative than other forms of analysis.[135]

Other kinds of statistical evidence sometimes considered include the race/sex/ethnic composition of the defendant's workforce

---

[130]*E.g.*, Bazemore v. Friday, 478 U.S. 385, 398–99, 41 FEP 92 (1986) (in one study, plaintiffs used only race, education, tenure, and job title as variables); Hemmings v. Tidyman's Inc., 285 F.3d 1174, 1183, 88 FEP 945 (9th Cir. 2002) (expert's statistical analysis included gender, salary, position, and time).

[131]*E.g.*, Greenspan v. Automobile Club, 495 F. Supp. 1021, 1062, 1064, 22 FEP 184 (E.D. Mich. 1980) (approximately 128 variables used); *cf.* Vuyanich v. Republic Nat'l Bank, 505 F. Supp. 224, 300, 24 FEP 128 (N.D. Tex. 1980) (over 20 factors), *vacated and remanded on other grounds*, 723 F.2d 1195, 33 FEP 1521 (5th Cir. 1984).

[132]Malave v. Potter, 320 F.3d 321, 326–27, 91 FEP 101 (2d Cir. 2003) (rejecting district court's ruling that plaintiff failed to establish prima facie case of disparate impact simply because plaintiff's statistical analysis "failed to conform to the preferred methodology described in *Wards Cove*, given the Supreme Court's express endorsement in that decision of alternative methodologies if the preferred statistics are 'difficult' or 'impossible' to obtain").

[133]A cohort analysis is a statistical methodology under which a group of employees who start together at the same level—"cohorts"—are surveyed over the course of a study period. The employees' comparative advancements in salary and promotions during that period then are evaluated. *See* Segar v. Smith, 738 F.2d 1249, 1262–63, 35 FEP 31 (D.C. Cir. 1984).

[134]*E.g.*, Berger v. Iron Workers Local 201, 170 F.3d 1111, 1122, 79 FEP 1018 (D.C. Cir. 1999) (rejecting union's assertion that the special master assigned to case failed to account for all union members as appropriate cohort group); O'Brien v. Sky Chefs, Inc., 670 F.2d 864, 866–67, 28 FEP 661, *amended*, 28 FEP 1690 (9th Cir. 1982) (finding persuasive cohort group study that revealed disparity between males and females in promotion); Valentino v. United States Postal Serv., 511 F. Supp. 917, 940–41, 25 FEP 24 (D.D.C. 1981) (cohort analysis compared advancement rates of men to those of women starting at same time, at same level, and with same general length of government service; analysis showed statistically indistinguishable relative advancement rates for similarly situated men and women, thereby refuting any inference of discrimination in promotion), *aff'd*, 674 F.2d 56 (D.C. Cir. 1982).

[135]*See, e.g.*, Pollard v. E.I. du Pont de Nemours, 338 F. Supp. 2d 863, 880 (W.D. Tenn. 2003) (rejecting cohort analysis as "containing significant flaws when applied in this case"); Trout v. Lehman, 702 F.2d 1094, 1105, 31 FEP 286 (D.C. Cir. 1983) (rejecting employer's cohort analysis), *vacated on other grounds*, 465 U.S. 1056, 34 FEP 76 (1984); Segar v. Civiletti, 508 F. Supp. 690, 698, 25 FEP 1452 (D.D.C. 1981) ("Cohort analysis is an untried method of statistical study, unsupported in any published statistical work or judicial decision.").

compared with the composition of workforces of similar employers in the same or similar geographic areas,[136] and the increase or
decrease in the race/sex/ethnic composition of the employer's
workforce over time.[137] In *Wards Cove Packing Co. v. Atonio*,[138]
however, the Supreme Court held that a mere statistical discrepancy between minority representation in upper- and lower-level jobs
in an organization will not alone make out a prima facie case of
adverse impact.[139] The key deficiency in the analysis, the Court
explained, was the failure to compare the composition of the upper-level jobs with the pool of qualified applicants.[140]

In some circumstances, it may be appropriate for a party to
compare an employer's workforce to similar workforces that extend beyond the defendant employer's geographic locale. In *Vitug
v. Multistate Tax Commission*,[141] for example, the Seventh Circuit
refused to find that an employer's reliance on subjective criteria
and word-of-mouth hiring had an adverse impact on minority applicants where the employer offered expert testimony that the percentage of minority auditors employed by the defendant exceeded
the "total percentage of minorities among accountants and auditors in the national workforce."[142]

The courts have also allowed statistical evidence to be presented where the expert's testimony included a "step analysis"[143]
approach. The plaintiff's expert "compared the number of women
to the number of men within each rank of Tidyman's management
hierarchy."[144] For the levels where there was representation of men
and women, which made comparison possible, the plaintiff's expert

---

[136]*E.g.*, Bridgeport Guardians, Inc. v. Members of Bridgeport Civil Serv. Comm'n,
482 F.2d 1333, 1335–36, 5 FEP 1344 (2d Cir. 1973) (percentage of African-American
and Hispanic policemen in Bridgeport, Connecticut, was compared to that found in
New Haven and Hartford, Connecticut); Chance v. Board of Exam'rs, 458 F.2d 1167,
1172, 4 FEP 596 (2d Cir. 1972) (comparison of African-American school principals in New York versus other major U.S. cities).

[137]*E.g.*, *Valentino*, 511 F. Supp. at 954 (evidence that number of women employed in higher positions increased whereas number of male employees in these
positions decreased rebuts any inference of discrimination in promotion).

[138]490 U.S. 642, 49 FEP 1519 (1989); *see also* Section III.D.4 *infra*.

[139]490 U.S. at 650.

[140]*Wards Cove*, 490 U.S. at 650–51.

[141]88 F.3d 506, 71 FEP 1445 (7th Cir. 1996).

[142]*Id.* at 514; *see also* Section IV *infra*.

[143]Hemmings v. Tidyman's Inc., 285 F.3d 1174, 1183, 88 FEP 945 (9th Cir. 2002)
(expert's statistical analysis included gender, salary, position, and time).

[144]*Id.*

found gender disparities in wages for many of the rankings. For example, at level four of the hierarchy, which included store manager, office manager, system analyst, and controller, the statistical evidence revealed that the average salary for women was $10,400 less than men.[145]

Finally, courts may apply *Daubert*[146] and *Kumho Tire*[147] to novel statistical approaches before an expert is allowed to testify before a jury.[148]

G. The Bottom-Line Concept and the Inexorable Zero

Application of a selection rate comparison to the overall employment process, rather than to a component part, is known as the "bottom-line" concept.[149] Plaintiffs and defendants alike have offered bottom-line statistics. In earlier years, plaintiffs used a bottom-line analysis, the "bottom-line *offense*," by alleging that an employment process is discriminatory where the process as a whole has a significant adverse impact on the plaintiff's protected group, even though no particular component part of the process is shown to have a significant adverse impact. Defendants used the bottom-line analysis, the "bottom-line *defense*," by asserting that an employment process that has one or more component parts with a proven adverse impact, nevertheless, is nondiscriminatory if the process as a whole has no statistically significant adverse impact.[150]

The Supreme Court in *Wards Cove* rejected the bottom-line offense.[151] The Court held that plaintiffs who allege adverse impact

---

[145]*Id.*

[146]Daubert v. Merrell Dow Pharms., 509 U.S. 579 (1993).

[147]Kumho Tire Co. v. Carmichael, 526 U.S. 137 (1999).

[148]*See* Adams v. Ameritech Servs., 231 F.3d 414, 425–28 (7th Cir. 2000) (evaluating whether plaintiff's statistical methodology was sound under *Daubert* and *Kumho Tire*); Sheehan v. Daily Racing Form, Inc., 104 F.3d 940, 942, 72 FEP 1390 (7th Cir. 1997) (in discriminatory discharge case, plaintiff's statistical analysis that failed to analyze all employees impacted by employer's layoff decisions and failed to correct for potential explanation of variables other than age "was not even admissible under the standard of *Daubert*"); Wyche v. Marine Midland Bank, 73 FEP 1600, 1601 (S.D.N.Y. 1997) (court rejected "Proportional Hazards Model" because it would not assist trier of fact and was not generally accepted within scientific community).

[149]United States v. County of Fairfax, 25 FEP 662, 668 (E.D. Va. 1981).

[150]The bottom-line concept is discussed more extensively in Chapter 3 (Adverse Impact).

[151]*Wards Cove*, 490 U.S. at 656–57.

discrimination must isolate the adverse effects of a particular employment practice, test, or criterion on their protected group. A demonstration that an employer's entire selection system has an adverse impact, the Court held, is insufficient.[152]

This particular holding of *Wards Cove* was codified in part and overruled in part by the Civil Rights Act of 1991, which allows an exception to the *Wards Cove* rule. Under the 1991 Act, the statistical attack must be on an identifiable component of the hiring process, except where the plaintiff "demonstrate[s] to the court that the elements of a respondent's decisionmaking process are not capable of separation for analysis."[153]

In disparate impact claims, courts have refused to base liability solely on bottom-line statistical imbalances in the employer's workforce. For example, in *EEOC v. Joe's Stone Crab, Inc.*,[154] the court held that the mere fact that a restaurant had hired no women, by itself, was insufficient to establish disparate impact liability.[155]

The bottom-line defense was endorsed, at least as a matter of prosecutorial discretion, in the EEOC's Uniform Guidelines on Employee Selection Procedures.[156] But the Supreme Court, in *Connecticut v. Teal*[157]—by a 5–4 margin—rejected the bottom-line defense in cases challenging criteria that act as a "pass-fail barrier" to further consideration in the selection process.[158] Since that decision, courts generally have refused to accept the bottom-line

---

[152]*Id.*

[153]Pub. L. No. 102-166, § 105(a), 1991 U.S.C.C.A.N. (105 Stat.) 1071, 1074 (codified at 42 U.S.C. § 2000e-2(k)(1)(A)(i), (B)(i) (2000)). *See generally* Chapter 3 (Adverse Impact). Nevertheless, some courts look to bottom-line statistics to buttress other evidence of discrimination. In *Waisome v. Port Authority*, 948 F.2d 1370, 1376, 57 FEP 567 (2d Cir. 1991), the plaintiff failed to show that a scored test had a cognizable adverse impact on African Americans where the African-American pass rate was greater than four-fifths that of whites. However, African-American passing scores were bunched at the bottom of the passing range. The overall African-American selection rate, based on a composite of written test and oral test scores, was 8%, compared to 14% for whites. Based on all the evidence, the court held that summary judgment should not have been granted to the defendant. *Id.* at 1379–80.

[154]220 F.3d 1263, 84 FEP 195 (11th Cir. 2000).

[155]*Id.* at 1276.

[156]29 C.F.R. § 1607.4C (2005). *See generally* Chapter 4 (Application of Adverse Impact to Employment Decisions), Section I.

[157]457 U.S. 440, 29 FEP 1 (1982).

[158]*Id.* at 443–45.

defense in employment discrimination cases.[159] In one case, however, bottom-line justification was accepted where the number of successful minorities far exceeded the expected number based on the qualified labor market.[160] In cases where a particular criterion is *not* a pass/fail barrier, however, the bottom line still may be determinative.[161]

The "inexorable zero" is another method used to establish discrimination based on data. Courts recognize that evidence of the "inexorable zero"[162]—a failure to hire any members of a protected class—by itself may support an inference of intentional discrimination under the disparate treatment theory.[163] The persuasiveness

---

[159]Woodman v. Haemonetics Corp., 51 F.3d 1087, 1093 n.3, 67 FEP 838 (1st Cir. 1995) (companywide statistics showing that workforce reduction process as whole did not have disproportionate impact on older employees did not refute claim of disparate treatment of individual employee); Anderson v. Douglas & Lomason Co., 26 F.3d 1277, 1291, 65 FEP 417, 69 FEP 131 (5th Cir. 1994) (comparison of percentage of African-American supervisors at company to African-American supervisors countywide found insufficient as bottom-line defense); United States v. Delaware, 91 FEP 1480 (D. Del. 2003) (finding aggregate data of pass/fail ratios between African Americans and whites as significantly compelling to reject state's bottom-line defense).

[160]Bailey v. DiMario, 925 F. Supp. 801, 813, 69 FEP 233, 243 (D.D.C. 1995) (where hiring of African Americans into disputed positions was 1½ to 5 times greater than percentage in qualified labor market, "[s]uch evidence demonstrates the absence of discrimination").

[161]See, e.g., Arnold v. United States Postal Serv., 863 F.2d 994, 998–99, 48 FEP 930 (D.C. Cir. 1988) (rule directing transfer of most senior inspectors not pass/fail barrier because inspectors also may volunteer to transfer); Brunet v. City of Columbus, 642 F. Supp. 1214, 1226, 42 FEP 1846 (S.D. Ohio 1986) (refusing to apply *Teal* rationale to multicomponent selection process for fire fighters, reasoning that *Teal* is limited by its terms to pass/fail barriers), *appeal dismissed*, 826 F.2d 1062 (6th Cir. 1987); *cf.* Sengupta v. Morrison-Knudsen Co., 804 F.2d 1072, 1076–77, 42 FEP 535 (9th Cir. 1986) (*Teal* inapplicable to case where layoff procedure consisted of one step); Costa v. Markey, 706 F.2d 1, 5, 30 FEP 593 (1st Cir. 1982) (distinguishing *Teal*; height requirement could have no adverse impact on women where only women were in competition for job).

[162]Teamsters v. United States, 431 U.S. 324, 342 n.23, 14 FEP 1514 (1977).

[163]See NAACP v. East Haven, 70 F.3d 219, 225, 69 FEP 500 (2d Cir. 1995) (reversing trial court for, inter alia, failing to consider "the 'inexorable zero'—evidence that an employer in an area with a sizeable black population has never hired a single black employee—which, by itself, supports an inference of discrimination") (citations omitted); EEOC v. O & G Spring & Wire Forms Specialty Co., 38 F.3d 872, 878, 65 FEP 1823 (7th Cir. 1994) (affirming district court's verdict in favor of EEOC based on defendant company's "inability to rebut the inference of discrimination [that] comes not from a measure of statistics but from the 'inexorable zero' ") (additional internal quotation marks and citation omitted); Loyd v. Phillips Bros., Inc., 25 F.3d 518, 524 n.4, 64 FEP 1513 (7th Cir. 1994) (reversing judgment for defendant and

of "the inexorable zero," however, depends on the circumstances of the case.[164]

IV. SOURCES OF STATISTICS

A. Statistical Data Sources

Understanding the sources of statistical data is critical to comprehending its significance to the facts of a particular case. Courts have followed the Supreme Court's cautionary words in *Teamsters v. United States*[165] that the usefulness of statistics depends on "the surrounding facts and circumstances."[166] As the Seventh Circuit has observed, "statistics, like any evidence, are not irrefutable; strong statistics may prove a case on their own, while shaky statistics may be insufficient unless accompanied by additional evidence."[167]

With respect to selection rate statistics, the basic choice is whether to base the comparison on "actual" or "potential" applicant flow data.[168] Both actual and potential applicant flow selection rate comparisons can be applied to any component of the employment process.[169] In a hiring case, there are many choices to be made

---

ordering that judgment be entered for plaintiff based, in part, on "inexorable zero" in hiring women for position); Victory v. Hewlett-Packard Co., 34 F. Supp. 2d 809, 823, 78 FEP 1718 (E.D.N.Y. 1999) (noting "evidence of the absence of a single minority employee being hired, labeled the 'inexorable zero,' would in and of itself support an inference of discrimination") (citations omitted).

[164]Frazier v. Ford Motor Co., 176 F. Supp. 2d 719, 724, 87 FEP 370 (W.D. Ky. 2001) (reasoning that use of "inexorable zero" is less persuasive in cases where courts consider objective quantitative jobs of "blue collar" positions than in cases where courts consider subjective job evaluations for professional positions).

[165]431 U.S. 324, 14 FEP 1514 (1977).

[166]*Id.* at 340; *see, e.g.*, Carter v. Ball, 33 F.3d 450, 456, 65 FEP 1414 (4th Cir. 1994) (citing Teamsters v. United States, 431 U.S. 324, 340, 14 FEP 1514 (1977)).

[167]*O & G Spring & Wire*, 38 F.3d at 876; *see also* Fisher v. Vassar Coll., 70 F.3d 1420, 1443, 1447, 70 FEP 1155 (2d Cir. 1995) (plaintiff's statistics were "merely organized anecdotes" and "[p]laintiff's statistical case is built on gerrymandered data and a series of statistical fallacies"), *aff'd on reh'g en banc*, 114 F.3d 1332, 74 FEP 109 (2d Cir. 1997).

[168]Potential applicant flow data are analytically identical to qualified workforce data, which are discussed *infra*.

[169]As noted in Section III.G *supra*, plaintiffs in most adverse impact cases are required to show the adverse impact of a particular selection device, as opposed to adverse impact in the overall selection process.

about which data to use, on both sides of the population/workforce comparison.

For the population ("left") side of the population/workforce comparison, the sources of data that might be proposed include (1) general population data, (2) general labor force data (civilian, nonfarm, or total), (3) qualified labor market data, (4) qualified and interested labor market data, (5) actual applicant flow data (sometimes used as a proxy for qualified and interested labor market data), (6) qualified actual applicant flow data, (7) the employer's own workforce composition, and (8) the employer's own qualified and interested workforce composition.

There are many subsidiary questions related to the sources of data used. For example, where qualified labor market, qualified applicant flow, or qualified workforce data are used, a determination must be made about which qualifications will be considered and how they will be measured. Where the data are limited to those "interested" in employment or promotion, a decision must be made about how that interest will be determined.[170]

For the workforce ("right") side of the population/workforce equation, the basic choice is whether to use a "time frame" or "static" analysis.[171] Another issue, once "availability" is defined, is whether availability should be compared to the actual hire or promotion rate or to the "offer" rate.[172]

B. Applicant Flow Data

In *Teamsters v. United States*,[173] the Supreme Court recognized the superiority, as a general rule, of actual applicant flow

---

[170]*See, e.g.*, Stender v. Lucky Stores, Inc., 803 F. Supp. 259, 304–09, 327–28 (N.D. Cal. 1992) (finding defendant's expert's job interest survey "unpersuasive").

[171]The time frame analysis is discussed in Section VI *infra*. In brief, the focus in a time frame analysis is on employment decisions made during the particular period relevant to the litigation and not on the composition of the workforce, which may have been determined largely by employment decisions made over a much longer period of time.

[172]The Fifth Circuit has stated: "The most statistically pure representation of discrimination would be the percentage of black versus white offers of promotion." Swint v. Pullman-Standard, 539 F.2d 77, 104, 13 FEP 604 (5th Cir. 1976); *see* Hill v. Seaboard Coast Line R.R., 885 F.2d 804, 812 n.15, 50 FEP 1751 (11th Cir. 1989) (fact that one African American was offered promotion, but did not accept it, should be considered in determining whether promotion system had adverse impact on African Americans).

[173]431 U.S. 324, 342 n.23, 14 FEP 1514 (1977); *accord* Moore v. Hughes Helicopters, Inc., 708 F.2d 475, 482, 32 FEP 97, 102 (9th Cir. 1983) ("Disparate impact

data,[174] although it also approved the use of general population (or potential applicant flow) data where the jobs at issue required no special skills and thus the general population approximated the qualified applicant pool.[175] In *Dothard v. Rawlinson*,[176] however, the Supreme Court noted that applicant flow data may be an improper measure when otherwise qualified persons are "discouraged from applying because of a self-recognized inability to meet the very standards being challenged as discriminatory."[177]

Defendants have successfully relied on actual applicant flow data to rebut prima facie cases established through the use of population/workforce comparisons or potential applicant flow selection rate comparisons.[178] Applicant flow statistics also have been relied on in fashioning remedies for proven discrimination (e.g.,

---

should always be measured against the actual pool of applicants or eligible employees unless there is a characteristic of the challenged selection device that makes use of the actual pool of applicants or eligible employees inappropriate."); Hester v. Southern Ry., 497 F.2d 1374, 1379, 8 FEP 646 (5th Cir. 1974) ("most direct route to proof of racial discrimination in hiring is proof of disparity between the percentage of blacks among those applying for a particular position and the percentage of blacks among those hired for the position"). *See generally* Elaine W. Shoben, *Differential Pass-Fail Rates in Employment Testing: Statistical Proof Under Title VII*, 91 HARV. L. REV. 793 (1978).

[174]Since *Teamsters*, courts have continued to recognize this general rule of preference for actual applicant flow data. *See, e.g.*, Hazelwood Sch. Dist. v. United States, 433 U.S. 299, 308 n.13, 15 FEP 1 (1977) (applicant flow data "very relevant"); Malave v. Potter, 320 F.3d 321, 326, 91 FEP 101 (2d Cir. 2003) ("in the context of promotions, we have held that the appropriate comparison is customarily between the composition of candidates seeking to be promoted and the composition of those actually promoted"); Bullington v. United Air Lines, Inc., 186 F.3d 1301, 1313, 80 FEP 926 (10th Cir. 1999) (applicant flow data "is generally considered probative because it reflects how the employer's hiring procedure actually operated"); Courtney v. Biosound, Inc., 42 F.3d 414, 420, 66 FEP 971 (7th Cir. 1994) (statistics insufficient to establish pretext where age plaintiff produced no evidence of applicant pool or any related evidence that substantial number of older workers actually applied for employment with defendant); Anderson v. Douglas & Lomason Co., 26 F.3d 1277, 1286–87, 69 FEP 131 (5th Cir. 1994) (appropriate labor market to use in statistical analysis of employer's hiring practices was composed of those persons who actually sought employment with company). *But see* Forehand v. Florida State Hosp., 89 F.3d 1562, 1574, 71 FEP 905 (11th Cir. 1996) (declining to adopt "per se rule that applicant flow data are the best measure of the pool from which applicants are selected").

[175]*See* Section IV.C.1 *infra*.

[176]433 U.S. 321, 15 FEP 10 (1977).

[177]*Id.* at 330 ("the application process might itself not adequately reflect the actual potential applicant pool").

[178]*E.g.*, Lee v. Washington County Bd. of Educ., 625 F.2d 1235, 1238, 23 FEP 1472 (5th Cir. 1980) (rebutting plaintiffs' prima facie case of discrimination in hiring for positions in athletic coaching and central office staffs by evidence of lack

to determine the number of positions discriminatorily denied to the protected group).[179]

Although courts often regard actual applicant flow data as the best source for selection rate and other comparisons,[180] there are a number of factors that may influence the quality, and therefore the value, of such data. Where actual applicant flow data are incomplete or flawed, courts have declined to apply the resulting statistical analysis.[181] Applicant flow data may be rejected where the employer did not keep accurate or complete personnel records;[182]

---

of African-American applicants for these positions); Falcon v. General Tel. Co., 611 F. Supp. 707, 720–22, 39 FEP 1116 (N.D. Tex. 1985) (defendant successfully rebutted plaintiff's charge of race discrimination with applicant flow data showing that it hired greater percentage of Mexican American applicants than it did white applicants), aff'd, 815 F.2d 317, 43 FEP 1040 (5th Cir. 1987).

[179]E.g., Berkman v. City of N.Y., 705 F.2d 584, 594–95, 31 FEP 767 (2d Cir. 1983) (relying on applicant flow data to determine number of fire fighter positions that would be offered to qualified women applicants). See generally Chapters 32 (Class Actions) and 40 (Monetary Relief).

[180]See, e.g., Bullington v. United Air Lines, Inc., 186 F.3d 1301, 1313, 80 FEP 926 (10th Cir. 1999) (applicant flow data "is generally considered probative because it reflects how the employer's hiring procedure actually operated"); Courtney v. Biosound, Inc., 42 F.3d 414, 420, 66 FEP 971 (7th Cir. 1994) (statistics insufficient to establish pretext where age plaintiff produced no evidence of applicant pool or any related evidence that substantial number of older workers actually applied for employment with defendant); Anderson v. Douglas & Lomason Co., 26 F.3d 1277, 1286–87, 65 FEP 417, 69 FEP 131 (5th Cir. 1994) (appropriate labor pool to use in statistical analysis of employer's hiring practices composed of those persons who actually sought employment with company).

[181]See, e.g., Johnson v. Penske Truck Leasing Co., 949 F. Supp. 1153, 1177 (D.N.J. 1996) (plaintiff failed to present statistical evidence showing number of promotions available, number of qualified female applicants, or number of qualified female applicants denied promotion) (quoting Ezold v. Wolf, Block, Schorr & Solis-Cohen, 983 F.2d 509, 60 FEP 849 (3d Cir. 1992)); Ashton v. City of Memphis, 49 F. Supp. 2d 1051, 1072 (W.D. Tenn. 1999) (rejecting applicant flow analysis that omitted number of classes of applicants for police jobs in Title VII reverse discrimination suit). But see EEOC v. Regency Windsor Mgmt. Co., 862 F. Supp. 189, 195, 65 FEP 1777 (W.D. Mich. 1994) (court accepted plaintiff's statistics as supporting claim of age discrimination even though evidence did not include ages of comparators hired and fired and did not indicate composition of pool of qualified applicants for open positions during relevant periods).

[182]Malave v. Potter, 320 F.3d 321, 326–27, 91 FEP 101 (2d Cir. 2003) (applicant flow data not required where data not available); EEOC v. Turtle Creek Mansion Corp., 70 FEP 899 (N.D. Tex. 1995) (applicant flow data rejected where employer did not maintain applicant flow log, and records did not indicate how long particular job was open, date job offer was made, who interviewed applicant, or for what position applicant applied), aff'd, 82 F.3d 414 (5th Cir. 1996). But see Anderson, 26 F.3d at 1287 n.13 (affirming use of employer's applicant flow data even though employer failed to preserve employment applications for 1 year, contrary to Uniform

where the sample size is too small to provide meaningful statistical analysis;[183] where the pool, as defined, omits applicants who were offered but declined the positions at issue;[184] or where the

---

Guidelines on Employee Selection Procedures). In some cases, it may be possible to extrapolate applicant flow data for earlier years based on the applicant flow data for the available years. *See, e.g.*, United States v. Fairfax County, 629 F.2d 932, 940, 23 FEP 485 (4th Cir. 1980) (extrapolated applicant flow data for earlier years was reliable). *But see* EEOC v. American Nat'l Bank, 652 F.2d 1176, 1195–97, 26 FEP 472 (4th Cir. 1981) ("Applicant flow data limited to one out of seven relevant years cannot . . . rebut a prima facie case based upon gross disparities revealed in static work force statistics over the period."). Frequently, there is incomplete information on the job or jobs for which applicants applied and on the race or possibly the sex of prior applicants, particularly where application is made by mail. *E.g.*, Phillips v. Joint Legislative Comm., 637 F.2d 1014, 1025, 25 FEP 120 (5th Cir. 1981) (actual applicant flow data unavailable because employer did not identify its applicants by race); Gay v. Waiters & Dairy Lunchmen's Local 30, 489 F. Supp. 282, 312, 22 FEP 281 (N.D. Cal. 1980) (rejecting applicant flow data because race coding was speculative and unreliable, records were kept intermittently and were incomplete, oral applications were not included, and applications not specified for job in question were included), *aff'd*, 694 F.2d 531, 29 FEP 1027 (9th Cir. 1982); *cf.* Hazelwood Sch. Dist. v. United States, 433 U.S. 299, 303 n.5, 15 FEP 1 (1977) ("parties disagree whether it is possible to determine from the present record exactly how many of the job applicants in each of the school years were [African Americans]"). One court facing this situation used estimation techniques to fill in gaps in available data. *See* Guardians Ass'n v. Civil Service Comm'n, 633 F.2d 232, 239–41 & n.14, 23 FEP 677 (2d Cir. 1980), *aff'd*, 463 U.S. 582, 32 FEP 250 (1983) (approving use of estimated applicant flow data for selection rate comparison where estimate was based on actual records of race for approximately 30% of applicants, results from questionnaires inquiring into race mailed to applicants, compilation of surnames by U.S. Bureau of Census, census tract data evidencing racial concentration with which applicants' addresses were matched, and telephone sample of applicants whose race remained unknown; distinguishing *New York City Transit Auth. v. Beazer*, 440 U.S. 568, 19 FEP 149 (1979), because record in *Beazer* lacked kind of data from which to derive reliable estimates of composition of applicant pool.).

[183]*See* Section VII.C *infra*; *see also* EEOC v. Joint Apprenticeship Comm., 186 F.3d 110, 118, 80 FEP 1518 (2d Cir. 1998) (district court inappropriately sanctioned application of four-fifths rule to fail ratio where sample would be too small to produce reliable results); Ward v. Gulfstream Aerospace Corp., 894 F. Supp. 1573, 1580 (S.D. Ga. 1995) (sample size of 11 candidates for departmental RIF not statistically compelling and of little relevance); Maidenbaum v. Bally's Park Place, Inc., 870 F. Supp. 1254, 1259, 68 FEP 1245 (D.N.J. 1994) (sample size of 16 discharged employees insufficient to evidence adverse impact), *aff'd*, 67 F.3d 291, 69 FEP 320 (3d Cir. 1995); Campbell v. Fasco Indus., 861 F. Supp. 1385, 1395, 72 FEP 33 (N.D. Ill. 1994) (group of nine too small), *aff'd*, 67 F.3d 301, 72 FEP 96 (7th Cir. 1995). *But see* Pietras v. Board of Fire Comm'rs, 180 F.3d 468, 474, 80 FEP 307 (2d Cir. 1999) (rejecting challenge to small sample size of seven female candidates for firefighting job where statistics were bolstered by other evidence of discrimination).

[184]*Anderson*, 26 F.3d at 1293 ("the statistics submitted by the plaintiffs are fatally flawed because they overlook the black employees who turned down promotions later offered to white employees"). *But cf.* Mangold v. California Pub. Utils.

data are distorted because of the defendant's reputation for discrimination,[185] recruiting criteria,[186] or recruiting practices[187] produces disproportionately few minority applicants. The same phenomenon also can occur in reverse, where exceptionally substantial affirmative action efforts produce disproportionately many minority applicants.[188] In effect, inadequate minority recruiting and chilling, on the one hand, and unusually extensive minority recruiting or affirmative action on the other, are opposite sides of the same coin:

Comm'n, 67 F.3d 1470, 1476, 69 FEP 48 (9th Cir. 1995) (plaintiff's statistics were admissible even though they did not factor out "repeaters" who failed but continued to take exam).

[185]*E.g.*, EEOC v. Rath Packing Co., 787 F.2d 318, 337, 40 FEP 580 (8th Cir. 1986) (employer's applicant flow data rejected where employer was one of few large employers in small community, and company's discriminatory employment record was known to community); EEOC v. Steamship Clerks Local 1066, 48 F.3d 594, 606, 67 FEP 629 (1st Cir. 1995) (court below "could have inferred causation, despite the dearth of actual applicants," in part because union policy discouraged potential minority candidates from applying); Lea v. Cone Mills Corp., 301 F. Supp. 97, 102, 2 FEP 12 (M.D.N.C. 1969) (comparison of hires to relevant applicant pool may be entirely inappropriate when employer's discriminatory practices are so well known throughout community that protected groups may be reluctant to apply), *aff'd in relevant part*, 438 F.2d 86, 3 FEP 137 (4th Cir. 1971); EEOC v. Rodriguez, 66 FEP 1649 (E.D. Cal. 1994) (court rejected defendant employer's argument that small number of African Americans applying for positions as auto salesmen was appropriate labor pool based on evidence that potential applicants understood they would not be hired, so did not apply).

[186]*See* Dothard v. Rawlinson, 433 U.S. 321, 330, 15 FEP 10 (1977) ("application process might itself not adequately reflect the actual potential applicant pool, since otherwise qualified people might be discouraged from applying because of a self-recognized inability to meet the very standards challenged as being discriminatory"); Reynolds v. Sheet Metal Workers Local 102, 498 F. Supp. 952, 964 n.12, 24 FEP 648 (D.D.C. 1980) (high school diploma requirement and arrest record inquiries may have dissuaded or "chilled" potential applicants), *aff'd*, 702 F.2d 221, 25 FEP 837 (D.C. Cir. 1981).

[187]*E.g.*, Van v. Plant & Field Serv. Corp., 672 F. Supp. 1306, 1317 (C.D. Cal. 1987) (reliance on word-of-mouth or walk-in applicants, when only applicants likely to walk in are members of majority group, "amounts to unlawful discrimination"), *aff'd mem.*, 872 F.2d 432 (9th Cir. 1989); EEOC v. Andrew Corp., 49 FEP 804, 811 (N.D. Ill. 1989) (rejecting applicant flow data as proper measure of minority availability because of employer's significant word-of-mouth recruitment), *modified*, 1989 U.S. Dist. LEXIS 16708 (N.D. Ill. Sept. 12, 1989); *see also* Kilgo v. Bowman Transp., 570 F. Supp. 1509, 1517, 31 FEP 1451 (N.D. Ga. 1983) (where applicant flow data were distorted by recruiting and hiring practices, general labor force statistics were used regarding truck driver position). *See generally* Chapter 15 (Hiring).

[188]Specifically, actual applicant flow data may not be the appropriate measure of availability where affirmative action efforts have generated a higher level of protected group applicants than would have been the case absent such affirmative

both may justify the conclusion that the applicant flow data are distorted and should be disregarded.

Employers almost always will find it helpful to separate actual applicant flow data by jobs for which applicants are applying[189] and refine the data to include only "qualified" applicants.[190]

---

action. *See, e.g.*, Hammon v. Barry, 826 F.2d 73, 78 n.7, 44 FEP 869 (D.C. Cir. 1987) (recent applicant flow may be skewed by recent recruiting campaigns targeted at minority applicants); Williams v. City of New Orleans, 729 F.2d 1554, 1562, 34 FEP 1009 (5th Cir. 1984) (en banc) (general population statistics were used where applicant flow was distorted by heavy recruiting of African-American applicants), *appeal dismissed*, 763 F.2d 667 (5th Cir. 1985); Carroll v. Sears, Roebuck & Co., 514 F. Supp. 788, 796, 30 FEP 1446 (W.D. La. 1981) (employer's applicant flow was affected by proximity of its personnel office to state employment office and by company's substantial recruitment efforts), *rev'd in part on other grounds*, 708 F.2d 183, 32 FEP 286 (5th Cir. 1983).

[189]EEOC v. Sears, Roebuck & Co., 839 F.2d 302, 322–24, 45 FEP 1257 (7th Cir. 1988) (plaintiff's pool of applicants for sales positions was inflated, and thus flawed, because it neither distinguished between commission and noncommission sales jobs nor accounted for differences in interest or qualifications among applicants); Vuyanich v. Republic Nat'l Bank of Dallas, 505 F. Supp. 224, 304–05, 24 FEP 128 (N.D. Tex. 1980) (plaintiff's comparison between proportions of minorities hired and applicants rejected in part because data failed to distinguish between those seeking exempt and nonexempt jobs and failed to account for requisite skill levels), *vacated in part on other grounds*, 723 F.2d 1195, 33 FEP 1521 (5th Cir. 1984).

[190]*E.g.*, Dorsey v. Pittsburgh Assocs., 90 Fed. Appx. 636 (3d Cir. 2004) (use of statistics to prove pretext must focus on appropriate labor pool and take into account legitimate, objective qualifications for job being analyzed; such statistics cannot be based on applicant pool including those lacking qualifications for relevant positions); Hill v. Mississippi State Employment Serv., 918 F.2d 1233, 1240, 54 FEP 997 (5th Cir. 1990) (statistics defective because they did not consider experience of some applicants); Croker v. Boeing Co., 437 F. Supp. 1138, 1184, 15 FEP 165 (E.D. Pa. 1977) (rejecting use of applicant flow data in part because of lack of evidence regarding qualifications of applicants), *aff'd*, 662 F.2d 975 (3d Cir. 1981) (en banc); Johnson v. Penske Truck Leasing Co., 949 F. Supp. 1153, 1177 (D.N.J. 1996) (plaintiff failed to present statistical evidence showing number of promotions available, number of qualified female applicants, or number of qualified female applicants denied position) (quoting Ezold v. Wolf, Block, Schorr & Solis-Cohen, 983 F.2d 509, 543, 60 FEP 849 (3d Cir. 1992)). *Compare* Bullington v. United Air Lines, Inc., 186 F.3d 1301, 1313, 80 FEP 926 (10th Cir. 1999) (plaintiff's statistical evidence raised genuine issue of material fact; analysis reliable because "each member of the applicant pool not only applied for the at-issue position, as is the usual case with applicant flow data, but actually interviewed for the at-issue position") *with* EEOC v. American Airlines, Inc., 48 F.3d 164, 172, 67 FEP 754 (5th Cir. 1995) (EEOC's statistics rejected where EEOC did not produce comparison of pilots hired to those qualified to be hired; statistics simply compared pilots hired to those who had applied and were disqualified by certain "obvious criteria"), Aiken v. Memphis, 37 F.3d 1155, 1165, 1167, 65 FEP 1757 (6th Cir. 1994) (on remand, district court required to consider

On the other hand, data can be overly refined; if all qualified applicants are not considered, applicant flow statistics may be rejected as underinclusive.[191]

A crucial question, then, is which applicants should be considered "qualified." Where it is the "qualifications" at issue that are said to cause adverse impact, several cases state that the qualifications should be disregarded.[192] In many cases, however, there are certain qualifications for a job that are not at issue, such as the ability to read and write, or the ability to type, for work that requires such skills or other special skills, education, or training.[193]

Applicant flow data can be further refined by excluding those individuals who voluntarily remove themselves from the application process, such as those who inquire about a job but never apply; who apply but fail to show up for an interview, test, or some other step of the process; or who fail some nondiscriminatory aspect of the total selection process.[194] Multiple applications from

---

whether racial makeup of qualified labor pool differed from general workforce) *and* Anderson v. Queen Carpet Corp., 68 FEP 83 (N.D. Ga. 1995) (court rejected plaintiff's statistics where, among other inadequacies, plaintiff did not provide court with pool of available and qualified applicants and any applicable requirements or limitations with regard to available positions). Analogous considerations arise in determining the qualified labor market in "potential applicant" and population/workforce comparisons. *See* Section IV.C.1 *infra*.

[191]*E.g.*, Butler v. Portland Gen. Elec. Co., 748 F. Supp. 783, 789–90, 54 FEP 357 (D. Or. 1990) (employee's statistical evidence unreliable because it did not include entire applicant pool), *aff'd sub nom.* Flynn v. Portland Gen. Elec. Co., 958 F.2d 377 (9th Cir. 1992).

[192]*See* Quigley v. Braniff Airways, Inc., 85 F.R.D. 74, 80, 23 FEP 1811 (N.D. Tex. 1979) (improper to consider "qualified" applicants to include only those selected for interviews when their selection was based on challenged qualifications); *cf.* Spurlock v. United Airlines, Inc., 475 F.2d 216, 218, 5 FEP 17 (10th Cir. 1972) (no requirement to use qualified labor market data where qualifications for job in question are what is at issue).

[193]The Supreme Court in *New York City Transit Authority v. Beazer*, 440 U.S. 568, 584–86, 19 FEP 149 (1979), noted that statistics should reflect persons "otherwise qualified" (possessing agreed-upon legitimate qualifications) for the job at issue. *See generally* Chapter 4 (Application of Adverse Impact to Employment Decisions), Section II.

[194]Vulcan Soc'y v. Civil Serv. Comm'n, 490 F.2d 387, 392–93, 6 FEP 1045 (2d Cir. 1973) (defendants had valid argument, in theory, that applicants who failed other, nonchallenged aspects of total selection process should be excluded from plaintiff's statistics, but here there was no showing that minorities failed those other criteria at greater rate than whites; therefore, excluding those applicants would have no effect on statistical result). In disparate treatment hiring and promotion cases, applying for

the same applicant also may cause actual applicant flow data to be unreliable.[195] Courts, however, treat with suspicion employers' arguments that minority applicants self-select out of the applicant pool for reasons not attributable to discrimination.[196]

C. Population/Labor Market Data

Where applicant flow data are unreliable, courts often look to "potential applicant flow" data. Potential applicant flow, as discussed earlier, is drawn from general population data or some subset of the general population data (e.g., qualified labor market data). Both plaintiffs[197] and defendants[198] may contend that potential applicant flow data should be used. As with any population/labor market data, potential applicant flow data are vulnerable to attack unless the

---

the desired position normally is a required element of the plaintiff's prima facie case. *E.g.*, Tagupa v. Board of Dirs., 633 F.2d 1309, 1312, 27 FEP 1041 (9th Cir. 1980) (in individual case, summary judgment properly granted because plaintiff failed to complete application process). *See generally* Chapters 15 (Hiring) and 16 (Promotion, Advancement, and Reclassification).

[195]*E.g.*, Robinson v. Union Carbide Corp., 538 F.2d 652, 658, 13 FEP 645 (5th Cir. 1976) (multiple applications by same individuals can produce unreliable data), *modified on rehearing on other grounds*, 544 F.2d 1258, 14 FEP 266 (5th Cir. 1977) (en banc); Progressive Officers Club, Inc. v. Metropolitan Dade County, 54 FEP 1161, 1173 (S.D. Fla. 1990) (analysis used misleading sample size by counting repeaters); Croker v. Boeing Co., 437 F. Supp. 1138, 1184, 15 FEP 165 (E.D. Pa. 1977) (multiple applications by various individuals can skew statistics), *aff'd in relevant part*, 662 F.2d 975, 26 FEP 1569 (3d Cir. 1981) (en banc). *But cf.* Reynolds v. Sheet Metal Workers Local 102, 498 F. Supp. 952, 965, 24 FEP 648 (D.D.C. 1980) (burden is on defendant to offer evidence that double counting of minority applications is so pervasive or significant as to undermine validity of applicant data).

[196]*See, e.g.*, EEOC v. O & G Spring & Wire Forms Specialty Co., 38 F.3d 872, 877, 65 FEP 1823 (7th Cir. 1994) (court rejected employer's argument that African Americans, who represented about 20% of actual walk-in applicant pool, self-selected out of pool because they preferred not to work with Polish and Spanish-speaking workers).

[197]*E.g.*, Berger v. Iron Workers Local 201, 843 F.2d 1395, 1414, 46 FEP 780 (D.C. Cir. 1988) (plaintiffs used proxy of job experience in crafting pool of potential applicants for union's journeyman examination); Hameed v. Iron Workers Local 396, 637 F.2d 506, 510–11, 24 FEP 352 (8th Cir. 1980) (general population statistics were used to establish prima facie case of adverse impact; union used high school diploma requirement for admission to apprenticeship program); *cf.* Lewis v. Bloomsburg Mills, Inc., 773 F.2d 561, 568, 38 FEP 1692, *amended*, 40 FEP 1615 (4th Cir. 1985) (employers improperly disposed of applications for relevant period; therefore, census data were used to determine available pool of minority applicants).

[198]*See, e.g.*, Patterson v. Western Dev. Labs., 13 FEP 772, 775 (N.D. Cal. 1976) (defendant used qualified labor force as benchmark to defeat plaintiff's adverse impact claim, which was based on actual applicant flow data).

data fairly represent the qualified available labor pool for the jobs in question.[199]

1. Qualified Labor Market Data

Following *Hazelwood* and *Teamsters*, lower courts generally have held that "qualified labor market" data should be used for population/workforce comparisons.[200] In *EEOC v. Turtle Creek*

---

[199]*See, e.g.*, Robinson v. Adams, 847 F.2d 1315, 1318, 49 FEP 1043 (9th Cir. 1987) ("We have consistently rejected the usefulness of general population statistics as a proxy for the pool of potential applicants where the employer sought applicants for positions requiring special skills."). In *Robinson v. City of Dallas*, 514 F.2d 1271, 1272 n.4, 10 FEP 1235 (5th Cir. 1975), the municipal employer had a written rule calling for discipline of employees who failed to pay their "just debts." The plaintiff (1) argued that such a rule by definition would most injure poor persons, and (2) proved that African Americans predominate among the impoverished persons in Dallas. However, the Fifth Circuit rejected the contention that statistics concerning the general population would make out a prima facie case:

> [T]he statistics offered by plaintiff indicate that he misconstrues the class. [The "just debts" rule] is imposed on employees of the city of Dallas, not on the population generally. If the city of Dallas refused to hire any individual who had ever failed to pay a just debt, statistics concerning the population as a whole would be relevant. But in the present case, the employment practice is applied only to employees of the city of Dallas. Thus the question is whether black *employees* of the city of Dallas fail to pay their just debts more frequently than white *employees* of the city of Dallas. The statistics offered by plaintiff are not helpful in answering this question.

Id. at 1273–74.

[200]*E.g.*, Lopez v. Laborers Local 18, 987 F.2d 1210, 1213–14, 61 FEP 876 (5th Cir. 1993) (without reference to qualified persons in relevant labor market, comparison of percentage of protected group members placed with employers under two different selection methods proved nothing); Scales v. Slater, 181 F.3d 703, 709 n.5, 82 FEP 485, 485 n.5 (5th Cir. 1999) (statistics are meaningless when they fail to account for qualifications); Kidd v. Illinois State Police, 167 F.3d 1084, 1102, 79 FEP 380 (7th Cir. 1999) ("[h]ad Kidd proffered the statistics to establish a pattern of discriminatory hiring, the relevant comparison would be one between the racial composition of ISP's cadet classes and the racial makeup of the workforce qualified for employment as ISP troopers"); Hopper v. Hallmark Cards, Inc., 87 F.3d 983, 989, 71 FEP 1362 (8th Cir. 1996) (plaintiff failed to show that those discharged "were similarly situated, qualified individuals," and, as such, court did not accept statistical proof); Forehand v. Florida State Hosp., 89 F.3d 1562, 1571–74, 71 FEP 905 (11th Cir. 1996) (plaintiff's statistics failed to control for competitive and noncompetitive promotions); Middleton v. Flint, 92 F.3d 396, 406, 71 FEP 962 (6th Cir. 1996) (plaintiffs challenged promotion plan that relied on racial quotas; court held that "raw" statistics based on general labor pool cannot justify hiring quota); Simon v. Youngstown, 73 F.3d 68, 72 (6th Cir. 1995) (court found that statistics, which assumed that all police officers in department rotated through assignments without

Mansion Corp.,[201] the court rejected the plaintiff's labor market statistics. The plaintiff tried to compare the percentage of women in the food service industry, based on census data, with the percentage in the defendant's luxury restaurant. The court found the data insufficient because they did not narrow the pool (which consisted of cocktail waitresses, room service waitresses, etc.) to those applicants having the specific qualifications required for the job in the defendant's restaurant.[202] So refined, defendants often offer

---

regard to qualification, were invalid); El Deeb v. University of Minn., 60 F.3d 423, 430–31, 68 FEP 1173, 1178 (8th Cir. 1995) (court found that doctor's statistical comparison of salaries was insufficient because it did not control for expertise); EEOC v. American Airlines, Inc., 48 F.3d 164, 172–73, 67 FEP 754 (5th Cir. 1995) (court rejected EEOC's statistical comparisons, which omitted important qualification criteria such as score on flight simulator test); Aiken v. Memphis, 37 F.3d 1155, 1165, 1167, 65 FEP 1757 (6th Cir. 1994) (on remand, district court was required to consider whether racial makeup of qualified labor pool differed from general workforce); Carter v. Ball, 33 F.3d 450, 456, 65 FEP 1414 (4th Cir. 1994) ("In the case of discrimination in hiring or promoting, the relevant comparison is between the percentage of minority employees and the percentage of potential minority applicants in the qualified labor pool."); McNairn v. Sullivan, 929 F.2d 974, 979, 55 FEP 1092 (4th Cir. 1991) (plaintiff failed to show that employees at GS-3 level were qualified to be promoted to GS-4 level); Mallory v. Booth Refrigeration Supply Co., 882 F.2d 908, 912, 50 FEP 1066 (4th Cir. 1989) (adverse impact not established where evidence did not disclose how many clerical employees were qualified to become supervisors); Smith v. General Scanning, Inc., 876 F.2d 1315, 1321, 50 FEP 58 (7th Cir. 1989) (statistics failed to show discrimination; there was no evidence regarding qualified potential applicants from relevant labor market); Pegues v. Mississippi State Employment Serv., 699 F.2d 760, 766–67, 31 FEP 257 (5th Cir. 1983) (comparison to general population was valueless where qualifications must be considered, such as "work preferences, experience, education, and the state of the job market"); O'Neal v. Riceland Foods, 684 F.2d 577, 580, 29 FEP 956 (8th Cir. 1982) (general population statistics not indicative even where clerical duties are involved); Piva v. Xerox Corp., 654 F.2d 591, 596–97, 26 FEP 1267 (9th Cir. 1981) (disparity between percentage of employer's regional sales representatives who were women and percentage of women in general workforce not highly probative absent evidence that most workers would be qualified to be sales representatives); Patterson v. American Tobacco Co., 634 F.2d 744, 753, 754 & n.14, 24 FEP 531 (4th Cir. 1980) (en banc) (if special qualifications for supervisory positions exist "beyond those commonly possessed or readily acquired" by general population, then most probative evidence will be qualified labor market data), *vacated on other grounds*, 456 U.S. 63 (1982).

[201]70 FEP 899 (N.D. Tex. 1995) (census data that indicated percentage of female waitresses in general population not probative in determining percentage of waitresses with requisite qualifications for fine dining establishment), *aff'd*, 82 F.3d 414 (1996).

[202]*Id.* at 904–06.

qualified labor market data to refute a plaintiff's prima facie case based on general population data.[203]

In order to estimate the qualified labor market, parties have turned to various sources, including census data[204] and unemployment data.[205] Even with these sources, though, census data may not be categorized specifically enough for the job in question,[206] and the timing of the census snapshot may not provide an accurate picture of availability in years hence.[207] Evidence that shows

---

[203]E.g., Garcia v. Rush-Presbyterian-St. Luke's Med. Ctr., 660 F.2d 1217, 1224–25, 26 FEP 1556 (7th Cir. 1981) (hospital prevailed based on its study, which compared representation of Latinos in skilled and licensed jobs at hospital with their availability in identical jobs in national health field labor force); see also Jimerson v. Kisco Co., 542 F.2d 1008, 1009–10, 13 FEP 977 (8th Cir. 1976) (per curiam) (65% African-American workforce compared to 40.9% African-American general population); Robinson v. Union Carbide Corp., 538 F.2d 652, 658, 13 FEP 645 (5th Cir. 1976) (33% African-American hires compared to 26% African-American labor force), modified on reh'g on other grounds, 544 F.2d 1258, 14 FEP 266 (5th Cir. 1977) (en banc); Carton v. Trustees of Tufts Coll., 25 FEP 1114, 1123 (D. Mass. 1981) (hiring of women by university for full-time positions exceeded percentage of women in available pool).

[204]E.g., Long v. City of Saginaw, 911 F.2d 1192, 1199, 53 FEP 1025 (6th Cir. 1990) (U.S. Census Data and Commerce Department's report of job classifications used).

[205]E.g., Phillips v. Joint Legislative Comm., 637 F.2d 1014, 1025–26, 25 FEP 120 (5th Cir. 1981) (plaintiff used statistics showing racial percentage of persons registering with State Employment Security Commission for professional, technical, or managerial employment and for clerical or sales jobs); cf. Neloms v. Southwestern Elec. Power Co., 440 F. Supp. 1353, 1361–62, 18 FEP 1683 (W.D. La. 1977) (defendant's qualified labor market data were flawed because they did not include unemployed persons).

[206]See, e.g., Long, 911 F.2d at 1200 (noting problem with use of "job titles" in Standard Occupational Classification Manual where category "Protective Services" includes not only police but also bouncers, camp guards, school crossing guards, "meter maids," railroad crossing guards, flaggers, and building security officers).

[207]Older census data may miss demographic shifts. E.g., United States v. Fairfax County, 629 F.2d 932, 941, 23 FEP 485 (4th Cir. 1980) (use of 1970 census data in late 1970s tends to distort availability of minorities and women); EEOC v. Akron Nat'l Bank & Trust Co., 497 F. Supp. 733, 747–48, 22 FEP 1665 (N.D. Ohio 1980) ("It is clear that the more active role taken by females in the workforce during the early 1970s would have a large effect on the continued validity of the . . . statistics relied upon."); Greenspan v. Automobile Club, 495 F. Supp. 1021, 1028–29, 22 FEP 184 (E.D. Mich. 1980) ("employment information which is nearly ten years old may not adequately reflect the current distribution of women in the work force"); Smith v. Union Oil Co., 17 FEP 960, 967 (N.D. Cal. 1977) (increase in percentage of minorities from 1960 to 1970 suggests that 1970 census figures should be adjusted upward in mid-1970s). Moreover, at best, census data reflect the number of persons employed, or experienced and unemployed, in a given job category as of the census

that the defendant employer employed a lower proportion of minority employees than similarly situated employers may be admitted, however.[208]

2. Qualified and Interested Labor Market Data

In many situations, "qualified" may not be a sufficient refinement of the left side of the population/workforce equation, because not all qualified persons *want* the job at issue. In *Wards Cove Packing Co. v. Atonio*,[209] for example, the Supreme Court held that one segment of the employer's job force—cannery workers—did not constitute the relevant labor pool for another segment—unskilled noncannery workers—in part for lack of indicia of interest:

> [I]solating the cannery workers as the potential "labor force" for unskilled noncannery positions is . . . too broad because the vast majority of these cannery workers did not seek jobs in unskilled noncannery positions; there is no showing that many of them would have done so even if none of the arguably "deterring" practices existed.[210]

The Seventh Circuit, in *EEOC v. Chicago Miniature Lamp Works*,[211] similarly determined that interest is a crucial factor in defining the relevant labor market.[212] *Chicago Miniature* involved

---

date. Thus, some courts have rejected the use of detailed census statistics to show the availability of qualified applicants because such statistics indicate the number of individuals *employed* in the positions in question rather than those with the qualifications and interest *to be employed* in such positions. Thus, the census "presents a picture of occupational background rather than qualification." *Smith, supra*, 17 FEP at 967. To combat the former problem, the Current Population Survey (CPS) is available from the Census Bureau, providing certain updated information. But some courts have rejected the use of such "updated data," finding they are less accurate than census data. *E.g.*, Gay v. Waiters & Dairy Lunchmen's Local 30, 489 F. Supp. 282, 304 & n.24, 22 FEP 281 (N.D. Cal. 1980) (more recent data determined to be less reliable than census), *aff'd*, 694 F.2d 531, 29 FEP 1027 (9th Cir. 1982).

[208]Wyche v. Marine Midland Bank, 73 FEP 1600 (S.D.N.Y. 1997) (plaintiff was allowed to introduce bank documents that compared percentages of minorities at defendant bank with higher percentages at "top 50 banks"); *see also* Vitug v. Multistate Tax Comm'n, 88 F.3d 506, 514, 71 FEP 1445 (7th Cir. 1996) (adverse impact rejected where percentage of auditors employed by defendant exceeded "total percentage among accountants and auditors in the national workforce").

[209]490 U.S. 642, 49 FEP 1519 (1989).

[210]*Id.* at 653–54.

[211]947 F.2d 292, 57 FEP 408 (7th Cir. 1991).

[212]*Id.* at 301.

a challenge by African Americans to recruiting practices that allegedly resulted in an underrepresentation of African Americans in the employer's workforce, to the benefit of Hispanics and Asians. The court held that the EEOC's "impressive litany of high standard deviations" (using all of Chicago as the relevant labor market) ignored the fact that the employer did not have an English fluency requirement. Common sense, the court held, dictated that a nondiscriminating employer with no English fluency requirement will attract a disproportionate number of applications from non-English-speaking persons.[213]

The "interest" element underscores why many courts look to qualified applicant flow, if that is untainted by discrimination, as the preferred source of data on the interested labor pool.[214] One court rejected income level as a valid indicator or indication of interest.[215] Courts are divided over the use of "job interest surveys" as a substitute for an applicant flow analysis in an attempt to identify the "interested" workforce. In one case, the defendant successfully relied on a job interest survey in order to rebut the plaintiff's statistical evidence.[216] In another case, the court rejected an employer's use of a job interest survey in a disparate treatment case; allowing the survey results to insulate the employer from liability, the court

---

[213]*Id.* at 300–01.

[214]*E.g.*, Mister v. Illinois Cent. Gulf R.R., 832 F.2d 1427, 1435, 45 FEP 178, 184 (7th Cir. 1987) ("Studies based on Census labor pool data rarely overcome studies based on actual applicants."); Markey v. Tenneco Oil Co., 707 F.2d 172, 174–75, 32 FEP 148 (5th Cir. 1983) (applicant flow should be used to determine relevant labor market unless skewed by discriminatory recruiting practices); Payne v. Travenol Labs., Inc., 673 F.2d 798, 823–24, 28 FEP 1212 (5th Cir. 1982) (applicant flow data are superior to census or general labor market statistics); United States v. Fairfax County, 629 F.2d 932, 940, 23 FEP 485 (4th Cir. 1980) (applicant flow data are most salient proof of labor market); *see* Hazelwood Sch. Dist. v. United States, 433 U.S. 299, 308 n.13, 15 FEP 1 (1977) (applicant flow statistics "very relevant"). *But cf.* United States v. Gregory, 871 F.2d 1239, 1243, 50 FEP 1568 (4th Cir. 1989) (applicant flow data not required to prove discrimination through statistics).

[215]*See, e.g., Gay*, 489 F. Supp. at 304–05 (rejecting use of income to define relevant interested market pool because of multitude of other factors that influence job preference).

[216]EEOC v. Sears, Roebuck & Co., 839 F.2d 302, 320–21, 45 FEP 1257 (7th Cir. 1988). The court emphasized that the EEOC's failure to present the testimony of any alleged victims of discrimination "confirmed the weaknesses of the EEOC's statistical evidence." *Id.* at 310.

decided, would be "to accept that an employer is permitted to discriminate against the minority of women who are interested in seeking non-traditional employment as long as the majority of women are not interested in such work."[217]

3. General Population Data

The Supreme Court approved the use of general population data for population/workforce comparisons in *Teamsters v. United States*[218]—a pattern-or-practice disparate treatment case—where the job skills in question were ones that "many persons possess or can fairly readily acquire."[219] Where the conditions of *Teamsters* are met[220]—but only then[221]—the general population can be a fair proxy for the qualified labor force. Population/workforce comparisons

---

[217]Stender v. Lucky Stores, Inc., 803 F. Supp. 259, 326, 62 FEP 11 (N.D. Cal. 1992).

[218]431 U.S. 324, 14 FEP 1514 (1977).

[219]*Id.* at 339, 340 & n.20; *accord Hazelwood*, 433 U.S. at 308 n.13 ("In *Teamsters*, the comparison between the percentage of Negroes on the employer's work force and the percentage in the general areawide population was highly probative, because the job skill there involved—the ability to drive a truck—is one that many persons possess or can fairly readily acquire. When special qualifications are required to fill particular jobs, comparisons to the general population . . . may have little probative value."); EEOC v. Rath Packing Co., 787 F.2d 318, 336, 40 FEP 580 (8th Cir. 1986) (where employer has not established that job in question requires any special qualifications not possessed or readily acquirable by general population, general population statistics are appropriate measure of extent of employer's discrimination); EEOC v. Radiator Specialty Co., 610 F.2d 178, 185, 21 FEP 351 (4th Cir. 1979) ("In some cases, the fact that no special qualifications exist will be manifest as a matter of law from the mere identification by the plaintiff of the job positions in question. . . . In such cases, a court may properly look to general population statistics in assessing plaintiff's *prima facie* proof.").

[220]*See* Wards Cove Packing Co. v. Atonio, 490 U.S. 642, 651 n.6, 49 FEP 1519 (1989) ("[W]here 'figures for the general population might . . . accurately reflect the pool of qualified job applicants,' we have even permitted plaintiffs to rest their prima facie cases on such statistics as well.") (quoting Teamsters v. United States, 431 U.S. 324, 340 n.20, 14 FEP 1514 (1977)).

[221]*E.g.*, Moore v. Hughes Helicopters, Inc., 708 F.2d 475, 482, 32 FEP 97 (9th Cir. 1983) ("General population statistics are useful as a proxy for the pool of potential applicants, if ever, only when the challenged employer practice screens applicants for entry level jobs requiring little or no specialized skills."); Middleton v. Flint, 92 F.3d 396, 406, 71 FEP 962 (6th Cir. 1996) (questioning district court's acceptance of statistics that compared number of minority group members in general labor pool and number of minority group members in local police force).

utilizing general population data thus generally are used by plaintiffs only in cases involving unskilled entry-level jobs,[222] in unusual cases where there is an overwhelming underrepresentation in the labor force,[223] or in cases where more refined data were unavailable.[224]

Some courts have held that general population data also may be used where the qualifications themselves are in question,[225] and one has held similarly where the qualifications are subjective and difficult to quantify.[226]

---

[222]*See, e.g.,* Bradley v. Pizzaco of Neb., Inc., 926 F.2d 714, 716, 55 FEP 347 (8th Cir. 1991) (pizza deliverer); *see also* EEOC v. United Va. Bank/Seaboard Nat'l, 615 F.2d 147, 154 n.4, 21 FEP 1405 (4th Cir. 1980) ("Absent other proof, we assume that those in the general labor force are generally qualified to hold operative and service jobs."); Kraszewski v. State Farm Gen. Ins. Co., 38 FEP 197, 217 (N.D. Cal. 1985) (relevant labor market to consider for insurance company trainees does not need to be controlled for personal characteristics, because there are none that screen out more women than men and no special skills are required to become insurance company trainee).

[223]*E.g., Hazelwood,* 433 U.S. at 307–08 ("Where gross statistical disparities can be shown, they alone in a proper case constitute prima facie proof of a pattern or practice of discrimination."); *Teamsters,* 431 U.S. at 342 n.23 ("[F]ine tuning of the statistics could not have obscured the glaring absence of minority line drivers. As the Court of Appeals remarked, the company's inability to rebut the inference of discrimination came not from a misuse of statistics but from 'the inexorable zero.' ") (citation omitted); *Radiator Specialty Co.,* 610 F.2d at 184 n.7 ("When the statistical disparities are 'gross,' it may be unnecessary to 'fine tune' the statistics.").

[224]For example, the Eleventh Circuit upheld the district court's reliance on general workforce data for individuals aged 18–55 in a case involving entry-level positions in the fire department. Peightal v. Metropolitan Dade County 26 F.3d 1545, 1555, 71 FEP 1107 (11th Cir. 1994) (challenge to fire department's affirmative action program by white male who was passed over for hiring whereas minorities with lower scores were hired). Although the employer allegedly had minimum education and language proficiency standards, the court found the lack of reliable raw data a persuasive reason to rely on general workforce statistics. *See* United States v. City of Warren, 138 F.3d 1083, 1093, 79 FEP 1603 (6th Cir. 1998) (where data on qualified applicant pool were unavailable, "the United States presented statistical evidence reflecting the racial composition of the population from which Warren would have recruited its workers absent discrimination").

[225]*E.g.,* Spurlock v. United Airlines, Inc., 475 F.2d 216, 218, 5 FEP 17 (10th Cir. 1972) (no requirement to use qualified labor market data where qualifications for flight officer were claimed to be discriminatory). *See generally* Chapter 3 (Adverse Impact).

[226]*E.g.,* Boyd v. Bechtel Corp., 485 F. Supp. 610, 619–20, 20 FEP 944 (N.D. Cal. 1979) (plaintiff not required to control for nonquantifiable factors). *But see* Williams v. New Orleans S.S. Ass'n, 466 F. Supp. 662, 677, 28 FEP 1001 (E.D. La. 1979) (rejecting plaintiff's statistical comparison of earnings of African-American

Some courts have refined general population data somewhat by looking to "civilian labor force" data rather than general population data.[227] The former eliminates children (who are not eligible to work), retired persons (who generally have decided that they no longer want to work), and persons in the military (who generally are ineligible for private employment and are disproportionately members of minority groups).[228]

4. Employer's Workforce Data

In some cases, especially cases involving claims of promotion and wage discrimination, the employer's own workforce database (or a portion thereof) may be the best source for data on the qualified labor market. But, as with other sources, such data cannot be used indiscriminately.

The Supreme Court addressed the issue of comparisons within an employer's workforce in *Wards Cove Packing Co. v. Atonio*.[229] The plaintiffs in *Wards Cove*, nonwhite workers in unskilled cannery jobs, challenged on adverse impact and disparate treatment grounds the employer's hiring and promotion process for mostly skilled, higher-paying noncannery jobs.[230] In support, the plaintiffs offered "statistics showing a high percentage of nonwhite workers in the cannery jobs and a low percentage of such workers in the noncannery positions."[231] The district and circuit courts held that such statistics sufficed to make out a prima facie case of adverse impact.

---

and white longshoremen in part because "a certain amount of skill at working certain cargoes or performing certain tasks is subjectively taken into account by superintendents when hiring foremen and their gangs"), *aff'd in relevant part*, 673 F.2d 742, 28 FEP 1092 (5th Cir. 1982).

[227]*Peightal*, 26 F.3d at 1555 (upholding district court's reliance on general workforce data for individuals aged 18 through 55 in case involving entry-level positions in fire department).

[228]*See, e.g.*, Alexander v. Machinists Lodge No. 735, 565 F.2d 1364, 1381–82, 15 FEP 1413 (6th Cir. 1977) (vacating and remanding decision of district court, which had relied on population as benchmark; on remand, court should consider using civilian labor force as comparative measure); *cf.* Marsh v. Flint Bd. of Educ., 708 F. Supp. 821, 824, 49 FEP 766 (E.D. Mich. 1989) (disparity between racial composition of student body and faculty not proper comparison).

[229]490 U.S. 642, 49 FEP 1519 (1989).

[230]*Id.* at 647–48.

[231]*Id.* at 650.

But the Supreme Court reversed, characterizing as "nonsensical" the comparison used by the plaintiffs and accepted by the lower courts.[232] The racial composition of unskilled cannery jobs, the Court noted, in no way reflects " 'the pool of *qualified* job applicants' or the '*qualified* population in the labor force.' "[233] The disparity reflected by the plaintiffs' statistics could be due entirely to legitimate reasons unrelated to the employer's selection processes—such as "a dearth of qualified nonwhite applicants [for noncannery positions] (for reasons that are not [the employer's] fault)."[234]

But *Wards Cove* did not hold that data from the employer's own workforce never can be used appropriately for the "left side" of the population/workforce analysis, or for the "potential applicant" pool in a selection rate analysis. Perhaps the most common use of employers' workforce statistics is in promotion cases.[235] Such

---

[232]*Id.* at 651. Accepting the plaintiffs' and the court of appeals' theory, the Court predicted, would lead to results contrary to the goals behind Title VII:

The Court of Appeals' theory, at the very least, would mean that any employer who had a segment of his work force that was—for some reason—racially imbalanced, could be haled into court. . . . The only practicable option for many employers would be to adopt racial quotas, insuring that no portion of their workforces deviated in racial composition from the other portions thereof; this is a result that Congress expressly rejected in drafting Title VII.

Id. at 652.

[233]*Id.* at 651. Even for *unskilled* noncannery jobs, for which most cannery workers would be qualified, "isolating the cannery workers as the potential 'labor force' . . . is at once both too broad and too narrow in its focus." *Id.* at 653. It is too broad because it would include uninterested cannery workers, and it is too narrow because it excludes potentially interested applicants outside the employer's workforce. *Id.* at 653–54.

[234]*Id.* at 651.

[235]*See, e.g.*, Hemmings v. Tidyman's, Inc., 285 F.3d 1174, 1185–86, 88 FEP 945 (9th Cir. 2002) (appropriate pool of candidates for promotion to management positions, when promotions are made from within company, is defendant's lower-level manager ranks); Shidaker v. Carlin, 782 F.2d 746, 750, 39 FEP 1768 (7th Cir. 1986) (for company that promotes from within, relevant labor pool for upper-level positions is group of employees from which promotees will be drawn; large disparity between composition of upper- and lower-level positions is sufficient to make out prima facie case of adverse impact), *vacated on other grounds sub nom.* Tisch v. Shidaker, 481 U.S. 1001, 43 FEP 640 (1987); Paxton v. Union Nat'l Bank, 688 F.2d 552, 564, 29 FEP 1233 (8th Cir. 1982) (general population figures irrelevant in promotion cases where majority of above-entry-level positions are filled from within employer's ranks); Gilbert v. City of Little Rock, 722 F.2d 1390, 1396, 33 FEP 557 (8th Cir. 1983) ("[b]ecause promotions were made from within, general population statistics [were] not probative"); Johnson v. Uncle Ben's, Inc., 628 F.2d 419, 42, 24 FEP 1 (5th Cir. 1980) (if employer hires employees from outside for upper-level

data must be refined, however. The employer's workforce data utilized on the "left side" of the equation must be limited to those employees who are qualified to be promoted to the upper-level job in question, as determined by skills, experience, historical flow pattern, or all three.[236] For example, employers often legitimately impose

---

positions, then relevant comparison for determining discrimination is qualified outside labor force, but if employer fills such positions by promotion, relevant comparison is within employer's internal workforce), *vacated and remanded on other grounds*, 451 U.S. 902, 25 FEP 737 (1981). *See generally* Chapter 16 (Promotion, Advancement, and Reclassification).

[236]*See, e.g., Hemmings*, 285 F.3d at 1186 (plaintiffs' statistical analysis appropriately compared employer's lower-level managers, from whose ranks promotions in question were drawn, to those actually promoted); McNairn v. Sullivan, 929 F.2d 974, 979, 55 FEP 1092 (4th Cir. 1991) (plaintiff failed to show that GS-3 workers were qualified to be promoted to GS-4); Mallory v. Booth Refrigeration Supply Co., 882 F.2d 908, 912, 50 FEP 1066 (4th Cir. 1989) (mere recitation of employee and minority composition in supervisory and clerical positions insufficient where there is no evidence of how many employees in pool were qualified to become supervisors); Rivera v. City of Wichita Falls, 665 F.2d 531, 540–41, 27 FEP 1352 (5th Cir. 1982) (*Hazelwood* requires that comparisons with respect to skilled jobs focus only on those who have skills in question; proper analysis differentiates between those incumbents who truly are part of pool from which promotions would be made; raw comparison of percentages of minorities in lower levels versus upper levels insufficient); Ste. Marie v. Eastern R.R. Ass'n, 650 F.2d 395, 400–01, 26 FEP 167 (2d Cir. 1981) (statistics showing underrepresentation of women in managerial and technical positions and overrepresentation in clerical positions of more than four standard deviations does not establish evidence of discrimination where statistics concerning clerical category include secretarial and stenographic jobs that do not provide training that could lead to advancement); Pack v. Energy Research & Dev. Admin., 566 F.2d 1111, 1113, 16 FEP 987 (9th Cir. 1977) (per curiam) (95% female lower-grade professionals compared to 2% female higher-grade professionals held not probative because "[n]o evidence whatsoever was introduced to demonstrate that the lower-grade professional women were qualified to occupy the higher positions"); *cf.* Davis v. Califano, 613 F.2d 957, 963–64, 21 FEP 272 (D.C. Cir. 1979) ("[O]nly the *minimum objective qualifications* necessary for one to be eligible for promotion must be considered in the statistical data presented initially by a plaintiff; not every conceivable factor relevant to a promotion decision must be included in the statistical presentation in order to make out a *prima facie* case."); EEOC v. Radiator Specialty Co., 610 F.2d 178, 186, 21 FEP 351 (4th Cir. 1979) (where "no special qualifications are required for the upper level positions, defendant's lower level work force is the appropriate labor pool. [But where] special skills are required for the promotion jobs, the [plaintiff] must produce evidence of the number of qualified blacks in lower level positions [in the employer's work force.]"). *But cf.* Fisher v. Procter & Gamble Mfg. Co., 613 F.2d 527, 544, 22 FEP 356 (5th Cir. 1980) (plaintiff's use of statistical comparisons between racial makeup in key positions and racial composition of workforce approved where employer based promotion on training received and skills developed through employment); Hemmings v. Tidyman's, Inc., 285 F.3d

length-of-service requirements, which, if not unlawful,[237] legitimately eliminate some employees from consideration for promotion.[238] Therefore, only a portion of the employer's lower-level workforce normally should be used for comparisons,[239] unless all members legitimately can be presumed qualified and interested. That might be the case, for example, where the desired position demands no special skills, is the next step in the normal line of progression,[240] or where a challenged rule or policy applies to everyone.[241]

Where a position is available only to current employees, a court will usually find that the qualified portion of the employer's workforce is the proper pool for comparison in any statistical analysis.[242] However, a plaintiff who relies on comparisons within an employer's workforce must take care to distinguish between groups of employees that may be subject to different policies.[243] For example, statistics concerning salaried and temporary employees may be irrelevant to bargaining unit employees who are subject to specific work rules and discharge policies.[244] On the other hand, when

---

1174, 1185–87, 88 FEP 945 (9th Cir. 2002) (where plaintiffs alleged discriminatory practice regarding employer's internal promotions from lower management to upper management positions, pool of all management employees of employer was proper basis for comparison even if plaintiffs not qualified for certain management positions).

[237]See generally Chapter 17 (Seniority).

[238]See generally Chapter 16 (Promotion, Advancement, and Reclassification).

[239]E.g., MacDissi v. Valmont Indus., Inc., 856 F.2d 1054, 1057–58, 47 FEP 1418 (8th Cir. 1988) (traffic department, rather than entire company, was relevant labor pool). See generally Chapter 16 (Promotion, Advancement, and Reclassification).

[240]See Stender v. Lucky Stores, Inc., 803 F. Supp. 259, 273, 333, 62 FEP 11 (N.D. Cal. 1992) (appropriate to compare movement of males and females from entry-level into apprenticeship programs in different grocery departments when evidence showed this was normal job progression).

[241]E.g., McAlester v. United Air Lines, Inc., 851 F.2d 1249, 1257–58, 47 FEP 512 (10th Cir. 1988) (proper labor pool was entire workforce because challenged disciplinary rule applies to all). See generally Chapter 16 (Promotion, Advancement, and Reclassification).

[242]Aiken v. Memphis, 37 F.3d 1155, 1163, 65 FEP 1757 (6th Cir. 1994) (finding statistical makeup of current fire department more probative than general workforce statistics).

[243]See, e.g., Kovacevich v. Kent State Univ., 224 F.3d 806, 832, 83 FEP 1306, 1323 (6th Cir. 2000) (court properly excluded plaintiff's statistical study that was based on entire university faculty at seven different campuses when each college determined merit raises in its own way); Forehand v. Florida State Hosp., 89 F.3d 1562, 1572–73, 71 FEP 905, 915 (11th Cir. 1996) (plaintiffs failed to distinguish applicant pools for positions filled through different procedures).

[244]See Plair v. E.J. Brach & Sons, Inc., 105 F.3d 343, 349, 73 FEP 1575 (7th Cir. 1997).

a plaintiff complains that a practice has a disparate impact on the entire workforce, it may be inappropriate to focus on only subsets of that workforce.[245]

Statistics derived from the employer's workforce composition also have been used in cases that involve alleged discrimination in departmental assignments,[246] pay practices,[247] layoffs,[248] and other terminations.[249]

---

[245]Smith v. Xerox Corp., 196 F.3d 358, 368–69, 81 FEP 343, 348–49 (2d Cir. 1999) (analysis of impact of decision-making process used for companywide RIF flawed because it focused on only certain groups of employees).

[246]E.g., Teamsters v. United States, 431 U.S. 324, 337, 342 n.23, 14 FEP 1514 (1977) (segregation of truck drivers); Bruno v. W.B. Saunders Co., 882 F.2d 760, 766–67, 50 FEP 898 (3d Cir. 1989) (statistical evidence concerning transfers is "relevant"); EEOC v. Korn Indus., Inc., 17 FEP 954, 959 (D.S.C. 1978) (segregated job categories), remanded in part on other grounds, 662 F.2d 256, 27 FEP 13 (4th Cir. 1981); Sears v. Atchison, Topeka & Santa Fe Ry., 454 F. Supp. 158, 170–71, 17 FEP 1138 (D. Kan. 1978) (African-American porters and white brakemen), aff'd in relevant part, 645 F.2d 1365, 25 FEP 337 (10th Cir. 1981); Domingo v. New Eng. Fish Co., 445 F. Supp. 421, 429, 19 FEP 253 (W.D. Wash. 1977) (segregated cannery workers), aff'd, 727 F.2d 1429, 34 FEP 584, modified on other grounds, 742 F.2d 520, 37 FEP 1303 (9th Cir. 1984). But see Wards Cove Packing Co. v. Atonio, 490 U.S. 642, 650 & n.5, 49 FEP 1519 (1989) (mere disparities in racial composition of different segments of employer's workforce not enough to make out prima facie case of adverse impact without proof of qualified labor market).

[247]Rudebusch v. Hughes, 313 F.3d 506, 516 (9th Cir. 2002) (concerns regarding plaintiff's regression analysis because it did not account for various performance factors); Siler-Khodr v. University of Tex. Health Sci. Ctr., 261 F.3d 542, 547, 86 FEP 1078, 1082 (5th Cir. 2002) (plaintiff's study of salaries for professors at medical school sufficient to prove disparate pay where study reflected salaries schoolwide and did not break down salaries into medical subspecialties). But see Keyes v. Lenoir Rhyne Coll., 15 FEP 914, 924 (W.D.N.C. 1976) (no discrimination shown because plaintiff failed to show salary disparity by job, discipline, or department), aff'd, 552 F.2d 579, 15 FEP 925 (4th Cir. 1977); Patterson v. Western Dev. Labs., 13 FEP 772, 775 (N.D. Cal. 1976) (discrimination in compensation).

[248]E.g., Rose v. Wells Fargo & Co., 902 F.2d 1417, 1425, 52 FEP 1430 (9th Cir. 1990) (plaintiff's statistics, showing that 73.5% of workers over age 50, 34.1% of those between 40 and 49, and 28.2% of those under 40 were terminated during RIF concentrated on management-level employees insufficient to overcome summary judgment where "[t]he statistical disparity . . . is explained by the fact older persons tend to occupy these key management positions"); Taylor v. Teletype Corp., 648 F.2d 1129, 1133–34, 26 FEP 124 (8th Cir. 1981) (prima facie case of discrimination in layoffs established by comparing percentage of laid-off employees who were African American with percentage of African Americans in employer's workforce).

[249]E.g., Pouncy v. Prudential Ins. Co., 499 F. Supp. 427, 465–66, 23 FEP 1349 (S.D. Tex. 1980) (comparing percentage of terminations received by African Americans with percentage of African Americans in defendant's workforce), aff'd, 668 F.2d 795, 28 FEP 121 (5th Cir. 1982); Agarwal v. Arthur G. McKee & Co., 19 FEP 503, 518 (N.D. Cal. 1977) (turnover of minorities roughly comparable to composition of internal workforce and new hires), aff'd, 644 F.2d 803, 25 FEP 1565 (9th Cir. 1981).

V. PROPER GEOGRAPHIC SCOPE OF STATISTICS

The geographic area from which data are drawn often is crucial.[250] The objective in determining the relevant geographic area is to help define which persons would be likely to apply, absent discrimination.[251] Because the determination of the geographic scope can have a significant effect on the results of a statistical comparison, substantial effort frequently is spent on establishing the appropriate geographic scope.[252]

---

[250]Only where the statistics involve a comparison of the selection rates of actual applicants for the job in question would the geographic scope question not arise; in applicant flow cases, normally the proper geographic base is implicitly determined automatically, by the act of actually applying for the job or actually taking the test in question. See Section IV.A *supra*. Even in some cases involving actual applicants, though, an issue as to geographic scope might arise. For example, where the employer has multiple facilities, the parties may disagree as to whether applicants at one facility should be deemed to be applicants at the employer generally. *See, e.g.,* Kirkland v. New York State Dep't of Corr. Servs., 520 F.2d 420, 425, 11 FEP 38 (2d Cir. 1975) (question as to whether applicant statistics should be taken from just one or all of defendant's facilities).

[251]*See, e.g.,* Bennett v. Roberts, 295 F.3d 687, 89 FEP 439 (7th Cir. 2002) (unsuccessful black applicant for teaching position failed to consider commuting patterns when comparing racial composition of teachers hired by suburban school district with composition of teachers employed in entire Chicago metropolitan area); Chicago Firefighters Local 2 v. City of Chi., 249 F.3d 649, 654, 85 FEP 1305, 1307 (7th Cir. 2001) (suggesting that, in case involving discriminatory practices of city's fire department, comparison to city's proportion of minority residents not appropriate even though department had city residency requirement, because department applicants could move to city's suburbs after submitting applications); Johnson v. Goodyear Tire & Rubber Co., 491 F.2d 1364, 1371, 7 FEP 627 (5th Cir. 1974) (employer's geographic statistics "conveniently ignore the recognized mobility of today's black labor force"); United States v. Iron Workers Local 86, 443 F.2d 544, 551 n.19, 3 FEP 496 (9th Cir. 1971) (statistics were limited to city of Seattle because it is area from which union most likely would draw vast majority of its workers for apprenticeship, referral, and membership purposes).

[252]In *Stone v. Federal Communications Commission,* 466 F.2d 316, 332, 7 FEP 225 (D.C. Cir. 1972), for example, the plaintiff sought to make a prima facie case from the fact that 7% of the employer's workforce was African American, whereas the general population of the District of Columbia was 70% African American. However, the District of Columbia Circuit found that the relevant geographic area was the entire Washington, D.C., metropolitan area, which was approximately 24% African American. With the geographic scope thus modified, "approximately 7% blacks out of this total metropolitan area is within the zone of reasonableness." Similarly, in *Hester v. Southern Railway,* 497 F.2d 1374, 1379 n.6, 8 FEP 646 (5th Cir. 1974), the plaintiff sought to make its prima facie case by comparing the employer's data-typist workforce, which was 16.4% African American, with the general population of the city of Atlanta (51% African American). However, the Fifth Circuit

The Supreme Court, in *Hazelwood School District v. United States*,[253] clarified the importance of defining the proper geographic scope of statistics as well as several relevant factors for making such determinations.[254] In *Hazelwood* (a pattern-or-practice disparate treatment case), the plaintiffs alleged that the Hazelwood School District discriminated against African Americans in its hiring of teachers. During the 1972–73 and 1973–74 school years, 3.7 percent of all teachers hired by Hazelwood were African American. The significance of this number—whether it weakened or bolstered the plaintiffs' other evidence of discrimination—depended on the relevant labor market used for comparison.[255] In the combined area of the city of St. Louis and St. Louis County, census figures showed that 15.4 percent of all teachers were African American. But in St. Louis County alone, excluding the city of St. Louis, only 5.7 percent of teachers were African American.[256] Finding that neither the district court nor the court of appeals had properly weighed the factors relevant to determining the proper geographic scope, the Supreme Court remanded the case for the district court to do so, focusing on the following:

> (i) whether the racially based hiring policies of the St. Louis City School District were in effect as far back as 1970, the year in which the census figures were taken; (ii) to what extent those policies have changed the racial composition of that district's teaching staff from what it would otherwise have been; (iii) to what extent St. Louis' recruitment policies have diverted to the city teachers who might otherwise have applied to Hazelwood; (iv) to what extent Negro teachers employed by the city would prefer employment in other districts such as Hazelwood; and (v) what the experience in other school districts in St. Louis County indicates about the validity of excluding the City School District from the relevant labor market.[257]

---

pointed out that "the applicant pool . . . was composed of individuals from the greater Atlanta metropolitan area," which was approximately 22% African American, so that no prima facie showing of discrimination had been made.

[253]433 U.S. 299, 15 FEP 1 (1977).

[254]*Id.* at 310–13.

[255]*Id.* at 311–12.

[256]The school district argued that "because the city of St. Louis has made special attempts to maintain a 50% Negro teaching staff, inclusion of that school district in the relevant market area distorts the comparison." *Id.* at 310.

[257]*Id.* at 312. Both the district court and the court of appeals previously considered erroneous comparisons. The former based its holding for the employer on a comparison of African-American *students* to teachers in Hazelwood. The latter based its

Several factors frequently found relevant to the proper geographic scope include the scope of the employer's actual recruiting practices[258] (as long as that territory is not discriminatorily determined);[259] the skills required and the level of compensation;[260] special aspects of the employer's business that might give applicants an incentive to travel farther;[261] and the commuting patterns and availability of public transportation.[262] One commonly used measure of the appropriate geographic scope is the residence area of actual job applicants[263] or, in the absence of such data, the residence of

---

holding for the plaintiffs on a static workforce comparison of the percentage of African-American teachers in Hazelwood's workforce (as opposed to hirings since 1972—the date Hazelwood fell within Title VII's coverage) to the percentage of African-American teachers in the relevant labor market. *Id.* at 308–09; *see* Section VI *infra.*

[258]*Compare* Castaneda v. Pickard, 781 F.2d 456, 463–64, 40 FEP 154 (5th Cir. 1986) (inappropriate to define relevant labor market for district school teachers as "the nation" where most new teachers are recruited from just five universities) *with* Quigley v. Braniff Airways, Inc., 85 F.R.D. 74, 81 n.5, 23 FEP 1811 (N.D. Tex. 1979) (nationwide statistics used because defendant recruited nationally).

[259]*See* Mays v. Motorola, Inc., 22 FEP 799, 801–02 (N.D. Ill. 1979) (rejecting use of employer's actual recruiting area, which consisted predominantly of white suburb, because employer reasonably could be expected to recruit from broader area).

[260]*See id.*

[261]*See, e.g.,* EEOC v. Chicago Miniature Lamp Works, 947 F.2d 292, 299–300, 57 FEP 408 (7th Cir. 1991) (because of lack of job opportunities, non-English speakers more likely than persons fluent in English to travel great distance to work for employer that does not have English fluency requirement); *cf. Hazelwood*, 433 U.S. at 312 (recruiting practices of competing employers may affect defendant's ability to recruit African Americans).

[262]*See, e.g.,* Bennett v. Roberts, 295 F.3d 687, 697, 89 FEP 439 (7th Cir. 2002) (criticizing plaintiff's statistical analysis for failing to take commuting patterns into account); *Chicago Miniature*, 947 F.2d at 302 (cost of commuting to job site is relevant factor in determining relevant geographic scope of statistics—especially for lower-paying jobs); United States v. Fairfax County, 629 F.2d 932, 939–40, 23 FEP 485 (4th Cir. 1980) (lack of adequate mass transportation made it difficult for African Americans living in District of Columbia to apply for jobs).

[263]*E.g.,* Markey v. Tenneco Oil Co., 635 F.2d 497, 501, 24 FEP 1675 (5th Cir. 1981) (rejecting use of residence of employees at time of hire but approving use of residence of applicants: "Absent discriminatory recruiting practices, the percentage of applicants from a particular parish may be probative of the willingness of individuals in that parish to travel to the [employer's] plant and of the relative accessibility of the plant to residents of the parish, and thus be [an] . . . accurate measure of that parish's contribution to [the employer's] labor pool."); Reynolds v. Sheet Metal Workers Local 102, 498 F. Supp. 952, 969, 24 FEP 648 (D.D.C. 1980) (proper geographic area for determining relevant labor pool is where most applications originate), *aff'd*, 702 F.2d 221, 25 FEP 837 (D.C. Cir. 1981).

current employees.[264] Where school recruiting is an important source of new employees, courts have looked at the location of universities that produce significant numbers of applicants.[265]

In applying the various factors, courts variously have relied on the Standard Metropolitan Statistical Area (SMSA) (now referred to as the Metropolitan Statistical Area, or MSA),[266] the city

---

[264]*E.g.*, Clark v. Chrysler Corp., 673 F.2d 921, 928, 28 FEP 342 (7th Cir. 1982) (best evidence of availability for hiring is weighted average of availability based on demographics of areas from which employer actually draws its employees, absent evidence of illegal recruiting patterns); Donnell v. General Motors Corp., 576 F.2d 1292, 1296 n.5, 17 FEP 712 (8th Cir. 1978) (using residence of current employees). *But see* EEOC v. E.I. du Pont de Nemours & Co., 445 F. Supp. 223, 236–37, 16 FEP 847, *supplemented*, 16 FEP 881 (D. Del. 1978) (rejecting use of rated concentric circles based on residence of employees at time of hire because actual commuting patterns not considered).

If the residence of current employees is used, it should be their residence at the time they applied (usually available from their employment application), rather than their residence at the time the study is done. Reason: many employees tend to move closer to their places of employment once hired, and the purpose of determining the proper geographic scope is to determine the areas from which job *applicants* are likely to come.

[265]*E.g.*, Castaneda v. Pickard, 781 F.2d 456, 463–64, 40 FEP 154 (5th Cir. 1986) (trial court did not commit clear error when it held that school district's relevant labor market consisted of teachers graduating from five college campuses in counties corresponding to two of state education agency's regions).

[266]*E.g., Donnell,* 576 F.2d at 1296 n.5 (SMSA used based on zip code distribution of employee residences); Gibson v. Longshoremen (ILWU) Local 40, 543 F.2d 1259, 1268, 13 FEP 997 (9th Cir. 1976) (metropolitan area, not city, is relevant labor market for union in which 30% of its members live outside city); Drayton v. City of St. Petersburg, 477 F. Supp. 846, 857–58, 20 FEP 1495 (M.D. Fla. 1979) (SMSA data based on residence of employees and applicants); Croker v. Boeing Co., 437 F. Supp. 1138, 1183 n.7, 15 FEP 165 (E.D. Pa. 1977) (Philadelphia SMSA was used, rather than county in which employer was located, because "a substantial portion of [the employer's] workforce does come from other counties"), *vacated in part on other grounds*, 662 F.2d 975 (3d Cir. 1981). *But see* United States v. Fairfax County, 629 F.2d 932, 939–40, 23 FEP 485 (4th Cir. 1980) (approving district court's rejection of SMSA as measure of labor market, because it encompassed areas unlikely to produce applicants); *Bennett,* 295 F.3d at 697 (rejecting MSA as measure of labor market where plaintiff did not consider degree to which Chicago primary MSA residents would be interested in commuting to defendant's school district in Chicago suburbs); Gay v. Waiters & Dairy Lunchmen's Local 30, 489 F. Supp. 282, 302–03, 22 FEP 281 (N.D. Cal. 1980) (rejecting use of unmodified SMSA data because more precise measure of percentage of African Americans in relevant workforce is available for particular jobs at issue by weighting counties on basis of applicant flow data), *aff'd*, 694 F.2d 531, 29 FEP 1027 (9th Cir. 1982).

and county in which the employer is located,[267] an entire state,[268] and sometimes even the entire nation.[269] The geographic area normally will be at its smallest for lower-paying jobs and at its largest for high-level executive positions for which an applicant rationally might relocate.[270]

Some courts have found it useful, in determining the relevant geographic scope, to consider availability statistics drawn from areas defined by concentric circles around the employer's facility (weighted or unweighted)[271] or by looking at counties on

---

[267]*E.g.*, Thomas v. Washington County Sch. Bd., 915 F.2d 922, 926, 53 FEP 1754 (4th Cir. 1990) (county data); Detroit Police Officers Ass'n v. Young, 608 F.2d 671, 688, 20 FEP 1728 (6th Cir. 1979) (choosing city data over SMSA data because police department adopted legitimate residency requirement and police department serves city-only population); Sethy v. Alameda County Water Dist., 545 F.2d 1157, 1162–63, 13 FEP 845 (9th Cir. 1976) (county data); United States v. Iron Workers Local 86, 443 F.2d 544, 552, 3 FEP 496 (9th Cir. 1971) (city data); NAACP v. Town of Harrison, 749 F. Supp. 1327, 1331–32, 53 FEP 1499 (D.N.J. 1990) (four-county area), *aff'd*, 940 F.2d 792, 56 FEP 680 (3d Cir. 1991).

[268]*E.g.*, Griggs v. Duke Power Co., 401 U.S. 424, 430 n.6, 3 FEP 175 (1971) (state of North Carolina); Greenspan v. Automobile Club of Mich., 495 F. Supp. 1021, 1028, 22 FEP 184 (E.D. Mich. 1980) (state of Michigan); Lim v. Citizens Sav. & Loan Ass'n, 430 F. Supp. 802, 809, 15 FEP 113 (N.D. Cal. 1976) (state of California).

[269]Quigley v. Braniff Airways, Inc., 85 F.R.D. 74, 79–80, 23 FEP 1811 (N.D. Tex. 1979) (relevant geographic market is defined as entire nation because defendant recruits and hires nationally); Movement for Opportunity & Equality v. General Motors Corp., 18 FEP 557, 582 (S.D. Ind. 1978) (nationwide statistics used for jobs filled by recent college graduates), *aff'd*, 622 F.2d 1235, 22 FEP 1010 (7th Cir. 1980); *cf.* Kilgo v. Bowman Transp., Inc., 789 F.2d 859, 870, 40 FEP 1415 (11th Cir. 1986) (where trucking company hired throughout southeastern United States, nationwide area was appropriate, absent evidence that regional figures would differ significantly from nationwide figures).

[270]*See, e.g.*, Vittug v. Multistate Tax Comm'n, 88 F.3d 506, 71 FEP 1445 (7th Cir. 1996) (accepting employer's statistical comparison of percentage of auditors employed at defendant's firm with percentage of auditors in nationwide workforce).

[271]*Compare* EEOC v. O & G Spring & Wire Forms Specialty Co., 705 F. Supp. 400, 403–04, 406, 48 FEP 1540, *amended*, 52 FEP 1685 (N.D. Ill. 1988) (EEOC presented statistics on relevant labor market and availability as, alternatively, (1) one-mile ring surrounding employer's plant; (2) extent of minority operatives working for EEO-1 reporting employers within defendant employer's zip code and eight zip codes surrounding defendant; and (3) census data for employer's city, county, and SMSA; EEOC demonstrated in all situations significant statistical disparity; although court agreed in part with defendant's rebuttal and acknowledged that EEOC's data might be skewed; "no explanation [was] sufficient to overcome the inexorable zero employment of blacks ... from 1979 to 1985") *with* EEOC v. Andrew Corp., 49 FEP 804, 815–16 (N.D. Ill. 1989) (EEOC presented statistics on relevant labor market as population of all zip codes within 15- or 20-mile zone surrounding employer's

a weighted basis (the more proximate counties being given a heavier "weight").[272]

Weighted statistics are used to reflect more accurately the geographic areas in which applicants historically reside. In other words, it may be inaccurate to give the same weight to statistics from geographic areas far away from, or less accessible to, the employer's job site as statistics from more accessible geographic areas. *Gay v. Waiters & Dairy Lunchmen's Local 30*[273] provides a good example:

> Because the percentage of black residents varies among the counties in the SMSA, the percentage of blacks in the relevant labor market will vary depending on the geographic definition of the market. Dr. Pencavel chose to use data from the San Francisco/Oakland SMSA, weighted in accordance with the ratio of applications for all waiter positions received from within and without San Francisco, respectively. Of all waiter applications which were retained by the St. Francis and the Hilton, approximately 85 percent came from residents of the City and County of San Francisco, 13% came from other counties in the SMSA, and 2% came from outside the SMSA. Thus, Dr. Pencavel weighted the San Francisco data by a factor of 85/98 and the data from other counties in the SMSA by 13/98.[274]

Even where it is agreed that a proper analysis must focus on the employer's own workforce, differences in approach still may arise. Where an employer has multiple facilities, for example, should the employer's workforce statistics be confined to one facility, or should they reflect all of those facilities? The answer, according to some courts, depends on the similarity of the employment practices

---

plant; court rejected analysis for several reasons, including EEOC's failure to weight zip code data by proximity to employer's plant).

[272]*E.g.*, Markey v. Tenneco Oil Co., 635 F.2d 497, 500–01, 24 FEP 1675 (5th Cir. 1981) (using weighted parishes); *Movement for Opportunity & Equality*, 18 FEP at 582 (using weighted average of SMSA counties based on actual residences of employees holding lower-level positions). *See generally* Joseph L. Gastwirth & Sheldon E. Haber, *Defining the Labor Market for Equal Employment Standards*, 99 MONTHLY LAB. REV. 32 (Mar. 1976) (advocating weighted average approach using residences of current employees).

[273]489 F. Supp. 282, 302, 22 FEP 281 (N.D. Cal. 1980).

[274]*Id.* at 302; *see also* EEOC v. O & G Spring & Wire Forms Specialty Co., 38 F.3d 872, 65 FEP 1823 (7th Cir. 1994) (finding that series of statistical analyses, which used variety of pools based on slightly different geographic areas, provided "sufficiently accurate range against which the district court could evaluate [the employer's] hiring record").

at the various facilities, the interchange (or lack thereof) of employees among the facilities, or both.[275]

The U.S. Department of Labor has developed a complex methodology for analyzing geographic scope issues for contractors covered by Executive Order 11246. That methodology is extensively reviewed elsewhere.[276]

VI. THE PROPER TIME FRAME FOR STATISTICS

In *Hazelwood School District v. United States*,[277] the Supreme Court recognized the superiority of "time-frame" or "flow" statistics over static statistics.[278] Time frame statistics focus on employment

---

[275]*Compare* Regner v. City of Chi., 789 F.2d 534, 538, 40 FEP 1027 (7th Cir. 1986) (district court erred in considering workforce data from both main library and branch libraries where promotion of minorities may have been concentrated in branch libraries), Stastny v. Southern Bell Tel. & Tel. Co., 628 F.2d 267, 278–79, 23 FEP 665 (4th Cir. 1980) (court rejected plaintiff's statistics challenging statewide promotion practices where plaintiff made no showing of extent to which, if at all, overall disparities were paralleled in separate facilities; each facility had substantial autonomy in making its own employment decisions), Bradley v. Pizzaco of Neb., Inc., 51 FEP 811, 813–14 (D. Neb. 1989) (nationwide statistics do not apply just because franchisor operates throughout nation), *rev'd in part on other grounds*, 939 F.2d 610, 68 FEP 242 (8th Cir. 1991) *and* EEOC v. Sears, Roebuck & Co., 628 F. Supp. 1264, 1316, 39 FEP 1672 (N.D. Ill. 1986) (plaintiff erroneously performed its statistical analysis as though every applicant at one store simultaneously was applicant at every other store), *aff'd*, 839 F.2d 302, 45 FEP 1257 (7th Cir. 1988) *with* Paige v. California, 291 F.3d 1141, 1148–49, 88 FEP 1666 (9th Cir. 2002) (statistical analyses run on aggregated data may be highly relevant and more probative than subdivided data, depending on particular facts of case), Eldredge v. Carpenters 46 N. Cal., 833 F.2d 1334, 1339 n.7, 57 FEP 151 (9th Cir. 1987) (affirming use of data aggregated over time where challenged policy remained unchanged during that period), Kirkland v. New York State Dep't of Corr. Servs., 520 F.2d 420, 425, 11 FEP 38 (2d Cir. 1975) (rejecting defendant's effort to limit statistics to only one of its facilities; facilities shared hiring practices, and there was interfacility mobility of defendant's employees), Brown v. Marriott Corp., 33 FEP 550, 551 (N.D. Ga. 1983) (allowing plaintiff to discover promotion practices in divisions other than one at which he worked because defendant commonly transferred employees, and promotion patterns and practices at different divisions overlapped) *and* Haykel v. G.F.L. Furniture Leasing Co., 76 F.R.D. 386, 390–91, 22 FEP 507 (N.D. Ga. 1976) (ordering discovery regarding branch stores as well as defendant's main facility because main facility made certain decisions that affected the others). Discovery scope issues are covered more extensively in Chapter 33 (Discovery).

[276]*See generally* Chapter 38 (Federal Contractor Affirmative Action Compliance).

[277]433 U.S. 299, 15 FEP 1 (1977).

[278]*Id.* at 309.

decisions made during the relevant time period rather than the composition of the employer's workforce at a fixed point in time.[279] The *Hazelwood* Court recognized that snapshot statistics may reflect the effects of discrimination before the employer became subject to Title VII; they also may reflect the effects of decisions outside the limitations period. Therefore, time frame statistics limited to the relevant time period, the *Hazelwood* Court held, should be used.[280] Following *Hazelwood*, most courts prefer, if not require, time frame statistics.[281]

A plaintiff who offers only a static comparison yielding a gross disparity is at risk that the defendant will come forward with more particularized time frame statistics showing that decisions made during the relevant time period resulted in no significant adverse impact, either because there is not a sufficient disparity[282] or because

---

[279]For example, assume an employer with one job classification and 1,000 employees. Because of prior discrimination, no African Americans were employed as of January 1, 1990. Assume that African Americans constituted 20% of the applicant flow and relevant workforce in the relevant area. Assume that new management took over on January 1, 1990, abolishing the practice of hiring discrimination. There was a turnover of 50 employees each year thereafter, and 20% of the 50 employees hired each year (i.e., 10 employees) were African Americans. At the end of 1990, therefore, the company had 10 African-American employees; at the end of 1991, approximately 20 African-American employees; and at the end of 1992, approximately 30 African-American employees (assuming little or no turnover of the African-American employees). Further assume a discrimination charge in 1992 and immediate litigation thereon. Under a "static" analysis, the 20% availability figure would be compared to the 3% African-American composition of the workforce. Under a time frame analysis, the relevant time frame would be some portion of the 1990–92 period, and the 20% availability figure would be compared to the 20% African-American hiring figure.

[280]*Hazelwood*, 433 U.S. at 309.

[281]*E.g.*, Hill v. Seaboard Coast Line R.R., 885 F.2d 804, 812–13, 50 FEP 1751 (11th Cir. 1989) (evidence that focused on percentage of African Americans on fixed date failed to demonstrate that promotions during recent period had adverse impact on African Americans); Smith v. Western Elec. Co., 770 F.2d 520, 527–28, 38 FEP 1605 (5th Cir. 1985) (plaintiff's promotion and termination statistics were unpersuasive because they were based primarily on facts that occurred outside liability period); Eubanks v. Pickens-Bond Constr. Co., 635 F.2d 1341, 1348, 24 FEP 897 (8th Cir. 1980) (in promotion case, focus should not be on percentage of African Americans in job in question, but on number of African Americans selected for promotion during relevant time period). *But cf.* EEOC v. American Nat'l Bank, 652 F.2d 1176, 1189, 26 FEP 472 (4th Cir. 1981) ("gross statistical disparities in the static work force during the relevant period may alone constitute prima facie proof of the discriminatory practice").

[282]*E.g.*, Lieberman v. Gant, 630 F.2d 60, 69, 23 FEP 505 (2d Cir. 1980) (although statistics showed that 11.9% of members of English department were women,

too few decisions were made during the relevant time period to create an inference of discrimination.[283]

In *Hazelwood*, the focus of the "relevant time period" debate was on employment decisions that occurred before 1972, when Title VII was amended to cover public employers.[284] In most cases these days, the relevant time period will be the potential liability period, as limited by the applicable statute of limitations. One exception is for cases involving allegations of a "continuing violation"—a course of illegal conduct occurring over a period of time that can be considered one unlawful practice, such as the maintenance of a hostile work environment.[285] Additionally, pre-liability period evidence may be relevant even in instances where it cannot give rise to liability. In *United Air Lines, Inc. v. Evans*,[286] the Supreme Court explained that acts occurring before the charge-filing period are analytically the same as acts occurring before Title VII was passed, but nonetheless may be considered:

---

whereas women make up 31% of nation's Ph.D.s in English, any inference of discrimination was dispelled by proof that women filled two-thirds of new positions in English department during 6-year period before claim arose); Movement for Opportunity & Equality v. General Motors Corp., 622 F.2d 1235, 1244–45, 22 FEP 1010 (7th Cir. 1980) (prima facie case based on snapshot statistics successfully rebutted by time frame statistics). *But cf.* Parson v. Kaiser Aluminum & Chem. Corp., 575 F.2d 1374, 1386 n.27, 17 FEP 1272 (5th Cir. 1978) (defendant has burden of proving lack of turnover to refute use of static statistics).

[283]*E.g.*, Ste. Marie v. Eastern R.R. Ass'n, 650 F.2d 395, 402, 26 FEP 167 (2d Cir. 1981) (after positions that were filled prior to relevant time period were excluded, any discrepancy between expected figures and actual numbers lacked statistical significance because of small sample size); *see also* Teamsters v. United States, 431 U.S. 324, 341, 14 FEP 1514 (1977) (defendant can refute disparity in static statistics by showing that it did virtually no new hiring during relevant time period).

[284]*Hazelwood*, 433 U.S. at 309–10 n.15.

[285]*See* National R.R. Passenger Corp. v. Morgan, 536 U.S. 101, 115, 118, 122, 88 FEP 1601 (2002) (no continuing violation theory may apply in cases alleging discrete incident of discrimination, such as hiring, promotion, or discharge; all acts that are part of hostile work environment claim, however, constitute one unlawful practice, and employer may be liable for all acts that are part of claim, even those arising before limitations period, so long as employee files charge within 180 or 300 days of any act that is part of hostile work environment). In *Morgan*, the Court declined to address the applicability of the continuing violation theory to pattern-or-practice claims. *Id.* at 115 n.9. At least one post-*Morgan* decision has concluded that the continuing violation theory still applied in a case alleging a pattern-or-practice claim. *See* Dandy v. United Parcel Serv., Inc., 388 F.3d 263, 270, 94 FEP 1156 (7th Cir. 2004) (continuing violation theory applies in Title VII and § 1981 cases alleging pattern or practice of discrimination). *See generally* Chapter 26 (Timeliness).

[286]431 U.S. 553, 14 FEP 1510 (1977).

A discriminatory act which is not made the basis for a timely charge is the legal equivalent of a discriminatory act which occurred before the statute was passed. It may constitute relevant background evidence in a proceeding in which the status of a current practice is at issue, but separately considered, it is merely an unfortunate event in history which has no present legal consequences.[287]

Because Title VII requires that a charge of discrimination be filed within 180 (or 300) days[288] of the alleged unlawful employment practice, the relevant time frame is the period commencing 180 (or 300) days before the filing of an EEOC charge upon which the Title VII litigation is based,[289] unless the case involves a continuing violation.[290] For claims under the Reconstruction-era Civil Rights Acts,[291] the relevant time frame is the period before the filing

---

[287]*Id.* at 558.

[288]42 U.S.C. § 2000e-5(e). *See generally* Chapter 26 (Timeliness).

[289]*Evans*, 431 U.S. at 558 (limiting hiring and promotion statistics to statutory period before filing charge); Hill v. Seaboard Coast Line R.R., 885 F.2d 804, 812, 50 FEP 1751 (11th Cir. 1989) (clearly no adverse impact in promotions made within 6-month period preceding filing of EEOC charge); EEOC v. Sears, Roebuck & Co., 839 F.2d 302, 315, 45 FEP 1257 (7th Cir. 1988) (relevant time period was based on EEOC commissioner charge); Smith v. Western Elec. Co., 770 F.2d 520, 528, 38 FEP 1605 (5th Cir. 1985) (plaintiffs' statistical study failed to "isolate and evaluate" terminations that occurred during liability period); Ste. Marie v. Eastern R.R. Ass'n, 650 F.2d 395, 401–02, 26 FEP 167 (2d Cir. 1981) (statistics purporting to demonstrate discrimination in promotion must exclude those positions that were filled more than 180 days before filing of plaintiff's EEOC charge); Patterson v. American Tobacco Co., 634 F.2d 744, 752 n.10, 24 FEP 531 (4th Cir. 1980) (en banc) (relevant time period commenced no earlier than effective date of Act, and "[u]nder *Evans*, of course, the beginning of the relevant time period may be at later times set by limitation periods for charging violations"), *vacated on other grounds*, 456 U.S. 63, 28 FEP 713 (1982); Movement for Opportunity & Equality v. General Motors Corp., 622 F.2d 1235, 1245, 22 FEP 1010 (7th Cir. 1980) (employment decisions made more than 300 days before filing of EEOC charge should be excluded from statistical comparison); Pouncy v. Prudential Ins. Co., 499 F. Supp. 427, 444, 23 FEP 1349 (S.D. Tex. 1980) (relevant statistics for purposes of analyzing adverse impact claims are those that reflect defendant's personnel actions taken during relevant time period: (1) statute of limitations period for claims under § 1981, and (2) 180 days before filing of EEOC charge), *aff'd*, 668 F.2d 795, 28 FEP 121 (5th Cir. 1982).

[290]Paige v. California, 291 F.3d 1141, 1149, 88 FEP 1666 (9th Cir. 2002) (plaintiffs who alleged continuing violation could use data taken from employer's eligibility lists that expired before start of liability period; pre-*Morgan* decision); Rendon v. AT & T Techs., 883 F.2d 388, 395–96, 50 FEP 1587 (5th Cir. 1989) (recognizing that, in continuing violation case, evidence prior to relevant period is admissible; pre-*Morgan* decision).

[291]42 U.S.C. §§ 1981, 1983, 1985(3). *See generally* Chapter 35 (The Civil Rights Acts of 1866 and 1871).

of the lawsuit that corresponds to the applicable statute of limitations.[292] With the passage of 28 U.S.C. § 1658, Congress enacted a four-year catch-all statute of limitations for actions arising under federal statutes enacted after December 1, 1990, that do not contain their own specific statute of limitations. In *Jones v. R.R. Donnelly & Sons Co.*,[293] the Supreme Court concluded that § 1981 actions brought pursuant to the amendments to § 1981 contained in the Civil Rights Act of 1991 were encompassed by § 1658.[294] For causes of action brought under these statutes but not encompassed by § 1658, however, the applicable statute of limitations remains the most analogous state limitations period.[295] Furthermore, as explained earlier, statistical proof relating to earlier time periods in some circumstances may be admissible as "background evidence," which may arguably constitute circumstantial evidence of violations occurring within the relevant time period.[296]

---

[292]*See* Wilson v. Garcia, 471 U.S. 261, 275–76 (1985) (in case preceding passage of 28 U.S.C. § 1658, statute of limitations for § 1983 actions is most analogous state limitations period for state in which lawsuit was filed; here that was limitations period for tort actions for recovery of personal injuries); Johnson v. Railway Express Agency, Inc., 421 U.S. 454, 462, 10 FEP 817 (1975) ("Since there is no specifically stated or otherwise relevant federal statute of limitations for a cause of action under § 1981, the controlling period would ordinarily be the most appropriate one provided by state law."); *Movement for Opportunity & Equality*, 622 F.2d at 1245 (relevant time period for statistical comparison should not include employment decisions made prior to applicable statute of limitations under § 1981); Davis v. Los Angeles County, 566 F.2d 1334, 1336–37, 16 FEP 396 (9th Cir. 1977) (same; §§ 1981, 1983), *vacated for mootness*, 440 U.S. 625, 19 FEP 282 (1979). *See generally* Chapter 26 (Timeliness).

[293]541 U.S. 369 (2004).

[294]*Id.* at 382.

[295]*Id.* at 371.

[296]Hazelwood Sch. Dist. v. United States, 433 U.S. 299, 309 n.15, 15 FEP 1 (1977) (statistics relating to earlier time period "might in some circumstances" be relevant, especially if little change had been made in employment practices being challenged); United Air Lines, Inc. v. Evans, 431 U.S. 553, 558, 14 FEP 1510 (1977) (discriminatory act not made basis for timely charge "may constitute relevant background evidence in a proceeding in which the status of a current practice is at issue"); NAACP v. City of Mansfield, 866 F.2d 162, 168 n.4, 48 FEP 1444 (6th Cir. 1989) (evidence of past hiring practices admissible, regardless of whether it is outside statute of limitations period, so long as it is relevant); Lewis v. Bloomsburg Mills, Inc., 773 F.2d 561, 568 n.12, 38 FEP 1692, *amended*, 40 FEP 1615 (4th Cir. 1985) (precharge period data relevant "for the limited purpose of inferring from it the continuation of the practice into the charge period"); Coates v. Johnson & Johnson, 756 F.2d 524, 540, 37 FEP 467 (7th Cir. 1985) (plaintiff's statistical evidence, which included data prior to class liability cutoff date, not necessarily unreliable, though

A second time frame issue concerns the determination of the most recent date for which statistics are deemed acceptable. Although many courts have allowed statistics that cover periods after suit was filed, and even up to the time of trial, without discussing the issue,[297] some courts have rejected the introduction of statistics covering the period following the filing of the suit. They reason that such statistics will be distorted by changes in the employment process brought about by the filing of suit and therefore offer little probative value on the issue of whether the defendant discriminated at the time that the cause of action arose.[298] Also, one district court has ruled that it may consider the plaintiff's statistical analysis for a period of years in which no historical data are

---

less probative than data focusing on practices after liability cutoff date); Grant v. Bethlehem Steel Corp., 635 F.2d 1007, 1017–18, 24 FEP 798 (2d Cir. 1980) (evidence of long history of discrimination against African Americans in hiring of iron workers can support inference of discrimination during relevant time period). *But see* Forman v. Small, 271 F.3d 285, 294, 87 FEP 526, 533 (D.C. Cir. 2001) (data for period prior to plaintiff's denial of promotion not relevant because no evidence supports inference that statistical trends continued to year of denial of promotion).

[297]*E.g.*, Croker v. Boeing Co., 437 F. Supp. 1138, 1153–65, 15 FEP 165 (E.D. Pa. 1977), *aff'd*, 662 F.2d 975, 26 FEP 1569 (3d Cir. 1981).

[298]*See, e.g.*, Teamsters v. United States, 431 U.S. 324, 341–42, 14 FEP 1514 (1977) (minority hiring after 1971 not relevant to finding of liability for prior period); Hameed v. Iron Workers Local 396, 637 F.2d 506, 512 n.7, 24 FEP 352 (8th Cir. 1980) (statistics drawn from period following defendant's change in its selection policies not relevant to issue of whether defendant's earlier policies violated Title VII); Johnson v. Uncle Ben's, Inc., 628 F.2d 419, 422–23, 24 FEP 1 (5th Cir. 1980) (ascribing no affirmative legal significance to defendant's increase in number of Mexican American employees after filing of suit), *vacated and remanded on other grounds*, 451 U.S. 902, 25 FEP 737 (1981); Donnell v. General Motors Corp., 576 F.2d 1292, 1298 n.11, 17 FEP 712 (8th Cir. 1978) ("subsequent employment practices may bear upon the remedy, but they are not relevant to the determination of whether the employer had previously violated Title VII"); Rich v. Martin Marietta Corp., 522 F.2d 333, 346, 11 FEP 211 (10th Cir. 1975) (rejecting post-complaint statistics because they do not constitute cogent evidence of any lack of pre-filing discrimination; indeed, if taken into account at all, statistics might tend to show existence of prior discrimination in effort to repair harm after discovery); Rice v. Gates Rubber Co., 521 F.2d 782, 784–85, 11 FEP 986 (6th Cir. 1975) (refusing to consider increase in percentage of minorities after filing of charge or lawsuit); Parham v. Southwestern Bell Tel. Co., 433 F.2d 421, 425, 2 FEP 1017 (8th Cir. 1970) ("The crucial issue in a lawsuit of this kind is whether the plaintiff establishes hiring bias at the time of his rejection for employment and subsequent complaint to the EEOC, not the employment practices utilized two years later."); Patterson v. Youngstown Sheet & Tube Co., 440 F. Supp. 409, 413, 22 FEP 1289 (N.D. Ind. 1977) (rejecting employer's statistics, which included the period up to trial, because they concealed pre-charge discrimination), *aff'd*, 659 F.2d 736, 28 FEP 1434 (7th Cir. 1981).

available if such data were unavailable because the employer failed to keep them.[299]

VII. THE PROPER WEIGHT TO BE GIVEN STATISTICAL PROOF

A. Reliability Standards

Raw statistics, unaccompanied by expert analysis of their relationship to the disputed issue, generally are found to be irrelevant.[300] Assuming that the analysis properly accounts for other legitimate nondiscriminatory factors, the reliability of inferences from statistics is directly dependent on two factors: (1) the degree of the disparity, and (2) the sample size.

B. Degree of the Disparity

For a statistic to have probative value so that an inference of discrimination can be drawn, the court must conclude that the statistic did not result from mere chance—e.g., that there is a reasonably high level of probability that a disparity between African Americans and whites resulted from discrimination rather than a series of random occurrences.[301] Because chance never can be totally ruled out as the cause of any numerical disparity, the question becomes what level of risk of error courts are willing to run

---

[299]Sims v. Montgomery County Comm'n, 873 F. Supp. 585, 601 (M.D. Ala. 1994) (court focused on entire period of decree, in effect since 1973, where defendant only produced data from 1981 through 1988, not data from 1973 through 1980, which court opined "would more than likely have been very incriminating").

[300]E.g., Williams v. Cerberonics, Inc., 871 F.2d 452, 455 n.1, 49 FEP 695 (4th Cir. 1989) (affirming trial court's exclusion of evidence; plaintiffs sought to introduce statistical evidence without expert testimony about how statistics were compiled in relation to employees' claims); Frazier v. Consolidated Rail Corp., 851 F.2d 1447, 1451–52, 47 FEP 720 (D.C. Cir. 1988) (presentation of raw statistics without expert or other supporting evidence of available workforce meaningless).

[301]Rivera v. City of Wichita Falls, 665 F.2d 531, 545, 27 FEP 1352 (5th Cir. 1982) ("It is axiomatic that statistical significance may be attributed to an observed discrepancy only upon reduction to an acceptable level of the possibility that such a variation would, in the normal course of events, reasonably be expected to occur simply by random chance.").

in drawing inferences from statistics. Put differently, the question is: How statistically significant[302] must a disparity be before the court will infer that it is the result of discrimination?[303]

If the statistics are finely tuned (accounting for relevant qualifications, the relevant geographic scope, and the proper time frame), the parties most commonly argue for the applicability of any of at least three possible tests of statistical significance: (1) the 0.05 level of statistical significance; (2) the *Hazelwood* "two or three standard deviations" test; or (3) for selection rate comparisons only, the EEOC's four-fifths (80 percent) rule.

The 0.05 level of statistical significance means that the probability of the statistical disparity occurring by chance is 5 percent, or 1 chance in 20. It has become a convention in the social sciences to accept, as statistically significant, values that have a probability of occurring by chance of 5 percent or less and to

---

[302]The role of a test of statistical significance has been explained as follows:

[T]he statistical test can say nothing about causation. The test does, however, provide relevant evidence on which an inference about causation can properly be based. For, if the observed result would occur by chance only 1 time out of 100 in a random system, the occurrence of the result observed in the case before the court would have to be considered a rare event (unless the system were not random), thereby suggesting chance was not the cause. And if bias is the only other plausible explanation for the result, one's belief that the defendant intentionally discriminated will be strengthened.

[E]ven if such a result would happen only 1 out of 100 times in a purely random system, a statistical test cannot measure the likelihood that a particular outcome was or was not a chance result. The test of significance states the likelihood of seeing evidence of the type observed over the long run, if the system were effectively blind to [any form of bias such as] color or sex. It simply does not follow that the chances are 99 out of 100 that the result in the instant case was not a chance result, let alone intentionally caused.

DAVID C. BALDUS & JAMES W.L. COLE, STATISTICAL PROOF OF DISCRIMINATION § 9.42, at 320–21 (1980).

[303]*See* Wards Cove Packing Co. v. Atonio, 490 U.S. 642, 655, 49 FEP 1519 (1989) ("Since the statistical disparity relied on by the Court of Appeals did not suffice to make out a prima facie case, any inquiry by us into whether the specific challenged employment practices of petitioners caused that disparity is pretermitted . . . ."); Taylor v. Teletype Corp., 648 F.2d 1129, 1133, 26 FEP 124 (8th Cir. 1981) (if disparity is established as statistically significant and race is only evident variable separating two groups, court may infer that racial considerations are responsible for results); MacRae v. McCormick, 458 F. Supp. 970, 980, 21 FEP 100 (D.D.C. 1978) (evidence of disparity without evidence bearing on statistical significance is "of little probative value"), *aff'd mem.*, 69 FEP 320 (D.C. Cir. 1979).

reject those that fail the 5 percent test.[304] Many courts have cited with approval this conventional standard,[305] but others have allowed some flexibility in close cases.[306] Some courts have suggested that a "two-tailed" test[307] be used instead of a "one-tailed" test;[308] the

---

[304]*See, e.g.*, Contreras v. City of L.A., 656 F.2d 1267, 1273 n.3, 25 FEP 866, *amended*, 29 FEP 1045 (9th Cir. 1981) (0.05 level of statistical significance generally recognized as point at which statisticians draw conclusions from statistical data).

[305]*E.g.*, Albemarle Paper Co. v. Moody, 422 U.S. 405, 430, 437, 10 FEP 1181 (1975) (referencing testimony and charts of statistical experts analyzing disparity under 0.05 and 0.01 levels of statistical confidence); Palmer v. Shultz, 815 F.2d 84, 96, 43 FEP 452 (D.C. Cir. 1987) (0.05 significance level sufficient to support inference of discrimination); McBride v. Seidman, 49 FEP 1333, 1340 (D.D.C. 1989) (using 0.05 significance test). *See generally* DAVID C. BALDUS & JAMES W.L. COLE, STATISTICAL PROOF OF DISCRIMINATION § 9.221, at 308 n.36 (1980); NORMAN H. NIE ET AL., STATISTICAL PACKAGE FOR THE SOCIAL SCIENCES (2d ed. 1975); Marcy M. Hallock, *The Numbers Game—The Use and Misuse of Statistics in Civil Rights Litigation*, 23 VILL. L. REV. 5, 13 (1977–78); Note, *Beyond the Prima Facie Case in Employment Discrimination Law: Statistical Proof and Rebuttal*, 89 HARV. L. REV. 387, 400 & n.58 (1975).

[306]*E.g.*, Kadas v. MCT Systemwide Corp., 255 F.3d 359, 362, 85 FEP 1720 (7th Cir. 2001) (rejecting rigid adherence to 5% significance test, labeling it "arbitrary," and explaining that "litigation generally is not fussy about evidence; much eyewitness and other nonquantitive evidence is subject to significant possibility of error, yet no effort is made to exclude it if it doesn't satisfy some counterpart to the 5 percent significance test"); United States v. Georgia Power Co., 474 F.2d 906, 915, 5 FEP 587 (5th Cir. 1973) (5% level is "a desirable goal and not a prerequisite"); Reynolds v. Sheet Metal Workers Local 102, 498 F. Supp. 952, 967, 24 FEP 648 (D.D.C. 1980) (significance at 5% level is conventional standard, but 6% or more may be sufficient under certain circumstances), *aff'd*, 702 F.2d 221, 25 FEP 837 (D.C. Cir. 1981); Pennsylvania v. Rizzo, 466 F. Supp. 1219, 1231, 20 FEP 130 (E.D. Pa. 1979) (where significance level is near 5%, other evidence, statistical and nonstatistical, should be considered); *cf.* Watkins v. Scott Paper Co., 530 F.2d 1159, 1187 n.40, 12 FEP 1191 (5th Cir. 1976) (10% level of significance rather than statisticians' more conventional and more stringent 5% level "*might*" be acceptable" in context of validity of job tests under Title VII).

[307]A two-tailed test refers to both sides of the bell curve; a one-tailed test to just one side of it. Thus, a two-tailed test looks for disparity in either direction. For example, in testing a hypothesis concerning the representation of women in a particular company, a two-tailed test would consider the possibility that women are overrepresented as well as the possibility that they are underrepresented. Here, the 5% significance level, rather than comprising just one of the tails of the bell curve, must comprise both. This has the effect of requiring a greater disparity between the expected number of women in the workforce and the actual number of women in the workforce before one concludes that discrimination has taken place. *See* ROBERT N. GOLDMAN & JOEL S. WEINBERG, STATISTICS, AN INTRODUCTION 353–55 (1985).

[308]*See, e.g., Palmer*, 815 F.2d at 92–93 (two-tailed test more appropriate where, as here, "statistically significant deviations in either direction from an equality in selection rates would constitute a prima facie case of unlawful discrimination"; one group of employees, for example, might view position in question as desirable, but another might view it as undesirable—employer then is subject to liability if its

former decreases the likelihood that a statistically significant disparity will be found.[309]

A close cousin to the 0.05 level of statistical significance is the two- or three-standard-deviations test,[310] which the Supreme Court first applied in an employment discrimination case in *Hazelwood School District v. United States*.[311] In *Hazelwood*, the Court held that the presence of an adverse impact of greater than "two or three" standard deviations between the expected number of the protected class in a given pool and the actual number in the pool "would undercut the hypothesis that decisions were being made randomly with respect to race."[312]

The difference between two or three standard deviations can be meaningful.[313] The two-standard-deviations test roughly is comparable

---

selection rate of protected group is either significantly overinclusive or significantly underinclusive); *cf.* EEOC v. Federal Reserve Bank, 698 F.2d 633, 655–56, 30 FEP 1137 (4th Cir. 1983) (noting criticisms of one-tailed test as way for plaintiffs to "beef up" their statistics, but not indicating general preference for either test), *rev'd on other grounds sub nom.* Cooper v. Federal Reserve Bank, 467 U.S. 867, 35 FEP 1 (1984); Stender v. Lucky Stores, Inc., 803 F. Supp. 259, 323, 62 FEP 11 (N.D. Cal. 1992) ("Two-tailed tests are appropriate when there is a possibility of both overselection and underselection in the populations that are being computed. One-tailed tests are most appropriate when one population is consistently overselected over another"; not deciding which test is most appropriate.). *But see* Brunet v. City of Columbus, 642 F. Supp. 1214, 1230, 42 FEP 1846 (S.D. Ohio 1986) ("Although defendants question this use of a one-tailed test, the Court concludes that it is appropriate where, as here, the raw numbers indicate that women are selected at a lesser rate than men."), *appeal dismissed*, 826 F.2d 1062 (6th Cir. 1987).

[309]*See, e.g.*, ROBERT N. GOLDMAN & JOEL S. WEINBERG, STATISTICS, AN INTRODUCTION, at 353–55 (1985).

[310]A standard deviation analysis tests the hypothesis that underrepresentation of a protected group in any sample made up of a protected and nonprotected group (binomial distribution) might be attributable to normal fluctuations of chance rather than to discrimination (or to other factors not accounted for in the analysis). The difference between the actual number of the protected group in such a sample and the number that would be expected in a perfectly proportional process of selection from the appropriate pool then can be expressed in terms of standard deviations. Standard deviations can be expressed in terms of the mathematical probability that chance is the cause of the disparities measured. As the number of standard deviations increases, the probability of chance as the cause of underrepresentation diminishes. The standard deviation test is based on two factors: (1) the extent of departure from what would be expected to be the norm, and (2) the sample size. The larger the sample size, the lower the difference must be to equal a standard deviation.

[311]433 U.S. 299, 308–11 & nn.14 & 17, 15 FEP 1 (1977). *See generally* Chapter 4 (Application of Adverse Impact to Employment Decisions).

[312]*Id.* at 311 n.17.

[313]*See* Adams v. Ameritech Servs., Inc., 231 F.3d 414, 424, 84 FEP 178 (7th Cir. 2000) (commenting that "[t]wo standard deviations is normally enough to show

to the 0.05 level of statistical confidence.[314] The three-standard-deviations test roughly corresponds to a 0.01 level of statistical confidence.[315] Courts have denied summary judgment for defendants where the plaintiffs' reliable statistical analyses revealed two or more standard deviations.[316]

More controversial is the four-fifths (or 80 percent) "rule of thumb" set forth in the EEOC's Uniform Guidelines on Employee Selection Procedures, under which adverse impact is presumed if the selection rate for the protected group in question is less than four-fifths, or 80 percent, of the selection rate for the most favored group.[317]

---

that it is extremely unlikely . . . that the disparity is due to chance, giving rise to a reasonable inference that the hiring was not race neutral; the more standard deviations away, the less likely the factor in question played no role in the decisionmaking process"). *But see* Rudebusch v. Hughes, 313 F.3d 506, 515, 90 FEP 865 (9th Cir. 2002) (noting that standard deviations of 1.3 and 2.46 were not enough to make inference of discrimination without other evidence) (citing Gay v. Waiters & Dairy Lunchmen's Local 30, 694 F.2d 531, 551, 30 FEP 605, (9th Cir. 1982)).

[314]To be more precise, the 0.05 level of statistical confidence equates with 1.96 standard deviations using a two-tailed test. Palmer v. Shultz, 815 F.2d 84, 92, 43 FEP 452 (D.C. Cir. 1987).

[315]In other words, it roughly equates to no more than one chance in a hundred that the observed disparity occurred by chance. DAVID C. BALDUS & JAMES W.L. COLE, STATISTICAL PROOF OF DISCRIMINATION § 9.03, at 297 (1980).

[316]Malave v. Potter, 320 F.3d 321, 327, 91 FEP 101 (2d Cir. 2003) (vacating summary judgment for employer and remanding for consideration of whether plaintiff can show statistically significant disparity of at least two standard deviations); *Adams*, 231 F.3d 424–26 (reversing summary judgment for defendants, applying rule that two standard deviations ordinarily suffice to support inference of discriminatory treatment); Anderson v. Zubieta, 180 F.3d 329, 339–40, 80 FEP 765 (D.C. Cir. 1999) (same); Smith v. Xerox Corp., 196 F.3d 358, 366, 81 FEP 343 (3d Cir. 1999) (recognizing rule that two standard deviations will ordinarily suffice for inference of discrimination) (citing Ottaviani v. State Univ. of N.Y., 875 F.2d 365, 371–72 (2d Cir. 1989)); Peightal v. Metropolitan Dade County, 26 F.3d 1545, 1555–56, 71 FEP 1107 (11th Cir. 1994) (finding that there was strong evidence of discrimination where difference between expected and actual percentage of Hispanics in fire department was 17.6 standard deviations); Sperling v. Hoffman-La Roche, Inc., 924 F. Supp. 1346, 1383, 72 FEP 1401 (D.N.J. 1996) (finding that reasonable jury could find statistics persuasive where standard deviation was in 4 to 5 range); Butler v. Home Depot, Inc., 1997 WL 605754 (N.D. Cal. Aug. 29, 1997) (denying summary judgment based on statistical analyses showing greater than two standard deviations). *But see* Scott v. Goodyear Tire & Rubber Co., 160 F.3d 1121, 1125, 1129, 78 FEP 705 (6th Cir. 1998) (reversing grant of summary judgment for defendant based on, inter alia, plaintiff's statistical evidence showing with "marginal" statistical significance membership in protected class correlated to adverse treatment in employment); Kadas v. MCI Systemhouse Corp., 255 F.3d 359, 362–63, 85 FEP 1720 (7th Cir. 2001) (statistical evidence admissible in trying to show discrimination even if it is not significant at 5% significance level).

[317]29 C.F.R. § 1607.4(D) (2005).

The 80 percent rule has received mixed acceptance by the courts[318] and has been sharply criticized by commentators.[319] Courts are particularly likely to reject the 80 percent rule when the sample size is small[320] or the selection rate of the favored group is low.[321] Some courts, though, have found persuasive a defendant's use of the 80 percent rule to disprove appreciable adverse impact.[322]

---

[318]*Compare* Isabel v. City of Memphis, 404 F.3d 404, 412–13, 95 FEP 801 (6th Cir. 2005) ("we are grateful for statistics beyond the four-fifths rule analysis because we prefer to look to the sum of statistical evidence to make a decision in these kinds of cases") *and* Clady v. Los Angeles County, 770 F.2d 1421, 1428, 38 FEP 1575 (9th Cir. 1985) (rejecting 80% test; Uniform Guidelines do not have force of law) *with* Boston Police Superior Officers Fed'n v. City of Boston, 147 F.3d 13, 21–23, 91 FEP 803 (1st Cir. 1998) (quoting Sheet Metal Workers Local 28 v. EEOC, 478 U.S. 421, 478, 41 FEP 107 (1986) (plurality opinion)) *and* Smith, 196 F.3d at 365 (applying four-fifths rule to assess disparate impact). *See generally* Chapter 4 (Application of Adverse Impact to Employment Decisions).

[319]*E.g.*, Elaine W. Shoben, *Differential Pass-Fail Rates in Employment Testing: Statistical Proof Under Title VII*, 91 HARV. L. REV. 793, 805–11 (1978) (criticizing four-fifths rule for failing to take into account differences in sample size and magnitude of differences in pass rates, comparing only ratios).

[320]*See* Mems v. City of St. Paul, 224 F.3d 73, 740–41, 81 FEP 962 (8th Cir. 2000) (refusing to apply 80% rule to sample size too small to be statistically significant); NAACP v. City of Mansfield, 866 F.2d 162, 168, 48 FEP 1444 (6th Cir. 1989) ("[T]his court has been cautious about giving too much weight to 'four-fifths' computations where the sample base is of less than significant proportions."); Frazier v. Consolidated Rail Corp., 851 F.2d 1447, 1451, 47 FEP 720 (D.C. Cir. 1988) (approving district court's rejection of 80% rule where sample size was small); Black v. City of Akron, 831 F.2d 131, 134, 44 FEP 1858 (6th Cir. 1987) ("[I]f [the employer] chooses 3 blacks out of 5 applicants and 4 whites out of 5 applicants, [the 80% rule is not met, even though] both common sense and rigorous statistical analysis tell us that it is much more likely that mere chance is the controlling factor."); Fudge v. City of Providence Fire Dep't, 766 F.2d 650, 658, 659 & n.10, 38 FEP 648 (1st Cir. 1985) (four-fifths rule not accurate test of adverse impact when sample size is small); Nash v. Jacksonville, 895 F. Supp. 1536, 1542–43 (M.D. Fla. 1995) (where only two African-American candidates were eligible for promotion, application of 80% rule would not be statistically significant), *aff'd*, 85 F.3d 643 (11th Cir. 1996). *But see* Pietras v. Board of Fire Comm'rs, 180 F.3d 468, 474, 80 FEP 307 (2d Cir. 1999) (sample size of seven not too small for application of 80% rule when corroborated with other evidence of gender bias).

[321]For example, if the selection rate for whites is 4%, the 80% rule would suggest adverse impact even if the selection rate for African Americans was 3%. The First Circuit has held that a probability analysis (like the standard deviation analysis of *Castaneda*), rather than a mere comparison of selection rates, should be used in such cases: "Where a plaintiff relies exclusively on a narrow base of data, . . . it is crucial for the court to consider the possibility that chance could account for the observed disparity." *Fudge*, 766 F.2d at 658.

[322]*See, e.g.*, Cox v. City of Chi., 868 F.2d 217, 221–22, 48 FEP 1674 (7th Cir. 1989) (eligibility rate for minority persons was 83% of that of whites); Thompson v. Mississippi State Pers. Bd., 674 F. Supp. 198, 206, 45 FEP 530 (N.D. Miss. 1987)

Other statistical tests also have been used on occasion to determine whether a disparity is statistically significant and what inferences should be drawn from such disparity.[323]

A virtue of tests of statistical significance, as opposed to the 80 percent rule's raw-numbers approach, is that significance tests take into account the number of persons in question—the "sample size"—and produce results more reliable than raw numbers alone. The degree of the observed disparity is not the same as the probability level or number of standard deviations. It is possible for a small disparity to be statistically significant if the sample size is very large, just as it is possible for a large disparity not to be statistically significant if the sample size is small. Some courts, though, simply have ruled, without statistical analysis, that a particular disparity was or was not "substantial."[324]

C. Size of the Statistical Sample

Courts have recognized that statistical evidence often is unreliable when the sample size is small.[325] Courts tend to characterize

---

(80% rule test proved there was no adverse impact). *But cf.* Waisome v. Port Auth., 948 F.2d 1370, 1378–80, 57 FEP 567 (2d Cir. 1991) (although defendant showed that African Americans passed its scored test at rate greater than 80% that of whites, their passing scores were bunched at lower levels, and overall selection rate of African Americans—based on composite of test and interview scores—was 8%, compared to 14% of whites; summary judgment should not have been granted to defendant); Sanchez v. City of Santa Ana, 928 F. Supp. 1494, 1501–02 (C.D. Cal. 1995) (employer who lowered passing score on employment test to ensure compliance with 80% rule manipulated rule in a way not consistent with Title VII's purpose of ensuring equal opportunity in employment).

[323]*See, e.g.,* Bernard v. Gulf Oil Corp., 890 F.2d 735, 744, 51 FEP 1126 (5th Cir. 1989) ("cluster analysis" used to determine correlation coefficient between test scores and job performance); Markey v. Tenneco Oil Co., 439 F. Supp. 219, 233 & n.59, 17 FEP 1807 (E.D. La. 1977) ("test of proportions" considered), *rev'd on other grounds,* 635 F.2d 497, 24 FEP 1675 (5th Cir. 1981); Mistretta v. Sandia Corp., 15 FEP 1690, 1705 (D.N.M. 1977) (age discrimination case where court used plaintiff's sophisticated Kolmogorov-Smirnov test). *See generally* DAVID C. BALDUS & JAMES W.L. COLE, STATISTICAL PROOF OF DISCRIMINATION chs. 9 & 9A (1980 & Supp. 1981).

[324]*Compare* Griggs v. Duke Power Co., 401 U.S. 424, 430–31 & n.6, 3 FEP 175 (1971) (implying that disparity between whites with high school diplomas (34%) and African Americans with such diplomas (12%) in North Carolina was substantial, without speaking of statistical significance at all) *with Waisome,* 948 F.2d at 1376 (disregarding finding of statistical significance—2.68 standard deviations—where African-American pass rate was 87% of white pass rate and finding of significance would have been removed if two additional African Americans had passed examination). *See generally* Chapter 3 (Adverse Impact).

[325]*See, e.g., Mems,* 224 F.3d at 740–41 (refusing to find discrimination based on sample of three to seven, which court concluded was too small to be statistically

statistical evidence based on small samples as nothing more than anecdotal evidence.[326] Where the disparity is great or the plaintiff presents other evidence of discrimination, however, some courts have held that even smaller sample sizes can give rise to significant statistical results.[327] If the sample size is marginal, sophisticated statistical techniques can be attempted to improve the level

---

significant); Pollis v. New Sch. for Soc. Research, 132 F.2d 115, 121, 76 FEP 173 (2d Cir. 1997) (refusing to draw inferences from statistical analysis using sample size of five employees, finding that the "smaller the sample, the greater the likelihood that an observed pattern is attributable to other factors and accordingly less persuasive the inferences of discrimination to be drawn from it"); Tinker v. Sears, Roebuck & Co., 127 F.3d 519, 524, 75 FEP 380 (6th Cir. 1997) (holding sample of 13 too small); Shutt v. Sandoz Crop Prot. Corp., 944 F.2d 1431, 1432–34, 57 FEP 144 (9th Cir. 1991) (statistics showing that five out of six terminated persons from smaller company after merger were over age 40 did not show discrimination, because sample size was too small; if one looked at all terminated employees from both companies, statistical disparity was not compelling); Frazier, 851 F.2d at 1451 (district court properly rejected application of four-fifths rule to sample of 11 women and 70 African Americans); Gillespie v. Wisconsin, 771 F.2d 1035, 1044, 38 FEP 1487 (7th Cir. 1985) ("the number of employees taking the pretest was so small that a correlation between the test scores and job performance would be statistically meaningless"); Contreras v. City of L.A., 656 F.2d 1267, 1273 n.4, 25 FEP 866, amended, 29 FEP 1045 (9th Cir. 1981) ("Statistics are not trustworthy when minor numerical variations produce significant percentage fluctuations."); Williams v. Tallahassee Motors, Inc., 607 F.2d 689, 693, 21 FEP 626 (5th Cir. 1979) ("While there is no numerical cutoff point for statistical significance, the smaller the sample size, the greater the likelihood that the underrepresentation reflects chance rather than discriminatory practices."); Bridgeport Guardians, Inc. v. Bridgeport Civil Serv. Comm'n, 482 F.2d 1333, 1338–39, 5 FEP 1344 (2d Cir. 1973) (statistics had no probative value where only 20 nonwhites out of pool of over 200 had taken test being challenged); see also Teamsters v. United States, 431 U.S. 324, 339, 340 & n.20, 14 FEP 1514 (1977) ("Considerations such as small sample size may, of course, detract from the value of such [statistical] evidence."); Mayor of Phila. v. Educational Equality League, 415 U.S. 605, 620–21 (1974) (same).

[326]See Kuhn v. Ball State Univ., 78 F.3d 330, 332, 70 FEP 449 (7th Cir. 1996); see also Disher v. Vassar Coll., 70 F.3d 1420, 1442–47, 70 FEP 1155 (2d Cir. 1995) (statistical evidence rejected in part because it treated "anecdotes as statistics").

[327]See, e.g., EEOC v. Steamship Clerks Local 1066, 48 F.3d 594, 67 FEP 629 (1st Cir. 1995) (small sample size did not invalidate statistical evidence where there was evidence that all 36 new union members who were admitted in 6-year period were white and related to existing members); Thomas v. Washington County Sch. Bd., 915 F.2d 922, 925–26, 53 FEP 1754 (4th Cir. 1990) (teaching applicant, despite inadequacy of statistical database, proved her case by showing at least 46 examples of nepotism); McAlester v. United Air Lines, Inc., 851 F.2d 1249, 1258, 47 FEP 512 (10th Cir. 1988) (district court did not abuse its discretion in finding that sample of 63 terminations in employer's facility was probative; sample of eight terminations in ramp service was probative when it could be compared with whole facility); EEOC v. American Nat'l Bank, 652 F.2d 1176, 1194, 26 FEP 472 (4th Cir. 1981) (where charge of discrimination runs to several categories of differently qualified employees, so that proof must be assessed separately as to each, it is "entirely proper in gauging the danger of unfair

of statistical significance.[328] If the sample size is too small because, for example, too few applicants took the test in question during the relevant time frame, plaintiffs should contend that data from earlier periods should be introduced for purposes of allowing a reasonable opportunity to show statistical significance, at least where the same selection criteria were used during those earlier periods.[329] Courts at times may allow a plaintiff to aggregate different categories of minority employees to create a sufficient number for statistical significance, provided that there is evidence that the alleged discrimination affected all of the minority groups included.[330]

The issue of sample size, and particularly how it relates to a plaintiff's ability to establish a prima facie case of adverse impact, is discussed further in Chapter 3 (Adverse Impact).

D. Conflicting Statistical Conclusions

Today, virtually all well-litigated class action cases present the problem of conflicting statistical conclusions. One comparison typically demonstrates a substantial disparity, whereas the other refutes the existence of a substantial disparity. These conflicts,

---

inferences from small numbers in respect of one category to take into account for this limited purpose any patterns inferable from the total range of hiring decisions affecting all categories during a charged period of discrimination"); Dendy v. Washington Hosp. Ctr., 581 F.2d 990, 992, 17 FEP 1227 (D.C. Cir. 1978) (per curiam) (sample of 35; "While the numbers involved may have appeared small, statistical analysis showed them to reflect a discriminatory impact that could not reasonably be ascribed to chance alone."); Chicano Police Officers Ass'n v. Stover, 526 F.2d 431, 439, 11 FEP 1056 (10th Cir. 1975) (sample involving 26 persons sufficient to be evaluated as significant; if such small samples were rejected, "the tendency would be to deny employees in small plants the type of protection the civil rights statutes afford"), *vacated and remanded mem. on other grounds*, 426 U.S. 944 (1976).

[328]*E.g.*, *McAlester*, 851 F.2d at 1258–59 (plaintiff's expert correctly used binomial distribution formula in order to take into account small sample size). *See generally* DAVID C. BALDUS & JAMES W.L. COLE, STATISTICAL PROOF OF DISCRIMINATION §§ 9.1, 9A.1 (1980).

[329]*Cf.* United Air Lines, Inc. v. Evans, 431 U.S. 553, 558, 14 FEP 1510 (1977) (although liability cannot be based on acts occurring prior to charge-filing period, such acts may constitute relevant background evidence). *Evans* is discussed in Section VI *supra*.

[330]*See, e.g.*, Kohn v. Minneapolis Fire Dep't, 583 N.W.2d 7, 14, 84 FEP 1079 (Minn. Ct. App. 1998) (allowing aggregation of minority employees in different racial groups for statistical assessment of discrimination).

although vexing at first blush,[331] become more understandable in light of the great variety of possible sources of statistics, the numerous geographic and time frame possibilities, and the various tests that can be applied to the resulting data. The Supreme Court, in *Hazelwood School District v. United States*,[332] for example, recognized that the district court on remand would have to evaluate the range of available data—including population/workforce and actual applicant selection rate comparisons.[333]

In well-litigated cases, the parties can be counted on to point out the deficiencies in the other side's analyses. But in weighing conflicting statistical conclusions, some courts have taken the initiative sua sponte to test the strength of a party's statistical evidence.[334]

Examination of the cases in which courts have dealt with conflicting statistical conclusions reveals three generalizations that can be drawn: (1) statistics that account for relevant factors are more probative than generalized statistics;[335] (2) time frame statistics normally are far more probative than static or snapshot statistics;[336]

---

[331]*Cf.* West v. Swift, Hunt & Wesson, 847 F.2d 490, 492 n.2, 46 FEP 1531 (8th Cir. 1988) (" 'lies, damn lies, and statistics' ") (citation omitted).

[332]433 U.S. 299, 15 FEP 1 (1977).

[333]*Id.* at 308 n.13. A classic situation of conflicting statistical conclusions arises in selection rate comparisons when the selection rates are very high or very low. In such cases, whether selection or rejection rates are compared makes a dramatic difference. For example, if the selection rate for African Americans is 98%, and that for whites is 99%, a comparison of pass rates shows little difference. But, on the other hand, a comparison of rejection rates—2% compared to 1%—reflects a rejection rate of African Americans that is *twice* that of whites. This issue is discussed more extensively in Chapter 3 (Adverse Impact).

[334]*E.g.*, Tagatz v. Marquette Univ., 861 F.2d 1040, 1045, 50 FEP 99 (7th Cir. 1988) (judges are not "wallflowers or potted plants," and judge may rework statistical table); Dalley v. Michigan Blue Cross/Blue Shield, Inc., 612 F. Supp. 1444, 1448 n.10, 38 FEP 301 (E.D. Mich. 1985) (district court retained its own expert to assist in understanding conflicting statistical evidence presented by parties).

[335]Virtually all the text discussion and cited cases in this chapter demonstrate that the more probative statistics will be those that are more finely tuned, as long as the statistics can be shown to be reliable and undistorted. *E.g.*, Latinos Unidos de Chelsea en Accion (LUCHA) v. Secretary of Hous. & Urban Dev., 799 F.2d 774, 787, 41 FEP 838 (1st Cir. 1986) ("We conclude that the [general population statistics] here do not add up to a prima facie case of intentional discrimination, and note that the plaintiffs do not challenge any specific employment practice as causing a discriminatory impact.").

[336]*See* Section VI *supra.* Further, short-term recent time frame statistics normally are more probative than long-term time frame statistics. *See, e.g.*, Kypke v. Burlington

and (3) nonstatistical proof—such as anecdotal or comparative evidence[337]—offered by either party to buttress (or to rebut) proffered statistical proof enhances (or undercuts) the impact of the statistics on the decision maker.[338]

The district court has the authority and responsibility for ensuring that the jury understands its role in assessing statistics critically. In *Considine v. Newspaper Agency Corp.*,[339] the Tenth Circuit held that it was not error for the court to give a jury instruction informing the jury that the "usefulness or weight of statistical evidence depends on all the surrounding facts and circumstances" and "must not be accepted uncritically."[340] The district court had also denied the plaintiff's request for an instruction stating that statistical evidence "alone may be sufficient for you to find that age was a determinative factor in denying plaintiff's employment."[341]

VIII. OTHER CATEGORIES OF EXPERTS IN EMPLOYMENT CASES

A. Industrial Psychologists and Human Resources Experts

In employment discrimination cases, plaintiffs and defendants are increasingly relying on the testimony of industrial psychologists[342] or experts in human resources and employment practices

---

N. R.R., 928 F.2d 285, 288, 55 FEP 804 (8th Cir. 1991) (statistical evidence offered by older employee does not make out prima facie case of age discrimination, even though mean age for company dropped 1.77 years between 1980 and 1985, where average employee age actually increased between 1981 and 1985 and there was further increase for years 1985–87).

[337]*See generally* Chapter 2 (Disparate Treatment).

[338]*Teamsters*, for example, noted that testimony from individuals on their personal discriminatory experiences "brought the cold numbers convincingly to life." Teamsters v. United States, 431 U.S. 324, 339, 14 FEP 1514 (1977). In addition to Chapter 2 (Disparate Treatment), the various chapters on different bases of discrimination (e.g., age) should be consulted for examples of types of nonstatistical evidence.

[339]43 F.3d 1349, 69 FEP 1732 (10th Cir. 1994).

[340]*Id.* at 1367.

[341]*Id. But see* EEOC v. O & G Spring & Wire Forms Specialty Co., 38 F.3d 872, 876, FEP 1823 (7th Cir. 1994) (employer used word-of-mouth and walk-in applications to fill positions to hire 87 employees, none of which were African American; "statistical evidence by no means diminishes the plaintiff's obligation to prove discriminatory intent—but in some cases, statistical disparities alone may prove intent").

[342]Industrial psychology (often referred to as industrial-organizational psychology) is a branch of psychology that focuses on "the application of psychological

to either defend or attack an employer's employment practices. Courts have allowed these types of expert witnesses to testify on subjects such as the validity of an employer's selection procedures,[343] the ability of a particular employee to do a specific job,[344] the adequacy of an employer's procedures for dealing with complaints of harassment,[345] or the propriety and design of an employer's RIF.[346] Although many courts have treated these experts as they would any other, some courts have been more reluctant to allow or consider such testimony.[347]

---

principles to workplace phenomena." Ann Marie Ryan, *Defining Ourselves: I-O Psychology's Identity Quest*, INDUS.-ORGANIZATIONAL PSYCHOLOGIST, July 2003, at 24. Industrial psychologists employ scientific methods, including research and testing, to analyze and improve employee performance and organizational structures within the workplace. *Id.*; *see also* Society for Indus. & Organizational Psychology Inc., *Building Better Organizations; Industrial-Organizational Psychology in the Workplace* (2003), *available at* http://siop.org/visibilitybrochure/memberbrochure.htm (last visited Nov. 17, 2003).

[343]*See, e.g.*, Vulcan Pioneers, Inc. v. New Jersey Dep't of Civil Serv., 625 F. Supp. 527, 540, 51 FEP 1291 (D.N.J. 1985) (crediting testimony of plaintiff's expert industrial psychologist concerning validity of defendant's promotional examination), *aff'd*, 832 F.2d 811 (3d Cir. 1987); Graffam v. Scott Paper Co., 60 F.3d 809, 71 FEP 736 (1st Cir. 1995) (finding that employer established business necessity defense through industrial psychologist who testified that selection procedures measured job behaviors necessary for managerial positions); EEOC v. Mississippi, 654 F. Supp. 1168, 1178–79, 43 FEP 222 (S.D. Miss. 1987) (crediting testimony of EEOC's expert industrial psychologist in age discrimination case where plaintiffs challenged mandatory retirement age for state employees in wildlife department), *aff'd*, 837 F.2d 1398 (5th Cir. 1988).

[344]*See, e.g.*, DiPompo v. West Point Military Acad., 770 F. Supp. 887, 890–92, 56 FEP 1140 (S.D.N.Y. 1991) (granting judgment for defendant in Rehabilitation Act claim and crediting testimony of defendant's expert industrial psychologist concerning plaintiff's qualifications, with or without reasonable accommodation, for fire fighter position).

[345]*See, e.g.*, Kimzey v. Wal-Mart Stores, Inc., 107 F.3d 568, 571, 73 FEP 87 (8th Cir. 1997) (allowing expert witness to offer opinion that open door policy was inadequate and that employer had not properly trained employees to conduct sexual harassment investigations).

[346]*See, e.g.*, Gonzales v. Conoco, Inc., 81 FEP 225 (S.D. Tex. 1999).

[347]*See, e.g.*, Wilson v. Muckala, 303 F.3d 1207, 1218–19, 89 FEP 1217 (10th Cir. 2002) (court did not abuse its discretion by not allowing testimony of plaintiff's expert on adequacy of defendant hospital's response plan for handling sexual harassment complaints); Lewis v. NLRB, 750 F.2d 1266, 1276, 36 FEP 1338 (5th Cir. 1985) (rejecting plaintiffs' expert industrial psychologist's testimony that rating system that defendant used for promotional purposes was discriminatory because it allowed for too much subjectivity); Davis v. Frank, 711 F. Supp. 447, 452, 50 FEP 1188 (N.D. Ill. 1989) (characterizing testimony of defendant's expert industrial psychologist as "vague, speculative, and conjectural").

In determining whether to admit such testimony, courts should first determine whether the expert's testimony is reliable. In *Bryant v. City of Chicago*,[348] plaintiffs challenged the reliability of the expert's testimony concerning the content validity of a test used by the employer for promotion purposes, characterizing it as "inadmissible conjecture."[349] The court of appeals found that the testimony was properly admitted, noting that the expert had authored approximately 50 articles about employee selection and promotion testing for peer-reviewed journals and had "extensive academic and practical experience in designing employment evaluations."[350]

Some courts have rejected the testimony of human resources experts as being unreliable.[351] More often, instead of challenging the qualifications of human resources experts or the soundness of their methodology, parties will instead argue that testimony from these experts is unnecessary because jurors can determine these matters for themselves.[352] For example, in *Wilson v. Muckala*,[353] the Tenth Circuit considered whether the district court abused its discretion by excluding the testimony of the plaintiff's human resources expert in a sexual harassment lawsuit.[354] This expert would

---

[348]200 F.3d 1092 (7th Cir. 2000).

[349]*Id.* at 1097–98.

[350]*Id.*; *see also* Butler v. Home Depot, Inc., 984 F. Supp. 1257, 1266 (N.D. Cal. 1997) (admitting in sex discrimination case testimony of plaintiffs' human resources expert concerning (1) employee job interests and proper means of assessing them, and (2) impact of Home Depot's 95-pound weight-lifting requirement for merchandising jobs); EEOC v. Pacific Mar. Ass'n, 87 FEP 1182 (D. Or. 2001) (excluding testimony of EEOC's human resources expert because EEOC failed to comply with Rule 26(a)(2) of Federal Rules of Civil Procedure); Crenshaw v. Bozeman Deaconess Hosp., 693 P.2d 487, 501–03 (Mont. 1984) (holding in wrongful discharge case that court properly admitted testimony of plaintiff's expert on personnel management concerning propriety of procedures defendant hospital followed in discharging plaintiff).

[351]*Davis*, 711 F. Supp. at 452 (characterizing testimony of defendant's expert industrial psychologist as "vague, speculative, and conjectural," and granting judgment for plaintiff in Rehabilitation Act claim).

[352]*See, e.g.*, Green v. Kinney Shoe Corp., 715 F. Supp. 1122, 1124–25, 49 FEP 1283 (D.D.C. 1989) (expert testimony about employer's promotion criteria and its lack of affirmative action policy would not aid jury in its determination); Cirner v. True-Valu Credit Union, 429 N.W.2d 820, 822–23 (Mich. Ct. App. 1988) (expert testimony that employer should have used progressive discipline improperly admitted into evidence because "[t]here was nothing so exceptional in the record of this case as to require an expert opinion on the ultimate issue for the jury").

[353]303 F.3d 1207 (10th Cir. 2002).

[354]*Id.* at 1218–19.

have testified concerning the adequacy of the defendant hospital's
response plan in cases of sexual harassment and the reasonableness
of the hospital's response to the plaintiff's sexual harassment complaint.[355] The district court found that this testimony was relevant,
but excluded it nonetheless, finding that the facts were not so complicated that expert testimony would help the jury.[356] The Tenth
Circuit held that this decision was not an abuse of discretion, noting that the issues to which the expert would have testified "were
not so impenetrable as to require expert testimony."[357] Earlier, in
Corneveaux v. CUNA Mutual Insurance Group,[358] the Tenth Circuit considered the district court's exclusion of the testimony of
two experts offered by the plaintiff in support of her age discrimination claim.[359] The court found that an expert who would have
testified about the tests that the employer had used should not have
been excluded because test results were "beyond the common experience of the jury."[360] The court held, however, that the plaintiff's
second proposed expert, a professor of psychology who would have
testified about how the plaintiff's supervisor's bias against older
workers manifested itself in his behavior, was properly excluded.[361]

Besides initial admissibility issues, courts have also considered whether a human resources expert's proposed testimony is
sufficient to create a fact issue to enable the plaintiff to survive
summary judgment.[362]

B. Mental Health Experts

Because of the availability of compensatory damages under
the Civil Rights Act of 1991, § 1981, and certain state laws, courts

---

[355]*Id.* at 1218.
[356]*Id.*
[357]*Id.* at 1219.
[358]76 F.3d 1498, 70 FEP 247 (10th Cir. 1996).
[359]*Id.* at 1504–05.
[360]*Id.*
[361]*Id.*
[362]*See, e.g.*, Engstrand v. Pioneer Hi-Bred Int'l, Inc., 946 F. Supp. 1390, 1403–
04 (S.D. Iowa 1996) (expert testimony that large organizations such as defendant's
tend to be populated by male employees who are ignorant of human aspects of running business did not create fact issue concerning whether discrimination played role
in plaintiff's termination); *see also* EEOC v. McDonnell Douglas Corp., 17 F. Supp.

have often allowed mental health experts to testify about plaintiffs' emotional distress damages and how those damages were likely caused by the employer's illegal discrimination.[363] At least one court has held that the exclusion of such evidence is reversible error.[364] Some courts, however, have been reluctant to allow experts to testify that discrimination has caused emotional distress.[365] To establish the plaintiff's entitlement to front pay, in lieu of reinstatement, the testimony of mental health experts may also be relevant.[366] Mental health experts are typically not permitted to offer an opinion as to a plaintiff's credibility, however, or to try to explain inconsistencies in the plaintiff's testimony on the basis of mental

---

2d 1048, 1053 (E.D. Mo. 1998) (holding that testimony of EEOC's human resources expert concerning existence of "cultural focus of youth" at defendant company did not suffice to establish prima facie case of age discrimination).

[363]*See, e.g., Wilson*, 303 F.3d at 1218 ("Expert testimony on the psychological and emotional traits of abuse victims is typically admissible."); Hurley v. Atlantic City Police Dep't, 174 F.3d 95, 112–13, 79 FEP 808 (3d Cir. 1999) (court did not abuse its discretion by allowing psychologist to testify that plaintiff had suffered "psychological assault" at hands of defendant that caused severe pain comparable to physical touching); Skidmore v. Precision Printing & Packaging, Inc., 188 F.3d 606, 617–18, 81 FEP 1252 (5th Cir. 1999) (holding that district court did not abuse its discretion by admitting testimony of plaintiff's psychiatrist, who testified that plaintiff suffered from posttraumatic stress disorder and depression as result of defendant's conduct); Nichols v. American Nat'l Ins. Co., 154 F.3d 875, 881–82, 77 FEP 1338 (8th Cir. 1998) (summarizing testimony of plaintiff's psychologist concerning emotional distress plaintiff suffered as result of defendant's alleged harassment); Phillips v. Smalley Maint. Servs., Inc., 711 F.2d 1524, 1528, 32 FEP 975 (11th Cir. 1983) (plaintiff introduced testimony of physician and psychiatrist to show that plaintiff's anxiety was related to her termination); Webb v. Hyman, 861 F. Supp. 1094, 1113–15, 67 FEP 1425 (D.D.C. 1994) (allowing testimony of psychologist that sexually abusive conduct by plaintiff's supervisor destroyed plaintiff's coping mechanisms).

[364]Busby v. City of Orlando, 931 F.2d 764, 782, 55 FEP 1466 (11th Cir. 1991) (per curiam) (testimony of psychological counselor directly relevant to issue of damages).

[365]*See, e.g.,* Bohen v. City of E. Chi., 622 F. Supp. 1234, 1243 (N.D. Ind. 1985) (refusing to allow "expert on sexual harassment" to testify that harassment caused plaintiff's emotional maladies); Collier v. Bradley Univ., 113 F. Supp. 2d 1235, 1242–49, 83 FEP 1576 (C.D. Ill. 2000) (court precluded social psychologist from testifying that plaintiff suffered emotional distress as result of racial discrimination, harassment, and retaliation).

[366]*See, e.g.,* Gotthardt v. National R.R. Passenger Corp., 191 F.3d 1148, 1155–56, 80 FEP 1528 (9th Cir. 1999) (court did not clearly err in awarding plaintiff front pay instead of ordering reinstatement in light of expert testimony that plaintiff suffered from posttraumatic stress disorder caused in large part by defendant employer).

health theories.[367] Such testimony is considered to invade the province of the jury and to be unduly prejudicial.[368]

C. Economic Damages Experts

The admissibility of expert testimony about economic damages tends to be less controversial, and courts frequently allow plaintiffs' economic experts to testify concerning the amount of wages a plaintiff lost as a result of an adverse employment action.[369] Even when the economic analysis is flawed, it may be admitted. For example, in *Cummings v. Standard Register Co.*,[370] the First Circuit considered whether the district court erred in admitting the testimony of the plaintiff's economic expert concerning the plaintiff's future lost wages.[371] The plaintiff's expert testified on direct examination that

---

[367]Wilson v. Muckala, 303 F.3d 1207, 1218 (10th Cir. 2002) ("We find no error in the trial court's ruling that the expert [psychiatrist] could testify to [the plaintiff]'s condition, but not give his opinion on her credibility."); *Skidmore*, 188 F.3d at 618 (noting that credibility determinations fall within jury's province, but finding that plaintiff's psychiatrist's testimony that he did not think plaintiff had fabricated her psychiatric symptoms was not improper); *Nichols*, 154 F.3d at 881–84 (holding that defendant's psychiatric expert should not have been permitted to testify that plaintiff had poor "psychiatric credibility" and that "recall bias, secondary gain, and malingering had influenced her story"); Karibian v. Columbia Univ., 930 F. Supp. 134, 140–44, 71 FEP 325 (S.D.N.Y. 1996) (excluding testimony of plaintiff's mental health expert, a social worker, explaining inconsistencies in plaintiff's testimony, because such testimony "was not necessary nor would it have been helpful for the jury, and indeed would have been unduly prejudicial"). *But see* Snider v. Consolidated Coal Co., 973 F.2d 555, 559–60, 59 FEP 1143 (7th Cir. 1992) (stating that court could properly have relied on testimony of plaintiff's expert explaining plaintiff's failure to complain about alleged sexual harassment in reaching its judgment for plaintiff where defendant did not challenge admissibility of this testimony).

[368]*Karibian*, 930 F. Supp. at 144.

[369]*See, e.g.*, O'Neal v. Ferguson Constr. Co., 237 F.3d 1248, 1256–57, 84 FEP 1491 (10th Cir. 2001) (district court's instruction to jury concerning lost employment benefits supported by testimony of plaintiff's economist); Prine v. Sioux City Cmty. Sch. Dist., 95 F. Supp. 2d 1005, 1013–14, 82 FEP 1716 (N.D. Iowa 2000) (relying on testimony of plaintiff's economist to calculate plaintiff's entitlement to lost fringe benefits as part of front-pay award); Reginelli v. Motion Indus., Inc., 987 F. Supp. 1137, 1140–41 (E.D. Ark. 1997) (holding that jury's back-pay award was not excessive even though it exceeded amount suggested by plaintiff's expert); Webb v. Hyman, 861 F. Supp. 1094, 1115, 67 FEP 1425 (D.D.C. 1994) (holding that it was not error to admit testimony of plaintiff's economist concerning plaintiff's pension loss).

[370]265 F.3d 56, 87 FEP 1190 (1st Cir. 2001).

[371]*Id.* at 61, 64–65.

the plaintiff's future lost wages amounted to $656,867.00.[372] On cross-examination, the expert realized that he had made a mathematical error in applying an estimated 3.9 percent salary increase per year.[373] The correct front-pay amount, accounting for this error, should have been $494,712.00, but the expert never explicitly stated this corrected figure.[374] The defense moved to strike the expert's testimony, but the court denied the motion.[375] The First Circuit found that the district court did not err in denying the motion to strike the testimony.[376] The court reasoned that the defense had availed itself of the opportunity to point out errors in the expert's calculations and that these errors were only relevant to assessing the weight, not the admissibility, of the testimony.[377]

D. Other Experts

Following the Supreme Court's opinion in *Price Waterhouse v. Hopkins*,[378] citing the trial court's reliance on a social psychologist's testimony that the defendant's decision to deny the plaintiff a promotion was likely influenced by sex stereotyping,[379] some courts have allowed experts to testify about the effects of stereotyping on employment decisions.[380] One court refused to allow such testimony because it would be too speculative and would usurp

---

[372]*Id.* at 61.

[373]*Id.*

[374]*Id.* The expert also admitted not using data specific to the defendant in making certain calculations and to using the plaintiff's salary in a higher-than-average earnings year as his baseline figure. *Id.* at 61–62.

[375]*Id.* at 62.

[376]*Id.* at 64–65.

[377]*Id.* at 65.

[378]490 U.S. 228, 49 FEP 954 (1989).

[379]*Id.* at 235–36.

[380]*See, e.g.*, Butler v. Home Depot, Inc., 984 F. Supp. 1257, 1262–65 (N.D. Cal. 1997) (denying defendant's motion to exclude trial expert's testimony that subjective decision making allows gender stereotyping to influence hiring decisions); Hurst v. F.W. Woolworth, 75 FEP 530 (S.D.N.Y. 1997) (admitting expert testimony on age stereotyping); Flavel v. Svedala Indus., Inc., 875 F. Supp. 550, 557–58, 75 FEP 915 (E.D. Wis. 1994) (expert testimony on stereotyping allowed because age discrimination may arise from "*unconscious* application of stereotyped notions of ability rather than from a deliberate desire to remove older workers from the workplace"); Stender v. Lucky Stores, Inc., 803 F. Supp. 259, 301–03, 62 FEP 11 (N.D. Cal. 1992) (allowing for expert testimony about influence of gender stereotyping on managers' personnel decisions); Robinson v. Jacksonville Shipyards, Inc., 760 F. Supp.

the jury's role as fact finder.[381] In several disability discrimination cases, parties have offered expert testimony regarding the existence or extent of the plaintiff's disability.[382] Courts typically allow this testimony, finding that it meets the requirements of *Daubert* and will help the jury. However, even when such expert testimony is admitted, courts still must determine what probative weight it carries. In *Mason v. Frank*,[383] for example, the Eighth Circuit found that the testimony of the plaintiff's vocational expert was not sufficient to rebut the defendant's showing that the plaintiff could not perform the requirements of his job as a distribution clerk, even with reasonable accommodations.[384] The court affirmed the lower court's judgment for the defendant, noting that the plaintiff's expert was not a medical doctor and had never observed a distribution clerk at work.[385]

1486, 1502, 57 FEP 971 (M.D. Fla. 1991) (expert allowed to testify about sexual stereotyping).

[381]Lipsett v. University of P.R., 740 F. Supp. 921, 925 (D.P.R. 1990).

[382]*See, e.g.*, Smith v. City of Des Moines, 99 F.3d 1466, 1472–73, 72 FEP 628 (8th Cir. 1996) (finding that testimony of plaintiff's experts did not establish fact issue regarding defendant's proof of business necessity defense); Robinson v. Neodata Serv., Inc., 94 F.3d 499, 502, 5 AD 1441 (8th Cir. 1996) (noting that plaintiff's own medical expert had testified that plaintiff had only 6% impairment rating and this minor impairment rating would have little impact on her ability to perform major life activities); Lanni v. New Jersey, 177 F.R.D. 295, 302–03 (D.N.J. 1998) (allowing defendant's expert, forensic psychiatrist, to testify that plaintiff did not have learning disability despite expert's lack of any special training in diagnosing learning disabilities); DiPompo v. West Point Military Acad., 770 F. Supp. 887, 891–92, 56 FEP 1140 (S.D.N.Y. 1991); Davis v. Frank, 711 F. Supp. 447, 451, 50 FEP 1188 (N.D. Ill. 1989) (admitting testimony of plaintiff's and defendant's experts concerning plaintiff's ability to communicate in workplace).

[383]32 F.3d 315, 3 AD 835 (8th Cir. 1994).

[384]*Id.* at 319.

[385]*Id.*; *see also Smith*, 99 F.3d at 1472–73 (affirming summary judgment for defendant and finding that testimony of plaintiff's medical experts did not create fact issue on whether defendant was entitled to defense of business necessity); *DiPompo*, 770 F. Supp. at 891–92 (granting judgment for defendant in plaintiff's Rehabilitation Act claim and crediting testimony of defendant's experts, a reading specialist and an industrial psychologist, concerning plaintiff's qualifications for structural fire-fighter position, with or without reasonable accommodation); *Davis*, 711 F. Supp. at 451 (characterizing testimony of defendant's industrial psychologist as "speculation and conjecture" and granting judgment for plaintiff in Rehabilitation Act claim).

Part VI

Other Sources of Protection

CHAPTER 35

THE CIVIL RIGHTS ACTS OF 1866 AND 1871

I. INTRODUCTION

During the Reconstruction Era, Congress enacted a series of civil rights statutes designed to advance the goals of the newly ratified Thirteenth, Fourteenth, and Fifteenth Amendments.[1] Four of these statutes—now codified at 42 U.S.C. §§ 1981, 1983, 1985, and 1986—have been used to attack employment discrimination. Although Title VII of the Civil Rights Act of 1964, the Age Discrimination in Employment Act of 1967 (ADEA), and the Americans with Disabilities Act of 1990 (ADA) dominate the field of employment discrimination law, the Civil Rights Acts of 1866 and 1871 still are invoked to avoid those statutes' procedural requirements and pitfalls and, in some circumstances, to provide access to additional damages.

---

[1]For a discussion of the legislative history of these Acts, see *Jett v. Dallas Indep. Sch. Dist.*, 491 U.S. 701, 713–31, 50 FEP 27 (1989), and Michael Reiss, *Requiem for an "Independent Remedy": The Civil Rights Acts of 1866 and 1871 as Remedies for Employment Discrimination*, 50 S. CAL. L. REV. 961 (1977).

II. Scope and Coverage of the Civil Rights Act of 1866, 42 U.S.C. § 1981

A. Statutory Authority

Subsection (a) of § 1981 provides:

All persons within the jurisdiction of the United States shall have the same right . . . to make and enforce contracts, to sue, be parties, give evidence, and to the full and equal benefit of all laws and proceedings for the security of persons and property as is enjoyed by white citizens, and shall be subject to like punishment, pains, penalties, taxes, licenses, and exactions of every kind, and to no other.[2]

This subsection and its companion, § 1982, originally were enacted as § 1 of the Civil Rights Act of 1866,[3] pursuant to the Thirteenth Amendment, which was ratified in 1865. After the Fourteenth Amendment was ratified in 1868, the statute was reenacted in 1870[4] in order to remove any doubt of Congress' constitutional authority to pass such legislation. Thus, the statute has been referred to as the Civil Rights Act of 1866, the Civil Rights Act of 1870, or, most commonly, simply § 1981.

Section 1981 was amended by the Civil Rights Act of 1991[5] to provide two additional subsections:

(b) For purposes of this section, the term "make and enforce contracts" includes the making, performance, modification, and termination of contracts, and the enjoyment of all benefits, privileges, terms, and conditions of the contractual relationship.

(c) The rights protected by this section are protected against impairment by nongovernmental discrimination and impairment under color of State law.[6]

Subsection (b) was designed to overturn the U.S. Supreme Court's 1989 decision in *Patterson v. McLean Credit Union*,[7] which had

---

[2]42 U.S.C. § 1981(a) (2000).

[3]Act of Apr. 9, 1866, ch. 31, § 1, 14 Stat. 27.

[4]Act of May 31, 1870, ch. 114, §§ 16, 18, 16 Stat. 144.

[5]Pub. L. No. 102-166, § 101, 1991 U.S.C.C.A.N. (105 Stat.) 1071, 1072 (codified at 42 U.S.C. § 1981a (2000)).

[6]42 U.S.C. §§ 1981(b), (c) (2000).

[7]491 U.S. 164, 180–81, 49 FEP 1814 (1989).

narrowly construed § 1981 to address only claims of racially discriminatory hiring and those promotion disputes in which "a new and distinct" contractual relationship was at issue.[8] In 1994 the Supreme Court held that the amendments to § 1981 in the 1991 Act applied only prospectively, not retroactively.[9]

Subsection (c) reaffirms that § 1981 reaches both public and private intentional race discrimination. The history of that issue is traced in the next section.

B. Cognizable Defendants Under § 1981

1. Private Entities

In *Jones v. Alfred H. Mayer Co.*,[10] the Supreme Court recognized a purely private right of action under the 1866 Act.[11] Although *Jones* by its terms involved § 1982, its rationale thereafter was applied to § 1981 as well. In 1975, in *Johnson v. Railway Express Agency*,[12] the Supreme Court confirmed that a private right of action exists under § 1981: "[I]t is well settled among the Federal Courts of Appeals—and we now join them—that § 1981 affords a federal remedy against discrimination in private employment on the basis of race."[13] The Court in *Johnson* stressed the separate and independent nature of § 1981 and Title VII, pointing out that the two statutes differ in their coverage, jurisdictional prerequisites, procedures, and available relief. Section 1981 contains no restriction regarding the size of a covered employer, unlike Title VII, which applies only to employers of 15 or more persons. The

---

[8]*Id.* at 181 (holding, prior to 1991 Civil Rights Act, claim of racial harassment not actionable under § 1981). Prior to the Civil Rights Act of 1991, all circuits that considered the question construed *Patterson* to preclude actions for discriminatory discharges and other post-employment claims. *See, e.g.*, Taggart v. Jefferson County Child Support Enforcement Unit, 935 F.2d 947, 948, 55 FEP 1545 (8th Cir. 1991) (en banc) (discharge claim dismissed).

[9]Rivers v. Roadway Express, Inc., 511 U.S. 298, 311–13, 64 FEP 842 (1994) (no retroactive application).

[10]392 U.S. 409, 437–38 (1968).

[11]The earlier law had not been so clear. In 1883, the Supreme Court indicated that Congress did not have the power under the Thirteenth or Fourteenth Amendments to reach private incidents of discrimination and suggested that § 1981 be limited to incidents of "state action." The Civil Rights Cases, 109 U.S. 3, 16 (1883); *accord* Hurd v. Hodge, 334 U.S. 24, 31 (1948).

[12]421 U.S. 454, 10 FEP 817 (1975).

[13]*Id.* at 459–60.

Supreme Court in *Runyon v. McCrary*[14] and again in *Patterson v. McLean Credit Union*[15] reaffirmed § 1981's application to private conduct. In 1991, Congress nevertheless eliminated any doubt of the statute's application to private conduct by adding subsection (c) to § 1981.

A parent corporation may, under certain circumstances, be liable under § 1981 for the discriminatory acts of its subsidiary.[16] Moreover, employees such as supervisors who make or recommend employment decisions may be subject to individual liability under § 1981.[17] No personal liability, however, may be imposed on a corporate official when the official is not alleged to have participated in the actual discrimination.[18]

Additionally, some courts have ruled that third parties can be liable for intentionally and discriminatorily interfering with contractual rights protected by § 1981.[19] Also, courts generally have held that § 1981 employment claims are actionable against private clubs.[20] A district court has even held that a claim under § 1981

---

[14]427 U.S. 160, 168, 173–75 (1976).

[15]491 U.S. 164, 171–72, 49 FEP 1814 (1989).

[16]*See, e.g.*, Kim v. Dial Serv. Int'l, Inc., 73 FEP 1139, 1144 (S.D.N.Y. 1997) (denying motion to dismiss parent corporation where plaintiff alleged parent sent subsidiary money every month, made all personnel decisions, made financial decisions, controlled detailed operations, and was owned by same person); Richard v. Bell Atl. Corp., 946 F. Supp. 54, 61–64, 73 FEP 1257 (D.D.C. 1996) (applying integrated enterprise test).

[17]*See, e.g.*, Williams v. United Dairy Farmers, 20 F. Supp. 2d 1193, 1202, 78 FEP 15 (S.D. Ohio 1998); *Kim*, 73 FEP at 1139; *Richard*, 946 F. Supp. at 74; Vakharia v. Little Co. of Mary Hosp. & Health Care Ctrs., 917 F. Supp. 1282, 1293 (N.D. Ill. 1996); Leige v. Capitol Chevrolet, Inc., 895 F. Supp. 289, 293 (M.D. Ga. 1994).

[18]*See, e.g.*, Daulo v. Commonwealth Edison, 892 F. Supp. 1088, 1091, 72 FEP 1566 (N.D. Ill. 1995).

[19]*See, e.g.*, Lewis-Kearns v. Mayflower Transit, Inc., 932 F. Supp. 1061, 1070 (N.D. Ill. 1996) (citing Vakharia v. Swedish Covenant Hosp., 765 F. Supp. 461, 471 (N.D. Ill. 1991)).

[20]*See* Cook v. Twin Oaks Country Club, 122 F. Supp. 2d 1064, 1065, 84 FEP 545 (W.D. Mo. 2000) (Title VII's private club exception not applicable to § 1981); Crawford v. Willow Oaks Country Club, Inc., 66 F. Supp. 2d 767, 769 (E.D. Va. 1999) (neither Title VII's private club exception nor Title II's private club exception applies to employment discrimination cases brought under § 1981); Graham v. Leavenworth Country Club, 15 F. Supp. 2d 1062, 1064, 78 FEP 301 (D. Kan. 1998) (same); Baptiste v. Cavendish Club, Inc., 670 F. Supp. 108, 110, 44 FEP 1684 (S.D.N.Y. 1987) (same); Konicki v. Piedmont Driving Club, 44 FEP 486, 487 (N.D. Ga. 1987) (same). *But see* Hudson v. Charlotte Country Club, Inc., 535 F. Supp. 313, 315, 28 FEP 1208 (W.D.N.C. 1982) (private clubs impliedly exempted from liability under § 1981); Kemerer v. Davis, 520 F. Supp. 256, 257, 26 FEP 1652 (E.D. Mich. 1981) (same).

can be maintained against a medical board that administers examinations and awards certifications.[21]

Furthermore, in *Danco, Inc. v. Wal-Mart Stores, Inc.*,[22] the First Circuit upheld a jury verdict that found Wal-Mart liable under § 1981 for discrimination against an independent contractor who maintained Wal-Mart's parking lots. In reaching this conclusion, the appeals court specifically concluded that § 1981, as amended in 1991, encompasses claims for hostile work environment discrimination and that such claims can be pursued by an independent contractor.[23]

2. The Federal Government[24]

The Supreme Court in *Brown v. General Services Administration*[25] held that § 717 of Title VII provides the exclusive remedy for most federal employees. Section 1981 protects federal employees only in those few cases where discrimination in federal employment is not covered by Title VII.[26]

3. State and Local Governments

Section 1981 provides a remedy for discrimination against state and municipal employees, but it is subject to the same limitations

---

[21]*See* Morrison v. American Bd. of Psychiatry & Neurology, Inc., 908 F. Supp. 582, 588, 69 FEP 1217 (N.D. Ill. 1996) (motion to dismiss denied where physician alleged that, without certification, she would not be able to contract with medical facilities that require board certification).

[22]178 F.3d 8, 79 FEP 1689 (1st Cir. 1999).

[23]*Id.* at 13; *see also* Webster v. Fulton County, 283 F.3d 1254, 1257 (11th Cir. 2002) (holding that independent contractor can raise valid retaliation claim under § 1981 against county).

[24]Section 1981's applicability to discrimination against federal employees is primarily discussed in Chapter 31 (Federal Employee Litigation).

[25]425 U.S. 820, 835, 12 FEP 1361 (1976).

[26]*See, e.g.*, Lee v. Hughes, 145 F.3d 1272, 1277, 77 FEP 1491 (11th Cir. 1998) (§ 1981 does not provide cause of action against individuals acting under color of federal law); Belhomme v. Widnall, 127 F.3d 1214, 1217, 79 FEP 739 (10th Cir. 1997) ("[A] federal employee may not assert a claim for racial discrimination in his employment relationship except through the mechanism provided in [Title VII]."); Haynes v. Department of Health & Human Servs., 879 F. Supp. 127, 129 (D.D.C. 1995) (federal employee may not assert §§ 1981, 1985, or 1986 claims if covered by Title VII), *aff'd*, 1997 WL 362503 (D.C. Cir. May 6, 1997); Carlton v. Ryan, 916 F. Supp. 832, 838 (N.D. Ill. 1996); *see also* Johnson v. Hoffman, 424 F. Supp. 490, 493, 16 FEP 371 (E.D. Mo. 1977) (because Title VII does not cover uniformed military personnel, § 1981 can be used), *aff'd sub nom.* Johnson v. Alexander, 572 F.2d 1219, 16 FEP 894 (8th Cir. 1978).

that apply in § 1983 actions.[27] In *Jett v. Dallas Independent School District*,[28] the Supreme Court held that, in suits against municipalities, § 1981 liability must be based on official municipal policy and not on the doctrine of respondeat superior. Therefore, as with § 1983 actions, a § 1981 claimant must show that the violation was caused by a custom or policy of the municipality or agency.[29]

There is a split in the courts, however, regarding the impact of the 1991 Civil Rights Act on one of *Jett*'s primary holdings—that § 1983 is the exclusive federal remedy for violations of § 1981 by governmental entities. Several courts have interpreted subsection 1981(c), created by the 1991 amendments, to permit direct causes of action against governmental actors for violations of § 1981, thus finding that the 1991 amendments overruled this aspect of *Jett*.[30] Other courts still consider this holding of *Jett* to remain the law.[31] However, even those courts that have permitted § 1981 claims against government actors have continued to uphold the other holding in *Jett*, that liability may not be imposed on governmental entities based on respondeat superior.

---

[27]*See* Jett v. Dallas Indep. Sch. Dist., 491 U.S. 701, 710–11, 731–36, 50 FEP 27 (1989); *see* Section III.B.3 *infra*.

[28]491 U.S. at 712.

[29]*Id.* at 735, 738–39 (Scalia, J., concurring); *see also* Evans v. City of Houston, 246 F.3d 344, 358 (5th Cir. 2001) (applying *Monell v. Department of Soc. Servs.*, 436 U.S. 658 (1978), standard for municipal liability to § 1981 claims without reaching issue of whether § 1981 provided independent cause of action against governmental entity); Smith v. Chicago Sch. Reform Bd. of Trs., 165 F.3d 1142, 1148, 79 FEP 288 (7th Cir. 1999) (en banc) ("plaintiff must show that the body's official policy or custom was discriminatory"); Federation of African Am. Contractors v. City of Oakland, 96 F.3d 1204, 1215 (9th Cir. 1996) (same); Dennis v. County of Fairfax, 55 F.3d 151 (4th Cir. 1995) (same). *See* Section III.B.3 *infra*.

[30]*See* Oden v. Oktibbeha County, Miss., 246 F.3d 458, 463 (5th Cir. 2001); *Federation of African Am. Contractors*, 96 F.3d at 1214; *Powell*, 143 F. Supp. 2d at 112; Johnakin v. City of Phila., 1996 WL 18821, at *4 (E.D. Pa. Jan. 18, 1996) (unpublished); Jackson v. City of Chi., 1996 WL 734701, at *8 (N.D. Ill. Dec. 18, 1996) (unpublished); Robinson v. Colonie, 878 F. Supp. 387, 405 n.13 (N.D.N.Y. 1995).

[31]*See* Butts v. County of Volusia, 222 F.3d 891, 894, 83 FEP 1247 (11th Cir. 2000); *Dennis*, 55 F.3d at 156; Dill v. Pennsylvania, 3 F. Supp. 2d 583, 587 (E.D. Pa. 1998); McPhaul v. Board of Comm'rs of Madison County, 976 F. Supp. 1190 (S.D. Ind. 1997); Lewis v. Delaware Dep't of Pub. Instruction, 948 F. Supp. 352, 365 (D. Del. 1996). *Compare* Artis v. Francis Howell N. Band Booster Ass'n, 161 F.3d 1178, 1181 (8th Cir. 1998) (failing to discuss import of subsection (c) of § 1981, but holding that "[a] federal action to enforce rights under § 1981 against a state actor may only be brought pursuant to § 1983"); Anderson v. Conboy, 156 F.3d 167, 178 n.19 (2d Cir. 1998) (noting "ambiguity" of whether subsection (c) may create implied cause of action against state actors, but not resolving issue).

Although § 1981 covers *local* governmental entities and officials,[32] several courts have held that the Eleventh Amendment grants *state* governmental entities sovereign immunity from suits for damages.[33] The Eleventh Amendment bars actions under § 1981 against state employees in their official capacities, although it does not bar suits for damages against state officials in their individual capacities.[34] Additionally, state officials may be sued under § 1981, as under § 1983, for injunctive relief.[35]

---

[32]*Jett*, 491 U.S. at 737; *see, e.g.*, Garner v. Giarrusso, 571 F.2d 1330, 1337–38, 20 FEP 1314 (5th Cir. 1978) (under § 1981, city not immune from liability for monetary damages).

[33]*See, e.g.*, Johnson v. University of Cincinnati, 215 F.3d 561, 570–71, 82 FEP 1767 (6th Cir. 2000) (Eleventh Amendment bars suit under § 1981 against university, an arm of state); Blankenship v. Warren County, 931 F. Supp. 447, 449, 74 FEP 1459 (W.D. Va. 1996) (Eleventh Amendment bars only claim for monetary recovery against state actors; injunctive relief permissible); Gorman v. Roberts, 909 F. Supp. 1479, 1489 (M.D. Ala. 1995) (Eleventh Amendment applies in § 1981 litigation); Khan v. Maryland, 903 F. Supp. 881, 888 (D. Md. 1995) (§ 1981 claim against state agency prohibited by Eleventh Amendment); Minetos v. City Univ. of N.Y., 875 F. Supp. 1046, 1053, 68 FEP 355 (S.D.N.Y. 1995) (Eleventh Amendment bars claims against state university under § 1981 or § 1983); *see also* Daisernia v. New York, 582 F. Supp. 792, 795–96, 34 FEP 626 (N.D.N.Y. 1984) (§ 1981 does not abrogate sovereign immunity of State of New York or its agencies); Wong v. Calvin, 87 F.R.D. 145, 147, 23 FEP 447 (N.D. Fla. 1980) (Eleventh Amendment bars damages claim brought under § 1981 and § 1983 against state officials acting in their official capacities); Gibson v. Wisconsin Dep't of Health, 489 F. Supp. 1048, 1050–51, 27 FEP 1334 (E.D. Wis. 1980) (state department of health and social services immune from suit under § 1981); Henry v. Texas Tech Univ., 466 F. Supp. 141, 145–46, 23 FEP 406 (N.D. Tex. 1979) (Texas Tech University and Medical School is alter ego of state and thus protected from suit under § 1981 and § 1983 by Eleventh Amendment); *cf.* Quern v. Jordan, 440 U.S. 332, 336–46 (1979) (extensive review of cases finding state entity sovereign immunity under § 1983); Alabama v. Pugh, 438 U.S. 781, 781–82 (1978) (Alabama Board of Corrections shielded by Eleventh Amendment from suit under § 1983). Eleventh Amendment immunity is discussed extensively in Section III.B.3 *infra*.

[34]*See, e.g., Johnson*, 215 F.3d at 571; Foulks v. Ohio Dep't of Rehab. & Corr., 713 F.2d 1229, 1231, 32 FEP 829, 831–32 (6th Cir. 1983) (state officials can be sued under § 1981 in their individual capacities for individual acts violating § 1981); *Gorman*, 909 F. Supp. at 1489; Roberson v. Bowie State Univ., 899 F. Supp. 235, 237, 72 FEP 899 (D. Md. 1995); Philippeaux v. North Cent. Bronx Hosp., 871 F. Supp. 640, 656, 68 FEP 223 (S.D.N.Y. 1994), *aff'd*, 104 F.3d 353 (2d Cir. 1996); Culler v. South Carolina Dep't of Soc. Servs., 33 FEP 1590, 1595 (D.S.C. 1984) (state officials may be sued as individuals under § 1981 but may be immune from liability if they acted in good faith); *cf.* Hafer v. Melo, 502 U.S. 21, 29–30, 57 FEP 241 (1991) (state officials sued in their individual capacities are "persons" for purposes of § 1983); *see* Sections III.B.3 and III.B.4 *infra*.

[35]Freeman v. Michigan Dep't of State, 808 F.2d 1174, 1179, 42 FEP 1090 (6th Cir. 1987) (action for injunctive relief may be brought against state officials under § 1981 despite sovereign immunity defense); *see also Hafer*, 502 U.S. at 27 (same; § 1983 action).

4. Indian Tribes

The Fourth and Eleventh Circuits held that Indian tribes are immune from employment discrimination suits under § 1981.[36]

C. Types of Discrimination Prohibited by § 1981

In jurisdictions that have addressed the issue, courts have uniformly determined that an at-will employment relationship is a contract for purposes of § 1981, thereby permitting at-will employees to pursue § 1981 claims against their employers.[37] Employment discrimination claims, however, may not be viable under § 1981 when brought by testers[38] or by organizations

---

[36]*See* Yashenko v. Harrah's NC Casino Co., LLC, 446 F.3d 541, 553 (4th Cir. 2006) (case dismissed because employee could not pursue claim against casino without joining tribe as an indispensable party, but tribe has sovereign immunity); Taylor v. Alabama Intertribal Council Title IV J.T.P.A., 261 F.3d 1032, 1036, 86 FEP 714 (11th Cir. 2001) (inter-tribal council immune from § 1981 suit).

[37]*See, e.g.*, Walker v. Abbott Labs, 340 F.3d 471, 478 (7th Cir. 2003); Skinner v. Maritz, Inc., 253 F.3d 337, 341 (8th Cir. 2001); Lauture v. International Bus. Machs. Corp., 216 F.3d 258, 259–60, 83 FEP 286 (2d Cir. 2000); Perry v. Woodward, 199 F.3d 1126, 1132–33, 81 FEP 838 (10th Cir. 1999); Spriggs v. Diamond Auto Glass, 165 F.3d 1015, 1018–19, 78 FEP 1398 (4th Cir. 1999), *appeal after remand*, 242 F.3d 179, 85 FEP 342 (4th Cir. 2001); Fadeyi v. Planned Parenthood Ass'n of Lubbock, Inc., 160 F.3d 1048, 1049–50, 78 FEP 675 (5th Cir. 1998); McClease v. R.R. Donnelley & Sons Co., 226 F. Supp. 2d 695, 702 (E.D. Pa. 2002); Hill v. Textron Auto. Interiors, Inc., 2001 WL 276972, at *5–6 (D.N.H. Mar. 17, 2001) (unpublished); Copley v. Bax Global, Inc., 80 F. Supp. 2d 1342, 1346–47 (S.D. Fla. 2000); LaFate v. Chase Manhattan Bank, 123 F. Supp. 2d 773, 783 (D. Del. 2000); Joseph v. Wentworth Inst. Tech., 120 F. Supp. 2d 134, 144 (D. Mass. 2000); Williams v. United Dairy Farmers, 20 F. Supp. 2d 1193, 1202, 78 FEP 15 (S.D. Ohio 1998); Lane v. Ogden Entm't, Inc., 13 F. Supp. 2d 1261, 1272, 78 FEP 843 (M.D. Ala. 1998); Henry v. Trammell Crow SE, Inc., 34 F. Supp. 2d 629, 634 (W.D. Tenn. 1998).

[38]*See* Kyles v. J.K. Guardian Sec. Servs., Inc., 222 F.3d 289, 301, 83 FEP 404 (7th Cir. 2000) (employment testers have standing to sue under Title VII, but not under § 1981); Fair Empl. Council v. BMC Mktg. Corp., 28 F.3d 1268, 1271, 65 FEP 512 (D.C. Cir. 1994) (employment testers do not have standing to sue under § 1981, but do have valid Title VII claim). In the housing discrimination context several courts have held that testers have standing to bring claims under § 1981. *See* Meyers v. Pennypack Woods Home Ownership Ass'n, 559 F.2d 894, 898 (3d Cir. 1977) ("Even assuming arguendo that [the tester's] application to Pennypack was in fact motivated solely by his desire to test the legality of Pennypack's policies, such a purpose is sufficient to confer standing."), *overruled on other grounds*, Goodman v. Lukens Steel Co., 777 F.2d 113, 39 FEP 658 (3d Cir. 1985); Coel v. Rose Tree Manor Apartments, Inc., 1987 WL 18393, at *6 (E.D. Pa. Oct. 13, 1987) (court found tester had standing under § 1981 notwithstanding testers' lack of "particular interest in actually entering into" contract); Leadership Council for Metro. Open Cmtys. v. City of Chi. Sw. Holiday Inn Operators Oak Lawn Lodge, Inc., 1986

whose injuries derive only from the violation of others' civil rights.[39]

1. Race Discrimination

From § 1981's express language—"[a]ll persons . . . shall have the same right[s] . . . as [are] enjoyed by white citizens"—and from its historical context as a post–Civil War civil rights act, it is evident that § 1981 prohibits race discrimination against African Americans.[40] Furthermore, § 1981 is a vehicle for bringing "hostile environment" racial harassment claims.[41] Race-based claims of constructive discharge are also actionable under § 1981.[42]

The Supreme Court has held that § 1981, in certain circumstances, also protects whites and others who allege race discrimination. In *McDonald v. Santa Fe Trail Transportation Co.*,[43] the Supreme Court conceded that the phrase "as is enjoyed by white

---

WL 5651, at *4 (N.D. Ill. May 6, 1986) (testers have standing under § 1981); *see also* Watts v. Boyd Properties, Inc., 758 F.2d 1482, 1485 (11th Cir. 1985) ("[E]ven if a tester is motivated solely by the desire to challenge the legality of allegedly discriminatory practices, this is a sufficient purpose to confer standing [under § 1982]."). There would not seem to be a logical basis for treating tester standing under § 1981 differently depending on whether the claim arises in the housing or employment discrimination context.

[39]*BMC Mktg.*, 28 F.3d at 1279. *But see* NAACP v. City of Springfield, 139 F. Supp. 2d 990, 993 (C.D. Ill. 2001) (associations have standing to bring Title VII and § 1981 claims on behalf of their members under standard set by U.S. Supreme Court in *Hunt v. Washington State Apple Advertising Comm'n*, 432 U.S. 333 (1997)).

[40]*See* Johnson v. Railway Express Agency, 421 U.S. 454, 460, 10 FEP 817 (1975) (African American subjected to race discrimination in employment has remedies under § 1981 as well as Title VII).

[41]*See, e.g.*, Patterson v. Oneida, 375 F.3d 206, 225, 94 FEP 129 (2d Cir. 2004); Manatt v. Bank of Am., 339 F.3d 792, 797 (9th Cir. 2003); Whidbee v. Garzarelli Food Specialties, Inc., 223 F.3d 62, 69 (2d Cir. 2000); Danco, Inc. v. Wal-Mart Stores, Inc., 178 F.3d 8, 13 (1st Cir. 1999); Witt v. Roadway Express, 136 F.3d 1424, 1432, 76 FEP 1705 (10th Cir. 1998) (Civil Rights Act of 1991 amended § 1981 to provide cause of action for racial harassment); Jackson v. Motel 6 Multipurpose, Inc., 130 F.3d 999, 1008 n.17 (11th Cir. 1997); Dennis v. County of Fairfax, 55 F.3d 151, 155 (4th Cir. 1995); Johnson v. Uncle Ben's Inc., 965 F.2d 1363, 1372 (5th Cir. 1992); Harley v. McCoach, 928 F. Supp. 533, 541, 72 FEP 1725 (E.D. Pa. 1996).

[42]*See, e.g.*, Brown v. Ameritech Corp., 128 F.3d 605, 607, 75 FEP 226 (7th Cir. 1997) ("A [§ 1981] constructive discharge claim requires the plaintiff to show that his conditions of work were so intolerable, in a discriminatory way (for this kind of case), that a reasonable person would have been compelled to resign."); Tidwell v. Meyer's Bakeries, Inc., 93 F.3d 490, 494 (8th Cir. 1996); Reynolds v. School Dist. No. 1, Denver, Colo., 69 F.3d 1523, 1534, 72 FEP 485 (10th Cir. 1995); Jones v. School Dist. of Phila., 19 F. Supp. 2d 414, 419 (E.D. Pa. 1998), *aff'd*, 198 F.3d 403 (3d Cir. 1999); Villines v. Carpenters, 999 F. Supp. 97, 104–05 (D.D.C. 1998).

[43]427 U.S. 273, 12 FEP 1577 (1976).

citizens" lent support for the proposition that § 1981 was not intended to protect whites.[44] However, after an exhaustive analysis of the legislative history,[45] the Court concluded that § 1981 was intended "to proscribe discrimination in the making or enforcement of contracts against, or in favor of, any race."[46] Section 1981 also prohibits discrimination based on a white plaintiff's association with a member of a racial minority group.[47] In a "reverse" discrimination context, however, some courts have required majority plaintiffs to identify background circumstances that would justify applying to them the same presumption of discrimination upon proof of a prima facie case under the *McDonnell Douglas* paradigm, as afforded to minority plaintiffs.[48]

---

[44]*Id.* at 285–87.

[45]*See id.* at 287–96.

[46]*Id.* at 295; *accord* Jett v. Dallas Indep. Sch. Dist., 491 U.S. 701 (1989) (white football coach transferred by African-American principal can state § 1981 claim); *see also* Bellairs v. Coors Brewing Co., 907 F. Supp. 1448, 1455, 76 FEP 1071 (D. Colo. 1995), *aff'd*, 107 F.3d 880 (10th Cir. 1997).

[47]*See, e.g.*, Deffenbaugh-Williams v. Wal-Mart Stores, Inc., 156 F.3d 581, 588–89, 77 FEP 1699 (5th Cir. 1998) (white employee discriminated against because she was dating African-American man stated valid § 1981 claim), *vacated*, 169 F.3d 215 (5th Cir.), *reinstated except as to issue of punitive damages*, 182 F.3d 333 (5th Cir. 1999); Alizadeh v. Safeway Stores, Inc., 802 F.2d 111, 114, 42 FEP 226 (5th Cir. 1986) (terminated white plaintiff could state claim under § 1981 when discrimination was based on her marriage to man of Iranian descent); Parr v. Woodmen of the World Life Ins. Co., 791 F.2d 888, 890, 41 FEP 22 (11th Cir. 1986) (discrimination against white individual based on his interracial marriage actionable under § 1981); Fiedler v. Marumsco Christian Sch., 631 F.2d 1144, 1149–50 (4th Cir. 1980) (expulsion of white female for dating African-American male student violates § 1981); DeMatteis v. Eastman Kodak Co., 511 F.2d 306, 311–12, 10 FEP 153 (2d Cir. 1975) (white man forced to retire because he sold his house to African American may maintain § 1981 action); Jones v. Adams County, 297 F. Supp. 2d 1132, 1137 (W.D. Wis. 2003) (if white plaintiff can prove that defendant knew of her interracial marriage and this knowledge influenced employment decision, plaintiff will have satisfied § 1981 prerequisite for establishing racial discrimination); Ticali v. Roman Catholic Diocese of Brooklyn, 41 F. Supp. 2d 249, 265 (E.D.N.Y.), *aff'd*, 201 F.3d 432 (2d Cir. 1999).

[48]*See* Reynolds v. School Dist. No. 1, Denver, Colo., 69 F.3d 1523, 1534, 72 FEP 485 (10th Cir. 1995) (white plaintiff suing employer under § 1981 may not rely on *McDonnell Douglas* prima facie case to raise presumption of discrimination absent showing that defendant is unusual employer who discriminates against majority); DeWeese v. Daimler Chrysler Corp., 120 F. Supp. 2d 735, 747 (S.D. Ind. 2000) (same); Hardmann v. University of Akron, 100 F. Supp. 2d 509, 519 (N.D. Ohio 2000), *aff'd*, 40 Fed. Appx. 116 (6th Cir. 2002). *But see* Bass v. Board of County Comm'rs, 256 F.3d 1095, 1102–03 (11th Cir. 2001) (white plaintiff suing employer under § 1981 may rely on *McDonnell Douglas* prima facie case to raise the presumption of discrimination, and is not required to demonstrate that defendant is unusual employer who discriminates against majority).

Courts apply a broad definition of race for § 1981 claims, allowing cases of discrimination based on ancestry or ethnic characteristics, race, or color.[49] Courts have permitted individuals of differing ethnic backgrounds to proceed under § 1981 if they allege discrimination based on their color.[50] In *Saint Francis College v. Al-Khazraji*,[51] the Supreme Court reiterated that, although § 1981 does not apply to national origin discrimination,[52] it does

---

[49]*See* Manatt v. Bank of Am., 339 F.3d 792, 798 (9th Cir. 2003) (employee of Chinese descent could proceed with § 1981 claim); Amini v. Oberlin Coll., 259 F.3d 493, 503 (6th Cir. 2001) (Iranian-born Muslim male stated § 1981 claim when he alleged discrimination based on Middle Eastern race); Ramirez v. Department of Corr., 222 F.3d 1238, 1244, 83 FEP 1786 (10th Cir. 2000) (Hispanics of Mexican-American origin stated § 1981 claim); Magana v. Commonwealth of N. Mariana Islands, 107 F.3d 1436, 1446–47 (9th Cir. 1997) (plaintiff's allegation that she was discriminated against "because she was from the Philippines" sufficient to state Filipino-based race claim); Bisciglia v. Kenosha Unified Sch. Dist. No. 1, 45 F.3d 223, 229–30 (7th Cir. 1995) ("Congress intended to protect from discrimination identifiable classes of persons who are subjected to intentional discrimination solely because of their ancestry or ethnic characteristics"; court held that historical research suggested that Italians may be considered identifiable race and, thus, reversed district court's dismissal of § 1981 claim); Dolnaire v. NME Hosp., Inc., 27 F.3d 507, 509, 65 FEP 674 (11th Cir. 1994) (Filipino who alleged discrimination because of "ancestry or ethnic characteristics" satisfied pleading requirement of § 1981); Daemi v. Church's Fried Chicken, Inc., 931 F.2d 1379, 1387 n.7 (10th Cir. 1991) (plaintiff protected under § 1981 as person of Iranian descent); Lopez v. S.B. Thomas, Inc., 831 F.2d 1184, 1188 (2d Cir. 1987) (§ 1981 claim could be asserted by persons of Puerto Rican descent); Cantu v. Nocona Hills Owners Ass'n, 2001 WL 898437, at *4 (N.D. Tex. July 30, 2001) (Mexican American considered racial minority for purposes of § 1981); Copley v. Bax Global, Inc., 97 F. Supp. 2d 1164, 1167–68 (S.D. Fla. 2000) (termination of Caucasian employee so that employer could fill position with Hispanic employee actionable under § 1981); Stephens v. City of Topeka, 33 F. Supp. 2d 947, 957 (D. Kan.) (plaintiff who identified his race and national origin as "Jamaican" stated viable claim under § 1981), *aff'd*, 1999 U.S. App. LEXIS 20009 (10th Cir. 1999); Singer v. Denver Sch. Dist. No. 1, 959 F. Supp. 1325, 1331 (D. Colo. 1997) (Jews are distinct racial group for purposes of § 1981); Lovell v. Brinker Int'l, Inc., 71 FEP 417, 418 (W.D. Mo. 1996) (Chinese woman who alleged discrimination based on her national origin could state race discrimination claim under § 1981).

[50]*See, e.g.*, Gonzalez v. Stanford Applied Eng'g, Inc., 597 F.2d 1298, 1299, 19 FEP 1661 (9th Cir. 1979) (Mexican-Americans of brown color can sue under § 1981); Aponte v. National Steel Serv. Ctr., 500 F. Supp. 198, 202–03, 24 FEP 609 (N.D. Ill. 1980) (§ 1981 applies to Hispanics because they frequently are identified as "nonwhites"); Vasquez v. McAllen Bag & Supply Co., 21 FEP 1123, 1124–25 (S.D. Tex. 1979) (same); Saad v. Burns Int'l Sec. Servs., Inc., 456 F. Supp. 33, 37, 18 FEP 516 (D.D.C. 1978) (same).

[51]481 U.S. 604, 613, 43 FEP 1305 (1987).

[52]*See* Sagana v. Tenorio, 384 F.3d 731, 739–40 (9th Cir. 2004) (§ 1981 applies to claims of alienage discrimination, which is distinguishable from national origin discrimination), *cert. denied*, 543 U.S. 1149 (2005); *see also* Maldonado v. City of Altus, 433 F.3d 1294, 97 FEP 257 ("English-only" rule at work deemed discrimination on basis of both race and national origin). *See generally* Chapter 7 (National Origin and Citizenship).

apply to intentional discrimination based on "ancestry or ethnic characteristics."[53] According to the Court, "[s]uch discrimination is racial discrimination . . . , whether or not it would be classified as racial in terms of modern scientific theory."[54] Thus, in that case an Arab, although technically Caucasian, was permitted to state a § 1981 claim for race discrimination.[55]

The same day, the Supreme Court held in *Shaare Tefila Congregation v. Cobb*[56] that a Jew could state a § 1982 claim for intentional race discrimination based solely on his ancestry or ethnic characteristics. The Court stated that "Jews and Arabs were among the peoples then considered [by Congress when it enacted §§ 1981 and 1982] to be distinct races and hence within the protection of the statute."[57]

2. Retaliation[58]

The federal courts of appeals uniformly have held that § 1981 covers retaliation claims premised on the assertion of rights protected by § 1981.[59] Some courts that have permitted such claims have limited them to situations where the retaliation is either racially

---

[53]481 U.S. at 613.

[54]*Id.*

[55]*Id.*; *see also* Fonseca v. Food Servs. of Ariz., Inc., 374 F.3d 840, 849 (9th Cir. 2004) (although § 1981 does not apply to national origin discrimination, Hispanic employee could proceed with claim based on "ancestry or ethnic characteristics").

[56]481 U.S. 615, 43 FEP 1309 (1987).

[57]*Id.* at 617–18.

[58]*See generally* Chapter 14 (Retaliation).

[59]*See* Humphries v. CBDCS W., Inc., 474 F.3d 387, 398, 99 FEP 872 (7th Cir. 2007) (retaliation claim may be asserted under § 1981); Manatt v. Bank of Am., 339 F.3d 792, 799–801 (9th Cir. 2003) (recognizing retaliation claim as viable under § 1981); Foley v. University of Houston Sys., 355 F.3d 333, 338–39 (5th Cir. 2003) (same); Ajayi v. Aramark Bus. Servs., Inc., 336 F.3d 520, 533 (7th Cir. 2003) (same—Title VII and § 1981 case); O'Neal v. Ferguson Constr. Co., 237 F.3d 1248, 1257–58, 84 FEP 1491 (10th Cir. 2001) (same); Spriggs v. Diamond Auto Glass, 242 F.3d 179, 190 n.14 (4th Cir. 2001) (same); Johnson v. University of Cincinnati, 215 F.3d 561, 570 (6th Cir. 2000) (same); Anjelino v. New York Times Co., 200 F.3d 73, 98 (3d Cir. 1999) (same); Hawkins v. 1115 Legal Serv. Care, 163 F.3d 684, 693, 78 FEP 882 (2d Cir. 1998); Kim v. Nash Finch Co., 123 F.3d 1046, 1059, 75 FEP 1741 (8th Cir. 1997); Powell v. City of Pittsfield, 143 F. Supp. 2d 94, 127 (D. Mass. 2001); Zezulewicz v. Port Auth. of Allegheny County, 290 F. Supp. 2d 583, 598 (W.D. Pa. 2003); Glymph v. District of Columbia, 211 F. Supp. 2d 152, 154 (D.D.C. 2002) (same); *cf.* Andrews v. Lakeshore Rehab. Hosp., 140 F.3d 1405, 1411–13, 76 FEP 1617 (11th Cir. 1998) (alleged retaliatory discharge due to filing claim of race discrimination with EEOC actionable under § 1981); Little v. United Tech., Carrier Transicold Div., 103 F.3d 956, 960–61 (11th Cir. 1997) (no prima facie case of retaliation under § 1981

motivated or is designed to perpetuate a discriminatory condition.[60] Several courts have recognized retaliation claims of employees alleging retaliatory conduct based on efforts to protect the rights of individuals other than the plaintiff.[61]

---

where white plaintiff claimed retaliatory discharge for complaining about co-worker's derogatory remarks about African Americans).

Before *Patterson v. McLean Credit Union*, 491 U.S. 164, 49 FEP 1814 (1989) (discussed in Section II.A *supra*), courts were split on the issue of whether race-related retaliation claims could be brought under § 1981. *Compare* Sherpell v. Humnoke Sch. Dist. No. 5, 874 F.2d 536, 540, 49 FEP 1405 (8th Cir. 1989) (retaliation claim may be brought under § 1981), *aff'd mem.*, 985 F.2d 566 (8th Cir. 1991) *and* Goff v. Continental Oil Co., 678 F.2d 593, 597–98, 29 FEP 79 (5th Cir. 1982) (§ 1981 applicable to claims of retaliation based on plaintiff's opposition to racial discrimination) *with* Tafoya v. Adams, 816 F.2d 555, 557–58, 43 FEP 929 (10th Cir. 1987) (§ 1981 retaliation claim would not be entertained where Mexican Americans alleged that they were discharged for filing EEOC charges, absent allegations of racial discrimination). After *Patterson*, but before the 1991 Act, most courts dismissed § 1981 post-hire retaliation claims, reasoning that retaliation does not involve the right to "make and enforce" a contract. *See, e.g.*, McKnight v. General Motors Corp., 908 F.2d 104, 112, 53 FEP 505 (7th Cir. 1990) (rejecting employee's claim of retaliatory discharge for filing claims of racial discrimination); Williams v. First Union Nat'l Bank, 920 F.2d 232, 234, 55 FEP 799 (4th Cir. 1990) (rejecting employee's claim of being subjected to discriminatory conditions of employment in retaliation for filing EEOC charge). During that period, however, a few courts held that retaliatory conduct was actionable under § 1981 if it affected the right to enforce contracts through the legal process. *See, e.g.*, Mozee v. American Commercial Marine Serv. Co., 940 F.2d 1036, 1052, 56 FEP 1155 (7th Cir. 1991).

[60]*See, e.g., Manatt*, 339 F.3d at 800; *see also* O'Neal v. Ferguson Constr. Co., 237 F.3d 1248, 1257–58, 84 FEP 1491 (10th Cir. 2001) (retaliation claim under § 1981 requires proof that retaliation was product of "racial animus").

[61]*See, e.g.*, Foley v. University of Houston Sys., 355 F.3d 333, 340–41 (5th Cir. 2003) (implicitly assuming professor's retaliation claim for supporting colleague's allegations of race discrimination actionable under § 1981, but granting summary judgment to defendant based on qualified immunity); *Johnson*, 215 F.3d 561 (vice-president's efforts to advocate for affirmative action process and minority hires protected conduct under § 1981); Jackson v. Motel 6 Multipurpose, Inc., 130 F.3d 999, 1007 (11th Cir. 1997) (plaintiffs' § 1981 retaliation claim allowed to proceed based on allegations that plaintiffs were fired for refusing to participate in employer's discrimination against nonwhite customers); Skinner v. Total Petroleum, Inc., 859 F.2d 1439, 1447, 48 FEP 151 (10th Cir. 1988) (employee subjected to retaliation because of his efforts to vindicate rights of racial minorities may bring § 1981 claim); Hagemann v. Molinari, 14 F. Supp. 2d 277, 286 (E.D.N.Y. 1998) (white employee can pursue § 1981 claim for retaliation based on efforts to vindicate rights of racial minorities, but rejecting specific claim in this instance because minority whose rights plaintiff was attempting to vindicate was not employee and did not have contract with employer). *But see Little*, 103 F.3d 956, 961, 72 FEP 1560 (11th Cir. 1997) (where white plaintiff did not allege discrimination against him based on his race, but based retaliation claim solely on rights exercised under Title VII's opposition clause, § 1981 claim properly dismissed).

3. Other Types of Discrimination

Section 1981 applies to discrimination based only on race, as defined broadly by the Supreme Court in *Saint Francis College v. Al-Khazraji*.[62] Other bases generally have been rejected.

The Supreme Court in *Al-Khazraji* held that an Arab and a Jew, respectively, could state *race* but not national origin or religion discrimination claims under § 1981.[63] Thus, generally, a § 1981 claim based on allegations of national origin[64] or religious[65] discrimination cannot be maintained.

Early decisions held that § 1981 prohibited discrimination based on alienage.[66] Later cases, however, have been split. For example, the Fifth Circuit, sitting en banc in *Bhandari v. First National Bank*,[67]

---

[62]481 U.S. 604, 609 (1987).

[63]*Id.* at 613 (§ 1981 claim); *see also* Shaare Tefila Congregation v. Cobb, 481 U.S. 615, 617, 43 FEP 1309 (1987) (§ 1982 claim).

[64]*See* Betkerur v. Aultman Hosp. Ass'n, 78 F.3d 1079, 1095 n.11, 78 FEP 1765 (6th Cir. 1996); Chaiffetz v. Robertson Research Holding, Ltd., 798 F.2d 731, 735, 41 FEP 1097 (5th Cir. 1986) (§ 1981 does not encompass claim based on national origin); Anooya v. Hilton Hotels Corp., 733 F.2d 48, 49–50, 34 FEP 1529 (7th Cir. 1984) (alleged discrimination because of Iraqi background solely based on national origin fails to state cause of action under § 1981); Shah v. Mt. Zion Hosp., 642 F.2d 268, 272, 27 FEP 772 (9th Cir. 1981) ("[§] 1981 only prohibits racial discrimination" and does not apply to a Caucasian of East Indian descent); Rawlins-Roa v. United Way of Wyandotte County, Inc., 977 F. Supp. 1101, 1106–07, 75 FEP 294 (D. Kan. 1997); Hyman v. First Union Corp., 980 F. Supp. 46, 52–53 (D.D.C. 1997); Cardona v. American Express Travel Related Servs. Co., 720 F. Supp. 960, 961–62, 50 FEP 1510 (S.D. Fla. 1989); Ohemeng v. Delaware State Coll., 676 F. Supp. 65, 46 FEP 495 (D. Del. 1988), *aff'd mem.*, 862 F.2d 309, 58 FEP 1584 (1988). The issue is discussed further in Chapter 7 (National Origin and Citizenship).

[65]*See* Pennington v. City of Huntsville, 261 F.3d 1262 n.1 (11th Cir. 2001) (discrimination based on religious beliefs not covered under § 1981); Simmons v. Sports Training Inst., 692 F. Supp. 181, 182, 47 FEP 801 (S.D.N.Y. 1988) (same); *cf.* Runyon v. McCrary, 427 U.S. 160, 167 (1976) ("[Plaintiffs] do not present any question of the right of a private school to limit its student body to boys, to girls, or to adherents of a particular religious faith, since 42 U.S.C § 1981 is in no way addressed to such categories of selectivity.").

[66]*See, e.g.*, Ortega v. Merit Ins. Co., 433 F. Supp. 135, 138 (N.D. Ill. 1977); Jones v. United Gas Improvement Corp., 68 F.R.D. 1, 12, 12 FEP 344 (E.D. Pa. 1975); Mohamed v. Parks, 352 F. Supp. 518, 519–20, 5 FEP 494 (D. Mass. 1973); Lopez v. White Plains Hous. Auth., 355 F. Supp. 1016, 1025–26 (S.D.N.Y. 1972). *But see* De Malherbe v. Elevator Constructors Local 8, 438 F. Supp. 1121, 1131–32, 19 FEP 1581 (N.D. Cal. 1977) (stating in dictum that § 1981 does not necessarily prohibit alienage discrimination by federal government).

[67]887 F.2d 609, 55 FEP 226 (5th Cir. 1989) (en banc).

held that § 1981 prohibits only race, not alienage, discrimination.[68] *Al-Khazraji* arguably supports that distinction. Other courts, however, have concluded that § 1981 prohibits discrimination based on citizenship status.[69]

Section 1981 is not applicable to discrimination on the basis of age,[70] disability[71] or gender, including claims of sexual harassment.[72]

III. SCOPE AND COVERAGE OF THE CIVIL RIGHTS ACT OF 1871, 42 U.S.C. § 1983

A. Statutory Authority

Section 1983 provides that:

> Every person who, under color of any statute, ordinance, regulation, custom or usage, of any State or Territory, . . . subjects, or causes to be subjected, any citizen of the United States or other person within the jurisdiction thereof to the deprivation of any rights, privileges, or immunities secured by the Constitution and laws, shall be liable to the party injured in an action at law, suit in equity, or other proper proceeding for redress.[73]

---

[68]*Id.* at 610; *see also* Van Abrahams v. Pioneer Elecs. USA, Inc., 52 FEP 1010, 1011 (C.D. Cal. 1989) (citizenship bias not sufficiently indicative of race bias).

[69]*See, e.g.*, Sagana v. Tenorio, 384 F.3d 731, 739–40 (9th Cir. 2004) (§ 1981 applies to claims of alienage discrimination); Anderson v. Conboy, 156 F.3d 167, 77 FEP 1278 (2d Cir. 1998) (§ 1981 prohibits private discrimination based on alienage); Duane v. Geico, 37 F.3d 1036, 1040, 1044 (4th Cir. 1994) (§ 1981 covers citizenship discrimination); *see also* Chacko v. Texas A&M Univ., 960 F. Supp. 1180 (S.D. Tex. 1997) (same), *aff'd*, 149 F.3d 1175 (5th Cir. 1998) (unpublished). The issue is discussed further in Chapter 7 (National Origin and Citizenship).

[70]*See* Aramburu v. Boeing Co., 112 F.3d 1398, 1141, 77 FEP 238 (10th Cir. 1997); Barge v. Anheuser-Busch, Inc., 87 F.3d 256, 258, 72 FEP 426 (8th Cir. 1996); Williamson v. Hartmann Luggage Co., 34 F. Supp. 2d 1056, 1063 (M.D. Tenn. 1998).

[71]*See* Sherlock v. Montefiore Med. Ctr., 84 F.3d 522, 527, 70 FEP 1377 (2d Cir. 1996); Kilcrease v. Coffee County, 951 F. Supp. 212, 215 (M.D. Ala. 1996) (citing Kodish v. United Air Lines, Inc., 628 F.2d 1301 (10th Cir. 1980)).

[72]*See, e.g.*, Runyon v. McCrary, 427 U.S. 160, 194–95 (1976) (dictum; § 1981 does not apply to discrimination based on sex); Hawkins v. 1115 Legal Serv. Care, 163 F.3d 684, 693, 78 FEP 882 (2d Cir. 1998); *Sherlock*, 84 F.3d at 527; Bratton v. Roadway Package Sys., Inc., 77 F.3d 168, 177, 70 FEP 178 (7th Cir. 1996); Jones v. Bechtel, 788 F.2d 571, 574, 40 FEP 1067 (9th Cir. 1986); Manzanares v. Safeway Stores, Inc., 593 F.2d 968, 971, 19 FEP 191 (10th Cir. 1979).

[73]42 U.S.C. § 1983 (2000).

This statute, along with the conspiracy statutes that now appear at 42 U.S.C. §§ 1985 and 1986, originally was enacted as § 1 of the Civil Rights Act of 1871, also known as the Ku Klux Klan Act.[74] The statute was passed pursuant to § 5 of the Fourteenth Amendment, which empowers Congress to enforce its provisions.

B. Cognizable Defendants Under § 1983

1. The State Action Requirement and Private Discrimination

By its terms, § 1983 reaches only persons acting "under color of" state law. The statute does not reach purely private conduct, nor does it reach conduct of federal agencies and officials in most instances.[75] The requirement that defendants in a § 1983 action must have acted under color of state law has come to be known as the state action requirement.[76]

The state action requirement presents no real obstacles where discriminatory practices have been implemented by governmental agencies and officials.[77] Thus, § 1983 has been used to reach employment discrimination involving police[78] and fire[79]

---

[74]Act of Apr. 20, 1871, ch. 22, § 1, 17 Stat. 13 (codified at 42 U.S.C. § 1983 (2000)).

[75]See Section III.B.2 infra. See generally Chapter 31 (Federal Employee Litigation).

[76]There is extensive literature in the legal journals discussing the issue of state action. Some of the most significant pieces in this area were written in the early 1960s, prior to the passage of the Civil Rights Act of 1964. See, e.g., Charles L. Black, Jr., Foreword: "State Action," Equal Protection, and California's Proposition 14, 81 HARV. L. REV. 69 (1967); Vern Countryman, The Constitution and Job Discrimination, 39 WASH. L. REV. 74 (1964); Harold L. Horowitz, The Misleading Search for "State Action" Under the Fourteenth Amendment, 30 S. CAL. L. REV. 208 (1957); Kenneth L. Karst & William W. Van Alstyne, Comment: Sit-Ins and State Action—Mr. Justice Douglas Concurring, 14 STAN. L. REV. 762 (1962); Thomas P. Lewis, The Meaning of State Action, 60 COLUM. L. REV. 1083 (1960); William W. Van Alstyne & Kenneth L. Karst, State Action, 14 STAN. L. REV. 3 (1961); Harry H. Wellington, The Constitution, the Labor Union, and "Governmental Action," 70 YALE L.J. 345 (1961); Jerre S. Williams, The Twilight of State Action, 41 TEXAS L. REV. 347 (1963).

[77]See Section III.B.3 infra.

[78]See, e.g., Mandell v. County of Suffolk, 316 F.3d 368, 384–85, 90 FEP 1328 (2d Cir. 2003) (evaluating alleged retaliation against former deputy police inspector for exercise of free speech rights); Phillips v. Bowen, 278 F.3d 103, 110 (2d Cir. 2002) (similar); Gustafson v. Jones, 290 F.3d 895, 910–13 (7th Cir. 2002) (similar).

[79]See, e.g., Washington v. Normandy Fire Prot. Dist., 328 F.3d 400, 404 (8th Cir. 2003) (plaintiff, former assistant fire chief, submitted adequate proof to support

departments, public schools, colleges and universities,[80] and public hospitals.[81]

The more difficult cases arise where a *private* institution is arguably so involved with the state that state action is alleged to exist. Allegations of state involvement sometimes are based on licensing, regulation, receipt of public funds, location in state-owned facilities, the carrying out of functions normally exercised by the state, the existence of a state-supported monopoly, or some combination of these factors.

The Supreme Court in *Brentwood Academy v. Tennessee SSAA*[82] stated that "no one fact can function as a necessary condition across the board for finding state action."[83] The Court described the "judicial obligation" in this area as "not only to 'preserv[e] an area of individual freedom by limiting the reach of federal law' and 'avoi[d] the imposition of responsibility on a State for conduct it could not control,' but also to assure that constitutional standards are invoked 'when it can be said that the State is *responsible* for the specific conduct of which the plaintiff complains.' "[84] The Court

---

claim of retaliation for exercise of free speech rights); Greenawalt v. Sun City West Fire Dist., 250 F. Supp. 2d 1200, 1217 (D. Ariz. 2003) (plaintiff fire fighter adequately pled § 1983 claim of discharge in violation of due process rights).

[80]*See, e.g.*, Hulen v. Yates, 322 F.3d 1229, 1238–44 (10th Cir. 2003) (finding that associate professor's statements were protected under First Amendment, but that professor's procedural due process claim failed); Lockridge v. Board of Trustees of Univ. of Ark., 315 F.3d 1005, 1010, 90 FEP 1319 (8th Cir. 2003) (en banc) (state university chancellor immune from suit in individual capacity on employee's claim of race discrimination in promotion process where faculty member acknowledged he did not apply for position); Vukadinovich v. Board of Sch. Trs. of North Newton Sch. Corp., 278 F.3d 693, 700–701 (7th Cir. 2002) (discharged public school teacher failed to show he was denied procedural due process or that his discharge was in retaliation for protected free speech).

[81]*See, e.g.*, Ulrich v. City and County of S.F., 308 F.3d 968, 981–85 (9th Cir. 2002) (physician at city hospital stated claim of alleged retaliation in violation of First Amendment and alleged violation of due process); Jenkins v. County of Riverside, 25 Fed. Appx. 607, 609 (9th Cir. 2002) (county hospital employee demonstrated she had position that required procedural due process before her termination; summary judgment reversed for county).

[82]531 U.S. 288 (2001).

[83]*Id.* at 295.

[84]*Id.* The Supreme Court cited both *National Collegiate Athletic Ass'n v. Tarkanian*, 488 U.S. 179 (1988), and *Blum v. Yaretsky*, 457 U.S. 991, 1004 (1982). In *Tarkanian*, the Court found no state action on the part of the NCAA, in part because the Association's policies were shaped not by a single state, but by organizations from private institutions and many other states, leaving the ties to the state of

described its earlier cases as standing for the propositions that state action may be found (1) where the state exercises "coercive power";[85] (2) where the state provides "significant encouragement, either overt or covert" or when a private entity acts as a "willful participant either in joint activity with the state or its agents";[86] (3) where a private action is controlled by an "agency of the state";[87] (4) where the state delegates a public function to a private entity;[88] or (5) when the private action is "entwined with governmental policies" or when government is "entwined in [its] management or control."[89]

The Court in *Brentwood* found the Tennessee SSAA to be a state actor, given what the Court called the "pervasive entwinement of public institutions and public officials in its composition and workings."[90] The Tennessee SSAA is a private association that regulated interscholastic sports among the public and private member high schools in Tennessee. The "pervasive entwinement" was based on the fact that 84 percent of the Association's membership was from public schools, state board of education members served ex officio on the Association's board of control and legislative council, and the Association's ministerial employees were eligible for membership in the state retirement system.[91]

One of the more common state action issues in the employment context concerns privately owned but publicly subsidized universities. In *Rendell-Baker v. Kohn*,[92] the Supreme Court considered whether § 1983 was applicable to the employment practices of a privately owned school that received over 90 percent of

---

Nevada too insubstantial to ground a state action claim. 488 U.S. at 193. The Court held in *Blum* that "a State normally can be held responsible for a private decision only when it has exercised coercive power or has provided such significant encouragement, either overt or covert, that the choice must in law be deemed to be that of the State." 457 U.S. at 1004.

[85]531 U.S. at 296 (citing Blum v. Yaretsky, 457 U.S. 991, 1004 (1982)).

[86]*Id.* (citing Blum v. Yaretsky, 457 U.S. 991 (1982) and Lugar v. Edmonson Oil Co., 457 U.S. 922, 941 (1982)).

[87]*Id.* (citing Pennsylvania v. Board of Dirs. of City Trusts of Phila., 353 U.S. 230, 231 (1957)).

[88]*Id.* (citing Edmondson v. Leesville Concrete Co., 500 U.S. 614, 627–28 (1991)).

[89]*Id.* (citing Evans v. Newton, 382 U.S. 296, 299 (1966)).

[90]*Id.* at 298.

[91]*Id.* at 300.

[92]457 U.S. 830, 842 (1982).

its funds from state and federal agencies through tuition funding plans. Even though at least one of the plaintiffs was hired pursuant to a grant administered by a state committee, the Court found no state action, declaring that "since the school's fiscal relationship with the state is not any different from that of many contractors performing services for the government, there is no symbiotic relationship between the school and the state."[93]

Similarly, even substantial state funding and regulation have been held not to convert the conduct of hospitals,[94] utilities,[95] or an Indian tribe social services agency[96] into state action for purposes of § 1983.

---

[93]*Id.* at 840–43; *accord* Cohen v. Illinois Inst. of Tech., 524 F.2d 818, 824, 11 FEP 659 (7th Cir. 1975) (university not acting under color of state law and thus dismissal for failure to state claim under § 1983 granted). *But see* Pennsylvania v. Board of Dirs. of City Trusts of Phila., 353 U.S. 230, 231 (1957) (privately endowed Girard College was state actor because consistent with terms of settlor's gift, college's board of directors was state agency established by state law); *cf.* Burton v. Wilmington Parking Auth., 365 U.S. 715 (1961) (restaurant leased to private enterprise by publicly owned and operated facility was state actor because of several factors that collectively amounted to "symbiotic relationship").

[94]*See, e.g.*, Rockwell v. Cape Cod Hosp., 26 F.3d 254, 258 (1st Cir. 1994) (government regulation and receipt of federal funds insufficient to show hospital acted under color of state law); Mendez v. Belton, 739 F.2d 15, 17, 35 FEP 625 (1st Cir. 1984) (§ 1983 not applicable to highly regulated private, nonprofit hospital that received Medicare and Medicaid funds); Black v. Barberton Citizens Hosp., 8 F. Supp. 2d 697, 701 (N.D. Ohio 1998) (less than majority of hospital trustees were public officials, so hospital was not state actor).

[95]*See, e.g.*, Martin v. Pacific Nw. Bell Tel. Co., 441 F.2d 1116, 1118, 3 FEP 519 (9th Cir. 1971) ("The fact that a private corporation, such as Pacific Bell, enjoys an economic monopoly which is protected and regulated by the state does not necessarily bring its every action within the purview of Section 1983."); Stoutt v. Southern Bell Tel. & Tel. Co., 598 F. Supp. 1000, 1001, 36 FEP 1778 (S.D. Fla. 1984) (fact that defendant's operations are subject to state regulation or that it is granted quasi-monopoly status does not transform company's conduct into state action).

[96]E.F.W. v. St. Stephen's Indian High Sch., 264 F.3d 1297, 1305–06 (10th Cir. 2001) (employees of Indian tribe social services agency that receive state funds to provide services to reservation children and that agreed to use state rules and regulations as their own not acting under color of state law and not subject to suit under § 1983); *see also* Schnabel v. Abramson, 232 F.3d 83, 86–87, 84 FEP 779 (2d Cir. 2000) (legal aid society not state actor amenable to suit under § 1983 given lack of governmental control over or interference with society's affairs, notwithstanding receipt of substantial government funds); Dowe v. Total Action Against Poverty, 145 F.3d 563, 568–59, 77 FEP 151 (4th Cir. 1998) (public funding and state regulation do not turn entity into state actor); Sherlock v. Montefiore Med. Ctr., 84 F.3d 522, 527 (2d Cir. 1996) (fact that municipality is responsible for providing medical attention to persons held in its custody does not make independent contractor rendering services

Even where a private institution is brought within the scope of § 1983 by some state action theory or by conspiring with a state actor, it is insulated from respondeat superior liability, as are municipalities, under *Monell v. Department of Social Services.*[97] The institution can be held liable under § 1983 only for its own actions, customs, or policies.[98]

Courts have held that government subsidies and regulation will not convert private entities into state actors.[99] A not-for-profit organization that counseled rape victims and received public funding was not thereby converted into a state actor for § 1983 purposes.[100] A private attorney hired to consult with a public school

---

for municipality state actor with respect to its employment decisions); Downey v. Coalition Against Rape and Abuse, Inc., 143 F. Supp. 2d 423, 437–40 (D.N.J. 2001) (mere receipt of public funds did not convert nonprofit into state actor; plaintiff had to show that state was sole source of referred clientele, that state had power to hire or fire employees, or that state could require public official to be named to board in order to show state action); Reil v. Clinton County, 75 F. Supp. 2d 37, 40–41 (N.D.N.Y. 1999) (not-for-profit development corporation not state actor for purposes of § 1983 claim, even though corporation received county funds, where state had no involvement in allocation of organization's resources); Henderson v. Center for Cmty. Alternatives, 911 F. Supp. 689, 707 (S.D.N.Y. 1996).

[97]436 U.S. 658, 691, 17 FEP 873 (1978); *see* Section III.B.3.a *infra*.

[98]Sanders v. Sears, Roebuck & Co., 984 F.2d 972, 975 (8th Cir. 1993) (department store not subject to respondeat superior liability under § 1983); Rojas v. Alexander's Dep't Store, Inc., 924 F.2d 406, 408 (2d Cir. 1990) (private employers not liable under § 1983 based on respondeat superior); DeVargas v. Mason & Hanger-Silas Mason Co., 844 F.2d 714, 723, 53 FEP 1232 (10th Cir. 1988) ("the rationale of [*Monell's*] holding applies equally to corporate defendants"); Iskander v. Village of Forest Park, 690 F.2d 126, 128 (7th Cir. 1982) ("a private corporation is not vicariously liable under § 1983 for its employees' deprivations of others' civil rights"); Powell v. Shopco Laurel Co., 678 F.2d 504, 506 (4th Cir. 1982) (*Monell's* holding "equally applicable to the liability of private corporations").

[99]*Schnabel*, 232 F.3d at 86–87 (legal aid society not state actor amenable to suit under § 1983 given lack of governmental control over or interference with society's affairs, notwithstanding receipt of substantial government funds); *Sherlock*, 84 F.3d at 527 (fact that municipality is responsible for providing medical attention to persons held in its custody does not make independent contractor rendering services for municipality state actor with respect to its employment decisions); *Reil*, 75 F. Supp. 2d at 40–41 (not-for-profit development corporation not state actor for purposes of § 1983 claim, even though corporation received county funds, where state had no involvement in allocation of organization's resources).

[100]*See Dowe*, 145 F.3d at 658–59 (public funding and state regulation do not turn entity into state actor); *Downey*, 143 F. Supp. 2d at 437–40 (mere receipt of public funds did not convert nonprofit into state actor; plaintiff had to show that state was sole source of referred clientele, that state had power to hire or fire employees, or that state could require public official to be named to board in order to show state action).

board was found not to be acting under color of state law.[101] Nor do labor organizations and their officials become state actors simply by virtue of their normal dealings with state agencies and officials.[102] Moreover, a union president was found not to be acting under color of state law for § 1983 purposes where the plaintiff could not establish a common, unconstitutional goal between the union president and state officials.[103]

2. The Federal Government

Section 1983 does not apply to discrimination by the federal government.[104] Therefore, the actions of federal officials, unless taken in conjunction with state officials or pursuant to local custom, law, or regulation, cannot be challenged in a § 1983 suit.[105] In a footnote in *Wheeldin v. Wheeler*,[106] the Supreme Court explained the breadth of § 1983:

> Congress made liable in civil suits "every person" who "under color" of any state or territorial law deprives anyone of a right "secured by the Constitution and laws" of the United States. But respondent [an investigator for the House Un-American Activities Committee] was not acting "under color" of state or territorial law.[107]

Wheeldin has since been cited in support of the proposition that § 1983 "applies only to persons acting under color of state or territorial law. Therefore, the statute cannot apply to federal officers . . . who act only under federal law."[108]

---

[101]Raines v. Indianapolis Pub. Sch., 52 Fed. Appx. 828, 830 (7th Cir. 2002).

[102]Commodari v. Long Island Univ., 62 Fed. Appx. 28, 30 (2d Cir. 2003) (absent concert of action between union and state, union's action did not constitute state action as required for union member's § 1983 action).

[103]*See* Stagman v. Ryan, 176 F.3d 986, 1003, 161 LRRM 2204 (7th Cir. 1999).

[104]*See generally* Chapter 31 (Federal Employee Litigation).

[105]Redding v. Christian, 161 F. Supp. 2d 671, 675 (W.D.N.C. 2001) (federal employee does not act under color of state law even if he works with state actors in pursuing particular investigation).

[106]373 U.S. 647 (1963).

[107]*Id.* at 650 n.2 (citations omitted).

[108]LaRouche v. City of N.Y., 369 F. Supp. 565, 567 (S.D.N.Y. 1974) (Central Intelligence Agency and its director cannot be sued under § 1983); *see also* Franklin v. Henderson, 15 Fed. Appx. 205, 206 (6th Cir. 2001) (Postmaster General not subject to suit under § 1983). *But cf.* Walker v. Washington, 627 F.2d 541, 545 (D.C. Cir. 1980) (employees of District of Columbia not employees of United States for purposes of federal court jurisdiction).

3.   State and Local Governments

By its terms, § 1983 applies to "persons" who act under color of state law. Who is such a "person"? Although Congress can expressly create a right of action directly against state and local governments—as it did with the 1972 amendments to Title VII[109]—it did not do so with § 1983. The Supreme Court therefore initially held, in *Monroe v. Pape*,[110] that § 1983 did not cover governmental *entities*, as opposed to government *officials*, because government entities are not "persons." However, as discussed below, the Supreme Court later changed its mind, at least with regard to municipalities.

a. Local Governments. In *Monell v. Department of Social Services*,[111] the Supreme Court overruled *Monroe* as it applied to local governments.[112] The Court held that municipalities and individual municipal agents acting in their official capacities[113] may be sued under § 1983 for both damages and injunctive relief.[114] The petitioners in *Monell*, female employees of the New York Department of Social Services and Board of Education, challenged under § 1983 the city's policy requiring pregnant employees to take unpaid leaves of absence. The district court and the court of appeals held that the municipal entities were not cognizable defendants under § 1983 because they were "municipalities" within the meaning of *Monroe v. Pape*. The Supreme Court reversed, declaring that:

---

[109]*See* Fitzpatrick v. Bitzer, 427 U.S. 445, 456–57, 12 FEP 1586 (1976) (Congress properly exercised its power under § 5 of Fourteenth Amendment in extending Title VII coverage to state governments, thereby abrogating Eleventh Amendment immunity).

[110]365 U.S. 167, 190–92 (1961).

[111]436 U.S. 658, 663, 17 FEP 873 (1978).

[112]Not all courts agree that *Monell* applies to all forms of relief. In *Chaloux v. Killeen*, 886 F.2d 247, 250 (9th Cir. 1989), the Ninth Circuit held that *Monell* does not apply to claims for prospective injunctive relief. Although several courts have rejected *Chaloux*, *see* Duranne v. Brooklyn Police Dep't, 315 F.3d 65, 71 & n.4 (1st Cir. 2002), the Colorado Supreme Court has followed *Chaloux*. *See* Jackson v. State, 966 F.2d 1046, 1054 (Colo. 1998).

[113]The liability of individual government officials under § 1983 in their *individual* capacities is discussed in Section III.B.4 *infra*.

[114]*Monell*, 436 U.S. at 690. In *City of Newport v. Fact Concerts, Inc.*, 453 U.S. 247, 268–71 (1981), the Court held that punitive damages could not be awarded against municipalities under § 1983.

Our analysis of the legislative history of the Civil Rights Act of 1871 compels the conclusion that Congress *did* intend municipalities and other local government units to be included among those persons to whom § 1983 applies. Local governing bodies, therefore, can be sued directly under § 1983 for monetary, declaratory, or injunctive relief where, as here, the action that is alleged to be unconstitutional implements or executes a policy statement, ordinance, regulation, or decision officially adopted and promulgated by that body's officers.[115]

The "official policy" restriction is significant. The restriction bars respondeat superior liability against local governmental bodies for their employees' unauthorized misconduct.[116] It allows recovery, however, "for constitutional deprivations visited pursuant to governmental 'custom' even though such a custom has not received formal approval through the body's official decisionmaking channels."[117]

Courts have generally developed three different ways of establishing the existence of an official policy or custom. First, a municipal employee can be found to have acted pursuant to a formal government policy or a standard operating procedure long accepted within the government entity.[118] Second, as the Supreme Court concluded in *Pembaur v. City of Cincinnati*,[119] liability attaches to the local government where the accused individual has policy-making authority, making the individual's conduct an act of official government policy.[120] The Court explained that:

---

[115]436 U.S. at 690 (footnotes omitted).

[116]*Id.* at 691–95 ("Congress did not intend municipalities to be held liable unless action pursuant to official municipal policy of some nature caused a constitutional tort. In particular, we conclude that a municipality cannot be held liable *solely* because it employs a tortfeasor—or, in other words, a municipality cannot be held liable under § 1983 on a respondeat superior theory.").

[117]*Id.* at 690–91.

[118]Jett v. Dallas Indep. Sch. Dist., 491 U.S. 701, 737 (1989); *see also* Board of County Comm'rs v. Brown, 520 U.S. 397, 403–04 (1997) ("Locating a 'policy' ensures that a municipality is held liable only for those deprivations resulting from the decisions of its duly constituted legislative body or of those officials whose acts may fairly be said to be those of the municipality."); Brown v. District of Columbia, 251 F. Supp. 2d 152, 164 (D.D.C. 2003) (municipality's alleged failure to train its employees not official policy or custom where alleged failure not " 'deliberate' and 'conscious' ").

[119]475 U.S. 469 (1986).

[120]*Id.* at 480–81 (plurality opinion); *see also* Jeffes v. Barnes, 208 F.3d 49, 57, 16 IER 333 (2d Cir. 2000) ("the official in question need not be a municipal policymaker for all purposes . . . . Thus, the Court must ask whether the governmental official is a final policymaker for the local government in a particular area, or on the particular issue involved in the action.").

Municipal liability attaches only where the decisionmaker possesses final authority to establish municipal policy with respect to the action ordered. The fact that a particular official—even a policymaking official—has discretion in the exercise of particular functions does not, without more, give rise to municipal liability based on an exercise of that discretion.[121]

Third, an official with policy-making authority can ratify the unconstitutional actions of a subordinate, converting the behavior into official policy for liability purposes.[122]

The latter two methods for circumventing the official policy limitation on municipal liability require that "the trial judge must identify those officials or governmental bodies who speak with final policymaking authority for the local governmental actor concerning the action alleged to have caused the particular constitutional or statutory violation at issue."[123] Whether an official speaks with final policy-making authority is a question of state law.[124] The Supreme Court has found that a municipality could not be held liable under § 1983 for a non–policy maker's wrongful conduct unless the plaintiff could demonstrate that the "need for action by the policymaker [was] so obvious that the failure to act [rose] to deliberate indifference."[125]

---

[121]*Pembaur*, 475 U.S. at 481–82.

[122]City of St. Louis v. Praprotnik, 475 U.S. 112, 128 (1988) (plurality opinion); *see also* Randle v. Aurora, 69 F.3d 441, 447, 69 FEP 489 (10th Cir. 1995) (only those officials with "final policymaking authority" can subject municipality to liability; question of whether official has "final policymaking authority" is question of state law).

[123]Jett v. Dallas Indep. Sch. Dist., 491 U.S. 701, 737 (1989).

[124]Ulrich v. City and County of S.F., 308 F.3d 968, 985 (9th Cir. 2002) (city charter delegated personnel authority to director of health; individual who was not director of health did not have final policy-making authority); Horwitz v. Board of Educ. of Avoca Sch. Dist. 37, 260 F.3d 602, 619, 86 FEP 688 (7th Cir. 2001) (nothing in Illinois School Code allowed court to infer that superintendent or principal had been delegated final policy-making authority); Bechtel v. City of Belton, Mo., 250 F.3d 1157, 1161 (8th Cir. 2001) (fire chief did not have final policy-making authority where his actions were subject to review of city administrator).

[125]*See, e.g.*, Board of County Comm'rs of Bryan County v. Brown, 520 U.S. 397, 418 (1997). Under certain circumstances, a supervisor or authoritative policy maker's actions, even if contrary to the municipality's published policies, may give rise to § 1983 liability if the plaintiff can prove that the alleged misconduct was so pervasive among the employees of the municipality as to constitute a custom or usage with the force of law. *See also* Jeffes v. Barnes, 208 F.3d 49, 57, 16 IER 333 (2d Cir. 2000); Vela v. Village of Sauk Village, 218 F.3d 661, 665, 83 FEP 227 (7th Cir. 2000); Blair v. City of Pomona, 223 F.3d 1074, 1079 (9th Cir. 2000); Greensboro

A facially proper policy is not controlling where a contrary custom or practice is proven.[126] Where formal policy-making authority is vested exclusively in a particular city or county agency, however, and where that agency has promulgated a nondiscrimination policy, the intentionally discriminatory acts of the head of the agency normally do not by themselves constitute official policy.[127] But where a municipality looks the other way and where acceptance of harassment becomes an ongoing accepted practice, then it may be said that such harassment was an unconstitutional policy or custom.[128]

These rules regarding § 1983 municipal liability, although relatively easy to articulate, are difficult to apply, particularly in employment cases.[129] In the employment relationship, as a practical matter, some public official will inevitably make most day-to-day personnel decisions,[130] yet, by statute or regulation, final theoretical

---

Prof'l Fire Fighters Ass'n Local 3157 v. City of Greensboro, 64 F.3d 962, 966, 150 LRRM 2261 (4th Cir. 1995); McGautha v. Jackson County, 36 F.3d 53, 56 (8th Cir. 1994).

[126]A municipality with a facially constitutional policy may nonetheless be liable under § 1983 if the injury occurred through the municipality's failure to train its officials, and "if the need for more or different training is so obvious, and the inadequacy so likely to result in the violation of constitutional rights, that the policymakers of the city can reasonably be said to have been deliberately indifferent to the need." Canton v. Harris, 489 U.S. 378, 390 (1989).

[127]See Carrero v. New York City Hous. Auth., 890 F.2d 569, 577 (2d Cir. 1989); Crowley v. Prince George's County, 890 F.2d 683, 686–87 (4th Cir. 1989).

[128]See Back v. Hastings on Hudson Union Free Sch. Dist., 365 F.3d 107, 128 (2d Cir. 2004) (school district could be liable if it was "deliberately indifferent" to gender discrimination, but finding that district's actions in this case did not constitute deliberate indifference); Griffin v. City of Opa-Locka, 261 F.3d 1295, 1308 86 FEP 1295 (11th Cir. 2001) ("Sexual harassment was the on-going, accepted practice at the City and . . . the City Commission, Mayor, and other high-ranking officials knew of, ignored, and tolerated the harassment. As such, we are persuaded that the jury's conclusion that sexual harassment was so persistent and widespread as to amount to an unconstitutional policy or custom is amply supported by the evidence."); see also Bohen v. City of East Chi., Ind., 799 F.2d 1180, 1187–89 (7th Cir. 1986) (similar).

[129]See, e.g., Brown v. City of Fort Lauderdale, 923 F.2d 1474, 1480–81, 55 FEP 211 (11th Cir. 1991) (remanded to determine who or what exactly is policy-making authority).

[130]See Ulrich v. City and County of S.F., 308 F.3d 968, 985–86 (9th Cir. 2002) (city hospital's bylaws gave "Director of Health" final policy-making authority, so medical director, even one who has discretion to make decisions, could not bind municipality; but court remanded to trial court to resolve whether any defendants had been delegated final policy-making authority over decisions at issue or whether

authority generally is vested in a governing board or commission.[131] In *Hull v. Cuyahoga Board of Education*,[132] the plaintiff sued the school board and certain individual representatives, including the school superintendent who recommended that the board not renew her contract. The board, which under Ohio law had final authority to establish employment policy and to make contract renewal decisions, accepted the superintendent's recommendation. The plaintiff presented no evidence that the board knew that the recommendation was discriminatory. On motion for summary judgment, the court dismissed the board as a defendant because the plaintiff failed to show that the board had a policy to discriminate or that the board ratified the alleged discriminatory acts.[133] The action against the superintendent in his individual capacity was allowed to proceed, but that action was subject to a potential qualified immunity defense that would not be available to the board.[134]

Local legislators are absolutely immune from suit under § 1983 for their legislative activities.[135] This immunity also applies to nonlegislative officials acting in a legislative capacity.[136] In order to qualify as legislative, "the act in question must be both substantively and procedurally legislative in nature."[137] An act is substantively legislative where it involves "policymaking of a general purpose" or "line drawing."[138] An act is procedurally legislative if it is undertaken by "legislative procedures."[139] Courts have found

those decisions were ratified by officials with final policy-making authority); *see also* Christie v. Iopa, 176 F.3d 1231, 1236–37 (9th Cir. 1999) (official may be delegated final policy-making authority where "the official's discretionary decisionmaking is [not] 'constrained by policies not of that official's making' and . . . [not] 'subject to review by the municipality's authorized decisionmakers' ").

[131]*See* Horwitz v. Board of Educ. of Avoca Sch. Dist. 37, 260 F.3d 602, 619–20 (7th Cir. 2001) (claims against superintendent and principal fail where state school code vests final authority in board of education; claim against board failed where complaint failed to allege board was liable on any theory other than respondeat superior, which cannot support § 1983 liability).

[132]926 F.2d 505, 55 FEP 269 (6th Cir. 1991).

[133]*Id.* at 511–12.

[134]*See* Section III.B.4 *infra*.

[135]*See* Bogan v. Scott-Harris, 523 U.S. 44, 49 (1998).

[136]*See* Aitchison v. Rafiani, 708 F.2d 96, 99–100 (3d Cir. 1983) (extending legislative immunity to mayor who voted to pass ordinance and attorney who advised in drafting of ordinance).

[137]*In re* Montgomery County, 215 F.3d 367, 376 (3d Cir. 2000).

[138]*Id.* (quoting Carver v. Foerster, 102 F.3d 96, 100 (3d Cir. 1996)).

[139]*Id.*

that the decision to reorganize departments that resulted in the elimination of positions was entitled to absolute legislative immunity.[140] However, when the facts used to make a decision relate to particular individuals or situations and the decision impacts or singles out specific individuals, the decision of a legislative board is administrative, not legislative, in nature and is not entitled to legislative immunity.[141]

 b. State Governments. A completely different set of issues arises in actions against state governmental agencies. Foremost among these is the Eleventh Amendment to the U.S. Constitution, which states that:

> The Judicial power of the United States shall not be construed to extend to any suit in law or equity, commenced or prosecuted against one of the United States by Citizens of another State, or by Citizens or Subjects of any Foreign State.

 In *Edelman v. Jordan*,[142] the Supreme Court held that the Eleventh Amendment bars a private suit in federal court "seeking to impose a liability which must be paid from public funds in the state treasury."[143] That bar applies to suits for damages in federal court against a state by its own citizens as well as suits by the citizens of other states,[144] suits for "equitable restitution" as well as for damages,[145] and suits for damages where the state itself is sued or individual state officials are sued in their official capacities.[146] A state's waiver of immunity to suit on state-law claims in

---

[140]*See* Macuba v. DeBoer, 193 F.3d 1316, 1321, 16 IER 1680 (11th Cir. 1999).

[141]*See* Fortner v. City of Archie, 70 F. Supp. 2d 1028, 1030 (W.D. Mo. 1999); *see also* Katzenmoyer v. City of Reading, 158 F. Supp. 491, 501 (E.D. Pa. 2001) (creation of "hit list" of city employees intended for termination by mayor and city's human resource manager not legislative action and not entitled to absolute immunity); Campana v. City of Greenfield, 38 F. Supp. 2d 1043, 1049 (E.D. Wis. 1999) (city council's vote to allow mayor to suspend treasurer not legislative action, but administrative act, depriving council of absolute immunity); Parks v. City of Brewer, 56 F. Supp. 2d 89, 101 (D. Me. 1999) (municipality could be held liable for decisions of its legislative body where majority of legislators harbored impermissible motives for retaliation against city manager).

[142]415 U.S. 651 (1974).

[143]*Id.* at 663.

[144]*Id.* at 662–63; *accord* Papasan v. Allain, 478 U.S. 265, 276 (1986).

[145]415 U.S. at 665–66.

[146]*Id.* at 663.

state courts does not have the effect of waiving immunity to suit in federal court;[147] the state "must specify the State's intention to subject itself to suit in *federal court*."[148] Thus, a plaintiff who has both state-law and federal-law claims against a state may not bring them all in federal court, but must choose between proceeding in both court systems on the same facts, with the earlier decision possibly binding on common issues, or bringing both federal and state claims in state court. However, where a state removes a claim from state court to federal court, the Supreme Court has found that the state waives its immunity.[149]

A state is not divested of Eleventh Amendment immunity even when it is being indemnified by the federal government for costs of litigation as well as the costs of an adverse judgment.[150]

Although the Eleventh Amendment bars suits against states for damages, it does not bar suits for *prospective* relief against a state that is sued through an appropriate official,[151] even if compliance with the injunction will cost the state money or the injunction directly requires the state to pay money for a prospective program of relief.[152] The Eleventh Amendment also does not bar an award, in appropriate suits, of litigation costs or expenses, including attorney's fees,[153] or of prejudgment or postjudgment interest on back pay.[154]

---

[147]*See, e.g.*, Pennhurst State Sch. & Hosp. v. Halderman, 465 U.S. 89, 99 n.9 (1984); Smith v. Robinson, 468 U.S. 992, 1002 n.6 (1984).

[148]Atascadero State Hosp. v. Scanlon, 473 U.S. 234, 241, 38 FEP 97 (1985).

[149]Lapides v. Board of Regents of Univ. Sys. of Ga., 535 U.S. 613, 624 (2002) ("We conclude that the state's action joining the removing of this case to federal court waived its Eleventh Amendment immunity.").

[150]*See* Regents of Univ. of Cal. v. Doe, 519 U.S. 425, 431 (1997).

[151]Edelman v. Jordan, 415 U.S. 651, 663–34 (1974). A federal court injunction directly requiring the state to pay money for a past wrong, however, would violate the Eleventh Amendment even though framed as an injunction. *Id.* at 666–67.

[152]*See, e.g.*, Missouri v. Jenkins, 495 U.S. 33, 56 n.20 (1990) ("the Eleventh Amendment does not bar federal courts from imposing on the States the costs of securing prospective compliance with a desegregation order"); Milliken v. Bradley, 433 U.S. 267, 289 (1977) ("[The Eleventh Amendment] permits federal courts to enjoin state officials to conform their conduct to requirements of federal law, notwithstanding a direct and substantial impact on the state treasury.").

[153]Hutto v. Finney, 437 U.S. 678, 689–700 (1978).

[154]*See* Missouri v. Jenkins, 491 U.S. 274, 280–84, 50 FEP 17 (1989) (rejecting argument that, because federal government enjoys immunity from such awards, states should as well).

The Eleventh Amendment has no application to suits in state court[155] and no application to Supreme Court review of state court judgments.[156] As discussed earlier, it does not apply to suits against municipalities and other political subdivisions that "are not considered part of the State for Eleventh Amendment purposes."[157] It also does not bar actions brought by the United States, even where the United States seeks restitution on behalf of individuals who would be barred by the Eleventh Amendment from seeking relief themselves.[158]

The Enforcement Clause of the Fourteenth Amendment, § 5, allows Congress to abrogate the states' Eleventh Amendment immunity.[159] Congress exercised this power, for example, in extending the coverage of Title VII to state governments and subjecting them to the back pay remedy.[160]

Whether a statute is passed pursuant to the Fourteenth Amendment or pursuant to the Commerce Clause became significant when the Supreme Court, in *Seminole Tribe v. Florida*,[161] emphasized

---

[155]*See* Nevada v. Hall, 440 U.S. 410, 420–21 (1979) (State of Nevada not protected by Eleventh Amendment immunity from suit by California citizens in California state court involving automobile accident that occurred in California; Eleventh Amendment limits power of Article III federal courts, not state courts).

[156]*See* McKesson Corp. v. Division of Alcoholic Beverages & Tobacco, 496 U.S. 18, 27 (1990) ("We have repeatedly and without question accepted jurisdiction to review issues of federal law arising in suits brought against States in state court.").

[157]Monell v. Department of Soc. Servs., 436 U.S. 658, 691 n.54 (1978); *accord* Mt. Healthy City Sch. Dist. Bd. of Educ. v. Doyle, 429 U.S. 274, 280–81 (1977) (Because "a local school board . . . is more like a county or city than it is like an arm of the State . . . it [is] not entitled to assert any Eleventh Amendment immunity from suit in the federal courts.").

[158]Employees of Dep't of Public Health & Welfare v. Department of Pub. Health & Welfare, 411 U.S. 279, 286 (1973) ("suits by the United States against a State are not barred by the Constitution"; although Congress did not lift states' sovereign immunity under Fair Labor Standards Act, Secretary of Labor authorized to bring suit on behalf of aggrieved employees for unpaid wages).

[159]Section 5 of the Fourteenth Amendment is an affirmative grant of legislative power that gives Congress the " 'authority both to remedy and to deter violation of [Fourteenth Amendment] rights . . . by prohibiting a somewhat broader swath of conduct, including that which is not itself forbidden by the Amendment's text.' " Nevada Dep't of Human Res. v. Hibbs, 538 U.S. 721, 727 (2003) (quoting Board of Trustees of Univ. of Ala. v. Garrett, 531 U.S. 356, 365 (2001)); *see also* Fitzpatrick v. Bitzer, 427 U.S. 445, 456–57, 12 FEP 1586 (1976) ("We think that Congress may [under § 5] provide for private suits against States or state officials which are constitutionally impermissible in other contexts.").

[160]*See Fitzpatrick*, 427 U.S. at 456 n.11 ("[R]espondent state officials do not contend that the substantive provisions of Title VII as applied here are not a proper exercise of congressional authority under [§ 5].").

[161]517 U.S. 44, 59–73 (1996).

that statutes enacted only pursuant to the Commerce Clause generally are ineffective in waiving state Eleventh Amendment immunity. After *Seminole Tribe*, the Supreme Court in *Kimel v. Board of Regents*[162] found that the ADEA did not validly abrogate states' Eleventh Amendment immunity, rejecting numerous decisions of lower courts to the contrary.[163] The Court noted that no congressional act passed solely under the Commerce Clause could abrogate states' Eleventh Amendment immunity.[164] Congress generally can abrogate Eleventh Amendment immunity under § 5 of the Fourteenth Amendment, but the Court found that the ADEA was not a valid use of § 5.[165] The Court stated in *Kimel* that because

> "[o]ur Constitution permits states to draw lines on the basis of age when they have a minimal basis for doing so on a class-based level that it is clear that the ADEA is "so out of proportion to a supposed remedial or preventive object that it cannot be understood as responsive to, or designed to prevent, unconstitutional behavior."[166]

The Court followed *Kimel* with *Board of Trustees of the University of Alabama v. Garrett*,[167] where it found that the employment provisions of Title I of the ADA also did not validly abrogate states' Eleventh Amendment immunity.[168] The Court again found that Title I of the ADA was not validly passed pursuant to § 5 of the Fourteenth Amendment.[169] The Court stated that:

> Congress is the final authority as to desirable public policy, but in order to authorize private individuals to recover money damages against the States, there must be a pattern of discrimination by the States which violates the Fourteenth Amendment, and the remedy imposed by Congress must be congruent and proportional to the targeted violation. Those requirements are not met here, and to uphold the Act's application to the States would allow Congress to rewrite the Fourteenth Amendment law laid down by this Court

---

[162]528 U.S. 62 (2000).

[163]*Id.* at 91. Among the cases rejected were *Cooper v. New York State Office of Mental Health*, 162 F.3d 770 (2d Cir. 1998), *Migneault v. Peck*, 158 F.3d 1131 (10th Cir. 1998), *Coger v. Board of Regents of State of Tenn.*, 154 F.3d 296 (6th Cir. 1998), *Keeton v. University of Nev. Sys.*, 150 F.3d 1055 (9th Cir. 1998), *Scott v. University of Miss.*, 148 F.3d 493 (5th Cir. 1998), and *Gotashby v. Board of Trustees of Univ. of Ill.*, 141 F.3d 761 (7th Cir. 1998).

[164]528 U.S. at 78–80.

[165]*Id.* at 86.

[166]*Id.* (quoting City of Boerne v. Flores, 521 U.S. 507, 532 (1997)).

[167]531 U.S. 356 (2001).

[168]*Id.* at 373.

[169]*Id.*

in *Cleburne*. Section 5 does not so broadly enlarge congressional authority.[170]

A different conclusion was reached by the Supreme Court in *Nevada Department of Human Resources v. Hibbs*,[171] where it found that the Family and Medical Leave Act (FMLA) was properly promulgated pursuant to § 5 of the Fourteenth Amendment and that states therefore could be sued in federal court for violations of the law.[172] The key difference from the ADEA and the ADA, the Court found, was that: "The States' record of unconstitutional participation in, and fostering of, gender-based discrimination in the administration of leave benefits is weighty enough to justify its enactment of prophylactic legislation."[173]

An issue distinct from the *source* of congressional power to abrogate Eleventh Amendment immunity is whether Congress sufficiently made clear its intent to *exercise* that power. In *Atascadero State Hospital v. Scanlon*,[174] the Court reaffirmed prior decisions holding that Congress would not be held to have intended the abrogation of the states' Eleventh Amendment immunity unless there is no room for doubt. "Congress may abrogate the States' constitutionally secured immunity from suit only by making its intention unmistakably clear in the language of the statute."[175] Such a congressional intent may be clear either from the express language of the statute or by necessary implication, but it must be present in the statutory language itself.[176] Applying this principle, the Court in *Atascadero* held that Congress had not abrogated the Eleventh Amendment immunity of the states in enacting § 504 of the Rehabilitation Act of 1973; the states' acceptance of funds under the Rehabilitation Act did not constitute a waiver of Eleventh Amendment immunity.[177] The following year, however, Congress amended Title VI of the Civil Rights Act of 1964 to express the required unequivocal intent with respect to a series of laws, including the Rehabilitation Act:

---

[170]*Id.*
[171]538 U.S. 721 (2003).
[172]*Id.* at 740.
[173]*Id.* at 735.
[174]473 U.S. 234, 38 FEP 97 (1985).
[175]*Id.* at 242.
[176]*Id.* at 238–40, 243.
[177]*Id.* at 244–47.

(1) A State shall not be immune under the Eleventh Amendment of the Constitution of the United States from suit in Federal court for a violation of section 504 of the Rehabilitation Act of 1973, Title IX of the Education Amendments of 1972, the Age Discrimination Act of 1975, Title VI of the Civil Rights Act of 1964, or the provisions of any other Federal statute prohibiting discrimination by recipients of Federal financial assistance.

(2) In a suit against a State for a violation of a statute referred to in paragraph (1), remedies (including remedies both at law and in equity) are available for such a violation to the same extent as such remedies are available for such a violation in the suit against any public or private entity other than a State.[178]

The Supreme Court has not found in § 1983 a congressional foreclosure of the states' Eleventh Amendment immunity, nor has Congress amended the statute to accomplish that. Only 10 days after it decided *Monell*,[179] the Supreme Court held that state governments are insulated by Eleventh Amendment immunity from suit under § 1983. *Alabama v. Pugh*[180] involved a § 1983 action by prison inmates against the State of Alabama, its board of corrections, and its prison officials, seeking only injunctive relief. Nonetheless, the Court stated:

> There can be no doubt . . . that suit against the State and its Board of Corrections is barred by the Eleventh Amendment, unless Alabama has consented to the filing of such a suit. Respondents do not contend that Alabama has consented to this suit, and it appears that no consent could be given under Art. 1, § 14, of the Alabama Constitution, which provides that "the State of Alabama shall never be made a defendant in any court of law or equity."[181]

In *Quern v. Jordan*,[182] the Court explained its decisions in *Monell* and *Pugh*, reiterating that *Monell* was " 'limited solely to local government units which are not considered part of the State for Eleventh Amendment purposes.' "[183] The Court found no indication

---

[178]Pub. L. No. 99-506, § 1003, 1986 U.S.C.C.A.N. (100 Stat.) 1807, 1845 (codified at 42 U.S.C. § 2000d-7(a)). The reference in the quoted language to the Age Discrimination Act of 1975 is to the prohibition of age discrimination in federally assisted programs. *See* 42 U.S.C. § 6101 et seq.

[179]Monell v. Department of Soc. Servs., 436 U.S. 658 (1978).

[180]438 U.S. 781 (1978).

[181]*Id.* at 782 (citations omitted).

[182]440 U.S. 332 (1979).

[183]*Id.* at 338 (quoting Monell v. Department of Soc. Servs., 436 U.S. 658, 690 n.54 (1978)).

that Congress, when enacting § 1983, meant specifically to authorize actions against a state,[184] as it had when enacting Title VII. In *Will v. Michigan Department of State Police*,[185] the Court rejected the argument that the "state action" concept of § 1983 necessarily contemplated subjecting the states themselves to liability:

> But the intent of Congress to provide a remedy for unconstitutional state action does not without more include the sovereign States among those persons against whom § 1983 actions would lie. Construing § 1983 as a remedy for "official violation of federally protected rights" does no more than confirm that the section is directed against state action—action "under color of" state law. It does not suggest that the State itself was a person that Congress intended to be subject to liability.[186]

The Court in *Will* also settled the question of whether suits against state officials in their "official capacity" could be maintained under § 1983. The Court reiterated its earlier holdings that a *damages* action against a state official in his or her official capacity is "no different than a suit against the state itself,"[187] but that "a State official in his or her official capacity, when sued for *injunctive* relief, would be a person under § 1983 because 'official capacity actions for prospective relief are not treated as actions against the State.' "[188]

This does not mean, however, that an individual who is the victim of illegal discrimination perpetrated by a state actor has no damages recourse under § 1983. As discussed below, government officials who implement such discrimination can be sued for damages under § 1983 in their individual capacities.

---

[184]*See id.* at 342–43. The language in *Quern* would appear to apply equally to actions brought under §§ 1981, 1985, and 1986. District courts dealing with this issue since *Quern* have ruled that the Eleventh Amendment bars actions against the states under these sections as well. *See, e.g.*, Ellis v. University of Kan. Med. Ctr., 163 F.3d 1186, 1196, 78 FEP 1802 (10th Cir. 1998) (§§ 1981, 1983, 1985); Zelinski v. Pennsylvania State Police, 282 F. Supp. 2d 251, 264 (M.D. Pa. 2003) (§§ 1983, 1985), *aff'd in part, rev'd in part*, 2004 U.S. App. LEXIS 21235 (3d Cir. Aug. 11, 2004); Golthy v. Alabama, 287 F. Supp. 2d 1259, 1262–63 (M.D. Ala. 2003) (§§ 1981, 1983), *aff'd*, 104 Fed. Appx. 153 (11th Cir. 2004); Hill v. Taconic Dev. Disabilities Servs. Office, 181 F. Supp. 2d 303, 322 (S.D.N.Y. 2002) (§§ 1981, 1983), *vacated and remanded*, 57 Fed. Appx. 9 (2d Cir. 2003).

[185]491 U.S. 58, 68–69, 49 FEP 1664 (1989).

[186]*Id.* at 68.

[187]*Id.* at 71.

[188]*Id.* at 71 n.10 (quoting Kentucky v. Graham, 473 U.S. 159, 167 n.14 (1985)).

4. State and Local Governmental Officials in Their Individual Capacities

State and local governmental officials may be sued in their individual capacities under 42 U.S.C. § 1983 for actions taken under color of state law,[189] without any requirement that official policy or custom be shown.[190] Such officials may be sued in their personal capacities even for acts committed in the exercise of their official powers.[191]

Government officials,[192] however, do enjoy personal immunity from suit. In rare cases they enjoy absolute immunity; more commonly though, they are awarded qualified immunity.[193] The Supreme Court "has refused to extend absolute immunity beyond a very limited class of officials, including the President of the United States, legislators carrying out their legislative functions, and judges carrying out their judicial functions, 'whose special functions or constitutional status requires complete protection from suit.' "[194] In *Bogan v. Scott-Harris*,[195] the Supreme Court held that a mayor and city council member were immune from civil liability for their legislative action of eliminating the job of an African American who had complained about race discrimination.[196]

---

[189]*See* Hafer v. Melo, 502 U.S. 21, 25–26, 57 FEP 241 (1991) (claims for punitive as well as compensatory damages allowed against state official sued in her personal capacity).

[190]*Id.* at 25; *accord* Kentucky v. Graham, 473 U.S. 159, 166 (1985).

[191]*See Graham*, 473 U.S. at 167–68.

[192]Individuals sued for damages under § 1983 have no right to qualified immunity unless they are public officials. *See* Wyatt v. Cole, 504 U.S. 158, 168 (1992).

[193]*See* Burns v. Reed, 500 U.S. 478, 485–86 (1991); *see also* Tobin for Governor v. Illinois State Bd. of Elections, 268 F.3d 517, 521–23 (7th Cir. 2001) (finding members of board of elections entitled to absolute immunity because they functioned in quasi-adjudicatory role); Butz v. Economou, 438 U.S. 478, 512–13 (1978) (similar); Crenshaw v. Baynerd, 180 F.3d 866, 868 (7th Cir. 1999) (similar).

[194]Hafer v. Melo, 502 U.S. 21, 29, 57 FEP 241 (1991) (quoting Harlow v. Fitzgerald, 457 U.S. 800, 807 (1982)). *But see* Scheuer v. Rhodes, 416 U.S. 232, 248–49 (1974) (*state* executive officials not entitled to absolute immunity under § 1983 for their official actions). However, the President of the United States is not entitled to immunity from suit or even a delay in an action for claims based on alleged misconduct that occurred *before* the individual became President. Clinton v. Jones, 520 U.S. 681, 706–10 (1997).

[195]523 U.S. 44, 76 FEP 146 (1998).

[196]*Id.* at 49. *But see* Canary v. Osborn, 211 F.3d 324, 331, 16 IER 462 (6th Cir. 2000) (individual school board members not entitled to legislative immunity for role in voting against renewal of employee's contract for "budgetary reasons" where board

Absolute immunity is also available to those members of quasi-judicial adjudicatory bodies when they perform duties that are comparable to those of a judicial officer. However, when officials otherwise entitled to absolute immunity act on administrative matters, such as making employment decisions, they are entitled only to qualified immunity.[197]

Other state and local governmental officials sued for damages in their personal capacities enjoy qualified, or "good faith," immunity: "While the plaintiff in a personal-capacity suit need not establish a connection to governmental 'policy or custom,' officials sued in their personal capacities, unlike those sued in their official capacities, may assert personal immunity defenses such as objectively reasonable reliance on existing law."[198] Qualified immunity is an affirmative defense that must be pled by the defendant; the plaintiff is not required to put good faith in issue by pleading bad faith.[199]

In *Harlow v. Fitzgerald*,[200] the Supreme Court expressed great dissatisfaction with the subjective good faith defense because it allowed too many claims to be subject to discovery and go to trial, with the attendant disruption of the public business. Instead, the Court opted for an "objective" test: "We therefore hold that government officials performing discretionary functions generally are

---

minutes and other circumstances indicated that board was making personalized assessments of employees, rather than engaging in impersonal budgetary analysis of various positions); Meek v. County of Riverside, 183 F.3d 962, 966, 16 IER 406 (9th Cir. 1999) (judge's decision to terminate commissioner of courts allegedly administrative act, not judicial act, and did not qualify for immunity).

[197]*Hafer*, 502 U.S. at 29 ("In several instances, moreover, we have concluded that no more than a qualified immunity attaches to administrative employment decisions, even if the same official has absolute immunity when performing other functions."); *see also* Forrester v. White, 484 U.S. 219, 227–28, 45 FEP 1112 (1988) (state court judge acting in administrative capacity, not judicial capacity, when he demoted and then discharged probation officer and court employee; judge therefore not entitled to absolute judicial immunity for his actions); Riley v. Buckner, 1 Fed. Appx. 130, 134–45 (4th Cir. 2001) (state court judge not entitled to even qualified immunity for alleged sexual harassment of court employee). *Compare* Imbler v. Pachtman, 424 U.S. 409, 424–26 (1976) (state prosecuting attorney entitled to absolute immunity from suit regarding initiation and pursuit of criminal prosecution) *with* Buckley v. Fitzsimmons, 509 U.S. 259, 271 (1993) (state prosecuting attorney not absolutely immune from liability for pre-indictment investigative work).

[198]*Hafer*, 502 U.S. at 25; *accord* Kentucky v. Graham, 473 U.S. 159, 166–67 (1985); Owen v. City of Independence, 445 U.S. 622, 637–38 (1980).

[199]*See* Gomez v. Toledo, 446 U.S. 635, 639–41 (1980).

[200]457 U.S. 800, 815–19 (1982).

shielded from liability for civil damages insofar as their conduct does not violate clearly established statutory or constitutional rights of which a reasonable person would have known."[201]

The Court later stated that this two-step inquiry was designed to "provide ample protection to all but the plainly incompetent or those who knowingly violate the law."[202] Put another way, the Supreme Court has called the standard one of "objective legal reasonableness,"[203] that is, whether it was objectively reasonable for a defendant to believe that the challenged conduct did not violate the plaintiff's clearly established rights.

The Court held that immunity was a threshold question and should be determined prior to discovery; it involves immunity from *suit*, not just immunity from *damages*.[204] A denial of immunity by the district court is immediately appealable where the claim of qualified immunity turns on an issue of law.[205] Denials of qualified immunity by the district court may be appealed multiple times where appropriate, as, for example, both at the denial of a motion to dismiss stage and at the denial of summary judgment stage.[206]

Courts have found that constitutional rights are clearly established "if controlling precedent has recognized the right in a 'concrete and factually defined context.' "[207] Case law must have "staked

---

[201]*Id.* at 818. *Harlow* represented a sharp break from the prior immunity standard and its reliance on common law principles. *See* Wyatt v. Cole, 504 U.S. 158, 166 (1992) ("*Harlow* completely reformulated qualified immunity along principles not at all embodied in the common law.") (quoting Anderson v. Creighton, 483 U.S. 635 (1987)).

[202]Malley v. Briggs, 475 U.S. 335, 341 (1986).

[203]Behrens v. Pelletier, 516 U.S. 299, 306 (1996).

[204]*Harlow*, 457 U.S. at 818.

[205]*See* Mitchell v. Forsyth, 472 U.S. 511, 526–28 (1985) (doctrine provides immunity from burdens of litigation, including discovery); *see also* Johnson v. Jones, 515 U.S. 304, 319 (1995). There is no immediate appeal if the qualified immunity issue turns on a factual dispute.

[206]*See Behrens*, 516 U.S. at 309–10. It is not necessary to appeal after denial of a motion to dismiss in order to appeal after denial of a motion for summary judgment. *See* Vega v. Miller, 273 F.3d 460, 465 (2d Cir. 2001) ("multiple appeals will often be necessary due to the different posture of the case at the pleading stage and at summary judgment . . . *Behrens* makes clear that an appeal is available from denials of an immunity defense at both the pleading and summary judgment stages, and nothing in that decision suggests that a defendant is required to appeal an initial denial at the pleading stage in order to appeal a subsequent denial on summary judgment. Such an approach would precipitate many needless appeals.").

[207]Chesser v. Sparks, 248 F.3d 1117, 1122 (11th Cir. 2001) (quoting Lassiter v. Alabama A&M Univ. Bd. of Trs., 28 F.3d 1146, 1149 (11th Cir. 1994) (en banc)). The

out a bright line" in order to put governmental officials on notice of clearly established rights.[208] In analyzing whether an individual defendant is entitled to qualified immunity, a court may not consider developments in the law that occur after the alleged violation of protected rights.[209]

In *Owen v. City of Independence*,[210] the Supreme Court held that a *municipality* sued under § 1983 is not entitled to qualified immunity from liability despite the good faith of its municipal officials.[211] In *Owen*, a discharged former police chief sued the city

---

court in *Chesser* found that an employee allegedly terminated for complaining about the county's failure to pay overtime wages was speaking on a matter only of private concern—not of public concern—and so she did not show that such conduct violated clearly established constitutional rights. 248 F.3d at 1123.

[208]*See* Post v. City of Fort Lauderdale, 7 F.3d 1552, 1557 (11th Cir. 1993). A plaintiff "need not offer up a federal case which precisely mirrors the facts of [the] case," but must "at a minimum" point to a closely analogous case decided prior to the challenged conduct. Sonnleitner v. York, 304 F.3d 704, 716 (7th Cir. 2002).

[209]The Second Circuit, in *African Trade Information v. Abromatis*, 294 F.3d 355 (2d Cir. 2002), described the standard as follows: "Three factors are considered in evaluating whether a right was clearly established at the time a Section 1983 defendant acted: '(1) whether the right in question was defined with reasonable specificity; (2) whether the decisional law of the Supreme Court and the applicable circuit court supports the existence of the right in question; and (3) whether under preexisting law a reasonable defendant official would have understood that his or her acts were unlawful.' " *Id.* at 360 (quoting Shechter v. Comptroller of N.Y., 79 F.3d 265, 271 (2d Cir. 1996)). In *African Trade Information*, the court found that it was not clearly established at the time that unsuccessful applicants for government contracts were protected by the First Amendment from retaliation based on speech, and hence the defendant had qualified immunity. *Id.* at 361–62; *see also Sonnleitner*, 304 F.3d at 719 (individual defendants entitled to qualified immunity because there was no clearly established right to pre-demotion hearing as to all relevant charges associated with demotion); Vega v. Miller, 273 F.3d 460, 467–68 (2d Cir. 2001) (qualified immunity to discipline teacher for allowing vulgarities in class because it was not clearly established at time that this was unlawful); Lynch v. City of Boston, 180 F.3d 1, 13, 15 IER 305 (1st Cir. 1999) (employee entitled to qualified immunity where it was not reasonable for governmental official to have known that denial of uncompensated position could be unlawful retaliation for protected speech); Blake v. Wright, 179 F.3d 1003, 1007, 15 IER 297 (6th Cir. 1999) (government officials entitled to immunity where law regarding administrative monitoring of police phone lines was unclear at time of alleged unlawful tapping of phone lines); Bishop v. Avera, 177 F.3d 1233, 1234, 80 FEP 53 (11th Cir. 1999) (no qualified immunity in suit alleging reverse race discrimination brought by former deputy police chief because police chief knew or should have known acts were unlawful).

[210]445 U.S. 622 (1980).

[211]Municipalities sued under § 1983 must respond to bare allegations and engage in discovery and the other normal proceedings in litigation without plaintiffs having to plead malice. *See* Leatherman v. Tarrant County, 507 U.S. 163, 167 (1993).

of Independence and its elected officials. Both the district court and the court of appeals found for the defendants and ruled that all the defendants (including the city) were entitled to immunity from liability because the officials had acted in good faith and without malice. The Supreme Court reversed:

> We believe that today's decision, together with prior precedents in this area, properly allocates these costs among the three principals in the scenario of the § 1983 cause of action: the victim of the constitutional deprivation; the officer whose conduct caused the injury; and the public, as represented by the municipal entity. The innocent individual who is harmed by an abuse of governmental authority is assured that he will be compensated for his injury. The offending official, so long as he conducts himself in good faith, may go about his business secure in the knowledge that a qualified immunity will protect him from personal liability for damages that are more appropriately chargeable to the populace as a whole. And the public will be forced to bear only the costs of injury inflicted by the "execution of a government's policy or custom, whether made by its lawmakers or by those whose edicts or acts may fairly be said to represent official policy."[212]

In *Richardson v. McKnight*,[213] the Supreme Court held that employees of a private prison management firm were not entitled to qualified immunity under § 1983. The Court noted, however, that it had not been asked to decide whether the employees could be held liable under § 1983 because they were employed by a private firm.[214]

C. Bases of Discrimination Prohibited by § 1983

1. Introduction

Unlike § 1981, § 1983 "[does] not provide for any substantive rights—equal or otherwise," but was enacted to provide a federal remedy for violation of federally protected rights,[215] including certain

---

[212]*Owen*, 445 U.S. at 657 (quoting Monell v. Department of Soc. Servs., 436 U.S. 658, 694 (1978)).

[213]521 U.S. 399 (1997).

[214]*See id.* at 413 ("it is for the district court to determine whether, under this Court's decision in *Lugar v. Edmondson Oil Co.*, 457 U.S. 922 (1982), defendants actually acted 'under color of state law' ") (citations omitted).

[215]*See* Albright v. Oliver, 510 U.S. 266 (1994); Chapman v. Houston Welfare Rights Org., 441 U.S. 600, 617–18 (1979); *accord* Bruneau v. South Kortright Cent.

federal statutory rights.[216] Title VII, however, has its own compre-hensive enforcement scheme; § 1983 does not provide a supple-mental remedy for a violation of rights created under Title VII.[217]

The sections that follow review the three principal constitu-tional provisions invoked in support of § 1983 employment dis-crimination claims.

2. Equal Protection

The Equal Protection Clause of the Fourteenth Amendment provides the basis for § 1983 liability against state action even though Title VII (violation of which is not sufficient to establish § 1983 liability) also prohibits race and other forms of discrimi-nation.[219] Thus, where the defendant acts under color of state law, § 1983 reaches intentional discrimination based on any of the five

---

Sch. Dist., 163 F.3d 749, 756 (2d Cir. 1998) (it is well established that § 1983's procedural mechanism for asserting federal rights and documents does not in itself create any substantive rights).

[216]See Maine v. Thiboutot, 448 U.S. 1, 4 (1980) ("[T]he § 1983 remedy broadly encompasses violations of federal statutory as well as constitutional law.").

[217]See Schroeder v. Hamilton Sch. Dist., 282 F.3d 946, 951 (7th Cir. 2002) (finding no equal protection claim because plaintiff could not show that defendants "acted either intentionally or with deliberate indifference" to plaintiff's complaints of ha-rassment because of homosexuality; standards of proof for § 1983 equal protection claims and for Title VII claims are very different, and homosexuality is not pro-tected class under Title VII); Reed v. Connecticut Dep't of Transp., 161 F. Supp. 2d 73, 85–86 (D. Conn. 2001) (plaintiff can only concurrently assert Title VII cause of action with § 1983 cause of action if some law other than Title VII is source of right alleged to have been denied).

[218][reserved].

[219]See Booth v. Maryland, 327 F.3d 377, 382–83 (4th Cir. 2003) ("Title VII does not preclude a public sector employee from bringing a § 1983 action based on al-leged violations of the Equal Protection Clause"); Pennington v. City of Huntsville, 261 F.3d 1262 (11th Cir. 2001) (allowing Title VII and § 1983 claims to proceed concurrently and noting that mixed-motive defense to retaliation claim is still proper defense under both Title VII and §1983 even after passage of 1991 Civil Rights Act); English v. Colorado Dep't of Corr., 248 F.3d 1002, 1007–08 (10th Cir. 2001) (rec-ognizing validity of pleading both Title VII and § 1983 race discrimination claims). But see Lakoski v. James, 66 F.3d 751, 753 (5th Cir. 1995) (Title VII is exclusive remedy for victims of discrimination who seek money damages, but possibly not exclusive remedy for plaintiffs who seek only declaratory or injunctive relief); Jackson v. City of Atlanta, 73 F.3d 60, 63, 69 FEP 1505 (5th Cir. 1996) ("Congress intended for Title VII—with its own substantive requirements, procedural rules, and remedies—to be the exclusive means by which an employee may pursue a discrimination claim. Allowing the plaintiff to state a discrimination claim under Section 1983 as well

bases set out in § 703 of Title VII—race and color,[220] sex[221] (including sexual harassment),[222] religion,[223] and national origin.[224] The right to be free from racial and gender discrimination, including sexual harassment, is clearly established under the Equal Protection Clause, the intentional violation of which will result in liability under § 1983.[225] Courts have determined that the Supreme Court's

---

would enable him to sidestep the detailed and specific provisions of Title VII."); Thigpen v. Bibb County, Ga., Sheriff's Dep't, 223 F.3d 1231, 1239 (11th Cir. 2000) ("[a] Section 1983 claim predicated on the violation of a right guaranteed by the Constitution—here the right to equal protection of the laws—can be pleaded exclusive of a Title VII claim"); Annis v. County of Westchester, 36 F.3d 251, 254–55 (2d Cir. 1994) (same); Saulpaugh v. Monroe Cmty. Hosp., 4 F.3d 134, 143, 62 FEP 1315 (2d Cir. 1993) (§ 1983 claim not barred by concurrent Title VII claim if former is based on substantive rights different from Title VII).

[220]See Cotter v. City of Boston, 323 F.3d 160, 167 (1st Cir. 2003); Harrison v. City of Akron, 43 Fed. Appx. 903 (6th Cir. 2002); Juniel v. Pathforest—Chi. Heights, 46 Fed. Appx. 853 (7th Cir. 2002); Barber v. County of Ventura, 45 Fed. Appx. 725 (9th Cir. 2002); Trusty v. Maryland, 28 Fed. Appx. 327 (4th Cir. 2002); Donahue v. City of Boston, 304 F.3d 110, 119, 89 FEP 1495 (1st Cir. 2002); Keyser v. Sacramento City Unified Sch. Dist., 265 F.3d 741, 755 (9th Cir. 2001); Carter v. Hawaii, 17 Fed. Appx. 658 (9th Cir. 2001); Mason v. Village of El Portal, 240 F.3d 1337, 1339 (11th Cir. 2001).

[221]See Back v. Hastings on Hudson Union Free Sch. Dist., 365 F.3d 107, 117 (2d Cir. 2004); Zalewska v. County of Sullivan, 316 F.3d 314, 323, 90 FEP 1193 (2d Cir. 2003); Mercer v. City of Cedar Rapids, 308 F.3d 840 (8th Cir. 2002); Bowers v. Board of Regents of Univ. of Wis., 33 Fed. Appx. 812 (7th Cir. 2002); Maitland v. University of Minn., 260 F.3d 959, 962–63, 86 FEP 1317 (8th Cir. 2001).

[222]See Rogers v. City County Health Dep't of Okla. County, 30 Fed. Appx. 883 (10th Cir. 2002); Moring v. Arkansas Dep't of Corr., 243 F.3d 452, 455, 86 FEP 49 (8th Cir. 2001); Murray v. Chicago Transit Auth., 252 F.3d 880, 887, 85 FEP 1231 (7th Cir. 2001).

[223]See Booth v. Maryland, 327 F.3d 377, 381 (4th Cir. 2003); Knight v. Connecticut Dep't of Public Health, 275 F.3d 156, 87 FEP 728 (2d Cir. 2001); Phillips v. Collings, 256 F.3d 843, 848, 86 FEP 411 (2d Cir. 2001); Pennington v. City of Huntsville, 261 F.3d 1262, 1267–68 (11th Cir. 2001).

[224]See Ramirez v. Kroonen, 44 Fed. Appx. 212 (9th Cir. 2002); Menchaca v. Ottenwalder, 18 Fed. Appx. 508 (9th Cir. 2001); Sharma v. Ohio State Univ., 25 Fed. Appx. 243 (6th Cir. 2001).

[225]See, e.g., Lankford v. Hobart, 73 F.3d 283, 286, 69 FEP 1149 (10th Cir. 1996) ("Sexual harassment can violate the Fourteenth Amendment right to equal protection of the laws."); Cross v. Alabama Dep't of Mental Health & Mental Retardation, 49 F.3d 1490, 1507 (11th Cir. 1995) (employees have constitutional right to be free from unlawful sex discrimination and sexual harassment in public employment); Smith v. Lomax, 45 F.3d 402, 407, 67 FEP 1005 (11th Cir. 1995) (intentional discrimination in workplace based on employee's race is patently and obviously illegal and gives rise to § 1983 liability); Annis v. County of Westchester, 36 F.3d 251, 254, 65 FEP 1657 (2d Cir. 1994), *aff'd in part and vacated in part*, 136

decisions in *Ellerth*[226] and *Faragher*[227] are applicable in § 1983 sexual harassment cases.[228] Liability for racial harassment also is cognizable under § 1983.[229]

Although an ADEA claim may not be brought against a state,[230] a § 1983 claim may be brought against a state officer based on age as an equal protection claim.[231] Courts are split on whether ADEA and § 1983 age-based claims may be brought against municipalities.[232]

To establish a cause of action under § 1983 for a violation of equal protection, plaintiffs are required to demonstrate intentional discrimination; mere adverse impact will not suffice.[233] Challenges

---

F.3d 239, 76 FEP 1039 (2d Cir. 1998); Beardsley v. Webb, 30 F.3d 524, 530, 65 FEP 696 (4th Cir. 1994) (sexual harassment has long been recognized as type of gender discrimination in contravention of Equal Protection Clause); Yeldell v. Cooper Green Hosp., 956 F.2d 1056, 1064, 66 FEP 607 (11th Cir. 1992) (race discrimination in public employment violates Fourteenth Amendment).

[226]Burlington Indus., Inc. v. Ellerth, 524 U.S. 742, 77 FEP 1 (1998).

[227]Faragher v. City of Boca Raton, 524 U.S. 775, 77 FEP 14 (1998).

[228]Molnar v. Booth, 229 F.3d 593, 600–01, 83 FEP 1756 (7th Cir. 2000).

[229]*See* Malesevic v. Tecom Fleet Servs. Inc., 72 F. Supp. 2d 932, 940 (N.D. Ind. 1998).

[230]*See* Kimel v. Board of Regents, 528 U.S. 62, 91 (2000).

[231]*See* Menchaca v. Ottenwalder, 18 Fed. Appx. 508 (9th Cir. 2001).

[232]*Compare* Purdy v. Town of Greenburgh, 166 F. Supp. 2d 850, 869, 87 FEP 1223 (S.D.N.Y. 2001) (citing cases), Jungels v. State Univ. Coll. of N.Y., 922 F. Supp. 779, 785, 77 FEP 635 (W.D.N.Y. 1996) (cognizable claims distinct from rights exclusively protected by Title VII and ADEA may be brought under § 1983), *aff'd*, 112 F.3d 504 (2d Cir. 1997) *and* Mummelthie v. Mason City, 873 F. Supp. 1293, 1312–29, 66 FEP 1393 (N.D. Iowa 1995) (facts giving rise to ADEA claim and constitutional violation may be prosecuted under § 1983), *aff'd*, 78 F.3d 589, 70 FEP 928 (8th Cir. 1996) *with* Zombro v. Baltimore City Police Dep't, 868 F.2d 1364, 1368–70, 49 FEP 297 (4th Cir. 1989) (Congress intended that ADEA be exclusive remedy). *Compare* LaFleur v. Texas Dep't of Health, 126 F.3d 758, 760, 75 FEP 225 (5th Cir. 1997) (same), Gregor v. Derwinski, 911 F. Supp. 643, 651–52, 75 FEP 797 (W.D.N.Y. 1996) (actions under § 1983 based on age are foreclosed by ADEA) *and* Tranello v. Frey, 758 F. Supp. 841, 850–51 n.3, 55 FEP 699 (W.D.N.Y 1991) (ADEA provides exclusive remedy for age discrimination), *aff'd in part, dismissed in part*, 962 F.2d 244, 58 FEP 1334 (2d Cir. 1992).

[233]*See, e.g.*, Personnel Admin. of Mass. v. Feeney, 442 U.S. 256, 274 (1979) (holding that "purposeful discrimination is the condition that offends the Constitution"); Zalewska v. County of Sullivan, 316 F.3d 314, 323 (2d Cir. 2003) (it is "purposeful discrimination" that triggers Equal Protection Clause); Government Employees (NAGE) v. City Pub. Serv. Bd. of San Antonio, 40 F.3d 698, 714–15, 67 FEP 1013 (5th Cir. 1994); Lewellen v. Metropolitan Gov't of Nashville, 34 F.3d 345, 348–51 (6th Cir. 1994) (§ 1983 action can only be based on intentional deprivation of protected constitutional right; negligent or grossly negligent conduct on state actor's part will not trigger § 1983 liability).

can be successful only where the challenged conduct fails to satisfy the constitutional standard (e.g., strict scrutiny, rational basis) applicable to that suspect classification.[234]

A white plaintiff generally does not have standing under § 1983 solely for the purpose of vindicating the rights of minorities who have suffered from racial discrimination.[235] An exception exists, however, where the employer retaliates against a non-minority employee for assisting or interacting with minorities.[236]

Discrimination against family members is not unlawful discrimination under § 1983.[237] A violation of the Veterans' Preference Act likewise cannot form the basis of a § 1983 claim.[238] Furthermore, a general claim of retaliation where there is no violation of the U.S. Constitution or other federal law other than Title VII does not implicate the Equal Protection Clause.[239]

3. Speech

The public sector employment relationship is a fertile source of tension between the management prerogatives of government

---

[234]In order to show a violation of equal protection, the plaintiff must show dissimilar treatment of similarly situated individuals. Where "a § 1983 plaintiff compares government employees who are not similarly situated, and the dissimilarities do not result from suspect classifications, any different treatment is justified if it is rationally related to a legitimate government interest." Mercer v. City of Cedar Rapids, 308 F.3d 840, 844 (8th Cir. 2002) (quoting Post v. Harper, 980 F.2d 491, 495 (8th Cir. 1992)). Courts have found that the *McDonnell Douglas* analytical framework used in Title VII claims applies equally to § 1983 claims based on allegations of race discrimination in violation of the Equal Protection Clause. *See* English v. Colorado Dep't of Corrs., 248 F.3d 1002, 1007 (10th Cir. 2001); *see also* Russell v. Drabik, 24 Fed. Appx. 408, 413–14 (6th Cir. 2001).

[235]*See* Maynard v. City of San Jose, 37 F.3d 1396, 1402, 66 FEP 123 (9th Cir. 1994).

[236]*See id.* at 1403 (white plaintiff has standing under § 1983 where plaintiff asserts own right to be free from retaliation, alleges injuries that are personal to him, and is only effective plaintiff who can bring suit).

[237]*See* Columbus v. Biggio, 76 F. Supp. 2d 43, 52 (D. Mass. 1999); Roche v. Town of Wareham, 24 F. Supp. 2d 146 (D. Mass. 1998). However, favoritism of family members (nepotism) may violate § 1983 if the defendant cannot offer "some measure of justification." Backlund v. Hessen, 104 F.3d 1031, 1034 (8th Cir. 1997).

[238]*See* Philippeaux v. North Cent. Bronx Hosp., 871 F. Supp. 640, 647 (S.D.N.Y. 1994); *see also* Satterfield v. Borough of Schuylkill Haven, 12 F. Supp. 2d 423, 437 (E.D. Pa. 1998).

[239]*See* Lollar v. Baker, 196 F.3d 603, 608–09 (5th Cir. 1999); Strouss v. Michigan Dep't of Corr., 75 F. Supp. 2d 711, 734, 81 FEP 1618 (E.D. Mich. 1999), *aff'd*, 250 F.2d 336, 85 FEP 1250 (6th Cir. 2001); Price v. Delaware Dep't of Corr., 40 F. Supp. 2d 544, 558, 84 FEP 1155 (D. Del. 1999).

officials and the First Amendment rights of those they supervise.[240] An employee's right to speak on matters of public concern in the workplace is determined by balancing the employee's interests against the employer's interests in controlling its work environment.[241] Speech on matters purely of private concern is unprotected.[242]

---

[240]*See generally* Connick v. Myers, 461 U.S. 138, 153–54 (1983) (discharge of state employee for distributing questionnaires concerning internal office affairs did not violate First Amendment); Mt. Healthy City Sch. Dist. Bd. of Educ. v. Doyle, 429 U.S. 274, 283 (1977) (setting forth allocation and burdens of proof in speech cases where employer had mixed motives—one being employee's protected speech, other being legitimate); Pickering v. Board of Educ., 391 U.S. 563, 574 (1968) (dismissing teacher for writing letter to newspaper critical of school board violated teacher's right of free speech; setting forth "*Pickering* balancing test," used by subsequent cases to balance public employer and private interests involved).

[241]*See Pickering*, 391 U.S. at 568. *Compare* Branton v. City of Dallas, 272 F.3d 730, 742–43 (5th Cir. 2001) (internal affairs investigative officer had valid First Amendment claim for adverse employment action allegedly in retaliation for making report about what she perceived to be dishonest testimony of another police officer) *and* Cockrel v. Shelby County Sch. Dist., 270 F.3d 1036, 1051–54 (6th Cir. 2001) (under *Pickering* balancing test, teacher's speech protected because interests of school district, superintendent, and principal in efficient operations of public school and harmonious workplace did not outweigh teacher's interests in speaking to her class about benefits of industrial hemp) *with* Skaarup v. City of N. Las Vegas, 320 F.3d 1040, 1043 (9th Cir. 2003) (fire marshal properly demoted for making derogatory statements about firefighters union and deputy city manager; when those working relationships are essential to fulfilling public responsibilities; wide degree of deference to employer's judgment appropriate), Brochu v. City of Riviera Beach, 304 F.3d 1144, 1158, 89 FEP 1552 (11th Cir. 2002) (police officer's role in creation and dissemination of virtually secret plan to overthrow existing police administration and put himself and his friends in charge not protected speech; discharge not protected by First Amendment) *and* Sharp v. Lindsey, 285 F.3d 479, 486 (6th Cir. 2002) (interests of public school superintendent in having tension-free relationship with school principal outweighed principal's free speech rights in criticizing superintendent; principal's demotion did not violate principal's free speech rights). *See generally* Chapter 14 (Retaliation). When an employee's statements are made pursuant to carrying out "their official duties, the employees are not speaking as citizens for First Amendment purposes, and the Constitution does not insulate their communications from employer discipline." Garcetti v. Ceballos, 126 S. Ct. 1951, 1960 (2006).

[242]*See Connick*, 461 U.S. at 147 ("[W]hen a public employee speaks . . . upon matters only of personal interest, . . . a federal court is not the appropriate forum in which to review the wisdom of a personnel decision taken by a public agency allegedly in reaction to the employee's behavior."). Cases applying this principle give some guidance. *Compare* Charvat v. Eastern Ohio Reg'l Wastewater Auth., 246 F.3d 607, 615–17 (6th Cir. 2001) (letter from employee of authority sent to board of authority setting out numerous environmental and regulatory violations was matter of public concern under *Connick*) *and* Baldassare v. New Jersey, 250 F.3d 188, 194–96 (3d Cir. 2001) (internal police investigator's expressions in his internal investigation of fellow law enforcement officer were matter of public concern given strong

The employer is to be judged on what it reasonably *believed* was said, after conducting a reasonable inquiry, rather than on what the employee actually said.[243] In conducting a balancing of interests, the employer need not necessarily show an *actual* interference with the work environment, only a *likelihood* of such interference.[244] Speculative assertions of wrongful disruption are insufficient to establish a government interest in terminating speech.[245] However, "the closer the employee's speech reflects on matters of public concern, the greater must be the employer's showing that the speech is likely to be disruptive before it may be punished."[246]

Courts apply the balancing test established by the Supreme Court in *Pickering v. Board of Education*[247] and *Connick v. Myers*[248] when considering whether a public employee's speech is protected and whether the employee has been retaliated against for such speech.[249] A claim that a public sector employee was retaliated

---

public interest in uncovering wrongdoing by public employees) *with* Lunow v. City of Okla. City, 61 Fed. Appx. 598, 604–05 (10th Cir. 2003) (fire fighter's participation in safety and health committee and on behalf of union in lawsuit not sufficient to show matters of public concern) *and* Huntsinger v. Board of Dirs. of E-470 Pub. Hwy. S., 35 Fed Appx. 749, 755–56 (10th Cir. 2003) (speech by state agency employee respecting her attempts to resolve potential conflict of interest arising from promissory note issued to her husband by bidder for state contracts could not fairly be characterized as speech on matter of public concern).

[243]*See* Waters v. Churchill, 511 U.S. 661, 677 (1994).

[244]*See* Jeffries v. Harleston, 52 F.3d 9, 13 (2d Cir. 1995) ("the government's burden is to make a substantial showing of likely interference and not [of] an actual disruption").

[245]*See* Finn v. New Mexico, 249 F.3d 1241, 1249 (10th Cir. 2001); *see also* Gardetto v. Mason, 100 F.3d 803, 815–16 (10th Cir. 1996) (employer cannot rely on "purely speculative allegations that contain statements that caused or will cause disruption"); *see also* Wulf v. City of Wichita, 883 F.2d 842, 862 (10th Cir. 1989) (similar).

[246]*Jeffries*, 52 F.3d at 13.

[247]391 U.S. 563, 1 IER 8 (1968).

[248]461 U.S. 138, 1 IER 178 (1983).

[249]*See, e.g.*, Pappas v. Giuliani, 290 F.3d 143, 146 (2d Cir. 2002); Worley v. Board of County Comm'rs of Park County, 44 Fed. Appx. 892, 894 (10th Cir. 2002); Warren v. Ohio Dep't of Pub. Safety, 24 Fed. Appx 259, 267–68 (6th Cir. 2001); Cutts v. Peed, 17 Fed. Appx 132, 135 (4th Cir. 2001); Hale v. Mann, 219 F.3d 61, 70 (2d Cir. 2000); Johnson v. University of Cincinnati, 215 F.3d 561, 584, 82 FEP 1767 (6th Cir. 2000); Cochran v. City of L.A., 222 F.3d 1195, 1200, 16 IER 1230 (9th Cir. 2000); Lighton v. University of Utah, 209 F.3d 1213, 1224, 16 IER 345 (10th Cir. 2000); Maggio v. Sipple, 211 F.3d 1346, 1351 (11th Cir. 2000).

against because of his or her advocacy of minority issues may give rise to a claim under § 1983, even where the employee directed his or her complaints internally rather than to the general public.[250]

State or local government officials may not discriminate against public employees on the basis of their political affiliation,[251] unless "party affiliation is an appropriate requirement for the effective performance of the public office involved."[252] Similarly, a viable § 1983 claim may exist where non-policy-making public sector employees suffer adverse employment decisions because of the positions they take during an election campaign for civic officials.[253] Further, a number of courts have found it unlawful to retaliate against a public employee based on the speech or political affiliation of the employee's family member.[254]

---

[250]*See Johnson*, 215 F.3d at 579; *see also* Collin v. Rector & Bd. of Visitors of Univ. of Va., 873 F. Supp. 1008, 1016 (W.D. Va. 1995) (employee must show that retaliation was result of speech on matter of public concern), *aff'd*, 1998 U.S. App. LEXIS 21267 (4th Cir. Aug. 31, 1998).

[251]*See, e.g.*, Rutan v. Republican Party, 497 U.S. 62, 79–80, 5 IER 673 (1990); Branti v. Finkel, 445 U.S. 507, 516–18, 1 IER 91 (1980); Elrod v. Burns, 427 U.S. 347, 372–73, 1 IER 60 (1976). The court in *Hobler v. Brueher*, 325 F.3d 1145, 1151 (9th Cir. 2003), applied the *Branti* test and analyzed whether being a county prosecutor's secretary made her a "confidential employee" and whether that political contact was an "appropriate requirement for the effective performance of the public office involved." The court concluded that it is consistent with the First Amendment for a confidential secretary to a policy maker to be replaced by the policy maker's successor for political reasons. *See also* Aucoin v. Haney, 306 F.3d 268, 276 (5th Cir. 2002) (political loyalty from assistant district attorney was prerequisite to district attorney's effective performance of duties of his office).

[252]*Branti*, 445 U.S. at 517–18.

[253]*See* Hager v. Pike County Bd. of Educ., 286 F.3d 366, 377, 18 IER 1105 (6th Cir. 2002) (school district's teacher coordinator for gifted and talented children was not policy-making official and so her reassignment for supporting losing candidate for school superintendent was violative of First Amendment if allegation were true); *see also* Armour v. County of Beaver, 271 F.3d 417, 433, 18 IER 178 (3d Cir. 2001) (reversing summary judgment for county commissioner; commissioner may have violated former secretary's right to free speech for political purposes by discharging her based on her political affiliations); Hatfield Bermudez v. Ray Hernandez, 245 F. Supp. 2d 383, 386 (D.P.R. 2003) (similar).

[254]*See* Kipps v. Caillier, 205 F.3d 203, 206 (5th Cir. 2000) (en banc); Sowards v. Louden County, 203 F.3d 426, 433, 16 IER 213 (6th Cir. 2000); Adler v. Pataki, 185 F.3d 35, 44, 15 IER 490 (2d Cir. 1999); Morris v. Lindau, 196 F.3d 102, 111 (2d Cir. 1999); Sutton v. Village of Valley Stream, 96 F. Supp. 2d 189, 193 (E.D.N.Y. 2000). *But see* Wieland v. City of Arnold, 100 F. Supp. 2d 984, 990, 16 IER 823 (E.D. Mo. 2000) (police officer properly instructed to terminate his personal relationship with city resident on probation for felony offense; city's interest in maintaining strict order and efficiency in its police department outweighed officer's associational interest in continuing dating relationship with felon-probationer).

4. Due Process

The third principal constitutional provision invoked in support of § 1983 discrimination claims is the Fourteenth Amendment's Due Process Clause. Two types of due process claims arise: procedural and substantive.

In the employment context, procedural due process claims are the more common. The threshold issue in any *procedural* due process case is whether the plaintiff has shown that he or she was deprived of an interest (life, liberty, or property) protected by the Fourteenth Amendment.[255] In employment cases, plaintiffs typically claim the deprivation of either (1) a property interest in continued employment with the employer-defendant or (2) a liberty interest in future employment with other employers.

Not every discharged public employee who has been deprived of a property or liberty interest is entitled to due process protection. The Supreme Court in *Board of Regents v. Roth*[256] defined when such interests arise. The plaintiff in *Roth*, a nontenured assistant professor, claimed that the university's decision not to renew his contract at the end of his first year of employment violated procedural due process because the university gave him no reason for its nonrenewal decision and no opportunity to be heard.[257] The Court never reached the procedural issue. It found, rather, that the plaintiff failed to show that there was a "deprivation of interests encompassed by the Fourteenth Amendment's protection of liberty and property."[258]

The Court in *Roth* disposed of the plaintiff's liberty deprivation claim first. "Liberty," the Court said, includes " 'the right of [an] individual to contract [or] to engage in . . . the common occupations of life.' "[259] An employee's liberty interest might be compromised in an appropriate failure-to-reemploy case if the employer

---

[255]U.S. CONST. amend. XIV, § 1 ("nor shall any State deprive any person of life, liberty, or property without due process of law"). Title VII, unlike the Fourteenth Amendment, has no general "due process," or "fairness," component. *See* Archuleta v. Colorado Dep't of Insts., 936 F.2d 483, 487, 56 FEP 317 (10th Cir. 1991) ("Title VII does not ensure that employees will always be treated fairly or that they will be discharged only for meritorious reasons.").

[256]408 U.S. 564, 1 IER 23 (1972).

[257]*Id.* at 572–73.

[258]*Id.* at 569.

[259]*Id.* at 572 (quoting Meyer v. Nebraska, 262 U.S. 390, 399 (1923)) (alterations added).

(1) charges the employee with dishonesty or immorality so that his or her " 'good name, reputation, honor, or integrity is at stake' "[260] or (2) "impos[es] on [the employee] a stigma or other disability that foreclose[s] [the employee's] freedom to take advantage of other employment opportunities"—for example, if the university in *Roth* "barred the [plaintiff] from all other public employment in state universities."[261] The Court concluded that neither occurred in *Roth*: "It stretches the concept too far to suggest that a person is deprived of 'liberty' when he simply is not rehired in one job but remains as free as before to seek another."[262]

The plaintiff's property deprivation claim likewise failed. "To have a property interest in a benefit," the Court held that:

> a person clearly must have more than an abstract need or desire for it. He must have more than a unilateral expectation of it. He must, instead, have a legitimate claim of entitlement to it.
>
> . . . .
>
> Property interests . . . are not created by the Constitution. Rather they are created and their dimensions are defined by existing rules or understandings that stem from an independent source, such as state law—rules or understandings that secure certain benefits and that support claims of entitlement to those benefits.[263]

---

[260]408 U.S. at 573 (quoting Wisconsin v. Constantineau, 400 U.S. 433, 437 (1971)).

[261]*Id.*

[262]*Id.* at 575. Occupational liberty is a form of liberty under the Due Process Clause, and the dissemination of false information that renders a person unemployable is a constitutional tort if done without due process of law. *See* Eddings v. City of Hot Springs, 325 F.3d 596, 601–02 (8th Cir. 2003); Atwell v. Lisle Park Dist., 286 F.3d 987, 993, 18 IER 901 (7th Cir. 2002); Abramson v. Pataki, 278 F.3d 93, 103, 169 LRRM 2336 (2d Cir. 2002); Wojcik v. Massachusetts State Lottery Comm'n, 300 F.3d 92, 103 (1st Cir. 2002); Garcia v. Kankakee County Hous. Dist., 279 F.3d 532, 535, 18 IER 470 (7th Cir. 2002); Hawkins v. Rhode Island Lottery Comm'n, 238 F.3d 112, 115 (1st Cir. 2001).

[263]408 U.S. at 577. *Compare* Cleveland Bd. of Educ. v. Loudermill, 470 U.S. 532, 538, 1 IER 424 (1985) (state's civil service statute, providing that civil service employees may be terminated only for good cause and are entitled to administrative review of termination decisions, created for such employees protected property interest in continued employment), Hulen v. Yates, 322 F.3d 1229, 1243 (10th Cir. 2003) (professor had property interest in his departmental assignment based on terms and conditions of his appointment and provisions of faculty manual) *and* Sharp v. Lindsay, 285 F.3d 479, 487–88 (6th Cir. 2002) (principal had protected property interest in his position based on terms of his contract) *with* Meyer v. City of Joplin, 281 F.3d 759, 761 (8th Cir. 2002) (police sergeant had no property interest in promotion by city to rank of lieutenant), Moore v. Muncie Police & Fire Merit Comm'n, 312 F.3d 322, 327–28 (7th Cir. 2002) (applicant for fire-fighter position had no

The Court considered (and distinguished) several prior decisions where it found that certain public university employees had protected property interests in their jobs: for example, "a public college professor dismissed from an office held under tenure provisions,"[264] "college professors and staff members dismissed during the terms of their contracts,"[265] and "a teacher recently hired without tenure or a formal contract, but nonetheless with a clearly implied promise of continued employment."[266] By contrast, "the terms of [the *Roth* plaintiff's] appointment secured absolutely no interest in re-employment for the next year."[267] The Court concluded, therefore, that the *Roth* plaintiff was not deprived of a property interest for which he would be entitled to due process.

Once a plaintiff establishes the deprivation of a protected property or liberty interest, the next hurdle in any procedural due process case is to prove that the employer violated due process. The Supreme Court in *Cleveland Board of Education v. Loudermill*[268] held that the two procedural protections required to satisfy minimal procedural due process in the employment context are (1) notice (written or oral) of the anticipated adverse employment decision and (2) an opportunity for the affected employee to be heard *before* the adverse decision comes into effect, provided this is "coupled with [more extensive] post-termination administrative procedures."[269] The pre-termination opportunity to be heard, however, need not be extensive—" 'something less' than a full evidentiary hearing is sufficient"—and it "need not definitively resolve the propriety of

---

property interest in prospective employment), McMenemy v. City of Rochester, 241 F. 3d 279, 286–88, 85 FEP 237 (2d Cir. 2001) (city fire fighter did not have property interest in competitive examination for promotion) *and* Leventhal v. Knapek, 266 F.3d 64, 77–78, 17 IER 1697 (2d Cir. 2001) (state agency employee did not have property interest in maintaining job grade where he had been placed in that grade on "contingent permanent" basis).

[264]408 U.S. at 576 (citing Slochower v. Board of Higher Educ., 350 U.S. 551 (1956)).

[265]408 U.S. at 576–77 (citing Wieman v. Updegraff, 344 U.S. 183 (1952)).

[266]408 U.S. at 577 (citing Connell v. Higginbotham, 403 U.S. 207 (1971)). *But see* Schultea v. Wood, 47 F.3d 1427, 1429, 10 IER 623 (5th Cir. 1995) (allegations that city manager made oral agreement with plaintiff—former police chief—not to remove him without cause did *not* establish due process property interest of continued employment).

[267]408 U.S. at 578.

[268]470 U.S. 532, 1 IER 424 (1985).

[269]*Id.* at 542.

the discharge."[270] Although state law determines whether there is a property or liberty right, "it is purely a matter of federal constitutional law whether the procedure afforded is adequate."[271] The employee need only be given "[t]he opportunity to present reasons, either in person or in writing, why proposed action should not be taken."[272] Where pre-termination proceedings exist but are somewhat deficient, post-termination proceedings can make up for alleged deficiencies in pre-termination proceedings and thus satisfy procedural due process.[273]

In some instances, no pre-deprivation process need be given. In *Gilbert v. Homer*,[274] the Supreme Court noted that there are circumstances where "a state must act quickly, or where it would be impractical to provide predeprivation process, [and so] post-deprivation process satisfies the requirements of the Due Process Clause."[275] The Court found that the state had a significant interest

---

[270]*Id.* at 545.

[271]Hulen v. Yates, 322 F.3d 1229, 1247 (10th Cir. 2003). This principle is demonstrated by cases such as *Hulen*, where the court rejected a procedural due process claim based on the notion that the defendant violated procedures negotiated in a collective bargaining agreement. The court in *Hulen* quoted the decision in *Levitt v. University of Texas*, 759 F.2d 1224, 1229 (5th Cir. 1985), which stated that: "Even if the University failed to follow its own rules, it nevertheless gave [the professor] all the process to which he was entitled under the Constitution."

[272]*Loudermill*, 470 U.S. at 546. In *Loudermill*, the Court reversed dismissal of the plaintiffs' complaint because it properly alleged that the plaintiffs were given no pre-termination opportunity to be heard. *Id.*; *see also Hulen*, 322 F.3d at 1247–48 (employee afforded due process where, before transfer, he twice met with decision maker, lodged written complaints, and engaged attorney in attempt to prevent transfer, and then had access to grievance process after transfer); Vukadinovich v. Board of Sch. Trs., 278 F.3d 693, 700–01 (7th Cir. 2002) (employee's due process rights not violated by having hearing in front of same school board members he had criticized in letter, absent evidence of actual or potential bias); Otero v. Bridgeport Hous. Auth., 297 F.3d 142, 151–52 (2d Cir. 2002) (pre-termination process need not be elaborate or approach level of evidentiary hearing but requires only oral or written notice of charges, explanation of employer's evidence, and opportunity for employee to explain).

[273]470 U.S. at 547 n.12; *see, e.g.*, Adams v. Sewell, 946 F.2d 757, 764–65, 57 FEP 433 (11th Cir. 1991) (where plaintiff—accused sexual harasser—was given pretermination hearing and chance to respond to accusation but was given no notice of or opportunity to prepare for hearing, county's post-termination grievance procedures satisfied any lack of pre-termination procedural due process).

[274]520 U.S. 924, 12 IER 1473 (1997).

[275]*Id.* at 930.

in promptly suspending a police officer with felony charges pending against him, given that the position is one of "great public trust and high public visibility."[276]

In *O'Neill v. Baker*,[277] the First Circuit considered whether a plaintiff was denied procedural due process when her employer, a social services department, sent her a termination letter before conducting a pre-termination meeting. The plaintiff complained that she did not have specific notice that the purpose of the meeting was to discuss her impending termination, that the decision to terminate her was made prior to the meeting, and that the termination letter was drafted, signed, and mailed prior to the meeting.[278] The court held that the letters and memoranda provided to the plaintiff in connection with her prior suspensions and work plans provided the essential elements of due process: (1) notice that termination could result if she failed to improve her attendance and tardiness and (2) the right to be represented by her union at the "meeting," which the letter described as a "hearing."[279] Furthermore, the court found that "there was no constitutional infirmity" in this procedure because the plaintiff had the opportunity to give her side of the story at the hearing, and the plaintiff's supervisor testified that she would have reconsidered the decision to discharge the plaintiff if the plaintiff had offered "compelling reasons indicating that the contemplated discharge was unwarranted."[280]

Where a collective bargaining agreement confers on employees a property interest in their positions, procedural due process requires that the employees receive a pre-deprivation hearing before being transferred.[281] In order to state a claim for failure to provide due process, however, a plaintiff must have taken advantage

---

[276]*Id.* at 932; *see also* Patel v. Midland Mem'l Hosp. & Med. Ctr., 298 F.3d 333, 339–41 (5th Cir. 2002) (hospital could suspend physician without pre-suspension due process if it had ample reason to believe doctor posed risk to patient safety); Caine v. Hardy, 943 F.2d 1406, 1412 (5th Cir. 1991) (en banc) (similar).

[277]210 F.3d 41, 48–49 (1st Cir. 2000).

[278]*Id.* at 48.

[279]*Id.* at 49.

[280]*Id.*

[281]*See* Leary v. Daeschner, 228 F.3d 729, 742–43, 16 IER 1249 (6th Cir. 2000).

of these processes, unless they are unavailable or inadequate.[282] As such, an employee who fails to avail himself or herself of a grievance procedure is precluded from showing that he or she was denied procedural due process with respect to alleged deprivation of property rights.[283]

Different rules apply in *substantive* due process cases, where an employer's reasons for a particular employment decision, rather than its procedures, are challenged.[284] Not all "bad" or even "pretextual" decisions warrant substantive due process protection. The Supreme Court has made clear that the substantive component of the Due Process Clause is much more narrowly construed in the employment context than its procedural counterpart:

> *The federal court is not the appropriate forum in which to review the multitude of personnel decisions that are made daily by public agencies.* We must accept the harsh fact that numerous individual mistakes are inevitable in the day-to-day administration of our affairs. The United States Constitution cannot feasibly be construed to require federal judicial review for every such error. In the absence of any claim that the public employer was motivated by a desire to curtail or to penalize the exercise of an employee's constitutionally protected rights, we must presume that official action was regular and, if erroneous, can best be corrected in other ways.

---

[282]*See* Rivera v. Bernalillo County, 51 Fed. Appx. 828, 831–32 (9th Cir. 2002); *see also* Catlett v. Woodfin, 13 Fed. Appx. 412, 416 (7th Cir. 2001) (pre-termination due process does not require that employee be allowed to cross-examine or present witnesses; however, cross-examination and presentation of witnesses was to be permitted at arbitration of employee's grievance); Alvin v. Suzuki, 227 F.3d 107, 116 (3d Cir. 2000) (failure to use available grievance procedure defeats claim of violation of procedural due process).

[283]*See* O'Neill, 210 F.3d at 49.

[284]*See* Collins v. City of Harker Heights, 503 U.S. 115, 125, 7 IER 233 (1992) ("the substantive component of the [Due Process Clause] . . . protects individual liberty against 'certain government actions *regardless* of the fairness of the procedures used to implement them.' ") (quoting Daniels v. Williams, 474 U.S. 327, 331 (1986)) (emphasis added); Gilmere v. City of Atlanta, 774 F.2d 1495, 1500 (11th Cir. 1985) (en banc) ("Unlike procedural due process claims, which challenge the adequacy of the procedures used by the government in deciding how to treat individuals, substantive due process claims allege that certain governmental conduct would remain unjustified even if it were accompanied by the most stringent of procedural safeguards.").

The substantive/procedural distinction is not always easy to apply, and some courts have confused it. *See, e.g.,* Archuleta v. Colorado Dep't of Institutions, 936 F.2d 483, 489–91, 56 FEP 317 (10th Cir. 1991) (rejecting temporarily laid-off

The Due Process Clause of the Fourteenth Amendment is not a guarantee against incorrect or ill-advised personnel decisions.[285]

Unlike procedural due process, which reaches all employment decisions adversely affecting a state law–created property or liberty interest, substantive due process reaches only those employment decisions affecting constitutionally protected "fundamental rights" of an employee, such as the rights found in the Bill of Rights.[286] An individual asserting a substantive due process claim

---

employee's "substantive" due process claim because she received post-termination hearing that was procedurally adequate and was reinstated with back pay).

[285]Bishop v. Wood, 426 U.S. 341, 349–50 (1976) (emphasis added); *accord* McKinney v. Pate, 20 F.3d 1550, 1560–61, 9 IER 1266 (11th Cir. 1994) (rejecting plaintiff's substantive due process claim regarding his facially adequate but allegedly biased termination; treating case, rather, as one for procedural due process); *see also* Nebbia v. New York, 291 U.S. 502, 525 (1934) (test is "unreasonable, arbitrary or capricious"); *Collins*, 503 U.S. at 128 (rejecting plaintiff's substantive due process claim regarding alleged failure of city to adequately train its employees about safety; even if right protected by substantive due process were at stake, Court held that it is "not persuaded that the city's alleged failure to train its employees, or to warn them about known risks of harm, was an omission that can properly be characterized as arbitrary, or conscience-shocking in a constitutional sense"). A special balancing test applies in speech deprivation cases, where the employee's speech interest is weighed against the government's interest in effectively managing its workplace. *See* Section III.C.3 *supra*.

[286]*See* Regents of the Univ. of Mich. v. Ewing, 474 U.S. 214, 229 (1985) (Powell, J., concurring) ("While property interests are protected by procedural due process even though the interest is derived from state law rather than the Constitution, substantive due process rights are created only by the Constitution.") (citation omitted); *McKinney*, 20 F.3d 1556 ("The substantive component of the Due Process Clause protects those rights that are 'fundamental,' that is, rights that are 'implicit in the concept of ordered liberty.' The Supreme Court has deemed that most—but not all— of the rights enumerated in the Bill of Rights are fundamental; certain unenumerated rights (for instance, the penumbral right of privacy) also merit protection.") (citations omitted); *cf. Collins*, 503 U.S. at 125 ("As a general matter, the Court has always been reluctant to expand the concept of substantive due process because guideposts for responsible decisionmaking in this unchartered area are scarce and open-ended.").

There is some disagreement on this issue. In *Harrah Independent School District v. Martin*, 440 U.S. 194 (1976), the Supreme Court emphasized that the plaintiff teacher's substantive due process claim did not warrant any heightened scrutiny because no fundamental right was involved, yet the Court went on to state that the plaintiff could prevail if she could show that the employment action in question was wholly arbitrary. *See also* Singleton v. Cecil, 176 F.3d 419, 430–33 (8th Cir. 1999) (Arnold, J., dissenting) (referring to Supreme Court's decision in *Harrah* to support contention that nonfundamental right substantive due process claim should be subject to rational basis review).

must allege deprivation of an interest in life, liberty, or property; a simple allegation of arbitrary government conduct is not sufficient.[287] It is only the deprivation of "fundamental" rights that will implicate substantive due process protection. Public employment is not a fundamental property interest entitled to substantive due process protection.[288] Nor does substantive due process protect "occupational liberty."[289]

A substantive due process claim lies where the government's actions concerning a fundamental right either "shock[] the conscience" or "offend[] judicial notions of fairness . . . or . . . human dignity."[290] To meet this burden, a plaintiff must demonstrate that the government action complained of is "truly irrational,"—"something more than . . . arbitrary, capricious, or in violation of state law."[291] Courts have held that neither allegations of sexual harassment nor allegations of malicious prosecution rise to the level of shocking the conscience and thus do not give rise to a substantive due process claim.[292] The Supreme Court has said that "only the most egregious official conduct can be said to be 'arbitrary in the constitutional sense.' "[293] In the employment discrimination context, the most commonly litigated fundamental right deprivation is alleged interference with an employee's free speech rights.[294] Another example is alleged interference with an employee's right to privacy and procreation.[295]

---

[287]See Gravitte v. North Carolina Div. of Motor Vehicles, 33 Fed. Appx. 45, 48–49 (4th Cir. 2002) (governmental policy requiring law enforcement officer to write quota of tickets is not violation of substantive due process).

[288]See Nicholas v. Pennsylvania State Univ., 227 F.3d 133, 140 (3d Cir. 2000) (citing other circuit court decisions).

[289]Singleton, 176 F.3d at 424.

[290]Riley v. St. Louis County, 153 F.3d 627, 631 (8th Cir. 1998) (citations omitted).

[291]Id.; see also Klein v. McGowan, 198 F. 3d 705, 710, 81 FEP 1771 (8th Cir. 1999).

[292]See Klein, 198 F.3d at 710 (sexual harassment); Merkle v. Upper Dublin Sch. Dist., 211 F.3d 782, 792, 16 IER 432 (3d Cir. 2000) (malicious prosecution).

[293]County of Sacramento v. Lewis, 523 U.S. 833, 845–46 (1998).

[294]See, e.g., Beville v. South Dakota Bd. of Regents, 687 F. Supp. 464, 467 (D.S.D. 1988) (university professor's claim that his employer terminated him in retaliation for exercising his First Amendment right to free speech could provide basis for claimed denial of substantive due process).

[295]See, e.g., Cameron v. Board of Educ., 795 F. Supp. 228, 236, 81 FEP 1219 (S.D. Ohio 1991) (refusing to renew unwed teacher's contract because of her artificial insemination would offend substantive due process).

IV. SCOPE AND COVERAGE OF THE CIVIL RIGHTS ACT OF 1871, 42 U.S.C. §§ 1985 AND 1986

A. Statutory Authority

Section 1985(3)[296] provides:

> If two or more persons in any State or Territory conspire, or go in disguise on the highway or on the premises of another, for the purpose of depriving, either directly or indirectly, any person or class of persons of the equal protection of the laws, or of equal privileges and immunities under the laws; or for the purpose of preventing or hindering the constituted authorities of any State or Territory from giving or securing to all persons within such State or Territory the equal protection of the laws; . . . [then,] if one or more persons engaged therein do, or cause to be done, any act in furtherance of the object of such conspiracy, whereby another is injured in his person or property, or deprived of having and exercising any right or privilege of a citizen of the United States, the party so injured or deprived may have an action for the recovery of damages, occasioned by such injury or deprivation, against any one or more of the conspirators.[297]

Section 1986 provides:

> Every person who, having knowledge that any of the wrongs conspired to be done, and mentioned in section 1985 of this title, are about to be committed, and having power to prevent or aid in preventing the commission of the same, neglects or refuses so to do, if such wrongful act be committed, shall be liable to the party injured, or his legal representatives, for all damages caused by such wrongful act, which such person by reasonable diligence could have prevented; and such damages may be recovered in an action on the case; and any number of persons guilty of such wrongful neglect or refusal may be joined as defendants in the action . . . .[298]

---

[296]Section 1985 has three subparts, of which only § 1985(3) (conspiracies to deprive persons of rights or privileges) is of interest in employment discrimination law. Subpart (1) makes unlawful conspiracies to prevent federal officers from performing their duties; subpart (2) makes unlawful conspiracies to obstruct justice. *See* 42 U.S.C. §§ 1985(1), (2).

[297]42 U.S.C. § 1985(3) (2000).

[298]Act of Apr. 20, 1871, ch. 22, §§ 2, 6, 17 Stat. 15 (codified at 42 U.S.C. § 1986 (2000)). These statutes, along with the present § 1983, were originally enacted in 1871 as part of the Ku Klux Klan Act. Like § 1983, they were passed pursuant to Congress' powers granted in § 5 of the Fourteenth Amendment.

Section 1985(3) creates no substantive rights; rather, like § 1983, it "merely provides a remedy for violation of the rights it designates."[299] Determining which "rights" it "designates," however, has proved to be exceedingly difficult.[300] Breaking down the statutory clauses into parts, the Supreme Court has set forth four elements of a typical § 1985(3) claim:

> (1) a conspiracy; (2) for the purpose of depriving, either directly or indirectly, any person or class of persons of the equal protection of the laws, or of equal privileges and immunities under the laws; and (3) an act in furtherance of the conspiracy; (4) whereby a person is either injured in his person or property or deprived of any right or privilege of a citizen of the United States.[301]

Section 1985's companion statute, § 1986, provides that any person who, with knowledge of a conspiracy and the ability to prevent it, neglects or refuses to do so can be held liable for all resulting damages. The threshold requirement for maintenance of a § 1986 action thus is the establishment of liability against someone under § 1985(3).[302] Then, in order to prevail under § 1986, the

---

[299]Great Am. Fed. Sav. & Loan Ass'n v. Novotny, 442 U.S. 366, 372, 382, 19 FEP 1482 (1979).

[300]As one commentator has observed:

Even after one hundred and sixteen years, four major Supreme Court opinions, colorful legislative history, and over five hundred lower court opinions, there is probably no other federal statute in such complete disarray, distortion, and confusion as that section of the Civil Rights Act of 1871 now codified at 42 U.S.C. § 1985(3).

Janis L. McDonald, *Starting From Scratch: A Revisionist View of 42 U.S.C. § 1985(3) and Class-Based Animus*, 19 CONN. L. REV. 471, 471 (1987). The Seventh Circuit likewise observed that "an enduring interpretation of such an opaque statute" may not be possible, as courts attempt "to avoid turning all state torts into federal offenses" yet give meaning to a statute "that if read naturally speaks only to state action and therefore duplicates § 1983." Stevens v. Tillman, 855 F.2d 394, 404 (7th Cir. 1988). In *Stevens*, the Seventh Circuit concluded that § 1985(3) reaches racially motivated (and perhaps other class-based) conspiracies: (1) to deprive persons of rights secured to all by federal law; (2) to deprive persons of rights secured to all by state law, where the deprivation interferes with the exercise of a federally protected right (e.g., the rights to travel, to associate, to speak, and to vote); and (3) to deprive persons of rights secured against only government action (such as free speech), provided that the defendants either are "state actors" or are seeking to influence the state to act in a prohibited manner. 855 F.2d at 404.

[301]Carpenters Local 610 v. Scott, 463 U.S. 825, 828–29 (1983).

[302]*See* Jensen v. Henderson, 315 F.3d 854, 863, 90 FEP 898 (8th Cir. 2002) (§ 1986 claims are dependent upon a valid § 1985 claim); Mian v. Donaldson, Lufkin, Jennette Secs. Corp., 7 F.3d 1085, 1088 (2d Cir. 1993) (same); Lewellen v. Raff,

plaintiff also must prove that the § 1986 defendant had actual knowledge of the conspiracy, was in a position to prevent its execution, and failed to take reasonable steps to do so.[303]

B. Cognizable Defendants

1. The Applicability of § 1985 to Private Discrimination

In *Griffin v. Breckenridge*,[304] the Supreme Court overruled prior cases[305] and concluded that § 1985(3) covers private as well as governmental conduct.

It does not follow, however, that state action is irrelevant in all § 1985(3) actions. Because § 1985(3)'s reach is derivative, courts have since determined that where the underlying violation requires state action, there can be no violation on which to base § 1985(3) liability absent such state action. For example, almost immediately following *Griffin*, the Seventh Circuit, in *Dombrowski v. Dowling*,[306] concluded, in an opinion by then Circuit Judge (later Supreme Court Justice) Stevens, that "a private conspiracy which arbitrarily denies

---

843 F.2d 1103, 1106 (8th Cir. 1988) (same); Karim-Panahi v. Los Angeles Police Dep't, 839 F.2d 621, 626, 46 FEP 287 (9th Cir. 1988) (claim can be stated under § 1986 only if complaint states valid claim under § 1985); Landrigan v. City of Warwick, 628 F.2d 736, 739 n.1 (1st Cir. 1980) ("As section 1985 does not apply, any claim under section 1986 must also fail."); Brawer v. Horowitz, 535 F.2d 830, 841 (3d Cir. 1976) ("Having failed to state a claim under § 1985(2), a fortiori appellants failed to state a claim under § 1986."); Hamilton v. Chaffin, 506 F.2d 904, 914 (5th Cir. 1975) (same).

[303]*See, e.g.*, Buck v. Board of Elections, 536 F.2d 522, 524 (2d Cir. 1976) (unsuccessful candidate for school board has no claim under § 1986 where she failed to allege that defendants were aware of discriminatory acts); Lieberman v. Gant, 474 F. Supp. 848, 875, 20 FEP 877 (D. Conn. 1979) (in teacher's suit against state university for tenure denial, board of trustees shielded from liability if it lacked actual knowledge of conspiracy among various lower administrative officials), *aff'd*, 630 F.2d 60, 23 FEP 505 (2d Cir. 1980).

[304]403 U.S. 88, 101, 9 FEP 1196 (1971) ("It is thus evident that all indicators—text, companion provisions, and legislative history—point unwaveringly to § 1985(3)'s coverage of private conspiracies.").

[305]The reasoning of prior cases had gone as follows: Because the Fourteenth Amendment prohibited certain conduct by the states, and because the civil rights legislation in question was passed pursuant to the Fourteenth Amendment, a statute such as § 1985 could reach only conspiracies under color of state law and did not embrace purely private conspiracies. *See, e.g.*, United States v. Cruikshank, 92 U.S. 542, 555–56 (1875); Collins v. Hardyman, 341 U.S. 651, 658 (1951).

[306]459 F.2d 190 (7th Cir. 1972).

[the plaintiff] access to private property does not abridge his Fourteenth Amendment rights."[307] The object of a § 1985(3) conspiracy must fall into that certain category of conduct prohibited by the statute; where that prohibition is limited to state action, such as the denial of a right protected by the Fourteenth Amendment, § 1985(3) simply does not reach purely private conspiracies.[308]

Although other courts were divided on the question,[309] the Supreme Court seems to have adopted the Seventh Circuit's position in *Great American Federal Savings & Loan Ass'n v. Novotny*.[310] *Novotny* involved a § 1985(3) claim by an officer-employee who asserted that he was terminated for supporting a protest against his employer's sex discrimination. The Court characterized the claim as, in effect, a Title VII § 704(a) retaliation claim and held that "deprivation of a right created by Title VII cannot be the basis for a cause of action under § 1985[(3)]."[311] In his concurring opinion, joined in relevant part by Justice Powell, Justice Stevens wrote:

---

[307]*Id.* at 196.

[308]*Id.* at 194. *Dombrowski* involved an alleged private conspiracy to refuse to rent office space to criminal lawyers. The plaintiffs alleged that this was because their clients largely were minorities; the defendants claimed that it was because they did not want alleged criminals in their building. Before analyzing § 1985(3), the court analyzed § 1983, noting that it contains "two quite distinct 'state involvement' requirements," namely, that the defendants must be acting "under color of" state law and, second, that the object must be deprivation "of any rights, privileges, or immunities secured by the Constitution and laws." *Id.* The court then turned to § 1985(3), which clearly does not, after *Griffin*, impose an "under color of" state-law requirement. However, as to the "plaintiff's protected interests," the court said, "the coverage of the two provisions is probably co-extensive." *Id.* The court noted that *Griffin* gave three categories of protected interests covered by § 1985(3): (1) "a black citizen's Thirteenth Amendment rights"; (2) the "federal right to travel interstate"; and (3) "rights protected by the Fourteenth Amendment." The object of the alleged conspiracy clearly did not involve African-American citizens' Thirteenth Amendment rights or the right to travel interstate, and the Fourteenth Amendment had no application to a right to rent property in a private building. *Id.* at 194–95.

[309]*Compare* Cohen v. Illinois Inst. of Tech., 581 F.2d 658, 663–64, 17 FEP 1552 (7th Cir. 1978) (state action required), Doski v. M. Goldseker Co., 539 F.2d 1326, 1333–34, 12 FEP 1751 (4th Cir. 1976) (same), Bellamy v. Mason's Stores, Inc., 508 F.2d 504, 506, 9 FEP 1 (4th Cir. 1974) (same) *and* Hilliard v. Ferguson, 30 F.3d 649, 652–53 (5th Cir. 1994) (plaintiff alleged that public school board conspired to deny convicted felons equal protection; court applied rational basis test to demonstrate that board had legitimate interest in protecting school children) *with* Weise v. Syracuse Univ., 522 F.2d 397, 406–08, 10 FEP 1331 (2d Cir. 1975) (no state action found) *and* Action v. Gannon, 450 F.2d 1227, 1235–36 (8th Cir. 1971) (same).

[310]442 U.S. 366, 19 FEP 1482 (1979).

[311]*Id.* at 378; *see, e.g.*, Jensen v. Henderson, 315 F.3d 854, 862, 90 FEP 898 (8th Cir. 2002) (describing holding in *Novotny* that "a litigant may not bring a § 1985(3) claim to redress violations of Title VII").

Some privileges and immunities of citizenship, such as the right to engage in interstate travel and the right to be free of the badges of slavery, are protected by the Constitution against interference by private action, as well as impairment by state action. Private conspiracies to deprive individuals of these rights are, as this Court held in *Griffin v. Breckenridge*, 403 U.S. 88, 9 FEP 1196 (1971), actionable under § 1985[(3)] without regard to any state involvement.

Other privileges and immunities of citizenship such as the right to due process of law and the right to the equal protection of the laws are protected by the Constitution only against state action. *Shelley v. Kraemer*, 334 U.S. 1, 13 (1948). If a state agency arbitrarily refuses to serve a class of persons—Chinese Americans, for example, see *Yick Wo v. Hopkins*, 118 U.S. 356 (1886)—it violates the Fourteenth Amendment. Or if private persons take conspiratorial action that prevents or hinders the constituted authorities of any State from giving or securing equal treatment, the private persons would cause those authorities to violate the Fourteenth Amendment; the private persons would then have violated § 1985[(3)].

If, however, private persons engage in purely private acts of discrimination—for example, if they discriminate against women or against lawyers with a criminal practice, see *Dombrowski v. Dowling*, 459 F.2d 190, 194–196 (1972)—they do not violate the Equal Protection Clause of the Fourteenth Amendment. The rights secured by the Equal Protection and Due Process Clauses of the Fourteenth Amendment are rights to protection against unequal or unfair treatment by the State, not by private parties. Thus, while [§ 1985(3)] does not require that a defendant act under color of state law, there still can be no claim for relief based on a violation of the Fourteenth Amendment if there has been no involvement by the State. The requirement of state action, in this context, is no more than a requirement that there be a constitutional violation.[312]

A majority of the Court adopted this view in *Carpenters Local 610 v. Scott*.[313] The alleged conspiracy in *Scott*—a physical assault by labor union supporters against a group of nonunion employees working for a nonunion contractor—allegedly had interfered with the associational rights of nonunion workers. The Court

---

[312]442 U.S. at 380, 383–85 (Stevens, J., concurring); *id.* at 379 (Powell, J., concurring); *accord* Thomas v. Rohner-Gehrig & Co., 582 F. Supp. 669, 673, 34 FEP 887 (N.D. Ill. 1984) (any violation of Fourteenth Amendment sought under § 1985(3) must be predicated on state action); Spirt v. Teachers Ins. & Annuity Ass'n, 475 F. Supp. 1298, 1314, 20 FEP 738 (S.D.N.Y. 1979) (same; quoting and relying on Judge Stevens' concurrence in *Dombrowski*). *But see* Stevens v. Tillman, 568 F. Supp. 289, 292–93, 36 FEP 1232 (N.D. Ill. 1983) (state action not required), *rev'd on other grounds*, 855 F.2d 394 (7th Cir. 1988).

[313]463 U.S. 825, 825 (1983).

held "that an alleged conspiracy to infringe First Amendment rights is not a violation of § 1985(3) unless it is proved that the State is involved in the conspiracy or that the aim of the conspiracy is to influence the action of the State."[314] The Court reaffirmed, however, that the state action requirement does not generally limit the interpretation of § 1985(3), which applies to wholly private conspiracies aimed at rights constitutionally protected against private as well as official encroachment.[315] The Court did not reach the question of "whether respondents' action could be sustained under § 1985(3) as involving a conspiracy to deprive respondents of rights, privileges, or immunities under *state* law"[316] because it held that conspiracies motivated by commercial or business animosity simply are not actionable under § 1985(3) in any event.[317]

Courts are divided on whether violations of federal rights secured by § 1981 may support a § 1985 claim.[318] An action under § 1985 may not be used to obtain relief for Title VII or ADEA violations.[319]

Under circumstances otherwise actionable under § 1985, interference with an at-will employment relationship can give rise to a claim for damages under § 1985.[320]

---

[314]*Id.* at 830.

[315]*Id.* at 833; *see* Hobson v. Wilson, 737 F.2d 1, 15 (D.C. Cir. 1984) ("In other words, the rights protected by section 1985(3) exist independently of the section and only to the extent that the Constitution creates them. Thus, when state action is involved, the whole spectrum of rights against state encroachment that the Constitution sets forth comes into play. When no state action is involved, only those constitutional rights that exist against private actors may be challenged under the section.").

[316]463 U.S. at 833–34 (emphasis added).

[317]*Id.* at 838–39. The four dissenting Justices (Marshall, Blackmun, Brennan, and O'Connor) contended that § 1985(3) provides "a remedy to any class of persons, whose beliefs or associations placed them in danger of not receiving equal protection of the laws from local authorities." The dissenters would have included in the classes of those who benefit from § 1985(3) those who suffer bias on the basis of race, religion, sex, and national origin, as they per se meet the requirements of § 1985(3). *Id.* at 853.

[318]*Compare* Wesley v. Howard Univ., 3 F. Supp. 2d 1 (D.D.C. 1998) (recognizing that § 1985 claim can succeed only to extent predicate § 1981 claim is successful) *with* Harris v. Niagara Mohawk Power Corp., 1998 WL 865566, at *6 (N.D.N.Y. Dec. 7, 1998) (unpublished) (declining to recognize § 1985 claim based on § 1981) (citing Ladson v. Ulltra East Parking Corp., 853 F. Supp. 699, 703–04 (S.D.N.Y. 1994)).

[319]*See, e.g.,* Sherlock v. Montefiore Med. Ctr., 84 F.3d 522, 527, 70 FEP 1377 (2d Cir. 1996) (extending reasoning in *Novotny* to preclude § 1985 claims predicated on ADEA); Causey v. Balog, 929 F. Supp. 900, 912–13, 71 FEP 643 (D. Md. 1996) (same), *aff'd*, 162 F.3d 795, 78 FEP 1241 (4th Cir. 1998).

[320]*See* Haddle v. Garrison, 525 U.S. 121, 124–25 (1998) (at-will employee injured in his "person or property" and thus stated cognizable § 1985 claim where he

2. *The Conspiracy Requirement*

For an action to be maintained under § 1985, like any other conspiracy statute, "two or more persons" must have conspired together.[321] In the employment context, the most common recurring issue is the extent to which a corporate employer and its supervisors or agents can constitute co-conspirators. Although the Supreme Court has not decided the issue,[322] most lower courts hold that the actions of a single employer and its representatives cannot constitute a conspiracy covered by § 1985(3).[323] Some have relied on the restraint-of-trade conspiracy cases, which hold that:

---

alleged conspiracy to fire him in retaliation for obeying federal grand jury subpoena and to deter him from testifying).

[321]A civil "conspiracy" under § 1985(3) is defined as an agreement between two or more persons to participate in an unlawful act, or a lawful act in an unlawful manner. Hobson v. Wilson, 737 F.2d 1, 55 (D.C. Cir. 1984) (§ 1985(3) applies to conspiracy by Federal Bureau of Investigation to limit First Amendment rights); *see also* Grimes v. Louisville & Nashville Ry., 583 F. Supp. 642, 649–50, 35 FEP 1369 (S.D. Ind. 1984) (alleged conspiracy between employer and union fails for lack of agreement), *aff'd mem.*, 767 F.2d 925 (7th Cir. 1985).

[322]*See* Great Am. Fed. Sav. & Loan Ass'n v. Novotny, 442 U.S. 366, 372 n.11 (1979) ("For the purposes of this question, we assume but certainly do not decide that the directors of a single corporation can form a conspiracy within the meaning of § 1985(3)."); *see also* Hull v. Cuyahoga Valley Bd. of Educ., 926 F.2d 505, 509, 55 FEP 269 (6th Cir. 1991) (corporation cannot conspire with its own agents or employees).

[323]*See, e.g., Hull*, 926 F.2d at 509 (school district superintendent, executive director, and school administrator were not distinct "people" and thus could not form conspiracy); Buschi v. Kirven, 775 F.2d 1240, 1252 (4th Cir. 1985) (doctrine that no intracorporate conspiracy may be alleged is available even if suit is brought against individual employees and not corporation); Cross v. General Motors Corp., 721 F.2d 1152, 1156, 40 FEP 418 (8th Cir. 1983) (dismissing claim of conspiracy against corporation and its employees); Cohen v. Illinois Inst. of Tech., 581 F.2d 658, 663–64, 17 FEP 1552 (7th Cir. 1978) (corporation cannot conspire with itself as long as officers and employees acted within scope of their employment and without personal reasons); Herrmann v. Moore, 576 F.2d 453, 457, 17 FEP 1523 (2d Cir. 1978) (same); Baker v. Stuart Broadcasting Co., 560 F.2d 389, 391, 15 FEP 394 (8th Cir. 1977) (same); Girard v. 94th St. & Fifth Ave. Corp., 530 F.2d 66, 70–71 (2d Cir. 1976) (same); Givan v. Greyhound Lines, 616 F. Supp. 1223, 1224, 39 FEP 123 (S.D. Ohio 1985) (corporation and individually named employees who acted within scope of their employment cannot be sued under 42 U.S.C. § 1985(3) because they comprise single legal entity not capable of conspiring). *Contra* Stathos v. Bowden, 728 F.2d 15, 21, 34 FEP 142 (1st Cir. 1984) (where series of acts as opposed to single act was involved, conspiracy among corporate agents can be challenged under § 1985(3)); Novotny v. Great Am. Fed. Sav. & Loan Ass'n, 584 F.2d 1235, 1257, 17 FEP 1252 (3d Cir. 1978) (officers and directors of corporation can constitute conspiracy when purpose of their concerted action is violation of federal statute), *vacated on other grounds*, 442 U.S. 366; Padway v. Palches, 665 F.2d 965, 968–69, 27 FEP 1403 (9th Cir. 1982) (dictum; "[W]e have never held that it is impossible to

> A corporation cannot conspire with itself any more than a private individual can, and it is the general rule that the acts of the agent are the acts of the corporation. . . . In the absence of any allegation whatever to indicate that the agents of the corporation were acting in other than their normal capacities, plaintiff has failed to state a cause of action based on conspiracy . . . .[324]

In *Dombrowski v. Dowling*,[325] the Seventh Circuit summarized this position, declaring that the conspiracy requirement of § 1985

> is not satisfied by proof that a discriminatory business decision reflects the collective judgment of two or more executives of the same firm. . . . [I]f the challenged conduct is essentially a single act of discrimination by a single business entity, the fact that two or more agents participated in the decision or in the act itself will normally not constitute the conspiracy contemplated by this statute.[326]

The conspiracy requirement represents a significant limitation on employment discrimination cases brought under § 1985(3). Courts have consistently held that intracorporate communications and actions may not form the basis of a conspiracy within the meaning of § 1985(3).[327] Because, at common law, a corporation could not conspire with itself, courts typically held that the actions of employees of a single company that are within the scope of their employment cannot form the basis of a conspiracy under § 1985(3).[328]

---

have a conspiracy between trustees (or directors) and employees of a single corporation. It may be possible under some circumstances.").

[324]Nelson Radio & Supply Co. v. Motorola, 200 F.2d 911, 914 (5th Cir. 1952) (civil conspiracy cannot be committed by single corporation); *accord* Zelinger v. Uvalde Rock Asphalt Co., 316 F.2d 47, 52 (10th Cir. 1963).

[325]459 F.2d 190 (7th Cir. 1972).

[326]*Id.* at 196.

[327]*See, e.g.*, Denney v. City of Albany, 247 F.3d 1172, 1190 (11th Cir. 2001); McAndrew v. Lockheed Martin Corp., 206 F.3d 1031, 1036 (11th Cir. 2000) (en banc); Wright v. Illinois Dep't of Children & Family Servs., 40 F.3d 1492, 1508–09 (7th Cir. 1994); Godby v. Montgomery County Bd. of Educ., 996 F. Supp. 1390 (M.D. Ala. 1998); Kyle v. Morton High Sch. Dist. 201, 1997 WL 222870, at *5 (N.D. Ill. Apr. 24, 1997), *aff'd*, 144 F.3d 448 (7th Cir. 1998); Baldwin v. University of Tex. Med. Branch at Galveston, 945 F. Supp. 1022 (S.D. Tex. 1996), *aff'd mem.*, 122 F.3d 1066 (5th Cir. 1997); Baker v. American Juice, Inc., 870 F. Supp. 878, 883, 68 FEP 52 (N.D. Ind. 1994).

[328]*See, e.g.*, Johnson v. Hills & Dales Gen. Hosp., 40 F.3d 837, 838, 66 FEP 504 (6th Cir. 1994). The Supreme Court cast some doubt on the continuing validity of this line of authority in *Haddle v. Garrison*, 525 U.S. 121, 14 IER 1057 (1998). There, the Court held that an individual who was discharged from his at-will job with a medical services corporation had a viable § 1985(3) claim against the corporation and two of its officers. The plaintiff claimed that the defendants had

In *Baker v. Stuart Broadcasting Co.*,[329] the Eighth Circuit, citing *Dombrowski*, affirmed the dismissal of a § 1985(3) employment discrimination action brought against a radio broadcasting company, two of its stockholders, and its president, on the ground that the company could not conspire with itself or its personnel acting in their official capacities.[330]

Actions of employees of a single company that take place outside the scope of the alleged conspirators' employment are subject to § 1985(3).[331] Some courts have allowed alleged corporate conspiracies to be brought under § 1985(3) where, for example, the corporation is alleged to have conspired with a *former* employee[332]

---

conspired to terminate his employment because he had cooperated with federal agents investigating possible Medicare fraud. The Court's decision did not discuss, or even acknowledge, the intracorporate conspiracy problem, and its brief opinion in the case is devoted entirely to the question of whether the plaintiff was obligated to show a "constitutionally protected property interest" in continued employment as a threshold requirement for such a claim. The Court answered this question in the negative.

After the Supreme Court decision in *Haddle*, courts have continued to apply the theory that intracorporate communications will not support a § 1985 conspiracy claim. *See* McAndrew v. Lockheed Martin Corp., 206 F.3d 1031, 1036 (11th Cir. 2000); Jackson v. City of Columbus, 194 F.3d 737, 753 (6th Cir. 1999), *overruled in part by* Swierkiewicz v. Sorema, N.A., 534 U.S. 506 (2002); Linder v. City of N.Y., 263 F. Supp. 2d 585, 591 (S.D.N.Y. 2003); Everson v. New York City Transit Auth., 216 F. Supp. 2d 71, 76 (E.D.N.Y. 2002); Rhyce v. Martin, 173 F. Supp. 2d 521, 532–33 (E.D. La. 2001); Ibarra v. Houston Indep. Sch. Dist., 84 F. Supp. 2d 825, 838 (S.D. Tex. 1999). *But see* Quinn v. Nassau County Police Dep't, 53 F. Supp. 2d 347, 360 (E.D.N.Y. 1999) (exception to intracorporate conspiracy doctrine exists where individuals within single entity are pursuing personal interests wholly apart from entity). One court has held that a university cannot conspire with its own employees in violation of § 1985(3). *See* Roberson v. Bowie State Univ., 899 F. Supp. 235, 72 FEP 899 (D. Md. 1995).

   [329]505 F.2d 181, 182–83, 8 FEP 1241 (8th Cir. 1974).

   [330]*Id.* at 183; *see also* Bass v. E.I. du Pont de Nemours & Co., 324 F.3d 761, 765 (4th Cir. 2003) (affirming dismissal of claim that du Pont conspired with EEOC to impede EEOC investigations of EEOC charge, where du Pont "had a right to engage in the actions Bass alleged, and those actions caused her no cognizable injury"). *But see* Rebel Van Lines v. City of Compton, 663 F. Supp. 786, 792–93 (C.D. Cal. 1987) (intracorporate conspiracy exception should not apply to conspiracies within single governmental entity); Diem v. City & County of S.F., 686 F. Supp. 806, 809, 51 FEP 242 (N.D. Cal. 1988) (same).

   [331]*See Hills & Dales Gen. Hosp.*, 40 F.3d at 838, 841; *see also* Reese v. Southfield, 162 F.3d 1162 (6th Cir. 1998) (trier of fact could find that employees acted outside scope of employment if they committed acts of intentional race discrimination) (unpublished opinion).

   [332]*See, e.g.*, Novak v. World Bank, 703 F.2d 1305, 1308, 32 FEP 424 (D.C. Cir. 1983) (suit against World Bank, local bank, and their agents asserted conspiracy

or a union.[333] The issue most commonly litigated is where the corporation's representative is alleged to have acted outside the scope of his or her employment capacity. In these circumstances, some[334] but not all[335] courts allow the action to proceed. Courts allowing the claim in theory, though, note that proof of such ultra vires actions or ulterior motives may be a substantial hurdle.[336] Police officers who conspire with one another have been held liable under § 1985(2) for conspiracy to retaliate against a fellow officer for speech protected by the First Amendment.[337] Where a hospital employee had a sufficient "personal interest" in the challenged employment action, one court held that the employee's "unity of interest" with the defendant hospital was destroyed and therefore "render[ed] him capable of conspiring with it."[338] Another court

between more than one entity; thus, plaintiff not precluded from bringing action for age discrimination under § 1985(3)).

[333]See, e.g., Thompson v. Machinists, 580 F. Supp. 662, 668, 35 FEP 845 (D.D.C. 1984) (union and its officers alleged to have engaged in § 1985(3) conspiracy with plaintiff's employer).

[334]See, e.g., Alder v. Columbia Historical Soc'y, 690 F. Supp. 9, 14–15, 46 FEP 1622 (D.D.C. 1988) (if employees act outside scope of employment for personal reasons, liability may be found); Pavlo v. Stiefel Lab., Inc., 22 FEP 489, 494–95 (S.D.N.Y. 1979) (refusing to dismiss claim brought under § 1985(3) where reasonable minds might differ as to whether official's actions were outside scope of employment); Pantchenko v. C.B. Dolge Co., 18 FEP 686, 687–88 (D. Conn. 1977) (finding sufficient claim of harassment by company and its individual employees), aff'd in relevant part, 581 F.2d 1052, 18 FEP 691 (2d Cir. 1978); Rackin v. University of Pa., 386 F. Supp. 992, 1005–06, 10 FEP 1318 (E.D. Pa. 1974) (same); Coley v. M & M Mars, Inc., 461 F. Supp. 1073, 1076–77, 18 FEP 1809 (M.D. Ga. 1978) (same).

[335]See Cross v. General Motors Corp., 721 F.2d 1152, 1156–57, 40 FEP 418 (8th Cir. 1983) (corporation not liable for § 1985 conspiracy where alleged acts of corporate agents in furtherance of conspiracy were arguably within scope of their employment); Weaver v. Gross, 605 F. Supp. 210, 214–15, 37 FEP 1602 (D.D.C. 1985) (where all officers, directors, and stockholders adopt allegedly discriminatory policy, plaintiff's recourse must be against corporation as entity; thus § 1985 claim fails).

[336]See, e.g., Chambers v. Omaha Girls Club, 629 F. Supp. 925, 936–37, 40 FEP 362 (D. Neb. 1986) (although intracorporate conspiracies are actionable under § 1985(3) where individuals act outside scope of employment or for personal reasons, lack of evidence of individual acts of animus or harassment precludes finding of conspiracy), aff'd, 834 F.2d 697, 45 FEP 698 (8th Cir. 1987).

[337]Dooley v. City of Phila., 153 F. Supp. 2d 628, 661–62 (E.D. Pa. 2001), aff'd in part and vacated in part, 161 F. Supp. 2d 592 (E.D. Pa. 2001).

[338]Johnson v. Nyack Hosp., 954 F. Supp. 717, 725 (S.D.N.Y. 1997).

found no intracorporate ban where the conspiracy was alleged to be " 'part of some broader discriminatory pattern [that] permeated the ranks of the organization's employees.' "[339]

Public agencies cannot be sued under § 1985 for conspiring with their own agents because a public agency is not a covered "person."[340]

3. Federal and State Governments

Like both §§ 1981 and 1983, §§ 1985 and 1986 do not apply to federal employment.[341] States would appear to be immune from

---

[339]Zoch v. City of Chi., 1997 WL 89231, at *56 (N.D. Ill. Feb. 4, 1997) (unpublished) (where plaintiffs alleged continued complaints that were deliberately ignored, allegations went beyond defendants' "lawful business" and permeated ranks of organization's employees) (quoting Wright v. Illinois Dep't of Children & Family Servs., 40 F.3d 1492 (7th Cir. 1994)).

[340]*See, e.g.,* Zombro v. Baltimore City Police Dep't, 868 F.2d 1364, 1370–71, 49 FEP 297 (4th Cir. 1989) (police officer may not pursue claim under § 1985(3) that police commissioner conspired with police department to deny him equal protection; department is not "person" and therefore police commissioner cannot be held to have entered into conspiracy with department); Santiago v. New York State Dep't of Corr. Servs., 725 F. Supp. 780, 783, 52 FEP 482 (S.D.N.Y. 1989) (corrections department is not "person" capable of participation in conspiracy in violation of 1871 Civil Rights Act; neither state nor its agencies are persons under §§ 1983 and 1985), *rev'd on other grounds,* 945 F.2d 25 (2d Cir. 1991); Locus v. Fayetteville State Univ., 49 FEP 655, 655–56 (E.D.N.C. 1988) (intracorporate conspiracy doctrine bars female faculty member from litigating claim that state university and its officials conspired to deprive her of promotion where officials are employees of university), *aff'd mem.,* 870 F.2d 655 (4th Cir. 1989). *But see* Diem v. City & County of S.F., 686 F. Supp. 806, 809, 51 FEP 242 (N.D. Cal. 1988) (city and its employees can conspire to satisfy requirements of "two persons" in equal protection action; Jewish fire-fighter's charges of pattern of bias and harassment on basis of religion, rising to level of official custom or policy, would establish violation of U.S. Constitution redressable under § 1985(3), apart from any remedy available under Title VII).

[341]*See* Newbold v. United States Postal Serv., 614 F.2d 46, 46, 23 FEP 1768 (5th Cir. 1980) ("as Title VII is 'an exclusive, pre-emptive administrative and judicial scheme for the redress of federal employment discrimination,' " no claim may be brought under §§ 1981, 1983, 1985, or 1986 against federal agency, its individual agents, or federal employee's union) (quoting Brown v. Government Servs. Admin., 425 U.S. 820, 829 (1976)); Ornellas v. Lammers, 631 F. Supp. 522, 526 (D.N.H. 1986) (dismissing §§ 1985 and 1986 claims against federal employer, as "Title VII is the exclusive remedy for alleged discrimination in federal employment"); Ringgold v. United States Postal Serv., 19 FEP 857, 858–60 (S.D. Cal. 1978) (Title VII is exclusive remedy for Postal Service employee's claims of job-related discrimination; denying plaintiff's request to amend to add claim under § 1985(3)). *See generally* Chapter 31 (Federal Employee Litigation).

suit under these sections, at least insofar as they are immune from suit under § 1983.[342]

The Eleventh Amendment precludes actions for damages against state governments and their employees in their official capacity,[343] although state employees may be liable for damages in their individual capacities.[344] The Eleventh Amendment, however, does not bar § 1985(3) claims for injunctive and prospective declaratory relief against state officials.[345]

C. Bases of Discrimination Prohibited by §§ 1985 and 1986

The Supreme Court has held that § 1985(3) requires "class-based animus":

> That the statute was meant to reach private action does not, however, mean that it was intended to apply to all tortious, conspiratorial interferences with the rights of others. For, though the supporters of the legislation insisted on coverage of private conspiracies, they were equally emphatic that they did not believe, in the words of Representative Cook, "that Congress has a right to punish an assault and battery when committed by two or more persons within a State." The constitutional shoals that would lie in the path of interpreting § 1985(3) as a general federal tort law can be avoided by giving full effect to the congressional purpose— by requiring, as an element of the cause of action, the kind of

---

[342]Because these sections were part of the same act as § 1983, the same interpretations with respect to Eleventh Amendment immunity logically would apply. *See* Section III.B.3 *supra*; Parents for Quality Educ. with Integration, Inc. v. Fort Wayne Cmty. Schs. Corp., 662 F. Supp. 1475, 1479–81 (D. Ind. 1987) (unlike with Title VII, "Congress did not abrogate the state's Eleventh Amendment immunity" by enacting §§ 1981, 1983, and 1985).

[343]*See, e.g.*, McCrary v. Ohio Civ. Serv. Employees Ass'n Local 11 (AFL-CIO), 18 Fed. Appx. 281, 283 (6th Cir. 2001); Taylor v. Alabama, 95 F. Supp. 2d 1297, 1311 (M.D. Ala. 2000); Cohen v. Nebraska Dep't of Admin. Servs. Div. of Gen. Data Processing, 83 F. Supp. 2d 1043, 1044–45 (D. Neb. 2000); Gorman v. Roberts, 909 F. Supp. 1479, 1489 (M.D. Ala. 1995). *But see* Johnson v. City of Fort Lauderdale, 126 F.3d 1372 (11th Cir. 1997) (qualified immunity as defense to § 1985(3) claim not available where governmental employees sued in their individual capacities).

[344]Lilliard v. Shelby County Bd. of Educ., 76 F.3d 716, 726 (6th Cir. 1996); Johnson v. City of Fort Lauderdale, 126 F.3d 1372 (11th Cir. 1997) (qualified immunity as defense to § 1985(3) claim not available where governmental employees sued in their individual capacities).

[345]*See* Hayes v. Reed, 1997 WL 125742, at *7 (E.D. Pa. Mar. 13, 1997); Horton v. Marovich, 925 F. Supp. 540 (N.D. Ill. 1996).

invidiously discriminatory motivation stressed by the sponsors of the limiting amendment. . . . The language requiring intent to deprive of *equal* protection, or *equal* privileges and immunities, means that there must be some racial, or perhaps otherwise class-based, invidiously discriminatory animus behind the conspirators' action. The conspiracy, in other words, must aim at a deprivation of the equal enjoyment of rights secured by the law to all.[346]

But what kind of class-based animus is required? After *Griffin* eliminated the absolute requirement of state action under § 1985, it initially appeared to some courts that, assuming a conspiracy could be established, § 1985 (and, derivatively, § 1986) could reach all bases of discrimination and all conduct covered by Title VII (and perhaps other statutes).[347] But in *Great American Federal Savings & Loan Ass'n v. Novotny*,[348] the Supreme Court held that §§ 1985 and 1986 cannot be used to enforce rights created solely by Title VII or other federal acts[349] containing a remedial scheme that Congress intended to be exclusive.[350] Then, in *Carpenters Local*

---

[346]Griffin v. Breckenridge, 403 U.S. 88, 101–02 (1971) (citation omitted; emphasis added).

[347]For a comprehensive listing of the claims and classes initially recognized, see Canlis v. San Joaquin Sheriff's Posse Comitatus, 641 F.2d 711, 719 n.15 (9th Cir. 1981); Harrison v. KVAT Food Mgmt., Inc., 766 F.2d 155, 158–59 (4th Cir. 1985).

[348]442 U.S. 366, 372, 19 FEP 1482 (1979).

[349]Courts thus have applied *Novotny*'s reasoning to § 1985 suits brought to enforce ADEA rights. *See, e.g.*, Tranello v. Frey, 758 F. Supp. 841, 849–50, 55 FEP 699 (W.D.N.Y. 1991) (passage of ADEA supplanted any cause of action under §§ 1983 and 1985 for age bias, as ADEA provides exclusive remedy for such claims), *aff'd*, 962 F.2d 244, 58 FEP 1334 (2d Cir. 1992); Hill v. General Elec. Co., 34 FEP 1757, 1758–59 (W.D. Ky. 1984) (action under § 1985(3) may not be used as vehicle to obtain relief for ADEA violations); Wippel v. Prudential Ins. Co. of Am., 33 FEP 412, 413–14 (D. Md. 1982) (violation of ADEA cannot be asserted through § 1985; to allow such procedure would enable individuals to bypass completely administrative process that is crucial to ADEA scheme); *cf.* Lyon v. Temple Univ., 543 F. Supp. 1372, 1373–74, 30 FEP 1030 (E.D. Pa. 1982) (conspiracy to deprive plaintiff of rights under Equal Pay Act cannot be basis for claims under §§ 1985(3) and 1986); Hudson v. Teamsters Local 957, 536 F. Supp. 1138, 1143, 30 FEP 990 (S.D. Ohio 1982) (claims under § 1981, but not under § 301 of Labor Management Relations Act, may be enforced under § 1985(3)). *But see* Price v. Erie County, 654 F. Supp. 1206, 1207–08, 43 FEP 273 (W.D.N.Y. 1987) (former county employee who claimed that he was wrongfully deprived of his property interest in his employment and that his termination because of his age violated equal protection may sue county officials under §§ 1983 and 1985(3), even though ADEA provides exclusive remedy for age bias, because his causes of action are not based on ADEA).

[350]*Novotny*, 442 U.S. at 376–78; *accord* Long v. Laramie County Cmty. Coll. Dist., 840 F.2d 743, 751–52, 46 FEP 264 (10th Cir. 1988) (§ 1985 claim based on

610 v. Scott,[351] the Supreme Court declined to determine whether
§ 1985(3) reaches conspiracies motivated by other than racial bias.[352]

Some lower courts have allowed § 1985(3) suits, where state
action exists,[353] alleging a class-based animus against whites,[354]
religious groups,[355] women,[356] and persons of a particular national
origin.[357] One court has held that a white plaintiff has standing under
§ 1985 where the employee alleges that he or she was subjected

---

antiretaliation provision of Title VII not permitted); Vuksta v. Bethlehem Steel Corp.,
540 F. Supp. 1276, 1281–82, 32 FEP 1874 (E.D. Pa. 1982) (Title VII religious and
national origin claims may not be pursued under § 1985(3)), *aff'd mem.*, 707 F.2d
1405 (3d Cir. 1983).

[351]463 U.S. 825 (1983).

[352]The dissenters, however, all agreed that § 1983(3) reaches, through the Equal
Protection Clause, conspiracies based on race, religion, sex, and national origin. *Id.*
at 853 (Marshall, Blackmun, Brennan, and O'Connor, JJ., dissenting).

[353]*See* Section IV.B.1 *supra.*

[354]*See, e.g.*, Triad Assocs., Inc. v. Chicago Hous. Auth., 892 F.2d 583, 591–93
(7th Cir. 1989) (allowing white contractor's § 1985(3) claim that minority "set-aside"
statute discriminated on basis of race).

[355]*See, e.g.*, Diem v. City & County of S.F., 686 F. Supp. 806, 809–10, 51 FEP
242 (N.D. Cal. 1988) (Jewish fire-fighter's claim of harassment based on religion
may be redressed under § 1985(3)); St. Agnes Hosp. v. Riddick, 668 F. Supp. 478,
482–83 (D. Md. 1987) (religious group is protected class under § 1985(3)).

[356]*See* Lyes v. City of Riviera Beach, 166 F.3d 1332, 1339, 79 FEP 330 (11th
Cir. 1999) (en banc) (joining seven other circuits to squarely consider issue and holding
that § 1985(3) applies to conspiracies motivated by sex-based animus); *see also* Zoch
v. City of Chi., 1997 WL 89231 (N.D. Ill. Feb. 4, 1997) (plaintiffs stated cognizable § 1985 claim where they alleged they suffered intentional sexual harassment
that deprived them of equal protection of law); New York State NOW v. Terry, 886
F.2d 1339, 1358–59 (2d Cir. 1989) (conspiracies against women as class are inherently invidious and encompassed under § 1985); Volk v. Coler, 845 F.2d 1422, 1434–
35, 46 FEP 1287 (7th Cir. 1988) (recognizing constitutionally protected right to be
free of sex discrimination, sexual harassment, and retaliation); Way v. Mueller Brass
Co., 840 F.2d 303, 307–08, 46 FEP 558 (5th Cir. 1988) (upholding § 1985 claim
alleging conspiracy based on sex discrimination); Munson v. Friske, 754 F.2d 683,
695 (7th Cir. 1985) (§ 1985(3) extends to conspiracies to discriminate against persons based on sex, religion, ethnicity, or political loyalty); Wymer v. New York State
Div. for Youth, 671 F. Supp. 210, 213, 44 FEP 1785 (W.D.N.Y. 1987) (§ 1985(3)
applies to sex-based discrimination); Eggleston v. Prince Edward Volunteer Rescue
Squad, 569 F. Supp. 1344, 1352 (E.D. Va. 1983) ("Section 1985(3) protects against
conspiracies to deprive persons of equal protection because of some discrete, insular, or immutable characteristic they possess such as race, national origin, or sex."),
aff'd mem., 742 F.2d 1448 (4th Cir. 1984).

[357]*See, e.g.*, Garza v. City of Omaha, 814 F.2d 553, 556–57, 43 FEP 572 (8th
Cir. 1987) (alleging personal bias by city officials against Mexican Americans); Photos
v. Township High Sch. Dist. 211, 639 F. Supp. 1050, 1054–55, 41 FEP 667 (N.D.
Ill. 1986) (discrimination based on Greek ancestry actionable under § 1985(3)).

to retaliation for assisting minorities.[358] Some courts recognize § 1983 as an independent means to challenge (through the Equal Protection Clause) discrimination otherwise prohibited by Title VII.[359] The courts theorize that the § 1985 claims could also be brought under Title VII and that such claims also have an independent constitutional basis under the Equal Protection Clause and could be pleaded as conspiracies to deprive equal protection, not Title VII, rights.[360] Other courts, though, have extended *Novotny* to preempt any claim brought under § 1985(3) that is based on the same facts as a separate Title VII claim[361] or that *could have been* brought under Title VII.[362]

---

[358]*See* Maynard v. City of San Jose, 37 F.3d 1396, 1403 (9th Cir. 1994).

[359]*See* Section III.C.1 *supra*.

[360]*See, e.g.*, Roybal v. City of Albuquerque, 653 F. Supp. 102, 105–06, 42 FEP 1635 (D.N.M. 1986) (female police department employee who alleged that city and its officials conspired to deprive her of equal protection of laws and discriminated against her because of her sex may maintain action under § 1985(3), despite Supreme Court's decision in *Novotny*, where she alleged violation of Fourteenth Amendment); Smith v. Private Indus. Council, 622 F. Supp. 160, 164–65, 39 FEP 702 (W.D. Pa. 1985) (action under § 1985(3) not barred merely because same facts would constitute violation of both § 1985(3) and Title VII); Drake v. City of Ft. Collins, 927 F.2d 1156, 1162, 55 FEP 600 (10th Cir. 1991) (§ 1985(3) claims must rest on basis independent of Title VII); *cf.* Skadegaard v. Farrell, 578 F. Supp. 1209, 1218–19, 33 FEP 1528 (D.N.J. 1984) (Fourteenth Amendment does not preclude state agency employee from obtaining relief under §§ 1983 and 1985(3) against state officials, even though private sector employees would not have these additional statutory rights).

[361]Alexander v. Chicago Park Dist., 773 F.2d 850, 856, 38 FEP 1685 (7th Cir. 1985) (comparing Title VII's preemption of § 1985(3) to Title VI's preemption of § 1983); Rochon v. Federal Bureau of Investig., 691 F. Supp. 1548, 1555–56, 47 FEP 872 (D.D.C. 1988) (every fact alleged in African-American FBI employee's complaint was basis for both Title VII and § 1985(3) claims; court could not single out facts for each claim and dismissed both claims); Torres v. Wisconsin Dep't of Health & Social Servs., 592 F. Supp. 922, 927, 35 FEP 1041 (E.D. Wis. 1984) (plaintiffs contend that Title VII did not preempt their §§ 1985(3) and 1986 claims because defendant also violated Fourteenth Amendment; court applied *Novotny* and dismissed two claims); Marchwinski v. Oliver Tyrone Corp., 83 F.R.D. 606, 608, 25 FEP 1730 (W.D. Pa. 1979) (plaintiff's § 1985(3) claim did not survive because of Title VII preemption based on *Novotny*).

[362]*See, e.g.*, Richards v. New York Dep't of Corr. Servs., 572 F. Supp. 1168, 1175, 46 FEP 763 (S.D.N.Y. 1988) (claim by African-American corrections officer that employer acted in concert and wrongfully deprived him of privileges and immunities of public employment on basis of race could have been raised under Title VII and thus may not be brought under § 1985); Polisoto v. Weinberger, 638 F. Supp. 1353, 1368–69, 47 FEP 1186 (W.D. Tex. 1986) (fact that ex-Air Force employee's sex bias claims are cognizable under Title VII bars her from litigating claims under

In any event, as § 1985 plaintiffs stray farther from the proto-typical racial animus claim, courts look closely at the "class-based animus" requirement to see whether § 1985 applies.[363] In *Bray v. Alexandria Women's Health Clinic*,[364] the Supreme Court held that opposition to abortion does not qualify "alongside race discrimi-nation as an 'otherwise class-based, invidiously discriminatory animus . . .' as is required under *Griffin v. Breckenridge*." Articu-lating a standard, however, has proven difficult. The Ninth Circuit said (somewhat circularly) that, to state a claim under § 1985(3), "the plaintiff must be a member of a class that requires special federal assistance in protecting its civil rights."[365] The Third Cir-cuit has joined the Second Circuit, contrary to the view of the Seventh and Tenth Circuits, to hold that mentally retarded indi-viduals, as a class, are entitled to protection under § 1985(3).[366]

---

§ 1985(3), despite charge of conspiracy to deprive her of equal protection of laws); Davis v. Devereux Found., 644 F. Supp. 482, 486, 40 FEP 1560 (E.D. Pa. 1986) (claims within scope of Title VII preclude redress under § 1985(3)).

[363]*See, e.g.*, Franklin v. Henderson, 15 Fed. Appx. 205, 207 (6th Cir. 2001) (upholding dismissal of § 1985(3) claim for failure to allege plaintiff "was a mem-ber of a protected class or that the defendant was acting on a class-based discrimi-natory animus"); D'Amato v. Wisconsin Gas Co., 760 F.2d 1474, 1486, 37 FEP 1092 (7th Cir. 1985) (allegation must involve "historically suspect class").

[364]506 U.S. 263, 269 (1993).

[365]*See, e.g.*, McCalden v. California Library Ass'n, 919 F.2d 538, 546 (9th Cir. 1990) ("holocaust revisionists" not covered) (citing Gerritsen v. De la Madrid Hurtado, 819 F.2d 1511, 1519 (9th Cir. 1987) (protester alleging interference by Mexican authorities not protected)); *see also* Maynard v. City of San Jose, 37 F.3d 1396, 1403 (9th Cir. 1994) (plaintiffs have standing under § 1985 only if they can show that they are members of class that government has determined " 'require[s] and warrant[s] special federal assistance in protecting their civil rights' ") (quoting Sever v. Alaska Pulp Corp., 978 F.2d 1529, 1536–37, 141 LRRM 2678 (9th Cir. 1992)).

[366]Lake v. Arnold, 112 F.3d 682, 686 (3d Cir. 1997); *see also* Wilhelm v. Con-tinental Title Co., 720 F.2d 1173, 1176–77, 33 FEP 385 (10th Cir. 1983) (class of "handicapped persons" not in contemplation of Congress in 1871 and not included as class in what is now § 1985(3)); D'Amato v. Wisconsin Gas Co., 760 F.2d 1474, 1485–86, 37 FEP 1092 (7th Cir. 1985) (employment discrimination on basis of disability outside scope of § 1985(3); permitting handicap discrimination claim under § 1985(3) would intrude impermissibly on statutory scheme of both § 503 of Re-habilitation Act and § 1985(3)); Corkery v. SuperX Drugs Corp., 602 F. Supp. 42, 44–45, 36 FEP 1815 (M.D. Fla. 1985) (same). *Contra* Tyus v. Ohio Dep't of Youth Servs., 606 F. Supp. 239, 246–47, 38 FEP 921 (S.D. Ohio 1985) (disabled indi-viduals constitute class especially meriting protection under § 1985(3)); Stewart v. Suwol, 55 FEP 422, 427 (D. Or. 1991) (jury could find that state officials con-spired under § 1985(3) to deprive plaintiff of employment based on handicap; summary judgment denied).

There is no consensus regarding whether conspiracies to discriminate based on political association are actionable under § 1985(3).[367] Courts have rejected miscellaneous other putative "classes."[368]

V. LITIGATION, PROOF, PROCEDURE, AND REMEDIES

A. Jurisdiction and Venue

Actions arising under §§ 1981, 1983, 1985, and 1986 may be properly brought in either federal district court or a state court of general jurisdiction.[369]

Federal district courts have jurisdiction over suits based on the Civil Rights Acts of 1866 and 1871, without regard to the amount

---

[367]*See, e.g.*, Aulson v. Blanchard, 83 F.3d 1, 4–6 (1st Cir. 1996) (collecting cases and refusing to recognize class comprised of members opposed to "politics of the old guard" as sufficiently distinct to constitute protected class); Smith v. Turner, 764 F. Supp. 632 (N.D. Ga. 1991) (declining to recognize wholly political conspiracies "not accompanied by racially motivated animus" under § 1985).

[368]*See, e.g.*, Schultz v. Sundberg, 759 F.2d 714, 718 (9th Cir. 1985) (class of state representatives not covered); DeSantis v. Pacific Tel. & Tel. Co., 608 F.2d 327, 333, 19 FEP 1493 (9th Cir. 1979) (gays not covered); Lopez v. Arrowhead Ranches, 523 F.2d 924, 926–28, 11 FEP 636 (9th Cir. 1975) (legally admitted aliens not covered). Courts have differed as to whether political affiliation can give rise to "class-based" status under § 1985(3). *Compare* Lewis v. Board of Educ. of Talbot County, 262 F. Supp. 2d 608, 617 (D. Md. 2003) (those politically opposed to gun control are not discrete and insular minority protected by § 1985(3)) *with* McLean v. International Harvester Co., 817 F.2d 1214, 1219 (5th Cir. 1987) (§ 1985 protects those characterized by some inherited immutable characteristic as well as those characterized by political beliefs or associations), Herhold v. City of Chi., 723 F. Supp. 20, 34, 36, 51 FEP 72 (N.D. Ill. 1989) (§ 1985(3) does not extend to conspiracy to retaliate against person based on that person's speech on particular issue) *and* Rodriguez v. Nazario, 719 F. Supp. 52, 56–57 (D.P.R. 1989) (party members not protected class).

[369]*See* DeHorney v. Bank of Am. Nat'l Trust & Sav. Ass'n, 879 F.2d 459, 463, 50 FEP 558 (9th Cir. 1989) (state courts have concurrent jurisdiction over actions brought under § 1981); Brown v. Pitchess, 531 P.2d 772, 777 (Cal. 1975) (providing exhaustive analysis of jurisdiction under 1866 and 1871 Acts). *See generally* Yellow Freight Sys., Inc. v. Donnelly, 494 U.S. 820, 821 (1990) (holding that "Congress did not divest the state courts of their concurrent authority to adjudicate federal claims"). Section 1981 originally provided for federal jurisdiction "exclusively of the courts of the several states," Act of Apr. 9, 1866, § 3, 14 Stat. 27, but that limitation on state court jurisdiction was repealed. Federal jurisdiction over § 1981 claims now is based on 28 U.S.C. § 1343(a)(4), which provides "original," but not "exclusive," jurisdiction.

in controversy, under 28 U.S.C. § 1343.[370] Venue is governed by 28 U.S.C. § 1391.[371] One court has held that where Title VII and § 1981 claims are joined, the Title VII claim should be considered the principal cause of action and its narrower venue provisions should control.[372]

---

[370]28 U.S.C. § 1343 (2000) provides:

The district courts shall have original jurisdiction of any civil action authorized by law to be commenced by any person:

(1) To recover damages for injury to his person or property, or because of the deprivation of any right or privilege of a citizen of the United States, by any act done in furtherance of any conspiracy mentioned in section 1985 of Title 42;

(2) To recover damages from any person who fails to prevent or to aid in preventing any wrongs mentioned in section 1985 of Title 42 which he had knowledge were about to occur and power to prevent;

(3) To redress the deprivation, under color of any State law, statute, ordinance, regulation, custom or usage, of any right, privilege or immunity secured by the Constitution of the United States or by any Act of Congress providing for equal rights of citizens or of all persons within the jurisdiction of the United States;

(4) To recover damages or to secure equitable or other relief under any Act of Congress providing for the protection of civil rights, including the right to vote.

Citing its earlier decision in *Hague v. C.I.O.*, 307 U.S. 496, 507–14 (1939), the Supreme Court in *Douglas v. City of Jeannette*, 319 U.S. 157, 161 (1943), held that 28 U.S.C. § 1343 (then 28 U.S.C. § 41) provides the federal district courts with jurisdiction over cases based on the Civil Rights Act of 1871 "without the allegation or proof of any jurisdictional amount."

[371]*See* Helder v. Hitachi Power Tools, 764 F. Supp. 93, 95, 56 FEP 380 (E.D. Mich. 1991) (venue for § 1981 purposes determined under general venue statute, 28 U.S.C. § 1391(b); proper venue is where claim arose). Section 1391(b) provides:

A civil action wherein jurisdiction is not founded solely on diversity of citizenship may, except as otherwise provided by law, be brought only in (1) a judicial district where any defendant resides, if all defendants reside in the same State, (2) a judicial district in which a substantial part of the events or omissions giving rise to the claim occurred, or a substantial part of property that is the subject of the action is situated, or (3) a judicial district in which any defendant may be found, if there is no district in which the action may otherwise be brought.

[372]*See* Hayes v. RCA Serv. Co., 546 F. Supp. 661, 665, 31 FEP 246 (D.D.C. 1982) (narrower venue provisions of Title VII control; otherwise, Congress' intent that Title VII actions be confined to certain districts could be "effectively written out of the statute by using a companion cause of action under 42 U.S.C. § 1981 as a basis for venue"); *accord* Washington v. General Elec. Corp., 686 F. Supp. 361, 362, 47 FEP 1225 (D.D.C. 1988) (suit of civil rights claimant, who stated in open court that her Title VII claim was principal claim on which she relied, could go forward only if venue was proper under Title VII venue provisions).

B. Timeliness

The Civil Rights Acts of 1866 and 1871 specify no limitations period. Historically, federal courts have looked to state law for the limitations period applicable to such actions.[373] But which state-law limitations period? The Supreme Court held in *Wilson v. Garcia*[374] that § 1983 claims are best characterized as personal injury actions; the state personal injury statute of limitations therefore applies. In *Goodman v. Lukens Steel Co.*,[375] the Court extended this reasoning to § 1981 claims. The Court held that where state law provides multiple statutes of limitations for different types of personal injury actions, the state's general or residual personal injury statute is the one that applies.[376]

The 1991 Civil Rights Act amendments to § 1981 changed the way the statute of limitations for § 1981 claims is applied. On December 1, 1990, Congress enacted 28 U.S.C. § 1658,[377] creating a four-year statute of limitations for all claims arising out of any federal law enacted after § 1658's enactment that does not specify its own limitations period. The Supreme Court decided in *Jones v. R.R. Donnelley & Sons, Co.*[378] that this includes claims made possible by post-1990 amendments to existing statutes, including claims arising under the 1991 Civil Rights Act amendments to § 1981.[379] The Court in *Jones* found that the plaintiff's

---

[373]*See, e.g.*, Burnett v. Grattan, 468 U.S. 42, 45–46, 49–50, 35 FEP 15 (1984) (state law being applied must take into account practicalities involved in litigating civil rights claims based on broadly inclusive language of Civil Rights Acts); Johnson v. Railway Express Agency, 421 U.S. 454, 462, 10 FEP 817 (1975) (citing prior Supreme Court decisions applying state limitations periods to claims brought under other federal statutes).

[374]471 U.S. 261, 265 (1985).

[375]482 U.S. 656, 44 FEP 1 (1987).

[376]*Id.* at 660; *see also* Owens v. Okure, 488 U.S. 235, 245–49 (1989).

[377]Section 1658 states that "a civil action arising under an Act of Congress enacted after the date of enactment of this section may not be commenced later than 4 years after the cause of action accrues."

[378]541 U.S. 369 (2004).

[379]*Id.* at 381. This decision resolved a split in the circuit courts regarding whether a post-1990 amendment to an existing statute qualified as a post-1990 enactment. *Compare* Harris v. Allstate Ins. Co., 300 F.3d 1183, 1189–93 (10th Cir. 2002), Hill v. Textron Auto. Interiors, Inc., 2001 WL 276972, at *5 (D.N.H. Mar. 17, 2001) (unpublished), Nealey v. University Health Servs., Inc., 114 F. Supp. 2d 1358, 1365–66 (S.D. Ga. 2000), Pitts v. Chester County Hosp., 81 FEP 1599, 1600 (E.D. Pa.

hostile work environment, wrongful termination, and failure-to-transfer claims arose under the 1991 Act's amendments to Title VII.[380] The Court did not answer, however, whether the four-year provision of § 1658 would apply to claims brought under § 1981 that were unaltered by the 1991 Act, such as traditional claims of alleged failure to hire that arise under the "make and enforce contracts" provision existing in § 1981 before it was amended.[381] Following *Jones*, the Tenth Circuit held in *Cross v. Home Depot*[382] that the four-year provision of § 1658 applies to failure-to-promote claims where the promotion would not result in a new and distinct relationship between the employer and employee.[383] In *Cross*, the court held that a promotion from assistant store manager to store manager would not create a "meaningful, qualitative change in the contractual relationship," despite expanded career opportunities and increased pay resulting from the promotion, because the qualifications for and duties of both positions were practically identical and both were paid a salary rather than hourly wages.[384] The Fifth Circuit subsequently held that a refusal-to-rehire claim essentially alleges a failure to enter into a new contract, and as such, the relevant state personal injury statute of limitations, not § 1658, applies.[385]

Tolling issues arise with some frequency. As discussed in the next section, the filing of a charge with the Equal Employment Opportunity Commission (EEOC) is not a procedural prerequisite to suit. The filing of a state or federal administrative charge therefore

---

2000), Rodgers v. Apple S., Inc., 35 F. Supp. 2d 974, 977 (W.D. Ky. 1999) *and* Miller v. Federal Express Corp., 56 F. Supp. 2d 955 (W.D. Tenn. 1999) *with* Madison v. IBP, Inc., 257 F.3d 780, 797–98 (8th Cir. 2001), *vacated on other grounds*, 536 U.S. 919, 88 FEP 1887 (2002), Zubi v. AT&T Corp., 219 F.3d 220, 221–26 (3d Cir. 2000), Campbell v. National R.R. Passenger Corp., 163 F. Supp. 2d 19, 23 (D.D.C. 2001), Lane v. Ogden Entm't, Inc., 13 F. Supp. 2d 1261, 1269, 78 FEP 843 (M.D. Ala. 1998), Jackson v. Motel 6 Multipurpose, Inc., 1997 WL 724429, at *2 (M.D. Fla. Nov. 6, 1997), Chawla v. Emory Univ., 1997 WL 907570, at *12–14 (N.D. Ga. Feb. 13, 1997) (unpublished) *and* Davis v. California Dep't of Corr., 1996 WL 271001, at *18–20 (E.D. Cal. Feb. 23, 1996).

[380]*Jones*, 541 U.S. at 384.
[381]*Id.*
[382]390 F.3d 1283, 94 FEP 1537 (10th Cir. 2004).
[383]*Id.* at 1289.
[384]*Id.*
[385]Johnson v. Crown Enters., Inc., 398 F.3d 339, 341–42, 95 FEP 88 (5th Cir. 2005).

normally does not toll the running of the statute of limitations for actions under the Civil Rights Acts of 1866 and 1871.[386] Otherwise, state tolling rules should be borrowed, so long as the result does not offend federal policy.[387]

In general, Title VII timeliness case law extends to cases brought under the nineteenth-century Civil Rights Acts. Several courts have applied Title VII's continuing violation theory to §§ 1981 and 1983 actions.[388] The limitations period begins to run when the plaintiff knows or has reason to know that the *act* providing the basis for the cause of action has occurred; the limitations period

---

[386]*See, e.g.*, Johnson v. Railway Express Agency, 421 U.S. 454, 465–66, 10 FEP 817 (1975); Carter v. District of Columbia, 14 F. Supp. 2d 97, 102 (D.D.C. 1998) (limitations period on § 1983 claim not tolled by pendency of administrative action on Title VII claim).

[387]*See* Chardon v. Fumero Soto, 462 U.S. 650, 662 (1983) (state law generally governs tolling in class action brought under § 1983); Board of Regents v. Tomanio, 446 U.S. 478, 483–85 (1980) (in action under § 1983 where state limitations period is borrowed, state tolling statute also should be borrowed); Griffen v. Big Spring Indep. Sch. Dist., 706 F.2d 645, 650–52, 31 FEP 1750 (5th Cir. 1983) (Texas "wrong court" tolling statute applies to § 1983 claim); Garrison v. International Paper Co., 714 F.2d 757, 759 n.2, 32 FEP 1278 (8th Cir. 1983) (state-law savings clause, which allows 1 year to refile after dismissal without prejudice, applies to § 1981 action); Conerly v. Westinghouse Elec. Corp., 623 F.2d 117, 119, 23 FEP 318 (9th Cir. 1980) (in § 1981 action, when state statute of limitations is borrowed, state tolling statute also is borrowed).

[388]*See* Madison v. IBP, 330 F.3d 1051, 1061 (8th Cir. 2003) (if one act of hostile work environment claim falls within § 1981's limitations period, party may recover for all illegal acts that made up hostile work environment claim); Shields v. Fort James Corp., 305 F.3d 1280, 1282–83 (11th Cir. 2002) (holding that § 1981 claim must be reviewed in its entirety if one of events complained of falls within statute of limitations); Gutowsky v. County of Placer, 108 F.3d 256, 259 (9th Cir. 1997) (applying continuing violation theory to § 1983 claim against county for gender discrimination in employment); Hull v. Cuyahoga Valley Bd. of Educ., 926 F.2d 505, 510–11, 55 FEP 269 (6th Cir. 1991); Petrosky v. New York State Dep't of Motor Vehicles, 72 F. Supp. 2d 39, 63, 84 FEP 259 (N.D.N.Y. 1999) (finding Second Circuit would apply continuing violation theory to § 1983 civil rights actions); Reyes v. Municipality of Guaynabo, 59 F. Supp. 2d 305, 308 (D.P.R. 1999); Moore v. Allstate Ins. Co., 928 F. Supp. 744, 753, 75 FEP 983 (N.D. Ill. 1996); *see also* Lane v. Ogden Entm't, 13 F. Supp. 2d 1261, 1269 (M.D. Ala. 1998) (although recognizing that continuing violation theory may apply to § 1981 claim, court refused to do so where alleged race discrimination constituted discrete acts by employer); Harel v. Rutgers State Univ., 5 F. Supp. 2d 246, 267, 79 FEP 547 (D.N.J. 1998), *aff'd*, 191 F.3d 444 (3d Cir. 1999) (two denials of tenure did not constitute continuing violation under § 1983; claim was time-barred by New Jersey's 2-year limitations period). For a more extensive treatment of the continuing violation theory, in general, see Chapter 26 (Timeliness).

is not tolled until the plaintiff receives "unequivocal notice" that his or her challenge of an adverse employment action has been rejected, such as in an internal grievance proceeding.[389]

C. Procedural Prerequisites

The procedural prerequisites to filing suit under Title VII—the timely filing of a valid charge with the EEOC and the timely filing of a complaint after receiving the statutory right-to-sue notice[390]—do not apply in cases under the Civil Rights Acts of 1866 and 1871.[391] Parties therefore may be named as defendants even if not named in an EEOC charge,[392] and the scope of the action may exceed the scope of an EEOC charge filed by the plaintiff or the Commission's investigation thereof.[393] Similarly, as the Supreme Court held in *Patsy v. Board of Regents*,[394] the exhaustion of *state* administrative remedies is not a prerequisite to bringing a § 1983 action in federal court.

The Supreme Court has held that the President of the United States is not entitled, as a result of that individual's office, to the stay of a lawsuit brought under §§ 1983 and 1985 until the President's term of office is completed.[395] The Court observed that, "if properly managed by the District Court, it appears . . . unlikely [that such a case would] occupy any substantial amount of the [President's] time."[396]

---

[389]*See, e.g.*, Smith v. City of Enid, 149 F.3d 1151, 1156 (10th Cir. 1998); Collyer v. Darling, 98 F.3d 211, 220 (6th Cir. 1996); *Carter*, 14 F. Supp. 2d at 102.

[390]*See* Chapters 26 (Timeliness) and 28 (Title VII Litigation Procedure).

[391]*See Railway Express*, 421 U.S. at 461 (stressing independent nature of § 1981 remedy).

[392]*See, e.g.*, Sabala v. Western Gillette, Inc., 516 F.2d 1251, 1254–55, 11 FEP 98 (5th Cir. 1975) (allowing § 1981 claims to proceed against unions who were not named in plaintiff's EEOC charge), *vacated and remanded on other grounds*, 431 U.S. 951 (1977).

[393]*See, e.g.*, Jenkins v. Blue Cross Mut. Hosp. Ins., Inc., 538 F.2d 164, 166–68, 13 FEP 52 (7th Cir. 1976) (en banc) (former employee may maintain action under § 1981 challenging recruiting, hiring, promotion, appearance, job assignment, and salary policies, even though he cannot do so under Title VII because those claims were not in EEOC charge); *cf.* Hawkins v. Groot Indus., Inc., 210 F.R.D. 226, 232–33 (N.D. Ill. 2002) (African Americans who filed class action may add Hispanic plaintiffs to class on their § 1981 claim, but not on their Title VII claim, because Hispanic employees did not file charge with EEOC). *See generally* Chapter 28 (Title VII Litigation Procedure).

[394]457 U.S. 496, 507–10, 29 FEP 12 (1982).

[395]*See* Clinton v. Jones, 520 U.S. 681, 73 FEP 1548 (1997).

[396]*Id.* at 702.

If an employee has agreed to arbitrate all grievances he or she has with the employer, including discrimination claims, any suit filed by the plaintiff pursuant to § 1981 may be stayed pending arbitration[397] so long as the arbitration agreement allows for the full range of remedies available under § 1981 and is otherwise valid under state contract law.[398] However, courts have held that an adverse arbitration award under a collective bargaining agreement does not preclude a plaintiff from bringing an action under § 1981 involving the identical set of facts and issues.[399] Also, the Supreme Court has held that a collective bargaining agreement does not require a union member to arbitrate statutory claims unless the contract explicitly so requires.[400]

D. Proof

The Supreme Court established in *Washington v. Davis*[401] that in cases based on the Equal Protection Clause (as are most § 1983 employment discrimination cases),[402] proof of discriminatory purpose or intent is required. In § 1985(3) actions, similarly, a conspiratorial

---

[397]*See* Johnson v. Circuit City Stores, 148 F.3d 373, 378–79, 77 FEP 139 (4th Cir. 1998) (arbitration agreement contained in employment application enforceable where both applicant and employer agreed to be bound; § 1981 claim proper for arbitration); Pitter v. Prudential Life Ins. Co. of Am., 906 F. Supp. 130, 131, 138 (E.D.N.Y. 1995) (citing Gilmer v. Interstate/Johnson Lane Corp., 500 U.S. 20, 26–27, 55 FEP 1116 (1991)). *See generally* Chapter 42 (Alternative Dispute Resolution).

[398]*See* Circuit City Stores v. Adams, 279 F.3d 889, 892, 87 FEP 1509 (9th Cir. 2002) (arbitration clause unconscionable under California law; "general contract defenses such as fraud, duress, or unconscionability, grounded in state contract law, may operate to invalidate arbitration agreements"); Johnson v. Circuit City Stores, 203 F.3d 821 (4th Cir. 2000) (unpublished); Wright v. Circuit City Stores, Inc., 82 F. Supp. 2d 1279, 1287–88, 83 FEP 877 (N.D. Ala. 2000) (pursuant to severability provisions, arbitration clause modified to allow for full range of § 1981 remedies). *See generally* Chapter 42 (Alternative Dispute Resolution).

[399]*See* Peterson v. BMI Refractories, 132 F.3d 1405, 1411–12, 75 FEP 1322 (11th Cir. 1998) (mandatory arbitration clause did not bar § 1981 claim where employee did not agree individually to contract; union agreeing on behalf of employee during collective bargaining insufficient); Humphrey v. Council of Jewish Fed'ns, 901 F. Supp. 703, 710, 69 FEP 201 (S.D.N.Y. 1995) (declining to dismiss § 1981 suit alleging some facts on basis of which plaintiff lost in arbitration). *But see* Brownlee v. City of Chi., 983 F. Supp. 776, 784–86 (N.D. Ill. 1997) (where arbitration conducted pursuant to collective bargaining agreement determined that employee did not have property interest in his job, employee's subsequent § 1983 claim in which he alleged that city violated his procedural due process rights failed; arbitral decision resolved very same question as in § 1983 suit).

[400]*See* Wright v. Universal Maritime, 525 U.S. 70, 159 LRRM 2769 (1998).

[401]426 U.S. 229, 12 FEP 1415 (1976).

[402]*See* Section III.C.1 *supra*.

intent must be shown, requiring proof of a purpose to discriminate on the basis of some invidious, class-based characteristic.[403] In *General Building Contractors Ass'n v. Pennsylvania*,[404] the Supreme Court thoroughly analyzed the legislative history and concluded that § 1981 likewise can be violated "only by purposeful discrimination."[405] Therefore, only cases alleging disparate treatment may be brought under the Civil Rights Acts of 1866 and 1871; cases alleging disparate impact may not.[406]

The disparate treatment analytical framework developed under Title VII is equally applicable to proof of intentional discrimination under the nineteenth century Civil Rights Acts.[407] The

---

[403]*E.g.*, Dozier v. Chupka, 395 F. Supp. 836, 847, 11 FEP 1331 (S.D. Ohio 1975) ("Discriminatory intent is an essential element of a § 1985(3) claim."). In *Griffin v. Breckenridge*, 403 U.S. 88, 102 n.10, 9 FEP 1196 (1971), the Supreme Court stated that the intent requirement of § 1985(3) "focuses not on scienter in relation to deprivation of rights but on invidiously discriminatory animus." *Id.* at 102 n.10.

[404]458 U.S. 375, 29 FEP 139 (1982).

[405]*Id.* at 391.

[406]*See generally* Chapter 3 (Adverse Impact).

[407]*See* Patterson v. Oneida, 375 F.3d 206, 225–27, 94 FEP 129 (2d Cir. 2004) (§§ 1981 and 1983 require proof of intentional discrimination; most core substantive standards applicable to disparate treatment claims apply under Title VII, § 1981, and § 1983); Swinton v. Potomac Corp., 270 F.3d 794, 806, 87 FEP 65 (9th Cir. 2001) (§ 1981 requires proof of intentional discrimination but does not necessarily require proof that white employees were not subject to same sort of conduct as plaintiff); Bickhem v. United Parcel Serv., 949 F. Supp. 630, 634 (N.D. Ill. 1996) (§ 1981 plaintiff must establish intentional discrimination); *see also* Deffenbaugh-Williams v. Wal-Mart Stores, Inc., 156 F.3d 581, 587, 77 FEP 1699 (5th Cir. 1998) (applying *McDonnell Douglas* burden-shifting paradigm), *vacated and remanded on other grounds*, 169 F.3d 215 (5th Cir. 1999); Kim v. Nash Finch Co., 123 F.3d 1046, 1055, 1056, 75 FEP 1741 (8th Cir. 1997) (same); Betkerur v. Aultman Hosp. Ass'n, 78 F.3d 1079, 1093, 78 FEP 1765 (6th Cir. 1996) (same); Bratton v. Roadway Package Sys., Inc., 77 F.3d 168, 175–76, 70 FEP 178 (7th Cir. 1996) (same); Singh v. Shoney's, Inc., 64 F.3d 217, 219, 68 FEP 1288 (5th Cir. 1995) (same); Barbour v. Merrill, 48 F.3d 1270, 1276, 67 FEP 369 (D.C. Cir. 1995) ("A plaintiff may establish a violation of this section using the same three-step framework of proof used to establish racial discrimination under Title VII."); Turner v. AmSouth, N.A., 36 F.3d 1057, 1060, 66 FEP 340 (11th Cir. 1994) (same).

Likewise, under § 1983, an analysis similar under § 1981 applies. *See, e.g.*, Coleman v. Houston Indep. Sch. Dist., 113 F.3d 528, 533, 74 FEP 697 (5th Cir. 1997) (plaintiff must demonstrate intentional discrimination to state claim under § 1983); Lipsett v. University of P.R., 864 F.2d 881, 896, 54 FEP 230 (1st Cir. 1988).

Under § 1985, discriminatory animus must be proven. *See* Park v. City of Atlanta, 120 F.3d 1157, 1161 (11th Cir. 1997) (§ 1985(3) conspiracy requires discriminatory animus); *see also* Haddle v. Garrison, 525 U.S. 121 (1998) (employee stated cause of action under § 1985(2) when he alleged that former corporate officers induced employer to terminate his at-will employment in retaliation for obeying federal grand jury subpoena and to deter him from testifying at federal criminal trial); *see also* Chavis v. Clayton County Sch. Dist., 300 F.3d 1288 (11th Cir. 2002) (on

McDonnell Douglas burden-shifting analysis also pertains to § 1983 claims.[408] A § 1981 plaintiff can also prove his or her case by invoking the mixed-motive standard.[409] A plaintiff may attempt to prove discriminatory intent through the employer's failure to follow established policies.[410] A plaintiff need not prove that the defendant acted with racial animus (that is, ill will, enmity, or hostility) to prove an intent to discriminate.[411]

To the extent that a plaintiff has articulated a valid disparate treatment cause of action under Title VII, courts have found that the plaintiff has sufficiently alleged a violation of § 1981.[412] However, there are significant differences between Title VII and § 1981. For example, under Title VII, individuals are not subject to suit personally, although they may be individually liable under § 1981.[413]

---

issue of first impression, § 1985(2) supports cause of action for allegation that African-American teacher was demoted in retaliation for appearing at a criminal proceeding to testify on behalf of white co-worker accused of sex crime).

Under § 1986, courts have applied a negligence standard, focusing on whether the defendant knew of the § 1985(3) conspiracy, was in a position to prevent it, and neglected or refused to do so. *See, e.g., Park, supra*, 120 F.3d at 1160–63 (in non-employment context, court held that party need not be participant in § 1985(3) conspiracy to be liable under § 1986). *See generally* Chapter 2 (Disparate Treatment).

[408]*See* Causey v. Baloy, 162 F.3d 795, 804, 78 FEP 1241 (4th Cir. 1998); Arrington v. Cobb County, 139 F.3d 865, 872, 76 FEP 1270 (11th Cir. 1998); Richardson v. Leeds Police Dep't, 71 F.3d 801, 805, 69 FEP 795 (11th Cir. 1995); Cross v. Alabama State Dep't of Mental Health & Mental Retardation, 49 F.3d 1490, 1508, 67 FEP 844 (11th Cir. 1995).

[409]*See* Walker v. Northwest Airlines, Inc., 2004 WL 114977, at *5–6 (D. Minn. Jan. 14, 2004) (applying *Desert Palace*'s mixed-motive standard to plaintiff's § 1981 claims); *see also* Desert Palace Inc. v. Costa, 539 U.S. 90, 101–02 (2003) (addressing Title VII claim).

[410]*See* Landon v. Northwest Airlines, Inc., 72 F.3d 620, 625, 72 FEP 675 (8th Cir. 1995) (supervisor's failure to follow drug testing policy created genuine issue of material fact as to whether decision to administer drug test was racially motivated under § 1981).

[411]*See* Ferrill v. Parker Group, Inc., 168 F.3d 468, 473, 79 FEP 161 (11th Cir. 1999) (under *Goodman v. Lukens Steel Co.*, 482 U.S. 656 (1987), § 1981 liability "requires only that decisions be premised on race, not that decisions be motivated by invidious hostility or animus"); LaRoche v. Denny's Inc., 62 F. Supp. 2d 1375, 1384 (S.D. Fla. 1999) (same). *But see Park*, 120 F.3d at 1161 (§ 1985(3) conspiracy required discriminatory animus).

[412]*See, e.g.*, Humphrey v. Council of Jewish Fed'ns, 901 F. Supp. 703, 710, 69 FEP 201 (S.D.N.Y. 1995).

[413]*See, e.g*, Patterson v. Oneida, 375 F.3d 206, 226, 94 FEP 129 (2d Cir. 2004) (individuals may be liable under § 1981 and § 1983 for discriminatory acts giving rise to hostile work environment); Preyer v. Dartmouth Coll., 968 F. Supp. 20, 25 (D.N.H. 1997) (dismissing Title VII claim but not § 1981 claim against two supervisors); Grimes v. Superior Home Health Care of Middle Tenn., Inc., 929 F. Supp. 1088, 1095, 74 FEP 1539 (M.D. Tenn. 1996) (individual defendants may be held

In addition, adverse impact theory is not available under the Civil Rights Acts of 1866 and 1871.[414] An important difference between Title VII claims and § 1983 actions is that under § 1983 an employer has an affirmative defense to liability where the employer can show it would have reached the same adverse employment decision even in the absence of the employer's alleged discriminatory intent.[415] Under the 1991 amendments to Title VII, on the other hand, the court may still award declaratory and injunctive relief, attorney's fees, and costs, even where the employer can show it would have reached the same decision in the absence of discrimination.[416]

One issue that continues to trouble some courts is the relationship, if any, between Title VII and the 1866 and 1871 Acts with respect to seniority systems. In *Teamsters v. United States*,[417] a Title VII case, the Supreme Court held that even though a seniority system may have an adverse impact or perpetuate the effects of past discrimination, a bona fide seniority plan is not unlawful.[418] The Court there relied, of course, on Title VII's § 703(h), which protects bona fide seniority systems. Section 1981, by contrast, does not contain language analogous to § 703(h). Plaintiffs therefore may attempt to argue that a seniority system that does not violate Title VII because of § 703(h) might nevertheless violate § 1981, at least if it perpetuated prior intentional discrimination and could be attacked without reliance on the adverse impact theory. Most courts, however, hold that a seniority system that is lawful under Title VII does not violate § 1981.[419]

It remains an open issue whether a plaintiff may maintain a § 1983 action in addition to or in lieu of a cause of action under

---

liable under § 1981) (citing Johnson v. Railway Express Agency, Inc., 421 U.S. 454, 461, 10 FEP 817 (1975)).

[414]*See, e.g.,* Majeske v. Fraternal Order of Police Local Lodge 7, 94 F.3d 307, 310–12, 71 FEP 1307 (7th Cir. 1996) (requirement under §§ 1983 and 1985(3) of purposeful discrimination not satisfied by adverse impact alone). *Contra* Smith v. Texaco, Inc., 951 F. Supp. 109, 111 (E.D. Tex. 1997) (prima facie case of racial discrimination under § 1981 may be shown by demonstrating that African Americans are adversely impacted by employer's wage and promotion policies).

[415]Mt. Healthy City Sch. Dist. Bd. of Educ. v. Doyle, 429 U.S. 274, 286 (1977).

[416]*See* Desert Palace Inc. v. Costa, 539 U.S. 90, 94–95 (2003).

[417]431 U.S. 324, 14 FEP 1514 (1977).

[418]*Id.* at 352–53. *See generally* Chapter 17 (Seniority).

[419]*See, e.g.,* NAACP, Detroit Branch v. Detroit Police Officers Ass'n, 900 F.2d 903, 912–14, 52 FEP 1001 (6th Cir. 1990) (§ 703(h) applies); Freeman v. Motor Convoy, 700 F.2d 1339, 1348–49, 31 FEP 517 (11th Cir. 1983) (§ 703(h) limits a

the Rehabilitation Act of 1973 or the ADA if the only "alleged deprivation" is of the employee's rights created by either act.[420]

E. Remedies

The Supreme Court in *Johnson v. Railway Express Agency, Inc.*[421] stressed the independence of actions brought under the Civil Rights Acts of 1866 and 1871 from those brought under Title VII. It follows, therefore, that remedies derived from these acts may differ from those available under Title VII.[422] Specifically, the Court said: "An individual who establishes a cause of action under § 1981 is entitled to both equitable and legal relief, including compensatory and, under certain circumstances, punitive damages."[423] Thus, a back pay award under § 1981 is not subject to the two-year limitation applicable under Title VII.[424] Presumably the analysis would

---

§ 1981 claim); Pettway v. American Cast Iron Pipe Co., 576 F.2d 1157, 1191 n.37, 17 FEP 1712 (5th Cir. 1978) ("Congress intended section 703(h) to accord absolute protection to pre-Act seniority rights which accrued under bona fide seniority systems."); Johnson v. Ryder Truck Lines, Inc., 575 F.2d 471, 473–74, 17 FEP 571 (4th Cir. 1978) (§ 1981 gives African Americans no more rights than whites, so facially neutral seniority system is valid under § 1981; further, 42 U.S.C. § 1988 directs courts to enforce § 1981 "in conformity with the laws of the United States, so far as such laws are suitable"); Waters v. Wisconsin Steel Works of Int'l Harvester Co., 502 F.2d 1309, 1322 n.4, 8 FEP 577 (7th Cir. 1974) (seniority system that passes muster under Title VII does not violate § 1981).

[420]*See* Lollar v. Baker, 196 F.3d 603, 610 (5th Cir. 1999) (§ 1983 action not an affirmative method to enforce Rehabilitation Act); Alsbrook v. City of Maumelle, 184 F.3d 999, 1011 (8th Cir. 1999) ("the ADA's comprehensive remedial scheme bars" § 1983 claims); Holbrook v. City of Alpharetta, 112 F.3d 1522, 1530–31, 6 AD 1409 (11th Cir. 1997) (§ 1983 not available "in lieu of—or in addition to—a Rehabilitation Act or ADA cause of action"). *But see* Johnson v. City of Fort Lauderdale, 148 F.3d 1228, 1230–31, 77 FEP 794 (11th Cir. 1998) (Civil Rights Act of 1991 did not render Title VII and § 1981 exclusive causes of action for public sector employment discrimination, thereby preempting constitutional claim under § 1983); Arrington v. Cobb County, 139 F.3d 865, 872, 76 FEP 1270 (11th Cir. 1998) (plaintiff who claimed that county violated her Fourteenth Amendment right of equal protection stated claim under § 1983 separate from her claim of gender discrimination under Title VII).

[421]421 U.S. 454, 460–61, 10 FEP 817 (1975).

[422]*Id.* at 461 ("[T]he remedies available under Title VII and under § 1981, although related, and although directed to most of the same ends, are separate, distinct, and independent.").

[423]*Id.* at 460 (citations omitted); *see, e.g.,* Runyon v. McCrary, 427 U.S. 160, 164–66 (1976) (affirming award of compensatory damages for "embarrassment, humiliation and mental anguish"); Harris v. Richards Mfg. Co., 511 F. Supp. 1193, 1205–06, 25 FEP 720 (W.D. Tenn. 1981) (awarding punitive damages), *aff'd in part, rev'd in part on other grounds*, 675 F.2d 811, 28 FEP 1343 (6th Cir. 1982).

[424]*E.g., Railway Express*, 421 U.S. at 460.

be the same for actions brought under §§ 1983 or 1985. And although under §§ 1981 and 1983 a court has wide discretion to award equitable relief,[425] compensatory damages such as for emotional distress caused by the deprivation of civil rights may be awarded only when the complainant submits proof of actual injury.[426]

Although the Court in *Johnson* stressed the then-considerable differences in remedies under Title VII and the Civil Rights Acts of 1866 and 1871, those differences no longer are as great. Since the Civil Rights Act of 1991, Title VII provides for compensatory and punitive damages (subject to caps).[427] And, even before the 1991 Act, the courts had construed the nineteenth century Civil Rights Acts (which were not specific as to the remedies available thereunder) to allow many of the same remedies specifically authorized under Title VII. Declaratory and injunctive relief—including instatement or reinstatement and other forms of specific relief for the aggrieved individual—as well as goals and timetables for an affected class, are generally all available as remedies under the Civil Rights Acts of 1866 and 1871.[428] Back-pay awards also are available,[429] as are attorney's fees.[430]

---

[425]*See* Barbour v. Merrill, 48 F.3d 1270, 1278, 67 FEP 369 (D.C. Cir. 1995); *see also* McDaniel v. Princeton City Sch. Dist. Bd. of Educ., 114 F. Supp. 2d 658, 661–62 (S.D. Ohio 2000) (§ 1983 prevailing plaintiff entitled to back wages and compensation for lost fringe benefits, which included pension contributions and vacation pay, as well as costs incurred by plaintiff in maintaining health insurance coverage).

[426]*See* Carey v. Piphus, 435 U.S. 247, 264 (1978) (holding that § 1983 requires proof of actual injury to sustain award of compensatory damages); Patterson v. PHP Healthcare, 90 F.3d 927, 940 (5th Cir. 1996) (extending *Carey* to § 1981 claims).

[427]Pub. L. No. 102-66, § 101, 1991 U.S.C.C.A.N. (105 Stat.) 1071, 1072 (codified at 42 U.S.C. § 1981a (2000)). *See generally* Chapter 40 (Monetary Relief).

[428]*See, e.g.*, Catlett v. Missouri Highway & Transp. Comm'n, 828 F.2d 1260, 1272, 45 FEP 1627 (8th Cir. 1987) (equitable remedies under Title VII and § 1983 are almost identical); *cf.* Carter v. Gallagher, 452 F.2d 315, 329–31, 3 FEP 900 (in class action alleging discriminatory practices in determining qualifications of fire department applicants, affirming lower court's mandate that minority persons be hired in 1:2 ratio), *modified on other grounds en banc*, 452 F.2d 327, 4 FEP 121 (8th Cir. 1971). *See generally* Chapter 39 (Injunctive and Affirmative Relief).

[429]*See, e.g.*, Sabala v. Western Gillette, Inc., 516 F.2d 1251, 1263–67, 11 FEP 98 (5th Cir. 1975) (upholding district court's award of back pay against defendant employer after finding discriminatory seniority system in Title VII/§ 1981 action), *vacated and remanded on other grounds*, 431 U.S. 951 (1977). *See generally* Chapter 40 (Monetary Relief).

[430]*See* 42 U.S.C. § 1988 (2000); *see also* Nydam v. Lennerton, 948 F.2d 808, 812–13 (1st Cir. 1991) (prevailing civil rights plaintiff entitled to recover attorney's fees);

Moreover, although injury to reputation, standing alone, does not provide a basis for an action under § 1983, persons who sustain such injury in connection with a termination of employment may claim compensatory damages.[431]

In cases under §§ 1981 and 1983, punitive damages are proper only on a showing of "evil motive or intent, or . . . reckless or callous indifference to the federally protected rights of others."[432] To impose punitive damages on the employer, it must have knowledge of malicious or reckless conduct or authorize, ratify, or approve an employee's malicious or reckless conduct.[433] In the employment

---

Schofield v. Trustees of Univ. of Pa., 919 F. Supp. 821, 825 (E.D. Pa. 1996) ("The Civil Rights Attorney's Fees Awards Act of 1976, 42 U.S.C. § 1988, confers upon the court the discretion to award to the prevailing party 'a reasonable attorney's fee as part of the costs.' "); Mason v. Oklahoma Tpk. Auth., 115 F.3d 1442, 1460 (10th Cir. 1997) (awarding successful § 1983 plaintiff reasonable attorney's fees under § 1988 as determined by district court and accounting for degree of success obtained); Fauntleroy v. Staszak, 3 F. Supp. 2d 234, 236 (N.D.N.Y. 1998) (where § 1981 claim involving issuance of public assistance benefits was settled by consent decree that found plaintiffs were prevailing parties, plaintiffs were entitled to attorney's fees); Wagner v. City of Memphis, 971 F. Supp. 308, 322 (W.D. Tenn. 1997) (awarding prevailing § 1983 plaintiff reasonable attorney's fees). *See generally* Chapter 41 (Attorney's Fees).

[431]*See* Carrero v. New York City Hous. Auth., 890 F.2d 569, 581, 51 FEP 596 (2d Cir. 1989); *see also* Campbell v. Pierce County, 741 F.2d 1342, 1346 (11th Cir. 1984) (awarding damages in case involving denial of due process and deprivation of "liberty").

[432]Smith v. Wade, 461 U.S. 30, 56 (1983) (§ 1983 action); *accord* Goodwin v. St. Louis County Cir. Ct., 729 F.2d 541, 547, 34 FEP 347 (8th Cir. 1984) (§ 1983 sex discrimination case in which court held that award of actual damages is not prerequisite to award of punitive damages); Garza v. City of Omaha, 814 F.2d 553, 556, 43 FEP 572 (8th Cir. 1987) (§ 1983 punitive damages recoverable where defendant exhibits oppression, malice, gross negligence, willful misconduct, or reckless disregard for plaintiff's civil rights); *cf.* EEOC v. Gaddis, 733 F.2d 1373, 1380, 34 FEP 1210 (10th Cir. 1984) (§ 1981 punitive damages appropriate where defendant's actions were "malicious, willful and in gross disregard of [the charging party's] rights"); *see also* Williams v. Brimeyer, 116 F.3d 351, 354 (8th Cir. 1997) (§ 1983); Merriweather v. Family Dollar Stores of Ind., 103 F.3d 576, 583, 76 FEP 1251 (7th Cir. 1996) (upholding assessment of punitive damages against employer in § 1981 action; evidence established that employer displayed reckless indifference in illegal discharge of employee); Fitzgerald v. Mountain States Tel. & Tel. Co., 68 F.3d 1257, 1263 (10th Cir. 1995) (punitive damages in § 1981 action requires that discrimination must have been malicious, willful, and in gross disregard of plaintiff's rights; claim for punitive damages dismissed where no evidence existed that employer authorized employee's actions); Barbour v. Merrill, 48 F.3d 1270, 1277 (D.C. Cir. 1995). Other constitutional due process requirements relating to punitive damages awards are discussed in Chapter 40 (Monetary Relief).

[433]*See Fitzgerald*, 68 F.3d at 1263 (applying standard requiring conduct that is malicious, willful, and in gross disregard of plaintiff's rights); Cooper v. Paychex,

context, the Third Circuit in *Keenan v. City of Philadelphia*,[434] a sexual harassment case under § 1983, affirmed awards of punitive damages against three levels of management in a police department: (1) the supervisor who sexually harassed the plaintiff; (2) the supervisor of the harasser, for failing to take adequate action in the face of known complaints and for approving certain discriminatory actions of the harasser; and (3) the harasser's supervisor's boss, also for implicitly condoning the known sexual harassment. The court refused to permit punitive damages to be awarded against a fourth level of the command structure—the police commissioner—who merely acknowledged that he was responsible for the conduct of his subordinates, but who himself had neither engaged in nor condoned discriminatory conduct.[435]

In June 1999, the Supreme Court decided *Kolstad v. American Dental Association*,[436] which addressed the propriety of awarding punitive damages in a Title VII sexual discrimination case. The Court held that under the Civil Rights Act of 1991, a plaintiff need not show that the employer engaged in egregious or outrageous acts to prove the malice and reckless indifference necessary to prevail on a claim of punitive damages.[437] The Court also held that, "in the punitive damages context, an employer may not be vicariously liable for the discriminatory employment decisions of managerial agents where such decisions are contrary to the employer's 'good faith efforts to comply with Title VII.' "[438] The nineteenth century Civil Rights Acts are not subject to the Civil Rights Act of 1991 punitive damages provision.[439] However, several courts have applied the *Kolstad* standard for recovery of punitive damages to § 1981 and § 1983 claims.[440] Any award of

---

Inc., 960 F. Supp. 966, 972 (E.D. Va. 1997) (supervisor's conduct supported punitive damages award against employer in Title VII/§ 1981 action where supervisor acted within scope of his authority), *aff'd*, 163 F.3d 598 (4th Cir. 1998).

[434]983 F.2d 459, 469–72, 60 FEP 719 (3d Cir. 1992).

[435]*Id.* at 470–71.

[436]527 U.S. 526, 79 FEP 1697 (1999).

[437]*Id.* at 536–40.

[438]*Id.* at 545 (citations omitted).

[439]*See, e.g.*, Deffenbaugh-Williams v. Wal-Mart Stores, 156 F.3d 581, 598, 77 FEP 1699 (5th Cir. 1998); Kim v. Nash Finch Co., 123 F.3d 1046, 1061 (8th Cir. 1997) (Title VII's statutory cap on damages (§ 1981a(b)(3)) does not apply to claims under § 1981, although court reduced grossly excessive jury award for § 1981 violation).

[440]*See* DiMarco-Zappa v. Cabanillas, 238 F.3d 25, 37–38 (1st Cir. 2001) (applied *Kolstad* to § 1983 punitive damages claim); Pearson v. Ramos, 237 F.3d 881,

punitive damages must also comply with the criteria established by the Supreme Court to determine the reasonableness of a punitive damage award.[441]

Although local government entities are subject to liability under §§ 1981 and 1983, they are immune from punitive damages. The Supreme Court in *City of Newport v. Fact Concerts*[442] held that a municipality is immune from punitive damages in a claim brought under § 1983. In *Jett v. Dallas Independent School District*,[443] the Court held that the § 1983 remedies also govern § 1981 claims against local public agencies.[444]

A plaintiff has an obligation to use reasonable efforts to mitigate damages under §§ 1981 and 1983.[445]

F. Jury Trial

Plaintiffs suing for damages under the Civil Rights Acts of 1866 and 1871 are entitled by the Seventh Amendment to a jury trial.[446]

886–87 (7th Cir. 2001) (same); Lowery v. Circuit City Stores, 206 F.3d 431, 441–42, 82 FEP 353 (4th Cir. 2000) (applied *Kolstad* to § 1983 claims); Alexander v. Fulton County, 207 F.3d 1303, 1337–38, 92 FEP 858 (11th Cir. 2000) (same); Copley v. Bax Global, Inc., 97 F. Supp. 2d 1164, 1168 n.4 (S.D. Fla. 2000) (same).

[441]*See* State Farm Mut. Auto. Ins. Co. v. Campbell, 538 U.S. 408, 419 (2003) ("the most important indicium of reasonableness of punitive damages award is the degree of reprehensibility"); BMW of N. Am., Inc. v. Gore, 517 U.S. 559 (1996) (factors to be considered in determining whether punitive damage award was reasonable are (1) degree of reprehensibility of defendant's conduct; (2) disparity between harm suffered and damage award; and (3) difference between damages awarded in this case and comparable cases).

[442]453 U.S. 247, 263–71 (1981).

[443]491 U.S. 701, 50 FEP 27 (1989).

[444]*Id.* at 712–23; *see also* Busby v. City of Orlando, 931 F.2d 764, 771 n.6, 55 FEP 1466 (11th Cir. 1991) (§ 1981 claim merged in § 1983 claim by operation of law) (citing Jett v. Dallas Indep. Sch. Dist., 491 U.S. 701, 735, 50 FEP 27 (1989)).

[445]*See, e.g.,* Deffenbaugh-Williams v. Wal-Mart Stores, 156 F.3d 581, 591, 77 FEP 1699 (5th Cir. 1998) (no reversible error in permitting jury in § 1983 case to consider awarding lost earnings after December 1994 despite plaintiff voluntarily quitting her subsequent employment; mitigation was fact question hinging on reasonableness, similarity, and diligence); Cooper v. Paychex, Inc., 960 F. Supp. 966, 973 (E.D. Va. 1997) (upholding plaintiff's back pay award of $200,272; jury verdict significantly reduced back pay for years after plaintiff's discharge while he was in law school, evidencing consideration of mitigation doctrine), *aff'd*, 163 F.3d 598 (4th Cir. 1998); Coleman v. Lane, 949 F. Supp. 604, 611–12 (N.D. Ill. 1996) (successful § 1983 plaintiff failed to exercise reasonable diligence in attempting to locate alternative job following reinstatement order).

[446]*See* Lytle v. Household Mfg., Inc., 494 U.S. 545, 550, 52 FEP 423 (1990) (jury must resolve § 1981 claim before court considers pre–1991 Act Title VII claims); Keller v. Prince George's County, 827 F.2d 952, 954–55, 44 FEP 1065 (4th Cir. 1987)

However, a plaintiff is not entitled to a jury trial if the only relief sought is equitable in nature.[447]

G. Res Judicata

The preclusive effect of prior litigation is primarily discussed elsewhere.[448] In *Migra v. Warren City School District Board of Education*,[449] the Supreme Court held that the preclusive effect of an earlier state court decision, where claims under §§ 1983 and 1985 could have been raised but were not, is to be decided by reference to state-law preclusion principles. Lower federal courts have dismissed on res judicata grounds numerous actions brought under the Civil Rights Acts of 1866 and 1871 that could have been raised in prior state court proceedings.[450] However, where an employee first brings suit in small claims court for unpaid wages and benefits, lower courts have not found preclusion on res judicata grounds where the small claims court lacked the equitable power

---

(persons seeking monetary damages under § 1983 have right to jury trial); Setser v. Novack Inv. Co., 638 F.2d 1137, 1139–42, 24 FEP 1793 (8th Cir. 1981) (parties are constitutionally entitled to jury trials under § 1981 on all claims for legal relief), *modified en banc on other grounds*, 657 F.2d 962, 26 FEP 513 (8th Cir. 1981).

[447]*See, e.g.*, Moore v. Sun Oil Co., 636 F.2d 154, 156, 24 FEP 1072 (6th Cir. 1980) (plaintiff not entitled to jury trial on equitable issue of back pay); Saad v. Burns Int'l Sec. Servs., Inc., 456 F. Supp. 33, 38, 18 FEP 516 (D.D.C. 1978) (same); Miller v. Doctor's Gen. Hosp., 76 F.R.D. 136, 142, 18 FEP 825 (W.D. Okla. 1977) (same); Flores v. Electrical Workers (IBEW) Local 25, 407 F. Supp. 218, 220, 12 FEP 185 (E.D.N.Y. 1976) (same).

[448]*See generally* Chapter 27 (Jurisprudential Bars to Action).

[449]465 U.S. 75, 33 FEP 1345 (1984).

[450]*Compare* Takahashi v. Lincoln Union Sch. Dist., 783 F.2d 848, 850–51, 40 FEP 267 (9th Cir. 1986) (affirming res judicata determination by district court in § 1983 action because of prior unsuccessful litigation in California state court), Nilsen v. City of Moss Point, 701 F.2d 556, 562–64, 31 FEP 612 (5th Cir. 1983) (dismissal of Title VII action for untimeliness bars subsequent § 1983 claim), Poe v. John Deere Co., 695 F.2d 1103, 1105–06, 30 FEP 827 (8th Cir. 1982) (determination of § 1981 action bars subsequent action asserting state-law claims) *and* Pillow v. Schoemehl, 620 F. Supp. 360, 360–61, 39 FEP 438 (E.D. Mo. 1985) (giving res judicata effect to decisions of state circuit court and appellate court; racial discrimination issue raised in § 1981 action should have been raised in state proceedings), *aff'd mem.*, 802 F.2d 462 (8th Cir. 1986) *with* Foulks v. Ohio Dep't of Rehab. & Corr., 713 F.2d 1229, 1231–32, 32 FEP 829 (6th Cir. 1983) (plaintiffs' prior state human rights and state court actions against their employer do not preclude § 1981 action against their supervisors) *and* Novak v. World Bank, 703 F.2d 1305, 1307–10, 32 FEP 424 (D.C. Cir. 1983) (res judicata does not bar § 1985 action against alleged conspirator who was not party to original discrimination suit).

to order the reinstatement sought in a subsequent § 1983 action.[451] Furthermore, an employee who lost a Title VII action against his university employer was not precluded under res judicata from relitigating the same claim in the form of a § 1983 action against the university's employees, where the court found that privity was lacking between employees in their individual capacities and the university.[452]

Even where a claim is not extinguished by res judicata, collateral estoppel may limit what factual issues remain to be litigated. In pre–1991 Act cases, for example, jury determinations of factual issues under § 1981 and § 1983 have been held to bar contrary rulings by the court on equitable issues in a companion Title VII claim.[453] However, the Supreme Court held in *Lytle v. Household Manufacturing, Inc.*[454] that the reverse is not true: where the district court had erroneously dismissed the plaintiff's legal claims under § 1981, its factual findings regarding the plaintiff's equitable Title VII claim did not collaterally estop contrary jury findings following reversal by an appellate court of the dismissal of those legal claims.[455]

The rules governing nonjudicial adjudications are less clear. The Supreme Court has held that an unreviewed arbitration award is not preclusive in a § 1983 action; 28 U.S.C. § 1738 does not apply to such arbitration awards.[456] The findings of fact from a

---

[451]*See* Ortiz v. Costilla County Bd. of Comm'rs, 11 F. Supp. 2d 1254, 1256 (D. Colo. 1998).

[452]*See* DeLlano v. Berglund, 183 F.3d 780, 781, 80 FEP 719 (8th Cir. 1999).

[453]*See* Garza v. City of Omaha, 814 F.2d 553, 557, 43 FEP 572 (8th Cir. 1987) (jury verdict in § 1983 action in favor of plaintiff controls Title VII determination); King v. Emerson Elec. Co., 746 F.2d 1331, 1332 n.2, 38 FEP 1666 (8th Cir. 1984) ("The factual question of discrimination *vel non* is, of course, common to both the § 1981 and Title VII claims. A jury verdict on this issue in the context of a § 1981 claim is normally conclusive on the same issue in the Title VII context as well."); Goodwin v. St. Louis County Cir. Ct., 729 F.2d 541, 549 n.11, 34 FEP 347 (8th Cir. 1984) ("Ordinarily, when § 1983 and Title VII claims are tried jointly, the § 1983 theory to the jury and the Title VII theory to the court, a jury verdict on the issue of discrimination would collaterally estop the parties with respect to that issue on the Title VII claim."); Brooks v. Carnation Pet Food Co., 38 FEP 1663, 1664–65 (W.D. Mo. 1985) (special jury verdicts in § 1981 action preclude contrary findings on identical Title VII issues).

[454]494 U.S. 545, 52 FEP 423 (1990).

[455]*Id.* at 552–53.

[456]*See* McDonald v. City of W. Branch, 466 U.S. 284, 290–92 (1984) (federal court may not, in § 1983 actions, accord res judicata or collateral estoppel effect to unappealed award in arbitration proceeding); *see also* Alexander v. Gardner-Denver

state administrative proceeding *may* be entitled to preclusive effect in a subsequent § 1983 suit.[457] In *University of Tennessee v. Elliott*,[458] the Supreme Court held that even *unreviewed* agency factual findings, where the agency acted in a judicial capacity and resolved "disputed issues of fact properly before it which the parties have had an adequate opportunity to litigate," in some instances can collaterally estop litigation in a subsequent suit brought under the nineteenth century Civil Rights Acts.[459] But not all unreviewed agency findings qualify. In *Astoria Federal Savings & Loan Ass'n v. Solimino*,[460] the Court held that a state agency's judicially unreviewed findings had no preclusive effect on an ADEA claim. The Court reasoned: "Although administrative estoppel is favored as a matter of general policy, its suitability may vary according to

---

Co., 415 U.S. 36, 48–52, 7 FEP 81 (1974) (employee's statutory right under Title VII to trial de novo not foreclosed by prior submission of claim to final arbitration; federal courts have final responsibility for enforcement of Title VII).

[457]*See* Baez-Cruz v. Municipality of Comerio, 140 F.3d 24, 30 (1st Cir. 1998) (where employees chose to proceed first before administrative agency that satisfied minimum procedural requirements of Fourteenth Amendment's Due Process Clause, court applied issue preclusion to § 1983 suit); Alexander v. Pathfinder, Inc., 91 F.3d 59, 62 (8th Cir. 1996) (outlining standards for determining preclusive effect of state agency's findings of fact); Schlimgen v. City of Rapid City, 83 F. Supp. 2d 1061, 1069 (D.S.D. 2000) (city estopped from relitigating whether retaliation for exercise of First Amendment rights was factor in termination, where earlier administrative agency decision had found employee was terminated for exercising free speech rights); Harrison v. Arlington Cent. Sch. Dist., 60 F. Supp. 2d 186, 189–90 (S.D.N.Y. 1999) (administrative agency's quasi-judicial determination adverse to plaintiff has collateral estoppel preclusive effect). *But see* Campbell v. Arkansas Dep't of Corr., 155 F.3d 950, 960 (8th Cir. 1998) (refusing to apply issue preclusion in § 1983 case to prohibit retaliation claim based on evidence in state grievance hearing because hearing was not sufficiently like judicial proceeding).

[458]478 U.S. 788, 41 FEP 177 (1986).

[459]*Id.* at 799. The Court distinguished Title VII claims, however, holding that unreviewed agency findings do not have collateral estoppel effect on a subsequent Title VII action. The Court reasoned that in light of the language of § 706(b), which requires the EEOC to give "substantial weight" to the findings of state or local EEO authorities, "it would make little sense for Congress to write such a provision if state agency findings were entitled to preclusive effect in Title VII actions in federal court." *Id.* at 795; *see, e.g.*, DeCintio v. Westchester County Med. Ctr., 821 F.2d 111, 116–19, 44 FEP 33 (2d Cir. 1987) (§ 1981 and § 1983 claims, but not Title VII claims, barred by state agency decision); Buckhalter v. Pepsi-Cola Gen. Bottlers, 820 F.2d 892, 894–97, 43 FEP 1615 (7th Cir. 1987) (same); Abramson v. Council Bluffs Cmty. Sch. Dist., 62 FEP 3, 3–4 (8th Cir. 1987) (although Title VII action not precluded, § 1983 action is).

[460]501 U.S. 104, 110–11, 55 FEP 1503 (1991).

the specific context of the rights at stake, the power of the agency, and the relative adequacy of agency procedures."[461]

The decision of a state *court* reviewing an administrative determination clearly is res judicata and bars a subsequent action under §§ 1981, 1983, or 1985.[462]

---

[461]*Id.* at 109–10.

[462]*See, e.g.*, Brown v. St. Louis Police Dep't, 691 F.2d 393, 395–96, 30 FEP 18 (8th Cir. 1982) (giving res judicata effect to state court's affirmance of state board's determination that good cause existed for plaintiff's termination); Lee v. City of Peoria, 685 F.2d 196, 198–99, 29 FEP 892 (7th Cir. 1982) (same); Davis v. United States Steel Corp., 688 F.2d 166, 174–76, 29 FEP 1202 (3d Cir. 1982) (giving res judicata effect to state court's reversal of agency determination); Capers v. Long Island R.R., 31 FEP 668, 669–70 (S.D.N.Y. 1983) (same); Stitzer v. University of P.R., 617 F. Supp. 1246, 1252–53, 38 FEP 1419 (D.P.R. 1985) (giving res judicata and collateral estoppel effect to state superior court decision upholding administrative findings); *cf.* Kremer v. Chemical Constr. Corp., 456 U.S. 461, 467–71, 28 FEP 1412 (1982) (28 U.S.C. § 1738 mandates that full faith and credit be given in Title VII action to prior state court determination on plaintiff's appeal of adverse administrative ruling).

Chapter 36

THE NATIONAL LABOR RELATIONS ACT

I. INTRODUCTION

The National Labor Relations Act (NLRA)[1] declares that it is the policy of the United States to encourage "the practice and procedure of collective bargaining" and to protect "the exercise by workers of full freedom of association, self-organization, and designation of representatives of their own choosing, for the purpose

---

[1] Act of July 5, 1935, 49 Stat. 449, as reenacted by Act of June 23, 1947, Pub. L. No. 80-101, 1947 U.S.C.C.A.N. (61 Stat. 136) 135, amended by Act of Sept. 14, 1959, Pub. L. No. 86-257, 1959 U.S.C.C.A.N. (73 Stat. 519) 565, amended by Act of July 26, 1974, Pub. L. No. 93-360, 1974 U.S.C.C.A.N. (88 Stat. 395) 444 (codified as amended at 29 U.S.C. §§ 151–168).

of negotiating the terms and conditions of their employment or other mutual aid or protection."[2]

Section 7 of the NLRA[3] guarantees employees the right to organize, the right to bargain collectively, and the right to engage in strikes, picketing, and other concerted activities for their mutual aid and protection, or to refrain from such activities. Section 9[4] sets forth the procedure under which employees may select (or reject) by secret ballot a labor organization to act as their exclusive representative for the purpose of collective bargaining.

This scheme is tied together by § 8,[5] which, among other things, makes it an unfair labor practice for an employer to interfere with employees in the exercise of the rights guaranteed by the NLRA,[6] or to discriminate against an employee because the employee engaged in any of the activities protected by the NLRA,[7] or to refuse to bargain with a union selected by the employees as their exclusive representative.[8] It also makes it an unfair labor practice for unions to restrain or coerce employees in the exercise of their rights guaranteed by the NLRA,[9] or to cause or attempt to cause employers to discriminate against employees who engage in or refuse to engage in protected concerted activity,[10] or to refuse to bargain in good faith with employers.[11]

The National Labor Relations Board (NLRB or Board) was created to enforce the NLRA by issuing cease-and-desist orders against those found to have violated the NLRA and to supervise and conduct representation elections. Section 10(b)[12] requires that charges of unfair labor practices be filed with the NLRB within six months of their occurrence.

This chapter focuses on the relationship of the NLRA to the employment discrimination laws.[13]

---

[2]29 U.S.C. § 151 (2000).
[3]Id. § 157.
[4]Id. § 159.
[5]Id. § 158.
[6]§ 8(a)(1) (codified at 29 U.S.C. § 158(a)(1) (2000)).
[7]§ 8(a)(3) (codified at 29 U.S.C. § 158(a)(3) (2000)).
[8]§ 8(a)(5) (codified at 29 U.S.C. § 158(a)(5) (2000)).
[9]§ 8(b)(1)(A) (codified at 29 U.S.C. § 158(b)(1)(A) (2000)).
[10]§ 8(b)(2) (codified at 29 U.S.C. § 158(b)(2) (2000)).
[11]§ 8(b)(3) (codified at 29 U.S.C. § 158(b)(3) (2000)).
[12]29 U.S.C. § 160(b) (2000).
[13]Section 8(a)(3) of the NLRA makes it unlawful for an employer to discriminate against an employee (interpreted to include a job applicant) who has engaged in conduct protected by the Act. See 29 U.S.C. § 158(a)(3) (2000). As the Supreme

II. REMEDIES AGAINST UNIONS[14]

A. General Statutory Obligations

The NLRA does not expressly prohibit discrimination.[15] Nonetheless, over the years, the Board has addressed allegations of race discrimination by unions.

Court has noted, this provision is not intended to "outlaw all discrimination in employment as such; only such discrimination as encourages or discourages membership in a labor organization is proscribed." Radio Officers v. NLRB, 347 U.S. 17, 43, 33 LRRM 2417 (1954).

    In most cases, proof of a violation of § 8(a)(3) requires a showing that the employer's conduct was motivated by union animus. *See* Wright Line, Wright Line Div., 251 NLRB 1083, 105 LRRM 1169 (1980), *enforced*, 662 F.2d 899, 108 LRRM 2513 (1st Cir. 1981). Examples of employer conduct requiring independent proof of union animus include situations involving hiring, firing, or discipline of individual employees. A § 8(a)(3) violation requires proof that the employer was aware of the aggrieved employee's union activities or union support at the time of the adverse employment action. *See* Leyendecker Paving, 247 NLRB 28, 103 LRRM 1107 (1980).

    In certain cases, however, the employer's conduct is so "inherently destructive" of employee § 7 rights that no independent proof of antiunion motive is necessary. In *NLRB v. Erie Resistor Corp.*, 373 U.S. 221, 53 LRRM 2121 (1963), the Supreme Court found that an employer's grant of superseniority to striker replacements and strikers who crossed the picket line "carried its own indicia of intent and [was] barred by the [NLRA] unless saved from illegality by an overriding business purpose justifying the invasion of union rights." *Id.* at 231; *see* Aztech Elec. Co., 335 NLRB No. 25, 168 LRRM 1073 (2001) (employer's policy of excluding job applicants, who had previously earned 30% more than the employer's starting wage, to be so inherently destructive of § 7 rights, that no additional proof of motive was necessary); *see also* NLRB v. Great Dane Trailers, 388 U.S. 26, 65 LRRM 2465 (1967) (setting forth the burden of proof in discrimination cases arising under the NLRA).

    Section 8(b)(2) prohibits labor organizations from inducing employers to discriminate against employees who are not union members. *See* 29 U.S.C. §158(b)(3). Under § 8(b)(2), it is an unfair labor practice for a labor organization to "cause or attempt to cause an employer to discriminate against an employee with respect to whom membership in such organization has been denied or terminated on some ground other than his failure to tender the periodic dues and the initiation fees uniformly required as a condition of acquiring or retaining membership."

    The NLRB has jurisdiction to remedy claims of discrimination under §§ 8(a)(3) and 8(b)(2) of the NLRA. For further discussion of discrimination issues arising under § 8 of the NLRA, see AMERICAN BAR ASSOCIATION, SECTION OF LABOR & EMPLOYMENT LAW, THE DEVELOPING LABOR LAW (John E. Higgins, Jr. ed., 5th ed. BNA 2006), Chapter 7, "Discrimination in Employment."

    [14]*See generally* Chapter 22 (Unions) (extensive discussion of the general scope and coverage of employment discrimination laws as they pertain to unions).

    [15]*See* S. REP. NO. 105, 80th Cong., 1st Sess. 20 (1947); *see also* Bernard D. Meltzer, *The National Labor Relations Act and Racial Discrimination: The More Remedies, the Better?* 42 U. CHI. L. REV. 1, 12 n.63 (1974) ("[W]hen the Wagner Act of 1935 was being considered, civil rights organizations proposed amendments that would have prohibited a bargaining order in favor of a union discriminating on

The NLRB first confronted race discrimination in representation cases. In 1938, the NLRB ruled that it would not grant an all-white union's request for an election limited to white employees because "no evidence was introduced to show . . . a basis for separation of the white and colored employees."[16] Later, the Board declined to deny certification to a parent union that maintained separate black and white locals, but indicated it would consider rescinding or denying certification to any local that engaged in racial discrimination.[17]

Although not arising under the NLRA,[18] the case of *Steele v. Louisville & Nashville Railroad*[19] expresses the rationale that forms much of the basis for the NLRB's authority to remedy union discrimination. In *Steele*, the Supreme Court considered whether a union could lawfully discriminate on the basis of race in the negotiation or administration of a collective bargaining agreement. The Court declined to reach the constitutional issue,[20] basing its decision instead on statutory grounds. The Court noted that Congress made the union the exclusive bargaining representative of the bargaining unit. The union's status as exclusive representative carried with it "a duty to exercise the power in th[e] interest and behalf" of all represented persons.[21] It follows, the Court held, that Congress intended "to impose on the bargaining representative . . . the duty to exercise fairly the power conferred upon it . . . without hostile discrimination,"[22] based on race or other "irrelevant" characteristics.[23]

---

the basis of race, color, or creed. *See* 1 LEGISLATIVE HISTORY OF THE NATIONAL LABOR RELATIONS ACT 1036, 1059–60 (1949). Those proposals were not even considered in the debates.").

[16]American Tobacco Co., 9 NLRB 579, 583, 3 LRRM 308 (1938).

[17]*See* Larus & Bros. Co., 62 NLRB 1075, 1076–77, 16 LRRM 242 (1945), *overruled in part by* Independent Metal Workers Local 1 & 2 (Hughes Tool Co.), 147 NLRB 1573, 56 LRRM 1289 (1964).

[18]*Steele* arose under the Railway Labor Act (RLA). The RLA, administered by the National Mediation Board, governs labor relations in the railroad and airline industries.

[19]323 U.S. 192, 199–203, 9 FEP 381 (1944).

[20]323 U.S. at 207.

[21]*Id.* at 202.

[22]*Id.* at 202–03. Justice Murphy, concurring, would have held that the result was constitutionally compelled. *Id.* at 208–09.

[23]*Id.* at 203.

After *Steele*, a union's status as exclusive representative became the basis, under the NRLA, for attacking various forms of invidious discrimination by unions.[24] The *Steele* doctrine led to several lines of cases imposing remedies against, or denying remedies in favor of, unions that discriminate:

(1) Denial of access to NLRB processes, particularly to a § 8(a)(5) bargaining remedy;

(2) Denial or rescission of certification;

(3) Finding an unfair labor practice for a breach of the duty of fair representation; and

(4) Finding an unfair labor practice where a union opposes an employer's efforts to remedy discrimination.

B. Denial of Access to NLRB Remedies

In *NLRB v. Mansion House Center Management Corp.*,[25] the employer lost a representation election and refused to bargain with the prevailing union. The employer defended its refusal to bargain on the ground that the union had engaged in racial discrimination in its membership practices. The court found that the evidence proffered to the NLRB was sufficient to establish the union's violation of Title VII,[26] and held that the violation precluded the union from availing itself of the NLRB's normal remedies.[27] The Eighth Circuit reasoned that to permit the union access to the NLRB would result in unconstitutional "federal complicity" in invidious discrimination.[28]

Notwithstanding *Mansion House*, it is rare that NLRB remedies will be denied to a union even where it is shown to be in violation of Title VII or other discrimination laws. The overt discrimination formerly practiced by many unions now generally has ceased. Moreover, *Mansion House* is not uniformly followed; the

---

[24]*See* Ford Motor Co. v. Huffman, 345 U.S. 330, 337, 31 LRRM 2548 (1953) (dictum making it clear that the *Steele* doctrine applies in cases under the NLRA); *see also* Railroad Trainmen v. Howard, 343 U.S. 768, 773, 9 FEP 414 (1952) (same result as *Steele*, even though African Americans were in separate unit).

[25]473 F.2d 471, 9 FEP 358 (8th Cir. 1973).

[26]*Id.* at 477.

[27]*Id.*

[28]*Id.*

District of Columbia Circuit has specifically rejected it[29] and no other court has fully embraced it. The NLRB itself declines to follow *Mansion House*[30] and will not deny certification because of a union's pre-certification discrimination.[31] The Fifth and Ninth Circuits have cited *Mansion House* without disapproval, but they generally require a substantial and specific prima facie showing of discrimination.[32]

---

[29]*See* Bell & Howell Co. v. NLRB, 598 F.2d 136, 139 n.1, 18 FEP 1204 (D.C. Cir. 1979) (court was compelled to disagree with *Mansion House*); *see also* NLRB v. Mangurian's, Inc., 566 F.2d 463, 464, 97 LRRM 2477 (5th Cir. 1978) (allegation of union racial and other invidious discrimination was not properly considered as an affirmative defense to a § 8(a)(1) unfair labor practice charge against employer).

[30]*E.g.*, Nomad Div. Skyline Corp., 240 NLRB 737, 737–38, 100 LRRM 1312 (1979) (allegations of discrimination cannot constitute a defense to a § 8(a)(5) proceeding), *enforced*, 613 F.2d 1328, 103 LRRM 3003 (5th Cir. 1980); Heavy Lift Serv., Inc., 234 NLRB 1078, 1079, 98 LRRM 1177 (1978) (NLRB was not under a constitutional mandate to consider allegations of union discrimination in either representation or refusal-to-bargain proceedings), *enforced*, 607 F.2d 1121, 102 LRRM 3061 (5th Cir. 1979); FDI, Inc., 231 NLRB 1010, 1010–11 & n.5, 96 LRRM 1628 (1977) (issues involving alleged union discrimination were prematurely raised in representation or refusal-to-bargain proceedings), *enforced sub nom. In re* Bel Air Chateau Hosp., 611 F.2d 1248, 104 LRRM 2976 (9th Cir. 1979). *But see* Pioneer Bus Co., 140 NLRB 54, 55, 51 LRRM 1546 (1962) (pre-*Mansion House* decision in which NLRB indicated that it would deny to a racially discriminatory union the benefit of the "contract-bar rules"). However, this sanction appears applicable only where unlawful discrimination is apparent on the face of the contract. *See* St. Louis Cordage Mills, 168 NLRB 981, 982, 67 LRRM 1017 (1967) (NLRB was unable to determine without extrinsic evidence whether or not sex-segregated seniority lists were justified as BFOQ; therefore, the clause was not unlawful on its face).

[31]*See* Section II.C *infra*.

[32]*See, e.g.*, Skyline Corp. v. NLRB, 613 F.2d 1328, 1335 n.4, 103 LRRM 3003 (5th Cir. 1980) (employer could not defend its refusal to bargain based on the union's failure to provide information relative to union's racial and sexual composition, because the employer failed to present prima facie evidence of union discrimination); NLRB v. Heavy Lift Serv., Inc., 607 F.2d 1121, 1123–24, 102 LRRM 3061 (5th Cir. 1979) (employer seeking to defend its refusal to bargain on basis of the union's race discrimination was not entitled to a NLRB hearing on the issue absent a prima facie showing of union discrimination); Natter Mfg. Corp. v. NLRB, 580 F.2d 948, 951–52 n.2, 99 LRRM 2963 (9th Cir. 1978) (where employer failed to proffer specific evidence constituting prima facie showing of union discrimination, employer could not defend its refusal to bargain on basis of NLRB's refusal to conduct hearing on alleged discrimination); NLRB v. Sumter Plywood Corp., 535 F.2d 917, 929–30, 14 FEP 191 (5th Cir. 1976) (NLRB may properly consider union discrimination in certification proceedings or when asserted as an affirmative defense in refusal-to-bargain proceeding; however, a prima facie showing is a prerequisite to a hearing on the issue); NLRB v. Bancroft Mfg. Co., 516 F.2d 436, 446–47, 10 FEP 1429 (5th Cir. 1975) (employer was not entitled to have its subpoena of union statistical data enforced in a refusal-to-bargain proceeding absent a prima facie showing of union discrimination; employer's allegations of discrimination

C. Challenges to Certification

The NLRB has considered several times whether a discriminatory union may obtain or retain Board certification. In *Independent Metal Workers Union Locals Nos. 1 & 2 (Hughes Tool Co.)*,[33] a union effectively divided its bargaining unit in two and secured the company's consent to segregate by race certain plant jobs. When an African-American employee sought to bid on "white" jobs, the company, following the labor contract, selected others. The employee sought to grieve the matter, but the union declined to do so. The NLRB held that the union committed an unfair labor practice by refusing to process the grievance,[34] and wrote in strong dictum that the negotiation of a discriminatory contract was an independent unfair labor practice.[35] The NLRB rescinded the certification of the offending union, on the dual grounds of (1) "execut[ing] contracts based on race and administer[ing] the contracts so as to perpetuate racial discrimination in employment,"[36] and (2) "discriminat[ing] on the basis of race in determining eligibility for full and equal membership, and segregat[ing] their members on the basis of race."[37]

Although the NLRB has reiterated its willingness to rescind the certification of a union that discriminates,[38] in practice it rarely has taken this action. Indeed, to the extent such an action was taken in the context of a supposedly non-adversarial representation proceeding, for which no direct judicial review exists, a serious procedural due process question could be presented.[39]

---

in union's sister locals was insufficient); *In re* Bel Air Chateau Hosp., 611 F.2d 1248, 1253, 104 LRRM 2976 (9th Cir. 1979) (affirming NLRB's refusal to enforce employer's request to subpoena documents concerning possible discrimination by union; there was no proffer of specific evidence constituting a prima facie showing of discrimination).

[33] 147 NLRB 1573, 56 LRRM 1289 (1964).

[34] 147 NLRB at 1574.

[35] *Id.*

[36] *Id.* at 1577.

[37] *Id.*

[38] *See, e.g.*, Bell & Howell Co., 230 NLRB 420, 423, 95 LRRM 1333 (1977) (NLRB may revoke certification in § 8(b) proceeding), *enforced*, 598 F.2d 136, 18 FEP 1204 (D.C. Cir. 1979).

[39] *Hughes Tool* arose in a dual posture case (unfair labor practice complaint and representation case) and, therefore, was in fact an adversary proceeding reviewable by an appellate court as provided by § 10(f) of the NLRA, 29 U.S.C. § 160(f).

Constitutional considerations formed the basis for the NLRB's short-lived 1974 holding in *Bekins Moving & Storage Co.*[40] In *Bekins*, the Board concluded that it lacked the constitutional power to certify a discriminatory union. Thus, it held that if objections to a union-won election are filed alleging that the union engaged in unlawful discrimination, the NLRB would conduct a pre-certification inquiry and would not certify the union if it found the allegations to be true.[41]

In *Handy Andy, Inc.*,[42] the NLRB overruled *Bekins* and announced that it would no longer consider evidence of union discrimination before certifying a union:

> We now conclude that the policies of the Act are better effectuated by considering allegations that a labor organization practices invidious discrimination in appropriate unfair labor practice rather than representation proceedings. Accordingly, . . . the *Bekins* decision is overruled.[43]

The NLRB further concluded in *Handy Andy* that it is not constitutionally required to consider evidence of discrimination during the certification process and that the NLRA does not authorize it to withhold certification of a labor organization duly selected by a majority of the unit employees.

The NLRB's present rule and its rationale are stated in *Bell & Howell Co.*[44] In that case, an employer refused to bargain with a newly certified union. The company sought to justify its refusal by alleging that the union discriminated against women in benefit plans, membership requirements, and certain job opportunities. The

---

[40]211 NLRB 138, 86 LRRM 1323 (1974), *overruled by* Handy Andy, Inc., 228 NLRB 447, 94 LRRM 1354, *supplemented*, 94 LRRM 1554 (1977).

[41]*Bekins*, 211 NLRB at 141.

[42]228 NLRB 447, 94 LRRM 1354, *supplemented*, 94 LRRM 1554 (1977).

[43]228 NLRB at 448. Notwithstanding the NLRB's pronouncements, several courts of appeals have opined that the *Handy Andy* rule does not completely foreclose denial of union certification because of discrimination. *See, e.g.*, Skyline Corp. v. NLRB, 613 F.2d 138, 1335 n.4, 103 LRRM 3003 (5th Cir. 1980) (citing, inter alia, *Mansion House*; denial of union certification upon proof of union discrimination is not completely foreclosed); Bell & Howell Co. v. NLRB, 598 F.2d 136, 150 n.46, 18 FEP 1204 (D.C. Cir. 1979) (court left open the question of whether union's constitution or bylaws, or explicit conduct that establishes that union will engage in discrimination, requires pre-certification inquiry); Natter Mfg. Corp. v. NLRB, 580 F.2d 948, 951–52 n.2, 99 LRRM 2963 (9th Cir. 1978) (correctness of Board's *Handy Andy* rule remains an open question).

[44]230 NLRB 420, 95 LRRM 1333 (1977).

NLRB found that the employer's refusal constituted a § 8(a)(5) violation. In doing so, the NLRB noted that it was not condoning the alleged discrimination. It held, however, that even if the discrimination allegations were true, it was preferable that employees follow the "statutorily prescribed method of redress designed to permit elimination of the offending practices while preserving the collective-bargaining relationship."[45] The NLRB reaffirmed the rule in *Hughes Tool* that a certification could be *revoked* if discrimination persisted,[46] but it did not directly confront the resulting anomaly: that discrimination could be enough to warrant revocation of certification at a later time, but not enough to justify denying certification *in the first place*. Thus, the NLRB held that, in general, discrimination should be "dealt with in a statutorily prescribed way by employees whose rights are infringed,"[47] rather than by permitting the employer to avoid honoring its collective bargaining responsibilities.

Despite *Bell & Howell*, the NLRB has indicated that it will continue to consider evidence of union discrimination when the discrimination manifests itself in a way that jeopardizes the fairness of the election process.[48] Thus, clear union discrimination, coupled with irrelevant and inflammatory appeals to prejudice directed to employees, if significant enough to affect the fairness of the election, may be a basis for setting aside election results.[49]

---

[45]*Id.* at 421. The NLRB identified the mechanisms by which discrimination could be attacked under the NLRA, Title VII, and otherwise. *Id.* at 422 n.19.

[46]*Id.* at 423 & n.20.

[47]*Id.* at 422 & n.19.

[48]*See* Handy Andy, 228 NLRB 447, 454, 94 LRRM 1354, *supplemented*, 94 LRRM 1554 (1977).

[49]*Id.*; *see* YKK (U.S.A.), 269 NLRB 82, 84, 115 LRRM 1186 (1984) (relying on Sewell Mfg. Co., 138 NLRB 66, 72, 50 LRRM 1532 (1962)); *see also* NLRB v. Silverman's Men's Wear, 656 F.2d 53, 59 & n.11, 26 FEP 876 (3d Cir. 1981) (per curiam) (union appeals to racial prejudice on matters unrelated to election issues destroyed prerequisite "laboratory conditions" for a fair election). Refusal to certify when there are serious flaws in the electoral process is consistent with the primary purpose of the electoral machinery established by § 9, namely, to determine the true wishes of a majority of the unit. *See* NLRB v. A.J. Tower Co., 329 U.S. 324, 330–31, 19 LRRM 2128 (1946) (decided under the Wagner Act). Nevertheless, the cases permitting and denying certification when discrimination allegations are made are not easily harmonized. *Compare* KI (U.S.A.) Corp. v. NLRB, 35 F.3d 256, 258–60, 147 LRRM 2275 (6th Cir. 1994) (applying standard established by NLRB in *Sewell Mfg. Co.*, 140 NLRB 220, 51 LRRM 1611 (1962), Sixth Circuit sustained objection of employer, a wholly owned subsidiary of a Japanese corporation,

based on union's distribution of literature on day before the election in which Japanese businessman with no connection to employer expressed "very negative views regarding American workers"), Zartic, Inc., 315 NLRB 495, 497–98, 147 LRRM 1201 (1994) (election set aside based on union's sustained and inflammatory appeal to ethnic sensibilities of employer's Hispanic employees) *and* NLRB v. Eurodrive, Inc., 724 F.2d 556, 558–59, 33 FEP 1361 (6th Cir. 1984) (relying upon *Sewell*, denying enforcement where union representative, shortly before a representation election, made racial statements that had exacerbated racial tensions and interfered with employees' freedom of choice) *with* NLRB v. Foundry Div., 260 F.3d 631, 635–37, 86 FEP 661 (6th Cir. 2001) (African-American employee's use of racial epithet in addressing another African-American employee did not constitute improper appeal by union proponent to racial prejudice, and thus did not warrant overturning of election), Pacific Micronesia Corp., 326 NLRB 458, 458, 164 LRRM 1225 (1998) (supervisor's statements not objectionable absent evidence that statements were disseminated to voters), Shepherd Tissue, Inc., 326 NLRB 369, 159 LRRM 1253 (1998) (Gould, C., concurring) (campaigning that takes race into account is not *per se* objectionable), Catherine's, Inc., 316 NLRB 186, 189–90, 148 LRRM 1181 (1995) (no interference when union representative told employees that employer's law firm was Jewish firm, and that Jews "would fight you hard, but when you beat them, they would sit down and negotiate a contract with you"; statements "were isolated and lacked inflammatory appeal") *and* NLRB v. Utell Int'l, 750 F.2d 177, 179, 36 FEP 897 (2d Cir. 1984) (distinguishing *Eurodrive* and enforcing NLRB order; racial statements made by employees were not deliberately inflammatory).

For cases decided in favor of the union, see NLRB v. Chicago Tribune Co., 943 F.2d 791, 798, 138 LRRM 2510 (7th Cir. 1991) (charges of union racial discrimination were no defense to refusal to bargain unless related to unfairness of election itself); DID Building Servs. v. NLRB, 915 F.2d 490, 498–500, 53 FEP 1844 (9th Cir. 1990) (union member's "reprehensible" and "vile" anti-Semitic remarks, under totality of the circumstances, did not taint election where member was not an agent of union); Tony Scott Trucking v. NLRB, 821 F.2d 312, 315–16, 125 LRRM 2910 (6th Cir. 1987) (per curiam) (enforcing the NLRB's order, despite racial slurs and threats invoking Ku Klux Klan against employee who refused to sign authorization card, where employer failed to produce evidence that any employee was affected by the alleged threats or that the outcome of the election was affected); Del Rey Tortilleria, 272 NLRB 1106, 1115, 117 LRRM 1449 (1984) (union organizer did not inject inflammatory ethnic or racial issues into election campaign by making statements that employer tipped off immigration authorities about undocumented aliens at its plants; statement was opinion and "arguable comment" on a public event), *enforced*, 787 F.2d 1118, 122 LRRM 2111 (7th Cir. 1986); Vitek Elecs., 268 NLRB 522, 527–28, 115 LRRM 1075 (1984) (union did not interfere with election when prounion African-American employee made derogatory racial remarks to antiunion African-American employee in presence of others, since such conduct was not intended to inflame racial feelings of employees; African-American union representative's letter did not intimidate employees or appeal to racial prejudice, and therefore did not interfere with the election), *enforced in relevant part*, 763 F.2d 561, 119 LRRM 2699 (3d Cir. 1985); NLRB v. Carl Weissman & Sons, 849 F.2d 449, 450–52, 128 LRRM 2756 (9th Cir. 1988) (per curiam) (no abuse of discretion in NLRB's scheduling rerun election 67 days after union official's anti-Semitic remark that was basis for overturning the first election); Arlington Hotel Co. v. NLRB, 712 F.2d 333, 338, 113 LRRM 3381 (8th Cir. 1983) (remarks having racial overtones did not impermissibly inject race into representative election campaign).

For cases decided in favor of the employer, see M & M Supermkts., Inc. v. NLRB, 818 F.2d 1567, 1573–74, 125 LRRM 2918 (11th Cir. 1987) (denying enforcement

Courts will not overturn the NLRB's decision to certify a bargaining unit where such references are demonstrably relevant and accurate, or did not constitute an inflammatory appeal to prejudices or create an atmosphere where a reasoned election choice was impossible.[50] When pre-election statements referencing race or other protected classifications are made by employees, but cannot be attributed to the union, election results will not be overturned unless the rumor so inflamed and tainted the atmosphere in which the election was held as to make a reasoned choice impossible.[51]

D. Remedies for Breach of the Duty of Fair Representation

The concept of the union's duty of fair representation was created initially to combat racial discrimination by labor unions.[52] Union liability to a member who is not also an employee of the union is limited to instances where it fails to discharge its duty of fair

---

due to anti-Semitic and racial remarks by an employee to 3 out of 17 employees in the bargaining unit, even though remarks were not attributable to the union); NLRB v. Katz, 701 F.2d 703, 705–06, 31 FEP 319 (7th Cir. 1983) (Catholic priest made remarks at union meeting about employer being Jewish and rich while employees were poor; other ethnic and religious references also were made during the campaign).

[50]See Family Serv. Agency S.F. v. NLRB, 163 F.3d 1369, 1377–79, 78 FEP 1453 (D.C. Cir. 1999) (affirming NLRB certification where union's comments to the press regarding employer's "English-only" policy, were reasonably accurate descriptions of workplace and not calculated to spark racial prejudice or drive wedge between African-American and Latino co-workers); Clearwater Transp., Inc. v. NLRB, 133 F.3d 1004, 1007–09, 157 LRRM 2281 (7th Cir. 1998) (alleged anti-Semitic remark made by third party and not by either employer or union, or their respective agents, did not render results of union representation election invalid where improper remarks did not create such an atmosphere of fear and reprisal that rational, uncoerced selection of bargaining representative was made impossible); Case Farms of N.C., Inc. v. NLRB, 128 F.3d 841, 844–49, 75 FEP 140 (4th Cir. 1997) (specifically distinguishing Zartic Inc., 315 NLRB 495, 147 LRRM 1201 (1994), and holding that union flyer accusing employer of firing Amish workers because Latinos could be paid less and treated worse did not constitute inflammatory appeal to racial or ethnic prejudices and did not create condition that made reasoned election choice impossible).

[51]See Cross Pointe Paper Corp., 330 NLRB 658, 659–60 (2000) (refusing to set aside election based on election day rumor that company's director of operations hoped that the "f-ing Mexicans" voted against the union, where there was no evidence that union was responsible for rumor and alleged remark was not "inflammatory"); see also NLRB v. Flambeau Airmold Corp., 178 F.3d 705, 707–08, 79 FEP 1517 (4th Cir. 1999) (although 94–92 vote in favor of union may have been affected by a rumor that racial epithets were used at a supervisors' meeting, NLRB's certification of the election upheld because the rumors could not be attributed to the union and did not so inflame racial tensions as to make a reasoned choice impossible).

[52]See Steele v. Louisville & Nashville R.R., 323 U.S. 192, 9 FEP 381 (1944).

representation.[53] A union violates its duty of fair representation when it engages in "invidious" discrimination.[54] "Discrimination is invidious if it is based upon impermissible or immutable classifications such as race or other constitutionally protected categories, or arises from prejudice or animus."[55] The union's duty of fair representation, however, extends only to the bargaining units it represents.[56]

Most courts hold that the union has no affirmative duty to prevent or remedy known discrimination when not presented with a discrimination grievance.[57] The failure to process a discrimination

---

[53]*See* Mack v. Otis Elevator Co., 326 F.3d 116, 129, 91 FEP Cases 1009 (2d Cir.) ("To establish a breach of duty of fair representation the union's conduct must, first, have been arbitrary, discriminatory or in bad faith, and second, it must have seriously undermined the arbitral process."), *cert. denied*, 540 U.S. 1017 (2003); *see also* Cooper v. Chemical Workers Local 143C, 106 F. Supp. 2d 479 (S.D.N.Y. 2000) (Title VII provides proper foundation for a duty of fair representation lawsuit where a plaintiff alleges the union failed to assist in processing a grievance concerning the employer's underlying discrimination and/or where the underlying grievance does not involve actionable discrimination, but the union itself acted discriminatorily in failing to prosecute the grievance). A union's refusal to process a discrimination grievance based upon a good-faith belief that the grievance lacks merit, however, is not a violation of the duty of fair representation. *See, e.g.*, Greenslade v. Chicago Newspaper Guild, 112 F.3d 853 (7th Cir. 1997) (union did not violate duty when it decided not to pursue sex discrimination grievance after investigation); Eichelberger v. NLRB, 765 F.2d 851 (9th Cir. 1985) (enforcing NLRB finding that union's refusal to arbitrate grievance that, in part, protested sexual harassment was not arbitrary and did not violate duty); Bowe v. Pulitzer Publ'g Co., 646 F.2d 1281, 1283 (8th Cir. 1981) ("Where a union determines, in good faith, that a particular grievance lacks merit, it does not breach its duty of fair representation when it fails to take that grievance to arbitration."); Teamsters Local 307, 238 NLRB 1450 (1978) (union's decision not to pursue grievance protesting quid pro quo sexual harassment was not arbitrary).

[54]*See, e.g.*, Jeffreys v. Communications Workers, 354 F.3d 270, 276 (4th Cir. 2003) (duty of fair representation prohibits only "invidious" discrimination such as discrimination based on race or gender or arising "from animus or prejudice"); *see also* Air Line Pilots Ass'n Int'l v. O'Neill, 499 U.S. 65, 81 (1991) (same); Considine v. Newspaper Agency Corp., 43 F.3d 1349, 1359 (10th Cir. 1994) (same). *But see* Simo v. Union of Needletrades, Industrial & Textile Employees, Sw. Dist. Council, 322 F.3d 602, 638 (9th Cir. 2003) (suggesting that the holdings in *O'Neill* and *Considine* are too narrow).

[55]Cooper v. TWA Airlines, 274 F. Supp. 2d 231, 243 (E.D.N.Y. 2003) (citing *Considine*, 43 F.3d 1349, 1359–60); *see also Jeffreys*, 354 F.3d at 276 (a union's choice between competing contract interpretations that benefits and disadvantages competing groups of employees is not discriminatory, absent ill will or improper motive).

[56]Bensel v. Allied Pilots Ass'n, 2004 U.S. App. LEXIS 22262, at *36 (3d Cir. Oct. 26, 2004), *cert. denied*, 544 U.S. 1018 (2005).

[57]*See, e.g.*, EEOC v. Pipefitters Ass'n Local 597, 334 F.3d 656, 659–60 (7th Cir. 2003) ("we reject the EEOC's contention that unions have an affirmative duty

grievance when the union knows discrimination exists, however, violates the duty of fair representation.[58]

It is well settled that the NLRB may find a § 8(b)(1)(A), § 8(b)(2), or § 8(b)(3) violation arising out of a union's discriminatory practices toward its members. In *Rubber Workers Local 12 v. NLRB*,[59] the Fifth Circuit considered what remedies were available against a union that declined on the basis of race to process grievances. The court had little difficulty enforcing a Board order finding violations of § 8(b)(1)(A), § 8(b)(2), and § 8(b)(3). Similarly, in *Glass Bottle Blowers Ass'n (Owens-Illinois, Inc.)*,[60] the maintenance of male and female locals, which represented the same bargaining unit and that processed grievances separately, was held to violate § 8(b)(1)(A). Cases after *Rubber Workers* have established that discrimination

---

to prevent racial harassment or other forms of unlawful discrimination in the workplace," although selective inaction or failure to process a discrimination grievance when requested may be unlawful); Thorn v. Transit Union, 305 F. 826, 832–33, 89 FEP 1783 (8th Cir. 2002) (unions are prohibited from causing or assisting unlawful discrimination by an employer; but have no affirmative duty to investigate and take steps to remedy employer discrimination); *Mack*, 326 F.3d at 129 (no violation of duty of fair representation because, although the plaintiff complained to a steward about racial and sexual harassment, she neither filed a grievance nor requested that the steward do so on her behalf); York v. AT&T, 95 F.3d 948, 955–57 (10th Cir. 1996) (mere inaction insufficient—must prove union knowledge that prohibited discrimination may have occurred and decision not to assert the discrimination claim); Anspach v. Tompkins Indus., 51 F.3d 285 (10th Cir. 1995) (union not vicariously liable whenever employer liable); Martin v. Local 1513, 859 F.2d 581, 51 FEP 1802 (8th Cir. 1988) (union not liable for mere acquiescence, including failure to bargain about alleged employer sex discrimination). In *Goodman v. Lukens Steel Co.*, 482 U.S. 656 (1987), the Supreme Court expressly declined to address whether "mere union passivity in the face of employer [race] discrimination renders the union liable under Title VII." *Id.* at 665–66. (case against the union "was much stronger than one of mere acquiescence").

[58]*See Goodman*, 482 U.S. at 665–67 (1987) (union liable under Title VII, even if its leaders were pro-minority, for intentionally refusing to file or process race discrimination and harassment grievances it knew were meritorious, whether in order not to antagonize the employer or in deference to its white membership); *see also* Marquart v. Machinists Lodge 837, 26 F.3d 842, 851 (8th Cir. 1994) (union may be liable for failing to process meritorious complaints of sexual harassment); Woods v. Graphic Commc'ns, 925 F.2d 1195, 1201 (9th Cir. 1991) (union violated duty of fair representation when it intentionally failed to file grievance protesting known racial harassment because of concern for implicating white members).

[59]368 F.2d 12, 23–24, 9 FEP 294 (5th Cir. 1966).

[60]210 NLRB 943, 948, 86 LRRM 1257 (1974), *enforced*, 520 F.2d 693, 10 FEP 1426 (6th Cir. 1975).

based on race,[61] sex,[62] age,[63] alienage,[64] religion,[65] or disability[66] violates the duty of fair representation. Duty of fair representation lawsuits, as the *Rubber Workers* court recognized, may be asserted in state or federal court under § 301 of the Labor Management Relations Act.[67]

---

[61]*See, e.g., Woods*, 925 F.2d 1195, 136 LRRM 2660, 2665 ("Racial discrimination in grievance processing constitutes primary violation of the duty.").

[62]*See, e.g.*, Farmer v. ARA Servs., 660 F.2d 1096 (6th Cir. 1981) (union breached duty of fair representation when it negotiated contractual job class certification system that perpetual sex discriminatory job assignments); Bell & Howell Co., 230 NLRB 420, 423, 95 LRRM 1333 (1977) (duty of fair representation includes duty not to discriminate based on sex; dictum), *enforced*, 598 F.2d 136, 18 FEP 1204 (D.C. Cir. 1979); Peterson v. Rath Packing Co., 461 F.2d 312, 316, 9 FEP 1054 (8th Cir. 1972) (sustaining finding that union breached duty of fair representation when it refused to process female employees' grievance challenging company's refusal to transfer them to jobs in a category established for male employees); Farmer v. Hotel Workers Local 1064, 21 FEP 1599, 1617–21 (E.D. Mich. 1978) (action for violation of duty of fair representation under § 301 of the LMRA, 29 U.S.C. § 185, based on union's negotiation of and agreement to collective bargaining agreements that discriminate against female employees in wages, promotions, transfers, and seniority); *see also* Auto Workers Local 122 (Chrysler Corp.), 247 NLRB 400, 401–02, 103 LRRM 1170 (1980) (although a union's sexual harassment may violate § 8(b)(1)(A), the allegation was not proved in the instant case).

[63]*See* Graphic Commc'ns Local 51, 240 NLRB 25, 27–28, 100 LRRM 1225 (1979) (union acquiescence in employer age discrimination would violate its duty of fair representation; however, evidence in the instant case failed to establish that the union did so); *cf.* EEOC v. Air Line Pilots, 489 F. Supp. 1003, 1009–10, 22 FEP 1609 (D. Minn. 1980) (union that agreed to contract provision that violated Age Discrimination in Employment Act held jointly liable with the employer for damages), *rev'd on other grounds*, 661 F.2d 90, 26 FEP 1615 (8th Cir. 1981).

[64]Actors' Equity, 247 NLRB 1193, 1196, 103 LRRM 1494 (1980) (union violated § 8(b)(2) by maintaining and enforcing disparate dues structure against nonresident alien members working under union security agreement), *enforced*, 644 F.2d 939, 106 LRRM 2817 (2d Cir. 1981).

[65]*Cf.* Beam v. General Motors Corp., 21 FEP 85, 88 (N.D. Ohio 1979) (union did not breach its duty of fair representation in failing to process employees' grievances alleging failure of the employer to accommodate their religious beliefs, since the union did not act arbitrarily or in bad faith).

[66]NLRB Memorandum on Collective Bargaining and ADA, *reprinted in* ADA MAN. (BNA) 70:1021, 701:1023 (Sept. 1992). This includes union discrimination based on disability, perceived disability, or a record of a disability. 42 U.S.C. § 12101 et seq. *See generally* Chapter 13 (Disability). Controversies, however, may arise where a union declines to sacrifice contractual rights or procedures—typically, seniority preferences—in response to a demand for reasonable accommodation by an applicant or employee. The union, however, is not required to grant an accommodation request that would violate the collective bargaining agreement. *See* U.S. Airways, Inc. v. Barnett, 535 U.S. 391, 12 AD 1729 (2002).

[67]29 U.S.C. § 185 (2004). The federal courts have concurrent jurisdiction with the NLRB under § 301 even if the claim of breach of duty of fair representation might also be characterized as an unfair labor practice over which, as the Supreme Court ruled in *San Diego Building Trades Council v. Garmon*, 359 U.S. 236, 245,

E. Union Opposition to Employer Efforts to Remedy Discrimination

A union's opposition to an employer's efforts to eliminate discrimination may constitute an unfair labor practice. Thus, where a labor agreement contained a departmental seniority system that had its genesis in racial discrimination, which perpetuated the effects of past discrimination, and the union refused to accede to employer proposals designed to end such effects, the employer might be able to obtain NLRA relief.[68]

An employer's efforts to accommodate employees with disabilities may conflict with the provisions in a labor agreement. A union's attempt to enforce provisions that inhibit accommodating disabilities may expose the union to charges of discrimination or breach of the duty of fair representation. Further, a union's refusal to bargain with an employer over a proposed accommodation may result in a § 8(b)(3) charge.[69] However, the duty to accommodate does not require a union to acquiesce in a violation of a collective bargaining agreement.[70]

III. EMPLOYER DISCRIMINATION

A. Overview

The NLRB has been reluctant to find NLRA authority for remedying employer discrimination based on race, color, religion,

---

43 LRRM 2838 (1959), the NLRB has exclusive jurisdiction. *See* Breininger v. Sheet Metal Workers, 493 U.S. 67, 80–84, 132 LRRM 3001 (1989) (discrimination charge based on hiring hall practices was cognizable in federal court, even though the alleged violation also would be an unfair labor practice in violation of §§ 8(b)(2) or (3)). *See generally* Chapter 22 (Unions).

[68]*See* Quarterly Report of NLRB General Counsel for Third Quarter 1974, DAILY LABOR REP. (BNA) at D-1, D-7 (Jan. 31, 1975) (union's refusal of an employer's offer to rectify past discrimination violates § 8(b)(1)(A)); *see also* Graphic Arts v. NLRB, 596 F.2d 904, 911–12, 101 LRRM 2664 (9th Cir. 1979) (a party cannot lawfully demand an illegal contractual provision). *See generally* Chapter 17 (Seniority).

[69]NLRB Memorandum on Collective Bargaining and ADA (Sept. 1992), *reprinted in* ADA MAN. (BNA) 70:1021. Of course, the union's duty to bargain does not require that the union agree to whatever accommodation is proposed by the employer, any more than its duty of fair representation requires that it strike in order to obtain whatever accommodation is sought by the employee, and a union may itself seek relief under the Act on the grounds that the employer has not satisfied its own bargaining obligations regarding proposed accommodations.

[70]*See* U.S. Airways, Inc. v. Barnett, 535 U.S. 391, 12 AD 1729 (2002).

sex, or national origin. In *Packinghouse Workers v. NLRB*,[71] however, the District of Columbia Circuit held that "a policy and practice of discrimination [by an employer] against its employees on account of their race or national origin . . . violates Section 8(a)(1) of the Act."[72] Finding that the legislative history indicated that Title VII was not intended to oust the NLRB's jurisdiction,[73] and observing that there exist numerous instances where courts had held that a union's discrimination violated the NLRA, the court concluded that "[n]o reason appears why employer discrimination is exempted from Board scrutiny."[74] Indeed, the court said, racial or national origin discrimination inherently interferes with § 7 rights because it creates a clash of interests between groups of workers, reducing their effectiveness in working together, and because it engenders apathy in the victims of discrimination.[75]

In 1973, in *Jubilee Manufacturing*, the NLRB rejected the *Packinghouse* rationale, explaining its reasons for viewing race, religion, and sex discrimination by employers, standing alone, as beyond the reach of the NLRA.[76] It was alleged in *Jubilee* that the employer granted wage increases to males on the basis of sex, and insisted to the point of impasse on a contractual provision that permitted the employer to grant unilateral wage increases. The NLRB focused on the specific allegations: violations of § 8(a)(1) (general interference with § 7 rights), § 8(a)(3) (discrimination based on concerted activity), and § 8(a)(5) (refusal to bargain in good faith). The NLRB held:

> [D]iscrimination based on race, color, religion, sex, or national origin, standing alone, . . . is not "inherently destructive" of employees' Section 7 rights and therefore is not violative of Section 8(a)(1) and (3) of the Act. There must be actual evidence, as opposed to

---

[71]416 F.2d 1126, 9 FEP 317 (D.C. Cir. 1969).

[72]*Id.* at 1130.

[73]*Id.* at 1133 n.11.

[74]*Id.* at 1135.

[75]*Id.* On remand, however, the NLRB found no discrimination despite evidence that only 12–15% of the workforce was white; whites held all supervisory positions and 85% of the highest-paying jobs.

[76]Jubilee Mfg. Co., 202 NLRB 272, 82 LRRM 1482 (1973), *enforced mem. sub nom.* Steelworkers v. NLRB, 504 F.2d 71, 87 LRRM 3168 (D.C. Cir. 1974). Many collective bargaining agreements themselves prohibit discrimination. Employees covered by such contracts may challenge discriminatory conduct by employers in violation of the provisions of the agreement via grievances pursued through their union representatives, or under § 301 of the Labor Management Relations Act, 29 U.S.C. § 185. *See* Woods v. Dunlop Tire Corp., 972 F.2d 36, 37, 59 FEP 887 (2d Cir. 1992).

speculation, of a nexus between the alleged discriminatory conduct and the interference with, or restraint of, employees in the exercise of those rights . . . .[77]

The *Jubilee* Board noted, however, that discrimination in some circumstances could be the basis for an NLRA violation: "Appeals to racial prejudice" during an election campaign may be a basis for setting aside the election under § 8(a)(1);[78] employees who band together to protest discrimination thereby engage in protected concerted activity and are protected under § 8(a)(1) and § 8(a)(3);[79] an employer that refuses to bargain over the elimination of a discriminatory contract provision violates § 8(a)(5);[80] and the discharge of women, in an effort to frustrate or even moot a union's campaign to negotiate better working standards for them, violates § 8(a)(3).[81] As none of those things were found in *Jubilee*, the Board held that, "standing alone," employer discrimination did not violate the NLRA.[82]

An employer may not differentiate in its treatment of employee groups not recognized or certified under the NLRA. In *Black Grievance Committee v. NLRB*,[83] an employer refused to grant to an African-American-dominated minority union the same grievance-procedure privileges accorded a larger independent union that also had not been formally recognized or certified. The Third Circuit set aside the NLRB's order dismissing an unfair labor practice complaint, which had been based on the distinction between different treatment of the two organizations as opposed to disparate treatment on the basis of race:

> We are not holding that an employer violates section 8(a)(1) merely when it refuses to listen to or accord special status to the grievances

---

[77]202 NLRB at 272. The Board found factually unsupported the District of Columbia Circuit's conclusions that discrimination inevitably created a "clash of interests between groups of workers" that inevitably frustrated concerted action, and "apathy or docility which inhibits" the assertion of legal rights. *Id.*

[78]*Id.* at 273.

[79]*Id.*

[80]*Id.*

[81]Jubilee Mfg. Co., 202 NLRB 272, 273, 82 LRRM 1482 (1973), *enforced mem. sub nom.* Steelworkers v. NLRB, 504 F.2d 71, 87 LRRM 3168 (D.C. Cir. 1974).

[82]*Id.* at 273. The union filed for review of the Board's *Jubilee* decision in the District of Columbia Circuit—the court that had decided *United Packinghouse*. Even though the court's reasoning in *United Packinghouse* was specifically repudiated in *Jubilee*, the court affirmed *Jubilee* without opinion. *See* Steelworkers v. NLRB, 504 F.2d 271, 87 LRRM 3168 (D.C. Cir. 1974). The NLRB has not opined on extending *Jubilee* to ADA and ADEA allegations.

[83]749 F.2d 1072, 36 FEP 787 (3d Cir. 1984).

of a minority labor organization, even if that refusal will affect the ability of that organization to attract members. Rather, we are holding that when an employer accords one non-majority employee group privileged status over another non-majority group, and thus encourages membership in the former while discouraging it in the latter, he unlawfully interferes with the section 7 rights of employees to band together in the group of their choice, even though neither organization seeks section 9(a) exclusive representative status.[84]

Courts have consistently held that Title VII and the NLRA offer overlapping remedies for retaliation claims. In *Pelech v. Klaff-Joss, LP*,[85] the court held that a plaintiff's Title VII claim of retaliatory discharge and on-going retaliation was not preempted by §§ 7 and 8 of the NLRA. The court observed that the preemption doctrine articulated in *San Diego Building Trades Council v. Garmon*[86] is intended to guard against conflicts between state and federal systems for regulating labor activity. "Not only is [this] danger not presented by Title VII claims," the *Pelech* court observed, "but *Garmon* has never been applied to preempt the hearing of a federal, as opposed to a state, claim."[87] Although courts protect the NLRB's jurisdiction over labor disputes, Congress has clearly mandated that federal courts have jurisdiction to decide employment discrimination cases. Thus, Title VII and the NLRA offer some concurrent remedies.

Overlapping remedies also exist between disability discrimination claims and the NLRA. In *Smith v. National Steel & Shipbuilding Co.*,[88] the Ninth Circuit held that the *Garmon* preemption doctrine was inapplicable to the plaintiffs' claims that their former employer's layoff policy violated the ADA, because the conflict presented was between two federal statutes:

> Just as federal courts are ill-equipped to displace the role of the NLRB, the NLRB is not suited to balance the competing federal interests presented by these two statutes. To permit the NLRB to decide claims in which an employer's reasonable accommodation may violate the NLRA would leave the interpretation of the ADA to the NLRB. This judicial function certainly exceeds that agency's expertise and authority.[89]

---

[84]*Id.* at 1077.
[85]828 F. Supp. 525, 65 FEP 1011 (N.D. Ill. 1993).
[86]359 U.S. 236, 43 LRRM 2838 (1959).
[87]*Pelech*, 828 F. Supp. at 530.
[88]125 F.3d 751, 754–57, 156 LRRM 2257 (9th Cir. 1997).
[89]125 F.3d at 757.

Likewise, a plaintiff's claims under the ADA will not preempt the provisions of a collective bargaining agreement entered into under the authority of the NLRA.[90] Numerous federal courts have held that an employee's proposed accommodation pursuant to the ADA is per se unreasonable if it squarely conflicts with a bona fide seniority system under a collective bargaining agreement.[91] The EEOC, however, saw the issue differently. In its 1999 "Enforcement Guidance: Reasonable Accommodation and Undue Hardship Under the Americans with Disabilities Act," the EEOC rejected the position that a reasonable accommodation imposes an undue hardship simply because it violates a collective bargaining agreement (CBA), and asserted that in such circumstances the employer and union might be required to negotiate a variance to the CBA.[92] Following the U.S. Supreme Court's decision in *U.S. Airways, Inc. v. Barrett*,[93] however, the EEOC modified that enforcement guidance, which now provides

> Generally, it will be "unreasonable" to reassign an employee with a disability if doing so would violate the rule of a seniority system. . . . Seniority systems governing job placement give employees

---

[90]*See* Willis v. Pacific Maritime Ass'n, 244 F.3d 675, 680–81, 11 AD 1046 (9th Cir. 2001) (accommodation contrary to the seniority rights of other employees as set forth in collective bargaining agreement, would be unreasonable *per se*); *cf.* U.S. Airways, Inc. v. Barnett, 535 U.S. 391, 12 AD 1729 (2002) (normally, even seniority rights not founded in a collective bargaining agreement may not be ignored in providing reasonable accommodation).

[91]*See Willis*, 244 F.3d at 677; Davis v. Florida Power & Light Co., 205 F.3d 1301, 1307, 10 AD 492 (11th Cir. 2000) (enactment of ADA showed no intent to alter the special status afforded collectively bargained seniority rights); Feliciano v. Rhode Island, 160 F.3d 780, 787, 8 AD 1520 (1st Cir. 1998) (failure to reassign employee in violation of collectively bargained seniority rights of another employee does not violate ADA); Aldrich v. Boeing Co., 146 F.3d 1265, 1271 n.5, 8 AD 424 (10th Cir. 1998) (ADA does not require transfer in contravention of seniority provisions of collective bargaining agreement); Kralik v. Durbin, 130 F.3d 76, 83, 7 AD 1040 (3d Cir. 1997) ("an accommodation to one employee which violates the seniority rights of other employees in a collective bargaining agreement simply is not reasonable"); Foreman v. Babcock & Wilcox Co., 117 F.3d 800, 810, 7 AD 331 (5th Cir. 1997) (ADA does not require employer to make accommodation that impinges on rights granted to other employees under collective bargaining agreement); Eckles v. Consolidated Rail Corp., 94 F.3d 1041, 1051, 5 AD 1367 (7th Cir. 1996) ("[T]he ADA does not require disabled individuals to be accommodated by sacrificing the collectively bargained, bona fide seniority rights of other employees."); *cf. Barnett*, 535 U.S. 391, 12 AD 1729 (2002) (even seniority rights not founded in collective bargaining agreement may not be ignored in providing reasonable accommodation).

[92]*Enforcement Guidance: Reasonable Accommodation and Undue Hardship Under the Americans with Disabilities Act*, DAILY LAB. REP. (BNA) at E-23 (Mar. 2, 1999).

[93]535 U.S. 391, 12 AD 1729 (2002).

expectations of consistent, uniform treatment[,] expectations that would be undermined if employers had to make the type of individualized, case-by-case assessment required by the reasonable accommodation process.[93a]

B. Concerted Activity Protesting Alleged Discrimination

The NLRB has consistently held that employees who strike in violation of a no-strike agreement lose the protection of § 7.[94] That is, even though employees may be engaged in concerted activity (striking) in order to call their employer's attention to legitimate grievances relating to their wages, hours, and working conditions, such activity is not protected by § 7 if there is a valid, binding, no-strike agreement in effect.[95]

In *The Emporium*,[96] the Board ruled that concerted activity to protest an employer's racial policies was not protected by the NLRA where such activity was prohibited by a no-strike agreement negotiated by the union, the employees' exclusive representative. The District of Columbia Circuit reversed,[97] but the Supreme Court reinstated the Board's holding.[98] The employees argued, among other things, that the public policy against discrimination authorized them to picket and even to strike over their perception of discrimination. The Court held, however:

> This argument confuses the employees' substantive right to be free of racial discrimination with the procedures available under the

[93a]"Enforcement Guidance: Reasonable Accommodation and Undue Hardship Under the Americans with Disabilities Act" (Oct. 17, 2002 revision), *available at* http://www.eeoc.gov/policy/docs/accommodation.html (last visited Mar. 29, 2007).

[94]*See, e.g.*, Joseph Dyson & Sons, Inc., 72 NLRB 445, 446–47, 19 LRRM 1187 (1947); Scullin Steel Co., 65 NLRB 1294, 1317–18, 17 LRRM 286 (1946), *enforced as modified*, 161 F.2d 143, 20 LRRM 2058 (8th Cir. 1947). At least one court has held that such strikes are also not protected by § 704(a) of Title VII. *See* King v. Illinois Bell Tel. Co., 476 F. Supp. 495, 501, 21 FEP 501 (N.D. Ill. 1978).

[95]*But cf.* Mastro Plastics Corp., 103 NLRB 511, 556–59, 31 LRRM 1494 (1953) (strike during term of collective bargaining contract with no-strike clause was protected, since it was in protest of serious unfair labor practices), *enforced*, 214 F.2d 462, 34 LRRM 2484 (2d Cir. 1954), *aff'd*, 350 U.S. 270, 37 LRRM 2587 (1956).

[96]192 NLRB 173, 177, 77 LRRM 1669 (1971).

[97]*See* Western Addition Cmty. Org. v. NLRB, 485 F.2d 917, 926–32, 9 FEP 363 (D.C. Cir. 1973).

[98]*See* Emporium Capwell Co. v. Western Addition Cmty. Org., 420 U.S. 50, 72–73, 9 FEP 195 (1975). The Ninth Circuit had earlier reached a result contrary to the District of Columbia Circuit. NLRB v. Tanner Motor Livery, Ltd., 419 F.2d 216, 221–22, 9 FEP 331 (9th Cir. 1969) (discharge of an employee for picketing to induce additional minority hiring does not violate the NLRA).

NLRA for securing these rights . . . . [T]hey cannot be pursued at the expense of the orderly collective-bargaining process contemplated by the NLRA.[99]

Subsequent decisions of the Board and courts have found protected other, lesser forms of concerted activity, which protest an employer's alleged discrimination. In some circumstances there may be a remedy for retaliation for opposing discrimination, in addition to that provided in § 704 of Title VII. Thus, complaints by one or more employees[100] concerning race[101] and sex[102] discrimination

---

[99]*Emporium Capwell*, 420 U.S. at 69. If it were otherwise, the Court declared, there would be chaos:

> With each group able to enforce its conflicting demands—the incumbent employees by resort to contractual processes and the minority employees by economic coercion—the probability of strife and deadlock is high; the likelihood of making headway against discriminatory practices would be minimal.

Id. at 68–69.

[100]Whether the activities engaged in by *one* employee are protected "concerted" activity has been the subject of much litigation. The employee is now required to demonstrate that the action was authorized by other employees or intended to induce group action. *See* Meyers Indus., 281 NLRB 882, 888–89, 123 LRRM 1137 (1986) (no violation of § 8(a)(1) when discharging employee for reporting unsafe condition because the action was not concerted), *aff'd*, 835 F.2d 1481, 127 LRRM 2415 (D.C. Cir. 1987).

[101]*See, e.g.*, Dearborn Big Boy No. 3, Inc., 328 NLRB No. 92 (1999) (upholding administrative law judge's finding that employee was unlawfully discharged for engaging in protected concerted activity of protesting racial discrimination); Franklin Iron & Metal Corp., 315 NLRB 819, 822–26, 148 LRRM 1246 (1994) (employer violated § 8(a)(1) of Act by retaliating against African-American employees because of their protected concerted activity, which included protesting alleged payment of higher wage rate to white employees who had less seniority and then filing complaints with state FEPC), *enforcement granted*, 83 F.3d 156 (6th Cir. 1996); Continental Pet Techs., 291 NLRB 290, 302, 131 LRRM 1470 (1988) (employer violated §§ 8(a)(1) and (3) by discharging a white employee who had accused African-American shift leaders of brutality and favoring African-American employees); Vought Corp., 273 NLRB 1290, 1291–92, 118 LRRM 1271 (1984) (employer violated §§ 8(a)(1) and (3) when it disciplined employee for spreading a rumor to African-American employees that a white employee might be promoted over an African American and suggesting that they take the issue up at the next meeting between African Americans and management; in communicating the rumor, employee's remarks were related to group action concerning possible racial discrimination), *aff'd*, 788 F.2d 1378, 122 LRRM 2168 (8th Cir. 1986); United States Postal Serv., 245 NLRB 901, 902–03, 102 LRRM 1522 (1979) (employee protests of racial discrimination and contact with EEOC were protected activities).

[102]*See, e.g.*, NLRB v. Magnetics Int'l, 699 F.2d 806, 813, 30 FEP 1524 (6th Cir. 1983) (unfair labor practice to discharge employee for prosecuting sex discrimination action); *cf.* Sioux City Foundry, 241 NLRB 481, 484–86, 100 LRRM 1564 (1979) (discharge of two employees, allegedly because their employment was contrary to employer's policy against hiring strikers, violated § 8(a)(1) where real reason for their discharge was to avoid or defend sex discrimination charges

and sexual harassment[103] by the employer have been held to be protected concerted activity.[104] In *Hollings Press*,[105] the Board qualified this position by holding that in order to constitute concerted activity the pursuit of a sexual harassment claim must be for the purpose of a collective goal.[106] Thus, when the employee in *Hollings Press* induced another employee to testify by threatening to "[hit] her with a subpoena," she was found to be pursuing her own interests rather than the interests of the group.[107] In *Ellison Media Co.*,[108] the Board held that one female employee who had reported sexual harassment to management was engaged in protected activity when she encouraged another employee to report comments he had experienced. The Board distinguished *Hollings Press*, stating that the employee in that case sought help from an employee who "was unconcerned with [her] complaint and uninterested in supporting it."[109] By contrast, the employee in *Ellison Media* sought the help of other employees who also were experiencing sexual harassment.[110]

In *Frank Briscoe, Inc. v. NLRB*,[111] the employer allegedly failed to recall laid-off employees because some of them had filed EEOC

---

threatened by an applicant purportedly rejected because she was then a striker at another company).

[103] *See, e.g.*, NLRB v. Downslope Indus., 676 F.2d 1114, 1119–20, 110 LRRM 2261 (6th Cir. 1982) (violation of § 8(a)(1) for discharge of group of nonsupervisory employees and one supervisor for concerted protest of sexual harassment), *enforcing in part*, 246 NLRB 948, 103 LRRM 1041 (1979); Continental Pet Techs., 291 NLRB 290, 302, 131 LRRM 1470 (1988) (employer violated §§ 8(a)(1) and (3) by discharging white employee who accused African-American shift leaders of sexually harassing white employees). *But cf.* Blaw-Knox Foundry, 247 NLRB 333, 345–51, 103 LRRM 1222, *enforcement denied*, 646 F.2d 113, 116, 107 LRRM 2037 (4th Cir. 1980) (although the NLRB found both male and female employees were engaged in protected concerted activity when they sought to register a complaint with their foreman about his alleged misconduct toward the female employees, the Fourth Circuit concluded that the male employees' protest was merely a "personal mission").

[104] This protection likely will be extended to concerted activity against disability discrimination violative of the ADA. *See* NLRB Memorandum on Collective Bargaining and ADA, *reprinted in* ADA MAN. (BNA) 70:1021, 70:1023 (Sept. 1992).

[105] 343 NLRB No. 435, 175 LRRM 1449 (2004).

[106] *Id.* at 9.

[107] *Id.* at 10.

[108] 344 NLRB No. 136 (2005).

[109] *Id.* at 11.

[110] *Id.*

[111] 637 F.2d 946, 949–50, 24 FEP 1175 (3d Cir. 1981), *enforcing* 247 NLRB 13, 103 LRRM 1110 (1980); *see also* King Soopers, Inc., 222 NLRB 1011, 1018, 91 LRRM 1292 (1976) (employer violated LMRA when it discharged employee for filing charge with EEOC alleging failure to promote because of race).

charges. The Third Circuit affirmed the NLRB's conclusion that filing discrimination charges is protected concerted activity:

> concerted activity directed toward ending alleged discriminatory employment practices . . . deserves protection under section 7, at least as long as it does not violate another important principle of labor law, such as the principle of exclusive representation.[112]

The court explicitly held that § 704(a) of Title VII is not the exclusive remedy for employees who suffer employer retaliation for engaging in conduct that is protected by both § 7 of the NLRA and § 704(a) of Title VII.[113]

C. Employer's Duty to Bargain and to Furnish Union With Workforce Demographics

Section 8(a)(5) makes it an unfair labor practice for an employer to refuse to bargain collectively with the exclusive representative of its employees. As a component of the duty to bargain, an employer upon request must provide the union with certain information relevant to the union's role as exclusive representative.[114]

In *Electrical Workers (IUE) v. NLRB*,[115] the District of Columbia Circuit considered an employer's obligation to furnish statistical and other data concerning the race, national origin, and gender of the employer's workforce.[116] The court affirmed the

---

[112]637 F.2d at 950.

[113]*Id.* at 1018; *accord* Magnetics Int'l, 254 NLRB 520, 529, 106 LRRM 1133 (1981) (NLRA is violated when an employee is discharged because she filed suit under Title VII), *enforced*, 699 F.2d 806, 30 FEP 1524 (6th Cir. 1983).

[114]*See* Detroit Edison Co. v. NLRB, 440 U.S. 301, 303, 100 LRRM 2728 (1979); NLRB v. Acme Indus. Co., 385 U.S. 432, 435–36, 64 LRRM 2069 (1967); NLRB v. Truitt Mfg. Co., 351 U.S. 149, 153–54, 38 LRRM 2042 (1956); *see also* NLRB v. New Jersey Bell Tel. Co., 936 F.2d 144, 150–52, 137 LRRM 2739 (3d Cir. 1991) (company's investigative reports must be disclosed to the union to facilitate processing of a grievance); Olivetti Office U.S.A., Inc. v. NLRB, 926 F.2d 181, 188–89, 136 LRRM 2601 (2d Cir. 1991) (to withhold information on confidentiality grounds, employer must prove that relevant information should not be disclosed to union because the need for confidentiality outweighs union's right to the information).

[115]648 F.2d 18, 24 FEP 627 (D.C. Cir. 1980).

[116]In *Electrical Workers*, two Board decisions were consolidated for review: *Westinghouse, Inc.*, 239 NLRB 106, 99 LRRM 1482 (1978), and *General Motors Corp.*, 243 NLRB 186, 101 LRRM 1461 (1979) (both cases *enforced as modified sub nom.* Electrical Workers (IUE) v. NLRB, 648 F.2d 18, 24 FEP 627 (D.C. Cir. 1980)). In *Westinghouse*, the Board had held that statistical data relating to employment practices are presumptively relevant to the collective bargaining process, but that

Board's holding that the employers were obliged to produce: (1) data showing the distribution and extent of advancement of women and minorities,[117] under the theory that such data "is presumptively relevant to the Union's collective bargaining duties"[118] and (2) certain components of the workforce analysis section of their affirmative action plans (AAPs).[119] The court refused, however, to order production of the entire AAPs[120] and also refused to require production of actual copies of discrimination complaints filed.[121] As for the AAPs, the court noted that the union's access right "must be

---

such presumption did not attach to data pertaining to non-bargaining unit employees, discrimination complaints, and charges filed against the employer, or the employer's affirmative action programs, as to which a more specific showing of relevance had to be made. *Westinghouse*, 239 NLRB at 109. The Board has issued similar rulings in a number of other decisions. *See, e.g.*, Lucky Mkts., Inc., 251 NLRB 836, 838, 105 LRRM 1320 (1980) (statistical data were presumptively relevant; the union also established relevance of those portions of the affirmative action plan upon which the employer sought to justify its award of full-time status to a less-senior employee); Wellman Indus., Inc., 248 NLRB 325, 340, 103 LRRM 1483 (1980) (union was entitled to "admittedly relevant" equal employment data); Kentile Floors, Inc., 242 NLRB 755, 757, 101 LRRM 1236 (1979) (race and sex data pertaining to unit employee complement were presumptively relevant to the union's administration of the contract; however, neither the employer's affirmative action program nor a list of discrimination complaints is presumptively relevant, and the union failed to establish relevance); Bendix Corp., 242 NLRB 1005, 1005, 101 LRRM 1459 (1979) (race and sex data pertaining to unit employees are presumptively relevant; union also established relevance of a list of discrimination complaints and charges, but failed to demonstrate relevance of copies of reports filed pursuant to Executive Order 11,246); Automation & Measurement Div., 242 NLRB 62, 63, 101 LRRM 1118 (1979) (race and sex data pertaining to job applicants and unit employees were presumptively relevant); East Dayton Tool & Die Co., 239 NLRB 141, 142, 99 LRRM 1499 (1978) (union was entitled to race and sex data pertaining to job applicants and hires; however, the employer need not respond to union query as to employer's reason for allegedly employing few females and African Americans); Safeway Stores, Inc., 240 NLRB 836, 838, 100 LRRM 1328 (1979) (employer did not violate § 8(a)(5) when it refused to provide information concerning employer's alleged failure to place women in managerial positions; information was not relevant to the union's statutory duties and obligations).

[117]*Electrical Workers*, 648 F.2d at 24. The court also held, however, that "no reason appears for requiring an employer to recast all of its data into a particular, union-designed format." *Id.* at 26.

[118]*Id.* at 24–26. The court dismissed the companies' contention that the union's request was simply to obtain through the "back door" information that "might prove useful in litigation." *Id.* at 26. If such litigation occurs, it will be up to the trial judge "to control the actual use of information in the litigation." *Id.*

[119]*Id.* at 27–28.

[120]*Id.* at 28.

[121]*Id.* at 27.

balanced [against] the desirability of confidential, frank self-analysis on the part of the employer," which would be "necessarily chilled by a foreknowledge that the results of that analysis must be disclosed."[122] As for the discrimination complaints, the court held (overruling the Board) that the union was entitled only to "a compilation of the numbers, types, dates and alleged bases of the complaints filed."[123]

Subsequently, in *Minnesota Mining & Manufacturing Co.*, the NLRB reaffirmed its position that only certain statistics contained in the workforce analysis portion of an employer's affirmative action plan are presumptively relevant to collective bargaining.[124] The union may obtain information that does not enjoy the presumption, but only on a particularized showing of relevance.[125]

In *NLRB v. United States Postal Service*,[126] the Third Circuit reviewed the NLRB's findings regarding an employer's refusal to supply information or bargain over the elimination of two new hiring procedures that were alleged to be unlawfully discriminatory. The court stated that an employer's obligation to bargain is not triggered until the union adduces sufficient evidence in support of its allegations of discrimination. The union must first make a demand and communicate information to the employer indicating that it has an objective basis for alleging discrimination. The court noted, however, that a separate analysis is required with respect to the duty to provide information. A union has the burden of showing that information concerning persons that it does not represent is necessary to the performance of its representational responsibilities. The union may meet this burden when it has a rational basis for believing that the hiring practice *may* discriminate, i.e., "information sufficiently probative of discrimination to support a belief

---

[122]*Id.* at 28.

[123]*Id.* at 27.

[124]261 NLRB 27, 28–29, 109 LRRM 1345 (1982) (to obtain other portions of the AAP, union must demonstrate relevance), *enforced sub nom.* Oil, Chemical, & Atomic Workers Local 6-418 v. NLRB, 711 F.2d 348, 113 LRRM 3163 (D.C. Cir. 1983).

[125]*See, e.g.*, Safeway Stores v. NLRB, 691 F.2d 953, 958, 111 LRRM 2745 (10th Cir. 1982) (employer required to provide union with list of complaints; information concerning members, distribution, and status of employees in protected classes; workforce analysis; and copies of actual complaints, with complainants' names deleted).

[126]18 F.3d 1089, 145 LRRM 2705, 64 FEP 305 (3d Cir. 1994).

that further inquiry is justified."[127] The employer is obligated to respond to the information request once that burden is satisfied.[128]

In *Frito-Lay, Inc.*,[129] the employer refused to provide the union with information regarding the racial make-up of its nonunion facilities. The union's reasons for requesting this information were that (1) the employer appeared to pay the lowest wages at the union-represented Jackson, Mississippi, facility, which was 90 percent African American; and (2) the employer's other facilities appeared to be "less black." The NLRB deemed these to be relevant inquiries because the information would allow the union to bargain knowledgeably about the employer's wage policy in Jackson.[130]

Conflicts have occurred between employers' bargaining obligations under the NLRA and employers' duties to provide reasonable accommodations to individuals with disabilities. These issues include:

> the extent to which the NLRA requires bargaining with the union in the selection of an effective reasonable accommodation; whether an employer violates the NLRA if it negotiates directly with a bargaining unit employee, rather than a union representative, about reasonable accommodation; the limitations, if any, that the confidentiality provisions of the ADA impose on the duty to furnish information to the union necessary to bargaining; and whether an employer can provide a reasonable accommodation that involves a

---

[127]18 F.3d at 1101.

[128]*Id.* In *NLRB v. United States Postal Service*, 128 F.3d 280, 156 LRRM 2955 (5th Cir. 1997), the Fifth Circuit noted that the Postal Service is covered by the Privacy Act of 1974, which limits the liberal disclosure standards of the NLRA by prohibiting the disclosure of employee information unless certain exceptions are met. The court denied enforcement of the NLRB's order requiring the employer to comply with the union's request for the entire contents of two employees' personnel files in connection with a grievance alleging that one employee's promotion was based on favoritism. The court held that the NLRB's finding that the entire contents of such files were relevant to the union's collective bargaining duties was not supported by substantial evidence. *Id.* at 283–84; *see also* Hertz Corp. v. NLRB, 105 F.3d 868, 872–74, 154 LRRM 2276 (3d Cir. 1997) (per curiam) (employer had no duty to furnish information regarding applicants who were not part of bargaining unit where union failed to demonstrate a rational basis for its belief that the hiring practice at issue was discriminatory).

[129]333 NLRB No. 154, 167 LRRM 1065 (2001).

[130]167 LRRM at 1066; *see also* Corporation for Gen. Trade, 330 NLRB No. 92 (2000) (union had right to information related to employer's AAP because the information sought was relevant to union's statutory and contractual right to make a good faith effort to correct discrimination).

mid-term modification of a collective bargaining agreement without the union's approval.[131]

A related issue is the tension between a request that an employer make an accommodation to an employee with a disability, and the undue hardship that might be created where the requested accommodation would violate a labor agreement.[132] According to EEOC Guidelines, the terms of a collective bargaining agreement may be relevant to, but not determinative of, whether a particular accommodation is an undue hardship.[133] If, however, an employer unilaterally implements a reasonable accommodation that effects a material, substantial, or significant change in working conditions, it may violate § 8(a)(5).[134]

In 2002, the Supreme Court held, in *US Airways, Inc. v. Barnett*,[135] that an employer's showing that a requested accommodation conflicts with applicable seniority provisions is generally sufficient to support a claim that a requested accommodation under the ADA is not reasonable.[136] However, the Court also stated that an employee might present evidence of special circumstances that would make an exception to the seniority provision reasonable under the specific facts presented.[137] The *Barnett* Court suggested that evidence that an employer frequently and unilaterally modified its seniority system, thus reducing employee expectations that the system will be followed, might support a showing that one more exception to the system would not be unreasonable.[138]

In *Dilley v. SuperValu*, the Tenth Circuit held that a potential, as opposed to a certain, violation of a collective bargaining agreement's seniority provisions does not render an employee's

---

[131]EEOC Legal Counsel Memorandum on Americans with Disabilities Act and National Labor Relations Act, DAILY LAB. REP. (BNA) at D-1 (Aug. 18, 1992).

[132]*See* Sections II.D and II.E *supra*.

[133]29 C.F.R. § 1630.15(d) (2005); *see* EEOC TECHNICAL ASSISTANCE MAN. tit. I § 7.11(a), *reprinted in* ADA MAN. (BNA) 90:0566, 90:0566–67 (Feb. 1992).

[134]NLRB Memorandum on Collective Bargaining and ADA, *reprinted in* ADA MAN. (BNA) 70:1021 (Sept. 1992).

[135]535 U.S. 391 (2002). This case arose under the Railway Labor Act, 45 U.S.C. §§ 151–188; its holding, however, is equally applicable to cases arising under the NLRA. For additional discussion of the *Barnett* decision, *see* Section III.A *supra*. *See generally* Chapter 13 (Disability).

[136]*Id.* at 405.

[137]*Id.*

[138]*Id.*

requested accommodation under the ADA unreasonable.[139] The court interpreted the Supreme Court's *Barnett* holding in a limited fashion, finding that it applies only to requested accommodations that would result in a "direct violation" of a seniority system.[140]

IV. ARBITRATION OF STATUTORY CLAIMS UNDER COLLECTIVE BARGAINING AGREEMENTS

The 1960 Supreme Court rulings in the Steelworkers' Trilogy[141] established a presumption in favor of arbitration of disputes arising out of collective bargaining agreements. Despite this presumption in favor of arbitration, in 1974 the Supreme Court in *Alexander v. Gardner-Denver Co.*[142] held that an arbitration clause contained in a collective bargaining agreement does not preclude individual employees from bringing an action in court based on alleged discriminatory conduct.[143]

In 1991, in *Gilmer v. Interstate/Johnson Lane Corp.*,[144] the Supreme Court addressed the issue of arbitration in an employment discrimination case, in the context of an arbitration agreement not found within a collective bargaining agreement. In *Gilmer*, the Court held that a plaintiff's Age Discrimination in Employment Act claims were arbitrable under an arbitration clause contained in a securities dealers' registration application. The Court held that *Gardner-Denver* did not control, in part because the employee in *Gilmer* had himself agreed to arbitrate statutory claims and because the arbitration would not occur under a collective

---

[139]296 F.3d 958, 963 (10th Cir. 2002).

[140]*Id.* (relying on Aldrich v. Boeing Co., 146 F.3d 1265, 1272 n.5 (10th Cir. 1998) ("had Boeing transferred Aldrich to any of the last three disputed jobs ... it would have violated seniority provisions of the collective bargaining agreement")).

[141]United Steelworkers v. American Mfg. Co., 363 U.S. 564 (1960); United Steelworkers v. Warrior & Gulf Navigation Co., 363 U.S. 574, 46 LRRM 2416 (1960); United Steelworkers v. Enterprise Wheel & Car Corp., 363 U.S. 593, 46 LRRM 2423 (1960).

[142]415 U.S. 36, 7 FEP 81 (1974).

[143]*Id.* at 51 (because Title VII rights are conferred on individuals, these rights are not susceptible to "prospective waiver" through a collective bargaining agreement). The Court adhered to its *Gardner-Denver* analysis in two subsequent cases: *McDonald v. City of West Branch*, 466 U.S. 284, 115 LRRM 3646 (1984), and *Barrentine v. Arkansas-Best Freight Sys.*, 450 U.S. 728, 24 WH 1284 (1981).

[144]500 U.S. 20, 55 FEP 1116 (1991).

bargaining agreement, eliminating the possibility that the plaintiff's interests could be subordinated by the union.[145] The majority of circuits continue to treat *Gardner-Denver* and *Gilmer* as distinct lines of authority, applying *Gardner-Denver* to collectively bargained agreements to arbitrate, and *Gilmer* to arbitration agreements entered into by individuals.[146]

The Supreme Court revisited the arbitration of statutory claims pursuant to collectively bargained agreements in *Wright v. Universal Maritime Service Corp.*[147] The employee in *Wright* filed suit alleging that his employer violated the ADA. The employer argued that the claim was barred by the arbitration clause contained in the collective bargaining agreement, which provided for the arbitration of all "[m]atters under dispute," and did not expressly limit the arbitrator to interpreting and applying the contract.[148]

The *Wright* Court found that the arbitration clause of the collective bargaining agreement did not bar the plaintiff from pursuing his statutory claim in court. The Court's decision was based, in part, on the fact that the agreement did not contain a clear and unmistakable waiver of statutory claims,[149] as to which the Court stated: "We do not reach the question of whether such a waiver would be enforceable."[150] Thus, the Court left open the ultimate question whether collectively bargained provisions can mandate arbitration of individual statutory claims.

---

[145]Numerous circuits have extended *Gilmer* to Title VII claims. *See, e.g.*, Seus v. John Nuveen & Co., 146 F.3d 175, 182, 77 FEP 751 (3d Cir. 1998); Metz v. Merrill Lynch, Pierce, Fenner & Smith, Inc., 39 F.3d 1482, 1487–88, 66 FEP 439 (10th Cir. 1994); Bender v. A.G. Edwards & Sons, Inc., 971 F.2d 698, 700, 59 FEP 1231 (11th Cir. 1992) (per curiam); Mago v. Shearson Lehman Hutton Inc., 956 F.2d 932, 935, 58 FEP 178 (9th Cir. 1992); Willis v. Dean Witter Reynolds, Inc., 948 F.2d 305, 308–10, 57 FEP 386 (6th Cir. 1991); Alford v. Dean Witter Reynolds, Inc., 939 F.2d 229, 230, 56 FEP 1046 (5th Cir. 1991).

[146]*See* Penny v. United Parcel Serv., 128 F.3d 408, 412–14, 7 AD 718 (6th Cir. 1997); Brisentine v. Stone & Webster Eng'g Corp., 117 F.3d 519, 6 AD 1878 (11th Cir. 1997); Harrison v. Eddy Potash, Inc., 112 F.3d 1437, 1452–54, 73 FEP 1384 (10th Cir. 1997), *vacated on other grounds*, 524 U.S. 947 (1998); Pryner v. Tractor Supply Co., 109 F.3d 354, 363–65, 73 FEP 615 (7th Cir. 1997).

[147]525 U.S. 70, 159 LRRM 2769 (1998).

[148]*Id.* at 81. Wright, a stevedore, clearly was employed in the transportation industry and therefore was excluded from the coverage of the Federal Arbitration Act.

[149]*Id.* at 79–81.

[150]*Id.*

Since *Wright*, courts generally have declined to bar statutory discrimination claims on the basis of a collective bargaining agreement containing a broad arbitration clause and general antidiscrimination provisions.[151]

The Supreme Court reiterated in *Circuit City Stores, Inc. v. Adams*[152] that the advantages of arbitration are not lost in the employment context, though not in the context of a collective bargaining agreement. Thereafter, the Fourth Circuit in *Safrit v. Cone Mills Corp.*[153] held that a valid "clear and convincing" marker could occur in two different ways: "First, the [collective bargaining] agreement can contain an explicit arbitration clause in which the parties agree to submit to arbitration of all federal causes of action arising out of employment. Second, a general clause requiring arbitration under the agreement can be coupled with a provision which makes 'unmistakably clear that the discrimination statutes at issue are part of the agreement.' "[154] The *Safrit* court found that

---

[151]*See, e.g.*, Rogers v. New York Univ., 220 F.3d 73, 75–76, 164 LRRM 2854 (2d Cir. 2000) (per curiam) (neither the arbitration clause nor the antidiscrimination clause, which prohibited discrimination "as defined by applicable Federal" law, demonstrated explicit agreement by employees to submit all federal claims to arbitration); Kennedy v. Superior Printing Co., 215 F.3d 650, 653–54, 164 LRRM 2609 (6th Cir. 2000) (general antidiscrimination provision insufficient to compel arbitration of ADA claim; ADA not specifically mentioned in the CBA); Bratten v. SSI Servs., Inc., 185 F.3d 625, 631, 161 LRRM 2985 (6th Cir. 1999) (clause prohibiting discrimination because of "presence of a disability or handicap," expressly mentioning Title VII, does not require arbitration of an ADA claim; "a statute must specifically be mentioned" in an agreement to meet the "clear and unmistakable standard"); Quint v A.E. Staley Mfg. Co., 172 F.3d 1 (1st Cir. 1999) ("in the present case, CBA articles 5 & 6, neither of which explicitly mentions employee rights under the ADA or any other federal antidiscrimination statute, pose no bar to the instant action"); Brown v. ABF Freight Sys., Inc., 183 F.3d 319, 322–23, 161 LRRM 2769 (4th Cir. 1999) ("parties must make 'unmistakably clear' their intent to incorporate in their entirety the 'discrimination statutes at issue' "); Paris v. Dallas Airmotive, Inc., 130 F. Supp. 2d 844, 847 (N.D. Tex. 2001) (CBA not "clear and unmistakable" waiver of right to bring Title VII action). *But see* Carson v. Giant Food, Inc., 175 F.3d 325, 331, 79 FEP 976 (4th Cir. 1999) (collective bargaining agreement that contains a clear and unmistakable agreement to arbitrate all federal causes of action arising out of employment *or* a broad arbitration clause coupled with explicit incorporation of statutory antidiscrimination requirements can require the arbitration of civil rights claims; the agreement at issue in this case met neither requirement and therefore arbitration was not required).

[152]532 U.S. 105, 85 FEP 266 (2001).

[153]248 F.3d 306, 85 FEP 833 (4th Cir. 2001) (per curiam).

[154]*Id.* at 307–08 (citations omitted); *see also* Clarke v. UFI, Inc., 98 F. Supp. 2d 320, 336–37, 82 FEP 1681 (E.D.N.Y. 2000) (Title VII claims precluded by arbitration decision pursuant to contractual grievance procedure).

a valid waiver had been established where the collective bargaining agreement provided that the employer "will not discriminate against any employee with regard to race, color, religion, age, sex, national origin or disability," "will abide by the requirements of Title VII of the Civil Rights Act of 1964," and, in the same section of the agreement, provided that "unresolved grievances arising under this Section are the proper subjects for arbitration."[155]

---

[155]248 F.3d at 307; *see also* Singletary v. Enersys, Inc., 57 Fed. Appx. 161, 164 (4th Cir. 2003) (finding "clear and unmistakable" waiver of employee's right to bring separate ADA claim in federal court where collective bargaining agreement explicitly provided that "Any and all claims . . . under any federal or state employment law shall be exclusively addressed by an individual employee or the Union under the grievance and arbitration provisions of this Agreement"); *Carson*, 175 F.3d 325, 331 (collective bargaining agreement that contains a clear and unmistakable agreement to arbitrate all federal causes of action arising out of employment or a broad arbitration clause coupled with explicit incorporation of statutory antidiscrimination requirements can require the arbitration of civil rights claims; the agreements at issue in *Carson* met neither requirement, and therefore arbitration was not required); Saunders v. Longshoremen (ILA), 265 F. Supp. 2d 624, 627, 172 LRRM 2922 (E.D. Va. 2003) (finding waiver of right to pursue Title VII claims in federal court where agreement provided that all alleged violations of Title VII "shall be brought before the Contract Board" for a final and binding decision, and the parties "waive any rights they may otherwise have to pursue such disputes . . . in any judicial forum"), *aff'd*, 2004 U.S. App. LEXIS 2445 (4th Cir. Feb. 13, 2004); Neppl v. Signature Flight Support Corp., 234 F. Supp. 2d 1016, 1020 n.6 (D. Minn. 2002) (citing *Safrit* for the proposition that the collective bargaining agreement may require the arbitration of Title VII claims); Kemp v. California Fed'n of Teachers, 2002 U.S. Dist. LEXIS 24308, at *13 (N.D. Cal. Dec. 13, 2002) (same); Washington v. Park'N'Fly, 2001 U.S. Dist. LEXIS 20590 (E.D. La. Nov. 30, 2001) (finding no waiver where provision did not explicitly make compliance with federal antidiscrimination statutes an obligation under the agreement, as opposed to the agreement's explicit reference to Title VII in *Safrit*).

CHAPTER 37

"REVERSE" DISCRIMINATION
AND AFFIRMATIVE ACTION

I. INTRODUCTION

One area of persistent controversy in the area of employment law is that of so-called "reverse" discrimination.[1] May employers lawfully consider race, sex, religion, or national origin when making employment decisions? Are claims of disparate treatment brought by members of majority groups to be given any less credence than those advanced by minority groups? And, if race or sex may be a factor in employment decisions, how much of a factor and in what situations?

The complexity of these issues is reflected in the multitude of legal decisions involving them. The legislative history of Title VII, set forth in pertinent part in the majority and dissenting opinions in *United Steelworkers of America, AFL-CIO v. Weber*,[2] could be read to support the view that *any* preferential treatment based on race is illegal. During Title VII debates, members of Congress expressed fear that the statute would be interpreted to require the correction of racial imbalance through the granting of preferential treatment to minorities. In response to this concern, § 703(j) was added to Title VII. Section 703(j) reads in relevant part:

> Nothing contained in this [subsection] shall be interpreted to require any employer . . . to grant preferential treatment to any individual or to any group because of the race, color, religion, sex, or national origin of such individual or group on account of an imbalance which may exist with respect to the total number or percentage of persons of any race, color, religion, sex, or national origin

---

[1] The term "reverse discrimination" refers to any discrimination against a member of a majority group—typically whites and males—whether or not prohibited by law in any particular case. As discussed below, courts have held that some consideration of race or gender pursuant to a lawful affirmative action plan is consistent with Title VII.

[2] 443 U.S. 193, 202–07 (majority opinion), 230–52 (dissenting opinion), 20 FEP 1 (1979).

employed by any employer . . . in comparison with the total number or percentage of persons of such race, color, religion, sex, or national origin in any . . . area, or in the available work force in any . . . area.[3]

In construing Title VII and the other laws forbidding discrimination in employment, however, the Supreme Court has held that Congress did not intend to prohibit all race- or sex-conscious actions taken voluntarily by employers and unions. It established a series of limits on race- or sex-conscious affirmative action plans to ensure that such plans were consistent with the intent of Congress and did not undermine the basic principle of nondiscrimination. In enacting the Civil Rights Act of 1991, Congress provided that nothing in the Act "shall be construed to affect court-ordered remedies, affirmative action, or conciliation agreements, that are in accordance with the law."[4] But the critical question has not changed. In what factual circumstances are preferences "in accordance with the law"?

II. "REVERSE" DISCRIMINATION OUTSIDE THE CONTEXT OF AFFIRMATIVE ACTION PROGRAMS

A. Prohibited Bases for Discrimination

Title VII indisputably applies to all people, regardless of race, gender, or national origin. In *Griggs v. Duke Power Co.*,[5] a unanimous Supreme Court stated:

[T]he Act does not command that any person be hired simply because he was formerly the subject of discrimination, or because he is a member of a minority group. Discriminatory preference for any group, minority or majority, is precisely and only what Congress has proscribed.

---

[3]42 U.S.C. § 2000e-2(j) (2000). The Supreme Court in *Teamsters v. United States*, 431 U.S. 324 (1977), explained that "[e]vidence of longlasting and gross disparity between the composition of a work force and that of the general population . . . may be significant even though § 703(j) makes clear that Title VII imposes no requirement that a work force mirror the general population." *Id.* at 339–40 n.20.

[4]Pub. L. No. 102-166, § 116, 1991 U.S.C.C.A.N. (105 Stat.) 1071, 1079 (*see* notes to 42 U.S.C. § 1981).

[5]401 U.S. 424, 430–31, 3 FEP 175 (1971).

In keeping with the spirit of *Griggs*, courts have recognized "reverse" discrimination claims not only on the basis of race, but also based on gender[6] and national origin.[7]

Claims of "reverse" discrimination apply to the same range of employment actions as traditional discrimination claims, including hiring,[8] discharge,[9] promotion,[10] demotion,[11]

---

[6]Schoenfeld v. Babbitt, 168 F.3d 1257, 1268, 79 FEP 497 (11th Cir. 1999) (male applicant stated prima facie case of gender discrimination by pointing to tacit admission by employer that gender was factor in rejecting his application for vacant position).

[7]Stern v. Trustees of Columbia Univ., 131 F.3d 305, 306–07, 75 FEP 1423 (2d Cir. 1997) (reversing district court's grant of summary judgment against white plaintiff who alleged that he was passed over for position managing Spanish language program in favor of an individual of Hispanic descent); Preda v. Nissho Iwai Am. Corp., 128 F.3d 789, 791, 75 FEP 371 (2d Cir. 1997) (per curiam) (reversing district court's grant of summary judgment in favor of Japanese employer on Title VII claims for national origin and race discrimination brought by white, naturalized American citizen).

[8]*See, e.g.*, Rudin v. Lincoln Land Cmty. Coll., 420 F.3d 712, 722–24 (7th Cir. 2005) (reversing summary judgment on unsuccessful white female applicant's Title VII claims of race and sex discrimination in hiring for instructor position); Wheeler v. Missouri Highway & Transp. Comm., 348 F.3d 744 (8th Cir. 2003) (affirming jury verdict for male employee who alleged "reverse" discrimination in hiring), *cert. denied*, 541 U.S. 1043 (2004); McGarry v. Board of County Comm'rs, 175 F.3d 1193, 79 FEP 964 (10th Cir. 1999) (white applicant for building maintenance worker position raised fact issue entitling him to trial on claim that county denied his application due to preference for minority hires).

[9]*See, e.g.*, Mastro v. Potomac Elec. Power Co., 447 F.3d 843, 98 FEP 193 (D.C. Cir. 2006) (reversing summary judgment for employer on termination claim brought by white employee); Hunt v. City of Markham, 219 F.3d 649 (7th Cir. 2000) (white police officers raised fact issue on discharge claim); Canup v. Chipman-Union, Inc., 123 F.3d 1440, 75 FEP 220 (11th Cir. 1997) (jury award in favor of white male employee whose discharge was in part motivated by his race); Greenslade v. Chicago Sun-Times, Inc., 112 F.3d 853, 863–64, 73 FEP 1674 (7th Cir. 1997) (male employee failed to state prima facie case of sex discrimination since he could not show that similarly situated female employee received preferential treatment and since he was replaced by male).

[10]*See, e.g.*, Zambetti v. Cuyahoga Cmty. Coll., 314 F.3d 249 (6th Cir. 2002) (reversing summary judgment granted to employer on promotion claims of white employee); Babbar v. Ebadi, 216 F.3d 1086 (table), 2000 WL 702428 (10th Cir. 2000) (sex discrimination claim brought by male professor who was denied tenure); Reynolds v. School Dist. No. 1, Denver, Colo., 69 F.3d 1523, 1534–35, 72 FEP 485 (10th Cir. 1995) (white employee who was denied promotion established prima facie case by showing that she was only white employee in her department and supervisors who denied her promotions were Hispanic).

[11]*See, e.g.*, Weberg v. Franks, 229 F.3d 514 (6th Cir. 2000) (white employee established claim of "reverse" discrimination in suspension and demotion through direct evidence); Lynn v. Deaconess Med. Ctr.-W. Campus, 160 F.3d 484, 488, 78 FEP 595 (8th Cir. 1998) (hospital not entitled to summary judgment on male nurse's

compensation,[12] and transfer.[13] Courts have also recognized hostile work environment claims based upon racial harassment of majority group members by minority supervisors and co-workers.[14]

Title VII also prohibits retaliation by employers against majority group employees who complain of discrimination against minorities.[15] Similarly, plaintiffs continue to state successful claims based on discrimination by employers against white employees involved in interracial relationships.[16]

---

discrimination claim as female nurses were disciplined less harshly for similar conduct); Morrow v. Wal-Mart Stores, Inc., 152 F.3d 559, 561–63, 77 FEP 1446 (7th Cir. 1998) (male employee discharged for sexual harassment failed to establish claim of "reverse" discrimination because he did not show that female employees were disciplined differently).

[12]See, e.g., Gagnon v. Sprint Corp., 284 F.3d 839, 848 (8th Cir. 2002) (summary judgment was improper; comment by supervisor that "I'm not going to pay him. He's just a white guy." is direct evidence of "reverse" discrimination); Harrington v. Harris, 118 F.3d 359, 368, 75 FEP 1303 (5th Cir. 1997) (jury verdict in favor of white law school professor affirmed based on evidence of discriminatory policy of not giving white professors equal credit and consideration for their scholarship and research, which caused African-American professors to receive consistently higher merit pay increases); Reynolds v. Dallas Area Rapid Transit, 2000 WL 1586444 (N.D. Tex. Oct. 20, 2000) (white plaintiff created issue of disputed fact with respect to pay discrimination claim).

[13]See, e.g., Douglas v. Evans, 888 F. Supp. 1536, 1546, 68 FEP 472, 478 (M.D. Ala. 1995) (white employee met prima facie standard of discriminatory transfer by showing that she routinely received above-average evaluations and that African American ultimately replaced her). In Douglas, summary judgment was later granted due to plaintiff's failure to establish a prima facie case that she was qualified for the position. See Douglas v. Evans, 916 F. Supp. 1539, 1547 (M.D. Ala. 1996), aff'd, 116 F.3d 492 (11th Cir. 1997).

[14]See, e.g., Huckabay v. Moore, 142 F.3d 233, 240–41, 77 FEP 172 (5th Cir. 1998) (white county employee defeated summary judgment by offering proof that he was subjected to continuing pattern of verbal and nonverbal harassment by African-American county commissioner); Pickens v. Runyon, 128 F.3d 1151, 1156, 75 FEP 433 (7th Cir. 1997) (white postal carrier entitled to new trial on claims of racial and sexual harassment by African-American co-workers).

[15]See, e.g., Olmsted v. Taco Bell Corp., 141 F.3d 1457, 1461, 76 FEP 1833 (11th Cir. 1998) (upholding jury verdict in favor of white Taco Bell employee based on allegation that Taco Bell retaliated against him after he complained of racial discrimination); Lamberson v. Six West Retail Acquisition, Inc., 122 F. Supp. 2d 502, 511 (S.D.N.Y. 2000) (plaintiff presented triable issue of fact as to whether he was terminated in retaliation for complaining that reassignment of African-American employee was racially discriminatory).

[16]See, e.g., Madison v. IBP, Inc., 257 F.3d 780 (8th Cir. 2001); Deffenbaugh-Williams v. Wal-Mart Stores, Inc., 156 F.3d 581, 589, 77 FEP 1699 (5th Cir. 1998) (Title VII prohibits discrimination against white employees because of their

B. Proof of "Reverse" Discrimination

In the traditional Title VII disparate treatment case, a minority plaintiff can prove a prima facie case of discrimination based on indirect evidence, through the burden-shifting scheme set forth by the Supreme Court in *McDonnell Douglas Corp. v. Green*.[17] In *McDonald v. Santa Fe Trail Transportation Co.*,[18] the Supreme Court did not alter the prima facie *McDonnell Douglas* test for cases of alleged "reverse" discrimination, but rather stated that the requirement of a plaintiff belonging to a racial minority "was set out only to demonstrate how the racial character of the discrimination could be established in the most common sort of case, and not as an indication of any substantive limitation of Title VII's prohibitions."[19]

Courts remain divided over whether the first prong of the *McDonnell Douglas* prima facie test—establishing that the plaintiff is a member of a minority group—should be modified, replaced, or eliminated in "reverse" discrimination Title VII cases. Indeed, courts reviewing the issue have set forth a variety of theories. A clear majority of the lower courts that have considered the issue have accepted the test established in *Parker v. Baltimore & Ohio Railroad*,[20] otherwise known as the "background circumstances" test.[21] The *Parker* court's background circumstances test is an alteration of the first prong of the *McDonnell Douglas* burden-shifting

---

relationship with minorities; upholding jury verdict for white plaintiff discharged for dating African American), *vacated and reh'g en banc granted*, 169 F.3d 215, 79 FEP 1770 (5th Cir.), *opinion reinstated on reh'g*, 182 F.3d 333, 80 FEP 704 (5th Cir. 1999). *But see* Drake v. Minnesota Mining & Mfg. Co., 134 F.3d 878, 883–85, 76 FEP 48 (7th Cir. 1998) (recognizing validity of associational race discrimination claims but affirming summary judgment against white plaintiffs' claims of race discrimination due to friendship with African-American co-worker as facts did not establish inference plaintiffs were harassed on basis of race).

[17]411 U.S. 792, 5 FEP 965 (1973). *See generally* Chapter 2 (Disparate Treatment), Section I.

[18]427 U.S. 273, 12 FEP 1577 (1976). In *McDonald*, two white employees claimed racial discrimination after being discharged for participating in criminal activity against their employer, while an African-American co-worker was retained.

[19]*Id.* at 279 n.6.

[20]652 F.2d 1012 (D.C. Cir. 1981).

[21]*See* Mastro v. Potomac Elec. Power Co., 447 F.3d 843, 98 FEP 193 (D.C. Cir. 2006) (applying *Parker* background evidence analysis); Hague v. Thompson Distrib. Co., 436 F.3d 816, 820–21, 97 FEP 545 (7th Cir. 2006); Leadbetter v. J. Wade Gilley, 385 F.3d 683 (6th Cir. 2004) (same); Stover v. Martinez, 382 F.3d 1064 (10th Cir. 2004) (same); Woods v. Perry, 375 F.3d 671 (8th Cir. 2004) (same).

presumption, whereby a plaintiff must establish that "background circumstances support the suspicion that the defendant is that unusual employer who discriminates against the majority."[22] The types of background circumstances that might support this type of inference are: (1) evidence indicating that the employer has some reason or inclination to discriminate invidiously against the majority group, or (2) evidence from which an inference of discrimination can otherwise be drawn.[23]

A significant minority of circuits, however, has declined to apply any additional requirements to "reverse" discrimination claims. The Third Circuit, in *Iadimarco v. Runyon*,[24] criticized *Parker* and its progeny and held that "all that should be required to establish a prima facie case in the context of ' "reverse" discrimination' is for the plaintiff to present sufficient evidence to allow a fact finder to conclude that the employer is treating some people less favorably than others based upon a trait that is protected under Title VII."[25] The Fourth, Fifth, and Eleventh Circuits have determined that the *McDonnell Douglas* test in a "reverse" discrimination case simply requires proof that the plaintiff is a member of any race or

---

[22]652 F.2d at 1017–18.

[23]*Mastro*, 447 F.3d at 847 (citing Harding v. Gray, 9 F.3d 150, 153 (D.C. Cir. 1993)). *Background evidence found*: Sutherland v. Michigan Dep't of Treasury, 344 F.3d 603 (6th Cir. 2003) (statistical evidence of promotion of blacks at a higher rate than expected given their representation in workforce was sufficient to establish background evidence); Zambetti v. Cuyahoga Cmty. Coll., 314 F.3d 249 (6th Cir. 2002) (substantial background evidence of "reverse" discrimination; minority decision maker ignored recommendation of advisory committee and promoted minority candidates who were substantially less qualified than white plaintiff); Bass v. Board of County Comm'rs, 256 F.3d 1095 (11th Cir. 2001) (variety of background evidence found to exist; white candidate for position was most senior and should have received position under union contract; interview panel was made up entirely of minority employees, several of whom professed support for affirmative action; one of the minority candidates selected did not even meet minimum qualifications for position; plaintiff proved existence and application of an improper affirmative action plan). *No background evidence*: Woods, 375 F.3d 671 (similar rates of promotion for women and men demonstrated there was no background evidence of reverse gender discrimination, even though women were promoted over men in some circumstances); *Leadbetter*, 385 F.3d 683 (public statements of general intent to promote women and minorities insufficient to satisfy background evidence requirement); Yeager v. General Motors Corp., 265 F.3d 389 (6th Cir. 2001) (statistical evidence that whites were vast majority of employees selected for apprenticeship program demonstrated no background evidence of "reverse" discrimination).

[24]190 F.3d 151, 80 FEP 1294 (3d Cir. 1999).

[25]*Id.* at 161.

gender group—thus analyzing all claims of discrimination pursuant to the same analytical framework.[26]

III. "REVERSE" DISCRIMINATION PURSUANT TO AFFIRMATIVE ACTION PROGRAMS

A. Introduction

Claims of "reverse" discrimination related to affirmative action programs, particularly constitutional challenges, have garnered a high degree of public attention and generated significant controversy for many years. Despite the number of times that the Supreme Court has addressed these questions, this is still an unsettled area of law.

B. Affirmative Action Under the Equal Protection Clause

The Supreme Court first addressed the constitutionality of affirmative action under the Fourteenth Amendment's Equal Protection Clause in *University of California Regents v. Bakke*,[27] which

---

[26]*See* Bass v. Board of County Comm'rs, 256 F.3d 1095, 1102–03 (11th Cir. 2001) ("Sometimes this type of claim, where a white employee alleges to be the victim of discrimination, is referred to as a reverse discrimination claim. Whatever the rhetorical effect of that phrase in the ongoing public debate over affirmative action may be, it has no place in the legal analysis of the alleged governmental action before us. Discrimination is discrimination no matter what the race, color, religion, sex or national origin of the victim."); Byers v. Dallas Morning News, Inc., 209 F.3d 419, 426 (5th Cir. 2000) ("This Court finds that *Singh* marks a retreat from the 'racial minority' requirement to the 'protected group' requirement for cases of reverse race discrimination.") (citing Singh v. Shoney's, Inc., 64 F.3d 217, 219 (5th Cir. 1995)); Brown v. McLean, 159 F.3d 898, 78 FEP 225 (4th Cir. 1998). *But see* Weeks v. Union Camp Corp., 215 F.3d 1323 (table), 2000 WL 727771 (4th Cir. June 7, 2000) (recognizing split among circuits regarding standard of proof in "reverse" discrimination claims and declining to "take a position on the issue").

[27]438 U.S. 265 (1978). This section of the chapter addresses *voluntarily* adopted affirmative action plans and consent decrees by public agencies. Most courts have assessed the constitutionality of such consent decrees by reference to the same standards applied to affirmative action plans voluntarily adopted outside the litigation context and have rejected the position that consent decrees, having been judicially approved, should be subject to less exacting scrutiny. *See, e.g.*, Aiken v. City of Memphis, 37 F.3d 1155, 1161–62 (6th Cir. 1994). *But cf.* Donaghy v. City of Omaha, 933 F.2d 1448, 1459 (8th Cir. 1991) ("While the entry of an affirmative action consent decree does not guarantee that the decree serves a remedial purpose or is narrowly tailored, the heightened judicial oversight inherent in a properly entered decree helps attain that end.").

The Constitution does not generally compel "affirmative action" as that term is commonly understood. *See, e.g.*, Austin Black Contractors v. Austin, 78 F.3d 185,

involved a race-based preferential university admissions plan. Since *Bakke*, the Supreme Court has addressed the constitutionality of raced-based affirmative action plans against " 'reverse' discrimination" challenges in a variety of contexts: *Wygant v. Jackson Board of Education*[28] addressed a collectively bargained preferential layoff plan in public employment; *Fullilove v. Klutznick*[29] and *City of Richmond v. J.A. Croson Co.*[30] addressed minority contractor set-aside plans involving federal and municipal contracting authorities, respectively; *United States v. Paradise*[31] addressed court-ordered affirmative relief for proven instances of unlawful discrimination in employment; *Metro Broadcasting, Inc. v. FCC*[32] addressed preferential licensing policies by a federal regulatory agency; *Adarand Constructors, Inc. v. Peña*[33] revisited the issue of federal minority preferences in the construction industry and established that all governmental racial classifications are subject to "strict scrutiny"; and *Grutter v. Bollinger*[34] and *Gratz v. Bollinger*,[35] a pair of 2003 decisions, returned to the issue of preferential admissions policies in higher education first addressed 25 years earlier in *Bakke*.[36]

Although *Wygant* and *Paradise* are the Court's only cases dealing directly with the issue of affirmative action in the employment context, the Court's other affirmative action decisions address issues that arise in nearly all affirmative action cases—including, not least, the constitutional standard of review governing race- and sex-based preferences and the permissible ends to which federal, state, and local governments may direct such preferences.[37]

---

186 (5th Cir. 1996). Race-conscious remedies, on the other hand, may sometimes be required. *See, e.g.*, City of Richmond v. J.A. Croson Co., 488 U.S. 469, 524 (1989) (Scalia, J., concurring). *See generally* Chapter 39 (Injunctive and Affirmative Relief).

[28]476 U.S. 267, 40 FEP 1321 (1986).

[29]448 U.S. 448 (1980).

[30]488 U.S. 469, 53 FEP 197 (1989).

[31]480 U.S. 149, 43 FEP 1 (1987). *See generally* Chapter 39 (Injunctive and Affirmative Relief).

[32]497 U.S. 547, 53 FEP 161 (1990).

[33]515 U.S. 200, 67 FEP 1828 (1995); *see* Section III.B.2 *infra*.

[34]539 U.S. 306, 91 FEP 1761 (2003).

[35]539 U.S. 244, 91 FEP 1803 (2003).

[36]For a detailed discussion of the Supreme Court's affirmative action cases prior to *Grutter* and *Gratz*, see GIRARDEAU A. SPANN, THE LAW OF AFFIRMATIVE ACTION (2000).

[37]A threshold issue that sometimes arises in cases challenging adverse employment actions undertaken pursuant to an affirmative action plan (whether at the federal, state, or local level), but on which courts seldom focus, is whether the plaintiff or the defendant bears the burden of proof. *Wygant* held that the "ultimate burden remains with the employee to demonstrate the unconstitutionality of an affirmative

1. Voluntary State and Local Government Plans

a. Race-Based Plans.[38] In *Bakke*, the Court addressed whether a medical school admissions plan that set aside 16 slots for disadvantaged minorities in each entering class violated Title VI of the Civil Rights Act of 1964[39] or the Equal Protection Clause. The purpose of the plan was to remedy societal discrimination, not to redress the school's own discrimination (of which there was no evidence).[40] Bakke, a white applicant, was rejected for admission.

---

action program." 476 U.S. at 277–88; *cf.* Johnson v. Transp. Agency, 480 U.S. 616, 626 (1987) (under Title VII, as under the Constitution, the plaintiff bears the burden of establishing the invalidity of the plan). The lower courts have generally imposed on the plaintiff the ultimate burden of proof—as distinct from the burden of producing evidence supporting the plan's constitutionality, which generally lies with the defendant. *See, e.g.,* Contractors Ass'n of E. Pa. v. City of Phila., 91 F.3d 586, 598–99 (3d Cir. 1996); Aiken v. City of Memphis, 37 F.3d 1155, 1162 (6th Cir. 1994). Some courts have questioned whether, on the burden of proof issue, *Wygant's* holding survives *Croson* and *Adarand,* which mandate the application of strict judicial scrutiny to state/local and federal affirmative action plans, respectively. *See, e.g.,* Hill v. Ross, 183 F.3d 586, 590 (7th Cir. 1999) (Easterbrook, J.).

Another threshold issue that sometimes arises in the employment context is whether and how the *McDonnell Douglas* burden-shifting scheme applies where a race-based preference is undertaken pursuant to an affirmative action plan. In *Johnson v. Transportation Agency,* 480 U.S. 616 (1987), a case decided under Title VII, the Court held that affirmative action cases fit "readily" into the *McDonnell Douglas* framework: the invocation of an affirmative action plan discharges the defendant's burden of production, and it is then incumbent on the plaintiff to prove that the "employer's justification is pretextual and the plan is invalid." *Id.* at 626; *see also Hill,* 183 F.3d at 590. But a number of courts have concluded in the equal protection context that *McDonnell Douglas'* pretext analysis does not apply where the defendant admits that it made a race- or sex-based decision but defends the decision by invoking the authority of an affirmative action plan. *See, e.g.,* Bass v. Board of County Comm'rs, 256 F.3d 1095, 1111 n.7 (11th Cir. 2001); Thigpen v. Bibb County, 223 F.3d 1231, 1241 (11th Cir. 2000); *see also* Smith v. Virginia Commonwealth Univ., 84 F.3d 672, 683 n.5 (4th Cir. 1996) (Luttig, J., concurring). One court has held that a pretext analysis is appropriate if the plaintiff proceeds on the theory that the plan was adopted with an "intent unrelated" to remedying past discrimination. Contractors Ass'n of E. Pa. v. City of Phila., 91 F.3d 586, 597 (3d Cir. 1996). In nearly all of the cases discussed in this chapter, though, the key issue is the validity of the plan, not the defendant's motive or intent in adopting it.

[38]Courts have subjected plans drawn around national origin classifications to the same degree of judicial scrutiny as plans drawn around racial classifications. *See, e.g.,* Jana-Rock Constr., Inc. v. New York State Dep't of Econ. Dev., 438 F.3d 195, 200 n.1 (2d Cir. 2006).

[39]42 U.S.C. § 2000d (2000) (prohibiting race discrimination in federally funded programs).

[40]*See* University of Cal. Regents v. Bakke, 438 U.S. 265, 309–10 (1978).

He claimed that, but for the minority set-aside, he would have been admitted.

Bakke divided the Court, yielding six decisions and two separate majorities. Chief Justice Burger and Justices Powell, Stevens, Stewart, and Rehnquist concluded that the medical school improperly denied Bakke admission because of his race.[41] Only Justice Powell, though, grounded his decision on the Equal Protection Clause; the other four Justices relied exclusively on Title VI. Applying strict scrutiny, Justice Powell concluded that remedying "societal discrimination" does not constitute a compelling state interest.[42]

But a separate majority of the Court, which consisted of Justice Powell and the four dissenting Justices who voted to uphold the affirmative action plan under review, concluded that an educational institution may sometimes employ race-based preferences in making admissions decisions, even if it has not itself discriminated in the past.[43] Of the five Justices, though, only Justice Powell demanded that every affirmative action plan undergo strict scrutiny;[44] the four other Justices would have applied intermediate scrutiny.[45] Justice Powell opined that a race-based admissions preference could survive strict scrutiny if its purpose was either to remedy the plan sponsor's own discrimination (assuming the existence of an adequate factual predicate) or, in the absence of such discrimination, to promote diversity, so long as the preference was narrowly tailored to achieve its objective.[46] With the first possibility foreclosed

---

[41]*See id.* at 271 (Powell, J., announcing the judgment of the Court); *id.* at 421 (Stevens, J., joined by Burger, C.J., and Stewart and Rehnquist, JJ., concurring in part).

[42]*See id.* at 307–10 (opinion of Powell, J.).

[43]*See id.* at 311–20 (opinion of Powell, J.); *id.* at 324–26, 369 (Brennan, J., with whom Blackmun, Marshall, and White, JJ., joined, concurring in part and dissenting in part).

[44]*See id.* at 288–305 (opinion of Powell, J.).

[45]*See* University of Cal. Regents v. Bakke, 438 U.S. 265, 356–62 (1978) (Brennan, J., with whom Blackmun, Marshall, and White, JJ., joined, concurring in part and dissenting in part). *See generally* Kathleen M. Sullivan, *Sins of Discrimination: Last Term's Affirmative Action Cases*, 100 HARV. L. REV. 78 (1986) (arguing that the Court had taken an unduly restrictive view of affirmative action by allowing it only as a remedy for past discrimination rather than a prospective program to achieve racial integration).

[46]*See Bakke*, 438 U.S. at 307–08.

on the record before the Court, Justice Powell turned to the second and asked whether the plan at issue was narrowly tailored to achieve diversity. He concluded that it was not. The infirmity in the plan, according to Justice Powell, was its use of a rigid, race-based quota. Race can only be used in higher education admissions, he concluded, as a "plus-factor," and then only in the context of an individualized, flexible, and nonmechanical review of an applicant such that no minority candidate is insulated from competition with non-minority candidates and no non-minority candidate is foreclosed from being considered for any slot.[47]

More than 25 years later, in *Grutter* and *Gratz*, Justice Powell's position in *Bakke* was adopted by a majority of the Supreme Court, and thus became the clearly governing law of race-based affirmative action in the context of admissions in public higher education. *Grutter* and *Gratz* addressed the constitutionality of two University of Michigan affirmative action plans—the law school's admissions plan (*Grutter*) and the undergraduate admissions plan (*Gratz*)—both of which gave preferences in one form or another to minority applicants. The objective of the plans was not to remedy actual discrimination in the University's admissions system or even societal discrimination in general, but instead to ensure diversity in the student body—in particular, to enroll in each entering class a "critical mass" of students from underrepresented minority groups.

But the undergraduate and law school plans, though similar in their objectives, differed in a key respect. Under the undergraduate plan, applicants from underrepresented racial and ethnic groups were automatically awarded 20 of the 100 total points that an applicant needed to gain admission, with the result that all or nearly all minority applicants who met the minimum qualification standards set by the University were, unlike non-minority applicants, guaranteed admission. Under the law school plan, by contrast, minority applicants were given no "mechanical, predetermined diversity 'bonuses' based on [their] race or ethnicity."[48] Each applicant—minority and non-minority alike—was given individualized consideration as a part of a "holistic" review.[49] One important factor, to be weighed subjectively along with other factors,

---

[47]*See id.* at 316–20.
[48]Grutter v. Bollinger, 539 U.S. 306, 337, 91 FEP 1761 (2003).
[49]*Id.*

was an applicant's contribution to diversity. Although the law school put particular weight on racial and ethnic diversity, with the objective of enrolling a "critical mass" of underrepresented minority students in each entering class, it recognized other bases of diversity and eschewed strict quotas on minority enrollment.[50]

As a threshold matter, the Court reemphasized the principle—already well established as a result of the cases discussed below—that all "racial classifications by government" " 'must be analyzed by a reviewing court under strict scrutiny.' " They are therefore "constitutional only if they are narrowly tailored to further compelling governmental interests."[51]

The Court then went on to hold, for the first time, that the attainment of a diverse student body along racial and ethnic lines is a compelling governmental interest that can, if achieved through narrowly tailored means, justify a university's consideration of race and ethnicity in making admissions decisions.[52] The Court thereby rejected the argument, endorsed by some lower courts and even suggested by some of the Court's own post-*Bakke* dicta, that "the only governmental use of race that can survive strict scrutiny is remedying past discrimination."[53] In justifying its conclusion, the

---

[50]*See id.* at 316.

[51]*Id.* at 326 (citations omitted). This is true even with respect to racial classifications that purport to benefit members of historically disadvantaged groups. *See id.*

[52]*See id.* at 328. It remains unclear after *Grutter* and *Gratz* whether diversity can constitute a compelling state interest in education below the college or university level, let alone outside the educational context (e.g., employment). *Compare* Cavalier v. Caddo Parish Sch. Bd., 403 F.3d 246, 259 n.15 (5th Cir. 2005) (questioning *Grutter*'s and *Gratz*'s applicability to education "at or below the high school level") *with* Comfort v. Lynn Sch. Comm., 418 F.3d 1, 14–16 (1st Cir. 2005) (upholding diversity-promoting plan under which school system took race into account in evaluating high school students' applications to transfer out of neighborhood schools), Parents Involved in Cmty. Sch. v. Seattle Sch. Dist. No. 1, 426 F.3d 1162, 1175–77 (9th Cir. 2005) (en banc) (under *Grutter* and *Gratz* diversity can be a compelling interest at the high school level), *cert. granted*, 126 S. Ct. 2351 (2006) *and* McFarland v. Jefferson County Pub. Schs., 330 F. Supp. 2d 834 (W.D. Ky. 2004) (relying on *Grutter* and *Gratz* in upholding public school student assignment plan whose purpose was to increase diversity in and racial integration of the student body), *aff'd*, 416 F.3d 513 (6th Cir. 2005), *cert. granted*, 126 S. Ct. 2351 (2006).

[53]Grutter v. Bollinger, 539 U.S. 306, 328, 91 FEP 1761 (2003). That narrow view of the permissibility of affirmative action in higher education was endorsed most strongly by the Fifth Circuit. *See* Hopwood v. State of Tex., 78 F.3d 932 (5th Cir. 1996); *see also* Podberesky v. Kirwan, 38 F.3d 147 (4th Cir. 1994) (holding unconstitutional a university scholarship program open only to African-American

Court noted that diversity "promotes 'cross-racial understanding,' helps to break down racial stereotypes and 'enables [students] to better understand persons of different races' "—benefits that not only serve important educational functions, but also, because education prepares students "for work and citizenship," important civic and social functions.[54]

The Court then went on in *Grutter* and *Gratz* to decide the key question—whether the two affirmative action plans were narrowly enough tailored to achieve permissibly the University's interest in diversity. "To be narrowly tailored," the Court held in *Grutter*,

> a race-conscious admissions plan cannot "insulat[e] each category of applicants with certain desired qualifications from competition with all other applicants." Instead, a university may consider race or ethnicity only as a "plus in a particular applicant's file," without "insulat[ing] the individual from comparison with all other candidates for the available seats." In other words, an admissions policy must be "flexible enough to consider all pertinent elements of diversity in light of the particular qualifications of each applicant, and to place them on the same footing for consideration, although not necessarily according them the same weight."[55]

The Court added that a race-conscious admissions plan "must remain flexible enough to ensure that each applicant is evaluated as an individual and not in any way that makes an applicant's race or ethnicity the defining feature of his or her application. The importance of this individualized consideration . . . is paramount."[56]

In addition, the Court emphasized that, to be narrowly tailored, a "race-conscious" affirmative action plan must not "unduly burden" non-minority candidates for admission.[57] At the same time,

---

students, the purpose of which was to address the continuing effects of the university's past discrimination, because it was not narrowly tailored to achieve its objective). Most lower courts had at least left open the possibility that diversity could provide a compelling state interest. *See, e.g.,* Johnson v. Board of Regents of Univ. of Ga., 263 F.3d 1234, 1244–45 (11th Cir. 2001); Brewer v. West Irondequoit Cent. Sch. Dist., 212 F.3d 738, 747–52 (2d Cir. 2000); Eisenberg v. Montgomery County Pub. Schs., 197 F.3d 123, 130 (4th Cir. 1999); Tuttle v. Arlington County Sch. Bd., 195 F.3d 698, 704 (4th Cir. 1999); Wessmann v. Gittens, 160 F.3d 790, 796 (1st Cir. 1998).

[54]539 U.S. at 330–31 (modifications in original; citations omitted).

[55]*Id.* at 334 (citations omitted) (modifications in original).

[56]*Id.* at 337.

[57]*Id.* at 341.

however, the Court cautioned that "[n]arrow tailoring does not require the exhaustion of every conceivable race-neutral alternative"—just "serious, good faith consideration of workable race-neutral alternatives that will achieve . . . diversity."[58] No less importantly, the Court emphasized that "race-conscious admissions policies must be limited in time," and it suggested that this requirement could be satisfied "by sunset provisions" and "periodic reviews to determine whether racial preferences are still necessary to achieve student body diversity."[59] Finally, the Court commended to universities for consideration "race-neutral alternatives" "as they develop,"[60] and it identified several such alternatives already in existence at other universities.[61]

Not surprisingly, the Court held that the law school affirmative action plan at issue in *Grutter* (with its emphasis on individualized determinations) passed constitutional muster,[62] but the undergraduate plan at issue in *Gratz* (which awarded fixed points to every minority applicant) did not. Neither conclusion, however, drew a consensus of the Justices. Four Justices (Chief Justice Rehnquist and Justices Kennedy, Scalia, and Thomas) dissented in *Grutter*,[63]

---

[58]Grutter v. Bollinger, 539 U.S. 306, 339, 91 FEP 1761 (2003).

[59]*Id.* at 342. As the Court explained in full: "We are mindful . . . that '[a] core purpose of the Fourteen Amendment was to do away with all governmentally imposed discrimination based on race.' Accordingly, race-conscious admissions policies must be limited in time. This requirement reflects that racial classifications, however compelling their goals, are potentially so dangerous that they may be employed no more broadly than the interest demands. Enshrining a permanent justification for racial preferences would offend this fundamental equal protection principle. We see no reason to exempt race-conscious admissions programs from the requirement that all government use of race must have a logical end point." *Id.* (emphasis and modifications in original; citations omitted).

[60]*Id.*

[61]*See id.*

[62]Relying on *Grutter* and *Gratz*, the Ninth Circuit in *Smith v. University of Washington*, 392 F.3d 367 (9th Cir. 2004), upheld the University of Washington Law School's race-based admissions plan, which similarly provided for individualized, holistic decision making. *See id.* at 375–82.

[63]Justices Scalia and Thomas staked out the most absolute position. Both strongly rejected the proposition that diversity is a compelling state interest. *See* Grutter v. Bollinger, 539 U.S. 306, 347, 91 FEP 1761 (2003) (Scalia, J., joined by Thomas, J., dissenting); *id.* at 349 (Thomas, J., joined by Scalia, J., dissenting); *see also* Gratz v. Bollinger, 539 U.S. 244, 281, 91 FEP 1803 (2003) (Thomas, J., dissenting) (contending that "a State's use of racial discrimination in higher education admissions is categorically prohibited by the Equal Protection Clause"). Chief Justice Rehnquist

and three Justices (Ginsburg, Souter, and Stevens) dissented in *Gratz*.[64]

Outside the context of higher education admissions policies, the Supreme Court first addressed a challenge to an affirmative action plan under the Equal Protection Clause in its 1986 decision in *Wygant v. Jackson Board of Education*.[65] *Wygant* involved a school board's layoff of tenured non-minority teachers and retention of minority teachers with less seniority under a collectively bargained plan.[66] The school board defended the implementation of the plan not on the ground that the board had itself discriminated in the past, but instead on the ground that the board was providing models for its minority students to alleviate the effects of societal discrimination. A five-member majority of the Court concluded that the plan was unconstitutional.[67]

Justice Powell's plurality opinion subjected the challenged racial classification to strict scrutiny, thereby requiring it to " 'be justified by a compelling governmental interest,' "[68] and " 'narrowly tailored to the achievement of that goal.' "[69] Applying the first criterion, the plurality rejected the school board's argument that its interest in providing role models for its minority students to alleviate the effects of societal discrimination was sufficiently compelling. The plurality concluded that a government employer could justify affirmative action only if it possessed, at the time it undertook the affirmative action, "convincing evidence that remedial action is warranted. That is, it must have sufficient evidence to

---

and Justice Kennedy limited their dissents in *Grutter* to the less categorical argument that the law school plan, being little more than a "naked effort to achieve racial balancing," was not narrowly tailored enough to survive strict scrutiny. *See id.* at 379 (Rehnquist, C.J., joined by Kennedy, Scalia, and Thomas, JJ., dissenting); *see also id.* at 387 (Kennedy, J., dissenting) (contending that the Court failed to subject the law school's plan—and, in particular, the means by which the law school sought to achieve racial diversity—to sufficiently strict scrutiny, as required by Justice Powell's *Bakke* opinion).

[64]Justice Stevens dissented only on the narrow ground that the petitioners lacked standing to sue. *See* 539 U.S. at 282 (Stevens, J., joined by Souter, J., dissenting).

[65]476 U.S. 267, 40 FEP 1321 (1986).

[66]*See id.* at 270.

[67]The majority included Chief Justice Burger and Justices O'Connor, Powell, and Rehnquist.

[68]*Id.* at 274 (quoting Palmore v. Sidoti, 466 U.S. 429, 432 (1984)).

[69]*Id.* (quoting Fullilove v. Klutznick, 448 U.S. 448, 480 (1980)).

justify the conclusion that there has been prior discrimination."[70] The government need not, however, establish in court that it was right in its conclusion; a mistaken conclusion supported by "strong evidence" will suffice.[71] Justice O'Connor similarly contended in her concurring opinion that, although a "public employer must have a firm basis for determining that affirmative action is warranted,"[72] "a contemporaneous or antecedent finding of past discrimination by a court or other competent body is not a constitutional prerequisite" to a public employer's lawful use of affirmative action.[73] Justice White supplied the fifth vote against the plan. Concurring only in the judgment, Justice White provided little explanation for his vote except to note that the justification asserted by the board was inadequate and that the impact on non-minorities too high a price to justify the board's use of race-based preferences.[74]

The *Wygant* plurality also rejected the school board's plan because it was not narrowly tailored to achieve its objective. According to the plurality, "the means chosen to accomplish the State's asserted purpose must be specifically and narrowly framed to accomplish that purpose."[75] In concluding that the plan did not satisfy this requirement, the plurality stressed the difference between hiring plans and lay-off plans and its preference for the former:

> [T]he means chosen to achieve the Board's asserted purposes is that of laying off nonminority teachers with greater seniority in

---

[70]Wygant v. Jackson Bd. of Educ., 476 U.S. 267, 277, 40 FEP 1321 (1986).

[71]*See id.* ("In such a case, the trial court must make a factual determination that the employer had a strong basis in evidence for its conclusion that remedial action was necessary."). The Court's four dissenters (Justices Brennan, Blackmun, Marshall, and Stevens) agreed with this point. *See id.* at 305 (Marshall, J., joined by Blackmun and Brennan, JJ., dissenting) ("The Court is correct to recognize, as it does at least implicitly today, that formal findings of past discrimination are not a necessary predicate to the adoption of affirmative-action policies, and that the scope of such policies need not be limited to remedying specific instances of identifiable discrimination."); *id.* at 305 (Stevens, J., dissenting) ("In my opinion, it is not necessary to find that the Board of Education has been guilty of racial discrimination in the past to support the conclusion that it has a legitimate interest in employing more black teachers in the future.").

[72]*Id.* at 292 (O'Connor, J., concurring).

[73]*Id.* at 289. Justice O'Connor noted that "[t]he imposition of a requirement that public employers make findings that they have engaged in illegal discrimination before they engage in affirmative action plans would severely undermine public employers' incentive to meet voluntarily their civil rights obligations." *Id.* at 290.

[74]*See id.* at 295 (White, J., concurring).

[75]Wygant v. Jackson Bd. of Educ., 476 U.S. 267, 280, 40 FEP 1321 (1986).

order to retain minority teachers with less seniority. We have previously expressed concern over the burden that a preferential-layoffs scheme imposes on innocent parties. In cases involving valid *hiring* goals, the burden to be borne by innocent individuals is diffused to a considerable extent among society generally. Though hiring goals may burden some innocent individuals, they simply do not impose the same kind of injury that layoffs impose. Denial of a future employment opportunity is not as intrusive as loss of an existing job. There are cases involving alteration of strict seniority layoffs, but they do not involve the critical element here—layoffs based on race. The Constitution does not require layoffs to be based on strict seniority. But it does require the State to meet a heavy burden of justification when it implements a layoff plan based on race. . . . While hiring goals impose a diffuse burden, often foreclosing only one of several opportunities, layoffs impose the entire burden of achieving racial equality on particular individuals, often resulting in serious disruption of their lives. That burden is too intrusive. We therefore hold that, as a means of accomplishing purposes that otherwise may be legitimate, the Board's layoff plan is not sufficiently narrowly tailored. Other, less intrusive means of accomplishing similar purposes—such as the adoption of hiring goals—are available.[76]

The Supreme Court applied and reaffirmed the *Wygant* strict-scrutiny approach to racial preferences in *City of Richmond v. J.A. Croson Co.*[77] *Croson* arose out of an equal protection challenge to a Richmond, Virginia ordinance requiring that 30 percent of all city construction contracts be awarded to minority-owned subcontractors.[78] In support of the set-aside, Richmond cited a statistical disparity between the percentage of minorities in the general population and the number of minority firms receiving city construction contracts. But the city did not, according to the Court, justify the ordinance with any "direct evidence of race discrimination on the part of the city in letting contracts or any evidence that the city's prime contractors had discriminated against minority-owned subcontractors."[79] The Court rejected the city's recitation of the

---

[76]*Id.* at 282–84 (emphasis added).

[77]488 U.S. 469, 492–94, 53 FEP 197 (1989).

[78]The Court did not address the "market participation" doctrine under which a state is accorded more deference when it spends through public contracting than when it regulates directly. *See* Kathleen M. Sullivan, City of Richmond v. J.A. Croson Co., *The Backlash Against Affirmative Action*, 64 Tul. L. REV. 1609, 1621–22 (1990).

[79]488 U.S. at 480.

ordinance's remedial purpose as being entitled to "little or no weight."[80]

Justice O'Connor's plurality opinion emphasized, at the outset, that only by applying strict scrutiny could the Court differentiate between benign (permissible) racial classifications and invidious (impermissible) racial classifications, and that strict scrutiny is not dependent on the race of the beneficiary of the preference. It applies equally to race-based classifications favoring whites as well as those favoring minority groups.[81] Although Justice Scalia did not join this part of Justice O'Connor's opinion, he agreed—indeed, emphasized—in a separate concurring opinion that *all* racial classifications are subject to strict scrutiny.[82] Five Justices thus agreed that strict scrutiny governed Richmond's affirmative action plan.

Applying strict scrutiny, the Court held Richmond's ordinance unconstitutional. Justice O'Connor's plurality opinion (which commanded a majority of the Justices with respect to its key conclusions) stated that the city failed to demonstrate a compelling government interest justifying the plan and that the plan was not narrowly tailored to remedy the effects of prior discrimination. The problem was that Richmond had not sufficiently established the factual predicate necessary to undertake affirmative action.[83] Justice O'Connor emphasized that the city had failed even to establish a "prima facie case of a constitutional or statutory violation by *anyone* in the Richmond construction industry."[84] Mere evidence of general "societal discrimination," Justice O'Connor added, is insufficient to justify race-based preferences, as is an "amorphous claim that there has been past discrimination in a particular industry."[85] Rather, the government must identify actual discrimination in the particular industry to which the plan applies,[86] and it must do so "with some specificity."[87] Justice Scalia later characterized

---

[80]*Id.* at 499–500.

[81]*See id.* at 492–94.

[82]*See* City of Richmond v. J.A. Croson Co., 488 U.S. 469, 520, 53 FEP 197 (1989) (Scalia, J., concurring).

[83]*See id.* at 498–99.

[84]*Id.* at 500 (emphasis in original).

[85]*Id.* at 499.

[86]*Id.* at 505.

[87]*Id.* at 504.

Croson as adopting a "strong basis in evidence" standard,[88] an assessment supported by language in *Croson* and other cases.[89]

Although Richmond had identified a disparity between the number of prime contracts awarded to minority firms and the minority population of the city, it had not identified a disparity between the number of prime contracts awarded to minority firms and the number of minority firms *qualified* to perform the contracts. Only the latter, Justice O'Connor suggested, could give rise to an "inference of discrimination."[90] Drawing on the Court's employment discrimination cases, Justice O'Connor concluded that, when special qualifications are necessary, the relevant comparator group is not the minority population at large, but the minority population qualified to perform the function at issue.[91] Justice O'Connor also found insufficient certain general, conclusory statements by Richmond city council members regarding the level of discrimination in the city's construction industry.[92]

At the same time, Justice O'Connor did stress that a public agency undertaking affirmative action need not have directly discriminated itself for its race-based preferences to survive strict scrutiny.[93] A city's "passive participation" in a system of private sector racial discrimination in the construction industry would be justification enough for undertaking affirmative action, even if the city did not itself actively discriminate in its contracting decisions. Joined by Chief Justice Rehnquist and Justice White on this point, Justice O'Connor stated that:

---

[88]Concrete Works of Colo., Inc. v. Denver, 540 U.S. 1027 (2003) (Scalia, J., joined by Rehnquist, C.J., dissenting from denial of certiorari).

[89]*See Croson*, 488 U.S. at 510 (citing to *Wygant*'s "strong basis in evidence" standard).

[90]*Id.* at 509.

[91]*See id.* at 501–03. *See generally* Chapters 3 (Adverse Impact) and 34 (Statistical and Other Expert Proof).

[92]*See* City of Richmond v. J.A. Croson Co., 488 U.S. 469, 499, 53 FEP 197 (1989). Justice O'Connor did not accord much weight to congressional findings of nationwide discrimination in the construction industry, *see id.* at 499–500, noting that "Congress explicitly recognized that the scope of the problem would vary from market area to market area," *id.* at 503.

[93]The Fourth Circuit had concluded below, by contrast, that the discrimination finding must concern " 'prime discrimination by the government unit involved.' " 822 F.2d 1355, 1358 (quoting Wygant v. Jackson Bd. of Educ., 476 U.S. 267, 274, 40 FEP 1321 (1986)). Several other lower federal courts had reached the same conclusion. *See, e.g.*, Associated Gen. Contractors of Cal. v. San Francisco, 813 F.2d 922, 931–32 (9th Cir. 1987).

if the city could show that it had essentially become a "passive participant" in a system of racial exclusion practiced by elements of the local construction industry, we think it clear that the city could take affirmative steps to dismantle such a system. It is beyond dispute that any public entity, state or federal, has a compelling interest in assuring that public dollars, drawn from the tax contributions of all citizens, do not serve to finance the evil of private prejudice.[94]

Elsewhere in her plurality opinion Justice O'Connor suggested that, under some limited circumstances at least, the existence of private discrimination in the construction industry might alone supply the necessary factual predicate for affirmative action, without referring to the city's participation in the discrimination.[95] Whether there

---

[94]488 U.S. at 492 (Kennedy, J., concurring). In a separate concurring opinion, Justice Kennedy substantially agreed with this point, writing that a city can discriminate "either by intentional acts or by passive complicity in acts of discrimination by the private sector." *Id.* at 519. Justice Scalia, also concurring, took the more absolutist position that the Equal Protection Clause allows states to "act by race 'to undo the effects of discrimination' only [1] where it is necessary to eliminate their own maintenance of a system of racial classification," *id.* at 529 (Scalia, J., concurring), or [2] to remedy harms suffered by identified victims of discrimination, *see id.* at 526; *see also* Adarand Constructors, Inc. v. Peña, 515 U.S. 200, 239, 67 FEP 1828 (1995) (Scalia, J., concurring). *See generally* GIRARDEAU A. SPANN, THE LAW OF AFFIRMATIVE ACTION 220 n.19 (2000) (noting that Justice Scalia has not taken the more extreme position that "racial classifications should be limited to the actual victims of discrimination"). *But cf.* Kathleen M. Sullivan, *The Jurisprudence of the Rehnquist Court*, 32 NOVA L. REV. 741, 746 n.25 (1998) (noting that Justice Scalia would allow for "race-conscious measures extending beyond remediation for [only] identified victims of discrimination"). The three dissenters (Justices Blackmun, Brennan, and Marshall) concluded that Richmond had a compelling interest to undertake the minority contractor set-aside—namely, the "prospective . . . one of preventing the city's own spending decisions from reinforcing and perpetuating the exclusionary effects of past discrimination." 488 U.S. at 537–38 (Marshall, J., joined by Blackmun and Brennan, JJ., dissenting, arguing for application of intermediate scrutiny).

[95]488 U.S. at 509 ("If the city of Richmond had evidence before it that nonminority contractors were systematically excluding minority businesses from subcontracting opportunities it could take action to end the discriminatory exclusion. Where there is a significant statistical disparity between the number of qualified minority contractors willing and able to perform a particular service and the number of such contractors actually engaged by the locality or the locality's prime contractors, an inference of discriminatory exclusion could arise. Under such circumstances, the city could act to dismantle the closed business system by taking appropriate measures against those who discriminate on the basis of race or other illegitimate criteria. In the extreme case, some form of narrowly tailored racial preference might be necessary to break down patterns of deliberate exclusion.") (citations omitted). *See generally* Ian Ayres & Fredrick E. Vars, *When Does Private Discrimination Justify Public Affirmative Action?*, 98 COLUM. L. REV. 1577 (1998).

is any substantive difference here—that is, between a government undertaking affirmative action in its contracting decisions to address private discrimination among the parties with which it contracts and undertaking affirmative action to address its "passive participation" in that discrimination—is not altogether clear and may, in any event, be a question of only theoretical interest.

In addition to finding that Richmond lacked a compelling state interest to undertake affirmative action, the Court also concluded that Richmond's plan was not sufficiently narrowly tailored to survive strict scrutiny. Two principal reasons underlay this conclusion. First, Richmond had failed to consider the use of "race-neutral" alternatives, among them offering financing to small contractors to help them compete in the construction market.[96] Second, the "30% quota" set by the city was not calculated to achieve any defensible objective and was not "tied to any injury suffered by anyone";[97] instead it rested on the indefensible assumption that, absent discrimination, minorities will join a particular trade in proportion to their representation in the general population.[98]

In the wake of Croson, the lower courts have consistently applied Croson's strict scrutiny approach to race-conscious affirmative action plans and consent decrees, with the exception only of plans that provide for outreach-type efforts but do not actually provide for tangible preferences in favor of minorities.[99] Although

---

[96]See 488 U.S. at 507. The Court noted that in Fullilove it "found that Congress had carefully examined and rejected race-neutral alternatives before enacting the MBE set-aside." Id.

[97]City of Richmond v. J.A. Croson Co., 488 U.S. 469, 499, 53 FEP 197 (1989).

[98]See id. at 507–08. In Cone Corp. v. Hillsborough County, 908 F.2d 908 (11th Cir. 1990), the Eleventh Circuit found constitutional the Hillsborough County MBE plan, which established a 25% annual goal for the participation of MBEs in county construction projects. The Eleventh Circuit emphasized the significant differences between Hillsborough's plan and the Richmond plan declared unconstitutional in Croson, including that Hillsborough's plan was put in place only after the County's previous voluntary plan failed to remedy discrimination in the award of construction dollars, and that the County had established a prima facie case of discrimination through a carefully prepared statistical analysis. See id. at 915–17.

[99]A number of courts have refused to apply strict scrutiny to employment outreach plans that, although they are organized around racial classifications, do not actually authorize or encourage minority preferences. See, e.g., Hill v. Ross, 183 F.3d 586, 589 (7th Cir. 1999) ("Affirmative action plans may be arranged along a spectrum. On the one end are detailed hiring quotas designed to overcome past discrimination. On the other end are the sort of plans that all federal contractors must adopt, under President Johnson's Executive Order 11246, a directive enforced by the Office of Federal Contract Compliance Programs. Plans of the latter kind promise to search intensively for minority candidates and to ensure equal opportunity by

some affirmative action plans[100] have survived *Croson*'s heightened standard of review,[101] many have not.

---

clearing away barriers to employment; they do not entail preferential treatment for any group in making offers of employment."). Courts that have approved outreach plans have usually done so on the ground that they do not receive any heightened scrutiny because they do not discriminate on the basis of race. *See, e.g.*, Duffy v. Wolle, 123 F.3d 1026, 1038–39, 75 FEP 1637 (8th Cir. 1997); Sussman v. Tanoue, 39 F. Supp. 2d 13, 24–25 (D.D.C. 1999), *aff'd*, 64 Fed. Appx. 248 (D.C. Cir. 2003); *cf.* Parents Involved in Cmty. Sch. v. Seattle Sch. Dist. No. 1, 426 F.3d 1162, 1194 (9th Cir. 2005) (Kozinski, J., concurring) (arguing that not all race-based classifications in aid of affirmative action should be subject to strict scrutiny, only those that raise core Fourteenth Amendment concerns), *cert. granted*, 126 S. Ct. 2351 (2006). *But see* Virdi v. Dekalb County Sch. Dist., 135 Fed. Appx. 262, 267 (11th Cir. 2005) (applying strict scrutiny to contractor outreach plan that, although it provided for specific numerical goals, required a race-neutral selection procedure; noting that strict scrutiny "applies to *all* racial classifications, not just those creating binding racial preferences") (emphasis in original); MD/DC/DE Broadcasters Ass'n v. FCC, 236 F.3d 13, 84 FEP 1376 (D.C. Cir. 2001) (invalidating minority outreach program under strict scrutiny in part on ground that it deprived non-minorities of the opportunity to compete for positions); Lutheran Church-Missouri Synod v. FCC, 141 F.3d 344, 353–56, 76 FEP 857 (D.C. Cir. 1998) (applying strict scrutiny to FCC regulations that required broadcasting licensees to implement race-based outreach efforts in hiring; emphasizing "that any regulation encouraging broad outreach to, as opposed to actual hiring of, a particular race would necessarily trigger strict scrutiny"); *see also* Florida A.G.C. Council, Inc. v. Florida, 303 F. Supp. 2d 1307, 1316 (N.D. Fla. 2004) (subjecting plan to strict scrutiny even though its hiring goals were "precatory" instead of "compulsory" because the plan nevertheless induced race-based decision making by its incentive structure) (citing *Lutheran Church-Missouri Synod*, 141 F.3d at 354). *See generally* Johnson v. California, 543 U.S. 499, 505–06 (2005) (emphasizing that strict scrutiny applies to all race-based classifications).

[100]Affirmative action can also, on rare occasion, be undertaken successfully outside the context of a formal plan. *See, e.g.*, Boston Police Superior Officers Fed'n v. City of Boston, 147 F.3d 13, 24–25, 91 FEP 803 (1st Cir. 1998) (upholding promotion of single African-American employee, in disregard of standard qualification procedures, in order to remediate past discrimination under special circumstances).

[101]*See, e.g.*, Petit v. City of Chi., 352 F.3d 1111, 1117, 92 FEP 1731 (7th Cir. 2003) ("standardization" of police department promotional exams to eliminate disparate impact on African-American and Hispanic applicants), *cert. denied*, 541 U.S. 1074 (2004); Majeske v. City of Chi., 218 F.3d 816, 824, 85 FEP 1713 (7th Cir. 2000) (remedial promotions in police department to redress past discrimination); Edwards v. City of Houston, 37 F.3d 1097, 1112–14 (5th Cir. 1994) (same); Peightal v. Metropolitan Dade County, 26 F.3d 1545, 1562, 71 FEP 1107 (11th Cir. 1994) (preferential treatment for minority firefighter applicants); Officers for Justice v. Civil Serv. Comm'n, 979 F.2d 721, 728, 62 FEP 868 (9th Cir. 1992) (promotional preferences in police department); Mackin v. City of Boston, 969 F.2d 1273, 1278, 59 FEP 474 (1st Cir. 1992) (preferential treatment of minority firefighter applicants); Jansen v. City of Cincinnati, 977 F.2d 238, 245, 64 FEP 1655 (6th Cir. 1992) (same); Stuart v. Roache, 951 F.2d 446, 450–51, 57 FEP 902 (1st Cir. 1991) (consent decree establishing goals and timetables for promotion); Donaghy v. City of Omaha, 933 F.2d 1448, 1461, 55 FEP 1547 (8th Cir. 1991) (promotion of African American over a higher-ranking white employee in police department under consent decree); Cone Corp. v. Hillsborough

Plans have most often been invalidated because the sponsoring state or local government agencies have failed to establish a compelling state interest justifying resort to race-based preferences—namely, the presence of unremedied past discrimination or current, ongoing discrimination.[102] Nearly all of the lower courts have, in particular, held that evidence of general "societal discrimination" (or the desire to prevent discrimination) will not, standing alone, justify race-based preferences. Instead, the sponsoring government agency must (at least outside the context of admissions policies in higher education) introduce evidence of its own discrimination or (outside the employment context) industry-wide discrimination in which it has been a passive participant.[103] On the fact-specific issue

---

County, 908 F.2d 908, 916–18 (11th Cir. 1990) (minority set-aside for municipal construction contracts); *see also* Howard v. McLucas, 871 F.2d 1000, 1011, 56 FEP 387 (11th Cir. 1989) (in case decided 4 months after *Croson*, upholding preferential treatment of minorities in promotions, but failing to cite *Croson*); *cf.* Ensley Branch, NAACP v. Seibels, 31 F.3d 1548, 1578, 1582 (11th Cir. 1994) (requiring modifications to consent decree to bring it into line with current standards and requiring an examination of the current factual predicate for race- and sex-conscious relief).

[102]*See, e.g.,* Contractors Ass'n of E. Pa. v. City of Phila., 91 F.3d 586, 569–605 (3d Cir. 1996) (set-asides for minority contractors); Middleton v. City of Flint, 92 F.3d 396, 407–09 (6th Cir. 1996) (requirement that 50% of all officers promoted to certain rank in police department be minorities); Brunet v. City of Columbus, 1 F.3d 390, 406, 64 FEP 1215 (6th Cir. 1993) (consent decree denying men the right to compete for all firefighter positions); Maryland Troopers Ass'n, Inc. v. Evans, 993 F.2d 1072, 1074, 61 FEP 1171 (4th Cir. 1993) (consent decree designed to ensure that African Americans constituted a fixed percentage of the state police). Already-remedied past discrimination is likewise insufficient, *see, e.g., Middleton*, 92 F.3d 396 at 409, as is compliance with a federal regulation, *see* Biondo v. City of Chi., 382 F.3d 680, 684, 94 FEP 513 (7th Cir. 2004) (compliance with EEOC regulations governing employment testing procedures), *cert. denied*, 543 U.S. 1152 (2005); *see also* Messer v. Meno, 130 F.3d 130, 136, 75 FEP 838 (5th Cir. 1997) ("the Supreme Court has rejected the notion that a state actor's compliance with federal mandates insulates the state from liability for discrimination").

[103]*See, e.g.,* Rothe Dev. Corp. v. U.S. Dep't of Defense, 262 F.3d 1306, 1317 (Fed. Cir. 2001) (government bears initial burden of establishing " 'strong basis in evidence' to believe that remedial action based on race was necessary") (quoting *Wygart*, 476 U.S. at 277); Airth v. City of Pomona, 216 F.3d 1082 (table), 2000 WL 425006 (9th Cir. Apr. 19, 2000) (same); *Majeske*, 218 F.3d at 820 (city "presented" persuasive statistical evidence of past discrimination and impact on current staffing); Engineering Contractors Ass'n v. Metropolitan Dade County, 122 F.3d 895, 911 (11th Cir. 1997) (plan can be supported by evidence that county is a " 'passive participant' in a system of racial exclusion practiced by elements of the local construction industry"); Monterey Mech. Co. v. Wilson, 125 F.3d 702, 712–13 (9th Cir. 1997); Associated Gen. Contractors v. New Haven, 41 F.3d 62, 66 (2d Cir. 1994); Davis v. Waterloo, 551 N.W.2d 876, 882, 71 FEP 988 (Iowa 1996).

as to what evidence is needed to prove discrimination sufficient to undertake affirmative action, however, the lower courts have not taken a consistent approach.[104]

Some generalizations are possible. Statistical evidence of an imbalance, without evidence of a causal connection to discrimination, will not supply the necessary factual predicate for affirmative action;[105] and, in the employment context, any statistical disparities must be evaluated using the appropriate labor pool, not simply by looking at general population statistics.[106] Similarly, anecdotal evidence of discrimination without valid statistical evidence will rarely, if ever, justify a race-based preference, although anecdotal evidence does have strong evidentiary value where it supplements other evidence.[107] Courts have concluded that a strong link between the plan and the discrimination further supports the existence of a factual predicate.[108] Whatever the proffered evidence,

---

[104]*See* Dallas Fire Fighters Ass'n v. City of Dallas, 526 U.S. 1046 (1999) (Breyer, J., joined by Ginsburg, J., dissenting from denial of certiorari) (noting arguable circuit split with respect to nature of evidentiary submission); *see also* Concrete Works of Colo., Inc. v. Denver, 540 U.S. 1027 (2003) (Scalia, J., joined by Rehnquist, C.J., dissenting from denial of certiorari) (noting failure of some circuits to require a sufficient factual predicate under *Croson*'s heightened scrutiny standard by requiring only an "inference of discrimination instead of a finding of actual discrimination").

[105]*See, e.g., Engineering Contractors Ass'n*, 122 F.3d at 926 (statistical evidence, by itself or in combination with anecdotal evidence, was insufficient); Dallas Fire Fighters Ass'n v. City of Dallas, 150 F.3d 438, 442, 77 FEP 1025 (5th Cir. 1998) (consent decree and statistical finding of underrepresentation of minorities, without more, does not establish past discrimination). Justice Breyer, dissenting from the subsequent denial of certiorari in *Dallas Fire Fighters*, argued that there may well have been sufficient evidence of discrimination on the record to justify resort to affirmative action, that at least several circuits appeared to have upheld affirmative action plans based on similar records, and that the circuits were divided concerning the "means of proving discrimination." 526 U.S. 1046 (1999) (Breyer, J., joined by Ginsburg, J., dissenting from denial of certiorari); *see also* Austin Black Contractors v. Austin, 78 F.3d 185, 186 (5th Cir. 1996) (dismissing contractors association's claim that city had to adopt an affirmative action plan based on minority underutilization in construction industry).

[106]*See, e.g., Middleton*, 92 F.3d at 406; *see also Contractors Ass'n of E. Pa.*, 91 F.3d at 606–07; Coral Constr. Co. v. King County, 941 F.2d 910, 917 (9th Cir. 1991) (upholding the lower court's exclusion of data from a neighboring jurisdiction and warning that "data sharing presents the risk that data of 'societal discrimination' will become the factual basis for an MBE plan").

[107]*See, e.g., Majeske*, 218 F.3d at 822, 85 FEP 1713; Wessmann v. Gittens, 160 F.3d 790 (1st Cir. 1998); McNamara v. City of Chi., 138 F.3d 1219, 1224, 76 FEP 668 (7th Cir. 1998); *Engineering Contractors Ass'n*, 122 F.3d at 925–26.

[108]*See, e.g.,* Concrete Works of Colo., Inc. v. Denver, 36 F.3d 1513, 1520–22 (10th Cir. 1994).

courts generally scrutinize it carefully and often have remanded cases for further development of a factual record or to resolve factual disputes (thereby often making summary judgment more difficult for government agencies to obtain).[109]

Nearly all of the post-*Croson* lower court cases were decided before the Supreme Court's 2003 university admissions affirmative action cases—*Gratz* and *Grutter*. Those cases raise the question whether factual predicates other than actual discrimination (in particular, diversity) will support affirmative action in the employment context. After *Croson* but before *Gratz* and *Grutter*, several circuits answered this question "no" and rejected the suggestion that the achievement of racial diversity constitutes a compelling state interest that will justify racial preferences for underrepresented minorities.[110]

In *Petit v. City of Chicago*,[111] the Seventh Circuit relied on *Grutter* and *Gratz* in holding that the Chicago police department's race-based promotions were justified by "compelling need" to have a diverse police force in a "racially and ethnically divided" city.[112] The court cited the need for public trust in the police across racial and ethnic lines and for internal cooperation within the department— which in turn help to increase "police effectiveness in protecting the city."[113] To similar effect is the Seventh Circuit's pre-*Gratz* and

---

[109]*See, e.g.*, Aiken v. City of Memphis, 37 F.3d 1155, 1158, 65 FEP 1757 (6th Cir. 1994); Billish v. City of Chi., 989 F.2d 890, 893–94, 61 FEP 678 (7th Cir. 1993); United States v. City of Miami, 2 F.3d 1497, 1507–08, 62 FEP 1474 (11th Cir. 1993) (en banc).

[110]*See* Lutheran Church-Missouri Synod v. FCC, 141 F.3d 344, 354, 76 FEP 857 (D.C. Cir. 1998) (in context of holding unconstitutional FCC regulations mandating that licensees undertake employment-related affirmative action with objective of increasing broadcasting diversity; seemingly rejecting proposition that diversity can constitute a compelling state interest); Back v. Carter, 933 F. Supp. 738, 756 (N.D. Ind. 1996) (diversity is not a compelling state interest in the employment context); *see also* Hayes v. Northern State Law Enforcement Officers Ass'n, 10 F.3d 207, 217, 63 FEP 374 (4th Cir. 1993) (declining to decide whether diversity provides a compelling state interest in the employment context). *But see* Hunter v. Regents of Univ. of Cal., 190 F.3d 1061, 1065–67 (9th Cir. 1999) (laboratory school for primary education run by state university could consider race of applicants as part of narrowly tailored plan to conduct research about multicultural, urban education).

[111]352 F.3d 1111, 92 FEP 1731 (7th Cir. 2003), *cert. denied*, 541 U.S. 1074 (2004).

[112]352 F.3d at 1114.

[113]*Id.* at 1115; *see also* Kohlbek v. City of Omaha, 447 F.3d 552, 97 FEP 1742 (8th Cir. 2006) (remanding for assessment whether workforce diversity was compelling interest with respect to firefighters).

Grutter decision in *Wittmer v. Peters*,[114] where the court rejected as dicta language from *Croson* and Fifth Circuit case law[115] that the only type of racial preference that can survive strict scrutiny is that which is designed to remedy past discrimination by the sponsor of the plan. "A judge would be unreasonable to conclude," the Seventh Circuit stated, "that no other consideration except a history of discrimination could ever warrant a discriminatory measure unless every other consideration had been presented to and rejected by him."[116] In *Wittmer*, the Seventh Circuit upheld the selection of an African-American lieutenant in a prison boot camp because it credited an expert's analysis that there was a need for an African-American lieutenant or authority figure in order to encourage the African-American inmates to participate in the "correctional game of brutal drill sergeant and brutalized recruit."[117] Distinguishing its rationale from the "role model" theory that the Supreme Court rejected in *Wygant*, the Seventh Circuit emphasized that boot camp inmates were not seeking to become correctional officers.[118] Another context in which courts may, under some circumstances, recognize diversity as a compelling state interest in employment is in the hiring of teachers.[119]

Just as a plan can be invalidated because the sponsoring government agency has not established a compelling state interest (the first prong of *Croson*), it can also be invalidated because it is not

---

[114]87 F.3d 916, 919, 71 FEP 312 (7th Cir. 1996).

[115]*See, e.g.,* Messer v. Meno, 130 F.3d 130, 75 FEP 838 (5th Cir. 1997). In *Messer*, the Fifth Circuit extended its antiaffirmative action university admissions decision in *Hopwood v. Texas*, 78 F.3d 932 (5th Cir. 1996) to the employment context. *See* 130 F.3d at 136.

[116]87 F.3d at 919; *see also* Petit v. Chicago, 31 F. Supp. 2d 604 (N.D. Ill. 1998) (the "attempt to avoid discrimination in violation of Title VII could be another such compelling interest").

[117]87 F.3d at 919.

[118]*See id. But see* McNamara v. City of Chi., 138 F.3d 1219, 1222 (7th Cir. 1998) (declining to extend *Wittmer* to the context of employment in an urban fire department absent compelling evidence that white firefighters could not be effective in minority neighborhoods); Ferrill v. Parker Group, Inc., 168 F.3d 468, 475–76, 79 FEP 161 (11th Cir. 1999) (rejecting employer's reliance on *Wittmer* to justify company's decision to assign African-American telemarketers to call on African-American potential voters).

[119]*See* University & Cmty. Coll. Sys. of Nevada v. Farmer, 930 P.2d 730, 735, 75 FEP 953 (Nev. 1997) (university had compelling interest in fostering culturally and ethnically diverse faculty).

"narrowly tailored" (the second prong of *Croson*). Sometimes courts interchange the two inquiries.[120] A common reason that a plan fails the narrowly-tailored requirement is that it unduly trammels on the rights of non-beneficiaries, either by seeking racial parity rather than merely an end to discrimination, or by continuing race-conscious affirmative action longer than necessary to eliminate discrimination.[121] The duration issue will take on greater significance given the Supreme Court's admonition in *Grutter* that all "*race-conscious admissions plans must be limited in time.*"[122] A related ground on which a plan may not satisfy the narrowly-tailored requirement is that the government has failed to consider less restrictive means to achieve its objectives, including, where appropriate, racially neutral alternatives.[123]

---

[120]*See, e.g.*, Kohlbek v. City of Omaha, 447 F.3d 552 (8th Cir. 2006) (plan was not narrowly tailored because the employer's declared underutilization of minorities was not statistically significant and thus did not establish a prima face case justifying race-based classifications).

[121]*See, e.g.*, Virdi v. Dekalb County Sch. Dist., 135 Fed. Appx. 262, 268 (11th Cir. 2005) ("unlimited duration of racial goals" under affirmative action plan applicable to contractors "demonstrates a lack of narrow tailoring"); Ensley Branch, NAACP v. Seibels, 31 F.3d 1548, 1571–74 & n.12 (11th Cir. 1994) (district court's failure to impose a reasonable deadline for developing job-related selection procedures, and defendant's failure to implement such procedures for 13 years, unjustifiably resulted in discrimination against non-beneficiaries of plan); Crumpton v. Bridgeport Educ. Ass'n, 993 F.2d 1023, 1030–31, 61 FEP 1295 (2d Cir. 1993) (modification of a consent decree in order to give absolute preference to minority-group teachers in a layoff not narrowly tailored); Detroit Police Officers Ass'n v. Young, 989 F.2d 225, 228, 61 FEP 577 (6th Cir. 1993) (19-year term in a promotion plan was excessive since the plan's long-term goal had largely been achieved); Hayes v. Northern State Law Enforcement Officers Ass'n, 10 F.3d 207, 215–17, 63 FEP 374 (4th Cir. 1993) (racial preference of unlimited duration designed to maintain, rather than attain, a specific racial composition within a job classification was not narrowly tailored). As the Eleventh Circuit explained in *Ensley Branch*, long-term racial goals are improper because "they are designed to create parity between the racial composition of the labor pool and the race of the employees in each job position." 31 F.3d at 1570–71.

[122]Grutter v. Bollinger, 539 U.S. 306, 342, 91 FEP 1761 (2003) (emphasis in original).

[123]*See, e.g., Virdi*, 135 Fed. Appx. at 268 (holding unconstitutional race-based awards of contracts because school district had failed to consider race-neutral alternatives to increase minority representation, including nonpreferential outreach plans); *cf.* Walker v. City of Mesquite, 169 F.3d 973, 987 (5th Cir. 1999) (holding unconstitutional provision in court's remedial order calling for construction or acquisition of units of public housing in "predominantly white" neighborhoods because promising, nonracially discriminatory ways existed to desegregate public housing); Contractors Ass'n of E. Pa. v. City of Phila., 91 F.3d 586, 609–10 (3d Cir. 1996) (invalidating city ordinance creating set-asides for minority subcontractors in order

Yet another ground on which a plan may not satisfy the narrowly-tailored requirement is that it is over-inclusive because it confers benefits not only on those minorities who have been discriminated against, but also those who have not been. A plan may fail in this regard, for instance, because it benefits all minority groups even though only evidence of actual discrimination against a single minority group justifies the plan's existence.[124] By contrast, a plan will not fail strict scrutiny because it is underinclusive—that is, it does not extend affirmative action preferences to all disadvantaged minority groups—as long as the exclusion of groups was not motivated by a discriminatory purpose and a rational basis exists for the exclusion.[125]

---

to achieve "participation goals" because the set-aside failed to include either race-neutral or less burdensome remedies to encourage minority subcontractor participation); Engineering Contractors Ass'n v. Metropolitan Dade County, 122 F.3d 895, 927 (11th Cir. 1997) (invalidating plan because county failed to consider race-neutral remedies, such as elimination of bureaucratic barriers or passage of local ordinances prohibiting discrimination).

[124]*See* Jana-Rock Constr., Inc. v. New York State Dep't of Econ. Dev., 438 F.3d 195, 208 (2d Cir. 2006); *see also* Alexander v. Estepp, 95 F.3d 312, 316, 71 FEP 1279 (4th Cir. 1996) (invalidating plan because it benefited all minority groups rather than merely discriminated-against African Americans); *Contractors Ass'n of E. Pa.*, 91 F.3d at 607 (affirmative action plan was not narrowly tailored in part because it benefited groups of minorities against which no discrimination had been established); Black Fire Fighters' Ass'n v. City of Dallas, 19 F.3d 992, 995–97, 64 FEP 764 (5th Cir. 1994) (rejecting a "skip promotion" remedy, which provided for promotions of "qualified blacks" over higher-scoring white candidates, because there were identifiable victims of past discrimination still employed by fire department who would not necessarily benefit from this remedy, while African Americans who were not injured by past discrimination would benefit; noting, however, that an affirmative action plan would not necessarily always fail the narrowly tailored requirement merely because it might confer benefits on nonvictims of discrimination); Coral Constr. Co. v. King County, 941 F.2d 910, 925 (9th Cir. 1991) (reversing summary judgment on grounds of overbreadth because affirmative action plan permitted participation by businesses that had no prior contact with the county that sponsored the plan); *cf.* Hershell Gill Consulting Eng'g v. Miami-Dade County, 333 F. Supp. 2d 1305, 1326–30 (S.D. Fla. 2004) (finding municipal affirmative action plan unconstitutional in part because some of its beneficiary groups, though they constituted minorities at the federal and state level, constituted majorities in the local communities where the preferences operated).

[125]*See, e.g., Jana-Rock Constr.*, 438 F.3d at 207, 210–12 (exclusion from the definition of "Hispanic" people of Spanish or Portuguese descent who were not also of Latin American descent, with respect to an affirmative action plan benefiting Hispanics and other minorities, passed constitutional muster under deferential rational basis review; strict scrutiny would only be applied to such an exclusion if the plaintiffs presented evidence that a discriminatory purpose motivated the exclusion).

A plan also can fail the narrowly tailored requirement because it sets goals disproportionate to the actual discrimination suffered by the minority group it is intended to benefit. This can happen either because the plan sets numerical goals without due consideration for the relevant labor pool[126]—a defect that also, of course, deprives the plan of the necessary factual predicate—or by setting goals beyond those that are necessary to remedy the actual discrimination that provides the factual predicate for the plan in the first place.[127] As the Seventh Circuit has explained, the question is whether a numeric goal represents "a plausible lower-bound estimate of a shortfall in minority representation."[128]

b. Sex-Based Plans. For three decades the Supreme Court has held (outside the employment discrimination context) that sex-based distinctions by public agencies are subject to the more deferential intermediate standard of review.[129] *Croson* did not modify the intermediate standard of review applicable to sex-based classifications.[130] Most circuits have held that sex-based affirmative action

---

[126]*See, e.g., Contractors Ass'n of E. Pa.*, 91 F.3d at 606–07 (3d Cir. 1996) (plan was not narrowly tailored in part because its numerical goals were based on percentage of minorities in the general population and not the applicable labor pool); Middleton v. City of Flint, 92 F.3d 396, 406, 71 FEP 962 (6th Cir. 1996) (same); Back v. Carter, 933 F. Supp. 738, 756 (N.D. Ind. 1996) (same); Mallory v. Harkness, 895 F. Supp. 1556, 1560 (S.D. Fla. 1995) (same), *aff'd*, 109 F.3d 771 (11th Cir. 1997).

[127]The plan in *Croson* suffered from this defect. *See* City of Richmond v. J.A. Croson Co., 488 U.S. 469, 499, 53 FEP 197 (1989); *see also* Kohlbek v. City of Omaha, 447 F.3d 552, 557 (8th Cir. 2006) (plan was not narrowly tailored in part because its methodology for declaring "underutilization" "trigger[ed]" racial classifications in more situations than if a test of statistical significance were used to determine whether racial discrimination has occurred"); *Mallory*, 895 F. Supp. at 1560 (holding unconstitutional a statute requiring that one-third of all appointees to judicial commissions be women or minorities because there was no correlation between numerical quota and injury); *cf.* Dallas Fire Fighters Ass'n v. City of Dallas, 885 F. Supp. 915, 923 (N.D. Tex. 1995) (plan was not narrowly tailored because it set a single uniform promotion goal across all ranks of fire fighters without taking into account the number of qualified candidates in the feeder pool, which varied for each rank), *aff'd in part and rev'd in part*, 150 F.3d 438, 77 FEP 1025 (5th Cir. 1998).

[128]Majeske v. City of Chi., 218 F.3d 816, 823, 85 FEP 1713 (7th Cir. 2000).

[129]*See, e.g.,* Craig v. Boren, 429 U.S. 190, 197 (1976).

[130]*See* Contractors Ass'n of E. Pa. v. City of Phila., 6 F.3d 990, 1010, 3 AD 167 (3d Cir. 1993) ("Logically, a city must be able to rely on less evidence in enacting a gender preference than a racial preference because applying *Croson*'s evidentiary standard to a gender preference would eviscerate the difference between strict and intermediate scrutiny."). Dissenting in *Adarand Constructors, Inc. v. Peña,* 515 U.S. 200, 67 FEP 1828 (1995), Justice Stevens noted what he perceived to be

plans are subject only to intermediate scrutiny.[131] The Sixth Circuit, by contrast, has applied strict scrutiny to plans that give preferences to women and has applied intermediate scrutiny only to plans that are sex-"conscious" but do not accord actual preferences to women.[132] The Second Circuit has reserved the question,[133] and legal commentators are divided.[134]

Under intermediate scrutiny, a sex-based preference "may be upheld so long as it is substantially related to an important government objective."[135] Very few case cases, however, have addressed the key issue of the nature of the government's evidentiary burden.[136]

---

the anomalous result that affirmative action benefiting women would be more easily justified than affirmative action benefiting African Americans, "even though the primary purpose of the Equal Protection Clause was to end discrimination against the former slaves." *Id.* at 2122.

[131]*See* Danskine v. Miami Dade Fire Dep't, 253 F.3d 1288, 1295–1301 (11th Cir. 2001); Engineering Contractors Ass'n v. Metropolitan Dade County, 122 F.3d 895, 907 (11th Cir. 1997); Concrete Works of Colo., Inc. v. Denver, 36 F.3d 1513, 1519 (10th Cir. 1994); Ensley Branch, NAACP v. Seibels, 31 F.3d 1548, 1579–80 (11th Cir. 1994); *Contractors Ass'n of E. Pa.*, 6 F.3d at 1000–01; Coral Constr. Co. v. King County, 941 F.2d 910, 931 (9th Cir. 1991); Back v. Carter, 933 F. Supp. 738, 755 (N.D. Ind. 1996).

[132]*See* Brunet v. City of Columbus, 1 F.3d 390, 403–04, 64 FEP 1215 (6th Cir. 1993); Conlin v. Blanchard, 890 F.2d 811, 816, 51 FEP 707 (6th Cir. 1989).

[133]*See* Harrison & Burrowes Bridge Constructors, Inc. v. Cuomo, 981 F.2d 50, 61–62 (2d Cir. 1992).

[134]*See, e.g.*, Jason M. Skaggs, *Justifying Gender-Based Affirmative Action Under* United States v. Virginia*'s "Exceedingly Persuasive Justification" Standard*, 86 CALIF. L. REV. 1169 (1998); Rebecca L. Berkeley, *Gender Based Affirmative Action: A Journey That Has Only Just Begun*, 50 WASH. U. J. URB. & CONTEMP. L. 353 (1996); Deborah L. Brake, *Sex as a Suspect Class: An Argument for Applying Strict Scrutiny to Gender Discrimination*, 6 SETON HALL CONST. L.J. 953 (1996); John Galotto, *Strict Scrutiny for Gender, via* Croson, 93 COLUM. L. REV. 508 (1993); Peter Lurie, Comment, *The Law as They Found It: Disentangling Gender-Based Affirmative Action Plans From* Croson, 59 U. Chi. L. REV. 1563 (1992).

[135]*Engineering Contractors Ass'n*, 122 F.3d at 908.

[136]*See Contractors Ass'n of E. Pa.*, 6 F.3d at 1010, 3 AD 167 ("Few cases have considered the evidentiary burden needed to satisfy intermediate scrutiny in this context and there is no *Croson* analogue to provide a ready reference point."). The courts have not for the most part offered much guidance on the means by which discrimination must be proven. *See id.* ("In particular, it is unclear whether statistical evidence as well as anecdotal evidence is required to establish the discrimination necessary to satisfy intermediate scrutiny, and if so, how much statistical evidence is necessary. The Supreme Court gender-preference cases are inconclusive. The Court has never squarely ruled on the necessity of statistical evidence of gender discrimination."). The Ninth Circuit sanctioned affirmative action in one case based largely on an affidavit containing little statistical evidence. *See* Coral Constr. Co. v. King County, 941 F.2d 910, 931 (9th Cir. 1991). *But cf.* Hershell Gill Consulting Eng'g v. Miami-Dade County, 333 F. Supp. 2d 1305, 1333 (S.D. Fl. 2004) (finding sex-based

Most recently, the Eleventh Circuit has held that although a sex-based preference must rest on evidence of past discrimination against women, the evidence need not meet *Croson*'s "strong basis in evidence" standard but instead a less exacting "sufficient basis in evidence" standard.[137] Conceding that this standard eludes precise definition, the Eleventh Circuit offered two "guidelines."[138] First, the proponent of affirmative action must " 'demonstrate some past discrimination, . . . but not necessarily discrimination by the government itself, . . . in the economic sphere at which the affirmative action plan is directed.' "[139] Second, the proponent must show that its resort to affirmative action is the " 'product of analysis rather than a stereotyped reaction based on habit,' " although it need not defend the affirmative action as a necessary " 'last resort.' "[140] The Eleventh Circuit also made clear that a sex-based plan need not necessarily tie its goals to the proportion of women in the qualified market, and otherwise be as narrowly tailored to achieve the government's objective as a race-based plan.[141]

2. Congressionally Sanctioned Affirmative Action

A divided Supreme Court held in *Adarand Constructors, Inc. v. Peña*[142] that the Due Process Clause of the Fifth Amendment mandates the application of strict scrutiny to federal congressionally enacted racial preferences, just as the Fourteenth Amendment mandates the application of strict scrutiny to preferences adopted by state and local governments.[143] *Adarand* marked a departure from

---

contractor set-aside plan unconstitutional because the sponsor had no evidence as to "who is discriminating and where the discrimination is taking place").

[137]Danskine v. Miami-Dade Fire Dep't, 253 F.3d 1288, 1294 (11th Cir. 2001). In *Danskine*, the Eleventh Circuit seemed to place much of the burden of persuasion on the plaintiffs. *See id.* at 1296–98; *cf. Contractors Ass'n of E. Pa.*, 6 F.3d at 1011 (seemingly placing burden of persuasion on government).

[138]253 F.3d at 1294.

[139]*Id.* (quoting Engineering Contractors Ass'n of S. Fla., Inc. v. Metropolitan Dade County, 122 F.3d 895, 908–11 (11th Cir. 1997)); *see also Coral Constr.*, 941 F.2d at 932 ("Unlike the strict standard of review applied to race-conscious plans, intermediate scrutiny does not require any showing of governmental involvement, active or passive, in the discrimination it seeks to remedy.").

[140]*Danskine*, 253 F.3d at 1294.

[141]*See id.* at 1299.

[142]515 U.S. 200, 67 FEP 1828 (1995).

[143]*See id.* at 227. The majority opinion in *Adarand* stated that it was unnecessary to address the Justices' "different views of the authority § 5 of the Fourteenth

the Court's prior, more-deferential approach to congressionally sanctioned affirmative action. In *Fullilove v. Klutznick*,[144] a six-member majority of the Court approved a 10 percent "minority business enterprise" set-aside enacted by Congress, declaring that Congress has "broad remedial powers" to which the Court must defer once Congress has acted after appropriate consideration, although a majority did not endorse a single standard of review.[145] A decade later, in *Metro Broadcasting, Inc. v. FCC*,[146] a divided Court upheld the FCC's racial preferences in broadcast licensing on the grounds that "they serve the important governmental objective of broadcast diversity" and "are substantially related to the achievement of that objective."[147] *Adarand* overruled both *Fullilove* and *Metro Broadcasting* to the extent that they had applied intermediate scrutiny.[148]

Adarand arose from a challenge by a non-minority subcontractor that, although it was the lowest bidder, lost a federal subcontract to

---

Amendment confers upon Congress to deal with the problem of racial discrimination, and the extent to which courts should defer to Congress' exercise of that authority." *Id.* at 230. Three of the dissenting Justices agreed on that point. *See id.* at 255 n.11 (Stevens, J., joined by Breyer and Ginsburg, JJ., dissenting). Justice Souter stated in his dissent that "it is also worth noting that nothing in today's opinion implies any view of Congress's § 5 power and the deference due its exercise." *Id.* at 268.

[144]448 U.S. 448 (1980).

[145]*See id.* at 483–84 (Burger, C.J., joined by Powell and White, JJ.); *id.* at 522 (Marshall, J., joined by Brennan and Blackmun, JJ., concurring). According to Chief Justice Burger and Justice White, the racial preference survived constitutional challenge whether the Court applied strict scrutiny or (as Justices Blackmun, Brennan, and Marshall contended was the applicable standard of review) intermediate scrutiny. *See id.* at 491–92 (Burger, C.J., joined by White, J.); *id.* at 518–19 (Marshall, J., joined by Blackmun and Brennan, JJ. concurring). Neither Chief Justice Burger nor Justice White committed to one or the other. Justice Powell, on the other hand, contended that strict scrutiny applied, *see id.* at 496 (Powell, J., concurring), as did the three dissenting justices, *see id.* at 528–30 (Stewart, J., joined by Rehnquist, J., dissenting) and at 548–51 (Stevens, J. dissenting).

[146]497 U.S. 547, 53 FEP 161 (1990).

[147]*Id.* at 566. Anticipating the dissolution of the *Metro Broadcasting* majority, the District of Columbia Circuit ruled in *Lamprecht v. FCC*, 958 F.2d 382 (D.C. Cir. 1992), that the federal government may not give preferential treatment to women in awarding broadcast licenses. *Lamprecht* arose from a challenge by a male broadcaster to the FCC's award of a license to a female broadcaster, who had been given preferential treatment under the same FCC affirmative action policy at issue in *Metro Broadcasting*. The court's opinion relied on statistics that purportedly showed that stations owned by women would not increase "women's planning" to the same extent that ownership by a racial minority would increase "minority planning." *Id.* at 395.

[148]*See* Adarand Constructors, Inc. v. Peña, 515 U.S. 200, 67 FEP 1828 (1995); *id.* at 225–27 (overruling *Metro Broad.*); *id.* at 237 (overruling *Fullilove*).

a minority-owned small business solely because of a federal affir-mative action incentive offered to the prime contractor to subcon-tract with minority-owned small businesses.[149] The contractor "receive[d] additional compensation [for] hir[ing] subcontractors certified as small businesses controlled by 'socially and economi-cally disadvantaged individuals.' "[150] The *Adarand* plaintiff chal-lenged, in particular, the statutory presumption that "socially and economically disadvantaged individuals include Black Americans, Asian Pacific Americans, and other minorities."[151] The trial court applied *Metro Broadcasting's* intermediate scrutiny standard and granted summary judgment for the government. The Tenth Circuit affirmed.[152]

The Supreme Court reversed and remanded. Writing for the majority, Justice O'Connor reviewed the Court's prior equal pro-tection cases and found—*Metro Broadcasting* aside—three areas of common ground:

> First, *skepticism*: "[a]ny preference based on racial or ethnic crite-ria must necessarily receive a most searching examination." Second, *consistency*: "the standard of review under the Equal Protection Clause is not dependent on the race of those burdened or benefited by a particular classification," *i.e.*, all racial classifications reviewable under the Equal Protection Clause must be strictly scrutinized. And third, *congruence*: "[e]qual protection analysis in the Fifth Amend-ment area is the same as that under the Fourteenth Amendment."[153]

"Taken together," Justice O'Connor stated, "these three propositions lead to the conclusion that any person, of whatever race, has the right to demand that any government actor subject to the Consti-tution justify any racial classification subjecting that person to un-equal treatment under the strictest judicial scrutiny."[154] No special deference is to be given to federal race-based preferences, Justice O'Connor added, just because they may appear "benign" rather than "invidious" by favoring traditionally disadvantaged minorities.[155]

---

[149]*See id.* at 205–10.

[150]*Id.* at 205.

[151]*Id.* at 204–06.

[152]16 F.3d 1537 (10th Cir. 1994).

[153]Adarand Constructors, Inc. v. Peña, 515 U.S. 200, 223–24, 67 FEP 1828 (1995) (modifications in original; citations omitted).

[154]*Id.* The Court's formulation in *Adarand* of the strict-scrutiny standard is con-sistent with the standards set forth in *Wygant, Croson*, and other cases: "[Racial classifications] are constitutional only if they are narrowly tailored measures that further compelling government interests." *Id.* at 227.

[155]*Id.* at 226–29.

At the same time, Justice O'Connor made clear that strict scrutiny would not necessarily lead to the invalidation of all race-based preferences—that strict scrutiny is not, as some commentators and courts have observed, "strict in theory, but fatal in fact."[156] "When race-based action is necessary to further a compelling interest, such action is within constitutional constraints if it satisfies the 'narrow tailoring' test this Court has set out in previous cases."[157] Justice O'Connor also noted that factors such as a plan's intent to benefit members of a traditionally discriminated-against group may be considered in determining whether the plan is narrowly tailored.[158] The five-Justice majority remanded *Adarand* to the lower court to test the challenged plan under strict scrutiny.[159]

Several congressionally sanctioned affirmative action plans—most of them involving minority set-asides for Department of Transportation contracts—have survived strict scrutiny post-*Adarand*.[160] The one federal employment affirmative action plan to have come

---

[156]*Id.* at 237.

[157]*Id.* Chief Justice Rehnquist and Justice Kennedy joined Justice O'Connor's opinion in part. *See id.* at 202–03 (Rehnquist, C.J., joined by Kennedy, J., concurring). Justice Scalia agreed with Justice O'Connor's adoption of strict scrutiny as the governing standard, but differed with her with respect to what it would mean in application. According to Justice Scalia, "government can never have a 'compelling interest' in discriminating on the basis of race in order to 'make up' for past racial discrimination in the opposite direction. . . . [U]nder our Constitution there can be no such thing as either a creditor or a debtor race. . . . In the eyes of government, we are just one race here. It is American." *Id.* at 239 (Scalia, J., concurring in the judgment) (citations omitted). Justice Thomas, although also joining Justice O'Connor's opinion in part, seemed to agree with Justice Scalia on this point. He too doubted whether any race-based preference could survive strict scrutiny: "In my mind, government-sponsored racial discrimination based on benign prejudice is just as noxious as discrimination inspired by malicious prejudice. In each instance, it is racial discrimination, plain and simple." *Id.* at 241 (Thomas, J., concurring in part and concurring in the judgment) (footnote omitted). According to Justice Ginsburg, all of the Justices other than Justices Scalia and Thomas believe that, no matter what standard of review is applied, some race-based affirmative action plans are constitutional. *See id.* at 271–76 (Ginsburg, J., dissenting, joined by Breyer, J.).

[158]*See Adarand Constructors*, 515 U.S. at 227, 67 FEP 1828; *see also id.* at 242 (Stevens, J., joined by Ginsburg, J., dissenting); *id.* at 271–74 (Ginsburg, J., joined by Breyer, J., dissenting).

[159]*Id.* at 239.

[160]*See, e.g.*, Western States Paving Co. v. Washington State Dep't of Transp., 407 F.3d 983, 1002–03 (9th Cir. 2005) (upholding facial constitutionality of Transportation Equity Act for the twenty-first century, but not application thereof by State of Washington), *cert. denied*, 126 S. Ct. 1332 (2006); Adarand Constructors, Inc. v. Slater, 228 F.3d 1147, 1186–87 (10th Cir. 2000) (although original plan was not narrowly tailored, present plan passes scrutiny as to program on its face; nevertheless, remand required for development of facts regarding program implementation); Sherbrooke Turf,

before a federal appellate court, on the other hand, did not survive *Adarand*'s strict scrutiny standard. In *Lutheran Church-Missouri Synod v. FCC*,[161] the District of Columbia Circuit held unconstitutional an FCC regulation that required radio stations to maintain workplaces that mirrored the racial breakdown of their metropolitan statistical audiences. The FCC argued in support of the regulation that the diverse workplace would result in diverse broadcast planning. The court held that, even assuming plan diversity constitutes a compelling interest, the regulations' inclusion of lower-level employees was not narrowly tailored to that interest given the absence of evidence that those employees participated in broadcasting decisions.[162]

Although *Adarand* has certainly blurred the historical distinction between congressionally sanctioned and state and local affirmative action plans, Congress may be entitled to some deference to which state and local governments are not when undertaking affirmative action under Congress' Fourteenth Amendment enforcement authority.[163] The matter is not settled, and the Justices in the *Adarand* majority declined to address it specifically.[164] The Supreme Court initially agreed in one post-*Adarand* case to address the standard applicable to federal legislation undertaken to remedy race discrimination under Congress' Fourteenth Amendment remedial authority, but it later dismissed the grant of certiorari.[165]

Inc. v. Minnesota Dep't of Transp., 345 F.3d 964, 972–73 (8th Cir. 2003) (DOT regulations pass narrow tailoring requirements on their face and as applied by two states), *cert. denied*, 541 U.S. 1041 (2004). *But see* Rothe Dev. Corp. v. U.S. Dep't of Defense, 324 F. Supp. 2d 840 (W.D. Tex. 2004) (holding unconstitutional congressionally established Department of Defense plan under which "small disadvantaged businesses" received preferences under contracting system because Congress failed to consider whether statistical evidence established discrimination in the private sector contracting practices to which the plan applied, but upholding a later reauthorization of the same plan because it was predicated on statistical findings of discrimination).

[161]141 F.3d 344, 76 FEP 857 (D.C. Cir. 1998).

[162]*See id.* at 352.

[163]*See, e.g.*, Cortez III Serv. Corp. v. NASA, 950 F. Supp. 357, 361–63 (D.D.C. 1996). *But cf. Rothe Dev. Corp.*, 262 F.3d at 1321 ("no greater deference accorded to determination of Congress than would be given to a state or municipal racial classification").

[164]Adarand Constructors, Inc. v. Peña, 515 U.S. 200, 231, 67 FEP 1828 (1995).

[165]Adarand Constructors, Inc. v. Mineta, 532 U.S. 967 (2001) (granting certiorari on the question "Whether the court of appeals misapplied the strict scrutiny standard in determining if Congress had a compelling interest to enact legislation [under the Fourteenth Amendment's enforcement clause] designed to remedy the effects of racial discrimination.").

C. Voluntary Affirmative Action Plans Under Title VII

1. Legality of Affirmative Action Under Title VII

One year after *Bakke*, the Supreme Court decided *Steelworkers v. Weber*,[166] the first "reverse" discrimination case involving an affirmative action plan to come before the Court under Title VII. In 1974, Kaiser Aluminum and the United Steelworkers entered into a collective bargaining agreement that provided for the establishment of an on-the-job program to train employees for craft jobs. This program replaced the previous requirement of prior experience for entrance into craft jobs. For every two training vacancies, one African American and one white employee were to be selected from race-segregated lists of employees. Each list ranked employees by seniority. This 50 percent selection ratio was to be maintained until the percentage of African-American craft workers at Kaiser approximated the percentage of African Americans in the local labor force surrounding each Kaiser plant.

Weber, a white production worker, challenged the plan under Title VII after he was passed over for participation in the training program in favor of an African-American employee with less seniority. The Supreme Court found that the Kaiser-Steelworkers plan passed muster under Title VII. A majority of the Justices concluded that Title VII could not be construed to bar "all private, voluntary, race-conscious" efforts to abolish "traditional patterns of racial segregation."[167] A "literal construction" of §§ 703(a) and (d)—which prohibit discrimination in employment and employer-sponsored training programs, respectively—was "misplaced" in light of the remedial purpose behind Title VII and the background against which it was enacted.[168] As for § 703(j), the Court concluded that it only prevents the federal government from *requiring* preferential treatment; it does not, as Weber argued, prohibit all voluntary affirmative action.[169]

---

[166]443 U.S. 193, 20 FEP 1 (1979).

[167]*Id.* at 204.

[168]*Id.* at 201, 206–07. *But see id.* at 230–52 (Rehnquist, J., dissenting) (contending that Congress' intention was to bar voluntary, private sector affirmative action).

[169]*Id.* at 205–07. *But cf.* McDonald v. Santa Fe Trail Transp. Co., 427 U.S. 273, 12 FEP 1577 (1976) (holding that Title VII prohibits discrimination against white employees).

2. Requirements for a Valid Plan

a. *The Supreme Court's Evolving View—From* Weber *to* Johnson. Although *Weber* declined to draw a precise line between permissible and impermissible affirmative action, the case has been widely read to establish a three-part test[170] for evaluating the legality of voluntary affirmative action plans and employment actions taken under them.[171]

First, there must be a factual predicate for a voluntary affirmative action plan. In *Weber*, the evidence showed a clear statistical disparity: African Americans constituted 39 percent of the surrounding labor market, but filled only 1.83 percent of Kaiser's craft positions.[172] This raised a strong presumption of discrimination under *International Brotherhood of Teamsters v. United States*[173] and *Hazelwood School District v. United States*,[174] both of which had endorsed reliance upon a statistically significant disparity as a basis for a finding of discrimination. The Court also took judicial notice of governmental and academic findings that African Americans had historically been excluded from craft positions, with the result that African-American applicants were disadvantaged when employers used past experience as a selection criterion for such positions.[175] What the Court did not say, however, was whether the validity of an affirmative action plan depends upon a past history of discrimination by the actual employer whose plan is being challenged as opposed to general societal discrimination. The Court noted only that the Kaiser plan had been adopted "to eliminate traditional patterns of racial segregation"[176] and "falls within the area of discretion left by Title VII to the private sector voluntarily to adopt affirmative action plans designed to eliminate conspicuous

---

[170]The precise manner in which the test is stated varies a bit from court to court. *See, e.g.*, Doe v. Kamehameha Schs., 416 F.3d 1025, 1041 (9th Cir. 2005).

[171]*Weber* addressed only *voluntary* plans. *See* Steelworkers v. Weber, 443 U.S. 193, 204–07, 20 FEP 1 (1979). Court-ordered remedies are considered in Chapter 39 (Injunctive and Affirmative Relief).

[172]*See* 443 U.S. at 198–99. The *Weber* majority did not decide how underutilization should be measured. *But see id.* at 214 (Blackmun, J., concurring) (assuming that the relevant comparison is between minority representation in the applicable employer's workforce and minority representation in the general labor force).

[173]431 U.S. 324, 14 FEP 1514 (1977).

[174]433 U.S. 299, 15 FEP 1 (1977).

[175]*See Weber*, 443 U.S. at 198.

[176]*Id.* at 201.

racial imbalance in traditionally segregated job categories."[177] The Court did not, however, provide a standard to measure "traditional patterns" or "conspicuous racial imbalances."

Second, the plan must be temporary.[178] The temporary nature of the plan ensures that it is "not intended to maintain racial balance, but simply to eliminate a manifest racial imbalance."[179] In *Weber*, the Court offered no guidance as to how long the plan could be maintained, although it is clear that the plan the Court approved there would take over a decade to achieve its goal.

Third, the plan must not "unnecessarily trammel the interests of the white employees" by requiring their discharge or by creating an absolute bar to the advancement of white employees.[180]

The Supreme Court considered the legality of consent decrees providing for minority preferences in two post-*Weber* decisions: *Firefighters Local 1784 v. Stotts*,[181] and *Firefighters Local 93 v. City of Cleveland*.[182] In *Stotts*, the Court set aside a lower court order that had modified a Title VII consent decree over the objection of the defendant. The modification took the form of an injunction requiring the Memphis Fire Department to suspend its "last-hired, first-fired" seniority system during a layoff in order to preserve the percentage of African-American firefighters employed in the department. The Sixth Circuit upheld the district court's injunction. The Supreme Court reversed, directing that the original consent decree be left unmodified, even though the effect of layoffs in reverse seniority order would be to reduce the percentage of African-American firefighters. The majority opinion rested on both § 703(h) (which protects bona fide seniority systems)[183] and § 706(g) (which identifies the court's remedial powers):[184]

---

[177]*Id.* at 209.

[178]*See id.* The Ninth Circuit has cast this prong in somewhat more general terms in recent decisions. *See, e.g., Kamehameha Schs.*, 416 F.3d 1025, 1041 (explaining that a plan may not "do more than is necessary to achieve a balance") (citing Rudebusch v. Hughes, 313 F.3d 506, 520–21 (9th Cir. 2002)).

[179]*Weber*, 443 U.S. at 208.

[180]*Id.*

[181]467 U.S. 561, 34 FEP 1702 (1984).

[182]478 U.S. 501, 41 FEP 139 (1986).

[183]Section 703(h) provides: "[I]t shall not be an unlawful employment practice for an employer to apply different standards of compensation, or different terms, conditions, or privileges of employment pursuant to a bona fide seniority or merit system ... provided that such differences are not the result of an intention to discriminate because of race, color, religion, sex, or national origin." 42 U.S.C. § 2000e-2(h) (2000).

[184]42 U.S.C. § 2000e-5(g) (2000).

Here, there was no finding that any of the blacks protected from layoff had been a victim of discrimination . . . . Our ruling in *Teamsters [v. United States]* that a court can award competitive seniority only when the beneficiary of the award has actually been a victim of illegal discrimination is consistent with the policy behind § 706(g) of Title VII . . . . That policy, which is to provide make-whole relief only to those who have been actual victims of illegal discrimination, was repeatedly expressed by the sponsors of the Act during the congressional debates.[185]

In *Firefighters Local 93*, by contrast, the Court upheld a consent decree that provided for a 50 percent promotion rate for minorities over a four-year period. The sole question was whether § 706(g) precludes the entry of a consent decree that benefits minorities who were not themselves victims of discrimination.[186] The Court upheld the consent decree on the limited ground that § 706(g) does not govern them.[187] The Court did not address the circumstances under which voluntary affirmative action is lawful, except to note generally that *Weber* permits an employer to take voluntary action that includes "reasonable race-conscious relief that benefits individuals who were not actual victims of discrimination."[188] As in *Stotts*, the Court did not address the factual predicate necessary to support such action.[189]

It was not until its 1987 decision in *Johnson v. Transportation Agency*[190] that the Court finally confronted the key question left unanswered in *Weber*: What factual predicate is needed to justify a voluntary affirmative action plan?

In *Johnson*, the Court upheld a voluntary affirmative action plan adopted by the Santa Clara County, California, Transportation

---

[185]467 U.S. at 579–80 (citations and footnotes omitted).

[186]*See Firefighters Local 93*, 478 U.S. at 504.

[187]The Court also reaffirmed the conclusion in *Stotts* that § 706(g) does apply to a court's modification of a consent decree. The Court stated that a court's exercise of its power to modify a consent decree over the objection of a party to the decree will subject the decree to § 706(g), but the mere existence of an unexercised power does not. *See* Firefighters Local 93 v. City of Cleveland, 478 U.S. 501, 523–24 & n.12, 41 FEP 139 (1986).

[188]*Id.* at 516.

[189]*See id.* at 517 n.8 ("Nor need we decide . . . what showing the employer would be required to make concerning possible prior discrimination on its part against minorities in order to defeat a challenge by nonminority employees based on § 703.").

[190]480 U.S. 616, 43 FEP 411 (1987). For an in-depth discussion of the case, see MELVIN I. UROFSKY, AFFIRMATIVE ACTION ON TRIAL: SEX DISCRIMINATION IN *JOHNSON V. SANTA CLARA COUNTY* (1997).

Agency. The plan provided that the sex or race of the qualified applicant might be considered as one of a number of factors in making promotions within job categories in which women or minorities had been "significantly underrepresented."[191]

Although no specific number of positions was set aside for women or minorities, the plan's goal was to achieve a yearly improvement in the hiring, training, and promotion of women and minorities in classifications in which they were underrepresented. Its long-term goal was "to attain a work force whose composition reflected the proportion of minorities and women in the area labor force."[192]

The plan challenged in *Johnson* stated that women were underrepresented in five of seven job categories—not as a result of discrimination by the employer, but rather due to societal discrimination. Women "had not been strongly motivated to seek training or employment in" the underrepresented classifications, the plan recited, " 'because of the limited opportunities that have existed in the past for them to work in such classifications.' "[193]

A promotional vacancy occurred for a skilled road dispatcher position. Of the 238 skilled craft worker positions, none was held by a woman. Twelve employees applied for the promotion. Nine were deemed qualified, and seven were certified as eligible on the basis of scoring at a two-person interview. At that interview, Paul Johnson tied for second with a score of 75, and Diane Joyce ranked next with a score of 73. After a second interview before three supervisors, Johnson was recommended for promotion. The county's affirmative action office, which Joyce had previously contacted, recommended that the agency's director promote her. The director subsequently chose Joyce from among the seven applicants certified as eligible.

Johnson challenged the denial of the promotion under Title VII. The district court found the plan invalid on the ground that it did not satisfy *Weber's* temporary requirement. Reversing, the Ninth Circuit held that the plan was temporary because its express purpose was to attain, not maintain, a balanced workforce and that "[i]mplicit in the plan is the intent to stop taking sex into account

---

[191]*Johnson*, 480 U.S. at 620–21.
[192]*Id.* at 621–22.
[193]*Id.* at 621.

once the long-range percentage goals are attained."[194] Affirming the Ninth Circuit, the Supreme Court agreed that the plan was sufficiently temporary, and, more importantly, the Court found in the substantial underrepresentation of women in traditionally male jobs a sufficient factual predicate for the plan.

Johnson resolved several important issues concerning the lawfulness of voluntary affirmative action under Title VII.[195] Among them was the Court's conclusion that the same legal standards govern the legality of both private and public sector affirmative action under Title VII.[196] The Court also indicated that its approach to sex-based preferences would also govern race-based preferences.[197] More importantly for purposes of this chapter, though, the Court provided guidance as to the specific requirements (especially the factual predicate) necessary to support voluntary affirmative action under Title VII.[198]

b. The Necessary Factual Predicate. Johnson held that the employer need not admit prior discrimination to support a voluntary affirmative action program. Rather, a statistical showing of a "manifest imbalance" between minorities or women in an employer's workforce and the applicable labor market will suffice.[199] The Court

---

[194]770 F.2d 752, 757, 36 FEP 725 (9th Cir. 1984), *aff'd*, 480 U.S. 616 (1987).

[195]Because no constitutional issue "was either raised or addressed in litigation below," the case was decided solely under Title VII. Johnson v. Transportation Agency, 480 U.S. 616, 620 n.2, 43 FEP 411 (1987). The Court cautioned, however, that "where the issue is properly raised, public employers must justify the adoption and implementation of a voluntary affirmative action plan under the Equal Protection Clause." *Id.*

[196]*Id.* at 628 n.6.

[197]*See id.* at 635 n.13.

[198]*Id.* at 632–33. *Johnson* drew a clear distinction between the factual predicate necessary to sustain affirmative action under the Constitution's Equal Protection Clause and the less-rigorous standard required by Title VII: "The fact that a public employer must also satisfy the Constitution does not negate the fact that the *statutory* prohibition with which that employer must contend was not intended to extend as far as that of the Constitution." *Id.* at 628 n.6 (emphasis in original). Thus, although the Court in *Wygant* held that a public employer may not constitutionally extend preferential treatment to minority employees solely to remedy the effects of societal discrimination, in *Johnson* the Court held that an employer may implement race- or sex-conscious preferences under Title VII to correct manifest imbalance in "traditionally segregated" job categories—arguably without regard to whether the imbalance resulted from societal discrimination or actual prior discrimination by the employer extending the preferences.

[199]*Johnson*, 480 U.S. at 633 n.11. *But cf.* Shuford v. Alabama State Bd. of Educ., 897 F. Supp. 1535 (M.D. Ala. 1995) (holding that historical and anecdotal evidence can suffice).

further concluded that a "manifest imbalance" need not rise to the level of a prima facie case of Title VII discrimination.[200]

The Court's precedents, taken together, suggest that three factual predicates will support voluntary affirmative action under Title VII: first, actual past discrimination by the employer; second, the existence of a statistical disparity that would suffice to establish a prima facie "pattern or practice" Title VII case, without regard to whether the employer (or union) has actually discriminated;[201] and third, a "manifest imbalance" in "traditionally segregated" job categories.[202]

As for the third and oftentimes key category, *Johnson* suggests that any assessment of the legal significance of an imbalance must account for the skills required for the particular jobs at issue. Where the job requires no particular skills or qualifications, or where training opportunities are at issue, as in *Weber*, the existence of a manifest imbalance can be determined by comparing the percentage of minorities or women in the employer's workforce with the percentage of minorities or women in the area's general labor market. Where the job in question requires special skills, however, the applicable comparison is between the percentage of

---

[200]Johnson v. Transportation Agency, 480 U.S. 616, 632–33, 43 FEP 411 (1987). Four Justices disagreed. Justice Scalia, joined by Chief Justice Rehnquist, would have overruled *Weber* entirely and severely limited the circumstances under which an employer may undertake voluntary affirmative action. Taking a more moderate position, Justice O'Connor in concurrence and Justice White in dissent argued that the *Johnson* majority had misread *Weber* in concluding that the legality of affirmative action does not depend on whether the employer that engages in the affirmative action has itself discriminated in the past. Justice O'Connor reiterated her view that *Weber* interpreted Title VII as "permitting affirmative action only as a remedial device to eliminate actual or apparent discrimination or the lingering effects of this discrimination." 480 U.S. at 649. Unlike Justice White, however, Justice O'Connor concurred in the Court's judgment because she concluded that the statistical disparity established in *Johnson* "would have been sufficient for a prima facie Title VII case brought by unsuccessful women job applicants." *Id.* at 656. Justice O'Connor's concurring opinion largely tracked her position in *Wygant*. The Court's majority there concluded that "some showing of prior discrimination by the governmental unit involved" is required to support an affirmative action plan under the Equal Protection Clause. Wygant v. Jackson Bd. of Educ., 476 U.S. 267, 274, 40 FEP 1321 (1986). Although she concurred in the judgment, Justice O'Connor rejected the *Wygant* majority's position that an actual finding of discrimination is necessary; she took the position that a public employer may employ voluntary race-conscious programs if the statistical evidence establishes a prima facie case of discrimination under Title VII. *See id.* at 289 (O'Connor, J., concurring).

[201]*See Johnson*, 480 U.S. at 633 n.11.

[202]*See id.* at 632.

minority or female workers in the job with the percentage of minorities or women in the area who are qualified for the job.[203]

Several post-*Johnson* courts of appeals decisions illustrate how the "manifest imbalance" test has generally been applied. In *Higgins v. City of Vallejo*,[204] the Ninth Circuit upheld the city's race-based, promotion-centered affirmative action plan largely because the city had shown a "manifest [racial] imbalance" under *Johnson*. The court accepted the city's reliance on findings by the California Fair Employment Practices Commission (FEPC) several years prior to adoption of the plan "that minorities were conspicuously lacking in the City's work force,"[205] as 11.4 percent of municipal employees were minorities compared to 30 percent among the city's population. It approved the use of generalized statistical comparisons between the percentage of minorities in the city's population and the municipal workforce. The court also noted the FEPC's findings that blacks earned "considerably less" money than whites employed by the city and that the city's personnel practices "facilitate[d] discrimination."[206] The court added that "[t]he record also shows a racial imbalance within the City fire department."[207] Finally, the court found that the city adopted the plan in response to the FEPC investigation and that "the record provides abundant evidence that the City of Vallejo engaged in past discrimination."[208]

In *Hammon v. Barry*,[209] decided soon after *Johnson*, the District of Columbia Circuit construed the *Johnson* requirement of a "manifest imbalance" as actually requiring evidence of at least the effects of *the employer's* past or current discrimination.[210] The

---

[203]*See id.* at 631–32; *see also* City of Richmond v. J.A. Croson Co., 488 U.S. 469, 53 FEP 197 (1989) (considering the relevant statistical comparison under the Equal Protection Clause).

[204]823 F.2d 351, 44 FEP 676 (9th Cir. 1987).

[205]*Id.* at 356.

[206]*Id.*

[207]*Id.*

[208]*Id.* at 358.

[209]826 F.2d 73, 44 FEP 869 (D.C. Cir. 1987).

[210]*See id.* at 74–75 & n.1. The District of Columbia Circuit drew on Justice O'Connor's concurring opinion in *Johnson* to reach the conclusion that *Johnson* did not " 'demolish' " the District of Columbia Circuit's pre-*Johnson* position that "discrimination is a predicate to remediation" through affirmative action. *See id.* at 74–75 & n.1 ("Although the [*Johnson*] majority rejected Justice O'Connor's *prima facie* case standard, it did not quarrel with her conclusion that, although an employer need not

District of Columbia Circuit declined to reconsider its pre-*Johnson* decision in the same case finding unlawful the District of Columbia's affirmative action plan, which required that 60 percent of each entering class of firefighters be African American. It held that *Johnson* did not call for a different result in large part because the factual situations in *Hammon* and *Johnson* were "light years" apart.[211] The court first noted that the entry-level hiring rates for African Americans had averaged 50 percent for 18 years, and since 1981 had exceeded 75 percent; thus, by 1984, 37 percent of the firefighting force was African American.[212] The court rejected the district court's findings that vestiges of discrimination remained from officially sanctioned segregation in the past, stating that "something more recent should serve as a predicate for remedial action right now."[213] The court also rejected the district court's statistical findings, holding that the proper comparison was between the percentage of African Americans in the workforce of the District of Columbia fire department and the corresponding percentage in the entire Washington metropolitan area, rather than the District itself, because approximately half of the District's entry-level firefighters came from the suburbs. By using the broader geographical area

---

admit or prove that it had acted discriminatorily, evidence of the effects of *its past or current discrimination* is a prerequisite to lawful race conscious employment decisions.") (emphasis added; citations omitted). Only one judge on the panel, however, actually endorsed this reading of *Johnson*—Judge Starr. Judge Mikva dissented and took strong issue, in particular, with the court's statement that a showing of discrimination is a necessary predicate for affirmative action. *See id.* at 90 (Mikva, J., dissenting) ("For Title VII purposes, there need be no showing at all regarding the employer's past or current discrimination, although such a showing certainly strengthens the employer's justification for adopting an affirmative action plan. The Court held in *Johnson* that it is sufficient for . . . [an employer] to show *manifest statistical imbalance* . . . to meet Title VII's requirement that the employer's affirmative action plan be remedial.") (emphasis in original). The third judge on the panel, Judge Silberman, although he agreed with Judge Starr that the D.C. plan violated Title VII, confessed "uncertain[ty] as to the meaning of 'manifest imbalance,' " which he characterized as "the imprecise term used by the Supreme Court interpreting Title VII of the Civil Rights Act in *Johnson v. Transportation Agency*." *Id.* at 81 (Silberman, J., concurring) (citations omitted). Judge Silberman appeared not to read *Johnson*, as did Judge Starr, as requiring discrimination by the employer. *See id.* at 86. At the same time, however, Judge Silberman did not read *Johnson* as sanctioning affirmative action to nearly the same extent as Judge Mikva.

[211]*Id.* at 76–77.
[212]*See id.*
[213]*Id.* at 77 (emphasis omitted).

as its benchmark, the court found that there was no "manifest imbalance."[214]

In *Taxman v. Board of Education of Township of Piscataway*,[215] the Third Circuit rejected a voluntary affirmative action plan that did not satisfy the requirements of *Weber* and *Johnson*. The Third Circuit noted that the employer had not adopted its affirmative action plan in order to address a manifest imbalance in its employment practices.[216] Indeed, the parties stipulated that the plan was not "intended to remedy the results of any prior discrimination or identified underrepresentation" of minority candidates within the applicable workforce.[217] Rather, the board had justified its existing, discretionary affirmative action plan as an anticipatory measure, designed to ensure that its business department was not staffed by an all-white faculty when deciding which of two equally qualified teachers to lay off.[218] According to the Third Circuit, although the board's stated interest in ensuring a "racially diverse faculty" may have been laudatory, it was not sufficient under *Weber* and *Johnson*.[219]

Several cases have addressed the statistical methods used to establish a manifest imbalance. In *Smith v. Virginia Commonwealth University*,[220] an appeal from the district court's grant of summary judgment in favor of the defendant, the Fourth Circuit considered a university's use of "multiple regression analysis" to demonstrate the existence of a manifest imbalance in the salaries of male and female employees.[221] The court found that the Supreme Court's decision in *Bazemore v. Friday*,[222] although it permits the use of multiple regression analysis, requires that such analysis be evaluated

---

[214]*Id.* at 78.

[215]91 F.3d 1547, 71 FEP 848 (3d Cir. 1996). *See generally* Linda Greenhouse, *Settlement Ends High Court Case in Preferences: Tactical Retreat*, N.Y. TIMES, Nov. 22, 1997, at A6.

[216]*See* 91 F.3d at 1563.

[217]*Id.*

[218]*Id.*

[219]*Id.* at 1563–65. The Third Circuit likewise rejected the use of an affirmative action plan in *Schurr v. Resorts International Hotel, Inc.* to favor a minority applicant because the plan was not supported by either a finding of historical discrimination or a manifest imbalance in the employer's workforce. 196 F.3d 486, 497–98 (3d Cir. 1999).

[220]84 F.3d 672, 70 FEP 1248 (4th Cir. 1996).

[221]84 F.3d at 676.

[222]478 U.S. 385, 41 FEP 92 (1986).

in "light of all the evidence in the record."[223] The Fourth Circuit concluded that the lower court's grant of summary judgment was improper, as there was a dispute of material fact regarding whether the multiple regression analysis could establish a manifest imbalance under the facts of the case.[224]

Similarly, in *Maitland v. University of Minnesota*,[225] the Eighth Circuit reversed the district court's grant of a summary judgment in favor of a university that invoked its affirmative action plan to defeat a Title VII sex discrimination claim by a male professor challenging his pay. The Eighth Circuit concluded that the district court improperly resolved at the summary judgment stage a factual dispute over the validity and significance of three statistical models upon which the university relied to establish a manifest or conspicuous imbalance in pay.[226] The court also rejected the notion that a 1989 court-ordered consent decree implementing the salary plan relieved the employer of the burden of establishing that the plan served an appropriate remedial purpose and was narrowly tailored, noting that no finding of intentional discrimination accompanied the court's order entering the decree.[227]

c. Permissible Scope of a Voluntary Plan. (i.) Considering the rights of non-minority and male applicants and employees. Johnson and other decisions make clear that, even where the necessary predicate for affirmative action has been established, an affirmative action plan will not survive Title VII scrutiny if the rights of nonfavored employees are unreasonably infringed. Drawing on *Weber*, the *Johnson* Court asked whether the plan at issue "unnecessarily trammeled the rights of [non-minority or] male employees or created an absolute bar to their [employment or] advancement."[228]

---

[223]*Smith*, 84 F.3d at 676. The court also noted that the particular multiple regression analysis under consideration failed to account for "performance factors" and that "*Bazemore* and common sense require that any multiple regression analysis used to determine pay disparity must include all the *major* factors on which pay is determined." *Id.* (emphasis in original).

[224]*Id.* at 676–77.

[225]155 F.3d 1013, 77 FEP 1661 (8th Cir. 1998).

[226]*Id.* at 1017 (the use or omission of variables in a multiple regression analysis affecting the size of the salary disparity and the general significance of statistics must be evaluated by a jury).

[227]*Id.* at 1018.

[228]Johnson v. Transportation Agency, 480 U.S. 616, 637–38, 43 FEP 411 (1987).

It follows that a basic requirement of lawful voluntary affirmative action, which is closely bound up with the distinction between permissible "goals" and impermissible "quotas," is that a plan should extend preferential treatment only to *qualified* minorities or women.[229] Thus, the *Johnson* Court emphasized that the plan required supervisors to consider the number of qualified women available for particular job categories, rather than the availability of women in the general workforce.[230] The Court noted that the plan set aside no positions for women and imposed no quotas, but "merely authorizes that consideration be given to affirmative action concerns when evaluating qualified applicants."[231] The Court cautioned that if

> a plan failed to take distinctions in qualifications into account in providing guidance for actual employment decisions, it would dictate mere blind hiring by the numbers, for it would hold supervisors to "achievement of a particular percentage of minority employment or membership . . . regardless of circumstances such as economic conditions or the number of available qualified minority applicants . . . ."[232]

Thus, in rejecting the hiring plan at issue in *Hammon*, the District of Columbia Circuit explained that the District of Columbia's plan,

---

[229]*See, e.g.*, United States v. Paradise, 480 U.S. 149, 177–78, 183, 43 FEP 1 (1987) (plurality opinion); *id.* at 188 (Powell, J., concurring); Sheet Metal Workers Local 28 v. EEOC, 478 U.S. 421, 447, 41 FEP 107 (1986) (plurality opinion); *id.* at 494–95 (O'Connor, J., concurring in part and dissenting in part); *cf.* Martin v. Wilks, 490 U.S. 755, 776–77, 49 FEP 1641 (1989) (dissenting opinion). *But cf.* Lutheran Church-Missouri Synod v. FCC, 141 F.3d 344, 391, 76 FEP 857 (D.C. Cir. 1998) ("We do not think it matters whether a government hiring program imposes hard quotas, soft quotas, or goals. Any one of these techniques induces an employer to hire with an eye to meeting the numerical target. As such, they can and surely will result in individuals being granted a preference because of their race.").

[230]*See* 480 U.S. at 631–32; *see also* EEOC General Counsel Memorandum, *Goals and Timetables Provisions in Proposed Title VII Consent Decrees* (Oct. 6, 1987), EEOC COMPL. MAN. (BNA) N:3341 (providing that goals in EEOC consent decrees must be based upon the market availability of the benefited group for the position in question).

[231]480 U.S. at 638. Similarly, in approving the city of Vallejo's plan in *Higgins v. City of Vallejo*, the Ninth Circuit emphasized that "the city manager had discretion to choose among the top three applicants." 823 F.2d 351, 357, 44 FEP 676 (9th Cir. 1987); *see also* Conlin v. Blanchard, 890 F.2d 811, 816–17, 51 FEP 707 (6th Cir. 1989) (emphasizing as an important factor in assessing whether a plan is narrowly tailored the extent to which the preferred minority (or female) candidate holds the same qualifications as the disfavored non-minority (or male) candidate).

[232]480 U.S. at 636–37 (quoting *Sheet Metal Workers*, 478 U.S. at 495 (O'Connor, J., concurring in part and dissenting in part)).

which required that 60 percent of entering firefighters be African American, employed a "tell-tale, single-factor, rigid quota."[233] The plan bore "no resemblance to the 'moderate, flexible, case-by-case approach' . . . at issue in *Johnson*."[234] By contrast, in *Gilligan v. Department of Labor*,[235] the Ninth Circuit approved an affirmative action plan under which gender was a factor, but not the exclusive factor.[236] The Ninth Circuit cautioned that a plan's reliance on gender as the exclusive criterion would violate Title VII.[237]

Least objectionable to non-minorities and males, of course, are minority and female outreach programs commonly used among private sector employers—especially federal contractors[238]—and illustrated in, among other cases, the Eighth Circuit's decision in *Duffy v. Wolle*.[239] The plan there merely sought to increase the number of minorities and females in the applicant pool by employing various minority and female "outreach" or recruiting programs. It did not accord any actual preferences to minorities or females in making hiring decisions. Not surprisingly, the court concluded that the plan, because it did no more than require non-minority and male applicants to compete against a larger number of minority and female applicants than they would have in the absence of the plan, resulted in no cognizable harm to non-minorities and males.[240]

Most cases are far more difficult, though, than *Duffy*, in that they burden non-minorities or males in some respect and to some degree. Although *Weber* allows a plan to give preference to minorities and women over non-minorities and men without running afoul of Title VII[241]—assuming, of course, that the other criteria discussed above for a valid plan have been satisfied—there are limits

---

[233]Hammon v. Barry, 826 F.2d 73, 79, 44 FEP 869 (D.C. Cir. 1987).

[234]*Id.* at 80 (citation omitted).

[235]81 F.3d 835, 70 FEP 856 (9th Cir. 1996).

[236]*Id.* at 839. The Ninth Circuit also addressed whether an action consistent with, but not taken in reliance on, an affirmative action plan may be defended by reference to the plan. The court concluded that "in an institutional setting, it is not necessarily determinative whether the hiring officials actually relied upon the plan as long as they acted consistently with it." *Id.* at 839.

[237]*Id.* ("any affirmative action program which specifically provides for such discrimination or in practice results in such discrimination is illegal").

[238]*See* Chapter 38 (Federal Contractor Affirmative Action Compliance).

[239]123 F.3d 1026 (8th Cir. 1997).

[240]*See id.* at 1039; *accord* Hannon v. Chater, 887 F. Supp. 1303, 1316–18 (N.D. Cal. 1995).

[241]*Weber* upheld a plan that set aside half the openings in an internal training program for minorities. *But cf. In re* Birmingham Reverse Discrimination Employment

on how far a plan may go in this regard.[242] Unfortunately, there are no clear standards on which the courts have settled; much depends on the nature of the preference. In *Taxman v. Board of Education of Township of Piscataway*,[243] the Third Circuit rejected an affirmative action plan that lacked any "definition or structure" and failed even to define what goal of "racial diversity" it sought.[244] "[T]he Board's policy, devoid of goals and standards, is governed entirely by the Board's whim. . . . Such a policy unnecessarily trammels the interests of nonminority employees."[245] Especially troubling to the court was that the plan directly favored the retention of minority employees during layoffs. Loss of employment, the court concluded, was too great a price for non-minorities to pay so that the employer could achieve racial diversity.[246]

In *Rudebusch v. Hughes*,[247] by contrast, the Ninth Circuit held that a university's one-time pay adjustment program, which targeted minority and female professors for salary increases, "did not unnecessarily trammel the rights of" white male professors.[248] The court found the pay equity situation fundamentally different from the more traditional settings for Title VII claims—in particular,

---

Litig., 20 F.3d 1525, 1541, 1547, 1549, 64 FEP 1032 (11th Cir. 1994) (consent decree implementing a one-to-one promotion ratio was an unlawful quota; faulting the decree for requiring promotions to be made "woodenly and reflexively"; and emphasizing that a viable alternative would have been the elimination of seniority as a basis for promotion).

[242]*See* Johnson v. Transportation Agency, 480 U.S. 616, 638, 43 FEP 411 (1987); United States v. Paradise, 480 U.S. 149, 182, 43 FEP 1 (1987); Sheet Metal Workers Local 28 v. EEOC, 478 U.S. 421, 479, 41 FEP 107 (1986).

[243]91 F.3d 1547, 71 FEP 848 (3d Cir. 1996).

[244]*Id.* at 1564. The court noted that it did not intend to suggest that specific numerical goals must be set for an affirmative action plan to be acceptable. Rather, "[t]he absence of goals, while it may not have been fatal alone, is a factor contributing to the overall vagueness of the plan." *Id.* at 1564 n.15.

[245]*Id.*

[246]*Id.* (emphasizing that the loss of a job "is so substantial and the cost so severe that the Board's goal of racial diversity, even if legitimate under Title VII, may not be pursued in this particular fashion").

[247]313 F.3d 506 (9th Cir. 2002).

[248]*Id.* at 510. On remand, after 4 years had passed since the original salary adjustments, the district court found that the minority professors had been given increases that went beyond addressing the salary imbalances identified by the regression analysis, and awarded the white male professors back pay commensurate with these "more than remedial" increases. Rudebusch v. Arizona, 436 F. Supp. 2d 1058, 1066–67, 98 FEP 645 (D. Ariz. 2006).

hiring, promotion, and set-aside programs.[249] The court concluded that the salary increases did not appropriate any opportunity that might otherwise fall to white male professors because the program involved only a one-time adjustment, which did not affect the funds available to male and non-minority employees under the university's regular salary program.[250]

McNamara v. City of Chicago[251] involved a promotion claim. In upholding the plan, the court emphasized not only that it was sensitive to employee qualifications, but that giving preferences to minorities with respect to promotions imposes less of a burden on non-minority employees than giving preferences with respect to hiring and layoffs. " 'Denial of a future employment opportunity,'" the court stated, "is not as intrusive as loss of an existing job.' "[252] The court also emphasized that the policy did not serve as a permanent bar to promotion. Rather, it delayed, but did not bar, the promotion of non-minorities.[253]

As the above cases show, the type of employment decision with which an affirmative action plan concerns itself may determine its fate. A plan that confers special lay-off protection on minority or female employees (in particular, by giving them preferential seniority treatment) or provides for the discharge of non-minority or male employees to create opportunities for minorities and women would not likely pass muster under Title VII.[254] The Supreme Court looks more favorably on hiring goals, by contrast, because they are relatively diffuse in their impact and generally do not dislodge the settled employment expectations of non-minorities and males. Promotional goals fall somewhere in between. In *Johnson*, for

---

[249]*Id.* at 520–21.

[250]*Id.* at 522–23; *see* Airth v. City of Pomona, 2000 WL 425006 (9th Cir. Apr. 19, 2000) (unpublished disposition) (commenting approvingly on transfer plan that, although benefiting only minorities, involved a one-time initiative and did not result in the discharge or demotion of any non-minority employees; remanding case to district court, however, given the absence of discrimination suffered by the plan's beneficiary).

[251]867 F. Supp. 739, 750 (N.D. Ill. 1994) (granting summary judgment to city on Title VII and § 1981 claims of "reverse" discrimination by not strictly following rank-order of test results for promotions to captain).

[252]*Id.* at 751 (quoting United States v. Paradise, 480 U.S. 149, 43 FEP 1 (1987)).

[253]867 F. Supp. at 751–52.

[254]*See, e.g.*, Wygant v. Jackson Bd. of Educ., 476 U.S. 267, 275–78, 40 FEP 1321 (1986); Firefighters Local 1784 v. Stotts, 467 U.S. 561, 578–79, 34 FEP 1702 (1984).

instance, the Court noted that the plaintiff was only one of seven employees qualified for the disputed promotion and had no settled expectation of receiving it. Moreover, he "retained his employment with the Agency . . . and remained eligible for other promotions."[255]

As Justice Powell warned, however, it may not always be appropriate to evaluate the legality of an affirmative action plan by reference to the type of personnel action that it purports to regulate and the label assigned to the plan. A more searching, case-by-case inquiry into the facts may be necessary. In his concurrence in *Sheet Metal Workers Local 28 v. EEOC*,[256] where the Court upheld a court-ordered remedial plan, Justice Powell commented:

> [I]t is too simplistic to conclude from the combined holdings in *Wygant* and this case that hiring goals withstand constitutional muster whereas layoff goals and fixed quotas do not. There may be cases, for example, where a hiring goal in a particularly specialized area of employment would have the same pernicious effect as the layoff goal in *Wygant*. The proper constitutional inquiry focuses on the effect, if any, and the diffuseness of the burden imposed on innocent nonminorities, not on the label applied to the particular employment plan at issue.[257]

(ii.) Attaining, not maintaining, balanced workforces. The Supreme Court has emphasized that affirmative action plans are permissible only if designed to attain, not maintain, a balanced workforce.[258] In *Johnson*, the Court deemed the employer to have taken "a moderate, gradual approach" to affirmative action: "Given this fact, as well as the Agency's express commitment to 'attain' a

---

[255]Johnson v. Transportation Agency, 480 U.S. 616, 638, 43 FEP 411 (1987). The Ninth Circuit made the same point in *Higgins v. City of Vallejo*, 823 F.2d 351, 357, 44 FEP 676 (9th Cir. 1987); *cf.* Dallas Fire Fighters Ass'n v. City of Dallas, 885 F. Supp. 915, 926–27 (N.D. Tex. 1995) (plan providing for race-conscious promotion decisions unduly trammeled the rights of non-minorities because race was employed as a dispositive, exclusionary factor), *aff'd in part, rev'd in part*, 150 F.3d 438, 443 (5th Cir. 1998).

[256]478 U.S. 421, 41 FEP 107 (1986). In *Sheet Metal Workers*, the Court affirmed the authority of the district court to order a union to implement a race-conscious affirmative action plan that would benefit individuals who were not themselves actual victims of discrimination, in response to the union's continuing and egregious Title VII violations.

[257]478 U.S. at 488 n.3.

[258]In both of the cases to come before the Supreme Court where the avowed purpose of the preference was the maintenance of prior affirmative action gains— *Firefighters Local 1784 v. Stotts*, 467 U.S. 561, 34 FEP 1702 (1984), and *Wygant v. Jackson Board of Education*, 476 U.S. 267, 40 FEP 1321 (1986)—the Court disapproved the plans.

balanced work force, there is ample assurance that the Agency does not seek to use its Plan to maintain a permanent racial and sexual balance."[259]

An actual limitation on the duration of preferences may sometimes be required. As the Court suggested in *Johnson*, an explicit termination point may be especially important where the plan fixes an actual numerical goal: "Express assurance that a program is only temporary may be necessary if the program actually sets aside positions according to specific numbers."[260] Although the plan approved in *Johnson* had no express end date, it did not establish any specific set-asides for women. By contrast, the consent decree challenged in *Firefighters Local 93 v. City of Cleveland*,[261] which required promotion of a particular number of minorities, had a four-year duration, and the plan challenged in *Weber* was self-terminating once a specified balance was reached.[262]

In *Taxman v. Board of Education of Township of Piscataway*,[263] the Third Circuit rejected an affirmative action plan because it had no termination date. Rather than qualifying as the type of "temporary" affirmative action plan endorsed by the Court in *Johnson*, the plan was "an established fixture of unlimited duration, to be resurrected from time to time whenever the Board believes that

---

[259]480 U.S. at 640. *But cf.* Jansen v. City of Cincinnati, 977 F.2d 238, 244, 64 FEP 1655 (6th Cir. 1992) (rejecting a white applicant's contention that the employer could not defend against the applicant's failure-to-hire claim by reference to a consent decree because its goal of 18% minority representation had been achieved; noting that the 8% figure was a target, not a strictly enforceable ceiling).

[260]Johnson v. Transportation Agency, 480 U.S. 616, 639–40, 43 FEP 411 (1987). An EEOC consent decree must, under the EEOC's internal policies, provide for an appropriate timetable and, most importantly, "clearly state its termination date." EEOC General Counsel Memorandum, *Goals and Timetables in Proposed Title VII Consent Decrees* (Oct. 6, 1987), EEOC COMPL. MAN. (BNA) N:3341. The memorandum further provides that the duration of the decree should not normally exceed 3 years, at least not without providing for readjustment of the goals to allow for changes in labor market availability. *See id.* at 3341 n.10.

[261]478 U.S. 501, 512, 41 FEP 139 (1986).

[262]Steelworkers v. Weber, 443 U.S. 193, 208–09, 20 FEP 1 (1979). Over the objections of some of the parties, a district court in New York refused a request to increase the minority hiring goals of a consent decree, notwithstanding substantial increases in minority representation in the market, and dissolved an 18-year-old consent decree, because the goal of 25% minority employment had been reached: "The time has come for this Court to vacate the Consent Decree and allow the industry to self regulate; subject, of course, to the laws preventing racial discrimination." Patterson v. Newspaper & Mail Deliverers' Union, 797 F. Supp. 1174, 1181, 63 FEP 643 (S.D.N.Y. 1992), *aff'd*, 13 F.3d 33, 63 FEP 964 (2d Cir. 1993).

[263]91 F.3d 1547, 71 FEP 848 (3d Cir. 1996).

the ratio between Blacks and Whites in any Piscataway School is skewed."[264] The plan thus sought impermissibly to maintain—rather than attain—a racially balanced workforce contrary to the Supreme Court's position in *Weber*.[265]

In *University & Community College System of Nevada v. Farmer*,[266] by contrast, the Nevada Supreme Court affirmed an unwritten amendment to an affirmative action policy that allowed a department to hire an additional faculty member following the initial placement of a minority candidate. The court concluded that, with African Americans occupying just one percent of all faculty positions, the university permissibly sought to attain, rather than maintain, a racial balance.[267] To similar effect is the district court's decision in *McNamara v. City of Chicago*,[268] where the court approved a plan to evaluate candidates for promotion even though the plan did not contain a self-defined termination date. Critical to the court's conclusion was the fact that the employer did not use any given, position-specific list of promotion candidates for more than a year.[269]

Support for the proposition that affirmative action plans must have end dates may also be found in the Supreme Court's most recent pronouncement on the issue of affirmative action under the Equal Protection Clause. In *Grutter v. Bollinger*,[270] the Court emphasized at the conclusion of its decision approving a race-conscious

---

[264]*Id.* at 1564.

[265]*See id.*; *see also* Wessmann v. Gittens, 160 F.3d 790 (1st Cir. 1998) (rejecting school admissions policy on constitutional grounds because there was no evidence that any vestiges of past discrimination remained).

[266]930 P.2d 730, 75 FEP 953 (Nev. 1997); *cf.* Bernstein v. St. Paul Cos., 134 F. Supp. 2d 730, 738–39 & n.12 (D. Md. 2001) (granting summary judgment to employer on promotion discrimination claim; despite managerial bonus system predicated in part on success in supporting diversity, no evidence of quota system and no evidence bonus impacted by decision to select any specific candidate). *But see* Preston v. Wisconsin Health Fund, 397 F.3d 539, 542 (7th Cir. 2005) (evidence that those "running the company are under pressure from affirmative action plans, customers, public opinion, the EEOC, a judicial decree, or corporate superiors imbued with belief in 'diversity' to increase the proportion of [minorities] in the company's workforce" could satisfy the "background circumstances" standard required of "reverse" discrimination plaintiff); White v. Alcoa, Inc., 2006 U.S. Dist. LEXIS 17422 (S.D. Ind. 2006) (decision makers' disregard of interviewers' preferences and ranking in choosing female candidate sufficient evidence for "reverse" discrimination plaintiff to survive employer's motion for summary judgment).

[267]*Id.* at 735.

[268]867 F. Supp. 739 (N.D. Ill. 1994), *aff'd in part, rev'd in part sub nom.* Billish v. Chicago, 962 F.2d 1269 (7th Cir. 1992).

[269]*See McNamara* at 752.

[270]539 U.S. 306, 91 FEP 1761 (2003).

admissions program that the program "must be limited in time" and "have a logical end point."[271] The Court added that the "durational requirement can be met by sunset provisions in race-conscious admissions policies and periodic reviews" to determine the ongoing need for the plan.[272]

d. Consent Decrees. In *Firefighters Local 93 v. City of Cleveland*,[273] the Supreme Court held that consent decrees should be judged by the standards applicable to voluntary affirmative action and generally are not subject to the limitations on court-ordered relief set forth in § 706(g).[274] That was a significant conclusion because in its earlier decision in *Firefighters Local 1784 v. Stotts*[275] the Court had rejected the district court's modification of two consent decrees requiring the Memphis Fire Department to suspend its "last-hired, first-fired" seniority system in order to preserve minority employment gains. *Stotts* held that § 706(g) prohibited *courts* from awarding preferential treatment to persons not found to have been actual victims of discrimination, thereby raising a potential impediment to such affirmative action when it was embodied in a negotiated consent decree.[276]

In *Firefighters Local 93*, the Court distinguished *Stotts* and resolved the issue in favor of the legality of negotiated consent decrees providing for affirmative action outside the context of providing remedies to victims of actual discrimination. In *Firefighters*

---

[271]539 U.S. at 342.

[272]*Id.*

[273]478 U.S. 501, 512, 41 FEP 139 (1986).

[274]Section 706(g) provides:

If the court finds that the respondent has intentionally engaged in or is intentionally engaging in an unlawful employment practice charged in the complaint, the court may enjoin the respondent from engaging in such unlawful employment practice, and order such affirmative action as may be appropriate, which may include, but is not limited to, reinstatement or hiring of employees, with or without back pay . . . or any other equitable relief as the court deems appropriate. . . . No order of the court shall require the admission or reinstatement of an individual as a member of a union, or the hiring, reinstatement, or promotion of an individual as an employee, or the payment to him of any back pay, if such individual was refused admission, suspended, or expelled, or was refused employment or advancement or was suspended or discharged for any reason other than discrimination on account of race, color, religion, sex, or national origin or in violation of § 2000e-3(a) of this title.

42 U.S.C. § 2000e-5(g) (2000). *See generally* Chapter 39 (Injunctive and Affirmative Relief).

[275]467 U.S. 561, 34 FEP 1702 (1984).

[276]*Id.* at 579.

Local 93, an organization of African-American and Hispanic firefighters, the Vanguards of Cleveland, brought a class action against the city, alleging discrimination on the basis of race and national origin in hiring, assignment, and promotion.[277] Over the objections of the union, which intervened as a party-plaintiff, the city and the Vanguards negotiated a consent decree, which the district court approved.[278] The decree was to remain in place for four years and provided for the creation of a number of openings for promotion.

At the outset, the Court emphasized that the sole issue under review was whether § 706(g) precludes the entry of a consent decree that benefits individuals who were not the actual victims of the allegedly discriminatory practices of the employer-defendant.[279] Finding that a principal legislative objective embodied in § 706(g) was the protection of "management prerogatives and union freedoms"[280]—neither of which the Court deemed to be implicated by a voluntarily entered consent decree—the Court held § 706(g) does not apply to consent decrees at all.[281] The Court reasoned that "absent some contrary indication" in the language of Title VII, "there is no reason to think that voluntary, race-conscious affirmative action such as was held permissible in *Weber* is rendered impermissible by Title VII simply because it is incorporated into a consent decree."[282]

The Court thus implicitly confirmed in *Firefighters Local 93* that *Weber* permits an employer or union, unilaterally or through a consent decree, to take voluntary action that includes "race-conscious relief that benefits individuals who were not actual victims of discrimination."[283] The Court noted that it had no need, given the procedural posture of the case, to address what showing of prior discrimination would be necessary to sustain a consent decree under

---

[277]478 U.S. at 504.

[278]Firefighters Local 93 v. City of Cleveland, 478 U.S. 501, 509–12, 41 FEP 139 (1986).

[279]*Id.* at 513–14.

[280]*Id.* at 520 (quoting H.R. Rep. No. 914, 88th Cong., 1st Sess., pt. 2, at 29 (1963), *reprinted in* 1964 U.S.C.C.A.N. 2355).

[281]478 U.S. at 521–23. The Court noted that EEOC guidelines "plainly contemplate the use of consent decrees as an appropriate form of voluntary affirmative action." *Id.* at 517–18.

[282]*Id.* at 518.

[283]Firefighters Local 93 v. City of Cleveland, 478 U.S. 501, 516, 41 FEP 139 (1986).

Title VII.[284] Thus § 706(g) does not prohibit race-conscious preferences embodied in a consent decree simply because they have the imprimatur of the district court that enters the decree. It is important to emphasize, however, that the content of the decree remains subject to challenge and review under § 703 against the standards for affirmative action,[285] and that a district court's nonconsensual modification of a consent decree is subject to § 706(g).[286]

Since *Firefighters Local 93*, several courts have examined consent decrees under the standards for "voluntary" affirmative action programs set forth in *Weber* and *Johnson*. In *Plott v. General Motors Corp.*,[287] the Sixth Circuit considered and rejected an employee's objection to General Motor's adherence to a "Conciliation Agreement" entered in 1983 between General Motors and the EEOC. The plaintiff-employee alleged that he was not admitted into a skilled trade apprentice program because General Motors had adhered to—in fact had exceeded with regard to women— the percentage goals for the representation of minorities and women established in the conciliation agreement.[288] Because General Motors argued that it acted in reliance upon a letter from the EEOC concerning the effect of its good faith compliance with the conciliation agreement, the court examined whether General Motors had in fact acted in good faith.[289] The court first noted that General Motors had extended affirmative action only to those individuals who possessed, or were likely to develop, the required skills for the positions in question. Second, the court found that the percentages

---

[284]*See id.* at 517 n.8.

[285]*See id.* at 521 n.11. The EEOC General Counsel once directed regional attorneys to consider using goals and timetables in consent decrees "only in the absence of effective relief which has less impact on third parties." EEOC General Counsel Memorandum, *Goals and Timetables in Proposed Title VII Consent Decrees* (Oct. 6, 1987), EEOC COMPL. MAN. (BNA) N:3341, 3342. He stated that "it will often be prudent to ask the Court, prior to seeking judicial approval for a consent decree containing goals, to hold a fairness hearing in order to afford all affected individuals—both beneficiaries and potentially adversely affected individuals—an opportunity to comment on the proposed remedy." *Id.* He directed that "[e]xcept in extraordinary circumstances, goals should be set at . . . current labor market availability as measured by census work force data or nondiscriminatory applicant flow." *Id.* at 3341.

[286]*See* 478 U.S. at 527–28.

[287]71 F.3d 1190, 69 FEP 826 (6th Cir. 1995).

[288]71 F.3d at 1192–93.

[289]*Id.* at 1194.

contained in the conciliation agreement were goals, not quotas or fixed set-asides. Third, the court found that the conciliation agreement did not displace the seniority rights of non-minority or male employees, and did not require their replacement or mandate their ineligibility from participation in the apprenticeship program.[290]

In *People Who Care v. Rockford Board of Education*,[291] the Seventh Circuit affirmed a district court's finding that a school district's policies had resulted in past discrimination, but it rejected portions of the district court's consent decree because it amounted to "reverse" discrimination. "Violations of law must be dealt with firmly, but not used to launch the federal courts on ambitious schemes of social engineering."[292] The Seventh Circuit rejected, among other things, the use of racial quotas for teachers and super-seniority for minority teachers.[293]

Having decided that consent decrees should be judged by the Title VII standards applicable to "voluntary" affirmative action, the Supreme Court in *Martin v. Wilks*[294] considered the circumstances under which individuals who are not parties to the decree may assert private claims for "reverse" discrimination resulting from the employer's compliance with the decree. In *Martin*, white firefighters who were not parties to a consent decree between African-American firefighters and the city of Birmingham, Alabama, brought a "reverse" discrimination action against the city,

---

[290]*Id.* at 1194–95; *see* Killebrew v. Greenwood, 988 F. Supp. 1014 (N.D. Miss. 1997) (white firefighters would likely succeed in bringing an end to a consent decree entered by court in 1978 to remedy past discrimination against African Americans given that African Americans occupied a majority of positions within the fire department and were in no danger of being discriminated against absent consent decree); *see also* Dallas Fire Fighters Ass'n v. City of Dallas, 150 F.3d 438, 443 (5th Cir. 1998) (a consent decree and a statistical finding of underrepresentation of minorities does not, without more, establish lingering effects of past discrimination). Before terminating a consent decree, a district court must make sufficiently detailed findings of fact and conclusions of law supporting the termination. *See, e.g.*, Gonzales v. Galvin, 151 F.3d 526, 531, 77 FEP 1573 (6th Cir. 1998).

[291]111 F.3d 528 (7th Cir. 1997).

[292]*Id.* at 534.

[293]*Id.* at 534–35 ("The white teachers currently employed by the school district who will lose seniority rights [under the proposed Order], and future white applicants for teaching jobs who will be discriminated against in favor of minority applicants, cannot be deemed to owe their jobs, their job prospects, or their seniority to being beneficiaries against minorities.").

[294]490 U.S. 755, 49 FEP 1641 (1989).

alleging discriminatory denial of promotions. A divided Court held that the plaintiffs could challenge employment decisions made pursuant to the consent decree even though they had not intervened in the lawsuit in which the decree was entered. The Court rejected the "impermissible collateral attack doctrine," which several courts had used to protect consent decrees from such a challenge.[295] Under the Federal Rules of Civil Procedure, the Court explained, "[j]oinder as a party, rather than knowledge of a lawsuit and an opportunity to intervene, is the method by which potential parties are subjected to the jurisdiction of the court and bound by a judgment or decree."[296] The dissenters, by contrast, insisted that a party's compliance with a consent order remedying discrimination ordinarily should not risk further liability; "[a]ny other conclusion would subject large employers who seek to comply with the law by remedying past discrimination to a never-ending stream of litigation and potential liability."[297] The Civil Rights Act of 1991 modified the effect of *Martin*, and changed the rules governing the circumstances under which nonparties may challenge a consent decree.

3. The Effect of the Civil Rights Act of 1991

a. Martin v. Wilks. The dilemma faced by employers after *Martin* was directly addressed by the Civil Rights Act of 1991. Section 108 of the Act provides that employment actions taken in conformity with a consent decree (or judgment) may not be challenged by those affected if the affected parties had actual notice of the decree and a reasonable opportunity to object to its terms, or if their interests were adequately represented by another person who has already challenged the content of the decree.[298] The 1991 Act does not, however, prevent challenges to decrees obtained through collusion or fraud, decrees that are "transparently invalid," or decrees entered by a court without subject matter jurisdiction.[299] Nor

---

[295]*See id.* at 762–63.

[296]*Id.* at 765.

[297]*Id.* at 791 (Stevens, J., dissenting).

[298]Pub. L. No. 102-166, § 108, 1991 U.S.C.C.A.N. (105 Stat.) 1071, 1076 (codified at 42 U.S.C. § 2000e-2(n)(1)–(2)). The Act does not overrule *Martin*, but rather provides a means for parties to surface disagreements by other affected employees prior to approval of a consent decree.

[299]*Id.*

does the 1991 Act "authorize or permit the denial to any person of the due process of law required by the Constitution."[300] Additionally, § 108 does not apply retroactively to bar a nonparty's challenge to a consent decree entered before the Act's effective date.[301]

Where the specific notice provisions of § 108 have been followed, courts have precluded later challenges to consent decrees. In *Sims v. Montgomery County Commission*,[302] the court determined that notices to white officers regarding the proposed consent decree and invitations to object either in writing or at two fairness hearings barred later challenges to the decree.[303] In *Edwards v. City of Houston*,[304] the Fifth Circuit distinguished situations where nonparties seek to intervene in the litigation that produces the challenged decree from those where nonparties bring a separate "reverse" discrimination suit after being provided notice of the decree and an opportunity to object under § 108. The court held that nonparties are not precluded by § 108 from intervening in the litigation that produces the challenged decree.[305]

b. Burden of Proof. The 1991 Act also may affect the proof burden in "reverse" discrimination cases involving affirmative action plans. In *Johnson*, the Supreme Court indicated that the *McDonnell Douglas-Burdine* approach[306] applies in such cases.[307] The plaintiff must first establish a prima facie case that the employer took race or sex into account when making the challenged employment decision. That showing usually is easily made in the context of employment decisions made under an affirmative action plan as most such plans provide for express preferences for minority or female applicants or employees.[308] The burden of production then

[300]*Id.*

[301]*See, e.g.*, Rafferty v. Youngstown, 54 F.3d 278, 281–82 n.2, 67 FEP 1564 (6th Cir. 1995); Maitland v. University of Minn., 43 F.3d 357, 363, 66 FEP 796 (8th Cir. 1994). *But see* Aiken v. City of Memphis, 37 F.3d 1155, 1176–77, 65 FEP 1757 (6th Cir. 1994) (Jones, J., dissenting) (endorsing retroactive application in some circumstances).

[302]890 F. Supp. 1520 (M.D. Ala. 1995), *aff'd mem.*, 119 F.3d 9 (11th Cir. 1997).

[303]*Id.* at 1530.

[304]78 F.3d 983 (5th Cir. 1996).

[305]*Id.* at 997–98.

[306]*See generally* Chapter 2 (Disparate Treatment).

[307]*See* Johnson v. Transportation Agency, 480 U.S. 616, 626, 43 FEP 411 (1987).

[308]*See, e.g.*, Doe v. Kamehameha Schs., 416 F.3d 1025 (9th Cir. 2005) (discussing a school admissions affirmative action plan); *cf.* Rudin v. Lincoln Land Cmty. Coll.,

shifts to the employer to articulate a "nondiscriminatory rationale" for its action. In *Johnson*, the Court noted that "[t]he existence of an affirmative action plan provides such a rationale."[309] The burden then shifts back to the plaintiff to prove that the justification is "pretextual" because the plan is invalid. The ultimate burden of proving the plan's invalidity always lies with the plaintiff:

> As a practical matter, of course, an employer will generally seek to avoid a charge of pretext by presenting evidence in support of its plan. That does not mean, however, as petitioner suggests, that reliance on an affirmative action plan is to be treated as an affirmative defense requiring the employer to carry the burden of proving the validity of the plan. The burden of proving its invalidity remains on the plaintiff.[310]

But the Supreme Court's subsequent "mixed motive" decision in *Price Waterhouse v. Hopkins*,[311] and the enactment, in response to *Price Waterhouse*, of § 107 of the 1991 Act,[312] raises some questions about whether this aspect of *Johnson* remains good law. In *Price Waterhouse*, the Court held that once a plaintiff shows that the employer acted with an impermissible motive, the burden of persuasion shifts to the employer to prove that it would have made the same decision even in the absence of the impermissible motive.[313] A four-Justice plurality of the Court, however, noted that this mixed-motive doctrine does not apply in "the special context of affirmative action."[314] Although Justice O'Connor concurred in the Court's judgment, she agreed with Justice Kennedy's dissenting opinion[315] that no exception should be made for race- or sex-based employment actions undertaken pursuant to affirmative action plans.[316]

---

420 F.3d 712, 722 (7th Cir. 2005) (the existence of an affirmative action plan may be relevant to the issue of "discriminatory intent," but a "Title VII plaintiff must establish a link" between the plan and the challenged personnel action rather than pointing to the " 'mere existence' " of the plan) (citations omitted).

[309]*Id.; accord Kamehameha Schs.*, 416 F.3d at 1040.

[310]*Johnson*, 480 U.S. at 626–27.

[311]490 U.S. 228, 49 FEP 954 (1989). *See generally* Chapter 2 (Disparate Treatment).

[312]42 U.S.C. § 2000e-2(m) (2000).

[313]490 U.S. at 242. *See generally* Chapter 2 (Disparate Treatment).

[314]490 U.S. at 239 n.3.

[315]*Id.* at 293 n.4 (Kennedy, J., dissenting).

[316]*Id.* at 279 (O'Connor, J., concurring).

Section 107 of the 1991 Act codified *Price Waterhouse* to the extent that it shifts the burden of persuasion to the defendant to prove a nondiscriminatory motive for its actions once the plaintiff establishes that an impermissible motivation was at work. What is the effect of § 107, though, in a "reverse" discrimination case? In *Officers for Justice v. Civil Service Commission*,[317] the Ninth Circuit concluded that § 116 of the Act—the so-called "savings clause" for affirmative action—forecloses an interpretation of § 107 that would adversely affect affirmative action plans structured in compliance with Title VII law as it existed in 1991. The court thus held that the 1991 Act does not change the allocation of the burden of persuasion.[318]

Section 116 of the 1991 Act provides that "[n]othing in the amendments made by this Act shall be construed to affect court-ordered remedies, affirmative action, or conciliation agreements that are in accordance with the law."[319] Proponents of affirmative action will cite legislative history to the effect that § 116 was intended to leave affirmative action law as it was prior to the 1991 Act's passage, without affecting plans that are "otherwise in accordance with the law as previously established by Congress in Title VII and by the decisions of the United States Supreme Court."[320] Opponents will argue that, in enacting § 116, Congress

---

[317]979 F.2d 721, 725, 62 FEP 868 (9th Cir. 1992).

[318]The sponsors' memorandum on the 1991 Act is silent on this issue. *See* 137 CONG. REC. S15,483 (daily ed. Oct. 30, 1991). An interpretive memorandum submitted in the House by Representative Edwards, one of the House floor managers, explicitly stated that this section "is not intended to provide an additional method to challenge affirmative action." 137 CONG. REC. H9526, H9529 (daily ed. Nov. 7, 1991) (hereinafter "Edwards Memorandum"). An interpretative memorandum submitted by Senator Dole, however, "stresse[s]" that § 107 does apply "to cases involving challenges to unlawful affirmative action plans, quotas, and other preferences." 137 CONG. REC. S15,472, S15,476 (daily ed. Oct. 30, 1991) (hereinafter "Dole Memorandum").

[319]Pub. L. No. 102-166, § 116, 1991 U.S.C.C.A.N. (105 Stat.) 1071, 1079.

[320]Edwards Memorandum, 137 CONG. REC. at H9530. In *Officers for Justice*, the city of San Francisco banded test scores and considered race as a "plus" factor in promotion decisions. The union challenged the practice, arguing that § 107(a) of the 1991 Act prohibits consideration of race as a factor in employment decisions. The union further argued that § 116 did not save the practice because the term "in accordance with law" refers to the law as amended by the 1991 Act. The Ninth Circuit rejected the union's argument:

The Union's reading of the 1991 Act is predicated on an internal inconsistency: that Congress sought to protect affirmative action in section 116 while outlawing it in section 107. . . . [A] more natural reading of the phrase "in accordance

expressed no view on the legality of preferential treatment. Senator Dole emphasized that the legislation makes no change in the applicable sections of Title VII and therefore does not "purport to resolve the . . . legality . . . of affirmative action programs that grant preferential treatment" based on race, color, sex, or national origin.[321] Other legislative history, such as the 1991 Act's sponsors' memorandum,[322] is silent with respect to the meaning of § 116.[323]

In *Hannon v. Chater*,[324] the court considered the burden of proof in "reverse" discrimination cases in light of § 107.[325] Although stating that § 107's mixed-motive analysis is "arguably a direct anti-affirmative action provision,"[326] the court held that where the consideration of gender is consistent with an existing affirmative action plan § 107's mixed-motive analysis is inapplicable. In *Gilligan v. Department of Labor*,[327] the Ninth Circuit reached much the same result, concluding that the mixed-motive analysis comes into play only when gender is used as an impermissible consideration, not when it is used in accordance with a lawfully constituted affirmative action plan.[328]

c. Race-Norming. Section 106 of the 1991 Act prohibits "race-norming"—the practice of adjusting or using different cut-off scores,

---

with law" is that affirmative action programs that were in accordance with law *prior* to passage of the 1991 Act are unaffected by the amendments. *Id.* at 725 (emphasis in original).

[321] 137 CONG. REC. at S15,477–78. The Dole Memorandum states that the 1991 Act "should in no way be seen as expressing approval or disapproval" of *Weber, Johnson*, or any other affirmative action decision. *Id.* at S15,478.

[322] *See id.* at S15,483.

[323] In *Aiken v. City of Memphis*, 37 F.3d 1155, 65 FEP 1757 (6th Cir. 1994), the dissent interpreted § 116 as providing protection for consent decrees, stating that it is "prudent . . . to remain mindful of the quagmire that we create when we use laws which are intended to *remedy* past racial discrimination *against* the very people who have historically been made to bear the burden of legal and extra-legal racial discrimination." *Id.* at 1177 n.5 (Jones, J., dissenting).

[324] 887 F. Supp. 1303 (N.D. Cal. 1995).

[325] 42 U.S.C. § 2000e-2(m) (2000).

[326] *Hannon*, at 1315 n.48 (quoting Note, *The Continuing Evolution of Affirmative Action Under Title VII: New Directions After the Civil Rights Act of 1991*, 81 VA. L. REV. 565, 596 (1995)).

[327] 81 F.3d 835, 70 FEP 856 (9th Cir. 1996).

[328] 81 F.3d at 840. The key question before the Ninth Circuit was whether the employer had *relied* upon the affirmative action plan within the meaning of *Johnson*. The court concluded that it was unnecessary to answer this question because it was enough for the employer to show that it acted *consistent* with the plan. *See id.* at 839.

or otherwise altering the results of employment-related tests used in selecting or referring candidates for employment or promotion, on the basis of the candidate's race, color, religion, sex, or national origin.[329] This section would seem to prohibit affirmative action programs and judicial orders that require separate cut-off scores to meet "race, color, religion, sex, or national origin" hiring goals. The Dole Memorandum states that § 106 prohibits a court from ordering race-norming as part of a remedy or approving it in a consent decree "when done because of the disparate impact" of scores.[330]

In *Fioriglio v. New Jersey Department of Personnel*,[331] the court held that the employer did not violate § 106 when it rescored an examination pursuant to a consent decree and applied new criteria "evenhandedly to each and every score, not just to the scores of minority candidates."[332] In *Hayden v. County of Nassau*, the court held that an employer's effort to develop a valid test with the least adverse impact on racial minorities did not violate § 106.[333] And in *Chicago Firefighters Local 2 v. City of Chicago*, the Seventh Circuit held that "test banding"—i.e., the practice of treating test scores falling into certain ranges the same—under an affirmative action program did not constitute prohibited "race norming."[334]

d. Enhanced Damages. Section 102 of the Civil Rights Act of 1991[335] provides for the recovery of compensatory, and in some

---

[329]*See* 42 U.S.C. § 2000e-2(l) (2000); *see also* Dean v. City of Shreveport, 438 F.3d 448, 462–63, 97 FEP 454 (5th Cir. 2006) (finding "reverse" discrimination where those achieving minimum cut-off score separated into three lists; company considered all females and minorities that passed but only half of the men).

[330]Dole Memorandum, 137 CONG. REC. at S15,476. In interpreting § 106 to prohibit race-norming as part of the remedy in any case, the Dole Memorandum cited to *Bridgeport Guardians, Inc. v. City of Bridgeport*, 933 F.2d 1140, 55 FEP 1631 (2d Cir. 1991). In *Bridgeport Guardians*, the Second Circuit upheld the remedy ordered by the district court where the city's examination for promotion had an adverse impact on minorities. The remedy, called "banding," required selection of candidates for promotion based on a "range of [test] scores whose differences are not statistically significant and, within that band range, provides for promotions of candidates on the basis of considerations such as race or ethnicity, gender, work experience, past job dependability, and other factors that the hiring authorities deem pertinent." *Id.* at 1144.

[331]1996 WL 599400 (D.N.J. Oct. 15, 1996), *aff'd*, 166 F.3d 1205 (3d Cir. 1998).

[332]*Fioriglio*, 1996 WL 599400, at *5.

[333]180 F.3d 42, 53, 79 FEP 1874 (2d Cir. 1999).

[334]249 F.3d 649, 656, 85 FEP 1305 (7th Cir. 2001); *see also* Koski v. Gainer, 1995 WL 599052, at *16 (N.D. Ill. Oct. 5, 1995) (challenging race-norming pursuant to settlement agreement with EEOC).

[335]42 U.S.C. § 1981a (2000).

cases punitive, damages for intentional violations of Title VII (and certain other statutes) subject to caps tied to the size of the defendant's workforce. Such damages had not previously been available under Title VII.[336] Although the sponsors' memorandum does not address the application of this section to affirmative action-related "reverse" discrimination claims, Senator Dole stated that "the damages contemplated in this section are to be available in cases challenging unlawful affirmative action plans, quotas, and other preferences."[337]

Other legislative history states that the EEOC's affirmative action guidelines[338] establish a safe harbor for employers—that is, a defense for employers "who prove that their actions were taken in good faith, in reliance on, and in conformity with, written interpretations and opinions of the EEOC," or in compliance with a court order.[339] The EEOC's guidelines, issued in 1979 following *Weber*, purport to provide a defense, based on § 713(b)(1) of Title VII,[340] to employers and unions whose affirmative action efforts are challenged as "reverse" discrimination. The EEOC regulations provide that the defense applies in the affirmative action context if an employer conducts a "reasonable self analysis," has a "reasonable basis for concluding that [affirmative] action is appropriate," and takes "reasonable action" to resolve the problems disclosed by the "reasonable self analysis,"[341] provided that the "reasonable self analysis" and the affirmative action plan are in a written, dated document.[342] Several courts have recognized the availability of the § 713(b)(1) defense in other contexts.[343]

In *Plott v. General Motors Corp., Packard Electrical Division*,[344] the Sixth Circuit held that § 713(b)(1) insulated the employer from

---

[336]*See generally* Chapter 40 (Monetary Relief).

[337]Dole Memorandum, 137 CONG. REC. at S15,473.

[338]29 C.F.R. § 1608 (2005).

[339]137 CONG. REC. at H9527. *See generally* Chapter 40 (Monetary Relief).

[340]Section 713(b)(1) provides that "no person shall be subject to any liability or punishment if an act or omission was taken in good faith and in reliance upon a written interpretation or opinion of the Commission." 42 U.S.C. § 2000e-12(b)(1) (2000); *see also* 29 C.F.R. § 1608.2 (2005).

[341]29 C.F.R. § 1608.4 (2005).

[342]*Id.* § 1608.4(d).

[343]*See, e.g.*, Albemarle Paper Co. v. Moody, 422 U.S. 405, 423 n.17, 10 FEP 1181 (1975) (§ 713(b)(1) provides "a complete, but very narrow, immunity for employer conduct shown to have been undertaken 'in good faith, in conformity with, and in reliance on any written interpretation or opinion' " of the EEOC).

[344]71 F.3d 1190, 69 FEP 826 (6th Cir. 1995).

liability because the employer's affirmative action plan was a good faith attempt to comply with the employer's agreement with the EEOC, which was instituted in reliance on a previously issued EEOC opinion.[345]

---

[345]*Id.* at 1194.

FEDERAL CONTRACTOR AFFIRMATIVE ACTION COMPLIANCE

I. INTRODUCTION

Federal government contractors face legal requirements beyond those applicable to other businesses. Executive Order 11246 (the Executive Order),[1] § 503 of the Rehabilitation Act of 1973 (Rehabilitation Act),[2] and § 402 of the Vietnam Era Veterans' Readjustment Assistance Act of 1972 (Veterans Act)[3] impose nondiscrimination

---

[1]Exec. Order No. 11246 (1965), *reprinted as amended in* 1 AFFIRMATIVE ACTION COMPL. MAN. (BNA) 101.
[2]29 U.S.C. § 793 (2000).
[3]38 U.S.C. §§ 4211–4212 (2000 & Supp. III 2003).

and affirmative action obligations on holders of covered federal government contracts and subcontracts.[4] The Executive Order (1) prohibits discrimination based upon race, sex,[5] religion, and national origin, and (2) mandates affirmative action for minorities and women.[6] The Rehabilitation Act (1) prohibits discrimination against, and (2) mandates affirmative action with respect to, individuals with disabilities. The Veterans Act, similarly, (1) prohibits discrimination against, and (2) mandates affirmative action for, disabled veterans, veterans who served on active duty during a war or in a campaign or expedition for which a campaign badge has been authorized, veterans who participated in a military operation for which an Armed Forces service medal was awarded, and recently separated veterans.[7] Collectively, these requirements cover an estimated $184 billion in federal contracts, pursuant to which approximately 26 million individuals—approximately 22% of the national workforce—are employed.[8]

---

[4]The Executive Order, the Rehabilitation Act, and the Veterans Act are collectively referred to herein as "the three OFCCP programs."

[5]Exec. Order No. 11375 (1967), 3 C.F.R. § 684 (1966–70 Compl.), 32 Fed. Reg. 14,303 (1967) (added gender coverage).

[6]A nondiscrimination clause has been required in government contracts since 1941 when President Roosevelt issued an order mandating nondiscrimination in employment by defense contractors. Exec. Order No. 8802, 3 C.F.R. § 957 (1938–43 Compl.). The history of succeeding executive orders is detailed in *Contractors Ass'n of Eastern Pennsylvania v. Secretary of Labor*, 442 F.2d 159, 168–76, 3 FEP 395 (3d Cir. 1971). The only Executive Orders addressed in this chapter are Nos. 11246, 11375 (amending 11246 to prohibit sex discrimination), 11758 (authorizing the Secretary of Labor to adopt regulations governing the employment of qualified individuals with disabilities pursuant to § 503 of the Rehabilitation Act of 1973, 29 U.S.C. § 793), and 11701 (directing the Secretary of Labor to implement § 402 of the Veterans Act).

[7]38 U.S.C. §§ 4211–4212 (2000). The Veterans Employment Opportunities Act of 1998 (VEOA), Pub. L. No. 105-339, 112 Stat. 3182, 3188–89, amended the Veterans Act to add "other veterans who served on active duty during a war or in a campaign or expedition for which a campaign badge has been authorized." The Veterans Benefits and Health Care Improvement Act of 2000 (VBHCIA), Pub. L. No. 106-419, 114 Stat. 1822, expanded the Veterans Act to include "recently separated veterans." The Jobs for Veterans Act of 2002, Pub. L. No. 107-288, 116 Stat. 2033, altered the definition of veterans covered by affirmative action requirements under 38 U.S.C. §§ 4211–4212 by changing "special disabled veterans" to "disabled veterans," deleting "veterans of the Vietnam era," adding "veterans who, while serving on active duty in the Armed Forces, participated in a United States military operation for which an Armed Forces service medal was awarded," and changing the definition of "recently separated veteran" to "any veteran during the three-year period beginning on the date of such veteran's discharge or release from active duty." 38 U.S.C. §§ 4211–4212 (2000).

[8]*See* http://www.dol.gov/esa/regs/compliance/ofccp/aa.htm (last visited Dec. 5, 2005).

The Executive Order, the Rehabilitation Act, and the Veterans Act all delegate to the Secretary of Labor responsibility to administer their requirements.[9] The Secretary in turn has established the Office of Federal Contract Compliance Programs (OFCCP) within the Department of Labor[10] to administer and enforce their provisions.[11]

The Executive Order's requirements are set forth in the order itself and its implementing regulations.[12] The Rehabilitation Act and Veterans Act requirements are set forth in the respective statutes and their implementing regulations.[13] The OFCCP has developed a Federal Contract Compliance Manual (Compliance Manual), which interprets the regulations and specifies the agency's compliance processes for all three OFCCP programs.[14] Should conflicts exist between the Compliance Manual and the regulations, the latter prevail.[15] Decisions of administrative law judges (ALJs)

---

[9]Exec. Order No. 11246, § 201 (1965), *reprinted as amended in* 1 AFFIRMATIVE ACTION COMPL. MAN. (BNA) 101 (empowering the Secretary of Labor to "adopt such rules and regulations and issue such orders as are deemed necessary and appropriate" to achieve the purposes of the order); 41 C.F.R. §§ 60-250.4, -741.4 (2005).

[10]41 C.F.R. § 60-1.2 (2005). In 1978, Exec. Order No. 12086 consolidated within the OFCCP the enforcement and implementation functions previously performed by the government's different contracting agencies. 3 C.F.R. ch. 230 (1978 Compilation), 43 Fed. Reg. 46,501 (1978).

[11]Regulations issued by the OFCCP (regulations) are published at 41 C.F.R. ch. 60. They include: (1) Part 60-1 (general obligations of contractors and subcontractors, the required equal opportunity clause, and the enforcement, review, and complaint procedures applicable under the Executive Order); (2) Part 60-2, known as Revised Order No. 4 (affirmative action requirements applicable to nonconstruction contractors); (3) Part 60-3 (Uniform Guidelines on Employee Selection Procedures); (4) Part 60-4 (affirmative action requirements applicable to federal or federally assisted construction contracts); (5) Part 60-20 (sex discrimination guidelines); (6) Part 60-30 (rules of practice for administrative enforcement proceedings); (7) Part 60-40 (provisions pertaining to public disclosure by OFCCP of information submitted by contractors); (8) Part 60-50 (guidelines on religion and national origin discrimination); (9) Part 60-60 (evaluation procedures for supply and service contractors); (10) Part 60-250 (affirmative action requirements administered by the OFCCP under the Veterans Act); (11) Part 60-741 (affirmative action obligations administered by the OFCCP for individuals with disabilities under the Rehabilitation Act); and (12) Part 60-999 (OMB control numbers for the OFCCP's information-collection requirements).

[12]Exec. Order No. 11246 (1965), *reprinted as amended in* 1 AFFIRMATIVE ACTION COMPL. MAN. (BNA) 101; 41 C.F.R. pts. 60-1–60-60 (2005).

[13]29 U.S.C. § 793 (2000); 38 U.S.C. §§ 4211–4212 (2000); 41 C.F.R. pts. 60-250, -741 (2005).

[14]FED. CONTRACT COMPL. MAN., *reprinted in* 1 & 2 AFFIRMATIVE ACTION COMPL. MAN. (BNA). Portions of the Compliance Manual currently are out of date.

[15]41 C.F.R. § 60-2.34 (2005).

and the Secretary of Labor also provide guidance on the requirements of the three OFCCP programs.[16]

Section II of this chapter first summarizes the key coverage concepts generally applicable to the three OFCCP programs. Section III discusses coverage and compliance issues under the Executive Order. Sections IV, V, and VI discuss the applicability of, and coverage and compliance issues under, the Rehabilitation Act and the Veterans Act. Section VII explains the compliance evaluation and complaint investigation processes, from the desk audit letter through the exit conference, applicable to all three OFCCP programs. Section VIII sets forth the enforcement process and sanctions for noncompliance. Section IX explains how the Freedom of Information Act applies to OFCCP records. Finally, Section X discusses the legal basis for the OFCCP's assertion of jurisdiction, particularly in the context of the controversial areas of affirmative action and minority and gender preferences.

II. COVERAGE AND EXEMPTIONS

A. Contracts and Covered Subcontracts

Both prime contractors and subcontractors can be covered, as explained below.

1. Prime Contracts

The term "government contract" is defined by the regulations revised in 1997[17] as

---

[16]Most ALJ and Secretary of Labor decisions are available by writing to the Head Librarian, U.S. Department of Labor, 200 Constitution Avenue N.W., Washington, D.C. 20210.

[17]41 C.F.R. § 60-1.3 (2005); id. §§ 60-250.2(i), -741.2(i). The Rehabilitation Act and Veterans Act regulations add the parenthetical "(including construction)" after the phrase "personal property or nonpersonal services." 41 C.F.R. §§ 60-250.2(i), -741.2(1) (2005). The 1997 revisions to the regulations changed the definition of "government contract" to clarify that contracts covered by the affirmative action requirements include contracts under which the government is a seller of goods or services, as well as contracts under which the government is a purchaser. 62 Fed. Reg. at 44,175; 61 Fed. Reg. at 19,339. This change was merely technical because courts and administrative law judges have applied the requirements of the Executive Order, the Rehabilitation Act, and the Veterans Act to contracts in which the government was the seller.

any agreement or modification thereof between any contracting agency[18] and any person[19] for the purchase, sale or use of personal property[20] or non-personal services.[21]

Federal financial assistance agreements, such as grants, are not covered contracts.[22] However, federally assisted construction contracts are covered under all three OFCCP programs.[23] Contracts for purchases of personal property from the government also are covered.[24]

---

[18]The term "contracting agency" "means any department, agency, establishment or instrumentality of the United States, including any wholly owned Government corporation, which enters into contracts." 41 C.F.R. §§ 60-1.3, -250.2(i)(2), -741.2(i)(2) (2005).

[19]The term "person" "means any natural person, corporation, partnership or joint venture, unincorporated association, State or local government, and any agency, instrumentality, or subdivision of such a government." 41 C.F.R. §§ 60-1.3, -250.2(i)(3), -741.2(i)(3) (2005).

[20]The term "personal property" "includes supplies, and contracts for the use of real property (such as lease arrangements), unless the contract for the use of real property itself constitutes real property (such as easements)." 41 C.F.R. §§ 60-1.3, -250.2(i)(6), -741.2(i)(6) (2005).

[21]The term "nonpersonal services" "includes, but is not limited to, the following services: Utilities, construction, transportation, research, insurance, and fund depository." 41 C.F.R. §§ 60-1.3, -250.2(i), -741.2(1) (2005).

[22]OFCCP v. USAA Fed. Sav. Bank, No. 87-OFC-27, [1987–1993 Transfer Binder] OFCCP FED. CONT. COMPL. MAN. (CCH) ¶ 21,399, at 4057, 4059 (Oct. 4, 1990) (Recommended Decision). USAA Federal Savings Bank (FSB) refused to permit a compliance review by the OFCCP. FSB, arguing that it was not a federal contractor, contended that its only contractual link to the federal government was that it was a member of the Federal Home Loan Bank system and purchased deposit insurance from the Federal Savings and Loan Insurance Corporation. It sought a declaratory judgment from the district court. The Department of Labor successfully moved to dismiss, arguing that FSB had failed to exhaust its administrative remedies. The District of Columbia Circuit affirmed the dismissal on the ground that the OFCCP was prepared to allow FSB to challenge jurisdiction in an administrative proceeding. USAA Fed. Sav. Bank v. McLaughlin, 849 F.2d 1505, 1510, 47 FEP 229 (D.C. Cir. 1988). The administrative law judge (ALJ) subsequently held that such "financial assistance agreements" are not covered contracts. The ALJ noted, however, that federally assisted *construction* contracts are covered expressly by the Executive Order.

[23]*See* Crown Cent. Petroleum Corp. v. Kleppe, 424 F. Supp. 744, 750, 14 FEP 49 (D. Md. 1976) (lessee of oil and gas rights on the outer continental shelf is covered by Executive Order No. 11,246).

[24]*See* OFCCP v. Ozark Airlines, No. 80-OFCCP-24 (Dep't of Labor June 13, 1986) (purchases of space at airports owned by the U.S. government constitute "government contracts" under § 503); Department of Labor v. St. Regis Corp., No. 78-OFCCP-1, [1993–present Transfer Binder] OFCCP FED. CONT. COMPL. MAN. (CCH) ¶ 21,506, at 4647 (Mar. 2, 1994) (Final Decision) (a timber facility, specializing in

The OFCCP retains jurisdiction over contractors for enforcement purposes, even after work under a government contract has been completed, with respect to violations that occurred during the contract's term.[25]

2. Subcontracts

A "subcontract" subject to the OFCCP programs is defined in the regulations[26] as

> any agreement or arrangement between a contractor and any person (in which the parties do not stand in the relationship of an employer and an employee):
> (1) For the purchase, sale or use of personal property or nonpersonal services which, in whole or in part, is necessary to the performance of any one or more contracts; or
> (2) Under which any portion of the contractor's obligation under any one or more contracts is performed, undertaken or assumed.

A few cases have litigated the issue of coverage under the first test, addressing whether a subcontract is "necessary" to the performance of a government contract. The Fourth Circuit, in *Liberty Mutual Insurance Co. v. Friedman*,[27] held that workers' compensation policies issued to government contractors are covered subcontracts. The court reasoned that such insurance is "legally necessary" because all states require the employer either to supply

---

cutting, clearing, and processing, entered into a covered government contract by purchasing timber from the government; the Executive Order does not restrict coverage to contractors who sell supplies or services to the government; even though the company's only business transactions with the government consisted of timber purchases, it was covered by the Executive Order).

[25]*Compare* OFCCP v. Loffland Bros. Co., OEO 75-1, 1984 WL 484538, at *2 (Apr. 16, 1984) ("a past contractor who holds no current government contracts is not subject to any of the substantive provisions of the Executive Order or regulations after the contract is fully performed . . ."; however, it is subject to enforcement proceedings for violations committed while the contract was in effect) *with* OFCCP v. Priester Constr. Co., No. 78-OFCCP-11, 1983 WL 411026, [1979–1987 Transfer Binder] OFCCP FED. CONT. COMPL. MAN. (CCH) ¶ 21,191, at 3161 (Feb. 23, 1983) (Final Decision) (the OFCCP retains jurisdiction over a contractor for enforcement purposes after the work on the contract has been completed to resolve a violation that took place during the term of the contract).

[26]41 C.F.R. §§ 60-1.3, -250.2(1), -741.2(1) (2005). Rehabilitation Act and Veterans Act regulations add the parenthetical "(including construction)" after the phrase "personal property or nonpersonal services." *Id.* §§ 60-250.2(1), -741.2(1).

[27]639 F.2d 164, 166 (4th Cir. 1981).

its own through self insurance or to purchase a policy from an insurance company.[28]

In *Department of Labor v. Coldwell, Banker & Co.*,[29] the Secretary of Labor held covered as a "subcontractor" a company that managed buildings leased to federal executive agencies. Coldwell, Banker unsuccessfully contended that it was not covered because it acted only as the agent of the building owner in engaging service subcontractors. Coldwell Banker claimed that it furnished neither supplies nor services necessary to the government contract's performance. The Secretary of Labor disagreed; in arranging for building repairs and services, the Secretary said, Coldwell, Banker was performing a service "necessary" to satisfy the prime contractor's obligations to its federal government tenant. The Secretary further noted that the company would be a covered subcontractor if it did nothing more than hire employees for the building owner and contract for building utility and maintenance services on behalf of the owner, presumably because the services of such employees are required for contract performance.[30]

Several cases also have applied the second test: whether a subcontractor is undertaking performance of any portion of a contractor's obligation. In *OFCCP v. Loffland Brothers*,[31] the Secretary of Labor ruled that Loffland was not a subcontractor because the OFCCP failed to demonstrate that any of the oil Loffland supplied to a contractor was sold to the government; merely doing business with a government contractor was insufficient to trigger coverage.[32] To invoke the second test, the Secretary explained, the OFCCP must be able to "trace" the subcontractor's goods or services through the contractor and prove that they actually are used by the government.

---

[28]*Id.* at 167. Liberty Mutual unsuccessfully argued that a subcontract is covered only if it "is necessary" for the prime contractor to enter into a subcontract.

[29]44 FEP 850, 853 (Dep't of Labor 1987); *see also* OFCCP v. Coldwell, Banker & Co., 1987 WL 774232, [1979–1987 Transfer Binder] OFCCP FED. CONT. COMPL. MAN. (CCH) ¶ 21,307, at 3638 (Aug. 14, 1987) (Final Decision).

[30]44 FEP at 852–53.

[31]OEO 75-1, 1984 WL 484538 (Apr. 16, 1984).

[32]That Loffland had contracts to drill wells on land that a prime contractor leased from the government did not make its work necessary to the performance of the government contract, the Secretary ruled. *Id.* at *4.

By contrast, in *OFCCP v. Monongahela Railroad*,[33] a railroad was deemed a covered subcontractor because it hauled coal that eventually was used by Detroit Edison Company, a prime federal contractor. Monongahela argued that it was not a covered subcontractor under the Rehabilitation Act because it was not the sole source of Detroit Edison's coal supply; Monongahela's service was therefore not unique. Monongahela also contended that the amount of coal it supplied was minute, and therefore its services were not sufficiently connected to the government. An administrative law judge rejected both arguments. The judge held that the size of the contribution and the fact that others furnished the same service were irrelevant. It was of no import that the subcontractor was "large or small, significant or insignificant," provided that the other criteria of Executive Order 11246 were met.[34]

3. Extension of Coverage to Related Entities

Autonomous parent or subsidiary corporations (collectively "affiliates") of covered contractors generally are treated as separate and distinct entities. Thus, common ownership, without more, does not trigger coverage. However, where one corporation controls another, the OFCCP may treat the affiliates as a single entity, such that a government contract held by one triggers coverage as to both.[35]

What "controls" means is not clear. Several decisions have utilized the "actual control" test, based upon a consideration of five principal factors, to determine whether two units constitute a

---

[33]No. 85-OFC-2 (Apr. 2, 1986).

[34]*Id.*

[35]*See* OFCCP v. Texas Utils. Generating Co., No. 85-OFC-13, [1987–1993 Transfer Binder] OFCCP FED. CONT. COMPL. MAN. (CCH) ¶ 21,327, at 3684–85 (Mar. 2, 1988) (Recommended Decision) (a "captive supplier of 3 service companies all . . . owned by a single entity," not a supplier of unrelated goods, was required to comply with § 503; "to allow a contractor to circumvent the provisions of the Act . . . would be inconsistent with the Act's intent to assure that the government uses its spending power so as to improve employment opportunities for qualified [disabled] persons"); Department of Labor v. Interco, Inc., No. 86-OFC-2 (Mar. 10, 1987) (a company and its completely autonomous subsidiary were a single corporate entity because one was financially liable for debts incurred by the other and daily operations of one were subject to "rather close oversight" by the officers and directors of the other).

single entity.[36] The Fourth Circuit, however, applied an "ultimate authority" test, in *Board of Governors v. Department of Labor*.[37] The case arose from the University of North Carolina's refusal to permit the OFCCP to investigate its Asheville campus and the North Carolina School of the Arts on the grounds that neither of these schools held federal contracts. The Department of Labor contended that it had jurisdiction over all campuses because several other schools or campuses held such contracts. The Fourth Circuit, adopting the "ultimate authority" test, concluded that all 16 campuses constituted a single entity and were covered because at least one campus had a covered contract. Noncontracting campuses therefore fell within the OFCCP's compliance review jurisdiction.[38]

In practice, the "ultimate authority" test is significantly more tilted toward coverage than the "actual control" test, because a subsidiary almost always falls under the ultimate authority of its parent. Thus, the OFCCP often will contend that even if the noncontracting subsidiary's daily operations are essentially self-contained, the subsidiary will be covered by the affirmative action requirements if the parent company holds a covered federal contract and exercises some authority over the subsidiary.

4. Successor Liability

In evaluating the liability of a successor business enterprise for the noncompliance of its predecessor, the OFCCP typically weighs several factors.[39] These were articulated in, among other

---

[36]The OFCCP has considered the following five factors in determining whether two companies are a single entity: (1) common ownership; (2) common directors and/or officers; (3) *de facto* exercise of control; (4) unity of personnel policies emanating from a common source; and (5) dependency of operations. *See In re* Ernst-Theodore Arndt, Dec. B-170536, 52 Compl. Gen. 145, 146 (1972); Liberty Mut. Ins. Co. v. Friedman, 485 F. Supp. 695, 701 n.8, 21 FEP 1016 (D. Md. 1979), *rev'd on other grounds*, 639 F.2d 164 (4th Cir. 1981). In *Beverly Enterprises, Inc. v. Herman*, 130 F. Supp. 2d 1, 22 (D.D.C. 2000), the contractor refused to comply with a corporate management review. An administrative law judge sanctioned Beverly's subsidiaries for the misconduct of their parent company. The district court held that "if the plaintiff [parent] and its subsidiaries are considered one entity under the five-factor test established by the Secretary of Labor, the subsidiaries would have been adequately represented by the plaintiff in the hearing . . . [and] may be punished by the sanction levied against the plaintiff." *Id.*

[37]917 F.2d 812, 814, 54 FEP 136 (4th Cir. 1990).

[38]917 F.2d at 816–18.

[39]OFCCP Order No. 660b21, [1979–1987 Transfer Binder] OFCCP FED. CONT. COMPL. MAN. (CCH) ¶ 21,243, at 3383–84 (April 11, 1985).

cases, *EEOC v. MacMillan Bloedel Containers, Inc.*:[40] (1) whether the successor company had notice of the charge of discrimination; (2) whether the predecessor had the ability to provide relief; (3) whether there has been a substantial continuity of business operations; (4) whether the successor uses the same plant; (5) whether the successor uses the same or substantially the same workforce; (6) whether the successor uses the same or substantially the same supervisory personnel; (7) whether the same jobs exist under substantially the same working conditions; (8) whether the successor uses the same machinery, equipment, and methods of production; and (9) whether the successor produces the same product.[41]

B. Coverage Thresholds

1. Basic Threshold

There are two distinct coverage thresholds: the "basic threshold" and the "AAP threshold." The "basic threshold" requires nondiscrimination and affirmative action *practices*, but no written affirmative action *plans* (AAPs). The "AAP threshold" specifies which contractors and subcontractors[42] must prepare and maintain written AAPs.

A contractor satisfies the "basic threshold" under the Executive Order and the Rehabilitation Act if it has a single contract with the government or a covered subcontract that exceeds $10,000.[43] The Veterans' Employment Opportunities Act of 1998 (VEOA)[44] amended the Veterans Act to raise the basic threshold to $25,000,[45] while the Jobs for Veterans Act of 2002 raises the threshold for coverage to $100,000 for contracts or subcontracts entered into on or after December 1, 2003.[46]

---

[40]503 F.2d 1086, 8 FEP 897 (6th Cir. 1974).

[41]*Id.* at 1094. *See generally* Chapter 21 (Employers).

[42]The term "contractor" includes the term "subcontractor" throughout the remainder of this chapter; "contract" includes a covered "subcontract."

[43]41 C.F.R. §§ 60-1.5(a)(1), -741.4(a)(1) (2004).

[44]Veterans' Employment Opportunities Act of 1998, Pub. L. No. 105-339, 112 Stat. 3182, 3188.

[45]*Id.*

[46]38 U.S.C. § 4212(a)(1) (2000); Pub. L. 107-288, § 2(b)(1), 116 Stat. 2033 (2002) (providing that "the amendments made by this subsection [amending § 4212(a)] shall apply with respect to contracts entered into on or after the first day of the first month that begins 12 months after the date of the enactment of this Act").

For purposes of the Executive Order only, the basic threshold also is triggered (1) for a contractor that has government contracts (including subcontracts) with an aggregate total value or expected value that exceeds $10,000 in any 12-month period, even if no single contract equals or exceeds $10,000;[47] (2) for anyone having government bills of lading in any amount;[48] and (3) for any financial institution serving (a) as a depository of federal funds in any amount or (b) as an issuing and paying agent for U.S. savings bonds and savings notes.[49]

Contracts for indefinite quantities, including open end and requirements contracts, also meet the basic threshold for the Executive Order and the Rehabilitation Act unless the government contracting entity has reason to believe that the amount to be ordered in any year will not exceed $10,000. Coverage for the first year is determined at the time of the initial contract award and thereafter on an annual basis.[50]

The regulations exempt certain other contracts[51] from coverage:

> (1) work performed outside the United States by employees who were not recruited within or transferred from this country;[52]

---

[47]41 C.F.R. § 60-1.5(a) (2005). The Secretary of Labor has made clear that contracts otherwise are not aggregated to establish the threshold coverage. Department of Labor v. Bruce Church, Inc., No. 87-OFC-7, 1987 WL 774233, at *2, [1979–1987 Transfer Binder] OFCCP FED. CONT. COMPL. MAN. (CCH) ¶ 21,304, at 3631 (June 30, 1987) (Final Decision) (there is no aggregation of contracts other than as provided in the regulations); OFCCP v. Fulton Corp., No. 87-OFC-2 (July 23, 1987) (same); see also Burnett v. Brock, 806 F.2d 265, 267 (11th Cir. 1986) (per curiam) (in the absence of a master contract, individual purchase orders are considered individual contracts).

[48]41 C.F.R. § 60-1.5(a) (2005).

[49]Id.

[50]Id. §§ 60-1.5(a)(2), -741.4(a)(3). If the amount of any single order exceeds $10,000, coverage remains in effect for the duration of the contract, regardless of the amounts actually ordered in a year.

[51]In addition to those exemptions listed in the text, religiously oriented church-related schools, colleges, universities, and other educational institutions may employ persons of a particular religion. Id. § 60-1.5(a)(5). A contractor may extend a preference in employment to Indians living on or near an Indian reservation for employment opportunities on such reservation or within a reasonable commuting distance. However, no discrimination based upon religion, sex, or tribal affiliation is permitted. Id. § 60-1.5(a)(6).

[52]Id. §§ 60-1.5(a)(3), -250.3(a)(3), -741.4(a)(4). If a contractor cannot obtain a visa due to discrimination, it must notify the Department of State and the OFCCP Director. Id. § 60-1.10.

(2) work performed by a state or local government's agency, instrumentality, or subdivision (collectively "subdivision") which itself has no federal contract and does not participate in work on or under a federal contract held by another subdivision of that government;[53]

(3) contracts exempted by the OFCCP Director when "special circumstances in the national interest so require";[54]

(4) contracts exempted by the head of an agency because the exemption is necessary to the national security;[55] and

(5) work performed at a contractor's facilities which the OFCCP Director finds "in all respects separate and distinct from activities of the [prime contractor or subcontractor] related to the performance of the contract or subcontract," if such exemption will not impede the OFCCP's programs.[56]

If a contractor satisfies the basic threshold, it must not discriminate unlawfully based upon race, sex, religion, national origin, or status as a qualified individual with a disability.[57] Nor may it discriminate unlawfully against a Vietnam era veteran,[58] an otherwise

---

[53]*Id.* §§ 60-1.5(a)(4), -250.4(a)(4), -741.4(a)(5). For example, a county bureau of adoptions that has no federal contract would not be covered by any OFCCP program simply because another county agency is a party to such a contract. Agencies, instrumentalities, and subdivisions of a state or local government are not required to maintain a written AAP prescribed by the regulations or file an annual compliance report unless they are educational institutions or medical facilities. *Id.* § 60-1.5(a)(4).

[54]*Id.* §§ 60-1.5(b)(1), -250.4 (b)(1), -741.4(b)(1).

[55]*Id.* §§ 60-1.5(c), -250.4(b)(2), -741.4(b)(2).

[56]Exec. Order No. 11246, § 204 (1965), *reprinted as amended in* 1 AFFIRMATIVE ACTION COMPL. MAN. (BNA) 101, 102; 41 C.F.R. §§ 60-1.5(b)(2), -250.4(b)(3), -741.4(b)(3)(i) (2004). In practice, exemptions of separate facilities are virtually never granted. Executive Order 11246's predecessor, Exec. Order No. 10925, 3 C.F.R. 448 (1959–63 Compilation), issued in 1961, applied the equal employment clause only to employment practices "[i]n connection with the performance of work under [a] contract." *Id.* § 301.

[57]*See* Section IV *infra.*

[58]Section 505 of the Veterans' Benefits Improvement Act of 1996 changed the definition of "Vietnam era" to include those who served on active duty for more than 180 days and were discharged or released with other than a dishonorable discharge (or were discharged or released from active duty for a service-connected disability) if any part of such active duty occurred from February 28, 1961, through May 7, 1975, in the Republic of Vietnam, or from August 5, 1964, through May 7, 1975, in all other cases. Pub. L. No. 104-275, 110 Stat. 3342 (codified at 38 U.S.C. § 101(29)). The regulations track this statutory language. 41 C.F.R. § 60-250.2(p) (2005).

protected veteran (i.e., one who served on active duty during a war or in a campaign or expedition for which a campaign badge has been authorized),[59] a recently separated veteran,[60] or a special disabled veteran.[61] It also must take affirmative action (e.g., outreach recruiting, training, and other steps) as necessary to ensure equal employment opportunity. The OFCCP may investigate, conduct audits of, and if necessary take remedial action against such a covered contractor.[62] Unless specifically exempted (by one of the avenues listed above), each facility of a covered contractor must comply with these requirements, even if the facility is not performing any covered contract or subcontract work.[63]

2. AAP Threshold

The second threshold, the "AAP threshold," applies to each nonconstruction contractor that has (1) at least 50 employees, and (2) a federal contract of $50,000 or more.[64] Contractors that meet

---

[59]38 U.S.C. §§ 4211–4212 (2000). The Veterans Employment Opportunities Act of 1998 (VEOA), Pub. L. No. 105-339, 112 Stat. 3182, 3188–89, amended the Veterans Act to add "other veterans who served on active duty during a war or in a campaign or expedition for which a campaign badge has been authorized."

[60]The Jobs for Veterans Act of 2002, Pub. L. No. 107-288, 116 Stat. 2033, defines a recently separately veteran as "any veteran during the three-year period beginning on the date of such veteran's discharge or release from active duty."

[61]See Section V infra.

[62]41 C.F.R. § 60-1.26 (2005).

[63]E.g., OFCCP v. Burlington Indus., Inc., No. 90-OFC-10, [1987–1993 Transfer Binder] OFCCP FED. CONT. COMPL. MAN. (CCH) ¶ 21,459, at 4343 (Nov. 1, 1991) (Recommended Decision) ("a contract between a corporate owner of the plant and the government is enough, even though the particular plant may not be involved in government work"; the company's entire workforce was covered); OFCCP v. Priester Constr. Co., No. 78 OFCCP-11, 1983 WL 411026, at *20, [1979–1987 Transfer Binder] OFCCP FED. CONT. COMPL. MAN. (CCH) ¶ 21,191, at 3161 (Feb. 23, 1983) (Final Decision) (if a contractor has a direct federal contract or subcontract over $10,000, its entire workforce is covered).

[64]See OFCCP v. Star Mach. Co., No. 83-OFCCP-4, [1979–1987 Transfer Binder] OFCCP FED. CONT. COMPL. MAN. (CCH) ¶ 21,189, at 3157 (Sept. 21, 1983) (Secretary of Labor concluded that blanket purchase agreements are contracts within the meaning of 41 C.F.R. § 60-1.40; a blanket purchase contract is one contract with the total amount measured by the total amount of orders the parties reasonably anticipate to be placed during the life of the contract); see also OFCCP v. Safeco Ins. Co., No. 83-OFC-7, 1984 WL 484541, at *3, [1979–1987 Transfer Binder] OFCCP FED. CONT. COMPL. MAN. (CCH) ¶ 21,212, at 3293 (July 31, 1984) (Recommended Decision) (the value of Safeco's government contract for purposes of determining whether the threshold requirement had been met was governed by the bond premium it was to receive, not the penal amount of the bond).

the AAP threshold must (1) develop and adopt at each of its establishments *written* AAPs for minorities, women, individuals with disabilities, special disabled veterans, veterans who served on active duty during a war or in a campaign or expedition for which a campaign badge has been authorized, veterans who participated in a military operation for which an Armed Forces service medal was awarded, and recently separated veterans;[65] and (2) file annually a standard Form 100 (EEO-1) and VETS-100 report.[66]

Financial institutions that employ at least 50 employees and serve as depositories of federal funds in any amount or as issuing and redeeming agents for U.S. savings bonds and savings notes in any amount automatically are deemed to have met the AAP threshold, at least for purposes of the Executive Order.[67] So are holders of government bills of lading that in any 12-month period total or can reasonably be expected to total at least $50,000, if the holder employs at least 50 employees.[68]

III. EXECUTIVE ORDER 11246[69]

A. Mandates of the Order

Executive Order 11246 mandates that every nonexempt federal government contract obligate contractors and covered subcontractors: (1) not to discriminate against employees or applicants

---

[65]41 C.F.R. §§ 60-1.40, -2.1(b)(2), -741.40, -250.40 (2005). The Veterans Act regulations were updated to incorporate the new categories added by the 1998 and 2000 amendments on December 1, 2005. 70 Fed. Reg. 72,148, 72,151 (Dec. 1, 2005). The requirements for these programs are set forth at 41 C.F.R. pts. 60-2, -250, -741 (2005).

[66]*Id.* §§ 60-1.7, -250.6(c). For a discussion of the VETS-100 requirements, see Section V *infra*.

[67]*Id.* § 60-1.40(a). Although the regulations under the Veterans and Rehabilitation Acts do not by their terms say that these bases trigger coverage, the OFCCP nevertheless contends that such employers must comply with the AAP provisions of these Acts.

[68]*Id.*

[69]The balance of this chapter differs in at least two respects from the format followed elsewhere in this book. First, because readers of prior editions have suggested the need for more practical guidance for practitioners in this area, the chapter is drafted principally from the perspective of a lawyer who advises businesses with respect to OFCCP matters. Second, this area is unique in the relative paucity of case law to which to refer. The applicable regulations and the OFCCP's Compliance

because of race, color, religion, sex, or national origin; and (2) to take affirmative action to ensure that applicants and employees are employed without regard to such factors.[70]

The government's standard contract clause requires that each contractor agree to comply with provisions of the Executive Order and the rules, regulations, and orders of the Secretary of Labor issued thereunder; post notices setting forth provisions of the nondiscrimination clause; furnish required information and reports; permit access to its books and records for purposes of investigation by the Secretary of Labor; and include the equal employment opportunity clause in every subcontract or purchase order so that such provisions will be binding upon each subcontractor or vendor. It further provides that, in the event of noncompliance with the clause itself or with any rule, regulation, or order issued under the Executive Order, the contract may be canceled, terminated, or suspended. After a hearing, the contractor may be declared ineligible for further government contracts.

B. Components of the Executive Order 11246 Affirmative Action Program for Supply and Service Contractors

1. Basic Requirements

A written Executive Order 11246 AAP is required only when the AAP threshold (discussed above) is met.[71] A covered contractor must develop, update annually,[72] and at all times maintain a

---

Manual, now outdated in many respects, provide somewhat more guidance, but many employers believe that they offer only an incomplete picture. The reader therefore will find in this chapter—in contrast to the remainder of the book—a number of factual and tactical assertions unaccompanied by citations to authority. It should be emphasized, however, that the OFCCP maintains that contractors that deviate from the agency's regulations, Compliance Manual, and case precedents risk findings of noncompliance and possible sanctions.

[70]Exec. Order No. 11246, § 202(1) (1965), *reprinted as amended in* 1 AFFIRMATIVE ACTION COMPL. MAN. (BNA) 101; 41 C.F.R. § 60-1.4(a)(1) (2005). The threshold triggers for each of these requirements are set forth in Section II *supra*.

[71]*See* Section II.B.2 *supra*.

[72]AAPs must be updated annually. 41 C.F.R. § 60-2.31 (2005). Although the regulations provide that an AAP summary must be prepared and submitted annually to OFCCP on the AAP anniversary date, the OFCCP has never published the

written AAP setting forth action plans to achieve equal opportunity for women and men of all racial and ethnic groups.[73]

The OFCCP typically requires a separate AAP for each of the contractor's establishments (i.e., each single location or group of locations in the same local recruiting area). There are exceptions, however. Employees who work at an establishment where the contractor employs fewer than 50 employees may be included in any of the following: (1) an AAP that covers only their own establishment; (2) an AAP that "covers the location of the personnel function which supports the establishment"; or (3) an AAP that "covers the location of the official to whom they report."[74] Alternatively, a contractor may request approval of the Deputy Assistant Secretary, or his or her designee, to establish an AAP "based on functional or business units."[75] On March 21, 2002, the OFCCP issued a directive setting forth the procedures for processing and approving

---

requisite program summary format in the *Federal Register*, so this summary requirement has never been enforced. *Id.*

[73]*Id.* §§ 60-1.40, -1.12(b). For any record the contractor maintains pursuant to §§ 60-1.40 and 60-1.12, the contractor must be able to identify: (1) the gender, race, and ethnicity of each employee; and (2) where possible, the gender and race/ethnicity of each applicant. *Id.* § 60-1.12(c). Section II.B.4.b delineates the applicants from whom gender and race/ethnicity must be collected. Upon request, contractors must supply this information to the OFCCP. *Id.; see also id.* § 60-2.32 (describing requirement that contractors must provide to OFCCP documents maintained pursuant to §§ 60-1.12 and 60-2.10). "[T]he final rule recognizes that some job applicants refuse to divulge demographic information to identify themselves. Therefore, OFCCP wishes to be reasonable through inclusion of the 'where possible' phrase referring to applicants in Sec. 60-1.12(c)(1)(ii)." 65 Fed. Reg. at 68,023 (Nov. 13, 2000).

[74]41 C.F.R. § 60-2.1(d)(2) (2005). The regulations also provide that "employees who work at establishments other than that of the manager to whom they report, must be included in the [AAP] of their manager" and that "employees for whom selection decisions are made at a higher level establishment within the organization must be included in the [AAP] of the establishment where the selection decision is made." *Id.* § 60-2.1(d)(1), (3). If, pursuant to § 60-2.1(d)(1)–(3), an employee is included in an AAP for an establishment other than the one in which the employee is located, the organizational profile and job group analysis of the AAP in which the employee is included must be annotated to identify the actual location of such employee. *Id.* § 60-2.1(e). Moreover, if the establishment at which such employee is actually located also maintains an AAP, the organizational profile and job group analysis of that program must also be annotated to show the program in which such employee is included. *Id.*

[75]*Id.* § 60-2.1(d)(4).

a functional AAP.[76] However, agreements "allowing the use of functional or business unit [AAPs] cannot be construed to limit or restrict how the OFCCP structures its compliance evaluations."[77]

A separate AAP for each facility or locality has certain advantages for employers, even where the OFCCP permits a contractor to adopt a functional AAP or otherwise aggregate facilities, including: (1) the separate AAP facilitates evaluation of workforce availability by recruitment area, as the OFCCP mandates; (2) it results in an AAP that covers fewer employees, and thus fewer hires, promotions, and terminations;[78] and (3) it focuses more narrowly the likely scope of any ensuing OFCCP compliance evaluation of the AAP.[79] However, some employers prefer functional AAPs because they more easily allow management to hold a specific executive accountable for an organization's performance.

---

[76]See OFCCP Directive No. 254 (Mar. 21, 2002), *available at* http://www.dol.gov/esa/media/ reports/ofccp/directive/02aapdir.htm (last visited Dec. 5, 2005). The contractor must submit a written request explaining why it believes that use of a functional AAP would be most appropriate for an actual functional area or business unit that operates somewhat autonomously. *Id.* If the OFCCP neither approves nor disapproves the request within 120 calendar days after its receipt, it will be deemed approved by the Deputy Assistant Secretary and may be implemented. *Id.* Upon 90 calendar days' written notice, either the contractor or the OFCCP may terminate the functional AAP agreement. *Id.* These agreements automatically expire 5 years after approval, unless a renewal request is submitted by the contractor at least 120 days prior to the expiration date. *Id.* Renewal requests will be deemed accepted unless rejected in writing by the OFCCP within 60 calendar days of their receipt. *Id.*

[77]*Id.*

[78]In *OFCCP v. Coldwell, Banker & Co.*, No. 78-OFCCP-12, 1987 WL 774232, [1979–1987 Transfer Binder] OFCCP FED. CONT. COMPL. MAN. (CCH) ¶ 21,307, at 3638 (Aug. 14, 1987) (Final Decision), a decision that predated functional AAPs, the OFCCP filed an administrative complaint because Coldwell, Banker failed to develop, maintain, or submit acceptable AAPs for each of its 186 establishments. Although ruling against the company on other grounds, the ALJ recommended that the OFCCP regulations be interpreted to allow the company to submit one national or several regional AAPs. The Secretary of Labor held that "each physically separate facility is prima facie an 'establishment,' " but that several facilities could be grouped and treated as one establishment where the contractor could show "central authority for employment and personnel decisions, including the power to set wages and assign personnel to different locations." The Secretary further noted that facilities in different labor markets or recruiting areas should not be combined, but small facilities might be combined for goal-setting purposes where failure to combine would result in meaningless goals of a fraction of a person.

[79]See Doninger v. Pacific Nw. Bell, Inc., 564 F.2d. 1304, 1310–11 (9th Cir. 1997) (plaintiffs would have difficulty representing employees from various facilities in a class action as each facility had its own AAP and thus different patterns and practices).

2. Narrative Sections

The regulations require that the Executive Order AAP include various narrative and statistical sections. The narrative portions of an Executive Order 11246 AAP contain the contractor's equal opportunity/affirmative action policy and steps for its implementation. Narrative components are identified in the regulations[80] and discussed in detail below.

a. Background Issues. An AAP potentially is a liability document for an employer. It may create potential or actual liability for a contractor in OFCCP proceedings (if the contractor did not comply with the regulations) as well as in private discrimination and other employment litigation (particularly if the contractor failed to fulfill its AAP commitments).[81] In addition, absent appropriate disclaimers in the AAP, an employee in some jurisdictions arguably

---

[80]41 C.F.R. § 60-2.17 (2005).

[81]Most courts hold that the departure from an AAP may be relevant evidence, but not conclusive proof, of discrimination. *E.g.*, Mozee v. American Commercial Marine Serv. Co., 940 F.2d 1036, 1051, 56 FEP 1155 (7th Cir. 1991) (the employer's "noncompliance with its various affirmative-action plans [was] probative of discriminatory intent," but not conclusive to prove discrimination); Gonzales v. Police Dep't, City of San Jose, 901 F.2d 758, 760–62, 52 FEP 1132 (9th Cir. 1990) (remanding to the trial court to consider the defendant's violation of its AAP as evidence of potential discrimination, after noting that the plaintiff had been passed over for promotion in an apparent violation of the AAP; "Indeed, there might never have been a need for the claim had the Police Department followed the city's plan—even once."); Yatvin v. Madison Metro. Sch. Dist., 840 F.2d 412, 416, 45 FEP 1862 (7th Cir. 1988) (an employer's failure to adhere to its affirmative action plan may be evidence of discrimination); Lowe v. City of Monrovia, 775 F.2d 998, 1007 n.6, 39 FEP 350 (9th Cir. 1985), *as amended* by 784 F.2d 1407, 41 FEP 931 (9th Cir. 1986) ("In any particular case the significance of such a failure [to follow an AAP] may depend on the circumstances, including the reasons why the defendants failed to comply with the plan. Any evidence that indicates that a defendant intentionally circumvented an affirmative action plan would, of course, be probative regarding the defendant's motives in making a given employment decision."); Love v. Alamance County Bd. of Educ., 757 F.2d 1504, 1509, 37 FEP 633 (4th Cir. 1985) (the plaintiff claimed that the defendant's failure to adopt objective criteria as required by its AAP was evidence of continuing discrimination; in affirming judgment in favor of the defendant, the Fourth Circuit held that failure to follow the plan requirements was not *conclusive* evidence of racial discrimination); Craik v. Minnesota State Univ. Bd., 731 F.2d 465, 472–73, 34 FEP 649 (8th Cir. 1984) (evidence that the defendant failed to set goals and timetables in its AAP and that the affirmative action committee met irregularly is relevant to discriminatory intent). *But cf.* Gray v. University of Ark., 658 F. Supp. 709, 727, 43 FEP 1103 (W.D. Ark. 1987) (the defendant's failure

could base a breach of contract claim on unfulfilled commitments therein.[82] Plaintiffs may be able to obtain an AAP and supporting

---

strictly to comply with its AAP did not show that the plaintiff was terminated because of her sex), *aff'd*, 883 F.2d 1394, 50 FEP 1112 (8th Cir. 1989).

Compliance with OFCCP programs is measured by good faith efforts, not goal attainment. The OFCCP's 1995 Notice on "Numerical Goals under Executive Order 11246" clarified:

    f. Goals May Not Be Treated as a Ceiling or a Floor.

    The Executive Order does not require that contractors treat goals as either a ceiling or a floor for the employment of particular groups. Goals establish neither a minimum nor a maximum number of members of a group which must be employed. Either use of a numerical goal would be an impermissible quota.

    g. Compliance is Measured by Good Faith Effort.

    A contractor's compliance is measured by whether it has made good faith efforts to meet its goals. Failure to meet goals is not a violation of the Executive Order. Therefore, a contractor that has not met its goals will be found in compliance if it has made good faith efforts.

DAILY LAB. REP. (BNA) at E-2 (Aug. 11, 1995).

[82]*See* Holley v. Pansophic Sys., Inc., 1992 WL 137124, at *4 (N.D. Ill. June 12, 1992) (mem.) (Executive Order does not preempt a state breach of contract claim arising from an asserted violation of the affirmative action policy); Manuel v. International Harvester Co., 502 F. Supp. 45, 48, 23 FEP 1477 (N.D. Ill. 1980) (an aggrieved individual may sue under state contract law as a third-party beneficiary); *see also Yatvin*, 840 F.2d at 416 (court suggests in dictum that the plaintiff may have a cause of action for breach of contract if the defendant's AAP was found to be a part of plaintiff's employment contract); Stokes v. Northwestern Mem'l Hosp., 1990 U.S. Dist. LEXIS 14815, at *8 (N.D. Ill. Nov. 5, 1990) ("a reasonable jury could find that [AAP and other manuals] make it more (or less) likely that plaintiff's version of her contract is in fact true"; the court denied the employer's motion in limine to exclude the AAP in the breach of contract case arising from employment termination); Elstner v. Southwestern Bell Tel. Co., 659 F. Supp. 1328, 1341, 43 FEP 1437 (S.D. Tex. 1987) (the employer's failure to adhere to its AAP provides a basis for a breach of contract claim; because the nondiscrimination clause in the collective bargaining agreement incorporated the affirmative action plan, the court consolidated the plaintiff's breach of the CBA claim with the plaintiff's supposed "separate right of action that exists under the Affirmative Action Program"), *aff'd*, 863 F.2d 881, 49 FEP 650 (5th Cir. 1988); *cf.* Ferguson v. Veterans Admin., 723 F.2d 871, 873, 33 FEP 1525 (11th Cir. 1984) (absent a showing of discrimination, there is no Title VII cause of action for the failure of an employer to follow its AAP; court notes, however, that its decision would not control a breach of contract action). *Contra* NAACP v. Detroit Police Officers Ass'n, 821 F.2d 328, 331, 43 FEP 1786 (6th Cir. 1987) ("Judicial approval of a voluntary affirmative action plan does not create a contract of permanent employment or invalidate or modify a collective bargaining agreement providing for layoffs on the basis of seniority."); Robinson v. Jacksonville Shipyards, Inc., 760 F. Supp. 1486, 1532, 57 FEP 971 (M.D. Fla. 1991) (the plaintiff cannot sue as a third-party beneficiary of a government contract).

documents through discovery or a request under the Freedom of Information Act (FOIA).[83]

(i.) Appropriate prefatory language. Most employers choose to begin an AAP with a preface that includes appropriate qualifying language. For example, some contractors utilize one or more of the following statements: (1) the AAP does not create any express or implied contractual or other rights in or for any employee or prospective employee; (2) whenever the term "goal" is used, it does not provide a "justification to extend a preference to any individual, select an individual, or adversely affect an individual's employment status, on the basis of that person's race, color, religion, sex, or national origin";[84] (3) the AAP has been developed in accordance with and in reliance upon the EEOC's Guidelines on Affirmative Action;[85] (4) the terms "comparing incumbency to availability," "underutilization," and "problem area" appearing in the AAP are terms that government regulations require the contractor to use, and the criteria used in relation to these terms also are specified by the government; these terms have no independent legal or factual significance whatsoever; therefore, although the contractor will use the terms in good faith in connection with its AAP, such usage does not necessarily signify that the contractor agrees that these terms are properly applied to any particular factual situation; (5) the comparison of incumbency to availability is required by government regulations to be based on certain statistical comparisons, geographic areas, and sources of statistics; the contractor's use thereof does not indicate that the contractor agrees that the geographic areas are appropriate, that the sources of statistics are the most relevant, or that the resulting statistical comparisons are probative; indeed, the comparison of incumbency to availability

---

[83]5 U.S.C. § 552 (2000); *see* Section IX *infra.*

[84]41 C.F.R. § 60-2.16(e)(2) (2005). The regulations clearly establish that placement goals: (1) are not rigid or inflexible quotas that must be met; (2) are neither a ceiling nor a floor for the employment of particular groups; (3) do not create set-asides for specific groups; (4) do not entitle a contractor to extend a preference or adversely affect an individual's employment status on the basis of the individual's protected group status; and (5) do not have as a purpose the achievement of proportional representation or equal results. *Id.*

[85]*See* 29 C.F.R. § 1608 (2005).

and other statistical comparisons are intended to have no significance outside the context of the AAP;[86] and (6) the grouping of job titles into a given pay grade or job group does not suggest that the contractor believes the jobs so grouped are substantially the same or of comparable worth.

(ii.) *Making realistic commitments.* Most contractors attempt to include in their AAPs only realistically achievable qualitative numerical goals. Contractors also generally avoid using the following types of language: (1) extremes which are suggested by words like "all" and "fully" rather than the more cautious "as may be appropriate"; (2) language that suggests that the contractor has failed to engage in adequate affirmative action in the past, has committed unlawful discrimination, or has violated Executive Order 11246 or other laws or regulations; and (3) other phrases appearing to admit problems, such as "despite our efforts, we never have had a woman in this job" or "management needs to become more sensitive to these issues."

To ensure accountability, most contractors assign implementation responsibility to a designated employee.

(iii.) *Maintaining the confidentiality of AAPs.* Potential plaintiffs and/or civil rights organizations may seek to review the AAP to select targets for litigation or to support a breach of contract or discrimination claim. Thus, many contractors take steps to maintain the confidentiality of numerical data and analyses of progress and concerns. By limiting disclosure of such information to the executive team and human resources managers, the contractor more credibly can argue that it should not be required to divulge proprietary information in discovery[87] and that the OFCCP should be barred from releasing it under the FOIA.[88] Although contractors

---

[86]In an employment discrimination class action, the selection of the most appropriate statistics to determine availability often is crucial. *See generally* Chapters 2 (Disparate Treatment), 3 (Adverse Impact), and 34 (Statistical and Other Expert Proof). The suggested prefatory statement would support a contractor's argument that it should not be bound in subsequent employment discrimination litigation by the availability figures set forth in its AAP. However, the AAP statistics should be as precise as possible.

[87]*See generally* Chapter 33 (Discovery).

[88]*See* Section IX *infra.*

do not always prevail with these arguments, they are even less likely to do so if they have waived confidentiality.

Therefore, a carefully drafted Executive Order 11246 AAP typically will state that "the document contains confidential information which is subject to the provisions of 18 U.S.C. § 1905 and *Chrysler Corp. v. Brown*, 441 U.S. 281, 19 FEP 475 (1979), and is exempt from disclosure under the FOIA."[89] Contractors accordingly often stamp pages containing numerical data, analyses of status and progress, and action plans to address concerns with the legend "CONFIDENTIAL & PROPRIETARY: EXEMPT FROM FOIA DISCLOSURE" and place them in separate sections of the AAP.

Many contractors restrict disclosure of AAP documents to those who have a need to have them. Contractors, therefore, often separate the AAP for veterans/individuals with disabilities from the Executive Order AAP because the former must be available for inspection by any interested employee or applicant,[90] but the latter need not be disclosed. Similary, contractors typically give to individual managers and supervisors the Executive Order incumbency and goals for their respective departments only, a list of their individual responsibilities and action plans, and (possibly) the standard narrative sections. Many contractors do not include within the AAP self-critical analyses, such as standard deviation analyses of hiring, promotion, and termination data,[91] which they instead place in a separate confidential, proprietary document, access to which is restricted to those who have a need to know. Some companies seek to cover such analyses by the attorney-client privilege and maintain them in a confidential manner to preserve the privilege, recognizing that disclosure of similar nonprivileged impact analyses may be required by the OFCCP during a compliance evaluation.

Contractors often state in the preface, where appropriate, that (1) the AAP and supporting documents are made available on loan

---

[89]*See* 5 U.S.C. § 552 (2000); *see also* Section IX *infra.*

[90]*See* 41 C.F.R. §§ 60-250.41, -741.41 (2005).

[91]*See generally* Chapter 33 (Discovery). The regulations now require contractors to analyze applicant flow, hires, promotions, terminations, and other personnel actions to determine whether there are selection disparities. *Id.* § 60-2.17(b)(2).

to the U.S. government on the express condition that the government hold the information completely confidential and not release copies to anyone; (2) the AAP and supporting documents contain trade secrets, confidential statistical data, self-critical analysis, and other confidential commercial and financial data within the meaning of the FOIA, Title VII of the Civil Rights Act of 1964 (as amended), and the Uniform Trade Secrets Act,[92] the disclosure of which is prohibited by law; and (3) the contractor's chief executive officer should be notified if the government receives any FOIA request or otherwise contemplates the release of information.

Notwithstanding all such efforts, the data at issue may not, in fact, be deemed exempt from disclosure under the FOIA. Thus, even these actions to restrict access may not prevent release of the AAP by the government.

b. Required Narrative Sections. The Executive Order 11246 AAP must, at a minimum, include narrative sections that should bear at least[93] the following headings:

(1) designation of responsibilities for implementation of the contractor's AAP;[94]

(2) identification of problem areas by organizational units and job groups;[95]

---

[92]18 U.S.C. § 1905 (2000).

[93]Although a contractor is not required to indicate in its AAP the details of its compliance with the OFCCP's Guidelines on Discrimination Because of Sex or Religion and National Origin, 41 C.F.R. §§ 60-20, -50 (2005), the OFCCP typically audits such compliance. Therefore, contractors often include a section in the AAP confirming such compliance.

[94]*Id.* § 60-2.17(a). A contractor must provide for the implementation of the AAP, and of equal employment opportunity, by assigning responsibility and accountability to one of the organization's officials. "He or she must have the authority, resources, support of and access to top management to ensure the effective implementation of the [AAP]." *Id.*

[95]*Id.* § 60-2.17(b). At a minimum, a contractor must evaluate: (1) the workforce by organizational unit and job group to determine whether there are issues concerning minority or female utilization or distribution; (2) personnel activity (i.e., applicant flow, hires, promotions, terminations, and other personnel actions) to determine if there are selection disparities; (3) compensation systems to determine if there are race/ethnicity/sex disparities; (4) selection, recruitment, referral, and other personnel procedures to see if they cause disparities in employment or advancement of women or minorities; and (5) "any other areas that might impact the success" of an AAP. *See id.* However, these analyses should be reported carefully, because statements of this nature may be introduced in subsequent discrimination litigation.

(3) development and execution of action-oriented programs designed to correct any problem areas and further designed to attain established goals and objectives;[96] and

(4) design and implementation of internal audit and reporting systems to measure effectiveness of the total AAP.[97]

3. Statistical Sections

a. Introduction. The Executive Order 11246 AAP contains five statistical sections: organizational profile, job group analysis, availability, comparison of incumbency to availability, and placement goals.[98]

b. Organizational Profile.[99] The organizational profile "depict[s] the staffing pattern within an establishment" by organizational unit to help contractors "determine whether barriers to equal employment opportunity exist in their organizations" and identify units "where women or minorities are underrepresented or concentrated."[100] A contractor has the option to select one of two formats for the profile: (1) an "organizational display," or (2) the traditional "workforce analysis."[101]

The organizational display is a "detailed graphical or tabular chart, text, spreadsheet or similar presentation of the contractor's organizational structure."[102] It must identify each organizational unit (e.g., a department, division, section, group, branch, project team,

---

[96]*Id.* § 60-2.17(c). The regulations provide guidance as to how such action-oriented programs should be developed and executed: "the contractor must ensure that [programs] consist of more than following the same procedures which have previously produced inadequate results" and must show "good faith efforts to remove identified barriers, expand employment opportunities, and produce measurable results." *Id.* When writing action-oriented programs, a contractor should avoid making commitments that are not realistically achievable during the program year.

[97]*Id.* § 60-2.17(d). The auditing system should: (1) monitor records of all personnel activity to determine that nondiscriminatory policies are fulfilled; (2) require internal reporting on a scheduled basis as to the degree to which objectives are attained; (3) review report results with all levels of management; and (4) advise top management of the effectiveness of the AAP and provide recommendations for improving unsatisfactory performance. *See id.*

[98]*Id.* § 60-2.10(b)(1).

[99]*Id.* § 60-2.11.

[100]*See id.* § 60-2.11(a).

[101]*Id.* § 60-2.11(b).

[102]*Id.* § 60-2.11(b)(1).

job family, or similar component) in the establishment and show the relationship between the units.[103] For each unit listed, contractors must indicate: (1) the name of the unit; (2) the job title, gender, race, and ethnicity of any unit supervisors; (3) the total number of male and female incumbents; and (4) the total number of male and female incumbents in each of several listed minority groups: African Americans, Hispanics, Asians/Pacific Islanders, and American Indians/Alaskan Natives.[104] A sample organizational display is included in the *Federal Register*.[105]

The traditional "workforce analysis," which a contractor may use in lieu of the organizational display, is a breakdown of a contractor's current workforce by department or other similar organizational unit, gender, and race.[106] A contractor begins by listing each unit, including its supervision, within the facility covered by the AAP. For example, if a facility has employees in five units (e.g., design, production, maintenance, finance, and administration), a separate workforce analysis chart would be prepared for each. Each unit's chart must list each job title found therein, ranked by wage rate or salary range from the "lowest paid to the highest paid," including unit supervision.[107] If there are separate

---

[103]*See id.* § 60-2.11(b)(1), (2).

[104]*See id.* § 60-2.11(b)(3)(i)–(iv). On November 28, 2005, the EEOC published a notice that it has submitted to the Office of Management and Budget final revisions to the Employer Information Report (EEO-1) that would require reporting of male and female employees in the following seven categories effective with the 2007 EEO-1: Hispanic or Latino; White; Black or African American; Asians; Native Hawaiian or other Pacific Islander; American Indian or Alaska Native; and Two or More Races, Not Hispanic or Latino. 70 Fed. Reg. 71,294, 71,301 (Nov. 28, 2005). In the affirmative action program year following final approval, a contractor will modify the race/ethnic group categories in the affirmative action plan to correspond.

[105]*See* 65 Fed. Reg. 68,028 (Nov. 13, 2000). The preamble to the final rule indicates that this chart, which is a graphical representation, is merely illustrative and clarifies that the display need not be a graphical representation, but also may be a chart, text, spreadsheet, or other such textual representation. *Id.* at 68,026–27; 41 C.F.R. § 60-2.11(b) (2005).

[106]*See* 41 C.F.R. § 60-2.11(c) (2005).

[107]*Id.* Each job title employed at the facilities covered by the AAP must be listed, even if it is included for job group analysis and goal-setting purposes in a corporate or regional AAP, in which case it must be annotated to show the affirmative action program in which the employee is included. *See* FED. CONTRACT COMPL. MAN. § 2G01(a), *reprinted in* 1 AFFIRMATIVE ACTION COMPL. MAN. (BNA) 2:0005.

work units or lines of progression within an organizational unit, the contractor must prepare a separate list for each one.[108] Lines of progression should indicate the order of jobs in the line.[109]

For each job title, in each organizational unit or progression line, a contractor must list: (1) the total number of incumbents; (2) the total number of male and female incumbents; (3) the total number of male and female incumbents in each of the following groups: African American, Hispanic, Asian/Pacific Islander, and American Indian/Alaskan Native; and (4) the wage rate or salary range for each job title.[110] If a contractor prefers to keep wage or salary data confidential, it may code those rates or ranges with a letter or other designation and include only the codes on the work-force analysis.[111]

   c. Job Group Analysis.[112] A job group is a grouping of jobs with "similar content, wage rates, and opportunities."[113] The job group analysis is the "first step in the contractor's comparison of the representation of minorities and women in its workforce with the estimated availability of minorities and women qualified to be employed."[114]

The job group analysis differs from the organizational profile because (among other differences) the job group analysis is not divided along organizational unit lines. Thus, for example, executive secretaries in the production department would be counted as part of the same job group as executive secretaries in the administration department, even though they would not be counted together for purposes of the organizational profile.

---

[108]41 C.F.R. § 60-2.11(c)(2) (2005).

[109]*Id.*

[110]*Id.* § 60-2.11(d).

[111]*See* FED. CONTRACT COMPL. MAN. § 2G01(b)(2), *reprinted in* 1 AFFIRMA-TIVE ACTION COMPL. MAN. (BNA) 2:0005 (where wage rates or salary ranges are coded, contractors must give the OFCCP the key to the code during the on-site review; the codes must be consistent across department/unit lines and be arranged in order of the wage/salary).

[112]41 C.F.R. § 60-2.12 (2005).

[113]*See id.* § 60-2.12(b). "Similarity of content" means similarity in "the duties and responsibilities of the job titles which make up the job group." *Id.* "Similarity of opportunities" relates to "training, transfers, promotions, pay, mobility, and other career enhancement opportunities offered by the jobs within the job group." *Id.*

[114]41 C.F.R. § 60-2.12(a) (2005).

The design of job groups is one of the most important decisions a contractor will make in drafting an AAP. If the job groups are inappropriate, the statistical analyses based on them will be flawed. Although the identification of job groups is necessarily a subjective process in which the often-competing requirements of content, wage rate, opportunities, and size are balanced, the following general guidelines should be considered in grouping jobs.

A contractor begins by separating jobs covered by the AAP into the nine EEO-1 categories.[115] A single job group should not include jobs from more than one of these categories.[116] Thus, there will be at least nine job groups, assuming that a contractor has employees in each EEO-1 category. The regulations state explicitly that a contractor with fewer than 150 employees may utilize the EEO-1 categories as job groups.[117] A contractor with more employees normally is expected to subdivide at least some EEO-1 categories into two or more job groups, in order to ensure that the jobs categorized together in fact have similar content, wage rates, and opportunities.

In determining whether to subdivide an EEO-1 category into more than one job group, a contractor must balance the following four factors. First, each job group should have enough incumbents to permit meaningful statistical analysis. Typically, a contractor will not subdivide an EEO-1 category unless the resulting job groups each have at least 50 incumbents.

---

[115]The nine EEO-1 categories represent the nine occupational groups used in the Standard Form 100, the Employer Information EEO-1 survey. The categories are Officials and Managers; Professionals; Technicians; Sales; Office and Clerical; Craft Workers (skilled); Operatives (semi-skilled); Laborers (unskilled); and Service Workers. 41 C.F.R. § 60-2.12(e) (2005); 1 AFFIRMATIVE ACTION COMPL. MAN. (BNA) 419. The EEOC has proposed that effective with the 2007 EEO-1, there will be 10 EEO-1 categories; Officials and Managers will be subdivided into Executive/Senior Level Officials and Managers, and First/Mid Level Officials and Managers; Office and Clerical will be renamed Administrative Support Workers; and Laborers will be renamed Laborers and Helpers. See 70 Fed. Reg. 71,294, 71,298–300, 71,302–03 (Nov. 28, 2005). The Dictionary of Occupational Titles, published by the Department of Labor, codes job titles based on duties, requirements, and other factors, and may be useful in determining the appropriate group for a particular job. See FED. CONTRACT COMPL. MAN. § 2G02(b)(1), reprinted in 1 AFFIRMATIVE ACTION COMPL. MAN. (BNA) 2:0006.

[116]FED. CONTRACT COMPL. MAN. § 2G02(d)(2), reprinted in 1 AFFIRMATIVE ACTION COMPL. MAN. (BNA) 2:0006.

[117]41 C.F.R. § 60-2.12(e) (2005).

Second, although the number of job groups will vary depending upon the size and type of the business, most contractors attempt to limit the number to as few as possible, preferably between 9 and 18.[118] This not only increases the statistical power of any analyses, but also decreases the number of job groups that may require monitoring of goal attainment and good faith compliance efforts.

Third, a job group should contain jobs that have similar rates of pay, as well as similar opportunities for training, transfer, promotion, pay mobility, and other employment benefits. It is impossible to fully achieve this objective. However, a contractor generally should avoid combining senior professional jobs (e.g., those that pay more than $120,000) with entry professional positions (e.g., those that pay $30,000 per year) because their pay and opportunities are too dissimilar.

Once the appropriate job groups are determined, a contractor must include, for each job group, a list of the job titles that comprise

---

[118]For example, an AAP might have the following job groups:
Officials and Managers Job Groups
    Executives and Senior Management
    Middle Management
    Entry Management
Professionals Job Groups
    Senior Technical Professionals
    Senior Administrative Professionals
    Technical Professionals
    Administrative Professionals
Technicians Job Group
    Technicians
Sales Job Groups
    Field Sales
    Inside Sales
Administrative Support Job Groups
    Secretaries
    Senior Administrative Support
    Administrative Support
Skilled Craft Job Groups
    Electrical Skilled Craft
    Other Skilled Craft
Operatives Job Group
    Operatives
Laborers and Helpers Job Group
    Laborers and Helpers
Service Workers Job Group
    Service Workers

the group.[119] A contractor is required to separately state the percentage of minorities and the percentage of women it employs in each job group established.[120] The OFCCP prefers that the list also reflect the number of employees in each job title and their racial and gender composition.

d. *Determining Availability.*[121] A contractor then must separately determine the availability of minorities and women for each job group.[122] This is the appropriate percentage representation of women and minorities having the skills required to fill the positions in each job group.[123] In determining the availability of minorities and females under current regulations, a contractor must consider at least the following two factors:[124]

(1) "The percentage of minorities or women with requisite skills in the reasonable recruitment area," which is "the geographical area from which the contractor usually seeks *or reasonably could seek* workers to fill" the applicable position;[125] and

---

[119]*Id.* § 60-2.12(c). Additionally, if pursuant to §§ 60-2.1(d) and (e), the job group analysis contains jobs that are located at another establishment, the job group analysis must be annotated to identify the actual location of those jobs. *See id.* If the establishment at which the jobs are actually located also maintains an AAP, that job group analysis must also be annotated to identify the program in which the jobs are included. *See id.*

[120]41 C.F.R. § 60-2.13 (2005).

[121]*Id.* § 60-2.14.

[122]*Id.* § 60-2.14(b).

[123]*See id.* § 60-2.14(a). The purpose of this determination is to establish a benchmark against which the demographic composition of the incumbent workforce can be compared, in order to identify possible barriers to equal opportunity within particular job groups. *Id.*

[124]*Id.* § 60-2.14(c). A contractor should identify the source for each availability figure included in the analysis (e.g., most recent census for job titles in the job group, or representation of incumbents in feeder jobs). The requirements for statistical information are set out at 41 C.F.R. § 60-2.14(d) (2005), and specify that the contractor must use the most current and discrete statistical information available, such as census data, data from local job service offices, and data from colleges or other training institutions.

[125]*Id.* § 60-2.14(c)(1) (emphasis added). The most useful data on the availability of minorities/women with the requisite skills typically will be census data on more than 500 occupations. This information is available from the Bureau of Census and many private companies in printed form or on computer diskettes. Some states' employment security departments also provide more limited statistical information on certain categories of jobs. FED. CONTRACT COMPL. MAN. § 2G05(e), *reprinted in* 1 AFFIRMATIVE ACTION COMPL. MAN. (BNA) 2:0008.

(2) "The percentage of minorities or women among those promotable, transferable, and trainable within the contractor's organization." Trainable minorities or women are those "who could, with appropriate training which the employer is *reasonably* able to provide, become promotable or transferable during the AAP year."[126]

A contractor may not draw the "reasonable recruitment area" in a way that has the effect of excluding minorities or women.[127] Nor may it "define the pool of promotable, transferable, and trainable employees in such a way as to have the effect of excluding minorities or women."[128] The OFCCP explicitly refused to clarify that contractors will be in violation only if they draw recruitment areas or define pools of employees in a way *intended* to have an exclusionary effect.[129] The OFCCP asserted that such a change is not "necessary or desirable."[130] On the other hand, the OFCCP indicated that contractors who find that an unintentional discriminatory effect occurs from inaccurately drawing the reasonable recruitment area or improperly defining the pool of employees will be given an opportunity to correct errors before the conclusion of any compliance evaluation.[131]

---

[126]41 C.F.R. § 60-2.14(c)(2) (2005) (emphasis added).

[127]*Id.* § 60-2.14(e). For each job group, a contractor must identify the reasonable recruitment area and provide a brief explanation of the reasoning behind selection of that recruitment area. *Id.* The "reasonable recruitment area" will vary depending upon the types of jobs in the job group. For jobs that require minimal to intermediate skills, the reasonable recruitment area often will be only the geographic area from which employees may reasonably commute to the contractor's establishment. By contrast, jobs in the Officials and Managers, Professionals, and Sales (nonretail) EEO-1 categories often have larger reasonable recruitment areas. For these categories, national, state, or regional statistics may be appropriate. *See* FED. CONTRACT COMPL. MAN. § 2G04(c)(4), *reprinted in* 1 AFFIRMATIVE ACTION COMPL. MAN. (BNA) 2:0008.

[128]41 C.F.R. § 60-2.14(f) (2005). For each job group, a contractor must identify the pool of such employees and provide a short explanation of the reasoning behind selection of that pool. *Id.*

[129]65 Fed. Reg. at 68,032.

[130]*Id.* In discussing its rationale for drawing the reasonable recruitment area, the OFCCP states: "The objective . . . is to have the contractor compute, as accurately as possible, the availability of minorities and women for employment. Accurate computation of availability is essential to the entire goal setting process. Improper drawing of the reasonable recruitment area has the effect of misstating availability. The effect is the same, whether the improper drawing is intentional or inadvertent, and it cannot be accepted." *Id.*

[131]*Id.*

Where a job group is composed of job titles with different availability rates, contractors must prepare a composite availability figure in the manner set out at 41 C.F.R. § 60-2.14(g).[132] First, the contractor must separately determine the availability for each job title within the job group and determine the proportion of job group incumbents employed in each job title. Then, it must weight the availability for each job title by the proportion of job group incumbents employed in that job title. Finally, the contractor adds the weighted availability estimates for all job titles in the job group to calculate the composite availability for the job group.[133]

e. *Comparing Incumbency to Availability*.[134] The next step is a comparison of the percentage of minorities and women employed in each job group, determined pursuant to § 60-2.13, with the availability for those job groups, determined in accordance with § 60-2.14.[135] Placement goals must be established when the percentage of minorities or women actually employed in a job group is less than would "reasonably be expected" given their availability percentage in that particular job group.[136]

For many years, the OFCCP took the position that contractors must declare "underutilization" whenever the percentage of minorities or women employed is less than the percentage determined to be available, no matter how small the discrepancy might be. In *Firestone Synthetic Rubber & Latex Co. v. Marshall*,[137] however, the court held that the OFCCP could not lawfully insist that

---

[132]41 C.F.R. § 60-2.14(g) (2005).

[133]A detailed sample computation may be found in the preamble comments to the revised regulations and final rule. 65 Fed. Reg. at 68,033. A sample AAP, including statistical sections, is available on the OFCCP's website at http://www.dol.gov/esa/regs/compliance/ofccp/pdf/sampleaap.pdf (last visited Dec. 5, 2005).

[134]41 C.F.R. § 60-2.15 (2005). Section 60-2.15 replaces the former section regarding the "utilization analysis" and also replaces a portion of former § 60-2.11(b) (defining "underutilization" as "having fewer minorities or women in a particular job group than would reasonably be expected by their availability").

[135]*Id.*

[136]*Id.* § 60-2.15(b).

[137]507 F. Supp. 1330, 24 FEP 1699 (E.D. Tex. 1981). In a "technical guidance memorandum," the OFCCP had interpreted the former regulation's definition of "underutilization" to mean any numerical disparity between availability and utilization. *Id.* at 1331. According to the OFCCP, underutilization could exist even where the disparity was less than one person. Because Firestone's AAP at one facility failed to declare underutilization in each of the various job groups in which numerical disparities were found, the OFCCP asserted that the program was deficient. Firestone

contractors adopt this "any difference" standard for determining underutilization. The court held that the OFCCP's interpretation created a new obligation for contractors that the agency was required, but had failed, to subject to notice and comment procedures under the Administrative Procedure Act before implementation.[138] As an alternative and independent ground for vacating the decision of the Secretary of Labor, the court ruled that the OFCCP's interpretation was unreasonable, inconsistent with the regulations, and thus entitled to no weight.[139]

The OFCCP now has withdrawn its strict interpretation of underutilization and acknowledges a variety of methods to determine whether incumbency is lower than availability, including the following four tests:[140]

---

contended that it did not have to declare underutilization because the differences between availability and utilization were not statistically significant at the 5% level of significance. *Id.* In the administrative enforcement proceedings, the Secretary of Labor had maintained that the 5% test, which is used in many Title VII cases to infer whether a disparity between incumbency and availability occurred by chance, was an inappropriate basis for acknowledgment of underutilization, because that latter concept "carries no imputation of improper discriminatory motive"; in other words, according to the OFCCP, the concept of underutilization focuses on a statistical fact, not its cause. OFCCP v. Firestone Tire & Rubber Co., 23 FEP 215, 221 (Dep't of Labor 1980); *see also* Firestone Synthetic Rubber & Latex Co. v. Marshall, 23 FEP 526, 528 (E.D. Tex. 1980) (enjoining debarment pending decision on the merits).

Although an administrative law judge found in Firestone's favor, the Secretary stood by his interpretation of the regulations, overruling the recommended decision and ordering the contractor debarred for noncompliance. *Firestone*, 507 F. Supp. at 1333. On review, the district court set aside the order. The court rejected the Secretary's memorandum as legal authority for the "any disparity" rule because the OFCCP failed to comply with the notice and comment requirements of the Administrative Procedure Act, 5 U.S.C. § 553 (2000). *Firestone*, 507 F. Supp. at 1333. The court further ruled that the Secretary's interpretation of the regulation was unreasonable because the words "less women or minorities than would reasonably be expected by their availability" create a subjective standard by which underutilization is to be determined, not the objective, nondiscretionary standard urged by the OFCCP. *Id.* at 1336. The court noted that the contractor must consider the factors designated in the regulations in determining whether underutilization should be declared. However, a mere mathematical comparison between availability and utilization is not the sole consideration in determining underutilization. *Id.* at 1337. The court did not, however, express an opinion as to whether the 5% test was a proper alternative to the OFCCP's policies. The 5% test of statistical significance is discussed in Chapters 3 (Adverse Impact), 4 (Application of Adverse Impact to Employment Decisions) and 34 (Statistical and Other Expert Proof).

[138]507 F. Supp. at 1335.
[139]*Id.* at 1336.
[140]65 Fed. Reg. at 68,033–34.

(1) Any numerical difference between incumbency and availability.[141]

(2) A numerical difference of one person or more.

(3) Minority or female incumbency that is less than 80 percent of availability.[142]

(4) A disparity between the actual representation (incumbency) and expected representation (availability) for minorities or females that is statistically significant, namely −2.00 standard deviations or more.

The OFCCP declined to specify which method a contractor must use, asserting that the current practice of permitting various methods is the appropriate approach.[143]

f. Placement Goals.[144] Placement goals "serve as objectives or targets reasonably attainable by means of applying every good faith effort" to ensure that every aspect of the AAP works.[145] Placement goals also "measure progress toward achieving equal employment opportunity."[146] Contractor determinations that a placement goal is required under the regulations are not findings or admissions of discrimination.[147]

Where, pursuant to § 60-2.15, a contractor determines that it is required to establish a placement goal for a particular job group, it must establish an annual placement goal percentage at least equal to the availability figure derived for women or minorities for that job group.[148] A single goal for all minorities continues to be the standard. However, where there is a "substantial disparity"[149] between

---

[141]In other words, a contractor *may*, but is not required to, declare a shortfall requiring a goal if their minority incumbency (e.g., 18%) is less than the minority availability for the job group (e.g., 20%), even if that 2% difference amounts to a difference of less than one person, the availability and incumbency percentages are within 80% of each other, and the disparity is not statistically significant.

[142]For example, if female availability for a job group is 20%, a contractor would be required to declare a shortfall requiring a goal only if its female incumbency in the job group is less than 16% (80% of 20%).

[143]65 Fed. Reg. at 68,033–34.

[144]41 C.F.R. § 60-2.16 (2005). The revised regulations replace and streamline the former regulations referring to "goals and timetables," found in former § 60-2.12.

[145]41 C.F.R. § 60-2.16(a) (2005).

[146]*Id.*

[147]*Id.* § 60-2.16(b).

[148]*Id.* § 60-2.16(c).

[149]The term "substantial disparity" is used, but not defined in the regulations, Compliance Manual, or otherwise.

the incumbency and availability of a particular minority group or of men or women of a particular minority group, a contractor may be required to establish separate goals for such groups.[150]

A placement is an entry into a job group, typically through hire or promotion. A placement rate for a group is calculated by dividing the entries into the job group for that race or gender by the total entries into the group. For example, if a contractor hires 60 employees (including 30 women) and promotes 40 employees (including 10 women) into its "Senior Engineers" job group during the AAP year, the annual female placement rate would be calculated as follows:

$$\frac{\text{Female hires (30)} + \text{Female promotions (10)}}{\text{Total hires (60)} + \text{Total promotions (40)}} = \frac{40}{100} = 40\% \text{ female placement rate}$$

If the annual minority (or female) placement-rate percentage for a job group equals or exceeds the minority (or female) goal percentage for that group, the contractor has met its placement-rate goal. It will continue to set an annual minority (female) placement-rate goal until it no longer has a lower percentage of minority (female) incumbents than availability.[151]

---

[150]65 Fed. Reg. at 68,034; 41 C.F.R. § 60-2.16(d) (2005). In the preamble commentary, the OFCCP asserted that this is not intended to represent an approach different than that set out in the former regulations (former § 60-2.12(l)).

[151]The Ninth Circuit, in *Legal Aid Society v. Brennan*, 608 F.2d 1319, 21 FEP 605 (9th Cir. 1979), analyzed the former regulatory provisions on goals:

The regulations do not explicitly require that ultimate goals be fixed, but they do so by inescapable implication. Goals are to be directed toward achieving "Full and equal employment opportunity" by correcting "any identifiable deficiencies" in female or minority utilization. (Citations omitted.) Affirmative action programs must be "result-oriented," and the result to which they are to be directed under the current regulations is not merely "to increase materially the utilization of minorities and women" as it once was, 41 C.F.R. § 60-2.10 (1973), but "to achieve prompt and full utilization of minorities and women" in deficient segments of the contractor's work force. 41 C.F.R. § 60-2.10 (1978). Goals that must be stated in terms of "full utilization" and correction of "any deficiencies" can hardly be less than ultimate goals.

Similarly, although the regulations do not state in so many words that acceptable ultimate goals must reflect a level of female and minority employment in the contractor's establishment at least equal to the percentage of women and minorities available in the job group in the contractor's labor area, no other inference is consistent with what the regulations do state. . . . [A]bsent discrimination utilization will not be less than availability, and . . . to correct underutilization

A number of principles apply when establishing placement goals:[152]

(1) Placement goals may not be rigid and inflexible quotas, nor are they a ceiling or a floor for the employment of particular groups.

---

goals must be set to achieve parity with the level of available women and minority workers in the relevant labor pool. To say that compliance officials may accept employment goals lower than the level of qualified women or minority workers in the relevant labor area . . . is inconsistent with the simple central canon of the regulations that underutilization must be corrected.
Id. at 1341.

[152]41 C.F.R. § 60-2.16(e)(1)–(4) (2005). The *OFCCP Notice Reaffirming Affirmative Action Goals in Light of ADARAND Decision, Administrative Review,* DAILY LAB. REP. (BNA) at E-2 (Aug. 11, 1995), provides in relevant part:

b. Prohibition against Quotas and Preferential Treatment.

The numerical goals component of affirmative action programs is not designed to be, nor may it properly or lawfully be interpreted as, permitting unlawful preferential treatment and quotas with respect to persons of any race, color, religion, sex or national origin. The regulations at [former] 41 C.F.R. §§60-2.12(e), 60-2.15 and 60-2.30 [now found at 41 C.F.R. § 60-2.16(e)], specifically prohibit discrimination and the use of goals as quotas.

c. Goals are Neither Set-asides Nor a Device to Achieve Proportional Representation or Equal Results.

Numerical goals do not create set-asides for specific groups, nor are they designed to achieve proportional representation or equal results. Rather, the goal-setting process in affirmative action planning is used to target and measure the effectiveness of affirmative action efforts to eradicate and prevent discrimination. Moreover, the numerical benchmarks are realistically established based on the availability of qualified applicants in the job market or qualified candidates in the employer's workforce.

d. There is No Requirement, Under the Affirmative Action Component, to Fill any Position on the Basis of Race or Sex.

Goals under Executive Order 11246 do not require that any specific position be filled by a person of a particular race, gender or ethnicity, even where the phenomena of jobs traditionally segregated by race or sex remain substantially intact. Instead, the requirement is to engage in outreach and other efforts to broaden the pool of qualified candidates to include minorities and women.

e. The Use of Numerical Goals is Consistent with Principles of Merit.

In seeking to achieve its goals, an employer is never required to: 1) hire a person who does not have the qualifications needed to perform the job successfully; 2) hire an unqualified person in preference to another applicant who is qualified; or 3) hire a less qualified person in preference to a more qualified person. Unlike preferences and quotas, numerical goals recognize that persons are to be judged on individual ability, and are, therefore, consistent with the principles of merit hiring and promotion.

(2) Contractors must act in a nondiscriminatory manner in all employment decisions. This means placement goals do not provide a contractor with a justification to extend a preference to an individual, select an individual, or adversely affect an individual's employment status, on the basis of such individual's sex, race, color, religion, or national origin.

(3) Placement goals are not to create set-asides for specific groups, nor are they for the purpose of achieving proportional representation or equal results.

(4) Placement goals must not be used to supersede merit selection principles.

However, a contractor extending a publicly announced preference for Native Americans (authorized by 41 C.F.R. § 60-1.5(a)(6)) may reflect in its placement goals permissive employment preference for Native Americans living on or near a reservation.[153]

4. Good Faith Efforts

A contractor's compliance status will not be judged solely by whether it reaches its goals.[154] Instead, compliance with affirmative action obligations will be determined by reviewing the nature and extent of a contractor's "good faith affirmative action activities as required under § 60-2.17, and the appropriateness of those activities to identified equal employment opportunity problems."[155] The OFCCP determines a contractor's compliance with nondiscrimination obligations through an analysis of statistical data and other nonstatistical information that indicates if both employees and applicants are treated "without regard to their race, color, religion, sex, or national origin."[156]

5. Analysis of Hiring, Promotion, and Termination Practices

a. Introduction. A contractor is required to perform an in-depth analyses of its total employment process to determine whether and

---

[153]41 C.F.R. § 60-2.16(f) (2005).
[154]Id. § 60-2.35.
[155]Id.
[156]Id.

where impediments to equal employment opportunity arise.[157] At a minimum, this requires a contractor to evaluate and analyze:

(1) the workforce by organizational unit *and* job group to determine if there are shortfalls in minority or female utilization or inappropriate distribution;

(2) applicant flow, hires, terminations, promotions, and other personnel actions to determine if there are selection disparities;

(3) compensation systems to determine if there are disparities;

(4) selection, recruitment, referral, and other personnel procedures to ascertain whether they result in disparities in minority or female employment or advancement; and

(5) any other areas that could have an impact on the success of the AAP.[158]

Moreover, a contractor must develop and implement auditing systems that periodically measure the effectiveness of its AAPs.[159]

b. Hiring Rates. A hiring rate is calculated by dividing the number of persons hired by the number of applicants. For example, if 100 Hispanics apply for mechanic positions and 10 are hired, the Hispanic hiring rate would be 10 percent:

$$\frac{10 \text{ Hispanic hires}}{100 \text{ Hispanic applicants}} = 10\% \text{ Hispanic hiring rate}$$

Similarly, if 200 Caucasians apply for mechanic positions and 30 are hired, the Caucasian hiring rate would be 15 percent.

Using hiring rates, the OFCCP derives an impact ratio analysis (IRA). The IRA is the ratio of the selection rate for a minority group or women to the selection rate for non-minorities or men. In the example above, the IRA of Hispanics and Caucasians would be:

---

[157]*Id.* § 60-2.17(b).

[158]*Id.*

[159]*Id.* § 60-2.17(d). The regulations indicate that key activities for a successful AAP include: (1) monitoring records of all personnel activity, including referrals, placements, transfers, promotions, terminations, and compensation, at all levels; (2) internal reporting on a scheduled basis as to the degree to which equal employment opportunity and organizational objectives are met; (3) reviewing report results with management at all levels; and (4) advising top management of AAP effectiveness and submitting recommendations for improvement of problem areas. *See id.*

$$\frac{10\% \text{ Hispanic hiring rate}}{15\% \text{ Caucasian hiring rate}} = 66.7\% \text{ IRA for Hispanics}$$

Generally, the OFCCP flags for on-site investigation an IRA of less than 80 percent for hires or promotions. In other words, if the selection rate for minorities or women is less than 80 percent of the selection rate for Caucasians or men, the OFCCP examines the reasons.

Many OFCCP offices now use standard deviation analyses, rather than 80 percent analyses, to flag practices for on-site investigation. A standard deviation of –2.00 or greater typically triggers further investigation.

   c. *Definition of Applicant: Internet Applicants.* On October 7, 2005, after a decade of discussion and a full 18 months after publishing its Notice of Proposed Rulemaking (NPRM),[160] the OFCCP issued its final regulations on the definition of an Internet Applicant;[161] a federal contractor's obligation to solicit race, gender, and ethnicity data from Internet Applicants;[162] and record-keeping requirements for a contractor who solicits or accepts expressions of interest via the Internet or related technologies.[163] The regulations became effective on February 6, 2006.[164]

   (i.) Who is an Internet Applicant? An "Internet Applicant" is someone who fits the following four criteria:

---

[160]69 Fed. Reg. 16,446 (Mar. 29, 2004).

[161]Three weeks before the OFCCP issued its NPRM, the so-called Uniform Guidelines agencies (OFCCP, EEOC, DOJ and OPM) issued their own Notice of Proposed Rulemaking seeking to add four questions to the Q&As on the Uniform Guidelines, all related to the handling of Internet Applicants by all employers subject to Title VII of the Civil Rights Act. These Q&As have not yet been issued in final form. The new regulations apply only to federal contractors. 69 Fed. Reg. 10,152 (Mar. 4, 2004).

[162]A federal contractor ("contractor") is an entity that contracts with an executive branch agency, department, establishment, instrumentality, or wholly owned government corporation for the purchase, sale, or use of personal property or nonpersonal services, valued at over $10,000. *See* 41 C.F.R. §§ 1.3, 1.5 (2005). A subcontractor is an entity or person that provides a federal contractor with personal property or nonpersonal services that, in whole or in part, are necessary to the performance of any one or more federal contracts. 41 C.F.R. § 1.4 (2005).

[163]*See* Obligation to Solicit Race and Gender Data for Agency Enforcement Purposes, 70 Fed. Reg. 58,946 (Oct. 7, 2005) (to be codified at 41 C.F.R. pt. 60-1) (hereinafter the "regulations").

[164]70 Fed. Reg. at 58,960 (Oct. 7, 2005), Preamble ("OFCCP agrees . . . that contractors should be afforded sufficient time to implement . . . . Therefore, OFCCP has established an effective date of one-hundred twenty days after . . . publication."); *see also* 70 Fed. Reg. 64,895 (Oct. 31, 2005) (semiannual agenda of regulations identifying effective date).

(1) the individual submits an "expression of interest" in employ-
    ment through "the internet or related electronic data tech-
    nologies";

(2) the contractor "considers" the individual for employment
    in a particular position;

(3) the individual's expression of interest indicates that he or
    she possesses the "basic qualifications" for the position;
    and

(4) at no point in the selection process prior to receiving an
    offer of employment does the individual remove himself
    or herself from consideration or otherwise indicate that he
    or she is no longer interested in the position.

The discussion that accompanies the final regulations includes
guidance as to each of these components.[165]

(ii.) Submitting an "expression of interest." The OFCCP creates a distinction between "Internet Applicants" and traditional
"applicants." A contractor, however, may use both Internet and related electronic technology along with more traditional paper
methods (e.g., resumes mailed in or paper applications) to identify candidates for the same position. The regulations provide that
if a contractor uses both means to recruit, then all who make expressions of interest in that position will be considered "Internet
Applicants"[166] as long as the individuals meet all remaining elements of the definition.

The only time "applicants" are not "Internet Applicants" is
when the contractor solicits and accepts expressions of interest only
through methods other than the Internet or related data technologies.[167] The agency provides no definition of a non-Internet Applicant but, presumably, the basic qualifications test (discussed below) will *not* apply to traditional applicants. For those positions

---

[165]*Id.* at 58,961 (Oct. 7, 2005) (to be codified at 41 C.F.R. § 60-1.3, Definition
of Internet Applicant, subsection (1)).

[166]*Id.* at 58,961 (Oct. 7, 2005) (to be codified at 41 C.F.R. § 60-1.3, Definition
of Internet Applicant, subsections (2)(i), (ii)). This was a modification from the NPRM,
which would have required a contractor to deal separately with electronic expressions of interest and traditional expressions of interest, even if they related to the
same identified position.

[167]*Id.* at 58,962 (Oct. 7, 2005) (to be codified at 41 C.F.R. § 60-1.3, Definition
of Internet Applicant, subsection (2)(iii)).

where no electronic technology is involved, anyone who expresses an interest in employment in that position is in the applicant pool from which required demographic information must be solicited.[168]

The OFCCP intentionally left the term "related electronic data technologies" undefined so that the terminology would not be quickly outmoded by new technology.[169] The commentary states that the term includes expressions of interest submitted by e-mail and through resume databases, job banks, electronic scanning technology, applicant screeners, and applicant service providers.[170] As new technologies enter the market, the OFCCP intends this regulation to cover those technologies.[171]

In order to reduce and therefore more efficiently manage an applicant pool, a contractor may dictate the manner in which it chooses to receive expressions of interest for employment. Only those candidates who comply with the contractor's specified procedures will have properly "expressed interest" in a position.[172] Any such limitation must be applied uniformly and consistently.[173] Similarly, just as a contractor may decline to consider unsolicited paper submissions, so too may a contractor refuse to consider unsolicited electronic expressions of interest, as long as this is done uniformly and consistently.[174]

(iii.) "Considered for" employment. An individual is not an "Internet Applicant" unless he or she is "considered for" a particular position. An individual is not "considered" unless the contractor assesses the substantive information the individual provides about his or her qualifications for that position.[175]

---

[168]*Id.* at 58,959 (Oct. 7, 2005), Preamble ("OFCCP intends to make clear that . . . contractors are required to solicit race, ethnicity, and gender information from 'applicants' or 'Internet Applicants,' whichever is applicable to the particular position.").

[169]*Id.* at 58,951 (Oct. 7, 2005), Preamble ("OFCCP will not provide a precise definition of this term in recognition of rapid changes in technology in this area.").

[170]*Id.*

[171]*Id.*

[172]*Id.* at 58,962 (Oct. 7, 2005) (to be codified at 41 C.F.R. § 60-1.3, Definition of Internet Applicant, subsection (3)).

[173]*Id.* at 58,950 (Oct. 7, 2005), Preamble ("provided that the contractor has a consistently applied policy or procedure of not considering similarly situated job seekers").

[174]*Id.*

[175]*Id.* at 58,962 (Oct. 7, 2005) (to be codified at 41 C.F.R. § 60-1.3, Definition of Internet Applicant, subsection (3)).

The regulations provide a number of ways in which a contractor may limit the candidates that meet the "considered for" prong of the definition. In addition to establishing standard procedures for considering candidates for employment (e.g., the individual must indicate a particular position on the expression of interest and follow the application procedures specified), the regulations permit the use of data management techniques. Thus, a contractor may use random sampling or absolute numerical limits (e.g., taking the first 30 expressions of interest posted on hotjobs.yahoo.com or Monster.com), so long as the technique does not depend upon an assessment of an individual's qualifications.[176]

After the contractor applies its standard procedures and undertakes its data management strategies, the remaining pool of people will be deemed to have been "considered" for the position. Once an individual is "considered" for a position by the contractor, certain record-keeping obligations created by the new regulations are triggered,[177] regardless of whether the individual qualifies as an Internet Applicant.[178]

(iv.) Meeting "basic qualifications." An individual's expression of interest must reveal that the candidate meets the contractor's

---

[176]*Id.* (the regulations provide examples, "such as random sampling or absolute numerical limits, to reduce the number of expressions of interest to be considered, provided that the sample is appropriate in terms of the pool of those submitting expressions of interest"). The commentary to the regulations indicate that data management techniques are not "appropriate" if they are either not facially neutral or if they produce disparate impact based on race, gender, or ethnicity. The OFCCP may compare the percentage of women and minorities in the final applicant pool with labor force statistics in the relevant labor market to assess the contractor's recruitment and hiring practices. Data management techniques used by a contractor will likely come under scrutiny in such an assessment. *Id.* at 58,960, Preamble ("OFCCP intends to use [census and other labor market data] during compliance reviews to determine whether basic qualifications have an adverse impact").

[177]*See* Section III.B.5.c.vi *infra.*

[178]A contractor may be required to solicit and retain records of the demographics of individuals who take a test used to screen them for employment, even if they fail to qualify as Internet Applicants. The commentary to the final regulations provides the following example. First, if 100 people take an employment test, but the contractor only considers the test results of the 50 candidates who otherwise meet the basic qualifications for the job, the employer need only solicit race, gender, and ethnicity data from the 50 candidates whom it then considered. In contrast, if the contractor only reviews the basic qualifications of those candidates who passed the test, then the contractor must solicit the demographic data for all 100 who took the test, because in this situation the contractor used the test as a selection procedure.

established "basic qualifications" in order for him or her to be an Internet Applicant. Basic qualifications mean qualifications that

(a) the contractor advertises for a position (e.g., posts on its website), or

(b) the contractor establishes in advance before considering any expressions of interest, *and*

(c) are noncomparative, objective, and relevant to performance of the particular position and that "enable the contractor to accomplish business-related goals."[179]

Requiring three years of relevant experience is noncomparative; being among the candidates with the top five numbers of years of experience is comparative. Basic qualifications are objective if a third party, who has the benefit of the contractor's technical knowledge, would be able to evaluate whether the candidate possesses the qualification.[180] Relevant to the performance of the particular position does not mean "job related" as that term is used in the Civil Rights Act of 1991, but rather is intended to provide a reasonable limit on the nature of what constitutes a basic qualification.[181]

The contractor may use basic qualifications to limit the number of candidates who become "Internet Applicants." For example, a contractor may add basic qualifications sequentially when searching a resume database for candidates for a position in order to reduce a candidate pool to a manageable size. Thus, a contractor can initially keyword search (i) a Master's degree in engineering, (ii) certification in avionics engineering, and (iii) fluency in an advanced computer language, then add three years of experience to further reduce the pool, and, thereafter, add one year of supervisory experience to narrow the pool still further.[182] All five of these

---

[179]*Id.* at 58,962 (Oct. 7, 2005) (to be codified 41 C.F.R. § 60-1.3, Definition of Internet Applicant, subsection (4)).

[180]*Id.* at 58,962 (Oct. 7, 2005) (to be codified 41 C.F.R. § 60-1.3, Definition of Internet Applicant, subsection (4)(ii)(B)).

[181]*Id.* at 58,957 (Oct. 7, 2005), Preamble ("OFCCP agrees . . . that use of the term 'job-related' in the proposed definition of 'Internet Applicant' could cause confusion [with the CRA of 1991] . . . . Therefore, OFCCP has eliminated the term in the final rule and replaced it with the phrase, 'relevant to the performance of the particular position.' ").

[182]*Id.* at 58,954 (Oct. 7, 2005), Preamble (providing an example of screening for a bilingual emergency nursing supervisor by using a 4-year nursing degree, state

qualifications would have to have been identified in the job post-ing or otherwise established in advance of the keyword search, in order to be deemed "basic qualifications" under the regulations.[183]

(v.) Removal from consideration. An individual is not an Inter-net Applicant if the contractor concludes that he or she has removed himself or herself from further consideration or is otherwise no longer interested in the position.[184] A contractor is permitted to conclude that an individual is no longer interested in the position on the basis of statements made in the expression of interest that conflict with the features of the position. This includes geographic limitations, salary requirements, or other work requirements that are incompatible with the position.[185] Further, if a candidate is repeatedly non-responsive to inquiries from the contractor about interest in the position, the individual has removed himself or herself from consideration.[186] In order to remain in compliance, a contractor must consistently exclude from consideration individuals who in-dicate disinterest in the position in one of the ways described above.[187]

(vi.) Record-keeping requirements. A contractor must maintain certain records regarding each individual who makes "expressions of interest" through the Internet or related electronic technologies if the contractor "considers [the individual] for" a position—not only records of those who ultimately qualify as Internet Appli-cants.[188]

---

certification, English and Spanish fluency, 3 years of ER experience, and 2 years of supervisory experience).

[183]*Id.* at 58,962 (Oct. 7, 2005) (to be codified at 41 C.F.R. § 60-1.3, Definition of Internet Applicant, subsection (4)(i)(B)) (qualifications "[f]or which the contrac-tor establishes criteria in advance by making and maintaining a record of such quali-fications for the position prior to considering any expression of interest").

[184]*Id.* at 58,962 (Oct. 7, 2005) (to be codified at 41 C.F.R. § 60-1.3, Definition of Internet Applicant, subsection (5)).

[185]*Id.* (with the proviso that "the contractor has a uniformly and consistently applied policy or procedure of not considering similarly situated job seekers"). The commentary to the regulations states that salary or geographic requirements do not constitute a basic qualification, but rather enter into the definition only as a means by which a candidate removes himself or herself from consideration.

[186]*Id.* ("based on the individual's passive demonstration of disinterest shown through repeated non-responsiveness to inquires from the contractor").

[187]*Id.*

[188]*Id.* at 58,962 (Oct. 7, 2005) (to be codified at 41 C.F.R. § 60-1.12(a)).

For internal resume databases a contractor must:

(1) keep records identifying candidates contacted regarding their interest in a position;

(2) keep a record of each resume added to the database and the date it was added; and

(3) maintain a record of each search of the database, including the position for which the search was made, the substantive search criteria, and the date of the search.[189]

For external resume databases,[190] a contractor must retain for each position for which it uses the database:

(1) a record of each search;

(2) the substantive search criteria used;

(3) the date of the search;

(4) the resumes of any candidates who meet the basic qualifications for the position and who were "considered" by the contractor; and

(5) records identifying all candidates contacted regarding their interest in the position.[191]

(vii.) Solicitation of race, gender, and ethnicity data from Internet Applicants. The new regulations require contractors to solicit race, gender, and ethnicity data from all Internet Applicants (or from all applicants using traditional methods of expressing an interest, for those openings where those are the sole methods of making an expression of interest)—but does not specify a particular point in the hiring process when this must be done. Contractors may use the same methods of collecting this data on Internet Applicants that they have used for traditional applicants, including e-mail, a postcard, or an electronic "tear-off sheet."[192] Self-reporting

---

[189]*Id.*

[190]External resume databases are not a term defined by the regulations, but would include databases like hotjobs.yahoo.com, Monster.com, or America's Job Bank.

[191]70 Fed. Reg. at 58,962 (Oct. 7, 2005) (to be codified at 41 C.F.R. § 60-1.12(a)).

[192]*Id.* at 58,960 (Oct. 7, 2005), Preamble (referring to OFCCP's Policy Directive, ADM04-1 "Contractor Data Tracking Responsibilities," for OFCCP's policy on collecting demographic information).

or self-identification is the preferred method for collecting race, gender, and ethnicity data.[193]

If an Internet Applicant declines to self-identify, but appears in person during the hiring process, the contractor may gather the data through visual observation.[194] During a compliance evaluation, when reviewing a contractor's adverse impact analysis with respect to Internet hiring, the OFCCP will require only the records related to the analysis of Internet Applicants.[195] Where employment tests are used as an employee selection procedure, however, the OFCCP will require records necessary to determine the impact of the test, regardless of whether all members of the tested group are Internet Applicants.[196]

d. Promotion Rates. A promotion rate is calculated by dividing the number of persons promoted by the number who applied for the promotional opportunities. If there is no application process for promotional opportunities, the denominator for OFCCP purposes typically is the number of qualified persons in the feeder pay grade or job classifications from which the promotions were made unless other data on the pool of qualified, interested applicants are available.[197] The same tests used by the OFCCP to evaluate hiring rates are used to analyze promotions.[198]

e. Termination Rates. The analysis of termination rates is slightly different. A termination rate is calculated by dividing the number of employees who departed during the AAP year by the average number in the job group during the year. If the latter is difficult to calculate, the OFCCP typically will accept the number terminated divided by the number at the commencement of the year.

---

[193]*Id.* (referring to the Office of Management and Budget's 1997 and 2000 Guidance as prompting OFCCP's 2004 guidance).

[194]In April 2004, the OFCCP issued a Policy Directive regarding "Contractor Data Tracking Responsibilities." *See* OFCCP Order ADM 04-1. In that directive the agency clarified that a contractor is not required to guess at the race, gender, or ethnicity of an applicant who refused to self-identify. Such applicants should be logged as unknown and should not be included in any adverse impact analysis.

[195]70 Fed. Reg. at 58,963 (Oct. 7, 2005) (to be codified at 41 C.F.R. § 60-1.12(d)).

[196]*Id.*

[197]FED. CONTRACT COMPL. MAN. § 2415 Appendix 2A-2, *reprinted in* 1 AFFIRMATIVE ACTION COMPL. MAN. (BNA) 2:0335.

[198]*Id.*

For example, if 5 of 50 Hispanic employees depart and 8 of 100 Caucasian employees depart, their termination rates are 10 percent for Hispanics and 8 percent for Caucasians. From these rates an IRA can be derived as follows:

$$\frac{5 \div 50}{8 \div 100} = \frac{10\% \text{ Hispanic termination rate}}{8\% \text{ Caucasian termination rate}} = 1.25 \text{ IRA}$$

A termination IRA of more than 1.20, or greater than –2.00 standard deviations, typically is a flag for on-site investigation.

6. Equal Opportunity Survey[199]

Each year the OFCCP designates "a substantial portion"[200] of "nonconstruction contractor establishments" to prepare and file an equal opportunity survey (the EO Survey).[201] The purpose of the survey is to provide the OFCCP with compliance data early in the compliance evaluation process so that the OFCCP may more effectively identify contractors for further evaluation.[202]

Completing the EO Survey is time-intensive.[203] The completed survey must include information "that will allow for an accurate assessment of contractor personnel activities, pay practices, and affirmative action performance."[204] At a minimum, this includes information regarding applicants, hires, promotions, terminations, compensation, and tenure by race and gender.[205] Part-time employees are not included in the EO Survey.[206]

---

[199]*Id.* § 60-2.18. A sample EO survey form may be found on the OFCCP's website at http://www.dol.gov/esa/regs/compliance/ofccp/eosurvey/surveyform4.pdf (last visited Dec. 5, 2005).

[200]*See id.* A "substantial portion" is interpreted as "half of all nonconstruction contractor establishments." 65 Fed. Reg. at 68,038–39 (Oct. 7, 2005).

[201]*Id.*

[202]*See id.*

[203]*Id.* at 68,036 (Oct. 7, 2005).

[204]41 C.F.R. § 60-2.18(b) (2005).

[205]*See id.* The regulations state that, if the Department determines that any elements of the EO Survey should be altered or deleted, the Secretary must (1) demonstrate through statistical analyses of EO Survey submissions that the data element at issue is no longer of any value; and (2) follow notice and comment procedures. *See id.*; 65 Fed. Reg. at 68,037 (Nov. 13, 2000).

[206]65 Fed. Reg. at 68,038 (Nov. 13, 2000). Although recognizing that the exclusion of part-time employees from the EO Survey restricts the survey's effectiveness as a predictor of possible part-time employment problems and that contractors

The OFCCP allows reporting by job groups rather than by EEO-1 category, but only if the contractor (1) submits both personnel activity and compensation data by job groups; (2) submits the EO Survey via the Internet; (3) identifies the EEO-1 category to which each job group belongs; and (4) does not submit a job group that crosses EEO-1 category lines.[207]

In response to concerns from the contractor community regarding data confidentiality, the regulations now provide that EO Survey data will be treated as confidential "to the maximum extent the information is exempt from public disclosure under the Freedom of Information Act."[208]

7. Corporate Management Compliance Evaluations[209]

Corporate management compliance evaluations, patterned after the OFCCP's glass-ceiling reviews of the 1990s, are designed to determine whether individuals are faced with "artificial barriers to advancement into mid-level and senior corporate management."[210] The OFCCP typically examines succession plans, pipelines, and selection practices for these corporate management jobs. If the OFCCP discovers violations at establishments outside of corporate headquarters while conducting a corporate management compliance evaluation, the OFCCP may expand the evaluation beyond the headquarters and request relevant data for all areas of the corporation to ensure compliance with the Executive Order.[211]

---

must include such employees in AAP reporting systems, the OFCCP nevertheless concluded that inclusion would have increased the EO Survey's length by several pages and that potential discrimination against part-time employees would continue to be investigated during compliance evaluations. *See id.*

[207]*Id.* at 68,038 (Nov. 13, 2000). In fact, the regulations governing the EO Survey encourage all contractors to file the EO Survey via the Internet, although contractors using EEO-1 categories instead of job groups may also mail or fax the EO Survey. *Id.* at 68,039; 41 C.F.R. § 60-2.18(c) (2005).

[208]41 C.F.R. § 60-2.18(d) (2005). OFCCP's stated practice is not to release data where (1) the contractor is still in business; and (2) the contractor indicates, and through the Department of Labor review process it is determined, that data are confidential and sensitive and the release of such data would cause commercial harm to the contractor. *Id.*

[209]*Id.* § 60-2.30.

[210]*Id.*

[211]*See id.* § 60-2.30(b).

C. Construction Contractors

Different requirements apply to those who perform "federally assisted construction contracts." The term refers to "construction work which is paid for in whole or in part with funds obtained from the Government or borrowed in the credit of the Government pursuant to any Federal program."[212] "Construction work" includes construction, rehabilitation, alteration, extension, demolition, and repair of buildings, highways, and other real property, as well as supervision, inspection, and on-site functions incidental to construction.[213]

The principal requirements applicable to a construction contractor are (1) nondiscrimination based upon race, color, religion, sex, and national origin;[214] (2) a written affirmative action plan;[215] (3) posting of notices detailing the provisions of the nondiscrimination clause;[216] (4) compliance with the Executive Order and the Secretary of Labor's rules, regulations, and orders;[217] (5) providing the OFCCP access to the contractor's books, records, and accounts for purposes of compliance investigation;[218] and (6) inclusion of these provisions in every nonexempt subcontract or purchase order.[219]

The primary differences between affirmative action requirements for construction and nonconstruction contractors are that (1) the required construction AAP narrative is less complex; and (2) construction goals and timetables are set periodically on an areawide basis by the director of OFCCP, rather than self-generated by individual contractors.

A notice advises bidders for federally assisted construction contracts of the applicable goals and timetables for the area where the project will be located.[220] The goals are for minority and female participation in the contractor's aggregate construction workforce

---

[212]*Id.* § 60-1.3.
[213]*Id.*
[214]*Id.* § 60-1.4(b)(1).
[215]*Id.*
[216]*Id.*
[217]*Id.* § 60-1.4(b)(4).
[218]*Id.* § 60-1.4(b)(5).
[219]*Id.* § 60-1.4(b)(7).
[220]*Id.* § 60-4.2.

"in each trade on all construction work in the covered area"[221] and are expressed as percentages of total hours worked by the contractor's entire on-site construction workforce.[222] The OFCCP has established a single national goal (currently 6.9 percent)[223] for utilization of women in a contractor's on-site construction workforce (including workers who are not performing work on a federal or federally assisted construction contract or subcontract). Goals for minority construction employment are designated for each geographic area in the country.[224] Currently, the OFCCP has set the minority utilization goals equal to the percentage of minorities in the civilian labor force in the relevant area.[225]

As a condition of bidding, a contractor must agree to make a good faith effort to meet the specified goal, subscribe to an equal opportunity clause,[226] and satisfy certain other contract specifications.[227] These requirements apply to each contractor and subcontractor that holds any federal or federally assisted construction contract in excess of $10,000, and extend to all of the contractor's employees engaged in on-site construction, whether on a federal-related project or not.[228] If a contractor violates the order or regulations, the OFCCP

---

[221]*Id.* § 60-4.2(d).

[222]*Id.*

[223]*See* http://www.dol.gov/esa/regs/compliance/ofccp/aa.htm (last visited Dec. 5, 2005).

[224]41 C.F.R. pt. 60-4, App. A, *reprinted in* 1 AFFIRMATIVE ACTION COMPL. MAN. (BNA) 289. The OFCCP uses the Metropolitan Statistical Area (MSA), and the Economic Area (EA) for areas not within an MSA, as the geographic units for which goals are set. 41 C.F.R. pt. 60-4, App. B-80, *reprinted in* 1 AFFIRMATIVE ACTION COMPL. MAN. (BNA) 289–301.

[225]41 C.F.R. § 60-4.6.

[226]41 C.F.R. §§ 60-1.4(b), -4.3(a) (2005).

[227]*Id.* § 60-4.3(a). Chapter 4 of the Compliance Manual describes compliance reviews of construction contracts. 2 AFFIRMATIVE ACTION COMPL. MAN. (BNA) 4:0001–29. The equal opportunity clause requires a contractor, inter alia, to maintain a working environment free of harassment, intimidation, and coercion, in part by (where possible) assigning two or more women to each construction project; conduct and document special recruiting activities directed toward minorities and women; notify the OFCCP if any union referral process is impeding efforts to meet the affirmative action obligation; provide on-the-job training to women and minorities; disseminate the EEO policy; hold and maintain a written record of attendees at an annual review of affirmative action obligations of supervisors; conduct an annual inventory of minority and female personnel for purposes of promotion; and review annually supervisors' adherence to the EEO policies. *Id.*

[228]*Id.* § 60-4.1. The requirements also apply to construction work performed by construction contractors, and subcontractors of federal nonconstruction contractors,

issues a notice to show cause.[229] Enforcement proceedings may result from a contractor's failure to show good cause within 30 days.[230]

IV. SECTION 503 OF THE REHABILITATION ACT OF 1973

Section 503 of the Rehabilitation Act[231] requires that all nonexempt federal government contracts include the dual requirements of (1) nondiscrimination on the basis of disability and (2) affirmative action to employ and advance in employment qualified persons with disabilities. The statute covers a contract or subcontract of $10,000 or more "for the procurement of personal property and nonpersonal services (including construction)."[232]

The Rehabilitation Act protects a "qualified" individual with a disability: "any person who (1) has a physical or mental impairment which substantially limits one or more of such person's major life activities,[233] (2) has a record of such impairment, or (3) is regarded as having such an impairment,"[234] and who is "capable of performing a particular job, with reasonable accommodation to his or her handicap."[235]

The OFCCP has revised the definitions of "substantially limits," "reasonable accommodation," and "direct threat" to be consistent with the EEOC regulations adopted under the ADA.[236] The term "substantially limits" is defined[237] as

(i) Unable to perform a major life activity that the average person in the general population can perform;[[238]] or (ii) Significantly restricted as to the condition, manner or duration under which an individual can

---

if the construction work is necessary in whole or in part of the performance of the federal nonconstruction contract. *Id.*

[229]41 C.F.R. § 60-4.8 (2004).

[230]*Id.* For a discussion of enforcement proceedings, see Section VIII *infra.*

[231]29 U.S.C. § 793 (2000).

[232]*Id.* § 793(a); *see also* 41 C.F.R. § 60-741.1 (2005).

[233]41 C.F.R. § 741.2 (2005).

[234]*Id.*

[235]*Id.*

[236]61 Fed. Reg. at 19,340–41.

[237]41 C.F.R. § 60-741.2(q) (2005).

[238]"People have a range of abilities with regard to many major life activities such as walking, lifting, and bending, and a range of such abilities may be considered average. Thus, the term 'average' person in the general population does not

perform a particular major life activity as compared to the condition, manner, or duration under which the average person in the general population can perform that same major life activity.

The term "reasonable accommodation" is defined[239] as

(i) Modifications or adjustments to a job application process that enable a qualified applicant with a disability to be considered for the position such applicant desires;[[240]] or

(ii) Modifications or adjustments to the work environment, or to the manner or circumstances under which the position held or desired is customarily performed, that enable a qualified individual with a disability to perform the essential functions of that position; or

(iii) Modifications or adjustments that enable the contractor's employee with a disability to enjoy equal benefits and privileges of employment as are enjoyed by the contractor's other similarly situated employees without disabilities.

A contractor is not required to employ an individual with a disability who poses a "direct threat," which is defined[241] as

a significant risk of substantial harm to the health or safety of the individual or others that cannot be eliminated or reduced by reasonable accommodation.

The Act's AAP requirements are described in Section VI below. Complaint procedures and enforcement actions are described in Section VII below.[242]

---

indicate a need to determine a precise average ability, but rather reflects that a range of abilities may be considered average." *Id.* § 60-741.2.(q) n.1.

[239]*Id.* § 60-741.2(v).

[240]"A contractor's duty to provide a reasonable accommodation with respect to applicants with disabilities is not limited to those who ultimately demonstrate that they are qualified to perform the job in issue. Applicants with disabilities must be provided a reasonable accommodation with respect to the application process if they are qualified with respect to that process (*e.g.*, if they present themselves at the correct location and time to fill out an application)." *Id.* § 60-741.2(v) n.2.

[241]*Id.* § 60-741.2(y). Any determination that an individual with a disability poses a "direct threat" must be based on "an individualized assessment of the individual's present ability to perform safely the essential functions of the job. This assessment shall be based on a reasonable medical judgment that relies on the most current medical knowledge and/or on the best available evidence." *Id.* Factors to consider include the duration of the risk, the nature and severity of the potential harm, the likelihood that the potential harm will occur, and the imminence of the potential harm. *See id.*

[242]For a further discussion of the substantive law of disability discrimination and reasonable accommodation, see Chapter 13 (Disability).

V. The Veterans Act

A federal contractor is barred from discriminating against, and is required to take affirmative action to employ and advance in employment, qualified:[243]

(1) Disabled veterans;

(2) Veterans who served on active duty in the Armed Forces during a war or in a campaign or expedition for which a campaign badge has been authorized;

(3) Veterans who, while serving on active duty in the Armed Forces, participated in a U.S. military operation for which an Armed Forces service medal was awarded pursuant to Executive Order No. 12985; and

(4) Recently separated veterans.[244]

The term "disabled veteran" means:

(a) a veteran who is entitled to compensation (or who but for the receipt of military retired pay would be entitled to compensation) under laws administered by the Secretary, or (b) a person who was discharged or released from active duty because of service-connected disability.[245]

---

[243]The term "qualified" means "having the ability to perform the essential functions of the position with or without reasonable accommodation for an individual with a disability." *Id.* § 4212(a)(3)(B).

Further changes were made to the statute by the Veterans Benefits and Health Care Improvement Act of 2000 (VBHCIA), Pub. L. No. 106-419, 114 Stat. 1822, which expanded the class of veterans covered to include "recently separated veterans," defined as "any veteran during the one-year period beginning on the date of such veteran's discharge or release from active duty." *Id.*

The Jobs for Veterans Act of 2002, Pub. L. No. 107-288, 116 Stat. 2033, further altered the definition of veterans covered by affirmative action requirements under 38 U.S.C. §§ 4211–4212 by changing "special disabled veterans" to "disabled veterans," deleting "veterans of the Vietnam era," adding "veterans who, while serving on active duty in the Armed Forces, participated in a United States military operation for which an Armed Forces service medal was awarded," and changing the definition of "recently separated veteran" to "any veteran during the three-year period beginning on the date of such veteran's discharge or release from active duty." 38 U.S.C. §§ 4211–4212 (2000). The regulations, however, have not yet been amended to reflect these statutory changes.

[244]38 U.S.C. § 4212(a)(3)(A) (2000).

[245]42 U.S.C. § 4211(3) (2000).

The term "recently separated veteran" means:

any veteran during the three-year period beginning on the date of such veteran's discharge or release from active duty.[246]

Pursuant to the Jobs for Veterans Act of 2002, every nonexempt federal government contract of at least $100,000 must include the dual requirements of nondiscrimination against and affirmative action to employ and advance these qualified categories of veterans.[247]

The Act's AAP requirements are described in Section VI below. Complaint procedures and enforcement actions are described in Section VII.

VI. AFFIRMATIVE ACTION PROGRAMS FOR VETERANS AND INDIVIDUALS WITH DISABILITIES

The Veterans and Rehabilitation Acts require a contractor with at least 50 employees and a contract of at least $50,000 in the case of the Rehabilitation Act (and $100,000 in the case of the Veterans Act) to prepare,[248] within 120 days of contract commencement,[249] an AAP covering individuals with disabilities,[250] disabled veterans, veterans who served on active duty in the Armed Forces during a war or in a campaign or expedition for which a campaign badge has been authorized, veterans who, while serving on active duty in the Armed Forces, participated in a U.S. military operation for which an Armed Forces service medal was awarded pursuant to Executive Order No. 12985, and recently separated veterans.[251] Unlike the Executive Order AAP, this AAP must be available for inspection upon request by any applicant or employee.[252] Further, the contractor must post at each facility the location and hours during

---

[246]*Id.* § 4211(6).

[247]Pub. L. No. 107-288, 116 Stat. 2033 (2002). The original $10,000 threshold was increased to $25,000 by the VEOA, Pub. L. No. 105-339, 112 Stat. 3182 (1998), and then to $100,000 by the Jobs for Veterans Act of 2002.

[248]41 C.F.R. §§ 60-250.40(a), -741.40(a) (2005).

[249]*Id.* §§ 60-250.40(b), -741.40(b).

[250]*See* Section IV *supra.*

[251]*See* Section V *supra.*

[252]41 C.F.R. §§ 60-250.41, -741.41 (2005). For this reason, the Executive Order AAP should be a separate document.

which this AAP may be "obtained."[253] The contractor must review and update the AAP annually.[254]

Each contractor must invite all covered veterans and individuals with disabilities to identify themselves in order to benefit under the AAP. The Veterans Act allows contractors to invite veterans to self-identify before or after a job offer is extended.[255] The contractor should issue the invitation to self-identify a disability or disabled veteran status after the contractor has made an offer of employment but before the applicant begins his or her employment.[256] However, the contractor may, but is not required to, invite an individual with a disability or a disabled veteran to self-identify before an offer of employment if the invitation is made when the contractor is undertaking affirmative action at the pre-offer stage or if the invitation is made pursuant to federal, state, or local law requiring affirmative action for individuals with disabilities.[257]

The invitation to self-identify must summarize the relevant portions of the appropriate Act as well as the contractor's AAP.[258] It must state that the information is provided voluntarily, will be kept confidential, and will be used only in accordance with law, and that refusal to provide it will not lead to adverse treatment.[259] The invitation also must contain a statement informing the individual that his or her request can be made immediately upon receipt of the invitation and/or at any time in the future.[260] Upon receipt of a self-identification, the contractor, after extending the job offer, is required to seek the individual's input regarding proper placement within the organization and reasonable accommodation.[261]

---

[253]*Id.*

[254]*Id.* §§ 60-250.40(c), -741.40(c).

[255]*Id.* § 60-250.42. The sample invitation to self-identify, contained in Appendix B to the regulations, reflects this exception.

[256]*Id.* § 60-741.42. These requirements comply with the ADA's provisions regarding preemployment inquiries. 61 Fed. Reg. at 19,344–45, 19,367 (May 1, 1996). The Veterans Act follows these Rehabilitation Act regulations for special disabled veterans. 63 Fed. Reg. at 59,634–36, 59,649 (Nov. 4, 1998); *see* 41 C.F.R. § 60-250.42 (2005).

[257]61 Fed. Reg. at 19,344–45 (May 1, 1996).

[258]41 C.F.R. §§ 60-250.42(c), -741.42(b) (2005).

[259]*Id.* However, the individual's failure to identify disability status does not relieve the contractor from its nondiscrimination obligation or its obligation to take affirmative action, if it has actual knowledge of the disability. *Id.* §§ 60-250.42(f), -741.42(c).

[260]*Id.* §§ 60-250.42(c), -741.42(c).

[261]*Id.* §§ 60-250.42(d), -741.42(b).

The contractor may also make additional inquiries into the abilities of the individual to the extent they are consistent with the ADA.[262]

The Veterans and Rehabilitation Acts list specific employment actions that constitute prohibited discrimination.[263] Moreover, the revised regulations also address the direct threat defense,[264] medical examinations and inquiries,[265] drug and alcohol policies,[266] and issues relating to health insurance, life insurance, and other benefit plans.[267]

The veterans and disabilities AAPs contain no statistical analyses. Because their narrative sections are very similar, most contractors combine these AAPs into a single document[268] containing the following sections:

(1) "Policy statement."[269]

(2) "Review of personnel processes."[270]

---

[262]*Id.* These include asking applicants to describe or demonstrate how they would perform the job. *Id.*

[263]*Id.* §§ 60-250.21, -741.21. The actions outlined in each Act are substantially similar.

[264]*Id.* §§ 60-250.22, -741.22.

[265]*Id.* §§ 60-250.23, -741.23.

[266]*Id.* §§ 60-250.24, -741.24.

[267]*Id.* §§ 60-250.25, -741.25.

[268]The Compliance Manual explicitly allows this combination. FED. CONTRACT COMPL. MAN. § 2C02, *reprinted in* 1 AFFIRMATIVE ACTION COMPL. MAN. (BNA) 2:0003.

[269]41 C.F.R. §§ 60-250.44(a), -741.44(a) (2005). The policy communicates the contractor's prohibition of discrimination and its establishment of affirmative action in all levels of employment and all employment practices listed in 41 C.F.R. §§ 60-250.20, -741.20 (2005) (e.g., hiring, upgrading, demotion, transfer, recruitment, layoff, termination, compensation, and selection for training). *Id.* §§ 60-250.43, -741.43. This equal employment opportunity statement should: (1) indicate the chief executive officer's attitude on affirmative action; (2) provide for an audit and reporting system; (3) assign overall responsibility for implementation of affirmative action; and (4) contain a statement that the contractor will recruit, hire, train, and promote persons in all job titles and ensure that all employment decisions are based on nondiscriminatory job requirements. The policy must state that employees and applicants will not be subject to harassment, intimidation, threats, coercion, or discrimination because they have engaged in activities protected by the Rehabilitation Act or Veterans Act, or any other federal, state, or local law requiring equal employment opportunity for individuals with disabilities. The contractor should post this policy statement on company bulletin boards and ensure that the applicants and disabled and veteran employees are aware of the contents of the policy statement. *Id.* §§ 60-250.44, -741.44.

[270]*Id.* §§ 60-250.44(b), -741.44(b). In this section, the contractor periodically reviews personnel processes to determine whether they assure systematic consideration

(3) "Physical and mental qualifications."[271]

(4) "Reasonable accommodation to physical and mental limitations."[272]

(5) "Harassment."[273]

(6) "External dissemination of policy, outreach and positive recruitment."[274]

---

of the job qualifications of known disabled and covered veteran applicants and employees for all available hiring, promotion, and training opportunities. If not, the contractor develops new procedures. The appendices to the regulations set forth suggested procedures.

[271]*Id.* §§ 60-250.44(c), -741.44(c). This section requires a schedule for the periodic review of all physical or mental job qualification requirements to ensure that those that tend to screen out qualified individuals with disabilities and disabled veterans are job-related and consistent with business necessity (e.g., required for safe job performance). The contractor bears the burden of demonstrating that the job requirements satisfy these requirements. The contractor may defend against allegations of violations of this section by demonstrating, inter alia, that the individual poses a direct threat to the health or safety of those in the workplace or the individual himself or herself. *See* § 60-250.2(u) (definition of "direct threat"). Comprehensive medical examinations may be conducted after a job offer has been extended or a change in employment status occurs, to the extent permitted by the Americans with Disabilities Act (ADA). *See generally* Chapter 13 (Disability).

[272]41 C.F.R. §§ 60-250.44(d), -741.44(d) (2005). In this section, the contractor sets forth its commitment to reasonably accommodate the physical and mental limitations of covered veterans and individuals with disabilities unless the contractor can show that the accommodations would impose an undue hardship on the operation of its business. If an employee with a known disability is having significant difficulty performing his or her job and it is reasonable to conclude that the performance problem may be related to the known disability, the OFCCP takes the position that the contractor must confidentially notify the employee of the performance problem and inquire whether the problem is related to the employee's disability. If the employee responds affirmatively, the contractor is required to confidentially ask the employee if he or she needs a reasonable accommodation.

[273]*Id.* §§ 60-250.44(e), -741.44(e). The contractor must produce and implement a statement regarding procedures to ensure that employees with disabilities are not harassed because of their disability or covered veteran status.

[274]*Id.* §§ 60-250.44(f), -741.44(f). Here the contractor commits to a review of its employment practices to determine whether personnel programs provide the required affirmative action for the employment and advancement of qualified individuals with disabilities and covered veterans. Appropriate outreach and recruitment activities, based on results of this review and the contractor's size and resources, are then required.

Suggested activities include: enlistment of assistance and support of recruiting and on-the-job training sources (41 C.F.R. § 60-250.44(f)(1) (2005) lists veterans' offices, agencies, representatives, and service organizations; 41 C.F.R. § 60-741.44(1) (2005) lists state and national labor, employment, and education agencies); recruitment efforts in educational institutions that make a special effort to reach students who are covered veterans or who have disabilities; establishment of meaningful contacts with appropriate veterans' service organizations, social service agencies,

(7)   "Internal dissemination of policy."[275]

(8)   "Audit and reporting system."[276]

(9)   "Responsibility for implementation."[277]

(10) "Training."[278]

---

and organizations of and for the disabled, that can provide referral of potential employees, advice, and technical assistance, including guidance on placement, recruitment, training, and accommodations; inclusion of disabled individuals when employees are pictured in consumer, promotional, or help-wanted advertising and the participation of covered veterans and disabled individuals in career days and other related activities in the community; notification to subcontractors, vendors, and suppliers of company policy and a request for appropriate action on their part; consideration of qualified individuals, not currently in the workforce, who have the requisite skills and can be recruited through affirmative action measures; and in the hiring context, consideration of applicants who are known covered veterans or who have known disabilities for all available positions for which they may be qualified to the extent that each position applied for is unavailable.

[275]*Id.* §§ 60-250.44(g), -741.44(g). This section sets forth steps the contractor will take to disseminate its policy internally in order to engender adequate internal support from supervisory and management-level personnel and other employees. Recommended actions include: print the policy in the policy manual; periodically inform employees and prospective employees of the contractor's commitment to affirmative action and schedule meetings with employees to discuss the policy and explain individual employee responsibilities; publicize the policy in the contractor's newspaper, magazine, annual report, and other media; conduct meetings with executive, management, and supervisory personnel to explain the intent of the policy and individual responsibility for effective implementation, emphasizing the chief executive officer's attitude; discuss the policy thoroughly in both employee orientation and management training programs; meet with union officials to inform them of the policy and request their cooperation; include articles on accomplishments of disabled and veteran employees in company publications; and include disabled and veteran employees in employee handbooks or publications when employees are featured.

[276]*Id.* §§ 60-250.44(h), -741.44(h). The contractor is obligated to design and implement an audit and reporting system that will do the following: measure the effectiveness of the contractor's AAP; indicate any need for remedial action; determine the degree to which the contractor's objectives have been attained; determine whether known disabled or known veteran individuals have had the opportunity to participate in all company-sponsored educational, training, recreational, and social activities; and measure the contractor's compliance with the AAP's specific obligations. *Id.* §§ 60-250.44(h)(1), -741.44(h)(1). If the AAP is determined deficient, the contractor must take action to bring the program into compliance. *Id.* §§ 60-250.44(h)(2), -741.44(h)(2).

[277]*Id.* §§ 60-250.44(i), -741.44(i). This section reflects the designation of an executive as director or manager of the affirmative action activities; indicates the executive should be given top-managerial support to implement the programs; and states that his or her identity will appear both on internal and external communications regarding the AAP.

[278]*Id.* §§ 60-250.44(j), -741.44(j). This section requires the contractor to commit to train all personnel involved in the recruitment, screening, selection, promotion,

Additionally, the Veterans Act requires the contractor to list "all of its employment openings with the appropriate employment service delivery system."[279] The statute further provides that the contractor "may also list such openings with one-stop career centers under the Workforce Investment Act of 1998, other appropriate service delivery points, or America's Job Bank."[280] However, the contractor is not required to list openings for "executive and senior management positions,"[281] those that will be filled from within the contractor's organization,[282] and positions lasting three days or less.[283]

Contractors must file annually a Federal Contractor Veterans Employment Report (VETS-100) with the Office of the Assistant

---

disciplinary, and related processes to help ensure that the contractor's AAP obligations are implemented.

[279]38 U.S.C. § 4212(a)(2)(A) (2000).

[280]*Id.* America's Job Bank is a computerized, nationwide listing of job openings that links the state employment service offices. The Job Bank may be accessed on the Internet at http://www.ajb.dni.us/ (last visited Dec. 5, 2005). 63 Fed. Reg. at 59,633.

[281]38 U.S.C. § 4212(a)(2)(A) (2000). The term "executive and senior (formerly 'top') management" has a restrictive definition with five requirements, all of which must be met. It includes any employee:

(a) Whose primary duty consists of the management of the enterprise in which he or she is employed or of a customarily recognized department or subdivision thereof; and (b) who customarily and regularly directs the work of two or more other employees therein; and (c) who has the authority to hire or fire other employees or whose suggestions and recommendations as to the hiring or firing and as to the advancement and promotion or any other change of status of other employees will be given particular weight; and (d) who customarily and regularly exercises discretionary powers; and (e) who does not devote more than 20 percent, or, in the case of an employee of a retail or service establishment who does not devote as much as 40 percent, of his or her hours of work in the work week to activities which are not directly and closely related to the performance of the work described in (a) through (d) of this paragraph.

41 C.F.R. § 60-250.5(a)(6)(ii) (2005). An employee who is in sole charge of an independent establishment or a physically separated branch establishment, or who owns at least a 20% interest in the employer, is exempted from the limitation of working only up to 20% (or up to 40%, as the case may be) in nonmanagement duties. *Id.*

[282]*Id.* § 60-250.5(a)(6)(iii). Positions that will be filled from within the contractor's organization include:

employment openings for which no consideration will be given to persons outside the contractor's organization (including any affiliates, subsidiaries, and parent companies) and includes any openings which the contractor proposes to fill from regularly established "recall" lists. The exception does not apply to a particular opening once an employer decides to consider applicants outside of his or her own organization.

Id.

[283]*Id.* § 60-250.5(a)(6)(i).

Secretary for Veterans Employment and Training. The 2005 version of this report reflects the number of special disabled veterans, the number of veterans of the Vietnam era, and the number of other protected veterans in the contractor's workforce, by job category and hiring location. It shows the total number of new employees, special disabled veterans, veterans of the Vietnam era, newly separated veterans, and other protected veterans who were hired during the period covered by the report.[284] The VETS-100 also highlights the maximum and minimum number of the contractor's employees at each hiring location during the period covered by the report.[285]

VII. COMPLIANCE EVALUATION AND COMPLAINT INVESTIGATION PROCESS: DESK AUDIT LETTER THROUGH EXIT CONFERENCE

A. Compliance Evaluation

A compliance evaluation consists of a wide range of actions taken by the OFCCP when auditing a federal contractor or subcontractor's compliance with the nondiscrimination and affirmative action obligations imposed by Executive Order 11246 and the Veterans and Rehabilitation Acts.[286] A compliance evaluation may consist of any one or a combination of the following: (1) a compliance review, (2) an off-site review of records, (3) a compliance check, and (4) a focused review.[287] OFCCP will treat the information it obtains in the course of a compliance evaluation "as confidential to the maximum extent the information is exempt from public disclosure" under FOIA.[288]

---

[284]See http://www.vets100.cudenver.edu/vetsform.pdf (last visited Dec. 5, 2005).

[285]38 U.S.C. § 4212(d)(1) (2000); see also http://www.vets100.cudenver.edu/vetsform.pdf (last visited Dec. 5, 2005).

[286]41 C.F.R. §§ 60-1.3, -1.20, -250.2, -250.60, -741.2, -741.60 (2005).

[287]Id.

[288]41 C.F.R. § 60-1.20(g) (2005). On June 22, 2005, the OFCCP added to its final rule its practice "not to release data where the contractor is still in business, and the contractor indicates, and through the Department of Labor review it is determined, that the data are confidential and sensitive and that the release of data would subject the contractor to commercial harm." Id.

1. Compliance Review

A compliance review is a comprehensive analysis and evaluation by the OFCCP of a contractor's employment practices regarding nondiscrimination and affirmative action obligations of the facility in which the audit takes place.[289] The review typically focuses on three broad issues:

(1) Has the contractor discriminated against a minority group, women, individuals with disabilities, or covered veterans, in hiring, promotion, transfer, training, compensation, benefits, or termination?

(2) Has the contractor taken the required affirmative action to recruit, train, and advance in the organization/members of these groups?

(3) Has the contractor complied with all of the OFCCP's regulations regarding postings, maintenance of records, AAP content, recruitment, and other personnel practices?[290]

The OFCCP usually divides a compliance review of a supply or service contractor into the following phases: (1) a "desk audit" review, in which the OFCCP reads and analyzes the contractor's written AAP and support data;[291] (2) an on-site review, in which the OFCCP visits the contractor's premises to conduct further investigation;[292] (3) when necessary, a further off-site review of information obtained;[293] and (4) in some cases an exit conference to review findings with the contractor.[294]

---

[289]If the contractor's AAP covers multiple facilities, all facilities the AAP encompasses may be included in the review.

[290]*Id.* § 60-1.20(a)(1)–(2).

[291]*Id.* § 60-1.20(a)(1)(i). During the desk audit, the OFCCP determines whether the AAP meets agency standards of reasonableness and acceptability. The OFCCP conducts a pre-award desk audit at the contractor's establishment, but the remainder of desk audits at OFCCP offices. *Id.*

[292]*Id.* § 60-1.20(1)(ii). The on-site review usually includes an entrance conference with the chief executive or designee, a tour of the facility, a review and perhaps copying of records, and interviews with employees, supervisors, and human resources staff. The OFCCP is tasked with investigating unresolved problem areas identified during the desk audit, verifying that the AAP has been implemented, ascertaining whether the contractor has complied with the regulatory obligations that it is not required to spell out in the AAP, and investigating discrimination.

[293]*Id.* § 60-1.20(a)(1)(iii).

[294]*Id.*

2. Off-Site Review

An off-site review of records consists of:

[a]n analysis and evaluation of the AAP (or any part thereof) and supporting documentation, and other documents related to the contractor's personnel policies and employment actions that may be relevant to a determination of whether the contractor has complied with the requirements of the Executive Order and regulations.[295]

The scope of the off-site review of records is similar to the scope of the desk audit.[296]

3. Compliance Check

A compliance check is:

[a] determination of whether the contractor has maintained records consistent with § 60-1.12;[[297]] at the contractor's option the documents may be provided either on-site or off-site.[298]

---

[295]*Id.* §§ 60-1.20(a)(2), -250.60(a)(2), -741.60(a)(2).

[296]62 Fed. Reg. at 44,180 (Aug. 19, 1997). For a more thorough discussion of the desk audit, see Section VII.D *infra.*

[297]41 C.F.R. §§ 60-1.12 and 60-250.80 (2005) add a record retention provision. These provisions require contractors to retain personnel or employment records for 2 years if the contractor has more than 150 employees or has a government contract of at least $150,000. If the contractor has fewer than 150 employees or does not have a government contract of at least $150,000, the contractor is required to retain the records for 1 year. This provision also specifies that failure to retain the required records constitutes noncompliance with the contractor's obligations under the Executive Order and regulations and that destruction or failure to retain the records may lead to the presumption that the information would have been unfavorable to the contractor. This presumption will not apply if the contractor demonstrates that the destruction or failure to retain records results from circumstances beyond the contractor's control. *Id.* §§ 60-1.12, -250.80.

A longer record retention period may be required or appropriate to ensure compliance with other federal, state, and local laws, to effectively defend employment claims that have a long statute of limitations, and to comply with document preservation requirements once a charge or lawsuit has been filed. *See id.* § 60-741.80 (contractor's duty to maintain records once it is on notice that a complaint has been filed, an enforcement action commenced, or a compliance evaluation has been initiated). *See generally* Chapter 26 (Timeliness).

[298]41 C.F.R. § 60-1.20(a)(3) (2005). On June 22, 2005, the OFCCP issued a final rule eliminating the on-site visit requirement for compliance checks. 70 Fed. Reg. 36,262, 36,263, 36,264, 36,265 (June 22, 2005).

4. Focused Review

A focused review is:

[a]n on-site review restricted to one or more components of the contractor's organization or one or more aspects of the contractor's employment practices.[299]

The OFCCP has indicated that it intends to follow the standards already established for the frequency and duration of the compliance review and that it will establish similar standards for the off-site review of records, compliance check, and focused review to ensure they are not overly intrusive.[300] The OFCCP also has indicated that it would not use any new methods of evaluation until after the Compliance Manual is updated to include policy and procedural guidance and is made public.[301]

B. Selection for Evaluation

Although the OFCCP may select a contractor for a compliance evaluation for any number of reasons,[302] there are five common triggers.

1. Federal Contractor Selection System

In July 2004, the OFCCP implemented on a trial basis the new Federal Contractor Selection System (FCSS), replacing the former Equal Employment Data System (EEDS) used to select

---

[299]41 C.F.R. §§ 60-1.20(a)(4), -250.60(a)(4), -741.60(a)(4) (2005).

[300]62 Fed. Reg. at 44,180 (Aug. 19, 1997).

[301]*Id.* In 1998, the OFCCP published on its website limited updates to the Compliance Manual regarding compliance check and compliance evaluation procedures. Those updates may be found at http://www.dol.gov/esa/regs/compliance/ofccp/directives/dir227.htm; http://www.dol.gov/esa/regs/compliance/ofccp/directives/dir230.htm (last visited Dec. 5, 2005). The update regarding compliance evaluation procedures only addresses procedures to ensure maintenance of records consistent with 41 C.F.R. § 60-1.12 (2005). The OFCCP has indicated that it is in the process of updating the entire Compliance Manual to reflect the current status of the law.

[302]After the Fifth Circuit found that the OFCCP's selection of a contractor for a compliance review was arbitrary, and therefore void, in *United States. v. New Orleans Public Service Co.*, 734 F.2d 226, 229, 34 FEP 1801 (5th Cir. 1984) (per curiam), the OFCCP has attempted to be more "objective" in selecting contractors for review. In practice, however, selection remains largely within the agency's discretion.

contractors for compliance reviews.[303] The FCSS, based upon re-search conducted by an outside data collection and analysis firm, reportedly compares the workforce profiles of a contractor's establishments to others in the same industry and to the local labor market based on the 2000 Census.[304] Contractors are ranked on what the OFCCP considers their likelihood of discrimination based upon past relationships between EEO-1 workforce profiles and historical OFCCP findings of discrimination.[305]

During the summer of 2004, the OFCCP selected a sample of approximately 700 "top-ranked establishments" for compliance reviews to validate the model. Under the new system, no contractor will have more than 25 establishments audited annually and the OFCCP will attempt to avoid several reviews of the same contractor at the same time.[306]

The OFCCP informed the contractor community in August 2004 that it would "give serious consideration to any remedial action voluntarily undertaken" by a particular establishment prior to an OFCCP review and noted that such action "may mitigate any relief sought by OFCCP, to the extent the remedial action completely corrects the problem(s) at issue."[307]

2. Pre-Award Review

The second trigger for a compliance evaluation may be a contract award of at least $10 million or a first-tier subcontract of $10 million or more.[308] A contractor will not be subject to a pre-award review if the OFCCP has issued a finding of compliance within the previous 24 months.[309] Within 15 days of the awarding agency's notice to the OFCCP of its intent to award a contract, the OFCCP

---

[303]In *Copus v. Rougeau*, 504 F. Supp. 534, 537, 26 FEP 1665 (D.D.C. 1980), the court held that the OFCCP was not required under the Freedom of Information Act to disclose which companies were targets for review pursuant to the OFCCP's then-existing priority compliance-review targeting system.

[304]*See* http://www.dol.gov/esa/regs/compliance/ofccp/faqs/fcssfaqs.htm (last visited Nov. 21, 2006).

[305]*Id.*

[306]*Id.*

[307]August 21, 2004 letter from Charles E. James Sr., Deputy Assistant Secretary for Federal Contract Compliance, *available at* http://www.dol.gov/esa/ofccp/pdf/FCSS_04.pdf (last visited Nov. 21, 2004).

[308]41 C.F.R. § 60-1.20(d) (2005).

[309]*Id.*

must inform the awarding agency of its intention to conduct a pre-award compliance evaluation. If the OFCCP fails to do so, the awarding agency can presume clearance and proceed with the award.[310] If the OFCCP notifies an awarding agency of its intention to conduct a pre-award compliance evaluation, it must then inform the awarding agency of its conclusions within 20 days;[311] if the OFCCP fails to do so, the awarding agency may presume clearance and proceed with the award.[312] The OFCCP typically combines into its on-site visit the desk audit phase of a pre-award review.[313] Because the OFCCP does not have the resources to fulfill every pre-award request for review, it gives review priority to those contractors that have poor EEO-1 profiles or have never been reviewed.[314]

3. Discrimination Complaint

A discrimination complaint, or series of discrimination complaints, may trigger a compliance evaluation. Anyone claiming a violation of the Executive Order must file an administrative complaint with the OFCCP "within 180 days of the alleged violation unless the time for filing is extended by the Deputy Assistant Secretary for good cause shown."[315] The Rehabilitation Act and the Veterans Act allow a filing period of 300 days, unless the time for filing is extended by the OFCCP for good cause shown.[316]

---

[310]*Id.*

[311]*Id.*

[312]*Id.*

[313]FED. CONTRACT COMPL. MAN. § 2A00, *reprinted in* 1 AFFIRMATIVE ACTION COMPL. MAN. (BNA) 2:0001.

[314]As neither the Rehabilitation Act nor the Veterans Act provides for a pre-award review, the OFCCP will not address deficiencies under these laws during such a review. Nevertheless, the OFCCP will note apparent violations so that a subsequent compliance review encompassing these areas can be scheduled. *See* FED. CONTRACT COMPL. MAN. § 3C, *reprinted in* 1 AFFIRMATIVE ACTION COMPL. MAN. (BNA) 3:002.

[315]41 C.F.R. § 60-1.21 (2005).

[316]*Id.* §§ 60-250.61(a), -741.61(b). The OFCCP allows this elongated deadline in order to establish a uniform national standard consistent with the complaint filing period under the ADA. 61 Fed. Reg. at 19,346 (May 1, 1996). The required contents of a complaint as well as complaint procedures under the Veterans Act and the Rehabilitation Act are delineated in 41 C.F.R. §§ 60-250.61, -741.61 (2005).

Veterans' complaints may also be filed with the Veterans' Employment and Training Service of the Department of Labor directly or through the Local Veterans' Employment Representative (LVER) or his or her designee at the local employment service office. *Id.* § 60-250.61(a).

A complaint must be in writing, signed either personally or by an authorized representative of the complainant, and contain the following:

(1) The name, address, and telephone number of the complainant;

(2) The name and address of the contractor or subcontractor who committed the alleged violation;

(3) A description of the acts alleged to constitute a violation, including the pertinent dates;

(4) For Rehabilitation Act complaints, the facts showing that either (a) the individual has a disability, has a history of a disability; or (b) the individual was regarded by the contractor as having an impairment. For Veterans Act complaints, a certification, within one year of the complaint filing date, indicating the percent of disability and whether the veteran has been determined by the Department of Veteran Affairs to have a serious employment handicap under 38 U.S.C. § 3106; and

(5) Any other pertinent and available information that would assist in the investigation and resolution of the complaint, including the name of any federal agency with which the contractor is known to have contracted.[317]

If the OFCCP deems the complaint incomplete or decides further documentation regarding the "disability" status of the complainant is necessary, the complainant may be required to provide additional information.[318] The case may be closed if the complainant does not furnish the requested information within 60 days.[319]

The Rehabilitation Act and the Veterans Act permit the authorized representative of the aggrieved party to file a complaint that does not reveal the aggrieved party's name.[320] The authorized representative must provide the name of the aggrieved person to the OFCCP so that the investigator can confirm that the aggrieved person authorized the filing of the complaint. However, the OFCCP

---

[317]*Id.* §§ 60-1.23(a), -250.61(b)(1), -741.61(c)(1).
[318]*Id.* §§ 60-1.23(b), -250.61(c), -741.61(d).
[319]*Id.*
[320]*Id.* §§ 60-250.61(b)(2), -741.61(c)(2).

will attempt to keep the aggrieved person's name confidential if possible.

The OFCCP will then initiate a prompt investigation of each complaint.[321] At a minimum, the OFCCP will create an investigation case record consisting of the name, address, and telephone number of each person interviewed, the interview statements, copies, transcripts, or summaries of pertinent documents, a reference to at least one covered contract, and a narrative summary of the evidence disclosed in the investigation.[322] The complainant and the contractor must be notified if the OFCCP investigation uncovers no violation or the Deputy Assistant Secretary declines to refer the matter to the Solicitor of Labor for enforcement proceedings.[323] The Deputy Assistant Secretary may, on his or her own initiative, reconsider his or her determination or that of any designated officers who have authority to issue Notifications of Results of Investigation.[324]

If the OFCCP investigation indicates that the contractor has failed to comply with its obligations under the Executive Order, the Rehabilitation Act, or the Veterans Act, the parties first must attempt conciliation to secure compliance within a reasonable time.[325] According to the regulations, the failure of conciliation efforts under Executive Order obligations permits the OFCCP to proceed with an enforcement action.[326] But, an OFCCP decision not to take enforcement action on a complaint under these circumstances is immune from judicial review.[327] The Veterans and Rehabilitation Acts' regulations provide that if a violation has not been corrected in accordance with conciliation procedures, or if the OFCCP determines that referral for consideration of formal enforcement (rather

---

[321]*Id.* §§ 60-1.24(b), -250.61(d), -741.61(e).

[322]*Id.* § 60-1.24(b).

[323]*Id.* §§ 60-250.61(e)(1), -741.61(f)(1).

[324]*Id.* Should the Deputy Assistant Secretary decide to reconsider, prompt notification of such intent to reconsider is required, as well as the final determination after reconsideration. *Id.* §§ 60-250.61(e)(3), -741.61(f)(3).

[325]*Id.* §§ 60-1.24(c)(2), -250.62, -741.62.

[326]*Id.* § 60-1.24(c)(3). The language indicates that the OFCCP "shall" proceed with an enforcement action. *Id.*

[327]Andrews v. Consolidated Rail Corp., 831 F.2d 678, 685–87, 44 FEP 786 (7th Cir. 1987) (" 'an agency's decision not to take enforcement action should be presumed immune from judicial review' ") (citations omitted). *But see* Section VIII.C.3 *infra* (citizens may sue OFCCP to enjoin failure to perform nondiscretionary tasks).

than settlement) is appropriate, it may refer the matter to the Solicitor of Labor with a recommendation to institute enforcement proceedings.[328]

The OFCCP and EEOC have overlapping, but not co-extensive, jurisdiction.[329] Pursuant to a revised memorandum of understanding (MOU) between the agencies,[330] the OFCCP normally will retain, investigate, and attempt to resolve systemic or class discrimination allegations as well as individual complaints alleging discrimination against or failure to accommodate persons with disabilities or covered veterans.[331] It will refer to the EEOC allegations of individual discrimination on the basis of Title VII violations in dual-filed complaints/charges under Executive Order 11246.[332] However, the

---

[328]41 C.F.R. §§ 60-250.65, -741.65 (2005).

[329]The EEOC is the lead agency to coordinate federal agencies' enforcement of equal employment obligations. Exec. Order No. 12,067, 3 C.F.R. ch. 206 (1978 Compilation), 43 Fed. Reg. 28,967 (1978). The EEOC later published regulations providing for interagency coordination and development of uniform standards, policies, and procedures. 45 Fed. Reg. 68,361 (1980), 29 C.F.R. pt. 1690. All agency "issuances" of this kind, including regulations and policy directives, must be submitted to the EEOC for clearance. 45 Fed. Reg. at 68,362, 29 C.F.R. § 1690.107(f), subpt. C (2005).

[330]Coordination of Functions; Memorandum of Understanding, 64 Fed. Reg. 17,664 (1999).

[331]Under coordinating regulations issued by the EEOC and OFCCP regarding the agencies' overlapping jurisdiction with respect to the Americans with Disabilities Act, 42 U.S.C. §§ 12101–12213 (ADA) and § 503 of the Rehabilitation Act, the OFCCP will retain jurisdiction of disability discrimination complaints, unless the complaint also includes: (1) an EEOC priority litigation issue (*see generally* Chapter 29 (EEOC Litigation)); (2) allegations of individual-type race, color, religion, sex, or national origin discrimination; or (3) allegations of age discrimination. If complaints within any of the above categories also contain allegations that the contractor violated the affirmative action requirements under § 503, the OFCCP will bifurcate the complaint and retain jurisdiction over those affirmative action issues. 29 C.F.R. § 1641.5(e) (2004); 41 C.F.R. § 60-742.5(e) (2005).

[332]Memorandum of Understanding, 64 Fed. Reg. at 17,664–66 (MOU). "Complaints of employment discrimination filed with OFCCP under Executive Order 11246 will be considered charges simultaneously filed under Title VII whenever the complaints also fall within the jurisdiction of Title VII." MOU, ¶ 7, 64 Fed. Reg. at 17,666. This de facto simultaneous filing can be of critical importance in determining whether a complaint has been timely filed, because the date the matter was received by OFCCP will be deemed to be the date it was received by EEOC. *See generally* Chapter 26 (Timeliness).

The revisions modify a memorandum of understanding originally published at 46 Fed. Reg. 7435 (1981). One case noted that the 1981 memorandum, by its terms, provides only that a charge of discrimination filed with the OFCCP shall be deemed a charge filed jointly with the EEOC *if* the OFCCP *actually refers* the complaint to the EEOC. *See* Walker v. Novo Nordisk Pharm. Indus., Inc., 2000 WL 1012960, at

OFCCP may retain these individual complaints or charges "so as to avoid duplication and assure effective law enforcement,"[333] and in so doing act as EEOC's agent to process and resolve the claims.[334] The OFCCP is only authorized to act as such an agent with respect to Title VII claims or charges because the EEOC's enforcement authority does not extend to compliance evaluations.[335] Moreover, information shared by the EEOC with the OFCCP is subject to the confidentiality provisions of the Trade Secrets Act and Privacy Act.[336]

C. Contractor Precompliance Review Preparation

A self-audit is essential before the OFCCP's arrival. A contractor typically works with legal counsel to establish audit processes and scope, as well as requirements for data collection and analysis. Although documents prepared by or on behalf of counsel in anticipation of potential litigation arising out of the OFCCP's examination of compliance with the Executive Order should be protected as work product[337] or covered by attorney-client privilege, employers often still take additional precautions because a court may disagree. Thus, many employers afix to all self-audit and other self-critical documents, including those stored in computers, labels reflecting accurately the nature of their content. These labels include: "ATTORNEY-CLIENT PRIVILEGE," "ATTORNEY WORK PRODUCT," "SELF-CRITICAL ANALYSIS PRIVILEGE,"[338] and/or

---

*4 (4th Cir. July 24, 2000) (per curiam). An earlier, similar memorandum, 39 Fed. Reg. 35,855 (1974), has been upheld by the courts. *See* Emerson Elec. Co. v. Schlesinger, 609 F.2d 898, 904, 907, 21 FEP 475 (8th Cir. 1979) (the memorandum, procedural in nature, did not violate the Administrative Procedure Act (APA), Federal Reports Act, Trade Secrets Act, or privilege against disclosure of self-critical analysis documents); Reynolds Metals Co. v. Rumsfeld, 564 F.2d 663, 669, 15 FEP 1185 (4th Cir. 1977) (memorandum is not invalid under the APA even though it was not promulgated in accordance with the APA's notice and comment requirement since it does not have a substantive impact on a government contractor; it neither diminishes nor increases a contractor's rights and duties under the Executive Order and Title VII).

[333]MOU, ¶ 7(b)–(c), 64 Fed. Reg. at 17,666 (Apr. 12, 1999).

[334]MOU, ¶ 7(d), 64 Fed. Reg. at 17,666 (Apr. 12, 1999).

[335]64 Fed. Reg. at 17,665 (Apr. 12, 1999).

[336]MOU, ¶ 8, 64 Fed. Reg. at 17,665–66 (Apr. 12, 1999).

[337]*See* Abdallah v. Coca-Cola Co., 2000 WL 33249254, at *4–5 (N.D. Ga. Jan. 25, 2000).

[338]Documents prepared voluntarily by a contractor should be contrasted with those prepared because they are *mandated* by the OFCCP. Even in those jurisdictions

"CONFIDENTIAL & PROPRIETARY—EXEMPT FROM FOIA DISCLOSURE."[339] Employers generally retain these documents in secure, confidential files to which only authorized individuals have access.

Although the requirements in the Compliance Manual span hundreds of pages, the OFCCP, in practice, appears to focus on 12 areas. An understanding of those significant areas, and thorough precompliance review preparation with respect to them, are important.

1. An AAP That Satisfies the OFCCP's Technical Requirements

Each organization should designate someone to master the regulations and Compliance Manual. Using those authorities, that expert should audit the AAP and its supporting data for technical compliance. During this phase of the internal audit,[340] the auditor typically will:

(1) Inspect the employment lobby and all employee bulletin boards to be certain that the following are displayed: the required federal and state EEO/AA posters, current policy statements, invitations for self-identification and requests for accommodation of a disability, and the notice that the veterans/individuals-with-disabilities AAP is available for inspection.

(2) Review all outstanding charges of discrimination with federal and state agencies.

---

that endorse the privilege of self-critical analysis, documents prepared because they are required by a government agency are unlikely to be covered by this privilege. *See, e.g.*, Reid v. Lockheed Martin Aeronautics Co., 199 F.R.D. 379 (N.D. Ga. 2001). *But see* Johnson v. United Parcel Serv., Inc., 206 F.R.D. 686 (M.D. Fla. 2002) (declining to recognize a qualified privilege for self-critical analysis under any circumstances and directly refusing to follow *Reid*); Freiermuth v. PPG Indus., Inc., 218 F.R.D. 694 (N.D. Ala. 2003) (finding that recognizing a self-critical analysis privilege is questionable and declining to apply such a privilege to documents that contain no subjective analysis).

[339]*See* Section IX *infra*. *See generally* Chapter 33 (Discovery).

[340]Nothing in the discussion that follows should be read to suggest that the recommendations herein should be heeded only upon notice of a compliance review. Human resources and corporate legal departments should constantly monitor compliance. Nevertheless, even in the most careful companies, a prereview self-audit is prudent.

(3) Collect responses to the disability/veterans self-identification invitations, and compile a list of reasonable accommodations requested, declined, and made.

(4) Verify that the contractor has listed and is listing its employment openings with the appropriate local office of the state employment service (and America's Job Bank or equivalent if the contractor desires).[341]

(5) Verify that the contractor has made timely submission of the VETS-100 report.[342]

(6) Collect the I-9[343] forms for inspection by the OFCCP. Be certain that the contractor has all required forms and that each form is complete.

(7) Verify that the affirmative action clause is incorporated into covered contracts, subcontracts, and purchase orders.

(8) Verify that the contractor has fulfilled all commitments made in prior letters of commitment and conciliation agreements.

(9) Plan the facility tour to highlight the employer's compliance with the Executive Order and the OFCCP Guidelines.

(10) Arrange offices or work space for the OFCCP.

If the self-audit discloses that the contractor has failed to fulfill certain obligations, the employer generally will want to consult legal counsel for advice.

2. Enhance the Knowledge of and Commitment to Affirmative Action and Nondiscrimination on the Part of All Persons With Supervisory or Human Resources Responsibility

Training and information bulletins for all persons with supervisory responsibility are important.[344] A briefing session may include topics such as the nature of the review, standards the OFCCP expects

---

[341]See Section VI supra.

[342]Id.

[343]The Immigration Reform and Control Act of 1986, 8 U.S.C. § 1324(a) (2000), requires preparation and maintenance of documentation that each new hire has a legal right to work in the United States.

[344]The term "supervisory," as used in this chapter, includes all supervisors from first-line forepersons through the chief executive.

the employer to meet, supervisors' affirmative action responsibilities, applicable goals, the typical questions the OFCCP asks during an on-site review, and the tone and approach management should take with the OFCCP.

Most contractors conduct separate preparation sessions with supervisors who are likely to be interviewed regarding potential discrimination or adverse impact concerns in their organizations so that they can articulate persuasively the legitimate, nondiscriminatory reasons for their actions.[345]

Supervisors often will be asked to:

(1) Identify and explain the necessity for the published minimum qualifications for a job.
(2) Explain the value added by the "additional" qualifications that the most desirable candidates (including current incumbents) possess.
(3) Explain the job-related criteria that caused the supervisor to select particular candidates as the best qualified for certain vacancies.
(4) Explain how affirmative action was and is part of the recruiting and selection process.

During interviews with supervisors the OFCCP typically (1) checks the interviewee's knowledge of and attitude toward affirmative action; (2) ascertains the interviewee's knowledge of underutilization and affirmative action goals applicable to the work unit; (3) attempts to determine why a particular suspected substantive deficiency (e.g., discrimination) in the unit exists; (4) obtains descriptions of how personnel decisions in the unit are made and the criteria used; (5) determines who else in the unit might know or have information concerning certain specific personnel decisions; (6) ascertains the affirmative action commitments for which the unit was responsible; (7) determines what opportunities (vacancies) the supervisor had during the past two years; and (8) gathers facts about actual EEO accomplishments.

Supervisors in these interviews are frequently asked the following types of questions:

(1)   What is the difference between equal employment opportunity and affirmative action?

---

[345]It is important, of course, to review supervisory decisions periodically to ensure that those decisions are in fact supported by legitimate nondiscriminatory reasons.

(2) What are the major nondiscrimination laws?

(3) Who is protected by these laws?

(4) Does the company have a harassment/discrimination complaint procedure?

(5) What does the harassment/discrimination complaint procedure say? Where does one take a complaint?

(6) Have you personally received any complaints of harassment or discrimination from employees?

(7) If so, what actions did you take?

(8) Who is responsible for implementing the company's AAP?

(9) Have you reviewed the AAP or any portions of it? Which ones? What do they say?

(10) What is a goal?

(11) What goals are applicable to your unit?

(12) Are you involved in goal setting?

(13) What placement (hiring and promotion) opportunities have you had during the past two years?

(14) Did you achieve your goals? If not, why not, and what good faith efforts have you made?

(15) What steps are you required to take when you have an opening in a job group for which a goal has been set?

(16) What difficulties, if any, are you encountering in achieving your affirmative action goals?

(17) Why was candidate X not hired and candidate Y hired instead?

(18) What were the minimum qualifications for these jobs? What are the desired qualifications? What are the job's essential functions? Other functions?

(19) Are the interview questions or evaluation factors the same for each applicant or employee? What questions did you ask? What tests did you give?

(20) Have you been trained with regard to interviewing and making hiring or promotion decisions? When? What did you learn?

(21) Do you document your hiring and promotion decisions? How? What information do you record?

(22) Are your hiring or promotion decisions reviewed by anyone else?

(23) What affirmative action recruiting was conducted for this opening?

(24) Was the job posted? If not, why not? If not, what did you do to identify and consider qualified minorities and women?

(25) Do you attend meetings on AAP goal progress? When was the last one? What was discussed?

(26) Have you attended AAP training? When? What was covered?

(27) What jobs do women and minorities hold in your unit? Have you taken any steps to help them advance? What steps?

(28) Do you do succession planning? If so, what documents do you fill out? To whom do you send them? What selection criteria do you apply in succession planning? Who has been selected/not selected as successors in your organization? What special training, preference, assignments, or other benefits do persons named in the succession plan receive? Do you consider affirmative action goals in selecting persons for succession planning lists? What consideration do you give?

(29) Do you play a role in setting compensation? What factors do you consider in setting starting compensation? What factors do you consider in determining eligibility for and the amount of pay raises?

(30) Why does the compensation of employees *X* and *Y* differ?

(31) Are supervisors rated on their EEO efforts?

3. Regular Involvement of Top Executives in Designing, Monitoring Progress Under, and Holding Supervisors Accountable for Performance Under the AAPs Applicable to Their Organization

Contractors often will prepare a briefing paper of key points for executives to make with the OFCCP. This briefing paper may include affirmative action accomplishments, current activities to address incumbency that is lower than availability, good faith efforts to increase minority/female representation in management positions, and the executive's personal commitment to and involvement in the monitoring progress.

Executives often are asked to identify the information they receive on the affirmative action performance of each supervisor each year, how they use that information to evaluate subordinates' performance in this area, and how it affects subordinates' compensation and prospects for advancement.

4. Representation in Each Job Group Compared to the Availability of Minorities and Women With the Requisite Skills

A contractor typically will review its minority/female incumbency versus availability in each job group,[346] in order to be prepared to explain the reasons for any apparent disparity. Typical issues to consider include, for example: (a) reliability of external availability statistics for the jobs at issue;[347] and (b) whether layoffs and recalls have impacted progress toward goals.

5. Documentation of Systematic Affirmative Action Recruiting

When underutilization exists, a contractor should take special steps to identify and use recruiting sources that reach minorities and women.[348] Efforts to recruit individuals with disabilities and veterans are mandated as well.[349] Recruiting sources should know the company, its job application and selection processes, the types of openings it typically has, and its interest in referrals of protected-group applicants.

In a corporate management review of a contractor's headquarters,[350] the OFCCP typically will identify the outside sources from which current executives have been recruited, determine whether the contractor has articulated to these sources its commitment to affirmative action at high-management levels, examine whether the contractor has tracked the number and percentage of referrals by

---

[346]For an explanation of the availability analysis and comparison of incumbency to availability, see Sections III.B.3.d–e, *supra.*

[347]Contractors experience particular difficulty in estimating minority/female availability for management jobs because the 2000 Census sets forth the number of persons employed in various types of management jobs but fails to divide them by compensation level. For example, the census heading "financial managers" includes managers earning $30,000 as well as those earning more than $1 million per year.

[348]FED. CONTRACT COMPL. MAN. § 5082, *reprinted in* 1 AFFIRMATIVE ACTION COMPL. MAN. (BNA) 5:0088.

[349]*Id.*

[350]Chapter 5 of the Compliance Manual specifies additional requirements for a compliance review of a corporate headquarters. FED. CONTRACT COMPL. MAN. Ch. 5, *reprinted in* 2 AFFIRMATIVE ACTION COMPL. MAN. (BNA) 5:0001–32.

race and gender from each source, and evaluate whether the contractor has added recruiting sources likely to generate minority and female candidates.[351]

6. A Well-Documented Internal System of Advertising Openings and Screening Applicants

A contractor should be able to explain and justify its internal selection processes. Such a justification is significantly assisted by a system under which the contractor has posted its openings and/or carefully identified qualified minorities and women within its workforce, examined their respective qualifications, and considered them. Some contractors that do not post high-level positions instead use a centralized management selection committee for each high-management opening; this committee is responsible for identifying and considering potentially qualified minority and women employees, including those at subsidiaries or outlying divisions. Other contractors have a pre-registration system that allows employees to designate job classifications for which they would like to be considered during the year.

7. Placement-Rate Goals for Hiring and Promoting Minorities and Women Consistent With Their Percentage Availability

For each job group in which the percentage utilization of minorities and women is less than their availability, a contractor should identify placement-rate goals for hiring and promotion. The OFCCP expects supervisors to participate, at least annually, in such goal setting and in evaluating progress toward goals.[352] Supervisors will be asked about the applicable goals, and progress toward them, during past and current years.

8. Narrative Descriptions of the Good Faith Efforts Made Toward Goal Achievement During the Year

Good faith efforts to achieve goals—by recruiters, supervisors, and others—not only should occur, but also should be documented, as jobs are filled.[353]

---

[351]*Id.* § 5H, *reprinted in* 2 AFFIRMATIVE ACTION COMPL. MAN. (BNA) 5:0007–09.
[352]For goal-setting requirements, see Section III.B.3.e *supra.*
[353]For a discussion of documenting good faith efforts, see Section III.B.4 *supra.*

9. Explanations for Any Statistically Significant Disparities in Hiring, Promotion, and Termination Rates[354]

Where statistical disparities exist, and particularly where disparities are statistically significant,[355] the OFCCP will ask for an explanation. Thus, a contractor typically will seek to ascertain the reasons and be prepared to articulate them.

Each supervisor may be asked about his or her hiring and promotion decisions for the past two years and to explain the job-related reasons for selecting—and not selecting—particular candidates. The OFCCP inspects closely the rates at which women versus men, and minorities versus Caucasians, are promoted out of particular job levels (particularly in the management ranks).[356]

10. Analyze Compensation for Both Sexes and Each Race in Each Pay Grade for Persons of Comparable Performance, Skill, and Seniority

In November 2000, the OFCCP issued a final rule adopting several new affirmative action program requirements.[357] One required contractors to evaluate their "[c]ompensation system(s) to determine whether there are gender-, race- or ethnicity-based disparities."[358] However, the agency issued no guidance on the standards for these analyses, other than to leave their selection to the contractor.[359]

During its subsequent compliance reviews of federal contractors, the OFCCP focused on attempting to prove systemic pay discrimination under a disparate treatment, pattern-or-practice theory

---

[354]For computation and analysis methods, see Section III.B.5 *supra*.

[355]*See generally* Chapter 3 (Adverse Impact).

[356]FED. CONTRACT COMPL. MAN. § 2043, *reprinted in* 1 AFFIRMATIVE ACTION COMPL. MAN. (BNA) 2:0003 ("The normal liability period for a compliance review is the full two years preceding the date the contractor received the Scheduling Letter."); FED. CONTRACT COMPL. MAN. § 7081(g), *reprinted in* 1 AFFIRMATIVE ACTION COMPL. MAN. (BNA) 7:0011(g) (inspection of rates of men versus women and minorities versus Caucasians); 41 C.F.R. § 60-2.30 (compliance evaluations are designed to ascertain whether individuals are encountering artificial barriers to advancement into mid-level and senior corporate management, i.e., glass ceilings).

[357]65 Fed. Reg. 68,022 (Nov. 13, 2000).

[358]*Id.* at 68,046 (referencing 41 C.F.R. § 60-2.17(b)(3)).

[359]65 Fed. Reg. at 68,036 (Nov. 13, 2000).

of discrimination by showing that discrimination was a contractor's standard operating procedure.[360]

On November 16, 2004, the OFCCP published a notice of proposed standards for analyzing potential systemic compensation discrimination under Executive Order 11246,[361] along with a notice of proposed guidelines for self-evaluation of compensation practices.[362] The notices contained important substantive information about OFCCP's current and intended practices, as well as explanatory comments that may be informative to federal government contractors faced with systemic pay discrimination claims.[363]

The notices explain that Executive Order 11246 and the Department of Labor's Sex Discrimination Guidelines[364] prohibit "systemic compensation discrimination involving dissimilar treatment of individuals who are similarly situated."[365] The determination of employees who are "similarly situated" for purposes of comparing contractor pay decisions will focus on the similarity of the work performed, the levels of responsibility, and the skills and qualifications involved in the positions.[366] In making its determination as to whether "employees are similarly situated . . . , *actual facts* regarding employees' work activities, responsibility, and skills and qualifications are determinative."[367] The OFCCP will ascertain those "actual facts" by considering job descriptions and interviewing employees.[368] Pay grades, AAP job groups, and other preexisting groupings "may be relevant only to the extent that they do in fact

---

[360]*See* Teamsters v. United States, 431 U.S. 324, 336 (1977); Bazemore v. Friday, 478 U.S. 385, 398 (1986). Under the OFCCP's proposed standards, " 'systemic compensation discrimination' is discrimination under a pattern or practice theory of disparate treatment." 69 Fed. Reg. at 67,251 (Nov. 16, 2004).

[361]69 Fed. Reg. 67,246 (Nov. 16, 2004).

[362]*Id.* at 67,252.

[363]The OFCCP invokes Title VII standards for determining compliance with the nondiscrimination requirements of the Executive Order. *See id.* at 67,246 n.1.

[364]41 C.F.R. pt. 60-20, 35 Fed. Reg. 8888 (June 9, 1970).

[365]69 Fed. Reg. 67,249 (Nov. 16, 2004).

[366]The agency will consider employees to be "similarly situated with respect to pay decisions" if they "perform similar work, have similar responsibility levels, and occupy positions involving similar qualifications and skills." *Id.* at 67,251. The notice acknowledges that the agency will consult with the Solicitor's Office to address this issue on a case-by-case basis because some courts hold that "the Equal Pay Act's standard of 'substantial equality' applies to gender-based pay discrimination claims under Title VII" only "absent direct evidence of discrimination." *Id.* n.9.

[367]*Id.* at 67,251 (emphasis added).

[368]*Id.* at 67,252.

group employees with similar work, skills and qualifications and responsibility levels."[369]

The notices further provide that the OFCCP has formed a Division of Statistical Analysis and hired expert-level statisticians who will use multiple regression analyses to account for the difference that legitimate factors play in compensation.[370] The agency proposes several specifications for regression analyses:

(1) The regression model "must include those factors that are important to how the contractor in practice makes pay decisions."[371]

(2) Potential regression factors may include, but are not limited to, "education, work experience with previous employers, seniority in the job, time in a particular salary grade, performance ratings," "productivity, location," and the "categories or groupings of jobs that are similarly situated."[372]

(3) The regression should not use factors that are " 'tainted' by discrimination."[373] "OFCCP may reject inclusion of such a factor upon proof that the factor was actually tainted by the employer's discrimination."[374] However, the agency will not conclude there is taint by virtue of the "fact that the factor has an influence on the outcome of a regression model that includes the factor."[375]

(4) Since the factors that influence pay decisions may not bear the same relationship to compensation for all categories of jobs in the employer's workforce, the contractor should either:

(i) "perform separate regressions for each category of jobs in which the relationship between the factors and compensation is similar (while including category factors in each regression that control for groupings of employees

---

[369]*Id.* at 67,251.

[370]*Id.* at 67,249; *see also id.* at 67,251 ("The determination of whether there are statistically significant compensation disparities between similarly situated employees after taking into account such legitimate factors must be based on a multiple regression analysis.").

[371]*Id.* at 67,250.

[372]*Id.* at 67,250, 67,251.

[373]*Id.*

[374]*Id.* at 67,252.

[375]*Id.* at 67,250–51.

who are similarly situated based on work performed, responsibility level, and skills and qualifications);" or

(ii) "[i]f separate regressions by categories of jobs would not permit OFCCP to assess the way the contractor's compensation practices impact on a significant number of employees, OFCCP may perform a 'pooled' regression."[376]

(a) "OFCCP will determine whether a pooled regression model is appropriate based on two factors: (i) the contractor should include at least 80% of the employees (in the workforce subject to OFCCP's compliance review) in some regression analysis; and (ii) there should be enough incumbent employees in a particular regression to produce statistically meaningful results."[377]

(b) A pooled regression combines categories of jobs into a single regression (that contains a factor controlling for groupings of employees who are similarly situated based on work performed, responsibility level, and skills and qualifications). However, a pooled regression "must include appropriate 'interaction terms'[[378]] . . . to account for differences in the effects of certain factors by job category."[379]

(c) "If a pooled regression is required, OFCCP will conduct statistical tests generally accepted in the statistics profession (*e.g.*, the 'Chow test'), to determine which interaction terms should be included in the pooled regression model."[380]

(5) Only disparities that are "statistically significant" can support a systemic discrimination finding. "To ensure uniformity and predictability, OFCCP will conclude that a compensation disparity is statistically significant . . . if it is

---

[376]*Id.*

[377]*Id.* at 67,252.

[378]*Id.* at 67,251 n.11 ("An 'interaction term' is a factor used in the regression model whose value is the result of a combination of subfactors, which allows the factor to vary based on the combined effect of the subfactors. For example, a performance by job level interaction term would allow performance to have a different impact on compensation depending on the job level.").

[379]*Id.* at 67,251.

[380]*Id.* at 67,252; *see also id.* at 67,251 ("If a pooled regression model is used, this must be accompanied by statistical tests generally accepted in the statistics profession (*e.g.*, the 'Chow test'), to determine which interaction terms should be included in the pooled regression model.").

significant at a level of two or more standard deviations, based on measures of statistical significance that are generally accepted in the statistics profession."[381]

(6) "OFCCP will seldom make a finding of systemic discrimination based on statistical analysis alone, but will obtain anecdotal evidence to support the statistical evidence."[382]

Under the proposed standards, a contractor has two options: (1) conduct a self-evaluation "in good faith" that "reasonably" implements the OFCCP's prescribed methodology, in which case the contractor will be deemed in compliance with 41 C.F.R. § 60-2.17(b)(3), or (2) select its own forms of analysis to comply with the regulatory requirements, recognizing the OFCCP will evaluate the contractor's compensation practices without regard to the contractor's own analysis.[383]

To meet the OFCCP's proposed standards for a compensation self-evaluation:

(1) The contractor's self-evaluation must be performed by groupings of employees who are similarly situated (Similarly Situated Employee Groupings, or SSEGs) so that the contractor combines those who perform work that is actually "similar in content, responsibility, and requisite skill and qualifications."[384] Job titles and classifications, pay grades or ranges, and AAP job groupings are not dispositive.

(2) The contractor must make a reasonable attempt to produce SSEGs that are large enough for meaningful statistical analysis (i.e., generally "at least 30 employees overall," with "five or more incumbents who are members of either of the following pairs: male/female or minority/non-minority").[385]

(3) The contractor may eliminate from the statistical evaluation process small numbers of employees who are not sufficiently similarly situated to other employees to permit them to be grouped in an SSEG, but must conduct a self-evaluation of pay decisions related to those employees using nonstatistical methods.[386]

---

[381]*Id.* at 67,251–52.
[382]*Id.*
[383]*Id.* at 67,252–53.
[384]*Id.*
[385]*Id.* at 67,254.
[386]*Id.*

(4) The contractor's statistical analyses must encompass a significant majority of the employees in the particular AAP or workplace. OFCCP will carefully scrutinize when "the statistical analyses do not encompass at least 80% of the employees in the [AAP] or workplace."[387]

(5) The contractor must conduct a statistical analysis annually in a manner that accounts for factors that legitimately affect the compensation of the members of the SSEGs under the contractor's compensation system, such as experience, education, performance, productivity, location, and other factors. Contractors with at least 250 employees must use a multiple regression analysis that conforms with the standards set forth above.[388]

(6) Where a contractor finds a statistical disparity of two or more standard deviations from a zero disparity level, it must determine whether the disparity is explained by legitimate factors or otherwise not the product of unlawful discrimination.[389] It also must provide "appropriate remedies" for statistical disparities it cannot so explain.[390] With respect to the initial self-evaluation, the contractor is expected to make adjustments based on both current disparities and prior disparities, using a "two-year window for back pay corrections."[391] Thereafter,

---

[387]*Id.*

[388]*Id.* (inappropriate to use a regression factor if there is evidence showing it is tainted; "[c]orrelation between such a factor and a protected characteristic does not automatically disqualify the factor, if the employer has implemented formal standards to constrain subjective decisionmaking," *id.* at 67,254; must include recognized tests of statistical significance).

[389]*Id.*

[390]*Id.*

[391]*Id.* The OFCCP acknowledges that contractors run a risk of liability when they make corrective compensation adjustments under a self-evaluation process, including (i) claims by minorities or women based on the theory that the employer's own self-evaluation study established that it engaged in discrimination or that the employer did not make sufficient compensation adjustments to remedy discrimination. *Id.* (citing Cullen v. Indiana Univ., 338 F.3d 693, 701–04 (7th Cir. 2003) (female professor sued university alleging compensation discrimination and basing her claim, in part, on university's pay equity study)); and (ii) claims by male or non-minority employees alleging violation of Title VII because the employer gave salary adjustments to female or minority employees under the compensation self-evaluation. 69 Fed. Reg. at 67,253 (citing Rudebusch v. Hughes, 313 F.3d 506, 515–16 (9th Cir. 2002) (employer's self-audit, regression analysis was not technically sufficient to foreclose male professor's discrimination claim against the employer));

"the remedy would involve correcting current disparities."[392]

In addition, the contractor must contemporaneously create, retain, and make available to OFCCP during a compliance review:

(1) Documents necessary to explain and justify its decisions with respect to SSEGs, exclusion of certain employees from the regression, factors included in the statistical analyses, and the form of the statistical analyses;

(2) The data used in the statistical analyses and the results of the statistical analyses for two years from the date that the statistical analyses are performed;

(3) The data and documents explaining the results of the non-statistical methods that the contractor used to evaluate pay decisions regarding those employees who were eliminated from the statistical evaluation process; and

(4) Documentation (for two years from the date that the follow-up investigation is performed) as to any follow-up investigation into statistically significant disparities, the conclusions of such investigation, and any pay adjustments made to remedy such disparities.[393]

Under the proposed standards, the OFCCP will determine during a compliance review whether the contractor's self-evaluation comports with these standards. If so, the OFCCP will consider the contractor's compensation practices to be in compliance with Executive Order 11246.[394] The agency may suggest in writing that the contractor make prospective modifications to improve the self-evaluation system's conformity with the OFCCP's standards if the agency concludes that the self-evaluation system is only marginally reasonable under the guidelines.[395] In such cases, the OFCCP will assess during future compliance reviews whether

---

Maitland v. University of Minn., 155 F.3d 1013, 1016–18 (8th Cir. 1998) (same); Smith v. Virginia Commonwealth Univ., 84 F.3d 672, 676–77 (4th Cir. 1996) (same).

[392]69 Fed. Reg. at 67,254 (Nov. 16, 2004).

[393]*Id.* The OFCCP may also review any personnel records and conduct any employee interviews it deems necessary to determine the accuracy of any representation the contractor has made in such documentation or data. *Id.*

[394]*Id.*

[395]*Id.*

the contractor made the suggested changes, and may review documents and data to so determine.[396] If the OFCCP finds that the contractor has not made those changes, it will no longer accept the contractor's self-evaluation system.[397]

If the contractor selects its own form of analysis to comply with § 60-2.17(b)(3)'s compensation analysis requirement,[398] the proposed standards call for the OFCCP to audit the contractor's compensation de novo. The standards recognize that "some contractors may take the position, based on advice of counsel, that their compensation self-evaluation is subject to certain protections from disclosure, such as the attorney client privilege or attorney work product doctrine, and that these protections would be waived if the contractor disclosed the self-evaluation."[399] The OFCCP takes no position regarding the applicability of these protections, but "will permit the contractor to certify its compliance with 41 CFR § 60-2.17(b)(3) in lieu of producing the methodology or results of its compensation self-evaluation analyses to OFCCP during a compliance review."[400] That certification must be in writing, signed by a duly authorized officer of the contractor under penalty of perjury. It must state that the contractor has performed, at the direction of counsel, a compensation self-evaluation with respect to the AAP or workplace at issue, and that counsel has advised the contractor that the compensation self-evaluation analyses and results are subject to the attorney-client privilege and/or the attorney work product doctrine.[401]

A contractor's attorney-client-privileged audit also should examine starting salaries and annual salary increases. The contractor also should assess whether there are individuals who are paid above or below the published pay range for a grade, which is a particularly significant issue for the OFCCP. Such employees should either be reclassified or have their compensation adjusted.

In corporate management evaluations, the OFCCP will pay particular attention to executive compensation systems, including

---

[396]*Id.* at 67,254–55.

[397]*Id.* at 67,254.

[398]*Id.*

[399]*Id.* at 67,255.

[400]*Id.*

[401]*Id.* The OFCCP-prescribed disclosure itself compels the contractor to disclose information that may itself be privileged, which raises concerns of a potential waiver of privilege.

cash compensation, incentive cash bonuses, stock option programs, and executive perquisites such as vehicles, financial consulting, club memberships, annual physical examinations, and travel benefits. The OFCCP examines whether the criteria for participation are applied consistently regardless of race or gender; whether the size of the benefit granted (e.g., number of stock options) to similarly situated individuals is comparable; and whether the contractor monitors discretionary decisions to ensure the absence of bias.[402]

11. Identify a Systematic Program for Moving Minorities and Women Into Mid- and Top-Management Positions

The OFCCP typically evaluates hiring rates; promotion rates; succession plans; training, education, and mentoring programs; participation in task forces, committees, and other assignments that provide exposure to management; compensation; and benefits for management employees. Supervisors interviewed by the OFCCP frequently will be asked to describe what steps they have taken to identify minorities and women for advancement to higher management, to mentor and train them, and to critique their performance so that they can continue to develop.[403]

A contractor often is asked to explain how it conducts succession planning and what documents, if any, reflect the process. The OFCCP looks for instructions setting forth the job-related objective and subjective factors that supervisors should consider in selecting successors. A contractor should be prepared to explain how it considers affirmative action in the process and attempts to ensure that the resulting decisions do not discriminate unlawfully against any group.[404]

The compliance evaluation often includes an examination of actual management succession or "high potential" lists. The OFCCP evaluates whether minorities and women are selected for inclusion in management succession plans at a rate appropriate to their representation in the levels from which such individuals are drawn. The OFCCP also considers whether, once included in succession plans, minorities and women progress at the rate that Caucasians

---

[402]FED. CONTRACT COMPL. MAN. § 5J, *reprinted in* 2 AFFIRMATIVE ACTION COMPL. MAN. (BNA) 5:0014–17.

[403]*Id.* § 5I, *reprinted in* 2 AFFIRMATIVE ACTION COMPL. MAN. (BNA) 5:0009–14.

[404]*Id.* § 5I, *reprinted in* 2 AFFIRMATIVE ACTION COMPL. MAN. (BNA) 5:0009–10.

and men do. Key focus areas are: (1) opportunities for training, education, and development; and (2) actual promotion rates.[405]

12. A Well-Documented Internal Complaint Procedure

The OFCCP sometimes reviews internal complaints of harassment and discrimination, as well as the contractor's files reflecting the investigation and resolution of such complaints.[406]

D. The Desk Audit

1. Purpose of the Desk Audit

Most compliance evaluations of supply and service contractors[407] start with a desk audit by an OFCCP Compliance Officer (CO) away from the contractor's worksite.[408] During this phase, the CO reviews the contractor's paperwork to ascertain compliance with affirmative action and equal opportunity obligations at the particular establishment being audited. Specifically, the CO: (1) examines the contractor's basic organizational structure, personnel policies, and procedures; (2) reviews, for technical compliance, the contractor's AAP; (3) identifies areas in which the contractor has made little progress in increasing protected-group representation, where further investigation on-site may be necessary to evaluate the contractor's good faith efforts; and (4) identifies areas for an in-depth investigation of potential discrimination, such as adverse impact in hiring, promotion, or termination rates, as well as underrepresentations or concentrations of minorities or women in particular organizational units.[409]

---

[405]*Id.*

[406]FED. CONTRACT COMPL. MAN. § 6052, *reprinted in* 1 AFFIRMATIVE ACTION COMPL. MAN. (BNA) 6:0002.

[407]Compliance reviews of construction contractors are somewhat different. *See* FED. CONTRACT COMPL. MAN. Ch. 4, *reprinted in* 2 AFFIRMATIVE ACTION COMPL. MAN. (BNA) 4:0001–34.

[408]41 C.F.R. § 60-1.20(a)(1)(i) (2005). Desk audits generally are conducted at OFCCP offices. In the case of pre-award reviews, however, the desk audit is conducted at the contractor's establishment. *Id.*

[409]FED. CONTRACT COMPL. MAN. § 2A01, *reprinted in* 1 AFFIRMATIVE ACTION COMPL. MAN. (BNA) 2:0001. Adverse impact computations are described in Section III.B.5 *supra.* For an explanation of underrepresentation and concentration, see Section VII.C.4 *supra.*

2. The OFCCP's Activities Preceding the Desk Audit

a. Initial Contact With Contractor. Before commencing the compliance evaluation, the CO typically contacts the contractor by telephone to obtain the name of the chief executive officer of the facility under review, the name of the person responsible for AAP preparation and implementation, the correct mailing address, and the identity of any federal contracts or subcontracts. The same information is requested for any larger corporate entity of which the facility is a part.[410]

If the contractor chooses to be represented by legal counsel or a consultant during the compliance evaluation, the contractor, either at this point in the process or thereafter, should inform the CO of the representation. The CO requires written confirmation of the representation, including: (1) the representative's name, address, and telephone number; (2) the scope of the representative's authority; (3) whether all contacts, including routine ones, should be made through the representative; and (4) whether the contractor should be sent copies of correspondence mailed to the representative.[411]

During this initial telephonic contact, the CO typically determines whether the evaluation should be cancelled or postponed due to any special circumstances. For example, the OFCCP may delay the evaluation if the contractor is having a large layoff,[412] or if the contractor's key representative has scheduling conflicts.

b. The Scheduling Letter. The OFCCP then issues the official "scheduling letter" notifying the contractor of the compliance evaluation and requesting the contractor's AAP[413] and supporting documentation.[414] The letter may also request examples of job

---

[410]FED. CONTRACT COMPL. MAN. § 2B02(a), *reprinted in* 1 AFFIRMATIVE ACTION COMPL. MAN. (BNA) 2:0002. The OFCCP now endeavors to give contractors advance notice that it intends to send a compliance review scheduling letter.

[411]*Id.* § 2B02(b), *reprinted in* 1 AFFIRMATIVE ACTION COMPL. MAN. (BNA) 2:0002.

[412]*Id.* § 2B02(c), *reprinted in* 1 AFFIRMATIVE ACTION COMPL. MAN. (BNA) 2:0002.

[413]Most contractors will have two AAPs: one for the Executive Order, the other for veterans and individuals with disabilities. The term "AAP" as used herein refers to both. The importance of a separate Executive Order AAP is explained in Section VI *supra.*

[414]FED. CONTRACT COMPL. MAN. § 2B03, *reprinted in* 1 AFFIRMATIVE ACTION COMPL. MAN. (BNA) 2:0002.

advertisements (including listings with state employment services) and examples of accommodations made for persons with disabilities.[415] The letter includes an itemized checklist of the information the contractor is required to submit within 30 days of receipt of the letter. The OFCCP sometimes—though not routinely—grants extensions of time for the submission of these materials, and generally will allow an additional five calendar days to allow their receipt by OFCCP, if informed by the contractor that the materials are in the mail.[416]

c. Contact With EEOC, State and Local FEP Agencies, and VETS. The CO sends a standard inquiry letter to the district office of the EEOC and to state and local fair employment practices (FEP) agencies, requesting information on complaints filed against the contractor. In evaluating the information received, the CO looks for patterns in the types of complaints filed that might indicate potential systemic discrimination.[417] In addition, the CO contacts the Veterans Employment and Training Service (VETS) representative at the appropriate state employment security office. The VETS representative is invited to provide information pertinent to the evaluation, such as affirmative action recruiting efforts by the contractor.[418]

d. Review of Previous Compliance Actions. If the contractor has been audited previously, the CO examines at least the prior case file for violations and other problems identified, as well as commitments made to resolve the audit. Files reflecting investigations of prior OFCCP complaints against the contractor also are reviewed.

---

[415]*See* Sample Scheduling Letter in revised compliance materials, found on the OFCCP website at http://www.dol.gov/esa/regs/compliance/ofccp/fccm/ofcpch2.htm (last visited Dec. 5, 2005).

[416]FED. CONTRACT COMPL. MAN. § 2C00, *reprinted in* 1 AFFIRMATIVE ACTION COMPL. MAN. (BNA) 2:0003.

[417]*Id.* § 2B09, *reprinted in* 1 AFFIRMATIVE ACTION COMPL. MAN. (BNA) 2:0002–03. The Compliance Manual defines "systemic discrimination" as:

Employment policies or practices that serve to differentiate or to perpetuate a differentiation in terms or conditions of employment of applicants or employees because of their status as members of a particular group. Such policies or practices may or may not be facially neutral, and intent to discriminate may or may not be involved. Systemic discrimination, sometimes called class discrimination or a pattern or practice of discrimination, concerns a recurring practice or continuing policy rather than an isolated act of discrimination.

Id. § 1B, *reprinted in* 1 AFFIRMATIVE ACTION COMPL. MAN. (BNA) 1:0010.

[418]*Id.* § 2B05(b), *reprinted in* 1 AFFIRMATIVE ACTION COMPL. MAN. (BNA) 2:0002.

As the evaluation progresses, the CO seeks to determine whether past problems have remained unremedied or have recurred.[419]

3. The Contractor's Response to the Scheduling Letter

Upon receipt of the scheduling letter, a contractor should review its government contracts. If the contractor does not meet the threshold limits for the development of an AAP, it should so advise the OFCCP.

If the contractor is covered, it should submit the information requested in the scheduling letter within 30 days. Failure to timely submit the data may result in the issuance of a notice to show cause why enforcement proceedings should not be brought against the contractor.[420]

4. The OFCCP's Initial Review of the AAP and Supporting Data

The CO preliminarily reviews the contractor's submission for currency, completeness, reasonableness, and acceptability. The latter three criteria sound redundant, but they in fact are analytically distinct.

a. Currency and Completeness. The CO initially reviews the contractor's AAP and support data for currency[421] and completeness. If the AAP has not been updated within the past year, the CO treats the omission as a wholesale failure to submit an AAP and issues a notice to show cause.[422] If the AAP is current, the CO

---

[419]*Id.* § 2B08, *reprinted in* 1 Affirmative Action Compl. Man. (BNA) 2:0002.

[420]*Id.* § 2C01, *reprinted in* 1 Affirmative Action Compl. Man. (BNA) 2:0003. Enforcement proceedings are described in Section VIII *infra.* Contractors are ill advised to submit their materials belatedly. Although the OFCCP is unlikely to base enforcement proceedings on an issue such as timeliness—which can be cured before the enforcement proceedings begin—as a practical matter a tardy submission begins the review process on the wrong note and places at risk the contractor's credibility, upon which the contractor may need to draw in later discussions of substantive issues.

[421]Each AAP must be updated annually. 41 C.F.R. §§ 60-2.1(c), -250.40(c), -741.40(c) (2005).

[422]Fed. Contract Compl. Man. § 2E00, *reprinted in* 1 Affirmative Action Compl. Man. (BNA) 2:0004. The Compliance Manual defines a show cause notice as:

A letter from OFCCP to the contractor ordering it to show cause why enforcement proceedings should not be instituted. A show cause notice follows OFCCP's

determines whether all the other materials requested in the scheduling letter and itemized listing have been submitted.

The CO then determines whether the submission contains all components required by the regulations.[423] For example, if the contractor's Executive Order AAP fails to include an organizational profile, comparison of incumbency to availability, or goals for areas declared underutilized, the OFCCP automatically considers the submission defective, suspends the desk audit, and issues a show cause notice. If these components are included in the Executive Order AAP, the CO next evaluates them for reasonableness.[424]

b. Review of the Executive Order AAP for Reasonableness. To be deemed reasonable, the Executive Order AAP organizational profile, comparison of incumbency to availability, and goals development must meet the standards specified in the Compliance Manual. The organizational profile, for example, must list all jobs at the establishment by title and by organizational unit, showing at least total employees, total women, and total minorities for each job title. The comparison of incumbency to availability must demonstrate: (1) an attempt to combine job titles into job groups (one or more jobs with similar content, wage rates, and opportunities); (2) an attempt to establish separate availability estimates for minorities and women for each such job group; and (3) a comparison of availability to current incumbency to determine the existence of underutilization. The submission also must reflect an attempt to establish goals for those job groups in which minorities or women are underutilized. If the OFCCP deems the Executive Order AAP reasonable, it and its supporting data then will be reviewed for acceptability. If not, the agency issues a notice to show cause.[425]

---

issuance of a notice of violation and failure of conciliation. The show cause notice provides that the contractor must come into compliance within 30 days or OFCCP will recommend the institution of enforcement proceedings.

Id. § 1B, *reprinted in* 1 AFFIRMATIVE ACTION COMPL. MAN. (BNA) 1:0009; *see also* 41 C.F.R. §§ 60-1.28, -250.64, -741.64 (2005). The enforcement process is covered in Section VIII *infra*.

[423]FED. CONTRACT COMPL. MAN. § 2E01, *reprinted in* 1 AFFIRMATIVE ACTION COMPL. MAN. (BNA) 2:0004.

[424]*Id.* § 2E02, *reprinted in* 1 AFFIRMATIVE ACTION COMPL. MAN. (BNA) 2:0004–05.

[425]*Id.* § 2F03, *reprinted in* 1 AFFIRMATIVE ACTION COMPL. MAN. (BNA) 2:0012.

c. Review of Executive Order AAP for Acceptability. Once the Executive Order AAP has been deemed reasonable, the CO evaluates the acceptability of each of its required components.[426] Deficiencies identified at this stage typically are reflected in a notice of violations issued at the conclusion of the evaluation.[427]

d. Review of Executive Order Support Data for Acceptability. (i.) Personnel activity data. The itemized listing enclosed with the scheduling letter requests information on personnel activities for the prior AAP year (and the current year, if at least six months have elapsed).[428] To be acceptable, the data must be presented either by job group (as requested) or by job title. For each job group or title, the support data for applicants, hires, promotions, and terminations must include at least: (1) the total number of transactions (e.g., the total of all persons of all races and both genders who applied or were hired, promoted, or terminated); (2) the total number of women; and (3) the total number from *each* racial group (i.e., Caucasians, African Americans, Hispanics, Asian/Pacific Islanders, and American Indians/Alaskan Natives separately designated).[429]

If the contractor does not submit the required personnel activity data for applicants, hires, promotions, or terminations, the OFCCP will issue a show cause notice.[430] When the format of the data submitted is unacceptable, the CO calls the contractor and requests that the appropriate changes be made and the data resubmitted within 10 calendar days. If data are not submitted in an acceptable form within 10 calendar days, the OFCCP will issue a show cause notice.[431]

(ii.) Goals and good faith efforts. The itemized listing also requests summary data and information indicating the numerical and other results of affirmative action goals for each job group for the current AAP year and for the preceding year.[432] Current-year

---

[426]*See* Section III.B *supra.*

[427]*See* Section VII.E.5 *infra.*

[428]FED. CONTRACT COMPL. MAN. § 2H01, *reprinted in* 1 AFFIRMATIVE ACTION COMPL. MAN. (BNA) 2:0014–15.

[429]*Id.* § 2H01(c), *reprinted in* 1 AFFIRMATIVE ACTION COMPL. MAN. (BNA) 2:0015.

[430]*Id.* § 2H01(a), *reprinted in* 1 AFFIRMATIVE ACTION COMPL. MAN. (BNA) 2:0014.

[431]*Id.* § 2H01(d), *reprinted in* 1 AFFIRMATIVE ACTION COMPL. MAN. (BNA) 2:0015.

[432]*Id.* § 2L00, *reprinted in* 1 AFFIRMATIVE ACTION COMPL. MAN. (BNA) 2:0017–18.

data are required only if the contractor is six months or more into its current AAP year at the time it receives the scheduling letter.[433]

The contractor's report on prior year goals typically will specifically list (1) the percentage placement goals for total minorities and women for each job group for which a goal was required; (2) the total number of placements into each job group for which a goal was established; and (3) the number and percentage of minority and female placements into each of those job groups.[434] For each goal it failed to meet, the contractor should describe its good faith efforts in sufficient detail for the CO to evaluate their adequacy.

The CO begins the investigation of good faith efforts at the desk audit stage by: (1) examining how much progress the contractor made in eliminating underutilization in job groups for which the contractor had both goals and actual placement opportunities;[435] and (2) evaluating the contractor's overall placement-rate goals performance (e.g., how many annual minority and female placement-rate goals were achieved; how many were missed; and, for those missed, how close the contractor's actual placement rate was to its percentage placement goal for that job group).[436] If the contractor achieved placement-rate goals in a job group, but nevertheless made little or no progress in moving minority and female utilization closer to availability, the OFCCP examines whether the reasons from OFCCP's standpoint are positive (e.g., promotions of minorities or women out of that job group) or negative (e.g., a disproportionately high number of minority or female terminations).[437]

The evaluation of the contractor's good faith effort takes into account several factors. The CO considers, for example, whether the contractor made progress in most job groups for which goals were established, and whether deficiencies in one area were outweighed by strong performance in similar but higher-level jobs.

---

[433]*Id.* § 2H00, *reprinted in* 1 AFFIRMATIVE ACTION COMPL. MAN. (BNA) 2:0014.

[434]*Id.* § 2H00(a), *reprinted in* 1 AFFIRMATIVE ACTION COMPL. MAN. (BNA) 2:0014.

[435]For example, if the contractor's utilization of women in a job group was 20% at the beginning of an AAP year, its female goal was 30%, and it had four openings, the OFCCP expects to see the 20% female utilization increase during the AAP year.

[436]FED. CONTRACT COMPL. MAN. § 2L, *reprinted in* 1 AFFIRMATIVE ACTION COMPL. MAN. (BNA) 2:0017–18.

[437]*Id.* § 2L00(c), *reprinted in* 1 AFFIRMATIVE ACTION COMPL. MAN. (BNA) 2:0018.

The OFCCP also notes whether the contractor over multiple years has repeatedly failed to meet annual placement-rate goals.[438]

For each goal missed, the CO reviews the contractor's narrative description of the good faith efforts made. The audit then attempts to identify the probable reason(s) why goals were not met, identifies the type of affirmative action that may correct the problem, and evaluates whether other AAP narrative and statistical commitments were fulfilled.[439]

If there is insufficient desk audit information to assess the adequacy of the contractor's good faith effort toward any particular goal, the CO lists additional information needed during the on-site review. This may include, for example, verifying that the contractor used affirmative action recruitment sources for openings. (This particularly is true where the contractor's failure to meet a particular goal appears to be due to few protected-group applicants.[440]) The regulations explicitly note:

> No contractor's compliance will be judged alone by whether it reaches its goals. The composition of the contractor's workforce (*i.e.*, employment of minorities or women at a percentage rate below, or above, the goal level) does not, by itself, serve as a basis to impose [ ] sanctions . . . . Each contractor's compliance with its affirmative action obligations will be determined by reviewing the nature and extent of the contractor's good faith affirmative action activities . . . and the appropriateness of those activities to identified equal employment opportunity problems. [A]n analysis of statistical data and other non-statistical information [that] would indicate whether employees and applicants are treated [in a nondiscriminatory manner will be completed in order to determine a contractor's compliance].[441]

e. Review, for Acceptability, of AAPs for Individuals With Disabilities and Veterans. As with the Executive Order AAP, the CO evaluates for acceptability, at the desk audit stage, the contractor's Rehabilitation Act and Veterans Act AAPs.[442] To be

---

[438]*Id.* § 2L01(a), *reprinted in* 1 AFFIRMATIVE ACTION COMPL. MAN. (BNA) 2:0018.

[439]*Id.* § 2L01(b), *reprinted in* 1 AFFIRMATIVE ACTION COMPL. MAN. (BNA) 2:0018.

[440]*Id.* § 2L02, *reprinted in* 1 AFFIRMATIVE ACTION COMPL. MAN. (BNA) 2:0018.

[441]41 C.F.R. § 60-2.35 (2005).

[442]FED. CONTRACT COMPL. MAN. § 2I00, *reprinted in* 1 AFFIRMATIVE ACTION COMPL. MAN. (BNA) 2:0015.

acceptable, these AAPs must address at least those items listed in the implementing regulations for the two statutes.[443]

5. Overview of Personnel Activity, EEO Trends, and Workforce Structure/Personnel Practices

a. *Summary of Personnel Activity.* During the desk audit, the CO prepares an overview, by EEO-1 category, of the contractor's personnel activity during the prior year.[444] For example, for each EEO-1 category, the CO charts out the number of male and female employees; the number of Caucasian, African-American, Hispanic, Asian/Pacific Islander, and Native American/Alaskan Native employees by gender; and the number of applicants, hires, promotions, and terminations in each of those racial and gender groups.

b. *EEO Trend Analysis.* The CO also prepares statistical and narrative summaries of trends in the contractor's workforce by EEO-1 categories. The current representation is compared with the contractor's EEO-1 profiles approximately five years earlier (to indicate long-term trends) and approximately one year earlier (to indicate short-term trends). The OFCCP notes the direction and magnitude of changes, for all races and both genders, in the total workforce and in particular EEO-1 categories.[445] The CO may perform separate analyses to determine the type of activity (e.g., promotions) that likely created any disparity.[446]

c. *Workforce Structure/Personnel Practices.* The CO prepares a narrative description of the contractor's organization, operations,

---

[443]*Id.* § 2I01, *reprinted in* 1 AFFIRMATIVE ACTION COMPL. MAN. (BNA) 2:0015; *see* 41 C.F.R. §§ 60-250.44(a)–(j), -741.44(a)–(j) (2005).

[444]FED. CONTRACT COMPL. MAN. § 2K00, *reprinted in* 1 AFFIRMATIVE ACTION COMPL. MAN. (BNA) 2:0017.

[445]*Id.* § 2K01(a), *reprinted in* 1 AFFIRMATIVE ACTION COMPL. MAN. (BNA) 2:0017. Contractors should be aware that major changes in the size of particular EEO-1 categories, with little or no corresponding personnel activity, will be viewed with suspicion. The CO investigates further to determine if such changes are due to the reclassification of jobs concentrated with minorities or women from one EEO-1 category to another. *Id.* § 2K01(b), *reprinted in* 1 AFFIRMATIVE ACTION COMPL. MAN. (BNA) 2:0017. Accordingly, if many changes are made, the contractor should note the justification for them in its AAP or a letter to the OFCCP accompanying the desk audit submission.

[446]*Id.* § 2K01(c), (d), *reprinted in* 1 AFFIRMATIVE ACTION COMPL. MAN. (BNA) 2:0017.

pay structure, and human resources policies, particularly those relating to selection and promotion.[447]

6. Preliminary Discrimination Analyses

a. General Considerations. The OFCCP follows principles derived from Title VII of the Civil Rights Act of 1964 (Title VII)[448] in conducting analyses of potential discrimination under the Executive Order.[449] Generally, the analyses are performed for women and for total minorities. However, if there appears to be a substantial disparity in the representation of a particular minority group, the CO may conduct separate discrimination analyses for that minority group as well as for total minorities.[450]

b. Review of the Organizational Profile or Workforce Analysis. The OFCCP conducts an overview of the organizational profile or workforce analysis. The CO looks for apparent disparities in the contractor's distribution of minorities and women by organizational unit (e.g., department) or by level of job (e.g., professional versus clerical workers). Flags for further investigation on site may include, for example, men supervising work units composed predominantly of women, or a concentration of the contractor's Hispanics in one department.[451]

Aspects of the OFCCP's review of the organizational profile or workforce analysis are set forth below.

(i.) Job area acceptance range analysis of underrepresentations and concentrations. The OFCCP looks for evidence of "concentrations" and "underrepresentations." "Concentrations" occur when minorities or women are represented in a particular "job area" of a contractor's workforce in numbers "substantially" greater than would be expected by their overall representation in the relevant

---

[447]*Id.* § 2K02, *reprinted in* 1 AFFIRMATIVE ACTION COMPL. MAN. (BNA) 2:0017.

[448]42 U.S.C. § 2000e et seq. (2000).

[449]FED. CONTRACT COMPL. MAN. § 2M00, *reprinted in* 1 AFFIRMATIVE ACTION COMPL. MAN. (BNA) 2:0018. For principles governing on-site investigation and resolution of discrimination issues, see Section VII.E *infra.*

[450]FED. CONTRACT COMPL. MAN. § 2M01, *reprinted in* 1 AFFIRMATIVE ACTION COMPL. MAN. (BNA) 2:0018. For a discussion of "substantial disparity," see Section III.B.3 *supra.*

[451]FED. CONTRACT COMPL. MAN. § 2N00, *reprinted in* AFFIRMATIVE ACTION COMPL. MAN. (BNA) 2:0019.

workforce "sector." "Underrepresentations," on the other hand, occur when minorities or women are represented in a particular "job area" in numbers "substantially" fewer than would be expected by their overall representation in the relevant workforce "sector."[452] For example, if minorities filled approximately 40 percent of the secretarial jobs in departments *A* and *B*, but only 5 percent of the secretarial jobs in department *C*, the OFCCP likely will want an explanation for the lower minority representation in department *C*.

The terms "job area" (referring to a subgroup), "workforce sector" (referring to the total group), and "substantially" greater (or fewer) have no fixed definition.[453] Consequently, the process for designating appropriate "workforce sectors" and "job areas" is ill defined, and the resulting statistical analyses often are flawed.

The CO may employ a statistical method known as the job area acceptance range (JAAR) to identify, for further on-site investigation, the particular job areas in which there is a concentration or underrepresentation of minorities or women, perhaps suggestive of discrimination.[454] The JAAR, based on the "80 percent" (four-fifths) rule, assumes that the percentage representation of minorities or women in a particular *job area* normally will fall in a range that is plus or minus 20 percent of that group's representation in the relevant *workforce sector*.[455]

To compute the JAAR for a particular workforce sector (e.g., the facility), the percentage of minorities (or women) in that sector is multiplied by 0.80 and 1.20 to determine the minority (or female) percentage representation range that the OFCCP generally will expect to see in job areas within that sector. For example, for a workforce sector composed of 50 percent minorities, the JAAR

---

[452]*Id.* § 2N02, *reprinted in* 1 AFFIRMATIVE ACTION COMPL. MAN. (BNA) 2:0019.

[453]The Compliance Manual gives the following examples: workforce as sector, departments as job area; workforce as sector, lines of progression as job area; department as sector, lines of progression within department as job area; department as sector, job title within department as job area; EEO category as sector, job classifications as job area; line of progression as sector, job title in line of progression as job area; and job title as sector, job title within department as job area. FED. CONTRACT COMPL. MAN. § 2N03(c), *reprinted in* 1 AFFIRMATIVE ACTION COMPL. MAN. (BNA) 2:0019–20.

[454]*Id.* § 2N03(e), (f), *reprinted in* 1 AFFIRMATIVE ACTION COMPL. MAN. (BNA) 2:0020.

[455]*Id.* § 2N03(f)(1), *reprinted in* 1 AFFIRMATIVE ACTION COMPL. MAN. (BNA) 2:0020.

would be calculated by multiplying 50 percent by both 0.80 (to produce a lower range of 40 percent) and 1.20 (to produce an upper range of 60 percent). The minority (or female) percentage in each job area (e.g., department) within the workforce sector then is compared to the range of 40 percent to 60 percent. If the percentage of minorities (or women) in the job area falls below the JAAR, the area is considered underrepresented; if it exceeds the range, the job area is considered concentrated.[456] This finding is not dispositive; it simply flags the area for further examination during the on-site review. At that time, for example, the OFCCP may question whether similar qualifications applied to openings in the underrepresented and concentrated job areas and whether there was an employment policy or system in effect that created or maintained such disparity.[457]

(ii.) Comparison of recent personnel activity data with the organizational profile or workforce analysis. The CO compares the organizational profile or workforce analysis with the analysis of more recent hires, promotions, and terminations. High priorities for on-site scrutiny include areas in which relatively few minorities or women are employed and relatively few been hired and promoted during the past two years.[458]

   c. Audit of Impact Ratio Analyses (IRAs) of Personnel Activity. The CO also performs impact ratio analyses[459] of selection rates (i.e., hiring, promotion, transfer, and termination rates) by job group to identify personnel activity that should be investigated in more detail on site. Generally, the CO flags for investigation on site those

---

[456]*Id.* § 2N03(f)(2), (3), *reprinted in* 1 AFFIRMATIVE ACTION COMPL. MAN. (BNA) 2:0020.

[457]Ultimately, the JAAR normally has little probative value because it compares the composition of jobs that involve different skills and qualifications. *See* Wards Cove Packing Co. v. Atonio, 490 U.S. 642, 650, 49 FEP 1519 (1989) (declaring the respondents' use of statistics to be defective). *See generally* Chapter 34 (Statistical and Other Expert Proof).

[458]FED. CONTRACT COMPL. MAN. § 2N03(g), *reprinted in* 1 AFFIRMATIVE ACTION COMPL. MAN. (BNA) 2:0020.

[459]Instructions for calculating IRAs are set forth in Section III.B.5 *supra.* In brief, for positive personnel actions, such as hires or promotions, the IRA is calculated by dividing the minority or female rate by the rate for others. The IRA for negative personnel actions, such as terminations, is calculated by dividing the rate for others by the minority or female rate. FED. CONTRACT COMPL. MAN. § 2001, *reprinted in* 1 AFFIRMATIVE ACTION COMPL. MAN. (BNA) 2:0021.

hiring, promotion, and transfer activities yielding IRAs for minorities or women that are less than 80 percent (or two standard deviations negative).[460]

The CO decides what information is needed during the on-site review to determine whether the facially troublesome IRAs in fact represent discrimination.[461] Although contractors submit selection rates by job group, not job title, the CO may request, of contractors with more than 100 employees, the relevant adverse impact determinations for each job title within each job group having an adverse IRA.[462] The CO also may request information about the contractor's selection process. This will include the contractor's description of: (1) the steps in the selection process; (2) the decision makers for each step; (3) the criteria used; (4) how the criteria are applied; and (5) what records are maintained. The CO typically attempts to corroborate the contractor's statements through document reviews, applicant or employee interviews, and, if possible, observation of the process by which applicants are screened and selected.[463]

If the contractor has not maintained detailed records so that the job titles causing the adverse rate within the job group can be identified, the OFCCP may cite the contractor for a violation.[464] If the minority group or gender, for which the IRA is adverse, also is underutilized for that job group, the consequences may be substantive as well: the OFCCP may draw an inference of adverse impact from the contractor's failure to maintain, by job title, the required data.[465] Even in these circumstances, however, the adverse inference is only a preliminary indicator of potential discrimination; "[o]nly further investigation onsite can determine whether discrimination has occurred."[466]

---

[460]*Id.* § 2000, *reprinted in* 1 AFFIRMATIVE ACTION COMPL. MAN. (BNA) 2:0020–21.

[461]*Id.* § 2004, *reprinted in* 1 AFFIRMATIVE ACTION COMPL. MAN. (BNA) 2:0021.

[462]*Id.* § 2004(a)(3), *reprinted in* 1 AFFIRMATIVE ACTION COMPL. MAN. (BNA) 2:0021–22.

[463]*Id.* § 2004(b), *reprinted in* 1 AFFIRMATIVE ACTION COMPL. MAN. (BNA) 2:0022.

[464]*See* 41 C.F.R. §§ 60-3.4, -3.15 (2005) (requiring maintenance of data by job title).

[465]*Id.* § 60-3.4(D); FED. CONTRACT COMPL. MAN. § 3K03(a), *reprinted in* 1 AFFIRMATIVE ACTION COMPL. MAN. (BNA) 3:0013.

[466]FED. CONTRACT COMPL. MAN. § 2OO3, *reprinted in* 1 AFFIRMATIVE ACTION COMPL. MAN. (BNA) 2:0021.

Where any of the contractor's IRAs show adverse impact for a gender or minority group, the contractor is required to analyze the individual components of the selection process for adverse impact.[467] Therefore, in a multistep or multicriterion selection process with overall adverse impact, the CO requests the contractor's records showing at what step (e.g., written test, oral interview, background check) or by what criterion (e.g., degree requirement) minorities and women are disproportionately screened out.[468]

d. Compensation Analyses. In reviewing the contractor's workforce analysis for potentially discriminatory patterns, the CO is attentive to disparities between the compensation of minorities and women in underrepresented areas as compared to concentrated areas.[469] Although this apples-to-oranges comparison may yield results that are not statistically meaningful, the CO flags perceived problems for further investigation on site.[470]

More meaningfully, the CO identifies during the desk audit those job families or job titles that reflect significant negative results for minorities or women and examines on site the reasons for specific pay decisions.[471] The contractor should be prepared to present an explanation for individual compensation rates where a multiple regression analysis reflects significant negative results for minorities or women.[472]

e. Summary of Potential Discrimination Problems and On-Site Investigative Plan. At the end of the desk audit, the CO summarizes on the OFCCP's Standard Compliance Review Report (SCRR) form each potential discrimination problem that has been identified during the desk audit, and the corresponding on-site investigative plan. The plan typically lists specific documents and data the CO will review and individuals the CO will interview.[473]

---

[467]41 C.F.R. §§ 60-3.4(C), -3.15(A)(2) (2005).
[468]FED. CONTRACT COMPL. MAN. § 2O04(c)(1), *reprinted in* 1 AFFIRMATIVE ACTION COMPL. MAN. (BNA) 2:0022.
[469]*Id.* § 2P00, *reprinted in* 1 AFFIRMATIVE ACTION COMPL. MAN. (BNA) 2:0022.
[470]*Id.* § 2P01, *reprinted in* 1 AFFIRMATIVE ACTION COMPL. MAN. (BNA) 2:0022.
[471]*Id.* § 2P02, *reprinted in* 1 AFFIRMATIVE ACTION COMPL. MAN. (BNA) 2:0022.
[472]For suggested methods of analysis, see Section VII.C.10 *supra.*
[473]FED. CONTRACT COMPL. MAN. § 2Q, *reprinted in* 1 AFFIRMATIVE ACTION COMPL. MAN. (BNA) 2:0022.

If potential problems have not been identified during the desk audit, the OFCCP may issue a compliance letter or may continue with the on-site phase of the review; some contractor AAP commitments cannot be evaluated without an on-site inspection, including corroborating interviews.[474]

E. The On-Site Review

1. Scope

In general, the on-site review[475] will include investigation of findings made during the desk audit; evaluation of the contractor's implementation of AAP commitments; and review of its compliance with (1) regulatory obligations, such as the guidelines on religion, national origin, and sex discrimination; (2) affirmative action and nondiscrimination requirements covering individuals with disabilities and veterans; and (3) miscellaneous technical requirements, including lawful collection and retention of the contractor's I-9 forms.[476]

2. Notice of the On-Site Review

The Compliance Manual requires the CO to establish the date and time of the on-site review through a telephone conference with the contractor's designated representative.[477] During this contact, the CO typically requests that the contractor make available, at the beginning of the on-site review, additional required information.[478]

---

[474]*Id.* § 2R00, *reprinted in* 1 AFFIRMATIVE ACTION COMPL. MAN. (BNA) 2:0023.

[475]Although the OFCCP cannot come to the contractor's facility without its consent, the agency is authorized to seek an injunction to enforce its right of access either in federal district court or in an administrative proceeding. 41 C.F.R. § 60-1.26(b), (c) (2005) (the OFCCP may refer the matter to the Solicitor of Labor with a recommendation to initiate administrative proceedings or refer the matter to the Attorney General, who may bring a civil action in an appropriate district court). The Fifth Circuit has held that the inspection provision does not run afoul of the Fourth Amendment because the regulations provide the safeguard of an adversarial hearing in federal court before an inspection can be mandated. United States v. Mississippi Power & Light Co., 638 F.2d 899, 907, 25 FEP 250 (5th Cir. 1981).

[476]FED. CONTRACT COMPL. MAN. §§ 2R01, 2R03, 2R06(c), *reprinted in* 1 AFFIRMATIVE ACTION COMPL. MAN. (BNA) 2:0023, 2:0024.

[477]*Id.* § 2S, *reprinted in* 1 AFFIRMATIVE ACTION COMPL. MAN. (BNA) 2:0024.

[478]*Id.* § 2S00, *reprinted in* 1 AFFIRMATIVE ACTION COMPL. MAN. (BNA) 2:0024.

At this time, the CO generally will identify, if requested, the potential problems identified and the CO's plan for reviewing records and conducting interviews during the on-site review.

The CO then sends an on-site confirmation letter specifying the date and time the review will commence. The letter provides the required three-day notice of I-9 form inspection.[479] It also typically lists materials that the contractor should make available at the start of the on-site review. This list may include materials related to specific areas of potential discrimination, documents required but not included in the original submission, I-9 forms, the VETS-100 Report, and a list of the names of applicants and employees who have responded to the contractor's invitation to self-identify (or who otherwise have become known to the contractor) as individuals with disabilities or covered veterans.[480] The CO is required to send the confirmation letter by certified mail, return receipt requested, sufficiently in advance of the on-site date to ensure that the letter arrives at least three days before the on-site review commences.[481]

3. Components of the On-Site Review

The on-site phase typically includes the activities described below.

a. Entrance Conference. The entrance conference generally is the first item of business. The OFCCP prefers to commence the on-site review with a get-acquainted meeting with the highest executive, generally the chief executive officer.[482] During this initial conference, the OFCCP typically will attempt to:

(1) Arrange access to data, employees (including managers), and facilities (both for a tour and to obtain a place to work);

---

[479]*Id.* § 2S01, *reprinted in* 1 AFFIRMATIVE ACTION COMPL. MAN. (BNA) 2:0024–25.

[480]*Id.* § 2S01(a), *reprinted in* 1 AFFIRMATIVE ACTION COMPL. MAN. (BNA) 2:0024–25.

[481]*Id.* § 2S01(b), *reprinted in* 1 AFFIRMATIVE ACTION COMPL. MAN. (BNA) 2:0025.

[482]In many reviews, an informal meeting with knowledgeable human resources managers is held weeks before the entrance conference to gather additional information about the contractor's organization, policies, and records.

(2) Form an impression of the executive's understanding of and attitude toward equal employment opportunity and affirmative action, and familiarity with and involvement in the organization's AAP; and

(3) Determine the executive's view of the role the organization's affirmative action manager should and does play. During this interview, the OFCCP is interested in an explanation of the corporate organizational structure (e.g., headquarters, subsidiaries) and recent and anticipated changes therein.

b. Human Resources Meeting. The OFCCP often discusses with the persons responsible for an organization's affirmative action efforts the specific deficiencies in the AAP uncovered during the desk audit and the OFCCP's desire to investigate potential discrimination issues. The OFCCP at this meeting typically attempts to:

(1) Obtain a description (sometimes a step-by-step walk-through) of how recruitment, hires, transfers, promotions, succession planning, training, compensation decisions, and terminations occur;

(2) Determine the existence of, and obtain access to, personnel files, human resources records, pay and benefits records, and additional information needed for the review;

(3) Request specific information needed to respond to issues raised during the desk audit;

(4) Review areas where good faith efforts were perceived to be lacking, or areas where discrimination seems to have occurred, and ask the representative to explain what might have caused them;

(5) Identify personnel processes that are likely impediments to equal employment opportunity and affirmative action;

(6) Identify the criteria used in, and the decision makers responsible for, specific personnel decisions that particularly appear to be at issue;

(7) Determine where a specific item of information can be found in the contractor's records;

(8) Arrange to interview other supervisors and employees;

(9) Schedule a tour of the facility;

(10) Arrange for a private place to work and for necessary logistical support (e.g., access to a calculator and telephone—not typing or photocopying);

(11) Form an impression of the human resources representative's role in and attitude toward the facility's affirmative action status and programs; and

(12) Learn about, and evaluate, the contractor's internal audit and reporting systems for EEO and affirmative action matters. For example, the CO may ask whether the contractor prepares written reports; if so, how often; who prepares and who reads them; and what else, if anything, the contractor does with them.

c. Facility Tour. The next stage of the on-site investigation is the tour of the facility. If the OFCCP has identified work units in which minorities or women are concentrated, the agency usually will include these areas as part of the tour. The work areas with concentrations of protected-group members will be compared with those where protected groups are underrepresented. If the working conditions in concentrated areas are less desirable than those in underrepresented areas, the OFCCP may attempt to use this as evidence of discrimination against protected-group members. Some compliance officers conduct informal interviews with employees as they pass through work areas during the tour.[483]

During this walk-through, the OFCCP confirms that the following have been posted: the federal EEOC/OFCCP poster, the contractor's policy statements, the invitations for self-identification of disability status, and the notice of the times and places where the AAPs for veterans and individuals with disabilities can be reviewed.[484] The agency is alert during the tour for signs of sexual, racial, or other unlawful harassment.[485] The CO also examines whether the facility is accessible to individuals with disabilities, including those in wheelchairs (or others with mobility impairments) and those with hearing, sight, and other disabilities.[486]

---

[483]FED. CONTRACT COMPL. MAN. §§ 3D02, 3E04, *reprinted in* 1 AFFIRMATIVE ACTION COMPL. MAN. (BNA) 3:0002, 3:0003.

[484]*Id.* § 3D02, *reprinted in* 1 AFFIRMATIVE ACTION COMPL. MAN. (BNA) 3:0002.

[485]*Id.* § 3G01(h)(3), *reprinted in* 1 AFFIRMATIVE ACTION COMPL. MAN. (BNA) 3:0005.

[486]*Id.* § 3E04, *reprinted in* 1 AFFIRMATIVE ACTION COMPL. MAN. (BNA) 3:0003.

d. Investigation of Potential Discrimination. The fourth stage of the on-site review is the investigation of potential discrimination. This usually is the major focus of the on-site review and takes the most time. During this stage, the OFCCP conducts interviews and examines documents such as personnel records.

e. Management Interviews. The OFCCP often is most interested in speaking with supervisors in work units that have (1) concentrations;[487] (2) underrepresentations;[488] (3) incumbency of minorities or women below availability;[489] and/or (4) apparent adverse impact against minority groups or women in hiring and/or promotion.[490]

The contractor is entitled to be represented during interviews of supervisors, so long as the interviewee is speaking for management and not as a potential discriminatee.[491]

The CO often asks interviewees to read, sign, and date the CO's interview notes and attest that they are accurate.[492] Where such a request is made, the CO will permit the interviewee to take the statement out of the interview room, take whatever time is needed to consider it and ensure its accuracy, and to make appropriate changes and additions before signing. No witness can be forced to sign a statement.

f. Employee Interviews. The OFCCP also interviews nonsupervisory employees. The OFCCP's Compliance Manual does not give a contractor a right to be present at interviews of employees who

---

[487]*See* Section VII.D.6.b.(i) *supra.* Concentration refers to a substantially higher percentage representation of a protected group in a particular department than in the contractor's workforce as a whole. Conversely, underrepresentation typically reflects a substantially lower percentage representation of a protected group in a particular department than in the contractor's workforce as a whole.

[488]*Id.*

[489]*See* Section III.B.3.d *supra.* Underutilization means that the percentage representation of a protected group in a job group is lower than the protected group's percentage availability for such jobs.

[490]*See* Section III.B.5 *supra.*

[491]FED. CONTRACT COMPL. MAN. § 3D03(c), *reprinted in* 1 AFFIRMATIVE ACTION COMPL. MAN. (BNA) 3:0002.

[492]*Id.* § 3D03(d), *reprinted in* 1 AFFIRMATIVE ACTION COMPL. MAN. (BNA) 3:0002.

do not have supervisory or policymaking authority, unless the employee requests such representative's presence.[493]

During these employee interviews, the OFCCP often attempts to:

(1) Verify the employee's background and qualifications;

(2) Determine the employee's views of how personnel practices work, what the contractor's policies are, and how and why individual decisions were made (e.g., training and mentoring opportunities);

(3) Verify the contractor's version of some decision or event in which the employee was involved;

(4) Determine what the employee knows about the contractor's AAP;

(5) Ascertain the employee's view of the contractor's AAP commitment and performance;

(6) Learn about the duties of a given job and ascertain what qualifications actually are needed for competent performance;

(7) Inquire whether the employee or identifiable others have been victims of discrimination or harassment; and

(8) Assess the employee's view of his or her future opportunities with the contractor.

The OFCCP is likely to interview those who have information concerning some potential discrimination issue that the OFCCP is exploring or who appear to be members of potential affected classes. In particular, the OFCCP may want to interview minorities and women who have current discrimination or harassment complaints or who during the review approach the OFCCP with a complaint.

g. Hiring/Recruiting/Compensation Manager Interview. The OFCCP also interviews those responsible for recruitment, selection, compensation, and benefits practices in order to:

(1) Obtain descriptions of recruiting, hiring, transfer, promotion, training, compensation, and termination processes;

---

[493]FED. CONTRACT COMPL. MAN. §§ 5073, 6067(d), *reprinted in* 1 AFFIRMATIVE ACTION COMPL. MAN. (BNA) 5:0006, 6:0005(d).

(2) Get copies of policies and procedures;

(3) Obtain job descriptions;

(4) Determine criteria for selecting, promoting, and terminating employees;

(5) Ascertain how the contractor sets starting-pay levels and determines raises; and

(6) Determine whether the human resources staff is familiar with and has specific responsibilities under the AAP.[494]

h. Document Review. The OFCCP has a broad right to review records—and typically exercises it—during an on-site review. The regulations require the contractor to permit the OFCCP access to its premises, books, records (including computerized records),[495] accounts, and other material, "as may be relevant to the matter under investigation and pertinent to compliance with the Order."[496] Denial of access is cause for, and likely to lead to, initiation of an enforcement proceeding.[497]

Documents typically inspected include recruitment activity records; personnel activity logs for applicant flow, new hires, promotions, transfers, and terminations; procedures; policy statements; job advertisements and requisitions; position descriptions; training activity records; compensation records; benefits policies and records; application forms; personnel files of current employees; purchase orders and subcontracts; tests; lists of persons tested; adverse impact records on tests; test validation studies; a termination roster designating name, race, and gender, and the reasons for termination; personnel files of terminated employees; succession plans; and lists of "high potential" employees. The OFCCP also looks for written proof of good faith efforts, action plan achievement, and other compliance.

---

[494]FED. CONTRACT COMPL. MAN. § 2P03, *reprinted in* 1 AFFIRMATIVE ACTION COMPL. MAN. (BNA) 2:0022.

[495]The regulation does not require a contractor to reprogram its computers in order to generate responsive data to an OFCCP request; rather, it simply requires access to existing records and data in computerized forms. 62 Fed. Reg. at 44,186 (Aug. 19, 1997).

[496]41 C.F.R. § 60-1.43 (2005).

[497]*Id.* § 60-1.26(a). Interference with an investigation also may be a basis for the imposition of sanctions. *Id.* § 60-1.32.

A contractor may refuse to photocopy documents, but the CO's likely response is to offer to remove the documents from the contractor's premises to allow photocopying by the OFCCP, or to subpoena them. Once a document is in the OFCCP's files, the public may attempt to obtain it under the Freedom of Information Act.[498] Thus, contractors often attempt to reach agreement with the OFCCP to keep sensitive records at the contractor's premises.

i. Predetermination Notice and Response. If the OFCCP finds a pattern or practice of discrimination,[499] its Compliance Manual specifies that it will issue a predetermination notice before the evaluation is concluded, identifying the alleged discrimination, the employment action(s) giving rise to the allegation, whether the agency is proceeding on a disparate treatment and/or adverse impact theory, and the deadline for the contractor's response.[500] In practice, however, the OFCCP has abandoned this step but generally gives the contractor informally the same type of information before an official notice of violations is issued.

At the conclusion of the evaluation (generally, but not always, before the exit conference), the OFCCP issues a notice of violations listing all unrebutted pattern-or-practice issues, individual discrimination findings, and any other deficiencies identified during the evaluation.[501]

j. Exit Conference. The final stage of the on-site review is the exit conference. Here the OFCCP brings to the contractor's attention problems that have been identified in a notice of violations and requests that the contractor resolve them.[502] If the government finds any victims of discrimination, it will require the contractor to make each victim whole, including back pay and benefits, and to place the victim in the job from which he or she was discriminatorily denied placement. A date for the contractor's response and

---

[498]*See* Section IX *infra.*

[499]For a discussion of discrimination investigations, findings, and resolution, see Sections VII.E.4 and VII.E.5 *infra.*

[500]FED. CONTRACT COMPL. MAN. §§ 3P01, 3P02, *reprinted in* 1 AFFIRMATIVE ACTION COMPL. MAN. (BNA) 3:0019.

[501]*Id.* § 3P04(b), *reprinted in* 1 AFFIRMATIVE ACTION COMPL. MAN. (BNA) 3:0020.

[502]*Id.* § 3S, *reprinted in* 1 AFFIRMATIVE ACTION COMPL. MAN. (BNA) 3:0021. For a description of the notice of violations and enforcement process, see Sections VII.E.5 and VIII *infra.*

subsequent "conciliation" meetings may be scheduled at this time. If the agency finds no violations, it will so inform the contractor.

4. On-Site Investigation of Potential Discrimination

a. Employment Discrimination Theories. The OFCCP assesses whether a contractor has engaged in discrimination based upon standards and precedents established under Title VII of the Civil Rights Act of 1964.[503] "Individual" discrimination cases are based upon one or more events adversely affecting an identified individual. The most common way the OFCCP develops an individual case is by reconstructing a selection or other personnel decision and making a one-on-one comparison of the alleged victim against a better-treated comparator. In a promotion case, for example, the alleged discriminatee's qualifications and other merits are compared to those of the successful candidate. The agency refers to this as "cohort analysis."[504]

"Pattern-or-practice" cases examine how members of a minority group or women, as a group, are affected by the contractor's policies and practices. A pattern-or-practice case usually is developed through the use of statistics to show the "impact" of the contractor's employment policies or practices on women or members of a minority group.[505]

If the agency has reason to believe a contractor may have engaged in either individual or pattern-or-practice discrimination, the CO examines statistical and other relevant information for a two-year period preceding the date the contractor received the scheduling letter.[506]

b. Investigation of Alleged Individual Discrimination. Most selection decisions involve several candidates competing for a

---

[503]42 U.S.C. §§ 2000e–2000e-17 (2000). The standards for determining discrimination under the Rehabilitation Act are those applied under Title I of the Americans with Disabilities Act, 42 U.S.C. §§ 12111–12117, 12201–12204, 12210. FED. CONTRACT COMPL. MAN. § 1E, reprinted in 1 AFFIRMATIVE ACTION COMPL. MAN. (BNA) 101.

[504]FED. CONTRACT COMPL. MAN. § 3K05(a), reprinted in 1 AFFIRMATIVE ACTION COMPL. MAN. (BNA) 3:0013–14.

[505]Id. § 3K05(b), reprinted in 1 AFFIRMATIVE ACTION COMPL. MAN. (BNA) 3:0014.

[506]Id. § 2C03(b), reprinted in 1 AFFIRMATIVE ACTION COMPL. MAN. (BNA) 2:0003.

particular job opening and a comparison of their relative qualifications to determine who is the best qualified. Therefore, in investigating individual discrimination, the CO attempts to determine (1) the minimum objective criteria a person must meet to be considered and (2) what factors are most important in choosing among those who meet the minimum qualifications.[507]

To evaluate instances of potential individual disparate treatment, the CO usually obtains the applications of the minority-group members (or women) rejected and those of the persons selected. From those records, the following information is noted: (1) the date each minority (or woman) applied; (2) the date each non-minority (or male) was selected; and (3) each person's relative qualifications, based on the contractor's objective criteria. This information allows the CO to make a preliminary assessment of whether each minority or woman rejected was at least as well qualified as the person selected on the basis of objective qualifications. The CO then asks the contractor the reason the non-minority (or male) was selected and leaves it to the contractor to raise any subjective elements in response. The OFCCP ultimately determines whether the contractor's response is a pretext for discrimination (i.e., is not true, and the real reason is discrimination).[508]

In a small number of cases, the selection criteria have a foreseeable adverse impact on a minority group or women based on societal data (e.g., minimum height requirements), but there is no statistically significant adverse impact at the instant contractor because the criteria were applied to very few individuals. In such cases, the OFCCP proceeds with an "individual [adverse] impact" case and seeks relief for the minorities or women involved, unless

---

[507]*Id.* § 3L01, *reprinted in* 1 AFFIRMATIVE ACTION COMPL. MAN. (BNA) 3:0014.

[508]*Id.* § 3L03, *reprinted in* 1 AFFIRMATIVE ACTION COMPL. MAN. (BNA) 3:0014–15. The Compliance Manual refers only to the first prong, whether the reason advanced by the contractor is true. In view of the OFCCP's pledge to apply Title VII principles, a contractor may argue that the OFCCP should be required to find not only that the contractor's proffered reason was false, but also that discrimination was the reason. *See* St. Mary's Honor Ctr. v. Hicks, 509 U.S. 502, 512 n.4, 62 FEP 96 (1993) (burden is on plaintiff to prove "*both* that the reason [for the adverse action] was false, *and* that discrimination was the real reason") (emphasis in original). *But see* Reeves v. Sanderson Plumbing Prod., Inc., 530 U.S. 133, 147–48, 82 FEP 1748 (2000) (holding that in appropriate circumstances, "it is permissible for the trier of fact to infer the ultimate fact of discrimination from the falsity of the employer's explanation"). *See generally* Chapter 2 (Disparate Treatment).

the contractor can establish evidence of job relatedness and consistency with business necessity.[509]

The OFCCP gives contractors initial notice of claimed individual discrimination allegations in a notice of violations.[510]

 c. Investigation of Alleged Pattern-or-Practice of Discrimination. The focus of the pattern-or-practice investigation is on whether the disparities being investigated were caused by legitimate factors or by discrimination.[511] The OFCCP employs both adverse impact and disparate treatment analysis in pattern-or-practice cases.

The CO's first objective in any pattern-or-practice case is to identify all the steps and decision points involved in getting the job or opportunity under investigation. If the process involves a series of "pass/fail points," the CO evaluates each one to determine whether members of a minority group (or women) are disproportionately eliminated at that point.

Where a contractor does not eliminate candidates at distinct steps, but instead makes a final decision based upon aggregate performance during the selection process, the process as a whole is evaluated. The contractor is asked to describe the importance of each step (or factor) in the selection decision. If data are available on how candidates fare as to each step (or factor), the CO may weight the analysis in an attempt to determine the particular factor that disproportionately eliminated members of a minority group (or women).[512]

---

[509]FED. CONTRACT COMPL. MAN. § 3L02, *reprinted in* 1 AFFIRMATIVE ACTION COMPL. MAN. (BNA) 3:0014. The Compliance Manual offers the following "definition" of "business necessity":

 An [*sic*] defense available when the employer has a criterion for selection that is facially neutral but which excludes members of one sex, race, national origin or religious group at a substantially higher rate than members of other groups (thus creating adverse impact). The employer must prove that its requirement having the adverse impact is job-related and consistent with business necessity. See Manual Section 7E08.

Id. § 1B, *reprinted in* 1 AFFIRMATIVE ACTION COMPL. MAN. (BNA) at 1:0002. The manual does not define "job-related." *See generally* Chapter 3 (Adverse Impact).

[510]FED. CONTRACT COMPL. MAN. § 3K05(a), *reprinted in* 1 AFFIRMATIVE ACTION COMPL. MAN. (BNA) 3:0013–14.

[511]*Id.* § 3M00(a), *reprinted in* 1 AFFIRMATIVE ACTION COMPL. MAN. (BNA) 3:0015.

[512]*Id.* § 3M01(b), *reprinted in* 1 AFFIRMATIVE ACTION COMPL. MAN. (BNA) 3:0016.

If the contractor failed to maintain adequate data to ascertain at which step and by which criterion members of a minority group or women were disproportionately screened out, the CO cites the contractor for a recordkeeping violation.[513] The substantive discrimination evaluation then is performed on the "bottom line" effect of the entire selection process.[514]

The second step in the investigation of pattern-or-practice discrimination involves analysis of the contractor's selection criteria. The CO distinguishes between objective and subjective selection criteria, and then analyzes the objective criteria first to determine that they were, in fact, used to make selections and were required both of members of a minority group (or women) and of others.[515] The CO examines the personnel files of the persons selected and notes whether they satisfied each criterion. When those selected do not satisfy a particular criterion, the CO discounts the employer's statement that the criterion actually formed the basis for the selection decision. If the contractor used the criteria in a nonuniform manner (i.e., applied different standards to minorities (or women)), the CO may infer disparate treatment.[516]

(i). Adverse impact analysis. Adverse impact analysis of a pattern-or-practice case consists of two steps: "(1) calculating the adverse impact of the criterion and the statistical significance of that impact; and (2) determining whether the contractor can justify use of the criterion based on job relatedness or business necessity."[517] The OFCCP does not require evidence of discriminatory intent—such as discriminatory remarks or other anecdotal proof.

The adverse impact calculation compares a pass or success rate for each gender and racial/ethnic group. The difference in pass

---

[513]*Id.* § 3M01(d), *reprinted in* 1 Affirmative Action Compl. Man. (BNA) 3:0015; *see* 41 C.F.R. pt. 60-3; Wards Cove Packing Co. v. Atonio, 490 U.S. 642, 658 & n.10, 49 FEP 1519 (1989) (noting the Uniform Guidelines' recordkeeping provisions).

[514]Fed. Contract Compl. Man. § 3M01(d), *reprinted in* 1 Affirmative Action Compl. Man. (BNA) 3:0015.

[515]*Id.* § 3M02, *reprinted in* 1 Affirmative Action Compl. Man. (BNA) 3:0016.

[516]*Id.* § 3N01, *reprinted in* 1 Affirmative Action Compl. Man. (BNA) 3:0016.

[517]*Id.* § 3N02, *reprinted in* 1 Affirmative Action Compl. Man. (BNA) 3:0017. Elsewhere the Compliance Manual uses the phrase "job related and necessary to the safe and efficient operation of [the] business." *Id.* § 7E08, *reprinted in* 2 Affirmative Action Compl. Man. (BNA) 7:0007. The latter is similar to the phrase used in the Civil Rights Act of 1991. *See generally* Chapter 3 (Adverse Impact).

rates then is tested for adverse impact and statistical significance.[518] This may involve the use of a weighted calculation, known as multiple regression, to separate out which criterion is (or which criteria are) causing the adverse impact. If adverse impact is shown, the CO requests the contractor to respond with evidence showing the criterion or criteria to be job-related and consistent with business necessity.[519] If the contractor accomplishes this, the CO considers whether there are alternative selection procedures with less adverse impact.[520] If the CO cannot establish the latter, the matter is dropped.

(ii.) Disparate treatment analysis. A disparate treatment analysis of a pattern-or-practice case is different. The OFCCP works only with the pool of persons who met the criteria, comparing the selection rate for qualified minorities (or women) with the selection rate for qualified non-minorities (or men). The difference in the rates then is tested for statistical significance. In forming the pool of qualified individuals, the CO considers the contractor's stated minimum objective criteria. However, if the CO determines that the contractor did not apply a stated criterion, the CO forms the pool based on the criteria actually used.[521]

If the difference in selection rates among qualified minorities (or women) and others is greater than would be expected by chance (i.e., statistically significant), then the CO presumes that the difference is due to discrimination. In the disparate treatment case, the CO seeks additional evidence, including biased remarks by decision makers, anecdotal comparative evidence of differences in

---

[518]FED. CONTRACT COMPL. MAN. § 3N02(a), *reprinted in* 1 AFFIRMATIVE ACTION COMPL. MAN. (BNA) 3:0017. The term "statistical significance" relates to the likelihood that a result occurred by chance. If this likelihood is 5% (0.05) or less (i.e., the result would occur by chance only 5% of the time or less), then the result normally is considered statistically significant; an assumption then is made that some factor such as discrimination must have caused the result. The 5% level is approximately equal to 2.00 standard deviations. The greater the number of standard deviations, the less likely the result could have occurred by chance. *Id.* § 3K00(e), *reprinted in* 1 AFFIRMATIVE ACTION COMPL. MAN. (BNA) 3:0012. *See generally* Chapters 3 (Adverse Impact), 4 (Application of Adverse Impact to Employment Decisions), and 34 (Statistical and Other Expert Proof).

[519]FED. CONTRACT COMPL. MAN. § 3N02(c), *reprinted in* 1 AFFIRMATIVE ACTION COMPL. MAN. (BNA) 3:0017.

[520]*Id.* § 3N02(d), *reprinted in* 1 AFFIRMATIVE ACTION COMPL. MAN. (BNA) 3:0017.

[521]*Id.* § 3N03(a), (b), *reprinted in* 1 AFFIRMATIVE ACTION COMPL. MAN. (BNA) 3:0017.

treatment of similarly situated individuals, and a longstanding history of disparate results, to support a finding of intentional discrimination. The CO then documents the supporting evidence and requests the contractor's explanation of the difference in selection rates. The contractor typically will defend its position by showing that it hired the most qualified individual.[522]

(iii.) Analysis of subjective criteria/processes. Subjective selection criteria and processes are subject to both disparate treatment and adverse impact analysis.[523] The CO first determines whether the stated subjective criteria actually are being used and then whether they are being applied in a uniform manner to both minorities (or women) and others. If not, a disparate treatment finding may result; if so, the CO seeks to establish a statistical adverse impact case.[524]

In evaluating whether the subjective criteria are applied lawfully, the CO looks for specific safeguards the contractor has instituted to avoid inconsistent application of the selection criteria. For example, the CO will examine whether the contractor used predetermined, consistent interview questions. Other factors considered in evaluating subjective criteria are the existence of guidelines, documentation procedures, decision-making review processes, and methods of ensuring that decision makers know the jobs' requirements and the candidates' qualifications to perform them.[525] If the process has relatively few safeguards, the CO may seek to establish disparate treatment by collecting nonstatistical evidence of discriminatory intent. Where there are many safeguards and the system is well documented, but minorities (or women) still are selected at a statistically significant lower rate, the CO may allege adverse impact.[526]

---

[522]The contractor may wish to attack the OFCCP's findings on other grounds as well, for example, by disputing the relevance of the CO's statistical analysis and/or perhaps by demonstrating that in each case the persons hired had superior qualifications to the candidate selected. FED. CONTRACT COMPL. MAN. § 3N03(c)–(f), *reprinted in* 1 AFFIRMATIVE ACTION COMPL. MAN. (BNA) 3:0017–18.

[523]*See* Watson v. Fort Worth Bank & Trust Co., 487 U.S. 977, 990–91, 47 FEP 102 (1988). *See generally* Chapter 4 (Application of Adverse Impact to Employment Decisions).

[524]FED. CONTRACT COMPL. MAN. § 3001, *reprinted in* 1 AFFIRMATIVE ACTION COMPL. MAN. (BNA) 3:0018.

[525]*Id.* § 3004, *reprinted in* 1 AFFIRMATIVE ACTION COMPL. MAN. (BNA) 3:0018.

[526]*Id.* § 3005, *reprinted in* 1 AFFIRMATIVE ACTION COMPL. MAN. (BNA) 3:0018–19.

(iv.) Predetermination notices. If the OFCCP finds a pattern or practice of discrimination, the Compliance Manual states that it will issue a predetermination notice.[527] Although the OFCCP generally has abandoned this in practice, most OFCCP offices still provide an equivalent preliminary notice describing the alleged pattern or practice by identifying the class, the employment action giving rise to the allegation, and the basis for the liability determination (i.e., disparate treatment or adverse impact). The notice typically offers the contractor the opportunity to respond in writing by a given date.[528]

The contractor normally should respond in a timely fashion to the notice, as it becomes increasingly difficult to persuade the OFCCP of errors in its approach as the formality of proceedings increases. If, however, there is no response, the CO issues a notice of violations, citing the contractor's failure to rebut the pattern-or-practice allegation and proposing a remedy. The notice of violations also addresses any affirmative action deficiencies or individual discrimination discovered in the evaluation and describes proposed corrective action.[529] The notice of violations is discussed more extensively below.

d. The Contractor's Response to Discrimination Findings. The contractor should prepare a comprehensive brief in response to any discrimination allegation, setting forth the relevant facts and applicable legal principles. Legal authorities may include the regulations, OFCCP case law and administrative decisions, and case law under Title VII and other analogous statutes. To the extent that facts are in dispute, documentary evidence from business records and declarations should be attached as exhibits in support of the brief. The contractor may at this stage attempt to explain the cause of the statistical results.

The CO reviews the response and may request additional information. Analysis of that information may be conducted either on site or off site. The CO considers not only whether the contractor's

---

[527]*Id.* § 3P01, *reprinted in* 1 AFFIRMATIVE ACTION COMPL. MAN. (BNA) 3:0019. No predetermination notice is issued for individual cases of discrimination. The OFCCP asserts those claims initially in the notice of violations.

[528]*Id.* § 3P02, *reprinted in* 1 AFFIRMATIVE ACTION COMPL. MAN. (BNA) 3:0019.

[529]*Id.* § 3P03, *reprinted in* 1 AFFIRMATIVE ACTION COMPL. MAN. (BNA) 3:0019.

response offers a nondiscriminatory explanation, but also whether the response is a pretext for discrimination.[530] If the contractor points out factual errors on the part of the agency, the CO evaluates the contractor's responses and attempts to correct any use of erroneous data or misunderstanding of the employment process. The OFCCP may seek expert review of contractor contentions concerning correct statistical analysis or formal validation studies. The CO also evaluates any assertion by the contractor of job relatedness and/or business necessity. If the contractor makes an adequate showing of this kind, the CO may attempt to show pretext by identifying another method that accomplishes the contractor's purpose but has less adverse impact.[531]

Where the allegation is a pattern or practice of disparate treatment, the contractor may assert that: (1) the CO overlooked a selection criterion in constructing the pool of minimally objectively qualified candidates; (2) the CO based the analysis on the wrong applicant pools or feeder groups and, thus, identified the wrong selection pool; (3) the wrong statistical test was employed or the statistics were not calculated correctly; (4) the best-qualified candidate was selected in each case;[532] and/or (5) there is no evidence of discriminatory intent other than an inference arising from the statistics.[533] If a court or another agency is considering or has considered the issue, the contractor may consider arguing that the OFCCP should defer to the other forum.[534]

In response, the CO typically investigates the contractor's allegations concerning overlooked selection criteria by determining whether the individuals actually selected possessed the asserted

---

[530]*Id.* § 3P04, *reprinted in* 1 AFFIRMATIVE ACTION COMPL. MAN. (BNA) 3:0019–20.

[531]*Id.* § 3Q00(b), (c), *reprinted in* 1 AFFIRMATIVE ACTION COMPL. MAN. (BNA) 3:0020.

[532]*See* Section VII.E.4.c *supra.*

[533]*Id.* § 3Q01(a), *reprinted in* 1 AFFIRMATIVE ACTION COMPL. MAN. (BNA) 3:0020.

[534]*Cf. In re* University of Tex., 38 FEP 886, 888 (Dep't of Labor 1985) (Secretary of Labor dismissed an Executive Order complaint alleging sex discrimination, holding it was barred under the doctrine of collateral estoppel by a district court decision on a Title VII claim based on the same facts). *But cf.* Department of Labor v. Coldwell, Banker & Co., 44 FEP 850, 853–54 (Dep't of Labor 1987) (prior consent decree would have to cover all aspects of affirmative action dealt with in the Executive Order to relieve contractor of its duties under the Order).

qualifications at the time of their selection.[535] If so, the CO may consider changing theories and review the selection process for adverse impact. If the contractor's allegations concerning applicant pools or feeder groups are correct, the CO often conducts a new analysis based on the proper pools.[536]

If the contractor adequately rebuts the pattern-or-practice allegation, the OFCCP accepts the response. If at least some issues are not rebutted, the OFCCP issues a notice of violations[537] regarding the unrebutted pattern-or-practice issues, any individual discrimination violations, and other deficiencies found during the compliance evaluation.[538]

5. Notice of Violations, Contractor Responses, and Conciliation Agreements

For each pattern-or-practice issue, the notice of results of investigation restates the problem, analyzes the contractor's response, and states that the contractor may present any legitimate defenses available regarding liability and those entitled to relief. It also describes the proposed remedy in class terms, including the type and scope of relief, and the time period involved. This notification specifically requires termination of the identified discriminatory practice (if that has not occurred already). It also states that resolution of the pattern-or-practice violation, and any other violations included in the notice, must be memorialized in a conciliation agreement.[539]

Under the OFCCP's proposed rules, any notice of results of investigation alleging systemic discrimination with respect to compensation practices must be based on the OFCCP's published standards.[540] Except in "unusual cases," the OFCCP will not issue a

---

[535]FED. CONTRACT COMPL. MAN. § 3Q01(b), *reprinted in* 1 AFFIRMATIVE AC-TION COMPL. MAN. (BNA) 3:0021.

[536]*Id.* § 3Q01(a)(2), *reprinted in* 1 AFFIRMATIVE ACTION COMPL. MAN. (BNA) 3:0020.

[537]This notice officially is known as a "notice of results of investigation" (NRI), which may be a finding of violations or no violations.

[538]FED. CONTRACT COMPL. MAN. § 3P04, *reprinted in* 1 AFFIRMATIVE ACTION COMPL. MAN. (BNA) 3:0019–20.

[539]*Id.* § 3T00, *reprinted in* 1 AFFIRMATIVE ACTION COMPL. MAN. (BNA) 3:0021.

[540]*Id.*

notice of results of investigation for systemic compensation discrimination unless it has (1) anecdotal evidence, (2) supporting a statistically significant compensation disparity, (3) that is based on a multiple regression analysis, (4) "that compares similarly situated employees . . . and controls for factors that OFCCP's investigation reveal were used in making pay decisions."[541] With each such notice, the OFCCP will attach its regression analysis results and a summary of its anecdotal evidence.[542] The OFCCP "may assert a systemic discrimination violation based only on anecdotal evidence, if such evidence presents a pattern or practice of compensation discrimination."[543]

The OFCCP also cautions that it may find a compensation discrimination violation where the contractor uses a market survey in a manner that pays the full market rate for predominantly male-occupied jobs, but pays below the market rate for predominantly female- or minority-occupied jobs, or otherwise makes "wage-rate decisions based on the sex, race or ethnicity of the incumbent employees that predominate in each job."[544]

The notice for individual discrimination issues not involving a pattern or practice includes a complete description of the violation and a statement of the remedy required.[545]

A conciliation agreement is a formal resolution of alleged violations that contains three parts. Part I consists of mandatory provisions. These, inter alia, purport to allow the OFCCP to reopen the audit and initiate enforcement proceedings. Part II specifies the violations and remedies. Part III states the term of the agreement and typically requires semiannual reports for up to two years from execution.[546] The OFCCP Director must approve any provision that precludes the OFCCP from issuing a press release or otherwise publicizing the results of compliance actions.[547]

---

[541]69 Fed. Reg. at 67,252 (Nov. 16, 2004).

[542]*Id.*

[543]*Id.*

[544]*Id.*

[545]FED. CONTRACT COMPL. MAN. § 3T01, *reprinted in* 1 AFFIRMATIVE ACTION COMPL. MAN. (BNA) 3:0021.

[546]*Id.* § 8F01(a), *reprinted in* 2 AFFIRMATIVE ACTION COMPL. MAN. (BNA) 8:0007.

[547]*Id.* § 8F01(d), *reprinted in* 2 AFFIRMATIVE ACTION COMPL. MAN. (BNA) 8:0007.

"[P]roof of compliance or noncompliance with conciliation agreements may be admitted in Title VII actions as circumstantial evidence of discriminatory intent."[548] Most cases hold that individuals who are beneficiaries of relief provided under a conciliation agreement may sue to obtain it.[549]

In a proceeding involving an alleged violation of a conciliation agreement, the OFCCP does not have to present proof of the underlying violation resolved by the agreement when seeking enforcement of the agreement.[550]

Letters of commitment were once used to resolve minor technical violations that generally could be corrected within 10 to 15 days of inspection.[551] However, the OFCCP has discontinued the use of such letters.[552] Conciliation agreements continue to be used for major and substantive violations of OFCCP regulations. Minor technical violations typically are included in the OFCCP's "notice of review completion, minor deficiencies resolved."[553]

---

[548]*E.g.*, Langland v. Vanderbilt Univ., 589 F. Supp. 995, 1016, 36 FEP 200 (M.D. Tenn. 1984), *aff'd*, 772 F.2d 907 (6th Cir. 1985).

[549]*See* Eatmon v. Bristol Steel & Iron Works, Inc., 769 F.2d 1503, 1505, 1516, 38 FEP 1364 (11th Cir. 1985) (the plaintiffs, 14 former employees and one former applicant, named in a conciliation agreement between a contractor and the OFCCP, did not receive all the back pay provided for in the agreement because the contractor unilaterally made deductions for the interim earnings of the class; the plaintiffs were permitted to enforce the conciliation agreement on a third-party beneficiary theory and to pursue an action for breach of release agreements to which they were parties); Amalgamated Clothing & Textile Workers Union v. S. Lichtenberg & Co., 54 FEP 635, 638 (S.D. Ga. 1990) (although the plaintiffs were not expressly named, they nevertheless could pursue their rights as intended third-party beneficiaries of the Executive Order's nondiscrimination provisions); *cf.* Terry v. Northrop Worldwide Aircraft Servs., Inc., 786 F.2d 1558, 1561, 40 FEP 985 (11th Cir. 1986) (conciliation agreement could not be enforced by its third-party beneficiaries where the contractor, after signing the agreement, invoked the regulations' protest procedures, 41 C.F.R. § 60-1.24(c)(4) (2005), which enable a contractor to challenge demands made by the OFCCP without subjecting itself to a sanctions proceeding; since the agency had agreed to stay implementation of the agreement pending resolution of the protest, neither it nor the third-party beneficiaries could enforce it). *But cf.* Robinson v. Jacksonville Shipyards, Inc., 760 F. Supp. 1486, 1532, 57 FEP 971 (M.D. Fla. 1991) (third-party beneficiary theory was "merely derivative" of private cause of action theory, and the former could not be entertained because the latter was not cognizable).

[550]41 C.F.R. § 1.34 (2005).

[551]Letters of commitment were written by the contractor and described each violation, the corrective action which was to be taken, and a timetable or completion date.

[552]70 Fed. Reg. 36,262, 36,263 (June 22, 2005).

[553]FED. CONTRACT COMPL. MAN. § 3V(b)(1), Figure 8-15, *reprinted in* 1 AFFIRMATIVE ACTION COMPL. MAN. (BNA) 3:0022 and 2 AFFIRMATIVE ACTION COMPL. MAN. (BNA) 8:0034.

If the contractor declines to enter into a conciliation agreement, and instead wishes to contest, in whole or in part, any alleged violation or proposed remedy, it typically will submit a thorough letter brief. Therein, the contractor generally sets forth its affirmative action accomplishments, along with the material facts and applicable law and regulations in support of its position on each contested violation. Absent some negotiated resolution following receipt of the contractor's response, the OFCCP either will withdraw its allegations as improvidently made or send the matter for formal enforcement proceedings to the Solicitor of Labor, through the Associate Solicitor of Labor for Civil Rights or the Regional Solicitor.[554]

6. Notices of Review Completion

If the OFCCP has not identified any violations, it issues a "notice of review completion—no deficiencies found," commonly referred to as a letter of compliance. When the compliance evaluation closure letter has identified and resolved minor deficiencies, the evaluation concludes with a "notice of review completion, minor deficiencies resolved."[555] If the contractor and the OFCCP have executed a conciliation agreement to resolve all issues, the agency issues a "notice of review completion, major deficiencies voluntarily resolved."[556] Any of these officially concludes the compliance evaluation of a supply and service contractor.[557]

VIII. ENFORCEMENT PROCEDURES AND SANCTIONS FOR NONCOMPLIANCE

If a compliance evaluation or complaint investigation asserts a violation that is not resolved by a conciliation agreement, administrative enforcement proceedings normally follow.[558] Violations

---

[554]See Section VIII infra.

[555]FED. CONTRACT COMPL. MAN. § 3V(b)(1), Figure 8-15, reprinted in 1 AFFIRMATIVE ACTION COMPL. MAN. (BNA) 3:0022 and 2 AFFIRMATIVE ACTION COMPL. MAN. (BNA) 8:0034.

[556]Id. § 3V(b)(2), Figs. 8-13, 8-14, reprinted in 1 AFFIRMATIVE ACTION COMPL. MAN. (BNA) 3:0022 and 2 AFFIRMATIVE ACTION COMPL. MAN. (BNA) 8:0032–33.

[557]Id. § 3V(a), reprinted in 1 AFFIRMATIVE ACTION COMPL. MAN. (BNA) 3:0022.

[558]41 C.F.R. § 60-1.26(a)(1) (2005).

may be based, inter alia, on a contractor's refusal to submit an AAP; its refusal to allow an on-site evaluation or to provide data for an off-site review; its refusal to maintain and supply records as required; its alteration or falsification of required records; deficiencies in an AAP; the results of the OFCCP's investigation of affirmative action compliance or discrimination; or "any substantial or material violation or the threat of substantial or material violation of the contractual provisions of the Order, or of the rules or regulations or orders issued pursuant thereto."[559]

The Executive Order and the regulations implementing the Rehabilitation and Veterans Acts enumerate the sanctions that may be imposed for noncompliance. These include administrative determinations to cancel, terminate, or suspend a contract, or to provide, as the ultimate sanction, "debarment"—after which contracting agencies refrain from entering into further contracts with non-complying contractors.[560]

In addition, at the OFCCP's recommendation, the federal government may institute judicial proceedings to enforce the OFCCP programs and to obtain injunctive relief against those persons who prevent compliance, directly or indirectly.[561] The OFCCP also may recommend to the EEOC or the Justice Department that proceedings be instituted under Title VII.[562]

A. Administrative Enforcement

The OFCCP relies heavily on its power to negotiate conciliation agreements as a method of resolving complaints administratively.[563] Through such negotiation, the OFCCP has secured substantial

---

[559]*Id.* § 60-1.26(a)(1)(i)–(x).

[560]Exec. Order No. 11246, § 209(a), *reprinted as amended in* 1 AFFIRMATIVE ACTION COMPL. MAN. (BNA) 101, 103; 41 C.F.R. §§ 60-1.4(b)(6), -250.66, -741.66 (2005). Moreover, the regulations implementing the Veterans Act and the Rehabilitation Act provide that, "[w]ith the prior approval of the Deputy Assistant Secretary, so much of the accrued payment due on the contract or any other contract between the Government contractor and the Federal Government may be withheld as necessary to correct any violations." *Id.* §§ 60-250.66(a), -741.66(a).

[561]Exec. Order No. 11246, § 209(a)(2) (1965), *reprinted as amended in* 1 AFFIRMATIVE ACTION COMPL. MAN. (BNA) 101, 103; 41 C.F.R. §§ 60-1.26(a)(1), -250.65(a)(1), -741.65(a)(2) (2004).

[562]Exec. Order No. 11246, § 209(a)(3) (1965), *reprinted as amended in* 1 AFFIRMATIVE ACTION COMPL. MAN. (BNA) 101, 103.

[563]41 C.F.R. § 60-30.13 (2005).

monetary and nonmonetary relief from contractors for the benefit of alleged victims of discrimination. When relief includes back pay, the regulations governing the Executive Order, the Rehabilitation Act, and the Veterans Act require that interest on the pay be calculated from the date of the loss and compounded quarterly, instead of allowing simple interest.[564]

When conciliation fails, the OFCCP may commence administrative enforcement proceedings "to enjoin violations, to seek appropriate relief, and to impose appropriate sanctions."[565] In proceedings under the Executive Order, the contractor generally is first entitled to a 30-day show cause notice, providing a last opportunity to avert the institution of enforcement proceedings.[566] The Rehabilitation and Veterans Acts give the Deputy Assistant Secretary

---

[564]41 C.F.R. §§ 60-1.26(a)(2), -250.65(a)(1), -741.65(a)(1) (2005).

[565]*Id.* § 60-1.26(b)(1). The relief sought may include back pay for an affected class. *See* Section X.B *infra; see also* 41 C.F.R. §§ 60-250.65(a)(1), -741.65(a)(1) (2005).

[566]*Id.* §§ 60-1.28, -250.64, -741.64. However, if the contractor is alleged to have violated the terms of a conciliation agreement, it has only 15 days to demonstrate in writing that no violation has occurred. The OFCCP may designate a shorter period if a delay would result in irreparable injury to employment rights of affected applicants or employees. *Id.* §§ 60-1.34(a), -250.63(a)(1), -741.63(a)(1).

In the 1970s, several cases addressed whether an administrative hearing must be held before the OFCCP declares a company "ineligible" for a particular government contract. The Executive Order regulations appear to allow, and the OFCCP many years ago followed, the practice of declaring a company to be "nonresponsible"—and thus ineligible for government contracts—without a hearing, because of alleged deficiencies in (or substantial deviation from) its AAP. *Id.* § 60-2.2(b). In procurement law terms, the designation "nonresponsible" means that the company does not have the capability to perform the contract and therefore is ineligible for its award. Once a company has been passed over for two contracts, the regulations require the OFCCP to provide notice and a hearing. *Id.*

Contractors argued, however, that such a "passover" was a de facto debarment contravening the terms of the Executive Order, which require a hearing before debarment or suspension. They also argued that the practice imposed a penalty without a hearing and violated constitutional due process protections. Most courts agreed with one or both of the contractors' contentions. *Compare* Illinois Tool Works, Inc. v. Marshall, 601 F.2d 943, 948, 20 FEP 359 (7th Cir. 1979), Sundstrand Corp. v. Marshall, 17 FEP 432, 435 (N.D. Ill. 1978), Pan Am. World Airways, Inc. v. Marshall, 439 F. Supp. 487, 496, 15 FEP 1607 (S.D.N.Y. 1977) *and* Crown Zellerbach Corp. v. Wirtz, 281 F. Supp. 337, 340, 1 FEP 274 (D.D.C. 1968) *with* Crown Zellerbach Corp. v. Marshall, 441 F. Supp. 1110, 1118, 15 FEP 1628 (E.D. La. 1977) (no hearing required because nonresponsibility determination is not a retributive sanction based on past misconduct) *and* Commercial Envelope Mfg. Co. v. Dunlop, 11 FEP 117, 119–20 (S.D.N.Y. 1975) (no hearing required before finding of nonresponsibility). In any event, although the passover provision remains in the regulations, the OFCCP has abandoned this practice.

discretion to issue a 30-day show cause notice when he or she has reasonable cause to believe that the contractor has violated the Act.[567]

Administrative enforcement controversies under all OFCCP programs are resolved initially by an administrative law judge. This normally occurs in an evidentiary hearing under the OFCCP's rules of practice, which parallel the Federal Rules of Civil Procedure and Evidence.[568] The OFCCP may choose to employ an expedited hearing procedure designed "to dispose of uncomplicated issues in an uncomplicated proceeding."[569] The hearing then is conducted on an accelerated schedule without an opportunity for extended discovery.[570] In an administrative proceeding, the contractor may present evidence, argument, and briefing before the administrative law judge issues recommended findings, conclusions, and a decision. In a normal proceeding, the contractor and the OFCCP have 14 days following receipt of that decision to appeal by filing "exceptions." However, this time is shortened to 10 days under the regulations governing expedited proceedings.[571] The Administrative Review Board,[572] U.S. Department of Labor, rules on the exceptions and issues a final order on an Executive Order complaint.[573]

A contractor, but not the OFCCP, may appeal the order[574] of the Administrative Review Board to the U.S. District Court under

---

[567]41 C.F.R. §§ 60-250.64, -741.64 (2005). Issuing such a notice is not a prerequisite to instituting enforcement proceedings. *See id.*

[568]*Id.* pt. 60-30.

[569]44 Fed. Reg. 77,000, 77,002 (1979) (preamble to regulations).

[570]41 C.F.R. §§ 60-30.31 to -30.37 (2005).

[571]*See id.* § 60-30.36.

[572]The Secretary of Labor established the Administrative Review Board in 1996 to succeed the former Office of Administrative Appeals and gave it the authority to issue final agency decisions. 61 Fed. Reg. 19,978 (1996).

[573]41 C.F.R. §§ 60-30.30, -30.37 (2005).

[574]Before a final administrative decision, however, contractors have encountered substantial obstacles to judicial review. Citing the doctrine of exhaustion of administrative remedies, several courts have refused to entertain suits for a declaratory judgment or preliminary injunction. *E.g.*, St. Regis Paper Co. v. Marshall, 591 F.2d 612, 615, 18 FEP 1635 (10th Cir. 1979) (upholding dismissal, prior to an administrative hearing, of a contractor's suit challenging the validity of the OFCCP regulations that require "affected class" relief; the possibility of permanent debarment at the administrative level, without assurance that a stay will be granted pending judicial review, is insufficient to trigger any exception to the exhaustion requirement, in part because the possibility of irreparable injury was too speculative and tenuous); Uniroyal, Inc. v. Marshall, 579 F.2d 1060, 1064, 17 FEP 1207 (7th Cir. 1978)

the Administrative Procedure Act.[575] Either party thereafter has the right to file an appeal with the U.S. Court of Appeals and, thereafter, a petition with the U.S. Supreme Court.[576]

B. Cancellation, Debarment, and Other Sanctions Following Administrative Hearing

The Executive Order and the regulations implementing the Veterans and Rehabilitation Acts authorize the Secretary of Labor to preclude a noncomplying contractor from working on or receiving payment under government contracts. The Secretary may:

(contractor's pre-enforcement challenge to the OFCCP's discovery regulation was properly dismissed for failure to exhaust administrative remedies). *But cf.* National Bank of Commerce v. Marshall, 628 F.2d 474, 479, 24 FEP 98 (5th Cir. 1980) ("The general rule is that where the plaintiff 'enter[s] the federal courthouse prematurely . . . the district court should [dismiss].' On consideration, we think an exception to this rule should be made when the exercise of jurisdiction and the granting of preliminary relief will prevent irreparable injury to the plaintiff. If the court's actions will not, however, prevent such injury, we think a court must dismiss the action to avoid unnecessarily entangling itself in ongoing administrative proceedings.") (citations omitted); Liberty Mut. Ins. Co. v. Friedman, 485 F. Supp. 695, 700, 21 FEP 1016 (D. Md. 1979) (court permits, without comment, contractor's declaratory judgment action to determine if it is subject to OFCCP jurisdiction), *rev'd on other grounds*, 639 F.2d 164 (4th Cir. 1981).

[575]5 U.S.C. § 701 et seq (2000). A reviewing court is required to hold unlawful and set aside agency action, findings, and conclusions found to be (1) arbitrary, capricious, an abuse of discretion, or otherwise not in accordance with law; (2) contrary to constitutional rights; (3) in excess of statutory jurisdiction or authority; (4) in violation of procedures required by law; (5) unsupported by substantial evidence; or (6) unwarranted by the facts to the extent that the facts are subject to trial de novo by the reviewing court. *Id.* § 706(2); *see, e.g.,* Timken Co. v. Vaughan, 413 F. Supp. 1183, 1192, 12 FEP 1140 (N.D. Ohio 1976) (setting aside an order debarring Timken; there was not substantial evidence to support the agency's decision that the contractor's availability estimate was improper because it failed to assume, in calculating availability, that residents of a town located beyond a 15-mile radius would commute to its plant); Commercial Envelope Mfg. Co. v. Dunlop, 11 FEP 117, 119 (S.D.N.Y. 1975) (rejected low bidder, who was declared nonresponsible because of its failure to meet Executive Order 11246 affirmative action requirements, has standing under the Administrative Procedure Act to seek review of the finding of nonresponsibility); *see also* Firestone Synthetic Rubber & Latex Co. v. Marshall, 507 F. Supp. 1330, 1336, 24 FEP 1699 (E.D. Tex. 1981) (challenging debarment for failure to calculate underutilization according to OFCCP interpretation).

[576]*Compare* American Airlines, Inc. v. Herman, 176 F.3d 283 (5th Cir. 1999) *and* Nationsbank Corp. v. Herman, 174 F.3d 424 (4th Cir. 1999) (OFCCP appeals of judgments in favor of contractors) *with* Trinity Indus., Inc. v. Herman, 173 F.3d 527 (4th Cir. 1999) *and* Partridge v. Reich, 141 F.3d 920 (9th Cir. 1998) (contractor appeals of judgments in favor of Department of Labor).

(1) Withhold as much of the accrued payment due on a government contract as is necessary to correct any violations;

(2) Cancel or terminate, in whole or in part, the government contract in question; and/or

(3) Debar from, or declare a contractor ineligible for, future contracts, for failing to comply with the equal opportunity/affirmative action clause.[577]

An accused contractor has a right to a hearing if the Deputy Assistant Secretary proposes (1) the cancellation or termination of a contract; (2) the withholding of progress payments, either in whole or in part; and/or (3) a declaration that the contractor should be debarred or ineligible for future contracts.[578]

The regulations governing the Executive Order, the Rehabilitation Act, and the Veterans Act allow debarment for an indefinite term *or* a fixed minimum period of at least six months.[579] The Rehabilitation and Veterans Acts impose a maximum period of three years for a fixed debarment.[580] The Deputy Assistant Secretary decides the length of a fixed-term debarment on a case-by-case basis, considering such factors as the nature and severity of the violations, the contractor's compliance history, and whether the violations can be remedied in the absence of a fixed-term debarment.[581]

A debarred or ineligible contractor may request reinstatement in a letter to the Deputy Assistant Secretary. A contractor debarred for an indefinite period may file a request for reinstatement at any time after the effective date of debarment.[582] A contractor debarred for a fixed period under the Executive Order may file a request 30 days before the period ends, while a contractor under the regulations governing the Rehabilitation and Veterans Acts must wait six

---

[577]Exec. Order No. 11246, § 209(a)(6) (1965), *reprinted as amended in* 1 AFFIRMATIVE ACTION COMPL. MAN. (BNA) 101, 103; 41 C.F.R. §§ 60-1.4(a)(6), -1.26, -1.27 (2004).

[578]Exec. Order No. 11246, § 208(b) (1965), *reprinted as amended in* 1 AFFIRMATIVE ACTION COMPL. MAN. (BNA) 101, 102–03; 41 C.F.R. §§ 250.65–66, -741.65–66 (2004) (hearing required); *cf. id.* §§ 60-1.26, -2.2(b) (providing for a hearing only if the Deputy Assistant Secretary determines that substantial issues of law or fact exist).

[579]41 C.F.R. §§ 60-1.27(b), -250.66(c), -741.66(c) (2005).

[580]*Id.* §§ 60-250.66(c), -741.66(c).

[581]*Id.* §§ 60-250.68(a), -741.68(a).

[582]*Id.* §§ 60-1.31, -250.68(a), -741.68(a).

months from the effective date of the debarment.[583] To secure re-instatement, the contractor must show that it has come into, and will maintain, compliance.[584]

Debarment has been used not only as a sanction for actual discrimination or other violations proven in an administrative hearing, but also where a contractor denies that it is even covered by the Executive Order and on that basis refuses to prepare an AAP[585] or to cooperate with the OFCCP compliance-review efforts.[586] The extent of the Secretary's authority to invoke the debarment sanction was first illustrated in *Uniroyal, Inc. v. Marshall*.[587] The Department of Labor initiated an administrative enforcement proceeding against Uniroyal, alleging that the company had discriminated against minorities and women at one of its plants. After some discovery had been taken, Uniroyal advised the government that it considered the Secretary's prehearing discovery regulations invalid[588] and would not comply with them. Uniroyal sued in federal court to be relieved from compliance, but the action was dismissed for failure to exhaust administrative remedies.[589] In the administrative proceeding, the government successfully moved to have Uniroyal's government contracts terminated because of its refusal to allow discovery. The Labor Secretary so ordered. Seeking to enjoin this action, Uniroyal again sued, contending that the administrative law judge lacked authority under the Executive Order to compel discovery, or, even if such authority existed, the refusal to comply with the discovery regulations could not be punished by debarment through an administrative proceeding.[590]

---

[583]*Id.*

[584]*Id.* §§ 60-1.31, -250.69, -741.68.

[585]*See, e.g.*, Department of Labor v. Coldwell, Banker & Co., 44 FEP 850, 852 (Dep't of Labor 1987) (respondent claimed it was not a covered subcontractor and refused to submit an AAP); Department of Labor v. Interco, Inc., No. 86-OFC-2 (Mar. 10, 1987) (respondent claimed its autonomous divisions were not subject to the Executive Order and refused to submit an AAP).

[586]*See, e.g.*, OFCCP v. Monongahela R.R., No. 85-OFC-2 (Apr. 2, 1986) (Recommended Decision) (employer claimed it was not a subcontractor under § 503 and refused to grant OFCCP access to its establishment).

[587]482 F. Supp. 364, 375, 20 FEP 437 (D.D.C. 1979).

[588]*See* 41 C.F.R. §§ 60-30.9 to 30.11 (2005).

[589]Uniroyal, Inc. v. Marshall, 579 F.2d 1060, 1064, 17 FEP 1207 (7th Cir. 1978).

[590]Uniroyal contended that the Secretary's recourse was to seek enforcement of its discovery requests in federal court. *Uniroyal*, 482 F. Supp. at 373.

The district court rejected Uniroyal's arguments. It held that the administrative law judge had power derived from validly promulgated Executive Order discovery rules to require Uniroyal to produce documents and participate in depositions and other discovery.[591] The court further observed:

> The government's position as to the authority of the Executive Order is further strengthened by the principle . . . that its authority with respect to contractors is extensive and that it may set the terms upon which those wishing to deal with it must operate. . . . Here, the government, acting through the President's Executive Order and the Secretary of Labor's regulations has determined that one wishing to do business with the government must agree to mutual prehearing discovery. While, to be sure, the government has no power by contract to bind others to abide by invalid regulations, regulations are likely to be regarded as reasonable and valid if they operate in an area where the government has extensive authority, and the field of government contracts is, obviously, such an area.[592]

The court then rejected Uniroyal's contentions that the authority to debar extended only to violations of the substantive nondiscrimination provisions of the Executive Order.[593]

Turning to the merits, the court found that debarment was not an abuse of the Secretary's discretion, given that Uniroyal had refused to provide the government access to documents for several years, and its "recalcitrance and discriminatory policies had already been the subject of judicial proceedings and had been documented in court opinions."[594] Similarly, in *Department of Labor v. Bruce Church, Inc.*,[595] the Secretary reaffirmed immediate debarment as

---

[591]*Id.* at 367.

[592]Uniroyal, Inc. v. Marshall, 482 F. Supp. 364, 370, 20 FEP 437 (D.D.C. 1979) (citations omitted).

[593]*Id.* at 374. However, the court held that because Uniroyal was debarred for failure to comply with the Secretary's prehearing discovery regulations and orders, it was entitled to be relieved from debarment upon compliance with those same regulations and orders. "The remedy of debarment must be coextensive with the violation." *Id.* at 376.

[594]*Id.* at 374. Following this decision, Uniroyal remained debarred for 3 months, during which time it attempted to comply with the discovery demands. The government, however, deemed Uniroyal's submission unsatisfactory. Eventually, Uniroyal signed a settlement and consent decree providing $5.2 million in back pay and other benefits. DAILY LAB. REP. (BNA) at A-17 (Oct. 29, 1979); *see also* Uniroyal, Inc. v. Marshall, 20 FEP 446 (D.C. Cir. 1979) (per curiam) (injunction pending appeal denied).

[595]No. 87-OFC-7 [1979–1987 Transfer Binder] OFCCP FED. CONT. COMPL. MAN. (CCH) ¶ 21,304, at 3631–32 (June 30, 1987) (Final Decision).

an appropriate remedy against a contractor that refused to prepare a written AAP.

The Secretary's debarment orders have been reversed several times. In *Firestone Synthetic Rubber & Latex Co. v. Marshall*,[596] the Secretary had debarred a contractor because of a dispute regarding the proper statistical method for determining underutilization in its AAP. But the district court overturned the debarment.[597] In *Timken Co. v. Vaughan*,[598] the Secretary debarred a contractor because it disputed the appropriate recruiting area for goal-setting purposes. That order, too, was overturned.[599] These cases illustrate the dilemma a contractor faces when confronted by an OFCCP position that the contractor considers to be groundless or unreasonable. The contractor can abandon its contentions and comply;[600] or it can resist and argue its case in an enforcement proceeding. The danger associated with the latter course is that the contractor is at peril of debarment if it loses. In practice, however, the contractor often is given—and it normally accepts—a new opportunity to correct the violation and settle. Such a second chance is particularly likely where the contractor's failure to comply resulted from a misunderstanding of its obligations. In *First Alabama Bank of Montgomery, N.A. v. Donovan*,[601] the Eleventh Circuit modified a district court's immediate debarment order to permit First Alabama to rectify its refusal to cooperate with the OFCCP's compliance review. In so holding, the court explained, "the purpose of debarment is limited to encouraging compliance and is not intended for use as punishment for non-compliance."[602] Similarly, in *OFCCP v. Priester Construction Co.*,[603] the Secretary of Labor rejected the OFCCP's argument for mandatory debarment of contractors that

---

[596]507 F. Supp. 1330, 1333, 24 FEP 1699 (E.D. Tex. 1981).

[597]*Id.* at 1338.

[598]413 F. Supp. 1183, 1188, 12 FEP 1140 (N.D. Ohio 1976).

[599]*Id.* at 1192.

[600]41 C.F.R. § 60-1.24(c)(4) (2005) sets forth a procedure by which the contractor can comply under protest with an OFCCP demand but request a hearing before the Director on the issue.

[601]692 F.2d 714, 30 FEP 448 (11th Cir. 1982).

[602]*Id.* at 722. *See generally* Department of Labor v. Coldwell, Banker & Co., 44 FEP 850, 857 (Dep't of Labor 1987) (Final Decision) (30 days given to comply); OFCCP v. Monongahela R.R., No. 85-OFC-2 (Apr. 2, 1986) (Recommended Decision) (same).

[603]No. 78-OFCCP-11 (Feb. 22, 1983), *reprinted in* 2 AFFIRMATIVE ACTION COMPL. MAN. (BNA) D:7361.

violate the Executive Order, noting the "harsh and anticonciliatory nature" of such an approach.

The OFCCP, in practice, has no firm standards for deciding when to seek debarment or, alternatively, a lesser penalty such as withholding payments on or canceling a single contract. The agency evaluates the facts and circumstances of the current violations and the contractor's history. After enforcement actions result in an order to debar, the Deputy Assistant Secretary is required to notify the heads of all contracting governmental agencies.[604]

C. Judicial Enforcement

1. Justice Department Actions

The regulations authorize the OFCCP to refer a matter to the Justice Department to enforce the contractual provisions of the Executive Order, to seek injunctive relief, and to seek such additional relief as may be appropriate.[605] Judicial enforcement appears to be used only where administrative debarment would be impracticable or ineffective as a negotiating tool or sanction. For example, the Justice Department may sue, rather than seek to debar, public utilities, banks,[606] companies that are the sole source of needed supplies or services, or contractors that are essential to national defense. The OFCCP also may prefer judicial enforcement where government contracts are too insignificant to the contractor's business to make debarment an effective sanction.

In *United States v. Whitney National Bank of New Orleans*,[607] the district court reaffirmed the Justice Department's authority to sue to enforce the Executive Order's provisions. The court held that the Executive Order lawfully imposes a back-pay obligation

---

[604]41 C.F.R. §§ 60-1.30, -250.67, -741.67 (2005).

[605]*Id.* §§ 60-1.26, -250.65, -741.65. The regulations also purport to authorize the Department of Justice to seek back pay as a remedy. *See generally* Chapter 30 (Justice Department Litigation).

[606]The OFCCP's policy is that it will not seek to terminate banks' deposit insurance. *See, e.g.,* 46 Fed. Reg. 42,968, 42,970 (1981); 45 Fed. Reg. 86,216 (1980); 45 Fed. Reg. 11,856, 11,857 (1980); *cf.* OFCCP v. First Ala. Bank, 25 FEP 347, 348 (Dep't of Labor), *vacated sub. nom.* First Ala. Bank v. Marshall, 26 FEP 388 (N.D. Ala. 1981), *vacated and remanded by* 692 F.2d 714, 722 (11th Cir. 1982).

[607]671 F. Supp. 441, 45 FEP 983 (E.D. La. 1987).

on government contractors found liable for discriminatory employment policies.[608]

2. No Private Enforcement Against Contractors

Enforcement of the terms of the Executive Order or the other OFCCP programs rests with the government; protected individuals themselves have no direct action against contractors under the Executive Order,[609] § 503 of the Rehabilitation Act,[610] or the Veterans Act.[611] A private right of action, courts say, would undermine the conciliation and administrative enforcement mechanism

---

[608]*Id.* at 442; *see also* United States v. Commercial Lovelace Motor Freight, Inc., 31 FEP 499, 502 (S.D. Ohio 1983) (although the Justice Department no longer had jurisdiction over pattern-or-practice suits under Title VII, the Attorney General retained authority to enforce Executive Order).

[609]*See, e.g.*, Women's Equity Action League v. Cavazos, 906 F.2d 742, 750–52 (D.C. Cir. 1990); Cohen v. Illinois Inst. of Tech., 524 F.2d 818, 822 n.4, 11 FEP 659 (7th Cir. 1975); Brug v. National Coalition for Homeless, 45 F. Supp. 2d 33 (D.D.C. 1999) (Executive Order); McPartland v. American Broad. Cos., 623 F. Supp. 1334, 1339–40, 42 FEP 286 (S.D.N.Y. 1985); Bey v. Schneider Sheetmetal, Inc., 603 F. Supp. 450, 452 n.1, 38 FEP 1139 (W.D. Pa. 1985); Hubbard v. Council for Advancement & Support of Educ., 38 FEP 1690, 1691 (D.D.C. 1983). *But cf.* Stiles v. Delta Airlines, Inc., 23 FEP 1829, 1833 (N.D. Ga. 1980) (relief denied for failure to exhaust administrative remedies; court reserves decision on whether private cause of action should be implied in plaintiff's favor as an intended beneficiary of antidiscrimination mandate).

A private action also was denied under Exec. Order No. 10925, 3 C.F.R. pt. 448 (1959–1963 Compilation), issued by President Kennedy on March 6, 1961. *See* Farkas v. Texas Instrument, Inc., 375 F.2d 629, 633, 1 FEP 890 (5th Cir. 1967); Farmer v. Philadelphia Elec. Co., 329 F.2d 3, 10, 1 FEP 36 (3d Cir. 1964) (both relying in part on plaintiff's failure to exhaust administrative remedies). Executive Order No. 11141, prohibiting age discrimination by government contractors, also does not create a private cause of action. Kodish v. United Air Lines, Inc., 628 F.2d 1301, 1303, 23 FEP 1221 (10th Cir. 1980).

[610]*E.g.*, Fisher v. City of Tucson, 663 F.2d 861, 867, 1 AD 286 (9th Cir. 1981); Davis v. United Air Lines, Inc., 662 F.2d 120, 127, 26 FEP 1527 (2d Cir. 1981); Simon v. St. Louis County, 656 F.2d 316, 319, 1 AD 268 (8th Cir. 1981); Rogers v. Frito-Lay, Inc., 611 F.2d 1074, 1078, 1084, 1 AD 131 (5th Cir. 1980); Simpson v. Reynolds Metals Co., 629 F.2d 1226, 1237–38, 1 AD 206 (7th Cir. 1980); Hoopes v. Equifax, Inc., 611 F.2d 134, 135, 22 FEP 957 (6th Cir. 1979); *cf.* Bryant v. New Jersey Dep't of Transp., 998 F. Supp. 438, 446 (D.N.J. 1998) (granting plaintiffs standing to assert claim because they were in "zone of interest" affected by Title VI statute).

[611]*E.g.*, Tolliver v. Xerox Corp., 918 F.2d 1052, 1056, 54 FEP 629 (2d Cir. 1990); Harris v. Adams, 873 F.2d 929, 931–32, 1 AD 1475 (6th Cir. 1989); Barron v. Nightingale Roofing, Inc., 842 F.2d 20, 22, 127 LRRM 2996 (1st Cir. 1988).

contemplated by the Executive Order.[612] On the other hand, where administrative proceedings have run their course and a conciliation agreement is in existence, a private action by a beneficiary may be available.[613] The distinction is that such an action is a contractual one by a third-party beneficiary, not a direct suit under the statute or order.

3. Third-Party Standing to Sue the OFCCP

Some courts have held that citizens may sue federal officials to compel performance of their obligations under the Executive Order.[614] The most instructive of these cases is *Legal Aid Society*

---

[612]Utley v. Varian Assocs., 811 F.2d 1279, 1286, 43 FEP 191 (9th Cir. 1987) (although the court recognized that private actions under the Executive Order would further promote equal employment opportunity, it noted that the Executive Order "envisions achievement of this goal through conciliation—not confrontation").

[613]*See* Holley v. Pansophic Sys., Inc., 1992 WL 137124, at *4 (N.D. Ill. June 12, 1992) (mem.) (Executive Order does not preempt a state breach of contract claim arising from an asserted violation of the affirmative action policy); Manuel v. International Harvester Co., 502 F. Supp. 45, 48, 23 FEP 1477 (N.D. Ill. 1980) (an aggrieved individual may sue under state contract law as a third-party beneficiary; *see also* Yatvin v. Madison Metro. Sch. Dist., 840 F.2d 412, 416, 45 FEP 1862 (7th Cir. 1988) (court suggests in dictum that the plaintiff may have a cause of action for breach of contract if the defendant's AAP was found to be a part of plaintiff's employment contract); Stokes v. Northwestern Mem'l Hosp., 1990 U.S. Dist. LEXIS 14815, at *8 (N.D. Ill. Nov. 5, 1990) ("a reasonable jury could find that [AAP and other manuals] make it more (or less) likely that plaintiff's version of her contract is in fact true"; the court denied the employer's motion in limine to exclude the AAP in the breach of contract case arising from employment termination); Elstner v. Southwestern Bell Tel. Co., 659 F. Supp. 1328, 1341, 43 FEP 1437 (S.D. Tex. 1987) (the employer's failure to adhere to its AAP provides a basis for a breach of contract claim; because the nondiscrimination clause in the collective bargaining agreement incorporated the affirmative action plan, the court consolidated the plaintiff's breach of the CBA claim with the plaintiff's supposed "separate right of action that exists under the Affirmative Action Program"), *aff'd*, 863 F.2d 881, 49 FEP 650 (5th Cir. 1988); *cf.* Ferguson v. Veterans Admin., 723 F.2d 871, 873, 33 FEP 1525 (11th Cir. 1984) (absent a showing of discrimination, there is no Title VII cause of action for the failure of an employer to follow its AAP; court notes, however, that its decision would not control a breach of contract action). *Contra* NAACP v. Detroit Police Officers Ass'n, 821 F.2d 328, 331, 43 FEP 1786 (6th Cir. 1987) ("Judicial approval of a voluntary affirmative action plan does not create a contract of permanent employment or invalidate or modify a collective bargaining agreement providing for layoffs on the basis of seniority."); Robinson v. Jacksonville Shipyards, Inc., 760 F. Supp. 1486, 1532, 57 FEP 971 (M.D. Fla. 1991) (the plaintiff cannot sue as a third-party beneficiary of a government contract).

[614]*E.g.*, Castillo v. Usery, 14 FEP 1240, 1250–54 (N.D. Cal. 1976) (in a suit by a civil rights organization against the Secretary of Labor, the court ordered the OFCCP (1) to issue a notice of proposed sanctions whenever a contractor fails to show good

v. *Brennan*.[615] Organizations and citizens sued federal officials, alleging they had failed to discharge their duty to review AAPs and had regularly approved ones that did not comply with the regulations. The district court granted plaintiffs' motion for partial summary judgment, declaring that the OFCCP had approved 10 specific AAPs that violated the regulations. It also enjoined officials from approving programs that did not comply with the Executive Order. The federal officials filed, then withdrew, a notice of appeal, and ultimately appeared before the Ninth Circuit in support of the judgment. The remaining appellants were some of the contractors whose AAPs were at issue.[616] They contended, inter alia, that the terms of the Executive Order and its regulations are not enforceable in the courts. The Ninth Circuit disagreed, holding that nothing in the Executive Order precludes judicial review; indeed, the order appears to anticipate such review by preserving remedies "as otherwise provided by law."[617]

Other courts, however, have taken a contrary view.[618] And even *Legal Aid Society v. Brennan* seemed to limit its holding to the

---

cause for past noncompliance, even if the contractor is willing to develop an acceptable AAP; and (2) to enter into written conciliation agreements covering all violations and deficiencies disclosed and resolved by the parties); Percy v. Brennan, 384 F. Supp. 800, 805–06, 8 FEP 1213 (S.D.N.Y. 1974) (minority-group members can sue federal officials seeking injunctive relief and declaration of invalidity of "New York Plan" governing affirmative action in federal- and state-assisted construction projects without first exhausting administrative remedies with the EEOC and OFCCP).

[615]608 F.2d 1319, 21 FEP 605 (9th Cir. 1979).

[616]They were not parties to the proceedings below. The district court had denied their motion to intervene and reopen the proceedings, but permitted their intervention for the purpose of appeal. *Legal Aid Soc'y*, 608 F.2d at 1328.

[617]Exec. Order No. 11246, § 202(6) (1965), *reprinted as amended in* 1 AFFIRMATIVE ACTION COMPL. MAN. (BNA) 101.

[618]Women's Equity Action League v. Cavazos, 906 F.2d 742, 750–51 (D.C. Cir. 1990) (court held Executive Order 11246 does not contain an implied right of action against the federal government officers charged with monitoring and enforcing compliance with the Executive Order); *cf.* Hadnott v. Laird, 463 F.2d 304, 304, 307–10 & n.12, 4 FEP 374 (D.C. Cir. 1972) (class action, on behalf of the employees and applicants for employment at paper factories, to enjoin the Secretary of Defense and Administrator of General Services Administration from awarding a contract to paper suppliers until racially discriminatory employment practices were terminated, dismissed because plaintiffs failed to exhaust administrative complaint remedies); Freeman v. Shultz, 468 F.2d 120, 120, 122, 4 FEP 1245 (D.C. Cir. 1972) (class action, by current and former employees and applicants seeking injunctive and declaratory relief against allocation of government contracts to an aerospace employer pending elimination of alleged racial discrimination, held precluded by plaintiffs' failure to exhaust administrative remedies by filing a formal administrative complaint).

performance of nondiscretionary responsibilities, such as disapproving AAPs that do not contain the elements mandated by the regulations.[619]

4. Suits Against Unions

Attempts to sue unions under the Executive Order have resulted in inconsistent rulings. In *United States v. East Texas Motor Freight System, Inc.*,[620] the Fifth Circuit ruled that a union, not being a government contractor or subcontractor, could not be subject to an independent action under the Executive Order.[621] Yet, in *United States v. Operating Engineers Local 701*,[622] another court enjoined a union from interfering with Executive Order compliance. The union had engaged in work stoppages against government contractors that refused to yield to the union's demands to discharge African-American employees hired from sources other than the union referral system provided for in the collective bargaining agreement. Issuing an injunction, the court ruled that "[i]t is unlawful for a union to interfere with the obligations of contractors and subcontractors under Executive Order 11246."[623]

---

[619]Clear, mandatory terms of the regulations then at issue identified elements that must be included in AAPs before they could be deemed acceptable by compliance officials, thus creating nondiscretionary obligations in the court's view: "As Revised Order No. 4 [a portion of the Executive Order regulations] recognizes, the complex task of 'transform[ing] . . . paper commitments [into] equal employment opportunity' requires leeway for the operation of discretion and good faith. But 'developing and judging' the initial adequacy of the paper commitments can be carried out according to clearly stated criteria. 41 C.F.R. § 60-2.1(a)." *Legal Aid Soc'y*, 608 F.2d at 1331 n.21 (citation omitted).

[620]564 F.2d 179, 16 FEP 163 (5th Cir. 1977).

[621]*Id.* at 184. The court noted that, if a union discriminates while engaged in work on a government contract, the union would be subject to a Title VII action. *Id.*; *cf.* United States v. Building & Constr. Trades Council, 271 F. Supp. 447, 451–52, 1 FEP 897 (E.D. Mo. 1966) (dismissing suit by government for an injunction restraining unions from tortiously interfering with a contractor's performance of obligations under the Executive Order, holding that there was no federal common law remedy for tortious interference with such obligations).

[622]14 FEP 1400 (D. Or. 1977).

[623]*Id.* at 1407; *see also* Exec. Order No. 11246, § 207 (1965), *reprinted as amended in* 1 AFFIRMATIVE ACTION COMPL. MAN. (BNA) 101, 102 (the Secretary of Labor is to use his or her best efforts to secure cooperation and compliance of labor unions and is authorized to notify the EEOC or the Justice Department of a Title VII violation); 41 C.F.R. § 60-1.26(c)(2) (2004) (authorizing injunctive actions against unions that seek to thwart purposes of the Executive Order); *id.* § 60-1.9

IX. DISCLOSURE OF INFORMATION TO THIRD PARTIES PURSUANT TO THE FREEDOM OF INFORMATION ACT

Because government records often must be made available to the public under the Freedom of Information Act (FOIA), the OFCCP's recordkeeping requirements and record-retention practices have given rise to considerable contractor concern, and some litigation. A complete dissertation on the FOIA is beyond the scope of this book. Set forth below is an introduction to the FOIA issues that most often arise in OFCCP proceedings.

A. General Provisions

The FOIA gives the public access to certain government records so that governing bodies can be held accountable to the people they serve.[624] The statute mandates that the federal government release to the public certain categories of agency records.[625] It exempts other categories from *mandatory* disclosure, but gives the agency in possession the *discretion* to release them, unless disclosure is otherwise prohibited by law.[626]

(authorizing hearings by the Director to aid in securing compliance by labor unions and by recruiting and training agencies). *See generally* Chapter 22 (Unions).

[624]*See, e.g.*, NLRB v. Robbins Tire & Rubber Co., 437 U.S. 214, 242 (1978) ("basic purpose of FOIA is to ensure an informed citizenry, vital to the functioning of a democratic society, needed to check against corruption and to hold the governors accountable to the governed").

[625]*See* 5 U.S.C. § 552(a) (2000) (e.g., final opinions, statements of policy, staff manuals, rules). In *Forsham v. Harris*, 445 U.S. 169 (1980), the Supreme Court held that data files maintained by a government grantee need not be produced because they were not "agency records" within the scope of the FOIA, even though the government had a right of access to the data. The Court explained that the FOIA applied to records that have in fact been obtained, not to records that merely could have been obtained under a right of access. *Id.* at 186. The Court did not, however, explain what agency conduct would constitute "obtaining" documents. This decision would seem to preclude disclosure under the FOIA of a contractor's AAPs that never have been submitted to the OFCCP. Thus, in its decision debarring the University of California at Berkeley, the Department of Labor cited *Forsham* in dismissing the university's concerns about disclosure of faculty review records pursuant to the FOIA. OFCCP v. University of Cal., 23 FEP 1117, 1128–29 (Dep't of Labor 1980).

[626]5 U.S.C. § 552(b) (2000) describes the categories of information that an agency need not disclose under the FOIA. Exemptions of greatest interest to contractors are: "(4) trade secrets and commercial or financial information obtained from a person

The OFCCP is an agency subject to the FOIA.[627] Accordingly, documents submitted to the OFCCP by government contractors are "agency records" within the meaning of the statute. As such, they are subject to potential disclosure.[628]

FOIA litigation involving the OFCCP has arisen in two primary procedural postures. The first set of cases is those seeking disclosure of AAPs and supporting information submitted to the OFCCP by government contractors. The second set of cases is those filed by contractors seeking to enjoin OFCCP release of information submitted in conjunction with a compliance review or complaint investigation.

B. OFCCP Guidelines for Disclosure of Contractor Records

The OFCCP has issued regulations regarding disclosure of records in response to FOIA requests.[629] Generally, the agency has taken a pro-disclosure stance. Unless disclosure is prohibited by law, the OFCCP will release all records submitted pursuant to its programs, provided that the release will further the public interest[630] and will not impede the agency's functioning.[631] The regulations by their terms provide for the release of: AAPs, "imposed" and "hometown" plans applicable to construction contractors,[632]

---

and privileged or confidential"; "(6) personnel and medical files and similar files the disclosure of which would constitute a clearly unwarranted invasion of personal privacy"; and "(7) records or information compiled for law enforcement purposes," to the limited extent specified in the regulation.

[627]5 U.S.C. § 552 (2000).

[628]*See, e.g.*, Chrysler Corp. v. Brown, 441 U.S. 281, 292, 19 FEP 475 (1979) ("By its terms, [the FOIA] demarcates the agency's obligation to disclose; it does not foreclose disclosure.").

[629]41 C.F.R. pt. 60-40 (2005). On October 12, 2001, the Bush administration issued a memorandum reaffirming the government's commitment to the principles of the FOIA. *See* Thomas M. Susman & Harry A. Hammitt, *Business Uses of the Freedom of Information Act*, 14-3rd CORP. PRAC. SERIES (BNA), Wkst. 8 (2001) (reprinting the memorandum).

[630]The Supreme Court has held that the only "public interest in disclosure" relevant to the FOIA is "the extent to which disclosure would . . . contribut[e] significantly to public understanding of the operations or activities of the government." U.S. Dep't of Def. v. FLRA, 510 U.S. 487, 495, 145 LRRM 2513 (1994) (citation omitted).

[631]41 C.F.R. § 60-40.2 (2005).

[632]*See id.* § 60-4.5.

final conciliation agreements, validation studies of preemployment selection methods, dates and times of scheduled compliance evaluations,[633] and EEO-1 reports.[634]

The regulations also delineate the types of documents or parts thereof that should not be released, because disclosure either does not further the public interest or may impede the discharge of any OFCCP functions:

(1) Those portions of affirmative action plans such as goals and timetables which would be confidential commercial or financial information because they indicate, and only to the extent that they indicate, that a contractor plans major shifts or changes in his personnel requirements and he has not made this information available to the public. A determination to withhold this type of information should be made only after receiving verification and a satisfactory explanation from the contractor that the information should be withheld.

(2) Those portions of affirmative action plans which constitute information on staffing patterns and pay scales but only to the extent that their release would injure the business or financial position of the contractor, would constitute a release of confidential financial information of an employee or would constitute an unwarranted invasion of the privacy of an employee.

(3) The names of individual complainants.

(4) The assignments to particular contractors of named compliance officers if such a disclosure would subject the named compliance officers to undue harassment or would affect the efficient enforcement of the [OFCCP program].

(5) Compliance investigation files including the standard compliance review report and related documents, during the course of the review to which they pertain or while enforcement action against the contractor is in progress or contemplated within a reasonable time. Therefore, these reports and related files shall not be disclosed only to the extent that information contained therein constitutes trade secrets and confidential commercial or financial information. Inter-agency or intra-agency memoranda or letters which would not be available by law to a private party in litigation with the agency, personnel and medical files and similar files the disclosure of which would constitute a clearly unwarranted invasion of personal privacy, data which would be exempt from mandatory disclosure pursuant to the

---

[633]*Id.* § 60-40.2(b)(1)–(5).
[634]*Id.* § 60-40.4.

2688 EMPLOYMENT DISCRIMINATION LAW CH. 38.IX.B

"informant's privilege" or such information the disclosure of which is prohibited by statute.

(6) Copies of pre-employment selection tests used by contractors.[635]

The regulations allow the OFCCP to withhold other records, consistent with the FOIA, on a case-by-case basis.[636] On occasion, the agency exercises this right.[637]

C. Contractor Objections to Disclosure

When the OFCCP receives a FOIA request, the contractor that submitted the documents requested under the FOIA will receive notification where the contractor in good faith has denoted the information as commercially or financially sensitive, or where the OFCCP has reason to believe the disclosure could cause substantial competitive harm.[638]

Upon notification, the contractor must timely[639] object in writing to the agency's release of records. The objection should detail all the facts demonstrating that the information is exempt from disclosure (e.g., a trade secret or commercial or financial information that is privileged or confidential).[640] The Solicitor of Labor will consider the contractor's timely objections before deciding whether to release the requested records. Should the OFCCP decide to disclose the materials, written notice of that decision will

---

[635]*Id.* § 60-40.3(a).

[636]*Id.* § 60-40.3(b).

[637]*See, e.g.,* Gulf Oil Corp. v. Brock, 778 F.2d 834, 841, 39 FEP 892 (D.C. Cir. 1985) ("in recent years OFCCP has withheld [AAPs] that were requested under FOIA, which is testimony to the flexibility of the regulations"); Brinkerhoff v. Montoya, 26 FEP 436, 437 (N.D. Tex. 1981) (affirming the OFCCP's decision not to release records reflecting charges made against a contractor, on the ground that the documents were "investigatory" under the meaning of Exemption 7 of the FOIA); Copus v. Rougeau, 504 F. Supp. 534, 537, 26 FEP 1665 (D.D.C. 1980) (upholding the OFCCP's decision to withhold quarterly compliance review forecasts as "predecisional" and thus immune from mandatory disclosure under Exemption 7).

[638]29 C.F.R. § 70.26(d)(1) (2005).

[639]The notification specifies the deadline for filing an objection, typically 10 to 14 days.

[640]5 U.S.C. § 552(b)(4) (2000). In *CNA Financial Corp. v. Donovan*, 830 F.2d 1132, 1152, 44 FEP 1648 (D.C. Cir. 1987), the court required a showing that the contractor was engaged in "actual competition" and would likely suffer "substantial competitive injury." Note, however, that the objection itself may be susceptible to FOIA disclosure.

be given to the contractor[641] and will specify a period of time (generally 10–14 days) to appeal the decision.[642]

D. Suits to Compel and Prohibit Disclosure of Documents in Possession of the OFCCP

The FOIA expressly provides that suit may be brought to force the production of records an agency is refusing to release.[643] Few claims of this nature have been filed against the OFCCP, perhaps because the OFCCP itself generally has taken a pro-disclosure stance.

Conversely, contractors have filed a number of so-called "reverse-FOIA" suits to preclude disclosure of AAPs and related data. In *Chrysler Corp. v. Brown*,[644] the Supreme Court identified § 10 of the Administrative Procedure Act[645] as the authority for an aggrieved submitter's legal challenge to the release of records. The Court explained three significant principles. First, the FOIA is designed to affect a disclosure of agency records, and thus the FOIA provides no private right of action for a submitter to challenge release of information.[646] In fact, the statute affirmatively precludes disclosure only if the agency itself decides not to release information it holds. Second, although the Trade Secrets Act[647] imposes criminal

---

[641]29 C.F.R. § 70.26(f) (2005).

[642]The appeal must be submitted to the Solicitor of Labor. Upon receipt of the appeal, the reviewer may request additional information from the contractor in support of the objection. If the appeal is denied, the reviewer will notify the contractor that the information requested under the FOIA will be released within a specified time frame. The contractor then may appeal the decision through the federal courts. *See* Section IX.D *supra*; 29 C.F.R. §§ 70.22, -.26 (2005). In practice, a contractor's unsuccessful objection to the OFCCP, and then its administrative appeal, will cause disclosure of records to be delayed from 60 days to more than 1 year. The period of delay depends upon the agency's backlog, the nature and number of documents requested, and the number of contractors covered by the request.

[643]5 U.S.C. § 552(a)(4)(B) (2000).

[644]441 U.S. 281, 19 FEP 475 (1979).

[645]5 U.S.C. § 702 (2000). Section 10(a) of the APA provides that "[a] person suffering legal wrong because of agency action, or adversely affected or aggrieved by agency action . . . , is entitled to judicial review thereof."

[646]*Chrysler*, 441 U.S. at 292.

[647]18 U.S.C. § 1905 (2000) provides:

Whoever, being an officer or employee of the United States or of any department or agency thereof . . . publishes, divulges, discloses, or makes known in

penalties for the unlawful disclosure of certain types of information, such as trade secrets and confidential statistical data, it does not afford a private right to judicial review.[648] Third, however, § 10 of the APA allows an aggrieved contractor to obtain judicial review of the OFCCP's decision to release records if such disclosure would violate the Trade Secrets Act.

The inquiry then becomes: When does the government's disclosure of contractor information violate that Act? The answer appears to be: unless disclosure is otherwise "authorized by law,"[649] documents may not be released if they come within Exemption 4 of the FOIA,[650] which covers trade secrets and confidential commercial or financial information.[651]

Post-*Chrysler* courts typically have upheld the OFCCP's disclosure of AAPs, EEO-1 reports, and other records compiled under the Executive Order.[652] However, portions of such records containing

---

any manner or to any extent not authorized by law any information coming to him in the course of his employment or official duties or by reason of any examination or investigation made by, or return, report or record made to or filed with, such department or agency or officer or employee thereof, which information concerns or relates to the trade secrets, processes, operations, style of work, or apparatus, or to the identity, confidential statistical data, amount or source of any income, profits, losses, or expenditures of any person, firm, partnership, corporation, or association; or permits any income return or copy thereof or any book containing any abstract or particulars thereof to be seen or examined by any person except as provided by law; shall be fined not more than $1,000, or imprisoned not more than one year, or both; and shall be removed from office or employment.

[648]*Chrysler*, 441 U.S. at 316–17.

[649]The OFCCP's regulations do not "authorize" the disclosure of records covered by this exemption. *See* Chrysler Corp. v. Brown, 441 U.S. 281, 315–16, 19 FEP 475 (1979); 5 U.S.C. § 552(b)(3) (2000); General Dynamics Corp. v. Marshall, 572 F.2d 1211, 1217 n.7, 16 FEP 898 (8th Cir. 1978) (§ 1905 is not a basis for exemption under 5 U.S.C. § 552(b)(3)); Crown Cent. Petroleum Corp. v. Kleppe, 424 F. Supp. 744, 750–53, 14 FEP 49 (D. Md. 1976) (§ 709(e) of Title VII and § 1905 are not exempting statutes). *But see* Burroughs Corp. v. Brown, 501 F. Supp. 375, 382–83, 21 FEP 1455 (E.D. Va. 1980) (§ 1905 is a statutory exemption under Exemption 3), *vacated and remanded on other grounds sub nom.* General Motors Corp. v. Marshall, 654 F.2d 294, 26 FEP 571 (4th Cir. 1981).

[650]*Chrysler*, 441 U.S. at 319 n.49; *see also General Motors Corp.*, 654 F.2d at 297 ("[W]e have held that 'the scope of § 1905 and Exemption 4 of the FOIA are, . . . "the same," or, . . . "coextensive." Accordingly, material qualifying for exemption under (b)(4) falls within the material, disclosure of which is prohibited under § 1905.' ").

[651]*Chrysler*, 441 U.S. at 291; 5 U.S.C. § 552(b)(4) (2000).

[652]*See, e.g.*, CNA Fin. Corp. v. Donovan, 830 F.2d 1132, 1159, 44 FEP 1648 (D.C. Cir. 1987) (it was appropriate for the OFCCP to release documents submitted

"confidential" information[653] have been withheld where disclosure would be prohibited by law.[654]

The same result is likely with respect to Exemption 6 for "personnel and medical files and similar files the disclosure of which could constitute a clearly unwarranted invasion of personal privacy."[655]

Most courts have held that contractors cannot base a reverse-FOIA action on Exemption 3, for matters "specifically exempted from disclosure by statute."[656]

Chrysler did not specify whether a court reviewing a disclosure decision must rely on the factual record compiled by the agency; it did, however, observe that de novo review "is ordinarily not necessary."[657] Courts, on occasion, have engaged in de novo review of agency decisions where the agency's actions are arbitrary

---

and created in accordance with the Executive Order); United Tech. Corp. v. Marshall, 464 F. Supp. 845, 855, 24 FEP 929 (D. Conn. 1979) (upholding the release of EEO-1 reports); *see also Crown Cent. Petroleum Corp.*, 424 F. Supp. at 753 (affirming the OFCCP's decision to disclose EEO-1 reports where doing so would not violate the Trade Secrets Act).

[653]"Confidential" is defined in 29 C.F.R. § 70.26(b) and Exec. Order No. 12600 § 2(a) as information, the disclosure of which "could reasonably be expected to cause substantial competitive harm." Information that previously has been disclosed to the public cannot qualify as confidential.

[654]*See, e.g.*, National Org. for Women, Wash., D.C. Chapter v. Social Sec. Admin., 736 F.2d 727, 732, 34 FEP 1514 (D.C. Cir. 1984) (per curiam) (enjoining the disclosure of workforce analyses, department lists, and projected promotions data contained in AAPs and compliance-review reports as exempt under Exemption 4 of the FOIA; but allowing the disclosure of EEO-1 reports, and the remaining portions of the AAPs and compliance-review reports).

[655]5 U.S.C. § 552(b)(6) (2000). One pre-*Chrysler* court denied disclosure of an AAP section that identified minorities and females who were eligible for upgrade and promotion or possessed college degrees. Hughes Aircraft Co. v. Schlesinger, 384 F. Supp. 292, 298, 8 FEP 1163 (C.D. Cal. 1974), *vacated mem.*, 20 FEP 1422 (9th Cir. 1979). Another court, however, found it appropriate to release (1) comments as to reasons applicants were not hired or reasons for employee terminations; (2) comments concerning promotions; and (3) service, termination, and promotion dates. Sears, Roebuck & Co. v. General Servs. Admin., 402 F. Supp. 378, 384, 11 FEP 727 (D.D.C. 1975).

[656]5 U.S.C. § 522(b)(3) (2000); *see, e.g.*, General Dynamics Corp. v. Marshall, 572 F.2d 1211, 1217 n.7, 16 FEP 898 (8th Cir. 1978) (§ 1905 is not a basis for exemption under 5 U.S.C. § 522(b)(3)), *vacated*, 441 U.S. 919 (1979); Crown Cent. Petroleum Corp. v. Kleppe, 424 F. Supp. 744, 750–53, 14 FEP 49 (D. Md. 1976) (§ 709(e) of Title VII and § 1905 are not exempting statutes). *But see* Burroughs Corp. v. Brown, 501 F. Supp. 375, 382–83, 21 FEP 1455 (E.D. Va. 1980) (§ 1905 is statutory exemption under Exemption 3), *vacated and remanded on other grounds sub nom.* General Motors Corp. v. Marshall, 654 F.2d 294, 26 FEP 571 (4th Cir. 1981).

[657]Chrysler Corp. v. Brown, 441 U.S. 281, 318, 19 FEP 475 (1979).

and capricious or its fact-finding procedures are inadequate.[658] In practice, however, the likelihood of de novo review of an OFCCP disclosure decision is remote.[659]

X. VALIDITY OF THE EXECUTIVE ORDER AND RESULTING ACTIONS

A. Validity of the Executive Order and Implementing Regulations

Courts repeatedly have upheld the basic authority of the President to require a nondiscrimination clause in government contracts,[662] and—at least on that issue—have accorded the Executive Order the force and effect of law, over contentions that it is unconstitutional and in conflict with other statutes.[663] In fact, some authorities suggest

---

[658]*See* Camp v. Pitts, 411 U.S. 138, 142 (1973) (recognizing de novo review in cases where adjudication by agency is " 'arbitrary, capricious, an abuse of discretion, or otherwise not in accordance with law,' as specified in 5 U.S.C. § 706(2)(A)"); Citizens to Preserve Overton Park, Inc. v. Volpe, 401 U.S. 402, 415 (1971) (de novo review is appropriate when the action is "adjudicatory in nature and the agency factfinding procedures are inadequate" under 5 U.S.C. § 706(2)(F)); *cf.* General Motors Corp. v. Marshall, 654 F.2d 294, 300, 26 FEP 571 (4th Cir. 1981) (de novo review may be appropriate where the agency does not offer a "fully reasoned basis for its decision"); General Dynamics Corp. v. Marshall, 607 F.2d 234, 235, 21 FEP 568 (8th Cir. 1979) (per curiam) (review based on the agency's record; under *Chrysler*, the agency must determine whether disclosure would be in the public interest and would not impede agency functions and, in the event the agency finds disclosure desirable, whether disclosure is forbidden by the Trade Secrets Act).

[659]*See, e.g.*, CNA Fin. Corp. v. Donovan, 830 F.2d 1132, 1159, 44 FEP 1648 (D.C. Cir. 1987) (the OFCCP employed adequate procedures even where the submitter was denied an evidentiary hearing).

[660][reserved].

[661][reserved].

[662]As discussed more fully in Chapter 37 ("Reverse" Discrimination and Affirmative Action), the Supreme Court has provided guidelines on the permissible scope of goal-oriented AAPs that benefit protected-group members who have not been shown themselves to be the victims of prior discrimination. These decisions generally have not focused directly on the validity of the AAPs mandated by Executive Order 11246. *Cf.* Smith v. Harvey, 648 F. Supp. 1103, 1115, 42 FEP 796 (M.D. Fla. 1986) (AAP for firefighters deemed constitutional pursuant to statutory challenge); Parker v. Baltimore & Ohio R.R., 641 F. Supp. 1227, 1234, 41 FEP 761 (D.D.C. 1986) (AAP implemented under Executive Order 11246 held constitutional).

[663]*See, e.g.*, Utley v. Varian Assocs., 811 F.2d 1279, 1285 n.4, 43 FEP 191 (9th Cir. 1987) (separation of powers requires that an executive order be "rooted" in an

that the Constitution *compels* the government to impose the basic condition of nondiscrimination in its contracts.[664]

Nevertheless, the precise source of the President's authority to carry out the contract compliance program has not been conclusively agreed upon.[665] Most courts identify the procurement power granted by the Federal Property and Administrative Services Act of 1949[666] as the sole or principal basis for the Executive Order.[667] Other courts have found additional statutory support for the Executive Order in Title VII itself or its 1972 amendments.[668] The source of authority selected is important in determining the validity of particular regulations or actions.

---

appropriate grant of congressional authority); First Ala. Bank of Montgomery, N.A. v. Donovan, 692 F.2d 714, 721–22, 30 FEP 448 (11th Cir. 1982) (due process challenge to the Executive Order summarily rejected; bank had challenged the order's administrative procedures that permit quasi-judicial hearings to be conducted by administrative law judges who are employed by the same agency that initiates review); United States v. Mississippi Power & Light Co., 638 F.2d 899, 905, 25 FEP 250 (5th Cir. 1981) (proposition that the Executive Order has the force and effect of law is well established).

[664]*See* NAACP v. Federal Power Comm'n, 520 F.2d 432, 444–46, 10 FEP 3 (D.C. Cir. 1975) (Federal Power Commission has a constitutional duty under the Fifth Amendment to prohibit employment discrimination by regulatees), *aff'd*, 425 U.S. 662 (1976); Castillo v. Usery, 14 FEP 1240, 1250 (N.D. Cal. 1976) ("Eradication of employment discrimination is a national policy of 'the highest priority.' In the federal compliance program the policy has constitutional dimensions since public funds may not constitutionally be used to subsidize employment discrimination.") (citations omitted).

[665]*See* Chrysler Corp. v. Brown, 441 U.S. 281, 304–06, 19 FEP 475 (1979) (discussing possible sources of authority for the Executive Order).

[666]Federal Property and Administrative Services Act of 1949, ch. 288, 64 Stat. 377 (codified as amended in scattered sections of U.S.C. titles 40, 41, 44, and 50).

[667]*See* United States v. East Tex. Motor Freight Sys., 564 F.2d 179, 184, 16 FEP 163 (5th Cir. 1977) ("The order is authorized by the broad grant of procurement authority."); Contractors Ass'n of E. Pa. v. Secretary of Labor, 442 F.2d 159, 170, 3 FEP 395 (3d Cir. 1971) ("it is in the interest of the United States in all procurement to see that its suppliers are not over the long run increasing its costs and delaying its programs by excluding from the labor pool available minority workmen"); Farkas v. Texas Instruments, Inc., 375 F.2d 629, 632 n.1, 1 FEP 890 (5th Cir. 1967) ("We would be hesitant to say that the antidiscrimination provisions of Executive Order No. 10925 are so unrelated to the establishment of 'an economical and efficient system for . . . the procurement and supply' of property and services, 40 U.S.C.A. § 471, that the order should be treated as issued without statutory authority.").

[668]*See* Eatmon v. Bristol Steel & Iron Works, Inc., 769 F.2d 1503, 1516, 38 FEP 1364 (11th Cir. 1985) (Executive Order 11246 is authorized by Title VII) (citing *Contractors Ass'n of E. Pa.*, 442 F.2d at 171); United States v. New Orleans Pub. Serv., Inc., 553 F.2d 459, 467, 14 FEP 1734 (5th Cir. 1977) (legislative history of Title VII and the 1972 Act indicates the congressional intent that the Executive Order

1. Validity of Particular Regulations

The validity of a particular implementing regulation or its administrative application under the Executive Order is a recurring question. In *Chrysler Corp. v. Brown*,[669] the Supreme Court considered the validity of OFCCP regulations calling for public disclosure, pursuant to the FOIA, of information submitted by contractors to the government. In its decision, the Court explained:

> The origins of the congressional authority for Executive Order 11246 are somewhat obscure and have been roundly debated by commentators and courts. . . . For purposes of this case, it is not necessary to decide whether Executive Order 11246 as amended is authorized by the Federal Property and Administrative Services Act of 1949, Titles VI and VII of the Civil Rights Act of 1964, the Equal Employment Opportunity Act of 1972, or some more general notion that the Executive can impose reasonable contractual requirements in the exercise of its procurement authority. The pertinent inquiry is whether under any of the arguable *statutory* grants of authority the OFCCP disclosure regulations relied on by the [government] are reasonably within the contemplation of that grant of authority. We think that it is clear that when it enacted these statutes, Congress was not concerned with public disclosure of trade secrets or confidential business information, and, unless we were to hold that any federal statute that implies some authority to collect information must grant *legislative* authority to disclose that information to the public, it is simply not possible to find in these statutes a delegation of the disclosure authority asserted by the [government] here.
>
> The relationship between any grant of legislative authority and the disclosure regulations becomes more remote when one examines § 201 of the Executive Order. It speaks in terms of rules and regulations "necessary and appropriate" to achieve the purposes of the Executive Order. Those purposes are an end to discrimination in employment by the Federal Government and those who deal with the Federal Government. One cannot readily pull from the logic and purposes of the Executive Order any concern with the public's

---

program continue and that Title VII not be the exclusive federal remedy in this area), *vacated and remanded on other grounds*, 436 U.S. 942, 17 FEP 897 (1978); Legal Aid Soc'y v. Brennan, 608 F.2d 1319, 1329 n.14, 21 FEP 605 (9th Cir. 1979) (essential features of affirmative action regulations were effectively ratified by Congress in adopting the 1972 Act because frontal attacks on OFCCP goal-and-timetable enforcement system were defeated).

[669]441 U.S. 281, 19 FEP 475 (1979). For a further discussion of this case, the arguments raised by Chrysler, and the FOIA, see Section IX *supra*.

access to information in Government files or the importance of protecting trade secrets or confidential business statistics.

The "purpose and scope" section of the disclosure regulations indicates two underlying rationales: OFCCP's general policy "to disclose information to the public," and its policy "to cooperate with other public agencies as well as private parties seeking to eliminate discrimination in employment." 41 C.F.R. § 60-40.1 (1978). The [government] argue[s] that "[t]he purpose of the Executive Order is to combat discrimination in employment, and a disclosure policy designed to further this purpose is consistent with the Executive Order and an appropriate subject for regulation under its aegis." Were a grant of legislative authority as a basis for Executive Order 11246 more clearly identifiable, we might agree with the [government] that this "compatibility" gives the disclosure regulations the necessary legislative force. But the thread between these regulations and any grant of authority by the Congress is so strained that it would do violence to established principles of separation of powers to denominate these particular regulations "legislative" and credit them with the "binding effect of law."[670]

In light of *Chrysler*, therefore, the validity of a particular regulation is contingent upon some grant of legislative authority.

Failure to properly use or to exhaust administrative remedies can be fatal to challenges to the OFCCP's enforcement actions. In *Trinity Industries v. Herman*,[671] the company maintained that the OFCCP lacked jurisdiction to conduct a compliance review at a facility that had no involvement with the company's federal contract work. The local agency office advised the company that such an issue could be addressed only by requesting a waiver from the Deputy Assistant Secretary. The company took no further action to request a waiver. The agency then filed an administrative complaint against the company, seeking to compel compliance with the reporting requirement. An administrative law judge held for the agency, and the Administrative Review Board affirmed. The company subsequently filed an action in federal district court contesting this order, and the district court granted summary judgment in

---

[670]*Chrysler*, 441 U.S. at 304–08 (footnotes and some citations omitted).

[671]173 F.3d 527, 79 FEP 854 (4th Cir. 1999); *see also* Goya de Puerto Rico, Inc. v. Herman, 115 F. Supp. 2d 262 (D.P.R. 2000) (government contractor required to exhaust administrative remedies with the OFCCP prior to filing suit challenging constitutionality of AAP under Rehabilitation Act, VEVRAA, and the Executive Order, even though agency did not have jurisdiction to consider constitutional questions).

favor of the Secretary of Labor. On appeal, the appellate court upheld the waiver provisions of the regulations. It concluded that the company had not used the proper administrative route and, in any event, had filed suit in court in the absence of final agency action.[672]

In *NationsBank Corp. v. Herman*,[673] the bank and its subsidiaries challenged the constitutionality of the OFCCP's selection of certain of the bank's offices for compliance reviews. Soon after notifying the bank of alleged violations of the Executive Order at one of its branches, the agency initiated compliance reviews at two other bank offices in different states. The bank refused to cooperate unless the agency revealed what criteria it had used in selecting these two new offices. When the agency did not respond, the bank filed an action for declaratory and injunctive relief in federal district court, alleging that the document searches incident to the compliance reviews were unreasonable, in violation of the Fourth Amendment, because the agency had not used neutral selection criteria. The district court denied the agency's motion to dismiss and subsequent motion for summary judgment, which were based on the bank's failure to exhaust administrative remedies, and granted the bank's motion for a preliminary injunction. On appeal, the appellate court quickly dispatched the bank's arguments and reversed, holding that the bank "must exhaust administrative remedies before bringing its Fourth Amendment suit against the OFCCP."[674]

2. *Validity of the Affirmative Action Requirement*

A broader question—and, today, one much debated—is the validity of the affirmative action requirement. The order does not define the concept "affirmative action." It simply refers to affirmative action as a commitment "to ensure that applicants are employed . . . without regard to their race, color, religion, sex or national origin."[675] Thus, it is possible to read the term narrowly,

---

[672]173 F.3d at 529–31.

[673]174 F.3d 424, 79 FEP 1113 (4th Cir. 1999).

[674]*Id.* at 426–28; *see also* Volvo GM Heavy Truck Corp. v. U. S. Dep't of Labor, 118 F.3d 205, 211–12, 74 FEP 399 (4th Cir. 1997); *Goya de P.R., Inc.*, 115 F. Supp. 2d at 267–68.

[675]Exec. Order No. 11246, § 202(1) (1965), *reprinted as amended in* 1 AFFIRMATIVE ACTION COMPL. MAN. (BNA) 101.

as only requiring action to assure that employment *discrimination* does not occur. For many years, however, the OFCCP has interpreted the Executive Order to require affirmative action to *increase* the utilization of women and minorities. AAPs mandated by the present regulations must contain provisions to achieve both objectives.[676]

The constitutional and legal status of affirmative action under the Executive Order is unresolved. A number of early decisions rejected constitutional and statutory challenges to the validity of government-imposed AAPs requiring goals and timetables in the construction industry.[677] These cases, however, predate significant developments in the Supreme Court's development of a "reverse discrimination" jurisprudence.[678] It remains an open question whether OFCCP-mandated AAPs, which are required even without a finding of past discrimination by the contractor, are permissible under Title VII and consistent with equal protection. Lower courts have found no unlawful discrimination when contractors have defended employment actions based upon Executive Order AAP commitments, but these cases also predate many, if not most, of the major Supreme Court precedents. In *McLaughlin v. Great Lakes Dredge & Dock Co.*,[679] a white male alleged that he was discriminated against, in violation of Title VII and the Fifth and Fourteenth Amendments, when a less-experienced minority applicant was re-

---

[676]The Executive Order AAP must be designed to achieve full utilization of minorities and women. 41 C.F.R. § 60-2.10 (2004). It also must contain provisions to monitor personnel actions "to ensure the nondiscriminatory policy is carried out." *See id.* § 60-2.17(d).

[677]*E.g.*, Southern Ill. Builders Ass'n v. Ogilvie, 471 F.2d 680, 686–87, 5 FEP 229 (7th Cir. 1972) (the "Ogilvie Plan" for recruitment, placement, and training of minority group members in the highway construction industry did not violate the Fifth and Fourteenth Amendments); Contractors Ass'n of E. Pa. v. Secretary of Labor, 442 F.2d 159, 177, 3 FEP 395 (3d Cir. 1971) (upholding the "Philadelphia Plan" for utilization of minorities in construction trades).

[678]*See generally* Chapter 37 ("Reverse" Discrimination and Affirmative Action). For example, *Fullilove v. Klutznick*, 448 U.S. 448 (1980), involved a congressional set-aside of federal funds for the promotion of minority business participation in local public works projects. Congress itself explicitly authorized the set-aside. According to one of the concurring opinions in *Fullilove*, for race-conscious remedies to be constitutional they must be imposed by an appropriate governmental body authorized to act in this area, following findings that demonstrate the existence of illegal discrimination. *Id.* at 498 (Powell, J., concurring). The Executive Order is an administrative, rather than a legislative, program. Its principal source of legislative authority, the procurement law, makes no mention of affirmative action.

[679]495 F. Supp. 857, 23 FEP 1295 (N.D. Ohio 1980).

called ahead of him from layoff. The district court held that an AAP was "adopted voluntarily" by the contractor (even though it was required by the company's government contract) and did not create unlawful reverse discrimination.[680] Other cases are to the same effect.[681] However, litigants are likely to challenge the assumption in *McLaughlin* that AAPs mandated by the Executive Order are voluntary, particularly in view of the fact that the OFCCP asserts jurisdiction[682] over contractors who in fact have *not* consented to the equal opportunity clause.

In defending its program, the government may rely on *United States v. New Orleans Public Service, Inc.*[683] The defendant, New Orleans Public Service, Inc. (NOPSI), a public utility, challenged the government's authority to impose Executive Order obligations on NOPSI when it had not agreed to be bound. NOPSI supplied gas and electric services to various federal agencies within its territory. The Fifth Circuit held that the government could compel NOPSI to comply with the Executive Order even though the company had not consented to be so bound. The court stated that NOPSI's lack of consent was irrelevant: "The regulation incorporating by

---

[680]*Id.* at 861.

[681]*See also* Freeze v. ARO, Inc., 503 F. Supp. 1045, 1048, 24 FEP 837 (E.D. Tenn. 1980) (no Title VII violation in granting an African-American employee preferential seniority pursuant to Executive Order conciliation agreement with Secretary of Labor), *aff'd mem.*, 708 F.2d 723 (6th Cir. 1982); Tangren v. Wackenhut Servs., Inc., 480 F. Supp. 539, 547, 21 FEP 570 (D. Nev. 1979) (upholding, under the *Weber* criteria, a seniority override provision in favor of minorities; it was established to bring the contractor into compliance with the Executive Order), *aff'd*, 658 F.2d 705 (9th Cir. 1981); *cf.* Hunter v. St. Louis-San Francisco Ry., 639 F.2d 424, 426, 24 FEP 1601 (8th Cir. 1981) (railroad did not violate Title VII by rejecting a white female applicant in favor of African-American male applicants pursuant to an Executive Order AAP valid under the *Weber* criteria; by articulating a racial criterion that was permissible under Title VII, the railroad stated a nondiscriminatory reason).

[682]*See* Liberty Mut. Ins. Co. v. Friedman, 639 F.2d 164, 168–71, 24 FEP 1168 (4th Cir. 1981); United States v. New Orleans Pub. Serv., Inc., 553 F.2d 459, 467–68, 14 FEP 1734 (5th Cir. 1977), *vacated and remanded on other grounds*, 436 U.S. 942, 17 FEP 897 (1978). The OFCCP takes the position that banks and other financial institutions are parties to covered government contracts by reason of their subscription to federal deposit and share insurance. 45 Fed. Reg. 86,216, 86,218 (1980). Because the purchase of such insurance from the government is required of federally chartered financial institutions, coverage under the order virtually becomes automatic. The banks must acquiesce in the assertion of OFCCP jurisdiction, and comply with the affirmative action obligation, or forego an essential service.

[683]553 F.2d 459, 14 FEP 1734 (5th Cir. 1977), *vacated and remanded on other grounds*, 436 U.S. 942, 17 FEP 897 (1978).

operation of the Order the nondiscrimination clause into every government contract would be a dead letter if the Government could not apply it to a government contractor like NOPSI, merely because the company refused to consent."[684] There was no unfairness, the court said, in NOPSI's lack of choice as to whether to accept the government's business. A utility in a monopoly situation cannot force upon the government the dilemma of either acquiescing or going without necessary services by refusing to consent.[685] The court concluded that "equal employment goals themselves, reflecting important national policies, validate the use of the procurement power in the context of the [Executive] Order."[686]

Consider, on the other hand, *Liberty Mutual Insurance Co. v. Friedman*.[687] That case involved a company that unknowingly became a subcontractor within the meaning of the Executive Order, because it did business with a covered prime contractor that had not identified the work as necessary or even related to a government contract. In *Liberty Mutual*, the company sought a declaratory judgment defining its status under the Executive Order. Plaintiff had no prime government contracts. It did, however, provide workers'

---

[684]533 F.2d at 468.

[685]*Id.* at 470. Following the intervening decision in *Chrysler Corp v. Brown*, 441 U.S. 281, 19 FEP 475 (1979), the Fifth Circuit reaffirmed its holding that the Executive Order had proper statutory authority and could validly be applied to the utilities:

> *Chrysler* does not undermine our holding that E.O. 11246 is itself firmly rooted in congressionally delegated authority. . . . The regulation is an evocation of the strict policy that the affirmative action obligation is an understood and unalterable part of doing business with the government. If the federal government has the power to impose the affirmative action obligation at all, it must certainly have the power to impose it without exception. . . . [T]he regulation does "nothing more than give teeth to the mandate of the Order."

United States v. Mississippi Power & Light Co., 638 F.2d 899, 905–06, 25 FEP 250 (5th Cir. 1981) (citations omitted).

[686]*New Orleans Pub. Serv., Inc.*, 553 F.2d at 467; *cf.* AFL-CIO v. Kahn, 618 F.2d 784, 796 (D.C. Cir. 1979) (the Procurement Act gave the President the authority to condition the letting of contracts in excess of $5 million on the contractor's compliance with wage and price guidelines); Contractors Ass'n of E. Pa. v. Secretary of Labor, 442 F.2d 159, 176, 3 FEP 395 (3d Cir. 1971) (sustaining the validity of the "Philadelphia Plan"; the source of the affirmative action requirement was a voluntary contractual agreement: "Plaintiffs . . . are merely being invited to bid on a contract with terms imposed by the source of the funds. The affirmative action covenant is no different in kind than other covenants specified in the invitation to bid. . . . The Plan . . . exacts a covenant for present performance.").

[687]639 F.2d 164, 24 FEP 1168 (4th Cir. 1981).

compensation insurance to several companies that held prime contracts with the government. Liberty Mutual's insurance agreements
with those contractors did not contain the equal opportunity clause.
Liberty Mutual's clients purchased a single workers' compensation insurance policy to cover employees who both worked on
federal contracts and those who did not, without distinction between the two.

The district court held that Liberty Mutual was a government
subcontractor,[688] following *United States v. New Orleans Public
Service, Inc.* But the Fourth Circuit reversed, concluding that application of the Executive Order to Liberty Mutual was not reason-
ably within the contemplation of any statutory grant of authority.
Specifically, the court held that the general procurement power of
Congress as delegated to the executive branch by the Federal Property and Administrative Services Act[689] was not a source of agency
authority for imposing the Executive Order on Liberty Mutual; the
Act does not even mention employment discrimination.[690] Citing
Chrysler, the court held that Titles VI and VII of the Civil Rights
Act of 1964 are not sources of statutory authorization for the
Executive Order because neither title contains any express delegation of substantive lawmaking authority to the President.[691] The
1972 amendments did not supply that delegation either, the court
held; that Congress rejected a series of amendments that would
have cut back the Executive Order program does not establish a
grant of authority to extend the Executive Order to companies like
Liberty Mutual, even assuming *arguendo* that the Executive Order
could lawfully be applied to some prime contractors.

B. Validity of the Back-Pay Remedy

Claims for back pay under the Executive Order have arisen in
two distinct situations. First, the government has sought back pay
as a remedy in a lawsuit or an administrative enforcement proceeding

---

[688]Liberty Mut. Ins. Co. v. Friedman, 485 F. Supp. 695, 708, 21 FEP 1016 (D.
Md. 1979), *rev'd*, 639 F.2d 164 (4th Cir. 1981).

[689]Federal Property and Administrative Services Act of 1949, ch. 288, 63 Stat.
377 (codified as amended in scattered sections of 40, 41, 44 and 50 U.S.C.).

[690]*Liberty Mut.*, 639 F.2d at 169–70.

[691]*Id.* at 172.

in which the contractor is found to have engaged in discrimination in violation of the equal employment clause of its government contract.[692] In *United States v. Duquesne Light Co.*,[693] a district court refused to strike a claim for back pay from an action brought by the Attorney General to enforce Duquesne Light's Executive Order and contractual obligations. The court held that there was statutory authority, or inherent executive authority, for the government to seek back pay, because such "restitutionary relief" would provide an incentive to eliminate discriminatory employment practices that increase the costs of government contracts.[694] Yet, in *American Airlines v. Herman*,[695] a federal district court held that the OFCCP had no authority under the Rehabilitation Act to seek back pay or other remedies on behalf of alleged victims of disability discrimination for acts occurring prior to the 1992 effective date of that statute. On appeal, however, the Fifth Circuit reversed and remanded, finding that the district court lacked jurisdiction because American Airlines had failed to exhaust administrative remedies prior to bringing its action for declaratory relief.[696]

Second, the OFCCP has sought back pay for an "affected class."[697] The OFCCP takes the position that an " 'affected class'

---

[692]41 C.F.R. § 60-1.26(a)(2) (2005).

[693]423 F. Supp. 507, 13 FEP 1608 (W.D. Pa. 1976).

[694]*Id.* at 509.

[695]971 F. Supp. 1096, 1097–98, 7 AD 1 (N.D. Tex. 1997), *rev'd*, 176 F.3d 283 (5th Cir. 1999).

[696]American Airlines v. Herman, 176 F.3d 283, 294, 9 AD 516 (5th Cir. 1999).

[697]*See* 41 C.F.R. §§ 60-1.26(a)(2), -1.33, -250.62(a), -741.62(a) (2005). In 1987, the OFCCP clarified that back pay may be awarded for violations that occur within 2 years of the time the contractor is notified of a compliance review. OFCCP Order No. 640a5, [1979–1987 Transfer Binder] OFCCP FED. CONT. COMPL. MAN. (CCH) ¶ 21,293, at 3550 (Feb. 23, 1982). There is a suggestion in a few earlier Recommended Decisions that back pay may be sought for violations prior to the 2-year period if a continuing violation exists. *See* Department of Labor v. St. Regis Corp., No. 78-OFCCP-1 (Dec. 28, 1984) (Recommended Decision) (utilizing the formula stated in Title VII, the ALJ proposed that back-pay entitlement for affected employees be retroactive to the date of the new year following the original compliance review that revealed continuing hiring deficiencies); Department of Labor v. Harris Trust & Sav. Bank, No. 78-OFCCP-2, [1979–1987 Transfer Binder] OFCCP FED. CONT. COMPL. MAN. (CCH) ¶ 21,281, at 3515 (Dec. 22, 1986) (Recommended Decision) (recommending a classwide back-pay remedy, retroactive to a date prior to the 2-year period). This view is inconsistent with the subsequent position expressed by the Department of Labor in OFCCP Order No. 640a5 and, thus, should not be considered authoritative. These decisions also provide, however, that the 2-year period

problem" must be remedied—i.e., there must be no continuing effects of discrimination—in order for a contractor to be in compliance. Contractors have disputed this position, claiming it goes beyond the authority of the Executive Order. These challenges to date have been unsuccessful.[698]

---

should be shortened to exclude any period covered by a compliance review that has been approved by the Department of Labor or not acted upon by the Director of the OFCCP within 45 days of the execution of a conciliation agreement.

[698]*See, e.g.*, United States v. Whitney Nat'l Bank, 671 F. Supp. 441, 442, 45 FEP 983 ("Executive Order 11246 lawfully imposes a back pay obligation on government contractors allegedly guilty of discriminatory employment practices."); United States v. Commercial Lovelace Motor Freight, Inc., 31 FEP 499, 502 (S.D. Ohio 1983) (court refuses to dismiss plaintiff's back-pay claim on summary judgment).

Part VII

Remedies and Resolution

CHAPTER 39

INJUNCTIVE AND AFFIRMATIVE RELIEF

I. STATUTORY AUTHORITY AND OBJECTIVES

Title VII authorizes injunctive and affirmative relief.[1] Section 706(g)(1) of Title VII provides, in relevant part:

> If the court finds that the respondent has intentionally engaged in or is intentionally engaging in an unlawful employment practice charged in the complaint, the court may enjoin the respondent from engaging in such unlawful employment practice, and order such affirmative action as may be appropriate, which may include, but

---

[1]The Age Discrimination in Employment Act (ADEA) and the Americans with Disabilities Act (ADA) also provide for injunctive relief. *See* 29 U.S.C. § 626(b) (2000) (making injunctive relief available under ADEA and stating in relevant part that "[i]n any action brought to enforce this chapter the court shall have jurisdiction to grant such . . . equitable relief as may be appropriate to effectuate the purposes of this chapter, including without limitation judgments compelling employment, reinstatement or promotion"); 42 U.S.C. § 12117(a) (2000) (making injunctive relief available under ADA by incorporating remedies of § 2000e-5 of Title VII).

is not limited to, reinstatement or hiring of employees, . . . or any other equitable relief as the court deems appropriate.[2]

Section 706(g)(2)(B), added by the Civil Rights Act of 1991, generally allows a court to order relief for a plaintiff in cases where race, color, religion, sex, or national origin is found to be *a* motivating factor—i.e., mixed-motive cases.[3] In some mixed-motive cases, however, the availability of affirmative relief is limited. Where the "respondent demonstrates that the respondent would have taken the same action in the absence of the impermissible motivating factor," the court may not "issue an order requiring any admission, reinstatement, hiring, [or] promotion."[4] In such mixed-motive situations the court may order declaratory relief and certain types of injunctive relief, and attorney's fees and costs.[5]

---

[2]42 U.S.C. § 2000e-5(g)(1) (2000). Although § 706(g)(1) specifies the remedies in cases where the employer "has intentionally engaged in an unlawful employment practice," the Supreme Court has held that § 706(g) relief is also available in adverse impact cases. *See* Albemarle Paper Co. v. Moody, 422 U.S. 405, 415–23, 10 FEP 1181 (1975).

[3]Pub. L. No. 102-166, § 107(a), 1991 U.S.C.C.A.N. (105 Stat.) 1071, 1075 (codified at 42 U.S.C. § 2000e-2(m) (2000)). An employee need not present direct evidence of discrimination in a mixed-motive case, but need only "present sufficient evidence for a reasonable jury to conclude, by a preponderance of the evidence, that 'race, color, religion, sex, or national origin was a motivating factor for any employment practice.' " Desert Palace, Inc. v. Costa, 539 U.S. 90, 95–96 (2003).

[4]Pub. L. No. 102-166, § 107(b) (codified at 42 U.S.C. § 2000e-5(g)(2)(B)(ii)); *see also Desert Palace*, 539 U.S. at 94 (in mixed-motive case "the employer has a limited affirmative defense that does not absolve it of liability, but restricts the remedies available to a plaintiff . . . [to] include only declaratory relief, certain types of injunctive relief, and attorney's fees and costs"); Gagnon v. Sprint Corp., 284 F.3d 839, 847–48, 88 FEP 417 (8th Cir. 2002) (whether defendant would have reached same employment decision absent any discrimination "only relevant to determine whether the court may award full relief"), *cert. denied*, 537 U.S. 1001 (2002); Weston-Smith v. Cooley Dickinson Hosp., Inc., 282 F.3d 60, 64, 88 FEP 716 (1st Cir. 2002) (employer may avoid liability for monetary damages and reinstatement if it can show that it "would have taken the same action in the absence of the impermissible motivating factor"); Arnold v. United States Dep't of Interior, 213 F.3d 193, 197, 82 FEP 1786 (5th Cir. 2000) (relief limited where "mixed motive defense" is established).

[5]42 U.S.C. § 2000e-5(g)(2)(B)(i), (ii) (2000) (in mixed-motive cases, courts may grant attorney's fees, declaratory relief, and injunctive relief, except orders requiring any admission, reinstatement, hiring, or promotion); *see also* Garcia v. City of Houston, 201 F.3d 672, 678, 82 FEP 1 (5th Cir. 2000) (awarding attorney's fees where plaintiff proved race discrimination but employer established mixed-motive defense; injunction not issued because of absence of continuing harm); Norris v. Sysco Corp., 191 F.3d 1043, 1050–52 (9th Cir. 1999) (awarding attorney's fees on Title VII gender claim although employer established mixed-motive defense; failing to award

Congress vested courts with broad authority to fashion appropriate relief.[6] Although the decision to grant or deny injunctive relief is a matter for the trial court's discretion,[7] that discretion must be exercised in a manner consistent with the purposes of the Act.[8] Two related but distinct purposes underlie the Act: (1) to eradicate discrimination and thereby achieve equality of employment opportunity,[9] and (2) to "make whole" actual victims of discrimination by restoring them, so far as practicable, to where they would have been but for the unlawful discrimination.[10]

The Supreme Court, in *Albemarle Paper Co. v. Moody*,[11] held that district courts have "not merely the power but the duty to render a decree which will so far as possible eliminate the discriminatory effects of the past as well as bar like discrimination in the future."[12] Thus, where courts decline to grant relief that is generally available under Title VII, they should "carefully articulate" their reasons for doing so,[13] and those reasons must be ones that,

---

injunctive and declaratory relief); Gudenkauf v. Stauffer Commc'ns, Inc., 158 F.3d 1074, 1077, 77 FEP 1742 (10th Cir. 1998) (denying injunctive relief but awarding attorney's fees to plaintiff); Peoples v. Florida Dep't of Children & Families, 24 F. Supp. 2d 1268, 1276 (N.D. Fla. 1998) (enjoining defendant from considering race in promotion applications and from engaging in subjective promotion procedures in mixed-motive Title VII race discrimination promotions case after jury finding of liability as well as finding that defendant would have made same decision absent discrimination). *See generally* Chapters 40 (Monetary Relief) and 41 (Attorney's Fees).

Courts are divided over the applicability of the mixed-motive provisions of the 1991 Civil Rights Act to mixed-motive retaliation cases. *See generally* Chapter 14 (Retaliation), Section IV.E.

[6]*E.g.*, Sheet Metal Workers Local 28 v. EEOC, 478 U.S. 421, 446, 41 FEP 107 (1986); Bruso v. United Airlines, Inc., 239 F.3d 848, 863, 84 FEP 1780 (7th Cir. 2001) ("district court is given broad discretion to fashion an equitable remedy").

[7]*See* 42 U.S.C. § 2000e-5(g)(2)(B) (2000).

[8]*See* Franks v. Bowman Transp. Co., 424 U.S. 747, 770–71, 12 FEP 549 (1976); Albemarle Paper Co. v. Moody, 422 U.S. 405, 415–17, 10 FEP 1181 (1975); *see also* Garrison v. Baker Hughes Oilfield Operations, Inc., 287 F.3d 955, 961 (10th Cir. 2002) ("The court's discretion is to be exercised in light of the purposes of the statute on which [the] plaintiff's suit is based.") (quoting Roe v. Cheyenne Mountain Conference Resort, Inc., 124 F.3d 1221, 1230, 7 AD 779 (10th Cir. 1997)).

[9]*Franks*, 424 U.S. at 771; *Albemarle Paper*, 422 U.S. at 417, 421.

[10]*Franks*, 424 U.S. at 763–64; *Albemarle Paper*, 422 U.S. at 418–19.

[11]422 U.S. 405, 10 FEP 1181 (1975).

[12]*Id.* at 418 (quoting Louisiana v. United States, 380 U.S. 145, 154 (1965)); *accord Franks*, 424 U.S. at 770.

[13]*Albemarle Paper*, 422 U.S. at 421 n.14; *see also Franks*, 424 U.S. at 774. A failure to articulate such reasons, however, need not be considered abuse of discretion

if generally applied, would not frustrate the purposes of the Act.[14] Indeed, many courts apply liberally the language in *Albemarle Paper*.[15]

Despite the broad language in *Albemarle Paper*, injunctive relief cases may present difficult issues. Where job opportunities are limited, for example, *affirmative relief* for one individual can be an *impediment* to job opportunity for another. Section 706(g) itself suggests a limitation on the circumstances in which affirmative relief is proper under Title VII:

> No order of the court shall require the admission or reinstatement of an individual as a member of a union or the hiring, reinstatement, or promotion of an individual as an employee, or the payment to him of any back pay, if such individual was refused admission, suspended, or expelled, or was refused employment or advancement

---

requiring reversal and remand. *See* Barbano v. Madison County, 922 F.2d 139, 146–47, 54 FEP 1287 (2d Cir. 1990) (although it would have been better for district court to state its reasons for denying both appointment to next vacancy and front pay, its failure to do so, under circumstances of case, was not abuse of discretion); *cf.* McKnight v. General Motors, Inc., 908 F.2d 104, 116, 53 FEP 505 (7th Cir. 1990) ("make-whole" language of *Albemarle Paper* was dictum).

[14]*Albemarle Paper*, 422 U.S. at 421; *Franks*, 424 U.S. at 771, 774.

[15]*See, e.g.*, Pollard v. E.I. du Pont de Nemours & Co., 532 U.S. 843, 849–50, 853–54, 85 FEP 1217 (2001) (front pay may be awarded in lieu of reinstatement given remedies authorized under Title VII); Teamsters v. United States, 431 U.S. 324, 364–67, 14 FEP 1514 (1977) (failure to apply for job does not automatically bar award of retroactive seniority, based on remedial principles of *Albemarle Paper* and *Franks*); Morrison v. Circuit City Stores, Inc., 317 F.3d 646, 670, 90 FEP 1697 (6th Cir. 2003) (arbitration agreement provision that limited remedies was unenforceable because it significantly undermined remedial purposes of Title VII); Newark Branch, NAACP v. Town of Harrison, 940 F.2d 792, 806–07, 56 FEP 680 (3d Cir. 1991) (affirming order requiring affirmative recruitment of African-American police officers and fire fighters because *Albemarle Paper* gives district court broad power to order most complete relief possible to eliminate effects of discrimination and bar like discrimination in future); EEOC v. Gurnee Inn Corp., 914 F.2d 815, 817, 53 FEP 1425 (7th Cir. 1990) (affirming order that prohibited future discrimination and required policy effectively banning sexual harassment; under *Albemarle Paper*, trial court has wide discretion to fashion complete remedy to eliminate effects of past discrimination and bar like discrimination in future); Ingram v. Missouri Pac. R.R., 897 F.2d 1450, 1456–57 (8th Cir. 1990) (district court order reinstating employee at higher rate of pay, subject to nondiscriminatory consideration for even higher job, was inadequate; in view of mandate to provide fullest possible make-whole relief, defendant should be ordered to promote employee to first available vacancy); Hopkins v. Price Waterhouse, 920 F.2d 967, 975–77, 54 FEP 750 (D.C. Cir. 1990) (affirming award of professional partnership; applying remedial principles of *Albemarle Paper* and *Franks*); Brown v. Trustees of Boston Univ., 891 F.2d 337, 359–60, 51 FEP 815 (1st Cir. 1989) (affirming grant of reinstatement with academic tenure, based on *Albemarle Paper*'s mandate to provide most complete relief possible in making victim whole).

The teaching of *Albemarle Paper* has been extended to cases under the ADEA. *See, e.g.*, Farber v. Massillon Bd. of Educ., 917 F.2d 1391, 1396–97, 54 FEP 1063

or was suspended or discharged for any reason other than discrimination . . . .[16]

The U.S. Supreme Court, faced with that language, has sent different messages about what limits § 706(g) places on the circumstances under which a court can order affirmative relief. In 1984, the Court suggested that "make whole" relief that protects persons from layoffs is available only to actual victims of unlawful discrimination.[17] Just two terms later, however, the Court held that affirmative relief designed to eliminate the effects of discrimination is not always so limited; in appropriate cases, beneficiaries of such relief need not be shown to have been actual victims.[18]

With these caveats, this chapter will explore court-ordered affirmative relief.[19] Courts that find unlawful discrimination have entered injunctions that fall generally into three categories: (1) orders

---

(6th Cir. 1990) (reversing and remanding district court's denial of reinstatement to successful age discrimination plaintiff, in light of *Albemarle Paper*'s mandate that equitable relief should be denied only for carefully articulated reasons that, if generally applied, will not frustrate statutory goals of eradicating discrimination and making persons whole); Morgan v. Arkansas Gazette, 897 F.2d 945, 953–54, 52 FEP 431 (8th Cir. 1990) (affirming order of reinstatement; reinstatement often is best way to effectuate purposes of ADEA; under *Albemarle Paper*, relief should be denied only for reasons that, if generally applied, would not frustrate statutory goals of eradicating discrimination and making victims whole); Verbraeken v. Westinghouse Elec. Corp., 881 F.2d 1041, 1052, 50 FEP 1099 (11th Cir. 1989) (remanding case to district court to carefully articulate its rationale for denying requested equitable relief).

[16]42 U.S.C. § 2000e-5(g)(2)(A) (2000).

[17]Fire Fighters Local 1784 v. Stotts, 467 U.S. 561, 576 n.9, 37 FEP 1702 (1984) ("Title VII precludes a district court from displacing a non-minority employee with seniority under the contractually established seniority system absent either a finding that the seniority system was adopted with discriminatory intent or a determination that such a remedy was necessary to make whole a proven victim of discrimination").

[18]Sheet Metal Workers Local 28 v. EEOC, 478 U.S. 421, 474 (1986) (plurality opinion) ("The purpose of affirmative action is not to make identified victims whole, but rather to dismantle prior patterns of employment discrimination and to prevent discrimination in the future. Such relief is provided to the class as a whole rather than to individual members; no individual is entitled to relief, and beneficiaries need not show that they were themselves victims of discrimination."); *id.* at 483 (Powell, J., concurring in part and concurring in judgment) ("I further agree that § 706(g) does not limit a court in all cases to granting relief only to actual victims of discrimination."); *id.* at 499 (White, J., dissenting) ("But I agree that § 706(g) does not bar relief for nonvictims in all circumstances."). On the same day that *Sheet Metal Workers* was decided, the Court decided *Fire Fighters (IAFF) Local 93 v. City of Cleveland*, 478 U.S. 501 (1986), in which the Court held that § 706(g) did not apply to voluntary actions undertaken pursuant to a consent decree.

[19]Voluntary actions pursuant to a consent decree or an affirmative action plan are addressed in Chapter 37 ("Reverse" Discrimination and Affirmative Action).

that enjoin either specific discriminatory practices or any further discrimination on the part of the defendant;[20] (2) orders that provide "make-whole" relief to victims of discrimination;[21] and (3) orders that mandate affirmative relief to eliminate the effects of past discrimination.[22] Each of these categories is discussed in turn.

II. ENJOINING PRACTICES FOUND TO BE UNLAWFUL

The most straightforward kind of affirmative relief often is an injunction against the use of specific, unlawful employment practices. Thus, for example, following a finding that they are discriminatory, courts have enjoined height and weight requirements,[23] scored tests,[24] educational requirements,[25] unlawful nepotism practices,[26] age limits,[27] and various other practices.[28] In addition, courts

---

[20]*See* Section II *infra.*

[21]*See* Section III *infra.*

[22]*See* Section IV *infra.*

[23]*See, e.g.*, United States v. Virginia, 22 FEP 936, 941 (E.D. Va. 1978) (enjoining height and weight standards), *aff'd in relevant part*, 620 F.2d 1018, 22 FEP 942 (4th Cir. 1980); Mieth v. Dothard, 418 F. Supp. 1169, 1185, 13 FEP 1412 (M.D. Ala. 1976) (enjoining height and weight standards), *aff'd in relevant part sub nom.* Dothard v. Rawlinson, 433 U.S. 321, 15 FEP 10 (1977).

[24]*See, e.g.*, Vulcan Pioneers, Inc. v. New Jersey Dep't of Civil Serv., 832 F.2d 811, 816–17, 53 FEP 703 (3d Cir. 1987) (affirming injunction against use of test scores as basis for promotion); Easley v. Anheuser-Busch, Inc., 758 F.2d 251, 263, 37 FEP 549 (8th Cir. 1985) (enjoining racially discriminatory preemployment test); Guardians Ass'n v. Civil Serv. Comm'n, 630 F.2d 79, 109, 23 FEP 909 (2d Cir. 1980) (enjoining written test for police officers); Legault v. aRusso, 842 F. Supp. 1479, 1492, 64 FEP 170 (D.N.H. 1994) (enjoining use of agility and obstacle course tests that had adverse impact on female firefighter applicants).

[25]*See, e.g.*, Carpenter v. Stephen F. Austin State Univ., 706 F.2d 608, 622–23, 31 FEP 1758 (5th Cir. 1983) (ordering employer to reevaluate its educational standards for promotion); James v. Stockham Valves & Fittings Co., 559 F.2d 310, 354–55, 15 FEP 827 (5th Cir. 1977) (enjoining use of high school diploma requirement).

[26]*See, e.g.*, Thomas v. Washington County Sch. Bd., 915 F.2d 922, 926, 53 FEP 1754 (4th Cir. 1990) (enjoining hiring preference for relatives of incumbent employees).

[27]*See, e.g.*, State Police for Automatic Ret. Ass'n v. Difava, 317 F.3d 6, 15, 90 FEP 1363 (1st Cir. 2003) (affirming enforceability of permanent injunction against mandatory retirement age of 55 for state police); EEOC v. Johnson & Higgins, Inc., 91 F.3d 1529, 1542, 71 FEP 818 (2d Cir. 1996) (affirming injunction against mandatory retirement of employee-directors at age 60 or 62); Criswell v. Western Airlines, Inc., 709 F.2d 544, 547, 558, 32 FEP 1204 (9th Cir. 1983) (affirming injunction against mandatory retirement of second officers at age 60), *aff'd*, 472 U.S. 400 (1985).

[28]*See, e.g.*, Roe v. Cheyenne Mountain Conference Resort, 124 F.3d 1221, 1231, 7 AD 779 (10th Cir. 1997) (remanding for lower court to instate injunction against

have implemented a variety of affirmative measures to remedy unlawful practices.[29] Courts also have enjoined defendants from discriminating or retaliating in the future against the plaintiffs[30] or others in the same protected class.[31]

---

employer policy requiring employees to disclose prescription drug use); Eldredge v. Carpenters 46 N. Cal. Counties Joint Apprenticeship & Training Comm., 94 F.3d 1366, 1369–70, 71 FEP 1385 (9th Cir. 1996) (enjoining use of applicant list by name for apprenticeship system as having disparate impact on women, requiring use of numerical referral list, and ordering 20% affirmative action program); Newark Branch, NAACP v. Town of Harrison, 940 F.2d 792, 805, 56 FEP 680 (3d Cir. 1991) (enjoining use of municipal residency hiring requirement and eligibility lists compiled while such requirement was in effect); Evans v. Harnett County Bd. of Educ., 684 F.2d 304, 306, 29 FEP 672 (4th Cir. 1982) (reversing district court's refusal to enjoin practice of appointing whites as principals of formerly white schools and African Americans as principals of formerly African-American schools); Garland v. USAir, Inc., 56 FEP 377, 378 (W.D. Pa. 1991) (enjoining use of separate, preferential track for recruiting, interviewing, and hiring candidates referred by influential persons); Flight Attendants v. Pan Am World Airways, Inc., 50 FEP 1698, 1706 (N.D. Cal. 1987) (enjoining double standard on maximum-weight guidelines and "appearance checks" that discriminate against women).

[29]See, e.g., Newark Branch, NAACP, 940 F.2d at 807 (affirming injunction requiring affirmative recruiting measures in race hiring class action); EEOC v. Townley Eng'g & Mfg. Co., 859 F.2d 610, 621 & n.18, 47 FEP 1601 (9th Cir. 1988) (determining employer must excuse religious objectors from requirement that they attend employer's religious services); Berger v. Iron Workers Local 201, 843 F.2d 1395, 1439, 46 FEP 780 (D.C. Cir. 1988) (holding union must permit all class members with 3,000 hours of experience in trade to take journeyman's exam); EEOC v. Gurnee Inn Corp., 48 FEP 871, 883–84 (N.D. Ill. 1988) (ordering employer to adopt training program for supervisory employees, post notice informing employees about court's judgment, and prepare companywide policy prohibiting sexual harassment), aff'd, 914 F.2d 815 (7th Cir. 1990). But see EEOC v. HBE Corp., 135 F.3d 543, 557–58, 76 FEP 543 (8th Cir. 1998) (reversing portion of injunctive relief requiring appointment of monitor as too broad and addressing speculative future harm).

[30]See Bruso v. United Airlines, Inc., 239 F.3d 848, 864, 84 FEP 1780 (7th Cir. 2001) (remanding for entry of injunction against future retaliation); Rau v. Apple-Rio Mgmt. Co., 85 F. Supp. 2d 1344 (N.D. Ga. 1999) (enjoining employer from providing negative evaluation of employee to prospective employers, although refusing to require issuance of positive reference letter); Malarkey v. Texaco, Inc., 983 F.2d 1204, 1215, 61 FEP 421 (2d Cir. 1993) (enjoining employer from future retaliation against plaintiff); Brown v. Trustees of Boston Univ., 891 F.2d 337, 361 & n.23, 51 FEP 815 (1st Cir. 1989) (holding successful tenure-discrimination plaintiff is entitled to injunction barring future discrimination against her in promotion, salary, or benefits); Pecker v. Heckler, 801 F.2d 709, 710, 41 FEP 1485 (4th Cir. 1986) (enjoining further discrimination or retaliation against plaintiff).

[31]See, e.g., EEOC v. Frank's Nursery & Crafts, Inc., 177 F.3d 448, 468, 79 FEP 936 (6th Cir. 1999) (affirming injunction to protect individual or group of employees from future discrimination); EEOC v. Ilona of Hungary, Inc., 108 F.3d 1569, 1578–79, 73 FEP 528 (7th Cir. 1996) (affirming injunction against future religious discrimination against Jewish employees); EEOC v. Gurnee Inn Corp., 914 F.2d 815, 816–17, 53 FEP 1425 (7th Cir. 1990) (affirming order that "prohibited [defendant]

Where there is evidence of consistent past discrimination, injunctive relief often is imposed unless the employer clearly establishes that further noncompliance is unlikely.[32] However, courts have declined to issue injunctive relief where the employer has shown that its discrimination ceased well before the entry of judgment,[33] where the plaintiff or the perpetrator is no longer employed by the defendant and is unlikely to be reinstated,[34] and where the

---

from engaging in future discrimination"); EEOC v. Beverage Canners, Inc., 897 F.2d 1067, 1068, 52 FEP 878 (11th Cir. 1990) (affirming injunction against race discrimination); EEOC v. Hacienda Hotel, 881 F.2d 1504, 1518–19, 50 FEP 877 (9th Cir. 1989) (affirming injunction against discrimination on basis of sex, religion, or opposition to discriminatory practices); Criswell v. Western Airlines, Inc., 709 F.2d 544, 547, 558, 32 FEP 1204 (9th Cir. 1983) (affirming injunction against violations of ADEA); Robinson v. Jacksonville Shipyards, Inc., 760 F. Supp. 1486, 1541, 57 FEP 971 (M.D. Fla. 1991) (enjoining continued maintenance of sexually hostile work environment).

[32]See United States v. Gregory, 871 F.2d 1239, 1246–47, 50 FEP 1568 (4th Cir. 1989) (district court has "no discretion to deny injunctive relief completely"); Hacienda Hotel, 881 F.2d at 1519 (injunctive relief should be ordered unless employer proves that it is unlikely to repeat challenged practice); Cox v. American Cast Iron Pipe Co., 784 F.2d 1546, 1561, 40 FEP 678 (11th Cir. 1986) (where consistent past discrimination is shown, injunctive relief mandatory absent clear and convincing proof that there is no reasonable probability of further noncompliance); James v. Stockham Valves & Fittings Co., 559 F.2d 310, 354–55, 15 FEP 827 (5th Cir. 1977) (injunctive relief mandatory "absent clear and convincing proof of no reasonable probability of further noncompliance").

[33]See, e.g., Dole v. Shenandoah Baptist Church, 899 F.2d 1389, 1401, 54 FEP 501 (4th Cir. 1990) (denial of injunctive relief not abuse of discretion where defendant had ceased challenged practice of paying "head of household" salary supplement in 1986 and thereafter had been in compliance with Equal Pay Act); Walls v. Mississippi State Dep't of Pub. Welfare, 730 F.2d 306, 324–25, 34 FEP 1114 (5th Cir. 1984) (vacating injunction against offending selection procedure, which had been discontinued 11 years before district court's order); Daines v. City of Mankato, 754 F. Supp. 681, 704–05, 54 FEP 41 (D. Minn. 1990) (denying injunctive relief where defendant had advertised and interviewed for all pertinent positions since charges were filed in 1984 and had operated under "thorough and aggressive" affirmative action policy since 1988).

[34]See, e.g., Cardenas v. Massey, 269 F.3d 251, 265, 87 FEP 19 (3d Cir. 2001) (denying injunction requiring employer to implement specific antidiscrimination policies because plaintiff no longer employed); Amirmokri v. Baltimore Gas & Elec. Co., 60 F.3d 1126, 1132, 68 FEP 809 (4th Cir. 1995) (denying injunction against future harassment where plaintiff no longer employed, although noting it would be appropriate if plaintiff were reinstated); Spencer v. General Elec., 894 F.2d 651, 660–61, 51 FEP 1725 (4th Cir. 1990) (affirming denial of injunction against sexual harassment where harassing supervisor was no longer employed and company had implemented comprehensive policy against sexual harassment); McKinney v. Illinois, 720 F. Supp. 706, 709, 50 FEP 1625 (N.D. Ill. 1989) (denying injunction where plaintiff no longer works for defendant, and thus no likelihood that she will again

employer otherwise has shown that injunctive relief is unnecessary to prevent future noncompliance.[35] An injunction in some cases may be denied if its enforcement would unnecessarily interfere with a defendant's legitimate operations[36] or injure or significantly burden an innocent individual or entity.[37] Neither the cessation of the discriminatory practices nor the adoption of corrective measures, however, automatically precludes injunctive relief. Courts retain the power to enter injunctive relief after the discontinuance of unlawful practices,[38] especially where necessary to provide a complete remedy and prevent recurrence. In particular, many courts

---

be subjected to sexual harassment by defendant). *But see* EEOC v. Gurnee Inn Corp., 914 F.2d 815, 817, 53 FEP 1425 (7th Cir. 1990) (holding injunction prohibiting future discrimination proper despite termination of employee who engaged in discriminatory conduct, based on evidence company had tolerated improper behavior and failed to respond to complaints).

[35]*See, e.g.*, Griffith v. Colorado Div. of Youth Servs., 17 F.3d 1323, 1330, 64 FEP 206 (10th Cir. 1994) (affirming denial of injunction where employer not shown to have pattern or practice of discrimination and it acted promptly to rid workplace of hostile work environment); Domingo v. New Eng. Fish Co., 727 F.2d 1429, 1438, 34 FEP 584 (determining injunctive relief not available because company no longer in operation), *modified on other grounds*, 742 F.2d 520, 37 FEP 1303 (9th Cir. 1984); Payne v. Travenol Labs. Inc., 673 F.2d 798, 28 FEP 1212 (5th Cir. 1982) (denying injunction because employer modified hiring procedure so as to remove its discriminatory character); Lawson v. Lapeka, Inc., 1991 WL 49775, at *3, 55 FEP 987, 990 (D. Kan. Mar. 19, 1991) (denying injunction where defendant company no longer in business, individual defendant is only co-owner of successor company, and 1986 reduction in force (RIF) was isolated instance of age discrimination); Ingram v. Madison Square Garden Ctr., 535 F. Supp. 1082, 1094, 32 FEP 548 (S.D.N.Y. 1982) (finding no need for order limiting union's future role in hiring and referral, as union had ceased to play any role in hiring of laborers), *modified*, 709 F.2d 807 (2d Cir. 1983).

[36]*See In re* National Airlines, Inc., 700 F.2d 695, 699, 31 FEP 369 (11th Cir. 1983) (denying injunctive relief that would prohibit air carrier's use of its maternity leave policy, where such injunction would impede carrier's efforts to consolidate flight attendant system on routewide basis).

[37]*See, e.g.*, General Bldg. Contractors Ass'n v. Pennsylvania, 458 U.S. 375, 397–402, 29 FEP 139 (1982) (where employer has not been found liable, court cannot allocate costs for implementing decree to employer or grant affirmative relief against employer under 42 U.S.C. §1981; rather, employer may be subject only to ancillary injunctive orders necessary to grant complete relief from union's discrimination); Walls v. Mississippi Dep't of Pub. Welfare, 730 F.2d 306, 326, 34 FEP 1114 (5th Cir. 1984) (federal agencies innocent of Title VII violations may not be compelled to contribute to costs of implementing decree to remedy another party's Title VII violations).

[38]Section 706(g) by its terms authorizes a court to "enjoin the respondent from engaging in [an] unlawful employment practice" upon a finding that the respondent "*has* intentionally engaged in or *is* intentionally engaging in" such a practice. 42 U.S.C. §2000e-5(g) (emphasis added). *See* EEOC v. Ilona of Hungary, Inc., 108 F.3d

have rejected arguments against injunctive relief where defendants changed their practices only in response to being sued.[39]

The scope of a prohibitory injunction generally is determined by the scope of the unlawful conduct at issue; it normally is limited to enjoining the specific conduct found to violate the law.[40]

1569, 1578–79 (7th Cir. 1996) (affirming injunction against future religious discrimination because of court's concern for possibility of future discrimination); Dombeck v. Milwaukee Valve Co., 40 F.3d 230, 238, 66 FEP 497 (7th Cir. 1994) (approving injunctive relief in hostile environment case where plaintiff and harasser had been assigned to separate work areas, because employer could subsequently alter work assignments in absence of injunctive relief); United States v. Gregory, 871 F.2d 1239, 1246, 50 FEP 1568 (4th Cir. 1989) (district court has authority to grant injunctive relief even after unlawful practices apparently have ceased).

[39]See, e.g., EEOC v. Astra U.S.A., Inc., 94 F.3d 738, 745, 71 FEP 1267 (1st Cir. 1996) (affirming injunction against employer's future settlement agreements including clause prohibiting employees from assisting in EEOC investigations despite defendant's "attempts to reinterpret the operative provisions of its agreements when under siege"); EEOC v. Hacienda Hotel, 881 F.2d 1504, 1518–19, 50 FEP 877 (9th Cir. 1989) (affirming injunction against future discrimination on basis of sex, religion, or opposition to discriminatory practices, despite absence of recent EEOC charges, where employer's corrective efforts came only after being sued); EEOC v. Goodyear Aerospace Corp., 813 F.2d 1539, 1544, 43 FEP 875 (9th Cir. 1987) ("[a]n employer that takes curative actions only after it has been sued fails to provide sufficient assurances that it will not repeat the violation to justify denying an injunction"); NAACP v. City of Evergreen, 693 F.2d 1367, 1370, 30 FEP 925 (11th Cir. 1982) (reversing denial of injunctive relief as abuse of discretion where discriminatory practices ended only in response to EEOC charge and suit); James v. Stockham Valves & Fittings Co., 559 F.2d 310, 354–55, 15 FEP 827 (5th Cir. 1977) (corrective actions taken in response to lawsuit offer "insufficient assurance that the practice sought to be enjoined will not be repeated"). But see Spencer v. General Elec. Co., 894 F.2d 651, 660–61, 51 FEP 1725 (4th Cir. 1990) (rejecting view that remedial measures undertaken after litigation is filed never can be adequate to obviate injunctive relief and affirming denial of injunction where harasser had been forced to resign and company had instituted comprehensive sexual harassment policy).

[40]See, e.g., United States v. Criminal Sheriff, 19 F.3d 238, 239–40, 64 FEP 813 (5th Cir. 1994) (narrowing injunction against sex discrimination in hiring, promotion, and recruitment to injunction against discriminatory job assignments, which parties had stipulated was only claim at issue); Mitchell v. Seaboard Sys. R.R., 883 F.2d 451, 454, 57 FEP 619 (6th Cir. 1989) (injunction against all future violations of Title VII not sufficiently specific, although racial harassment plaintiff entitled to broad injunction barring race discrimination against *him* "with respect to his compensation, term, conditions or privileges of employment"); Davis v. Richmond, Fredericksburg & Potomac R.R., 803 F.2d 1322, 1328, 42 FEP 69 (4th Cir. 1986) (injunction against "committing further violations of Title VII" overbroad); Easley v. Anheuser-Busch, Inc., 758 F.2d 251, 263, 37 FEP 549 (8th Cir. 1985) (ordering injunction against racially discriminatory hiring practices at bottling plant at which plaintiffs worked and holding that injunction encompassing any form of race discrimination at any of defendant's plants was too broad); EEOC v. Wooster Brush

Because courts differ in how they define the scope of what is "at issue," the scope of an injunction may vary correspondingly.[41] Where a particular practice is found to be unlawful, it may be enjoined to the benefit of all affected individuals, regardless of whether the suit was brought as a class action.[42] Thus, practices found to be discriminatory may be enjoined for the benefit of others even where the employer rebuts an individual plaintiff's claim for relief by showing that it would have reached the same decision without regard to the discriminatory motive or practice.[43] Where no discriminatory pattern or practice is at issue, however, courts may limit the benefit of injunctive relief to the individual plaintiff.[44] Courts may also limit the scope of an injunction when it is believed to be "more

---

Co. Employees Relief Ass'n, 727 F.2d 566, 576, 33 FEP 1823 (6th Cir. 1984) (rejecting injunction against any future sex discrimination as overbroad where claims at issue involved denial of equal disability benefits for pregnancy and narrowing injunction to prohibition against fringe benefit policies that violate Pregnancy Discrimination Act).

[41]*Compare* Gaddy v. Abex Corp., 884 F.2d 312, 318, 50 FEP 1333 (7th Cir. 1989) (reversing injunction against future retaliation as improper where discrimination plaintiff never had alleged retaliation) *and* Brady v. Thurston Motor Lines Corp., 726 F.2d 136, 146–47, 33 FEP 1370 (4th Cir. 1984) (where plaintiffs showed discrimination in transfers, promotions, termination, and work assignments, but not in initial job placement, injunction should not extend to initial job placement) *with* Bennun v. Rutgers State Univ., 737 F. Supp. 1393, 1401, 1410, 54 FEP 875 (D.N.J. 1990) (granting injunction prohibiting national origin discrimination and retaliation, although plaintiff lost retaliation claim at trial), *aff'd in part and rev'd in part*, 941 F.2d 154 (3d Cir. 1991) *and* Brown v. Trustees of Boston Univ., 891 F.2d 337, 361 & n.23, 51 FEP 815 (1st Cir. 1989) (affirming injunction against discrimination in promotion, salary, and other benefits even though plaintiff showed discrimination only in tenure decision).

[42]*See* Criswell v. Western Airlines, Inc., 709 F.2d 544, 547, 558, 32 FEP 1204 (9th Cir. 1983) (affirming systemwide relief from mandatory retirement policy and injunction, despite defendant's claim that relief should be limited to individual plaintiffs); Evans v. Harnett County Bd. of Educ., 684 F.2d 304, 306, 29 FEP 672 (4th Cir. 1982) (reversing denial of injunction even though employer argued that absence of class certification made injunction inappropriate).

[43]*See* 42 U.S.C. § 2000e-5(g)(2)(B) (2000) (in these circumstances courts "may grant . . . injunctive relief" but may not "issue an order requiring any admission, reinstatement, hiring or promotion"); Thomas v. Washington County Sch. Bd., 915 F.2d 922, 924–26, 53 FEP 1754 (4th Cir. 1990) (non–class action plaintiff entitled to injunction against future nepotism and failure to post vacancies even though employer showed that its failure to hire *her* was for nondiscriminatory reason).

[44]*See, e.g.*, Brown v. Trustees of Boston Univ., 891 F.2d 337, 361, 51 FEP 815 (1st Cir. 1989) (reversing order enjoining sex discrimination in faculty appointment, promotion, and tenure decisions as overbroad because individual plaintiff showed discrimination only against herself).

burdensome to the defendant than necessary to provide complete relief to the plaintiffs."[45] In extreme circumstances, courts may enjoin even lawful conduct where that conduct serves as a catalyst for discriminatory behavior. In *EEOC v. Wilson Metal Casket Co.*,[46] for example, a sexual harassment case, the Sixth Circuit affirmed an injunction that prohibited the defendant from leaving the business premises with any female employee. The court reasoned that the proper scope of an injunction can include even lawful conduct that is shown to be closely related to the proven unlawful conduct.[47]

III. RELIEF FOR IDENTIFIABLE VICTIMS OF UNLAWFUL EMPLOYMENT PRACTICES

Following *Albemarle Paper*'s instruction to make victims whole, courts have tailored remedies to restore victims to the positions they would have held in the absence of discrimination. For example, in *Franks v. Bowman Transportation Co.*,[48] a class action, the Supreme Court held that retroactive seniority for victims of discrimination in hiring is a presumptively correct remedy, one that can be denied in particular cases "only on the basis of unusual adverse impact arising from facts and circumstances that would not be generally found in Title VII cases."[49] The Court specifically

---

[45]*See* EEOC v. Astra U.S.A., Inc., 94 F.3d 738, 746, 71 FEP 1267 (1st Cir. 1996) (vacating portion of injunction prohibiting defendant from entering into settlement agreements with employees that prohibited them from filing charges of discrimination) (citing Califano v. Yamasaki, 442 U.S. 682 (1979)); *see also* EEOC v. HBE Corp., 135 F.3d 543, 557–58, 76 FEP 495 (8th Cir. 1998) (vacating portion of affirmative relief requiring appointment of monitor).

[46]24 F.3d 836, 842, 64 FEP 1402 (6th Cir. 1994).

[47]*Accord* Garrison v. Baker Hughes Oilfield Operations, Inc., 287 F.3d 955, 961–62, 12 AD 1825 (10th Cir. 2002) (affirming denial of injunction of lawful activity, although noting court's ability to enjoin lawful activity in appropriate context, stating: " 'A federal court's equity jurisdiction affords it the power to enjoin otherwise lawful activity when necessary and appropriate in the public interest to correct or dissipate the evil effects of past unlawful conduct.' ") (quoting United States v. Holtzman, 762 F.2d 720, 724 (9th Cir. 1985)); Kentucky Fried Chicken Corp. v. Diversified Packaging Corp., 549 F.2d 368, 390 (5th Cir. 1977) ("In fashioning relief against a party who has transgressed the governing legal standards, a court of equity is free to proscribe activities that, standing alone, would have been unassailable.").

[48]424 U.S. 747, 12 FEP 549 (1976).

[49]424 U.S. at 780 n.41.

rejected the view that such relief should be denied because of its impact on "other, arguably innocent, employees," because this reasoning "would if applied generally frustrate the central 'make whole' objective of Title VII."[50]

Specific make-whole remedies seen in cases after *Franks* include hiring,[51] transfer,[52] promotion,[53] reinstatement,[54] retroactive seniority,[55]

---

[50]*Id.* at 774.

[51]*See, e.g.*, Hartman v. Duffey, 88 F.3d 1232, 1239 (D.C. Cir. 1996) (ordering set number of slots to be filled by job applicant class members); Rivers v. Washington County Bd. of Educ., 770 F.2d 1010, 1012 (11th Cir. 1985) (ordering applicant placed in next available vacancy); Easley v. Anheuser-Busch, 758 F.2d 251, 263, 37 FEP 549 (8th Cir. 1985) (awarding positions to successful Title VII litigants who were wrongfully denied jobs); Darnell v. City of Jasper, 730 F.2d 653, 657, 37 FEP 1315 (11th Cir. 1984) (hiring ordered, conditional on applicant passing civil service exam); Garza v. Brownsville Indep. Sch. Dist., 700 F.2d 253, 254–56, 31 FEP 403 (5th Cir. 1983) (reversing denial of hiring order).

[52]*See, e.g.*, Harrison v. Dole, 643 F. Supp. 794, 795, 797, 55 FEP 1419 (D.D.C. 1986) (ordering transfer to position with greater potential for upward mobility).

[53]*See, e.g.*, Malarkey v. Texaco, Inc., 983 F.2d 1204, 1214, 61 FEP 421 (2d Cir. 2003) (affirming award of promotion with commensurate salary increase as equitable relief); Ingram v. Missouri Pac. R.R., 897 F.2d 1450, 1456–57, 52 FEP 571 (8th Cir. 1990) (reversing award of "fair consideration" for promotion rather than retroactive promotion); Taylor v. Home Ins. Co., 777 F.2d 849, 860, 39 FEP 769 (4th Cir. 1985) (affirming order promoting ADEA plaintiff); Paxton v. Union Nat'l Bank, 688 F.2d 552, 573, 574, 29 FEP 1233 (8th Cir. 1982) (ordering plaintiff and class members promoted); Bennun v. Rutgers State Univ., 737 F. Supp. 1393, 1409–10, 54 FEP 875 (D.N.J. 1990) (ordering retroactive promotion to rank of full professor), *aff'd in relevant part*, 941 F.2d 154, 56 FEP 746 (3d Cir. 1991); Evans v. Secretary of Energy, 52 FEP 347, 350 (D.D.C. 1990) (ordering promotion of victim of racial harassment); Edwards v. Hodel, 738 F. Supp. 426, 431–32, 53 FEP 13 (D. Colo. 1990) (ordering retroactive promotion).

[54]*See, e.g., In re* Pan Am World Airways, Inc., 905 F.2d 1457, 1460, 1464–65, 53 FEP 707 (11th Cir. 1990) (ordering reinstatement for flight attendant discharged because of unlawful pregnancy policy and refusing to order plaintiff to show she would have complied with lawful pregnancy policy); Morgan v. Arkansas Gazette, 897 F.2d 945, 953–54, 52 FEP 431 (8th Cir. 1990) (affirming reinstatement of ADEA plaintiff); Carrero v. New York City Hous. Auth., 890 F.2d 569, 579, 51 FEP 596 (2d Cir. 1989) (reinstating demoted plaintiff).

[55]*See, e.g.*, Sands v. Runyon, 28 F.3d 1323, 1329, 3 AD 660 (2d Cir. 1994) (district court clearly erred in denying plaintiff's claim for retroactive seniority because plaintiff met burden of demonstrating that, but for defendant's discrimination in hiring process, he would be at increased salary level); EEOC v. Rath Packing Co., 787 F.2d 318, 334–35, 40 FEP 580 (8th Cir. 1986) (reversing denial of retroactive seniority to victims of hiring discrimination, even though such remedy would require bumping long-term employees to inferior jobs and could impair employee morale); Morris v. American Nat'l Can Corp., 730 F. Supp. 1489, 1497, 52 FEP 210 (E.D. Mo. 1989) (granting constructively discharged sexual harassment plaintiff seniority retroactive to date of her initial hire), *aff'd in relevant part*, 952 F.2d 200, 57 FEP 946

tenure,[56] restoration of benefits,[57] salary adjustment,[58] expunging adverse material from personnel files,[59] and letters of commendation.[60] Where appropriate, more creative remedies have been crafted to make victims whole, such as freezing promotions until victims of hiring discrimination are eligible to compete for promotion.[61] Ordering

---

(8th Cir. 1991). *But see* Romasanta v. United Air Lines, Inc., 717 F.2d 1140, 1147–56, 32 FEP 1545 (7th Cir. 1983) (no abuse of discretion to deny retroactive competitive seniority in consideration of unusual and extreme adverse impact on incumbents).

[56]*See, e.g.*, Brown v. Trustees of Boston Univ., 891 F.2d 337, 359–61, 51 FEP 815 (1st Cir. 1989) (awarding tenure); Kunda v. Muhlenberg Coll., 621 F.2d 532, 535, 546–51, 22 FEP 62 (3d Cir. 1980) (awarding retroactive tenure to college instructor upon completion of master's degree within 2 years). *But see* Gutzwiller v. Fenik, 860 F.2d 1317, 1333, 48 FEP 395 (6th Cir. 1988) (tenure should be awarded only where reinstated plaintiff would not receive fair tenure reconsideration).

[57]*See, e.g.*, Banks v. Travelers Cos., 180 F.3d 358, 365–66, 80 FEP 30 (2d Cir. 1999) (restoration of benefits, including pension credits, was equitable remedy appropriate for submission to court); Scarfo v. Cabletron Sys., 54 F.3d 931, 956, 959–60, 67 FEP 1474 (1st Cir. 1995) (affirming award of prospective relief in value of stock options plaintiffs would have received but for unlawful discrimination).

[58]*See, e.g.*, Rudebusch v. Hughes, 313 F.3d 506, 523, 90 FEP 865 (9th Cir. 2002) (discussing scope of equity pay adjustments made pursuant to sex discrimination class action); Gumbhir v. Curators of Univ. of Mo., 157 F.3d 1141, 1144–45, 78 FEP 296 (8th Cir. 1998) (affirming grant of prospective salary adjustment).

[59]*See, e.g.*, Bruso v. United Airlines, Inc., 239 F.3d 848, 863, 84 FEP 1780 (7th Cir. 2001) (reversing lower court's refusal "to expunge from [plaintiff's] personnel records all references to United's investigation into his reports of Sporer's sexual harassment and any disciplinary action taken against him as a result of those reports"); EEOC v. HBE Corp., 135 F.3d 543, 557–58, 76 FEP 495 (8th Cir. 1998) (affirming order for employer to expunge plaintiffs' employment records of references to their discharge); Hayes v. Shalala, 933 F. Supp. 21, 27, 71 FEP 1240 (D.D.C. 1996) (ordering correction of plaintiff's personnel file and other records to reflect jury's verdict in favor of plaintiff and equitable relief provided by court). *But see* Cardenas v. Massey, 269 F.3d 251, 265, 87 FEP 19 (3d Cir. 2001) (denying request to modify personnel records to reflect, "contrary to fact," higher pay grade and more favorable performance evaluations); Sands v. Runyon, 28 F.3d 1323, 1331–32, 3 AD 660 (2d Cir. 1994) (affirming district court's denial of order directing defendant to expunge negative information from plaintiff's personnel file where there was lack of specific evidence of incidents of purposeful discrimination that caused plaintiff harm); Jones v. Rivers, 732 F. Supp. 176, 178, 52 FEP 550 (D.D.C. 1990) (denying request to expunge where plaintiff failed specifically to identify any adverse materials).

[60]*Compare* EEOC v. HBE Corp., 135 F.3d 543, 557–58, 76 FEP 495 (8th Cir. 1998) (affirming order requiring employer to provide letters of recommendation for plaintiffs) *with Sands*, 28 F.3d at 1330–31 (affirming denial of plaintiff's request for letter of commendation and stating that "[c]ircumstances are few in which a court can properly order an employer to sweeten a plaintiff's personnel file with praise of the employee's talents, abilities, and work habits—which affirmations might not even be true").

[61]*See* Association Against Discrimination in Employment, Inc. v. City of Bridgeport, 647 F.2d 256, 287–88, 25 FEP 1013 (2d Cir. 1981) (affirming district court

accommodation of an employee's disability is another form of affirmative relief.[62]

At least one court has awarded a professional partnership as part of a make-whole remedy.[63] In *Hopkins v. Price Waterhouse*,[64] the district court (on remand from the Supreme Court) ordered instatement of the plaintiff as a partner. The District of Columbia Circuit affirmed, relying on the general rule that "Title VII authorizes courts to put a victim of discrimination in the position that she or he would have been in but for the unlawful discrimination."[65] Because the injury suffered was a discriminatory denial of partnership, "it is apparent that an invitation to join the . . . partnership would be 'the most complete relief possible' and in fact the *only* possible relief that would restore Ann Hopkins to 'the situation [s]he would have occupied if the wrong had not been committed.' "[66] In upholding the award, the court held that such affirmative relief was permissible, even though the award, upon receipt, "may place the beneficiary beyond Title VII's protective reach."[67] The court rejected the employer's arguments that the award (1) violated the partners' constitutional rights of free association; (2) violated the rule against enforcement of personal-service contracts;

---

order prohibiting city from giving any promotional exams; fire fighters hired from lists generated by discriminatory tests should not be promoted until discriminatees ordered hired became qualified for promotion).

[62]*See, e.g.*, Ralph v. Lucent Techs., Inc., 135 F.3d 166, 172, 7 AD 1345 (1st Cir. 1998) (affirming award of accommodation permitting employee to work part-time on temporary basis); Muller v. Costello, 997 F. Supp. 299, 305, 9 AD 179 (N.D.N.Y. 1998) (granting reinstatement with accommodation for plaintiff's disability and stating court's goal is to place plaintiff in position in which she would have been absent discrimination). The ADA and accommodation issues are addressed in Chapter 13 (Disability).

[63]Hopkins v. Price Waterhouse, 920 F.2d 967, 975–79, 54 FEP 750 (D.C. Cir. 1990) (affirming award of accountancy partnership). The same remedy has been ordered in a law firm partnership case, although the Third Circuit reversed the liability determination on the merits, thus eliminating any need to discuss the appropriateness of the remedy. *See* Ezold v. Wolf, Block, Schorr & Solis-Cohen, 983 F.2d 509, 513, 547, 60 FEP 849 (3d Cir. 1992).

[64]920 F.2d 967.

[65]*Id.* at 976.

[66]*Id.* at 977 (citations omitted).

[67]*Id.* at 978. In *Clackamas Gastroenterology Associates v. Wells*, 538 U.S. 440 (2003), the Supreme Court clarified that whether a shareholder-director (or a partner) is an employee for the purposes of Title VII depends on " 'all of the incidents of the relationships.' " *Id.* at 451 (citations omitted) (citing Justice Powell's concurrence in Hishon v. King & Spalding, 467 U.S. 69, 80 n.2 (1984) ("an employer may not evade the strictures of Title VII simply by labeling its employees as 'partners' ")).

and (3) was an abuse of discretion, given the plaintiff's subsequent misconduct.[68] The court noted that unlimited front pay (in lieu of partnership) was too speculative and potential hostility was insufficient to deny the award of partnership.[69]

Although reinstatement is the strongly preferred remedy in cases of discriminatory discharge,[70] it will not be ordered where it would produce a dysfunctional working environment or excessive friction, hostility, or antagonism.[71] Because hostility is inherent in any litigation, the party opposing reinstatement must point to hostility

---

[68]*Price Waterhouse*, 920 F.2d at 979–81.

[69]*Id.* at 981.

[70]*See* Tadlock v. Powell, 291 F.3d 541, 548, 88 FEP 1734 (8th Cir. 2002) (stating that "[r]einstatement is the typical remedy" and holding it appropriate where no evidence of extreme animosity); Slayton v. Ohio Dep't of Youth Servs., 206 F.3d 669, 680, 82 FEP 289 (6th Cir. 2000) ("reinstatement is an appropriate remedy when a hostile environment prevented an employee from adequately performing her job"); Duke v. Uniroyal, Inc., 928 F.2d 1413, 1424, 55 FEP 816 (4th Cir. 1991) (reinstatement is "much preferred" remedy); Spulak v. K-Mart Corp., 894 F.2d 1150, 1157, 51 FEP 1652 (10th Cir. 1990) (reinstatement is preferred remedy under ADEA); Jackson v. City of Albuquerque, 890 F.2d 225, 231–35, 51 FEP 669 (10th Cir. 1989) (reinstatement is presumptive, preferred remedy).

[71]*See, e.g.*, Farley v. Nationwide Mut. Ins. Co., 197 F.3d 1322, 1338, 81 FEP 1775 (11th Cir. 1999) (awarding front pay in lieu of reinstatement based on discord and antagonism between parties, despite plaintiff's desire for reinstatement as preferred remedy); Kirsch v. Fleet St., Ltd., 148 F.3d 149, 169, 77 FEP 318 (2d Cir. 1998) (affirming denial of reinstatement, in part because of hostility between parties described at trial); Cowan v. Strafford R-VI Sch. Dist., 140 F.3d 1153, 1160, 77 FEP 1834 (8th Cir. 1998) (affirming denial of reinstatement based on evidence of damaged relationship between parties); Simpson v. Ernst & Young, 100 F.3d 436, 445, 72 FEP 343 (6th Cir. 1996) (reinstatement highly impractical based on evidence in record indicating underlying hostility between parties); Paperworkers Local 274 v. Champion Int'l Corp., 81 F.3d 798, 805 (8th Cir. 1996) (affirming denial of reinstatement where district court found that there was "[s]ubstantial hostility, above that normally incident to litigation," but noting that reinstatement not foreclosed on remand as passage of time may soften acrimonious relationship); Lewis v. Federal Prison Indus., Inc., 953 F.2d 1277, 1283, 58 FEP 127 (11th Cir. 1992) (front pay rather than reinstatement appropriate where there was psychiatric and medical evidence that discrimination "disabled" plaintiff and that return to former job would result in antagonism with supervisors and increased depression, agitation, and other physiological complaints; court rejected employer's attempt to "paint a rosy picture" of warm relationships with employees and open arms with which it awaited plaintiff's return); Spulak v. K Mart Corp., 894 F.2d 1150, 1157–58, 51 FEP 1652 (10th Cir. 1990) (plaintiff's request for front pay in lieu of reinstatement properly granted given antagonism, humiliation of plaintiff in front of his subordinates, and his fear of retaliation); Starrett v. Wadley, 876 F.2d 808, 815, 51 FEP 608 (10th Cir. 1989) (affirming denial of reinstatement when atmosphere of hostility would be detrimental to plaintiff's health).

well above and beyond that which is inevitable in hard-fought litigation before reinstatement may be denied.[72]

Courts have found reinstatement inappropriate if some intervening nondiscriminatory event would have ended the plaintiff's employment;[73] if there have been substantial changes in the company

---

[72]*See, e.g.*, Bruso v. United Airlines, Inc., 239 F.3d 848, 862, 84 FEP 1780 (7th Cir. 2001) ("[w]e do not believe, however, that the angry reaction of United's management to Mr. Bruso's success before the jury can, standing alone, justify denying reinstatement"); Philipp v. ANR Freight Sys., 61 F.3d 669, 674, 70 FEP 1347 (8th Cir. 1995) (friction arising from litigation not alone sufficient to deny reinstatement; "a court might deny [employment] in virtually every case if it considered the hostility engendered from litigation as a bar to relief") (citation omitted); Squires v. Bonser, 54 F.3d 168, 175 (3d Cir. 1995) ("[i]n order to deny reinstatement, more than the ordinary tensions accompanying an unconstitutional discharge lawsuit must be present"); Hutchison v. Amateur Elec. Supply, Inc., 42 F.3d 1037, 1045–46, 66 FEP 1275 (7th Cir. 1994) (mere employer hostility developed during litigation cannot alone defeat reinstatement); Morgan v. Arkansas Gazette, 897 F.2d 945, 953–54, 52 FEP 431 (8th Cir. 1990) (refusing to reverse reinstatement order because of antagonism between parties that is "the natural bi-product of any litigation"); Farber v. Massillon Bd. of Educ., 917 F.2d 1391, 1396, 54 FEP 1063 (6th Cir. 1990) (denial of affirmative relief can be justified only where workplace tensions are "so serious as to manifest themselves in the public function of the employer"); McKnight v. General Motors, 908 F.2d 104, 116, 53 FEP 505 (7th Cir. 1990) (hostility by employer and its supervisory personnel is "no ground for denying reinstatement"; to hold otherwise "would arm the employer to defeat the court's remedial order"); *Jackson*, 890 F.2d at 234–35 (where hostility was of defendant's making and denial of reinstatement would allow defendant to accomplish its goal of ousting plaintiff, court's denial of reinstatement on grounds of hostility must be reversed).

[73]*Compare* McKennon v. Nashville Banner Publ'g Co., 513 U.S. 352, 361–62, 66 FEP 1192 (1995) (although after-acquired evidence of misconduct does not totally defeat discrimination claim, it does bar prospective relief), Crapp v. City of Miami Beach, 242 F.3d 1017, 1021, 85 FEP 353 (11th Cir. 2001) (affirming, in race discrimination case, district court's order vacating reinstatement of police officer because of intervening suspension by police board for "conduct unbecoming an officer"), O'Day v. McDonnell Douglas Helicopter Co., 79 F.3d 756, 763–64, 70 FEP 615 (9th Cir. 1996) (ADEA plaintiff not entitled to remedies where defendant established that it would have discharged plaintiff for subsequently acquired evidence that plaintiff rifled through supervisor's office and copied confidential documents, which plaintiff then showed to co-worker) *and* Neufeld v. Searle Labs., 884 F.2d 335, 341, 50 FEP 1126 (8th Cir. 1989) (employer can avoid award of reinstatement by proving that "some new development—such as a reduction in the sales force or termination of operations—would have ended [plaintiff's] employment") *with* Medlock v. Ortho Biotech, Inc., 164 F.3d 545, 555, 78 FEP 1592 (10th Cir. 1999) (evidence of misconduct during unemployment hearing subsequent to plaintiff's discharge did not preclude finding of front pay under *McKennon* doctrine) *and* Delli Santi v. CNA Ins. Cos., 88 F.3d 192, 204–05, 71 FEP 143 (3d Cir. 1996) (rejecting district court's determination that plaintiff's alleged theft rendered her ineligible for front pay; alleged theft known by employer at time plaintiff was discharged was not after-acquired evidence).

that have made reinstatement impracticable;[74] if, in a mixed-motive case, the defendant proves that the plaintiff would not have been (for example) hired, promoted, or retained even in the absence of discrimination;[75] if the plaintiff is not capable of performing the job in question;[76] or if the relief sought plainly would place the plaintiff in a better position than he or she would have occupied in the absence of discrimination.[77] In some circumstances courts may consider the employee's success in finding other work as a factor relevant to whether or not to grant reinstatement.[78]

---

[74]*See, e.g.*, Kelewae v. Jim Meagher Chevrolet, Inc., 952 F.2d 1052, 1055, 57 FEP 1199 (8th Cir. 1992) (current adverse financial position of defendant militated against award of reinstatement or front pay); Williams v. Pharmacia Opthalmics, Inc., 926 F. Supp. 791, 795, 71 FEP 628 (N.D. Inc. 1996) (declining to order reinstatement in light of pending merger and reorganization, which would result in elimination of plaintiff's position). *But see* Banks v. Travelers Cos., 180 F.3d 358, 364–65, 80 FEP 30 (2d Cir. 1999) (reversing lower court's denial of reinstatement or front pay, based on company's assertion that plaintiff would have been eliminated in RIF; plaintiff produced evidence that she would have survived RIF).

[75]42 U.S.C. § 2000e-5(g)(2)(B) (2000).

[76]*See, e.g.*, Doane v. City of Omaha, 115 F.3d 624, 630, 6 AD 1553 (8th Cir. 1997) (burden shifts to employer during remedial phase to show that plaintiff is not qualified for reinstatement); Thurman v. Yellow Freight Sys., 90 F.3d 1160, 1171–72, 72 FEP 657 (6th Cir. 1996) (district court did not abuse discretion in denying instatement where plaintiff injured himself and was unable to do heavy lifting required for position). Although the plaintiff's application for and receipt of Social Security disability insurance (SSDI) does not create a special legal presumption against liability or damages, *see* Cleveland v. Policy Mgmt. Sys. Corp., 526 U.S. 795, 805, 9 AD 491 (1999) (receipt of SSDI benefits does not create special legal presumption preventing plaintiff from pursuing claims or claiming damages), when this evidence relates to the plaintiff's ability to perform the job in question or to mitigate his or her damages, it may affect an award of reinstatement or front pay. *See* Christou v. Hyatt Regency-O'Hare, 996 F. Supp. 811, 814–15, 8 AD 1781 (N.D. Ill. 1998) (finding, in pre-*Cleveland* case, that plaintiff's application for SSDI benefits submitted more than 1 month after his discriminatory discharge precluded any award of reinstatement or front pay). *See generally* Chapter 13 (Disability).

[77]*See, e.g.*, McKnight v. General Motors, Inc., 973 F.2d 1366, 1370–71, 64 FEP 1071 (7th Cir. 1992) (affirming lower court's denial of reinstatement, which was based on its determination that plaintiff sought placement in different job and relocation in new city); Fong v. Lawn, 851 F.2d 1559, 1561, 47 FEP 614 (9th Cir. 1988) ("[t]he purpose of Title VII is to 'make whole' the victims of discrimination . . . not to place them in a position superior to the status quo ante").

[78]*See, e.g.*, Roush v. KFC Nat'l Mgmt. Co., 10 F.3d 392, 398, 63 FEP 609 (6th Cir. 1993) (listing whether plaintiff has found other work as one factor that may negatively affect reinstatement or front pay); Baker v. John Morrell & Co., 263 F. Supp. 2d 1161 (N.D. Iowa 2003) (describing, as one factor affecting reinstatement, whether plaintiff has found similar work). *But see* Dilley v. Supervalu, Inc., 296 F.3d 958, 967, 13 AD 486 (10th Cir. 2002) (reversing lower court's denial of reinstatement based on plaintiff's failure to mitigate damages, stating that mitigation was relevant only to back pay and front pay).

Where reinstatement is not feasible, some courts allow front pay in lieu of reinstatement.[79] For example, front pay in lieu of reinstatement may be granted when no comparable position is available[80] or when the plaintiff's approaching retirement makes

---

[79]*See* Williams v. Pharmacia, Inc., 137 F.3d 944, 952, 76 FEP 310 (7th Cir. 1998) (front pay is "substitute remedy" where reinstatement is inappropriate); EEOC v. HBE Corp., 135 F.3d 543, 555, 76 FEP 495 (8th Cir. 1998) (affirming front-pay award in lieu of reinstatement where there was evidence of animosity between parties); Reed v. A.W. Lawrence & Co., 95 F.3d 1170, 1182, 72 FEP 1345 (2d Cir. 1996) (upholding front-pay award where antagonism between parties made reinstatement inappropriate and plaintiff made good-faith effort to mitigate damages but was unable to obtain comparable alternative employment); Paperworkers Local 274 v. Champion Int'l Corp., 81 F.3d 798, 805 (8th Cir. 1996) (front pay generally appropriate when reinstatement must be denied); Doll v. Brown, 75 F.3d 1200, 1205, 5 AD 369 (7th Cir. 1996) (district court should have awarded front pay, equitable substitute for reinstatement, if court had determined that reinstatement would be inequitable); Suggs v. ServiceMaster Educ. Food Mgmt., 72 F.3d 1228, 1234, 69 FEP 1270 (6th Cir. 1996) (front pay generally awarded when reinstatement is infeasible; "[t]hus, the remedies of reinstatement and front pay are alternative, rather than cumulative"); Weaver v. Amoco Prod. Co., 66 F.3d 85, 88, 70 FEP 931 (5th Cir. 1995) (front pay appropriate award in ADEA action if reinstatement is not feasible; court should articulate basis for its conclusion that reinstatement was not feasible); Philipp v. ANR Freight Sys., 61 F.3d 669, 674, 70 FEP 1347 (8th Cir. 1995) (no abuse of discretion in ordering reinstatement rather than front pay where no showing that reinstatement impracticable or impossible); Scarfo v. Cabletron Sys., 54 F.3d 931, 954, 67 FEP 1474 (1st Cir. 1995) (district court has discretion to award front pay in Title VII case when reinstatement is "impracticable or impossible"); Avitia v. Metropolitan Club, 49 F.3d 1219, 1232, 2 WH 2d 993 (7th Cir. 1995) (plaintiff may seek front pay in lieu of reinstatement when reinstatement infeasible); Hadley v. VAM P T S, 44 F.3d 372, 376, 67 FEP 186 (5th Cir. 1995) (equitable remedy of front pay appropriate when reinstatement not feasible); Feldman v. Philadelphia Hous. Auth., 43 F.3d 823, 832 (3d Cir. 1994) (front pay is alternative remedy when reinstatement not appropriate because of irreparable animosity between parties); Smith v. World Ins. Co., 38 F.3d 1456, 1466, 66 FEP 13 (8th Cir. 1994) (front pay may be awarded under ADEA "in lieu of, but not in addition to, reinstatement"); *cf.* Squires v. Bonser, 54 F.3d 168, 176 (3d Cir. 1995) (jury award of front-pay damages does not preclude remand for entry of order of reinstatement, but that "the issue of double recovery should be resolved by a new trial on compensatory damages"). *But see* Wildman v. Lerner Stores Corp., 771 F.2d 605, 616, 38 FEP 1377 (1st Cir. 1985) (front pay in lieu of reinstatement inappropriate when plaintiff received adequate compensatory and liquidated damages under state law); Bingman v. Natkin & Co., 937 F.2d 553, 558, 56 FEP 570 (10th Cir. 1991) (rejecting plaintiff's appeal of award of reinstatement, as opposed to front pay, where testimony showed that plaintiff was able to work and had good relations with supervisors and co-workers; defendant needed employees, had flexible employee relations, and showed no animosity toward plaintiff, and workplace would not be unduly hostile upon plaintiff's return).

[80]*See, e.g.*, Deloach v. Delchamps, Inc., 897 F.2d 815, 822, 52 FEP 1121 (5th Cir. 1990) (affirming front pay in lieu of reinstatement where employee had been replaced and reinstatement would disrupt employment of others); Whittlesey v. Union Carbide Corp., 742 F.2d 724, 728, 35 FEP 1089 (2d Cir. 1984) (front pay in lieu of reinstatement may be appropriate where no position is available).

the front-pay period of short duration.[81] A court's failure to articulate reasons for granting front pay in lieu of reinstatement may result in a remand for reconsideration of appropriate equitable relief.[82] Although front pay and reinstatement are often described as mutually exclusive remedies, courts may award a combination of reinstatement and front pay in order to provide a "make-whole" remedy.[83] Front pay is discussed more extensively in Chapter 40 (Monetary Relief).

That affirmative relief such as instatement or reinstatement may be *ordered* does not resolve the issue of when the order should be *effective*. In many cases the position sought by a successful Title VII litigant is occupied by another individual. Since the early days of Title VII, courts generally have refused to displace an incumbent employee in order to place the discrimination victim immediately in that position.[84] As the Supreme Court observed, "[l]ower courts have uniformly held that relief for actual victims does not extend to bumping employees previously occupying jobs."[85] Instead, the standard make-whole remedy in such cases has involved an

---

[81]*See* Chace v. Champion Spark Plug Co., 732 F. Supp. 605, 610, 52 FEP 721 (D. Md. 1990) (where ADEA plaintiff plans to retire in 1 month, reinstatement impracticable and front pay award appropriate).

[82]*See, e.g.*, Kucia v. Southeast Ark. Cmty. Action Corp., 284 F.3d 944, 948, 88 FEP 861 (8th Cir. 2002) (vacating award of front pay and remanding for further consideration of appropriate equitable relief where lower court gave no reasons for its award of front pay as opposed to reinstatement); EEOC v. W&O, Inc., 213 F.3d 600, 619, 83 FEP 117 (11th Cir. 2000) (lower court erred in ordering front pay in lieu of reinstatement; "[w]hile it may be implicit in the district court's award of front pay that the court credited the EEOC's claims of antagonism toward Nuesse and discounted W&O's claims that reinstatement was a viable option, we must require the district court to make explicit findings on this issue").

[83]*See* Selgas v. American Airlines, Inc., 104 F.3d 9, 15, 72 FEP 1457 (1st Cir. 1997) (award of both front pay and reinstatement may be appropriate as long as there is no duplication of awards); Nedder v. Rivier Coll., 972 F. Supp. 81, 82, 6 AD 1378 (D.N.H. 1997) (front pay and reinstatement not mutually exclusive so long as there is no duplication of remedies). For example, front pay may be ordered until such time as the plaintiff can be reinstated.

[84]*See, e.g.*, Paperworkers Local 189 v. United States, 416 F.2d 980, 988, 1 FEP 875 (5th Cir. 1969) (describing remedy that would avoid displacing innocent incumbent union employees); Patterson v. American Tobacco Co., 535 F.2d 257, 267–70, 12 FEP 314 (4th Cir. 1976) (and cases cited therein) (articulating importance of providing make-whole relief to discrimination victims while recognizing precedents disfavoring bumping innocent incumbents), *vacated on other grounds*, 456 U.S. 63 (1982).

[85]Fire Fighters Local 1784 v. Stotts, 467 U.S. 561, 579 n.11, 34 FEP 1702 (1984).

order awarding the next available vacancy and requiring the continuation of back pay or front pay until such time as the job becomes available.[86] Bumping has been permitted only when, after a judgment or settlement awarding the plaintiff the next available vacancy, the defendant nevertheless awarded subsequent positions to other individuals.[87]

Those rules generally continue to apply,[88] but exceptions have been made in some circumstances. The Eleventh Circuit authorized the bumping of an incumbent because of four unique factors:[89]

> the defendants' repeated instances of racial discrimination against plaintiff; (2) the defendants' recalcitrance as evidenced by subsequent retaliatory acts of discrimination; (3) the uniqueness of the

---

[86]*Patterson*, 535 F.2d at 269 (even employee unlawfully denied promotion must await vacancy); Spagnuolo v. Whirlpool Corp., 717 F.2d 114, 121, 32 FEP 1382 (4th Cir. 1983) (employee should be permitted to obtain next available vacancy); Briseno v. Central Technical Cmty. Coll. Area, 739 F.2d 344, 348, 37 FEP 57 (8th Cir. 1984) (if no vacancy exists, plaintiff is entitled to monthly payments—less mitigation—until placed in comparable position).

[87]*See, e.g., Spagnuolo*, 717 F.2d at 121–22 (although bumping is not permissible remedy for discrimination, it is permissible to remedy noncompliance with prior order); Brewer v. Muscle Shoals Bd. of Educ., 790 F.2d 1515, 1522–24, 40 FEP 1580 (11th Cir. 1986) (bumping permitted to enforce terms of prior settlement).

[88]*See, e.g.*, Hudson v. Reno, 130 F.3d 1193, 1202, 75 FEP 1011 (6th Cir. 1997) (denying reinstatement where it would require displacing innocent employee), *overruled in part on other grounds*, Pollard v. E.I. du Pont de Nemours & Co., 532 U.S. 843 (2001); Avita v. Metropolitan Club, 49 F.3d 1219, 1230–31 (7th Cir. 1995) (affirming denial of reinstatement in Fair Labor Standards Act case where it would require "bumping" innocent employee and relationship between parties was "poisoned"); Ray v. Iuka Special Mun. Separate Sch. Dist., 51 F.3d 1246, 1254–55, 67 FEP 1348 (5th Cir. 1995) (affirming district court's denial of reinstatement, concluding that (1) reinstatement infeasible where no vacancies exist; (2) reinstatement would require bumping incumbent employee; (3) plaintiff secured substantially similar employment; and (4) because of consolidation, plaintiff's former position no longer exists); *accord* Doll v. Brown, 75 F.3d 1200, 1205, 5 AD 369 (7th Cir. 1996) (although court has power to order innocent incumbent to be bumped as part of equitable relief, effect on incumbent is factor that may weigh negatively against order of reinstatement as opposed to front pay); Carrero v. New York City Hous. Auth., 890 F.2d 569, 579, 51 FEP 596 (2d Cir. 1989) (deferring reinstatement of demoted employee); Walsdorf v. Board of Comm'rs, 857 F.2d 1047, 1053–54, 48 FEP 209 (5th Cir. 1988) (refusing to order bumping); Pecker v. Heckler, 801 F.2d 709, 712 & n.7, 41 FEP 1485 (4th Cir. 1986) (race discrimination victim entitled only to next available deputy manager position because "[u]nder the law of this circuit, the innocent incumbent may not be displaced"), *overruled*, Laber v. Harvey, 438 F.3d 404, 410 (4th Cir. 2006).

[89]Walters v. City of Atlanta, 803 F.2d 1135, 1148–50, 42 FEP 387 (11th Cir. 1986) ("reverse" discrimination cases).

position wrongfully denied plaintiff; and (4) the defendants' ability to minimize the harm suffered by the "bumped" employee.[90]

The District of Columbia Circuit likewise has approved a bumping order where a plaintiff was demoted in retaliation for his opposition to affirmative action.[91] The court noted, however, that "[t]he necessity for the bumping remedy only arises with unique, typically higher-level, jobs that have no reasonable substitutes."[92] Some lower courts have begun to issue bumping orders more frequently.[93]

IV. AFFIRMATIVE RELIEF BENEFITING PERSONS OTHER THAN IDENTIFIED VICTIMS OF DISCRIMINATION

Some of the most controversial issues of injunctive relief involve affirmative remedies for persons who are not themselves identified discrimination victims. Third parties, and sometimes defendant employers, argue that such relief should be judged by entirely different standards because, by definition, it is not "make-whole" relief to an actual victim, it may injure innocent third parties, and courts should be loath to impose substantial injunctive burdens

---

[90]*Id.* at 1150 (footnote omitted). The court noted that this list "is not exhaustive, nor is any one factor controlling." *Id.* at 1150 n.15. The court also noted that the current occupant of the unique position was the direct beneficiary of the discrimination and was aware of the litigation prior to taking the position. *Id.*

[91]Lander v. Lujan, 888 F.2d 153, 155–58, 51 FEP 157 (D.C. Cir. 1989).

[92]*Id.* at 156.

[93]*See, e.g.*, Allen v. Barram, 215 F. Supp. 2d 184, 192, 89 FEP 1287 (D.D.C. 2002); Hayes v. Shalala, 933 F. Supp. 21, 25, 71 FEP 1240 (D.D.C. 1996) (ordering retroactive appointment of plaintiff despite fact that it will result in "bumping" of incumbent employee, as "the District of Columbia Circuit has indicated that bumping is authorized and appropriate in precisely the kind of situation presented by this case"); Shea v. Icelandair, 925 F. Supp. 1014, 1031, 70 FEP 1544 (S.D.N.Y. 1996) (ordering reinstatement despite potential displacement of another employee, stating that factors such as uniqueness of position denied plaintiff, ability to minimize harm to "bumped" employee, and frequency of discriminatory acts may weigh in favor of reinstatement that results in "bumping" of another employee); Underwood v. District of Columbia Armory Bd., 58 FEP 45, 49 (D.D.C. 1992) (in awarding reinstatement, court explained that defendant who sanctioned discrimination was in best position to reduce harm to incumbent by transfer, monetary compensation, or other relief); Jones v. Rivers, 732 F. Supp. 176, 178–80, 52 FEP 550 (D.D.C. 1990) (ordering bumping remedy for victim of sex discrimination); Quicker v. American V. Mueller, 712 F. Supp. 824, 829, 49 FEP 1319 (D. Colo. 1989) (ordering bumping remedy for victim of age and disability discrimination).

on parties not found liable for discrimination.[94] Plaintiffs respond that in these circumstances the employer is *not* an innocent party; this kind of relief is a necessary race- or gender-conscious remedy designed to address the systemic underutilization of minorities or women. This section explores these sensitive issues.[95]

A. Race- or Gender-Neutral Affirmative Relief

Where discriminatory practices are well-entrenched or involve more than isolated or sporadic incidents of discrimination, courts have issued affirmative decrees requiring adherence to particular procedures for admission and hiring,[96] promotion,[97] and testing.[98]

---

[94]General Bldg. Contractors Ass'n, Inc. v. Pennsylvania, 458 U.S. 375, 397–402, 29 FEP 139 (1982) (where only union was liable for discriminatory operation of hiring hall, contractors could not be required to meet minority hiring goals, to establish training program, or to share in overall financial cost of compliance with decree). However, courts may subject such parties to "such minor and ancillary provisions of an injunctive order as the District Court might find necessary to grant complete relief to [the plaintiffs] from the discrimination they suffered at the hands of the [discriminating party]." *Id.* at 399; *see also* Zipes v. Trans World Airlines, Inc., 455 U.S. 385, 399–400, 28 FEP 1 (1982) (retroactive seniority contrary to collective bargaining agreement may be ordered where employer, but not union, was found guilty of discrimination); Darnell v. City of Jasper, 730 F.2d 653, 656, 37 FEP 1315 (11th Cir. 1984) (district court should have ordered nonparty civil service board to administer exam to plaintiff). For example, an injunction modifying provisions of a collective bargaining agreement may run against both the employer and the union although only one of them was found liable for discrimination. *General Building Contractors*, 458 U.S. at 400.

[95]The related but distinct issue of voluntary affirmative action is discussed in Chapter 37 ("Reverse" Discrimination and Affirmative Action).

[96]*E.g.*, Eldredge v. Carpenters 46 N. Cal. Counties Joint Apprenticeship & Training Comm., 94 F.3d 1366, 1370–72, 71 FEP 1385 (9th Cir. 1996) (order requiring labor-management committee to adopt specific procedures to eliminate impermissible adverse impact on women seeking admission to carpentry apprenticeship program, including eliminating hunting license system, requiring all applicants to use sequential referral list to satisfy first-job requirement, implementing 20% affirmative action program, and appointing monitor); Thomas v. Washington County Sch. Bd., 915 F.2d 922, 926, 53 FEP 1754 (4th Cir. 1990) (order to publicly advertise job vacancies); Garland v. USAir, Inc., 56 FEP 377, 378–79 (W.D. Pa. 1991) (order specifying detailed rules for recruitment and hiring of flight officers).

[97]*E.g.*, Paxton v. Union Nat'l Bank, 688 F.2d 552, 572–74, 29 FEP 1233 (8th Cir. 1982) (requiring employer to develop written job descriptions and selection standards that are reasonably objective and job-related, use written supervisory evaluations in promotion decisions that are administered in accordance with written guidelines, and post notices of job vacancies and permit employees to request promotions).

[98]*E.g.*, Bridgeport Guardians, Inc. v. City of Bridgeport, 933 F.2d 1140, 1145–46, 1149, 55 FEP 1631 (2d Cir. 1991) (requiring "banding" of test scores, designating

In cases of sexual or racial harassment, courts have required employers to adopt antiharassment policies and complaint procedures or to implement other policies designed to prevent future harassment.[99] Other forms of affirmative relief have been tailored to remedy particular discriminatory practices.[100]

Courts generally have refused, however, to order affirmative injunctive relief beyond make-whole relief where the plaintiff has shown only an isolated incident of discrimination[101] or

---

group that will make selections from among applicants whose scores are in same band, and specifying criteria upon which such selections must be based); Gilbert v. City of Little Rock, 799 F.2d 1210, 1215, 44 FEP 509 (8th Cir. 1986) (requiring validation of any future oral exam for police promotions). *See generally* Chapter 4 (Application of Adverse Impact to Employment Decisions).

[99]*E.g.*, EEOC v. Gurnee Inn Corp., 914 F.2d 815, 816–17, 53 FEP 1425 (7th Cir. 1990) (ordering defendant to adopt policy prohibiting sexual harassment and procedure to enforce that policy); Davis v. City & County of San Francisco, 890 F.2d 1438, 1449–52, 51 FEP 1542 (9th Cir. 1989) (requiring specified officers, on pain of contempt, to inspect station houses and remove and destroy any racially or sexually inflammatory materials); Spina v. Forest Preserve Dist., 2002 U.S. Dist. LEXIS 14016, at *13 (N.D. Ill. July 31, 2002) (enjoining district from permitting sexual harassment, discrimination, or retaliation, and directing it to issue comprehensive harassment/discrimination policy incorporating zero tolerance, to offer comprehensive training program, and to implement complaint and investigation procedure); Morris v. American Nat'l Can Corp., 730 F. Supp. 1489, 1498, 52 FEP 210 (E.D. Mo. 1989) (requiring employer to develop staff training program and to establish and publicize grievance procedure for sexual harassment complaints), *aff'd in relevant part*, 952 F.2d 200, 57 FEP 946 (8th Cir. 1991).

[100]*E.g., Spina*, 2002 U.S. Dist. LEXIS 14016, at *10–11 (directing forest preserve district whose male law enforcement officers had sexually harassed female officer to provide separate locker facilities); EEOC v. Wal-Mart Stores, Inc., 83 FEP 833, 836–37 (S.D. Ill. 2000) (ordering defendant to notify EEOC office of any employee discharged within next 2 years and requiring posting of result of trial, including verdict against defendant and reminder of employee rights under federal antidiscrimination laws); Hammon v. Kelly, 830 F. Supp. 11 (D.D.C. 1993) (enjoining district from demoting, without cause, for period of 6 years, fire fighters who were promoted under settlement agreement and consent decree); EEOC v. Ackerman, Hood & McQueen, Inc., 758 F. Supp. 1440, 1456, 55 FEP 668 (W.D. Okla. 1991) (requiring defendant to develop and implement written policy concerning leaves and schedule adjustments that does not discriminate against pregnant employees), *aff'd*, 956 F.2d 944 (10th Cir. 1992); Daniels v. Pipefitters Ass'n Local 597, 53 FEP 1669 (N.D. Ill. 1990) (special master appointed to recommend new, nondiscriminatory method of referring union members to jobs), *aff'd*, 945 F.2d 906 (7th Cir. 1991).

[101]*E.g.*, Hopkins v. Price Waterhouse, 737 F. Supp. 1202, 1216, 52 FEP 1275 (D.D.C.) (one atypical case does not provide basis for affirmative injunctive relief), *aff'd*, 920 F.2d 967, 54 FEP 750 (D.C. Cir. 1990). *But see* EEOC v. Northwest Airlines, Inc., 188 F.3d 695, 701 (6th Cir. 1999) (EEOC may obtain general injunctive relief even where only one or a handful of aggrieved employees is identified and need not demonstrate pattern or policy of discrimination).

where the defendant has otherwise shown that affirmative relief is unnecessary.[102]

B. Race- or Gender-Conscious Affirmative Relief

The Supreme Court, in *Fire Fighters (IAFF) Local 1784 v.
Stotts*,[103] addressed the issue of race-conscious affirmative relief
for persons who are not themselves victims of discrimination. *Stotts*
arose from a consent order that required the city to use its best
efforts to increase the percentage of African Americans in the fire
department. When budgetary problems ensued, the district court
enjoined the city from conducting layoffs in accordance with its
seniority system, thereby preventing the layoff of African Americans. The Supreme Court, however, ruled that a court must respect
bona fide seniority systems during layoffs even though the effect
is to undo the results of a prior Title VII consent decree. The Court
reasoned that, because the African-American fire fighters aided by
the decree were not themselves proven victims of discrimination,
the district court lacked the authority to modify the consent decree so as to override the seniority provisions of the collective
bargaining agreement.[104]

Just two terms later, however, a sharply divided Court upheld
race-conscious affirmative relief to nonvictims, based on longstanding, egregious discrimination practiced by the defendant union,
as to which the trial court had made extensive factual findings. In
Sheet Metal Workers Local 28 v. EEOC,[105] the relief at issue was
not designed to "make whole" any identifiable victim, but rather
to eradicate the effects of a proven history of discrimination. The
lower court in *Sheet Metal Workers* had found the union local in
continuing violation of Title VII and in contempt of prior remedial orders and had entered an order imposing a 29.23 percent

---

[102]*E.g.*, Webb v. Missouri Pac. R.R., 98 F.3d 1067 (8th Cir. 1996) (district court
abused its discretion by granting injunction where evidence of discriminatory treatment was over 4 years old and uncontested evidence demonstrated employer's effective implementation of comprehensive antidiscrimination programs); Daines v.
City of Mankato, 754 F. Supp. 681, 704–05, 54 FEP 41 (D. Minn. 1990) (affirmative relief inappropriate where defendant has advertised and interviewed for all relevant positions for 6 years and has operated under thorough and aggressive affirmative action policy for 2 years).

[103]467 U.S. 561, 34 FEP 1702 (1984).

[104]*Id.* at 578–79.

[105]478 U.S. 421, 41 FEP 107 (1986).

minority membership goal (based on minority labor market avail-ability). The order also required the creation of a fund to be used for minority recruitment, counseling, training, and financial assis-tance. The Supreme Court affirmed. In doing so, the Court rejected the view that affirmative relief must be limited to make-whole relief for identified victims of discrimination. Instead, the Court held that courts "may, in appropriate circumstances, order preferential re-lief benefiting individuals who are not the actual victims of dis-crimination as a remedy for violations of Title VII."[106] The plural-ity opinion in *Sheet Metal Workers* cautioned, however, that, "[a]lthough we conclude that § 706(g) does not foreclose a dis-trict court from instituting some sorts of racial preferences where necessary to remedy past discrimination, we do not mean to sug-gest that such relief is always proper."[107] Indeed, the plurality said, race-conscious relief to nonvictims would not be needed in "the majority of Title VII cases."[108] Without attempting to list all possible circumstances that would justify exceptions from the normal rule, the plurality held that such relief may be warranted where there has been "persistent or egregious discrimination" or where needed "to dissipate the lingering effects of pervasive discrimination."[109]

Several factors seemed most persuasive to the *Sheet Metal Workers* plurality. First, relief to nonvictims was "necessary to remedy [the defendant's] pervasive and egregious discrimination" and "to combat the lingering effects of past discrimination."[110] The district court had determined that the union had a pervasive his-tory of and reputation for discrimination, such that minorities were discouraged even from applying for membership.[111] Second, the

---

[106]*Id.* at 482 (plurality opinion); *see also id.* at 483 (Powell, J., concurring in part and concurring in judgment) ("[I]n cases involving particularly egregious con-duct a district court may fairly conclude that an injunction alone is insufficient to remedy a proven violation of Title VII."); *id.* at 499 (White, J., dissenting) ("[T]he general policy under Title VII is to limit relief for racial discrimination in employ-ment practices to actual victims of the discrimination. But I agree that § 706(g) does not bar relief for nonvictims in all circumstances.").

[107]478 U.S. at 475.

[108]*Id.* at 476.

[109]*Id.* at 475–76.

[110]*Id.* at 476.

[111]*Id.* at 477. In his opinion concurring in the judgment, Justice Powell explic-itly relied on the "history of petitioners' contemptuous racial discrimination and their successive attempts to evade all efforts to end that discrimination" to support his

district court flexibly applied the membership goal, twice adjusting the deadline and accommodating legitimate reasons for failure to meet the goal. This demonstrated that it had been adopted as a compliance benchmark and not simply to achieve and maintain racial balance.[112] Moreover, the district court expressly disavowed any reliance on the failure to meet the goal as the basis for its ruling.[113] Third, the relief was temporary in that it would end when goals were met and the relief was no longer needed.[114] Finally, it did not "unnecessarily trammel" the interests of white employees, because it would neither require the layoff of existing employees nor absolutely bar whites seeking union membership.[115]

Race-based hiring preferences inevitably shift some of the burden of remediation to innocent persons and thus should not remain in place for any longer than necessary to alleviate the effects of past discrimination.[116] This issue is particularly significant in promotion cases. There, relief to minorities who are not themselves discrimination victims poses a greater risk of undue interference with the legitimate expectations of other (usually white or male) workers.[117] Even in this context, however, such relief may

---

belief that the remedy did not violate Title VII. *Id.* at 484 (Powell, J., concurring in part and concurring in judgment).

[112]478 U.S. at 478.

[113]*See id.*

[114]*Id.* at 479.

[115]*Id.* at 476–79.

[116]Quinn v. City of Boston, 325 F.3d 18, 27 (1st Cir. 2003); *see also* Grutter v. Bollinger, 539 U.S. 306, 341–42 (2003) (race-conscious admissions policies must be limited in time to ensure that "deviation from the norm of equal treatment of all races and ethnic groups is a temporary matter").

[117]*See, e.g.*, Rudebusch v. Hughes, 313 F.3d 506, 522 (9th Cir. 2002) ("In the circumstance of a promotion, where there is competition for a finite position or where the benefits of promotion will have lasting employment consequences, appropriating the opportunity exclusively for purposes of alleviating racial or gender-based disparities may trammel upon the excluded employee's legitimate expectation to compete equally for the position."); United States v. City of Chi., 870 F.2d 1256, 1260, 50 FEP 682 (7th Cir. 1989) (successful white female exam takers had "not a 'vested' right, not a property right . . . , but a confident expectation of being promoted"; this was sufficient expectancy to entitle them to intervention as of right under Fed. R. Civ. P. 24(a)(2); district court previously had found discrimination under promotion exam, and its remedial orders altered proposed intervenors' chances for promotion); *cf. Sheet Metal Workers*, 478 U.S. at 488 n.3 (Powell, J., concurring in part and concurring in judgment) ("The proper constitutional inquiry focuses on the effect, if any, and the diffuseness of the burden imposed on innocent nonminorities . . . ."); United States v. Paradise, 480 U.S. 149, 186, 43 FEP 1 (1987) (Powell, J., concurring)

be permissible. For example, in *United States v. Paradise*,[118] the Supreme Court upheld, against an equal protection challenge, an order that required the Alabama Department of Public Safety to promote one African-American state trooper for every white promoted until the rank to which promotions were being made was 25 percent African American or until the department had developed nondiscriminatory procedures for promotion to that rank.[119] The plurality opinion first asserted that the government "unquestionably has a compelling interest in remedying past and present discrimination by a state actor" sufficient to warrant the use of race-conscious measures.[120] The four-member plurality then set forth the following factors to be used in assessing whether, in a particular case, race-conscious relief is appropriate:

> In determining whether race-conscious remedies are appropriate, we look to several factors, including the necessity for the relief and the efficacy of alternative remedies; the flexibility and duration of the relief, including the availability of waiver provisions; the relationship of the numerical goals to the relevant labor market; and the impact of the relief on the rights of third parties.[121]

Applying these factors, the plurality found that the 50 percent promotion order was necessary under the circumstances to remedy the effects of the department's "long-term, open, and pervasive" discrimination and its refusal to obey prior court orders to implement nondiscriminatory promotion procedures.[122] The plurality also found it important that the one-for-one promotion ratio was

---

("[T]he promotion requirement at issue in this case does not 'impose the entire burden of achieving racial equality on particular individuals,' and does not disrupt seriously the lives of innocent individuals."). *But cf.* Vulcan Pioneers v. New Jersey Dep't of Civil Serv., 832 F.2d 811, 816–17, 53 FEP 703 (3d Cir. 1987) (Candidates who scored well on an invalid exam "do not have an 'absolute right' to or even a 'legitimate firmly rooted expectation' of the promotion . . . . [B]urdens placed on these candidates simply do not rise to an impermissible level.").

[118]480 U.S. 149, 43 FEP 1 (1987).

[119]*Id.* at 163, 185–86 (plurality opinion of Brennan, J., joined by Marshall, Blackmun, and Powell, J.J.); *id.* at 195 (Stevens, J., concurring in judgment).

[120]*Id.* at 166–67.

[121]*Id.* at 171. Justice Stevens, the fifth vote for the judgment affirming the decree, would not have required that even these factors be considered. According to Justice Stevens, any court decree, regardless of whether it involves race-conscious relief, should be evaluated under a "reasonableness" standard. *Id.* at 192–93 (Stevens, J., concurring in judgment).

[122]*Id.* at 171.

imposed only once and that alternative measures would not have satisfied the same goals.[123] The plurality was satisfied that the promotion order was sufficiently flexible and limited in duration because the order by its terms was effective only until the department adopted nondiscriminatory procedures, or until the 25 percent goal was met, and because the 50 percent requirement was subject to the availability of qualified African-American candidates.[124] Finally, the plurality found that the order did not unduly burden innocent third parties, in view of the following factors: the promotion ratio was temporary, it did not impose an absolute bar to white advancement, it did not require the layoff or discharge of white employees, it postponed rather than precluded the promotion of qualified whites, and it did not require the passing over of qualified whites in favor of unqualified African Americans.[125]

Three of the four dissenting Justices said that the remedy failed to meet the strict scrutiny standard.[126] The dissenters reasoned that the one-to-one promotion order was not narrowly tailored to its stated purpose of causing the department to develop promotion procedures that did not have an adverse impact. The dissenters also faulted the district court—unlike the district court in *Sheet Metal Workers*—for not considering alternative remedies that were less likely to interfere with the rights and frustrate the legitimate expectations of non-minority employees.[127]

Before *Sheet Metal Workers* and *Paradise*, every court of appeals had upheld the use of race- or gender-conscious relief in at least some circumstances.[128] Subsequently, courts have continued

[123]*Id.* at 171–72.
[124]*Id.* at 177–79.
[125]*Id.* at 182–83.
[126]*Id.* at 201 (O'Connor, J., joined by Rehnquist, C.J., and Scalia, J., dissenting). Justice White, the fourth dissenter, wrote simply that he agreed with "much" of Justice O'Connor's dissenting opinion and that "the District Court exceeded its equitable powers in devising a remedy in this case." *Id.* at 196 (White, J., dissenting).
[127]*Id.* at 199–200.
[128]*E.g.*, Boston Chapter, NAACP, Inc. v. Beecher, 504 F.2d 1017, 1026–28, 8 FEP 855 (1st Cir. 1974) (affirming race-conscious fire fighter hiring ratios); Association Against Discrimination in Employment, Inc. v. City of Bridgeport, 647 F.2d 256, 279–84, 25 FEP 1013 (2d Cir. 1981) (affirming race-conscious relief, including order requiring priority hiring of 102 minority fire fighters); United States v. City of Buffalo, 633 F.2d 643, 646–47, 24 FEP 313 (2d Cir. 1980) (affirming interim hiring ratios of 50% minority and 25% women, even though those figures were higher than workforce availability or applicant flow); United States v. Elevator

to order such relief where it was warranted under the principles set forth in *Sheet Metal Workers* and *Paradise*.[129] Where the necessary predicate was not established, courts have denied such relief.[130]

Constructors Local 5, 538 F.2d 1012, 1017–20, 13 FEP 81 (3d Cir. 1976) (affirming order prescribing 23% African-American union membership goal and 33% African-American job referrals); Chisholm v. United States Postal Serv., 665 F.2d 482, 498–99, 27 FEP 425 (4th Cir. 1981) (affirming hiring and promotion goals based on African-American workforce availability); Williams v. City of New Orleans, 729 F.2d 1554, 1557–58, 34 FEP 1009 (5th Cir. 1984) (en banc) (imposition of quota to remedy past discrimination not forbidden by Title VII, even where it is not limited to actual victims of discrimination); United States v. Masonry Contractors Ass'n, 497 F.2d 871, 877–78, 8 FEP 159 (6th Cir. 1974) (affirming requirement that at least 5% of bricklayer hours be worked by African-American bricklayers); United States v. City of Chi., 663 F.2d 1354, 1362, 25 FEP 1271 *and* 27 FEP 177 (7th Cir. 1981) (en banc) (adopting 25% minority police promotion ratio); Firefighters Inst. for Racial Equality v. City of St. Louis, 616 F.2d 350, 362–64, 21 FEP 1140 (8th Cir. 1980) (remanding for entry of order requiring immediate promotion to fire captain of eight African Americans, and subsequent promotions based on ratio of one African American for every two whites); United States v. Iron Workers Local 86, 443 F.2d 544, 548, 552–54, 3 FEP 496 (9th Cir. 1971) (affirming race-conscious relief); United States v. Lee Way Motor Freight, Inc., 625 F.2d 918, 943–45, 20 FEP 1345 (10th Cir. 1979) (affirmative hiring relief available under Title VII); Paradise v. Prescott, 767 F.2d 1514, 1524, 1538, 38 FEP 1094 (11th Cir. 1985) (affirming 1 to 1 interim promotion order), *aff'd sub nom.* United States v. Paradise, 480 U.S. 149, 43 FEP 1 (1987); McKenzie v. Sawyer, 684 F.2d 62, 80, 29 FEP 633 (D.C. Cir. 1982) (goals do not overreach their usefulness). *But see* Segar v. Smith, 738 F.2d 1249, 1293–94, 35 FEP 31 (D.C. Cir. 1984) (race-conscious promotion goals and timetables, although permissible remedy, not warranted in this case); Thompson v. Sawyer, 678 F.2d 257, 294, 28 FEP 1614 (D.C. Cir. 1982) (although interim quotas are permissible form of Title VII relief, 3 to 1 ratio not appropriate in this case because it did not focus on unlawful practices and ignored rights of nonminorities).

[129]Newark Branch, NAACP v. Town of Harrison, 940 F.2d 792, 805–08, 56 FEP 680 *and* 1688 (3d Cir. 1991) (affirming, under *Sheet Metal Workers* and *Paradise*, goal that African Americans be recruited and hired in proportion to labor market availability and order requiring affirmative recruiting targeted to African-American audiences); Pennsylvania v. Operating Eng'rs Local 542, 807 F.2d 330, 334–39, 42 FEP 836 (3d Cir. 1986) (affirming, under *Sheet Metal Workers*, 40% minority goal for hiring-hall referrals in geographic district with 18% minority availability); Eldredge v. Carpenters 46 N. Cal. Counties Joint Apprenticeship & Training Comm., 94 F.3d 1366, 1370, 71 FEP 1385 (9th Cir. 1996) (adopting, under *Sheet Metal Workers* and *Paradise*, plan requiring one out of every five applicants dispatched under job referral list to be woman until women constitute 20% of apprentices).

[130]Catlett v. Missouri Highway & Transp. Comm'n, 828 F.2d 1260, 1268–69, 45 FEP 1627 (8th Cir. 1987) (because *Sheet Metal Workers* and *Paradise* require court to consider alternate remedies before imposing numerical goal, female hiring goal must be vacated; record does not show that general injunction against discrimination would be ineffective); McKenzie v. Kennickell, 825 F.2d 429, 433–37, 44 FEP 657 (D.C. Cir. 1987) (reversing order requiring promotion of class member to meet previously ordered 4-year promotion goal; African Americans had received

In its 1995 landmark decision, *Adarand Constructors, Inc. v. Peña*,[131] the Supreme Court reiterated that federal courts may order affirmative action to remedy an employer's "pervasive, systematic, and obstinate discriminatory conduct,"[132] and held that a strict scrutiny standard should be used to review race-based voluntary affirmative action programs.[133] *Adarand* unleashed a torrent of challenges to government action, including employment preferences,[134] government contract set-aside and incentive programs,[135]

---

approximately 80% of promotions, and defendant's failure to meet goal was due only to low job vacancy rate; lower court's order failed to reflect flexibility and concern for rights of non-minority employees required by *Sheet Metal Workers* and *Paradise*).

[131]515 U.S. 200, 67 FEP 1828 (1995).

[132]*Id.* at 237.

[133]*Id. See generally* Chapter 37 ("Reverse" Discrimination and Affirmative Action).

[134]*See, e.g.*, Chicago Firefighters Local 2 v. City of Chi., 249 F.3d 649, 85 FEP 1305 (7th Cir. 2001) (challenging fire fighter affirmative action promotion practices and exams); Danskine v. Miami Dade Fire Dep't, 253 F.3d 1288 (11th Cir. 2001) (challenging fire department's hiring goal for women); Majeske v. City of Chi., 218 F.3d 816 (7th Cir. 2000) (challenging police officer affirmative action promotion plan); Schurr v. Resorts Int'l Hotel, Inc., 196 F.3d 486, 81 FEP 364 (3d Cir. 1999) (challenging casino's affirmative action hiring plan); Hayden v. County of Nassau, 180 F.3d 42, 79 FEP 1874 (2d Cir. 1999) (challenging police department's use of entrance examination designed to eliminate differential effects suffered by minorities); Boston Police Superior Officers Fed'n v. City of Boston, 147 F.3d 13 (1st Cir. 1998) (challenging race-based promotion); MD/DC/DE Broadcasters Ass'n v. Federal Commc'ns Comm'n, 236 F.3d 13, 84 FEP 1376 (D.D.C. 2001) (challenging EEO rule requiring race-conscious recruiting efforts); Barnhill v. City of Chi., 2001 WL 243410 (N.D. Ill. Mar. 12, 2001) (challenging police department's use of merit component in promotions as mask for illegal affirmative action program); Patrolmen's Benevolent Ass'n v. City of N.Y., 74 F. Supp. 2d 321, 80 FEP 1701 (S.D.N.Y. 1999) (challenging police department's racially and ethnically conscious involuntary transfer decision), *aff'd*, 310 F.3d 43 (2d Cir. 2002).

[135]*See, e.g.*, Builders Ass'n v. County of Cook, 256 F.3d 642 (7th Cir. 2001) (challenging county set-aside ordinance favoring minority- and women-owned enterprises); Adarand Constructors, Inc. v. Slater, 228 F.3d 1147 (10th Cir. 2000) (challenging federal subcontracting clause that used race-conscious presumption designed to favor minority enterprise and other disadvantaged business enterprises); W.H. Scott Constr. Co. v. City of Jackson, 199 F.3d 206 (5th Cir. 1999) (challenging city set-aside policy encouraging minority participation in city construction contracts); Government Employees (AFGE) v. United States, 104 F. Supp. 2d 58 (D.D.C. 2000) (challenging Air Force preference in favor of Native American firms for civil engineering and maintenance work at two Air Force bases); Concrete Works of Colo., Inc. v. City & County of Denver, 86 F. Supp. 2d 1042 (D. Colo. 2000) (challenging ordinances requiring use of certified minority- and women-owned business on city construction contracts), *rev'd and remanded*, 321 F.3d 950 (10th Cir. 2003); Rothe Dev. Corp. v. United States Dep't of Def., 49 F. Supp. 2d 937 (W.D. Tex. 1999)

school admission programs,[136] and court orders and consent decrees.[137]

Though few courts have addressed the issue of race-conscious, court-ordered relief, nearly every court to have done so has applied a strict scrutiny standard.[138] This standard obliges a court to make a finding that the race-based relief is not only justified by a compelling governmental purpose but also narrowly drawn to fit the contours of that purpose.[139] Some question may remain,

---

(challenging government contract preference for socially and economically disadvantaged persons).

[136]*See, e.g.*, Grutter v. Bollinger, 539 U.S. 306 (2003) (challenging law school's use of race as factor in student admissions); Gratz v. Bollinger, 539 U.S. 244 (2003) (challenging university's use of racial preferences for undergraduate admissions); Hopwood v. Texas, 236 F.3d 256 (5th Cir. 2000) (challenging law school's race-based admission program); Smith v. University of Wash. Law Sch., 233 F.3d 1188 (9th Cir. 2000) (challenging law school's racially conscious admission program); Brewer v. West Irondequoit Cent. Sch. Dist., 212 F.3d 738 (2d Cir. 2000) (challenging public school's race-conscious interdistrict school transfer program); Eisenberg v. Montgomery County Pub. Schs., 197 F.3d 123 (4th Cir. 1999) (challenging racial preference in public magnet school's transfer policy); Parents Involved in Cmty. Schs. v. Seattle Sch. Dist. No. 1, 137 F. Supp. 2d 1224 (W.D. Wash. 2001) (challenging high school's use of race as tiebreaker to award spaces in oversubscribed schools), *rev'd*, 285 F.3d 1236 (9th Cir. 2002); Johnson v. Board of Regents, 106 F. Supp. 2d 1362 (S.D. Ga. 2000) (challenging university's use of race and gender in admission decisions), *aff'd*, 263 F.3d 1234 (11th Cir. 2001); Comfort v. Lynn Sch. Comm., 100 F. Supp. 2d 57 (D. Mass. 2000) (challenging school district's racially conscious transfer policy).

[137]*See, e.g.*, United States v. Secretary of Housing & Urban Dev., 239 F.3d 211 (2d Cir. 2001) (affirming consent decree with race-conscious remedy under strict scrutiny); Albright v. City of New Orleans, 2001 WL 725354 (E.D. La. June 26, 2001) (challenging racially conscious promotions allegedly given under consent decree); Allen v. Alabama State Bd. of Educ., 190 F.R.D. 602 (M.D. Ala. 2000) (amending consent decree regarding race-conscious certification exams); Ashton v. City of Memphis, 49 F. Supp. 2d 1051 (W.D. Tenn. 1999) (race-conscious remedial decree does not stand up under strict scrutiny).

[138]*See, e.g.*, Quinn v. City of Boston, 325 F.3d 18, 28 (D. Mass. 2003) ("[B]ecause this litigation challenges a judicial decree affording race-based relief, any interpretation of the decree or any application of it in practice must survive strict scrutiny."); Ehrenberg v. Goord, 2001 WL 314598 (2d Cir. Mar. 30, 2001); *Ashton*, 49 F. Supp. 2d at 1051; *Albright*, 2001 WL 725354; Killebrew v. City of Greenwood, 1999 U.S. Dist. LEXIS 13363 (N.D. Miss. July 8, 1999). *But see* United States v. New York City Bd. of Educ., 85 F. Supp. 2d 130 (E.D.N.Y. 2000) (court only needs to decide whether settlement agreement is substantially related to objective of eliminating discrimination and does not unnecessarily trammel interests of third parties), *vacated and remanded sub nom.* Brennan v. New York City Bd. of Educ., 260 F.3d 123 (2d Cir. 2001).

[139]*See Grutter*, 539 U.S. at 3 ("racial classifications imposed by the government . . . are constitutional only if they are narrowly tailored to further compelling

however, regarding the appropriate standard of scrutiny for a judicial decree.[140]

Where a party challenges a district court's race-conscious remedial measure, the party defending the measure bears the initial burden of producing evidence that the measure is constitutional, although the challenging party bears the ultimate burden of proving that the measure is unconstitutional.[141] A consent decree that does not admit that the state participated in racial discrimination in the past cannot be used to justify a race-conscious state action not mandated by the decree.[142]

The standard of scrutiny to be applied to gender-based, court-ordered relief also remains unclear. Generally, however, gender-based programs are analyzed under an intermediate level of scrutiny.[143]

---

governmental interests"); Adarand Constructors, Inc. v. Peña, 515 U.S. 200, 235, 67 FEP 1828 (1995) ("Federal racial classifications . . . must serve a compelling governmental interest, and must be narrowly tailored to further that interest.").

[140]*See Housing & Urban Development*, 239 F.3d at 218–19 (level of scrutiny to be applied to race-conscious judicial remedies is undecided, but applying strict scrutiny and declining to decide question); Allen v. Alabama State Bd. of Educ., 164 F.3d 1347, 1352 n.2 (11th Cir. 1999) (rejecting broad reading of *Adarand*); Lutheran Church-Mo. Synod v. Federal Commc'ns Comm'n, 154 F.3d 494, 497 (D.C. Cir. 1998) (same); Raso v. Lago, 135 F.3d 11, 16 (1st Cir. 1998) (limiting *Adarand* to government actions distributing benefits "preferentially favorable to one race"); Monterey Mech. Co. v. Wilson, 125 F.3d 702, 711 (9th Cir. 1997) (limiting *Adarand* to government actions subjecting "person to unequal treatment").

[141]Majeske v. City of Chi., 218 F.3d 816, 820 (7th Cir. 2000); Walker v. City of Mesquite, 169 F.3d 973, 982 (5th Cir. 1999); *Raso*, 135 F.3d at 20. *But see* Bass v. Board of County Comm'rs, 256 F.3d 1095, 1114–15 (11th Cir. 2001) (suggesting that intervening decisional law in Supreme Court may have shifted burden to employer to prove validity).

[142]*See* Hiller v. County of Suffolk, 977 F. Supp. 202, 206 (E.D.N.Y. 1997) (citing Wygant v. Jackson Board of Educ., 476 U.S. 267, 274 (stating that there must be some "showing of prior discrimination by the governmental unit involved before allowing limited use of racial classifications in order to remedy such discrimination")).

[143]*See Adarand Constructors*, 515 U.S. at 247 (Stevens, J. dissenting) ("[A]s the law currently stands, the Court will apply 'intermediate scrutiny' to cases of invidious gender discrimination and 'strict scrutiny' to cases of invidious race discrimination . . . even though the primary purpose of the Equal Protection Clause was to end discrimination against the former slaves."); Danskine v. Miami Dade Fire Dep't, 253 F.3d 1288 (11th Cir. 2001) (upholding fire department's gender-based affirmative action plan under intermediate scrutiny); Dallas Fire Fighters Ass'n v. City of Dallas, 150 F.3d 438, 441–42 (5th Cir. 1998) (holding fire department's gender-based promotions unconstitutional while "[a]pplying the less exacting intermediate scrutiny analysis applicable to gender-based affirmative action"); Engineering Contractors Ass'n v. Metropolitan Dade County, 122 F.3d 895, 905 (11th Cir. 1997) (noting that

V. MONITORING THE COURT DECREE

Courts often retain jurisdiction in injunction cases to monitor and ensure compliance with their orders.[144] Courts may require that an employer maintain records and make reports[145] or allow access

---

race- or ethnicity-conscious remedies are subject to strict scrutiny and that gender-conscious remedies are subject to intermediate scrutiny); *see also Monterey Mechanical Co.*, 125 F.3d at 712 (applying intermediate scrutiny while also indicating that sex-based classifications must be justified by "exceedingly persuasive justification"); Cohen v. Brown Univ., 101 F.3d 155, 181, 183–84 (1st Cir. 1996) (analyzing gender-based challenge to college sports funding under intermediate scrutiny, but noting that *Adarand* did not mandate level of scrutiny to be applied to gender-conscious government action). *See generally* Deborah L. Brake, *Sex as a Suspect Class: An Argument for Applying Strict Scrutiny to Gender Discrimination*, 6 SETON HALL CONST. L.J. 953 (1996).

[144]*See* Bridgeport Guardians, Inc. v. Delmonte, 248 F.3d 66, 73 (2d Cir. 2001) (specifically retaining jurisdiction in court decree to "insure complete and continuing compliance"); EEOC v. Northwest Airlines, Inc., 188 F.3d 695, 698–99 (6th Cir. 1999) (noting transfer of venue to district court that entered consent decree for enforcement of subsequent actions arising out of decree); Eldredge v. Carpenters 46 N. Cal. Counties Joint Apprenticeship & Training Comm., 94 F.3d 1366, 1370–72, 71 FEP 1385 (9th Cir. 1996) (in ordering implementation of system for admitting women applicants to apprenticeship program, court appointed monitor until 20% of apprentices were women); Darnell v. City of Jasper, 730 F.2d 653, 656, 37 FEP 1315 (11th Cir. 1984) (district court should retain jurisdiction after remand so that it may order plaintiff instated as policy officer if he passes exam and meets other valid qualifications for position); Allen v. Alabama State Bd. of Educ., 190 F.R.D. 602, 620 (N.D. Ala. 2000) (specifically retaining jurisdiction in consent decree); Querim v. EEOC, 111 F. Supp. 2d 259, 266 (S.D.N.Y. 2000) (same), *aff'd*, 9 Fed. Appx. 35 (2d Cir. 2001); Kilgo v. Bowman Transp., 576 F. Supp. 600, 601, 604, 40 FEP 1412 (N.D. Ga. 1984) (retaining jurisdiction over trucking company to ensure compliance and to consider hiring goals if company fails to make special efforts to recruit women for over-the-road positions), *aff'd*, 789 F.2d 859 (11th Cir. 1986). *But see* Holland v. Department of Corr., 246 F.3d 267, 281 (3d Cir. 2001) (holding that district court did not have jurisdiction to modify decree beyond 4-year jurisdictional period provided for in consent decree); J. G. v. Board of Educ., 193 F. Supp. 2d 693 (W.D.N.Y. 2002) (no jurisdiction to enforce where consent decree expired by its own terms), *aff'd*, 53 Fed. Appx. 157 (2d Cir. 2002).

[145]*See* Teamsters v. United States, 431 U.S. 324, 361, 14 FEP 1514 (1977) (court that finds pattern or practice of discrimination may order employer to "keep records of its future employment decisions and file periodic reports with the court"); EEOC v. Plumbers & Pipefitters Local 120, 235 F.3d 244, 248 (6th Cir. 2000) (required recordkeeping and annual report to court); EEOC v. Iron Workers Local 40, 76 F.3d 76, 81 (2d Cir. 1996) (union required to keep permanent records of hiring hall activities); Brady v. Thurston Motor Lines, 726 F.2d 136, 147, 33 FEP 1370 (4th Cir. 1984) (affirming order that required company to "make periodic reports for two years about its implementation of decree"); Williams v. Montgomery County Sheriff's Dep't, 99 F. Supp. 2d 1330, 1332 (M.D. Ala. 2000) (employer required to submit policies and procedures for judicial approval).

to review records or the employer's premises.[146] They also may appoint third parties to monitor compliance and make reports.[147] Failure to comply may lead to sanctions.[148]

Modifications or amendments to a decree may be necessary to enforce compliance or to accommodate changed circumstances.[149]

---

[146]*See Iron Workers Local 40*, 76 F.3d at 81 (EEOC given access to variety of records); Robinson v. Jacksonville Shipyards, Inc., 760 F. Supp. 1486, 1545, 57 FEP 971 (M.D. Fla. 1991) (order in sexual harassment case gave plaintiff's counsel access to workplace to monitor compliance; court reserved right to appoint its own representative to monitor compliance; names and phone numbers of monitors to be posted and circulated so that employees have ability to contact monitors).

[147]*See Bridgeport Guardians*, 248 F.3d at 69 (decree appointed special master to review disciplinary actions taken by employer and to receive and investigate complaints of racial discrimination); Pennsylvania v. Operating Eng'rs Local 542, 807 F.2d 330, 332–33, 42 FEP 836 (3d Cir. 1986) (district court appointed special master to oversee implementation, appointed hiring hall monitor); Ingram v. Coca-Cola Co., 200 F.R.D. 685 (N.D. Ga. 2001) (creation of independent task force to review policies and investigate complaints and to provide court and employer with annual written report regarding compliance; employer to hire ombudsperson to monitor complaints); EEOC v. Iron Workers Local 580, 139 F. Supp. 2d 512, 517 (S.D.N.Y. 2001) (decree required special master to monitor compliance and establishment of record-keeping system); EEOC v. Joe's Stone Crab, Inc., 15 F. Supp. 2d 1364, 1381 (S.D. Fla. 1998) (requiring court-appointed monitor to attend and report on "roll-call" of applicants and requiring employer to hire industrial psychologist to complete criterion-related validation study of hiring evaluation criteria), *vacated and remanded on other grounds*, 220 F.3d 1263 (11th Cir. 2000), *ratified and reinstated*, 136 F. Supp. 2d 1311 (2001); EEOC v. Sheet Metal Workers Local 638, 889 F. Supp. 642, 687 (S.D.N.Y. 1995) (ordering defendants to pay appointed monitor and statistical experts to prepare compliance reports), *aff'd in pertinent part*, 81 F.3d 1162 (2d Cir. 1996); Stewart v. Rubin, 948 F. Supp. 1077 (D.D.C. 1996) (to assist parties in monitoring compliance with settlement agreement, defendant would retain expert who was mutually acceptable to parties to produce report analyzing employment data to determine whether employment practices had adverse impact on African-American employees), *aff'd mem.*, 124 F.3d 1309 (D.C. Cir. 1997); *cf.* A&M Records, Inc. v. Napster, Inc., 284 F.3d 1091, 1097 (9th Cir. 2002) (court appointed technical advisor to assist it).

[148]*See* Reynolds v. McInnes, 338 F.3d 1201, 1208 (11th Cir. 2003) (consent decree enforceable through contempt power); *Sheet Metal Workers Local 638*, 889 F. Supp. at 685; *A&M Records*, 284 F.3d 1091, 1098–99 (district court had authority to modify injunction to require shutdown of service in intellectual property case).

[149]*See* Holland v. Department of Corr., 246 F.3d 267, 270–71 (3d Cir. 2001) (recognizing court's power to extend duration of decree or to modify decree based on change of circumstances); EEOC v. Plumbers & Pipefitters Local 120, 235 F.3d 244, 254–55 (6th Cir. 2000) (upholding modification of consent decree requiring third-party contractors to be subject to recordkeeping requirements of consent decree even though they were not parties to original lawsuit); Vanguard v. City of Cleveland, 23 F.3d 1013, 64 FEP 1611 (6th Cir. 1994) (extending consent decree 2 years because of lower than expected minority pass rates); *Pennsylvania v. Operating Eng'rs Local 542*, 807 F.2d at 332–39, 42 FEP 836 (2-year extension

Additional violations are not necessarily required to trigger a modification of the original decree.[150] Where a requested modification imposes new obligations because of changed circumstances, it may be necessary to

(1) provide specific notice that the court is contemplating imposing additional obligations;

(2) allow the parties to present relevant evidence on the need for and character of the additional obligations; and

(3) issue specific findings that will support that a modification was warranted.[151]

A court also has the authority to dissolve or weaken a prior decree.[152] The Supreme Court has considered this issue mostly in school desegregation cases. Defendants generally argue that these

---

because of noncompliance). *But see* Reynolds v. Roberts, 207 F.3d 1288, 1300–01 (11th Cir. 2000) (acknowledging strong public policy against rewriting consent decrees); EEOC v. Iron Workers Local 40, 76 F.3d 76, 80 (2d Cir. 1996) (district court had no power, especially in absence of continuing jurisdiction clause, to enforce decree 12 years after expiration, even though union agreed to take on other responsibilities).

[150]*See* Bridgeport Guardians, Inc. v. Delmonte, 248 F.3d 66, 73 (2d Cir. 2001) ("Decrees may be modified even in the absence of additional violations or changes in law or fact."); EEOC v. Sheet Metal Workers Local 28, 753 F.2d 1172, 1185, 36 FEP 1466 (2d Cir. 1985) (where district court retained jurisdiction, additional violations not necessary to trigger modifications of original orders).

[151]Querim v. EEOC, 111 F. Supp. 2d 259, 256–66 (S.D.N.Y. 2000); Allen v. Alabama State Bd. of Educ., 190 F.R.D. 602, 606 (M.D. Ala. 2000) (requiring notice and hearing to all interested parties before approving party's requested amendment to consent decree).

[152]*See, e.g.,* Patterson v. Newspaper & Mail Deliverers of N.Y., 13 F.3d 33, 39, 63 FEP 964 (2d Cir. 1993) ("Application of the flexible standard for modifying decrees in the context of this lawsuit seeking broad remedies to change hiring practices entitles a court of equity to focus on the dominant objective of the decree and to terminate the entire decree once that objective has been reached."); Williams v. Montgomery County Sheriff's Dep't, 99 F. Supp. 2d 1330, 1334 (M.D. Ala. 2000) (discussing three factors to consider in terminating consent decrees, as articulated in *Freeman v. Pitts*, 503 U.S. 467, 490 (1992)); United States v. City of Buffalo, 721 F. Supp. 463, 468–69, 50 FEP 1693 (W.D.N.Y. 1989) (removing 50% hiring ratio because goal of raising minority representation to level of workforce availability had been substantially met; however, court also added new requirement that each police and fire recruit class must reflect applicant flow rate of African Americans, Hispanics, and women until city validated its selection procedures); United States v. New York, 711 F. Supp. 699, 699–703, 49 FEP 1195 (N.D.N.Y. 1989) (dissolving 40% minority hiring goal for state troopers where goal had been in place 10 years and had achieved its purpose).

cases are analogous,[153] whereas plaintiffs assert that the area is sui generis. In *Freeman v. Pitts*,[154] the Court held that district courts have the authority to withdraw their supervision and control:

> Just as a court has the obligation at the outset of a desegregation decree to structure a plan so that all available resources of the court are directed to comprehensive supervision of its decree, so too must a court provide an orderly means for withdrawing from control when it is shown that the school district has attained the requisite degree of compliance.[155]

The Court listed several factors a district court should consider in determining whether to dissolve or weaken a prior decree: whether there has been full or satisfactory compliance with the decree in those areas where supervision will be withdrawn, whether retention of judicial control is necessary to achieve compliance with other parts of the decree, and whether there has been a good faith commitment to those provisions of the law that were predicate for judicial intervention in the first place.[156] Where advisable, a court's withdrawal of supervision can occur in stages.[157]

Often, third parties may be affected by court orders in this area, and they have used two avenues to challenge decrees: § 108 of the Civil Rights Act of 1991,[158] and Rule 24 of the Federal Rules of Civil Procedure. However, under § 108, a prior decree cannot be challenged in a subsequent action:

> (i) by a person who, prior to the entry of the judgment or order . . . , had —
> > (I) actual notice of the proposed judgment or order sufficient to apprise such person that such judgment or order might

---

[153]*See Patterson*, 13 F.3d at 38–39, 63 FEP 964 ("[T]he flexible standard outlined in [school desegregation and institutional reform cases] is not limited to cases in which institutional reform is achieved in litigation brought directly against a governmental entity. The 'institution' sought to be reformed need not be an instrumentality of government.").

[154]503 U.S. 467 (1992).

[155]*Id.* at 489–90; *see also* Board of Educ. v. Dowell, 498 U.S. 237, 248 (1991) ("[Injunctions]. . . are not intended to operate in perpetuity.").

[156]503 U.S. at 491.

[157]*Id.* at 490–91.

[158]Pub. L. No. 102-166, § 108, 1991 U.S.C.C.A.N. (105 Stat.) 1071, 1076 (codified at 42 U.S.C. § 2000e-2(n)(1)). This section was enacted to protect, to the extent provided in the Act, any "employment practice that implements and is within the scope of a litigated or consent judgment or order that resolves a claim of employment discrimination under the Constitution or federal civil rights laws." *Id.*

adversely affect the interests and legal rights of such person and that an opportunity was available to present objections to such judgment or order by a future date certain; and

(II) a reasonable opportunity to present objections to such judgment or order; or

(ii) by a person whose interests were adequately represented by
another person who had previously challenged the judgment
or order on the same legal grounds and with a similar factual
situation, unless there has been an intervening change in law
or fact.[159]

A limited exception also permits subsequent suits where the
original judgment was obtained through collusion or fraud, is transparently invalid, or was entered by a court that lacked subject matter
jurisdiction.[160]

Any lawful challenge under these provisions must be brought
in the same court and, if possible, before the same judge, that entered the original order.[161]

---

[159]42 U.S.C. § 2000e-2(n)(1)(B) (2000); *see, e.g.*, Steans v. Combined Ins. Co.,
148 F.3d 1266, 1269 n.13 (11th Cir. 1998) (applying criteria); Rutherford v. City of
Cleveland, 137 F.3d 905, 910, 76 FEP 505 (6th Cir. 1998) (same); EEOC v. Federal
Express Corp., 268 F. Supp. 2d 192 (E.D.N.Y. 2003) (office of attorney general not
barred from bringing claims on behalf of others); Allen v. Alabama State Bd. of Educ.,
190 F.R.D. 602, 606 (M.D. Ala. 2000) (acknowledging requirements of § 108); Querim
v. EEOC, 111 F. Supp. 2d 259, 264–65 (S.D.N.Y. 2000) (holding that § 108 barred
third party from challenging decree); Williams v. Montgomery County Sheriff's Dep't,
99 F. Supp. 2d 1330, 1333–34 (M.D. Ala. 2000) (providing notice of motion to terminate decree to all affected persons subject to court decree appropriate); Stewart
v. Rubin, 948 F. Supp. 1077, 1097 (D.D.C. 1996) (§ 108 would not have preclusive
effect on future claims by class member that may develop as result of settlement
agreement); United States v. City of Hialeah, 899 F. Supp. 603, 607 (S.D. Fla. 1994)
(court complied with § 108 by publishing notice of hearing and proposed settlement,
which allowed challenges to settlement agreement), *aff'd*, 140 F.3d 968 (11th Cir.
1998); Sims v. Montgomery County Comm'n, 890 F. Supp. 1520, 1528 (M.D. Ala.
1995) (notices and fairness hearings sufficient under § 108 with respect to non-class
members where notices were sent to all employees not represented by plaintiffs,
inviting all employees to respond in writing, and where notices were posted in conspicuous places).

[160]42 U.S.C. § 2000e-2(n)(2)(C).

[161]*Id.* § 2000e-2(n)(3). It appears that § 108 has no retroactive application. *See*
EEOC v. Plumbers & Pipefitters Local 120, 235 F.3d 244, 254 n.4 (6th Cir. 2000)
(§ 108 does not apply retroactively to challenges commenced prior to enactment in
1991); Maitland v. University of Minn., 43 F.3d 357, 363, 66 FEP 796 (8th Cir. 1994)
(same). *But see* Aiken v. City of Memphis, 37 F.3d 1155, 1175–78, 65 FEP 1757
(6th Cir. 1994) (Jones J. dissenting) (favoring retroactive application to protect
longstanding remedial policy).

If a third party fails to meet the § 108 requirements, they may still be able to move under Rule 24.[162] That rule, unlike §108, provides nonparty nonintervenors a right to appeal.[163]

A third party who seeks to enforce an order may arguably have standing to do so under Rule 71 of the Federal Rules of Civil Procedure, which provides, in part, that a nonparty who is an intended beneficiary of a court decree or order may enforce the order as if it were an original party.[164]

VI. PRELIMINARY INJUNCTIONS

A. Rule 65 Preliminary Relief

Pursuant to Rule 65 of the Federal Rules of Civil Procedure, preliminary injunctions are available in employment discrimination cases. Most but not all cases hold that district courts have jurisdiction to grant preliminary injunctions under Title VII during the pendency of administrative procedures.[165] However, where

---

[162]*See, e.g.*, EEOC v. Iron Workers Local 580, 139 F. Supp. 2d 512, 518–20 (S.D.N.Y. 2001) (allowing nonparty union members to intervene to enforce court decree).

[163]*See* Johnson v. Reno, 1994 WL 189071, at *1 (D.D.C. Apr. 19, 1994).

[164]*See Iron Workers Local 580*, 139 F. Supp. 2d at 520–21 (nonparty union members may enforce court decree pursuant to Fed. R. Civ. P. 71). *But see* Tucker v. Troy State Univ., 82 FEP 1300 (M.D. Ala. 2000) (nonparty seeking to enforce consent decree does not have standing).

[165]*See* Wagner v. Taylor, 836 F.2d 566, 570–75, 45 FEP 1184 (D.C. Cir. 1987) (district court has jurisdiction to enjoin retaliation during pendency of administrative proceedings); Holt v. Continental Group, Inc., 708 F.2d 87, 89–90, 31 FEP 1468 (2d Cir. 1983) (district court has jurisdiction to consider request for restoration of status quo ante through reinstatement of plaintiff who alleged retaliatory discharge, even before conclusion of state administrative procedures); Duke v. Langdon, 695 F.2d 1136, 1137, 30 FEP 1059 (9th Cir. 1983) (district court has jurisdiction to grant preliminary injunction maintaining status quo prior to completion of administrative process); Drew v. Liberty Mut. Ins. Co., 480 F.2d 69, 72, 5 FEP 1077 (5th Cir. 1973) (individual litigant, not just EEOC, may seek injunctive relief to preserve status quo before completion of EEOC process); *see also* Aronberg v. Walters, 755 F.2d 1114, 1115–16, 45 FEP 522 (4th Cir. 1985) (district court has jurisdiction to grant preliminary injunction against retaliatory reassignment to preserve status quo pending appeal, notwithstanding failure to meet administrative exhaustion requirement on retaliation claim); Bailey v. Delta Air Lines, Inc., 722 F.2d 942, 943–45, 33 FEP 713 (1st Cir. 1983) (on appeal from dismissal for lack of jurisdiction, suggesting that district court may have jurisdiction to order preliminary relief prior to conclusion

an employee is "no longer in harm's way," such as when the movant is no longer employed by the employer and there are no serious prospects of the movant's return, a request for preliminary injunctive relief may be moot.[166]

Where a plaintiff fails to make an adequate showing under the appropriate standard, injunctive relief will be denied.[167] However, where the standard for granting preliminary relief is met, courts will grant relief to maintain the status quo during the pendency of

---

of EEOC process, but declining to so hold because these plaintiffs failed to meet standards for such relief). *But see* Knopp v. Magaw, 9 F.3d 1478, 1479–80, 63 FEP 353 (10th Cir. 1993) (unless needed to enjoin retaliation, district court lacks subject matter jurisdiction to order preliminary relief prior to exhaustion of EEOC procedures; distinguishing contrary cases; reversing district court's grant of preliminary injunction enjoining employer from carrying out alleged discriminatory transfer ending EEOC processes).

[166]Taylor v. Resolution Trust Corp., 56 F.3d 1497, 1502, 1504 (D.C. Cir. 1995) (employee who voluntarily chooses to permanently leave workplace bears responsibility for matter becoming moot and must forgo injunctive relief in favor of damages); Hudson v. Reno, 130 F.3d 1193, 1207 (6th Cir. 1997) (preliminary injunction to prevent adverse action became moot where plaintiff resigned while claiming constructive discharge), *overruled in part on other grounds*, Pollard v. E.I. du Pont de Nemours & Co., 532 U.S. 843 (2001).

[167]*See* Zervos v. Verizon N.Y., Inc., 252 F.3d 163, 173–74 (2d Cir. 2001) (failure to show either likelihood of success on ADA, Title VII, and Employee Retirement Income Security Act claims or sufficiently serious question going to merits of litigation); Gonzales v. National Bd. of Med. Exam'rs, 225 F.3d 620, 632 (6th Cir. 2000) (failure to prove strong likelihood of success on merits in ADA action); Gaines v. White River Envtl. P'ship, 202 F.3d 273 (7th Cir. 2000) (table) (failure to make any showing regarding irreparable harm or likelihood to prevail on merits); Black Firefighters Ass'n v. Dallas, 905 F.2d 63, 65–66 (5th Cir. 1990) (insufficient statistical analysis presented); Castro v. United States, 775 F.2d 399, 408–09, 39 FEP 162 (1st Cir. 1985) (terminated employee's allegations of inability to find other employment and loss of credit insufficient to demonstrate irreparable damage); O'Connor v. Peru State Coll., 728 F.2d 1001, 1003, 34 FEP 85 (8th Cir. 1984) (no showing of irreparable harm, and balance of equities did not favor plaintiff); Shaffer v. Globe Prot., Inc., 721 F.2d 1121, 1123–24, 33 FEP 450 (7th Cir. 1983) (no showing of irreparable injury); United States v. Jefferson County, 720 F.2d 1511, 1519–20, 33 FEP 829 (11th Cir. 1983) (same); Anderson v. U.S.F. Logistics (IMC), Inc., 2001 WL 114270, at *13–14, 84 FEP 1581, 1591–92 (S.D. Ind. Jan. 30, 2001) (plaintiff failed to prove that employer did not accommodate her religious beliefs; thus unlikely to succeed on merits); Moore v. Summers, 113 F. Supp. 2d 5, 27 (D.D.C. 2000) (failure to prove discriminatory promotions); Stuart v. Roache, 739 F. Supp. 54, 57 FEP 902 (D. Mass. 1990) (no irreparable injury where police sergeant's promotion eligibility list was revoked because it would conflict with consent decree; plaintiffs will have opportunity to take another test in future), *aff'd*, 951 F.2d 446 (1st Cir. 1991).

the litigation[168] or to restore the status quo where it has been upset by discriminatory practices.[169]

In reviewing motions for preliminary injunctions in employment cases, courts typically apply the traditional four-part analysis: (1) a strong likelihood of success on the merits, (2) the presence of irreparable injury to the plaintiff, (3) harm to others, and (4) whether the public interest will be furthered by issuing an injunction.[170] However, some circuits apply a variant of the traditional analysis. For example, the Second Circuit requires that the movant establish "(a) irreparable harm in the absence of an injunction and (b) either (i) a likelihood of success on the merits or (ii) sufficiently serious questions going to the merits to make them

---

[168]EEOC v. Hawaii, 764 F. Supp. 158, 162, 55 FEP 1357 (D. Haw. 1991) (enjoining mandatory retirement of judge); EEOC v. Lockheed Corp., 54 FEP 1632, 1634 (C.D. Cal. 1991) (enjoining removal of pilot at age 60); EEOC v. City of Bowling Green, 607 F. Supp. 524, 525–27, 37 FEP 963 (W.D. Ky. 1985) (enjoining involuntary retirement).

[169]EEOC v. Chrysler Corp., 733 F.2d 1183, 1184, 34 FEP 1401 (6th Cir. 1984) (affirming preliminary injunction giving forced retirees same option as younger employees: to be placed on layoff status with possibility of recall); Paige v. California, 2001 WL 128439, at *1–3 (C.D. Cal. Jan. 19, 2001) (enjoining hiring practices and decisions of highway patrol); *Moore*, 113 F. Supp. 2d at 27 (requiring curative e-mail message to be sent to employees promising no retaliation for participation in discrimination lawsuit); Bonds v. Heyman, 950 F. Supp. 1202, 1215 (D.D.C. 1997) (enjoining RIF termination of 58-year-old employee); Golden v. Lutheran Family Servs., 601 F. Supp. 383, 383–85, 39 FEP 1422 (W.D.N.C. 1984) (ordering plaintiff reinstated to position he held at time he filed race discrimination charge); EEOC v. Pacific Sw. Airlines, Inc., 587 F. Supp. 686, 696, 698, 34 FEP 1430 (N.D. Cal. 1984) (ordering reinstatement of skycaps and prohibiting contracting out of their work pending completion of EEOC proceedings); York v. Alabama State Bd. of Educ., 581 F. Supp. 779, 780–81, 787, 39 FEP 548 (M.D. Ala. 1983) (ordering preliminary injunction, in race discrimination class action, prohibiting use of challenged test and requiring reemployment of former teachers who would have been reemployed but for their test scores).

[170]Gonzales v. National Bd. of Med. Exam'rs, 225 F.3d 620, 625 (6th Cir. 2000); Black Firefighters Ass'n v. City of Dallas, 905 F.2d 63, 65, 53 FEP 613 (5th Cir. 1990); Cox v. City of Chi., 868 F.2d 217, 219, 48 FEP 1674 (7th Cir. 1989); Wagner v. Taylor, 836 F.2d 566, 575, 45 FEP 1184 (D.C. Cir. 1987); Castro v. United States, 775 F.2d 399, 407, 39 FEP 162 (1st Cir. 1985); United States v. Jefferson County, 720 F.2d 1511, 1519, 33 FEP 829 (11th Cir. 1983); Oburn v. Shapp, 521 F.2d 142, 147, 11 FEP 58 (3d Cir. 1975) (plaintiff generally must show probability of success and irreparable injury; where relevant, court should also consider harm to others and public interest); Crozier v. Howard, 772 F. Supp. 1192, 56 FEP 878 (W.D. Okla. 1991) (Tenth Circuit standard).

fair grounds for litigation and a balance of hardships tilting decidedly towards the plaintiff."[171] The Seventh Circuit requires a plaintiff to satisfy the first two parts of the traditional test before looking to the remaining parts.[172] The Ninth Circuit allows application of alternative tests. The movant can either establish the four traditional requirements or show "*either* a combination of probable success on the merits and the possibility of irreparable injury *or* that serious questions are raised and the balance of hardships tips sharply in [their] favor."[173]

With regard to irreparable injury, the Fifth and Eleventh Circuits have held that it is presumed where plaintiffs have exhausted their administrative remedies.[174] Where irreparable injury must be shown, generally courts hold that loss of a job or job opportunity

[171]Zervos v. Verizon N.Y., Inc., 252 F.3d 163, 172 (2d Cir. 2001); Jayaraj v. Scappini, 66 F.3d 36, 38 (2d Cir. 1995); Karmel v. City of N.Y., 200 F. Supp. 2d 361, 364 (S.D.N.Y. 2002) (noting that challenges to governmental policies implemented through "reasoned democratic processes" cannot rely on less rigorous "serious questions" alternative); Hartzog v. Reebok Int'l, 77 F. Supp. 2d 475, 476 (S.D.N.Y. 1999) (applying same test, although not requiring party to show sufficiently serious questions).

[172]*Compare* Ferrell v. United States Dep't of Hous. & Urban Dev., 186 F.3d 805, 811 (7th Cir. 1999) *and* Abbott Labs. v. Mead Johnson & Co., 971 F.2d 6, 11 (7th Cir. 1992) *with* Gaines v. White River Envtl. P'ship, 2000 WL 6199, at *1 (7th Cir. Jan. 3, 2000) (citing to first two parts of traditional test without reference to remaining requirements), NAACP v. City of Springfield, 139 F. Supp. 2d 990, 994 (C.D. Ill. 2001) (same) *and* Kiel v. City of Kenosha, 236 F.3d 814, 815–16 (7th Cir. 2000) (establishing similar five-part test).

[173]*See* Johnson v. California State Bd. of Accountancy, 72 F.3d 1427, 1430 (9th Cir. 1995) (preliminary injunction sought to enjoin state board from taking disciplinary action against plaintiff for violating state regulations); Sharr v. Department of Transp., 247 F. Supp. 2d 1208, 1213 (D. Or. 2003) (court also notes that movant must meet more stringent standard when seeking injunction going beyond status quo); *see also* A&M Records v. Napster, 239 F.3d 1004, 1013 (9th Cir. 2001) (applying alternative test in intellectual property case); Duke v. Langdon, 695 F.2d 1136 (9th Cir. 1983).

[174]Baker v. Buckeye Cellulose Corp., 856 F.2d 167, 169, 47 FEP 1697 (11th Cir. 1988) (plaintiff should have been given presumption of irreparable harm); EEOC v. Cosmair, Inc., 821 F.2d 1085, 1090–91, 44 FEP 569 (5th Cir. 1987) (extending presumption of irreparable harm to ADEA retaliation cases); Middleton-Keirn v. Stone, 655 F.2d 609, 612, 26 FEP 1154 (5th Cir. 1981) (applying presumption where plaintiff had exhausted administrative remedies). *But cf.* Black Firefighters Ass'n v. City of Dallas, 905 F.2d 63, 66–67, 53 FEP 613 (5th Cir. 1990) (majority found it unnecessary to reach applicability of presumption, but concurring opinion would overrule prior circuit decisions reciting presumption); White v. Carlucci, 862 F.2d 1209, 1211–13 (5th Cir. 1989) (refusing to apply any presumption in federal employee case); United States v. Jefferson County, 720 F.2d 1511, 1520, 33 FEP 829 (11th Cir. 1983) (refusing to apply any presumption where plaintiffs had not pursued administrative remedies).

is not sufficient.[175] Courts are divided over whether financial hardship, humiliation, emotional stress, damage to reputation, or diminished ability to obtain other employment are sufficient to demonstrate irreparable injury.[176]

Where an employer's retaliatory actions have a chilling effect on employees' ability to exercise their own rights, however, irreparable injury has been found.[177]

---

[175]*See* Cox v. City of Chi., 868 F.2d 217, 223, 48 FEP 1674 (7th Cir. 1989) (delay in promotion not irreparable harm); Castro v. United States, 775 F.2d 399, 408, 39 FEP 162 (1st Cir. 1985) (termination from job not irreparable harm); *Jefferson County*, 720 F.2d at 1520 (loss of promotion not irreparable harm); *Duke*, 695 F.2d at 1127 (impending termination not irreparable harm); Oburn v. Shapp, 521 F.2d 142, 151, 11 FEP 58 (3d Cir. 1975) (failure to be hired not irreparable harm).

[176]*See Castro*, 775 F.2d at 408 (loss of credit, inability to obtain other employment, and loss of children's health insurance coverage do not constitute irreparable harm); Stewart v. U.S. Immigration & Naturalization Serv., 762 F.2d 193, 199–200, 37 FEP 1357 (2d Cir. 1985) (humiliation, damage to reputation and self-esteem, and financial hardship because of suspension without pay do not constitute irreparable injury); Holt v. Continental Group, Inc., 708 F.2d 87, 90–91, 31 FEP 1468 (2d Cir. 1983) (financial distress and inability to find work because of discharge do not constitute irreparable injury absent truly extraordinary circumstances); Moore v. Summers, 113 F. Supp. 2d 5 (D.D.C. 2000) (financial loss not irreparable). *But see* EEOC v. Chrysler Corp., 733 F.2d 1183, 1186, 34 FEP 1401 (6th Cir. 1984) (forced retirees showed irreparable harm where they suffered loss of work and future prospects for work as well as emotional distress, depression, increased drug use, decrease in feelings of useful life, contracted social life, increased cigarette consumption, lassitude, sexual problems, and reduced sense of well-being); Bonds v. Heyman, 950 F. Supp. 1202 (D.D.C. 1997) (preliminary injunction granted preventing termination by RIF pending outcome of discrimination suit where employee had no marketable skills and little prospect of obtaining other employment); EEOC v. City of Bowling Green, 607 F. Supp. 524, 527, 37 FEP 963 (W.D. Ky. 1985) (impending involuntary retirement would cause irreparable harm because plaintiff would not be able to keep up with current policy department matters and would suffer anxiety and emotional problems); Golden v. Lutheran Family Servs., 601 F. Supp. 383, 384, 39 FEP 1422 (W.D.N.C. 1984) (involuntarily terminated employee shows irreparable harm where he suffers not only loss of wages and benefits but also loss of reputation, which makes it difficult or impossible for him to find other work); York v. Alabama State Bd. of Educ., 581 F. Supp. 779, 787, 39 FEP 548 (M.D. Ala. 1983) (teachers denied reemployment because of allegedly discriminatory test suffer irreparable harm because of their removal from their professional environment and inability to advance their careers).

[177]*See* Marxe v. Jackson, 833 F.2d 1121, 1125–28, 45 FEP 557 (3d Cir. 1987) (where retaliatory discharge threatens plaintiff's ability to prove her case by intimidating potential witnesses, plaintiff can show irreparable harm, but danger of intimidation will not be presumed); Garcia v. Lawn, 805 F.2d 1400, 1405–06, 42 FEP 873 (9th Cir. 1986) (retaliatory discharge's chilling effect on other employees' willingness to exercise their rights or testify for plaintiff constitutes irreparable harm); *Holt*, 708 F.2d at 91 (risk that retaliatory discharge may deter other employees from

If the movant is challenging governmental action or seeking an injunction that goes beyond the status quo, a heightened showing is generally required.[178]

B. Section 706(f)(2) Preliminary Relief

Section 706(f)(2) of Title VII gives the EEOC authority to seek preliminary relief.[179] The main issue of controversy is whether the EEOC must satisfy the traditional requirement of establishing irreparable harm or whether a more relaxed standard is applicable.[180]

Most courts that insist on irreparable harm hold that injury can be shown as to either the charging party or the EEOC itself.[181] Irreparable injury to the EEOC can be established by showing that

---

protecting their rights or providing testimony for plaintiff may be found to constitute irreparable injury, although irreparable injury will not be presumed in every retaliatory discharge case); Karmel v. City of N.Y., 200 F. Supp. 2d 361 (S.D.N.Y. 2002) (internal interrogation of plaintiff would interfere with constitutional right); *Moore*, 113 F. Supp. 2d at 27 (e-mail message to employees condemning Title VII lawsuit found to have chilling effect on employees' desire to exercise their statutory rights); *see also Bonds*, 950 F. Supp. at 1215 (acknowledging that employment actions that have "chilling effect" on other employees' decisions to pursue their rights under Title VII constitute irreparable harm).

[178]*See* NAACP v. Town of E. Haven, 70 F.3d 219, 223 (2d Cir. 1995) (attempt to enjoin hiring of police officers and fire fighters); Sharr v. Department of Transp., 247 F. Supp. 2d 1208, 1209 (D. Or. 2003) (challenge to government policy); *Bonds*, 950 F. Supp. at 1214 (preliminary injunctive relief against federal government employers requires showing of extraordinary irreparable harm); *see also Moore*, 113 F. Supp. 2d at 18 (discussing but not concluding that heightened standard applies).

[179]42 U.S.C. § 2000e-5(f)(2) (2000). *See generally* Chapter 29 (EEOC Litigation).

[180]*Compare* EEOC v. Astra U.S.A., Inc., 94 F.3d 738, 743 (1st Cir. 1996) (lower standard, chilling effect on EEOC's ability to investigate claims), EEOC v. Pacific Press Publ'g Ass'n, 535 F.2d 1182, 1187, 12 FEP 1312 (9th Cir. 1976) (stating in dictum that irreparable injury requirement is relaxed where EEOC seeks preliminary relief under § 706(f)(2)) *and* Garcia v. Lawn, 805 F.2d 1400, 1405, 42 FEP 873 (9th Cir. 1986) (reiterating in dictum that, under *Pacific Press*, EEOC need not show irreparable harm) *with EEOC* v. Anchor Hocking Corp., 666 F.2d 1037, 1039, 27 FEP 809 (6th Cir. 1981) (EEOC must show irreparable harm), EEOC v. Norris, 81 FEP 175, 176 (N.D. Okla. 1999) (rejecting lower standard), EEOC v. Chateau Normandy, Inc., 658 F. Supp. 598, 603, 43 FEP 1652 (S.D. Ind. 1987) (must show irreparable harm) *and* EEOC v. Howard Univ., 1983 WL 519, at *2–4, 32 FEP 331, 332 (D.D.C. June 14, 1983) (same).

[181]*Anchor Hocking*, 666 F.2d at 1043 (irreparable harm may be shown as to either EEOC or charging party); *Chateau Normandy*, 658 F. Supp. at 603–04 (same); EEOC v. Target Stores, Inc., 1984 WL 1071, at *2, 36 FEP 543, 544 (D. Minn. Sept. 21, 1984) (same); *Howard Univ.*, 1983 WL 519, at *4, 32 FEP at 333 (same).

the failure to grant preliminary relief will discourage other employees from cooperating with the EEOC's investigation or from filing their own claims.[182]

---

[182]*Anchor Hocking*, 666 F.2d at 1043–44 (irreparable harm requirement satisfied where EEOC shows that alleged retaliation has chilling effect on other employees' willingness to cooperate and thus impedes EEOC's ability to prosecute charge; here, however, EEOC failed to make that showing); *Target Stores*, 1984 WL 1071, at *2, 36 FEP at 544 (temporary restraining order granted where, absent relief, retaliatory discharge would discourage employees from opposing discriminatory practices or participating in EEOC processes). *But see Howard Univ.*, 1983 WL 519, at *4, 32 FEP at 333 (preliminary injunction denied because defendant had not threatened employees or students or discouraged them from cooperating with EEOC).

CHAPTER 40

MONETARY RELIEF

I. Introduction

Before the Civil Rights Act of 1991,[1] back pay (and, in some cases, front pay) was the primary monetary relief available under Title VII and other federal antidiscrimination statutes.[2] Now, compensatory and punitive damages also are recoverable in cases of proven intentional discrimination. This chapter first discusses the different types of monetary relief, including back pay, front pay, compensatory and punitive damages, and liquidated damages. Next, it considers the right to a jury trial on monetary issues, defenses to monetary relief, and, finally, individual back-pay claims in class or collective proceedings.

II. Back Pay

A. A Discriminatee's Right to Back Pay in General

Section 706(g) authorizes back-pay relief in actions under Title VII[3] and, by incorporation, Title I of the ADA.[4] As amended, § 706(g)(1) provides:

> If the court finds that the respondent has intentionally engaged in or is intentionally engaging in an unlawful employment practice charged in the complaint, the court may enjoin the respondent from engaging in such unlawful employment practice, and order such affirmative action as may be appropriate, which may include, but is not limited to, reinstatement or hiring of employees, with or without back pay (payable by the employer, employment agency, or labor organization, as the case may be, responsible for the unlawful employment practice), or any other equitable relief as the court deems appropriate. Back-pay liability shall not accrue from a date more than two years prior to the filing of a charge with the

---

[1]Pub. L. No. 102-166, 1991 U.S.C.C.A.N. (105 Stat.) 1071 (codified in various sections of the U.S. Code, including 42 U.S.C. § 1981(a) (making compensatory and punitive damages available for violations of Title VII).

[2]The ADEA and Equal Pay Act were exceptions, pursuant to which a successful plaintiff could obtain liquidated damages for "willful" violations. *See* Section IV *infra*. The other chief exception was 42 U.S.C. § 1981, which permits an award of compensatory and/or punitive damages. *See generally* Chapter 35 (The Civil Rights Acts of 1866 and 1871).

[3]42 U.S.C. § 2000e-5(g) (2000).

[4]Pub. L. No. 101-336, § 107(a), 1990 U.S.C.C.A.N. (104 Stat.) 327, 336 (codified at 42 U.S.C. § 12117(a) (2000)).

Commission. Interim earnings or amounts earnable with reasonable diligence by the person or persons discriminated against shall operate to reduce the back pay otherwise allowable.[5]

Back-pay relief also is available in actions brought under the ADEA,[6] the Equal Pay Act,[7] § 504 of the Rehabilitation Act of 1973,[8] the Vietnam Era Veterans' Readjustment Assistance Act of 1974,[9] the Uniformed Services Employment and Reemployment Rights Act of 1994,[10] the Energy Reorganization Act of 1974,[11] the Export Administration Act of 1979,[12] and under at least some

---

[5]42 U.S.C. § 2000e-5(g)(1) (2000). In *Albemarle Paper Co. v. Moody*, 422 U.S. 405, 419, 10 FEP 1181 (1975), the Supreme Court stated that the legislative history makes clear that "[t]he [Title VII] back pay provision was expressly modeled on the back pay provision of the National Labor Relations Act." Thus, where there is inadequate Title VII authority on back-pay issues, a party may cite precedent under the National Labor Relations Act as persuasive authority. *See* Brady v. Thurston Motor Lines, Inc., 753 F.2d 1269, 1279 (4th Cir. 1985) (relying on NLRB precedent).

[6]Pub. L. No. 90-202, § 7(b), 1967 U.S.C.C.A.N. (81 Stat. 602) 658, 661 (codified as amended at 29 U.S.C. § 626(b) (2000)) (incorporating by reference the remedies of the Fair Labor Standards Act (FLSA), 29 U.S.C. § 216); *see* Taylor v. Home Ins. Co., 777 F.2d 849, 858, 39 FEP 769 (4th Cir. 1985); Rodriguez v. Taylor, 569 F.2d 1231, 1240, 16 FEP 533 (3d Cir. 1977). *See generally* Chapter 12 (Age).

[7]Pub. L. No. 88-382, 1963 U.S.C.C.A.N. (77 Stat. 56) 59 (codified as amended at 29 U.S.C. § 206 (2000)) (added as an amendment to the FLSA, and thus allowing for remedies available under the FLSA); *see* Lusted v. San Antonio Indep. Sch. Dist., 741 F.2d 817, 818 (5th Cir. 1984) (district court awarded back pay under the EPA). *See generally* Chapter 18 (Compensation).

[8]Pub. L. No. 93-112, § 504, 1973 U.S.C.C.A.N. (87 Stat. 355) 409, 454 (codified as amended at 29 U.S.C. § 794 (2000)); *see* Consolidated Rail Corp. v. Darrone, 465 U.S. 624, 631, 34 FEP 79 (1984) (§ 505(a)(2) of the Rehabilitation Act "provides to plaintiffs under § 504 the remedies set forth" in Title VII). *See generally* Chapter 13 (Disability).

[9]Pub. L. No. 90-508, 1974 U.S.C.C.A.N. (88 Stat. 1578) 1818 (codified as amended at scattered sections of 38 U.S.C.); *see* Hanna v. American Motors Corp., 724 F.2d 1300, 1305, 115 LRRM 2393 (7th Cir. 1984); Carr v. RCA Rubber Co., 609 F. Supp. 526, 529, 118 LRRM 3249 (N.D. Ohio 1985). *See generally* Chapter 13 (Disability).

[10]Pub. L. No. 103-353, § 2(a), 1993 U.S.C.C.A.N. (108 Stat. 3149 (codified at 38 U.S.C. § 4323 (2000)); *see* Rogers v. City of San Antonio, 2003 U.S. Dist. LEXIS 4314 (W.D. Tex. Mar. 4, 2003), *aff'd in part and reversed in part*, 392 F.3d 758 (5th Cir. 2004), *cert. denied*, 545 U.S. 1129 (2005).

[11]Pub. L. No. 93-438, 1974 U.S.C.C.A.N. (88 Stat. 1233) 1401 (codified as amended at 42 U.S.C. §§ 5801–5891 (2000)); *see* Blackburn v. Martin, 982 F.2d 125, 130 (4th Cir. 1992).

[12]Pub. L. No. 96-72, 1979 U.S.C.C.A.N. (93 Stat.) 503 (codified as amended at 50 U.S.C. app. §§ 2401–2420 (2000)); *cf.* Abrams v. Baylor Coll. of Med., 581 F. Supp. 1570, 1582, 34 FEP 229 (S.D. Tex. 1984) (denying economic damages under the EAA, where it would duplicate an award of back pay under Title VII), *rev'd in part on other grounds*, 805 F.2d 528, 42 FEP 806 (5th Cir. 1986).

circumstances, Title IX of the Education Amendments of 1972.[13] Back-pay relief also may be awarded in actions brought under 42 U.S.C. § 1981[14] and, in cases of government employers, § 1983.[15]

In *Albemarle Paper Co. v. Moody,*[16] the Supreme Court established a strong presumption in favor of back-pay awards to victims of employment discrimination under Title VII. While acknowledging that "back pay is not an automatic or mandatory remedy"[17] under the language of § 706(g), the Court found that back pay is an integral part of the "primary objective" of Title VII to deter unlawful employment practices;[18] further, according to the Court, "[i]t is . . . the purpose of Title VII to make persons whole for injuries suffered on account of unlawful employment discrimination."[19]

> It follows that, given a finding of unlawful discrimination, back pay should be denied only for reasons which, if applied generally, would not frustrate the central statutory purposes of eradicating discrimination throughout the economy and making persons whole for injuries suffered through past discrimination.[20]

Before *Albemarle,* courts felt free to deny back pay.[21] But *Albemarle* left district courts with extremely limited discretion to

---

[13]Pub. L. No. 92-318, 1972 U.S.C.C.A.N. (86 Stat. 235) 278 (codified as amended at 20 U.S.C. §§ 1681–1688 (2000)). In *Franklin v. Gwinnett County Public Schools,* 503 U.S. 60, 75–76, 59 FEP 213 (1992), the Supreme Court recognized a "damages remedy" that could include back pay. The Court stated that "[t]he general rule . . . is that absent clear direction to the contrary by Congress, the federal courts have the power to award any appropriate relief in a cognizable cause of action brought pursuant to a federal statute." In *Jackson v. Birmingham Bd. of Education,* 125 S. Ct. 1497 (2005), the Supreme Court found a private right of action under Title IX for retaliation because of complaints of sex discrimination, which includes a right to monetary damages.

[14]*See* Gunby v. Pennsylvania Elec. Co., 840 F.2d 1108, 1119, 45 FEP 1818 (3d Cir. 1988); *see also* Johnson v. Railway Express Agency, Inc., 421 U.S. 454, 460, 10 FEP 817 (1975) ("An individual who establishes a cause of action under § 1981 is entitled to both equitable and legal relief . . . . And a back pay award under § 1981 is not restricted to the two years specified for back pay recovery under Title VII.") (citations omitted). *See generally* Chapter 35 (The Civil Rights Acts of 1866 and 1871).

[15]*See* Gurmankin v. Costanzo, 626 F.2d 1115, 1124, 23 FEP 301 (3d Cir. 1980). *See generally* Chapter 35 (The Civil Rights Acts of 1866 and 1871).

[16]422 U.S. 405, 421, 10 FEP 1181 (1975).

[17]*Id.* at 415.

[18]*Id.* at 417.

[19]*Id.* at 418.

[20]*Id.* at 421 & n.14 ("It is necessary, therefore, that if a district court does decline to award back pay, it carefully articulate its reasons.").

[21]*See* Norman v. Missouri Pac. R.R., 497 F.2d 594, 597, 8 FEP 156 (8th Cir. 1974) (affirming denial of back-pay relief where damages were not proved with

deny back-pay relief to prevailing plaintiffs.[22] The *Albemarle* presumption remains the standard in employment discrimination cases[23] once the plaintiff establishes that discrimination caused the loss.[24]

---

sufficient certainty); United States v. N.L. Indus., Inc., 479 F.2d 354, 379–80, 5 FEP 823 (8th Cir. 1973) (refusing to award back pay because the law was not sufficiently developed to give the defendants notice that their particular practice was unlawful).

[22]*See* Isabel v. City of Memphis, 404 F.3d 404, 95 FEP 801 (6th Cir. 2005) (city failed to present evidence to rebut presumptive remedy of retroactive instatement and back pay); EEOC v. Joint Apprenticeship Comm., 186 F.3d 110, 122 (2d Cir. 1999) (applicant denied employment in violation of Title VII is ordinarily entitled to an award of back pay from the date of the discriminatory action to the date of judgment); EEOC v. Massey Yardley Chrysler Plymouth, Inc., 117 F.3d 1244, 1251, 74 FEP 847 (11th Cir. 1997) ("once liability for harassment and constructive discharge on the basis of age is established, the injured victim is presumptively entitled to back pay from the date of the discriminatory discharge until the date of judgment, unless the victim obtains or could have obtained substantially equivalent work before that time"); United States v. County of Fairfax, 629 F.2d 932, 942, 23 FEP 485 (4th Cir. 1980) ("[I]f proof is offered of identifiable economic injury to [the plaintiffs] who have suffered from the [employer's] discriminatory practices, [the district court] should grant back pay or retroactive seniority or both."); Pegues v. Mississippi State Employment Serv., 899 F.2d 1449, 1457 (5th Cir. 1990) ("once a plaintiff establishes a violation of [Title VII], 'the instances wherein [a back-pay award] is not granted are exceedingly rare' "); Gaddy v. Abex Corp., 884 F.2d 312, 318, 50 FEP 1333 (7th Cir. 1989) ("Once plaintiff has established that her employment was terminated as a result of unlawful discrimination on the part of the employer, a presumption in favor of full relief arises.").

[23]*See* Faragher v. City of Boca Raton, 524 U.S. 775, 808 (1998) (relying on *Albemarle*, the Court reaffirmed that Title VII seeks "to make persons whole for injuries suffered on account of unlawful employment discrimination"); McKennon v. Nashville Banner Publ'g Co., 513 U.S. 352, 358 (1995) ("Congress designed the remedial measures in these statutes to serve as a 'spur or catalyst' to cause employers 'to self-examine and to self-evaluate their employment practices and to endeavor to eliminate, so far as possible, the last vestiges' of discrimination") (quoting *Albemarle*); Johnson v. Spencer Press of Me., Inc., 364 F.3d 368, 382 (1st Cir. 2004) ("*Albemarle* taught that back pay is a presumptive entitlement of a victim of discrimination and that the discriminating employer is responsible for all wage losses that result from its unlawful discrimination, at least until the time of judgment."); *see also* Kneisley v. Hercules, Inc., 577 F. Supp. 726, 735, 33 FEP 1579 (D. Del. 1983) (the identical objectives of ending discrimination and compensating injured victims underlie the remedy of back pay under both Title VII and the ADEA); Gurmankin v. Costanzo, 626 F.2d 1115, 1120–21, 23 FEP 301 (3d Cir. 1980) (§ 1983 case).

[24]*See* Fox v. General Motors Corp., 247 F.3d 169, 181, 11 AD 1121 (4th Cir. 2001) (reversing award of unpaid overtime to ADA plaintiff because the jury's award conflicted with its finding that defendant had not intentionally discriminated against plaintiff but had subjected him to a hostile work environment); Hertzberg v. SRAM Corp., 261 F.3d 651, 657–61, 88 FEP 165 (7th Cir. 2001) (reversing award of back pay and front pay because the jury rejected plaintiff's claim as to her discharge and the sexual harassment against her did not result in lost earnings), *cert. denied,*

Some courts have applied *Albemarle* to deny requests for a partial denial of back pay.[25] A defendant's lack of bad faith or evil motive will not operate to preclude or reduce an award of back pay.[26] Once the plaintiff has established discrimination, courts have cited few circumstances that justify denying back pay other than the plaintiff's failure to mitigate damages.[27]

---

534 U.S. 1130 (2002); Mallinson-Montague v. Pocrnick, 224 F.3d 1224, 1236–37, 83 FEP 1746 (10th Cir. 2000) (affirming the judgment for the Title VII sexual harassment plaintiffs and the denial of back pay because the plaintiffs had resigned from the jobs, and the jury had rejected their constructive-discharge claim); Martinez v. El Paso County, 710 F.2d 1102, 1106, 32 FEP 747 (5th Cir. 1983) (the court is not bound by a pretrial stipulation as to the amount of back pay where it found that, even if the plaintiff received the desired transfer, he would have been laid off in 3 months).

[25]*See* Nord v. United States Steel Corp., 758 F.2d 1462, 1472–73, 37 FEP 1232 (11th Cir. 1985) (it is reversible error not to include in the back-pay period the 4 months from the court's oral findings to the date of judgment); EEOC v. Korn Indus., Inc., 662 F.2d 256, 262–64, 27 FEP 13 (4th Cir. 1981) (reversible error to limit relief and to deny de minimis relief of $50 or less); Laffey v. Northwest Airlines, Inc., 567 F.2d 429, 471, 13 FEP 1068 (D.C. Cir. 1976) (the authority for partial denial of back pay "must be as narrowly construed as authority to totally deny; its exercise, therefore, must be supported by reasons faithful to the dual purpose attributed to the back pay remedy by the *Albemarle* Court").

[26]*See* Dutton v. Johnson County Bd., 868 F. Supp. 1260, 1264 (D. Kan. 1994) (employer's alleged good faith attempt to accommodate plaintiff's disability, and the claimed unsettled nature of the law regarding the application of the ADA, are not special circumstances that warrant the denial of back pay) (citing Robinson v. Lorillard Corp., 444 F.2d 791, 804 (4th Cir. 1971) and Waters v. Wisconsin Steel Works, 502 F.2d 1309, 1321 (7th Cir. 1974)).

[27]*See* Acevedo-Garcia v. Monroig, 351 F.3d 547, 571 (1st Cir. 2003) (rejecting defendants' arguments that a jury's award for back pay was excessive because it exceeded the amount of lost earnings that had been proven); EEOC v. Rath Packing Co., 787 F.2d 318, 330, 40 FEP 580 (8th Cir. 1986) (back pay should not be denied on the basis of adverse economic consequences either to the employer or to employee-stockholders in the corporation); Salinas v. Roadway Express, Inc., 735 F.2d 1574, 1578, 35 FEP 533 (5th Cir. 1984) ("Difficulty in calculating the precise amount of back pay does not defeat the right itself."); Carpenter v. Stephen F. Austin State Univ., 706 F.2d 608, 631–32, 31 FEP 1758 (5th Cir. 1983) (neither that injunctive relief prospectively would correct discriminatory practices nor that a back-pay award might financially weaken the employer—a state university financed by the public—justified denial of back pay); Seep v. Commercial Motor Freight, Inc., 575 F. Supp. 1097, 1109, 45 FEP 203 (S.D. Ohio 1983) (that plaintiff expressed interest in a position but never actually bid on it and offered no proof that she would have been successful in such bid did not bar an award of back pay). *But see* City of L.A. Dep't of Water & Power v. Manhart, 435 U.S. 702, 719–23, 17 FEP 395 (1978) (liability would have a devastating effect on the fund, which would "fall in large part on innocent third parties"); EEOC v. Ilona of Hung., Inc., 108 F.3d 1569, 1579–80, 73 FEP 528 (7th Cir. 1997) (back pay denied for charging party who had planned

In *Hoffman Plastics Compounds, Inc. v. NLRB*,[28] the Supreme Court held that an undocumented alien could not be awarded back pay under the National Labor Relations Act, although he was discharged for engaging in protected activity. The Court concluded that "such relief is foreclosed by federal immigration policy, as expressed by Congress in the Immigration Reform and Control Act of 1986 (IRCA)."[29] Courts have not yet established conclusively, however, whether the *Hoffman* principle applies to undocumented aliens who are discharged in violation of antidiscrimination statutes,[30] particularly for those who subsequently attain legal work status.[31]

That an employee has signed a mandatory arbitration agreement does not limit the remedies available to the EEOC.[32] The EEOC may seek in an enforcement action victim-specific relief, such as back pay, without the alleged victim's consent.[33] The alleged victim's

to quit her job even before being discharged; "the award of back pay to [plaintiff] places her in a better position than she would have occupied had the discrimination not occurred, because she would have quit anyway" and "[w]e cannot sanction such a result"); EEOC v. O & G Spring & Wire Forms Specialty Co., 38 F.3d 872, 880, 65 FEP 1823, 1829 (7th Cir. 1994) (court has discretion to alter back-pay award if full award would bankrupt defendant); Trujillo v. County of Santa Clara, 775 F.2d 1359, 1369–70, 44 FEP 954 (9th Cir. 1985) (the plaintiff, who already received an award of back pay under state law, could not seek a duplicate back-pay remedy in federal court).

[28]535 U.S. 137, 169 LRRM 2769 (2002).
[29]*Id.* at 140. The IRCA is codified at 8 U.S.C. § 1324a (2000). *See generally* Chapter 7 (National Origin and Citizenship).
[30]*See* Rivera v. NIBCO, Inc., 364 F.3d 1057, 1069 (9th Cir. 2004) ("The differences between the two statutes persuade us that *Hoffman* does not resolve the question whether federal courts may award back pay to undocumented workers who have been discharged in violation of Title VII."), *cert. denied*, 125 S. Ct. 1603 (2005).
[31]*See Rivera*, 364 F.3d at 1069–70 (limiting discovery on whether plaintiffs are documented workers because back pay was not being sought); Escobar v. Spartan Sec. Serv., 281 F. Supp. 2d 895, 897 (S.D. Tex. 2003) (undocumented worker not entitled to back pay on sexual harassment and retaliation claims, but "fact that Escobar is now a documented worker certainly means that he is not ineligible for re-employment" or front pay); *see also* EEOC v. First Wireless Group, Inc., 225 F.R.D. 404, 407 (E.D.N.Y. 2004) (barring discovery on immigration status, since there was no record evidence showing that the employer had inquired into the plaintiffs' immigration status at the time of hiring or that employer knew of plaintiffs' alleged illegal immigration status); Flores v. Amigon, 233 F. Supp. 2d 462, 463 (E.D.N.Y. 2002) (wages already earned while employed are not rendered unpayable to the undocumented worker).
[32]EEOC v. Waffle House, Inc., 534 U.S. 279, 297 (2002) (claim under the ADA).
[33]*Id.* at 291 (this is true even if the employee disavows any desire to seek relief).

acceptance of a monetary settlement, however, will limit the EEOC's ability to recover back pay for the victim.[34]

B. Calculation of the Back-Pay Award

1. Elements of a Back-Pay Award

Back-pay awards normally reflect not just lost wages or salary, but also other benefits lost due to discrimination.[35]

a. *Wages and Salary.* The prevailing plaintiff bears the burden of establishing the value of the lost salary. However, a court may award a successful Title VII plaintiff back pay even if the plaintiff's lost wages are not susceptible to exact dollar calculations,[36] as the court should resolve any uncertainties in the calculation of back pay against the discriminating employer.[37]

This core component of back pay has been interpreted to include such items of lost compensation as overtime,[38] shift differentials,[39]

---

[34]*Id.* at 296–97. Once the EEOC has begun its enforcement action, the employer may not compel the employee to arbitrate the underlying claims. *See* EEOC v. Circuit City Stores, Inc., 285 F.3d 404, 407 (6th Cir. 2002).

[35]*See* Albemarle Paper Co. v. Moody, 422 U.S. 405, 421–42, 10 FEP 1181 (1975); Hartley v. Dillard's, Inc., 310 F.3d 1054, 91 FEP 1217 (8th Cir. 2002) (not error to include in back and front-pay awards such benefits as insurance, 401(k), accrued vacation pay, value of employee discount, COBRA); Pettway v. American Cast Iron Pipe Co., 494 F.2d 211, 263, 7 FEP 1115 (5th Cir. 1974) ("the ingredients of back pay should include more than 'straight salary.' Interest, overtime, shift differentials, and fringe benefits such as vacation and sick pay are among the items which should be included in back pay. Adjustment to the pension plan for members of the class who retired during this time should also be considered on remand.").

[36]*See* Acevedo-Garcia v. Monroig, 351 F.3d 547, 571 (1st Cir. 2003) (jury award of back pay slightly in excess of proven lost wages was acceptable); Durham Life Ins. Co. v. Evans, 166 F.3d 139, 156 (3d Cir. 1999) (held that back pay may be awarded even if figures are inexact; the "court may estimate what a claimant's earnings would have been without discrimination, and uncertainties are resolved against a discriminating employer").

[37]*See* Lowe v. Southmark Corp., 998 F.2d 335, 337 (5th Cir. 1993); Stewart v. General Motors Corp., 542 F.2d 445, 452 (7th Cir. 1976).

[38]*See* United States v. City of Warren, 138 F.3d 1083, 1097 (6th Cir. 1998) (lost overtime pay "should be included in back pay"); Kossman v. Calumet County, 800 F.2d 697, 703, 41 FEP 1355 (7th Cir. 1986) (overtime benefits should be considered in a back-pay award), *overruled in part on other grounds*, Coston v. Plitt Theatres, Inc., 860 F.2d 834, 48 FEP 248 (7th Cir. 1988).

[39]*See* Cox v. American Cast Iron Pipe Co., 784 F.2d 1546 (11th Cir. 1986) (the back-pay award in a Title VII case should take into account interest, overtime, shift differentials, vacation and sick pay, pension benefits, bonuses and interest, as well as straight salary); Sinclair v. Automobile Club, 733 F.2d 726, 729, 34 FEP 1206

commissions,[40] tips,[41] cost-of-living increases,[42] merit increases,[43] and raises due to promotions,[44] so long as the plaintiff can prove that he or she would have earned those items absent discrimination. Courts will deny recovery of items, such as anticipated future pay raises, if they are too speculative or if the plaintiff did not adequately prove the actual loss of the items.[45] Bonuses are includable in back pay if not speculative.[46]

(10th Cir. 1984) (the salary differential plus raises and bonuses should be included).

[40]*See* Gilchrist v. Jim Slemons Imps., Inc., 803 F.2d 1488, 1501, 42 FEP 314 (9th Cir. 1986) (approving use of a former employee's last year of commission revenues to estimate lost earnings); Goldstein v. Manhattan Indus., Inc., 758 F.2d 1435, 1146–47, 37 FEP 1217 (11th Cir. 1985) (lost sales commissions should be included).

[41]*See* EEOC v. House of Prime Rib, 31 FEP 981, 984 (N.D. Cal. 1983) (bartenders are entitled to tips as a component of back-pay awards), *aff'd*, 735 F.2d 1369, 35 FEP 736 (9th Cir. 1984).

[42]*See* Sands v. Runyon, 28 F.3d 1323, 1328 (2d Cir. 1994) (refusal to hire disabled worker, recovery under the Rehabilitation Act of 1973); Virgo v. Riviera Beach Assocs., 30 F.3d 1350, 1364 (11th Cir. 1994) (sexual harassment of sales representative; expert's assumed annual cost-of-living increase was reasonable); EEOC v. Liggett & Myers, 690 F.2d 1072, 1077–78, 40 FEP 1285 (4th Cir. 1982) (a female employee should be compensated for salary increases that a comparable male employee would have received); Kumar v. University of Mass. Bd. of Trs., 34 FEP 1231, 1237 (D. Mass. 1984) (cost-of-living increases, merit increases, and an additional 4% per year to reflect value of all fringe benefits should be included), *rev'd*, 774 F.2d 1, 38 FEP 1734 (1st Cir. 1985).

[43]*See* Zerilli v. New York City Transit Auth., 973 F. Supp. 311, 315 (S.D.N.Y. 1997), *aff'd in part, vacated in part*, 162 F.3d 1149 (2d Cir. 1998) (unpublished) (merit increase included in back pay as part of remedy for denial to promote based on gender); Morris v. American Nat'l Can Corp., 730 F. Supp. 1489, 1497, 52 FEP 210 (E.D. Mo. 1989) (back pay includes any increases that would have been received during the relevant period), *aff'd in relevant part*, 952 F.2d 200, 57 FEP 946 (8th Cir. 1991).

[44]*See* Saunders v. Claytor, 629 F.2d 596, 597, 26 FEP 1734 (9th Cir. 1980) (noting the district court's back-pay award included amounts for promotions and step increases).

[45]*See* Neufeld v. Searle Lab., 884 F.2d 335, 342, 50 FEP 1126 (8th Cir. 1989) (denial of recovery of future bonuses affirmed as speculative); Waters v. Wisconsin Steel Works of Int'l Harvester Co., 502 F.2d 1309, 1321–22, 8 FEP 577 (7th Cir. 1974) (claim for wages from second job, that the plaintiff claimed he could have held had he been employed by the defendant, rejected as speculative and remote). *But cf.* Willis v. Watson Chapel Sch. Dist., 899 F.2d 745, 747, 52 FEP 903 (8th Cir. 1990) ("Mere difficulty in calculating damages is not sufficient reason to deny relief."); Kossman v. Calumet County, 849 F.2d 1027, 1033, 47 FEP 236 (7th Cir. 1988) (the back-pay award properly included overtime earnings based on total employee averages; it was speculative to assume that the plaintiffs would have worked less overtime than average employees), *overruled in part on other grounds*, Coston v. Plitt Theatres, Inc., 860 F.2d 834, 48 FEP 248 (7th Cir. 1988).

[46]*Compare* Zhang v. American Gem Seafoods, Inc., 339 F.3d 1020, 1040 (9th Cir. 2003) (history of bonuses justified award), Dailey v. Societe Generale, 915 F. Supp. 1315, 1325 (S.D.N.Y. 1996) (jury free to include the value of bonuses in back-pay award), *affirmed in relevant part*, 108 F.3d 451, 458 (2d Cir. 1997) *and* Taylor v. Central Pa. Drug & Alcohol Servs., 890 F. Supp. 360, 372, 72 FEP 1315 (M.D.

b. Fringe Benefits. Back-pay awards routinely include fringe benefits. These include vacation pay,[47] pension and retirement benefits,[48] stock options and bonus plans,[49] savings plan contributions,[50] cafeteria plan benefits,[51] and profit-sharing benefits.[52] Some courts in appropriate circumstances have included sick pay,[53] the cost of

---

Pa. 1995) (plaintiffs entitled to have Christmas bonuses included in back-pay award where they would have received bonuses but for unlawful discrimination) *with* Hodgson v. Ideal Corrugated Box Co., 10 FEP 744, 752 (N.D.W. Va. 1974) (denying recovery of bonuses) *and* Holthaus v. Compton & Sons, Inc., 71 F.R.D. 18, 19, 11 FEP 333 (E.D. Mo. 1975) (refusing to award a bonus even though the plaintiff had received bonuses in past years; the bonus was "optional with management, depending on the work performed by its employees").

[47]*See* O'Neal v. Ferguson Constr. Co., 237 F.3d 1248, 1256–57 (10th Cir. 2001) (upholding jury award of vacation benefits); Munoz v. Oceanside Resorts, Inc., 223 F.3d 1340, 1348 (11th Cir. 2000) (affirming jury award of vacation pay for ADEA plaintiff); United States v. Burke, 504 U.S. 229, 238, 58 FEP 1323 (1992) (back pay is defined as "an amount equal to the wages the employee would have earned from the date of discharge to the date of reinstatement, along with lost fringe benefits such as vacation pay and pension benefits"); Gutzwiller v. Fenik, 860 F.2d 1317 (6th Cir. 1988) (a back-pay award appropriately should account for vacation pay); Bowe v. Colgate-Palmolive Co., 489 F.2d 896, 903 (7th Cir. 1973). If vacation benefits are paid by the employer upon termination, and if those benefits normally would not have been convertible to cash, absent termination of employment, some courts have held that they can be deducted from a back-pay award. *See* Section II.B.2.b *infra.*

[48]*See O'Neal*, 237 F.3d at 1256–57 (upholding jury award of retirement benefits); Sharkey v. Lasmo (AUL Ltd.), 214 F.3d 371, 374–75, 84 FEP 967 (2d Cir. 2000) (holding that relief without pension benefits was not a make-whole remedy); Johnson v. Spencer Press of Me., Inc., 364 F.3d 368, 383 (1st Cir. 2004) (full relief includes pension benefits); Gaworski v. ITT Commercial Fin. Corp., 17 F.3d 1104 (8th Cir. 1994) (401(k) contributions); *cf.* Sands v. Runyon, 28 F.3d 1323, 1330 (2d Cir. 1994) (employee's voluntary withdrawal from savings plan to finance litigation warranted exclusion from make-whole remedy).

[49]Greene v. Safeway Stores, Inc., 210 F.3d 1237, 1243–44, 82 FEP 1306 (10th Cir. 2000) (ADEA jury verdict, awarding unrealized stock option appreciation); Cline v. Roadway Express, Inc., 689 F.2d 481, 490 (4th Cir. 1982) (stock bonus plan).

[50]*See* Tidwell v. American Oil Co., 332 F. Supp. 424, 437, 3 FEP 1007 (D. Utah 1971).

[51]Dutton v. Johnson County Bd., 868 F. Supp. 1260, 1264, 3 AD 1614 (D. Kan. 1994).

[52]*See* Ross v. Buckeye Cellulose Corp., 980 F.2d 648, 652 (11th Cir. 1993) (affirming award of profit-sharing benefits, which were shares of stock); Whatley v. Skaggs Cos., 707 F.2d 1129, 1140 (10th Cir. 1983) (profit sharing is appropriately included in a remedy); Dickerson v. Deluxe Check Printers, Inc., 703 F.2d 276 (8th Cir. 1983) (appropriately included as equitable relief).

[53]*See* O'Neal v. Ferguson Constr. Co., 237 F.3d 1248, 1256–57 (10th Cir. 2001) (upholding jury award of sick leave benefits); Pettway v. American Cast Iron Pipe Co., 494 F.2d 211, 263, 7 FEP 1115 (5th Cir. 1974); Bowe v. Colgate-Palmolive Co., 489 F.2d 896, 903, 6 FEP 1132 (7th Cir. 1973); *cf.* Satty v. Nashville Gas Co., 522 F.2d 850, 855, 11 FEP 1 (6th Cir. 1975) (affirming an "order[ ] that plaintiff recover sick leave benefits that should have been paid during her maternity leave"), *vacated and remanded in part on other grounds*, 434 U.S. 136 (1977).

cleaning uniforms,[54] reduced cost of meals,[55] and hotel accommodations.[56]

Medical[57] and life insurance[58] also can be components of back pay. Courts disagree about the proper method of calculating the

[54]*See* Laffey v. Northwest Airlines, Inc., 642 F.2d 578, 589, 23 FEP 1628 (D.C. Cir. 1980).

[55]Munoz v. Oceanside Resorts, Inc., 223 F.3d 1340, 1348 (11th Cir. 2000) (affirming jury award of reduced cost of meals for ADEA plaintiff, who was a room service waiter).

[56]*Laffey*, 642 F. 2d at 588–89 (the difference between the expense of a double hotel room provided to female airline employees on layovers as opposed to the single rooms provided to male employees). *But cf.* Long v. Ringling Brothers-Barnum & Bailey Combined Shows, Inc., 882 F. Supp. 1553, 1562, 67 FEP 1685, 63 FEP 289 (D. Md. 1995) (refusing to reimburse travel and transportation costs, such as the cost of a rental car, to a plaintiff discriminatorily denied the chance even to interview for a 4-month international position).

[57]*See* EEOC v. Dial Corp., 2006 U.S. App. LEXIS 28507 (8th Cir. Nov. 17, 2006) (affirming jury award of medical benefits); *O'Neal*, 237 F.3d at 1256–57 (upholding jury award of medical benefits); *Munoz*, 223 F.3d at 1348 (affirming jury award of medical coverage for ADEA plaintiff); Muller v. Costello, 997 F. Supp. 299, 305 (N.D.N.Y. 1998), *aff'd*, 187 F.3d 298 (2d Cir. 1999) (granting medical insurance); Thornton v. Kaplan, 961 F. Supp. 1433 (D. Colo. 1996) (reimbursement for medical premiums); EEOC v. Domino's Pizza, 909 F. Supp. 1529, 1537 (M.D. Fla. 1995) (out-of-pocket expenditures for medical insurance are recoverable), *aff'd mem.*, 113 F.3d 1249 (11th Cir. 1997). Courts differ, however, on whether such benefits should be included where the plaintiff neither purchased substitute insurance nor had compensable medical expenses during the back-pay period. *Compare* Brownlow v. Edgcomb Metals Co., 49 FEP 331, 346 (N.D. Ohio 1987) (the plaintiff is entitled to recover lost insurance benefits notwithstanding that he neither purchased alternative coverage nor incurred out-of-pocket expenses that would have been compensable under the employer's insurance plan), *rev'd on other grounds*, 867 F.2d 960, 49 FEP 346 (6th Cir. 1989) *with* McMillan v. Massachusetts SPCA, 140 F.3d 288 (1st Cir. 1998) (to recover damages representing benefits, a plaintiff must show that she actually incurred insurance or medical care expenses), Proulx v. Citibank, N.A., 681 F. Supp. 199, 205, 49 FEP 664 (S.D.N.Y. 1988) (a plaintiff who acted unreasonably in not pursuing alternative employment is not entitled to recover the cost of health insurance benefits where he had no need of such benefits during the back-pay period), *aff'd*, 862 F.2d 304, 55 FEP 351 (2d Cir. 1988), Jackson v. City of Independence, 40 FEP 1466, 1467 (W.D. Mo. 1986) (the city is not required to pay past health insurance benefits for a job applicant absent showing that she suffered damage from not receiving benefits from the date she was denied employment to judgment) *and* Spagnuolo v. Whirlpool Corp., 550 F. Supp. 432, 434, 32 FEP 1377 (W.D.N.C. 1982) (a plaintiff who acquired coverage with his present employer was entitled to any costs he incurred to acquire comparable medical coverage, plus any payments he made to cover costs not covered by current insurance that the former employer's plan would have covered, less the insurance costs borne by employees of the former employer), *rev'd in part on other grounds*, 717 F.2d 114, 32 FEP 1382 (4th Cir. 1983).

[58]*See* Aledo-Garcia v. Puerto Rico Nat'l Guard Fund, Inc., 887 F.2d 354, 356, 51 FEP 9 (1st Cir. 1989) (the value of fringe benefits such as life insurance should be added to "the amount of wages that could have been earned"); Fariss v. Lynchburg

value of lost insurance. Courts have based their calculations on the cost of the insurance to the employer;[59] the out-of-pocket expenses to the plaintiff in obtaining substitute coverage;[60] and the out-of-pocket expenditures actually incurred that would have been covered by the insurance.[61]

The plaintiff carries the burden to show the value and the actual loss of the benefit.[62] Where the plaintiff did not elect to participate in the employer's retirement plan during employment, one court held that the plaintiff could not recover projected employer contributions to the plan.[63]

Foundry, 769 F.2d 958, 965–67 (4th Cir. 1985) (heir to ADEA discriminatee entitled to premium cost and not face value of life insurance policy, but this and lumpsum pension benefits offset back pay that was due); *see also* Sposato v. Electronic Data Sys., 188 F.3d 1146, 1147, 80 FEP 918 (9th Cir. 1999) (relying on make-whole policy of Title VII, where wrongfully discharged employee died during litigation, heirs were entitled to face value of life insurance policy that would have been in effect but for discharge).

[59]*See Fariss*, 769 F.2d at 965–67 (premium cost of insurance and not policy value is compensable); *Aledo-Garcia*, 887 F.2d at 356 ("[t]he amount of wages that could have been earned includes the value of any fringe benefits such as life insurance [and] medical insurance" that are generally provided by the employer); Blackwell v. Sun Elec. Corp., 696 F.2d 1176, 1185–86, 30 FEP 1177 (6th Cir. 1983) (awarding the plaintiff the dollar amount of health benefits he would have received had he not been illegally discharged).

[60]*See* Berndt v. Kaiser Aluminum & Chem. Sales, Inc., 604 F. Supp. 962, 965, 38 FEP 182 (E.D. Pa. 1985), *aff'd*, 789 F.2d 253 (3d Cir. 1986); *see also* Kossman v. Calumet County, 800 F.2d 697, 703–04, 41 FEP 1355 (7th Cir. 1986) (the employer must reimburse the cost of alternate insurance actually purchased, or any proper medical expenses incurred that would have been covered by insurance formerly provided by the employer), *overruled in part on other grounds*, Coston v. Plitt Theatres, Inc., 860 F.2d 834, 48 FEP 248 (7th Cir. 1988).

[61]*See* Weiss v. Parker Hannifan Corp., 747 F. Supp. 1118, 1132, 57 FEP 216 (D.N.J. 1990) (awarding actual unreimbursed medical expenses); Davis v. Ingersoll Johnson Steel Co., 628 F. Supp. 25, 29, 39 FEP 1197 (S.D. Ind. 1985) (awarding the plaintiff medical bills that would have been covered by the defendant's group insurance policy but for the termination); Foster v. Excelsior Springs City Hosp. & Convalescent Ctr., 631 F. Supp. 174, 175, 40 FEP 1616 (W.D. Mo. 1986) (if age discrimination is established, the widow of a former employee who died without life insurance may recover proceeds under the life insurance policy as if he had died while still employed, rather than just premiums the employer paid on that policy; noting plaintiff's medical history and age made the cost of life insurance "prohibitively expensive").

[62]Barbour v. Merrill, 48 F.3d 1270, 1278, 67 FEP 369 (D.C. Cir. 1995) (prevailing Title VII plaintiff not entitled to car allowance given to successful applicant where record contained no evidence that allowance was regular part of compensation package or that plaintiff would have received allowance).

[63]EEOC v. Domino's Pizza, Inc., 909 F. Supp. 1529, 1537, 69 FEP 570 (M.D. Fla. 1995).

Courts differ on whether to award the plaintiff fringe benefits in kind or their cash value, and whether the value of the benefit should be offset against back pay.[64] Where a benefit restored in kind is one for which the employee would have been obligated to pay part of the cost, that portion of the cost has been deducted from the award.[65]

One court included an amount to account for the difference in the quality of company-provided housing for white employees as opposed to nonwhites.[66] Some plaintiffs under the ADEA have received compensation to restore lost Social Security benefits.[67]

c. Interest. The Supreme Court held in *Loeffler v. Frank*[68] that, consistent with the "make-whole" remedial scheme of § 706(g), "Title VII authorizes prejudgment interest as part of the back pay remedy in suits against private employers."[69] Although there continues to be a strong presumption that prejudgment interest on back-pay awards should be granted in employment discrimination

---

[64]*Compare* Doyne v. Union Elec. Co., 953 F.2d 447 (8th Cir. 1992) (no offset for pension benefits under the ADEA), EEOC v. O'Grady, 857 F.2d 383, 391 (7th Cir. 1988) (pension not to be offset, since it is a collateral source like unemployment in ADEA cases, but can be offset in other cases if the employer is the source of the benefit) *and* McDowell v. Avtex Fibers, Inc., 740 F.2d 214 (3d Cir. 1984) (pension benefits are collateral benefits not to be used as an offset) *vacated and remanded on other grounds*, 469 U.S. 1202 (1985) *with* Fariss v. Lynchburg Foundry, 769 F.2d 958, 965–67 (4th Cir. 1985) (heir to ADEA discriminatee entitled to premium cost and not face value of life insurance policy; this and lump-sum pension benefits offset back pay that was due) *and* EEOC v. Sandia Corp., 639 F.2d 600, 626 (10th Cir. 1980) (offset of severance allowance).

[65]*See Fariss*, 769 F.2d at 965–67 (heir to ADEA discriminatee entitled to premium cost and not face value of life insurance policy; this and lump-sum pension benefits offset back pay that was due); *Sandia Corp.*, 639 F.2d at 626 (10th Cir. 1980) (offset of severance allowance).

[66]*See* Domingo v. New Eng. Fish Co., 727 F.2d 1429, 1446, 34 FEP 584 (9th Cir. 1984) (measurable differences in the quality of housing is a wage differential because room and board provided to employees is part of compensation), *modified on other grounds*, 742 F.2d 520, 37 FEP 1303 (9th Cir. 1984).

[67]*See* Hawks v. Ingersoll Johnson Steel Co., 38 FEP 93, 96 (S.D. Ind. 1984) (the employee is entitled to compensation for lower Social Security benefits resulting from the fact he worked fewer months than he would have worked had he not been illegally terminated).

[68]486 U.S. 549, 46 FEP 1659 (1988).

[69]*Id.* at 557–58; *see* Hunter v. Allis-Chalmers Corp., 797 F.2d 1417, 1426, 41 FEP 721 (7th Cir. 1986) (an award of back pay plus interest is necessary to put a former employee in the monetary position he or she would have been in but for the discharge).

actions,[70] appellate courts hesitate to disturb the discretion of trial courts that have denied prejudgment interest awards.[71] Some courts consider an award of punitive damages as a factor militating against

---

[70]*See* Hutchison v. Amateur Elec. Supply, Inc., 42 F.3d 1037, 1046, 66 FEP 1275 (7th Cir. 1994) ("Prejudgment interest is an element of complete compensation and a normal incident of relief under Title VII."); Shore v. Federal Express Corp., 42 F.3d 373, 380 (6th Cir. 1994) (reversing trial court's finding that prejudgment interest could not be granted but holding no interest for periods of delay caused by the plaintiff); Dailey v. Societe Generale, 889 F. Supp. 108, 114, 68 FEP 345 (S.D.N.Y. 1995) ("The purposes of Title VII—to deter violations of the statute and to make the plaintiff whole—are both served by a prejudgment interest award on the back pay portion of the damage award."), *aff'd in part and rev'd and remanded on other grounds*, 108 F.3d 451, 74 FEP 1428 (2d Cir. 1997).

In addition to the "make-whole" rationale, the Sixth Circuit has held that "an award of prejudgment interest is appropriate under circumstances where a party fails to negotiate a good faith settlement." Simpson v. Ernst & Young, 100 F.3d 436, 445, 72 FEP 343 (6th Cir. 1996).

[71]*See* Rhodes v. Guiberson Oil Tools, 82 F.3d 615, 619, 623, 71 FEP 83 (5th Cir. 1996) (district court did not abuse its discretion in deciding not to award prejudgment interest in ADEA action where it determined that, in awarding damages for back pay, front pay, and pension benefits offset by interim earnings, projected future earnings, and pension benefits already paid, plaintiff was made whole without award of prejudgment interest); Gloria v. Valley Grain Prods., Inc., 72 F.3d 497, 500, 69 FEP 1163 (5th Cir. 1996) (district court's decision to refuse prejudgment interest award in Title VII action was not abuse of discretion where plaintiff's only argument to establish abuse of discretion was that district court ignored "make-whole" policies of Title VII; "[a] general rule that prejudgment interest on every back pay award must be granted would obliterate the discretion of the district court"); Hogan v. Bangor & Aroostook R.R., 61 F.3d 1034, 1038, 4 AD 1251 (1st Cir. 1995) (district court did not abuse its discretion in not awarding ADA plaintiff prejudgment interest "where the award of damages is almost three times the size of the back pay award"); Philipp v. ANR Freight Sys., Inc., 61 F.3d 669, 675, 70 FEP 1347 (8th Cir. 1995) (it was within district court's discretion to deny age discrimination plaintiff prejudgment interest based on defendant company's " 'continued financial plight' and the fact that 'liability was far from clear in this case' "); *cf.* Scarfo v. Cabletron Sys., Inc., 54 F.3d 931, 961, 67 FEP 1474 (1st Cir. 1995) ("A trial court has discretion whether to award prejudgment interest on a successful Title VII claim."); Hadley v. VAMPTS, 44 F.3d 372, 376 (5th Cir. 1995) (award of prejudgment interest is left to the discretion of the trial court); Maksymchuk v. Frank, 987 F.2d 1072, 1077 (4th Cir. 1993) (prejudgment interest is left to the sound discretion of the trial court). *Contra* Sharkey v. Lasmo, 214 F.3d 371, 375, 84 FEP 967 (2d Cir. 2000) (reversing district court's denial of prejudgment interest where the plaintiff had received a "surprising[ly] generous" jury award, had made "desultory efforts" to mitigate, and had received a "considerable settlement" of his severance claims; it is ordinarily an abuse of discretion not to include prejudgment interest where damages representing compensation for lost wages have been awarded; prejudgment interest cannot be denied as a substitute for reducing an excessive award); Thurman v. Yellow Freight Sys., Inc., 90 F.3d 1160, 1170, 72 FEP 657 (6th Cir.) (although prejudgment interest should be excluded for delays specifically attributable to plaintiff, the trial court abused its

the propriety of prejudgment interest, but others[72] have held that it is an abuse of discretion to refuse, without adequate justification, a request for prejudgment interest.[73]

Public employers present certain different issues. The states may be sued under Title VII,[74] but have immunity from private actions under the ADEA[75] and the employment provisions of the ADA.[76] Local units of government, however, enjoy no such immunity and may be sued under these statutes.[77]

Most courts continue to hold that prejudgment interest may be awarded against public employer defendants,[78] although one court

---

discretion by denying prejudgment interest altogether rather than reducing interest award when plaintiff delayed case by requesting extensions to respond to summary judgment motion), *amended on other grounds*, 97 F.3d 833 (6th Cir. 1996).

[72]*See* Emmel v. Coca-Cola Bottling Co., 904 F. Supp. 723, 736 (N.D. Ill. 1995) ("[P]rejudgment interest is disfavored in the Seventh Circuit when punitive damages have been awarded."), *aff'd*, 95 F.3d 627, 72 FEP 1811 (7th Cir. 1996); Greene v. Safeway Stores, Inc., 210 F.3d 1237, 1247, 82 FEP 1306 (10th Cir. 2000) (holding to the same effect); Hurley v. Atlantic City Police Dep't, 933 F. Supp. 396, 431, 72 FEP 1828 (D.N.J. 1996) (after sex discrimination plaintiff received "adequate compensation for her injuries" and $700,000 in punitive damages, which court characterized as "pure windfall," court declined to exercise its discretion "to increase the size of that windfall" and award prejudgment interest). *Contra* Luciano v. Olsten Corp., 912 F. Supp. 663, 676, 73 FEP 221 (E.D.N.Y. 1996) ("In the Court's view, to award the plaintiff prejudgment interest, even where she has recovered punitive damages, will not overcompensate her.").

[73]*See* Sellers v. Delgado Cmty. Coll., 839 F.2d 1132, 1140, 46 FEP 464 (5th Cir. 1988) (discretion was abused in denying prejudgment interest "on the basis that [the employer] did not intend by its actions that [the employee] resign or be fired").

[74]Fitzpatrick v. Bitzer, 427 U.S. 445 (1976); *cf.* Nevada Dep't of Human Res. v. Hibbs, 538 U.S. 721, 730 (2003) (Congress properly abrogated the states' immunity in enacting the FMLA).

[75]Kimel v. Florida Bd. of Regents, 528 U.S. 62 (2000).

[76]Board of Trs. of the Univ. of Ala. v. Garrett, 531 U.S. 356 (2001). But an action may be brought against the state under Title II of the ADA, the "access" provisions of the Act applicable to public entities. *See* Tennessee v. Lane, 541 U.S. 509 (2004).

[77]*Garrett*, 531 U.S. at 369.

[78]*See* Winbush v. Iowa, 66 F.3d 1471, 1483, 69 FEP 1348 (8th Cir. 1995) (holding as a matter of first impression "that under Title VII courts have the power to award prejudgment interest against state defendants"); Pegues v. Mississippi State Employment Serv., 899 F.2d 1449, 1454 (5th Cir. 1990) (the Eleventh Amendment does not bar a court from including prejudgment interest with a back-pay award levied against a state agency under Title VII); EEOC v. County of Erie, 751 F.2d 79, 81 (2d Cir. 1984) ("we cannot see that an employee whose wages have unlawfully been withheld is any the less injured because her employer was a municipal entity rather than a private entity. We thus see no valid reason to distinguish between municipal employers and private employers in determining what award should be made to the

has held that the waiver of sovereign immunity will not be applied retroactively to permit such an award of interest.[79] Since 1987, interest has been available in at least some Title VII actions against the federal government, pursuant to the Back Pay Act;[80] previously, such interest had been unavailable because of sovereign immunity.[81]

Courts have used a variety of formulas to determine the appropriate interest rate to apply, giving rise to with conflicts not only between circuits, but also within the circuits.[82]

victims of the employer's discriminatory practices."); Jones v. Washington Metro. Area Transit Auth., 946 F. Supp. 1023, 1032–33 (D.D.C. 1996) (public contractor enjoyed governmental immunity when dealing in discretionary capacity with other contractors; however, it was "liable for, as opposed to immune from, discrimination against its employees on the basis of sex," and, therefore, plaintiff was entitled to prejudgment interest), aff'd in part and vacated in part on other grounds, 205 F.3d 428, 82 FEP 628 (D.C. Cir. 2000). But cf. Coleman v. Kaye, 87 F.3d 1491, 1512, 71 FEP 236 (3d Cir. 1996) ("[T]he New Jersey Tort Claims Act 'specifically prohibits prejudgment interest against government tortfeasors.' ").

[79]Brown v. Secretary of Army, 78 F.3d 645, 647, 72 FEP 595 (D.C. Cir. 1996) ("We hold that sovereign immunity bars application of the interest provision retroactively to this case.").

[80]Continuing Appropriations, Fiscal Year 1988, Pub. L. No. 100-202, § 623, 1987 U.S.C.C.A.N. (101 Stat.) 1329, 1329–428 (codified at 5 U.S.C. § 5596 (2000)); see Woolf v. Bowles, 57 F.3d 407, 410–11, 68 FEP 161 (4th Cir. 1995) (allowing interest in a Title VII case); Brown v. Secretary of Army, 918 F.2d 214, 218, 68 FEP 485 (D.C. Cir. 1990) (although the Back Pay Act amendments waived sovereign immunity as to prejudgment interest for Title VII violations that also come within the scope of the Back Pay Act, denials of promotion are not covered by the Back Pay Act, and prejudgment interest accordingly may not be awarded as to such denials); Edwards v. Lujan, 40 F.3d 1152, 1154, 68 FEP 32 (10th Cir. 1994) (same); see also Loeffler v. Frank, 486 U.S. 549, 554, 46 FEP 1659 (1988) (Congress waived the Postal Service's immunity from interest awards; recovery of interest is available to the extent that interest was recoverable against a private party). Section 114(2) of the Civil Rights Act of 1991, 42 U.S.C. § 200e-16d (2000), abrogates federal immunity to interest on Title VII awards. See Trout v. Secretary of Navy, 317 F.3d 286, 91 FEP 187 (D.C. Cir. 2003).

[81]Library of Congress v. Shaw, 478 U.S. 310, 318–21, 41 FEP 85 (1986).

[82]See Conetta v. National Hair Care Ctrs., Inc., 236 F.3d 67, 78 (1st Cir. 2001) (district court did not abuse its discretion in using higher state interest rate instead of federal rate prescribed by 28 U.S.C. § 961a); Jones v. UNUM Life Ins. Co. of Am., 223 F.3d 130, 140 (2d Cir. 2000) (remanding for trial court to address why a rate higher than the federal rate is not appropriate to make the plaintiff whole); Taxman v. Board of Educ., 91 F.3d 1547, 1566, 71 FEP 848 (3d Cir. 1996) (court did not abuse its discretion in using IRS adjusted prime rate, codified in 26 U.S.C. § 6621, to calculate prejudgment interest rather than post-judgment rate set forth in 28 U.S.C. § 1961a); Berger v. Iron Workers Local 201, 170 F.3d 1111, 79 FEP 1018 (D.C. Cir. 1999) (affirming district court's use of a rate previously agreed to by the parties that was not tied to a state or federal rate); Gelof v. Papineau, 829 F.2d 452, 456, 45

Under the Equal Pay Act[83] and the ADEA,[84] which incorporate the remedial scheme of the Fair Labor Standards Act, the circuits differ over whether prejudgment interest should be awarded only in lieu of liquidated damages.

Although plaintiffs must always comply with procedural rules to preserve the possibility of recovering prejudgment interest, courts usually resolve questionable situations in favor of the presumption supporting prejudgment interest.[85] Nevertheless, a plaintiff who

---

FEP 83 (3d Cir. 1987) (approving use of the state judgment rate); EEOC v. Guardian Pools, Inc., 828 F.2d 1507 (11th Cir. 1987) (directing that the IRS prime rates are to be used); Conway v. Electro Switch Corp., 825 F.2d 593, 602, 44 FEP 753 (1st Cir. 1987) (awarding interest at the federal judgment rate); EEOC v. Rath Packing Co., 787 F.2d 318, 334 (8th Cir. 1986) (IRS prime rates are acceptable but not mandated); EEOC v. County of Erie, 751 F.2d 79, 81 (2d Cir. 1984) (prime rate). One court has held that prejudgment interest must be compounded in order to make the plaintiff whole. *See* Saulpaugh v. Monroe Cmty. Hosp., 4 F.3d 134, 145, 62 FEP 1315 (2d Cir. 1993).

[83]*See* Linn v. Andover Newton Theological Sch., Inc., 874 F.2d 1, 7 n.8, 49 FEP 1176 (1st Cir. 1989) ("It is well settled that under the FLSA, prejudgment interest may not be awarded on top of liquidated damages because the latter were meant to compensate successful plaintiffs for a variety of harms, including loss due to delay.").

[84]*See* Starceski v. Westinghouse Elec. Corp., 54 F.3d 1089, 1102–03, 67 FEP 1184 (3d Cir. 1995) (acknowledging split among circuits over whether prejudgment interest may be awarded along with liquidated damages and following reasoning of those circuits that permit awards of both liquidated damages and prejudgment interest); Powers v. Grinnell Corp., 915 F.2d 34, 40, 42, 53 FEP 1814 (1st Cir. 1990) (reaffirming prior First Circuit precedent; the district court properly held that an award of liquidated damages precluded an award of prejudgment interest); Kossman v. Calumet County, 800 F.2d 697, 703, 41 FEP 1355 (7th Cir. 1986) (vacating the prejudgment interest award in light of the liquidated damages award so that retirees would not receive surplus compensation); Heiar v. Crawford County, 746 F.2d 1190, 1202, 35 FEP 1458 (7th Cir. 1984) (if liquidated damages are awarded, prejudgment interest would be duplicative; liquidated damages are compensatory rather than punitive); Rose v. National Cash Register Corp., 703 F.2d 225, 230, 31 FEP 706 (6th Cir. 1983) (a plaintiff awarded liquidated damages under the ADEA is not also entitled to an award of prejudgment interest); Castle v. Sangamo Weston, Inc., 837 F.2d 1550, 1562–63, 46 FEP 139 (11th Cir. 1988) (authorizing an award of prejudgment interest where liquidated damages are awarded because the latter are punitive in nature); Lindsey v. American Cast Iron Pipe Co., 810 F.2d 1094, 1102, 43 FEP 139 (11th Cir. 1987) (because ADEA liquidated damages are punitive in nature, both prejudgment interest and liquidated damages may be awarded); Criswell v. Western Airlines, Inc., 709 F.2d 544, 556–57, 32 FEP 1204 (9th Cir. 1983) (awarding prejudgment interest on the portion of damages representing actual loss, but not on liquidated damages under ADEA), *aff'd*, 472 U.S. 400 (1985).

[85]*See* Dalal v. Alliant Techsystems, 72 F.3d 177 (10th Cir. 1995) (Rule 54(c) of the Federal Rules of Civil Procedure allows an award of prejudgment interest, although not requested in the complaint or the pretrial order); Sellers v. Delgado Cmty. Coll., 781 F.2d 503, 505, 39 FEP 1766 (5th Cir. 1986) (a former instructor preserved her claim to interest and fringe benefits by giving pro se notice of appeal of the

fails to do so may lose the opportunity to recover prejudgment interest.[86]

After an award of back pay, post-judgment interest routinely is allowed.[87] Deciding an issue of first impression, the Sixth Circuit has held that post-judgment interest accrues from the date the district court enters a judgment memorializing a verdict, rather than from the date the district court enters a final judgment.[88]

d. Expenses Incurred in Mitigating Damages. Some damage awards account for either increased expenses or expense savings associated with a discharged plaintiff's new position. Strictly speaking, these adjustments are not true elements of the back-pay award. Rather, they are factors to be considered in modifying a plaintiff's gross back-pay award to account for mitigation earnings.[89] One district court has even allowed the jury to award more than the amount requested by the plaintiff to account for expenses incurred in the plaintiff's efforts to obtain new employment.[90]

---

back-pay award); Woodson v. Scott Paper Co., 898 F. Supp. 298, 309, 68 FEP 947 (E.D. Pa. 1995) (where counsel stipulated to "a total back pay award of $150,000" and during closing plaintiff's counsel referred to amount as " '$150,000 worth of past losses,' " prejudgment interest was nevertheless added to verdict), *aff'd in part and rev'd in part on other grounds*, 109 F.3d 913, 73 FEP 1237 (3d Cir. 1996).

[86]*See* Bunch v. Bullard, 795 F.2d 384, 399, 41 FEP 515 (5th Cir. 1986) (the prevailing plaintiffs' failure to appeal or cross-appeal from the lower court's judgment precludes them from challenging a back-pay award that denied prejudgment interest); Goodman v. Heublein, Inc., 682 F.2d 44, 45, 43 FEP 247 (2d Cir. 1982) (prejudgment interest is barred in an ADEA action where the prevailing plaintiff had not moved to alter or amend the judgment within 10 days, as is required by Fed. R. Civ. P. 59(e)); *cf.* Andre v. Bendix Corp., 38 FEP 1817, 1818–19 (N.D. Ind. 1984) (a former employee who did not file suit until 2 years after she was eligible to is not entitled to prejudgment interest).

[87]28 U.S.C. § 1961 (2000); *see* EEOC v. Gurnee Inns, Inc., 956 F.2d 146, 149, 58 FEP 120 (7th Cir. 1992); Johnson v. Ryder Truck Lines, Inc., 30 FEP 659, 669 (W.D.N.C. 1980); United States v. Lee Way Motor Freight, Inc., 15 FEP 1385, 1388 (W.D. Okla. 1977), *remanded in part on other grounds*, 625 F.2d 918, 20 FEP 1345 (10th Cir. 1979). For claims against the United States, however, post-judgment interest is available "only under a contract or Act of Congress expressly providing for payment thereof." 28 U.S.C. § 2516(a) (2000).

[88]Skalka v. Fernald Envtl. Restoration Mgmt. Corp., 178 F.3d 414, 427–29 (6th Cir. 1999).

[89]*See* Section II.B.2.b *infra*.

[90]Luciano v. Olsten Corp., 912 F. Supp. 663, 674, 73 FEP 221 (E.D.N.Y. 1996) (in addition to $2,500 for job search expenses and $3,538 for early withdrawal tax penalty from her IRA account, which plaintiff expressly sought, court also allowed the jury to award other incidental monetary losses, such as $11,675 that plaintiff paid in taxes on money she withdrew from retirement account).

Some courts have included as part of these mitigation expense awards the plaintiff's expenses incurred in moving or traveling to seek interim employment.[91] Similarly, courts have adjusted awards to account for differences in commuting expenses. One court denied back pay where a lower interim salary was more than offset by a savings in commuting expenses.[92] Where commuting to the new employment is more expensive, courts have differed as to whether the additional commuting expenses should be included in a back-pay award.[93]

---

[91]*See, e.g.*, Williams v. Albemarle Bd. of Educ., 5 FEP 814, 819, 822 (M.D.N.C.) (awarding expenses incident to seeking and holding alternative employment), *aff'd in relevant part*, 485 F.2d 232, 6 FEP 966 (4th Cir. 1973), *aff'd on rehearing en banc*, 508 F.2d 1242, 10 FEP 585 (4th Cir. 1974); Wall v. Stanly County Bd. of Educ., 378 F.2d 275, 278, 9 FEP 1095 (4th Cir. 1967) (Fourteenth Amendment action; a damages award should include moving expenses to a new job); NLRB v. Miami Coca-Cola Bottling Co., 360 F.2d 569, 574–75 (5th Cir. 1966) (hiring hall fees are deductible from interim earnings as expenses incurred seeking new employment); Nabors v. NLRB, 323 F.2d 686, 692, 54 LRRM 2259 (5th Cir. 1963) (job hunting expenses are deductible from interim earnings); Thomas v. Cooper Indus., Inc., 627 F. Supp. 655, 668, 39 FEP 1825 (W.D.N.C. 1986) (awarding costs of commuting and setting up a second household); Milton v. Bell Labs., Inc., 428 F. Supp. 502, 515, 15 FEP 1751 (D.N.J. 1977) (if an appeals court found that discrimination occurred, back pay would terminate at the time the plaintiff took a job in another city, but moving expenses incurred to move to the new location should be awarded); American Casting Serv., Inc., 177 NLRB 105, 107 & n.13 (1969) (expenses incurred in a given quarter looking for work are compensable only to the extent they can be offset against earnings in the same quarter); Mastro Plastics Corp., 136 NLRB 1342, 1348, 50 LRRM 1006 (1962) (expenses incurred looking for work are compensable only to the extent they can be offset against interim earnings); *cf.* Jackson v. Wheatley Sch. Dist. No. 28, 489 F.2d 608, 612–13, 6 FEP 1277 (8th Cir. 1973) (§ 1981 action; affirming denial of an award for travel expenses while the employees were searching for interim employment because no clear evidence was offered that the expenses actually were incurred). *But see* Lyons v. Allendale Mut. Ins. Co., 484 F. Supp. 1343, 1344, 23 FEP 537 (N.D. Ga. 1980) (consequential damages, including those incurred in securing employment in another state and selling one's home, cannot be awarded under the ADEA); Culp v. General Am. Transp. Corp., 8 FEP 460, 466 (N.D. Ohio 1974) (Title VII action; travel expenses not allowed), *aff'd mem.*, 517 F.2d 1404 (6th Cir. 1975).

[92]*See, e.g.*, Mitchell v. West Feliciana Parish Sch. Bd., 507 F.2d 662, 666 & n.7 (5th Cir. 1975).

[93]*Compare* McDowell v. Mississippi Power & Light, 641 F. Supp. 424, 431, 44 FEP 1088 (S.D. Miss. 1986) (awarding expenses for renting a mobile home and making 230-mile round trips to the family home) *and* American Mfg. Co., 167 NLRB 520, 523, 66 LRRM 1122 (1967) (subtracting the miles the plaintiff would have traveled to his former employer from the additional commuting expenses) *with* Butta v. Anne Arundel County, 473 F. Supp. 83, 89, 20 FEP 24 (D. Md. 1979) (not allowing additional commuting expenses as part of back-pay award).

e. Negative Tax Consequences. Courts differ on whether a successful plaintiff may be awarded additional back pay to compensate them for the tax effects of receiving a lump-sum back-pay amount in a single year.[94] In one case, the district court allowed a plaintiff to recover an amount to compensate for the negative tax consequences suffered as a result of receiving an ADEA award of back pay and front pay in a single tax year.[95] To support this award, however, expert testimony was provided specifying the award's tax consequences.[96]

2. The Period of Recovery

a. Commencement of the Back-Pay Period.[97] Because back pay is viewed as an equitable remedy of restitution,[98] the underlying premise for awarding back pay is that, absent the employer's unlawful conduct, the employee would have remained in the specified position at the designated rate of pay.[99] As a general matter

---

[94]Sears v. Atchison, Topeka & Santa Fe Ry., 749 F.2d 1451, 1456, 36 FEP 783 (10th Cir. 1984) (although the tax component may not be appropriate in a *typical* Title VII case, the award of a large lump sum covering over 17 years' back pay warrants an added tax component) *and* Gelof v. Papineau, 829 F.2d 452, 455 & n.2, 45 FEP 83 (3d Cir. 1987) (awarding tax component where the defendant did not dispute that the judgment properly should include an extra component to cover the negative tax impact of the lump-sum back-pay award) *with* Blim v. Western Elec. Co., 731 F.2d 1473, 1480, 34 FEP 757 (10th Cir. 1984) (damages should not be awarded for the increased tax liability caused by a back-pay award; noting the existence of a 5-year averaging provision in the tax law resulting in no "significant tax penalty").

[95]O'Neill v. Sears, Roebuck & Co., 108 F. Supp. 2d 443, 447 (E.D. Pa. 2000). *But see* Morris v. Lee, 83 FEP 1790 (E.D. La. 2000) (court refused to increase damage award to reflect increased tax liability since it was not clear whether the jury had already considered such liability).

[96]*O'Neill,* 108 F. Supp. 2d at 447.

[97]The back-pay rules under the ADEA and the Equal Pay Act, both of which incorporate the enforcement provisions of the FLSA, are discussed elsewhere.

[98]*See* EEOC v. Steamfitters Local 638, 542 F.2d 579 (2d Cir. 1976); Rosen v. Public Serv. Elec. & Gas Co., 477 F.2d 90 (3d Cir 1973); United States v. Georgia Power Co., 474 F.2d 906 (5th Cir. 1973), *vacated on other grounds,* 634 F.2d 929 (5th Cir. 1981); Rogers v. Loether, 467 F.2d 1110 (7th Cir.1972), *aff'd,* 415 U.S. 189 (1974); United States v. N.L. Indus. Inc., 479 F.2d 354, 379 (8th Cir. 1973); Head v. Timken Roller Bearing Co., 486 F.2d 870, 876 (6th Cir. 1973).

[99]*See* Albemarle Paper Co. v. Moody, 422 U.S. 405, 417–18 (1975) (quoting United States v. N.L. Indus. Inc., 479 F.2d 354, 379 (8th Cir. 1973)); Fadhl v. City & County of S.F., 741 F.2d 1163 (9th Cir. 1984) (back-pay damages not warranted

therefore, back-pay liability begins at the point that there is a discriminatory act causing the plaintiff to suffer an economic injury.[100] This starting point is often identified as the time when "a choice is . . . made [by the employer]—for example in a decision on hiring or promotion,"[101] or when the plaintiff is first deterred from making an application for the position.[102] This is not to say, however, that the starting point for the accrual of the back-pay award absolutely begins at the point of the employer's illegal action. The discretionary nature of the award will allow courts some latitude in deciding when the accrual of back pay is to begin.[103] On appeal, the district court's determination as to when the back-pay period commences will be reviewed for an abuse of discretion.[104]

Back pay will not typically begin to accrue unless the employee is actually ready, willing, and able to assume the position, but for the employer's discriminatory practices.[105] From an evidentiary standpoint, some courts have looked to the application

---

based on a showing that the prospective employee would not have been hired absent discrimination).

[100]*See* Thorne v. City of El Segundo, 802 F.2d 1131, 1136, 46 FEP 1651 (9th Cir. 1986); Dillon v. Coles, 746 F.2d 998, 1006 (3d Cir. 1984); Martinez v. El Paso County, 710 F.2d 1102, 1106 (5th Cir. 1983); Wooldridge v. Marlene Indus. Corp., 875 F.2d 540, 547–48 (6th Cir. 1989); EEOC v. Safeway Stores, 634 F.2d 1273, 1281 (10th Cir. 1980); Gurmankin v. Costanzo, 626 F.2d 1115, 1125 (3d Cir. 1980); Taylor v. Philips Indus., 593 F.2d 783, 786–87 (7th Cir. 1979).

[101]Croker v. Boeing Co., 23 FEP 1783, 1786 (E.D. Pa. 1979).

[102]*See* EEOC v. Joe's Stone Crab, Inc., 296 F.3d 1265, 1276, 89 FEP 522 (11th Cir. 2002), *cert. denied*, 539 U.S. 941 (2003).

[103]*See, e.g., Thorne*, 802 F.2d at 1136; Kober v. Westinghouse Elec. Corp., 480 F.2d 240 (3d Cir. 1973).

[104]*See* Giles v. General Elec. Co., 245 F.3d 474 (5th Cir. 2001) (courts review back-pay awards for abuse of discretion); *cf.* United States v. City of Warren, 138 F.3d 1083, 1094–96 (6th Cir. 1998) ("in a pattern or practice case, the back pay period should begin whenever the United States provides the employer with notice and information comparable to that normally contained in a charge of discrimination filed with the EEOC"); Head v. Timken Roller Bearing Co., 486 F.2d 870 (6th Cir. 1973).

[105]*See, e.g.,* Wooldridge v. Marlene Indus. Corp., 875 F.2d 540 (6th Cir. 1989) (proof of qualification for the position and availability to work create presumption of entitlement to back pay); Younger v. Glamorgan Pipe & Foundry Co., 561 F.2d 563 (4th Cir. 1977); Howard v. University of S. Miss., 30 FEP 1614, 1621 (S.D. Miss. 1980) (the discrimination began when the plaintiff first requested the promotion at issue); EEOC v. Blue & White Serv. Corp., 674 F. Supp. 1579, 1581, 45 FEP 963 (D. Minn. 1987) (awarding back pay from the date the position first opened after the affiant applied), *aff'd*, 863 F.2d 613 (8th Cir. 1988); Saracini v. Missouri Pac. R.R., 431 F. Supp. 389, 397, 14 FEP 1604 (E.D. Ark. 1977) (no back pay awarded where the employee would not have received the position even in the absence of

submitted by the plaintiff for a particular position to establish the plaintiff's willingness and ability to work.[106]

The beginning point for the accrual of back pay is further limited by §706(g) of Title VII, which provides that "[b]ack pay liability shall not accrue from a date more than two years prior to the filing of a charge with the Commission."[107] Thus, Title VII precludes the recovery of back-pay damages allegedly suffered more than two years before the plaintiff filed a charge of discrimination with the EEOC.[108] One recognized exception to this two-year limitation, however, is in the case of a pattern-or-practice claim.

In a claim asserting a pattern or practice of discrimination, §707(e) provides that the EEOC shall proceed "in accordance with the procedures set forth in [§ 706]."[109] Where a true "continuing violation" exists,[110] however, a defendant is not protected from back-pay liability simply because the defendant's first discriminatory act occurred outside the two-year look-back period.[111] Rather, a

---

discrimination); Milton v. Bell Labs., Inc., 428 F. Supp. 502, 515, 15 FEP 1751 (D.N.J. 1977) (monetary relief, if any, should be awarded from the time when employment would have commenced following the applicant's graduation from law school, not from the earlier time when the plaintiff applied for the job).

[106]See Meadows v. Ford Motor Co., 510 F.2d 939 (6th Cir. 1975). In some circumstances, however, an application may not be necessary. In *Teamsters v. United States*, 431 U.S. 324, 369–71, 14 FEP 1514 (1977), the Supreme Court held that an employee's failure to apply for a position will not bar a claim for individual relief if the employee can carry the burden of showing that he or she was qualified and would have applied but for the known and pervasive discriminatory practices of the employer. *Id.* at 369–71; *see* Claiborne v. Illinois Cent. R.R., 583 F.2d 143, 151, 18 FEP 536 (5th Cir. 1978) (ordering the district court to consider whether a nonapplicant plaintiff should be treated as an applicant in light of the employers' "discriminatory policies, the [employees'] qualifications, and the potential costs and benefits of accepting promotion"). *See generally* Chapter 15 (Hiring).

[107]42 U.S.C. § 2000e-5(g)(1) (2000).

[108]Goodwin v. General Motors Corp., 275 F.3d 1005 (10th Cir. 2002), *cert. denied*, 537 U.S. 941 (2002).

[109]42 U.S.C. § 2000e-6(e) (2000).

[110]In *National Railroad Passenger Corp. v. Morgan*, 536 U.S. 101, 88 FEP 1601 (2002), the Supreme Court distinguished between "discrete acts," such as hiring, firing, promotion, etc., as to which there can be no continuing violation, at least in an individual case, and hostile environment harassment claims, in which a single event generally does not rise to the level of a violation. *Id.* at 117. The Court expressly reserved ruling on the proper interpretation of continuing violations in the context of a case alleging a pattern or practice of intentional discrimination. *Id.* at 111.

Cases regarding the continuing violation theory that preceded *Morgan* should be analyzed carefully through the lens of the Supreme Court's opinion in that case.

[111]See generally* Chapter 26 (Timeliness).

court will be permitted to "take[] into account the effects" occurring within the two-year period to determine whether they may have stemmed from acts of discrimination occurring more than two years before.[112]

   b. Termination of the Back-Pay Period. Because an award of back pay compensates the plaintiff for economic losses caused by the illegal discrimination, the back-pay accrual period ends when the plaintiff no longer suffers the economic effects of the discrimination.[113] In many cases this means that the back-pay accrual period

---

   [112]*See, e.g., Goodwin,* 275 F.3d at 1011 ("Relief back to the beginning of the limitations period strikes a reasonable balance between permitting redress of an ongoing wrong and imposing liability for conduct long past."); Thompson v. Sawyer, 678 F.2d 257, 290–91, 28 FEP 1614 (D.C. Cir. 1982) ("We therefore hold that it is proper to allow acts of illegal discrimination lying beyond the two-year period of Title VII back pay accrual to affect the measurement of the award."); Crawford v. Western Elec. Co., 614 F.2d 1300, 1309, 22 FEP 819 (5th Cir. 1980) ("Of course, back pay relief under Title VII is limited to the two years preceding the filing of a charge with the EEOC. However, *liability* of the employer for back pay may be based on acts occurring outside the two-year period if a current violation is shown.") (emphasis in original; citation omitted); United States v. Lee Way Motor Freight, Inc., 625 F.2d 918, 933–34, 20 FEP 1345 (10th Cir. 1979) (the 2-year back-pay limitation is irrelevant to claims asserting a pattern and practice of discrimination); Acha v. Beame, 570 F.2d 57, 65, 16 FEP 526 (2d Cir. 1978) ("A continuously maintained illegal employment policy may be the subject of a valid complaint until a specified number of days after the *last occurrence* of an instance of that policy. . . . Furthermore, where an illegal policy is so maintained, relief for injuries sustained even before the beginning of the limitations period is appropriate.") (emphasis in original). In *Cantrell v. Knoxville Community Development Corp.,* 60 F.3d 1177, 1181, 68 FEP 536 (6th Cir. 1995), the district court had awarded back pay at the rate it felt the plaintiff should have been receiving but for the employer's discriminatory conduct prior to the discharge. The appellate court opined that this approach "effectively affords Cantrell relief for a disparate pay claim that he failed to pursue." *Id.* Also, the court noted that whether a back-pay award includes the value of enhanced income has been addressed only in the context of a continuing violation, and since "[t]here is not authority in support of or in opposition to basing a damages award for a discrete act of discriminatory discharge on non-actionable prior acts of discrimination," the court remanded to allow the district to recalculate the award based on the plaintiff's actual wages at the time of the discharge. *Id.*
   [113]*See, e.g.,* Alexander v. Laborers Local 496, 177 F.3d 394 (6th Cir. 1999) (termination date for damages was when applicants' attorneys were in position to request injunctive relief regarding future referrals); Bolden v. Pennsylvania State Police, 30 FEP 689 (E.D. Pa. 1979) (back-pay period ends on the date of the Appeal Board's decision that Bolden was not presently qualified for admission into the next class of cadets).

ends on either the date judgment is rendered,[114] or the date that the jury returns its verdict.[115]

There are, however, other events that will terminate the back-pay accrual period.[116] One court has let stand a jury's determination

---

[114]*See, e.g.*, Suggs v. Servicemaster Educ. Food Mgmt., 72 F.3d 1228, 1233, 69 FEP 1270 (6th Cir. 1996) ("general rule is to award back pay through the date of judgment"); Daniels v. Loveridge, 32 F.3d 1472, 1476–78, 65 FEP 1052 (10th Cir. 1994) (defendant argued that plaintiff should receive back pay from date of her discharge to date of her first subsequent employment; however, court awarded back pay through date of judgment); *cf.* Thomas v. National Football League Players Ass'n, 131 F.3d 198, 207, 76 FEP 1590 (D.C. Cir. 1997) (affirming district court's decision to end plaintiff's back-pay award in December 1989, "by which time, it found, she should have secured employment"), *vacated in part*, 1998 U.S. App. LEXIS 3634 (D.C. Cir. Feb. 25, 1998); Anderson v. Group Hospitalization, Inc., 820 F.2d 465, 473, 43 FEP 1840 (D.C. Cir. 1987) (award to employee directing employer to pay benefits that would have accrued to employee between date of jury verdict and judgment was permissible award of back pay); Thorne v. City of El Segundo, 802 F.2d 1131, 1136, 46 FEP 1651, 1654 (9th Cir. 1986) ("Absent compelling circumstances, when an employer has refused to hire an employee in violation of that employee's rights under Title VII, the court should compute the backpay award from the date of the discriminating act until the date of final judgment."); Nord v. United States Steel Corp., 758 F.2d 1462, 1472–73, 37 FEP 1232 (11th Cir. 1985) (ending back-pay period on the date of the court's oral findings, over 4 months before judgment was entered, was contrary to the make-whole purpose of Title VII, and therefore constitutes error); Wells v. North Carolina Bd. of Alcoholic Control, 714 F.2d 340, 342, 46 FEP 1766 (4th Cir. 1983) (award of back pay accruing to the date of judgment was proper); Gathercole v. Global Assocs., 560 F. Supp. 642, 647, 31 FEP 736 (N.D. Cal. 1983) (a plaintiff wrongfully discharged under the ADEA may recover those wages and benefits to which plaintiff would have been entitled had he remained employed by defendant until the trial date), *rev'd on other grounds*, 727 F.2d 1485, 34 FEP 502 (9th Cir. 1984).

[115]*E.g.*, Koyen v. Consolidated Edison Co., 560 F. Supp. 1161, 1164, 31 FEP 488 (S.D.N.Y. 1983). As discussed in Section III *infra*, an award of front pay may compensate for ongoing economic harm beyond the verdict or date of judgment.

[116]*See, e.g.*, Taylor v. Invacare Corp., 64 Fed. Appx. 516 (6th Cir. 2003) (back pay cut off at point plaintiff was no longer able to work); Kirsch v. Fleet St., Ltd., 148 F.3d 149, 167–68, 77 FEP 318 (2d Cir. 1998) (back pay cut off at date of plaintiff's retirement); Boehms v. Crowell, 139 F.3d 452, 461–62, 76 FEP 1368 (5th Cir. 1998) (award of back pay cut off as of date of plaintiff's resignation; constructive-discharge analogy used to determine ending date of back-pay award); EEOC v. Massey Yardley Chrysler Plymouth, Inc., 117 F.3d 1244, 1252 (11th Cir. 1997) (back-pay period ran until plaintiff rejected employer's pretrial offer of reinstatement); Harper v. Godfrey Co., 45 F.3d 143, 149, 66 FEP 1258 (7th Cir. 1995) ("Regardless of whether the discrimination had occurred plaintiffs would have been fired in early 1987 for their misconduct. Accordingly, the district court correctly restricted their awards of back pay to the time preceding termination and disallowed their reinstatements."); Saladin

that the back-pay award could be cut off when the evidence showed that it was reasonably unlikely that the plaintiff would have remained employed by the defendant for any extended period.[117] Regardless of the event triggering the termination of back pay, the employer maintains the burden of proof on this issue.[118]

(i.) *Reemployment.* The back-pay accrual period typically will end when a plaintiff assumes a comparable position[119] or

---

v. Turner, 936 F. Supp. 1571, 1581–82 (N.D. Okla. 1996) (back pay cutoff at expiration of employer's offer of reinstatement because plaintiff's rejection due to "mere recitation of hostility" was unreasonable); EEOC v. Domino's Pizza, Inc., 909 F. Supp. 1529, 1537, 69 FEP 570 (M.D. Fla. 1995) (although plaintiff is presumptively entitled to back pay from date of discharge to date of judgment, less interim earnings, court found that plaintiff was "made whole" with award of damages from date of discharge up to date he enrolled in college to change careers), *aff'd mem.*, 113 F.3d 1249 (11th Cir. 1997); EEOC v. Regency Architectural Metals Corp., 896 F. Supp. 260, 271 (D. Conn. 1995) (cutoff point for recovering back pay is date when shop where plaintiff was working went out of business), *aff'd*, 1997 U.S. App. LEXIS 9570 (2d Cir. Apr. 29, 1997); Taylor v. Central Pa. Drug & Alcohol Servs. Corp., 890 F. Supp. 360, 371, 72 FEP 1315 (M.D. Pa. 1995) ("the calculation period for back pay terminates if the former employer establishes that the plaintiff's position would have been eliminated at some point during the alleged entitlement period for business reasons or other unrelated factors"); Roberson v. Mullins, 876 F. Supp. 100, 104 (W.D. Va. 1995) (plaintiff entitled to recover back pay accruing only until date on which he had announced he was planning to retire); *see also* Criado v. IBM Corp., 145 F.3d 437, 445, 8 AD 336 (1st Cir. 1998) (district court's award of back pay affirmed notwithstanding employer's argument that back-pay period should have ended earlier when plaintiff would have lost her job in RIF even if there had been no discrimination); Odima v. Westin Tucson Hotel, 53 F.3d 1484, 1495–96, 67 FEP 1222 (9th Cir. 1995) (employee who has been discriminatorily denied an opportunity for promotion typically may not collect back pay for periods beyond the employee's voluntary resignation unless the employee shows constructive discharge; this doctrine, however, does not apply when the employee was preparing to enter a completely different career with the same employer; employer's refusal to offer the employee a new position would be considered a refusal to rehire rather than a refusal to promote and back pay should extend beyond the date the employee quit).

[117]Taylor v. Airborne Freight Corp., 155 F. Supp. 2d 287 (E.D. Pa. 2001) (evidence sufficient to restrict back-pay damage award to $1,200 where uncontroverted evidence demonstrated that plaintiff only remained in a series of prior jobs less than 6 months).

[118]Richardson v. Restaurant Mktg. Assocs., Inc., 527 F. Supp. 690, 697, 31 FEP 1562 (N.D. Cal. 1981) ("The burden of showing that an otherwise appropriate back pay award should be limited in some way is on the defendant.").

[119]*See, e.g.*, Hammond v. Northland Counseling Ctr., 218 F.3d 886 (8th Cir. 2000) (plaintiff who suffered no lost earnings and was immediately employed was not entitled to recovery of back-pay damages); Smith v. American Serv. Co., 38 FEP 377, 378–79 (N.D. Ga. 1985) (the back-pay period for an unlawfully rejected applicant for receptionist ended when she accepted employment as a cosmetologist), *aff'd in relevant part*, 796 F.2d 1430, 41 FEP 802 (11th Cir. 1986). Where earnings

higher-paying[120] employment. If the plaintiff subsequently decides to voluntarily leave the new employment,[121] or is terminated from the new position for cause,[122] the accrual of additional back-pay

---

from subsequent employment are less than the plaintiff would have earned from the defendant/employer, the plaintiff may be entitled to compensation for the difference.

[120]*See, e.g.*, Franzoni v. Hartmarx Corp., 89 FEP 934, 938 (7th Cir. 2002) (denial of back pay was proper when plaintiff was transferred to a position where he did not suffer any loss in salary or benefits until he was properly terminated); Skalka v. Fernald Envtl. Restoration Mgmt. Corp., 178 F.3d 414, 426 (6th Cir. 1999) (no back pay during period in which plaintiff earned higher salary but back pay should be paid for period of unemployment with no deductions made for the salary increase from the new job); Harkless v. Sweeny Indep. Sch. Dist., 466 F. Supp. 457, 469, 22 FEP 1557 (S.D. Tex. 1978) (the back-pay period terminates when the plaintiff obtains a better-paying job; but the defendant is not entitled to a credit toward an earlier period of lesser pay simply because greater amounts were earned in a later period of higher pay), *aff'd mem.*, 608 F.2d 594, 22 FEP 1571 (5th Cir. 1979); Somers v. Aldine Indep. Sch. Dist., 464 F. Supp. 900, 903, 22 FEP 1097 (S.D. Tex. 1979) (an unlawfully discharged teacher is entitled to back pay for the remainder of the school year even though she earned more the following year than she would have had she continued in defendant's employ), *aff'd*, 620 F.2d 298, 23 FEP 778 (5th Cir. 1980); Reid v. Memphis Publ'g Co., 369 F. Supp. 684, 690–91, 7 FEP 13 (W.D. Tenn. 1973) (back pay awarded until the higher-paying job was obtained), *rev'd in part on other grounds*, 521 F.2d 512, 11 FEP 129 (6th Cir. 1975).

[121]*E.g.*, Sennello v. Reserve Life Ins. Co., 667 F. Supp. 1498, 1514, 1518–19, 48 FEP 1328 (S.D. Fla. 1987) (the plaintiff's resignation from comparable employment because of a vague dispute with the new employer was a failure to mitigate), *aff'd*, 872 F.2d 393, 49 FEP 1159 (11th Cir. 1989); EEOC v. Domino's Pizza, Inc., 34 FEP 1075, 1076 (E.D. Mich. 1983) (the back-pay period did not resume when the plaintiff voluntarily quit a better-paying job); Griffin v. George B. Buck Consulting Actuaries, Inc., 566 F. Supp. 881, 882, 32 FEP 1884 (S.D.N.Y. 1983) (the back-pay period terminated on the date the plaintiff obtained new employment, even though he shortly thereafter left the new job in part because the discriminatory experiences with the defendant left him disillusioned with actuarial companies; the court concluded it was still a voluntary quit). *But cf.* EEOC v. Delight Wholesale Co., 973 F.2d 664, 670, 59 FEP 1222 (8th Cir. 1992) (the claimant's voluntary quits for personal reasons, such as taking care of her health and spending more time with her child, toll the back-pay period between quits and the next position); Quintanilla v. K-Bin, Inc., 8 F. Supp. 2d 928, 937 (S.D. Tex.1998) (resignation of subsequent position is not determinative of the termination of the accrual of back-pay damages); EEOC v. Riss Int'l Corp., 35 FEP 423, 425–26 (W.D. Mo. 1982) (the plaintiff's voluntary quit because of personal preferences tolls the back-pay period; however, voluntary quit does not end the back-pay period when justification is reasonable).

[122]*E.g.*, Brady v. Thurston Motor Lines, Inc., 753 F.2d 1269, 1277–79, 36 FEP 1805 (4th Cir. 1985) (a subsequent discharge for cause tolls the back-pay period; the plaintiff must exercise reasonable diligence in maintaining subsequent employment). *Contra* EEOC v. Stone Container Corp., 548 F. Supp. 1098, 1107 n.1, 30 FEP 134 (W.D. Mo. 1982) (the back-pay period did not end when the discriminatee was discharged for cause from a subsequent employer).

damages may be cut off if the plaintiff is deemed not to have exercised reasonable diligence in retaining the new position.[123] Likewise, in a failure-to-promote or other case where the plaintiff is able to continue working for the defendant, the period of liability will normally end—absent a finding of constructive discharge—if the plaintiff voluntarily resigns.[124] Courts are reluctant to find, however, that a plaintiff failed to exercise reasonable diligence merely because he or she was terminated or left a new position that is an inferior job.[125]

---

[123]*Compare* Deffenbaugh-Williams v. Wal-Mart Stores, Inc., 156 F.3d 581 (5th Cir. 1998) (because award of back pay is an equitable remedy designed to make the injured party whole, injured party has duty under both § 1981 and Title VII to use reasonable diligence in maintaining substantially similar employment), *opinion vacated by* Williams v. Wal-Mart Stores, Inc., 169 F.3d 215 (5th Cir. 1999), *opinion reinstated on rehearing by* 182 F.3d 333 (5th Cir. 1999) *with* Hare v. H&R Indus., 67 Fed. Appx. 114 (3d Cir. 2003) (plaintiff that voluntarily quit new employment was entitled to back pay because the harassment suffered by plaintiff was the primary cause of the psychological condition leading to her quitting of the new job).

[124]*Compare* Jurgens v. EEOC, 903 F.2d 386, 389 (5th Cir. 1990) (where employer's discriminatory denial of a promotion ultimately precipitates the employee's retirement, the employee does not receive back-pay compensation for any time after his retirement unless he can show (i) that his retirement was the result of objectively intolerable working conditions constituting a constructive discharge and (ii) that there is a sufficient nexus or causal link between the denial and the employee's subsequent resignation—i.e., that at the time of the denial, the employer reasonably could have foreseen that the employee would face intolerable conditions forcing him to resign) *and* Muller v. United States Steel Corp., 509 F.2d 923, 929–30, 10 FEP 323 (10th Cir. 1975) (where discriminatory job assignments were not intended to force resignation, back pay terminated on resignation) *with* Nobler v. Beth Israel Med. Ctr., 715 F. Supp. 570, 572, 573, 55 FEP 1531 (S.D.N.Y. 1989) (once someone else was appointed as director of radiation, there was no purpose for a rejected applicant to stay and work out the dispute because no other equivalent position existed; although not constructively discharged, the employee could receive back pay calculated according to the difference between the appointee's salary and the plaintiff's actual salary after resigning or the old salary, whichever is less) *and* Taylor v. Ford Motor Co., 392 F. Supp. 254, 256–57, 8 FEP 253 (W.D. Mo. 1974) (back pay did not terminate on resignation where the job was "distasteful" to the plaintiff and "sometimes injurious to his health").

[125]*See* Mathieu v. Gopher News Co., 273 F.3d 769 (8th Cir. 2001) (refusal of three different jobs offered by former employer did not decrease back-pay award when any of the jobs offered would have been a demotion because of their lower pay and lack of benefits); Sellers v. Delgado Cmty. Coll., 839 F.2d 1132, 1137, 46 FEP 464 (5th Cir. 1988) (duty to mitigate damages did not require claimant to remain in non-comparable position accepted while claim pending; requiring claimant to remain in such a position, once accepted, would deter claimant from seeking or accepting any type of non-comparable work); Wheeler v. Snyder Buick, Inc., 794 F.2d 1228, 1234, 41 FEP 341 (7th Cir. 1986) (voluntary resignation from a job in

(ii.) Failure to mitigate. A plaintiff has an affirmative duty to mitigate lost wages by taking reasonable measures[126] to locate comparable or substantially equivalent employment.[127] Although the plaintiff is normally the party charged with the burden of proving his or her damages, the burden of pleading and establishing the

---

the insurance field did not preclude the claimant's entitlement to back pay because the job was not comparable, especially financially, to her original job, and the claimant's failure to secure work in her original field was excusable because of her supervisor's threat to blackball her in that business); *see also* EEOC v. Guardian Pools, 828 F.2d 1507, 1511, 44 FEP 1824 (11th Cir. 1987) (the duty to mitigate does not require that the claimant remain in a new job with which she is dissatisfied).

[126]*Compare* Yancey v. Weyerhaeuser Co., 277 F.3d 1021 (8th Cir. 2002) (plaintiff who had a ninth grade education, limited job skills, and who lived in a small town reasonably mitigated by reviewing classifieds and enrolling in national job search), Dilley v. SuperValu, 296 F.3d 958 (10th Cir. 2002) ($43,968 reduction in back-pay award due to plaintiff's failure to mitigate), Hunter v. Allis-Chalmers Corp., 797 F.2d 1417, 1427–28, 41 FEP 721 (7th Cir. 1986) (very limited work and only 16 applications for employment over 5 years warrants a reduction of back pay from 5 to 3 years), Munoz v. Oceanside Resorts, Inc., 223 F.3d 1340 (11th Cir. 2000), Weatherspoon v. Andrews & Co., 32 FEP 1226, 1229 (D. Colo. 1983) (the plaintiff failed to mitigate damages upon ceasing to seek alternative employment; the back-pay period terminates at that time), Coley v. Consolidated Rail Corp., 561 F. Supp. 645, 652, 34 FEP 129 (E.D. Mich. 1982) (the plaintiff's failure to seek employment terminates the back-pay period at the point when the plaintiff's inaction no longer is attributable to her former supervisor's sexual harassment) *and* Hayes v. Shelby Mem'l Hosp., 546 F. Supp. 259, 266–67, 29 FEP 1173 (N.D. Ala. 1982) (the back-pay award is reduced where the claimant unreasonably assumed that any effort to obtain employment would be futile because of her pregnancy), *aff'd*, 726 F.2d 1543, 34 FEP 444 (11th Cir. 1984) *with* Baggett v. Program Res., Inc., 806 F.2d 178, 182, 42 FEP 648 (8th Cir. 1986) (a discriminatee is entitled to back pay if a "good faith effort" to find work is made; the district court's determination, that the plaintiff made such efforts after she resigned her job to move to another state where she got married, was not clearly erroneous), Maxfield v. Sinclair Int'l, 766 F.2d 788, 796, 38 FEP 442 (3d Cir. 1985) (a 65-year-old claimant's failure to seek alternate employment was reasonable in view of his income from Social Security and other sources), Nord v. United States Steel Corp., 758 F.2d 1462, 1471, 37 FEP 1232 (11th Cir. 1985) (abandonment of an unsuccessful 2½-year search for employment, to set up a business for her husband that would provide future employment, does not terminate the claimant's back-pay period), Brady v. Thurston Motor Lines, Inc., 753 F.2d 1269, 1274, 36 FEP 1805 (4th Cir. 1985) (abandonment of a job search after 1 year to accept a lower-paying job does not terminate the back-pay period) *and* Thorkildson v. Insurance Co. of N. Am., 631 F. Supp. 372, 374, 40 FEP 813 (D. Minn. 1986) (refusing to conclude without further information that an employee who was 61 years old at the time of discharge failed to mitigate damages as a matter of law; she stopped looking for work only after her husband became ill).

[127]*See* Ford Motor Co. v. EEOC, 458 U.S. 219, 231, 29 FEP 121 (1982) (the duty of a plaintiff in a job discrimination case to mitigate damages "requires the claimant to use reasonable diligence in finding other suitable employment"; this

affirmative defense that the plaintiff failed to mitigate his or her damages is on the defendant.[128]

There is a split among the circuits as to the elements required for a defendant to establish that the plaintiff failed to reasonably mitigate.

Some courts require what can be interpreted as a two-step analysis. The defendant must prove *both* (1) that the claimant was not reasonably diligent in seeking other employment, and (2) that, with the exercise of reasonable diligence, the claimant had a reasonable chance of finding comparable employment.[129] The Fourth,

---

includes jobs with the same employer); *accord* Payne v. Security Sav. & Loan Ass'n, 924 F.2d 109, 110, 55 FEP 96 (7th Cir. 1991) (ADEA); Blake v. J.C. Penney Co., 894 F.2d 274, 282, 51 FEP 1564 (8th Cir. 1990) (ADEA); Johnson v. Chapel Hill Indep. Sch. Dist., 853 F.2d 375, 383, 47 FEP 1498 (5th Cir. 1988) (§§ 1981 and 1983); *see also* Sellers v. Delgado Cmty. Coll., 839 F.2d 1132, 1136–38 (5th Cir. 1988) (duty to locate comparable or substantially equivalent employment does not require a claimant to remain in a non-comparable position); Walters v. City of Atlanta, 803 F.2d 1135, 1145, 42 FEP 387 (11th Cir. 1986) (§ 1981); Huegel v. Tisch, 683 F. Supp. 123, 125, 49 FEP 742 (E.D. Pa. 1988) (the Rehabilitation Act); *cf.* EEOC v. Board of Regents, 288 F.3d 296 (7th Cir. 2002) (court did not require plaintiffs to reapply for jobs with former employer); NLRB v. Future Ambulette, Inc., 903 F.2d 140, 144–45, 134 LRRM 2654 (2d Cir. 1990) (NLRA).

[128]*E.g.*, Peyton v. DiMaro, 287 F.3d 1121 (D.C. Cir. 2002) (back-pay award was not an abuse of discretion when defendant failed to show that plaintiff was attending school full time and did not adequately seek additional employment); Dailey v. Societe Generale, 108 F.3d 451, 455 (2d Cir. 1997); Normand v. Research Inst. of Am., 927 F.2d 857, 865, 55 FEP 875 (5th Cir. 1991) ("The employer in a Title VII case has a burden of proving that the plaintiff has not exercised due diligence in seeking comparable employment after an unlawful discharge."); *Sellers*, 902 F.2d at 1193; Gaddy v. Abex Corp., 884 F.2d 312, 318, 50 FEP 1333 (7th Cir. 1989) (the defendant has the burden "[t]o demonstrate the affirmative defense of a plaintiff's failure to mitigate damages"); Jackson v. Shell Oil Co., 702 F.2d 197, 202, 31 FEP 686 (9th Cir. 1983) ("defendant bears the burden of showing failure to mitigate"); Maturo v. National Graphics, Inc., 722 F. Supp. 916, 928, 55 FEP 325 (D. Conn. 1989) ("Defendants carry the burden of proving that plaintiff failed to exercise reasonable diligence in seeking equivalent employment in mitigation of her damages.").

[129]*See, e.g.*, Conetta v. National Hair Care Ctrs., 236 F.3d 67 (1st Cir. 2001) (defendant met burden of proof showing plaintiff's failure to mitigate by showing plaintiff's less than diligent job search and the availability of substantially equivalent positions; pursuing one job application and reviewing newspaper ads daily was not an adequate job search); Carey v. Mount Desert Island Hosp., 156 F.3d 31, 41, 77 FEP 861 (1st Cir. 1998) (district court's decision to reduce plaintiff's back pay affirmed; court properly weighed testimony of competing experts and concluded that plaintiff did not exercise reasonable diligence in seeking comparable employment and comparable employment was shown to be available); Quint v. A.E. Staley Mfg. Co., 172 F.3d 1, 16 (1st Cir. 1999) ("the defendant-employer [should be relieved]

Fifth, Eighth, and Eleventh Circuits, on the other hand, require the employer to show only that the plaintiff did not make reasonable efforts to obtain other work.[130] These courts reason that it is the plaintiff's failure to act that cuts off back pay; the employer does not also have to affirmatively show that comparable work was

---

of the burden to prove the availability of substantially equivalent jobs in the relevant geographic area once it has been shown that the former employee made no effort to secure suitable employment"), *cert. denied*, 535 U.S. 1023 (2002); Van Le v. University of Pa., 321 F.3d 403 (3d Cir. 2003) (defendant met burden of proof showing plaintiff's failure to mitigate by showing plaintiff's less than diligent job search and the availability of substantially equivalent positions); Booker v. Taylor Milk Co., 64 F.3d 860, 866, 71 FEP 525 (3d Cir. 1995) ("The duty of a successful Title VII claimant to mitigate damages is *not* met by using reasonable diligence to obtain *any* employment. Rather, the claimant must use reasonable diligence to obtain *substantially equivalent employment*."); Tubari Ltd., Inc. v. NLRB, 959 F.2d 451, 454 (3d Cir. 1992) (absent a showing that employee exercised diligence to find comparable employment, evidence of a scarcity of work and the possibility that none would have been found even with the use of diligence is irrelevant); Wheeler v. Snyder Buick, Inc., 794 F.2d 1228, 1234, 41 FEP 341 (7th Cir. 1986) ("To prevail, the employer must prove both that the employee was not reasonably diligent in seeking other employment, and that with the exercise of reasonable diligence there was a reasonable chance the employee might have found comparable employment."); EEOC v. Farmer Bros. Co., 31 F.3d 891, 906, 65 FEP 857 (9th Cir. 1994) (to prevail on summary judgment motion, defendant had to prove that during time in question there were substantially equivalent jobs available and that plaintiff failed to use reasonable diligence in pursuing them); *Jackson*, 702 F.2d at 202 (same); Ali v. City of Clearwater, 915 F. Supp. 1231, 1242 (M.D. Fla. 1996) (while defendant city advanced evidence of plaintiff's failure to use reasonable diligence, defendant failed to point out any factual basis that there were suitable positions available; therefore, defendant failed to meet burden on its affirmative defense of failure to mitigate), *aff'd*, 138 F.3d 956 (11th Cir. 1999); Shpargel v. Stage & Co., 914 F. Supp. 1468, 1479, 5 AD 1558 (E.D. Mich. 1996) (because plaintiff demonstrated prima facie case of discrimination and presented evidence on issue of damages, "the burden is on the defendants to prove that there were substantially equivalent jobs available to the plaintiff but that he failed to exercise reasonable diligence in seeking such jobs").

[130]Greenway v. Buffalo Hilton Hotel, 143 F.3d 47, 54 (2d Cir. 1998) ("The underlying rationale [for the exception] is that an employer should not be saddled by a requirement that *it* show other suitable employment in fact existed—the threat being that if it does not, the employee will be found to have mitigated his damages—when the employee, who is capable of finding replacement work, failed to pursue employment at all.") (emphasis in original); Miller v. AT&T Corp., 250 F.3d 820, 838, 85 FEP 578 (4th Cir. 2001) ("Failure to diligently seek new [substantially equivalent] employment precludes an award of back pay for the period during which employment was not sought."); *cf.* NLRB v. Pepsi Cola Bottling Co., 258 F.3d 305, 310 (4th Cir. 2001) ("Where an employer 'demonstrates that an employee did not exercise reasonable diligence in his or her efforts to secure interim employment, then it has established that the employee has not properly mitigated his or her damages.' ").

actually available.[131] Regardless of whether the analysis is a one-
or two-step process, most courts agree that a plaintiff who abandons the search for new employment or fails to pursue new employment with reasonable diligence will be held to have cut off
his or her right to any further recovery of back pay.[132] Many courts
have in fact reduced back-pay awards by the amount the plaintiff
could have earned with reasonable diligence.[133] In some,[134] but not

---

[131]*See, e.g.*, West v. Nabors Drilling U.S.A., Inc., 330 F.3d 379 (5th Cir. 2003)
(no attempts to find substantially equivalent employment sufficiently demonstrated
a failure to mitigate); Wagner v. Dillard Dep't, Inc., 17 Fed. Appx. 141 (4th Cir.
2001) (while defendant must ordinarily present evidence that comparable work was
available, no such evidence is necessary if the plaintiff makes little or no effort to
seek employment); Weaver v. Casa Gallardo, Inc., 922 F.2d 1515, 1527, 55 FEP 27
(11th Cir. 1991) ("If . . . 'an employer proves that the employee has not made reasonable efforts to obtain work, the employer does not also have to establish the
availability of substantially comparable employment.' ") (quoting Sellers v. Delgado
Cmty. Coll., 839 F.2d 1132, 1139, 46 FEP 464 (5th Cir. 1988)); *cf.* Duty v. Norton-
Alcoa Proppants, 293 F.3d 481 (8th Cir. 2002) (affirming ADA case where district
court determined that the jury could disregard plaintiff's alleged failure to mitigate
even absent evidence of the availability of other positions that plaintiff could assume).
[132]*See, e.g.*, Kirsch v. Fleet St., Ltd., 148 F.3d 149 (2d Cir. 1998) (employment
discrimination plaintiff may not simply abandon his job search and continue to recover back pay); Tubari Ltd., Inc. v. NLRB, 959 F.2d 451, 454 (3d Cir. 1992) (absent a showing that employee exercised diligence to find comparable employment,
evidence of a scarcity of work and the possibility that none would have been found
even with the use of diligence is irrelevant).
[133]*See, e.g.*, Landgraf v. USI Film Prods., 511 U.S.244, 253 n.5 (1994) (interim
earnings or amounts earnable with reasonable diligence by the person or persons
discriminated against shall operate to reduce the back pay otherwise allowable); Troy
v. Bay State Computer Group, Inc., 141 F.3d 378, 382 (1st Cir. 1998) (back-pay award
must be reduced by any compensation that plaintiff actually received during the same
period and any additional amount that she would have received through reasonable
efforts to mitigate her damages); EEOC v. Delight Wholesale Co., 765 F. Supp. 583,
588, 59 FEP 1212 (W.D. Mo. 1991) ("The amounts plaintiff did earn, or reasonably
should have earned, in mitigation are deducted from the backpay award."), *aff'd*, 973
F.2d 664, 59 FEP 1222 (8th Cir. 1992); *cf.* 42 U.S.C. § 2000e-5(g)(1) (2000).
[134]*See, e.g.*, EEOC v. Gurnee Inn Corp., 914 F.2d 815, 818 n.4, 53 FEP 1425
(7th Cir. 1990) (failure of a 15-year-old high school student and a 20-year-old college student to look for employment after their constructive discharges due to being sexually harassed did not bar an award of back pay; the district court could
conclude that the students would feel "gun shy" about looking for similar positions);
Maturo v. National Graphics, Inc., 722 F. Supp. 916, 925–26, 55 FEP 325 (D. Conn.
1989) (the plaintiff was unable to obtain work for 6 months due to depression and
emotional debilitation resulting from sexual harassment and later left a position for
"reasons directly related to emotional injuries sustained from the sexual harassment");
EEOC v. FLC & Bros. Rebel, Inc., 663 F. Supp. 864, 870, 44 FEP 362 (W.D. Va.
1987) (the plaintiff's failure to take a job she could not reach with public transportation

all,[135] cases, however, courts may allow the plaintiff to argue that otherwise deficient mitigation efforts should be excused because of the psychological or economic injuries inflicted by the employer's conduct.[136]

Courts typically will not require the plaintiff to pursue mitigation efforts beyond employment opportunities that are "substantially equivalent" to the plaintiff's former position.[137] Although a plaintiff need not accept significantly inferior employment in order to satisfy his or her duty to mitigate,[138] the fact that no two jobs are identical often means that the plaintiff must accept a job even though the position differs in some respects. "Substantially equivalent" employment is most often defined as employment that affords similar promotional opportunities, compensation, job responsibilities, working conditions, and status.[139] Yet, after the passage

---

did not terminate her former employer's back-pay liability where her automobile had been repossessed after loss of her job), *aff'd mem.*, 846 F.2d 70 (4th Cir. 1988).

[135]*E.g.*, Bossalina v. Lever Bros. Co., 47 FEP 1264, 1267 (D. Md. 1986) (the plaintiffs' claim that they were unfit to look for other work due to emotional distress from their discharges "as a matter of law" is an insufficient excuse for failing to mitigate under the ADEA, *aff'd mem.*, 849 F.2d 604 (4th Cir. 1988).

[136]*E.g.*, Hine v. Mineta, 238 F. Supp. 2d 497 (E.D.N.Y. 2003) (jury rejected testimony by plaintiff and her psychologist that she could not work again as an air traffic controller because of the emotional distress she suffered due to post-traumatic stress disorder and the symptoms arising from that ailment); *cf.* Conetta v. National Hair Care Ctrs., 236 F.3d 67 (1st Cir. 2001).

[137]*See, e.g.*, Van Le v. University of Pa., 321 F.3d 403, 91 FEP 310 (3d Cir. 2003) (in order to meet its burden on insufficient plaintiff mitigation, "an employer must demonstrate that 1) substantially equivalent work was available, and 2) the . . . claimant did not exercise reasonable diligence to obtain the employment"); Booker v. Taylor Milk Co., 64 F.3d 860, 866, 71 FEP 525 (3d Cir. 1995) (same).

[138]*See* Ford Motor Co. v. EEOC, 458 U.S. 219, 231 (1982) ("the unemployed or underemployed claimant need not go into another line of work, accept a demotion, or take a demeaning position"); Wheeler v. Snyder Buick, Inc., 794 F.2d 1228, 1234–35, 41 FEP 341 (7th Cir. 1986) (the duty to mitigate damages does not require the discriminatee to stay in a job in a "different business that pays substantially less money"); Long v. Trans World Airlines, Inc., 761 F. Supp. 1320, 1331 n.16 (N.D. Ill. 1991) ("The Court agrees with plaintiffs that they were not required to mitigate damages by accepting any employment they could find, but rather by finding substantially equivalent employment.").

[139]*See, e.g.*, Sharkey v. Lasmo, 214 F.3d 371 (2d Cir. 2000) (59-year-old plaintiff with limited education and specialized skills reasonably mitigated when he placed about 50 calls in the industry, pursued an outplacement service, and followed other tips on possible employment); Weaver v. Casa Gallardo, Inc., 922 F.2d 1515, 1527 (11th Cir. 1991) (" 'Substantially equivalent employment' is employment that affords virtually identical promotional opportunities, compensation, job responsibilities,

of a reasonable period of time searching for a nearly identical job, the plaintiff may have "to lower his/her sights" and accept the best available job.[140] An employee who was earning an above-market salary will nevertheless have a duty to seek and obtain employment at the lower market rate.[141]

Even though it may not be considered "substantially equivalent" work in all respects, subsequent work in an unrelated field may in some cases satisfy the mitigation requirement.[142] A plaintiff's full-time enrollment in school has been held to remove the plaintiff from the job market, thereby terminating the back-pay period. There is not, however, a *"per se* rule that finds inherently incompatible the duty of a Title VII plaintiff to use reasonable diligence in securing comparable employment and such a plaintiff's decision to attend school on a full-time basis."[143] In determining whether part-time employment satisfies the mitigation requirement, courts will often consider the availability of comparable jobs and the plaintiff's diligence in seeking employment.[144] A former employee's

working conditions, and status to those available to employees holding the position from which the Title VII claimant has been discriminatorily terminated.").

[140]*Weaver*, 922 F.2d at 1527; *see also* Walters v. City of Atlanta, 803 F.2d 1135, 1145, 42 FEP 387 (11th Cir. 1986) (extensive efforts to obtain only the particular position discriminatorily denied the plaintiff are insufficient; the plaintiff is obligated to seek employment in other fields); Coleman v. City of Omaha, 714 F.2d 804, 808, 33 FEP 1462 (8th Cir. 1983) (a former deputy police chief was not required to apply for police chief jobs in two small towns, but his failure to apply for a position with a local security company presents a jury issue); Arline v. School Bd., 692 F. Supp. 1286, 1292, 47 FEP 530 (M.D. Fla. 1988) (the plaintiff failed to mitigate damages where she made only minimal efforts to locate employment outside the teaching field).

[141]*See* Hutchison v. Amateur Elec. Supply, Inc., 42 F.3d 1037, 1067, 66 FEP 1275 (7th Cir. 1994) (employee who received above-market "abuse premium" had duty to seek and accept comparable "nonabusive" employment at market rate).

[142]*See* Suggs v. Servicemaster Educ. Food Mgmt., 72 F.3d 1228, 1234, 69 FEP 1270 (6th Cir. 1996) (plaintiff previously employed as director at corporate/institutional food catering service satisfied mitigation requirement by immediately securing alternative employment as substitute teacher for 2 years and then working at Head Start program up to time of trial).

[143]Dailey v. Societe Generale, 108 F.3d 451, 454–57, 74 FEP 1428 (2d Cir. 1997) ("We believe that a fact-finder may, under certain circumstances, conclude that 'one who chooses to attend school only when diligent efforts to find work prove fruitless,' . . . satisfies his or her duty to mitigate."); *see also* Miller v. AT&T Corp., 250 F.3d 820, 838–39 (4th Cir. 2001) (finding no failure to mitigate when plaintiff enrolled in school only after a diligent but unsuccessful job search).

[144]*Compare* Meyer v. United Air Lines, 950 F. Supp. 874, 876, 73 FEP 202 (N.D. Ill. 1997) (attorney formerly employed in arbitration department of airline's legal

discharge for cause from subsequent employment will not in most cases constitute a failure to mitigate damages where the former employee did not act intentionally and did not commit a "gross or egregious wrong."[145]

No matter what is deemed to be "substantially equivalent employment," courts have consistently held that the plaintiff's job search must be more than a passive search through want ads.[146] The plaintiff must take a proactive approach to obtaining new employment; otherwise, the courts will hold that the plaintiff failed to mitigate sufficiently his or her damages.[147] This proactive effort may include the pursuit of self-employment so long as the business venture is viewed as being reasonable, even if it ultimately fails.[148] But, where the plaintiff, preferring self-employment, fails

---

department failed to satisfy mitigation requirement by accepting part-time position in county State's Attorney office "preparing appellate briefs and doing other related appellate work") *with* EEOC v. Northwestern Mem'l Hosp., 858 F. Supp. 759, 767, 73 FEP 742 (N.D. Ill. 1994) (plaintiff satisfied mitigation requirement by securing part-time work on "as needed" basis from one hospital 3 months after discharge and ultimately obtained full-time position at another hospital fewer than 2 years later).

[145]Thurman v. Yellow Freight Sys., 90 F.3d 1160, 1169, 72 FEP 657 (6th Cir. 1996) (employee fired for cause from subsequent employment for driving truck under underpass that was too low and bending exhaust pipe as result did not fail to mitigate damages where plaintiff did not act willfully and did not commit "gross or egregious wrong"); *cf.* NLRB v. Pepsi Cola Bottling Co., 258 F.3d 305, 310 (4th Cir. 2001) ("An employee who loses employment by engaging in 'deliberate or gross misconduct' is not entitled to back pay for a resulting earning loss.").

[146]*See, e.g.,* Booker v. Taylor Milk Co., 64 F.3d 860, 865–66, 71 FEP 525 (3d Cir. 1995) (plaintiff's "constant" and "continuous" review of want ads was insufficient where in 3 ½ years following discharge plaintiff failed to submit any applications in response to want ads that advertised positions substantially similar to plaintiff's previous position). In fact, want ads alone may not even provide sufficient evidence that substantially similar positions were available. *See* Shpargel v. Stage & Co., 914 F. Supp. 1468, 1480, 5 AD 1558 (E.D. Mich. 1996) (defendants' mere proffering of want ads at summary judgment did not establish that positions were substantially similar to plaintiff's previous position).

[147]*See* EEOC v. Service News Co., 898 F.2d 958, 963, 52 FEP 677 (4th Cir. 1990) ("Looking through want ads for an unskilled position, without more, is insufficient to show mitigation, and the back pay award should accordingly be reduced.").

[148]*See* Smith v. Great Am. Rests., Inc., 969 F.2d 430, 438–39, 59 FEP 646 (7th Cir. 1992) (opening a restaurant after 1 week of searching for a job and continuing the business despite losses was not unreasonable; upholding jury award of 34 months of back pay); Carden v. Westinghouse Elec. Corp., 850 F.2d 996, 1005–06, 47 FEP 446 (3d Cir. 1988) (plaintiff's decision to enter into his own business was a reasonable effort to mitigate damages where no evidence showed otherwise and the plaintiff had searched unsuccessfully for alternative employment for nearly a year); Taylor v. Central Pa. Drug & Alcohol Servs., 890 F. Supp. 360, 367, 373, 72 FEP 1315

to pursue positions comparable to the one formerly held or where there is evidence that the plaintiff planned to quit her job and pursue self-employment prior to the discriminatory act,[149] the plaintiff's choice may curtail a back-pay award.[150] A plaintiff who abandons his or her profession and unsuccessfully begins employment in a completely unrelated field may be found to have failed to make adequate mitigation efforts.[151]

The Third Circuit has held that an examination of the plaintiff's reasonable diligence requires an individualized evaluation of the plaintiff's characteristics and the job market, and that a failure to mitigate alone is insufficient to overcome the presumption in favor of prejudgment interest on the ultimate back-pay award.[152] The Seventh Circuit has held that a jury's finding that the Title VII plaintiff partially failed to mitigate her damages does not defeat the presumption in favor of prejudgment interest.[153]

(M.D. Pa. 1995) (plaintiff twice attempted to start her own business, and both ventures failed; plaintiff's "attempt to mitigate her back pay damages by starting her own businesses when no offers of employment were forthcoming was a laudable effort and should not be used against her to cut off her right to receive back pay"); *see also* Teichgraeber v. Memorial Union Corp., 932 F. Supp. 1263, 1265–67 (D. Kan. 1996) (former employee's claim for back pay and assertion of self-employment as mitigation made relevant, and therefore discoverable, all documents reflecting compensation paid to any person who performed labor for former employee's business).

[149]*See* EEOC v. Ilona of Hung., Inc., 108 F.3d 1569, 1579 (7th Cir. 1996) (reversing district court's award of back pay where evidence showed that plaintiff planned to quit her job prior to discharge; plaintiff had acquired site and applied for zoning permit for Subway sandwich shop franchise more than 1 month before her discharge and planned to "be [her] own boss" and run store herself).

[150]*See, e.g.*, Hansard v. Pepsi-Cola Metro. Bottling Co., 865 F.2d 1461, 1468, 49 FEP 197 (5th Cir. 1989) (it was unreasonable for the plaintiff to abandon his job search to run a flea market booth on a weekend basis).

[151]*See, e.g.*, McIntosh v. Jones Truck Lines, Inc., 767 F.2d 433, 435, 38 FEP 710 (8th Cir. 1985) (a trucking company's back-pay liability ended when the claimant ceased looking for employment in the trucking industry); Johnson v. Memphis Police Dep't, 713 F. Supp. 244, 249, 50 FEP 211 (W.D. Tenn. 1989) (a plaintiff who abandoned a law enforcement career to unsuccessfully sell safety supplies failed reasonably to mitigate damages). *But cf.* Ellis v. Ringgold Sch. Dist., 832 F.2d 27, 30, 45 FEP 137 (3d Cir. 1987) (for purposes of reinstatement, the plaintiff did not abandon a teaching career by taking a better-paying industrial job).

[152]*See* Booker v. Taylor Milk Co., 64 F.3d 860, 865, 869, 71 FEP 525 (3d Cir. 1995) (plaintiff's reduced back-pay award reflects his failure to mitigate his damages and even if plaintiff had satisfied his duty to mitigate, he would not have been made whole absent some award of back pay; therefore, he is entitled to prejudgment interest for loss of use of amount included in back-pay award).

[153]*See* Hutchison v. Amateur Elec. Supply, Inc., 42 F.3d 1037, 66 FEP 1275 (7th Cir. 1994). The district court in *Hutchison* concluded that a reasonable jury could

The fact finder must determine what constitutes a reasonable geographical scope for the search for a substantially equivalent position. Although it can be argued that the employee's decision to relocate demonstrates a failure to mitigate, most,[154] but not every[155] court has held that a plaintiff's decision to move should not be grounds for eliminating or reducing back pay, as long as the employee continues to seek work. Indeed, some courts have required the plaintiff to seek out substitute employment in locations other than where the employee is currently located.[156]

---

have believed defendants' expert's opinion that plaintiff did not act diligently in failing to utilize employment placement services. Also, given that plaintiff was being paid a "premium" above-market rate to tolerate her supervisor's abuse, the Seventh Circuit held that the district court did not abuse its discretion in determining that the jury acted within the law in concluding that the plaintiff had a duty to seek and accept compensation at the market rate. However, the district court did abuse its discretion in denying prejudgment interest altogether based on the jury's determination that the plaintiff abandoned the job market. "In any event, the amount of back pay on which interest is to be awarded in this case is not uncertain—the jury awarded $80,000. The fact that the jury had to make implicit calculations to reach that amount does not defeat the presumption in favor of prejudgment interest." *Id.* at 1047.

[154]*See, e.g.*, Stone v. D.A. & S. Oil Well Servicing, Inc., 624 F.2d 142, 144, 23 FEP 157 (10th Cir. 1980) (finding no lack of reasonable diligence where the plaintiff terminated noncomparable employment and moved away to find comparable employment); Di Salvo v. Chamber of Commerce, 568 F.2d 593, 598, 20 FEP 825 (8th Cir. 1978) (upholding back pay to a plaintiff who quit a subsequent job to move to Miami; the district court found the plaintiff would have stayed in Kansas City had she received a nondiscriminatory salary and that the move was "based on mitigative motives" rather than a personal decision to accompany her then-husband there); NLRB v. Robert Haws Co., 403 F.2d 979, 981, 69 LRRM 2730 (6th Cir. 1968) (the claimant's move to another location to look for work is irrelevant); Tidwell v. American Oil Co., 332 F. Supp. 424, 437, 3 FEP 1007 (D. Utah 1971) (the plaintiff's move to another location to remain with her husband is irrelevant since she moved only after unsuccessfully seeking other employment).

[155]*See, e.g.*, NLRB v. Rice Lake Creamery Co., 365 F.2d 888, 891, 62 LRRM 2332 (D.C. Cir. 1966) (the claimant's move to another location for personal reasons terminates the back-pay period); Ryan v. Raytheon Data Sys. Co., 601 F. Supp. 243, 253, 39 FEP 1398 (D. Mass. 1985) (terminating back pay when the claimant moved from Massachusetts to Florida).

[156]*See, e.g.*, Ford v. Nicks, 866 F.2d 865, 874, 48 FEP 1657 (6th Cir. 1989) (a former college faculty member failed to mitigate damages when she refused to accept a comparable position 70 miles away; she and her husband could have moved and lived midway between their respective employers), *aff'd in part on other grounds sub nom.* Minority Employees of Tennessee Dep't of Employment Sec. v. Tennessee Dep't of Employment Sec., 901 F.2d 1327 (6th Cir. 1990); Sowers v. Kemira, Inc., 701 F. Supp. 809, 827, 46 FEP 1825 (S.D. Ga. 1988) (the plaintiff's refusal of a job offer that would have required relocation from Macon, Georgia, to Savannah, Georgia, was reasonable under the circumstances).

(iii.) Refusal of an unconditional offer of reinstatement. The employee's duty to mitigate carries with it the obligation to seek "substantially similar employment." Courts have recognized that this duty can in some cases require the employee to consider reinstatement with the defendant-employer. Because reinstatement cannot be overlooked as a required mitigation effort, employers sometimes use unconditional offers of reinstatement (or instatement) as a strategic litigation maneuver to cut off the accrual of back-pay damages. In *Ford Motor Co. v. EEOC*[157] the Supreme Court held that a claimant's unreasonable rejection of an employer's unconditional offer of reinstatement constitutes a failure to mitigate that will end the accrual of back pay.[158] An unreasonable rejection will also prevent the court from awarding reinstatement or front pay in lieu thereof.[159]

To be a valid offer of reinstatement, the employer must: (a) show that the employment offered, even if not precisely identical

---

[157]458 U.S. 219, 29 FEP 121 (1982).

[158]*Id.* at 238–39; *see also* EEOC v. Massey Yardley Chrysler Plymouth, Inc., 117 F.3d 1244, 1252 (11th Cir. 1997) (back-pay period ran until plaintiff rejected employer's pretrial offer of reinstatement); Lewis Grocer Co. v. Holloway, 874 F.2d 1008, 1012, 4 IER 781 (5th Cir. 1989) (looking to analogous Title VII law in the context of a claim under the Surface Transportation Assistance Act; "[A]n unconditional offer of reinstatement ordinarily tolls an employer's back-pay liability."); Giandonato v. Sybron Corp., 804 F.2d 120, 124, 42 FEP 219 (10th Cir. 1986) ("Under *Ford Motor Co.*, an employee is obligated to minimize his damages by accepting his employer's offer of reinstatement to his previous job or a job that is 'substantially equivalent' to his previous job."); Patterson v. Youngstown Sheet & Tube Co., 659 F.2d 736, 740, 28 FEP 1434 (7th Cir. 1981) (the back-pay period ended when members of the claimants' class were offered the opportunity to become apprentices in jobs previously denied discriminatees); Bahadirli v. Domino's Pizza, Inc., 873 F. Supp. 1528, 1235, 71 FEP 1615 (M.D. Ala. 1995) ("According to the Supreme Court, where a Title VII defendant unconditionally offers the plaintiff the position she previously applied for, doing so immediately cuts off liability for back pay from the date of the offer."); Bragalone v. Kona Coast Resort Joint Venture, 866 F. Supp. 1285, 1296, 66 FEP 65 (D. Haw. 1994) (plaintiff's rejection of unconditional offer of reinstatement was unreasonable where rejection was based on belief that it "would require her to return to a stressful allegedly harassing work environment").

[159]*E.g.*, Lewis Grocer Co. v. Holloway, 874 F.2d 1008, 1012, 4 IER 781 (5th Cir. 1989) ("We agree with our colleagues in the Tenth Circuit that [an unconditional offer of reinstatement] precludes a subsequent order of reinstatement.") (citing Giandonato v. Sybron Corp., 804 F.2d 120, 125, 42 FEP 219 (10th Cir. 1986)); Stanfield v. Answering Serv., Inc., 867 F.2d 1290, 1296, 50 FEP 1151 (11th Cir. 1989) ("by refusing the company's offer of reinstatement, [the plaintiff] waived her right to resume her former position, and the district court could not order [the plaintiff] reinstated").

to the prior job, was at least sufficiently comparable,[160] and (b) that the offer was unconditional, i.e., that the plaintiff was not required to waive or compromise his or her legal claims, or provide anything of value to the employer, as a condition of accepting the offer.[161] Although a plaintiff is not obligated to accept unreasonable

---

[160]*See* Boehms v. Crowell, 139 F.3d 452, 459–60 (5th Cir. 1998) (back-pay award affirmed; ADEA plaintiff not required to accept inferior position with defendant in order to mitigate his damages); EEOC v. Accurate Mech. Contractors, Inc., 863 F. Supp. 828, 835–36 (E.D. Wis. 1994) (offer of night-shift work was not offer of comparable employment and therefore did not toll accrual of back-pay liability where night-shift pipefitters were required to do more work with less supervision and night shift was statistically more dangerous than day shift, even though pay was higher for night shift); Graefenhain v. Pabst Brewing Co., 870 F.2d 1198, 1203–04, 49 FEP 829 (7th Cir. 1989) (the offer did not guarantee the employee a position substantially comparable to his previous job); Shore v. Federal Express Corp., 777 F.2d 1155, 1158, 39 FEP 809 (6th Cir. 1985) (the claimant's refusal of reinstatement was reasonable where differences in responsibilities between the claimant's former job and the offered job rendered them incomparable); Dickerson v. Deluxe Check Printers, Inc., 703 F.2d 276, 282, 31 FEP 621 (8th Cir. 1983) (even assuming the claimant was offered a position, her refusal to accept a position that she had no background or interest in would not end the back-pay period); Spagnuolo v. Whirlpool Corp., 548 F. Supp. 104, 108, 32 FEP 1372 (W.D.N.C. 1982) (the *Ford Motor Co.* rule is not applicable where the employer failed to offer the claimant his or her original job or one substantially equivalent to it), *aff'd in relevant part*, 717 F.2d 114, 32 FEP 1382 (4th Cir. 1983); Loubrido v. Hull Dobbs Co., 526 F. Supp. 1055, 1057–58, 30 FEP 1243 (D.P.R. 1981) (an offer is not bona fide where the new job is less prestigious and the compensation system is more speculative; noting that fringe benefits should be substantially similar); *cf.* NLRB v. Ryder Sys., Inc., 983 F.2d 705, 711–12, 142 LLRM 2290 (6th Cir. 1993) (the rehiring of an unlawfully discharged truck driver on probation without his former seniority did not constitute sufficient reinstatement to toll back-pay liability).

[161]*See, e.g.*, Odima v. Westin Tucson Hotel, 53 F.3d 1484, 1495–96, 67 FEP 1222 (9th Cir. 1995) (offer of employment conditioned on plaintiff relinquishing his discrimination claims against employer was not "unconditional offer" and plaintiff's rejection did not constitute failure to mitigate damages); Gerardi v. Hofstra Univ., 897 F. Supp. 50, 57–58 n.6 (E.D.N.Y. 1995) (university's settlement offer to job applicant made during administrative process could not be considered unconditional so as to limit university's back-pay liability under ADEA because offer specified that applicant would be required to provide full and complete release of all claims); Bruno v. W.B. Saunders Co., 882 F.2d 760, 770, 50 FEP 898 (3d Cir. 1989) (evidence supported the jury's finding that the reinstatement offer was invalid because it contemplated that plaintiff drop her EEOC claim). Thus, an *unconditional* offer of reinstatement differs meaningfully from a *settlement* offer that includes reinstatement. *See, e.g.*, Orzel v. City of Wauwatosa Fire Dep't, 697 F.2d 743, 757 n.26, 30 FEP 1070 (7th Cir. 1983) (an unconditional reinstatement offer can be admitted into evidence on the issue of mitigation, over Rule 408 objections); Thomas v. Resort Health Related Facility, 539 F. Supp. 630, 638, 31 FEP 65 (E.D.N.Y. 1982) (a defendant may offer evidence that it made an unconditional offer of reinstatement, even

or conditional offers of reinstatement,[162] only "special" or "exceptional" circumstances will permit the rejection of a valid unconditional offer without foreclosing any further back-pay recovery.[163]

Ford Motor did not specifically identify all the circumstances constituting the "special," "exceptional" basis under which an unconditional offer may be rejected without penalty.[164] Some direction as to such circumstances, however, may be drawn from cases where the court orders reinstatement, notwithstanding a plaintiff's request for front pay in lieu thereof.[165] Constructive discharge cases may also provide some guidance as to what is a "special," "exceptional" circumstance justifying a rejection.[166] But, it is well settled

---

though the offer was made at a meeting in which they also discussed settlement of the entire case, despite claimant's counsel's insistence that all the discussions were "without prejudice").

[162]*See, e.g.,* Berger v. Iron Workers Local 201, 170 F.3d 1111, 1135, 79 FEP 1018 (D.C. Cir. 1999) (no failure to mitigate when plaintiffs failed to accept interim jobs with their former employer where they would have been forced to leave good jobs that paid close to the same salary); Hawkins v. 1115 Legal Serv. Care, 163 F.3d 684, 695–96, 78 FEP 882 (2d Cir. 1998) ("[A]lthough an unemployed claimant would generally forfeit her right to back pay if she refused a job substantially equivalent to the one she was denied, she 'need not go into another line of work, accept a demotion, or take a demeaning position.' . . . Similarly, a claimant who voluntarily resigned from comparable employment for personal reasons would not have adequately mitigated damages, but 'a voluntary quit does not toll the back pay period when it is motivated by unreasonable working conditions or an earnest search for better employment.' . . . Self-employment, if it is undertaken in good faith and is a reasonable alternative to seeking other comparable employment, may be considered permissible mitigation."); Smith v. World Ins. Co., 38 F.3d 1456, 1465, 66 FEP 13 (8th Cir. 1994) (district court erred in failing to provide specific jury instruction on effect of plaintiff's rejection of defendant's unconditional offer of reinstatement); Mertig v. Milliken & Michaels of Del., Inc., 923 F. Supp. 636, 648 (D. Del. 1996) ("an applicant or discharged employee is not required to accept a job [offered] by the employer on the condition that the employee's claims against the employer be compromised"); Wilcox v. Stratton Lumber Co., 921 F. Supp. 837, 843 (D. Me. 1996) (sexual harassment plaintiff who feared continued harassment reasonably declined offer of reinstatement; therefore, offer did not toll accrual of back-pay liability); Lesko v. Clark Publisher Servs., 904 F. Supp. 415, 421 (M.D. Pa. 1995) (defendants' letters to plaintiff offering her opportunity to apply and interview were not unconditional offers of employment that would toll back-pay liability); Talada v. International Serv. Sys., Inc., 899 F. Supp. 936, 958 (N.D.N.Y. 1995) (defendants' offer of reinstatement without back pay and with implicit understanding that plaintiff would drop sexual harassment charges was not unconditional and would not limit back-pay award).

[163]*Ford Motor Co.,* 458 U.S. at 238 & n.7.

[164]*Id.*

[165]*See* Section III *infra. See generally* Chapter 39 (Injunctive and Affirmative Relief).

[166]*See generally* Chapter 20 (Discharge and Reduction in Force).

that the absence of retroactive seniority or accrued back pay does not constitute "special," "exceptional" circumstances that justify a rejection of an otherwise valid offer; the employee can accept the offer of employment and continue his or her suit to recover those benefits.[167] Moreover, merely offering the claimant the opportunity to interview, or "to apply," for a position is generally insufficient to constitute an unconditional offer of employment.[168]

One issue that is often litigated is whether a fear of hostility upon returning to the workplace is sufficiently "special" and/or "exceptional" so as to allow a rejection of the offer without consequence.[169] Courts have also had a mixed response where the offer

---

[167]*Ford Motor Co.*, 458 U.S. at 241.

[168]*See* EEOC v. Manville Sales Corp., 27 F.3d 1089, 1097 n.7, 65 FEP 804 (5th Cir. 1994) ("[a]n offer to interview is not tantamount to an unconditional job offer and therefore the plaintiff's refusal to interview does not automatically toll the plaintiff's accrual of damages"); Lesko v. Clark Publisher Servs., 904 F. Supp. 415, 421 (M.D. Pa. 1995) (neither employer's offer to employee to submit application nor employer's invitation to interview are offers of employment that end accrual of potential back-pay liability under Title VII); Bahadirli v. Domino's Pizza, Inc., 873 F. Supp. 1528, 1535–36, 71 FEP 1615 (M.D. Ala. 1995) (employer's statement to EEOC that employer was "willing to employ [plaintiff] at the location with the next available driver position" was not job offer that would warrant dismissal for failure to mitigate damages although it could limit back-pay recovery); *see also* Kilgo v. Bowman Transp., Inc., 789 F.2d 859, 879, 40 FEP 1415 (11th Cir. 1986) (an offer " 'to submit an application' " for one of an unknown number of openings, stating that the claimant stood a " 'good chance' " of being hired if she were " 'minimally qualified' " does not amount to an unconditional offer of reinstatement) (quoting the offer); Rasimas v. Michigan Dep't of Mental Health, 714 F.2d 614, 625, 32 FEP 688 (6th Cir. 1983) (a form letter inviting a claimant to interview for a position is not an unconditional offer of employment); *cf.* Orzel v. City of Wauwatosa Fire Dep't, 697 F.2d 743, 757, 30 FEP 1070 (7th Cir. 1983) (the claimant's refusal of an offer conditioned on taking and passing a physical arranged by the employer, given prior questionable settlement conduct by the employer, did not toll the back-pay period); Dickerson v. Deluxe Check Printers, Inc., 703 F.2d 276, 281, 31 FEP 621 (8th Cir. 1983) (conflicting evidence of the offer's existence precludes a legal determination and leaves only jury questions). Even where an offer is insufficiently concrete to be "unconditional," failure to pursue a meaningful opportunity may be evidence of a failure to mitigate. *See* Slack v. Havens, 7 FEP 885 (S.D. Cal. 1973) (the plaintiffs' refusal to return for an interview at the request of the employer cut off the back-pay period as of the time their interviews could have been processed and they could have been reemployed), *rev'd in part on other grounds*, 522 F.2d 1091, 11 FEP 27 (9th Cir. 1975).

[169]*Compare* Saladin v. Turner, 936 F. Supp. 1571, 1581 (N.D. Okla. 1996) (mere recitation of hostility does not render rejection of unconditional reinstatement offer reasonable; antagonism between parties is natural byproduct of any litigation) *with* Naylor v. Georgia-Pacific Corp., 875 F. Supp. 564, 581 (N.D. Iowa 1995) (fear of continuing racial harassment created material issue of fact as to reasonableness of

is of a job in another city.[170] In other cases, however, the lower courts have been more consistent in holding that the following contentions are not "special" and/or "exceptional" circumstances justifying rejection of an employer's unconditional offer: that the plaintiff no longer felt comfortable working at the prior employer or for the prior supervisor,[171] that insufficient time was allowed to consider the offer,[172] or that the offer was imprecise in some of its details.[173]

Ultimately, the courts continue to apply the Supreme Court's holding in *Ford Motor Co. v. EEOC*[174] and will terminate the accrual of back pay when it is found that a claimant's rejection of an employer's unconditional offer of employment is unreasonable.[175]

---

plaintiff's rejection of reinstatement offer, precluding summary judgment) *and* Miano v. AC & R Adver. Inc., 875 F. Supp. 204, 223–24, 227, 66 FEP 1603 (S.D.N.Y. 1995) (rejection of unconditional reinstatement offer reasonable where "exceptional circumstances existed whereby plaintiffs reasonably concluded their return to AC & R would be greeted by suspicion and antagonism, notwithstanding reassurances to the contrary . . . the work environment to which they were invited to return would have been one of serious discord and suspicion in a business where trust and open communication were essential").

[170]*Compare* Ford Motor Co. v. EEOC, 458 U.S. 219, 238 n.7, 29 FEP 121 (1982) (dictum; one exceptional circumstance might be that the plaintiff "had already move[d] a great distance to find a replacement job") *with* Cowen v. Standard Brands, Inc., 572 F. Supp. 1576, 1581–82 (N.D. Ala. 1983) (the offer still was valid, even though the job was in another city).

[171]*E.g.*, Giandonato v. Sybron Corp., 804 F.2d 120, 124, 42 FEP 219 (10th Cir. 1986) (a salesman is not justified in rejecting an unconditional reinstatement offer on grounds that his wife is ill and that he did not want to work under the manager who had criticized his performance); Fiedler v. Indianhead Truck Line, Inc., 670 F.2d 806, 808–09, 28 FEP 849 (8th Cir. 1982) (the claimant's failure to accept the reinstatement offer terminated the back-pay period notwithstanding personal reasons for rejection, which are not relevant in evaluating the reasonableness of refusal; however, rejection of the offer had no effect on damages accrued from the date of termination until the date the offer expired). *But cf.* Lewis v. Federal Prison Indus., Inc., 953 F.2d 1277, 1281, 58 FEP 127 (11th Cir. 1992) (the claimant was entitled to reject reinstatement because the discrimination caused such distress that he was unfit to return to his old job).

[172]*E.g., Cowen*, 572 F. Supp. at 1581–82 (the offer of a comparable position, giving the plaintiff 1 day to respond, is sufficient to terminate back-pay liability).

[173]*E.g.*, Davis v. Ingersoll Johnson Steel Co., 628 F. Supp. 25, 28–29, 39 FEP 1197 (S.D. Ind. 1985) (the claimant's refusal of a reinstatement offer tolled accrual of back-pay liability even though the offer was vague as to which shift the claimant would work, since he already had been subject to transfer to any shift when he was an employee).

[174]458 U.S. 219, 238–39, 29 FEP 121 (1982).

[175]*Id.* at 238–39; Lightfoot v. Union Carbide Corp., 110 F.3d 898, 908–09, 75 FEP 355 (2d Cir. 1997) (plaintiff's entitlement to back pay terminated when he rejected defendants' unconditional offer of reinstatement into job from which he had been discharged).

(iv.) After-acquired evidence of employee misconduct or fraud.
In *McKennon v. Nashville Banner Publishing Co.*,[176] the Supreme
Court settled a split among several circuits regarding the effect of
after-acquired evidence of employee misconduct.[177] The Court in
McKennon held that sufficient evidence of employee misconduct
will, in most cases, cut off the accrual of back-pay damages. The
plaintiff in *McKennon*, a 62-year-old former secretary, sued her
former employer under the ADEA for discriminatory discharge.[178]
During discovery, the employer learned (from the plaintiff's own

---

[176]513 U.S. 352, 360–61, 66 FEP 1192 (1995).

[177]Before *McKennon*, the circuits, for the most part, took one of three positions:
(1) Sufficient after-acquired evidence of employee misconduct warranting
discharge (whether prehire fraud or on-the-job misconduct) constitutes an
affirmative defense to employer discrimination and grounds for summary
judgment, barring all relief to the employee. *E.g.*, Summers v. State Farm
Mut. Auto. Ins. Co., 864 F.2d 700, 708, 709, 48 FEP 1107 (10th Cir. 1988)
(on-the-job falsification of documents; the seminal after-acquired evidence
case); *accord* Welch v. Liberty Mach. Works, Inc., 23 F.3d 1403, 1405–
06, 3 AD 385 (8th Cir. 1994) (after-acquired evidence of resume/application
fraud bars recovery for discriminatory discharge only if the employer had
a predated policy of never hiring an employee who made misrepresentations on his or her resume or application); Milligan-Jensen v. Michigan
Technological Univ., 975 F.2d 302, 304–05, 59 FEP 1249 (6th Cir. 1992)
(falsified employment application).
(2) Sufficient after-acquired evidence does not entirely insulate an employer
from liability for its discriminatory acts—rather it cuts off liability for
monetary and nonmonetary relief as of the date of discovery. *E.g.*, Kristufek
v. Hussmann Foodservice Co., 985 F.2d 364, 369, 371, 61 FEP 72 (7th
Cir. 1993) (falsified educational qualifications at the time of hire); *accord*
EEOC Office of Legal Counsel, *Revised Enforcement Guidance on Recent
Developments in Disparate Treatment Theory* (July 1992), 3 EEOC COMPL.
MAN. (BNA) N:2135, :2138–39 n.6, :2154–55.
(3) Sufficient after-acquired evidence cuts off prospective relief as of the date
of judgment. *E.g.*, Mardell v. Harleysville Life Ins. Co., 31 F.3d 1221, 1239–
40, 65 FEP 734 (3d Cir. 1994) (providing an exception for information
that would have inevitably been discovered independent of the discrimination investigation and proceedings), *vacated*, 514 U.S. 1034 (1995);
Wallace v. Dunn Constr. Co., 968 F.2d 1174, 1182, 59 FEP 997 (11th Cir.
1992) (same), *vacated*, 514 U.S. 1034 (1995).
On one point, the circuits agreed: where an employee's misconduct would warrant
firing, reinstatement and front pay never are appropriate remedies, regardless of when
the misconduct was discovered. *See, e.g.*, Smith v. General Scanning, Inc., 876 F.2d
1315, 1319 n.2, 50 FEP 58 (7th Cir. 1989) ("[I]t would hardly make sense to order
[the plaintiff] reinstated to a job which he lied to get and from which he properly
could be discharged for that lie."); *cf. Mardell*, 31 F.3d at 1240 ("[W]here an equitable remedy, such as reinstatement, would be particularly invasive of the employer's 'traditional management prerogatives,' the after-acquired evidence may bar that
remedy.") (citation omitted).

[178]*McKennon*, 513 U.S. at 354.

deposition testimony) "that, during her final year of employment, she had copied several confidential documents bearing upon the company's financial condition. . . . Her motivation, she averred, was an apprehension she was about to be fired because of her age."[179] Upon learning this, the employer promptly sent the plaintiff a letter informing her that her actions violated company policy, reiterating that she was terminated.[180] The Sixth Circuit subsequently affirmed summary judgment for the employer[181] based on this after-acquired evidence.[182]

Even though it unanimously reversed the Sixth Circuit's decision, the Supreme Court recognized that the after-acquired evidence was relevant to the damages calculations in the case. The Court articulated the conflicting policy considerations involved: "[A] violation of the ADEA cannot be . . . altogether disregarded,"[183] as the defense would have it, but "that does not mean . . . the employee's own misconduct is irrelevant to all the remedies otherwise available under the statute."[184] Upon weighing these considerations, the Court concluded that after-acquired evidence of employee misconduct, if "of such severity that the employee in fact would have been terminated on those grounds alone if the employer had known of it at the time of the discharge,"[185] goes not to liability, but to the relief available to the plaintiff.[186]

---

[179]*Id.* at 354–55.

[180]*Id.*

[181]9 F.3d 539, 542 & n.6, 63 FEP 354 (6th Cir. 1993).

[182]797 F. Supp. 604, 608 (M.D. Tenn. 1992).

[183]*McKennon*, 513 U.S. at 354–55.

[184]*Id.* at 360–61. The Court specifically outlined the common important public policy—eliminating invidious discrimination in the workplace—behind the ADEA and Title VII. *Id.* at 357. There is no reason, therefore, to limit the Supreme Court's holding in *McKennon* to ADEA actions, as compared to other federal antidiscrimination statutes. On the other hand, state common law claims, such as those for breach of contract or covenant of good faith and fair dealing, lack grounding in such fundamental public policies. The *McKennon* rule need not apply in an employment contract case brought by an employee who procured his job using a falsified resume. In such a case, normal fraudulent-inducement-of-contract argument may apply.

[185]*Id.* at 360–63. The "would have been terminated" standard is consistent with the predominent view of circuit courts pre-*McKennon*.

[186]*Id.* at 358–60. The Court distinguished "mixed-motives" cases as inapposite because, in *after*-acquired evidence cases, by definition, the lawful motive was unknown at the time of the decision. *Id.* at 358. Therefore, the mixed-motives provisions of Title VII do not apply to after-acquired evidence cases. *See* 42 U.S.C. §§ 2000e-2(m), 2000e-5(g)(2)(B) (2000).

In its holding, the Court established three guidelines[187] for the trial courts to use in deciding the relief to be awarded plaintiffs in cases involving after-acquired evidence of wrongdoing:

(1) "[A]s a general rule . . . neither reinstatement nor front pay is an appropriate remedy."[188]

(2) "The beginning point in the trial court's formulation of a remedy should be calculation of back pay from the date of the unlawful discharge to the date the new information was discovered."[189]

(3) The resulting back pay award can be adjusted up or down to account for "extraordinary equitable circumstances that affect the legitimate interests of either party."[190]

Courts continue to apply the Supreme Court's holding in *McKennon*[191] that back-pay liability ends when sufficient evidence of employee misconduct that precedes the discriminatory act is discovered.[192] The after-acquired evidence doctrine does not apply to misconduct occurring post-employment.[193] It is the employer's

---

[187]The Court allowed some leeway for courts to determine the "proper boundaries of remedial relief . . . in the ordinary course of further decisions." 513 U.S. at 360–61.

[188]*Id.* at 360–61 ("It would be both inequitable and pointless to order the reinstatement of someone the employer would have terminated, and will terminate, in any event and upon lawful grounds.").

[189]*Id. McKennon* did not address the effect of after-acquired evidence of material wrongdoing on a plaintiff's entitlement to liquidated damages or compensatory damages for emotional distress. The Fourth Circuit in *Russell v. Microdyne Corp.*, 65 F.3d 1229, 1241, 68 FEP 1602 (4th Cir. 1995), held that after-acquired evidence of material wrongdoing has *no* effect on a plaintiff's entitlement to compensatory damages. The EEOC is in accord. DAILY LAB. REP. (BNA) at E-8 (Dec. 15, 1995) (*McKennon* does not bar punitive or liquidated damages either).

[190]513 U.S. at 360–61.

[191]*Id.* at 360–63.

[192]*E.g.*, Crapp v. City of Miami Beach, 242 F.3d 1017 (11th Cir. 2001) (state agency's suspension of police officer retroactive to day he was terminated for discriminatory reason and made after district court's award of back pay and reinstatement was after-acquired evidence justifying the vacating of the district court's award).

[193]*See, e.g.*, Carr v. Woodbury County Juvenile Detention Ctr., 905 F. Supp. 619, 629, 69 FEP 1101 (N.D. Iowa 1995) (after-acquired evidence doctrine does not apply to former employee's post-employment marijuana use); Ryder v. Westinghouse Elec. Corp., 879 F. Supp. 534, 537 (W.D. Pa. 1995) (after-acquired evidence doctrine does not apply to former employee's alleged post-employment disclosure of confidential information).

burden to prove that it would have discharged the employee for such misconduct.[194]

Although after-acquired evidence does not give the employer the right to summary judgment on liability,[195] such evidence can significantly affect the accrual of monetary relief.[196] Back-pay liability can be limited to a period from the date of the unlawful discharge to the date the after-acquired evidence of misconduct was discovered, and precludes front pay or reinstatement.[197] Nothing in *McKennon* precludes a motion limiting damages under Federal Rule of Civil Procedure 56(d),[198] or an appropriate motion in limine

---

[194]*See, e.g.*, O'Day v. McDonnell Douglas Helicopter Co., 79 F.3d 756, 761, 70 FEP 615 (9th Cir. 1996) (employer must prove by preponderance of evidence that it would have discharged employee for that misconduct); Castle v. Rubin, 78 F.3d 654, 659, 72 FEP 1701 (D.C. Cir. 1996) (court may not deny reinstatement based on after-acquired evidence of misconduct if employer could not have lawfully discharged employee for that conduct).

[195]That is to say, in the ordinary *statutory discrimination case*, summary judgment is not appropriate. A different analysis may apply to nonstatutory contract claims, where the doctrine of "fraud in the inducement," at least in cases of later-discovered prehire fraud, arguably would bar any contractual remedies. *See* Massey v. Trump's Castle Hotel & Casino, 828 F. Supp. 314, 325, 63 FEP 21 (D.N.J. 1993) ("[U]nder New Jersey law, an employer may not be held liable for breach of an employment contract, if it can show that it had the power to void the contract due to reliance on material misrepresentations, even where the employer was unaware of that power when the breach occurred. Unlike the policies underlying the antidiscrimination statutes, there is no competing policy under ordinary contract principles to discourage an employer's breach of contract."); *cf.* Fair Employment Council of Greater Wash., Inc. v. BMC Mktg. Corp., 28 F.3d 1268, 1270–71, 65 FEP 512 (D.C. Cir. 1994) (testers lack standing to sue an employment agency under 42 U.S.C. § 1981 because their "conscious and material misrepresentations" regarding their credentials and intentions would have rendered any contract void); Camp v. Jeffer, Mangels, Butler & Marmaro, 41 Cal. Rptr. 2d 329, 338, 10 IER 1147 (Cal. Ct. App. 1995) (affirming summary judgment for the employer on the employees' public policy wrongful discharge claims based on after-acquired evidence that the employees lied on their employment applications in denying prior felony convictions; in this case, the employer's government contract required that none of its employees be felons).

[196]*See, e.g.*, Schnidrig v. Columbia Mach., Inc., 80 F.3d 1406, 1412, 71 FEP 1763 (9th Cir. 1996) (employer's discovery of after-acquired evidence of employee misconduct did not warrant summary judgment in favor of employer); *Ryder*, 879 at 536 (W.D. Pa. 1995) (after-acquired evidence doctrine does not bar all damages to former employee).

[197]*O'Day*, 79 F.3d at 764 (under *McKennon*, if the plaintiff prevails on his discrimination claim, he would at very least be entitled to back pay from date of his wrongful discharge to date that his former employer learned of his misconduct, as well as to any other remedies not precluded by *McKennon*).

[198]Under Fed. R. Civ. P. 56(d), a court may "make an order specifying the facts that appear without substantial controversy, including the extent to which the amount of damages or other relief is not in controversy." *E.g.*, Reynolds v. S & D Foods,

and/or jury instruction on damages.[199] Thus, in order to discover after-acquired evidence, employers may propound reasonable discovery[200] on matters of employee misconduct.

The courts have applied the reasoning of *McKennon* with equal force when the after-acquired evidence concerns an employee's fraud in the application process.[201] Like evidence of misconduct, after-acquired evidence of application fraud will not completely bar relief or warrant summary judgment for the employer in a discrimination case, despite the argument that the employer never would have hired the employee had it known of the application fraud at the time of hiring.[202] Where the employer proves that it would have discharged the employee when it learned of the fraud in the application,[203] back pay is limited to the period from the date of the unlawful discharge to the date the new information was discovered.[204] A

Inc., 822 F. Supp. 705, 706–07, 708 (D. Kan. 1993) (on the defendant's motion, ordering partial summary judgment of the plaintiff's damages claim; "When ruling on a partial summary judgment motion, the district court may indicate the extent to which the amount of damages is not in controversy.").

[199]For a discussion of motions in limine in general, see 1 JOHN W. STRONG, MCCORMICK ON EVIDENCE § 52, at 202–04 (4th ed. 1992). Such motions have been used, for example, to preclude a plaintiff from presenting evidence regarding front pay in the presence of the jury where the court had determined that the court, rather than the jury, should compute front pay. *E.g.*, Chace v. Champion Spark Plug Co., 725 F. Supp. 868, 871, 51 FEP 542 (D. Md. 1989).

[200]*Cf.* McKennon v. Nashville Banner Publ'g Co., 513 U.S. 352, 362, 66 FEP 1192 (1995) ("The concern that employers might as a routine matter undertake extensive discovery into an employee's background or performance on the job to resist claims under the Act is not an insubstantial one, but we think the authority of the courts to award attorney's fees, mandated under the statute, 29 U.S.C. §§ 216(b), 626(b), and appropriate to invoke the provisions [of Rule 11] of the Federal Rules of Civil Procedure will deter most abuses.").

[201]*See, e.g.*, Russell v. Microdyne Corp., 65 F.3d 1229, 1240, 68 FEP 1602 (4th Cir. 1995) (applying *McKennon* to after-acquired evidence of misrepresentations in resume and application); Wallace v. Dunn Constr. Co., 62 F.3d 374, 379, 68 FEP 990 (11th Cir. 1995) (*McKennon* applies to after-acquired evidence of falsification of employment application regarding prior criminal convictions).

[202]*See, e.g.*, Shattuck v. Kinetic Concepts, Inc., 49 F.3d 1106, 1108, 67 FEP 798 (5th Cir. 1995) (rejecting argument that plaintiff should be barred from recovery because he never would have been hired if employer had known of fraud at time of application); DiPuccio v. United Parcel Serv., 890 F. Supp. 688, 693, 5 AD 561 (N.D. Ohio 1995) (same); McCray v. DPC Indus., 875 F. Supp. 384, 387, 68 FEP 909 (E.D. Tex. 1995) (same).

[203]*Wallace*, 62 F.3d at 379 n.8 (pertinent inquiry is whether employee would have been discharged upon discovery of wrongdoing, not whether he would have been hired in first place).

[204]Russell v. Microdyne Corp., 65 F.3d 1229, 1240, 68 FEP 1602 (4th Cir. 1995); *Wallace*, 62 F.3d at 380.

plaintiff will not be entitled to reinstatement, front pay, and/or injunctive relief where the employee has committed application fraud that would have led to his or her discharge.[205]

(v.) Other events terminating the back-pay period. In termination cases, the accrual of back pay generally will end on the day that the plaintiff would otherwise have been laid off[206] or discharged for some other nondiscriminatory reason.[207] In the context of the closure or sale of a business, the back-pay period will end at the point of the sale or closure[208] unless the plaintiff can

---

[205]*Wallace*, 62 F. 3d at 380–81 (partial summary judgment in favor of employer was appropriate because reinstatement, front pay, and injunctive relief were unavailable in light of after-acquired evidence; summary judgment denied as to back pay because after-acquired evidence limits but does not bar back-pay liability).

[206]*See* EEOC v. Cherry-Burrell Corp., 35 F.3d 356, 361–63, 66 FEP 1749 (8th Cir. 1994) (illustrating the practical difficulties associated with determining whether and when employee would have been laid off absent discrimination); *see also* Criado v. IBM Corp., 145 F.3d 437, 445, 8 AD 336 (1st Cir. 1998) (district court's award of back pay affirmed notwithstanding employer's argument that back-pay period should have ended earlier when plaintiff would have lost her job in RIF even if there had been no discrimination); Bartek v. Urban Redevelopment Auth., 882 F.2d 739, 746–47, 50 FEP 964 (3d Cir. 1989) (an employee is not entitled to back pay after the date on which the position was eliminated); Bhaya v. Westinghouse Elec. Corp., 709 F. Supp. 600, 605, 49 FEP 1369 (E.D. Pa. 1989) ("If plaintiffs would have been laid off for permissible reasons sometime after [their discriminatory discharges], then plaintiffs' damages should have been limited accordingly."), *aff'd*, 922 F.2d 184, 54 FEP 1078 (3d Cir. 1990); Meschino v. IT&T Corp., 661 F. Supp. 254, 257, 43 FEP 1560 (S.D.N.Y. 1987) ("A prevailing plaintiff in an ADEA action may not recover damages for the period after which he would have been terminated for a nondiscriminatory reason."); Nash v. City of Houston Civic Ctr., 39 FEP 1512, 1515 (S.D. Tex. 1985) (tolling back-pay liability as of the date the claimant's position was eliminated in a reorganization, there being no evidence that he was qualified for a position under the reorganization plan), *aff'd in relevant part*, 800 F.2d 491, 41 FEP 1480 (5th Cir. 1986).

[207]*See, e.g.*, Harper v. Godfrey Co., 45 F.3d 143, 149, 66 FEP 1258 (7th Cir. 1995) (ending back-pay liability at time that plaintiffs would have been discharged for misconduct); Cosgrove v. Sears, Roebuck & Co., 68 FEP 1006 (S.D.N.Y. 1995) (ending back-pay period at time plaintiff would have been discharged for poor performance under procedures in employer's management manual), *aff'd*, 72 FEP 192 (2d Cir. 1996); Welch v. University of Tex., 659 F.2d 531, 535, 26 FEP 1725 (5th Cir. 1981) (the back-pay period is cut off when the grant that had funded the plaintiff's position ended); Kiper v. Louisiana State Bd. of Elementary & Secondary Educ., 592 F. Supp. 1343, 1358, 38 FEP 1432 (M.D. La. 1984) (the back-pay period for a plaintiff not named to a temporary position ceased to run once that temporary position ceased to exist, i.e., when a permanent employee was hired), *aff'd mem.*, 778 F.2d 789, 40 FEP 984 (5th Cir. 1985).

[208]*See, e.g.*, Slack v. Havens, 522 F.2d 1091, 1095, 11 FEP 27 (9th Cir. 1975) (sale cuts off the seller's liability; the question of liability (if any) of the buyer is

establish that he or she would have been retained elsewhere in the employer's business[209] or by the purchaser.[210] Where a fixed-term employment contract exists, the expiration of the fixed term often is held to mark the end of the back-pay period.[211] In some circumstances, however, a plaintiff may be entitled to back pay beyond the duration of even a fixed-term employment relationship where the evidence shows that a renewal or other continuation of the employment was likely, but was denied for a discriminatory reason.[212]

---

not before the court); Helbling v. Unclaimed Salvage & Freight Co., 489 F. Supp. 956, 963, 22 FEP 1620 (E.D. Pa. 1980) (the back-pay period ends on date the store closed).

[209]*See, e.g.*, Taylor v. Central Pa. Drug & Alcohol Servs., 890 F. Supp. 360, 375, 72 FEP 1315 (M.D. Pa. 1995) (back pay terminated at time defendant ceased operations).

[210]*E.g.*, Hill v. Spiegel, Inc., 708 F.2d 233, 238, 31 FEP 1532 (6th Cir. 1983) (ADEA plaintiff properly was awarded back pay past the date on which his position was eliminated pursuant to a reorganization, since the plaintiff's successor continued employment with the defendant beyond that date); Gibson v. Mohawk Rubber Co., 695 F.2d 1093, 1098–99, 30 FEP 859 (8th Cir. 1982) (whether plant closure will terminate the back-pay period is a question of fact, but the claimant has the burden of proving that he would have been transferred to another facility within the company's operations); Bonura v. Chase Manhattan Bank, N.A., 629 F. Supp. 353, 356, 43 FEP 163 (S.D.N.Y. 1986) (the sale of the bank department in which the claimants had worked did not toll back-pay liability where evidence indicated that, but for discrimination, the claimants would have retained their positions after the sale or that the defendant would have retained them in another of its departments), *aff'd*, 795 F.2d 276 (2d Cir. 1986). *But cf.* Jackson v. Shell Oil Co., 702 F.2d 197, 202, 31 FEP 686 (9th Cir. 1983) (the back-pay period was not terminated by the claimant's refusal to accept an offer of employment by the purchaser of the plant; the new job was not substantially equivalent to the old position).

[211]*E.g.*, Fitzgerald v. Green Valley Area Educ. Agency, 589 F. Supp. 1130, 1139, 39 FEP 899 (S.D. Iowa 1984) (the back-pay period ended for an instructor upon termination of the school year for which he was unlawfully denied employment, as there was no evidence that the position would have been available for the succeeding school year).

[212]*See* Kirsch v. Fleet Street, Ltd., 148 F.3d 149, 167–68, 77 FEP 318 (2d Cir. 1998) (back pay cut off at date of plaintiff's retirement); Boehms v. Crowell, 139 F.3d 452, 461–62, 76 FEP 1368 (5th Cir. 1998) (back-pay award cut off as of date of plaintiff's resignation; constructive-discharge analogy used to determine ending date of back-pay award); Roberson v. Mullins, 876 F. Supp. 100, 104 (W.D. Va. 1995) (back pay stopped at date on which plaintiff had stated he would retire); Wangsness v. Watertown Sch. Dist. 14-4, 541 F. Supp. 332, 339–40, 29 FEP 375 (D.S.D. 1982) (the back-pay period is not limited to the term of the claimant's fixed-term teaching contract); *see also* Walker v. Ford Motor Co., 684 F.2d 1355, 1361–62, 29 FEP 1259 (11th Cir. 1982) (it is only a rebuttable presumption that the back-pay period terminates at the end of a fixed-term contract).

Back pay will also end if the plaintiff dies,[213] retires,[214] or otherwise becomes ineligible for continuing employment.[215] Some courts have terminated the back-pay period based on a theory that it would be speculative to assume that the plaintiff would have continued working for the defendant longer than an average employee would.[216] Therefore, evidence that other employees work for the employer only for a specified period of time may, in some cases, cut off back-pay damages. Whether back pay is permanently terminated when an employee is fired for misconduct or voluntarily quits interim employment remains a contested issue.[217]

III. FRONT PAY

To compensate for future damages, reinstatement (or instatement) is the preferred, presumptive remedy for a discrimination victim; it makes the plaintiff whole by putting him or her in the position he or she would have occupied in the absence of discrimination.[218] But where reinstatement is not feasible, an award of front

---

[213]*E.g.*, Hodgson v. Ideal Corrugated Box Co., 10 FEP 744, 752–53 (N.D.W. Va. 1974) (ADEA).

[214]*E.g., Hodgson*, 10 FEP at 752.

[215]*See, e.g.*, Mims v. Wilson, 514 F.2d 106, 110 n.6, 10 FEP 1359 (5th Cir. 1975) (if a plaintiff commits a crime that would be cause for discharge, back pay would terminate as of date of crime). Deductions and offsets for periods of unavailability are discussed in Section IV.C.4.c *infra*.

[216]*E.g.*, EEOC v. Mike Smith Pontiac GMC, Inc., 896 F.2d 524, 530, 52 FEP 729 (11th Cir. 1990) (limiting back pay to the average tenure of sales employees); EEOC v. Spokane Concrete Prods., 534 F. Supp. 518, 526, 28 FEP 423 (E.D. Wash. 1982) (terminating the back-pay period based on the defendant's high employee turnover rate caused by the physically demanding nature of the position).

[217]*See* Johnson v. Spencer Press of Me., Inc., 364 F.3d 368, 382 (1st Cir. 2004) (back pay is not permanently terminated because "[h]ad there been no discrimination at employer A, the employee would never have come to work (or have been fired from employer B")); *cf.* EEOC v. Dial Corp., 2006 U.S. App. LEXIS 28507 (8th Cir. Nov. 17, 2006) (genuine issue of material fact whether employee would have been terminated under screening policy that employer asserted would have detected previously undisclosed felony conviction); Patterson v. P.H.P. Healthcare Corp., 90 F.3d 927 (5th Cir. 1996) (involuntary termination ended entitlement to back pay until there is new interim employment); Brady v. Thurston Motor Lines, Inc., 753 F.2d 1269, 1279 (4th Cir. 1985) (back pay is terminated if employee unjustifiably quits interim employment and resumes with new interim employment).

[218]*See, e.g.*, Julian v. City of Houston, 314 F.3d 721, 728, 90 FEP 887 (5th Cir. 2002) (district court required to first determine whether employee could be instated

pay—in essence, a continuation of back pay under § 706(g) beyond the date of judgment[219]—may be appropriate to compensate the plaintiff for the future effects of discrimination.[220]

---

to position to which city failed to promote him, in violation of the ADEA, before it court could consider front pay instead of reinstatement); Kucia v. Southeast Cmty. Action Corp., 284 F.3d 944, 948–49, 88 FEP 861 (8th Cir. 2002) (front pay is an exceptional award under Title VII; reinstatement should be the norm); Squires v. Bonser, 54 F.3d 168, 172 (3d Cir. 1995) ("Reinstatement advances the policy goals of make-whole relief and deterrence in a way which money damages cannot."); Goldstein v. Manhattan Indus., Inc., 758 F.2d 1435, 1449, 37 FEP 1217 (11th Cir. 1985) (reinstatement rather than front pay is appropriate since the employer was willing to reemploy the discharged plaintiff in a job in which he could function effectively); Blim v. Western Elec. Co., 731 F.2d 1473, 1479, 34 FEP 757 (10th Cir. 1984) (front pay should be avoided whenever possible, and reinstatement should be ordered; there existed no undue hostility between the parties); Shea v. Icelandair, 925 F. Supp. 1014, 1030, 70 FEP 1544 (S.D.N.Y. 1996) ("Courts strongly favor reinstatement over alternative forms of relief."); *see also* Ramos v. Davis & Geck, Inc., 167 F.3d 727, 733 (1st Cir. 1999) (affirming denial of front pay under Puerto Rico law, court stated: "To collect front pay in the absence of a request for reinstatement, [plaintiff] had to prove that he could not return to work . . . because of the discriminatory acts of the [employer]."). *See generally* Chapter 39 (Injunctive and Affirmative Relief).

[219]*See* Cassino v. Reichhold Chems., Inc., 817 F.2d 1338, 1346 (9th Cir. 1987) ("Front pay is an award of future lost earnings to make a victim of discrimination whole.").

[220]*See* Bruso v. United Airlines, Inc., 239 F.3d 848, 862, 84 FEP 1780 (7th Cir. 2001) ("[w]hen reinstating a successful Title VII plaintiff is not feasible, front pay is usually available as an alternative remedy"); Gotthardt v. National R.R. Passenger Corp., 191 F.3d 1148, 1156, 80 FEP 1528 (9th Cir. 1999) (where sexual harassment resulted in posttraumatic stress syndrome, district court did not abuse discretion by ordering front pay in lieu of reinstatement); Kelley v. Airborne Freight Corp., 140 F.3d 335, 352–54, 76 FEP 1340 (1st Cir. 1998) (front-pay award affirmed along with district court's finding that reinstatement was "impracticable in the extreme"); Walther v. Lone Star Gas Co., 952 F.2d 119, 127, 59 FEP 848 (5th Cir. 1992) (if the plaintiff shows that reinstatement is not feasible, front pay can be awarded); Duke v. Uniroyal, Inc., 928 F.2d 1413, 1423, 55 FEP 816 (4th Cir. 1991) ("When reinstatement is not appropriate, then other remedies may be considered. We join virtually all circuits that have considered the subject in concluding that front pay is an available remedy to complete the panoply of remedies available to avoid the potential of future loss."); Blum v. Witco Chem. Corp., 829 F.2d 367, 373–74, 46 FEP 306 (3d Cir. 1987) (front pay is available as an equitable remedy under the ADEA when reinstatement does not fully compensate the victim or is impractical); *Cassino*, 817 F.2d at 1346 (the court may elect to award front pay under the ADEA if reinstatement is not feasible); Nord v. United States Steel Corp., 758 F.2d 1462, 1473, 37 FEP 1232 (11th Cir. 1985) (front pay is proper if the court determines that, due to extraordinary circumstances, reinstatement is inappropriate); Shea v. Icelandair, 925 F. Supp. 1014, 1030, 70 FEP 1544 (S.D.N.Y. 1996) ("[R]einstatement does not always afford a practicable remedy for either the plaintiff or the defendant."). *But cf.* McKnight v. General Motors Corp., 908 F.2d 104, 116, 53 FEP 505 (7th Cir.

Factors considered by the courts in determining whether reinstatement, rather than front pay, should be ordered include whether the employer is still in business, whether the parties agree that reinstatement is a viable remedy, whether the plaintiff has acquired other work,[221] whether the plaintiff's career goals have changed, and whether the plaintiff is able to return to work.[222] Courts have allowed front pay as a remedy for plaintiffs whose inability to return to work is the result of the employer's unlawful conduct.[223]

Occasionally, even where injunctive relief is granted, continuing injury may occur that front pay can redress.[224] For example, courts have awarded both front pay and reinstatement so long as they do

---

1990) (dictum; although "[t]he logic of [front pay], if the purpose of Title VII's remedial scheme is indeed to make the plaintiff whole, is undeniable[,] . . . the premise can be doubted, as can the propriety, under a statute confined to equitable relief, of an award of what is realistically damages for lost future earnings—a legal rather than an equitable remedy"). Front pay under the ADEA is discussed extensively in Chapter 12 (Age).

[221]*See* Brocklehurst v. PPG Indus., Inc., 865 F. Supp. 1253, 1266, 66 FEP 545 (E.D. Mich. 1994) (within months of his discharge, plaintiff obtained better-paying job, and while benefits at subsequent job were not as great, this is not controlling on issue of propriety of front pay), *rev'd on other grounds*, 123 F.3d 890, 74 FEP 984 (6th Cir. 1997).

[222]*See* Ogden v. Wax Works, Inc., 29 F. Supp. 2d 1003, 1017, 78 FEP 973 (N.D. Iowa 1998) (reinstatement would be counterproductive to defendant and an empty remedy to plaintiff who suffered a devastating blow to her self-esteem as a result of her dismissal), *aff'd*, 214 F.3d 999, 82 FEP 1821 (8th Cir. 2000).

[223]*See* Salitros v. Chrysler Corp., 306 F.3d 562, 572, 13 AD 1057 (8th Cir. 2002) (successful ADA plaintiff could recover front pay for the time he was unable to work because employer's retaliatory acts rendered him psychologically unable to return to the workplace); Farley v. Nationwide Mut. Ins. Co., 197 F.3d 1322, 1339, 10 AD 87 (11th Cir. 1999) ("we find that Farley's hostile work environment, coupled with his stress-induced disabilities, created sufficient special circumstances to support the trial court's award of front pay in lieu of reinstatement"); Gotthardt v. National R.R. Passenger Corp., 191 F.3d 1148, 1156, 80 FEP 1528 (9th Cir. 1999) (despite being treated for PTSD for a short period prior to the discrimination alleged, testimony from treating and expert psychologist rendered it plausible that the hostile work environment caused plaintiff's disability); Prine v. Sioux City Cmty. Sch. Dist., 95 F. Supp. 2d 1005, 1012, 82 FEP 1716 (N.D. Iowa 2000) ("[t]he court also finds—on the basis of Prine's testimony and the testimony of her psychiatrist—that Prine's ability to work full-time is presently foreclosed by the physical, mental and emotional trauma she continues to suffer as a result of post-traumatic stress disorder").

[224]*See* United States v. Lee Way Motor Freight, Inc., 625 F.2d 918, 932–33, 20 FEP 1345 (10th Cir. 1979) (rejecting the argument that back pay should terminate on the date of a preliminary injunction); EEOC v. Steamfitters Local 638, 542 F.2d 579, 590–91, 13 FEP 705 (2d Cir. 1976) (it is reversible error to terminate back pay on the date of court-ordered injunctive relief).

not provide compensation for the same period of time.[225] In class action suits concerning promotion discrimination, front pay has been awarded where it was expected that a significant time would elapse before the discriminatees could assume their "rightful place" in the workplace.[226] In individual cases, front pay has been awarded where there was no vacancy to which the plaintiff could be promoted immediately,[227] or where reinstatement would displace or disrupt the employment of plaintiff's replacement.[228]

---

[225]*See* Selgas v. American Airlines, Inc., 104 F.3d 9, 13, 72 FEP 1457 (1st Cir. 1997) (awards of both front pay and reinstatement appropriate since each covered separate and distinct periods of time).

[226]*E.g.*, Thompson v. Sawyer, 678 F.2d 257, 293, 28 FEP 1614 (D.C. Cir. 1982) (front pay, while appropriate, should persist "only until the wrongs for which the plaintiffs are owed back pay have been righted"; suggesting, in remanding the matter, that front pay should terminate at the point where the plaintiffs received 50% of the total number of openings that had occurred, and had been filled by males, during the actual period of discrimination); Wattleton v. Ladish Co., 520 F. Supp. 1329, 1349, 1350, 1356, 29 FEP 1307 (E.D. Wis. 1981) (in the context of discriminatory union seniority systems, an award of front pay is appropriate until the discriminatees obtain their rightful place by being allowed to transfer between union jurisdictions without loss of carryover seniority), *aff'd sub nom.* Wattleton v. Boiler Makers, 686 F.2d 586, 29 FEP 1389 (7th Cir. 1982); Chewning v. Seamans, 28 FEP 1735, 1740–41 (D.D.C. 1979) (a class member is entitled to front pay until he or she reaches his or her "rightful place" of equivalent grade, or refuses promotion to the same); Stamps v. Detroit Edison Co., 30 FEP 1805, 1813–14 (E.D. Mich. 1978) (a class member is entitled to front pay until he or she reaches his or her rightful position or its equivalent, or refuses promotion to the same, or to any job in the relevant job progression line, or to any job paying more than the entitlement rate).

[227]*See, e.g.*, Gaddy v. Abex Corp., 884 F.2d 312, 319, 50 FEP 1333 (7th Cir. 1989) (reinstatement is warranted absent exceptional circumstances demonstrating that the position is no longer available or where a continued reduction in force occurs); Pitre v. Western Elec. Co., 843 F.2d 1262, 1278–79, 51 FEP 656 (10th Cir. 1988) ("Front pay is a substitute for immediate promotion, which cannot occur because there are no positions currently available."); Briseno v. Central Technical Cmty. Coll. Area, 739 F.2d 344, 348, 37 FEP 57 (8th Cir. 1984) (a Mexican American discriminatorily denied a full-time position is entitled to front pay until assigned to that position or a comparable one); Velez v. Devine, 28 FEP 671, 674 (D.D.C. 1982) (a female employee discriminatorily denied promotion is entitled to pay and benefits of the position sought until promoted to an equivalent position).

[228]*See* Ray v. Iuka Special Mun. Separate Sch. Dist., 51 F.3d 1246, 1254, 67 FEP 1348 (5th Cir. 1995) (facts that there were no current openings in school district such that reinstatement would mandate displacement of existing employee and that plaintiff almost immediately found substantially similar employment were properly relied upon by district court in denying reinstatement). *But see* Shea v. Icelandair, 925 F. Supp. 1014, 1030, 70 FEP 1544 (S.D.N.Y. 1996) (reinstatement ordered despite the need to move the plaintiff's replacement to another position).

Some courts have justified front pay upon receipt of proof that reinstatement would not be feasible due to antagonism or hostility between the plaintiff and the employer.[229] Further, courts have awarded front pay as a remedy for an employer's aggravated or vindictive behavior.[230]

Front pay will be denied where the employer can prove that, for some legitimate, nondiscriminatory reason, the plaintiff would

---

[229]*E.g.*, Tadlock v. Powell, 291 F.3d 541, 548, 88 FEP 1734 (8th Cir. 2002) ("Before awarding front pay, a district court must find 'the animosity is so extreme that it makes an amicable and productive work relationship impossible.' ") (citing Cox v. Dubuque Bank & Trust Co., 163 F.3d 492, 498, 78 FEP 1229 (8th Cir. 1998)); Green v. Administrators of Tulane Educ. Fund, 284 F.3d 642, 658, 89 FEP 582 (5th Cir. 2002) (court appropriately awarded front pay to successful Title VII plaintiff, former university employee who alleged that her supervisor sexually harassed her after their consensual sexual relationship ended: reinstatement was not feasible due to the discord); Spulak v. K Mart Corp., 894 F.2d 1150, 1157–58, 51 FEP 1652 (10th Cir. 1990) (front pay, rather than reinstatement, was appropriate where the employee was forced to retire because he would be unable properly to supervise the employees in front of whom he was humiliated, and the antagonism between the parties had increased as a result of litigation characterized by the district court as " 'bitterly contested' "); Brooks v. Woodline Motor Freight, Inc., 852 F.2d 1061, 1066, 47 FEP 654 (8th Cir. 1988) (front pay is appropriate because "substantial animosity" existed between the plaintiff and his employer, their "relationship was not likely to improve, and the nature of the business required a high degree of mutual trust and confidence"); Goss v. Exxon Office Sys. Co., 747 F.2d 885, 890, 36 FEP 344 (3d Cir. 1984) (after the case generated acrimony, front pay is appropriate because of the likelihood of continuing disharmony between the female plaintiff holding a sensitive job as a sales representative and her employer); Whittlesey v. Union Carbide Corp., 742 F.2d 724, 729, 35 FEP 1089 (2d Cir. 1984) (reinstatement was inappropriate because of hostility generated by the litigation); Fadhl v. City & County of S.F., 741 F.2d 1163, 1167, 35 FEP 1291 (9th Cir. 1984) (a plaintiff properly is awarded front pay if the plaintiff is found otherwise qualified for permanent employment and if reinstatement would not be appropriate in light of antagonism between her and her employer), *overruled on other grounds by* Price Waterhouse v. Hopkins, 490 U.S. 228 (1989). *Contra* Philipp v. ANR Freight Sys., 61 F.3d 669, 674, 70 FEP 1347 (8th Cir. 1995) (given that new manager, who was not employed when plaintiff was discharged, agreed to work hard to make plaintiff part of management team and that plaintiff got along well with only other remaining supervisor, court found insufficient showing of animosity or friction to disturb lower court's award of reinstatement); Squires v. Bonser, 54 F.3d 168, 174–75 (3d Cir. 1995) (finding that factors considered by district court in denying reinstatement, such as incidents of poor performance by plaintiff, tension that would result from plaintiff resuming work with defendants, and plaintiff's ability to secure other employment, did not present special circumstances justifying denial of reinstatement).

[230]*See* Mota v. University of Tex. Houston Health Sci. Ctr., 261 F.3d 512, 527 (5th Cir. 2001) (affirming 15-year front-pay award for retaliation claim where president, after losing trial, sent e-mail to all 8,000 university employees stating that despite adverse verdict, plaintiff "was not fired, but rather failed to return to his faculty duties upon expiration of leave that he had requested and was granted by UT-Houston"); Whittlesey v. Union Carbide Corp., 742 F.2d 724, 729, 35 FEP 1089 (2d Cir. 1984)

no longer have been employed at the time of judgment, particularly where the employer experienced a reduction in workforce,[231] the employer closed the facility in which the plaintiff worked or sought work,[232] the position sought by the plaintiff was eliminated,[233] or the plaintiff is otherwise unavailable for reemployment by no fault of defendant.[234] On the other hand, the fact that employment was "at-will" does not alone make an award of front pay inherently speculative.[235]

Front pay typically will be denied (as will reinstatement) when an employer discovers, after the discriminatory act, that the employee engaged in either sufficient prehire fraud that would have justified not hiring the plaintiff, or that post-hire misconduct would have led to his or her discharge.[236] The severity of the misconduct

---

(reinstatement was inappropriate because of hostility generated by the litigation). *See generally* Chapter 39 (Injunctive and Affirmative Relief).

[231]*See, e.g.*, Burns v. Texas City Ref., Inc., 890 F.2d 747, 753, 51 FEP 1029 (5th Cir. 1989) (front pay denied where the employer's sale of its assets resulted in termination of nearly all employees). *But see* Davis v. Combustion Eng'g, Inc., 742 F.2d 916, 922–23, 35 FEP 975 (6th Cir. 1984) (the 59-year-old plaintiff properly was awarded 6 years' front pay notwithstanding potential layoff in the employer's workforce).

[232]*See, e.g.*, Tyler v. Union Oil Co. of Cal., 304 F.3d 379, 89 FEP 1226 (5th Cir. 2002) (front pay properly cut off at date that plaintiffs' former unit went out of business); Schrand v. Federal Pac. Elec. Co., 851 F.2d 152, 159, 47 FEP 273 (6th Cir. 1988) (front pay denied because the employee would have been terminated when the office in which he worked closed); Dillon v. Coles, 746 F.2d 998, 1006, 36 FEP 159 (3d Cir. 1984) (plaintiff properly denied front pay because the government employer closed the juvenile detention camp and there were disputed issues as to the applicant's competency and ability to get along with co-workers and a supervisor).

[233]*See, e.g.*, Bartek v. Urban Redevelopment Auth., 882 F.2d 739, 747, 50 FEP 964 (3d Cir. 1989) (in a promotion denial case, the last position that discriminatorily was denied the plaintiff had been eliminated by the time of judgment, and the plaintiff failed to identify a comparable position that existed after that time). *But see* Williams v. Pharmacia, Inc., 137 F.3d 944, 951, 76 FEP 310 (7th Cir. 1998) (noting for the first time in the Seventh Circuit that front pay is an appropriate remedy where reinstatement was unavailable because subsequent merger had eliminated plaintiff's position); Woodhouse v. Magnolia Hosp., 92 F.3d 248, 257, 71 FEP 1804 (5th Cir. 1996) (although plaintiff's previous position was eliminated, district court did not err in ordering reinstatement: plaintiff was qualified for a variety of jobs that were available, defendant did not show that rehiring plaintiff for a different position was infeasible, plaintiff requested reinstatement, and the parties were free to negotiate front pay instead of reinstatement).

[234]Schick v. Illinois Dep't of Human Servs., 307 F.3d 605, 90 FEP 78 (7th Cir. 2002) (incarcerated plaintiff could not be reinstated, therefore front pay was inappropriate).

[235]Julian v. City of Houston, Tex., 314 F.3d 721, 90 FEP 887 (5th Cir. 2002) (employment-at-will doctrine does not function as a bar to front pay, or render such an award speculative).

[236]*See* McKennon v. Nashville Banner Publ'g Co., 513 U.S. 352, 361–362, 66 FEP 1192 (1995) (front pay inappropriate where an employee engaged in wrongdoing

will determine whether an award of front pay (or reinstatement) is appropriate.[237]

Front pay also has been denied where, as of the time of trial, the plaintiff was unavailable for employment because he or she had entered school full time,[238] refused reinstatement,[239] or failed to seek substantially equivalent employment with reasonable diligence.[240] Front pay may also be denied if the court determines that front pay would result in a windfall for the plaintiff.[241] Courts are

---

for which the employer establishes he or should would have been terminated on those grounds alone); *see also* Section II.B.2.b.iv *supra*.

[237]*Compare* Moore v. University of Notre Dame, 22 F. Supp. 2d 896, 906, 78 FEP 62 (N.D. Ind. 1998) (the after-acquired evidence doctrine does not bar front pay to discharged employee where alleged wrongdoing standing alone was not severe enough to justify discharge) *with* Wallace v. Dunn Constr. Co., 62 F.3d 374, 380, 68 FEP 990 (11th Cir. 1995) (neither reinstatement nor front pay appropriate remedy for employee who was found to have lied on employment application).

[238]*E.g.*, Floca v. Homcare Health Servs., 845 F.2d 108, 113, 46 FEP 1433 (5th Cir. 1988) (the plaintiff entered law school prior to judgment and therefore was not available for employment).

[239]*E.g.*, Stanfield v. Answering Serv., 867 F.2d 1290, 1295–96, 50 FEP 1151 (11th Cir. 1989) (the plaintiff refused the employer's offer of reinstatement for personal reasons not within the employer's control); *cf.* Kucia v. Southeast Ark. Cmty. Action Corp., 284 F.3d 944, 88 FEP 861 (8th Cir. 2002) (remand for district court to enter proper findings supporting decision to award 2 years' front pay, in light of employer's unconditional offer to rehire her). *But see* Lewis v. Federal Prison Indus., Inc., 953 F.2d 1277, 1281, 58 FEP 127 (11th Cir. 1992) (the claimant is entitled to reject reinstatement and to collect front pay where the discrimination caused such distress that the claimant was unfit for the job).

[240]*E.g.*, Sellers v. Delgado Cmty. Coll., 902 F.2d 1189, 1196, 53 FEP 127 (5th Cir. 1990) ("In view of the magistrate's finding of fact that [the plaintiff] did not exercise reasonable diligence to obtain substantially equivalent employment and his conclusion that she was consequently not entitled to back pay for most of the period after she left [the defendant-employer], we uphold the magistrate's denial of front pay."); Fournerat v. Beaumont Indep. Sch. Dist., 6 F. Supp. 2d 612, 614 (E.D. Tex. 1998) (equitable remedy of front pay may be denied or reduced where employee fails to mitigate damages); Griffin v. George B. Buck Consulting Actuaries, Inc., 566 F. Supp. 881, 882, 32 FEP 1884 (S.D.N.Y. 1983) (front pay is unavailable to an unlawfully rejected job applicant who is no longer seeking employment). *But see* Maxfield v. Sinclair Int'l, 766 F.2d 788, 796, 38 FEP 442 (3d Cir. 1985) (upholding front-pay award notwithstanding the failure of a 65-year-old employee receiving Social Security and other income to seek employment); Gotthardt v. National R.R. Passenger Corp., 191 F.3d 1148, 1156–57, 80 FEP 1528 (9th Cir. 1999) (no clear error in court's award of front pay upon its finding that plaintiff could not mitigate due to health conditions brought about by post-traumatic stress syndrome).

[241]*See* Ford v. Rigidply Rafters, Inc., 984 F. Supp. 386, 392 (D. Md. 1997) ("Because front pay can result in an unfair windfall for the plaintiff, it must be granted sparingly.").

divided on whether an award of liquidated damages may adversely affect a plaintiff's entitlement to front pay.[242]

Where front pay is appropriate, it is calculated in many respects in the same manner as back pay, with "the front pay pool [constructed] as a continuation of the back pay pool."[243] Accordingly, lost pension and other fringe benefits may be recoverable as part of front pay,[244] as may anticipated bonuses and profit sharing, if not speculative and if adequately proved.[245] Front pay will be

---

[242]*Compare* Hadley v. VAM PTS, 44 F.3d 372, 376 (5th Cir. 1995) (in ADEA and Title VII cases, substantial liquidated or punitive damage award may indicate that additional award of front pay is inappropriate or excessive), Powers v. Grinnell Corp., 915 F.2d 34, 43, 53 FEP 1814 (1st Cir. 1990) (the district court properly considered its award of liquidated damages as a factor to deny front pay) *and* Graefenhain v. Pabst Brewing Co., 870 F.2d 1198, 1205, 49 FEP 829 (7th Cir. 1989) (a substantial liquidated damages award would make front pay less appropriate) *with* Price v. Marshall Erdman & Assocs., Inc., 966 F.2d 320, 326, 59 FEP 462 (7th Cir. 1992) ("while previous cases . . . suggest that the presence or absence of a liquidated damages award is material in determining entitlement to front pay, we think it should play only a very small role in that determination"), Castle v. Sangamo Weston, Inc., 837 F.2d 1550, 1562, 46 FEP 139 (11th Cir. 1988) (liquidated damages may not be factored into the front-pay determination because the punitive nature of such damages means "they are awarded to plaintiffs in addition to compensatory or actual damages") *and* Ogden v. Wax Works, Inc., 29 F. Supp. 2d 1003, 1018–19, 78 FEP 973 (N.D. Iowa 1998) (an award of punitive damages in Title VII case should be neutral factor not affecting court's decision to award front pay), *aff'd*, 214 F.3d 999, 82 FEP 1821 (8th Cir. 2000).

[243]Thompson v. Sawyer, 678 F.2d 257, 292–93, 28 FEP 1614 (D.C. Cir. 1982) ("The front pay formula must mirror the back pay formula."); *see also* Wattleton v. Ladish Co., 520 F. Supp. 1329, 1356, 29 FEP 1307 (E.D. Wis. 1981) (front pay should be calculated in a manner similar to that utilized for back pay), *aff'd sub nom.* Wattleton v. Boiler Makers, 686 F.2d 586, 29 FEP 1389 (7th Cir. 1982).

[244]*E.g.*, Fite v. First Tenn. Prod. Credit Ass'n, 861 F.2d 884, 894, 48 FEP 449 (6th Cir. 1988) (retirement benefits included), *overruled in part on other grounds*, Davis v. Mutual Life Ins. Co., 6 F.3d 367 (6th Cir. 1993); Johnson v. Philadelphia Elec. Co., 709 F. Supp. 98, 104, 49 FEP 1535 (E.D. Pa. 1989) (future lost pay and benefits awarded to the prevailing Title VII plaintiff).

[245]*See* Sharkey v. Lasmo, 214 F.3d 371, 375, 84 FEP 967 (2d Cir. 2000) (plaintiff entitled to equitable relief to compensate for lost pension entitlement); Skalka v. Fernald Envtl. Restoration Mgmt. Corp., 178 F.3d 414, 425 (6th Cir. 1999) (defendant presented insufficient evidence that the pension component of the damages was speculative, thus, pension benefits were awarded as part of front pay); Lussier v. Runyon, 50 F.3d 1103, 1105, 4 AD 265 (1st Cir. 1995) (holding that it is within trial court's discretion to tailor front-pay award to Rehabilitation Act plaintiff to incorporate increase in Veterans Administration benefits generated by adverse employment action); Partington v. Broyhill Furniture Indus., Inc., 999 F.2d 269, 273, 62 FEP 534 (7th Cir. 1993) (allowing a monetary award that included the employee's estimate of bonuses and profit sharing, but criticizing the employee's proof, which

denied if a calculation or accounting would be "hopelessly speculative."[246] Lost opportunities for promotion may affect the proper
level of front pay.[247]

---

consisted only of the employee's assumption that he would have continued to receive bonuses and profit sharing at the same level as in his last years at the company); Moore v. University of Notre Dame, 22 F. Supp. 2d 896, 905, 78 FEP 62
(N.D. Ind. 1998) (in ADEA suit brought by discharged football coach, court may
consider loss of benefits in front-pay analysis).

[246]Peyton v. DiMario, 287 F.3d 1121, 1128–29, 88 FEP 1041 (D.C. Cir. 2002)
(award of 26 years of front pay to a 34-year-old non-incapacitated former employee
was unduly speculative—subjective intent to remain at the job until retirement did
not justify an award for remainder of work life); Davoll v. Webb, 194 F.3d 1116,
1143, 9 AD 1533 (10th Cir. 1999) (front pay must specify end date based on more
than mere guesswork; however, district court abused discretion in awarding only 2
years' front pay, where plaintiff's expert gave uncontested testimony suggesting longer
period might be appropriate); Williams v. Pharmacia, Inc., 137 F.3d 944, 954, 76
FEP 310 (7th Cir. 1998) (front-pay award must be limited in duration, demonstrating
with reasonable degree of certainty how long plaintiff would have been expected to
work for defendant, based upon reasonable period of time in which plaintiff, using
reasonable diligence, should have found comparable employment); Suggs v.
ServiceMaster Educ. Food Mgmt., 72 F.3d 1228, 1235, 69 FEP 1270 (6th Cir. 1996)
("the court must make its award of front pay reasonably specific as to duration and
amount"); McKnight v. General Motors Corp., 973 F.2d 1366, 1372, 64 FEP 1071
(7th Cir. 1992) (the longer the period of time for which award is sought, the more
speculative it becomes); Ogden v. Wax Works, Inc., 29 F. Supp. 2d 1003, 1012, 78
FEP 973 (N.D. Iowa 1998) (though front-pay award will have some degree of speculation, it should not be "unduly speculative"), aff'd, 214 F.3d 999, 82 FEP 1821 (8th
Cir. 2000); Emmenegger v. Bull Moose Tube Co., 13 F. Supp. 2d 980, 1001 (E.D.
Mo. 1998) (court will not award front pay based on guesswork); Ward v. Papa's Pizza
To Go, Inc., 907 F. Supp. 1535, 1543–44 (S.D. Ga. 1995) (where plaintiff sought
monetary relief but not reinstatement, there was no definable terminating point for
calculating front-pay award; therefore, court declined "to allow computation of an
award spanning the rest of Plaintiff's working life"), aff'd in part, vacated in part
and remanded on other grounds, 197 F.3d 929 (8th Cir. 1999). But see Gotthardt v.
National R.R. Passenger Corp., 191 F.3d 1148, 1156–57, 80 FEP 1528 (9th Cir. 1999)
(11-year front-pay period not speculative where plaintiff testified about her intention
to work until her 70th birthday); Morse v. Southern Union Co., 174 F.3d 917, 927,
79 FEP 1317 (8th Cir. 1999) (no abuse of discretion to award front pay in light of
conflicting testimony about how long plaintiff would have continued to work); Barbour
v. Merrill, 48 F.3d 1270, 1280, 67 FEP 369 (D.C. Cir. 1995) ("[A] district court should
not refuse to award front pay merely because some speculation about future earnings
is necessary, or because the parties have introduced conflicting evidence."); Mitchell
v. Sisters of Charity, 924 F. Supp. 793, 803 (S.D. Tex. 1996) ("Calculations of front
pay cannot be totally accurate because they are prospective and necessarily speculative in nature."); Young v. Lukens Steel Co., 881 F. Supp. 962, 976–77, 71 FEP 739
(E.D. Pa. 1994) (employer not entitled to reduction of front-pay award despite argument that total economic loss figure from employee's discharge date up to age 65
included back pay; it was beyond district court's discretion "to attempt to enter the
jury deliberation room and guess how and why the jury used" the specific figure).

[247]See Abuan v. Level 3 Commc'ns, Inc., 353 F.3d 1158, 93 FEP 94 (10th Cir.
2003) (district court did not abuse discretion in finding that reinstatement was

As with back pay, the court may reduce front pay by the amount of any post-termination payments that otherwise would not have been received.[248]

Front pay differs from back pay in one important respect: it by definition is a remedy for losses that have not yet occurred. Front pay therefore creates a tension between two core principles of damages assessment: (1) that the incentive to mitigate damages be preserved,[249] and (2) that monetary awards not be unduly speculative.[250] Some courts, accordingly, have reversed long-term front-pay awards.[251] Periods of allowable front pay vary, with the determination normally based on facts such as the plaintiff's skills, age,

---

infeasible, but erred in calculating sum by not taking into account effect of discriminatory acts on plaintiff's rate of promotion).

[248]*See, e.g.,* Potence v. Hazleton Area Sch. Dist., 357 F.3d 366, 93 FEP 193 (3d Cir. 2004) (jury may, but is not required, to exclude retirement benefits from front-pay award); Graefenhain v. Pabst Brewing Co., 870 F.2d 1198, 1210, 49 FEP 829 (7th Cir. 1989) (remanded for determination of the proper setoff for certain pension plan payments).

[249]*Suggs,* 72 F.3d at 1235 n.4 (if district court determines that reinstatement is inappropriate and front pay is warranted, the court may wish to consider continued court-monitoring approach); Whittlesey v. Union Carbide Corp., 742 F.2d 724, 728, 35 FEP 1089 (2d Cir. 1984) ("an award of front pay in lieu of reinstatement does not contemplate that a plaintiff will sit idly by and be compensated for doing nothing, because the duty to mitigate damages by seeking employment elsewhere significantly limits the amount of front pay available") (citation omitted); Stafford v. Electronic Data Sys. Corp., 749 F. Supp. 781, 791–92 (E.D. Mich. 1990) (ordering court-monitored installment payments of future damages—in lieu of a lump-sum award of 23 years' front pay—to ensure that the plaintiff "fulfills his continuing duty to mitigate his losses in the future").

[250]*See, e.g.,* Julian v. City of Houston, Tex., 314 F.3d 721, 729, 90 FEP 887 (5th Cir. 2002) (district court abused its discretion by determining that the fact of at-will employment rendered any award of front pay speculative; at-will employment is merely a factor to consider, and not an absolute bar, to an award of front pay); Hybert v. Hearst Corp., 900 F.2d 1050, 1056, 1057, 52 FEP 1238 (7th Cir. 1990) (affirming jury verdict finding age discrimination, but vacating 5-year front-pay award as "impermissibly speculative"; " '[t]he longer the front pay period, the more speculative the front pay award' ") (citation omitted).

[251]*E.g.,* Biondo v. City of Chi., 382 F.3d 680, 691, 94 FEP 513 (7th Cir. 2004), *cert. denied,* 543 U.S. 1152 (2005) (reversing 12 years of front-pay award to 19 white candidates who lost promotional opportunity because of reservation of slots for minority candidates; 12 years is unduly speculative and exceeds equitable discretion); Cassino v. Reichhold Chems., Inc., 817 F.2d 1338, 1347, 47 FEP 865 (9th Cir. 1987) (noting the jury received no instruction on mitigation, the court reversed the front pay awarded "in effect" from the time of trial to the time a plaintiff then in his mid-50s would have retired; "the plaintiff's duty to mitigate must serve as a control on front pay damage awards"); Rodgers v. Fisher Body Div., 739 F.2d 1102, 1106–07, 35 FEP 349 (6th Cir. 1984) (reversing as "extremely speculative" a front-pay award equal to income at the time of wrongful termination, projected forward

the job market, and the nature of the position at issue.[252] Because
of the inherent speculation involved in calculating front-pay awards,

---

13 years, less present alternative income projected for the same period); Vance v.
Southern Bell Tel. & Tel. Co., 672 F. Supp. 1408, 1416, 44 FEP 1079 (M.D. Fla.
1987) ("Because it is a short-term alternative, front pay is computed on the basis of
a few months or years . . . . In the case *sub judice*, the front pay award was computed for plaintiff's remaining working life, or for twenty-seven years. This award
is unreasonable."), *aff'd in relevant part*, 863 F.2d 1503, 50 FEP 742 (11th Cir. 1989);
Dominic v. Consolidated Edison Co., 652 F. Supp. 815, 820, 44 FEP 1865 (S.D.N.Y.
1986) (jury front-pay award for a 52-year-old covering salary differential projected
until age 70 vacated as "highly speculative" and reduced to 2 years' differential),
aff'd, 822 F.2d 1249, 44 FEP 268 (2d Cir. 1987). *But see* Meacham v. Knolls Atomic
Power Lab., 381 F.3d 56, 94 FEP 602 (2d Cir. 2004) (affirming front-pay awards 9
to 12 years out), *vacated and remanded*, 544 U.S. 957 (2005); Sellers v. Mineta,
358 F.3d 1058, 93 FEP 417 (8th Cir. 2004) (8-year award); Buckley v. Reynolds
Metals Co., 690 F. Supp. 211, 216–17, 55 FEP 1508 (S.D.N.Y. 1988) (awarding 9
years of front pay to a 56-year-old sales representative who had worked for his
employer for 25 years and asserted he intended to remain there until his retirement).
   [252]*E.g.*, Johnson v. Spencer Press of Me., Inc., 364 F.3d 368, 93 FEP 939 (1st
Cir. 2004) (error to exclude back and front pay as a matter of law on the ground that
plaintiff was fired for cause from an intervening job; such an intervening event tolls
the back-pay period until reemployment); Ollie v. Titan Tire Corp., 336 F.3d 680,
688, 14 AD 993 (8th Cir. 2003) (award of 2 years of front pay appropriate where
plaintiff was relatively young; "Longer terms of front pay are usually awarded when
it is unlikely that the plaintiff will ever be able to achieve the level of income and
responsibility that he enjoyed in his earlier position or when it would take the plaintiff a significant number of years to gain the level of seniority and responsibility equivalent to the job lost."); Reneau v. Wayne Griffin & Sons, Inc., 945 F.2d 869, 871 (5th
Cir. 1991) (factors for determining relevant time period for award of front pay include the length of the prior employment, permanency of the position held, nature of
the work, age and physical condition of the employee, possible consolidation of jobs,
and other nondiscriminatory factors that could validly affect the possible post-dis-
charge employment relationship); Baker v. John Morrell & Co., 263 F. Supp. 2d 1161,
1185 (N.D. Iowa 2003) (cutting a 20-year front-pay award to 3 years because it was
"unduly speculative and otherwise excessive"); *Dominic*, 652 F. Supp. at 820 (vacating jury award of $378,000 front pay constituting salary differential until age 70,
and awarding instead $34,000 for 2 years' salary differential to the 52-year-old plain-
tiff); Snow v. Pillsbury Co., 650 F. Supp. 299, 300–01, 42 FEP 1391 (D. Minn. 1986)
(3 years of front pay); Reeder-Baker v. Lincoln Nat'l Corp., 649 F. Supp. 647, 664,
42 FEP 1567 (N.D. Ind. 1986) (2-years' wage differential as front pay), *aff'd*, 834
F.2d 1373, 45 FEP 985 (7th Cir. 1987); Hopkins v. City of Jonesboro, 578 F. Supp.
137, 142, 39 FEP 1000 (E.D. Ark. 1983) (3 months of front pay); Toth v. American
Greetings Corp., 40 FEP 1768, 1775 (N.D. Ohio 1985) (6 months of front pay), *aff'd
mem.*, 811 F.2d 608 (6th Cir. 1986); *cf.* Eivins v. Adventist Health System/Eastern &
Middle Am., Inc., 660 F. Supp. 1255, 1263–64, 43 FEP 1536 (D. Kan. 1987) (entering jury verdict of $180,000 in front pay to the 57-year-old plaintiff "nearing the usual
age of retirement").

expert testimony commonly is offered,[253] but according to several courts not necessarily required,[254] to prove what the plaintiff would have received in future earnings.

Awarding front pay can be complicated by the fact that present dollar valuation differs from future dollar valuation. Courts have taken a variety of approaches to the adjustment issue.[255] The process of calculating present versus future dollar valuations can be simplified by pre-verdict stipulations, which have been held to be enforceable.[256]

---

[253]*See, e.g.*, Hartley v. Dillard's, Inc., 310 F.3d 1054, 1063, 91 FEP 1217 (8th Cir. 2002) (expert testimony that, given the plaintiff's age, education, and employment history, it was unlikely plaintiff would find comparable employment supported the 4-year front-pay award representing earnings until anticipated date of retirement); Davoll v. Webb, 194 F.3d 1116, 1144, 9 AD 1533 (10th Cir. 1999) (vocational economic expert used to support front pay in excess of 2 years); Scarfo v. Cabletron Sys., 54 F.3d 931, 954, 67 FEP 1474 (1st Cir. 1995) (court awarded front pay based in part on testimony of plaintiff's expert that plaintiff only had 10% chance of returning to full employment at equivalent salary); Gonzales v. Sandoval County, 2 F. Supp. 2d 1442, 1447 (D.N.M 1998) (absence of testimony from economist warranted reduction of jury verdict of front pay from $450,000 to zero).

[254]*See* Cassino v. Reichhold Chems., Inc., 817 F.2d 1338, 1348, 47 FEP 865 (9th Cir. 1987) (a former employee's testimony based on his prior periodic pay increases was "sufficient to establish the loss of future earnings and benefits"); Maxfield v. Sinclair Int'l, 766 F.2d 788, 797, 38 FEP 442 (3d Cir. 1985) (future damages were available even though no expert testified as to projected earnings or reduced those damages to present value; 10% reduction approved); Paolella v. Browning-Ferris, Inc., 158 F.3d 183, 195, 14 IER 705 (3d Cir. 1998) (absence of expert testimony does not render jury's calculation of front pay improper).

[255]*See* Rhodes v. Guiberson Oil Tools, 82 F.3d 615, 622, 71 FEP 83 (5th Cir. 1996) (reaffirming Fifth Circuit's requirement that fact finders calculate damages for lost future earnings applying a below-market-discount rate to account for inflation); Suggs v. ServiceMaster Educ. Food Mgmt., 72 F.3d 1228, 1235, 69 FEP 1270 (6th Cir. 1996) (reiterating need to use discount tables to reduce amount of award to present value); Newhouse v. McCormick & Co., Inc., 910 F. Supp. 1451, 1457 (D. Neb. 1996) (court utilizes "total-offset" method where no discount to present value is required, on theory that any interest rate that might otherwise drive discount would be totally offset by such things as price inflation and real wage increases), *aff'd in part and rev'd and remanded on other grounds*, 110 F.3d 635, 73 FEP 1496 (8th Cir. 1997).

[256]*See, e.g.*, Woodson v. Scott Paper Co., 898 F. Supp. 298, 309, 68 FEP 947 (E.D. Pa. 1995), *aff'd in part and rev'd in part on other grounds*, 109 F.3d 913, 73 FEP 1237 (3d Cir. 1996) (although employee argued that state law did not require future earnings award to be reduced to present worth, award would be reduced pursuant to pre-verdict stipulation agreed upon between parties in lieu of present worth instruction to jury).

The plaintiff's entitlement vel non to front pay almost universally is held to be for the court's determination; the theory is that, as a substitute for the equitable remedy of reinstatement, front pay in effect is an equitable remedy.[257] Courts generally hold that the amount of front pay is also for the court's determination.[258]

IV. DEFENSES TO EQUITABLE FORMS OF MONETARY RELIEF

A. The Mixed-Motive Defense

The Civil Rights Act of 1991[259] limits available relief in mixed-motive cases, i.e., those where the plaintiff shows that at least one

---

[257]*E.g.*, Julian v. City of Houston, 314 F.3d 721, 728–29 (5th Cir. 2002) (under the ADEA, the appropriateness of front pay, an equitable remedy, should be determined by the district court rather than the jury); Duke v. Uniroyal, Inc., 928 F.2d 1413, 1424, 55 FEP 816 (4th Cir. 1991) ("[W]hether front pay is to be made available to a plaintiff under the ADEA is a matter left to the discretion of the trial judge who must consider a host of factors, including whether reinstatement is practical."); Fite v. First Tenn. Prod. Credit Ass'n, 861 F.2d 884, 892, 48 FEP 449 (6th Cir. 1988) (same), *overruled in part on other grounds*, Davis v. Mutual Life Ins. Co., 6 F.3d 367 (6th Cir. 1993); Cassino v. Reichhold Chems., Inc., 817 F.2d 1338, 1347, 47 FEP 865 (9th Cir. 1987) ("the decision whether to order the equitable remedy of reinstatement or, in the alternative, to award front pay, is a decision for the trial court").

[258]*See* EEOC v. W&O, Inc., 213 F.3d 600, 618 (11th Cir. 2000) (front pay is a form of equitable relief; as such, the decision to grant it, and, if granted, what form it should take, lies in the discretion of the court); Banks v. Travelers Cos., 180 F.3d 358, 364–65, 80 FEP 30 (2d Cir. 1999) (front pay and pension credits are form of injunctive relief that is awarded by court, not jury); Excel Corp. v. Bosley, 165 F.3d 635, 639, 78 FEP 1844 (8th Cir. 1999) ("The issue of front pay is not an issue for the jury to decide, rather it is a form of equitable relief which must be determined by the district court after considering all aspects of the case."); McCue v. Kansas Dep't of Human Res., 165 F.3d 784, 791–92, 78 FEP 1183 (10th Cir. 1999) (award of front pay in Title VII case vacated and remanded where district court allowed jury to determine amount to be awarded); Allison v. Citgo Petroleum Corp., 151 F.3d 402, 423 n.19 (5th Cir. 1998) (the right to jury trial provided by § 1981 does not include power to determine availability of front pay); Newhouse v. McCormick & Co., 110 F.3d 635, 642, 73 FEP 1496 (8th Cir. 1997) (choice between two equitable remedies of reinstatement and front pay clearly belongs to court); Wells v. New Cherokee Corp., 58 F.3d 233, 238, 68 FEP 284 (6th Cir. 1995) (district court erred in letting jury determine propriety of front-pay award, although error was harmless). *But see* Skalka v. Fernald Envtl. Restoration Mgmt. Corp., 178 F.3d 414, 427 (6th Cir. 1999) (front pay in ADEA case is for jury to decide); Gatti v. Community Action Agency of Greene County, Inc., 263 F. Supp. 2d 496, 507–11 (N.D.N.Y. 2003) (ADEA permits district court to fashion equitable remedies that can include front pay for loss of future earnings and court may receive advisory verdict from jury on issue of front pay), *aff'd*, 86 Fed. Appx. 478 (2d Cir. 2004).

[259]Pub. L. No. 102-166, § 107, 1991 U.S.C.C.A.N. (105 Stat.) 1071, 1075–76.

of the motivating factors for the employment decision was unlawful discrimination.[260] Pursuant to § 107 of the Act, a court "shall not award damages" if an employer can show that it would have taken the same action regardless of its impermissible discriminatory motivation.[261] Proof that discrimination was one of the motivating factors in the employer's decision will, in Title VII cases, allow a plaintiff to pursue only (1) declaratory relief, (2) injunctive relief (except instatement, reinstatement, or promotion), and (3) attorney's fees and costs directly attributable to pursuing the claim.[262]

Before the Civil Rights Act of 1991, an employer's proof that it would have taken the same action regardless of its impermissible discriminatory motivation operated as a complete bar to the plaintiff's right to recover any monetary relief.[263] Since the enactment of the Civil Rights Act of 1991, an employer can no longer

---

[260]42 U.S.C. § 2000e-2(m) (2000). *See generally* Chapter 2 (Disparate Treatment).

[261]42 U.S.C. § 2000e-5(g)(2)(B)(ii) (2000); *see also* Hennessy v. Penril Datacomm Networks, Inc., 69 F.3d 1344 (7th Cir. 1995) (back-pay award upheld when employer failed to show that the same employment decision would have been made even if there had been no impermissible motivating factor); Saracini v. Missouri Pac. R.R., 431 F. Supp. 389, 397, 14 FEP 1604 (E.D. Ark. 1977) (no back pay awarded where the employee would not have received the position even in the absence of discrimination); Patterson v. Greenwood School Dist. 50, 696 F.2d 293 (4th Cir. 1982); Rogers v. EEOC, 551 F.2d 456 (D.C. Cir. 1977) (where both selection officer of EEOC and district court found that plaintiff, a black male, was not best qualified applicant for EEOC district director position, plaintiff was not entitled to damages, even if race was one factor in selection officer's choice not to appoint plaintiff). *But see* Cohen v. West Haven Bd. of Police Comm'rs, 638 F.2d 496, 503, 24 FEP 1133 (2d Cir. 1980) (women denied placement on a police officer appointment list because they failed a discriminatory test should not be denied back pay because they failed a nondiscriminatory test 1½ years later; the defendant failed to prove that the plaintiffs would have failed the nondiscriminatory test had it been administered at the earlier date; applying Title VII standards to a Revenue Sharing Act suit); Rodriguez v. Taylor, 569 F.2d 1231, 1240–41, 16 FEP 533 (3d Cir. 1977) (even though the plaintiff, who illegally was not permitted to take a civil service examination because of his age, failed the examination after the court ordered the employer-city to administer it, back pay properly was awarded for the period between the time the first applicant was hired after the plaintiff's rejection and the time of the district court's final order).

[262]42 U.S.C. § 2000e-5(g)(2)(B)(i) (2000).

[263]Price Waterhouse v. Hopkins, 490 U.S. 228, 242, 49 FEP 954 (1989); Smith v. F.W. Morse & Co., Inc., 76 F.3d 413, 419 n.3 & 420–22, 69 FEP 1687 (1st Cir. 1996) (*Price Waterhouse* framework applicable where events that formed basis of plaintiff's claim occurred prior to effective date of the Civil Rights Act of 1991); *accord* Bristow v. Drake St., Inc., 41 F.3d 345, 419 n.3 & 421, 66 FEP 739 (7th Cir. 1994) (plaintiff cannot obtain damages if trier of fact is convinced that plaintiff would have been discharged even if sex had played no role in decision; she has suffered no harm by reason of sex that she would not have suffered anyway); Chenault v. United States Postal Serv., 37 F.3d 535, 536, 3 AD 1185 (9th Cir. 1994) (Civil Rights Act of 1991 section that permits finding that employer has committed an unlawful

completely avoid liability by proving that it would have made the same decision for nondiscriminatory reasons; such an employer now can limit the plaintiff's remedies.[264] The employer generally will be entitled to a mixed-motive jury instruction in any case "where the evidence is sufficient to allow a trier to find both forbidden and permissible motives."[265]

In *Tanca v. Nordberg,*[266] the First Circuit concluded that § 107 "explicitly applies only to discrimination claims,"[267] and does not also apply to retaliation cases.[268] The plaintiff in *Tanca*, a white male, was a long-term employee of defendant Massachusetts Department of Employment (DET). After several minority employees were promoted into positions for which Tanca had applied, Tanca complained to high-level DET managers. He believed that he was better qualified than the promoted employees and that their promotions were due to reverse discrimination. When a position became available in DET's Hyannis office, where Tanca worked, he applied. Instead of offering him the Hyannis position, however, DET offered him a similar position in New Bedford. Tanca sued DET, alleging that it had retaliated against him for making his complaints—a protected activity—by refusing him the Hyannis position and offering him the New Bedford one. Because of the distance between Hyannis, where Tanca lived, and New Bedford, he described the offered position as significantly less desirable. DET maintained that the decision was

---

employment practice whenever an improper consideration is a motivating factor in an employment decision, regardless of whether the employer would have taken the same action in the absence of the improper consideration, may not be applied retroactively); Preston v. Virginia *ex rel.* New River Cmty. Coll., 31 F.3d 203, 207, 65 FEP 877 (4th Cir. 1994) (employer has committed an unlawful employment practice whenever improper consideration is a motivating factor, irrespective of whether the employer would have taken the same action absent improper consideration).

[264]*See, e.g.,* Fuller v. Phipps, 67 F.3d 1137, 1142, 69 FEP 111 (4th Cir. 1995) (Civil Rights Act of 1991 overruled *Price Waterhouse* to extent that employer can no longer avoid liability by proving that it would have made same decision for nondiscriminatory reasons; such proof only limits plaintiff's remedies), *overruled in part by* Desert Palace, Inc. v. Costa, 539 U.S. 90 (2003); Russell v. Microdyne Corp., 65 F.3d 1229, 1237, 68 FEP 1602 (4th Cir. 1995) (same).

[265]Medlock v. Ortho Biotech, Inc., 164 F.3d 545, 553, 78 FEP 1592 (10th Cir. 1999); *see also* Thomas v. Denny's, Inc., 111 F.3d 1506, 1512, 73 FEP 1333 (10th Cir. 1997) (African-American employee entitled to mixed-motive instruction in § 1981 retaliation claim, even though he did not request instruction, where employee presented evidence that several people involved in promotion process stated that employee would not be considered for promotion because of his discrimination complaint).

[266]98 F.3d 680, 72 FEP 166 (1st Cir. 1996).

[267]*Id.* at 682–83.

[268]*Id.* at 680.

based solely on legitimate concerns regarding Tanca's management abilities and DET's ability to supervise Tanca in New Bedford.[269]

A jury found that Tanca had engaged in good faith activity protected under Title VII, that the activity was a motivating factor in DET's decision (and thus that DET had retaliated against Tanca), but that Tanca would not have received the Hyannis position even absent the illegitimate consideration. The court then granted the defendant's motion for judgment as a matter of law, holding that *Price Waterhouse* governed the parties' dispute and that, under that case, because the jury found that DET would have reached the same decision absent any retaliatory motives, DET was not liable.[270] On appeal, the First Circuit focused on the statutory language:

> As always, we begin our analysis with the plain language of the statute. By doing so, we immediately encounter Tanca's fundamental problem: as a retaliation claim, his suit was brought under section 2000-e(3), and although section 107(b) specifically addresses section 107(a), it makes no mention of section 2000-e(3). Indeed, section 107(b) plainly states that it applies to "a claim in which an individual proves a violation under § 2000e-2(m) [107(a)]." Section 107(a), in turn, specifies that "an unlawful employment practice is established when the complaining party demonstrates that race, color, religion, sex, or national origin was a motivating factor." There is no reference to section 2000-e(3) or retaliation claims in either provision. As the district court found, "nothing in the 1991 Act would appear to change any rule with respect to retaliation claims which existed prior to its enactment." ... On its face, then, the statute seems to express an intent not to preclude application of *Price Waterhouse* in the context of mixed-motive retaliation cases.[271]

In so holding, the First Circuit in *Tanca* noted that "[w]e are conscious that our decision in this case goes against those of some federal courts that have looked at this issue."[272] However, the court

---

[269]*Id.* at 681.

[270]*Id.*

[271]*Tanca v. Nordberg*, 98 F.3d 680, 682–83, 72 FEP 166 (1st Cir. 1996) (citations and footnotes omitted) (citing *Riess v. Dalton*, 845 F. Supp. 742, 744, 72 FEP 577 (S.D. Cal. 1993) (rejecting application of § 107(b) to Title VII mixed-motive retaliation claim as contrary to the plain meaning of the statute)); *see also* Kramer v. Banc of Am. Secs., LLC, 355 F.3d 961, 15 AD 141 (7th Cir. 2004) (42 U.S.C. § 1981a(a)(2) does not allow compensatory and punitive damages or a jury trial for retaliation claims under the ADA), *cert. denied*, 542 U.S. 932 (2004).

[272]*Tanca*, 98 F.3d at 684 (citing *Beinlich v. Curry Dev., Inc.*, 54 F.3d 772 (4th Cir. 1995) (table)); *Hall v. City of Brawley*, 887 F. Supp. 1333, 1345, 68 FEP 1343 (S.D. Cal. 1995) (court ordered parties to brief whether defendant's liability on plaintiff's retaliation claim was barred by *Price Waterhouse*; without analyzing statutory language, court held that 1991 Act does not preclude liability but limits damages).

concluded, an examination of these cases "reveals that, although all of them would apply § 107(b) to Title VII mixed-motive retaliation claims, and some of them examined the legislative history in drawing that conclusion, none of them weighed the plain language of the statute prior to borrowing the provision."[273] Ultimately, the *Tanca* court held that § 107 should not be expanded and that *Price Waterhouse* continues to apply to retaliation claims.[274] Since the First Circuit's decision in *Tanca,* other federal courts have issued decisions agreeing with *Tanca*'s rationale.[275]

B. Reliance on an EEOC Interpretation or Opinion

Section 713(b) of Title VII provides a defense for an employer that relies on an EEOC "written interpretation or opinion."[276] Both the EEOC's own regulations[277] and the judicial

---

[273]*Tanca*, 98 F.3d at 684. The *Tanca* court also observed that "the only case we found that examined the statute under traditional statutory interpretation methods supports our conclusions here." *Id.* (citing Riess v. Dalton, 845 F. Supp. 742, 744–45, 72 FEP 577 (S.D. Cal. 1993)).

[274]*Id.* at 682–83; *accord* Woodson v. Scott Paper Co., 109 F.3d 913, 935, 73 FEP 1237 (3d Cir. 1996) (§ 107 does not apply to retaliation claims); *cf.* Veprinsky v. Fluor Daniel, Inc., 87 F.3d 881, 893, 71 FEP 170 (7th Cir. 1996) (applying *Price Waterhouse* to retaliation claim arising after effective date of Civil Rights Act of 1991 without addressing impact of § 107 of 1991 CRA).

[275]*See* Norbeck v. Basin Elec. Power Coop., 215 F.3d 848 (8th Cir. 2000) (the Civil Rights Act of 1991 did not change the analysis applicable to retaliation claims; the district court erred in awarding Norbeck attorney's fees), *aff'd in part and rev'd in part on other grounds*, 248 F.3d 781 (8th Cir. 2001), *cert. denied*, 534 U.S. 1115 (2002); Lewis v. Young Men's Christian Ass'n, 208 F.3d 1303, 1305 (11th Cir. 2000) (the Civil Rights Act of 1991 does not makes reference to ADEA retaliation claims in § 2000e-2(m) and therefore § 2000e-5(g)(2)(B) does not change the treatment of mixed-motive cases of retaliation under the ADEA); Kubicko v. Ogden Logistics Serv., 181 F.3d 544, 552 n.7 (4th Cir. 1999) (§ 107(a) of Civil Rights Act of 1991 does not expressly overrule *Price Waterhouse*'s application to retaliation claims); McNutt v. Board of Trs., 141 F.3d 706, 708–09 (7th Cir. 1998) (in order to prove retaliation under Title VII, *Price Waterhouse* still requires plaintiffs to establish that the alleged discrimination was the "but for" cause); *Woodson*, 109 F.3d at 935 (§ 107 does not apply to retaliation cases).

[276]42 U.S.C. § 2000e-12(b) (2000); *see, e.g.*, Stryker v. Register Publ'g Co., 423 F. Supp. 476, 480, 14 FEP 748 (D. Conn. 1976) (employer would be immune from liability for back pay for denial of equal opportunity to earn overtime pay during period that state statute limited working hours of women in manufacturing or mechanical establishments if the employer made a bona fide decision to comply with a state statute in reliance on interpretation of EEOC that state protective laws regarding women were unaffected by and constituted exceptions to federal law).

[277]29 C.F.R. § 1601.93 (2005) (formerly § 1601.33) provides that only the following can constitute a "written interpretation or opinion" of the Commission within the meaning of § 713: (1) a letter entitled an "opinion letter" signed by the Legal

interpretations[278] of § 713(b), however, limit the application of this section. For example, in *Robinson v. Lorillard Corp.,*[279] the EEOC had issued a written decision stating that there was "no reasonable cause" to believe that the employment practice in question violated Title VII. The defendant, asserting reliance on the EEOC's determination as justification for its continuation of the practice, argued that it was entitled to immunity under § 713(b). The Fourth Circuit held that a "no reasonable cause" determination was not a "written interpretation or opinion of the Commission" under § 713(b), and therefore rejected the defense.[280]

In a similar case, *Erhart v. Libbey-Owens-Ford Co.,*[281] the defendant employer and the government had negotiated a consent order that allowed the defendant to maintain the same physical and nonphysical requirements for entry-level jobs as had existed before the suit was commenced, with the exception that a different minimum-weight requirement would apply for females. The district court held that the consent order constituted a "written interpretation or opinion" within the meaning of § 713(b), on which the defendant justifiably could have relied.[282] Relying on *Robinson,* however, the Seventh Circuit reversed, stating:

> [E]xpanding Section 713(b) to the case at hand would undermine the EEOC's system for granting immunity under that section. The EEOC's system "simply insures that the only Commission interpretations and opinions which will be given binding effect . . . are

---

Counsel or, in litigation, by the General Counsel, respectively, on behalf of and as approved by the Commission, (2) matter published in the *Federal Register* and specifically designated as the Commission's written interpretation or opinion, including the Commission's Guidelines on Affirmative Action, and (3) determinations of no reasonable cause made pursuant to § 1608.10 of the Commission's Guidelines on Affirmative Action that contain a statement that they are written interpretations or opinions of the Commission. The EEOC has ruled that General Counsel opinions issued before December 9, 1970, do not constitute a "written interpretation or opinion of the Commission" within the meaning of § 713(b). 35 Fed. Reg. 18,692 (1970).

[278]*See, e.g.,* Paperworkers Local 189 v. United States, 416 F.2d 980, 997, 1 FEP 875 (5th Cir. 1969) (letters and statements by EEOC officials, as opposed to "opinion letters" and material appearing in the *Federal Register,* do not give rise to a defense); United States v. New York, 475 F. Supp. 1103, 1107, 21 FEP 1286 (N.D.N.Y. 1979) (test found invalid where the state agency "utilized" the validation strategies of "consultants" from the U.S. Civil Service Commission).

[279]444 F.2d 791, 800–01, 3 FEP 653 (4th Cir. 1971).

[280]*Id.* at 801.

[281]482 F. Supp. 357, 359, 21 FEP 690 (N.D. Ill. 1979), *rev'd,* 616 F.2d 278, 22 FEP 13 (7th Cir. 1980).

[282]482 F. Supp. at 361, 363–64.

those based either upon a solid factual foundation or upon the most thorough considerations of the potential factual situations to which the rule might apply."[283]

By contrast, where the government's participation goes substantially beyond mere acquiescence or indication of approval, a denial of back pay might be justified to avoid substantial injustice to the defendant. In *Stevenson v. International Paper Co.*,[284] for example, in response to complaints by the African-American employees, the then-Office of Federal Contract Compliance (OFCC)[285] negotiated a change in the employer's seniority practices to create more opportunities for African Americans. After the new practices were in effect for less than a year, the unions contended that the employer went further than necessary in implementing the OFCC agreement and thereby had engaged in reverse discrimination. The OFCC, asked to resolve the dispute, modified the agreement, "restricting some of the opportunities previously available" to the African Americans, who later sued the employer and unions. When these plaintiffs challenged the district court's determination that the seniority system reflected in the agreement met Title VII requirements, the Fifth Circuit concluded that, unlike cases in which the government merely acquiesced in discrimination, the government here did much more. The court (though ultimately remanding to the trial court to resolve the issue) suggested: "[i]t may be that this 'government imposed' discrimination will tip the scales in favor of finding 'substantial injustice,' which would relieve [the employer] of the requirement to make restitution . . . by payment of back pay."[286]

In *Plott v. General Motors Corp.*,[287] the Sixth Circuit considered GM's defense to the plaintiff's reverse discrimination claim under Title VII based on GM's adoption of an EEOC conciliation

---

[283]616 F.2d at 282 (quoting *Robinson*, 444 F.2d at 801).

[284]516 F.2d 103, 107–08, 10 FEP 1386 (5th Cir. 1975).

[285]The OFCC later became the Office of Federal Contract Compliance Programs (OFCCP). *See generally* Chapter 38 (Federal Contractor Affirmative Action Compliance).

[286]516 F.2d at 113. The following year, however, the Fifth Circuit suggested that *Stevenson* is limited to its facts and that, as a general rule, OFCC intervention does not constitute a sufficiently compelling reason to deny back pay. *See* Watkins v. Scott Paper Co., 530 F.2d 1159, 1195, 12 FEP 1191 (5th Cir. 1976).

[287]71 F.3d 1190, 69 FEP 826 (6th Cir. 1995).

agreement setting forth minority and female participation goals for apprenticeship openings.[288] In the year following adoption of the conciliation agreement, the EEOC sent GM a letter stating, in pertinent part, that:

> [i]t is the opinion of the Commission that any action or omission of General Motors Corporation . . . , or any of [its] officers, agents or employees, that is or shall be taken in a good faith attempt to comply with the affirmative action or other provisions of the Conciliation Agreement . . . will not constitute a violation of any of the provisions of Title VII.[289]

The court held "[t]he letter met all the requirements of 29 CFR § 1601.93 (1995) and therefore qualified as an EEOC opinion under section 713(b)."[290]

C. Equitable Defenses to Monetary Relief

1. Laches

In its holding in *Albemarle Paper Co. v. Moody*[291] that district courts have only limited discretion to deny back pay,[292] the Supreme Court left open the equitable defense of laches.[293] As indicated in *Albemarle,* laches may be invoked to bar all or part of a back-pay claim.[294]

---

[288]*Id.* at 1193.

[289]*Id.* at 1194.

[290]*Id.*

[291]422 U.S. 405, 421, 10 FEP 1181 (1975).

[292]*See* Section I *supra.*

[293]"To deny back pay because a particular cause has been prosecuted in an eccentric fashion, prejudicial to the other party, does not offend the broad purposes of Title VII." 422 U.S. at 424 (emphasis deleted); *see also* Occidental Life Ins. Co. v. EEOC, 432 U.S. 355, 373, 14 FEP 1718 (1977) (when a defendant is prejudiced by inordinate EEOC delay, the court has the "discretionary power 'to locate a "just result" in light of the circumstances peculiar to the case' ") (citations omitted); EEOC v. Massey-Ferguson, Inc., 622 F.2d 271 (7th Cir. 1980) (recourse to the doctrine of laches is appropriate only if the EEOC has unduly, inexcusably, unreasonably, or inordinately delayed asserting a claim and that delay has substantially, materially, or seriously prejudiced the company's ability to conduct its defense); EEOC v. Peterson, Howell & Heather, Inc., 702 F. Supp. 1213 (D. Md. 1989) (undue prejudice sufficient to sustain the defense of laches may include unfairly accentuated potential monetary damages directly attributable to plaintiff's unreasonable delays, as well as harm to defendant's ability to succeed on merits at trial).

[294]422 U.S. at 423–25 (remanding with directions to determine whether all or part of the back-pay claim should be barred because of delays and inconsistencies

A laches defense requires both unreasonable delay[295] and prejudice.[296] What constitutes "unreasonable delay" varies depending on whether the defense is being asserted in a private lawsuit[297] or a lawsuit by the EEOC.[298] The prejudice element is most often satisfied by proof that evidence or witnesses have become unavailable due to the unreasonable delay.[299] Courts would reject claims of laches, regardless of delay, where no prejudice is shown[300] or

---

in asserting the claim); *see also* Kamberos v. GTE Automatic Elec., Inc., 603 F.2d 598, 603, 20 FEP 602 (7th Cir. 1979) (the back-pay period properly was reduced by the time between the availability of a right-to-sue letter and actual receipt of a right-to-sue letter). *See generally* Chapters 26 (Timeliness) and 29 (EEOC Litigation).

[295]*See, e.g.*, Whitfield v. Anheuser-Busch, Inc., 820 F.2d 243, 245, 43 FEP 1534 (8th Cir. 1987) (10-year delay; in this circuit laches can apply whether the delay was caused by the plaintiff or by an administrative agency); Jeffries v. Chicago Transit Auth., 770 F.2d 676, 680, 38 FEP 1282 (7th Cir. 1985) (10-year delay; claim barred); EEOC v. Bray Lumber Co., 478 F. Supp. 993, 998, 21 FEP 510 (M.D. Ga. 1979) (4½-year delay; declining to use the specific term "laches" in finding the claim barred due to unreasonable delay and resulting prejudice); EEOC v. C & D Sportswear Corp., 398 F. Supp. 300, 302–03, 10 FEP 1131 (M.D. Ga. 1975) (6-year delay; claim barred); EEOC v. J.C. Penney Co., 12 FEP 640, 641 (N.D. Ala. 1975) (a 4-year delay warrants dismissal unless explained).

[296]*See* Occidental Life Ins. Co. v. EEOC, 432 U.S. 355, 373, 14 FEP 1718 (1977) ("[W]hen a Title VII defendant is in fact prejudiced by a private plaintiff's unexcused conduct of a particular case, the trial court may restrict or even deny back pay relief."); Zelazny v. Lyng, 853 F.2d 540, 543 (7th Cir. 1988) (the required showing for delay and amount of prejudice are inversely proportional).

[297]*See generally* Chapters 26 (Timeliness) and 28 (Title VII Litigation Procedure).

[298]*See generally* Chapter 29 (EEOC Litigation).

[299]*E.g.*, Cleveland Newspaper Guild Local 1 v. Plain Dealer Publ'g Co., 839 F.2d 1147, 1154 (6th Cir. 1988) (because the earlier EEOC notice to retain personnel records was too "ambiguous to serve as a valid command," the prejudice caused by lost witnesses and documentary evidence was not of the defendant's "own making"); EEOC v. Alioto Fish Co., 623 F.2d 86, 88–89 (9th Cir. 1980) (finding prejudice where all three employees with the ability to hire were dead, only one of 16 food servers was still working, and the EEOC investigator and conciliator were unavailable; the employer had retained no job applications or complete employment records for approximately 2½ years after the claim was originally filed; further finding prejudice for a pattern-or-practice claim where the employment practices of the local restaurant industry had significantly changed since the time of the original charge); *Bray Lumber Co.*, 478 F. Supp. at 997–98, finding that the EEOC's unreasonable delay prejudiced a defendant not familiar with EEOC procedures; the defendant had not taken "particular pains" to preserve evidence and would have had to locate former employees who left during the 4½ years after the charges initially were filed).

[300]*See* Cornetta v. United States, 851 F.2d 1372, 1378–80 (Fed. Cir. 1988) (prejudice cannot be presumed); *see also* EEOC v. Delight Wholesale Co., 973 F.2d 664, 669–70, 59 FEP 1222 (8th Cir. 1992) (back pay should not be reduced due to the

where the prejudice was self-inflicted.[301] Ultimately, however, whether a laches defense is successful will depend on the specific facts at issue, with some cases finding laches,[302] and others not.[303]

The delay element often occurs during the EEOC administrative process—after a charge of discrimination is filed, but before the EEOC files suit or issues to the complainant a right-to-sue letter (which triggers the statutory limitations period for bringing suit). Some courts have rejected laches claims under such circumstances, refusing to attribute EEOC delay to the plaintiff.[304] A court that applied laches to a preadministrative filing delay to bar the subsequent lawsuit later vacated its opinion and held that laches could not be applied when the charge was timely under the express statute

---

EEOC's 3½-year delay in bringing suit since no prejudice to the defense was demonstrated); EEOC v. Sheet Metal Workers Local 638, 401 F. Supp. 467, 490–91, 12 FEP 712 (S.D.N.Y.) (even though the demand for back pay was not made until after trial, the tardiness did not prejudice the defendants—the court, however, limited relief to claimants with adequate records; not using the term "laches"), *supplemented*, 421 F. Supp. 603, 12 FEP 742 (S.D.N.Y. 1975), *aff'd as modified on other grounds*, 532 F.2d 821, 12 FEP 755 (2d Cir. 1976).

[301]*See, e.g.*, Rozen v. District of Columbia, 702 F.2d 1202, 1204, 31 FEP 618 (D.C. Cir. 1983) (per curiam) (noting any prejudice in lost records resulted from the employer's own actions in refusing to deny litigation on the basis that the records were difficult to retrieve and observing that because a charge had been filed, any destruction thereof violated EEOC regulations).

[302]McLemore v. Interstate Motor Freight Sys., Inc., 33 FEP 1384, 1391, 1393 (N.D. Ala. 1984) (in applying laches, noting the 8-year delay, dimming of memories of key witnesses, and destruction of some records); EEOC v. Bray Lumber Co., 478 F. Supp. 993, 997–98, 21 FEP 510 (M.D. Ga. 1979) (choosing no specific name (such as "laches") for the doctrine, but finding a 4½-year delay by the EEOC leading to loss of documents and witnesses was prejudicial to the defendant that had little experience with EEOC proceedings); EEOC v. C & D Sportswear Corp., 398 F. Supp. 300, 302–03, 10 FEP 1131 (M.D. Ga. 1975) (a Title VII discharge case is entirely barred by laches because of a 6-year delay; citing prejudice to the witnesses' memory); EEOC v. J.C. Penney Co., 12 FEP 640, 64 (N.D. Ala. 1975) (a long delay and inconsistent findings by the EEOC made laches appropriate).

[303]Seaman v. Spring Lake Park Indep. Sch. Dist. No. 16, 387 F. Supp. 1168, 1176, 10 FEP 31 (D. Minn. 1974) (a 1-year delay is not sufficient for laches where the plaintiff provided notice of its intent to press its demand).

[304]*E.g.*, Bernard v. Gulf Oil Co., 619 F.2d 459, 463, 23 FEP 20 (5th Cir. 1980) (en banc) (a delay is not unreasonable if the plaintiff was awaiting the conclusion of EEOC processes), *aff'd*, 452 U.S. 89, 25 FEP 1377 (1981); *see* EEOC v. Joint Apprenticeship Comm., 8 FEP 176, 177–78 (N.D. Cal. 1974) (considering the "backlog which has plagued the Commission" in refusing to strike a back-pay claim pursued after a 6-year delay but indicating that the delay would be "considered" in fashioning any back-pay relief); *cf.* NLRB v. Rutter-Rex Mfg. Co., 396 U.S. 258, 264–65 (1969) (a 3-year delay by the NLRB in enforcing a court decision does not bar back pay).

of limitations.[305] But other courts have allowed claims of unreasonable delay, holding that EEOC delay does not excuse plaintiffs from actively pursuing their claims.[306]

2. Good Faith

Good faith has not been a notably successful defense to Title VII back-pay liability.[307] "The mere absence of bad faith simply

---

[305]Ashley v. Boyle's Famous Corned Beef Co., 48 F.3d 1051, 1054–55, 67 FEP 208 (8th Cir.) ("[T]he same rationale supporting the laches defense for delays following administrative filing, applies equally as strong to delays prior to the administrative filing. The same potential prejudice to the defendant, e.g., loss of witnesses or evidence in support of a position, failing witness memory, etc., can occur regardless of whether the delay is before or after an administrative charge is made. In fact, we are inclined to agree with Boyle's that application of the laches doctrine may make more sense in pre-charge delay because once a charge has been filed with the EEOC, the company is at least put on notice that it is facing a claim. Without an administrative charge being filed, the defendant is wholly lacking in notice"; holding that although "no amount of time is per se unreasonable," here 6-year delay between time that employer classified employee's position as nonunion and resisted allowing female workers to become union members, and time that employee filed administrative charge with EEOC was unreasonable and defendant was prejudiced by delay, during which two key defense witnesses died.), *opinion vacated on reh'g en banc*, 66 F.3d 164, 167–70, 68 FEP 1261 (8th Cir. 1995) (rejecting laches defense where claim was timely filed under continuing violation doctrine as challenge to ongoing practice, and holding that "separation of power principles dictate that federal courts not apply laches to bar a federal statutory claim that is timely filed under an express statutory federal statute of limitations").

[306]*See* Cleveland Newspaper Guild Local 1 v. Plain Dealer Publ'g Co., 839 F.2d 1147, 1154, 45 FEP 1869 (6th Cir. 1988) (a 10-year delay was not excused by the plaintiff's reliance on the EEOC process where "there was little EEOC activity [for eight years] which could explain plaintiff's failure to act"); EEOC v. Alioto Fish Co., 623 F.2d 86, 88, 23 FEP 251 (9th Cir. 1980) (noting that an agency backlog of cases is not an excuse for unreasonable delay in holding that the "district court did not err in finding as a matter of law that the EEOC's delay" of 62 months in commencing a lawsuit was unreasonable); Lynn v. Western Gillette, Inc., 564 F.2d 1282, 1287, 16 FEP 337 (9th Cir. 1977) (plaintiffs "should not be permitted to prejudice the employer by taking advantage of the Commission's slowness in processing claims"). *But see* Rozen v. District of Columbia, 702 F.2d 1202, 1203–04, 31 FEP 618 (D.C. Cir. 1983) (per curiam) (a 21-month delay as the pro se plaintiff was awaiting a promised suit letter is not unreasonable); Wangsness v. Watertown Sch. Dist. No. 14-4, 541 F. Supp. 332, 340–41, 29 FEP 375 (D.S.D. 1982) (the back-pay period is not suspended for the 5-year period that the case was pending before the EEOC because the plaintiff did not know he could request a right-to-sue letter from the EEOC and he did not retain an attorney until after the EEOC finally sent his right-to-sue letter).

[307]*See, e.g.*, Rasimas v. Michigan Dep't of Mental Health, 714 F.2d 614, 626, 32 FEP 688 (6th Cir. 1983) (generally, good faith of the defendant employer is not

opens the door to equity; it does not depress the scales in the employer's favor."[308]

Reliance on state law is not a defense to federal law liability when the state law conflicts with the federal law.[309]

3. Unclean Hands

The Supreme Court in *McKennon v. Nashville Banner Publishing Co.*[310] rejected the application of the unclean hands to Title VII back-pay liability.

---

an "exceptional circumstance" warranting denial of back pay); Sims v. Mme. Paulette Dry Cleaners, 638 F. Supp. 224, 229, 41 FEP 193 (S.D.N.Y. 1986) (same). Good faith may, however, be relevant in determining entitlement to other relief. For example, under the EPA, "good faith" is part of an express statutory defense to a claim for liquidated damages. *See* 29 U.S.C. § 260; Thompson v. John L. Williams Co., 686 F. Supp. 315, 321, 46 FEP 1378 (M.D. Ga. 1988); *see also* Section IV *supra.*

[308]Albemarle Paper Co. v. Moody, 422 U.S. 405, 422, 10 FEP 1181 (1975). The Court pointed to the provisions of § 713(b) of Title VII, pursuant to which good faith reliance on an EEOC opinion letter is an affirmative defense, and noted: "It is not for the courts to upset this legislative choice to recognize only a narrowly defined 'good faith' defense." *Id.* at 423 n.17. *Albemarle* did leave open the possibility of a good faith defense to back-pay liability where the employer acted in accordance with state "female protective" legislation. *Id.* at 423 n.18. Given current state law, however, it is likely that *Albemarle*'s dictum is of historical significance only. *See* Alaniz v. California Processors, Inc., 785 F.2d 1412, 1417, 40 FEP 768 (9th Cir. 1986) (the employer is immunized from liability for back pay where it relied in good faith upon an order by a state commission prohibiting employers from assigning female employees to any job requiring lifting of more than 25 pounds); Horn v. Duke Homes, 755 F.2d 599, 606, 37 FEP 228 (7th Cir. 1985) (a special factor that could preclude a back-pay award is state legislation that conflicts with Title VII); Le Beau v. Libbey-Owens-Ford Co., 727 F.2d 141, 150, 33 FEP 1700 (7th Cir. 1984) (back pay should not be awarded where the employer relied on the Illinois Female Employment Act in placing all female employees in two areas not requiring overtime, before that Act was declared unconstitutional), *rev'd on other grounds*, 799 F.2d 1152 (7th Cir. 1986). *See generally* Chapter 10 (Sex).

[309]*See, e.g.,* Quinones v. City of Evanston, 58 F.3d 275, 280, 69 FEP 791 (7th Cir. 1995) (invalidating state law providing that local government employees are ineligible to receive pension benefits if hired at age 35 or older as in conflict with ADEA); United States v. Board of Trs. of Ill. State Univ., 944 F. Supp. 714, 722, 72 FEP 382 (C.D. Ill. 1996) (fact that voluntary affirmative action program was established pursuant to state law held no defense, because program violated Title VII).

[310]513 U.S. 352, 358–59, 66 FEP 1192 (1995) ("[E]quity's maxim that a suitor who engaged in his own reprehensible conduct in the course of the transaction at issue must be denied equitable relief because of unclean hands, a rule which in conventional formulation operated *in limine* to bar the suitor from invoking the aid of the equity court, has not been applied where Congress authorizes broad equitable relief to serve important national policies. We have rejected the unclean hands defense

4. Deductions and Offsets

a. Interim Earnings. Section 706(g)(1) of Title VII provides: "Interim earnings or amounts earnable with reasonable diligence by the person or persons discriminated against shall operate to reduce the back pay otherwise allowable."[311] This provision is consistent with the common law requirement that a plaintiff mitigate damages resulting from a breach of contract.[312]

In addition to a plaintiff's failure to comply with the general obligation to mitigate,[313] other deductions are considered under the statutory provision.

Amounts earned from employment that takes the place of employment denied or lost due to discrimination are credited against the back-pay award.[314] Interim earnings are not limited to net taxable income and may include the value of in-kind compensation for services rendered.[315]

'where a private suit serves important public purposes.' "). In a First Amendment case, however, one court has barred an award of back pay based on the unclean hands doctrine. *See* Byron v. Clay, 867 F.2d 1049, 1051–52 (7th Cir. 1989) (plaintiff, who was discharged for political reasons, was not entitled to reinstatement and back pay where his former position existed solely for political patronage purposes and had no legitimate function). *But see* Robinson v. Southeastern Pa. Transp. Auth., 982 F.2d 892, 898–99, 64 FEP 250 (3d Cir. 1993) (rejecting comparative fault based on plaintiff's contribution to the "decay" of his relationship with his employer as a basis for reducing the award).

[311]42 U.S.C. § 2000e-5g (2000); *see* Starceski v. Westinghouse Elec. Corp., 54 F.3d 1089, 1101, 67 FEP 1184 (3d Cir. 1995) (" 'an employer . . . need not reimburse the plaintiff for salary loss attributable to the plaintiff' ").

[312]Ochoa v. American Oil Co., 338 F. Supp. 914, 919, 4 FEP 361 (S.D. Tex. 1972) ("Title VII literally codifies the common law measure of damages for wrongful discharge.").

[313]*See* Section II.B.2.b.ii *supra.*

[314]*See* Nord v. United States Steel Corp., 758 F.2d 1462, 1471–72, 37 FEP 1232 (11th Cir. 1985) (interim earnings, no matter how small, must be deducted from a back-pay award); Horn v. Duke Homes, 755 F.2d 599, 608, 37 FEP 228 (7th Cir. 1985) (earnings from babysitting, housecleaning, and sewing should be deducted from the back-pay award); Rodriguez v. Taylor, 569 F.2d 1231 (3d Cir. 1977) (interim earnings will be deducted from the back-pay award under the ADEA).

[315]*See* McCluney v. Joseph Schlitz Brewing Co., 540 F. Supp. 1100, 1103–04, 29 FEP 1294 (E.D. Wis. 1982) (the value of ownership interests in oil, coal, and gas exploration ventures received by the plaintiff should be deducted from awardable back pay; the value of in-kind compensation at the time received, not the value at the time of trial, is the amount to be deducted from back pay), *aff'd,* 728 F.2d 924 (7th Cir. 1984). *Compare* Scott v. Oce Indus., Inc., 536 F. Supp. 141, 148–49,

   In addition, back pay may be reduced by the amount the employee gained,[316] or the expenses the employee avoided,[317] by virtue of not being employed by the defendant in the position at issue.

   Where total interim earnings exceed the gross back-pay award, back pay properly can be denied.[318] Some courts, though, have calculated back pay on a yearly[319] or quarterly[320] basis where the

---

36 FEP 1226 (N.D. Ill. 1982) (reducing the back-pay award by the value of services performed for a company in exchange for an equity interest) *with Nord*, 758 F.2d at 1472 (the back-pay award should not be reduced by the value of services performed in setting up the business of a claimant's spouse where the business was not earning money and no compensation was received).

[316]*See* Officers for Justice v. Civil Serv. Comm'n, 688 F.2d 615, 629–30, 29 FEP 1473 (9th Cir. 1982) ("hazard pay" received by a police officer discriminatorily denied a promotion to sergeant should be deducted from the back-pay award because the police officer "in all probability" would not have remained on the detail entitled to hazard pay as a sergeant).

[317]*See* Sabala v. Western Gillette, 516 F.2d 1251, 1265, 11 FEP 98 (5th Cir. 1975) (10% deducted for avoided employment-related expenses), *vacated and remanded on other grounds sub nom.* Teamsters Local 988 v. Sabala, 431 U.S. 951, 14 FEP 1686 (1977); Mitchell v. West Feliciana Parish Sch. Bd., 507 F.2d 662, 666 n.7 (5th Cir. 1975) (the plaintiff suffered no financial loss because lower travel expenses in commuting offset the lower interim salary). *But cf.* EEOC v. Hacienda Hotel, 881 F.2d 1504, 1518 n.12, 50 FEP 877 (9th Cir. 1989) (it was within the court's discretion not to deduct for "speculative and unproven work related expenses such as child-care and transportation").

[318]*See* EEOC v. New York Times Broad. Serv., Inc., 542 F.2d 356, 359, 13 FEP 813 (6th Cir. 1976) (where the plaintiff's interim earnings exceeded the amount she would have earned if she had worked for the defendant, back-pay relief was properly denied). *But cf.* Jennings v. Dumas Pub. Sch. Dist., 763 F.2d 28, 33 (8th Cir. 1985) (the back-pay award should not be reduced by the enhanced earning capacity realized by the plaintiff after the back-pay period on account of a master's degree obtained during the back-pay period following the discriminatory discharge); Matthews v. A-1, Inc., 748 F.2d 975, 978, 36 FEP 894 (5th Cir. 1984) (back pay that accrued while working at a lower-paying job is not reduced by the amounts subsequently earned at a higher-paying job).

[319]*See* Leftwich v. Harris-Stowe State Coll., 702 F.2d 686, 693–94, 31 FEP 376 (8th Cir. 1983) (the district court erred in denying back pay to the plaintiff whose total earnings over 3 years exceeded total lost back pay for that period; the court should have calculated entitlement on a year-by-year basis and awarded back pay for 2 of the 3 years during which the plaintiff's earnings were less than lost income); Brown v. Colman-Cocker Co., 16 FEP 1046, 1050 (W.D.N.C. 1975) (back pay computed on a year-by-year basis), *aff'd mem.*, 113 F.3d 1249 (11th Cir. 1997); EEOC v. Domino's Pizza, Inc., 909 F. Supp. 1529, 1537–38, 69 FEP 570 (M.D. Fla. 1995) (yearly basis), *aff'd mem.*, 113 F.3d 1249 (11th Cir. 1997); Brocklehurst v. PPG Indus., Inc., 865 F. Supp. 1253, 1264–66, 66 FEP 545 (E.D. Mich. 1994) (yearly basis).

[320]*See* Godinet v. Management & Training Corp., 56 Fed. Appx. 865, 872, 91 FEP 1024 (10th Cir. 2003) (periodic approach is well supported by law, and the district court has the discretion to decide which approach to employ); Darnell v. City of

discriminatee has had fluctuating earnings during the back-pay period. The effect of doing so favors the plaintiff because periods of low earnings are not offset against periods in which the plaintiff earned more than when employed by the defendant.[321]

The deductibility of "moonlighting" earnings depends on whether they could have been earned if the complainant had not suffered discrimination. Thus, where the "moonlighting" job could not (or would not) have been held if the plaintiff had remained in the job at issue, any back-pay award should be reduced by such earnings.[322] But where the part-time job could have (and likely would have) been held while working for the defendant, arguably no deduction from the back-pay award should be made.[323]

Jasper, 730 F.2d 653, 657 & n.4, 37 FEP 1315 (11th Cir. 1984) (approving the quarterly earnings formula favored by the NLRB); Hartman v. Duffey, 8 F. Supp. 2d 1, 6 (D.D.C. 1998) (periodic method is the preferred method); Mays v. Motorola, Inc., 22 FEP 803, 805 (N.D. Ill. 1979) (computing back pay on a quarterly basis). *Contra* Brady v. Thurston Motor Lines, Inc., 753 F.2d 1269, 1280, 36 FEP 1805 (4th Cir. 1985) (rejecting the NLRB's quarterly approach; "[T]he statute, 42 U.S.C. § 2000e-5(g), requires a credit for all earnings, so computing that figure quarterly as the NLRB does, should not apply.").

[321]Regardless of the period for computation, one court held that as a matter of law, the interim earnings should not be prorated to take into account that plaintiffs had to work longer hours at interim employment in order to earn the same amount as they previously had earned. Harkless v. Sweeny Indep. Sch. Dist., 466 F. Supp. 457, 458–59, 469, 22 FEP 1557 (S.D. Tex.) (adjusting for the number of days worked by former teachers would be impractical), *aff'd*, 608 F.2d 594, 22 FEP 1571 (5th Cir. 1979); *cf.* East Texas Steel Castings Co., 116 NLRB 1336, 1358 (1956) (where the claimant worked 7 days a week at the interim job and 6 days a week at the prior job, the full, not pro rata, amount of interim earnings should be deducted from the back-pay award), *enforced per curiam*, 255 F.2d 284, 42 LRRM 2109 (5th Cir. 1958).

[322]*See* Bing v. Roadway Express, Inc., 485 F.2d 441, 454, 6 FEP 677 (5th Cir. 1973) (moonlighting pay properly was deducted as interim earnings since the plaintiff could not have held the moonlighting job in addition to the job discriminatorily denied); *accord* Chesser v. Illinois, 895 F.2d 330, 337–38, 52 FEP 148 (7th Cir. 1990) (following *Bing*, and deducting earnings from private investigative work that would have been precluded if the plaintiff had remained with the state police); Whatley v. Skaggs Cos., 707 F.2d 1129, 1139, 31 FEP 1202 (10th Cir. 1983) (back pay reduced because the incentives and responsibilities of the management position "create the likelihood that plaintiff would have continued to work long hours" that would have precluded moonlighting); Laugesen v. Anaconda Co., 510 F.2d 307, 317–18, 10 FEP 567 (6th Cir. 1975) (teaching and lecturing income could be deducted only to the extent it exceeded the amount that the plaintiff would have earned from such activities if the plaintiff had remained employed by the defendant).

[323]*See* Wilson v. Peña, 79 F.3d 154, 168 (D.C. Cir. 1996) (no deduction should be made if the employee can show that he could hold the supplemental job and his

It remains an open question whether amounts received in lieu of earnings, such as unemployment, workers' compensation, and Social Security benefits, should be treated as interim earnings and deducted from back pay or as payments from a collateral source and not deducted. A number of courts have found that the issue is within the trial court's discretion.[324] As a result, no clear trend has emerged.[325]

---

full-time job simultaneously and that there was reason to believe that he would); Gaworski v. ITT Commercial Fin. Corp., 17 F.3d 1104, 1111 (8th Cir. 1994) (court refused to deduct $7,345.00 Gaworski had earned doing free-lance consulting work during the back-pay period, determining that this was part-time moonlighting income that he could have earned even if he had remained employed with ITT); Selgas v. American Airlines, Inc., 858 F. Supp. 316, 323, 69 FEP 655 (D.P.R. 1994) (no deduction where defendant did not allow moonlighting but plaintiff presented evidence that other employees engaged in moonlighting), *aff'd in part, vacated in part*, 69 F.3d 1205, 69 FEP 944 (1st Cir. 1995); Lilly v. City of Beckley, 615 F. Supp. 137, 140, 40 FEP 1213 (S.D. W. Va. 1985) (the applicant's earnings from secondary employment are not offset from the back-pay award because he established that such earnings could have been maintained had he been hired by the defendant), *aff'd*, 797 F.2d 191, 41 FEP 772 (4th Cir. 1986); Behlar v. Smith, 719 F.2d 950, 954, 33 FEP 92 (8th Cir. 1983) (per curiam) (amounts earned by the plaintiff faculty members during the summer and in evenings during the school term did not offset their back-pay awards); Buck v. Board of Educ., 27 FEP 461, 466 (E.D.N.Y. 1975) (earnings from family rental properties that plaintiff periodically helped manage are not deductible because the plaintiff was not paid and she could have continued working even while holding her full-time position), *aff'd in relevant part*, 553 F.2d 315 (2d Cir. 1977); Bing v. Roadway Express, Inc., 485 F.2d 441, 454, 6 FEP 677 (5th Cir. 1973) ("[I]f an [employee] can hold his supplemental job and his desired full time job simultaneously and there is reason to believe he will do so, the supplemental job assumes a permanent rather than an interim nature. Those earnings would be independent of the position sought and should not be taken into account in back pay calculations.").

[324]*See, e.g.*, Dailey v. Societe Generale, 108 F.3d 451, 459–61 (2d Cir. 1997) ("[T]he decision whether or not to deduct unemployment benefits from a Title VII back pay award rests in the sound discretion of the district court. We do not believe that the rule . . . requiring the deduction of these collateral benefits is appropriate, particularly in view of the compelling reasons, expressed by many of our sister circuits, that a district court might decline to deduct unemployment insurance from back pay."); EEOC v. Wyoming Ret. Sys., 771 F.2d 1425, 1431, 38 FEP 1544 (10th Cir. 1985) (because it is within a trial court's discretion to deduct collateral sources of income, it was not an abuse to deduct Social Security payments from a back-pay award to state employees; the trial court concluded that the public treasury should not bear the burden of providing windfalls to employees); *cf.* Hamlin v. Charter Twp. of Flint, 165 F.3d 426, 433 (6th Cir. 1999) (appeals court reviews the decision to deduct collateral benefits under the de novo standard of review).

[325]*Deduction not allowed*: Salitros v. Chrysler Corp., 306 F.3d 562, 573 (8th Cir. 2002) (no deduction for workers' compensation, Social Security payments, and

Courts giving the defendant the benefit of the offset typically do so to avoid requiring the defendant to make the plaintiff more than

---

disability payments that plaintiff was receiving); *Hamlin*, 165 F.3d at 432–36, 8 AD 1688 (reversed lower court's deduction of collateral pension benefits from plaintiff's undifferentiated damages award; "[a]pplying the collateral source rule in the employment discrimination context prevents the discriminatory employer from avoiding liability and experiencing a windfall, and also promotes the deterrence functions of discrimination statutes"); Arneson v. Callahan, 128 F.3d 1243, 1247–48 (8th Cir. 1997) (plaintiff's Civil Service Retirement System disability retirement benefits should not be deducted from plaintiff's back-pay award as interim earnings); Dominguez v. Tom James Co., 113 F.3d 1188, 1191, 73 FEP 1418 (11th Cir. 1997) (Social Security retirement benefits should not be deducted from ADEA award of back pay, front pay, and liquidated damages); *Dailey*, 108 F.3d at 459–61 (2d Cir. 1997) (trial court did not abuse discretion by not allowing deduction of unemployment benefits); EEOC v. Kentucky State Police Dep't, 80 F.3d 1086, 1100, 71 FEP 1495 (6th Cir. 1996) (following circuit precedent in declining to offset unemployment compensation but stating that not allowing such offset makes little sense where state is both employer and party administering and financing unemployment compensation, as payments are not truly collateral); Daniels v. Loveridge, 32 F.3d 1472, 65 FEP 1052 (10th Cir. 1994) (offset of unemployment benefits is within court's discretion, but will not be exercised in absence of evidence on manner in which defendant contributes to unemployment compensation fund); Johnson v. Chapel Hill Indep. Sch. Dist., 853 F.2d 375, 382, 47 FEP 1498 (5th Cir. 1988) (declining to deduct unemployment compensation benefits or retirement benefits from back pay); Hunter v. Allis-Chalmers Corp., 797 F.2d 1417, 1429, 41 FEP 721 (7th Cir. 1986) (upholding the decision by the lower court not to deduct unemployment compensation benefits from the back-pay award); Brown v. A.J. Gerrard Mfg. Co., 715 F.2d 1549, 1550–51, 32 FEP 1701 (11th Cir. 1983) (en banc) (per curiam) (unemployment compensation benefits, even if supported by a tax on employers, as a matter of law may not be deducted); Protos v. Volkswagen of Am., Inc., 615 F. Supp. 1513, 1519, 38 FEP 1292 (W.D. Pa. 1985) ("Unemployment compensation benefits are not deductible from an award of back pay against a private employer in a Title VII action in this jurisdiction . . . ."), *rev'd in part on other grounds*, 797 F.2d 129, 41 FEP 598 (3d Cir. 1986); Ackerman v. Western Elec. Co., 643 F. Supp. 836, 855, 48 FEP 1354 (N.D. Cal. 1986) (unemployment compensation is not an offset), *aff'd*, 860 F.2d 1514, 56 FEP 1806 (9th Cir. 1988).

Deduction allowed: McLean v. Runyon, 222 F.3d 1155–57 (9th Cir. 2000) (benefits paid under the Federal Employees Compensation Act were properly offset from plaintiff's back-pay award, since Postal Service pays both back pay and workers' compensation benefits); Flowers v. Komatsu Mining Sys., 165 F.3d 554, 558 (7th Cir. 1999) (award of back pay to ADA plaintiff vacated and remanded); Swanks v. Washington Metro. Area Transit Auth., 116 F.3d 582, 587, 6 AD 1544 (D.C. Cir. 1997) (ADA back-pay award could be reduced to take into account plaintiff's receipt of Social Security disability benefits, in order to avoid double recovery); Townsend v. Grey Line Bus Co., 597 F. Supp. 1287, 1293, 36 FEP 577 (D. Mass. 1984) (unemployment compensation deducted), *aff'd*, 767 F.2d 11, 38 FEP 483 (1st Cir. 1985).

whole.[326] Other courts, however, have found (or have upheld lower courts' discretion to find) that unemployment benefits are collateral earnings not for the benefit of the discriminator-defendant;[327] recoupment of unemployment benefits by the state is a preferable method of remedying any possible windfall to the plaintiff.[328]

Courts likewise disagree on whether public assistance benefits,[329] Social Security benefits,[330] and pension benefits[331] should be deducted from back pay.

---

[326]*See, e.g., Komatsu Mining Sys.*, 165 F.3d at 558 ("The purpose of the collateral source rule is 'not to prevent the plaintiff from being overcompensated but rather to prevent the tortfeasor from paying twice.' ").

[327]*See* EEOC v. Ford Motor Co., 645 F.2d 183, 195–96, 25 FEP 774 (4th Cir. 1981) (upholding the district court's decision not to deduct unemployment benefits; citing with approval *NLRB v. Gullett Gin Co.*, 340 U.S. 361, 364–65 (1951), wherein the Supreme Court held, under the NLRA, that unemployment benefits are collateral, and "failure to take them into account in ordering back pay does not make the employees more than 'whole' "), *rev'd on other grounds*, 458 U.S. 219, 29 FEP 121 (1982).

[328]*See* Craig v. Y & Y Snacks, 721 F.2d 77, 85, 33 FEP 187 (3d Cir. 1983) ("In summary, we adopt the rule of nondeductibility of unemployment benefits because we conclude that the legislative history and *Gullett Gin* are persuasive, that the primary prophylactic policy of Title VII would thereby be better served, that the rule would foster uniformity in applying the back pay remedy, and that the recoupment of unemployment benefits by the state is the better way of dealing with any possible unfairness as between the state and recipient."); *cf.* EEOC v. United Air Lines, Inc., 575 F. Supp. 309, 311, 37 FEP 33 (N.D. Ill. 1983) (no offset where state law would require the plaintiff to repay unemployment benefits), *rev'd on other grounds*, 755 F.2d 94, 37 FEP 36 (7th Cir. 1985). *But cf.* Dillon v. Coles, 746 F.2d 998, 1007, 36 FEP 159 (3d Cir. 1984) (where the state is the defendant, it would be a waste of public funds to require the state to institute a separate recoupment action; offset allowed).

[329]*Deduction allowed: Dillon*, 746 F.2d 998, 1007, 36 FEP 159 (3d Cir. 1984) (public assistance benefits should be deducted because the state considers the benefits a loan to be repaid).
Deduction not allowed: Littlejohn v. Null Mfg. Co., 45 FEP 1882, 1887 (W.D.N.C. 1983) (benefits under the Aid to Families with Dependent Children Act), *aff'd*, 732 F.2d 150, 45 FEP 1888 (4th Cir. 1984); Lilly v. Harris-Teeter Supermkt., 545 F. Supp. 686, 720, 33 FEP 98 (W.D.N.C. 1982) (welfare benefits), *rev'd and remanded in part on other grounds*, 720 F.2d 326, 33 FEP 195 (4th Cir. 1983).

[330]*Deduction allowed*: EEOC v. Wyoming Ret. Sys., 771 F.2d 1425, 1432, 38 FEP 1544 (10th Cir. 1985); Acevedo Martinez v. Coatings Inc., 286 F. Supp. 2d 107, 116 (D.P.R. 2003).
Deduction not allowed: Salitros v. Chrysler Corp., 306 F.3d 562, 573 (8th Cir. 2002) (no deduction for workers' compensation, Social Security payments, and disability payments that plaintiff was receiving); Guthrie v. J.C. Penney Co., 803 F.2d 202, 209, 42 FEP 185 (5th Cir. 1986); Maxfield v. Sinclair Int'l, 766 F.2d 788, 795, 38 FEP 442 (3d Cir. 1985).

[331]*Deduction allowed*: Giles v. GE, 245 F.3d 474, 494 (5th Cir. 2001) (disability pension and long-term disability benefits offset front pay, since employer paid

b. Separation Payments. Separation payments, such as severance pay, normally are deductible from back pay, because the
employee would not have received them but for the discharge. Thus,
the amount of any severance pay,[332] or similar separation payment

---

for these benefits); McMahon v. Libbey-Owens-Ford Co., 870 F.2d 1073, 1079, 49
FEP 620 (6th Cir. 1989) (not abuse of discretion to decrease awards to terminated
employees who prevailed on age discrimination claim by subtracting retirement benefit
from back-pay award; employees would not have received retirement benefit had
they remained employed); Fariss v. Lynchburg Foundry, 769 F.2d 958, 966–67, 38
FEP 992 (4th Cir. 1985) (lump-sum pension payment employee received upon
termination would be offset from damages claimed in action brought under the ADEA
where payment would not have been made at all if employee had continued working until his death 2 years following termination, because he had declined survivor-
ship option offered by employer).
   Deduction not allowed: Smith v. World Ins. Co., 38 F.3d 1456, 1465–66, 66
FEP 13 (8th Cir. 1994) (offset not allowed unless back-pay award includes pension
contributions that plaintiff would have received if plaintiff had not been discharged);
Doyne v. Union Elec. Co., 953 F.2d 447 (8th Cir. 1992) (no offset for pension benefits under the ADEA); EEOC v. O'Grady, 857 F.2d 383, 389–91, 47 FEP 1678 (7th
Cir. 1988) (refusal to offset amount of pension benefits corrections officers had
received since their retirement against back-pay award for age discrimination under
FLSA was not an abuse of discretion, even though benefits were paid from fund to
which employer had contributed); Dreyer v. Arco Chem. Co., 801 F.2d 651, 653 n.1,
41 FEP 1450 (3d Cir. 1986) (district court decision was in line with precedent disallowing reduction from ADEA back-pay awards of Social Security benefits);
McDowell v. Avtex Fibers, 740 F.2d 214, 217–18, 35 FEP 371 (3d Cir. 1984) (it
would be improper for a court to permit either unemployment compensation benefits or pension plan benefits to be deducted from ADEA back-pay awards), *vacated
and remanded on other grounds*, 469 U.S. 1202, 37 FEP 64 (1985).
   [332]*See* Rhodes v. Guiberson Oil Tools, 82 F.3d 615, 622, 71 FEP 83 (5th Cir.
1996) (deduction proper because plaintiff would not have received severance benefits in absence of discharge); Berndt v. Kaiser Aluminum & Chem. Sales, 604 F.
Supp. 962, 964, 38 FEP 182 (E.D. Pa. 1985) (back pay is measured by the difference between the salary an employee would have received but for a violation of the
ADEA, less severance pay, and the salary actually received from other employment),
aff'd, 789 F.2d 253 (3d Cir. 1986); Ryan v. Raytheon Data Sys., 601 F. Supp. 243,
253, 39 FEP 1398 (D. Mass. 1985) (1 month's salary severance compensation deducted from award of back pay); Hawks v. Ingersoll Johnson Steel Co., 38 FEP 93,
96 (S.D. Ind. 1984) (plaintiff entitled to back wages through the date of judgment
offset by severance pay and his total alternative earnings through the date of judgment); Francoeur v. Corroon & Black Co., 552 F. Supp. 403, 414, 34 FEP 323
(S.D.N.Y. 1982) (defendant is liable for an amount equivalent to 1 year's salary less
3 weeks severance pay that plaintiff has already received); Smith v. Flesh Co., 512
F. Supp. 46, 53, 35 FEP 448 (E.D. Mo. 1981) (deductions from plaintiff's recovery
should be made for her severance pay); EEOC v. Pacific Press Publ'g Ass'n, 482 F.
Supp. 1291, 1317–18, 21 FEP 848 (N.D. Cal. 1979) (since the purpose of the front-pay

such as sick pay or vacation pay that would not normally be convertible to cash,[333] will be deducted from any back-pay award. However, leave time accumulated by an employee before termination and paid to the employee upon termination is not deducted if the plaintiff would have been contractually entitled to it anyway.[334]

    c. Periods of Unavailability. Periods where the plaintiff was unavailable to work,[335] whether because of child bearing or family care,[336]

---

award in this case is to place Tobler in the same position as if she had been reinstated, credit for severance pay appropriate), *aff'd*, 676 F.2d 1272, 28 FEP 1596 (9th Cir. 1982). *But cf.* Jacobson v. Pitman-Moore, Inc., 582 F. Supp. 169, 179, 34 FEP 1267 (D. Minn. 1984) (the jury's refusal to deduct severance pay from the back-pay award was justified by the employer's failure of proof on the issue), *aff'd mem.*, 786 F.2d 1172 (8th Cir. 1986).

[333]*See* Cline v. Roadway Express, Inc., 689 F.2d 481, 490, 29 FEP 1365 (4th Cir. 1982) (the value of company stock received upon involuntary termination may under some circumstances be deducted from back pay); Naton v. Bank of Cal., 649 F.2d 691, 700, 27 FEP 510 (9th Cir. 1981) (accumulated sick pay and vacation benefits properly are deducted since they are not normally convertible to cash); EEOC v. Sandia Corp., 639 F.2d 600, 626–27, 23 FEP 799 (10th Cir. 1980) (layoff allowance deducted); Mistretta v. Sandia Corp., 639 F.2d 588, 598, 24 FEP 316 *and* 26 FEP 218 (10th Cir. 1980) (same); Laugesen v. Anaconda Co., 510 F.2d 307, 317, 10 FEP 567 (6th Cir. 1975) (severance pay); Combes v. Griffin Television, Inc., 421 F. Supp. 841, 844, 13 FEP 1455 (W.D. Okla. 1976) (reducing the back-pay period by the period covered by vacation and severance payments).

[334]*See* Coleman v. City of Omaha, 714 F.2d 804, 808 n.5, 33 FEP 1462 (8th Cir. 1983) ("[T]he amount [the plaintiff] received in compensation for his accumulated leave time could not be deducted from a back pay award" because "[the plaintiff] was entitled to it in addition to his regular salary.").

[335]*See* Shick v. Illinois Dep't of Human Servs., 307 F.3d 605, 614 (7th Cir. 2002) (front pay not awardable, since plaintiff's incarceration was not due to employer's conduct).

[336]*See* Caudle v. Bristow Optical Co., Inc., 224 F.3d 1014, 1021 (9th Cir. 2000) (plaintiff withdrew from workforce to care for young child); Winbush v. Iowa, 66 F.3d 1471, 1481, 69 FEP 1348 (8th Cir. 1995) (care of infirm mother); EEOC v. Delight Wholesale Co., 973 F.2d 664, 670, 59 FEP 1222 (8th Cir. 1992) (back pay is not awardable during times that the plaintiff quit and was off work for personal reasons, including poor health and the need to spend time with her child); Walston v. School Bd., 566 F.2d 1201, 1206, 16 FEP 728 (4th Cir. 1977) (no back pay awarded for the period when the claimant was unavailable due to childbearing); Baker v. John Morrell & Co., 263 F. Supp. 2d 1161, 1185 (N.D. Iowa 2003) (care of ailing brother); Reiner v. Family Ford, Inc., 146 F. Supp. 2d 1279 (M.D. Fla. 2001) (no back pay awarded where plaintiff quit jobs over child care needs). *But see* Harper v. Thiokol Chem. Corp., 619 F.2d 489, 493–94, 23 FEP 61 (5th Cir. 1980) (the back-pay period is not reduced by the period of plaintiff's pregnancy, which occurred 6 months after termination).

illness or injury,[337] or other disability,[338] have been excluded from the back-pay period. Some courts have estimated likely unavailability—by, for example, considering the claimant's history of absenteeism—and deducted back pay accordingly.[339] But where the plaintiff's unavailability has been caused by the employer's conduct, back pay may be awarded.[340]

---

[337]*See* Berger v. Iron Workers Local 201, 170 F.3d 1111, 1131–32, 79 FEP 1018 (D.C. Cir. 1999) (remanding action to district court to determine average injury time for plaintiffs to build into benchmark figures for damages); Flowers v. Komatsu Mining Sys., 165 F.3d 554, 558 (7th Cir. 1999) (award of back pay to ADA plaintiff vacated and remanded; statements in application for Social Security disability benefits may be relevant to determination of plaintiff's ability to work during parts of back-pay period); Ostapowicz v. Johnson Bronze Co., 541 F.2d 394, 401, 13 FEP 517 *and* 14 FEP 261 (3d Cir. 1976) (no back pay awarded for the period where the claimants were unemployable due to illness); NLRB v. Kolpin Bros. Co., 379 F.2d 488, 491, 65 LRRM 2190 (7th Cir. 1967) (reducing the back-pay award by the periods that ill health would have prevented the claimant from working).

[338]*See* Johnson v. Spencer Press of Me., Inc., 364 F.3d 368, 384 (1st Cir. 2004) (plaintiff's disability was not caused by defendant's conduct and therefore, no back pay); Starceski v. Westinghouse Elec. Corp., 54 F.3d 1089, 1101, 67 FEP 1184 (3d Cir. 1995) (" 'as a general rule, [an employment discrimination plaintiff] will not be allowed back pay during any periods of disability' ") (citation omitted); EEOC v. Riss Int'l Corp., 35 FEP 423, 425 (W.D. Mo. 1982) (the back-pay period terminates when the claimant's disability renders him or her unavailable for employment); Peters v. Missouri-Pacific R.R., 3 FEP 792, 793 (E.D. Tex. 1971) (deducting from back pay the periods when the plaintiffs were unable to work), *aff'd*, 483 F.2d 490, 6 FEP 163 (5th Cir. 1973). *But see* Blockel v. J.C. Penney Co., 337 F.3d 17, 14 AD 1107 (1st Cir. 2003) (back pay a permissible remedy, despite plaintiff's total disability, where record showed that disability was caused by employer's failure to accommodate her); Wells v. North Carolina Bd. of Alcoholic Control, 714 F.2d 340, 342, 46 FEP 1766 (4th Cir. 1983) (the back-pay period is not terminated on the date the plaintiff failed to return to work after receiving a negative response to his most recent request for lighter duty to accommodate his back injury, because it could be reasonably inferred that the plaintiff would not have been injured had he been granted the promotion denied him); White v. Carolina Paperboard Corp., 564 F.2d 1073, 1091, 16 FEP 44 (4th Cir. 1977) (if the disability that prevented the claimant from doing strenuous work occurred after he likely would have been promoted to less strenuous work, back pay should be computed as if the malady never existed).

[339]*See* Reiner v. Family Ford, Inc., 146 F. Supp. 2d 1279 (M.D. Fla. 2001) (excessive quitting of and absenteeism during interim employment); Bowe v. Colgate-Palmolive Co., 272 F. Supp. 332, 369, 1 FEP 201 (S.D. Ind. 1967) (reducing the back-pay award by the estimated period of absenteeism), *rev'd in part on other grounds*, 416 F.2d 711, 2 FEP 121 (7th Cir. 1969); *cf.* Robinson Freight Lines, 129 NLRB 1040, 1042, 47 LRRM 1127 (1960) (reducing the back-pay award by the employee's rate of absenteeism).

[340]Johnson v. Spencer Press of Me., Inc., 364 F.3d 368, 384 (1st Cir. 2004) (an employee who cannot mitigate damages because of the unlawful actions of the

Courts have reached different conclusions regarding the effect of a plaintiff's decision to attend college; often, the deciding factor is whether the student continued to seek employment while attending school.[341]

---

employer can still receive back pay); Lathem v. Department of Children & Youth Servs., 172 F.3d 786 (11th Cir. 1999) (back-pay award affirmed where employer conduct caused plaintiff's disability); Durham Life Ins. Co. v. Evans, 166 F.3d 139, 157 (3d Cir. 1999) ("Because [the employer's] conduct affirmatively impaired [the employee's] ability to mitigate her damages, it would be inequitable to reduce her back pay award in this case.").

[341]*Compare* David v. Caterpillar, Inc., 324 F.3d 851, 866 (7th Cir. 2003) (back pay proper where promotions were denied due to lack of college degree), Green v. Administrators of Tulane Educational Fund, 284 F.3d 642, 89 FEP 587 (5th Cir. 2002) (affirming jury finding on mitigation; plaintiff could obtain back pay, even though plaintiff returned to school part of the time), Dailey v. Societe Generale, 108 F.3d 451, 457 (2d Cir. 1997) (jury could reasonably conclude that after a diligent, but unsuccessful, job search, employee could no longer support herself where job was located and went to school to earn greater income in the future), Gaddy v. Abex Corp., 884 F.2d 312, 319, 50 FEP 1333 (7th Cir. 1989) (back pay is appropriate for the plaintiff where the "defendants failed to produce any evidence to contradict plaintiff's testimony that she remained at all times 'ready, willing, and available to accept employment' during the time she pursued her education" on a part-time basis) (citation omitted), Smith v. American Serv. Co., 796 F.2d 1430, 1432, 41 FEP 802 (11th Cir. 1986) (the plaintiff's decision to attend school did not terminate back pay in light of the plaintiff's reasonable efforts to mitigate), Nord v. United States Steel Corp., 758 F.2d 1462, 1471, 37 FEP 1232 (11th Cir. 1985) (the plaintiff's enrollment in college does not foreclose her availability for employment in light of her continued search for a full-time position and the fact that she took courses both before and after her termination), Brady v. Thurston Motor Lines, 753 F.2d 1269, 1274, 36 FEP 1805 (4th Cir. 1985) (the back-pay period continues, despite the plaintiff's enrollment in college, where the plaintiff continued to search for full-time employment and would have quit school had a position become available) *and* Hanna v. American Motors Corp., 724 F.2d 1300 (7th Cir. 1984) (back pay awarded, attendance at college after fruitless job search, to obtain veterans income benefits and a chance for greater employment opportunities while remaining available for employment) *with* Floca v. Homcare Health Servs., Inc., 845 F.2d 108, 113, 46 FEP 1433 (5th Cir. 1988) ("The time a person spends in school learning a new career is an investment for which future benefits are expected"; thus, front pay is not available where the plaintiff began law school before the judgment.), Miller v. Marsh, 766 F.2d 490, 492–93, 38 FEP 805 (11th Cir. 1985) (back pay properly was denied during the period that the full-time law student was unavailable for alternative employment while in law school), Washington v. Kroger Co., 671 F.2d 1072, 1079, 29 FEP 1739 (8th Cir. 1982) (full-time attendance in college precludes a back-pay award for the same period, but no deduction should be taken for actual part-time wages earned during that period) *and* Taylor v. Safeway Stores, Inc., 524 F.2d 263, 267–68, 11 FEP 449 (10th Cir. 1975) (attending school to "reap greater future earnings" precludes the "double benefit" of a back-pay award while attending).

d. Taxes. Tax issues affect both back-pay awards and settle-ments.[342] There are two distinct tax issues. First, is the payment "income" to the recipient? Second, is the payment "wages" sub-ject to employer withholding? The answers to these issues are much clearer than they once were.

In *United States v. Burke*,[343] the Supreme Court held that back pay received for disparate impact gender discrimination under Title VII was not excludable from gross income as damages received on account of personal injuries under Internal Revenue Code § 104(a)(2),[344] as it existed at that time. The Court reasoned that Title VII was designed to restore lost wages and not to compen-sate for a broad range of traditional tort harms.[345]

Three years later, in *Commissioner v. Schleier*,[346] the Supreme Court held that back pay and liquidated damages received to settle a claim under the ADEA are not excludable from gross income under former § 104(a)(2). The Court concluded that former § 104(a)(2) and its regulations set forth two requirements for a recovery to be ex-cludable from gross income: (1) it must be based on tort or tort-type rights, and (2) it must be received "on account of personal injuries or sickness."[347] The Court held that back pay and liquidated dam-ages received under the ADEA meet neither requirement because (1) the ADEA does not compensate for any of the other traditional tort harms associated with personal injury, (2) the back pay is completely independent of the existence or extent of any personal injury, and (3) the ADEA liquidated damages are punitive in nature.[348]

---

[342]*See generally* Chapter 43 (Settlement). The following discussion of tax-related issues is intended to be expository only, and is not intended as the provision of tax advice to any individual.

[343]504 U.S. 229 (1992).

[344]26 U.S.C. § 104(a)(2).

[345]Following *Burke*, the Internal Revenue Service issued Rev. Rul. 93-88, 1993-2 C.B. 61, which provided that compensatory damages and back pay are excludable from gross income as damages for personal injury under former § 104(a)(2) when received for: (1) disparate treatment gender discrimination under Title VII, as amended in 1991; (2) racial discrimination under § 16 of the Civil Rights Act of 1870, 42 U.S.C. § 1981 and Title VII; and (3) disparate treatment discrimination under the Americans with Disabilities Act, 42 U.S.C. §§ 12101–12213, as amended in 1991. According to the IRS, all three of these statutes provided a broad range of compen-satory damages of the type the Supreme Court focused upon in *Burke*.

[346]515 U.S. 323 (1995).

[347]*Id.* at 333–34.

[348]*Id.* at 335–37.

As a result of the Court's decision in *Schleier,* the IRS formally "suspended" Revenue Ruling 93-88.[349] Congress responded by amending § 104(a) with the Small Business Job Protection Act of 1996.[350] The "Job Act" provides generally that gross income does not include the amount of any damages received (whether by suit or agreement) on account of personal physical injuries or physical sickness. Section 104(a) further provides that emotional distress is not treated as a physical injury or physical sickness except to the extent of damages paid for medical care attributable to emotional distress.[351]

The IRS issued Revenue Ruling 96-65 in response to the Job Act.[352] It provides that back pay and compensation for emotional distress received in satisfaction of Title VII claims must be included in gross income. Only damages attributed to medical care for emotional distress may be excluded from income.

If a payment constitutes "wages," a withholding obligation is imposed on the employer.[353] An employer that fails properly to withhold faces interest[354] and penalties[355] in addition to the taxes due.

As for punitive damages, Congress in 1989 already had amended Internal Revenue Code § 104(a) to provide that "[p]unitive

---

[349]I.R.S. Notice 95-45, 1995-34 I.R.B. 1.

[350]110 Stat. 1755, 1838, § 1605.

[351]The covered "medical care" is described in IRC § 213(d)(1)(A) and (B), 26 U.S.C. §213(d)(1)(A) and (B). It includes "the diagnosis, cure, mitigation, treatment, or prevention of disease, or for the purpose of affecting any structure or function of the body," and "for transportation primarily for and essential to [the foregoing] medical care." The Job Act amendments to § 104(a) applied to amounts received after August 20, 1996, but not to amounts received under a written binding agreement, court decree, or mediation award in effect on (or issued on or before) September 13, 1995.

[352]1996-2 C.B. 6 (IRB 1996).

[353]A comprehensive treatment of withholding requirements is beyond the scope of this book. The following is only a very brief, and not comprehensive, synopsis. In general, monetary awards fall within one of three categories raising corresponding tax responsibilities: (1) not includable in income of the recipient; (2) includable as wage income by the recipient; and (3) includable as nonwage income by the recipient. The first category requires no withholding or reporting. The second, wage income, not only requires the employer to pay FUTA (Federal Unemployment Tax Act), I.R.C. §§ 3301–3322, and FICA (Social Security), I.R.C. §§ 3101–3128, taxes but necessitates FICA and wage withholding from the employee, I.R.C. §§ 3401–3406, and must be reported by the employer. Nonwage income may be subject to backup withholding, I.R.C. § 3406, and must be reported by the payer.

[354]26 U.S.C. §§ 6621, 6601 (2000).

[355]*Id.* §§ 6664, 6665, & 6671.

damages in connection with a case not involving physical injury or physical sickness" are not excluded from income as damages received on account of personal injuries.[356] The circuit courts have generally held that punitive damages in employment cases will not be excludable.[357] However, the employer has no obligation to withhold, as such payments are not "wages."[358]

To the extent that any part of a judgment now can be considered nontaxable, one court has held that it is reversible error to refuse to give a jury instruction so stating.[359]

V. COMPENSATORY AND PUNITIVE DAMAGES

A. Statutory Bases for Compensatory and Punitive Damages

1. Title VII

Neither compensatory nor punitive damages were recoverable under Title VII prior to the 1991 Act.[360] The original remedial provisions of Title VII were patterned after the National Labor Relations Act,[361] and for decades the law has been settled that

---

[356]Omnibus Budget Reconciliation Act of 1989, Pub. L. No. 101-239, § 7641(a), 1989 U.S.C.C.A.N. (103 Stat.) 2106, 2379 (codified at 26 U.S.C. § 104(a) (2000)).

[357]*See* Hawkins v. United States, 30 F.3d 1077, 1083–84 (9th Cir. 1994) (the § 104(a) exception does not "apply to punitive damages which bear no relationship to actual injuries, do not even purport to compensate the victim for actual losses, and cannot rationally be characterized as anything but a windfall"); *accord* Wesson v. United States, 48 F.3d 894, 896 (5th Cir. 1995); Commissioner v. Miller, 914 F.2d 586 (4th Cir. 1990). *But see* Horton v. Commissioner, 33 F.3d 625 (6th Cir. 1994) (punitive damages are excludable; not an employment case). A Tax Court opinion has held that punitive damages awarded in a sexual harassment case are not excludable from income. Shaltz v. Commissioner, T.C. Memo 2003-173 (U.S. Tax Court Memos 2003).

[358]*See* 26 U.S.C. § 3401(a) (2000) ("For purposes of [withholding], the term 'wages' means all remuneration . . . *for services performed* by an employee for his employer . . . .") (emphasis added).

[359]Allred v. Maersk Line, Ltd., 35 F.3d 139, 142 (4th Cir. 1994) (James Act case; "It is logical for juries to assume that . . . sources of non-wage income (such as pain and suffering awards in lawsuits) are also taxable.").

[360]In *United States v. Burke*, 504 U.S. 229, 238, 58 FEP 1323 (1992), the Supreme Court noted that the pre-1991 Title VII "does not allow awards for compensatory or punitive damages."

[361]*See* Albemarle Paper Co. v. Moody, 422 U.S. 405, 419 & n.11, 10 FEP 1181 (1975) (the back-pay provision of Title VII "was expressly modeled on the backpay provision of the National Labor Relations Act").

compensatory and punitive damages are not available under the NLRA.[362]

Section 102 of the Civil Rights Act of 1991[363] established 42 U.S.C. § 1981a, a purely remedial provision that created no additional bases for liability, and which can be invoked only by persons who have proven claims under the applicable statutes and who have satisfied the administrative prerequisites to suit.[364] Subject to caps graduated according to the size of the employer,[365] § 1981a provides for compensatory and punitive damage awards against private defendants for intentional[366] violations of Title VII, the Americans with Disabilities Act,[367] and § 501[368] of the Rehabilitation Act of 1973.[369] The 1991 Act also provides for awards of compensatory,[370] but not punitive,[371] damages against federal, state, and local government agencies.

Section 1981a(1) provides:

> In an action brought by a complaining party under section 706 or 717 of the Civil Rights Act of 1964 [42 U.S.C.A. §§ 2000e-5 or 2000e-16] against a respondent who engaged in unlawful intentional discrimination (not an employment practice that is unlawful

---

[362]*See* Consolidated Edison Co. v. NLRB, 305 U.S. 197, 235–36, 3 LRRM 645 (1938) (the National Labor Relations Act does not confer upon the Board punitive jurisdiction).

[363]Pub. L. 102-166, § 102, 1991 U.S.C.C.A.N. (105 Stat.) 1071, 1072–74 (codified at 42 U.S.C. § 1981a (2000)). The Supreme Court has held that § 1981a does not apply to conduct occurring before November 21, 1991. *See* Landgraf v. USI Film Prods., 511 U.S. 244, 286, 64 FEP 820 (1994).

[364]*See generally* Chapters 25 (EEOC Administrative Process), 26 (Timeliness), and 28 (Title VII Litigation Procedure).

[365]*See* Section V.D *infra.*

[366]The remedies and jury trial provisions of § 1981a do not apply to claims of adverse impact discrimination. 42 U.S.C. § 1981a(a)(1)–(2) (2000). *See generally* Chapter 3 (Adverse Impact).

[367]Pub. L. No. 101-336, 1990 U.S.C.C.A.N. (104 Stat.) 327 (codified as amended at 42 U.S.C. §§ 12101–12213 (2000)).

[368]Pub. L. No. 93-112, 1973 U.S.C.C.A.N. (87 Stat.) 355, 409 (codified as amended at 29 U.S.C. § 791 (2000)).

[369]These damages provisions do not apply in ADA or Rehabilitation Act reasonable-accommodation cases where the employer demonstrates that it has negotiated in good faith potential accommodations with the individual with a disability. 42 U.S.C. § 1981a(a)(3) (2000). *See generally* Chapter 13 (Disability).

[370]*See* 137 CONG. REC. S15,483–84 (daily ed. Oct. 30, 1991) (interpretive memorandum of Senator Danforth and co-sponsors).

[371]42 U.S.C. § 1981a(b)(1) (2000).

because of its disparate impact) prohibited under section 703, 704, or 717 of the Act [42 U.S.C.A. §§ 2000e-2, 2000e-3, or 2000e-16], and provided that the complaining party cannot recover under section 1981 of this title, the complaining party may recover compensatory and punitive damages as allowed in subsection (b) of this section, in addition to any relief authorized by section 706(g) of the Civil Rights Act of 1964, from the respondent.[372]

Courts have wrestled with the "cannot recover" language in § 1981a(a)(1).[373] In *Dunning v. General Electric Co.*,[374] the court noted that there are three ways to interpret "cannot recover."[375] First, it can be interpreted simply to exclude compensatory and punitive damages for plaintiffs who are already covered by § 1981, irrespective of whether relief is actually available to them under § 1981 (i.e., to

---

[372]42 U.S.C. § 1981a(a)(1) (2000).

[373]As stated by Senator Danforth, one of the principal drafters and co-sponsors of the 1991 Act, the phrase "cannot recover" was utilized so as to disallow double recovery for the same harm. Senator Danforth and his original Republican co-sponsors (joined by Senator Kennedy on most issues, including the following) stated in an interpretive memorandum: "The complaining party need not prove that he or she does not have a cause of action under section 1981 in order to recover damages in the section 1981a action." They went on to state that a complaining party may recover damages under both § 1981 and the new provision where there are "demonstrably different harms under each of the statutes," such as where a woman suffers both race discrimination and sexual harassment. 137 CONG. REC. S15,484 (daily ed. Oct. 30, 1991). Representative Edwards stated in his Section-by-Section Analysis: "While these plaintiffs may proceed under both sections, they, of course, cannot recover double damages for the same harm arising out of the same facts and circumstances." Where the causes of action are independent, Representative Edwards continued, plaintiffs "may proceed under both sections and recover damages under both sections for the independent causes of action." 137 CONG. REC. H9526–27 (daily ed. Nov. 7, 1991).

The damages provision of the 1991 Act provides that nothing in the Act shall be construed to limit available relief under § 1981. 42 U.S.C. § 1981a(b)(4) (2000). Representative Edwards' Section-by-Section Analysis states: "No party is under any obligation to proceed under one or the other statute or to waive any cause of action under either statute as a condition of proceeding." 137 CONG. REC. H9527 (daily ed. Nov. 7, 1991). The EEOC has announced that it will seek damages, at least for purposes of charge processing, "even if the complaining party has an ongoing § 1981 court action, as long as the complaining party has not recovered under § 1981." Office of Legal Counsel, *Enforcement Guidance: Compensatory and Punitive Damages Available Under § 102 of the Civil Rights Act of 1991* (July 1992), 3 EEOC COMPL. MAN. (BNA) N:6071, 6073.

[374]892 F. Supp. 1424 (M.D. Ala. 1995).

[375]*Id.* at 1427; *see* Roberts v. Roadway Express, Inc., 149 F.3d 1098, 1110, 77 FEP 398 (10th Cir. 1998) (where court recognized, without deciding, two of the three possible interpretations recognized in *Dunning*).

preclude such damages under Title VII for all claims of race and ethnic discrimination). Second, it can be interpreted to include compensatory and punitive damages for all plaintiffs, including those asserting claims of race and ethnic discrimination, unless compensatory and punitive damages are actually available to them under § 1981 (such that a plaintiff asserting such claims would be entitled to recover under Title VII if § 1981 damages are unavailable, as, for example, if the plaintiff's § 1981 claims are time-barred). Third, it can be interpreted to provide that a plaintiff who is covered by § 1981 because of race or ethnicity but also covered by Title VII because of sex or religion is not entitled to compensatory and punitive damages under Title VII even for the discrimination reached by Title VII (so that a plaintiff who alleged both race and sex discrimination would not be entitled to recover damages under Title VII, because he or she could recover under § 1981 for the race discrimination).[376] The *Dunning* court ultimately adopted the second interpretation, holding that the "cannot recover" language allows Title VII claims for compensatory and punitive damages when, at the time the Title VII claim is brought, relief under § 1981 is unavailable.[377] In *Dunning,* this meant that the plaintiff was able to seek relief under Title VII because the statute of limitations had run on the plaintiff's § 1981 claim.[378]

2. Civil Rights Acts of 1866 and 1871

a. Private Employers. Compensatory and punitive damages can be awarded against private employers and unions[379] for intentional

---

[376]*Dunning*, 892 F. Supp. at 1427–28.

[377]*Id.* at 1430; *see* Johnson v. Metropolitan Sewer Dist., 926 F. Supp. 874, 876 n.2, 74 FEP 683 (E.D. Mo. 1996) (the "cannot recover" restriction of § 1981(a)(1) is intended to prevent double recovery by a person already entitled to recover under § 1981).

[378]*Dunning*, 892 F. Supp. at 1431; *cf.* Bradshaw v. University of Me. Sys., 870 F. Supp. 406, 408, 66 FEP 806 (D. Me. 1994) (plaintiff who could have pleaded race discrimination claim under § 1981 but did not do so is not barred from recovering Title VII race discrimination damages under § 1981a).

[379]Although punitive damages may not be awarded against a union for breach of the duty of fair representation, Electrical Workers (IBEW) v. Foust, 442 U.S. 42, 52, 101 LRRM 2365 (1979), punitive damages may be awarded against a union that violates § 1981. *See* Woods v. Graphic Commc'ns, 925 F.2d 1195, 1204, 55 FEP 242 (9th Cir. 1991); *see also* Allen v. Transit Union Local 788, 554 F.2d 876, 883–84, 14

discrimination in violation of § 1981 of the 1866 Act.[380] Section
1983 of the 1871 Act, on the other hand, requires "state action"
and is not normally applicable to private employers.[381] In certain
circumstances, private defendants may be held liable under § 1981
for compensatory and punitive damages for the actions of their
officials.[382]

    b. Public Employers. Compensatory, but not punitive,[383] dam-
ages may be awarded against local (municipal) government agency
employers for violations of §§ 1981[384] and 1983,[385] subject to the

---

FEP 1494 (8th Cir. 1977) (since punitive damages have been awarded under § 1982,
the court sees no reason for denying a punitive award under § 1981); Daniels v.
Pipefitters Local 597, 53 FEP 1669, 1675 (N.D. Ill. 1990) (court not prepared to set
aside jury's determination that $150,000 is an adequate award of punitive damages
against the union), *aff'd*, 945 F.2d 906, 57 FEP 128 (7th Cir. 1991). *See generally*
Chapter 22 (Unions).

[380]*See* Patterson v. McLean Credit Union, 491 U.S. 164, 182 n.4, 49 FEP 1814
(1989) ("under § 1981 a plaintiff may be entitled to plenary compensatory damages,
as well as punitive damages in an appropriate case"); Johnson v. Railway Express
Agency, Inc., 421 U.S. 454, 460, 10 FEP 817 (1975) ("An individual who establishes a cause of action under § 1981 is entitled to both equitable and legal relief,
including compensatory and, under certain circumstances, punitive damages.").

[381]*See generally* Chapter 35 (The Civil Rights Acts of 1866 and 1871).

[382]*E.g.*, Flanagan v. Aaron E. Henry Cmty. Health Servs. Ctr., 876 F.2d 1231,
1235–36, 51 FEP 1483 (5th Cir. 1989) (the agency relationship between the employer and its officials was sufficiently close to support an award of damages against
the employer); Vance v. Southern Bell Tel. & Tel. Co., 863 F.2d 1503, 1514–15, 50
FEP 742 (11th Cir. 1989) (an employer is liable for the acts of an employee who
acts as its agent "in creating a hostile work environment"); Mitchell v. Keith, 752
F.2d 385, 390–91, 36 FEP 1443 (9th Cir. 1985) (punitive damages may be imposed
on a corporation for the discrimination of one of its officials, even if the employer
was unaware of the nature of the acts giving rise to the award, if that official acts in
a "managerial capacity"); EEOC v. Gaddis, 733 F.2d 1373, 1375, 1380, 34 FEP 1210
and 36 FEP 1592 (10th Cir. 1984) (en banc) (affirming an award of compensatory
and punitive damages against the individual employer for the actions of his managerial employee). Issues of employer responsibility for employee acts arise most
frequently in the harassment area, where an individual arguably acts outside the course
and scope of employment. *See generally* Chapter 19 (Sexual and Other Forms of
Harassment).

[383]Municipalities generally are immune from awards of punitive damages under § 1983. *See* City of Newport v. Fact Concerts, Inc., 453 U.S. 247, 270–71 (1981).
Punitive damages may be awarded against individual defendants under §§ 1981 and
1983. *See* Smith v. Wade, 461 U.S. 30, 56 (1983).

[384]Section 1981 cannot be invoked against *federal* agency employers where Title
VII provides the exclusive remedy. *See* 42 U.S.C. § 2000e-16 (2000). *See generally*
Chapter 31 (Federal Employee Litigation).

[385]On its face, § 1983 applies only to persons acting under color of *state* law.
See Monell v. Department of Social Servs., 436 U.S. 658, 690, 17 FEP 873 (1978)

requirement that the plaintiff prove that the discrimination occurred pursuant to an official policy or custom of the defendant.[386]

3. Title IX

In *Franklin v. Gwinnett County Public Schools,*[387] the Supreme Court relied on what it described as the traditional common law presumption that all "appropriate relief" (including damages) is available to remedy intentional statutory violations, unless Congress has limited such relief under the statute in question. Applying that presumption, the Court held that compensatory and punitive damages are available to remedy intentional violations of Title IX of the Education Amendments of 1972.[388]

4. Title VI, the ADA, and the Rehabilitation Act

Although Title VI generally has been interpreted consistently with Title IX,[389] the Supreme Court in *Barnes v. Gorman*[390] refused

---

(Congress also intended to include municipalities and other local governments as persons who potentially could be reached under § 1983). Compensatory damages may not be awarded against state agency employers or state officials sued in their *official* capacities for violations of 42 U.S.C. § 1983. *See* Will v. Michigan Dep't of State Police, 491 U.S. 58, 71, 49 FEP 1664 (1989) ("neither a State nor its officials acting in their official capacities are 'persons' under § 1983"). However, that limitation does not affect damages suits against state and local officials sued in their *individual* capacities for having engaged in intentional discrimination in the course of their work. *See* Hafer v. Melo, 502 U.S. 21, 31, 57 FEP 241 (1991) (state officials). Section 1983 does not generally reach federal agencies and officers. *See generally* Chapters 31 (Federal Employee Litigation) and 35 (The Civil Rights Acts of 1866 and 1871).

[386]*See* Jett v. Dallas Indep. Sch. Dist., 491 U.S. 701, 735–36, 50 FEP 27 (1989) (§ 1981 case); *cf. Monell,* 436 U.S. at 694 (a local government may be responsible for its execution of policy or custom under § 1983; choosing not to "address[] what the full contours of municipal liability under § 1983 may be"). This limitation applies only with respect to monetary relief; a court may award nonmonetary equitable relief without regard to the "official policy" requirement.

[387]503 U.S. 60, 70–71, 59 FEP 213 (1992).

[388]*Id.* at 73–76; *see also* Haynes v. Glen Mills Sch., 59 FEP 566, 567–68 (E.D. Pa. 1992) (a former employee may sue for uncapped damages under Title IX even though she has a remedy under Title VII; noting the plaintiff would not be entitled to compensatory damages under the latter if it were assumed that the pre-1991 Act applied).

[389]*See* Cannon v. University of Chi., 441 U.S. 677, 703 (1979) ("we have no doubt that Congress intended to create Title IX remedies comparable to those available under Title VI").

[390]536 U.S. 181, 13 AD 193 (2002).

to employ "the traditional presumption in favor of any appropriate relief for violation of a federal right" as stated in *Franklin*. Instead, the Court limited the remedies available for violations of Title VI to only those for which the funding recipient would have been on notice.[391] Thus, the Court limited the plaintiff's Title VI recovery to compensatory damages and injunctive relief, expressly disallowing any award of punitive damages.[392] The Court held that this same limitation applied under § 202 of the ADA and § 504 of the Rehabilitation Act.[393]

B. The Entitlement to, and Calculation of, Compensatory Damages

The availability of noneconomic damages does not mean that their recovery is automatic whenever a plaintiff prevails. To qualify, a plaintiff must prove that he or she sustained noneconomic injuries, such as emotional distress, pain and suffering, harm to reputation, and other consequential injury, caused by the defendant's unlawful conduct.[394]

---

[391]*Id.* at 187–88.

[392]*Id.* at 187.

[393]*Id.* at 189.

[394]*See* Salinas v. O'Neill, 286 F.3d 827, 830, 89 FEP 491 (5th Cir. 2002) ("any award for emotional injury . . . must be supported by evidence of the character and severity of the injury to the plaintiff's emotional well-being"); Carey v. Piphus, 435 U.S. 247, 266–67 (1978) (absent proof that the student-plaintiffs suffered actual harm when the defendant unlawfully suspended them from school without procedural due process, the plaintiffs are entitled to only nominal damages); Wright v. Sheppard, 919 F.2d 665, 669 (11th Cir. 1990) (the court did not err in rejecting the claim of a post-incident stroke, which was not proven to have resulted from an unlawful beating, but needed to address "evidence relate[d] to non-physical injuries such as humiliation, emotional distress, mental anguish and suffering that, if found to be present, are within the ambit of compensatory damages"); Rogers v. Kelly, 866 F.2d 997, 999, 1000 (8th Cir. 1989) (refusing to award compensatory damages to a plaintiff who was denied a pretermination hearing where he suffered "no actual injury" because he would have been " 'fired even if he had been accorded procedural due process' " anyway) (citation omitted); Vance v. Southern Bell Tel. & Tel. Co., 863 F.2d 1503, 1516, 50 FEP 742 (11th Cir. 1989) (affirming the district court's finding that a $500,000 award for mental distress was grossly excessive, where "there were many other unpleasant factors in her life which almost certainly contributed to her mental distress" and she was currently capable of working and leading a normal life); Edwards v. Jewish Hosp., 855 F.2d 1345, 1352–53, 47 FEP 1331 (8th Cir. 1988) (where race was a substantial and motivating factor in firing the plaintiff, but he would lawfully have been discharged anyway, the award of $50,000 in compensatory

There exists no one required way to prove emotional distress. "[G]enuine injury in this respect may be evidenced by one's conduct and observed by others."[395] Some courts have said that the testimony of the plaintiff alone can suffice.[396] But additional testimony of relatives, friends, and business associates plainly is helpful,[397] as bare-bones, conclusory, or vague references to emotional

---

damages should be reduced to $1); Hamilton v. Rodgers, 791 F.2d 439, 444–45, 40 FEP 1814 (5th Cir. 1986) (reversing an award of $50,000 for injury to the decedent's emotional and physical health, because given his preexisting physical conditions, racial discrimination at most "could have been a factor" in the decline in his health; on remand, compensatory damages are to be calculated with reference only to his emotional injury); Bennun v. Rutgers State Univ., 737 F. Supp. 1393, 1409, 54 FEP 875 (D.N.J. 1990) (compensatory damages denied where the plaintiff did not credibly establish emotional or mental harm), rev'd in part on other grounds, 941 F.2d 154, 56 FEP 746 and 1066 (3d Cir. 1991). But see Foster v. MCI Telecommc'ns Corp., 773 F.2d 1116, 1120–21, 39 FEP 698 (10th Cir. 1985) (substantial damages can be presumed under Carey where there is a deprivation of substantive rights, such as the right under § 1981 not to be discharged because of one's race; upholding the award of $50,000 in general damages, and observing that the trial judge was permitted to take a " 'reasonably spacious approach to a fair compensatory award' ") (citation omitted).

[395]Carey, 435 U.S. at 264 n.20.

[396]E.g., United States v. Balistrieri, 981 F.2d 916, 930–33 (7th Cir. 1992) (although characterizing the testers' testimony in a housing case as "somewhat general and conclusory (and strikingly consistent)," a court noted that given the indignity the plaintiffs suffered it would defer to the jury's evaluation that the testimony supported modest awards for emotional distress); Chalmers v. City of L.A., 762 F.2d 753, 761 (9th Cir. 1985) (a street vendor, harassed for the sale of t-shirts, "testified at trial to the anguish, embarrassment, anxiety, and humiliation which she suffered"); cf. Stallworth v. Shuler, 777 F.2d 1431, 1435, 39 FEP 983 (11th Cir. 1985) (upholding a $100,000 award based on the testimony that the plaintiff "suffered emotional stress, loss of sleep, marital strain and humiliation" because of racial discrimination against him, notwithstanding defendants' objection that he did not consult professional help, did not miss work, "and did not slip[] in his relationships with his students or coworkers"; plaintiff explained he "was being very careful not to give the school system any ammunition to use against him"); Seaton v. Sky Realty Co., 491 F.2d 634, 636 (7th Cir. 1974) (Given the circumstances, a housing discrimination plaintiff adequately supported his claim by testifying: "I was humiliated. I was intimidated, not only as a person, but as a man. He stripped me of my right as a father to my kids.").

[397]See Farfaras v. Citizens Bank & Trust, 433 F.3d 558, 97 FEP 391 (7th Cir. 2006) (in support of claim for emotional distress damages, lay witness may describe employee as "depressed"); Cline v. Wal-Mart Stores, Inc., 144 F.3d 294, 304, 8 AD 154 (4th Cir. 1998) (testimony of plaintiff and wife that he was "very upset and down in the dumps" over demotion held sufficient to sustain award for emotional distress); Blackburn v. Martin, 982 F.2d 125, 132, 8 IER 273 (4th Cir. 1992) (the plaintiff was entitled to compensatory damages for emotional distress where the employee, his wife, and his father testified; the court noted that "at least a portion of" the testimony of each "attributed his loss of self esteem and emotional problems to the

distress will not support a damages claim.[398] Even more specific proof of injury is needed when the actions causing the injury are

---

fact that he was fired, apart from any financial consequences of the termination"); Tallarico v. Trans World Airlines, Inc., 881 F.2d 566, 571 (8th Cir. 1989) (reversing the denial of emotional distress damages in a disability discrimination case under the Air Carriers Access Act where the distress was supported by testimony of the parents, the assistant director for the disabled child's school, and a limousine driver; reinstating emotional distress damages of $78,650). The EEOC favors testimony in addition to that by the plaintiff or other evidence of physical manifestations to support compensatory awards. Office of Legal Counsel, EEOC, *Policy Guide on Compensatory and Punitive Damages Under 1991 Civil Rights Act*, 8 LABOR REL. REP. (BNA) 405:7091, 7097 (July 1992).

[398]*E.g.*, Akouri v. Florida Dep't of Transp., 408 F.3d 1338, 95 FEP 1217 (11th Cir. 2005) (record reflected absence of any testimony on emotional distress; district court reduced award to nominal damages), *vacated in part and revised*, 2005 U.S. App. LEXIS 11427 (11th Cir. June 7, 2005); Brady v. Fort Bend County, 145 F.3d 691, 719 (5th Cir. 1998) (vague, conclusory, and uncorroborated testimony of emotional distress will not support award of compensatory damages); Patterson v. P.H.P. Healthcare Corp., 90 F.3d 927, 938–41, 72 FEP 613 (5th Cir. 1996) (compensatory damages award set aside where there was no evidence of any specific discernable injury to claimants' emotional states and no corroborating testimony or medical or psychological evidence); Hetzel v. County of Prince William, 89 F.3d 169, 171–72, 71 FEP 520 (4th Cir. 1996) ($500,000 compensatory damage award for emotional distress based solely on plaintiff's own testimony concerning stress and headaches held excessive as matter of law where there was no corroborating testimony and plaintiff never saw doctor, therapist, or counselor, and remained employee in good standing), *rev'd on other grounds*, 523 U.S. 208, 76 FEP 417 (1998); Biggs v. Village of Dupo, 892 F.2d 1298, 1304–05 (7th Cir. 1990) (rejecting the distress claim of a discharged police officer where he merely "testified that he was affected emotionally by being fired, and that he was concerned over 'the idea of my family going through it' "); Erebia v. Chrysler Plastic Prods. Corp., 772 F.2d 1250, 1259, 37 FEP 1820 (6th Cir. 1985) (reducing the award of $10,000 for emotional distress in a hostile work environment case to nominal damages where the "plaintiff's only proof of emotional harm consisted of his statements that he was 'highly upset' about the slurs and that 'you can only take so much' "); Davis v. Mansfield Metro. Hous. Auth., 751 F.2d 180, 186 (6th Cir. 1984) (testimony that the plaintiff was "kind of angry" that her application for housing was denied is not enough to support an award of damages for emotional distress); Nekolny v. Painter, 653 F.2d 1164, 1172–73 (7th Cir. 1981) ("A single statement by a party that he was 'depressed,' 'a little despondent,' or even 'completely humiliated' (the latter in the context of explaining why other employment was not sought), is not enough to establish injury . . . ."). *But see* Atchley v. Nordam Group, Inc., 180 F.3d 1143, 1149–50, 79 FEP 1818 (10th Cir. 1999) ($8,000 award for emotional distress supported by evidence of difficulties with family and marital relationships and stress of unemployment); Meyers v. City of Cincinnati, 14 F.3d 1115, 1119 (6th Cir. 1994) ($25,000 award affirmed where plaintiff testified that he lost weight, had insomnia, and was under doctor's care for stomach problems); Berger v. Iron Workers Local 201, 170 F.3d 1111, 1138–39, 79 FEP 1018 (D.C. Cir. 1999) (awards of $2,500 to $25,000 for emotional distress warranted when experienced iron workers were required, because of their race, to take on unnecessary

relatively mild. The contrapositive also is true—where the actions are egregious, less specific proof of effects may be adequate[399]—but compensable emotional distress is not to be presumed based solely on the importance of the rights at stake.[400] Qualified medical, psychological, and other professional testimony can help establish the existence or nonexistence and the degree of emotional injury.[401] Indeed, some courts have held that the exclusion of such evidence is reversible error.[402]

---

training and wait up to 2 years to take union entrance exam); Migis v. Pearle Vision, Inc., 135 F.3d 1041, 1046–47, 78 FEP 1379 (5th Cir. 1998) (plaintiff's testimony of anxiety, sleeplessness, stress, marital hardship, and loss of self-esteem was sufficiently detailed to justify award for emotional distress).

[399]See United States v. Balistrieri, 981 F.2d 916, 932 (7th Cir. 1992) (Fair Housing Act case; "The more inherently degrading or humiliating the defendant's action is, the more reasonable it is to infer that a person would suffer humiliation or distress from that action; consequently, somewhat more conclusory evidence of emotional distress will be acceptable to support an award for emotional distress."); cf. Seaton v. Sky Realty Co., 491 F.2d 634, 636 (7th Cir. 1974) ("Humiliation can be inferred from the circumstances as well as established by the testimony"; § 1983 claim based on Fair Housing Act.).

[400]See Memphis Cmty. Sch. Dist. v. Stachura, 477 U.S. 299, 310, 312–13 (1986) (judgment for compensatory damages in a teacher-suspension case must be reversed where it is impossible to separate the award for emotional distress from the award for the abstract value of the constitutional rights at stake); Gunby v. Pennsylvania Elec. Co., 840 F.2d 1108, 1122, 45 FEP 1818 (3d Cir. 1988) (reversing an award of $15,000 for emotional distress arising from denial of promotion where the plaintiff offered no proof of such injury; such distress cannot be presumed); Piver v. Pender County Bd. of Educ., 835 F.2d 1076, 1082, 2 IER 1382 (4th Cir. 1987) ("The award must focus on the real injury sustained and not on either the abstract value of the constitutional right at issue, see Carey, or the importance of the right in our system of government, see Stachura.").

[401]See Keenan v. City of Phila., 983 F.2d 459, 469, 60 FEP 719 (3d Cir. 1992) (affirming compensatory damages; in addition to lay testimony, "an expert witness[] stated that each plaintiff suffered emotional stress related to the transfer out of the Homicide Unit. [One plaintiff] required continuing therapy."); Brady v. Gebbie, 859 F.2d 1543, 1558 (9th Cir. 1988) (affirming compensatory damages; a psychiatrist testified that plaintiff's symptoms—including "severe and malignant insomnia, anxiety, suicidal fantasies, quiet and severe depression and anxiety" and permanent psychological damage—resulted from the plaintiff's failure to get a hearing and the events surrounding his termination). But cf. Deloughery v. City of Chi., 422 F.3d 611, 96 FEP 768 (7th Cir. 2005) (affirming compensatory award of $175,000; employee could prove emotional distress on her own testimony, without expert); Bolden v. Southeastern Pa. Transp. Auth., 21 F.3d 29, 36, 9 IER 676 (3d Cir. 1994) (a public sector employee need not submit expert medical evidence in a § 1983 case to prove that unconstitutional drug testing by his employer resulted in severe emotional distress).

[402]See Busby v. City of Orlando, 931 F.2d 764, 782–84, 55 FEP 1466 (11th Cir. 1991) (per curiam) (the testimony of a psychological counselor regarding "the

A jury's award of compensatory damages is subject to review for both adequacy[403] and, more commonly, excessiveness.[404] Compensatory damages awards for the distress and humiliation of discrimination can vary widely.[405] The trial court has the discretion

---

psychological impact of the termination on [the plaintiff] is directly relevant to the issue of damages" and should have been admitted). *But see* Tallarico v. Trans World Airlines, Inc., 881 F.2d 566, 572 (8th Cir. 1989) (plaintiff's failure to both identify the expert witness and make the witness available for deposition within the time allowed justified exclusion of the expert's testimony).

[403]*E.g.*, Blackburn v. Martin, 982 F.2d 125, 131–33, 8 IER 273 (4th Cir. 1992) (reversing Secretary of Labor's denial of compensatory damages to employee terminated in violation of Energy Reorganization Act (ERA); there was substantial evidence that employee's emotional distress was due, at least in part, to wrongful discharge itself); *see* Haley v. Wyrick, 740 F.2d 12, 14 (8th Cir. 1984) ("[i]nadequate verdicts are subject to the same procedural rules that govern excessive verdicts"; however, where the issue was not adequately preserved, a verdict that the court of appeals believes to be "inadequate but . . . not monstrous or shocking" will be upheld).

[404]Congress clearly contemplated such review in enacting § 102 of the Civil Rights Act of 1991. Senator Danforth and his original co-sponsors, with the agreement of Senator Kennedy (on most issues including the following), stated in his Interpretive Memorandum:

Judges currently serve as an adequate check on the discretion of juries to award damages. Consistent with the requirements of the Seventh Amendment, they can and do reduce awards which are excessive in light of a defendant's discriminatory conduct or a plaintiff's resulting loss.

137 CONG. REC. S15,484 (daily ed. Oct. 30, 1991). But in his Section-by-Section Analysis, Representative Edwards cautioned:

The sponsors recognize the limited role of the judiciary in reviewing jury awards and intend that only this well-established supervisory role be applied to the review of jury awards under section 1977A [§ 102 of the Act]. This legislation in no way suggests or authorizes any new or additional judicial authority in this area.

Id. at H9,527 (daily ed. Nov. 7, 1991).

[405]*See, e.g.*, Gagliardo v. Connaught Labs., Inc., 311 F.3d 565, 573–74, 13 AD 1345 (3d Cir. 2002) (upholding an award of $1.55 million in compensatory damages for pain and suffering of employee with multiple sclerosis where the testimony of co-workers and family members established "reasonable probability" that employee incurred the emotional damages); Tyler v. Bethlehem Steel Corp., 958 F.2d 1176, 1190, 59 FEP 875 (2d Cir. 1992) (an award of $18,000 under state law for emotional distress is not "conscience-shocking"); Kinsey v. Salado Ind. Sch. Dist., 916 F.2d 273, 281–82 (5th Cir. 1990) (upholding an award of $250,000 to a suspended school superintendent for emotional distress, loss of reputation, personal expenses, and other monetary injuries), *vacated en banc on other grounds*, 950 F.2d 988 (5th Cir. 1992); Moody v. Pepsi-Cola Metro. Bottling Co., 915 F.2d 201, 210–11, 56 FEP 1491 (6th Cir. 1990) (upholding a $150,000 award for emotional distress in an age discrimination case under Michigan's Elliott-Larsen Civil Rights Law); Brady v. Gebbie, 859 F.2d 1543, 1558 (9th Cir. 1988) (upholding an award of $300,000 for deprivation of a liberty interest—removal from the position of state medical examiner under charges implicating the plaintiff's honesty and morality—without due

to order remittitur or a new trial[406] when the award falls outside of the range of permissible awards.[407] In performing this review, many

process, where the plaintiff's distress arose in part from being denied the opportunity to "tell his side of the story," and included "severe and malignant insomnia, anxiety, suicidal fantasies, quiet and severe depression"); Rowlett v. Anheuser-Busch, Inc., 832 F.2d 194, 204–05, 44 FEP 1617 (1st Cir. 1987) (upholding an award of $123,000 for emotional distress, where the plaintiff's treating psychiatrist testified as to his emotional distress and the plaintiff was taking antidepressant medication); Pathways Psychosocial v. Town of Leonardtown, Md., 223 F. Supp. 2d 699, 715–16 (D. Md. 2002) ("courts tend to defer to a jury's award of damages for intangible harms, such as emotional distress, because such harm is subjective and depends considerably on the demeanor of the witness") (citation omitted); Doe v. District of Columbia, 796 F. Supp. 559, 573, 2 AD 197 (D.D.C. 1992) (awarding $25,000 for the rejection of an HIV-positive fire department applicant); Blaine v. Board of Trustees, 57 FEP 800, 810 (N.D.N.Y. 1991) (awarding $6,500 for "emotional distress, humiliation, and loss of professional reputation" for denial of a position); Bucci v. Chromalloy Am. Corp., 60 FEP 405, 410 (N.D. Cal. 1989) (noting it earlier had awarded $55,000 under California employment law for mental distress and physical pain as a result of gender harassment by "persistent verbal abuse"), aff'd mem., 927 F.2d 608 (9th Cir. 1991).

[406]See Gasperini v. Center for Humanities, Inc., 518 U.S. 415, 433 (1996) (federal trial judges can grant new trial if verdict is against the weight of the evidence; their discretion enables them to overturn a verdict for excessiveness and order a new trial without qualification, or conditioned on verdict winner's refusal to agree to a reduction); Vadie v. Mississippi State Univ., 218 F.3d 365, 376–77, 84 FEP 977 (5th Cir. 2000) (either remittitur or new trial was required for excessive mental anguish damages of $300,000: injury was from employer retaliation in violation of Title VII; however, the only evidence of the emotional injury was the employee's testimony and the employee made no claim for front pay and, hence, the evidence supported no more than a $10,000 award); Kirsch v. Fleet St., Ltd., 148 F.3d 149, 165 (2d Cir. 1998) (the district court can enter conditional order of remittitur, compelling plaintiff to choose between reduction of excessive verdict and new trial); Fitzgerald v. Mountain States Tel. & Tel. Co., 68 F.3d 1257, 1266, 69 FEP 163 (10th Cir. 1995) (jury verdict of $250,000 for emotional distress damages found to be clearly excessive in sex discrimination case); Smith v. Monsanto Co., 9 F. Supp. 2d 1113, 1118–19 (E.D. Mo. 1998) (award of $500,000 for Title VII plaintiff's emotional suffering was excessive where aspects of plaintiff's personal life contributed to her emotional pain and mental suffering); Valentin v. Crozer-Chester Med. Ctr., 986 F. Supp. 292, 305 (E.D. Pa. 1997) (new trial was required on damages unless plaintiff accepted remittitur on emotional damages where jury award was grossly excessive); Hurley v. Atlantic City Police Dep't, 933 F. Supp. 396, 424–25, 72 FEP 1828 (D.N.J. 1996) (finding jury's award of compensatory damages of $575,000 so "excessive as to shock the judicial conscience" and remitting award to $175,000); Newhouse v. McCormick & Co., 910 F. Supp. 1451, 1456–59 (D. Neb. 1996) (granting remittitur for excessive front-pay award), aff'd in part and rev'd and remanded on other grounds, 110 F.3d 635, 73 FEP 1496 (8th Cir. 1997).

[407]Indeed, many of the cases discussed above that stressed the limited review of the amount of damages verdicts went on to order a new trial or remittitur. See, e.g., Peoples Bank & Trust Co., 978 F.2d at 1071 (remanding a compensatory damages

courts consider awards in comparable cases.[408] In determining
whether a particular case is sufficiently comparable to the case at
bar, courts consider the severity of the conduct[409] as well as the

---

award of $650,000 for a "substantial" remittitur, where the "outward manifestation"
of the plaintiff's emotional distress "was limited to avoiding other people for a few
days and a temporary loss of a certain blithe cheerfulness, apparently typical of her
personality, which one witness described as a loss of the 'sparkle' in her eyes").

[408]*See, e.g.*, EEOC v. AIC Sec. Investigations, Ltd., 55 F.3d 1276, 1285–86, 4
AD 693 (7th Cir. 1995) (comparing other emotional damages awards in discrimina-
tory discharge cases to determine if $50,000 jury verdict was "roughly comparable");
Webb v. City of Chester, Ill., 813 F.2d 824, 837, 43 FEP 507 (7th Cir. 1987) ($20,250
for emotional distress in a sex discrimination case involving the discharge of a police officer is "not out of line with other awards in similar cases"); Kim v. Nash
Finch Co., 123 F.3d 1046, 1067, 75 FEP 1741 (8th Cir. 1997) (finding award of
$100,000 for emotional distress appropriate when compared with comparable cases);
Caldarera v. Eastern Airlines, Inc., 705 F.2d 778, 785 (5th Cir. 1983) (based on awards
in other cases, $250,000 is the maximum amount that could be awarded a plaintiff
of this age for emotional distress over the loss of a spouse); Hurley v. Atlantic City
Police Dep't, 933 F. Supp. 396, 423–25, 72 FEP 1828 (D.N.J. 1996) (noting that
awards in discrimination cases "in the realm of $500,000 have generally involved
measurable economic damages," which were not present in this case, thus warranting remittitur); Luciano v. Olsten Corp., 912 F. Supp. 663, 674, 73 FEP 221 (E.D.N.Y.
1996) (noting that emotional damages award was not so excessive as to shock court's
conscience when there is case law to support higher award); Lightfoot v. Union
Carbide Corp., 901 F. Supp. 166, 169–70, 71 FEP 269 (S.D.N.Y. 1995) (reviewing
New York cases to determine that damage verdict of $750,000 was "material devia-
tion from the norm" and remitting to $75,000).

[409]*E.g.*, Thomas v. Department of Criminal Justice, 297 F.3d 361, 369, 89 FEP
452 (5th Cir. 2002) (jury award of $30,000 for past emotional distress for sex and
race discrimination affirmed, as this amount fits within the range of damages established by the court; award of $100,000 for future emotional distress damages re-
versed because precedent does not support such an award based on insubstantial
injuries); Salinas v. O'Neill, 286 F.3d 827, 830, 89 FEP 491 (5th Cir. 2002) ("[a]
mainstay of the excessiveness determination is comparison to awards for similar
damages"; concluding that award of $300,000 is too high because the court's other
decisions point to $100,000–$150,000 as the proper award); Evans v. Port Auth. of
N.Y. & N.J., 273 F.3d 346, 354, 87 FEP 510 (3d Cir. 2001) (remitting award of $1.15
million to $375,000 where plaintiff could not cite any other discrimination case where
an award approaching the jury's verdict was sustained); Moody v. Pepsi-Cola Metro.
Bottling Co., 915 F.2d 201, 211, 56 FEP 1491 (6th Cir. 1990) (cautioning against
mechanically comparing the size of the verdict with the sizes of verdicts in other
cases, but finding that the verdict of $150,000 under Michigan's Elliott-Larsen Civil
Rights Act for emotional distress for a discriminatory discharge was in line with
the realm of other awards upheld by Michigan appellate courts); Walters v. City of
Atlanta, 803 F.2d 1135, 1146, 42 FEP 387 (11th Cir. 1986) (upholding a $150,000
emotional distress damages award to a plaintiff who repeatedly had been denied a
position he was well qualified for at a place he had a "lifelong desire" to work; the
court compared it to an award of $100,000 in another case where the plaintiff like-
wise had been passed over repeatedly for promotion).

nature and extent of proof of its effect on the victim.[410] However, reduction of a compensatory damages award cannot be made without offering the plaintiff the alternative of a new trial, in the form of a remittitur.[411] Appellate courts will disturb a damages award that

---

[410]*E.g.*, Fox v. General Motors Corp., 247 F.3d 169, 180, 11 AD 1121 (4th Cir. 2001) ($200,000 compensatory award not excessive where plaintiff "testified that he suffered anxiety, severe depression, and a worsening of his already-fragile physical condition as a result of the constant harassment and humiliation he experienced at the hands of his supervisors at GM" and both neurologist and psychiatrist corroborated testimony); Dodoo v. Seagate Tech., Inc., 235 F.3d 522, 532, 84 FEP 933 (10th Cir. 2000) ($125,000 emotional damages upheld where plaintiff testified that "he has trouble sleeping and wakes up with his heart pounding, not knowing where he is"); Cline v. Wal-Mart Stores, Inc., 144 F.3d 294, 305–06, 8 AD 154 (4th Cir. 1998) (award of $117,500 found excessive and reduced to $10,000 where evidence failed to show that plaintiff's emotional trauma persisted or that he required counseling or medical treatment); Kim v. Nash Finch Co., 123 F.3d 1046, 1065, 75 FEP 1741 (8th Cir. 1997) (award of $100,000 for emotional distress not excessive when supported by testimony from plaintiff, his wife, and son regarding anxiety, sleeplessness, stress, depression, high blood pressure, headaches, and humiliation he suffered after he was not promoted and filed charge of employment discrimination); EEOC v. AIC Sec. Investigations, Ltd., 55 F.3d 1276, 1285–86, 4 AD 693 (7th Cir. 1995) (award of $50,000 for emotional distress was not "grossly excessive" in discriminatory discharge case where, though plaintiff did not undergo any formal psychological treatment, "the emotional burden on a person dying of cancer, perceiving himself as unable to adequately provide for his family, is considerably greater than that suffered by the ordinary victim of a wrongful discharge"); Wulf v. City of Wichita, 883 F.2d 842, 874–75 (10th Cir. 1989) (after comparing the $250,000 emotional distress verdict for a police lieutenant fired for his membership in the Fraternal Order of Police with awards in cases where "plaintiffs suffered emotional distress of a magnitude comparable" to the lieutenant, the court remanded the case with instructions that the award should not exceed $50,000); Luciano v. Olsten Corp., 912 F. Supp. 663, 673–74, 73 FEP 221 (E.D.N.Y. 1996) (upholding jury award of $11,400 for emotional distress where plaintiff testified that as result of her discharge she was "hurt, shocked, upset, overcome with sadness and depression, that she cried, worried about finances, had trouble sleeping and eating and felt purposeless"); Webb v. Hyman, 861 F. Supp. 1094, 1115–16, 67 FEP 1425 (D.D.C. 1994) (jury verdict awarding plaintiff $225,000 and $75,000 against respective defendants was not "inordinately large or shocking to the conscience" given sexual harassment plaintiff's emotional trauma). *But cf.* Schneider v. National R.R. Passenger Corp., 987 F.2d 132, 137 (2d Cir. 1993) (rejecting proffered comparable cases because they did not involve injuries as severe or long lasting as the plaintiff's injuries); Ramsey v. American Air Filter Co., 772 F.2d 1303, 1313–14, 38 FEP 1612 (7th Cir. 1985) (after "[a] review of mental distress awards in discrimination cases from this and other circuits," ordering remittitur of the $75,000 mental distress award to $35,000 and of the $150,000 punitive damages award to $20,000).

[411]Hetzel v. Prince William County, Va., 523 U.S. 208, 76 FEP 417 (1998) (failure to offer remittitur before reducing a compensatory damages award violates the Seventh Amendment).

has survived meaningful trial court review only on the "strongest of showings."[412]

---

[412]In *Caldarera v. Eastern Airlines, Inc.*, 705 F.2d 778 (5th Cir. 1983), the Fifth Circuit summarized the standard of review of damages awards as follows:

> We do not reverse a jury verdict for excessiveness except on "the strongest of showings." The jury's award is not to be disturbed unless it is entirely disproportionate to the injury sustained. We have expressed the extent of distortion that warrants intervention by requiring such awards to be so large as to "shock the judicial conscience," "so gross or inordinately large as to be contrary to right reason," so exaggerated as to indicate "bias, passion, prejudice, corruption, or other improper motive," or as "clearly exceed[ing] that amount that *any* reasonable man could feel the claimant is entitled to." Nonetheless, when a jury's award exceeds the bounds of any reasonable recovery, we must suggest a remittitur ourselves or direct the district court to do so. Our power to grant a remittitur is the same as that of the district court. We determine the size of the remittitur in accordance with this circuit's "maximum recovery rule," which prescribes that the verdict must be reduced to the maximum amount the jury could properly have awarded.

Id. at 784 (footnotes omitted; brackets in original); *see* Lampley v. Onyx Acceptance Corp., 340 F.3d 478, 483–84, 92 FEP 722 (7th Cir. 2003) (when assessing propriety of compensatory damages award, relevant inquiries may include whether award is monstrously excessive, whether there is no rational connection between award and evidence, and whether award is roughly comparable to awards made in similar cases); Starceski v. Westinghouse Elec. Corp., 54 F.3d 1089, 1100, 67 FEP 1184 (3d Cir. 1995) ("The trial judge's decision to grant or withhold a remittitur cannot be disturbed absent a manifest abuse of discretion."); Schneider v. National R.R. Passenger Corp., 987 F.2d 132, 137 (2d Cir. 1993) (a verdict is excessive if it is so high as to shock the judicial conscience); Keenan v. City of Phila., 983 F.2d 459, 469, 60 FEP 719 (3d Cir. 1992) ("We may grant a new trial or remittitur only if the verdict awarded by the district court is so grossly excessive as to shock the judicial conscience."); Peoples Bank & Trust Co. v. Globe Int'l Publ'g, Inc., 978 F.2d 1065, 1070 (8th Cir. 1992) ("Our scope of review over a damage award is extremely narrow, and we may not reverse except for a manifest abuse of discretion."); Brunnemann v. Terra Int'l, Inc., 975 F.2d 175, 178, 60 FEP 12 (5th Cir. 1992) (an ADEA verdict is excessive if shown to exceed " 'any rational appraisal or estimate of the damages that could be based' " on the record) (citation omitted); Nydam v. Lennerton, 948 F.2d 808, 810 (1st Cir. 1991) (noting its "reluctance to alter a jury damages award"); Brady v. Gebbie, 859 F.2d 1543, 1557–58 (9th Cir. 1988) ("[T]he jury's award of $300,000 damages to [the plaintiff] should not be overturned or decreased unless it is clearly unsupported by the evidence or 'shocks the conscience.' "); *In re* Air Crash Disaster Near New Orleans, 767 F.2d 1151, 1155 (5th Cir. 1985) ("[I]n this area [damages for grief and emotional distress] the appellate court should step lightly or not at all."); Carter v. Duncan-Huggins, Ltd., 727 F.2d 1225, 1238, 34 FEP 25 (D.C. Cir. 1984) ("In reviewing the actual amount of a jury's award, our task is limited and a reluctance to interfere is our touchstone."); *see also* Hetzel v. County of Prince William, 89 F.3d 169, 171, 71 FEP 520 (4th Cir. 1996) ("A jury's award of compensatory damages will be set aside on the grounds of excessiveness only if 'the verdict is against the clear weight of evidence, or is based upon evidence which is false, or will result in a miscarriage of justice.' "), *rev'd on other grounds*, 523 U.S. 208, 76 FEP 417 (1998); Delli Santi v. CNA Ins. Cos., 88 F.3d 192, 206, 71 FEP 143 (3d Cir. 1996)

C. The Entitlement to, and Calculation of, Punitive Damages

1. Willfulness

Subject to graduated caps based upon the size of the employer,[413] punitive damages are available against nongovernmental entities under 42 U.S.C. § 1981a for cases of disparate treatment where "the respondent engaged in a discriminatory practice or discriminatory practices with malice or with reckless indifference to the federally protected rights of an aggrieved individual."[414] This standard is virtually identical to the traditional standard for punitive damages liability under 42 U.S.C. §§ 1981 and 1983.[415] Fed-

---

(declining to disturb district court's discretion against backdrop of "severely limited" nature of appellate review and additional deference mandated by fact that district court already granted remittitur); McKinnon v. Kwong Wah Rest., 83 F.3d 498, 506, 70 FEP 1037 (1st Cir. 1996) (stating that court "will not override a damage determination unless the award is unsupported by the evidence, grossly excessive, or shocking to the conscience"); Fitzgerald v. Mountain States Tel. & Tel. Co., 68 F.3d 1257, 1261, 69 FEP 163 (10th Cir. 1995) (" '[A]bsent an award so excessive as to shock the judicial conscience and to raise an irresistible inference that passion, prejudice, corruption or other improper cause invaded the trial, the jury's determination of the damages is considered inviolate.' ") (citing Malandris v. Merrill Lynch, 703 F.2d 1152, 1168 (10th Cir. 1981) (en banc)); Hogan v. Bangor & Aroostook R.R., 61 F.3d 1034, 1037, 4 AD 1251 (1st Cir. 1995) (stating that generousness of jury's award alone does not justify appellate court in setting it aside; rather, award of compensatory damages is excessive if it exceeds rational appraisal of damages actually incurred); EEOC v. AIC Sec. Investigations, Ltd., 55 F.3d 1276, 1285, 4 AD 693 (7th Cir. 1995) (stating that court will inquire whether award is "monstrously excessive," rationally connected to evidence, and roughly comparable to awards made in similar cases).

[413]*See* Section V.D *infra*.

[414]42 U.S.C. § 1981a(b)(1) (2000).

[415]"We hold that a jury may be permitted to assess punitive damages in an action under § 1983 when the defendant's conduct is shown to be motivated by evil motive or intent, or when it involves reckless or callous indifference to the federally protected rights of others. We further hold that this [standard] applies even [where] the underlying standard of liability for compensatory damages is one of recklessness." Smith v. Wade, 461 U.S. 30, 56 (1983); *accord* Barbour v. Merrill, 48 F.3d 1270, 1277, 67 FEP 369 (D.C. Cir. 1995) ("in section 1981 actions, as in section 1983 actions, punitive damages are proper only on a showing of 'evil motive or intent, or . . . reckless or callous indifference to the federally protected rights of others' ") (citing *Smith*); *see also Keenan*, 983 F.2d 459, 470, 60 FEP 719 (Punitive damages " 'must be reserved, we think, for cases in which the defendant's conduct amounts to something more than a bare violation justifying compensatory damages or injunctive relief.' ") (quoting Cochetti v. Desmond, 572 F.2d 102, 106, 98 LRRM 2393 (3d Cir. 1978)). *See generally* Walters v. City of Atlanta, 803 F.2d 1135, 1147, 42 FEP 387 (11th Cir. 1986) ("Punitive damages are disfavored by the law and are awarded solely to punish defendants and deter future wrongdoing.").

eral, not state, law governs the determination of punitive damages under the federal civil rights laws.[416]

Prior to the Supreme Court's decision in *Kolstad v. American Dental Ass'n*,[417] there was a split of authority whether a plaintiff seeking punitive damages had to prove that the intentional discrimination, in addition to being knowing, was also outrageous or egregious. In *Kolstad*, the Court noted that the standard for imposing punitive damages is more demanding than that required to obtain compensatory damages, but rejected any requirement for a demonstration of outrageous or egregious conduct.[418] Discussing the structure of the 1991 Act, the Court observed that the Act establishes two separate standards for recovery of compensatory and punitive damages and opined that:

> The very structure of § 1981a suggests a congressional intent to authorize punitive awards in only a subset of cases involving intentional discrimination. Section 1981a(a)(1) limits compensatory and punitive awards to instances of intentional discrimination, while § 1981a(b)(1) requires plaintiffs to make an additional "demonstrat[ion]" of their eligibility for punitive damages. Congress plainly sought to impose two standards of liability—one for establishing a right to compensatory damages and another, higher standard that a plaintiff must satisfy to qualify for a punitive award.[419]

Having concluded that Congress sought to impose a "higher standard" for recovery of punitive damages in workplace discrimination cases, the Court considered what the terms of the Act required. As traditionally used, "the terms 'malice' and 'reckless' ultimately focus on the actor's state of mind."[420] Although egregious misconduct may certainly be "evidence of the requisite mental state, . . . § 1981a does not limit plaintiffs to this form of evidence, and the section does not require a showing of egregious or outrageous discrimination independent of the employer's state of mind."[421] "The terms 'malice' and 'reckless indifference' pertain to the employer's knowledge that it may be acting in violation of federal law, not its awareness that it is engaging in discrimination."[422]

---

[416]Jackson v. Pool Mortgage Co., 868 F.2d 1178, 1181, 59 FEP 1611 (10th Cir. 1989).

[417]527 U.S. 526, 79 FEP 1697 (1999).

[418]527 U.S. at 534–35.

[419]*Id.* at 534.

[420]*Id.* at 535.

[421]*Id.*

[422]Kolstad v. American Dental Ass'n, 527 U.S. 526, 535, 79 FEP 1697 (1999).

The Court majority interpreted § 1981a to require proof that the employer discriminated "in the face of a perceived risk that its actions [would] violate federal law to be liable in punitive damages."[423] Thus, while "egregious or outrageous acts may serve as evidence supporting an inference of the requisite 'evil motive,' " they do not determine the plaintiff's eligibility for such an award.[424] The Court observed that when Congress drafted § 1981(a), it modeled the language on that employed in a prior Supreme Court decision regarding the availability of punitive damages arising under 42 U.S.C. § 1983.[425] The Court interpreted the relevant statutory terms in lockstep with its understanding of the parallel language in *Smith v. Wade.*[426]

Relying upon *Kolstad,* the Tenth Circuit in *Knowlton v. Teltrust Phones, Inc.*[427] reversed a directed verdict against the plaintiff on the issue of punitive damages. The record revealed that company management "was unmistakably aware that the environment at the three Teltrust entities, and specifically [the supervisor's] behavior, was rife with foul language, sexual innuendo, and sexual advances which could be reasonably labeled as sexual harassment" and that management was "unresponsive" to plaintiff's complaints.[428] In another post-*Kolstad* case, the Ninth Circuit affirmed a punitive award of $300,000 in *Pavon v. Swift Transportation Co.,*[429] where "the jury could have found that racial insults and slurs were a common occurrence on [the] shop floor and that management was aware of this behavior and took no meaningful steps to stop it."[430]

---

[423]*Id.* at 536.

[424]*Id.* at 538.

[425]*Id.* at 535 (referring to Smith v. Wade, 461 U.S. 30 (1983)).

[426]*Kolstad,* 527 U.S. at 535–36. Accordingly, courts in § 1983 cases now also treat *Kolstad* as applicable authority. *See* Iacobucci v. Boulter, 193 F.3d 14, 25 n.7 (1st Cir. 1999) (affirming district court's rejection of jury's punitive damage award based on authority of *Kolstad*).

[427]189 F.3d 1177, 80 FEP 1062 (10th Cir. 1999).

[428]*Id.* at 1187.

[429]192 F.3d 902, 80 FEP 1557 (9th Cir. 1999).

[430]*Id.* at 909; *see also* Rowe v. Hussmann Corp., 381 F.3d 775, 94 FEP 520 (8th Cir. 2004) (punitive award supported by harasser's outrageous conduct—contact verging on rape, threats of violence, etc.—and company's failure to take action); MacGregor v. Mallinckrodt, Inc., 373 F.3d 923, 94 FEP 35 (8th Cir. 2004) (punitive damages supported by evidence that plaintiff complained about manager's sex-biased comments, investigation was minimal, manger was not reprimanded, and plaintiff was never informed of outcome); Lampley v. Onyx Acceptance Corp., 340 F.3d 478, 92 FEP 722 (7th Cir. 2003) (jury could find against employer's good faith

Courts have also held that equal employment opportunity training may provide the requisite notice of illegal conduct under *Kolstad.*[431]

On the other hand, the *Kolstad* opinion suggested instances that would not meet the burden required to sustain an award of punitive damages:

> There will be circumstances where intentional discrimination does not give rise to punitive damages liability under this standard. In some instances, the employer may simply be unaware of the relevant federal prohibition. There will be cases, moreover, in which the employer discriminates with the distinct belief that its discrimination is lawful. The underlying theory of discrimination may be novel or otherwise poorly recognized, or an employer may reasonably believe that its discrimination satisfies a bona fide occupational qualification defense or other statutory exception to liability.[432]

---

defense, because it could have credited evidence that defendant (1) doctored the plaintiff's employment records before presenting them to the EEOC; (2) invented the existence of a written reprimand of plaintiff (of which no copy could be located); and (3) had no plan to fire plaintiff prior to the filing of the EEOC complaint); Fine v. Ryan Int'l Airlines, 305 F.3d 746, 89 FEP 1541 (7th Cir. 2002) (evidence was sufficient that principals involved in decision knew about antidiscrimination law and company management ratified decision to fire plaintiff); Anderson v. G.D.C., Inc., 281 F.3d 452, 88 FEP 309 (4th Cir. 2002) (plaintiff should have been allowed trial on punitive damages, where record in light most favorable to plaintiff showed that company lacked antidiscrimination policy and manager was aware of poster at worksite informing readers that sex harassment violates federal law, commented that plaintiff would have to get used to harassment because "that was the way of G.D.C.," and exploited his authority to perpetrate harassment); Hemmings v. Tidyman's Inc., 285 F.3d 1174, 88 FEP 945 (9th Cir. 2002) (punitive damage award upheld on evidence concerning employer's awareness of antidiscrimination laws and actions in face of that awareness).

[431]*See* EEOC v. Heartway Corp., 466 F.3d 1156 (10th Cir. 2006) (district court erred in granting judgment as a matter of law on punitive damages where there was evidence supervisor had been trained in and was aware of ADA prohibitions); Zimmerman v. Associates First Capital Corp., 251 F.3d 376, 385, 85 FEP 1505 (2d Cir. 2001) ("training in 'equal opportunity' may now fairly be understood to convey some awareness of Title VII requirements"); *see also* DiMarco-Zappa v. Cabanillas, 238 F.3d 25, 38 (1st Cir. 2001) ("[t]he extent of federal statutory and constitutional law preventing discrimination on the basis of ethnicity or race suggests that defendants had to know that such discrimination was illegal"); Molnar v. Booth, 229 F.3d 593, 604, 83 FEP 1756 (7th Cir. 2000) (noting that punitive damages were appropriate because "[t]he events here took place in 1994, long after the law of sexual harassment had become well established by the Supreme Court").

[432]Kolstad v. American Dental Ass'n, 527 U.S. 526, 536–37, 79 FEP 1697 (1999).

2. *Vicarious Liability and Good Faith as a Defense*

In a second part of the *Kolstad* opinion, the Court held that "[t]he inquiry does not end with a showing of the requisite 'malice or . . . reckless indifference' . . . on the part of certain individuals."[433] The Court stated that liability must be imputed to the employer in order for punitive damages to be assessed and that "agency principles place limits on vicarious liability for punitive damages."[434] The Court cited the Restatement (Second) of Agency § 217C as a starting point for determining appropriate agency principles for imputing liability for punitive damages.[435] Although agreeing with most of the Restatement's agency principles, the Court expressly recognized that applying the Restatement's "scope of employment" rule in a Title VII punitive damages context would run counter to the purposes underlying Title VII.[436]

> Recognizing Title VII as an effort to promote prevention as well as remediation, and observing the very principles underlying the Restatement's strict limits on vicarious liability for punitive damages, we agree that, in the punitive damages context, an employer may not be vicariously liable for the discriminatory employment decisions of managerial agents where these decisions are contrary to the employer's "good-faith efforts to comply with Title VII."[437]

Courts, post-*Kolstad,* have considered what degree of authority an agent of the employer must have to subject the employer to liability for punitive damages and what actions constitute "good-faith efforts" so as to insulate an employer from punitive damages. In weighing the employer's "good-faith efforts," courts have noted that the existence of an antidiscrimination policy, standing by itself, will not insulate an employer from punitive damages.[438] However, punitive damages awards have been rejected where an

---

[433]*Id.* at 539.
[434]*Id.*
[435]*Id.* at 542–43.
[436]*Id.* at 544–45.
[437]*Id.* at 545.
[438]*Zimmerman*, 251 F.3d at 386, 85 FEP 1505 (testimony about training in equal opportunity "does not establish as a matter of law the existence of such a policy, much less good faith enforcement of such a policy"); Lowery v. Circuit City Stores, Inc., 206 F.3d 431, 446, 82 FEP 353 (4th Cir. 2000) (written antidiscrimination policy does not automatically establish good faith enforcement).

employer had an extensively implemented antidiscrimination policy, established a grievance policy, assured employees that no retaliation would occur for making complaints, had a carefully developed diversity training program, and voluntarily monitored departmental demographics as part of an ongoing effort to keep the employee base reflective of the pool of potential employees.[439]

In *Deffenbaugh-Williams v. Wal-Mart Stores*,[440] a case remanded in the wake of *Kolstad,* the Fifth Circuit held that a store manager named Gipson "had authority to make personnel decisions regarding Deffenbaugh and others in her department and in those of five other stores. In sum, substantial evidence existed from which a jury could reasonably find that Gipson was a managerial agent, acting in the scope of employment."[441] The court rejected the employer's good faith defense, finding there was no evidence of any actions by Wal-Mart directed at "requiring its managers to obey Title VII," or of Wal-Mart's response to the plaintiff's complaint or anything beyond a general nondiscrimination policy encouraging employees to contact higher management with grievances.[442]

---

[439]*See* Bryant v. Aiken Reg'l Med-Ctrs., Inc., 333 F.3d 536, 548–49, 92 FEP 233 (4th Cir. 2003), *cert. denied,* 540 U.S. 1106 (2004); *see also* Cooke v. Stefani Mgmt. Servs., Inc., 250 F.3d 564, 568–69, 85 FEP 1295 (7th Cir. 2001) (punitive damage award overturned where employer had written harassment policies and was unaware of manager's conduct; manager was motivated by a desire to amuse himself and not to benefit the employer).

[440]188 F.3d 278, 80 FEP 1357 (5th Cir. 1999).

[441]*Id.* at 285–86.

[442]*Id.* at 286; *see* Hertzberg v. SRAM Corp., 261 F.3d 651, 663–64 (7th Cir. 2001) (employer made no real responses to complaints about 100+ gender-related comments to plaintiff in 4 months), *cert. denied,* 534 U.S. 1130 (2004); Knowlton v. Teltrust Phones, Inc., 189 F.3d 1177, 1187, 80 FEP 1062 (10th Cir. 1999) (company's management was unmistakably aware of offensive conduct of supervisor and was unresponsive to complaints); EEOC v. Wal-Mart Stores, Inc., 187 F.3d 1241, 1248–49, 9 AD 1057 (10th Cir. 1999) ("[o]ur review of the record leaves us unconvinced that Wal-Mart made a good faith effort to educate its employees about the ADA prohibitions"); Kimbrough v. Loma Linda Dev. Inc., 183 F.3d 782, 785, 80 FEP 782 (8th Cir. 1999) (failure to investigate repeated complaints regarding supervisor's sexual harassment); Blackmon v. Pinkerton Sec. & Investigative Servs., 182 F.3d 629, 637, 80 FEP 137 (8th Cir. 1999) (employer took only minimal action to investigate and address complaints of sexual harassment); *see also* EEOC v. Indiana Bell Tel. Co., 256 F. 3d 516, 528, 86 FEP 1 (7th Cir. 2001) (en banc) (citing *Kolstad,* court holds that district court erred in denying admission of employer's collective bargaining agreement as evidence of absence of malice, for purposes of punitive damages award, regarding its failure to respond more quickly to complaints of harassment).

Similarly, the Ninth Circuit has held that if a manager is sufficiently senior, he or she may be a proxy for the corporation and punitive damages may be imposed despite the good faith efforts described in *Kolstad*.[443]

3. Due Process Concerns

The Supreme Court, although expressing concern with the magnitude of some punitive damages awards, has not articulated a clear constitutional basis for reviewing them. Constitutional due process[444] is satisfied, according to the Court, when the punitive damages award is made after consideration of the character and the degree of the wrong as shown by the evidence, for purposes only of deterrence and retribution,[445] as long as the fact finder's exercise of its discretion is subject to meaningful judicial review.[446]

---

[443]*See* Passantino v. Johnson & Johnson Consumer Prods., 212 F.3d 493, 517–17 (9th Cir. 2000) ("while *Kolstad* established that, under some circumstances, corporations may not be subject to punitive damages for actions taken by their 'managerial' employees, it did nothing to eliminate the rule established in earlier cases that an individual sufficiently senior in the corporation must be treated as the corporation's proxy for purposes of liability"); Hemmings v. Tidyman's, Inc., 285 F.3d 1174, 1198 (9th Cir. 2002) (affirmative defense of good faith efforts is unavailable to an employer for the actions of agents sufficiently senior to be considered proxies), *cert. denied*, 537 U.S. 1110 (2003).

[444]*Cf.* Browning-Ferris Indus. v. Kelco Disposal, Inc., 492 U.S. 257, 263–64 (1989) (the excessive fines clause does not apply to punitive damages awarded to plaintiffs in private suits).

[445]*See* Pacific Mut. Life Ins. Co. v. Haslip, 499 U.S. 1, 19–21 (1991) (the state court imposing punitive damages may consider only the conduct of the defendant against its *own* citizens, i.e., "a state may not impose economic sanctions on violators of its laws with the intent of changing the tortfeasors' lawful conduct in other states"); BMW of N. Am., Inc. v. Gore, 517 U.S. 559, 574 (1996) ("The award must be analyzed in the light of [conduct that occurred within Alabama], with consideration given only to the interests of Alabama consumers, rather than those of the entire Nation."). Several cases have rejected the argument that punitive damages should be denied or reduced where an errant employee has departed the company, because there is less need for punishment. Bouman v. Block, 940 F.2d 1211, 1234, 60 FEP 1000 (9th Cir. 1991) (retirement of the sheriff does not vitiate the deterrent function of a punitive damages award, because other members of the department will be deterred from engaging in such conduct); Wright v. Sheppard, 919 F.2d 665, 671 (11th Cir. 1990) (an award of punitive damages against a deputy sheriff who left the department will "deter him from [again] abusing innocent persons" if he ever seeks to engage in law enforcement work again, and will deter other officers from engaging in similar conduct).

[446]Honda Motor Co. v. Oberg, 512 US. 415, 430–32 (1994) (Oregon's failure to provide judicial review of the size of punitive damages awards violates the Due Process Clause).

The Supreme Court's decisions in *State Farm Mutual Automobile Insurance Co. v. Campbell*,[447] and its predecessors, *BMW of North America, Inc. v. Gore*,[448] *TXO Production Corp. v. Alliance Resources Corp.*,[449] and *Pacific Mutual Life Insurance Co. v. Haslip*,[450] represent an attempt to set forth a standard for such meaningful review of punitive damages awards.

In *Haslip*, the Court endorsed the standards that the Alabama Supreme Court had announced in reviewing the award below: (a) whether there is a reasonable relationship between the punitive damages award and the harm likely to result from the defendant's conduct as well as the harm that actually has occurred; (b) the degree of reprehensibility of the defendant's conduct; (c) the profitability to the defendant of the wrongful conduct; (d) the "financial position" of the defendant; and (e) all the costs of litigation; as mitigated by (f) the imposition of criminal sanctions on the defendant for its conduct; and (g) the existence of other civil awards against the defendant for the same conduct.[451] In *TXO Production Corp.*, the Court employed the *Haslip* standards in upholding a punitive damages award of $10 million where the compensatory award was only $19,000. In *BMW*, the Court distilled these standards into three "guideposts" for reviewing whether the amount of punitive damages was properly awardable in a given case: "the degree of reprehensibility of the [defendant's conduct]; the disparity between the harm or potential harm suffered by [the plaintiff] and his punitive damages award; and the difference between this remedy and the civil penalties authorized or imposed in comparable cases."[452] More recently, the Court reaffirmed that *BMW*'s first "guidepost," the degree of reprehensibility, is "the most important indicium of a punitive damages award's reasonableness."[453]

---

[447]538 U.S. 408 (2003).
[448]517 U.S. 559 (1996).
[449]509 U.S. 443 (1993).
[450]499 U.S. 1 (1991).
[451]*Id.* at 21–22.
[452]*BMW*, 517 U.S. at 575 (reversing a $2 million punitive damages award that failed constitutional scrutiny under the three guideposts).
[453]State Farm Mut. Auto. Ins. Co. v. Campbell, 538 U.S. 408, 418–19 (2003) (In determining a defendant's reprehensibility, courts are instructed to consider whether "the harm was physical as opposed to economic; the tortious conduct evinced an indifference to or a reckless disregard of the health or safety of others; the target of the conduct had financial vulnerability; the conduct involved repeated actions or was an isolated incident; and the harm was the result of intentional malice, trickery, or

There is no clear constitutional rule of proportionality between an award of compensatory damages and an award of punitive damages.[454] The *State Farm* Court, however, while declining to impose a bright-line maximum ratio, stated that "in practice, few awards exceeding a single-digit ratio between punitive and compensatory damages, to a significant degree, will satisfy due process."[455] The Court cited cases in which it had previously approved the ratio of 4-to-1; a ratio the Court described as "instructive."[456] Nevertheless,

---

deceit, or mere accident. The existence of any one of these factors weighing in favor of a plaintiff may not be sufficient to sustain a punitive damages award; and the absence of all of them renders any award suspect. It should be presumed a plaintiff has been made whole for his injuries by compensatory damages, so punitive damages should only be awarded if the defendant's culpability, after having paid compensatory damages, is so reprehensible as to warrant the imposition of further sanctions to achieve punishment or deterrence."), *cert. denied*, 543 U.S. 874 (2004).

[454]In dealing with challenges to punitive damages awards based on both due process concerns and the application of statutory caps, courts generally first apply the statutory cap, and only then determine any remaining due process issues. *See, e.g.*, Millaazzo v. Universal Traffic Serv., Inc., 289 F. Supp. 2d 1251, 1255, 92 FEP 1532 (D. Colo. 2003) (applying the statutory cap before conducting the constitutional analysis comports with and accommodates the remedial purpose of Title VII and the Supreme Court's due process concerns); Parrish v. Sollecito, 280 F. Supp. 2d 145, 154, 158, 92 FEP 1021 (S.D.N.Y. 2003) (court considers statutory cap before conducting constitutional analysis).

[455]538 U.S. at 424–25 (award of $145 million in punitive damages on $1 million compensatory judgment violated due process). The Court did not address the split among the circuits as to whether a plaintiff under 42 U.S.C. § 1981a must obtain a compensatory or back-pay award before he or she can obtain punitive damages. *Compare* Quint v. A.E. Staley Mfg. Co., 172 F.3d 1, 14 n.10, 9 AD 242 (1st Cir. 1999) (must receive award of compensatory damages or back pay as condition to punitives), *cert. denied*, 535 U.S. 1023 (2002) *with* Cush-Crawford v. Adchem Corp., 271 F.3d 352, 357, 87 FEP 456 (2d Cir. 2001) (an award of actual or nominal damages is not a prerequisite for an award of punitive damages in Title VII cases) *and* Timm v. Progressive Steel Treating, Inc., 137 F.3d 1008 (7th Cir. 1998) (no requirement of compensatory or back-pay award).

[456]*Id.* A number of federal courts that have since addressed the issue of the proportionality between punitive and compensatory damages have attached significance to the 4-to-1 ratio referenced in *State Farm. See* Patterson v. County of Oneida, 440 F.3d 104, 97 FEP 1057 (2d Cir. 2006) ($20,000 punitive award on $1 nominal damage award did not violate due process, but was excessive in light of individual defendant's difficult economic circumstances); Williams v. ConAgra Poultry Co., 378 F.3d 790, 796, 94 FEP 266 (8th Cir. 2004) (punitive damage award in excess of $6 million overturned as unconstitutional; ratio of punitive damages to compensatory damages (10:1) far exceeds the levels the Supreme Court has suggested are consistent with due process); Bogle v. McClure, 332 F.3d 1347, 1361–62 (11th Cir. 2003) (upholding punitive damages award of $2 million for each plaintiff where the compensatory award was $500,000: "the ratio between punitive and compensatory damages in this case is in the neighborhood of 4:1, a range which the Supreme Court has found to be 'instructive' "), *cert. dismissed*, 540 US. 1158 (2004); Rhone Poulenc

the *State Farm* Court stated that the precise award must be based upon the facts of the case.[457] Where "a particularly egregious act has resulted in only a small amount of economic damages," or where the monetary value of the economic harm is difficult to determine, the Due Process Clause may permit greater ratios.[458] The Court also addressed the issue of consideration of a defendant's wealth in relation to a punitive damages award, holding that "the wealth

---

Agro, S.A. v. DeKalb Genetics Corp., 345 F.3d 1366, 1371–72 (Fed. Cir. 2003) (upholding punitive damages award of $50 million where compensatory damages award was $15 million, "[t]hat ratio. . . not even reaching the 4-to-1 ratio mentioned by the [*State Farm*] Court as a threshold where the punitive award becomes suspect"); Parrish v. Sollecito, 280 F. Supp. 2d 145, 154, 164, 92 FEP 1021 (S.D.N.Y. 2003) (reducing ratio from 33 times the $15,000 compensatory damages award to just under four times damages based on the facts of the case). *But see* Mathias v. Accor Economy Lodging, Inc., 347 F. 3d 672, 675–76 (7th Cir. 2003) (Upholding punitive damages award of $186,000 where compensatory award was $5,000: "The Supreme Court did not, however, lay down a 4-to-1 or single digit ratio rule—it said merely that 'there is a presumption against an award that has a 145-to-1 ratio.' "); Zhang v. American Gem Seafoods, Inc., 339 F.3d 1020, 1044 (9th Cir. 2003) (in holding that a punitive damages award more than seven times the amount of the compensatory award was not excessive, the court cited *State Farm* only for the proposition that "single-digit multipliers are more likely to [comply] with due process"), *cert. denied*, 541 U.S. 902 (2004); Jones v. Rent-A-Center, Inc., 281 F. Supp. 2d 1277, 1289–90, 92 FEP 1097 (D. Kan. 2003) (support for affirming a punitive damages award in a sexual harassment case that was 29 times the amount of compensatory damages awarded was found in *State Farm*'s recognition that there may be instances where particularly egregious conduct that happened to cause little actual economic damage may support a higher ratio of punitive to compensatory damages).

Some courts have held that the ratio of compensatory to punitive damages referenced in *State Farm* does not generally concern Title VII, under which compensatory and punitive damages are capped by law. *See* Lust v. Sealy, Inc., 383 F.3d 580, 590, 94 FEP 645 (7th Cir. 2004) ("When Congress sets a limit, and a low one, on the total amount of damages that may be awarded, the ratio of punitive to compensatory damages in a particular award ceases to be an issue of constitutional dignity."); Romano v. U-Haul Int'l, 233 F.3d 655, 673 (1st Cir. 2000) ("a punitive damages award that comports with a statutory cap provides strong evidence that a defendant's due process rights have not been violated").

[457]*State Farm*, 538 U.S. at 424–25 ("The precise award in any case, of course, must be based upon the facts and circumstances of the defendant's conduct and the harm to the plaintiff.").

[458]State Farm Mut. Auto. Ins. Co. v. Campbell, 538 U.S. 408, 424–25 (2003); *accord* Lincoln v. Case, 340 F.3d 283, 294 (5th Cir. 2003) (holding in a housing discrimination action that a punitive damages award in the amount of $55,000, where compensatory damages award was only $500, was not excessive given the small amount of actual damages, the difficulty in determining actual damages in housing discrimination cases, and the important goal of deterring future wrongdoing) (citing *State Farm*).

of a defendant cannot justify an otherwise unconstitutional punitive damages award."[459]

D. Statutory Caps

Section 1981a(b)(3) establishes the following caps for compensatory and punitive damages combined:[460] (a) $50,000 for

---

[459]*State Farm*, 538 U.S. at 425–26. A review of the few lower court opinions
that have addressed this aspect of the decision reveals the existence of some confusion as to whether or not it is still permissible for a jury to consider the wealth of
a defendant in determining an appropriate punitive damages award. *Compare* Eden
Elec., Ltd. v. Amana Co., L.P., 258 F. Supp. 2d 958, 972 (N.D. Iowa 2003) (interpreting *State Farm* to mean only that "the fact that [the] defendant is a wealthy
corporation does not mean that [the] court is free to disregard the *Gore* analysis of
determining of whether an award is violative of the Fourteenth Amendment. . . . if
punitive damages are to continue to serve the broader functions of deterrence and
retribution [citations omitted], the defendant's wealth must be a consideration in
calculating any award"), *aff'd*, 370 F. 3d 824 (2004) *with* McClain v. Metabolife
Int'l, Inc., 259 F. Supp. 2d 1225, 1229 (N.D. Ala. 2003) (in reducing the punitive
damages award, the court expressed confusion as to whether or not an inquiry into
the financial impact of punitives was still permissible given the holding of *State Farm*:
"Before *State Farm*, the financial impact of punitive damages had been universally
thought of as an important criterion for deciding what is and what is not appropriate for accomplishing the purpose of deterrence. . . . Now, this court is not sure whether
the financial impact on a defendant is a thing to be considered.") *and Mathias*, 347
F.3d at 676–77 (defendant's net worth is relevant to the determination of punitives
because wealth, "in the sense of resources," can allow a defendant to mount an
extremely aggressive defense and so deter plaintiffs from bringing legitimate claims).

[460]42 U.S.C. § 1981a(b)(3)(A) (2000) ("sum of the amount of compensatory
damages . . . *and* the amount of punitive damages awarded under this section . . .
shall not exceed, for each complaining party") (emphasis added). The caps are to
be applied by the court, and the jury is not to be informed of the limitations on
recovery. *See* 42 U.S.C. § 1981a(c)(2) (2000); EEOC v. AIC Sec. Investigations, Inc.,
55 F.3d 1276, 1279, 4 AD 693 (7th Cir. 1995) ("the statute forbids the court to inform the jury of that limit"). The reason for not advising juries of the caps is to
ensure that "no pressure, upward or downward, will be exerted on the amount of
jury awards by the existence of the statutory limitations." 137 CONG. REC. S15,484
(daily ed. Oct. 30, 1991) (interpretive memorandum of Senator Danforth and his
original co-sponsors). When awards of both compensatory and punitive damages are
made, the court will have to decide which type of award to cut, and the respective
amount of each cut if both types are to be cut. Prior to the IRS' 1997 determination
that emotional distress damages awarded in Title VII cases should be included in
the plaintiff's gross income, *see* Section II.B.1.e *supra*, both sides ordinarily found
it in their interest to reduce the punitive damages award instead of the compensatory damages award in an effort to reduce their taxes. The 1997 revenue ruling makes
the distinction less important. Still, employers' insurance policies may reimburse
employers for awards of compensatory damages, but for reasons of public policy
rarely reimburse them for awards of punitive damages. In an early case under the

respondents[461] who have from 15 to 100 employees[462] "in each of 20 or more calendar weeks in the current or preceding calendar year";[463] (b) $100,000 for respondents with 101 to 200 employees over that period;[464] (c) $200,000 for respondents with 201 to 500 employees over that period;[465] and (d) $300,000 for respondents with more than 500 employees over that period.[466] At least one court has held that the statutory caps apply to each complaining party,[467]

1991 Act, the court reduced the punitive damages award to bring the jury's award within the cap, leaving the compensatory damages award untouched. *See* EEOC v. AIC Sec. Investigations, Ltd., 823 F. Supp. 571, 576, 2 AD 890 (N.D. Ill. 1993), *rev'd and remanded in part on other grounds*, 55 F.3d 1276 (7th Cir. 1995); *see also* Lust v. Sealy, Inc., 383 F.3d 580, 587–88, 94 FEP 645 (7th Cir. 2004) (when faced with uncapped verdict amount, judge should determine maximum awardable compensatory damages, subtract that from $300,000, and denote the rest as punitives).

[461]Unions, employment agencies, and joint apprenticeship programs are not exempt from damages awards under the Act but the extent of their liability is determined by the sizes of their own workforces. *See* Office of Legal Counsel, EEOC, *Enforcement Guidance: Compensatory and Punitive Damages Available Under § 102 of the Civil Rights Act of 1991* (July 1992), 3 EEOC COMPL. MAN. (BNA) N:6071, 6071 n.3 (citing the definition of respondent under 42 U.S.C. § 2000e(n), which includes an "employment agency, labor organization, joint labor-management committee controlling apprenticeship or other training or retraining program"). The EEOC has taken the position that such respondents that are covered by Title VII but have fewer than 15 employees in each of 20 or more calendar weeks are neither immune from damages nor exposed to unlimited damages, but will be subject to the $50,000 cap. *Id.* at N:6071, 6075.

[462]The EEOC has determined that part-time and temporary employees are to be included in this count, even though sometimes they cannot be included in the count for purposes of determining whether the employer meets the jurisdictional requirement of 15 employees, because the "for each working day" limitation in the definition of "employer" in § 701(b) (42 U.S.C. § 2000e(b)) was not carried over into § 1981a. *Id.* at N:6071, 6074 n.6. *See generally* Chapter 21 (Employers).

[463]42 U.S.C. § 1981a(b)(3)(A) (2000).

[464]*Id.* § 1981a(b)(3)(B).

[465]*Id.* § 1981a(b)(3)(C).

[466]*Id.* § 1981a(b)(3)(D).

[467]42 U.S.C. § 1981a(b)(3) (2000). The term "complaining party" is defined in § 1981a(d)(1) to include the EEOC, the Attorney General, and persons who may bring an action or proceeding under the statutes creating the substantive rights for which this section provides a remedy (Title VII, § 505 (29 U.S.C. § 794a) of the Rehabilitation Act of 1973, the ADA). Because the persons for whom the EEOC is seeking relief *may* seek to intervene, and because even nonfiling class members *may* move to intervene in a class action, plaintiffs may contend that each such person and each such class member is a "complaining party" for purposes of the caps; under this analysis, the respondent's total exposure would be the product of the number of persons who join, the number of their distinct causes of action, and the amount of the cap. *See* Office of Legal Counsel, EEOC, *Enforcement Guidance: Compensatory and Punitive Damages Available Under § 102 of the Civil Rights Act of 1991* (July 1992), 3 EEOC COMPL. MAN. (BNA) N:6071, 6076 n.8.

rather than to each distinct claim brought by a party.[468] The legislative history arguably supports an interpretation allowing a separate cap for each distinct cause of action, though not permitting a double recovery "for the same harm arising out of the same facts and circumstances."[469]

It is vital to understand what the caps do—and do not—cover. The caps are "in addition to" relief awarded under § 706(g) of Title VII.[470] Nor will the caps operate to limit recoveries based on violations of state law.[471] Section 706(g) relief includes back pay and prejudgment interest, and possibly certain other out-of-pocket economic losses as well.[472] The Supreme Court, resolving a conflict

---

[468]*See, e.g.*, Jones v. Rent-A-Center, Inc., 281 F. Supp. 2d 1277, 1280, 92 FEP 1097 (D. Kan. 2003) (describing "the prevailing view of the Tenth Circuit that § 1981a(b)(3)'s cap applies 'for each complaining party,' rather than to each claim").

[469]The Interpretive Memorandum signed by Senator Danforth and his original Republican co-sponsors, and endorsed by Senator Kennedy (on most issues including the following), introduced the discussion of the caps and other limitations on recovery with the following statement: "In addition to the above-cited restrictions, the following limitations also are placed on the damages available to each individual complaining party for each cause of action brought under section 1981a . . . ." 137 CONG. REC. S15,484 (daily ed. Oct. 30, 1991). The Section-by-Section Analysis of Representative Edwards, one of the chief sponsors and floor managers of the 1991 Act in the House, stated: "The sponsors acknowledge the limitations on damages awards in the legislation which apply to the damages available to each individual complaining party for each cause of action brought under Section 1981a." 137 CONG. REC. H9,527 (daily ed. Nov. 7, 1991). Representative Edwards earlier had used the phrase "cause of action" in the context of a possible cause of action for racial discrimination and a different possible cause of action for sex discrimination. *Id.* Thus, the legislative history suggests that a plaintiff with more than one distinct cause of action does not need to bring more than one lawsuit in order to obtain the benefit of a separate cap for each claim. However, there may not be double recovery "for the same harm arising out of the same facts and circumstances," no matter how many claims combined to produce that injury. 137 CONG. REC. H9,526; *accord id.* at S15,484.

[470]Section 1981a(a)(1) authorizes recovery of damages for intentional violations of Title VII "in addition to any relief authorized by section 706(g) of the Civil Rights Act of 1964."

[471]*See* Gagliardo v. Connaught Labs., Inc., 311 F.3d 565, 570, 13 AD 1345 (3d Cir. 2002) (§ 1981 does not prevent a plaintiff from recovering greater damages under a state law claim that is virtually identical to a capped federal claim); Passantino v. Johnson & Johnson Consumer Prods., 212 F.3d 493, 510 (9th Cir. 2000) (same); Martini v. Federal Nat'l Mortgage Ass'n, 178 F.3d 1336, 1349–50 (D.C. Cir. 1999) (same); *cf.* Rodriguez-Torres v. Caribbean Forms Mfg., Inc., 399 F.3d 52, 95 FEP 353 (1st Cir. 2005) (allocation of damages between federal and Puerto Rican law claims that maximized award to plaintiff not erroneous).

[472]Section 1981a(b)(2) states: "Compensatory damages under this section shall not include back pay, interest on back pay, or any other type of relief authorized under section 706(g) of the Civil Rights Act of 1964." The EEOC has taken the view that past expenses for psychiatric treatment can be recovered under § 706(g) and are

between the circuits, has held that front pay is not an element of compensatory damages, but is rather an equitable remedy under § 706(g), and therefore is not subject to the caps in § 1981a(b)(3).[473]

Courts are divided about whether the amount of damages awarded within the statutory cap should be adjusted on a sliding scale, according to egregiousness.[474]

VI. RIGHT TO JURY TRIAL

In Title VII,[475] ADA,[476] and § 1981[477] cases, either party may demand a jury trial where the plaintiff seeks compensatory or punitive damages.[478] In *City of Monterey v. Del Monte Dunes at*

---

not subject to the caps, but that future psychiatric expenses are to be treated as damages, and will thus be subject to the caps. Office of Legal Counsel, EEOC, *Enforcement Guidance: Compensatory and Punitive Damages Available Under § 102 of the Civil Rights Act of 1991* (July 1992), 3 EEOC COMPL. MAN. (BNA) N:6071, 6077.

[473]*See* Pollard v. E.I. du Pont de Nemours & Co., 532 U.S. 843, 85 FEP 1217 (2001) (in cases of intentional discrimination in employment, front pay is not considered compensatory damages under the Civil Rights Act of 1991, and thus is not subject to the Act's statutory cap).

[474]*Compare* Peyton v. DiMario, 287 F.3d 1121, 1127, 88 FEP 1041 (D.C. Cir. 2002) (rejecting argument "that 42 U.S.C. § 1981a(b) in essence requires a sliding scale") *and* Hennessy v. Penril Datacomm Networks, Inc., 69 F.3d 1344, 1355–56, 69 FEP 398 (7th Cir.1995) (sliding scale not appropriate) *with* McDonough v. City of Quincy, 452 F.3d 8, 98 FEP 481 (1st Cir. 2006) (noting split in circuits regarding calibration of award under cap).

[475]42 U.S.C. § 1981a(c) (2000).

[476]*Id.*

[477]*See* Moore v. Sun Oil Co., 636 F.2d 154, 157, 24 FEP 1072 (6th Cir. 1980) (plaintiff "was entitled to a jury insofar as he was asserting a legal remedy for compensatory and punitive damages"); *see also* Setser v. Novack Inv. Co., 638 F.2d 1137, 1140, 24 FEP 1793 (8th Cir.) (there is a constitutional right to jury trial for all legal claims based on § 1981; legal rights include "compensatory and, under certain circumstances, punitive damages") (citation omitted), *vacated in part en banc on other grounds*, 657 F.2d 962, 26 FEP 513 (8th Cir. 1981).

[478]*See* Allison v. Citgo Petroleum Corp., 151 F.3d 402, 423, 81 FEP 501 (5th Cir. 1998) (both parties have right to demand jury trial when compensatory and punitive damages are sought in intentional discrimination claims under Title VII); EEOC v. HBE Corp., 135 F.3d 543, 551, 76 FEP 495 (8th Cir. 1998) (where Title VII plaintiffs seek money damages, jury trial is proper); Harrington v. American Nat'l Red Cross St. Louis, 31 F. Supp. 2d 703, 706 (E.D. Mo. 1999) (plaintiff entitled to punitive damages and jury trial because American Red Cross is not governmental agency or political subdivision); *cf.* Landgraf v. USI Film Prods., 511 U.S. 244, 64 FEP 820 (1994) (Civil Rights Act of 1991 provisions for compensatory damages and jury trial do not apply retroactively to Title VII case pending when statute was enacted). *But see* Lutz v. Glendale Union High Sch., 403 F.3d 1061, 16 AD 1031 (9th Cir. 2005) (failure to demand jury trial for liability under Title VII may limit jury role to awarding damages).

Monterey,[479] the Supreme Court held that an action under § 1983 seeking legal relief is an "action at law" within the meaning of the Seventh Amendment's grant of a right to trial by jury.

Under the ADEA[480] and the Equal Pay Act,[481] there is a right to trial by jury of some issues against private employers and local governments, but not against federal government agency employers.[482] Lost wages[483]—which in ADEA cases are not subject to the equitable discretion of the court—and liquidated damages[484] are legal issues subject to jury trial under these standards. The issue of "willfulness" is also a legal issue subject to jury trial.[485]

Courts are divided over whether the amount of front-pay awards in ADEA cases is for the jury's determination. Because front pay is awarded, if at all, in lieu of the plainly equitable remedy of reinstatement, some courts have held that front-pay determinations are to be made by the court, not by a jury.[486] Other courts have

---

[479]526 U.S. 687, 709 (1999).

[480]29 U.S.C. § 626(c)(2) (2000) (if the EEOC has not commenced an ADEA action, "a person shall be entitled to a trial by jury of any issue of fact in any such action for recovery of amounts owing as a result of a violation of this chapter, regardless of whether equitable relief is sought by any party in such action").

[481]*See* EEOC v. Chicago Hous. Auth., 725 F. Supp. 392, 395, 51 FEP 883 (N.D. Ill. 1989) (EEOC has a right to jury trial against city housing authority in Equal Pay Act cases); EEOC v. Sizes Unlimited, Inc., 723 F. Supp. 1195, 1196, 51 FEP 343 (E.D. Mich. 1989) (EEOC is entitled to a jury trial on its EPA claim); Polay v. West Co., 629 F. Supp. 899, 903, 45 FEP 1345 (E.D. Pa. 1986) (the only issues that could properly be presented to a jury are plaintiff's Equal Pay Act claims).

[482]*See* Lehman v. Nakshian, 453 U.S. 156, 168–69, 26 FEP 65 (1981) (ADEA); Walker v. Thomas, 678 F. Supp. 164, 167, 46 FEP 832 (E.D. Mich. 1987) (EPA).

[483]*See* Lorillard v. Pons, 434 U.S. 575, 582–84, 16 FEP 885 (1978) (ADEA).

[484]*See* Sailor v. Hubbell, Inc., 4 F.3d 323, 326 & n.5, 62 FEP 1444 (4th Cir. 1993) ("Even if a jury was not needed to determine the amount of liquidated damages, [the plaintiff] was entitled to have a jury determine [the employer's] liability for liquidated damages because liquidated damages are a legal remedy"; ADEA.); Lindsey v. American Cast Iron Pipe Co., 810 F.2d 1094, 1097 n.3, 43 FEP 143 (11th Cir. 1987) (the plaintiff "was entitled to a jury trial for all factual issues of his ADEA claim, including his claim for liquidated damages"); Goodman v. Heublein, Inc., 645 F.2d 127, 129 n.2, 25 FEP 645 (2d Cir. 1981) ("Because liquidated damages are in the nature of legal relief, it is manifest that a party is entitled to have the factual issues underlying such a claim decided by a jury.") (citing H.R. CONF. REP. NO. 950, 95th Cong., 2d Sess. 14 (1978), *reprinted in* 1978 U.S.C.C.A.N. 535).

[485]*See* Dominic v. Consolidated Edison Co., 822 F.2d 1249, 1257, 44 FEP 268 (2d Cir. 1987).

[486]*See* Kirsch v. Fleet St., Ltd., 148 F.3d 149, 169, 77 FEP 318 (2d Cir. 1998) ("The question of whether front pay should be awarded under the ADEA is one as to which the parties had no right to a jury trial."); Downes v. Volkswagen of Am., Inc., 41 F.3d 1132, 1141, 69 FEP 11 (7th Cir. 1994) (rejecting suggestion that jury plays role in determining amount of front pay); Denison v. Swaco Geolograph Co.,

held that, although the court in the first instance must determine whether an award of front pay is more appropriate than an order of reinstatement, the determination of the amount of front pay is left to the jury.[487]

For factual questions common to both jury and nonjury claims, the jury's factual determinations on jury claims are binding on the court's determination of equitable claims.[488] Except in the "most imperative circumstances" a court cannot try the equitable claim first and bind the jury with its bench findings, because doing so would in effect defeat the right to jury trial.[489] The proper remedy for such an error is relitigation of the common issues before the jury.[490]

VII. LIQUIDATED DAMAGES

Where an Equal Pay Act[491] or ADEA[492] violation is found to be "willful," liquidated damages are available up to the amount of back pay. The ADEA provides that liquidated damages are mandatory for willful violations,[493] but the EPA provides that such

---

941 F.2d 1416, 1426, 59 FEP 795 (10th Cir. 1991) (same); Deloach v. Delchamps, Inc., 897 F.2d 815, 823 (5th Cir. 1990) (same); Duke v. Uniroyal, Inc., 928 F.2d 1413, 1424, 55 FEP 816 (4th Cir. 1991) (same); Wildman v. Lerner Stores Corp., 771 F.2d 605, 616, 38 FEP 1377 (1st Cir. 1985) (same).

[487]See Wells v. New Cherokee Corp., 58 F.3d 233, 237, 68 FEP 284 (6th Cir. 1995) (determination of amount of front pay is jury question, but determination of propriety of front pay is matter for court that ordinarily must precede submission of case to jury); Fite v. First Tenn. Prod. Credit Ass'n, 861 F.2d 884, 893, 48 FEP 449 (6th Cir. 1988), overruled in part on other grounds, Davis v. Mutual Life Ins. Co., 6 F.3d 367, 382 (6th Cir. 1993); Cassino v. Reichhold Chems., Inc., 817 F.2d 1338, 1347, 47 FEP 865 (9th Cir. 1987); Maxfield v. Sinclair Int'l, 766 F.2d 788, 796, 38 FEP 442 (3d Cir. 1985).

[488]See Lytle v. Household Mfg., Inc., 494 U.S. 545, 551, 52 FEP 423 (1990).

[489]Beacon Theatres, Inc. v. Westover, 359 U.S. 500, 510–11 (1959) ("circumstances which in view of the flexible procedures of the Federal Rules we cannot now anticipate").

[490]See Lytle, 494 U.S. at 553–54.

[491]See generally Chapter 18 (Compensation).

[492]See generally Chapter 12 (Age).

[493]The ADEA, 29 U.S.C. § 626(b) (2000), authorizes courts to apply the remedies set forth in 29 U.S.C. § 216(b)–(e) (2000), which is part of the Fair Labor Standards Act (FLSA). There is no judicial discretion as to the award of liquidated damages under the ADEA; liquidated damages must be awarded if the statutory "willfulness" standard is met. See Tyler v. Union Oil Co. of Cal., 304 F.3d 379, 89 FEP 1226 (5th Cir. 2002) (district court erred in reducing liquidated damages to

awards in some circumstances are discretionary.[494] The liquidated damages remedy is available against the federal government in Equal Pay Act cases,[495] but not in ADEA cases.[496]

$2,500; as a matter of law doubling of back-pay award is mandatory); Greene v. Safeway Stores, Inc., 210 F.3d 1237, 1246 (10th Cir. 2000) ("Once a violation of the ADEA is determined to be willful, an award of liquidated damages is mandatory."); Lee v. Rapid City Area Sch. Dist. No. 51-4, 981 F.2d 316, 319–20, 60 FEP 577 (8th Cir. 1992) (en banc) (where willfulness has been proven under the ADEA, there is no discretion to reduce the amount of liquidated damages); Spanier v. Morrison's Mgmt. Servs., Inc., 822 F.2d 975, 979, 44 FEP 628 (11th Cir. 1987) ("We hold that the existence of a jury issue of willfulness under the [Trans World Airlines, Inc. v. Thurston, 469 U.S. 111, 36 FEP 977 (1985)] standard divests the district court of discretion to reduce an ADEA liquidated damages award.").

[494]29 U.S.C. § 260 (2000) (Portal-to-Portal Act) (providing that if the employer can prove a good faith defense—that its act or omission was in good faith and that it had reasonable grounds to believe it did not violate FLSA—the court has the discretion to award any amount of liquidated damages ranging from none to the maximum amount specified); *see also* Brinkley-Obu v. Hughes Training, Inc., 36 F.3d 336, 357, 65 FEP 1840 (4th Cir. 1994) ("[A]n employer in violation of the Equal Pay Act will be liable for liquidated damages, equal to and in addition to compensatory damages, unless the employer demonstrates to the satisfaction of the court that the act or omission giving rise to such action was in good faith and that he had reasonable grounds for believing that his act or omission was not violative of the Act. Under 29 U.S.C. § 260, the district court has the discretion to decline to award liquidated damages when good faith is established."); EEOC v. Cherry-Burrell Corp., 35 F.3d 356, 363–64 (8th Cir. 1994) (no liquidated damages awarded where district court properly found that employers did not violate EPA knowingly or with reckless disregard of its provisions); Peters v. City of Shreveport, 818 F.2d 1148, 1166–67, 43 FEP 1822 (5th Cir. 1987) (§ 260 was satisfied where the defendant relied in good faith on a gender-neutral state law; "the court below was well within its discretion in refusing to award liquidated damages"); *cf.* Lowe v. Southmark Corp., 998 F.2d 335, 337–38, 62 FEP 1087 (5th Cir. 1993) (an award of liquidated damages, equal to the amount awarded as back pay and retaliation damages, is mandatory where the defendant did not have reasonable grounds to believe that its action was lawful, and thus did not act in good faith). This provision of the FLSA was not incorporated into the ADEA. Hill v. Spiegel, Inc., 708 F.2d 233, 238, 31 FEP 1532 (6th Cir. 1983) (holding that § 11 of the Portal-to-Portal Act, 29 U.S.C. § 260, did not apply to ADEA liquidated damages claims and that "[t]he court need not . . . make an independent determination of good faith of the employer"; "the district court was correct insofar as it held that it was without discretion, once the jury found willfulness, to award liquidated damages in an amount other than that equal to the award for compensatory damages").

[495]*See* Thompson v. Sawyer, 678 F.2d 257, 279–82, 28 FEP 1614 (D.C. Cir. 1982) (affirming an award of liquidated damages under 29 U.S.C. § 216 in an Equal Pay Act case against the Government Printing Office).

[496]*See* Edwards v. Shalala, 846 F. Supp. 997, 1001 n.8, 68 FEP 1410 (N.D. Ga. 1994) ("Though liquidated damages and attorney's fees are provided for in the private-action portion of the ADEA, such relief is not available when proceeding against the federal government under § 633a."), *aff'd*, 64 F.3d 601, 68 FEP 1414 (11th Cir.

Under the ADEA, conduct is "willful" if the employer " 'knew or showed reckless disregard for the matter of whether its conduct was prohibited by the ADEA.' "[497] Under the ADEA, "willful" conduct may be imputed.[498] Willfulness has been found where an employer altered or destroyed documents that may have indicated an EPA violation,[499] and where a plaintiff's supervisor—whose employer faced a genuine need to reduce the workforce—"believed that older workers are inferior" and lied about the plaintiff's skills in recommending his discharge.[500] Willfulness has been found in a variety of circumstances.[501]

1995); Smith v. Office of Pers. Mgmt., 778 F.2d 258, 263, 39 FEP 1851 (5th Cir. 1985) (there is no mention of liquidated damages in 29 U.S.C. § 633a, which creates federal employee causes of action against the federal government). ADEA cases may not be brought against the states. *See* Kimel v. Florida Bd. of Regents, 528 U.S. 62 (2000).

[497]Trans World Airlines, Inc. v. Thurston, 469 U.S. 111, 126, 36 FEP 977 (1985); Hazen Paper Co. v. Biggins, 507 U.S. 604 (1993).

[498]*See* Starceski v. Westinghouse Elec. Corp., 54 F.3d 1089 n.12, 67 FEP 1184 (3d Cir. 1995) (intent of second-level manager who was final decision maker on selection of people for discharge was imputed to company for determining ADEA violation and whether it was willful for purposes of liquidated damages); Tompulis v. Schwartz & Freeman, 66 FEP 1544, 1546 (N.D. Ill. 1994) (fact that defendant was law firm "is a relevant factor [as to willfulness] since law firm administrators should be more apt to have knowledge of the various laws that apply to all employment decisions"); *cf.* Wiehoff v. GTE Directories Corp., 61 F.3d 588, 593–94, 68 FEP 639 (8th Cir. 1995) (difference between willful violation and basic ADEA violation is in state of mind and in remedy, not in conduct).

[499]*See* Soto v. Adams Elevator Equip. Co., 941 F.2d 543, 551, 56 FEP 1270 (7th Cir. 1991) (after it hired a male "senior buyer," the employer changed a female employee's title from "senior buyer" to "buyer" on internal documents).

[500]*See* Gusman v. Unisys Corp., 986 F.2d 1146, 1147, 61 FEP 382 (7th Cir. 1993) ("An employer cannot escape responsibility for willful discrimination by multiple layers of paper review, when the facts on which the reviewers rely have been filtered by a manager determined to purge the labor force of older workers."); *cf. Starceski*, 54 F.3d at 1099–1100, 67 FEP 1184 (willfulness finding affirmed where the plaintiff's evidence showed that a manager told a subordinate supervisor "to set up the 'senior' engineers in [the] plaintiff's department for permanent layoff").

[501]*See* McGinty v. New York, 193 F.3d 64, 69 (2d Cir. 1999) (imposition of liquidated damages depends on finding of willful conduct); Smith v. Berry Co., 165 F.3d 390, 395, 79 FEP 52 (5th Cir. 1999) (company memo characterizing older workers as "very difficult group" and "more difficult to terminate" supported jury finding of willful violation, exposing company to liquidated damages); Paolitto v. John Brown E.&C., Inc., 151 F.3d 60, 67–68, 77 FEP 1351 (2d Cir. 1998) (under plain language of ADEA, plaintiff was entitled to doubling of his $100,000 in actual loss for willful violation by employer); Stolzenburg v. Ford Motor Co., 143 F.3d 402, 405, 76 FEP 1244 (8th Cir. 1998) (to receive liquidated damages, plaintiff must show employer either knew or showed reckless disregard for matter of whether its

Reductions in the back-pay award—e.g., offsets for interim earnings or failure to mitigate—should be subtracted from the back-pay award before calculating liquidated damages.[502] Front pay ordinarily is excluded from the calculation of liquidated damages on the basis that it is not yet due, and so cannot be an "amount owing"[503] under § 626(b) as a result of a violation of the ADEA.

---

conduct was prohibited by ADEA); Chiaramonte v. Fashion Bed Group, Inc., 129 F.3d 391, 402, 76 FEP 251 (7th Cir. 1997) (evidence that employer sought to have its personnel department ensure that discharges did not violate applicable laws negates claim of willful discrimination justifying liquidated damages); Weaver v. Amoco Prod. Co., 66 F.3d 85, 88, 70 FEP 931 (5th Cir. 1995) (upholding award of liquidated damages after review of record revealed evidence of taped conversation between employee and his supervisor illustrating knowing decision to force employee's retirement); Beshears v. Asbill, 930 F.2d 1348, 1356 (8th Cir. 1991) (willfulness warranting liquidated damages is found when "the people making the employment decision know that age discrimination is unlawful and if there is direct evidence of . . . age-based animus").

[502]See EEOC v. White & Son Enters., 881 F.2d 1006, 1012, 50 FEP 1076 (11th Cir. 1989) (interim earnings); Linn v. Andover Newton Theological Sch., Inc., 874 F.2d 1, 9, 49 FEP 1176 (1st Cir. 1989) (deducting pension benefits received by the plaintiff from the back-pay award before calculating liquidated damages). But see Jordan v. United States Postal Serv., 379 F.3d 1196, 1202 (10th Cir. 2004) (no deduction for full back pay restored before trial); Kossman v. Calumet County, 849 F.2d 1027, 1030 (7th Cir. 1988) (no deduction where employer paid portion of the amounts due before trial).

[503]See Olitsky v. Spencer Gifts, Inc., 964 F.2d 1471, 1479, 61 FEP 1507 (5th Cir. 1992) (district court did not err in refusing to double Olitsky's front-pay award); Wheeler v. McKinley Enters., 937 F.2d 1158, 1163 n.2, 56 FEP 504 (6th Cir. 1991) (even when front pay is recoverable, it cannot figure in the calculation of liquidated damages); Graefenhain v. Pabst Brewing Co., 870 F.2d 1198, 1210, 49 FEP 829 (7th Cir. 1989) (award of front-pay damages is not "amount owing" within meaning of statute providing for doubling of amounts owing as result of willful violation of ADEA since front pay is prospective remedy); Cooper v. Asplundh Tree Expert Co., 836 F.2d 1544, 1556–57, 45 FEP 1386 (10th Cir. 1988) (because the authority to grant front pay as a remedy stems not from the "amounts owing" language but from the additional power to grant appropriate legal and equitable relief, the statute does not contemplate the doubling of front-pay awards as liquidated damages in cases of willful violations); Blum v. Witco Chem. Corp., 829 F.2d 367, 382–83, 46 FEP 306 (3d Cir. 1987) (a front-pay award is the monetary equivalent of the equitable remedy of reinstatement; given its tenor, court declines to extend the liquidated damages provision of the ADEA to double this equitable award); Dominic v. Consolidated Edison Co., 822 F.2d 1249, 1258–59, 44 FEP 268 (2d Cir. 1987) (front pay is not within the meaning of "amounts owing" in § 626(b); accordingly, a discharged employee has no entitlement to liquidated damages equal to his front-pay award); Cassino v. Reichhold Chems., Inc., 817 F.2d 1338, 1348–49, 47 FEP 865 (9th Cir. 1987) (the jury should be instructed to award as liquidated damages, if it determines such an award appropriate, an amount not to exceed the back pay and benefits award amounts).

The circuits differ on whether liquidated damages are "compensatory"[504] or "punitive"[505] in nature, and thus whether equitable relief such as front pay and prejudgment interest should be denied or limited where substantial liquidated damages have been awarded.

VIII. INDIVIDUAL BACK-PAY CLAIMS IN COLLECTIVE PROCEEDINGS[506]

A. Determining Individual Back-Pay Damages

1. Introduction

In *Teamsters v. United States*,[507] a pattern-or-practice disparate treatment case brought by the Justice Department, the Supreme

---

[504]Starceski v. Westinghouse Elec. Corp., 54 F.3d 1089, 1102 (3d Cir. 1995) (permitting awards of both liquidated damages and prejudgment interest); Lindsey v. American Cast Iron Pipe Co., 810 F.2d 1094, 1102 (11th Cir. 1987) (same); Criswell v. Western Airlines, Inc., 709 F.2d 544, 556–57, 32 FEP 1204 (9th Cir. 1983) (liquidated damages are punitive and prejudgment interest is compensatory, so both properly may be awarded in the same case), *aff'd*, 472 U.S. 400, 37 FEP 1829 (1985).

[505]*See* Greene v. Safeway Stores, Inc., 210 F.3d 1237, 1247 (10th Cir. 2000) ("prejudgment interest is not available under the ADEA if plaintiffs receive liquidated damages"); Powers v. Grinnell Corp., 915 F.2d 34, 42–43, 53 FEP 1814 (1st Cir. 1990) (liquidated damages are partly compensatory and therefore may be used to justify the denial of prejudgment interest and front pay); Hamilton v. 1st Source Bank, 895 F.2d 159, 166, 51 FEP 1874 (4th Cir.) (a plaintiff cannot "recover prejudgment interest as well as liquidated damages"), *rev'd in part en banc on other grounds*, 928 F.2d 86, 54 FEP 1019 (4th Cir. 1990) (en banc); McCann v. Texas City Ref., Inc., 984 F.2d 667, 673, 61 FEP 288 (5th Cir. 1993) ("In an ADEA case where liquidated damages are awarded, a court may not award prejudgment interest on either the back pay or the liquidated damage award."); *Linn*, 874 F.2d 1, 7 n.9, 49 FEP 1176 ("It makes no difference that the interest was awarded under state law."); Wildman v. Lerner Stores Corp., 771 F.2d 605, 616, 38 FEP 1377 (1st Cir. 1985) (affirming denial of front pay where the plaintiff received back pay, liquidated damages, double damages under the Puerto Rico Anti-Discrimination Statute, and additional damages under the Puerto Rico severance pay statute); *cf.* Cross v. New York City Transit Auth., 417 F.3d 241, 96 FEP 239 (2d Cir. 2005) (although liquidated damages are punitive in nature, ADEA expressly permits punitive damages against public employers, waiving their common law immunity); Walther v. Lone Star Gas Co., 952 F.2d 119, 127–28, 59 FEP 848 (5th Cir. 1992) (front-pay awards are subject to equitable discretion, and "a substantial liquidated damage award may indicate that an additional award of front pay is inappropriate or excessive"; remanding for a "greater explanation" of the court's rationale in allowing "sizeable awards" of front pay and liquidated damages).

[506]Chapter 32 (Class Actions) discusses procedural devices for determining classwide relief, such as bifurcation, appointment of a special master, and the use of proof-of-claim forms. This section by contrast, concentrates on substantive class monetary relief issues. Other issues related to collective proceedings are discussed in Chapters 29 (EEOC Litigation) and 30 (Justice Department Litigation).

[507]431 U.S. 324, 14 FEP 1514 (1977).

Court discussed, in some detail, how individual back-pay claims are resolved in a collective action after discrimination against a protected group has been shown.[508] Such cases typically are bifurcated: Stage I proceedings focus on liability, and Stage II proceedings, if necessary, focus on relief. If classwide liability is proven during Stage I, "the force of that proof does not dissipate at the remedial stage of the trial."[509] In hiring, transfer, and promotion cases, "the burden [during Stage II] rests on the employer to demonstrate that the individual applicant was denied an employment opportunity for lawful reasons."[510] The basic task of the district court in Stage II back-pay proceedings is as follows:

> Initially, the court will have to make a substantial number of individual determinations in deciding which of the minority employees were actual victims of the company's discriminatory practices. After the victims have been identified, the court must, as nearly as possible, "recreate the conditions and relationships that would have been had there been no" unlawful discrimination. This process of recreating the past will necessarily involve a degree of approximation and imprecision. Because . . . more than one minority employee may have been denied each . . . vacancy, the court will be required to balance the equities of each minority employee's situation in allocating the limited number of vacancies that were discriminatorily refused to class members.[511]

The calculation of individual back-pay claims in class actions is not an exact science; yet back pay cannot be denied following a finding of class discrimination simply because back-pay determinations are imprecise or difficult.[512] As the Seventh Circuit observed in *Stewart v. General Motors Corp.*:

> In light of the uncertainty which clouds the task before us, we must set down three general rules: (1) unrealistic exactitude is not required; (2) ambiguities in what an employee or group of employees would have earned but for the discrimination should be resolved against the discriminating employer; (3) the district court, far closer

---

[508]The discussion in this section applies equally to class actions under Fed. R. Civ. P. 23 and to actions prosecuted by the EEOC or the Justice Department involving a pattern or practice of discrimination.

[509]*Teamsters*, 431 U.S. at 361–62.

[510]*Id.* at 362.

[511]*Id.* at 371–72 (citation omitted).

[512]There is no de minimis exception to the obligation to award full back pay, even if the employer has to spend more identifying and locating claimants than the individual awards are worth. *See* EEOC v. Korn Indus., Inc., 662 F.2d 256, 264, 27 FEP 13 (4th Cir. 1981) (reversing a denial of back pay to those whose awards would be less than $50).

to the facts of the case than we can ever be, must be granted wide discretion in resolving ambiguities.[513]

The following four steps normally should be followed to determine the employer's total back-pay liability and which class members are entitled to a share of the award.

2. When Did the Period of Liability Commence?

Ascertaining when the back-pay liability period commenced depends on the date a charge of discrimination was filed. In fact, the date on which a class member filed the initial EEOC charge containing class allegations is crucial in determining (a) whether the charge is timely at all;[514] (b) the start of the statutory back-pay period (which is, at most, two years before the date of the charge);[515] and (c) according to most courts, the persons eligible for inclusion within the class.

Under the "single-filing rule," each member of the class is not required to have filed a separate charge with the EEOC.[516] The rationale behind the "single filing rule" is the belief that it would be wasteful for numerous employees with the same grievances to file identical complaints with the EEOC.[517] Class membership is limited, however, to those discriminatees who timely *could have* filed a charge with the EEOC on the date on which the earlier

---

[513]542 F.2d 445, 452, 13 FEP 1035 (7th Cir. 1976); *accord* Segar v. Smith, 738 F.2d 1249, 1291, 35 FEP 31 (D.C. Cir. 1984) ("If effective relief for the victims of discrimination necessarily entails the risk that a few non-victims might also benefit from the relief, then the employer, as a proven discriminator, must bear that risk."); Domingo v. New Eng. Fish Co., 727 F.2d 1429, 1445, 34 FEP 584 (9th Cir. 1984) ("All uncertainties should be resolved against the employer."); Pettway v. American Cast Iron Pipe Co., 576 F.2d 1157, 1223, 17 FEP 1712 (5th Cir. 1978) (the court should not substitute 1 hour of efficiency for 1 moment of justice); Hairston v. McLean Trucking Co., 520 F.2d 226, 232–33, 11 FEP 91 (4th Cir. 1975) (difficulty in assessing back pay is a function of the subtlety of the discrimination, and is not a defense; the employer must bear the risks of the necessary speculation and uncertainty).

[514]*See generally* Chapters 26 (Timeliness) and 32 (Class Actions).

[515]*See* Section II.B.2.a *supra*.

[516]*See* Albemarle Paper Co. v. Moody, 422 U.S. 405, 414 n.8, 10 FEP 1181 (1975). *See generally* Chapter 32 (Class Actions).

[517]*See* EEOC v. Wilson Metal Casket Co., 24 F.3d 836, 840, 64 FEP 1402 (6th Cir. 1994) ("Where a substantially related non-filed claim arises out of the same time frame as a timely filed claim, the complainant need not satisfy Title VII's filing requirement to recover.").

charge was filed—i.e., those who were employed or affected by discrimination within the time period starting 180 (or, in a deferral state, 300) days before the actual filing.[518] Likewise, class membership in § 1981 and § 1983 suits is limited to those who were harmed within the applicable limitations period.[519]

3. How Many Available Positions Did Class Members Lose?

Where an employer rejected more class members than it had positions available, plainly it would be improper to award each class member full back-pay relief[520]—because, by definition, some of the class members would not have been selected even in the absence of discrimination. In cases involving selection for hire,

---

[518]The leading case on this point is *Wetzel v. Liberty Mutual Insurance Co.*, 508 F.2d 239, 9 FEP 211 (3d Cir. 1974), which held that the timely filing requirement for EEOC charges is a jurisdictional prerequisite to suit under Title VII:

> A plaintiff may bring a class action on behalf of those who have not filed charges with the EEOC. . . . This tolls the statute of limitations for all members of the class. . . . But [the named plaintiffs] cannot represent those who could not have filed a charge with the EEOC at the time they filed their charges.

Id. at 246; *accord* Long v. Florida, 805 F.2d 1542, 1546, 42 FEP 1058 (11th Cir. 1986) ("Under Title VII the discriminatory event against each employee must take place within the requisite time frame before such an employee can be included in the class."), *rev'd on other grounds*, 487 U.S. 223, 47 FEP 7 (1988); Domingo v. New England Fish Co., 727 F.2d 1429, 1442–43, 34 FEP 584 (9th Cir. 1984) (to include in the class persons who were not discriminated against within the period beginning 300 days prior to the filing of the earliest EEOC charge "would effectively read the limitation period out of the statute, which we cannot do"); Payne v. Travenol Lab., Inc., 673 F.2d 798, 813–14, 28 FEP 1212 (5th Cir. 1982) ("The opening date for membership in a class for a Title VII claim should be set by reference to the earliest charge filed by a named plaintiff."); Laffey v. Northwest Airlines, Inc., 567 F.2d 429, 472, 13 FEP 1068 (D.C. Cir. 1976) ("That filing, it seems clear, however, cannot revive claims which are no longer viable at the time of the filing.").

The various issues related to the timely filing of EEOC charges are discussed extensively in Chapter 26 (Timeliness).

[519]*E.g., Payne*, 673 F.2d at 813–14 (§ 1981); Selzer v. Board of Educ., 113 F.R.D. 165, 170–71, 45 FEP 870 (S.D.N.Y. 1986) (§ 1983).

[520]*See* Evans v. City of Evanston, 881 F.2d 382, 386, 50 FEP 612 (7th Cir. 1989) (in a class action brought by women who failed a firefighters' agility test, district court judge awarded minimal back pay where only 1.2% of all applicants passing the agility test actually are hired). Claims for noneconomic damages, on the other hand, may not be limited by the number of vacancies but may be recoverable by all class members who suffered such injuries. *Cf.* Jordan v. Dellway Villa of Tenn., Ltd., 661 F.2d 588, 592–94 (6th Cir. 1981) (housing discrimination case; the number of available apartments, 244, did not limit the number of class members entitled to damages relief).

promotion, or transfer, therefore, the court must ascertain the number of vacancies filled from which class members were excluded.[521] The court must also determine what percentage of these vacancies would have been filled by class members, as opposed to others, absent discrimination.[522] The length of time that class members likely would have worked in the available positions, if they had been selected, also should be estimated.[523] If no vacancies occurred during the relevant time frame, normally there can be no back-pay liability at all,[524] except where the discriminatory practice prevented a vacancy from arising and being filled.[525]

---

[521]*See* Teamsters v. United States, 431 U.S. 324, 371–72, 14 FEP 1514 (1977) (the court must recreate, as nearly as possible, the conditions and relationships that would have existed in the absence of discrimination); Segar v. Smith, 738 F.2d 1249, 1292–93, 35 FEP 31 (D.C. Cir. 1984) (the trial court must limit relief to positions denied during the actionable period). The same principle applies in cases involving discriminatory referrals by employment agencies or unions. *E.g.*, Pegues v. Mississippi State Employment Serv., 899 F.2d 1449, 1451–52, 1454–56 (5th Cir. 1990) (parties entered into stipulations relating to the relevant job orders listed with the employment agency); Hameed v. Iron Workers, 637 F.2d 506, 520, 24 FEP 352 (8th Cir. 1980) (court determined size of class of discriminatees by determining the percentage of applicants who were black, applied that percentage to the number of positions available on an annual basis, determined damages for the number of positions denied applicants, and then divided that among the class on a pro-rata basis.)

[522]*See* Association Against Discrimination in Employment, Inc. v. City of Bridgeport, 647 F.2d 256, 284–87, 25 FEP 1013 (2d Cir. 1981) (remedial relief should be granted only to those class members who would have filled vacancies absent discrimination); Ingram v. Madison Square Garden Ctr., Inc., 709 F.2d 807, 811–12, 32 FEP 641 (2d Cir. 1983) (the district court erred in assuming without factual basis that class members would have filled all available positions).

[523]*Pegues*, 899 F.2d at 1454–56 (turnover must be taken into account, but the period of back-pay recovery for past violations does not end when the defendant stopped committing new violations, because the victims of past violations would have continued working); Domingo v. New England Fish Co., 727 F.2d 1429, 1444, 34 FEP 584 (9th Cir. 1984) (the award should reflect the seasons class members would have worked but for the discrimination); Sledge v. J.P. Stevens & Co., 50 EPD ¶ 38,985, at 57,268 (E.D.N.C. 1989) (shortfall calculations should be combined with the calculation of attrition to arrive at the total number of positions denied to class members during each year).

[524]Bishopp v. District of Columbia, 57 F.3d 1088, 1092–93 (D.C. Cir. 1995) (because fire marshal position never opened, "plaintiffs did not, and indeed could not, allege illegal discrimination in the filling of that position"); Bing v. Roadway Express, Inc., 485 F.2d 441, 451–52, 6 FEP 677 (5th Cir. 1973) (the lack of job openings bars relief for the periods of time prior to the occurrence of openings); *see also* Patterson v. Youngstown Sheet & Tube Co., 475 F. Supp. 344, 355, 24 FEP 1087 (N.D. Ind. 1979) (only one vacancy would have been filled by a member of the plaintiff class), *aff'd*, 659 F.2d 736, 28 FEP 1434 (7th Cir. 1981).

[525]*See Pegues*, 899 F.2d at 1456 (affirming a back-pay award for referrals not made because the employment service " 'might have been able to fill them by referring enough applicants' ") (quoting the district court).

Although the typical approach is that set forth above—assessing a defendant's liability by the number of available vacancies that would have gone to class members in the absence of discrimination—it is not the only approach. Where it is possible to make reasonably accurate determinations as to whether particular vacancies would (or would not) have been filled by particular class members, and where the amount at stake justifies the increased expense, it may be more appropriate in some cases to use an individual-by-individual approach as to all vacancies.[526]

4. Which Class Members Experienced Discrimination?

Even when classwide discrimination occurred, not every class member is an actual discrimination victim. That may be so, for example, where the employer had a manifestly legitimate, nondiscriminatory reason for an individual action or where the employer can establish that only one member of the class would have received a promotion absent discrimination.[527] Stage I of the trial determines whether class members *collectively* were discriminated against. Plaintiffs' success at Stage I, however, establishes only a rebuttable presumption of discrimination for each class member: "[T]he burden then rests on the employer to demonstrate that the individual applicant was denied an employment opportunity for lawful reasons."[528] Stage II proceedings thus, of necessity, are individualized.

---

[526]In *Kraszewski v. State Farm General Insurance Co.*, 41 FEP 1088 (N.D. Cal. 1986), *aff'd in part and rev'd in part*, 912 F.2d 1182 (9th Cir. 1990), for example, the defendant was found liable for discriminating against women for positions as insurance agents. There was a shortfall of 214 positions for women out of 1,250 filled. The defendant argued for a classwide approach, so as to cap its liability at 214 positions. Plaintiffs argued for an individualized approach, believing that the qualifications of the rejected female applicants would have led to hires of far more than 214 women if selections had been nondiscriminatory. *Id.* at 1091–92. The court held that an individualized approach was feasible and should take only 2 to 3 years. "[W]here large sums of money are at stake, the presumption in favor of individualized hearings would appear to be critical." *Id.* at 1090. In these circumstances, the court held that limiting plaintiffs to a ceiling of 214 positions would in effect adopt the "bottom-line" approach forbidden by *Connecticut v. Teal*, 457 U.S. 440, 29 FEP 1 (1982).

[527]*See* Bishopp v. District of Columbia, 57 F.3d 1088, 1093 (D.C. Cir. 1995) ("Here, where only one position was filled in a discriminatory manner, and the district court was able to conclude that another member of the plaintiffs' class would have received the promotion absent discrimination," then the "remaining class members are entitled to nothing.").

[528]Teamsters v. United States, 431 U.S. 324, 362, 14 FEP 1514 (1977) ("The proof of the pattern or practice supports an inference that any particular employment

Nonapplicants have an extra hurdle to overcome at this second stage. *Teamsters* concluded that, although nonapplicants are not per se barred from consideration for individual relief,[529] they must meet "the not always easy burden of proving that [they] would have applied for the job" had that been feasible.[530] For example, courts have allowed relief to nonapplicants where (a) the employer picks employees for promotion or other opportunities without soliciting applications,[531] (b) the employer accepts only word-of-mouth referrals,[532] and (c) an application for promotion or transfer would

---

decision, during the period in which the discriminatory policy was in force, was made in pursuit of that policy."); *see also* Sledge v. J.P. Stevens & Co., 585 F.2d 625, 637–38, 18 FEP 261 (4th Cir. 1978) (named plaintiffs should not have had their claims dismissed without the benefit of the presumption).

[529]*See* Winbush v. Iowa, 66 F.3d 1471, 1481, 69 FEP 1348 (8th Cir. 1995) (court noted that reason class members did not apply for promotions was "either that they did not know how or when to apply or that they were led to believe that applying would do no good"); EEOC v. O & G Spring & Wire Forms Specialty Co., 38 F.3d 872, 879 n.9, 65 FEP 1823 (7th Cir. 1994) (back-pay award for hiring shortfall included lost wages and benefits for number of positions that would have been filled by African Americans absent discriminatory word-of-mouth recruitment practice); Eldred v. Consolidated Freightways Corp., 898 F. Supp. 928, 938, 71 FEP 33 (D. Mass. 1995) ("failure to apply formally for a job opening when there is no formal application process will not preclude a Title VII plaintiff from establishing a prima facie case, as long as the plaintiff made a reasonable attempt to convey her interest in the job to the employer").

[530]431 U.S. at 367–68; *see, e.g.,* EEOC v. Metal Serv. Co., 892 F.2d 341, 348–51, 51 FEP 1238 (3d Cir. 1990) (the EEOC made out a prima facie case of discrimination on behalf of charging parties who never filled out applications with the employer but reasonably had informed the employer of their interest in its jobs). Relying on *Teamsters*, the Sixth Circuit has held that, in nonapplicant cases, general findings of deterrence or futility made during the liability stage do not create any presumption at the back-pay stage that each nonapplicant class member would have sought the desired position. Mitchell v. Mid-Continent Spring Co., 583 F.2d 275, 283–84, 17 FEP 1594 (6th Cir.), *modified on other grounds,* 587 F.2d 841, 23 FEP 787 (6th Cir. 1978). Rather, each class member must make an individual showing that he or she would have applied for that position. *Id.* At least where evidence indicates that the jobs in question had enough drawbacks to raise doubt that all class members would have wanted them, the Sixth Circuit's approach is sensible. In *Teamsters,* for example, the Court required individual determinations because the defendants' lawful seniority system would have imposed substantial temporary disadvantages on class members transferring to the higher-paid positions in question. 431 U.S. at 368–71.

[531]*E.g.,* Jones v. Firestone Tire & Rubber Co., 977 F.2d 527, 533, 60 FEP 456 (11th Cir. 1992) ("Jones does not argue that he applied for the Dahlem vacancy. Under the law of this circuit he need not make such a showing. Firestone uses an informal promotion system under which it does not post openings or take applications for positions.").

[532]*E.g.,* Cox v. American Cast Iron Pipe Co., 784 F.2d 1546, 1560, 40 FEP 678 (11th Cir. 1986) (an employer using an informal or word-of-mouth system should

have been futile because, for example, the employer used widely known policies, such as educational or height-and-weight requirements, that are not validated as job-related.[533]

Once the universe of putative discriminatees is known, the employer may choose to offer proof that it refused to hire a particular class member for entirely legitimate reasons. *Teamsters* did not characterize the necessary quantum of proof, and lower courts are divided on this issue. Some have held that the defendant can discharge its burden only by clear and convincing evidence,[534]

---

have considered each plaintiff for any and all positions for which they can show it reasonably was on notice). *See generally* Chapter 15 (Hiring).

[533]*See* Dothard v. Rawlinson, 433 U.S. 321, 330, 15 FEP 10 (1977) ("otherwise qualified people might be discouraged from applying because of a self-recognized inability to meet the very standards challenged as being discriminatory"); *Teamsters*, 431 U.S. at 365 ("A consistently enforced discriminatory policy can surely deter job applications from those who are aware of it and are unwilling to subject themselves to the humiliation of explicit and certain rejection."). *See generally* Chapters 4 (Application of Adverse Impact to Employment Decisions) and 10 (Sex).

[534]The Fifth Circuit in *Baxter v. Savannah Sugar Refining Corp.*, 495 F.2d 437, 8 FEP 84 (5th Cir. 1974), explained this view:

[T]he initial burden will be on the individual discriminatee to show that he was available for promotion and possessed the general characteristics and qualifications which are shown by Savannah to be possessed by the higher paid white employees and are job related. Once this burden is met, the employer must demonstrate by clear and convincing evidence that any particular employee would have never been advanced because of that individual's particular lack of qualifications for a more difficult position or for other good and sufficient reasons such employee would never have been promoted. It is apparent that whether any particular individual would have been advanced under a color-blind system cannot now be determined with 100% certainty. The court on remand will have to deal with probabilities. Any substantial doubts created by this task must be resolved in favor of the discriminatee who has produced evidence to establish a prima facie case . . . .

Id. at 444–45; *accord* United States v. City of Chi., 853 F.2d 572, 575, 47 FEP 859 (7th Cir. 1988) (to defeat a Title VII plaintiff's claim for damages, the employer must prove that the plaintiff was not an actual victim of discrimination; the employer must provide clear and convincing evidence to meet its burden); Jauregui v. City of Glendale, 852 F.2d 1128, 1136–37, 47 FEP 1860 (9th Cir. 1988) (once discrimination in an employment decision is shown, the disadvantaged applicant should be awarded the position retroactively unless the defendant shows by clear and convincing evidence that even in the absence of discrimination the rejected applicant would not have been selected for the open position); *Cox*, 784 F.2d 1546, 1559 (once a pattern and practice of discrimination is established, a rebuttable presumption arises that plaintiff was discriminated against because of her sex and is entitled to recovery; the employer may overcome this presumption only with clear and convincing evidence that job decisions made when the discriminatory policy was in force were not made in pursuit of that policy); McKenzie v. Sawyer, 684 F.2d 62, 77–78, 29 FEP 633 (D.C. Cir. 1982) (district court properly concluded that Office Press Section

whereas others have held that the defendant satisfies its burden with proof by a preponderance of the evidence.[535] Plaintiffs, in attacking the defendant's proof, may contend that the facts or circumstances the defendant claims to have relied upon are pretextual, such as by showing that they were not consistently applied.[536]

5. What Deductions Should Be Taken From Each Class Member's Damages?

Once the back-pay period, the number of available openings, and the eligible members of the class are determined, the court must

---

(OPS) of the Government Printing Office should be required to rebut the plaintiffs' individual showings by clear and convincing evidence; because OPS was a proven discriminator, individual members of the plaintiff class were presumptively entitled to relief upon a showing that they applied or would have applied for the positions at issue); *see also* 29 C.F.R. 1614.501(b)(1)(i), (c)(1), (c)(2) (EEOC approves the clear and convincing standard where the employer is a federal agency).

[535]*E.g.*, Wooldridge v. Marlene Indus. Corp., 875 F.2d 540, 549, 49 FEP 1455 (6th Cir. 1989) (unnecessary to impose a clear and convincing proof requirement because Sixth Circuit guidelines for back-pay awards under Title VII have effectively shifted the risk of error in favor of the back-pay claimant); Craik v. Minnesota State Univ. Bd., 731 F.2d 465, 470 n.8, 34 FEP 649 (8th Cir. 1984) (because the court does not believe that the public and private interests involved require altering that distribution of the risk of error between the litigants, the court finds that the normal standard of proof in civil litigation should apply); Sledge v. J.P. Stevens & Co., 585 F.2d 625, 637, 18 FEP 261 (4th Cir. 1978) (burden that shifts to the employer is based on a preponderance of the evidence standard); *cf.* Price Waterhouse v. Hopkins, 490 U.S. 228, 252–54, 49 FEP 954 (1989) (a Title VII defendant in a mixed-motive case, involving both legitimate and unlawful motives for the challenged action, can defeat liability by proving by a preponderance of the evidence that it would have reached the same decision in the absence of discrimination; rejecting the lower courts' requirement that this burden must be discharged by clear and convincing evidence); EEOC v. O & G Spring & Wire Forms Specialty Co., 38 F.3d 872, 878, 65 FEP 1823 (7th Cir. 1994) (employer may rebut prima facie case of discrimination by preponderance of evidence).

[536]*See* Franks v. Bowman Transp. Co., 424 U.S. 747, 773 n.32, 12 FEP 549 (1976) (evidence of the individual's lack of qualification for the jobs in question "under nondiscriminatory standards *actually applied* by [the employer] to individuals who were in fact hired" would be relevant) (emphasis in original); Chisholm v. United States Postal Serv., 665 F.2d 482, 496–97, 27 FEP 425 (4th Cir. 1981) (the Postal Service's asserted reliance on the greater length of service of white promotees is invalid where there is no evidence demonstrating that promotions were controlled by seniority, and where less senior whites sometimes were promoted over more senior African Americans); *cf. Baxter*, 495 F.2d 437, 444, 8 FEP 84 ("Of course, only those qualifications possessed by white workers which are established by Savannah to be job related should be considered."). *See generally* Chapter 2 (Disparate Treatment).

calculate the class back-pay award. Just as in individual back-pay awards,[537] interim earnings must be taken into account in class back-pay awards. In failure-to-promote cases, where the defendant has a record of the plaintiff's earnings, this presents little difficulty; in other cases, the defendant could look to the Social Security Administration's records, which show covered earnings.[538] Although there is some authority that the class's interim earnings should be deemed to be the interim earnings of the class member who has the least amount of interim earnings,[539] courts generally calculate classwide interim earnings based on the average interim earnings of the class members eligible for a particular position.[540] In calculating the average interim earnings, plaintiffs may argue that class members who did not suffer economic injury at all (i.e., those whose interim earnings equaled or exceeded the earnings anticipated absent discrimination) should be excluded before performing the classwide calculation.[541] Defendants may argue, on the other hand, that excluding any class members leads to an inaccurate calculation of the average, which by definition must reflect *all* eligible class members' interim earnings. Alternatively, defendants may contend, if the high earners (with little or no damages) are excluded from the calculation, so should the low (or non) earners (with the most damages) be excluded.

---

[537]*See* Section II.B.1 *supra.*

[538]*See, e.g.*, Pegues v. Mississippi State Employment Serv., 698 F. Supp. 116 (N.D. Miss. 1988) (taking Social Security Administration reports of earnings into account), *rev'd in part on other grounds*, 899 F.2d 1449 (5th Cir. 1990).

[539]*E.g.*, United States v. United States Steel Corp., 520 F.2d 1043, 1056, 11 FEP 553 (5th Cir. 1975) ("This method involves a distribution across the affected group of the sum which represents the largest loss suffered by a group member who, as likely as any other, could have occupied the vacancy in question but for discrimination.").

[540]*See, e.g., Pegues*, 698 F. Supp. at 120. The use of average earnings conceptually is a more accurate measure of the economic harm suffered by the class than is the use of earnings figures based upon extreme high-earning or low-earning members of the class.

[541]*Pegues*, 698 F. Supp. at 120 (N.D. Miss. 1988). This is roughly analogous to the situation in which an individual plaintiff, in some but not all years, earns more at another job than he or she would have earned from the defendant employer in the absence of discrimination. The "excess earnings" may stop the back-pay period from running or disqualify some years from inclusion in the back-pay award, but according to some courts do not operate to reduce the defendant's back-pay liability as to earlier time periods. *See* Section II.B.1.a *supra.*

Demonstrated failures to mitigate also should be taken into account in addition to interim earnings. As in individual actions, the defendant in a class action normally must prove by a preponderance of the evidence that a class member failed reasonably to mitigate his or her loss.[542] A court normally does not presume a failure to mitigate merely because a class member did not earn as much as the highest-earning class member, or as much as the average class member; courts instead generally rely on individual evidence of mitigation.[543] A few courts, however, have calculated on a classwide basis the monetary setoff for reasonable mitigation. This may be done using workforce statistics on the unemployment rate and average earnings of demographic groups, to derive the approximate amount of interim income that the class should have been able to earn in mitigation.[544]

B. Dividing a Classwide Award Among Class Members

Several techniques are used to divide classwide awards among class members. Distributing the awards pro rata among members

---

[542]*E.g.*, EEOC v. Gurnee Inn Corp., 914 F.2d 815, 818–19, 53 FEP 1425 (7th Cir. 1990) (the employer must prove both that the claimants were not reasonably diligent in seeking other work and that, with the exercise of reasonable diligence, there was a reasonable chance they would have found other employment); *see* Wooldridge v. Marlene Indus. Corp., 875 F.2d 540, 548, 49 FEP 1455 (6th Cir. 1989) ("Thus, there is no practical distinction between an individual action and a class action for the purpose of determining the issue of mitigation.").

[543]*See* United States v. Lee Way Motor Freight, 625 F.2d 918, 936–38, 20 FEP 1345 (10th Cir. 1979) (distinguishing and rejecting the "best man" or "best woman" approach and the approach of automatically presuming failure of mitigation from the failure to earn as much as the average class member).

[544]In *Pegues*, 698 F. Supp. at 118 (N.D. Miss. 1988), for example, the district court considered that the unemployment rate for African-American men was 13.5%, and for African-American women was 17.8%, rates which "approximated that of the United States in the depths of the Great Depression." Accordingly, the court held that a class member would be considered to have failed to mitigate losses if he or she earned, in 3 or more of the 5 years in question, less than 20% of the wages of a full-time minimum-wage position. Class members found to have failed to mitigate would be credited with at least 20% of the minimum wage as interim earnings for any year in which they had a lower amount of reported earnings. *Id.* at 118; *see also* Green v. United States Steel Corp., 640 F. Supp. 1521, 1539–43, 46 FEP 693 (E.D. Pa. 1986) (estimating interim earnings based on age, sex, and education), *vacated in part on other grounds sub nom.* Green v. USX Corp., 843 F.2d 1511, 46 FEP 720 (3d Cir. 1988).

of the class is within the discretion of the court whenever (1) the number of qualified claimants exceeds the number of openings lost to the class through discrimination, and (2) identification of the individuals entitled to relief would lead to "a quagmire of hypothetical judgment."[545] As the Fifth Circuit explained: "For instance in this case, actually to assume that employee #242 would have been promoted in three years to such-and-such job instead of employee #354 is so speculative as to unfairly penalize employee #354."[546]

Courts have employed different approaches to determine the method of allocation among class members. In one instance, the

---

[545]*See, e.g.*, Pettway v. American Cast Iron Pipe Co., 494 F.2d 211, 260–61, 7 FEP 1115 (5th Cir. 1974) ("unrealistic exactitude" is not required and back-pay awards need not be determined on an individualized basis where to do so would involve a "quagmire of hypothetical judgment"). In *White v. Carolina Paperboard Corp.*, 564 F.2d 1073, 16 FEP 44 (4th Cir. 1977), the Fourth Circuit held that, in the absence of a seniority or similar system that would make it possible to determine which employees would have been promoted in the absence of discrimination, "we believe that requiring the company to divide the damages among all those who might have been entitled thereto is preferable." *Id.* at 1087; *accord* Catlett v. Missouri Highway & Transp. Comm'n, 828 F.2d 1260, 1267, 45 FEP 1627 (8th Cir. 1987) ("A court, however, retains equitable discretion to fashion an appropriate remedy when, for example, the number of qualified class members exceeds the number of openings lost to the class through discrimination and identification of the individuals entitled to relief would 'drag the court into "a quagmire of hypothetical judgments"' and result in 'mere guesswork.'") (quoting Segar v. Smith, 738 F.2d 1249, 1289–90, 35 FEP 31 (D.C. Cir. 1984)); Domingo v. New Eng. Fish Co., 727 F.2d 1429, 1444, 34 FEP 584 (9th Cir.) (although individualized remedies are the general rule, departure from it is appropriate " '[when] the class size or the ambiguity of promotion or hiring practices or the illegal practices continued over an extended period of time calls forth [a] quagmire of hypothetical judgment' ") (quoting *Pettway*, 494 F.2d at 261), *modified on other grounds*, 742 F.2d 520, 37 FEP 1303 (9th Cir. 1984); *see* Dougherty v. Barry, 869 F.2d 605, 615, 49 FEP 289 (D.C. Cir. 1989) (where the district court was unable to determine which of several plaintiffs would have received two promotions absent discrimination, it "should have awarded each [plaintiff back pay equal to] a fraction of the promotions' value commensurate with the likelihood of his receiving one of the promotions" and, if unable to evaluate the plaintiffs against one another, simply divided the monetary value of the two promotions equally among them). *Contra* Mitchell v. Mid-Continent Spring Co., 583 F.2d 275, 283 n.11, 17 FEP 1594 (6th Cir.) ("If it is true that individual determinations are impossible, the class action aspects of this case should forthwith be dismissed. No individual should ever be permitted to recover damages in a case which he or she finds it is impossible to prove."), *modified on other grounds*, 587 F.2d 841, 23 FEP 787 (6th Cir. 1978).

[546]*Pettway*, 494 F.2d at 262 n.152.

Seventh Circuit determined the method of apportioning $380,000 in back pay to 451 eligible class members by multiplying the total wages and benefits of the employees hired by the employer (87 in total) by the percentage of the African-American hiring shortfall (17 out of 87) and then multiplying that by the percentage of the African-American unemployment rate in the relevant market (22 percent).[547]

Another approach is to allocate the award among class members in proportion to their individual economic loss.[548] In *United States v. United States Steel Corp.*,[549] the Fifth Circuit stated:

> Individual awards can be computed for each member of the group by the use of a linear progression formula. For example, if during a given period white A, with less plant seniority, occupied a job at which he earned $15,000, but blacks B, C, D, E, and F, with respective earnings in lower jobs of $10,000, $11,000, $12,000, $13,000, and $14,000, each were equally capable and substantially equal in superior plant seniority, then their pro rata recoveries for the period could be computed as follows: $5x + 4x + 3x + 2x + x = \$5,000$. The variable, x, comes to roughly $333. Thus B, whose hypothetical loss is five times greater than F's, recovers about $1,665; C recovers $1,332; D takes $999; E recovers $666; while F, who suffered the least economic injury, recovers $333. The defendants may wish to argue that under no circumstances would employee F, the one with the most damages, or for that matter any of the other discriminatees, have succeeded to the job ahead of A, or ahead of another black. The defendants have the burden of persuasion on the point . . . .[550]

Still another technique is mutual agreement. The parties may be able to agree on at least some of the standards by which back-pay

---

[547]EEOC v. O & G Spring & Wire Forms Specialty Co., 38 F.3d 872, 880, 65 FEP 1823 (7th Cir. 1994). The 22% adjustment using the unemployment rate was made in order to approximate the proper offset to recovery for mitigation of damages, because all but 22% of the plaintiffs could be presumed to have found comparable entry-level jobs. *Id.*

[548]In one case where three white state police troopers were discriminated against with respect to one promotion, the lower court used the "lost chance" theory and decided that the three plaintiffs, respectively, had a 45%, a 30%, and a 15% chance of receiving the promotion in a nondiscriminatory environment, and therefore awarded that proportion of back pay. The circuit court approved this method, indicating that although the approach was "more art than science" it was "the likeliest way to arrive at a just result." Bishop v. Gainer, 272 F.3d 1009, 1016–17, 87 FEP 920 (7th Cir. 2001), *cert. denied*, 534 U.S. 1058 (2002).

[549]520 F.2d 1043, 11 FEP 553 (5th Cir. 1975).

[550]*Id.* at 1056.

claims should be evaluated, perform the evaluations in consultation with each other, and present agreed orders to the court dismissing, limiting, or accepting particular claims.[551] In such cases, the court may require that notice be given to each disqualified or limited class member, along with the opportunity to reject the agreement and seek judicial determination of his or her own right to relief.[552] Class members who do not avail themselves of that opportunity are bound by the agreement of counsel. This approach allows a great deal of individualized consideration of class members' claims while avoiding the burden of individual hearings for the vast majority of claimants.

The appointment of a special master to apportion class relief and the use of proof-of-claim forms are other useful procedural devices.[553]

---

[551]*See, e.g.*, Pegues v. Mississippi State Employment Serv., 698 F. Supp. 116 (N.D. Miss. 1988) (the parties were able to investigate and stipulate to most of the class back-pay issues, leaving the court to determine questions of law and make the ultimate award), *rev'd in part on other grounds*, 899 F.2d 1449 (5th Cir. 1990). In an earlier proceeding in the same case, the court reproduced relevant portions of the agreement:

10. To avoid the burden of individualized litigation over each claimant's period of availability, the parties agree that it would be reasonable and fair to use the classwide presumption [of each claimant's availability, based on data specified in other parts of the agreement] for each claimant described above, subject to notice to the claimant and the claimant's right to make a timely contention that he or she was an active applicant, and available for referrals during lengthier or additional periods. Such a contention is in effect a rejection of the classwide approach by that claimant, and the MSES defendants would in that event reserve the right to rely on any evidence of shorter periods of availability . . . .

Pegues v. Mississippi State Employment Serv., 36 EPD ¶ 34,976, at 36,377 (N.D. Miss. 1985).

[552]*See* FED. R. CIV. P. 23(d)(2). *See generally* Chapter 32 (Class Actions).

[553]*See generally* Chapter 32 (Class Actions).

CHAPTER 41

ATTORNEY'S FEES

I. Introduction

The general rule in the United States is that each party to a lawsuit bears its own legal fees.[1] Congress has modified this

---

[1]Buckhannon Bd. & Care Home, Inc. v. West Virginia Dep't of Health & Human Res., 532 U.S. 598, 602 (2001) ("In the United States, parties are ordinarily required to bear

"American Rule" in employment discrimination and other civil rights actions by expressly authorizing an award of attorney's fees to a prevailing party.[2] The statutes that authorize such fee shifting may be mandatory, permitting the court no discretion to deny a reasonable attorney's fee once certain prerequisites are met, or discretionary, authorizing the court to grant or deny attorney's fees to the prevailing party. Further, the statute may authorize awards only to a prevailing plaintiff, or to either a prevailing plaintiff or defendant. Courts that apply the fee-shifting statutes that are used most frequently in employment discrimination cases—§ 706(k) of Title VII[3] and the Civil Rights Attorney's Fees Awards Act of 1976[4]—utilize a different standard in determining when a prevailing plaintiff, as opposed to a prevailing defendant, is entitled to an award of attorney's fees.

II. THE PREVAILING PLAINTIFF'S RIGHT TO ATTORNEY'S FEES

A. Statutory Authorization

1. Title VII

Section 706(k) of Title VII[5] provides:

In any action or proceeding under this subchapter the court, in its discretion, may allow the prevailing party, other than the [Equal Employment Opportunity] Commission or the United States, a reasonable attorney's fee (including expert fees) as part of the costs, and the Commission and the United States shall be liable for costs the same as a private person.

2. 42 U.S.C. § 1988

Section 1988 of the Civil Rights Attorney's Fees Awards Act of 1976[6] provides:

---

their own attorney's fees—the prevailing party is not entitled to collect from the loser. Under this 'American Rule,' we follow a general practice of not awarding fees to a prevailing party absent explicit statutory authority." (quotation marks and citations omitted)).

[2]*Id.* ("Congress, however, has authorized the award of attorney's fees to the 'prevailing party' in numerous statutes in addition to those at issue here.") (enumerating statutes).

[3]42 U.S.C. § 2000e-5(k) (2000).

[4]*Id.* § 1988.

[5]*Id.* § 2000e-5(k).

[6]*Id.* § 1988. Section 1988 was the legislative response to *Alyeska Pipeline Service Co. v. Wilderness Society*, 421 U.S. 240, 10 FEP 826 (1975), in which the Supreme

> In any action or proceeding to enforce a provision of [42 U.S.C.] sections 1981, 1981a, 1982, 1983, 1985, and 1986 of this title, . . . the court, in its discretion, may allow the prevailing party, other than the United States, a reasonable attorney's fee as part of the costs.

The standards for determining a reasonable attorney's fee pursuant to § 1988 are identical to those utilized for attorney's fee awards under § 706(k) of Title VII.[7]

3. The Age Discrimination in Employment Act and the Equal Pay Act

Attorney's fees are available to prevailing plaintiffs under the Age Discrimination in Employment Act (ADEA),[8] which incorporates selected provisions, including those pertaining to attorney's fees, of the Fair Labor Standards Act (FLSA).[9] The Equal Pay Act (EPA) is part of the FLSA,[10] and the recovery of attorney's fees in EPA cases is thus also governed by the attorney's fees provision of the FLSA. Unlike under Title VII and § 1988, where the court retains some discretion, an award of reasonable fees to a prevailing plaintiff[11] in an ADEA or EPA case is mandatory.[12] In other

---

Court held that under the "American Rule," an award of attorney's fees normally cannot be granted to prevailing parties in the absence of specific statutory authorization.

[7]See Hensley v. Eckerhart, 461 U.S. 424, 433 n.7, 31 FEP 1169 (1983) ("The standards set forth in this opinion are generally applicable in all cases in which Congress has authorized an award of fees to a prevailing party."); Davis v. City & County of S.F., 976 F.2d 1536, 1541 n.1, 61 FEP 440 (9th Cir. 1992).

[8]29 U.S.C. § 621 et seq. (2000).

[9]29 U.S.C. § 626(b) (2000) expressly incorporates a number of Fair Labor Standards Act (FLSA) provisions, including 29 U.S.C. § 216(b), which states in relevant part: "The court in such an action shall, in addition to any judgment awarded to the plaintiff or plaintiffs, allow a reasonable attorney's fee to be paid by the defendant, and costs of the action."

[10]29 U.S.C. § 206(d) (2000). See generally Chapter 18 (Compensation).

[11]Although Title VII allows attorney's fees to a prevailing party (42 U.S.C. § 2000e-5(k)), the FLSA by its terms allows attorney's fees only to a prevailing plaintiff (29 U.S.C. § 216(b)). For a discussion of awards under Title VII to parties other than plaintiffs, see Sections IV and V infra.

[12]See, e.g., Eddleman v. Switchcraft, Inc., 927 F.2d 316, 317, 55 FEP 483 (7th Cir. 1991) (ADEA); Hagelthorn v. Kennecott Corp., 710 F.2d 76, 86, 33 FEP 977 (2d Cir. 1983) (ADEA); Detje v. James River Paper Corp., 167 F. Supp. 2d 248, 250 (D. Conn. 2001) (attorney's fees are mandatory under ADEA to prevailing party); Herndon v. William A. Straub, Inc., 17 F. Supp. 2d 1056, 1065 (E.D. Mo. 1998) (award of reasonable attorney's fees and costs to prevailing party is mandatory under EPA). The difference arises from the use of the word "shall" in 29 U.S.C. § 216(b); 42 U.S.C. § 2000e-5(k), by contrast, uses the word "may."

respects, however, attorney's fee awards under the ADEA and EPA are generally subject to the same considerations applicable to Title VII cases and cases raising claims under 42 U.S.C. §§ 1981, 1983, and 1985.[13]

4. The Equal Access to Justice Act

Pursuant to the Equal Access to Justice Act (EAJA),[14] attorney's fees may be awarded to some plaintiffs who prevail against the United States.[15] The Act provides in part:

> Unless expressly prohibited by statute, a court may award reasonable fees and expenses of attorneys . . . to the prevailing party in any civil action brought by or against the United States or any agency or any official of the United States acting in his or her official capacity in any court having jurisdiction of such action. The United States shall be liable for such fees and expenses to the same extent that any other party would be liable under the common law or under the terms of any statute which specifically provides for such an award.[16]

There is a significant limitation. A prevailing party may be awarded attorney's fees under this statute only if it establishes that "the position of the United States was not substantially justified."[17]

5. The Americans with Disabilities Act

Title I of the Americans with Disabilities Act (ADA)[18] incorporates the remedial provisions of Title VII, including § 706.[19] Thus, the standards and procedures for recovering attorney's fees in employment cases under the ADA are the same as under Title VII.

---

[13]See Hensley v. Eckerhart, 461 U.S. 424, 433 n.7, 31 FEP 1169 (1983) (standards generally apply to all statutes authorizing fee award to prevailing party); Spulak v. K Mart Corp., 894 F.2d 1150, 1159–60, 51 FEP 1652 (10th Cir. 1990) (ADEA; as in Title VII cases, usual billing rate of attorney and quality of services are proper factors to be considered in awarding attorney's fees); Blum v. Witco Chem. Corp., 888 F.2d 975, 977 n.1, 51 FEP 386 (3d Cir. 1989) (ADEA; defining lodestar fee).
[14]28 U.S.C. § 2412 (2000).
[15]28 U.S.C. § 2412(b) (2000).
[16]Id.
[17]Id. § 2412(d)(1)(B).
[18]42 U.S.C. § 12101 et seq. (2004).
[19]Id. § 12107(a).

6. The Family and Medical Leave Act

The Family and Medical Leave Act (FMLA)[20] requires awards of attorney's fees to prevailing plaintiffs: "The court in such an action shall, in addition to any judgment awarded to the plaintiff, allow a reasonable attorney's fee, reasonable expert witness fees, and other costs of the action to be paid by the defendant."[21]

B. The General Fee Rule for Prevailing Plaintiffs

Although most federal employment discrimination and civil rights statutes leave the award of attorney's fees to judicial discretion, the general rule is that a prevailing plaintiff should be awarded reasonable attorney's fees absent unusual circumstances.[22] Therefore, courts must sometimes determine whether the plaintiff achieved enough success in the lawsuit to be considered the prevailing party. The question, "Who is a prevailing plaintiff?" arises most frequently in cases where the plaintiff achieved only partial success.

1. Who Is a Prevailing Plaintiff?

a. The Relevance of Minimal Success. In *Texas State Teachers Ass'n v. Garland Independent School District*,[23] the U.S. Supreme Court articulated the standard for determining whether a party has "prevailed" in an action. The circuits earlier had been divided on this issue. Some had required that a party succeed on the "central issue" in the litigation and "achieve the primary relief sought" in order to be eligible for a fee award.[24] Others had applied a less demanding standard, "requiring only that a party succeed on a significant issue and receive some of the relief sought in the lawsuit to qualify for a fee award."[25]

---

[20]29 U.S.C. § 2601 et seq. (2000).

[21]29 U.S.C. § 2607 (2000).

[22]*See, e.g.,* Hensley v. Eckerhart, 461 U.S. 424, 429, 31 FEP 1169 (1983) (prevailing plaintiff "should ordinarily recover an attorney's fee unless special circumstances would render such an award unjust").

[23]489 U.S. 782, 49 FEP 465 (1989).

[24]*See, e.g.,* Simien v. City of San Antonio, 809 F.2d 255, 258, 42 FEP 1657 (5th Cir. 1987).

[25]*Texas State Teachers Ass'n*, 489 U.S. at 784; *see also* Lampher v. Zagel, 755 F.2d 99, 102 (7th Cir. 1985).

In *Texas State Teachers Ass'n*,[26] the Court adopted the latter view. The teachers' organization and its members had sued a school district under 42 U.S.C. § 1983, alleging that various school district policies that governed communications between employee organizations and teachers violated the teachers' First and Fourteenth Amendment rights. Although the teachers prevailed on some issues, they failed to prove their central claim that the First Amendment required the school district to allow union representatives access to school facilities during school hours.[27] The district court denied the teachers' application for attorney's fees because the plaintiffs lost the "central issue" in the case. The Fifth Circuit affirmed.[28]

But the Supreme Court reversed, relying on its earlier analysis in *Hensley v. Eckerhart*:[29]

> We think it clear that the "central issue" test applied by the lower courts here is directly contrary to the thrust of our decision in *Hensley*. Although respondents are correct in pointing out that *Hensley* did not adopt one particular standard for determining prevailing party status, *Hensley* does indicate that the *degree* of the plaintiff's success in relation to the other goals of the lawsuit is a factor critical to the determination of the size of a reasonable fee, not to eligibility for a fee award at all.[30]

The Court then described the minimum threshold for a fee recovery:

> If the plaintiff has succeeded on "any significant issue in litigation which achieve[d] some of the benefit the parties sought in bringing suit," the plaintiff has crossed the threshold to a fee award of some kind. . . . Thus, at a minimum, to be considered a prevailing party within the meaning of § 1988, the plaintiff must be able to point to a resolution of the dispute which changes the legal relationship between itself and the defendant. . . . Beyond this absolute limitation, a technical victory may be so insignificant, . . . as to be insufficient to support prevailing party status. For example, in the context of this litigation, the District Court found that the requirement that nonschool hour meetings be conducted only with prior approval from the local school principal was unconstitutionally

---

[26]489 U.S. 782 (1989).
[27]*Id.* at 787.
[28]837 F.2d 190, 192–93, 130 LRRM 2938 (5th Cir. 1988).
[29]461 U.S. 424, 31 FEP 1169 (1983).
[30]489 U.S. at 790 (emphasis added).

vague. . . . The District Court characterized this issue as "of minor significance" and noted that there was "no evidence that the plaintiffs were ever refused permission to use school premises during non-school hours.". . . . If this had been petitioners' only success in the litigation, we think it clear that this alone would not have rendered them "prevailing parties" within the meaning of § 1988. Where the plaintiff's success on a legal claim can be characterized as purely technical or *de minimis*, a district court would be justified in concluding that even the "generous formulation" we adopt today has not been satisfied. . . . The touchstone of the prevailing party inquiry must be the material alteration of the legal relationship of the parties in a manner which Congress sought to promote in the fee statute. Where such a change has occurred, the degree of the plaintiff's overall success goes to the reasonableness of the award under *Hensley*, not to the availability of a fee award *vel non*.[31]

The Supreme Court revisited the standard for achieving "prevailing party" status in *Farrar v. Hobby*.[32] The plaintiffs in *Farrar* asserted civil rights claims against government officials in connection with criminal proceedings against the plaintiffs. Although the plaintiffs initially sought injunctive relief and $17 million in damages, the jury found that there were only technical violations of the plaintiffs' due process rights and that these violations were not proximate causes of any injuries.

The district court entered judgment for the plaintiffs on their due process claim, denied compensatory damages, and awarded $1 nominal damages. Despite awarding only nominal damages, the court awarded the plaintiffs $280,000 in attorney's fees, plus $27,932 in costs and $9,730 in prejudgment interest.

A divided Fifth Circuit panel reversed the fee award. After considering prior Supreme Court decisions, the appellate court held that the recovery of $1 nominal damages, after seeking $17 million, was a "technical victory . . . so insignificant . . . as to be insufficient to support prevailing party status."[33]

The Supreme Court affirmed the Fifth Circuit, but on different grounds. The Court expressly *reversed* the appellate court's conclusion that the plaintiffs were not prevailing parties. The Court held that "a plaintiff 'prevails' when actual relief on the merits of

---

[31]*Id.* at 791–93 (citations omitted).
[32]506 U.S. 103, 60 FEP 633 (1992).
[33]Estate of Farrar v. Cain, 941 F.2d 1311, 1315 (5th Cir. 1991).

his claim materially alters the legal relationship between the parties by modifying the defendant's behavior in a way that directly benefits the plaintiff."[34] That standard was met in *Farrar*, the Court explained:

> We therefore hold that a plaintiff who wins nominal damages is a prevailing party under § 1988. When a court awards nominal damages, it neither enters judgment for defendant on the merits nor declares the defendant's legal immunity to suit. . . . A judgment for damages in any amount, whether compensatory or nominal, modifies the defendant's behavior for the plaintiff's benefit by forcing the defendant to pay an amount of money he otherwise would not pay. As a result, the Court of Appeals for the Fifth Circuit erred in holding that petitioners' nominal damages award failed to render them prevailing parties.[35]

As noted earlier, however, the *Farrar* Court nevertheless affirmed the judgment denying attorney's fees. Although the plaintiffs were prevailing parties for purposes of fee *entitlement*, the Court explained that the *amount* of the fee award may be limited by the extent of the plaintiffs' success. In cases such as this one, marked by a "failure to prove an essential element of his claim for monetary relief," a majority held that "the only reasonable fee is usually no fee at all."[36]

Justice O'Connor wrote a separate concurring opinion explaining more fully why, in her view, the facts of that case made it appropriate to award nothing for attorney's fees.[37] She identified three factors that should be considered in determining whether a fee is justified: (1) the extent of the relief sought and won, (2) the significance of the legal issue, and (3) the public purpose served by bringing the case.[38]

---

[34]506 U.S. at 104.

[35]*Id.* at 112–13.

[36]*Id.* at 115; *see also* Bonner v. Guccione, 178 F.3d 581, 593 (2d Cir. 1999) (no entitlement to fees under Title VII where plaintiff recovered only on state-law claim); Salvatori v. Westinghouse Elec. Corp., 190 F.3d 1244, 1245, 80 FEP 1778 (11th Cir. 1999) (per curiam) (fees denied to plaintiff who obtained favorable verdict on ADEA claim but was awarded no damages).

[37]503 U.S. at 116–22. Justices White, Blackmun, Stevens, and Souter joined in a separate opinion concurring in part and dissenting in part. These Justices agreed that an award of nominal damages was sufficient to warrant prevailing party status but believed that the matter should have been remanded back to the lower courts for a determination of the amount of a reasonable fee. *Id.* at 122–24.

[38]*Id.* at 121–22; *see also* Murray v. City of Onawa, 323 F.3d 616, 619–20 (8th Cir. 2003) ((1) amount plaintiff sought and amount she received ($500,000 and $1,

Courts after *Farrar* have construed challenges to the degree of relief actually obtained by the plaintiff as properly directed to the *amount* of the attorney's fee award, rather than to the plaintiff's *entitlement* to an award.[39] The relationship between the magnitude of success and the amount of the fee is discussed further in Section III *infra*.

Thus, courts generally find that prevailing party status exists if the plaintiff has obtained either an award of greater than "nominal" damages[40] *or* a judgment that vindicates important personal or public constitutional or statutory rights.[41] By contrast, courts

---

respectively) "not an outrageous split"; (2) plaintiff raised significant legal issues by compelling at least cursory investigations into serious allegations of misconduct; and (3) case served "clear public policy" by putting police departments and cities on notice that they cannot ignore sexual harassment and other allegations); Jones v. Lockhart, 29 F.3d 422, 424 (8th Cir. 1994) (plaintiffs entitled to fee award where (1) they sought $860,000 and won $2, (2) they vindicated significant constitutional rights, and (3) their civil rights lawsuit served important public purpose).

[39]*See, e.g.*, Webb v. Sloan, 330 F.3d 1158, 1168 (9th Cir. 2003) (extent of plaintiff's success crucial factor in determining proper amount of award of attorney's fees under § 1988), *cert. denied*, 540 U.S. 1189 (2004); Truesdell v. Philadelphia Hous. Auth., 290 F.3d 159, 166 (3d Cir. 2002) (when there is material alteration in legal relationship of parties, degree of plaintiff's overall success goes to reasonableness of the attorney's fee award, not to availability of fee award vel non); Coutin v. Young & Rubicam Pub. Relations, Inc., 124 F.3d 331, 336 n.2, 74 FEP 1463 (1st Cir. 1997) (district court's references to degree of success obtained and "equities" between parties more properly addressed as part of fee adjustment factors rather than in determination of prevailing party status); Hetzel v. County of Prince William, 89 F.3d 169, 173–74, 71 FEP 520 (4th Cir. 1996) (fact that plaintiff received only insignificant portion of relief originally requested, failed to prevail on most consequential claims, and will receive only "pittance" of her original damages request goes to amount of fees properly awarded, not plaintiff's entitlement to award of fees).

[40]*See, e.g.*, Payne v. Milwaukee County, 288 F.3d 1021, 1025, 18 IER 988 (7th Cir. 2002) (plaintiff awarded damages of $10,400 was prevailing party); Sheehan v. Donlen Corp., 173 F.3d 1039, 1048, 79 FEP 540 (7th Cir. 1999) (plaintiff who obtained $30,000 jury verdict on claims under Pregnancy Discrimination Act was prevailing party); *Coutin*, 124 F.3d at 340 (Title VII plaintiff who obtains damage award of $45,000, roughly three times her annual salary, was prevailing party entitled to fee award); Bridges v. Eastman Kodak Co., 102 F.3d 56, 59, 72 FEP 948 (2d Cir. 1996) (plaintiff awarded no damages under Title VII because of failure to mitigate nevertheless entitled to attorney's fees because she obtained damages in related state court action); Caban-Wheeler v. Elsea, 71 F.3d 837, 842, 69 FEP 1193 (11th Cir. 1996) (plaintiff who obtained valid judgment on her national origin and race discrimination claims and was awarded $1 in nominal damages and $100,000 in punitive damages was prevailing party).

[41]*See, e.g.*, Murray v. City of Onawa, 323 F.3d 616, 619–20 (8th Cir. 2003) (plaintiff was prevailing party entitled to attorney's fees under § 1988 because case furthered clear public policy); Richard S. v. Department of Developmental Servs.

have denied attorney's fees altogether in cases where the plaintiff recovered *only* nominal monetary damages[42] or in cases where the nonmonetary relief obtained did not alter the legal relationship between the parties or otherwise vindicate important personal or public constitutional or statutory rights.[43]

   b. The Relevance of Judicial Involvement. For some time there was a split in the circuits regarding whether the plaintiff's success must include some form of *judicial* relief or whether "prevailing party" includes a plaintiff who asserts that it has prevailed by being a "catalyst," causing the defendant to voluntarily change its conduct in response to the plaintiff's lawsuit. In *Buckhannon Board & Care Home, Inc. v. West Virginia Department of Health & Human Resources*,[44] the Supreme Court answered that question. In a 5–4 decision, over a vigorous dissent, the Court held that the "catalyst" theory, which was previously recognized by almost every circuit,[45]

---

of State of Cal., 317 F.3d 1080, 1086–87, 14 AD 26 (9th Cir. 2003) (ADA plaintiffs were prevailing parties because their settlement achieved protection for disabled persons in community); Brandau v. Kansas, 168 F.3d 1179, 1181–83, 79 FEP 31 (10th Cir. 1999) ($1 award for Title VII hostile work environment sexual harassment claim, although not significant monetarily, did serve larger public purpose and would thus support award of $41,598.13 in attorney's fees and expenses); Koopman v. Water Dist. No. 1 of Johnson County, Kan., 41 F.3d 1417, 1420–21 (10th Cir. 1994) (plaintiff is prevailing party, despite award of only nominal damages, because district court's judgment in her favor had significant implications by ensuring that other public employees would be guaranteed constitutionally adequate predischarge and postdischarge hearings).

   [42]*See, e.g.*, Pouillon v. Little, 326 F.3d 713, 717–18 (6th Cir. 2003) (arrestee awarded nominal damages in § 1983 action against police officers denied attorney's fees although he obtained finding of officers' liability); Barber v. T.D. Williamson, Inc., 254 F.3d 1223, 1230–31, 86 FEP 187 (10th Cir. 2001) (employee who received award of $1 not prevailing party); Pino v. Locascio, 101 F.3d 235, 238–39, 72 FEP 875 (2d Cir. 1996) (former employee not prevailing party where individual was awarded only $1 and no causal connection existed between former employee's suit and resignations of supervisor and administrator connected with former employee's claims).

   [43]*See, e.g.*, Barnes v. Broward County Sheriff's Office, 190 F.3d 1274, 1279, 9 AD 1341 (11th Cir. 1999) (permanent injunction against preemployment psychological testing does not entitle plaintiff to attorney's fees where he neither won damages nor personally benefitted from injunction); Pedigo v. P.A.M. Transp., Inc., 98 F.3d 396, 398, 6 AD 389 (8th Cir. 1996) (former employee who recovered no monetary damages not prevailing party because relief obtained did not alter behavior of defendant toward plaintiff).

   [44]532 U.S. 598 (2001).

   [45]*See, e.g.*, Stanton v. Southern Berkshire Reg'l Sch. Dist., 197 F.3d 574, 577 n.2 (1st Cir. 1999); Morris v. West Palm Beach, 194 F.3d 1203, 1207 (11th Cir. 1999);

is "not a permissible basis for the award of attorney's fees under the [Fair Housing Amendments Act of 1988, 42 U.S.C. § 3613(C)(2)] and ADA, 42 U.S.C. § 12205."[46] The Court reached this conclusion after reasoning that a "defendant's voluntary change in conduct, although perhaps accomplishing what the plaintiff sought to achieve by the lawsuit, lacks the necessary judicial *imprimatur* on the change."[47] Thus, the Court concluded that in order for the plaintiff to be a prevailing party, there must be a "corresponding alteration" in the legal relationship of the parties.[48]

The plaintiffs in *Buckhannon* sued the state of West Virginia and various state actors over a state law requiring that all residents of residential board and care homes be capable of moving themselves from dangerous situations, such as fire.[49] The West Virginia statute, they alleged, violated the Fair Housing Amendments Act of 1988[50] and the ADA.[51]

While the lawsuit was pending and before the district court ruled on the merits, the West Virginia Legislature eliminated the allegedly offensive provisions, and the district court dismissed the case as moot.[52] The plaintiffs nevertheless sought attorney's fees under the

---

Marbley v. Bane, 57 F.3d 224, 234 (2d Cir. 1995); Kilgour v. Pasadena, 53 F.3d 1007, 1010 (9th Cir. 1995); Baumgartner v. Harrisburg Housing Auth., 21 F.3d 541, 546–50 (3d Cir. 1994); Payne v. Board of Educ., 88 F.3d 392, 397 (6th Cir. 1996); Zinn v. Shalala, 35 F.3d 273, 276 (7th Cir. 1994); Little Rock Sch. Dist. v. Pulaski County Sch. Dist. No. 1, 17 F.3d 260, 263 n.2 (8th Cir. 1994); Beard v. Teska, 31 F.3d 942, 951–52 (10th Cir. 1994).

[46]*Buckhannon*, 532 U.S. at 610. Even though *Buckhannon* was not an employment discrimination case, the Court noted in dicta that its decision should apply to the "prevailing party" fee-shifting provisions of the Civil Rights Act of 1964, 42 U.S.C. § 2000e-5(k), and the Civil Rights Attorney's Fees Awards Act of 1976, 42 U.S.C. § 1988, which are phrased nearly identically to those of the fee-shifting provision of the Fair Housing Amendments Act (FHAA) and ADA, which were at issue in *Buckhannon*. *Id.* at 602–03; *see also* Dennis v. Columbia Colleton Med. Ctr., 290 F.3d 639, 652–53, 88 FEP 1460 (4th Cir. 2002) (applying *Buckhannon* to fee award under Title VII); Johnson v. ITT Aerospace Commc'ns Div. of ITT Indus., Inc., 272 F.3d 500, 87 FEP 553 (7th Cir. 2001) (same); Bennett v. Yoshina, 259 F.3d 1097 (9th Cir. 2001) (applying *Buckhannon* to fee award under 42 U.S.C. § 1988); Griffin v. Steeltek, Inc., 261 F.3d 1026, 1029 (10th Cir. 2001) (applying *Buckhannon* to fee award in ADA employment case).

[47]*Buckhannon*, 532 U.S. at 605.
[48]*Id.*
[49]*Id.* at 600.
[50]42 U.S.C. § 3601 et seq. (2000).
[51]*See* 532 U.S. at 601.
[52]*Id.*

"catalyst theory," because the lawsuit achieved the desired result when the legislature acted to change the law.[53] Because the Fourth Circuit did not recognize the "catalyst theory," the district court denied the attorney's fees petition. In an unpublished per curiam opinion, the Fourth Circuit upheld the denial of fees.[54]

Affirming the Fourth Circuit, the Supreme Court stated that the "clear meaning of 'prevailing party' " is "one who has been awarded some relief *by the court.*"[55] The Court distinguished enforceable judgments on the merits and settlements enforceable through consent decrees, each of which constitute a "court-ordered 'change [in] the legal relationship between [the plaintiff] and the defendant' "[56] and "create the 'material alteration of the legal relationship of the parties' necessary to permit an award of attorney's fees,"[57] from private settlements and voluntary changes in conduct, which "do not entail the judicial approval and oversight involved in consent decrees."[58]

Following *Buckhannon*, courts have split over the issue of what constitutes an "alteration in the legal relationship of the parties"[59] sufficient to give rise to an award of attorney's fees to the prevailing plaintiff. The questions that have stirred the most controversy are whether a private settlement agreement or a preliminary injunction provide a sufficient basis for conferring "prevailing party" status on the plaintiff.[60]

---

[53]*Id.*

[54]*Id.* (order reported at 203 F.3d 819 (4th Cir. 2000)).

[55]532 U.S. at 603 (citations omitted, emphasis added); *id.* at 610.

[56]*Id.* at 604 (quoting Texas State Teachers Ass'n v. Garland Indep. Sch. Dist., 489 U.S. 782, 792, 49 FEP 465 (1989)).

[57]*Id.* (quoting Texas State Teachers Ass'n v. Garland Indep. Sch. Dist., 489 U.S. 782, 792–93, 49 FEP 465 (1989)).

[58]532 U.S. at 604 n.7.

[59]*Id.* at 605.

[60]*Private Settlement Agreement or Preliminary Injunction Not Enough to Confer Prevailing Party Status: See* Atomic Workers v. Department of Energy, 288 F.3d 452, 454–58 (D.C. Cir. 2002) (attorney's fee award reversed because order approving parties' terms of dismissal was mere formality, not decision on merits, and did not alter parties' legal relationship); Richardson v. Miller, 279 F.3d 1, 4–5 (1st Cir. 2002) (attorney's fee award reversed following *Buckhannon*: "Although we approved the catalyst theory in the past, we are constrained to follow the Court's broad directive and join several of our sister circuits in concluding that the catalyst theory may no longer be used to award attorney's fees under the Fees Act.") (citing New York State Fed'n of Taxi Drivers, Inc. v. Westchester County Taxi & Limousine Comm'n, 272 F.3d 154, 158 (2d Cir. 2001)); Dubuc v. Green Oak Twp., 312 F.3d 736, 753–55 (6th Cir. 2002) (preliminary injunction insufficient to support award

In *Smyth ex rel. Smyth v. Rivero*,[61] the Fourth Circuit reversed an attorney's fee award to plaintiffs who sued the state in a § 1983 action that challenged a new paternity identification policy for welfare applicants.[62] The district court granted a preliminary injunction barring enforcement of the paternity identification policy against the plaintiffs. While the plaintiffs' summary judgment motion was pending, the state agreed not to seek repayment of benefits paid to the plaintiffs[63] and also modified its policy so that it no longer applied to the plaintiffs. The district court dismissed the plaintiffs' claims as moot and in its dismissal order declared that the state was unable to seek repayment of the benefits because of the parties' agreement.[64]

Finding that the plaintiffs had received a judgment against the defendant in the form of a preliminary injunction and a partial settlement, which materially altered the legal relationship between the parties, the district court awarded attorney's fees to the plaintiffs.[65]

---

of fees and, in light of *Buckhannon*, plaintiff not entitled to fees based on catalyst theory; trial court's award of fees to defendant an abuse of discretion).

Private Settlement Agreement or Preliminary Injunction Enough to Confer Prevailing Party Status: See Roberson v. Giuliani, 346 F.3d 75, 80–82 (2d Cir. 2003) (judicial action other than a judgment on the merits or a consent decree, such as a private settlement agreement with continuing jurisdiction for enforcement, can support an award of attorney's fees); Richard S. v. Department of Dev. Servs., 317 F.3d 1080, 1088 (9th Cir. 2003) (favorable settlement agreement that is binding and enforceable and filed with court sufficient to confer prevailing party status, even without court retaining jurisdiction; preliminary injunction is also sufficient for prevailing party status); Barrios v. California Interscholastic Fed'n, 277 F.3d 1128, 1134 (9th Cir. 2002) (legally enforceable settlement agreement confers prevailing party status); Truesdell v. Philadelphia Housing Auth., 290 F.3d 159, 165 (3d Cir. 2002) (settlement memorialized in court order that contained mandatory language and was signed by judge sufficient to confer prevailing party status); American Disability Ass'n v. Chmielarz, 289 F.3d 1315, 1320 (11th Cir. 2002) (district court's incorporation of settlement terms into order of dismissal, or express retention of jurisdiction to enforce settlement, constitutes judicially sanctioned change in parties' legal relationship sufficient for prevailing party status); *see also* Johnson v. District of Columbia, 190 F. Supp. 2d 34, 44 (D.D.C. 2002) (*Buckhannon* "did not . . . resolve the issue of whether a plaintiff who enters a private settlement agreement could be considered a prevailing party, but did arguably express skepticism that such a private settlement could alter the legal relationship between the parties.").

[61]282 F.3d 268, 277–78 (4th Cir. 2002).
[62]*Id.* at 271.
[63]*Id.* at 272–73.
[64]*Id.* at 273.
[65]*Id.* at 273–74.

The Fourth Circuit reversed the award of fees, citing *Buckhannon*, which was decided while the case was pending on appeal.[66]

The appellate court analogized "a preliminary injunction to the examples of judicial relief deemed insufficient in *Buckhannon*."[67] The court reasoned that, under Fourth Circuit standards, a preliminary injunction is at most a prediction of the probable but yet uncertain outcome of the case; it is not a determination on the merits and is therefore not a sufficient basis for finding prevailing party status.[68]

In addition, the agreement referenced in the court's order was insufficient to qualify the plaintiffs as prevailing parties.[69] The Fourth Circuit explained that a private settlement can serve as the basis for prevailing party status when it has the essential function of a consent decree: (1) it is embodied in a court order "such that the obligation to comply with its terms is court-ordered, [and (2)] the court's approval and the attendant judicial over-sight (in the form of continuing jurisdiction to enforce the agreement)" is apparent.[70] The district court's order in *Smyth* fell short of this test because it failed to make the obligation to comply with the terms of the settlement agreement part of the order and failed to retain jurisdiction to enforce the agreement.[71] As a result, the Fourth Circuit concluded that the district court's award of attorney's fees violated the "admonition in *Buckhannon*" that fees may not be awarded to a plaintiff who fails to obtain any judicial relief.[72]

The Ninth Circuit has taken the opposite position. In *Barrios v. California Interscholastic Federation*,[73] the Ninth Circuit held that a plaintiff who obtains a judicially enforceable settlement, even one resulting in a dismissal, can be a prevailing party entitled to an attorney's fee award because the settlement agreement provides the plaintiff with relief on the merits and materially alters the legal relationship between the parties. Further, the court concluded

---

[66]*Id.* at 270, 274.
[67]*Id.* at 276.
[68]*Id.* at 276–77.
[69]*Id.* at 283–85.
[70]*Id.* at 281.
[71]*Id.* at 283–84.
[72]*Id.* at 285.
[73]277 F.3d 1128, 1134 (9th Cir. 2002).

that when parties to a settlement agree that the district court will retain jurisdiction over the issue of attorney's fees, they have provided sufficient judicial oversight to justify an award of attorney's fees and costs.[74] In reaching these conclusions, the Ninth Circuit described as dictum the *Buckhannon* footnote suggesting "that a plaintiff 'prevails' only when he or she receives a favorable judgment on the merits or enters into a court-supervised consent decree."[75]

In *Barrios*, a baseball coach with paraplegia brought ADA and state-law discrimination claims against two high school athletic foundations that refused to let him coach from his wheelchair on the field.[76] The case was settled before the court ruled on the plaintiff's request for a temporary restraining order. The court entered a judgment and order, which was then vacated on the defendants' motion.[77]

The trial court concluded that the plaintiff was the prevailing party but denied his request for attorney's fees because he had obtained only de minimis success.[78] The Ninth Circuit reversed the trial court, holding that the plaintiff's victory, a settlement payment of $10,000 and an agreement that prohibited the defendants from excluding him from on-field coaching, was not de minimis as a matter of law.[79]

The Ninth Circuit has also held that a plaintiff who obtains a preliminary injunction is a prevailing party entitled to a fee award because the plaintiff has achieved the benefit sought in bringing the lawsuit.[80]

---

[74]*Id.* at 1134 n.5; *see also* Noyes v. Grossmont Union High Sch. Dist., 331 F. Supp. 2d 1233, 1240–41 (S.D. Cal. 2004) (legally enforceable settlement agreement sufficient for plaintiff to be considered prevailing party).

[75]277 F.3d at 1134 n.5 (citing Buckhannon Bd. & Care Home, Inc. v. West Virginia Dep't of Health & Human Res., 532 U.S. 598, 604 n.7 (2001) ("private settlements do not entail the judicial approval and oversight involved in consent decrees. And federal jurisdiction to enforce a private contractual settlement will often be lacking unless the terms of the agreement are incorporated into the order of dismissal.")); *see also* Roberson v. Giuliani, 346 F.3d 75, 81–82 (2d Cir. 2003) (interpreting *Buckhannon* footnote as providing but two examples of the types of dispositions that can support a statutory attorney's fee award, leaving the door open for an award of fees in additional situations that may be deemed judicially sanctioned).

[76]277 F.3d at 1130–32.

[77]*Id.* at 1133.

[78]*Id.* at 1135.

[79]*Id.*

[80]Richard S. v. Department of Dev. Servs., 317 F.3d 1080, 1088 (9th Cir. 2003).

c. *Mixed-Motive Cases.* "Mixed-motive" cases present a dilemma in awarding attorney's fees. A mixed-motive case involves a plaintiff who succeeds in proving that the defendant based an employment decision in part on an impermissible factor (such as race or sex), but who receives no monetary damages because the defendant demonstrates that it would have made the same decision absent the impermissible factor. Following the changes to Title VII made by the Civil Rights Act of 1991,[81] courts have struggled to harmonize the *Farrar*[82] Court's skepticism toward awarding attorney's fees where no actual damages were recovered with their post-1991 discretionary Title VII authority to award attorney's fees to the plaintiff who has prevailed on a mixed-motive claim even though monetary damages are not, by statute, available.[83]

Some courts, focusing on the permissive language in §§ 2000e-5(g)(2)(B), 2000e-5(k),[84] and 1988,[85] which state that the court "in its discretion may allow" prevailing parties to recover reasonable attorney's fees, have concluded that the *Farrar* standards also apply to a court's analysis of a successful plaintiff's prevailing party status in a mixed-motive case.[86] In *Sheppard v. Riverview Nursing*

---

[81]Section 107 of the Civil Rights Act of 1991 in part overruled the Supreme Court's decision in *Price Waterhouse v. Hopkins*, 490 U.S. 228, 49 FEP 954 (1989), and established that a violation of Title VII does in fact occur where an impermissible characteristic "was a motivating factor for any employment practice." *See* 42 U.S.C. § 2000e-2(m) (2000).

[82]Farrar v. Hobby, 506 U.S. 103, 60 FEP 633 (1992).

[83]Under amended Title VII, the court "may grant . . . attorney's fees and costs demonstrated to be directly attributable only to the pursuit of a [mixed-motive] claim under section 2000e-2(m)." 42 U.S.C. § 2000e-5(g)(2)(B) (2000).

[84]Section 2000e-5(k) provides, in pertinent part, that "the court, in its discretion, may allow the prevailing party . . . a reasonable attorney's fee as a part of the costs." 42 U.S.C. § 2000e-5(k) (2000).

[85]Section 1988 provides, in pertinent part, that "the court, in its discretion, may allow the prevailing party . . . a reasonable attorney's fee as a part of the costs." 42 U.S.C. § 1988 (2000).

[86]*See* Norris v. Sysco Corp., 191 F.3d 1043, 1051–52, 9 AD 1262 (9th Cir. 1999) (district court has discretion to determine whether to award attorney's fees in Title VII mixed-motive action in which jury finds that gender is factor in employer's adverse employment decision but that employer would have made adverse employment decision anyway); Canup v. Chipman-Union, Inc., 123 F.3d 1440, 1442–43, 75 FEP 220 (11th Cir. 1997) (denying employee's requests for attorney's fees where employer prevailed on mixed-motive defense and employee recovered no damages and failed to obtain declaratory or injunctive relief); Sheppard v. Riverview Nursing Ctr., Inc., 88 F.3d 1332, 1335–37, 71 FEP 218 (4th Cir. 1996) (remanding case to district court to reconsider fee award where district court had erroneously concluded

Center, Inc.,[87] the Fourth Circuit explained its conclusion that the *Farrar* standards are applicable to fee requests in mixed-motive cases under § 2000e-5(g)(2)(B):

> In appropriate cases, for instance, courts should consider the reasons why injunctive relief was or was not granted, or the extent and nature of any declaratory relief. Moreover, *Farrar*'s concern was not only with whether the extent of recovery accords with the amount of attorney's fees. The decision suggested a more general proportionality consideration as well: whether the public purposes served by resolving the dispute justifies the recovery of fees.
>
> . . . .
>
> Such an analysis should apply here. By definition, an illicit factor will have played some role in cases subject to § 2000e-5(g)(2)(B). *See* 42 U.S.C. § 2000e-2(m). But within that category of cases, there are large differences. Some mixed-motive cases will evidence a widespread or intolerable animus on the part of a defendant; others will illustrate primarily the plaintiff's unacceptable conduct which, by definition, will have justified the action taken by the defendant. The statute allows the district court to distinguish among cases that in reality are quite different.[88]

In Title VII *retaliation* mixed-motive cases, courts generally have concluded that a finding that the same action would have been taken even absent the impermissible factor acts as a complete bar to the retaliation claim, precluding any and all relief, including an award of attorney's fees.[89]

---

that fees were mandatory under § 2000e-5(g)(2)(B) and without regard to *Farrar*); Snell v. Reno Hilton Resort, 930 F. Supp. 1428, 1431–32, 78 FEP 1236 (D. Nev. 1996) (reducing attorney's fees by 50% to recognize policy objectives of § 2000e-5(g)(2)(B) and degree of success considerations articulated by *Farrar*).

[87]88 F.3d 1332, 71 FEP 218 (4th Cir. 1996).

[88]*Id.* at 1336; *see also* Garcia v. City of Houston, 201 F.3d 672, 82 FEP 1 (5th Cir. 2000) (Title VII mixed-motive case affirming award of one-fourth attorney's fee requested despite failure to obtain injunctive relief or damages); Bonner v. Guccione, 178 F.3d 581, 601 (2d Cir. 1999) (employee not entitled to attorney's fees and costs expended on her Title VII claim where jury returned finding of liability without awarding any damages); Akrabawi v. Carnes Co., 152 F.3d 688, 696, 77 FEP 1203 (7th Cir. 1998) (attorney's fees properly denied based on evidence that invidious discrimination was minimal and employee's misconduct was serious); *Canup*, 123 F.3d at 1442–43 (district court, in denying employee's fee request, did not improperly consider *Farrar* factors in mixed-motive case).

[89]*See, e.g.*, Speedy v. Rexnord Corp., 243 F.3d 397, 406, 85 FEP 541 (7th Cir. 2001) (Civil Rights Act of 1991 does not permit injunctive relief and award of attorney's fees, costs, or both in mixed-motive retaliation case); Matima v. Celli, 228 F.3d 68, 81, 83 FEP 1660 (2d Cir. 2000) (citing to identical holdings in other circuits).

Other courts have held that the more "restrictive" *Farrar* fee standards simply do not apply to these mixed-motive cases following the 1991 amendments to Title VII.[90] Rejecting the applicability of the *Farrar* standards to fee claims in mixed-motive cases, the Tenth Circuit reasoned:

> A verdict for a plaintiff in a mixed motive Title VII case constitutes a victory on a significant legal issue that furthers a public goal, a goal that is advanced notwithstanding the fact that a plaintiff recovers no damages . . . . Accordingly, we conclude that recovery of damages is not a proper factor upon which to assess the propriety of granting a fee award in a mixed motive case. Moreover, . . . as under section 2000e-5(k), a plaintiff who prevails under section 2000e-2(m) should ordinarily "be awarded attorney's fees in all but special circumstances."[91]

Furthermore, attorney's fees may not be available in mixed-motive cases under the ADEA. Thus, one court has held that attorney's fees are not available in mixed-motive ADEA cases because the 1991 amendments to Title VII do not apply to the ADEA, and the ADEA does not provide for an award of attorney's fees to the plaintiff if the defendant prevails on an affirmative defense.[92] In addition, a pair of Eleventh Circuit cases under the ADEA held that a finding of liability, but without damages or equitable relief, will not support an award of attorney's fees.[93]

In a case under the FMLA, the district court in *McDonnell v. Miller Oil Co.*[94] ruled that different considerations are involved in resolving the "prevailing party" issue under the FMLA because of the statutory language concerning the plaintiff's entitlement to

---

[90]Gudenkauf v. Stauffer Commc'ns, 158 F.3d 1074, 1085, 77 FEP 1742 (10th Cir. 1998) (attorney's fee reduced by 50% to account for degree of success on mixed-motive claim); de Llano v. North Dakota State Univ., 951 F. Supp. 168, 170–71, 73 FEP 55 (D.N.D. 1997); Hall v. Brawley, 887 F. Supp. 1333, 1346 n.5, 68 FEP 1343 (S.D. Cal. 1995).

[91]*Gudenkauf*, 158 F.3d at 1081 (quoting Fogerty v. Fantasy, Inc., 510 U.S. 517, 535 (1994)).

[92]*See* Donovan v. Dairy Farmers of Am., Inc., 53 F. Supp. 2d 194, 198–99, 80 FEP 914 (N.D.N.Y. 1999), *aff'd*, 243 F.3d 584 (2d Cir. 2001).

[93]*See* Salvatori v. Westinghouse Elec. Corp., 190 F.3d 1244, 1245, 80 FEP 1778 (11th Cir. 1999); Nance v. Maxwell Fed. Credit Union, 186 F.3d 1338, 1343, 80 FEP 960 (11th Cir. 1999).

[94]968 F. Supp. 288, 3 WH 2d 1877 (E.D. Va. 1997), *remanded on other grounds*, 134 F.2d 638, 4 WH 2d 545 (4th Cir. 1998); *see also* Sherry v. Protection, Inc., 14 F. Supp. 2d 1055, 1057, 4 WH 2d 1598 (N.D. Ill. 1998).

fees.[95] First, noting that Congress used the word "shall" in the FMLA's attorney's fee provision rather than "may," as is used in § 1988 and Title VII, the court concluded that the FMLA's attorney's fee provision makes mandatory the award of reasonable attorney's fees if the statutory conditions are met.[96] Second, after comparing the FMLA's "in addition to any judgment" criteria for determining the entitlement to attorney's fees with the words "prevailing" or "successful" party as is used in other statutes, the court concluded that the FMLA's attorney's fee provision may be simultaneously broader and more narrow than the provisions under § 1988 and Title VII:

> The FMLA's attorney's fee provision may be more narrow because it apparently requires a judgment, rather than a mere settlement. . . . Second, the FMLA's attorney's fee provision is certainly more narrow than "prevailing party" because it is unilateral: only *plaintiffs* are eligible for attorney's fees. . . . [T]he FMLA's attorney's fee provision is broader because "*any* judgment" likely includes such limited and even Phyrric victories for a plaintiff that might fail to meet the Supreme Court's test of a "prevailing party."[97]

d. The Attorney's Entitlement to Fees. Questions sometimes arise as to the relationship between, and the rights and responsibilities of, the prevailing party and counsel. Only the prevailing party, not the party's attorney, has standing to seek attorney's fees under § 1988[98] or Title VII.[99] However, what if lawyer and client

---

[95]29 U.S.C. § 2601 et seq. (2000). The FMLA's fee provision provides: "The court in such an action shall, in addition to any judgment awarded to the plaintiff, allow a reasonable attorney's fee, reasonable expert witness fees, and other costs of the action to be paid by the defendant." *Id.* § 2607.

[96]968 F. Supp. at 292–93.

[97]*Id.* at 293 (citations omitted).

[98]United States *ex rel.* Virani v. Jerry M. Lewis Truck Parts & Equip., Inc., 89 F.3d 574, 577 (9th Cir. 1996) (if client does not ask for fees, attorney lacks standing to request them under § 1988); Benitez v. Collazo-Collazo, 888 F.2d 930, 933 (1st Cir. 1989) (prevailing party language "makes it patently obvious that it is the prevailing party, not the party's counsel, who is entitled to be awarded fees" and, because attorney's fees belong initially to prevailing party, only party and not attorney has standing); Brown v. General Motors Corp., 722 F.2d 1009, 1011, 33 FEP 417 (2d Cir. 1983) (where client fired attorney before settlement, attorney lacked standing to seek fees in his own name under § 1988).

[99]Soliman v. Ebasco Servs., Inc., 822 F.2d 320, 323, 51 FEP 1067 (2d Cir. 1987) (independent of client, attorney has no personal right to attorney's fees under Title VII); Keesee v. Orr, 816 F.2d 545, 546–47, 43 FEP 952 (10th Cir. 1987) (attorney

are one and the same? The Supreme Court held that a lawyer who represents himself or herself in a successful civil rights action may not recover attorney's fees.[100] The rationale for this rule is that "Congress contemplated an attorney-client relationship as the predicate for an award under § 1988," and "the overriding statutory concern is the interest in obtaining independent counsel for victims of civil rights violations."[101]

Courts refuse to permit a lawyer who represents himself or herself in a successful civil rights action to recover attorney's fees, regardless of the statutory authority relied on.[102] In addition, fee awards are not available to nonattorney pro se litigants who prevail in employment discrimination cases,[103] and fees may not be awarded under the fee-shifting statutes against opposing counsel in a Title VII action.[104]

2. In What Forum Must the Plaintiff Prevail?

The preceding cases helped to clarify *who* the prevailing party was; they did not, however, address the question of the *forum* in which it was necessary to prevail. The Supreme Court resolved that issue in *North Carolina Department of Transportation v. Crest Street Community Council.*[105] The Court held that attorney's fees under § 1988 may only be awarded if a court action to enforce civil rights laws has been initiated.[106] Attorney's fees may be awarded

---

dismissed before settlement was reached could not bring suit for fees; court lacked Title VII jurisdiction); Bandera v. City of Quincy, 220 F. Supp. 2d 26, 45 (D. Mass. 2002) (ability to apply for attorney fees under Title VII belongs to client and not his attorney); *cf.* Sinyard v. Commissioner, 268 F.3d 756, 759, 86 FEP 1417 (9th Cir. 2001) (in ADEA action, party rather than lawyer eligible for award of fees).

[100]Kay v. Ehrler, 499 U.S. 432, 435–38, 55 FEP 737 (1991); *see also* Krislov v. Rednour, 97 F. Supp. 2d 862, 866 (N.D. Ill. 2000) (pro se plaintiff, even one who is attorney, not entitled to award of attorney's fees under § 1988).

[101]*Kay*, 499 U.S. at 436–37.

[102]*See, e.g.*, Prewitt v. Alexander, 173 F.R.D. 438, 440 (N.D. Miss. 1996) (§ 1988); Hannon v. Chater, 900 F. Supp. 1276, 1284 n.23 (N.D. Cal. 1995) (Title VII); Roepsch v. Bentsen, 846 F. Supp. 1363, 1370 (E.D. Wis. 1994) (ADEA).

[103]*See, e.g.*, Hawkins v. 1115 Legal Serv. Care, 163 F.3d 684, 695, 78 FEP 882 (2d Cir. 1998).

[104]*See, e.g.*, Corneveaux v. CUNA Mut. Ins. Group, 76 F.3d 1498, 1508–09, 70 FEP 247 (10th Cir. 1996).

[105]479 U.S. 6, 42 FEP 177 (1986).

[106]*Id.* at 15 ("Under the plain language and legislative history of § 1988, however, only a court in an action to enforce one of the civil rights laws listed in § 1988

under § 1988 for administrative proceedings "when those proceedings are part of or followed by a lawsuit."[107]

With respect to claims for attorney's fees incurred for work on administrative proceedings in connection with court actions to enforce the civil rights laws covered by Title VII, the ADA, and § 1988, the key factor in determining whether such fees may be awarded to the prevailing party is whether the work on administrative proceedings was necessary to, or an integral part of, the civil rights action.[108] However, where a Title VII action is brought only to request attorney's fees for work performed as a part of an EEOC administrative proceeding that resolved the complaint on the merits prior to the filing of a federal court action, one court has held that it did not have subject matter jurisdiction over the claim for attorney's fees alone.[109] The court reasoned that "[t]he jurisdictional grant in 42 U.S.C. § 2000e-5(f)(3) refers to legal proceedings in a court of law to enforce the substantive rights guaranteed by Title VII . . . [and] does not extend to an independent action solely for attorney's fees and costs incurred during the course of the Title VII administrative process."[110]

---

may award attorney's fees."); *see also* Martin v. Mabus, 734 F. Supp. 1216, 1223 (S.D. Miss. 1990) (plaintiffs not entitled to recover attorney's fees for administrative activities as opposed to litigation).

[107]*North Carolina Dep't of Transp.*, 479 U.S. at 14; *see also* Section I.E *infra*.

[108]*Compare* Lambert v. Fulton County, 151 F. Supp. 2d 1364, 1371–72, 84 FEP 994 (N.D. Ga. 2000) (allowing attorney's fees for county employees' appeal of race discrimination complaint to county's personnel board), Spradley v. Notami Hosps., 892 F. Supp. 1459, 1463 (M.D. Fla. 1995) (allowing attorney's fees before Florida Commission on Human Relations to prevailing plaintiff where filing of complaint with state administrative agency is prerequisite to filing suit in federal court under ADEA) *and* Stover v. Riley, 30 F. Supp. 2d 501, 505–06 (E.D. Pa. 1998) (allowing attorney's fees under Title VII for work done in mandatory administrative proceeding that was jurisdictional prerequisite to commencement of Title VII action) *with* Reynolds v. U.S.X. Corp., 170 F. Supp. 2d 530, 532, 87 FEP 307 (E.D. Pa. 2001) (barring recovery of attorney's fees for work related to employee's unemployment compensation hearings), Castle v. Bentsen, 872 F. Supp. 1062, 1067, 66 FEP 1498 (D.D.C. 1995) (excluding from attorney's fee award time spent preparing for administrative hearing, which plaintiff cancelled, and pursuing unsuccessful complaint to bar counsel during administrative proceedings; such time did not contribute to litigation before court) *and* Williams v. Secretary of Navy, 853 F. Supp. 66, 69, 64 FEP 1709 (E.D.N.Y. 1994) (refusing award of attorney's fees for time spent solely on internal Navy Adverse Action Appeal as those administrative proceedings were not integral part of plaintiff's Title VII action).

[109]Chris v. Tenet, 221 F.3d 648, 655, 83 FEP 724 (4th Cir. 2000).

[110]*Id.*

In a slightly different twist, the court in *DiRussa v. Dean Witter Reynolds, Inc.*[111] refused to vacate a security industry arbitrator's denial of an award of attorney's fees to a successful ADEA complainant as a "manifest disregard of the law," despite the clearly mandatory nature of the right to attorney's fees for a prevailing plaintiff under the ADEA. The court reasoned that the ADEA's statutory entitlement to attorney's fees for a prevailing plaintiff was not "capable of being readily and instantly perceived" by the average National Association of Securities Dealers arbitrator and noted that the plaintiff's counsel had failed to make any mention to the arbitrator of the plaintiff's entitlement to fees under the statutory language of the ADEA.[112] However, in *DeGaetano v. Smith Barney, Inc.*,[113] the court did vacate an arbitration panel's refusal to award fees to a successful plaintiff in an arbitration proceeding where the arbitration panel had been "notified unequivocally by all parties of the governing legal principles granting attorney's fees to prevailing plaintiffs" and the arbitration panel applied the wrong legal standards in reaching its conclusion.[114]

3. Discretion in Denying Attorney's Fees

Newman v. Piggie Park Enterprises, Inc.[115] is the leading case establishing that a civil rights plaintiff acts as a "private attorney general" and is thus normally entitled to fees if statutorily authorized.[116] Although *Newman* arose under Title II[117] (the public accommodations title) of the Civil Rights Act of 1964, the attorney's fees provision of Title II[118] is almost identical to that of Title VII. And, indeed, the Supreme Court made clear in *Albemarle Paper Co. v. Moody*[119] and

---

[111]936 F. Supp. 104, 71 FEP 1002 (S.D.N.Y. 1996), *aff'd*, 121 F.3d 818, 74 FEP 726 (2d Cir. 1997).

[112]*Id.* at 106.

[113]983 F. Supp. 459, 75 FEP 579 (S.D.N.Y. 1997).

[114]*Id.* at 462–64.

[115]390 U.S. 400, 402 (1968).

[116]As noted earlier, in proceedings governed by the attorney's fees provision of the FLSA, the award of attorney's fees to a prevailing plaintiff is mandatory. *See* Section II.A.3 *supra*.

[117]42 U.S.C. § 2000a (2000).

[118]*Id.* § 2000a-3b.

[119]422 U.S. 405, 415, 10 FEP 1181 (1975) ("While the Act appears to leave Title II fee awards to the district court's discretion . . . , the court [in *Newman*] determined that the great public interest in having injunctive actions brought could be

New York Gaslight Club, Inc. v. Carey[120] that the *Newman* standard is applicable to Title VII. Thus, a plaintiff who prevails in a Title VII or other civil rights suit normally will be awarded attorney's fees unless special circumstances render such an award unjust.[121]

Thus, even where the fee statute speaks in permissive rather than mandatory terms, courts have made clear that no finding of the defendant's bad faith is required for an award of fees to plaintiffs. This is so because the primary purpose of the fee award is to encourage litigation that might vindicate important public rights, not to punish the defendant. As the Court in *Newman* explained:

> When the Civil Rights Act of 1964 was passed, it was evident that enforcement would prove difficult and that the Nation would have to rely in part upon private litigation as a means of securing broad compliance with the law. A Title II suit is thus private in form only. When a plaintiff brings an action under that Title, he cannot recover damages. If he obtains an injunction, he does so not for himself alone but also as a "private attorney general," vindicating a policy that Congress considered of the highest priority. If successful plaintiffs were routinely forced to bear their own attorneys' fees, few aggrieved parties would be in a position to advance the public interest by invoking the injunctive powers of the federal courts. Congress therefore enacted the provision for counsel fees—

---

vindicated only if successful plaintiffs, acting as 'private attorneys general,' were awarded attorneys' fees in all but very unusual circumstances. There is, of course, an equally strong public interest in having injunctive actions brought under Title VII, to eradicate discriminatory employment practices. But this interest can be vindicated by applying the [*Newman*] standard to the attorneys' fees provision of Title VII.") (citations omitted).

[120]447 U.S. 54, 68, 22 FEP 1642 (1980) ("We ... find no merit in petitioners' suggestion that denial of a fee award was within the District Court's discretion. . . . [T]he court's discretion to deny a fee award to a prevailing plaintiff is narrow. Absent 'special circumstances,' see *Newman v. Piggie Park Enterprises*, . . . fees should be awarded.") (internal citation omitted).

[121]*See, e.g.*, Hensley v. Eckerhart, 461 U.S. 424, 433 n.7, 31 FEP 1169 (1983) (§ 1988) ("The standards set forth in this opinion are generally applicable in all cases in which Congress has authorized an award of fees to a 'prevailing party.' "); Roadway Express, Inc. v. Piper, 447 U.S. 752, 762, 23 FEP 12 (1980) (in describing both § 1988 and § 2000e-5(k), Court said: "Prevailing plaintiffs in civil rights cases win [attorney's] fee awards unless special circumstances would render such an award unjust.' ") (citing *Newman*); *see* S. REP. NO. 1011, 94th Cong., 2d Sess. 5, *reprinted in* 1976 U.S.C.C.A.N. 5908, 5912 ("It is intended that the standards for awarding fees be generally the same [under § 1988] as under the fee provisions of the 1964 Civil Rights Act. A party seeking to enforce the rights protected by the statutes . . . , if successful, 'should ordinarily recover an attorney's fee unless special circumstances would render such an award unjust.' ").

not simply to penalize litigants who deliberately advance arguments they know to be untenable but, more broadly, to encourage individuals injured by racial discrimination to seek judicial relief under Title II.[122]

Courts in employment discrimination cases[123] have rejected many claims that "special circumstances" warrant denial of attorney's fees to prevailing plaintiffs. In *Carey*,[124] the Supreme Court rejected two such claims. The plaintiff in *Carey* had litigated a sex discrimination claim before a state fair employment practices agency prior to filing in federal court. She was represented by a public interest group throughout, even though the state agency was willing to provide a staff attorney to prosecute her complaint before the agency. After the plaintiff prevailed on the merits, the defendant contended that "special circumstances" made an award of attorney's fees unjust, because the plaintiff did not need to obtain her own counsel. In the alternative, the defendant argued that no fee should be awarded because the plaintiff's counsel was a public interest group.

The Supreme Court rejected both arguments. With respect to the former, the Court held that counsel fees should be awarded because "the private attorney has an important role to play in preserving and protecting federal rights and interests"[125]—a role distinct from that played by the lawyer for the state agency. With respect

---

[122]390 U.S. 400, 401–02 (1968) (citations and footnote omitted).

[123]Courts more frequently have found special circumstances in cases not involving employment discrimination, where the fee issue was litigated under § 1988. *See, e.g.,* Cunningham v. County of L.A., 879 F.2d 481, 491 (9th Cir. 1988) (balance of equities strongly disfavored award of attorney's fees, because plaintiff failed to produce evidence to support allegations against four of seven defendants); Aho v. Clark, 608 F.2d 365, 367 (9th Cir. 1979) (where consent agreement was silent on question of attorney's fees with no reservation of rights to petition for award, court would not alter terms of compromise agreement); Buxton v. Patel, 595 F.2d 1182, 1185 (9th Cir. 1979) (appellants' chance of success sufficiently high to attract competent counsel, and adequate compensation to counsel was provided from damages awarded plaintiffs); Zarcone v. Perry, 581 F.2d 1039, 1044 (2d Cir. 1978) (prospects for financial recovery were good, and it was apparent that counsel fees would not present significant barrier to prosecution of action; defendant's conduct was unlikely to recur, and plaintiff sued to redress "an essentially private injury"). *But see* Lawrence v. Bowsher, 931 F.2d 1579, 1580, 55 FEP 1284 (D.C. Cir. 1991) (special circumstances did not exist to preclude award of attorney's fees even though plaintiff took litigation position that court believed was harmful to civil rights of others).

[124]447 U.S. 54, 22 FEP 1642 (1980).

[125]*Id.* at 70.

to the latter argument, the Court cited legislative history of § 1988 indicating that Congress wanted counsel fees to be available to public interest groups.[126]

The Fourth Circuit rejected another claim of special circumstances in *Lea v. Cone Mills Corp.*[127] The district court there had denied attorney's fees to the prevailing plaintiffs on the ground that they were seeking only a test case and were not actually interested in employment. The court of appeals reversed, holding that the motivation of the plaintiffs was not relevant to their entitlement to attorney's fees.[128]

Courts have rejected a variety of other "special circumstances" as grounds for denying fees:

(1) the defendant acted in good faith;[129]

(2) the defendant relied on EEOC interpretations and protective laws;[130]

(3) the defendant took prompt action in remedying the discrimination;[131]

(4) the lawyer already had been paid, pursuant to a private fee arrangement;[132]

(5) it would be impracticable to divide up counsel's hours between the issue on which the plaintiff prevailed and others on which the plaintiff did not prevail;[133]

(6) the plaintiff was fully able to afford the cost of the suit;[134]

---

[126]*Id.* at 70 n.9.

[127]438 F.2d 86, 3 FEP 137 (4th Cir. 1971).

[128]*Id.* at 87–88.

[129]Walker v. City of Mesquite, 313 F.3d 246, 248–49 (5th Cir. 2002); Martin v. Heckler, 773 F.2d 1145, 1150 (11th Cir. 1985); Ortiz de Arroyo v. Barcelo, 765 F.2d 275, 281 (1st Cir. 1985); Holley v. Lavine, 605 F.2d 638, 646 (2d Cir. 1979); Teitelbaum v. Sorenson, 648 F.2d 1248, 1250–51 (9th Cir. 1981); *see also* Coalition for Basic Human Needs v. King, 691 F.2d 597, 602 (1st Cir. 1982) (§ 1988).

[130]Rosenfeld v. Southern Pac. Co., 519 F.2d 527, 529, 10 FEP 1439 (9th Cir. 1975).

[131]Tyler v. Corner Constr. Corp., 167 F.3d 1202, 1205 (8th Cir. 1999); Fields v. City of Tarpon Springs, 721 F.2d 318, 321–22 (11th Cir. 1983) (per curiam).

[132]Venegas v. Mitchell, 495 U.S. 82, 90, 52 FEP 849 (1990); Blanchard v. Bergeron, 489 U.S. 87, 93, 49 FEP 1 (1989); *see also* Sargeant v. Sharp, 579 F.2d 645, 649 (1st Cir. 1978) (§ 1988 case).

[133]Nadeau v. Helgemoe, 581 F.2d 275, 278–79 (1st Cir. 1978).

[134]Jones v. Wilkinson, 800 F.2d 989, 991 (10th Cir. 1986), *aff'd*, 480 U.S. 926 (1987); International Soc'y for Krishna Consciousness, Inc. v. Collins, 609 F.2d 151, 151 (5th Cir. 1980).

(7) the financial burden of any fee would fall on the tax-payers;[135]

(8) the plaintiff failed to engage in meaningful settlement discussions;[136]

(9) the case was "simple" or could be "routinely handled";[137]

(10) the attorney's fees requested exceed the amount of damages awarded on the merits;[138]

(11) the plaintiff failed to take into account his or her limited degree of success, made a "grossly excessive" fee request, or both;[139]

(12) the plaintiff received a "generous award" of damages[140] or an award that was "disproportionately high";[141] and

(13) the issue resolved was "novel" under the ADA, the violation was not knowing or purposeful, and the plaintiff had increased the cost of litigation by pursuing "additional and unnecessary" claims.[142]

On occasion, however, courts find sufficient "special circumstances" to warrant the complete denial of an award of attorney's fees to the prevailing plaintiff. In *United States ex rel. Averback v. Pastor Medical Associates*,[143] the court stated that the absence of an attorney's detailed, contemporaneous time records would, in egregious cases, warrant a complete disallowance of fees.[144]

---

[135]Copeland v. Marshall, 641 F.2d 880, 894–96, 23 FEP 967 (D.C. Cir. 1980) (en banc); Rodriguez v. Taylor, 569 F.2d 1231, 1249 n.32, 16 FEP 533 (3d Cir. 1977).

[136]*See, e.g.*, Shott v. Rush-Presbyterian-St. Luke's Med. Ctr., 338 F.3d 736, 744, 747 (7th Cir. 2003); NAACP v. Town of E. Haven, 259 F.3d 113, 119–20, 87 FEP 1319 (2d Cir. 2001); Moore v. University of Notre Dame, 22 F. Supp. 2d 896, 909, 78 FEP 62 (N.D. Ind. 1998); Schofield v. Trustees of Univ. of Pa., 919 F. Supp. 821, 827 n.2 (E.D. Pa. 1996).

[137]Jackson v. Pennsylvania Hous. Auth., 858 F. Supp. 464, 471 (E.D. Pa. 1994).

[138]Fair Housing of Marin v. Combs, 285 F.3d 899, 908 (9th Cir. 2002); Abrams v. Lightolier, Inc., 50 F.3d 1204, 1222, 67 FEP 543 (3d Cir. 1995).

[139]St. Louis Fire Fighters Ass'n v. St. Louis, 96 F.3d 323, 331–32, 71 FEP 1513 (8th Cir. 1996).

[140]Sasaki v. Class, 92 F.3d 232, 243, 71 FEP 709 (4th Cir. 1996).

[141]Lockard v. Pizza Hut, Inc., 162 F.3d 1062, 1076, 78 FEP 1026 (10th Cir. 1998).

[142]Roe v. Cheyenne Mountain Conference Resort, Inc., 124 F.3d 1221, 1231–33, 7 AD 779 (10th Cir. 1997), *aff'd*, 172 F.3d 879 (10th Cir. 1999).

[143]224 F. Supp. 2d 342 (D. Mass. 2002).

[144]*Id.* at 347–48.

In addition, in *Mindler v. Clayton County*,[145] the court found that the plaintiff's untimely request for an award of attorney's fees in the amount of $120,000, filed 45 days after the time had expired for the defendant to appeal the jury's $49,000 verdict for the plaintiff, was a "special circumstance" warranting the complete denial of an award of attorney's fees. The court reasoned that the untimely request for fees unduly prejudiced the defendant because, had the defendant been aware he was paying a judgment of $169,000 rather than $49,000, he might well have chosen to appeal that judgment.[146]

Poor performance of the plaintiff's counsel is usually a factor in determining the *amount* of attorney's fees, rather than a special circumstance justifying a denial of fees altogether.[147] But some early cases found poor performance to be a basis for denying attorney's fees to the prevailing party altogether.[148]

C. Awards to Prevailing Plaintiffs in Actions Against State Governments

In the past, states argued that the Eleventh Amendment barred Title VII awards against them for back pay or attorney's fees. But in *Fitzpatrick v. Bitzer*,[149] the Supreme Court held that, because Title VII was enacted pursuant to § 5 of the Fourteenth Amendment (which specifically authorized Congress to enforce it by appropriate legislation), any otherwise existing constitutional restrictions on such monetary awards were not applicable.[150]

After *Fitzpatrick*, it was clear that prevailing plaintiffs in Title VII actions against state governments could recover reasonable attorney's fees under § 706(k). *Hutto v. Finney*[151] similarly held

---

[145]864 F. Supp. 1329 (N.D. Ga. 1994), *aff'd*, 63 F.3d 1113 (11th Cir. 1995); *see also* Hipps v. Steelworkers, 85 FEP 367, 368 (N.D. Ga. 2001).

[146]*Mindler*, 865 F. Supp. at 1331.

[147]*See* Section III.B.2.d *infra*.

[148]Drake v. Southwestern Bell Tel. Co., 553 F.2d 1185, 1189 n.4, 15 FEP 577 (8th Cir. 1977) (failure of plaintiff's counsel to respond to motion contributed to district court's erroneous ruling); Johnson v. Shreveport Garment Co., 422 F. Supp. 526, 544, 13 FEP 1677 (W.D. La. 1976) (plaintiffs prevailed on their individual but not class claims; no fee awarded, "because so much of plaintiffs' failing must be attributed to their attorneys"), *aff'd mem.*, 577 F.2d 1132 (5th Cir. 1978).

[149]427 U.S. 445, 12 FEP 1586 (1976).

[150]*Id.* at 456.

[151]437 U.S. 678, 694–95 (1978).

that § 1988, like § 706(k), authorizes awards of attorney's fees for plaintiffs who prevail in actions against state governments. In *Missouri v. Jenkins*,[152] another § 1988 case, the Supreme Court further held that the Eleventh Amendment does not prohibit enhancement of an attorney's fee award against a state to compensate for delay in payment when the award is ancillary to prospective injunctive relief.

Although plaintiffs may sue state actors for violations of Title VII and the FMLA,[153] the Supreme Court has held that states are immune from employment discrimination suits seeking back pay under the ADEA[154] and the ADA[155] because Congress did not validly abrogate the states' Eleventh Amendment immunity from suit in enacting the latter two statutes.

D. Awards to Prevailing Plaintiffs in Suits Against the Federal Government

Although Title VII clearly authorizes awards of attorney's fees against the United States,[156] courts are split over the rationale for allowing prevailing plaintiffs to recover attorney's fees against the federal government in ADEA actions. Some courts hold that such a prevailing plaintiff may recover attorney's fees under the ADEA because § 633a(c) of the ADEA contains an affirmative waiver of the government's sovereign immunity.[157]

Other courts find that a prevailing plaintiff may not recover attorney's fees from a federal government defendant under the ADEA,

---

[152]491 U.S. 274, 280–84, 50 FEP 17 (1989).

[153]Nevada Dep't of Human Res. v. Hibbs, 538 U.S. 721, 724–25 (2003).

[154]Kimel v. Florida Bd. of Regents, 528 U.S. 62, 92 (2000).

[155]Board of Trustees of Univ. of Ala. v. Garrett, 531 U.S. 356, 360 (2001).

[156]*See, e.g.*, Adcock v. Secretary of Treasury, 227 F.3d 343, 351–52 (6th Cir. 2000) (plaintiff entitled to recover attorney's fee award under Title VII against U.S. Secretary of Treasury and U.S. Secret Service).

[157]*Compare* Nowd v. Rubin, 76 F.3d 25, 27–28, 69 FEP 1587 (1st Cir. 1996) (ADEA does not authorize award of attorney's fees against U.S. Department of Treasury or for any federal employee; generalized statutory language insufficient to overcome either American Rule or sovereign immunity) *and* Gregor v. Derwinski, 911 F. Supp. 643, 656, 75 FEP 797 (W.D.N.Y. 1996) (ADEA does not authorize award of attorney's fees against federal Veterans Affairs medical center or for any federal employee, absent express congressional authorization) *with* Craig v. O'Leary, 870 F. Supp. 1007, 1009, 69 FEP 452 (D. Colo. 1994) (reaching contrary result and citing cases).

yet nevertheless conclude that an award of attorney's fees is authorized under the Equal Access to Justice Act (EAJA).[158] To recover under the EAJA, however, the party seeking fees must show that "the position of the agency was not substantially justified."[159] Where that test can be met, sovereign immunity does not apply, as the EAJA waived sovereign immunity in cases to which the Act applies.[160]

E. Awards to Prevailing Plaintiffs Before Administrative Agencies

In *New York Gaslight Club, Inc. v. Carey*,[161] the Supreme Court addressed whether, under Title VII, a federal court may allow the prevailing party attorney's fees for legal services performed in prosecuting a Title VII claim in state administrative and judicial proceedings. The Court held that the answer is yes: "Congress' use of the broadly inclusive disjunctive phrase 'any action or proceeding' in § 706(k) indicates an intent to subject the losing party to an award of attorney's fees and costs that includes expenses incurred for administrative proceedings."[162] State agency proceedings

---

[158]28 U.S.C. § 2412 (2000); *see, e.g.*, Boehms v. Crowell, 139 F.3d 452, 462–63, 76 FEP 1368 (5th Cir. 1998) (ADEA does not permit award of attorney's fees against federal government, but EAJA enables award of attorney's fees against federal government in ADEA cases); *Nowd*, 76 F.3d at 28; *see also* Section II.A.4 *supra*.

[159]5 U.S.C. § 504(a)(2) (2000).

[160]*In re* Sealed Case 00-5116, 254 F.3d 233, 237 (D.C. Cir. 2001) (EAJA acts as waiver of sovereign immunity but is construed strictly in favor of sovereign); Maritime Mgmt., Inc. v. United States, 242 F.3d 1326, 1331–32, 1336 (11th Cir. 2001) (EAJA waives sovereign immunity by making United States liable for attorney's fees to same extent that any other party would be liable under common law or any statute specifically providing for such award, but waiver must be strictly construed); Resolution Trust Corp. v. Gaudet, 192 F.3d 485, 487 (5th Cir. 1999) (as waiver of sovereign immunity, provision of EAJA authorizing award of attorney's fees against United States is to be strictly construed); Lauritzen v. Lehman, 736 F.2d 550, 554 n.4 (9th Cir. 1984) (EAJA waived sovereign immunity); *cf.* Scarborough v. Principi, 319 F.3d 1346, 1348 (Fed. Cir. 2003) (EAJA amounts to partial waiver of sovereign immunity), *rev'd and remanded*, 541 U.S. 401, 93 FEP 1096 (2004). Pre-Act cases on sovereign immunity thus probably are no longer valid authority. *See, e.g.*, Knights of Ku Klux Klan v. East Baton Rouge Parish Sch. Bd., 643 F.2d 1034, 1037–39 (5th Cir.), *vacated*, 454 U.S. 1075 (1981); NAACP v. Civiletti, 609 F.2d 514, 518 (D.C. Cir. 1979); Shannon v. United States Dep't of Hous. & Urban Dev., 577 F.2d 854, 856 (3d Cir. 1978) (Title VI). Indeed, the *Ku Klux Klan* decision was expressly vacated by the Supreme Court in light of the adoption of the EAJA. 454 U.S. 1075 (1981).

[161]447 U.S. 54, 22 FEP 1642 (1980).

[162]*Id.* at 55.

must be included, the Court reasoned, because Title VII created
the system of required deferral to state and local agencies:

> Congress envisioned that Title VII's procedures and remedies would
> "mes[h] nicely, logically, and coherently with the State and city leg-
> islation," and that remedying employment discrimination would be an
> area in which "[t]he Federal Government and the State governments
> could cooperate effectively." . . . It is clear from this scheme of inter-
> related and complementary state and federal enforcement that Congress
> viewed proceedings before the EEOC and in federal court as supple-
> ments to available state remedies for employment discrimination.[163]

A few early decisions held that attorney's fees may be awardable in some circumstances for time expended by a prevailing plaintiff pursuing remedies collateral to a Title VII suit, such as debarment proceedings before the Office of Federal Contract Compliance
Programs (OFCCP).[164] But Title VII does not support an award of
attorney's fees for an optional internal grievance procedure that is
not a prerequisite to filing a Title VII action.[165]

Some courts have expanded on the reasoning of *Carey* and
awarded counsel fees for state *court* proceedings.[166]

---

[163]*Id.* at 63–65 (citations omitted).

[164]Chrapliwy v. Uniroyal, Inc., 670 F.2d 760, 766, 28 FEP 19 (7th Cir. 1982)
(where work in inducing OFCCP to institute debarment proceedings was instrumental
to favorable settlement of Title VII litigation, fees may be awarded for work with
respect to both Title VII suit and OFCCP department). *But see* Harmon v. San Diego County, 664 F.2d 770, 772, 28 FEP 28 (9th Cir. 1981) (time spent pursuing
unsuccessful efforts to intervene in lawsuit brought by Justice Department excluded
from fee award).

[165]Manders v. Oklahoma *ex rel.* Dep't of Mental Health, 875 F.2d 263, 266, 49
FEP 1188 (10th Cir. 1989); Mertz v. Marsh, 786 F.2d 1578, 1579–81, 40 FEP 1110
(11th Cir. 1986) (plaintiff not entitled to attorney's fees for time spent processing
pre-complaint grievance).

[166]Lampher v. Zagel, 755 F.2d 99, 103–04 (4th Cir. 1985) (court applied reasoning of *Carey* to § 1988 action); Bartholomew v. Watson, 665 F.2d 910, 912–13
(9th Cir. 1982) (attorney's fees could be awarded under § 1988 for services performed
in state courts where state court action was initiated and pursued under *Pullman*
abstention doctrine); Beltran Rosas v. County of San Bernardino, 260 F. Supp. 2d
990, 993–94 (C.D. Cal. 2003) (plaintiff suing under § 1983 may recover compensatory damages for attorney's fees expended in defending prior criminal action in state
court where defense was necessary for success on § 1983 claim). *Contra* Schneider
v. Colegio de Abogados de P.R., 187 F.3d 30, 32–33 (1st Cir. 1999) (no entitlement
to attorney's fees for work done in courts of Commonwealth of Puerto Rico before
plaintiffs filed their federal lawsuit under § 1983); Cooper v. Williamson County Bd.
of Educ., 820 F.2d 180, 183 (6th Cir. 1987) (citing *Carey*; fees for defending state
court dismissal proceedings denied because they were not part of Title VII "scheme").

As for § 1983 actions, in *Webb v. Board of Education*[167] the Supreme Court held that attorney's fees cannot be automatically recovered for earlier pursuit of state administrative remedies; these are an independent avenue of relief,[168] and state proceedings are not mandatory. Some courts say that these fees may be recoverable, however, if the trial court finds that the state administrative hearings or suits are an integral part of the successful federal court action.[169]

F. Awards to Prevailing Plaintiffs Represented by Public Interest Law Firms

Carey, as noted earlier, resolved that prevailing plaintiffs may be awarded attorney's fees when they are represented by a public interest law firm.[170] The Supreme Court thereafter also held that the measure of "reasonable fees" to be awarded is governed by prevailing market rates in the community, regardless of whether the plaintiff is represented by a conventional private law firm or by a nonprofit public interest or legal services organization.[171]

The Third Circuit has held that a contractual provision that purported to preclude legal services attorneys from seeking fee awards payable by the state is unenforceable and against public policy.[172]

---

[167]471 U.S. 234, 241–42, 37 FEP 785 (1985).

[168]Even before *Webb*, the Second, Third, Fifth, Eighth, and Eleventh Circuits had determined that, when a plaintiff has been made whole in a state administrative proceeding for a § 1983 violation, he or she cannot then file in federal court for an award of attorney's fees under § 1988. Latino Project, Inc. v. City of Camden, 701 F.2d 262, 265 (3d Cir. 1983); Estes v. Tuscaloosa County, 696 F.2d 898, 900 (11th Cir. 1983); Horacek v. Thone, 710 F.2d 496, 499 (8th Cir. 1983); Blow v. Lascaris, 668 F.2d 670, 671 (2d Cir. 1982); Redd v. Lambert, 674 F.2d 1032, 1034 (5th Cir. 1982).

[169]*E.g.*, Stathos v. Bowden, 728 F.2d 15, 22 (1st Cir. 1984) (plaintiff awarded attorney's fees for defense of state court action, because such defense was necessary to succeed in § 1983 case); *cf. Webb*, 471 U.S. at 243 (because plaintiff here did not claim administrative legal work was "useful" or "necessary to advance the civil rights litigation . . . the District Court correctly held . . . [it] was not compensable").

[170]New York Gaslight Club, Inc. v. Carey, 447 U.S. 54, 70–71, 22 FEP 1642 (1980).

[171]*See* Blum v. Stenson, 465 U.S. 886, 895, 34 FEP 417 (1984). Fee calculation issues are discussed in further detail in Section III *infra*.

[172]*See* Shadis v. Beal, 685 F.2d 824, 830 (3d Cir. 1982) ("It is well settled that Congress intended legal service programs, like private attorneys, to receive fees under the Fees Awards Act."); *cf.* Westchester Legal Servs., Inc. v. Westchester County,

G. Awards to Prevailing Plaintiffs in Negotiated Settlements

As discussed earlier, some courts have interpreted the Supreme Court's decision in *Buckhannon Board & Care Home, Inc. v. West Virginia Department of Health & Human Resources*[173] to preclude an award of attorney's fees where the plaintiff achieved success through a negotiated settlement agreement.[174] The rationale for denying fees in this context is that the plaintiff did not receive relief *from the court* so as to qualify the plaintiff as a prevailing party.[175]

Several courts have held that where the settlement agreement is embodied in a court order, or where the court explicitly retains jurisdiction to enforce the terms of the settlement agreement, the agreement is functionally equivalent to a consent decree because the obligation to comply with its terms is court-ordered and the court's approval and oversight is readily apparent.[176] In those circumstances, *Buckhannon*'s requirement that the plaintiff's victory bear a judicial imprimatur is met.[177]

In addition, some courts have held that *Buckhannon*'s discussion of private settlement agreements is nonbinding dictum. Those courts have continued to uphold attorney's fee awards to plaintiffs who obtained an enforceable settlement agreement but no other judicial relief.[178]

Rule 23(e) of the Federal Rules of Civil Procedure states that "the court must approve any settlement, . . . or compromise of the claims . . . of a certified class," and that such approval should be granted "only on finding that the settlement . . . or compromise is fair, reasonable and adequate."[179] The Eighth Circuit held that this

---

607 F. Supp. 1379, 1383 n.2 (S.D.N.Y. 1985) ("The Court does not accept the defendants' contention that they have a genuine concern and question as to whether it is ethical for a group which receives funding from a government entity to engage in litigation against that source of funding.").

[173]532 U.S. 598 (2001).

[174]*See* Section II.B.1.b *supra*.

[175]*See Buckhannon*, 532 U.S. at 605.

[176]*See* Smyth *ex rel.* Smyth v. Rivero, 282 F.3d 268, 279–81 (4th Cir. 2002).

[177]*Id.*; *see also* American Disability Ass'n, Inc. v. Chmielarz, 289 F.3d 1315, 1320 (11th Cir. 2002) (plaintiff qualifies as prevailing party where court either incorporates settlement terms in dismissal order or expressly retains jurisdiction to enforce settlement).

[178]*See* Section II.B.1.b *supra*.

[179]FED. R. CIV. P. 23(e)(1)(A), (C).

type of review is "merely an exercise in compliance with Rule 23(e)," which "fails to impose the necessary *imprimatur* on the agreement" to qualify the plaintiffs as prevailing parties.[180] The court added that the district court's retention of jurisdiction to enforce the agreement is also "not enough to establish judicial '*imprimatur*' on the settlement contract."[181]

In contrast, the Ninth Circuit held that *Buckhannon*'s judicial imprimatur requirement was met in a class action where the district court approved a legally enforceable settlement agreement and retained jurisdiction to enforce the agreement.[182]

H. Awards for Interim Success

Federal courts may allow an interim fee award to a plaintiff who has prevailed on the merits at an interim stage.[183]

In *Hanrahan v. Hampton*,[184] the Supreme Court considered the circumstances in which an interim award of attorney's fees would be appropriate under § 1988. In that case, the plaintiffs on appeal had succeeded in overturning directed verdicts against them in their suit for damages resulting from an allegedly unlawful search for weapons in an apartment. However, as the case came to the Supreme Court, the plaintiffs had not prevailed on the merits of any of their claims. The Court explained that no fee had yet been earned:

> It is evident also that Congress contemplated the award of fees *pendente lite* in some cases. But it seems clearly to have been the intent of Congress to permit such an interlocutory award only to a party who has established his entitlement to some relief on the merits of his claims, either in the trial court or on appeal. The congressional Committee Reports described what were considered to be appropriate circumstances for such an award by reference to two

---

[180]*E.g.*, Christina A. v. Bloomberg, 315 F.3d 990, 992 (8th Cir. 2003) (quotation and citations omitted).

[181]*Id.* at 993.

[182]Richard S. v. Department of Dev. Servs., 317 F.3d 1080, 1888 (9th Cir. 2003) (citing Watson v. County of Riverside, 300 F.3d 1092, 1096 (9th Cir. 2002)). The Second Circuit has noted that the Eighth Circuit, in *Christiana A. v. Bloomberg*, "is the only circuit to squarely adopt such a narrow reading of *Buckhannon*, and it did so over a vigorous and persuasive dissent by Judge Melloy." Roberson v. Giuliani, 346 F.3d 75, 82 n.7 (2d Cir. 2003).

[183]*See, e.g.*, Hensley, 461 U.S. 424, 452 n.9 (Brennan, J., concurring); Marks v. Clarke, 102 F.3d 1012, 1034 (9th Cir. 1996).

[184]446 U.S. 754 (1980).

cases—*Bradley v. Richmond School Board*, 416 U.S. 696, 94 S.
Ct. 2006, 40 L. Ed. 2d 476 (1974) and *Mills v. Electric Auto-Lite
Co.*, 396 U.S. 375, 90 S. Ct. 616, 24 L. Ed. 2d 593 (1970). In each
of those cases the party to whom fees were awarded had established the liability of the opposing party, although final remedial
orders had not been entered. The House Committee Report, moreover, approved the standard suggested by this Court in *Bradley*,
that " 'the entry of any order that determines substantial rights of
the parties may be an appropriate occasion upon which to consider
the propriety of an award of counsel fees . . . ,' " quoting *Bradley
v. Richmond School Board*, supra, 416 U.S. at 723 n.28, 94 S. Ct.
at 2022 n.28. Similarly, the Senate Committee Report explained
that the award of counsel fees *pendente lite* would be "especially
appropriate where a party has prevailed on an important matter in
the course of litigation, even when he ultimately does not prevail
on all issues." It seems apparent from these passages that Congress
intended to permit the interim award of counsel fees only when a
party has prevailed on the merits of at least some of his claims.
For only in that event has there been a determination of the "substantial rights of the parties," which Congress determined was a
necessary foundation for departing from the usual rule in this country
that each party is to bear the expense of his own attorney.[185]

In *Bradley v. Richmond School Board*,[186] a lengthy and complicated school desegregation case, the Supreme Court approved
an interim fee award because delaying consideration of the fee issue
until the completion of remedial proceedings, anticipated to take
years, "would work a substantial hardship on plaintiffs and their
counsel."[187]

After the Supreme Court's decision in *Buckhannon*, some courts
have held that a preliminary injunction lacks the judicial imprimatur required for a plaintiff to qualify as a prevailing party, whereas
others have affirmed that granting the plaintiff's request for preliminary injunction confers prevailing party status.[188] Courts have

---

[185]*Id.* at 757–58 (citations to legislative history omitted).
[186]416 U.S. 696 (1974).
[187]*Id.* at 723–24.
[188]*Compare* Smyth ex rel. Smyth v. Rivero, 282 F.3d 268, 276–77 (4th Cir. 2002)
(preliminary injunction is at best prediction of probable outcome, not determination
on merits) *with* Richard S. v. Department of Dev. Servs., 317 F.3d 1080, 1088–89 (9th
Cir. 2003) (plaintiff who obtains preliminary injunction can be deemed prevailing party)
and Wyner v. Struhs, 179 Fed Appx. 566, 569 (11th Cir. 2006) (plaintiffs entitled to
award of fees under 42 U.S.C. § 1988 where they obtained preliminary injunction on
merits, which was primary relief they sought), *cert. granted*, 127 S. Ct. 1055 (2007).

also applied the *Farrar*[189] standards to interim claims for fees following the granting of temporary or preliminary injunctive relief, again basing the decision concerning the plaintiff's eligibility for an award of fees on the degree of relief obtained.[190]

In the Ninth Circuit, a prevailing plaintiff may be awarded attorney's fees at an interlocutory stage of the proceedings (i.e., appeal) if the "party prevails on the merits as to one or more of his or her claims."[191] To obtain such fees, courts hold that it is not necessary that the party win a judgment that ends the litigation on the merits and leaves nothing for the court to do but execute the judgment: "The fact that the dispute between the parties may continue does not preclude a fee award."[192]

---

[189]Farrar v. Hobby, 506 U.S. 103, 60 FEP 633 (1992).

[190]*Compare* Scelsa v. City Univ. of N.Y., 827 F. Supp. 1073, 1075–76, 71 FEP 707 (S.D.N.Y. 1993) (plaintiff who achieved preliminary injunction keeping both institute that he ran and teaching position in place for upcoming school year, as well as order prohibiting discrimination against Italian Americans pending trial, was prevailing party under *Farrar* because he modified defendant's behavior in significant way to his benefit, even though that interim success was later negated by loss on merits at trial) *with* Hudson v. Reno, 130 F.3d 1193, 1207–08, 75 FEP 1011 (6th Cir. 1997) (court denies fee request for obtaining successful temporary restraining order where order was dissolved on appeal and plaintiff ultimately lost case on underlying merits of claim) *and* NAACP Detroit Branch v. Detroit Police Officers Ass'n, 46 F.3d 528, 531, 66 FEP 1569 (6th Cir. 1995) (plaintiffs who obtained preliminary injunction preventing imminent lapse of contractual recall rights pending full trial on merits not prevailing parties simply by virtue of that order; plaintiffs ultimately lost their challenge to prevent lapse of contractual recall rights provision at issue and no officer was returned to work because of temporary preservation of contractual recall right in question).

[191]Marks v. Clarke, 102 F.3d 1012, 1034 (9th Cir. 1996) (internal quotations and citations omitted) (fees awarded under § 1988 and question of amount of fees remanded to district court for determination).

[192]*Id.*; Atlanta Journal & Const. v. Atlanta Dep't of Aviation, 6 F. Supp. 2d 1359, 1366–67 (N.D. Ga. 1998) ("An award of attorneys' fees under 42 U.S.C. § 1988 does not require a favorable judgment following a full trial on the merits.") (*citing* Hanrahan v. Hampton, 446 U.S. 754, 757 (1980)); *cf.* Belk v. Charlotte-Mecklenburg Bd. of Educ., 233 F.3d 232, 278 (4th Cir. 2000) (to be considered "prevailing party," there must be "some defendant in the case who has been 'prevailed against . . . with a material alteration of the legal relationship' between that defendant and the party seeking fees"); Harper v. City of Chi. Heights, 223 F.3d 593, 603 (7th Cir. 2000) (to achieve "prevailing party" status, plaintiff must have "succeeded on any significant issue in litigation which achieved some of the benefit the parties sought in bringing suit").

The Tenth Circuit denied attorney's fees associated with work done after the entry of a consent decree where the consent decree failed to provide for such fees.[193]

I. Awards to Prevailing Plaintiffs for Services on Appeal

Courts award attorney's fees to prevailing plaintiffs for work defending[196] or prosecuting[197] an appeal. Included in such awards are fees incurred by a prevailing plaintiff during an individual defendant's interlocutory appeal.[198]

---

[193]*See* Sinajini v. Board of Educ. of San Juan Sch. Dist., 233 F.3d 1236, 1240 (10th Cir. 2000) (fees not allowed for efforts to monitor enforcement of consent decree absent proof that monitoring efforts were necessary).

[194][reserved].

[195][reserved].

[196]*See, e.g.*, Rizzo v. Children's World Learning Ctrs., Inc., 173 F.3d 254, 263, 9 AD 436 (5th Cir. 1999) (ADA plaintiff awarded $20,625 in attorney's fees for appellate work), *aff'd on unrelated grounds after rehearing en banc*, 213 F.3d 209 (5th Cir. 2000) (en banc); Quarantino v. Tiffany & Co., 166 F.3d 422, 428, 78 FEP 1849 (2d Cir. 1999) (employee entitled to reasonable attorney's fee under Title VII's fee-shifting provisions for services rendered in successful appeal of district court's fee calculation); Jenkins v. Missouri, 127 F.3d 709, 719–20 (8th Cir. 1997) (awarding fees for services performed on unsuccessful appeal that was nonetheless "integrally related to the underlying case"); Eskra v. Provident Life & Accident Ins. Co., 125 F.3d 1406, 1418, 76 FEP 1745 (11th Cir. 1997) (plaintiff entitled to attorney's fees for successfully defending, on appeal, judgment for plaintiff); Roe v. Cheyenne Mountain Conference Resort, Inc., 124 F.3d 1221, 1234, 7 AD 779 (10th Cir. 1997) (employee who successfully challenged district court's denial of injunction and attorney's fees in ADA case entitled to appellate fees and costs), *aff'd*, 172 F.3d 879 (10th Cir. 1999). *But see* Barjon v. Dalton, 132 F.3d 496, 503 (9th Cir. 1997) (denying fees for services on appeal where plaintiff recovered only $90 additional to award made administratively); Corder v. Gates, 104 F.3d 247, 250 (9th Cir. 1996) (civil rights plaintiffs not entitled to attorney's fees on appeal because they were not prevailing parties on appeal).

[197]*See* Perry v. Bartlett, 231 F.3d 155, 163 (4th Cir. 2000) (award of attorney's fees to nonprofit organization for its work on interlocutory appeal from denial of preliminary injunction not abuse of discretion, even though plaintiff did not prevail on its interlocutory appeal, because plaintiff ultimately prevailed in case in chief). *But see* U&I Sanitation v. City of Columbus, 112 F. Supp. 2d 902, 906–07 (D. Neb. 2000) (refusing to rule on prevailing plaintiff's request for attorney's fees incurred in connection with successful appeal on ground that any award of such fees was for appellate court to decide).

[198]*See* Brady v. Fort Bend County, 145 F.3d 691, 716–17 (5th Cir. 1998) (court allowed recovery of attorney's fees incurred during interlocutory appeal of qualified immunity issue).

The fact that an appellate court dismisses an appeal of an interim attorney's fee award by a plaintiff's attorney as premature does not necessarily mean that the plaintiff is not "successful" and thus not entitled to attorney's fees for that appeal. In such a situation, one court has found that the fees requested by attorneys for that appeal were reasonably incurred because the defendant also appealed the interim order, and the decision to appeal was not unreasonable when made in view of the agreement among the parties and the district court judge that immediate appeal was in everyone's best interest.[199]

An appellate court has granted attorney's fees to a prevailing plaintiff for work defending an appeal even when the case is remanded for review of an original award for front pay.[200]

J. Awards to Prevailing Plaintiffs for Time Spent on the Fee Claim

Although the Supreme Court has cautioned that "[a] request for attorney's fees should not result in a second major litigation,"[201] prevailing plaintiffs who are awarded fees may also be awarded fees for time preparing an attorney's fee application.[202] As the Fifth Circuit has explained, absent special circumstances a prevailing plaintiff should be awarded fees for the time expended on the fee claim "as a matter of course."[203] A district court's decision not to include such amounts in an attorney's fee award is reviewed for

---

[199]See People Who Care v. Rockford Bd. of Educ., Sch. Dist. No. 205, 90 F.3d 1307, 1314 (7th Cir. 1996).

[200]See Weaver v. Amoco Prod. Co., 66 F.3d 85, 89, 70 FEP 931 (5th Cir. 1995).

[201]Hensley v. Eckerhart, 461 U.S. 424, 437, 31 FEP 1169 (1983).

[202]See Cruz v. Hauck, 762 F.2d 1230, 1233 (5th Cir. 1982) ("it is settled that a prevailing plaintiff is entitled to attorney's fees for the effort entailed in litigating a fee claim and securing compensation"); see also Weyant v. Okst, 198 F.3d 311, 316–17 (2d Cir. 1999) (reasonable fee should be awarded to successful § 1983 plaintiff for time reasonably spent in preparing and defending an application for attorney's fees); Miller v. Artistic Cleaners, 153 F.3d 781, 784–85, 78 FEP 510 (7th Cir. 1998) (attorney's fees incurred in litigating fee issues recoverable); Gates v. Rowland, 39 F.3d 1439, 1448 (9th Cir. 1994) (affirming award of $177,603 for work on fee application); Baird v. Boies, Schiller & Flexner LLP, 219 F. Supp. 2d 510, 525 (S.D.N.Y. 2002) (time spent preparing initial fee applications unreasonably excessive; plaintiffs billed nearly one-third of total number of hours expended on case for time spent preparing and defending fee application).

[203]Cruz, 762 F.2d at 1233.

abuse of discretion, but a court's authority to deny such fees is "exceedingly narrow."[204] Reversal or remand on the question is generally the action taken by the reviewing appellate tribunal.[205]

One federal appellate court has allowed a contingency multiplier to be applied to a "fees-on-fees" award where both state and federal discrimination claims were decided by the jury in favor of the plaintiff and the request for fees was made pursuant to a state statute. The court upheld use of the multiplier under state law even though such multipliers are unavailable under federal fee-shifting statutes.[206]

K. Awards of Costs

Costs and litigation expenses are awarded to prevailing plaintiffs pursuant to the same standards and principles as attorney's fees.[207] In any action in federal court that proceeds to judgment, courts may award the prevailing party the fees of the court clerk and marshal, transcript costs, witness fees, copy costs, docket fees, expenses of court-appointed experts, and interpreter fees.[208] In addition, the civil rights fee-shifting statutes authorize courts to

---

[204]*Id.*

[205]*See, e.g.*, Quarantino v. Tiffany & Co., 166 F.3d 422, 428, 78 FEP 1849 (2d Cir. 1999) (vacating district court's fee award order and remanding with directions to calculate and award fees for time spent on fee application itself); Eskra v. Provident Life & Accident Ins. Co., 125 F.3d 1406, 1418, 76 FEP 1745 (11th Cir. 1997) (granting appellate attorney's fees to prevailing ADEA party and remanding to district court with instructions to assess amount of appellate attorney's fees to be awarded). *But see* Delph v. Dr. Pepper Bottling Co., 130 F.3d 349, 358–59, 75 FEP 886 (8th Cir. 1997) (affirming district court's fee award as within bounds of its discretion where district court had accepted all time claimed except for time spent preparing fee application); Reed v. A.W. Lawrence & Co., 95 F.3d 1170, 1183–84 (2d Cir. 1996) (reversing order reducing award of attorney's fees incurred in litigating fee application and remanding for recomputation of attorney's fees in manner consistent with opinion).

[206]Mangold v. California Pub. Utils. Comm'n, 67 F.3d 1470, 1479, 69 FEP 48 (9th Cir. 1995).

[207]Dowdell v. City of Apopka, 698 F.2d 1181, 1188 (11th Cir. 1983); *see also* O'Rourke v. City of Providence, 77 F. Supp. 2d 258, 271, 85 FEP 1123 (D.R.I. 1999), *aff'd in relevant part*, 235 F.3d 713, 85 FEP 1135 (1st Cir. 2001) (awards of costs and expenses committed to trial court's sound discretion); Simi Inv. Co. v. Harris County, 236 F.3d 240, 256 (5th Cir. 2000) (court of appeals reviews awards of expert fees under abuse of discretion standard); Selgas v. American Airlines, Inc., 1994 WL 528068, at *6, 69 FEP 938 (D.P.R. Aug. 22, 1994) (reasonableness standard applies to award of expert expenses).

[208]28 U.S.C. § 1920 (2000).

award such reasonable out-of-pocket expenses incurred by the attorney as are normally charged to a fee-paying client in the course of providing legal services.[209] As the Eleventh Circuit has explained:

> [R]easonable attorneys' fees under the Act must include reasonable expenses because attorneys' fees and expenses are inseparably intertwined as equally vital components of the costs of litigation. The factually complex and protracted nature of civil rights litigation frequently makes it necessary to make sizeable out-of-pocket expenditures which may be as essential to success as the intellectual skills of the attorneys. If these costs are not taxable, and the client, as is often the case, cannot afford to pay for them, they must be borne by counsel, reducing the fees award correspondingly.[210]

Accordingly, courts otherwise awarding attorney's fees will reimburse reasonable litigation expenses and out-of-pocket costs as part of the prevailing plaintiff's fee award, unless special circumstances make such an award unjust.[211]

In the Civil Rights Act of 1991, Congress amended Title VII to make clear that reasonable expert fees are among the fees and expenses that a court may award the prevailing party.[212] Congress similarly amended 42 U.S.C. § 1988 to allow courts to include reasonable expert fees as part of the attorney's fee awarded in successful actions brought to enforce § 1981 or § 1981a.[213] By contrast, there is no express authority in the ADEA or FLSA to

---

[209]*See* 42 U.S.C. § 2000e-5(k) (2000); 42 U.S.C. § 1988 (2000); *see also* Mota v. University of Tex. Houston Health Sci. Ctr., 261 F.3d 512, 529, 86 FEP 1140 (5th Cir. 2001).

[210]*Dowdell*, 698 F.2d at 1190.

[211]*Id.* at 1188; *see, e.g.*, Snell v. Reno Hilton Resort, 930 F. Supp. 1428, 1434, 78 FEP 1236 (D. Nev. 1996) (denying request for expert's fees where prevailing plaintiff achieved only mixed-motive verdict and was not entitled to damages, back pay, or front pay, and experts were retained to testify about damages issues); Marshall v. New York Div. of State Police, 31 F. Supp. 2d 100, 106–07 (N.D.N.Y. 1998) (prevailing plaintiff in Title VII gender discrimination case not entitled to recover costs associated with retention of economics expert where parties had previously stipulated to amount of back-pay damages prior to trial without aid of expert and plaintiff failed to recover damages relating to front pay and emotional distress).

[212]*See* 42 U.S.C. § 2000e-5(k) (2000) (court may award "reasonable attorney's fee (including expert fees) as part of the costs") (superseding in part West Virginia Univ. Hosp., Inc. v. Casey, 499 U.S. 83, 87, 55 FEP 353 (1991)).

[213]*See* 42 U.S.C. § 1988(c) (2000) ("in awarding an attorney's fee under subsection (b) of this section in any action or proceeding to enforce a provision of section 1981 or 1981a of this title, the court in its discretion may include expert fees as part of the attorney's fee").

award expert witness fees other than for court-appointed experts,[214] and Congress has not amended either the ADEA or the FLSA[215] to address the recovery of expert fees. Hence, in ADEA cases courts may reject requests to recover the fees of experts beyond the per diem and travel expense limits set forth in 28 U.S.C. § 1821.[216] The exception to this rule in ADEA cases, however, can be found in those decisions where courts use their "equitable discretion" to award expert witness fees beyond the statutory amount because the "expert's testimony is indispensable to the determination of the case."[217]

Courts also typically award reasonable out-of-pocket expenses incurred by the attorney that are normally charged to a fee-paying client in the course of providing legal services, such as postage, photocopying, long-distance telephone charges, travel costs, computerized legal research, mediator fees, deposition transcripts, and paralegal and law clerk services.[218]

---

[214]*See* Tyler v. Union Oil Co. of Cal., 304 F.3d 379, 404–05 (5th Cir. 2002) (no express statutory authority in ADEA or FLSA to award expert witness fees for other than court-appointed expert witnesses); Cush-Crawford v. Adchem Corp., 94 F. Supp. 2d 294, 303, 82 FEP 1554 (E.D.N.Y. 2000), *aff'd*, 271 F.3d 352 (2d Cir. 2001).

[215]*See* 42 U.S.C. § 2000e-5 (2000).

[216]*See, e.g., Tyler*, 304 F.3d at 404; Zotos v. Lindbergh Sch. Dist., 121 F.3d 356, 363, 74 FEP 1055 (8th Cir. 1997); Padro v. Puerto Rico, 100 F. Supp. 2d 99, 109–10 (D.P.R. 2000) (general provision for taxation of costs does not allow for expert fees in excess of $40 per day, amount set in applicable statute), *aff'd in part and modified in part sub nom.* Gay Officers Action League v. Puerto Rico, 247 F.3d 288 (1st Cir. 2001).

[217]*See* Becker v. ARCO Chem. Co., 15 F. Supp. 2d 621, 636 (E.D. Pa. 1998) (in ADEA case, "the Court finds that the testimony of the plaintiff's expert was important to plaintiff's presentation regarding the issue of whether damages were suffered by the plaintiff" and "the expert witness' fee shall be appropriately considered as part of the costs").

[218]*See* Mota v. University of Tex. Houston Health Sci. Ctr., 261 F.3d 512, 529 (5th Cir. 2001) (postage, photocopying, paralegal services, long-distance telephone charges, investigation fees, and travel costs awardable under § 2000e-5(k), and deposition transcripts awardable under 28 U.S.C. § 1920(2)); EEOC v. W&O, Inc., 213 F.3d 600, 620–21, 623–24 (11th Cir. 2000) (award of deposition and photocopying costs affirmed and request for process server fees remanded for reevaluation); Sussman v. Patterson, 108 F.3d 1206, 1213 (10th Cir. 1997) ("photocopying, mileage, meals, and postage" awarded under § 1988); Downes v. Volkswagen of Am., Inc., 41 F.3d 1132, 1144, 69 FEP 11 (7th Cir. 1994) (expenses of litigation that are distinct from either statutory costs or costs of lawyer's time reflected in hourly billing rates and expenses for such things as postage, long-distance phone calls, photocopying, travel, paralegals, and expert witnesses part of reasonable attorney's fee allowed by § 1988); Davis v. City & County of S.F., 976 F.2d 1536, 1556, 61 FEP 440 (9th Cir. 1992)

Costs and expenses must be documented to be recoverable.[219]

("we have continued to hold that attorney's fees awards [under Title VII and § 1988] can include reimbursement for out-of-pocket expenses including travel, courier, and copying costs"); Jackson v. Austin, 267 F. Supp. 2d 1059, 1070 (D. Kan. 2003) (recovery of online research expenses proper because online research more efficient); Dumas v. Tyson Foods, Inc., 139 F. Supp. 2d 1243, 1249 (N.D. Ala. 2001) (allowing prevailing plaintiff to recover mediation expenses as taxable cost); Hogan v. General Elec. Co., 144 F. Supp. 2d 138, 143 (N.D.N.Y. 2001) (prevailing parties in ADEA action may recover all reasonable out-of-pocket expenses that are normally charged to clients, including travel, hotels, and meals to meet with statistical experts; travel expenses for statistical expert; and photocopying costs); O'Rourke v. City of Providence, 77 F. Supp. 2d 258, 271 (D.R.I. 1999) (constable costs and transcript fees incurred by plaintiff awarded as "these costs were necessarily incurred as part of the litigation"), aff'd in relevant part, 235 F.3d 713, 85 FEP 1135 (1st Cir. 2001). But see Brisco-Wade v. Carnahan, 297 F.3d 781, 782–83 (8th Cir. 2002) (district court abused its discretion in taxing mediator's fee against prison officials in prisoner's § 1983 lawsuit, because taxation of costs statute did not list mediation fees as taxable costs and local rules did not permit prisoner civil rights cases to be referred for mediation); Mota, 261 F.3d at 529–30 (denying requests for award of plaintiff's share of mediator's fee and videotaped depositions as taxable expenses under Title VII); Migis v. Pearle Vision, Inc., 135 F.3d 1041, 1048–49, 78 FEP 1379 (5th Cir. 1998) (district court has broad discretion in taxing costs and did not abuse its discretion by disallowing process service fees for certain witnesses, legal research, couriers, postage, and copying expenses and costs of videotape in addition to transcript of plaintiff's deposition, where plaintiff did not demonstrate need for incurring such costs); Spegon v. Catholic Bishop of Chi., 175 F.3d 544, 550, 559, 5 WH2d 457 (7th Cir. 1999) (affirming lower court's refusal to tax $150 filing fee as costs to plaintiff because case could have been resolved by telephone call rather than filing of suit and bulk of time spent was inappropriate); UNI-Systems, Inc. v. Delta Air Lines, Inc., 2002 WL 505914, at *2 (D. Minn. Mar. 28, 2002) (court unable to determine whether transcripts for which plaintiff claims fees were used in trial, necessary for trial, or merely investigatory); Omnipoint Commc'ns, Inc. v. Planning & Zoning Comm'n of Town of Wallingford, 91 F. Supp. 2d 497, 500 (D. Conn. 2000) (routine overhead costs, such as duplicating, postage, and telephone costs not recoverable; pursuant to local rule; computerized legal research fees and express mail services also not recoverable); Searles v. Van Bebber, 64 F. Supp. 2d 1033, 1041 (D. Kan. 1999) (prevailing plaintiff in civil rights litigation not entitled to recover full cost of computerized legal research where much of research could have been done manually at lower cost), vacated on other grounds, 251 F.3d 869 (10th Cir. 2001); Moore v. University of Notre Dame, 22 F. Supp. 2d 896, 912, 78 FEP 62 (N.D. Ind. 1998) (in ADEA action, court reduced computer research charges by 20% because of unreasonable number of hours spent); Perdue v. City Univ. of N.Y., 13 F. Supp. 2d 326, 348 (E.D.N.Y. 1998) (no entitlement to recover costs for faxes absent evidence that faxes were sent outside of metropolitan New York area); Bleimehl v. Eastman Kodak Co. Clinical Diagnostic Div., 1997 WL 33322218, at *21 (S.D. Iowa Jan. 27, 1997) (three depositions that "were primarily designed to assist discovery and were investigatory in nature" not recoverable expenses); Ryther v. KARE 11, 864 F. Supp. 1525, 1534, 70 FEP 1701 (D. Minn. 1994) (court refused to award costs of discovery depositions that "were investigatory in nature" and were not reasonably necessary for litigation of case).

[219]See Jackson v. Austin, 267 F. Supp. 2d 1059, 1070 (D. Kan. 2003) (no reimbursement of expenses for faxes or local and express delivery where plaintiff failed

III. COMPUTATION OF ATTORNEY'S FEES FOR PREVAILING PLAINTIFFS

A. General Principles

1. The Johnson Criteria

Johnson v. Georgia Highway Express, Inc.[220] was long considered the leading case setting forth factors to be considered in computing an attorney's fee. *Johnson* held that courts should evaluate fee requests in light of 12 criteria. *Johnson* was decided before the Supreme Court adopted the "lodestar" method (described later) in *Hensley v. Eckerhart*[221] as the starting point for determining reasonable attorney's fees.[222] Nevertheless, a review of the *Johnson* criteria is essential for a full understanding of attorney's fee jurisprudence. *Johnson* explained that the 12 key criteria for determining a reasonable attorney's fee are as follows:

> (1) The time and labor required. Although hours claimed or spent on a case should not be the sole basis for determining a fee, they are a necessary ingredient to be considered. The trial judge should weigh the hours claimed against his own knowledge, experience, and expertise of the time required to complete similar activities. If more than one attorney is involved, the possibility of duplication of effort along with the proper utilization of time should be scrutinized. The time of two or three lawyers in a courtroom or conference when one would do, may obviously be discounted. It is appropriate to distinguish between legal work, in the strict sense, and investigation, clerical work, compilation of facts and statistics and other work which can often be accomplished by non-lawyers but which a lawyer may do because he has no other help available.

---

to provide explanation for those expenses); Alexander v. CIT Tech. Fin. Servs., Inc., 222 F. Supp. 2d 1087, 1089–91 (N.D. Ill. 2002) (prevailing employer in employment discrimination action could not recover any photocopying charges from plaintiff as costs where employer failed to provide number of pages copied, rate per page used to calculate such costs, and descriptions of documents copied, nor could employer recover court reporter deposition attendance fees where employer failed to indicate number of hours spent by court reporter or hourly rate charged); *cf.* Lambert v. Fulton County, 151 F. Supp. 2d 1364, 1376–77, 84 FEP 994 (N.D. Ga. 2000) (photocopying costs recoverable where prevailing plaintiffs' counsel established that it had used internal procedures to track amount of expenses incurred for photocopying).

[220]488 F.2d 714, 717–19, 7 FEP 1 (5th Cir. 1974).

[221]461 U.S. 424, 31 FEP 1169 (1983).

[222]*See Hensley*, 461 U.S. at 433; *see also* Pennsylvania v. Delaware Valley Citizens' Council, 483 U.S. 711, 734, 45 FEP 1750 (1987); Blum v. Stenson, 465 U.S. 886, 888, 34 FEP 417 (1984); Kerr v. Screen Extras Guild, Inc., 526 F.2d 67, 70 (9th Cir. 1975) (adopting 12 factors).

Such non-legal work may command a lesser rate. Its dollar value is not enhanced just because a lawyer does it.

(2) The novelty and difficulty of the questions. Cases of first impression generally require more time and effort on the attorney's part. Although this greater expenditure of time in research and preparation is an investment by counsel in obtaining knowledge which can be used in similar later cases, he should not be penalized for undertaking a case which may "make new law." Instead, he should be appropriately compensated for accepting the challenge.

(3) The skill requisite to perform the legal service properly. The trial judge should closely observe the attorney's work product, his preparation, and general ability before the court. The trial judge's expertise gained from past experience as a lawyer and his observation from the bench of lawyers at work become highly important in this consideration.

(4) The preclusion of other employment by the attorney due to acceptance of the case. This guideline involves the dual consideration of otherwise available business which is foreclosed because of conflicts of interest which occur from the representation, and the fact that once the employment is undertaken the attorney is not free to use the time spent on the client's behalf for other purposes.

(5) The customary fee. The customary fee for similar work in the community should be considered. It is open knowledge that various types of legal work command differing scales of compensation. . . .

(6) Whether the fee is fixed or contingent. The fee quoted to the client or the percentage of the recovery agreed to is helpful in demonstrating the attorney's fee expectations when he accepted the case. But . . .

> the statute does not prescribe the payment of fees to the lawyers. It allows the award to be made to the prevailing party. Whether or not he agreed to pay a fee and in what amount is not decisive. Conceivably, a litigant might agree to pay his counsel a fixed dollar fee. This might be even more than the fee eventually allowed by the court. Or he might agree to pay his lawyer a percentage contingent fee that would be greater than the fee the court might ultimately set. Such arrangements should not determine the court's decision. The criterion for the court is not what the parties agreed but what is reasonable. . . .[223]

(7) Time limitations imposed by the client or the circumstances. Priority work that delays the lawyer's other legal work is entitled to some premium. This factor is particularly important when a new counsel is called in to prosecute the appeal or handle other matters at a late stage in the proceedings.

---

[223]*Johnson*, 488 F.2d at 718 (quoting Clark v. American Marine Corp., 320 F. Supp. 709, 711 (E.D. La. 1970)).

(8) The amount involved and the results obtained. Title VII permits the recovery of damages in addition to injunctive relief. Although the Court should consider the amount of damages, or back pay awarded, that consideration should not obviate court scrutiny of the decision's effect on the law. If the decision corrects across-the-board discrimination affecting a large class of an employer's employees, the attorney's fee award should reflect the relief granted.

(9) The experience, reputation, and ability of the attorneys. Most fee scales reflect an experience differential with the more experienced attorneys receiving larger compensation. An attorney specializing in civil rights cases may enjoy a higher rate for his expertise than others, providing his ability corresponds with his experience. Longevity per se, however, should not dictate the higher fee. If a young attorney demonstrates the skill and ability, he should not be penalized for only recently being admitted to the bar.

(10) The "undesirability" of the case. Civil rights attorneys face hardships in their communities because of their desire to help the civil rights litigant. Oftentimes his decision to help eradicate discrimination is not pleasantly received by the community or his contemporaries. This can have an economic impact on his practice which can be considered by the Court.

(11) The nature and length of the professional relationship with the client. A lawyer in private practice may vary his fee for similar work in the light of the professional relationship of the client with his office. The Court may appropriately consider this factor in determining the amount that would be reasonable.

(12) Awards in similar cases. The reasonableness of a fee may also be considered in the light of awards made in similar litigation within and without the court's circuit.[224]

2. The "Lodestar" Evolution

Experience proved that the *Johnson* factors were difficult to administer because they are vague and overlapping.[225] Appellate courts found that trial judges citing *Johnson* were setting fees without identifying the analysis used to reach the particular dollar amount.[226] One of the most persuasive critiques of the *Johnson* approach was set forth by Judge McGowan, speaking for the District of Columbia Circuit en banc, in *Copeland v. Marshall*,[227] who

---

[224]488 F.2d at 717–19.

[225]*See, e.g.*, Copeland v. Marshall, 641 F.2d 880, 890, 23 FEP 967 (D.C. Cir. 1980) (en banc); Samuel R. Berger, *Court-Awarded Attorneys' Fees: What Is "Reasonable"?* 126 U. PA. L. REV. 281, 286–87 (1977).

[226]*See, e.g.*, Gay v. Board of Trs., 608 F.2d 127, 128, 23 FEP 1569 (5th Cir. 1979) (recitation by district court that it had considered *Johnson* factors insufficient).

[227]641 F.2d 880, 23 FEP 967 (D.C. Cir. 1980) (en banc).

noted that simply articulating the 12 factors did not "conjure up a reasonable dollar figure" and that many district court judges have had difficulty applying the factors.[228]

The *Copeland* court then elected to follow the "lodestar" method earlier articulated by the Third Circuit:

> Any fee-setting inquiry begins with the "lodestar": the number of hours reasonably expended multiplied by a reasonable hourly rate. The figure generated by that computation is the basic fee from which a trial court judge should work . . . .
>
> When a law firm seeks a fee, it should document the amount of work performed. The District Court then . . . can segregate into categories the kinds of work performed by each participating attorney. . . .
>
> Compiling raw totals of hours spent, however, does not complete the inquiry. It does not follow that the amount of time actually expended is the amount of time reasonably expended. In the private sector, "billing judgment" is an important component in fee setting. It is no less important here. Hours that are not properly billed to one's *client* also are not properly billed to one's *adversary* pursuant to statutory authority. . . .
>
>   . . . .
>
> The remaining element in fixing a "lodestar" fee is the reasonable hourly rate.
>
> The reasonable hourly rate is that prevailing in the community for similar work. . . . [T]here may be more than one reasonable hourly rate for each of the attorneys, and for each of the kinds of work, involved in the litigation. After receiving documentation and other submissions, and perhaps holding a hearing, the trial judge [should determine the lodestar by taking the reasonable hourly rate(s) and multiplying the rate(s) by the hours reasonably expended].[229]

The Supreme Court later endorsed this general approach. In *Hensley v. Eckerhart*,[230] the prevailing plaintiffs had obtained only partial success. The Court therefore had to consider the relationship between the results obtained and a reasonable fee. There is no better way to understand the Court's analysis than to reprint the opinion in relevant part. The *Hensley* Court explained:

> The most useful starting point for determining the amount of a reasonable fee is the number of hours reasonably expended on

---

[228]*Id.* at 890.
[229]*Id.* at 891–92 (citations and footnotes omitted).
[230]461 U.S. 424, 31 FEP 1169 (1983).

the litigation multiplied by a reasonable hourly rate. This calculation provides an objective basis on which to make an initial estimate of the value of a lawyer's services. The party seeking an award of fees should submit evidence supporting the hours worked and rates claimed. Where the documentation of hours is inadequate, the district court may reduce the award accordingly.

The district court also should exclude from this initial fee calculation hours that were not "reasonably expended." S.Rep. No. 94-1011, p. 6 (1976). Cases may be overstaffed, and the skill and experience of lawyers vary widely. Counsel for the prevailing party should make a good-faith effort to exclude from a fee request hours that are excessive, redundant, or otherwise unnecessary, just as a lawyer in private practice ethically is obligated to exclude such hours from his fee submission. . . .

The product of reasonable hours times a reasonable rate does not end the inquiry. There remain other considerations that may lead the district court to adjust the fee upward or downward, including the important factor of the "results obtained." This factor is particularly crucial where a plaintiff is deemed "prevailing" even though he succeeded on only some of his claims for relief. In this situation two questions must be addressed. First, did the plaintiff fail to prevail on claims that were unrelated to the claims on which he succeeded? Second, did the plaintiff achieve a level of success that makes the hours reasonably expended a satisfactory basis for making a fee award?

In some cases a plaintiff may present in one lawsuit distinctly different claims for relief that are based on different facts and legal theories. In such a suit, even where the claims are brought against the same defendants—often an institution and its officers, as in this case—counsel's work on one claim will be unrelated to his work on another claim. Accordingly, work on an unsuccessful claim cannot be deemed to have been "expended in pursuit of the ultimate result achieved." *Davis v. County of Los Angeles*, 8 E.P.D. at 5049 (C.D. Cal. 1974). The congressional intent to limit awards to prevailing parties requires that these unrelated claims be treated as if they had been raised in separate lawsuits, and therefore no fee may be awarded for services on the unsuccessful claim.

It may well be that cases involving such unrelated claims are unlikely to arise with great frequency. Many civil rights cases will present only a single claim. In other cases the plaintiff's claims for relief will involve a common core of facts or will be based on related legal theories. Much of counsel's time will be devoted generally to the litigation as a whole, making it difficult to divide the hours expended on a claim-by-claim basis. Such a lawsuit cannot be viewed as a series of discrete claims. Instead the district court should focus on the significance of the overall relief obtained by the plaintiff in relation to the hours reasonably expended on the litigation.

Where a plaintiff has obtained excellent results, his attorney should recover a fully compensatory fee. Normally this will encompass all hours reasonably expended on the litigation, and indeed in some cases of exceptional success an enhanced award may be justified. In these circumstances the fee award should not be reduced simply because the plaintiff failed to prevail on every contention raised in the lawsuit. See *Davis v. County of Los Angeles*, supra, at 5049. Litigants in good faith may raise alternative legal grounds for a desired outcome, and the court's rejection of or failure to reach certain grounds is not a sufficient reason for reducing a fee. The result is what matters.

If, on the other hand, a plaintiff has achieved only partial or limited success, the product of hours reasonably expended on the litigation as a whole times a reasonable hourly rate may be an excessive amount. This will be true even where the plaintiff's claims were interrelated, nonfrivolous, and raised in good faith. Congress has not authorized an award of fees whenever it was reasonable for a plaintiff to bring a lawsuit or whenever conscientious counsel tried the case with devotion and skill. Again, the most critical factor is the degree of success obtained.

Application of this principle is particularly important in complex civil rights litigation involving numerous challenges to institutional practices or conditions. This type of litigation is lengthy and demands many hours of lawyers' services. Although the plaintiff often may succeed in identifying some unlawful practices or conditions, the range of possible success is vast. That the plaintiff is a "prevailing party" therefore may say little about whether the expenditure of counsel's time was reasonable in relation to the success achieved. . . .

There is no precise rule or formula for making these determinations. The district court may attempt to identify specific hours that should be eliminated, or it may simply reduce the award to account for the limited success. The court necessarily has discretion in making this equitable judgment. This discretion, however, must be exercised in light of the considerations we have identified.
. . . .

. . . It remains important, [also], for the district court to provide a concise but clear explanation of its reasons for the fee award. When an adjustment is requested on the basis of either the exceptional or limited nature of the relief obtained by the plaintiff, the district court should make clear that it has considered the relationship between the amount of the fee awarded and the results obtained.[231]

---

[231]461 U.S. at 433–40 (footnotes omitted).

3. Lodestar Enhancements?

The following year, in *Blum v. Stenson*,[232] the Supreme Court considered whether and under what circumstances the degree of a plaintiff's success warranted an *enhancement* of the amount derived from the basic lodestar calculation. The Court reaffirmed the lodestar method as the proper foundation for the derivation of a reasonable fee.[233] The Court also declared it settled that reasonable fees "are to be calculated according to the prevailing market rates in the relevant community, regardless of whether plaintiff is represented by private or nonprofit counsel."[234] The principal issue in dispute in *Blum* was whether the district court abused its discretion by awarding a 50 percent upward adjustment in the lodestar. The Court held that upward adjustments may be appropriate under 42 U.S.C. § 1988 and stated that "an enhanced award may be justified 'in some cases of exceptional success.' "[235] The Court explained that many of the criteria sometimes used to justify enhancements may already be reflected in the lodestar, as they were in that case, and that the fee applicant bore the burden to support the requested upward adjustment:

> The burden of proving that such an adjustment is necessary to the determination of a reasonable fee is on the fee applicant. The record before us contains no evidence supporting an upward adjustment to fees calculated under the basic standard of reasonable rates times reasonable hours. The affidavits of respondents' attorneys do not claim, or even mention, entitlement to a bonus or upward revision. Respondents' brief to the District Court merely states in conclusory fashion that an upward adjustment to the fee is necessary because the issues were novel, the litigation was complex, and the results were of far-reaching significance to a large class of people. The District Court, without elaboration, accepted these conclusory reasons for approving the upward adjustment and supplied additional reasons of its own. In awarding the 50% increase, the court referred to the complexity of the litigation, the novelty of the issues, the high quality of representation, the "great benefit" to the class, and the "riskiness" of the law suit. . . .

---

[232]465 U.S. 886, 34 FEP 417 (1984).
[233]*Id.* at 888.
[234]*Id.* at 895.
[235]*Id.* at 897 (quoting Hensley v. Eckerhart, 461 U.S. 424, 435, 31 FEP 1169 (1983)).

The reasons offered by the District Court to support the upward adjustment do not withstand examination. The novelty and complexity of the issues presumably were fully reflected in the number of billable hours recorded by counsel and thus do not warrant an upward adjustment in a fee based on the number of billable hours times reasonable hourly rates. There may be cases, of course, where the experience and special skill of the attorney will require the expenditure of fewer hours than counsel normally would be expected to spend on a particularly novel or complex issue. In those cases, the special skill and experience of counsel should be reflected in the reasonableness of the hourly rates. Neither complexity nor novelty of the issues, therefore, is an appropriate factor in determining whether to increase the basic fee award.

[Similarly, t]he "quality of representation" . . . generally is reflected in the reasonable hourly rate. It, therefore, may justify an upward adjustment only in the rare case where the fee applicant offers specific evidence to show that the quality of service rendered was superior to that one reasonably should expect in light of the hourly rates charged and that the success was "exceptional." See *Hensley*, 461 U.S., at 435, 103 S. Ct., at 1940. Respondents offered no such evidence in this case, and on this record the District Court's rationale for providing an upward adjustment for quality of representation is a clear example of double counting. . . .

The 50% upward adjustment also was based in part on the District Court's determination that the ultimate outcome of the litigation "was of great benefit to a large class of needy people." 512 F. Supp. at 685. The court did not explain, however, exactly how this determination affected the fee award. "Results obtained" is one of the twelve factors identified in *Johnson v. Georgia Highway Express*, 488 F.2d, at 718, as relevant to the calculation of a reasonable attorney's fee. It is "particularly crucial where a plaintiff is deemed 'prevailing' even though he succeeded on only some of his claims for relief." *Hensley, supra*, at 434, 103 S. Ct. at 1940 (fee award must be reduced by the number of hours spent on unsuccessful claims). Because acknowledgment of the "results obtained" generally will be subsumed within other factors used to calculate a reasonable fee, it normally should not provide an independent basis for increasing the fee award. . . .

Finally, the District Court included among its reasons for an upward adjustment a statement that the "issues presented were novel and the undertaking therefore risky." 512 F. Supp., at 685. Absent any claim in the affidavits or briefs submitted in support of respondent's fee request, seeking such an adjustment, we cannot be sure what prompted the court's statement. Nowhere in the affidavits submitted in support of respondents' fee request, nor in their brief to the District Court, did respondents identify any risks associated with the litigation or claim that the risk of nonpayment required an upward adjustment to provide a reasonable fee. On this record, therefore, any upward adjustment for the contingent nature of the litigation was unjustified.[236]

Blum thus resolved that the *Johnson* factor of novelty and difficulty or complexity of the issues is not an appropriate basis for enhancing the lodestar; stated that the factors of exceptional quality of representation and success, and exceptional result obtained may, in rare cases, provide the basis for enhancement; and left open the question of whether, on a proper record, enhancement may be appropriate to compensate for assuming the risk of nonpayment.[237] In *Pennsylvania v. Delaware Valley Citizens' Council*,[238] the Supreme Court took up the risk-of-nonpayment issue. *Delaware Valley* resulted in a decision by a divided Court, in which Justice O'Connor provided the pivotal vote. In the plurality opinion, four Justices (White, Rehnquist, Powell, and Scalia) believed that the use of a risk multiplier is improper under federal fee-shifting statutes;[239] in the dissenting opinion, four Justices (Blackmun, Brennan, Marshall, and Stevens) believed that the use of a risk multiplier is almost always appropriate when it appears that the market would compensate the attorney for assuming the risk of nonpayment. Justice O'Connor, in her concurring opinion, held that although Congress did not intend to foreclose consideration of contingent risk in setting a reasonable fee, a risk enhancement was not warranted by the record in that case.[240] Justice O'Connor's concurring opinion was recognized by many[241] but not all[242] lower

---

[236]465 U.S. at 898–901 (footnotes omitted).

[237]*Id.* at 901 n.17.

[238]483 U.S. 711, 45 FEP 1750 (1987).

[239]The plurality (joined on this issue by Justice O'Connor) distinguished between, on the one hand, "delay" in the payment of attorney's fees and, on the other hand, the "risk of nonpayment." The plurality agreed that adjustments for delay may be consistent with fee-shifting statutes. *Id.* at 716. *See* Section III.B.2.a *infra*.

[240]483 U.S. at 731–34 (O'Connor, J., concurring in part and concurring in judgment).

[241]*See, e.g.,* Alberti v. Klevenhagen, 896 F.2d 927, 935 (5th Cir.), *vacated in part*, 903 F.2d 352 (5th Cir. 1990); Lattimore v. Oman Const., 868 F.2d 437, 439 n.4, 49 FEP 472 (11th Cir. 1989); Blum v. Witco Chem. Corp., 888 F.2d 975, 981, 51 FEP 386 (3d Cir. 1989); Islamic Ctr. v. City of Starkville, 876 F.2d 465, 471 n.26 (5th Cir. 1989) (citing cases).

[242]King v. Palmer, 950 F.2d 771, 794–95, 60 FEP 525 (D.C. Cir. 1991) (en banc) (halting practice of enhancing attorney's fee awards in civil rights litigation to compensate for risk of losing; there is no practical middle ground between providing enhancement in every case and not providing one in any case).

courts as representing the holding of the Court, preserving the right of lower courts to award contingent risk multipliers in appropriate cases.

But in *City of Burlington v. Dague*,[243] a Supreme Court majority rejected fee multipliers in a case involving the fee-shifting provision of the federal Clean Water Act, 33 U.S.C. § 1365(d), and stated that "case law construing what is a 'reasonable' fee applies uniformly" to other similar federal fee-shifting statutes.[244] The Court reasoned as follows:

> The Court of Appeals held, and Dague argues here, that a "reasonable" fee for attorneys who have been retained on a contingency-fee basis must go beyond the lodestar, to compensate for risk of loss and of consequent nonpayment. Fee-shifting statutes should be construed, he contends, to replicate the economic incentives that operate in the private legal market, where attorneys working on a contingency-fee basis can be expected to charge some premium over their ordinary hourly rates. Petitioner Burlington argues, by contrast, that the lodestar fee may not be enhanced for contingency.
>
> We note at the outset that an enhancement for contingency would likely duplicate in substantial part factors already subsumed in the lodestar. The risk of loss in a particular case (and, therefore, the attorney's contingent risk) is the product of two factors: (1) the legal and factual merits of the claim, and (2) the difficulty of establishing those merits. The second factor, however, is ordinarily reflected in the lodestar—either in the higher number of hours expended to overcome the difficulty, or in the higher hourly rate of the attorney skilled and experienced enough to do so. *Blum, supra,* 898–899, 104 S. Ct. at 1548–1549. Taking account of it again through lodestar enhancement amounts to double-counting. *Delaware Valley II,* 483 U.S., at 726–727, 107 S. Ct. at 3087–3088 (plurality opinion).
>
> The first factor (relative merits of the claim) is not reflected in the lodestar, but there are good reasons why it should play no part in the calculation of the award. It is, of course, a factor that always exists (no claim has a 100% chance of success), so that computation of the lodestar would never end the court's inquiry in contingent-fee cases. *See id.* at 740, 107 S. Ct. at 3094 (Blackmun, J., dissenting). Moreover, the consequence of awarding contingency

---

[243]505 U.S. 557, 60 FEP 11 (1992).

[244]*Id.* at 562. A word about terminology: With the evolution of the Supreme Court's attorney's fees jurisprudence has come a corresponding evolution in nomenclature. What in the 1970s and early 1980s were called fee "multipliers" came to be known as "contingent risk premiums" or "risk enhancements" justified by the risk of "nonpayment."

enhancement to take account of this "merits" factor would be to provide attorneys with the same incentive to bring relatively meritless claims as relatively meritorious ones. Assume, for example, two claims, one with underlying merit of 20%, the other of 80%. Absent any contingency enhancement, a contingent-fee attorney would prefer to take the latter, since he is four times more likely to be paid. But with a contingency enhancement, this preference will disappear: the enhancement for the 20% claim would be a multiplier of 5 (100/20), which is quadruple the 1.25 multiplier (100/80) that would attach to the 80% claim. Thus, enhancement for the contingency risk posed by each case would encourage meritorious claims to be brought, but only at the social cost of indiscriminately encouraging nonmeritorious claims to be brought as well. We think that an unlikely objective of the "reasonable fees" provisions. "These statutes were not designed as a form of economic relief to improve the financial lot of lawyers." *Delaware Valley I*, 478 U.S. at 565, 106 S. Ct. at 3098.[245]

4. The Primacy of the Lodestar

As the Supreme Court announced in *Hensley v. Eckerhart*,[246] "the most useful starting point for determining a reasonable fee is the number of hours reasonably expended on the litigation multiplied by a reasonable hourly rate."[247] There is a strong presumption that the lodestar figure represents a reasonable fee.[248] Although the original 12 *Johnson* criteria retain vitality and are still addressed in most fee decisions,[249] the analysis of these factors is now generally

---

[245]505 U.S. at 562–63.

[246]461 U.S. 424, 31 FEP 1169 (1983).

[247]*Id.* at 433; *see also* Staton v. Boeing Co., 327 F.3d 938, 965 (9th Cir. 2003) ("Under a fee-shifting statute, the court must calculate awards for attorneys' fees using the 'lodestar' method.") (quotation omitted).

[248]Watkins v. Fordice, 7 F.3d 453, 459 (5th Cir. 1993); Chalmers v. City of L.A., 796 F.2d 1205, 1210 (9th Cir. 1986).

[249]*See* Hamlin v. Charter Twp. of Flint, 165 F.3d 426, 438–39, 8 AD 1688 (6th Cir. 1999) (reciting 12 *Johnson* factors and holding that trial court's reduction of attorney's fees to prevailing ADA plaintiff by 50% was abuse of discretion); Hadley v. Vam P T S, 44 F.3d 372, 375–76, 67 FEP 186 (5th Cir. 1995) ("Although the district judge's recitation of the reasons why he reduced the requested fee is not fulsome, it does evidence the required examination of the *Johnson* factors."); Hatley v. Store Kraft Mfg. Co., 859 F. Supp. 1257, 1267–69, 70 FEP 1361 (D. Neb. 1994) (court applied *Johnson* criteria to fee application of successful plaintiff in sex harassment case); *cf.* Law v. National Collegiate Athletic Ass'n, 2001 U.S. App. LEXIS 3066, at *9, 2001 Colo. J.C.A.R. 1127 (10th Cir. Feb. 27, 2001) ("we have never held that a district court abuses its discretion by failing to specifically address each *Johnson* factor").

subsumed within the lodestar, except in extraordinary cases.[250] A lodestar analysis is not necessary where the prevailing plaintiff only achieves nominal success; the district court may permissibly "award low fees or no fees" without the lodestar analysis in such circumstances.[251]

B. Applying the General Criteria

Certain fee issues recur and are addressed *infra*.[252]

1. Lodestar Components

The lodestar consists of the reasonable hourly rate multiplied by the number of hours reasonably expended.[253]

a. Rates. The standard for rates is well settled: the court selects an appropriate hourly rate based on prevailing rates in the relevant forum community for attorneys of similar skill, reputation, and experience in cases of comparable complexity.[254] Courts

---

[250]Barnes v. City of Cincinnati, 401 F.3d 729, 745–47 (6th Cir. 2005) (affirming 1.75 fee multiplier granted on basis of *Johnson* factors); Geier v. Sundquist, 372 F.3d 784, 792–95 (6th Cir. 2004) (*Johnson* factors presumably reflected in lodestar, but not certainly so); Gudenkauf v. Stauffer Commc'ns, 158 F.3d 1074, 1083, 77 FEP 1723 (10th Cir. 1998) (*Johnson* factors should guide fee determination but not all of them need to be considered); Perdue v. City Univ. of N.Y., 13 F. Supp. 2d 326, 348, 79 FEP 259 (E.D.N.Y. 1998) (court stated in Title VII and EPA case that plaintiff's attorneys were fully compensated by court's lodestar calculation because *Johnson* factors were subsumed in lodestar calculation); Tabech v. Gunter, 869 F. Supp. 1446, 1457 (D. Neb. 1994) (court explained that *Johnson* factors are subsumed into lodestar calculation); Spradley v. Notami Hosps., 892 F. Supp. 1459, 1461 (M.D. Fla. 1995) (court in ADEA case held that 12 *Johnson* factors can be considered to determine reasonable hourly rate); EEOC v. Accurate Mech. Contractors, Inc., 863 F. Supp. 828, 838, 74 FEP 1351 (E.D. Wis. 1994) (court considered *Johnson* factors in computing lodestar). *But see Hamlin*, 165 F.3d at 437 ("This court has held that the trial court may apply the *Johnson* factors either after the court's initial valuation of the hours reasonably expended at a reasonable rate or during its initial valuation.").

[251]Farrar v. Hobby, 506 U.S. 103, 115 (1992); *see* Section III.B.2.b *infra*.

[252]Older cases, especially those from lower courts, must be read with caution in light of the refinements in the law imposed by the Supreme Court in *Hensley, Blum, Delaware Valley, Dague,* and *Farrar.*

[253]*E.g.,* Hensley v. Eckerhart, 461 U.S. 424, 433, 31 FEP 1169 (1983).

[254]Blum v. Stenson, 465 U.S. 886, 891–95, 34 FEP 417 (1984); *Geier*, 372 F.3d at 791–92 (when determining reasonable hourly rate, district court must consider evidence submitted by prevailing plaintiffs attesting to rates charged by lawyers of comparable skill and experience in relevant locale); Denesha v. Farmers Ins. Exch.,

also award fees for the work of law clerks and paralegals at prevailing market rates.[255] The "prevailing rate" standard applies to private attorneys and to attorneys working in nonprofit legal services organizations as well.[256] This standard results in widely different rates in different communities and over time.[257] Many of

---

161 F.3d 491, 501, 78 FEP 691 (8th Cir. 1998) (District court's award of local rates upheld even though employer's counsel's rate was lower: "The record indicates, however, that the charges are consistent with rates in the Kansas City market, and that the fees charged by Farmers' attorneys are below market rate."); Washington v. Philadelphia County Ct. of Common Pleas, 89 F.3d 1031, 1035 (3d Cir. 1996) ("reasonable hourly rate is calculated according to prevailing market rates in the community"); Wells v. New Cherokee Corp., 58 F.3d 233, 239–40, 68 FEP 284 (6th Cir. 1995) (in ADEA case, district court chose plaintiff's theory that rate should be determined from affidavits of trial counsel and experienced local practitioner over defendant's theory that rate should be average of that awarded in four allegedly similar cases over 4 years); Alberti v. Klevenhagen, 896 F.2d 927, 930 (appropriate hourly rate is based on prevailing community standards for attorneys of similar experience in similar cases), *vacated in part on other grounds*, 903 F.2d 352 (5th Cir. 1990); Moore v. University of Notre Dame, 22 F. Supp. 2d 896, 910, 78 FEP 62 (N.D. Ind. 1998) (requested rates must be "in line with those prevailing in the community for similar services by lawyers of reasonably comparable skill, experience and reputation"); Perdue v. City Univ. of N.Y., 13 F. Supp. 2d 326, 344–45, 79 FEP 259 (E.D.N.Y. 1998) (court based rates on other fee awards in that district and attorney's lack of experience with employment cases).

[255]*See, e.g.*, Case v. Unified Sch. Dist. No. 233, Johnson County, 157 F.3d 1243, 1249 (10th Cir. 1998) (court may award fees for law clerk and paralegal services and should scrutinize reported hours and suggested rates in same manner it scrutinizes lawyer time and rates); Barjon v. Dalton, 132 F.3d 496, 503 (9th Cir. 1997) (in fee award under § 1988, reasonable hourly rate for law clerk properly determined by prevailing market rate in forum in which district court sits); System Mgmt., Inc. v. Loiselle, 154 F. Supp. 2d 195, 204 (D. Mass. 2001) (court may award fees for paralegals and law clerks consistent with rates and practices prevailing in relevant market); *see also* Spegon v. Catholic Bishop of Chi., 175 F.3d 544, 553, 5 WH2d 457 (7th Cir. 1999) (relevant inquiry for requested paralegal fees is whether work was sufficiently complex to justify efforts of paralegal as opposed to employee at next rung lower on pay-scale ladder).

[256]*Blum*, 465 U.S. at 895 n.11; Blanchard v. Bergeron, 489 U.S. 87, 94 (1989) (same standard applies to attorneys who handle cases on contingent risk basis and therefore have no standard billing rate); Copeland v. Marshall, 641 F.2d 880, 900 (D.C. Cir. 1980) (public interest attorneys entitled to same rate as private firm lawyers of similar caliber).

[257]*E.g., Geier*, 372 F.3d at 791–92 (vacating district court's award of attorney's fees based on hourly rate of $250 when plaintiff's evidence showed attorneys of comparable skill, reputation, and experience in relevant community commanded $400 to $450 per hour); McNabola v. Chicago Transit Auth., 10 F.3d 501, 519, 63 FEP 1064 (7th Cir. 1993) ($210 per hour for lead attorney; $100 per hour for junior attorney); Davis v. City & County of S.F., 976 F.2d 1536, 1546–47, 61 FEP 440 (9th Cir. 1992) ($235 per hour for senior attorney; $110 per hour for junior attorney),

the *Johnson* factors influence the determination of rates that are considered "reasonable," including the level of the attorney's skill and experience,[258] the attorney's normal billing rate or the fee quoted to the client,[259] and rates awarded in similar cases.[260]

---

vacated on other grounds, 984 F.2d 345, 61 FEP 457 (9th Cir. 1993); Hendrickson v. Brandstad, 934 F.2d 158, 164 (8th Cir. 1991) ($180 per hour); Spulak v. K Mart Corp., 894 F.2d 1150, 1160, 51 FEP 1652 (10th Cir. 1990) ($100 per hour); Associated Builders & Contractors v. Orleans Parish Sch. Bd., 919 F.2d 374, 379 (5th Cir. 1990) (upholding hourly rates of $175 and $165 for two partners and $100 for associate); Herrington v. County of Sonoma, 883 F.2d 739, 746–47 (9th Cir. 1989) ($200 per hour for senior partner; $150 per hour for senior associate; total fee of $41,854); Cabrales v. County of L.A., 875 F.2d 740, 740–41 (9th Cir. 1989) (range between $175 and $225 per hour; total fee of $47,256); Baird v. Boies, Schiller & Flexner, 219 F. Supp. 2d 510, 523, 89 FEP 1524 (S.D.N.Y. 2002) ($375, $300, and $60 per hour for partner with 14 years' experience, associate with 10 years' experience, and paralegal, respectively, were reasonable); Park v. Howard Univ., 881 F. Supp. 653 (D.D.C. 1995) (rate of $300 per hour justified by experience and expertise); Knight v. Alabama, 824 F. Supp. 1022, 1031–32 (N.D. Ala. 1993) (range between $150 and $225 per hour); Cuban Museum of Arts & Culture, Inc. v. City of Miami, 771 F. Supp. 1190, 1193 (S.D. Fla. 1991) (range between $175 and $275 per hour); United States v. City & County of S.F., 748 F. Supp. 1416, 1430, 1442 (N.D. Cal. 1990) (range between $70 per hour for paralegals and $235 per hour for attorneys; total fee of $1,694,076), *vacated on other grounds*, 984 F.2d 345, 61 FEP 457 (9th Cir. 1993); Williams v. City of N.Y., 728 F. Supp. 1067, 1071 (S.D.N.Y. 1990) ($200 per hour; total fee of $24,378).

[258]Mathur v. Board of Trs. of S. Ill. Univ., 317 F.3d 738, 743, 90 FEP 1537 (7th Cir. 2003) (attorney's hourly rate may be higher than community average if she possesses unusual skill, abilities, or qualities); Gudenkauf v. Stauffer Commc'ns, 158 F.3d 1074, 1082, 77 FEP 1742 (10th Cir. 1998) (district court properly assessed prevailing market rates and experience, skill, reputation, and performance of plaintiff's attorneys in setting hourly rates in Pregnancy Discrimination Act case); Luciano v. Olsten Corp., 109 F.3d 111, 116 (2d Cir. 1997) (court relied on attorney's experience and expertise).

[259]*Mathur*, 317 F.3d at 743 (attorney's actual billing rate presumptively appropriate to use as market rate); St. Louis Fire Fighters Ass'n v. City of St. Louis, 96 F.3d 323, 332 n.9, 71 FEP 1513 (8th Cir. 1996) ("We do not believe that the hourly rate previously agreed upon by a party with its counsel is dispositive for determining a reasonable award of fees. We note, however, that such a previously agreed upon fee may well be strongly indicative of what constitutes a 'reasonable' fee, and may be properly considered by the district court in its analysis.") (citations omitted); Islamic Ctr. of Miss., Inc. v. City of Starkville, 876 F.2d 465, 469 (5th Cir. 1989) (when attorney's actual billing rate is rate at which attorney requests lodestar be computed and that rate is within range of prevailing market rates, court should consider this rate when fixing fee award).

[260]Dang v. Cross, 422 F.3d 800, 814 (9th Cir. 2005) (district court did not abuse its discretion in awarding plaintiff fees based on hourly rate of $400 rather than requested rate of $550 per hour when evidence of rates of other attorneys in similar practices, awards in similar cases, market rates, and plaintiff's counsel's experience and reputation justified lower rate); Thorne v. Welk Inv., Inc., 197 F.3d 1205, 1213, 82 FEP 367 (8th Cir. 1999) ("When . . . the amount sought by the prevailing party

Courts may distinguish not only the experience of different attorneys, but also the different tasks performed, the level of difficulty of those tasks, whether those tasks were or could be performed by paralegals, and the complexity of the legal issues.[261] In determining the hourly rate, courts have relied on testimony and affidavits of other counsel,[262] on the court's own knowledge of rates

---

is far more than one would expect for a case of its complexity and novelty, the court should reference awards in similar cases."); Spegon v. Catholic Bishop of Chi., 175 F.3d 544, 557 (7th Cir. 1999) (evidence of "fee awards from prior similar cases is relevant to . . . determination of a reasonable hourly rate and cannot be ignored"); *Luciano*, 109 F.3d at 116 (rates awarded are in line with rates recently awarded in same district).

[261]*See* Case v. Unified Sch. Dist. No. 233, 157 F.3d 1243, 1249 (10th Cir. 1998) (As to services provided by nonlawyers, if "law clerk and paralegal services are . . . not reflected in the [attorney's fee], the court may award them separately as part of the fee for legal services. The court should scrutinize the reported hours and the suggested rates in the same manner it scrutinizes lawyer time and rates."); Thomlison v. Omaha, 63 F.3d 786, 791, 4 AD 1319 (8th Cir. 1995) (court affirmed district court's reduction in reasonable hourly rate from $160 to $125 because case did not present "high level of difficulty"); Johnston v. Harris County Flood Control Dist., 869 F.2d 1565, 1583 (5th Cir. 1989) (district court properly reviewed requested attorney's fees by examining such issues as attorney work that should have been done by paralegals and duplication of effort); Stathos v. Bowden, 728 F.2d 15, 21, 34 FEP 142 (1st Cir. 1984) ($125 per hour for in-court work; $85 per hour for out-of-court work); Johnson v. Georgia Highway Express, Inc., 488 F.2d 714, 717, 7 FEP 1 (5th Cir. 1974) (court should "distinguish between legal work, in the strict sense, and investigation, clerical work, compilation of facts and statistics and other work which can often be accomplished by non-lawyers"); Miller v. Kenworth of Dothan, Inc., 117 F. Supp. 2d 1247, 1261 (M.D. Ala. 2000) (when reviewing application for attorney's fees, court may appropriately consider "whether the work performed was 'legal work in the strict sense' or was merely clerical work that happened to be performed by a lawyer"); Reed v. Rhodes, 934 F. Supp. 1492, 1503 (N.D. Ohio 1996) (no novel or difficult issues confronted the applicants), *aff'd*, 179 F.3d 453 (6th Cir. 1999); Hyland v. Kenner Prods. Co., 13 FEP 1647, 1652–53 (S.D. Ohio 1976) ($50 per hour for out-of-court work; $60 per hour for all other work); Firebird Soc'y v. Board of Fire Comm'rs, 433 F. Supp. 752, 755–56, 14 FEP 741 (D. Conn. 1976) (distinguishing between time spent in court, for which $50 per hour was allowed, and time attributed to research and related services, for which hourly rates of $35 and $25 were allowed), *aff'd*, 556 F.2d 642, 15 FEP 1090 (2d Cir. 1977); Foster v. Boise-Cascade, Inc., 420 F. Supp. 674, 691–92, 1 FEP 578 (S.D. Tex. 1976) ($50 an hour for pretrial work, including conferences, $65 an hour for courtroom time, and $35 an hour for time spent on telephone and other communications), *aff'd per curiam*, 577 F.2d 335, 17 FEP 1336 (5th Cir. 1978).

[262]*See, e.g.*, Harper v. City of Chi. Heights, 223 F.3d 593, 605 (7th Cir. 2000) (attorneys' own affidavits and affidavits from other attorneys practicing in field sufficient to satisfy plaintiff's burden of reasonableness of their rates); Washington v. Philadelphia County Ct. of Common Pleas, 89 F.3d 1031, 1037 (3d Cir. 1996) (affidavits of attorneys met prima facie burden and where opposing party offered no contradictory evidence, it was abuse of discretion to adjust requested rate downward).

in the community, and on a published survey of the state's lawyers' fees.[263]

Courts are divided as to what constitutes the "relevant community," especially when counsel is from a different community from the court.[264] Some courts use the attorney's normal rate or the market rate in his or her big-city or national practice,[265] whereas other courts award only local rates, regardless of where the attorney normally practices or what he or she usually charges.[266] Courts are likely to award fees at higher than local market rates if evidence establishes that competent local counsel is not available.[267]

---

[263]Smith v. Norwest Fin. Acceptance, 129 F.3d 1408, 1418, 75 FEP 1274 (10th Cir. 1997) (court reasonably looked to published survey of rates of lawyers in state and is "uniquely qualified to establish hourly rate because of familiarity with case and with prevailing rates in the community"); Miele v. New York State Teamsters Conference Pen. & Ret. Fund, 831 F.2d 407, 409 (2d Cir. 1987) (district judge may rely on own knowledge of private law firm hourly rates in the community).

[264]See Blum v. Stenson, 465 U.S. 886, 895 (1984).

[265]E.g., Adcock-Ladd v. Secretary of Treasury, 227 F.3d 343, 351, 83 FEP 1400 (6th Cir. 2000) (local rate in Tennessee forum did not apply to Washington, D.C., counsel hired by plaintiff to take deposition in Washington; district court abused discretion by reducing Washington attorney's hourly rate from $300 to $150); Rum Creek Coal Sales, Inc. v. Caperton, 31 F.3d 169, 178–79 (4th Cir. 1994) (Richmond, Virginia, attorneys awarded higher Richmond rates for complex case litigated in Charleston, West Virginia); Gates v. Deukmejian, 977 F.2d 1300, 1313–14 (9th Cir. 1992) (San Francisco attorneys awarded higher San Francisco rates for complex case litigated in Sacramento, California); Chrapliwy v. Uniroyal, Inc., 670 F.2d 760, 764, 28 FEP 19 (7th Cir. 1982) ("an out-of-town specialist may be able to command a somewhat higher price for his talents, both because of his specialty and because he is likely to be from a larger city, where rates are higher"; "The legal profession no longer operates in a strictly local product market, and the attorney's fee provision of Title VII cannot be utilized to unrealistically tie the fees paid to the locality's wage scale."); Maceira v. Pagan, 698 F.2d 38, 40 (1st Cir. 1983).

[266]E.g., Hudson v. Reno, 130 F.3d 1193, 1208, 75 FEP 1011 (6th Cir. 1997) ("[T]his Court has made it clear that it is not an abuse of discretion for a court to apply local market rates."); Luciano v. Olsten Corp., 109 F.3d 111, 115–16 (2d Cir. 1997) (district court should consider prevailing rates in district in which court sits); Andrade v. Jamestown Hous. Auth., 82 F.3d 1179, 1190 (1st Cir. 1996) (affirming reduction of hourly rate to that customary in forum community); Avalon Cinema Corp. v. Thompson, 689 F.2d 137, 141 (8th Cir. 1982) (en banc) ("plaintiff could have found adequate counsel closer to the situs of the case for substantially less" per hour); Ramos v. Lamm, 713 F.2d 546, 555 (10th Cir. 1983) (absent unusual circumstances, "the fee rates of the local area should be applied even when the lawyers seeking fees are from another area"); Polk v. New York State Dep't of Corr. Servs., 722 F.2d 23, 24–25 (2d Cir. 1983) ("the skill and expertise of plaintiff's counsel, which might have warranted some increase, was balanced by the simplicity of the issues," causing court to award fee calculated at local rate).

[267]See Mathur v. Board of Trustees of S. Ill. Univ., 317 F.3d 738, 744, 90 FEP 1537 (7th Cir. 2003) (Chicago attorneys litigating in southern Illinois entitled

b. Hours. As the Supreme Court stated in *Hensley*, "the appropriate number of hours [in the lodestar calculation] includes all time reasonably expended in pursuit of the ultimate result achieved in the same manner that an attorney traditionally is compensated by a fee-paying client for all time reasonably expended on a matter."[268] The prevailing party bears the burden of demonstrating the reasonableness of the number of hours claimed.[269] Once the successful party has documented the appropriate hours, the opposing party bears the burden of submitting specific evidence challenging the accuracy and reasonableness of the hours charged.[270] In calculating the reasonableness of the hours expended, the court may eliminate duplicative and unnecessary time.[271] However, in

---

to higher Chicago hourly rates because plaintiff had tried and failed to find attorney in local area who could handle case; plaintiff need not demonstrate there was no local counsel willing to represent him); Hadix v. Johnson, 65 F.3d 532, 535–36 (6th Cir. 1995) (reversing award of fees based on hourly rate of nationally known, nonlocal counsel absent showing that competent, local counsel was not available); *Adcock-Ladd*, 227 F.3d at 350 ("trial court erroneously concluded that the hourly rate prevailing within the venue of the court wherein the case was commenced will always constitute the maximum allowable reasonable hourly rate for legal work performed by a foreign counselor in a venue other than the jurisdiction wherein the case was commenced") (citations omitted); Bostic v. American Gen. Fin., Inc., 87 F. Supp. 2d 611, 616 (S.D. W. Va. 2000) (" 'The community in which the court sits is the first place to look to in evaluating the prevailing market rate.' If a matter is so complex or specialized that 'no attorney, with the required skills, is available locally,' a court may, of course, award fees for counsel located elsewhere.") (citations omitted).

[268]Hensley v. Eckerhart, 461 U.S. 424, 431, 31 FEP 1169 (1983).

[269]Leroy v. City of Houston, 831 F.2d 576, 586 (5th Cir. 1987).

[270]Gates v. Gomez, 60 F.3d 525, 534–35 (9th Cir. 1995).

[271]*See* Luciano v. Olsten Corp., 109 F.3d 111, 117 (2d Cir. 1997) (court affirmed 15% reduction of hours spent on unnecessary contentious conduct by plaintiff's attorney); EEOC v. Clear Lake Dodge, 60 F.3d 1146, 1154, 68 FEP 663 (5th Cir. 1995) (attorney's fees must not be awarded for attorney hours that are excessive, redundant, or otherwise unnecessary); Carter v. Sedgewick County, 36 F.3d 952, 957, 65 FEP 1585 (10th Cir. 1994) (district court abused its discretion when it reduced hourly rate and number of compensable hours to account for duplication in services; district court "corrected twice for a single problem"); Alberti v. Klevenhagen, 896 F.2d 927, 932 ("It is not the case that all claimed time is a fortiori reasonably expended [even] if the *total hours* claimed by counsel appear to reflect sound legal judgment and resulted in satisfactory results."), *vacated on other grounds*, 903 F.2d 352 (5th Cir. 1990); Sims v. Jefferson Downs Racing Ass'n, 778 F.2d 1068, 1084 (5th Cir. 1985) (unnecessary, duplicative, or excessive hours may be disallowed); Furtado v. Bishop, 635 F.2d 915, 920 (1st Cir. 1980) (in setting fee, court should "eliminat[e] time beyond that consistent with a standard of reasonable efficiency and productivity"); Riter v. Moss & Bloomberg, Ltd., 2000 U.S. Dist. LEXIS 14470, at *18 (N.D. Ill. Sept. 26, 2000) ("[C]ourt finds that a moot court practice session is a

order to meet its burden of supporting an objection concerning duplication of hours, the fee opponent must show that the prevailing party's attorneys were *"unreasonably* doing the *same* work."[272] Unreasonable duplication may result from the inadequate supervision of junior attorneys[273] or the use of multiple attorneys on the same task.[274] However, the presence of more than one attorney may be appropriate and reasonable in some circumstances.[275] Federal

---

reasonable use of time but could have been accomplished with one additional attorney. It therefore reduces the total hours allowed to 36.1, granting each defendant a reduction of 18.05 hours. It also strikes as duplicative the 19.6 hours that a less-senior attorney devoted to reanalyzing the cases for oral argument when another attorney actually argued the case."); Summerville v. Trans World Airlines, 1999 U.S. Dist. LEXIS 21890, at *8 (E.D. Mo. Sept. 28, 1999) ("A court should deduct redundant hours."); Moore v. University of Notre Dame, 22 F. Supp. 2d 896, 911, 78 FEP 62 (N.D. Ind. 1998) (court reduced fee award by 20% for "unrelated legal services provided to plaintiff, excessive conference time, and media related time"); Perdue v. City Univ. of N.Y., 13 F. Supp. 2d 326, 343 (E.D.N.Y. 1998) (court should exclude excessive, redundant, or otherwise unnecessary hours or hours dedicated to unsuccessful claims; reducing fee application by 20% for redundancy and unrelated expenses for general education in employment law); Vallo v. Great Atl. & Pac. Tea Co., 16 FEP 967, 969–71 (W.D. Pa. 1977) (disallowing 10% of claimed hours because overlapping work was done when new lawyers took over case in "midstream").

[272]Johnson v. University Coll., 706 F.2d 1205, 1208 (11th Cir. 1983).

[273]*E.g.*, Copeland v. Marshall, 641 F.2d 880, 902–03, 23 FEP 967 (D.C. Cir. 1980) (en banc) (time-wasting "may occur, for example, when young associates' labors are inadequately organized by supervising partners").

[274]*E.g.*, Lanni v. New Jersey, 259 F.3d 146, 151 (3d Cir. 2001) (presence of two named partners at ADA trial excessive; fee disallowed for second partner); Marisol v. Guiliani, 111 F. Supp. 2d 381 (S.D.N.Y. 2000) (court orders small reduction in fees to plaintiffs for practice of sending multiple attorneys and staff to court conferences in which they played no meaningful role); Fleming v. Kane County, 686 F. Supp. 1264, 1275 (N.D. Ill. 1988) (attorney brought into suit late cannot bill his time of coming "up to speed" on case; "the lawyers already in place should have been competent to handle the case"), *aff'd*, 898 F.2d 553 (7th Cir. 1990); Clanton v. Allied Chem. Corp., 416 F. Supp. 39, 43, 13 FEP 288 (E.D. Va. 1976) (inappropriate to charge for time spent by more than two counsel for "either the taking of depositions or argument on motions"); *cf.* Hensley v. Eckerhart, 461 U.S. 424, 434, 31 FEP 1169 (1983) ("Counsel for the prevailing plaintiff should make a good faith effort to exclude from a fee request hours that are excessive, redundant, or otherwise unnecessary.").

[275]Democratic Party of Wash. v. Reed, 388 F.3d 1281, 1286 (9th Cir. 2004) (presence of more than one attorney at hearings may be appropriate to assist lawyer arguing case); Webner v. Titan Distrib., Inc., 267 F.3d 828, 837, 12 AD 513 (8th Cir. 2001) (awarding fees in case where two attorneys attended depositions; "[t]he district court reasoned that it was not unreasonable for both attorneys to be present at the depositions and was actually more efficient because the ADA and retaliation issues were closely related"); O'Rourke v. City of Providence, 235 F.3d 713, 737, 85 FEP 1135 (1st Cir. 2001) (reversing, as abuse of discretion, denial of fee to second

courts also generally recognize that a team approach is often necessary in complex litigation.[276] Additionally, courts acknowledge that the hours necessarily expended in a case will often "vary in direct proportion to the ferocity of [its] adversaries' handling of the case."[277] Because the initial "burden of proof of reasonableness

---

attorney at Title VII trial); Lockard v. Pizza Hut, Inc., 162 F.3d 1062, 1077, 78 FEP 1026 (10th Cir. 1998) (time spent on same task not duplicative per se and careful preparation often requires collaboration and rehearsal); Kurowski v. Krajewski, 848 F.2d 767, 776 (7th Cir. 1988) ("The use of two (or more) lawyers, which solvent clients commonly pay for because they believe extra help beneficial, may well reduce the total expenditures by taking advantage of the division of labor."); Norman v. Housing Auth., 836 F.2d 1292, 1302 (11th Cir. 1988) ("there is nothing inherently unreasonable about a client having multiple attorneys, and they may all be compensated if they are not unreasonably doing the same work and are being compensated for the distinct contribution of each lawyer"); *Summerville*, 1999 U.S. Dist. LEXIS 21890, at *8 ("While certain hours spent by multiple attorneys may be too duplicative to be reasonable, 'there is nothing inherently unreasonable about a client having multiple attorneys, and they may all be compensated if they are not unreasonably doing the same work and are being compensated for the distinct contribution of each lawyer.' ") (quoting *Norman*, 836 F.2d at 1301); Altman v. Port Auth. of N.Y. & N.J., 879 F. Supp. 345, 354, 67 FEP 1355 (S.D.N.Y. 1995) (court refused to reduce fee award because two attorneys tried age discrimination and retaliation case); Wahad v. Coughlin, 870 F. Supp. 506, 507 (S.D.N.Y. 1994) (court in civil rights action permitted fees for conferences between attorneys, finding that billing entries were sufficiently specific and detailed regarding such conferences).

[276]*See Johnson*, 706 F.2d at 1208; Davis v. City & County of S.F., 976 F.2d 1536, 1544 (9th Cir. 1992) ("broad based class litigation often requires the participation of multiple attorneys").

[277]*See* Rodriguez-Hernandez v. Miranda-Velez, 132 F.3d 848, 860 (1st Cir. 1998) (in determining reasonable attorney's fee, district courts should not reward defendant for vehement "Stalingrad defense") (quoting Lipsett v. Blanco, 975 F.2d 934, 939 (1st Cir. 1992) (fee award in amount higher than damages awarded justified by defendant's "Stalingrad defense"; hardnosed litigation tactics required plaintiff to respond in kind)); *see also* Safer Display Tech., Ltd. v. Tatung Co., 227 F.R.D. 435, 435–36 (E.D. Va. 2004) ("The Stalingrad Defense, in which the proponent tries to wear down the adversary until he succumbs to the depths of a longsome, frigid winter, cannot be implemented without severe cost to the proponent himself. Indeed, '[w]hile this hard-nosed approach to litigation may be viewed as effective trench warfare, it must be pointed out that such tactics have a significant downside. The defendants suffer the adverse effects of that downside here. There is a corollary to the duty to defend to the utmost—the duty to take care to resolve litigation on terms that are, overall, the most favorable to a lawyer's client. Although tension exists between the two duties, they apply concurrently. When attorneys blindly pursue the former, their chosen course of action may sometimes prove to be at the expense of the latter.' ") (quoting Lipsett v. Blanco, 975 F.2d 934, 941 (1st Cir. 1992)); Ramos v. Davis & Geck, 976 F. Supp. 108, 109 (D.P.R. 1997) ("a 'Stalingrad Defense' may prove costly in the end to an employer by requiring the victorious employee's attorney(s) to battle every step of the way" and thus be compensated for time necessarily expended).

of the number of hours is on the fee applicant,"[278] claimed hours
may be reduced where detailed, contemporaneous time records are
not available.[279] However, in some cases, reconstructed or "conglomerated" records may be considered adequate,[280] and where hours
are documented, the district court may abuse its discretion if it
disallows hours without a supporting rationale.[281]

To recover for time incurred by law clerks and paralegals, the
petitioning attorney must specifically identify the tasks completed
and adequately document the charges.[282]

---

[278]*E.g.*, Leroy v. City of Houston, 831 F.2d 576, 586 (5th Cir. 1987).

[279]Hensley v. Eckerhart, 461 U.S. 424, 433, 31 FEP 1169 (1983) ("where the
documentation of hours is inadequate, the district court may reduce the award accordingly"); Harper v. City of Chi. Heights, 223 F.3d 593, 605 (7th Cir. 2000) (within
district court's power to reduce fee award based on reconstructed records since it is
not supported by contemporaneous time records); Kirsch v. Fleet Street, Ltd., 148
F.3d 149, 173, 77 FEP 318 (2d Cir. 1998) (reducing attorney's fee award by 20% in
part because of deficient billing records in ADEA case); Walker v. United States
Dep't of Hous. & Urban Dev., 99 F.3d 761, 773 (5th Cir. 1996) (rejecting fee request in its entirety because time records inadequately documented activities);
Blanchard v. Bergeron, 893 F.2d 87, 90 (5th Cir. 1990) (court "refused to award a
recovery of fees for the vaguely enumerated hours"); Alberti v. Klevenhagen, 896
F.2d 927, 931–34 (5th Cir.) (vacating district court's finding that all hours billed
were appropriate; no contemporaneous time records), *vacated on other grounds*, 903
F.2d 352 (5th Cir. 1990); National Ass'n of Concerned Veterans v. Secretary of Def.,
675 F.2d 1319, 1327, 28 FEP 114 (D.C. Cir. 1982) ("the better practice is to prepare detailed summaries based on contemporaneous time records").

[280]Kline v. Kansas City Fire Dep't, 245 F.3d 707, 709, 86 FEP 266 (8th Cir.
2001) (rejecting imposition of per se rule that submission of reconstructed time records
rather than contemporaneous time accounts requires reduction of attorney's fees);
Cadena v. Pacesetter Corp., 224 F.3d 1203, 1215, 83 FEP 1645 (10th Cir. 2000)
(despite "block billing," fee award proper); Brady v. Fort Bend County, 145 F.3d
691, 716 (5th Cir. 1998) (despite complaint that daily time entries were vague and
conglomerated, they adequately described activity on which time was expended);
Washington v. Philadelphia County Ct. of Common Pleas, 89 F.3d 1031, 1037–38
(3d Cir. 1996) (reversing and remanding district court's reduction of plaintiff's attorneys' hours because of improperly documented time where appellate court found
time records specifying date of work performed, attorney performing work, and nature
of work to be sufficiently detailed).

[281]Steelworkers v. Phelps Dodge Corp., 896 F.2d 403, 407, 133 LRRM 2636
(9th Cir. 1990) (hours actually expended cannot be disallowed without supporting
rationale); Walje v. City of Winchester, 773 F.2d 729, 732, 120 LRRM 2714 (6th
Cir. 1985) ("[A] district court must indicate the [attorney] hours eliminated and its
reasons for their elimination, and must in general explain why and how the fee was
reduced.").

[282]*See, e.g.*, Becker v. ARCO Chem. Co., 15 F. Supp. 2d 621, 635 (E.D. Pa.
1998) (costs awarded to counsel for prevailing plaintiff in ADEA case would not
include claimed charge for paralegal and support personnel where counsel failed to

c. The Partially Prevailing Plaintiff. Identifying reasonable hours may be problematic where the plaintiff prevails in part, because such a plaintiff may be awarded either full fees or a reduced amount from which time spent on distinct or unrelated unsuccessful claims has been deducted. Often a plaintiff attacks several allegedly discriminatory practices or espouses several legal theories and succeeds only with respect to one or a few, or succeeds on pendent state-law or on nonfee federal claims in addition to fee-generating claims. The Supreme Court in *Hensley v. Eckerhart*[283] provided general guidance for cases in which there is partial success, distinguishing between those suits involving separable claims and those including different theories of attack on essentially the same practice or injury. The Court explained:

> Where the plaintiff has failed to prevail on a claim that is distinct in all respects from his successful claims, the hours spent on the unsuccessful claim should be excluded in considering the amount of a reasonable fee. Where a lawsuit consists of related claims, a plaintiff who has won substantial relief should not have his attorney's fee reduced simply because the district court did not adopt each contention raised. But where the plaintiff achieved only limited success, the district court should award only that amount of fees that is reasonable in relation to the results obtained.[284]

Thus, often there is no need to mechanically apportion the fee award on the basis of success or failure on interrelated theories.[285] The court may also allow fees if the prevailing party succeeds on a nonfee claim if it arose out of a common nucleus of operating fact

---

identify any of tasks completed by such individuals); Reynolds v. U.S.X. Corp., 170 F. Supp. 2d 530, 532, 87 FEP 307 (E.D. Pa. 2001) (prevailing employee in Title VII action entitled to recover fees for 34.7 paralegal hours where hours were reasonable and well documented); *cf.* Spegon v. Catholic Bishop of Chi., 175 F.3d 544, 553, 5 WH2d 457 (7th Cir. 1999) (district court did not abuse its discretion in reducing paralegal hours requested in fee application where tasks performed, such as organizing file folders, document preparation, and copying documents, could have been performed by legal secretary).

[283]461 U.S. 424, 434–35, 31 FEP 1169 (1983).

[284]*Id.* at 440.

[285]*E.g., id.* at 438; *see also* Wal-Mart Stores, Inc. v. Barton, 223 F.3d 770, 773, 84 FEP 1181 (8th Cir. 2000) (time spent on unsuccessful pendent state tort claim deemed compensable); Failla v. Passaic, 146 F.3d 149, 160, 8 AD 275 (3d Cir. 1998) (district court did not abuse its discretion by declining to deduct time to reflect plaintiff's unsuccessful claims and his limited success because all claims are from common core of facts); Dunning v. Simmons Airlines, Inc., 62 F.3d 863, 874, 68 FEP 785 (7th Cir. 1995) (district court did not abuse its discretion in awarding plaintiff

with the fee-generating federal claim.[286] On the other hand, many cases have disallowed compensation for time spent litigating distinct claims on which the party seeking compensation did not ultimately prevail.[287]

---

attorney's fees because claims for retaliation (successful), sex harassment (unsuccessful), and gender discrimination (dismissed before trial) were interrelated); Thorne v. City of El Segundo, 802 F.2d 1131, 1140–41, 46 FEP 1651 (9th Cir. 1986) (trial court must ascertain whether claims were essentially same or instead segregated); Cinevision Corp. v. City of Burbank, 745 F.2d 560, 581 (9th Cir. 1984) (fees were properly awarded even though same counsel also represented another party, which lost on directed verdict); Altman v. Port Auth. of N.Y. & N.J., 879 F. Supp. 345, 354, 67 FEP 1355 (S.D.N.Y. 1995) (fees did not have to be reduced where evidence regarding plaintiff's age discrimination claim, which was dropped at trial, was intertwined with evidence of plaintiff's retaliation claim).

[286]Webb v. Sloan, 330 F.3d 1158, 1168 (9th Cir. 2003) (successful and unsuccessful claims are related if they share common law or facts; claims are unrelated if they are " 'distinctly different' both legally and factually"); Robinson v. City of Edmond, 160 F.3d 1275, 1283 (10th Cir. 1998) ("litigants should be given breathing room to raise alternative legal grounds without fear that merely raising an alternative theory will threaten the attorney's subsequent compensation"); Thomlinson v. City of Omaha, 63 F.3d 786, 791 (8th Cir. 1995) (error to reduce fee for partial success when plaintiff won full relief and "strong interrelationship" existed between successful and unsuccessful claims); Vukadinovich v. McCarthy, 595 F.3d 58, 60–61 (7th Cir. 1995) (prevailing party entitled to fees incurred collecting judgment, even though collection procedures are not pursuant to Civil Rights Act); Munson v. Milwaukee Bd. of Sch. Dirs., 969 F.2d 266, 271–72 (7th Cir. 1992) (prevailing party entitled to fees for work on unsuccessful pendent state claim that is factually or legally related to successful civil rights claim); Leroy v. City of Houston, 906 F.2d 1068, 1085–86 (5th Cir. 1990) (awarding fees for collecting judgment); Carreras v. City of Anaheim, 768 F.2d 1039, 1050 (9th Cir. 1985) (plaintiffs entitled to attorney's fees even though they prevailed in pendent state claims rather than their federal claims); McDonald v. Doe, 748 F.2d 1055, 1056–57 (5th Cir. 1984) (plaintiff may qualify for fees when he succeeds on nonfee federal or state claim joined with fee-generating federal claim when both arise out of common nucleus of operative fact); Lamphere v. Brown Univ., 610 F.2d 46, 47, 21 FEP 824 (1st Cir. 1979) ("[I]t was not error to award fees for the time spent by counsel in an unsuccessful attempt to broaden the scope of remedies available under the decree. This issue was all part and parcel of one matter—counsel should not be penalized for every lost motion. This is not the same as a case where claims are truly fractionable."); Park v. Howard Univ., 881 F. Supp. 653, 661, 71 FEP 1830 (D.D.C. 1995) (party entitled to fees for all hours where plaintiff prevailed on core allegations and other allegations were interrelated).

[287]Thomas v. NFL Players Ass'n, 273 F.3d 1124, 1128–29 (D.C. Cir. 2001) (district court did not abuse discretion in awarding partial fees on finding that plaintiff's claim of discrimination could not succeed, but that her "pattern and practice claim of discriminatory failure to promote was 'distinctly different' from her other claims"; award of approximately $338,000 not "unreasonable in relation to the overall result achieved" given length of litigation and "dilatory" defense waged); Iqbal v. Golf Course Superintendents Ass'n, 900 F.2d 227, 228, 52 FEP 961 (10th Cir. 1990) (court did not abuse its discretion in reducing lodestar by 30% to reflect limited success achieved by plaintiff); Rendon v. AT & T Techs., 883 F.2d 388, 399, 50 FEP 1587

To assist the appellate court in reviewing an award, the district court should state its reasoning on the multiple-claims issue.[288]

When a reviewing court has disagreed with the lower court on the merits of a claim and altered the judgment below, the assessment of attorney's fees often is remanded to reflect the new outcome.[289]

2. Adjustments to the Lodestar

The burden of justifying a deviation from the lodestar rests on the party proposing it.[290] The Supreme Court decisions have

---

(5th Cir. 1989) (reduction of lodestar proper where there was limited success); Johnson v. Nordstrom-Larpenteur Agency, Inc., 623 F.2d 1279, 1282, 23 FEP 284 (8th Cir. 1980) ("In redetermining the amount of fees to which appellant's attorney is entitled, the district court may, on remand, take into account appellant's limited success."); Hardy v. Porter, 613 F.2d 112, 114, 26 FEP 1260 (5th Cir. 1980) (district court correctly stated that attorneys are not entitled to fees for time spent unsuccessfully pursuing claim on which they did not prevail, but record was not clear on whether court considered possibility that some evidence gathered with respect to unsuccessful claim was also relevant to claim on which plaintiffs prevailed); EEOC v. Safeway Stores, Inc., 597 F.2d 251, 252–53, 23 FEP 273 (10th Cir. 1979) (plaintiff prevailed on discriminatory suspension claim but lost on claims of discriminatory work assignment and constructive discharge; fee award of $550 upheld); Nadeau v. Helgemoe, 581 F.2d 275, 279 (1st Cir. 1978) (nonemployment case; "[t]he amount of attorney's fees [prevailing plaintiffs] receive should be based on the work performed on the issues in which they were successful"); Sweeney v. Board of Trs. of Keene State Coll., 569 F.2d 169, 180, 16 FEP 378, 386 (1st Cir.) (fee reduction of 20% upheld in light of plaintiff's partial recovery), *vacated and remanded on other grounds*, 439 U.S. 24, 18 FEP 520 (1978) (per curiam).

[288]Coutin v. Young & Rubicam Pub. Relations, Inc., 124 F.3d 331, 337, 74 FEP 1463 (1st Cir. 1997) (court's drastic reduction of fees because of limited success without performing lodestar analysis was abuse of discretion); Black Grievance Comm. v. Philadelphia Elec. Co., 802 F.2d 648, 653–54, 41 FEP 1820 (3d Cir. 1986) (no abuse of discretion where trial court made 25% reduction for limited success), *vacated and remanded on other grounds*, 483 U.S. 1015, 45 FEP 1895 (1987); Richardson v. Byrd, 709 F.2d 1016, 1022, 32 FEP 603 (5th Cir. 1983) (vacating fee award and remanding; trial court did not explain how it dealt with issue of unsuccessful claims); King v. McCord, 707 F.2d 466, 467–68, 35 FEP 831 (11th Cir. 1983) (per curiam) (although court of appeals earlier had vacated $2,000 fee award, made without analysis of relevant factors, on remand trial court had conducted "detailed" analysis, discounting the hours by 70/191 to reflect work on claims as to which plaintiff did not prevail).

[289]*E.g.*, Holsey v. Armour & Co., 743 F.2d 199, 218, 35 FEP 1064 (4th Cir. 1984) (because part of judgment was vacated, "district court must reconsider the award of attorneys' fees"); *cf.* Domingo v. New Eng. Fish Co., 727 F.2d 1429, 1446, 34 FEP 584 (9th Cir.) (attorney's fees had to be reconsidered because district court needed to determine if additional relief was owed to class members), *modified*, 742 F.2d 520, 37 FEP 1303 (9th Cir. 1984).

[290]*E.g.*, Blum v. Stenson, 465 U.S. 886, 898, 34 FEP 417 (1984).

established that adjustments to the lodestar will be permissible in only limited circumstances. Indeed, in *Dague*, the Supreme Court reaffirmed the " 'strong presumption' that the lodestar represents the 'reasonable' fee, and [has] placed upon the fee applicant who seeks more than that the burden of showing that 'such an adjustment is *necessary* to the determination of a reasonable fee.' "[291] Similarly, downward adjustments for limited success are applied only where the circumstances make a full lodestar fee award unjust.[292]

The various circumstances where an adjustment to the lodestar may be warranted are discussed below.

a. Contingency. In *Dague*, the Supreme Court held that enhancements to the lodestar to compensate for risk of nonpayment are not available under most federal "prevailing party" fee-shifting statutes.[293] Even after *Dague*, however, some federal courts have awarded a risk premium when there is a supplemental or pendent *state*-law claim, in a state that continues to recognize the validity of contingent risk enhancements.[294] Although *Dague* restricts what can be awarded by the courts in fees *from the defendant* under a fee-shifting statute, it may not affect what the attorney can recover by way of contract with the client[295] or from the class in a "common fund" class situation.[296] Although enhancement because of

---

[291]City of Burlington v. Dague, 505 U.S. 557, 562, 60 FEP 11 (1992) (citations omitted).

[292]*See* Farrar v. Hobby, 506 U.S. 103, 114–15, 60 FEP 633 (1992).

[293]*Dague*, 505 U.S. at 567.

[294]Mangold v. California Pub. Util. Comm'n, 67 F.3d 1470, 1479, 69 FEP 48 (9th Cir. 1995) (affirming award of contingent risk enhancement to employment discrimination claimant under pendent state-law claim where California law provided for enhancement); Davis v. Mutual Life Ins. Co., 6 F.3d 367, 383 (6th Cir. 1993) (awarding risk multiplier under Ohio law when plaintiff prevailed on state-law claims, even though *Dague* prevented enhancement on plaintiff's claim under Racketeer Influenced and Corrupt Organizations Act); Hurley v. Atlantic City Police Dep't, 933 F. Supp. 396, 430, 72 FEP 1828 (D.N.J. 1996) (court gave one-third contingency enhancement to lodestar fee under New Jersey law), *aff'd in part, vacated in part on other grounds*, 174 F.3d 95, 79 FEP 808 (3d Cir. 1999).

[295]*See* Venegas v. Mitchell, 495 U.S. 82, 90, 52 FEP 849 (1990) (attorney can enforce private contingency fee agreement even if it involves fee exceeding amount court orders losing defendant to pay); *cf.* Curry v. Del Priore, 941 F.2d 730, 731, 56 FEP 1010 (9th Cir. 1991) (federal courts have ancillary jurisdiction to adjudicate contractual fee disputes between counsel and client).

[296]*See* Staton v. Boeing Co., 327 F.3d 938, 967 (9th Cir. 2003) ("in common fund cases . . . the court can apply a risk multiplier when using the lodestar approach"); Brytus v. Spang, 203 F.3d 238, 247 (3d Cir. 2000) (district court did not abuse its discretion to deny enhancement of attorney's fees for contingent nature of

contingent risk is unavailable, courts have also held that it is clear error to *reduce* the attorney's fee award solely because of a plaintiff's contingency fee arrangement.[297]

b. Results Achieved. The results achieved constitute a permissible factor in adjusting the lodestar either downward or upward. The Supreme Court has held that "in some cases of exceptional success an enhancement award may be justified."[298] In *City of Riverside v. Rivera*,[299] the Supreme Court held that fee awards under

---

undertaking and result obtained out of common fund after making lodestar award under ERISA but not foreclosing possibility); Cook v. Niedert, 142 F.3d 1004, 1015 (7th Cir. 1998) (application of multiplier did not result in double compensation for riskiness of litigation because unenhanced lodestar does not reflect possibility of no recovery; defendants in common fund cases cannot be characterized as subsidizing unsuccessful lawsuits against other defendants); In re Washington Pub. Power Supply Sys. Sec. Litig., 19 F.3d 1291, 1299–1302 (9th Cir. 1994) (district court abused its discretion in refusing to award risk multiplier from common fund created by settlement of class securities litigation; *Dague* applies only to statutory fee-shifting cases, not to common fund cases); Alexander v. Chicago Park Dist., 927 F.2d 1014, 1024–25 (7th Cir. 1991) (approving payment of fees from common fund created by settlement of employment discrimination class action); McClendon v. Continental Group, Inc., 872 F. Supp. 142, 156 (D.N.J. 1994) (concluding that common fund fee awards need not be governed by statutory fee cases because they are governed by significantly different standards; granting multiplier of 1.5 based on contingency); In re Oracle Sec. Litig., 852 F. Supp. 1437, 1455–56 (N.D. Cal. 1994) (same); Parker v. Anderson, 667 F.2d 1204, 1213–14, 28 FEP 788 (5th Cir. 1982) (same); Robinson v. Klassen, 553 F. Supp. 76, 77 (E.D. Ark. 1982) ("the common fund approach, employed by the parties in the settlement agreement, is an acceptable way of dealing with fees and costs in civil rights actions"). *But see* Evans v. City of Evanston, 941 F.2d 473, 479, 57 FEP 281 (7th Cir. 1991) (rejecting enhancement and recovery from both defendants and common fund and noting "the widespread use of common-fund recoveries as a source of fees for lawyers in Title VII or civil rights cases would not only skew the incentives of plaintiffs' lawyers toward damages rather than equitable remedies, but also toward class actions rather than suits by individuals").

[297]Ross v. Douglas County, 244 F.3d 620, 622–23 (8th Cir. 2001); Hamlin v. Charter Twp. of Flint, 165 F.3d 426, 430, 8 AD 1688 (6th Cir. 1999); Park v. Howard Univ., 881 F. Supp. 653, 661, 71 FEP 1830 (D.D.C. 1995) (court awarded fee under lodestar calculation at $300 per hour despite contingent fee agreement in which client agreed to pay $125 per hour).

[298]Blum v. Stenson, 465 U.S. 886, 901, 34 FEP 417 (1984) (citation omitted); *see also* Barnes v. City of Cincinnati, 401 F.3d 729, 746, 95 FEP 994 (6th Cir. 2005) (prevailing plaintiff, pre-operative transsexual police officer who sued city for sex discrimination because he was demoted for failing to conform to sexual stereotypes, entitled to enhanced fee award based in part on extraordinary result achieved in highly controversial case); Daggitt v. Food & Commercial Workers Local 304A, 245 F.3d 981, 990, 85 FEP 666 (8th Cir. 2001) (25% enhancement not abuse of discretion given complexity of case and modest nature of lodestar, bringing total fee to $33,547).

[299]477 U.S. 561, 41 FEP 65 (1986).

the civil rights statutes are not necessarily limited to a proportion of the damages award, particularly because civil rights cases involve a public benefit.[300] In upholding a fee award of $243,343 to plaintiffs who had recovered only $33,350 in a § 1983 police misconduct case, the Court stated:

> Unlike most private tort litigants, a civil rights plaintiff seeks to vindicate important civil and constitutional rights that cannot be valued solely in monetary terms. And, Congress has determined that "the public as a whole has an interest in the vindication of the rights conferred by the statutes enumerated in § 1988, over and above the value of a civil rights remedy to a particular plaintiff. . . ." *Hensley*, 461 U.S., at 444, n. 4 (Brennan, J., concurring in part and dissenting in part).
>
> . . . .
>
> Because damage awards do not reflect fully the public benefit advanced by civil rights litigation, Congress did not intend for fees in civil rights cases, unlike most private law cases, to depend on obtaining substantial monetary relief. Rather, Congress made clear that it "intended that the amount of fees awarded under [§ 1988] be governed by the same standards which prevail in other types of equally complex Federal litigation, such as antitrust cases and *not be reduced because the rights involved may be nonpecuniary in nature.*" Senate Report, at 6 (emphasis added). "[C]ounsel for prevailing parties should be paid, as is traditional with attorneys compensated by a fee-paying client, *'for all time reasonably expended on a matter.'* "[301]

---

[300]*Id.* at 574.

[301]*Id.* at 574–75 (some citations omitted); *accord* Lytle v. Carl, 382 F.3d 978, 989 (9th Cir. 2004) (affirming fee award of $239,268, where damages award totaled $75,000); Thomas v. NFL Players Ass'n, 273 F.3d 1124, 1129, 87 FEP 894 (D.C. Cir. 2001) (affirming fee award of $338,000, where damages came to $73,390 and stating that fact "that the fees awarded are nearly five times the amount of plaintiff's recovery does not make them excessive"); Lipsett v. Blanco, 975 F.2d 934, 938–40, 59 FEP 1498 (1st Cir. 1992) (fee award, though higher than damages, is justified by employer's "Stalingrad defense"; hard-nosed litigation tactics necessarily required plaintiff to respond in kind); Cowan v. Prudential Ins. Co., 935 F.2d 522, 526, 56 FEP 229 (2d Cir. 1991) ("A presumptively correct 'lodestar' figure should not be reduced simply because a plaintiff recovered a low damage award."); Thorne v. City of El Segundo, 802 F.2d 1131, 1143, 46 FEP 1651 (9th Cir. 1986) ("there is no absolute requirement that attorneys' fees in civil rights cases be proportionate to the damages awarded"); *see* Singer v. City of Waco, 324 F.3d 813 (5th Cir. 2003) (fact that fire fighters in FLSA case sought $5 million and collected only $180,000 did not require district court to reduce lodestar); Green v. Administrator of Tulane Educ. Fund, 284 F.3d 642, 661, 89 FEP 587 (5th Cir. 2002) (attorney's fee award does not need to be commensurate with actual amount of damages; amount of damages

Earlier decisions from the lower courts thus focused on such factors as the significance of injunctive relief ordered[302] or the precedential significance of the decision[303] as a factor in determining whether an adjustment was appropriate.

As for lodestar reductions, in *Hensley v. Eckerhart*[304] the Supreme Court explained that, although a partially prevailing plaintiff

---

plaintiff recovers is only one of many factors court must consider); *Thomas*, 273 F.3d at 1129 (that fees awarded are nearly five times amount of plaintiff's recovery does not make them excessive); Hollowell v. Orleans Reg'l Hosp., 217 F.3d 379, 392 (5th Cir. 2000) (low damages only one factor and should not alone lead district court to reduce fee award in ERISA case); Spegon v. Catholic Bishop of Chi., 175 F.3d 544, 588 (7th Cir. 1999) (in FLSA case, failure to obtain every dollar sought does not automatically mean that lodestar should be reduced); *Hamlin*, 165 F.3d at 436–38 (district court abused discretion by cutting fee award by 50% because plaintiff, in "close" case, received only half of damages requested; court reinstated 100% of fee on appeal); Riley v. City of Jackson, 99 F.3d 757, 759–60 (5th Cir. 1996) (district court abused its discretion by awarding only $2,500 in attorney's fees—where plaintiffs had requested $86,000—when plaintiffs were awarded injunctive relief as well as nominal damages); Patterson v. PHP Health Care Corp., 90 F.3d 927 (5th Cir. 1996) (affirming attorney's fee award greater than total monetary award); Casey v. City of Cabool, 12 F.3d 799, 805–06 (8th Cir. 1993) (fee of $66,000 approved despite jury award of only $19,000); Finch v. Hercules, Inc., 941 F. Supp. 1395, 1426, 75 FEP 1709 (D. Del. 1996) (when calculating results obtained and fixing lodestar amount, court may not diminish counsel fees by merely quantifying proportionate ratio based on amount of damages recovered), *aff'd*, 124 F.3d 186 (3d Cir. 1997); EEOC v. Accurate Mech. Contractors, Inc., 863 F. Supp. 828, 839, 74 FEP 1351 (E.D. Wis. 1994) ("Although the amount of damages a plaintiff recovers is relevant to an award of attorney's fees for that recovery, the size of the award does not dictate that the attorney's fee allowed must be proportional to the damage award."); *see also* Staton v. Boeing, 327 F.3d 938, 973 (9th Cir. 2003) (dicta; value of injunctive relief may be basis for enhancing lodestar); Zabkowicz v. West Bend Co., 789 F.2d 540, 549, 40 FEP 1171 (7th Cir. 1986) (total denial of fees may be abuse of discretion).

[302]*E.g.*, Copeland v. Marshall, 641 F.2d 880, 888, 23 FEP 967 (D.C. Cir. 1980) (en banc) ("While the actual cash awards to individual members of the class were in this instance relatively small in relation to the total fee claim, this was basically an equity action which was intended to and did achieve benefits that cannot be measured solely in monetary terms. The judgment . . . established an entirely new pattern of training and promotion for female employees in an important segment of the Department of Labor. . . . The benefits of the litigation will be felt for many years to come.") (quoting trial court); Davis v. County of L.A., 8 FEP 244, 246 (C.D. Cal. 1974) ($7,193 bonus for significant injunctive relief; $60,000 counsel fee awarded where "excellent" results were obtained for represented class), *aff'd in relevant part*, 13 FEP 1217 (9th Cir. 1976).

[303]Rosenfeld v. Southern Pac. Co., 519 F.2d 527, 530, 10 FEP 1439 (9th Cir. 1975) (precedent-setting opinion).

[304]461 U.S. 424, 436, 31 FEP 1169 (1983) ("If . . . a plaintiff has achieved only partial or limited success, the [lodestar] may be an excessive amount.").

was a "prevailing party" presumptively entitled to an attorney's fee, the extent of the plaintiff's success plays a key role in fee calculation. Subsequently, in *Texas State Teachers Ass'n v. Garland Independent School District*,[305] the Court reaffirmed that "the degree of the plaintiff's overall success goes to the reasonableness of the award."[306] Later, in *Farrar v. Hobby*[307]—a § 1988 case—the Court held that a party, even one who prevailed, might have the fee reduced or even denied entirely based on the results of the litigation. In *Farrar*, the plaintiffs sought $17 million in damages against six defendants, but ultimately established only a technical violation by one defendant and recovered only $1 in nominal damages. In such cases, "the only reasonable fee is usually no fee at all."[308] Courts are divided as to *Farrar*'s implications for mixed-motive cases,[309] which apply a different attorney's fee provision.[310]

---

[305]489 U.S. 782, 49 FEP 465 (1989) (emphasis omitted).

[306]489 U.S. at 793.

[307]506 U.S. 103, 60 FEP 633 (1992).

[308]*Id.* at 115.

[309]*See* Sheppard v. River View Nursing Ctr., 88 F.3d 1332, 1335–36, 71 FEP 218 (4th Cir. 1996) (same considerations of proportionality addressed in *Farrar* should guide decision whether to award fees and amount of fees under 42 U.S.C. § 2000(e)-5(g)(2)(B); describing factors that should inform district court's exercise of its discretion in awarding attorney's fees in mixed-motive cases: why injunctive relief was or was not granted; nature of any declaratory relief granted; public purpose served by resolving dispute; and whether defendant's actions demonstrated widespread or intolerable animus or were justified by plaintiff's unacceptable behavior); *see also* Norris v. Cysco Corp., 191 F.3d 1043, 1051 (9th Cir. 1999) (adopting *Sheppard* factors); Akrabawi v. Carnes Co., 152 F.3d 688, 695–96, 77 FEP 1203 (7th Cir. 1998) (adopting *Sheppard* factors in weighing whether to award fees); Canup v. Chipman-Union, Inc., 123 F.3d 1440, 1444, 75 FEP 220 (11th Cir. 1997) (starting point for fee request under § 2000e-5(g)(2)(B) must be degree of success obtained by plaintiff). *Compare* Gudenkauf v. Stauffer Commc'ns, 158 F.3d 1074, 1081, 77 FEP 1723 (10th Cir. 1998) (recovery of damages not proper factor upon which to assess propriety of granting fee award in mixed-motive case; plaintiff who prevails under § 2000e-2(m) should ordinarily be awarded attorney's fees in all but special circumstances) *with* Garcia v. City of Houston, 201 F.3d 672, 679, 82 FEP 1 (5th Cir. 2000) (affirming award of $18,000 in fees and costs when $67,000 was requested in mixed-motive case where district court applied *Sheppard* factors and noted that attorney's fees should be awarded in mixed-motive cases in all but special circumstances because of plaintiff's role in helping to end unlawful discrimination in workplace).

[310]Section 2000e-5(g)(2)(B) of the Civil Rights Act of 1991 provides:

On a claim in which an individual proves a violation under §2000e-2(m) of this Title and a respondent demonstrates that the respondent would have taken the same action in the absence of the impermissible motivating factor, the court may grant declaratory relief, injunctive relief (except as provided in clause (ii)), and attorney's fees and costs demonstrated to be directly attributable only to the pursuit of a claim under §2000e-2(m) of this Title . . . .

The extent of a plaintiff's success is a factor in the calculation of any fee award, and courts may therefore reduce the lodestar based on the plaintiff's lack of success.[311] A negative multiplier based on partial success may be inappropriate, however, if the number of hours used to calculate the lodestar already has been

---

[311]Dalal v. Alliant Techsystems, Inc., 182 F.3d 757, 761–62 (10th Cir. 1999) (where partial success under ADEA supported fee award and plaintiff received judgment amount significantly below pretrial Rule 68 offer of judgment, award of full fees up to rejection of offer of judgment and half of the fees afterward was within court's discretion); Gumbhir v. Curators of Univ. of Mo., 157 F.3d 1141, 1147, 78 FEP 296 (8th Cir. 1998) (although pro rata fee reductions based on relationship between damages requested and damages awarded are often inappropriate, in this case it was generous method of determining appropriate reduction for limited success when plaintiff lost claims for equitable relief and all damage claims except one, and recovered 43% of requested damages); Migis v. Pearle Vision, Inc., 135 F.3d 1041, 1047–48, 78 FEP 1379 (5th Cir. 1998) (although district court reduced fee by 10% for limited success, it "did not give adequate consideration to the eighth *Johnson* factor, the amount involved and the result obtained"); Pino v. Locascio, 101 F.3d 235, 239 (2d Cir. 1996) (in case where plaintiff recovered $1 in damages, appeals court reversed trial court's fee award, observing that "the vast majority of civil rights litigation does not result in ground-breaking conclusions of law, and therefore, will only be appropriate candidates for fee awards if a plaintiff recovers some significant measure of damages or other meaningful relief"); McGinnis v. Kentucky Fried Chicken of Cal., 51 F.3d 805, 810, 4 AD 352 (9th Cir. 1994) (district court erred by not reducing fee award where plaintiff claimed fees of $138,672 on verdict of $34,000 in compensatory damages); Williams v. Trans World Airlines, Inc., 660 F.2d 1267, 1274, 27 FEP 487 (8th Cir. 1981) (attorney's fee must bear realistic relationship to right at issue; 450 hours claimed in case involving less than $1,000 totally unreasonable); Beazer v. New York City Transit Auth., 558 F.2d 97, 100, 17 FEP 226 (2d Cir. 1977) (eliminating "premium" awarded in part because no monetary fund was recovered for plaintiff class), *rev'd on other grounds*, 440 U.S. 568 (1979); Baird v. Boies, Schiller & Flexner, 219 F. Supp. 2d 510, 524–25, 89 FEP 1524 (S.D.N.Y. 2002) (imposing overall 60% reduction to plaintiffs' initial fee request and awarding fees in amount of $50,000 where case was launched with great fanfare but plaintiffs accepted offer of judgment 4 months later); Finch v. Hercules, Inc., 941 F. Supp. 1395, 1427, 75 FEP 1709 (D. Del. 1996) (court reduced lodestar by 35% because plaintiff did not achieve "excellent results" where plaintiff only recovered 5% of relief sought and failed to prove willful violation, entitlement to front pay, or stock losses); Cragen v. Barnhill, 859 F. Supp. 566, 574–75 (N.D. Fla. 1994) (plaintiff in pregnancy discrimination case had fees reduced 50% because of her limited success: she recovered no punitive damages, compensatory damages recovered were only small fraction of those requested, and individual defendant was found not liable); Carey v. Rudeseal, 721 F. Supp. 294, 298–99 (N.D. Ga. 1989) (adjustment of lodestar figure appropriate where client received only $1,000 and legal theories of case did not require exceptional legal ability to develop); *cf.* Quarantino v. Tiffany & Co., 166 F.3d 422, 427, 78 FEP 1849 (2d Cir. 1999) (reduction of lodestar because of only partial success in obtaining monetary relief inappropriate because all claims intertwined; not appropriate for court to apply "billing judgment" to lodestar).

reduced to account for time expended on distinct unsuccessful claims.[312]

Courts have been divided on the propriety of limiting an attorney's fee based on the prospect of a prefiling settlement. In *NAACP v. Town of East Haven*,[313] the Second Circuit found that a district court committed clear error in limiting an attorney's fee award under Title VII to fees incurred prior to the NAACP's receipt of a presuit letter from the defendant's counsel about possible settlement terms. The court held that prevailing circuit law "prohibit[ed] the use of informal negotiations as a basis for reducing fee awards in order to avoid just this sort of hindsight scrutiny of a litigant's tactical decisions that would 'improperly dissuade []' 'plaintiffs with meritorious claims . . . from pressing forward with their litigation.' "[314] The Seventh Circuit, by contrast, in *Spegon v. Catholic Bishop*,[315] affirmed a reduction of a fee award in an FLSA case where the plaintiff's attorney failed to pursue a prefiling settlement with the employer, even though the amount of overtime back pay sought by the plaintiff was "limited."[316] "[W]hether a fee-paying client in Spegon's shoes would have expected counsel to contact the Diocese prior to filing suit is a permissible factor for the district court to consider in determining the reasonableness of the hours subsequently expended in pursuit of the litigation."[317]

c. Delay. The Supreme Court has recognized the propriety of enhancements for delay in payment.[318] In some circumstances, courts

---

[312]*See* Corder v. Gates, 947 F.2d 374, 378 (9th Cir. 1991).

[313]259 F.3d 113 (2d Cir. 2001).

[314]*Id.* at 119 (citing Ortiz v. Regan, 980 F.2d 138 (2d Cir. 1992)); *see also* Gudenkauf v. Stauffer Commc'ns, 158 F.3d 1074, 1084, 77 FEP 1723 (10th Cir. 1998) ("Congress . . . clearly did not intend a district court to reduce a mixed motives plaintiff's fee award on the basis of a rejected pretrial settlement"); Canup v. Clupman-Union, 123 F.3d 1440, 1445, 75 FEP 220 (11th Cir. 1997) (rejection of settlement offer may be considered but should not be controlling factor in assessing fee request in mixed-motive case).

[315]175 F.3d 544 (7th Cir. 1999).

[316]*Id.* at 552 and n.4.

[317]*Id.* at 552.

[318]Pennsylvania v. Delaware Valley Citizens' Council, 483 U.S. 711, 716, 45 FEP 1750 (1987); *see also* Missouri v. Jenkins, 491 U.S. 274, 286, 50 FEP 17 (1989) ("an appropriate adjustment for delay in payment—whether by the application of current rather than historic hourly rates or otherwise—is within the contemplation of [§ 1988]").

have enhanced fee awards because of delay in payment,[319] either by basing the award on current rates or by adjusting upward a fee based on historical rates to reflect its present value, but not both.[320] Such enhancements are available in actions against the states, notwithstanding the Eleventh Amendment.[321] Before the Civil Rights Act of 1991, sovereign immunity barred enhancement for delay in all cases brought against the United States.[322] As amended in 1991, however, Title VII explicitly provides that "the same interest to compensate for delay in payment" is available in actions brought by federal employees against the United States "as in cases involving nonpublic parties."[323]

It may be necessary to distinguish between prejudgment and postjudgment payment delays. The former are dealt with in the manner described earlier. Several cases have held that the only way to deal with delay between the time fee eligibility is established and the fee is actually paid is through statutory post-judgment interest under 28 U.S.C. § 1961.[324]

---

[319]Gierlinger v. Gleason, 160 F.3d 858, 882, 78 FEP 989 (2d Cir. 1998) (district court ordered to consider current market rates where delay in trial attributed mostly to court); Walker v. United States Dep't of Hous. & Urban Dev., 99 F.3d 761, 773 (5th Cir. 1996) (awarding enhancement to compensate for delay in payment by adjusting upward fee based on historical rates); Marinelli v. Erie, 25 F. Supp. 2d 674, 683–84 (W.D. Pa. 1998) (court stated that although upward enhancement in lodestar for delay may be proper in rare cases, it was not warranted because plaintiff provided no evidence of costs incurred by his counsel as result of any delay in payment of attorney's fees), *vacated on other grounds*, 216 F.3d 354 (3d Cir. 2000); Finch v. Hercules, 941 F. Supp. 1395, 1427–28, 75 FEP 1709 (D. Del. 1996) (court permitted fee enhancement to compensate for delay in payment for time gap between time services were rendered and fee award); Tabech v. Gunter, 869 F. Supp. 1446, 1462 (D. Neb. 1994) (court addressed delay in payment of fees by increasing reasonable rate for case that was 7 years old).

[320]It would be double counting to use current hourly rates (which presumably are higher than historical rates), and then to award an enhancement on top of the lodestar to reflect delay in payment. *E.g.*, Copeland v. Marshall, 641 F.2d 880, 893 & n.23, 23 FEP 967 (D.C. Cir. 1980).

[321]*Jenkins*, 491 U.S. at 278–84.

[322]Library of Congress v. Shaw, 478 U.S. 310, 319–20, 41 FEP 85 (1986) (no interest on fee award).

[323]42 U.S.C. § 2000e-16 (2000).

[324]Corder v. Brown, 25 F.3d 833, 838 (9th Cir. 1994) ("a delay in payment occasioned by appeal is redressable solely by an award of interest"); Islamic Ctr. v. City of Starkville, 876 F.2d 465, 473 (5th Cir. 1989) (If lodestar is calculated using historical billing rates, "the court should compensate for belated payment by increasing the lodestar by the rate of inflation from the time services were provided to the date

d. Quality. Although the Supreme Court has noted that the quality of representation normally is reflected in the hourly rate used to compute the lodestar,[325] some courts grant enhancements[326] or impose reductions[327] to reflect the quality of representation.

e. Undesirability of Case. Although rarely awarded, undesirability is treated as a possible enhancement factor in cases that pose a particular hardship to the prevailing party's attorney. Undesirability has been cited as a relevant enhancement factor in cases that are particularly unpopular in the community, either because of the identity of the represented party or the nature of the litigation.[328]

---

of judgment. Post-judgment interest should then be awarded under 28 U.S.C. § 1961 for the period following the determination of the fee until its actual payment."); Black Grievance Comm. v. Philadelphia Elec. Co., 802 F.2d 648, 655–56 (3d Cir. 1986) ("The period following the fee determination . . . is covered by post-judgment interest provided for in section 1961 of title 28 of the United States Code."), *vacated and remanded on other grounds*, 483 U.S. 1015 (1987).

[325]*See, e.g.*, Blum v. Stenson, 465 U.S. 886, 899–900, 34 FEP 417 (1984) (cautioning against double counting); Eddleman v. Switchcraft, Inc., 965 F.2d 422, 424–26, 59 FEP 151 (7th Cir. 1992) (it would be double counting in reverse to use low hourly rate for computing lodestar and then to discount fees further for inadequate representation; proper approach is to use regular, prevailing hourly rate and then to adjust lodestar downward); National Ass'n of Concerned Veterans v. Secretary of Def., 675 F.2d 1319, 28 FEP 1134 (D.C. Cir. 1982) (quality adjustment appropriate only if representation is unusually good or bad, taking into account level of skill normally expected of attorney commanding hourly rate used to compute lodestar).

[326]*See* Barnes v. City of Cincinnati, 401 F.3d 729, 746, 95 FEP 994 (6th Cir. 2005) (in successful Title VII action brought by pre-operative transsexual police officer against city, 1.75 multiplier justified in part by "the immense skill requisite to conducting this case properly"); McKenzie v. Kennickell, 875 F.2d 330, 338–39 (D.C. Cir. 1989) (5% quality enhancement for exceptional performance over 15 years proper); Hollowell v. Gravett, 723 F. Supp. 107, 110 (E.D. Ark. 1989) (75% quality enhancement to counsel appointed 3 days before jury trial); Allen v. Freeman, 694 F. Supp. 1554, 1556 (S.D. Fla. 1988) (45% enhancement for superior quality of representation).

[327]*E.g.*, Lanasa v. City of New Orleans, 619 F. Supp. 39, 51 (E.D. La. 1985) (25% reduction for negative quality of work; pro se plaintiff, who was also attorney, could have reached settlement much earlier and showed poor judgment in pursuing too zealously claim that did not merit such intensive effort); Barrett v. Kalinowski, 458 F. Supp. 689, 707 (M.D. Pa. 1978) (fees of three most active counsel reduced by 25% to reflect poor quality of work; performance of legal services inefficient, and settlement probably could have been reached earlier).

[328]*See* Barnes v. City of Cincinnati, 401 F.3d 729, 746, 95 FEP 994 (6th Cir. 2005) (awarding enhancement based in part on undesirability of controversial case brought against city by pre-operative transsexual police officer; affidavits testified that few lawyers locally or nationally would take such a case); Gomez v. Gates, 804 F. Supp. 69, 75 (C.D. Cal. 1992) (undesirability enhancement appropriate in case involving accused felons who alleged excessive force claims against police department).

C. Procedure

Procedural controversies may arise in litigating the attorney's fee question.

1. Discovery

Although the Supreme Court has admonished that fee disputes "should not result in a second major litigation"[329] and that, ideally, the fee issue will be settled by the parties,[330] some discovery often is inevitable.

The extent of permissible discovery sometimes is disputed. Defendants who contend that a plaintiff's request is excessive or that the submittal is deficient may seek discovery by interrogatory or document request.[331] But discovery may work the other way as well; if the defendant asserts that the plaintiff's rates are unreasonable or that the plaintiff's time expenditures were duplicative or excessive, the plaintiff is likely to seek discovery of the fees paid by the defendant to its own counsel in the litigation. The rationale for the discovery is that the amount of time expended and rates charged by counsel for the unsuccessful *defendant* may be relevant to whether counsel for the successful *plaintiff* expended excessive time or charged unreasonable rates.[332] Some courts allow[333]

---

[329]Hensley v. Eckerhart, 461 U.S. 424, 437, 31 FEP 1169 (1983) ("A request for attorney's fees should not result in a second major litigation.").

[330]*Id.* at 437 ("Ideally . . . litigants will settle the amount of a fee.").

[331]*E.g.*, Kemp v. Williams, 30 FEP 701, 702 (D.D.C. 1981) (plaintiff's attorney required to answer interrogatories pertaining to fee arrangement with client, despite objections based on lack of relevance and attorney-client privilege).

[332]Chalmers v. City of L.A., 796 F.2d 1205, 1214 (1986), *amended*, 808 F.2d 1373 (9th Cir. 1987); Chrapliwy v. Uniroyal, Inc., 670 F.2d 760, 768 n.18, 28 FEP 19 (7th Cir. 1982); Murray v. Stuckey's Inc., 153 F.R.D. 151, 152–53 (N.D. Iowa 1993) (hours expended by attorneys for defendants must be disclosed because defendants resisted plaintiff's fee claim on basis of number of hours claimed); Coalition to Save Our Children v. State Bd. of Educ., 143 F.R.D. 61, 64–66 (D. Del. 1992) (whether discovery is appropriate depends in part on objections raised by opponent to fee petition; ordering defendant to disclose its attorneys' billing rates and time spent on case); Corder v. Gates, 688 F. Supp. 1418, 1421–22 (C.D. Cal. 1988), *rev'd in part on other grounds*, 947 F.2d 374 (9th Cir. 1991); Real v. Continental Group, Inc., 116 F.R.D. 211, 213 (N.D. Cal. 1986).

[333]*E.g.*, Gaines v. Dougherty County Bd. of Educ., 775 F.2d 1565, 1571 n.12 (11th Cir. 1985); Brown v. Rollins, Inc., 397 F. Supp. 571, 579–80, 16 FEP 271 (W.D.N.C. 1974) (absent settlement on attorney's fees, "defendants are directed to

and others disallow[334] such discovery. The result often depends on
the relevance of the defendant's records to the particular fee dispute or the extent of the plaintiff's access to relevant information
through other readily accessible means. The Eleventh Circuit, for
example, has held that refusal to allow discovery of the defendant's
fee records, upon a proper showing of relevance, constitutes an
abuse of the trial court's discretion.[335]

2. Documentation

Courts require detailed billing records and affidavits or other
evidence to support a fee application.[336] Similarly, once the prevailing

---

file a statement with the court setting forth the bases on which they have compensated
their counsel"); Stastny v. Southern Bell Tel. & Tel. Co., 77 F.R.D 662, 664, 23 FEP
631 (W.D.N.C. 1978) (rejecting claim of attorney-client privilege and requiring defendant to provide number of attorney hours and description of time spent.); cf. Blowers
v. Lawyers Co-op. Publ'g Co., 526 F. Supp. 1324, 1325, 27 FEP 1224 (W.D.N.Y.
1981) (defendant must disclose number of attorney hours but not hourly rates).

[334]E.g., Martinez v. Schock Transfer & Warehouse Co., 789 F.2d 848, 849–50
(10th Cir. 1986) (no abuse of discretion in denying discovery regarding defendant
attorney's fees); Mirabal v. General Motors Acceptance Corp., 576 F.2d 729, 731 (7th
Cir. 1978) (comparing fees of counsel for both sides of case "ignores the fact that a
given case may have greater precedential value for one side than the other"); Samuel
v. University of Pittsburgh, 80 F.R.D. 293, 294–95 (W.D. Pa. 1978) (comparing number of hours spent on case and hourly rates of counsel for plaintiffs and defendants
will not produce relevant evidence on reasonableness of fees); Payne v. Travenol Labs.,
Inc., 23 FEP 1079, 1080 (N.D. Miss. 1976) (Denying plaintiff's motion to compel
discovery of defendants' fee arrangement with their counsel; "The court has the authority to compel the discovery sought by plaintiffs should the court determine that
the information obtainable through such source would be helpful in arriving at a fair
and just award. The granting of such discovery, however, would invade the privacy of
counsel['s] relationship with their clients and should be avoided unless the need for
the information outweighs the protection of the privacy mentioned."); Spell v.
McDaniel, 616 F. Supp. 1069, 1100 n.44 (E.D.N.C. 1985) (court declined to intrude
on defense counsel's privacy by requiring disclosure of their respective hours billed),
vacated in part on other grounds, 824 F.2d 1380 (4th Cir. 1987).

[335]See Henson v. Columbus Bank & Trust, 770 F.2d 1566, 1574–75 (11th Cir.
1985); Gaines v. Dougherty County Bd. of Educ., 775 F.2d 1565, 1571 n.12 (11th
Cir. 1985).

[336]See Gunter v. Ridgewood Energy Corp., 223 F.3d 190, 192 (3d Cir. 2000)
(jurisprudence in this area requires a " 'thorough judicial review of fee applications
. . . in all class action settlements' " (citations omitted)); Washington v. Philadelphia County Ct. of Common Pleas, 89 F.3d 1031, 1035–36, 76 FEP 151 (3d Cir.
1996) (plaintiff met his prima facie burden by submitting affidavits of other attorneys and billing statements); Perkins v. Mobile Housing Bd., 847 F.2d 735, 738 (11th
Cir. 1988) ("sworn testimony that, in fact, it took the time claimed is evidence of
considerable weight on the issue of the time required"); Northern Ind. Gun & Outdoor

party has documented his or her fee claim, courts require the opposing party's objections to be particularized and supported by evidence as well.[337] In a decision involving two Freedom of Information Act cases and one Title VII case against the federal government, the District of Columbia Circuit promulgated exacting standards for the documentation of fee applications and fee oppositions. In *National Ass'n of Concerned Veterans v. Secretary of Defense*,[338] the court held that (1) an attorney's fee applicant is required to provide specific evidence of the prevailing community rate for the type of work for which the award is sought, not generalized, conclusory, or "information and belief" affidavits from friendly attorneys; (2) the preferred practice for documenting the number of hours spent is to prepare detailed summaries based on contemporaneous time records indicating the work performed by each attorney for whom fees are sought;[339] (3) when seeking an adjustment to the lodestar figure, a fee applicant should clearly identify the specific circumstances of the case that support the requested adjustment; and (4) a party opposing a fee request is entitled to discovery of information it reasonably requires to appraise the reasonableness of the fee requested and to present any legitimate challenges to the fee application.[340]

Shows, Inc. v. Hedman, 111 F. Supp. 2d 1020, 1029 (N.D. Ind. 2000) (party may submit affidavits to respond to any objections regarding reasonableness of proposed fee and its supporting evidence; burden of initially establishing requested fee requires that any affidavit supporting reasonableness of that fee be filed contemporaneously with petition for fees); Moore v. University of Notre Dame, 22 F. Supp. 2d 896, 911, 78 FEP 62 (N.D. Ind. 1998) (reducing award by 20% for inadequate documentation). *But see* Norris v. Sysco Corp., 191 F.3d 1043, 1052, 9 AD 1262 (9th Cir. 1999) (district court did not abuse discretion by awarding fees in Title VII and ADA case despite poor records, though court stated it was in no way encouraging poor recordkeeping).

[337]*See* McGrath v. County of Nev., 67 F.3d 248, 255 (9th Cir. 1995) (fee opponent "bears the burden of providing specific evidence to challenge the accuracy and reasonableness of the hours charged"); Steelworkers v. Phelps Dodge Corp., 896 F.2d 403, 407, 133 LRRM 2636 (9th Cir. 1990) ("hours actually expended in the litigation are not to be disallowed without a supporting rationale"); Wooldridge v. Marlene Indus. Corp., 898 F.2d 1169, 1176 n.14 (6th Cir. 1990) (fee opponent's objections should be specific).

[338]675 F.2d 1319, 28 FEP 1134 (D.C. Cir. 1982).

[339]In *Hensley v. Eckerhart*, 461 U.S. 424 (1983), the Supreme Court noted that "plaintiff's counsel, of course, is not required to record in great detail how each minute of his time was expended. But at least counsel should identify the general subject matter of his time expenditures." *Id.* at 437 n.12.

[340]675 F.2d at 1324–29; *accord* McClure v. Mexia Indep. Sch. Dist., 750 F.2d 396, 403–04, 36 FEP 1402 (5th Cir. 1985) (recommending same procedure).

The District of Columbia Circuit further held that the party opposing an attorney's fee application should be equally detailed in setting forth the specific bases for its opposition.[341]

3. Hearing

If written briefing and supporting and opposing documentation are complete, it may not be necessary to hold an evidentiary hearing.[342] If, however, a party desires a hearing, it should request one, lest the issue be deemed waived.[343] It may constitute an abuse of discretion if the district court significantly departs from the lodestar without giving the relevant party an opportunity to be heard.[344]

4. Timing

Federal Rule of Civil Procedure 54(d)(2)(B) requires a motion for attorney's fees to be filed within 14 days after the entry of judgment, "unless otherwise provided by statute or order of court." Therefore, a motion for attorney's fees filed more than 14 days after judgment is untimely unless a local rule provides for a greater period of time.[345]

---

[341]675 F.2d at 1326.

[342]E.g., Calhoun v. Acme Cleveland Corp., 801 F.2d 558, 561, 41 FEP 1515 (1st Cir. 1986) (hearing often helpful and prudent but not mandatory); Copeland v. Marshall, 641 F.2d 880, 905, 23 FEP 967 (D.C. Cir. 1980) (en banc) (no hearing necessary where district court "ruled on the fee question ... with the benefit of substantial briefs from both sides"); Konczak v. Tyrrell, 603 F.2d 13, 18–19 (7th Cir. 1979) (same).

[343]See Kargman v. Sullivan, 589 F.2d 63, 67 (1st Cir. 1978) ("having sought no hearing on [the attorney's fee] motion, counsel could hardly have been surprised when none was held").

[344]Hutchinson v. Amateur Elec. Supply, Inc., 42 F.3d 1037, 1048, 66 FEP 1275, 1282 (7th Cir. 1994) (where defendant objected generally to fee request but did not specifically challenge any provisions and court did not hold hearing, it was abuse of discretion to drastically reduce lodestar).

[345]Planned Parenthood v. Attorney Gen. of N.J., 297 F.3d 253, 257 (3d Cir. 2002) (local rule constitutes "order of the court"; therefore, motion for attorney's fees filed 28 days after judgment pursuant to local rule not untimely); Weyent v. Okst, 198 F.3d 311, 315 (2d Cir. 1999) (motion for attorney's fees in connection with opposing defendant's post-trial motions was timely because it was filed within 14 days of resolution of those motions); Jones v. Central Bank, 161 F.3d 311, 313 (5th Cir. 1998) (motion for attorney's fees timely when filed 15 days after judgment but within 30-day limit for filing such motion under local rule); King v. Town of Hanover, 72 FEP 120, 121 (D.N.H. 1996) (motion for attorney's fees 17 days after entry of judgment untimely).

5. Effect of Settlement

To extinguish the prevailing party's claim for attorney's fees, the parties to a settlement must do so specifically and expressly within the terms of the agreement.[346]

IV. THE PREVAILING DEFENDANT'S RIGHT TO ATTORNEY'S FEES

Section 706(k) of Title VII provides that "the court, in its discretion, may allow the prevailing party . . . a reasonable attorney's fee."[347] The statute, by using the term "prevailing *party*," as opposed to "prevailing *plaintiff*," suggests that prevailing defendants should be entitled to fees on the same basis as prevailing plaintiffs. This interpretation, however, was rejected by the Supreme Court in *Christiansburg Garment Co. v. EEOC.*[348] In noting that prevailing plaintiffs are different from prevailing defendants, the Court declared:

> First, . . . the plaintiff is the chosen instrument of Congress to vindicate "a policy that Congress considered of the highest priority." Second, when a district court awards counsel fees to a prevailing plaintiff, it is awarding them against a violator of federal law. As the Court of Appeals clearly perceived, "these policy considerations which support the award of fees to a prevailing plaintiff are not present in the case of a prevailing defendant."[349]

On the other hand, the *Christiansburg Garment* Court declared, Congress plainly intended to discourage groundless actions. Examining the legislative history, the Court detected sentiment that

> allowance of awards to defendants would serve "to deter the bringing of lawsuits without foundation," "to discourage frivolous suits," and

---

[346]Torres v. Metropolitan Life Ins. Co., 189 F.3d 331, 335 (3d Cir. 1999) (Title VII settlement agreement silent on issue of attorney's fees will not be deemed to constitute waiver); Hartsoe v. Kmart Retail Distrib. Ctr., 2000 U.S. Dist. LEXIS 4789 (E.D. Pa. Apr. 17, 2000) (when parties to settlement agreement dispute whether prevailing party waived its statutory right to attorney's fees, "the burden is on the losing party to show that the settlement agreement clearly waived" this right).

[347]42 U.S.C. § 2000e-5(k) (2000).

[348]434 U.S. 412, 16 FEP 502 (1978).

[349]*Id.* at 418–19 (citations omitted).

2964 EMPLOYMENT DISCRIMINATION LAW CH. 41.IV

"to diminish the likelihood of unjustified suits being brought." If anything can be gleaned from these fragments of legislative history, it is that while Congress wanted to clear the way for suits to be brought under the Act, it also wanted to protect defendants from burdensome litigation having no legal or factual basis.[350]

Balancing the competing considerations, the Court held that a trial court "may in its discretion award attorney's fees to a prevailing defendant in a Title VII case upon a finding that the plaintiff's action was frivolous, unreasonable, or without foundation, even though not brought in subjective bad faith."[351]

The Court further explained that its fees test could be applied both when the litigation was *brought*, and also as it *evolved*; fees thus can be awarded if

a court finds that [the plaintiff's] claim was frivolous, unreasonable, or groundless, *or that the plaintiff continued to litigate after it clearly became so.* And, needless to say, if a plaintiff is found to have brought *or continued* such a claim in bad faith, there will be an even stronger basis for charging him with the attorney's fees incurred by the defense.[352]

Following the standard enunciated in *Christiansburg Garment*, courts have awarded defendants attorney's fees in cases where a plaintiff's claims were "frivolous, unreasonable, or without foundation, even though not brought in subjective bad faith."[353]

---

[350]*Id.* at 420 (footnotes omitted).

[351]*Id.* at 421.

[352]*Id.* at 422 (emphasis added).

[353]*Id.* at 421; *see, e.g., First Circuit*: EEOC v. Caribe Hilton Int'l, 821 F.2d 74, 76 (1st Cir. 1987) (plaintiff not credible and employer had tried to accommodate his religion). *Second Circuit*: Prate v. Freedman, 583 F.2d 42, 48, 17 FEP 1572 (2d Cir. 1978) (action found to be vexatious and unreasonable within meaning of *Christiansburg Garment*). *Third Circuit*: Quiroga v. Hasbro, Inc., 934 F.2d 497, 504–05, 57 FEP 1320 (3d Cir. 1991) (action so frivolous that case was remanded to consider Rule 11 award). *Fourth Circuit*: Arnold v. Burger King Corp., 719 F.2d 63, 66 (4th Cir. 1983) (frivolous lawsuit by plaintiff fired for persistent sexual harassment). *Fifth Circuit*: Dean v. Riser, 240 F.3d 505, 511 (5th Cir. 2001) (vacating and remanding denial of defendant's attorney's fees to determine prevailing party status and apply *Christiansburg Garment* standards). *Sixth Circuit*: Wilson-Simmons v. Lake County Sheriff's Dep't, 207 F.3d 818, 823–24 (6th Cir. 2000) (awarding attorney's fees against both plaintiff and her attorneys who failed to advise plaintiff against pursuing unfounded claim or to terminate her action when its futility was obvious). *Seventh Circuit*: Adkins v. Briggs & Stratton Corp., 159 F.3d 306, 307, 8 AD 1298 (7th Cir. 1998) (reversing district court's denial of attorney's fees to prevailing defendant, stating "a district court cannot, however, backpedal from a frivolous finding on a motion to dismiss to

Although determining whether a plaintiff's claims are frivolous, unreasonable, or without foundation must be done on a case-by-case basis, the Eleventh and Third Circuits have identified three factors to guide the inquiry: (1) whether the plaintiff established a prima facie case; (2) whether the defendant offered to settle; and

---

avoid imposing fees"). *Eighth Circuit*: Meriwether v. Caraustar Packaging Co., 326 F.3d 990, 994, 91 FEP 978 (8th Cir. 2003) (affirming award of attorney's fees to defendant under *Christiansburg Garment* standard where material contradictions existed in plaintiff's submissions). *Ninth Circuit*: EEOC v. Bruno's Rest., 59 FEP 1516, 1518–19 (9th Cir. 1992) (witnesses not credible and success depended on their credibility). *Tenth Circuit*: Allen v. Lucero, 108 F.3d 1388 (table), 1997 WL 143712 (10th Cir. Mar. 31, 1997) (upholding district court's award of attorney's fees to prevailing defendant under § 1988 where district court accurately determined that plaintiff's underlying claim was groundless and without foundation in law or fact). *Eleventh Circuit*: Baker v. Alderman, 158 F.3d 516, 525 (11th Cir. 1998) (upholding district court's award of attorney's fees to prevailing defendant under § 1988 where plaintiff failed to establish prima facie case, defendant did not offer to settle, and district court granted summary judgment in defendant's favor). *D.C. Circuit*: Harris v. Group Health Ass'n, 662 F.2d 869, 874, 26 FEP 969 (D.C. Cir. 1981) (fees awarded for appeal because appellant had no legal or factual basis for appeal). *But see First Circuit*: Bercovitch v. Baldwin Sch., Inc., 191 F.3d 8, 11–12, 9 AD 1210 (1st Cir. 1999) (denying fees applying *Christiansburg Garment* standard to nonemployment ADA case). *Second Circuit*: Parker v. Sony Pictures Ent'mt, Inc., 260 F.3d 100, 111–12, 12 AD 1 (2d Cir. 2001) (reversing award of fees where disability claim was strong enough to get to jury). *Third Circuit*: EEOC v. L.B. Foster Co., 123 F.3d 746, 753, 78 FEP 485 (3d Cir. 1997) (finding some factual basis for each claim, reversing award of fees for defendant where district court merely rejected EEOC's evidence). *Fourth Circuit*: Glymph v. Spartanburg Gen. Hosp., 783 F.2d 476, 479–80 (4th Cir. 1986) (plaintiff's claim not frivolous where defendant lost its summary judgment motion and court denied motion for dismissal after plaintiff presented evidence at trial). *Fifth Circuit*: Alizadeh v. Safeway Stores, Inc., 910 F.2d 234, 239 (5th Cir. 1990) (attorney's fee award to defendant vacated and remanded in § 1988 case). *Sixth Circuit*: Wrenn v. Gould, 808 F.2d 493, 504–05, 42 FEP 1133 (6th Cir. 1987) (reversing award of defendant's fees in § 1988 case where facts disputed and law unsettled). *Seventh Circuit*: Johnson v. Artim Transp. Sys., 826 F.2d 538, 551 (7th Cir. 1987) (prevailing union not entitled to attorney's fees because plaintiff's arguments not entirely groundless). *Eighth Circuit*: EEOC v. Kenneth Balk & Assocs., 813 F.2d 197, 198 (8th Cir. 1987) (reversing defendant's award of attorney's fees because EEOC had some basis for claims; no summary judgment or directed verdict sought). *Ninth Circuit*: Summers v. Teichert & Sons, Inc., 127 F.3d 1150, 1154, 7 AD 830 (9th Cir. 1997) (attorney's fees to prevailing defendant denied under 42 U.S.C. § 12205 given *Christiansburg Garment* standard). *Tenth Circuit*: Figures v. Board of Pub. Utils., 967 F.2d 357, 362 (10th Cir. 1992) (employment discrimination action not frivolous in light of racial remarks made by board members). *Eleventh Circuit*: Bonner v. Mobile Energy Servs. Co., 246 F.3d 1303, 1305, 85 FEP 1182 (11th Cir. 2001) (though racial discrimination claim was abandoned when opposing summary judgment and plaintiffs adduced no admissible evidence to support gender discrimination claim, action not so "patently devoid of merit as to be frivolous").

(3) whether the trial court dismissed the case prior to trial or held a full-blown trial on the merits.[354] In determining whether a plaintiff's claims are frivolous, courts have also examined whether the claims were factually or legally groundless.[355]

Courts have also applied the *Christiansburg Garment* standard to award fees to defendants when it becomes apparent during the pendency of the action that the plaintiff's claims are not well taken[356]—even, in some instances, after a trial on the merits[357]—or

---

[354]*See* Quintana v. Jenne, 414 F.3d 1306, 1309, 95 FEP 1761 (11th Cir. 2005); Sullivan v. School Bd. of Pinellas County, 773 F.2d 1182, 1189, 39 FEP 53 (11th Cir. 1985); EEOC v. L.B. Foster Co., 123 F.3d 746, 751, 78 FEP 485 (3d Cir. 1997) (citing *Sullivan*); *see also* Sayers v. Stewart Sleep Ctr., Inc., 140 F.3d 1351, 1354, 76 FEP 1399 (11th Cir. 1998) (citing Walker v. NationsBank of Fla., 53 F.3d 1548, 1558–59, 68 FEP 314 (11th Cir. 1995) (citing *Sullivan*)).

[355]*See, e.g.*, Bruce v. City of Gainesville, 177 F.3d 949, 951–52, 9 AD 734 (11th Cir. 1999) (case not so legally and factually groundless as to justify attorney's fees); Adkins v. Briggs & Stratton Corp., 159 F.3d 306, 307, 8 AD 1298 (7th Cir. 1998) (finding plaintiff's ADA claim frivolous where neither plaintiff nor employer knew of plaintiff's disability until well after plaintiff's termination); Newhouse v. McCormick & Co., 130 F.3d 302, 304, 75 FEP 648 (8th Cir. 1997) (plaintiff continued to litigate in face of controlling precedent that removed every colorable basis in law for plaintiff's position).

[356]*See* Turner v. Sungard Bus. Sys., Inc., 91 F.3d 1418, 1423 (11th Cir. 1996) (fact that plaintiff may have had reasonable basis for suit when filed insufficient to avoid fee award where claims became frivolous during pendency of case); Marquart v. Lodge 837, 26 F.3d 842, 849, 64 FEP 1789 (8th Cir. 1994) (prevailing defendant entitled to fees if suit is frivolous when filed or if it becomes so during course of proceedings).

[357]*See* No Barriers, Inc. v. Brinker Chili's Texas, Inc., 262 F.3d 496, 499–500 (5th Cir. 2001) (defendant awarded fees after bench trial on nonemployment ADA claim where plaintiff failed to sue proper party and failed to present evidence supporting its theory at trial); Flowers v. Jefferson Hosp. Ass'n, 49 F.3d 391, 393 (8th Cir. 1995) (rejecting argument that denial of summary judgment precludes award of fees to defendant; "it may sometimes be necessary for defendants to 'blow away the smoke screens the plaintiff had thrown up' before the defendants may prevail"); Introcase v. Cunningham, 857 F.2d 965, 967 (4th Cir. 1988) (awarding defendant's attorney's fees after jury trial on merits); Little v. Ford Motor Co., 9 AD 830, 830 (W.D. Mo. 1999) (awarding defendant attorney's fees on one of two claims after jury trial because evidence revealed no foundation in law or facts for plaintiff's disability claim); Torretto v. I.B. Diffusion, L.P., 1997 U.S. Dist. LEXIS 15989, at *10 (N.D. Ill. Sept. 30, 1997) (prevailing defendant awarded attorney's fees where trial judge found plaintiff's quid pro quo sexual harassment and hostile work environment claims under Title VII embodied wanton, malicious, and vexatious litigation and abuse of process); Daramola v. Westinghouse Elec. Corp., 872 F. Supp. 1418, 1420 (W.D. Pa. 1995) (awarding fees to defendant after trial on merits based on plaintiff's "willingness to lie and fabricate evidence so as to use this to punish Westinghouse").

where an appeal is groundless.[358] The EEOC may also be held liable for fees upon an appropriate showing.[359]

Christiansburg Garment fee awards, because they are "costs," normally run against the opposing party, not counsel.[360]

Although a plaintiff sometimes may be entitled to a fee for *securing* interim relief,[361] it does not necessarily follow that a defendant is entitled to a fee for successfully *resisting* interim relief.[362] A plaintiff's voluntary dismissal requires an initial determination that the defendant was a prevailing party before the *Christiansburg Garment* standard applies to the fees request.[363]

---

[358]*E.g.*, Bugg v. Industrial Workers (AIW) Local 507, 674 F.2d 595, 600 n.10, 28 FEP 40 (7th Cir.) (proper focus is on frivolity of appeal; district court determination that original action was frivolous not necessary), *appeal dismissed*, 459 U.S. 805 (1982); *see also* Hilmon Co. v. Hyatt Int'l, 899 F.2d 250, 254 (3d Cir. 1990) ($23,393 award for frivolous appeal); Bacon v. State, County, & Mun. Employees No. 13, 795 F.2d 33, 34–35, 42 FEP 1520 (7th Cir. 1986) (fees awarded on appeal even though not requested); Reynolds v. Humko Prods., 756 F.2d 469, 473–74, 37 FEP 294 (6th Cir. 1985) (case remanded to determine damages or costs against plaintiff or his attorney, or both, for frivolous appeal); *cf.* Johnson v. Allyn & Bacon, Inc., 731 F.2d 64, 74, 34 FEP 804 (1st Cir. 1984) (defendant awarded recovery of double costs on appeal but no attorney's fees). *But cf.* Wrenn v. Gould, 808 F.2d 493, 504–05, 42 FEP 1133 (6th Cir. 1987) (although plaintiff was overly litigious, court did not find appeal frivolous, unreasonable, or unfounded).

[359]EEOC v. Hendrix Coll., 53 F.3d 209, 211, 76 FEP 465 (8th Cir. 1995) (EEOC litigated ADEA action in bad faith); EEOC v. Bruno's Rest., 59 FEP 1516, 1518–19 (9th Cir. 1992) (witnesses not credible and success depended on their credibility); EEOC v. Caribe Hilton Int'l, 821 F.2d 74, 76 (1st Cir. 1987) (EEOC acted unreasonably and without foundation in bringing case).

[360]*E.g.*, Corneveaux v. CUNA Mut. Ins. Group, 76 F.3d 1498, 1509, 70 FEP 247 (10th Cir. 1996) (Title VII does not permit recovery from counsel); Smith v. Detroit Fed'n of Teachers Local 231, 829 F.2d 1370, 1374 (6th Cir. 1987) (award under § 1988 can only be charged against losing party, not counsel); Hamer v. County of Lake, 819 F.2d 1362, 1370 (7th Cir. 1987) (same); Durrett v. Jenkins Brickyard, Inc., 678 F.2d 911, 915 (11th Cir. 1982) (same); Prate v. Freedman, 583 F.2d 42, 48, 17 FEP 1572 (2d Cir. 1978) ("[i]n our legal system, an attorney is his client's agent and representative; the client retains ultimate authority over the conduct of the litigation"). *But cf.* Quiroga v. Hasbro, Inc., 934 F.2d 497, 503–04, 57 FEP 1320 (3d Cir. 1991) (district court's award of $10,000 in attorney's fees proper, but case was remanded to determine whether award should be levied against plaintiff or his attorney).

[361]*See* Section II.H *supra*.

[362]Howard v. Roadway Express, Inc., 726 F.2d 1529, 1536, 34 FEP 341 (11th Cir. 1984) (defendant who defeats one recovery theory presented as part of request for summary judgment relief is not yet entitled to recover fees and costs).

[363]Dean v. Riser, 240 F.3d 505, 511 (5th Cir. 2001) (requiring demonstration that plaintiff voluntarily withdrew claim to avoid disfavorable judgment on merits). *But cf.* Marquart v. Lodge 837, 26 F.3d 842, 852 (8th Cir. 1994) (requiring favorable judicial determination on merits for prevailing party status).

A Title VII defendant cannot recover attorney's fees in costs recovered pursuant to a Rule 68 offer of judgment because by definition the plaintiff must prevail in some measure before the rule goes into effect.[364]

The ADEA fee section, in contrast to Title VII, specifies that "in addition to any judgment awarded to the plaintiff or plaintiffs," the court shall "allow a reasonable attorney's fee to be paid by the defendant, and costs of the action."[365] As this section addresses only prevailing plaintiffs, rather than "prevailing parties," courts usually decline to award attorney's fees to prevailing defendants in ADEA cases except when the plaintiff proceeded in bad faith.[366] In ADEA cases brought by the EEOC, courts apply the Equal Access to Justice Act,[367] which allows the defendant an attorney's fee where the government's position was not substantially justified.[368]

Once a defendant's *entitlement* to fees is established, courts take different approaches to the *calculation* of them. Some courts say that the calculation of fees is the same for defendants as for plaintiffs.[369] However, other courts consider the financial status of

---

[364]Le v. University of Pa., 321 F.3d 403, 411 (3d Cir. 2003) (Rule 68 does not apply if defendant wins lawsuit, and some victory by plaintiff belies claim that plaintiff's claim was frivolous).

[365]29 U.S.C. § 216(b) (2000).

[366]*See, e.g.*, Turlington v. Atlanta Gas Light Co., 135 F.3d 1428, 1437–38 (11th Cir. 1998) (vacating award of fees to prevailing defendant in ADEA case and remanding for determination of bad faith); EEOC v. Hendrix Coll., 53 F.3d 209, 211, 76 FEP 465 (8th Cir. 1995) (defendant in ADEA case awarded fees only where plaintiff litigated in bad faith); Gray v. New Eng. Tel. & Tel. Co., 792 F.2d 251, 260 & n.1 (1st Cir. 1986) (fee award under ADEA must be based on bad faith of plaintiff); Morgan v. Union Metal Mfg., 757 F.2d 792, 796, 37 FEP 625 (6th Cir. 1985) (plaintiff maintained suit in bad faith after he summarily rejected offer of reinstatement, full seniority, and back pay); Richardson v. Alaska Airlines, Inc., 750 F.2d 763, 767 (9th Cir. 1984) (prevailing defendants may not recover fees under ADEA). *But see* Colbert v. Yadkin Valley Tel. Membership Corp., 960 F. Supp. 84, 86 (M.D.N.C. 1997) (awarding fees under *Christiansburg Garment* standard to prevailing defendant on assumption that it is comparable to bad faith standard).

[367]28 U.S.C. § 2412 (2000).

[368]EEOC v. O & G Spring & Wire Forms Specialty Co., 38 F.3d 872, 883 (7th Cir. 1994) (no award of fees to employer that defended ADEA claim against EEOC pursuant to EAJA); EEOC v. Clay Printing Inc., 13 F.3d 813, 817 (4th Cir. 1994) (because ADEA is silent as to attorney's fees for prevailing defendant, EAJA standard applies).

[369]*E.g.*, Miller v. Los Angeles County Bd. of Educ., 827 F.2d 617, 621 (9th Cir. 1987) (requiring court to analyze fee award under 12-factor test); Arnold v. Burger King Corp., 719 F.2d 63, 67, 32 FEP 1769 (4th Cir. 1983) (court simply arrived at fee "by multiplying the number of hours spent on each party's defense by a reasonable hourly attorney's fee").

the plaintiff as a basis for reducing the level of fees,[370] but not denying fees entirely.[371] Some courts also adjust costs for the same reason.[372]

---

[370]Gibbs v. Clements Food Co., 949 F.2d 344, 345 (10th Cir. 1991) (plaintiff's financial condition relevant factor in award of attorney's fees to prevailing defendant); Alizadeh v. Safeway Stores, Inc., 910 F.2d 234, 239 (5th Cir. 1990) ($33,750 attorney's fee award to defendant vacated and remanded for reconsideration in light of plaintiff's limited financial resources and ability to pay); Miller, 827 F.2d at 621 (after calculation of lodestar and 12-factor test, court should consider financial resources of plaintiff); Charves v. Western Union Tel. Co., 711 F.2d 462, 465 (1st Cir. 1983) ("The district court was quick to recognize that an award of attorney's fees to a prevailing defendant must not be oblivious of a plaintiff's financial capacity."); Faraci v. Hickey-Freeman Co., 607 F.2d 1025, 1029, 20 FEP 1777 (2d Cir. 1979) ("the court below should have ascertained whether, in light of [the plaintiff's] ability to pay, a lesser sum assessed would have fulfilled the statute's deterrent purpose without subjecting him to financial ruin"; $200 fee awarded). But cf. Munson v. Friske, 754 F.2d 683, 697 (7th Cir. 1985) (amount of award is equitable matter, but with due consideration of plaintiff's financial circumstances, entire award stands); National Org. for Women v. Bank of Cal., 680 F.2d 1291, 1293–94, 29 FEP 300 (9th Cir. 1982) (upholding lower court's finding that plaintiffs could afford attorney's fees awarded to prevailing defendant).

[371]Alizadeh, 910 F.2d at 238 (plaintiff's financial status not proper factor to consider in determining whether to award attorney's fees against that party; however, nonprevailing party's inability to pay should be considered when determining amount of attorney's fees to be awarded against that party); Miller, 827 F.2d at 621 (court should not refuse to award fees solely because of plaintiff's indigence); Durrett v. Jenkins Brickyard, Inc., 678 F.2d 911, 917, 29 FEP 58 (11th Cir. 1982) (when awarding attorney's fees to defendant, district court should consider plaintiff's financial resources, but should not deny fees entirely solely because of plaintiff's insolvency); Smith v. Continental Ins. Corp., 747 F. Supp. 275, 285, 61 FEP 640 (D.N.J. 1990) ("Lest a $1,000.00 penalty not adequately convey the message it is intended to convey, I will be blunt: while this court is, as it must be, solicitous of pro se litigants, pro se status will not insulate an individual when he or she, dragging opposing counsel along the way, determines to make this court her personal playground."), aff'd mem., 941 F.2d 1203 (3d Cir. 1991). But see Marquardt v. North Am. Car Corp., 652 F.2d 715, 719 (7th Cir. 1981) (dictum in ERISA case, stating that "[a] party's ability personally to satisfy a fee award, especially that of a plaintiff of limited means, has been held, in and of itself, to be an adequate basis for denying a defendant's motion for attorney's fees") (citing Wooten v. New York Tel. Co., 485 F. Supp. 748, 762 (S.D.N.Y. 1980)).

[372]Chapman v. AI Transport, 229 F.3d 1012, 1040, 83 FEP 1849 (11th Cir. 2000) (court has discretion to consider proof of nonprevailing party's financial condition in setting costs award, but is not required to do so); Smith v. Southeastern Pa. Transp. Auth., 47 F.3d 97, 100 (3d Cir. 1995) (same); Wrighten v. Metropolitan Hosps., Inc., 726 F.2d 1346, 1357–58, 33 FEP 1714 (9th Cir. 1984) (case remanded with instructions to reassess costs based on plaintiff's limited financial resources and fact that plaintiff should have prevailed on issue of retaliatory discharge); Badillo v. Central Steel & Wire Co., 717 F.2d 1160, 1165, 32 FEP 1679 (7th Cir. 1983) (proper for court to consider plaintiff's indigency). But see Cherry v. Champion Int'l Corp., 186 F.3d

V. INTERVENORS AND ATTORNEY'S FEES

A. Prevailing Intervenors

Courts have discretion to award attorney's fees to prevailing intervenors.[373] For example, an intervening plaintiff who seeks and obtains modification of a consent decree that increases the relief provided under the decree may recover attorney's fees.[374] One case even allowed fees to persons whose motion to intervene was denied as untimely, under the theory that the putative intervenors' arguments benefited the class by improving the settlement.[375]

B. Unsuccessful Intervenors

In *Flight Attendants v. Zipes*,[376] the Supreme Court held that the *Christiansburg Garment* standard governed awards of attorney's

---

442, 446 (4th Cir. 1999) (court must have sound basis to deny full costs to prevailing party, and modest means of plaintiff did not support denial); Corder v. Lucent Techs., Inc., 162 F.3d 924, 929, 8 AD 1611 (7th Cir. 1998) (plaintiff's unsupported allegations of indigence insufficient to reduce award of costs).

[373]*Compare* EEOC v. Clear Lake Dodge, 25 F.3d 265, 272, 65 FEP 376 (5th Cir. 1994) (attorney's fees denied to intervenor in EEOC-initiated suit that was relatively simple; because EEOC already was paying attorneys to prosecute it, it would have been windfall to pay for another lawyer), *aff'd in part*, 60 F.3d 1146, 68 FEP 663 (5th Cir. 2005) *and* Grove v. Mead Sch. Dist. No. 354, 753 F.2d 1528, 1535 (9th Cir. 1985) (§ 1988 attorney's fee awards to intervenors should not be granted unless intervenor plays significant role in litigation) *with* St. Louis Fire Fighters Ass'n v. City of St. Louis, 96 F.3d 323, 331 (8th Cir. 1996) (remanding case for determination of reasonable attorney's fee award for intervenors where success in Title VII and § 1981 action was more than de minimus) *and* Davis v. Board of Sch. Comm'rs, 600 F.2d 470, 475, 22 FEP 1579 (5th Cir. 1979) (intervenors allowed attorney's fees for establishing violation of Title VII even though their individual claims fail).

[374]Ensley Branch, NAACP v. Seibels, 31 F.3d 1548, 1582–83 (11th Cir. 1994) (where class of male nonblack employees sought to intervene to modify consent decrees and court modified decrees, intervenors were entitled to attorney's fees); Miller v. Staats, 706 F.2d 336, 342, 31 FEP 976 (D.C. Cir. 1983) ("threshold of discrimination" test applied to fee claimants improper; they deserved to be awarded their fees based on their successful role in obtaining modifications in consent decree).

[375]Alaniz v. California Processors, Inc., 13 FEP 738, 742 (N.D. Cal. 1976) (formal "party" status not necessary to be treated as "prevailing party" under Title VII). *But see* Latin Am. Law Enforcement Ass'n v. City of L.A., 29 F.3d 633 (table), 1994 WL 383884 (9th Cir. July 21, 1994) (rare instance where attorney's fees assessed against third-party intervenors for unsuccessful appeal where they challenged denial based on untimeliness without meaningful explanation for failure to bring timely motion to intervene or any argument to support their position).

[376]491 U.S. 754, 759–61, 50 FEP 47 (1989).

fees against losing intervenors. Thus, such awards will be made "only where the intervenors' action was frivolous, unreasonable, or without foundation."[377]

Most cases that have applied the *Christiansburg Garment* standard have denied fee requests against intervenors.[378] Pre-*Zipes* cases that awarded fees[379] may be persuasive but are not necessarily authoritative.

One case holds that a losing intervenor in an ADEA suit cannot be held liable for fees at all.[380]

VI. Income Tax Consequences of a Plaintiff's Attorney's Fee Award

The tax status of awards of attorney's fees and costs to successful plaintiffs in employment discrimination cases has caused substantial litigation.[380a] Prior to October 2004, the Internal Revenue Service took the position that such awards, whether achieved by judgment or settlement, could not be excluded from the plaintiff's gross income where the attorney represented the plaintiff on a contingent fee arrangement. Accordingly, such an award could be treated only as a miscellaneous itemized deduction for the plaintiff, often resulting in very adverse tax consequences because of both the limitations on

---

[377]*Id.* at 760.

[378]*E.g.*, Davis v. City & County of S.F., 890 F.2d 1438, 1452, 51 FEP 1542 (9th Cir. 1989) (attorney's fees not awarded against intervening union whose intervention was not frivolous, unreasonable, or without foundation); Paradise v. Prescott, 626 F. Supp. 117, 118, 39 FEP 1744 (M.D. Ala. 1985) (pre-*Zipes* case; plaintiffs could not be awarded attorney's fees incurred in defeating defendant-intervenors because intervenors were "functionally plaintiffs," and plaintiffs failed to show that intervenors' claims were "frivolous," "unreasonable," or "without foundation").

[379]*E.g.*, Thompson v. Sawyer, 586 F. Supp. 635, 638, 34 FEP 1327 (D.D.C. 1984) (plaintiffs awarded $37,461 in attorney's fees expended in defeating union's three attempts to intervene); Vulcan Soc'y v. Fire Dep't, 533 F. Supp. 1054, 1058–59, 1063–65, 34 FEP 1691 (S.D.N.Y. 1982) (attorney's fees awarded to prevailing plaintiff against defendant and intervenors; allocation based on relative responsibilities of defendant and intervenors in incurring those fees).

[380]Richardson v. Alaska Airlines, Inc., 750 F.2d 763, 765, 36 FEP 986 (9th Cir. 1984) (labor union held not liable; ADEA does not provide for recovery of attorney's fees from anyone except employer).

[380a]The following discussion of tax-related issues is intended to be expository only, and is not intended to provide tax advice to any individual.

such deductions and the alternative minimum tax.[381] As a result, some plaintiffs actually ended up paying more in federal income taxes than they personally received in the judgment or settlement.

Congress addressed this inequity in the American Jobs Creation Act of 2004. The Act, which went into effect on October 22, 2004, allows a taxpayer in computing adjusted gross income to deduct "attorney fees and court costs paid by, or on behalf of, the taxpayer in connection with any action involving a claim of unlawful discrimination."[382] The Act defines "unlawful discrimination" broadly to include any discrimination claim arising under a federal, state, or local civil rights statute; the FLSA; a federal whistleblower statute; and any federal, state, or local law "regulating any aspect of the employment relationship . . . or prohibiting the discharge of any employee, the discrimination against an employee, or any other form of retaliation or reprisal against an employee for asserting rights or taking other actions permitted by law."[383] Thus, where an attorney's fee award is considered income to the plaintiff in an employment case, it must be reported on the plaintiff's tax return as income, but it is then fully deductible. The Act applies to all fees and costs paid in cases settled or reaching judgment after October 22, 2004.[384]

Prior to the Act, the circuits were divided over whether such a fee award could be excluded from a taxpayer's gross income.[385] A few months after Congress passed the Act, the Supreme Court took up the issue in *Commissioner v. Banks*.[386] *Banks* involved two separate actions. In one, the plaintiff, Banks, filed a federal civil rights

---

[381]*See generally* Internal Revenue Code § 104, 26 U.S.C. § 104 (2000).

[382]Internal Revenue Code, 26 U.S.C.A. § 62(a)(20) (Supp. 2006).

[383]*Id.* § 62(e)(18).

[384]Pub. L. No. 108-357, Title VII, § 703(c) (Oct. 22, 2004), 118 Stat. 1548 ("The amendments made by this section shall apply to fees and costs paid after the date of the enactment of this Act with respect to any judgment or settlement occurring after such date.").

[385]*See* Kenseth v. Commissioner, 259 F.3d 881, 885 (7th Cir. 2001) (gross income includes fee award); Young v. Commissioner, 240 F.3d 369, 378–39 (4th Cir. 2001) (same); Baylin v. United States, 43 F.3d 1451, 1454–55 (Fed. Cir. 1995) (same). *But see* Davis v. Commissioner, 210 F.3d 1346, 1347 (11th Cir. 2000) (under Alabama law regarding attorneys' liens, portion of judgment paid to attorneys pursuant to contingency arrangement not income to taxpayer).

[386]125 S. Ct. 826 (2005).

suit. In the other, the plaintiff, Banaitis, sued in state court alleging employment-related tort claims. Both plaintiffs settled their cases and paid their attorneys pursuant to the terms of their contingency fee retainer agreements. Neither plaintiff reported as income on his tax return the portion of the settlement recovery that he paid to his attorney as a contingency fee. Both plaintiffs were held liable by the U.S. Tax Court for filing deficient returns.

On review, the Supreme Court noted that "had the [American Jobs Creation Act of 2004] been in force for the transactions under review, these cases likely would not have arisen. The Act is not retroactive, however, so while it may cover future taxpayers in respondents' position, it does not pertain here."[387] The Court went on to address the proper resolution of the issue for pre-Act awards.

The Court reasoned that the Internal Revenue Code defines gross income for federal tax purposes as "all income from whatever source derived."[388] In the case of litigation recovery, the income-generating asset is the cause of action that derives from the plaintiff's injury.[389] A contingency fee agreement is an anticipatory assignment to the attorney of the plaintiff's income from the litigation recovery; in other words, the contingency fee is still a portion of the plaintiff's income.[390] Thus, when a plaintiff settles his or her statutory or tort claims and calculates the attorney's fee solely on the basis of the contingent fee agreement, the entire settlement amount, including the portion that is to be paid to counsel as attorney's fees, constitutes the plaintiff's taxable income.[391]

Banks, the federal civil rights plaintiff, had argued that treating the attorney's fees as the plaintiff's income would be inconsistent with the purpose of statutory fee-shifting provisions because it could lead to the perverse result of the plaintiff losing money by winning the suit. The Court declined to address that claim and did not determine whether attorney's fees awarded by a court under

---

[387]*Id.* at 831.

[388]*Id.* (citing 26 U.S.C. § 61(a)). *But* see Murphy v. IRS, 460 F.3d 79 (D.C. Cir. 2006) (taxation of noneconomic damages for emotional distress and loss of reputation violates Sixteenth Amendment to U.S. Constitution), *vacated*, 2006 U.S. App. LEXIS 32293 (D.C. Cir. Dec. 22, 2006).

[389]125 S. Ct. at 832.

[390]*Id.* at 831.

[391]*Id.* at 834.

a fee-shifting statute constitute the plaintiff's taxable income.[392] The Court similarly declined to address whether a contingent fee paid to the attorney in lieu of statutory fees must be included in the plaintiff's taxable income.[393]

---

[392]125 S. Ct. at 834.

[393]*Id.* The Court also did not address attorney's fees paid or awarded to plaintiffs' counsel in class actions, where fees generally are paid pursuant to a court order rather than a retainer agreement. Under the reasoning in *Banks*, absent contingent fee agreements with absent class members granting the attorney a portion of the class members' awards, there would be no anticipatory assignment of income to the attorney, and the fees therefore would not be reportable as class members' income. This analysis, however, may not apply with respect to named plaintiffs in a class action, or nonnamed plaintiffs who actually have a representation agreement with plaintiffs' counsel, depending on the nature of their respective retention agreements.

CHAPTER 42

ALTERNATIVE DISPUTE RESOLUTION

I. INTRODUCTION

For decades, private settlement efforts between opposing counsel constituted the only meaningful form of alternative dispute resolution (ADR) used in employment cases. In more recent years, however, both mediation and arbitration have played an increasingly important role in the resolution of discrimination claims. The substantive issues involved in settling employment disputes are addressed in Chapter 43 (Settlement). This chapter deals predominantly with the issues arising from the spread of private arbitration agreements and with the use of neutrals or judicial officers to mediate employment claims.

II. AUTHORITY FOR ARBITRATION

A. The Federal Arbitration Act

The law of claim adjudication and resolution through arbitration has deep roots in traditional labor law, but only since the Supreme Court's 1991 decision in *Gilmer v. Interstate/Johnson Lane Corp.*[1] has arbitration been applied to discrimination claims in nonunionized settings. An agreement to arbitrate claims is contractual and allows parties to resolve statutory claims outside of a judicial forum.[2] As the U.S. Supreme Court confirmed in *Circuit City Stores, Inc. v. Adams*,[3] private employment arbitration agreements are enforceable by virtue of the Federal Arbitration Act (FAA),[4] subject to the limitations imposed by the FAA and general state contract law on formation and enforceability of contracts.

---

[1]500 U.S. 20, 24, 55 FEP 1116 (1991).

[2]*See* Mitsubishi Motors Corp. v. Soler Chrysler-Plymouth, Inc., 473 U.S. 614, 623 (1985).

[3]532 U.S. 105, 85 FEP 266 (2001) (FAA applies to contracts of employment in interstate commerce, except for interstate transportation workers).

[4]9 U.S.C. § 1 et seq. (2000).

In *Gilmer*, the Supreme Court observed that arbitration affects only the choice of forum, not substantive rights.[5] Hence, "so long as the prospective litigant effectively may vindicate [his or her] statutory cause of action in the arbitral forum, . . . [the arbitration of statutory claims] will continue to serve both its remedial and deterrent function."[6]

The FAA is the principal statutory scheme that governs individual agreements to arbitrate.[7] Congress enacted the FAA to reverse the longstanding judicial hostility to arbitration agreements that American courts had adopted and to place arbitration agreements on the same footing as other contracts.[8] The provisions of the FAA "manifest a liberal federal policy favoring arbitration agreements."[9]

---

[5]500 U.S. at 26 (quoting Mitsubishi Motors Corp. v. Soler Chrysler-Plymouth, Inc., 473 U.S. 614, 623 (1985)).

[6]500 U.S. at 28 (quoting *Mitsubishi Motors*, 473 U.S. at 628); *see also* Circuit City Stores, Inc. v. Adams, 532 U.S. 105, 123 (2001) (reciting same standard).

[7]Congress enacted the FAA in 1925, reenacted it in 1947, and codified it at 9 U.S.C. § 1 et seq. The FAA's primary substantive provisions are contained in §§ 1 through 4 of the Act:

Section 1. "Maritime transactions" and "commerce" defined; exceptions to operation of title. "Maritime transactions," as herein defined, means charter parties, bills of lading of water carriers, . . . or any other matters in foreign commerce which, if the subject of controversy, would be embraced within admiralty jurisdiction; "commerce," as herein defined, means commerce among the several States . . . but nothing herein contained shall apply to contracts of employment of seamen, railroad employees, or any other class of workers engaged in foreign or interstate commerce.

Section 2. Validity, irrevocability, and enforcement of agreements to arbitrate. A written provision in any maritime transaction or a contract evidencing a transaction involving commerce to settle by arbitration a controversy . . . arising out of such a contract, . . . shall be valid, irrevocable, and enforceable, save upon such grounds as exist at law or in equity for the revocation of any contract.

Section 3. Stay of proceedings where issue therein referable to arbitration. If any suit or proceeding be brought in any of the courts of the United States upon any issue referable to arbitration under an agreement in writing for such arbitration, the court . . . shall on application of one of the parties stay the trial of the action until such arbitration has been had . . . .

Section 4. Failure to arbitrate under agreement; petition to United States court having jurisdiction for order to compel arbitration; notice and service thereof; hearing and determination. A party aggrieved by the alleged failure, neglect, or refusal of another to arbitrate under a written agreement for arbitration may petition any United States district court . . . for an order directing that such arbitration proceed in the manner provided for in such agreement . . . .

[8]*Gilmer*, 500 U.S. at 24.

[9]*Id.* at 25 (citations omitted).

B. The Supreme Court Decisions Concerning Private Employment Arbitration

In *Alexander v. Gardner-Denver Co.*,[10] the plaintiff alleged that he was wrongfully discharged because of his race. The Court had to decide whether the plaintiff's Title VII statutory right to a trial de novo could be foreclosed where he had earlier submitted his dispute to final arbitration under the nondiscrimination clause of a collective bargaining agreement (CBA).[11]

The Supreme Court found that the CBA's nondiscrimination clause was a contractual right, not a statutory right, and did not exclude a civil action.[12] The Court reasoned that, at trial, the employee was asserting a statutory right independent of the arbitration process, as opposed to judicial review of the arbitrator's decision. Accordingly, the employee was permitted to pursue both remedies.[13] The Court stated that "arbitral procedures, while well suited to the resolution of contractual disputes, make arbitration a comparatively inappropriate forum for the final resolution of rights created by Title VII."[14]

In *Mitsubishi Motors Corp. v. Soler Chrysler-Plymouth, Inc.*,[15] a case involving transnational corporations' claims against each other, the Court opined that "we are well past the time when judicial suspicion of the desirability of arbitration and of the competence of arbitral tribunals inhibited the development of arbitration as an alternative means of dispute resolution."[16] The Court found nothing inherent in the FAA to support disfavoring agreements to arbitrate statutory claims.[17] The Court noted that by agreeing to arbitrate a statutory claim, a party does not forgo the substantive rights afforded by the statute.[18] Instead, the party trades the procedures and opportunity for review of the courtroom for the "simplicity, informality and expedition of arbitration."[19] The Supreme

---

[10]415 U.S. 36, 7 FEP 81 (1974).
[11]*Id.* at 38.
[12]*Id.* at 47.
[13]*Id.* at 52, 54, 59–60.
[14]*Id.* at 56.
[15]473 U.S. 614 (1985).
[16]*Id.* at 627.
[17]*Id.*
[18]*Id.* at 628.
[19]*Id.*

Court continued to endorse expansion of arbitration in *Dean Witter Reynolds, Inc. v. Byrd*,[20] *Shearson/American Express, Inc. v. McMahon*,[21] and *Rodriguez de Quijas v. Shearson/American Express, Inc.*[22]

The first case to reach the Supreme Court regarding the enforceability of a private arbitration agreement in an employment setting, but not involving a collective bargaining agreement, was *Gilmer v. Interstate/Johnson Lane Corp.*[23] The issue in *Gilmer* was whether a claim brought under the Age Discrimination in Employment Act (ADEA) could be subjected to compulsory arbitration.[24] Gilmer, a broker, had executed a Uniform Application for Securities Industry Registration or Transfer (Form U-4), as mandated by the National Association of Securities Dealers (NASD), which required him to submit any employment claims to arbitration.[25] The Supreme Court reiterated its position that statutory claims were subject to arbitration agreements and that where the parties have made a bargain to arbitrate, they should be held to their bargain, unless Congress itself "evinced an intention to preclude a waiver of judicial remedies for the statutory rights at issue."[26] These intentions, in turn, will be found in the text of the statutory claim, its legislative history, or in the case of "inherent conflict between arbitration and the [statute's] underlying purposes."[27] Gilmer could not show that anything in the text of the ADEA or its legislative history explicitly precluded arbitration.[28] The Court also rejected

---

[20]470 U.S. 213 (1987) (state law securities claims).

[21]482 U.S. 220 (1987) (federal securities claims and claims under the Racketeer Influenced and Corrupt Organizations Act (RICO)).

[22]490 U.S. 477 (1989) (federal securities claims).

[23]500 U.S. 20, 55 FEP 1116 (1991).

[24]*Id.* at 23.

[25]The Form U-4 is a contract between the registrant and the NASD, not between the registrant and his or her firm. *Id.* at 25 n.2. Amendments to NASD Rule 10201 and New York Stock Exchange (NYSE) Rules 347 and 600, effective January 1, 1999, provide that the NASD and NYSE will not arbitrate statutory employment discrimination claims based solely on the mandatory arbitration provisions contained in a Form U-4. *See* Order Granting Approval to Proposed Rule Change Relating to the Arbitration of Employment Discrimination Claims, Exchange Act Release No. 40,109 (June 22, 1998), 63 Fed. Reg. 35,299 (June 29, 1998); Order Approving Proposed Rule Change by the New York Stock Exchange, Inc. Relating to Arbitration Rules, Exchange Act Release No. 40,858 (Dec. 29, 1998), 64 Fed. Reg. 1051 (Jan. 7, 1999).

[26]*Gilmer*, 500 U.S. at 26 (internal quotes and citations omitted).

[27]*Id.* at 26 (internal quotes and citations omitted).

[28]*Id.* at 26–27.

Gilmer's contentions that because the ADEA was designed not only to address individual claims, but also to further important social policies, it would be undermined by the arbitration process[29] or that arbitration would undermine the role of the Equal Employment Opportunity Commission (EEOC) in enforcing the ADEA.[30] The Court also rejected Gilmer's generalized attacks on the adequacy of arbitration procedures, finding them "out of step with our current strong enforcement of . . . this method of resolving disputes."[31] The Court thus erased the generalized criticisms of arbitration of employment discrimination disputes voiced in *Gardner-Denver* and opened the door to the wholesale use of individual arbitration agreements in employment relationships.

Following *Gilmer*, courts of appeals have upheld the general enforceability of mandatory arbitration agreements for claims based on Title VII, the Americans with Disabilities Act (ADA), and other civil rights statutes.[32] Many issues have arisen, however, regarding enforceability with respect to the circumstances and characteristics of particular employers' agreements.

In *Wright v. Universal Maritime Service Corp.*,[33] the issue was "whether a general arbitration clause in a [CBA] requires an employee to use the arbitration procedure for an alleged violation

---

[29]*Id.* at 27.

[30]*Id.* at 28.

[31]*Id.* at 30 (citation omitted).

[32]*See* EEOC v. Luce, Forward, Hamilton & Scripps, 345 F.3d 742, 748–53, 92 FEP 1121 (9th Cir. 2003) (en banc) (ADA and Title VII) (overruling Duffield v. Robertson Stephens & Co., 144 F.3d 1182, 76 FEP 1450 (9th Cir. 1998)); Rosenberg v. Merrill Lynch, Pierce, Fenner & Smith, Inc., 170 F.3d 1, 7 (1st Cir. 1999) (Title VII); Koveleskie v. SBC Capital Mkts., Inc., 167 F.3d 361, 368, 79 FEP 73 (7th Cir. 1999) (Title VII); Desiderio v. National Ass'n of Secs. Dealers, 191 F.3d 198, 206, 80 FEP 1731 (2d Cir. 1999) (Title VII); Seus v. John Nuveen & Co., 146 F.3d 175, 182, 77 FEP 751 (3d Cir. 1998) (Title VII), *abrogated on other grounds by* Blair v. Scott Specialty Gases, 283 F.3d 595, 599–602 (3d Cir. 2002); Patterson v. Tenet Healthcare, Inc., 113 F.3d 832, 837, 73 FEP 1822 (8th Cir. 1997) (Title VII and Missouri Human Rights Act); Cole v. Burns Int'l Sec. Servs., 105 F.3d 1465, 1482–83, 72 FEP 1775 (D.C. Cir. 1997) (Title VII); Austin v. Owens-Brockway Glass Container, Inc., 78 F.3d 875, 882, 70 FEP 272 (4th Cir. 1996) (Title VII); Metz v. Merrill Lynch, Pierce, Fenner & Smith, Inc., 39 F.3d 1482, 1487, 66 FEP 439 (10th Cir. 1994) (Title VII); Bender v. A.G. Edwards & Sons, Inc., 971 F.2d 698, 700, 59 FEP 1231 (11th Cir. 1992) (Title VII); Alford v. Dean Witter Reynolds, Inc., 939 F.2d 229, 230, 56 FEP 1046 (5th Cir. 1991) (Title VII); Willis v. Dean Witter Reynolds, Inc., 948 F.2d 305, 307, 57 FEP 386 (6th Cir. 1991) (Title VII).

[33]525 U.S. 70, 8 AD 1429 (1998).

of statutory protections against discrimination." Wright sought to pursue an ADA claim in federal court, bypassing (on his union's recommendation) the collectively bargained grievance procedure. On the basis of its prior decision in *Austin v. Owens-Brockway Glass Container, Inc.*,[34] that an arbitration provision in a CBA could preclude a civil action under Title VII, the Fourth Circuit affirmed the dismissal of Wright's claim.[35]

The Supreme Court sidestepped the tension between its holdings in *Gardner-Denver* and *Gilmer*, finding instead that the particular CBA in *Wright* did not create a "clear and unmistakable waiver" of the right to a judicial forum, as required by the Labor-Management Relations Act (LMRA),[36] and therefore did not preclude litigation in the federal court.[37] The *Wright* Court observed that its decision in *Gardner-Denver* "at least stands for the proposition that the right to a federal judicial forum is of sufficient importance to be protected against less-than-explicit union waiver in a CBA."[38] The Court declined, however, to "reach the question whether such a waiver would [ever] be enforceable."[39]

In *Circuit City Stores, Inc. v. Adams*,[40] the Supreme Court resolved another issue that *Gilmer* left unanswered: whether the FAA's exclusion from coverage of "contracts of employment of seamen, railroad employees, or any other class of workers engaged in foreign or interstate commerce" applies to *all* contracts of employment.[41] The Ninth Circuit Court of Appeals found that the FAA did not apply to contracts of employment and therefore the arbitration agreement between Adams and Circuit City was not subject to the FAA.[42] The Supreme Court applied the maxim ejusdem

---

[34]78 F.3d 875, 70 FEP 272 (4th Cir. 1996).

[35]Wright v. Universal Mar. Serv. Corp., 121 F.3d 702 (4th Cir. 1997).

[36]29 U.S.C. § 185 et seq. (2000).

[37]*Wright*, 525 U.S. at 79–80 (citing Metropolitan Edison Co. v. NLRB, 460 U.S. 693, 708 (1983)).

[38]525 U.S. at 80; *see also* Eastern Associated Coal Corp. v. Massey, 373 F.3d 530 (4th Cir. 2004) (coal miner need not arbitrate his statutory discrimination claims because CBA did not expressly waive right to litigate).

[39]525 U.S. at 82.

[40]532 U.S. 105, 85 FEP 266 (2001).

[41]*Id.* at 112; *see also* Gilmer v. Interstate/Johnson Lane Corp., 500 U.S. 20, 25 n.2, 55 FEP 1116 (1991).

[42]Circuit City Stores, Inc. v. Adams, 194 F.3d 1070, 81 FEP 720 (9th Cir. 1999) (Adams' agreement to arbitrate was contained in his employment application). Nine

generis to the residual phrase "any other class of workers engaged in . . . commerce" following specific reference to "seamen" and "railroad employees." Rather than giving the phrase open-ended construction, which would subsume those specific categories of workers within the phrase "engaged in . . . commerce," the Court found that § 1 of the FAA exempts only contracts of employment of transportation workers.[43] The Court recognized that its holding would mean that state laws restricting or limiting arbitration agreements between employees and employers would be preempted by the FAA.[44] Further expanding the FAA's reach, the Court found that although its earlier cases, such as *Gilmer*, concerned federal statutory rights, judicial enforcement of a state statute must also await the outcome of arbitration.[45] Thus, other than bona fide transportation workers and the hypothetical case that may be deemed beyond interstate commerce, federal law would appear to govern the enforcement of all private agreements to arbitrate employment disputes not asserted pursuant to a CBA[46] and to preempt state arbitration law concerning such disputes.[47]

---

other circuits reached the opposite conclusion. *See Adams*, 532 U.S. at 111; McWilliams v. Logicon, Inc., 143 F.3d 573, 575–76, 8 AD 225 (10th Cir. 1998); O'Neil v. Hilton Head Hosp., 115 F.3d 272, 274, 12 IER Cases 1579 (4th Cir. 1997); Pryner v. Tractor Supply Co., 109 F.3d 354, 358, 73 FEP 615 (7th Cir. 1997); Cole v. Burns Int'l Sec. Servs., 105 F.3d 1465, 1470–72, 72 FEP 1775 (D.C. Cir. 1997); Rojas v. TK Commc'ns, Inc., 87 F.3d 745, 747–48, 71 FEP 664 (5th Cir. 1996); Asplundh Tree Expert Co. v. Bates, 71 F.3d 592, 596–601 (6th Cir. 1995); Erving v. Virginia Squires Basketball Club, 468 F.2d 1064, 1069 (2d Cir. 1972); Dickstein v. DuPont, 443 F.2d 783, 785 (1st Cir. 1971); Tenney Eng'g, Inc. v. Electrical Workers (UE), 207 F.2d 450 (3d Cir. 1953).

[43]*Adams*, 532 U.S. at 119.

[44]*Id*. at 122.

[45]*Id*. at 119; *see, e.g.*, Marcus v. Superior Court of Cal. for County of Orange, 75 Cal. App. 3d 204, 209 (Cal. Ct. App. 1977) (court may stay pending state actions until arbitration is completed in accordance with order to arbitrate).

[46]Additional sources of federal law governing arbitration under CBAs include decades of administrative and decisional law under the Railway Labor Act, 45 U.S.C. § 151 et seq., and § 301 of the Labor Management Relations Act (LMRA), 29 U.S.C. § 185. Although a survey of traditional labor law as applied to individuals is beyond the purview of this book, we note here that when an employment discrimination claim would require a court to interpret or alter a CBA term, the case may fall within the preemptive sweep of federal labor law.

[47]*See, e.g.*, Oblix, Inc. v. Winiecki, 374 F.3d 488, 492, 93 FEP 1833 (7th Cir. 2004) ("if a state . . . imposes on form arbitration clauses more or different requirements from those imposed on other clauses, then its approach is preempted by § 2" of the FAA); Adkins v. Labor Ready, Inc., 303 F.3d 496, 506 (4th Cir. 2002) (West

The *Circuit City* Court did not, however, decide which employees are "engaged in commerce" and thus are not subject to FAA coverage. In *Harden v. Roadway Package Systems, Inc.*,[48] a Ninth Circuit panel held that a driver employed by a nationwide pickup and delivery service who handled packages coming into and going out of state could not be compelled to arbitrate his discrimination claims.[49]

In *EEOC v. Waffle House*,[50] the Supreme Court affirmed that, notwithstanding a private arbitration agreement, the EEOC may pursue victim-specific remedies for individual employees through civil litigation. The Court overruled the holding of some circuits

---

Virginia law purporting to bar compulsory arbitration of West Virginia Human Rights Act claims preempted by federal law); Whitley v. Carolina Neurosurgical Assocs., 2002 WL 1009721, at *2 (M.D.N.C. Feb. 6, 2002) (doctors in local medical practice must arbitrate under FAA where practice "treats patients from other states, accepts payments from out-of-state and multi-state insurance carriers, and receives goods from out-of-state vendors"); Meyer v. Starwood Hotels & Resorts Worldwide, Inc., 85 FEP 878 (S.D.N.Y. 2001) (employee in hotel within interstate commerce for FAA purposes); Topf v. Warnaco, Inc., 942 F. Supp. 762, 772 (D. Conn. 1996) (provision in Connecticut Employment Practices Act expressly permitting suit notwithstanding arbitration clause preempted); *cf.* Johnson v. Apna Ghar, Inc., 330 F.3d 999, 1003 (7th Cir. 2003) (not-for-profit employer that provides residential, social, and legal services for the poor held to be "a person engaged in an industry affecting commerce" under Title VII), *cert. denied*, 124 S. Ct. 482 (2003).

[48]249 F.3d 1137, 85 FEP 1604 (9th Cir. 2001).

[49]*Id.* at 1142; *see also* Hill v. Rent-a-Center, Inc., 398 F.3d 1286, 1290, 95 FEP 245 (11th Cir. 2005) (FAA's "engaged in commerce" exemption applies to class of workers employed in transportation industry who actually engage in transportation of goods in interstate commerce; exemption does not extend to account manager who makes incidental deliveries of merchandise out of state in employer's truck); Palcko v. Airborne Express, Inc., 372 F.3d 588, 593–94, 596, 93 FEP 1775 (3d Cir. 2004) (rejecting employer's argument that "engaged in commerce" exemption is limited to employee truck drivers who physically move packages, holding that FAA's exemption applies to truck drivers' direct supervisor whose job duties include " 'monitoring and improving the performance of drivers under [her] supervision to ensure timely and efficient delivery of packages,' " but finding agreement enforceable under state law), *cert. denied*, 543 U.S. 1049 (2005); Brown v. Nabors Offshore Corp., 339 F.3d 391, 393–94 (5th Cir. 2003) (seaman falls within exception); Valdes v. Swift Transp. Co., 292 F. Supp. 2d 524 (S.D.N.Y. 2003) (finding interstate motor carrier driver exempt from FAA, but enforcing agreement under state law); Gagnon v. Service Trucking, Inc., 266 F. Supp. 2d 1361, 1364 (M.D. Fla. 2003) (because parties were engaged in interstate commerce, FAA preempted Florida's Arbitration Act, but owner-operators of tractor trailers were exempt from FAA because they transported goods across state lines; arbitration agreement unenforceable), *vacated*, 2004 U.S. Dist. LEXIS 2217 (Feb. 3, 2004).

[50]534 U.S. 279 (2002).

limiting the EEOC under such circumstances to purely injunctive or classwide relief.[51]

C. Other Federal and State Sources of Arbitration Law

Supreme Court decisions outside the employment context also establish that the FAA generally supersedes conflicting state law that is specifically directed at arbitration. The sweep of this preemption is very broad. In *Doctor's Associates, Inc. v. Casarotto*,[52] the Supreme Court invalidated a state statute that required references to arbitration in a contract to be in bold print on the ground that it was preempted by the FAA's strong policy in favor of arbitration. Moreover, the Supreme Court has held that § 2 of the FAA extends to the limits of Congress' Commerce Clause power.[53] Further, in *Southland Corp. v. Keating*,[54] the Court held that the FAA applies not only to cases in federal court but also to state-law claims in state court proceedings, and preempts all contrary state law concerning the enforceability of arbitration agreements.[55]

The arbitration of employment discrimination disputes nevertheless continues to proceed under state arbitration law in some circumstances. Public employee disputes, for instance, may be subject to arbitration under local rules.[56] Or the parties may have consented to application of a state law rather than federal arbitration procedure, an approach specifically countenanced by the Supreme Court in *Volt Information Sciences, Inc. v. Board of Trustees of Leland Stanford Junior University*.[57] In *Little v. Auto Stiegler, Inc.*,[58] the California Supreme Court held that in an employment case involving mandatory arbitration, the FAA did not preempt a

---

[51]*See* EEOC v. Kidder, Peabody & Co., 156 F.3d 298, 77 FEP 1212 (2d Cir. 1998) (allowing EEOC to pursue injunctive relief in federal court but precluding monetary relief); Merrill Lynch, Pierce, Fenner & Smith, Inc. v. Nixon, 210 F.3d 814 (8th Cir. 2000) (same).

[52]517 U.S. 681 (1996).

[53]Allied-Bruce Terminix Cos. v. Dobson, 513 U.S. 265, 277 (1995).

[54]465 U.S. 1 (1984).

[55]*Id.* at 6.

[56]*See, e.g.*, City of New Bedford v. Massachusetts Comm'n Against Discrimination, 440 Mass. 450, 455, 799 N.E.2d 578, 583 (2003) (police officer).

[57]489 U.S. 468, 478–79 (1989) (parties to arbitration agreement may incorporate state law procedures even when their operation may be inconsistent with FAA).

[58]29 Cal. 4th 1064, 63 P.3d 979, 130 Cal. Rptr. 2d 892 (Cal. 2003).

state court decision that an arbitration agreement silent on fees imposes costs entirely on the employer. The court so held notwithstanding the U.S. Supreme Court's decision in *Green Tree Financial Corp.-Alabama v. Randolph*,[59] eschewing such a categorical rule.[60]

Although state arbitration law is generally superseded by the FAA, under § 2 of the FAA state contract law governs the validity and interpretation of, and defenses to, arbitration agreements.[61]

There is a split in the circuits on preemption under the Railway Labor Act (RLA). In *Brown v. Illinois Central Railroad*,[62] the Seventh Circuit considered the clash of the RLA with the ADA. The RLA compels arbitration of claims statutorily designated as "minor disputes," defined as claims "grow[ing] out of grievances or out of the interpretation or application of agreements covering rates of pay, rules, or working conditions."[63] In *Brown*, the plaintiff trainman requested, as an accommodation of a psychiatric condition, that he be permitted to take off two days a week. He was instead found by the employer to be medically disqualified for employment because he was not available seven days a week, as the employer contended was required by the CBA. The Seventh Circuit held that since the availability of a reasonable accommodation in this case inevitably required consideration of the CBA, the controversy constituted a "minor dispute" that was statutorily consigned to arbitration, even though the source of the claim itself was a civil rights statute. Emphasizing to readers the "limited scope of [its] holding," the court stated that a "claim brought under an independent federal statute is precluded by the RLA only if it can be dispositively resolved through an interpretation of a CBA."[64] By contrast, the Ninth Circuit in *Saridakis v. United Airlines*[65] denied preemption of the ADA in the face of a claim by a former drug user that he was unlawfully discharged under a "last chance agreement" in the wake of a positive drug test. The court held that although the ADA claim hinged on whether the plaintiff was properly

---

[59]531 U.S. 79 (2000).
[60]*Little*, 29 Cal. 4th at 1085.
[61]9 U.S.C. § 2 (2000); *see* Section III.B.2 *infra*.
[62]254 F.3d 654 (7th Cir. 2001).
[63]45 U.S.C. § 151a (2000).
[64]*Brown*, 254 F.3d at 668.
[65]166 F.3d 1272 (9th Cir. 1999).

fired under the CBA, its resolution depended on legal standards extrinsic to the CBA itself and thus was not preempted by the RLA.[66]

In *Humble v. Boeing Co.*,[67] the Ninth Circuit also rejected a preemption argument under § 301 of the LMRA. The plaintiff there sought relief under the state of Washington's Law Against Discrimination.[68] As in *Brown*, the plaintiff raised a reasonable accommodation claim that the employer violated its obligations under a CBA to maintain a seniority system for transferring to lighter duty work. The Ninth Circuit held that "the mere need to refer to a CBA to determine the jobs for which a disabled employee might be eligible may not be sufficient to trigger § 301 preemption, even if such consultation is certain to occur."[69] Where such an inquiry is "only potential and limited," the court held, there was no preemption.[70]

III. PROCEDURES AND ENFORCEMENT OF ARBITRATION AGREEMENTS

A. Introduction

In the wake of *Circuit City Stores, Inc. v. Adams*,[71] federal courts face a wide array of issues concerning the enforceability of mandatory predispute agreements to arbitrate individual employment claims. The bulk of the cases discussed below arose in the context of motions to dismiss or to compel arbitration where the plaintiff sought to have the entire arbitration agreement declared unenforceable. In some cases, courts have allowed claims to proceed to arbitration even in the face of doubt, reserving issues of fairness and reasonableness of the procedures for the arbitrator and

---

[66]*Id.* at 1276–77; *see also* Bates v. Long Island R.R., 997 F.2d 1028, 1034–35 (2d Cir. 1993) (RLA did not preclude Rehabilitation Act claim even though it implicated portions of CBA; "absent the same rights and procedures provided in federal court, arbitration should not be the sole forum for final resolution of federal civil rights claims").

[67]305 F.3d 1004 (9th Cir. 2002).

[68]WASH. REV. CODE § 49.60.020 (1995).

[69]305 F.3d at 1010.

[70]*Id.* at 1011.

[71]532 U.S. 105, 85 FEP 266 (2001).

subsequent judicial review.[72] As this is a developing area of law, the issues discussed below may take on a new cast with a fully developed arbitral record.[73]

B. Formation of Arbitration Agreements

1. Arbitration Required as a Condition of Employment

Since *Gilmer*, the Supreme Court has implicitly endorsed the employers' requirement of arbitration agreements as a condition of employment. In *Circuit City Stores, Inc. v. Adams*[74] and *EEOC v. Waffle House*,[75] the Court again implicitly, though not expressly, approved the use of mandatory arbitration agreements. A number of circuit courts have reviewed arbitration agreements imposed as a condition of employment when determining whether the agreements were procedurally unconscionable or otherwise void. They have reached divergent results.

In *Circuit City Stores, Inc. v. Adams*,[76] on remand from the Supreme Court, the Ninth Circuit concluded that the employer's

---

[72]*See, e.g.*, Great W. Mortgage Corp. v. Peacock, 110 F.3d 222, 229–30, 73 FEP 856 (3d Cir. 1997) (arbitration agreement included provisions waiving employee's right to attorney's fees and punitive damages and imposing 1-year statute of limitations on discrimination claims; court did not hold terms unenforceable as matter of law, but instead referred matters to arbitrator to determine validity of waivers); Johnson v. Hubbard Broad., Inc., 940 F. Supp. 1447, 1462, 73 FEP 8 (D. Minn. 1996) (upholding enforceability of agreement, but noting that if arbitrator finds that provision requiring both parties to bear own attorney's fees would bar award of fees to prevailing plaintiff, then agreement would violate federal law and be unenforceable).

[73]*See, e.g.*, Brown v. ITT Consumer Fin. Corp., 211 F.3d 1217, 1223, 82 FEP 1388 (11th Cir. 2000) (arbitrator did not engage in manifest disregard of law by applying possibly erroneous standard for proof of retaliation); Williams v. Cigna Fin. Advisors, Inc., 197 F.3d 752, 81 FEP 747 (5th Cir. 1999) (expanding its narrow review of arbitration awards, court adopted "manifest disregard of the law standard" under which arbitration award will be upheld if, on basis of information available to court, it is not manifest that arbitrator acted contrary to applicable law; if it is concluded that arbitrator did act in manifest disregard of law, award should still be upheld unless it would result in significant injustice); Halligan v. Piper Jaffray, 148 F.3d 197, 203–04, 77 FEP 182 (2d Cir. 1998) (overwhelming evidence against employer combined with lack of written opinion supports finding that arbitrator's decision was in manifest disregard of law); DeGaetano v. Smith Barney, Inc., 983 F. Supp. 459, 462–64, 75 FEP 579 (S.D.N.Y. 1997) (arbitrator's failure to award attorney's fees to prevailing plaintiff after award was requested was in manifest disregard of law).

[74]532 U.S. 105, 109, 85 FEP 266 (2001).

[75]534 U.S. 279, 281 (2002).

[76]279 F.3d 889, 893 (9th Cir. 2002).

arbitration agreement, which was contained in its application for employment, was unenforceable. The court found that the agreement—which was drafted by a party with superior bargaining power and provided the weaker party the option of adhering to its terms or rejecting it (in which case the employer would not consider the application for employment)—was a procedurally unconscionable contract of adhesion.[77] In another *Circuit City* case that applied Ohio's contract law, the Sixth Circuit found a similar version of Circuit City's arbitration agreement not to be procedurally unconscionable.[78] Ohio law directs courts to consider the age, education, and intelligence of the parties when evaluating whether an agreement process is procedurally unconscionable. In doing so, the court reasoned that although the bargaining power of the parties was unequal (the agreement was drafted by Circuit City and was not open to negotiation), it was not unconscionable because the plaintiff was a well-educated graduate of the Air Force Academy who held a master's degree.[79]

The enforceability of employer-imposed arbitration agreements depends on the governing state's contract law[80] and the facts of the individual cases, including the prominence and clarity of the arbitration agreement,[81] whether the employee acknowledged the

---

[77]*Id.* at 891–93.

[78]Morrison v. Circuit City Stores, Inc., 317 F.3d 646, 666, 90 FEP 1697 (6th Cir. 2003); *see also* Oblix, Inc. v. Winiecki, 374 F.3d 488, 490–91, 93 FEP 1833 (7th Cir. 2004) (standard form arbitration agreement offered on take-it-or-leave-it basis not per se unconscionable).

[79]*Morrison*, 317 F.3d at 666–67.

[80]*See* Section III.B.2 *infra*.

[81]*See* Rosenberg v. Merrill Lynch, Pierce, Fenner & Smith, Inc., 170 F.3d 1, 20–21 (1st Cir. 1999) (finding *Wright*'s requirement that union's waiver of right to judicial forum must be "clear and unmistakable" requires some "minimal level of notice" that an employee's statutory claims are subject to arbitration); Eastern Associated Coal Corp. v. Massey, 373 F.3d 530 (4th Cir. 2004) (arbitration agreement not enforced as CBA did not expressly waive right to litigate). *But see* Hadnot v. Bay, Ltd., 344 F.3d 474, 478, 92 FEP 1090 (5th Cir. 2003) (arbitration agreement as condition for accepting job application enforceable).

Cases declining to enforce arbitration agreements: Penn v. Ryan's Family Steak Houses, Inc., 269 F.3d 753 (7th Cir. 2001) (contract too vague about commitment of arbitration firm hired to provide services); Bailey v. Federal Nat'l Mortgage Ass'n, 209 F.3d 740, 82 FEP 1089 (D.C. Cir. 2000) (employee did not intend to be bound by new arbitration policy promulgated post-employment); Kummetz v. Tech Mold, Inc., 152 F.3d 1153, 1156 (9th Cir. 1998) (employee handbook not arbitration agreement where "clear implication of these clauses [in acknowledgment] is that the Booklet contained a set of non-contractual policies unilaterally established by Tech Mold"); Nelson v.

arbitration requirement,[82] whether the employee had a "meaningful choice,"[83] and whether the employee was well-educated.[84]

Cyprus Bagdad Copper Corp., 119 F.3d 756, 760–62 (9th Cir. 1997) ("Complaint Resolution Policy" provisions in employee handbook, which in some cases required arbitration, insufficiently clear and unambiguous to constitute waiver of rights); Sherry v. Sisters of Charity Med. Ctr., 5 WH 2d 1132 (E.D.N.Y. 1999) ("grievance procedure" in employee handbook that is avowedly not compulsory is not arbitration agreement); Trumbull v. Century Mktg. Corp., 12 F. Supp. 2d 683, 686–88, 77 FEP 571 (N.D. Ohio 1998) (failure to include language that clearly states that statutory claims will be arbitrated makes agreement invalid); Sportelli v. Circuit City Stores, Inc., 1998 WL 54335 (E.D. Pa. Jan. 13, 1998) (finding that employee opted out of company arbitration program); J.M. Davidson, Inc. v. Webster, 2003 Tex. LEXIS 527 (Tex. Dec. 31, 2003) (remanding case where it was unclear whether employer could terminate arbitration policy unilaterally); Davis v. Powertel, Inc., 776 So. 2d 971, 975 (Fla. Dist. Ct. App. 2000) (cell phone provider "attempted to modify its contracts with customers after the fact, by including an insert in the customer's bill stating the terms of the existing contracts would be changed to add an arbitration provision as of a certain date").

[82]*See* Marino v. Dillard's, Inc., 2005 WL 1439892 (5th Cir. June 21, 2005) (Louisiana law did not require employee's written consent to arbitration policy); May v. Higbee Co., 372 F.3d 757, 94 FEP 44 (5th Cir. 2004) (employee assented to arbitration both by signing acknowledgment of receiving policy and by continuing to work for employer); Blair v. Scott Specialty Gases, 283 F.3d 595, 603–04 (3d Cir. 2002) (arbitration clause in employee handbook acknowledged by employee enforceable); Hightower v. GMRI, Inc., 272 F.3d 239, 87 FEP 461 (4th Cir. 2001) (employee who attended meeting about company's new arbitration plan, signed acknowledgment, and continued his employment assented to plan); Johnson v. Circuit City Stores, 148 F.3d 373, 77 FEP 139 (4th Cir. 1998) (agreements under which job applicant and employer agree to arbitration held binding), *aff'd*, 203 F.3d 821 (4th Cir. 2000); McWilliams v. Logicon, Inc., 143 F.3d 573 (10th Cir. 1998) (arbitration agreement signed in job-acceptance letter held binding). *But see* Campbell v. General Dynamics Gov't Sys. Corp., 407 F.3d 546, 16 AD 1361 (1st Cir. 2005) (e-mail notice to employees of mandatory arbitration policy did not create binding agreement where e-mail did not require return acknowledgment, failed to inform employee that policy waived judicial forum, and lacked clarity about whether arbitration term was contractual in nature); Mouton v. Metropolitan Life Ins. Co., 147 F.3d 453, 78 FEP 1697 (5th Cir. 1998) (arbitration clause need not refer directly to employment disputes to require arbitration of Title VII claims); Rojas v. TK Commc'ns, Inc., 87 F.3d 745, 71 FEP 664 (5th Cir. 1996) (broad arbitration clause covering "any other disputes" required arbitration of Title VII claims); Nghiem v. NEC Elec., Inc., 25 F.3d 1437, 1439–40, 64 FEP 1669 (9th Cir. 1994) (enforcing policy in employment manual); Bishop v. Smith Barney, Inc., 1998 WL 50210 (S.D.N.Y. Feb. 6, 1998) (enforcing arbitration clause in employee manual without individual assent; written company policy sufficient under FAA); Leonard v. Clear Channel Commc'ns, I, 1997 WL 581439 (W.D. Tenn. Jul. 24, 1997) (enforcing unsigned, unacknowledged arbitration agreement in employment manual).

[83]*See* Potts v. Baptist Health Sys., Inc., 853 So. 2d 194 (Ala. 2002) (plaintiff's failure to show she would have been able to find other employment were she to be fired for failing to sign agreement does not constitute lack of "meaningful choice" under Alabama law).

[84]Morrison v. Circuit City Stores, Inc., 317 F.3d 646, 666–67, 90 FEP 1697 (6th Cir. 2003) (well-educated plaintiff with master's degree).

2. Contract Law: Unconscionability and Mutuality

Because the FAA "directs courts to place arbitration agreements on equal footing with other contracts," they are subject to the same defenses to enforcement that apply to contracts generally.[85] Therefore, when evaluating the validity of an agreement, federal courts "should apply ordinary state law principles that govern the formation of contracts."[86] That includes the forum state's choice-of-law rules,[87] which vary significantly among states.

Courts are divided over whether relinquishment of the federal judicial forum and jury right requires a knowing and voluntary waiver or is governed instead by ordinary contract principles. Most courts have applied a contract standard, holding that arbitration must be compelled if the parties agreed to the term and it is supported by consideration.[88]

Two circuits, the Ninth and the First, have taken different approaches. The Ninth Circuit, in *Prudential Insurance Co. of America v. Lai*,[89] held that the "text and legislative history of Title VII" require that an employee "knowingly agree[] to submit such disputes to arbitration."[90] Thus, in the Ninth Circuit, courts must determine whether employees knowingly and voluntarily waived

---

[85]Ingle v. Circuit City Stores, Inc., 328 F.3d 1165, 1170, 91 FEP 1426 (9th Cir. 2003), *cert. denied*, 124 S. Ct. 1169 (2004).

[86]*Ingle*, 328 F.3d at 1170 (citing First Options of Chi., Inc. v. Kaplan, 514 U.S. 938, 944 (1995)); *see also* Gold v. Deutsche Aktiengesellschaft, 365 F.3d 144, 149, 93 FEP 1125 (2d Cir. 2004) (general principles of contract law determine whether an employee's claims are subject to mandatory arbitration), *cert. denied*, 543 U.S. 874 (2004).

[87]*See* Cap Gemini Ernst & Young, U.S. v. Nackel, 346 F.3d 360, 365 (2d Cir. 2003).

[88]*See, e.g.*, Gold v. Deutsche Aktiengesellschaft, 365 F.3d 144, 149–50, 93 FEP 1125 (2d Cir. 2004) (declining to follow contrary approach of First Circuit); Seus v. John Nuveen & Co., 146 F.3d 175, 183–84 n.2, 77 FEP 751 (3d Cir. 1998); Patterson v. Tenet Healthcare, Inc., 113 F.3d 832, 834–35, 73 FEP 1822 (8th Cir. 1997); Great W. Mortgage Corp. v. Peacock, 110 F.3d 222, 229–30, 73 FEP 856 (3d Cir. 1997); Hart v. Canadian Imperial Bank of Commerce, 43 F. Supp. 2d 395, 400–01, 81 FEP 31 (S.D.N.Y. 1999); Beauchamp v. Great W. Life Assurance Co., 918 F. Supp. 1091, 1097–98, 73 FEP 361 (E.D. Mich. 1996); Maye v. Smith Barney, Inc., 897 F. Supp. 100, 107, 68 FEP 1648 (S.D.N.Y. 1995); *cf.* Gibson v. Neighborhood Health Clinics, Inc., 121 F.3d 1126, 1129–30, 8 AD 483 (7th Cir. 1997) (noting split authority).

[89]42 F.3d 1299, 66 FEP 933 (9th Cir. 1994).

[90]*Id.* at 1304–05.

their right to a judicial forum.[91] In *Rosenberg v. Merrill Lynch, Pierce, Fenner & Smith, Inc.*,[92] the First Circuit appeared to split the difference between the opposing "contract versus waiver" views. It held that § 118 of the Civil Rights Act of 1991 governed the standard of review and that the court must determine whether the arbitration clause is "appropriate" under the facts of the case. Thus, in *Rosenberg*, where the employer failed to provide the employee with the NASD rules for arbitration (as required by Form U-4 at the time the agreement is signed), the employee's waiver was deemed not "appropriate" under the circumstances, and therefore she was not bound by the arbitration clause.[93]

A contract will not be enforced in any jurisdiction if it is found to be unconscionable, although what is unconscionable varies by jurisdiction. Under California law, for example, unconscionability is an absence of meaningful choice on the part of one party, together with contract terms that unreasonably favor the other party.[94] In other jurisdictions, the employee must show (1) an absence of meaningful choice, (2) unreasonably unfavorable contractual terms, (3) unequal bargaining power, and (4) oppressive or unfair terms in the contract.[95]

In *Armendariz v. Foundation Health Psychcare Services, Inc.*,[96] the California Supreme Court held that although arbitration agreements may be enforced against employees, such agreements may constitute unlawful adhesion contracts unless they preserve substantial statutory rights, such as those under the state's Fair Employment and Housing Act. The court explained that the judicially

---

[91]*See, e.g.*, Kummetz v. Tech Mold, Inc., 152 F.3d 1153, 1155 (9th Cir. 1998); Nelson v. Cyprus Bagdad Copper Corp., 119 F.3d 756, 760–61 (9th Cir. 1997); Renteria v. Prudential Ins. Co. of Am., 113 F.3d 1104, 1105–06, 73 FEP 1581 (9th Cir. 1997).

[92]170 F.3d 1 (1st Cir. 1999).

[93]*Id.* at 19–21.

[94]*See* Armendariz v. Foundation Health Psychcare Servs., Inc., 24 Cal. 4th 83, 99 Cal. Rptr. 2d 745, 6 P.3d 669, 690, 83 FEP 1172 (Cal. 2000).

[95]Potts v. Baptist Health Sys., Inc., 853 So. 2d 194, 204–05 (Ala. 2002); *see also* Cooper v. MRW Inv. Co., 367 F.3d 493, 503–05, 93 FEP 1290 (6th Cir. 2004) (burden is on party seeking to show arbitration agreement should not be enforced to affirmatively demonstrate party lacked meaningful choice; employment agreements on their face are not adhesion contracts; unequal bargaining power alone does not make an agreement unconscionable).

[96]24 Cal. 4th 83, 99 Cal. Rptr. 2d 745, 6 P.3d 669, 83 FEP 1172 (Cal. 2000).

created doctrine of unconscionability begins with an inquiry into whether the contract is one of adhesion—i.e., a standardized contract imposed by the party with superior bargaining power, relegating to the other party the opportunity only to adhere to the contract or reject it.[97] Then the courts look at whether other factors are present that would render the agreement unenforceable.[98] In *Armendariz*, the court found that the agreement was unconscionable "because it require[d] only employees to arbitrate their wrongful termination claims against the employer, but [did] not require the employer to arbitrate claims it may have against the employees."[99] The court reasoned that a lack of mutuality does not render such an agreement invalid on its face,[100] but there must still be a "modicum of bilaterality."[101] The court opined that an agreement imposed in an adhesive context that requires one contracting party but not the other to be bound to arbitration lacks basic fairness and mutuality.[102]

In *Circuit City Stores, Inc. v. Adams*,[103] after remand from the Supreme Court, the Ninth Circuit followed *Armendariz* to support its conclusion that, although arbitration agreements may be enforceable under the FAA, the agreement before it was unconscionable and, therefore, unenforceable. The court found that because the agreement (1) unilaterally forced arbitration; (2) bound only the employees to seek arbitration of their claims and, therefore, deprived the employees of any "modicum of bilaterality;" and (3) required employees to split the forum fees (unless the arbitrator found otherwise), it exemplified both procedural and substantive unconscionability under state law and was therefore unenforceable.[104]

---

[97]*Armendariz*, 6 P.3d at 689.

[98]*Id.*

[99]*Id.* at 691.

[100]*Id.* at 692.

[101]*Id.*

[102]*Id.* at 694; *see also* Perez v. Hospitality Ventures-Denver, 245 F. Supp. 2d 1172, 1173–74 (D. Colo. 2003) (because agreement included provision where employer retained unilateral right to modify, add, revise, or delete any and all policies in it and only employee executed arbitration agreement, it was illusory; if it does not bind both parties, contract is void; terms could not be severed as agreement lacked severability or savings clause that would allow court jurisdiction to enforce revised version).

[103]279 F.3d 889 (9th Cir. 2002).

[104]*Id.* at 896.

In *Ingle v. Circuit City Stores, Inc.*,[105] the Ninth Circuit once again evaluated the evolving Circuit City arbitration agreement for procedural and substantive unconscionability. This agreement, like the one in *Adams*, was found to be oppressive because it gave considerably more bargaining power to the employer and was thus procedurally unconscionable.[106] Pursuant to the analysis applied by the Ninth Circuit, substantive unconscionability occurs where the terms of the agreement "are so one-sided as to shock the conscience,"[107] prohibit a legal claim available in another judicial forum,[108] deprive the employee a possibility of relief under the continuing violations doctrine or otherwise tamper with the statute of limitations,[109] require the employee to pay a mandatory fee that is not the type of expense the employee would have to bear in another judicial forum, blatantly violate basic principles of fairness,[110] limit remedies properly available in that forum, or allow unilateral termination or modification of the agreement.[111]

In *Circuit City Stores, Inc. v. Ahmed*,[112] the Ninth Circuit considered a revised Circuit City arbitration agreement, which allowed employees a meaningful opportunity to opt out of the arbitration program within 30 days of receipt of the policy, and concluded that the agreement was not unconscionable.[113]

Courts have found that arbitration agreements that bind both employees and employers to the process are supported by mutuality,[114]

---

[105]328 F.3d 1165, 91 FEP 1426 (9th Cir. 2003), *cert. denied*, 124 S. Ct. 1169 (2004).

[106]328 F.3d at 1179 ("insidious pattern" within Circuit City's arbitration agreements furthered court's conclusion that unenforceable clauses were not severable and that entire contract was wholly unenforceable).

[107]*Id.* at 1172.

[108]In *Ingle*, the contract did not permit class actions.

[109]328 F.3d at 1174 (in *Ingle*, Circuit City policy shortened statute of limitations period).

[110]*Id.* at 1178.

[111]*Id.* at 1179.

[112]283 F.3d 1198, 88 FEP 626 (9th Cir. 2002).

[113]*Id.* at 1200; *see also* Circuit City Stores, Inc. v. Mantor, 335 F.3d 1101, 1106 (9th Cir. 2003) (explaining that "meaningful opportunity to opt out" requires reasonable notice that employee or applicant can negotiate or reject terms of contract and actual, meaningful, and reasonable choice to exercise that discretion), *cert. denied*, 540 U.S. 1160 (2004).

[114]Michalski v. Circuit City Stores, 177 F.3d 634, 636, 79 FEP 1160 (7th Cir. 1999) (following Wisconsin law, agreement to arbitrate upheld where employer agreed

but there is a split of authority over whether agreements that bind only the employee are valid.[115] Some courts have refused to enforce arbitration agreements where there is no mutual promise or where the employer's promise is illusory.[116] In *Jenkins v. United Healthcare*,[117] a court declined to mandate arbitration for lack of consideration because the defendant could alter, amend, modify, or revoke the agreement without notice. In *Snow v. BE&K Construction Co.*,[118] an employee handbook that permitted an employer to modify or discontinue its unilaterally imposed arbitration mechanism was held to be unenforceable because it failed to create an agreement of mutual assent.[119]

A provision that, although facially neutral, in effect applies to only one side may also be stricken as unconscionable. In *Ting v. AT&T*,[120] the Ninth Circuit (following California law in a consumer

---

to be bound by arbitration of employee's claim, even though employer had not agreed to arbitrate its claims against employee); Koveleskie v. SBC Capital Mkts., Inc., 167 F.3d 361, 368, 79 FEP 73 (7th Cir. 1999) (agreement to arbitrate upheld as it bound both parties); Johnson v. Circuit City Stores, 148 F.3d 373, 378, 77 FEP 139 (4th Cir. 1998) (employer's promise to be bound by process and results of arbitration of employee's claims provided requisite consideration), *aff'd*, 203 F.3d 821 (4th Cir. 2000); Wilson v. Darden Rests., 82 FEP 266, 269 (E.D. Pa. 2000); Bauer v. Morton's of Chi., 82 FEP 286, 287–88 (N.D. Ill. 2000) (both employer and employee bound by arbitration).

[115]*Compare* Gibson v. Neighborhood Health Clinics, Inc., 121 F.3d 1126, 1131–32 (7th Cir. 1997) (under Indiana law, no consideration for employee's unilateral commitment to arbitration against employer) *and* Trumbull v. Century Mktg. Corp., 12 F. Supp. 2d 683, 686, 77 FEP 571 (N.D. Ohio 1998) (noting absence of mutuality) *with* Harris v. Green Tree Fin. Corp., 183 F.3d 173, 183 (3d Cir. 1999), Doctor's Assocs., Inc. v. Distajo, 66 F.3d 438, 451–53 (2d Cir. 1995) (arbitration clause enforceable, even though one party reserves right to bring civil action) *and* J.M. Davidson, Inc. v. Webster, 2003 Tex. LEXIS 527 (Tex. Dec. 31, 2003) (remanding case where it was unclear whether employer could unilaterally terminate arbitration policy).

[116]*See* Floss v. Ryan's Family Steak Houses, Inc., 211 F.3d 306, 315, 6 WH 2d 17 (6th Cir. 2000) ("Where a promissor retains an unlimited right to decide later the nature or extent of his performance, the promise is too indefinite for legal enforcement."); *see also* Penn v. Ryan's Family Steak Houses, Inc., 269 F.3d 753, 761 (7th Cir. 2001) (finding policy unenforceable because there was no mutuality of obligation).

[117]82 FEP 984 (D.C. Super. Ct. 2000).

[118]126 F. Supp. 2d 5, 84 FEP 1260 (D. Me. 2001).

[119]126 F. Supp. 2d at 10; *see also* Smith v. Chrysler Fin. Corp., 101 F. Supp. 2d 534, 538 (E.D. Mich. 2000) (agreement that "reserves the right to amend, modify, suspend, or terminate all or part of this [employee dispute resolution process] at any time in [employer's] sole discretion" makes arbitration provision unenforceable under Michigan law).

[120]319 F.3d 1126 (9th Cir. 2003).

case) held that an arbitration agreement that banned the use of class action procedures was unconscionable, noting that it is "difficult to imagine AT&T bringing a class action against its customers."[121] The court also struck a provision that required confidentiality, because the defendant "placed itself in a far superior legal posture by ensuring that none of its potential opponents have access to precedent, while, at the same time, [it] accumulates a wealth of knowledge on how to negotiate the terms of its own unilaterally crafted contract."[122]

C. Procedural Issues

1. Enforceability

The FAA mandates that the arbitral forum permit a claimant to "effectively vindicate" a statutory cause of action.[123]

2. Selection of the Arbitrator

An arbitration provision that unfairly tilts the selection of the arbitrator in favor of the employer may be struck down as invalid. In *McMullen v. Meijer, Inc.*,[124] the employee challenged her discharge through the employer's two-step binding arbitration process, which expressly incorporated the American Arbitration Association (AAA) procedures. Once the arbitration hearing was requested, the employer had the right to unilaterally select a pool of five neutral arbitrators.[125] The employer and employee alternately struck arbitrators from that pool until only one remained. However, because the employer controlled the pool of arbitrators, the parties ultimately selected an arbitrator that had already served in seven of the employer's arbitrations. The employee challenged the fairness of the selection process in a declaratory judgment action

---

[121]*Id.* at 1150.
[122]*Id.* at 1151.
[123]*See* Gilmer v. Interstate/Johnson Lane Corp., 500 U.S. 20, 28 55 FEP 1116 (1991) ("so long as the prospective litigant effectively may vindicate [his or her] statutory cause of action in the arbitral forum, the statute will continue to serve both its remedial and deterrent function") (quoting Mitsubishi Motors Corp. v. Soler Chrysler-Plymouth, Inc., 473 U.S. 614, 637 (1985)).
[124]355 F.3d 485 (6th Cir. 2004).
[125]*Id.* at 488.

in state court; the employer removed the action to federal court under federal question jurisdiction. The issue before the court was then whether the employer's exclusive control over the pool of potential arbitrators rendered the arbitral forum so fundamentally unfair that it prevented the employee from effectively vindicating her statutory rights and thus precluded the court's enforcement of the predispute agreement. The employer argued that the employee could only escape from the arbitration agreement upon a showing of "fraud, duress or mistake."[126] The court, however, found that an agreement may be voided where it leaves the employee with no ability to "effectively vindicate" his or her statutory cause of action.[127] The court found that the employer's unilateral control over the pool of potential arbitrators prevented its program from being an effective substitute for a judicial forum because it inherently lacked neutrality. Because the arbitrator selection process was therefore fundamentally unfair, that provision of the agreement was unenforceable.[128]

3. Allocation of Fees and Costs

In *Green Tree Financial Corp. v. Randolph*,[129] a consumer loan case, the Supreme Court was asked to decide whether an arbitration agreement that was silent on the issue of forum costs could be enforced over the moving party's objections that she could not afford to vindicate her statutory rights in private arbitration. Although the Court recognized that large arbitration costs could preclude a litigant from effectively vindicating his or her federal statutory rights, it held that the plaintiff had not affirmatively shown that she would be unable to bear the costs.[130] That arbitration costs could exceed those in court was not deemed sufficient to invalidate the arbitration agreement. Thus, the Court declined to impose a per se rule that would invalidate mandatory arbitration agreements where the plaintiff may have to bear costs in excess of those required in court.[131]

---

[126]*Id.* at 490.
[127]*Id.* at 491.
[128]*Id.* at 493–95.
[129]531 U.S. 79 (2000).
[130]*Id.* at 90–92.
[131]*Id.* at 90.

Subsequently, a number of courts have cited *Randolph* when evaluating whether to invalidate an employment-related arbitration agreement that either requires fee splitting[132] or contains a loser-pays provision.[133] Appellate courts are split on how to interpret and apply *Randolph*; they have generally adopted one of three approaches: (1) a per se invalidation of fee-splitting or "loser pays" provisions;[134] (2) an "arbitrate first" rule that requires the claimant

---

[132]*See, e.g.*, Spinetti v. Service Corp. Int'l, 324 F.3d 212, 91 FEP 745 (3d Cir. 2003) (provision requiring employees to pay their own attorney's fees and split arbitration costs—win or lose—invalidated and severed, leaving remainder of agreement enforceable); Perez v. Hospitality Ventures-Denver, 245 F. Supp. 2d 1172 (D. Colo. 2003) (arbitration provision requiring employees to pay half arbitration costs and all of their attorney's fees unenforceable; acknowledging *Randolph*, court credited plaintiff's demonstration that costs of arbitration, which she could not afford and would not incur in judicial forum, would prevent her from vindicating her federal statutory rights).

[133]*See* Musnick v. King Motor Co. of Ft. Lauderdale, 325 F.3d 1255 (11th Cir. 2003) (once arbitrator reaches issues of fees and costs, matter will no longer be speculative and will be ripe for decision); *see also* Cole v. Burns Int'l Sec. Servs., 105 F.3d 1465, 1478–86 (D.C. Cir. 1997) (holding employee not required to arbitrate public law claims as condition of employment if he were required to pay all or part of arbitration expenses, but interpreting language incorporating AAA Rules as requiring employer to pay all fees).

[134]The Ninth Circuit generally has applied the per se invalidation approach. *See* Adams v. Circuit City Stores, Inc., 279 F.3d 889, 891, 87 FEP 1509 (9th Cir. 2002) (where arbitration agreement required claimant to split arbitration costs, arbitration agreement not enforced because it denied claimant benefit of full range of civil remedies available to plaintiff in action under California Fair Employment and Housing Act; arbitration agreement limited available remedies to injunctive relief, up to 1 year of back pay and 2 years of front pay, compensatory damages, and punitive damages up to $5,000, but in civil court damages for emotional distress also would have been available; severance of multiple unconscionable provisions would have resulted in rewriting contract); *see also* Ting v. AT&T, 319 F.3d 1126, 1151 (9th Cir. 2003). *But see* Armendariz v. Foundation Health Psychcare Servs., Inc., 24 Cal. 4th 83, 99, 99 Cal. Rptr. 2d 745, 6 P.3d 669, 83 FEP 1172 (2000) (individualized inquiry "whether and to what extent the arbitration agreement [is] unconscionable or contrary to public policy").

Since *Randolph*, the District of Columbia, Tenth, and Eleventh Circuits have moved away from their prior apparent adherence to a per se rule toward a case-by-case approach. The District of Columbia Circuit initially adopted a per se rule against fee splitting in matters involving statutory claims under Title VII, reasoning "it would undermine Congress's intent to prevent employees who are seeking to vindicate statutory rights from gaining access to a judicial forum and then require them to pay for the services of an arbitrator when they would never be requested to pay for a judge in court." *Cole*, 105 F.3d at 1483–85. The court in *Cole* further held that although such provisions may be unenforceable, they can also be "blue-penciled" out to save the balance of the agreement. *Id.* at 1485. *But see* Brown v. Wheat First Secs., Inc., 257 F.3d 821, 17 IER 1410 (D.C. Cir. 2001) (declining to extend *Cole* beyond statutory causes of action, holding fee provisions enforceable for common law, "public policy" tort action). Subsequently, however, another panel of the District of Columbia Circuit affirmed an award of more than $8,000 in costs against a partially prevailing employee, assessed as her share of "the reasonable costs of filing fees and other administrative expenses arising from arbitration of statutory claims." LaPrade v. Kidder, Peabody & Co., 246 F.3d 702, 85 FEP 779 (D.C. Cir. 2001). In *LaPrade*, a securities representative sued her former employer for both statutory and common law claims. After numerous arbitral sessions, the panel dismissed the statutory claims but awarded LaPrade $65,000 for her contractual claim. LaPrade was ordered to pay 12% of the forum costs, which she challenged. Noting that "the party seeking to vacate or otherwise modify the arbitration award bears the burden of demonstrating that the arbitration panel acted in manifest disregard of the law," the court found the award reasonable because LaPrade failed to show that she would not be liable for those costs in a federal forum. 246 F.3d at 705. The court also rejected LaPrade's argument that the award contravened *Cole*, because the amount at issue could not be characterized as arbitrators' compensation but was in the nature of the costs and administrative expenses that would be incurred in federal court. The court further distinguished *Cole* by concluding that the assessment against LaPrade might have been associated with the nonstatutory claims. Finally, citing *Randolph*, the court noted that LaPrade made no showing that the possibility of a large assessment prevented her from attempting to vindicate her rights. *LaPrade*, 246 F.3d at 708.

In decisions rendered before *Randolph*, the Tenth and Eleventh Circuits also adhered to a per se invalidation rule, finding that arbitration agreements that required a Title VII plaintiff to pay all or part of an arbitrator's fee are unenforceable because they do not provide for a forum where litigants can effectively vindicate their statutory rights. *See* Shankle v. B-G Maint. Mgmt. of Colo., Inc., 163 F.3d 1230, 1234–35, 78 FEP 1057 (10th Cir. 1999) (finding arbitration agreement unenforceable when it required arbitration, therefore prohibiting use of judicial forum, but contained fee-splitting provision that rendered arbitration cost-prohibitive); Paladino v. Avnet Computer Techs., Inc., 134 F.3d 1054, 1058, 76 FEP 1315 (11th Cir. 1998) ("the presence of an unlawful provision in an arbitration agreement may serve to taint the entire arbitration agreement, rendering the agreement completely unenforceable"). Subsequent to *Randolph*, the Eleventh Circuit held that an arbitration agreement providing that all of the fees and costs of the arbitration will be shared equally is unenforceable because Title VII provides that prevailing parties are entitled to fees and costs. Perez v. Globe Airport Sec. Servs., Inc., 253 F.3d 1280, 86 FEP 613 (11th Cir. 2001), *vacated*, 294 F.3d 1275 (11th Cir. 2002). However, in *Musnick v. King Motor Co. of Fort Lauderdale*, 325 F.3d 1255, 1259–60 (11th Cir. 2003), the Eleventh Circuit noted the developing trend among the other circuits applying a case-by-case analysis, focusing on whether the arbitral forum is an adequate and accessible substitute for the individual claimant, and held that the party seeking to avoid arbitration must establish that enforcement of the agreement would preclude him or her from effectively vindicating his or her federal statutory right in the arbitral forum. The Eleventh Circuit also stated its belief that the Tenth Circuit's decision in *Shankle* supports a case-by-case approach because, "despite articulating what sounds like a *per se* rule that mandatory fee-splitting 'clearly undermines the remedial and deterrent functions of the federal anti-discrimination laws,' the court then went on to examine the facts and circumstances of that plaintiff's ability to pay the costs of arbitration and invalidated the agreement because he could not afford to pay for access to the arbitral forum." *Musnick*, 325 F.3d at 1259 (citing Shankle v. B-G Maint. Mgmt. of Colo., Inc., 163 F.3d 1230, 1235, 78 FEP 1057 (10th Cir. 1999)).

to present to the arbitration panel any objections to costs;[135] or (3) a prearbitration case-by-case analysis.[136]

---

[135]The First Circuit introduced the "arbitrate first" approach in *Rosenberg v. Merrill Lynch, Pierce, Fenner & Smith, Inc.*, 170 F.3d 1, 16 (1st Cir. 1999) (NYSE arbitrators possess discretion to award costs and fees when they decide dispute). The First Circuit determined in *Rosenberg* that because an award had not already been granted, the fee issue was not yet ripe and that a claimant could challenge an arbitrator's unreasonable award of attorney's fees in federal court if and when that issue matured. At the time of Rosenberg's employment as a financial consultant, the NYSE required arbitration of all disputed claims, but Rosenberg alleged that the NYSE's arbitration procedures inadequately accounted for attorney's fees with respect to his Title VII claims. The court stated that although Rosenberg may be correct regarding the accounting of fees, it did not render the system inadequate because the argument could be presented to a reviewing court. Thereafter, the First Circuit reaffirmed the *Rosenberg* decision in *Thompson v. Irwin Home Equity*, 300 F.3d 88, 92 (1st Cir. 2002) (to address merits of attorney's fees provision would be premature when award is yet to be granted). Other courts have adopted a similar approach. *See* Bradford v. Rockwell Semiconductor Sys., Inc., 238 F.3d 549, 558–59, 84 FEP 1358 (4th Cir. 2001) (affirming award ordering employee to pay $4,470.88 in forum fees); Williams v. Cigna Fin. Advisors, Inc., 197 F.3d 752, 81 FEP 747 (5th Cir. 1999) (affirming award ordering employee to pay half of all fees, totaling $3,150); Koveleskie v. SBC Capital Mkts., Inc., 167 F.3d 361, 366, 79 FEP 73 (7th Cir. 1999) (noting that when employees are required to pay filing fee, expenses, or administrative fee, these fees are often waived because of hardship); DiRussa v. Dean Witter Reynolds Inc., 121 F.3d 818, 74 FEP 726 (2d Cir. 1997) (failure of arbitrator to award attorney's fees to prevailing plaintiff did not violate public policy); Arakawa v. Japan Network Group, 56 F. Supp. 2d 349, 353–55, 83 FEP 1097 (S.D.N.Y. 1999) (adopting position of First and Seventh Circuits); Howard v. Anderson, 36 F. Supp. 2d 183, 187, 83 FEP 1225 (S.D.N.Y. 1999) (upholding $500 fee imposed on employee).

[136]Most courts of appeals appear to follow a case-by-case analysis when deciding the enforceability of a fee provision in arbitration agreements. The Third Circuit, interpreting *Randolph*, adopted a case-by-case analysis in *Blair v. Scott Specialty Gases*, 283 F.3d 595, 609 (3d Cir. 2002). The court agreed that the claimant should be entitled to make an appropriate showing of financial hardship before being forced to incur the expenses of arbitration, even though *Randolph* placed the burden of proof that arbitration would be prohibitively expensive on the party resisting arbitration. *Id.* at 610; *see* Valdes v. Swift Transp. Co., Inc., 292 F. Supp. 2d 524 (S.D.N.Y. 2003) (applying *Randolph* and finding plaintiff failed to meet her burden of showing likelihood of actually incurring unreasonable costs); *see also* Spinetti v. Service Corp. Int'l, 324 F.3d 212, 217 (3d Cir. 2003) (employer also should be afforded opportunity to show that arbitration would be prohibitively expensive).

The Fourth, Eighth, and Eleventh Circuits, post-*Randolph*, also adhere to the case-by-case approach. *See Bradford*, 238 F.3d 549 (focusing on whether arbitral forum is adequate and accessible substitute for individual claimant); Murray v. Food & Commercial Workers, 289 F.3d 297, 302 (4th Cir. 2002) (citing *Bradford* for proposition that "crucial inquiry is whether the particular claimant has an adequate and accessible substitute forum in which to resolve his statutory rights"); Faber v.

D. Contractual Limitations of Claims or Procedures

1. Damages

As the Supreme Court recognized in *Gilmer* and reiterated in *Circuit City*, the parties to a predispute arbitration agreement do "not forgo the substantive rights afforded by the statute; [the agreement] only submits to their resolution in an arbitral, rather than a judicial, forum."[137] In line with this admonition, some courts have held that contractual limitations on remedies or one-sided procedures can render the entire arbitration agreement unenforceable;[138]

Menard, Inc., 367 F.3d 1048, 1054, 93 FEP 1730 (8th Cir. 2004) (party seeking to avoid arbitration should present specific evidence of likely arbitrators' fees and its financial ability to pay those fees so that court can determine whether arbitral forum is accessible to party); Lyster v. Ryan's Family Steak Houses, Inc., 239 F.3d 943, 947, 91 FEP 1477 (8th Cir. 2001) (recognizing potential that substantial arbitration fees may make arbitration agreement unconscionable but requiring plaintiff to prove unconscionability); Musnick v. King Motor Co. of Ft. Lauderdale, 325 F.3d 1255, 1259–60 (11th Cir. 2003) (following *Bradford*, requiring individual to offer evidence of fees he or she would be likely to incur and inability to pay those fees in order to demonstrate that arbitration would effectively preclude individual from vindicating his or her Title VII rights). The Sixth Circuit has further revised and applied the case-by-case approach to "similarly situated claimants." In *Morrison v. Circuit City Stores, Inc.*, 317 F.3d 646 (6th Cir. 2003), the Sixth Circuit noted that courts should look beyond the interests and conduct of an individual plaintiff and that nothing in *Randolph* forbade such an analysis. *Morrison* involved the application of a fee-sharing provision in an arbitration agreement to a class of plaintiffs; the court looked to whether the provision would "deter a substantial number of similarly situated potential litigants." 317 F.3d at 663. The Sixth Circuit said that the case-by-case analysis should include the actual plaintiff's income and resources as representative of [the] class's ability to bear the costs of arbitration; the typical or average costs of arbitration; whether the litigants will incur any additional expense; whether that level of expense would deter potential litigants; and whether the potential cost to arbitrate exceeds the potential cost to litigate. The court reasoned that such an analysis would determine whether the provision itself undermines the deterrent effect of the antidiscrimination statutes, essentially dissuading plaintiffs with fewer resources from raising meritorious claims. *Id.*; *see also* Cooper v. MRM Inv. Co., 367 F.3d 493, 93 FEP 1290 (6th Cir. 2004) (remanding to allow plaintiff to show that costs of arbitration are likely to be so high as to deter her and others similarly situated to proceed; defendant could not moot cost issue by offering to pay claimant's arbitration costs after litigation began).

[137]Circuit City Stores Inc. v. Adams, 532 U.S. 105, 123 (2001) (quoting Gilmer v. Interstate/Johnson Lane Corp., 500 U.S. 20, 26, 55 FEP 1116 (1991)); *see also* Mitsubishi Motors Corp. v. Soler Chrysler-Plymouth, Inc., 473 U.S. 614, 628 (1985).

[138]*See, e.g.*, Ting v. AT&T, 319 F.3d 1126, 1151 (9th Cir. 2003) (unenforceable fee-splitting scheme under California law); Perez v. Globe Airport Sec. Serv., Inc., 253 F.3d 1280, 1286–87 (11th Cir. 2001) (contract that apparently bars fee shifting

others have enforced agreements that contain such provisions while ordering modifications.[139]

The Third Circuit has held that it is the arbitrator, not the court, that decides the enforceability of such provisions in the first instance. In *Great Western Mortgage Corp. v. Peacock*,[140] the arbitration agreement included provisions that waived the employee's right to attorney's fees and punitive damages and imposed a one-year statute of limitations on her discrimination claims. The Third

---

for prevailing party cannot be enforced); Hooters of Am., Inc. v. Phillips, 39 F. Supp. 2d 582, 612, 76 FEP 1757 (D.S.C. 1998), *aff'd*, 173 F.3d 933, 938–39 (4th Cir. 1999) (extensive list of restrictions on employees in arbitration proceedings); Shankle v. B-G Mgmt. of Colo., 163 F.3d 1230, 1235 & n.6, 78 FEP 1057 (10th Cir. 1999) (rejecting employer's suggestion to sever fee-splitting provision and enforce reminder); Paladino v. Avnet Computer Techs., Inc., 134 F.3d 1054, 1060–62, 76 FEP 1315 (11th Cir. 1998) (arbitration clause that provides only for award of contract damages denies plaintiff meaningful relief) (Cox and Tjoflat, JJ., concurring); Alcaraz v. Avnet, Inc., 933 F. Supp. 1025, 1027–28, 71 FEP 68 (D.N.M. 1996) (employee's Title VII and ADA claims not subject to arbitration because agreement did not provide full range of statutory damages); Derrickson v. Circuit City Stores, 81 FEP 1533 (D. Md. 1999) (agreement that does not provide all remedies under § 1981 will not be enforced); *Armendariz*, 24 Cal. 4th at 99–101 (to be enforced, agreement must include full range of statutory remedies, including punitive damages and attorney's fees to prevailing plaintiff); *see also* Pinedo v. Premium Tobacco Stores, Inc., 85 Cal. App. 4th 774, 84 FEP 1090 (Cal. Ct. App. 2000) (where agreement barred employee but not employer from litigating claims, limited back pay to 6 months, and required employee to pay for costs of arbitration, court found agreement unconscionable and unenforceable).

[139]*See* Booker v. Robert Half Int'l, Inc., 413 F.3d 77 (D.C. Cir. 2005) (district court had power to sever unenforceable provision barring punitive damages and enforce remainder of agreement); Hadnot v. Bay, Ltd., 344 F.3d 474, 478, 92 FEP 1090 (5th Cir. 2003) (bar to punitive damages severed); Spinetti v. Service Corp. Int'l, 324 F.3d 212, 223, 91 FEP 745 (3d Cir. 2003) (enforcing agreement but severing fee-splitting provision); Morrison v. Circuit City Stores, Inc., 317 F.3d 646, 675, 90 FEP 646 (6th Cir. 2003) (finding unenforceable cost-splitting and limitation on remedies provisions severable and enforcing remaining provisions); Gannon v. Circuit City Stores, Inc., 262 F.3d 677, 86 FEP 755 (8th Cir. 2001) (limitation on punitive damages can be severed, leaving rest of agreement intact); DeGaetano v. Smith Barney, Inc., 983 F. Supp. 459, 464–70, 75 FEP 579 (S.D.N.Y. 1997) (provision barring award of statutory attorney's fees struck from agreement); Johnson v. Hubbard Broad., Inc., 940 F. Supp. 1447, 1462, 73 FEP 8 (D. Minn. 1996) (upholding enforceability of agreement but noting that if arbitrator finds that provision requiring both parties to bear own attorney's fee bars award of fee to prevailing plaintiff, agreement would violate federal law and be unenforceable); *see also* Mastrobuono v. Shearson Lehman Hutton, Inc., 514 U.S. 52 (1995) (nonemployment case; punitive damage award by arbitrator upheld based on agreement of parties to make punitive damages arbitrable; FAA requires that such agreement be enforced even if state law would exclude punitive damages).

[140]110 F.3d 222, 73 FEP 856 (3d Cir. 1997).

Circuit did not hold the terms to be unenforceable as a matter of law, but instead referred the matters to the arbitrator to determine whether the plaintiff had in fact agreed to abandon statutory rights.[141]

The law with regard to punitive damages remains unclear. The Fourth Circuit has held that an arbitrator may not award punitive damages in a proceeding under a CBA unless the agreement expressly permits such an award that would be available in litigation.[142] Where arbitration agreements purport to prohibit or limit punitive damage awards, the courts have reached conflicting conclusions about whether such clauses render the agreements unenforceable.[143] More recent decisions have rejected efforts to limit the scope of statutory relief otherwise available. In *Circuit City Stores, Inc. v. Ingle*,[144] Circuit City sought to limit the arbitrator to granting awards of injunctive relief, up to one year of back pay, up to two years of front pay, and, punitive damages up to $5,000. The court, applying California law, found that the arbitration agreement was substantively unconscionable, in part, because it failed to provide for all of the relief that would have been available in court.[145] Thus, an issue that may arise where an arbitration agreement purports to limit remedies will be whether the entire agreement will be void and unenforceable or whether the court will be able to sever the provision that attempts to limit an employee's recovery.[146] In *Clary v. Stanley Works*[147] the court recognized that

---

[141]*Id.* at 231–32; *see also* Kinnebrew v. Gulf Ins. Co., 67 FEP 189, 191 (N.D. Tex. 1994) (referring claim to arbitration even though arbitration policy does not expressly provide for punitive damages, injunctive relief, and attorney's fees).

[142]*See* Island Creek Coal Co. v. Mine Workers (UMW) District 28, 29 F.3d 126, 146 LRRM 2773 (4th Cir. 1994) (under standard CBA, arbitrator may not award punitive damages unless agreement expressly permits such award).

[143]*Compare Kinnebrew*, 67 FEP at 191 (enforcing arbitration agreement that did not provide for punitive damages) *with Hubbard Broad.*, 940 F. Supp. at 1461–62 (court would consider arbitration agreement unenforceable as unconscionable if arbitrator interpreted agreement to preclude punitive damages).

[144]328 F.3d 1165 (9th Cir. 2003), *cert. denied*, 124 S. Ct. 1169 (2004).

[145]328 F.3d. at 1178–79.

[146]*See id.* at 1180 (ameliorating unconscionable terms would require court to "assume the role of contract author rather than an interpreter"); *cf.* Booker v. Robert Half Int'l, Inc., 2005 WL 1540796 (D.C. Cir. July 1, 2005) (allowing district court to sever provision barring punitive damages); Hadnot v. Bay, Ltd., 344 F.3d 477, 478, 92 FEP 1090 (5th Cir. 2003) (deciding to sever term purporting to restrict arbitrator's power to award exemplary and punitive damages).

[147]2003 WL 21728865, 8 WH 2d 1649 (D. Kan. Jul. 24, 2003).

a term specifically limiting available relief can be severed or can result in an unenforceable contract.[148] The *Clary* court declined to sever the offending term, stating "an over eagerness to sever offending provisions will encourage [employers] to load their arbitration agreements with questionable or even clearly unlawful provisions."[149]

The Ninth Circuit's *Ingle* decision differs from the outcome in a parallel Eighth Circuit case, *Gannon v. Circuit City Stores, Inc.*,[150] which was decided under Missouri law. The panel in *Gannon* held, with one judge dissenting, that the agreement was not unconscionable, save for the provisions that limited damages that the panel deemed severable. It will pose a challenge in future litigation, especially for nationwide enterprises like Circuit City, to navigate the variable laws of the 50 states that govern the interpretation of arbitration agreements. Furthermore, it is uncertain how the Supreme Court can resolve such disparate results that depend so intimately on state law and therefore generally elude Supreme Court review.

2. *Limitations Periods*

In the employment arena, courts have been chary about arbitration agreements that unduly shorten the limitations periods provided by the federal civil rights laws.[151] Courts generally hold that employees must be afforded the same limitations period for proceeding in an arbitral forum that the employee would enjoy in state or federal court under the relevant statutes or cause of action. In *Ingle*, the agreement required the employee to submit claims to

---

[148]*Id.* at *6.

[149]*Id.*

[150]262 F.3d 677, 86 FEP 755 (8th Cir. 2001).

[151]*See* Krahel v. Owens-Brockway Glass Container, Inc., 971 F. Supp. 440, 452–53, 74 FEP 465 (D. Or. 1997) (finding invalid requirement that employee give notice of Title VII claim within 3 days); Salisbury v. Art Van Furniture, 938 F. Supp. 435, 437–38 (W.D. Mich. 1996) (finding employment application that imposed 6-month deadline on filing of action challenging failure to hire unconscionable as applied to ADA claim where statute prescribed 180-day minimum conciliation period); *cf.* Howsam v. Dean Witter Reynolds, Inc., 537 U.S. 79, 85–86 (2002) (application of time-limit rules is presumptively procedural question for arbitrator to decide); Great W. Mortgage Corp. v. Peacock, 110 F.3d 222, 228 (3d Cir. 1997) (holding that arbitrator is to determine validity of shortened statute of limitations).

arbitration within one year of the date that the employee became aware of the facts giving rise to the claim.[152] Believing that this limitation undermined the "continuing violations doctrine" and insulated the employer from potential damages, the court found the term unconscionable under California law.[153] Similarly, in *Circuit City Stores, Inc. v. Mantor*,[154] the Ninth Circuit rejected Circuit City's "modified and improved" arbitration agreement, which attempted to comport with *Ingle*[155] and with *Adams'*[156] holding that the agreements were unconscionable. Because the new agreement failed to excise the statute of limitations restriction, however, it was again found to be substantively unconscionable.[157]

3. Discovery

Arbitration agreements are often written to limit the scope and extent of discovery.[158] In *Gilmer v. Interstate/Johnson Lane Corp.*,[159] the plaintiff, a securities representative registered with the New York Stock Exchange (NYSE), had "agreed" to arbitrate any dispute, claim, or controversy between him and his employer.[160] The Court rejected Gilmer's argument that the NYSE's limited discovery provisions would make it too difficult to prove discrimination.[161] The Court dismissed the concern, believing it unlikely that age discrimination cases require more discovery than antitrust claims and claims under the Racketeer Influenced and Corrupt Organizations Act (RICO)—both of which are arbitrable.[162] The Court noted that although the procedures may not be as extensive as those available in federal courts, one "trades the procedures and the opportunity for review of the courtroom for the simplicity, informality, and

---

[152]Ingle v. Circuit City Stores, Inc., 328 F.3d 1165, 1175, 91 FEP 1426 (9th Cir. 2003), *cert. denied*, 124 S. Ct. 1169 (2004).

[153]*Id.*

[154]335 F.3d 1101 (9th Cir. 2003), *cert. denied*, 124 S. Ct. 1169 (2004).

[155]328 F.3d at 1178–79.

[156]279 F.3d 889, 894 (9th Cir. 2002).

[157]*Mantor*, 335 F.3d at 1107.

[158]*See, e.g.*, Morrison v. Circuit City Stores, Inc., 317 F.3d 646, 655 (6th Cir. 2003) (limiting claimant to personnel file, 20 interrogatories, and three depositions).

[159]500 U.S. 20, 55 FEP 1116 (1991).

[160]*Id.* at 24.

[161]*Id.* at 31.

[162]*Id.*

expedition of arbitration."[163] Similarly, the AAA directs the arbitrator to "order such discovery, by way of deposition, interrogatory, document production, or otherwise, as the arbitrator considers necessary to a full and fair exploration of the issues in dispute, *consistent with the expedited nature of arbitration*."[164]

Unfairly truncated discovery terms may still be unenforceable.[165] In *Armendariz v. Foundation Health Psychcare Services, Inc.*,[166] the California Supreme Court noted that an arbitration agreement in the employment area must generally permit sufficient discovery procedures to vindicate statutory rights and that the employer must bear the expense of administering the program.[167]

E. Effect of Arbitration on Public Enforcement Agencies

In *Gilmer*, the plaintiff unsuccessfully argued that enforcement of employment-based arbitration agreements would undermine the EEOC's enforcement role.[168] The Supreme Court was unpersuaded, noting that the EEOC's role in combating discrimination is not dependent on the filing of a charge, because it has independent authority to investigate discrimination[169] and can bring its own actions seeking classwide and equitable relief.[170]

Almost 11 years later, in *EEOC v. Waffle House, Inc.*,[171] the Court addressed whether the EEOC could be barred from pursuing victim-specific relief where the employee signed an agreement to arbitrate employment-related disputes. The Fourth Circuit held that although the EEOC was not a party to the contract, it was precluded from seeking victim-specific relief because the strong public policy favoring arbitration, as expressed in the FAA, required it

---

[163]*Id.* (citations omitted); *see also* Rosenberg v. Merrill Lynch, Pierce, Fenner & Smith, Inc., 170 F.3d 1, 16 (1st Cir. 1999) (relying on *Gilmer* and dismissing plaintiff's claim that arbitration discovery is inadequate).

[164]AMERICAN ARBITRATION ASS'N, AAA NATIONAL RULES FOR THE RESOLUTION OF EMPLOYMENT DISPUTES § 7 (2004) (emphasis added).

[165]*See, e.g.*, Hooters of Am., Inc. v. Phillips, 173 F.3d 933, 938, 79 FEP 629 (4th Cir. 1999) (only employee was obliged to provide discovery).

[166]24 Cal. 4th 83, 99 Cal. Rptr. 2d 745, 6 P.3d 669, 83 FEP 1172 (Cal. 2000).

[167]*Id.* at 104–13.

[168]500 U.S. 20, 28, 55 FEP 1116 (1991).

[169]*Id.*

[170]*Id.* at 32.

[171]534 U.S. 279 (2002).

to give effect to the individual employee's agreement to arbitrate.[172] The Court granted the EEOC's petition for certiorari to resolve a conflict among the circuit courts; the Second and Eighth Circuit had limited the EEOC's ability to seek monetary relief in such circumstances, whereas the Sixth Circuit held that the EEOC's authority was not affected by an employee's agreement to arbitrate.[173]

The Supreme Court found, based on the history of the amendments to Title VII, that Congress unambiguously intended to authorize the EEOC to bring suits for injunctive relief, reinstatement, back pay, and compensatory and punitive damages.[174] Although the 1991 amendments expanded remedies available to the EEOC in enforcement actions, they in no way suggested "that the existence of an arbitration agreement between private parties materially changes the EEOC's statutory function or the remedies that are otherwise available."[175]

Thus, despite the policy favoring arbitration, the Supreme Court declined to bind the EEOC to a contract that it had not agreed to accept.[176] The Court found that the "detailed enforcement scheme" that Congress created to enable the EEOC to vindicate the public interest or to pursue entirely victim-specific relief would be undermined if the arbitration agreement between private parties were given greater effect.[177] The Court left open the question of whether and to what extent the individual employee's conduct—e.g., settlement, actual arbitration of the claim, failure to mitigate, etc.—could affect the validity of the EEOC's claim or the character of the relief it could seek.[178]

---

[172]*Id.* at 284.

[173]*Id.* at 285. *Compare* EEOC v. Kidder, Peabody & Co., 156 F.3d 298, 300–01, 77 FEP 1212 (2d Cir. 1998) ("allowing the EEOC to pursue injunctive relief in the federal forum, but precluding the EEOC from seeking purely monetary relief for employees") *and* Merrill Lynch, Pierce, Fenner and Smith, Inc. v. Nixon, 210 F.3d 814, 819, 82 FEP 1080 (8th Cir. 2000) (affirming district court's decision to enjoin state FEP agency from seeking individual monetary remedies on behalf of employee who had previously submitted claim to arbitration) *with* EEOC v. Frank's Nursery & Crafts, Inc., 177 F.3d 448, 461, 79 FEP 936 (6th Cir. 1999) (allowing EEOC to seek monetary relief on behalf of individual who signed arbitration agreement would neither undermine FAA nor *Gilmer* holding).

[174]*Waffle House*, 534 U.S. at 286–87.

[175]*Id.* at 288.

[176]*Id.* at 294.

[177]*Id.* at 296.

[178]*Id.* at 297.

F. Collective Bargaining Issues Related to Discrimination Claims

In the unionized setting, a CBA generally requires grievances to be resolved through binding arbitration. Where an individual union member seeks to vindicate statutory rights outside of the grievance process, the question becomes whether the CBA actually covers the right that the employee seeks to enforce, and if so, whether the union can waive the individual's right to a judicial forum. This tension first arose in *Alexander v. Gardner-Denver Co.*,[179] where the Court found that the CBA did not effectively waive the employee's right to a judicial forum because the statutory right that the employee sought to vindicate was distinct from the contractual right that was subject to arbitration.[180]

In *Wright v. Universal Maritime Services Corp.*,[181] the Supreme Court addressed whether a general arbitration clause in a CBA requires the employee to use the arbitration procedure to pursue a claim under the ADA. The Court noted that there is a presumption of arbitrability, unless it is clear that the "arbitration clause is not susceptible of an interpretation that covers the asserted dispute."[182] The presumption is justified because "arbitrators are in a better position than courts to interpret the terms of a CBA."[183] The Court found that the arbitration clause in question, however, was intended to cover "wages, hours and other terms and conditions of employment," not rights under a federal statute.[184] The Court concluded that a union-negotiated waiver of an employees' statutory right to a judicial forum for claims of employment discrimination must be clear and unmistakable.[185]

Following *Wright*, employers generally have not been successful in compelling the arbitration of employment discrimination claims

---

[179]415 U.S. 36, 7 FEP 81 (1974).

[180]415 U.S. at 47.

[181]525 U.S. 70 (1998).

[182]*Id.* at 78 (internal quotations and citations omitted).

[183]*Id.*

[184]*Id.* at 79 (distinguishing *Gardner-Denver*, where employee pursued his grievance to arbitration under CBA's nondiscrimination clause).

[185]*Id.* at 80 (referring to *Gardner-Denver*'s seemingly absolute prohibition of union waiver of employees' federal forum right).

pursuant to a CBA clause purporting to waive a judicial forum.[186] In *Safrit v. Care Mills*,[187] however, the Fourth Circuit found that the CBA provided a clear and unmistakable waiver of the employee's statutory rights to a federal forum on her Title VII sex discrimination claim.[188]

G. Judicial Enforcement

1. Statutory Standards Under the FAA

Section 10 of the FAA provides that a court may vacate an arbitration award in cases of corruption, fraud, misconduct, or where

---

[186]*See* O'Brien v. Town of Agawam, 350 F.3d 279, 285–86 (1st Cir. 2003) (reference to "grievances" in agreement limited to violations of CBA, not statutory claims); Rogers v. New York Univ., 220 F.3d 73, 76 (2d Cir. 2000) (waiver was not "clear and unmistakable"); Kennedy v. Superior Printing Co., 215 F.3d 650, 654–55 (6th Cir. 2000) (same); Bratten v. SSI Servs., Inc., 185 F.3d 625, 631–32 (6th Cir. 1999) (same); Carson v. Giant Food, Inc., 175 F.3d 325, 329–31 (4th Cir. 1999) (CBAs did not unmistakably consign statutory claims to arbitration where broad clauses require arbitration to resolve disputes "regarding the terms of this Agreement" and "concerning the interpretation of the provisions of this Agreement"); Quint v. A.E. Staley Mfg. Co., 172 F.3d 1, 9 ("CBA Articles 5 & 6, neither of which explicitly mentions employee rights under the ADA or any other federal anti-discrimination statute, pose no bar to the instant action."); Durham Life Ins. Co. v. Evans, 166 F.3d 139, 159–60, 79 FEP 160 (3d Cir. 1999) (expired CBA did not bind plaintiff to use arbitration in sex harassment case where employer indicated its intention not to be bound); Kelly v. Classic Rest. Corp., 2003 U.S. Dist. LEXIS 15211, at *8, 92 FEP 1222 (S.D.N.Y. Sept. 2, 2003) (although CBA clause prohibited age discrimination, arbitration clause not enforceable because it did not clearly and unmistakably indicate deferral age claim subject to arbitration); Ozolins v. Northwood-Kensett Cmty. Sch. Dist., 40 F. Supp. 2d 1055, 1067 (N.D. Iowa 1999) ("it is not clear that the CBA, by incorporating the FMLA with the qualification that the FMLA 'in no way replace[d], reduce[d], or change[d] any articles' in the CBA, constituted an agreement to arbitrate claims under the FMLA"); Taylor v. Lockheed Martin Corp., 6 Cal. Rptr. 3d 358, 359 (Cal. Ct. App. 2003) (arbitration decision will preclude later civil action for retaliatory discharge only if CBA clearly and unmistakably provides for binding arbitration of statutory claim at issue and if arbitration is conducted in manner that allows for full litigation and fair adjudication of statutory claim); *cf.* Air Line Pilots v. Northwest Airlines, Inc., 199 F.3d 477, 81 FEP 830 (D.C. Cir. 1999) (arbitration clause not mandatory subject of bargaining under RLA; therefore, employer not required to negotiate with union over such clause), *reh'g en banc granted, judgment vacated, judgment reinstated*, 211 F.3d 1312 (D.C. Cir. 2000).
    [187]248 F.3d 306 (4th Cir. 2001).
    [188]*Id.* at 308; *see also* Brown v. ABF Freight Sys., Inc., 183 F.3d 319, 321 (4th Cir. 1999) ("broad but nonspecific" arbitration clause will not require arbitration of statutory claims when agreement does not establish with "requisite degree of clarity" that discrimination statutes are part of agreement); Carson v. Giant Foods, Inc.,

the arbitrators exceed their powers.[189] There is a split in the circuits regarding whether the parties may contract for additional grounds of judicial review not otherwise provided by this section.[190]

Under § 10(a)(1), the party challenging the award ordinarily must establish that the corruption, fraud, or undue means was (1) not discoverable upon the exercise of due diligence prior to the arbitration, (2) materially related to an issue in the arbitration, and (3) established by clear and convincing evidence.[191] In *Pacific & Arctic Railway & Navigation Co. v. United Transportation Union*,[192] the Ninth Circuit affirmed the vacating of an arbitration award on finding that the union arbitrator took part in extensive ex parte communications, accepted undisclosed gratuities, and essentially ignored the employer's entire factual record.[193] In another case that involved alleged fraud by a witness, the Eighth Circuit held that

---

175 F.3d 325, 331 (4th Cir. 1999) (CBA provision to arbitrate statutory claims must be "clear and unmistakable").

[189]9 U.S.C. § 10 (2000):

(a) In any of the following cases the United States court in and for the district wherein the award was made may make an order vacating the award upon the application of any party to the arbitration—

(1) Where the award was procured by corruption, fraud, or undue means.

(2) Where there was evident partiality or corruption in the arbitrators, or either of them.

(3) Where the arbitrators were guilty of misconduct in refusing to postpone the hearing, upon sufficient cause shown, or in refusing to hear evidence pertinent and material to the controversy; or of any other misbehavior by which the rights of any party have been prejudiced.

(4) Where the arbitrators exceeded their powers, or so imperfectly executed them that a mutual, final, and definite award upon the subject matter submitted was not made.

[190]*Compare* Harris v. Parker Coll. of Chiropractic, 286 F.3d 790, 792–93, 88 FEP 663 (5th Cir. 2002) *and* Roadway Package Sys., Inc. v. Kayser, 257 F.3d 287, 292–93 (3d Cir. 2001) (parties may augment standard of review under FAA) *with* Kyocera Corp. v. Prudential-Bache Trade Servs., Inc., 341 F.3d 987, 996–1000 (9th Cir. 2003) (en banc), *cert. dismissed*, 124 S. Ct. 980 (2004) *and* Bowen v. Amoco Pipeline Co., 254 F.3d 925, 933–36 (10th Cir. 2001) (parties cannot alter FAA standard of review).

[191]*See* MidAmerican Energy Co. v. Electrical Workers (IBEW) Local 499, 345 F.3d 616, 622 (8th Cir. 2003) (enumerating test for determining whether arbitration award was procured by fraud); Gingiss Int'l, Inc. v. Bormet, 58 F.3d 328, 333 (7th Cir. 1995) (same); A.G. Edwards & Sons, Inc. v. McCollough, 967 F.2d 1401, 1404 (9th Cir. 1992) (same); Bonar v. Dean Witter Reynolds, Inc., 835 F.2d 1378, 1383 (11th Cir. 1988) (same).

[192]952 F.2d 1144 (9th Cir. 1991).

[193]*Id.* at 1148.

management's challenge to the award presented a triable issue of fact, "[g]iven these statements [in the written findings] regarding how crucial the arbitrator felt that honesty and truthfulness were and given the fact that, if fraud is proven, the entirety of [the witness'] involvement in the arbitration process would be shown to be a sham."[194] An opponent's use of counsel unlicensed in the jurisdiction, however, advanced as a species of "undue means," was held to be insufficient grounds for vacating an award.[195]

To constitute "evident partiality" under § 10(a)(2) requires more than a mere appearance of impropriety.[196] An aggrieved party must point to "specific facts that indicate improper motives."[197] Yet, as the Supreme Court emphasized in *Commonwealth Coatings Corp. v. Continental Casualty Co.*,[198] courts should "be even more scrupulous to safeguard the impartiality of arbitrators than judges, since the former have completely free rein to decide the law as well as the facts and are not subject to appellate review."[199] Accordingly, arbitrators must disclose actual conflicts of interest.[200] The command

---

[194]*MidAmerican Energy*, 345 F.3d at 622–23.

[195]Sirotzky v. New York Stock Exch., 347 F.3d 985, 990 (7th Cir. 2003) (fitness of counsel to represent party subject to arbitrator's discretion; if party showed up at hearing with pit bull rather than with lawyer to extort panel, however, opponent "would have grounds for objection").

[196]*See* Lifecare Int'l Inc. v. CD Med., Inc., 68 F.3d 429, 433 (11th Cir. 1995) ("mere appearance of bias or partiality is not enough to set aside an arbitration award"); Consolidation Coal Co. v. Mine Workers (UMW) Local 1643, 48 F.3d 125, 129 (4th Cir. 1995) ("mere appearance" not enough); Schmitz v. Zilveti, 20 F.3d 1043, 1046 (9th Cir. 1994) (rejecting "appearance of bias" standard); Health Servs. Mgmt. Corp. v. Hughes, 975 F.2d 1253, 1264 (7th Cir. 1992) (evident partiality "means more than a mere appearance of bias").

[197]Remmey v. PaineWebber, Inc., 32 F.3d 143, 148–49 (4th Cir. 1994); *see also Hughes*, 975 F.2d at 1264 (requiring "direct and definite" evidence of partiality; evidence in transcript that arbitrator cut short party's presentation of motion and otherwise indicated personal doubts about viability of defense not enough).

[198]393 U.S. 145 (1968).

[199]*Id.* at 149.

[200]*Compare* University Commons-Urbana, Ltd. v. Universal Constructors Inc., 304 F.3d 1331, 1341–44 (11th Cir. 2002) (ordering remand for factual hearing because of arbitrator's relationship with one party's lawyers and inappropriate ex parte contact with that party) *and* Olson v. Merrill Lynch, Pierce, Fenner & Smith, Inc., 51 F.3d 157, 159 (8th Cir. 1995) (business relationship between arbitrator and investment firm should have been disclosed) *with* Montez v. Prudential Secs., Inc., 260 F.3d 980, 984 (8th Cir. 2001) (failure to disclose arbitrator's prior relationship with law firm representing party, which ended 5 years earlier, not sufficient), ANR Coal Co. v. Cogentrix of N.C., Inc., 173 F.3d 493, 502 (4th Cir. 1999) ("[a] trivial

of neutrality, however, is subject to waiver by the parties, as by an agreement to use party-appointed arbitrators.[201]

Section 10(a)(3) covers circumstances where the arbitrator engages in conduct that unduly favors one party. An award for a union was vacated on this ground where the arbitrator refused to consider the employer's evidence of a positive drug test by the employee and had misled the employer into believing that the test was already admitted into evidence.[202] Section 10(a)(3), however, is not a vehicle for challenging the arbitrator's inherently discretionary decisions, such as a failing to grant a continuance,[203] cutting off testimony,[204] denying leave to file a reply brief before issuing a decision,[205] or limiting discovery.[206]

Review under § 10(a)(4) "focuses on whether the arbitrators had the power, based on the parties' submissions or the arbitration agreement, to reach a certain issue, not whether the arbitrators correctly decided that issue."[207] Awards that are clearly at odds with the arbitrator's express authority under the contract are subject to

---

relationship, even if undisclosed, will not justify vacating an arbitration award"), Lifecare Int'l Inc. v. CD Med., Inc., 68 F.3d 429, 434 (11th Cir. 1995) (arbitrator's prior contentious relationship with law firm representing one party not sufficient) *and Consolidation Coal*, 48 F.3d at 129 (undisclosed sibling relationship between arbitrator and employee of one of the parties not grounds for vacating arbitrator's decision).

[201]*See* Sphere Drake Ins. Ltd. v. All Am. Life Ins. Co., 307 F.3d 617, 620 (7th Cir. 2002); Delta Mine Holding Co. v. AFC Coal Props., Inc., 280 F.3d 815, 821 (8th Cir. 2001); Sunkist Soft Drinks, Inc. v. Sunkist Growers, Inc., 10 F.3d 753, 759–60 (11th Cir. 1993).

[202]*See* Gulf Coast Indus. Workers Union v. Exxon Co., USA, 70 F.3d 847, 850 (5th Cir. 1995); *see also* Tempo Shain Corp. v. Bertek, Inc., 120 F.3d 16, 20 (2d Cir. 1997) (claimant not permitted to introduce broad range of evidence concerning allegedly fraudulent representations).

[203]*See, e.g.*, El Dorado Sch. Dist. #15 v. Continental Cas. Co., 247 F.3d 843, 848 (8th Cir. 2001); DVC-JPW Investors v. Gershman, 5 F.3d 1172, 1174 (8th Cir. 1993).

[204]*See, e.g., Delta Mine Holding Co.*, 280 F.3d at 822–23; Morani v. Landenberger, 196 F.3d 9, 11–12 (1st Cir. 1999); Kiewit/Atkinson/Kenny v. Electrical Workers (IBEW) Local 103, 76 F. Supp. 2d 77, 80–81 (D. Mass. 1999).

[205]*See, e.g.*, Sav-A-Trip, Inc. v. Belfort, 164 F.3d 1137, 1139 (8th Cir. 1999).

[206]*See, e.g.*, Nationwide Mut. Ins. Co. v. Home Ins. Co., 278 F.3d 621, 624–25 (6th Cir. 2002).

[207]DiRussa v. Dean Witter Reynolds Inc., 121 F.3d 818, 824, 74 FEP 726 (2d Cir. 1997); *see also* Kergosian v. Ocean Energy, Inc., 390 F.3d 346, 354 (5th Cir. 2004) (arbitrator's powers determined by arbitration agreement and scope of parties' submissions).

review under § 10(a)(4), although limitations on the arbitrator's authority are construed narrowly and all doubts are resolved in favor of the award.[208] Awards have been vacated under § 10(a)(4) where the arbitrator (1) awarded relief to or against a nonparty,[209] (2) entered an award beyond the limits set by the agreement,[210] (3) rejected procedures chosen expressly by the parties,[211] or (4) reached an issue expressly excluded from the scope of the arbitration agreement.[212]

Awards will not be vacated under § 10(a)(4) where the arbitrator disregarded the losing side's evidence.[213] In *DiRussa v. Dean Witter Reynolds Inc.*,[214] the Second Circuit held that although an arbitrator's failure to award attorney's fees to a prevailing employee in an ADEA case was an "obvious legal error," the decision was unreviewable under § 10(a)(4) because it was not an action in excess of the arbitrator's authority under the arbitration agreement.[215]

---

[208]*See* Mastrobuono v. Shearson Lehman Hutton, 514 U.S. 52, 62 (1995); *see also* Action Indus., Inc. v. U.S. Fid. & Guar. Co., 358 F.3d 337, 343 (5th Cir. 2004) ("A reviewing court examining whether arbitrators executed their powers must resolve all doubts in favor of arbitration."); Banco de Seguros del Estado v. Mutual Marine Office, Inc., 344 F.3d 255, 262–63 (2d Cir. 2003) (finding that arbitrator could demand party post prehearing security where agreement did not expressly preclude it).

[209]*See* AGCO Corp. v. Anglin, 216 F.3d 589, 594 (7th Cir. 2000) (arbitrators lacked authority to award relief against nonsignatories); NCR Corp. v. SAC-CO, Inc., 43 F.3d 1076 (6th Cir. 1995) (award of punitive damages to nonparty causes court to vacate award); Eljer Mfg., Inc. v. Kowin Dev. Corp., 14 F.3d 1250, 1256–57 (7th Cir. 1994) (vacating award to third party for separate transaction unrelated to arbitration agreement).

[210]*See* Missouri River Servs., Inc. v. Omaha Tribe of Neb., 267 F.3d 848, 855–56 (8th Cir. 2001) (arbitrator erased geographical and gaming limitations agreed to by parties in dispute over casino revenues); Coady v. Ashcraft & Gerel, 223 F.3d 1, 10 (1st Cir. 2000) (where parties stipulated to method of calculating law partner's bonus, arbitrators erred by rejecting stipulation and generating their own formula).

[211]*See* Morrison v. Circuit City Stores, Inc., 317 F.3d 646, 688, 90 FEP 1697 (6th Cir. 2003) (en banc) (discrepancies between AAA procedures and procedures in arbitration agreement demonstrated that there was no meeting of minds with regard to arbitration procedures).

[212]*See* Katz v. Feinberg, 290 F.3d 95, 97–98 (2d Cir. 2002) (arbitrator erroneously decided valuation issue that had been reserved to panel of accountants); Roadway Package Sys. v. Kayser, 257 F.3d 287, 301–02 (3d Cir. 2001) (arbitrator improperly ruled on fairness of procedures rather than whether party breached agreement).

[213]Mays v. Lanier Worldwide, Inc., 115 F. Supp. 2d 1330, 1346–47 (M.D. Ala. 2000) (in race discrimination case, arbitrator did not exceed authority by ignoring "much favorable evidence" in favor of employee).

[214]121 F.3d 818, 74 FEP 726 (2d Cir. 1997).

[215]*Id.* at 824.

2. Judicial Exceptions: Manifest Disregard of the Law and Public Policy

In addition to the statutory grounds provided by the FAA to vacate an arbitration award, courts widely recognize two nonstatutory standards: the arbitrator's "manifest disregard of the law" and "public policy."

The Supreme Court considered the "manifest disregard" standard in *Wilko v. Swan*[216] and more recently in *First Options of Chicago Inc. v. Kaplan*,[217] but has yet to rule on its scope.

Courts of appeal have articulated the scope of manifest disregard in a variety of ways, and although the standard is universally recognized as difficult to meet, it is a higher standard in some circuits than others. In *Williams v. CIGNA Financial Advisors Inc.*,[218] an ADEA case, the Fifth Circuit articulated a two-part inquiry that courts must undertake in applying the doctrine to cases arising under the employment laws. The first part is similar to that used in other circuits, namely, "where on the basis of the information available to the court it is not manifest that the arbitrators acted contrary to the applicable law, the award should be upheld."[219] The second part, however, is unique to the Fifth Circuit. If a court finds that the award was, in fact, rendered in contravention to the applicable law, the court must then decide whether the award "would result in significant injustice, taking into account all the circumstances of the case, including powers of arbitrators to judge norms appropriate to the relations between the parties."[220] If "significant injustice" would result, the award should be overturned; otherwise, it should stand.

---

[216]346 U.S. 427, 436–37 (1953) ("the interpretations of the law by the arbitrators in contrast to manifest disregard are not subject, in the federal courts, to judicial review for error in interpretation"), *overruled on other grounds by* Rodriguez de Quijas v. Shearson/Am. Express, Inc., 490 U.S. 477 (1989).

[217]514 U.S. 938, 942 (1995) (parties bound by arbitrator's decision, which is not in "manifest disregard" of law).

[218]197 F.3d 752, 81 FEP 747 (5th Cir. 1999).

[219]*Id.* at 762.

[220]*Id.; see also* Kergosian v. Ocean Energy, Inc., 390 F.3d 346, 355 (5th Cir. 2004) (applying two-part test and concluding that arbitrator did not commit manifest disregard of law when going outside administrative record in reviewing ERISA plan administrator's decisions; although federal court could not look outside record, parties to arbitration were not in federal court).

In *Koveleskie v. SBC Capital Markets, Inc.*,[221] the Seventh Circuit recognized "manifest disregard" as a valid basis for setting aside an arbitration award in a Title VII case.[222] In a nonemployment case, however, the Seventh Circuit held that manifest disregard of the law will be found only in cases where an arbitrator has "direct[ed] the parties to violate the law."[223] The court suggested, for example, that an arbitral award that required a party to employ unlicensed truck drivers would be in manifest disregard of the law.[224] In an FLSA case, the Eleventh Circuit has held that manifest disregard will only be found where the arbitrator is "conscious of the law and deliberately ignore[s] it."[225] The Eighth Circuit, in *Gas Aggregation Services, Inc. v. Howard Avista Energy*,[226] held that an arbitration panel that awarded attorney's fees under a state consumer fraud statute committed manifest disregard of the law where the panel itself recognized in its findings that the statute did not apply to the transaction.

In *Halligan v. Piper Jaffray, Inc.*,[227] the Second Circuit sanctioned a more searching standard of judicial review, at least in employment discrimination cases. The court there reversed an arbitrator's award for the employer in an ADEA case. In view of what the court termed "overwhelming evidence" of age discrimination,[228] it held that the arbitrators had "ignored the law or the evidence or both."[229] The court stated:

> In view of the strong evidence that Halligan was fired because of his age and the agreement of the parties that the arbitrators were correctly advised of the applicable legal principles, we are inclined to hold that they ignored the law or the evidence or both. Moreover, the arbitrators

---

[221]167 F.3d 361, 79 FEP 73 (7th Cir. 1999).

[222]167 F.3d at 366.

[223]George Watts & Son, Inc. v. Tiffany & Co., 248 F.3d 577, 580 (7th Cir. 2001).

[224]*Id.* at 581.

[225]*See* Brown v. ITT Consumer Fin. Corp., 211 F.3d 1217, 1223, 82 FEP 1388 (11th Cir. 2000); Montes v. Shearson Lehman Bros., Inc., 128 F.3d 1456, 1461 (11th Cir. 1997). The Ninth Circuit appears to follow the Eleventh Circuit standard. *See* Luong v. Circuit City Stores, Inc., 356 F.3d 1188 (9th Cir. 2004) ("arbitrators recognized the applicable law and then ignored it").

[226]319 F.3d 1060, 1069 (8th Cir. 2003).

[227]148 F.3d 197, 77 FEP 182 (2d Cir. 1998). In *GMS Group v. Benderson*, 326 F.3d 75, 79 (2d Cir. 2003), the Second Circuit expressly confined *Halligan* to "the unique concerns at issue with employment discrimination claims."

[228]148 F.3d at 203.

[229]*Id.* at 204.

did not explain their award . . . . At least in the circumstances here, we believe that when a reviewing court is inclined to hold that an arbitration panel manifestly disregarded the law, the failure of the arbitrators to explain the award can be taken into account. Having done so, we are left with the firm belief that the arbitrators here manifestly disregarded the law or the evidence or both.[230]

District courts within the Second Circuit have since applied *Halligan* both to affirm and to vacate awards in employment cases for manifest disregard.[231]

In *Cole v. Burns International Security Services*,[232] the District of Columbia Circuit, although noting that courts ordinarily defer to arbitrators' awards, held that the manifest disregard standard is somewhat elastic and "must be defined in light of the bases underlying the Court's decisions in *Gilmer*-type cases."[233] The court noted:

> The nearly unlimited deference paid to arbitration awards in the context of collective bargaining is not required, and not appropriate, in the context of employees' statutory claims. In this context, the Supreme Court has assumed that arbitration awards are subject to judicial review sufficiently rigorous to ensure compliance with statutory law.[234]

Thus, "there will be some cases in which novel or difficult legal issues are presented demanding judicial judgment. In such cases, the courts are empowered to review an arbitrator's award to ensure that its resolution of public law issues is correct."[235]

The other nonstatutory standard for vacating an arbitration award, "public policy," has been reviewed repeatedly by the Supreme Court, which in successive opinions has narrowed the standard's scope. The "public policy" exception bars arbitrators from compelling activity that violates either positive law or a well-defined

---

[230]*Id.* (internal citations omitted).

[231]*Compare* Raiola v. Union Bank of Switz., 230 F. Supp. 2d 355 (S.D.N.Y. 2002) (finding no manifest disregard in Title VII case), Sobol v. Kidder, Peabody & Co., Inc., 49 F. Supp. 2d 208, 83 FEP 35 (S.D.N.Y. 1999) (same) *and* Campbell v. Cantor Fitzgerald & Co., 21 F. Supp. 2d 341 (S.D.N.Y. 1998) (same), *aff'd*, 205 F.3d 1321 (2d Cir. 1999) *with* Neary v. Prudential Ins. Co. of Am., 63 F. Supp. 2d 208 (D. Conn. 1999) (finding manifest disregard of record by arbitration panel in state-law whistleblowing case).

[232]105 F.3d 1465, 1485, 72 FEP 1775 (D.C. Cir. 1997).

[233]*Id.* at 1487.

[234]*Id.* at 1468–69.

[235]*Id.* at 1487.

public interest. In the Supreme Court's first case involving the public policy exception, *W.R. Grace & Co. v. Rubber Workers Local 759*,[236] the employer challenged as a violation of public policy back-pay arbitration awards to male employees who were laid off in the wake of an EEOC conciliation agreement that required the company to lay off male and female employees proportionally. The Court noted that public policy challenges to arbitration awards are "ultimately . . . for resolution by the courts" rather than arbitrators, and that if a contract as interpreted by an arbitrator "violates some explicit public policy, we are obliged to refrain from enforcing it."[237] The Court then laid down the key standard: "Such a public policy, however, must be well defined and dominant, and is to be ascertained by reference to the laws and legal precedents and not from general considerations of supposed public interests."[238] Although recognizing that "obedience to judicial orders is an important public policy,"[239] the Court held that the CBA as interpreted by the arbitrator did not compel the employer to violate the injunction. Rather, the arbitrator found that the company assumed the risk of loss (in the form of back pay for the male employees) if it chose to lay off employees under the terms of the conciliation agreement.

In two subsequent cases that involved firing employees from safety-sensitive jobs—*Paperworkers v. Misco, Inc.*[240] and *Eastern Associated Coal Corp. v. Mine Workers (UMW) District 17*[241]—the Supreme Court further narrowed the public policy exception. In *Misco*, an employee who worked with heavy cutting equipment was found in his white Cutlass automobile in the plant parking lot, in the company of two other men, with a smoldering marijuana joint propped in the ashtray. The employer fired the employee for possession of drugs on plant property, in violation of work rules, but the arbitrator reinstated him. The Court ultimately sustained the arbitrator's award. The Court held that the employer failed to identify either a "well-defined and dominant" policy or a clear violation of such a policy by the arbitration award. The policy against intoxicated operation of

---

[236]461 U.S. 757 (1983).
[237]*Id.* at 766.
[238]*Id.* (quoting Muschany v. United States, 324 U.S. 49, 66 (1945)).
[239]*Id.*
[240]484 U.S. 29 (1985).
[241]531 U.S. 57 (2000).

heavy equipment, although "firmly rooted in common sense," lacked any foundation in existing laws and precedents.[242]

In *Eastern Associated*, the employee truck driver tested positive on two marijuana tests. His discharge was reversed by the arbitrator because the employee had a solid 17-year record, suffered a momentary relapse in his drug use, and could be rehabilitated with tight supervision (including a lengthy, unpaid suspension).[243] The Supreme Court again upheld the award. Although the Court recognized "in principle" that "the public policy exception is not limited solely to instances where the arbitration award itself violates positive law,"[244] here both the Congress and the U.S. Department of Transportation, in the Omnibus Transportation Employee Testing Act of 1991,[245] laid out detailed guidance for how to treat drivers who test positive for illegal drug use, the provisions of which did not compel the instant discharge of employees who tested positive for drug use.[246] *Eastern Associated* essentially halted the practice of federal courts vacating reinstatement awards for safety-sensitive positions.[247]

Courts have recognized a public policy against reinstatement of employees responsible for sex or race harassment in the workplace.[248] But, as with public safety cases, courts seldom reverse

---

[242]*Misco*, 484 U.S. at 44.

[243]*Eastern Associated*, 531 U.S. at 60–61.

[244]*Id.* at 63. The concurring opinion, by Justices Scalia and Thomas, eschewed this reservation as dicta and would have held that arbitration awards must violate positive law before the public policy exception could apply.

[245]Pub. L. No. 102-143, 105 Stat. 952 (codified as amended at 49 U.S.C. §§ 31301, 31306 (2000)).

[246]*Eastern Associated*, 531 U.S. at 67.

[247]*See* Southern Cal. Gas Co. v. Utility Workers Local 132, 265 F.3d 787, 796–97 (9th Cir. 2001) (employees' drug tests not reliable because they did not comport with Department of Transportation regulations); Boston Med. Ctr. v. Service Employees Local 285, 260 F.3d 16, 23–27 (1st Cir. 2001) (reversing vacatur of award reinstating nurse to hospital duty after investigation of infant death; although recognizing that "egregious" conduct by health professional might raise public policy concerns, here investigation turned up no evidence of willful or callous misconduct); Teamsters Local 58 v. BOC Gases, 249 F.3d 1089, 1093–94 (9th Cir. 2001) (arbitrator found that truck driver carting hazardous materials was fit to perform duties); Pan Am. Airways Corp. v. Air Line Pilots, 206 F. Supp. 12, 23–24 (D.D.C. 2002) (reinstatement of pilot termed "insubordinate" by management).

[248]*See* EEOC v. Indiana Bell Tel. Co., 256 F.3d 516, 524, 86 FEP 1 (7th Cir. 2001) (en banc) (in harassment case, court plurality notes that no award that required employer to tolerate ongoing violation of Title VII could be enforced).

reinstatement awards when there is a plausible basis for the arbitrator's decision, such as the potential for rehabilitation.[249]

H. Scope of the Arbitration

An agreement to arbitrate may be limited to particular issues and exclude others.[250] Class claims may be found to be not arbitrable, depending on the terms of the agreement.[251]

Broadly defined arbitration agreements that cover any dispute or controversy have been enforced.[252] However, an arbitration agreement that used the phrase "claims under this agreement" has been interpreted to *exclude* statutory claims and applied only to the claims based on the employment agreement.[253] The scope of arbitrability, as with other interpretive questions, is governed by state contract law.[254]

---

[249]*See* Weber Aircraft Inc. v. General Warehouse & Helpers Local 767, 253 F.3d 821, 825–27 (5th Cir. 2001) (reinstatement without back pay appropriate treatment of accused harasser); Westvaco Corp. v. Paperworkers, 171 F.3d 971, 977, 79 FEP 595 (4th Cir. 1999) ("because [harassment] misconduct often differs in degree, there is no universal punishment that fits every case"); Communications Workers v. Southeastern Elec. Coop., 882 F.2d 467, 470 (10th Cir. 1989) (affirming award allowing 19-year veteran with previously clean record to return to work after harassment incident); Communications Workers v. Bell Atlantic-W. Va., Inc., 27 F. Supp. 2d 66, 70–71, 78 FEP 630 (D.D.C. 1998) (companies seeking broader right to terminate harassers must assure that definition of "just cause" under CBA allows such latitude). *But see* Newsday, Inc. v. Long Island Typographical Union No. 915, 915 F.2d 840, 845, 54 FEP 24 (2d Cir. 1990) (vacating reinstatement of alleged harasser where employee was repeat sexual offender who had been reinstated following prior incident of sexual harassment with warning by that arbitrator that any further harassing behavior "shall be grounds for immediate discharge"); Brookdale Hosp. Med. Ctr. v. Health & Human Serv. Employees Local 1199, 107 F. Supp. 2d 283, 292–93 (S.D.N.Y. 2000) (record doubtful on circumstances supporting award to reinstate putative harasser; court remands to arbitrator to make factual findings).

[250]*E.g.*, Keymer v. Management Recruiters Int'l Inc., 169 F.3d 501, 504, 78 FEP 1864 (8th Cir. 1999) (issues arising from discharge may be litigated in ADEA case where arbitration agreement specifically excluded such claims); Brennan v. King, 139 F.3d 258, 265–66 (1st Cir. 1998) (dispute over tenure not covered by arbitration agreement).

[251]*See* Ting v. AT&T, 319 F.3d 1126, 1150 (9th Cir. 2003) (form contract's class action ban violated California's unconscionability law); Olde Discount Corp. v. Hubbard, 4 F. Supp. 2d 1268, 1270–71, 77 FEP 618 (D. Kan. 1998) (NASD rules did not allow class action to be arbitrated), *aff'd*, 172 F.3d 879 (10th Cir. 1999).

[252]*See* Oldroyd v. Elmira Sav. Bank, 134 F.3d 72 (2d Cir. 1998).

[253]*See* Boone v. Etkin, 771 So. 2d 557, 83 FEP 1765 (Fla. Dist. Ct. App. 2000) (arbitration agreement not enforced; applying state law that phrase "claims and questions regarding the rights and obligations of the parties under the terms of this agreement" did not include sexual harassment).

[254]*See, e.g.*, First Options of Chi., Inc. v. Kaplan, 514 U.S. 938, 944 (1995) (to decide "whether the parties agreed to arbitrate a certain matter," courts apply "ordinary

In addition to whether parties agreed to subject a particular claim to arbitration, courts have addressed the subsidiary question of whether the issue of arbitrability should be resolved by the court or the arbitrator. In *Green Tree Financial Corp. v. Bazzle*,[255] a four-Justice plurality of the Supreme Court confronted this issue with respect to a consumer lender's arbitration clause, which provided that "[a]ll disputes . . . arising from or relating to this contract or the relationships which result . . . shall be resolved by binding arbitration by one arbitrator selected by [the lender] with consent of you."[256]

A majority of the Court in *Bazzle* agreed that the contract did not clearly forbid class action treatment, as the South Carolina Supreme Court had held. Nonetheless, the Supreme Court held that it was for the arbitrator, rather than the court, to decide whether a class action procedure could be applied.[257]

The *Bazzle* opinion went on to cite threshold issues presumed to belong to the courts rather than arbitrators "in the absence of 'clea[r] and unmistakabl[e]' evidence to the contrary,"[258] "such as whether the parties have a valid arbitration agreement and whether a concededly binding arbitration clause applies to a certain type of controversy."[259] The lower courts have read this language to ordinarily require courts to construe issues concerning arbitrability of a claim.[260]

---

state-law principles that govern the formation of contracts"); Mastrobuono v. Shearson Lehman Hutton, Inc., 514 U.S. 52, 62–63 (1995) (applying New York and Illinois law); Volt Info. Scis., Inc. v. Board of Trs. of Leland Stanford Junior Univ., 489 U.S. 468, 475–76 (1989) ("general state-law principles of contract interpretation [apply] to the interpretation of an arbitration agreement"); Perry v. Thomas, 482 U.S. 483, 492 (1987) ("state law, whether of legislative or judicial origin, is applicable *if* that law arose to govern issues concerning the validity, revocability, and enforceability of contracts generally").

[255]539 U.S. 444 (2003).

[256]*Id.* at 448.

[257]*Id.* at 454 (remanding case for further arbitration proceedings). Justice Stevens authored a brief dissenting opinion contending that the South Carolina Supreme Court's interpretation of the clause to permit classwide arbitration had been correct and that he would vote to affirm the decision below. *Id.* at 454–55.

[258]*Id.* at 452 (quoting AT&T Techs., Inc. v. Communications Workers, 475 U.S. 643, 649 (1986)).

[259]*Id.*; *see also* Howsam v. Dean Witter Reynolds, Inc., 537 U.S. 79, 84 (2002) ("a gateway dispute about whether the parties are bound by a given arbitration clause raises a 'question of arbitrability' for a court to decide").

[260]*See, e.g.*, Marie v. Allied Home Mortgage Corp., 402 F.3d 1, 13–14, 95 FEP 737 (1st Cir. 2005) (arbitrator is to decide application of time limitations clause, but court decides whether employer's delay in demanding arbitration constitutes waiver

IV. MEDIATION

Mediation is a supervised settlement conference presided over by a neutral intermediary or a judge who assists the parties in reaching a settlement. A mediator does not have the authority to make a binding decision or award. Employers may use mediation before arbitration as part of a multistep alternative dispute resolution (ADR) program.[261] Unlike arbitration, the mediation process does not contemplate the testimony of witnesses or admission of evidence, and the mediator does not rule on questions of law or fact or render any decisions.[262]

Pursuant to the Alternative Dispute Resolution Act of 1988,[263] some federal district courts have adopted specific rules for court-ordered mediation. The First Circuit, in *In re Atlantic Pipe Corp.*,[264] affirmed the inherent authority of a federal district court to order private mediation. The court in *Atlantic Pipe Corp.* determined that the mediation program affords "procedural and substantive safeguards to ensure fairness to all parties involved," including reasonable limits on duration and expenses.[265]

---

of right to arbitration); Anders v. Hometown Mortgage Servs., Inc., 346 F.3d 1024, 1027 (11th Cir. 2003) (use of terms "any" and "all" to describe claims covered under arbitration clause communicates full breadth of arbitrability); Ciago v. Ameriquest Mortgage Co., 295 F. Supp. 2d 324, 330 (S.D.N.Y. 2003) (clause that includes "all claims" but specifically excludes workers' compensation claims, unemployment claims, and employers' claims for unfair competition or theft of trade secrets applies to FLSA and state law claims).

[261]*See, e.g.*, Potts v. Baptist Health Sys. Inc., 853 So. 2d 194 (Ala. 2002) (employer's program provided right to be heard by supervisory structure and/or by peer-review committee in effort to resolve disputes before proceeding to arbitration).

[262]The EEOC launched a national mediation program in 1999. Under the program, charges filed against employers participating in this program are referred to the EEOC's mediation unit before the Commission launches an investigation into the charge.

[263]28 U.S.C. § 651(b) (2000) (directing each district court to "devise and implement its own [ADR] program, by local rule adopted under [28 U.S.C.] section 2071(a), to encourage and promote the use of [ADR] in its district"); *see, e.g.*, Nick v. Morgan's Foods, Inc., 270 F.3d 590, 595 (8th Cir. 2001) (affirming sanctions against party for failing to participate in court-ordered mediation under Eastern District of Missouri Local Rule 6.01); Turner v. Young, 205 F.R.D. 592, 595 (D. Kan. 2002) (compelling attendance at private mediation under District of Kansas Local Rule 16.3).

[264]304 F.3d 135 (1st Cir. 2002).

[265]*Id.* at 147. *But see In re* African-American Slave Descendants' Litig., 272 F. Supp. 2d 755, 759 (N.D. Ill. 2003) (although "the court does have the inherent power to order the parties to submit to non-binding mediation," court declined to do so where "such an order would not facilitate an expeditious end to the litigation").

A number of courts have considered a "mediation privilege" that precludes discovery of communications made during mediation.[266] The Fourth Circuit observed that some degree of confidentiality "is essential to the integrity and success of the Court's mediation program, in that confidentiality encourages candor between the parties and on the part of the mediator, and confidentiality serves to protect the mediation program from being used as a discovery tool."[267]

---

[266]*Compare* Folb v. Motion Picture Indus. Pension & Health Plans, 16 F. Supp. 2d 1164, 1179 (C.D. Cal. 1998) (privileging from discovery "information disclosed in conjunction with mediation proceedings with a neutral"), *aff'd*, 216 F.3d 1082 (9th Cir. 2000) *and In re* Grand Jury Subpoena Dated Dec. 17, 1996, 148 F.3d 487, 493 (5th Cir. 1998) (refusing to recognize privilege where grand jury demands mediation communications) *with* Smith v. Smith, 154 F.R.D. 661, 675 (N.D. Tex. 1994) (declining to recognize federal mediator's privilege in RICO, securities fraud, and common law fraud case despite existence of such privilege under Texas law), *aff'd mem.*, 132 F.3d 1454 (5th Cir. 1997).

[267]*In re* Anonymous, 283 F.3d 627, 636–37 (4th Cir. 2002) (upon request by lawyer for authorization to disclose communications during mediation in disciplinary proceedings, court adopts standard "disallowing disclosure unless the party seeking such disclosure can demonstrate that 'manifest injustice' will result from non-disclosure").

CHAPTER 43

SETTLEMENT

The U.S. Supreme Court has noted that "[i]n enacting Title VII, Congress expressed a strong preference for encouraging voluntary settlement of employment discrimination claims."[1] Employers and other respondents enter into settlement agreements to avoid the costs of litigation, to avert the disruption inherent in the litigation process, and to obviate the risk of liability and damages.

---

[1]Carson v. American Brands, Inc., 450 U.S. 79, 88 n.14, 25 FEP 1 (1981) (district court's order refusing to enter proposed consent decree immediately appealable under 28 U.S.C. § 1292(a)(1) as order refusing injunction; order may have "serious, perhaps irreparable, consequence" on employees in that they might lose their opportunity to settle their case on negotiated terms); *accord* Alexander v. Gardner-Denver Co., 415 U.S. 36, 44, 7 FEP 81 (1974) ("Cooperation and voluntary compliance were selected as the preferred means for achieving [equality of opportunity]. To this end, Congress created the Equal Employment Opportunity Commission . . . to settle disputes through conference, conciliation, and persuasion before the aggrieved party was permitted to file a lawsuit."); United States v. Allegheny-Ludlum Indus., Inc., 517 F.2d 826, 847, 11 FEP 167 (5th Cir. 1975) (noting deference to be accorded processes of voluntary conciliation and settlement as expressed in *Gardner-Denver*); Hutchings v. United States Indus., Inc., 428 F.2d 303, 309, 2 FEP 725 (5th Cir. 1970) ("[f]rom a reading of the provisions enacted to effectuate [§ 703(a) of Title VII], it is clear that Congress placed great emphasis upon private settlement and the elimination of unfair practices without litigation, . . . on the ground that voluntary compliance is preferable to court action").

Complainants enter into settlement agreements to obtain immediate monetary and other consideration and to avoid the stress, uncertainty, and inevitable delay of litigation.

I. VALIDITY OF WAIVERS OF DISCRIMINATION CLAIMS

Virtually all settlements of discrimination claims involve a release or waiver of claims by the complainant; indeed, this typically is the most important element of consideration to the employer. A large body of Title VII case law has developed that addresses the circumstances under which a privately negotiated release of claims will be upheld. In the Older Workers Benefit Protection Act (OWBPA),[2] in part building on and in part abrogating that case law, Congress specified the elements required for a valid waiver of age discrimination claims under the Age Discrimination in Employment Act (ADEA). This section discusses waiver rules that are applicable in discrimination cases generally. The OWBPA's requirements are discussed in Section II.

A. Knowing and Voluntary Waivers of Past Claims Are Valid

Knowing, voluntary releases of preexisting claims repeatedly have been upheld by the courts.

1. Waivers of Past Claims Are Valid

The Supreme Court noted in dictum in *Alexander v. Gardner-Denver Co.*[3] that an employee may waive causes of action under Title VII as part of a voluntary settlement. The Court added, however, that "[i]n determining the effectiveness of any such waiver, a court would have to determine at the outset that the employee's consent to the settlement was voluntary and knowing."[4]

In *United States v. Allegheny-Ludlum Industries*,[5] the Fifth Circuit considered a challenge to a proposed consent decree that

---

[2]Pub. L. No. 101-433, § 201, 1990 U.S.C.C.A.N. (104 Stat.) 1509 (codified as amended at 29 U.S.C. §§ 623, 626, 630 (2000)). The OWBPA is discussed in greater detail in Section II *infra* and in Chapter 12 (Age).

[3]415 U.S. 36, 52, 7 FEP 81 (1974).

[4]*Id.* at 52 n.15.

[5]517 F.2d 826, 11 FEP 167 (5th Cir. 1975).

provided for individual releases.[6] It held that an employee may waive both monetary and injunctive relief on claims that "arise from antecedent discriminatory events, acts, patterns, or practices, or the 'continuing' or 'future' effects thereof so long as such effects are causally rooted—in origin, logic, and factual experience—in discriminatory acts or practices which antedate the execution of the release."[7] To decide otherwise, the court noted, would be illogical; Title VII lawsuits then could be resolved only in the courtroom.[8] The court emphasized, however, that the release must be "executed voluntarily and with adequate knowledge."[9]

2. The Waiver Must Be Knowing and Voluntary

The courts of appeals have articulated two different tests to determine whether a waiver was executed "knowingly and voluntarily." The Fourth, Sixth, and Eighth Circuits apply "ordinary contract principles" in determining whether a release was given knowingly and voluntarily.[10] The First, Second, Third, Fifth, Seventh, Tenth, and Eleventh Circuits apply a "totality of the circumstances" standard.[11] The differences between the two tests may be more

---

[6]*Id.* at 837–38.

[7]*Id.* at 853.

[8]*Id.* at 858–59 ("[W]e cannot conceive of how any employment discrimination dispute could ever be resolved outside, or indeed inside, the courtroom, if defendants were forbidden to obtain binding, negotiated settlements. No defendant would ever deliver money, promises, or any other consideration—not even a peppercorn—except after entry of a contested, final court order.").

[9]*Id.* at 853.

[10]*E.g.*, Morrison v. Circuit City Stores, Inc., 317 F.3d 646, 668, 90 FEP 1697 (6th Cir. 2003) ("In reviewing whether a waiver of prospective claims was valid, we apply ordinary contract principles."); Warnebold v. Union Pac. R.R., 963 F.2d 222, 223, 58 FEP 1664 (8th Cir. 1992) (court applies "ordinary contract principles" in determining validity of release as a knowing and voluntary waiver of claims); O'Shea v. Commercial Credit Corp., 930 F.2d 358, 362, 55 FEP 973 (4th Cir. 1991) (better approach is to utilize ordinary contract principles). *But see* Todd v. Blue Ridge Legal Servs., Inc., 175 F. Supp. 2d 857, 862 (W.D. Va. 2001) (court acknowledged that OWBPA had superseded by statute Fourth Circuit's application of "ordinary contract principles" test in age discrimination cases in favor of "totality of the circumstances" test, but applied "ordinary contract principles" test in case under Equal Pay Act).

[11]*See* Myricks v. Federal Reserve Bank of Atlanta, 2007 WL 675341, at *4 (11th Cir. Mar. 7, 2007) ("To release a cause of action under Title VII, the employee's consent to the settlement must be voluntary and knowing based on the totality of the circumstances."); Bachiller v. Turn on Prods., Inc., 86 Fed. Appx. 465, 466–67, 93 FEP 479 (2d Cir. 2004) (applying the "totality of the circumstances" test to determine whether release was invalid for failure to meet the specific requirements for a knowing and voluntary waiver); Wastak v. Lehigh Valley Health Network, 342 F.3d

superficial than tangible.[12] Although cases that apply "ordinary contract principles" generally consider the circumstances surrounding the execution of the release, the clarity of the release, and whether the complainant was represented by counsel,[13] the courts that apply

---

281, 295, 92 FEP 1079 (3d Cir. 2003) (courts must inquire into the totality of the circumstances "to determine factually whether the execution of a waiver was 'knowing and voluntary' "); Smith v. Amedisys, Inc., 298 F.3d 434, 441, 89 FEP 874 (5th Cir. 2002) ("[i]n determining whether a release was knowingly and voluntarily executed, this court has adopted a 'totality of the circumstances' approach"); Melanson v. Browning-Ferris Indus., Inc., 281 F.3d 272, 274, 88 FEP 286 (1st Cir. 2002) ("our precedent leaves little room for doubt that a [Title VII] release, like a release of other federal statutorily-created rights, must be knowing and voluntary, as evidenced by the totality of the circumstances"); Bennett v. Coors Brewing Co., 189 F.3d 1221, 1228, 80 FEP 1197 (10th Cir. 1999) ("a court must look to the 'totality of the circumstances' to determine if the release of an employment discrimination claim is knowing and voluntary"); Pierce v. Atchison, Topeka & Santa Fe Ry., 65 F.3d 562, 571, 68 FEP 1270 (7th Cir. 1995) (*Pierce I*) ("While we recognize the critical role that the plain language of the contract plays, our inquiry into knowledge and voluntariness cannot end there. . . . The totality of the circumstances approach is consistent with the strong congressional purpose underlying the ADEA to eradicate discrimination in employment." (citation omitted)); Beadle v. City of Tampa, 42 F.3d 633, 635, 66 FEP 1540 (11th Cir. 1995) (factors to be considered include "the plaintiff's education and business experience; the amount of time the plaintiff considered the agreement before signing it; the clarity of the agreement; the plaintiff's opportunity to consult with an attorney; the employer's encouragement or discouragement of consultation with an attorney; and the consideration given in exchange for the waiver when compared with the benefits to which the employee was already entitled"); *cf.* Stroman v. West Coast Grocery Co., 884 F.2d 458, 462–63, 50 FEP 1204 (9th Cir. 1989) (in determining whether waiver was voluntary court considered clarity and lack of ambiguity of the agreement, the employee's education and business experience, and whether the employee had the benefit of legal counsel).

[12]For example, in *Coventry*, 856 F.2d at 522–23 n.9, the Third Circuit noted that although the Sixth Circuit in *Runyan*, 787 F.2d at 1044–46, had purported to apply "ordinary contract principles," it really considered the totality of the circumstances, including the fact that the plaintiff himself was a lawyer who was knowledgeable in labor law and employment discrimination matters. Indeed, in another case, *Adams v. Philip Morris, Inc.*, 67 F.3d 580, 583, 71 FEP 1025 (6th Cir. 1995), the Sixth Circuit purported to apply "ordinary contract principles" in determining the validity of the waiver but then listed factors to consider that expressly included the "totality of the circumstances." Similarly, in *Lancaster v. Buerkle Buick Honda Co.*, 809 F.2d 539, 541, 42 FEP 1472 (8th Cir. 1987), the Eighth Circuit invoked "ordinary contract principles" but in fact considered the totality of the circumstances, including the plaintiff's possession of the agreement for 5 days, that the agreement contained no ultimatums or deadlines, that the agreement was clear and unambiguous, that significant favorable additions were negotiated, and that the plaintiff was a well-paid management employee who in his lifetime had signed numerous contracts.

[13]*See, e.g.*, Pilon v. University of Minn., 710 F.2d 466, 467–68, 32 FEP 508 (8th Cir. 1983) (where plaintiff was represented by an attorney, the release language was clear, and there was no claim of fraud or duress, release upheld).

the "totality of the circumstances" standard have found the following factors to be relevant:

(1) the plaintiff's education and business experience,

(2) the amount of time the plaintiff had possession of or access to the agreement before signing it,

(3) the role of the plaintiff in deciding or negotiating the terms of the agreement,

(4) the clarity of the agreement,

(5) whether the plaintiff was represented by or consulted with an attorney,

(6) whether an employer encouraged or discouraged the plaintiff to consult an attorney, and

(7) whether the plaintiff had a fair opportunity to consult an attorney.[14]

Courts have examined a number of agreements that utilize either of the two tests to determine whether the waiver of claims was knowing and voluntary. In most[15]

---

[14]Riley v. American Family Mut. Ins. Co., 881 F.2d 368, 372, 50 FEP 668 (7th Cir. 1989); *see also* EEOC v. American Express Publ'g Corp., 681 F. Supp. 216, 219, 47 FEP 1596 (S.D.N.Y. 1988) (identifying additional factor of "whether the consideration given in exchange for the waiver exceeds employee benefits to which the employee was already entitled by contract or law").

[15]*First Circuit*: Melanson v. Browning-Ferris Indus., Inc., 281 F.3d 272, 277, 88 FEP 286 (1st Cir. 2002) (employee had capacity to make knowing and voluntary waiver despite history of depression and treatment for bulimia; court noted that "incapacity to knowingly and voluntarily execute a release will not be inferred simply from the showing, standing alone, that the [employee] suffered from some psychiatric disorder. . . . Nor may incapacity or duress, without more, be inferred from merely the emotional and financial stress associated with loss of a job"); Rivera-Flores v. Bristol-Myers Squibb Caribbean, 112 F.3d 9, 12–13 (1st Cir. 1997) (court noted that heightened judicial scrutiny is warranted where person asserts that he was disabled at time release was signed, but cautioned that not all disabilities inherently involve question about capacity to act; release held valid where language was "clear and unmistakable" and where ADA was specifically mentioned, even though there was little room for negotiation and plaintiff lacked business sophistication).

Second Circuit: Vital v. Interfaith Med. Ctr., 168 F.3d 615, 622, 80 FEP 281 (2d Cir. 1999) (holding waiver of Title VII claims was knowing and voluntary release when examined in light of totality of circumstances); Bormann v. AT&T Commc'ns, Inc., 875 F.2d 399, 403, 49 FEP 1622 (2d Cir. 1989) (dismissal of ADEA claims upheld based on district court's findings that appellants "were experienced executives familiar with reading and analyzing contracts"; "release itself is written in clear and unambiguous language" that specifically referred to age discrimination claims; included statement that signer was aware of right to consult attorney; appellants had "sufficient time to consider the release"; and "there was no economic duress"; although it did not appear that there was opportunity to negotiate release terms, this fact, although relevant, did not require trial on "voluntariness").

Third Circuit: Cirillo v. Arco Chem. Co., 862 F.2d 448, 452–53, 48 FEP 678 (3d Cir. 1988) (validity of release was upheld even though plaintiff was not represented by counsel because he was "literate, well-educated man" who took 1 month to sign, which is reasonable time to deliberate; text was "straightforward, clear and specific" and "was presented to employees in a manner and context that signalled the importance of the matter, explained the nature of the claims that would be released, and counseled mature consideration with the help of an attorney").

Fourth Circuit: O'Shea v. Commercial Credit Corp., 930 F.2d 358, 362, 55 FEP 973 (4th Cir. 1991) (release upheld applying ordinary contract principles; plaintiff's decision was "voluntary, deliberate, and informed"; waiver of age discrimination claims was unambiguous, and consideration was substantial).

Fifth Circuit: Smith v. Amedisys, Inc., 298 F.3d 434, 89 FEP 874 (5th Cir. 2002) (enforcing contract where plaintiff was high school graduate, generally understood terms of release, had weeks to review it, and contract used plain language); O'Hare v. Global Natural Res., Inc., 898 F.2d 1015, 1016–18, 52 FEP 1139 (5th Cir. 1990) (employee was attorney with contract experience who consulted three attorneys while in possession of draft copy before signing release 1 month later and had received consideration); Rogers v. General Elec. Co., 781 F.2d 452, 455–56, 39 FEP 1581 (5th Cir. 1986) (affirming summary judgment; release in sex discrimination case was knowingly and voluntarily signed, because it was unambiguous and labeled as release, plaintiff was advised both orally and in writing that she could consult attorney, and she admitted that no one had forced her to sign release); Fulgence v. J. Ray McDermott & Co., 662 F.2d 1207, 1209–10, 27 FEP 799 (5th Cir. 1981) (oral settlement agreement upheld; it was negotiated by attorney with plaintiff's approval, and there was no evidence of fraud, coercion, or overreaching or incompetence of counsel).

Sixth Circuit: Adams v. Phillip Morris, Inc., 67 F.3d 580, 583 (6th Cir. 1995) (release valid where waiver was plain, unambiguous, and easily understandable by someone with plaintiff's abilities, plaintiff was given 5 days to consider whether to sign and was advised to consult with attorney, and plaintiff received approximately twice as much in benefits as he would otherwise have been entitled to receive); Shaheen v. B.F. Goodrich Co., 873 F.2d 105, 107–08, 49 FEP 1060 (6th Cir. 1989) (release of ADEA claims upheld where plaintiff was given 3 months to decide among options and consulted with attorney; release supported by consideration independent of pension entitlements described in employee handbook); Runyan v. National Cash Register Corp., 787 F.2d 1039, 1044, 40 FEP 807 (6th Cir. 1986) (en banc) (settlement upheld because Runyan was "well-paid, well-educated, labor lawyer with many years of experience" and was well aware of his legal rights); Kendrick v. Kmart Corp., 24 EB 2141 (E.D. Mich. 2000) (applying *Adams* and rejecting defense of economic duress where plaintiff had bachelor's degree, had over 20 years of experience as store manager, could have taken 45 days to consider agreement, was expressly told to obtain legal counsel, and was given substantial consideration ($12,250), COBRA subsidies, and use of relocation services); Parker v. Key Plastics, Inc., 68 F. Supp. 2d 818, 826–27 (E.D. Mich. 1999) (following *Adams* and rejecting economic duress argument even though employee wrote "under duress" next to his signature; economic pressure and protestations of innocence do not establish that agreement was anything other than knowing and voluntary).

Seventh Circuit: Riley, 881 F.2d at 373–74 (settlement upheld where plaintiff signed unambiguous release supported by consideration while represented by counsel;

but not all[16] of these cases, the agreement has been

---

inaccurate conveyance of effect of release or inadequate protection of rights by counsel may be remedied through malpractice action).

Eighth Circuit: Lancaster, 809 F.2d at 541 (unambiguous release valid because Lancaster was well-paid management employee with much contracting experience; he had 5 days to consider agreement, which had no ultimatums or deadlines, and he chose not to consult attorney); Worthy v. McKesson Corp., 756 F.2d 1370, 1372–73, 37 FEP 539 (8th Cir. 1985) (oral settlement agreement enforced where plaintiff was represented by counsel who discussed settlement with him for more than 1 hour; plaintiff had expressly agreed to release all claims; confidentiality and no-reemployment terms were not so significant that they could be used to abrogate agreement); *Pilon*, 710 F.2d at 467–68 (affirming summary judgment; settlement agreement valid where waiver was unambiguous and plaintiff was represented by counsel).

Ninth Circuit: Stroman v. West Coast Grocery Co., 884 F.2d 458, 462–63, 50 FEP 1204 (9th Cir. 1989) (release of claims upheld despite absence of lawyers; agreement was unambiguous, and Stroman's army training and business management–related community college degree were indicative of education and skills necessary to understand that he waived all legal claims).

Eleventh Circuit: Freeman v. Motor Convoy, Inc., 700 F.2d 1339, 1352, 31 FEP 517 (11th Cir. 1983) (conciliation agreement binding on employee who, although unrepresented by counsel, received advice from Equal Employment Opportunity Commission (EEOC) representative, read agreement, and obtained relief specified).

[16]*Second Circuit*: Gorman v Earmark, Inc., 968 F. Supp. 58, 64 (D. Conn. 1997) (plaintiff, although experienced businessman, asserted that he was given only 10 minutes to review release, that he was unaware he would need to sign release, and that there was no independent consideration; court held that "jury could reasonably conclude that the release was an eleventh-hour addition to the agreement, extracted . . . without negotiation and additional consideration, and thus not enforceable").

Third Circuit: Coventry, 856 F.2d at 524–25 (reversing district court finding that appellant had "knowingly and willfully" released age discrimination claims; appellant given "Hobson's choice" of automatic layoff or early retirement without ADEA rights, indicating that his choice was not free of duress, and there was no evidence that appellant had been encouraged to consult attorney or that he had done so).

Fifth Circuit: Mosley v. St. Louis S.W. Ry., 634 F.2d 942, 945–46, 24 FEP 1366 (5th Cir. 1981) (release invalid where settlement terms did not address plaintiffs' discrimination claims and amounted to "precious little more" than promise of nonretaliation, which is statutory right; EEOC representative supervised execution of agreements even though she knew that plaintiffs were represented by counsel, required that they sign immediately to avoid formal proceedings, and intimated that if plaintiffs sued they might be held liable for attorney's fees).

Sixth Circuit: Lyght v. Ford Motor Co., 643 F.2d 435, 439–40, 25 FEP 246 (6th Cir. 1981) (plaintiff's back-pay claims not knowingly and voluntarily waived because he was unrepresented, did not participate in settlement negotiations, signed no release, and was never told that acceptance of promotion constituted waiver).

Seventh Circuit: Pierce I, 65 F.3d 562, 571, 68 FEP 1270 (7th Cir. 1995) (although employee must specifically challenge release as not "voluntary and knowing," ultimate burden of proof that employee has knowingly and voluntarily waived claims properly placed on employer); Pierce v. Atchison, Topeka & Santa Fe Ry., 110 F.3d 431, 438, 73 FEP 1062 (7th Cir. 1997) (*Pierce II*) (employee given short time to sign release, and parties disagreed whether employer's representative ever

upheld.[17] Conceivably, there may be a disputed issue of material fact bearing on the validity of the release, which would require a trial before the release may be enforced.[18]

Settlement agreements and releases that are executed by an unrepresented complainant before litigation begins are more closely scrutinized than agreements entered into by a represented complainant after a charge or complaint has been filed.[19]

B. Waivers of Future Claims Are Invalid

The Supreme Court in *Alexander v. Gardner-Denver Co.*[20] stated that "there can be no prospective waiver of an employee's rights under Title VII."[21] In *United States v. Allegheny-Ludlum Industries*,[22] the court upheld consent decrees in the steel industry but noted

---

corrected initial statement to employee that release did not include discrimination claims).

Tenth Circuit: Torrez v. Public Serv. Co., 908 F.2d 687, 690, 53 FEP 764 (10th Cir. 1990) (question of fact whether waiver was knowing and voluntary based on evidence that employee was high school educated, unfamiliar with law, unrepresented by counsel, and may have been placed under unfair economic pressure; in addition, he did not realize that release, which he did not negotiate, waived possible discrimination claims even though it did not mention employment discrimination).

[17]In *Cirillo v. Arco Chemical Co.*, 862 F.2d 448, 48 FEP 678 (3d Cir. 1988), the court was particularly impressed by the release it was reviewing and quoted it in full, noting that if this release were found to be inadequate, "we would be hard-pressed to prescribe an adequate one." However, this release no longer would be an effective waiver of age discrimination claims because it predated the OWBPA and did not comply with its terms. 862 F.2d at 452.

[18]*See, e.g.*, Bandera v. City of Quincy, 344 F.3d 47, 92 FEP 1014 (1st Cir. 2003) (issues of fact bearing on whether plaintiff was coerced into settlement agreement or whether second agreement existed; case remanded for evidentiary hearing on these issues).

[19]Some have argued that an employer's unaccepted offer to "settle" all claims, made before any claims are actually asserted by a complainant, should be admissible as evidence of discrimination, notwithstanding Federal Rule of Evidence 408. *See* Cassino v. Reichhold Chems., Inc., 817 F.2d 1338, 1342–43, 47 FEP 865 (9th Cir. 1987); *cf.* Josephs v. Pacific Bell, 443 F.3d 1050, 17 AD 1465 (9th Cir. 2006) (admitting evidence of settlements of grievances of other employees not in protected class as evidence of an adverse action). *But see* Mundy v. Household Fin. Corp., 885 F.2d 542, 546–47, 50 FEP 1303 (9th Cir. 1989) (distinguishing *Cassino*; employer's unaccepted offer inadmissible under Rule 408, where it was made after termination of employment and employee had retained legal counsel).

[20]415 U.S. 36, 7 FEP 81 (1974).

[21]*Id.* at 51.

[22]517 F.2d 826, 11 FEP 167 (5th Cir. 1975).

that "the release cannot preclude a suit for any form of appropriate relief for *subsequent* injuries caused by *future* acts or undertakings."[23] Accordingly, the court explained, defendants would be fully liable for any discrimination occurring after the dates of the releases executed by the employees.[24] Any settlement of a discrimination claim thus should be entered into with full awareness that the employer will be liable for any future discrimination, including any future acts of harassment and retaliation against the complainant for pursuing the settled claim.[25] These issues particularly arise where the settlement contemplates instatement or reinstatement.[26] In these circumstances, an employer is well advised to take appropriate steps to review proposed discipline of the former claimant in order to ensure that discrimination or retaliation claims are defensible on the merits.[27]

Other issues also can arise when the employer has a continuing relationship with the claimant after the settlement is executed. In *Wagner v. Nutrasweet Co.*,[28] the plaintiff, a human resources officer, signed an agreement that provided, in part, that her employment would continue for six months following the execution of the release. The agreement also provided that at the end of the retention period the plaintiff would receive two months' "redeployment pay," outplacement assistance, and severance benefits worth more than $46,000. Shortly before its expiration, the plaintiff was presented with a second release covering the six-month retention period. She refused to sign, claiming she had been discriminated against in compensation during the retention period. The district

---

[23]*Id.* at 854 (emphasis added).

[24]*Id.* at 854–55; *see* Rogers v. General Elec. Co., 781 F.2d 452, 454, 39 FEP 1581 (5th Cir. 1986) (release that waives prospective Title VII claims invalid as violative of public policy); Williams v. Vukovich, 720 F.2d 909, 925, 33 FEP 238 (6th Cir. 1983) (consent decree containing waivers of future discrimination claims invalid).

[25]*See, e.g.*, Miller v. Fairchild Indus., 885 F.2d 498, 501, 58 FEP 915 (9th Cir. 1989) (claims of "breach of contract, tortious breach of the implied covenant of good faith and fair dealing and fraud," and negligent and intentional infliction of emotional distress after entering into settlement agreement that relinquished right to sue for discrimination under Title VII).

[26]*See, e.g.*, Munday v. Waste Mgmt., 858 F. Supp. 1364, 1369, 1376 (D. Md. 1994) (settlement agreement included reinstatement; employer liable for subsequent discrimination), *aff'd in part and rev'd in part*, 126 F.3d 239, 74 FEP 1478 (4th Cir. 1997).

[27]*See generally* Chapter 14 (Retaliation).

[28]95 F.3d 527, 533–34, 72 FEP 284 (7th Cir. 1996).

court held that her compensation claims were barred by the earlier release because the rate of pay she earned during the retention period was based on the rate of pay earned prior to her execution of the first release, the time period as to which she had released all claims. Relying on a continuing violation theory, the appeals court reversed and stated that each paycheck received during the retention period was the basis for a separate claim. The court noted that even if it were possible to waive prospective claims, the fact that the company asked for a second release "speaks volumes" about whether the parties even intended the release to reach prospective claims.[29]

Courts have suggested that it is sometimes difficult to determine whether subsequent claims of discrimination are barred as the result of a prior settlement or consent decree or whether the claims are new ones that could not have lawfully been included within the scope of the prior resolution.[30] In *Adams v. Philip Morris, Inc.*,[31] the plaintiff signed a settlement agreement that waived "any and all right to assert any claim or demand for reemployment or tenure with the company or for any benefits, etc., not specifically enunciated herein."[32] The plaintiff applied for rehire, was rejected, and sued, contending that the provision in the settlement agreement amounted to an unlawful waiver of a prospective claim. The district court granted summary judgment to the employer, but the court of appeals reversed. It noted that not every settlement agreement that refers to postsettlement conduct results in a prospective waiver and that a settlement agreement may lawfully release claims for the future effects of past discrimination.[33] The appeals court held, however, that the district court needed to determine whether the employer had discriminated anew or whether the refusal to consider the plaintiff's application related back or

---

[29]*Id.* at 533.

[30]*See, e.g.*, Huguley v. General Motors Corp., 52 F.3d 1364, 1366 (6th Cir. 1995) (*Huguley II*) ("The [consent] decree purported to settle all past claims of discrimination as well as all claims arising from the future effects of past discrimination. However, distinguishing between past acts of discrimination, the future effects of past discrimination and new acts of alleged discrimination has proved quite challenging."); Huguley v. General Motors Corp., 35 F.3d 1052 (6th Cir. 1994) (*Huguley I*) (failure to transfer following consent decree independently actionable).

[31]67 F.3d 580, 71 FEP 1025 (6th Cir. 1995).

[32]*Id.* at 582.

[33]*Id.* at 584 (citing court's holding in *Huguley II*).

was a continuing effect of the alleged age discrimination that prompted the settlement agreement.[34]

In *Kendall v. Watkins*,[35] the Tenth Circuit considered the lawfulness of refusing to hire a former employee who had signed a settlement agreement providing that the employer had "no further obligation to [the former employee]."[36] The court held that the employer's reason for not rehiring the plaintiff was the employer's reliance on the terms of the settlement agreement, a nondiscriminatory reason not prohibited by Title VII; accordingly, no prospective waiver of a Title VII claim was at issue.[37] The court noted, however, that a valid retaliation claim would have been stated if the reason for the failure to rehire had been simply the fact that the employee had earlier filed a Title VII claim, which the employer had to settle, as opposed to the employer's interpretation of the specific terms of the settlement agreement.[38]

C. Extinguishment of Claims of Nonparties by Entry of Consent Decree

In *Martin v. Wilks*,[39] the Supreme Court articulated and followed the general rule that an individual's legal rights are not adjudicated in a suit to which he or she is not a party.[40] In *Martin*, a plaintiff class of African-American fire fighters had entered into

---

[34]*Id.* at 584–85.

[35]998 F.2d 848, 62 FEP 681 (10th Cir. 1993).

[36]*Id.* at 849.

[37]*Id.* at 851–52.

[38]*Id.* These cases should be contrasted with cases holding that, generally, to be actionable, a claim for discriminatory failure to rehire into the same position from which a discriminatory discharge allegedly occurred must stem from a new and discrete act of discrimination; a request for reinstatement to redress the original discriminatory discharge is not such a new and discrete act. Burnam v. Amoco Container Co., 755 F.2d 893, 894, 45 FEP 1180 (11th Cir. 1985) (per curiam) (to hold otherwise would permit plaintiff to indefinitely extend statute of limitations by making repeated requests for reinstatement); Hargett v. Valley Fed. Sav. Bank, 60 F.3d 754, 763–64, 68 FEP 852 (11th Cir. 1995) (following *Burnam* and holding that statute of limitations on alleged discriminatory failure-to-rehire claim began to run at time of layoff); Lauderdale v. Johnston Indus., Inc., 139 F. Supp. 2d 1315, 1324–25 (M.D. Ala. 2001) (applying concept to claim for discriminatory failure to rehire where discharge claim involving same position was previously settled), *aff'd in part and rev'd in part*, 31 Fed. Appx. 940 (11th Cir. 2002).

[39]490 U.S. 755, 49 FEP 1641 (1989).

[40]*Id.* at 759.

consent decrees with the city providing for hiring and promotion goals. White fire fighters had notice of the lawsuit but did not intervene. After African-American fire fighters were promoted, the white fire fighters sued, alleging that the promotions pursuant to the consent decree constituted impermissible racial discrimination. Although the district court dismissed the suit as an "impermissible collateral attack" on the consent decree, the Supreme Court disagreed, holding that the white fire fighters were not bound by the consent decree. The Court stated that joinder as a party, rather than knowledge, is the key to being bound. Thus, the Court found that a voluntary settlement in the form of a consent decree between one group of employees and their employer cannot settle the conflicting claims of other groups of employees who are not parties to the decree.

Congress, however, changed the rules. The Civil Rights Act of 1991[41] provides that an employment practice that is within the scope of litigated or consent judgments or orders may not be challenged:

> (i) by a person who, prior to the entry of the judgment or order described in subparagraph (A), had—
>
>> (I) actual notice of the proposed judgment or order sufficient to apprise such person that such judgment or order might adversely affect the interests and legal rights of such person and that an opportunity was available to present objections to such judgment or order by a future date certain; and
>>
>> (II) a reasonable opportunity to present objections to such judgment or order; or
>
> (ii) by a person whose interests were adequately represented by another person who had previously challenged the judgment or order on the same legal grounds and with a similar factual situation, unless there has been an intervening change in law or fact.[42]

D. Choice of Law

There is a split of authority over whether to apply federal common law or the forum state's law to interpret an agreement to settle a federal law employment discrimination claim.[43] Some courts

---

[41]Pub. L. No. 102-166, 1991 U.S.C.C.A.N. (105 Stat.) 1071.

[42]42 U.S.C. § 2000e-2(n)(1)(B)(i), and (ii) (2000).

[43]*Compare* Snider v. Circle K Corp., 923 F.2d 1404, 1407, 58 FEP 723 (10th Cir. 1991) (applying federal common law to Title VII settlement agreement), Heuser

have sidestepped the issue, finding either that the parties themselves did not contest the applicable law or that there was no material difference between the standards.[44]

II. WAIVER OF AGE DISCRIMINATION CLAIMS AFTER THE OLDER WORKERS BENEFIT PROTECTION ACT

A. Requirements Applicable to All OWBPA Waivers

1. General Standards

The OWBPA[45] permits waiver of ADEA claims, but only if minimum procedural standards are met. The OWBPA establishes that conforming waivers of ADEA claims are enforceable even without supervision by the Equal Employment Opportunity Commission (EEOC) or a court.[46]

---

v. Kephart, 215 F.3d 1186, 1190 (10th Cir. 2000) (following *Snider*), Brewer v. Muscle Shoals Bd. of Educ., 790 F.2d 1515, 1519, 40 FEP 1580 (11th Cir. 1986) (Title VII settlement agreements construed according to federal common law) *and* Fulgence v. J. Ray McDermott & Co., 662 F.2d 1207, 1209 (5th Cir. 1981) (applying federal law to determine validity of oral settlement agreement in Title VII case; "federal courts are competent to determine whether a settlement exists without resort to state law") *with* Makins v. District of Columbia, 277 F.3d 544, 548, 87 FEP 1379 (D.C. Cir. 2002) (local law applies to determine enforceability of Title VII release), Resnick v. Uccello Immobilien GMBH, Inc., 227 F.3d 1347, 1350, 10 AD 1802 (11th Cir. 2000) (state law applied to ADA release), Horton v. Norfolk S. Corp., 102 F. Supp. 2d 330, 339, 164 LRRM 3038 (M.D.N.C. 1999) ("[t]o analyze a release of a federal discrimination claim, this court looks to the appropriate state's law regarding the validity of the releases") (citing O'Shea v. Commercial Credit Corp., 930 F.2d 358, 362 (4th Cir. 1991)) *and* Morgan v. South Bend Cmty. Sch. Corp., 797 F.2d 471, 476–77, 41 FEP 736 (7th Cir. 1986) (noting but finding it unnecessary to resolve tension in prior circuit court decisions, holding that, even when federal common law applies, the court should adopt state law as rule of decision; state law was applied with respect to issue of who has authority to settle case).

[44]Ciaramella v. Reader's Digest Ass'n, Inc., 131 F.3d 320, 322, 7 AD 1035 (2d Cir. 1997) (no material difference between applicable state law and federal common law standard); Sheng v. Starkey Labs., Inc., 117 F.3d 1081, 1083 n.1, 74 FEP 278 (8th Cir. 1997) (no dispute because both parties and district court assumed state law controlled); Bowden v. United States, 106 F.3d 433, 439, 73 FEP 395 (D.C. Cir. 1997) (same result regardless of which standard is used).

[45]Pub. L. No. 101-433, 1990 U.S.C.C.A.N. (104 Stat.) 1509 (amending ADEA, 29 U.S.C. § 621 et seq.). The requirements of the OWBPA are explained generally here; for a more complete discussion, see Chapter 12 (Age).

[46]Controversy had developed regarding the legality of unsupervised ADEA waivers in light of the incorporated enforcement procedures of the Fair Labor Standards Act, which includes a requirement of agency or court supervision in certain

The requirements for a valid waiver differ depending on the circumstances. The key variables are (1) whether the waiver is sought before or after litigation (an EEOC charge or court action) has commenced; and (2) as for precharge and prelitigation agreements, whether the waiver is sought "in connection with an exit incentive or other employment termination program offered to a group or class of employees."[47]

There are five basic requirements for a knowing and voluntary waiver applicable in *all* instances. They are:

(1) the waiver must be part of an agreement written in such a way that it is calculated to be understood by the individual to whom it applies or by the average individual eligible to participate;[48]

(2) the waiver must refer specifically to rights or claims under the ADEA;[49]

(3) the waiver cannot cover prospective claims;[50]

(4) the waiver must be contractually valid—i.e., the employee must receive valuable consideration for the waiver in addition to any benefits or amounts to which the employee already was entitled;[51] and

(5) the employee must be "advised in writing to consult with an attorney prior to executing the agreement."[52]

---

situations. *See, e.g.,* Runyan v. National Cash Register Corp., 787 F.2d 1039, 1041–44, 40 FEP 807 (6th Cir. 1986) (en banc).

[47]29 U.S.C. §§ 626(f)(1)(F)(ii), (H), 626(f)(2) (2000).

[48]*Id.* § 626(f)(1)(A).

[49]*Id.* § 626(f)(1)(B).

[50]*Id.* § 626(f)(1)(C); *see* Foster v. United States, 249 F.3d 1275, 1279 n.7 (11th Cir. 2001) ("We recognize the circuit split on this issue. The Fifth and Sixth Circuits have applied the [*Cotnam v. Commissioner of Internal Revenue,* 263 F.2d 119 (5th Cir. 1959)] ruling, while the Third, Fourth, Ninth, and Federal Circuits included contingency fees in a taxpayer's gross income. *See* Srivastava v. Commissioner, 220 F.3d 353, 365 (5th Cir. 2000); Estate of Clarks v. United States, 202 F.3d 854, 858 (6th Cir. 2000); O'Brien v. Commissioner, 38 T.C. 707, 712 (U.S. Tax Ct. 1962), *aff'd,* 319 F.2d 532 (3d Cir. 1963); Young v. Commissioner, 240 F.3d 369, 372 (4th Cir. 2001); Coady v. Comm'r, 213 F.3d 1187, 1187 (9th Cir. 2000); Baylin v United States, 43 F.3d 1451, 1452 (Fed. Cir. 1995). [*Cotnam* is] binding precedent in our circuit, *Bonner v. City of Prichard,* 661 F.2d 1206, 1209 (11th Cir. 1981), and has been upheld in *Davis v. Commissioner,* 210 F.3d 1346, 1347 n.4 (11th Cir. 2000).").

[51]29 U.S.C. § 626(f)(1)(D) (2000). Some plaintiffs contend that this requirement means that an offer to an over-40 claimant—for example, one laid off in a reduction in force—must be larger than that offered to a similarly situated under-40 counterpart. The Third Circuit, in *Dibiase v. SmithKline Beecham Corp.,* 48 F.3d 719, 721, 67 FEP 58 (3d Cir. 1995), reversed a trial court decision so holding.

[52]29 U.S.C. § 626(f)(1)(E) (2000).

The EEOC issued regulations entitled "Waiver of Rights and Claims Under the Age Discrimination in Employment Act," effective July 6, 1998 (known as the waiver regulations).[53] The EEOC subsequently issued regulations that interpret *Oubre v. Entergy Operations, Inc.*,[54] which became effective January 10, 2001 (known as the *Oubre* regulations).[55]

Since passage of the OWBPA, the courts have provided some guidance with respect to the requirements of the OWBPA generally and with respect to the five criteria applicable to all OWBPA waivers. These requirements are also addressed in the waiver regulations.

2. Written in a Manner to Be Understood

The waiver regulations provide that the waiver must be in writing, that the employer should take into consideration the "level of comprehension and education of typical participants," and that this consideration will usually "require the limitation or elimination of technical jargon and of long, complex sentences."[56] In addition, the waiver agreement "must not have the effect of misleading, misinforming, or failing to inform participants and affected individuals. Any advantages or disadvantages described shall be presented without either exaggerating the benefits or minimizing the limitations."[57]

Similarly, § 7(f)(1)(H) of the ADEA[58] requires that exit incentive and group employment termination programs be conveyed in writing in a manner calculated to be understood by the average participant.[59]

In *Lloyd v. Brunswick Corp.*,[60] a patent attorney claimed that the release he signed was not written in an easy-to-understand manner. The court found that there was nothing unclear about the waiver and stated: "On top of this, Lloyd is a lawyer. We have a

---

[53]63 Fed. Reg. 30,624 (June 5, 1998) (codified at 29 C.F.R. § 1625.22 (2005)).
[54]522 U.S. 422, 75 FEP 1255 (1998).
[55]65 Fed. Reg. 77,438 (Dec. 11, 2000) (codified at 29 C.F.R. § 1625.23 (2005)).
[56]29 C.F.R. § 1625.22(b)(3) (2005).
[57]*Id.* § 1625.22(b)(4) (2005).
[58]29 U.S.C. § 626(f)(1)(H) (2000).
[59]29 C.F.R. § 1625.22(b)(5) (2005).
[60]180 F.3d 893, 80 FEP 126 (7th Cir. 1999).

hard time imagining that someone with a law degree would be unable to understand a simple letter deal like this."[61] In *Kinghorn v. Citibank*,[62] the court distinguished the concepts of nondisclosure and clarity, finding that the alleged failure to disclose the consequences of the application of benefit plan provisions referenced in the agreement was irrelevant to the question of whether the language was ambiguous.

In *Thomforde v. International Business Machines Corp.*,[63] the Eighth Circuit found unenforceable a release that was not written in a manner calculated to be understood by the participants. The agreement included both a covenant not to sue (that expressly excluded ADEA claims) and a release (that referenced the ADEA). When the employee asked the employer's in-house counsel, prior to signing the agreement, what the apparent conflict in the two provisions meant, the attorney refused to answer the question. The court stated:

> We can easily see how a participant under this Agreement could construe the statement that "[t]his covenant not to sue does not apply to actions based solely under the [ADEA]" as an exception to the general release, not just an exception to the covenant not to sue. Given the lack of clarity in the Agreement, and IBM's declination to tell Thomforde what it meant by the language, we hold that the Agreement is not written in a manner calculated to be understood by the intended participants as required by the OWBPA.[64]

3. Specific Reference to the ADEA

The waiver regulations provide that the requirement that the waiver specifically refer to rights or claims under "this Act"[65] means that "the waiver agreement must refer to the Age Discrimination in Employment Act (ADEA) by name in connection with the waiver."[66] Thus, in order to comply with the regulations, releases must expressly spell out "Age Discrimination in Employment Act

---

[61]*Id.* at 895.

[62]1999 WL 30534, at *3 (N.D. Cal. Jan. 20, 1999).

[63]406 F.3d 500, 95 FEP 1145 (8th Cir. 2005).

[64]*Id.* at 504; *see also* Syerson v. International Bus. Machs. Corp., 461 F.3d 1147, 98 FEP 1345 (9th Cir. 2006) (adopting Eighth Circuit's reasoning and invalidating same release).

[65]29 U.S.C. § 626(f)(1)(B) (2000).

[66]29 C.F.R. § 1625.22(b)(6) (2005).

(ADEA)." In *Carr v. Armstrong Air Conditioning, Inc.*,[67] the failure to specifically identify age discrimination claims was one of several reasons for the court's conclusion that OWBPA requirements had not been met.

4. The Release May Not Reach Future Claims

Consistent with the case law under Title VII[68] and the requirements of the OWBPA,[69] the waiver may not release future claims. The waiver regulations provide, however, that this does not bar the enforcement of agreements "to perform future employment-related actions such as the employee's agreement to retire or otherwise terminate employment at a future date."[70]

In *Kinghorn v. Citibank*,[71] the court refused to grant summary judgment for the defendants regarding the validity of the release under the OWBPA, finding that it was not clear whether the release reached future claims. The release language was silent regarding any limitation to claims arising prior to its effective date.

5. Consideration

The waiver regulations provide that "consideration in addition" means "anything of value in addition to that to which the individual is already entitled in the absence of a waiver."[72] They also provide:

> If a benefit or other thing of value was eliminated in contravention of law or contract, express or implied, the subsequent offer of such benefit or thing of value in connection with a waiver will not constitute "consideration" .... Whether such elimination as to one employee or group of employees is in contravention of law or contract as to other employees, or to that individual employee at some later time, may vary depending on the facts and circumstances of each case.[73]

---

[67]817 F. Supp. 54, 61 FEP 332 (N.D. Ohio 1993).

[68]*See* Section I.B *supra*.

[69]29 U.S.C § 626(f)(1)(C) (2000).

[70]29 C.F.R. § 1625.22(c)(2) (2005); *see* Lauderdale v. Johnston Indus., Inc., 139 F. Supp. 2d 1315, 1318–21 (M.D. Ala. 2001) (articulating rule).

[71]1999 WL 30534, at *4 (N.D. Cal. Jan. 20, 1999).

[72]29 C.F.R. § 1625.22(d)(2) (2005).

[73]*Id.* § 1625.22(d)(3).

The waiver regulations state that an employer is not required to give a person age 40 or older a greater amount of consideration than one under the age of 40 solely because the person over 40 is a member of a protected class under the ADEA.[74] The waiver regulations thus are in accord with the Third Circuit's holding in *Dibiase v. SmithKline Beecham Corp.*,[75] which held that an employer can offer enhanced benefits to all terminated employees without providing extra consideration to workers protected by the ADEA.[76] The Eleventh Circuit has followed the Third Circuit's reasoning.[77]

6. Consultation With an Attorney

In *American Airlines, Inc. v. Cardoza-Rodriguez*,[78] the waiver of age discrimination claims was attacked because it did not comply with the requirement of 29 U.S.C. § 626(f)(1)(E) that an individual be advised to consult with an attorney. The release stated only: "I have had reasonable and sufficient time and opportunity to consult with an independent legal representative of my own choosing before signing this Complete Release of All Claims."[79] According to the court, the voluntary early retirement agreement itself, "although it advised employees to consult financial and tax advisors, to seek advice from local personnel representatives, and to attend retirement seminars, . . . said nothing about seeking independent legal advice prior to making the election to retire and agreeing to execute the release as the statute dictates."[80] The court further observed:

> Given the burden OWBPA places on employers to demonstrate their agreements contain the required information, the reference contained in the release is insufficient to satisfy § 626(f)(1)(E). "Congress' intent in enacting § 626 was to compel employers to provide data so that an employee considering waiving ADEA rights could assess, *with the assistance of counsel*, the viability of an ADEA claim." *Raczak*, 103 F.3d at 1259 (emphasis supplied). For this purpose, § 626(f)(1)(E) provides that a waiver is not knowing and voluntary

---

[74]*Id.* § 1625.22(d)(4).

[75]48 F.3d 719, 721, 67 FEP 58 (3d Cir. 1995).

[76]*Id.* at 726.

[77]Griffin v. Kraft Gen. Foods, Inc., 62 F.3d 368, 374, 68 FEP 1072 (11th Cir. 1995) (no additional consideration needed).

[78]133 F.3d 111, 75 FEP 1217 (1st Cir. 1998).

[79]*Id.* at 114.

[80]*Id.* at 118 (footnote omitted).

unless "the individual is advised in writing to consult with an attorney prior to executing the agreement." To advise is to caution, warn, or recommend. . . . This statutory requirement could not be more clear, nor its purpose more central to the statutory scheme at issue, especially in light of Congress' concern with discrimination in the suspect context of group exit programs.

. . . .

We read § 626(f)(1)(E) to mean what it says: employers must advise employees in writing to consult an attorney prior to executing a release of ADEA claims. The failure to advise the employees to consult with counsel goes to the heart of the statute's purpose. . . . Because American failed to directly advise their employees to consult a lawyer before making the election, we rule, as a matter of law, that American failed to meet its burden under the OWBPA.[81]

7. Degree of Compliance Necessary

In *Raczak v. Ameritech Corp.*,[82] the court focused on whether the information provided was sufficient to allow an individual to understand and gauge the prospects of an ADEA claim; because § 626(f)(1)(H) of the OWBPA, which requires disclosure of information regarding individuals in the same "job classification or organizational unit," is ambiguous, the court found that "a rigid and mechanical interpretation of that provision is inappropriate."[83]

In *American Airlines, Inc. v. Cardoza-Rodriguez*,[84] the court recognized that some violations of the OWBPA may be so technical as to be de minimis and thus may not invalidate an otherwise valid release of ADEA claims. However, it found that American's failure to adequately advise the affected employees to obtain counsel was not de minimis.[85] In *Howlett v. Holiday Inns, Inc.*,[86] the court, noting that OWBPA requirements should not be difficult for most

---

[81]*Id.* (footnotes omitted); *see also* Carr v. Armstrong Air Conditioning, Inc., 817 F. Supp. 54, 57, 61 FEP 332 (N.D. Ohio 1993) (court held that waiver was not knowing and voluntary under OWBPA; among other deficiencies, including failure to refer specifically to claims arising under ADEA and failure to provide 21-day consideration period and 7-day revocation period, court noted that release was deficient in that it failed to state that employee was advised to consult with attorney before signing waiver—even though plaintiff admitted that he had actually consulted with attorney).

[82]103 F.3d 1257, 72 FEP 1357 (6th Cir. 1997).

[83]*Id.* at 1259.

[84]133 F.3d 111, 75 FEP 1217 (1st Cir. 1998).

[85]*Id.* at 118 n.6.

[86]120 F.3d 598, 74 FEP 1875 (6th Cir. 1997).

employers to meet, stated that "the courts should read these requirements in a common-sense manner and not dogmatically."[87]

The Seventh Circuit held in *Adams v. Ameritech Services, Inc.*[88] that the employer's OWBPA waiver furnished too little information about the job titles to be of use to employees: "Congress's use of the term 'job title' indicates that it wanted that information to be quite specific (that is, more literal and particular than the functional approach for which the defendants are arguing, which would have been adequate for a statistician)."[89]

8. OWBPA Requirements Are Minimum Requirements

In *Griffin v. Kraft General Foods, Inc.*,[90] a case involving a prelitigation waiver in the context of a group discharge program, the court held that the statutory requirements of the OWBPA that must be met for a release of age discrimination claims to be valid are not exclusive. It stated that the OWBPA sets forth *minimum* requirements and that factors examined in pre-OWBPA cases to determine whether a waiver is knowing and voluntary (such as allegations of fraud, duress, or coercion) also must be considered. The case was remanded to the district court to consider whether the release was valid under the totality of the circumstances as well as under the OWBPA.[91] Similarly, in *Bennett v. Coors*,[92] the court reversed summary judgment and remanded for trial on the issue of whether the plaintiffs' releases were procured by fraud where the employer represented that the plaintiffs' jobs were eliminated in a

---

[87]*Id.* at 603–04. *But see* Butcher v. Gerber Prods. Co., 8 F. Supp. 2d 307, 314, 77 FEP 339 (S.D.N.Y. 1998) ("Since the OWBPA establishes minimum or threshold requirements, absolute technical compliance with its provisions is required."). The *Butcher* court cited to *Griffin v. Kraft General Foods, Inc.*, 62 F.3d 368, 373, 68 FEP 1072 (11th Cir. 1995); however, in *Griffin*, the court merely held that the decisional unit could be broader than a single facility. *See also* Suhy v. AlliedSignal, 44 F. Supp. 2d 432, 436, 79 FEP 1010 (D. Conn. 1999) (following *Butcher* in the context of disclosure providing age ranges rather than actual ages). In *Oubre v. Entergy Operations, Inc.*, 522 U.S. 422, 75 FEP 1255 (1998), the Supreme Court described the OWBPA as implementing Congress' policy "via a strict, unqualified statutory stricture on waivers." *Id.* at 427.
[88]231 F.3d 414, 84 FEP 178 (7th Cir. 2000).
[89]*Id.* at 431.
[90]62 F.3d 368, 371–73, 68 FEP 1072 (11th Cir. 1995).
[91]*Id.* at 373–74.
[92]189 F.3d 1221, 1230, 80 FEP 1197 (10th Cir. 1999).

reduction in force but there was evidence that the company hired replacements shortly after the downsizing.

Other courts have also found that the OWBPA requirements are merely minimum threshold requirements and that an employee may challenge a waiver's validity on grounds in addition to OWBPA noncompliance.[93] This is in accord with the OWBPA's legislative history.[94]

9. Burden of Proof

In cases disputing the validity of the waiver under the OWBPA, the party asserting validity has the burden of proving that the waiver was knowing and voluntary.[95]

In *Pierce v. Atchison, Topeka & Santa Fe Railway*,[96] the court discussed burdens of proof, noting that in *Pierce I*[97] it had held that an employee " 'must come forward with specific evidence sufficient to raise a question as to the validity of the release.' "[98] It then held: "Once the employee has made the requisite showing, the employer then bears the burden of proving that the release was knowing and voluntary."[99]

10. Effect of OWBPA Noncompliance on the Release of Non-ADEA Claims

Courts have grappled with how to handle non-ADEA claims that are released in the same document as ADEA claims when the

---

[93]*See* Lauderdale v. Johnston Indus., Inc., 139 F. Supp. 2d 1315, 1321 (M.D. Ala. 2001) (considering and rejecting fraudulent inducement claim); Kendrick v. Kmart Corp., 2000 WL 246582, at *4 (E.D. Mich. Feb. 25, 2000) (adjudicating economic duress defense despite finding of OWBPA compliance).

[94]*See* S. REP. NO. 263, 101st Cong., 2d Sess. 32, *reprinted in* 1990 U.S.C.C.A.N. 1509, 1537 ("The Committee expects that courts reviewing the 'knowing and voluntary' issue will scrutinize carefully the complete circumstances in which the waiver was executed. The Committee expresses (sic) support for the [totality of the circumstances] approach taken on this limited issue in *Cirillo v. Arco Chemical Co.*, 862 F.2d 448 (3d Cir. 1988), and disapproves the [ordinary contract principles] approach adopted in *Lancaster v. Buerkle Buick Honda Co.*, 809 F.2d 539 (8th Cir. 1987).").

[95]29 U.S.C. § 621(f)(3) (2000).

[96]110 F.3d 431, 438, 73 FEP 1062 (7th Cir. 1997) (*Pierce II*).

[97]Pierce v. Atchison, Topeka & Santa Fe Ry., 65 F.3d 562, 68 FEP 1270 (7th Cir. 1995).

[98]65 F.3d at 572.

[99]110 F.3d at 437–38.

release does not comply with OWBPA requirements. In *Oubre v. Entergy Operations, Inc.*,[100] the Court apparently assumed that a release that is invalid with respect to ADEA claims might remain valid as to other claims, stating that "these questions [claims for restitution, recoupment, or setoff] may be complex where a release is effective as to some claims but not as to ADEA claims."[101]

In *Long v. Sears, Roebuck & Co.*,[102] the court found the release defective (and found pre-*Oubre* that there was no tender-back requirement and that retention of the settlement proceeds did not constitute ratification), and therefore remanded the case to the district court to determine how to handle the non-ADEA claims.[103] In contrast, in *Howlett v. Holiday Inns, Inc.*,[104] the court found that the release did not comply with the OWBPA and therefore the plaintiff's age discrimination claims had not been waived. The court then proceeded to invalidate the release as to all claims, not just age claims, stating that

> [i]t would be extremely difficult, if not impossible, for the district court to identify all the potential theories of liability that these former employees have waived in consideration for money payments. And it would be impossible to assign meaningful values to all those potential claims and then apportion some of the consideration for the ADEA claims, and the rest for the remaining claims.[105]

Other courts have held that the fact that a waiver is invalid under the ADEA does not render the release ineffective as to state law claims.[106]

---

[100]522 U.S. 422 (1998); *see* Bennett v. Coors, 189 F.3d 1221, 1234, 80 FEP 1197 (10th Cir. 1999) (interpreting *Oubre*).

[101]522 U.S. at 429. In the proposed *Oubre* regulations, 64 Fed. Reg. 19,952, 19,956 (1999) (proposed Apr. 23, 1999), the EEOC suggested that in determining the amount of restitution, recoupment, or setoff that is appropriate, contractual allocation among ADEA and non-ADEA claims should be considered; if not expressly apportioned, the apportionment should be done on an equitable basis. The final regulations do not contain the list of factors to be considered in restitution, recoupment, and setoff situations, but there was no indication that the EEOC has changed its views in this regard.

[102]105 F.3d 1529, 72 FEP 1860 (3d Cir. 1997).

[103]*Id.* at 1545; *see also* American Airlines, Inc. v. Cardoza-Rodriguez, 133 F.3d 111, 121–22, 75 FEP 1217 (3d Cir. 1998) (vacating district court's "declaration" that release barred non-ADEA claims and remanding case to provide parties adequate opportunity to litigate issue).

[104]120 F.3d 598, 74 FEP 1875 (6th Cir. 1997).

[105]*Id.* at 602.

[106]*See* Bennett v. Coors, 189 F.3d 1221, 1237, 80 FEP 1197 (10th Cir. 1999) (possible invalidity of ADEA release does not affect release of state law claims);

The requirement of "tender back" also is at issue in these cases.[107] In *Wright v. Heritage Environmental Services*,[108] a Title VII case where the plaintiff sued after signing a waiver, the court held that the OWBPA and *Oubre* did not apply and that the plaintiff was required to tender back consideration in order to maintain her suit.

B. Prelitigation Releases

1. General Standards

In cases where a prelitigation release is sought, two additional requirements must be met besides the five listed earlier. First, the agreement must provide that the individual may revoke the agreement for a period of at least 7 days following the execution of the agreement; it does not become effective or enforceable until the revocation period has expired.[109]

Second, the offer must allow a defined time period for consideration of the release. The time depends on whether the prelitigation waiver is sought in connection with an exit incentive or other employment termination program offered to a group or class of employees. Where the prelitigation waiver sought is *not* in connection with such an employment termination program, the individual must be given at least 21 days within which to consider the agreement.[110] Where the prelitigation waiver sought *is* in connection with such an employment termination program, the individual

---

Branker v. Pfizer, Inc., 981 F. Supp. 862 (S.D.N.Y. 1997) (employer's failure to provide information required by OWBPA in release form does not invalidate waiver of New York state-law claims); Burch v. Fluor Corp., 867 F. Supp. 873, 878, 70 FEP 165 (E.D. Mo. 1994) (elements for knowing and voluntary waiver under ADEA will not be read into Missouri Human Rights Act).

[107]*See* Section II.D *infra.*

[108]2000 WL 1474410, at *4 (N.D. Ill. Oct. 4, 2000) (following the pre-*Oubre* Seventh Circuit precedent in *Fleming v. United States Postal Service AMF O'Hare,* 27 F.3d 259, 260–62, 66 FEP 627 (7th Cir. 1994)); *see also* Livingston v. Bev-Pak, Inc. d/b/a Adirondack Beverages, 112 F. Supp. 2d 242, 249 (N.D.N.Y. 2000) (ratification of release, allegedly invalid due to mental incapacity and/or duress, found where plaintiff did not tender back or offer to tender back in order to pursue race claim). *But see* Rangel v. El Paso Natural Gas Co., 996 F. Supp. 1093, 1097–99, 76 FEP 445 (D.N.M. 1998) (applying *Oubre* to release of Title VII claims based upon policy considerations).

[109]29 U.S.C. § 626(f)(1)(G) (2000).

[110]*Id.* § 626(f)(1)(F)(i).

must be given at least 45 days (not 21) within which to consider the agreement.[111]

Where the 45-day rule is applicable, an additional requirement applies as well. The employer must make a written disclosure, calculated to be understood by the average individual eligible to participate in the employment termination program, containing the following information:

> (1) the class, unit, or group of individuals covered by such program, any eligibility factors for such program, and any time limits applicable to such program;[112] and
>
> (2) the job titles and ages of all individuals eligible or selected for the program, and the ages of all individuals in the same job classification or organizational unit who are not eligible or selected for the program.[113]

Thus, where a class of employees is being asked to waive rights, the employer in effect must give each member of the class preliminary discovery as to the impact of the program on older workers (called an "adverse impact disclosure"). Also, this information must be given at the "commencement of the period"[114] that the employee is given to consider the waiver. In other words, the employer must either provide the adverse impact disclosure at the same time it gives the employee the release or extend the consideration period until at least 45 days following the disclosure.[115]

The waiver regulations address a number of the issues that were left unresolved in the OWBPA itself. In addition, the courts have decided some issues relative to OWBPA requirements for prelitigation waivers. These issues are explored below.

---

[111]*Id.* § 626(f)(1)(F)(ii); *see* EEOC v. Sears, Roebuck & Co., 857 F. Supp. 1233, 1236–38, 1240, 65 FEP 479 (N.D. Ill. 1994) (Sears argued that the decision to resign, which it required under its severance plan to be made within 5 days, was distinguishable from the decision to waive ADEA claims, for which, under the OWBPA, the employee was entitled to 45 days; the court rejected this distinction, holding that the term "agreement," as used in § 626(f), refers generally to the agreement to participate in the severance plan, not just to the part of the agreement waiving ADEA claims).

[112]29 U.S.C. § 626(f)(1)(H)(i) (2000).

[113]*Id.* § 626(f)(1)(H)(ii).

[114]*Id.*

[115]*See* Tung v. Texaco, Inc., 150 F.3d 206, 209, 77 FEP 670 (2d Cir. 1998) (waiver of ADEA claim not valid where employer failed to provide the adverse impact disclosure until the day the employee signed the release).

2. Time Periods for Consideration/Revocation

With respect to time periods, the waiver regulations specifically provide:

- The 21- and 45-day consideration periods run from the date of the employer's final offer.[116]
- If material changes are made to the offer, the 21- and 45-day periods begin to run anew, unless the parties agree to the contrary.[117]
- The 7-day revocation period cannot be shortened, even by agreement of the parties.[118]
- The 21- and 45-day consideration periods are waivable, such that the employee may sign an agreement before the expiration of the applicable period, provided that the employee's acceptance of the shortened period is "knowing and voluntary."[119]

In *Ellison v. Premier Salons International, Inc.*,[120] the Eighth Circuit held that an employer has the right to withdraw or revoke the offer during the 21-day consideration period—there is no irrevocable right of acceptance on the part of the employee. The employer and its chief financial officer, Ellison, had negotiated over the terms of a severance package, and Premier's president, Sanders, gave a "Separation Agreement and Release of Claims" to Ellison. Age claims were among those released. The document was signed by Sanders. Several days later, Ellison gave Sanders a copy of the agreement with numerous longhand changes. Ellison subsequently contended that the changes were suggestions, whereas Sanders testified that Ellison stated that he would not sign the agreement unless the changes were made. Shortly thereafter, Sanders telephoned Ellison and told him that, as a result of defamatory remarks that Sanders had learned that Ellison had made, Sanders would send Ellison a new less valuable agreement. Sanders testified that he advised Ellison that the earlier agreement was revoked. Ellison signed the earlier agreement within 21 days of receiving it. The company refused to perform under the earlier "agreement."

---

[116]29 C.F.R. § 1625.22(e)(4) (2005).
[117]*Id.*
[118]*Id.* § 1625.22(e)(5).
[119]*Id.* § 1625.22(e)(6).
[120]164 F.3d 1111 (8th Cir. 1999).

Ellison then sued for breach of contract and violation of the OWBPA. Ellison contended that the OWBPA creates an irrevocable power of acceptance for 21 days and that offers under the OWBPA, unlike offers governed by common law contract principles, cannot be rejected or revoked by the employer during the 21-day period. The court rejected this contention, noting that there was no basis for the argument in the statutory language; the OWBPA simply provides that an employee be given 21 days within which to consider an offer if the waiver of ADEA claims is to be considered knowing and voluntary. The court also rejected Ellison's contention that the Supreme Court in *Oubre* had held that the OWBPA preempts all contract law principles. It stated: "Because the OWBPA is concerned only with the validity of agreed upon waiver agreements, it does not preempt contract formation principles such as rejection and revocation."[121]

In *Kinghorn v. Citibank*,[122] the release provided that the plaintiff had 21 days from first receiving the agreement to execute it. Typographical changes were subsequently made. The court found the plaintiff's claim that he was thus denied a full 21-day period to consider the release to be frivolous.

In *Wamsley v. Champlin Refining & Chemicals, Inc.*,[123] the plaintiffs contended that the employer instructed them to sign their releases prior to the expiration of the 45-day consideration period. The employer denied these allegations, but stated that it had informed employees that they could avoid an interruption in payroll if they signed their releases before their discharge date, which, in turn, was prior to the expiration of the 45-day period. The court indicated that the plaintiffs' claims created an issue of fact as to whether they had been given adequate time to consider the waivers. The court concluded that this issue was immaterial, however, because the plaintiffs ratified their releases as a matter of law (a result that would not have been reached post-*Oubre*).

In *Lloyd v. Brunswick Corp.*,[124] the plaintiff's attorney contended that the plaintiff's ADEA rights had not been knowingly and voluntarily waived because he had not seen the employer's letter containing the waiver until the day before he signed it. The court rejected the assertion, noting that the plaintiff had seen prior

---

[121]*Id.* at 1115; *see also* Marks v. New York Univ., 61 F. Supp. 2d 81 (S.D.N.Y. 1999).

[122]1999 WL 30534, at *3 (N.D. Cal. Jan. 20, 1999).

[123]11 F.3d 534, 539–40 (5th Cir. 1993).

[124]180 F.3d 893, 80 FEP 126 (7th Cir. 1999).

drafts, some of which he had written; the prior drafts unambiguously referred to a release of *all* claims (even if the prior drafts had not specifically referred to the ADEA); the employer provided him with 45 days to consider whether to sign; and the plaintiff himself chose to sign the release on the spot.[125]

In *Kendrick v. Kmart Corp.*,[126] the court rejected the contention that a waiver was invalid because the plaintiff was allegedly told to sign it immediately. The plaintiff was required to have his signature notarized and to mail the release back to the company, such that a consideration period was "built into" the process. The court found that the fact that the plaintiff chose not to read the document in full and to mail it back the same day did not mean the waiver was invalid. Relying on the *Lloyd* determination that even "on-the-spot" signing does not necessarily render the waiver invalid when the agreement on its face permits a 45-day consideration period,[127] the court found that "the employee did not need to *take* the 45 days in order for the agreement to become effective."[128] Therefore, the 45 days needed only be *provided*, not *used*.

3. Required Disclosures for Group Discharge Programs

a. Definition of "Exit Incentive" and "Other Employment Termination Programs." The waiver regulations address at length the disclosure requirements applicable to exit incentive and other discharge programs under the OWBPA.[129]

The waiver regulations provide that "[u]sually an 'exit incentive program' is a voluntary program offered to a group or class of employees where such employees are offered consideration in addition to anything of value to which the individuals are already entitled . . . in exchange for their decision to resign voluntarily and sign a waiver," whereas "[u]sually 'other termination program' refers to a group or class of employees who were involuntarily terminated and who are offered additional consideration in return for their decision to sign a waiver."[130]

---

[125]*Id.* at 895.

[126]2000 U.S. Dist. LEXIS 2307 (E.D. Mich. Feb. 25, 2000).

[127]180 F.3d at 895.

[128]*Kendrick*, 2000 U.S. Dist. LEXIS 2307, at *10.

[129]*Id.*

[130]29 C.F.R. § 1625.22(f)(1)(iii)(A) (2005).

Whether a "program" exists will be decided based on the facts and circumstances of each case.[131] A "program" exists "when an employer offers additional consideration for the signing of a waiver pursuant to an exit incentive or other employment termination (e.g., a reduction in force) to two or more employees."[132] The waiver regulations state:

> Typically, an involuntary termination program is a standardized formula or package of benefits that is available to two or more employees, while an exit incentive program typically is a standardized formula or package of benefits designed to induce employees to sever their employment voluntarily. In both cases, the terms of the programs generally are not subject to negotiation between the parties.[133]

In *Burch v. Fluor Corp.*,[134] decided before the promulgation of the waiver regulations, the court interpreted the term "employment termination program" in light of the legislative history to include a 25 percent reduction in force where the plaintiffs received a standard package of benefits that varied only in the amount of severance pay.

In *Blackwell v. Cole Taylor Bank*,[135] the court considered the meaning of the terms "exit incentive" and "group termination" programs, holding that "an outright termination is merely the extreme case of creating an exit incentive."[136] The employer offered a group of employees two choices: (1) they could quit immediately and be given a bonus of one month's pay—they were also given 21 days to sign a release in exchange for one month's severance pay; or (2) they could attempt to perform in an alternative job—within the first 90 days they could elect to quit and still receive one month's severance pay by signing the release within 21 days of leaving. Certain employees accepted the "quit now" option and signed the release; others tried the new job but elected to quit within the 90-day period and signed the releases. Some of the employees then

---

[131]*Id.* § 1625.22(f)(1)(iii)(B); Burlison v. McDonald's Corp., 455 F.3d 1242, 98 FEP 778 (11th Cir. 2006) (affirming this regulation, in light of "ambiguous" statutory language).

[132]*Id.*

[133]*Id.*

[134]867 F. Supp. 873, 70 FEP 165 (E.D. Mo. 1994).

[135]152 F.3d 666, 78 FEP 95 (7th Cir. 1998).

[136]*Id.* at 669.

filed lawsuits alleging age discrimination. At issue was whether the program was an "exit incentive" or "termination program" under the OWBPA such that a 45-day rather than a 21-day consideration period should have been provided and such that the information concerning ages, job titles, and the like should have been distributed. The lower court granted summary judgment to the employer.

The court of appeals concluded that "[t]he 'new position' option, especially in juxtaposition with the 'quit now' option, could be found to constitute the requisite incentive (not compulsion) to resign."[137] Accordingly, the court found that it would have had to remand the case for a trial on the validity of the waivers but for the fact that it found, alternatively, that there was no evidence of age discrimination and "the mere fact the reconfigured job was less attractive to older than to younger workers would not establish a violation."[138]

In *Campbell v. Amana Co.*,[139] the court, examining legislative history and relevant cases, upheld summary judgment for the plaintiffs and rejected the argument that the informational requirements of the OWBPA apply only to situations where employee terminations are optional. It also rejected the argument that because the decision-making process was decentralized and because there were no "eligibility" factors, there was no exit incentive or other termination program.

In *Carpenter v. General Motors Corp.*,[140] the plaintiff separately negotiated consideration in addition to that provided in the standard package. He signed a separate agreement with a release waiving ADEA claims. The court held that the failure to provide him with the disclosures mandated for group discharge programs did not invalidate the second release because it was individually negotiated. The fact that the individual release agreement and the group release agreement contained integration clauses did not affect the analysis.

b. To Whom Information Must Be Provided. The required information must be provided to each employee in the "decisional

---

[137]*Id.* at 671.
[138]*Id.* at 672–73.
[139]125 F. Supp. 2d 1129 (N.D. Iowa 2001).
[140]188 F.3d 506 (6th Cir. 1999).

unit" who is asked to sign a waiver agreement.[141] The terms "class," "unit," "group,"[142] and "job classification or organizational unit"[143] in the OWBPA are examples and not exclusive listings.[144] The "decisional unit" must be determined in each case based on an employer's organizational structure and decision-making process.[145] It is "that portion of the employer's organizational structure from which the employer chose the persons who would be offered consideration for the signing of a waiver and those who would not be offered consideration for the signing of a waiver."[146] The decisional unit may be composed of multiple facilities.[147] Examples of common decisional units used in involuntary reductions in force are provided in the waiver regulations:

(A) Facility-wide: Ten percent of the employees in the Springfield facility will be terminated within the next ten days;

(B) Division-wide: Fifteen of the employees in the Computer Division will be terminated in December;

(C) Department-wide: One-half of the workers in the Keyboard Department of the Computer Division will be terminated in December;

(D) Reporting: Ten percent of the employees who report to the Vice President of Sales, wherever the employees are located, will be terminated immediately;

(E) Job Category: Ten percent of all accountants, wherever the employees are located, will be terminated next week.[148]

According to the EEOC, the decisional units are "(A) The Springfield facility; (B) The Computer Division; (C) The Keyboard department; (D) All employees reporting to the Vice President of Sales; and (E) All accountants."[149]

In *Adams v. Moore Business Forms, Inc.*,[150] the plaintiffs contended that the decisional unit encompassed another facility because

---

[141]29 C.F.R. § 1625.22(f)(1)(iv)(2) (2005).
[142]29 U.S.C. § 626(f)(1)(H)(i) (2000).
[143]*Id.* § 626(f)(1)(H)(ii).
[144]29 C.F.R. § 1625.22(f)(3)(i)(A) (2005).
[145]*Id.* § 1625.22(f)(3)(i)(B).
[146]*Id.*
[147]*Id.* § 1625.22(f)(3)(ii)(E).
[148]*Id.* § 1625.22(f)(3)(iii)(A)–(E).
[149]*Id.* § 1625.22(f)(3)(iv)(A)–(E).
[150]224 F.3d 324, 83 FEP 1241 (4th Cir. 2000).

the company may have transferred work to that facility and there had been past competitions with respect to productivity between the plants. The court, citing the EEOC regulations, found that there was no evidence that the company had actually considered employees at other plants for layoffs or had considered other plants for closure.[151]

    c. Information to Be Provided. The waiver regulations address the OWBPA requirement that an employer conducting a group discharge program provide a listing of the job titles and ages of employees selected and the ages of all employees in the same job classification or organizational unit who are not selected[152] as follows:

- Age information cannot be presented in bands greater than one year.[153]
- If there are established grade levels or other established subcategories within a job category or title, information needs to be broken down by grade level or subcategory as well.[154]
- If information about voluntary and involuntary discharges is included, the information presented must distinguish between the two.[155]
- Information provided concerning involuntary discharge programs that occur in increments over a period of time must be cumulative, but there is no obligation to supplement information given to earlier dischargees.[156]
- A sample disclosure form is included for guidance.[157]

The courts have also begun to address the technical requirements of the OWBPA in the context of exit incentive and group discharge programs.

    In *Griffin v. Kraft General Foods, Inc.,*[158] decided prior to the promulgation of the waiver regulations, the court examined the sufficiency of the information provided to employees about a group discharge program offered in connection with a plant closure. The

---

[151]*Id.* at 328.
[152]29 U.S.C. § 626(f)(1)(H)(ii) (2000).
[153]29 C.F.R. § 1625.22(f)(4)(ii) (2005).
[154]*Id.* § 1625.22(f)(4)(iii).
[155]*Id.* § 1625.22(f)(4)(iv).
[156]*Id.* § 1625.22(f)(4)(vi).
[157]*Id.* § 1625.22(f)(4)(vii).
[158]62 F.3d 368, 68 FEP 1072 (11th Cir. 1995).

court held that the OWBPA does not restrict the terms "job classification" and "organizational unit" to employees in the same plant. Because no facts were presented with respect to employees at other plants, summary judgment concerning compliance with the OWBPA's notice requirements was inappropriate.[159] In *Raczak v. Ameritech Corp.*,[160] also decided prior to the promulgation of the waiver regulations, the court rejected the determination of the district court, in the context of a summary judgment motion, that because the employer had provided required OWBPA information organized by salary grade instead of by job title, the OWBPA was violated. Instead, the court held that "a rigid and mechanical interpretation of [the OWBPA's disclosure requirements] is inappropriate."[161] It continued: "Holding an employer strictly accountable for what might be a technical violation of these imprecise terms, with no indication that this would facilitate the provision's purpose and might even hamper it, is untenable and would elevate form over substance."[162]

In *Suhy v. AlliedSignal*,[163] the court concluded that providing information about the ages of those eligible and ineligible in age ranges does not satisfy the requirements of § 626(f)(1)(H)(ii).

> The requirements of the OWBPA are clear and unambiguous: the employer must provide "the job titles and ages of *all* individuals eligible or selected for the program, and the ages of *all* individuals in the same job classification" not selected. . . . If Congress intended to allow employers to satisfy this requirement with ranges of ages, it could have made this distinction in the statute.[164]

---

[159]*Id.* at 371–73.

[160]103 F.3d 1257, 72 FEP 1357 (6th Cir. 1997).

[161]*Id.* at 1259.

[162]*Id.* at 1260; *see also* Tung v. Texaco, Inc., 150 F.3d 206, 209, 77 FEP 670 (2d Cir. 1998) (plaintiff was supplied with information required by 29 U.S.C. § 626(f)(1)(H) on the day he signed release; noting that required information must be provided at commencement of period employee is given to consider waiver, court found release invalid); Branker v. Pfizer, Inc., 981 F. Supp. 862, 867 (S.D.N.Y. 1997) (where job titles were not matched with work units or ages such that employee could not derive ages of those not included in separation program and whether those not included were in same job classification or work unit, disclosure not in compliance with OWBPA); Eye v. Fluor Corp., 952 F. Supp. 635 (E.D. Mo. 1997) (invalidating releases where group of discharged employees not supplied with required information).

[163]44 F. Supp. 2d 432, 79 FEP 1010 (D. Conn. 1999).

[164]*Id.* at 435; *see also* Butcher v. Gerber Prods. Co., 8 F. Supp. 2d 307, 315, 77 FEP 339 (S.D.N.Y. 1998) (listing number of individuals over 40 and over 50 not sufficient compliance; providing information after fact does not cure failure to disclose).

C. Waivers as Part of Settlement of an EEOC Charge or Court Action

If the waiver is part of a settlement of an EEOC charge under the ADEA or an ADEA court action, it is considered knowing and voluntary if, at a minimum, the five basic requirements set out earlier are met and the individual is "given a reasonable period of time within which to consider the settlement agreement."[165]

The waiver regulations provide that the term "reasonable time within which to consider the settlement agreement"[166] means "reasonable under all the circumstances, including whether the individual is represented by counsel or has the assistance of counsel."[167] If the requirements for time periods specified in the OWBPA for prelitigation releases[168] are satisfied, the time will automatically be deemed reasonable, although compliance with these time periods is not mandatory outside of the prelitigation context.[169]

Presumably, courts will look to the pre-OWBPA cases in determining "reasonableness under all the circumstances." In *Manning v. New York University*,[170] the court addressed the applicability of the OWBPA waiver requirements to releases reached on the record in court. Although finding that the OWBPA requirements for unsupervised releases had been met, the court held that the OWBPA waiver requirements do not apply to judicially supervised on-the-record settlements.[171]

D. *Oubre*: Tender-Back and Ratification

Whether an employee must return monetary consideration received under a release of ADEA claims as a precondition to challenging the enforceability of the release for OWBPA noncompliance has been resolved by the Supreme Court. In *Oubre v. Entergy*

---

[165]29 U.S.C. § 626(f)(2)(B) (2000). Presumably, this "reasonable period" is shorter than the 21 days applicable to prelitigation releases. *See* Section II.B.2 *supra*. Pre-OWBPA cases on this issue also may be instructive.

[166]29 U.S.C. § 626(f)(2)(B) (2000).

[167]29 C.F.R. § 1625.22(g)(4) (2005).

[168]29 U.S.C. § 626(f)(1) (2000).

[169]29 C.F.R. § 1625.22(g)(5) (2005).

[170]86 FEP 1240 (S.D.N.Y. 2001).

[171]*Id.* at 1252.

Operations, Inc.,[172] the Court held that a release that did not comply with the OWBPA did not bar the plaintiff's ADEA lawsuit even though the plaintiff had not returned or promised to return the money she received in return for signing the release. Nor did retention of the payments constitute ratification of the invalid release. However, through one concurring and two dissenting opinions, five Justices intimated that once suit is filed, the employer may be able to make a counterclaim for restitution of the ADEA release consideration, seek a setoff as to such consideration, or pursue relief from ongoing obligations under the now-rejected ADEA release.[173]

The EEOC issued final regulations regarding the enforceability of ADEA releases following the *Oubre* decision, which became effective January 10, 2001.[174] These regulations provide that an individual who challenges the validity of an ADEA release need not first tender back the consideration provided under the release,[175] and that employers may not contractually impose a tender-back requirement.[176]

---

[172]522 U.S. 422, 75 FEP 1255 (1998).

[173]*Id.* at 431–35. In his concurring opinion, Justice Breyer described the settlement contract as voidable, not void, and expressed the view that "[o]nce [the employee] has sued . . . nothing in the statute prevents his employer from asking for restitution of his reciprocal payment or relief from any ongoing reciprocal obligation." *Id.* at 432. According to Justice Breyer, "five or more Justices" take the view "that the statute's provisions are consistent with viewing an invalid release as voidable, rather than void." *Id.* Note, however, that ratification as a result of a failure to return consideration received may be found with respect to state law claims. *See* Bennett v. Coors Brewing Co., 189 F.3d 1221, 1236, 80 FEP 1197 (10th Cir. 1999); Hodge v. New York Coll. of Podiatric Med., 157 F.3d 164, 167, 78 FEP 80 (2d Cir. 1998) (plaintiff did not ratify invalid ADEA release by continuing to work for 1 year after signing settlement); *see also* Aikins v. Tosco Ref. Co., 1999 WL 179686, at *5 (N.D. Cal. Mar. 26, 1999) (ratification applied to Title VII release, but plaintiff presented issue of fact, precluding summary judgment, where plaintiff testified that he knew of other employees who did not sign release but received benefits anyway).

[174]65 Fed. Reg. 77,438 (Dec. 11, 2000) (codified at 29 C.F.R. § 1625.23 (2005)).

[175]29 C.F.R. § 1625.23(a) (2005).

[176]*Id.* § 1625.23(b). The regulations also provide that if a plaintiff successfully challenges an ADEA release and prevails on an ADEA claim, the court may set off against the plaintiff's monetary recovery the consideration provided under the release, 29 C.F.R. § 1625.23(c), and that an employer must continue to perform its obligations under the release even if the employee successfully challenges the validity of the release, *id.* § 1625.23(d).

In *Butcher v. Gerber Products Co.*, 8 F. Supp. 2d 307, 77 FEP 339 (S.D.N.Y. 1998), the court interpreted *Oubre* as permitting an employer to assert an appropriate defense or to make an appropriate motion at the end of litigation, but not as

E. Violation of § 626(f) as an Independent Basis for Action

The Tenth Circuit found that there is nothing in the language or the legislative history of the OWBPA that suggests that a noncompliant waiver alone could support an independent cause of action.[177] Other courts have agreed.[178] The court in *Massachusetts v. Bull HN Information Systems, Inc.*,[179] however, held that the Commonwealth of Massachusetts could state an independent cause of action for declaratory and injunctive relief against an employer that violates § 626(f) even in the absence of an actual discrimination action. In so deciding, the court relied on § 626(c)'s language, which provides that "[a]ny person aggrieved may bring a civil action in any court of competent jurisdiction for such legal and equitable relief as will effectuate the purposes of this chapter."[180] The *Bull HN* court rejected the employer's argument that the sole remedy for a plaintiff-employee who has signed a nonconforming waiver is that the waiver is ineffective as a defense in an age discrimination lawsuit.

Among the cases criticized by the court in the *Bull HN* case is *EEOC v. Sears, Roebuck & Co.*[181] In an action by the EEOC challenging waivers associated with Sears' severance pay plan, the

---

permitting an employer to engage in "self-help" by ceasing payments during the pendency of litigation. *Id.* at 316. In *Isaacs v. Caterpillar, Inc.*, 702 F. Supp. 711, 712–13, 49 FEP 607 (C.D. Ill. 1988), the plaintiffs signed a general release in exchange for special payments but then sued for age discrimination, claiming that the releases were void. Caterpillar counterclaimed for breach of the settlement agreement, seeking damages in the amount of the special payments plus attorney's fees and costs. The court characterized the release as purely "defensive" and dismissed the counterclaim, holding that Caterpillar should have drafted the release to give it an "offensive" right of action in the event of a lawsuit if it wished to retain the right to sue for damages. The court rejected Caterpillar's argument that this result would mean that it had received nothing in exchange for its payments: "Caterpillar obtained Plaintiffs' departure from its employment, and it obtained releases which, if valid, may be used to defend against litigation." *Id.* at 715. The court alternatively concluded that the ADEA preempts any state law allowing recovery of damages for breach of a defensive release, in that such a law would discourage ADEA plaintiffs from asserting their rights. *Id.* at 715.

[177]Whitehead v. Oklahoma Gas & Elec. Co., 187 F.3d 1184, 1191–92, 80 FEP 790 (10th Cir. 1999).

[178]*See, e.g.*, EEOC v. Brinson, Inc., 2003 U.S. Dist. LEXIS 570, at *11 (S.D.N.Y. Jan. 15, 2003).

[179]16 F. Supp. 2d 90, 77 FEP 1523 (D. Mass. 1998).

[180]16 F. Supp. 2d at 105.

[181]883 F. Supp. 211, 70 FEP 175 (N.D. Ill. 1995).

EEOC argued that a violation of § 626(f) gives rise to a separate cause of action. The court found no support for the assertion in the legislative history of the OWBPA. Noting that Congress expressly provided that the effect of an invalid release is to bar an employer from relying on the release as a defense, it refused to "read into" the statute a separate cause of action.[182]

In *Williams v. General Motors Corp.*,[183] individual plaintiffs included not only a claim for substantive age discrimination but also one for violation of the subsection (f) waiver provisions. In contrast to the *Bull HN* case, this court dismissed the second claim, refusing to find that violation of the OWBPA's procedural requirements "may be extrapolated into a holding that a substantive cause of action for age discrimination exists."[184] Another court held that an employer's severance pay offer, including a waiver and release of ADEA claims that did not comply with the OWBPA, does not give rise to an inference of age discrimination.[185]

One court affirmed a jury determination that a release, which concededly did not comply with the OWBPA, supported equitable estoppel of a statute of limitations defense by an employer that used the defective release.[186]

III. TERMS OF THE SETTLEMENT AGREEMENT

A. General and Special Releases

Although some courts have found so-called "standard" general release language sufficiently comprehensive to cover all possible

---

[182]883 F. Supp. at 215; *see also* EEOC v. Sara Lee, 923 F. Supp. 994, 999, 70 FEP 57 (W.D. Mich. 1995) (relying on *Sears Roebuck*, court held that failure to meet OWBPA requirements does not constitute separate cause of action and is not violation of ADEA; EEOC could not state claim and could not seek injunctive relief to enjoin future use of nonconforming waivers).

[183]901 F. Supp. 252, 69 FEP 445 (E.D. Mich. 1995).

[184]*Id.* at 255.

[185]Waldemar v. American Cancer Soc'y, 971 F. Supp. 547, 554 (N.D. Ga. 1996).

[186]Tyler v. Union Oil Co. of Cal., 304 F.3d 379, 390–91, 89 FEP 1226 (5th Cir. 2002) (jury instruction was: "For each of the following plaintiffs, do you find that the defendant's conduct induced him to refrain from filing his claim with the EEOC within 300 days of the alleged unlawful practices?"; jury answered "yes" with regard to each plaintiff).

claims,[187] other courts have ruled that the absence of language specifically identifying the statutory employment discrimination claims being released may undercut the effectiveness of the release.[188] A release that fails to state explicitly whether it is a general release encompassing any and all claims of whatever nature may result in finding that the release covers a narrow group of claims or that the waiver is wholly or partially invalid.[189] A release

---

[187]*See* Stroman v. West Coast Grocery Co., 884 F.2d 458, 461, 50 FEP 1204 (9th Cir. 1989) ("[a]n agreement need not specifically recite the particular claims waived in order to be effective"); Lancaster v. Buerkle Buick Honda Co., 809 F.2d 539, 540–41, 42 FEP 1472 (8th Cir. 1987) (pre-OWBPA case; upholding release of ADEA claim even though ADEA was not expressly mentioned; release extended to "each and every claim of any kind"); EEOC v. American Express Publ'g Corp., 681 F. Supp. 216, 219 n.5, 47 FEP 1596 (S.D.N.Y. 1988) (pre-OWBPA case; although issue of fact existed whether waiver was knowing and voluntary, court found release language itself did not suffer from ambiguity even though it did not explicitly mention that it was intended to apply to ADEA claims; "standard" general release language was utilized). Of course, as discussed earlier, the OWBPA requires specific reference to claims arising under the ADEA as a condition of a valid waiver. Pre-OWBPA cases presumably still have vitality in the context of other claims, such as race or sex.

[188]*E.g.*, Pierce v. Atchison (*Pierce II*), 110 F.3d 431, 439 (7th Cir. 1997) (jury entitled to consider absence of specific language); Torrez v. Public Serv. Co., 908 F.2d 687, 690, 53 FEP 764 (10th Cir. 1990) (material issues of fact precluded entry of summary judgment in favor of defendant; "[t]he language of the release, although clear and unambiguous, failed to mention specifically waiver of employment discrimination claims"); Thiessen v. General Elec., 232 F. Supp. 2d 1230, 1236 (D. Kan. 2002) ("the waiver must be part of a written settlement agreement which specifically identifies that rights and claims under the ADEA are being waived"); Mashman v. Universal Match Corp., 727 F. Supp. 941, 944–45, 51 FEP 1387 (E.D. Pa. 1989) (salesman's release of "all claims" rising out of employment did not bar age or disability discrimination claims, which were not separately enumerated in release).

[189]*Compare* McElroy v. Union Pac. R.R., 961 F.2d 1397, 1399, 58 FEP 1052 (8th Cir. 1992) (summary judgment for employer inappropriate in absence of unequivocal waiver of all of employee's claims; separation agreement stated only that employer's performance of terms of agreement fulfills "all of its obligations" to discharged employee) *and* Kawatra v. Medgar Evers Coll., 700 F. Supp. 648, 651–52, 62 FEP 1243 (E.D.N.Y. 1988) (Although plaintiff relinquished right to initiate further suits, agreement did not explicitly address whether plaintiff was precluded from continuing then-pending complaints in judicial rather than administrative forum: "If the defendants wanted to make sure that the settlement agreement would bar any lawsuit growing out of the then-pending administrative proceedings, they could have made that crystal clear in the agreement. They did not. Accordingly, no such waiver will be inferred.") *with American Express Publishing*, 681 F. Supp. at 219 (that there was no explicit mention of application to ADEA claims did not render agreement ambiguous; pre-OWBPA case).

that fails to specify whether it is intended to release "known and unknown" claims may not cover claims not expressly known to the employee;[190] some state statutes presumptively disfavor waivers of unknown claims.[191]

Similarly, a failure to spell out nonmonetary terms with precision may result in future litigation.[192]

B. Covenants Not to File Charges or to Assist in the Future Prosecution of Claims

In negotiating a settlement agreement, some employers have bargained for a promise that the complainant will not cause any claim to be filed with the EEOC or any other federal, state, or local administrative agency on any matter related to the matters released in the settlement agreement. In *EEOC v. Cosmair, Inc.*,[193] an employee filed a discrimination charge with the EEOC after executing a general release pursuant to which he had begun to receive severance payments to which he was not otherwise entitled. Cosmair ceased making payments, claiming that the employee breached the agreement by filing the charge. The employee then filed a retaliation charge. The EEOC, after finding that reasonable cause existed to believe that unlawful retaliation had occurred, filed for an injunction, seeking, among other matters, an order that barred Cosmair from suspending the severance payments.[194] The Fifth Circuit found that the release did not, by its terms, bar the filing of the charge. Alternatively, however, it held that if the release had

---

[190]*See* Wagner v. Nutrasweet Co., 95 F.3d 527, 533, 72 FEP 284 (7th Cir. 1996) (holding that release that covered all claims, "known and unknown," including claims that an employee did not know about and that, the employee alleged, she could not have known about at the time of signing the release, was nevertheless valid and had been entered into knowingly and voluntarily).

[191]*See, e.g.*, CAL. CIV. CODE § 1542.

[192]*See, e.g.*, Pardi v. Kaiser Permanente Hosp., 389 F.3d 840, 848, 16 AD 289 (9th Cir. 2004) (meaning of terms "accept the voluntary resignation" and "become effective" under settlement agreement unclear; summary judgment reversed on breach of contract claim); Holmes v. Potter, 384 F.3d 356, 94 FEP 737 (7th Cir. 2004) (district court conducted hearing over meaning of term "saved grade" in settlement agreement with agency; district court did not clearly err in finding that contract did not require Postal Service to confer noncompetitive transfer on plaintiff).

[193]821 F.2d 1085, 44 FEP 569 (5th Cir. 1987).

[194]*Id.* at 1087.

so provided, the waiver would have been against public policy and therefore void. The court, in granting the requested preliminary injunction, reasoned that "[a]llowing the filing of charges to be obstructed by enforcing a waiver of the right to file a charge could impede EEOC enforcement of the civil rights laws."[195] The court, however, noted that although an agreement to waive the right to file a charge is void, the waiver of the employee's right to file suit and recover thereon or to recover in a suit brought by the EEOC on his or her behalf is valid.[196] The OWBPA specifically provides that a release of age discrimination claims in a privately negotiated settlement agreement does not affect the EEOC's "rights and responsibilities to enforce [the ADEA]. No waiver may be used to justify interfering with the protected right of an employee to file a charge or participate in an investigation or proceeding conducted by the Commission."[197]

In *EEOC v. Astra, Inc.*,[198] Astra challenged a preliminary injunction that barred it from entering into or enforcing any settlement agreements containing provisions that prohibited settling employees from filing charges with the EEOC and from assisting the EEOC in the investigation of EEOC charges. Astra had entered into at least 11 settlement agreements that contained provisions, among others, that the settling employees agreed not to file charges with the EEOC (the nonfiling clause), that the settling employees agreed not to assist others who filed EEOC charges (the nonassistance clause), and that the settling employees agreed not to discuss the incidents that gave rise to the claims (the confidentiality clause). The First Circuit held that the nonassistance and confidentiality clauses were void as against public policy, to the

---

[195]*Id.* at 1090.

[196]*Id.* at 1091; *see also* EEOC v. United States Steel Corp., 921 F.2d 489, 496–97, 54 FEP 1044 (3d Cir. 1990) ("[I]ndividuals who fully litigated their own claims under the ADEA are precluded by res judicata from obtaining individual relief in a subsequent EEOC action based on the same claims. As the Commission concedes, the district court also erred in awarding interest to those individuals who previously settled their claims with USX."); EEOC v. Goodyear Aerospace Corp., 813 F.2d 1539, 1543–45, 43 FEP 875 (9th Cir. 1987) (employee's settlement mooted EEOC's claim for back pay on behalf of employee but did not moot EEOC's right of action to seek injunctive relief).

[197]29 U.S.C. § 626(f)(4) (2000).

[198]94 F.3d 738, 71 FEP 1267 (1st Cir. 1996).

extent they prohibited communication with the EEOC, and upheld the preliminary injunction with respect to them.[199] Without determining the validity vel non of the nonfiling clause, the court found that the EEOC had not demonstrated that inclusion and enforcement of the clause would cause it to suffer irreparable injury absent a preliminary injunction. The court did note that it viewed the validity of the nonfiling clause as a close question.[200]

Subsequently, in 1997, the EEOC published "Guidance on Waivers Under Civil Rights Laws,"[201] stating its position that employers may not limit individuals' rights to file charges or participate in EEOC proceedings by requiring employees to sign agreements relinquishing these rights. The EEOC contends that such agreements are void and that they may amount to separate and discrete violations of the antiretaliation provisions of the civil rights laws. The EEOC notes, however, that if an individual signs a valid waiver and then files an EEOC charge, the employer will be shielded against any further recovery by the employee.[202]

A related issue is whether the employer can extract a promise by the signatory employee not to counsel or assist in the prosecution of claims, whether on behalf of the employee or others. The EEOC has argued, generally successfully, that such promises are contrary to public policy.[203] Employers have had better success where the release prohibits only voluntary acts by the employee and permits testimony under subpoena.[204]

---

[199]*Id.* at 744–45.

[200]*Id.* at 746.

[201]*EEOC Policy Guidance on Waivers Under Civil Rights Laws, reprinted in* 8 FEP MAN. (BNA) 405:7491.

[202]*Id.* at 405:7495.

[203]For example, in *EEOC v. United States Steel Corp.*, 671 F. Supp. 351, 354, 44 FEP 1801 (W.D. Pa.), *supplemented*, 728 F. Supp. 1167, 51 FEP 739 (W.D. Pa. 1987), *rev'd on other grounds*, 921 F.2d 489, 54 FEP 1044 (3d Cir. 1990), the employer was enjoined from using and enforcing a provision in a release whereby an employee promised "not to counsel or assist in the prosecution of such claim whether on his behalf or on the behalf of others." The court stated that "[t]he mere possibility that this provision would deter individuals from participating in any ADEA claims is sufficient to render it violative of § 4(d) [prohibiting retaliation] and public policy." *Id.* at 358.

[204]*E.g.*, Hoffman v. United Telcomms., Inc., 687 F. Supp. 1512 (D. Kan. 1988) (settlement with original named plaintiff in class action prohibited plaintiff from further participation in case, with exception of testifying pursuant to subpoena; provision

With respect to the waiver of age discrimination claims, the OWBPA is consistent with the EEOC's 1997 Guidance on these issues. It provides: "No waiver agreement may affect the Commission's rights and responsibilities to enforce the Act. No waiver may be used to justify interfering with the protected right of an employee to file a charge or participate in an investigation or proceeding conducted by the Commission."[205]

The OWBPA waiver regulations also expressly address the validity of settlement provisions purporting to prohibit the filing of EEOC charges and assisting the EEOC:

> (2) No waiver agreement may include any provision prohibiting any individual from:
>
> (i) Filing a charge or complaint, including a challenge to the validity of the waiver agreement, with EEOC, or
>
> (ii) Participating in any investigation or proceeding conducted by EEOC.
>
> (3) No waiver agreement may include any provision imposing any condition precedent, any penalty, or any other limitation adversely affecting any individual's right to:
>
> (i) File a charge or complaint, including a challenge to the validity of the waiver agreement, with EEOC, or
>
> (ii) Participate in any investigation or proceeding conducted by EEOC.[206]

In *American Airlines, Inc. v. Cardoza-Rodriguez*,[207] the First Circuit noted that the release at issue prohibited employees from maintaining "any legal proceedings of any nature whatsoever against American *et al.* before any court or administrative agency" and required employees to " 'direct that agency or court to withdraw from or dismiss the matter with prejudice' if the agency assumes jurisdiction on their behalf."[208] The court found that this provision was "deficient" under the OWBPA.[209]

---

was found lawful under circumstances, given plaintiff's prior testimony, many years that case was pending, her availability to testify upon subpoena, and her interest in settling case and receiving monetary compensation).

[205]29 U.S.C. § 626(f)(4) (2000).

[206]29 C.F.R. § 1625.22(h)(2) (2005).

[207]133 F.3d 111, 75 FEP 1217 (1st Cir. 1998).

[208]*Id.* at 118.

[209]*Id.* at 118 n.7. *But see* Wastak v. Lehigh Valley Health Network, 324 F.3d 281, 92 FEP 1079 (3d Cir. 2003) (OWBPA release that purported to bar filing of

C. Attorney's Fees and Retainer Agreements

Plaintiffs' counsel often do not receive hourly fees; their sole prospect for compensation is either through a contingency fee arrangement with the client or through fees recovered under either 42 U.S.C. § 1988 or the attorney's fee provision of § 706(k) of Title VII. Ethical considerations can be presented by simultaneous negotiation of attorney's fees and the substantive terms of the settlement. The ethical issue arises because there are substantial pressures on the attorney to concede benefits that might be obtained for the plaintiff (or plaintiffs) in exchange for attorney's fee concessions.[210]

Courts generally hold that the failure to include in the settlement agreement a release of the claimant's attorney's fees results in no release of a claim for attorney's fees in an employment discrimination case.[211]

In *Torres v. Metropolitan Life Insurance Co.*,[212] the Third Circuit held that a written settlement agreement that is silent as to attorney's fees will not be deemed to constitute a waiver of the statutory entitlement to such fees in a national origin/retaliation Title VII case. The court so held even though the release language was very broad and the plaintiff had released any rights and claims under Title VII and the Civil Rights Act of 1991. Similarly, the Ninth Circuit has stated that "we, like the Third Circuit, have made it clear that any party wishing to foreclose a suit for § 1988 fees must negotiate a provision waiving attorneys' fees."[213] However,

---

EEOC charges nevertheless could be enforced, with offending clause severed); Hansen v. Vanderbilt Univ., 961 F. Supp. 1149, 73 FEP 1866 (M.D. Tenn. 1997) (requiring employee to withdraw EEOC charge as part of settlement of ADEA claim not adverse action that will support retaliation claim).

[210]*See* Evans v. Jeff D., 475 U.S. 717, 737–38, 40 FEP 860 (1986) (class action settlement conditioned on waiver of fees does not violate Civil Rights Attorney's Fees Awards Act of 1976, 42 U.S.C. § 1988; district court may approve consent decree with fee waiver provision).

[211]*See, e.g.*, Ellis v. University of Kan. Med. Ctr., 163 F.3d 1186, 1200, 78 FEP 1802 (10th Cir. 1998) (also citing Sixth and Ninth Circuit cases) (as settlement agreement was silent regarding plaintiff's right to recover fees and expenses, plaintiff did not waive her right to pursue fees and expenses).

[212]189 F.3d 331 (3d Cir. 1999). This decision is consistent with the Third Circuit decisions in *El Club Del Barrio, Inc. v. United Community Corps.*, 735 F.2d 98 (3d Cir. 1984), and *Ashley v. Atlantic Richfield Co.*, 794 F.2d 128, 41 FEP 255 (3d Cir. 1986).

[213]Muckleshoot Tribe v. Puget Sound Power & Light Co., 875 F.2d 695, 698 (9th Cir. 1989) (citations omitted).

the Ninth Circuit also stated that it will permit the defendant to go beyond the written instrument to prove that both parties intended to waive attorney's fees.[214] In *Wray v. Clarke*,[215] the Eighth Circuit held that attorney's fees could be waived by silence when they were not raised in a settlement conference before a magistrate judge, during which conference an agreement was reached. In *Gilbert v. Monsanto Co.*,[216] however, the Eighth Circuit held that a plaintiff who settled an ADEA case and then successfully enforced the settlement agreement was a "prevailing party" entitled to attorney's fees in the absence of express waiver, under a theory of "monitoring" the ADEA judgment.[217]

IV. TAX CONSIDERATIONS

A. Introduction

The net value to the plaintiff of a monetary settlement is substantially greater if the employee is not required to pay taxes on all or a portion of it. Thus, whether amounts paid pursuant to a settlement agreement may be excluded from income under the tax laws has been an important factor in settlement negotiations.

B. Allocation Issues

On August 20, 1996, Congress passed the Small Business Job Protection Act of 1996,[218] significantly affecting the tax treatment of settlements in employment discrimination cases. Following that revision, the Internal Revenue Code provides that punitive damages are taxable to the recipient, regardless of whether they are related to a physical injury or physical sickness.[219] The Supreme Court reached the same result in *O'Gilvie v. United States*,[220] in which the Court interpreted the tax law before the amendment.

---

[214]*Id.* In *Ellis*, 163 F.3d at 1107, the Tenth Circuit held that an evidentiary hearing concerning the parties' intent should be held.

[215]151 F.3d 807 (8th Cir. 1998).

[216]216 F.3d 695, 83 FEP 531 (8th Cir. 2000).

[217]*Id.* at 702–04.

[218]Pub. L. No. 104-188, 110 Stat. 1838 (1996).

[219]26 U.S.C. § 104(a)(2) (2000).

[220]519 U.S. 79, 84 (1996).

Further, even with respect to nonpunitive damages, the exclusion from gross income is now restricted to "personal physical injuries or sickness."[221] This means that, in the typical employment case, which involves only claims for back pay, front pay, and/or compensatory damages for emotional distress, but no actual physical injury to the plaintiff, the proceeds of a settlement will not be excludable from gross income and therefore will be taxable.[222]

Because settlements in most employment discrimination cases will not be attributable to personal injuries or sickness and thus will be taxable, the parties must decide whether the settlement amounts should be treated as wages subject to payroll tax withholding. The authorities are not definitive, and the appropriate result generally depends on the nature of the specific claims alleged and damages incurred.

C. Attorney's Fees

Another issue with which the parties must grapple is the proper tax handling of attorney's fees. After substantial bipartisan lobbying, Congress included within the American Jobs Creation Act of 2004 (the JOBS Act) a provision designed to rectify the inequity caused by the decisions requiring that attorney's fees be included in a plaintiff's gross income, subject only to a generalized "below the line" deduction. Section 703 of the JOBS Act established an "above the line" deduction from gross income for attorney's fees and court costs incurred by an individual in an action involving a claim of unlawful discrimination, certain claims against the federal government, or private causes of action under the Medicare

---

[221]26 U.S.C. § 104(a)(2) (2000).

[222]Emotional distress damages not attributable to physical injury or sickness may be excluded from income to the extent of amounts actually paid for medical care attributable to emotional distress. 26 U.S.C. § 104(a) (2000). *But* see Murphy v. IRS, 460 F.3d 79 (D.C. Cir. 2006) (taxation of non-economic damages for emotional distress and loss of reputation violates Sixteenth Amendment to U.S. Constitution). For any cases governed by the pre-August 1996 law, the Supreme Court decision in *Commissioner of Internal Revenue v. Schleier*, 515 U.S. 323, 337 (1995), governs the interpretation of the exclusion for damages or settlement proceeds "on account of personal injuries or sickness," as § 104(a)(2) read prior to the 1996 amendment. In *Schleier*, the Court found that a recovery under the ADEA was taxable, holding that a recovery can be excluded only when it is both (1) received through prosecution or settlement of an action "based upon tort or tort type rights" and (2) received "on account of personal injuries or sickness." *Id.*

secondary payer statute. The deduction is limited to no more than the amount included in gross income for the year as a result of the claim. The term "unlawful discrimination" is defined to include illegal acts under a long list of federal statutes, including civil rights, fair labor standards, age discrimination, rehabilitation, ERISA, education, family and medical leave, fair housing, disabilities, and whistle-blower protection. The law became effective for fees and costs paid after October 22, 2004, with respect to judgments or settlements occurring after that date.[223]

In *Commissioner v. Banks*,[224] the Supreme Court resolved a circuit split[225] on this issue. In *Banks*, decided after the passage of

---

[223]Tax issues are further addressed in Chapters 12 (Age) and 40 (Monetary Relief).

[224]543 U.S. 426 (2005).

[225]*See* Foster v. United States, 249 F.3d 1275, 1279 n.7 (11th Cir. 2001) ("We recognize the circuit split on this issue. The Fifth and Sixth Circuits have applied the [*Cotnam v. Commissioner of Internal Revenue*, 263 F.2d 119 (5th Cir. 1959)] ruling, while the Third, Fourth, Ninth, and Federal Circuits include contingency fees in a taxpayer's gross income. *See* Srivastava v. Commissioner, 220 F.3d 353, 365 (5th Cir. 2000); Estate of Clarks v. United States, 202 F.3d 854, 858 (6th Cir. 2000); O'Brien v. Commissioner, 38 T.C. 707, 712 (1962), *aff'd*, 319 F.2d 532 (3d Cir. 1963); Young v. Commissioner, 240 F.3d 369, 372 (4th Cir. 2001); Coady v. Comm'r, 213 F.3d 1187, 1187 (9th Cir. 2000); Baylin v. United States, 43 F.3d 1451, 1452 (Fed. Cir. 1995). [*Cotnam* is] binding precedent in our circuit, *Bonner v. City of Prichard*, 661 F.2d 1206, 1209 (11th Cir. 1981), and has been upheld in *Davis v. Commissioner*, 210 F.3d 1346, 1347 n.4 (11th Cir. 2000).").

In *Alexander v. Internal Revenue Service*, 72 F.3d 938 (1st Cir. 1995), the parties settled claims for breach of contract, breach of implied pension contract, and age discrimination for $350,000; $100,000 was allocated to the age discrimination claim and $250,000 to the remaining claims. (At the time, the parties considered the $100,000 payment to be tax-free.) The taxpayers incurred $258,000 in attorney's fees and allocated $245,100 of that to the settlement of the contract and pension claims. They offset the $245,100 against the $250,000 and reported income of $4,900. The IRS did not challenge the allocation of attorney's fees between the claims; it did not state, for example, that the fees needed to be allocated to the nontaxable portion of the settlement in the same percentage as the nontaxable portion of the settlement bore to the whole settlement. However, the IRS took the position, upheld by the court, that the full amount of the taxable portion of the settlement should have been reported as income and that the attorney's fees had to be taken as an itemized deduction, subject to the 2%-of-adjusted-gross-income limitation. Moreover, this treatment triggered the operation of the alternative minimum tax.

Similarly, in *Sinyard v. Commissioner of Internal Revenue*, 268 F.3d 756, 86 FEP 1417 (9th Cir. 2001), the Ninth Circuit held that attorney's fees paid in settlement of an age discrimination claim are income to the plaintiff or class member taxpayer, even if paid by separate check directly to the attorney. The court held that

the JOBS Act but involving a factual situation that arose before that Act, an employee sued his former employer for employment discrimination. He hired an attorney on a 30 percent contingency fee. The case settled with the employee being awarded $464,000, of which the employer paid $314,000 to the employee and $150,000 to his lawyer.[226] The employee paid taxes on the $314,000, and the lawyer paid taxes on the $150,000. The IRS, however, contended that the employee must declare as income the full $464,000 award, subject to appropriate "below-the-line" deductions. Citing 26 U.S.C. § 61(a) for the proposition that gross income is defined as "all income from whatever source derived," the Court unanimously held that the employee must include the full $464,000 in his income.[227] The Court relied on the "anticipatory assignment of income" doctrine, pursuant to which the individual who earns or has control of income cannot escape being taxed on that income even if he or she assigns it to someone else.[228] Employees thus must report as income the full amount of the award, but may take a "below the line" deduction for the full amount paid to their attorneys.

In consequential settlements, the rule adopted in *Banks* had a very adverse impact on the plaintiff, particularly by bringing into play the alternative minimum tax. As the Supreme Court noted in *Banks*, Congress had already addressed these issues prospectively in the JOBS Act.[229]

---

the amounts were constructively received by the taxpayer and that the payments were paid in satisfaction of the indebtedness of the taxpayer to his attorney. *Id.* at 758–59; *see also* Hukkanen-Campbell v. Commissioner, 2000 WL 748170 (U.S. Tax Court 2000) (same); Kenseth v. Commissioner, 114 T.C. 399, 82 FEP 1512 (U.S. Tax Court 2000) (same), *aff'd*, 259 F.3d 881 (7th Cir. 2001); Benci-Woodward v. Commissioner, T.C. Memo. 1998-395 (1998) (same), *aff'd*, 219 F.3d 941 (9th Cir. 2000); Brewer v. Commissioner, T.C. Memo. 1997-542 (1997), *aff'd in unpublished disposition*, 172 F.3d 875 (9th Cir. 1999) (same); Frederickson v. Commissioner, T.C. Memo. 1997-542 (1997), *aff'd in unpublished disposition*, 172 F.3d 875 (9th Cir. 1999) (same). *But see Cotnam*, 263 F.2d at 125–26 (attorney's fees may be directly offset against plaintiff's recovery); *Srivastova*, 220 F.3d 353 (portion of defamation settlement payable to taxpayer's attorney pursuant to contingent fee agreement not included as gross income for tax purposes).

[226]*Banks*, 543 U.S. at 430.
[227]*Id.* at 433.
[228]*Id.*
[229]Pub. L. No. 108-357, 118 Stat. 1418 (Oct. 22, 2004).

V. RULE 68 OFFERS OF JUDGMENT

Rule 68 of the Federal Rules of Civil Procedure provides as follows:

> At any time more than 10 days before the trial begins, a party defending against a claim may serve upon the adverse party an offer to allow judgment to be taken against the defending party for the money or property or to the effect specified in the offer, with costs then accrued. If within 10 days after the service of the offer the adverse party serves written notice that the offer is accepted, either party may then file the offer and notice of acceptance together with proof of service thereof and thereupon the clerk shall enter judgment. An offer not accepted shall be deemed withdrawn and evidence thereof is not admissible except in a proceeding to determine costs. If the judgment finally obtained by the offeree is not more favorable than the offer, the offeree must pay the costs incurred after the making of the offer. The fact that an offer is made but not accepted does not preclude a subsequent offer. When the liability of one party to another has been determined by verdict or order or judgment, but the amount or extent of the liability remains to be determined by further proceedings, the party adjudged liable may make an offer of judgment, which shall have the same effect as an offer made before trial if it is served within a reasonable time not less than 10 days prior to the commencement of hearings to determine the amount or extent of liability.

A Rule 68 offer allows the complainant to obtain judgment against the employer in a specified amount. If a Rule 68 offer is not accepted within a period of 10 days, however, it is deemed withdrawn, and subsequent settlement negotiations legally can proceed without reference to it. A Rule 68 offer of judgment need not be filed with the court unless accepted or until after trial, thereby not prejudicing the employer's case.

Trial courts normally have discretion as to whether to award costs, but no discretion exists where the conditions of Rule 68 are satisfied. Where a Rule 68 offer is made but not accepted and the judgment finally obtained by the plaintiff is less favorable than the offer, the plaintiff must pay the defendant's costs incurred after the making of the offer.[230] In addition, the insufficiently successful

---

[230]*See, e.g.,* Hopper v. Euclid Manor Nursing Home, Inc., 867 F.2d 291, 295 (6th Cir. 1989) (reversing district court's decision to vacate award of nominal damages in order to avoid Rule 68).

plaintiff is not entitled to recover his or her post-offer costs and post-offer attorney's fees, even in litigation under a statute (like Title VII) that defines costs to include attorney's fees.[231]

Rule 68 does not apply if the employer prevails entirely.[232] The anomalous result is that a defendant who loses, but in an amount less than the Rule 68 offer, will recover its post-offer costs from the insufficiently successful plaintiff as a matter of right, whereas a defendant who prevails totally may, in the discretion of the trial court, be denied its costs.[233]

In *Marek v. Chesny*,[234] the Supreme Court held that a Rule 68 offer can be made in one lump sum, including attorney's fees, costs, and damages.[235] A Rule 68 offer silent on whether it is inclusive or exclusive of costs and attorney's fees may give the plaintiff an opportunity to accept the offer and later claim attorney's fees as the prevailing party.[236]

---

[231]Marek v. Chesny, 473 U.S. 1, 7–8, 38 FEP 124 (1985) (applicable statute defined recoverable costs to include attorney's fees). One court has held that following the Civil Rights Act of 1991 the rule differs for claims of mixed-motive discrimination. *See* Sheppard v. Riverview Nursing Ctr., Inc., 870 F. Supp. 1369, 1384, 66 FEP 996 (D. Md. 1994) (mixed-motive case arising after Civil Rights Act of 1991; "awarding plaintiff post-offer attorney's fees because the plaintiff in [a mixed-motive] case rejected a Rule 68 offer of judgment that was higher than the judgment finally obtained at trial, she must bear her own post-offer costs under the rule. However, the plaintiff's post-offer attorney's fees are not part of these 'costs.' "), *vacated and remanded*, 88 F.3d 1332, 71 FEP 218 (4th Cir. 1996).

[232]Delta Air Lines, Inc. v. August, 450 U.S. 346, 353, 25 FEP 233 (1981) (court rejected contention that "offer of [even] one penny should trigger the cost-shifting provision" of Rule 68 if the defendant prevails).

[233]*See id.* at 362 (Powell, J., concurring in judgment) (noting anomaly); *id.* at 379–80 (Rehnquist, J., dissenting) (same).

[234]473 U.S. 1, 38 FEP 124 (1985).

[235]*Id.* at 5–6.

[236]*E.g.*, James v. Webb, 147 F.3d 617, 622–23 (7th Cir. 1998) (plaintiff in ADA action accepted Rule 68 offer silent with respect to costs and attorney's fees; plaintiff was allowed to recover both in addition to receiving Rule 68 amount); Lyte v. Sara Lee Corp., 950 F.2d 101, 104–05, 57 FEP 746 (2d Cir. 1991) (plaintiff in Title VII race discrimination case who accepts Rule 68 offer of judgment is "prevailing party" and therefore may be awarded attorney's fees; "No adjudication of rights or admission of fault is necessary for a fee award."); David v. AM Int'l, 131 F.R.D. 86, 89, 53 FEP 17 (E.D. Pa. 1990) (plaintiff's acceptance of defendant's offer of judgment entitled plaintiff, as prevailing party, to recover attorney's fees as part of his costs); Sas v. Trintex, 709 F. Supp. 455, 457–58, 49 FEP 842 (S.D.N.Y. 1989) (employer made offer of judgment for $5,000; employee accepted offer and then sought substantial attorney's fees; court found that acceptance of offer entitled employee to attorney's fees as prevailing party). *But see* Nusom v. Comh Woodburn,

In *Sheppard v. Riverview Nursing Center, Inc.*,[237] the court considered the language added to Title VII by the Civil Rights Act of 1991, which provides that a court may award "attorney's fees and costs" in mixed-motive cases.[238] It held that, unlike the general remedy language found at § 2000e-5(k) of Title VII, which provides that attorney's fees may be awardable "as part of costs," attorney's fees are not includable as costs under 42 U.S.C. § 2000e-5(g)(2)(B).[239] Accordingly, the plaintiff, who had rejected a Rule 68 offer and who did not obtain a more favorable judgment than the Rule 68 offer, was still permitted to recover post-offer attorney's fees. The court, however, held that the rejection of the offer was a permissible factor to be considered by the district court in exercising its discretion in determining the amount of the fee award.[240]

Several courts have held that attorney's fees are not included as part of "costs" in Americans with Disabilities Act (ADA) cases.[241]

The court dealt with a classic Rule 68 situation in *Van Le v. University of Pennsylvania*,[242] in which the plaintiff alleged national origin harassment and retaliation under Title VII. The plaintiff rejected the defendant's Rule 68 offer for $50,000 plus costs then

---

Inc., 122 F.3d 830, 834 (9th Cir. 1997) (permitting plaintiff to recover attorney's fees after Rule 68 offer in Truth-in-Lending Act case; court noted that its ruling was not unfair because defendant may explicitly state that Rule 68 offer, if accepted, does not permit plaintiff to recover attorney's fees); Erdman v. Cochise County, 926 F.2d 877, 879–80 (9th Cir. 1991) ("with costs" interpreted by court to mean, in "plain language," "plus costs" (attorney's fees to be added) rather than "including costs"); cf. Scheeler v. Crane Co., 21 F.3d 791, 792–93, 64 FEP 627 (8th Cir. 1994) (offer of judgment of $15,000 in sexual harassment action not more favorable than eventual judgment of $12,500; plaintiff had incurred $3,500 in attorney's fees by time of offer, and she would have had to pay her attorney's fees and other costs out of amount offered). *But see* Radecki v. Amoco Oil Co., 858 F.2d 397, 403 (8th Cir. 1988) (Rule 68 offer void because of ambiguity regarding inclusion of attorney's fees, and therefore no mutual assent existed to support purported acceptance).

[237]88 F.3d 1332, 71 FEP 218 (4th Cir. 1996).

[238]42 U.S.C. § 2000e-5(g)(2)(B) (2000).

[239]88 F.3d at 1337.

[240]*Id.; see also* Gudenkauf v. Stauffer Commc'ns, Inc., 158 F.3d 1074, 1083–84, 77 FEP 1742 (10th Cir. 1998) (fees to successful plaintiff in mixed-motives case not reduced on basis of rejected pretrial settlement offer, even though monetary relief did not exceed amount of settlement offer).

[241]*See* James v. Webb, 147 F.3d 617, 622–23 (7th Cir. 1998); Foster v. Kings Park Cent. Sch. Dist., 174 F.R.D. 19, 24 (E.D.N.Y. 1997).

[242]321 F.3d 403, 91 FEP 310 (3d Cir. 2003) (affirming 2001 WL 849707 (E.D. Pa. July 13, 2001)).

accrued. The plaintiff recovered $35,000 on the retaliation claim at trial and nothing on the national origin claim. Finding that "costs" under Title VII includes attorney's fees, the district court awarded the plaintiff costs and attorney's fees through the date of the Rule 68 offer, but refused to award attorney's fees for work performed thereafter. The court found the offer and judgment "readily comparable" and rejected the plaintiff's claim that the Rule 68 offer was deficient because it did not separately apportion between the national origin and retaliation claims and because it was on behalf of two defendants.[243] The court awarded the defendant the costs it had incurred post-offer, but excluded any recovery for the defendant's post-offer attorney's fees. Summarizing authorities, the court noted that the Supreme Court in *Marek*[244] had held that only the costs "properly awardable" under the underlying statute are shifted under Rule 68.[245] Relying on the reasoning of the First Circuit in *Crossman v. Marcoccio*,[246] the court held that the defendant's post-offer attorney's fees were not properly awardable to the defendant because there had been no showing that the action was frivolous or unreasonable under *Christiansburg Garment Co. v. EEOC*.[247] The Third Circuit affirmed.

Apart from the attorney's fee issue, another question that arises in the Rule 68 context is whether the plaintiff has been sufficiently "successful" to avoid the effects of Rule 68 in comparing the offer of judgment with the final judgment. At least one court has held that the plaintiff cannot claim credit for changes wrought by nonjudgment relief.[248] This point may be important where the plaintiff's lawsuit has induced the employer to modify its procedures but where that modification was not required by the final judgment that is being compared to the Rule 68 offer.[249] On the other hand, courts are

---

[243]2001 WL 849707, at *2.
[244]Marek v. Chesny, 473 U.S. 1, 9, 38 FEP 124 (1985).
[245]2001 WL 849707, at *2.
[246]806 F.2d 329 (1st Cir. 1996).
[247]434 U.S. 412, 16 FEP 502 (1978).
[248]Spencer v. General Elec. Co., 894 F.2d 651, 662–63, 51 FEP 1725 (4th Cir. 1990), *overruled on other grounds*, 506 U.S. 103 (1992) (plaintiff who proved that employer maintained sexually hostile environment and who served as catalyst for employer's voluntary development of comprehensive sexual harassment policy was prevailing party, but because actual judgment was less favorable than Rule 68 offer, plaintiff not entitled to any post-offer fees).
[249]894 F.2d at 663.

required to assess some value for injunctive relief, such as reinstatement to a more responsible position after a demotion, or restoration of nonmonetary benefits, such as the use of a private secretary.[250]

One court has held that Rule 68 offers do not apply in a Title VII class action, reasoning that the disproportionate risk that otherwise would be imposed on the class representatives would discourage the filing of putative class actions under Title VII.[250a]

VI. "BUSTED" SETTLEMENTS[251]

It is not uncommon for the parties (normally speaking through counsel) to reach a verbal (or written but unsigned) agreement, only to have one party deny the existence of, or repudiate, the deal. The parties' legal relationship when this occurs is commonly misunderstood.

Verbal settlements of Title VII claims[252] are enforceable on the same terms as other contracts, although courts do not uniformly agree on how to enforce verbal agreements in this context.[253] The

---

[250]*See* Reiter v. MTA N.Y. City Transit Auth., 457 F.3d 224, 98 FEP 968 (2d Cir. 2006).

[250a]*See* Gay v. Waiters' & Dairy Lunchmen's Union Local 30, 86 F.R.D. 500, 503–04, 22 FEP 1249 (N.D. Cal. 1980).

[251]The term, and the practical suggestions summarized herein, are drawn from Paul W. Cane, Jr., *Staying at "Yes": How to Avoid a Busted Settlement*, LOS ANGELES LAWYER, Sept. 1992, at 26.

[252]In light of the OWBPA, different rules apply to settlements of age claims. *See* Section II *supra*.

[253]*See, e.g.,* Gilbert v. Monsanto Co., 216 F.3d 695, 700, 83 FEP 531 (8th Cir. 2000) (enforcing oral settlement because employee detrimentally relied on oral representations by employer's counsel); Ciaramella v. Reader's Digest Ass'n, 131 F.3d 320, 323 (2d Cir. 1997) ("This court has articulated four factors to guide the inquiry regarding whether parties intended to be bound by a settlement agreement in the absence of a document executed by both sides. We must consider (1) whether there has been an express reservation of the right not to be bound in the absence of a signed writing; (2) whether there has been partial performance of the contract; (3) whether all of the terms of the alleged contract have been agreed upon; and (4) whether the agreement at issue is the type of contract that is usually committed to writing.") (citations omitted); Porter v. Chicago Bd. of Educ., 981 F. Supp. 1129, 1133–34 (N.D. Ill. 1997) (enforcing oral settlement reached at pretrial settlement conference conducted by magistrate, but refusing to incorporate into settlement "boilerplate terms" that were included in draft written settlement agreement but that had not been discussed at pretrial settlement conference); Lobeck v. City of Riviera Beach, 976 F. Supp. 1460, 1464 (S.D. Fla. 1997) (noting that Eleventh and Fifth Circuits apply

courts repeatedly have enforced supposedly "busted" discrimination settlements,[254] frequently invoking the "powerful federal interest in enforcing Title VII settlement agreements."[255] Unsigned settlements are easiest to enforce when there is no contention that an attorney acted without authorization, yet such settlements may be enforced even in the face of such a contention.[256]

By contrast, a party can, by the terms of its offer or acceptance, insist that execution of documentation be a condition precedent to the formation of the settlement contract.[257]

Courts differ on whether the party who refuses to comply with an enforceable agreement can be held liable for damages related to that breach.[258]

---

federal common law in determining scope and validity of settlement agreements in Title VII cases and that oral agreements are enforceable; however, court will not infer existence of agreement by piecing together documents capable of differing interpretations, so summary judgment is inappropriate as to existence of settlement).

[254]"Federal law does not require . . . that the settlement be reduced to writing. Absent a factual basis rendering it invalid, an oral agreement to settle a Title VII claim is enforceable against a plaintiff who knowingly and voluntarily agreed to the terms of the settlement or authorized his attorney to settle the dispute." Fulgence v. J. Ray McDermott & Co., 662 F.2d 1207, 1209 (5th Cir. 1981); *accord* Brockman v. Sweetwater County Sch. Dist., 25 F.3d 1055, 1994 WL 170795, at *2 (10th Cir. May 5, 1994) (unpublished decision) (oral settlement agreement as binding as written one where terms are mutually understood and agreed upon in all respects); Alexander v. Industries of the Blind, Inc., 901 F.2d 40, 41, 52 FEP 1110 (4th Cir. 1990) (improper to deny enforcement of settlement agreement simply because it was oral); Taylor v. Gordon Flesch Co., 793 F.2d 858, 862, 41 FEP 56 (7th Cir. 1986) (oral settlement agreement enforceable even though plaintiff's attorney agreed at settlement conference to prepare initial draft); Worthy v. McKesson Corp., 756 F.2d 1370, 1373, 37 FEP 539 (8th Cir. 1985) (oral settlement agreement enforceable where plaintiff, upon reconsideration, decides that he is dissatisfied with deal; this is true even in extreme case where "the amount of the settlement is 'paltry' "); Whittaker v. Morgan State Univ., 42 FEP 878, 880–82 (D. Md. 1986) (court enforced settlement agreement even though it was not yet in writing, where terms had been decided and plaintiff simply changed her mind).

[255]*E.g.*, EEOC v. Safeway Stores, Inc., 714 F.2d 567, 571–73, 32 FEP 1465 (5th Cir. 1983) (citing Melendez v. Horizon Cellular Tel. Co., 841 F. Supp. 687, 694, 64 FEP 85 (E.D. Pa. 1994)).

[256]*E.g.*, *Worthy*, 756 F.2d at 1373 (oral agreement enforced despite plaintiff's allegation that attorney lacked authority to bind him to agreement); Yanchor v. Kagan, 22 Cal. App. 3d 544, 550, 99 Cal. Rptr. 367 (Cal. Ct. App. 1971) (unsigned agreement enforced where plaintiff contended that his attorney had no authority).

[257]*E.g.*, *Taylor*, 793 F.2d at 862 (enforcing verbal agreement; parties could have but did not condition settlement on acceptance and execution of written formulation of agreement).

[258]*Compare* Astor v. International Bus. Machs. Corp., 7 F.3d 533, 540, 17 EB 1377 (6th Cir. 1993) (employees who sued in derogation of settlement were liable

Where the plaintiff sues in derogation of an enforceable settlement, after the settlement proceeds already have been turned over to the plaintiff, some courts have concluded that the plaintiff's continued retention of the benefits constitutes ratification, an accord and satisfaction, or a waiver.[259]

The Supreme Court's decision in *Oubre v. Entergy Operations, Inc.*,[260] that a plaintiff need not "tender back" funds received in exchange for signing a release as a precondition to bringing an ADEA action, obviously impacts all prior ADEA cases holding to the contrary or based on the reasoning rejected in *Oubre*. However, the decision may not have implications for non-ADEA cases, because the holding was predicated on the mandatory requirements for a valid waiver of ADEA claims found in the OWBPA's statutory language. In *Fleming v. United States Postal Service AMF O'Hare*,[261] a pre-*Oubre* case, the court distinguished cases involving statutes such as the OWBPA, which limit releases, from cases

---

for employer's attorney's fees) *with* Isaacs v. Caterpillar, Inc., 702 F. Supp. 711, 713–14, 49 FEP 607 (C.D. Ill. 1988) (employer has no right to sue for damages, even where plaintiff sues in breach of release, unless release so specified).

[259]*See, e.g.*, Wamsley v. Champlin Ref. & Chems., Inc., 11 F.3d 534, 539–40, 63 FEP 821 (5th Cir. 1993) (retention of benefits received in exchange for release of ADEA claims manifests "intention to be bound by the waiver and thus, [makes] a new promise to abide by [its] terms"); Botefur v. City of Eagle Point, 7 F.3d 152, 158, 8 IER 1546 (9th Cir. 1993) (plaintiff's claim was barred by the doctrine of accord and satisfaction where plaintiff had entered into a written release agreement and accepted and retained its proceeds); O'Shea v. Commercial Credit Corp., 930 F.2d 358, 362, 55 FEP 973 (4th Cir. 1991) (even if release was invalid, "appellant's subsequent acceptance of severance pay demonstrated an intent to ratify the agreement"; in such circumstances, "retention of the benefits of a voidable contract may constitute ratification"); Cumberland & Ohio Co. v. First Am. Nat'l Bank, 936 F.2d 846, 850 (6th Cir. 1991) ("releasor who retains the consideration after learning that the agreement is voidable effectively ratified the release and may not later avoid its terms"); Grillet v. Sears, Roebuck & Co., 927 F.2d 217, 220, 55 FEP 709 (5th Cir. 1991) ("A party cannot be permitted to retain the benefits received under a contract and at the same time escape the obligations imposed by the contract. If a releasor, therefore, retains the consideration after learning that the release is voidable, her continued retention of the benefits constitutes a ratification of the release.").

[260]522 U.S. 422, 75 FEP 1255 (1998).

[261]27 F.3d 259, 66 FEP 627 (7th Cir. 1994); *see also* Reid v. IBM Corp., 74 FEP 332 (S.D.N.Y. 1997) (pre-*Oubre*; collecting cases and upholding tender-back requirement in Title VII case). A slightly different approach was taken in *Kristoferson v. Otis Spunkmeyer, Inc.*, 965 F. Supp. 545, 73 FEP 1863 (S.D.N.Y. 1997), also pre-*Oubre*, where the court held that, in light of the "wave of dubious and potentially extortionate discrimination cases currently flooding the federal docket," it would

brought under Title VII and the Rehabilitation Act and held that the plaintiff's release could not be rescinded because she had failed to tender back the consideration received. A contrary conclusion was reached by the court in *Rangel v. El Paso Natural Gas Co.*,[262] however. The district court, post-*Oubre*, looked to the similar remedial purposes of Title VII and the ADEA. Noting the general willingness of the courts to look at the totality of the circumstances in determining whether waivers are knowing and voluntary rather than strictly adhering to principles of contract law, the court refused to require that consideration be returned.

Although the *Oubre* holding was based on the OWBPA's statutory language and its mandated minimum standards for a valid ADEA release, the majority opinion in *Oubre* left open the issue of whether ratification or tender-back would ever apply to an equitable action under Title VII and other employee-protective statutes, but cast doubt on that proposition. The Court stated:

> These general [ratification and tender back] rules may not be as unified as the employer asserts. And in equity, a person suing to rescind a contract, as a rule, is not required to restore the consideration at the very outset of the litigation. Even if the employer's statement of the general rule requiring tender back before one files suit were correct, it would be unavailing. The rule cited is based simply on the course of negotiation of the parties and the alleged later ratification. The authorities cited do not consider the question raised by statutory standards for releases and a statutory declaration making non-conforming releases ineffective. It is the latter question we confront here.[263]

---

henceforth require a written undertaking by a plaintiff bringing a Title VII lawsuit after signing a settlement agreement, promising to return the consideration received if the release was later found to be invalid. *Id.* at 548.

[262]996 F. Supp. 1093, 76 FEP 445 (D.N.M. 1998). The *Rangel* opinion noted that the reasoning in the Seventh Circuit's decision in *Fleming*, the principal Title VII case requiring tender-back, was "highly questionable" in the wake of *Oubre*. *Rangel*, 996 F. Supp. at 1097; *see also* Riddell v. Medical Inter-Ins. Exch., 18 F. Supp. 2d 468, 475–76 (D.N.J. 1998) (no tender-back required to challenge Family and Medical Leave Act release).

[263]*Oubre*, 522 U.S. at 426 (internal citations omitted).

TABLE OF CASES

Cases are referenced to chapter and footnote number(s): e.g., *32:* 407, 409 indicates the case is cited in Chapter 32, at footnotes 407 and 409. Entries beginning with numerals are alphabetized as if spelled out. Alphabetization is letter-by-letter (e.g., "Fortner" precedes "Fort Worth Club"). Cites to BNA's reporter *Fair Employment Practices* (FEP) have been added to the table as parallel citations whenever possible.

A

A&M Records, Inc. v. Napster, Inc.
—239 F.3d 1004, 57 USPQ 2d 1729 (9th Cir. 2001) *39:* 173
—284 F.3d 1091, 62 USPQ 2d 1221 (9th Cir. 2002) *39:* 147, 148
AARP v. EEOC, 383 F. Supp. 2d 705, 95 FEP 748, 96 FEP 994 (E.D. Pa.), *vacated*, 390 F. Supp. 2d 437, 96 FEP 994 (E.D. Pa. 2005) *12:* 521
Abbasi v. Herzfeld & Rubin, P.C., 1995 WL 303603 (S.D.N.Y. May 17, 1995) *13:* 253
Abbe v. Allen's Store for Men, Inc., 94 F.R.D. 295, 31 FEP 60 (N.D. Ill. 1982) *12:* 321
Abbott v. Federal Forge, Inc., 912 F.2d 867, 53 FEP 1382 (6th Cir. 1990) *3:* 179; *12:* 502
Abbott Labs.
—v. Gardner, 387 U.S. 136 (1967) *27:* 144, 161, 163, 164
—v. Mead Johnson & Co., 971 F.2d 6 (7th Cir. 1992) *39:* 172
Abdallah v. Coca-Cola Co.
—186 F.R.D. 672, 79 FEP 1409 (N.D. Ga. 1999) *29:* 318; *32:* 407, 410, 413, 416, 422, 427–30, 432, 433
—1999 WL 527835 (N.D. Ga. July 16, 1999) *32:* 361
—2000 WL 33249254 (N.D. Ga. Jan. 25, 2000) *38:* 337

Abdu-Brisson v. Delta Air Lines, Inc., 239 F.3d 456, 85 FEP 161 (2d Cir. 2001) *12:* 411, 452; *28:* 144, 152
Abdullah v. Philadelphia Hous. Auth., 2000 WL 377796 (E.D. Pa. Mar. 29, 2000) *9:* 129, 131, 138
Abeita v. TransAmerica Mailings, Inc., 159 F.3d 246, 78 FEP 364 (6th Cir. 1998) *28:* 115
Abel
—v. Dubberly, 210 F.3d 1334, 82 FEP 1407 (11th Cir. 2000) *12:* 434
—v. Merrill Lynch & Co., 1993 WL 33348 (S.D.N.Y. Feb. 4, 1993) *33:* 67
Abercrombie v. Bi-Lo, Inc., 21 FEP 1252 (D.S.C. 1979) *32:* 386
Aberman v. J. Abouchar & Sons, 160 F.3d 1148, 8 AD 1496 (7th Cir. 1998) *23:* 107; *24:* 38
Able v. United States, 88 F.3d 1280, 71 FEP 419 (2d Cir. 1996), *rev'd on remand*, 155 F.3d 628 (2d Cir. 1998) *11:* 182, 196, 200, 202, 203
Abraham v. Graphic Arts Int'l Union, 660 F.2d 811, 26 FEP 818 (D.C. Cir. 1981) *10:* 452
Abrahamson v. Board of Educ., 374 F.3d 66, 94 FEP 25 (2d Cir.), *cert. dismissed*, 543 U.S. 984 (2004) *12:* 140, 560, 661, 666, 670, 759
Abram v. United Parcel Serv., Inc., 200 F.R.D. 424 (E.D. Wis. 2001) *2:* 140; *3:* 145; *33:* 74

Bahadirli v. Domino's Pizza, Inc., 873 F. Supp. 1528, 71 FEP 1615 (M.D. Ala. 1995) *40:* 158, 168

Bahl v. Royal Indem. Co., 115 F.3d 1283, 74 FEP 1060 (7th Cir. 1997) *20:* 20

Bailey
—v. Binyon, 583 F. Supp. 923, 36 FEP 1236 (N.D. Ill. 1984) *20:* 74, 86, 117, 119
—v. Delta Air Lines, Inc., 722 F.2d 942, 33 FEP 713 (1st Cir. 1983) *26:* 278; *39:* 165
—v. DiMario, 925 F. Supp. 801, 69 FEP 233 (D.D.C. 1995) *34:* 160
—v. Federal Nat'l Mortgage Ass'n, 209 F.3d 740, 82 FEP 1089 (D.C. Cir. 2000) *42:* 81
—v. Georgia-Pacific Corp., 306 F.3d 1162, 13 AD 1066 (1st Cir. 2002) *13:* 883
—v. Great Lakes Canning Co., 908 F.2d 38, 59 FEP 1647 (6th Cir. 1990) *32:* 560
—v. Runyon, 167 F.3d 466, 79 FEP 225 (8th Cir. 1999) *19:* 307
—v. Southeastern Area Joint Apprenticeship Comm., 561 F. Supp. 895 (N.D.W. Va. 1983) *15:* 134
—v. United Airlines, 279 F.3d 194, 88 FEP 22 (3d Cir. 2002) *12:* 167; *26:* 105; *28:* 172

Bailey Co.; EEOC v., 563 F.2d 439, 15 FEP 972 (6th Cir. 1977) *24:* 3, 86; *29:* 53, 196–98

Baird
—v. Boies, Schiller & Flexner LLP, 219 F. Supp. 2d 510, 89 FEP 1524 (S.D.N.Y. 2002) *41:* 202, 257, 311
—ex rel. Baird v. Rose, 192 F.3d 462 (4th Cir. 1999) *13:* 752

Bak v. United States Postal Serv., 52 F.3d 241, 67 FEP 795 (9th Cir. 1995) *31:* 320

Baker
—v. Alderman, 158 F.3d 516 (11th Cir. 1998) *41:* 353
—v. American Juice, Inc., 870 F. Supp. 878, 68 FEP 52 (N.D. Ind. 1994) *35:* 327

—v. Buckeye Cellulose Corp., 856 F.2d 167, 47 FEP 1697 (11th Cir. 1988) *14:* 246; *39:* 174
—v. California Land Title Co., 507 F.2d 895, 8 FEP 1313 (9th Cir. 1974) *10:* 627
—v. Carr, 369 U.S. 186 (1962) *27:* 146
—v. Delta Air Lines, Inc., 6 F.3d 632, 62 FEP 1588 (9th Cir. 1993) *12:* 734
—v. Detroit, City of, 483 F. Supp. 930, 24 FEP 1728 (E.D. Mich. 1979), *aff'd,* 704 F.2d 878, 31 FEP 465 (6th Cir.), *vacated,* 712 F.2d 222, 31 FEP 1795 (6th Cir. 1983) *4:* 274
—v. John Morrell & Co.
——249 F. Supp. 2d 1138 (N.D. Iowa 2003) *20:* 105
——263 F. Supp. 2d 1161 (N.D. Iowa 2003) *39:* 78; *40:* 252, 336
—v. Runyon, 922 F. Supp. 1296, 75 FEP 621 (N.D. Ill. 1996), *rev'd,* 114 F.3d 668, 74 FEP 160 (7th Cir. 1997) *13:* 943; *31:* 52, 359, 360
—v. Stuart Broad. Co., 560 F.2d 389, 15 FEP 394 (8th Cir. 1977) *23:* 40, 100; *35:* 323, 329, 330

Bakrim v. Sony Elecs., Inc., 216 F.3d 1082, 2000 U.S. App. LEXIS 8057 (9th Cir. Apr. 20, 2000) *15:* 122

Balazs v. Liebenthal, 32 F.3d 151, 65 FEP 993 (4th Cir. 1994) *14:* 6; *26:* 95; *28:* 20

Balcerzak v. Milwaukee Police Dep't, 163 F.3d 993, 78 FEP 512 (7th Cir. 1998) *27:* 17, 23

Baldassare v. New Jersey, 250 F.3d 188 (3d Cir. 2001) *14:* 367–69; *35:* 242

Balderas v. La Casita Farms, Inc., 500 F.2d 195, 8 FEP 686 (5th Cir. 1974) *7:* 34; *14:* 93

Balderston v. Fairbanks Morse Engine
—2003 WL 342124, 90 FEP 1673 (W.D. Wis. 2003) *12:* 143
—Div. of Coltec Indus., 328 F.3d 309 (7th Cir. 2003) *2:* 242; *12:* 14, 346, 353, 364, 373, 392, 394, 453

Baldwin v. University of Tex. Med. Branch at Galveston, 945 F. Supp. 1022 (S.D. Tex. 1996), *aff'd,* 122 F.3d 1066 (5th Cir. 1997) *35:* 327

Barbano v. Madison County, 47 FEP 1872 (N.D.N.Y. 1988), *aff'd*, 922 F.2d 139, 54 FEP 1287 (2d Cir. 1990) *15:* 136; *39:* 13

Barber

—v. American Airlines, Inc., 791 F.2d 658, 40 FEP 1565 (8th Cir. 1986) *12:* 406

—v. CSX Distrib. Servs., 68 F.3d 694, 69 FEP 81 (3d Cir. 1995) *14:* 90, 95; *16:* 1

—v. Lovelace Sandia Health Sys., 409 F. Supp. 2d 1313 (D.N.M. 2005) *7:* 171

—v. T.D. Williamson, Inc., 254 F.3d 1223, 86 FEP 187 (10th Cir. 2001) *41:* 42

—v. Ventura, County of, 45 Fed. Appx. 725 (9th Cir. 2002) *35:* 220

Barbera v. Metro-Dade County Fire Dep't, 117 F. Supp. 2d 1331 (S.D. Fla. 2000) *4:* 268; *10:* 731, 732; *15:* 103

Barbosa v. Baxter Healthcare Corp., 2000 WL 1739309 (D.P.R. Nov. 15, 2000) *12:* 93

Barbour v. Merrill, 48 F.3d 1270, 67 FEP 369 (D.C. Cir. 1995) *35:* 407, 425, 432; *40:* 62, 246, 415

Barefield v. Chevron U.S.A., Inc.

—44 FEP 1885 (N.D. Cal. 1987) *32:* 98, 178, 179

—48 FEP 907 (N.D. Cal. 1988) *32:* 196, 205, 294, 316, 320, 509

Barela v. United Nuclear Corp., 462 F.2d 149, 4 FEP 831 (10th Cir. 1972) *14:* 31

Barge v. Anheuser-Busch, Inc., 87 F.3d 256, 72 FEP 426 (8th Cir. 1996) *35:* 70

Barjon v. Dalton, 132 F.3d 496 (9th Cir. 1997) *41:* 196, 255

Barker

—v. Menominee Nation Casino, 897 F. Supp. 389 (E.D. Wis. 1995) *8:* 104–06

—v. Taft Broad. Co., 549 F.2d 400, 14 FEP 697 (6th Cir. 1977) *10:* 627

—v. YMCA of Racine, 18 Fed. Appx. 394 (7th Cir. 2001) *20:* 106

Barlow v. AVCO, 527 F. Supp. 269, 51 FEP 1420 (E.D. Va. 1981) *21:* 42

Barnard v. Jackson County, 43 F.3d 1218, 10 IER 323 (8th Cir. 1995) *14:* 360

Barnes

—v. Broward County Sheriff's Dep't. *See* Barnes v. Cochran

—v. Broward County Sheriff's Office, 190 F.3d 1274, 9 AD 1341 (11th Cir. 1999) *41:* 43

—v. Cincinnati, City of

——401 F.3d 729, 95 FEP 994 (6th Cir. 2005) *2:* 97, 100, 170, 225; *10:* 658; *11:* 45; *41:* 250, 298, 326, 328

——2002 U.S. Dist. LEXIS 26207 (S.D. Ohio Mar. 8, 2002) *11:* 167

—v. Cochran, 944 F. Supp. 897, 5 AD 1685 (S.D. Fla. 1996), *aff'd sub nom.* Barnes v. Broward County Sheriff's Dep't, 130 F.3d 443 (11th Cir. 1997) *13:* 428, 700

—v. Colonial Life & Accident Ins. Co., 818 F. Supp. 978, 68 FEP 685 (N.D. Tex. 1993) *24:* 40

—v. Costle, 561 F.2d 983, 15 FEP 345 (D.C. Cir. 1977) *19:* 6

—v. GenCorp, Inc., 896 F.2d 1457, 56 FEP 1203 (6th Cir. 1990) *2:* 244; *3:* 80; *12:* 10, 369; *20:* 49

—v. Goodyear Tire & Rubber Co., 48 S.W.3d 698 (Tenn. 2000) *13:* 225, 244

—v. Gorman, 536 U.S. 181, 13 AD 193 (2002) *13:* 42, 893, 909, 910, 950, 951, 957, 958, 960–62; *40:* 390–93

—v. Hewlett-Packard Co., 846 F. Supp. 442, 64 FEP 302 (D. Md. 1994) *10:* 464

—v. Levitt, 118 F.3d 404 (5th Cir. 1997) *28:* 5, 12

—v. McDowell, 848 F.2d 725 (6th Cir. 1988) *27:* 32

—v. Rourke, 8 FEP 1112 (M.D. Tenn. 1973) *23:* 54, 69, 74

—v. Small, 840 F.2d 972, 46 FEP 412 (D.C. Cir. 1988) *14:* 23

Bethel
—v. Dixie Homecrafters, Inc., 192 F.R.D. 320, 82 FEP 345 (N.D. Ga. 2000) *33:* 116
—v. Garland, City of, 1997 WL 325983 (N.D. Tex. June 11, 1997) *13:* 617
—v. Jefferson, 589 F.2d 631, 18 FEP 789 (D.C. Cir. 1978) *31:* 26
Bethesda Lutheran Homes & Servs., Inc. v. Leean, 165 F.R.D. 87 (W.D. Wis. 1996) *32:* 157
Bethlehem Steel Corp.
—EEOC v., 765 F.2d 427, 38 FEP 345 (4th Cir. 1985) *29:* 46, 175
—United States v., 446 F.2d 652, 3 FEP 589 (2d Cir. 1971) *3:* 156; *17:* 106, 107, 111, 114, 115
Betkerur v. Aultman Hosp. Ass'n, 78 F.3d 1079, 78 FEP 1765 (6th Cir. 1996) *15:* 40; *35:* 64, 407
Bettcher v. Brown Schs., Inc., 262 F.3d 492, 86 FEP 929 (5th Cir. 2001) *12:* 158, 292; *26:* 258; *28:* 118
Betton v. Yellow Transp., Inc., 2003 U.S. Dist. LEXIS 8682 (E.D. Tenn. May 1, 2003) *13:* 784
Betts
—v. Hamilton County Bd. of Mental Retardation & Dev. Disabilities, 848 F.2d 692, 46 FEP 1608 (6th Cir. 1988), *rev'd sub nom.* Public Employees Ret. Sys. v. Betts, 492 U.S. 158, 50 FEP 104 (1989) *12:* 21, 140, 162, 515, 554; *25:* 40
—v. Iowa Dep't of Natural Res., 2002 U.S. Dist. LEXIS 3538 (S.D. Iowa Feb. 25, 2002) *18:* 65
Bevan
—v. Honeywell, Inc., 118 F.3d 603, 75 FEP 255 (8th Cir. 1997) *12:* 315
—v. New York State Teachers' Ret. Sys., 345 N.Y.S. 2d 921, 7 FEP 74 (N.Y. Sup. Ct. 1973), *aff'd as modified,* 355 N.Y.S.2d 185, 8 FEP 283 (N.Y. App. Div. 1974) *13:* 168
Beverage Canners, Inc.; EEOC v., 897 F.2d 1067, 52 FEP 878 (11th Cir. 1990) *39:* 31

Beverly Enters., Inc. v. Herman, 130 F. Supp. 2d 1 (D.D.C. 2000) *38:* 36
Beville v. South Dakota Bd. of Regents, 687 F. Supp. 464 (D.S.D. 1988) *35:* 294
Bevins v. Dollar Gen. Corp., 952 F. Supp. 504 (E.D. Ky. 1997) *12:* 225
Bew v. City of Chi.
—252 F.3d 891, 85 FEP 1675 (7th Cir. 2001) *4:* 272, 273, 275
—979 F. Supp. 693, 75 FEP 625 (N.D. Ill. 1997) *4:* 81
Bey v. Schneider Sheetmetal, Inc., 603 F. Supp. 450, 38 FEP 1139 (W.D. Pa. 1985) *38:* 609
Bhandari v. First Nat'l Bank of Commerce, 829 F.2d 1343, 45 FEP 126 (5th Cir. 1987), *vacated & remanded,* 492 U.S. 901, 50 FEP 96, *reinstated,* 887 F.2d 609, 55 FEP 226 (5th Cir. 1989) *22:* 167; *35:* 67, 68
Bhaya v. Westinghouse Elec. Corp., 709 F. Supp. 600, 49 FEP 1369 (E.D. Pa. 1989), *aff'd,* 922 F.2d 184, 54 FEP 1078 (3d Cir. 1990) *40:* 206
Bhella v. England, 91 Fed. Appx. 835 (4th Cir. 2004) *7:* 186
Bialas v. Greyhound Lines, Inc., 59 F.3d 759, 68 FEP 552 (8th Cir. 1995) *12:* 351, 450
Bianchi v. City of Philadelphia, 183 F. Supp. 2d 726, 87 FEP 1728 (E.D. Pa. 2002), *aff'd,* 80 Fed. Appx. 232 (3d Cir. 2003) *2:* 99
Biank v. National Bd. of Med. Exam'rs, 130 F. Supp. 2d 986, 11 AD 925 (N.D. Ill. 2000) *13:* 663
Bibby v. Philadelphia Coca-Cola Bottling Co., 260 F.3d 257, 86 FEP 553 (3d Cir. 2001), *cert. denied,* 534 U.S. 1155, 89 FEP 1888 (2002) *2:* 106; *11:* 2–6, 11, 18, 29; *19:* 110, 112
Bice of Chicago; EEOC v., 229 F.R.D. 581 (N.D. Ill. 2005) *33:* 81, 101
Bickerstaff v. Vassar Coll., 992 F. Supp. 372, 76 FEP 440 (S.D.N.Y. 1998), *aff'd,* 196 F.3d 435, 81 FEP 624 (2d Cir. 1999) *16:* 63, 64, 137, 143; *34:* 128

Blount
—v. Alabama Co-op. Extension Serv., 869 F. Supp. 1543, 66 FEP 889 (M.D. Ala. 1994) *18:* 186
—v. Shalala, 1999 WL 978892 (4th Cir. Oct. 28, 1999) *31:* 300
Blow
—v. Lascaris, 668 F.2d 670 (2d Cir. 1982) *41:* 168
—v. San Antonio, City of, 236 F.3d 293, 84 FEP 1268 (5th Cir. 2001) *2:* 21, 190
Blowers v. Lawyers Co-op. Publ'g Co.
—526 F. Supp. 1324, 27 FEP 1224 (W.D.N.Y. 1981) *41:* 333
—11 FEP 1119 (W.D.N.Y.), *aff'd*, 527 F.2d 333, 11 FEP 1316 (2d Cir. 1975) *29:* 257, 258, 261, 264, 266
—25 FEP 1425 (W.D.N.Y. 1981) *2:* 231
Blue v. Department of Army, 914 F.2d 525 (4th Cir. 1990) *31:* 371
Blue & White Serv. Corp.; EEOC v., 674 F. Supp. 1579, 45 FEP 963 (D. Minn. 1987), *aff'd*, 863 F.2d 613 (8th Cir. 1988) *40:* 105
Bluebeard's Castle Hotel v. Government of V.I., 786 F.2d 168, 40 FEP 603 (3d Cir. 1986) *2:* 230
Blue Bell Boots, Inc. v. EEOC, 418 F.2d 355, 2 FEP 228 (6th Cir. 1969) *25:* 338
Blue Cross Blue Shield; EEOC v., 30 F. Supp. 2d 296 (D. Conn. 1998) *15:* 139
Blue Ox Rest.; EEOC v., 1986 U.S. Dist. LEXIS 29263 (N.D. Ill. Feb. 14, 1986) *29:* 188
Bluitt
—v. Arco Chem. Co., 777 F.2d 188 (5th Cir. 1985) *33:* 9
—v. Houston Indep. Sch. Dist., 236 F. Supp. 2d 703 (S.D. Tex. 2002) *12:* 113, 263
Blum
—v. Gulf Oil Corp., 597 F.2d 936, 20 FEP 108 (5th Cir. 1979) *11:* 2; *33:* 74

—v. Stenson, 465 U.S. 886, 34 FEP 417 (1984) *41:* 171, 222, 232–37, 252, 254, 256, 264, 290, 298, 325
—v. Witco Chem. Corp.
——829 F.2d 367, 46 FEP 306 (3d Cir. 1987) *40:* 220, 503
——888 F.2d 975, 51 FEP 386 (3d Cir. 1989) *41:* 13, 241
—v. Yaretsky, 457 U.S. 991 (1982) *35:* 84–86
Blumenthal v. Merrill Lynch, Pierce, Fenner & Smith, Inc., 910 F.2d 1049 (2d Cir. 1990) *27:* 102
BMG Music v. Martinez, 74 F.3d 87 (5th Cir. 1996) *28:* 164
BMW of N. Am., Inc. v. Gore, 517 U.S. 559 (1996) *35:* 441; *40:* 445, 448, 452
Board of County Comm'rs
—v. EEOC, 405 F.3d 840, 95 FEP 897 (10th Cir. 2005) *24:* 70
—v. Umbehr, 518 U.S. 668, 11 IER 1393 (1996) *14:* 319, 368
Board of County Comm'rs of Bryan County v. Brown, 520 U.S. 397 (1997) *35:* 118, 125
Board of Educ.
—v. Dowell, 498 U.S. 237 (1991) *39:* 155
—v. National Gay Task Force, 470 U.S. 903, 37 FEP 505 (1985) *11:* 174
—United States v.
——50 FEP 71 (E.D. Pa. 1989), *aff'd in part*, 911 F.2d 882, 53 FEP 1077 (3d Cir. 1990) *21:* 42
——52 FEP 653 (N.D. Ill. 1990) *33:* 69
Board of Educ., Garfield Heights; United States v., 581 F.2d 791 (6th Cir. 1978) *30:* 11
Board of Governors
—v. Department of Labor, 917 F.2d 812, 54 FEP 136 (4th Cir. 1990) *38:* 37, 38
—EEOC v.
——957 F.2d 424, 58 FEP 292 (7th Cir. 1992) *22:* 104; *31:* 191
——706 F. Supp. 1377, 50 FEP 126 (N.D. Ill. 1989) *12:* 212

Bowen—*Contd.*
—v. Parking Auth. of City of Camden, 214 F.R.D. 188, 91 FEP 1200 (D.N.J. 2003)   *33:* 116
Bowens v. Big K-Mart Corp., 117 F. Supp. 2d 288 (E.D.N.Y. 2000)   *12:* 257; *26:* 324
Bower v. Federal Express Corp., 287 F. Supp. 2d 840, 14 AD 1674 (W.D. Tenn. 2003)   *13:* 513
Bowers
—v. Bethany Med. Ctr., 959 F. Supp. 1385 (D. Kan. 1997)   *13:* 583
—v. Board of Regents of Univ. of Wis., 33 Fed. Appx. 812 (7th Cir. 2002)   *35:* 221
—v. Hardwick, 478 U.S. 186 (1986)   *11:* 78, 157, 180, 203
—v. NCAA, 118 F. Supp. 2d 494, 11 AD 415 (D.N.J. 2000), *amended*, 130 F. Supp. 2d 610 (2001)   *13:* 104, 110
Bowling v. Proctor-Silex, Inc., 50 FEP 871 (W.D. Pa. 1989)   *32:* 185
Bowling Green, City of; EEOC v., 607 F. Supp. 524, 37 FEP 963 (W.D. Ky. 1985)   *29:* 295; *39:* 168, 176
Bowman
—v. Bank of Del., 712 F. Supp. 1150, 49 FEP 1634 (D. Del. 1989)   *7:* 178
—v. EPA, 712 F. Supp. 375 (S.D.N.Y. 1989)   *14:* 248
Box v. A&P Tea Co., 772 F.2d 1372, 38 FEP 1509 (7th Cir. 1985)   *34:* 42
Boyce v. Moore, 314 F.3d 884 (7th Cir. 2002)   *28:* 165
Boyd
—v. Bechtel Corp., 485 F. Supp. 610, 20 FEP 944 (N.D. Cal. 1979)   *32:* 551; *34:* 226
—v. Borg-Warner Protective Servs., 1999 U.S. Dist. LEXIS 13974 (S.D. Fla. July 21, 1999)   *13:* 252
—v. Harding Acad. of Memphis, 88 F.3d 410, 71 FEP 300 (6th Cir. 1996)   *9:* 151; *10:* 386, 387
—v. Illinois State Police, 2001 U.S. Dist. LEXIS 3792 (N.D. Ill. Mar. 27, 2001)   *18:* 346, 365, 375, 377

—v. O'Neill, 273 F. Supp. 2d 92 (D.D.C. 2003)   *31:* 340
—v. Ozark Air Lines, Inc., 419 F. Supp. 1061, 13 FEP 529 (E.D. Mo. 1976), *aff'd*, 568 F.2d 50, 17 FEP 827 (8th Cir. 1977)   *10:* 703
—v. United States Postal Serv., 752 F.2d 410, 1 AD 686 (9th Cir. 1985)   *13:* 63, 65, 955; *31:* 300
—v. Wilmington, City of, 943 F. Supp. 585 (E.D.N.C. 1996)   *15:* 75, 76
Boyer v. Cordant Techs., Inc., 316 F.3d 1137, 90 FEP 1249 (10th Cir. 2003)   *26:* 152
Boykin
—v. ATC/Vancom of Colo., 247 F.3d 1061, 11 AD 1204 (10th Cir. 2001)   *13:* 577, 810
—v. Georgia-Pacific Corp., 706 F.2d 1384, 32 FEP 25 (5th Cir. 1983)   *3:* 139
—v. Mobile, City of, 2000 WL 360233 (S.D. Ala. Mar. 23, 2000)   *16:* 26
Boze v. Branstetter, 912 F.2d 801, 53 FEP 1630 (5th Cir. 1990)   *20:* 71, 80, 81, 126
Brack v. Shoney's, Inc., 249 F. Supp. 2d 938 (W.D. Tenn. 2003)   *2:* 93, 94, 308; *6:* 7, 8
Braden v. Cargill, Inc., 176 F. Supp. 2d 1103 (D. Kan. 2001)   *19:* 191
Bradford
—v. Norfolk S. Corp., 54 F.3d 1412, 71 FEP 259 (8th Cir. 1995)   *20:* 83
—v. Peoples Natural Gas Co., 60 F.R.D. 432, 6 FEP 1336 (W.D. Pa. 1973)   *11:* 1
—v. Rockwell Semiconductor Sys., Inc., 238 F.3d 549, 84 FEP 1358 (4th Cir. 2001)   *12:* 760; *42:* 135, 136
Bradley
—v. Americold Servs., Inc., 75 FEP 8 (D. Kan. 1997)   *27:* 82
—v. Arkansas Dep't of Educ., 189 F.3d 745 (8th Cir. 1999)   *21:* 217
—v. Harcourt, Brace & Co., 104 F.3d 267, 77 FEP 303 (9th Cir. 1996)   *12:* 441

Byrnie v. Cromwell Bd. of Educ., 243
F.3d 93, 85 FEP 323 (2d Cir. 2001)
2: 135; *12:* 323, 344, 420, 436, 495,
506; *15:* 120; *18:* 253; *25:* 87; *33:*
28
Byron v. Clay, 867 F.2d 1049 (7th Cir.
1989) *40:* 310

C

Caban v. Sedgwick Co. Sheriff's Dep't,
2001 WL 487905 (D. Kan. Apr. 19,
2001) *16:* 37
Caban-Wheeler v. Elsea
—904 F.2d 1549, 53 FEP 885 (11th Cir.
1990) *2:* 200; *14:* 218
—71 F.3d 837, 69 FEP 1193 (11th Cir.
1996) *41:* 40
Cabell v. Chavez Salido, 454 U.S. 432,
27 FEP 1129 (1982) *7:* 82, 83
Cable v. Ivy Tech State Coll., 200 F.3d
467 (7th Cir. 1999) *28:* 98
Cabot Corp.; EEOC v., 48 FEP 1136
(E.D. Pa. 1988) *29:* 100
Cabrales v. County of L.A., 875 F.2d
740 (9th Cir. 1989) *41:* 257
Cabrera v. Jakabovitz, 24 F.3d 372, 64
FEP 1239 (2d Cir. 1994) *2:* 281,
282, 284; *28:* 206
Cada v. Baxter Healthcare Corp., 920
F.2d 446, 54 FEP 961 (7th Cir.
1990) *12:* 186; *26:* 104, 193, 234
Cadbury Beverages v. NLRB, 160 F.3d
24, 159 LRRM 2775 (D.C. Cir. 1998)
14: 284
Cadena v. Pacesetter Corp., 224 F.3d
1203, 83 FEP 1645 (10th Cir. 2000)
41: 280
Cady v. Bristol-Myers Squibb Co.,
1998 WL 822732 (9th Cir. Nov. 17,
1998) *11:* 90
Cage v. IMFS, Inc., 36 FEP 1085 (W.D.
Tenn. 1984) *15:* 15, 29
Caggiano v. Fontoura, 804 A.2d 1193,
89 FEP 838 (N.J. Super. Ct. App.
Div. 2002) *26:* 159
Cain v. Hyatt, 101 B.R. 440, 50 FEP
195 (E.D. Pa. 1989) *24:* 24

Caine v. Hardy, 943 F.2d 1406 (5th Cir.
1991) *35:* 276
Caines v. Village of Forest Park
—2003 U.S. Dist. LEXIS 11153 (N.D.
Ill. June 30, 2003) *11:* 23
—2003 WL 21518558 (N.D. Ill. July
2, 2003) *19:* 117
Caldarera v. Eastern Airlines, Inc., 705
F.2d 778 (5th Cir. 1983) *40:* 408,
412
Caldeira v. County of Kauai, 866 F.2d
1175 (9th Cir. 1989) *27:* 109
Calder v. TCI Cablevision of Mo., Inc.,
298 F.3d 723, 89 FEP 910 (8th Cir.
2002) *12:* 338, 454
Calderon
—v. Martin County, 639 F.2d 271, 25
FEP 553 (5th Cir. 1981) *21:* 84
—v. Presidio Valley Farmers Ass'n, 863
F.2d 384 (5th Cir. 1989) *32:* 344
Caldwell
—v. Federal Express Corp., 908 F.
Supp. 29, 69 FEP 1055 (D. Me.
1995) *12:* 172
—v. ServiceMaster Corp., 966 F. Supp.
33 (D.D.C. 1997) *23:* 93, 120–22
Calef v. Gillette Co., 322 F.3d 75, 14
AD 110 (1st Cir. 2003) *13:* 342,
529, 850
Calero-Cerezo v. U.S. Dep't of Justice,
355 F.3d 6 (1st Cir. 2004) *13:* 624,
629
Calhoun
—v. Acme Cleveland Corp., 801 F.2d
558, 41 FEP 1515 (1st Cir. 1986)
41: 342
—v. Federal Nat'l Mortgage Ass'n, 823
F.2d 451, 44 FEP 761 (11th Cir.
1987) *26:* 104
Califano v. Yamasaki, 442 U.S. 682
(1979) *39:* 45
California Ass'n of the Physically
Handicapped v. FCC, 721 F.2d 667,
1 AD 358 (9th Cir. 1983) *13:* 92
California Brewers Ass'n v. Bryant, 444
U.S. 598, 22 FEP 1 (1980) *17:* 11,
43, 45–49
California Fed. Sav. & Loan Ass'n v.
Guerra, 758 F.2d 390, 37 FEP 849

Casillas
—v. Federal Express Corp., 140 F. Supp. 2d 875 (W.D. Tenn. 2001) *10:* 180; *12:* 615
—v. United States Navy, 735 F.2d 338, 34 FEP 1493 (9th Cir. 1984) *4:* 441; *16:* 115, 117
Cason v. Builders FirstSource-Se. Group, Inc., 159 F. Supp. 2d 242 (W.D.N.C. 2001) *33:* 41
Cassells v. University Hosp., 740 F. Supp. 143, 62 FEP 964 (E.D.N.Y. 1990) *7:* 14
Casseus v. Kessler Inst. of Rehab., 36 Fed. Appx. 707 (3d Cir.), *opinion replaced*, 45 Fed. Appx. 167 (3d Cir. 2002) *2:* 152; *15:* 120
Cassiday v. Greenhorne & O'Mara, Inc., 220 F. Supp. 2d 488, 89 FEP 1434 (D. Md. 2002), *aff'd*, 63 Fed. Appx. 169 (4th Cir. 2003) *12:* 622, 631
Cassidy v. Detroit Edison Co., 138 F.3d 629, 8 AD 326 (6th Cir. 1998) *13:* 574, 580, 598; *22:* 129
Cassimy v. Board of Educ., 461 F.3d 932, 18 AD 647 (7th Cir. 2006) *14:* 159
Cassino v. Reichhold Chems., Inc., 817 F.2d 1338, 47 FEP 865 (9th Cir. 1987) *12:* 315; *40:* 219, 220, 251, 254, 257, 487, 503; *43:* 19
Castaneda
—v. Partida, 430 U.S. 482 (1977) *3:* 82, 83
—v. Pickard
——648 F.2d 989 (5th Cir. 1981) *15:* 28
——781 F.2d 456, 40 FEP 154 (5th Cir. 1986) *34:* 258, 265
Casteel v. Local 703 Teamsters Executive Bd., 272 F.3d 463, 87 FEP 557 (7th Cir. 2001) *10:* 179; *12:* 190, 495; *17:* 91
Castellano v. City of N.Y., 142 F.3d 58, 9 AD 67 (2d Cir. 1998) *12:* 593; *13:* 657
Castille v. Teletech Customer Mgmt., Inc., 2003 WL 245634 (10th Cir.),

cert. denied, 540 U.S. 836 (2003) *16:* 109
Castillo v. Usery, 14 FEP 1240 (N.D. Cal. 1976) *38:* 614, 664
Castle
—v. Bentsen
——867 F. Supp. 1, 3 AD 1449 (D.D.C. 1994) *13:* 284
——872 F. Supp. 1062, 66 FEP 1498 (D.D.C. 1995) *41:* 108
—v. Rubin, 78 F.3d 654, 72 FEP 1701 (D.C. Cir. 1996) *40:* 194
—v. Sangamo Weston, Inc.
——837 F.2d 1550, 46 FEP 139 (11th Cir. 1988) *12:* 353, 678, 743; *40:* 84, 242
——31 FEP 324 (M.D. Fla. 1983), *rev'd*, 744 F.2d 1464, 36 FEP 113 (11th Cir. 1984) *29:* 249
Castleman v. Acme Boot Co., 959 F.2d 1417, 58 FEP 969 (7th Cir. 1992) *20:* 13
Castner
—v. Colorado Springs Cablevision, 979 F.2d 1417, 60 FEP 566 (10th Cir. 1992) *27:* 85, 86
—v. United States Dep't of Energy, 897 F. Supp. 481, 68 FEP 1642 (D. Or. 1995) *2:* 144
Castro
—v. Beecher, 334 F. Supp. 930, 4 FEP 51 (D. Mass. 1971), *rev'd in part*, 459 F.2d 725, 4 FEP 700, *modified*, 4 FEP 1223 (1st Cir. 1972) *3:* 99; *4:* 340, 377; *7:* 21
—v. Child Psychiatry Ctr., 1997 WL 141860 (E.D. Pa. Mar. 25, 1997) *13:* 514
—v. United States, 775 F.2d 399, 39 FEP 162 (1st Cir. 1985) *12:* 114; *39:* 167, 170, 175, 176
Casucci v. Faughnan, 109 Fed. Appx. 450 (2d Cir. 2004) *14:* 350
Catagnus v. Aramark Corp., 235 F. Supp. 2d 413 (E.D. Pa. 2002) *28:* 66
Caterpillar, Inc.
—EEOC v., 409 F.3d 831, 95 FEP 1371 (7th Cir. 2005) *28:* 97; *29:* 199

Chavero v. Transit Union Local 241, 787 F.2d 1154, 40 FEP 766 (7th Cir. 1986) **22:** 3

Chavez
—v. Arvada, City of, 88 F.3d 861, 71 FEP 320 (10th Cir. 1996) **14:** 181
—v. New Mexico, 397 F.3d 826, 95 FEP 434 (10th Cir. 2005) **19:** 95
—v. Tempe Union High Sch. Dist., 565 F.2d 1087, 16 FEP 674 (9th Cir. 1977) **24:** 78

Chavis v. Clayton County Sch. Dist., 300 F.3d 1288 (11th Cir. 2002) **35:** 407

Chawla v. Emory Univ., 1997 WL 907570 (N.D. Ga. Feb. 13, 1997) (unpublished) **35:** 379

Che v. Massachusetts Bay Transp. Auth., 342 F.3d 31, 92 FEP 895 (1st Cir. 2003) **2:** 218; **6:** 38; **28:** 188

Cheek v. Peabody Coal Co., 97 F.3d 200, 71 FEP 1775 (7th Cir. 1996) **2:** 214

Chemisco, Inc.; EEOC v.
—216 F. Supp. 2d 940, 88 FEP 1651 (E.D. Mo. 2002) **9:** 38, 85
—203 F.R.D. 432, 87 FEP 278 (E.D. Mo. 2001) **29:** 147, 316

Chemtech Int'l Corp.; EEOC v., 4 AD 1465 (S.D. Tex. 1995) **29:** 147, 316, 317

Chen v. County of Orange, 96 Cal. App. 4th 926 (2002) **14:** 145

Chenault v. U.S. Postal Serv., 37 F.3d 535, 3 AD 1185 (9th Cir. 1994) **40:** 263

Cheng v. Metropolitan Life Ins. Co., 1995 WL 37843 (S.D.N.Y.), aff'd, 71 F.3d 404 (2d Cir. 1995) **12:** 257

Chenoweth v. Hillsborough County, 250 F.3d 1328, 11 AD 1421 (11th Cir. 2001), cert. denied, 534 U.S. 1131 (2002) **13:** 258

Cherokee Nation; EEOC v., 871 F.2d 937, 49 FEP 1074 (10th Cir. 1989) **8:** 84; **12:** 98

Cherosky v. Henderson, 330 F.3d 1243, 14 AD 673 (9th Cir. 2003) **31:** 292

Cherry
—v. Champion Int'l Corp., 186 F.3d 442 (4th Cir. 1999) **41:** 372
—v. University of Wis. Sys. Bd. of Regents, 265 F.3d 541, 86 FEP 1302 (7th Cir. 2001) **10:** 739; **18:** 36

Cherry-Burrell Corp.; EEOC v., 35 F.3d 356, 66 FEP 1749 (8th Cir. 1994) **14:** 181; **18:** 294; **40:** 206, 494

Chesapeake & Ohio Ry. Co.
—EEOC v., 577 F.2d 229, 17 FEP 815 (4th Cir. 1978) **29:** 180, 200
—United States v., 471 F.2d 582, 5 FEP 308 (4th Cir. 1972) **4:** 453

Cheshewalla v. Rand & Son Constr. Co., 415 F.3d 847, 96 FEP 171 (8th Cir. 2005), cert. denied, 126 S. Ct. 1033 (2006) **19:** 231

Chesser
—v. Illinois, 895 F.2d 330, 52 FEP 148 (7th Cir. 1990) **40:** 322
—v. Sparks, 248 F.3d 1117, 17 IER 883, 6 WH 2d 1736 (11th Cir. 2001) **35:** 207

Chester v. American Tel. & Tel. Co., 907 F. Supp. 982 (N.D. Tex. 1994), aff'd, 68 F.3d 470 (5th Cir. 1995) **12:** 273

Cheung
—v. Collier, 55 FEP 834 (W.D.N.Y. 1991) **7:** 13
—v. Merrill Lynch, Pierce, Fenner & Smith, Inc., 913 F. Supp. 248, 77 FEP 1475 (S.D.N.Y. 1996) **7:** 105; **11:** 58

Chevron USA, Inc.
—v. Echazabal, 536 U.S. 73, 13 AD 97 (2002), remanded, 336 F.3d 1023, 14 AD 1089 (9th Cir. 2003) **13:** 10, 435, 830, 832, 836, 839
—v. Natural Res. Def. Council, 467 U.S. 837 (1984) **3:** 57; **13:** 4, 40, 106, 896; **25:** 45, 46; **26:** 326

Chewning v. Seamans, 28 FEP 1735 (D.D.C. 1979) **40:** 226

Cheyenne Mtn. Conference Resort, Inc.; Roe v., 124 F.3d 1221, 7 AD 779, 13 IER 257 (10th Cir. 1997),

Dachman v. Shalala, 9 Fed. Appx. 186 (4th Cir. 2001) **2:** 151; **9:** 95

Daemi v. Church's Fried Chicken, Inc., 931 F.2d 1379, 59 FEP 395 (10th Cir. 1991) **7:** 11; **35:** 49

Daggett v. Blind Enters. of Or., 1996 U.S. Dist. LEXIS 22465 (D. Or. Apr. 18, 1996) **32:** 54

Daggitt v. Food & Commercial Workers Local 304A, 245 F.3d 981, 85 FEP 666 (8th Cir. 2001) **22:** 3; **24:** 59; **41:** 298

Dahill v. Police Dep't of Boston, 434 Mass. 233, 748 N.E.2d 956 (2001) **13:** 141

Dahl v. Secretary of Navy, 830 F. Supp. 1319, 62 FEP 1373 (E.D. Cal. 1993) **11:** 191

Dailey v. Societe Generale
—889 F. Supp. 108, 68 FEP 345 (S.D.N.Y. 1995), *aff'd in part & rev'd in part*, 108 F.3d 451, 74 FEP 1428 (2d Cir. 1997) **40:** 70, 128, 143, 322, 325, 341
—915 F. Supp. 1315 (S.D.N.Y. 1996), *aff'd in part*, 108 F.3d 451, 74 FEP 428 (2d Cir. 1997) **40:** 46

Daimler-Chrysler Corp. v. NLRB, 288 F.3d 434, 169 LRRM 3217 (D.C. Cir. 2002) **14:** 281

Daines v. City of Mankato, 754 F. Supp. 681, 54 FEP 41 (D. Minn. 1990) **16:** 87, 160; **39:** 33, 102

Dais v. Mobil Oil Corp., 20 FEP 874 (S.D.N.Y. 1979) **28:** 133

Daisernia v. New York, 582 F. Supp. 792, 34 FEP 626 (N.D.N.Y. 1984) **35:** 33

Daka, Inc. v. McCrae, 839 A.2d 682, 93 FEP 33 (D.C. 2003) **11:** 90

Dalal v. Alliant Techsystems, Inc.
—72 F.3d 177 (10th Cir. 1995) **40:** 85
—927 F. Supp. 1374 (D. Colo. 1996), *aff'd*, 182 F.3d 757 (10th Cir. 1999) **12:** 722; **41:** 311

Dale v. Chicago Tribune Co., 797 F.2d 458, 41 FEP 714 (7th Cir. 1986) **20:** 27

D'Alema v. Appalachian Heritage Cmtys., Inc., 55 FEP 1426 (N.D. Ga. 1991) **18:** 70

Dalessandro v. Monk, 864 F.2d 6, 48 FEP 912 (2d Cir. 1988) **12:** 203, 205

Daley v. Koch, 892 F.2d 212 (2d Cir. 1989) **13:** 201

Dallas v. England, 846 S.W.2d 957 (Tex. Ct. App. 1993) **11:** 132

Dallas Fire Fighters Ass'n v. City of Dallas, 885 F. Supp. 915, 75 FEP 451 (N.D. Tex. 1995), *aff'd in part & rev'd in part*, 150 F.3d 438, 77 FEP 1025 (5th Cir. 1998), *cert. denied*, 526 U.S. 1046, 75 FEP 511 (1999) **4:** 267, 294, 296; **16:** 175, 178; **37:** 104, 105, 127, 255, 290; **39:** 143

Dalley v. Michigan Blue Cross/Blue Shield, Inc., 612 F. Supp. 1444, 38 FEP 301 (E.D. Mich. 1985) **16:** 141; **34:** 334

Dalmau v. Vicao Aerea Rio-Grandense, S.A., 337 F. Supp. 2d 1299 (S.D. Fla. 2004) **7:** 142–45, 147

Dalton
—v. Palatine, Village of, 1997 WL 189301 (N.D. Ill. Apr. 15, 1997) **4:** 169
—v. Subaru-Isuzu Auto., Inc., 141 F.3d 667, 7 AD 1872 (7th Cir. 1998) **13:** 419, 545, 580, 582

D'Amato v. Wisconsin Gas Co., 760 F.2d 1474, 37 FEP 1092 (7th Cir. 1985) **35:** 363, 366

Dambrot v. Central Mich. Univ., 55 F.3d 1177, 10 IER 1130 (6th Cir. 1995) **14:** 357

Dammen v. Unimed Med. Ctr., 236 F.3d 978, 84 FEP 1417 (8th Cir. 2001) **2:** 185, 193

Damon v. Fleming Supermkts., 196 F.3d 1354, 82 FEP 899 (11th Cir. 1999) **2:** 321; **12:** 14, 344, 419

Damron v. Yellow Freight Sys., 18 F. Supp. 2d 812 (E.D. Tenn. 1998), *aff'd*, 188 F.3d 506 (6th Cir. 1999) **7:** 58

Dattoli v. Principi, 332 F.3d 505, 91 FEP 1665 (8th Cir. 2003) *19:* 92, 117

Daubert v. Merrell Dow Pharms.

—509 U.S. 579 (1993) *3:* 108; *4:* 306; *19:* 430; *32:* 392; *34:* 13, 15, 17, 18, 146

—43 F.3d 1311 (9th Cir. 1995) *34:* 19

Daugherty

—v. Daley, 370 F. Supp. 338, 11 FEP 617 (N.D. Ill. 1974) *10:* 132

—v. El Paso, City of, 56 F.3d 695, 4 AD 993 (5th Cir. 1995) *13:* 435, 592

Daughtry v. King's Dep't Stores, Inc., 608 F.2d 906, 21 FEP 333 (1st Cir. 1979) *26:* 183, 201

Daulo v. Commonwealth Edison, 892 F. Supp. 1088, 72 FEP 1566 (N.D. Ill. 1995) *28:* 114; *35:* 18

Davey v. City of Omaha, 107 F.3d 587, 73 FEP 205 (8th Cir. 1997) *3:* 166

David

—v. AM Int'l, 131 F.R.D. 86, 53 FEP 17 (E.D. Pa. 1990) *43:* 236

—v. Caterpillar, Inc., 324 F.3d 851, 91 FEP 528 (7th Cir. 2003) *2:* 217, 257; *14:* 189; *16:* 83, 85; *40:* 341

David Gomez & Assocs.; EEOC v., 1997 U.S. Dist. LEXIS 3269 (N.D. Ill. Mar. 17, 1997) *23:* 67, 73

Davidson

—v. America Online, Inc., 337 F.3d 1179, 14 AD 1185 (10th Cir. 2003) *13:* 353, 749; *26:* 133, 139, 152

—v. Board of Governors, 920 F.2d 441, 54 FEP 956 (7th Cir. 1990) *12:* 188; *18:* 375

—v. Franciscan Health Sys. of the Ohio Valley, Inc., 82 F. Supp. 2d 768 (S.D. Ohio 2000) *10:* 351, 352, 381, 461

—v. Midelfort Clinic, Ltd., 133 F.3d 499, 8 AD 77 (7th Cir. 1998) *13:* 318; *14:* 209

—v. United States Postal Serv., 24 F.3d 223 (Fed. Cir. 1994) *31:* 279

Davila

—v. Delta Air Lines, Inc., 326 F.3d 1183, 14 AD 304 (11th Cir. 2003) *27:* 70–72

—v. Qwest Corp., 2004 WL 2005915 (10th Cir. Sept. 9, 2004) *13:* 509

Davis

—v. American Soc'y of Civil Eng'rs, 330 F. Supp. 2d 647 (E.D. Va. 2004), *aff'd,* 123 Fed. Appx. 139 (4th Cir. 2005) *15:* 113

—v. Board of Sch. Comm'rs, 600 F.2d 470, 22 FEP 1579 (5th Cir. 1979), *aff'd,* 616 F.2d 893, 22 FEP 1583 (5th Cir. 1980) *16:* 120; *41:* 373

—v. Boykin Mgmt. Co., 57 FEP 1737 (W.D.N.Y. 1992) *12:* 249

—v. Bucher, 451 F. Supp. 791, 17 FEP 918 (E.D. Pa. 1978) *13:* 163

—v. Burlington Indus., Inc., 34 FEP 917 (N.D. Ga. 1983) *33:* 56

—v. Calgon Corp., 627 F.2d 674, 23 FEP 796 (3d Cir. 1980) *12:* 180

—v. Califano, 613 F.2d 957, 21 FEP 272 (D.C. Cir. 1979) *34:* 236

—v. California Dep't of Corr., 1996 WL 271001 (E.D. Cal. Feb. 23, 1996) *35:* 379

—v. Chicago Transit Auth., 2003 U.S. Dist. LEXIS 3776 (N.D. Ill. Mar. 12, 2003) *18:* 128, 131

—v. Coastal Int'l Secs., 275 F.3d 1119, 87 FEP 1263 (D.C. Cir. 2002) *11:* 14, 24; *19:* 114

—v. Combustion Eng'g, Inc., 742 F.2d 916, 35 FEP 975 (6th Cir. 1984) *40:* 231

—v. Commissioner, 210 F.3d 1346 (11th Cir. 2000) *41:* 385; *43:* 50, 225

—v. Dallas, City of, 777 F.2d 205, 39 FEP 744 (5th Cir. 1985) *4:* 340, 403, 432, 433

—v. Dallas Area Rapid Transit

——383 F.3d 309, 94 FEP 665 (5th Cir. 2004) *16:* 1, 59

——2003 WL 21501899 (N.D. Tex. June 24, 2003) *16:* 24

—v. Devereux Found., 644 F. Supp. 482, 40 FEP 1560 (E.D. Pa. 1986) *35:* 362

—v. Florida Power & Light Co., 205 F.3d 1301, 10 AD 492 (11th Cir. 2000) *13:* 606, 826; *36:* 91

EMPLOYMENT DISCRIMINATION LAW

Dominguez-Cruz v. Suttle Caribe, Inc., 202 F.3d 424, 83 FEP 21 (1st Cir. 2000) *12:* 436; *20:* 48

Dominguez-Curry v. Nevada Transp. Dep't, 424 F.3d 1027, 96 FEP 744 (9th Cir. 2005) *2:* 200, 201, 305, 308; *19:* 172; *28:* 144, 153

Dominic v. Consolidated Edison Co., 652 F. Supp. 815, 44 FEP 1865 (S.D.N.Y. 1986), *aff'd,* 822 F.2d 1249, 44 FEP 268 (2d Cir. 1987) *12:* 315; *40:* 251, 252, 485, 503

Domino's Pizza, Inc.; EEOC v.
—870 F. Supp. 655, 66 FEP 888 (D. Md. 1994) *29:* 227
—909 F. Supp. 1529, 69 FEP 570 (M.D. Fla. 1995), *aff'd,* 113 F.3d 1249 (11th Cir. 1997) *40:* 57, 63, 116, 319
—34 FEP 1075 (E.D. Mich. 1983) *40:* 121

Donaghy v. City of Omaha, 933 F.2d 1448, 55 FEP 1547 (8th Cir. 1991) *32:* 34; *37:* 27, 101

Donahoo v. Ohio Dep't of Youth Servs., 237 F. Supp. 2d 844 (N.D. Ohio 2002) *16:* 80

Donahue
—v. Boston, City of
——304 F.3d 110, 89 FEP 1495 (1st Cir. 2002) *35:* 220
——371 F.3d 7, 93 FEP 1618 (1st Cir.), *cert. denied,* 543 U.S. 987 (2004) *24:* 22
—v. Consolidated Rail Corp., 224 F.3d 226, 10 AD 1505 (3d Cir. 2000) *13:* 540, 570, 812, 840
—v. Pendleton Woolen Mills, Inc., 719 F. Supp. 149, 57 FEP 1577 (S.D.N.Y. 1988) *12:* 173

Donaldson
—v. Cafritz Co., 30 FEP 436 (D.D.C. 1981) *12:* 213; *28:* 14
—v. Microsoft Corp., 205 F.R.D. 558 (W.D. Wash. 2001) *32:* 112, 114, 175
—v. Taylor Prod. Div. of Tecumseh Prod. Co., 620 F.2d 155, 27 FEP 1439 (7th Cir. 1980) *22:* 68, 92

Donato v. American Tel. & Tel. Co., 767 So. 2d 1146, 81 FEP 1302 (Fla. 2000) *10:* 586

Dondore v. NGK Metals Corp., 152 F. Supp. 2d 662 (E.D. Pa. 2001) *29:* 318

Doninger v. Pacific Nw. Bell, Inc., 564 F.2d 1304, 16 FEP 316 (9th Cir. 1997) *27:* 97; *38:* 79

Donlon v. Group Health, Inc., 85 FEP 705 (S.D.N.Y. 2001) *14:* 189

Donnell
—v. General Motors Corp., 576 F.2d 1292, 17 FEP 712 (8th Cir. 1978) *4:* 335; *22:* 152; *34:* 264, 266, 298
—v. National Guard Bureau, 568 F. Supp. 93, 32 FEP 589 (D.D.C. 1983) *28:* 131

Donnellon v. Fruehauf Corp., 794 F.2d 598, 41 FEP 569 (11th Cir. 1986) *14:* 208

Donnelly
—v. Glickman, 159 F.3d 405, 78 FEP 724 (9th Cir. 1998) *27:* 60
—v. Rhode Island Bd. of Governors for Higher Educ., 929 F. Supp. 583, 71 FEP 363 (D.R.I. 1996), *aff'd,* 110 F.3d 2, 73 FEP 972 (1st Cir. 1997) *3:* 129, 170; *4:* 122; *20:* 60

Donovan
—v. Agnew, 712 F.2d 1509, 26 WH 466 (1st Cir. 1983) *18:* 34; *21:* 328
—v. Coeur d'Alene, 751 F.3d 1113 (9th Cir. 1985) *8:* 80
—v. Dairy Farmers of Am., Inc., 53 F. Supp. 2d 194, 80 FEP 914 (N.D.N.Y. 1999), *aff'd,* 243 F.3d 584, 85 FEP 65 (2d Cir. 2001) *41:* 92
—v. Fasgo, Inc., 25 WH 332 (E.D. Pa. 1981) *33:* 85
—v. First Fed. Sav. & Loan Ass'n, 26 WH 108 (S.D. Iowa 1982) *33:* 85
—v. Forbes, 614 F. Supp. 124, 27 WH 669 (D. Vt. 1985) *33:* 85
—v. Grim Hotel, 747 F.2d 966 (5th Cir. 1984) *21:* 327
—v. Milk Mktg., Inc., 243 F.3d 584, 85 FEP 65 (2d Cir. 2001) *12:* 487
—v. OSHRC, 713 F.2d 918 (2d Cir. 1983) *14:* 302

—v. Veterans Admin., 723 F.2d 871, 33 FEP 1525 (11th Cir. 1984) *38:* 82, 613

Fernandes v. Costa Bros. Masonry, Inc., 199 F.3d 572, 81 FEP 1149 (1st Cir. 1999) *6:* 1

Fernandez

—v. Allstate Ins. Co., 1998 WL 416034 (9th Cir. July 1, 1998) *23:* 100

—v. Chardon, 681 F.2d 42 (1st Cir. 1982), *aff'd sub nom.* Chardon v. Soto, 462 U.S. 650 (1983) *32:* 344; *35:* 387

—v. Georgia, 716 F. Supp. 1475, 50 FEP 565 (M.D. Ga. 1989) *7:* 60, 61

—v. Wynn Oil Co., 653 F.2d 1273, 26 FEP 815 (9th Cir. 1981) *9:* 194

Ferraro v. General Motors Corp., 105 F.R.D. 429 (D.N.J. 1984) *33:* 110

Ferrel v. Harvard Indus., 2001 WL 1301461 (E.D. Pa. Oct. 23, 2001) *14:* 27

Ferrell

—v. United States Dep't of Hous & Urban Dev., 186 F.3d 805 (7th Cir. 1999) *39:* 172

—v. West Bend Mut. Ins. Co., 393 F.3d 786 (8th Cir. 2005) *12:* 767

Ferrill v. Parker Group, Inc., 168 F.3d 468, 79 FEP 161 (11th Cir. 1999) *2:* 307; *6:* 30, 74–78; *21:* 39; *35:* 411; *37:* 118

Ferris v. Delta Air Lines, Inc., 277 F.3d 128, 87 FEP 899 (2d Cir. 2001) *19:* 159, 307, 308

Ferroni v. Teamsters Local 222, 297 F.3d 1146, 89 FEP 801 (10th Cir. 2002) *18:* 125; *22:* 2, 3

Ferry v. Roosevelt Bank, 883 F. Supp. 435, 4 AD 476 (E.D. Mo. 1995) *13:* 515

Fesel v. Masonic Home, 428 F. Supp. 573, 14 FEP 860 (D. Del. 1977) *21:* 77

Fester v. Farmer Bros. Co., 49 Fed. Appx. 785 (10th Cir. 2002) *12:* 741

Ficek v. Griffith Labs., Inc., 67 FEP 1396 (N.D. Ill. 1995) *19:* 184

Ficken v. Alvarez, 146 F.3d 978, 77 FEP 293 (D.C. Cir. 1998) *25:* 265

Fickling v. New York State Dep't of Civil Serv., 909 F. Supp. 185 (S.D.N.Y. 1995) *3:* 91; *4:* 92, 141, 185, 213, 214, 321

Fidelity & Guar. Co.; EEOC v., 13 FEP 1005 (4th Cir. 1976) *26:* 81

Fiedler

—v. Indianhead Truck Line, Inc., 670 F.2d 806, 28 FEP 849 (8th Cir. 1982) *40:* 171

—v. Marumsco Christian Sch., 631 F.2d 1144 (4th Cir. 1980) *35:* 47

Fielder v. UAL Corp., 218 F.3d 973, 83 FEP 493 (9th Cir. 2000), *vacated*, 536 U.S. 919 (2002) *26:* 114

Fields

—v. Beech Aircraft Corp., 95 F.R.D. 1, 38 FEP 1239 (1981), *modified on reh'g*, 39 FEP 582 (D. Kan. 1982) *29:* 138

—v. Bolger, 723 F.2d 1216, 33 FEP 1109 (6th Cir. 1984) *10:* 357

—v. Hallsville Indep. Sch. Dist., 906 F.2d 1017, 53 FEP 877 (5th Cir. 1990) *4:* 25; *21:* 4, 57; *23:* 107, 108

—v. Skokie, Village of, 502 F. Supp. 456, 24 FEP 834 (N.D. Ill. 1980) *26:* 277

—v. Tarpon Springs, City of, 721 F.2d 318 (11th Cir. 1983) *41:* 131

Fierros v. Texas Dep't of Health, 274 F.3d 187, 87 FEP 503 (5th Cir. 2001) *14:* 162

Fifth Third Bank; EEOC v., 2004 U.S. Dist. LEXIS 3410 (N.D. Ill. Mar. 5, 2004) *29:* 211

Figgous v. Allied/Bendix Corp., 906 F.2d 360, 53 FEP 295 (8th Cir. 1990) *14:* 181; *20:* 17

Figueira v. Black Entm't Television, Inc., 944 F. Supp. 299, 76 FEP 1850 (S.D.N.Y. 1996) *25:* 253

Figuero v. Buccaneer Hotel, Inc., 188 F.3d 172, 80 FEP 938 (3d Cir. 1999) *26:* 259

Hedrick v. Western Reserve Care Sys., 355 F.3d 444, 15 AD 1, 93 FEP 167 (6th Cir.), *cert. denied*, 543 U.S. 817, 15 AD 1856, 94 FEP 832 (2004) *12:* 390; *13:* 419, 458, 577, 598, 758

Heiar v. Crawford County, 746 F.2d 1190, 35 FEP 1458, *amended*, 36 FEP 112 (7th Cir. 1984) *12:* 192, 547; *40:* 84

Heideman v. PFL, Inc., 904 F.2d 1262, 53 FEP 92 (8th Cir. 1990) *12:* 198

Heilweil v. Mount Sinai Hosp., 32 F.3d 718, 3 AD 964 (2d Cir. 1994) *13:* 283

Hein
—v. All Am. Plywood Co., 232 F.3d 482 (6th Cir. 2000) *13:* 302, 303
—v. Oregon Coll. of Educ., 718 F.2d 910, 33 FEP 1538 (9th Cir. 1983) *18:* 67, 123

Heinemeier v. Chemetco, Inc., 246 F.3d 1078, 85 FEP 902 (7th Cir. 2001) *12:* 89

Heiniger v. City of Phoenix, 625 F.2d 842, 23 FEP 709 (9th Cir. 1980) *26:* 50

Heintzelman v. Runyon, 120 F.3d 143 (8th Cir. 1997) *13:* 277

Heise v. Genuine Parts Co., 900 F. Supp. 1137, 4 AD 1551 (D. Minn. 1995) *13:* 368

Helbling v. Unclaimed Salvage & Freight Co., 489 F. Supp. 956, 22 FEP 1620 (E.D. Pa. 1980) *40:* 208

Held v. Missouri Pac. R.R., 373 F. Supp. 996, 7 FEP 789 (S.D. Tex. 1974) *22:* 182

Helder v. Hitachi Power Tools, 764 F. Supp. 93, 56 FEP 380 (E.D. Mich. 1991) *35:* 371

Helgeson v. American Int'l Group, 44 F. Supp. 2d 1091 (S.D. Cal. 1999) *20:* 110

Helland v. South Bend Cmty. Sch. Corp., 93 F.3d 327, 71 FEP 1621 (7th Cir. 1996) *9:* 117

Heller
—v. Columbia Edgewater Country Club, 195 F. Supp. 2d 1212, 88 FEP 1586 (D. Or. 2002) *2:* 99; *11:* 30; *19:* 110
—v. EBB Auto Co., 8 F.3d 1433, 63 FEP 505 (9th Cir. 1993) *9:* 56

Hellinger v. Eckerd, 67 F. Supp. 2d 1359 (S.D. Fla. 1999), *revised in part, appeal dismissed in part*, 75 F.3d 825 (2d Cir. 1996) *9:* 98

Helm v. California, 722 F.2d 507, 50 FEP 7 (9th Cir. 1983) *12:* 50

Helt v. Metropolitan Dist. Comm'n, 113 F.R.D. 7, 42 FEP 1561 (D. Conn. 1986) *33:* 67

Hemmings v. Tidyman's, Inc., 285 F.3d 1174, 88 FEP 945 (9th Cir. 2002), *cert. denied*, 537 U.S. 1110, 90 FEP 1696 (2003) *2:* 358; *3:* 139; *4:* 448; *9:* 57; *16:* 99, 118, 122, 133, 137, 138, 146, 147, 150, 152, 154; *34:* 112, 113, 124, 125, 130, 143–45, 235, 236; *40:* 430, 443

Henderson
—v. Anne Arundel County Bd. of Educ., 54 F. Supp. 2d 481 (D. Md. 1998) *28:* 6, 26
—v. Ardco, Inc., 247 F.3d 645, 11 AD 1333 (6th Cir. 2001) *13:* 427
—v. Center for Cmty. Alternatives, 911 F. Supp. 689 (S.D.N.Y. 1996) *35:* 96
—v. Eastern Freight Ways, Inc., 460 F.2d 258, 4 FEP 726 (4th Cir. 1972) *26:* 293
—v. International Union, 263 F. Supp. 2d 1245 (D. Kan. 2003) *12:* 141; *22:* 59
—v. Kennedy, 265 F.3d 1072 (D.C. Cir. 2001) *9:* 45
—v. New York Life, 991 F. Supp. 527 (N.D. Tex. 1997) *13:* 555
—v. Rice, 407 F. Supp. 2d 47 (D.D.C. 2005) *7:* 142–45
—v. Simmons Foods, Inc., 217 F.3d 612, 83 FEP 279 (8th Cir. 2000) *19:* 446; *20:* 82, 88

Hendrickson v. Brandstad, 934 F.2d 158 (8th Cir. 1991) *41:* 257

Hendricks-Robinson v. Excel Corp.
—154 F.3d 685, 8 AD 875 (7th Cir. 1998) *13:* 546–48, 625, 683; *25:* 39

Hollowell—*Contd.*
—v. Orleans Reg'l Hosp. LLC, 217 F.3d 379 (5th Cir. 2000) *21:* 27; *41:* 301
Holly D. v. California Inst. of Tech., 339 F.3d 1158, 92 FEP 705 (9th Cir. 2003) *19:* 249, 256, 294, 302, 303
Holman v. Indiana, 211 F.3d 399, 82 FEP 1287 (7th Cir. 2000) *11:* 23; *19:* 90, 97, 103, 115, 117
Holmberg v. Baxter Healthcare Corp., 901 F.2d 1387, 52 FEP 1452 (7th Cir. 1990) *2:* 230
Holmes
—v. Aurora, City of, 4 AD 1781 (N.D. Ill. 1995) *13:* 505
—v. California Army Nat'l Guard, 124 F.3d 1126 (9th Cir. 1997) *11:* 200, 202
—v. Continental Can Co., 706 F.2d 1144, 31 FEP 1707 (11th Cir. 1983) *32:* 205, 206, 292, 576
—v. Marion County Office of Family & Children, 184 F. Supp. 2d 828, 87 FEP 1665 (S.D. Ind. 2002), *vacated sub nom.* Endres v. Indiana State Police, 2003 U.S. App. LEXIS 13027 (7th Cir. June 27, 2003) *18:* 37
—v. Potter, 384 F.3d 356, 94 FEP 737 (7th Cir. 2004) *43:* 192
—v. West Palm Beach Hous. Auth., 309 F.3d 752, 89 FEP 1852 (11th Cir. 2002) *16:* 169
—v. World Wildlife Fund, Inc., 908 F. Supp. 19, 69 FEP 1181 (D.D.C. 1995) *26:* 322
Holness v. Penn State Univ., 1999 WL 270388 (E.D. Pa. May 5, 1999) *7:* 185
Holowecki v. Federal Express Corp., 440 F.3d 558, 97 FEP 1037 (2d Cir. 2006) *12:* 167, 293; *28:* 119
Holsey v. Armour & Co., 743 F.2d 199, 35 FEP 1064 (4th Cir. 1984) *14:* 76; *26:* 378; *32:* 182, 192; *41:* 289
Holt
—v. Continental Group, Inc., 708 F.2d 87, 31 FEP 1468 (2d Cir. 1983) *26:* 275; *27:* 138, 140; *39:* 165, 176, 177

—v. JTM Indus., Inc., 89 F.3d 1224, 71 FEP 809 (5th Cir. 1996) *14:* 29; *24:* 91; *27:* 159
—v. KMI-Continental, Inc., 95 F.3d 123, 73 FEP 1615 (2d Cir. 1996) *2:* 149; *16:* 61; *33:* 50
—v. Olmsted Twp. Bd. of Trs., 43 F. Supp. 2d 812 (N.D. Ohio 1998) *13:* 823, 824
—v. Welch Allyn, Inc., 3 WH 2d 1622 (N.D.N.Y. 1997) *19:* 374, 400
Holthaus v. Compton & Sons, Inc.
—514 F.2d 651, 10 FEP 601 (8th Cir. 1975) *10:* 470
—71 F.R.D. 18, 11 FEP 333 (E.D. Mo. 1975) *40:* 46
Holtz v. Rockefeller & Co., 258 F.3d 62, 86 FEP 305 (2d Cir. 2001) *12:* 446; *28:* 108, 115
Holtzclaw v. DSC Commc'ns Corp., 255 F.3d 254, 12 AD 178, 86 FEP 777 (5th Cir. 2001) *12:* 777; *13:* 407
Holtzman; United States v., 762 F.2d 720 (9th Cir. 1985) *39:* 47
Holz v. Nenana City Pub. Sch. Dist., 347 F.3d 1176, 92 FEP 1464 (9th Cir. 2003) *21:* 236
Hom v. Squire, 81 F.3d 969 (10th Cir. 1996) *14:* 355
Home Ins. Co.; EEOC v., 672 F.2d 252, 27 FEP 1665 (2d Cir. 1982) *12:* 192, 652
Homemakers, Inc. v. Division of Indus. Welfare, 509 F.2d 20, 10 FEP 633 (9th Cir. 1974) *10:* 147
Home of Econ., Inc.; EEOC v., 712 F.2d 356, 32 FEP 599 (8th Cir. 1983) *18:* 284; *25:* 88; *29:* 110
Homesley v. Freightliner Corp., 61 Fed. Appx. 105, 2003 U.S. App. LEXIS 7545 (4th Cir. Apr. 22, 2003) *19:* 169
Honda Motor Co. v. Oberg, 512 U.S. 415 (1994) *40:* 446
Honeywell Int'l, Inc. Sec. Litig., In re, 2003 U.S. Dist. LEXIS 20602 (S.D.N.Y. Nov. 18, 2003) *32:* 366

Horney v. Westfield Gage Co.
—95 F. Supp. 2d 29 (D. Mass. 2000)
  21: 49
—211 F. Supp. 2d 291 (D. Mass. 2002),
  rev'd in part, 77 Fed. Appx. 24 (1st
  Cir. 2003) *18:* 113, 128
Hornick v. Borough of Duryea, 507 F.
  Supp. 1091, 24 FEP 482 (M.D. Pa.
  1980) *3:* 111, 140
Horton
—v. Board of Trs., 1996 WL 277962
  (N.D. Ill. May 16, 1996), *aff'd*, 107
  F.3d 873 (7th Cir. 1997) *13:* 515
—v. Commissioner, 33 F.3d 625 (6th
  Cir., 1994) *40:* 357
—v. Jackson County Bd. of County
  Comm'rs, 343 F.3d 897, 92 FEP 929
  (7th Cir. 2003) *32:* 321
—v. Marovich, 925 F. Supp. 540 (N.D.
  Ill. 1996) *35:* 345
—v. Norfolk S. Corp., 102 F. Supp. 2d
  330, 164 LRRM 3038 (M.D.N.C.
  1999) *43:* 43
—v. Rockwell Int'l Corp., 93 F. Supp.
  2d 1048 (N.D. Iowa 2000) *15:* 122
Horvath
—v. Keystone Health Plan E., Inc., 333
  F.3d 450 (3d Cir. 2003) *28:* 180
—v. Rimtec Corp., 102 F. Supp. 2d 219
  (D.N.J. 2000) *12:* 93
Horwitz v. Board of Educ. of Avoca
  Sch. Dist. 37, 260 F.3d 602, 86 FEP
  688, 7 WH 2d 207 (7th Cir. 2001)
  12: 464; *35:* 124, 131
Hoskins v. Oakland County Sheriff's
  Dep't, 227 F.3d 719, 10 AD 1417
  (6th Cir. 2000) *13:* 444, 540, 545,
  577, 732
Hosler v. Greene, 5 F. Supp. 2d 99
  (N.D.N.Y. 1998) *21:* 46
Hotchkins v. Fleet Delivery Serv., 25 F.
  Supp. 2d 1141 (D. Or. 1998) *2:* 208
Hou v. Pennsylvania Dep't of Educ.,
  573 F. Supp. 1539, 33 FEP 513
  (W.D. Pa. 1983) *7:* 178
Houck
—v. Prairie Vill., City of, 977 F. Supp.
  1128 (D. Kan. 1997), *aff'd*, 166 F.3d
  1221 (10th Cir. 1998) *15:* 47, 49

—v. Virginia Polytechnic Inst., 10 F.3d
  204, 63 FEP 188 (4th Cir. 1993)
  18: 58
Houghton
—v. McDonnell Douglas Corp.
——553 F.2d 561, 14 FEP 1594 (8th
  Cir. 1977). *See* Brennan v. McDonnell Douglas Corp.
——627 F.2d 858, 23 FEP 757 (8th Cir.
  1980) *12:* 678
—v. Sipco, Inc., 38 F.3d 953, 66 FEP
  97 (8th Cir. 1994) *3:* 161; *12:* 780
Houlton Band of Maliseet Indians v.
  Maine Human Rights Comm'n, 960
  F. Supp. 449, 76 FEP 1379 (D. Me.
  1997) *8:* 112
House v. Cannon Mills Co., 713 F. Supp.
  159 (M.D.N.C. 1988) *21:* 327
House of Prime Rib; EEOC v., 31 FEP
  981 (N.D. Cal. 1983), *aff'd*, 735 F.2d
  1369, 35 FEP 736 (9th Cir. 1984)
  40: 41
Houseton v. Nimmo, 670 F.2d 1375
  (9th Cir. 1982) *31:* 341
Housley v. Boeing Co., 177 F. Supp.
  2d 1209 (D. Kan. 2001), *aff'd*, 50
  Fed. Appx. 934 (10th Cir. 2002)
  16: 47
Houston v. Sidley & Austin, 185 F.3d
  837, 80 FEP 417 (7th Cir. 1999)
  26: 312
Houston Area Sheet Metal Joint Ap-
  prenticeship Comm.; EEOC v., 2002
  WL 1263893, 13 AD 214 (S.D. Tex.
  May 31, 2002) *13:* 435
Houston Chapter of the Int'l Ass'n of
  Black Professional Firefighters v.
  City of Houston, 1991 U.S. Dist.
  LEXIS 13391, 56 FEP 445 (S.D. Tex.
  May 6, 1991) *4:* 242
Hover v. Florida Power & Light Co.,
  67 FEP 34 (S.D. Fla. Dec. 9, 1994)
  9: 33, 80, 81, 83; *21:* 39
Howard
—v. Anderson, 36 F. Supp. 2d 183, 83
  FEP 1225 (S.D.N.Y. 1999) *42:* 135
—v. Board of Educ., 2003 WL
  21518725 (6th Cir. July 1, 2003) *6:*
  41

Hyman v. First Union Corp., 980 F. Supp. 46 (D.D.C. 1997) *35:* 64

Hypes v. First Commerce Corp., 134 F.3d 721, 7 AD 1546 (5th Cir. 1998) *13:* 399

Hysten v. Burlington N. & Santa Fe Ry. Co., 296 F.3d 1177, 89 FEP 814 (10th Cir. 2002) *14:* 180

I

Iacampo v. Hasbro, Inc., 929 F. Supp. 562, 5 AD 1075 (D.R.I. 1996) *13:* 77–79

Iacobucci v. Boulter, 193 F.3d 14 (1st Cir. 1999) *40:* 426

Iadimarco v. Runyon, 190 F.3d 151, 80 FEP 1294 (3d Cir. 1999) *2:* 84, 85; *10:* 624; *37:* 24, 25

Ianetta v. Putnam Invs., Inc., 183 F. Supp. 2d 415, 87 FEP 1812 (D. Mass. 2002) *2:* 99–101, 103

Ibarra v. Houston Indep. Sch. Dist., 84 F. Supp. 2d 825 (S.D. Tex. 1999) *35:* 328

IBP, Inc.
—EEOC v., 824 F. Supp. 147, 61 FEP 1351 (C.D. Ill. 1993) *9:* 38
—v. Mercantile Bank of Topeka, 6 F. Supp. 2d 1258 (D. Kan. 1998) *28:* 163

Ibrahim
—v. American Univ., 80 FEP 97 (D.D.C. 1999) *33:* 5
—v. New York State Dep't of Health, 904 F.2d 161, 54 FEP 1219 (2d Cir. 1990) *2:* 71, 225

ICON Benefit Adm'rs, Inc.; EEOC v., 91 FEP 116 (W.D. Tex. 2003) *28:* 131

Ilhardt v. Sara Lee Corp., 118 F.3d 1151, 74 FEP 273 (7th Cir. 1997) *2:* 68; *3:* 14, 90; *10:* 611

Illinois; EEOC v., 69 F.3d 167, 69 FEP 306 (7th Cir. 1995) *12:* 87; *24:* 48

Illinois Dep't of Employment Sec.; EEOC v.
—995 F.2d 106, 61 FEP 1385 (7th Cir. 1993) *25:* 341; *33:* 45
—6 F. Supp. 2d 784, 77 FEP 107 (N.D. Ill. 1998) *29:* 50

Illinois State Univ. Bd, of Trs.; United States v., 944 F. Supp. 714 (C.D. Ill. 1996) *30:* 40–43

Illinois Tool Works, Inc. v. Marshall, 601 F.2d 943, 20 FEP 359 (7th Cir. 1979) *38:* 566

Ilona of Hung., Inc.; EEOC v., 108 F.3d 1569, 73 FEP 528 (7th Cir. 1997) *9:* 99; *39:* 31, 38; *40:* 27, 149

IMAGE v. Bailar
—518 F. Supp. 800, 28 FEP 770 (N.D. Cal. 1981) *3:* 176
—78 F.R.D. 549, 24 FEP 1410 (N.D. Cal. 1978) *32:* 138

Imbler v. Pachtman, 424 U.S. 409 (1976) *35:* 197

Immigration & Naturalization Serv. v. Chadha, 462 U.S. 919 (1983) *18:* 281; *29:* 4

IMPACT v. Firestone, 893 F.2d 1189, 52 FEP 71 (11th Cir. 1990) *2:* 126; *24:* 10; *25:* 179

Impervious Paint Indus., Inc. v. Ashland Oil, 508 F. Supp. 720 (W.D. Ky. 1981) *32:* 408, 411, 425

Increase Minority Participation by Affirmative Change Today of Nw. Fla., Inc. v. Firestone, 24 FEP 572 (N.D. Fla. 1980), *rev'd*, 893 F.2d 1189, 52 FEP 71 (11th Cir. 1990) *32:* 323

Independent Metal Workers Union Locals Nos. 1 & 2 (Hughes Tool Co.), 147 NLRB 1573, 56 LRRM 1289 (1964) *36:* 17, 33–37

Indest v. Freeman Decorating, Inc., 164 F.3d 258, 78 FEP 1527 (5th Cir. 1999) *19:* 288–93

Indiana Bell Tel. Co.; EEOC v., 256 F.3d 516, 86 FEP 1 (7th Cir. 2001) *19:* 325; *22:* 168; *27:* 102; *28:* 50; *40:* 442; *42:* 248

Indianapolis, City of v. Wright, 371 N.E.2d 1298 (Ind.), *appeal dismissed*, 439 U.S. 804 (1978) *10:* 133

Ingersoll-Rand Co. v. McClendon, 498 U.S. 133 (1990) *27:* 184

Ingle v. Circuit City Stores, Inc., 328 F.3d 1165, 91 FEP 1426 (9th Cir. 2003), *cert. denied*, 124 S. Ct. 1169 (2004) *42:* 85, 86, 105–11, 144–46, 152, 153, 155

Krauel v. Iowa Methodist Med. Ctr., 95 F.3d 674, 5 AD 1503, 71 FEP 1326 (8th Cir. 1996) *3:* 87; *10:* 327, 328, 352, 370, 371, 374, 392; *13:* 200, 652

Kraus v. Sobel Corrugated Containers, Inc., 915 F.2d 227, 53 FEP 1691 (6th Cir. 1990) *12:* 383

Krause v. Dresser Indus., Inc., 910 F.2d 674, 53 FEP 771 (10th Cir. 1990) *12:* 382

Kravec v. Chicago Pneumatic Tool Co., 579 F. Supp. 619, 36 FEP 266 (N.D. Ga. 1983) *28:* 138

Krchnavy v. Limagrain Genetics Corp., 294 F.3d 871, 89 FEP 289 (7th Cir. 2002) *12:* 351

Kremer v. Chemical Constr. Corp., 456 U.S. 461, 28 FEP 1412 (1982) *26:* 86, 87; *27:* 6, 8–12, 39, 40, 122, 123; *35:* 462

Krempel v. Prairie Island Indian Cmty., 125 F.3d 621, 74 FEP 1449 (8th Cir. 1997) *8:* 130

Krenik v. Le Sueur, 47 F.3d 953, 67 FEP 312 (8th Cir. 1995) *12:* 434

Kresefsky v. Panasonic Commc'ns & Sys. Co., 169 F.R.D. 54, 74 FEP 905 (D.N.J. 1996) *32:* 191, 193; *33:* 3

Kresge v. Circuitek, Div. of TDI, 958 F. Supp. 223, 6 AD 959 (E.D. Pa. 1997) *15:* 139

Kreshik v. St. Nicholas Cathedral of Russian Orthodox Church, 363 U.S. 190 (1960) *9:* 165

Kresko v. Rulli, 432 N.W.2d 764 (Minn. Ct. App. 1988) *33:* 61

Kriescher v. Fox Hills Golf Resort & Conference Ctr., 384 F.3d 912, 94 FEP 1007 (7th Cir. 2004) *19:* 366

Krisa v. Equitable Life Assurance Soc'y, 196 F.R.D. 254 (M.D. Pa. 2000) *34:* 24

Krislov v. Rednour, 97 F. Supp. 2d 862 (N.D. Ill. 2000) *41:* 100

Kristoferson v. Otis Spunkmeyer, Inc., 965 F. Supp. 545, 73 FEP 1863 (S.D.N.Y. 1997) *43:* 261

Kristufek v. Hussmann Foodservice Co., 985 F.2d 364, 61 FEP 72 (7th Cir. 1993) *40:* 177

Krocka
—v. Bransfield, 969 F. Supp. 1073 (N.D. Ill. 1997), *aff'd sub nom.* Krocka v. City of Chic., 203 F.3d 507, 10 AD 289 (7th Cir. 2000) *13:* 259, 330, 706
—v. Riegler, 958 F. Supp. 1333, 8 AD 682 (N.D. Ill. 1997) *13:* 455

Krodel v. Young, 748 F.2d 701, 36 FEP 468 (D.C. Cir. 1984) *12:* 461, 474

Kromnick v. School Dist., 739 F.2d 894, 35 FEP 538 (3d Cir. 1984) *17:* 129

Kroneberger v. Science Applications Int'l Corp., 161 F.3d 13 (9th Cir. 1998) *15:* 102

Kronisch v. United States, 150 F.3d 112 (2d Cir. 1998) *33:* 121

Krouse v. American Sterilizer Co., 126 F.3d 494, 7 AD 662 (3d Cir. 1997) *14:* 181, 206

Kruchowski v. Weyerhaeuser Co.
—423 F.3d 1139, 96 FEP 914 (10th Cir. 2005) *12:* 606
—446 F.3d 1090 (10th Cir. 2006) *12:* 626

Krueger v. New York Tel. Co.
—163 F.R.D. 433, 80 FEP 873 (S.D.N.Y. 1995) *32:* 94
—163 F.R.D. 446 (S.D.N.Y. 1995) *33:* 111

Kruger v. Pacific Benefits Group N.W., 228 F. Supp. 2d 1143 (D. Or. 2001) *10:* 366

Krulik v. Board of Educ. of N.Y., 781 F.2d 15, 39 FEP 1448 (2d Cir. 1986) *16:* 79, 115

Krumwiede v. Mercer County Ambulance Serv., Inc., 116 F.3d 361, 74 FEP 188 (8th Cir. 1997) *2:* 143

Kubicko v. Ogden Logistics Servs., 181 F.3d 544, 79 FEP 1591 (4th Cir. 1999) *14:* 229; *40:* 275

Kucia v. Southeast Ark. Cmty. Action Corp., 284 F.3d 944, 88 FEP 861 (8th Cir. 2002) *39:* 82; *40:* 218, 239

Kuhar v. Greensburg-Salem Sch. Dist., 616 F.2d 676, 22 FEP 80 (3d Cir. 1980) *12:* 126

EMPLOYMENT DISCRIMINATION LAW

Lanigan v. Bartlett & Co. Grain, 466
F. Supp. 1388, 19 FEP 1039 (W.D.
Mo. 1979) *10:* 641, 642
Lankford v. Hobart, 73 F.3d 283, 69
FEP 1149 (10th Cir. 1996) *35:* 225
Lanman v. Johnson County, 393 F.3d
1151, 16 AD 449 (10th Cir. 2004)
13: 636
Lanni v. New Jersey
—259 F.3d 146, 12 AD 1064 (3d Cir.
2001) *41:* 274
—177 F.R.D. 295 (D.N.J. 1998) *34:*
382
Lanning v. Southeastern Pa. Transp.
Auth., 181 F.3d 478, 80 FEP 221
(1999), *aff'd,* 308 F.3d 286, 90 FEP
49 (3d Cir. 2002) *3:* 159, 160, 170;
4: 179, 277, 292, 372–76; *10:* 691,
726, 727; *15:* 100
Lanza v. Sugarland Run Homeowners
Ass'n, 97 F. Supp. 2d 737, 6 WH 2d
175 (E.D. Va. 2000) *14:* 300
Lape v. Pennsylvania, 157 Fed. Appx.
491 (3d Cir. 2005), *cert. denied*, 127
S. Ct. 35 (2006) *14:* 355
LaPerriere v. Auto Workers, 348 F.3d
128 (6th Cir. 2003) *22:* 67
Lapides v. Board of Regents of Univ.
Sys. of Ga., 535 U.S. 613, 18 IER
961 (2002) *21:* 252, 268, 270, 271;
35: 149
LaPorta v. Wal-Mart Stores, Inc., 163
F. Supp. 2d 758 (W.D. Mich. 2001)
10: 372; *13:* 200
LaPrade v. Kidder, Peabody & Co., 246
F.3d 702, 85 FEP 779, 17 IER 869
(D.C. Cir. 2001) *42:* 134
LaQuaglia v. Rio Hotel & Casino, Inc.,
186 F.3d 1172, 80 FEP 848 (9th Cir.
1999) *26:* 79, 96
Larimer
—v. Dayton Hudson Corp., 137 F.3d
497, 77 FEP 1545 (7th Cir. 1998)
16: 63
—v. International Bus. Machs. Corp.,
370 F.3d 698, 15 AD 1070 (7th Cir.),
cert. denied, 125 S. Ct. 477 (2004)
13: 677

Larkin
—v. Pullman-Standard Div., 854 F.2d
1549, 47 FEP 1732 (11th Cir. 1988),
vacated & remanded sub nom. Swint
v. Pullman-Standard, Inc., 493 U.S.
929, 51 FEP 112 (1989) *17:* 86; *21:*
8; *24:* 147; *32:* 324
—v. West Hartford, Town of, 891 F.
Supp. 719 (D. Conn. 1995), *aff'd,*
101 F.3d 109 (2d Cir. 1996) *20:* 81,
86
Laro v. New Hampshire, 259 F.3d 1, 7
WH 2d 262 (1st Cir. 2001) *10:* 450
LaRocca v. Precision Motorcars, Inc.,
45 F. Supp. 2d 762 (D. Neb. 1999)
6: 25
LaRoche v. Denny's, Inc., 62 F. Supp.
2d 1375 (S.D. Fla. 1999) *35:* 411
LaRouche v. New York City, 369 F.
Supp. 565 (S.D.N.Y. 1974) *35:* 108
Larsen
—v. Frederiksen, 277 F.3d 1040 (8th
Cir. 2002) *31:* 377
—v. U.S. Navy, 346 F. Supp. 2d 122
(D.D.C. 2004) *9:* 46
Larus & Bros. Co., 62 NLRB 1075, 16
LRRM 242 (1945) *36:* 17
Lassiter v. Alabama A&M Univ. Bd. of
Trs., 28 F.3d 1146 (11th Cir. 1994)
35: 207
Latham v. Office of Attorney Gen., 395
F.3d 261, 94 FEP 1798 (6th Cir.),
cert. denied, 126 S. Ct. 420 (2005)
14: 339
Lathem v. Department of Children &
Youth Servs., 172 F.3d 786 (11th Cir.
1999) *40:* 340
Lathram v. Snow, 336 F.3d 1085, 92
FEP 609 (D.C. Cir. 2003) *16:* 108
Latimore v. Citibank F.S.B., 151 F.3d
712 (7th Cir. 1998) *2:* 305
Latin Am. Law Enforcement Ass'n v.
City of L.A., 29 F.3d 633, 1994 WL
383884 (9th Cir. July 21, 1994) *41:*
375
Latino Police Officers Ass'n v. City of
N.Y., 209 F.R.D. 79 (S.D.N.Y. 2002)
32: 46, 97, 113, 118, 120, 277

Lockard
—v. GMC, 2002 U.S. App. LEXIS 25787 (6th Cir. Dec. 11, 2002) *13:* 731, 767
—v. Pizza Hut, Inc., 162 F.3d 1062, 78 FEP 1026 (10th Cir. 1998) *19:* 327, 328, 332; *41:* 141, 275
Locke v. Davey, 540 U.S. 712 (2004) *9:* 152
Lockhart v. Westinghouse Credit Corp., 879 F.2d 43, 50 FEP 216 (3d Cir. 1989) *12:* 296
Lockheed Corp.
—EEOC v., 54 FEP 1632 (C.D. Cal. 1991) *39:* 168
—v. Spink, 517 U.S. 882, 70 FEP 1633 (1996) *12:* 592–94
Lockheed Martin Corp.; EEOC v., 70 FEP 1457 (D. Md. 1996), *aff'd,* 116 F.3d 110, 74 FEP 202 (4th Cir. 1997) *25:* 347; *29:* 49
Lockridge v. Board of Trs. of Univ. of Ark., 315 F.3d 1005, 90 FEP 1319 (8th Cir. 2003) *16:* 38, 41, 43, 44, 120; *35:* 80
Lococo v. Barger, 958 F. Supp. 290 (E.D. Ky. 1997), *aff'd in part, rev'd in part,* 234 F.3d 1268 (6th Cir. 2000) *24:* 67
Locus v. Fayetteville State Univ., 49 FEP 655 (E.D.N.C. 1988), *aff'd,* 870 F.2d 655 (4th Cir. 1989) *35:* 340
Loeb v. Textron, Inc., 600 F.2d 1003, 20 FEP 29 (1st Cir. 1979) *20:* 26
Loeffler v. Frank, 486 U.S. 549, 46 FEP 1659 (1988) *32:* 465; *40:* 68, 69, 80
Loffland Bros. Co.; OFCCP v., OEO 75-1, 1984 WL 484538 (Apr. 16, 1984) *38:* 25
Logan
—v. Denny's Inc., 259 F.3d 558 (6th Cir. 2001) *20:* 127
—v. Kotex Textron N. Am., 259 F.3d 635, 86 FEP 609 (7th Cir. 2001) *2:* 149
—v. St. Luke's Hosp. Ctr., 428 F. Supp. 127, 14 FEP 1370 (S.D.N.Y. 1977) *4:* 358

Logue v. International Rehab. Ass'n, 837 F.2d 150, 45 FEP 1382 (3d Cir. 1988) *2:* 169
Loiseau v. Department of Human Res., 567 F. Supp. 1211, 39 FEP 289 (D. Or. 1983) *7:* 177; *16:* 131
Lollar v. Baker, 196 F.3d 603 (5th Cir. 1999) *35:* 239, 420
Lomascolo v. Otto Oldsmobile-Cadillac, Inc., 253 F. Supp. 2d 354, 91 FEP 780 (N.D.N.Y. 2003) *33:* 7
Long
—v. Eastfield Coll., 88 F.3d 300, 71 FEP 750 (5th Cir. 1996) *14:* 189
—v. First Union Corp., 894 F. Supp. 933, 68 FEP 917 (E.D. Va. 1995), *aff'd mem.,* 86 F.3d 1151, 71 FEP 736 (4th Cir. 1996) *3:* 87; *7:* 171; *20:* 89
—v. Florida, 805 F.2d 1542, 42 FEP 1058 (11th Cir. 1986), *rev'd,* 487 U.S. 223, 47 FEP 7 (1988) *40:* 518
—v. Frank, 22 F.3d 54, 64 FEP 782 (2d Cir. 1994) *12:* 113; *31:* 78
—v. Georgia Kraft Co., 450 F.2d 557, 3 FEP 1222 (5th Cir. 1971), *aff'd,* 455 F.2d 331 (5th Cir. 1972) *17:* 108
—v. Laramie County Cmty. Coll. Dist., 840 F.2d 743, 46 FEP 264 (10th Cir. 1988) *14:* 199, 269; *27:* 43; *35:* 350
—v. Ringling Bros.-Barnum & Bailey Combined Shows, Inc., 9 F.3d 340, 63 FEP 289 (4th Cir. 1993), *on remand,* 882 F. Supp. 1553, 67 FEP 1685 (D. Md. 1995) *2:* 248; *40:* 56
—v. Saginaw, City of, 911 F.2d 1192, 53 FEP 1025 (6th Cir. 1990) *34:* 204, 206
—v. Sapp, 502 F.2d 34, 8 FEP 1079 (5th Cir. 1974) *32:* 76
—v. Sears, Roebuck & Co., 105 F.3d 1529, 72 FEP 1860 (3d Cir. 1997) *12:* 638, 782; *43:* 102, 103
—v. Trans World Airlines, Inc., 761 F. Supp. 1320 (N.D. Ill. 1991) *40:* 138
Longariello v. School Bd. of Monroe County, 987 F. Supp. 1440 (S.D. Fla.

Love
—v. Alamance County Bd. of Educ., 757 F.2d 1504, 37 FEP 633 (4th Cir. 1985) *2:* 135; *38:* 81
—v. Pullman Co., 404 U.S. 522, 4 FEP 150 (1972), *motion to intervene denied*, 12 FEP 330 (D. Colo. 1973) *12:* 221; *26:* 21–23, 25–27, 82; *29:* 251, 264, 269
—v. RE/MAX of Am., Inc., 738 F.2d 383, 35 FEP 565 (10th Cir. 1984) *14:* 208
—v. Turlington, 733 F.2d 1562 (11th Cir. 1984) *32:* 372
Lovejoy-Wilson v. NOCO Motor Fuel, Inc., 263 F.3d 208, 12 AD 340 (2d Cir. 2001) *13:* 713, 845; *14:* 255; *16:* 83; *25:* 39
Lovell
—v. Brinker Int'l, Inc., 71 FEP 417 (W.D. Mo. 1996) *35:* 49
—v. Chandler, 303 F.3d 1039, 13 AD 918 (9th Cir. 2002), *cert. denied*, 537 U.S. 1105, 13 AD 1632 (2003) *13:* 931
—v. Comsewogue Sch. Dist., 214 F. Supp. 2d 319, 89 FEP 1189 (E.D.N.Y. 2002) *11:* 167
Lowe
—v. Alabama Power Co., 244 F.3d 1305, 11 AD 1038 (11th Cir. 2001) *2:* 131; *13:* 363, 835
—v. Angelo's Italian Foods, Inc.
——87 F.3d 1170, 71 FEP 339 (10th Cir. 1996) *10:* 637; *13:* 255
——3 AD 1654 (D. Kan. 1994) *13:* 284
—v. Commack Union Free Sch. Dist., 886 F.2d 1364, 50 FEP 1400 (2d Cir. 1989) *12:* 506
—v. J.B. Hunt Transp., Inc., 963 F.2d 173, 59 FEP 74 (8th Cir. 1992) *2:* 265, 273; *12:* 411
—v. Monrovia, City of, 775 F.2d 998, 39 FEP 350 (9th Cir. 1985), *amended*, 784 F.2d 1407, 41 FEP 931 (9th Cir. 1986) *38:* 81
—v. Southmark Corp., 998 F.2d 335, 62 FEP 1087 (5th Cir. 1993) *14:* 298; *40:* 37, 494

—v. Wolin-Levin, Inc., 2003 U.S. Dist. LEXIS 1646 (N.D. Ill. Feb. 5, 2003) *21:* 13
Lowery
—v. Circuit City Stores, Inc., 158 F.3d 742, 77 FEP 1319 (4th Cir. 1998), *vacated & remanded*, 527 U.S. 1031, 80 FEP 64 (1999), *aff'd in part*, 206 F.3d 431, 82 FEP 353 (4th Cir. 2000) *16:* 36, 115, 125, 137, 145, 150, 151; *34:* 7, 33, 120; *35:* 440; *40:* 438
—v. Hazelwood Sch. Dist., 244 F.3d 654, 11 AD 1057 (8th Cir. 2001) *13:* 614
Lowrey
—v. Texas A&M Univ. Sys., 117 F.3d 242 (5th Cir. 1997) *10:* 804, 805
—v. WMC-TV, 658 F. Supp. 1240, 43 FEP 972, *vacated*, 661 F. Supp. 65 (W.D. Tenn. 1987) *6:* 17
Loya v. Desert Sands Unified Sch. Dist., 721 F.2d 279, 33 FEP 739 (9th Cir. 1983) *26:* 337
Loyd v. Phillips Bros., Inc., 25 F.3d 518, 64 FEP 1513 (7th Cir. 1994) *10:* 226; *16:* 42, 48, 131; *18:* 410; *34:* 163
Lu v. Woods, 717 F. Supp. 886, 50 FEP 536 (D.D.C. 1989) *7:* 186
Lubkeman v. Commonwealth Edison Co., 877 F. Supp. 1180, 67 FEP 514 (N.D. Ill. 1995) *12:* 344
Lucarelli v. Conrail, 2002 U.S. Dist. LEXIS 12201 (E.D. Pa. Mar. 26, 2002) *13:* 805
Lucas
—v. Dole, 835 F.2d 532, 45 FEP 971 (4th Cir. 1987) *2:* 84
—v. Dover Corp., 857 F.2d 1397, 47 FEP 1713 (10th Cir. 1988) *10:* 210; *12:* 395; *20:* 33
—v. Miami County, 9 Fed. Appx. 809 (10th Cir. 2001) *2:* 213
—v. Wheeler Mach. Co., 53 FEP 1729 (D. Utah 1989) *25:* 411
—v. W.W. Grainger, Inc., 257 F.3d 1249, 11 AD 1761 (11th Cir. 2001) *2:* 63; *13:* 347, 576

Maturo v. National Graphics, Inc., 722 F. Supp. 916, 55 FEP 325 (D. Conn. 1989) *40:* 128, 134

Matvia v. Bald Head Island Mgmt., Inc., 259 F.3d 261, 86 FEP 803 (4th Cir. 2001) *19:* 278, 304; *20:* 71, 74

Matzo v. Postmaster Gen., 685 F. Supp. 260, 1 AD 1137 (D.D.C. 1987), *aff'd,* 861 F.2d 1290, 1 AD 1339 (D.C. Cir. 1988) *13:* 393

Matzo Food Prods. Litig., In re, 156 F.R.D. 600 (D.N.J. 1994) *32:* 582

Maudlin v. Wal-Mart Stores, Inc., 2002 WL 2022334, 89 FEP 1600 (N.D. Ga. Aug. 23, 2002) *10:* 326; *32:* 94

Mauro v. Southern New Eng. Telecomm., 208 F.3d 384, 82 FEP 1054 (2d Cir. 2000) *2:* 152; *12:* 416; *16:* 1, 38, 62, 91

Mauro, Estate of v. Burgess Med. Ctr., 137 F.3d 398, 7 AD 1571 (6th Cir. 1998) *13:* 840, 842, 859

Mauter v. Hardy Corp., 825 F.2d 1554, 45 FEP 116 (11th Cir. 1987) *2:* 208

Mawhinney v. GMAC Commercial Mortgage Corp., 2002 WL 511503 (E.D. Pa. Apr. 2, 2002) *10:* 624, 654, 655

Maxfield v. Sinclair Int'l, 766 F.2d 788, 38 FEP 442 (3d Cir. 1985) *12:* 315; *40:* 126, 240, 254, 330, 487

Maxwell v. City of Tucson, 803 F.2d 444, 42 FEP 205 (9th Cir. 1986) *18:* 103

May

—v. Higbee Co., 372 F.3d 757, 94 FEP 44, 21 IER 587 (5th Cir. 2004) *42:* 82

—v. Shuttle, Inc., 129 F.3d 165, 82 FEP 1395, 156 LRRM 2820 (D.C. Cir. 1997) *2:* 144; *12:* 232, 776

May & Co.; EEOC v., 572 F. Supp. 536 (N.D. Ga. 1983) *29:* 172, 174

Mayberry v. Vought Aircraft Co., 55 F.3d 1086, 68 FEP 401 (5th Cir. 1995) *2:* 68

Maye v. Smith Barney, Inc., 897 F. Supp. 100, 68 FEP 1648 (S.D.N.Y. 1995) *42:* 88

Mayer v. Nextel W. Corp., 318 F.3d 803, 90 FEP 1750 (8th Cir. 2003) *12:* 337, 381, 410; *20:* 15, 23, 42

Mayfield

—v. Meese, 669 F. Supp. 1123, 53 FEP 1301 (D.D.C. 1987) *24:* 23

—v. President Riverboat Casino, 84 FEP 318 (E.D. Mo. 2000) *33:* 83

Maynard

—v. Nygren, 372 F.3d 890, 15 AD 1121 (7th Cir. 2004), *cert. denied,* 543 U.S. 1049 (2005) *33:* 9

—v. Pneumatic Prods. Corp., 256 F.3d 1259, 11 AD 1790 (11th Cir. 2001) *25:* 134; *26:* 34, 69

—v. Revere Copper Prods., Inc., 773 F.2d 733 (6th Cir. 1985) *22:* 148

—v. San Jose, City of, 37 F.3d 1396, 66 FEP 123 (9th Cir. 1994) *24:* 86; *35:* 235, 236, 358, 365

Mayorga v. Donnelley Mktg., Inc., 1996 WL 28483, 70 FEP 670 (N.D. Ill. Jan. 24, 1996) *10:* 466; *20:* 89, 138

Mayor of Philadelphia v. Educational Equality League, 415 U.S. 605 (1974) *34:* 325

Mays

—v. Chicago Sun-Times, 865 F.2d 134, 48 FEP 1425, *amended,* 49 FEP 288 (7th Cir. 1989) *22:* 89

—v. Lanier Worldwide, Inc., 115 F. Supp. 2d 1330 (M.D. Ala. 2000) *42:* 213

—v. Motorola, Inc., 22 FEP 799 (N.D. Ill.), *final decree entered,* 22 FEP 803 (N.D. Ill. 1979) *15:* 60; *34:* 259, 260; *40:* 320

—v. Principi, 301 F.3d 866, 13 AD 985 (7th Cir. 2002) *13:* 444, 488, 630

Maziarka v. Mills Fleet Farm, Inc., 245 F.3d 675, 11 AD 1140 (8th Cir. 2001) *13:* 392, 732

McAdams v. Reno, 858 F. Supp. 945 (D. Minn. 1994), *aff'd,* 64 F.3d 1137, 91 FEP 1381 (8th Cir. 1995) *14:* 389; *31:* 278

McAlester v. United Air Lines, Inc., 851 F.2d 1249, 47 FEP 512 (10th Cir.

Menchaca
—v. American Med. Response of Ill., Inc., 6 F. Supp. 2d 971 (N.D. Ill. 1998) *26:* 284
—v. Ottenwalder, 18 Fed. Appx. 508 (9th Cir. 2001) *35:* 224, 231
Mendez
—v. Belton, 739 F.2d 15, 35 FEP 625 (1st Cir. 1984) *35:* 94
—v. Gearan, 947 F. Supp. 1364 (N.D. Cal. 1996) *13:* 969, 970
Mendoza
—v. Borden, Inc., 195 F.3d 1238, 81 FEP 470 (11th Cir. 1999) *19:* 88, 103
—v. Miami, City of, 483 F.2d 430, 6 FEP 492 (5th Cir. 1973) *7:* 79
Mercado v. Ritz-Carlton San Juan Hotel, Spa & Casino, 410 F.3d 41, 95 FEP 1464 (1st Cir. 2005) *26:* 211
Mercer v. City of Cedar Rapids, 308 F.3d 840, 90 FEP 11 (8th Cir. 2002) *35:* 221, 234
Mercy Health Ctr.; EEOC v., 1982 WL 3108, 29 FEP 159 (W.D. Okla. Feb. 2, 1982) *10:* 91, 110
Meredith
—v. Beech Aircraft Corp., 18 F.3d 890, 64 FEP 473 (10th Cir. 1994) *27:* 127
—v. Louisiana Fed'n of Teachers, 1996 WL 137632 (E.D. La. Mar. 26, 1996) *12:* 130
Mereish v. Walker, 359 F.3d 330, 93 FEP 608 (4th Cir. 2004) *12:* 393, 455, 486, 523
Merit v. Southeastern Pa. Transit Auth., 276 F. Supp. 2d 382 (E.D. Pa. 2003) *26:* 226
Meritor Sav. Bank v. Vinson, 477 U.S. 57, 40 FEP 1822 (1986) *10:* 7, 784; *14:* 121; *19:* 7–15, 17–19, 22, 36, 48, 61, 67, 143, 204, 265, 371, 372; *21:* 47; *25:* 39; *32:* 42; *33:* 96
Meriwether v. Caraustar Packaging Co., 326 F.3d 990, 91 FEP 978 (8th Cir. 2003) *19:* 202; *41:* 353
Merkle v. Upper Dublin Sch. Dist., 211 F.3d 782, 16 IER 432 (3d Cir. 2000) *35:* 292

Merrick v. Farmers Ins. Group, 892 F.2d 1434, 51 FEP 1391 (9th Cir. 1990) *2:* 154, 210
Merrill v. Cintas Corp., 941 F. Supp. 1040, 76 FEP 1059 (D. Kan. 1996) *18:* 64, 235, 335, 336
Merrill Lynch, Pierce, Fenner & Smith, Inc.
—EEOC v., 677 F. Supp. 918, 58 FEP 1778 (N.D. Ill. 1987) *25:* 67
—v. ENC Corp., 446 F.3d 1019 (9th Cir. 2006) *28:* 76
—v. Nixon, 210 F.3d 814, 82 FEP 1030 (8th Cir. 2000) *27:* 111; *42:* 51, 173
Merritt v. Dillard Paper Co., 120 F.3d 1181, 74 FEP 1511 (11th Cir. 1997) *14:* 21, 34
Merriweather
—v. American Cast Iron Pipe Co., 362 F. Supp. 670, 6 FEP 1242 (N.D. Ala. 1973) *4:* 405
—v. Family Dollar Stores of Ind., 103 F.3d 576, 76 FEP 1251 (7th Cir. 1996) *35:* 432
Merry v. A. Sulka & Co., 953 F. Supp. 922, 8 AD 946 (N.D. Ill. 1997) *13:* 455
Mertig v. Milliken & Michaels of Del., Inc., 923 F. Supp. 636 (D. Del. 1996) *40:* 162
Mertz v. Marsh, 786 F.2d 1578, 40 FEP 1110 (11th Cir. 1986) *41:* 165
Merwine v. Board of Trs. for State Insts. of Higher Learning, 754 F.2d 631, 37 FEP 340 (5th Cir. 1985) *4:* 338
Mesa Airlines v. United States, 951 F.2d 1186 (10th Cir. 1991) *30:* 71
Meschino v. IT&T Corp., 661 F. Supp. 254, 43 FEP 1560 (S.D.N.Y. 1987) *40:* 206
Mesnick v. General Elec. Co., 950 F.2d 816, 57 FEP 822 (1st Cir. 1991) *2:* 137; *12:* 411; *14:* 180, 186
Messer v. Meno, 936 F. Supp. 1280, 71 FEP 1372 (W.D. Tex. 1996), *aff'd in part, rev'd in part,* 130 F.3d 130, 75 FEP 838 (5th Cir. 1997) *16:* 61; *37:* 102, 115

Michas v. Health Cost Controls, 209 F.3d 687 (7th Cir. 2000) **20:** 32, 42

Michelson v. Exxon Research & Eng'g Co., 808 F.2d 1005, 42 FEP 1031 (3d Cir. 1987) **12:** 166, 168

Michigan State Employees Ass'n v. Civil Serv. Comm'n, 441 N.W.2d 423, 50 FEP 473 (Mich. Ct. App. 1989) **12:** 49

Mickel v. Employment Sec. Comm'n, 3 FEP 81 (D.S.C. 1970) **23:** 26

Mickelson v. New York Life Ins. Co., 460 F.3d 1304, 98 FEP 1485 (10th Cir. 2006) **14:** 159; **18:** 103, 235; **28:** 153

Mico Oil Co.; EEOC v., 48 FEP 1206 (D. Kan. 1988) **29:** 20

MidAmerican Energy Co. v. Electrical Workers (IBEW) Local 499, 345 F.3d 616, 173 LRRM 2353 (8th Cir. 2003) **42:** 191, 194

Middleton v. City of Flint, 92 F.3d 396, 71 FEP 962 (6th Cir. 1996) **3:** 99, 108; **34:** 200, 221; **37:** 102, 106, 126

Middleton-Keirn v. Stone, 655 F.2d 609, 26 FEP 1154 (5th Cir. 1981) **26:** 281; **39:** 174

Miecznikowski v. UPS, 1998 U.S. Dist. LEXIS 21581 (M.D. Fla. Sept. 30, 1998), aff'd, 196 F.3d 1260 (11th Cir. 1999) **13:** 252

Miele v. New York State Teamsters Conference Pension & Ret. Fund, 831 F.2d 407 (2d Cir. 1987) **41:** 263

Mieth v. Dothard, 418 F. Supp. 1169, 13 FEP 1412 (M.D. Ala. 1976), aff'd in part sub nom. Dothard v. Rawlinson, 433 U.S. 321, 15 FEP 10 (1977) **39:** 23

Migis v. Pearle Vision, Inc., 135 F.3d 1041, 78 FEP 1379 (5th Cir. 1998) **40:** 398; **41:** 218, 311

Migneault v. Peck, 158 F.3d 1131, 78 FEP 600 (10th Cir. 1998), vacated, 528 U.S. 1110, reaff'd, 204 F.3d 1004 (10th Cir. 2000) **12:** 127; **35:** 163

Migra v. Warren City Sch. Dist. Bd. of Educ., 465 U.S. 75, 33 FEP 1345 (1984) **27:** 16–18; **35:** 449

Miguel v. Guess, 112 Wash. App. 536, 51 P.3d 89 (Wash. Ct. App. 2002) **11:** 167

Mike Fink Corp.; EEOC v., 1998 WL 34078445 (M.D. Tenn. July 17, 1998) **10:** 109

Mikels v. City of Durham, 183 F.3d 323, 80 FEP 248 (4th Cir. 1999) **19:** 231, 285

Mike Smith Pontiac GMC, Inc.; EEOC v., 896 F.2d 524, 52 FEP 729 (11th Cir. 1990) **40:** 216

Milbert v. Koop, 830 F.2d 354, 1 AD 1148 (D.C. Cir. 1987) **13:** 65

Milburn v. West, 854 F. Supp. 1 (D.D.C. 1994), aff'd, 1995 WL 117983 (D.C. Cir. Feb. 7, 1995) **31:** 212

Miles
—v. Boeing Co., 154 F.R.D. 117 (E.D. Pa. 1994) **33:** 27
—v. Dell, Inc., 429 F.3d 480, 96 FEP 1639 (4th Cir. 2005) **2:** 19, 54; **14:** 16
—v. Department of Army, 881 F.2d 777, 50 FEP 1006 (9th Cir. 1989) **25:** 264
—v. M.N.C. Corp., 750 F.2d 867, 36 FEP 1289 (11th Cir. 1985) **2:** 119, 198

Millaazzo v. Universal Traffic Serv., Inc., 289 F. Supp. 2d 1251, 92 FEP 1532 (D. Colo. 2003) **40:** 454

Millage v. Sioux City, 258 F. Supp. 2d 976, 14 AD 504 (N.D. Iowa 2003) **13:** 787; **26:** 20

Millbrook v. IBP, Inc., 280 F.3d 1169, 88 FEP 297 (7th Cir. 2002) **2:** 134, 185, 193, 258; **4:** 441; **15:** 120; **16:** 62, 115, 116, 124

Miller
—v. Airborne Express, 1999 WL 47242 (N.D. Tex. Jan. 22, 1999) **13:** 251, 253
—v. Aluminum Co., 679 F. Supp. 495, 45 FEP 1775 (W.D. Pa.), aff'd, 856 F.2d 184, 52 FEP 1472 (3d Cir. 1988) **18:** 107
—v. American Family Mut. Ins. Co., 203 F.3d 997, 82 FEP 113 (7th Cir. 2000) **10:** 431; **14:** 94, 125

Mitchell—*Contd.*
—v. Hutchings, 116 F.R.D. 481, 44 FEP 615 (D. Utah 1987) *19:* 396; *33:* 97, 99
—v. Jefferson County Bd. of Educ., 936 F.2d 539, 56 FEP 644 (11th Cir. 1991) *17:* 52; *18:* 179, 317, 381
—v. Jones Truck Lines, Inc., 754 F. Supp. 584, 55 FEP 1211 (W.D. Tenn. 1990) *3:* 127, 128
—v. Keith, 752 F.2d 385, 36 FEP 1443 (9th Cir. 1985) *40:* 382
—v. Los Angeles Cmty. Coll., 861 F.2d 198 (9th Cir. 1988) *21:* 234, 237
—v. Mid-Continent Spring Co.
——466 F.2d 24, 4 FEP 1144 (6th Cir. 1972) *26:* 30, 50
——583 F.2d 275, 17 FEP 1594 (6th Cir.), *modified,* 587 F.2d 841, 23 FEP 787 (6th Cir. 1978) *40:* 530, 545
—v. Mobil Oil Corp., 896 F.2d 463, 52 FEP 374 (10th Cir. 1990) *12:* 571; *20:* 93
—v. Seaboard Sys. R.R., 883 F.2d 451, 57 FEP 619 (6th Cir. 1989) *39:* 40
—v. Secretary of Commerce, 715 F. Supp. 409, 68 FEP 482 (D.D.C. 1989), *aff'd sub nom.* Brown v. Secretary of Army, 918 F.2d 214, 68 FEP 485 (D.C. Cir. 1990) *31:* 199; *40:* 80
—v. Sisters of Charity, 924 F. Supp. 793 (S.D. Tex. 1996) *40:* 246
—v. Toledo Hosp., 964 F.2d 577, 59 FEP 76 (6th Cir. 1992) *2:* 228, 230; *20:* 15, 19
—v. Vanderbilt Univ., 389 F.3d 177, 94 FEP 1290 (6th Cir. 2004) *12:* 138
—v. Washingtonville Cent. Sch. Dist., 190 F.3d 1, 9 AD 1123 (2d Cir. 1999) *13:* 541, 583
—v. West Feliciana Parish Sch. Bd., 507 F.2d 662 (5th Cir. 1975) *40:* 92, 317
—v. Worldwide Underwriters Ins. Co., 967 F.2d 565, 59 FEP 754 (11th Cir. 1992) *20:* 15, 32
Mitchom v. Bi-State Dev. Agency, 43 Fed. Appx. 958 (7th Cir. 2002) *12:* 138

Mitroff v. Xomox Corp., 797 F.2d 271, 41 FEP 290 (6th Cir. 1986) *12:* 743
Mitsubishi Motor Mfg. of Am., Inc.; EEOC v.
—960 F. Supp. 164 (C.D. Ill. 1997) *29:* 319
—990 F. Supp. 1059, 75 FEP 1379 (C.D. Ill. 1998) *19:* 217; *25:* 230; *26:* 379; *29:* 125, 126; *32:* 43, 52, 352
Mitsubishi Motors Corp. v. Soler Chrysler-Plymouth, Inc., 473 U.S. 614 (1985) *42:* 2, 5, 6, 15–19, 123, 137
Mixson v. Southern Bell Tel. & Tel. Co., 334 F. Supp. 525, 4 FEP 27 (N.D. Ga. 1971) *10:* 286–88
Mmubango v. Leavitt, 428 F. Supp. 2d 833 (N.D. Ill. 2006) *7:* 185
Mobayed v. Kleinfeld, 1999 WL 65139 (2d Cir. Feb. 8, 1999) *12:* 273
Mobil Exploration & Producing U.S., Inc. v. NLRB, 200 F.3d 230, 163 LRRM 2387 (5th Cir. 1999) *14:* 277
M.O.C.H.A. Soc'y, Inc. v. City of Buffalo, 199 F. Supp. 2d 40 (W.D.N.Y. 2002) *24:* 115
Mockler
—v. Multnomah County, 140 F.3d 808, 76 FEP 890 (9th Cir. 1998) *19:* 307
—v. Skipper, 1994 WL 41334 (D. Or. Feb. 3, 1994) *19:* 390, 392, 393
Mogilevsky v. Bally Total Fitness Corp., 311 F. Supp. 2d 212 (D. Mass. 2004) *12:* 764
Mohamed v. Parks, 352 F. Supp. 518, 5 FEP 494 (D. Mass. 1973) *35:* 66
Mohammed
—v. Callaway, 698 F.2d 395 (10th Cir. 1983) *16:* 47
—v. May Dep't Stores, 273 F. Supp. 2d 531, 92 FEP 540 (D. Del. 2003) *27:* 33
Mohasco Corp. v. Silver, 447 U.S. 807, 23 FEP 1 (1980) *25:* 134; *26:* 57–63
Mojica v. Gannett Co., 7 F.3d 552, 62 FEP 1561 (7th Cir. 1993) (1994) *7:* 3

Mole v. Buckhorn Rubber Prods., 165 F.3d 1212, 8 AD 1873 (8th Cir. 1999) *13:* 357, 449, 488, 540

Molerio v. FBI, 36 FEP 582 (D.D.C. 1983), *aff'd*, 749 F.2d 815, 36 FEP 586 (D.C. Cir. 1984) *7:* 195; *21:* 147, 148

Molin v. Chapario Perma Fiber Corp., 2003 U.S. App. LEXIS 18415 (2d Cir. 2003) *19:* 365

Molnar

—v. Booth, 229 F.3d 593, 83 FEP 1756 (7th Cir. 2000) *19:* 247; *21:* 49; *35:* 228; *40:* 431

—v. Ebasco Constructors, Inc., 986 F.2d 115, 61 FEP 598 (5th Cir. 1993) *12:* 395

Molovinsky v. Fair Employment Council of Greater Wash., Inc., 683 A.2d 142, 72 FEP 79 (D.C. 1996) *24:* 114, 127

Molski v. Gleich, 318 F.3d 937 (9th Cir. 2003) *32:* 125, 263–72, 560, 568, 570

Molthan v. Temple Univ.

—442 F. Supp. 448, 16 FEP 581 (E.D. Pa. 1977) *18:* 155

—83 F.R.D. 368, 24 FEP 282 (E.D. Pa. 1979) *32:* 204

—93 F.R.D. 585, 28 FEP 430 (E.D. Pa. 1982), *aff'd*, 778 F.2d 955, 39 FEP 816 (3d Cir. 1985) *29:* 264

Monaco v. American Gen. Assurance Co., 359 F.3d 296, 93 FEP 523 (3d Cir.), *cert. denied*, 543 U.S. 814, 94 FEP 832 (2004) *2:* 86

Monahan v. City of Wilmington, 2004 U.S. Dist. LEXIS 1322 (D. Del. Jan. 30, 2004) *32:* 346

Monarch Mach. Tool Co.; EEOC v., 737 F.2d 1444, 42 FEP 859 (6th Cir. 1980) *32:* 467

Monclova Twp.; EEOC v., 920 F.2d 360, 54 FEP 865 (6th Cir. 1990) *12:* 118

Mondy v. Secretary of Army, 845 F.2d 1051 (D.C. Cir. 1988) *31:* 259

Mondzelewski v. Pathmark Stores, Inc., 162 F.3d 778, 8 AD 1752 (3d Cir. 1998) *2:* 65; *13:* 219–21; *16:* 29

Monell v. New York City Dep't of Soc. Servs., 436 U.S. 658, 17 FEP 873 (1978) *7:* 71; *21:* 238, 310; *35:* 29, 97, 111, 114–17, 157, 179, 183, 212; *40:* 385, 386

Monette v. Electronic Data Sys. Corp., 90 F.3d 1173 (6th Cir. 1996) *13:* 732, 747–49

Monley v. Q Int'l Courier, Inc., 128 F. Supp. 2d 1155, 85 FEP 132 (N.D. Ill. 2001) *6:* 22, 23

Monnig v. Kennecott Corp., 603 F. Supp. 1035, 37 FEP 193 (D. Conn. 1985) *26:* 107

Monongahela R.R.; OFCCP v., No. 85-OFC-2 (Apr. 2, 1986) (Recommended Decision) *38:* 586, 602

Monreal v. Potter, 367 F.3d 1224, 93 FEP 1562 (10th Cir. 2004) *31:* 174, 175

Monroe

—v. Burlington Indus., 784 F.2d 568, 40 FEP 273 (4th Cir. 1986) *16:* 84

—v. Children's Home Ass'n, 128 F.3d 591, 75 FEP 417 (7th Cir. 1997) *12:* 762

—v. Pape, 365 U.S. 167 (1961) *35:* 110

—v. United Air Lines, Inc., 736 F.2d 394, 5 EB 1745, 34 FEP 1622 (7th Cir. 1984) *12:* 548

Monroe-Lord v. Hytche, 668 F. Supp. 979 (D. Md. 1987), *aff'd*, 854 F.2d 1317, 64 FEP 1632 (4th Cir. 1988) *18:* 166

Monsanto Co. v. EEOC, 2 FEP 50 (N.D. Fla. 1969) *25:* 345, 350

Montalvo v. Radcliffe, 167 F.3d 873, 9 AD 15 (4th Cir. 1999) *13:* 859

Montana

—v. First Fed. Sav. & Loan Ass'n, 869 F.2d 100, 49 FEP 269 (2d Cir. 1989) *12:* 353

—v. United States

——440 U.S. 147 (1979) *27:* 123

——445 U.S. 960 (1980) *8:* 124

——450 U.S. 544, 101 S. Ct. 1245 (1981) *8:* 126

Montandon v. Farmland Indus., Inc., 116 F.3d 355, 74 FEP 947 (8th Cir. 1997) *13:* 556; *16:* 29

Morgan
—v. Arkansas Gazette, 897 F.2d 945, 52 FEP 431 (8th Cir. 1990) *2:* 199; *12:* 684; *39:* 15, 54, 72
—v. Hilti, Inc., 108 F.3d 1319 (10th Cir. 1997) *13:* 747
—v. Jasper, City of, 959 F.2d 1542, 58 FEP 1406 (11th Cir. 1992) *14:* 194
—v. Massachusetts Gen. Hosp., 712 F. Supp. 242, 53 FEP 1647 (D. Mass. 1989), *aff'd*, 901 F.2d 186, 53 FEP 1780 (1st Cir. 1990) *14:* 196; *20:* 41, 53; *33:* 9
—v. Northwest Permanente, P.C., 989 F. Supp. 1330 (D. Or. 1997) *13:* 534
—v. Safeway Stores, Inc., 884 F.2d 1211, 50 FEP 1339 (9th Cir. 1989) *10:* 522
—v. Servicemaster Co., 57 FEP 1423 (N.D. Ill. 1992) *12:* 484
—v. South Bend Cmty. Sch. Corp., 797 F.2d 471, 41 FEP 736 (7th Cir. 1986) *25:* 179; *43:* 43
—v. Union Metal Mfg., 757 F.2d 792, 37 FEP 625 (6th Cir. 1985) *41:* 366
—v. United Parcel Serv. of Am., Inc.
——143 F. Supp. 2d 1143 (E.D. Mo. 2000), *aff'd*, 380 F.3d 459, 94 FEP 591 (8th Cir. 2004), *cert. denied*, 544 U.S. 999 (2005) *2:* 356; *3:* 40, 129
——169 F.R.D. 349, 77 FEP 165 (E.D. Mo. 1996) *32:* 174, 191, 296, 442, 507
—v. United States Postal Serv., 798 F.2d 1162, 1 AD 963 (8th Cir. 1986) *13:* 64, 66, 954; *31:* 345
Morgan Stanley & Co.; EEOC v.
—206 F. Supp. 2d 559, 89 FEP 245 (S.D.N.Y. 2002) *29:* 148, 319
—132 F. Supp. 2d 146, 86 FEP 100 (S.D.N.Y. 2000) *29:* 47, 232
—89 FEP 1791 (S.D.N.Y. 2002) *29:* 292
Moriarty v. Consolidated Funeral Servs., Inc., 65 F. Supp. 2d 853 (N.D. Ill. 1999) *28:* 72
Moring v. Arkansas Dep't of Corr., 243 F.3d 452, 86 FEP 49 (8th Cir. 2001) *35:* 222

Morisky v. Broward County, 80 F.3d 445, 5 AD 737 (11th Cir. 1996) *4:* 39; *13:* 195, 662
Mormol v. Costco Wholesale Corp., 364 F.3d 54, 93 FEP 1045 (2d Cir. 2004) *19:* 202
Morris
—v. Amalgamated Lithographers, 994 F. Supp. 161, 83 FEP 163 (S.D.N.Y. 1998) *22:* 73, 76
—v. American Nat'l Can Corp., 730 F. Supp. 1489, 52 FEP 210 (E.D. Mo. 1989), *aff'd in part*, 952 F.2d 200, 57 FEP 946 (8th Cir. 1991) *39:* 55, 99; *40:* 43
—v. Bianchini, 1987 WL 11822, 43 FEP 674 (E.D. Va. Feb. 24, 1987), *aff'd mem.*, 838 F.2d 467, 46 FEP 176 (4th Cir. 1988) *10:* 111
—v. Electrical Sys. Div., 54 FEP 292 (N.D. Ind. 1990) *33:* 67
—v. Hobart, City of, 39 F.3d 1105, 66 FEP 285 (10th Cir. 1994) *25:* 180
—v. Lee, 83 FEP 1790 (E.D. La. 2000) *40:* 95
—v. Lindau, 196 F.3d 102 (2d Cir. 1999) *35:* 254
—v. Rumsfeld, 420 F.3d 287, 16 AD 1852 (3d Cir. 2005), *cert. denied*, 126 S. Ct. 1769 (2006) *31:* 326
—v. Russell, Burdsall & Ward Corp., 577 F. Supp. 147, 38 FEP 1453 (N.D. Ohio 1983) *12:* 205
—v. Wallace Cmty. Coll., 125 F. Supp. 2d 1315 (S.D. Ala. 2001), *aff'd*, 34 Fed. Appx. 388 (11th Cir. 2002) *16:* 121
—v. Washington Metro. Area Transit Auth., 781 F.2d 218 (D.C. Cir. 1986) *21:* 234
—v. West Palm Beach, 194 F.3d 1203 (11th Cir. 1999) *41:* 45
Morrison
—v. American Bd. of Psychiatry & Neurology, Inc., 908 F. Supp. 582, 69 FEP 1217 (N.D. Ill. 1996) *4:* 35–38; *23:* 31; *35:* 21
—v. Amway Corp., 323 F.3d 920 (11th Cir. 2003) *23:* 41
—v. Circuit City Stores, Inc., 317 F.3d 646, 90 FEP 1697 (6th Cir. 2003)

Mowery v. Rite Aid Corp., 40 Fed.
Appx. 926 (6th Cir. 2002) *18:* 72
Moyo v. Gomez, 32 F.3d 1382, 65 FEP
821, *amended,* 40 F.3d 982, 68 FEP
1419 (9th Cir. 1994) *14:* 57; *24:* 90
Moysey v. Andrus, 481 F. Supp. 850,
21 FEP 836 (D.D.C. 1979) *31:* 3,
331
Mozee
—v. American Commercial Marine
Serv. Co., 940 F.2d 1036, 56 FEP
1155 (7th Cir. 1991), *supplemented,*
963 F.2d 929, 58 FEP 1201 (7th Cir.
1992) *2:* 361; *3:* 10, 80, 147; *4:*
460; *20:* 64, 65; *35:* 59; *38:* 81
—v. Jeffboat, Inc., 746 F.2d 365, 35
FEP 1810 (7th Cir. 1984) *14:* 127,
128; *16:* 73
Muckleshoot Tribe v. Puget Sound
Power & Light Co., 875 F.2d 695
(9th Cir. 1989) *43:* 213, 214
Mueller v. CBS, Inc.
—200 F.R.D. 242 (W.D. Pa. 2001)
33: 76, 77
—201 F.R.D. 425 (W.D. Pa. 2001)
12: 284, 286, 288
Muka v. Nicolet Paper Co., 24 FEP 671
(E.D. Wis. 1979) *29:* 262, 267
Mukaddam v. Permanent Mission of
Saudi Arabia, 111 F. Supp. 2d 457,
83 FEP 1587 (S.D.N.Y. 2000) *21:*
135
Mukaida v. Hawaii, 159 F. Supp. 2d
1211 (D. Haw. 2001), *aff'd,* 85 Fed.
Appx. 631 (9th Cir. 2004) *31:* 51
Mulhall
—v. Advance Sec., Inc., 19 F.3d 586,
64 FEP 938 (11th Cir. 1994) *18:*
61, 72, 108
—v. Ashcroft, 287 F.3d 543, 88 FEP
1209 (6th Cir. 2002) *14:* 185, 386;
31: 266, 314
Mull v. Arco Durethene Plastics, Inc.,
599 F. Supp. 158, 36 FEP 1052 (N.D.
Ill. 1984), *aff'd,* 784 F.2d 284, 40
FEP 311 (7th Cir. 1986) *26:* 107
Mullane v. Central Hanover Bank &
Trust Co., 339 U.S. 306 (1950) *32:*
521

Mullen v. Treasure Chest Casino,
L.L.C., 186 F.3d 620 (5th Cir. 1999)
32: 164, 166
Mullenberg v. United States, 857 F.2d
770 (Fed. Cir. 1989) *8:* 36, 37, 39
Mullenix v. Forsyth Dental Infirmary
for Children, 965 F. Supp. 120, 77
FEP 707 (D. Mass. 1996) *18:* 250
Muller
—v. Costello, 997 F. Supp. 299, 9 AD
179 (N.D.N.Y. 1998), *aff'd,* 187 F.3d
298 (2d Cir. 1999) *13:* 227, 244,
302; *39:* 62; *40:* 57
—v. First Unum Life Ins. Co., 23 F.
Supp. 2d 231 (N.D.N.Y. 1998) *13:*
152; *21:* 56
—v. Hotsy Corp., 917 F. Supp. 1389,
6 AD 35 (N.D. Iowa 1996) *13:* 369
—v. Lujan, 928 F.2d 207, 55 FEP 560
(6th Cir. 1991) *12:* 100, 126
—v. Oregon, 208 U.S. 412 (1908) *10:*
124
—v. U.S. Steel Corp., 509 F.2d 923,
10 FEP 323 (10th Cir. 1975) *40:*
124
Mullin v. Raytheon Co., 2 F. Supp. 2d
165, 78 FEP 1166 (D. Mass. 1998),
aff'd, 164 F.3d 696, 78 FEP 1174 (1st
Cir. 1999) *2:* 210; *12:* 463, 466,
495; *18:* 214
Mullins
—v. Crowell, 228 F.3d 1305 (11th Cir.
2000) *2:* 305; *13:* 244; *31:* 310
—v. Pfizer, Inc., 828 F. Supp. 139, 62
FEP 1007 (D. Conn. 1993), *aff'd in
part,* 23 F.3d 663, 64 FEP 1184 (2d
Cir. 1994) *12:* 572
Multi-Ad Servs., Inc. v. NLRB, 255
F.3d 363, 167 LRRM 2450 (7th Cir.
2001) *14:* 287
Mummelthie v. Mason City, 873 F.
Supp. 1293, 66 FEP 1393 (N.D. Iowa
1995), *aff'd,* 78 F.3d 589, 70 FEP
928 (8th Cir. 1996) *35:* 232
Munday v. Waste Mgmt., 858 F. Supp.
1364 (D. Md. 1994), *aff'd in part &
rev'd in part,* 126 F.3d 239, 74 FEP
1478 (4th Cir. 1997) *20:* 145; *43:*
26

National City Bank; EEOC v., 694 F. Supp. 1287, 47 FEP 401 (N.D. Ohio 1987), *rev'd*, 865 F.2d 1267, 49 FEP 656 (6th Cir. 1988)   *25:* 360; *29:* 57, 59, 182

National Cleaning Contractors, Inc.; EEOC v., 56 FEP 1081 (S.D.N.Y. 1991)   *29:* 209, 222

National Coalition Gov't of Union of Burma v. Unocal, Inc., 176 F.R.D. 329 (C.D. Cal. 1997)   *32:* 133

National Collegiate Athletic Ass'n
—v. Smith, 525 U.S. 459 (1999)   *10:* 764–66
—v. Tarkanian, 488 U.S. 179 (1988)   *10:* 768; *35:* 84

National Educ. Ass'n
—EEOC v., 422 F.3d 840, 96 FEP 556 (9th Cir. 2005)   *19:* 95
—v. South Carolina. *See* South Carolina; United States v.

National Elec. Benefit Fund; EEOC v., 12 FEP 1006 (D.D.C. 1976)   *25:* 347

National Farmers Union Ins. Cos. v. Crow Tribe, 471 U.S. 845 (1985)   *8:* 124, 129

National Gay Task Force v. Board of Educ. of Oklahoma City, 729 F.2d 1270, 34 FEP 459 (10th Cir. 1984), *aff'd*, 470 U.S. 903, 37 FEP 505 (1985)   *11:* 172, 173

National League of Cities v. Usery, 426 U.S. 833, 22 WH 1064 (1976)   *18:* 16

National Organization for Women v. *See* NOW

National R.R. Passenger Corp. v. Morgan, 536 U.S. 101, 88 FEP 1601 (2002)   *3:* 103; *6:* 48; *18:* 317, 386; *19:* 71–81, 343; *26:* 11, 110, 116, 117, 126, 138, 141–51, 153, 154, 161, 162, 186–88, 377; *28:* 6; *31:* 292, 305; *32:* 349; *34:* 285; *40:* 110

National Treasury Employees Union; United States v., 513 U.S. 454, 10 IER 452 (1995)   *14:* 361, 362

NationsBank Corp. v. Herman, 174 F.3d 424, 79 FEP 1113 (4th Cir. 1999)   *38:* 576, 673, 674

Nationwide Mut. Ins. Co.
—v. Darden, 503 U.S. 318 (1992)   *18:* 21; *24:* 32, 34, 56
—v. Home Ins. Co., 278 F.3d 621 (6th Cir. 2002)   *42:* 206

Naton v. Bank of Cal., 649 F.2d 691, 27 FEP 510 (9th Cir. 1981)   *12:* 296; *18:* 331; *40:* 333

Natter Mfg. Corp. v. NLRB, 580 F.2d 948, 99 LRRM 2963 (9th Cir. 1978)   *36:* 32, 43

Navajo Freight Lines, Inc.; United States v., 525 F.2d 1318, 11 FEP 787 (9th Cir. 1975)   *17:* 106; *22:* 135

Navajo Ref. Co.; EEOC v., 593 F.2d 988, 19 FEP 184 (10th Cir. 1979)   *4:* 333; *7:* 4

Navarro v. Pfizer Corp., 261 F.3d 90, 7 WH 2d 321 (1st Cir. 2001)   *25:* 39

Navy Fed. Credit Union; EEOC v., 424 F.3d 397, 96 FEP 641 (4th Cir. 2005), *cert. denied*, 126 S. Ct. 1629 (2006)   *29:* 170

Nawrot v. CPC Int'l, 277 F.3d 896, 12 AD 1138, 87 FEP 1414 (7th Cir. 2002)   *12:* 385, 386, 410; *13:* 209, 231, 303, 304, 723, 724

Nayar v. Howard Univ., 881 F. Supp. 15 (D.D.C. 1995)   *16:* 64

Naylor v. Ga.-Pac. Corp., 875 F. Supp. 564 (N.D. Iowa 1995)   *40:* 169

NCR Corp. v. SAC-CO, Inc., 43 F.3d 1076 (6th Cir. 1995)   *42:* 209

Neal
—v. Director, D.C. Dep't of Corr., 1995 U.S. Dist. LEXIS 11469 (D.D.C. Aug. 9, 1995)   *32:* 46
—v. Honeywell, Inc., 995 F. Supp. 889, 13 IER 1408 (N.D. Ill. 1998), *aff'd*, 191 F.3d 827 (7th Cir. 1999)   *20:* 146
—v. Moore
——1994 U.S. Dist. LEXIS 21336 (D.D.C. Aug. 25, 1994)   *32:* 277
——1994 U.S. Dist. LEXIS 21339 (D.D.C. Dec. 23, 1994)   *32:* 113
—v. Newspaper Holdings, Inc., 349 F.3d 363, 173 LRRM 2577 (7th Cir. 2003)   *22:* 79

Ochoa
—v. American Oil Co., 338 F. Supp. 914, 4 FEP 361 (S.D. Tex. 1972) *40:* 312
—v. Monsanto Co., 473 F.2d 318, 5 FEP 483 (5th Cir. 1973) *3:* 140
O'Connell v. Champion Int'l Corp., 812 F.2d 393, 48 FEP 504 (8th Cir. 1987) *12:* 293
O'Connor
—v. Consolidated Coin Caterers Corp., 517 U.S. 308, 70 FEP 486 (1996) *2:* 53; *12:* 9–12, 327, 342, 343, 370, 506; *20:* 8, 18, 23, 28
—v. Davis, 126 F.3d 112, 74 FEP 1561 (2d Cir. 1997) *24:* 31
—v. DePaul Univ., 123 F.3d 665, 75 FEP 1052 (7th Cir. 1997) *12:* 433, 436
—v. Northshore Int'l Ins. Servs., 61 Fed. Appx. 722 (1st Cir.), *cert. denied*, 540 U.S. 903 (2003) *2:* 77, 78
—v. PCA Family Health Plan, Inc., 200 F.3d 1349, 81 FEP 1112 (11th Cir.), *reh'g denied*, 211 F.3d 596 (11th Cir. 2000) *10:* 496
—v. Peru State Coll.
——728 F.2d 1001, 34 FEP 85 (8th Cir. 1984) *39:* 167
——781 F.2d 632, 39 FEP 1241 (8th Cir. 1986) *2:* 135
Oconomowoc Residential Programs, Inc. v. City of Milwaukee, 300 F.3d 775, 13 AD 681 (7th Cir. 2002) *13:* 794, 795
O'Day v. McDonnell Douglas Helicopter Co., 79 F.3d 756, 70 FEP 615 (9th Cir. 1996) *39:* 73; *40:* 194, 197
Oden v. Oktibbeha County, Miss., 246 F.3d 458, 85 FEP 1377 (5th Cir. 2001) *16:* 1, 24; *35:* 30
Odima v. Westin Tucson Hotel
—991 F.2d 595, 61 FEP 961 (9th Cir. 1993) *7:* 183
—53 F.3d 1484, 67 FEP 1222 (9th Cir. 1995) *2:* 208; *16:* 146, 149, 152, 170, 171; *40:* 116, 161

Odom v. Frank, 3 F.3d 839, 65 FEP 718 (5th Cir. 1993) *16:* 73
Odomes v. Nucare, Inc., 653 F.2d 246, 26 FEP 317 (6th Cir. 1981) *18:* 113, 221
O'Donnell
—v. Barry, 148 F.3d 1126, 14 IER 1510 (D.C. Cir. 1998) *14:* 367–69
—v. Burlington Coat Factory Warehouse, Inc., 656 F. Supp. 263, 43 FEP 150 (S.D. Ohio 1987) *10:* 637
O'Driscoll v. Hercules, Inc., 54 FEP 314 (D. Utah 1990) *18:* 180
Odum v. Beverly Enter. Miss., Inc., 1998 WL 173232 (N.D. Miss. Feb. 20, 1998), *aff'd*, 165 F.3d 23 (5th Cir. 1998) *20:* 118
Odunmbaku v. New York Blood Ctr., 72 FEP 202 (S.D.N.Y. Sept. 10, 1996), *adhered to on reconsideration*, 72 FEP 1564 (S.D.N.Y. 1996) *27:* 48
Oestman v. National Farmers Union Ins. Co., 958 F.2d 303, 58 FEP 426 (10th Cir. 1992) *12:* 65
Oestringer v. Dillard Store Servs., Inc., 92 Fed. Appx. 339, 2004 WL 259737 (7th Cir. Feb. 9, 2004) *13:* 449, 519
OFCCP v. *See name of opposing party*
Office of Senate Sgt. at Arms v. Office of Senate Fair Employment Practices, 95 F.3d 1102, 6 AD 1237 (Fed. Cir. 1996) *13:* 534
Officers for Justice v. Civil Serv. Comm'n
—979 F.2d 721, 62 FEP 868 (9th Cir. 1992) *37:* 101, 317
—395 F. Supp. 378, 11 FEP 815 (N.D. Cal. 1975) *4:* 177, 378; *10:* 721–25
—473 F. Supp. 801 (N.D. Cal. 1979), *aff'd*, 688 F.2d 615, 29 FEP 1473 (9th Cir. 1984) *10:* 691; *32:* 34, 205, 528, 549; *40:* 316
Ogborn v. Food & Commercial Workers Local 881, 305 F.3d 763, 13 ADA 1071, 8 WH 2d 243 (7th Cir. 2002) *22:* 2

Olson
—v. Dubuque Cmty. Sch. Dist., 137 F.3d 609, 7 AD 1598 (8th Cir. 1998) *13:* 259, 330
—v. General Elec. Astrospace, 101 F.3d 947, 6 AD 270 (3d Cir. 1996) *13:* 331
—v. Merrill Lynch, Pierce, Fenner & Smith, Inc., 51 F.3d 157 (8th Cir. 1995) *42:* 200
—v. Philco-Ford, 531 F.2d 474, 12 FEP 426 (10th Cir. 1976) *2:* 44
—v. Rembrandt Printing Co., 511 F.2d 1228, 10 FEP 27 (8th Cir. 1975) *26:* 135
Omaha Employees Betterment Ass'n v. City of Omaha, 883 F.2d 650, 50 FEP 1265 (8th Cir. 1989) *22:* 163
Omnipoint Commc'ns, Inc. v. Planning & Zoning Comm'n of Town of Wallingford, 91 F. Supp. 2d 497 (D. Conn. 2000) *41:* 218
Oncale v. Sundowner Offshore Servs., 83 F.3d 118, 70 FEP 1303 (5th Cir. 1996), *rev'd,* 523 U.S. 75, 76 FEP 221 (1998) *2:* 105, 107; *6:* 43; *9:* 131; *11:* 7–12, 36, 37; *19:* 16, 30, 33–42, 70, 89, 96, 99, 103, 106, 108, 146, 147, 161, 165, 199, 201
O'Neal
—v. Ferguson Constr. Co., 237 F.3d 1248, 84 FEP 1491 (10th Cir. 2001) *14:* 73, 262, 265; *34:* 369; *35:* 59, 60; *40:* 47, 48, 53, 57
—v. New Albany, City of, 293 F.3d 998, 13 AD 289, 89 FEP 221 (7th Cir. 2002) *13:* 692, 697; *15:* 124
—v. Riceland Foods, 684 F.2d 577, 29 FEP 956 (8th Cir. 1982) *33:* 67; *34:* 200
Oneida Indian Nation v. City of Sherrill, 337 F.3d 139 (2d Cir. 2003) *28:* 180
O'Neil
—v. Appel, 165 F.R.D. 479 (W.D. Mich. 1996) *32:* 165
—v. Hilton Head Hosp., 115 F.3d 272, 12 IER 1579 (4th Cir. 1997) *42:* 42

O'Neill
—v. Baker, 210 F.3d 41 (1st Cir. 2000) *35:* 277–80, 283
—v. New York Times Co., 2004 WL 1047941 (D. Mass. May 7, 2004) *12:* 571
—v. Sears, Roebuck & Co., 108 F. Supp. 2d 443, 90 FEP 201 (E.D. Pa. 2000) *12:* 311, 768, 771; *40:* 95, 96
Ong v. Cleland, 642 F.2d 316, 25 FEP 994 (9th Cir. 1981) *31:* 12
Onishea v. Hopper, 171 F.3d 1289 (11th Cir. 1999) *13:* 840, 859
Onuorah v. Kmart Corp., 102 F. Supp. 2d 992 (S.D. Ind. 1999) *16:* 42, 49
O'Patka v. Menasha Corp., 878 F. Supp. 1202, 70 FEP 11 (E.D. Wis. 1995) *19:* 120, 129, 130
Operating Eng'rs
—Locals 14 & 15; EEOC v., 13 FEP 1490 (S.D.N.Y. 1976), *aff'd in part,* 553 F.2d 251, 14 FEP 870 (2d Cir. 1977) *4:* 356, 384; *22:* 212
—Local 701; United States v., 14 FEP 1400 (D. Or. 1977) *22:* 212; *38:* 622, 623
Opinions of Justices to the Senate, In re, 440 Mass. 1201, 802 N.E.2d 565 (Mass. 2004) *11:* 146
Opsteen v. Keller Structures, Inc., 408 F.3d 390, 16 AD 1281 (7th Cir. 2005) *13:* 407
Optical Cable Corp.; EEOC v.
—169 F. Supp. 2d 539 (W.D. Va. 2001) *32:* 352
—76 FEP 1552 (W.D. Va. 1998) *29:* 49
Opuku-Boateng v. California, 95 F.3d 1461, 71 FEP 1849 (9th Cir. 1996) *9:* 54, 77, 96–98
O'Quinn v. New York Univ. Med. Ctr., 163 F.R.D. 226, 68 FEP 1798 (S.D.N.Y. 1995), *motion granted in part, denied in part,* 933 F. Supp. 341 (S.D.N.Y. 1996) *33:* 116
Oracle Sec. Litig., In re, 852 F. Supp. 1437 (N.D. Cal. 1994) *41:* 296

Premier Operator Servs., Inc.; EEOC v.
—75 F. Supp. 2d 550 (N.D. Tex. 1999) *29:* 165
—113 F. Supp. 2d 1066 (N.D. Tex. 2000) *7:* 169, 170
Presbyterian Ministries, Inc.; EEOC v., 788 F. Supp 1154 (W.D. Wash. 1992) *9:* 149
Presbytery of N.J. v. Florio, 40 F.3d 1454 (3d Cir. 1994), *aff'd sub nom.* Presbytery of N.J. v. Whitman, 99 F.3d 101 (3d Cir. 1996) *11:* 61
President
—v. Illinois Bell Tel. Co., 865 F. Supp. 1279, 3 AD 1218 (N.D. Ill. 1994) *22:* 77, 90
—v. Vance, 627 F.2d 353 (D.C. Cir. 1980) *31:* 248, 265
Presseisen v. Swarthmore Coll., 442 F. Supp. 593, 15 FEP 1466 (E.D. Pa. 1977), *aff'd mem.*, 582 F.2d 1275 (3d Cir. 1978) *34:* 129
Presta v. Southeastern Pa. Transp. Auth., 1998 WL 310735 (E.D. Pa. June 11, 1998) *13:* 215
Preston
—v. Virginia ex rel. New River Cmty. Coll., 31 F.3d 203, 65 FEP 877 (4th Cir. 1994) *10:* 798, 799; *40:* 263
—v. Wisconson Health Fund, 397 F.3d 539 (7th Cir. 2005) *37:* 265
Prevo's Family Mkt., Inc.; EEOC v., 135 F.3d 1089, 8 AD 401 (6th Cir. 1998) *13:* 635
Prewitt
—v. Alexander, 173 F.R.D. 438 (N.D. Miss. 1996) *41:* 102
—v. United States Postal Serv., 662 F.2d 292, 1 AD 273, 27 FEP 1043 (5th Cir. 1981) *2:* 28; *13:* 64, 370, 954, 955
Preyer v. Dartmouth Coll., 968 F. Supp. 20 (D.N.H. 1997) *35:* 413
Price
—v. Cannon Mills Co., 607 F. Supp. 1146, 39 FEP 708 (M.D.N.C. 1985) *14:* 80
—v. Chicago, City of, 2000 U.S. Dist. LEXIS 12447 (N.D. Ill. Aug. 29,

2000), *aff'd*, 251 F.3d 656, 85 FEP 1579 (7th Cir. 2001) *3:* 94; *16:* 76, 99
—v. Choctaw Glove & Safety Co., 459 F.3d 595, 98 FEP 1101 (5th Cir. 2006) *28:* 119
—v. Delaware Dep't of Corr., 40 F. Supp. 2d 544, 84 FEP 1155 (D. Del. 1999) *35:* 239
—v. Digital Equip. Corp., 846 F.2d 1026, 47 FEP 136 (5th Cir. 1988) *26:* 355
—v. Erie County
——654 F. Supp. 1206, 43 FEP 273 (W.D.N.Y. 1987) *35:* 349
——40 FEP 115 (W.D.N.Y. 1986) *33:* 55
—v. Federal Express Corp., 283 F.3d 715, 88 FEP 619 (5th Cir. 2002) *2:* 189, 193; *15:* 112; *16:* 61, 73
—v. Lockheed Space Operations Co., 856 F.2d 1503, 47 FEP 1851 (11th Cir. 1988) *18:* 210
—v. Marshall Erdman & Assocs., Inc., 966 F.2d 320, 59 FEP 462 (7th Cir. 1992) *40:* 242
—v. Social Sec. Admin., 398 F.3d 1322 (Fed. Cir. 2005) *31:* 159
—v. Southwestern Bell Tel. Co., 687 F.2d 74, 29 FEP 1584 (5th Cir. 1982) *12:* 167
Price Waterhouse v. Hopkins, 490 U.S. 228, 49 FEP 954 (1989) *2:* 97, 98, 102, 210, 312–15, 317, 350; *7:* 183; *10:* 192–98, 637, 662, 663; *11:* 26–29, 38, 39, 48; *12:* 478; *14:* 172, 173, 213–15, 222; *15:* 132; *16:* 10; *18:* 428; *28:* 225; *34:* 6, 7, 378, 379; *37:* 311, 313–16; *40:* 229, 263, 535; *41:* 81
Pridemore v. Rural Legal Aid Soc'y, 625 F. Supp. 1180 (S.D. Ohio 1985) *13:* 229
Priest v. Rotary
—634 F. Supp. 571, 40 FEP 208 (N.D. Cal. 1986) *10:* 640; *33:* 61
—98 F.R.D. 755, 32 FEP 1064 (N.D. Cal. 1983) *33:* 90, 98

Q

Rose—*Contd.*
—v. New York City Bd. of Educ., 257 F.3d 156, 86 FEP 380 (2d Cir. 2001) *12:* 446, 451; *28:* 192, 220
—v. Potter, 2002 WL 31738799 (N.D. Ill. Dec. 4, 2002) *9:* 84
—v. Stephens, 291 F.3d 917, 18 IER 1147 (6th Cir. 2002) *14:* 375
—v. Wells Fargo & Co., 902 F.2d 1417, 52 FEP 1430 (9th Cir. 1990) *20:* 32, 59; *34:* 248
Rosell v. Wood, 357 F. Supp. 2d 123 (D.D.C. 2004) *31:* 192
Rose-Maston v. NME Hosps., Inc., 133 F.3d 1104, 75 FEP 1534 (8th Cir. 1998) *16:* 1
Rosen
—v. Columbia Univ., 68 FEP 1190 (S.D.N.Y. 1995), *aff'd*, 101 F.3d 108 (2d Cir. 1996) *12:* 387
—v. Public Serv. Elec. & Gas Co., 477 F.2d 90, 5 FEP 709 (3d Cir. 1973) *10:* 280; *27:* 160; *40:* 98
Rosenberg
—v. Merrill Lynch, Pierce, Fenner & Smith, Inc., 170 F.3d 1, 79 FEP 707 (1st Cir. 1999) *12:* 632; *42:* 32, 81, 92, 93, 135, 163
—v. University of Cincinnati, 118 F.R.D. 591 (S.D. Ohio 1988) *32:* 193
Rosenblatt v. Bivona & Cohen, P.C., 946 F. Supp. 298, 72 FEP 945 (S.D.N.Y. 1996) *6:* 22; *24:* 89
Rosenfeld v. Southern Pac. Co.
—444 F.2d 1219, 3 FEP 604 (9th Cir. 1971) *10:* 23, 27, 126, 130, 136
—519 F.2d 527, 10 FEP 1439 (9th Cir. 1975) *41:* 130, 303
Ross
—v. Buckeye Cellulose Corp., 733 F. Supp. 363, 52 FEP 1208 (M.D. Ga. 1990), *rev'd*, 980 F.2d 648, 60 FEP 822 (11th Cir. 1993) *4:* 457; *26:* 123; *40:* 52
—v. Campbell Soup Co., 237 F.3d 701, 11 AD 577 (6th Cir. 2001) *13:* 331
—v. Communications Satellite Corp., 759 F.2d 355, 37 FEP 797 (4th Cir. 1985) *14:* 142; *27:* 18, 25

—v. Denver Dep't of Health & Hosps., 883 P.2d 516 (Colo. Ct. App. 1994) *11:* 137
—v. Douglas County
——234 F.3d 391, 84 FEP 791 (8th Cir. 2000) *6:* 44
——244 F.3d 620 (8th Cir. 2001) *41:* 297
—v. Kansas City Power & Light Co., 293 F.3d 1041, 88 FEP 1796 (8th Cir. 2002) *2:* 225, 227; *14:* 181; *16:* 62
—v. University of Tex., 139 F.3d 521, 79 FEP 788 (5th Cir. 1998) *12:* 387
Rossbach v. City of Miami, 371 F.3d 1354, 15 AD 1064, 93 FEP 1064 (11th Cir. 2004) *13:* 282
Rosser v. Laborers Local 438, 616 F.2d 221, 22 FEP 1274 (5th Cir. 1980) *14:* 141; *22:* 5
Rossini v. Ogilvy & Mather, Inc., 798 F.2d 590, 42 FEP 1615 (2d Cir. 1986) *33:* 55
Rossiter v. Potter, 357 F.3d 26, 93 FEP 129 (1st Cir. 2004) *12:* 113; *31:* 78, 244
Rossy v. Roche Prods., Inc., 880 F.2d 621, 50 FEP 822 (1st Cir. 1989) *16:* 91
Roth
—v. Koppers Indus., Inc., 993 F.2d 1058, 61 FEP 1387 (3d Cir. 1993) *27:* 42
—v. Rhode Island Hosp. Trust Nat'l Bank, 848 F. Supp. 15, 64 FEP 776 (D.R.I. 1994) *12:* 169
Rothe Dev. Corp. v. United States Dep't of Def.
—262 F.3d 1306 (Fed. Cir. 2001) *37:* 103, 163
—49 F. Supp. 2d 937 (W.D. Tex. 1999) *39:* 135
—324 F. Supp. 2d 840 (W.D. Tex. 2004) *37:* 160
Rothman v. Emory Univ., 123 F.3d 446, 7 AD 372 (7th Cir. 1997) *2:* 199
Rothmeier v. Investment Advisers, Inc., 85 F.3d 1328, 71 FEP 1458 (8th Cir. 1996) *12:* 433, 441, 442

3372   EMPLOYMENT DISCRIMINATION LAW

Scullin Steel Co., 65 NLRB 1294, 17 LRRM 286 (1946), *enforced as modified*, 161 F.2d 143, 20 LRRM 2058 (8th Cir. 1947) *36:* 94

Scully v. Summers, 2000 WL 1234588 (S.D.N.Y. Aug. 30, 2000) *16:* 145, 147, 148, 153

Scusa v. Nestle U.S.A. Co., 181 F.3d 958, 80 FEP 239 (8th Cir. 1999) *19:* 92, 103

SDDS, Inc., In re, 225 F.3d 970 (8th Cir. 2000) *21:* 273

S.D. Myers, Inc. v. City & County of San Francisco, 253 F.3d 461, 85 FEP 1802 (9th Cir. 2001) *11:* 63

Seaboard Lumber Co. v. United States, 308 F.3d 1283 (Fed. Cir. 2002) *34:* 27

Seabrook v. City of N.Y., 2001 WL 40767 (S.D.N.Y. Jan. 16, 2001) *9:* 109

Seafarers Union (SIU); EEOC v., 394 F.3d 197, 95 FEP 35 (4th Cir. 2005) *12:* 131; *25:* 39, 46

Sealed Case 00-5116, In re, 254 F.3d 233 (D.C. Cir. 2001) *41:* 160

Seaman
—v. C.S.P.H., Inc.
——179 F.3d 297 (5th Cir. 1999) *13:* 616
——1997 WL 538751 (N.D. Tex. Aug. 25, 1997) *13:* 215
—v. Spring Lake Park Indep. Sch. Dist. No. 16, 387 F. Supp. 1168, 10 FEP 31 (D. Minn. 1974) *40:* 303

Seamons v. Snow, 84 F.3d 1226 (10th Cir. 1996) *10:* 823

Searles v. Van Bebber, 64 F. Supp. 2d 1033 (D. Kan. 1999), *vacated*, 251 F.3d 869 (10th Cir. 2001) *41:* 218

Sears
—v. Atchison, Topeka & Santa Fe Ry.
——749 F.2d 1451, 36 FEP 783 (10th Cir. 1984) *40:* 94
——454 F. Supp. 158, 17 FEP 1138 (D. Kan.), *determination of remedies*, 19 FEP 1007 (D. Kan. 1978), *aff'd in part*, 645 F.2d 1365, 25 FEP 337 (10th Cir. 1981) *17:* 66, 68, 69, 72, 76, 77; *22:* 195; *34:* 246

—v. EEOC, 42 FEP 1890 (D.D.C. 1987) *28:* 8; *29:* 67

Sears, Roebuck & Co.
—EEOC v.
——650 F.2d 14, 25 FEP 1338 (2d Cir. 1981) *24:* 138; *29:* 93, 109
——233 F.3d 432, 11 AD 193 (7th Cir. 2000) *13:* 303; *20:* 96, 142
——243 F.3d 846, 85 FEP 525 (4th Cir. 2001) *2:* 121, 185, 190; *7:* 6
——490 F. Supp. 1245, 22 FEP 1479 (M.D. Ala. 1980) *24:* 138; *29:* 93
——504 F. Supp. 241, 24 FEP 325 (N.D. Ill. 1980), *aff'd*, 839 F.2d 302, 45 FEP 1257 (7th Cir. 1988) *24:* 138
——628 F. Supp. 1264, 39 FEP 1672 (N.D. Ill. 1986), *aff'd*, 839 F.2d 302, 45 FEP 1257 (7th Cir. 1988) *3:* 139, 145; *18:* 121, 347; *34:* 124, 189, 216, 275, 289
——857 F. Supp. 1233, 65 FEP 479 (N.D. Ill. 1994), *modified*, 883 F. Supp. 211, 70 FEP 175 (N.D. Ill. 1995) *12:* 567, 646; *43:* 111, 181, 182
——114 F.R.D. 615, 42 FEP 1358 (N.D. Ill. 1987) *29:* 344
——22 FEP 457, *motion granted*, 24 FEP 937 (N.D. Ga. 1980) *24:* 138; *25:* 223; *29:* 77
——50 FEP 1123 (N.D. Cal. 1989) *29:* 93
——1991 U.S. Dist. LEXIS 3321, 55 FEP 482 (D. Or. Mar. 12, 1991) *25:* 317; *27:* 30; *29:* 13
—v. EEOC, 581 F.2d 941, 17 FEP 897 (D.C. Cir. 1978) *33:* 39
—v. General Servs. Admin., 402 F. Supp. 378, 11 FEP 727 (D.D.C. 1975) *38:* 655

Seaton v. Sky Realty Co., 491 F.2d 634 (7th Cir. 1974) *40:* 396, 399

Seaworth v. Pearson, 203 F.3d 1056 (8th Cir. 2000) *9:* 63, 118, 119

Seay v. Tennessee Valley Auth., 339 F.3d 454, 92 FEP 577 (6th Cir. 2003) *16:* 103

Sherpell v. Humnoke Sch. Dist. No. 5, 874 F.2d 536, 49 FEP 1405 (8th Cir. 1989), *aff'd*, 985 F.2d 566 (8th Cir. 1991) *35:* 59

Sherrod
—v. American Airlines, 132 F.3d 1112, 7 AD 1298 (5th Cir.), *aff'd without opinion*, 163 F.3d 1356 (5th Cir. 1998), *aff'd without opinion*, 211 F.3d 592 (5th Cir. 2000) *13:* 319; *14:* 186, 188
—v. Philadelphia Gas Works, 209 F. Supp. 2d 443, 89 FEP 617, 7 WH 2d 1748 (E.D. Pa. 2002), *aff'd*, 57 Fed. Appx. 68 (3d Cir. 2003) *16:* 58
—v. Sears, Roebuck & Co., 785 F.2d 1312, 40 FEP 717 (5th Cir. 1986) *12:* 360

Sherry
—v. Protection, Inc., 14 F. Supp. 2d 1055, 4 WH 2d 1598 (N.D. Ill. 1998) *41:* 94
—v. Sisters of Charity Med. Ctr., 5 WH 2d 1132 (E.D.N.Y. 1999) *42:* 81

Sherwood Med. Indus., Inc.; EEOC v., 452 F. Supp. 678, 17 FEP 441 (M.D. Fla. 1978) *29:* 75, 99, 211

Shick v. Illinois Dep't of Human Servs., 307 F.3d 605, 90 FEP 78 (7th Cir. 2002) *40:* 234, 335

Shidaker v. Carlin, 782 F.2d 746, 39 FEP 1768 (7th Cir. 1986), *vacated sub nom.* Tisch v. Shidaker, 481 U.S. 1001, 43 FEP 640 (1987) *34:* 235

Shieh v. Lyng, 710 F. Supp. 1024, 50 FEP 1353 (E.D. Pa. 1989), *aff'd mem.*, 897 F.2d 523, 52 FEP 1184 (3d Cir. 1990) *7:* 186

Shield Club v. City of Cleveland, 838 F.2d 138, 45 FEP 1539 (6th Cir. 1987) *4:* 433

Shields
—v. BellSouth Adver. & Publ'g Co., 254 F.3d 986, 11 AD 1716 (11th Cir. 2001) *27:* 27
—v. Fort James Corp., 305 F.3d 1280, 89 FEP 1280, 89 FEP 1646 (11th Cir. 2002) *26:* 140, 166; *35:* 388

Shikles v. Sprint/United Mgmt. Co., 426 F.3d 1304, 96 FEP 1156 (10th Cir. 2005) *12:* 224; *25:* 150; *28:* 4, 5, 12

Shipes v. Trinity Indus., Inc.
—987 F.2d 311, 66 FEP 375 (5th Cir. 1993) *32:* 174, 476, 477
—40 FEP 1136 (E.D. Tex. 1981) *33:* 6

Shipp v. Tennessee Dep't of Employment Sec., 581 F.2d 1167, 17 FEP 1430 (6th Cir. 1978) *23:* 25

Shirey v. Devine, 670 F.2d 1188, 1 AD 298 (D.C. Cir. 1982) *13:* 72; *31:* 321

Shiring v. Runyon, 90 F.3d 827, 5 AD 1216 (3d Cir. 1996) *13:* 545, 598

Shirley v. Chrysler First, Inc., 970 F.2d 39, 59 FEP 1434 (5th Cir. 1992) *14:* 142

Shoney's, Inc.; EEOC v., 28 F.3d 1213, 1994 WL 325995 (6th Cir. July 5, 1994) *29:* 344

Shore v. Fed. Express Corp.
—777 F.2d 1155, 39 FEP 809 (6th Cir. 1985) *40:* 160
—42 F.3d 373 (6th Cir. 1994) *40:* 70

Shores v. Publix Super Mkts., Inc.
—1996 WL 407850 (M.D. Fla. Mar. 12, 1996) *16:* 52; *32:* 113, 194, 195, 296, 442; *34:* 61
—1996 WL 859985 (M.D. Fla. Nov. 25, 1996), *vacated*, 1997 U.S. Dist. LEXIS 16778 (M.D. Fla. Jan. 27, 1997) *29:* 152; *32:* 427

Shorette v. Rite Aid of Me., Inc., 155 F.3d 8, 78 FEP 736 (1st Cir. 1998) *2:* 213; *12:* 396, 450

Shott v. Rush-Presbyterian-St. Luke's Med. Ctr., 338 F.3d 736, 14 AD 1333 (7th Cir. 2003) *12:* 767; *41:* 136

Shotz v. City of Plantation, Fla., 344 F.3d 1161, 14 AD 1395 (11th Cir. 2003) *13:* 26; *14:* 256

Showalter v. University of Pittsburgh Med. Ctr., 190 F.3d 231, 80 FEP 1161 (3d Cir. 1999) *12:* 344, 364, 436

Snell—*Contd.*
—v. Suffolk County, 782 F.2d 1094, 39 FEP 1590 (2d Cir. 1986) *7:* 15
Snetsinger v. Montana Univ. Sys., 325 Mont. 148, 104 P.3d 445 (2004) *11:* 135
Snider
—v. Belvidere Twp.
——216 F.3d 616, 83 FEP 110 (7th Cir. 2000) *18:* 440
——1998 WL 920400 (N.D. Ill. Dec. 28, 1998) *18:* 34
—v. Circle K Corp., 923 F.2d 1404, 58 FEP 723 (10th Cir. 1991) *43:* 43
—v. Consolidated Coal Co., 973 F.2d 555, 59 FEP 1143 (7th Cir. 1992) *19:* 438; *34:* 367
—v. Jefferson State Cmty. Coll., 344 F.3d 1325, 92 FEP 1009 (11th Cir. 2003) *11:* 25
Snow
—v. BE&K Constr. Co., 126 F. Supp. 2d 5, 84 FEP 1260 (D. Me. 2001) *42:* 118, 119
—v. Pillsbury Co., 650 F. Supp. 299, 42 FEP 1391 (D. Minn. 1986) *40:* 252
Snyder v. Murray City Corp., 159 F.3d 1227 (10th Cir. 1998) *9:* 21
Snyder Doors; EEOC v., 844 F. Supp. 1020, 63 FEP 1292 (E.D. Pa. 1994) *14:* 48
Sobba v. Pratt Cmty. Coll. & Area Vocational Sch., 117 F. Supp. 2d 1043 (D. Kan. 2000) *18:* 170
Sobel v. Yeshiva Univ.
—839 F.2d 18, 45 FEP 1785, *amended,* 47 FEP 912 (2d Cir. 1988) *3:* 139; *34:* 124
—438 F. Supp. 625, 21 FEP 47 (S.D.N.Y. 1977) *29:* 255
Soble v. University of Md., 572 F. Supp. 1509, 33 FEP 611 (D. Md. 1983) *26:* 293
Sobol v. Kidder, Peabody & Co., 49 F. Supp. 2d 208, 83 FEP 35 (S.D.N.Y. 1999) *18:* 191, 233; *42:* 231
Social Servs. Union Local 535 v. County of Santa Clara, 609 F.2d 944,
21 FEP 684 (9th Cir. 1979) *22:* 199–201; *32:* 106
Society for Individual Rights, Inc. v. Hampton, 63 F.R.D. 399, 11 FEP 1243 (N.D. Cal. 1973), *aff'd,* 528 F.2d 905 (9th Cir. 1975) *32:* 162
Socks-Brunot v. Hirschvogel, 184 F.R.D. 113 (S.D. Ohio 1999) *19:* 407
Socorro; United States v., 25 FEP 815 (D.N.M. 1976) *14:* 29
Soderbeck v. Burnett County, 752 F.2d 285 (7th Cir. 1985) *14:* 375
Sofferin v. American Airlines, Inc., 923 F.2d 552, 56 FEP 338 (7th Cir. 1991) *25:* 99, 126; *26:* 67
Soileau v. Guilford of Me., Inc., 105 F.3d 12, 6 AD 437 (1st Cir. 1997) *13:* 259; *14:* 209
Sokol
—v. New United Motor Mfg., 9 AD 1767 (N.D. Cal. 1999) *32:* 57
—v. Smith, 671 F. Supp. 1243 (W.D. Mo. 1987) *10:* 517
Soledad v. U.S. Dep't of Treasury, 304 F.3d 500, 13 AD 865 (5th Cir. 2002) *13:* 752, 758; *16:* 24
Soliman v. Ebasco Servs., Inc., 822 F.2d 320, 51 FEP 1067 (2d Cir. 1987) *41:* 99
Solon
—v. Gary Cmty. Sch. Corp., 180 F.3d 844, 80 FEP 377 (7th Cir. 1999) *12:* 559
—v. Kaplan, 398 F.3d 629, 95 FEP 289 (7th Cir. 2005) *24:* 56
Solt v. Alpo Petfoods, Inc., 837 F. Supp. 681, 67 FEP 684 (E.D. Pa. 1993), *aff'd,* 30 F.3d 1488, 69 FEP 1601 (3d Cir. 1994) *12:* 34
Somers v. Aldine Indep. Sch. Dist., 464 F. Supp. 900, 22 FEP 1097 (S.D. Tex. 1979), *aff'd,* 620 F.2d 298, 23 FEP 778 (5th Cir. 1980) *10:* 462; *40:* 120
Sommers
—v. Budget Mktg., Inc., 667 F.2d 748, 27 FEP 1217 (8th Cir. 1982) *10:* 656; *11:* 31, 34, 35, 45

Thomas—*Contd.*
—v. National Football League Players Ass'n, 131 F.3d 198, 76 FEP 1590 (D.C. Cir. 1997), *vacated in part*, 1998 U.S. App. LEXIS 3634, 87 FEP 893 (D.C. Cir. Feb. 25, 1998), *rev'd*, 273 F.3d 1124, 87 FEP 984 (D.C. Cir. Dec. 11, 2001) *14:* 232; *40:* 114; *41:* 287, 301
—v. Resort Health Related Facility, 539 F. Supp. 630, 31 FEP 65 (E.D.N.Y. 1982) *40:* 161
—v. Review Bd. of Ind. Sec. Div., 450 U.S. 707, 25 FEP 629 (1981) *9:* 14
—v. Rite Aid Corp., 147 LRRM 2886 (E.D. Pa. 1994), *aff'd*, 68 F.3d 457 (3d Cir. 1995) *22:* 76, 81, 86, 165
—v. Rohner-Gehrig & Co., 582 F. Supp. 669, 34 FEP 887 (N.D. Ill. 1984) *35:* 312
—v. St. Francis Hosp. & Med. Ctr., 990 F. Supp. 81, 82 FEP 1379 (D. Conn. 1998) *16:* 92
—v. Texas Dep't of Criminal Justice, 297 F.3d 361, 89 FEP 452 (5th Cir. 2002) *16:* 149, 153; *40:* 409
—v. Union Indus., 98 Fed. Appx. 462 (6th Cir. 2004) *21:* 330
—v. Washington County Sch. Bd., 915 F.2d 922, 53 FEP 175 (4th Cir. 1990) *15:* 18, 41; *34:* 267, 327; *39:* 26, 43, 96
Thomas & Thomas Rodmakers, Inc. v. Newport Adhesives & Composites, Inc., 209 F.R.D. 159 (C.D. Cal. 2002) *32:* 394
Thomason v. Prudential Ins. Co. of Am., 866 F. Supp. 1329, 74 FEP 1841 (D. Kan. 1994) *24:* 40
Thomasson v. Perry, 80 F.3d 915 (4th Cir. 1996) *11:* 200, 202
Thomforde v. International Bus. Machs. Corp., 406 F.3d 500, 95 FEP 1145 (8th Cir. 2005) *12:* 620, 629; *43:* 63, 64
Thomlinson v. City of Omaha, 63 F.3d 786, 4 AD 1319 (8th Cir. 1995) *41:* 261, 286

Thompkins v. Morris Brown Coll., 752 F.2d 558, 37 FEP 24 (11th Cir. 1985) *20:* 11
Thompson
—v. Albuquerque, 950 F. Supp. 1098 (D.N.M. 1996) *18:* 72, 75
—v. Borg-Warner Prot. Servs. Corp., 1996 WL 162990 (N.D. Cal. Mar. 11, 1996) *13:* 683, 701
—v. Colorado, 278 F.3d 1020, 13 AD 192 (10th Cir. 2001) *13:* 174
—v. Irwin Home Equity, 300 F.3d 88 (1st Cir. 2002) *42:* 135
—v. John L. Williams Co., 686 F. Supp. 315, 46 FEP 1378 (M.D. Ga. 1988) *18:* 253, 292; *40:* 307
—v. Machinists, 580 F. Supp. 662, 35 FEP 845 (D.D.C. 1984) *35:* 333
—v. McDonnell Douglas Corp., 416 F. Supp. 972, 14 FEP 1573 (E.D. Mo. 1976), *aff'd*, 552 F.2d 220, 14 FEP 1582 (8th Cir. 1977) *4:* 486; *20:* 74
—v. Mississippi State Pers. Bd., 674 F. Supp. 198, 45 FEP 530 (N.D. Miss. 1987) *4:* 338, 358; *10:* 653; *34:* 76, 322
—v. Pharmacy Corp. of Am., Inc., 334 F.3d 1242, 92 FEP 129 (11th Cir. 2003) *16:* 62
—v. Prudential Ins. Co. of Am., 795 F. Supp. 1337, 59 FEP 263 (D.N.J. 1992), *aff'd*, 993 F.2d 226, 62 FEP 1056 (3d Cir. 1993) *12:* 188, 190, 484, 585
—v. Runyon, 4 AD 188 (W.D. Mo. 1994), *aff'd*, 46 F.3d 1136, 4 AD 512 (8th Cir. 1995) *13:* 372
—v. Sawyer
——678 F.2d 257, 28 FEP 1614 (D.C. Cir. 1982) *18:* 87, 122, 264, 299, 313; *39:* 128; *40:* 112, 226, 243, 495
——586 F. Supp. 635, 34 FEP 1327 (D.D.C. 1984) *41:* 379
Thoms v. ABF Freight Sys., 31 F. Supp. 2d 1119 (E.D. Wis. 1998) *13:* 350, 784
Thomsen v. Romeis, 198 F.3d 1022, 15 IER 1599 (7th Cir. 2000) *13:* 580

Walters
—v. Atlanta, City of, 803 F.2d 1135, 42 FEP 387 (11th Cir. 1986) *16:* 160, 161; *39:* 89, 90; *40:* 127, 140, 409, 415
—v. Metropolitan Educ. Enters., Inc., 519 U.S. 202, 72 FEP 1211 (1997) *12:* 78–80; *21:* 10–12; *23:* 39; *25:* 39
—v. Robert Bosch Corp., 683 F.2d 89 (4th Cir. 1982) *25:* 142
—v. Schuylkill County, 129 F. Supp. 2d 726 (M.D. Pa. 2001) *12:* 93
Walther v. Lone Star Gas Co., 952 F.2d 119, 59 FEP 848 (5th Cir. 1992) *12:* 473, 505; *40:* 220, 505
Waltman v. International Paper Co., 875 F.2d 468, 50 FEP 179 (5th Cir. 1989) *2:* 200; *19:* 181, 182
Walton
—v. Bisco Indus., Inc., 119 F.3d 368, 75 FEP 42 (5th Cir. 1997) *2:* 145
—v. Johnson & Johnson Servs., Inc., 347 F.3d 1272, 92 FEP 1284 (11th Cir. 2003), *cert. denied*, 541 U.S. 959 (2004) *19:* 304
—v. McDonnell Douglas Corp., 167 F.3d 423, 78 FEP 1854 (8th Cir. 1999) *12:* 449
—v. Mental Health Ass'n of Pa., 168 F.3d 661, 9 AD 34 (3d Cir. 1999) *13:* 447, 793, 794, 810
—v. Nalco Chem. Co., 272 F.3d 13, 87 FEP 492 (1st Cir. 2001) *2:* 216; *12:* 425, 447
Wambheim v. J.C. Penney Co.
—642 F.2d 362, 27 FEP 1495 (9th Cir. 1981) *10:* 296, 521
—705 F.2d 1492, 31 FEP 1297 (9th Cir. 1983) *10:* 294, 295, 297; *18:* 258, 259
Wamsley v. Champlin Ref. and Chems., Inc., 11 F.3d 534, 63 FEP 821 (5th Cir. 1993) *43:* 123, 259
W&O, Inc.; EEOC v., 213 F.3d 600, 83 FEP 117 (11th Cir. 2000) *10:* 347; *28:* 187, 188, 191; *29:* 145; *32:* 318, 471, 482, 486; *39:* 82; *40:* 258; *41:* 218

Wangsness v. Watertown Sch. Dist. No. 14-4, 541 F. Supp. 332, 29 FEP 375 (D.S.D. 1982) *40:* 212, 305
Wanpanoag Tribe of Gay Head (Aquinnah) v. Massachusetts Comm'n Against Discrimination, 63 F. Supp. 2d 119 (D. Mass. 1999) *8:* 107, 112
Ward
—v. EEOC, 719 F.2d 311 (9th Cir. 1983) *29:* 67
—v. Gulfstream Aerospace Corp., 894 F. Supp. 1573 (S.D. Ga. 1995) *34:* 183
—v. Massachusetts Health Research Inst., Inc., 209 F.3d 29, 10 AD 776 (1st Cir. 2000) *13:* 401, 533, 732
—v. Papa's Pizza To Go, Inc., 907 F. Supp. 1535 (S.D. Ga. 1995), *aff'd in part, vacated in part & remanded*, 197 F.3d 929 (8th Cir. 1999) *40:* 246
—v. Proctor & Gamble Paper Prods. Co., 111 F.3d 558, 73 FEP 1182 (8th Cir. 1997) *2:* 68
—v. Skinner, 943 F.2d 157, 1 AD 1881 (1st Cir. 1991) *13:* 336
—v. W&H Voortman, Ltd., 685 F. Supp. 231, 46 FEP 1490 (M.D. Ala. 1988) *21:* 2, 120
Wardle v. Ute Indian Tribe, 623 F.2d 670 (10th Cir. 1980) *8:* 94–96
Wards Cove Packing Co. v. Atonio, 490 U.S. 642, 49 FEP 1519 (1989), *on remand*, 1991 U.S. Dist. LEXIS 5486, 54 FEP 1623 (W.D. Wash. Apr. 12, 1991), *aff'd in later proceeding*, 231 F.3d 572, 84 FEP 474 (9th Cir. 2000) *3:* 36, 39, 42, 60, 62, 64, 101–06, 126, 127, 161; *4:* 80, 122, 347; *10:* 701; *12:* 498, 514; *13:* 760, 762; *15:* 8, 36, 158, 159; *16:* 126, 134, 137; *25:* 86; *32:* 33; *33:* 12; *34:* 87, 104, 105, 138–40, 151, 152, 209, 210, 220, 229–34, 246, 303; *38:* 457, 513
Wardwell v. School Bd. of Palm Beach County, Fla., 786 F.2d 1554 (11th Cir. 1986) *20:* 126
Ware v. Wyoming Bd. of Law Exam'rs, 973 F. Supp. 1339 (D. Wyo. 1997),

INDEX

*References are to chapter and section numbers (e.g., **13:** VI.C; **38:** VI.D.2 refers to Section VI.C in Chapter 13 and Section VI.D.2 in Chapter 38; **33:**II.B.n20 refers to text within footnote 20 of Section II.B. in Chapter 33). Alphabetization is word-by-word (e.g., "Construct validation of scored tests" precedes "Construction contractors").*

A

Ability tests
See also Scored tests for employment decisions
adverse impact claims, **4:** I.B.1
sex discrimination, **10:** X
Abortion, *10:* VII.A.3.b
Abrogation of sovereign immunity, *21:* II.B
See also Immunity
Absences
See also Attendance requirements; Leaves of absence
concerted absence, whether protected, **14:** III.D.6
disability discrimination (ADA), **13:** V.B.5
sick leave, pregnancy exclusion, **10:** VII.A.2
Academic privilege, *33:* III.A.1
Accent as basis for discrimination, *7:* III.C
Access for disabled employees, *13:* VI.D.2.a
Access to information
See also Confidential information
EEOC files, **25:** V.A
federal contractor records. *See* Federal contractors and subcontractors
Freedom of Information Act, **33:** II.B; **38:** III.B.2.a
See also Freedom of Information Act (FOIA)

Accommodation of disability. *See* Reasonable accommodation of disability
Accommodation of religion. *See* Religious accommodation
Accommodation of sex, *10:* II.B.3
Actions, civil. *See* Class actions; Litigation; Private right of action
ADA. *See* Americans with Disabilities Act
Addictions. *See* Drug use and abuse
ADEA. *See* Age Discrimination in Employment Act
Administrative employees
Equal Pay Act, applicability, **18:** II.A.2
Administrative enforcement
attorney's fees before administrative agencies, **41:** II.E
disability discrimination, **13:** VIII.A.1
federal aid recipients, **13:** VIII.B.3.a
exhaustion of remedies. *See* Exhaustion of administrative remedies
federal contractors, **38:** VIII.A
federal employees, **31:** II
IRCA enforcement, **7:** II.D.2
Title IX of Education Amendments of 1972, **10:** XI.A.2
Administrative law judges
federal employee cases
appeals in mixed cases, **31:** II.A.2.b.iii

offsets, *40:* IV.C.4
period of recovery, *40:* II.B.2
  commencement of period, *40:* II.B.2.a
  termination of period, *40:* II.B.2.b
promotion cases, *16:* IX
proof of failure to mitigate, *40:* II.B.2.b.ii
reduction of award for mitigation of damages, *40:* II.B.2.b.ii
reinstatement offer, effect, *40:* II.B.2.b.iii
Revenue Ruling 93-88, *40:* IV.C.4.d
sale of business, terminating coverage period, *40:* II.B.2.b.v
sexual harassment claims, *19:* IV.D.1
Small Business Job Protection Act of 1996, legislation on taxability, *40:* IV.C.4.d
tax consequences, *40:* II.B.1.e, IV.C.4.d
termination of period of recovery, *40:* II.B.2.b
unavailability for work, effect, *40:* IV.C.4.c
undocumented aliens, *7:* II.A.2.a
unemployment, deduction for, *40:* IV.C.4.a
withholding obligations, *40:* IV.C.4.d
workers' compensation, deduction for, *40:* IV.C.4.a
Bad debt information, *4:* II.D
Bakke* case, *37: III.B.1.a
Bankruptcy
automatic stay, effect on EEOC subpoena, *25:* IV.C; *29:* II.A.3
class actions against bankrupt employer, *32:* V.D
Title VII charges, effect, *24:* II.A
Bar doctrines. *See* Preclusion
Bargaining. *See* Collective bargaining; Collective bargaining agreements

Bars to actions
exhaustion of remedies, *27:* II
mootness, *27:* III.A.2
preclusion, *27:* I
  See also Preclusion
preemption, *27:* IV
ripeness, *27:* III.A.2
standing, *27:* III.A.1
Beards. *See* Personal appearance
Beneficial female protection laws, *10:* II.D.3
Benefit seniority, *17:* II.A
Benefits
See also specific benefit (e.g., Health insurance)
ADEA prohibition against denial due to age, *12:* V
age-based reductions, *12:* XI.D
back pay, calculation to include, *40:* II.B.1.b
disability discrimination, *13:* VI.F
essential job functions, effect of statements in applications for benefits on, *13:* V.C
pregnancy and childbirth, *10:* VII.D
property interest in, *13:* III.A.2
religion as BFOQ, *9:* VI.F
sex discrimination, *10:* VI
sexual orientation discrimination, *11:* II.D
Bennett Amendment, *10:* VI.A; *18:* III.B, IV.E
BFOQs. *See* Bona fide occupational qualifications
BIA (Bureau of Indian Affairs), *8:* II.B
Biased comments, *2:* II.C.2
Bidding on promotion openings, *16:* IV
Bifurcation of class actions, *32:* III.B.2, VIII.D.1
Birth. *See* Pregnancy and childbirth
Bisexuality
See also Sexual orientation discrimination
sexual harassment, *19:* II.B.4
Blacks. *See* Race and color discrimination

nondecisionmakers' statements, examples, *2:* II.C.2
pattern-or-practice cases, proof in, *2:* III; *3:* I
pregnancy and childbirth, *10:* VII.A.1
preponderance of evidence standard, *2:* II.E, II.G, III
presumption of discrimination, *2:* II.A.2, III
pretext, *2:* II.C
  generally, *2:* II.C.1
  biased comments, *2:* II.C.2
  comparative evidence, *2:* II.C.3
  employer's explanation, strength of, *2:* II.C.5
    honest belief, role of, *2:* II.C.5.c
    multiple explanations, *2:* II.C.5.b
    prior performance history, probativeness of, *2:* II.C.5.a
    same decisionmaker inference, *2:* II.C.5.d
  judgment as matter of law, *2:* II.C.1
  pretext-plus standard, *2:* II.C.1; *16:* V
  prior disparate treatment, *2:* II.C.6
  procedural irregularities, *2:* II.C.6
  statistics, *2:* II.C.4
  stray remarks, *2:* II.C.2
  summary judgment, *2:* II.B, II.C.1
prima facie case, *2:* II.A.2, II.F
  discharge, *20:* II.B
  prior instances of disparate treatment used in evidence, *2:* II.C.5.d
  promotion cases, *Ch.* 16
  See also Promotions
  delay as religious discrimination, *9:* IV
  prima facie case analysis, *16:* I
proof in class actions and pattern-or-practice cases, *2:* III
proof in individual cases, *2:* II

elements of case, *2:* II.A.2
employer's burden of proof, *2:* II.B; *15:* III.B
inference or rebuttal presumption of illegal discrimination, *2:* II.A.2
jury instructions, *2:* II.E, II.G
mixed-motive cases, *2:* II.E, II.G
order of proof, *2:* II.D
plaintiff's proof of pretext, *2:* II.C; *15:* III.B
promotion cases, *Ch.* 16
punitive damages, *2:* II.G; *3:* IV; *40:* V.C.1
qualification for job, *2:* II.A.2
reinstatement, *2:* II.G
religious corporations, Title VII exemptions, *9:* VI.B
religious discrimination, *9:* I, IV
reverse discrimination, *2:* II.A.4.a; *37:* II
scored tests for employment decisions, *4:* I.E.1
sexual orientation discrimination, *2:* II.A.4.d
statistical proof, *2:* II.C.4, III
  ADEA, *12:* X.B.3
  class actions, *2:* III
  pretext, *2:* II.C.4
  promotions, *16:* V
subjective criteria for employment decisions, *4:* III.A, III.C.1
summary judgment motions, *28:* VI.C
testing claims, *4:* I.E.1
theory, *2:* I
Disruptive conduct of employees, *14:* III.D, VI.C.2
District offices, EEOC, *25:* I.A
Doctors' staff privileges. *See* Hospitals
DOJ. *See* Justice Department
DOL. *See* Labor Department
Domestic Partner Rights and Responsibilities Act of 2003 (California), *11:* II.D
Domestic partners. *See* Marital status discrimination; Sexual orientation discrimination

Title VII—*Contd.*
pattern-or-practice suits. *See* Pattern-or-practice cases
personal staff exemption to qualify as charging party, ***24:*** II.C
policymaking appointees, exemption, ***21:*** I.B.3
posting requirements for EEOC notices, ***25:*** II.B
preclusion, ***27:*** I.A
See also Preclusion
preliminary injunctions, ***39:*** VI.B
private membership clubs, exemption, ***21:*** I.B.2
promotion cases, ***Ch.*** 16
See also Promotions
provisions of enforcement. *See this heading:* EEOC enforcement
public officials, exemption, ***21:*** I.B.3
public sector suits, ***30:*** I
race discrimination. *See* Race and color discrimination
reasonable cause determination, ***29:*** II.A.4
religious accommodation. *See* Religious accommodation
religious discrimination. *See* Religious discrimination
remedies. *See* Remedies; *specific type of remedy (e.g., Back pay)*
reporting requirements, ***25:*** II.C.1
respondents, ***21:*** I
employers as. *See this heading:* employers as respondents
retaliation cases
federal employees, ***14:*** VI.D
overlap with Section 1983, ***14:*** VI.C.1
reverse discrimination. *See* Reverse discrimination
right-to-sue notices, ***25:*** III.J.7, III.L
rulemaking powers of EEOC, ***25:*** II.A
scope, ***37:*** II.A
scope of charge limiting scope of lawsuit, ***28:*** IV
See also Charges
scored tests, use of, ***4:*** I.A, I.B
See also Scored tests for employment decisions
demographic norming, ***4:*** I.B.2
licensing examinations, ***4:*** I.B.3
Section 703(h), ***4:*** I.B.1
seniority issues, ***Ch.*** 17
See also Seniority systems
service of charge on respondent, ***25:*** III.F; ***29:*** II.A.2
settlements. *See* Settlements
sex discrimination. *See* Sex discrimination
sexual harassment. *See* Sexual harassment
sexual orientation discrimination, protection unavailable, ***11:*** I.A
standing issues, ***15:*** II.H
state and local government suits, ***30:*** I
state licensing examinations not covered by, ***4:*** I.B.3
agencies not covered as employers, ***21:*** I.A.3.d
statute of limitations, ***26:*** III.B; ***29:*** V.A.1
federal employees, ***31:*** II.A.1
subjective criteria for employment decisions. *See* Subjective criteria for employment decisions
suits in court by charging parties, ***25:*** III.M.2
summary judgment, ***28:*** VI
See also Summary judgment
testers as charging parties, ***24:*** VII
third-party challenges to court-ordered practices, ***39:*** V
undocumented aliens, remedies, ***7:*** II.A.2.a
Uniform Guidelines on Employee Selection Procedures. *See* Uniform Guidelines on Employee Selection Procedures
union stewards as charging parties, ***24:*** II.B.5